The V.C. and D.S.O.

VOL. III.

THE DISTINGUISHED SERVICE ORDER

A COMPLETE RECORD OF THOSE WHO FROM THE 1st OF JANUARY, 1916, TO THE PRESENT TIME HAVE BEEN AWARDED THE DECORATION OR WHO HAVE RECEIVED BARS TO THEIR D.S.O.'s, WITH DESCRIPTIONS OF THE SERVICES WHICH WON THE DISTINCTION AND WITH MANY BIOGRAPHICAL AND OTHER DETAILS

With 313 Portrait Illustrations

CONTENTS

PAGE

"The London Gazette" Notices from 1st January, 1916, to the Present Time of Awards of the D.S.O.; of Bars to the D.S.O., and of the Services which won the Distinctions 1

Index, including References to the "Gazette" Notices of Awards and Services, and also including Biographical and other Details 195

ERRATUM

The name R. H. Brittan and his record on page 212 should be deleted (see R. H. Britton and his record on same page).

The Distinguished Service Order was instituted 6th September, 1886. The Bar to the Order was instituted 23rd August, 1916.

The Distinguished Service Order

Appointments and Services as Gazetted from 1st January, 1916, to date, including all awards made during the same period, of Bars to D.S.O.'s

These Extracts from the Gazettes are arranged chronologically

London Gazette, 1 Jan. 1916.—"Admiralty, 1 Jan. 1916. The King has been graciously pleased to give orders for the following appointments to the undermentioned Officers, in recognition of their bravery and devotion to duty during mine-sweeping and mine-laying operations. To be Companions of the Distinguished Service Order."

WALTERS, RICHARD HUTH, Commander (Acting Capt.), R.N.
MORANT, EDGAR ROBERT, Commander, R.N
RIGG, WALTER GEOFFREY, Lieut.-Commander (Acting Commander), R.N.
HEATON, GERVASE WILLIAM HEATON, Lieut.-Commander (Acting Commander), R.N.
CARMICHAEL, JOHN, Engineer-Commander, R.N.R.
THURSTAN, NORMAN MALET COLQUHOUN, Lieut.-Commander, R.N.
RICE, WILLIAM VICTOR, Lieut., R.N.

London Gazette, 1 Jan. 1916.—"Admiralty, 1 Jan. 1916. The King has been graciously pleased to give orders for the appointment of the undermentioned Officers to be Companions of the Distinguished Service Order."

COODE, CHARLES PENROSE RUSHTON, Capt., R.N. For the services described in the London Gazette of the 16th Aug. 1915.
FITZMAURICE, RAYMOND, Commander, R.N. For his services in charge of the operation of blocking the Rufigi river to prevent the escape of the Königsberg on the 10th Nov. 1914. Commander Fitzmaurice was on board the collier Newbridge, which was sunk up the river, and was exposed to heavy fire at short range from both banks both when entering the river and again when returning in the steam cutter of H.M.S. Chatham.
SNEYD, RALPH STUART, Commander, R.N. For his services during operations in the Cameroons. Commander Sneyd has commanded several successful operations on the coast and up the rivers, notably on the Dibamba River on the 10th Sept. 1914, when he engaged and sank a large enemy launch, drove the enemy out of their post at Piti, and captured important defence plans.
HUGHES, ROBERT HERBERT WILFRID, Commander, R.D., R.N.R. For his services during operations in the Cameroons. At the beginning of the campaign Commander Hughes superintended the work of clearing a way through the wreck barrage and piloting H.M.S. Challenger to within bombarding distance of Duala, and he has subsequently, at considerable risk and frequently under fire, carried out survey work on the Sanaga, Njong and Campo Rivers, and continuously harassed the enemy's coast outposts.
BRUCE, KENNETH MERVYN, Lieut.-Commander, R.N. For his services in command of a submarine in the Sea of Marmora, where he made a prolonged cruise, during the course of which he inflicted much damage on enemy shipping and engaged and put to flight by gunfire a Turkish gunboat and a destroyer, and subsequently displayed much coolness and resource in extricating his boat from a difficult position.
PIRIE, WILFRID BAYLEY, Lieut., R.N. For his services in command of a submarine in the Sea of Marmora, where he inflicted much damage on enemy shipping, and co-operated with Lieut.-Commander Bruce in the chase of a Turkish gunboat.
BARR, EDWIN HAROLD, Capt., R.M.A. For services with the Royal Marine Artillery Anti-Aircraft Brigade in France.
LEAF, HENRY MEREDITH, Temporary Capt., R.M. For services with the Royal Naval Division Motor Transport Company in France.
FERRAND, JAMES BRIAN PATRICK, Flight Sub-Lieut., R.N. On the 28th Nov. 1915, accompanied by First Class Air Mechanic Oldfield as gunner, Flight Sub-Lieut. Ferrand attacked a hostile seaplane, which was accompanied by three more seaplanes and a destroyer, off the Belgian coast, and brought it down by gunfire into the water, where it immediately sank. He then attacked the destroyer, and only abandoned the attack after coming under heavy shell fire both from the destroyer and the shore batteries of Westende.
VINEY, TAUNTON ELLIOTT, Flight Sub-Lieut., R.N. For his services on the 28th Nov. 1915, when, accompanied by le Lieut. en second de Sinçay as observer, he destroyed a German submarine off the Belgian coast by bombs dropped from an aeroplane.

London Gazette, 10 Jan. 1916.—"Admiralty, 10 Jan. 1916. The King has been graciously pleased to give orders for the appointment of the undermentioned Officer. To be a Companion of the Distinguished Service Order."

DUFF-DUNBAR, KENNETH JAMES, Lieut.-Commander R.N. In recognition of his services in attacking and torpedoing a German auxiliary vessel on the 22nd Dec. 1915. The ship was protected by a screen consisting of a torpedo boat, a small sloop, four trawlers and several tugs and small craft, and Lieut.-Commander Duff-Dunbar showed great determination in prosecuting the attack through the screen.

London Gazette, 11 Jan. 1916.—"Admiralty, 11 Jan. 1916. His Majesty the King has been graciously pleased to give orders for the appointment of the following Officer to the Distinguished Service Order."

BOND, THOMAS ARTHUR, Lieut., R.A.N.R. In recognition of his services during the operations against the German possessions in the Western Pacific, 1914. On 11 Sept. 1914, during the attack upon the Wireless Station, Bita Paka, German New Guinea, Lieut. Bond displayed conspicuous ability and coolness under fire in leading his men through most difficult country and enforcing the terms of surrender whilst drawing off the attack by another body of the enemy. He showed great daring, when accompanied by only one officer and one man, in suddenly disarming eight Germans in the presence of 20 German native troops drawn up under arms, all of whom were then marched off and held prisoners. Later he personally captured five armed natives.

London Gazette, 12 Jan. 1916.—Officers (amongst others) specially recommended in the Despatch dated 3 Dec. 1915, of Vice-Admiral Sir Reginald H. S. Bacon, Commanding the Dover Patrol.

JOHNSON, C. D., Commodore, M.V.O., 6th Flotilla. In command of the Destroyer Flotilla, and has performed much valuable work during the whole of the operations, and directly responsible for the efficiency with which the patrol was conducted.
WIGRAM, E., Capt., H.M.S. Prince Eugene. Commanded the detached squadron during a successful attack on Zeebruge on 6 Sept., which caused considerable loss and inconvenience to the enemy.
BIRD, F. G., Capt., Dover Drifter Patrol. In personal charge of the drifters during five of the major attacks, and contributed materially to the success of the operations.
BOWRING, H. W., Flag Capt., Dover Patrol. Acted as Chief of my Staff during all the operations and afforded me most valuable assistance.
BICKFORD, W. G. H., Commander, Dover Patrol. In charge of the forward observation party under the close fire of the batteries during two attacks, and largely assisted in correcting the fire of the guns.

"Admiralty, 12 Jan. 1916. His Majesty the King has been graciously pleased to give orders for the following appointments to the undermentioned Officers in recognition of their services as mentioned in the foregoing despatch. To be Companions of the Distinguished Service Order."

JOHNSON, CHARLES DUNCAN, M.V.O., Commodore, R.N.
WIGRAM, ERNEST, Capt., R.N.
BIRD, FREDERIC GODFREY, Capt., R.N.
BOWRING, HUMPHREY WYKEHAM, Capt., R.N.
BICKFORD, WILLIAM GEORGE HASTINGS, Commander, R.N.

London Gazette, 14 Jan. 1916.—"War Office, 14 Jan. 1916. His Majesty the King has been graciously pleased to approve of the undermentioned Honours and Rewards for distinguished service in the field, with effect from 1 Jan. 1916, inclusive. To be Companions of the Distinguished Service Order."

BUTLER, THE HONOURABLE LESLEY JAMES PROBYN, Lieut.-Colonel, Irish Guards.
GREENE, WALTER RAYMOND, Temporary Lieut.-Colonel, 3rd County of London Yeomanry, Territorial Force.
HUTCHINSON, CHARLES ALEXANDER ROBERT, Major and Brevet Lieut.-Colonel, 41st Dogras, Indian Army.
HUTCHINSON, FREDERICK PIERREPONT, Lieut.-Colonel, Royal Artillery.
KAY, WILLIAM HEAPE, Lieut.-Colonel, Royal Artillery.
PLUMMER, EDMUND WALLER, Lieut.-Colonel, Royal Artillery.
SANDERSON, WILLIAM DENZILOE, Lieut.-Colonel, Loyal North Lancashire Regt.
SCOTT, ALEXANDER FRANCIS SINCLAIR, Lieut.-Colonel, Royal Artillery.
STENNETT, HARRY MARCH, Lieut.-Colonel, Northern Rhodesia Police.
WEEKES, HENRY WILSON, Lieut.-Colonel, Royal Engineers.
ABADIE, RICHARD NEVILE, Major, King's Royal Rifle Corps.
TROYTE, GILBERT JOHN ACLAND, Major, King's Royal Rifle Corps.
ADLERCRON, RODOLPH LADEVEZE, Major, Cameron Highlanders.
AGG, FREDERICK JOHN GARDNER, Major, Yorkshire Light Infantry.
AINSWORTH, RALPH BIGNELL, Major, Royal Army Medical Corps.
ALSTON, FRANCIS GEORGE, Major, Scots Guards.
ANDREWES, FRANCIS EDWARD, Major, Royal Artillery.
ASH, WILLIAM CLAUDIUS CASSON, Major, Middlesex Regt.
BAILEY, JOHN HENRY, Major (Temporary Lieut.-Colonel), Shropshire Light Infantry.
BAILEY, VIVIAN TELFORD, Major (Temporary Lieut.-Colonel), Liverpool Regt. (Service Battn.).
BAKER, EDWARD MERVYN, Major, The Royal Fusiliers.
BAKER-CARR, CHRISTOPHER D'ARCY BLOOMFIELD SALTERN, Temporary Major, Commandant, Machine Gun School.
BARKER, ERNEST FRANCIS WILLIAM, Major, Yorkshire Light Infantry (attached 14th Divisional Signal Company, Royal Engineers).
BECK, EDWARD ARCHIBALD, Major, Royal Scots Fusiliers.
BELGRAVE, JOHN DALRYMPLE, Major, Royal Artillery.
BERKLEY, JAMES, Major, Reserve of Officers, Royal Artillery.
BLAMEY, EDWIN HERBERT, Major, Army Service Corps.
BLENCOWE, EDWARD PROWETT, Major, Army Service Corps.
BLOIS, DUDLEY GEORGE, Major, Royal Artillery.
BOOTH, ERNEST BRABAZON, Major, M.D., Royal Army Medical Corps.
BOUSFIELD, HUGH DELABERE, Major, West Yorkshire Regt., Territorial Force.
BOWDLER, BASIL WILFRED BOWDLER, Major, Royal Engineers.
BRADLEY, CECIL GUSTAVOS (name Gustavos corrected to Gustave, London Gazette, 28 Jan. 1916), Major, Yorkshire Light Infantry, Territorial Force.

A 1

BRAINE, HERBERT EDMUND REGINALD RUBENS, Major, Royal Munster Fusiliers.
BRANDON, OSCAR GILBERT, Major, Royal Engineers.
BROWN, GEORGE HERBERT JAMES, M.B., Major, Royal Army Medical Corps.
BROWN, HENRY ROBERT, Capt. and Brevet Major (Temporary Major), Cameron Highlanders (Special Reserve) (attached Service Battn.).
BROWN, JAMES PEARSON, M.B., Major, Royal Army Medical Corps, Territorial Force.
BROWN, PERCY WILSON, Major (Temporary Lieut.-Colonel), Gordon Highlanders.
BROWNE, JAMES CLENDINNING, Major, Army Service Corps.
BRUCE, GEORGE DAVID, Major, 61st King George's Own Pioneers, Indian Army.
BUCHANAN, KENNETH GRAY, Major, Seaforth Highlanders.
BUDGE, PHILIP PRIDEAUX, Major, Royal Artillery.
BULLOCK, REGINALD LAUNCELOT, Major, 1st West Riding Brigade, Royal Field Artillery, Territorial Force Reserve.
BURKE, BERNARD BRUCE, Major, Royal Army Medical Corps.
BURNE, EDWARD ROBERT, Major, Royal Artillery.
CAMERON, JAMES SAUMAREZ, Major, Royal Sussex Regt.
CAMPBELL, HARRY LA TROBE, Major, 1st West Lancashire Field Company, Royal Engineers, Territorial Force.
CAMPBELL, JAMES HAMILTON, M.B., Major, Royal Army Medical Corps.
CAMPBELL, ROBERT WEMYSS, Temporary Major, The Royal Scots (Lothian Regt.), Service Battn.
CARLYON, TRISTREM, Major, Royal Artillery.
CASSON, WILFRID FRANCIS SEYMOUR, Major, 27th Light Cavalry, Indian Army.
CAVENDISH, FREDERICK WILLIAM LAWRENCE SHEPPARD HART, Major, 9th Lancers.
CHAMPION DE CRESPIGNY, CLAUDE RAUL, Major, Grenadier Guards.
CHANCE, OSWALD KESTEVEN, Major (Temporary Lieut.-Colonel), 5th Lancers.
CHAPMAN, ROBERT, Major, 4th Durham (Howitzer) Battery, Royal Field Artillery, Territorial Force.
CLARKE, ARTHUR LIONEL CRISP, Major, Argyll and Sutherland Highlanders.
CLAYTON, EDWARD ROBERT, Major, Oxfordshire and Buckinghamshire Light Infantry.
COLBECK, BERNARD BOWLES, Major, Royal Artillery.
COLLINGWOOD, CLENNELL WILLIAM, Major, Royal Artillery.
COMMINGS, PERCY RYAN CONWAY, Major, South Staffordshire Regt.
COMYN, LEWIS JAMES, Major (Temporary Lieut.-Colonel), Connaught Rangers.
CONWAY, ARTHUR SEPTIMUS, Major, North Staffordshire Regt.
COPEMAN, HUGH CHARLES, Major (Reserve of Officers), Essex Regt. (Service Battn.).
COURTICE, JAMES GEORGE, Major, Army Ordnance Department.
COWAN, SAMUEL HUNTER, Major, Royal Engineers.
CRAWFORD, JAMES NORMAN, Major, Royal Inniskilling Fusiliers.
CRAWFORD, ROBERT DUNCAN, Major, Royal Artillery.
CROFTON, MALBY, Major, Royal Artillery.
CUFFE, JAMES ALOYSIUS FRANCIS, Major, Royal Munster Fusiliers.
CUNNINGHAM, AYLMER BASIL, Major, Royal Engineers.
CUNNINGHAM, HAROLD TWEEDALE, Major, Royal Artillery and Army Ordnance Department.
CURRIE, RYVES ALEXANDER MARK, Major (Temporary Lieut.-Colonel), Somerset Light Infantry.
DANSEY, FRANCIS HENRY, Major (Temporary Lieut.-Colonel), Wiltshire Regt.
DAVIDSON, NORMAN RANDALL, Major, Royal Artillery.
DAVIES, WALTER PERCY LIONEL, Major (Temporary Lieut.-Colonel), Royal Artillery.
DEACON, HENRY ROBERT GORDON, Major (Temporary Lieut.-Colonel), Connaught Rangers.
DICKINS, VERNON WILLIAM FRANK, Major (Temporary Lieut.-Colonel), 9th (County of London) Battn. The London Regt., Territorial Force.
DOBBIN, LEONARD GEORGE WILLIAM, Major (Temporary Lieut.-Colonel), The Northamptonshire Regt.
DOIG, CLAUDE PRENDERGAST, Major (Temporary Lieut.-Colonel), Seaforth Highlanders (attached Oxfordshire and Buckinghamshire Light Infantry, Territorial Force).
DORAN, JOHN CRAMPTON MORTON, Major, Army Service Corps.
DOYLE, JOHN FRANCIS INNES HAY, Major (Temporary Lieut.-Colonel), Royal Artillery.
DREYER, JOHN TUTHILL, Major, Royal Artillery.
DRUMMOND, THE HONOURABLE MAURICE CHARLES ANDREW, Major, Royal Highlanders.
DUFF, GARDEN BEAUCHAMP, Major, Cameron Highlanders.
DUTHIE, ARTHUR MURRAY, Major, Royal Artillery.
EASTON, PHILIP GEORGE, Major, Royal Army Medical Corps.
ETON, ERNEST, Major, 21st County of London (Howitzer) Battery, Royal Field Artillery, Territorial Force.
FERGUSSON, VIVIAN MOFFAT, Major, Royal Artillery.
FITZGERALD, MORDAUNT JOHN FORTESCUE, Major, Royal Artillery.
FLEMING, JOHN GIBSON, Major, Royal Engineers.
FOLLETT, ROBERT SPENCER, Major, The Rifle Brigade.
FORESTIER-WALKER, ROLAND STUART, Major, Royal Monmouthshire Royal Engineers (Special Reserve).
FORSYTH, JAMES ARCHIBALD CHARTERIS, Major, Royal Artillery.

FRANKLIN, HAROLD SCOTT ERSKINE, Major, 15th Ludhiana Sikhs, Indian Army.
FRY, PETER GEORGE, Major, 2nd Wessex Field Company, Royal Engineers, Territorial Force.
GAGE, MORETON FOLEY, Major (Temporary Lieut.-Colonel), 5th Dragoon Guards.
GEARY, JOHN ALEXANDER, Major, Royal Artillery.
GEPP, ERNEST CYRIL, Major, Duke of Cornwall's Light Infantry (Special Reserve).
GILES, FRANK LUCAS NETLAM, Major, Royal Engineers.
GODMAN, LAWRENCE, Major, Royal Artillery.
GORDON-HALL, GORDON CHARLES WILLIAM, Major, Yorkshire Light Infantry.
GRAZEBROOK, GEORGE CHARLES, Major, Royal Inniskilling Fusiliers.
GREEN, WILLIAM, Major, Royal Highlanders.
GRIFFITHS, JOHN NORTON, Major, 2nd Regt., King Edward's Horse.
GUY, ROBERT FRANCIS, Major, Wiltshire Regt.
GWYNN, REGINALD SNOW, Major (Temporary Lieut.-Colonel), South Wales Borderers.
HAIG, ALAN GORDON, Major, Royal Artillery.
HALL, CHARLES HENRY TORRINGTON BYNG, Temporary Major, Motor Machine Gun Service.
HANAFIN, PATRICK JOHN, Major, Royal Army Medical Corps.
HANSON, HARRY ERNEST, Major, 2nd East Riding Battery, Northumbrian Brigade, Royal Field Artillery, Territorial Force.
HARDING, DANIEL LITTON, F.R.C.S.I., Major, Royal Army Medical Corps.
HARDWICK, PHILIP EDWARD, Major, 1st Royal Dragoons.
HARRISON, JAMES MURRAY ROBERT, Major, Royal Artillery.
HARTIGAN, JAMES ANDREW, M.B., Major, Royal Army Medical Corps.
HAWKSLEY, JOHN PLUNKETT VERNEY, Major, Royal Artillery.
HAY, CHARLES JOHN BRUCE, Major, Queen Victoria's Own Corps of Guides (Frontier Force) (Lumsden's), Indian Army.
HEADLAM, EDWARD JAMES, Commander, Royal Indian Marine.
HESKETH, GEORGE, Major (Temporary Lieut.-Colonel), Loyal North Lancashire Regt., Territorial Force.
HEWLETT, ERNEST, Major, Devonshire Regt.
HIGGINS, CHARLES GRÆME, Major, Oxfordshire and Buckinghamshire Light Infantry.
HIGGINSON, HAROLD WHITLA, Major (Temporary Lieut.-Colonel), Royal Dublin Fusiliers.
HILDYARD, HAROLD CHARLES THOROTON, Major, Reserve of Officers, Royal Artillery.
HILL, CONWAY ROWLAY, Major, Royal Artillery.
HILL, GERALD ERNEST MONTAGUE, Major (Temporary Lieut.-Colonel) East Lancashire Regt.
HOBBS, CHARLES JAMES WILLOUGHBY, Major (Temporary Lieut.-Colonel), Nottinghamshire and Derbyshire Regt.
HOLLOND, SPENCER EDMUND, Major (Temporary Lieut.-Colonel), The Rifle Brigade.
HUDSON, PERCY, Major, Liverpool Regt.
HUDSON, ROBERT ARTHUR, Major, West Yorkshire Regt., Territorial Force.
HULSEBERG, HERBERT, Major, 127th (Queen Mary's Own) Baluchis Light Infantry (attached 129th Baluchis), Indian Army.
HUMPHREYS, ARTHUR SELDEN, Major, Army Service Corps.
HUMPHREYS, EDWARD THOMAS, Major, Lancashire Fusiliers.
INCLEDON-WEBBER, ADRIAN BEARE, Major (Temporary Lieut.-Colonel), Royal Irish Fusiliers.
INGHAM, ROBERT JOHN FITZGERALD, Major, Royal Artillery.
IRVINE, ARTHUR EDMUND STEWART, Major, Royal Army Medical Corps.
JACKSON, HENRY CHOLMONDELEY, Major, Bedfordshire Regt.
JEFFREYS, JOHN WILLIAM, Major (Temporary Lieut.-Colonel), Durham Light Infantry.
JESSE, JOHN LEONARD, Major (Temporary Lieut.-Colonel), Army Service Corps.
JONES, BRYAN JOHN, Major, Leinster Regt.
JONES, JOHN HENRY HILL, Major, Royal Artillery.
JONES, RICHARD CHARLES ROYNON, Major, Liverpool Regt.
KEEN, FREDERICK STEWART, Major, 45th Rattray's Sikhs, Indian Army.
KELSALL, THOMAS EDWARD, Major, Royal Engineers.
KENNEDY, JOHN, Major, Argyll and Sutherland Highlanders.
KERANS, GEORGE CHARLES LOVEL, Major, Indian Medical Service.
KERR, JAMES COLE MUNRO, Major, Scottish Signal Company, Royal Engineers, Territorial Force.
KIRKPATRICK, ALEXANDER RONALD YVONE, Major, Royal Artillery.
LAMONT, JOHN WILLIAM FRASER, Major (Temporary Lieut.-Colonel), Royal Artillery.
LANG, GODFREY GEORGE, Major (Temporary Lieut.-Colonel), West Yorkshire Regt.
LEE, HARRY HYLTON, Major, Scottish Rifles.
LEECH, ARTHUR GRAVES, Major, Royal Artillery.
LEWER, LEONARD WILLIAM, Major, Royal Artillery.
LEWES, CHARLES GEORGE, Major (Temporary Lieut.-Colonel), Essex Regt.
LEWIN, ERNEST ORD, Major, Royal Artillery.
LEWIS, HENRY LESTER, Major, Royal Engineers.
LIDDELL, JOHN STEWART, Major, Reserve of Officers, Royal Engineers.
LONGSTAFF, RALPH, Major, Royal Artillery, attached Royal Flying Corps.
LOW, NELSON, Major, Royal Army Medical Corps.
LYON, CHARLES HARRY, Major, North Staffordshire Regt.
MACFIE, WILLIAM COLVIN, Major, Royal Engineers.
McGOWAN, THORBURN, Major, Royal Artillery.

The Distinguished Service Order

McKENZIE, KENNETH McLEOD, Major, Army Veterinary Corps.
McTAGGART, MAXWELL FIELDING, Major (Temporary Lieut.-Colonel), 5th Lancers (attached Gordon Highlanders, Territorial Force).
MAKGILL-CRICHTON, HENRY COVENTRY MAITLAND, Major, Royal Scots Fusiliers.
MAJENDIE, BERNARD JOHN, Major, King's Royal Rifle Corps.
MANN, GEORGE DUNCAN, Major, Royal Artillery.
MARTIN, GERALD HAMILTON, Major, King's Royal Rifle Corps.
MAUGHAN, FRANCIS GILFRID, Major, Durham Light Infantry.
MAY, REGINALD SEABURNE, Major (Temporary Lieut.-Colonel), Royal Fusiliers.
MEADEN, ALBAN ANDERSON, Major, Royal Army Medical Corps.
MILDRED, SPENCER, Major, Royal Engineers.
MOORE, FRANCIS HAMILTON, Major, Royal Berkshire Regt.
MOORHOUSE, HARRY, Major, Yorkshire Light Infantry, Territorial Force.
MORGAN, ROSSLEWIN WESTROPP, Major, South Staffordshire Regt.
MORLEY, LIONEL ST. HELIERS, Major, Nottinghamshire and Derbyshire Regt.
MORTIMORE, CLAUDE ALICK, Major, Royal Artillery.
MOSLEY, HENRY SAMUEL, Major, Army Veterinary Corps.
MOWATT, CHARLES RYDER JOHN, Major, Northamptonshire Regt.
MURRAY, THE HONOURABLE ARTHUR CECIL, Major, 2nd Regt., King Edward's Horse.
MURRAY, BERTIE ELIBANK, Major, Shropshire Light Infantry.
MURPHY, JOHN JOSEPH, Temporary Major, Army Service Corps.
NEEDHAM, HENRY, Major, Gloucestershire Regt.
NEEDHAM, RICHARD ARTHUR, M.B., Major, Indian Medical Service.
NEWMAN, CHARLES RICHARD, Major, Royal Artillery.
NEWMAN, THOMAS GOULD WALKER, Major, 17th (County of London) Battn. The London Regt., Territorial Force.
NISBET, FRANCIS COURTENAY, Major (Temporary Lieut.-Colonel), Gloucestershire Regt.
NOOTT, CUTHBERT CECIL, Major, Royal Artillery.
NUGENT, FRANK HENRY (surname changed to Burnell-Nugent), Major (Temporary Lieut.-Colonel), The Rifle Brigade.
OGG, WILLIAM MORTIMER, Major (Temporary Lieut.-Colonel), Royal Artillery.
OSBORNE, GEORGE FREDERICK FOLGER, Major, Royal Engineers.
OVEY, RICHARD LOCKHART, Major, Oxfordshire and Buckinghamshire Light Infantry, Territorial Force.
OWEN, CHARLES HAROLD WELLS, Major, Royal Artillery.
PARKINSON, THOMAS WILLIAM, Major, York and Lancaster Regt.
PETERS, JOHN WESTON PARSONS, Major, Reserve of Officers, 7th Dragoon Guards.
PICKERING, CHARLES JAMES, Major (Temporary Lieut.-Colonel), West Riding Regt.
PINCHING, MINDEN CHARLES CARDIGAN, Major, 2nd Dragoon Guards.
POOLE, HENRY REYNOLD, Major, Royal Artillery.
POSTON, WILLIAM JOHN LLOYD, Major, Royal Artillery.
POWELL, RICHMOND FFOLLIOTT, Major, Royal Artillery.
PRANCE, ROBERT COURTENAY, Major, Royal Artillery.
PRATT, ALFRED GILBERT, Major, Essex Regt.
RAIKES, LAWRENCE TAUNTON, Major, Royal Artillery.
RAINSFORD-HANNAY, JOHN, Major, Royal West Surrey Regt.
RAMSAY, FRANK WILLIAM, Major (Temporary Lieut.-Colonel), Middlesex Regt.
RENDALL, FRANCIS HOLDEN SHUTTLEWORTH, Major, Duke of Cornwall's Light Infantry.
RITCHIE, MICHAEL BALFOUR HUTCHISON, M.B., Major, Royal Army Medical Corps.
RITCHIE, THOMAS FRASER, Major, Somerset Light Infantry.
ROBERTS, ARTHUR COLIN, Major (Temporary Lieut.-Colonel), Royal Fusiliers.
ROBERTS, FREDERICK EMILIUS, Major, Royal Army Medical Corps.
ROE, WILLIAM FRANCIS, Major, Royal Army Medical Corps, Territorial Force.
ROGERS, JAMES SAMUEL YEAMAN, M.B., Major, Royal Army Medical Corps, Territorial Force.
ROSE, RICHARD AUBREY DE BURGH, Major (Temporary Lieut.-Colonel) Worcestershire Regt.
ROYSTON-PIGOTT, GEORGE ARTHUR, Major, Northamptonshire Regt.
RYAN, EUGENE, Major, Royal Army Medical Corps.
ST. LEGER, STRATFORD EDWARD, Major, Royal Irish Regt.
SAMPSON, FRANCIS CORNELIUS, M.B., Major, Royal Army Medical Corps.
SCARLETT, THE HONOURABLE HUGH RICHARD, Major, Royal Artillery.
SCOBELL, SANFORD JOHN PALAIRET, Major, Norfolk Regt.
SCOTT, CHARLES WALKER, Major, Royal Artillery.
SEDGWICK, FRANCIS ROGER, Major, Royal Artillery (retired pay).
SEYMOUR, CHARLES HUGH NAPIER, Major, King's Royal Rifle Corps.
SIMPSON, HENRY CHARLES, Major, Royal Artillery.
SMALLMAN, ARTHUR BRITON, M.D., Major, Royal Army Medical Corps.
SMITH, DUNCAN VAUGHAN, Major, 1/1st Battn. The London Regt. (Royal Fusiliers), Territorial Force.
SPURRIER, GEORGE STRETTON, Temporary Major, Army Service Corps.
STACK, GEORGE HALL, Major, Royal Engineers.
STANTON, HUGH AURIOL STANTON, Major, Royal Scots (Lothian Regt.).
STENHOUSE, HERBERT WILSON, Major, Royal West Surrey Regt.
STEVENS, GEORGE ARCHIBALD, Major, Royal Fusiliers.
STREET, HAROLD, Major, Devonshire Regt.
STRONG, ADDINGTON DAWSONNE, Major, 10th Duke of Cambridge's Own Lancers (Hodson's Horse) (attached Jodhpur Imperial Service Lancers), Indian Army.
SULLIVAN, GEOFFREY ARNOLD, Major, Oxfordshire and Buckinghamshire Light Infantry.
TAYLOR, BROOK WILBRAHAM, Major, Royal Artillery.
TEACHER, NORMAN McDONALD, Major, Royal Scots Fusiliers.
THELLUSSON, THE HONOURABLE HUGH EDMUND, Major, Royal Artillery.
THEOBALD, ALFRED CHARLES LESTOURGEON, Major, Royal Artillery.
THOMPSON, RICHARD JAMES CAMPBELL, Major, Royal Army Medical Corps.
THORNE, AUGUSTUS FRANCIS ANDREW NICOL, Major, Grenadier Guards.
THORNHILL, JOHN EVELYN, Major, Seaforth Highlanders.
THORNTON, LESLIE HEBER, Major, The Rifle Brigade (Special Reserve).
THORNYCROFT, CHARLES MYLTON, Major, Manchester Regt. (Special Reserve).
THORP, HERBERT WALTER BECK, Major, Yorkshire Light Infantry.
TOLLER, WILLIAM SHIRLEY NORTON, Major, Leicestershire Regt., Territorial Force.
TOVEY, GEORGE STRANGWAYS, Major, Royal Artillery.
TRAILL, WILLIAM STEWART, Major, Royal Engineers.
TREDENNICK, JAMES PAUMIER, Major (Temporary Lieut.-Colonel), Royal Dublin Fusiliers.
TUFTON, THE HONOURABLE JOHN SACKVILLE RICHARD, Major, Royal Sussex Regt. (Special Reserve).
TURNER, ARTHUR MONTAGU, Major, 1st Dragoon Guards.
TURNER, CHARLES HAROLD, Major, Royal Army Medical Corps.
TYRWHITT, FREDERICK ST. JOHN, Major, Worcestershire Regt.
VIVIAN, VALENTINE, M.V.O., Major, Grenadier Guards.
WADLEY, EDWARD JOHN, Major, Army Veterinary Corps.
WALLINGER, JOHN ARNOLD, Temporary Major, Special List (General Staff Officer).
WALTER, BERTRAM, Major, Royal Artillery.
WATSON, HUGH WHARTON MYDDLETON, Major, King's Royal Rifle Corps.
WEBB, ANDREW HENRY, Major, Royal Artillery.
WESTMACOTT, GERALD PERCY, Temporary Major, Northumberland Fusiliers (Service Battn.).
WHITE, ALISON KINGSLEY GORDON, Major, Royal Artillery.
WHITE, ROBERT LYNCH, Major, Royal West Kent Regt.
WHITE, WILLIAM NICHOLAS, Major, Army Service Corps.
WHITTY, ALLEN, Quartermaster and Honorary Major, Worcestershire Regt.
WIGHTON, EDWARD, Major, Royal Artillery.
WILKINSON, SIDNEY JOHN, Major (Temporary Lieut.-Colonel), West Yorkshire Regt.
WILLETT, FREDERIC WILFRID BAGNALL, Major, Royal Sussex Regt.
WILSON, ARTHUR HOLT, Major (Reserve of Officers), East Surrey Regt. (Service Battn.).
WILSON, FRANCIS, Major, 1st East Anglian Field Company, Royal Engineers, Territorial Force.
WINTERBOTHAM, HAROLD ST. JOHN LOYD, Major, Royal Engineers.
WOLLASTON, FREDERICK HARGREAVES ARBUTHNOT, Major, The Rifle Brigade.
WOODS, BYRON JAMES GOODRICH, Major (Temporary Lieut.-Colonel) Army Service Corps.
WYNNE, HENRY ERNEST SINGLETON, Major, Royal Artillery.
ABSON, JOSEPH, F.R.C.V.S., Capt. (Temporary Major), Army Veterinary Corps, Territorial Force.
ALEXANDER, SIR LIONEL CECIL WILLIAM, Bart., Capt. (Temporary Major), 2nd London Divisional Signal Company, Royal Engineers, Territoria Force.
ALEXANDER, WILLIAM, Capt. (Temporary Major), Royal Highlanders, Territorial Force.
BARNES, FRANK PURCELL, Capt. (Temporary Lieut.-Colonel), Army Service Corps.
BATEMAN, CHARLES MALCOLM, Capt. (Temporary Major), West Riding Regt., Territorial Force.
BIRD, LAWRENCE WILFRID, Capt., Royal Berkshire Regt.
BRADFORD, THOMAS ANDREW, Capt., Durham Light Infantry, Territorial Force.
BROCK, HENRY LE MARCHANT, Capt., Royal Warwickshire Regt. and Royal Flying Corps.
BROOKE, CHARLES BERJEW, Capt., The Suffolk Regt., Special Reserve (attached Royal West Surrey Regt.).
BRYAN, CECIL CLIVE, Capt. (Temporary Major), 1st Home Counties Field Company, Royal Engineers, Territorial Force.
CARRINGTON, ROBERT HAROLD, Capt., Royal Artillery.
CHAPPLE, FRANCIS JOHN, Capt. (Temporary Major), Royal Garrison Artillery, Territorial Force.
CHASE, ARCHIBALD ALDERMAN, Capt., Royal Engineers.
CUMINE, GEORGE JAMES GORDON GERALD, Capt. (Temporary Major), Gordon Highlanders (Service Battn.).
DALY, LOUIS DOMINIC, Capt., Leinster Regt.
DAVIDSON, ALEXANDER ELLIOTT, Capt., Royal Engineers.
DOBBIE, WILLIAM GEORGE SHEDDEN, Capt., Royal Engineers.
DOWNIE, JOHN, M.B., Capt., Royal Army Medical Corps, Territorial Force.
EVANS, FRED EVAN, Capt. (Temporary Major), 17th (County of London) Battn. The London Regt., Territorial Force.
FLEMING, GEORGE, Capt., Somerset Light Infantry.
FORSYTH, CUSACK GRANT, Capt. (Temporary Major), Yorkshire Regt.

GASKELL, HERBERT STUART, Capt., Royal Engineers.
GLYN, RICHARD FITZGERALD, Temporary Capt. (Reserve of Officers, 1st Dragoons), Army Service Corps.
GOLD, ERNEST, Temporary Major, Special List (Meteorological Section).
HALDANE, LAURENCE AYLMER, Capt. (Temporary Major), Northamptonshire Regt.
HAMMOND, FREDERICK DAWSON, Capt. (Temporary Major), Royal Engineers.
HEARSON, JOHN GLANVILLE, Capt., Royal Engineers and Royal Flying Corps.
HILL, GERALD VICTOR WILMOT, Capt., Royal Irish Fusiliers.
HOLDICH, GODFREY WILLIAM VANRENEN, Capt., Royal Artillery.
HOUSTON, JOSEPH WILFRED, M.B., Capt., Royal Army Medical Corps.
IMBERT-TERRY, CLAUDE HENRY MAXWELL, Capt., Devonshire Regt.
JACKSON, BASIL, Capt. (Temporary Major), Yorkshire Regt., Territorial Force.
JOSEPH, REGINALD HERBERT, Capt. (Temporary Major), 1st London Field Company, Royal Engineers, Territorial Force.
KEANE, SIR JOHN, Bart., Capt., Reserve of Officers, Royal Artillery.
KENNEDY, ARCHIBALD ARROL, Capt. (Temporary Major), Scottish Rifles, Territorial Force.
KISCH, FREDERICK HERMANN, Capt., Royal Engineers.
LATHAM, FRANCIS, Capt., Leicestershire Regt.
LAURIE, PERCY ROBERT, Capt., 2nd Dragoons.
LYON, ALEXANDER, Capt. (Temporary Major), Gordon Highlanders, Territorial Force.
MACARTHUR, WILLIAM PORTER, M.D., F.R.C.P.I., Capt., Royal Army Medical Corps.
McDONALD, SAMUEL, Capt. (Temporary Major), Gordon Highlanders, Territorial Force.
McGILLYCUDDY, ROSS KINLOCH, Capt., 4th Dragoon Guards.
MACKENZIE, SIR VICTOR AUDLEY FALCONER, Bart., M.V.O., Capt., Scots Guards.
MACTAVISH, DUNCAN, Capt., The Gordon Highlanders (Special Reserve).
MITCHELL, ROBERT, Capt. (Temporary Major), 2nd Highland Field Company, Royal Engineers, Territorial Force.
NEAME, PHILIP, V.C., Capt., Royal Engineers.
NICHOLL, HUGH ILTID, Capt., Reserve of Officers, Bedfordshire Regt.
NOBLE, NORMAN DONCASTER, Capt., Royal Engineers.
NORTON, CECIL BARRINGTON, Capt. (Temporary Major) (Reserve of Officers), Duke of Cornwall's Light Infantry.
NORTON, GILBERT PAUL, Capt. (Temporary Major), West Riding Regt., Territorial Force.
O'NEILL, EDWARD MICHAEL, M.B., Capt., Royal Army Medical Corps.
O'SULLEVAN, JOHN JOSEPH, Capt. (Temporary Major), Northern Rhodesia Police.
PARRY, RICHARD ALLEN, Capt., Suffolk Regt., Territorial Force.
PELLY, RAYMOND THEODORE, Capt. (Temporary Lieut.-Colonel), Loyal North Lancashire Regt., Special Reserve (commanding Princess Patricia's Canadian Light Infantry.)
PENNYMORE, PERCY GEORGE, Capt. and Honorary Major, The Monmouthshire Regt., Territorial Force.
POLLARD, CYRIL ARTHUR, Capt. (Temporary Major), 2nd County of London (Howitzer) Battery, Royal Field Artillery, Territorial Force.
RAYMOND, EDWARD HUGH BROOME, Capt. (Temporary Major), Reserve of Officers, Royal Scots (Service Battn.).
RICH, CHARLES EDWIN FREDERICK, Capt. and Honorary Major, Lincolnshire Regt. (Special Reserve).
ROBINSON, DANIEL GEORGE, Capt., 46th Punjabis, Indian Army.
ROSS, RONALD CAMPBELL, Capt., 6th Jat Light Infantry, Indian Army.
SAUNDERS, HERBERT CECIL, Capt. (Temporary Major), Home Counties Divisional Signal Company, Royal Engineers, Territorial Force.
SAVILE, CLARE RUXTON UVEDALE, Capt. (Temporary Major), Royal Fusiliers.
SLADEN, GERALD CAREW, Capt. (Temporary Lieut.-Colonel), The Rifle Brigade.
STACEY, GERALD ARTHUR, Capt. (Temporary Major), 2nd (City of London) Battn. The London Regt., Territorial Force.
STEWART, WALTER PETER, Capt., Highland Light Infantry.
THRUSTON, BERTIE JOHN, Capt., Lincolnshire Regt.
TURNBULL, GEORGE OLIVER, Capt. (Temporary Major), 26th Punjabis, Indian Army (attached Royal Scots Fusiliers, Service Battn.).
WALTER, FRANCIS EDWARD, Capt. (Temporary Major), Reserve of Officers, Norfolk Regt. (Service Battn.).
WICKHAM, JOHN CHARLES, Capt., Royal Engineers (2nd Queen Victoria's Own Sappers and Miners, Indian Army).
WILBRAHAM, BERNARD HUGH, Capt., Royal Engineers.
WILSON, FRANK O'BRIEN, Capt., East African Mounted Rifles (formerly Royal Navy).
WORTHINGTON, FRANK, M.B., Capt., Royal Army Medical Corps.
ASHWELL, ARTHUR LINDLEY, Lieut. (Temporary Major), Nottinghamshire and Derbyshire Regt., Territorial Force.
BIRCH, ALLAN GRANT, Lieut. (Temporary Major), 3rd London Field Company, Royal Engineers, Territorial Force.
CHICHESTER-CONSTABLE, RALEIGH CHARLES JOSEPH, Lieut. (Temporary Capt.), The Rifle Brigade.
COTTRELL, JOSEPH, Lieut. (Temporary Capt.), Royal Welsh Fusiliers.
NEWINGTON, HERBERT ARCHER HAYES, Lieut. (Temporary Capt.), 14th (County of London) Battn. The London Regt., Territorial Force.
STEVEN, JOHN FRASER, M.B., Temporary Lieut., Royal Army Medical Corps.

AUSTRALIAN FORCE.

BURGESS, WILLIAM LIVINGSTONE HATCHWELL, Major, 9th Battery, Australian Artillery.
MARTYN, ATHELSTAN MARKHAM, Major, 2nd Field Company, Australian Engineers.
DEXTER, THE REVEREND WALTER ERNEST, M.A., Chaplain, 4th Class, Chaplains' Department.
FAHEY, THE REVEREND FATHER JOHN, Chaplain, 4th Class, Chaplains' Department.

CANADIAN FORCE.

COLQUHOUN, MALCOLM ALEXANDER, Lieut.-Colonel, 4th Canadian Infantry Battn.
HILL, FREDERICK WILLIAM, Lieut.-Colonel, 1st Canadian Infantry Battn.
MACLAREN, CHARLES HENRY, Lieut.-Colonel, 1st Canadian Field Artillery Brigade.
RATTRAY, JOHN GRANT, Lieut.-Colonel, 10th Canadian Infantry Battn.
RENNIE, ROBERT, M.V.O., Lieut.-Colonel, 3rd Canadian Infantry Battn.
SIMSON, WILLIAM AMOR, Lieut.-Colonel, 1st Canadian Divisional Train.
SWIFT, ALBERT EDWARD, Lieut.-Colonel, 2nd Canadian Infantry Battn.
ANDREWS, GEORGE WILLIAM, Major, 8th Canadian Infantry Battn.
BROWN, JAMES SUTHERLAND, Major, Royal Canadian Regt.
CLARK-KENNEDY, WILLIAM HEW, Major, 13th Canadian Infantry Battn.
DYER, HUGH MARSHAL, Major, 5th Canadian Infantry Battn.
GOODEVE, LESLIE CHARLES, Major, 1st Battery, Canadian Artillery.
HILLIAM, EDWARD, Major (Temporary Lieut.-Colonel), 5th Canadian Infantry Battn.
LEONARD, EDWIN WOODMAN, Major, 12th Battery, Canadian Artillery.
MAGEE, FRANK CORMACK, Major, Heavy Battery, Canadian Artillery.
PANET, EDOUARD DE BELLEFEUILLE, Major, Royal Canadian Artillery.
PROWER, JOHN MERVYN, Major, 8th Canadian Infantry Battn.
RAE, WILLIAM, Major, 30th Canadian Infantry Battn.
ASHTON, EDWARD JOHN (corrected to Edward James [London Gazette, 28 January, 1916]), Lieut., 9th Canadian Infantry Battn.

NEW ZEALAND FORCE.

FALLA, NORRIS STEPHEN, Major, New Zealand Artillery.
HASTINGS, NORMAN FREDERICK, Major, Wellington Mounted Rifles.

London Gazette, 22 Jan. 1916.—" War Office, 22 Jan. 1916. His Majesty the King has been graciously pleased to approve of the appointment of the undermentioned Officers to be Companions of the Distinguished Service Order, in recognition of their gallantry and devotion to duty in the field."
HOWARD, LEWIS CHARLES, Temporary Lieut.-Colonel, 8th Battn. Prince Albert's (Somerset Light Infantry). For conspicuous gallantry and ability on the night of 15th/16th Dec. 1915, near Armentières. He organized with the greatest energy and skill a successful raid by his battalion on the German trenches. His example inspired all ranks with enthusiasm and confidence. He displayed complete indifference to personal danger during the withdrawal of the raiding force under heavy fire. Lieut.-Colonel Howard has been previously brought to notice for gallant work near Loos on 26 Sept. 1915.
NEWCOMBE, STEWART FRANCIS, Major, Royal Engineers. For conspicuous gallantry and devotion to duty near Anzac, Gallipoli Peninsula, on 29 Oct. 1915. During rescue operations he entered a mine tunnel soon after the first casualties were reported, and, although suffering from the effects of fumes, he continued to lead rescue parties till he was completely disabled by the gas. One officer lost his life on this occasion in the attempt at rescue.
BELL-IRVING, MALCOLM McBEAN, Capt., Royal Flying Corps (Special Reserve). For conspicuous and consistent gallantry and skill during a period of nine months in France, notably on 19 Dec. 1915, between Lille and Ypres, when he successfully engaged three hostile machines. The first he drove off, the second he sent to the ground in flames, and the third nose-dived and disappeared. He was then attacked by three other hostile machines from above, but he flew off towards Ypres, and chased a machine he saw in that direction. He overhauled it and had got to within a hundred yards when he was wounded by a shell and had to return.
FINDLATER, ALEXANDER, M.D., Capt., 1st London Mounted Brigade Field Ambulance, Royal Army Medical Corps, Territorial Force. For conspicuous gallantry and devotion to duty on several occasions, notably on 29 Sept. 1915, at Chocolate Hill, Gallipoli Peninsula. He crossed over two hundred yards of open ground under very heavy shell fire to render aid to two wounded men. He saved the life of one, but the other was beyond help.
HUNTINGTON, RICHARD HALL, Temporary Capt., 8th Battn. Prince Albert's (Somerset Light Infantry). For conspicuous gallantry and skill on the night of 15/16 Dec. 1915, near Armentières. He was in command of a raiding party of his battalion, which, largely owing to his skill, entered the German trench undiscovered, and, after disposing of all the enemy found in the trench, were very ably withdrawn. Capt. Huntington was previously brought to notice for good work at the Chalk Pit, near Loos, on 26 Sept. 1915.
JACKSON, ERNEST CHARLES, Temporary Capt., 5th Canadian Infantry Battn. For conspicuous gallantry on 15 Dec. 1915. He commanded the attack on a German advanced barricade on the Messines road with great dash and determination. Previously, on 7 Nov. 1915, he displayed great daring in entering a German sap opposite our trenches on Hill 63, and in withdrawing under heavy fire.
EATON, ARTHUR ERNEST, Temporary Second Lieut., General List (late 7th Battn. Leicestershire Regt.), attached 184th Tunnelling Company, Royal Engineers. For conspicuous gallantry and determination near Moulin de Farguy on the night of 4/5 Jan. 1916. Lieut. Eaton made a most daring reconnaissance, remaining six and three-quarter hours behind the German lines and bringing back valuable information. He stunned a German sentry whom he believed to be aware of his presence and finally had to swim back to the point from which he started.

London Gazette, 2 Feb. 1916.—" War Office, 2 Feb. 1916. His Majesty the King has been graciously pleased to approve of the undermentioned rewards for Distinguished Service in the field. To be Companions of the Distinguished Service Order."
FIRTH, RICHARD ANSON, Lieut.-Colonel, 2/10th Gurkha Rifles (Indian Army).

The Distinguished Service Order

ALEXANDER, CHARLES TAYLOR, Major, Lancashire Fusiliers (Territorial Force).
ANDERSON, JAMES, Major (Temporary Lieut.-Colonel), Highland Light Infantry (Territorial Force).
BATTYE, WALTER ROTHNEY, M.B., F.R.C.S., Major, Indian Medical Service.
BENTINCK, LORD CHARLES CAVENDISH, Capt. and Brevet Major (Temporary Lieut.-Colonel), Reserve of Officers, late 9th Lancers.
CROCKER, HERBERT EDMUND, Major, Essex Regt. (attached Royal Engineers).
DODGSON, RAYMOND CHARLES, Major, Royal Artillery.
GORDON, WILLIAM ALEXANDER, C.M.G., Major, Special Reserve, Worcestershire Regt. (attached Royal Warwickshire Regt., Service Battn.).
HAWTHORN, GEORGE MONTAGUE PHILIP, Major (Temporary Lieut.-Colonel), Liverpool Regt., Commandant 1st Battn. The King's African Rifles.
HAY, STUART, Major, Cameron Highlanders.
MEINERTZHAGEN, RICHARD, Major, Royal Fusiliers.
MILLAR, WILLIAM JOHN, Major (Temporary Lieut.-Colonel), King's Own Scottish Borderers (Territorial Force).
MORGAN-OWEN, LLEWELLYN ISAAC GETHIN, Major, South Wales Borderers.
NELSON, HERBERT, Major (Temporary Lieut.-Colonel), Border Regt.
NEVILL, COSMOS CHARLES RICHARD, Major, Royal Warwickshire Regt (attached Service Battn.).
ROWAN-ROBINSON, HENRY, Major (Temporary Lieut.-Colonel), Royal Artillery.
ROSS, ARTHUR MURRAY, Major, West Yorkshire Regt.
SANDFORD, DANIEL ARTHUR, Major, Royal Artillery.
SHERWOOD-KELLY, JOHN, Temporary Major, Norfolk Regt. (Service Battn.).
SKELTON, DUDLEY SHERIDAN, Major, Royal Army Medical Corps.
SLAUGHTER, REGINALD JOSEPH, Major, Army Service Corps.
SMITH, HUGH WILFRID THOMAS, Major, Royal Artillery.
STEVENS, HERBERT LYNN, Major, Welsh Regt. (attached Service Battn.).
THORNTON, GODFREY ST. LEGER, Major, Royal Artillery.
WAGSTAFF, CYRIL MOSLEY, C.I.E., Major (Temporary Lieut.-Colonel) Royal Engineers.
WILKINSON, ROGER, Major (Temporary Lieut.-Colonel), Gloucestershire Regt. (attached Service Battn.).
WOLFF, ARNOLD JOHNSTON, Major (Temporary Lieut.-Colonel), Royal Engineers.
WOOD, MAXIMILIAN DAVID, Major, West Yorkshire Regt.
WORTHINGTON, CHARLES SWANWICK (name Charles corrected to Claude, London Gazette, 21 Feb. 1916), Major, Manchester Regt. (Territorial Force).
YOUNGHUSBAND, HAROLD, Major, Bedfordshire Regt.
BRIDGES, EDWARD CHARLES PHILIPPI, Capt. (Temporary Major) Reserve of Officers, South Staffordshire Regt.
DUCK, FRANCIS PONSONBY, Temporary Capt. (Temporary Major), 6th (Service) Battn. Lincolnshire Regt., attached Nottinghamshire and Derbyshire Regt. (Service Battn.).
FERRERS-GUY, MARMION CARR, Capt., Lancashire Fusiliers (Adjutant, Service Battn.).
MONEY, NOEL CAMPBELL KYRLE, Capt. (Temporary Major), 22nd Punjabis (Indian Army), attached Connaught Rangers (Service Battn.).
PHIPSON, EDWARD SELBY, M.B., Capt., Indian Medical Service.
PIKE, WILLIAM, Capt., Royal Inniskilling Fusiliers.
WARD, LANCELOT EDWARD SETH, Capt. (Temporary Lieut.-Colonel), Reserve of Officers, Oxfordshire and Buckinghamshire Light Infantry, attached Royal Artillery.

London Gazette, 4 Feb. 1916.—"War Office, 4 Feb. 1916. His Majesty the King has been graciously pleased to approve of the undermentioned reward for distinguished service in the field. To be an Honorary Companion of the Distinguished Service Order."

EGYPTIAN ARMY.

EL BIMBASHI MOHAMMED EFFENDI SHAHIM, Egyptian Cavalry.

London Gazette, 24 Feb. 1916.—"Admiralty, 24 Feb. 1916. The King has been graciously pleased to approve of the appointment of the undermentioned Officers to be Companions of the Distinguished Service Order."

LAURENCE, NOEL FRANK, Commander, R.N. For his services in charge of British submarines operating in the Baltic Sea.
DENNISTOUN, GEORGE HAMILTON, Lieut.-Commander, R.N. For his services on the occasion of the destruction of the German gunboat Hermann von Wissmann, at Sphinxhaven, on Lake Nyassa, on the 30th May, 1915.
GRAHAM, CHARLES WALTER, Flight Sub-Lieut., R.N. For his services on the 14th Dec. 1915, when with Flight Sub-Lieut. Ince as observer and gunner he attacked and destroyed a German seaplane off the Belgian coast.

London Gazette, 1 March, 1916.—"Admiralty, 1 March, 1916. The King has been graciously pleased to give orders for the appointment of the undermentioned Officer. To be a Companion of the Distinguished Service Order."

HODSON, GERALD LORD, Lieut.-Commander, R.N.

London Gazette, 14 March, 1916.—"Admiralty, S.W., 14 March, 1916. The King has been graciously pleased to give orders for the appointment of the undermentioned Officers to be Companions of the Distinguished Service Order."

WRAY, FAWCET, Capt., R.N. In command of H.M.S. Talbot, which was the mainstay of the supporting cruisers and light craft, especially at Suvla from 6 to 10 Aug.
McCLINTOCK, JOHN WILLIAM LEOPOLD, Capt., R.N. Was in command of H.M.S. Lord Nelson, and inflicted severe damage on the enemy in the operations of last May. Is mentioned for having handled his ship most ably.
VYVYAN, ARTHUR VYELL, Capt., R.N. Beachmaster at Anzac on 25 April and subsequently. Was frequently exposed to heavy shell-fire while carrying out his very arduous duties.
GODFREY, HARRY ROWLANDSON, Capt., R.N. Senior Officer afloat of the Destroyer Flotilla. Showed a fine example to all under him whilst sweeping and patrolling inside the Straits under heavy gunfire.
BEVAN, GEORGE PARKER, Commander, R.N. Has done continuous patrol work with great zeal and energy, and carried out valuable feints at landing in the Gulf of Xeros on 6 and 7 Aug. during the landing at Suvla.
SWABEY, GEORGE THOMAS CARLYLE, Commander, R.N. Rendered very valuable assistance to the Army as Naval Observation Officer. Strongly recommended by General Sir Francis Davies and General Sir William Birdwood.
DIX, CHARLES CABRY, Commander, R.N. Assistant Beachmaster, and later Beachmaster, at Anzac. Performed exceptionally good service under most trying conditions. Was twice wounded.
RAMSAY, THE HONOURABLE ALEXANDER R. M., Commander. Flag Commander to Vice-Admiral de Robeck, and has done exceptionally good service throughout the operations.
SEYMOUR, CLAUDE, Commander, R.N.
CUNNINGHAM, ANDREW BROWNE, Commander, R.N.
CAMPBELL, LEVESON GRANVILLE BYRON ALEXANDER, Lieut.-Commander, R.N.
WYLD, HERBERT WILLIAM, Lieut.-Commander, R.N.
BACCHUS, ROY, Lieut.-Commander, R.N.
CLARK, JAMES LENOX CONYNGHAM, Lieut.-Commander, R.N.

All Officers of the Destroyer Flotilla, and specially recommended for the good services they have performed.

CHANCE, GEORGE HAROLD DE PEYSTER, Lieut.-Commander, R.N. Has performed consistent good service on the Beaches.
HARDY, HENRY NOEL MARRYAT, Lieut.-Commander, R.N. Has performed exceptionally good service in command of a Trawler Flotilla inside the Straits, then in H.M.S. Folkestone, and lastly in H.M.S. Racoon.
GRATTAN, ERNEST LOFTUS COLLEY, Lieut.-Commander, R.N. In charge of Wireless Telegraphy at Cape Helles since 1 May. Admiral de Robeck reports that the work carried out by this Officer has been of inestimable service.
SEATH, GORDON HAMILTON, Lieut. (Temporary Capt.), R.M.L.I. Has acted as Naval Observation Officer at Helles since 1 May, 1915. Has shown great enterprise and resource in his duties under very heavy fire.
JONES, RONALD LANGTON, Lieut., R.N.R. Assistant Beachmaster at Helles since 30 May, 1915. Has set a magnificent example throughout.
SINCLAIR, JOHN LEWIS, Acting Lieut., R.N.R. Has rendered valuable service on patrols and on carrying out reconnaissances close inshore in very exposed positions.

London Gazette, 14 March, 1916.—"Admiralty, 14 March, 1916. The King has been graciously pleased to give orders for the appointment of the undermentioned Officers to be Companions of the Distinguished Service Order."

DAVIDSON, ALEXANDER PERCY, Capt., R.N. In charge of Suvla covering force.
TALBOT, HENRY FITZROY GEORGE, Capt., R.N. In general charge of vessels off the beach at Helles evacuation.
LAMBART, THE HONOURABLE LIONEL JOHN OLIVE, Commander (Acting Capt.), R.N. Performed good service on the staff of Rear-Admiral Wemyss at the evacuation of Suvla and Anzac, and previously.
SOMERVILLE, JAMES FOWNES, Commander, R.N. Fleet Wireless Officer. Has had duties of exceptional difficulty, which he has performed most efficiently.
HOOD, BASIL FREDERICK, Assistant Paymaster (Acting Paymaster), R.N. Secretary to Vice-Admiral de Robeck. Has carried out very heavy duties under arduous conditions.
MULOCK, GEORGE FRANCIS ARTHUR, Lieut.-Commander (Acting Commander), R.N. Mainly responsible for the evacuation of the great quantity of war material and animals, and for the comparative immunity from losses amongst beach craft at the final evacuation of Helles. Took a prominent part in Suvla and Helles evacuations.
BEVAN, RICHARD HUGH LORAINE, Lieut.-Commander, R.N. Performed meritorious service on the staff of Rear-Admiral Wemyss at evacuation of Suvla and Anzac.

London Gazette, 15 March, 1916.—"War Office, 15 March, 1916. His Majesty the King has been graciously pleased to approve of the appointment of the undermentioned Officers to be Companions of the Distinguished Service Order, in recognition of their gallantry and devotion to duty in the field."

HERBERT, GEORGE MELBOURNE, Major, 2nd Battn. The Dorsetshire Regt. For conspicuous gallantry and determination. He led his battalion forward against heavy odds after his senior officer had been severely wounded. On a later occasion he successfully covered a retirement with great skill and tenacity.
UTTERSON, HENRY KELSO, Major, 2nd Battn. The Dorsetshire Regt. For conspicuous gallantry and ability. He led his men with marked coolness and skill when assaulting a strong redoubt. He behaved very gallantly in several engagements, during one of which he took command of his battalion when all the senior Officers had been killed or wounded, and led a successful charge resulting in the capture of the enemy's trenches.
APTHORP, SHIRLEY EAST, Capt., 96th Berar Infantry, Indian Army. For conspicuous gallantry. During a retirement, when it was found that two wounded men had been left behind, he immediately volunteered with a private to return some 300 yards to their rescue in face of a heavy fire from the advancing enemy. A serjeant and private were guarding the wounded men, and between them all they brought them back into safety.
DE GREY, GEORGE, Capt., 2nd Battn. The Norfolk Regt. For conspicuous gallantry in the performance of his duties as Adjutant. He repeatedly crossed fire-swept zones in order to take orders, send up ammunition and direct reinforcements, until he was severely wounded. His cool bravery had twice previously been brought to notice.
JUKES, ANDREW HENRY, Capt., 9th Gurkha Rifles, Indian Army (Staff Capt.), 6th Canadian Infantry Brigade). For conspicuous good service and ability as a Staff Captain, Intelligence. Capt. Jukes organized on two occasions enterprises against the enemy trenches, with marked success. His enterprise and careful training has resulted in most excellent work on the part of the Scouts.
MACINTYRE, DUNCAN EBERTS, Capt., 28th Canadian Infantry Battn. For conspicuous gallantry when leading an assaulting party after personal reconnaissance. Having reached the enemy trenches, Capt. MacIntyre acted with great promptness, and later showed great coolness and presence of mind in the selection of a suitable line of retirement.

SWINBURNE, THOMAS ANTHONY STEWART, Capt., Royal Engineers. For conspicuous gallantry and continuous good work in action, notably when a mine was exploded by us in close proximity to the enemy. Directly our bombers had made good the near edge of crater, Capt. Swinburne organized and controlled the digging parties to consolidate it. This work was carried out under heavy fire. Later he explored the far edge of the crater and descended the mine shaft, as it appeared that some of the enemy had been entombed by the explosion.

TAYLOR, KENNETH CHURCHILL CRAIGIE, Capt., 29th Canadian Infantry Battn. For conspicuous gallantry when leading bombers in a raid on enemy trenches. Although wounded, Capt. Taylor jumped into the trench, and disposed of several of the enemy with bomb, revolver and bayonet. Later he withdrew his men most coolly, and assisted in taking back wounded.

KNOX, ROBERT UCHTRED EYRE, Temporary Lieut., 8th Battn. The Suffolk Regt. For conspicuous gallantry. When firing a "West" gun one of the grenades landed in our own parapet. Seeing that two of his men could not possibly get under cover, he rushed to pick up the grenade and throw it over the parapet. Just as he reached it it exploded. Although by an extraordinary chance he was only slightly injured, it was a fine example of bravery. He has several times undertaken tasks requiring coolness and daring.

WARDER, RICHARD OLIVER, Second Lieut. (Temporary Lieut.), A Battery, 78th Brigade, Royal Field Artillery (Special Reserve). For conspicuous gallantry. During a heavy bombardment, when the other Officers and many men were temporarily injured and three gun emplacements had been damaged, Lieut. Warder, with one bombardier, continued to fire the fourth gun. He personally brought up ammunition from a cellar which was under fire.

London Gazette, 28 March, 1916.—" War Office, 28 March, 1916. His Majesty the King has been graciously pleased to confer the undermentioned rewards for gallantry in connection with the engagement at Sollum, Egypt, 14 to 17 March, 1916. To be a Companion of the Distinguished Service Order."

WESTMINSTER (DUKE OF), HUGH RICHARD ARTHUR, G.C.V.O., Major, Cheshire Yeomanry, T.F.

London Gazette, 30 March, 1916.—" War Office, 30 March, 1916. His Majesty the King has been graciously pleased to approve of the appointment of the undermentioned Officers to be Companions of the Distinguished Service Order, in recognition of their gallantry and devotion to duty in the field."

BARKER, WILLIAM ARTHUR JOHN, Temporary Major, 8th Battn. The South Staffordshire Regt. For conspicuous gallantry and devotion to duty. When organizing a counter-attack he was wounded in four places by a bomb, but continued to command his battalion throughout the three following days till it was relieved.

CROSFIELD, GEORGE ROWLANDSON, Major, 4th Battn. The Prince of Wales's Volunteers (South Lancashire Regt.), Territorial Force (attached 2nd Battn.). For conspicuous gallantry and good service. He repeatedly visited the front line under heavy shell fire, and during the successful assault rallied and led back to the attack men who had suffered much from artillery fire. Previously he had made an excellent and daring reconnaissance of the enemy's position.

FISHER, JOHN WILFRED, Temporary Capt., 10th Battn. The Sherwood Foresters (Nottinghamshire and Derbyshire Regt.). For conspicuous gallantry. When the enemy blew up a portion of the front trench, he drove off their attack and skilfully organized the defence. He continued fighting long after he was wounded, and set a fine example to all around him.

GILLUM, WIDGWOOD WILLIAM, Capt., D Battery, 79th Brigade, Royal Field Artillery. For conspicuous gallantry and devotion to duty. When in charge of four forward guns, although wounded in the face and much shaken by the explosion of a heavy shell, he continued to encourage and direct his men under a fierce concentrated fire until he was a second time wounded.

GALE, ARTHUR WITHERBY, Lieut. (Temporary Capt.), (Reserve of Officers) 2nd Life Guards (Commanding Trench Mortars, 3rd Division). For conspicuous good service. He took command of all the trench mortars concentrated for an attack, and made all arrangements. The fine work done by the trench mortars under his direction contributed largely to the success of the assault.

LOCH, ALEXANDER ARTHUR FRANCIS, Lieut. (Temporary Capt.), 1st Battn. The South Wales Borderers. For conspicuous gallantry and determination. When the enemy had bombed our grenadiers out of a new post, he led a counter-attack up our sap, and with a machine-gun dispersed some thirty of the enemy who had collected. He was twice wounded, and the man by his side was killed, but he hung on till nightfall, and eventually made the post bullet-proof under very heavy fire.

MOZLEY, BERNARD CHARLES, Temporary Lieut., 6th Battn. The Dorsetshire Regt. For conspicuous gallantry. When the Officers of two companies had been killed or wounded he took command, and ably organized a withdrawal. Later, though badly wounded in the arm, he dragged into safety an Officer, who was also badly wounded, under heavy rifle and machine-gun fire.

TAYLEUR, CHARLES LANCELOT OLIVER, Lieut. (Temporary Capt.), 110th Battery, Royal Field Artillery. For conspicuous gallantry and good service throughout the campaign, notably on one occasion when an enemy H.E. shell had ignited several of our own H.E. shells in a gun pit. Capt. Tayleur rushed into the pit regardless of personal danger, and, by pouring buckets of water on the flames, put out the fire.

TRIPP, DONALD OWEN, Lieut. (Temporary Capt.), 3rd Battn. (attached 1st), The Loyal North Lancashire Regt. For conspicuous gallantry and determination. When he and several of his bombers had been wounded during an enemy bomb attack, he had his wounds hurriedly dressed, returned to his post, and with only a serjeant and two bombers kept the enemy at bay. When the two bombers were wounded he sent the serjeant back for reinforcements, and single-handed held up the enemy for twenty minutes till relieved.

HENDERSON, MALCOLM, Second Lieut. (Temporary Lieut.), 4th (Ross Highland) Battn. Seaforth Highlanders (Ross-shire Buffs, The Duke of Albany's), Territorial Force, and Royal Flying Corps. For conspicuous gallantry when, on photographic reconnaissance, his machine was struck by a shell from an enemy anti-aircraft gun. The shell passed through the nacelle of the machine, and took off his left leg just below the knee. In spite of this he succeeded in coming down from 7,000 feet, and landing 3,000 yards behind our line, thus saving his aeroplane and the life of the Observer.

SANDERSON, CHRISTOPHER, Temporary Second Lieut., 1st Battn. Gordon Highlanders. For conspicuous gallantry. During a successful assault he led the grenadiers and personally forced the enemy's machine-guns to retire. He then, by throwing bombs, put two enemy grenadier posts out of action, and was himself slightly wounded. Later, when two enemy grenadiers appeared from behind, he went out into the open and shot them both. The capture of the enemy trench was largely due to his gallantry. He had previously distinguished himself as a serjeant.

LYALL, EDWARD, Quartermaster and Honorary Lieut., 2nd Northumbrian Field Ambulance, Royal Army Medical Corps, Territorial Force (attached 185th Tunnelling Company, Royal Engineers). For conspicuous gallantry and devotion to duty. When a large camouflet was blown in by the enemy he hurried through a flooded gallery in the dark, and under heavy fire went for proto apparatus. Finding all the proto apparatus already in use, he hurried on and, although in an exhausted state, descended a shaft without any apparatus, assisted in the rescue of an officer, and then went further, rendered aid to two men, and made a most gallant effort to save two officers.

London Gazette, 31 March, 1916.—" Admiralty, S.W., 31 March, 1916. The King has been graciously pleased to give orders for the following appointments to the undermentioned Officers, in recognition of their services in the Patrol Cruisers, under the command of Rear-Admiral Sir Dudley R. S. De Chair, K.C.B., M.V.O., during the period ending the 31st Dec. 1915. To be Companions of the Distinguished Service Order."

LAWFORD, VINCENT ADRIAN, Fleet Paymaster, R.N.

GILLESPIE, EDWARD, Capt., R.M.L.I.

London Gazette, 4 April, 1916.—" War Office, 4 April, 1916. His Majesty the King has been graciously pleased to confer the undermentioned reward for gallantry and distinguished service in the field during the engagement on 26 Feb. 1916, at Agagir, Egypt. To be a Companion of the Distinguished Service Order."

SOUTER, HUGH MAURICE WELLESLEY, Major (Temporary Lieut.-Colonel), 14th Murray's Jat Lancers, Commanding Dorset Yeomanry, T.F.

London Gazette, 7 April, 1916.—" War Office, 7 April, 1916. His Majesty the King has been graciously pleased to confer the undermentioned reward for gallantry and distinguished service on the occasion of the attack on the Hartlepools by the German Fleet on the 16th Dec. 1914. To be a Companion of the Distinguished Service Order."

ROBSON, LANCELOT, Lieut.-Colonel, Durham Royal Garrison Artillery, T.F.

London Gazette, 7 April, 1916.—" Admiralty, 7 April, 1916. The King has been graciously pleased to give orders for the appointment of the undermentioned Officers to be Companions of the Distinguished Service Order."

BONE, REGINALD JOHN, Lieut., R.N., Flight Commander, R.N.A.S. In recognition of his services on the 19th March, 1916, when, flying a land machine and unaccompanied by an observer, he chased out to sea, and after bold and skilful manœuvring, disabled and brought down by gunfire a German seaplane, which had been engaged in a raid on the coast of Kent.

SMITH, CYRIL ALDIN, Lieut., R.N.V.R. For excellent work on the nights of the 13th–14th and 14th–15th March, 1916, in connection with enterprises against the enemy's trenches south of Verlorenhoek. This officer on two successive nights went forward to the enemy's wire, superintended the laying of torpedoes and blew gaps in the enemy's wire. His conduct and gallantry were conspicuous on both occasions.

London Gazette, 15 April, 1916.—" War Office, 15 April, 1916. His Majesty the King has been graciously pleased to approve of the appointment of the undermentioned Officers to be Companions of the Distinguished Service Order, in recognition of their gallantry and devotion to duty in the field."

ANNESLEY, ALBEMARLE CATOR, Major (Temporary Lieut.-Colonel), The Royal Fusiliers (City of London Regt.), Commanding 8th Battn. For conspicuous ability and energy when in command of his battalion during an attack. The success of the attack and the subsequent defeat of counter-attacks were due to his foresight, energy and example.

KEILY, FREDERICK PETER CHARLES, Major, 125th Napier's Rifles, Indian Army. For conspicuous gallantry on several occasions, notably when, after being wounded, he continued to lead his company with great coolness. Finally he escorted a badly wounded officer to a field ambulance under heavy fire, and returned at once to his post when his own wound was dressed. He has set a fine example.

OSBORN, WILLIAM LUSHINGTON, Major (Temporary Lieut.-Colonel), The Royal Sussex Regt., Commanding 7th Battn. For conspicuous ability in the performance of his duties. The excellent training of his battalion and the careful attention paid to all details of organization of defence, ensured that the captured position he took over on relief was securely held, in spite of constant counter-attacks. He showed great initiative in launching counter-attacks.

COPE, THOMAS GEORGE, Capt. (Temporary Major), The Royal Fusiliers (City of London Regt.), attached 8th Battn. For conspicuous ability in supporting his own line, affording help to captured craters and gaining valuable information. Though wounded, he remained on duty till the following day.

GUBBINS, STAMER, Capt. (Temporary Lieut.-Colonel), The Royal Fusiliers (City of London Regt.), Commanding 9th Battn. This officer commanded his battalion in an attack, the success of which was due to the excellent organization he had established in his battalion and to the fighting spirit he had fostered in it.

MACRAE, JOHN, Capt., 1st Battn. Seaforth Highlanders (Ross-shire Buffs, The Duke of Albany's). For conspicuous gallantry. He took command of his battalion at a critical moment when all the senior officers had become casualties, and by his coolness and energy saved a critical situation. At one time in the darkness he fell into the hands of the enemy, but escaped by the use of his fists.

HAMILTON, SACKVILLE WILLIAM SACKVILLE, Capt., 70th Field Company, Royal Engineers. For conspicuous gallantry and resource when in charge of Royal Engineers, consolidating captured craters. Capt. Hamilton's example under heavy shell and grenade fire, and his energetic dispositions, contributed largely to the success of the undertaking.

WEIR, DONALD LORD, Capt., 2nd Battn. The Leicestershire Regt. For conspicuous gallantry. He took command of his battalion when his Commanding Officer had been wounded, and led it with marked ability. Later he showed great skill and coolness in withdrawing his men in the dark under heavy fire.

ABERCROMBIE, ALEXANDER RALPH, Lieut., 1st Battn. The Queen's (Royal West Surrey Regt.). For conspicuous gallantry and devotion to duty. After an assault he found himself with one man only in the hostile saphead. Lieut. Abercrombie sent this man back for support, and bombed, meanwhile, along the sap. When his supply of bombs was exhausted, he fell back, and with rifle fire held the sap for three hours single-handed. He has done most excellent work.

DAWSON, WILLIAM ROBERT AUFRERE, Lieut. (Temporary Capt.), The Queen's Own (Royal West Kent Regt.), attached 6th Battn. For conspicuous gallantry. Though severely wounded, Capt. Dawson rejoined his company as soon as his wounds had been dressed, remained at his post till an attack had been repulsed and was again wounded later. His example of courage, endurance and devotion to duty was one of a very high order.

BEASLEY, WALTER HENRY, Temporary Second Lieut. (Temporary Capt.), 181st Tunnelling Company, Royal Engineers. For conspicuous gallantry. He was in charge of operations by which a large part of the enemy's gallery was destroyed. He explored their mining system until finally overcome by foul gas.

London Gazette, 17 April, 1916.—" War Office, 17 April, 1916. His Majesty the King has been graciously pleased to approve of the undermentioned rewards for services rendered in connection with military operations in the field, with effect from 1 Jan. 1916, inclusive. To be Companions of the Distinguished Service Order."

HICKMAN, CHARLIE STEWARD, Commander, Royal Indian Marine.
COTTER, HARRY JOHN, Major, Royal Artillery, Commandant 30th Mountain Battery, Indian Army.
LODGE, FRANCIS CECIL, Major, Norfolk Regt.
McLEOD, TORQUIL JOHN, Major, 2/7th Gurkha Rifles, Indian Army.
NELSON, JOHN WEDDALL, Major, Royal West Kent Regt.
RYBOT, NORMAN VICTOR LACEY, Major, 76th Punjabis, Indian Army.
STILWELL, WILLIAM BYRON, Major, 1/4th Battn. Hampshire Regt. (T.F.).
BHARUCHA, PHIROZSHAH BYRAMJI, F.R.C.S., Capt., Indian Medical Service.
BUTTERFIELD, EDWARD, Capt., Indian Army, attached 90th Punjabis.
COLAN, HARRY NORMAN, Capt., 67th Punjabis, Indian Army.
DENT, WILKINSON, Capt., 103rd Mahratta Light Infantry, Indian Army.
HEWETT, GEORGE, Capt., 48th Pioneers, Indian Army.
HIBBERT, OSWALD YATES, Capt., Royal West Kent Regt.
WILSON, ARNOLD TALBOT, C.M.G., Capt., Indian Army (Political Department).
WILSON, NIGEL MAITLAND, Capt., 2/7th Gurkha Rifles, Indian Army.

London Gazette, 18 April, 1916.—" War Office, 18 April, 1916. His Majesty the King has been graciously pleased to appoint the undermentioned Officers to be Companions of the Distinguished Service Order, in recognition of their distinguished service and devotion to duty at the Camp at Wittenberg, Germany, during the Typhus Epidemic which prevailed there from Feb. to June, 1915."

VIDAL, ALAN CUNLIFFE, Capt., R.A.M.C.
LAUDER JAMES LA FAYETTE, Temporary Capt., R.A.M.C.

London Gazette, 2 May, 1916.—" War Office, 2 May, 1916. His Majesty the King has been graciously pleased to approve of the undermentioned rewards for Distinguished Service in the field, with effect from the 1st Jan. 1916. To be Companions of the Distinguished Service Order."

GOSTLING, ERNEST VICTOR, Lieut.-Colonel, R.A.M.C., Territorial Force.
BELL, JOHN GRENVILL, M.B., Major, R.A.M.C.
BEST, THOMAS ANDREW DUNLOP, Major, Royal Inniskilling Fusiliers.
BOWEN, HUGH RICE, Major, Essex Regt.
CARR, HENRY ARBUTHNOT, Major, Worcestershire Regt.
GIBBON, JOHN HOUGHTON, Major, Royal Artillery.
GREENWAY, THOMAS CATTELL, Major, South Wales Borderers.
HAMILTON, NORMAN CHIVAS, Major, Army Service Corps (Lieut.-Colonel, New Zealand Imperial Force).
HARMAN, FRANK DE WINTON, Major, Norfolk Regt., attached Egyptian Army.
HORE-RUTHVEN, THE HONOURABLE ALEXANDER GORE ARKWRIGHT, V.C., Major (Temporary Lieut.-Colonel), Welsh Guards.
McALESTER, WILLIAM HENRY SOMERVILLE, Major, late King's Own Scottish Borderers.
FLOOD, RICHARD ELLES SOLLY, Major, Rifle Brigade.
WHIGHAM, ROBERT DUNDAS, Major, King's Own Scottish Borderers.
WORSLEY, RICHARD STANLEY, Major, Army Service Corps.
CRIPPS, HENRY HARRISON, Capt. (Temporary Major), Royal Fusiliers.
DEEDES, WYNDHAM HENRY, Capt., King's Royal Rifle Corps.
FESTING, HAROLD ENGLAND, Capt., Border Regt.
HUTTON, GEORGE FREDERICK, Capt., Royal Welsh Fusiliers.
MACAULAY, ROBERT KEITH AGNEW, Capt. (Temporary Major), Royal Engineers.
SHANNON, WILLIAM BOYD, Capt. (Temporary Major) (Reserve of Officers), York Regt., Service Battn.
TALLENTS, GODFREY EDWARD, Capt., Lancashire Fusiliers.

AUSTRALIAN IMPERIAL FORCE.

GELLIBRAND, JOHN, Major, Staff (Reserve of Officers, late Manchester Regt.).
FOSTER, WILLIAM JAMES, Capt., Staff.

London Gazette, 16 May, 1916.—" War Office, 16 May, 1916. His Majesty the King has been graciously pleased to approve of the appointment of the undermentioned Officers to be Companions of the Distinguished Service Order, in recognition of their gallantry and devotion to duty in the field."

SCOTT, WILLIAM HENRY, Major, 9th Light Horse Regt., Australian Imperial Force. For conspicuous ability and good work. He led a small column to reconnoitre a distant enemy post, attacked it, killed several of the enemy, and brought in thirty-eight prisoners, including the officer in command. His plans were so well laid that he effected this with the loss of only one man and one horse.

SUTHER, PERCIVAL, Major, 71st Heavy Battery, Royal Garrison Artillery. For conspicuous good work on more than one occasion as Forward Liaison Officer with the Infantry. His observations were very valuable, and greatly aided the successful work of the Artillery.

WILD, WILFRID HUBERT, Major (Temporary Lieut.-Colonel), 1st Battn. Northumberland Fusiliers. For conspicuous ability in the training and leading of his battalion. The successful capture and occupation with trifling loss of a portion of the enemy's position was mainly due to his fine example, skill, and the efficiency to which he has brought his command.

CONGREVE, WILLIAM LA TOUCHE, Capt., Rifle Brigade. For conspicuous gallantry. He consolidated a newly-won position under very difficult conditions at a critical moment, and by personal courage brought about the surrender of a considerable body of enemy officers and men.

HILL, ROBERT McCOWAN, M.B., Temporary Capt., R.A.M.C. (attached 2nd Battn., Argyll and Sutherland Highlanders). For conspicuous gallantry and devotion to duty. He went to an area which was under intense bombardment, amputated the leg of a wounded officer, and attended to other wounded under most difficult and dangerous circumstances. Finally, he accompanied two stretcher cases back under shell fire.

WILSON, ROBERT EDWARD, Capt., Royal Garrison Artillery (attached 30th Mountain Battery, Indian Army). For conspicuous gallantry during a retirement. He commanded a section of guns with great ability, and finally extricated them most skilfully, having to use his revolver on the enemy, who were within 50 yards.

TYNAN, JOHN, Second Lieut., Wiltshire Regt. (attached 6th Battn.). For conspicuous gallantry on patrol duty, notably when he took out a party and successfully rushed an enemy listening post within 30 yards of the enemy's lines, and obtained important information. On another occasion he brought in with his patrol an enemy officer, serjeant and private.

London Gazette, 31 May, 1916.—" War Office, 31 May, 1916. His Majesty the King has been graciously pleased to approve of the appointment of the undermentioned Officers to be Companions of the Distinguished Service Order, in recognition of their gallantry and devotion to duty in the field."

FREETH, JOSEPH CASHMORE, Lieut.-Colonel, 7th Battn. South African Infantry. For conspicuous gallantry and determination. With only eighteen men he established and held a position for several hours.

IRVINE, ALFRED ERNEST, Major (Temporary Lieut.-Colonel), 2nd Battn. Durham Light Infantry. For conspicuous gallantry and devotion to duty. During a critical period and continuous bombardment by the enemy lasting three days he was up with his front companies each night directing and organizing the defences. His energy, cheerfulness and splendid example were invaluable.

THOMPSON, WILLIAM JAMES, Major, 7th Battn. South African Infantry. For conspicuous gallantry. He successfully assaulted the enemy's position, compelled the enemy to retire, and held the position till dawn.

HOWARD, SAMUEL WILLIAM, Capt., 1st Battn. Connaught Rangers. For conspicuous gallantry when rallying parties of men who had become detached during operations. It was greatly due to his fine example that these men were safely withdrawn from within 80 yards of the enemy's trenches. He was also largely responsible for the capture of about fifty enemy prisoners.

INGRAM, THOMAS LEWIS, Temporary Capt., R.A.M.C. (attached 1st Battn. Shropshire Light Infantry). For conspicuous gallantry and devotion to duty. He collected and attended to the wounded under very heavy fire, and set a splendid example. Since the commencement of the war he has been conspicuous on all occasions for his personal bravery.

MOMBER, EDWARD MARIE FELIX, Capt. (Temporary Major), 176th Tunnelling Company, Royal Engineers. For conspicuous gallantry and skill in connection with mining operations. By his energy and determination he has achieved important successes over the enemy.

OWEN, GORONWY, Temporary Capt., 15th Battn. Royal Welsh Fusiliers. For conspicuous gallantry and determination in organizing and leading a successful raid on the enemy's trenches. Many of the enemy were accounted for, and Capt. Owen covered the withdrawal with great skill under heavy fire. Although slightly wounded, he gave assistance to wounded men.

PODMORE, HUBERT, Temporary Capt., 6th Battn. Northampton Regt. For conspicuous gallantry and ability during a night attack by the enemy. It was largely due to Capt. Podmore that his company held its own in spite of very heavy bombardment, and repelled every attack.

ROBERTS, ROBERT JESSE ADAMS, Temporary Capt., 10th Battn. Welsh Regt. For conspicuous gallantry. He led a party to lay a torpedo in the enemy's wire. When the torpedo failed to explode he made, with a lance-corporal, a very gallant attempt to get it back. When shown up by a bright flame emitted by the burning torpedo he was attacked at fifteen yards' distance by several of the enemy, but both he and his companion threw bombs which caused casualties, and got back safely. The torpedo was destroyed.

THOMPSON, HAROLD, Capt., Royal Scottish Fusiliers (Adjutant, 4th Battn. Territorial Force). For conspicuous gallantry and skill. He took up reinforcements to a point which was being attacked, assumed command, and, with great dash, led a counter-attack, which dispersed the enemy.

WYNTER, JOHN RAWSON, Capt., 52nd Sikhs (attached 59th Scinde Rifles), Indian Army. For conspicuous gallantry. Though shot through the shoulder, he continued to lead an attack on an enemy redoubt, entered it, and held his position for some time against bomb attacks from both flanks. He then covered a flank with marked ability during the retirement, although again hit twice.

HENDERSON, GEORGE STUART, Lieut. (Temporary Capt.), 1st Battn. Manchester Regt. For conspicuous gallantry and determination in an attack on an enemy redoubt. On entering the redoubt he organized and led bombing parties which cleared out the enemy, of whom he personally shot five. He subsequently covered our withdrawal, and was one of the last to leave the redoubt.

KERR, WILLIAM, Lieut. (Temporary Capt.), 2nd Battn. Border Regt. For conspicuous gallantry. During an intense bombardment and subsequent attacks by the enemy, it was mainly due to his coolness, bravery, and careful disposition that the enemy was driven off.

POPE, VYVYAN VAVASOUR, Lieut. (Temporary Capt.), 1st Battn. North Staffordshire Regt. For conspicuous gallantry and devotion to duty. When a party of the enemy broke into our trench, he at once organized a counter-attack, drove them out, and, although himself wounded in two places, remained at the point of danger till all was quiet. He then had his wounds dressed, but refused to leave his duties.

DRIVER, HARRY, Temporary Second Lieut., 7th Battn. Bedfordshire Regt. For conspicuous gallantry on several occasions, notably when leading a successful raid on the enemy's trenches. He forced the enemy back into their dug-outs, entered a deep dug-out and personally bombed the occupants, shot the sentry over another dug-out, and, though himself wounded in two places, remained at the point of exit till every man was reported present. He was wounded a third time on his way back to our trenches.

SWELL, ALBERT ERNEST, Second Lieut. (Temporary Lieut.), 1st Battn. Northampton Regt. For conspicuous gallantry and ability. He displayed great pluck in reconnoitring the enemy's trenches during several nights, and finally led a successful raid against them with great dash and skill.

London Gazette, 31 May, 1916.—"Admiralty, S.W., 31 May, 1916. The King has been graciously pleased to give orders for the appointment of the undermentioned Officers to be Companions of the Distinguished Service Order, in recognition of their services whilst employed on Transport duties at the Dardanelles."

LAMBERT, ROBERT CATHCART KEMBLE, Capt., R.N., H.M.S. Europa. As Beachmaster on " V " Beach on 25 April, 1915, and subsequent days, by his coolness under fire, zeal and energy, showed a magnificent example to his subordinates in a most difficult and dangerous position. Has since proved a most able assistant to the Principal Naval Transport Officer, Mudros.

MUIR, HENRY GEORGE, Commander, R.D., R.N.R., H.M.S. Sarnia. Sarnia has carried out the arduous duties of a ferry steamer, plying between Mudros and the peninsula, carrying troops and military stores, entailing constant moving and going alongside other ships. Commander Muir has handled his ship well, and it is owing to his zeal and attention to duty that the work has been satisfactorily performed under trying conditions.

EYERS, FRANK, Lieut.-Commander, R.N.R., M.F.A., Carrigan Head. Has performed meritorious service in the Eastern Mediterranean during the past nineteen months, including the saving of his unarmed ship when attacked by an enemy submarine.

London Gazette, 31 May, 1916.—" Admiralty, 31 May, 1916. The King has been graciously pleased to approve of the appointment of the undermentioned Officers to be Companions of the Distinguished Service Order."

SPICER-SIMSON, GEOFFREY BASIL, Commander, R.N. In recognition of his services in command of an Allied flotilla on Lake Tanganyika on the 9th Feb. 1916, when, after a chase and running fight lasting 3¼ hours, he sank the German gunboat Hedwig von Wissmann.

CROMIE, FRANCIS NEWTON ALLEN, Commander, R.N.

GOODHART, FRANCIS HERBERT HEAVENINGHAM, Commander, R. N.

In recognition of their services in command of British submarines operating in the Baltic Sea.

CAMPBELL, GORDON, Commander, R.N.

PEACE, ALFRED GEOFFREY, Lieut.-Commander, R.N.

BORTON, ARTHUR DRUMMOND, Lieut.-Commander, R.N.V.R.

In recognition of most valuable services in command of a detachment of R.M. machine guns in difficult and dangerous parts of the line in the Gallipoli Peninsula.

TEALE, JOSEPH WILLIAM, Temporary Major, R.M. In recognition of most valuable services throughout the whole of the evacuation of the Gallipoli Peninsula. With very limited resources he constructed the pier at which practically the whole of the guns and stores were embarked, and was in charge of the destruction of all ammunition, etc., which was left behind at Lancashire Landing.

London Gazette, 3 June, 1916.—" Admiralty, 3 June, 1916. The King has been graciously pleased to give orders for the appointment of the undermentioned Officers to be Companions of the Distinguished Service Order, in recognition of the services rendered by them in the prosecution of the war."

KEYES, ROGER JOHN BROWNLOW, Capt., C.B., C.M.G., M.V.O., A.D.C., R.N. (Commodore, 2nd Class).

TYRWHITT, REGINALD YORKE, Capt., C.B., R.N. (Commodore, 1st Class)

LITCHFIELD-SPEER, FREDERICK SHIRLEY, Capt., R.N.

London Gazette, 3 June, 1916.—" War Office, 3 June, 1916. His Majesty the King has been graciously pleased to approve of the undermentioned rewards for Distinguished Service in the field, dated 3 June, 1916. Awarded the Distinguished Service Order."

ACTON, WILLIAM MAXWELL, Major, Royal Irish Regt.

AITKEN, JOHN JAMES, Major (Temporary Lieut.-Colonel), Army Veterinary Corps.

AIREY, ROBERT BERKELEY, Major and Brevet Lieut.-Colonel, Army Service Corps.

ALEXANDER, JAMES WHITELAW, Major (Temporary Lieut.-Colonel), West Yorkshire Regt. (T.F.).

ALVES, HENRY MALCOLM JEROME, Capt., Royal Artillery.

ANNESLEY, CLIFFORD REGINALD TEMPLEMAN, Major (Temporary Lieut.-Colonel), Army Service Corps.

ARMITAGE, CHARLES CLEMENT, Major, Royal Artillery.

ARNOLD, HERBERT TOLLEMACHE, Major, Army Pay Department.

BAGSHAWE, HERBERT VALE, Major, Royal Army Medical Corps.

BARNETT, GEORGE HENRY, Major, King's Royal Rifle Corps.

BARTLETT, BASIL SORLEY, Major, Royal Army Medical Corps.

BAUMGARTNER, JOHN SAMUEL JOCELYN (surname changed to Percy), Lieut.-Colonel, East Lancashire Regt.

BAYLEY, ARTHUR GEORGE, Major (Temporary Lieut.-Colonel), Oxfordshire and Buckinghamshire Light Infantry.

BECKWITH, WILLIAM MABISSE, Capt., Reserve of Officers, late Coldstream Guards.

BEDDY, BERTRAM LANGDON, Major (Temporary Lieut.-Colonel), Army Service Corps.

BELL, ARTHUR HUGH, Major, Royal Engineers.

BENSKIN, JOSEPH, Capt., Royal Engineers.

BICKNELL, HENRY PERCY FRANK, Major (Temporary Lieut.-Colonel), Middlesex Regt.

BINGHAM, CHARLES HENRY MARION, Major, Army Service Corps.

BLACKBURN, CHARLES CAUTLEY, Capt., Reserve of Officers, late Norfolk Regt.

BLACKLOCK, CYRIL AUBREY, Temporary Lieut.-Colonel, King's Royal Rifle Corps., Service Battn.

BLUNT, GERALD CHARLES GORDON, Major, Army Service Corps.

BOONE, HENRY GRIFFITH, Major, Royal Artillery.

BOOTH, THOMAS MACAULAY, Major, Gordon Highlanders.

BOURKE, ERNEST ALBERT, Lieut.-Colonel, Royal Army Medical Corps.

BOWLES, JOHN DE VERE, Major, Royal Artillery.

BOYD, HENRY ALEXANDER, Major, Royal Artillery.

BRAND, THE HONOURABLE ROGER, Capt. (Temporary Major), Rifle Brigade, Special Reserve

BREWILL, ARTHUR WILLIAM, Major and Honorary Lieut.-Colonel (Temporary Lieut.-Colonel), Nottinghamshire and Derbyshire Regt. (T.F.).

BROOKE, EARDLEY WILMOT, Lieut.-Colonel, Army Service Corps.

BRUCE, PERCY ROBERT, Major, Nottinghamshire Yeomanry.

BULL, GEORGE, Capt. and Brevet Major (Temporary Lieut.-Colonel), Royal Irish Fusiliers, Commanding Service Battn. Royal Irish Rifles.

BURNETT, WILLIAM, Major (Temporary Lieut.-Colonel), North Staffordshire Regt. (T.F.).

BUTTERWORTH, REGINALD FRANCIS AMHURST, Major, Royal Engineers.

BUXTON, ANTHONY, Major, Essex Yeomanry.

BUXTON, JOHN LAURENCE (name Laurence changed to Lawrence), Major, Rifle Brigade.

CALDECOTT, ERNEST LAWRENCE, Major, Royal Artillery.

CAMPBELL, KEITH GORDON, Major, Royal Artillery, attached 26th Jacob's Mountain Battery, Indian Army.

CAMPBELL, NORMAN ST. CLAIR, Major, Royal Artillery.

CARPENTER, CHARLES MURRAY, Major (Temporary Lieut.-Colonel), Royal Engineers.

CARRINGTON, CHARLES RONALD BROWNLOW, Major, Royal Artillery.

CHALLINOR, WILLIAM FRANCIS, Major, Royal Field Artillery (T.F.).

CHAMBERLAYNE, EDWARD TANKERVILLE, Capt. (Temporary Major), Warwickshire Yeomanry.

CHESNEY, CLEMENT HOPE RAWDON, Capt., Royal Engineers.

CHILD, SIR SMITH HILL, Bart., Lieut.-Colonel, M.V.O., Royal Field Artillery (T.F.).

CHILES-EVANS, DAVID BRYNMOR, Capt., M.B., R.A.M.C. (T.F.).

CLARK, CECIL HORACE, Major, Royal Artillery.

CLISSOLD, HARRY, Major, Royal Engineers (T.F.).

COCKCRAFT, LOUIS WILLIAM LA TROBE, Major, Royal Artillery.

COHEN, JACOB WALEY, Major, 16th Battn. London Regt. (T.F.).

COLERIDGE, JOHN FRANCIS STANHOPE DUKE, Capt., 8th Gurkha Rifles, Indian Army.

COLLINS, DUDLEY STUART, Capt., Royal Engineers.

COLLINS, HAMILTON STRATFORD, Capt., Shropshire Light Infantry.

COLLINS, ROBERT JOHN, Major (Temporary Lieut. Colonel), Royal Berkshire Regt.

COLLISON, CHARLES SYDNEY, Lieut.-Colonel, Middlesex Regt., Special Reserve, Commanding Service Battn. Royal Warwickshire Regt.

CONDER, GERALD, Major, Army Veterinary Corps.

COOKE, BERTRAM HEWETT HUNTER, Major and Brevet Lieut.-Colonel (Temporary Brigadier-General), Rifle Brigade.

COTTON, HAROLD TEMPLE, Major (Temporary Lieut.-Colonel), South Lancashire Regt.

CRACROFT HUGH, Major (Temporary Lieut.-Colonel), Army Service Corps.

CRAWFURD, REGINALD BASKERVILLE JERVIS, Major, Coldstream Guards.

CRESWELL, EDMUND FRASER, Major, Royal Artillery.

CROOKSHANK, SYDNEY D'AGUILAR, Major (Temporary Lieut.-Colonel), C.I.E., M.V.O., R.E.

CROSLAND, GEORGE WILLIAM KILNER, Major, late West Riding Regt. (T.F.).

CUMMINS, ERNEST JACKSON, Major, Royal Artillery.

CUNNINGHAM, THOMAS LATIMER, Temporary Major, Cameron Highlanders, Service Battn.

CURTEIS, CYRIL SAMUEL SACKVILLE, Capt. (Temporary Major), Reserve of Officers, Royal Artillery.

DANFORD, BERTRAM WILLIAM YOUNG, Major (Temporary Lieut.-Colonel), Royal Engineers.

DARLING, JOHN CLIVE, Capt., 20th Hussars.

DARLING, JOHN MAY, Major, M.B., F.R.C.S., Special Reserve, Royal Army Medical Corps.

DAVENPORT, SAMUEL, Lieut.-Colonel, Gloucestershire Regt. (T.F.).

DAVIS, ARTHUR HENRY, Temporary Major, Army Service Corps.

DAVIS, GRONOW JOHN, Major (Temporary Lieut.-Colonel), 22nd Punjabis, Indian Army, Commanding Service Battn. King's Royal Rifle Corps.

DE BURGH, ERIC, Capt., 9th Hodson's Horse, Indian Army.

DELACOMBE, ADDIS, Major, Army Pay Department.

DE LA POER BERESFORD, MARCUS JOHN BARRE, Major (Temporary Lieut.-Colonel), Reserve of Officers, Commanding Service Battn. South Wales Borderers.

DENISON, HARRY, Major, Royal Artillery.

DE SATGE, HENRY VALENTINE BACHE, Major (Temporary Lieut.-Colonel), Royal Field Artillery (T.F.).

DIXON-NUTTALL, WILLIAM FRANCIS, Capt. (Temporary Major), Royal Engineers (T.F.).

DODD, WILFRID THOMAS, Capt. (Temporary Capt., Royal Engineers), Royal Engineers (T.F.).

DRURY-LOWE, WILLIAM DRURY, Major (Temporary Lieut.-Colonel), Capt., Reserve of Officers, Royal Field Artillery (T.F.).

DUNBAR, JOSEPH CAMERON, Major, Royal Artillery.

DUNCAN, KENNETH, Major, Royal Field Artillery (T.F.).

EAVES, FREDERICK, Capt. (Temporary Lieut.-Colonel), Royal Lancaster Regt. (T.F.).

EDEN, ARCHIBALD JAMES FERGUSSON, Lieut.-Colonel, Oxfordshire and Buckinghamshire Light Infantry.

EDWARDS, CHARLES WILLIAM, Capt. (Temporary Major), Army Service Corps.

ELLES, HUGH JAMIESON, Major, Royal Engineers.

ERSKINE, ARTHUR EDWARD, Major, Royal Artillery.

ERSKINE, SIR THOMAS WILFRED HARGREAVES JOHN, Bart., Major, Cameron Highlanders.

The Distinguished Service Order

ERSKINE-MURRAY, ARTHUR, Major, Royal Artillery.
EUGSTER, OSCAR LEWIS, Major, Honourable Artillery Company (T.F.).
EVERINGHAM, ARTHUR EDWARD, Quartermaster and Honorary Major, Royal Scots.
EVILL, CHARLES ARIEL, Capt. (Temporary Lieut.-Colonel), Monmouthshire Regt. (T.F.).
EXHAM, FRANK SIMEON, Major (Temporary Lieut.-Colonel), Army Ordnance Department.
FALCON, CHARLES GORDON, Major, Royal Engineers.
FALLE, PHILIP VERNON LE GEYT, Major, Army Service Corps.
FARQUHAR, JAMES, Major, Royal Artillery.
FARRANT, CHARLES, Major, Royal Army Medical Corps (T.F.).
FAWCETT, RALPH FRANKLAND MORRIS, Major (Temporary Lieut.-Colonel), Royal Army Medical Corps.
FETHERSTONHAUGH, TIMOTHY, Major (Temporary Lieut.-Colonel), Reserve of Officers, Commanding Service Battn. Seaforth Highlanders.
FITZGERALD, CHARLES ROBERT LEWIS, Capt. (Temporary Major), 126th Baluchis, Indian Army.
FLOWER, HORACE JOHN, Capt., King's Royal Rifle Corps.
FORREST, THOMAS HENDERSON, Lieut.-Colonel, M.B., Royal Army Medical Corps (T.F.).
FORSTER, DAVID, Major, Royal Engineers.
FORTUNE, VICTOR MORVEN, Capt. and Brevet Major, Royal Highlanders.
FOSTER, ARTHUR HERBERT BROOM, Major, Royal Lancaster Regt.
FRASER, ALASTAIR NORMAN, Major, M.B., Royal Army Medical Corps.
FRASER, GEORGE IRELAND, Major, Cameron Highlanders.
FREELAND, HENRY FRANCIS EDWARD, Major and Brevet Lieut.-Colonel (Temporary Colonel), M.V.O., Royal Engineers.
FRITH, GILBERT ROBERTSON, Major and Brevet Lieut.-Colonel, Royal Engineers.
GAIRDNER, ERIC DALRYMPLE, Capt., M.B., Royal Army Medical Corps (T.F.).
GALLIE, JAMES STUART, Lieut.-Colonel, Royal Army Medical Corps.
GATER, GEORGE HENRY, Temporary Major, Nottinghamshire and Derbyshire Regt., Service Battn.
GEMMELL, WILLIAM ALEXANDER STEWART, Major, Reserve of Officers, Royal Horse Artillery (T.F.).
GIBBONS, THOMAS, Capt. (Temporary Lieut.-Colonel), Essex Regt. (T.F.).
GILES, EDWARD DOUGLAS, Capt., 35th Scinde Horse, Indian Army
GLASFURD, ALEXANDER INGLIS ROBERTSON, Major, 46th Punjabis, Indian Army.
GLASGOW, ALFRED EDGAR, Major (Temporary Lieut.-Colonel), Royal Sussex Regt., Commanding Service Battn.
GOLDSMITH, HARRY DUNDAS, Major, Duke of Cornwall's Light Infantry.
GORDON, BERTRAND GORGES REGINALD, Major (Temporary Lieut.-Colonel), Gordon Highlanders.
GORDON, EVELYN BOSCAWEN, Major, Northumberland Fusiliers.
GORDON, EDWARD HYDE HAMILTON, Temporary Lieut.-Colonel, Commanding Service Battn. Gordon Highlanders.
GRANT, ARTHUR KENNETH, Major, Royal West Kent Regt.
GRANT, DUDLEY HARCOURT FLEMING, Major (Temporary Lieut.-Colonel), Lincolnshire Regt.
GRAY, CLIVE OSRIC VERE, Major, Seaforth Highlanders.
GRAY, JOHN ANSELM SAMUEL, Temporary Lieut.-Colonel, Special List.
GRECH, JOHN, Lieut.-Colonel, Royal Army Medical Corps.
GREEN, HENRY CLIFFORD RODES, Major (Temporary Lieut.-Colonel), King's Royal Rifle Corps, Commanding Service Battn.
GRIFFITH, JOHN JOSEPH, Major, F.R.C.V.S., Army Veterinary Corps.
HAMERSLEY, HAROLD ST. GEORGE, Capt. (Temporary Major), Army Service Corps.
HAMILTON, CLAUD LORN CAMPBELL, Lieut.-Colonel, Royal Artillery.
HAMILTON, JAMES MELVILL, Capt. and Brevet Major, Gordon Highlanders.
HAMILTON-STUBBER, ROBERT, Major, South Irish Horse, attached 1st Life Guards.
HAMMOND, REGINALD CHALMERS, Major, Royal Engineers.
HARMAN, ANTONY ERNEST WENTWORTH, Major (Temporary Lieut.-Colonel), 2nd Dragoon Guards, Commanding 18th Hussars.
HAYTER, HERBERT ROCHE, Major (Temporary Lieut.-Colonel), Army Service Corps.
HEDLEY, JOHN RAPH, Major (Temporary Lieut.-Colonel), Northumberland Fusiliers (T.F.), Commanding Territorial Battn. Border Regt.
HENDERSON, KENNETH, Major, 39th Garhwal Rifles, Indian Army
HENDERSON, PATRICK HAGART, Major, M.B., Royal Army Medical Corps.
HENLEY, THE HONOURABLE ANTHONY MORTON, Capt. and Brevet Major (Temporary Lieut.-Colonel), 5th Lancers.
HERBERT, LOUIS WILLIAM, Major, South Lancashire Regt., Special Reserve.
HERON, GEORGE WYKEHAM, Major, Royal Army Medical Corps.
HESLOP, ALFRED HERBERT, Capt., M.B., Royal Army Medical Corps.
HEWITT, THE HONOURABLE EVELYN JAMES, Capt., Dorset Regt.
HEYWOOD, CECIL PERCIVAL, Major (Temporary Lieut.-Colonel), Coldstream Guards.
HICKLING, CHARLES LAWRENCE, Major, Royal Artillery.
HILL, WALTER PITTS HENDY, Major, Royal Fusiliers.
HOARE, LIONEL LENNARD, Major, Army Ordnance Department.
HOBKIRK, CLARENCE JOHN, Major (Temporary Lieut.-Colonel), Essex Regt., Temporarily Commanding Service Battn.
HODGKINS, JOHN ROWLAND, Capt. (Temporary Major), F.R.C.V.S., Army Veterinary Corps.
HODSOLL, FRANK, Temporary Major, Army Service Corps.
HOGG, PHILIP GRANVILLE HARDINGE, Major, Royal Engineers.
HOLBROOK, ARTHUR ERNEST, Major, Army Service Corps.

HUGHES, EDMUND LOCOCK, Major, Northampton Regt.
HUNT, THOMAS EDWARD CAREW, Major, Royal Berkshire Regt.
HUNTER, CHARLES FINLAYSON, Major, 4th Dragoon Guards.
HUSBAND, GEORGE STAUNTON, Capt., M.B., Indian Medical Service.
INGPEN, PERCY LEIGH, Major (Temporary Lieut.-Colonel), West Yorkshire Regt.
INGRAM, JOHN O'DONNELL, Major, Gloucestershire Regt.
JACKSON, GEORGE SCOTT, Capt. (Temporary Lieut.-Colonel), Northumberland Fusiliers (T.F.).
JAMESON, EDMOND JAMES, Major, Leinster Regt., Special Reserve.
JARVIS, EDWARD HARVEY, Major, Royal Inniskilling Fusiliers, Special Reserve.
JELLICOE, RICHARD VINCENT, Major, Reserve of Officers, late Royal Engineers.
JENNER, LEOPOLD CHRISTIAN DUNCAN, Capt. (Temporary Major), Reserve of Officers, late King's Royal Rifle Corps.
JOHNSTON, FRANCIS GARVEN DILLON, Major, Royal Field Artillery (T.F.).
JONES, CONRAD ROUTH, Capt. (Temporary Lieut.-Colonel), Army Ordnance Department.
JONES, WILLIAM ALLEN FRERE, Major, Royal Artillery.
JUPE, PHILIP WALTER, Temporary Major, Motor Machine Gun Service.
KAYE, HAROLD SWIFT, Major, Yorkshire Light Infantry.
KELLNER, PHILIP TRAVICE RUBIE, Temporary Major, Royal Engineers.
KELLY, WILLIAM HYDE, Capt., Royal Engineers.
KENNEDY, HENRY BREWSTER PERCY LION, Major (Temporary Lieut.-Colonel), King's Royal Rifle Corps, Commanding 1/21st Battn. London Regt. (T.F.).
KING, WILLIAM ALBERT DE COURCY, Major, Royal Engineers.
KIRKE, WALTER MERVYN ST. GEORGE, Major and Brevet Lieut.-Colonel, Royal Artillery.
KIRKWOOD, JAMES GEORGE, Temporary Major, Gloucestershire Regt., Service Battn.
KITCHIN, CHARLES EDWARD, Capt. (Temporary Lieut.-Colonel), Reserve of Officers, Temporarily Commanding Service Battn. South Wales Borderers.
KNIGHT, CHARLES LOUIS WILLIAM MORLEY, Capt. (Temporary Lieut.-Colonel), late Reserve of Officers, Royal Artillery.
KNOTT, JAMES LEADBITTER, Temporary Major, West Yorkshire Regt., Service Battn.
LANG, BERTRAM JOHN, Major (Temporary Lieut.-Colonel), Argyll and Sutherland Highlanders.
LANYON, OWEN MORTIMER, Major, Royal Artillery.
LAW, FREDERICK WILLIAM BERNARDINE, Capt. (Temporary Lieut.-Colonel), South Staffordshire Regt. (T.F.).
LEA, PERCY GERALD PARKER, Major (Temporary Lieut.-Colonel), Army Service Corps.
LEWES, PRICE KINNEAR, Major, Royal Artillery.
LEWIS, ERNEST ALBERT, Major, Royal Engineers (T.F.).
LIDBURY, DAVID JOHN, Major, Royal Engineers, Special Reserve.
LISTER, FREDERICK HAMILTON, Major, Royal Artillery.
LUCEY, WALTER FRANCIS, Major, Royal Field Artillery (T.F.).
LYNCH, COLMER WILLIAM DONALD, Capt. (Temporary Lieut.-Colonel), Reserve of Officers, Commanding Service Battn. Yorkshire Light Infantry.
LYON, CLAUDE DARCY GEORGE, Major, Royal Artillery.
McALLISTER, EDMUND JOSEPH, Major (Temporary Lieut.-Colonel), Army Service Corps.
McCONAGHEY, MAURICE EDWIN, Major (Temporary Lieut.-Colonel), Royal Scots Fusiliers.
McCONAGHY, JOHN GERALD, Capt., 25th Cavalry, Indian Army.
MACDONALD, ARTHUR GABELL, Major, Royal Berkshire Regt.
MACDONALD, KENNETH LACHLAN, Major, 1st Lovat's Scouts, Yeomanry.
MACHELL, PERCY WILFRID, Capt. (Temporary Lieut.-Colonel), C.M.G (retired), Commanding Service Battn. Border Regt.
MACKENZIE, GEORGE BIRNIE, Major and Brevet Lieut.-Colonel, Royal Artillery.
McLACHLAN, JAMES DOUGLAS, Lieut.-Colonel (Temporary Brigadier-General), Cameron Highlanders.
MACLACHLAN, RONALD CAMPBELL, Lieut.-Colonel, Rifle Brigade, Commanding Service Battn.
MAGNIAC, MEREDITH, Major, Lancashire Fusiliers.
MAITLAND, CLAUD ARCHIBALD SCOTT, Major, Gordon Highlanders.
MAN, HUBERT WILLIAM, Major, Army Ordnance Department.
MARSHALL, HENRY SEYMOUR, Major, Royal Artillery.
MARTEL, GIFFARD LE QUESNE, Capt., Royal Engineers.
MASON, GLYN KEITH MURRAY, Capt., 14th Hussars.
MASSY, SEATON DUNHAM, Capt. and Brevet Major, Royal Flying Corps, Indian Army.
MATTHEWS, WALTER HUDSON, Lieut.-Colonel, 19th Battn. London Regt. (T.F.).
MEADE-WALDO, EDMUND RICHARD, Major, Rifle Brigade.
MELDON, PHILIP ALBERT, Major, Royal Artillery.
MELLOR, ABEL, Major, Royal Artillery.
MENZIES, GEORGE FEILDEN, Major (Temporary Lieut.-Colonel), Reserve of Officers, Commanding Service Battn. Durham Light Infantry.
MERRIMAN, ARTHUR DRUMMOND NAIRNE, Major, Royal Irish Rifles.
METCALFE, FRANCIS EDWARD, Temporary Major (Temporary Lieut.-Colonel), Temporarily Commanding Service Battn. Lincolnshire Regt.
MOBERLY, ARCHIBALD HENRY, Major, Royal Artillery.
MONTEAGLE-BROWNE, EDGAR, Temporary Lieut.-Colonel, Royal Munster Fusiliers, Service Battn.
MOORE, MAXTON, Major (Temporary Lieut.-Colonel), Army Service Corps.

MORRIS, GEORGE WILLIAM STERNE, Major, Royal Field Artillery, Special Reserve.
MORRISON, JAMES ARCHIBALD, Capt. (Temporary Major), Reserve of Officers, Grenadier Guards.
MOUSLEY, JOHN HAROLD, Capt. (Temporary Major), Royal Engineers (T.F.).
MOZLEY, EDWARD NEWMAN, Major, Royal Engineers.
MURRAY-THREIPLAND, WILLIAM, Lieut.-Colonel, Welsh Guards.
MUSGRAVE, EDWARD CHRISTOPHER, Temporary Major, King's Royal Rifle Corps, Service Battn.
MUSPRATT, SYDNEY FREDERICK, Capt. (Temporary Lieut.-Colonel), 12th Cavalry, Indian Army.
NEWELL, ETHELBERT MONK, Major and Brevet Lieut.-Colonel, Royal Engineers (T.F.).
NEWELL, STANLEY MONK, Major (Temporary Lieut.-Colonel), Royal Engineers (T.F.).
NEWTON, HENRY, Capt., Nottinghamshire and Derbyshire Regt. (T.F.).
NIBLETT, HERBERT, Temporary Major, Army Service Corps.
NICHOLSON, WALTER NORRIS, Major, Suffolk Regt.
NIVEN, OSWALD CARMICHAEL, Major, Royal Artillery.
NIXON, JAMES ARUNDEL, Major (Temporary Lieut.-Colonel), Royal Lancaster Regt.
NORMAN, EDWARD HUBERT, Major (Temporary Lieut.-Colonel), Royal West Kent Regt., Commanding 1/7th Battn. London Regt. (T.F.).
NORTHEN, ARTHUR, Major (Temporary Lieut.-Colonel), Army Service Corps.
NUGENT, WALTER VYVIAN, Major, Royal Artillery.
OLDHAM, GEORGE MUIR, Major, Royal Engineers.
ORMSBY, THOMAS, Major, Army Pay Department.
ORPEN-PALMER, REGINALD ARTHUR HERBERT, Major, Leinster Regt.
OSBURN, ARTHUR CARR, Major (Temporary Lieut.-Colonel), Royal Army Medical Corps.
O'SHEA, TIMOTHY, Quartermaster and Honorary Major, 9th Battn. London Regt. (T.F.).
OWEN, SYDNEY LLOYD, Major, Royal Engineers.
PACKE, WILLIAM VERE, Major, Royal Field Artillery, Special Reserve.
PAGE, CUTHBERT FREDERICK GRAHAM, Major, Royal Artillery.
PAGET, CECIL WALTER, Temporary Lieut.-Colonel, Royal Engineers.
PEIRS, HUGH JOHN CHEVALLIER, Temporary Major, Royal West Surrey Regt., Service Battn.
PELHAM, THE HONOURABLE DUDLEY ROGER HUGH, Capt. (Temporary Lieut.-Colonel), Reserve of Officers, late 10th Hussars.
PHIPPS, CHARLES FOSKETT, Major and Brevet Lieut.-Colonel, Royal Artillery.
PILKINGTON, WILLIAM NORMAN, Major, South Lancashire Regt. (T.F.).
POLLARD-LOWSLEY, HERBERT DE LISLE, Major, C.I.E., Royal Engineers.
POPE, SYDNEY BUXTON, Capt., 58th Vaughan Rifles, Indian Army.
POTTER, CLAUD FURNISS, Major, Royal Artillery.
POWELL, PHILIP LIONEL WILLIAM, Major, Welsh Regt.
PRENTICE, ROBERT EMILE SHEPHERD, Major (Temporary Lieut.-Colonel), Highland Light Infantry.
PRIOR, HAROLD ASTLEY SOMERSET, Temporary Major, Yorkshire Regt., Service Battn.
PRITTIE, THE HONOURABLE HENRY CORNELIUS O'CALLAGHAN, Major, Rifle Brigade.
PROWSE, CHARLES BERTIE, Major and Brevet Lieut.-Colonel (Temporary Brigadier-General), Somerset Light Infantry.
PURVIS, JOHN HENRY, Capt. and Brevet Major (Temporary Lieut.-Colonel), Reserve of Officers, Commanding Service Battn. Highland Light Infantry.
RADCLIFFE, PERCY POLLEXFEN DE BLAQUIERE, Major and Brevet Lieut.-Colonel (Temporary Brigadier-General), Royal Artillery.
RAMSAY, HILTON ALEXANDER, Major, Royal Artillery.
RAYMER, ROBERT RICHMOND, Major (Temporary Lieut.-Colonel), South Staffordshire Regt. (T.F.).
RAYNER, WILLIAM BRYAN FLEETWOOD, Major, Royal Fusiliers.
READMAN, JOHN JEFFREY, Capt., 2nd Dragoons.
REBSCH, WILLIAM KNOWLES, Capt., S. and T. Corps, Indian Army.
REID, FREDERIC JAMES, Major (Temporary Lieut.-Colonel), Army Service Corps.
RIGG, EDWARD HARRISON, Major (Temporary Lieut.-Colonel), Yorkshire Light Infantry.
ROBERTSON, ALEXANDER, Capt. (Temporary Major), Royal Engineers (T.F.).
ROGERS, HUGH STUART, Major, Shropshire Light Infantry.
ROLLAND, ALEXANDER, Major (Temporary Lieut.-Colonel), Royal Engineers.
ROSS, ARTHUR JUSTIN, Capt. and Brevet Major, Royal Engineers and Royal Flying Corps.
RUSSELL-BROWN, CLAUDE, Major and Brevet Lieut.-Colonel (Temporary Lieut.-Colonel), Royal Engineers.
SANDERS, ARTHUR RICHARD CARELESS, Major and Brevet Lieut.-Colonel, Royal Engineers.
SANGSTER, PATRICK BARCLAY, Major, 2nd Lancers, Indian Army.
SAUNDERS, REGINALD GEORGE FRANCIS, Temporary Major, Army Service Corps.
SAWYER, GUY HENRY, Major, Royal Berkshire Regt.
SCAFE, WILLIAM ERNEST, Major, Devonshire Regt.
SCAMMELL, ALFRED GEORGE, Major, Royal Field Artillery (T.F.).
SCOTT, JOHN CREAGH, Major, Argyll and Sutherland Highlanders.
SEWELL, EVELYN PIERCE, M.B., Lieut.-Colonel, Royal Army Medical Corps.
SEYMOUR, LORD HENRY CHARLES, Major (Temporary Lieut.-Colonel), Grenadier Guards.

SHANNON, WILLIAM JOHN, Major, 16th Lancers.
SHUTE, JOHN JOSEPH, Major (Temporary Lieut.-Colonel), Liverpool Regt. (T.F.).
SINCLAIR, JOHN NORMAN, Major, Royal Artillery.
SKINNER, EDWARD JOHN, Major, Royal Artillery.
SMALES, WILLIAM CLAYTON, Capt., Royal Army Medical Corps.
SMITH, GEORGE ALEXANDER, Major (Temporary Lieut.-Colonel), Gordon Highlanders (T.F.), Temporarily Commanding Service Battn. Royal Lancaster Regt.
SMITH, HARRY REGINALD WALTER MARRIOTT, Major (Temporary Lieut.-Colonel), Royal Artillery.
SMITH, JOHN GRANT, Major (Temporary Lieut.-Colonel), Seaforth Highlanders (T.F.).
SNOW, HUMPHRY WAUGH, Capt., Reserve of Officers, late Royal West Kent Regt.
SOWERBY, MAURICE EDEN, Capt. (Temporary Major), Royal Engineers.
SPARKES, WILLIAM MOORE BELL, Major, Royal Army Medical Corps.
STANBROUGH, LEONARD KENGON, Major, Royal Artillery.
STEWART, DAVISON BRUCE, Lieut.-Colonel, Royal Artillery.
SUGDEN, RICHARD EDGAR, Capt. (Temporary Major), West Riding Regt. (T.F.).
SUTTON, FREDERICK, Major, Royal Artillery.
SWAINSON, JOSEPH LEONARD, Major, Duke of Cornwall's Light Infantry.
SYDNEY-TURNER, CUTHBERT GAMBIER RYVES, Major (Temporary Lieut.-Colonel), Army Service Corps.
TAYLOR, MAURICE GROVE, Capt., Royal Engineers.
TEMPERLEY, ARTHUR CECIL, Major, Norfolk Regt.
THACKERAY, CHARLES BOUVERIE, Major, R.A.
THOMPSON, FREDERICK VIVIAN, Major, Royal Engineers.
THOMSON, CHARLES PINKERTON, Major, M.D., Royal Army Medical Corps.
THOMSON, NOEL ARBUTHNOT, Major (Temporary Lieut.-Colonel), Seaforth Highlanders, Commanding Service Battn.
THOMSON, ROGER GORDON, Major, Royal Artillery.
TORRENS, GEORGE LESLIE, Lieut. (Temporary Major), West Indian Regt. (employed Service Battn. Lancashire Fusiliers).
UNDERWOOD, JOHN PERCY DELABENE, Capt., North Lancashire Regt. (attached Nigeria Regt.).
VAUGHAN, EDWARD JAMES FORRESTER, Major, Devonshire Regt.
WACE, EDWARD GURTH, Major, Royal Engineers.
WAIT, HUGH GODFREY KILLIGREW, Major, Royal Engineers.
WALKER, JAMES, Capt. (Temporary Major), East Riding of Yorkshire Yeomanry (Temporary Lieut.-Colonel, Commanding Divisional Ammunition Column, Royal Artillery).
WALKER, REGINALD SELBY, Major, Royal Engineers.
WALLACE, HUGH ROBERT, Temporary Lieut.-Colonel, Commanding Reserve Garrison Battn. Suffolk Regt., late Gordon Highlanders, Service Battn.
WALLER, ROBERT JOCELYN ROWAN, Capt., Royal Artillery (attached Nigeria Regt.).
WALLINGER, ERNEST ARNOLD, Major, Royal Engineers.
WALTON, CUSACK, Major, Royal Engineers.
WANNELL, GEORGE EDWARD, Temporary Lieut.-Colonel, Commanding Service Battn. West Riding Regt.
WARRENDER, HUGH VALENTINE, Major (Temporary Lieut.-Colonel), London Regt. (T.F.).
WEBB-JOHNSON, ALFRED EDWARD, Capt. (Temporary Major), M.B., F.R.C.S., Royal Army Medical Corps (T.F.).
WEBBER, NORMAN WILLIAM, Major, Royal Engineers.
WEBER, WILLIAM HERMANN FRANK, Major (Temporary Lieut.-Colonel), Royal Artillery.
WESTLEY, JOSEPH HAROLD STOPS, Capt., Yorkshire Regt.
WETHERED, JOSEPH ROBERT, Major, Gloucestershire Regt.
WHINNEY, HAROLD FIFE, Major, Royal Fusiliers.
WHITE, GEOFFREY HERBERT ANTHONY, Lieut.-Colonel, Royal Artillery.
WHITEHEAD, JAMES, Capt. (Temporary Lieut.-Colonel), 1st Brahmans, Indian Army.
WIGAN, JOHN TYSON, Major (Temporary Lieut.-Colonel), Berkshire Yeomanry, late 13th Hussars.
WILLAN, ROBERT HUGH, Capt. (Temporary Major), King's Royal Rifle Corps (attached Signal Service, Royal Engineers).
WILLIAMS, ROBERT CARLISLE, Major, Royal Artillery.
WILLIS, MONTAGUE HARRY SHERWOOD, Capt., Suffolk Regt. (attached Nigeria Regt.)
WILSON, PATRICK HOGARTH, Major, Royal Artillery (attached Royal Field Artillery) (T.F.).
WINGFIELD, THE HONOURABLE MAURICE ANTHONY, Capt. and Brevet Major (Temporary Lieut.-Colonel), Rifle Brigade.
WYATT, LOUIS JOHN, Major (Temporary Lieut.-Colonel), North Staffordshire Regt., Commanding 4th Battn. York and Lancaster Regt. (T.F.).
YARDLEY, JOHN WATKINS, Lieut.-Colonel, retired pay.

AUSTRALIAN IMPERIAL FORCE.

DARE, CHARLES MORELAND MONTAGUE, Major, 14th Battn.
FITZGERALD, RICHARD FRANCIS, Major, 20th Battn.
FRANCIS, FREDERICK HOWARD, Major, Army Service Corps.
GRANVILLE, CECIL HORACE, Major, 1st Light Horse Regt.
HOLDSWORTH, ALBERT ARMYTAGE, Major, Army Service Corps.
LE MAISTRE, FRANK WILLIAM, Major, 5th Battn.
MARGOLIN, ELIAZAR LAZAR, Major, 16th Battn.
McLEAN, JOHN BARR, Major, Army Medical Corps.
TRAVERS, REGINALD JOHN ALBERT, Major, 17th Battn.

The Distinguished Service Order

WATTS, BERTRAM ALEXANDER GORDON, Major, Royal Australian Garrison Artillery.
WISDOM, EVAN ALEXANDER, Major, Commonwealth Military Forces.
BROWN, THOMAS FREDERICK, Capt., Army Medical Corps.
CAMPBELL, RANALD DOUGLAS, Capt. (Temporary Major), Army Medical Corps.
GRIFFITHS, THOMAS, Honorary Capt., Staff.
LEANE, RAYMOND LIONEL, Capt. (Temporary Lieut.-Colonel), 11th Battn.
LITTLER, CHARLES AUGUSTUS, Capt., 12th Battn.
MILNE, EDMUND OSBORN, Capt., Army Service Corps.
BRACEGIRDLE, LEIGHTON SEYMOUR, Acting Lieut.-Commander, Royal Australian Naval Bridging Train.

CANADIAN FORCE.

ADAMSON, AGAR STUART ALLAN MASTERTON, Major, Princess Patricia's Canadian Light Infantry.
ALLAN, WILLIAM DONALD, Lieut.-Colonel, 3rd Infantry Battn.
BROOK, REGINALD JAMES, Major, 3rd Infantry Battn.
BRUTINEL, RAYMOND, Lieut.-Colonel, Canadian Motor Machine Gun Brigade
BUCHANAN, VICTOR CARL, Lieut.-Colonel, 13th Infantry Battn.
CAMERON, ALEXANDER GEORGE, Major, 13th Infantry Battn.
CRITCHLEY, ALFRED CECIL, Major, Lord Strathcona's Horse.
DOCHERTY, MALCOLM, Major, Lord Strathcona's Horse.
ELMSLEY, JAMES HAROLD, Brevet Lieut.-Colonel, Royal Canadian Dragoons.
FORD, ELROYD, Major, 15th Divisional Signal Company (corrected to 1st Canadian Divisional Signal Company).
GRAY, DONALD FAVILIE BRANSTON, Major, Princess Patricia's Canadian Light Infantry.
HAINES, LESLIE EARLS, Major, 7th Infantry Battn.
IRVING, THOMAS CRAIK, Major, Canadian Engineers.
McAVITY, THOMAS MALCOLM, Major, 5th Canadian Infantry Brigade.
MILLS, JAMES EDGAR, Major, Royal Canadian Horse Artillery.
MITCHELL, CHARLES HAMILTON, Lieut.-Colonel, Canadian Force.
MORRISEY, THOMAS SYDNEY, Major, 13th Infantry Battn.
SHANLY, COOTE NISBITT, Lieut.-Colonel, Canadian Army Pay Corps.

NEW ZEALAND IMPERIAL FORCE.

GRIGOR, ROBERT RENTON, Lieut.-Colonel, Otago Mounted Rifle Regt.
AUSTEN, WILLIAM SEMMERS, Major, 1st Battn. New Zealand Rifle Brigade.
AVERY, HENRY ESAU, Major, No. 1 Company, Divisional Train.
HURST, HERBERT CLARENCE, Major, Canterbury Mounted Rifle Regt.
KING, GEORGE AUGUSTUS, Major, Staff Corps.
POWLES, CHARLES GUY, Capt. (Temporary Lieut.-Colonel), Staff Corps.
WYMAN, RALPH, Major, Auckland Mounted Rifle Regt.

SOUTH AFRICAN DEFENCE FORCES.

BAKER, JAMES MITCHELL, Major (Temporary Major in Army).

London Gazette, 22 June, 1916.—" Admiralty, S.W., 22 June, 1916. The King has been graciously pleased to give orders for the appointment of the undermentioned Officers to be Companions of the Distinguished Service Order."
CORBETT, ROBERT GWYNNE, Capt., R.N. In recognition of his services in the cruisers engaged in the North Atlantic Patrol since the outbreak of the war.
WARDLE, THOMAS ERSKINE, Capt., R.N. In recognition of his services in command of H.M.S. Alcantara on the 29th Feb. 1916, when he engaged and sank S.M.S. Greif.
GROVES, ROBERT MARSLAND, Commander, R.N. (Wing Commander, R.N.A.S.). In recognition of his services in command of a Wing of the Royal Naval Air Service at Dunkirk. Commander Groves has by his personal skill as a pilot, and also by his untiring zeal, effected a marked advancement in the general standard of flying on active service. He has on several occasions carried out successful reconnaissances to Ostend under fire, and by his own example has proved the utility and great importance of night flying.
GERRARD, EUGENE LOUIS, Capt. and Brevet Major (Temporary Lieut.-Colonel), R.M. (Wing Commander, R.N.A.S.). In recognition of his services in command of a Wing of the R.N.A.S. in the Eastern Mediterranean. The present efficiency of this Wing is due very largely to Wing Commander Gerrard, whose personal example and the manner in which he has encouraged the younger officers under his command are all that can be desired.
SMITH, HENRY FRANK, Engineer Commander, R.N. In recognition of his services in one of the cruisers engaged in the North Atlantic Patrol since the outbreak of war.
OLIVER, DOUGLAS AUSTIN, Lieut., R.N. (Squadron Commander, R.N.A.S.). In recognition of his services on the morning of the 25th April, 1916, when he pursued out to sea the enemy fleet which had bombarded Yarmouth, and flew along the line dropping bombs, being subjected to intense anti-aircraft fire.
WILLIAMS, CHARLES ALFRED NORTON, Engineer Lieut.-Commander, R.N.R. In recognition of his services in charge of the engine-room of H.M.S. Alcantara on the 29th Feb. 1916, during the action with S.M.S. Greif.
SAVORY, KENNETH STEVENS, Flight Lieut., R.N.A.S.
DICKINSON, RICHARD SEBASTIAN WILLOUGHBY, Flight Sub-Lieut., R.N.A.S.
In recognition of their services on the night of the 14th-15th April, 1916, when they carried out a flight to Constantinople and dropped bombs upon points of military importance, returning safely to their base after a long flight in rough and stormy weather.
MULOCK, REDFORD HENRY, Flight Lieut. (Acting Flight Commander), R.N.A.S. In recognition of his services as a pilot at Dunkirk. This officer has been constantly employed at Dunkirk since July, 1915, and has displayed indefatigable zeal and energy. He has on several occasions engaged hostile aeroplanes and seaplanes, and attacked submarines, and has carried out attacks on enemy air stations, and made long-distance reconnaissances.
DALBIAC, JOHN HENRY, Lieut., R.M.A. In recognition of his services as an aeroplane observer at Dunkirk since Feb. 1915. During the past year Lieut. Dalbiac has been continually employed in coastal reconnaissances and fighting patrols. The Vice-Admiral Commanding the Dover Patrol, in reporting on the work of the R.N.A.S. at Dunkirk, lays particular emphasis on the good work done by the observers.

London Gazette, 24 June, 1916.—" War Office, 24 June, 1916. His Majesty the King has been graciously pleased to approve of the appointment of the undermentioned Officers to be Companions of the Distinguished Service Order, in recognition of their gallantry and devotion to duty in the field."
GRIESBACH, WILLIAM ANTROBUS, Lieut.-Colonel, 49th Canadian Infantry Battn. For conspicuous gallantry and skill in the handling of his battalion during a heavy bombardment and subsequent attack by the enemy. On another occasion by his prompt action and fine example he was largely responsible for the rescue of several men who had been buried by shell fire.
PEACOCKE, WARREN JOHN, Temporary Major, 9th Battn. Royal Inniskilling Fusiliers. For conspicuous gallantry and ability. He organized and commanded with great skill a successful raid on the enemy's trenches, and displayed great coolness throughout. He succeeded in bringing in all his wounded in spite of heavy shell fire.
KNOTT, JOHN ESPENETT, Temporary Capt., 8th Battn. Royal Inniskilling Fusiliers. For conspicuous gallantry and devotion to duty. By his fine example and coolness during an enemy attack he kept up the discipline and fine spirit of his company under very difficult and trying circumstances.
MAXWELL, ARTHUR, Capt. (Temporary Lieut.-Colonel), 8th Battn. London Regt. (T.F.). For conspicuous gallantry and devotion to duty. When the enemy, after an intense bombardment, penetrated a portion of our trench, Lieut.-Colonel Maxwell, though wounded by shrapnel, personally organized two counter-attacks, and refused to leave his post till ordered next day to do so.
UNIACKE, EVELYN WILLIAM PIERREPONT, Capt. (Temporary Major), 2nd Regt., King Edward's Horse (attached 8th Battn. Royal Irish Fusiliers). For conspicuous gallantry and devotion to duty. When a party of the enemy had penetrated into an unoccupied portion of our trench, he organized bombing parties, one of which he led himself, and, though twice severely wounded continued to fight till the enemy were driven out.
BRUNGER, ROBERT, Lieut. (Temporary Capt.), 4th Battn. Suffolk Regt. (T.F.). For conspicuous gallantry when leading a successful raid on the enemy's trenches. Although the enemy were alert and offered a strong resistance he inflicted considerable loss, and finally withdrew skilfully with only few casualties.
HAPPOLD, FREDERICK CROSSFIELD, Temporary Second Lieut., 9th Battn. North Lancashire Regt. For conspicuous gallantry. When the enemy exploded a mine, he at once collected a few men, rushed up and out-bombed a far larger force of the enemy in the crater until reinforcements arrived. After being wounded he continued to lead and encourage his party.

London Gazette, 24 June, 1916.—" War Office, 24 June, 1916. The undermentioned Officers have been awarped the Distinguished Service Order, and the specific acts for which the rewards have been granted will be announced as soon as possible in the London Gazette." (See London Gazette, 27 July, 1916.)
KITSON, CHARLES EDWARD, Major and Brevet Lieut.-Colonel, 2nd Battn. Royal West Kent Regt.
ROSS, JOHN ALEXANDER, Major, 24th Canadian Infantry Battn.
BATTYE, BASIL CONDON, Capt. and Brevet Major, Royal Engineers.
DOPPING-HEPENSTAL, MAXWELL EDWARD, Major, 1st Battn. 1st Gurkha Rifles, Indian Army.
HUNT, HENRY RICHARD AUGUSTUS, Capt. and Brevet Major, 25th Punjabis, Indian Army (attached 142nd Infantry Brigade).
ATKINSON, GUY MONTAGUE, Capt. (Temporary Major), 1st Battn. King's Royal Rifle Corps.
CAMPBELL, ALEXANDER, Capt., 12th Field Company, Royal Engineers.
DAWSON, WALTER, Temporary Capt., M.B., Royal Army Medical Corps.
GOW, PETER FLEMING, Capt., M.B., Indian Medical Service.
HAMILTON, ERNEST GRAHAM, Capt., Connaught Rangers.
HOBART, PERCY CLEGHORN STANLEY, Capt., Royal Engineers (attached 1st Sappers and Miners, Indian Army).
MILLER, WILLIAM ARCHIBALD, Capt., M.B., Royal Army Medical Corps, Special Reserve (attached 22nd Battn. Royal Fusiliers).
HERD, HERBERT JAMES, Second Lieut. (Temporary Lieut.), 1/7th Battn. Royal Highlanders (T.F.).

London Gazette, 26 June, 1916.—" War Office, 26 June, 1916. His Majesty the King has been graciously pleased to approve of the undermentioned rewards for Distinguished Service in the field, dated 3 June, 1916. Awarded the Distinguished Service Order."
BATTYE, IVAN URMSTON, Major, Corps of Guides, Indian Army.
BEALE-BROWNE, DESMOND JOHN EDWARD, Major and Brevet Lieut.-Colonel (Temporary Brigadier-General), 9th Lancers.
BEAMAN, ARDERN ARTHUR HULME, Capt., 1st Lancers, Indian Army.
BROWN, ROBERT TILBURY, Major, M.D., Royal Army Medical Corps.
BUTLER, JOHN FITZHARDINGE PAUL, Capt., V.C., King's Royal Rifle Corps.
COLLINS, CHARLES BURY, Lieut.-Colonel, Royal Engineers.
COLSTON, EDWARD MURRAY, Major, M.V.O., Grenadier Guards.
CROOKENDEN, JOHN, Major, East Kent Regt.
DUNLOP, WILLIAM BRUCE, Capt. (Temporary Major), S. & T. Corps, Indian Army.
FANSHAWE, LIONEL ARTHUR, Major, Royal Artillery.
FINLAY, ROBERT FRANCIS, Major, 58th Rifles, Indian Army.
GALLAGHER, MICHAEL (name Michael corrected to Maurice), Honorary Major, Works Manager, Uganda Railway.
HAWTREY, HENRY COURTENAY, Capt. (Temporary Major), Royal Engineers.
HOLLAND-PRYOR, POMEROY, Lieut.-Colonel (Temporary Brigadier-General), M.V.O., 1st Lancers, Indian Army.
JOHNSTON, GEORGE NAPIER, Lieut.-Colonel (Temporary Brigadier-General), Royal Artillery.
KEBLE, ALFRED ERNEST CONQUER, Lieut.-Colonel (Temporary Colonel), Royal Army Medical Corps.
LINTON, CHARLES STRANGWAY, Major, Worcester Regt.
MOBERLY, MAURICE, Temporary Major, Egyptian Camel Transport Corps.

ROUTH, GUY MONTGOMERY, Major, Royal Artillery.

SKINNER, HENRY TERENCE, Capt., 29th Punjabis, Indian Army.

STORDY, ROBERT JOHN, Temporary Lieut.-Colonel, Army Veterinary Corps.

WATKINS, OSCAR FERRIS, Temporary Major, East Africa Transport Corps.

London Gazette, 14 July, 1916.—"Admiralty, 14 July, 1916. The Lords Commissioners of the Admiralty have received with much satisfaction from the officers in charge of the Auxiliary Patrol areas at home and abroad reports on the services performed by the officers and men serving under their orders during the period 1 Jan. 1915, to 31 Jan. 1916. These reports show that the officers and men serving in Armed Yachts, Trawlers and Drifters of the Auxiliary Patrol during the period in question have carried out their duties under extremely arduous and hazardous conditions of weather and exposure to enemy attack and mines with marked zeal, gallantry and success.

"The King has been graciously pleased to give orders for the following appointments to the Distinguished Service Order, in recognition of the services referred to in the reports mentioned above. To be Companions of the Distinguished Service Order."

HOWARD, WILLIAM VANSITTART, Capt., R.N.

SMITH, SUTTON, Commander, R.N.

BOOTHBY, EVELYN LEONARD BERIDGE, Commander, R.N.

MARSHALL, WILLIAM, Commander, R.D., R.N.R.

GIBB, ALFRED SPENCER, Commander, R.D., R.N.R.

ARCHER, HUGH EDWARD MURRAY, Lieut.-Commander, R.N.

VENN, GEORGE WILLIAM CAVENDISH, Lieut.-Commander (Acting-Commander), R.N.R.

"The King has also been graciously pleased to give orders for the following appointments to the Distinguished Service Order to the undermentioned Officers, in recognition of their services in connection with the evacuation of the Serbian Army and Italian troops from Durazzo in Dec. 1915, and Jan. and Feb. 1916. To be Companions of the Distinguished Service Order."

CRAMPTON, DENIS BURKE, Capt., M.V.O., R.N.

HATCHER, JAMES OLDEN, Commander, R.N.

COCHRANE, MORRIS EDWARD, Lieut.-Commander, R.N.

"The King has further been graciously pleased to approve of the following appointments to the Distinguished Service Order to the undermentioned Officers, in recognition of the services stated. To be Companions of the Distinguished Service Order."

BRIDGEMAN, THE HON. RICHARD ORLANDO BEACONSFIELD, Commander, R.N. Commander Bridgeman displayed great courage and coolness on the 19th Aug. 1915, in command of two whalers which proceeded into Tanga Harbour. The manner in which the whalers endeavoured, though subjected to a heavy and accurate fire, to carry out their orders and board the S.S. Markgraf was worthy of the best traditions of the Royal Navy.

BRIDGES, HENRY DALRYMPLE, Commander, R.N. Commander Bridges proceeded into Sudi Harbour with two whalers on the 11th April, 1916, and remained under fire with two vessels in a very hot corner, spotting the fall of shot from H.M.S. Hyacinth to enable her to destroy a store ship which was in the harbour. In order to reach the requisite position the whalers were obliged to run up a narrow harbour, where they were confronted with a heavy fire from 4-inch guns at close range.

London Gazette, 25 July, 1916.—"Admiralty, 25 July, 1916. Officers (amongst others) specially recommended in the Despatch dated 29 May, 1916, of Vice-Admiral Sir Reginald H. S. Bacon, Commanding the Dover Patrol, reporting the operations of the Dover Patrol since 3 Dec. 1915."

GIBBS, GEORGE LOUIS DOWNALL, Commander. Commanded a Division of Destroyers with marked ability and dash in action against the enemy.

OLIPHANT, HENRY GERARD LAURENCE, Commander, M.V.O. Commanded a Division of Destroyers in action and on patrol duties off the enemy's coast.

HANCOCK, REGINALD LIONEL, Commander. Carried out surveying operations of considerable importance under heavy gun fire off the enemy's coast.

"Admiralty, 25 July, 1916. The King has been graciously pleased to give orders for the following appointments to the undermentioned Officers, in recognition of their services as mentioned in the foregoing Despatch. To be Companions of the Distinguished Service Order."

GIBBS, GEORGE LOUIS DOWNALL, Commander, R.N.

HANCOCK, REGINALD LIONEL, Commander, R.N.

OLIPHANT, HENRY GERARD LAURENCE, Commander, M.V.O., Royal Navy.

London Gazette, 27 July, 1916.—"War Office, 27 July, 1916. His Majesty the King has been graciously pleased to approve of the appointment of the undermentioned Officers to be Companions of the Distinguished Service Order, in recognition of their gallantry and devotion to duty in the field."

BATTYE, BASIL CONDON, Capt. and Brevet Major, Royal Engineers. For conspicuous gallantry and ability during a period of active operations. His skill and energy in sending forward reinforcements and ammunition under very difficult circumstances tended much to the success of the operations. He had previously made a personal reconnaissance of great value.

DOPPING-HEPENSTAL, MAXWELL EDWARD, Major, 1st Battn. 1st Gurkha Rifles, Indian Army. For conspicuous gallantry when leading his battalion in the attack under heavy rifle and machine-gun fire.

HUNT, HENRY RICHARD AUGUSTUS, Capt. and Brevet Major, 25th Punjabis, Indian Army (attached 142nd Infantry Brigade). For untiring and invaluable work as Brigade Major during operations. He was continually exposed to shell fire in the performance of his duties.

KITSON, CHARLES EDWARD, Major and Brevet Lieut.-Colonel, 2nd Battn. Royal West Kent Regt. For conspicuous gallantry and devotion to duty during an attack on the enemy's trenches. He dug his men in under heavy shell, rifle and machine-gun fire, and later returned under heavy fire for a stretcher for a wounded officer. Though himself wounded by three bullets, he remained on duty till unable any longer to walk.

ROSS, JOHN ALEXANDER, Major, 24th Canadian Infantry Battn. For conspicuous gallantry. He volunteered for and carried out, with another officer, a very dangerous reconnaissance in face of heavy fire, and secured information of the utmost value regarding the enemy.

ATKINSON, GUY MONTAGUE, Capt. (Temporary Major), 1st Battn. King's Royal Rifle Corps. For conspicuous coolness and power of command. With his battalion he relieved another battalion under intense shell fire, and quickly got his men into assaulting fo· ation on an extremely difficult and open bit of ground.

CAMPBELL, ALEXAND R, Capt., 12th Field Company, Royal Engineers. For gallant conduct and ex ellent work during an important infantry enterprise. Capt. Campbell controlled the efforts of large working parties, and the work performed was of the greatest importance to our operations. His example and energy were remarkable. He went from point to point over ground heavily swept by fire.

DAWSON, WALTER, Temporary Capt., M.B., Royal Army Medical Corps. For conspicuous gallantry and devotion to duty when dressing the wounded and directing stretcher-bearers in the firing line. At dusk he searched the front himself under heavy rifle fire till every wounded man had been removed.

DENE, HUMPHREY, Capt., 1st Battn. Welsh Guards. For conspicuous gallantry and ability. When in command of an attack his arrangements were such that the enemy were taken by surprise, and he carried his objective without loss. When the enemy counter-attacked next morning, he went over the open to the front line under heavy fire, and controlled a difficult situation with great coolness and skill.

GOW, PETER FLEMING, Capt., M.B., Indian Medical Service. For conspicuous gallantry and devotion to duty on several occasions, notably when he took one end of a stretcher after three bearers had been hit, and brought in a wounded officer.

GRANT-DALTON, STUART, Capt., Yorkshire Regt. and Royal Flying Corps. For conspicuous gallantry and resource. When on return from escort duty his observer, Second Lieut. Paris, discovered one of our machines which had been forced to land in enemy country owing to damage by hostile fire. Capt. Grant-Dalton with great gallantry landed, destroyed the machine, which was past repair, and returned ninety miles to his aerodrome with his observer and the pilot of the other machine.

HAMILTON, ERNEST GRAHAM, Capt., Connaught Rangers. For conspicuous gallantry during an enemy counter-attack. He rallied men of different regiments at a critical time and under heavy rifle fire. His efforts were successful in stopping the enemy.

HOBART, PERCY CLEGHORN STANLEY, Capt., Royal Engineers (attached 1st Sappers and Miners, Indian Army). For conspicuous gallantry when carrying out a series of dangerous reconnaissances under fire, during which he collected much useful information. On one occasion he made gallant efforts to rescue one of his escort, who was wounded; on another occasion he was wounded himself.

HOWELL-PRICE, PHILIP LLEWELLYN, Capt., 1st Battn. Australian Imperial Force. For conspicuous gallantry when leading a party, which he had previously trained, in a successful raid on the enemy trenches. In face of heavy opposition and uncut wire he carried through his attack with great coolness and resource, and saw every officer and man back in our trenches before he returned.

MILLER, WILLIAM ARCHIBALD, Capt., M.B., Royal Army Medical Corps, Special Reserve (attached 22nd (S.) Battn. Royal Fusiliers). For conspicuous gallantry and devotion to duty. Capt. Miller followed the front line of our attack over ground swept by shell, machine gun and rifle fire. He searched in every direction for wounded, and gained valuable information regarding the situation. This he at once communicated and again continued his search for wounded. This officer has on previous occasions shown distinguished gallantry,

MURDIE, ROBERT, Capt., 5th Canadian Infantry Battn. For conspicuous gallantry and ability. During a long continued and very heavy bombardment of his trench by the enemy he set a fine example of cool courage, and by his skilful dispositions materially reduced the casualties.

ROWLETTE, LIONEL MATTHEW, Temporary Lieut., Royal Army Medical Corps (attached 1st Battn. Welsh Guards). For conspicuous gallantry and devotion to duty. During a heavy bombardment he crawled across the open for a considerable distance to attend to two wounded men. Later he went out again and, although twice wounded, dressed the wounds of seven wounded men and tended them till he had to be himself removed.

TOOP, FRANCIS HART, Lieut. (Temporary Capt.), Gloucestershire Regt. (attached 14th Battn.). For conspicuous gallantry and ability during a successful raid on the enemy. When his C.O. had become a casualty he took charge, behaved with great gallantry, and was largely responsible for the success of the operations.

FRAME, ANDREW CARMICHAEL, Second Lieut. (Temporary Capt.), 9th Battn. Highland Light Infantry (T.F.). For conspicuous gallantry and ability. He organized and carried out with great dash a successful raid on the enemy's trenches. Many of the enemy were killed, many prisoners taken and two machine guns destroyed.

HERD, HERBERT JAMES, Second Lieut. (Temporary Lieut.), 1/7th Battn. Royal Highlanders (T.F.). For conspicuous gallantry when in command of a raiding party. Accompanied by a wounded serjeant he completed work which his bombers had failed to do. Under very heavy fire Lieut. Herd carried a wounded serjeant to safety, and on three separate occasions went out under heavy fire to look for missing men.

McCUBBIN, GEORGE REYNOLDS, Second Lieut., Royal Flying Corps, Special Reserve. For conspicuous gallantry and skill. Seeing one of our machines about to engage two Fokkers he at once entered the fight, and his observer shot down one Fokker, which crashed to the ground. On another occasion when returning from a bombing raid he saw one of our machines being followed by a Fokker. He recrossed the lines to the attack and his observer shot down the Fokker. Although very badly wounded in the arm he successfully landed his machine well behind our lines.

MURRAY, SYDNEY, Second Lieut., 2nd Battn. Rifle Brigade. For conspicuous gallantry and determination when leading a raid on the enemy's trenches. He personally entered a dug-out and bombed the few remaining enemy who still offered fight. It was mainly owing to his skilful organization and dash that the raid was completely successful in spite of heavy opposition.

POTTER, JOHN, Temporary Second Lieut., 1st Battn. South Staffordshire Regt. For conspicuous gallantry. During the storming of an enemy position he was the first man to enter it, and then with his platoon captured and held under heavy fire till reinforced an hour later a point of great tactical importance. Later he took part in the assault on another position which was taken owing to his personal gallantry and fine leadership.

WANLISS, HAROLD BOYD, Second Lieut., 29th Battn. (attached 14th Battn)., Australian Imperial Force. For conspicuous gallantry and determination when leading an attacking party during a raid. He forced the wire which was uncut, entered the trench, inflicted heavy loss on the enemy and supervised the withdrawal. While forcing the wire he was wounded in the face, later he was wounded by a bullet in the neck, and finally when withdrawing he was again wounded and had to be carried in. He set a fine example to all with him.

NOTE.—The Officers who were awarded the Distinguished Service Order, as notified on page 6305 of the Gazette of 24th ultimo, are included in the foregoing list, with statement of services now specified.

London Gazette, 27 July, 1916.—" War Office, 27 July, 1916.—The undermentioned Officer has been awarded the Distinguished Service Order, and the specific act for which the reward has been granted will be announced as soon as possible in the London Gazette." (See London Gazette, 19 Aug. 1916.)

DAVIDSON, ADRIAN NORMAN, Capt., Gordon Highlanders, Special Reserve (attached 2nd Battn.).

London Gazette, 27 July, 1916.—" War Office, 27 July, 1916. Gazetted on this date as M.C. for the following services. The M.C. was cancelled and the D.S.O. awarded for the same service." (See London Gazette, 5 Aug. 1916.)

STANWAY, WILLIAM HENRY, Lieut. (Temporary Capt.), 2nd Battn. Royal Welsh Fusiliers. For conspicuous gallantry and ability. When the enemy exploded a large mine which wrecked some 75 yards of our trench, and then attacked in force after bombarding the spot heavily, several officers being incapacitated, Capt. Stanway, who commanded the next company, at once took charge, and after the enemy had been driven off, with great skill and coolness occupied the near lip of the crater and organized the defences.

London Gazette, 28 July, 1916.—" Admiralty, 28 July, 1916. The King has been graciously pleased to give orders for the following appointment to the Distinguished Service Order."

FULLER, CYRIL THOMAS MOULDEN, Capt., C.M.G., Royal Navy. In recognition of the ability and success with which he organized the naval operations in the Cameroons, where he was Senior Naval Officer throughout the campaign.

London Gazette, 5 Aug. 1916.—" War Office, 5 Aug. 1916. *Correction.*—The announcement of the award of the Military Cross in the London Gazette of 27 July, 1916, to Lieut. (Temporary Capt.) William Henry Stanway, 2nd Battn. Royal Welsh Fusiliers, is cancelled. The Distinguished Service Order was awarded, and not the Military Cross."

London Gazette, 18 Aug. 1916.—" War Office, 18 Aug. 1916. His Majesty the King has been graciously pleased to approve of the undermentioned rewards for Distinguished Service in the field. Awarded the Distinguished Service Order."

CHAMBERS, PHILIP ROPER, Brevet Major (Temporary Major), Indian Army.

CHATTERTON, GEORGE DAVENPORT LATHAM, Lieut.-Colonel, Indian Army.

COCHRAN, GEORGE WALKER, Capt. (Temporary Major), Indian Army.

COOK, CHARLES CHESNEY, Lieut.-Colonel, Indian Army.

DARLEY, JAMES RUSSELL, Lieut.-Colonel, Indian Army.

MACDONALD, ARTHUR CAMERON, Temporary Lieut.-Colonel, Royal Engineers.

MACRAE, JOHN CECIL, Capt., Indian Army.

OGG, ARTHUR CHARLES, Major, Indian Army.

RENNY-TAILYOUR, JOHN WINGFIELD, Major, Royal Artillery.

TOBIN, HARRY WALTER, Brevet Major (Temporary Major), Indian Army.

WILLIAMS, LESLIE GWATKIN, Capt., Indian Army.

EAST AFRICAN FORCE.

NUSSEY, ALBERT HENRY MORTIMER, Brevet Lieut.-Colonel, South African Mounted Brigade.

WILKENS, JACOB, Major, 1st South African Horse.

London Gazette, 19 Aug. 1916.—" War Office, 19 Aug. 1916. His Majesty the King has been graciously pleased to approve of the appointment of the undermentioned Officers to be Companions of the Distinguished Service Order, in recognition of their gallantry and devotion to duty in the field."

BIBBY, JAMES VICTOR, Temporary Capt., Northumberland Fusiliers. For conspicuous gallantry when, during operations, he held his own three days and two nights in an exposed position, organizing and leading successful bomb attacks, and being himself constantly attacked.

COBB, ERNEST CHARLES (name Ernest corrected to Edward, 29 Aug. 1916), Capt., Northampton Regt. For conspicuous gallantry and devotion to duty. When he was knocked into a shell hole and his leg was broken in two places by shrapnel, he collected some 20 men, and though himself unable to move, formed them into a bombing post and held his own under constant fire till dark.

DAVIDSON, ADRIAN NORMAN, Capt., Gordon Highlanders, Special Reserve. For conspicuous gallantry and determination during an attack on a strong enemy position. With 50 men he reached a point and held it for seven hours till reinforcements came up, when 600 of the enemy surrendered. His tenacity was largely instrumental in the final capture of the position.

FLETCHER, HERBERT PHILLIPS, Major, Yeomanry. For conspicuous ability and skill in the performance of his special duties, which have been carried out at great personal risk and devotion to duty at all times.

GIMSON, EDWARD CARWARDINE, Temporary Capt., Royal Army Medical Corps. For conspicuous gallantry when continually attending to the wounded under very heavy shell fire. He has displayed the greatest devotion to duty and contempt of personal danger.

GORDON-KIDD, ARTHUR LIONEL, Temporary Second Lieut., Special List and Royal Flying Corps. For conspicuous gallantry, skill and determination. On one occasion he dived his machine from a height of 7,500 feet to 900 feet, and placed a bomb on the enemy's ammunition train, which set it on fire and blocked the line. A few days afterwards he performed another very hazardous undertaking well within the enemy's lines, whilst exposed the whole time to all descriptions of heavy fire.

WATKIN-WILLIAMS, PENROSE LANYON, Temporary Capt., Royal Army Medical Corps. For conspicuous gallantry when tending the wounded for six hours in a shell crater under very heavy shell fire. He was twice knocked over by the explosion of shells, and his coat and putties were ripped by shrapnel.

CANADIAN FORCE.

DENISON, WALTER WALBRIDGE, Major, Canadian Mounted Rifles. For conspicuous gallantry. He held on to his position under an intense bombardment, and later, after retiring in order to make a stand at another post, collected a few men and went back to gather information.

DRAPER, DENIS COLBURN, Major (Temporary Lieut.-Colonel), Canadian Mounted Rifles. For conspicuous gallantry in face of the enemy. He led reinforcements to exposed points, and twice drove off determined hostile counter-attacks. Though himself wounded, he carried his mortally wounded C.O. from the firing line.

HILL, CLAUDE HARDINGE, Lieut.-Colonel, Canadian Infantry. For conspicuous gallantry when in command of his battalion. He repelled several attacks and displayed great coolness and courage in directing bodies of men under heavy fire.

HOBBINS, ALBERT KEEFE, Major, Canadian Infantry. For conspicuous gallantry in face of the enemy. He launched his battalion in counter-attack after his senior Officer had been wounded, and by his fine example and leading seized and held the position gained under heavy hostile fire.

MASON, DOUGLAS HERBERT CAMPBELL, Major, Canadian Infantry. For conspicuous gallantry when commanding an assault. He displayed great dash and, though wounded in the head and foot early in the attack, continued at his post till the objective was gained and secured.

McCALLUM, ERIC EDWARD NAPIER, Lieut., Canadian Infantry. For conspicuous gallantry. When on patrol with two scouts, one of the latter was killed and the other wounded. Although himself wounded three times in the back and once in the leg, he dressed the other man and carried him some 600 yards under shell fire into safety.

McMORDIE, STEWART PERCIVAL, Major, Canadian Pioneers. For conspicuous gallantry and devotion to duty, notably when assisting to consolidate some newly-won trenches. Though severely wounded in the head and arm, he stuck to his post till the company was withdrawn.

NIVEN, HUGH WILDERSPIN, Capt., Canadian Infantry. For conspicuous gallantry when in command of his company and holding an advanced position. He repulsed the enemy and hung on to his position when he was practically surrounded and the enemy were calling on him to surrender. He continued to direct operations after being wounded.

PERRY, KENNETH MEIKLE, Major, Canadian Infantry. For conspicuous gallantry on several occasions, notably when he commanded the two first lines in an attack. He led his men with great dash through a heavy barrage of fire up to the enemy's front line. Here he was wounded in the leg and back, and compelled to retire.

STYLES, ALFRED GAVILLER, Capt., Canadian Infantry. For conspicuous gallantry. When his men had suffered severely under a heavy bombardment and the mine explosions which followed, he reorganized the remainder and held a defensive post against numerous hostile attacks. Though himself blown some distance by the blast of a shell, he continued to carry on with great coolness.

VERRETT, HECTOR BACON, Major, Canadian Infantry. For conspicuous gallantry. Although wounded by shrapnel, he stuck to his command under most trying circumstances, and assisted greatly in strengthening the position He set a fine example to all under him.

London Gazette, 25 Aug. 1916.—" War Office, 25 Aug. 1916. His Majesty the King has been graciously pleased to approve of the appointment of the undermentioned Officers to be Companions of the Distinguished Service Order, in recognition of their gallantry and devotion to duty in the field."

ASTON, REV. BASIL, Temporary Chaplain to the Forces, 4th Class. For conspicuous gallantry during operations. For two days and a night he worked incessantly tending and clearing the wounded under shell fire. During the night, after he had been working twelve hours, he helped to carry a wounded man to the dressing station through trenches blown in and knee-deep in mud. He then immediately went back to rescue others.

BALDWIN, RAYMOND HENRY, Major (Temporary Lieut.-Colonel), East Surrey Regt. For conspicuous gallantry in action. He has displayed great coolness under fire as Battalion Commander, and his fine example has inspired his men. On one occasion he captured and held two lines of enemy trenches under very difficult circumstances.

BECK, EDWYN WALTER TYRRELL, Temporary Capt., Royal Fusiliers. For conspicuous gallantry in action. By his fine example of coolness and courage he steadied his company under an intense bombardment. In the enemy's trenches he did fine work, personally capturing two officers and twenty men of the enemy.

BIRCHALL, EDWARD VIVIAN DEARMAN, Capt., Oxfordshire and Buckinghamshire Light Infantry. For conspicuous gallantry and devotion to duty in action. He led forward his company with great dash under heavy fire, entered the enemy's trenches, and, though dangerously wounded, refused any assistance till assured that the position won was firmly held.

BRICKWOOD, ROBERT, Temporary Capt., Rifle Brigade. For conspicuous gallantry and determination during a raid. He reached the enemy trenches in the face of strong opposition and himself accounted for four of the enemy. When wounded he stuck to his command till forced by his wounds to go back. It was chiefly due to his leading that the raid was successful.

BRINSON, HAROLD NEILSON, Temporary Second Lieut. (Temporary Capt.), Liverpool Regt. For conspicuous gallantry in action. He led his company with great dash and skill across the open, dealt with the enemy's machine guns, and, after accounting for many of the enemy, consolidated his position and repelled a counter-attack. During the next twenty-four hours he repelled another counter-attack and did further fine work.

BROWN, OSBERT HAROLD, Temporary Capt., Suffolk Regt. For conspicuous gallantry in action. With only one orderly he proceeded to the enemy's third line, where, collecting details of all units, he drove off two hostile counter-attacks and repelled a strong bombing attack. He held his position till relieved.

CALLAGHAN, MICHAEL AUGUSTINE, Temporary Second Lieut., Lancashire Fusiliers. For conspicuous gallantry during operations. With a bombing party of 16 N.C.O.'s and men he went down an enemy trench repelling bombing attacks all day. Finally, owing to his vigorous and ceaseless attacks, two officers and 128 men of the enemy surrendered to him.

CALVERLEY, GEOFFREY WALTER, Lieut. (Temporary Capt.), Royal Irish Rifles. For conspicuous gallantry during several days of fighting. He led his company with great dash, and successfully beat off enemy counter-attacks. He helped to organize bombing attacks, which broke down the enemy's resistance, and led to the capture of a large number of prisoners.

CURRIN, RICHARD WILLIAM, Temporary Capt., York and Lancaster Regt. For conspicuous courage and ability in organizing the defence of front line trenches, and by personal example and total disregard of danger securing good work under heavy fire. He was instrumental in bringing in 80 wounded from exposed positions.

DEWING, ROBERT EDWARD, Capt., Royal Engineers. For conspicuous gallantry and devotion to duty when preparing for the offensive and later when consolidating positions won. Though wounded early one morning he stuck to his post all day, and drove off an enemy counter-attack with great determination.

HARRISON, AIDAN, Temporary Second Lieut., North Lancashire Regt. For conspicuous gallantry during several days of fighting. He displayed the greatest coolness and bravery in fighting his guns under heavy fire, and repeatedly rendered the greatest assistance to the infantry.

HARRISON, HAROLD CECIL, Lieut. and Temporary Capt., Royal Marine Artillery (attached South African Artillery, with rank of Temporary Major). For conspicuous gallantry during operations. He carried out two dangerous reconnaissances far in front of our foremost line, and brought back valuable reports. On both occasions he was under heavy shell and rifle fire. He had previously been observing from a tree when it was struck by a direct hit from an enemy gun.

HOBSON, FREDERICK GREIG Temporary Second Lieut. (Temporary Capt.) West Yorkshire Regt. For conspicuous gallantry and good work during operations. During 30 hours he continually organized parties for water and bomb carrying, and also for carrying the wounded. He collected men who had lost their way in the dark, and did fine work generally.

HUGHES, HUGH LLEWELLYN GLYN, Temporary Lieut., Royal Army Medical Corps. For conspicuous gallantry and devotion to duty during operations. He went out in broad daylight, under heavy fire, and bandaged seven wounded men in the open, lying out in an exposed spot for one and a half hours. At nightfall he led a party through a heavy barrage and brought the seven men back.

HUME-SPRY, CHARLES AUGUSTUS NELSON, Major, Royal Field Artillery. For conspicuous gallantry and devotion to duty. Having been ordered to demolish with fire certain wire in front of enemy trenches, this officer went out in front of our infantry position, accompanied by his telephonist only. He crawled along till he could see the wire and there remained till his work was done. He was under heavy fire and might have been rushed at any time by an enemy patrol.

HUNTER, DOUGLAS WILLIAM, Temporary Capt., M.B., Royal Army Medical Corps. For conspicuous gallantry in action. He tended the wounded incessantly in the open and in the front line trench under very heavy fire. When no combatant officer remained in the battalion he took command, rallied the men and set a splendid example. (See London Gazette, 26 Sept. 1916.)

JONES, DAVID ALEXANDER, Temporary Lieut., Lincolnshire Regt. For conspicuous gallantry in action and repeated fine work with his bombers. On one occasion he held an advanced post for 48 hours under heavy machine-gun fire. Throughout he showed the greatest determination.

LAMB, HENRY JOHN, Lieut.-Colonel, Canadian Local Forces. For conspicuous gallantry and good work during operations. As liaison officer to the three brigades of his division he rendered most valuable assistance to brigadiers when communications were broken down by shell fire. He displayed great courage and ability.

LOOKER, ARTHUR WILLIAM, Second Lieut., Cambridgeshire Regt. For conspicuous gallantry when leading a raid on the enemy's trenches. In face of heavy fire he forced his way through uncut wire and ran up and down the enemy's parapet firing in their faces. Though wounded in both hands, foot and abdomen, he refused assistance till quite close to our own trench.

MADDEN, JOHN GREVILE, Temporary Capt., Manchester Regt. For conspicuous gallantry in action. When the leading waves of attack were wavering after losing most of their officers, he pushed forward, rallied the men and led them into the village. Later he organized and led a party which repelled a counter-attack.

MAULE, WILLIAM HARRY FOWKE, Temporary Capt., North Lancashire Regt. For conspicuous gallantry when leading his company during operations. During several days' fighting he set a fine example of cheerfulness and cool courage to those around him. He was three times knocked down by the blast of shells.

MORIARTY, OLIVER NASH, Capt., Royal Garrison Artillery, Special Reserve. For conspicuous and consistent gallantry when reconnoitring and reporting under very trying conditions, constantly under heavy shell fire. On one occasion his pluck and enterprise prevented a premature attack.

MOULD, JAMES, Temporary Lieut., Worcestershire Regt. For conspicuous courage and ability in erecting a block in an advanced trench heavily enfiladed by fire. The prompt measures taken checked an enemy counter-attack, and he, in addition, inflicted heavy casualties with a Lewis gun.

OGILVIE, SHOLTO STUART, Temporary Lieut. (Temporary Capt.), Wiltshire Regt. For conspicuous gallantry and determination in action. He took command when his seniors became casualties, and by his energy and fine example inspired the depleted battalion, so that they maintained all the ground won against repeated counter-attacks and continuous shelling.

PEASE, HERBERT ERNEST, Temporary Capt., Durham Light Infantry. For conspicuous gallantry during four days of fighting. He set a fine example of dash and bravery when leading the battalion in the attack which led to the capture of the enemy's trench. Subsequently he did fine work in the consolidation of the positions won.

PETERSON, ARTHUR JAMES, Temporary Capt., Royal Field Artillery. For conspicuous gallantry in action. He fought his battery for five days and nights within 400 yards of the enemy's position, in spite of heavy retaliations, and rendered the greatest assistance to our infantry. His personal bravery and devotion to duty were beyond praise.

RAMSAY, STUART, Temporary Lieut., North Lancashire Regt. For conspicuous gallantry in action. When the enemy attacked our trenches in greatly superior numbers he repeatedly organized and led bombing attacks against them, keeping them at a distance. He frequently reconnoitred over the parapet, which was swept by machine-gun fire, and gave valuable information to our artillery.

REID, NOEL SPENCE, Lieut. (Temporary Capt.), Oxfordshire and Buckinghamshire Light Infantry. For conspicuous gallantry in action. By promptly bringing up his company he ensured the success of the leading troops, and, after assuming command when his senior officer became a casualty, did fine work in making good the position, in establishing connection with isolated troops on his right, and in repelling counter-attacks.

RICHARDSON, MORRIS ERNALD, Major (Temporary Lieut.-Colonel), Northumberland Fusiliers. For conspicuous gallantry in action. When he had received three wounds in the attack he refused to go back till he had given orders to his successor. He remained two hours in a dangerous spot, and then walked back to Brigade Headquarters, and personally reported the situation.

ROBINSON, HENRY HAROLD, Temporary Capt., Royal Army Medical Corps. For conspicuous gallantry and devotion to duty. After a raid in the enemy's trenches, he twice crawled out in broad daylight to assist wounded men under fire. They were brought in at night.

RUSSELL, GORDON BRUCE, Lieut. (Temporary Capt.), Wiltshire Regt. For conspicuous courage and ability in the capture, with his company, of an enemy trench. He subsequently repelled violent attacks. Regardless of all personal risk he organized and directed his company. He has consistently done most excellent work.

SIM, GEORGE EDWARD HERMAN, Capt., Royal Engineers. For conspicuous gallantry in action. He led forward his company with great bravery in the assault on a wood, and then advanced himself under heavy fire of all kinds to locate strong points for the defence of the wood. Finally, after putting his men to work, he was severely wounded.

SPARKS, HUBERT CONRAD, Second Lieut. (Temporary Capt.), London Regt. For conspicuous gallantry in action. During an assault on the enemy's trenches he took command when his senior officer was killed, and rallied his men, who were under heavy fire, and had expended nearly all their ammunition. With a handful of men he made a most determined stand, although nearly surrounded, and thus enabled the remainder to withdraw. He was the last to leave.

SPOONER, CECIL CHARTERS, Capt. (Temporary Major), Essex Regt. For conspicuous gallantry in action. He crossed over 400 yards under heavy shell and machine-gun fire to take back an accurate report of the situation. He has always shown an utter disregard of danger.

TRENCH, CHARLES FREDERICK, Capt., Lancers, Indian Army. For conspicuous gallantry. Capt. Trench, with another officer and a party of 13 Sowars, carried a very urgent message some 12 miles through country swarming with enemy horsemen and successfully delivered it.

WILDER-NELIGAN, MAURICE, Capt., Australian Infantry. For conspicuous gallantry when commanding a raid in force. His careful training and fine leading were responsible for the success attained. Fifty-three of the enemy were killed and 24 prisoners taken, besides a machine gun, many rifles and much equipment. Though wounded in the head he stuck to his command.

WINSER, CHARLES RUPERT PETER, Capt. (Temporary Lieut.-Colonel), Reserve of Officers, South Lancashire Regt. For conspicuous gallantry during operations. He led his battalion with great dash and ability during several days of hard fighting, and showed remarkable coolness and resource.

London Gazette, 6 Sept. 1916.—" Admiralty, 6 Sept. 1916. The King has been graciously pleased to give orders for the appointment of the undermentioned Officers to be Companions of the Distinguished Service Order."

DORMAN, THOMAS STEPHEN LEWIS, Lieut.-Commander, R.N. For his gallant conduct at Reshire on the 9th Sept. 1915, when he volunteered and endeavoured to bring a machine gun into action, exposed to a heavy fire from the enemy, at about 300 yards' range. A Yeoman of Signals who accompanied Lieut.-Commander Dorman was mortally wounded.

CLARKE, WILLIAM HOWARD, Engineer Lieut.-Commander, R.N. After his ship had been holed below the water-line in action off the Belgian coast, he kept the engines running under most difficult conditions.

EGERTON, WILLIAM MARKHAM, Lieut.-Commander, R.N.V.R.

FLEMING, ALOYSIUS FRANCIS, Staff Surgeon, R.N.

LOUGH, REGINALD DAWSON HOPCRAFT, Capt. (Temporary Major), R.M.L.I.

In recognition of their services with the Royal Naval Division in the Gallipoli Peninsula.

Extracts from despatch of Admiral Sir John R. Jellicoe, G.C.B., G.C.V.O., Commander-in-Chief, Grand Fleet, dated Iron Duke, 23rd Aug. 1916.

" SIR,—With reference to my despatch of 24th June, 1916, I have the honour to bring to the notice of the Lords Commissioners of the Admiralty the names of the following Officers who are recommended for honours and special commendation.

" Where all carried out their duties so well it is somewhat invidious and difficult to select officers for special recognition.

" THE REMARKS OF THE FLAG OR COMMANDING OFFICERS OF THE SQUADRONS CONCERNED, IN WHICH I CONCUR, HAVE BEEN INSERTED AFTER THE NAMES OF THE OFFICERS RECOMMENDED IN THE FOLLOWING LIST."

LIST OF OFFICERS RECOMMENDED FOR HONOURS FOR SERVICE IN THE BATTLE OF JUTLAND.

BLAKE, GEOFFREY, Commander, R.N. Gunnery and principal control office of H.M.S. Iron Duke, whose zeal, knowledge and devotion to duty throughout the war, and coolness and skill in action resulted in severe damage being inflicted by Iron Duke's 13.5-inch guns on a German battleship of the Koenig class in the action off the coast of Jutland on 31 May.

Remarks of Admiral Sir Cecil Burney.

CURREY, HUGH SCHOMBERG, Commander, R.N. Executive officer of Marlborough, whose untiring energy and skilful work greatly assisted in saving the ship after she was torpedoed.

SKELTON, REGINALD WILLIAM, Engineer Commander, R.N. A valuable officer whose department during the action reflected credit on his organization.

FINLAYSON, HENRY WILLIAM, M.B., Fleet Surgeon, R.N. A zealous and hardworking officer, who organized his department in an efficient manner for the action.

MURRAY, HERBERT PATRICK WILLIAM GEORGE, Staff Paymaster R.N. (Secretary to Second-in-Command). My Secretary, whose services were most valuable to me during the action.

KITSON, JAMES BULLER, Lieut.-Commander R.N My Flag Lieut.-Commander, who was of very great assistance to me during the action.

Remarks of Vice-Admiral Sir Martyn Jerram.

SANDERS, WILLIAM CORY, Engineer Commander, R.N. A very capable and zealous officer, who showed great ability throughout the action in the working of the engine-room department.

HORNE, RICHARD, Commander, R.N. An officer of great ability, who conned Orion throughout the action with ability and skill.

CARRINGTON, JOHN WALSH, Commander, R.N. An officer of great ability, who conned King George V. throughout the action with good judgment and prompt decision. He was navigating officer of H.M.S. Inflexible in the action off the Falkland Islands and in the Dardanelles.

Remarks of Vice-Admiral Sir Doveton Sturdee.

MOON, JOSEPH AGNEW, Fleet Surgeon, R.N. Was responsible for the excellent medical arrangements for dealing with the wounded in H.M.S. Benbow, which were very efficient.

JOHNSON, CYRIL SHELDON, Paymaster, R.N. Rendered valuable services as my Secretary in keeping records and generally assisting me during the action. His name was mentioned in despatches after the Falkland Islands action.

The Distinguished Service Order

SPENCE, ROBERT, Engineer Commander, R.N. By his general management of the machinery and stokers under his orders in H.M.S. Vanguard enabled the ship to be taken into and maintained in action in a most effective manner.

Remarks of Rear-Admiral Evan-Thomas.

WALWYN, HUMPHREY THOMAS, Commander, R.N. Commander Walwyn, from the moment the first shell struck the ship, managed to be everywhere where attention was necessary in putting out fires, plugging holes, shoring, etc., with the fire brigade and repair parties. Considering the size of the ship and the damage sustained, and also the fact that he was keeping the Captain fully informed of her condition, the work effected by Commander Walwyn in the short space of time was marvellous, and the Captain considers it greatly due to his prompt action that much water was prevented from access into the port wing and main engine rooms.

BROWNRIGG, HENRY JOHN STUDHOLME, Commander, R.N. Commander Brownrigg took charge of and conducted the operations in connection with dealing with fires and repairs to damage by shell. He was continually in positions of greatest danger, and where the conditions were most trying to the nerves. His example inspired all those under him, and he was largely instrumental in keeping the ship in effective fighting condition to the end of the action, notwithstanding the severe damage from shell fire.

Remarks of Rear-Admiral Herbert L. Heath.

INGHAM, JAMES GEOFFRY PENROSE, Commander, R.N.
KITCHING, HENRY WALTON, Engineer Commander, R.N.

Remarks of Commodore Charles E. Le Mesurier.

BICKFORD, BERTRAM RALEIGH, Staff Surgeon, R.N. For great gallantry and devotion to duty in action. This officer, though severely wounded by a shell splinter, persisted in attending to the wounded, only yielding to a direct order from myself to place himself on the sick list.

Remarks of Vice-Admiral Sir David Beatty.

SPICKERNELL, FRANK TODD, Acting Paymaster, R.N. (Secretary to the Vice-Admiral Commanding Battle Cruiser Fleet). For very valuable services in the action and throughout the war.

SEYMOUR, RALPH FREDERICK, Lieut.-Commander, R.N. (Flag Lieut.-Commander to Vice Admiral Commanding Battle Cruiser Fleet). For very valuable services in the action and throughout the war.

LONGHURST, GERALD FORTESCUE, Lieut.-Commander, R.N. (now Commander). Gunnery Officer of my Flagship. Controlled the fire of Lion with greatest coolness, courage and skill, and inflicted immense damage on the enemy. This is the third time he has controlled the fire of Lion in action.

MACLEAN, ALEXANDER, M.B., Fleet Surgeon, R.N. Performed his exhausting duties with the greatest zeal and courage. The medical staff was seriously depleted by casualties; the wounded and dying had to be dressed under very difficult conditions on the mess deck, which was flooded with a foot of water from damaged fire mains. Fleet Surgeon Maclean has suffered considerably since the action from his devotion to duty.

MARTELL, ALBERT ARTHUR GREEN, Engineer Lieut.-Commander, R.N. In charge of all fire and salvage parties, and directed and led them with complete success, setting an example of coolness and vigour of action which unquestionably prevented far more serious damage.

DANNREUTHER, HUBERT EDWARD, Commander, R.N. The senior of the two surviving officers of the Invincible. Up till the moment when the ship blew up Commander Dannreuther controlled the fire of Invincible in a manner which produced visible and overwhelming results on the enemy.

MACDONALD, MALCOLM HENRY SOMERLED, Commander, R.N. For his coolness in the night action, when he extinguished the fires on mess deck, and his prompt action in preventing the fore magazine from being flooded.

BAMFORD, EDWARD, Capt., R.M.L.I. In after control when it was blown to pieces by a shell burst. Slightly burnt in face and slightly wounded in leg. Then assisted to work one gun with a much reduced crew, and controlled another gun. Assisted in extinguishing a fire, and in general showed great coolness, power of command, judgment and courage, when exposed to a very heavy fire.

PALMER, LAURENCE REYNOLDS, Lieut.-Commander, R.N. For his gallantry, when his destroyer was disabled, in proceeding to the assistance of Onslow and taking her in tow under heavy shell fire. He succeeded in towing her in a heavy sea until relieved by tugs when in sight of land.

MOCATTA, JACK ERNEST ALBERT, Lieut., R.N. Supported Commander Bingham, of Nestor, in his gallant action against destroyers, battle-cruisers, and battleships, in the most courageous and effective manner.

ALISON, ROGER VINCENT, Lieut.-Commander, R.N. For promptness and gallantry in taking advantage of the opportunity of attacking the enemy's vessels with the torpedo on two occasions, as described in my original despatch.

LEGGE, MONTAGUE GEORGE BENTINCK, Lieut.-Commander, R.N. Having defeated the enemy destroyers, gallantly pressed home attack with torpedoes on the enemy battle-cruisers.

BLAKE, CUTHBERT PATRICK, Lieut.-Commander, R.N. Having defeated the enemy destroyers, gallantly pressed home attack with torpedoes on the enemy battle-cruisers.

Remarks of Capt. Percy M. R. Royds.

VACHER, CECIL CHARLES BRITTAIN, Lieut.-Commander, R.N. For controlling the fire from the ship in the coolest manner from a very exposed position under extremely heavy fire.

Remarks of Capt. Walter L. Allen.

COLES, GORDON ALSTON, Lieut.-Commander, R.N. The commander of his division speaks highly of the way he conned his ship. Ambuscade fired three torpedoes, and the rapid reloading under fire reflects great credit on all concerned, and proves the ship is in a high state of efficiency.

Remarks of Commodore James R. P. Hawkesley.

HOLMES, JAMES McALISTER, M.B., Staff Surgeon, R.N. For the very efficient manner in which the wounded were attended to whilst under fire and subsequently.

MOORE, HENRY RUTHVEN, Lieut.-Commander, R.N. For the assistance he gave the Commodore (F), both during the day and night action, and the manner in which he carried out his duties.

SULIVAN, HAROLD ERNEST, Commander, R.N. As second-in-command of the flotilla he manoeuvred his half very ably during the daytime, and at night, when Castor could make no signals owing to damage by gunfire, he very ably turned his half-flotilla and kept clear of the first half-flotilla manoeuvring.

Remarks of Capt. (D) Anselan J. B. Stirling.

CHAMPION, JOHN PELHAM, Commander, R.N. Handled his division with great ability whilst in action, and led his division to attack an enemy battle squadron with great gallantry.

CORSAR, JOHN KIRK, Engineer Lieut.-Commander, R.N. Kept his department in good order and kept the boiler water going in spite of evaporator being semi-disabled most of the time and out of action entirely for some period.

Remarks of Capt. Berwick Curtis.

TOSTEVIN, HAROLD BERTRAM, Engineer Lieut.-Commander, R.N. This officer's organization of the engine room department and general energy at all times, keeping the machinery of the ship in a thoroughly efficient state, contributed largely to the success of Abdiel's operations on the night of 31 May, observing that the ship proceeded at full speed for over six hours.

Staff of the Commander-in-Chief (with remarks of Admiral Sir John Jellicoe).

BEST, THE HON. MATTHEW ROBERT, M.V.O., Commander, R.N. Has performed valuable staff work during the war and services during the action.

FORBES, CHARLES MORTON, Commander, R.N. My Flag Commander, who has always afforded me great assistance. This officer was Executive Officer of H.M.S. Queen Elizabeth during the whole period that ship was employed at the Dardanelles.

WOODS, ALEXANDER RIALL WADHAM, Commander, R.N. Controlled the visual signal work with great coolness and accuracy.

NICHOLSON, RICHARD LINDSAY, Commander, R.N. Controlled the wireless telegraph work with great coolness and most marked efficiency, and reaped the reward of the excellent organization for which he is responsible.

London Gazette, 15 Sept. 1916.—"Admiralty, 15 Sept. 1916. The King has been graciously pleased to give orders for the following appointments to the Distinguished Service Order to the undermentioned Officers, in recognition of their services, as mentioned in the foregoing Despatch. To be Companions of the Distinguished Service Order."

SULIVAN, HAROLD ERNEST, Commander, R.N.
CURREY, HUGH SCHOMBERG, Commander, R.N.
HORNE, RICHARD, Commander, R.N.
BEST, THE HONOURABLE MATTHEW ROBERT, Commander, M.V.O., Royal Navy.
WALWYN, HUMPHREY THOMAS, Commander, R.N.
WOODS, ALEXANDER RIALL WADHAM, Commander, R.N.
CARRINGTON, JOHN WALSH, Commander, R.N.
FORBES, CHARLES MORTON, Commander, R.N.
BROWNRIGG, HENRY JOHN STUDHOLME, Commander, R.N.
MACDONALD, MALCOLM HENRY SOMERLED, Commander, R.N.
INGHAM, JAMES GEOFFREY PENROSE, Commander, R.N.
BLAKE, GEOFFREY, Commander, R.N.
DANNREUTHER, HUBERT EDWARD, Commander, R.N.
CHAMPION, JOHN PELHAM, Commander, R.N.
NICHOLSON, RICHARD LINDSAY, Commander, R.N.
LONGHURST, GERALD FORTESCUE, Commander, R.N.
COLES, GORDON ALSTON, Lieut.-Commander, R.N.
KITSON, JAMES BULLER, Lieut.-Commander, R.N.
LEGGE, MONTAGUE GEORGE BENTINCK, Lieut.-Commander, R.N.
ALISON, ROGER VINCENT, Lieut.-Commander, R.N.
SEYMOUR, RALPH FREDERICK, Lieut.-Commander, R.N.
BLAKE, CUTHBERT PATRICK, Lieut.-Commander, R.N.
PALMER, LAURENCE REYNOLDS, Lieut.-Commander, R.N.
MOORE, HENRY RUTHVEN, Lieut.-Commander, R.N.
VACHER, CECIL CHARLES BRITTAIN, Lieut.-Commander, R.N.
MOCATTA, JACK ERNEST ALBERT, Lieut., R.N.
SANDERS, WILLIAM CORY, Engineer Commander, R.N.
SPENCE, ROBERT, Engineer Commander, R.N.
SKELTON, REGINALD WILLIAM, Engineer Commander, R.N.
KITCHING, HENRY WALTON, Engineer Commander, R.N.
TOSTEVIN, HAROLD BERTRAM, Engineer Lieut.-Commander, R.N.
CORSAR, JOHN KIRK, Engineer Lieut.-Commander, R.N.
MARTELL, ALBERT ARTHUR GREEN, Engineer Lieut.-Commander, R.N.
MOON, JOSEPH AGNEW, Fleet Surgeon, R.N.
MACLEAN, ALEX., Fleet Surgeon, M.B., Royal Navy.
FINLAYSON, HENRY WILLIAM, Fleet Surgeon, M.B., Royal Navy.
BICKFORD, BERTRAM RALEIGH, Staff Surgeon, R.N.
HOLMES, JAMES McALISTER, Staff Surgeon, M.B., Royal Navy.
MURRAY, HERBERT PATRICK WILLIAM GEORGE, Staff Paymaster, R.N.
JOHNSON, CYRIL SHELDON, Paymaster, R.N.
SPICKERNELL, FRANK TODD, Assistant Paymaster (Acting Paymaster), R.N.
BAMFORD, EDWARD, Capt., R.M.L.I.

London Gazette, 22 Sept. 1916.—"War Office, 22 Sept. 1916. His Majesty the King has been graciously pleased to approve of the appointments of the undermentioned Officers to be Companions of the Distinguished Service Order, in recognition of their gallantry and devotion to duty in the field."

HOUBLON, RICHARD ARCHER, Capt., Royal Field Artillery. For conspicuous gallantry and devotion to duty during operations. He was wounded when wire-cutting under heavy shell fire, but stuck to his duty till two days later, when he was again seriously wounded. He has always shown great coolness and bravery.

BOURDILLON, LANCELOT GERARD, Temporary Capt., Royal Army Medical Corps. For conspicuous gallantry and devotion to duty. When an officer had been killed carrying in a wounded serjeant, Capt. Bourdillon went out in broad daylight, bandaged the serjeant's wounds, and only came in when certain that the latter could not live.

CANNAN, HORATIUS JAMES, Temporary Capt., Royal Field Artillery. For conspicuous gallantry, during a long period of operations, in going forward to observe before positions were consolidated. On several occasions he has come in personal contact with the enemy, and acquitted himself most courageously. His reconnaissances, carried out at great personal risk, have produced much valuable information.

CAMPBELL, WILLIAM KEALTY, Capt., M.B., Royal Army Medical Corps, Special Reserve. For conspicuous gallantry and devotion to duty. He went ahead of the bearers and dressed the wounded in the open under heavy shell fire. Whilst establishing advanced dressing stations he was wounded and half-blinded by the explosion of a shell, but carried on his work. He set a splendid example to those around him.

CARTER, THOMAS HEALY HUNTON, Capt. (Temporary), Royal Warwickshire Regt. For conspicuous gallantry. When the explosion of an enemy mine wrecked a portion of the defences, Capt. Carter, though dazed by the explosion, rallied the survivors under heavy shell fire and beat off a strong enemy attack. He has constantly shown great courage.

COLLEY, FRANK, Temporary Second Lieut., York and Lancaster Regt. For conspicuous gallantry in action. He led his men to the attack under very heavy fire, and, after being wounded in the face and shoulder and put out of action for some time, he insisted on returning to the front line. Here he continued to do fine work, and was only stopped by being hit again in both wrists.

DAVIS, SIDNEY ALFRED, Temporary Second Lieut. (Temporary Lieut.), General List, Commanding Trench Mortar Battery. For conspicuous gallantry in action. He worked his guns with great skill and courage, repelling three counter-attacks. Finally he carried his wounded to the dressing station under heavy fire.

ELLIS, ARCHIBALD JENNER, Major, Border Regt. For conspicuous gallantry in action. He led his reserve under very heavy machine-gun fire till he was severely wounded. After this he continued to direct operations and to reorganize men in "No Man's Land."

EVANS, HENRY COPE, Temporary Second Lieut., General List (attached Royal Flying Corps). For conspicuous gallantry and skill on many occasions in attacking hostile aircraft, frequently against large odds. In one fortnight he brought down four enemy machines, returning on one occasion with his machine badly damaged.

FRASER, ARTHUR WILLIAM, Temporary Second Lieut., Border Regt. For conspicuous gallantry in action. After suffering heavy casualties he led his company up to the enemy wire at a place where it was uncut. Though severely wounded, twice by bombs and once by rifle fire, he continued to direct the wire-cutting till he lost consciousness.

GALLAUGHER, HENRY, Temporary Lieut., Royal Inniskilling Fusiliers. For conspicuous gallantry in action. When other officers became casualties he took command and led on his men with great dash. Seeing the enemy firing on our wounded, he got into a shell hole with a private, and shot six enemy snipers with a rifle. Finally he volunteered and with 20 men rescued 28 wounded men under very heavy fire.

GLOVER, GEORGE WRIGHT, Second Lieut., Rifle Brigade. For conspicuous gallantry in action. Though twice wounded in the advance, he continued to lead his men forward under heavy machine-gun and artillery fire into the enemy's third line, where he organized the defences. Although his left arm was useless, he threw bombs as long as there was any supply. He set a splendid example all day.

GOUGH, ROLAND IVOR, Temporary Capt., Royal Warwickshire Regt. For conspicuous gallantry in action. He led his men with great dash under heavy machine-gun and rifle fire, and, though his company suffered severely, he reached the enemy's trenches, where he was dangerously wounded. Nevertheless he continued to direct his men until exhausted.

GRANT, IAN CAMERON, Capt., Cameron Highlanders. For conspicuous gallantry in action. When the attack was wavering he went forward into the front line and cheered on the troops till he was badly wounded. As Brigade Major he has set a fine example to all the officers in the brigade.

HALL, HENRY SIDNEY HOFFMAN, Temporary Capt., Royal Fusiliers. For conspicuous gallantry when leading his company in two attacks, and consolidating and holding a new line at a very critical time, until blinded by a wound, and forced to give up his command. He displayed the greatest coolness and bravery, and set a fine example to both officers and men.

HANCE, HENRY MALKIN, Second Lieut. (Temporary Major), Reserve of Officers, Indian Army. For conspicuous gallantry during mining operations. He has done fine work and has set an example of great courage and determination under very hazardous conditions.

HOBSON, ALLEN FABER, Second Lieut. (Temporary Major), Royal Engineers. For conspicuous gallantry and devotion to duty on many occasions. By his absolute coolness in danger he has set a magnificent example to his company and has carried out important work under trying conditions.

HOPKINSON, JOHN OLIVER, Major (Temporary Lieut.-Colonel), Seaforth Highlanders. For conspicuous gallantry in action. He led his battalion against the enemy trenches, captured them, and held his ground for 13 hours under heavy fire, repulsing constant attacks. He continued to command after being wounded.

JONES, JAMES WALKER, Capt., M.B., Indian Medical Service. For conspicuous gallantry and presence of mind in closing with a soldier who had lost his reason and was moving along a trench prior to an attack with a bomb in each hand. Realizing the situation, Capt. Jones closed with him, and wrenched one bomb from his hand. It immediately started to burn. Capt. Jones threw it some yards away, and it burst on touching the ground. Two officers were injured by the explosion, and several others might have been injured but for this prompt and courageous action.

KELLY, JOHN UPTON, Capt., Wiltshire Regt. and Royal Flying Corps. For conspicuous gallantry and skill on several occasions. When making a reconnaissance he came down to 700 feet under heavy fire, and obtained valuable information. Again, in attempting to observe through clouds, he flew over the enemy lines at 500 feet, and although severely wounded and almost blind, he brought his machine back to our lines.

LAURIE, JOHN EMILIUS, Capt., Seaforth Highlanders. For conspicuous gallantry in action. At a critical time he rallied men of various units who were without leaders, did fine work consolidating the position and helped to repel a bomb attack.

McCALLUM, JOHN DUNWOODY MARTIN, Temporary Capt., Royal Irish Rifles. For conspicuous gallantry in action. As senior officer with the battalion he controlled the operations with great skill and courage. He organized the consolidating of the position, moving about utterly regardless of personal danger and encouraging his men.

McCLYMONT, ROBERT ARTHUR, Major, Royal Field Artillery. For conspicuous gallantry. For several days he cut the enemy's wire, using an observation post which was exposed to heavy shell fire. Later, during an advance, he maintained communication with his battery, and was enabled to cut hostile wire and frequently to bring the fire of his battery to assist our infantry advance and to resist enemy counter-attacks.

McNAMARA, ARTHUR EDWARD, Major, Royal West Surrey Regt. For conspicuous gallantry during operations. When acting as liaison officer between divisional headquarters and brigades he visited all brigade and battalion headquarters under very heavy shell fire. When both his orderlies were wounded he dressed their wounds under fire. After returning with his report he went out again, and when another orderly was wounded dressed his wounds also. While doing so a piece of shrapnel passed through his own clothing.

MILES, LANCELOT GEORGE, Temporary Lieut. (Temporary Capt.), Royal Highlanders. For conspicuous gallantry during operations. He handled his company with great skill and coolness during a heavy bombardment. He also led his company with great dash in an assault during which he captured four machine guns. During the attack he was severely wounded by a bomb.

MILLER, ALLISTER MACKINTOSH, Temporary Capt., Cavalry, and Royal Flying Corps. For conspicuous gallantry and skill when attacking troops on the ground under heavy fire. On one occasion he flew close to the ground along a line of hostile machine guns, engaging them with his machine gun, drawing their fire, and enabling the cavalry to advance. Again, when alone, he engaged five enemy machines, bringing one down, and also successfully bombed a troop train, coming down to 300 feet to make sure of hitting.

MONTGOMERY, WILLIAM ALEXANDER, Temporary Capt., Royal Irish Rifles. For conspicuous gallantry in action. For five hours he fought a running fight in the trenches, and held up the enemy's advance. Eventually he threw bombs himself till utterly exhausted, when he had to be carried to our lines. He set a splendid example all day.

PAUL, COURTENAY TALBOT SAINT, Major, Royal Field Artillery. For conspicuous gallantry during operations. During two days his battery and observing station were subjected to very heavy shell-fire. His coolness and utter disregard of danger gave great confidence to his battery, and he carried out wire-cutting with great success.

RAIKES, GEOFFREY TAUNTON, Capt. (Temporary Major), South Wales Borderers. For conspicuous gallantry in action. He led forward his reserve under very great difficulty with the greatest coolness and courage. After dark he personally supervised the withdrawal of his wounded.

SANDYS, EDWIN THOMAS FALKINER, Major (Temporary Lieut.-Colonel), Middlesex Regt. For conspicuous gallantry when leading his battalion and keeping its direction during an attack under very heavy fire. Although wounded in several places, he continued to lead it until further wounds made it no longer possible to do so. The fine behaviour of the battalion was largely due to the Commanding Officer's personal qualities.

SLADE, ERNEST COWPER, Capt. (Temporary Major), Gloucestershire Regt. For conspicuous gallantry during operations. He organized with great skill bombing attacks, in order to reach two companies which were isolated in a trench further north. On another occasion he was twice buried by shells in one night, but dug himself out and carried on as if nothing had happened.

SUGDEN, JOHN EDWIN, Temporary Capt., Royal Irish Rifles. For conspicuous gallantry in action. He took command of a battalion when his C.O. was killed at a critical moment in the advance. Under heavy machine-gun and trench mortar fire he handled the two leading companies with great skill and courage. Later he went back to fetch the two remaining companies. By his courage and fine example he kept the battalion together and reached the enemy line.

VAUGHAN, PHILIP EDMUND, Major (Temporary Lieut.-Colonel), Worcestershire Regt. For conspicuous gallantry in action. After a long advance under very heavy machine-gun fire his battalion was held up by wire, but with another officer he forced his way through, got his men into a village, consolidated and held his position there, and captured over 150 prisoners and ten machine guns.

WESTERN, BERTRAM CHARLES MAXIMILIAN, Capt. (Temporary Major), East Lancashire Regt. For conspicuous gallantry in action. After a long advance over the open under heavy machine-gun fire, he assisted his C.O. to force a way through wire. They led on the men into a village, and held on to their position there, capturing over 150 prisoners and ten machine guns.

WILSON-CHARGE, JOHN ALEXANDER, Capt. (Temporary Major). Royal Warwickshire Regt. For conspicuous gallantry during operations. He organized a bombing attack which gained 220 yards of trench. After he had left it, the bombing party was driven back. He returned, and had succeeded in capturing some of the lost ground, when he was wounded.

AUSTRALIAN IMPERIAL FORCE.

COOPER, VIVIAN STEWART, Lieut., Australian Infantry. For conspicuous gallantry in action. He repulsed a strong enemy counter-attack, and, when his battalion was relieved, remained in the position. When the enemy attacked he opened fire on them from a point which he had selected, killing large numbers. Ninety-one prisoners were taken by his battalion, 20 surrendering to Lieut. Cooper.

KINGSMILL, HORACE FREDERICK, Major, Australian Artillery. For conspicuous gallantry and fine work during an attack, when acting as liaison officer, constantly under heavy fire. Without the clear and quick information supplied by him, the support given by the brigade would have been impossible.

LAWRANCE, STANLEY NORMAN, Capt., Australian Infantry. For conspicuous gallantry during an attack, when, although severely wounded, he continued to direct operations, and, in spite of great difficulties, consolidated and maintained his position, remaining at his post until overcome by loss of blood.

LODGE, AUGUSTINE BERNARD, Capt., Australian Infantry. For conspicuous gallantry and skill in reconnoitring a position under heavy fire prior to an attack, and subsequently in leading the attacking force to their place of assembly. After one company had lost all its officers, Capt. Lodge went forward, rallied the men, and cleared the trench which was obstructing the advance. Although wounded, he continued his work until the objective had been gained.

MATHER, LESLIE FRANK STRANG, Major, Australian Engineers. For conspicuous gallantry and consistent good work since the commencement of the campaign, and until he was wounded leading his company into action under heavy shell fire.

MEDCALF, FERDINAND GEORGE, Capt., Australian Infantry. For conspicuous gallantry when, in leading his company in an attack, he put the crew of a hostile machine gun out of action with a bomb and captured the gun. He showed unfailing courage and resource in holding captured ground. When wounded in three places, and unable to walk, he ordered the stretcher-bearers to take up a seriously wounded man, and to leave him to crawl to the rear.

MOORE, DONALD TICEHURST, Major, Australian Infantry. For conspicuous gallantry when leading his men during an attack under very heavy shell fire. He led through an intense barrage to an advanced position in the line just captured.

OATES, AUGUSTUS, Capt., Australian Infantry. For conspicuous gallantry during operations in holding the enemy at bay on several occasions with revolver fire, thus enabling the erection of barricades and the evacuation of the wounded. He also organized and led bombing attacks with great courage and skill.

SAVAGE, PERCIVAL JAMES, Capt. (Temporary Major), Australian Engineers. For conspicuous gallantry and ability during a period of operations under very heavy shell fire. The good work done by his company was due to his untiring energy and fine powers of leadership.

VOWLES, ALAN STEWART, Capt., Australian Infantry. For conspicuous gallantry and fine leadership during a period of operations, when he commanded the greater portion of three companies in the front line with great success and ability. His cool appreciation and handling of the situation enabled the position to be held against counter-attack, and under heavy shell fire.

CANADIAN FORCE.

KILMER, CHARLES EDWARD, Capt., Canadian Infantry. For conspicuous gallantry during operations. He led with great skill a successful daylight attack on the enemy's trenches. Though severely wounded, he was the last man to withdraw after all his party, including the wounded, had got clear.

London Gazette, 26 Sept. 1916.—" War Office, 26 Sept. 1916. His Majesty the King has been graciously pleased to approve of the appointments of the undermentioned Officers to be Companions of the Distinguished Service Order, in recognition of their gallantry and devotion to duty in the field."

BALL, ALBERT, Second Lieut. (Temporary Lieut.), M.C., Nottinghamshire and Derbyshire Regt. and Royal Flying Corps. For conspicuous gallantry and skill. Observing seven enemy machines in formation, he immediately attacked one of them and shot it down at 15 yards' range. The remaining machines retired. Immediately afterwards, seeing five more hostile machines, he attacked one at about ten yards' range and shot it down, flames coming out of the fuselage. He then attacked another of the machines, which had been firing at him, and shot it down into a village, when it landed on the top of a house. He then went to the nearest aerodrome for more ammunition, and, returning, attacked three more machines, causing them to dive under control. Being then short of petrol he came home. His own machine was badly shot about in these flights.

BRISCOE, GEORGE SETON, Capt. (Temporary Major), Worcestershire Regt. For conspicuous gallantry in action. During the attack he made untiring efforts under heavy shell fire to get consolidating parties forward to the newly-captured position. He led them personally until severely wounded.

BROUGHTON, NORMAN WALFORD, Temporary Capt., M.B., Royal Army Medical Corps. For conspicuous gallantry and devotion to duty during operations. During a very heavy bombardment he, on three occasions, helped to dig out men from blown-in dug-outs. Shells were bursting all round him, but he refused to take cover, and it was mainly due to his efforts that most of the buried men were rescued. He has done other fine and gallant work.

BUTCHER, HERBERT CECIL, Second Lieut. (Temporary Lieut.), Royal Lancashire Regt. For conspicuous gallantry in action. When the battalion was suffering severe casualties it was largely due to his courage and utter disregard of personal danger that there was no check in the advance. When his C.O. was wounded he took command of the battalion, and displayed the greatest coolness and devotion to duty at a critical time.

CARMICHAEL, IAN, Temporary Second Lieut., Highland Light Infantry. For conspicuous gallantry. He led a raid with great dash, jumped into the enemy's sap, killed two of the enemy, wounded another and took one prisoner. He was himself wounded. Subsequently he went out twice into " No Man's Land " and rescued wounded men.

CAZALET, GUY LANGSTON, Temporary Capt., M.C., Royal Fusiliers. For conspicuous gallantry in action. He led his company in the attack, and held 500 yards of the trench won, although twice heavily counter-attacked by the enemy, who used liquid fire, bombs and rifles. Though wounded, he cheered on his men and refused to leave the trench.

CROSHAW, OSWALD MOSLEY, Major, Yeomanry. For conspicuous gallantry in action. When attached to Brigade Headquarters, he twice voluntarily passed through a very heavy artillery and machine-gun barrage, and brought back accurate information of the situation.

FEARENSIDE, EDMUND, Temporary Capt., Manchester Regt. For conspicuous gallantry in action. He led up two companies of reinforcements, over some 1,800 yards of open ground swept by machine-gun fire, into a village. Here he rallied his men and organized a further attack. He displayed the greatest coolness and courage.

FIFOOT, EDGAR LYN, Temporary Second Lieut., Royal Fusiliers. For conspicuous gallantry in action. During the attack he made his way along a trench to get into touch with the battalion attacking on his right. He took several prisoners, and finally built a barricade when held up by the enemy's bombers. He was severely burnt in the enemy's liquid fire attack, but stuck to his duty and did further fine work.

FRASER-TYTLER, NEIL, Capt., Royal Horse Artillery. For conspicuous gallantry in action. On several occasions he displayed the greatest coolness and courage under heavy shell fire, when ranging his own and other batteries from exposed positions. He has done other fine work and has set a splendid example.

GILLSON, ROBERT MOORE THACKER, Major (Temporary Lieut.-Colonel) Wiltshire Regt. For conspicuous gallantry in action. Under very heavy fire he attacked and captured a wood. Though wounded himself he resumed command when he heard that the next senior officer had been killed, and remained on duty till loss of blood compelled him to hand over to his Adjutant.

GRINLINTON, JOHN LIESCHING, Major, Royal Garrison Artillery. For conspicuous gallantry during several days of operations. As F.O.O. he sent back invaluable information. He was twice knocked over by shell-bursts, and his pluck and cheerfulness exercised great influence on his battery.

HALL, JOHN HAMILTON, Major (Temporary Lieut.-Colonel), Middlesex Regt. For conspicuous gallantry in action. He led his battalion to consolidate a mine crater in the enemy's front line. In spite of very heavy casualties, he conducted the operation with the greatest determination, and succeeded in holding his position all day.

HILL, JOHN CHARLES HOLDEN, Second Lieut. (Temporary Lieut.), Worcestershire Regt. For conspicuous gallantry in action. When the attack was held up by flanking fire, he ordered his men back and was the last to re-enter our trenches. After rallying his men, he went out 100 yards into " No Man's Land " and partly carried and partly dragged a wounded man back into safety. The enemy were sniping at them the whole time.

JESSUP, WILLIAM HENRY GRAY, Temporary Second Lieut., Duke of Cornwall's Light Infantry. For conspicuous gallantry during operations. When the enemy launched a heavy bomb attack on the flank of our attacking troops, he met them with a party of eight bombers and drove them back. The whole party except himself and one man became casualties. But, collecting another party, he held on for 24 hours under continuous fire in his isolated position.

MACFARLANE, WILLIAM MACCALLUM, Temporary Major, Highland Light Infantry. For conspicuous gallantry during operations. Just as the relief of his company had been completed, the enemy made a strong bombing counter-attack, which drove back the relieving troops. Major Macfarlane at once led his company back to its original position, and repelled the counter-attack. He set a fine example of cool courage.

McKAY, ROBERT JAMES, Second Lieut. (Temporary Capt.), Argyll and Sutherland Highlanders. For conspicuous gallantry in action. Though wounded early in the attack, he stuck to his post and seized a portion of the enemy's line with a small party of about 20 men. This he held against repeated attacks till he was forced back by overwhelming numbers four hours later.

O'DONNELL, ALBERT BERNARD, Temporary Second Lieut., Royal Warwickshire Regt. For conspicuous gallantry in action. During an attack, when all his senior officers had become casualties, he took command, led the companies on, and captured the enemy's trench. He then reorganized the company and consolidated the defences. He himself shot six of the enemy in the trench.

PASK, ISAAC ARTHUR JAMES, Capt., M.C., Royal Garrison Artillery. For conspicuous gallantry in action. He displayed the greatest coolness during a very heavy bombardment, and carried on after a shell had blown him across a gunpit and slightly wounded him. His dugout has twice been hit, and he has constantly gone out through a heavy barrage to observe fire. He put out a fire, although surrounded by ammunition and under heavy fire.

PROCTOR, WILLIAM HOWARD, Temporary Lieut., North Lancashire Regt. For conspicuous gallantry in action. He supported a bomb attack on a strongly held trench. When the attack was checked, he at once joined in with great determination and carried the whole attack forward. Though wounded by a bullet through the jaw, he led his men on till exhausted by loss of blood.

PERKS, ROBERT CLEMENT, Temporary Second Lieut., West Riding Regt. For conspicuous gallantry during operations. When leading a bombing party, he was wounded in the face and rendered insensible. On recovering, he again took part in the attack. While throwing bombs he was again twice wounded, in the hand and foot, but continued to lead his men till rendered unconscious by a fourth wound in the face.

SELOUS, FREDERICK COURTENEY, Capt., Royal Fusiliers. For conspicuous gallantry, resource and endurance. He has set a magnificent example to all ranks, and the value of his services with his battalion cannot be overestimated.

TAYLOR, ARTHUR CHARLES, Temporary Second Lieut., Middlesex Regt. For conspicuous gallantry in action. Seeing a large number of men of another unit who had lost their bearings, he went out, and, finding that they had lost their officers, reorganized them, directed them where to dig in, and thus enabled the ground won to be held. Later, he did other fine work.

TURNER, ERNEST GILBERT, Second Lieut., Royal Scots. For conspicuous gallantry during operations. By a combined bombing operation with another platoon, he cut off and captured 63 of the enemy. Two days later he did fine and gallant work during an attack, and afterwards returned, under close machine-gun fire, and rescued wounded men.

WALSH, RICHARD KNOX, Major (Temporary Lieut.-Colonel), Royal Scottish Fusiliers. For conspicuous gallantry in action. He commanded the supporting battalion in the attack, and displayed great skill and courage. He was in charge of the captured village until relieved. Nine days later, when his battalion captured another position, he held on to it for 36 hours with great ability and determination. He has done other fine work.

WYNNE, FRANCIS GEORGE, Capt. (Temporary Major), North Lancashire Regt. For conspicuous gallantry and devotion to duty in action. When the enemy, in overwhelming numbers, attacked our trenches, he remained at his post, though wounded and unable to stand, until the enemy were beaten off. He not only commanded his own company, but took charge of another, the officers of which had become casualties.

AUSTRALIAN IMPERIAL FORCE.

BEARDSMORE, ROBERT HENRY, Major, Australian Infantry. For conspicuous gallantry in action. Though wounded early in the engagement, he proceeded, without waiting to have his wounds dressed, to organize his company as a working party, and supervised the work for about ten hours. He did fine work throughout, and displayed great coolness and courage.

COULTER, LESLIE JACK, Major, Australian Engineers. For conspicuous gallantry during operations. When a " Push Pipe " failed to explode he went out, accompanied by a corporal, under heavy shrapnel and machine-gun fire, and blew up the exposed portion of the " Push Pipe." Later, when the leads were cut by hostile shell fire, he went out under very heavy fire to try and light the fuse further down the sap. Though wounded he refused to be removed till the " Push Pipe " had been successfully exploded.

CURRIE, PATRICK, Major, Australian Infantry. For consistent gallantry and good work during operations, notably on one occasion, during an attack, when he jumped over the parapet exposed to heavy fire in order to cheer on his men. He was subsequently wounded.

DEVONSHIRE, WILLIAM PENDENNIS, Capt., Australian Infantry. For consistent good work during operations, notably when he took charge of all the men of his battalion in the first captured enemy trench, and, after repulsing a counter-attack, led them on and captured further enemy positions.

HARPER, ROBERT RAINY, Capt., Australian Infantry. For conspicuous gallantry in action. He led an attack on the enemy trenches, and, though wounded before reaching the enemy, stuck to his command and entered their trenches. He was almost immediately again wounded by a bomb, but remained at his post for over an hour. He refused to be removed till he had seen all his men in safety.

KENNEDY, REV. JOHN JOSEPH, Australian Army Chaplain Department. For conspicuous gallantry and devotion to duty. He carried wounded men from the front trenches to the dressing station under very heavy shell fire throughout the whole night, returning repeatedly to the firing line. He also assisted in dressing wounded men, and did most gallant work throughout.

MARSDEN, THOMAS ROY, Capt., Australian Infantry. For conspicuous gallantry during operations. He took charge of six guns in the front line, and remained in action all night. Finally with these guns he covered the retirement of our infantry, and then carried a wounded man back across " No Man's Land." Later he went forward again and carried in a serjeant.

MARSHALL, ALFRED, Lieut., Australian Infantry. For conspicuous gallantry during operations. He displayed great skill and courage as Adjutant, when guiding a battalion into its position for attack across " No Man's Land " under heavy shell fire. On another occasion he did fine work consolidating the captured trench.

MAUGHAN, JOHN MALBON, Major, Australian Infantry. For conspicuous gallantry during a bomb fight. He stood before the parapet firing a " Very " pistol, to light up the ground for his bombers. He was exposed to enemy snipers' fire from " No Man's Land," and the continual firing of his pistol showed his position. Finally he was wounded.

HUNTER, DOUGLAS WILLIAM, Temporary Capt., M.B., Royal Army Medical Corps. For exceptional gallantry and devotion to duty. This officer laboured incessantly tending and clearing the wounded in the open and in front line trenches under very heavy fire At a critical time when casualties had been heavy he steadied and reorganized his stretcher bearers by his magnificent example and skilful control. After the battalion had withdrawn he continued searching the battlefield for wounded. He showed absolute disregard of danger. (Substituted for the announcement published in the London Gazette dated 25 Aug. 1916.)

The undermentioned have been awarded a Bar to their Distinguished Service Order for subsequent acts of conspicuous gallantry.

BALL, ALBERT, Lieut., D.S.O., Nottinghamshire and Derbyshire Regt., and Royal Flying Corps. For conspicuous skill and gallantry. When on escort duty to a bombing raid he saw four enemy machines in formation. He dived on to them and broke up their formation, and then shot down the nearest one, which fell on its nose. He came down to about 500 feet to make certain it was wrecked. On another occasion, observing 12 enemy machines in formation, he dived in among them, and fired a drum into the nearest machine, which went down out of control. Several more hostile machines then approached, and he fired three more drums at them, driving down another out of control. He then returned, crossing the lines at a low altitude, with his machine very much damaged. (The award of the Distinguished Service Order is also announced in the Gazette of this date.)

GOSCHEN, ARTHUR ALEC, Major, D.S.O., Royal Field Artillery. For conspicuous gallantry during operations. When a heavy shell knocked out one of his guns and buried several men he immediately commenced to dig them out, under very heavy shell fire, and, with assistance, rescued them all. On another occasion, when a pile of H.E. ammunition was ignited by a shell, he succeeded in extinguishing the flames at very great personal risk. (The Distinguished Service Order was awarded in the London Gazette dated 27 Sept. 1901.)

London Gazette, 4 Oct. 1916.—" War Office, 4 Oct. 1916. His Majesty the King has been graciously pleased to appoint the undermentioned Officers, Companions of the Distinguished Service Order, in recognition of their gallantry and distinguished service in connection with the successful attack on Enemy Airships."

SOWREY, FREDERICK, Second Lieut., Royal Fusiliers, attached Royal Flying Corps.

BRANDON, ALFRED DE BATH, Second Lieut., M.C., Royal Flying Corps Special Reserve.

London Gazette, 13 Oct. 1916.—" War Office, 13 Oct. 1916. His Majesty the King has been graciously pleased to appoint the undermentioned Officer to be a Companion of the Distinguished Service Order, in recognition of conspicuous gallantry and devotion to duty in connection with the destruction of an Enemy Airship."

TEMPEST, WULSTAN JOSEPH, Second Lieut., General List and Royal Flying Corps.

London Gazette, 19 Oct. 1916.—" War Office, 19 Oct. 1916. His Majesty the King has been graciously pleased to approve of the undermentioned Honours and Rewards for distinguished service in the field, with effect from 3 June, 1916, inclusive. To be Companions of the Distinguished Service Order."

AYLEN, ERNEST VAUGHAN, Major, M.B., Royal Army Medical Corps.

BROWNE-MASON, HUBERT OLIVER BROWNE, Lieut.-Colonel, Royal Army Medical Corps.

CARLISLE, THOMAS ROGER MASSIE, Major, Royal Field Artillery.

CLIFFORD, REGINALD CHARLES, Capt., Indian Medical Service.

HILL, HAROLD CHARLES, Major, Mahratta Light Infantry.

MANNERS, CHARLES MOLYNEUX SANDYS, Capt., Rifles.

MATTHEWS, ALEC BRYAN, Lieut., Royal Engineers.

McKENNA, JAMES CHARLES, Capt. (Temporary Major), Rajputs.

MURPHY, LEO, Capt., Royal Army Medical Corps.

PEEL, BASIL GERARD, Capt., Pioneers.

REILLY, HUGH LAMBERT, Capt. and Brevet Major, Punjabis and Royal Flying Corps.

REYNE, GERARD VAN ROSSUM, Capt., Punjabis.

SMITH, HENRY BROKE, Lieut.-Colonel, Royal Field Artillery.

SWEET, ROY THORNHILL, Lieut., Gurkha Rifles.

THOMSON, HERBERT GUY, Major, Royal Field Artillery.

London Gazette, 20 Oct. 1916.—" War Office, 20 Oct. 1916. His Majesty the King has been graciously pleased to approve of the appointments of the undermentioned Officers to be Companions of the Distinguished Service Order, in recognition of their gallantry and devotion to duty in the field."

ALEXANDER, THE HONOURABLE HAROLD RUPERT LEOFRIC GEORGE, Capt., M.C., Irish Guards. For conspicuous gallantry in action. He was the life and soul of the attack, and throughout the day led forward not only his own men but men of all regiments. He held the trenches gained in spite of heavy machine-gun fire.

ANSTRUTHER, PHILIP NOEL, Capt., M.C., Royal West Kent Regt. For conspicuous gallantry in action. When sent forward to report on the situation, he found some 150 men scattered about the edge of a wood with no officers. He rallied them and pushed on to the final objective, consolidated his position, brought five machine guns into action, and maintained his position against attacks from three sides.

BAILEY, FRANCIS WILLIAM, Surgeon-Major, Royal Field Artillery (Medical Officer). For conspicuous gallantry and devotion to duty. When the batteries of his brigade came under heavy shell fire, he at once went out to tend the wounded and dying in the open with utter disregard of danger.

BARKER, RANDLE BARNETT, Capt. (Temporary Lieut.-Colonel), Royal Fusiliers. For conspicuous gallantry during operations. He took over and organized the defences of a wood with great skill, after making a personal reconnaissance of the whole wood under shell and machine-gun fire. He has done other fine work, and has displayed great personal bravery.

BARRINGTON-WARD, VICTOR MICHAEL, Temporary Major, Royal Engineers. For conspicuous gallantry. During a fire at an ammunition depôt he took an engine between sheds where ammunition was exploding, and brought back 15 men who were exposed to considerable danger.

BELL, MICHAEL CHARLES, Capt., M.C., Royal Fusiliers. For conspicuous gallantry and skilful handling of his company in attack. His organization and initiative were very marked. For ten days previous to this attack he had worked untiringly in preparation. He remained at duty though wounded.

BELLINGHAM, EDWIN HENRY CHARLES PATRICK, Temporary Lieut.-Colonel, Royal Dublin Fusiliers. For conspicuous gallantry in action. He took command of the two leading battalions when the situation was critical, and displayed the greatest determination under shell and machine-gun fire. The success of the operation was largely due to his quick appreciation of the situation, and his rapid consolidation of the position.

BOSCAWEN, THE HONOURABLE MILDMAY THOMAS, Capt., M.C., Rifle Brigade. For conspicuous gallantry in action. During two separate fights he showed great coolness and ability. He kept his C.O. informed of the situation by observing from a place which was heavily shelled all the time.

BROWNE-CLAYTON, ROBERT CLAYTON, Major (Temporary Lieut.-Colonel) (Reserve of Officers), South Irish Horse. For conspicuous gallantry and ability during five days of operations. He commanded his battalion with great coolness, and inspired his men with a fine fighting spirit.

BULL, PHILIP CECIL, Temporary Capt., Suffolk Regt. For conspicuous gallantry in action. When he alone was left out of the officers of two companies, he rallied both of them, organized the defences of the captured position, and held it with great determination. Later, he repelled an enemy bombing attack.

CARTER, WILLIAM HENRY, Lieut. (Temporary Major), M.C., South Staffordshire Regt. For conspicuous gallantry during operations. He commanded the battalion after his C.O. was wounded, and displayed great skill and personal courage. He went about everywhere encouraging his men and making personal reconnaissances during three days of heavy fighting. He set a fine example to his command.

CLAY, BERTIE GORDON, Major (Temporary Lieut.-Colonel), Dragoon Guards. For conspicuous ability and good service during prolonged operations. The success of his battalion in the attack was largely due to his fine personal example and resource.

COLQUHOUN, SIR IAIN, Bart., Capt., Scots Guards. For conspicuous gallantry in action. He led his company with the greatest dash during the day, and with a few men reached the enemy's second line, which was full of bombers. He personally accounted for six of them, and knocked over several others with a stick. He has done other fine work.

COSSART, ARTHUR RALEIGH BLANDY, Major (Temporary Lieut.-Colonel), Royal Field Artillery. For conspicuous gallantry and good service. He was in command of a group during two prolonged periods of operations, and was largely responsible for the accurate shooting and the success achieved by the artillery, owing to his skill and careful organization.

CROOK, FRANCIS JOHN FIELDING, Temporary Major, Lancashire Fusiliers. For conspicuous gallantry and ability when in command of a battalion. Covering the left flank of our Allies in attack he carried out a difficult task with much skill. The success of the operation was very largely due to his ability.

DENISON, EDWARD BRIDGEMAN, Major (Temporary Lieut.-Colonel), M.C., King's Royal Rifle Corps. For conspicuous gallantry in action. He led his battalion in the attack with great skill and courage, and was completely successful. He displayed an utter disregard of personal safety, and set a fine example to his command.

DOBBIN, HERBERT THOMAS, Major (Temporary Lieut.-Colonel), Royal Warwickshire Regt. (Corrected to Duke of Cornwall's Light Infantry, attached Gloucestershire Regt. [London Gazette, 10 Jan., 1917.]) For excellent handling of his battalion while temporarily in command, notably on two occasions, when he captured, respectively, 500 yards and 400 yards of the enemy's trenches.

FLUKE, WALTER GEORGE, Lieut. (Temporary Capt.), South Staffordshire Regt. For conspicuous gallantry during operations. He got up to the support line through a heavy barrage, and reorganized the line when all the officers had become casualties. On another occasion he led a bombing attack, although his company were much exhausted, and forced his way along the enemy trenches in an endeavour to reach a party of men who had been cut off. He showed an utter disregard of personal safety.

FOLLIT, CHARLES ALBERT ROY, Temporary Capt., Royal Welsh Fusiliers. For conspicuous gallantry during operations. During our deployment in a wood the enemy twice attacked, and we came under heavy fire. It was mainly due to Capt. Follit's fine work that the deployment was completed. He also did most gallant work reconnoitring the enemy wire.

FRANCIS, ROBERT, Second Lieut. (Temporary Capt.), Norfolk Regt. For conspicuous gallantry in action. Though wounded during the morning, he led his company in the attack in the afternoon with the greatest gallantry. When hung up by machine-gun fire, he moved backwards and forwards under heavy fire, bringing up men to the firing line. Though again wounded, he remained with his company for five hours in the open. On previous occasions he has shown similar gallantry.

GRENFELL, ARTHUR MORTON, Major, Yeomanry. For conspicuous gallantry. He rallied a considerable number of men who were retiring, and, with some of his own working party, led them forward and consolidated a position under heavy rifle and machine-gun fire. Later, while trying to get a wounded officer back to safety, he was himself wounded.

GWYNNE-JONES, ALLAN, Second Lieut., East Surrey Regt., Special Reserve. For conspicuous gallantry in action. He rallied the men of two companies which had lost their officers, and succeeded in gaining a footing in the enemy's position, gradually working the enemy out of it and consolidating his position under heavy shell-fire. On the previous day he carried out a daring reconnaissance and was slightly wounded.

HALL, PHILIP SARSFIELD, Temporary Major (Temporary Lieut.-Colonel), West Yorkshire Regt. During the short time he has been in command of a battalion he has, by his personal example and initiative, created a fine soldierly spirit throughout all ranks. He has shown conspicuous ability as a leader in all situations.

HARMAN, ALEXANDER RAMSAY, Lieut.-Colonel, Worcestershire Regt. For the excellent handling of his battalion, notably when clearing the enemy's trenches with great determination during several consecutive days.

HARRISSON, ROLAND DAMER, Major, Royal Field Artillery. For conspicuous gallantry in action. He commanded and fought his battery with great skill, and went out in front of our infantry advance posts in search of O.P.'s. During many days of operations he showed great courage and devotion to duty.

HEATON, DAVID RIMINGTON, Temporary Lieut. (Temporary Capt.), Royal West Surrey Regt. For conspicuous gallantry in action. When his battalion had suffered heavy casualties and was unsupported, he led a bombing party and drove the enemy up a communication trench. He then cleared the enemy third line trench, taking 163 prisoners. Finally he rallied all troops near him and led them on to the final objective.

HEWETT, EDWARD VINCENT OSBORNE, Major (Temporary Lieut.-Colonel), C.M.G., Reserve of Officers, South Wales Borderers. For consistent gallantry and good service. During a prolonged period of operations he has, by his fine example and good leading, done excellent work with his battalion.

HOARE, WALTER JOHN GERALD, Temporary Capt., Royal Fusiliers. For conspicuous gallantry during operations. With two serjeants, one of whom was wounded by the intense shell-fire, he dug out a buried serjeant and rescued him alive. He has done fine work throughout the operations.

HOPLEY, FREDERICK JOHN VANDER BYL, Lieut. (Temporary Capt.), Grenadier Guards, Special Reserve. For conspicuous gallantry in action. He showed fine leadership throughout the attack, in spite of being wounded himself, and of severe casualties among his men. He stuck to his position on the extreme flank throughout the day, though exposed to machine-gun fire, until the battalion was relieved.

HUNT, JOHN PATRICK, Temporary Capt., Royal Dublin Fusiliers. For conspicuous gallantry in action. He formed and held a defensive flank for ten hours, until relieved, under heavy machine-gun and rifle fire, thus frustrating the enemy's attempt to turn the flank.

PIGOT, ROBERT, Capt. and Brevet Major (Temporary Lieut.-Colonel), Rifle Brigade. For conspicuous gallantry and ability in action. During three days, operations he commanded his battalion with great skill and determination, and was entirely successful. During the operations three enemy officers and 79 men were captured, and also three machine guns.

INGLIS, ARTHUR MACULLOCH, Capt., Gloucestershire Regt. For conspicuous gallantry in action. He brought his "Tanks" forward over very difficult ground. Although one of the wheels of his own "Tank" was blown off early by a shell he succeeded in reaching his objective and manœuvring throughout the whole operation.

INGLIS, HAROLD JOHN, Lieut. (Temporary Capt.), M.C., South Wales Borderers. For conspicuous gallantry in action. He led his company with great dash in the attack. When checked he went forward with a serjeant and private and captured nine of the enemy, at the same time gaining another 80 yards of trench.

IRWIN, ALFRED PERCY BULTEEL, Capt. (Temporary Major), East Surrey Regt. For conspicuous gallantry in action. When the battalion was in danger of being hung up owing to heavy casualties and severe opposition he went forward, formed up the men as if on parade, and personally led them to the final objective.

JANION, CLAUDE WILSON, Temporary Second Lieut., East Surrey Regt. For conspicuous gallantry in action. When he was the only officer left in his company he led it on with great determination. He personally led bombing parties down the enemy's trenches and cleared the first four lines of them. It was due to his good leading and pluck that the company reached its objective.

KELLY, EDWARD HENRY, Capt., M.C., Royal Engineers. For conspicuous gallantry in action. He organized and directed the concentration and deployment of the brigade by night with great skill. When the attack was hung up by uncut wire he personally reconnoitred under very difficult conditions, and organized bombing attacks from both flanks. It was mainly due to his fine work that 1,000 yards of trench were taken and 300 prisoners captured.

KEMP-WELCH, MARTIN, Capt. (Temporary Major), M.C., Royal West Surrey Regt. For conspicuous gallantry and good service in action. When the battalion had suffered severely and matters had come to a standstill, he went forward, reorganized the battalion, restarted the attack, and carried it through to a successful conclusion.

LUCAS, LEONARD WAINWRIGHT, Major (Temporary Lieut.-Colonel), M.C., East Kent Regt. For conspicuous gallantry and ability when commanding his battalion, which captured in attack many prisoners and two machine guns. He displayed the greatest initiative and resource.

LYTTELTON, OLIVER, Lieut. (Temporary Capt.), Grenadier Guards. For conspicuous gallantry in action. He showed great bravery in the attack, led a company forward, and was largely instrumental in taking 100 prisoners. He stuck to his position for five hours under fire, till obliged to retire to prevent being surrounded.

MAHONEY, MICHAEL JOSEPH, Major, M.D., Royal Army Medical Corps. For conspicuous gallantry and devotion to duty in action. When his aid post was blown in he at once established another under heavy shell-fire, and tended the wounded for two days and nights. When relieved he took a few hours' rest and then returned to his gallant work.

MARTIN, CECIL WATSON, Capt., Royal Warwickshire Regt. For conspicuous gallantry in action. He led his company in the attack with great dash, repelled bombing attacks, and displayed great courage in endeavouring to consolidate the position.

MICKLEM, JOHN, Capt. (Temporary Lieut.-Colonel), M.C., Rifle Brigade. For the excellent handling of his battalion, notably on two occasions during heavy counter-attacks by the enemy.

MILBURN, BOOKER, Second Lieut. (Temporary Capt.), M.C., Hertfordshire Regt. For conspicuous gallantry and devotion to duty during operations. He has handled his machine-gun company with great skill and determination, and stuck to his duty after being wounded in many places.

MILNE, JOSEPH ELLIS, Capt., M.D., Royal Army Medical Corps. For conspicuous gallantry and devotion to duty during operations. He has repeatedly tended the wounded under heavy shell-fire, and has shown himself utterly regardless of personal safety.

MORGAN, FREDERICK JAMES, Temporary Lieut. (Temporary Capt.), Norfolk Regt. For conspicuous gallantry in action. When nearly all the officers had become casualties, he took command of the whole firing line, and, by his fine example, coolness and pluck, led the battalion on to its objective. On another occasion he did similar fine work.

NEGUS, RAYMOND EWINGS, Temporary Major (Temporary Lieut.-Colonel), Shropshire Light Infantry. For conspicuous gallantry in action. When unable to find an opening in the enemy's wire, he continued to hack his way through under very heavy rifle and machine-gun fire, till he was badly wounded. He set a fine example to his men.

OLIPHANT, PHILIP LAURENCE KINGTON BLAIR, Temporary Major, Royal Irish Rifles. For conspicuous gallantry in action. When there was great difficulty in getting information regarding the situation, owing to casualties among officers and runners and to the enemy's heavy barrage, he went forward under very heavy fire, organized scattered parties in the firing line, repelled a counter-attack, and brought back valuable information.

PAPILLON, PELHAM RAWSTORN, Temporary Lieut.-Colonel, Essex Regt. For conspicuous gallantry during operations. When leading his battalion a shell burst in front of him, knocked him down, and cut his eye, but he carried on with the greatest coolness. Next morning another shell severely bruised him and broke the drum of his ear, but he refused to leave his post. He set a fine example to his command.

PERCIVAL, EDGAR, Capt., M.B., Royal Army Medical Corps. For conspicuous gallantry and devotion to duty. He led a party of stretcher-bearers into a wood, and remained for over two hours searching for wounded under shell and machine-gun fire. On previous occasions he has done similar gallant work.

RICHARDSON, ARTHUR JOHNSTONE, Lieut.-Colonel, Reserve of Officers, South Lancashire Regt. For conspicuous devotion to duty when commanding a battalion in attack. Although injured, he carried out his duties unremittingly, and it was due to his personal example and perseverance that his battalion succeeded in holding a portion of the line subjected to constant heavy shell fire.

RYALLS, HARRY DOUGLAS, Temporary Lieut., Cheshire Regt. For conspicuous gallantry in action. He held on to his position during a very heavy bombardment. Though he had suffered heavy casualties, and was attacked by strong forces of the enemy on both flanks, he handled his company and machine guns with such skill that the attacks were repulsed with great loss.

SANDAY, WILLIAM DOUGLAS STOCK, Capt., M.C., Royal Flying Corps. For conspicuous gallantry and skill. He has led over 35 patrols with great gallantry. On one occasion a machine of his formation was attacked, but he charged and brought down the enemy machine in flames. He has destroyed at least four enemy machines.

SHELLARD, EDWIN, Capt. (Temporary Major), Gloucestershire Regt. For conspicuous gallantry in action. He led a successful attack on the enemy's front-line trenches, and, after their capture, reorganized the defences, consolidated the position, and held it against counter-attack.

SMITH, JACOB HARDY, Lieut. (Temporary Capt.), M.C., Rifle Brigade. For conspicuous gallantry in action. He led his company with great determination in two attacks, and it was mainly due to his training and fine example that the company did so well after losing very heavily. He was badly wounded in a fight with two enemy officers, both of whom he killed.

STAFFORD, RONALD SEMPILL HOWARD, Second Lieut. (Temporary Capt.), M.C., King's Royal Rifle Corps, Special Reserve. For conspicuous gallantry in action. He commanded his company in the attack with great skill and courage, and it was largely due to his fine example and good leadership that persistent counter-attacks and bomb-attacks were driven off. He also took command of another company which had lost its officers, and, under heavy fire of all kinds, held on to the captured ground and consolidated it.

THOMPSON, GEORGE ERNEST, Second Lieut., London Regt. For conspicuous gallantry when leading bombers in a raid. Though severely wounded, he continued to fight, and personally shot two of the enemy. He helped a wounded man back to our lines, and insisted on searching for a missing officer before his wounds were dressed.

TWEEN, ALFRED STUART, Temporary Capt., Essex Regt. For conspicuous gallantry in action. He took command of four companies after nearly all the officers had become casualties. By his fine example he held the men together, consolidated his position, and repulsed several counter-attacks.

VAUGHAN, EUGENE NAPOLEON ERNEST MALLET, Capt., Reserve of Officers, Grenadier Guards. For conspicuous gallantry in action. When in command of an isolated trench and attacked on front, flank and rear, he drove off the enemy, killing over 100 of them, and took 29 prisoners. His fine example has given great confidence to his men.

VERNON, HENRY ALBEMARLE, Major (Temporary Lieut.-Colonel), King's Royal Rifle Corps. For conspicuous gallantry in action. He led his battalion in the attack with great skill and courage, and was completely successful. He set a fine example to his command.

WARD, CLEMENT WYNDHAM, Temporary Second Lieut. (Temporary Capt.), Wiltshire Regt. For conspicuous gallantry in action. After a successful advance, he secured his flank with great ability, and, owing to the good information which he sent back, it was possible to organize further attacks. He showed a quick grasp of the situation at a time when reinforcements were badly needed elsewhere.

WILKINSON, ALAN MACHIN, Lieut. (Temporary Capt.), Hampshire Regt., and Royal Flying Corps. For conspicuous gallantry and skill. He has shown great dash in attacking enemy machines, and, up to the end of August, he had accounted for five. On one occasion while fighting a hostile machine he was attacked from behind, but out-manœuvred the enemy and shot him down. Finally he got back, his machine much damaged by machine-gun fire.

AUSTRALIAN IMPERIAL FORCE.

BOURNE, GEORGE HERBERT, Major, Australian Light Horse. For conspicuous gallantry in action. He held the outpost line against heavy odds for four hours, and then gradually and skilfully withdrew. A few days later he held the extreme flank with great determination at a critical time.

NICHOLAS, GEORGE MATSON, Capt., Australian Infantry. For conspicuous gallantry and initiative. Having whilst on reconnaissance discovered a machine gun, Capt. Nicholas went out again alone, and with great dash and initiative captured the gun.

CANADIAN FORCE.

HAGARTY, WILLIAM GRASETT, Major, Royal Canadian Artillery. For conspicuous gallantry during operations. After an excellent reconnaissance he succeeded in bringing his battery into position by night, over difficult ground and under heavy shell fire. He did fine work next morning.

NEWFOUNDLAND CONTINGENT.

FRANKLIN, WILL HODGSON, Major (Temporary Lieut.-Colonel), Newfoundland Regt. For conspicuous gallantry in action. He led his men in the attack with great dash, and directed a bombing party after being severely wounded.

The undermentioned Officers have been awarded a Bar to their Distinguished Service Order for subsequent acts of conspicuous gallantry.

DONE, HERBERT RICHARD, Brevet Lieut.-Colonel (Temporary Brigadier-General), D.S.O., Norfolk Regt. For conspicuous good service in action. He handled his brigade with great skill during two attacks, and showed great determination.

(The Distinguished Service Order was awarded in London Gazette dated 18 Feb. 1915.)

MORGAN, ROSSLEWIN WESTROPP, Major (Temporary Lieut.-Colonel), D.S.O., South Staffordshire Regt. For conspicuous gallantry during operations. When the C.O. and second in command of another battalion had become casualties, he took command of both battalions, organized his defences, and held his own against counter-attack and during a very heavy bombardment. He has always displayed the greatest bravery, and has set a fine example to his command.

(The Distinguished Service Order was awarded in London Gazette dated 14 Jan. 1916.)

SLADEN, GERALD CAREW, Major (now Temporary Brigadier-General), D.S.O., M.C., Rifle Brigade. For the excellent handling of his battalion, notably when he placed it at such a position as to cause the surrender of many of the enemy in a village. On another occasion he captured a whole system of enemy trenches and many prisoners.
(The Distinguished Service Order was awarded in London Gazette dated 14 Jan. 1916.)

London Gazette, 25 Oct. 1916.—" Admiralty, S.W., 25 Oct. 1916. The King has been graciously pleased to give orders for the appointment of the undermentioned Officers to be Companions of the Distinguished Service Order."
LEIR, ERNEST WILLIAM, Commander, R.N.
BENNING, CHARLES STUART, Commander, R.N.
In recognition of their services in submarines in enemy waters.
TURNER, ROBERT ROSS, Lieut.-Commander, R.N. In recognition of his gallantry and determination in carrying out submarine attacks on enemy ships.
RAIKES, ROBERT HENRY TAUNTON, Lieut.-Commander, R.N.
HARDEN, GEORGE ELLIOTT, Lieut., R.N. Lieut. Harden was temporarily in command of the river gunboat Comet during the attack on Ctesiphon and the subsequent withdrawal to Kut-el-Amara, and behaved with great coolness during the whole period. On the 1st Dec. 1915, when H.M.S. Firefly had grounded and been abandoned, he took a boat over from the armed launch Sumana under very heavy fire, and brought off the Firefly's crew.
ROBSON, HUMPHREY MAURICE, Lieut., R.N.
MACKENZIE, COLIN ROY, Flight Lieut., R.N.A.S. In recognition of his skill and gallantry in destroying a German kite balloon on the 7th Sept. 1916, under very severe anti-aircraft fire.

London Gazette, 28 Oct. 1916.—" War Office, 28 Oct. 1916. His Majesty the King has been graciously pleased to appoint the undermentioned Officer to be a Companion of the Distinguished Service Order."
ELKINGTON, JOHN FORD, Lieut.-Colonel, Royal Warwickshire Regiment.

London Gazette, 2 Nov. 1916.—" War Office, 2 Nov. 1916. His Majesty the King has been graciously pleased to award the Distinguished Service Order to the undermentioned Officers, in recognition of their distinguished service and devotion to duty during the spring and summer of last year in the Prisoners-of-War Camp at Gardelegen, Germany."
WILLIAMS, AUGUSTUS SCOTT, Capt., Royal Army Medical Corps.
BROWN, ARTHUR JAMES, Capt., Royal Army Medical Corps, Special Reserve.

London Gazette, 14 Nov. 1916.—" War Office, 14 Nov. 1916. His Majesty the King has been graciously pleased to approve of the appointments of the undermentioned Officers to be Companions of the Distinguished Service Order, in recognition of their gallantry and devotion to duty in the field."
ALLERTON, CLAUDE, Temporary Lieut., Suffolk Regt. For conspicuous gallantry in action. After his senior officers had become casualties in the attack, he took command of the battalion and carried on with coolness and judgment under heavy fire, until a senior officer arrived in the evening.
ASHTON, HENRY GORDON GOOCH, Temporary Capt., Welsh Guards. For conspicuous gallantry in action. Owing to several casualties he found himself in command of three companies and some 50 men of other units. For many hours he was fighting the enemy on all sides, and had his men facing front and rear in the same trench. His great determination and fine leadership were largely responsible for the holding of the position.
BAILEY, THE HONOURABLE WILFRED RUSSELL, Capt., Grenadier Guards. For conspicuous gallantry in action. Capts. Bailey and Harcourt-Vernon led a company out of the trench with great dash. They themselves led by at least 50 yards, and shot many of the enemy with their revolvers. About 60 of the enemy were accounted for, mainly with the bayonet, and 42 made prisoners.
BARNES, ANTHONY CHARLES, Temporary Major, Yorkshire Regt. For conspicuous gallantry in action. When in command of two companies he held his own with great determination under heavy fire for 36 hours, and later re-captured a lost position.
BARNETT, WILLIAM HAROLD LOUIS, Lieut. (Temporary Capt.), Bedfordshire Regt., Special Reserve. For conspicuous gallantry in action. He led his company with the greatest courage and determination. Later he led his company in the assault after suffering nine hours under barrage fire. His gallantry and initiative greatly assisted the success of the operations.
BAUGH, RUPERT STANTON, Lieut., Coldstream Guards, Special Reserve. For conspicuous gallantry in action. When cut off from his battalion he rallied the men of different units around him, and beat off three hostile counter-attacks. He hung on to his position for 48 hours, though himself twice blown up by high explosive shells, one of which rendered him unconscious.
BENFIELD, KARL VERE BARKER, Lieut., Royal Artillery. For conspicuous gallantry in action. When observation officer, he, with two men and a N.C.O., attacked a party of the enemy, killing several and capturing seven prisoners and a communication trench. He displayed the greatest courage and initiative throughout.
BLUNT, DUNCAN HAMILTON, Major (Temporary Lieut.-Colonel), Devonshire Regt. For conspicuous gallantry in action. He led his battalion with great dash in the attack and capture of a wood, and established his position in a captured enemy trench beyond. He thus greatly facilitated the further advance.
BRINDLEY, JAMES, Lieut. (Temporary Capt.), M.C., East Yorkshire Regt. For conspicuous gallantry in action. He led his company in the attack with the greatest courage and initiative, himself accounting for 12 of the enemy. Later, although wounded, he continued to advance, and with a small party captured 61 prisoners. He has previously done very fine work.
BUCKLEY, GEORGE ALEXANDER McLEAN, Temporary Lieut.-Colonel, Leinster Regt. For conspicuous gallantry in action. He led his battalion with the greatest courage and determination. He has on many previous occasions done very fine work.
CANGLEY, FREDERICK GEORGE, Temporary Second Lieut., Liverpool Regt. For conspicuous gallantry in action. He led his company under intense fire to support a battalion which had been held up, displaying the greatest courage and initiative. Later, he assumed command of the battalion, rallied it, and organized the defence with great ability.
CLARKE, ROBERT JOYCE, Lieut.-Colonel, Royal Berkshire Regt. For conspicuous gallantry in action. He has handled his battalion with great skill and determination. On three separate occasions his fine leading has achieved important success.

CLEMINSON, CHARLES ROBERT DAVIDGE, Temporary Capt., Liverpool Regt. For conspicuous gallantry in action. While leading troops to reinforce the attacking line, he saw the troops on his left retiring and leaving the flank of the division exposed. On his own initiative he at once took his two companies, and any other men he could gather, close to the position consolidated a defensive flank and held it till relieved.
CROSBIE, WALTER McCLELLAND, Major, Royal Munster Fusiliers. For conspicuous gallantry in action. He led two companies with the greatest courage and initiative. Later, he organized the position with great skill, displaying great coolness throughout. He was wounded.
DARELL, HARRY FRANCIS, Temporary Lieut.-Colonel, Rifle Brigade. For conspicuous gallantry in action. He organized a reinforcing attack, under heavy shell fire and when units were much mixed up. By his skill and good leading the attack reached its objective.
DAUBENY, GILES BULTEEL, Major, Royal Artillery. For conspicuous gallantry in action. He conducted the fire of his battery from the advanced trenches under heavy fire with great skill and determination. He also sent in accurate reports throughout the day.
DUNFORD, ROY CRAIG, Second Lieut. (Temporary Capt.), Northumberland Fusiliers. For conspicuous gallantry in action. For three days prior to an attack he directed the digging of assault trenches under heavy shell fire. During the attack his personal direction of his company resulted in heavy losses to the enemy and the capture of 150 prisoners. Finally he was shot through the body whilst organizing his defences.
FERGUSON, GEORGE DOUGLAS, Temporary Capt., M.B., Royal Army Medical Corps. For conspicuous gallantry and devotion to duty. He tended the wounded under very heavy fire, bringing in over 50 wounded men, and displaying the greatest courage and determination. His fearless bearing set a fine example.
FULLER, JOHN STEED, Second Lieut., Coldstream Guards, Special Reserve. For conspicuous gallantry in action. When his portion of the line was held up by rifle and machine-gun fire, he collected a party of his company and rushed the enemy's position in face of overwhelming odds, thus enabling the advance to proceed. Later he was seriously wounded.
GORELL, LORD (HENRY GORELL BARNES), Capt. (Temporary Major), Royal Artillery. For conspicuous gallantry in action. He pushed forward and handled his battery under very heavy fire with the greatest courage and skill. Later, he carried out a daring reconnaissance and obtained most valuable information.
GOW, ANDREW, Temporary Capt., Cameron Highlanders. For conspicuous gallantry in action. He took command of the whole of the forward operations and led the attack with great skill and determination. It was greatly due to his organizing powers and the excellent information he sent back that the operations were successful.
HARCOURT-VERNON, GRANVILLE CHARLES FITZHERBERT, Capt., Grenadier Guards. For conspicuous gallantry in action. Capts. Harcourt-Vernon and Bailey led a company out of the trench with great dash. They themselves led by at least 50 yards, and shot many of the enemy with their revolvers. About 60 of the enemy were accounted for, mainly with the bayonet, and 42 made prisoners.
HARGREAVES, THOMAS CHARLES, Capt. (Temporary Major), London Regt. For conspicuous gallantry in action. He led the advance with skill and determination when the attack was held up by machine-gun fire. Later, he set a fine personal example when beating off a counter-attack on an exposed flank. He was wounded.
HATFIELD, EDGAR RICHARD, Capt. (Temporary Major), Royal Artillery. For conspicuous gallantry in action. He handled his battery throughout with the greatest courage and determination. Later, with one N.C.O., he put out a fire among burning ammunition in a gun-pit at great personal risk.
HOPE, JOHN FREDERIC ROUNDEL, Capt. (Temporary Lieut.-Colonel), King's Royal Rifle Corps. For conspicuous gallantry in action. He commanded his battalion with great determination during two days of heavy enemy counter-attacks, and it was largely due to his personal example that the attacks were repulsed. He carried on after he had been blown from the parapet, nearly buried and much shaken.
JAMES, CHARLES KENNETH, Temporary Capt., Border Regt. For conspicuous gallantry in action. He led a party against the enemy with the greatest courage and skill, and put the enemy to flight. Later, he organized and led a bombing party, capturing a much greater position than he had set out to take. He has on many previous occasions done very fine work.
JAMES, ERIC GWYN, Second Lieut. (Temporary Capt.), Shropshire Light Infantry. For conspicuous gallantry during operations. He personally superintended, with great skill, all arrangements for two attacks on the enemy, and was dangerously wounded.
KIDD, GUY EGERTON, Major, Royal Artillery. For conspicuous gallantry in action. He commanded his battery with great skill and determination. Later he carried out a most valuable reconnaissance; during this he passed two trenches held by the enemy and captured two prisoners.
LANGAN-BYRNE, PATRICK ANTHONY, Second Lieut., Royal Artillery and Royal Flying Corps. For conspicuous skill and gallantry. He has shown great pluck in attacking hostile machines, often against large odds. He has accounted for several. On one occasion, with two other machines, he attacked seventeen enemy machines, shot down one in flames and forced another to land.
LEE, JOHN HENRY, Temporary Second Lieut., King's Royal Rifle Corps. For conspicuous gallantry in action. Although wounded he assumed command and led his company with the greatest courage and determination. Later, again being wounded, he remained on duty, establishing connection with neighbouring units, and consolidating ground won.
LEESE, OLIVER WILLIAM HARGREAVES, Lieut., Coldstream Guards. For conspicuous gallantry in action. He led the assault against a strongly-held part of the enemy's line, which was stopping the whole attack. He personally accounted for many of the enemy and enabled the attack to proceed. He was wounded during the fight.
LEONARD, REV. MARTIN PATRICK GRANGE, Temporary Chaplain, 4th Class, Army Chaplain Department (Royal Lancashire Regt.). For conspicuous gallantry and devotion to duty during protracted operations. He was always moving about among the wounded giving them encouragement. He assisted the medical officer in tending the wounded under heavy shell fire, and on one occasion carried a wounded man himself on a stretcher. His gallantry and devotion to duty has been beyond praise.
LONGUEVILLE, FRANCIS, Capt., M.C., Coldstream Guards. For conspicuous gallantry in action. He commanded his company with great determination throughout the fight. When the first objective was taken he collected men, and led the leading wave through an intense barrage to the second objective.

MACMILLAN, JAMES BONTHRON, Temporary Capt., Duke of Cornwall's Light Infantry. For conspicuous gallantry in action. He led the attacking force with the greatest courage and determination at all times, sending back most valuable information. Later, with both his flanks exposed, he held and consolidated the position against determined enemy bombing attacks.

MATHERS, DAVID, Major (Temporary Lieut.-Colonel), Royal Inniskilling Fusiliers. For conspicuous gallantry in action. He handled his battalion throughout the operations with the greatest courage and initiative, gaining his objective, and capturing two machine guns, three officers, and over 100 other ranks.

MINCHIN, THOMAS WILLIAM, Second Lieut., Grenadier Guards, Special Reserve. For conspicuous gallantry in action. He cleared an orchard, killing many of the enemy, and sited and organized a new line of defence under heavy rifle and machine-gun fire. He displayed the greatest coolness, and went back himself to report on the situation after four different runners had become casualties.

OAKLEY, RICHARD, Major (Temporary Lieut.-Colonel), Scottish Rifles. For conspicuous gallantry in action. He gallantly led his regiment and assisted to defeat two enemy counter-attacks. He set a splendid example of coolness and courage to his men. He was wounded.

PATTERSON, JOHN WILSON, Temporary Lieut., Royal Engineers. For conspicuous gallantry. While proceeding with two men to his working party, he suddenly saw a party of the enemy coming out of a deep dug-out. He and his two men rushed at them, disarmed about ten who had rifles, and took the whole party, two officers and 34 men, prisoners.

PORTER, HENRY COLIN MANSEL, Major, King's Royal Rifle Corps. For conspicuous gallantry in action. He assumed command of his battalion, and also of another unit, displaying the greatest courage and initiative. In order to exercise his extended command he went about in the open under very heavy fire.

PRESCOTT-WESTCAR, WILLIAM VILLIERS LEONARD, Major (Temporary Lieut.-Colonel), Rifle Brigade. For conspicuous gallantry in action. He led his battalion with the greatest courage and initiative, carrying the first, third and fifth objectives. Later, he personally supervised the reorganization and consolidation, and sending back most valuable information. He was severely wounded.

REYNOLDS, LEWIS LESLIE CLAYTON, Major (Temporary Lieut.-Colonel), Oxfordshire and Buckinghamshire Light Infantry. For conspicuous gallantry in action. He handled his battalion with great skill and determination. On two separate occasions his good leading has achieved important success.

RHODES, FREDERICK WILLIAM, Temporary Lieut., Shropshire Light Infantry. For conspicuous gallantry in action. When his battalion was held up, he organized a party and rushed a battery of enemy guns, capturing four officers and 20 other ranks, as well as four field guns. He displayed the greatest courage and initiative throughout.

RIDLEY, CLAUDE ALWARD, Second Lieut., M.C., Royal Fusiliers and Royal Flying Corps. For conspicuous gallantry and judgment in the execution of a special mission. When his machine was wrecked he showed great resource, and obtained valuable information.

SHAW, WILLIAM MAXWELL, Major, Royal Artillery. For conspicuous gallantry in action. He went forward to ascertain the exact situation of our advanced infantry. Later, with another officer and two bombers, he carried out a daring reconnaissance of a trench thought to be occupied by the enemy, thereby obtaining most valuable information.

SHEPPARD, EDGAR, Capt., M.C., Grenadier Guards. For conspicuous gallantry in action. He led his men to their objective with the greatest courage and initiative. Later, his left flank being unprotected, he threw back a defensive flank and got into touch with the troops on his left.

STEYN, PIERRE, Temporary Capt., Bedfordshire Regt. For conspicuous gallantry in action. In three separate fights he displayed great coolness and determination, and by his fine example greatly encouraged all ranks.

TAMPLIN, ROBERT JAMES ABBOTT, Temporary Capt. (Temporary Major), Connaught Rangers. For conspicuous gallantry in action. He led his company with the greatest courage and determination, and was instrumental in capturing the position. He was wounded.

THOMAS, GWYN, Major, Bengal Lancers. For conspicuous gallantry in action. He went forward to ascertain the situation, passed through a heavy barrage, rallied and collected the troops, and led them forward with great skill and determination, displaying splendid personal courage.

TRAILL, HENRY EDWARD O'BRIEN, Major, Royal Artillery. For conspicuous gallantry in action. He handled his battery throughout with the greatest courage and determination. His fearless bearing was of the greatest value, not only to his own battery, but to the batteries on either side of him. On several occasions he extricated wagons and teams from places of danger.

TROYTE-BULLOCK, CECIL JOHN, Major (Temporary Lieut.-Colonel), Somerset Light Infantry. For conspicuous gallantry in action. He led his battalion, which was in reserve, with great skill, and by his prompt reinforcement of the attacking line materially helped to beat off a counter-attack. Though wounded in the leg, he remained in command till the position was secured.

WATSON, SIDNEY TWELLS, Major (Temporary Lieut.-Colonel), Royal West Surrey Regt. For conspicuous gallantry and able leadership in action. Under his direction and initiative the enemy attack was driven back, the position won, and many prisoners taken.

AUSTRALIAN IMPERIAL FORCE.

BIDDLE, FRED LESLIE, Major, Field Artillery. For conspicuous gallantry during three days of operations. As liaison officer he did fine work, and when his telephone lines were repeatedly cut, passed through the barrage to telephone stations of other units in order to get his information through. He was himself wounded on the last day.

BLACK, PERCY, Major, Infantry. For conspicuous gallantry during operations. He led his company over "No Man's Land" against an enemy's strong point, which he captured and consolidated under very difficult circumstances, and under heavy artillery and machine-gun fire. On a subsequent occasion he did similar fine work.

BRETTINGHAM-MOORE, HERBERT MANSEL, Capt., Infantry. For conspicuous gallantry during operations. He cleared his trench of the enemy with great determination, and, hearing that some of the enemy wanted to surrender, he went towards them and drove them out of the dug-outs with his revolver to the part of the trench held by us, where they were taken by our men. He was wounded at the time.

FORTESCUE, CHARLES, Capt., Infantry. For conspicuous gallantry in action. He commanded his company with the greatest courage and skill. Later, although wounded, he greatly assisted in defeating several enemy counter-attacks. He showed a splendid example of coolness and initiative to his men.

HARWOOD, ROSS, Capt., Infantry. For conspicuous gallantry in action. He led his company with the greatest gallantry against two enemy strong points. Although wounded, he secured his objective and captured 150 prisoners. He set a splendid example of coolness and initiative to his men.

JEFFRIES, LEWIS WIBMER, Major, Army Medical Corps. For conspicuous gallantry and devotion to duty during operations. He tended the wounded and reorganized the stretcher-bearers in the front line at great personal risk. When only a few bearers were left, he himself assisted to carry back the wounded under heavy fire.

MURRAY, HENRY WILLIAM, Capt., Infantry. For conspicuous gallantry in action. Although twice wounded, he commanded his company with the greatest courage and initiative, beating off four enemy counter-attacks. Later, when an enemy bullet started a man's equipment exploding, he tore the man's equipment off at great personal risk. He set a splendid example throughout.

CANADIAN FORCE.

BODWELL, HOWARD LIONEL, Major, Pioneers. For conspicuous gallantry in action. He, with a small party, built a roadway under intense fire, displaying the greatest courage and initiative. He has on many previous occasions done very fine work.

BREDIN, CHARLES EDGAR ATHELING, Capt., Infantry. For conspicuous gallantry in action. He led his company in attack and captured an enemy strong point, which was holding up the attack, under intense artillery, rifle and machine-gun fire. Later he took over the companies of the whole line and consolidated the position with great skill and determination.

FAIRWEATHER, CHARLES EDWARD, Temporary Major, Infantry. For conspicuous gallantry in action. With his company he dug a trench 200 yards in front of the front line under intense fire, and thereby rendered the support necessary to ensure the safety of the ground gained by a flanking battalion. He displayed the greatest courage and initiative throughout.

HARDY, ETHELBERT BROWN, Lieut.-Colonel, Army Medical Corps. For conspicuous gallantry and devotion to duty during operations. He controlled the evacuation of the sick and wounded, and by his energy and courage kept up the spirits of the stretcher-bearers when they were much exhausted.

HARSTONE, JOHN BRUNTON, Capt. (Temporary Major), Infantry. For conspicuous gallantry in action. He led his company with great dash in the attack, and, when he had lost touch with his battalion commander, assumed command of all the troops round him, consolidated his position, and organized his defences. All this was under heavy fire.

HERON, LIONEL DALZIEL, Capt., M.C., Infantry. For conspicuous gallantry in action. He made a most valuable reconnaissance. Later he organized a bombing party, capturing many prisoners. These services he performed with splendid courage and skill, and greatly assisted the advance.

JACQUES, HARRY MERVILLE, Lieut.-Colonel, Army Medical Corps. For conspicuous gallantry and devotion to duty. He supervised the clearing of the front and controlled the work of the advanced and main dressing stations with great skill and personal courage.

MACLEOD, GEORGE WALKERS, Major, Infantry. For conspicuous gallantry during operations. He went forward into the fight and selected the ground to be consolidated, and, though severely wounded, made his way back under heavy fire, and rendered a complete report on the situation. He has always set a fine example of coolness and courage.

McDONALD, HAROLD FRENCH, Major, Infantry. For conspicuous gallantry during operations. He carried out a dangerous reconnaissance under heavy shell fire, and after a shell splinter had blown off his arm he reported the result of his reconnaissance before allowing the stretcher-bearers to remove him.

McELLIGOTT, ARNOLD E., Lieut., Infantry. For conspicuous gallantry in action. He took complete command of the front line of three companies, and with great skill and determination consolidated the line under intense fire and local attacks.

McKENZIE, JOHN ALLEN, Major, Infantry. For conspicuous gallantry during operations. He commanded his company with great skill and determination during the capture of a position, and, by his accurate reports, enabled preparations to be made by which a heavy counter-attack was beaten off. He has done other fine work.

McLAUGHLIN, LARNE T., Major, Infantry. For conspicuous gallantry in action. He led his men forward with great dash under machine-gun and rifle fire, consolidated his position, and repulsed frequent counter-attacks. On one occasion he personally led bombers to repulse an attack on his flank.

NORRIS, HERBERT, Lieut., Infantry. For conspicuous gallantry in action. The officers of the battalion having become casualties, he took command of the whole, and under very heavy fire organized and consolidated the position. He displayed high qualities of initiative and command.

REYNOLDS, CHARLES EDWARD, Lieut., Infantry. For conspicuous gallantry in action. He led his company with the greatest courage and initiative. Later, he led a small party against the enemy, himself shooting two enemy officers, and thereby enabling his company to advance. He set a splendid example of bravery and devotion to duty.

RICHARDSON, JOHN JAMES, Lieut., Infantry. For conspicuous gallantry in action. When his senior officers had become casualties, he led his men with great courage and determination to the final objective, and consolidated the position. Later, he captured many prisoners.

STEWART, CHARLES JAMES TOWNSEND, Major, Princess Patricia's Canadian Light Infantry. For conspicuous gallantry in action. He led an attack which captured two enemy trenches, and showed great determination, both in the attack and in the consolidation of the position won.

VANDERWATER, ROSCOE, Major, Infantry. For conspicuous gallantry in action. He commanded the attacking party with great determination, and held and consolidated the captured trench. He personally supervised the digging of the new communication trenches. On other occasions he has done fine work.

NEW ZEALAND FORCE.

STARNES, FRED, Capt., Canterbury Regt. For conspicuous gallantry in action. When, after heavy fighting, our men were exhausted, and being attacked in front and on both flanks, he rallied them and personally led a third and final attack with such determination that the enemy were swept back up their own communication trenches. Next day he beat off a strong counter-attack, with heavy loss.

SOUTH AFRICAN FORCE.

BURNE, NEWDIGATE HALFORD MARRIOTT, Lieut.-Colonel, Infantry. For conspicuous gallantry and ability in action. During the enemy's attack, which lasted eight hours, he selected his positions with great skill, inspired his officers and men by his fine example, and beat off the enemy with heavy loss.

The undermentioned have been awarded a Bar to their Distinguished Service Order for subsequent acts of conspicuous gallantry.

ALLASON, WALTER, Major (Temporary Lieut.-Colonel), D.S.O., Bedfordshire Regt. For conspicuous gallantry in action. He executed an attack with the greatest initiative and resource, thereby enabling a strong enemy position to be captured. He handled his battalion with great skill throughout the operations.

(The Distinguished Service Order was awarded in London Gazette dated 18 Feb, 1915.)

BIRCH, ALLAN GRANT, Capt. (Temporary Major), D.S.O., Royal Engineers. For conspicuous gallantry in action. With a small party he pushed forward on reconnaissance work under very heavy fire. The information gained was of great value. He was severely wounded.

(The Distinguished Service Order was awarded in London Gazette dated 14 Jan. 1916.)

BLACKLOCK, CYRIL AUBREY, Temporary Lieut.-Colonel, D.S.O., King's Royal Rifle Corps. For conspicuous gallantry in action. When in command of the left attack of the brigade, considerable bodies of the enemy emerged from underground defences in rear of the brigade. He at once detached parties to deal with the situation, thereby enabling the attack to be successfully carried out. Later he captured and consolidated five consecutive objectives, displaying he greatest courage and initiative.

(The Distinguished Service Order was awarded in London Gazette dated 3 June, 1916.)

HUGHES, HUGH LLEWELLYN GLYN, Temporary Capt., D.S.O., Royal Army Medical Corps. For conspicuous gallantry and devotion to duty during operations. On four separate days he showed an utter contempt for danger when collecting and tending the wounded under heavy shell fire.

(The Distinguished Service Order was awarded in London Gazette dated 25 Aug. 1916.)

London Gazette, 23 Nov. 1916.—" War Office, 23 Nov. 1916. His Majesty the King has been graciously pleased to approve of the undermentioned Honours and Rewards for distinguished service in the field, with effect from 3 June, 1916. To be Companions of the Distinguished Service Order."

ALLHUSEN, FREDERICK HENRY, Major (Temporary Lieut.-Colonel), Retired Pay, late 9th Lancers.

BASSETT, TARN PRITCHARD, Capt. and Brevet Major, Royal Engineers, attached Sappers and Miners, Indian Army.

BROADBENT, EDWARD NICHOLSON, Major and Brevet Lieut.-Colonel, King's Own Scottish Borderers.

BEACH, WILLIAM HENRY, Major and Brevet Lieut.-Colonel, Royal Engineers.

BROWN, JOHN NEWTON, Capt. and Brevet Major (Temporary Lieut.-Colonel), Manchester Regt. (T.F.).

CAMPBELL, WILLIAM, Capt., Supply and Transport Corps, Indian Army.

COOPER, JOHN, Temporary Major, Army Service Corps.

DENISON, GARNET WOLSELEY, Major, Royal Engineers.

ELLIOTT, GILBERT CHARLES EDWARD, Major (Temporary Lieut.-Colonel), Royal Engineers, employed under Commonwealth of Australia.

FREEMAN, WILFRID RHODES, M.C., Capt. (Temporary Lieut.-Colonel), Manchester Regt. and Royal Flying Corps.

FURNEAUX, CLAUDE HENRY, Major (Temporary Lieut.-Colonel), Army Service Corps.

HARTWELL, JOHN REDMOND, Capt., Gurkha Rifles, Indian Army.

BRAMLY, ALWYN WILLIAM JENNINGS, Lieut.-Colonel, employed with Egyptian Army.

LEEDS, THOMAS LOUIS, Major and Brevet Lieut.-Colonel (Temporary Lieut.-Colonel), 59th Scinde Rifles, Indian Army.

LUBBOCK, GUY, Major (Temporary Colonel), Royal Engineers.

MACPHERSON, ALEXANDER DUNCAN, Major (Temporary Lieut.-Colonel), Cameron Highlanders.

MATHEW-LANNOWE, BROWNLOW HENRY HAMILTON, Major (Temporary Lieut.-Colonel), 2nd Dragoon Guards, Commanding Argyll and Sutherland Highlanders (T.F.).

MELDRUM, DONALD ROY, Temporary Capt., Special List (Topographical Section).

RENNISON, ARTHUR JOHN, Capt. and Brevet Major (Temporary Major), Supply and Transport Corps, Indian Army.

ROBERTSON, ALEXANDER BROWN, Major (Temporary Lieut.-Colonel), Cameron Highlanders.

ROWAN-ROBINSON, JOHN ROWAN, Capt. (Temporary Major), Supply and Transport Corps, Indian Army.

RUDKIN, GERALD FITZGERALD, Capt. (Temporary Major), Royal Army Medical Corps.

SHEPPARD, HERBERT CECIL, Lieut.-Colonel (Temporary Brigadier-General), Royal Artillery.

SIMPSON, GEORGE SELDON, Major (Temporary Lieut.-Colonel), Royal Field Artillery (T.F.).

STALLARD, STACY FRAMPTON, Lieut.-Colonel (Temporary Brigadier-General), Royal Artillery.

THOMSON, ALAN FORTESCUE, Major (Temporary Lieut.-Colonel), Royal Artillery.

TODD, ARTHUR GEORGE, Major (Temporary Lieut.-Colonel), Army Veterinary Corps.

TRAVERS, HENRY CECIL, Major (Temporary Lieut.-Colonel), Army Ordnance Department.

VILLIERS, CHARLES WALTER, Lieut. (Temporary Lieut.-Colonel), Coldstream Guards, Special Reserve.

WIDDRINGTON, BERTRAM FITZHERBERT, Major (Temporary Brigadier-General), King's Royal Rifle Corps.

WALKER, GEORGE, Lieut.-Colonel (Temporary Brigadier-General), Royal Engineers.

WHITTALL, HUGH, Temporary Lieut., General List, formerly Royal Marines.

WIGGIN, WILLIAM HENRY, Capt. (Temporary Major), 1/1st Worcestershire Yeomanry.

YARDLEY, JOHN HENRY REGINALD, Capt., Royal Inniskilling Fusiliers, Special Reserve.

YATES, HUBERT PEEL, Major and Brevet Lieut.-Colonel, South Wales Borderers.

London Gazette, 25 Nov. 1916.—" War Office, 25 Nov. 1916. His Majesty the King has been graciously pleased to confer the undermentioned award for gallantry and distinguished service in the field. Distinguished Service Order.

BAXTER, GEORGE LEWIS, Capt. (Temporary Major), Cameron Highlanders. For gallantry and ability when in command of part of the force which was attacked by far superior numbers. Major Baxter showed great ability in the handling of his force, and repulsed the enemy with considerable losses. He showed great coolness, and rendered valuable assistance in bringing in a wounded officer under heavy rifle and machine-gun fire.

London Gazette, 25 Nov. 1916.—" War Office, 25 Nov. 1916. His Majesty the King has been graciously pleased to approve of the appointments of the undermentioned Officers to be Companions of the Distinguished Service Order, in recognition of their gallantry and devotion to duty in the field."

BARRY, REV. FRANK RUSSELL, Temporary Chaplain to the Forces, 4th Class, Army Chaplain Department. For conspicuous gallantry and devotion to duty. He tended and dressed the wounded under very heavy fire with the greatest courage and determination. He set a splendid example throughout the operations.

BEARD, GEORGE JOHN ALLEN, Major (Temporary Lieut.-Colonel), East African Division (South African Defence Force). For conspicuous good service. He was indefatigable in organizing and pushing forward supplies and ammunition, when the roads were quagmires. He carried out his difficult task with great success.

BLACKWELL, SAMUEL FREDERICK BAKER, Second Lieut., Norfolk Regt. For conspicuous gallantry in action. He led a reinforcement party over the open under very heavy fire, bombing back the enemy and maintaining his position against three enemy counter-attacks for 36 hours. Later he led a daring patrol, and proceeded over 100 yards along the enemy line and obtained valuable information.

CROSS, FRANK NOEL, Temporary Lieut., Liverpool Regt. For conspicuous gallantry in action. Although wounded, he led a bombing attack with the greatest courage and skill, capturing the enemy's position. Later, he greatly assisted in repulsing several counter-attacks.

FAWCETT, HUGH HERBERT JAMES, Major (Temporary Lieut.-Colonel), Royal Army Medical Corps. For conspicuous gallantry in action and devotion to duty. He tended the wounded continuously for 72 hours. He has on many previous occasions done very fine work.

FORBES, RICHARD ROBERT, Major (Temporary Lieut.-Colonel), Argyll and Sutherland Highlanders. For conspicuous gallantry and ability in leading an attack under heavy shell and enfilade rifle and machine-gun fire, capturing and consolidating the position, and repelling a counter-attack. His calmness and determination inspired his men and greatly assisted the success of the operations.

GEHRKE, RICHARD ARTHUR, Lieut., Royal Dublin Fusiliers. For conspicuous gallantry during a very heavy attack. He showed great coolness in mounting and using his gun in a position exposed to all-round fire, though his kit and cloths were cut by bullets. He remained at his post until nearly surrounded, and then saved his gun and tripod.

HARINGTON, WILLIAM GUY, Capt. (Temporary Major), Gurkha Rifles, Indian Army. For conspicuous gallantry in action. Although severely wounded, he commanded and handled his battalion with great courage and ability throughout the action.

HOBDAY, RUPERT EDMUND, Lieut. (Temporary Capt.), West Yorkshire Regt. For conspicuous gallantry in action. Accompanied by one man, he attacked a strongly-held enemy trench, clearing 200 yards of the trench and capturing 108 prisoners, and himself killing two of the enemy.

LONGBOURNE, HUGH RICHARD, Capt., Royal West Surrey Regt. For conspicuous gallantry in action. He crawled to within 25 yards of an enemy strong point and bombed the enemy with good effect. Later, with a serjeant and a private, he rushed the strong point, capturing a machine gun and 46 unwounded prisoners.

MARRIOTT, GUY BROOK, Major (Temporary Lieut.-Colonel), Royal Warwickshire Regt. For conspicuous gallantry in action. He handled his battalion with the greatest courage and ability, carrying out very difficult work under most trying conditions.

McCALL, RALPH LEYCESTER, M.C., Capt. (Temporary Major), Cameron Highlanders. For conspicuous gallantry and skill in an attack. After his commanding officer had been wounded he took command of the battalion, organized the defence of the captured position, and repelled counter-attacks by day and night, killing five of the enemy himself.

PAGE, GEOFFREY FAULDER, Capt., Lancashire Fusiliers. For conspicuous gallantry in action. He led his company with the greatest courage and initiative. He set a splendid example to his men throughout the operations, and greatly assisted in maintaining the line.

PECK, EDWARD GEORGE, Surgeon-Major, Royal Field Artillery. For conspicuous gallantry in action. He attended to wounded men under heavy fire, quite regardless of his own personal danger. Later, he again attended wounded men under heavy fire and personally superintended their evacuation. He displayed the greatest courage and determination throughout.

PRETORIUS, PHILIP JACOBUS, Temporary Lieut., East African Division. For conspicuous gallantry and good work during several months. On one occasion he tracked up a bombing party of the enemy and forced them to surrender.

REWCASTLE, GEORGE LYON DUNCAN, Second Lieut., Royal Garrison Artillery. For conspicuous gallantry and devotion to duty. Assisted by a gunner, he extinguished a fire in a store of mortar bombs and ammunition. Although twice knocked down by explosions, he succeeded in preventing the fire reaching the S.A.A. boxes, thus saving many lives.

RIDDEL, DONALD OLSON, M.B., Temporary Capt., Royal Army Medical Corps. For conspicuous gallantry and devotion to duty. He tended and dressed the wounded under intense fire, displaying the greatest courage and determination. Later, during a very heavy enemy bombardment, he walked up and down our trenches and administered to the wounded.

ROBSON, FREDERICK WILLIAM, Capt., Yorkshire Regt. For conspicuous gallantry in action. He assumed command of his battalion and carried out his duty with the greatest courage and initiative. He set a splendid example to his men throughout the operations.

ROMANES, JAMES GERALD PAGET, Capt. (Temporary Major), Royal Scots. For conspicuous gallantry in action. He led his battalion with the greatest courage and initiative. He set a splendid example throughout the operations.

ROSS, HUGH CAIRNS EDWARD, Capt., Scots Guards. For conspicuous gallantry in action. Although wounded, he remained in command of his company throughout the day, and went forward on two occasions to collect small parties of his men who were cut off, and place them in good positions.

RUSHBROOKE, WILLIAM PHILIP HENRY, Capt., Northumberland Fusiliers. For conspicuous gallantry in action. He led a successful attack against a village, and afterwards repulsed several enemy counter-attacks. He displayed the greatest courage and initiative throughout.

STOCKDALE, GEORGE VINCENT, M.B., Capt., Royal Army Medical Corps. For conspicuous gallantry and devotion to duty. He led his stretcher-bearers continuously for five days, under very heavy fire, and on several occasions rescued wounded men by himself. He has on many previous occasions done very fine work.

STREATFEILD-JAMES, RALPH, Capt., East Surrey Regt. For conspicuous gallantry in action. He led his company with the greatest courage and initiative, and greatly assisted in capturing the final objective.

TODD, CHESTER WILLIAM, Capt. (Temporary Major), Royal Field Artillery. For conspicuous gallantry in action. He handled his battery with the greatest courage and initiative throughout the operations. He carried out the most careful observations, enabling him to bring accurate fire to bear in support of the infantry.

WEBB, WILLIAM FRANCIS RICHMOND, Capt. and Brevet Major (Temporary Lieut.-Colonel), Punjabis, Indian Army. For conspicuous gallantry in action. Although wounded, he handled his battalion with the greatest courage and initiative. He set a splendid example to his men.

WRIGHT, REUBEN, Temporary Lieut., Yorkshire Light Infantry. For conspicuous gallantry in action. He assumed command of and led his battalion with the greatest courage and initiative. He succeeded in reorganizing and consolidating the position under very heavy fire.

AUSTRALIAN FORCE.

SHANAHAN, MICHAEL, Major, Light H.R. For conspicuous gallantry in action. He organized and maintained the outpost line with the greatest courage and determination. Later, he rescued several wounded men under very heavy fire. He was wounded.

CANADIAN FORCE.

COSGRAVE, LAWRENCE VINCENT MOORE, Major, Field Artillery. For conspicuous gallantry in action. He carried out several reconnaissances under very heavy fire, and explored the enemy's wire in daylight, displaying the greatest courage and ability throughout.

FOSTER, WILLIAM WASBROUGH, Major, Mounted Rifles. For conspicuous gallantry in action. He detailed two patrols, and himself led a third under heavy fire, and obtained most valuable information. Later, he carried out a successful attack, and captured his objective. He displayed the greatest courage and initiative throughout.

MACKAY, JOHN KEILER, Major, Field Artillery. For conspicuous gallantry in action. When the personnel of his O.P. had become casualties, he went forward under very heavy fire and re-established the O.P. 200 yards beyond our front line, and resumed communication with his battery. He remained forward all day, commanding his battery from this exposed position, and sending back most valuable information.

PATTERSON, WILLIAM REGINALD, Temporary Major, Mounted Rifles. For conspicuous gallantry in action. He led the attacking force with the greatest courage and determination, and captured two of the enemy's trenches. Later, he organized bombing attacks, and consolidated the position, sending back most valuable information.

THOMSON, ALEXANDER THOMAS, Temporary Major, Infantry. For conspicuous gallantry in action. He commanded and handled his battalion under very trying circumstances with the greatest courage and ability. He has previously done very fine work.

SOUTH AFRICAN CONTINGENT.

THACKÉRAY, EDWARD FRANCIS, C.M.G., Temporary Lieut.-Colonel, Infantry. For conspicuous gallantry in action. He commanded his own battalion and other units with the greatest courage and initiative, repulsing an enemy attack made by nine and a half battalions. He set a splendid example to his men throughout the operations.

TOMLINSON, LEONARD WARREN, Temporary Capt., Infantry. For conspicuous gallantry in action. He led his company against an enemy trench with the greatest courage and initiative, killing 32 of the enemy, and capturing two officers, 70 men and a machine gun. He was wounded.

The undermentioned has been awarded a second Bar to his Distinguished Service Order for a subsequent act of conspicuous gallantry.

BALL, ALBERT, D.S.O., M.C., Second Lieut. (Temporary Capt.), Nottinghamshire and Derbyshire Regt. For conspicuous gallantry in action. He attacked three hostile machines and brought one down, displaying great courage and skill. He has brought down eight hostile machines in a short period, and has forced many others to land.

(The Distinguished Service Order was awarded in London Gazette dated 26 Sept. 1916. First Bar was awarded in London Gazette dated 26 Sept. 1916.)

The undermentioned have been awarded a Bar to their Distinguished Service Order for subsequent acts of conspicuous gallantry.

GRANT-DALTON, STUART, D.S.O., Capt., Yorkshire Regt. For conspicuous gallantry in action. He attacked two hostile aeroplanes, although quite unsupported. Later, after being attacked by another enemy machine and wounded in three places, he brought his machine back and landed safely.

(The Distinguished Service Order was awarded in London Gazette dated 27 July, 1916.)

MAXWELL, FRANCIS AYLMER, V.C., C.S.I., D.S.O., Major and Brevet Lieut.-Colonel (Temporary Lieut.-Colonel), 18th Lancers, Indian Army. For conspicuous gallantry in action. He led his battalion with the greatest courage and initiative. Later, he reorganized three battalions and consolidated the position under very heavy fire. He has previously done very fine work.

(The Distinguished Service Order was awarded in the London Gazette dated 20 May, 1898.)

London Gazette, 5 Dec. 1916.—"Admiralty, 5 Dec. 1916. The King has been graciously pleased to give orders for the appointment of the following Officer to be a Companion of the Distinguished Service Order."

PULLING, EDWARD LASTON, Flight Sub-Lieut., R.N.A.S. In recognition of the skill and gallantry which he displayed on the morning of the 28th Nov. 1916, in pursuing out to sea, attacking at close range, and destroying a Zeppelin, which had been engaged in a raid on England. Flight Sub-Lieut. Pulling was exposed to machine-gun fire throughout the attack.

London Gazette, 11 Dec. 1916.—"War Office, 11 Dec. 1916. His Majesty the King has been graciously pleased to approve of the appointments of the undermentioned Officers to be Companions of the Distinguished Service Order, in recognition of their gallantry and devotion to duty in the field."

KNIGHT, ARTHUR GERALD, M.C., Second Lieut., Royal Flying Corps. For conspicuous gallantry in action. He led four machines against 18 hostile machines. Choosing a good moment for attack he drove down five of them and dispersed the remainder. He has shown the utmost dash and judgment as a leader of offensive patrols.

MESSITER, CHARLES BAYARD, Capt. (Temporary Lieut.-Colonel), Loyal North Lancashire Regt. For conspicuous gallantry in action. He led his battalion with great precision and determination. He secured his objective and consolidated his position very rapidly, taking a large number of prisoners. By his splendid example the whole operations were conducted in a most orderly manner.

METHUEN, JAMES ALLIN, Temporary Major, King's Royal Rifle Corps. For conspicuous gallantry in action. He showed untiring energy, sound judgment and fearlessness. He reorganized the line and consolidated the position, thereby enabling his men to endure a heavy barrage with little loss. He successfully evacuated many wounded under trying conditions.

MORRIS, ROBERT JOHN, Capt. (Temporary Major), South Staffordshire Regt. For conspicuous gallantry in action. He personally rallied men of other battalions who were near by, and, reinforcing his own battalion at a critical time, enabled them to capture the village. He displayed the greatest courage and initiative throughout.

RIDDELL, EDWARD PIUS ARTHUR, Major (Temporary Lieut.-Colonel), Rifle Brigade. For conspicuous gallantry in action. He showed the greatest skill and foresight in assembling his battalion and subsequently launching them to the attack without a casualty, in broad daylight, on ground observed by the enemy. His personal bravery, energy and example exercised great influence over all ranks.

ROBINSON, HENRY ABRAHALL, Temporary Capt., Royal Fusiliers. For conspicuous gallantry in action. Although wounded, he assisted in consolidating the position and getting other units up to the line. Later, he assisted in the capture of three enemy guns with their crews. He displayed the greatest courage and initiative throughout.

SAWYER, LEONARD, Temporary Capt. (Temporary Major), York and Lancaster Regt. For conspicuous gallantry in action. He organized and led a successful attack of two companies, displaying the greatest courage and determination. He directed his men from the top of the enemy trench, and was eventually wounded whilst throwing bombs into the enemy trench.

TURNER, CHARLES EDWARD, Capt. (Temporary Major), Gloucestershire Yeomanry. For conspicuous gallantry in action. He commanded his squadron with the greatest courage and skill. He defended an important point for over three hours, without support, against vastly superior numbers.

CANADIAN FORCE.

BURNETT, PHILIP, Major, Army Medical Corps. For conspicuous gallantry and devotion to duty. He took over the command of the bearers at the front and for 48 hours carried out his duties with great skill and determination under very heavy fire.

London Gazette, 15 Dec. 1916.—"His Majesty the King has been graciously pleased to appoint the undermentioned Officer to be a Companion of the Distinguished Service Order, in recognition of conspicuous gallantry and devotion to duty in connection with the destruction of an Enemy Airship."

PYOTT, IAN VERNON, Second Lieut., Royal Flying Corps.

London Gazette, 21 Dec. 1916.—"War Office, 21 Dec. 1916. The King has been graciously pleased to approve of the appointments of the following Officers to be Companions of the Distinguished Service Order, in recognition of their gallantry and devotion to duty in the field."

BARFF, WILLIAM HAROLD, Temporary Capt., Cheshire Regt.

BIRD, LENNOX GODFREY, Temporary Lieut.-Colonel., Lancashire Fusiliers.

CHALLINOR, EDWARD LACY, Major and Brevet Colonel (Temporary Lieut.-Colonel), Leicestershire Regt.

CLARK, ALEX. NEILSON, Capt., Durham Light Infantry.

DOUGLAS, JAMES WIGHTMAN, Temporary Major, Royal Engineers.

HOPKINS, RAWDON SCOTT, Capt. (Temporary Major), East Yorkshire Regt.

London Gazette, 22 Dec. 1916.—"War Office, 22 Dec. 1916. The King has been graciously pleased to approve of the award of the following Honours for distinguished service in the field in Mesopotamia, with effect from 3 June, 1916, inclusive. To be Companions of the Distinguished Service Order."

ANDERSON, BARTON EDWARD, Capt. and Brevet Major, 59th Rifles, Indian Army.

ANDERSON, JOHN FAULKENER HENNIKER, Capt. (Temporary Major added. [London Gazette, 17 April, 1917]), 31st Lancers (Remount Depôt), Indian Army.

ASHBURNER, HARLEY WENTWORTH, Major, 106th, attached 107th, Pioneers, Indian Army.

BARTTELOT, SIR WALTER BALFOUR, Major, Coldstream Guards.

BOND, GEORGE WESTON, Capt. (Temporary Major), Supply and Transport Corps, Indian Army.

BODY, JOHN, Capt., 1/5th Battn. East Kent Regt. (T.F.).

BROKE-SMITH, PHILIP WILLIAM LILIAN, Capt. (Temporary Major), Royal Engineers and Royal Flying Corps.

BROWNRIGG, WELLESLEY DOUGLAS, Capt. (Temporary Lieut.-Colonel), Nottinghamshire and Derbyshire Regt.

CAMPBELL, WILLIAM NEVILE, Major (Temporary Lieut.-Colonel) (retired), Indian Army.

CARNEGY, GERALD PATRICK OGILVY, Major, 7th Hariana Lancers, Indian Army.

CARTER, LINDSEY JAMES, Major, Oxfordshire and Buckinghamshire Light Infantry.

CROFTON, MALBY RICHARD HENRY, Major, Royal Field Artillery, attached 66th Battery.

DE LA MOTTE, REGINALD BARKER, Capt., Supply and Transport Corps, Indian Army.

DRYSDALE, ALEXANDER EDMOND, M.C., Capt. (corrected to Lieut. (Temporary Captain) Alexander Edward Drysdale [London Gazette, 17 April, 1917]), 47th Sikhs, Indian Army.

EVERETT, MAXWELL, Capt., Royal Engineers, 21st, attached 23rd, Company, S. and M., Indian Army.
GRASSIE, JAMES, Second Lieut., 2nd Battn. Royal Highlanders.
HAMER, MEREDITH ASHTON, M.C., Major, 129th Baluchis, Indian Army.
HAMILTON, WILLIAM HAYWOOD, Capt., Indian Medical Service.
HAROLD, AUSTIN EDWARD, Commander, Royal Indian Marines.
HARVEY, DOUGLAS, Capt., 31st Punjabis, Indian Army.
HAWES, CHARLES HOWARD, Major, 23rd Cavalry, Indian Army.
HERBERT, PERCY THOMAS COLTHURST, Major, Reserve of Officers, Royal Field Artillery.
HERRICK, ROBERT DE STRETTON BERKELEY, Capt., Indian Medical Service.
HEZLET, ROBERT KNOX, Major, Royal Field Artillery.
HOLDICH, HAROLD ADRIAN, Brevet Lieut.-Colonel, Gurkha Rifles, Indian Army.
HUME-SPRY, WILLIAM EDMOND, Capt. (Temporary Major), Supply and Transport Corps, Indian Army.
INSKIP, ROLAND DEBENHAM, M.C., Capt., Rifles, Indian Army.
IRWIN, REV. RONALD JOHN BERESFORD, M.C., M.A., Ecclesiastical Department, Bengal.
JOHNSTON, ROBERT, Capt. (Temporary Major) (rank corrected to Major [London Gazette, 17 April, 1917]), Cavalry, Indian Army.
KELSALL, ROBERT, M.B., Major, Indian Medical Service.
KINCH, ARTHUR GORDON, Lieut., Royal Indian Marines.
KNOX, ERNEST FRANCIS, Major (rank corrected to Lieut.-Col. [London Gazette, 17 April, 1917]), Sikhs, Indian Army.
MACDONALD, RODERICK WILLIAM, Capt. (Temporary Major), Sikhs, Indian Army.
MARSH, BRUCE CUNCLIFFE, Lieut., Royal Indian Marines.
MARSHALL, REV. GEORGE HERBERT, Army Chaplains' Department.
McWATTERS, HERBERT CLAUDE, Capt. (Temporary Major) (rank corrected to Major [London Gazette, 17 April, 1917]), Punjabis, Indian Army.
MINNS, ALAN NOEL, M.C., Temporary Capt., Royal Army Medical Corps.
MORPHETT, GEORGE CHARLES, Major, Royal Sussex Regt.
MORRIS, CHARLES OXLEY, Major, Supply and Transport Corps, Indian Army.
NIXON, CHARLES HOWARD FEATHERSTONEHAUGH, Capt., Punjabis, Indian Army.
NUGENT, JOHN FAGAN HENSLOWE, Lieut. (Temporary Capt.), Punjabis, Indian Army.
PETRE, HENRY ALOYSIUS, M.C., Capt., Australian Flying Corps.
POOLE, IVAN MAXWELL CONWAY, Major, Supply and Transport Corps, Indian Army.
PRESTON, WILLIAM JOHN PHAELIM, Major, Deccan Infantry, Indian Army.
REED, CHARLES, Major, Royal Artillery.
ROSS, GEORGE WHITEHILL, Major, Indian Army.
SCHOMBERG, REGINALD CHARLES FRANCIS, Capt., Seaforth Highlanders.
SCOTT, CHARLES ARTHUR, Lieut., Royal Indian Marines.
SMITH, HUBERT HAMILTON, Temporary Major (rank corrected to Major [London Gazette, 17 April, 1917]), Bhopal Infantry, Indian Army.
SPOWERS, ALLAN, M.C., Second Lieut., East Lancashire Regt., Special Reserve.
SQUIRES, ERNEST KER, M.C., Capt., Royal Engineers.
STRETCH, EDWARD ARTHUR, Temporary Capt., Welsh Fusiliers.
SWEET, ROBERT, M.B., Capt., Indian Medical Service.
TAYLOR, NORMAN CALLENDER, Capt., Punjabis, Indian Army.
WILSON-JOHNSTON, WALTER EDWARD, Capt. (Temporary Major) (rank corrected to Major [London Gazette, 17 April, 1917]), Sikhs, Indian Army.
WINTER, CLIFFORD BOARDMAN, Lieut.-Colonel, Infantry, Indian Army.

London Gazette, 1 Jan. 1917.—" Admiralty, S.W., 1 Jan. 1917. The King has been graciously pleased to give orders for the following appointments to the Distinguished Service Order to the undermentioned Officers, in recognition of their services in the Battle of Jutland."

PENFOLD, ERNEST ALFRED, M.B., Fleet Surgeon, Royal Navy. Was in the fore medical distributing station when a heavy shell burst just outside, killing and wounding many. He was knocked down, bruised and shaken, but personally assisted in the removal of the wounded, and tended them with unremitting skill and devotion for 40 hours without rest. His example was invaluable in keeping up the morale of the wounded and of the medical party under very trying conditions, the shell having destroyed instruments, dressings, etc.
HODGSON, JOHN COOMBE, Commander, R.N. Led destroyer attack on enemy battle cruisers, but, becoming engaged with enemy destroyers, was unable to get within range. On conclusion of gun attack, in which several hostile destroyers were sunk and the enemy beaten off, he attacked enemy battle fleet and fired four torpedoes under very hot fire of enemy battleships' secondary armament. His destroyer was struck and damaged by a shell.
THOMSON, EVELYN CLAUDE OGILVIE, Lieut.-Commander, R.N. Senior Officer of a division of destroyers, and having defeated the enemy destroyers, gallantly pressed home attack with torpedoes on enemy battle cruisers.
BLOUNT, HAROLD, Capt., R.M.A. Performed excellent service as officer of " Q " Turret on 31 May, as well as in the action off Heligoland in Aug. 1914, and at the Dogger Bank in Jan. 1915.

London Gazette, 1 Jan. 1917.—" Admiralty, 1 Jan. 1917. Mine Sweeping Operations. The King has been graciously pleased to give orders for the following appointments to the Distinguished Service Order to the undermentioned Officers, in recognition of their bravery and devotion to duty during minesweeping operations."

SEYMOUR, HUGH, Commander, R.N.
FISHER, LESLIE DREW, Lieut.-Commander (Acting Commander), R.N.
McDOWELL, DANIEL, Lieut.-Commander, R.N.

London Gazette, 1 Jan. 1917.—" Admiralty, 1 Jan. 1917. The King has been graciously pleased to give orders for the following appointments to the Distinguished Service Order to the undermentioned Officers, in recognition of their services."

STRONG, FREDERICK EDWARD KETELBY, Commander, R.N. For the successful manner in which he conducted H.M.S. Dwarf's actions with the armed yacht Herzogin Elizabeth, Joss Battery, and the armed vessel Nachtigall on the 9th, 11th and 16th Sept. 1914, respectively, as well as other important duties, which on several occasions brought him into contact with the enemy during the Cameroons Campaign.
GRENFELL, FRANCIS HENRY, Commander, R.N.
CHEETHAM, HERBERT CHARLES VALENTINE BERESFORD, R.D., Commander, Royal Naval Reserve. As Chief Transport Officer with the Cameroons Expeditionary Force, Commander Cheetham performed exceptional service under a heavy fire during the attacks on Jabassi on the 8th Oct. 1914, and in the subsequent embarkation of troops and retirement down stream of the flotilla after dark. He commanded the advanced detachments of the Nyong flotilla on the Edea Expedition, driving out a hostile party from Dehane, and thereby enabling the French troops to land without opposition.
MELLIN, ARTHUR ALURED, Lieut.-Commander, R.N.
JESSOP, JOHN DE BURGH, Lieut.-Commander, R.N. In recognition of the skill and determination which he showed in making a successful submarine attack on an enemy light cruiser on the 19th Oct. 1916.
WESTMORE, HENRY GEORGE GARDINER, R.D., Lieut.-Commander, Royal Naval Reserve.
PERCIVAL, JOHN, Lieut.-Commander, R.N.R. Lieut.-Commander Percival was Acting Director of Nigeria Marine at the commencement of hostilities in the Cameroons, and was largely responsible for the efficient manner in which the Nigeria Marine vessels were fitted out for duty with the expedition. He also performed valuable service as King's Harbour Master at Duala from the 28th Sept. to the 14th Dec. 1914, when he was appointed Director of the Nigeria Marine at Lagos, in which position he invariably assisted the Senior Naval Officer in every way possible throughout the campaign.

The undermentioned Officer has been awarded a Bar to his Distinguished Service Order.

LAURENCE, NOEL FRANK, D.S.O., Commander, Royal Navy. In recognition of the skill and determination he showed in making a submarine attack on an enemy battle squadron on the 5th Nov. 1916.
(The appointment to the Distinguished Service Order was announced in London Gazette dated 24 Feb. 1916.)

London Gazette, 1 Jan. 1917.—" War Office, 1 Jan. 1917. His Majesty the King has been graciously pleased to approve of the undermentioned rewards for distinguished service in the field, dated 1 Jan. 1917. Awarded the Distinguished Service Order."

ACKLOM, SPENCER, M.C., Capt. (Temporary Major), Highland Light Infantry, attached Northumberland Fusiliers.
AGER, FRANCIS GEORGE, Capt. (Temporary Major), Army Service Corps.
AINSLIE, CHARLES MARSHALL, Major (Temporary Lieut.-Colonel), Army Service Corps.
ALEXANDER, WILLIAM DALLAS, Major, Royal Artillery.
ALLARDYCE, JOHN GRAHAME BUCHANAN, Major (Temporary Lieut.-Colonel), Royal Field Artillery.
ALLEN, CECIL, Capt. (Temporary Major), Royal Field Artillery.
ALLEN, HAROLD, Major, Royal Artillery.
ALLETSON, GEORGE COVENTRY, Temporary Major, Remount Service.
ALLSUP, EDWARD SAUNDERS, Major, Royal Artillery.
ANDERSON, EDWARD PHILIP, Major, Royal Engineers.
ANLEY, WILLIAM BOWER, Major (Temporary Lieut.-Colonel), Royal Garrison Artillery.
ANNESLEY, WILLIAM HENRY, Capt., Reserve of Officers, late Royal West Kent Regt.
ARCHER, HENRY, Major, Royal Artillery.
ARCHIBALD, ROBERT GEORGE, M.B., Capt., Royal Army Medical Corps, employed Egyptian Army.
ARMITAGE, FRANK RHODES, M.B., Capt., Royal Army Medical Corps.
ARMYTAGE, GEORGE AYSCOUGH, Major and Brevet Lieut.-Colonel (Temporary Brigadier-General), King's Royal Rifle Corps.
ARNOLD, JOHN EFFINGHAM, Temporary Major, Army Service Corps.
ARNOTT, RALPH, Major, Royal Artillery.
ARTHUR, LIONEL FRANCIS, Major, Indian Army.
BABINGTON, MARCUS HILL, Lieut.-Colonel, Royal Army Medical Corps.
BADHAM-THORNHILL, GEORGE, Major, Royal Artillery.
BALD, PHILIP ROBERT, Major, Royal Engineers.
BALLINGALL, HARRY MILLER, Major, Royal Artillery.
BANNATYNE, EDGAR JAMES, Lieut. (Temporary Major), Hussars and Royal Flying Corps.
BARKER, MICHAEL GEORGE HENRY, Capt. and Brevet Major (Temporary Lieut.-Colonel), Lincolnshire Regt.
BARLEY, LESLIE JOHN, Capt., Scottish Rifles, Special Reserve.
BARNE, MILES, Major, Suffolk Yeomanry.
BARTHOLOMEW, WILLIAM HENRY, Major and Brevet Lieut.-Colonel (Temporary Lieut.-Colonel), Royal Artillery.
BARTON, WILLIAM HUGH, Major (Temporary Lieut.-Colonel), Army Service Corps.
BATESON, JOHN HOLGATE, Major, Royal Artillery.
BATTEN, JOHN BEARDMORE, Capt. (Temporary Lieut.-Colonel), Manchester Regt.
BAWDEN, VICTOR CECIL, Capt. (Temporary Major), London Regt.
BAYLAY, ATWELL CHARLES, Major, Royal Engineers.
BAYLY, EDWARD ARCHIBALD THEODORE, Major, Royal Welsh Fusiliers, attached Egyptian Army.
BEAMAN, WINFRED KELSEY, Capt. (Temporary Major), Royal Army Medical Corps.
BEARN, FREDERICK ARNOT, M.C., M.B., Capt., Royal Army Medical Corps, Special Reserve.

The Distinguished Service Order

BECHER, CECIL MORGAN LEY, Major (Temporary Lieut.-Colonel), Royal Irish Rifles.
BECKE, JOHN HAROLD WHITWORTH, Major (Temporary Lieut.-Colonel), Nottinghamshire and Derbyshire Regt. and Royal Flying Corps.
BELL, GAWAIN MURDOCH, Temporary Major, Hampshire Regt.
BELL, RICHARD CARMICHAEL, Lieut.-Colonel, Indian Army.
BELL, WILLIAM CORY HOWARD, Major, Reserve of Officers, Royal Artillery.
BENNETT, WILLIAM, M.B., Major (Temporary Lieut.-Colonel), Royal Army Medical Corps.
BENSON, ROBERT, Major, Royal Artillery.
BENSON, WILLIAM ARTHUR, Lieut.-Colonel, Royal Army Medical Corps.
BERNARD, DENIS JOHN CHARLES KIRWAN, Capt. and Brevet Major (Temporary Lieut.-Colonel), Rifle Brigade.
BEUTTLER, VALENTINE OAKLEY, Capt. (Temporary Major), Army Service Corps.
BICKERTON, REGINALD ERNEST, M.B., Capt. (Temporary Major), Royal Army Medical Corps.
BIDDER, MAURICE McCLEAN, A.M.I.C.E., Major, Royal Engineers.
BIDDULPH, HARRY, Major and Brevet Lieut.-Colonel (Temporary Lieut.-Colonel), Royal Engineers.
BIRD, CLARENCE AUGUST, Capt., Royal Engineers.
BIRD, ELLIOT BEVERLY, Major (Temporary Lieut.-Colonel), Royal Army Medical Corps.
BLACK, CLAUD HAMILTON GRIFFITH, Capt., Indian Army (corrected to Lancers [London Gazette, 1 Jan. 1917]).
BLACK, ROBERT BARCLAY, M.B., Major, Reserve of Officers, Royal Army Medical Corps.
BLACKER, STEWART WARD WILLIAM, Temporary Lieut.-Colonel, Royal Irish Fusiliers.
BLACKHAM, ROBERT JAMES, C.I.E., F.F.P.S., Lieut.-Colonel (Temporary Colonel), Royal Army Medical Corps.
BLACKWALL, JOHN EATON, Major (Temporary Lieut.-Colonel), Nottinghamshire and Derbyshire Regt.
BLAKISTON-HOUSTON, JOHN, Capt., Hussars.
BLISS, ERNEST WILLIAM, Lieut.-Colonel (Temporary Colonel), Royal Army Medical Corps.
BLUNT, CONRAD EDWARD GRANT, Major, Reserve of Officers.
BOARDMAN, THOMAS HENRY, Temporary Major, Royal Irish Fusiliers.
BODDAM-WHETHAM, SYDNEY ALEXANDER, M.C., Major, Royal Artillery.
BOND, HENRY HENDLEY, Lieut.-Colonel (Temporary Brigadier-General), Royal Field Artillery.
BONHAM-CARTER, CHARLES, Major (Brevet Lieut.-Colonel), Royal West Kent Regt.
BOLTON, AUBREY HOLMES, Major (Temporary Lieut.-Colonel), Gloucestershire Regt. (surname corrected to Boulton [London Gazette, 10 Jan., 1917]).
BOWEN, FRANCIS OSBORNE, Capt. (Temporary Lieut.-Colonel), Royal Irish Regt.
BOWER, CLAUDE EDWARD SYNDERCOMBE, Major, Royal Artillery.
BOWES, WILLIAM, Quartermaster and Honorary Major, Lancashire Fusiliers.
BOYCE, CHARLES EDWARD, Major, Royal Artillery.
BOYCE, HARRY AUGUSTUS, Lieut.-Colonel, Royal Field Artillery.
BOYLE, ERNEST CHARLES PATRICK, Capt. (Temporary Lieut.-Colonel), Honourable Artillery Company.
BRADFORD, EDWARD AUSTEN, Major, King's Royal Rifle Corps.
BRADSHAW, FREDERICK EWART, Major (Acting Lieut.-Colonel), Reserve of Officers, Rifle Brigade.
BRAY, ROBERT NAPIER, Major (Temporary Lieut.-Colonel), West Riding Regt.
BRIDGE, WILLIAM BASIL CHARLES, Capt. (Temporary Lieut.-Colonel), Reserve of Officers, Argyll and Sutherland Highlanders.
BRIERLEY, EUSTACE CARLILE, Capt. (Temporary Major), Reserve of Officers.
BRITTON, ARTHUR HENRY DANIEL, Temporary Major, Army Service Corps.
BROCK, HENRY JENKINS, Lieut.-Colonel (Temporary Brigadier-General), Royal Field Artillery.
BROOKE, ALAN FRANCIS, Major, Royal Field Artillery.
BROOKE, EDWARD WILLIAM SAURIN, Lieut.-Colonel, Royal Artillery.
BROOKE, GEOFFRY FRANCIS HEREMON, M.C., Capt., Lancers.
BROUSSON, FREDERICK, Major, Royal Artillery.
BROWN, CHARLES TURNER, Major, Royal Engineers.
BROWN, OSCAR, Honorary Major and Temporary Honorary Lieut.-Colonel, Army Ordnance Department.
BROWNE, ANDREW DUNCAN MONTAGUE, Major (Temporary Lieut.-Colonel), Royal Lancaster Regt.
BROWNE, GEORGE BUCKSTON, Capt. (Temporary Lieut.-Colonel), Royal Field Artillery.
BROWNE, JOHN GILBERT, Major (Temporary Lieut.-Colonel), Hussars.
BROWNE, WILLIAM THEODORE REDMOND, Major, Army Service Corps.
BROWNLOW, GUY JAMES, Capt. and Brevet Major (Temporary Lieut. Colonel), Rifle Brigade.
BRUCE, KENNETH HOPE, Major, Gordon Highlanders.
BRUCE, ROBERT, Major (Temporary Lieut.-Colonel), Gordon Highlanders.
BRUNSKILL, JOHN HANDFIELD, M.B., Major (Temporary Lieut.-Colonel), Royal Army Medical Corps.
BRYANT, ALAN, Major (Temporary Lieut.-Colonel), Gloucestershire Regt.
BRYDEN, RONALD ANDERSON, Major (Temporary Lieut.-Colonel), Royal Army Medical Corps.
BUDGEN, WILLIAM NAPIER, Major, Royal Artillery.
BULLER, JOHN DASHWOOD, Major (Temporary Lieut.-Colonel), Army Service Corps.
BULLOCH, RICHARD ARCHIBALD, Major, Royal Highlanders.

BURDETT, ARTHUR BURDETT, Major, York and Lancaster Regt. and Royal Flying Corps.
BURNSIDE, FREDERICK REGINALD, Capt., Hussars.
BURTON, COLIN, Major, Army Service Corps.
BUSH, HERBERT FULFORD, Temporary Major, Army Service Corps.
BUTCHART, JAMES ALEXANDER, Major, Royal Artillery.
BUTLER, PATRICK RICHARD, Capt., Royal Irish Regt.
BUZZARD, FRANK ANSTIE, Major (Temporary Lieut.-Colonel), Royal Field Artillery.
BYRNE, JOHN DILLON, Major, Royal Artillery.
CAIRNES, THOMAS ALGAR ELLIOTT, Capt. (Temporary Major), Dragoon Guards and Royal Flying Corps.
CALDER, HECTOR MACKAY, M.B., Capt., Royal Army Medical Corps.
CAMERON, CECIL AYLMER, Temporary Major, Intelligence Corps.
CAMPBELL, JAMES ALEXANDER, Capt. (Temporary Major), Suffolk Regt.
CAMPBELL, ROBERT, Major (Temporary Lieut.-Colonel), Cameron Highlanders.
CAMPBELL, RONALD BRUCE, Major, Gordon Highlanders.
CARDEW, GEORGE AMBROSE, Lieut.-Colonel, Royal Artillery.
CAREY, HAROLD EUSTACE, Lieut.-Colonel, Royal Field Artillery.
CAREY, WILFRID LEATHES DE MUSSENDEN, Capt. (Temporary Major), Royal Engineers.
CARR, CHARLES CATTLEY, Major (Temporary Lieut.-Colonel), Reserve of Officers.
CARR, GEORGE ARTHUR BUXTON, Major (Temporary Lieut.-Colonel), London Regt.
CARR, HARRIE GARDINER, Major, Royal Artillery.
CARR, LAWRENCE, Capt. and Brevet Major, Gordon Highlanders.
CARROLL, FREDERICK FITZGERALD, M.B., Lieut.-Colonel, Royal Army Medical Corps.
CARTER, LOUIS ALFRED LATIMER, Capt. (Temporary Major), Army Service Corps.
CASTLE, REGINALD WINGFIELD, Major (Temporary Lieut.-Colonel), Royal Garrison Artillery.
CHAMIER, JOHN ADRIAN, Capt. (Temporary Major), Indian Army and Royal Flying Corps.
CHAPMAN, GEORGE ARTHUR EMERSON, Major, East Kent Regt.
CHARLES, ERIC MONTAGU SETON, Major (Temporary Lieut.-Colonel), Royal Engineers.
CHARLTON, CLAUD EDWARD CHARLES GRAHAM, Lieut.-Colonel, Royal Artillery.
CHARRINGTON, SYDNEY HERBERT, Capt. (Temporary Major), Reserve of Officers, Hussars.
CHARTERIS, NIGEL KEPPEL, Major, Royal Scots.
CHEESEWRIGHT, WILLIAM FREDERICK, Lieut.-Colonel, Royal Engineers.
CHURTON, WILLIAM ARTHUR VERE, Capt. (Temporary Major), Cheshire Regt.
CLARK, CRAUFURD ALEXANDER GORDON, Major (Lieut.-Colonel, retired T.F.), London Regt.
CLARKE, SIR EDWARD HENRY ST. LAWRENCE, Bart., Lieut.-Colonel, West Yorkshire Regt.
CLARKE, EDWIN PERCY, Capt. (Temporary Major), Suffolk Regt.
CLARKE, MARSHAL FALCONER, Major (Temporary Lieut.-Colonel), Cheshire Regt.
CLARKE, MERVYN OFFICER, Major, Royal Fusiliers.
CLEAVER, FREDERICK HOLDEN, Temporary Major, Special List and Royal Flying Corps.
CLEMENTS, ROBERT WILLIAM, M.B., Lieut.-Colonel, Royal Army Medical Corps.
CLIFTON, PERCY JAMES, Capt. (Temporary Major), Royal Field Artillery.
CLOWES, GEORGE CHARLES KNIGHTS, Capt. (Temporary Major), London Regt.
COATES, PERCY LIONEL, Major (Temporary Lieut.-Colonel), Gloucestershire Regt.
COBBOLD, RALPH PATTESON, Capt. (Temporary Lieut.-Colonel), Reserve of Officers, Loyal North Lancashire Regt.
COBHAM, HORACE WALTER, Major (Temporary Lieut.-Colonel), Reserve of Officers, Liverpool Regt.
COCKRAM, FREDERICK SYDNEY, Capt., Middlesex Regt.
COFFIN, CLIFFORD, Lieut.-Colonel, Royal Engineers.
COLEMAN, GEORGE BURDETT, Major, Army Service Corps.
COLLACOTT, JOHN RICHARD, Honorary Major (Temporary Chief Inspector and Honorary Lieut.-Colonel), Army Ordnance Department.
COLLINSON, HAROLD, M.B., F.R.C.S, Lieut.-Colonel, Royal Army Medical Corps.
COLLUM, HERBERT WILLIAM ALLAN, Major (Temporary Lieut.-Colonel), Army Service Corps.
COLQUHOUN, JULIAN CAMPBELL, Capt. (Temporary Lieut.-Colonel), Leinster Regt.
COLVIN, GEORGE LETHBRIDGE, Capt. (Temporary Major), General List.
CONWAY, JOHN MARCUS HOBSON, F.R.C.S.I., Major, Royal Army Medical Corps.
COOKE, GEORGE STANLEY CURTIS, Major, Royal Engineers.
COOKE, HERBERT FOTHERGILL, Brevet Lieut.-Colonel (Temporary Brigadier-General), Indian Army.
COPLANS, MYER, M.D., Capt., Royal Army Medical Corps.
CORFIELD, FREDERICK ALLEYNE, Capt. (Temporary Major), Army Service Corps.
COTTON, ARTHUR EGERTON, Temporary Major, Rifle Brigade.
COURTNEY, FREDERICK HAROLD, Major (Temporary Lieut.-Colonel), Royal Garrison Artillery.
COWPER, MALCOLM GORDON, Capt. (Temporary Major) (Temporary Lieut.-Colonel), East Yorkshire Regt.

COX, CHARLES HENRY FORTNOM, Major, Royal Field Artillery.
COX, PATRICK GODFREY ASHLEY, Brevet Major (Temporary Lieut.-Colonel), Rifle Brigade.
CRAVEN, WALDEMAR SIGISMUND DACRE, Major (Temporary Lieut.-Colonel), Royal Field Artillery.
CRAWLEY, RICHARD PARRY, M.V.O., Major (Temporary Lieut.-Colonel), Army Service Corps.
CRAWSHAY, CODRINGTON HOWARD REES, Major (Temporary Lieut.-Colonel), Royal Welsh Fusiliers.
CROCKETT, BASIL EDWIN, Temporary Lieut.-Colonel, Hampshire Regt.
CROFT, WILLIAM DENMAN, Major (Temporary Lieut.-Colonel), Scottish Rifles.
CROFTS, LEONARD MARKHAM, Major (Temporary Lieut.-Colonel), Royal West Surrey Regt.
CROSBIE, JAMES DAYROLLES, Temporary Lieut.-Colonel (Temporary Brigadier-General), Lancashire Fusiliers.
CROSSE, REV. ERNEST COURTENAY, Army Chaplains' Department.
CROZIER, FRANK PERCY, Temporary Lieut.-Colonel (Temporary Brigadier-General), Royal Irish Rifles.
CUMMINS, CHARLES EDWARD, Temporary Major, Durham Light Infantry.
CUNNINGHAM-CUNNINGHAM, THOMAS, Major, Royal Artillery.
CUTBILL, REGINALD HEATON LOCKE, Major, Army Service Corps.
DAKEYNE, HENRY WOLRYCHE, Capt. (Temporary Major), Royal Warwickshire Regt.
DALBY, THOMAS GERALD, Major (Temporary Lieut.-Colonel), King's Royal Rifle Corps.
DANIELL, FRANK WILLIAM, Major (Temporary Lieut.-Colonel), Northumberland Fusiliers.
DANIELSEN, FREDERIC GUSTAVUS, Major (Temporary Lieut.-Colonel), Royal Warwickshire Regt.
DARWALL, ROBERT HENRY, Major, Royal Marines, attached Egyptian Army.
DAVIDSON, HUGH ALLAN, M.B., Major (Temporary Lieut.-Colonel), Royal Army Medical Corps.
DAVIES, PERCY MATCHAM, Lieut.-Colonel, Army Service Corps.
DAWES, GEORGE WILLIAM PATRICK, Major (Temporary Lieut.-Colonel), Royal Berkshire Regt. and Royal Flying Corps.
DAWNAY, ALAN GEOFFREY CHARLES, Capt., Coldstream Guards.
DAY, JOHN, Major, Royal Engineers.
DEAKIN, FREDERICK FARRER, Capt. (Temporary Lieut.-Colonel), retired pay, Yorkshire Hussars.
DEAN, ARTHUR CECIL HAMILTON, Major, Royal Garrison Artillery.
DE LA FONTAINE, HENRY VICTOR MOFFET, Major (Temporary Lieut.-Colonel), East Surrey Regt.
DENNISTOUN, JAMES GEORGE, Lieut.-Colonel, Royal Field Artillery.
D'ESTERRE, PHILIP OLIVER ELLARD, Major (Temporary Lieut.-Colonel), East Lancashire Regt.
DEVAS, THE REV. C. Army Chaplains' Department.
DE WINTON, RICHARD STRETTON, Lieut.-Colonel, Royal Garrison Artillery.
DICKIE, DAVID, F.R.C.S., Capt., Royal Army Medical Corps.
DIVE, GILBERT HENRY, Capt. (Temporary Major), Royal Army Medical Corps.
DIXON, FREDERICK ALFRED, Temporary Lieut.-Colonel, Royal Field Artillery.
DOBSON, ARTHUR CURTIS, Major, Royal Engineers.
DON, JOHN ARCHIBALD, Major, Royal Artillery.
DONALDSON-HUDSON, RALPH CHARLES, Capt. (Temporary Lieut.-Colonel), Territorial Force Reserve and Royal Flying Corps.
DRAFFEN, FREDERIC GEORGE WILLIAM, Major (Temporary Lieut.-Colonel), Scottish Rifles.
DRAGE, GILBERT, Lieut.-Colonel, Herefordshire Regt.
DRAGE, GODFREY, Capt. (Temporary Lieut.-Colonel), Royal Munster Fusiliers.
DUCKETT, JOHN STEUART, Temporary Capt. (Temporary Major), Lancers, Reserve of Officers.
DUKE, BASIL LAWRENCE, Major, Royal Artillery.
DUMBELL, CHARLES HAROLD, Major, Nottinghamshire and Derbyshire Regt.
DUNDAS, FREDERICK CHARLES, Major and Brevet Lieut.-Colonel, Argyll and Sutherland Highlanders.
DUNLOP, FRANK PASSY, Major (Temporary Lieut.-Colonel), Worcestershire Regt.
DUNMORE, EARL OF, ALEXANDER EDWARD, V.C., M.V.O., Major, Reserve of Officers, Lancers.
DUNN, HENRY MASON, M.B., Lieut.-Colonel (Temporary Colonel), Royal Army Medical Corps. (Christian name corrected to Henry Nason).
DU PRE, FRANCIS JAMES, Capt. (Temporary Major), Hussars.
DWYER, BERTIE CUNYNGHAME, Major and Brevet Lieut.-Colonel, Leicestershire Regt. (surname corrected to Dwyer-Hampton).
EAGLES, CHARLES EDWARD CAMPBELL, Capt. (Temporary Major), Royal Marine Light Infantry, Royal Marines.
EARDLEY-WILMOT, THEODORE, Major (Temporary Lieut.-Colonel), York and Lancaster Regt.
EDEN, SCHOMBERG HENLEY, Major, Royal Highlanders.
EDLMANN, FRANCIS JOSEPH FREDERICK, Temporary Major, Northumberland Fusiliers.
EDWARDS, GEORGIE BENNICK, Capt. (Temporary Major), Royal Army Medical Corps.
EDWARDS, GEORGE RICHARD OWEN, Temporary Major, Royal Field Artillery (correction: a Bar substituted for this award and the Distinguished Service Order awarded [London Gazette, 22 Aug. 1918]).
ELLIOTT, CHARLES ALLEN, Major (Temporary Lieut.-Colonel), Royal Engineers.
ELSNER, OTTO WILLIAM ALEXANDER, Lieut.-Colonel, Royal Army Medical Corps.

EMERSON, HENRY HORACE ANDREWS, M.B., Major, Royal Army Medical Corps.
ESTRIDGE, CECIL LORAINE, Capt. (Temporary Lieut.-Colonel), West Yorkshire Regt.
EVANS, ARTHUR PERCIVALE, Capt. (Temporary Major), King's Royal Rifle Corps.
EVANS, GEORGE FARRINGTON, Major, Royal Engineers.
EVANS, LLEWELYN, Major, Royal Engineers.
FAGAN, EDWARD ARTHUR, Major (Temporary Brigadier-General), Indian Army.
FAHMI, AHMED (Effendi), El Bimbashi (Major), Egyptian Army.
FAIR, CHARLES HERBERT, Lieut. (Temporary Major), London Regt.
FENN, HERBERT FRANCIS, Temporary Lieut.-Colonel, Lancaster Regt.
FETHERSTONHAUGH, WILLIAM ALBANY, Major (Temporary Lieut.-Colonel), Indian Army.
FIELD, KENNETH DOUGLAS, Major, Royal Garrison Artillery.
FIFE, ROBERT BAINBRIDGE, Lieut.-Colonel, Royal Garrison Artillery.
FINCH, LIONEL HUGH KNIGHTLEY, Capt. (Temporary Lieut.-Colonel), Cheshire Regt.
FISHE, ARTHUR FRANCIS BABINGTON, Major, Royal Garrison Artillery.
FISHER, HERBERT GEORGE, Major, Royal Field Artillery.
FITZGERALD, FITZGERALD GABBETT, Major and Brevet Lieut.-Colonel (Temporary Lieut.-Colonel), Royal Army Medical Corps.
FITZGERALD, PETER FRANCIS, Major, Shropshire Light Infantry.
FITZJOHN, TUDOR, Major (Temporary Lieut.-Colonel), Worcestershire Regt.
FITZPATRICK, ERNEST RICHARD, Major (Temporary Brigadier-General) North Lancashire Regt.
FLOWER, VICTOR AUGUSTINE, Capt. and Brevet Major (Temporary Lieut.-Colonel), London Regt.
FOORD, WILLIAM PERCY STILLES, Capt. (Temporary Lieut.-Colonel), Gloucestershire Regt.
FORBES, ATHEL MURRAY HAY, Major (Temporary Lieut.-Colonel), Royal Scots Fusiliers.
FORBES, RONALD FOSTER, Major (Temporary Lieut.-Colonel), Highland Light Infantry.
FORSTER, GEORGE NORMAN BOWES, Major (Temporary Lieut.-Colonel), Royal Warwickshire Regt.
FOSTER, RONALD THOMAS, Major, Nottinghamshire and Derbyshire Regt.
FRANKS, GEORGE DESPARD, Lieut.-Colonel, Hussars.
FRASER, ARTHUR ION, Capt. (Temporary Major), Indian Cavalry.
FRASER, PIERCE BUTLER, Major, Army Service Corps.
FREESTUN, WILLIAM HUMPHREY MAY, Major (Temporary Lieut.-Colonel), Somersetshire Light Infantry.
FREWEN, LATON, Temporary Capt. (Temporary Major), King's Royal Rifle Corps.
FULLER, CUTHBERT GRAHAM, Major and Brevet Lieut.-Colonel (Temporary Lieut.-Colonel), Royal Engineers.
FULLER, JOHN FREDERIC CHARLES, Major, Oxfordshire and Buckinghamshire Light Infantry.
FULLERTON, JOHN CAMPBELL, Major, Royal Field Artillery.
GALLAHER, ALEXANDER, Capt., Dragoon Guards.
GARSTIN, HENRY EDWARD, Lieut.-Colonel, Royal Artillery.
GEIGER, GERALD JOHN PERCIVAL, Major, Royal Welsh Fusiliers.
GETHIN, RICHARD WALTER ST. LAWRANCE, Major and Brevet Lieut.-Colonel, Royal Artillery.
GIBSON, BERTRAND DEES, Capt. (Temporary Lieut.-Colonel), Northumberland Fusiliers.
GILES, STANLEY EDMUND HERCULES, Major, Army Service Corps.
GILES, VALENTINE, Major, Royal Engineers.
GILL, DOUGLAS HOWARD, Major (Temporary Lieut.-Colonel), Royal Field Artillery.
GILL, GORDON HARRY, Capt. (Temporary Major), Army Service Corps.
GILLESPIE, HUGH JAMES, Temporary Major, Royal Field Artillery.
GILLESPIE, REGINALD HENRY, Capt. and Brevet Major (Temporary Lieut.-Colonel), Leicestershire Regt.
GILLETT, CHARLES RICHARD, Major, Royal Artillery.
GOODERSON, VALENTINE EDGAR, Temporary Major, Highland Light Infantry.
GOODWIN, WILLIAM RICHARD POWER, Major (Temporary Lieut.-Colonel), Royal Army Medical Corps.
GORDON, FRANCIS LEWIS RAWSON, Temporary Lieut.-Colonel, Royal Irish Rifles.
GORDON, HENRY WILLIAM, Major (Temporary Lieut.-Colonel), Royal Engineers.
GORE-BROWNE, STEWART, Major, Royal Artillery.
GOVER, CHARLES RHODES, Major, Royal Artillery.
GRAEME, JAMES ARCHIBALD, Capt., Royal Engineers.
GRAY, JAMES NEVILLE, Lieut. (Temporary Capt.), Special List.
GRAY, WALTER KER, Major (Temporary Lieut.-Colonel), Royal Field Artillery.
GRAY-CHEAPE, HUGH ANNESLEY, Major (Temporary Lieut.-Colonel), Yeomanry.
GREEN, ARTHUR FRANK UMFREVILLE, Major and Brevet Lieut.-Colonel (Temporary Brigadier-General), Royal Artillery.
GREEN, HERBERT WALTER, Major (Temporary Lieut.-Colonel), East Kent Regt.
GREENFIELD, THOMAS WARING BUNCE, Capt., Reserve of Officers, Irish Guards.
GREGORIE, HUGH GILBERT, Major (Acting Lieut.-Colonel), Royal Irish Regt.
GREGORY, ALFRED JOHN REGINALD, Major, Royal Garrison Artillery.
GRIMWOOD, JAMES, Temporary Lieut.-Colonel, South Wales Borderers.

The Distinguished Service Order

GRISSELL, BERNARD SALWEY, Major, Norfolk Regt.
GROGAN, SIR EDWARD ION BERESFORD, Bart., Lieut.-Colonel, Rifle Brigade.
GROGAN, GEORGE MEREDYTH, Major (Temporary Lieut.-Colonel), Reserve of Officers.
GROVE, THOMAS THACKERAY, Major, Royal Engineers.
GROVES, PERCY ROBERT CLIFFORD, Major (Temporary Lieut.-Colonel), Shropshire Light Infantry.
GRUTE, JOHN, Honorary Major, Army Ordnance Department.
GURNEY, CLEMENT HENDERSON, Temporary Major, York and Lancaster Regt.
GWYTHER, GRAHAM HOWARD, Major (Temporary Lieut.-Colonel), Royal Welsh Fusiliers.
HAIG, CLAUDE HENRY, Major (Temporary Lieut.-Colonel), Leicestershire Regt.
HAIG, WILLIAM, Major, Royal Army Medical Corps.
HALES, REV. JOHN PERCY, Army Chaplains' Department.
HALL, EDWARD, Major, Nottinghamshire and Derbyshire Regt.
HAMILTON, JOHN ALFRED, Major (Temporary Lieut.-Colonel), Army Service Corps.
HAMMICK, ROBERT TOWNSEND, Major, Royal Artillery.
HANNA, JOHN CONNOR, Major (Acting Lieut.-Colonel), Royal Garrison Artillery.
HARDCASTLE, EDWARD LEWIS, Major (Acting Lieut.-Colonel), Royal Garrison Artillery.
HARDIE, STEVEN JAMES LINDSAY, Lieut. (Temporary Capt.) (Temporary Major), Argyll and Sutherland Highlanders.
HARDING, COLIN, C.M.G., Temporary Lieut.-Colonel, Royal Warwickshire Regt.
HARDINGE, THOMAS SHEFFIELD NEWCOMBE, Major, Royal Garrison Artillery.
HARDMAN, REGINALD STANLEY, Lieut.-Colonel, Royal Field Artillery.
HARDRESS-LLOYD, JOHN, Temporary Capt. (Temporary Major), Royal Inniskilling Fusiliers.
HARDY, ERIC JOHN, Capt., Dragoons (corrected to 2nd Dragoons, Royal Scots Greys).
HARE, JOHN WILBERFORCE, Capt., Royal Garrison Artillery.
HARRIS, ALFRED, Capt. (Temporary Major), Royal Field Artillery.
HARRIS, THOMAS BIRKBECK, Capt., Royal Engineers.
HARRISON, GEORGE HYDE, Major (Temporary Lieut.-Colonel), Border Regt.
HARRISON, GEOFFREY BARNETT, Temporary Lieut.-Colonel, Royal Marines (name corrected to Geoffrey Harnett Harrisson [London Gazette, 1 June, 1917]).
HART, HERBERT PARSONS, Temporary Major, Scottish Borderers.
HARTY, THOMAS ERNEST, Major (Temporary Lieut.-Colonel), Royal Army Medical Corps.
HARVEY, FRANCIS HENRY, Major, East Yorkshire Regt.
HARVEY, WILLIAM JOHN SAUNDRY, Major (Temporary Lieut.-Colonel), Royal Army Medical Corps.
HASKARD, JOHN McDOUGALL, Major, Royal Dublin Fusiliers.
HASTINGS, WILLIAM HOLLAND, Capt. and Brevet Major, Indian Army.
HAWKES, CORLIS ST. LEGER GILLMAN, Lieut.-Colonel, Royal Field Artillery.
HAWKES, WILLIAM COTTER WILLIAMSON, Major (Temporary Lieut.-Colonel), Indian Army.
HAWTHORN, FRANK, M.D., Lieut.-Colonel, Royal Army Medical Corps.
HAY, ARTHUR KENNET, Major, Royal Artillery. (Christian name corrected to Arthur Kenneth [London Gazette, 9 July, 1917]).
HAYES, JOHN HIGSON, Major (Temporary Lieut.-Colonel), Shropshire Yeomanry.
HAYLEY, SYDNEY THOMAS, Major, Army Ordnance Department.
HAYMAN, WILLIAM MUIR, Temporary Major, Royal Engineers.
HEAD, ARTHUR EDWARD MAXWELL, Major (Temporary Lieut.-Colonel), Royal Field Artillery.
HEAD, CHARLES OCTAVIUS, Major (Temporary Lieut.-Colonel), Reserve of Officers, Royal Field Artillery.
HEARN, GORDON RISLEY, Major, Royal Engineers.
HENDERSON, HARRY ESMOND, Major, Royal Garrison Artillery.
HENDERSON, MALCOLM, Capt. and Brevet Major, Royal Scots.
HENEAGE, GODFREY CLEMENT WALKER, M.V.O., Major, Reserve of Officers.
HENNING, PHILIP WALTER BERESFORD, Lieut.-Colonel, Royal Field Artillery.
HERBERT, WILLIAM NORMAN, Major, Northumberland Fusiliers.
HERKLOTS, ARNOLD, Major, Army Service Corps.
HESELTINE, JOHN EDWARD NORFOR, Major, King's Royal Rifle Corps.
HEWETSON, HENRY, Lieut.-Colonel, Royal Army Medical Corps.
HEWITT, ALFRED SCOTT, Major, Royal West Kent Regt.
HEYMAN, ARTHUR AUGUSTUS INGLIS, Temporary Lieut.-Colonel, Highland Light Infantry.
HILL, SIR HENRY BLYTH, Bart., Capt. and Brevet Major, Reserve of Officers.
HILL, BASIL ALEXANDER, Major (Temporary Lieut.-Colonel), Army Ordnance Department.
HILL, HENRY WARBURTON, Major (Temporary Lieut.-Colonel), Royal Field Artillery.
HILL, WILLIAM JAMES MONTAGU, Capt., Reserve of Officers.
HIME, HENRY CHARLES RUPERT, M.B., Lieut.-Colonel, Royal Army Medical Corps.
HOARE, HENRY NOEL, Temporary Major, Army Service Corps.
HODDER, ANDREW EDWARD, M.B., Major (Temporary Lieut.-Colonel), Royal Army Medical Corps.

HOGG, CYRIL MINDON TROWER, Capt. (Temporary Major), Indian Army.
HOLDEN, CHARLES WALTER, Major (Temporary Lieut.-Colonel), Royal Army Medical Corps.
HOLLAND, HENRY WILLIAM, Capt., Special List.
HOLLAND, SAMUEL CLIFFORD, Capt. and Brevet Major, Reserve of Officers, late Dragoon Guards.
HOLMES, WILLIAM GEORGE, Capt. (Temporary Major), Royal Welsh Fusiliers.
HOLMES À COURT, RUPERT EDWARD, Major, Shropshire Light Infantry.
HOOD, THE HONOURABLE NEVILLE ALBERT, Capt. (Temporary Major), Reserve of Officers, Royal Garrison Artillery.
HOVIL, RICHARD, Major, Royal Field Artillery.
HOWARD, CHARLES ALFRED, Major (Temporary Lieut.-Colonel), King's Royal Rifle Corps.
HOWARD, FRANCIS JAMES LEIGH, Lieut.-Colonel, Army Service Corps.
HOWARD, HENRY CECIL LLOYD, Capt, and Brevet Major, Lancers.
HOWELL, FREDERICK DUKE GWYNNE, M.C., Capt., Royal Army Medical Corps.
HOWLETT, REGINALD, M.C., Major, Royal Fusiliers.
HOYSTED, DESMOND MURREE FITZGERALD, Brevet Lieut.-Colonel (Temporary Lieut.-Colonel), Royal Engineers.
HUDDLESTON, HUBERT JERVOISE, M.C., Major, Dorsetshire Regt.
HUDLESTON, WILFRID EDWARD, Lieut.-Colonel, Royal Army Medical Corps.
HUDSON, ARTHUR ROSS, Major (Temporary Lieut.-Colonel), Royal Field Artillery.
HUGGINS, ALFRED, Capt. (Temporary Lieut.-Colonel), Royal Flying Corps, Special Reserve.
HULKE, WALTER BACKHOUSE, Capt. (Temporary Lieut.-Colonel), York and Lancaster Regt., Reserve of Officers, Lincolnshire Regt.
HULL, CHARLES ROBERT INGHAM, Major (Temporary Lieut.-Colonel), Army Service Corps.
HUNT, GRANVILLE VERE, Major, Repair Unit, Army Service Corps.
HUTCHINSON, THOMAS MASSIE, Major, Army Service Corps.
HUTTON, VERNON MONTGOMERIE, Temporary Major, Army Service Corps.
HUTTON-SQUIRE, ROBERT HENRY EDMUND, Major, Royal Garrison Artillery.
HYDE, DERMOT OWEN, M.B., Major (Temporary Lieut.-Colonel), Royal Army Medical Corps.
HYNES, GEORGE BAYARD, Capt. (Temporary Major), Royal Artillery and Royal Flying Corps.
IEVERS, OSBURNE, M.B., Major, Royal Army Medical Corps.
IMPEY, GEORGE HASTINGS, Capt. (Temporary Lieut.-Colonel), Royal Sussex Regt.
INCHES, EDWARD JAMES, Major, Royal Field Artillery.
INGHAM, CHARLES ST. MAUR, Lieut.-Colonel, Royal Field Artillery.
INGLES, JOHN DARNLEY, Major and Brevet Lieut.-Colonel (Temporary Brigadier-General), Devonshire Regt.
INKSON, EDGAR THOMAS, V.C., Lieut.-Colonel, Royal Army Medical Corps.
INNES, SYDNEY ARMITAGE, Major (Temporary Lieut.-Colonel), Royal Highlanders.
JACK, EVAN MACLEAN, Major and Brevet Lieut.-Colonel, Royal Engineers.
JACKSON, FRANK WALTER FITTON, Major, Royal Field Artillery, Special Reserve.
JACKSON, VIVIAN ARCHER, Capt., York and Lancaster Regt.
JAMES, BOUCHER CHARLEWOOD, Temporary Lieut.-Colonel, Devonshire Regt.
JAMES, CECIL POLGLASE, Major (Temporary Lieut.-Colonel), Argyll and Sutherland Highlanders.
JERRAM, CHARLES FREDERIC, Capt. (Temporary Major), Royal Marine Light Infantry.
JOHNSON, EDMUND PERCY, Capt., Royal Field Artillery.
JOHNSON, FREDERICK EVANS, Major (Temporary Lieut.-Colonel), Army Service Corps.
JOHNSON, HENRY ALEXANDER, Major (Temporary Lieut.-Colonel), Army Service Corps.
JOHNSON, JAMES GERALD THEWLIS, Lieut. (Temporary Capt.), Yeomanry.
JOHNSON, JOHN TYRER, M.B., Major, Royal Army Medical Corps.
JOHNSON, RONALD MARR, Lieut.-Colonel, Royal Artillery.
JOHNSON, THOMAS HENRY FIELDER, Temporary Major, Dorsetshire Regt.
JOHNSON, THOMAS PELHAM, Lieut.-Colonel, Army Service Corps.
JOHNSTON, JOHN HERBERT, Capt. (Temporary Major), Royal Garrison Artillery.
JONES, HARRY LLEWELLYN, Capt. (Temporary Major), Hussars.
JONES, HOWARD PERCY, Capt. (Temporary Major), Royal Field Artillery.
JOUBERT DE LA FERTE, PHILIP BENNET, Capt. (Temporary Lieut.-Colonel), Royal Artillery and Royal Flying Corps.
JOURDIER, MAX. JAMES AUGUST, Capt., East Surrey Regt.
KAMBAL, BESHIR (Bey), El Miralai (Colonel), Egyptian Army.
KEEN, SYDNEY, Lieut.-Colonel, Royal Engineers.
KELLY, HARRY BEATTY, M.B., Major (Temporary Lieut.-Colonel), Royal Army Medical Corps.
KELLY, PHILIP JAMES VANDELEUR, Major (Temporary Lieut.-Colonel), Hussars, attached Egyptian Army.
KELLY, WALDRON HAROLD FLETCHER, Major (Temporary Lieut.-Colonel), Army Service Corps.
KEMBLE, HENRY HERBERT, M.C., Capt. (Temporary Lieut.-Colonel), London Regt.
KENNEDY, DONALD STUART, Temporary Major, Army Service Corps.
KING, DENNIS MALCOLM, M.C., Capt., Liverpool Regt.
KING, GILBERT EAST, Temporary Major, East Yorkshire Regt.
KING, GERALD HARTLEY, Major, Royal Artillery.

KIRK, JOHN WILLIAM CARNEGIE, Major (Temporary Lieut.-Colonel), Duke of Cornwall's Light Infantry.
KIRKE, KENNETH ST. GEORGE, Lieut.-Colonel, Royal Field Artillery.
KIRKLAND, TRAVERS, Major, Royal Field Artillery.
KNOLLES, RODERICK MACKENZIE, Major, Royal Artillery.
KNOTHE, HUGH, M.C., Lieut. (Temporary Major), Army Service Corps, Special Reserve.
KNOX, HARRY HUGH SIDNEY, Major and Brevet Lieut.-Colonel, Northampton Regt.
KNOX, JAMES MELDRUM, Major (Temporary Lieut.-Colonel), Royal Warwickshire Regt.
KNOX, ROBERT SINCLAIR, Temporary Major, Royal Inniskilling Fusiliers.
KOSTER, ROBERT HORACE, Capt., Reserve of Officers, South Lancashire Regt.
LAKE, BRUCE LAUNCELOT, Major, Army Veterinary Corps.
LAMB, ROGER MONTAGUE RADCLIFFE, Major, Northumberland Fusiliers.
LAMBERT, WALTER JOHN, Major (Temporary Lieut.-Colonel), Indian Army, attached Liverpool Regt.
LANGDON, JOHN FREDERICK PALTOCK, Major (Temporary Lieut.-Colonel), Reserve of Officers.
LANGSTAFF, JAMES WILLIAM, Lieut.-Colonel, Royal Army Medical Corps.
LARMOUR, FRANK CORDON, Major (Temporary Lieut.-Colonel), Army Ordnance Department.
LASCELLES, RONALD HASTINGS, Major, Royal Artillery.
LAW, WALTER HENRY PATRICK, Major (Temporary Lieut.-Colonel), Army Service Corps.
LEAHY, THOMAS BERNARD ARTHUR, Major (Temporary Lieut.-Colonel), Army Ordnance Department.
LEANING, AUGUSTINE, Major, Army Veterinary Corps.
LEDGARD, WILLIAM RIMINGTON, Temporary Capt., Royal Marine Artillery.
LEE, REGINALD TILSON, Capt. and Brevet Major, Royal West Surrey Regt.
LEESE, NEVILLE, Temporary Major, Army Service Corps.
LEGGE, REGINALD FRANCIS, Major (Temporary Lieut.-Colonel), Leinster Regt.
LEGGE, WILLIAM KAYE, Lieut.-Colonel, Essex Regt.
LEGGETT, ROBERT ANTHONY CLEGHORN LININGTON, Capt. (Temporary Colonel), Worcestershire Regt., Reserve of Officers.
LEMMON, CHARLES HERBERT, Capt. (Temporary Major), Royal Field Artillery.
LENOX-CONYNGHAM, HUBERT MAXWELL, F.R.C.V.S., Major (Temporary Colonel), Army Veterinary Corps.
LEVESON-GOWER, PHILIP, Lieut.-Colonel (Temporary Brigadier-General), Nottinghamshire and Derbyshire Regt.
LIARDET, CLAUDE FRANCIS, Major, Royal Garrison Artillery.
LIGERTWOOD, CHARLES EDWARD, M.D., Temporary Major (Temporary Lieut.-Colonel), Royal Army Medical Corps. (correction : a Bar was substituted for this award and the Distinguished Service Order awarded [London Gazette, 22 Aug. 1918].
LINDSAY, JAMES HOWARD, Major (Temporary Lieut.-Colonel), London Regt.
LINDSAY, MICHAEL EGAN, Capt.(Temporary Lieut.-Colonel), Dragoon Guards.
LINTOTT, ALFRED LORD, Capt. (Temporary Major), London Regt.
LITTLE, CECIL HUNTER, Major, Somersetshire Light Infantry, attached Egyptian Army.
LLOYD, HORACE, Major, Northampton Regt.
LOCKHART, ROBERT NORMAN, Major (Temporary Lieut.-Colonel), Royal Artillery.
LOGAN, FRANCIS DOUGLAS, Lieut.-Colonel, Royal Artillery.
LONGMORE, CHARLES MOORSOM, Major, Royal Field Artillery.
LOVELACE, EARL OF, LIONEL FORTESCUE KING, Temporary Major, Northumberland Fusiliers.
LOW, STUART, Major, Royal Garrison Artillery.
LOWIS, PENTON SHAKESPEAR, Major (Temporary Lieut.-Colonel), Royal Garrison Artillery.
LOWTHER, SIR CHARLES BINGHAM, Bart., Capt. (Temporary Major), Yeomanry.
LUCAS, CUTHBERT HENRY TINDALL, Major and Brevet Lieut.-Colonel (Temporary Brigadier-General), Royal Berkshire Regt.
LUCK, CYRIL MONTAGU, Temporary Major (Temporary Lieut.-Colonel), Royal Engineers.
LUMSDEN, FREDERICK WILLIAM, Major, Royal Marine Artillery.
LUMSDEN, WILLIAM FORBES, Major, Royal Garrison Artillery.
LUXMOORE, NOEL, Major (Temporary Lieut.-Colonel), Devonshire Regt.
MACCLELLAN, GORDON PONSONBY, Major, Royal Garrison Artillery.
McCALMONT, ROBERT CHAINE ALEXANDER, Lieut.-Colonel, Irish Guards.
McCORMICK, REV. WILLIAM PATRICK GLYN, Army Chaplains' Department.
McCRAE, SIR GEORGE, V.D., Temporary Lieut.-Colonel (Lieut.-Colonel, Territorial Force Reserve), Royal Scots.
McCOWAN, WILLIAM HEW, Major, Cameron Highlanders, employed Egyptian Army.
MACDONALD, CHARLES LESLIE, Capt. (Temporary Major), Unattached List, T.F., attached Manchester Regt.
McDONNELL, EDMOND, M.B., Major (Temporary Lieut.-Colonel), Royal Army Medical Corps.
McDOUGALL, WILLIAM ALLAN, F.R.C.V.S., Major (Temporary Lieut.-Colonel), Reserve of Officers, Army Veterinary Corps.
MACDOWELL, CHARLES CARLYLE, Major (Temporary Lieut.-Colonel), Royal Field Artillery.
McGRATH, ARTHUR THOMAS, Major, Royal Artillery.
MACKAY, JAMES DOULL, Lieut.-Colonel, Hampshire Regt.
MACKENZIE, COLIN MANSFIELD, Capt. (Temporary Lieut.-Colonel), London Regt.
MACKENZIE, DONALD FRANCIS, M.B., Capt. (Temporary Major), Royal Army Medical Corps.

MACKENZIE, ERIC DIGHTON, Lieut., Scots Guards.
MACKENZIE, JOHN HUGH, Major, Royal Scots.
MACKENZIE, WILLIAM SCOBIE, Major (Temporary Lieut.-Colonel), Army Ordnance Department.
MACKENZIE, FREDERICK WILLIAM, Lieut.-Colonel, Royal Field Artillery.
MACKESY, JOHN PIERSE, Major (Temporary Lieut.-Colonel), Royal Engineers.
MACKINNON, JAMES, Major (Temporary Lieut.-Colonel), Royal Army Medical Corps.
MACKINTOSH, ERNEST ELLIOT BUCKLAND, Major, Royal Engineers.
MACINTOSH, STANLEY HUGH, Temporary Major, Northumberland Fusiliers.
McLEOD, DONALD KENNETH, Capt., Indian Army.
McMAHON, FRANCIS RAYMOND, Temporary Major, Royal Engineers.
MACMICHAEL, HAROLD ALFRED, Temporary Capt., Sudan Civil Service, attached Egyptian Army.
MACNEECE, WILLIAM FOSTER, Capt. (Temporary Major), Royal West Kent Regt. and Royal Flying Corps.
McNICOLL, GRAHAM, Temporary Major, Durham Light Infantry.
McRAE, HENRY ST. GEORGE MURRAY, Capt. (Temporary Major), Indian Army.
MACRORY, FRANCIS SAMUEL NEEDHAM, Temporary Major (Temporary Lieut.-Colonel), Royal Inniskilling Fusiliers.
McVITTIE, CHARLES EDWIN, Major (Temporary Lieut.-Colonel), Army Service Corps, Reserve of Officers.
MAGAWLY CERATI DE CALRY, VALERIO AWLY, Capt. (Temporary Major), Dragoons.
MAIN, ARTHUR KERR, Major, Royal Artillery.
MAINPRISE, CECIL WILMOT, Lieut.-Colonel, Royal Army Medical Corps.
MAKGILL-CRIGHTON-MAITLAND, MARK EDWARD, Major (Temporary Lieut.-Colonel), Grenadier Guards.
MALLOCK, CHARLES HERBERT, Major, Special Reserve, Royal Field Artillery.
MALTBY, PAUL COPELAND, Capt. (Temporary Major), Royal Welsh Fusiliers and Royal Flying Corps.
MARKS, WILFRED OSBORNE, Major, Army Service Corps.
MARRYAT, RONALD, Major, Royal Field Artillery.
MARSHALL, FRANCIS JAMES, Major and Brevet Colonel (Temporary Brigadier-General), Seaforth Highlanders.
MARSHALL, JOHN DODDS, M.B., Temporary Capt., Royal Army Medical Corps.
MARTELLI, HORACE DE COURCY, Major (Temporary Lieut.-Colonel), Royal Artillery.
MASSY, EDWARD CHARLES, Lieut.-Colonel, Royal Field Artillery
MATHEW-LANNOWE, EDMUND BYAM, Major, Royal West Surrey Regt.
MATTHEW, JOHN SMART, Lieut.-Colonel, Army Service Corps.
MAUD, HARRY, Temporary Major, General List.
MAUDE, ALAN HAMER, Capt. (Temporary Major), Army Service Corps.
MAUGHAN, JOHN ST. AUBYN, Major, Royal Army Medical Corps.
MAXWELL, GEOFFREY ARCHIBALD PRENTICE, M.V.O., M.C., Capt. (Temporary Lieut.-Colonel), Royal Engineers.
MEARES, MERVYN, Major, Army Ordnance Department.
MEARS, ERNEST LENNOX, Lieut.-Colonel, Army Service Corps.
MEARS, TREVOR IRVINE NEVITT, Major (Temporary Lieut.-Colonel), Army Service Corps.
MEIKLEJOHN, JAMES ROSS CONRAD, Capt., Border Regt.
MENZIES, ALEXANDER HENRY, Capt. (Temporary Major), Highland Light Infantry.
METCALFE, CHRISTOPHER HENRY FRANK, Major, Bedfordshire Regt.
METCALFE, FENWICK HENRY, Lieut.-Colonel, Royal Garrison Artillery.
MEYNELL, FRANCIS HUGO LINDLEY, Capt. (Temporary Major), Royal Field Artillery.
MILLAR, CECIL ROY, Major, Royal Army Medical Corps.
MILLER, JOSEPH SIDNEY, Temporary Capt., Machine Gun Corps.
MILLER, ROBERT MOLYNEUX, Temporary Capt., Royal Army Medical Corps.
MILLIGAN, JOHN, Major, Royal Field Artillery.
MILLS, ARTHUR MORDAUNT, Capt. (Temporary Lieut.-Colonel), Indian Army.
MILMAN, OCTAVIUS RODNEY EVERARD, Major, Royal Garrison Artillery.
MILWARD, HERBERT MILWARD, Major (Temporary Lieut.-Colonel), Nottinghamshire and Derbyshire Regt.
MINSHULL-FORD, JOHN RANDLE MINSHULL, M.C., Brevet Lieut.-Colonel (Temporary Brigadier-General), Royal Welsh Fusiliers.
MITCHELL, CHARLES JOHNSTONE, Capt. (Temporary Major), Oxfordshire and Buckinghamshire Light Infantry, Reserve of Officers.
MITCHELL, JAMES THOMSON RANKIN, Temporary Major, Royal Scots.
MOBBS, EDGAR ROBERT, Temporary Lieut.-Colonel, Northampton Regt.
MOLESWORTH, HERBERT ELLICOMBE, Major (Temporary Lieut.-Colonel, Royal Garrison Artillery.
MONTAGUE-BATES, FRANCIS STEWART, Major and Brevet Lieut.-Colonel (Temporary Brigadier-General), East Surrey Regt.
MONTGOMERY, HUGH FERGUSON, Major, Royal Marine Light Infantry.
MOORE, LANCELOT GEOFFREY, Capt., King's Royal Rifle Corps.
MORANT, HUBERT HORATIO SHIRLEY, Major (Temporary Lieut.-Colonel), Durham Light Infantry.
MORPHEW, EDWARD MAUDSLEY, Lieut.-Colonel, Royal Army Medical Corps.
MORSHEAD, HENRY TREISE, Capt., Royal Engineers.
MOSS-BLUNDELL, FREDERICK BLUNDELL, Lieut.-Colonel, Royal Field Artillery.
MUNBY, JOSEPH ERNEST, Major, King's Own Yorkshire Light Infantry.

The Distinguished Service Order

MURPHY, CYRIL FRANCIS DE SALES, M.C., Capt. (Temporary Lieut.-Colonel), Royal Berkshire Regt. and Royal Flying Corps.
MURRAY, KENELM DIGBY BOLD, Capt., Indian Army.
MURRAY, LESLIE, Major (Temporary Lieut.-Colonel) (Capt., Reserve of Officers), Royal Warwickshire Regt.
MURROW, HENRY LLOYD, Major, Royal Garrison Artillery.
NEWCOMBE, EDWARD OSBORN ARMSTRONG, Capt., Reserve of Officers.
NICHOLLS, WILLIAM ASHLEY, Major, Royal Field Artillery.
NICOL-SMITH, ALEXANDER GEORGE, Capt. (Temporary Major), Army Service Corps.
NORMAN, WILLIAM WYLIE, Lieut.-Colonel (Brevet Colonel), Manchester Regt.
NORRIS, SAMUEL EDWARD, Major (Temporary Lieut.-Colonel), Liverpool Regt.
NOTT, THOMAS WALKER, Lieut. (Temporary Major), Gloucestershire Regt.
NORTH, EDWARD BUNBURY, Major, Royal Fusiliers.
NUTT, HERBERT JOHN, Lieut.-Colonel (Honorary Colonel), Royal Warwickshire Regt.
O'CONNELL, REV. MAURICE, Army Chaplains' Department.
OLDFIELD, ARTHUR RADULPHUS, Major (Temporary Colonel), Army Ordnance Department.
ORMEROD, GEORGE MILNER, Capt. (Temporary Lieut.-Colonel), Royal Field Artillery.
O'RORKE, THE REV. BENJAMIN GARNISS, M.A., Army Chaplains' Department.
OVEY, DARRELL, Major, Rifle Brigade.
PACKE, EDMUND CHRISTOPHER, Major (Temporary Lieut.-Colonel), Royal Fusiliers.
PAGE, LEWIS MEADOWS SHAW, Major, Army Service Corps.
LUIS-PALLANT, SANTIAGO, Major, Royal Army Medical Corps.
PALLIN, SAMUEL FARRER GODFREY, F.R.C.V.S., Major, Army Veterinary Corps.
PARKER, WILLIAM, Major (Temporary Lieut.-Colonel), London Regt.
PARKER, WILLIAM NEWTON, M.D., Temporary Capt., Royal Army Medical Corps.
PARRY, CLAUD FREDERICK PILLINGTON, Lieut.-Colonel, Royal Field Artillery.
PARSONS, CECIL, Capt., Royal West Surrey Regt., Reserve of Officers.
PARSONS, DURIE, Lieut.-Colonel, Army Service Corps.
PATERSON, ARTHUR WILLIAM SIBBALD, Major (Temporary Lieut.-Colonel), Somersetshire Light Infantry, attached Royal Irish Fusiliers.
PAYNTER, WILLIAM PATTINSON, Major, Royal Artillery.
PEARSE, SIDNEY ARTHUR, Major (Temporary Lieut.-Colonel), retired, Indian Army, attached East Lancashire Regt.
PECK, SYDNEY CAPEL, Major, Royal Artillery.
PEMBERTON, RYLAND TALBOT, Capt. (Temporary Major), Army Service Corps.
PENNINGTON, HUBERT STANLEY WHITMORE, Temporary Major, Army Service Corps.
PERY-KNOX-GORE, ARTHUR FRANCIS GORE, Major, Army Service Corps.
PEYTON, THOMAS HENRY, Capt. (Temporary Major), Royal Army Medical Corps.
PHILLPOTTS, BRIAN SURTEES, Major, Royal Engineers.
PICKERING, EMIL WILLIAM, Capt. (Temporary Major), Royal Field Artillery.
PICKERING, FRANCIS ALEXANDER UMFREVILLE, Capt., Dragoons.
PIGGOTT, FRANCIS STEWART GILDEROY, Major, Royal Engineers.
PILCHER, WILLIAM SPILMAN, Capt. (Temporary Major), Grenadier Guards.
PILKINGTON, GUY REGINALD, Capt., South Lancashire Regt.
PINKNEY, EDMUND WALKER PENNY, Lieut.-Colonel, Army Service Corps (Christian name Penny corrected to Renny [London Gazette, 13 Feb. 1917]).
PLEYDELL-BOUVERIE, THE HONOURABLE STUART, Lieut.-Colonel, Royal Field Artillery.
PLEYDELL-NOTT, JOHN GEORGE LATHAM, Capt. (Temporary Major), Army Service Corps, Special Reserve.
PLIMPTON, KELBURNE ARCHIBALD, Capt. (Temporary Major), East Yorkshire Regt.
POLLOCK, CHARLES EDWARD, Lieut.-Colonel (Temporary Colonel), Royal Army Medical Corps.
POLLITT, GEORGE PATON, Temporary Major, Royal Engineers.
POPE, EDWARD ALEXANDER, Major (Temporary Lieut.-Colonel), South Wales Borderers.
POPE, FRANCIS, Capt., Reserve of Officers, Northampton Regt.
POTTER, HUBERT CECIL, Major and Brevet Lieut.-Colonel (Temporary Brigadier-General), King's Liverpool Regt. (Christian name Hubert corrected to Herbert [London Gazette, 18 Feb. 1918]).
POTTER, WILLIAM ALLEN, Major, Army Service Corps.
POWELL, ROBERT MONTAGU, Major, Royal Artillery.
POWELL, WILLIAM HENRY, Lieut. (Temporary Capt.), Royal Field Artillery.
POYNTZ, HUGH STAINTON, Major (Temporary Lieut.-Colonel), Bedfordshire Regt.
POYSER, KENNETH ELLISTON, Temporary Capt., Yorkshire Light Infantry.
PRAGNELL, THOMAS WYKEHAM, Capt., Hussars.
PRATT, AUDLEY CHARLES, Major (Temporary Lieut.-Colonel) (Captain, Reserve of Officers), Inniskilling Fusiliers.
PRATT, ROBERT EDWARD BURTON, Capt., Royal Engineers.
PREEDY, FRANK, M.C., Capt. and Brevet Major (Temporary Lieut.-Colonel), Royal Engineers.
PRECHTEL, ALFRED FREDERICK, Lieut.-Colonel, Royal Field Artillery.
PRETOR-PINNEY, CHARLES FREDERICK, Temporary Lieut.-Colonel, Rifle Brigade.
PRICE, THOMAS HERBERT FRANCIS, Major and Brevet Lieut.-Colonel (Temporary Brigadier-General), Duke of Cornwall's Light Infantry.

PRICE, THOMAS ROSE CARADOC, Major, Welsh Guards.
PRIDHAM, GEOFFREY ROBERT, Major and Brevet Lieut.-Colonel (Temporary Lieut.-Colonel), Royal Engineers.
PRINGLE, HALL GRANT, Major and Brevet Lieut.-Colonel (Temporary Lieut.-Colonel), Royal Field Artillery.
PRITCHARD, CLIVE GORDON, Major (Temporary Lieut.-Colonel), Royal Garrison Artillery.
PROFEIT, CHARLES WILLIAM, M.B., Lieut.-Colonel (Temporary Colonel), Army Medical Service.
PRYNNE, HAROLD VERNON, F.R.C.S., Lieut.-Colonel (Temporary Colonel), Royal Army Medical Corps.
PUCKLE, BRUCE HALE, Temporary Major, Machine Gun Corps.
PURDON, WILLIAM BROOKE, M.C., M.B., Capt. (Temporary Major), Royal Army Medical Corps.
PURSER, LYDMAR MOLINE, M.B., Major, Royal Army Medical Corps.
PYE, KELLOW WILLIAM, Capt., Royal Engineers.
QUIRK, DOUGLAS, Temporary Major, York and Lancaster Regt.
RAINSFORD-HANNAY, ARCHIBALD GORDON, Capt., Royal Engineers, employed Egyptian Army.
RAINSFORD-HANNAY, FREDERICK, Major (Temporary Lieut.-Colonel), Royal Field Artillery.
RANDOLPH, ALGERNON FORBES, Major (Honorary Lieut.-Colonel), Reserve of Officers, Suffolk Regt.
RANSON, WILSON, F.R.C.S., Lieut.-Colonel, Royal Army Medical Corps.
RAY, MATTHEW BURROW, Major (Temporary Lieut.-Colonel), Royal Army Medical Corps.
READ, JOHN JAMES, Capt. (Temporary Major), Royal Field Artillery. (Christian names corrected to James John [London Gazette, 18 Jan., 1918]).
REES-MOGG, ROBERT JAMES, Major, Royal Irish Regt., employed Egyptian Army.
RETTIE, WILLIAM JOHN KERR, Lieut.-Colonel, Royal Field Artillery.
RHODES, GODFREY DEAN, Capt., Royal Engineers.
RICARDO, HENRY GEORGE, Major (Temporary Lieut.-Colonel), Royal Field Artillery, Retired.
RICHARDS, HAROLD ARTHUR DAVID, Major (Temporary Lieut.-Colonel), Army Service Corps.
RICKETTS, PERCY EDWARD, M.V.O., Lieut.-Colonel, Indian Army.
RICKMAN, ARTHUR WILMOT, Major (Temporary Lieut.-Colonel), Northumberland Fusiliers, Special Reserve.
RIDGWAY, JOHN HERBERT, Major, North Staffordshire Regt.
RISLEY, CRESCENT GEBHARD, Capt., Indian Army.
RITCHIE, THEODORE FRANCIS, M.B., Major (Temporary Lieut.-Colonel), Royal Army Medical Corps.
ROBERTS, ARTHUR HENRY, Major (Temporary Lieut.-Colonel), Army Service Corps.
ROBERTSON, CHARLES CHETWODE, Major (Temporary Lieut.-Colonel), Reserve of Officers, Royal Field Artillery.
ROBERTSON, NORMAN BETHUNE, Major, Royal Field Artillery.
ROBERTSON, WILLIAM, Major, Royal Engineers.
ROBINSON, ARCHIBALD TYRRELL, Major (Temporary Lieut.-Colonel), East Surrey Regt., attached Oxfordshire and Buckinghamshire Light Infantry.
ROBINSON, BEVERLY BEVERLY, Temporary Lieut.-Colonel, Yorkshire Light Infantry.
ROBINSON, EDWARD HEATON, Honorary Major and Honorary Lieut.-Colonel, Army Ordnance Department.
ROBINSON, FREDERICK WINWOOD, Major, Royal Field Artillery.
ROBINSON, LEONARD JOHN WHISHAW, Major, Royal Field Artillery.
ROBINSON, STRATFORD WATSON, Major and Brevet Lieut.-Colonel, Royal Artillery.
ROBINSON, WILLIAM PASLEY, Major, Army Service Corps.
ROCH, HORACE SAMSON, Lieut.-Colonel, Royal Army Medical Corps.
ROGERS, HENRY SCHOFIELD, Major, Reserve of Officers, Royal Engineers.
ROGERS, HUGH HENRY, Capt. (Temporary Lieut.-Colonel), Royal Artillery, Retired.
ROLLO, GEORGE, Temporary Lieut.-Colonel, Liverpool Regt.
ROLLS, STANLEY PERCY ASHBY, M.C., Capt., Dorsetshire Regt.
ROOKE, CRESSWELL PAILLET, Major, Middlesex Regt., Special Reserve.
ROSE, ALEXANDER MACGREGOR, M.B., Major (Temporary Lieut.-Colonel), Royal Army Medical Corps.
ROSE, HUGH ARTHUR, Temporary Lieut.-Colonel, Royal Scots.
ROSE, HUGH ALEXANDER LESLIE, Major, Royal Artillery.
ROYSTON-PIGOTT, WALTER MYTTON, Major, Army Service Corps.
RUSSELL, HENRY JOHN, Lieut.-Colonel, Army Service Corps.
RUSSELL, JAMES COSMO, Capt. (Temporary Lieut.-Colonel), Indian Army.
RUSSELL, WILLIAM CHAMBERS POMEROY, Major, Royal Garrison Artillery.
RUSSELL, WILLIAM KELSON, Major (Temporary Lieut.-Colonel), Royal Engineers.
ST. CLAIR, GEORGE JAMES PAUL, Capt., Royal Artillery.
ST. JOHN, EDMUND FARQUHAR, Major, Royal Engineers.
SAMUEL, FREDERICK DUDLEY, Lieut.-Colonel, London Regt.
SAMUEL, FREDERICK ALFARO, Temporary Major, Royal Welsh Fusiliers.
SANDILANDS, VINCENT CORBETT, Major (Temporary Lieut.-Colonel), Scottish Rifles.
SARGENT, ARTHUR EDWARD EVERY, M.C., Capt. (Temporary Major), Indian Army.
SARGENT, PERCY WILLIAM GEORGE, M.B., F.R.C.S., Lieut. (Temporary Colonel), Army Medical Service.
SAUNDERS, HAROLD CECIL RICH, Capt. (Temporary Major), East Yorkshire Regt.
SAVAGE, GERALD TAHOURDIN, Major, Army Service Corps.
SAVILE, LAWRENCE WREY, Major, Royal Artillery.

SAVORY, ARNOLD KENNETH MALCOLM CECIL WORDSWORTH, Temporary Major (Temporary Lieut.-Colonel), East Yorkshire Regt.
SCEALES, GEORGE ADINSTON McLAREN, Major (Temporary Lieut.-Colonel), Argyll and Sutherland Highlanders.
SCOTT, CHARLES ALEXANDER REID, Major, Reserve of Officers, Royal Artillery.
SCOTT, ERNEST, M.B., Temporary Capt., Royal Army Medical Corps.
SCOTT, JOHN WILLOUGHBY, Major (Temporary Lieut.-Colonel), Yeomanry.
SCOTT, ROBERT HAMILTON, Temporary Major, Royal Inniskilling Fusiliers.
SEAGRAM, TOM OGLE, Lieut.-Colonel, Royal Field Artillery.
SECKHAM, DOUGLAS THORNE, Major (Temporary Lieut.-Colonel), South Staffordshire Regt., Special Reserve.
SELIGMAN, HERBERT SPENCER, Lieut.-Colonel (Temporary Brigadier-General), Royal Artillery.
SEYMOUR, ARCHIBALD GEORGE, Major (Temporary Lieut.-Colonel), Dragoons.
SEYMOUR, EDWARD, M.V.O., Capt., Grenadier Guards, Reserve of Officers.
SHANAHAN, DANIEL DAVID, Lieut.-Colonel (Temporary Colonel), Royal Army Medical Corps.
SHAW, GORDON DONALD ARCHIBALD, Major, Royal Field Artillery.
SHAW-STEWART, BASIL HERON, Major, Royal Artillery.
SHELTON, ROBERT, Capt. (Temporary Major), Army Service Corps.
SHERER, JAMES DONNELLY, Lieut.-Colonel, Royal Garrison Artillery.
SILVER, JOHN PAYZANT, M.B., Lieut.-Colonel (Temporary Colonel), Royal Army Medical Corps.
SIMCOX, CHARLES THOMAS, Temporary Major, Duke of Cornwall's Light Infantry.
SIMNER, PERCY REGINALD OWEN ABEL, Temporary Major, West Riding Regt.
SIMONDS, JOHN DE LUZE, Capt., Royal Garrison Artillery.
SKINNER, PERCY CYRIAC BURRELL, Lieut.-Colonel (Temporary Brigadier-General), Northampton Regt.
SMALLEY, EDGAR, Temporary Lieut.-Colonel, Manchester Regt.
SMITH, GEORGE EDWARD, C.M.G., Lieut.-Colonel, Royal Engineers.
SMITH, REV. CANON MARTIN LINTON, D.D., Army Chaplains' Department.
SMITH, SIDNEY, Major, Royal Field Artillery and Royal Flying Corps.
SMYTH-OSBOURNE, GEORGE NOWELL THOMAS, Major (Temporary Lieut.-Colonel), Devonshire Regt.
SOLE, DENIS MAVISYN ANSLOW, Capt. (Temporary Major), Border Regt.
SOUTRY, TREVOR LLOYD BLUNDEN, Major, Royal Irish Rifles.
SPENCE, GILBERT ORMEROD, Lieut.-Colonel, Durham Light Infantry.
SPINKS, CHARLTON WATSON, Major (Temporary Lieut.-Colonel), Royal Artillery, employed Egyptian Army.
STANFORD, CHARLES EDWARD CORTIS, M.B., Staff Surgeon, Royal Navy, Royal Naval Division.
STANLEY, THE HONOURABLE FREDERICK WILLIAM, Capt. and Brevet Major (Temporary Major), Royal Artillery, Reserve of Officers, Hussars.
STEBBING, NIGEL AUSTIN, Major, Royal Field Artillery .
STERICKER, ARTHUR WILLIAM, Major, Duke of Cornwall's Light Infantry.
STEVENS, ARTHUR CORNISH JEREMIE, Major, Royal Engineers.
STEVENS, CECIL MORDANT HENRY, Major, Royal Artillery.
STEVENS, HAROLD RAPHAEL GAENATO, Major, Royal Garrison Artillery.
STEVENS, LEIGHTON MARLOW, Major (Temporary Lieut.-Colonel), Worcestershire Regt.
STEVENSON, PERCIVAL HENRY, Capt. (Acting Lieut.-Colonel), King's Own Scottish Borderers, Special Reserve.
STEWART, DOUGLAS, Major, Royal Field Artillery.
STIRLING, WILLIAM, Major (Temporary Lieut.-Colonel), Royal Field Artillery.
STOCKLEY, ERNEST NORMAN, Major (Temporary Lieut.-Colonel), Royal Engineers.
STOCKS, HARRIS LAWRENCE, Temporary Major, Royal Scots.
STOKOE, THOMAS RICHARD, Lieut.-Colonel, Duke of Cornwall's Light Infantry.
STONE, PERCY VERE POWYS, Capt. and Brevet Major (Temporary Lieut.-Colonel), Norfok Regt.
STORY, PHILIP FRANCIS, Temporary Major, Royal Engineers.
STOURTON, THE HONOURABLE EDWARD PLANTAGENET JOSEPH, Major, Yorkshire Light Infantry.
STRANACK, CYRIL EDWIN, Major, Royal Artillery.
STRATTON, FREDERICK JOHN MARTIN, Capt. (Temporary Major), Royal Engineers. (Christian name Martin corrected to Marrian [London Gazette, 18 July, 1917]).
STUBBS, GUY CLIFFORD, Capt. (Temporary Major), Suffolk Regt.
SUMMERHAYES, JOHN ORLANDO, Major, Royal Army Medical Corps.
SUMMERS, FRANK, D.S.C., Temporary Major, Machine Gun Corps.
SWENY, WILLIAM FREDERICK, Major and Brevet Lieut.-Colonel, Royal Fusiliers.
SWORD, DONALD CUTHBERTSON, Major (Temporary Lieut.-Colonel), Scottish Rifles.
SYNGE, MARK, Major (Temporary Lieut.-Colonel), Supply and Transport Corps, Indian Army.
TAYLOR, THOMAS GEORGE, Capt. (Temporary Major), Gordon Highlanders.
TEMPERLEY, ALFRED, Major, Northumberland Fusiliers.
TEMPEST, ROGER STEPHEN, Major and Brevet Lieut.-Colonel (Temporary Lieut.-Colonel), Scots Guards.
TENISON, WILLIAM PERCIVAL COSNAHAN, Major, Royal Artillery.
THACKERAY, FRANK STANIFORD, M.C., Capt., Highland Light Infantry.
THOMPSON, ALBERT GEORGE, M.B., Lieut.-Colonel, Royal Army Medical Corps.
THOMPSON, RICHARD LOVELL BRERETON, Major and Brevet Lieut.-Colonel, Royal Engineers.
THOMPSON, STEPHEN JOHN, Capt. (Temporary Major), Royal Field Artillery.

THOMSON, CHARLES GLENDENNING, Major, Royal Army Medical Corps.
THORP, AUSTIN, Major (Temporary Lieut.-Colonel), Royal Garrison Artillery.
THORPE, HAROLD, Major (Temporary Lieut.-Colonel), Yeomanry.
THORPE, EDWARD IVAN DE SAUSMAREZ, Major and Brevet Colonel (Temporary Lieut.-Colonel), Bedfordshire Regt.
THURSTON, LIONEL VICTOR, Major, Royal Army Medical Corps.
THWAITES, GUY, Major, Army Service Corps, employed Egyptian Army.
THYNNE, LORD ALEXANDER GEORGE, Major, Yeomanry.
TILNEY, NORMAN ECCLES, Lieut.-Colonel, Royal Artillery.
TOMKINSON, FRANCIS MARTIN, Major, Worcestershire Regt.
TOWNSEND, JAMES NEWMAN, Major, Royal Warwickshire Regt.
TRAILL, WILLIAM HENRY, Major, East Lancashire Regt.
TROWER, REGINALD GRAHAM, M.C., Temporary Major, Royal Engineers.
TRUMAN, CHARLES MONTAGU, Major (Temporary Lieut.-Colonel), Lancers.
TRUMP, FREDERICK JOSEPH, Capt. (Temporary Major) (Temporary Lieut.-Colonel), Monmouthshire Regt.
TUKE, GEORGE FRANCIS STRATFORD, Major, Royal Artillery.
TURNER, ERNEST VERE, Major and Brevet Lieut.-Colonel (Temporary Colonel), Royal Engineers.
TURNER, JOHN EAMER, Major, Scottish Rifles.
TWEEDIE, JOHN LANNOY FORBES, Major (Temporary Lieut.-Colonel), Gloucestershire Regt., attached Lancashire Fusiliers.
TWIDALE, WILLIAM CECIL ERASMUS, Major, Royal Artillery.
TWISS, EDWARD KEMTLE, Capt. and Brevet Major, Indian Army.
TWISS, FRANCIS ARTHUR, M.V.O., Major, Royal Artillery.
URMSTON, ARCHIBALD GEORGE BRABAZON, Major and Brevet Lieut.-Colonel (Temporary Lieut.-Colonel), retired pay.
UTTERSON, ARCHIBALD TITO LE MARCHANT, Capt. (Temporary Major), Leicestershire Regt.
VAN DER KISTE, FREEGIFT WILLIAM, Major, Royal Garrison Artillery.
VANDELEUR, THOMAS BOYLE, Major, Royal Irish Regt.
VELLACOTT, PAUL CAIRN, Temporary Major, South Lancashire Regt.
VINCE, ARTHUR NEVILLE, Temporary Lieut.-Colonel, Liverpool Regt.
WADE, HENRY OSWALD, Lieut.-Colonel, West Yorkshire Regt.
WADE, THOMAS STEWART HERSCHAL, Lieut.-Colonel, Lancashire Fusiliers.
WAKEFIELD, THOMAS MONTAGUE, Major, Royal Artillery.
WALCH, JOHN CROSBY, Major, Royal Field Artillery.
WALKER, HENRY WEST, Major, Royal Artillery.
WALKER, WILLIAM HERBERT, Capt. (Temporary Major), Army Veterinary Corps.
WALSHE, FREDERICK WILLIAM HENRY, Lieut.-Colonel (Temporary Brigadier-General), Royal Artillery.
WALWYN, CHARLES LAWRENCE TYNDALL, M.C., Major, Royal Artillery.
WARBURTON, WILLIAM MELVILL, Major (Temporary Lieut.-Colonel), Royal Field Artillery.
WARDEN, HUGH FAWCETT, Major (Temporary Lieut.-Colonel), Royal West Surrey Regt.
WARING, JOHN, Major, Royal Artillery.
WARTON, ROBERT BAKER, Major, Royal Artillery.
WARWICK, HUGH BRANSTON, Major, Army Ordnance Department.
WATLING, FRANCIS WYATT, Lieut.-Colonel, Royal Engineers.
WATSON, ANDREW ALEXANDER, Lieut.-Colonel, Royal Army Medical Corps.
WATTS, BRIAN, Lieut.-Colonel (Temporary Colonel), Royal Army Medical Corps.
WAY, BENJAMIN IRBY, Lieut.-Colonel, Retired Pay, North Staffordshire Regt.
WEBB, GEORGE AMBROSE CONGREVE, Capt. and Brevet Major (Temporary Lieut.-Colonel), Reserve of Officers.
WELDON, KENNETH CHARLES, Major, Royal Dublin Fusiliers.
WERE, HARRY HARRIS, Major, Reserve of Officers.
WEST, ALEXANDER HENRY DELAP, Major (Temporary Lieut.-Colonel), Royal Artillery.
WEST, FRANCIS GEORGE, Major (Temporary Lieut.-Colonel), Royal Artillery.
WESTON, JOHN LESLIE, Major, Army Service Corps.
WETHERED, HERBERT LAURENCE, Major (Temporary Lieut.-Colonel), Army Ordnance Department.
WHEATLEY, CYRIL MORETON, Major, General List.
WHITCOMBE, ROBERT HENRY, Major, Army Service Corps.
WHITE, ARTHUR CHARLES, Temporary Major, Yorkshire Light Infantry.
WHITE, GEORGE FREDERICK CHARLES, Major, Royal Artillery.
WHITE, OLIVER WOODHOUSE, Capt., Dorsetshire Regt.
WHITEHEAD, WILFRED JAMES, Lieut.-Colonel, London Regt.
WHITMORE, FRANCIS HENRY DOUGLAS CHARLTON, Lieut.-Colonel, Yeomanry.
WIGGIN, EDGAR ASKIN, Major and Brevet Lieut.-Colonel (Temporary Brigadier-General), Retired Pay.
WIGRAM, KENNETH, Major and Brevet Lieut.-Colonel, Indian Army.
WILEY, CHARLES JOSEPH, Capt. (Temporary Lieut.-Colonel), Royal Irish Rifles.
WILFORD, EDMUND ERNEST, Major (Temporary Lieut.-Colonel), Indian Army.
WILKINSON, CHARLES LEYBURN, Capt. (Temporary Major), Royal Field Artillery.
WILKINSON, HENRY BENFIELD DES VOEUX, Major (Temporary Lieut.-Colonel), Durham Light Infantry.
WILLAN, GEORGE THOMAS, Capt. (Temporary Lieut.-Colonel), Home Counties Field Ambulance, Royal Army Medical Corps.
WILLIAMS, JOHN CONDLIFF MODESLEY, Capt., Royal Field Artillery.

The Distinguished Service Order

WILSON, ARTHUR HARRY HUTTON, Major and Brevet Lieut.-Colonel Wiltshire Regt.
WILSON, ALEXANDER MORETON, Major (Temporary Lieut.-Colonel), Army Service Corps.
WILSON, GEORGE TYRIE BRAND, Lieut.-Colonel (Major, Retired Pay, Reserve of Officers), Argyll and Sutherland Highlanders, Special Reserve, attached King's Own Scottish Borderers.
WILSON, HENRY MAITLAND, Major, Rifle Brigade.
WILSON, WILLIAM HERBERT, Temporary Major, Royal Field Artillery.
WINDER, MAURICE GUY, Major (Temporary Lieut.-Colonel), Royal Army Medical Corps.
WINGATE, BASIL FENTON, Major (Temporary Lieut.-Colonel), Royal Army Medical Corps.
WINGFIELD, REV. WILLIAM EDWARD, Major (Temporary Lieut.-Colonel), Reserve of Officers, Royal Field Artillery.
WOOD, EDWARD ALLAN, Temporary Lieut.-Colonel, Shropshire Light Infantry.
WOODHOUSE, HUGO KENNETH STUART, Capt. (Temporary Major), Liverpool Regt.
WOODLEY, RICHARD NASON, Major, Royal Army Medical Corps.
WOODS, MAX, Capt. (Temporary Major), South Lancashire Regt.
WOODS, PHILIP JAMES, Temporary Major, 9th Battn. Royal Irish Rifles.
WORGAN, RIVERS BERNEY, Capt. and Brevet Major (Temporary Lieut.-Colonel), Indian Army.
WORTHINGTON-WILMER, GEOFFREY RAYMOND, Major, Scottish Rifles, employed Egyptian Army.
WOULFE FLANAGAN, EDWARD MARTYN, Major (Temporary Lieut.-Colonel), East Surrey Regt.
WRIGHT, WILLIAM GORDON, Capt. (Temporary Major), Royal Army Medical Corps.
WYATT, ERNEST ROBERT CALDWELL, Capt. (Temporary Major), Indian Army.
WYNNE, RICHARD OWEN, Capt., Bedfordshire Regt., Special Reserve.
YORKE, RALPH MAXIMILIAN, Major (Temporary Lieut.-Colonel), Yeomanry.
YOUNG, HERBERT NUGENT, Major (Temporary Lieut.-Colonel), Royal Inniskilling Fusiliers.
YOUNG, WALTER HERBERT, Lieut.-Colonel, Yorkshire Regt.
YOUNG, WILLIAM ALLAN, M.B., Temporary Capt., Royal Army Medical Corps.
YULE, GEORGE UDNY, Major, Royal Engineers.

AUSTRALIAN IMPERIAL FORCE.

ANDERSON, STUART MILLIGAN, Lieut.-Colonel, Australian Artillery.
ANNAND, FREDERICK WILLIAM GADSBY, Lieut.-Colonel, Australian Pioneer Battn.
BARBER, GEORGE WALTER, Lieut.-Colonel, Australian Army Medical Corps.
BLAMEY, THOMAS ALBERT, Major (Temporary Lieut.-Colonel), Commonwealth Military Forces.
BRUGGY, STEPHEN, Major, Commonwealth Military Forces.
CLARK, JAMES WILLIAM, Lieut.-Colonel.
COHEN, HAROLD EDWARD, Lieut.-Colonel, Australian Artillery.
COLLETT, HERBERT BRAYLEY, Lieut.-Colonel.
COULTER, GRAHAM, Lieut.-Colonel.
COXEN, WALTER ADAMS, Lieut.-Colonel, Australian Artillery.
COX-TAYLOR, HERBERT JAMES, Lieut.-Colonel, Australian Artillery.
DALY, CLARENCE WELLS DIDIER, Major.
DERHAM, FRANCIS PLUMLEY, Major, Field Artillery Brigade, Australian Artillery.
DODS, JOSEPH ESPIE, M.C., Major, Australian Army Medical Corps.
DURRANT, JAMES MURDOCH ARCHER, Lieut.-Colonel.
DWYER, ANDREW JAMES, Capt. (Temporary Major).
DYER, RICHARD JOHN, Major, Australian Engineers.
ELLIOTT, CHARLES HAZELL, Lieut.-Colonel.
EVANS, DANIEL EDWARD, Major, Australian Engineers.
FERGUSON, GEORGE ANDREW, Lieut.-Colonel.
FETHERS, WILFRID KENT, Lieut.-Colonel.
FEWTRELL, ALBERT CECIL, Lieut.-Colonel.
FORBES, FREDERICK WILLIAM DEMPSTER, Lieut.-Colonel.
FRY, HENRY KENNETH, Major, Australian Army Medical Corps.
FULLER, COLIN DUNMORE, Lieut.-Colonel, Australian Light Horse Regt.
GORDON, GROSVENOR GEORGE STUART, Major, Australian Engineers.
GRANT, WILLIAM, Lieut.-Colonel, Australian Light Horse Regt.
HARBOTTLE, FRANK, Major, Australian Artillery.
HARDY, CHARLES HENRY WILLIAM, V.D., Lieut.-Colonel (Temporary Colonel), Australian Army Medical Corps.
HARRIS, DOUGLAS RAWSON, Capt. (Temporary Major), Australian Artillery.
HENLEY, FRANK LE LEU, Major, Australian Army Service Corps.
HERRING, SYDNEY CHARLES EDGAR, Lieut.-Colonel.
HOWELL-PRICE, OWEN GLENDOWER, M.C., Lieut.-Colonel.
HUGHES, FRANCIS AUGUSTUS, Lieut.-Colonel, Australian Field Artillery.
JESS, CARL HERMAN, Lieut.-Colonel.
JOPP, ARTHUR HAROLD KEITH, Major, Australian Artillery.
LAYH, HERBERT THOMAS CHRISTOPHER, Lieut.-Colonel.
LILLIE, CYRIL McEACHERN, Capt.
LUXTON, DANIEL ASTON, Major, Australian Infantry.
McCONAGHY, DAVID McFIE, C.M.G., Lieut.-Colonel.
McDONALD, GEORGE ST. JOHN FANCOURT, Major, Australian Artillery.
MACKAY, IVEN GIFFORD, Lieut.-Colonel.
MACKENZIE, WILLIAM KENNETH SEAFORTH, Lieut.-Colonel.
MAGENIS, GEORGE CHARLES, Capt.
MANNING, CHARLES HENRY ERNEST, Lieut.-Colonel, Australian Army Service Corps.
MARKS, ALEXANDER HAMMETT, Major, Australian Army Medical Corps.
MARTIN, EDWARD FOWELL, Lieut.-Colonel.
MEREDITH, JOHN BALDWIN, Lieut.-Colonel, Australian Light Horse Regt.
MILES, CHARLES GORDON NORMAN, Major, Australian Divisional Artillery.
MILES, THE REV. FREDERIC JAMES, Australian Army Chaplains' Department.
MILLIGAN, STANLEY LYNALL, Major (Christian name corrected to Stanley Lyndal [London Gazette, 19 Nov. 1917]).
NICHOLSON, EDMUND JAMES HOUGHTON, Major (Temporary Lieut.-Colonel), Australian Pioneer Battn.
NUGENT, HECTOR ALEXANDER, Major, Australian Army Service Corps.
ONSLOW, GEORGE MACLEAY MACARTHUR, Lieut.-Colonel, Australian Light Horse Regt.
PHILLIPS, OWEN FORBES, Lieut.-Colonel, Australian Artillery.
PHIPPS, JOHN HARE, Lieut.-Colonel, Australian Army Medical Corps.
PLANT, ERIC CLIVE PEGUS, Major.
RADFORD, ERNEST GEORGE, Major, Australian Machine Gun Corps.
RALSTON, ALEXANDER WINDEYER, Lieut.-Colonel.
RIDLEY, JOHN CECIL THOMAS EDMUND CHARLES, Major, Australian Light Horse Regt.
ROBERTS, STEPHEN RICHARD, Lieut.-Colonel, Australian Infantry.
ROGERS, DAVID THOMPSON, Major, Australian Artillery.
ROSS, THOMAS GORDON, Lieut.-Colonel, Australian Army Medical Corps.
ST. CLAIR, WILLIAM HOWARD, Major, Australian Artillery.
SHAW, CHARLES GORDON, Lieut.-Colonel, Australian Army Medical Corps.
SMITH, ROBERT, Lieut.-Colonel.
SOMERVILLE, GEORGE CATTELL, Lieut.-Colonel, Staff.
STEELE, ALEXANDER, Major, Australian Machine Gun Co.
STEWART, JAMES CAMPBELL, Lieut.-Colonel.
STURDEE, VERNON ASLETON HOBART, Major, Australian Engineers.
TAYLOR, HERBERT JAMES COX, Lieut.-Colonel, Australian Field Artillery.
TOLL, FREDERICK WILLIAM, Lieut.-Colonel.
ULRICH, THEODORE FREDERICK, Major.
VINEY, HORACE GEORGE, Major, Light Horse Regt.
WALKER, JAMES, Lieut.-Colonel.
WEIR, STANLEY PRICE, Lieut.-Colonel.
WELCH, JOHN BASIL ST. VINCENT, Lieut.-Colonel, Australian Army Medical Corps.
WHITFELD, LESLIE CHARLES, Capt. (Temporary Major), Australian Army Veterinary Corps.
YOUNG, WILLIAM McKENZIE, Major.

CANADIAN CONTINGENT.

ALEXANDER, RONALD OKEDEN, Major, Canadian Infantry.
ALLEN, MERRILL VINCENT, Major, Canadian Mounted Rifles.
ANDERSON, WILLIAM BEAUMONT, Major and Brevet Lieut.-Colonel, Canadian Engineers (regiment corrected to Royal Canadian Engineers [London Gazette, 13 Feb. 1917]).
ANDREWES, WILLIAM, Major, Canadian Infantry.
ANDROS, RALPH CRAVEN, Lieut.-Colonel, Canadian Mounted Rifle Battn.
ARNOLDI, FRANK FARQUIER, Major, Canadian Field Artillery.
BALFOUR, WALTER MACKIE, Major, Canadian Mounted Rifle Battn.
BALL, JOHN CLEMENT, Major, Canadian Field Artillery.
BEEMAN, WILLIAM GILBERT, Major, Canadian Artillery.
BELL, ARTHUR HENRY, Lieut.-Colonel, Canadian Infantry.
BENT, CHARLES EDWARD, Lieut.-Colonel, Canadian Infantry.
BERTRAM, WILLIAM ROBERT, Major, Canadian Infantry.
BOAK, HENRY EVERSLEY, Major, Royal Canadian Horse Artillery.
BRITTON, RUSSELL HUBERT, Lieut.-Colonel, Canadian Field Artillery.
CANTLIE, GEORGE STEPHEN, Lieut.-Colonel, Canadian Infantry.
CARSCALLEN, HENRY GURNEY, Lieut.-Colonel, Canadian Field Artillery.
CONSTANTINE, CHARLES FRANCIS, Major, Royal Canadian Horse Artillery.
CORRIGAN, CHARLES ARTHUR, Temporary Major, Canadian Army Service Corps.
CREELMAN, JOHN JENNINGS, Lieut.-Colonel, Canadian Field Artillery.
DUBUC, ARTHUR EDOUARD, Major, Canadian Infantry.
FINDLAY, WILLIAM HENRI DE LA TOUR D'AUVERGNE, Lieut.-Col., Canadian Army Service Corps.
FOLGER, KARL CREIGHTON, Major, Canadian Ordnance Corps.
FORBES, JAMES WALLACE, Major, Canadian Infantry.
GASCOIGNE, FREDERICK ARTHUR DE LONG, Lieut.-Colonel, Canadian Infantry.
GENET, HARRY AUGUSTUS, Lieut.-Colonel, Canadian Infantry.
GIBSONE, WILLIAM WARING PRIMROSE, Temporary Lieut.-Colonel, Canadian Divisional Headquarters.
GORDON, HARRY DUNCAN LOCKHART, Lieut.-Colonel, Canadian Mounted Infantry.
GUNN, JOHN ALEXANDER, Lieut.-Colonel, Canadian Infantry.
HARBORD, HUGH WALTER, Major, Canadian Mounted Rifles.
HODGINS, FREDERICK OWEN, Major, Canadian Engineers (regiment corrected to Royal Canadian Engineers [London Gazette, 13 Feb. 1917]).
HOMER-DIXON, THOMAS FRASER, Lieut.-Colonel, Lord Strathcona's Horse.
HUGHES, WILLIAM ST. PIERRE, Lieut.-Colonel (Temporary Brigadier-General), Canadian Infantry.
HUNBLE, BERNARD MAYNARD, Major, Canadian Infantry (surname corrected to Humble [London Gazette, 26 Jan. 1917]).

JONES, ELMER WATSON, Lieut.-Colonel, Canadian Infantry.
JONES, TERENCE PERCIVAL, Major, Canadian Infantry.
KEMP, WALTER FREDERICK, Major, Canadian Infantry.
KIRKCALDY, JAMES, Lieut.-Colonel, Canadian Infantry.
McCRAIG, GEORGE ERIC, Lieut.-Colonel, Canadian Infantry (surname corrected to McCuaig).
MACDONALD, ERIC WHIDDEN, Major, Canadian Infantry.
MACDONELL, JAMES ALEXANDER, Major, Canadian Infantry.
McEWEN, ALAN BRETTELL, Major, Canadian Divisional Artillery.
McKENZIE, ARCHIBALD ERNEST GRAHAM, Lieut.-Colonel, Canadian Infantry.
MACKENZIE, JOHN PERCIVAL, Major, Canadian Infantry.
McDONALD, JOHN ANGUS, Major, Canadian Field Artillery.
McLENNAN, BARTLETT, Major, Canadian Infantry.
MANHARD, WILLIAM EDWARD, Capt., Canadian Engineers.
MILLIGAN, HENRY LINTON, Lieut.-Colonel, Canadian Infantry.
MORRISON, GORDON FRASER, Major, Canadian Infantry.
MORRISON, FRANK STANLEY, Major, Royal Canadian Dragoons.
PAGE, LIONEL FRANK, Major, Canadian Infantry.
PALMER, ROBERT HENRY, Major, Canadian Infantry.
PARSONS, JOHNSON LINDSAY ROWLETT, Major, Canadian Infantry.
POWERS, THOMAS EDWARD, Major, Canadian Divisional Signal Company.
ROSCOE, BARRY WENTWORTH, Major, Canadian Mounted Rifles.
ROSS, JOHN MUNRO, Major, Canadian Infantry.
ROSS, LORNE, Lieut.-Colonel, Canadian Infantry.
SHAW, JOHN ARTHUR, Lieut.-Colonel, Canadian Army Service Corps.
SNELL, ARTHUR EVANS, Temporary Colonel, Canadian Army Medical Corps.
STEWART, JOHN SMITH, Lieut.-Colonel, Canadian Field Artillery.
TREMBLAY, THOMAS LOUIS, Lieut.-Colonel, Canadian Infantry.
VILLIERS, PAUL FREDERICK, Major, Canadian Infantry.
WARE, FRANCIS BETHEL, Major, Canadian Infantry.
WEBSTER, WILLIAM, Lieut.-Colonel, Canadian Army Medical Corps.
WRIGHT, ROBERT PERCY, Lieut.-Colonel, Canadian Army Medical Corps.

NEW ZEALAND FORCE.

CUNNINGHAM, WILLIAM HENRY, Lieut.-Colonel.
FINDLAY, JOHN, C.B., Lieut.-Colonel, Canterbury Mounted Rifles.
LAMPEN, FRANCIS HENRY, Major, New Zealand Staff Corps.
MACKESY, CHARLES ERNEST RANDOLPH, Lieut.-Colonel, Auckland Mounted Rifles.
McGILP, CLYDE, Major, New Zealand Field Artillery.
McKENZIE, ALEXANDER GEORGE, Major.
MELDRUM, WILLIAM, C.M.G., Lieut.-Colonel, Wellington Mounted Rifles Regt.
MELVILL, CHARLES WILLIAM, Lieut.-Colonel, New Zealand Rifle Brigade.
MURRAY, DONALD NORMAN WATSON, Lieut.-Colonel, New Zealand Medical Corps.
POW, JAMES, Major, New Zealand Rifle Brigade.
ROGERS, VICTOR, Capt., New Zealand Field Artillery.
SAXBY, CONRAD GORDON, Major, New Zealand Pioneer Battn.
SMYTHE, ROBERT BARRINGTON, Major, New Zealand Signal Company.
STEWART, ALEXANDER EDWARD, Lieut.-Colonel, New Zealand Rifle Brigade.
STUDHOLME, JOHN, Major, Canterbury Mounted Rifles.

SOUTH AFRICAN CONTINGENT.

BRYDON, WALTER, Temporary Major, South African Heavy Artillery.
HARRISON, NORMAN, Major, South African Engineers.
MACLEOD, DONALD McLEAY, Major (Temporary Lieut.-Colonel), South African Infantry.
POWER, MICHAEL STANISLAUS, Temporary Major, South African Medical Corps.

London Gazette, 10 Jan. 1917.—" War Office, 10 Jan. 1917. His Majesty the King has been graciously pleased to approve of the appointments of the undermentioned Officers to be Companions of the Distinguished Service Order, in recognition of their gallantry and devotion to duty in the field."

BREARLEY, NORMAN, M.C., Second Lieut., Liverpool Regt. and Royal Flying Corps. For conspicuous gallantry in action. With another pilot he gallantly attacked seven hostile machines. Later, although severely wounded, he displayed great courage and determination in reaching our own lines.
CROFT, WILLIAM DENMAN, Major (Temporary Lieut.-Colonel), Royal Scots. For conspicuous gallantry in action. He showed great courage and initiative in organizing and supervising a successful attack. He established posts before dawn and joined them up the following night under heavy fire. He has previously done fine work. [The Distinguished Service Order was awarded London Gazette, 1 Jan. 1917. The award here should have been a first Bar (see London Gazette, 26 July, 1918, awarding second Bar)].
FOLLETT, GILBERT BURRELL SPENCER, M.V.O., Major (Temporary Lieut.-Colonel), Coldstream Guards. For conspicuous gallantry in action. Although wounded, he inspected the front-line trenches under heavy fire. Later, he remained with the battalion until they were relieved. He has on many previous occasions done fine work.
HARMAN, CHARLES, Major (Temporary Lieut.-Colonel), Leinster Regt. For conspicuous gallantry in action. He led his battalion throughout the action with great courage and initiative. He set a splendid example to his men, and materially assisted in the success of the operations.
HOTBLACK, FREDERICK ELLIOTT, M.C., Temporary Capt., Intelligence Corps, attached Machine Gun Corps. For conspicuous gallantry in action. He guided a Tank into action by walking in front of it under very heavy fire. He displayed great courage and determination throughout.
NASMITH, ARTHUR PLATER, Temporary Capt., Border Regt. For conspicuous gallantry in action. He displayed great courage and initiative in organizing and leading a successful attack. He set a splendid example throughout.
PARKER, GEORGE ALEC, M.C., Capt., Northampton Regt. and Royal Flying Corps. For conspicuous gallantry in action. He attacked hostile aeroplanes on three occasions during the same flight, killing an enemy observer. On another occasion he drove off three enemy machines, pursuing one of them down to 750 feet three miles behind the enemy's lines.
PENNINGTON, RICHARD, Temporary Second Lieut. (Acting Capt.), Lincolnshire Regt. For conspicuous gallantry in action. He led his men in the attack with great courage and initiative, himself killing at least seven of the enemy. He set a splendid example throughout, and materially assisted in the success of the operations.
ROBERTSON, JOSIAH JAMES, Capt. (Temporary Major), Seaforth Highlanders. For conspicuous gallantry in action. He reorganized several small parties under heavy fire, and drove off an enemy bombing attack. He formed with 20 men a strong post in the enemy's second line. Later, he led the men forward again and consolidated an advanced defensive line. He set a splendid example throughout.

AUSTRALIAN IMPERIAL FORCE.

SCOTT, WILLIAM JOHN RENDALL, Capt., Australian Infantry. For conspicuous gallantry in action. He organized the troops in the vicinity and formed a strong point, and by the judicious use of machine guns kept off several threatened enemy attacks, thereby saving a critical situation.

CANADIAN FORCE.

DREW, GEORGE LEMUEL, Major, Canadian Field Artillery. For conspicuous gallantry in action. Although crippled by rheumatism, he continued to command his battery under very trying conditions. He set a splendid example of courage and determination throughout the operations.
EDWARDS, CAMERON MACPHERSON, Lieut.-Colonel, Canadian Infantry. For conspicuous gallantry in action. He organized his battalion for attack, and carried out a dashing assault in a snow-storm with conspicuous success. He set a splendid example of courage and initiative throughout.
FROST, REGINALD WILLIAM, Lieut.-Colonel, Canadian Infantry. For conspicuous gallantry in action. He carried out a successful attack under very trying conditions. The entire objective was gained, and a strong patrol was sent forward, remaining out for 24 hours until ordered to withdraw. He set a splendid example of courage and coolness throughout.
HARVEY, VALENTINE VIVIAN, Major, Canadian Infantry. For conspicuous gallantry in action. He showed great coolness and power of organization during preparation, also in reorganizing and directing the consolidation under very heavy fire. He set a splendid example throughout, and materially assisted in the success of the operations.
KEMBALL, ARNOLD HENRY GRANT, C.B., Lieut.-Colonel, Canadian Infantry. For conspicuous gallantry in action. He led his battalion in the attack with conspicuous success, and carried out every task allotted to him. He set a splendid example of courage and good leadership throughout.
MACDOWELL, THAIN WENDELL, Capt., Canadian Infantry. For conspicuous gallantry in action. He led his company against an enemy position with great courage and initiative, capturing three machine guns and 50 prisoners. Later, although wounded, he remained at his post and greatly assisted in the success of the operations.
WARDEN, JOHN WEIGHTMAN, Lieut.-Colonel, Canadian Infantry. For conspicuous gallantry in action. He led his battalion in the attack with conspicuous success under the most trying conditions. He set a fine example of good leadership throughout.
WORSNOP, CHARLES BENSON, Major, Canadian Infantry. For conspicuous gallantry in action. He led his battalion in a night attack with conspicuous success, gained his objective, captured 32 prisoners and two machine guns, and successfully consolidated the position. He set a fine example throughout.

The undermentioned have been awarded a Bar to their Distinguished Service Order for subsequent acts of conspicuous gallantry.

BOOTH, THOMAS MACAULAY, D.S.O., Major (Temporary Lieut.-Colonel), Gordon Highlanders. For conspicuous gallantry in action. He led his battalion with great courage and determination throughout the operations. He set a splendid example to his men, and greatly assisted in clearing up a critical situation.
(The Distinguished Service Order was awarded in the London Gazette dated 3 Jan. 1916.)
COPE, THOMAS GEORGE, D.S.O., Capt. and Brevet Major (Temporary Lieut.-Colonel), Royal Fusiliers. For conspicuous gallantry in action. Although wounded, he continued to direct the operations, and, when the attack was momentarily checked, went out into " No Man's Land " under very heavy fire to reorganize his battalion. He was again wounded.
(The Distinguished Service Order was awarded in the London Gazette dated 15 April, 1916.)

London Gazette, 23 Jan. 1917.—" Admiralty, S.W., 23 Jan. 1917. A Bar to the Distinguished Service Order has been awarded to

SAMSON, CHARLES RUMNEY, D.S.O., Commander, Royal Navy.

London Gazette, 24 Jan. 1917.—" War Office, 24 Jan. 1917. His Majesty the King has been graciously pleased to approve of the undermentioned Honours and Rewards for valuable services rendered in connection with the War, with effect from 1 Jan. 1917, inclusive, except where otherwise stated. To be Companions of the Distinguished Service Order."

BLAIR, JAMES MOLESWORTH, Capt. (Temporary Lieut.-Colonel), Gordon Highlanders.
CHRISTIE, MALCOLM GRAHAME, M.C., Capt. (Temporary Major), Royal Flying Corps, Special Reserve.
HARRIS, GEORGE ARTHUR, Major, Unattached List (T.F.).
NEILSON, JOHN FRASER, Major, Hussars.
PRICE, IVON HENRY, Temporary Major, Special List.
QUIBELL, ARTHUR HOLMES, Capt., Nottinghamshire and Derbyshire Regt.
RAYNER, FRANK, Capt. (Temporary Lieut.-Colonel), Nottinghamshire and Derbyshire Regt.
SALT, SIR THOMAS ANDERDON, Bart., Major (Acting Lieut.-Colonel), retired pay, Reserve of Officers, late Hussars.
SOMERVILLE, HAROLD FOWNES, Major, Rifle Brigade.

The Distinguished Service Order

London Gazette, 26 Jan. 1917.—" War Office, 26 Jan. 1917. His Majesty the King has been graciously pleased to approve of the appointments of the undermentioned Officers to be Companions of the Distinguished Service Order, in recognition of their gallantry and devotion to duty in the field."

CLERK, AYLMER GUSTAVUS, M.C., Capt., Hertfordshire Regt. For conspicuous gallantry in action. He led his company in the attack with great courage and initiative. He organized the consolidation of the captured position under heavy fire. On another occasion he repelled an enemy counter-attack. He set a splendid example throughout the operations.

ELKINGTON, CHRISTOPHER GARRETT, Temporary Capt., Gloucestershire Regt. For conspicuous gallantry in action. With six men he attacked and silenced an enemy machine gun. Later, he displayed great courage and ability in organizing the defence of the position. He was twice wounded, but remained at duty directing operations until he was again severely wounded.

ELLIS, BERNARD HENRY, Temporary Lieut.-Commander, Royal Naval Volunteer Reserve. For conspicuous gallantry in action. When the attack was held up by heavy machine-gun fire, he pushed forward with some men and made a reconnaissance of the final position under very heavy fire. Later, he assumed command of and handled his battalion with marked courage and ability.

HERBERT-STEPNEY, CECIL CHAMPAGNE, Capt. (Temporary Lieut.-Colonel), Reserve of Officers, King's Royal Rifle Corps, attached Nottinghamshire and Derbyshire Regt. For conspicuous gallantry in action. He went forward under intense fire to ascertain that consolidation was proceeding satisfactorily. His preparations for the attack, and his action throughout the assembly, contributed very largely to the success of the operations.

MURRAY, THOMAS DAVID, Major, Hampshire Regt., attached Royal Highlanders, temporarily attached Cambridgeshire Regt. For conspicuous gallantry in action. He showed great skill and resource in handling his battalion over a very extended front and over a very difficult country. He seized all his objective, took many prisoners, and eventually consolidated the position won.

PENNANT, DYFRIG HUWS, Temporary Capt., Royal Army Medical Corps, attached Headquarters, Royal Field Artillery. For conspicuous gallantry and devotion to duty. He dressed and remained with three wounded men under the most intense fire. He has at all times set a splendid example of courage and coolness, and has on many occasions done fine work.

STERNDALE-BENNETT, WALTER, Temporary Lieut., Royal Naval Volunteer Reserve. For conspicuous gallantry in action. He assumed command of and handled his battalion with marked courage and ability. He personally collected a party and bombed the enemy out of part of their second line, where they might have held up the attack.

The undermentioned has been awarded a Bar to his Distinguished Service Order for a subsequent act of conspicuous gallantry.

STANWAY, WILLIAM HENRY, D.S.O., Lieut. (Temporary Capt.) (Acting Lieut.-Colonel), Royal Welsh Fusiliers, attached Cheshire Regt. For conspicuous gallantry in action. He handled his battalion in the attack with great courage and ability. He captured the position, inflicted much loss on the enemy, and took a large number of prisoners.

(The Distinguished Service Order was awarded in London Gazette dated 27 July, 1916.)

London Gazette, 1 Feb. 1917.—" War Office, 1 Feb. 1917. His Majesty the King has been graciously pleased to approve of the undermentioned Honours and Rewards for valuable services rendered in connection with military operations in the field, with effect from 1 Jan. 1917, inclusive. To be Companions of the Distinguished Service Order."

BATTEN, FREDERICK GRÆME, Colonel, Indian Army.

BENSON, WALLACE, M.B., Major (Temporary Lieut.-Colonel), Royal Army Medical Corps.

BOLTON, RICHARD EDMUND CORNFORTH, Engineer, Royal Indian Marine.

CHRISTIE, WILLIAM EDWARD TOLFREY, Major and Brevet Lieut.-Colonel, Army Service Corps.

DEALY, JOHN ANDERSON, C.M.G., Colonel (Temporary Brigadier-General), Royal Engineers.

DEY, REV. JAMES, Chaplain to the Forces, 3rd Class, Army Chaplains' Department.

DOBBS, CHARLES FAIRLIE, Major and Brevet Lieut.-Colonel, Indian Army.

FARFAN, ARTHUR JOSEPH THOMAS, Major, Royal Garrison Artillery, attached Indian Mountain Battery.

FORESTIER-WALKER, CLAUDE EDWARD, Lieut.-Colonel, Royal Garrison Artillery.

GRANT, HENRY FREDERICK LYALL, Major (Temporary Lieut.-Colonel), Royal Artillery.

GUNTER, FRANCIS ERNEST, M.B., Lieut.-Colonel (Temporary Colonel), Royal Army Medical Corps.

HEXT, GEORGE TREVOR BARKLEY, Capt. (Temporary Major), Indian Army.

HOME, GEORGE ARCHIBALD SWINTON, Major (Temporary Lieut.-Colonel), East African Protectorate Forces, Reserve of Officers, late Dragoon Guards.

JACKSON, ERNEST SOMERVILLE, Capt. (Temporary Major), Reserve of Officers, late Welsh Regt. (rank corrected to Capt. (Temporary Lieut.-Colonel) Reserve of Officers [London Gazette, 16 Aug. 1917]).

JOHNSTON, CHARLES ARTHUR, C.I.E., M.B., Lieut.-Colonel (Temporary Colonel), Indian Medical Service.

JOHNSON, GEORGE EDGAR ALLEN, Temporary Lieut. (Temporary Capt.), Army Ordnance Department.

KEANE, GERALD JOSEPH, M.D., Capt., Royal Army Medical Corps.

KEMPTHORNE, HENRY NOEL, Capt. (Temporary Major), Capt., Reserve of Officers, late Royal Scots Fusiliers, attached Royal Engineers.

KIRKE, EDWARD ST. GEORGE, Capt., Royal Engineers, attached Indian Army (christian name corrected to Edwards St. George [London Gazette, 3 March, 1917]).

LEAN, ALAN IVAN, Lieut.-Colonel, Army Pay Department.

LYALL, ROBERT ADOLPHUS, Major, Supernumerary List, Indian Army, attached Imperial Service Rifles.

MARSHALL, JOHN STUART, Capt., Indian Army.

McHARG, ALFRED ALEXIS, Major (Acting Lieut.-Colonel), Royal Engineers.

McKIE, JOHN, M.B., Lieut.-Colonel, Royal Army Medical Corps.

MITFORD, JOHN PHILIP, Capt., Indian Army.

MONEY, ERNLE FRANCIS DRUMMOND, Major, Indian Army.

MOUAT, GEORGE ELLIOTT DUNDAS, Capt. (Temporary Major), Indian Army.

PATTERSON, JOHN, Major, Royal Artillery.

ROBERTS, WILLIAM BRADLEY, Capt. (Temporary Major), Indian Army.

RUEL, WILLIAM GEORGE, Capt. (Temporary Major), Indian Army.

RUNDLE, FRANK PEVERIL, Major (Temporary Lieut.-Colonel), Royal Engineers.

SMELLIE, JOHN HUGH, Honorary Lieut.-Colonel, Railway Corps, Uganda.

SMITH, COLIN WALTER JOHNSTONE, Capt., Indian Army.

SUTHERLAND, JAMES, Temporary Lieut.-Colonel, Royal Engineers.

SWEENY, ROGER LEWIS CAMPBELL, M.C., Capt. (Temporary Major), Indian Army.

TATE, GERARD WILLIAM, M.B., Lieut.-Colonel (Temporary Colonel), Royal Army Medical Corps.

TILLARD, ELLIOT DOWELL, Major, Royal Engineers, attached Indian Army.

TURNER, REGINALD GEORGE, F.R.C.S., Lieut.-Colonel, Indian Medical Service.

TYNDALL, HENRY STUART, Major, Indian Army.

VENABLES, JAMES DOUGLAS, Major, Royal Welsh Fusiliers.

WATSON, CHARLES SCOTT MONCRIEFF CHALMERS, Major, Royal Engineers.

SOUTH AFRICAN FORCES.

BLANEY, JOHN ALBERT H., Capt. (Temporary Major), Permanent Force, South Africa.

BOTHA, PIETER SCHALK GROBBELAAR, Lieut.-Colonel, South African Horse.

BRINK, ANDRIES JACOB EKSTEEN, Major and Brevet Lieut.-Colonel (Temporary Colonel), Permanent Forces, South Africa.

BRINK, CHARLES, Temporary Lieut.-Colonel, Major, South African Defence Force.

BURGESS, CHARLES ROSCOE, Capt. and Brevet Major (Temporary Lieut.-Colonel), Permanent Forces, South Africa.

BYRON, JOHN JOSEPH, C.M.G., Lieut.-Colonel, South African Infantry.

ENSLIN, BAREND GOTTFRIED LEOPOLD, Temporary Brigadier-General. South African Defence Forces.

IRELAND, GEORGE, Temporary Major, South African Army Service Corps.

KOEN, JOHANNES JACOBUS, Lieut.-Colonel, South African Horse.

MOFFAT, HENRY ALFORD, Lieut.-Colonel, South African Medical Corps.

MOLYNEUX, GEORGE MARY JOSEPH, Lieut.-Colonel, South African Infantry.

MULLER, CHARLES HEROLD, M.B., Temporary Lieut.-Colonel, South African Medical Corps.

MURRAY-SMITH, WILLIAM, Lieut.-Colonel, South African Horse.

PEDLER, GEORGE HERBERT, Temporary Major, South African Army Service Corps.

SKINNER, WILLIAM BOOTH, M.B., Lieut.-Colonel, South African Medical Corps.

SMIT, BAREND JACOBUS JOHANNES, Lieut.-Colonel, South African Horse.

TAYLOR, ARTHUR JAMES, Lieut.-Colonel, South African Infantry.

TAYLOR, STANLEY SHERBOURNE, Lieut.-Colonel, South African Field Artillery.

WALLACE, GERARD PERCY, Temporary Major, Capt., South African Defence Force and Royal Flying Corps.

WHITEHEAD, JOHN HERBERT, Lieut.-Colonel, South African Medical Corps.

WHITELEY, PERCIVAL, Major, South African Pay Corps.

London Gazette, 13 Feb. 1917.—" War Office, 13 Feb. 1917. His Majesty the King has been graciously pleased to approve of the award of a Bar to the Distinguished Service Order to " :—

PAGE, FRANK, D.S.O., Major (Temporary Lieut.-Colonel), Hertfordshire Regt. For conspicuous gallantry in action. He handled his battalion in the attack with great courage and determination. Later, he showed marked ability and judgment in consolidating his final objective, thereby repelling any enemy attempts to counter-attack.

(The award of the Distinguished Service Order was published in London Gazette dated 23 June, 1915.)

" His Majesty the King has been graciously pleased to approve of the appointments of the undermentioned Officers to be Companions of the Distinguished Service Order, in recognition of their gallantry and devotion to duty in the field."

CARTWRIGHT, FRANCIS JOHN WINSOR, Major (Temporary Lieut.-Colonel), Royal Marines. For conspicuous gallantry in action. When the attack was held up by heavy machine-gun and rifle fire he went forward to the front line, where he reorganized and supervised mixed parties of men of different units and pushed forward to the objective.

EDWARDS, GEORGE ERIC, Second Lieut., Seaforth Highlanders. For conspicuous gallantry in action. Accompanied by a few men, he advanced through our barrage and held the entrance of a cave, thereby capturing 400 prisoners, but being unsupported he was forced to surrender by the enemy. Later, he was instrumental in the capture of many prisoners, and himself marched 12, including the Battalion Commander, back to Battalion Headquarters. He set a splendid example of courage and determination throughout.

HUTCHISON, ALEXANDER RICHARD HAMILTON, C.M.G., Lieut.-Colonel, Royal Marines. For conspicuous gallantry in action. When the attack was temporarily held up by heavy machine-gun fire, he rallied and reorganized the front line of the attack, and ably supervised the consolidation of the final objective reached by his battalion.

JAMESON, JOHN HENRY, Lieut. (Acting Capt.), Liverpool Regt., Special Reserve. For conspicuous gallantry in action. He handled his company in the attack with the greatest courage and skill, himself remaining out with a few men in an exposed position. He has at all times set a splendid example of gallantry and good leadership.

McPHERSON, ANDREW, Temporary Lieut. (Temporary Capt.), Highland Light Infantry. For conspicuous gallantry in action. He showed great resource under the most trying circumstances, and, although he had been wounded in two places before reaching the point of assembly, he launched his company on the attack and advanced with them. He set a fine example and was again wounded.

O'SHAUGNESSY, CUTHBERT LEO, Second Lieut., South Lancashire Regt., Special Reserve (surname corrected to O'Shaughnessy [London Gazette, 28 July, 1917]). For conspicuous gallantry in action. He took command of the three assaulting companies of his battalion after all the other officers had become casualties. He consolidated the captured position, and sent out bombing parties to assist the battalion on his right. He set a fine example of courage and coolness throughout.

PEASE-WATKIN, EDWARD HANDLEY PEASE, Major, Royal Field Artillery. For conspicuous gallantry in action. He carried out several daring reconnaissances at great personal risk and obtained information of the greatest value. He has consistently shown the greatest gallantry and initiative when commanding his battery, and has previously been brought to notice for good work.

RAMSAY-FAIRFAX, WILLIAM GEORGE ASTEL, Lieut.-Commander (Acting Commander), Emergency List, Royal Navy (rank corrected from Lieut.-Commander (Acting Commander) to Commander [London Gazette, 26 March, 1917]). For conspicuous gallantry in action. When the attack was temporarily held up, he reorganized the men and led a bombing attack, which cleared the enemy from a trench which threatened his flank. He afterwards organized an attack which was instrumental in capturing over 100 prisoners.

STOOKS, CHARLES SUMNER, Major, Indian Army. For conspicuous gallantry in action. He showed marked courage and skill in commanding the advanced guard under machine-gun and heavy rifle fire. He was severely wounded.

THORNTON, REV. STEPHEN AUGUSTIN LAWRENCE, Naval Chaplains' Department, attached Royal Dublin Fusiliers. For conspicuous gallantry and devotion to duty. He displayed great courage and determination in administering to the wounded under very heavy fire.

WARD, EDWARD FRANCIS, Capt. (Temporary Lieut.-Colonel), Reserve of Officers, King's Royal Rifle Corps. For conspicuous gallantry in action. He organized a counter-attack at a critical time, driving the enemy back and capturing 97 prisoners. He showed marked courage and initiative throughout.

WHITE, HENRY HERBERT RONALD, Temporary Major, Royal Fusiliers (late Capt., King's Royal Rifle Corps). For conspicuous gallantry in action. He displayed great courage and initiative in handling two companies under heavy fire. He has performed consistent good work throughout, and has at all times set a splendid example.

WHITTAKER, GORDON WILLIAM, Temporary Sub-Lieut., Royal Naval Volunteer Reserve. For conspicuous gallantry in action. He dashed forward in broad daylight, and, single-handed, put a machine gun and its crew out of action, thereby greatly assisting in the success of the operations. He was severely wounded.

WHITWORTH, HARRY, Second Lieut. (Temporary Capt.), Yorkshire Light Infantry. For conspicuous gallantry in action. He led his company in the attack with the greatest courage and initiative, and penetrated the enemy's second line. He was wounded. Previously he carried out several daring and successful reconnaissances.

WILKINSON, CHARLES WILLIAM, Lieut.-Colonel, Royal Engineers. For conspicuous gallantry in action. He displayed great courage and skill in handling a hastily improvised force under difficult conditions, and was largely instrumental in clearing parties of the enemy from the lines of communication.

SOUTH AFRICAN FORCE.

BRISCOE, JOHN EDWARD, Major, South African Medical Corps. For conspicuous gallantry and devotion to duty. Although himself wounded, he continued to tend wounded men under very heavy fire. He set a splendid example of courage and coolness throughout.

DOBSON, JOSEPH HENRY, Major, South African Pioneers. For conspicuous devotion to duty. He repaired a long stretch of railway, and converted motor lorries to run on rails, by means of which the difficult problem of rationing the force was much relieved. He has performed consistent good work throughout.

MONTGOMERY, JOHN WILLOUGHBY VERNER, Lieut.-Colonel, South African Infantry. For conspicuous gallantry in action. He led his battalion with great courage and skill against strong enemy positions, capturing the positions and causing the enemy to retire.

WOON, ERNEST W., Major, South African Infantry. For conspicuous gallantry in action. He repulsed a strong enemy attack, and saved the situation at a critical time. He displayed marked gallantry throughout, and materially assisted in the success of the operations.

London Gazette, 15 Feb. 1917.—"War Office, 15 Feb. 1917. His Majesty the King has been graciously pleased to approve of the undermentioned rewards for distinguished service in the field, with effect from 1 Jan. 1917, inclusive, except where otherwise stated. Awarded the Distinguished Service Order."

BEWSHER, WILLIAM DENT, Major (Temporary Lieut.-Colonel), Reserve of Officers.

DE BUTTS, FREDERICK CROMIE, M.C., Capt., Indian Army.

ISACKE, CHARLES VICTOR, Major, Army Pay Department.

MACKENZIE, HERBERT JOHN, Capt., Indian Army.

NISSEN, PETER NORMAN, Temporary Capt. (Acting Major), Royal Engineers.

POOLE, JOHN SANDERSON, Second Lieut., King's Royal Rifle Corps.

RAMSDEN, RICHARD ELMSLIE, Lieut.-Colonel, Royal Field Artillery.

RICHARDSON, ALEXANDER WHITMORE COLQUHOUN, Capt., Bedfordshire Regt.

ROBINSON, PERCY GOTCH, Major, Royal Artillery.

STORR, HENRY, Major (Temporary Lieut.-Colonel), Reserve of Officers.

STOREY, HENRY INNES, Major (Temporary Lieut.-Colonel), Devonshire Regt.

TORR, WILLIAM WYNDHAM TORRE, M.C., Capt., West Yorkshire Regt.

THUNDER, STUART HARMAN JOSEPH, M.C., Major (Temporary Lieut.-Colonel), Northampton Regt.

WILFORD, ARTHUR LUCIUS, Capt. (Temporary Major), Indian Army.

WINSLOE, HERBERT EDWARD, Major and Brevet Lieut.-Colonel, Royal Engineers.

WORSLEY, RONALD HENRY WARTON, Capt., King's Own Scottish Borderers, attached Egyptian Army.

CANADIAN FORCES.

BULLOCK, LAWRENCE NEWSAM BEVERLEY, Capt. (Temporary Major) Canadian Engineers.

DAVIS, ANGUS WARD, Temporary Major, Canadian Engineers.

London Gazette, 15 Feb. 1917.—"War Office, 15 Feb. 1917. His Majesty the King has been graciously pleased to approve of the undermentioned Honour for valuable services rendered in connection with the War, with effect from 1 Jan. 1917, inclusive. To be a Companion of the Distinguished Service Order."

LEE, ARTHUR NEALE, Major, Nottinghamshire and Derbyshire Regt.

London Gazette, 16 Feb. 1917.—Admiralty, 16 Feb. 1917. The King has been graciously pleased to give orders for the appointment of the undermentioned Officers to be Companions of the Distinguished Service Order.

ARMSTRONG, MATTHEW, Lieut., Royal Naval Reserve.

GOBLE, STANLEY JAMES, D.S.C., Flight-Lieut., Royal Naval Air Service. For conspicuous bravery and skill in attacking hostile aircraft on numerous occasions. On 7 Nov. 1916, he attacked an enemy scout and chased it down to 1,500 feet, when it was seen to land, crash into a fence, and turn over in a field. On 27 Nov. 1916, he attacked four hostile scouts, one of which he brought down in flames. On 4 Dec. 1916, on six different occasions during the same flight, he attacked and drove off hostile aircraft, whichth reatened the bombing machines which he was escorting, one of the hostile machines going completely out of control.

MAXWELL-SCOTT, MALCOLM RAPHAEL JOSEPH, Lieut.-Commander, Royal Navy.

SMYTH, HENRY HESKETH, Capt., Royal Navy.

London Gazette, 3 March, 1917.—"War Office, 3 March, 1917. His Majesty the King has been graciously pleased to approve of the award of a Bar to the Distinguished Service Order to":—

HUDDLESTON, HUBERT JERVOISE, D.S.O., M.C., Major, Dorsetshire Regt., attached Imperial Camel Corps. For conspicuous gallantry and the masterly manner in which he handled the final assault when light was failing, and a decision had become vitally necessary. He directed and led the final assault in the most gallant manner, and was directly responsible for its successful finish.

(The Distinguished Service Order was awarded in London Gazette dated 1 Jan. 1917.)

"His Majesty the King has been graciously pleased to approve of the appointments of the undermentioned Officers to be Companions of the Distinguished Service Order, in recognition of their gallantry and devotion to duty in the field."

BAILEY, GEORGE CYRIL, Second Lieut. (Temporary Capt.), Royal Flying Corps (Special Reserve). For conspicuous gallantry in action. He co-operated in an infantry raid by flying over the enemy's trenches at a height of only 1,500 feet for more than an hour and a half in very adverse weather conditions. He attacked the enemy in the trenches with machine-gun fire, and located 16 active enemy batteries during the flight. He has repeatedly done fine work.

DONOVAN, CHARLES OWEN, M.B., Temporary Capt., Royal Army Medical Corps, attached North Lancashire Regt. For conspicuous gallantry and devotion to duty. He displayed courage of a very high order over a period of 48 hours in attending to a large number of wounded of his own and other units, in a shallow muddy trench, which was continually subjected to heavy fire. On another occasion he dressed several wounded officers in the open. He was severely wounded.

ELEY, DENNIS RAMSAY AKERS, Capt. (Acting Major), Suffolk Regt. For conspicuous gallantry and brilliant leading of two companies during a night raid on the enemy lines. He broke through the opposing outpost line, inflicting severe losses on the enemy, and making 29 prisoners. The energy and skill of this officer largely contributed to the success of the raid.

GROUND, THOMAS LESLIE, Temporary Second Lieut., Royal Fusiliers. For conspicuous gallantry in action. He carried out a reconnaissance under most adverse conditions, established a few posts, and for 48 hours commanded the left-hand post within 50 yards of the enemy's lines. On a previous occasion he carried out a successful daylight raid on enemy trenches.

HERRING, JUSTIN HOWARD, M.C., Lieut. (Temporary Capt.), Royal Flying Corps, Special Reserve. For conspicuous gallantry in action. He displayed great courage and initiative in bombing an enemy gunboat which was towing a bridge upstream. He flew continuously for six hours under heavy rifle fire, and seriously harassed the enemy by preventing his bridging operations. On another occasion he carried out a successful raid and brought back most valuable information.

HIBBERT, CECIL BARCLAY, Second Lieut. (Temporary Lieut.), King's Royal Rifle Corps. Special Reserve, attached Machine Gun Corps. For conspicuous gallantry in action. When practically all the infantry officers were casualties, he gave most valuable assistance in organizing the defence, sending excellent reports back to Battalion Headquarters. Later, he went out with a serjeant and rescued a wounded officer under very heavy fire. He undoubtedly saved a critical situation.

KEOGH, JAMES BLAIR, Major, Lancers, Indian Army. For conspicuous gallantry in action. Although his horse was shot under him and he himself wounded, he remained in command, and by his personal example and skilful handling of his detachment extricated it with slight loss, whilst inflicting considerable punishment on an enemy force ten times his strength.

LLOYD, GEORGE AMBROSE, Lieut., Yeomanry. For conspicuous gallantry and devotion to duty. He has rendered valuable service as Liaison Officer. His duties, which have been carried out with the utmost skill, have been such as to place him in constant danger of his life.

MOORE, WILLIAM AGNEW, Major, Royal Garrison Artillery, attached Imperial Camel Brigade. For conspicuous gallantry in action. He handled his battery during the action with marked skill, thereby clearing a redoubt which was checking the infantry advance.

OWSTON, LEYCESTER VARLEY, Capt., Dragoon Guards, attached Motor Machine Gun Corps. For conspicuous gallantry and devotion to duty. He has rendered valuable service in command of armoured cars, and his personal gallantry has been on more than one occasion brought to notice.

SALMOND, WILLIAM GEOFFREY HANSON, Brevet Lieut.-Colonel (Temporary Brigadier-General), Royal Artillery and Royal Flying Corps. For conspicuous ability and devotion to duty when personally directing the work of the Royal Flying Corps during the action. The striking success attained was largely due to his magnificent personal example.

SEBASTIAN, ERROLL GRAHAM, Temporary Lieut. (Acting Capt.), East Kent Regt. For conspicuous gallantry and skill during a night attack. Under heavy artillery and rifle fire he maintained an effective fire control, and subsequently led a charge against a strongly-held position. Being unable to cut the wire, the attackers tore it up bodily, capturing the trench with considerable loss to the enemy.

STOCKS, JOHN LEOFRIC, Temporary Capt., King's Royal Rifle Corps. For conspicuous gallantry in action. He led his company with great gallantry during the assault. Later, when the other three Company Commanders had become

The Distinguished Service Order

casualties, he did most valuable work in reorganizing the companies. He was subsequently wounded.
WELLS, RUSSELL PRIMROSE, Capt., Hussars, attached Motor Machine Gun Corps. For conspicuous gallantry and devotion to duty. He has rendered valuable service in charge of armoured cars. The nature of his duties involve continued personal risk, and his personal gallantry has been several times brought to notice.

AUSTRALIAN IMPERIAL FORCE.

BIRKBECK, GILBERT, Major, Australian Light Horse Regt. For conspicuous gallantry in action. He displayed great initiative and excellent leadership in moving his squadron over most difficult country round the enemy's left flank, thereby materially assisting in the defeat of the enemy and preventing any escape.
BROOKS, JOSEPH JOHNSON, Major, Australian Light Horse Regt. For conspicuous gallantry in action. He handled his men in a most capable manner during a frontal attack under intense fire. He set a splendid example of courage and determination throughout.
MARKWELL, WILLIAM ERNEST, Major, Australian Light Horse Regt. For conspicuous gallantry in action. He gallantly led the final assault against both the enemy trenches and a redoubt, thereby completing the defeat of the enemy. He set a magnificent example to his men.
McKENZIE, KENNETH ALAN, Major, Australian Light Horse Regt. For conspicuous gallantry in action. He led his squadron in the attack with great gallantry, and was the first to reach the enemy's position. He has on many previous occasions done fine work.

CANADIAN CONTINGENT.

LAWS, BURNETT, Major, Canadian Mounted Rifle Battn. For conspicuous gallantry in action. Previous to the operation he personally carried out a successful reconnaissance in "No Man's Land." Later, he rendered most valuable service during the attack, and materially assisted in the success of the operations. He has previously done fine work.

London Gazette, 12 March, 1917.—"War Office, 12 March, 1917. His Majesty the King has been graciously pleased to approve of the award of a Bar to the Distinguished Service Order to":—

HAMILTON-BOWEN, ALFRED JOHN, D.S.O., Capt. (Temporary Lieut.-Colonel), Monmouthshire Regt. For conspicuous gallantry and devotion to duty. He, with great personal gallantry, supervised the difficult task of consolidation throughout the whole night, and continually went round his working parties. He was mainly responsible for the excellent work carried out.
(The Distinguished Service Order was awarded in London Gazette dated 3 July, 1915.)
LEGGETT, ARCHIBALD HERBERT, D.S.O., Brevet Major (Temporary Lieut.-Colonel), Reserve of Officers, late Royal Scots Fusiliers, Royal Scots Fusiliers. For conspicuous gallantry, coolness and resource when in command of an infantry battalion. He showed exceptional powers of leadership when attacked by the enemy, upon whom he inflicted a severe defeat.
(The Distinguished Service Order was awarded in London Gazette dated 27 Sept. 1901.)

"His Majesty the King has been graciously pleased to approve of the appointments of the undermentioned Officers to be Companions of the Distinguished Service Order, in recognition of their gallantry and devotion to duty in the field."
BURGESS, ALFRED, Second Lieut., Royal Berkshire Regt. For conspicuous courage and ability whilst commanding a raiding platoon which entered the enemy's trenches, and returned with two officers and 50 other ranks as prisoners. The success of the raid was largely due to the ability with which he conducted preparatory training, and also to his personal courage and example. He was severely wounded.
LONG, SELDEN HERBERT, M.C., Lieut. (Temporary Capt.), Durham Light Infantry and Royal Flying Corps. For great skill and daring in piloting his machine. He shot down an enemy machine, which fell in our lines, and the same day he forced another hostile machine to land in the enemy's lines. Later he shot down another enemy machine, which fell in our lines.
MASTERSON, THOMAS SAMUEL, Capt., General List. For conspicuous gallantry and devotion to duty in carrying out work of destruction. He passed through the rearguard of the retreating army and destroyed the remaining untouched works of value. He set a splendid example of courage and initiative throughout the operations.
MORRIS, FRANK GEORGE GRIER, Major (Temporary Lieut.-Colonel), Border Regt. For conspicuous gallantry and devotion to duty when commanding his battalion in the attack. He personally supervised the consolidation of the position, which he extended beyond the line specified in order to obtain better observation, and inspired his companies with his own determination and bravery.
MUTCH, GEORGE, Second Lieut. (Temporary Lieut.), Gordon Highlanders. For conspicuous gallantry and devotion to duty during a raid on the enemy's trenches. He rallied his men and led them forward under heavy fire. Later, with a few men he rushed an enemy post from the flank and captured the garrison. He was a magnificent example to his men, and to him was largely due the success of the raid.
SCALE, JOHN DYMOKE, Capt., Indian Army. For conspicuous gallantry and devotion to duty. He rode out beyond the rearguard until nearly surrounded by the enemy in order to convince the retreating troops that further delay was dangerous. Then, later, although the rearguard had retired, he stuck to his post until his work was completed.
WEBSTER, WALTER HENRY, Second Lieut., London Regt. For conspicuous gallantry and devotion to duty. At great personal risk he picked up an unexploded enemy projectile, and threw it over the parapet, where it at once exploded. He undoubtedly saved many lives.
WILKINSON, WILLIAM DALE, M.C., Temporary Capt., Yorkshire Regt. For conspicuous gallantry and devotion to duty. On entering the captured position he sent back clear and concise information, superintended the consolidation and blocking of the flanks, and remained complete master of the situation. It was mainly owing to his gallant leadership that the enemy's trench was captured and two officers and 78 other ranks taken prisoners.
WILSON, HERBERT DUCKWORTH, Major, Royal Field Artillery. For conspicuous gallantry and devotion to duty. He maintained observation throughout the day under very heavy fire. He was wounded on three different occasions during the day, but remained at his observation post until the light failed and his work was accomplished. He has on many previous occasions done fine work.

CANADIAN CONTINGENT.

FOSTER, HAROLD WILLIAM ALEXANDER, M.C., Capt. (Acting Major), Canadian Infantry. For conspicuous gallantry and devotion to duty when in command of one of the assaulting companies. Although wounded during the advance, he continued to direct his men throughout the whole operation, displaying great coolness and resource. When attacked by a party of the enemy, he personally accounted for two of them, and took a third prisoner.

London Gazette, 17 March, 1917.—"War Office, 17 March, 1917. His Majesty the King has been graciously pleased to approve of the undermentioned Honours for distinguished service in the field, in Mesopotamia, with effect from 10 March, 1917, inclusive."

Awarded a Bar to the Distinguished Service Order:
BODY, JOHN, D.S.O., Capt. (Acting Lieut.-Colonel), East Kent Regt. (D.S.O. gazetted 22 Dec. 1916.)

Awarded the Distinguished Service Order:
CHARLTON, FLORIAN HUBERT, Capt. (Temporary Lieut.-Colonel), South Lancashire Regt.
GIBBON, WILLIAM DUFF, M.C., Temporary Capt. (Acting Lieut.-Colonel), Worcestershire Regt.
INKSON, NORMAN LEOPOLD, Lieut., Indian Army, Reserve of Officers.
KIRBY, JOSEPH THOMAS, Capt., Supply and Transport Corps, Indian Army.
MORRIS, GEORGE MORTIMER, Lieut.-Colonel, Punjabis, Indian Army.
NISBET, THOMAS, Capt., Cavalry, Indian Army.

NOTE.—The acts of gallantry for which the following rewards have been conferred will be published in the London Gazette next month."

Awarded a Bar to the Distinguished Service Order:
CROFTON, MALBY RICHARD HENRY, D.S.O., Major, Royal Field Artillery (D.S.O. gazetted 22 Dec. 1916.) (See London Gazette, 17 April, 1917.)
SCOTT, HENRY ST. GEORGE STEWART, D.S.O., Capt. (Temporary Major), Gurkha Rifles, Indian Army. (D.S.O. gazetted 29 Oct. 1915.) (See London Gazette, 26 May, 1917.)

Awarded the Distinguished Service Order:
BAKER, ROBERT GEOFFREY, Major, Punjabis, Indian Army. (See London Gazette, 26 April, 1917.)
DE HAVILLAND, HEREWARD, Capt. (Temporary Major), Royal Flying Corps, Special Reserve. (See London Gazette, 26 May, 1917.)
DURNFORD, ROBERT CHICHESTER, Second Lieut., Hampshire Regt. See London Gazette, 18 June, 1917.)
FARRER, AUBREY DAVID MAPLETON, Temporary Capt., Royal Welsh Fusiliers. (See London Gazette, 26 April, 1917.)
GUNNING, ORLANDO GEORGE, C.M.G., Lieut.-Colonel and Brevet Colonel, Sikhs, Indian Army. (See London Gazette, 11 May, 1917.)
GORDON, DOUGLAS HAMILTON, Lieut., Sikhs, Indian Army. (See London Gazette, 17 April, 1917.)
HARRISON, WILLIAM RALPH ELLIOT, Capt., Royal Artillery. (See London Gazette, 11 May, 1917.)
HEMPSON, CLAUDE DAWSON, Temporary Capt., attached Suffolk Regt. (See London Gazette, 26 May, 1917.)
HORNOR, BASSETT FARDELL, Second Lieut., Norfolk Regt. (See London Gazette, 18 June, 1917.)
MYLES, EDGAR KINGHORN, V.C., Second Lieut., Welsh Regt. (See London Gazette, 26 April, 1917.)
O'CONNOR, CORNELIUS BERNARD, Temporary Second Lieut. (Acting Capt.), North Lancashire Regt. (See London Gazette, 26 May, 1917.)
PITMAN, CHARLES ROBERT SENHOUSE, Capt., Punjabis, Indian Army (See London Gazette, 18 June, 1917.)
RUSSELL, ROBERT TOR, Second Lieut., Indian Army Reserve of Officers. (See London Gazette, 18 June, 1917.)
SHEPHERD, CLAUDE INNES, Capt., Sikhs, Indian Army. (See London Gazette, 18 June, 1917.)
TOOGOOD, CYRIL GEORGE, Temporary Second Lieut., Gloucestershire Regt. (See London Gazette, 18 June, 1917.)
WATSON, ALLAN, M.B., Capt., Royal Army Medical Corps. (See London Gazette, 26 April, 1917.)

London Gazette, 23 March, 1917.—"Admiralty, 23 March, 1917. The King has been graciously pleased to give orders for the appointment of the undermentioned Officers to be Companions of the Distinguished Service Order."

MARX, JOHN LOCKE, M.V.O., Capt., Royal Naval Reserve.
HARMAR, CHARLES D'OYLY, Major, R.M.L.I.
KING, PHILIP WILFRED SIDNEY, Lieut.-Commander, R.N.
OLPHERT, WYBRANTS, D.S.C., Acting Lieut.-Commander, Royal Naval Reserve.
WILLIAMS, JOHN WHITTOW, Lieut.-Commander, R.N.R.
HAWKINS, ERNEST MORTIMER, Lieut., R.N.R.
DAVIES, EDWARD VAUGHAN, Lieut., R.N.R.
STUART, RONALD NEIL, Lieut., R.N.R.
LOVELESS, LEONARD SAMUEL, D.S.C., Engineer-Lieut., Royal Naval Reserve.

The undermentioned Officers have been awarded a Bar to the Distinguished Service Order, for subsequent acts of gallantry:
GRENFELL, FRANCIS HENRY, D.S.O., Commander, Royal Navy.
(The appointment to the Distinguished Service Order was announced in London Gazette dated 1 Jan. 1917.)
LOCKYER, EDMUND LAURENCE BRAITHWAITE, D.S.O., Commander, Royal Navy.
(The appointment to the Distinguished Service Order was announced in London Gazette dated 1 Jan. 1915.)
MELLIN, ARTHUR ALURED, D.S.O., Lieut.-Commander, Royal Navy.
(The appointment to the Distinguished Service Order was announced in London Gazette dated 1 Jan. 1917.)

London Gazette, 26 March, 1917.—" War Office, 26 March, 1917. His Majesty the King has been graciously pleased to approve of the appointments of the undermentioned Officers to be Companions of the Distinguished Service Order, in recognition of their gallantry and devotion to duty in the field."

ALGIE, WILLIAM, Temporary Second Lieut., Northumberland Fusiliers. For conspicuous gallantry and devotion to duty during a raid on the enemy's trenches. He led the assaulting party with great dash and inflicted many casualties on the enemy. He himself shot eight of the enemy with his revolver. Later, he skilfully withdrew his party under very heavy fire and assisted to bring in the wounded.

FORSYTH, MAXWELL HUNTER, M.C., Capt. (Temporary Major), Gordon Highlanders, attached Scottish Rifles. For conspicuous gallantry and devotion to duty when in command of a strong raiding party. He trained the party, and carried out the raid successfully, personally controlling it from the enemy's front line. The party entered the enemy's third line, captured 43 prisoners, two machine guns and a trench mortar.

GAMMELL, JAMES ANDREW HARCOURT, M.C., Capt., Royal Artillery. For conspicuous gallantry and devotion to duty when employed as Staff Officer to the Armoured Car Patrol. He displayed great coolness under heavy fire, and his energy and perseverance greatly assisted in the success of the operations.

PADWICK, HAROLD BOULTBEE, Temporary Surgeon, Royal Navy. For conspicuous gallantry and devotion to duty. He remained in the open, and continued to tend the wounded under very heavy fire. Later, he proceeded to Headquarters, and at great personal risk brought in many wounded men. He displayed great courage and determination throughout the operations.

PARTRIDGE, LLEWELLYN, Major, Yeomanry, attached Welsh Regt. For conspicuous gallantry and devotion to duty. He displayed great judgment and skill in the leadership of his three light patrols, and showed inexhaustible resource in overcoming the most serious physical obstacles. Later, in action he proved himself a dashing and competent leader.

PEREIRA, ARTHUR BERESFORD PHILEMON, Capt. (Temporary Major), Army Service Corps. For conspicuous gallantry and devotion to duty. He was untiring in his work, and kept the force supplied in its important requirements of petrol and water for the cars, as well as rations and water for personnel with conspicuous success. He displayed great coolness and resource in action.

PORCH, CECIL PORCH, Temporary Lieut.-Colonel, Northumberland Fusiliers. For conspicuous gallantry and able leading while in command of a raiding party. The success of the raid was largely due to his most careful work in preparing the details of the scheme and his own determined leading. Later, although wounded, he continued to direct operations, and personally superintended the removal of the wounded under heavy fire.

SOUTH AFRICAN FORCE.

CURRIE, JOHN, Second Lieut., South African Artillery. For conspicuous gallantry and devotion to duty. He, with another officer, organized and led forward a party of infantry at a critical time, thereby enabling an enemy strong point to be carried and over 100 prisoners taken. Later, he again took charge of parties of four different regiments, and succeeded in repelling an enemy counter-attack. He set a splendid example of courage and determination throughout.

Distinguished Service Order Award :
McKENZIE, WILLIAM SINCLAIR, Lieut. (rank corrected to Second Lieut. [London Gazette, 22 April, 1918]), Seaforth Highlanders.

The particulars of the act of gallantry in this case will be published next month in the London Gazette. This award was omitted from the Gazette dated 17 March, 1917, pending verification. (See London Gazette, 18 July, 1917.)

London Gazette, 11 April, 1917.—" Admiralty, 11 April, 1917. In addition to the honours notified in the Supplements to the London Gazette dated 14 March, 15th May (3rd Supplement), and 31 May, 1916 (3rd Supplement), the King has been graciously pleased to give orders for the following appointment to the Distinguished Service Order to the undermentioned Officer, in recognition of his services in the Eastern Mediterranean up to the 30th June, 1916."

CAMPBELL, ALEXANDER V., M.V.O., Capt., Royal Navy. Performed meritorious service whilst in command of H.M.S. Prince George, which took part in the actions of 25 Feb. and 18 March, 1915. Prince George supported the Army from inside the Straits between 25 April and 10 May, 1915, and also at Suvla for several weeks continuously under fire. Capt. Campbell also did good service during the evacuation.

London Gazette, 17 April, 1917.—" War Office, 17 April, 1917. His Majesty the King has been graciously pleased to approve of the award of a Bar to the Distinguished Service Order to " :—

*CROFTON, MALBY RICHARD HENRY, D.S.O., Major, Royal Field Artillery. For conspicuous gallantry and devotion to duty. He went forward under the most intense fire to a position 150 yards from the enemy's trenches, from where he controlled the fire of his battery with great skill.
(D.S.O. gazetted 22 Dec. 1916.)

HILL, GERALD VICTOR WILMOT, D.S.O., Capt. and Brevet Major (Temporary Lieut.-Colonel), Royal Irish Fusiliers, attached Suffolk Regt. For conspicuous gallantry and good leadership when in command of his battalion. He formed up his battalion under very heavy fire and under the most difficult conditions. The successful start of his battalion and the accomplishment of its task in the attack was in a great measure due to his personal example and fine leadership.
(D.S.O. gazetted 14 Jan. 1916.)

ROSS, RONALD CAMPBELL, D.S.O., Major, Jats, Indian Army. For conspicuous gallantry and good leadership when in command of his battalion. He gallantly led his battalion to the assault of the enemy's position, and the success of the operation was largely due to his fine example and able leadership. Later, while leading his men, he was severely wounded.
(D.S.O. gazetted 14 Jan. 1916.)

" His Majesty the King has been graciously pleased to approve of the appointments of the undermentioned Officers to be Companions of the Distinguished Service Order, in recognition of their gallantry and devotion to duty in the field."

ASQUITH, ARTHUR MELLAND, Temporary Lieut.-Commander, Royal Naval Volunteer Reserve. For conspicuous gallantry and devotion to duty. He obtained leave to go up to the front when he heard a fight was imminent. Later, although wounded, he returned to Brigade Headquarters and gave a clear account of the situation and of the fighting, which had been going on during the night. He has previously done fine work.

BROWN, KENNETH ARROWSMITH, Temporary Major, Devonshire Regt. For conspicuous gallantry during a raid. It was largely owing to his initiative and courage that the operations met with such success. Previous to the raid he carried out two reconnaissances close to the enemy's wire, and brought back most valuable information.

CUMBERLEGE, GEOFFREY FENWICK JOCELYN, Temporary Capt., Royal Fusiliers. For conspicuous gallantry and devotion to duty. He dashed along the line rallying his own battalion and men of other units. He succeeded in restoring order and in reorganizing the line at a most critical time. Throughout the day he inspired all ranks by his high example of courage and devotion to duty.

DEARDEN, JAMES FERRAND, M.C., Lieut. (Temporary Capt.), Royal Fusiliers. For conspicuous gallantry and devotion to duty in commanding his company. By his splendid example of courage and fine leadership several strong enemy counter-attacks were repulsed. At a critical stage he jumped on to the parapet with a machine gun and accounted for many of the enemy.

*GORDON, DOUGLAS HAMILTON, Lieut., Sikhs, Indian Army. For conspicuous gallantry and devotion to duty when in command of two platoons. He led his men to reinforce the right flank, and commenced bombing along the enemy trench, thereby regaining much lost ground. Later, he handled a machine gun with great skill, and succeeded in establishing a block under very heavy fire. He set a splendid example throughout the day.

GWYNNE, ROLAND VAUGHAN, Temporary Major, Sussex Yeomanry, attached Royal West Surrey Regt. For conspicuous gallantry and judgment in commanding and carrying out a daylight raid with his battalion. His personal example of courage and coolness was of great value throughout the operation. He personally went over to the enemy lines and supervised. He was wounded.

HAMMOND, JOHN MAXIMILIAN, M.B., Temporary Lieut., Royal Army Medical Corps, attached Devonshire Regt. For conspicuous gallantry and devotion to duty in evacuating a large number of wounded under the most difficult conditions. He was himself subsequently wounded, and although both his feet were practically blown off he ordered his stretcher-bearers to carry away another wounded man first.

MILDREN, WILLIAM FREDERICK, C.M.G., Lieut.-Colonel, London Regt. For conspicuous gallantry and devotion to duty when in command of a strong raiding party. He made admirable arrangements both as regards the preparation and the execution of the raid, and inspired his battalion with his own fine example.

MONTAGU, THE HONOURABLE LIONEL SAMUEL, Temporary Capt., Royal Marines. For conspicuous gallantry and devotion to duty. He led his company in the first attack and captured his objective. Later, under very heavy fire, he personally took out a covering party and kept his men consolidating the trenches for over 24 hours. On another occasion he single-handed captured 50 prisoners, and later, although wounded, remained at duty.

OZANNE, HAROLD, Major, Royal Marine Light Infantry. For conspicuous gallantry and devotion to duty. He directed the consolidation of the position with marked ability, and was largely responsible for holding the position against subsequent enemy counter-attacks. He displayed great courage and determination throughout the operations.

PRICE, THOMAS REGINALD, Second Lieut. (Temporary Lieut.), Northampton Regt. For conspicuous gallantry and devotion to duty. He took command of his battalion and led it from the first to the second objective. He organized two successive defensive positions under very heavy fire, thereby saving a critical situation. He inspired all ranks by his high example of courage and devotion to duty.

SHELTON, ROBERT HOWARD, Temporary Lieut.-Commander, Royal Naval Volunteer Reserve. For conspicuous gallantry and devotion to duty. He was repeatedly counter-attacked by the enemy, and some of his posts were driven in, and it was only by his personal bravery in placing himself at the head of his men and charging the enemy that the position was held.

WEST, CHARLES SKEFFINGTON, Temporary Lieut.-Commander, Royal Naval Volunteer Reserve. For conspicuous gallantry and devotion to duty. He rendered invaluable service by most ably guiding and placing companies of the battalion in their battle positions within 400 yards of the enemy. He worked continuously under heavy hostile shell-fire, and was largely responsible for the success of the operations.

WESTON, SPENCER VAUGHAN PERCY, M.C., Temporary Capt. (Acting Major), Royal Berkshire Regt. For conspicuous gallantry and devotion to duty in forming up the brigade in their assembly positions previous to an attack. He worked continuously under very heavy fire, and rendered invaluable assistance throughout.

WYLIE, JOHN PRICE, Capt. (Acting Major), Nottinghamshire and Derbyshire Regt. For conspicuous gallantry and devotion to duty when in command of a raiding party. He handled his party with great skill, and carried out the task allotted to him with conspicuous success. He has on many previous occasions done fine work.

CANADIAN CONTINGENT.

DAVIES, REGINALD DANBURY, Lieut.-Colonel, Canadian Infantry. For conspicuous gallantry and devotion to duty when in command of a strong raiding party. He personally superintended the assembly of all parties prior to the attack, and carried out the task allotted to him with conspicuous success. He has previously rendered excellent service on many occasions.

SOUTH AFRICAN FORCE.

ROSE, JOHN GEORGE, Temporary Lieut.-Colonel, Service Corps. For conspicuous devotion to duty and the able manner in which he organized and maintained the Motor Tractor Service. It was largely due to his energy and resource that the forces in the field were able to receive supplies, without which the success of the operations would have been impossible.

(The names marked with an asterisk appeared in the London Gazette dated 17 March, 1917, without deeds.)

London Gazette, 21 April, 1917.—" Admiralty, S.W., 21 April, 1917. The King has been graciously pleased to give orders for the following appointments to the Distinguished Service Order to the undermentioned Officers, in recognition of their services in the Patrol Cruisers, under the command of Vice-Admiral Reginald G. O. Tupper, C.B., C.V.O., during the period 1 July–31 Dec. 1916."

SMITH, HUMPHREY HUGH, Capt., R.N.

JORDAN, WALTER, Engineer Commander, R.N.R.

Honours for Royal Naval Air Service.

" The King has been graciously pleased to give orders for the appointment of the undermentioned Officer to be a Companion of the Distinguished Service Order."

BELL, BERTRAM CHARLES, Flight-Lieut. (Acting Flight-Commander), Royal Naval Air Service. For conspicuous bravery and skill in attacking hostile aircraft. Since 1 Feb. 1917, he has taken part in fourteen aerial combats, notably : On 17 March, 1917, on two different occasions during the same offensive patrol he attacked and drove down hostile machines, one completely out of control and the other in flames. On 24 March, 1917, he attacked a hostile machine which was diving on one of our machines. After he had fired about 30 rounds at a range of about 50 yards the hostile pilot fell back and his machine went down spinning and side-slipping completely out of control.

Honours for Miscellaneous Services.

"The King has been graciously pleased to give orders for the appointment of the undermentioned Officers to be Companions of the Distinguished Service Order."

HANAN, FRANCIS WILLIAM, Commander, R.N.

PARKER, JAMES SANDBACH, Lieut.-Commander, R.N.

FRANK, FREDERICK AUGUSTUS, Lieut. (now Acting Lieut.-Commander), R.N.R.

London Gazette, 26 April, 1917.—" War Office, 26 April, 1917. His Majesty the King has been graciously pleased to approve of the appointments of the undermentioned Officers to be Companions of the Distinguished Service Order, in recognition of their gallantry and devotion to duty in the field."

*BAKER, ROBERT GEOFFREY, Major, Punjabis, Indian Army. For conspicuous gallantry and devotion to duty. He showed a quick grasp of the situation, and with great ability secured his left flank at a critical time, rendering it possible to organize further attacks elsewhere. His fearless, personal example contributed largely to the success of a difficult operation.

*FARRER, AUBREY DAVID MAPLETON, Temporary Capt., Royal Welsh Fusiliers. For conspicuous gallantry and devotion to duty. He went forward alone a distance of 1,000 yards under very heavy fire to take command of an advanced post. Although wounded, he succeeded in reaching the post, and held it with marked skill and determination against great odds. Later in the day he was severely wounded.

GRIFFITHS, ALEXANDER HARCOURT, Capt., Duke of Cornwall's Light Infantry, attached King's African Rifles. For conspicuous gallantry and devotion to duty. He led his column in a most gallant manner against a strongly-entrenched position and captured a field gun. He has consistently shown great coolness and ability.

HITCHIN, HAROLD EVERETT, Temporary Second Lieut., Durham Light Infantry. For conspicuous gallantry and devotion to duty when in command of a bombing party. He made three most gallant attempts to force his way into the enemy's position and himself shot four of the enemy with his revolver. Later, he voluntarily joined in another company's attack, and rendered invaluable assistance. He was largely responsible for the final success of the operations.

KING, MARK, Second Lieut., Coldstream Guards, Special Reserve. For conspicuous gallantry and devotion to duty. He led his platoon through an intense hostile barrage, displaying the greatest bravery. Later, on reaching the first objective and finding his left flank exposed, he got his men out of the enemy's front line, formed front to the left, advanced 400 yards, and captured an enemy second-line trench, thereby saving a critical situation.

MURRAY, RONALD ERNEST, Lieut.-Colonel, British South Africa Police. For conspicuous gallantry and devotion to duty when in command of his column. He set a splendid example of gallantry and able leadership during a successful assault on very superior forces of the enemy.

*MYLES, EDGAR KINGHORN, V.C., Second Lieut., Welsh Regt., attached Worcestershire Regt. For conspicuous gallantry and devotion to duty. When all the officers except two had become casualties, he, for five hours, inspired confidence in the defence against two counter-attacks, and sent back most accurate and valuable reports of the situation. His courage and fine example were largely responsible for the steadiness of all ranks with him.

*WATSON, ALLAN, M.B., Capt., Royal Army Medical Corps. For conspicuous gallantry and devotion to duty. He went forward under very heavy fire, before his own unit was ordered to advance, and commenced to dress the wounded of another battalion. He worked untiringly under fire both day and night, never resting until all the wounded had been brought in.

AUSTRALIAN IMPERIAL FORCE.

CROWTHER, HENRY ARNOLD, Major, Infantry. For conspicuous gallantry and devotion to duty in leading the front line of his battalion during a reconnaissance in force on the enemy position. He repeatedly traversed the front line under heavy fire to superintend the action of the companies. Later in the day he personally directed the necessary movements to break off the action, showing marked ability and initiative.

(The names marked with an asterisk appeared in the London Gazette dated 7 March, 1917, without deeds.)

London Gazette, 4 May, 1917.—" War Office, 4 May, 1917. His Majesty the King has been graciously pleased to approve of the undermentioned Rewards for valuable services rendered in connection with Military operations in the field. Dated 1 Jan. 1917. To be Companions of the Distinguished Service Order."

FENNING, EDWARD GEORGE, Capt., Carrier Section, East Africa Transport Corps.

GUEST, THE HONOURABLE FREDERICK EDWARD, Capt., Reserve of Officers, late Life Guards.

PATTERSON, JOHN, Temporary Major, East African Pay Corps.

RIGBY, WALTER, Capt., Reserve of Officers, late Royal Irish Rifles and East African Police.

ANDERSON, ROY DUNLOP, Capt., Carrier Section, E. A. Transport Corps, was gazetted on this date as M.C. for the above-mentioned services, but this was cancelled and the D.S.O. substituted. (See London Gazette, 22 June, 1918.)

London Gazette, 10 May, 1917.—" Admiralty, S.W., 10 May, 1917."

Honours for Service in the Action between H.M. Ships Swift and Broke and German Destroyers, on the Night of the 20th to 21st April, 1917.

" The King has been graciously pleased to give orders for the appointment of the undermentioned Officers to be Companions of the Distinguished Service Order, in recognition of their services in command of H.M.S. Swift and H.M.S. Broke respectively, on the night of the 20th to 21st April, 1917, when they successfully engaged a flotilla of five or six German destroyers, of which two were sunk."

PECK, AMBROSE MAYNARD, Commander (now Capt.), R.N.

EVANS, EDWARD RATCLIFFE GARTH RUSSELL, C.B., Commander (now Capt.), Royal Navy.

London Gazette, 11 May, 1917.—" War Office, 11 May, 1917. His Majesty the King has been graciously pleased to award a Second Bar to the Distinguished Service Order to " :—

LUMSDEN, FREDERICK WILLIAM, D.S.O., Major, Royal Marine Artillery. For conspicuous gallantry and devotion to duty when in charge of a strong reconnaissance party. He carried out the task allotted to him with conspicuous success, and skilfully withdrew his party at a critical time. His conduct, rapid decision and good judgment saved many casualties.

(Distinguished Service Order gazetted 1 Jan. 1917. First Bar awarded in this Gazette.) (See next entry.)

" His Majesty the King has been graciously pleased to award a Bar to the Distinguished Service Order to " :—

LUMSDEN, FREDERICK WILLIAM, D.S.O., Major, Royal Marine Artillery. For conspicuous gallantry and devotion to duty. He made a reconnaissance of the enemy's position, moving over open ground under very heavy fire and bringing back most valuable information. He rendered invaluable services throughout the operations.

(Distinguished Service Order gazetted 1 Jan. 1917.)

MEIKLEJOHN, JAMES ROSS CONRAD, D.S.O., Major, Border Regt. For conspicuous gallantry and devotion to duty when he kept well in touch with battalions, moving about regardless of fire until severely wounded. After having his skull fractured by a shell splinter he continued at work until he had rendered a clear report on the situation.

(Distinguished Service Order gazetted 1 Jan. 1917.)

" His Majesty the King has been graciously pleased to approve of the appointments of the undermentioned Officers to be Companions of the Distinguished Service Order, in recognition of their gallantry and devotion to duty in the field."

BUCKLE, CHRISTOPHER GALBRAITH, M.C., Capt. (Acting Lieut.-Colonel), Northampton Regt. For conspicuous gallantry and devotion to duty when in command of his battalion. He visited the captured trenches during the action and gave orders regarding dispositions and consolidation. The dash of his battalion in the attack and their tenacity in holding the position won, were to a considerable extent due to his influence.

DUGUID, CHARLES FREDERICK, M.C., Temporary Capt., Manchester Regt. For conspicuous gallantry and devotion to duty. With 20 men of his company he fought his way through uncut enemy wire and established a strong point in a small length of hostile trench. He maintained his position there for 36 hours in spite of several strong enemy counter-attacks.

GROGAN, GEORGE WILLIAM ST. GEORGE, C.M.G., Major (Temporary Lieut.-Colonel), Worcestershire Regt. For conspicuous gallantry and devotion to duty when in command of his battalion. He visited the captured trenches during the action and gave instructions regarding dispositions and consolidation. He kept the brigade informed of the situation, and his reports were of great value. The spirit of his battalion owes much to his personal courage and cheerfulness.

*GUNNING, ORLANDO GEORGE, C.M.G., Lieut.-Colonel and Brevet Colonel, Indian Army. For conspicuous coolness and gallant leadership. He led his battalion through heavy enfilade rifle and machine-gun fire, and continued to command although twice wounded. By his example he retained the cohesion of his regiment and kept up their fighting spirit under very adverse circumstances.

*HARRISON, WILLIAM RALPH ELLIOT, Capt., Royal Artillery. For conspicuous gallantry and devotion to duty. He moved his observation ladder to within 700 yards of the enemy's trenches and remained up it throughout the day under very heavy fire. His accurate information was of the greatest value, and his initiative and utter disregard of personal safety beyond all praise.

STOREY, CHARLES ERNEST, Temporary Lieut., Machine Gun Corps. For conspicuous gallantry and initiative when in command of a Tank. He took his car up and down the enemy trenches, working until all his petrol was exhausted and only two of the crew were unwounded. He is reported as having been responsible for the taking of between 200 and 300 prisoners.

BYL, JOHN VANDER, Major (Temporary Lieut.-Colonel), Hussars. For conspicuous gallantry and devotion to duty when in command of an advanced squadron. Under very heavy fire he effected an entrance to the village, and shortly after assumed command of another squadron. He cleared the village of the enemy and seized the tactical points in advance. He held all the positions gained until relieved by the Infantry.

AUSTRALIAN IMPERIAL FORCE.

PYE, JOHN VANDER BYL, Major (Temporary Lieut.-Colonel), Australian Infantry. For conspicuous gallantry and initiative when in charge of the whole of the front line held by his battalion. He organized a successful attack and exhibited great energy and determination when meeting a counter-attack made by the enemy. He set a splendid example to those under him.

CANADIAN CONTINGENT.

BROWN, JOHN HECTOR INNES, Major, Canadian Infantry. For conspicuous gallantry during a raid on the enemy's trenches. He took charge of the assembly of the left assaulting wave and of three large offensive patrols. He carried out these duties with marked skill, and throughout set a magnificent example to his men. Later, he reorganized the dispositions of the companies in the front line and personally supervised the collection of a number of the wounded.

RORKE, HERBERT VICTOR, Major (Acting Lieut.-Colonel), Canadian Infantry. For conspicuous gallantry and devotion to duty when in command of a raiding party. By his untiring energy and carefully thought-out preparations he contributed in a very large degree to the splendid success of the operation. He personally superintended the assembly of all parties before the attack, and his arrangements were perfect and worked without a hitch.

WILSON, ALEXANDER DOUGLAS, Major, Canadian Infantry. For conspicuous gallantry and devotion to duty when in command of his battalion. Owing to his fearless leading and sound preliminary training his battalion carried out the task allotted to it with conspicuous success.

(The names marked with an asterisk appeared in the London Gazette dated 17 March, 1917, without deeds.)

" His Majesty the King has been graciously pleased to approve of the undermentioned Reward for distinguished service in the field. Awarded the Distinguished Service Order."

BROWN, JAMES HENRY (Christian name corrected to James Hardy), Temporary Sub-Lieut., Royal Naval Volunteer Reserve.

(The act of gallantry will be announced in a later Gazette). (See London Gazette, 18 July, 1917.)

London Gazette, 12 May, 1917.—" Admiralty, 12 May, 1917."

Honours for Royal Naval Air Service.

" The King has been graciously pleased to give orders for the appointment of the undermentioned Officers to be Companions of the Distinguished Service Order."

LAMBE, CHARLES LAVEROCK, Capt., R.N. For his valuable services in command of the R.N.A.S. units on the Belgian Coast; he is very largely responsible for the good service in the varied duties carried out by them against the enemy.

BROMET, GEOFFREY RHODES, Squadron-Commander, R.N. This officer commanded a squadron of the R.N.A.S., attached to the Flying Corps, with conspicuous ability and success. Under his command the squadron developed into a most efficient and formidable fighting force, which has brought great credit to the Royal Naval Air Service.

NEWTON-CLARE, EDWARD THOMAS, Squadron-Commander, R.N.A.S. During the past year he has led his squadron with conspicuous success in numerous bomb attacks, and on many occasions has engaged and driven down hostile machines.

Honours for Miscellaneous Services.

"The King has been graciously pleased to give orders for the appointments of the undermentioned Officers to be Companions of the Distinguished Service Order."

HALLWRIGHT, WILLIAM WYBROW, Lieut.-Commander, R.N. (since killed).
MATHESON, CHARLES GEORGE, Lieut.-Commander, R.N.R.
BRADSHAW, GEORGE FAGAN, Lieut., R.N.
HARRISON, FRANCIS CHARLES, Acting Lieut., R.N.
JONES, GERALD NORMAN, Lieut., R.N.R.
CHARLES, FRANK WATKIN, Lieut., R.N.R.
REED, ARCHIBALD DAYRELL, Lieut., R.N.R.

Honours to the Mercantile Marine.

"The King has been graciously pleased to approve the award of the Distinguished Service Order to the following Officers of the British Mercantile Marine, in recognition of zeal and devotion to duty shown in carrying on the trade of the country during the war."

WEBSTER, ALBERT ERNEST, Capt. (Lieut., R.N.R.).
MALING, FREDERICK MAUDE, Capt. (Lieut., R.N.R.).
LARGE, EDWARD RYDER, Capt. (Lieut., R.N.R.) (Christian name corrected to Edwin Ryder [London Gazette, 23 May, 1917]).

London Gazette, 23 May, 1917.—"Admiralty, S.W., 23 May, 1917."

Honours for Service in Destroyer Patrol Flotillas, Armed Boarding Steamers, etc.

"The King has been graciously pleased to give orders for the following appointments to the Distinguished Service Order to the undermentioned Officers, in recognition of their services in the Destroyer Patrol Flotillas, Armed Boarding Steamers, etc., during the period which ended on the 30th Sept. 1916."

BRUCE, ALAN CAMERON, Capt., R.N.
EDWARDS, EDWIN HAROLD, Capt., R.N.
YEATS-BROWN, ALAN MONTAGU, Commander, R.N.
COMPTON, WALTER BURDGE, M.V.O., Commander (now Acting Capt.), Royal Navy.
BETTY, ARTHUR KEMMIS, Commander, R.N.
ANDERSON, LIONEL JOHN GARFIT, Commander, R.N.
MONROE, HUBERT SEEDS, Commander, R.N.
CLUTTERBUCK, FRANCIS ALEXANDER, Commander, R.N.
PEEBLES, AUBREY WILLIAM, M.V.O., Commander, Royal Navy.
HUNT, WILFRID WARD, Commander, R.N.
COATES, WILLIAM HERBERT, R.D., Commander, Royal Naval Reserve.
BORLAND, JOHN McINNES, R.D., Commander, Royal Naval Reserve.
COATES, FRANCIS GEORGE CRAWSHAY, Lieut.-Commander, R.N.
BRENT, ERNEST CYRIL, Lieut.-Commander, R.N.
COOPER-KEY, ASTLEY DUNDAS COOPER, Lieut.-Commander, R.N.
McLEOD, JOHN KELTY, Lieut.-Commander, R.N.
WARNER, FREDERICK ARCHIBALD, Lieut.-Commander, R.N.
WOODWARD, HUGH JOSEPH, Lieut.-Commander, R.N.
BRIGGS, HERBERT GERALD, Lieut.-Commander, R.N.

Honours for Service in the Dover Patrol.

"The King has been graciously pleased to give orders for the following appointments to the Distinguished Service Order to the undermentioned Officers, in recognition of their services in vessels of the Dover Patrol, under the command of Vice-Admiral Sir Reginald H. S. Bacon, K.C.B., K.C.V.O., D.S.O., during the period from 1 July-31 Dec. 1916."

PATON, WILLIAM DOUGLAS, M.V.O., Capt., Royal Navy.
BLOUNT, GEORGE RONALD BEDDARD, Commander, R.N.
PULLIBLANK, JOHN BLACKLER, Engineer Lieut.-Commander, R.N.

Honours for Miscellaneous Services.

"The King has been graciously pleased to give orders for the appointment of the undermentioned Officers to be Companions of the Distinguished Service Order."

CURTIS, BERWICK, Capt., R.N.
GUY, BASIL JOHN DOUGLAS, V.C., Lieut.-Commander, Royal Navy.
FORBES, ARTHUR WALTER, Lieut., R.N.
BOLSTER, THOMAS CHARLES CARPENTER, Lieut.-Commander, R.N. In recognition of conspicuously gallant conduct on the 15th of April, 1917, when he took his destroyer into a mined area to rescue survivors from a hospital ship, which had been sunk by a mine, and from a patrol boat, which had struck a mine in proceeding to the assistance of the hospital ship. His handling of his destroyer in heavy weather and taking her alongside the wreck of the patrol boat was a splendid piece of seamanship.

Honours for Royal Naval Air Service.

"The King has been graciously pleased to give orders for the following appointment to the Distinguished Service Order."

MALONE, JOHN JOSEPH, Flight Sub-Lieut., Royal Naval Air Service. For successfully attacking and bringing down hostile aircraft on numerous occasions. At about 6.30 a.m. on 23 April, 1917, while on patrol, he attacked a hostile scout and drove it down under control. He then attacked a second scout, which, after the pilot had been hit, turned over on its back and went down through the clouds. A third scout, attacked by him from a distance of about 20 yards, descended completely out of control. While engaging a fourth machine he ran out of ammunition, so returned to the advanced landing ground, replenished his supply, and at once returned and attacked another hostile formation, one of which he forced down out of control. On the afternoon of 24 April, 1917, he engaged a hostile two-seater machine and, after badly wounding the observer, forced it to land on our side of the lines.

London Gazette, 26 May, 1917.—"War Office, 26 May, 1917. His Majesty the King has been graciously pleased to award a Bar to the Distinguished Service Order to":—

WILKINSON, ALLAN MACHIN, D.S.O., Lieut. (Temporary Capt.), Hampshire Regt. and Royal Flying Corps. For great skill and gallantry. He came down to a low altitude and destroyed a hostile scout which was attacking one of our machines, the pilot of which had been wounded, thereby saving it. In one day he shot down and destroyed six hostile machines. He has destroyed eight hostile machines during the past ten days and has displayed exceptional skill and gallantry in leading offensive patrols.
(Distinguished Service Order gazetted 20 Oct. 1916.)

*SCOTT, HENRY ST. GEORGE STEWART, D.S.O., Capt. (Temporary Major), Indian Army. For conspicuous gallantry and determination when with 250 men he captured 373 of the enemy. He was twice held up by strong entrenched picquets, who were covering parties attempting to cross the river in pontoons, but he pushed on under heavy fire, inflicting great loss on those crossing and prevented any further attempt at escape.
(Distinguished Service Order gazetted 29 Oct. 1915.)

"His Majesty the King has been graciously pleased to approve of the appointments of the undermentioned Officers to be Companions of the Distinguished Service Order, in recognition of their gallantry and devotion to duty in the field."

BEALE, CLIVE OLIVER BERTRAM, Temporary Second Lieut., General List and Royal Flying Corps. For conspicuous gallantry and devotion to duty. He made two most gallant attempts to carry out a special mission, which involved a night flight of about 50 miles, in very adverse weather. Although unsuccessful, he showed throughout the greatest courage and determination to achieve his mission.

BIRD, AUGUSTUS WIELAND, Temporary Second Lieut. (Temporary Capt.), General List and Royal Flying Corps. For conspicuous gallantry and devotion to duty on many occasions. When on artillery patrol he succeeded in reporting 13 active batteries, observing fire on and silencing several of them. On another occasion he attacked and scattered with machine-gun fire two parties of the enemy which were seen forming up. This operation was carried out for a period of 2½ hours in very adverse weather conditions.

CURRY, WILLIAM HORACE, Second Lieut., South Staffordshire Regt., Special Reserve. For conspicuous gallantry and devotion to duty. He collected men from three different companies and led them forward as far as it was possible to advance. Later, although nearly surrounded by the enemy, he succeeded in consolidating and maintaining his position. On another occasion he took command of two companies and handled them in a most able manner.

DAVIS, HAROLD JAMES NORMAN, Major (Temporary Lieut.-Colonel), Connaught Rangers, attached Highland Light Infantry. For conspicuous gallantry and devotion to duty when in command of his battalion. He took charge of a critical situation in the most able manner, and under very heavy fire personally directed the movements of his battalion. He successfully occupied and consolidated his objective.

*DE HAVILLAND, HEREWARD, Capt. (Temporary Major), Royal Flying Corps. Special Reserve. For conspicuous gallantry and skill. He attacked and drove down a hostile machine. This is the second enemy machine he has destroyed. He has rendered invaluable service throughout the operations, and has at all times set a magnificent example.

*HEMPSON, CLAUDE DAWSON, Temporary Capt., Suffolk Regt., attached Royal Lancaster Regt. For conspicuous gallantry and devotion to duty. Although his right flank was exposed, he held and consolidated the captured trenches for 16 hours against determined enemy bombing attacks. It was mainly owing to his untiring energy and organizing powers that the position was maintained and the enemy finally driven back.

JOHNSTON, WALTER MOWBRAY PERCIVAL, Temporary Capt. (Acting Major), Royal Field Artillery. For conspicuous gallantry and devotion to duty when in command of his battery. He established himself, before dawn, on the remains of a tree, a short distance from our front trenches, and, in full view of the enemy, remained there for several hours directing the fire of his battery by telephone until the whole of the enemy's wire had been effectively destroyed.

*O'CONNOR, CORNELIUS BERNARD, Temporary Second Lieut. (Acting Capt.), North Lancashire Regt. For conspicuous gallantry and devotion to duty. His company was exposed to heavy rifle and enfilade machine-gun fire. By his skilful handling he managed to consolidate the position, despite heavy casualties and several determined efforts on the part of the enemy to drive him out. He eventually captured 90 prisoners.

AUSTRALIAN IMPERIAL FORCE.

ROBINSON, JAMES ALEXANDER, Major, Australian Infantry. For conspicuous gallantry and devotion to duty. He supervised the assembly of the battalion previous to the attack. After the attack had been launched he went forward and sent back most valuable reports on the situation. He showed great bravery and coolness throughout, and his presence in the front line had a most cheering and marked effect on all present.

(* The names marked with an asterisk appeared in the London Gazette dated 17 March, 1917, without deeds.)

London Gazette, 4 June, 1917.—"Admiralty, 4 June, 1917. The King has been graciously pleased to give orders for the appointment of the undermentioned Officers to be Companions of the Distinguished Service Order, in recognition of their services in the prosecution of the war."

CHISHOLM-BATTEN, ALEXANDER WILLIAM, M.V.O., Admiral (Temporary Capt., Royal Naval Reserve).
DENISON, JOHN, Admiral (Temporary Capt., R.N.R.).
PAGET, SIR ALFRED WYNDHAM, K.C.B., K.C.M.G., Admiral (Temporary Capt., R.N.R.).
CLARKE, ARTHUR CALVERT, C.M.G., Vice-Admiral (Temporary Capt., Royal Naval Reserve).
PIKE, FREDERICK OWEN, Vice-Admiral (Temporary Capt., R.N.R.).
BENWELL, WILLIAM FRANCIS, Capt., R.N.
CARVER, EDMUND CLIFTON, Capt., R.N.
EGERTON, WION DE MALPAS, Commander, R.N.
BULLER, FRANCIS ALEXANDER WADDILOVE, Commander, R.N.
GOLDSMITH, MALCOLM LENNON, Commander, R.N.
WATSON, FISCHER BURGES, Commander, R.N.
BIRKETT, MILES BROCK, Commander, R.N.

The Distinguished Service Order

SMART, MORTON, Commander, R.N.V.R.
WATSON, BERTRAM CHALMERS, Lieut.-Commander, R.N.
MACMAHON, MAURICE, Acting Lieut.-Commander, R.N.R.

London Gazette, 4 June, 1917.—" War Office, 4 June, 1917. His Majesty the King has been graciously pleased to approve of the undermentioned rewards for distinguished service in the field."

Awarded a Bar to the Distinguished Service Order :

HARRIS, ARTHUR ELLIS FOWKE, D.S.O., Major (Temporary Lieut.-Colonel), Royal Berkshire Regt.
HULSEBERG, HERBERT, D.S.O., Major, Indian Army.
WILSON, WALTER CARANDINI, D.S.O., M.C., Capt. and Brevet Major, Leicestershire Regt.

To be Companions of the Distinguished Service Order :

AHERN, DAVID, Major (Temporary Lieut.-Colonel), Royal Army Medical Corps.
AHERNE, REV. DAVID, Temporary Chaplain to the Forces, 3rd Class, Army Chaplains' Department.
ALDERMAN, WILLIAM JOHN, Lieut. (Temporary Major), Royal West Kent Regt.
ALEXANDER, JOHN DONALD, M.B., Lieut.-Colonel (Temporary Colonel), Royal Army Medical Corps.
ALLAN, JAMES GIBB, Capt. (Temporary Major), Royal Engineers.
ALLDERIDGE, CHARLES DONALD, Capt. (Acting Major), Royal Garrison Artillery.
ALLFREY, EDWARD MORTIMER, Capt. (Temporary Major), Royal Berkshire Regt.
ALLGOOD, WILLIAM HENRY LORAINE, Lieut.-Colonel, H.P., late King's Royal Rifle Corps.
ANDERSON, THOMAS GAYER, Major, Royal Field Artillery.
ANDERSON, WILLIAM, M.C., Lieut. (Temporary Capt.), Northumberland Fusiliers.
ANDREWS, JOHN OWEN, Capt. (Temporary Major), Army Veterinary Corps.
ANSTRUTHER, ROBERT ABERCROMBIE, Major, Royal Field Artillery.
APLIN, HENRY, Temporary Major, Royal Munster Fusiliers.
ARCHDALE, ARTHUR SOMERVILLE, Major, Royal Field Artillery.
ARGYLE, EDWARD PERCY, Major, Army Veterinary Corps.
ARMSTRONG, EDWARD, Major (Temporary Lieut.-Colonel), Highland Light Infantry.
ASPINALL, CECIL FABER, C.M.G., Major and Brevet Lieut.-Colonel, Royal Munster Fusiliers.
ATKINSON, JOHN, Temporary Lieut.-Colonel, Army Service Corps (Capt., Army Service Corps, T.F.).
AXE, HENRY JOSEPH, Lieut.-Colonel (Temporary Colonel), Army Veterinary Corps.
BADCOCK, GERALD ELIOT, Capt. (Temporary Lieut.-Colonel), Army Service Corps.
BAHR, PHILIP HENRY, M.D., Temporary Capt., Royal Army Medical Corps. (surname changed to Manson-Bahr).
BAKER, WILLIAM HENRY GOLDNEY, Lieut. (Acting Lieut.-Colonel), Indian Army.
BALFOUR, ARTHUR MACINTOSH, Lieut.-Colonel, Royal Field Artillery.
BALFOUR, PERCY, Major (Temporary Lieut.-Colonel), Bedfordshire Regt., Special Reserve.
BALLANTINE-DYKES, FRECHEVILLE HUBERT, Capt., Retired List, late Scots Guards.
BAMBERGER, ARTHUR PRIER WOODBURN, Temporary Major, Army Service Corps.
BAMFIELD, HAROLD JOHN KINAHAN, Lieut.-Colonel, Indian Medical Service.
BANNERMAN, JOHN ARTHUR MURRAY, Major, Royal Warwickshire Regt.
BARNARD, WILLIAM GEORGE FREDERICK, Capt. (Acting Major), East Kent Regt., Special Reserve.
BARTON, NATHANIEL ALBERT DELAP, Major (Temporary Lieut.-Colonel), Army Service Corps, Retired Pay, late Connaught Rangers.
BATHER, EDWARD JOHN, Capt. (Acting Major), Royal Field Artillery.
BAUGH, GEORGE JOHNSTONE, Temporary Major, Royal Engineers.
BEASLEY, JAMES HENRY MOUNTIFORT, Major (Acting Lieut.-Colonel), Royal Garrison Artillery.
BEATTY, GUY ARCHIBALD HASTINGS, Lieut.-Colonel, Indian Army.
BEATTY-POWNALL, GEORGE ERNEST, Major (Acting Lieut.-Colonel), Border Regt. (surname corrected to Beaty-Pownall [London Gazette, 18 Feb. 1918]).
BECHER, HENRY WRIXON, Major (Temporary Lieut.-Colonel), Retired Pay, late West Riding Regt.
BEDDINGTON, EDWARD HENRY LIONEL, M.C., Capt. and Brevet Major (Temporary Lieut.-Colonel), Lancers.
BEHARRELL, JOHN GEORGE, Temporary Lieut.-Colonel, General List.
BELL, CHARLES FRANCIS, Temporary Major, Army Service Corps.
BELLAMY, CHARLES VINCENT, Temporary Major, Royal Engineers (late Major, T.F. Reserve).
BENN, WILLIAM WEDGWOOD, Temporary Capt., Yeomanry (attached Royal Naval Air Service).
BENT, PHILIP ERIC, Second Lieut. (Temporary Major and Acting Lieut.-Colonel), Leicestershire Regt.
BERKELEY, ROBERT ESME, Major, North Lancashire Regt.
BERNERS, RALPH ABERCROMBIE, Lieut.-Colonel (Temporary Brigadier-General), Royal Welsh Fusiliers.
BETTS, JAMES, Quartermaster and Honorary Lieut. (Temporary Capt.), Army Gymnasium Staff.
BINGHAM, RALPH CHARLES, Capt. (Temporary Lieut.-Colonel), Reserve of Officers, late Coldstream Guards (M.G. Guards).
BIRNEY, CHARLES FOLLIOTT, Major (Temporary Colonel), Royal Engineers.

BLEWITT, GUY, M.C., Capt. and Brevet Major, Oxford and Buckinghamshire Light Infantry.
BOND, GEORGE MONTGOMERY, Major, Yorkshire Light Infantry.
BORWICK, GEORGE OLDROYD, Major, Yeomanry.
BOWEN, ARTHUR WINHIETT NUNN, Lieut.-Colonel (Temporary Colonel), Royal Army Medical Corps.
BOYD-ROCHFORT, HAROLD, Capt., Lancers.
BOYLE, THE HONOURABLE JOHN DAVID, Capt. (Temporary Lieut.-Colonel), Rifle Brigade and Royal Flying Corps.
BRADY, JOHN BANKS, Capt., King's Royal Rifle Corps, Special Reserve.
BRAITHWAITE, JOHN, Temporary Major, Graves Registration Section.
BRANCKER, JAMES DONALDSON DULANY, Major, Royal Garrison Artillery.
BRETON, WALTER GUY NICHOLAS, Second Lieut. (Temporary Major), Royal Garrison Artillery.
BRIDCUTT, JOHN HENRY, Capt. (Temporary Major), Royal Irish Rifles.
BRIDGES, ARTHUR HOLROYD, Major and Brevet Lieut.-Colonel (Temporary Lieut.-Colonel), Indian Army (rank corrected to Lieut.-Colonel [London Gazette, 18 July, 1917]).
BRIDGES, ROLAND HARLEY, Major, Royal Army Medical Corps.
BRIGGS, ERNEST, Capt. (Temporary Major), Royal Engineers.
BRIMS, ROBERT WILSON, Temporary Capt. (Acting Major), Royal Engineers.
BROAD, CHARLES NOEL FRANK, Major, Royal Artillery.
BROOKE, GEORGE FRANK, Temporary Lieut.-Colonel, Retired List, late Connaught Rangers (rank corrected to Captain, Reserve of Officers, late Connaught Rangers, Temporary Lieut.-Colonel, Welsh Regt [London Gazette, 18 July, 1917]).
BROWN, REV. FREDERICK E., Temporary Chaplain to the Forces, 3rd Class, Army Chaplains' Department (Christian name corrected to Frederick Edmund).
BROWN, LOUIS NOEL FRANCIS, Capt. (Acting Major), Royal Garrison Artillery.
BROWN, WILLIAM REID, Capt. (Temporary Major), Royal Garrison Artillery.
BROWNLOW, CECIL ALEXANDER LITTLE, Capt. (Acting Major), Royal Field Artillery.
BRYANT, FREDERICK CARKEET, C.M.G., Major (Acting Lieut.-Colonel), Royal Field Artillery.
BUDDEN, ERNEST FREDERICK, Capt. (Acting Major), Royal Field Artillery.
BULLOUGH, CHARLES BERTHOLD, Capt. (Temporary Major), Retired Pay, late Royal Garrison Artillery.
BURKHARDT, VALENTINE RODOLPHE, Major, Royal Field Artillery.
BURNAND, NORMAN GEORGE, Major (Temporary Lieut.-Colonel), Leinster Regt.
BUSH, CHARLES GERALD, Temporary Major, Army Service Corps.
BUTLER, STEPHEN SEYMOUR, Major, South Staffordshire Regt.
CADELL, JOHN GEORGE, Major, Indian Army.
CADMAN, EDWARD CADMAN, Major (Temporary Lieut.-Colonel) Royal Lancaster Regt.
CAMERON, JAMES BLACK, Major, Royal Garrison Artillery.
CAMERON, ORFORD SOMERVILLE, Major, Retired Pay, late Royal Field Artillery.
CAMPBELL, ROBERT ORMUS, Temporary Lieut.-Colonel, Royal Welsh Fusiliers.
CAREY, ARTHUR BASIL, C.M.G., Major and Brevet Lieut.-Colonel (Temporary Lieut.-Colonel), Royal Engineers.
CARTWRIGHT, JOHN ROGERS, Capt. and Brevet Major, Devonshire Regt.
CASEMENT, FRANCIS, M.B., Capt., Royal Army Medical Corps.
CAZALET, CLEMENT H. LANGSTON, Temporary Major, General List.
CHADWICK, JAMES HENRY, Temporary Lieut.-Colonel, Manchester Regt. (Christain name corrected to James Haughton Henry).
CHANCE, KENNETH MILES, Temporary Major, Border Regt.
CHESTER-MASTER, RICHARD CHESTER, Capt. and Brevet Major (Temporary Lieut.-Colonel), Retired Pay, late King's Royal Rifle Corps.
CLARE, OLIVER CECIL, M.C., Temporary Major, East Surrey Regt.
CLARKE, ALBERT EDWARD STANLEY, M.V.O., Capt. and Brevet Major (Temporary Lieut.-Colonel), Retired List, late Scots Guards.
CLARKE, BOWCHER CAMPBELL SENHOUSE, Capt. and Brevet Major (Temporary Lieut.-Colonel), Worcestershire Regt.
CLARKE, CHARLES JAMES, Major, Royal Engineers.
CLEAVER, DOUGLAS WHYTE, Temporary Lieut. (Acting Major), Royal Garrison Artillery.
CLEGG-HILL, THE HONOURABLE ARTHUR REGINALD, Temporary Lieut.-Colonel, Cheshire Regt.
COKER, HARRY OLIVER, Major, Rhodesia Regt.
COLLINS, PERCY ROBERT MURDOCH, Capt. (Acting Major), Royal Garrison Artillery.
COMMON, LAURENCE ANDREW, Lieut. (Temporary Major), Royal Field Artillery.
COOPER, CLIFTON GRAHAM ASTLEY, Major (Acting Lieut.-Colonel), Royal Field Artillery.
COOPER, GORDON SAXTON, Major, Royal Artillery.
COOPER, LYALL NEWCOMEN, Temporary Capt. (Temporary Lieut.-Colonel), Royal Engineers.
COOPER, REGINALD ALFRED, Lieut. (Temporary Major), Yeomanry and Royal Flying Corps (late Capt., Dragoon Guards).
CORFE, ARTHUR CECIL, Major (Temporary Lieut.-Colonel), South African Defence Force (Commanding Battn. Royal West Kent Regt.).
CORNWALL, JAMES HANDYSIDE MARSHALL, M.C., Capt. and Brevet Major, Royal Field Artillery.
COSTIN, ERIC BOYD, Capt. (Temporary Major), West Yorkshire Regt.
COTGRAVE, THOMAS SCOTT, Major (Acting Lieut.-Colonel), Army Service Corps.
COTTEE, HERBERT, Second Lieut. (Acting Major), Royal Field Artillery.

COTTER, EDMOND BRIAN, Major (Acting Lieut.-Colonel), Royal Garrison Artillery.
COTTRELL, ARTHUR FOULKES BAGLIETTO, Capt. (Acting Major), Royal Field Artillery.
COX, FRANK THOMAS, Temporary Major, Army Service Corps.
COX, WILLIAM THOMAS, Lieut.-Colonel, Royal Field Artillery.
CRAIG, NEWMAN LOMBARD, Capt. (Temporary Major), Army Service Corps.
CRELLIN, WILLIAM ANDERSON WATSON, Capt. (Temporary Major), Nottinghamshire and Derbyshire Regt.
CRIPPS, CHARLES WILLIAM, Major, Royal Field Artillery.
CROSBIE, JOHN PATRICK GLANDORE, Major (Temporary Lieut.-Colonel), Rifle Brigade.
CROUCH, ERNEST, Second Lieut. (Acting Major), Durham Light Infantry.
CUMMING, HANWAY ROBERT, Lieut.-Colonel (Temporary Brigadier-General), Durham Light Infantry.
CUNNINGHAM, JOHN SYDNEY, Major, Middlesex Regt.
DANIELSEN, JOHN WILLIAM, Temporary Major (Acting Lieut.-Colonel), Royal Engineers (Capt., Royal Engineers, T.F.).
DARELL, LIONEL EDWARD HAMILTON MARMADUKE, Major, Life Guards.
DARLINGTON, ARTHUR JAMES, Major, Royal Engineers.
DAVIE, KEITH MAITLAND, Lieut.-Colonel, Gloucestershire Regt.
DAVSON, HARRY MILLER, Lieut.-Colonel, Royal Field Artillery.
DAWSON, HENRY KING, M.D., Capt. (Acting Lieut.-Colonel), Royal Army Medical Corps.
DAY, ROBERT WILLIAM, Temporary Major, General List, late Army Service Corps.
DE LA PRYME, PERCY CHRISTOPHER, Major (Temporary Lieut.-Colonel), Army Service Corps.
DELME-MURRAY, GEORGE ARTHUR, Major, Shropshire Light Infantry.
DICK, THOMAS SYDNEY, Temporary Major, Machine Gun Corps.
DICKENSON, REV. LENTHALL GREVILLE, Temporary Chaplain to the Forces, 3rd Class, Army Chaplains' Department (surname changed to Trotman-Dickenson).
DICKINSON, DOUGLAS POVAH, M.C., Capt., Welsh Regt.
DINWIDDIE, MELVILLE, M.C., Capt., Gordon Highlanders.
DOBBS, RICHARD CONWAY, Major, Royal Irish Fusiliers.
DOLPHIN, EDWARD JAMES, Capt., London Regt.
DONE, REGINALD JOHN, Major (Acting Lieut.-Colonel), Royal Engineers.
DONNELLY, THOMAS, Capt. (Acting Major), Royal Garrison Artillery.
DONOVAN, STEPHEN JOHN, Major (Acting Lieut.-Colonel), Army Service Corps.
DORMAN, LESLIE CLAUD, Major (Temporary Lieut.-Colonel), Worcestershire Regt.
DOUGLAS-JONES, STANLEY DOUGLAS, M.C., Capt., Royal Garrison Artillery.
DOWNEY, JOSEPH ALOYSIUS, Temporary Major, Durham Light Infantry.
DRESSER, PERCY BATES, Capt. (Acting Lieut.-Colonel), Royal Field Artillery.
DREW, JAMES SYME, M.C., Major, Cameron Highlanders.
DUNBAR, BENJAMIN HOWARD VELLA, M.D., Major (Temporary Lieut.-Colonel), Royal Army Medical Corps.
DUNCAN, JAMES FERGUS, Temporary Lieut.-Colonel, Royal Artillery (Capt., T.F.).
DUNDAS, JAMES COLIN, Major, Royal Field Artillery.
DUNLOP, ROBERT WILLIAM LAYARD, Temporary Lieut.-Colonel, Royal Field Artillery (Lieut.-Colonel and Honorary Colonel, Bombay Volunteer Rifles).
DUNNINGTON-JEFFERSON, JOHN ALEXANDER, Capt. and Brevet Major, Royal Fusiliers.
DU PORT, OSMOND CHARTERIS, Major (Temporary Lieut.-Colonel), Retired Pay, late Royal Artillery.
DUTTON, RICHARD BROADHURST, Major (Temporary Lieut.-Colonel), Royal Engineers.
DWYER, JAMES JAMESON, Temporary Capt., Royal Army Medical Corps.
DYSON, LOUIS MORGAN, Major (Temporary Lieut.-Colonel), Retired Pay, late Royal Artillery.
EDGEWORTH, KENNETH ESSEX, M.C., Major (Acting Lieut.-Colonel) Royal Engineers.
EDWARDS, HENRY MOLESWORTH, Capt. and Brevet Major, Royal Engineers.
ELKINGTON, ROBERT JAMES GOODALL, C.M.G., Lieut.-Colonel (Temporary Brigadier-General), Royal Artillery.
ELLIOTT, WILLIAM, Major (Temporary Lieut.-Colonel), Army Service Corps.
ELLIS, SHERMAN GORDON VENN, Major, West India Regt. (West India Regiment corrected to Indian Army [London Gazette, 18 July, 1917]).
ELTON, GORDON DAUBENY GRESLEY, M.C., Capt., Royal Irish Fusiliers.
ELVERY, PHILIP GORDON MOSS, M.C., Capt. (Acting Lieut.-Colonel), Royal Army Medical Corps.
ENGLISH, ERNEST ROBERT MALING, Major, Shropshire Light Infantry.
EVANS, EDWARD GEORGE, Lieut.-Colonel, Army Service Corps.
EVANS, FRANK SULIS, Temporary Major (Acting Lieut.-Colonel), Royal Field Artillery.
EYRE, MORELAND STANHOPE, Lieut.-Colonel, Royal Garrison Artillery.
FAIR, CHARLES HENRY, Major, Rhodesia Police.
FAIRCLOUGH, ERIC, Capt. (Temporary Major), South Lancashire Regt.
FALKNER, ERIC FELTON, Major, Army Service Corps.
FANE, OCTAVIUS EDWARD, M.C., Capt. (Acting Major), Royal Garrison Artillery.
FARMER, CYRIL, M.C., Capt. (Acting Major), Royal Field Artillery.
FAWCETT, PERCY HARRISON, Major (Temporary Lieut.-Colonel), Retired Pay, Reserve of Officers, late Royal Garrison Artillery.
FAWCUS, HAROLD BENN, C.M.G., M.B., Lieut.-Colonel, Royal Army Medical Corps.

FEILDING, ROWLAND CHARLES, Capt. (Temporary Lieut.-Colonel), Coldstream Guards, Special Reserve.
FELL, LOUIS FREDERICK RUDSTON, Capt. (Temporary Major), Royal Flying Corps, Special Reserve.
FENTON, GEORGE CECIL VERNER, Major, Royal Engineers.
FESSENDEN, JOHN HAMPDEN, Major (Temporary Lieut.-Colonel), Army Service Corps.
FIFE, RONALD D'ARCY, C.M.G., Major (Temporary Lieut.-Colonel), Retired Pay, late Yorkshire Regt.
FINCH, HAMILTON WALTER EDWARD, Lieut.-Colonel (Temporary Brigadier-General), Middlesex Regt.
FITZMAURICE, ROBERT, Lieut.-Colonel, Royal Field Artillery.
FLEMING, VALENTINE, Major, Yeomanry.
FRASER, ALEXANDER DONALD, M.C., M.B., Capt. (Acting Lieut.-Colonel), Royal Army Medical Corps.
FRASER, REV. DONALD, Temporary Chaplain to the Forces, 3rd Class, Army Chaplains' Department.
FRASER, HENRY, Major, Royal Field Artillery.
FRAZER, WILLIAM POOLEY BICKERTON, Capt., Royal Inniskilling Fusiliers.
FRIZELL, CHARLES WILLIAM, M.C., Capt. (Acting Lieut.-Colonel), Royal Berkshire Regt.
FULTON, HERBERT ALBRECHT, Major (Temporary Lieut.-Colonel), Worcestershire Regt. (Christian name corrected to Herbert Angus).
FUNNELL, HARRY ERNEST, Temporary Lieut.-Commander, Royal Naval Volunteer Reserve (Christian name corrected to Harry Edward).
GAILEY, JAMES HAMILTON, Temporary Major, Unattached List, East Africa Protectorate Forces.
GALBRAITH, JAMES EDWARD EVANS, Capt., Royal Fusiliers.
GARDNER, JAMES ANTHONY, Major, Royal Garrison Artillery.
GARNETT, WILLIAM BROOKSBANK, Major, Royal Welsh Fusiliers (corrected to Major (Temporary Lieut.-Colonel), Royal Irish Fusiliers).
GASK, GEORGE ERNEST, F.R.C.S., L.R.C.P., Major, Royal Army Medical Corps.
GIBBS, JOHN ANGEL, Temporary Capt. (Acting Major), Welsh Regt.
GIFFARD, GEORGE JAMES, Capt. (Acting Lieut.-Colonel), Royal West Surrey Regt.
GILCHRIST, HECTOR GORDON, M.C., Temporary Capt., Royal Engineers (Lieut., Royal Engineers, T.F.).
GILL, JAMES GEOFFREY, Lieut.-Colonel (Acting Colonel), Royal Army Medical Corps.
GILLAM, JOHN GRAHAM, Temporary Major, Army Service Corps.
GILLIBRAND, ALBERT, Temporary Major, Army Service Corps (Capt., Army Service Corps, T.F.).
GIRDLESTONE, REV. FREDERICK STANLEY PEARS LYNN, M.A., Temporary Chaplain to the Forces, 3rd Class, Army Chaplains' Department.
GODDARD, GERALD HAMILTON, Lieut.-Colonel, Royal Army Medical Corps.
GODFREY, WALTER, Temporary Major (Acting Lieut.-Colonel), Welsh Regt.
GODMAN, ARTHUR LOWTHIAN, Major, Yorkshire Regt. and Royal Flying Corps.
GOLDING, JOHN, Capt., Royal Army Medical Corps.
GOODWIN, HARVEY, Major, Middlesex Regt.
GORDON, WILLIAM FANSHAWE LOUDON, Major and Brevet Lieut.-Colonel (Temporary Lieut.-Colonel), Norfolk Regt.
GORT, VISCOUNT, JOHN STANDISH SURTEES PRENDERGAST VEREKER, M.V.O., M.C., Capt, and Brevet Major, Grenadier Guards.
GOSLING, SEYMOUR FREDERICK, Major (Temporary Lieut.-Colonel), Retired List, late Royal Artillery.
GOWLLAND, EDWARD LAKE, M.B., Temporary Major (Temporary Lieut.-Colonel), Royal Army Medical Corps (late Major, Royal Garrison Artillery T.F.).
GRAHAM, LORD DOUGLAS MALISE, M.C., Major, Royal Artillery.
GRAHAM, OGILVIE BLAIR, Capt. (Temporary Major), Rifle Brigade.
GRAHAM, REGINALD GUY, Major, Yorkshire Regt.
GRANGE, GEORGE ROCHFORD, M.C., Capt. (Temporary Major), Royal Engineers.
GRANT-DALTON, DUNCAN, Major (Temporary Lieut.-Colonel), West Yorkshire Regt.
GRANT-THOROLD, RICHARD STIRLING, Temporary Lieut.-Colonel, Welsh Regt.
GREEN, CHARLES JAMES SALKELD, M.C., Major, London Regt.
GREEN-WILKINSON, LEWIS FREDERIC, Major and Brevet Colonel (Temporary Brigadier-General), Retired Pay, late Rifle Brigade.
GREENE, JOHN, Capt. (Temporary Lieut.-Colonel), Dragoon Guards.
GREENLEY, WILLIAM ALFRED, Temporary Major, Army Service Corps.
GREER, FREDERICK AUGUSTUS, Lieut.-Colonel, Royal Irish Fusiliers.
GREVILLE, CHARLES HENRY, Capt., Grenadier Guards.
GRIERSON, WILLIAM ALEXANDER, Lieut. (Acting Major), North Lancashire Regt.
GRIFFIN, PETER GERALD, Major, Royal Field Artillery, Special Reserve.
GRIMWOOD, REGINALD FRANCIS, Capt., London Regt.
GROSE, DANIEL CHARLES EVANS, Lieut.-Colonel, Army Service Corps.
GROSS, ROBERT FERGUSON, Major (Temporary Lieut.-Colonel), South Wales Borderers.
HAIG-BROWN, ALAN RODERICK, Temporary Colonel, Unattached List (Commanding Battn. Middlesex Regt.).
HALL, DOUGLAS KEITH ELPHINSTONE, Major and Brevet Lieut.-Colonel (Temporary Lieut.-Colonel), Retired List, late Dorset Regt., Special Reserve.
HALL, HAROLD FLINTOFF, Capt. (Temporary Major), Royal Field Artillery.
HALLWARD, BERNARD MARSHAM, Second Lieut. (Temporary Major), Rifle Brigade, Special Reserve.
HAMILTON, GEORGE THEODORE, Major (Temporary Lieut.-Colonel), Royal Artillery.

The Distinguished Service Order

HAMMERTON, GEORGE HERBERT LEONARD, Major (Temporary Lieut.-Colonel), Royal Army Medical Corps.
HARDY, SYDNEY JAMES, Capt., Dragoons.
HARMAN, HENRY ALEXANDER AUGUSTUS FRANCIS, Capt. (Temporary Major), South Staffordshire Regt., Special Reserve.
HARRIS, EDWARD TEMPLE, M.B., Major, Indian Medical Service.
HARRISON, ARTHUR LIONEL, Temporary Major, Machine Gun Corps.
HART, GEORGE ALFRED, Second Lieut. (Acting Major), Royal Field Artillery.
HARTLEY, ALAN FLEMING, Capt. (Acting Major), Indian Army (rank corrected to Major (acting Lieut.-Colonel).
HAWES, GEORGE ERNEST, M.C., Major, Royal Fusiliers.
HAY, GEORGE LENNOX, Capt. (Temporary Lieut.-Colonel), Army Ordnance Department.
HAYES, WILLIAM, Capt. (Temporary Major), Royal West Surrey Regt.
HEATH, CHARLES PHILIP, Lieut. (Temporary Major), Royal Garrison Artillery.
HEDGES, KILLINGWORTH MICHAEL FENTHAM, Capt., Army Service Corps.
HEMELRYK, EDWARD VALENTINE, Major, Royal Field Artillery.
HENEAGE, ARTHUR PELHAM, Major, Royal Field Artillery.
HENVEY, RALPH, Lieut.-Colonel, Royal Artillery.
HERMON, ERNEST WILLIAM, Major (Temporary Lieut.-Colonel), Retired Pay, late Hussars (Christian name corrected to Edward William).
HERMON-HODGE, ROLAND HERMON, M.V.O., Capt. (Temporary Major), late Grenadier Guards.
HERRICK, HENRY, Lieut.-Colonel (Acting Colonel), Royal Army Medical Corps.
HERVEY-BATHURST, SIR FREDERICK EDWARD WILLIAM, Capt., Retired Pay, late Grenadier Guards.
HEWITT, RUPERT PATON, Temporary Major, Army Service Corps.
HEYLAND, HECTOR MILES, Capt. (Temporary Major), King's Royal Rifle Corps, Special Reserve.
HEYWOOD, MARCUS BERESFORD, M.B., Second Lieut. (Temporary Capt.) Yeomanry (correction, M.B. deleted [London Gazette, 9 Sept., 1917]).
HICKLING, HORACE CYRIL BENJAMIN, M.C., Temporary Capt. (Temporary Major), Royal Engineers.
HIGGINBOTHAM, THOMAS ALBERT, Lieut.-Colonel, Royal Field Artillery (surname corrected to Higginbottom [London Gazette, 18 July, 1917]).
HILDRETH, HAROLD CROSSLEY, F.R.C.S., Major (Temporary Lieut.-Colonel), Royal Army Medical Corps.
HILL, CLIFFORD, Major, East African Mounted Rifles.
HILL, DAVID JOHN JACKSON, Major (Temporary Colonel), Army Ordnance Department.
HILL, EDWARD RODEN, Lieut.-Colonel (Temporary Brigadier-General), Highland Light Infantry.
HINDLE, RALPH, Lieut.-Colonel, North Lancashire Regt.
HOARE, CHARLES HERVEY, Capt., Yeomanry.
HODGSON, PHILIP EGERTON, Major (Acting Lieut.-Colonel), Royal Engineers.
HODSON, EDMOND ADAIR, Capt. (Temporary Major), Rifle Brigade.
HOOD, EDWARD THESIGNER FRANKLAND, Major, Yeomanry (Temporary Major, Royal Field Artillery).
HOPKINS, LEWIS EGERTON, Major (Acting Lieut.-Colonel), Royal Engineers.
HOPWOOD, ALFRED HENRY, Major, Lincolnshire Regt.
HORN, ROBERT, M.C., Major (Temporary Lieut.-Colonel), Seaforth Highlanders.
HORWOOD, WILLIAM THOMAS FRANCIS, Capt. and Brevet Major (Temporary Brigadier-General), Retired Pay, late Lancers.
HOWKINS, CYRIL HENRY, Lieut.-Colonel, Royal Army Medical Corps.
HUDSON, NOEL, Capt. and Brevet Major (Acting Major), Royal Garrison Artillery.
HUGHES, HERBERT FRANCIS, Temporary Major, Army Service Corps.
HUME, JOHN ELGAR, Capt. (Temporary Major), Connaught Rangers.
HUNTER, JOHN, Temporary Capt. (Acting Major), Highland Light Infantry.
HUSKISSON, WILLIAM GORDON, Major (Temporary Lieut.-Colonel), Army Service Corps.
HUTCHINS, SAMUEL, Major (Temporary Lieut.-Colonel), Army Service Corps.
ILES, FREDERIC ARTHUR, Major (Acting Lieut.-Colonel), Royal Engineers.
IONIDES, PHILIP DENIS, Temporary Major, Middlesex Regt.
IRVINE, RICHARD ABERCROMBIE, C.M.G., Temporary Lieut.-Colonel, Commanding Battn., Lancashire Fusiliers (Honorary Major, Unattached List, late Militia).
JACKSON, ARCHIBALD HARDIE KNOWLES, M.C., Capt., Royal Warwickshire Regt.
JACKSON, ARNOLD NUGENT STRODE, Capt. (Acting Major), North Lancashire Regt. (name changed to Arnold Nugent Strode Strode-Jackson).
JACKSON, LAMBERT CAMERON, C.M.G., Major and Brevet Lieut.-Colonel (Temporary Lieut.-Colonel), Royal Engineers.
JANSON, JAMES THEODORE, Temporary Major, Yorkshire Light Infantry.
JARVIS, TALBOT McLEAVY, Temporary Major (Acting Lieut.-Colonel), Royal West Surrey Regt. (late Capt., 1st Royal Engineers Bedfordshire Volunteers).
JATAR, NILKRANTH SKRIRAM, Lieut., Indian Medical Service.
JAY, CHARLES DOUGLAS, Temporary Major, Machine Gun Corps.
JENNINGS, WALTON, Lieut.-Colonel, Royal Garrison Artillery.
JOHNSTON, ALEXANDER COLIN, M.C., Capt. and Brevet Major (Temporary Lieut.-Colonel), Worcestershire Regt.
JOHNSTON, HARRISON, Temporary Major, Cheshire Regt.
JOHNSON, PHILIP HENRY, Temporary Capt. (Acting Major), Machine Gun Corps.
JONES, BERNARD MOUNT, Temporary Capt., General List (Christian name corrected to Bernard Mouat).
KAY, REV. DAVID MILLER, Temporary Chaplain to the Forces, 3rd Class, Army Chaplains' Department.
KEDDIE, HERBERT WILLIAM GRAHAM, Lieut.-Colonel (Temporary Colonel), Army Ordnance Department.
KEITH, GEORGE THEODORE ELPHINSTONE, Capt., Royal Lancaster Regt.
KELLY, COURTENAY RUSSELL, Major and Brevet Lieut.-Colonel (Acting Lieut.-Colonel), Royal Garrison Artillery.
KELLY, WILLIAM DAVENPORT CRAWLEY, Major (Temporary Lieut.-Colonel), Royal Army Medical Corps.
KEMPSTER, REV. IVOR T., Temporary Chaplain to the Forces, 3rd Class, Army Chaplains' Department.
KENNEDY, JAMES, Lieut. (Acting Lieut.-Colonel), Royal Highlanders.
KENNEDY, NORMAN, Major, Royal Scots Fusiliers.
KENTISH, LEONARD WILLIAM, Capt., Royal Fusiliers, Special Reserve.
KERANS, EDWARD THOMAS JOHN, Capt. and Brevet Major (Temporary Lieut.-Colonel), Worcestershire Regt.
KEYWORTH, ROBERT GEOFFREY, Lieut.-Colonel, Royal Horse Artillery.
KINDERSLEY, DOUGLAS, Capt., Highland Light Infantry, Special Reserve.
KINGSMILL, ANDREW DE PORTAL, M.C., Capt. (Temporary Lieut.-Colonel), Reserve of Officers, late Grenadier Guards.
KIRBY, HAROLD, Major, Army Veterinary Corps.
KIRBY, WILLIAM LEWIS CLARK, Capt., Lancers.
KIRKPATRICK, HUGH CUNNINGHAM BRUCE, M.C., Capt., King's Own Scottish Borderers.
KIRKWOOD, JAMES RAMSAY NOTMAN, Temporary Major, Royal Engineers.
KITCHING, CHARLES HENRY, Capt. (Temporary Lieut.-Colonel), Retired Pay, Worcestershire Regt., Special Reserve.
KNAPP, REV. SIMON STOCK, M.C., Temporary Chaplain to the Forces, 3rd Class, Army Chaplains' Department.
KNIGHT, HENRY LEWKENO, Major and Brevet Lieut.-Colonel (Temporary Lieut.-Colonel), Royal Irish Fusiliers.
KNYVETT, FRANK BERNERS, Temporary Major, Royal Field Artillery.
KUHNE, CARL HANS, Temporary Major, Army Service Corps.
KYRKE, HENRY VERNON VENABLES, Major, Royal Welsh Fusiliers.
LAIRD, KENNETH MACGREGOR, Major, Argyll and Sutherland Highlanders
LAMONBY, ISAAC WANNOP, Temporary Major, Royal Engineers.
LANDEN, ARTHUR, Quartermaster and Honorary Major, Northumberland Fusiliers.
LANDON, CECIL WESTMORE, Temporary Major, Army Service Corps.
LANDON, JOSEPH HERBERT ARTHUR, Capt. (Temporary Major), Essex Regt. and Royal Flying Corps.
LANGFORD, EDWARD GILLIAT, Major, Royal Field Artillery.
LANGLEY, ARTHUR WINTON, M.C., Capt. (Acting Major), Royal Garrison Artillery (Christian name corrected to Arthur Wynton [London Gazette, 18 June, 1917]).
LARKIN, JOHN PETER, Temporary Capt. (Acting Major), King's Own Scottish Borderers.
LAST, ARTHUR JOHN, Honorary Major (Temporary Honorary Lieut.-Colonel), Army Ordnance Department.
LAWRENSON, REGINALD ROBERT, Major (Temporary Lieut.-Colonel), West Indian Regt.
LEAH, THOMAS COULSON, Major, Royal Garrison Artillery.
LECKY, MARCUS DALY, Capt. (Acting Major), Royal Garrison Artillery.
LEE, JAMES, Temporary Capt., General List.
LEFROY, HUGH PERCIVAL THOMSON, M.C., Major, Royal Engineers.
LENEY, CLAUD, Capt. (Temporary Major), Royal Garrison Artillery.
LEVENTHORPE, GRAHAM SYDNEY, Capt. (Acting Major), Royal Field Artillery.
LEWIS, HAROLD VICTOR, M.C., Capt., Indian Army.
LEWIS, WILLIAM ALFRED, Major, Monmouthshire Regt.
LEWIS, WILLIAM HERBERT, M.C., Capt. (Acting Lieut.-Colonel), Royal Garrison Artillery.
LIDDELL, ARTHUR ROBERT, Lieut.-Colonel, Army Service Corps.
LIGHTSTONE, HYMAN, M.C., Capt., Royal Army Medical Corps (Christian name corrected to Herbert).
LINDEMAN, CHARLES LIONEL, Temporary Major, General List (surname corrected to Lindemann).
LINDSAY, GEORGE MACKINTOSH, Major, Rifle Brigade.
LITTLE, WILLIAM BENJAMIN, M.C., Capt. (Acting Major), East Lancashire Regt.
LITTLEJOHNS, ARCHIBALD SMITH, Capt. (Acting Lieut.-Colonel), Royal Army Medical Corps.
LLOYD, GLYN, Capt., Army Veterinary Corps, Special Reserve.
LLOYD, JOHN HENRY, Major and Brevet Lieut.-Colonel (Temporary Brigadier-General), Royal Lancaster Regt., Special Reserve, Retired Pay.
LOCKHART-JERVIS, BERESFORD CLAYTON, Temporary Capt. (Acting Major), Royal Engineers.
LOGAN, DAVID DALE, M.D., Temporary Lieut.-Colonel, Royal Army Medical Corps.
LOMER, GODFREY, Temporary Capt. (Acting Major), Royal Field Artillery.
LORAINE, ROBERT, M.C., Capt. (Temporary Lieut.-Colonel), Royal Flying Corps, Special Reserve.
LORD, FRANK BAIGRIE, Lieut.-Colonel, Army Service Corps.
LUCK, BRIAN JOHN MICHAEL, Major, Royal Garrison Artillery.
LUMSDEN, ALFRED FORBES, Major (Acting Lieut.-Colonel), Royal Scots.
LUND, OTTO MARLING, Capt. (Acting Major), Royal Field Artillery.
LUNDIE, ROBERT CHARLES, Lieut. (Acting Major), Royal Engineers, Special Reserve.
LYELL, DAVID, Temporary Capt. (Temporary Colonel), Royal Engineers.
LYON, CYRIL ARTHUR, Major, Royal Garrison Artillery.
McCARTHY, JAMES JOSEPH, M.C., Major, Rhodesia Police.
McCLINTOCK, STANLEY ROBERT, Major (Temporary Lieut.-Colonel), Gordon Highlanders.

McCONNEL, DOUGLAS FITZGERALD, Capt. (Acting Major), Royal Field Artillery.
McGILDOWNY, WILLIAM, Capt. and Honorary Major (Temporary Major), Retired List, late Royal Garrison Artillery, Special Reserve.
McKAIG, JOHN BICKERTON, Capt. (Acting Lieut.-Colonel), Liverpool Regt.
MACKENZIE, DOUGLAS WILLIAM ALEXANDER DALZIEL, Capt., Seaforth Highlanders.
MACKESSACK, PETER, M.B., Lieut.-Colonel (Temporary Colonel), Royal Army Medical Corps.
MACKIE, GEORGE, Capt. (Acting Lieut.-Colonel), Royal Army Medical Corps.
MACKIE, JAMES CAMPBELL, Honorary Capt., Army Service Corps.
MACLEOD, NORMAN, Temporary Major, Cameron Highlanders.
McQUEEN, JOHN ARTHUR, M.C., Major, Royal Engineers.
McQUEEN, NORMAN, Capt. (Temporary Major), Argyll and Sutherland Highlanders, Special Reserve.
MADOCKS, WILLIAM ROBARTS NAPIER, C.M.G., Lieut.-Colonel, Royal Field Artillery.
MAGILL, ROBERT, M.B., Capt. (Acting Lieut.-Colonel), Royal Army Medical Corps, Special Reserve.
MAGRATH, MEYRICK MYLER, Capt. (Acting Major), Royal Field Artillery.
MAHON, BRIAN McMAHON, M.C., Capt., London Regt.
MAINGUY, ROGER FERDINAND, Major, Royal Engineers.
MAITLAND, REGINALD CHARLES FREDERICK, Major, Royal Horse Artillery.
MALET, HARRY CHARLES, Capt. (Temporary Lieut.-Colonel), Hussars, Special Reserve (Capt., Retired Pay).
MANNING, ROBERT CHARLES, M.C., Temporary Lieut. (Acting Major), Royal Engineers.
MARRACK, JOHN RICHARDSON, M.C., M.B., Temporary Capt., Royal Army Medical Corps.
MARRIOTT, EDWIN WALTER PURDY VERE, Lieut.-Colonel, Royal Army Medical Corps.
MARRIOTT, JOHN CHARLES OAKES, M.C., Lieut. (Temporary Capt.), Northamptonshire Regt.
MARSH, HOPTON ELIOTT, Lieut.-Colonel, Royal Garrison Artillery.
MARSHALL, EDWARD HILLIS, Lieut. (Temporary Major), Royal Field Artillery.
MARTIN, CUTHBERT THOMAS, Major (Acting Lieut.-Colonel), Highland Light Infantry.
MARTIN, HUGH, Temporary Capt. (Acting Major), Royal Field Artillery.
MASCALL, MAURICE EDWARD, Major, Royal Garrison Artillery.
MASSY, HUGH ROYDS STOKES, M.C., Major, Royal Field Artillery.
MASTER, GEORGE, Major, Royal Engineers.
MATHESON, ARCHIBALD, Temporary Capt., Royal Engineers, Special Reserve.
MATHIAS, THOMAS GILBERT, Major (Acting Lieut.-Colonel), Welsh Regt.
MATTHEWS, JOHN, Major (Temporary Lieut.-Colonel), Royal Army Medical Corps.
MEADE, GUY WARREN, M.C., Major, Royal Field Artillery.
MELLARD, REGINALD WILLIAM, Capt. (Temporary Major), Army Veterinary Corps.
MENZIES, JOHN, Major (Temporary Lieut.-Colonel), Highland Light Infantry.
MESSER, ARTHUR ALBERT, Temporary Lieut.-Colonel, Graves Registration Section.
MIDDLETON, WILLIAM HENRY, Major, Hampshire Regt.
MILES, ERIC GRANT, M.C., Capt., King's Own Scottish Borderers.
MILLER, CHARLES FREDERICK, Temporary Major, Duke of Cornwall's Light Infantry.
MILLS, GEORGE PILKINGTON, Temporary Major (Temporary Lieut.-Colonel), Bedfordshire Regt.
MILWARD, CLEMENT ARTHUR, Major (Acting Lieut.-Colonel), Indian Army.
MOIR, ALAN JAMES GORDON, Major and Brevet Lieut.-Colonel (Temporary Lieut.-Colonel), Royal Scots.
MOLLOY, LEONARD GREENHAM STAR, Major, Yeomanry.
MOLONY, WALTER WILLIAM, Major (Temporary Lieut.-Colonel), Army Service Corps.
MONCK-MASON, ROGER HENRY, Lieut.-Colonel, Royal Munster Fusiliers.
MONCKTON-ARUNDELL, THE HONOURABLE GEORGE VERE ARUNDELL, Major, Life Guards.
MOORE, REV. CHARLES WILFRED GWENNAP, M.A., Temporary Chaplain, Royal Navy.
MOORE, HERBERT DURIE, Major, Indian Army.
MORDAUNT, OSBERT CAUTLEY, Major (Acting Lieut.-Colonel), Somersetshire Light Infantry.
MORETON, PERCY CLIFFORD REYNOLDS, Capt. (Temporary Major), Royal Monmouthshire Engineers, Special Reserve.
MORGAN, FRANCIS ALAN STEWART, Major, Royal Garrison Artillery.
MORGAN, JOHN WILLIAM MOORE, Lieut.-Colonel, Army Service Corps.
MORGAN, WILLIAM HENRY, Second Lieut. (Acting Major), Royal Engineers Special Reserve.
MORIARITY, OISIN EVELEIGH, Temporary Lieut. (Temporary Capt.), Royal Field Artillery (late Lieut., Royal Garrison Artillery, Special Reserve).
MORRIS, ALFRED, Capt. (Temporary Major), Royal Fusiliers.
MORRIS, CHARLES READE MONROE, M.B., Capt. (Acting Lieut.-Colonel), Royal Army Medical Corps.
MORRIS, JOSEPH, Capt. (Temporary Major), Machine Gun Corps.
MUIRHEAD, JOHN ARTHUR, Capt. (Temporary Major), Indian Army.
MURCHISON, KENNETH DUNCAN, M.B., Capt. (Acting Lieut.-Colonel), Royal Army Medical Corps, Special Reserve.
MURRAY, JOHN ALEXANDER SHAKESPEAR, Lieut.-Colonel, Army Ordnance Corps.
MURRAY, WILLIAM ATHOL, Major, Royal Horse Artillery.

MURRAY-WHITE, RICHARD STEPHEN, Capt. (Temporary Lieut.-Colonel), Yeomanry.
NAISMITH, JOHN OLIVER, Capt. (Acting Major), Royal Field Artillery, Special Reserve.
NAPIER-CLAVERING, NOEL WARREN, Capt. (Acting Major), Royal Engineers.
NATION, JOHN JAMES HENRY, Major and Brevet Lieut.-Colonel (Temporary Colonel), Royal Engineers.
NEILL, FREDERICK AUSTIN, Capt. (Acting Major), Royal Engineers.
NEILSON, JOHN BEAUMONT, Major, Highland Light Infantry.
NEWBOLD, CHARLES JOSEPH, Temporary Capt., Royal Engineers.
NEWTON, HENRY LEIGH, Lieut. (Temporary Major), Royal Field Artillery.
NICOL, GEORGE GORDON, Temporary Capt. (Acting Major), Royal Engineers (rank and regiment corrected to Captain (Acting Major), Gordon Highlanders, attached R.E. [London Gazette, 18 July, 1917]).
NORMAN, COMPTON CARDEW, Major (Temporary Lieut.-Colonel), Royal Welsh Fusiliers.
NORNABELL, HENRY MARSHAL, Major, Royal Field Artillery.
NORTH, CYRIL BURTON, M.C., Temporary Lieut. (Temporary Major), Royal Engineers.
O'CARROLL, ARTHUR DROUGHT, M.B., Capt. (Acting Lieut.-Colonel), Royal Army Medical Corps.
OGLE, EDMUND CHALONER, Major (Temporary Lieut.-Colonel), West India Regt.
O'GRADY, STANDISH DE COURCY, M.B., Lieut.-Colonel (Temporary Colonel), Royal Army Medical Corps.
OLDHAM, FREDERICK HUGH LANGTON, Major, Royal Artillery.
ONSLOW, CRANLEY CHARLTON, C.M.G., Lieut.-Colonel (Temporary Brigadier-General), Bedfordshire Regt.
ORGAN, CHARLES ALEXANDER, Major, Army Service Corps.
ORMSTON, ERNEST WILLIAM, Temporary Capt. (Acting Major), Royal Engineers.
OUCHTERLONY, JOHN PALGRAVE HEATHCOTE, Major, Royal Engineers.
OWEN, DOUGLAS CHARLES, Major, Middlesex Regt.
PAINTER, GORDON WHISTLER ARNAUD, Lieut. (Acting Major), Royal Garrison Artillery.
PALLIN, WILLIAM ALFRED, F.R.C.V.S., Major (Temporary Colonel), Army Veterinary Corps.
PALMER, ALBERT JOHN, Major, Yeomanry.
PALMER, ALEXANDER EDWARD GUY, M.C., Capt., Yorkshire Regt.
PANET, ALPHONSE EUGENE, C.M.G., Lieut.-Colonel (Temporary Brigadier-General), Royal Engineers.
PARBURY, KEITH, Major, Royal Field Artillery.
PARSONS, WILLIAM FORSTER, Major, Royal Field Artillery.
PARSONS, WILLIAM FREDERIC, Major (Acting Lieut.-Colonel), Retired List, late Royal Field Artillery.
PASCOE, JAMES SYDNEY, Major, Royal Army Medical Corps.
PASKE, GEORGE FREDERICK, Major and Honorary Lieut.-Colonel, Oxfordshire and Buckinghamshire Light Infantry, Special Reserve.
PAULL, JOHN HICKS, Temporary Major (local Lieut.-Colonel), General List.
PAYNE, FRANK GERVAS, Temporary Major, Machine Gun Corps.
PEARLESS, CHARLES WILLIAM, Major and Brevet Lieut.-Colonel (Temporary Lieut.-Colonel), South Wales Borderers.
PEARSON, HAROLD LESLIE, Capt. (Temporary Major), Royal Field Artillery.
PEEBLES, HERBERT WALTER, Capt. (Temporary Major), Retired List, late Army Service Corps.
PEEL, THE HONOURABLE SIDNEY CORNWALLIS, Lieut.-Colonel, Yeomanry.
PEEL, WILLIAM RALPH, Temporary Major, Yorkshire Regt.
PERCEVAL, CHRISTOPHER PETER WESTBY, Capt. (Acting Major), Royal Field Artillery.
PERCY, LORD WILLIAM RICHARD, Capt. (Temporary Major), Grenadier Guards, Special Reserve.
PHILLIPS, FRANK ROFF, Major, Royal Artillery.
PHILLIPS, NOEL CLIVE, M.C., Capt. (Acting Lieut.-Colonel), North Lancashire Regt., Special Reserve.
PORTAL, JOHN LESLIE, Capt. (Temporary Major), Oxfordshire and Buckinghamshire Light Infantry.
PORTER, WILLIAM GUTHRIE, Capt. (Acting Major), Royal Field Artillery.
POTT, EDWARD HELME, Capt. (Temporary Major), Indian Army.
POWELL, JOHN EDWARD, Major (Temporary Lieut.-Colonel), Royal Army Medical Corps.
PRESCOTT-DECIE, CYRIL, Lieut.-Colonel (Temporary Brigadier-General), Royal Artillery.
PRESTON, THE HONOURABLE RICHARD MARTIN PETER, Major, Honourable Artillery Company.
PRESTON-WHYTE, ROBERT PRESTON, Temporary Major (Acting Lieut.-Colonel), Somersetshire Light Infantry.
PRICE, OWEN LLOYD, Major, Royal Garrison Artillery.
PRIESTLEY, JOSEPH HUBERT, Capt., Unattached List.
PRIOR, BERNARD HENRY LEATHES, Lieut.-Colonel, Norfolk Regt.
PRYCE, CARYL AP RHYS, Temporary Capt. (Acting Major), Royal Field Artillery.
PRYCE, HENRY EDWARD AP RHYS, C.M.G., Major and Brevet Lieut.-Colonel (Temporary Lieut.-Colonel), Indian Army.
PRYCE-JONES, HENRY MORRIS, M.C., Major (Temporary Lieut.-Colonel), Coldstream Guards.
PRYER, ALFRED AMOS, Capt., Army Veterinary Corps.
PUDDICOMBE, THOMAS PHARE, M.B., Major (Temporary Lieut.-Colonel), Royal Army Medical Corps.
PUGH, DAVID CHARLES, Lieut.-Colonel, Royal Artillery.
PUMPHREY, ARNOLD, Temporary Capt., Durham Light Infantry.

The Distinguished Service Order

PYM, REV. THOMAS WENTWORTH, Temporary Chaplain to the Forces, 3rd Class, Army Chaplains' Department.
PYMAN, GEOFFREY LEE, Temporary Capt., Yorkshire Light Infantry.
PYNE, FREDERICK SPARKE, Capt. (Acting Major), Royal Field Artillery.
RAMSBOTTOM, GORDON OPENSHAW, Temporary Major, Manchester Regt.
RATHBONE, HAROLD EUGENE FORD, Major, Royal Engineers.
RATTRAY, MALCOLM MACGREGOR, M.B., Lieut.-Colonel (Temporary Colonel), Royal Army Medical Corps.
REAY, TOM, Temporary Major, Northumberland Fusiliers.
REID, ALEXANDER DANIEL, Temporary Major (Lieut., Retired, Indian Army), attached Inniskilling Fusiliers.
REID, FRANCIS MAUDE, Lieut.-Colonel and Brevet Colonel, Retired Pay, late Highland Light Infantry (Commanding Battn., Royal Fusiliers).
REID, HECTOR GOWANS, Major and Brevet Lieut.-Colonel (Temporary Lieut.-Colonel), Army Service Corps.
REYNOLDS, JAMES PHILIP, Lieut.-Colonel, Royal Field Artillery.
RICARDO, WILFRID FRANCIS, Major, Yeomanry.
RICE, CECIL EDWARD, Major (Temporary Lieut.-Colonel), Yeomanry (Commanding Battn., Royal Fusiliers).
RICHARDS, FRANCIS HOWE, Capt. (Acting Major), Royal Field Artillery.
RICHMOND, JOHN DUNCAN, M.B., Major, Royal Army Medical Corps.
RIDEAL, JOHN GEORGE EDMUND, Capt. (Temporary Major), York and Lancaster Regt.
ROBERTS, HENRY CONSTABLE, Temporary Capt., Intelligence Corps.
ROBINSON, FRANCIS, Capt. (Acting Lieut.-Colonel), Royal Inniskilling Fusiliers.
ROBINSON, HUGH THOMAS KAY, Temporary Capt. (Acting Major), Royal Sussex Regt.
ROBINSON, JOHN POOLE BOWRING, Major, Royal Dublin Fusiliers.
ROGERS, HENRY, M.B., Major (Temporary Lieut.-Colonel), Royal Army Medical Corps.
ROGERS, WILFRID FRANK, Capt. (Acting Major), Royal Field Artillery.
RORIE, DAVID, M.D., Major (Temporary Lieut.-Colonel), Royal Army Medical Corps.
ROWAN-HAMILTON, GAWAINE BASIL, M.C., Capt., Royal Highlanders.
RUSHTON, HENRY WILLIAM, Lieut.-Colonel, Royal Engineers.
RYAN, AMBROSE WILLIAM, Lieut. (Acting Major), Royal Garrison Artillery.
SADLER, ALBERT, Temporary Major, Army Service Corps.
SADLER, HENRY KNIGHT, M.C., Major, Royal Field Artillery.
SANDILANDS, HAROLD RICHARD, Major, Northumberland Fusiliers.
SARGENT, JAMES, Major (Temporary Lieut.-Colonel), Lancashire Fusiliers.
SCOONES, GEOFFRY ALLEN PERCIVAL, M.C., Lieut., Indian Army.
SEDDON, EDWARD McMAHON, Lieut.-Colonel, Royal Garrison Artillery.
SELBY, CHARLES WESTROPE, M.C., Major, Royal Field Artillery.
SHAW, LAWRENCE DREW, Temporary Capt. (Acting Lieut.-Colonel), Royal Army Medical Corps.
SHEEHAN, GEORGE FABER, Major, Royal Army Medical Corps.
SHELDON, CLIFFORD DOMMETT, Lieut. (Temporary Capt.), Royal Engineers, Special Reserve.
SHEPHERD, GORDON STRACHEY, M.C., Capt. and Brevet Major (Temporary Brigadier-General), Royal Fusiliers (attached Royal Flying Corps).
SHEPHERD, GILBERT JOHN VICTOR, Capt., Royal Engineers.
SHEPHERD, WILLIAM KIDD OGILVIE, Major, Royal Field Artillery.
SHEPPARD, EUSTACE GRAHAM, M.V.O., Temporary Major, Royal Engineers (Capt., Royal Engineers, T.F.).
SHEPPARD, ROBERT OSBORNE, Major (Temporary Lieut.-Colonel), Army Ordnance Department.
SHERBROOKE, NEVILE HUGH CAIRNS, Major (Acting Lieut.-Colonel), Royal Horse Artillery.
SHERLOCK, DAVID JOHN CHRISTOPHER EUSTACE, Major, Royal Field Artillery.
SHERMAN, EDWIN COLLINGWOOD, Temporary Major, Army Service Corps.
SHERWOOD, OLIVER CATON, Major and Brevet Lieut.-Colonel (Temporary Lieut.-Colonel), Retired Pay, late Army Ordnance Department.
SHINKWIN, ION RICHARD STAVELEY, Major (Temporary Lieut.-Colonel), Army Service Corps.
SIDNEY, HENRY, Major, Yeomanry.
SIMPSON, CHARLES NAPIER, Lieut.-Colonel and Brevet Colonel, Retired Pay, Royal Field Artillery.
SIMPSON, LIGHTLY STAPLETON, Temporary Major, Royal Engineers.
SKEFFINGTON-SMYTH, RANDAL CHARLES EDWARD, Major (Temporary Lieut.-Colonel), Retired Pay, late Coldstream Guards.
SKIRROW, ARTHUR GEORGE WALKER, Temporary Major, General List.
SLOAN, ALLEN THOMSON, Temporary Capt. (Acting Major), Royal Field Artillery.
SMITH, REV. CHARLES WILLIAM, Chaplain to the Forces, 1st Class, Army Chaplains' Department.
SMITH, DOUGLAS KIRKE, Capt. (Temporary Major), Royal Field Artillery.
SMITH, FREDERICK WILLIAM, Temporary Lieut.-Colonel, Commanding Battn., Welsh Regt. (Honorary Lieut., Yeomanry).
SMITH, HERBERT CHARLES HYDE, Major, Scottish Rifles.
SMITH, SAMUEL BOYLAN, M.D., Major, Royal Army Medical Corps.
SMITH, TRISTRAM OSWALD, Lieut. (Acting Lieut.-Colonel), North Lancashire Regt. (christian name corrected to Thomas Oswald).
SMITH, WILLIAM MACKENZIE, Lieut.-Colonel, Yeomanry.
SMYTH, HUMPHREY ETWALL, Capt. (Temporary Major), Royal Artillery.
SMYTH, ROBERT RIVERSDALE, Major, Leinster Regt.
SOMERVILLE, WILLIAM JOHNSTON, Temporary Capt. (Acting Major), Royal Engineers.
SOREL, WYNDHAM LUCAS, Temporary Major (Acting Lieut.-Colonel), Army Service Corps.

SOUTHAM, LIONEL ARTHUR CLEMENT, Lieut.-Colonel, Royal Field Artillery.
SPENCER, RICHARD AUGUSTUS, Capt. (Acting Major), Royal Field Artillery.
SPENCER-PHILLIPS, JOHN CHARLES, Temporary Major, Army Service Corps (Capt., Army Service Corps, T.F.).
SPENCER-SMITH, GERALD MONTAGU, Major, Royal Field Artillery.
SPITTLE, GEORGE HERBERT, Temporary Major, Royal Engineers (late Royal Marines).
SPREULL, ANDREW, Capt. (Temporary Major), Army Veterinary Corps.
STANHOPE (EARL), JAMES RICHARD, M.C., Major, Royal West Surrey Regt. (late Capt., Grenadier Guards) (regiment corrected to Royal West Kent).
STANLEY, FREDERICK, Major (Acting Lieut.-Colonel), Royal Field Artillery.
STEPHENSON, DEREK CHARLES, M.C., Capt. (Acting Major), Royal Field Artillery.
STEPHENSON, ROBERT, Temporary Lieut.-Colonel, South Staffordshire Regt. (formerly Northumberland Fusiliers).
STEVENSON, GERALD HOEY, M.B., Capt. (Acting Lieut.-Colonel), Royal Army Medical Corps.
STEWART, HUGH, M.C., M.B., Major (Temporary Lieut.-Colonel), Royal Army Medical Corps.
STEWART, WILLIAM NORMAN, Capt. (Temporary Lieut.-Colonel), Yeomanry.
STOKES, RALPH SHELTON GRIFFIN, M.C., Temporary Major, Royal Engineers.
STREATFEILD, GRANVILLE EDWARD STEWART, Temporary Capt. Royal Engineers.
STREATFEILD, HENRY SIDNEY JOHN, Capt. (Temporary Major), London Regt. (late Lieut., Grenadier Guards) (rank corrected to Major (Acting Lieut.-Colonel)).
STRIEDINGER, OSCAR, Lieut.-Colonel (Temporary Colonel), Army Service Corps.
SYKES, CLEMENT ARTHUR, Lieut.-Colonel, Royal Field Artillery.
SYME, GILBERT ANDREW, M.C., Temporary Capt. (Temporary Major), Royal Engineers.
SYMONDS, GUY, Temporary Lieut.-Colonel, Royal Field Artillery.
SYNNOTT, WILFRID THOMAS, Major, Retired Pay, late Royal Garrison Artillery, attached Royal Field Artillery.
TAIT, JAMES, Capt. (Temporary Major), Royal Scots.
TALBOT, GEORGE JAMES FRANCIS, Major (Temporary Lieut.-Colonel), Retired Pay, late Royal Field Artillery.
TALLENTS, HUGH, Capt. (Temporary Major), Yeomanry.
TANDY, ERNEST NAPPER, Major and Brevet Lieut.-Colonel (Temporary Lieut.-Colonel), Royal Artillery.
TATTERSALL, REV. THOMAS NEWELL, Temporary Chaplain to the Forces, 2nd Class, Army Chaplains' Department.
TAYLER, HENRY PASCOE BLAIR, Temporary Major, General List (late Army Service Corps).
TAYLOR, MURRAY ROSS, M.D., Capt. (Acting Lieut.-Colonel), Royal Army Medical Corps, Special Reserve.
TAYLOR, RICHARD STOPFORD, M.B., F.R.C.S., Capt. (Temporary Major), Royal Army Medical Corps.
TERROT, CHARLES RUSSELL, Major (Temporary Lieut.-Colonel), Dragoons.
TETLEY, FRANK ERIC, Major, Lincolnshire Regt. (Christian name corrected to Francis Eric).
THEWLES, HORACE AUDLEY, Major (Temporary Lieut.-Colonel), East Kent Regt.
THICKNESSE, FRANCIS WILLIAM, Capt. (Acting Major), Royal Garrison Artillery.
THOMAS, ARNOLD NEWALL, M.B., Capt., Indian Medical Service.
THOMAS, GWYNNE CECIL, Quartermaster and Honorary Major, South Wales Borderers.
THOMAS, HUBERT ST. GEORGE, Lieut.-Colonel, Indian Army.
THOMPSON, AUBREY JULIAN, Major, Royal Garrison Artillery.
THOMPSON, WILLIAM GEORGE, Lieut.-Colonel, Royal Field Artillery.
THOMSON, ALEXANDER HENRY GOUGER, Lieut.-Colonel, Indian Army.
TILNEY, ROBERT HENRY, Lieut.-Colonel, Yeomanry.
TIMINS, REV. FRANCIS CHARLES, Temporary Chaplain to the Forces, 3rd Class, Army Chaplains' Department.
TOMKINSON, HENRY ARCHDALE, Major (Temporary Lieut.-Colonel), Dragoons.
TRENCH, DERRICK LE POER, M.C., Major, Royal Artillery.
TREW, EDWARD FYNMORE, Major (Temporary Lieut.-Colonel), Royal Marines.
TRIPP, WILLIAM HENRY LAINSON, Capt. (Temporary Major), Royal Marine Artillery.
TULLOCH, EWAN, M.C., Temporary Capt. (Temporary Major), Royal Engineers.
TURNBULL, DAVID OLIVER, Temporary Capt. (Temporary Major), Army Veterinary Corps.
TURNBULL, JOHN ARCHBOLD, Major, Royal Army Medical Corps.
TYLER, ARTHUR MALCOLM, Lieut.-Colonel, Royal Garrison Artillery.
TYLER, ROPER MAXWELL, Major, Durham Light Infantry.
TYRRELL, WILLIAM GRANT, Capt. (Temporary Major), Royal Engineers.
VALENTINE, JAMES, Capt. (Temporary Major), Royal Flying Corps, Special Reserve.
VAN STRAUBENZEE, ALEXANDER WILLIAM, Major, Royal Field Artillery.
VAUGHAN, EDWARD, Lieut.-Colonel, Manchester Regt.
VESEY, IVO LUCIUS BERESFORD, Major and Brevet Lieut.-Colonel (Temporary Lieut.-Colonel), Royal West Surrey Regt.
VICKRESS, WILLIAM HENRY, Temporary Major, Army Service Corps.
WALKER, CHARLES ERNEST, Lieut.-Colonel, Royal Field Artillery.
WALLACE, ROBERT BRUCE, M.B., Temporary Capt., Royal Army Medical Corps.
WARD, ARTHUR, Lieut.-Colonel, Indian Army.

WARDE-ALDAM, WILLIAM ST. ANDREW, Capt. (Temporary Lieut.-Colonel), Coldstream Guards.
WARING, ANTHONY HENRY, Lieut.-Colonel, Royal Army Medical Corps.
WARNER, EDWARD COURTENAY THOMAS, M.C., Capt., Scots Guards.
WATKINS, PHILIP SEYMOUR, Major, Royal Engineers.
WATSON, CHARLES HENRY, Major, Indian Medical Service.
WATSON, GEORGE EDMUND BORLASE, M.C., Capt. (Acting Major), Royal Field Artillery.
WAY, GERALD OSCAR, Capt., North Staffordshire Regt., Special Reserve.
WEBB-BOWEN, WILLIAM INCE, Major (Acting Lieut.-Colonel), Middlesex Regt.
WELLS, ALAN GEOFFRY, Capt. (Acting Lieut.-Colonel), Royal Army Medical Corps.
WEST, RICHARD MELBOURNE, M.D., Major (Temporary Lieut.-Colonel), Royal Army Medical Corps.
WESTON, WALTER JOHN, Major, Royal Army Medical Corps.
WHATFORD, STUART LUMLEY, Major (Temporary Lieut.-Colonel), Yorkshire Regt.
WHEATLEY, PHILIP, Lieut.-Colonel (Temporary Brigadier-General), Royal Artillery.
WHITE, MAURICE FITZGIBBON GROVE, Capt., Royal Engineers.
WHITE, JAMES ROSS, Major and Brevet Lieut.-Colonel (Temporary Lieut.-Colonel), Royal Engineers.
WHITEHEAD, JOHN JAMES, Temporary Major (Acting Lieut.-Colonel), Manchester Regt.
WHITTALL, PERCIVAL FREDERICK, Temporary Capt. (Acting Major), Royal Engineers (Capt., Reserve of Officers, late Lincolnshire Regt.).
WHITTINGHAM, CHARLES HERBERT, Lieut. (Temporary Lieut.-Colonel), Retired Pay, late Durham Light Infantry.
WHITTY, NOEL IRWINE, Capt. (Temporary Major), Royal West Kent Regt.
WIENHOLT, WILLIAM HUMPHREY MEYRICK, Temporary Major, North Lancashire Regt.
WILDE, LEONARD CLAY, Major, Manchester Regt.
WILLIAMS, HENRY JOHN, Major (Temporary Lieut.-Colonel), Dragoon Guards.
WILLIAMS, STANLEY HORATIO, Temporary Capt. (Acting Major), Royal Field Artillery.
WILLIS, SHERLOCK GEORGE RAMSAY, Major (Acting Lieut.-Colonel), Royal Field Artillery.
WILLOUGHBY, SIR JOHN CHRISTOPHER, Bart., Temporary Major, Army Service Corps (late Major, Royal Horse Guards).
WILLOUGHBY-OSBORNE, D'ARCY, Major, Royal Field Artillery.
WILLYAMS, EDWARD NEYNOE, Capt. (Temporary Major), Duke of Cornwall's Light Infantry.
WILSON, GEORGE, Quartermaster and Honorary Major, Royal Lancaster Regt.
WISE, PERCIVAL KINNEAR, Capt. (Temporary Lieut.-Colonel), Royal Warwickshire Regt. and Royal Flying Corps.
WOOD, CHARLES MICHELL ALOYSIUS, Major and Brevet Lieut.-Colonel, Northumberland Fusiliers.
WOOD, ERNEST, Lieut.-Colonel, Army Service Corps.
WOOD, HUGH REGINALD, Temporary Major (Acting Lieut.-Colonel), Welsh Regt.
WOOD, LOUIS, Lieut. (Acting Major), Royal Field Artillery.
WORSLEY, FRANK PICKFORD, Capt. and Brevet Major (Temporary Lieut.-Colonel), Retired Pay, late West Yorkshire Regt.
WOOTTEN, HERBERT EDWARD, Temporary Lieut.-Colonel, Border Regt.
WRAITH, EDWIN ARNOLD, Lieut.-Colonel, Royal Army Medical Corps.
WRAY, HENRY CECIL, Major, Royal Field Artillery.
WRIGHT, HAROLD LEE, Capt. (Acting Lieut.-Colonel), Royal Engineers.
WRIGHT, NICHOLAS IRWIN, Capt. (Temporary Lieut.-Colonel), Northumberland Fusiliers.
WRIGHT, THOMAS JAMES, Major (Temporary Lieut.-Colonel), Royal Army Medical Corps.
WYNFORD (LORD), PHILIP GEORGE, Major (Temporary Lieut.-Colonel), Royal Field Artillery.
YOUNG, JULIAN MAYNE, C.M.G., Lieut.-Colonel (Temporary Colonel), Army Service Corps.
YOUNG, REV. STANISLAUS DOMINIC, Temporary Chaplain to the Forces, 3rd Class, Army Chaplains' Department.
YUILL, HARRY HOGG, M.C., Temporary Capt., Royal Engineers.

AUSTRALIAN FORCE.

ADAMS, WILLIAM AFFLECK, Major, Pioneer Battn.
ALLSOP, WILLIAM GILLIAN, Lieut.-Colonel, Artillery.
BORWICK, THOMAS FAULKINER, Major, Australian Imperial Force.
BUTLER, CHARLES PHILIP, Major (Temporary Lieut.-Colonel), Australian Imperial Force.
BUTLER, HARRY NAIRN, Lieut.-Colonel, Australian Army Medical Corps.
BYRNE, GEORGE CUMMING, Major, Australian Army Medical Corps.
CADDY, HECTOR OSMAN, Lieut.-Colonel, Artillery.
COLE, GEORGE EDWARDS, Major, Australian Army Medical Corps.
DAVIS, CHARLES HERBERT, Lieut.-Colonel, Australian Imperial Force.
DE CRESPIGNY, CONSTANTINE TRENT CHAMPION, Lieut.-Colonel (Temporary Colonel), Australian Army Medical Corps.
DENHAM, HOWARD KYNASTON, Lieut.-Colonel, Australian Imperial Force.
DICKINSON, GEORGE FREDERICK, Major, Australian Imperial Force.
DIXON, OLIVER FRANCIS, Capt. (Temporary Major), Artillery.
DONNELLY, JOHN FRANCIS, Major, Infantry.
EDGLEY, JOHN MILTON, Major, Australian Imperial Force.
FANNING, RUPERT EDWARD, Capt. (Temporary Major), Artillery.
FRASER, JOHN EDWARD, Major, Engineers.
FRASER, WILLIAM ANGUS, Major, Australian Army Medical Corps.
GILES, FELIX GORDON, Major, Australian Imperial Force.
GODDARD, CHARLES JAMES, Major, Commanding Supply Company.
GREENWAY, HAROLD, Major, Engineers.
HEARNE, WILLIAM WESTON, Lieut.-Colonel (Temporary Colonel), Australian Army Medical Corps.
HOCKLEY, RUPERT REGINALD, Major (Temporary Lieut.-Colonel), Australian Imperial Force.
HUXTABLE, ROBERT BEVERIDGE, Lieut.-Colonel (Temporary Colonel), Australian Army Medical Corps.
IMLAY, ALEXANDER PETER, Major, Australian Imperial Force.
JOHNSTON, CHARLES MELBOURNE, Major, Australian Imperial Force.
KININMONTH, JAMES CARSTAIRS, Capt., Ordnance Corps.
LORD, JOHN EDWARD CECIL, Lieut.-Colonel, Australian Imperial Force (Christian name corrected to John Ernest Cecil).
LOUTIT, NOEL MEDWAY, Major, Australian Imperial Force.
MACINTOSH, CYRIL LESLIE STEWART, Major, Australian Army Medical Corps.
MATSON, THOMAS, Lieut.-Colonel, Australian Veterinary Corps.
MAXTED, GEORGE, Quartermaster and Honorary (Major Temporary Major) General List, Australian Imperial Force.
MAYGAR, LESLIE CECIL, V.C., Lieut.-Colonel, Light Horse.
McCAY, ROSS CAIRNS, Capt. (Temporary Major), Field Battery.
McSHARRY, TERENCE PATRICK, M.C., Lieut.-Colonel, Australian Imperial Force.
MORRELL, ROY, Major, Machine Gun Corps (surname corrected to Morell [London Gazette, 18 July, 1918]).
MORSE, RICHARD VICTOR, Major, Mining Section.
MORSHEAD, LESLIE JAMES, Lieut.-Colonel, Australian Imperial Force.
MULLEN, LESLIE MILTIADES, Lieut.-Colonel, Australian Imperial Force.
MUNRO, EDWARD JOY, Major, Army Service Corps.
MURPHY, GEORGE FRANCIS, Lieut.-Colonel, Australian Imperial Force.
PARSONS, JOHN WILLIAM, Major, Light Horse Regt.
PAUL, JOHN KEATING, Capt. (Temporary Major), Australian Artillery.
PECK, JOHN HENRY, Lieut.-Colonel, Australian Imperial Force.
PLAYFAIR, THOMAS ALFRED JACK, Capt. (Temporary Major), Australian Artillery.
POWELL, ARTHUR HUNTER, Capt., Australian Army Medical Corps.
RAFFERTY, RUPERT ANSTICE, Major, Australian Imperial Force.
ROBERTSON, HORACE CLEMENT HUGH, Capt., Light Horse Regt.
ROBERTSON, JAMES CAMPBELL, C.M.G., Colonel (Temporary Brigadier-General), Commanding Australian Infantry Brigade.
SALISBURY, ALFRED GEORGE, Lieut.-Colonel, Australian Imperial Force.
STACY, BERTIE VANDELEUR, Lieut.-Colonel, Australian Imperial Force.
TEBBUTT, ARTHUR HAMILTON, Lieut.-Colonel, Australian Army Medical Corps.
WAITE, WILLIAM CHARLES NIGHTINGALE, M.C., Lieut.-Colonel, Australian Artillery.
WALSH, ROY WILLIAM WHISTON, Major, Australian Army Medical Corps.
WALSTAB, JOHN, Lieut.-Colonel, Australian Imperial Force.
WELCH, HERBERT LOCKSLEY ST. VINCENT, Major, Australian Army Medical Corps.
WIECK, GEORGE FREDERICK GARDELLS, Major, Light Horse Regt.
WILLIAMS, THOMAS ISAAC CORNWALL, Major, Australian Artillery.
WILLIAMS, THOMAS RHYS, Major, Australian Engineers.
WILLIS, WILLIAM JAMES, Quartermaster and Honorary Major, Infantry Battn.
WOOTTEN, GEORGE FREDERICK, Major.

CANADIAN FORCES.

ANDERSON, SAMUEL BOYD, Lieut.-Colonel, Canadian Field Artillery.
CAPE, EDMUND GRAVES MEREDITH, Major, Canadian Artillery.
CLARK, JOHN ARTHUR, Lieut.-Colonel, Canadian Infantry.
GRERAR (correct name Crerar), HENRY DUNCAN GRAHAM, Major, Canadian Field Artillery.
CROSS, JAMES ALBERT, Major, Infantry.
DAWSON, HERBERT JOHN, Lieut.-Colonel, Infantry.
EVANS, WILLIAM BARNARD, Major (Acting Lieut.-Colonel), Infantry.
FORBES-MITCHELL, WILLIAM JOSEPH, Capt. (Acting Major), Infantry.
GILMAN, FREDERICK, Major, Dragoons.
GORSSLINE, RAYMOND MEYERS, Major, Canadian Army Medical Corps.
GRASSIE, WILLIAM, Lieut.-Colonel, Infantry.
HENDRY, WILLIAM BELFRY, Lieut.-Colonel, Canadian Army Medical Corps.
HODSON, GEORGE CUTHBERT, Lieut.-Colonel, Infantry.
HOGARTH, DONALD, Lieut.-Colonel, Canadian Army Service Corps.
HOLMES, WILLIAM JOSIAH HARTLEY, Lieut.-Colonel, Pioneer Battn.
JENKINS, JOHN STEPHEN, Major, Canadian Army Medical Corps.
LAFLECHE, LEO RICHER, Major, Infantry.
LATTA, WILLIAM SMITH, Major, Infantry.
LE FEVRE, ALFRED TULLY, Major (Temporary Lieut.-Colonel), Railway Construction Corps.
LINDSEY, CHARLES BETHUNE, Major, Infantry.
LYLE, HILLIARD, Capt. (Acting Major), Infantry.
MACFARLANE, ROBERT ALEXANDER, Major, Infantry.
MACKINNON, DANIEL ALBERT, Major, Infantry.
MASSIE, ALBERT EDWARD, Lieut.-Colonel, Canadian Army Service Corps.
McCOMBE, GAULT, Major (Acting Lieut.-Colonel), Infantry.
McFARLANE, GEORGE WHITLOCK, Major, Infantry.
McGUFFEN, CHESTER FISH, Lieut.-Colonel, Canadian Army Medical Corps (surname corrected to McGuffin [London Gazette, 18 June, 1917]).

The Distinguished Service Order

McQUEEN, JOHN DOUGLAS, Lieut.-Colonel, Canadian Army Medical Corps.
MARSHALL, KENRIC RUD, Capt. (Temporary Major), Infantry.
MITCHELL, JAMES HENRY, Lieut.-Colonel (Temporary Brigadier-General), Canadian Field Artillery.
O'DONAHOE, JAMES VINCENT PATRICK, Major, Infantry.
ORMOND, DANIEL MAWAT, Lieut.-Colonel, Infantry.
OSLER, STRATTON HARRY, Major (Temporary Lieut.-Colonel), Royal Canadian Engineers.
PECK, CYRUS WESLEY, Lieut.-Colonel, Infantry.
PORTER, CECIL GEORGE, Capt. (Acting Major), Infantry.
POUPORE, ALBERT GENELLE, Major, Infantry.
PROWSE, WALDREN BREWER, Major, Artillery.
RALSTON, GEORGE HARRAH, Lieut.-Colonel, Field Artillery.
ROSS, JAMES, Capt. (Acting Major), Infantry.
SPARLING, HERBERT C. Lieut.-Colonel, Infantry.
STEEL, FRANCIS MACDONALD, Major, Infantry.
SUTTON, ARTHUR CHRISTOPHER, Major, Pioneer Battn.
TEMPLETON, CHARLES PERRY, Lieut.-Colonel, Canadian Army Medical Corps.
TROTTER, CLIFFORD THACKWELL, Major, Canadian Engineers.
VAN DEN BERG, JOHN WILLIAM HENRY GERIT HOPMAN, Capt. (Acting Major), Infantry.
VANDERSLUYS, CHARLES HERMAN, Major, Infantry.
WANSBROUGH, CUTHBERT COLE, Major, Infantry.
WATSON, STANCLIFFE WALLACE, Capt. (Acting Major), Infantry.
WILGAR, WILLIAM PERCY, Major, Canadian Engineers.
WILLIAMS, EDWARD JOHNSTON, Lieut.-Colonel, Canadian Army Medical Corps.

NEW ZEALAND FORCE.

ACTON-ADAMS, PERCY MORLAND, Major, Mounted Rifles.
BUCK, PETER HENRY, Major, Pioneer Battn.
COOK, CHARLES FREDERICK DENMAN, Lieut.-Colonel, Infantry Regt.
DALTRY, HENRY JAMES, Major, Field Artillery.
DUIGAN, JOHN EVELYN, Major, Staff Corps.
GARD'NER, MURRAY MENZIES, Lieut.-Colonel, Field Artillery.
HERBERT, ALFRED HENRY, Lieut.-Colonel, Army Ordnance Corps.
ROACHE, JOSEPH GARRETT, Temporary Lieut.-Colonel, Rifle Brigade.
SAUNDERS, JOHN LLEWELLYN, Major.
STEWART, HUGH, M.C., Lieut.-Colonel.
STOUT, THOMAS DUNCAN MACGREGOR, Major, New Zealand Medical Corps.
SYMON, FRANK, C.M.G., Lieut.-Colonel, New Zealand Artillery.

SOUTH AFRICAN CONTINGENT.

BROWN, FREDERICK LESLIE, Temporary Major, South African Staff Corps.
CLARKE, COLIN, Major, South African Engineers.
GIRDWOOD, ROBERT LAURIE, Lieut.-Colonel, South African Medical Corps.
HOY, CHARLES NORMAN, Major.
KREFT, CARL JOHANNES, Major, South African Infantry.
LAUTH, JOACHIM FREDERICK REINHOLD, Major, South African Infantry.
MORRIS, GEORGE ABBOTT, Lieut.-Colonel.
MULLINS, ARTHUR GILBERT, Temporary Capt. (Acting Major), South African Artillery.
PARSON, GEORGE, Major.
PRINGLE, ROBERT NORMAN, Major (Acting Lieut.-Colonel), South African Medical Corps.
TATHAM, FREDERICK SPENCE, Temporary Major, General List (Lieut.-Colonel, Reserve of Officers, South African Defence Force).
TURNER, RALPH BERESFORD, Temporary Major, South African Forces.
VAUGHAN-WILLIAMS, HERBERT WYNNE, Lieut.-Colonel, South African Medical Corps.

London Gazette, 14 June, 1917.—"War Office, 14 June, 1917. His Majesty the King has been graciously pleased to approve of the undermentioned Rewards for gallantry and meritorious service on the occasion of the mining of a Hospital Ship. Awarded the Distinguished Service Order."

MEADOWS, ROBERT THORNTON, Major, Royal Army Medical Corps.

London Gazette, 15 June, 1917.—"Admiralty, 15 June, 1917. The King has been graciously pleased to give orders for the following appointments to the Distinguished Service Order to the undermentioned Officers, in recognition of their services in the operations described in the Commander-in-Chief's Despatch." (Despatch of Rear-Admiral E. Charlton, dated 28 Jan. 1917, describing the later coastal operations by His Majesty's Ships against German East Africa.)

WATSON, REGINALD JAMES NEWALL, Commander, R.N. Was in charge of landing party at Bagamoyo on 15 Aug. 1916, and displayed great dash and energy in the face of unexpectedly superior forces.
ROSKRUGE, FRANCIS JOHN, Engineer-Commander, R.N. Kept the squadron and H.M.S. Hyacinth in a state of continuous efficiency for over two years with the smallest possible allowance for necessary repairs.
MOON, EDWIN ROWLAND, Flight Lieut., R.N.A.S. (now prisoner of war). Since April, 1916, has carried out constant flights over the enemy's coast, including reconnaissances, bomb-dropping and spotting for gun fire in all weathers. Has shown great coolness and resource on all occasions.

"The King has further approved of the following appointment to the Distinguished Service Order to the undermentioned Officer, in recognition of his services with the East African Military Forces."

THORNLEY, GEORGE STANLEY, Commander, R.N., Senior Naval Officer, Lake Victoria Nyanza. Rendered most efficient assistance to the Military throughout the campaign.

London Gazette, 18 June, 1917.—"War Office, 18 June, 1917. His Majesty the King has been graciously pleased to award a Bar to the Distinguished Service Order to ":—

GIRDWOOD, AUSTIN CLAUDE, D.S.O., Major (Temporary Lieut.-Colonel), Northumberland Fusiliers, attached Border Regt. For conspicuous gallantry and devotion to duty when he made a daring and invaluable reconnaissance under heavy rifle and machine-gun fire. He concentrated his battalion in daylight, and organized a most successful attack over 200 yards of open ground.
(D.S.O. gazetted 27 Sept. 1901.)
HAIG, ROLAND, D.S.O., Major (Temporary Lieut.-Colonel), Rifle Brigade, attached Royal Berkshire Regt. For conspicuous gallantry and devotion to duty when in command of his battalion during an attack on the enemy's position. The success of this attack was due to the ability and energy with which he trained his battalion, made his preparations and handled the troops under his command during the battle.
(D.S.O. gazetted 18 Feb. 1915.)
HALL, JOHN HAMILTON, D.S.O., Major (Temporary Lieut.-Colonel), Middlesex Regt. For conspicuous gallantry and devotion to duty when in command of his battalion. His initiative and good leading and the determined way in which he pressed the attack of his battalion home greatly contributed to the success of the operations. The high moral of his battalion and its fine spirit in attacking qualities are greatly due to his personal efforts.
(D.S.O. gazetted 26 Sept. 1916.)

AUSTRALIAN IMPERIAL FORCE.

ELLIOTT, CHARLES HAZEL, D.S.O., Lieut.-Colonel, Infantry (Christian name corrected to Charles Hazell [London Gazette, 28 July, 1917]). For conspicuous gallantry and devotion to duty during an enemy attack. Although the enemy had penetrated our line and were within 500 yards of Battalion Headquarters, he took up a position with batmen, cooks and signallers, and checked the enemy's advance, thus enabling the counter-attacking force to come forward and drive the enemy back. His action at a most critical time turned what might have been a defeat into a victory.
(D.S.O. gazetted 1 Jan. 1917.)
GELLIBRAND, JOHN, D.S.O., Temporary Brigadier-General, Infantry Brigade. For conspicuous gallantry and devotion to duty. His brigade reached its third objective, but was ordered back owing to the division on the right being held up at the first objective. His brigade repelled several counter-attacks and held on when the brigade on the right was in difficulties. It was largely owing to his influence and presence in this advanced position that the operations were successful.
(D.S.O. gazetted 2 May, 1916.)
LOUTIT, NOEL MEDWAY, D.S.O., Major, Infantry. For conspicuous gallantry and devotion to duty in laying out the jumping-off tape under heavy shell and rifle fire. Later, he took forward a machine gun and platoon, and opened a surprise burst of fire into the enemy, thus relieving the pressure at a critical time. He did not leave the line until the whole front was secure.
(D.S.O. gazetted 4 June, 1917.)
MACKAY, IVEN GIFFARD, D.S.O., Lieut.-Colonel, Infantry. For conspicuous gallantry and devotion to duty. While acting as Brigadier, when the brigade on the right was broken into by the enemy, the battalion under his orders counter-attacked and assisted to drive out the enemy and restore the position. His action in repelling the counter-attack was of the utmost value, and his prompt action and extreme resolution showed leadership of a high order.
(D.S.O. gazetted 1 Jan. 1917.)
MURRAY, HENRY WILLIAM, V.C., D.S.O., Capt. (Temporary Major), Infantry. For conspicuous gallantry and devotion to duty. He gallantly led his company over 1,200 yards of fire-swept ground. Later, he went along the whole frontage, organizing the defence, encouraging the men of all units by his cheerfulness and bravery, and always moving to the points of danger. He is not only brave and daring, but a skilful soldier, possessing tactical instinct of the highest order.
(D.S.O. gazetted 14 Nov. 1916.)
SMITH, ROBERT, D.S.O., Colonel (Temporary Brigadier-General), Infantry. For conspicuous gallantry and initiative. By his skilful dispositions he met and held a powerful enemy attack, and personally conducting operations under heavy rifle fire, he counter-attacked, retook the lost ground, and pushed the enemy back for two miles at the point of the bayonet.
(D.S.O. gazetted 1 Jan. 1917.)

"His Majesty the King has been graciously pleased to approve of the appointments of the undermentioned Officers to be Companions of the Distinguished Service Order, in recognition of their gallantry and devotion to duty in the field."

AMBROSE, CHARLES FREDERICK NELSON, Temporary Second Lieut., Machine Gun Corps. For conspicuous gallantry and devotion to duty. After his tank had been badly damaged by shell fire, and all his gunners had become casualties, he continued to keep a brisk fire on the enemy, who were surrounding his tank and attacking it with bombs. His conduct throughout the action displayed the greatest courage.
BARRY, JOHN REDMOND, Capt. (Acting Major), Royal Field Artillery. For conspicuous gallantry and devotion to duty. He maintained his position at a very advanced observation post throughout the day, in order to cut wire preparatory to the infantry advancing. Later, he made a reconnaissance and handed in a report which was of the utmost value.
BERTIE, THE HONOURABLE ARTHUR MICHAEL, Temporary Capt., Rifle Brigade. For conspicuous gallantry and devotion to duty when in command of his company. When the attacking company was held up by intense machine-gun fire and the situation was becoming critical, he, taking a machine gun with him, advanced to a position where he could engage the enemy machine gun. He subsequently went back alone under the most intense fire and brought up ammunition for his gun. He set a magnificent example to his men.
BISHOP, WILLIAM AVERY, Capt., Canadian Cavalry and Royal Flying Corps. For conspicuous gallantry and devotion to duty. While in a single-seater he attacked three hostile machines, two of which he brought down, although in the meantime he was himself attacked by four other hostile machines. His courage and determination have set a fine example to others.
BURT, ALFRED, Lieut.-Colonel, Dragoon Guards. For conspicuous gallantry and devotion to duty. His regiment was ordered forward when the situation was most obscure, and by his skilful leading he was able to seize an important position and thus prevent the enemy from counter-attacking. His personal bravery was a fine example to all.
CAMPBELL, HUGH, Major, London Regt. For conspicuous gallantry and devotion to duty. The ammunition lorries were being heavily shelled when he personally drove two of them which were in flames out of the danger zone. He then organized a party to put the fire out and remove ammunition from the vicinity of the flames. This task was carried out under continuous shell fire, and by his prompt action and gallantry undoubtedly saved many lives and averted a disaster.

*DURNFORD, ROBERT CHICHESTER, Second Lieut., Hampshire Regt. For conspicuous gallantry and devotion to duty. Although severely wounded he continued to struggle on, encouraging his men for over a mile, when he was again hit, but he would not allow his wounds to be dressed until the position gained had been consolidated.

FITZGIBBON, FRANCIS, Major, Royal Field Artillery. For conspicuous gallantry and devotion to duty. He moved his battery up by daylight over exposed ground under shell fire, and came into action with the most successful results.

FORBES-ROBERTSON, JAMES, M.C., Capt. (Temporary Lieut.-Colonel), Border Regt. For conspicuous gallantry and devotion to duty when in command of his battalion during an enemy attack. He collected all the men he could find, and, taking up a position on the outskirts of the village, brought the hostile advance to an end by his fire. He undoubtedly saved a very critical situation by his promptness, bravery and example.

GREEN, GILBERT WARE M., M.C., Temporary Second Lieut. (Temporary Capt.), Royal Flying Corps. For conspicuous gallantry and devotion to duty. He has set a magnificent example by his gallant conduct in attacking the enemy's aeroplanes when in superior numbers. He brought down three enemy machines within 24 hours.

*HORNOR, BASSETT FARDELL, Second Lieut., Norfolk Regt., Special Reserve. For conspicuous gallantry in action. He was the first of his regiment to land on the left bank of the river, and displayed great courage and resource in promptly putting out of action single-handed an enemy machine gun which was about to open fire. Later, he gallantly led his company forward in the face of heavy fire and was responsible for the capture of three more machine guns.

JACK, JAMES LOCHHEAD, Capt. (Acting Lieut.-Colonel), Scottish Rifles, attached West Yorkshire Regt. For conspicuous gallantry and devotion to duty. He conducted the attack of his battalion with marked skill and foresight, and attained all his objectives in the minimum time and with very small loss. He has set a most inspiring example of gallantry to all.

LEY, EDWARD MARLBOROUGH, Temporary Lieut.-Colonel, King's Royal Rifle Corps. For conspicuous gallantry and devotion to duty when in command of his battalion. He handled his battalion with the greatest dash and judgment throughout and was largely responsible for the success of the operations. He showed great qualities as a leader.

OATES, JOHN SHERBROOKE COAFE, M.C., Lieut. (Temporary Capt.), Nottinghamshire and Derbyshire Regt. For conspicuous gallantry and devotion to duty. He displayed the greatest skill and gallantry while commanding the battalion at a critical period. During the day he repeatedly crossed the open a distance of 500 yards under continual sniping in order to superintend operations, and by his courage and determination succeeded in obtaining complete ascendency over the enemy.

PARRY, DULAS BENTLEY, Major (Acting Lieut.-Colonel), London Regt. For conspicuous gallantry and devotion to duty. He inspired all ranks with the greatest confidence, and thus materially assisted the battalion under his command to carry through a most difficult operation. He displayed great skill and untiring energy in training the battalion beforehand.

*PITMAN, CHARLES ROBERT SENHOUSE, M.C., Capt., Indian Army. For conspicuous gallantry and devotion to duty when in command of a raiding party. In spite of the most difficult conditions he succeeded in landing and reorganizing his party. He inflicted much damage on the enemy and brought back a trench mortar. It was owing to his coolness and good leading that the object of the raid was achieved and the whole party withdrawn with but few casualties.

PRIAULX, GEORGE KENDALL, Major (Acting Lieut.-Colonel), King's Royal Rifle Corps. For conspicuous gallantry and devotion to duty when in command of his battalion. With the utmost confidence and determination he fought his battalion through the village, overcoming all obstacles and gaining his objectives. He set a magnificent example throughout.

PRYOR, WALTER MARLBOROUGH, Capt. (Temporary Major), Hertfordshire Regt., attached Royal Warwickshire Regt. For conspicuous gallantry and devotion to duty. He rendered most valuable service in collecting parties of men who were lost and putting them on to the work of consolidating the position gained. It was largely due to his efforts that a strong position was created, thereby facilitating the dispersing of enemy counter-attacks. This task was accomplished at great personal risk from enemy machine-gun fire.

RICHMOND, GEORGE WILLIAM, Lieut. (Acting Capt.), Royal Engineers, Special Reserve. For conspicuous gallantry and determination while forcing a passage of the river. His coolness and resource were mainly responsible for the successful launching of the pontoons which effected the crossing, and his attitude was an inspiring example to all under his command. He has previously done fine work.

RODOCANACHI, THEODORE EMMANUEL, M.C., Capt., Oxfordshire and Buckinghamshire Light Infantry (Lieut., Hampshire Regt., Special Reserve). For conspicuous gallantry and devotion to duty. Although wounded he led his company with great gallantry and pressed on to his objective in the face of heavy fire. Although again wounded during the advance he continued to lead on into the hostile position, where he immediately organized the consolidation and continued to command his company until finally incapacitated by a third wound.

*RUSSELL, ROBERT TOR, Second Lieut., Indian Army Reserve of Officers. For conspicuous gallantry and devotion to duty in charging the enemy's trench, which was strongly held. He then led a bombing attack and cleared 200 yards of the trench. Later, he maintained his position for four hours, when reinforcements arrived.

*SHEPHERD, CLAUDE INNES, Capt., Indian Army. For conspicuous gallantry and devotion to duty during an enemy counter-attack. He rallied men who were without leaders, and by his personal example and leading saved a difficult situation. He was wounded in three places.

STORK, ERNEST STANLEY, Capt., M.B., Royal Army Medical Corps, attached Yeomanry. For conspicuous gallantry and devotion to duty. He displayed untiring energy and devotion to duty in evacuating a large number of wounded under heavy fire. He set a magnificent example of courage and determination.

*TOOGOOD, CYRIL GEORGE, Temporary Second Lieut., Gloucestershire Regt. For conspicuous gallantry and devotion to duty when in command of the first batch of pontoons to cross the river. On landing he so disposed his men and cleared the banks of the enemy that he was able to establish a foothold. In spite of heavy casualties, he held on for over six hours, thereby enabling a bridge to be built.

TURNER, ALFRED CHARLES FOSTER, M.B., Capt. (Temporary Major), Royal Army Medical Corps. For conspicuous gallantry and devotion to duty. He attended wounded under heavy fire day and night without rest. He was ever present along the line from the A.D.S. to the most advanced trenches, and on several occasions faced enemy artillery barrages in order that reserves of stretcher-bearers might reach their objectives.

WHITE, WILLIAM LAMBERT, Temporary Capt. (Acting Major), Royal Field Artillery. For conspicuous gallantry and devotion to duty when in command of his battery. He reconnoitred by daylight in front of our infantry outposts, and established an O.P. in a shell-hole 200 yards in front of our outposts, whence he controlled the wire-cutting operations all day. In addition to cutting wire, his battery carried out important bombardment tasks.

WOOD, WILLIAM FERGUSON, M.B., Capt., Royal Army Medical Corps, Special Reserve, attached Hussars. For conspicuous gallantry and devotion to duty. Under most trying circumstances and heavy fire he collected and tended the wounded without rest or food. He frequently made dangerous tours looking for wounded men.

AUSTRALIAN IMPERIAL FORCE.

SOMERVILLE, ROBERT SMITH, M.C., Capt., Infantry. For conspicuous gallantry and devotion to duty when in command of his company. He showed great skill in the handling of a delicate situation, and his cheerful courage under most trying circumstances inspired his men to the magnificent efforts which they undoubtedly made. He was severely wounded.

WOODMAN, HARROLD EUSTACE, Capt., Infantry. For conspicuous gallantry and devotion to duty. He prepared strong defences in carefully-chosen positions, and not only he, but all his officers and men, knew the ground thoroughly as the result of well-organized reconnaissances. At an early stage of the action he counter-attacked a large force of the enemy, and succeeded in holding up their advance until reinforcements arrived. He was largely responsible for saving a critical situation.

* The names marked with an asterisk appeared in the London Gazettes dated either the 17th March, 1917, or 26 April, 1917.

London Gazette, 22 June, 1917.—" Admiralty, S.W., 22 June, 1917.—Honours for Miscellaneous Services. The King has been graciously pleased to give orders for the appointment of the undermentioned Officers to be Companions of the Distinguished Service Order."

LEAKE, FRANCIS MARTIN, Capt., R.N.

DAY, SELWYN MITCHELL, Commander (now Capt.), R.D., R.N.R.

JONES, CHARLES HAROLD, Lieut.-Commander, R.N.

SWORDER, KENNETH FAVIELL, Lieut.-Commander, R.N.

WARBURTON, GEOFFREY, Lieut.-Commander, R.N.

WATKINS, GEOFFREY ROBERT SLADEN, Lieut.-Commander, R.N.

PRICE, THOMAS EDWARD, D.S.C., Lieut., Royal Naval Reserve.

PETERSON, FREDERICK HENRY, D.S.C., Lieut., Royal Naval Reserve.

BEATON, WILLIAM DONALD, Lieut., R.N.R.

The undermentioned Officers have been awarded a Bar to the Distinguished Service Order for subsequent acts of gallantry.

CAMPBELL, VICTOR LINDSAY ARBUTHNOT, D.S.O., Commander, Royal Navy.

(The appointment to the Distinguished Service Order was announced in London Gazette dated 3 June, 1915.)

RAIKES, ROBERT HENRY TAUNTON, D.S.O., Lieut.-Commander, Royal Navy.

(The appointment to the Distinguished Service Order was announced in London Gazette dated 25 Oct. 1916.)

" Honours for the Royal Naval Air Service.—The King has been graciously pleased to give orders for the following appointments to the Distinguished Service Order."

GALPIN, CHRISTOPHER JOHN, Flight Lieut., Royal Naval Air Service.

BRACKLEY, HERBERT GEORGE, D.S.C., Flight Lieut., Royal Naval Air Service. In recognition of his services on the morning of 14 April, 1917, when he carried out a raid on Bruges Harbour with good results in spite of difficult conditions. Great credit is due to him for his persistence and determination. He also dropped bombs on Ostend seaplane base on the night of 3-4 May, 1917, making two trips.

" Honours to the Mercantile Marine.—The King has been graciously pleased to approve the award of a Bar to the Distinguished Service Order to the undermentioned Officer of the British Mercantile Marine, in recognition of zeal and devotion to duty shown in carrying on the trade of the country during the war."

MALING, FREDERICK MAUDE, D.S.O., Capt. (Lieut., Royal Naval Reserve).

London Gazette, 27 June, 1917.—" Admiralty, S.W., 27 June, 1917.—Honours for Service in the Auxiliary Patrol. The King has been graciously pleased to give orders for the following appointments to the Distinguished Service Order to the undermentioned Officers, in recognition of their services in vessels of the Auxiliary Patrol between the 1st Feb. and 31st Dec. 1916."

HIGGINSON, ARCHIBALD BERTRAM WATSON, Commander, R.N.

NICHOLSON, BERTRAM WILLIAM LOTHIAN, Commander, R.N.

CAYLEY, HARRY FRANCIS, Commander, R.N.

CUSTANCE, FREDERICK HUME MUSGRAVE, Commander, R.D., R.N.R.

ROBERTS, JOHN, Commander, R.D., R.N.R.

SMITH, HENRY, Lieut.-Commander (Acting Commander), R.D., R.N.R.

BRADLEY, WILLIAM, Lieut.-Commander (Acting Commander), R.D., R.N.R.

STOCKWELL, HENRY, Lieut.-Commander (Acting Commander), R.D., R.N.R.

KELLY, WILLIAM HENRY, Lieut.-Commander, R.N.R.

COCKRELL, LEONARD C., Lieut. (Acting Lieut.-Commander), R.N.R.

London Gazette, 2 July, 1917.—" Admiralty, S.W., 2 July, 1917—Honours for Service in Mine-sweeping Operations. The King has been graciously pleased to give orders for the following appointments to the Distinguished Service Order to the undermentioned Officers, in recognition of their services in Mine-sweeping operations between the 1st July, 1916, and the 31st March, 1917."

DAWSON, FRANCIS EVELYN MASSY, Capt., R.N.

NAPIER, WILLIAM RAWDON, Capt., R.N.

DALGETY, ROBERT WILLIAM, Commander, R.N.

WIGRAM, RONALD SCOTT JERVOISE, Commander, R.N.

HARBORD, ERIC WALTER, Commander, R.N.

BROOKE, BASIL RICHARD, Commander, R.N.

FRANKLIN, CYRIL PRESCOTT, Lieut.-Commander, R.N.

GLEN, GRAHAM CUNNINGHAM, Lieut.-Commander, R.N.

Addendum to Admiralty List of Officers appointed Companions of the Distinguished Service Order, which appeared in the London Gazette dated 4 June, 1917.

"The King has been graciously pleased to give orders for the appointment of the undermentioned Officer to be a Companion of the Distinguished Service Order, in recognition of his services in the prosecution of the war."

CUMING, ROBERT STEVENSON DALTON, Admiral (Temporary Capt., R.N.R.).

London Gazette, 13 July, 1917.—"War Office, 13 July, 1917. Despatch on military operations of the Rhodesian Forces from the High Commissioner for South Africa to the Secretary of State for the Colonies, dated 10 March, 1917, states that the Distinguished Service Order and Special Promotion to Commander were awarded to":—

SPICER SIMSON, G. B., Commander, R.N. (for the Tanganyika Naval Expedition).

London Gazette, 18 July, 1917.—"War Office, 18 July, 1917. His Majesty the King has been graciously pleased to award a Second Bar to the Distinguished Service Order to":—

McLEAN, CHARLES WESLEY WELDON, D.S.O., Major, Royal Field Artillery. For conspicuous gallantry and devotion to duty. On two occasions in the same day he went forward at great personal risk into heavy barrage, machine-gun and rifle fire to reconnoitre and report upon the position of our infantry. The following day he led a party of officers and men under heavy shell fire to extinguish a fire which was threatening to cause grave casualties in his battery, he himself taking the chief part in saving the guns and ammunition. His fearlessness and disregard for personal safety was at all times most marked.
(D.S.O. gazetted 4 Nov. 1915; First Bar gazetted in this Gazette.)

"His Majesty the King has been graciously pleased to award a Bar to the Distinguished Service Order to":—

ASQUITH, ARTHUR MELLAND, D.S.O., Temporary Acting Commander, Royal Naval Volunteer Reserve. For conspicuous gallantry and determination in the attack and clearance of a village, when he personally captured ten of the enemy, and later organized its defence, and, by his contempt of danger under heavy fire, contributed greatly to the success of the operations and to the steadiness of all ranks with him.
(D.S.O. gazetted 17 April, 1917.)

BORRETT, OSWALD CUTHBERT, D.S.O., Major and Brevet Lieut.-Colonel (Temporary Lieut.-Colonel), Royal Lancaster Regt., attached Shropshire Light Infantry. For conspicuous gallantry and devotion to duty. He showed great initiative throughout the operations in handling his battalion. His personal bravery and energy under heavy fire were very great factors in the success of the advance. His grasp of the situation enabled this brigade to advance its line in the face of heavy opposition.
(D.S.O. gazetted 23 June, 1915.)

BRYANT, CHARLES EDGAR, D.S.O., Capt., Lancers and Royal Flying Corps. For conspicuous gallantry and devotion to duty. He has displayed the utmost gallantry and skill in leading photographic reconnaissances. In spite of overwhelming opposition by hostile aircraft, he has never failed to carry out his difficult task.
(D.S.O. gazetted 18 Feb. 1915.)

DAWSON, WILLIAM ROBERT AUFRERE, D.S.O., Capt. (Temporary Lieut.-Colonel), Royal West Kent Regt. For conspicuous gallantry and devotion to duty. When the situation was somewhat critical he displayed conspicuous bravery in organizing the defence. Although his troops were exhausted from prolonged exposure, he completely reorganized the line under heavy shell fire. His total disregard for personal danger was most marked.
(D.S.O. gazetted 15 April, 1916.)

GEPP, ERNEST CYRIL, D.S.O., Major, Duke of Cornwall's Light Infantry, Special Reserve. For conspicuous gallantry and devotion to duty. He several times visited the assaulting battalions and brought back valuable information. He had on each occasion to pass through heavy barrage and machine-gun fire. His splendid example of coolness and courage were of the greatest value.
(D.S.O. gazetted 14 Jan. 1916.)

GRIFFIN, CHRISTOPHER JOSEPH, D.S.O., Major and Brevet Lieut.-Colonel (Temporary Lieut.-Colonel), Lancashire Fusiliers. For conspicuous gallantry and devotion to duty. He commanded his battalion with great ability and determination. When the left brigade was out of touch he was mainly responsible for communication being re-established at a critical moment when conditions were most trying. The successful issue was largely due to his splendid example.
(D.S.O. gazetted 18 Feb. 1915.)

HAMILTON, SACKVILLE WILLIAM SACKVILLE, D.S.O., Major, Royal Engineers. For conspicuous gallantry and devotion to duty in siting first and support line trenches during an attack under heavy fire. His initiative enabled a situation which was confused owing to darkness to be cleared up, and after making a personal reconnaissance he returned with his information through heavy barrage and machine-gun fire. He subsequently made a further successful report on the whole situation under the same conditions, and displayed consummate ability and fearlessness.
(D.S.O. gazetted 15 April, 1916.)

HOLMES, WILLIAM GEORGE, D.S.O., Capt. (Acting Lieut.-Colonel), Royal Welsh Fusiliers. For conspicuous gallantry and devotion to duty. During the final stages of the fighting he was the soul of both defence and offence. He was placed in command of the remnants of all battalions in the vicinity, and it was mainly due to his gallantry and dash that the enemy counter-attack was defeated.
(D.S.O. gazetted 1 Jan. 1917.)

INNES, SYDNEY ARMITAGE, D.S.O., Major (Temporary Lieut.-Colonel), Royal Highlanders. For conspicuous gallantry and devotion to duty. Throughout the advance he commanded his battalion with the greatest skill and courage. His personal example and presence in the firing line, when the battalion had suffered heavy casualties, was of the utmost value and assistance to the men.
(D.S.O. gazetted 1 Jan. 1917.)

JACKSON, ARNOLD NUGENT STRODE, D.S.O. (name changed to Arnold Nugent Strode Strode-Jackson), Capt. (Temporary Major), Loyal North Lancashire Regt., attached Rifle Brigade. For conspicuous gallantry during lengthy operations, when he assumed command of the battalion and, although wounded on two separate occasions, was able to carry out most valuable work. By his skill and courage he offered a splendid example to all ranks with him.
(D.S.O. gazetted 4 June, 1917.)

McLEAN, CHARLES WESLEY WELDON, D.S.O., Major, Royal Field Artillery. For conspicuous gallantry and devotion to duty. He has commanded his battery with great skill and courage. He has observed fire and commanded the battery from an observation post under heavy fire with great coolness and accuracy.
(D.S.O. gazetted 4 Nov. 1915.)

PENNYCUICK, JAMES ALEXANDER CHARLES, D.S.O., Capt. (Temporary Major), Royal Engineers. For conspicuous gallantry and devotion during lengthy operations, when he was largely responsible for consolidating positions gained, constructing strong points and trenches in most exposed positions, and, notwithstanding heavy casualties, by his courage and skill he enabled the work to be successfully performed and the positions rendered secure.
(D.S.O. gazetted 9 Dec. 1914.)

POLLITT, GEORGE PATON, D.S.O., Temporary Major, Royal Engineers. For conspicuous gallantry and devotion to duty. He made constant and dangerous personal reconnaissances in connection with gas attacks. His close supervision and fearlessness in the front line contributed very largely to successful operations, and the men under his command owed their spirit and determination in no small degree to his magnificent example.
(D.S.O. gazetted 1 Jan. 1917.)

PORCH, CECIL PORCH, D.S.O., Capt. (Temporary Lieut.-Colonel), Reserve of Officers, East Surrey Regt., attached Northumberland Fusiliers. For conspicuous gallantry and devotion to duty. He led his battalion with the greatest gallantry and determination. He personally superintended the cutting of the enemy wire under continuous machine-gun and rifle fire. He set a very fine example of coolness and courage throughout.
(D.S.O. gazetted 26 March, 1917.)

RICE, CECIL EDWARD, D.S.O., Major (Temporary Lieut.-Colonel), Yeomanry. For conspicuous gallantry and devotion to duty in leading his battalion over ground that was under very heavy fire and in full view of the enemy. His splendid personal example inspired all ranks with confidence. Though severely wounded, he insisted on making his way to the dressing station unaided.
(D.S.O. gazetted 4 June, 1917.)

SHANNON, WILLIAM JOHN, D.S.O., Major, Lancers. For conspicuous gallantry and devotion to duty. He was commanding a dismounted party working on a cavalry track. By his skill in disposing his men and his personal energy under heavy fire, he succeeded in completing the track before the arrival of the Division, thereby performing most valuable service.
(D.S.O. gazetted 3 June, 1916.)

SMYTH, GERALD BRICE FERGUSON, D.S.O., Capt. and Brevet Major (Acting Lieut.-Colonel), Royal Engineers, attached King's Own Scottish Borderers. For conspicuous gallantry and devotion to duty. Although seriously wounded, he remained at the telephone in an ill-protected trench for many hours during a critical time to report the course of events to Brigade Headquarters. He realized that there was no officer of experience to replace him, and his sense of duty may cost him his remaining arm, the other having been amputated as the result of a previous wound. He was five times wounded.
(D.S.O. gazetted 11 Nov. 1914.)

STERNDALE-BENNETT, WALTER, D.S.O., Temporary Lieut.-Commander, Royal Naval Volunteer Reserve. For conspicuous gallantry and devotion to duty. On discovering the wire uncut except in a few places he went forward himself and led his battalion through the partially cut gaps. He finally gained his objective, and held on against very strong resistance. The success of the operation was almost entirely due to his personal example.
(D.S.O. gazetted 26 Jan. 1917.)

TOMKINSON, FRANCIS MARTIN, D.S.O., Capt. (Temporary Lieut.-Colonel), Worcestershire Regt. For conspicuous gallantry and ability in the handling of his battalion. He commanded in three attacks during the month, and on each occasion, after gaining his objective, was counter-attacked by considerable enemy forces. His determination and complete control of his unit enabled him in every instance to defeat the enemy.
(D.S.O. gazetted 1 Jan. 1917.)

AUSTRALIAN IMPERIAL FORCE.

PLANT, ERIC CLIVE PEGUS, D.S.O., Major, Australian Infantry. For conspicuous gallantry and devotion. When acting as Brigade Major he remained on duty continuously for over 48 hours, and his gallant work in reorganizing broken infantry, and later in rallying stragglers under heavy artillery fire, was invaluable.
(D.S.O. gazetted 1 Jan. 1917.)

"His Majesty the King has been graciously pleased to approve of the appointments of the undermentioned Officers to be Companions of the Distinguished Service Order, in recognition of their gallantry and devotion to duty in the field."

ALBAN, CLIFTON EDWARD RAWDON GRANT, Capt. (Acting Major), Liverpool Regt. For conspicuous gallantry and devotion to duty. When assembly trenches were ordered to be dug he reconnoitred the position, placed the tape, and superintended the digging of the trench. On a later date he carried out a daring reconnaissance of the enemy wire, and rendered most valuable reports.

ANDREWS, RICHARD JOHN, M.C., Temporary Second Lieut. (Acting Major), Devon Regt. (attached Welsh Regt.). For conspicuous gallantry and resource when in command of a brigade. Early in the operations he was wounded in the foot by a shell, but, with great courage and skill, he took effective measures to carry out an original plan, and subsequently directed a successful withdrawal. He personally supervised the retirement of the last supporting platoon in order to ensure, so far as possible, the safety of the wounded. He has been previously noted for gallantry and skill when in command of a battalion.

ARMITAGE, FRANCIS ARTHUR WILLIAM, Capt. (Acting Lieut.-Colonel) West Yorkshire Regt., attached Hampshire Regt. For conspicuous gallantry and devotion to duty. He commanded his battalion with the utmost skill and determination. Subjected to heavy shell fire throughout, he remained in close touch with the enemy, gaining his objective the first day. He successfully beat off an enemy counter-attack, and held on until relieved.

BARRY, JAMES HARDING, M.C., Temporary Capt., Royal Army Medical Corps, attached London Regt. For conspicuous gallantry and devotion to duty in attending to the wounded under exceptionally trying conditions. Under very heavy shell fire he dug out five men who were buried, and amputated two men's legs on the spot. He showed utter disregard of any personal risk, and his example was splendid.

BERESFORD, PERCY WILLIAM, Lieut.-Colonel, London Regt. For conspicuous gallantry and ability in command of his battalion during heavy enemy counter-attacks. The skill with which he handled his reserves was of the utmost assistance to the division on his right, and his determination enabled us to hold on to an almost impossible position. He repulsed three counter-attacks, and lost heavily in doing so.

BRIDGES, JOHN VICTOR, Capt. (Temporary Major), Worcestershire Regt., attached Northumberland Fusiliers. For conspicuous gallantry and devotion to duty. His display of untiring energy and devotion to duty was magnificent. He led his battalion with great skill and courage, and it was largely due to his initiative that the battalion gained its objectives.

BROWN, JAMES HARDY, Temporary Sub-Lieut., Royal Naval Volunteer Reserve. For conspicuous gallantry and devotion to duty throughout the campaign. He has navigated his ship at high speed, night and day, in all weathers, with marked zeal and determination. He has at all times set a magnificent example of courage and initiative.

(The award of the D.S.O. was announced in the Gazette of 11 May, 1917, without details of service. The second Christian name was incorrectly published therein.)

BURKE, THOMAS FRANCIS, Second Lieut., Scottish Rifles and Machine Gun Corps. For conspicuous gallantry and devotion to duty when in charge of machine guns during an attack upon enemy trenches. With great dash he personally captured an enemy machine gun and its team, and brought fire to bear on the retreating enemy with deadly effect. His promptness and courage were admirable.

CHILD-VILLIERS, THE HONOURABLE ARTHUR GEORGE, Capt. (Temporary Major), Yeomanry. For conspicuous gallantry and devotion to duty in making his way alone, through heavy shell fire, to a post that had been cut off by hostile fire. He at once reorganized the position, and remained in command, successfully conducting the defence, and by his courage and energy setting a splendid example to his men.

COLLINGS-WELLS, JOHN STANHOPE, Capt. (Acting Lieut.-Colonel), Bedfordshire Regt., Special Reserve. For conspicuous gallantry in command of a battalion which had gained its objective, holding it in spite of frequent and heavy counter-attacks. Later, in command of a composite battalion, it was owing to his powers of leadership and bravery that the battalion was formed up in darkness, on strange ground and under heavy shell fire, and subsequently achieved its object.

COMPTON-SMITH, GEOFFRY LEE, Capt. (Acting Lieut.-Colonel), Royal Welsh Fusiliers. For conspicuous gallantry and devotion to duty. He commanded his battalion with the greatest skill and determination. Immediately the objective was gained he moved forward to supervise consolidation and cover the advance of another brigade. Although wounded, he remained in the position, and his personal example was of the utmost value to all.

DANN, WILLIAM ROWLAND HARRIS, Major (Temporary Lieut.-Colonel), Bedfordshire Regt., attached London Regt. For conspicuous gallantry and devotion to duty when commanding a battalion. His personality and bravery enabled his battalion to carry out a most difficult relief at night, under very heavy shell fire. He was heavily counter-attacked on three successive occasions, but repulsed the enemy in spite of his own very severe losses.

ELLIOTT-COOPER, NEVILLE BOWES, M.C., Capt. (Temporary Lieut.-Colonel), Royal Fusiliers. For conspicuous gallantry and devotion to duty. At a critical moment, when his battalion had suffered heavily and was temporarily disorganized, he showed the greatest promptness and bravery in rallying the men and in clearing up and restoring the situation. He personally led forward a patrol of 20 men, under very heavy fire, and returned to his brigadier with 12 prisoners and very valuable information.

FELLOWES, RONALD TOWNSHEND, M.C., Capt. (Acting Lieut.-Colonel), Rifle Brigade. For conspicuous gallantry and devotion to duty. He led his battalion with great initiative and skill, capturing an important position and holding it against repeated counter-attacks. The fine spirit shown by the battalion under most trying conditions was largely due to his personal example.

FLETCHER, JAMES HENRY, M.C., Temporary Capt., Royal Army Medical Corps. For conspicuous gallantry and devotion to duty. He showed the utmost bravery and coolness when commanding the bearers. He worked continuously under artillery and machine-gun fire. It was largely due to his gallant conduct that so many wounded were safely evacuated.

FOLLETT, FRANCIS BERE, M.C., Major (Acting Lieut.-Colonel), Royal Warwickshire Regt., attached London Regt. For conspicuous gallantry and devotion to duty. He commanded his battalion with the utmost gallantry and skill. By his energy and grasp of the situation the brigade was enabled to reach its objective, having been previously held up by uncut wire and machine guns.

GOLD, CHARLES RENÉ, Second Lieut., Yeomanry, attached Durham Light Infantry. For conspicuous gallantry and devotion to duty. He showed the greatest gallantry and initiative in attacking an enemy strong point which had been a severe hindrance. He, with only a handful of men, rushed it from a flank, inflicting many casualties and capturing 20 prisoners and two machine guns.

HORSFALL, ALFRED GARNETT, Major (Acting Lieut.-Colonel), West Riding Regt. For conspicuous gallantry and devotion to duty. When in command of his battalion he displayed the greatest courage and determination. It was largely due to his personal example that the operations of his battalion were so successfully carried out.

HUTCHISON, HENRY OLIPHANT, M.C., Major, Royal Artillery. For conspicuous gallantry and devotion to duty. A battery was subjected to heavy shell fire, which set fire to the position and an ammunition dump close by. He at once dashed to where the fire was burning and, assisted by a gunner, succeeded in extinguishing the flames under continuous shell fire. By his prompt action the ammunition dump and gun were saved.

JERVIS, ERNEST CHARLES SCOTT, Capt. (Temporary Major), Reserve of Officers and Machine Gun Corps. For conspicuous gallantry and devotion to duty. He rendered most valuable service by his promptness in bringing machine guns into action. He invariably carried out personal reconnaissances of the situation.

KEMP, CHARLES MATTHEW, Temporary Capt. (Acting Major), Manchester Regt. For conspicuous gallantry when in command of his battalion. After an enemy attack, when some disorganization had set in, he rendered invaluable aid in collecting stragglers and leading them forward, under heavy fire, in a counter-attack. His coolness and bravery enabled him to successfully reorganize the troops at his disposal.

LEARMOUNT, LEONARD WRIGHT, M.C., Lieut. (Temporary Major), General List and Royal Flying Corps, Special Reserve. For conspicuous gallantry and devotion to duty. He has shown great skill and determination when on photographic reconnaissances. Despite continuous fire from the ground and attack from hostile aircraft, he has repeatedly effected a safe landing after completing his task.

MACCALLUM, HUGH, Temporary Capt., Royal Indian Marines. For conspicuous gallantry and devotion to duty throughout the campaign. He has navigated his ship at high speed, night and day, in all weathers, with marked zeal and determination. He has at all times set a magnificent example of courage and initiative.

MAJENDIE, VIVIAN HENRY BRUCE, Capt. (Acting Lieut.-Colonel), Somersetshire Light Infantry For conspicuous gallantry and devotion to duty. He commanded his battalion with the greatest skill and determination. His battalion was continuously in touch with the enemy and under heavy shell and machine-gun fire, and its grit and determination reflect the spirit of its commanding officer.

MILLER, LEONARD CHALLINOR, Temporary Lieut. (Acting Major), Royal Garrison Artillery. For conspicuous gallantry and devotion in maintaining his newly-formed battery in action, under heavy and accurate fire, until very serious casualties had been suffered and all the guns had been put out of action.

McCRACKEN, WILLIAM JAMES, M.C., Temporary Surgeon, R.N. For conspicuous gallantry and resource during operations, when, after attending wounded in captured dug-outs, he pushed forward into a village which was being heavily shelled, compelled a captured enemy M.O. to show the best enemy R.A.P., and then kept him, with 12 enemy Red Cross men, busy all day bringing in and dressing over 150 of our wounded, who otherwise could not have been treated, and then sending them down. He also searched the front line under a heavy fire for wounded.

*McKENZIE, WILLIAM SINCLAIR, Lieut., Seaforth Highlanders, Special Reserve (employed Indian Army Reserve of Officers). For conspicuous gallantry and devotion to duty. At a critical period during a strong enemy attack, when the left flank of his battalion was exposed, he, on his own initiative, collected a few men and rushed to the point of attack, encouraging those who had been temporarily dislodged to resume the offensive. It was due to his personal influence and courage that a critical situation was averted.

*(D.S.O. gazetted without deed 26 March, 1917.)

NEEVES, HORACE HUNTER, M.C., Temporary Second Lieut. (Acting Capt.), Northumberland Fusiliers. For conspicuous gallantry and devotion to duty in handling his company during an attack of the enemy position. His skilful leading and determined courage enabled him, in spite of enemy flanking and reverse fire, to get his men to within a few yards of the enemy's rear position. Owing to many casualties, however, he was compelled to withdraw. On his return he gave his battalion commander a full and lucid report on the situation—the only accurate one received. It was subsequently found that he had been wounded in the lungs early in the attack and had remained with his men under fire 23 hours after being wounded.

OSMOND, CHARLES FORTESCUE, Capt. (Acting Lieut.-Colonel), Honourable Artillery Company. For conspicuous gallantry in command of a battalion during operations. Owing to his coolness and courage under fire, and to his power of leadership, the enemy were held in check, and finally pushed back a considerable distance.

PORTAL, CHARLES FREDERICK ALGERNON, M.C., Temporary Lieut. (Temporary Capt.), Special Reserve, Royal Engineers and Royal Flying Corps. For conspicuous gallantry and devotion to duty. For many months he has done magnificent work in co-operation with the artillery. During an attack he succeeded in silencing nine active hostile batteries, ranging our artillery. His splendid example has been of the greatest value.

POTTS, JOHN, Temporary Second Lieut. (Acting Capt.), Durham Light Infantry. For conspicuous gallantry and devotion to duty when in command of a company. He himself rushed a machine gun, killed the team, and turned the gun on to the enemy. He held on in a very exposed position for some time, absolutely regardless of danger, and when his flanks were turned, and it became necessary to fight his way back, he personally covered the retirement of his men, leaving none behind.

PRIDEAUX-BRUNE, DENYS EDWARD, Capt. and Brevet Major (Temporary Lieut.-Colonel), Rifle Brigade. For conspicuous gallantry and devotion to duty. Owing to the weather and exhausted condition of the men it was not possible to carry out a prearranged plan. He took steps at once to meet the altered situation and repel a possible counter-attack. He finally returned through a heavy barrage and personally explained the situation to the Brigade Commander.

SHAW, RALPH, Second Lieut. (Temporary Lieut.), Royal Warwickshire Regt., Special Reserve. For conspicuous gallantry and ability in action. When all the senior officers of the brigade had become casualties he assumed charge of the whole line, and showed great courage and judgment under very heavy fire in organizing the consolidation.

SHIEL, FRANCIS ROBERT ARCHIBALD, Capt. (Acting Major), Royal Field Artillery. For conspicuous gallantry and devotion to duty. He showed great gallantry and initiative in organizing a party which succeeded in extinguishing a serious fire in the battery position. At the same time an ammunition dump close by caught fire. He alone rushed over, and assisted by the detachment succeeded in saving a large quantity of ammunition, thus preventing a disaster.

SPRING, FREDERICK GORDON, Major (Temporary Lieut.-Colonel), Lincolnshire Regt., attached Essex Regt. For conspicuous gallantry and devotion to duty. He has consistently shown a magnificent example under heavy fire. On occasions when his companies were counter-attacked he frequently went to the front and reorganized his men. His personal courage and coolness has been of the greatest value to all.

STANLEY, JOSEPH LOFTHOUSE, Temporary Second Lieut., West Yorkshire Regt. For conspicuous gallantry and determination during an enemy counter-attack. By his fearlessness in leading a bombing attack under very heavy fire he completely frustrated the enemy's attack upon our trenches, cut off their line of retreat, and captured 18 prisoners with the aid of two of his bombers.

STEARN, JOHN HOLDEN, Temporary Lieut., Durham Light Infantry. For conspicuous gallantry and devotion to duty. He led his men with great skill and determination, personally putting an enemy machine gun out of action. Later he commanded his company, and, although wounded himself, carried on for 16 hours in an exposed position.

TAYLOR, STUART CAMPBELL, Major (Temporary Lieut.-Colonel) (Retired Pay, Reserve of Officers), Yorkshire Light Infantry, Special Reserve. For conspicuous gallantry when in command of the right of an infantry attack. The attacking troops having been compelled to fall back, he collected the remnants of his battalion and about 100 men of other units, and, regardless of a heavy fire, he organized these in defence of a position, and by his fine example of courage and skill he successfully resisted three counter-attacks, and thus saved a critical situation.

THOM, JOHN GIBB, M.C., Temporary Major (Acting Lieut.-Colonel), Gordon Highlanders. For conspicuous gallantry and devotion to duty. He commanded one of the leading battalions, and throughout the operations he was with the leading companies, and personally led two attacks. He displayed a total disregard of personal safety, and by his fine example inspired his men to repeated efforts under most trying conditions.

TURNER, JAMES ALEXANDER, Lieut. (Temporary Capt.), Royal Scots. For conspicuous gallantry and devotion to duty whilst in charge of two companies under heavy machine-gun fire. With great skill and judgment he organized an assault on the machine-gun emplacement, and carried it through with such vigour that he captured the guns and teams. This happened at a very critical moment, and his coolness and skill were the direct means of averting very serious casualties. He was severely wounded two days later, after repeated acts of gallantry.

VIGNOLES, WALTER ADOLPH, Temporary Major, Lincolnshire Regt (rank and regiment corrected to Temporary Lieut.-Colonel, Northumberland Fusiliers). For conspicuous gallantry and devotion to duty during a hostile counter-attack upon the battalion, of which he was in temporary command. His prompt initiative and coolness at a most critical moment enabled him to rally his men, and to bring a heavy fire upon the advancing enemy, and subsequently to organize and carry out a counter-attack with complete success.

AUSTRALIAN IMPERIAL FORCE.

BOND, LIONEL WILFRED, Major, Australian Army Medical Corps. For conspicuous bravery and devotion to duty. When in charge of advanced collecting and forwarding posts, his total disregard of danger under a terrific hail of gas shells, H.E., and shrapnel fire, gained him the confidence of all ranks, and greatly assisted the evacuation of the wounded. Later, although wounded and partly gassed, he refused to leave his post, and his bravery and devotion saved a very critical situation.

BROWN, ARNOLD, M.C., Capt. (Temporary Major), Australian Infantry. For conspicuous gallantry and devotion to duty in organizing and leading bombing attacks. His sound judgment and determination were mainly instrumental in bringing about the success of these attacks, whilst his utter disregard of danger throughout set a splendid example to officers and men.

BROWNELL, HERBERT PERCIVAL, Major, Australian Army Medical Corps. For conspicuous gallantry and devotion to duty whilst attending to the wounded under heavy fire. His coolness in organizing matters amidst the greatest confusion enabled the wounded to be expeditiously treated, and he personally treated some hundreds of cases under heavy shell fire.

CONRICK, HORATIO VICTOR PATRICK, Major, Australian Army Medical Corps. For conspicuous gallantry and devotion to duty in attending to the wounded. He proceeded to the scene of an explosion under very heavy shell fire, and personally directed the removal of the wounded. His fearlessness and disregard for his personal safety has been marked on all occasions.

DENEHY, CHARLES ALOYSIUS, Lieut.-Colonel, Australian Infantry. For conspicuous gallantry and ability. When in command of a defence which was ceaselessly bombarded he was able, by his courage and fine example, to maintain the spirit of his men in spite of heavy losses, and later he organized and successfully carried through an attack, capturing 187 prisoners, and securing many machine guns and trench-mortars.

ELLIOTT, HAROLD EDWARD, C.M.G., Colonel (Temporary Brigadier-General). For conspicuous gallantry when in command of the advanced guards of the division during an advance. The successes during a long period of almost continuous fighting, the capture of several villages, which were held against frequent and violent counter-attacks, and the slightness of our losses compared to those of the enemy were largely due to his able leadership, energy and courage.

LECKY, CHARLES STUART, Major, Australian Infantry. For conspicuous gallantry and resource during an attack when in charge of the front line held by his battalion. Despite the heavy barrage and artillery bombardment, he handled the situation with great skill and courage, and his fine example greatly contributed to the steadiness of all ranks. Although wounded, he refused to leave the line until the attack had been repulsed and the position secured.

RAY, JOHN, Major, Australian Field Artillery. For conspicuous gallantry and devotion to duty. He showed great skill and initiative when the enemy obtained a footing to the rear of his battery. He pulled his guns out of their pits, reversed them, and opened fire on the enemy, inflicting heavy casualties, thus rendering valuable assistance at a critical moment.

TREW, WILLIAM MERRIMAN, Major, Australian Infantry. For conspicuous gallantry and devotion to duty in temporary command of his battalion. He organized the defence of a captured position in such a way that all counter-attacks were repulsed and heavy losses inflicted on the enemy. Though severely wounded, he remained on duty until the situation had cleared up.

YATES, WILLIAM THOMAS, Capt., Australian Infantry. For conspicuous gallantry and devotion to duty. He commanded a successful attack on an enemy strong point, and personally conducted the consolidation of the captured post. Later, under intense shell fire, he displayed the utmost gallantry and coolness in encouraging his men, and showing a fine disregard for personal safety.

CANADIAN FORCE.

ARCHAMBAULT, JOSEPH PIERRE URGEL, Capt. (Acting Major), Canadian Infantry. For conspicuous gallantry and devotion to duty. He showed great ability in organizing his company for the attack. During the advance he led his company with great courage and initiative until wounded. His personal courage was a splendid example to his men.

BLOIS, ARTHUR OSBORNE, Capt. (Acting Major), Canadian Infantry. For conspicuous gallantry and devotion to duty. Although wounded, he took command of the battalion, and superintended and continued to advance until relieved by another officer late at night. He showed the greatest gallantry throughout.

COLEMAN, THOMAS ROY, M.C., Temporary Major, Canadian Infantry. For conspicuous gallantry when commanding a company in an attack. When nearing the final objective a portion of the line was held up by enemy machine guns, whereupon he pushed forward and bombed the gun emplacement, continuing to clear the enemy trenches until wounded in the arm.

FEARMAN, HERBERT DOUGLAS, Capt. (Acting Major), Canadian Infantry. For conspicuous gallantry and devotion to duty. As Adjutant, he worked with untiring zeal and energy in organizing the details for the attack. After the operation, and during the consolidation of the position, he carried out a most difficult reconnaissance of the whole line, obtaining most valuable information.

LEONARD, CHARLES FRANKLIN, Capt. (Acting Major), Canadian Infantry. For conspicuous gallantry and devotion to duty. He led his company 2,500 yards across the open and dug in in daylight. He was most energetic in sending out patrols, and although his flank was exposed for several hours, took all possible steps to protect it. Throughout the advance he set a splendid example to his men.

McCRIMMON, KENNETH HOWARD, Capt. (Acting Major), Canadian Infantry. For conspicuous gallantry and devotion to duty. Under heavy artillery fire he superintended the laying out and the pumping of the trenches, and made a final reconnaissance in daylight of the position. Throughout he showed the greatest energy in organizing supplies, which proved of the utmost value to the men under severe weather conditions.

McMILLAN, ALEXANDER, Capt. (Acting Major), Canadian Infantry. For conspicuous gallantry and devotion to duty. He led his company with great skill and determination. By his personal example and disregard for his own safety, he gained his objective in the face of heavy shell and machine-gun fire. His bearing under heavy fire was most gallant.

MEREDITH, ALAN PICTON OSLER, Major, Canadian Infantry. For conspicuous gallantry and devotion to duty. As Brigade Major he personally, at great risk, reconnoitred ground along our front, thereby rendering invaluable assistance to his brigade commander in the attack which followed. He displayed the utmost fearlessness in personally superintending the work of patrols when it became necessary to push them forward.

MILLS, ARTHUR LENNOX STANLEY, Capt. (Acting Major), Canadian Infantry. For conspicuous gallantry and devotion to duty. He found a gap between his own and the next company which was strongly held by the enemy. At great personal risk he collected five men and, demoralizing the enemy, he assisted to capture 200 prisoners. Throughout he was most courageous and daring in handling the entire line of the battalion front.

PHILPOT, DAVID, Capt. (Acting Major), Canadian Infantry. For conspicuous gallantry and devotion to duty. The careful and painstaking manner in which he organized every detail contributed very largely to the remarkable success achieved by his battalion in an attack upon an enemy position. His reports were frequent and accurate, and proved invaluable as a means of appreciating the general situation.

RILEY, HAROLD JAMES, Major, Canadian Infantry. For conspicuous gallantry and devotion to duty. He led his company to the attack and consolidated his position under heavy shell fire. When the position was threatened by intense fire he advanced in front and encouraged his men and held on for 40 hours, suffering heavy casualties.

ROGERS, JOSEPH BARTLETT, M.C., Lieut.-Colonel, Canadian Infantry. For conspicuous gallantry and devotion to duty. He led his battalion in the attack with great tactical skill, and showed great promptness and sound judgment in dealing with the difficult situation which had arisen in consequence of the troops on his flank having failed to reach their objective.

ROSS, ALEXANDER, Lieut.-Colonel, Canadian Infantry. For conspicuous gallantry and devotion to duty. His preparation for the attack was perfected to a very high standard. During the advance he handled his battalion with the greatest skill and determination. The success of the operation was largely due to his fine leadership and example.

TAYLOR, FAWCETT GOWLER, Major, Canadian Rifles. For conspicuous gallantry. During an attack upon the enemy position he was the first man to reach the final objective, and his coolness and initiative in consolidating the position and reorganizing his unit were of the greatest assistance to his commanding officer.

TAUNTON, ARTHUR JOHN SHOWELL, Capt. (Acting Major), Canadian Infantry. For conspicuous gallantry and devotion to duty. He led his company in the face of very heavy fire at short range. By his coolness and courage the position was taken and three guns captured. The work of consolidation was carried out and the position maintained.

TUDOR, LORN PAULET OWEN, Major, Canadian Infantry. For conspicuous gallantry and devotion to duty. The magnificent success with which his battalion carried out its objective and consolidated the captured position was mainly due to his personal example of coolness and disregard of safety, and to the thoroughness with which all details had been prepared by him.

URQUHART, HUGH MACINTYRE, M.C., Major, Canadian Infantry. For conspicuous gallantry and devotion to duty. He showed remarkable tactical skill in preparing instructions for an attack, and when the attack had proved successful he displayed great coolness and bravery in selecting positions to be held and indicating action to be taken, the whole time under very heavy fire. He rendered a full and complete report of the situation on his return to brigade headquarters.

London Gazette, 20 July, 1917.—" Admiralty, 20 July, 1917.—Honours for Miscellaneous Services. The King has been graciously pleased to give orders for the appointment of the undermentioned Officers to be Companions of the Distinguished Service Order."

WILLS, CHARLES SAMUEL, Capt., R.N.

MACLEAN, COLIN KENNETH, Capt., R.N.

FRASER, JOHN STEWART GORDON, Commander, R.N.

BENN, ION HAMILTON, M.P., Commander, Royal Naval Volunteer Reserve.

BRUCE-GARDYNE, EVAN, Lieut.-Commander, R.N.

In recognition of their services in the bombardment of Zeebrugge on the 11th–12th May, 1917, and of Ostend on the 4th–5th June, 1917.

" Honours for Services in Action with Enemy Submarines.—The King has been graciously pleased to approve of the award of the following honours to Officers for services in action with enemy submarines. To be Companions of the Distinguished Service Order."

BERNAYS, LEOPOLD ARTHUR, C.M.G., Lieut.-Commander, Royal Navy.

HOLT, REGINALD VESEY, Lieut.-Commander, R.N.

WILSON, GRAHAM FRANCIS WINSTANLEY, Lieut.-Commander, R.N.

TURNBULL, RICHARD JAMES, D.S.C., Lieut., Royal Naval Reserve.

IRVINE, GEORGE, Lieut., R.N.R.

HEREFORD, FRANCIS ROBERT, D.S.C., Acting Lieut., Royal Naval R[illegible]

To receive a Bar to the Distinguished Service Order :

CAMPBELL, GORDON, V.C., D.S.O., Capt., Royal Navy.

" Honours for the Royal Naval Air Service.—The King has been g[illegible]usly pleased to give orders for the following appointments to the Distinguished Service Order."

MAITLAND, EDWARD MAITLAND, Wing Capt., Royal Naval Air Service. In recognition of valuable and gallant work in connection with airships and parachutes. He has carried out experiments at his own personal risk, and has made some descents under enemy fire.

BUTLER, CHARLES HENRY, D.S.C., Squadron Commander, Royal Naval Air Service. In recognition of his gallantry on the 5th June, 1917, when he fought single-handed two engagements with a number of powerful hostile machines. He attacked six hostile aeroplanes together over the Thames Estuary, and later attacked two off Ostend. On each occasion the machine selected for attack was compelled to dive.

HOBBS, BASIL DEACON, D.S.C., Flight Lieut., Royal Naval Air Service.

London Gazette, 26 July, 1917.—" War Office, 26 July, 1917. His Majesty the King has been graciously pleased to approve of the award of a Bar to the Distinguished Service Order to " :—

BARKER, RANDLE BARNETT, D.S.O., Capt. and Brevet Major (Temporary Lieut.-Colonel), Royal Fusiliers. For conspicuous gallantry and devotion to duty. During an assault his battalion was compelled to withdraw from its objective owing to heavy casualties and to its flank being unsupported. At this most critical moment he reorganized and rallied all the men of his brigade who were within reach, and by his promptitude and fine leadership won back most of the objective, and maintained it until relieved.

(D.S.O. gazetted 20 Oct. 1916.)

BROWN, HENRY ROBERT, D.S.O., Major (Temporary Lieut.-Colonel), Cameron Highlanders, Special Reserve. For conspicuous gallantry and devotion to duty. He led his battalion with great skill and precision in the attack. It was due to his skilful handling of the battalion under most trying conditions that the operations were carried through with complete success.

(D.S.O. gazetted 14 Jan. 1916.)

BUTTERWORTH, REGINALD FRANCIS AMHURST, D.S.O., Major (Acting Lieut.-Colonel), Royal Engineers. For conspicuous gallantry and devotion to duty when a fire occurred in an ammunition dump. He took charge of the arrangements and himself assisted in extinguishing the fire. His personal courage, example and work were of the greatest value.
(D.S.O. gazetted 3 June, 1916.)

CAMPBELL, ROBERT, D.S.O., Major (Acting Lieut.-Colonel), Cameron Highlanders, attached Argyll and Sutherland Highlanders. For conspicuous gallantry and devotion to duty. At a critical moment, when the enemy had pierced our line and were consolidating a position to our rear, he skilfully and energetically counter-attacked, forcing the enemy to surrender with heavy loss. He subsequently rendered valuable assistance to another unit by bringing enfilade fire to bear upon the enemy. His promptness and energy saved a very awkward situation.
(D.S.O. gazetted 1 Jan. 1917.)

HOPWOOD, ALFRED HENRY, D.S.O., Major, Lincolnshire Regt. For conspicuous gallantry and devotion to duty. He went forward to the front under the most intense fire and brought back invaluable information. He displayed great gallantry throughout the operations, and had a most inspiring effect on all ranks.
(D.S.O. gazetted 4 June, 1917.)

HORN, ROBERT, D.S.O., M.C., Major (Temporary Lieut.-Colonel), Seaforth Highlanders. For conspicuous gallantry and devotion to duty. He led his battalion with great ability and courage. It was largely due to his personal reconnaissance that many difficulties were overcome, and the objectives gained with complete success.
(D.S.O. gazetted 4 June, 1917.)

HOWARD, THOMAS NAIRNE SCOTT MONCRIEFF, D.S.O., Major and Brevet Lieut.-Colonel (Temporary Lieut.-Colonel), West Yorkshire Regt. For conspicuous gallantry and devotion to duty. He led his battalion through a heavy barrage, and was himself wounded. He established himself in the objective, and was a splendid example to the men.
(D.S.O. gazetted 24 July, 1917.)

IRWIN, ALFRED PERCY BULTEEL, D.S.O., Capt. (Temporary Major and Acting Lieut.-Colonel), East Surrey Regt. For conspicuous gallantry and devotion to duty. Owing to heavy casualties amongst officers, he personally took command of his own battalion and men of other units at a critical moment during an attack, and captured and held the final objective under very heavy fire. When compelled to withdraw after five hours, he did so with great skill, showing at all times a fine example of personal gallantry and coolness.
(D.S.O. gazetted 20 Oct. 1916.)

CANADIAN FORCE.

DYER, HUGH MARSHAL, D.S.O., Lieut.-Colonel, Infantry. For conspicuous gallantry and devotion to duty. His fine leadership and foresight of possible contingencies enabled his battalion to assault and capture its objectives in spite of almost impassable obstacles. At all times he showed a spirit of indomitable courage which communicated itself in marked degree to his officers and men. He assisted personally to dress the wounded under heavy shell fire, setting a splendid example to all ranks.
(D.S.O. gazetted 14 Jan. 1916.)

MACKENZIE, JOHN PERCIVAL, D.S.O., Major, Infantry. For conspicuous gallantry and devotion to duty. He showed very fine judgment and ability in handling his battalion during an attack, the success of which was very largely due to his quick grasp of every situation. He later made three personal reconnaissances of our advanced positions under intense hostile fire in order to obtain information for our artillery, and his reports were accurate and of great value.
(D.S.O. gazetted 1 Jan. 1917.)

WINTER, ORMONDE DE L'EPÉE, C.M.G., D.S.O., Lieut.-Colonel, Royal Field Artillery (amendment [London Gazette, 26 Sept. 1917], incorrectly shown under the heading "Canadian Force"). For conspicuous gallantry and devotion to duty in extinguishing a burning ammunition dump, aided by another officer, at great personal risk, thereby saving a large number of rounds and considerable loss of life.
(D.S.O. gazetted 8 Nov. 1915.)

"His Majesty the King has been graciously pleased to approve of the appointments of the undermentioned Officers to be Companions of the Distinguished Service Order, in recognition of their gallantry and devotion to duty in the field."

ABERCROMBY, SIR GEORGE WILLIAM, Bart., Temporary Major (Acting Lieut.-Colonel), Royal Highlanders. For conspicuous gallantry and devotion to duty. He led his battalion and gained his first two objectives, after considerable opposition, at the scheduled time. The success of the operation was largely due to his careful and continuous reconnaissances beforehand and to his skilful training and teaching of the battalion.

ANDREWS, JOHN OLIVER, M.C., Second Lieut. (Temporary Capt.), Royal Scots and Royal Flying Corps. For conspicuous gallantry and devotion to duty in leading offensive patrols with great dash and success on over 30 occasions, and taking part in over 22 combats. His skill and courage in attacking and destroying hostile aircraft have at all times been magnificent.

BARNES, DAVID THOMAS, Temporary Lieut. (Acting Capt.), Oxfordshire and Buckinghamshire Light Infantry. For conspicuous gallantry and devotion to duty. As commander of the leading waves in our attacks he personally superintended the passing of the companies through the gaps in enemy wire to their forward objective. This having been reached, he organized the whole of the defence with the utmost skill. His reports to headquarters were accurate and frequent, and throughout the operations his coolness, bravery, and initiative were most marked.

BAYNE-JARDINE, CHRISTIAN WEST, M.C., Capt. (Acting Major), Royal Field Artillery. For conspicuous gallantry and devotion to duty during an attack, in establishing and maintaining an observation post whence he was able to supply headquarters with constant and accurate information concerning our own advanced troops and the enemy. He was constantly exposed to fire, and his coolness and determination were most marked.

BRASH, JAMES, Second Lieut., Seaforth Highlanders, Special Reserve. For conspicuous gallantry and devotion to duty. When his platoon was consolidating their position he took six men to the assistance of a party on his flank and captured 40 prisoners. He then entered a hostile strong point and, killing the team, captured a machine gun.

BULLER, JAMES HENRY GEORGE, Capt. (Acting Major), Rifles, Indian Army. For conspicuous gallantry and devotion to duty. He gallantly led his men against superior forces of the enemy and captured a machine gun. He succeeded in penetrating to the enemy's second line, where he was wounded.

CAMPBELL, SIR JOHN BRUCE STEWART, Bart., Temporary Major, Royal Scots. For conspicuous gallantry and devotion to duty. He brought his battalion into action under very difficult circumstances and commanded it with conspicuous courage. He succeeded in evacuating all his wounded during the night, and only withdrew his battalion when this was complete.

COLEMAN, PERCY GEORGE, Second Lieut. (Temporary Lieut.), North Staffordshire Regt. For conspicuous gallantry and devotion to duty. He reached his objective with his platoon and was almost immediately severely wounded. Although isolated and hemmed in by the enemy he maintained his position and repulsed heavy attacks with great loss to the enemy.

COOPER, ARKWRIGHT RICHARD, Temporary Capt., Worcestershire Regt. For conspicuous gallantry and devotion to duty. He passed through the barrage several times when reorganizing his company and was severely wounded in doing so. He remained in command and personally led the assault and did not leave his men until the objective was gained.

D'ARCY, SAMUEL HOLLIS ALFRED, Second Lieut., Royal Flying Corps, Special Reserve. For conspicuous gallantry and devotion to duty, in continually attacking and dispersing hostile infantry and transport from a very low altitude. Whilst engaged in this he was wounded, but refused to return until he was almost unconscious. He also showed great courage and determination on several occasions in attacking hostile aircraft, destroying some and forcing others to descend.

DENE, ARTHUR POLLARD, Major and Brevet Lieut.-Colonel (Temporary Lieut.-Colonel), Duke of Cornwall's Light Infantry. For conspicuous gallantry and devotion to duty. He assumed command of an attacking force which captured its objective under difficult circumstances. Though himself wounded at the start he remained in command, and throughout acted with great coolness and courage.

FISHER, DONALD RUTHERFURD DACRE, Capt. (Acting Major), Royal Field Artillery. For conspicuous gallantry and devotion to duty. He commanded his battery with exceptional energy and skill. He advanced his battery with great steadiness under heavy shelling and reopened fire. Throughout he has performed his duties with the utmost courage and ability.

GREENSHIELDS, DAVID MACKENZIE, Second Lieut., Highland Light Infantry. For conspicuous gallantry and devotion to duty. After all company commanders had become casualties he took command of and reorganized his battalion, remaining in charge of the front line for two days. It was entirely due to his energy and cheerfulness that the position was so well maintained. He set a splendid example to all under him.

HAY, GEORGE HAROLD, Capt. (Temporary Major), Royal Scots. For conspicuous gallantry and devotion to duty. Commanding the battalion he led his men with great skill and courage. At each successive phase of the attack he reformed and led the men on again with such ability that all objectives were gained with comparatively small casualties.

KOEBEL, FRANK OSCAR, Major (Temporary Lieut.-Colonel), North Staffordshire Regt. For conspicuous gallantry and devotion to duty. He inspired his men to repeated efforts, and when most of his officers were casualties he collected the remainder of the men and was himself wounded in leading them to the final effort to capture the position.

LAYTON, EDWARD, Temporary Major, Argyll and Sutherland Highlanders. For conspicuous gallantry and devotion to duty. When all his officers had become casualties he reinforced his front line, and, by his courage and determination, carried the enemy second line, when he was severely wounded.

LEAKE, GEORGE ERNEST ARTHUR, Second Lieut. (Acting Capt.), London Regt. For conspicuous gallantry and devotion to duty when in command of his company. He showed a splendid example of coolness, disregard of danger, and cheerfulness, and, although wounded, he remained at duty. It was largely owing to his influence that all ranks showed such a splendid spirit under the most intense hostile barrage, which lasted for 14 hours.

LEWIS, NORMAN ALLEN, M.C., Temporary Capt., Royal Fusiliers. For conspicuous gallantry and devotion to duty. He acted with the greatest promptitude during an attack when direction had been lost, successfully organizing a bombing party to restore the situation, and re-establishing touch with another unit. He subsequently formed and held a strong point all day against enemy counter-attacks, working throughout with the greatest skill and gallantry and imparting his spirit to his men.

LOCK, JOHN MATTHEW BOYS, Second Lieut., Middlesex Regt., Special Reserve. For conspicuous gallantry and devotion to duty. He took charge of a bombing attack, and showed the utmost fearlessness and determination against strong opposition. His splendid leadership and courage under most difficult conditions rendered valuable assistance at a critical time.

MICKLE, KENNETH AUBREY, Second Lieut. (Acting Capt.), Royal Garrison Artillery, Special Reserve. For conspicuous gallantry and devotion to duty. He commanded a number of trench mortars with great ability and courage. He carried out all the wire cutting, organized supplies of ammunition, and carried out his duties under a continual hostile bombardment with great courage and coolness.

PIPON, ROBERT HENRY, M.C., Major (Acting Lieut.-Colonel), Royal Fusiliers. For conspicuous gallantry and devotion to duty in handling his battalion with great ability and sound judgment during an advance for the purpose of maintaining touch with the enemy. His personal courage and resource were invaluable to his battalion.

RASHLEIGH, REGINALD NICHOLAS, M.C., Capt. (Acting Major), Royal Field Artillery. For conspicuous gallantry and devotion to duty. He went forward to within 500 yards of the enemy's position, and for two hours, under very heavy fire, sent back invaluable reports on the situation. He has at all times set a fine example of courage, energy and devotion to duty.

RIGG, GEORGE SOUTHERTON, Second Lieut. (Temporary Lieut.), York and Lancaster Regt., Special Reserve. For conspicuous gallantry and devotion to duty. At an extremely critical moment, when the enemy had broken through on our flanks and were surrounding our line, he rallied the infantry and reorganized the line with such success that the enemy were repulsed on all sides and finally cut off in their attempt to retreat. His gallantry and initiative saved a very dangerous situation.

SPILLER, DUNCAN WILFRED LAMBERT, Major (Temporary Lieut.-Colonel), Royal Field Artillery. For conspicuous gallantry and devotion to duty in conducting most valuable reconnaissances of enemy wire, with a view to its being cut. He was heavily shelled, but carried on, and gained most valuable information. He has performed similar good work for his whole division on several occasions.

SUGARS, HAROLD SAUNDERSON, M.C., Temporary Capt., Royal Army Medical Corps. For conspicuous gallantry and devotion to duty. He showed magnificent disregard of personal safety in attending to the wounded under heavy fire for five days. On the fifth day his leg was broken, but this did not prevent him from going through heavy shell fire to save the life of a corporal whose main artery had been cut, and who required immediate attention. His fearlessness in crossing the open under continuous and heavy fire to save life or to alleviate suffering was most marked.

THORNTON-SMITH, ARTHUR DONALD, Temporary Second Lieut., King's Royal Rifle Corps. For conspicuous gallantry and devotion to duty. He carried out a daring reconnaissance of a village still occupied by the enemy. He went over a distance of 1,000 yards, and exposed to the enemy the whole way. His valuable information enabled the village to be captured with very light casualties.

TREASE, REGINALD ERNEST, M.C., Second Lieut., Royal Field Artillery, Special Reserve. For conspicuous gallantry and devotion to duty. He acted as artillery liaison officer during the attack. He was continuously in the front line, sending back most valuable information. When communications were cut he repeatedly brought back the information himself, having to go through a very heavy barrage on each occasion.

TREMLETT, ELIAS, Temporary Lieut., Machine Gun Corps. For conspicuous gallantry and devotion to duty. He organized a bombing attack, and succeeded in working his way down 500 yards of the enemy's trench. Throughout the attack he showed admirable coolness and resource, and greatly stimulated the men under his command.

WALSH, ROBERT HENRY, M.C., Major, Royal Field Artillery. For conspicuous gallantry and devotion to duty. He was observing from the front line, which was being heavily shelled, and, owing to casualties, the men were becoming disorganized. He collected and rallied these men, organizing a strong resistance against the enemy counter-attack. He then returned to R.A. headquarters and organized a concentrated fire upon the enemy.

WATSON, OSCAR CYRIL SPENCER, Major (Reserve of Officers), Yorkshire Light Infantry (Christian name corrected to Oliver Cyril Spencer). For conspicuous gallantry and devotion to duty. He reorganized men of all units, inspired them with his own coolness and confidence, and personally led them forward to a second attack. He was severely wounded.

WHEELER, CORDY, Temporary Major, Oxfordshire and Buckinghamshire Light Infantry. For conspicuous gallantry and devotion to duty. Although wounded, he assumed command of the battalion, which had no officer available, and organized an attack on the enemy's second line. By his energy and courage he inspired confidence in all ranks, and remained in command for four hours until relieved.

CANADIAN FORCE.

CRITCHLEY, WALTER RAMSAY, Major, Infantry. For conspicuous gallantry and devotion to duty. He took charge of the attack on the second objective, and displayed great skill and courage in capturing and consolidating the position, personally dealing with several of the enemy who offered resistance.

FERGUSON, HUGH CAMERON, Capt. (Acting Major), Infantry. For conspicuous gallantry and devotion to duty. When leading his company to the attack he was wounded, but continued on, handling his men with great skill and determination. He was wounded a second time, but carried on until the objective was captured. He remained with his company until the third and fourth waves had passed through the position.

FRENCH, JOHN POYNTZ, Capt. (Acting Major), Mounted Rifles. For conspicuous gallantry and devotion to duty. In spite of the most difficult conditions, he succeeded in gaining his objective, displaying a splendid example of courage and initiative. Later, he went forward under heavy fire, and made a most valuable report on the situation.

HUTCHISON, HARRY, Lieut. (Acting Major), Infantry. For conspicuous gallantry and devotion to duty. When in command of two companies he led them with great dash to the final objective, capturing a large number of the enemy, machine guns and mortars. He showed great initiative and resource in so disposing his forces, under heavy fire and with inadequate support, as to obtain and retain possession of high ground which was essential to the success of the attack. His coolness at a critical juncture was directly responsible for the safety of three battalions. His fearlessness in personally supervising the work of digging in under heavy barrage was most conspicuous, and his work throughout the engagement was splendid as an example to all ranks.

MAHAFFY, KENNETH A., M.C., Capt. (Acting Major), Infantry (Christian name corrected to Kenneth Arnold). For conspicuous gallantry and devotion to duty. After capturing his own objective, he took command of the second wave, which was without leaders, and led them to their objective, forming a defensive line 150 yards in front of it. Throughout his coolness and bravery were a striking example to all.

NORSWORTHY, STANLEY COUNTER, M.C., Major, Infantry. For conspicuous gallantry and devotion to duty when in command of his battalion. He went forward under very heavy fire and established a firm defensive flank. He continued in personal command for 36 hours, his example and forethought being an inspiration to his battalion and ensuring the success of operations at a critical time.

PEASE, EDSON RAYMOND, Capt. (Acting Major), Infantry. For conspicuous gallantry and devotion to duty when in command of his company. He consolidated the final objective with great skill, and maintained his position under the most difficult conditions. He has on many previous occasions rendered invaluable service.

REID, GEORGE ERIC, Capt. (Acting Major), Infantry. For conspicuous gallantry and devotion to duty. He led his company with great skill and energy. He finally led them to the successful assault of the guns, capturing four field guns, one machine gun, and over 50 prisoners. Throughout the advance he showed the utmost gallantry and good leadership, and set a splendid example to all.

ROSS, MALCOLM NUGENT, Major, Field Artillery. For conspicuous gallantry and devotion to duty. He showed great zeal and initiative in moving his battery forward and coming into action with the minimum loss of time. He also displayed great enterprise in repairing two captured howitzers and bringing them into action again.

SPARLING, ALBERT WALKER, Major, Infantry. For conspicuous gallantry and devotion to duty. Upon leaving the first objective he was the only officer of the two companies, and directed the capture and consolidation of the second objective. He was a most splendid example to all ranks under his command.

THORNLEY, JOSEPH HARRY, Major, Engineers (regiment corrected to Canadian Railway Troops). For conspicuous gallantry and devotion to duty in personally supervising repairs to a light railway upon which the supply of artillery ammunition entirely depended. It had been broken in twenty places by shell fire. He had previously shown great ability and courage whilst engaged in similar work under very trying circumstances.

WILLETS, CHARLES RICHARD EDWARD, Major, Infantry. For conspicuous gallantry and devotion to duty. He went forward to the front line under very heavy fire and organized the defence of the position with great skill. He has at all times displayed the greatest courage and initiative.

London Gazette, 8 Aug. 1917.—" War Office, 8 Aug. 1917. His Majesty the King has been graciously pleased to approve of the undermentioned Rewards for distinguished service in the field, dated 3 June, 1917. Awarded a Bar to the Distinguished Service Order."

ROSS, ARTHUR JUSTIN, D.S.O., Major, Royal Engineers and Royal Flying Corps.

To be Companions of the Distinguished Service Order:

BAZLEY-WHITE, RICHARD BOOTH LESLIE, Capt., Royal West Kent Regt.

CORNWALLIS, KINAHAN, Temporary Major, Special List.

HASTINGS, JOHN HENRY, Lieut.-Colonel, West Yorkshire Regt.

HOWARD, THOMAS NAIRNE SCOTT MONCRIEFF, Major and Brevet Lieut.-Colonel (Temporary Lieut.-Colonel), West Yorkshire Regt. (Commanding Battn., Devonshire Regt.).

McCLINTOCK, ARTHUR GEORGE, Major (Temporary Lieut.-Colonel), Lancers, Commanding Battn., Yorkshire Light Infantry.

NUTTALL, CHARLES MONTAGUE, Lieut.-Colonel, Royal Garrison Artillery.

WILSON, CYRIL EDWARD, Capt. and Brevet Major (Temporary Lieut.-Colonel) (Retired Pay), Reserve of Officers, late East Lancashire Regt.

London Gazette, 11 Aug. 1917.—" Admiralty, 11 Aug. 1917. The King has been graciously pleased to give orders for the appointment of the undermentioned Officers. To be Companions of the Distinguished Service Order."

TANDY, HENRY GEORGE HAMILTON, Lieut.-Commander, R.N. In recognition of the promptitude, courage and resource which he displayed when one of H.M. ships was torpedoed. Lieut.-Commander Tandy was in his bunk at the time of the explosion, but by the prompt and resourceful steps which he took on arriving on deck, succeeded in bringing his ship safely into harbour.

SCOTT, GILBERT BODLEY, Staff Surgeon, R.N. In recognition of his services with a Naval Armoured Car Squadron in France, Russia, Turkey and Roumania. On active service he has shown a devotion to duty and a forgetfulness of self which cannot be too highly praised.

KING, WILLIAM, Lieut., R.N.V.R.

SZULEZEWSKI, OSWALD, Lieut., R.N.V.R.

For gallant and devoted services with Inland Water Transport throughout the operations in Mesopotamia. They have navigated their ships at high speed, night and day, in all weathers with marked zeal and determination, and have often been under fire.

SMILES, WALTER DORLING, Lieut., R.N.V.R. In recognition of his services with a Naval Armoured Car Squadron in France, Belgium, Persia and Roumania. He was wounded on the 28th Nov. 1916, in the Dobrudja. On coming out of hospital he volunteered to lead a flying squadron for special duty round Braila, and his gallantry on this occasion was the chief factor of success. On one occasion, when in action with a light armoured car, he got out twice to start it up under heavy fire. Being struck by a bullet he rolled into a ditch and remained there all day under fire, having sent back a message to the Russian Colonel in command asking him to allow none of his soldiers in any circumstances to risk their lives to save his car. He did not escape until night.

To receive a Bar to the Distinguished Service Order:

WOODS, ALEXANDER RIALL WADHAM, D.S.O., Commander, R.N. In recognition of his services in command of the landing party at the capture of Salif on the 12th June, 1917. The place was attacked at dawn and captured after a three hours' resistance at the cost of only two casualties to the attacking force. This was largely due to the skilful manner in which Commander Woods conducted the advance.

" Honours for Services in Action with Enemy Submarines.—The King has been graciously pleased to approve of the award of the following honours to Officers for services in action with enemy submarines. To be a Companion of the Distinguished Service Order."

LAWRIE, JOHN, D.S.C., Lieut., Royal Naval Reserve.

" Honours for the Royal Naval Air Service.—The King has been graciously pleased to give orders for the appointments of the undermentioned Officers. To be Companions of the Distinguished Service Order."

LITTLE, ROBERT ALEXANDER, D.S.C., Flight Lieut., Royal Naval Air Service. For gallantry in action and for exceptional skill and daring in aerial combats. Since the 9th May, 1917, besides having driven off numerous artillery aeroplanes and damaged six hostile machines, he has destroyed six others. On the 26th June, 1917, an Aviatik being seen from the aerodrome he went up to attack it. He engaged it and fired a burst at close range, and the enemy machine stalled and went down in flames.

COLLISHAW, RAYMOND, D.S.C., Flight Lieut., Royal Naval Air Service. For conspicuous bravery and skill in successfully leading attacks against hostile aircraft. Since the 10th June, 1917, Flight Lieut. Collishaw has himself brought down four machines completely out of control and driven down two others with their planes shot away. Whilst on an offensive patrol on the morning of the 15th June, 1917, he forced down a hostile scout in a nose dive. Later, on the same day, he drove down one hostile two-seater machine completely out of control, one hostile scout in a spin, and a third machine with two of its planes shot away. On the 24th June, 1917, he engaged four enemy scouts, driving one down in a spin and another with two of its planes shot away; the latter machine was seen to crash.

To receive a Bar to the Distinguished Service Order:

BUTLER, CHARLES HENRY, D.S.O., D.S.C., Squadron Commander, Royal Naval Air Service. For the skill and gallantry with which he attacked a formation of 15 hostile machines returning from a raid on England. Closing on one machine, he engaged it at close quarters. Presently he saw this machine nose dive, crash into the sea and sink. Meanwhile he had engaged a second machine, but broke off the engagement to follow down the first machine. Afterwards he lost sight of the enemy formation and returned to his aerodrome.

London Gazette, 16 Aug. 1917.—" War Office, 16 Aug. 1917. His Majesty the King has been graciously pleased to award a Bar to the Distinguished Service Order to " :—

CHESTER-MASTER, RICHARD CHESTER, D.S.O., Capt. and Brevet Major (Temporary Lieut.-Colonel), Reserve of Officers, late King's Royal Rifle Corps, Commanding Battn. For conspicuous gallantry and devotion to duty. During operations for six days he displayed great courage and ability. His battalion was very short of officers, and he had no rest during that period. His splendid example and total disregard for safety inspired his men with great confidence. (D.S.O. gazetted 4 June, 1917.)

COLLEY, FRANK, D.S.O., Temporary Capt., York and Lancaster Regt. For conspicuous gallantry and devotion to duty. He personally led a bombing party and successfully attacked and captured a hostile machine gun and its team

Although wounded, he remained at duty for 36 hours, reorganizing his men and commanding his battalion, his Commanding Officer having been killed. He set a magnificent example, remaining in command until he fainted from loss of blood.
(D.S.O. gazetted 22 Sept. 1916.)

EVANS, WILFRID KEITH, D.S.O., Major (Temporary Lieut.-Colonel), Manchester Regt., Commanding Battn., Cheshire Regt. For conspicuous gallantry and devotion to duty. He led his battalion with great dash and initiative to their objective, capturing many guns and prisoners. He also repulsed strong hostile counter-attacks, and showed great coolness and promptitude in rallying and reorganizing troops who had been driven back through his line. His fine personal example saved a critical situation.
(D.S.O. gazetted 18 Feb. 1915.)

GAIRDNER, ERIC DALRYMPLE, D.S.O., M.B., Capt., Royal Army Medical Corps. For conspicuous gallantry and devotion to duty. He went forward under very heavy fire to attend to a wounded N.C.O., and was himself shot down. He has consistently displayed high courage and devotion to duty, and his example has been an inspiration to all ranks.
(D.S.O. gazetted 3 June, 1916.)

CANADIAN FORCE.

CLARK, JOHN ARTHUR, D.S.O., Lieut.-Colonel, Infantry. For conspicuous gallantry and devotion to duty. His preparations for the attack were most thorough, and successfully carried out. During the assault he displayed the utmost courage and ability, and personally carried out several important reconnaissances.
(D.S.O. gazetted 4 June, 1917.)

WANSBROUGH, CUTHBERT COLE. D.S.O., Major, Infantry. For conspicuous gallantry and devotion to duty. During the attack his company was twice held up. He promptly organized flanking parties under heavy fire, and captured the trench. He was severely wounded, but remained in action until the final objective had been gained.
(D.S.O. gazetted 4 June, 1917.)

"His Majesty the King has been graciously pleased to approve of the appointments of the undermentioned Officers to be Companions of the Distinguished Service Order, in recognition of their gallantry and devotion to duty in the field."

BARLOW, JOSEPH EDWARD, M.C., Second Lieut. (Temporary Capt.), Yorkshire Regt., Special Reserve, attached York and Lancaster Regt. For conspicuous gallantry and devotion to duty. During an attack he led his battalion with great skill and courage, restoring the direction which had been lost, and being the first to enter the objective. It was entirely due to him that a heavy hostile counter-attack was repulsed, and the following night he went through our own and the hostile barrage to re-establish communications. Although his men were badly shaken, he restored their confidence during a very critical situation, and his conduct was magnificent throughout.

BEACH, LIONEL HADWEN FLETCHER, Second Lieut. (Acting Major) Royal West Surrey Regt. For conspicuous gallantry and devotion to duty. He led his company forward to cover the withdrawal of the advanced troops, remaining under heavy rifle and shell fire for two hours, until the operation had been successfully carried out. He was severely wounded during the action.

CHURCH, DUDLEY ROSS, Second Lieut. (Temporary Capt.), Northamptonshire Regt. For conspicuous gallantry and devotion to duty. He led his company with great dash and determination through a heavy hostile barrage to a position within 500 yards of the enemy's trench. He organized and held this position until dusk, in spite of having been twice wounded himself and his company having suffered heavy casualties.

HALKETT, HUGH MARJORIBANKS CRAIGIE, Major (Temporary Lieut. Colonel), Highland Light Infantry, attached North Lancashire Regt. For conspicuous gallantry and devotion to duty. He led his battalion with great skill and determination to the final objective. The spirits and dash of his men in spite of very heavy casualties were largely due to his personality and the care with which he had previously trained them.

DRYNAN, WILLIAM BLAIR, Temporary Major, York and Lancaster Regt. For conspicuous gallantry and devotion to duty. During the advance his company came under heavy machine-gun fire and suffered severe casualties. He alone went forward and made a daring reconnaissance under heavy machine-gun fire. The information obtained enabled him to resume the advance and skilfully lead his men to their objective.

EARLE, FRANCIS WILLIAM, Major, Hampshire Regt. For conspicuous gallantry and devotion to duty. During the assault he was in temporary command of the battalion, and handled it with marked ability and determination. He succeeded in capturing and consolidating an enemy strong point containing four machine guns. His battalion captured 150 prisoners.

EWER, GEORGE GUY, Major, Essex Regt. For conspicuous gallantry and devotion to duty. He displayed great ability and resource under fire, organizing the ammunition and water supply of his brigade and supervising the collection of wounded and the disposal of prisoners. He performed invaluable services, and the success of the operations was largely due to his efforts.

FEW, ROBERT JEBB, Capt. (Temporary Major), Royal West Surrey Regt. For conspicuous gallantry and devotion to duty. He displayed fine judgment and great coolness in assisting to organize the withdrawal of an advanced section of our line under heavy shell fire.

FOULIS, DOUGLAS AINSLIE, Temporary Capt., Scottish Rifles. For conspicuous gallantry and devotion to duty. During the advance, regardless of heavy shell fire, he went about reorganizing and collecting men who had gone astray. By his coolness and example he inspired confidence in the men and largely contributed to the final success of the operations.

GATTIE, KENNETH FRANCIS DRAKE, M.C., Capt., Monmouthshire Regt. (Brigade Major). For conspicuous gallantry and devotion to duty. With great coolness he went through hostile barrage to consolidate communication between Brigade and Battalion Headquarters at a critical moment. His disregard of personal safety had a most reassuring effect on the men. He had previously rendered the greatest assistance in making preparations for the attack.

GREATWOOD, FRANCIS WILLIAM, Major (Acting Lieut.-Colonel), Lincolnshire Regt. For conspicuous gallantry and devotion to duty. He commanded his battalion with the utmost skill and courage throughout the operations, finally consolidating his position. This position was maintained throughout the day and following night under heavy shell fire. He was constantly rallying and encouraging his men under these trying conditions until he was seriously wounded.

GREEN, ARTHUR LLEWELLYN BALDWIN, Capt. (Temporary Major), Herefordshire Regt. For conspicuous gallantry and devotion to duty. He led his men with great dash and determination in an attack, and although wounded, refused to leave them until he received a further severe wound, which fractured his thigh.

HALLIDAY, WILLIAM JOHN FREDERICK, Major, Royal Field Artillery. For conspicuous gallantry and devotion to duty. He ran across to the battery next to his own when it was under heavy shell fire, and the men had been ordered away, and extinguished a serious fire which was involving the ammunition, guns and camouflage along the whole position. His gallantry and initiative saved serious disaster.

HOBLER, ARTHUR PRESTON, Capt. (Temporary Major), Middlesex Regt. (name and rank corrected to Major (Acting Lieut.-Colonel) Arthur Preston Hohler [London Gazette, 25 Aug. 1917]). For conspicuous gallantry and devotion to duty. After all company commanders had become casualties, he displayed the greatest courage and ability in collecting and reorganizing detachments of other units during our attack, in organizing the advance and in sending excellent reports to Headquarters.

HOWELL, JOHN ALDERNEY, M.C., Temporary Major, Cheshire Regt. For conspicuous gallantry and devotion to duty. He showed great powers of leadership and resource in commanding his battalion during an attack, and afterwards consolidated his position with great skill.

HUDGELL, GEORGE, Second Lieut. (Temporary Capt.), Yeomanry, attached Welsh Regt. For conspicuous gallantry and devotion to duty. After his Commanding Officer and second in command were wounded, he assumed command, although severely wounded himself, and kept his men going. He set a splendid example of courage and endurance, and although in considerable pain, remained in command until he was sent away.

HUDSON, CHARLES EDWARD, M.C., Temporary Major, Nottinghamshire and Derbyshire Regt. For conspicuous gallantry and devotion to duty. During an attack and before the objective was gained, he showed great promptitude and disregard for his own safety in reorganizing his battalion and leading it forward to the objective, which was secured and consolidated through his successful efforts. He has on many occasions showed capacity of the highest military value, notably in repulsing hostile counter-attacks upon his battalion at a critical moment.

KIRKWOOD, JOHN HENDLEY MORRISON, Temporary Major, Household Battn. For conspicuous gallantry and devotion to duty. The battalion under his command suffered heavy casualties, and was subjected to severe shell fire. Despite this he led them forward and gained his objective and consolidated the line. The success of the operation was largely due to his fine example and the able manner in which he handled his men.

KOEBEL, FREDERICK ERNEST, Major, Sikhs, Indian Army. For conspicuous gallantry and resource. He rallied his men when the left flank was seriously threatened, and by his energy and fine example saved the situation. He subsequently commanded his battalion with great ability. He has displayed marked gallantry in every action in which he has taken part.

LAURIE, RONALD MACDONALD, Major (Temporary Lieut.-Colonel) (now Lieut.-Colonel), Royal Field Artillery. For conspicuous gallantry and devotion to duty. He handled his brigade with marked ability and success, giving much needed assistance to the infantry brigades in their attack on the enemy's position.

LINTON, FREDERICK HENRY, Capt., Welsh Regt. For conspicuous gallantry and devotion to duty. During an attack he showed great courage and initiative in being one of the first to enter the enemy's lines, disarm prisoners and establish communication. He displayed the greatest gallantry and good leadership throughout.

MANN, WILLIAM EDGAR, Major, Royal Field Artillery. For conspicuous gallantry and devotion to duty. He commanded his battery with great skill and courage throughout three days of heavy fighting, during which his position was under intense shell fire, and, although wounded early in the attack, he continued at duty, setting an excellent example to all ranks by his good spirits and cheerfulness.

MILLS, FRANK, Capt. (Temporary Major), Royal Welsh Fusiliers. For conspicuous gallantry and devotion to duty. He showed the greatest coolness and skill when in charge of the firing line of his battalion during an attack, directing operations and sending back accurate messages under heavy fire. The success of the assault was due to his fine example.

NAUNTON, HUGH PARKER, Temporary Capt., East Surrey Regt. For conspicuous gallantry and devotion to duty. He led his company forward with great dash and courage, and with about 50 men successfully stormed an enemy strong point, capturing ten prisoners. Later, at a critical period he took command of the battalion, and carried through until the objective was gained.

NELSON, GEORGE ELLISS, Second Lieut. (Temporary Capt.), Cheshire Regt. For conspicuous gallantry and devotion to duty. At a critical moment, when our advance was held up, he collected sufficient men to move forward and straighten the line. By his fine example and disregard of danger under heavy fire he eventually led this line, which was composed of seven different units, into the enemy's position.

O'CONNOR, RICHARD NUGENT, M.C., Capt. and Brevet Major, Scottish Rifles. For conspicuous gallantry and resource. In consequence of a change in the situation a revision of plans became necessary, but, owing to darkness and heavy shelling, confusion arose. By his courage and promptness he quickly restored order, and organized a successful attack.

PARRY, THOMAS HENRY, Major, Royal Welsh Fusiliers. For conspicuous gallantry and devotion to duty. He showed great courage and skill whilst leading his company in an attack, and it was largely owing to his example that the attack made such good progress. Although twice wounded, he continued to command until put out of action by a third wound.

PYE-SMITH, CHARLES DERWENT, M.C., Temporary Capt. (Acting Lieut.-Colonel), Royal Army Medical Corps. For conspicuous gallantry and devotion to duty. When in charge of an advanced dressing station his Serjt.-Major and the whole of his staff were killed. He reorganized the work with the assistance of a Lance-Corporal, and, in consequence of his energy and presence of mind, the work was not delayed. He led his bearers continually into the front line, rescuing wounded under heavy shell fire, and working with great heroism for 60 hours, setting a splendid example to all.

RICHARDS, DARCY JOHN RIGBY, M.C., Capt. (Acting Major), Royal Garrison Artillery. For conspicuous gallantry and devotion to duty. The battery was under heavy shell fire, and an ammunition dump close to one of the gun pits was set on fire. In answer to a call he brought his battery into action and fought his guns, knowing the dump was likely to explode, which it did, while the guns were in action.

ROUND, HAROLD CECIL, M.C., Second Lieut., Rifle Brigade, Special Reserve. For conspicuous gallantry and devotion to duty. When our troops were forced to withdraw he collected a few men and made a strong point within 70 yards of the enemy trench. This position he held for two days without supplies of any kind. He was finally able to get a valuable report through, before being ordered to withdraw.

STABLE, ROBERT HENRY, Lieut., Infantry, Indian Army. For conspicuous gallantry and devotion to duty. He assumed command of his battalion early in the action, and displayed great coolness and courage under heavy fire. He set a magnificent example to his men throughout.

STOKES, JAMES GORDON, M.C., Capt., London Regt. For conspicuous gallantry and devotion to duty. He showed great skill and gallantry when in command of the forward defences under heavy shell fire, during which his dug-out was practically destroyed. By his courage and coolness he set a fine example to all ranks, and continued to supply battalion headquarters with very valuable information.

STOUT, PERCY WYFOLD, Temporary Lieut. (Acting Capt.), Motor Machine Gun Corps. For conspicuous gallantry and devotion to duty. At a critical moment, when a number of armoured cars were in danger of being cut off, he led the attack to their relief, and after two hours' heavy fighting gained the objective, after inflicting heavy losses upon the enemy.

TATTERSALL, PHILIP CHARLES PAUL, Capt., London Regt. For conspicuous gallantry and devotion to duty. When senior officer of his battalion, he led the front line forward to within 400 yards of the enemy's position. Although badly wounded in both legs, he continued to direct the fire until dusk. He refused to retire until all his men had been withdrawn.

THOMPSON, THOMAS JOHN CHICHESTER CONYNGHAM, Capt., Royal Irish Fusiliers, Special Reserve, attached Royal Irish Rifles. For conspicuous gallantry and devotion to duty. He led his company with great dash and success to their objective, afterwards by his initiative rendering valuable assistance to another unit by co-operating on their flank. The spirit and dash of his company were largely due to his personality and gallantry on this, as on all other occasions.

VON TREUENFELS, CARL OTTO, Lieut. (Temporary Capt. and Acting Major), Honourable Artillery Company, attached Royal Field Artillery. For conspicuous gallantry and devotion to duty. He showed the greatest disregard of danger in saving material and ammunition from burning buildings in which his battery was being heavily shelled. By his coolness and magnificent example the guns of his battery were saved, and heavy casualties of men and material were averted.

WALKER, EDWARD WILLIAM, Capt., Royal Welsh Fusiliers. For conspicuous gallantry and devotion to duty. He led his company forward and, assisted by an officer and a few men of another unit, captured an important point and held out against sharp counter-attacks until the remainder of the enemy position was won. He personally captured a machine gun and a large number of prisoners.

WALTON, LESLIE ARTHUR, M.C., Temporary Second Lieut., Welsh Regt. For conspicuous gallantry and devotion to duty. He showed a marked contempt for danger, and when the company was held up he was seriously wounded whilst engaging an enemy sniper. In spite of this he dashed forward at the head of his men, and was responsible for capturing 11 prisoners who had been holding up the advance.

WESTROP, SIDNEY ALBERT, M.C., Temporary Major, Machine Gun Corps. For conspicuous gallantry and devotion to duty. He commanded his company with marked ability and success. He carried out a reconnaissance of the captured ground, and it was due to his information that enemy machine guns were located and captured.

WILLIAMS, ALFRED ERNEST, Lieut.-Colonel, Royal Warwickshire Regt., Special Reserve, Commanding Battn., Wiltshire Regt. For conspicuous gallantry and devotion to duty. He handled his battalion during an attack with skill and decision, showing great resourcefulness under difficult circumstances.

WILSON, WILLIAM ERIC, Capt. (Temporary Major), Essex Regt. For conspicuous gallantry and devotion to duty. After leading his company with great gallantry in an assault, he took command of his battalion, his senior officers having become casualties, and carried out his duties with great ability, defeating a strong hostile counter-attack.

AUSTRALIAN IMPERIAL FORCE.

BOLINGBROKE, ARCHDALE GEORGE, Major, Cavalry. For conspicuous gallantry and devotion to duty. He showed great dash and initiative in leading troops forward to the capture of a hostile artillery observation post, afterwards taking an active part in a bayonet charge against enemy trenches.

CAMERON, DONALD CHARLES, Major, Cavalry. For conspicuous gallantry and devotion to duty. During an advance over difficult ground, he showed great skill in keeping touch with the brigade on his left, afterwards leading his squadron in a bayonet charge against the enemy trenches, thus enabling two captured enemy guns to be removed.

DEAN, EDWIN THEYER, Major, Artillery. For conspicuous gallantry and devotion to duty. He displayed the greatest fearlessness and gallantry in personally extinguishing three serious fires amongst his gun-pits and ammunition, working at the imminent risk of his own life. The following night he returned to a building which had just been wrecked by shell fire to search for missing men amongst the debris, thereby displaying a spirit of devotion towards his unit which has always been noticeable.

MACNEIL, ALEXANDER, Lieut., L.T.M. Battery. For conspicuous gallantry and devotion to duty. He handled his mortar with great courage and determination against an overwhelming attack. He held off the enemy with his revolver until his men had got the mortar away to safety. He then took part in the counter-attack, and did great execution with a machine gun.

WILLIAMS, RICHARD, Capt., Flying Corps. For conspicuous gallantry and devotion to duty. Flying at a low altitude under intense anti-aircraft fire, he attacked and dispersed enemy troops who were concentrating on our flank. On another occasion, whilst on a reconnaissance, he landed in the enemy's lines, and rescued a pilot of a machine which had been brought down by hostile fire.

CANADIAN FORCE.

CAREY, ALFRED BLAKE, Major, Infantry. For conspicuous gallantry and devotion in an attack, when he commanded the battalion with the greatest bravery and skill, secured all his objectives, and consolidated his position. Later, to clear up the situation, he made a valuable reconnaissance.

FRANCIS, MILTON JOHN, Major, Infantry. For conspicuous gallantry and devotion to duty. He has repeatedly shown fine qualities of leadership. In establishing an outpost line, the skill with which he took all possible advantage of the defeated enemy was most marked, and his personal courage at all times has been an inspiring example to his unit.

LINNELL, HENRY RUPERT, Major, Infantry. For conspicuous gallantry and devotion. After gaining his objective he took charge of a very critical situation, acting with the greatest bravery and skill, organized the defence with scattered forces, and under intense shell fire, and held the position for five days. He was the only officer of his battalion who was not killed or wounded.

STANLEY, HAROLD POOLE, Capt. (Acting Major), Infantry. For conspicuous gallantry in operations. He led his company with the greatest courage and skill, being the first into the enemy line, and he organized and led the party, which repulsed a counter-attack. Although wounded in two places he continued his work for several hours, displaying a courage and devotion of the highest order.

VICARS, DESMOND ODLUM, Lieut., Infantry. For conspicuous gallantry and devotion in operations. On reaching the objective only two of his platoon remained, but with the greatest coolness he attacked about 50 of the enemy, bayonetting several himself, causing numerous casualties, and taking eight prisoners, driving the rest away. His conduct throughout was magnificent.

WOOD, WILLIAM STEWART, Major, Infantry. For conspicuous gallantry and devotion to duty when in command of his battalion. He co-operated with another battalion in an attack with great courage and skill, materially assisting in the capture and subsequent consolidation of important positions.

NEW ZEALAND FORCE.

ALLEN, ROBERT CANDLISH, Lieut.-Colonel, Infantry. For conspicuous gallantry and devotion to duty. At a very critical moment and at great personal risk he rallied a number of men of another unit who were withdrawing under hostile barrage and prevented their further retirement. Although severely wounded he continued giving instructions for the continuance of the fight. He has at all times shown a very fine example of coolness and gallantry in action.

DIGBY-SMITH, ALFRED, Major, Infantry. For conspicuous gallantry and devotion to duty. Although severely wounded and suffering from gas, he successfully led his company to its objective, and remained until consolidation was well under way and the situation secure. He displayed great keenness and determination.

HARDIE, ROBERT DAVIES, Major, Machine Gun Corps. For conspicuous gallantry and devotion to duty. Although wounded in the eye during an advance he led his men through a heavy barrage into their positions, and continued with great skill and courage to direct the fire of his guns, remaining with them throughout the action, although he had every reason to suppose he had lost an eye. By his devotion to duty he set a splendid example to his men.

McGAVIN, DONALD JOHNSTONE, Lieut.-Colonel (Temporary Colonel), Medical Corps. For conspicuous gallantry and devotion to duty. While acting as A.D.M.S. to his division the successful evacuation of the wounded during our heavy offensive was due to the thoroughness of his preparations and his personal attention to the smallest details. He went into the advanced area at great personal risk to encourage the stretcher-bearers and superintend the removal of casualties, setting a splendid example to all ranks.

SOMMERVILLE, JOHN ADAM, Capt. (Temporary Major) (now Major), Mounted Rifles. For conspicuous gallantry and devotion to duty. He displayed fine leadership in the attack and capture of two enemy field guns.

WINTER-EVANS, ALFRED, Lieut.-Colonel, Infantry. For conspicuous gallantry and devotion to duty. During an attack and the subsequent consolidation of the captured position he showed the greatest coolness and energy, inspiring all ranks by his magnificent personal example and never sparing himself to make the operation of his battalion the success which it was. His work at all times has been of the same high standard.

London Gazette, 25 Aug. 1917.—" War Office, 25 Aug. 1917. His Majesty the King has been graciously pleased to award a Bar to the Distinguished Service Order to " :—

CARY-BARNARD, CYRIL DARCY VIVIEN, D.S.O., Major (Temporary Lieut.-Colonel), Wiltshire Regt. For conspicuous gallantry and devotion to duty. He handled his battalion with conspicuous success and ability on numerous occasions, inspiring all ranks with confidence by his fearless example.
(D.S.O. gazetted 1 Jan. 1915.)

HOWARD, HENRY CECIL LLOYD, D.S.O., Capt. and Brevet Major, Lancers. For conspicuous gallantry and devotion to duty as Brigade Liaison Officer. He went into the midst of a very heavy hostile barrage and remained there with the leading troops of the brigade until consolidation commenced and touch was established on the flanks. By his total disregard of danger he contributed largely to the success of the attack.
(D.S.O. gazetted 1 Jan. 1917.)

" His Majesty the King has been graciously pleased to approve of the appointments of the undermentioned Officers to be Companions of the Distinguished Service Order, in recognition of their gallantry and devotion to duty in the field."

BIRT, CHARLES WILLIAM HOWARD, Temporary Major (Acting Lieut.-Colonel), Border Regt. For conspicuous gallantry and devotion to duty. He made a dashing and successful reconnaissance of the ground in front of his outpost line, which enabled his battalion to make a successful attack on the following day. During this reconnaissance he encountered and wiped out a hostile picket which endeavoured to intercept his patrol, and, although wounded and very severely shaken by heavy shell fire, he displayed great personal courage and gallantry during the attack, as he had previously done on two other occasions.

CLARK, WILLIAM CHARLES, Temporary Lieut.-Colonel, Royal Fusiliers. For conspicuous gallantry and devotion to duty in leading his battalion with great coolness and ability under heavy fire. He has on all occasions proved himself a courageous and capable officer.

COLLAS, WILLIAM JOHN JERVOISE, Major (Temporary Lieut.-Colonel), South Staffordshire Regt. For conspicuous gallantry and devotion to duty when the enemy had gained possession of our assembly trenches by means of a counter-attack. He led his battalion against them under heavy fire, and recaptured the line, which he held later on, in spite of numerous bombing attacks, with great coolness and determination.

FLEMING, JAMES GEORGE GRANT, Temporary Second Lieut., Gordon Highlanders. For conspicuous gallantry and devotion to duty. During a night attack he successfully established his company in an important position at a critical moment after the right of his battalion had been driven back. He also displayed the greatest disregard of personal safety during a hostile counter-attack by running up and down a trench some 400 yards in length and rallying his men under very heavy shell and rifle fire. The following day he performed a similar act, largely compensating for the absence of any other officers in what was a very critical situation.

HILL, MURRAY VICTOR BURROW, M.C., Capt. (Temporary Lieut.-Colonel), Royal Sussex Regt. For conspicuous gallantry and devotion to duty. At a time when our advance was delayed by a " pocket " of the enemy, he skilfully enveloped them with his support company, thereby enabling the leading line to advance and reach their objective with only slight loss. His personal reconnaissances under fire and his arrangements for consolidation and protection have set a very fine example of both coolness and ability, and thoroughly gained the confidence of all under his command.

HOLLIDAY, FRED PARKINSON, Temporary Lieut., General List and Royal Flying Corps. For conspicuous gallantry and devotion to duty. By his initiative and skilful manœuvring he led six hostile machines to an encounter with our own formation, during which five out of the six hostile machines were destroyed and driven down. He had been equally successful the day before in misleading hostile aircraft, and his originality and fearless example were of the greatest value to his squadron.

MARTYN, ANTHONY WOOD, Major (Temporary Lieut.-Colonel), Reserve of Officers, Royal West Kent Regt. For conspicuous gallantry and devotion to duty in leading his battalion to the assault, which was completely successful. He superintended consolidation throughout the day, setting a very fine example of personal courage and good leadership.

MURPHY, ALFRED DURHAM, M.C., Capt. and Brevet Major (Acting Lieut.-Col.), Leinster Regt. For conspicuous gallantry and devotion to duty. With great presence of mind he moved up troops to fill a gap, which he had discovered by means of a personal reconnaissance, between his unit and the next division, afterwards handling his battalion with exceptional skill and personally selecting the best positions under heavy fire. His reports were invaluable and accurate, clearing up an obscure situation, and he has on all other occasions set a splendid example of fearlessness and ability.

PEARSON, BERTRAM LAMB, M.C., Temporary Lieut. (Acting Capt.), Yorkshire Regt. For conspicuous gallantry and devotion to duty in leading his company to their objective with great skill over difficult ground. He personally killed four of the enemy with his revolver, and, after being wounded for the second time, he lay in a shell hole giving all necessary orders until he fainted from loss of blood. He set a fine example of pluck and skilful leadership.

PHILIP, GEORGE MORRISON, M.C., Temporary Lieut., Northumberland Fusiliers. For conspicuous gallantry and devotion to duty. In spite of continued heavy shelling and machine-gun fire he spent the night in "No Man's Land," working right up to the enemy's wire, searching for and bringing in wounded. They had been lying out since dawn, and his gallantry and devotion enabled him to get at least 40 men back into our lines.

POTTER, KENNETH MITCHELL, Major, Royal Field Artillery. For conspicuous gallantry and devotion to duty. At a critical moment he restored order amongst transport that had been disorganized by shell fire, although it entailed removing his respirator under heavy gas-shell fire in order to make himself heard. After clearing the traffic he completely collapsed from the effect of the gas, and his gallant action was the means of saving the lives of many men and horses.

RICHARDSON, ARCHIBALD READ, Lieut.-Colonel, London Regt. For conspicuous gallantry and devotion to duty in organizing bombing parties for an unprotected flank. With these he beat off repeated enemy counter-attacks which were launched under heavy barrage, and it was owing to his skill and energy under most trying conditions that the troops on his right were able to hold on and consolidate their position. His fine personal example greatly encouraged all ranks in an extremely critical situation.

UMFREVILLE, RALPH BRUNTON, Temporary Major, Royal Lancaster Regt. For conspicuous gallantry and devotion to duty in organizing and successfully leading a difficult attack. He personally supervised and rallied his men under heavy shell fire. On the following day he was continuously in the front line, which was held at a critical period through his personal courage and example.

WARDELL, HENRY, Temporary Major, Royal West Surrey Regt. For conspicuous gallantry and devotion to duty when commanding his battalion in an attack. Although severely wounded in the leg, he bandaged it and continued with his battalion until stopped by a shell, which removed one eye and partially, if not completely, destroyed the other. The success of his battalion was in a very large degree due to his fine leadership.

AUSTRALIAN IMPERIAL FORCE.

ALLEN, ARTHUR SAMUEL, Capt. Infantry. For conspicuous gallantry and devotion to duty. He led his company with great dash and determination against enemy trenches, through heavy artillery and machine-gun barrage, and against a stubborn resistance of the garrison, of whom he captured 100 prisoners. He continued to rally and lead his men to the attack, gaining further ground by his aggressive spirit and setting a fine example of initiative and organizing ability.

BREMNER, NORMAN FREDERICK, Lieut., Infantry. For conspicuous gallantry and devotion to duty. He made his way through an intense enemy artillery barrage to a company which had become isolated and cut off from all communications, extricated it, and enabled it to capture the objective and 80 prisoners. He carried a wounded officer back under heavy fire of every description, during which he was attacked by five of the enemy, of whom he killed four and captured the fifth. His great gallantry saved the company and imbued fresh spirit into the men.

FURBER, RUPERT IGGULDEN, Major, Army Medical Corps. For conspicuous gallantry and devotion to duty. He had charge of an advanced dressing station for five days, during which it was under heavy shell fire most of the time. He displayed the greatest ability and devotion to duty in organizing the dressing and evacuation of a large number of the wounded, on several occasions helping to bring them in himself.

HERON, ALEXANDER ROBERT, Major, Infantry. For conspicuous gallantry and devotion to duty. He led his company to the relief of a battalion through extremely heavy shell fire, with great success and very few casualties. Throughout the operations, although under heavy barrage, he kept in touch and sent back information to his battalion headquarters. His skill and devotion contributed largely to the successful holding of our line, and throughout the whole period in the trenches his work has been consistently thorough.

HODGENS, SYDNEY FRANCIS, Major, Field Artillery. For conspicuous gallantry and devotion to duty. In spite of difficulties occasioned by destroyed roads, shell-torn ground and heavy shell fire, he kept his guns continually in action with an ample supply of ammunition, thereby giving most effective support to our infantry attack. He also did valuable service as forward observation officer, displaying great energy and resource in keeping up communication.

MAXWELL, ARTHUR MAINWARING, M.C., Capt., Infantry. For conspicuous gallantry and devotion to duty. He made a valuable reconnaissance at a critical moment to restore touch between two brigades, taking great risks under heavy shell fire, and leading his men with great skill and courage. Throughout the whole engagement his actions were marked by sound judgment and promptitude, especially when the command of his battalion had devolved upon himself.

MILNE, JOHN ALEXANDER, Lieut.-Colonel, Infantry. For conspicuous gallantry and devotion to duty. He showed great capacity and initiative in commanding his battalion when on carrying party duty. He kept the front line well supplied with stores, ammunition and water, and arranged for the relief of the parties in a most efficient manner, although constantly depleted by casualties and exhaustion.

PURDY, JOHN SMITH, Lieut.-Colonel, Army Medical Corps. For conspicuous gallantry and devotion to duty. Although continually under shell fire for seven days, he exercised close personal supervision over the evacuation of the wounded, and by his own example of courage and disregard of danger he animated all ranks with a similar attitude of mind. His work during preliminary preparations displayed the same untiring energy and devotion to duty.

RIDDELL, CONSETT CARRE, Major, Engineers. For conspicuous gallantry and devotion to duty. Although knocked down and stunned by shell fire, he continued to make most valuable and daring reconnaissances in advance of our front line. He has been wounded three times, but in spite of this his work has been consistently gallant throughout.

WHITE, HAROLD FLETCHER, Major, Infantry. For conspicuous gallantry and devotion to duty. He led his company to the attack with exceptional dash over difficult ground and under heavy gas shell bombardment. By his great cheerfulness and disregard of personal danger, he kept the morale of his men at its highest, under incessant artillery fire, repulsed a counter-attack and successfully organized the consolidation.

NEW ZEALAND FORCE.

THOMS, NATHANIEL WILLIAM BENJAMIN BUTLER, M.C., Major, Infantry. For conspicuous gallantry and devotion to duty in frequently moving forward under exceptionally heavy shell fire, personally reconnoitring the line and bringing back most valuable reports. He displayed exceptional courage and keenness throughout.

SOUTH AFRICAN FORCE.

KNAPP, ERLING, Temporary Major (Acting Lieut.-Colonel), Infantry. For conspicuous gallantry and devotion to duty. At very short notice he organized and carried out a successful raid upon the enemy, and his fine example and disregard of danger in commanding his battalion and supervising the consolidation of his captured objective, greatly inspired the men.

London Gazette, 25 Aug. 1917.—"War Office, 25 Aug. 1917. His Majesty the King has been graciously pleased to approve of the undermentioned Rewards for Distinguished Service in the field in Mesopotamia, dated 3 June, 1917. Awarded a Bar to the Distinguished Service Order."

HENDERSON, GEORGE STUART, D.S.O., M.C., Capt., Manchester Regt.

To be Companions of the Distinguished Service Order :

ALEXANDER, ROBERT DONALD THAIN, Capt. (Acting Major), London Regt.

ALLEN, HENRY ISHERWOOD, Capt. (Temporary Major), North Staffordshire Regt.

ANDREW, FREDERICK ANNESLEY, Lieut.-Colonel, Indian Army.

AUCHINLECK, CLAUD JOHN EYRE, Capt. (Acting Major), Indian Army.

BARNARD, ERIC, Temporary Capt. (Acting Major), Gloucestershire Regt.

BECKLEY, THOMAS HENRY, Major, Royal Artillery.

BELL-KINGSLEY, HAROLD EVELYN WILLIAM, Capt., Indian Army.

BINNEY, EDWARD VICTOR, Capt., Royal Engineers.

BIRCH, JOHN MORICE, Temporary Capt. (Acting Major), South Lancashire Regt.

BIRLEY, BEVIL LANGTON, Capt. (Acting Lieut.-Colonel), Royal Lancaster Regt.

BOND, JAMES HENRY ROBINSON, Lieut.-Colonel, Royal Army Medical Corps.

BOYD, STUART, Major, Royal Engineers.

BRIDGE, RICHARD EDWYN ATHOL, Capt., Indian Army.

BRIGGS, FREDERIC CECIL CURRER, Capt., Liverpool Regt.

BROMILOW, DAVID GEORGE, Capt., Indian Army.

BROOKE, ARTHUR CHARLES, Capt., Royal Artillery.

BROWSE, GEORGE, M.D., Major and Brevet Lieut.-Colonel, Indian Medical Service.

BULL, HARRY SPENCER, Temporary Major, East Lancashire Regt.

BURKE, EDMUND TYTLER, M.B., Capt. (Acting Lieut.-Colonel), Royal Army Medical Corps, Special Reserve.

BURNETT, ALLAN HARRINGTON, Capt., Indian Army.

CAPPER, ALFRED STEWART, Lieut.-Colonel, Indian Army.

CARLETON, HENRY ANTHONY, Lieut.-Colonel, Indian Army.

CASE, HORACE AKROYD, Major and Brevet Lieut.-Colonel (Acting Lieut.-Colonel), Dorsetshire Regt.

CATTY, THOMAS CLAUDE, Major, Indian Army.

CLARKSON, BERTIE ST. JOHN, C.M.G., Lieut.-Colonel, Dorsetshire Regt.

COLAN, WILLIAM ROBERT BOYLE, Lieut.-Colonel, Indian Army.

CONRAN, WILLIAM DOUGLAS BAYNES, Major, Royal Engineers.

COSTELLO, EDMOND WILLIAM, V.C., Major and Brevet Lieut.-Colonel, Indian Army.

CRUICKSHANK, ALEXANDER JOHN, Capt., Royal Engineers.

DARLEY, CECIL GEOFFRY, Capt., Hussars.

DE COURCY, THE HONOURABLE MICHAEL WILLIAM ROBERT, Capt., Indian Army.

DE SMIDT, GERALD EWALD OVERBECK, Temporary Capt., Royal Engineers.

DEWING, RICHARD HENRY, M.C., Capt., Royal Engineers.

DUNSFORD, FRANCIS PEARSON SHAW, Lieut.-Colonel (Temporary Brigadier-General), Indian Army.

EADIE, JOHN INGLIS, Major, Indian Army.

FAVIELL, WILLIAM FREDERICK OLIVER, Major (Temporary Lieut.-Colonel), Worcestershire Regt.

FISHER, CECIL JAMES, Capt. (Acting Major), Middlesex Regt.

FORBES, THE HONOURABLE DONALD ALEXANDER, M.V.O., Major, Royal Artillery.

FORBES, JOHN, Second Lieut., Seaforth Highlanders.

FOSTER, WILLIAM MONTAGUE ARNAUD, Capt., Indian Army.

FRY, ARTHUR BROWNFIELD, M.B., Major (Temporary Lieut.-Colonel), Indian Medical Service.

GAUNT, CECIL ROBERT, Major and Brevet Lieut.-Colonel (Temporary Lieut.-Colonel), Reserve of Officers, late Dragoon Guards.

GLENNIE, EDWARD AUBREY, Capt. (Acting Major), Royal Engineers.

GODKIN, SAMUEL ROBERT, F.R.C.S.I., Major, Indian Medical Service.

GREGSON, GEOFFREY KIRKES, Major, Royal Artillery.

GRIBBON, HENRY HUGH, Capt. (Acting Major), Hampshire Regt.

HAMILTON, HUGH WILLIAM ROBERTS, M.C., Capt., Royal Engineers.

HARLEY, ARTHUR BERTRAM, Major, Indian Army.

The Distinguished Service Order

HASELDINE, ROBERT HENRY, Major (Temporary Lieut.-Colonel), Liverpool Regt.
HASTED, JOHN ORD COBBOLD, Capt., Durham Light Infantry.
HAYDON, WILLIAM PITT, Lieut.-Colonel, Indian Army.
HEWITT, ROBERT WESTBROOK, Major (Temporary Lieut.-Colonel), Hussars.
HUGHES, HENRY BERNARD WYLDE, Capt. (Acting Major), Royal Engineers.
JACKSON, HUGH STANLEY, Major, Royal Artillery.
JOHNSON, ROBERT INGELOW BRADSHAW, Capt. (Temporary Lieut.-Colonel), Retired Pay, Reserve of Officers, late Royal Welsh Fusiliers.
KEENE, GEOFFREY GOLDNEY, Capt., Royal Artillery.
KENNEDY, ANDREW CAMPBELL, Lieut.-Colonel, Royal Garrison Artillery.
KETTLEWELL, LANCELOT, Temporary Capt., Wiltshire Regt.
KNOTT, REV. ALFRED ERNEST, Temporary Chaplain to the Forces, 1st Class, Army Chaplains' Department.
LEE, STANLAKE SWINTON, Capt., Royal Artillery.
LEESON, ALEXANDER NEVE, Lieut., Royal Artillery.
LENTAIGNE, EDWARD CHARLES, Capt., Indian Army.
LESLIE, WALTER STEWART, Major and Brevet Lieut.-Colonel, Indian Army.
LEY, JAMES WICKHAM, Major (Acting Lieut.-Colonel), North Staffordshire Regt.
LLOYD, CHARLES ROBERT, Major, Indian Army.
LOCK, FREDERICK ROBERT EDWARD, Lieut.-Colonel (Temporary Brigadier-General), Indian Army.
LYNN, GRAHAM RIGBY, M.B., Capt., Indian Medical Service.
MACKENZIE, CHARLES, Lieut.-Colonel, Indian Army.
MACLEOD, NORMAN, Major, Indian Army.
MACNAGHTEN, BALFOUR, Lieut.-Colonel, Lancers.
MAUDE, EUSTACE ARTHUR, Major, Indian Army.
MAYNE, ASHTON GERARD OSWALD MOSLEY, Capt., Indian Army.
McCOMBE, JOHN SMITH, M.B., Capt., Royal Army Medical Corps.
MOENS, ARTHUR WILLIAM HAMILTON MAY, Major and Brevet Lieut.-Colonel, Indian Army.
MORGAN, BERNARD EVAN, Major, Indian Army.
MORIN, ARCHIBALD HENRY, Major, Indian Army Reserve of Officers.
MORRISON, WILLIAM KENNETH, M.B., Capt., Royal Army Medical Corps.
MORTON, HUGH MURRAY, M.B., Lieut.-Colonel (Acting Colonel), Royal Army Medical Corps.
NORMAN, CLAUDE LUMSDEN, M.V.O., Major and Brevet Lieut.-Colonel, Indian Army.
NORMAN, WALTER HENRY, Lieut.-Colonel, Indian Army.
NORTH, HAROLD NAPIER, Major, Royal Engineers.
OGLE, NATHANIEL, Major, Indian Army.
PARMINTER, REGINALD HORACE ROGER, M.C., Capt., Manchester Regt.
PATCH, FRANCIS ROBERT, Lieut.-Colonel (Temporary Brigadier-General), Royal Artillery.
PATERSON, ADRIAN GORDON, M.C., Capt. (Acting Major), King's Own Scottish Borderers, attached Machine Gun Corps.
PATERSON, THOMAS GEORGE FERGUSON, M.B., Major, Indian Medical Service.
PECK, HENRY RICHARDSON, C.M.G., Lieut.-Colonel, Royal Artillery.
PEMBERTON, SHOLTO, M.C., Capt. and Brevet Major, Royal Engineers.
PERRY, EDMUND LUDLOW, Lieut.-Colonel, Indian Medical Service.
PETRE, RODERIC LORAINE, M.C., Capt., South Wales Borderers.
PHILIPS, JOHN LIONEL, Major, Royal Artillery.
PIM, DOUGLAS CHETHAM, M.B., Capt., Royal Army Medical Corps Special Reserve.
PONSONBY, DOUGLAS GORDON, Capt., Indian Army.
POTT, DOUGLAS, M.C., Capt., Indian Army.
RALSTON, WILLIAM HENRY, M.C., Capt., Indian Army.
RICHARDSON, JAMES JARDINE, Major (Temporary Lieut.-Colonel), Hussars.
RIDDELL, ARCHIBALD, Major, Indian Army.
RITCHIE, NEIL METHUEN, Lieut. (Acting Capt.), Royal Highlanders.
ST. JOHN, FREDERICK OLIVER, M.C., Capt., Royal Scots.
ST. JOHN, RICHARD STUKELEY, Major and Brevet Lieut.-Colonel (Temporary Brigadier-General), Indian Army.
SCOTT, HENRY LAWRENCE, M.C., Major, Indian Army.
SHEA, ALEXANDER GALLWEY, Major, Indian Army.
SHEWELL, EDEN FRANCIS, Major, Royal Artillery.
SUTHERLAND, ROBERT ORR, Major, Indian Army.
SWEET, EDWARD HERBERT, Lieut.-Colonel, Indian Army.
THOMAS, LEONARD RHYS, Temporary Major, Army Service Corps (Lieut., Unattached List).
THORNHILL, CHARLES MASSY, M.C., Capt., Indian Cavalry.
TURNER, ALFRED GRANVILLE BURNE, Lieut.-Colonel, Indian Army.
VENNING, FRANCIS ESMOND WINGATE, Capt., Indian Army.
WARD, JOHN CHAPPELL, Temporary Major, Royal Engineers (Lieut.-Commander, Royal Indian Marines).
WHEATLEY, WILLIAM PRESCOTT ROSS, Major, Indian Army.
WILLOUGHBY, DOUGLAS VERE, Major, Indian Army.
WITTS, FREDERICK VAVASOUR BROOME, M.C., Capt., Royal Engineers.
WOOD, CLEMENT BADDELEY, Lieut.-Colonel, Retired Pay, late Scottish Rifles.
WOOD, ERNEST JOSEPH MACFARLANE, Lieut.-Colonel, Indian Army.
WOODSIDE, WILLIAM ARTHUR, Lieut.-Colonel, Royal Army Medical Corps.
YOUNG, HENRY GEORGE, Lieut.-Colonel, Indian Army.
ZIEGLER, COLIN LOUIS, Major, Royal Field Artillery, Special Reserve.

London Gazette, 29 Aug. 1917.—" Admiralty, 29 Aug. 1917. The King has been graciously pleased to give orders for the following appointments to the Distinguished Service Order to the undermentioned Officers, in recognition of their services in the action in the Straits of Otranto on the 15th May, 1917."

TODD, GEORGE JAMES, Capt., R.N. For his services in command of H.M.S. Bristol during the action.
GOODWIN, FRANK RHEUBEN, Engineer Commander, R.N. For exceptional work under very trying conditions in bringing H.M.S. Dartmouth to port after she was torpedoed.

" Honours for Services in Action with Enemy Submarines.—The King has been graciously pleased to approve of the award of the following honours for services in action with enemy submarines. To be Companions of the Distinguished Service Order."

SIMPSON, SALISBURY HAMILTON, Lieut.-Commander, R.N.
HALLETT, JOHN IGNATIUS, Lieut.-Commander, R.N.
NAYLOR, CEDRIC, D.S.C., Lieut., Royal Naval Reserve.

" Honours for the Royal Naval Air Service.—The King has been graciously pleased to approve of the award of a Bar to the Distinguished Service Order to the undermentioned Officer."

SAVORY, KENNETH STEVENS, D.S.O., Squadron-Commander, Royal Naval Air Service. In recognition of his services on the night of the 9th July, 1917, when a successful attack was carried out against the Turkish-German fleet lying off Constantinople. When the Goeben, surrounded by warships (including submarines), had been located, the attack was made from a height of 800 feet. Direct hits were obtained on the Goeben and on the other enemy ships near her. Big explosions took place on board them, followed by a heavy conflagration. The War Office at Constantinople was also attacked, and a direct hit obtained.

London Gazette, 14 Sept. 1917.—" Admiralty, 14 Sept. 1917.—Honours for Miscellaneous Services. The King has been graciously pleased to give orders for the following appointments to the Distinguished Service Order."

DE BURGH, HUBERT HENRY, Commander, R.N. For his services in command of a destroyer in the action with enemy destroyers off the Belgian coast on the 5th June, 1917, when one of the enemy's destroyers, S. 20, was sunk, Commander de Burgh succeeded in saving seven men of S. 20's crew while under heavy fire from the shore batteries and with three German seaplanes hovering overhead.
BODDAM-WHETHAM, EDYE KINGTON, Lieut.-Commander, R.N. For his services in command of a destroyer in the action with enemy destroyers off the Belgian coast on the 5th June, 1917. He handled his ship well in the face of superior forces and under the fire of the shore batteries.
BROMLEY, FREDERICK WILLIAM, Engineer Lieut.-Commander, R.N.
SHARP, MAURICE JAMES ROGERS, Engineer Lieut.-Commander, R.N.
HUXHAM, HAROLD HUGH, Engineer Lieut.-Commander, R.N.
For their services in vessels of the Harwich Force during the war.

" Honours for Services in Action with Enemy Submarines.—The King has been graciously pleased to approve of the award of the following honour for services in action with enemy Submarines. To be a Companion of the Distinguished Service Order."

SANDERS, WILLIAM EDWARD, V.C., Lieut.-Commander, R.N.R. (since killed).

" Honours for the Royal Naval Air Service.—The King has been graciously pleased to approve of the award of a Bar to the Distinguished Service Order to the undermentioned Officer."

LITTLE, ROBERT ALEXANDER, D.S.O., D.S.C., Flight Lieut. (Acting Flight Commander), Royal Naval Air Service. For exceptional gallantry and skill in aerial fighting. On 16 July, 1917, he observed two Aviatiks flying low over the lines. He dived on the nearest one, firing a long burst at very close range. The enemy machine dived straight away, and Flight Lieut. Little followed him closely down to 500 feet, the enemy machine falling out of control. On 20 July, 1917, he attacked a D.F.W. After a short fight, the enemy machine dived vertically. Its tail plane seemed to crumple up, and it was completely wrecked. On 22 July, 1917, he attacked a D.F.W. Aviatik, and brought it down completely out of control. On 27 July, 1917, in company with another pilot, he attacked an Aviatik. After each had fired about 20 rounds, the enemy machine began to spin downwards. Flight Lieut. Little got close to it, and observed both the occupants lying back in the cock-pits, as if dead. The machine fell behind the enemy's lines, and was wrecked. Flight Lieut. Little has shown remarkable courage and boldness in attacking enemy machines.

London Gazette, 17 Sept. 1917.—" War Office, 17 Sept. 1917. His Majesty the King has been graciously pleased to award a Bar to the Distinguished Service Order to " :—

BURNETT, JAMES LAUDERDALE GILBERT, D.S.O., Major (Acting Lieut.-Colonel), Gordon Highlanders. For conspicuous gallantry and devotion to duty in commanding his battalion during the attack and capture of a position. The success of the attack was greatly due to his leadership and the confidence with which he inspired his men.
(D.S.O. gazetted 18 Feb. 1917.)   (This date corrected to 18 Feb. 1915.)
GATER, GEORGE HENRY, D.S.O., Major (Temporary Lieut.-Colonel), Nottinghamshire and Derbyshire Regt. For conspicuous gallantry and devotion to duty. He led his battalion with brilliant skill and resolution during an attack, minimizing their casualties during three days' intense shelling by his able dispositions and good eye for ground. He directed the consolidation, and remained in command for three days, although severely wounded in the face early in the action.
(D.S.O. gazetted 3 June, 1916.)
MATHERS, DAVID, D.S.O., Major (Temporary Lieut.-Colonel), Royal Inniskilling Fusiliers. For conspicuous gallantry and devotion to duty in commanding his battalion during an attack, remaining for two days at his post, although badly wounded and shaken by a shell. His example of fine leadership greatly inspired his battalion.
(D.S.O. gazetted 14 Nov. 1916.)
STUBBS, GUY CLIFFORD, D.S.O., Capt. (Acting Lieut.-Colonel), Suffolk Regt. For conspicuous gallantry and devotion to duty in holding captured trenches with his battalion for three days against hostile counter-attacks. He proceeded at a critical moment to the captured line, under heavy enemy barrage, to encourage his men and reorganize the defence, and shot several of the enemy who were in shell-holes. His gallant example and untiring energy inspired all ranks with the greatest enthusiasm.
(D.S.O. gazetted 1 Jan. 1917.)

"His Majesty the King has been graciously pleased to approve of the appointments of the undermentioned Officers to be Companions of the Distinguished Service Order, in recognition of their gallantry and devotion to duty in the field."

ANDERSON, LEWIS, M.B., Temporary Capt., Royal Army Medical Corps. For conspicuous gallantry and devotion to duty. He carried out his duties for 48 hours without relief, attending to over 100 cases and working under the most adverse conditions. He was exposed throughout to intense and heavy fire of shell and gas shells, which rendered it necessary for him to work in a mask. The following night, after his battalion had been withdrawn, he returned to search for wounded in the front line, which was still in close contact with the enemy, and, after working for several hours under heavy shell fire, he collected and evacuated all his wounded, having displayed magnificent devotion and the utmost contempt for danger throughout.

BATCHELOR, VIVIAN ALLAN Major, Royal Field Artillery. For conspicuous gallantry and devotion to duty at all times. During an intense bombardment of his battery, with H.E. by day and gas by night, he continually moved about, with an utter disregard of danger, extinguishing dumps that had been set on fire and warning his men at the outset of gas attacks. He brought his battery up in exceptionally quick time, and kept them in action by his magnificent example, and, although badly gassed and wounded, refused to leave them. He has also made daring and valuable personal reconnaissances on several occasions.

BEATTIE, MAURICE ALEXANDER, Major, Royal Garrison Artillery. For conspicuous gallantry and devotion to duty in commanding and fighting his battery splendidly for four days and nights under intense concentrated heavy fire. When three guns were rendered useless, he continued to fire with the fourth, until that was also hit. He displayed very great courage and endurance under most trying conditions.

BURNETT-STUART, GILBERT ROBERTSON, Major, Royal Field Artillery, Special Reserve. For conspicuous gallantry and devotion to duty under fire He commanded his battery with great skill and success, overcoming difficulties of observation for wire-cutting, and on one occasion going along the whole of the front line in his zone under heavy hostile fire to ascertain the position of our most advanced infantry. He successfully accomplished this, showing exceptional coolness and an utter disregard of personal safety.

CAMPBELL, WILLIAM CHARLES, M.C., Second Lieut. (Temporary Capt.), Royal Flying Corps, Special Reserve. For conspicuous gallantry and devotion to duty on numerous occasions whilst on offensive patrols. He has displayed the greatest courage and skill in attacking enemy aircraft at close range, destroying some and driving others down out of control. He has proved himself to be a scout leader of the highest class, and has destroyed 12 hostile machines and two balloons, besides taking part in many other combats during the last three months. By his fearlessness and offensive spirit he has set a splendid example to all ranks.

CLAUDET, GEOFFREY FRANCIS, Lieut. (Acting Capt.), Royal Field Artillery. For conspicuous gallantry and devotion to duty in taking over and commanding his battery under exceptionally difficult and trying conditions. Though his Battery Commander and two subalterns had been killed, and the battery had suffered heavily, two guns being damaged, as well as many of his men, he succeeded in bringing the remaining guns into action very shortly after assuming command. By his gallant conduct and great devotion to duty he set a splendid example to his men.

COCKBURN, GILBERT ERIC GRAHAM, M.C., Capt. (Temporary Major), Royal Irish Fusiliers. For conspicuous gallantry and devotion to duty. At a most critical and obscure period of an attack he was sent out with orders to clear up the situation, if possible, and to assume control of his battalion if he could reach his front line. This he eventually succeeded in doing, under heavy fire, during which he was shot through the right eye. Undeterred by this he stuck most gallantly to his mission, and although wounded again in the shoulder by a sniper, he displayed the most magnificent fearlessness and determination in reorganizing and leading his men against the enemy's position. Though under intense fire he sent in valuable and accurate reports on the situation, and remained directing operations until nightfall. His great gallantry and initiative and the example of devotion to duty which he set to all ranks were beyond all praise.

DEANE-DRUMMOND, JOHN DRUMMOND, M.C., Temporary Major, Cheshire Regt. For conspicuous gallantry and devotion to duty. When in charge of divisional machine guns his personal example and fearlessness had a splendid effect on all ranks during an attack. He successfully took his machine guns through our barrage and prevented the escape of two hostile field guns.

FRIEND, REGINALD STEWART IRVINE, Major (Acting Lieut.-Colonel), East Kent Regt., London Regt. For conspicuous gallantry and devotion to duty in personally supervising the consolidation of a captured position and pushing out important advanced posts. Although frequently under heavy shell fire he kept his men in splendid spirits by his personal example and energy.

GOODMAN, HARRY RUSSELL, Major (Acting Lieut.-Colonel), Royal Irish Rifles. For conspicuous gallantry and devotion to duty in commanding his battalion. The spirit and drive of his battalion during an attack and the splendid way in which they captured their own objective and then went to the assistance of another battalion that was temporarily in difficulties, are to be entirely attributed to the personal influence and initiative of this officer. By excellent training he has improved the fighting efficiency of his battalion beyond all recognition, and prior to the attack his patrols penetrated the enemy's lines on several occasions, inflicting heavy casualties and gaining much valuable information.

KENNEDY-COCHRAN-PATRICK, WILLIAM JOHN CHARLES, M.C., Lieut. (Temporary Capt.), Rifle Brigade and Royal Flying Corps. For conspicuous gallantry and devotion to duty on numerous occasions in destroying and driving down hostile machines, frequently engaging the enemy with great dash and a fine offensive spirit when encountered in superior numbers. By his cool judgment and splendid fearlessness he has instilled confidence in all around him, his brilliant leadership being chiefly responsible for his numerous successes.

MANN, HEATHCOTE UPFIELD, M.C., Capt., London Regt. For conspicuous gallantry and devotion to duty under heavy shelling and gas for a considerable period. The success of administrative preparations of the divisional front, carried out under considerable danger and difficulty, reflects great credit upon this officer.

MARK, ALAN WILLIAM DOBSON, M.C., Temporary Second Lieut., Northumberland Fusiliers. For conspicuous gallantry and devotion to duty in holding an extremely important point on the left of our line for 24 hours with his platoon, repeatedly beating off determined counter-attacks. After his party had been relieved the position was recaptured by the enemy, whereupon he moved up again on his own initiative and drove them out a second time, regaining the whole of the lost ground. He led his men with the utmost dash and fearlessness through heavy hostile barrage, setting a magnificent example by his own personal gallantry.

McKEE, JAMES, Temporary Capt., Royal Irish Rifles. For conspicuous gallantry and devotion to duty in leading his company in an attack. Although wounded he continued to advance until severely wounded for a second time, his leg being so badly shattered that it has since been amputated. He has at all times led his men with complete disregard of personal danger, and the splendid training which he had instilled into them beforehand proved its worth in enabling them to gain and hold their objective under trying circumstances.

PROBYN, HAROLD MELSOME, Second Lieut. (Temporary Capt.), Royal Warwickshire Regt. and Royal Flying Corps. For conspicuous gallantry and devotion to duty. At a critical time when hostile infantry had penetrated our trenches, he went up in unfavourable weather and under heavy machine-gun and anti-aircraft fire from guns of heavy calibre, and managed to locate and report with complete accuracy the position and progress of the enemy. To do this he had to fly at a very low altitude, during which his machine was seriously damaged by enemy fire. The following day he carried out another daring and successful reconnaissance of the enemy's line, bringing back information of the greatest value. He has already experienced a whole year's strenuous service flying, a fact which speaks for his gallantry and endurance on both of these particular occasions.

ROCHE-KELLY, EDMUND, Major (Temporary Lieut.-Colonel), Royal Irish Regt. For conspicuous gallantry and devotion to duty in commanding his battalion through an attack, in which he displayed great fearlessness and exceptional skill. He moved up through very heavy enemy barrage, personally reconnoitred two advanced positions, and supervised all details of consolidation, all the while exposed to very heavy shell fire. His splendid personal example and disregard of danger imbued all ranks with a spirit that swept away all opposition.

RUTHERFORD, NORMAN CECIL, M.B., F.R.C.S., Capt. (Temporary Lieut.-Colonel), Royal Army Medical Corps. For conspicuous gallantry and devotion to duty when in charge of an advanced dressing station. He worked continuously under heavy shell fire, evacuating the wounded from the forward area, and it was owing to his splendid example of devotion that the work was efficiently carried out.

SCOTT, WILLIAM DISHINGTON, M.C., Temporary Major, Highland Light Infantry. For conspicuous gallantry and devotion to duty under an intense bombardment, by which our communication and support trenches had been practically obliterated. He went forward to the front line and reorganized the defence of his sub-sector three times. It was entirely due to his magnificent example of pluck and total disregard of danger that the garrison showed such determination.

SHEPHERD, ALFRED SEYMOUR, M.C., Second Lieut., Royal Flying Corps, Special Reserve. For conspicuous gallantry and devotion to duty on numerous occasions when engaged in combat with hostile aircraft. Though surrounded by enemy machines, he continued to fight for nearly an hour with the utmost gallantry and determination against two hostile formations, finally bringing down one of the enemy out of control. Within a month he brought down seven hostile machines completely out of control.

SMITH, HERBERT FREDERICK EDGAR, Capt., King's Royal Rifle Corps, Special Reserve. For conspicuous gallantry and devotion to duty. During an enemy attack upon our trenches, he found himself blocked in a tunnel with 20 men. The only entrance that was not blown up was bombed by the enemy. With great coolness and control, however, he kept his men together, and at nightfall brought them through trenches held by the enemy and across a river. The escape of his party was entirely due to his initiative and resource.

STANNUS, THOMAS ROBERT ALEXANDER, Major (Acting Lieut.-Colonel) (Reserve of Officers, Leinster Regt., Special Reserve), Leinster Regt. For conspicuous gallantry and devotion to duty in commanding his battalion. Although severely wounded, and thereby unluckily precluded from leading them to the attack, his careful supervision and preliminary preparations undoubtedly ensured the success which his men attained. His adjutant was wounded at the same moment, but Lieut.-Colonel Stannus declined all aid until the other officer had been attended to. He had previously done splendid work when acting as O.C., on one occasion frustrating a raid with great loss to the enemy, entirely through his personal foresight and grasp of the situation.

WHEELDON, FREDERICK LAWRENCE, Temporary Second Lieut., East Lancashire Regt. For conspicuous gallantry and devotion to duty in leading his platoon to the attack under very heavy fire. He was the first to reach and to push into the enemy's trench, where he was opposed by four of the enemy, all of whom he killed single-handed, although severely wounded in both arms and legs by a bomb which one of them threw at him. He continued on until eight men were left out of his platoon. This alone shows what a splendid example of leadership he displayed during the operation.

WOODHOUSE, JOHN WHITAKER, M.C., Lieut. (Temporary Capt.), Royal Flying Corps, Special Reserve. For conspicuous gallantry and devotion to duty in carrying out special missions by night, during which he has frequently been compelled to face very bad weather. In the course of numerous bombing expeditions by night he invariably descended to very low altitudes in order to use his machine gun against hostile troops on the roads. He has consistently set a very fine example.

CANADIAN FORCE.

CONNOLLY, CHARLES EDWARD, Capt., Cavalry. For conspicuous gallantry and devotion to duty in commanding a raid upon four lines of enemy defences, in which heavy losses were inflicted upon the enemy and many prisoners captured, as well as a great number of dug-outs destroyed. He was wounded before reaching the enemy's wire, but he continued to direct the party with the greatest courage and skill, and after withdrawal he returned to the raided area with a Serjt.-Major to make sure that none of his wounded or dead were left behind.

LISTER, FRED, M.C., Capt. (Acting Major), Infantry. For conspicuous gallantry and devotion to duty in commanding his battalion for ten days in the trenches, during which they took part in five successful attacks on the enemy's lines, and resisted three vigorous counter-attacks. The success of the whole of this operation was due to his tireless supervision and the personal example which he set his men in preparing for the attacks, and consolidating the ground when it had been captured. He contributed largely to the capture of ground of the greatest tactical value, which had previously been unsuccessfully attacked.

NEW ZEALAND FORCE.

EVANS, CHARLES HELLIER DAVIS, Major, Infantry. For conspicuous gallantry and devotion to duty when in charge of a party which had to prepare a cavalry track. He reorganized his men when scattered by heavy shell fire, and continued to supervise the work, which by his fine personal example was rapidly completed under heavy fire, and proved subsequently invaluable to the success of our operations.

London Gazette, 17 Sept. 1917.—"War Office, 17 Sept. 1917. The King has been graciously pleased to approve of the following rewards for distinguished service in the field. Distinguished Service Order."

ARCHIBALD, GORDON KING, Capt. (Temporary Major), Army Service Corps.
CAHUSAC, CHARLES FITZROY, Capt., Indian Army.
CRAWFORD, JOHN DOUGLAS, M.C., Capt., Indian Army.

The Distinguished Service Order

EDGAR, DAVID KEITHOCH, Capt., Royal Engineers.
FERGUSSON, ARTHUR CHARLES, Lieut.-Colonel, Royal Artillery.
HUTSON, HENRY PORTER WOLSELEY, M.C., Lieut., Royal Engineers.
LELAND, FRANCIS WILLIAM GEORGE, Major (Temporary Lieut.-Colonel), Army Service Corps.
LLOYD, ROBERT ARCHER, M.D., Major, Indian Medical Service.
LOVEROCK, ROBERT CHARLES, Capt., Oxford and Bucks Light Infantry.
MACEWEN, NORMAN DUCKWORTH KERR, Major (Temporary Lieut.-Colonel), Argyll and Sutherland Highlanders and Royal Flying Corps.
NIXON, ERNEST JOHN, M.C., Capt., Royal Garrison Artillery.
O'CONNOR, JAMES LYNCH, Temporary Major, Army Service Corps.
OWEN, ALFRED DUDMAN, Inspector Mechanical Transport, 1st Class (Temporary Chief Inspector), and Honorary Capt., Army Service Corps.
PATTERSON, ARTHUR FREDERICK ISBELL, Lieut. (Temporary Capt.) Royal Army Medical Corps.
RAYMOND, EVELYN DALRYMPLE, M.C., Major, Indian Army.
TIMBRELL, THOMAS, Major (Temporary Lieut.-Colonel), Indian Army.
TOWNSEND, FREDERICK OWEN, Second Lieut. (Temporary Capt.), Indian Army Reserve of Officers.
TURNER, EDWARD GEORGE, Capt. (Acting Major), Army Veterinary Corps.

AUSTRALIAN IMPERIAL FORCE.
HILLARY, MICHAEL JAMES, Lieut., Engineers.

London Gazette, 21 Sept. 1917.—" Admiralty, 21 Sept. 1917.—Extracts from a Despatch of Vice-Admiral Sir Rosslyn E. Wemyss, K.C.B., C.M.G., M.V.O., late Commander-in-Chief, East Indies Station, covering a report by Capt. Wilfrid Nunn, C.M.G., D.S.O., R.N., on the operations of H.M. Gunboats in Mesopotamia from Dec. 1916, to March, 1917."

From Capt. Wilfrid Nunn's Report.—" I have the honour to submit the following for special mention, promotion, honours or awards " :—

H.M.S. Tarantula.
SHERBROOKE, HENRY G., Commander, R.N. For skilful handling of his ship, and especially on 26 Feb., when he contributed largely to the success of the operations.

H.M.S. Mantis.
BUXTON, BERNARD, Commander, R.N. For good work done on all occasions. His prompt action under heavy fire on 26 March saved H.M.S. Mantis from running aground in a critical position.

H.M.S. Moth.
HILL, FREDERICK G. E., Surgeon, R.N. Who, finding a man wounded on the battery deck, gallantly, under heavy fire, carried him into the sick bay to dress his wounds. Whilst doing this, the man received another wound through his throat, and Surgeon Hill himself received a nasty wound in his forearm. Nevertheless, although in considerable pain, and until his arm became too stiff to use it, he proceeded to dress and attend to all the wounded on board.

H.M.S. Gadfly.
ARBUTHNOT, ERNEST K., Commander, R.N. During the recent advance to Baghdad I have found this officer's knowledge and experience of great benefit, and he has shown great coolness under fire on all occasions.

London Gazette, 21 Sept. 1917.—" Admiralty, 21 Sept. 1917. The King has been graciously pleased to give orders for the following appointments to the Distinguished Service Order to the undermentioned Officers, in recognition of their services as mentioned in the foregoing Despatch."

BUXTON, BERNARD, Commander, R.N.
SHERBROOKE, HENRY G., Commander, R.N.
ARBUTHNOT, ERNEST K., Commander, R.N.
HILL, FREDERICK G. E., Surgeon, R.N.

London Gazette, 26 Sept. 1917.—" War Office, 26 Sept. 1917. His Majesty the King has been pleased to confer the undermentioned rewards for gallantry and distinguished service in the field. The acts of gallantry for which the decorations have been awarded will be announced in the London Gazette as early as practicable. Awarded a Second Bar to the Distinguished Service Order."

HILL, GERALD VICTOR WILMOT, D.S.O., Capt. and Brevet Major (Temporary Lieut.-Colonel), Royal Irish Fusiliers.
(D.S.O. gazetted 14 Jan. 1916.)
(First Bar gazetted 17 April, 1917.)

Awarded a Bar to the Distinguished Service Order :
BISHOP, WILLIAM AVERY, V.C., D.S.O., M.C., Lieut. (Temporary Capt.), Canadian Cavalry and Royal Flying Corps.
(D.S.O. gazetted 18 June, 1917.)
BRAND, THE HONOURABLE ROGER, D.S.O., Capt. and Brevet Major (Acting Lieut.-Colonel), Rifle Brigade, Special Reserve.
(D.S.O. gazetted 3 June, 1916.)
CLAY, BERTIE GORDON, D.S.O., Major and Brevet Lieut.-Colonel (Temporary Lieut.-Colonel), Dragoon Guards.
(D.S.O. gazetted 20 Oct. 1916.)
CORFE, ARTHUR CECIL, D.S.O., Major (Temporary Lieut.-Colonel), South African Defence Force.
(D.S.O. gazetted 4 June, 1917.)
DAUBENY, GILES BULTEEL, D.S.O., Major, Royal Garrison Artillery.
(D.S.O. gazetted 14 Nov. 1916.)
DENNIS, MICHAEL FREDERICK BEAUCHAMP, D.S.O., Temporary Major (Acting Lieut.-Colonel), King's Own Scottish Borderers.
(D.S.O. gazetted 4 Nov. 1915.)
FINCH, LIONEL HUGH KNIGHTLY, D.S.O., Capt. (Temporary Lieut.-Colonel), Cheshire Regt.
(D.S.O. gazetted 1 Jan. 1917.)
GORT, VISCOUNT, JOHN STANDISH SURTEES PRENDERGAST VEREKER, M.V.O., D.S.O., M.C., Capt. and Brevet Major (Acting Lieut.-Colonel), Grenadier Guards.
(D.S.O. gazetted 4 June, 1917.)
HANBURY-SPARROW, ARTHUR ALAN HANBURY, D.S.O., M.C., Capt. (Acting Lieut.-Colonel), Royal Berkshire Regt.
(D.S.O. gazetted 1 Dec. 1914.)
HINDLE, RALPH, D.S.O., Lieut.-Colonel, North Lancashire Regt.
(D.S.O. gazetted 4 June, 1917.)
INGPEN, PERCY LEIGH, D.S.O., Major (Temporary Lieut.-Colonel), West Yorkshire Regt.
(D.S.O. gazetted 3 June, 1916.)
MACDONALD, CHARLES LESLIE, D.S.O., Temporary Lieut.-Colonel, Manchester Regt.
(D.S.O. gazetted 1 Jan. 1917.)
MORIARTY, OLIVER NASH, D.S.O., Capt. (Acting Major), Royal Garrison Artillery, Special Reserve.
(D.S.O. gazetted 25 Aug. 1916.)
PEIRS, HUGH JOHN CHEVALLIER, D.S.O., Temporary Major, Royal West Surrey Regt.
(D.S.O. gazetted 3 June, 1916.)
PETERSON, ARTHUR JAMES, D.S.O., Temporary Capt. (Acting Major), Royal Field Artillery.
(D.S.O. gazetted 25 Aug. 1916.)
REYNOLDS, LEWIS LESLIE CLAYTON, D.S.O., Major, Oxfordshire and Buckinghamshire Light Infantry.
(D.S.O. gazetted 14 Nov. 1916.)
RIDDELL, EDWARD PIUS ARTHUR, D.S.O., Major (Temporary Lieut.-Colonel), Rifle Brigade.
(D.S.O. gazetted 11 Dec. 1916.)
ROGERS, JAMES SAMUEL YEAMAN, D.S.O., Major, Royal Army Medical Corps.
(D.S.O. gazetted 14 Jan. 1916.)
SAMUEL, FREDERICK DUDLEY, D.S.O., Lieut.-Colonel, London Regt.
(D.S.O. gazetted 1 Jan. 1917.)
WIENHOLT, WILLIAM HUMPHREY MEYRICK, D.S.O., Temporary Major, North Lancashire Regt.
(D.S.O. gazetted 4 June, 1917.)
WOOD, EDWARD ALLAN, D.S.O., Temporary Lieut.-Colonel, Shropshire Light Infantry.
(D.S.O. gazetted 1 Jan. 1917.)

Awarded the Distinguished Service Order :
ALEXANDER, THE HONOURABLE WILLIAM SIGISMUND PATRICK, Lieut. (Acting Capt.), Irish Guards.
ALLEN, LIONEL RAYMOND, Lieut., Nottinghamshire and Derbyshire Regt., Special Reserve.
ARCHER, HARRY, Lieut. (Acting Capt.), Devonshire Regt., Special Reserve.
BELLEW, FROUDE DILLON, M.C., Major, Somersetshire Light Infantry (surname changed to Trollope-Bellew).
BENNETT, THOMAS EDWIN, Major (Temporary Lieut.-Colonel), Army Service Corps.
BETHELL, HUGH KEPPEL, Capt. and Brevet Lieut.-Colonel (Temporary Brigadier-General), Hussars.
BOWELL, ROBERT HENRY, Second Lieut., Leicestershire Regt.
BOWIE, JOHN DARLING, Capt. (Acting Lieut.-Colonel), Royal Army Medical Corps.
BRADSHAW, WILLIAM PAT ARTHUR, Lieut. (Acting Capt.), Scots Guards.
BRYCE, EDWARD DANIEL, Capt. (Temporary Major), Tank Corps.
BUCKLEY, ALBERT, Capt. (Temporary Major), North Lancashire Regt.
CADE, ARTHUR GORDON, M.C., Capt. (Acting Major), Middlesex Regt.
COKE, THE HONOURABLE EDWARD, M.C., Capt. (Acting Lieut.-Colonel), Rifle Brigade.
CONINGHAM, ARTHUR, M.C., Second Lieut. (Temporary Capt.), Royal Flying Corps, Special Reserve.
DAVENPORT, FRED, M.C., Capt. (Temporary Major), Royal Field Artillery (rank corrected to Major [London Gazette, 18 Feb. 1918]).
DAVIDGE, GUY MORTIMER COLERIDGE, Major (Acting Lieut.-Colonel), Worcestershire Regt.
EATON, THE HONOURABLE FRANCIS ORMOND HENRY, Lieut. (Acting Capt.), Grenadier Guards.
EDWARDS, CHRISTOPHER VAUGHAN, Major (Acting Lieut.-Colonel), Yorkshire Regt.
EDWARDS, CYRIL GEORGE, Second Lieut., West Yorkshire Regt.
FORSTER, HAROLD THOMAS, M.C., Lieut., Royal Berkshire Regt.
FOULKES, JOHN SIMPSON, Temporary Major, Manchester Regt.
FURNESS, CHARLES CLIFFORD, Major, Royal Field Artillery.
GEDDES, GODFREY POWER, Temporary Lieut., Gordon Highlanders.
GLOVER, WILLIAM REID, Major (Acting Lieut.-Colonel), London Regt.
GORDON, LORD DUDLEY GLADSTONE, Temporary Major, Gordon Highlanders.
GOUGH, HORACE FREDERICK, Second Lieut., North Staffordshire Regt.
GUINNESS, THE HONOURABLE WALTER EDWARD, Major, Yeomanry.
HAMMILL, LONSDALE, M.C., Capt., South Lancashire Regt.
HANNAY, GEORGE MARTIN, Capt. (Temporary Lieut.-Colonel), Reserve of Officers, late King's Own Scottish Borderers.
HARVEY, ALBERT, Second Lieut., Liverpool Regt.
HENDERSON-ROE, CHRISTOPHER GORDON, Capt., Royal West Kent Regt., Special Reserve.
HORSFIELD, RICHARD MARSHALL, Major, Royal Field Artillery.
HUNKIN, SAMUEL LLEWELLYN, Temporary Major, Royal Welsh Fusiliers.
HUTCHESON, JOHN, M.C., Capt., Gordon Highlanders.
IRWIN, NORMAN LESLIE CROZIER, Temporary Capt., Royal Welsh Fusiliers.
JEFFERIES, HUGH ST. JOHN, Major (Acting Lieut.-Colonel), Worcestershire Regt.
JONES, REGINALD REES, Second Lieut., Welsh Guards.
KEWLEY, EDWARD RIGBY, M.C., Capt. (Acting Lieut.-Colonel), Rifle Brigade.
LANCE, EDWIN CHRISTOPHER, Second Lieut. (Temporary Capt.), Somersetshire Light Infantry.
LEECH, WILLIAM FREDERICK, Temporary Second Lieut., General List and Royal Flying Corps.

LEES, DAVID, M.B., Temporary Capt., Royal Army Medical Corps.
LE PREVOST, ALFRED PAUL HARRISON, Temporary Major (Acting Lieut.-Colonel), Nottinghamshire and Derbyshire Regt.
LEVEY, JOSEPH HENRY, Capt. (Temporary Lieut.-Colonel), Gordon Highlanders.
LLOYD, ERNEST GUY RICHARDS, Temporary Lieut. (Acting Capt.), Shropshire Light Infantry.
LOWCOCK, REGINALD JOHN, M.C., Lieut. (Temporary Capt.), Nottinghamshire and Derbyshire Regt. and Royal Flying Corps.
LYCETT, TIMOTHY, Second Lieut. (Temporary Capt.), King's Royal Rifle Corps.
MACLEAN, IVAN CLARKSON, M.C., Temporary Capt., Royal Army Medical Corps.
MACROBERTS, NOEL DE PUTRON, M.C., Temporary Lieut. (Acting Capt.), Royal Sussex Regt.
MAIR, BRODIE VALENTINE, M.C., Capt., Manchester Regt.
MAITLAND, WILLIAM BARCLAY, Second Lieut., Gordon Highlanders.
MARTIN, BERNARD WILLIAM JOHN HANKINS, Second Lieut., Royal Field Artillery, Special Reserve.
MARTIN, EDWARD CUTHBERT DE RENZY, M.C., Capt. (Temporary Lieut.-Colonel), Yorkshire Light Infantry.
MAY, HARRY, Second Lieut. (Temporary Lieut. and Acting Capt.), Royal Field Artillery.
McCARTHY-O'LEARY, HEFFERNAN WILLIAM DENIS, M.C., Capt. (Acting Lieut.-Colonel), Royal Irish Fusiliers.
MONTGOMERY-SMITH, EDWIN CHARLES, Major (Temporary Lieut.-Colonel), Royal Army Medical Corps.
NORTH, PIERS WILLIAM, Lieut.-Colonel, Reserve of Officers, Royal Berkshire Regt.
ORR, JOHN BOYD, M.C., M.B., Temporary Capt., Royal Army Medical Corps.
PALLANT, HUBERT ARNOLD, M.C., Temporary Capt., Royal Army Medical Corps.
PEGLER, SIDNEY JAMES, Temporary Second Lieut., Rifle Brigade.
PENNELL, RICHARD, Lieut. (Temporary Major), King's Royal Rifle Corps.
PETRIE, DAVID PARKER, Lieut., Scottish Rifles, Special Reserve.
POTTER, COLIN KYNASTON, M.C., Major (Acting Lieut.-Colonel), North Lancashire Regt.
PRIESTMAN, JOHN HEDLEY THORNTON, Capt., Lincolnshire Regt.
ROBINSON, ALBERT CHARLES HENRY, Temporary Second Lieut., attached Yorkshire Light Infantry.
SARGEAUNT, PERCY RICHARD, Capt. (Acting Major), Royal Garrison Artillery.
SHARLAND, ALAN ABBOTT, Capt. (Temporary Major and Acting Lieut.-Colonel), East Lancashire Regt.
SHERBROOKE, ROBERT LOWE, Capt. and Brevet Major (Temporary Lieut.-Colonel), Nottinghamshire and Derbyshire Regt.
SLADE, HAROLD ARTHUR, M.C., Temporary Capt., Rifle Brigade.
STEWART, ALEXANDER JOHN, Capt., Royal Highlanders.
STRANGE, JOHN STANLEY, M.C., Temporary Capt., Welsh Regt.
SUTHERLAND, THOMAS DOUGLAS, M.C., Temporary Capt., Lincolnshire Regt.
SUTTON, BERTINE ENTWISLE, M.C., Second Lieut. (Temporary Capt.), Yeomanry and Royal Flying Corps.
SYMON, JAMES ALEXANDER, Lieut. (Acting Capt.), Cameron Highlanders.
THOMAS, ALAN ERNEST WENTWORTH, Second Lieut. (Temporary Capt.) Royal West Kent Regt.
THOMAS, GWILYM IVOR, M.C., Capt. (Acting Major), Royal Field Artillery.
TRELOAR, GEORGE DEVINE, Lieut. (Acting Capt.), Coldstream Guards, Special Reserve.
TYSON, ERIC JAMES, M.C., Temporary Major, General List and Royal Flying Corps.
WARMAN, CLIVE WILSON, M.C., Second Lieut., General List and Royal Flying Corps.
WATKINS, GWELYM DAVID, Capt., Royal Army Medical Corps.
WATSON, CAMPBELL N. Temporary Major, Liverpool Regt.
WHALLEY, PERCY ROGER, Major (Acting Lieut.-Colonel), Worcestershire Regt.
WHEAL, SAMUEL, Second Lieut., East Lancashire Regt.
WHITE, JOHN DONALD, Capt., Middlesex Regt.
WILLIAMS, JESSE, Temporary Major, Royal Welsh Fusiliers.
WILSON, PERCY NORTON WHITESTONE, M.C., Capt., Royal Fusiliers.
YOUNG, KENNETH, Temporary Second Lieut., Lincolnshire Regt.

CANADIAN FORCE.

McKINERY, JOHN WILLIAM HERBERT, Lieut.-Colonel, Labour Battn.
PATERSON, ROBERT WALTER, Lieut.-Colonel, Cavalry.
RALSTON, JAMES LAYTON, Major, Infantry.

London Gazette, 1 Oct. 1917.—" Admiralty, 1 Oct. 1917. The King has been graciously pleased to give orders for the following appointments to the Distinguished Service Order and for the award of the decorations specified below to the undermentioned Officers. To be Companions of the Distinguished Service Order."

PETRE, WALTER REGINALD GLYNN, Capt., R.N.
LEITH, LOCKHART, Capt., R.N.
MAY, JOHN, Lieut.-Commander (Acting Commander), R.N.
MANN, JOHN, Engineer Commander, R.N.R.
QUINNE, JOHN, Engineer Lieut.-Commander, R.N.R.

To receive a Bar to the Distinguished Service Order :
CURTIS, BERWICK, D.S.O., Capt., Royal Navy.
MORANT, EDGAR ROBERT, D.S.O., Commander (Acting Capt.), Royal Navy.

" Honours for the Royal Naval Air Service.—The King has been graciously pleased to approve of the award of the following honours to Officers of the Royal Naval Air Service."

(1) For services on patrol duties and submarine searching in Home Waters :—
To be Companions of the Distinguished Service Order :

ROSS, ROBERT PEEL, Wing Commander, R.N.
MAGUIRE, OWEN HUGH KNOX, Acting Commander, R.N.

To receive a Bar to the Distinguished Service Order :
BIGSWORTH, ARTHUR WELLESLEY, D.S.O., Wing Commander, Royal Navy.

(2) For services in reconnaissance and bombing flights in the Eastern Mediterranean :—
To be a Companion of the Distinguished Service Order :
SCARLETT, FRANCIS ROWLAND, Wing Capt., R.N.

To receive a Bar to the Distinguished Service Order :
SMYTH-PIGOTT, JOSEPH RUSCOMBE WADHAM, D.S.O., Wing Commander, Royal Navy.
KILNER, CECIL FRANCIS, D.S.O., Squadron Commander, Royal Naval Air Service (Capt., Temporary Major, Royal Marine Light Infantry).

London Gazette, 17 Oct. 1917.—" War Office, 17 Oct. 1917. His Majesty the King has been graciously pleased to approve of the undermentioned rewards for distinguished service in the field, dated 3 June, 1917. To be Companions of the Distinguished Service Order."

CAMPBELL, ALAN JAMES, Lieut.-Colonel, Infantry, Indian Army.
COLLUM, JAMES ALFRED, Capt., Cavalry, Indian Army.
FARRAN, GEORGE LAMBERT, M.C., Major (Temporary Lieut.-Colonel), Cavalry, Indian Army.
HUNTER, FREDERICK FRASER, Major (Temporary Lieut.-Colonel), Indian Army.
POPHAM, EDWARD LEYBORNE, Major, Cavalry, Indian Army.
ROTHWELL, RICHARD SUTTON, Major, Royal Artillery.
SAUNDERS, MACAN, Capt. (Temporary Major), Sikhs, Indian Army.

London Gazette, 18 Oct. 1917.—" War Office, 18 Oct. 1917. His Majesty the King has been pleased to confer the undermentioned rewards for gallantry and distinguished service in the field. The acts of gallantry for which the decorations have been awarded will be announced in the London Gazette as early as practicable. Awarded a Bar to Distinguished Service Order."

ORMOND, DANIEL MAWAT, D.S.O., Lieut.-Colonel, Canadian Infantry.
(D.S.O. gazetted 4 June, 1917.)

Awarded Distinguished Service Order :
BENSON, CONSTANTINE EVELYN, Second Lieut., Grenadier Guards, Special Reserve.
CAMERON, JAMES FREDERICK CAMPBELL, M.C., Temporary Lieut., Argyll and Sutherland Highlanders.
CRAIG, ARCHIBALD HAY, M.C., Temporary Capt., Royal Scots.
DE MONTMORENCY, HERVEY FRANCIS, Temporary Capt. (Acting Major), Royal Field Artillery (rank corrected to Temporary Major [London Gazette, 17 Dec. 1917]).
GILL, JOHN HENRY, Temporary Major, West Yorkshire Regt.
HARDY, REV. THEODORE BAYLEY, Army Chaplains' Department.
KENNEDY, ARTHUR JULIUS RANN, Major, Royal Field Artillery.
MINET, ERNEST CHARLES TEMPLE, M.C., Temporary Lieut. (Acting Capt.), Machine Gun Corps.
MOBERLY, WALTER HAMILTON, Second Lieut., Oxfordshire and Buckinghamshire Light Infantry.
MUIR, JOHN BALDERSTONE, Major (Temporary Lieut.-Colonel), Royal Highlanders.
PARR, VICTOR HENRY, M.C., Temporary Capt., Royal Inniskilling Fusiliers.
REDMOND, WILLIAM ARCHER, Capt., Irish Guards, Special Reserve.
STORRIE, WILLIAM, Second Lieut., Highland Light Infantry, Special Reserve.
VIVIAN, THE HONOURABLE ODO RICHARD, M.V.O., Major, Yeomanry.
WENYON, HERBERT JOHN, Temporary Capt., Royal West Kent Regt.
WETHERALL, HARRY EDWARD DE ROBILLARD, M.C., Capt. (Temporary Lieut.-Colonel), Gloucestershire Regt.
WILSON, GAVIN LAURIE, M.C., Temporary Major, Argyll and Sutherland Highlanders.

CANADIAN FORCE.

BAILEY, CHARLES EDWARD, M.C., Lieut. (Acting Capt.), Infantry.
BROWN, WALTER RICHARD, Major (Acting Lieut.-Colonel), Infantry.
BURNHAM, SYDNEY SMITH, Major, Infantry.
COCKERAM, ALAN, Lieut., Infantry.
GILSON, WILLIAM FORBES, Capt. (Acting Lieut.-Colonel), Infantry.
JONES, LOUIS ELGIN, Major (Acting Lieut.-Colonel), Infantry.
McEACHERN, NORMAN ANGUS, Lieut., Infantry.
MILLER, ALBERT PETER, M.C., Capt. (Acting Major), Infantry.
MILLS, ARTHUR SAMUEL, Lieut. (Acting Major), Infantry.

SOUTH AFRICAN FORCE.

DURHAM, CORNEY GEORGE, Major, South African Force.

London Gazette, 27 Oct. 1917.—" War Office, 27 Oct. 1917. His Majesty the King has been pleased to confer the undermentioned rewards for gallantry and distinguished service in the field. The acts of gallantry for which the decorations have been awarded will be announced in the London Gazette as early as practicable. Awarded a Bar to the Distinguished Service Order."

DAVIDSON, NORMAN RANDALL, D.S.O., Major and Brevet Lieut.-Colonel, Royal Field Artillery.
(D.S.O. gazetted 14 Jan. 1916.)

The Distinguished Service Order

PRESTON, THE HONOURABLE RICHARD MARTIN PETER, D.S.O., Major, Royal Horse Artillery (formerly Honourable Artillery Company).
(D.S.O. gazetted 4 June, 1917.)

ROBINSON, HENRY ABRAHALL, D.S.O., Temporary Major, Royal Fusiliers.
(D.S.O. gazetted 11 Dec. 1916.)

Awarded the Distinguished Service Order.

DAVIDSON, THOMAS, Major, Royal Field Artillery.
DERVICHE-JONES, ARTHUR DANIEL, M.C., Capt. (Acting Lieut.-Colonel), Royal Lincolnshire Regt.
DRUMGOLD, ARTHUR, Second Lieut., Royal West Kent Regt., Special Reserve.
FOORD, ALEXANDER GUNNING, Major (Acting Lieut.-Colonel), Manchester Regt.
GRELLET, REGINALD CHARLES, Temporary Major, Yorkshire Regt.
HART, REGINALD SETON, Major (Acting Lieut.-Colonel), Nottinghamshire and Derbyshire Regt.
HENDERSON, GEORGE DUNNETT, M.C., Temporary Capt., Royal West Kent Regt.
HUDSON, HERBERT HENRY, M.C., Temporary Major, West Yorkshire Regt.
HUMPHREYS, HERBERT JOHN, M.C., Capt. (Acting Major), Royal Highlanders.
LETHBRIDGE, FRANCIS WASHINGTON, Temporary Major (Acting Lieut.-Colonel), West Riding Regt.
MASON, HAROLD LYALL, M.C., Lieut. (Acting Capt.), Royal Field Artillery, Special Reserve.
MILLWARD, WILLIAM COLSEY, Temporary Major (Acting Lieut.-Colonel), Royal Sussex Regt.
RHYS-DAVIDS, ARTHUR PERCIVAL FOLEY, M.C., Second Lieut., Royal Flying Corps, Special Reserve.
RITSON, JOHN ANTHONY SYDNEY, M.C., Capt. (Temporary Lieut.-Colonel), Durham Light Infantry.
SALE, JOHN CARUTHERS, M.C., Temporary Capt., Royal Army Medical Corps.
STEWART, PATRICK DOUGLAS, Capt. (Acting Lieut.-Colonel), Dragoon Guards.

AUSTRALIAN IMPERIAL FORCE.

ELLER, JOSEPH HENRY PETER, Major, Infantry.
ERREY, LEONARD GEORGE PRENTICE, M.C., Lieut., Infantry
McCLEAN, FREDERICK STEPHEN, Major, Pioneer Battn.

CANADIAN FORCE.

COLLIER, ERNEST VICTOR, Major, Infantry.
KING, WILLIAM HOPE, Lieut., Infantry.
McCORMICK, JAMES HANNA, Lieut., Infantry (Christian name James Hanna corrected to James).

London Gazette, 2 Nov. 1917.—"Admiralty, 2 Nov. 1917.—Honours for Services in Action with Enemy Submarines. The King has been graciously pleased to approve of the award of the following honours, for services in action with enemy submarines. To be Companions of the Distinguished Service Order."

BANNERMAN, BERTRAND, Lieut.-Commander, R.N.
DE BURGH, CHARLES, Lieut.-Commander, R.N.
NUNN, REGINALD ARTHUR, D.S.C., Assistant Paymaster, Royal Naval Reserve.

To receive a Bar to the Distinguished Service Order:
NAYLOR, CEDRIC, D.S.O., D.S.C., Lieut., Royal Naval Reserve (now Lieut., Royal Navy).

To receive a Second Bar to the Distinguished Service Order:
CAMPBELL, GORDON, V.C., D.S.O., Capt., Royal Navy.

"Honours for Service in Submarines.—The King has been graciously pleased to approve of the award of the following honours to the undermentioned Officers, in recognition of their services in submarines in enemy waters. To be Companions of the Distinguished Service Order."

COOPER, VINCENT MORSE, Lieut.-Commander, R.N.
SHOVE, HERBERT WILLIAM, Lieut.-Commander, R.N.
GLENCROSS, JOHN BULLER, Lieut.-Commander, R.N.
ACWORTH, BERNARD, Lieut.-Commander, R.N.
CARY, THE HONOURABLE BYRON PLANTAGENET, Lieut.-Commander, R.N. (since killed).
JOHNSON, BERNARD LEITCH, Lieut.-Commander, R.N.R.

To receive a Bar to the Distinguished Service Order:
TALBOT, CECIL PONSONBY, D.S.O., Commander, Royal Navy.
HORTON, MAX KENNEDY, D.S.O., Commander, Royal Navy.

"Honours for the Royal Naval Air Service.—The King has been graciously pleased to approve of the award of the following honour to an officer of the Royal Naval Air Service. To be a Companion of the Distinguished Service Order."

SMART, BERNARD ARTHUR, Flight Sub-Lieut., Royal Naval Air Service.

"Honours to the Mercantile Marine.—The King has been graciously pleased to approve of the award of the following honour to the undermentioned Officer of the British Mercantile Marine, in recognition of zeal and devotion to duty shown in carrying on the trade of the country during the war. To be a Companion of the Distinguished Service Order."

GEORGE, BENJAMIN WILLIAM, Capt. (Lieut., R.N.R.).

London Gazette, 17 Nov. 1917.—"Admiralty, 17 Nov. 1917.—Honours for Services in Action with Enemy Submarines. The King has been graciously pleased to approve of the award of the following honours to Officers of the Distinguished Service Order, for services in action with enemy submarines. To be Companions of the Distinguished Service Order."

BLACKWOOD, MAURICE BALDWIN RAYMOND, Commander, R.N.
TIPPET, ARTHUR GRENDON, Lieut.-Commander, R.N.
WORSLEY, FRANK HENRY, Lieut.-Commander, R.D., R.N.R. (Christian name corrected to Frank Arthur).
HALLIFAX, OSWALD ERNEST, Lieut., R.N.
JEFFREY, DOUGLAS GEORGE, Lieut., R.N.R.
GRAY, FREDERICK WILLIAM, Lieut., R.N.R.

"Honours to the Royal Naval Air Service.—The King has been graciously pleased to approve of the award of the following honours to Officers of the Royal Naval Air Service. To be Companions of the Distinguished Service Order."

GRAHAM, RONALD, D.S.C., Acting Flight Commander, Royal Naval Air Service. For conspicuous gallantry and devotion to duty in air fights and bombing raids. Since the award of a Bar to the Distinguished Service Cross, Acting Flight Commander Graham has carried out five night bombing raids, and attacked and brought down three enemy seaplanes. On one occasion he ascended at night for the purpose of attacking hostile machines, notwithstanding the fact that he had only returned a few hours previously from a successful action with hostile aircraft in superior numbers. He has always displayed remarkable skill and courage.

FISHER, PHILIP SIDNEY, D.S.C., Acting Flight Commander, Royal Naval Air Service. For conspicuous gallantry and devotion to duty in air fights and bombing raids. On one occasion, when very heavy fighting took place between eight machines of his squadron and about 20 Albatross scouts, he fought at least six combats single-handed, shooting down one of his opponents out of control. On another occasion, when he was acting as leader of a flight of five machines detailed for an offensive patrol, a general action took place with a number of Albatross scouts, in the course of which Acting Flight Commander Fisher was wounded whilst fighting with great gallantry. He has shown himself to be a most efficient and plucky flight leader, and has also taken part in numerous night bombing raids in addition to his day fighting.

London Gazette, 19 Nov. 1917.—"War Office, 19 Nov. 1917. His Majesty the King has been pleased to confer the undermentioned rewards for gallantry and distinguished service in the field. The acts of gallantry for which the decorations have been awarded will be announced in the London Gazette as early as practicable. Awarded a Second Bar to the Distinguished Service Order."

CORFE, ARTHUR CECIL, D.S.O., Major (Temporary Lieut.-Colonel), South African Defence Force and Royal West Kent Regt.
(D.S.O. gazetted 4 June, 1917. First Bar gazetted 26 Sept. 1917.)

Awarded a Bar to the Distinguished Service Order:
CLARK, WILLIAM CHARLES, D.S.O., Temporary Lieut.-Colonel, Royal Fusiliers.
(D.S.O. gazetted 25 Aug. 1917.)

CLEMSON, WILLIAM FLETCHER, C.M.G., D.S.O., Lieut.-Colonel (Temporary Brigadier-General), York and Lancaster Regt.
(D.S.O. gazetted 23 June, 1915.)

JARVIS, TALBOT McLEAVY, D.S.O., Temporary Lieut.-Colonel, King's Royal Rifle Corps (formerly Royal West Surrey Regt.).
(D.S.O. gazetted 4 June, 1917.)

PENNELL, RICHARD, D.S.O., Lieut. (Temporary Lieut.-Colonel), King's Royal Rifle Corps.
(D.S.O. gazetted 26 Sept. 1917.)

AUSTRALIAN IMPERIAL FORCE.

STEWART, JAMES CAMPBELL, D.S.O., Lieut.-Colonel, Infantry.
(D.S.O. gazetted 1 Jan. 1917.)

Awarded the Distinguished Service Order:

ARMSTRONG, GORDON WILSON, Temporary Capt., Royal Army Medical Corps.
BORROW, EDWARD, Temporary Major, Durham Light Infantry, attached West Riding Regt.
BOURNE, DENNIS KEMP, Temporary Lieut. (Acting Capt.), Welsh Regt.
CHRISTIE, MURRAY INGLIS, Temporary Second Lieut., attached Royal Fusiliers.
DENNISS, CYRIL EDMUND BARTLEY, Major, Royal Field Artillery.
EVANS, IVOR THOMAS, M.C., Temporary Capt., South Wales Borderers, attached Welsh Regt.
GALLIE, OSCAR EUGENE, M.C., Lieut., Royal Field Artillery, Special Reserve.
GAYER, AUBREY VIVIAN ARTHUR, Temporary Major (Acting Lieut.-Colonel), Middlesex Regt.
GRAY, EDWARD, M.C., Second Lieut. (Temporary Capt.), Durham Light Infantry.
HOWITT, THOMAS CECIL, Temporary Major, Leicestershire Regt.
JACKSON, DENNYS BRIAN MARRIOTT, Second Lieut. (Acting Capt.), Seaforth Highlanders.
HARDY, CLIVE, Capt., London Regt.
MAXWELL, ALLEN, Temporary Capt. (Acting Major), Royal Fusiliers.
McKIMM, DAVID SIDNEY ALEXANDER, M.C., Temporary Capt., Shropshire Light Infantry.
MOFFATT, FRANCIS JOHN CAMPBELL, Temporary Capt., Gordon Highlanders.
MUNRO, ALEXANDER, Second Lieut., Seaforth Highlanders.
PRIOR-WANDESFORDE, FERDINAND CHARLES RICHARD, Second Lieut., Royal Field Artillery, Special Reserve.
ROWBOTHAM, JAMES, M.C., Capt. (Acting Lieut.-Colonel), Highland Light Infantry, attached Gordon Highlanders.
WALKER, FREDERICK WILLIAM, Second Lieut., London Regt.
WARNER, THOMAS LOVELL, Temporary Major, Leicestershire Regt.
WELCH, HAROLD ECHALAZ, Temporary Major (Acting Lieut.-Colonel), Shropshire Light Infantry.
WILLIAMS, REES JOHN, Temporary Second Lieut. (Acting Capt.), Welsh Regt.

AUSTRALIAN IMPERIAL FORCE.

APPLEYARD, SYDNEY VERE, Major, Army Medical Corps.
BACHTOLD, HENRY, M.C., Major, Engineers.
FREEMAN, NEIL MACKENZIE, Major, Infantry.
JOHNSTON, WILLIAM WALLACE STEWART, M.C., Major, Army Medical Corps.

The Distinguished Service Order

MARSHALL, NORMAN, M.C., Lieut.-Colonel, Infantry.
MASON, CHARLES CONWAY, Lieut.-Colonel, Infantry.
TOLLEY, HOWARD GEORGE, Major, Engineers.

CANADIAN FORCE.

THOMPSON, WILLIAM WINFRED, Lieut. (Acting Capt.), Infantry.

London Gazette, 26 Nov. 1917.—" War Office, 26 Nov. 1917. His Majesty the King has been pleased to confer the undermentioned rewards for gallantry and distinguished service in the field. The acts of gallantry for which the decorations have been awarded will be announced in the London Gazette as early as practicable. Awarded a Bar to the Distinguished Service Order."

BEAUMAN, ARCHIBALD BENTLEY, D.S.O., Capt. and Brevet Major (Acting Lieut.-Colonel), South Staffordshire Regt.
(D.S.O. gazetted 6 Sept. 1915.)
HANAFIN, PATRICK JOHN, D.S.O., Major (Temporary Lieut.-Colonel), Royal Army Medical Corps.
(D.S.O. gazetted 14 Jan. 1916.)
HILL, ROBERT McCOWAN, D.S.O., M.B., Temporary Capt., Royal Army Medical Corps.
(D.S.O. gazetted 16 May, 1916.)
HUDSON, CHARLES EDWARD, D.S.O., M.C., Temporary Major, Nottinghamshire and Derbyshire Regt.
(D.S.O. gazetted 16 Aug. 1917.)
JAMES, CECIL POLGLASE, D.S.O., Major (Temporary Lieut.-Colonel), Argyll and Sutherland Highlanders.
(D.S.O. gazetted 1 Jan. 1917.)
KEARSLEY, EDWARD REGINALD, D.S.O., Capt., Royal Welsh Fusiliers.
(D.S.O. gazetted 4 Nov. 1915.)
LE PREVOST, ALFRED PAUL HARRISON, D.S.O., Temporary Major (Acting Lieut.-Colonel), Nottinghamshire and Derbyshire Regt.
(D.S.O. gazetted 26 Sept. 1917.)
LINTON, CHARLES STRANGWAY, D.S.O., M.C., Major (Acting Lieut.-Colonel), Worcestershire Regt.
(D.S.O. gazetted 26 June, 1916.)
SOMERVILLE, WILLIAM ARTHUR TENNISON BELLINGHAM, D.S.O., Major (Acting Lieut.-Colonel), Royal Lancaster Regt.
(D.S.O. gazetted 18 Feb. 1915.)

AUSTRALIAN IMPERIAL FORCE.

TOLL, FREDERICK WILLIAM, D.S.O., Lieut.-Colonel, Infantry.
(D.S.O. gazetted 1 Jan. 1917.)

Awarded the Distinguished Service Order:
ALDERSON, CHRISTOPHER, Major, Lancashire Fusiliers.
BAILEY, HERBERT, Capt. (Acting Major), East Lancashire Regt.
BEST, ALFRED JOHN, Second Lieut., Royal Engineers.
BRIGHTEN, GEORGE STANLEY, Lieut. (Acting Lieut.-Colonel), Liverpool Regt.
CLAYTON, MUIRHEAD COLLINS, Major, Cambridgeshire Regt.
DANE, JAMES AUCHINLECK, Major, Royal Field Artillery, Special Reserve.
DAVIES, CHARLES STEWART, Lieut.-Colonel, Leicestershire Regt.
DREW, FRANCIS WILLIAM MASSY, Major (Acting Lieut.-Colonel), South Lancashire Regt.
DUNN, JAMES CHURCHILL, M.C., M.D., Temporary Capt., Royal Army Medical Corps.
FULLARD, PHILIP FLETCHER, M.C., Temporary Capt., General List and Royal Flying Corps.
FURBER, CECIL TIDSWELL, Capt. (Acting Lieut.-Colonel), King's Own Scottish Borderers.
GARNSWORTHY, RANDALL, Second Lieut., attached Devonshire Regt.
GELSTHORPE, ALFRED MORRIS, Temporary Lieut. (Acting Capt.), Durham Light Infantry, attached Machine Gun Corps.
GOGARTY, HENRY EDWARD, Lieut.-Colonel, Worcestershire Regt.
GRIFFIN, ERNEST HARRISON, M.C., M.D., Temporary Capt., Royal Army Medical Corps.
HASSELL, LADAS LEWIS, M.C., Lieut. (Acting Capt.), South Staffordshire Regt.
HEATH, EDWARD CHARLES, Lieut.-Colonel, Liverpool Regt.
HESELTON, JOHN LISTER, Capt. (Acting Lieut.-Colonel), West Yorkshire Regt.
HOBBINS, WILFRED ALSTON, Capt. (Acting Lieut.-Colonel), Lancashire Fusiliers.
JOHNSTON, HOWARD RICHMOND, Temporary Second Lieut., attached Royal Lancashire Regt.
KING, HENRY JOHN, Temporary Lieut.-Colonel, Yorkshire Light Infantry.
LACON, SIR GEORGE HAWORTH USSHER, Bart., Capt. (Acting Lieut.-Colonel), Royal Warwickshire Regt., Special Reserve.
LIKEMAN, JOHN LONGHURST, Temporary Capt. (Acting Lieut.-Colonel), Gloucestershire Regt.
LINFOOT, HAROLD ANYON, M.C., Lieut. (Acting Capt.), Cheshire Regt.
McFEELY, CECIL MICHAEL, M.C., Lieut. (Acting Capt.), Royal Dublin Fusiliers.
MILLAR, JAMES WILLIAM JOSEPH, Second Lieut. (Temporary Lieut. and Acting Capt.), Nottinghamshire and Derbyshire Regt.
MORSHEAD, OWEN FREDERICK, M.C., Temporary Capt., Royal Engineers.
NADEN, FRANK, M.C., Second Lieut. (Temporary Lieut.), Cheshire Regt.
PANTON, HENRY FORBES, M.C., M.B., Capt. and Brevet Major, Royal Army Medical Corps.
PEDDIE, TOM ANDERSON, Second Lieut. (Temporary Major), Lincolnshire Regt.
PORTAL, WYNDHAM RAYMOND, Capt. (Temporary Lieut.-Colonel), Life Guards, Special Reserve.
PRESTON, JAMES, Second Lieut., Scottish Rifles, Special Reserve.
RADFORD, NORMAN HAROLD, M.C., Temporary Lieut. (Acting Capt.), Royal Welsh Fusiliers.
ROBINSON, ERNEST HAROLD, M.C., Temporary Capt., Shropshire Light Infantry.
SPRING, TREVOR COLERIDGE, Major (Acting Lieut.-Colonel), Hampshire Regt.
STUDDERT, ROBERT HALLAM, M.C., Capt. and Brevet Major (Acting Major), Royal Field Artillery.
TRON, REV. MAZZINI, M.C., Army Chaplains' Department.
WEBSTER, JOHN RYIE, M.C., Temporary Capt. (Acting Major), Nottinghamshire and Derbyshire Regt.
WILDE, REGINALD COLERIDGE, M.C., Second Lieut. (Acting Capt.), Liverpool Regt.

AUSTRALIAN IMPERIAL FORCE.

CRAIG, WILLIAM BANNERMAN, Major, Army Medical Corps.
HAILES, WILLIAM ALLAN, Major, Army Medical Corps.
LEE, HARRIE BERTIE, M.C., Major, Army Medical Corps.
McMASTER, ROBERT MAXWELL, Major, Army Medical Corps.
PURSER, MUIR, Lieut.-Colonel, Infantry.
ROBERTS, PERCIVAL THOMAS, Capt., Infantry.
SCALES, JOSEPH LINDLEY, Lieut., Infantry.
SLATER, HENRY ERNEST, Lieut., Infantry.
TRAILL, JOHN CHARLES MERRIMAN, M.C., Capt., Infantry.

NEW ZEALAND FORCE.

BLAIR, DUNCAN BARRIE, M.C., Lieut.-Colonel, Infantry.
COCKERELL, ALLAN RICHMOND, Second Lieut., Infantry.
COLQUHOUN, DUNCAN, Lieut.-Colonel, Infantry.
MACCORMICK, KENNETH, Major, Medical Corps.

SOUTH AFRICAN FORCE.

BROWNE, AMBROSE ROBIN INNES, Capt. (Temporary Major and Acting Lieut.-Colonel), South African Defence Force.
FORBES, ERNEST CRESPIN, Lieut., Infantry.
SPRENGER, LESLIE FRANCIS, M.C., Capt., Infantry.

London Gazette, 30 Nov. 1917.—" Admiralty, 30 Nov. 1917.—Honours for Services in Action with Enemy Submarines. The King has been graciously pleased to approve of the award of the following honour for services in action with enemy submarines. To be a Companion of the Distinguished Service Order."
LLOYD, ROBIN WYNELL MAYOW, Lieut.-Commander, R.N.

" Honours for Miscellaneous Services.—The King has been graciously pleased to approve of the award of the following honours to the undermentioned Officers. To be Companions of the Distinguished Service Order."
HIGGINS, HENRY GRAY, Lieut.-Commander, R.N. In recognition of his services in submarines.
BELT, FRANCIS WALTER, Lieut.-Commander (now Acting Commander), Royal Naval Volunteer Reserve. In recognition of his services with a Naval Armoured Car Squadron throughout the war. He conducted an expedition into Persia in trying circumstances with conspicuous success. He was later second-in-command of the squadron during the Dobrudja and Roumanian operations, where he was wounded. He has since done admirable work in Galicia. On all occasions he has shown himself to be a loyal and most reliable officer.

" Honours for the Royal Naval Air Service.—" The King has been graciously pleased to approve of the award of the following honours to Officers of the Royal Naval Air Service. To be Companions of the Distinguished Service Order."
COURTNEY, CHRISTOPHER LLOYD, Wing Commander, Royal Naval Air Service. In recognition of his services in command of a Wing of the Royal Naval Air Service at Dunkirk. Squadrons attached to his Wing have invariably shown a high standard of efficiency, and the success of the fighting squadrons generally is largely due to his knowledge and initiative.
GOW, RUSSELL WILLIAM, D.S.C., Observation Lieut., Royal Naval Air Service. For conspicuous gallantry and devotion to duty in carrying out a photographic reconnaissance of the Belgian coast under difficult conditions on the 15th Oct. 1917. Observation Lieut. Gow has also carried out a large amount of valuable spotting work for H.M. Monitors, both by day and night, including the successful operations against Zeebrugge on 12 May, 1917, and against Ostend on 5 June, 1917.

London Gazette, 17 Dec. 1917.—" War Office, 17 Dec. 1917. His Majesty the King has been pleased to confer the undermentioned rewards for gallantry and distinguished service in the field. The acts of gallantry for which the decorations have been awarded will be announced in the London Gazette as early as practicable. Awarded a Bar to the Distinguished Service Order."
PRETORIUS, PHILIP JACOBUS, D.S.O., Major, East African Protectorate Forces, attached Intelligence Department.
(D.S.O. gazetted 25 Nov. 1916.)
PYE-SMITH, CHARLES DERWENT, D.S.O., M.C., M.B., F.R.C.S., Temporary Capt. (Temporary Lieut.-Colonel), Royal Army Medical Corps.
(D.S.O. gazetted 16 Aug. 1917.)
ROBINSON, HUGH THOMAS KAY, D.S.O., Temporary Major (Acting Lieut.-Colonel), Royal Sussex Regt.
(D.S.O. gazetted 4 June, 1917.)
SUGDEN, RICHARD EDGAR, D.S.O., Lieut.-Colonel, West Riding Regt.
(D.S.O. gazetted 3 June, 1916.)
WORSLEY, FRANK PICKFORD, D.S.O., Capt. and Brevet Major (Temporary Lieut.-Colonel), Reserve of Officers, West Yorkshire Regt.
(D.S.O. gazetted 4 June, 1917.)

AUSTRALIAN FORCE.

IMLAY, ALEXANDER PETER, D.S.O., Lieut.-Colonel, Australian Infantry.
(D.S.O. gazetted 4 June, 1917.)
LEANE, RAYMOND LIONEL, D.S.O., M.C., Lieut.-Colonel, Australian Infantry.
(D.S.O. gazetted 3 June, 1916.)

The Distinguished Service Order

Awarded the Distinguished Service Order:
ANDERSON, FRANCIS, M.C., Capt., Royal Highlanders (Brigade Major, Infantry Brigade).
BOSANQUET, WILLIAM SYDNEY BENCE, Capt., Coldstream Guards, Special Reserve.
CLARK, PHILIP LINDSAY, Temporary Second Lieut. (Acting Capt.), Royal Sussex Regt.
CRAIG, DAVID, Second Lieut., Grenadier Guards, Special Reserve, attached Machine Gun Guards.
CRICHTON, ANDREW GAVIN MAITLAND MAKGILL, M.C., Temporary Capt. (Acting Lieut.-Colonel), Cameron Highlanders.
ELIOTT, RICHARD HEYMAN, Major, Royal Field Artillery.
HADOW, RONALD WALTER, Major (Acting Lieut.-Colonel), Reserve of Officers, Royal Highlanders.
JOHNSTONE, BEDE, Major (Acting Lieut.-Colonel), Royal West Kent Regt.
LAITHWAITE, ALLAN, Second Lieut., London Regt.
LISTER, WILLIAM HOWARD, M.C., Temporary Capt., Royal Army Medical Corps.
LOVEDAY, FRANCIS WILLIAM, Major, Royal Garrison Artillery.
MARTYN, MICHAEL CLEEVE, M.C., Major (Acting Lieut.-Colonel), Nottinghamshire and Derbyshire Regt.
MASKELL, WILLIAM CHARLES, M.C., Lieut. (Acting Major), Royal Field Artillery.
OAKMAN, WALTER GEORGE, Lieut., Coldstream Guards, Special Reserve.
OSWALD, KENNETH ALLAN, Major (Acting Lieut.-Colonel), Royal West Surrey Regt.
PEMBERTON, GEOFFREY HARRIS, Lieut., Lancashire Fusiliers.
PLACE, CHARLES GODFREY MORRIS, M.C., Temporary Capt. (Acting Major), East Surrey Regt.
RUSSELL, BERTIE ANGUS, Temporary Capt., Gloucestershire Regt.
STEELE, ROBERT CRAWFORD, Second Lieut., Royal Flying Corps, Special Reserve (Egypt).
TABERER, TRAVERS CHARLES MELVILLE, Second Lieut., Hampshire Regt., Special Reserve.
TETLEY, CHARLES HAROLD, Lieut.-Colonel, West Yorkshire Regt.
THOMPSON, HENRY CEDRIC ST. JOHN, Lieut. (Acting Capt.), Coldstream Guards.
WISTANCE, WILLIAM ALLSOP, M.C., Capt. (Temporary Major and Acting Lieut.-Colonel), South Staffordshire Regt.

AUSTRALIAN FORCE.
CHRISTIE, ROBERT, Major (Temporary Lieut.-Colonel), Australian Infantry.
COLLINS, WILLIAM HENRY, Capt., Australian Army Medical Corps.
FRASER, WILLIAM ARTHUR, Second Lieut., Australian Infantry.
HURRY, GEOFFREY, Major, Australian Infantry.
HUTCHINSON, ERIC LLOYD, Major, Army Medical Corps.
JAMES, TRISTRAM BERNARD WORDSWORTH, Major, Australian Field Artillery.
MANTON, RUSSELL FULTON, Major, Australian Field Artillery.
MAPLESTONE, PHILIP ALAN, Major, Australian Army Medical Corps.

NEW ZEALAND FORCE.
WICKENS, ROBERT CHARLES, Major, New Zealand Field Artillery.

SOUTH AFRICAN FORCE.
HEAL, FRANK HENRY, Lieut.-Colonel, South African Infantry Regt.

London Gazette, 18 Dec. 1917.—" War Office, 18 Dec. 1917. His Majesty the King has been pleased to confer the following rewards in recognition of gallantry and distinguished service in connection with Anti-Aircraft services in the United Kingdom. Awarded a Bar to Distinguished Service Order."
GREEN, GILBERT WARE MURLIS, D.S.O., M.C., Temporary Capt., General List, Royal Flying Corps.
Awarded the Distinguished Service Order:
THOMPSON, WILLIAM MAXWELL, Lieut.-Colonel, Royal Engineers.
HAYNES, WILLIAM HAROLD, Temporary Capt., Royal Flying Corps.

London Gazette, 19 Dec. 1917.—" Admiralty, 19 Dec. 1917.—Honours for Services in Action with Enemy Submarines. The King has been graciously pleased to approve of the award of the following honours for services in action with enemy submarines. To be a Companion of the Distinguished Service Order."
PHILLIPS, PHILIP ESMONDE, Lieut.-Commander, R.N.
To receive a Bar to the Distinguished Service Order:
WATKINS, GEOFFREY ROBERT SLADEN, D.S.O., Lieut.-Commander, Royal Navy.

" Honours for the Mercantile Marine.—The King has been graciously pleased to approve of the award of Honours to the undermentioned Officers of the British Mercantile Marine, in recognition of zeal and devotion to duty shown in carrying on the trade of the country during the war. To be Companions of the Distinguished Service Order."
MURRAY, GEORGE BADENOCH, Capt. (Lieut., R.N.R.).
MARTIN, JAMES, Chief Officer (Lieut., R.N.R.).

London Gazette, 1 Jan. 1918.—" War Office, 1 Jan. 1918. His Majesty the King has been graciously pleased to approve of the undermentioned rewards for distinguished service in the field. Dated 1 Jan. 1918. Awarded a Bar to the Distinguished Service Order."
ALEXANDER, WILLIAM NATHANIEL STUART, D.S.O., Major (Temporary Lieut.-Colonel), Connaught Rangers.
BARKER, MICHAEL GEORGE HENRY, D.S.O., Capt. and Brevet Major (Temporary Lieut.-Colonel), Lincolnshire Regt.
BEST, THOMAS ANDREW DUNLOP, D.S.O., Major (Temporary Lieut.-Colonel), Royal Inniskilling Fusiliers.
BOYD, JOHN DOPPING, D.S.O., Capt. and Brevet Major, Royal West Surrey Regt.
DOWDEN, CHARLES HENRY, D.S.O., M.C., Lieut. (Temporary Capt.), King's Royal Rifle Corps.
ELLIS, ARCHIBALD JENNER, D.S.O., Major (Acting Lieut.-Colonel), Border Regt.
FERGUSON, HENRY GASPARD DE LAVALETTE, D.S.O., Major and Brevet Lieut.-Colonel (Temporary Lieut.-Colonel), Retired Pay, Reserve of Officers, attached Norfolk Regt.
FERRERS-GUY, MARMION CARR, D.S.O., Major, Lancashire Fusiliers.
FORBES, RONALD FOSTER, D.S.O., Major (Temporary Lieut.-Colonel), Highland Light Infantry.
FRANCIS, SIDNEY GOODALL, D.S.O., Major and Brevet Lieut.-Colonel (Temporary Lieut.-Colonel), West Yorkshire Regt.
GRAHAM, JOHN MALISE ANNE, D.S.O., Lieut.-Colonel, Royal Lancashire Regt., Special Reserve.
GREEN, WILLIAM, D.S.O., Major (Temporary Lieut.-Colonel), Royal Highlanders.
GREENLEES, JAMES ROBERTSON CAMPBELL, D.S.O., M.B., Temporary Capt. (Acting Lieut.-Colonel), Royal Army Medical Corps.
HERBERT-STEPNEY, CECIL CHAMPAGNE, D.S.O., Capt. (Temporary Lieut.-Colonel), Reserve of Officers, King's Royal Rifle Corps.
HIGGINS, CHARLES GRAEME, D.S.O., Major and Brevet Lieut.-Colonel (Temporary Brigadier-General), Oxfordshire and Buckinghamshire Light Infantry.
HILL, CLIFFORD, D.S.O., Major, East African Mounted Rifles.
JACKSON, SIR THOMAS DARE, Bart., M.V.O., D.S.O., Major and Brevet Lieut.-Colonel, Royal Lancaster Regt.
JOHNSTON, ALEXANDER COLIN, D.S.O., M.C., Capt. and Brevet Major (Temporary Lieut.-Colonel), Worcestershire Regt.
MACLACHLAN, ALEXANDER FRASER CAMPBELL, D.S.O., Major and Brevet Lieut.-Colonel (Temporary Lieut.-Colonel), King's Royal Rifle Corps.
McDONALD, SAMUEL, D.S.O., Major (Acting Lieut.-Colonel), Gordon Highlanders.
MATURIN, REGINALD GEORGE, D.S.O., Major (Temporary Lieut.-Colonel), Royal Field Artillery.
MAXWELL, ARTHUR, D.S.O., Major (Acting Lieut.-Colonel), London Regt.
MILWARD, HERBERT MILWARD, D.S.O., Major (Temporary Lieut.-Colonel), Nottinghamshire and Derbyshire Regt.
MONEY, NOEL ERNEST, D.S.O., Major (Temporary Lieut.-Colonel), Shropshire Yeomanry.
MORANT, HUBERT HORATIO SHIRLEY, D.S.O., Major (Lieut.-Colonel), Durham Light Infantry.
MURRAY, RONALD ERNEST, D.S.O., Lieut.-Colonel, British South African Police.
OGILVIE, SHOLTO STUART, D.S.O., Temporary Major (Acting Lieut.-Colonel), Wiltshire Regt.
PARSONS, GEORGE, D.S.O., Major, British South African Police.
PEACOCKE, WARREN JOHN, D.S.O., Temporary Lieut.-Colonel, Royal Inniskilling Fusiliers.
SPARKES, WILLIAM MOORE BELL, D.S.O., Major (Temporary Lieut.-Colonel), Royal Army Medical Corps.
UNIACKE, GERALD LAWRENCE, D.S.O., Capt. and Brevet Major (Temporary Lieut.-Colonel), Reserve of Officers, Royal Lancaster Regt. and 2nd Nigeria Regt.
WARD, LANCOLET EDWARD SETH, D.S.O., Capt. (Temporary Lieut.-Colonel), Reserve of Officers, late Oxfordshire and Buckinghamshire Light Infantry.
WATT, DONALD MUNRO, D.S.O., Major and Brevet Lieut.-Colonel (Temporary Brigadier-General), Gurkha Rifles, Indian Army.
WESTERN, BERTRAM CHARLES MAXIMILIAN, D.S.O., Capt. and Brevet Major (Acting Lieut.-Colonel), East Lancashire Regt.
WHATFORD, STUART LUMLEY, D.S.O., Major (Temporary Lieut.-Colonel), Yorkshire Regt.
WICKHAM, THOMAS EDMUND PALMER, D.S.O., Major (Acting Lieut.-Colonel), Royal Artillery.
WORTHINGTON, FRANK, D.S.O., M.B., Capt. (Acting Lieut.-Colonel), Royal Army Medical Corps.

AUSTRALIAN FORCE.
TODD, THOMAS JOHN, D.S.O., Lieut.-Colonel, Light Horse Regt.
TRAVERS, REGINALD JOHN ALBERT, D.S.O., Lieut.-Colonel, Infantry.

CANADIAN FORCE.
PROWER, JOHN MERVYN, D.S.O., Lieut.-Colonel, Infantry.
ROSS, JOHN MUNRO, D.S.O., Lieut.-Colonel (Temporary Brigadier-General), Infantry.

NEW ZEALAND FORCE.
KING, GEORGE AUGUSTUS, D.S.O., Lieut.-Colonel, Canterbury Regt.
STEWART, HUGH, D.S.O., Lieut.-Colonel, Canterbury Regt.
WHYTE, JAMES HENRY, D.S.O., Lieut.-Colonel, Wellington Mounted Rifles.

Awarded the Distinguished Service Order:
ADAIR, HENRY SHAFTO, Major, Cheshire Regt.
ADAMS, HENRY RAINIER, Major, Royal Garrison Artillery.
AINSWORTH, JOHN, C.M.G., Local Colonel, East African Forces.
ADLER, REV. MICHAEL, Chaplain to the Forces, 3rd Class, Army Chaplains' Department.
AITKEN, NIGEL WOODFORD, M.C., Major, Royal Garrison Artillery.
AKERMAN, WILLIAM PHILIP JOPP, M.C., Capt. (Acting Major), Royal Field Artillery.
ALDERSON, EDMUND, M.D., Capt. (Acting Lieut.-Colonel), Royal Army Medical Corps.
ALLAN, PERCY STUART, Major and Brevet Lieut.-Colonel (Temporary Lieut.-Colonel), Gordon Highlanders.
ALLDEN, STANLEY GUY, Capt. (Temporary Major), Army Service Corps.

ALLEN, LEWIS ARTHUR, Lieut.-Colonel, Army Service Corps.
ALLFREY, HENRY IRVING RODNEY, M.C., Major, Somersetshire Light Infantry.
ANDERSON, ARTHUR EMILIUS DAVID, M.C., Capt., King's Own Scottish Borderers, Special Reserve.
ANDERSON, CHARLES ABBOT, Major (Acting Lieut.-Colonel), Manchester Regt.
ANDERSON, CECIL FORD, Major and Brevet Lieut.-Colonel (Temporary Lieut.-Colonel), Royal Engineers.
ANDERSON, CHARLES AGNEW, Temporary Major, South African Water Supply Corps (corrected to South African Staff Corps and name should have been placed under "South African Force" in this Gazette notice [London Gazette, 18 Jan. 1918]).
ANDERSON, JOHN, Temporary Capt., Royal Army Medical Corps.
ARMITAGE, THOMAS WILLIAM, Temporary Major, South African Staff Corps (correction, name should have been placed under "South African Force" in this Gazette notice [London Gazette, 18 Jan. 1918]).
ARMITAGE, WALTER ALEXANDER, Capt. (Temporary Major), Special Reserve, York and Lancaster Regt. and Machine Gun Corps.
ARNOLD, BENING MOURANT, Major, Hampshire Royal Garrison Artillery.
ARNOLD-FOSTER, FRANCIS ANSON, Major, Royal Field Artillery (Christian name corrected to Frederick Anson [London Gazette, 8 March, 1918]).
ARNOTT, KENNETH HUGH LOWDEN, M.C., Capt. (Acting Lieut.-Colonel), East Lancashire Regt.
ARROWSMITH-BROWN, JAMES ARNOLD, Major, Royal Engineers.
ASCHWANDEN, SYDNEY WILLIAM LOUIS, Lieut.-Colonel, Royal Field Artillery (surname changed to Ashwanden).
ATKINSON, FREDERIC ST. JOHN, Major, Horse, Indian Army.
AUBREY-FLETCHER, HENRY LANCELOT, M.V.O., Capt., Grenadier Guards.
AYLWIN-FOSTER, ERIC WILLIAM FANE, Capt., Army Service Corps.
BABINGTON, STAFFORD CHARLES, Lieut.-Colonel, Royal Engineers.
BAILEY, EDWARD ALEC HORSMAN, Major (Acting Lieut.-Colonel), Royal Field Artillery.
BAINES, REV. CHARLES FREDERICK, M.A., Chaplain to the Forces, First Class, Army Chaplains' Department.
BAKER, SIR RANDOLF LITTLEHALES, Bart., Major (Temporary Lieut.-Colonel), Yeomanry.
BAMFORD, ROBERT CECIL, Temporary Major, West Yorkshire Regt.
BARGE, KENNETH, M.C., Capt., Cavalry, Indian Army.
BARKER, FREDERIC EDWARD LLOYD, Lieut.-Colonel (Temporary Brigadier-General), Royal Field Artillery.
BARNWELL, ARCHIBALD STONHAM, Major, Royal Field Artillery, Special Reserve.
BARRINGTON-WARD, ROBERT McGOWAN, M.C., Temporary Capt., General List.
BARRON, NETTERVILLE GUY, Lieut.-Colonel (Temporary Brigadier-General), Royal Garrison Artillery.
BARROW, HAROLD PERCY WALLER, C.M.G., Lieut.-Colonel (Temporary Colonel), Royal Army Medical Corps
BARTLETT, ALFRED JAMES NAPIER, Capt. and Brevet Major (Acting Lieut.-Colonel), Oxfordshire and Buckinghamshire Light Infantry.
BASSETT, JOHN CHANNON, Major, Royal Garrison Artillery.
BATEMAN, HAROLD HENRY, M.C., Capt. (Acting Major), Royal Engineers.
BATES, AUSTIN GRAVES, M.C., Capt. (Acting Major), Royal Field Artillery.
BATES, CECIL ROBERT, M.C., Major, Reserve of Officers, Royal Field Artillery.
BEADON, LANCELOT RICHMOND, Major (Temporary Lieut.-Colonel), Army Service Corps.
BEASLEY, ROBERT LONGFIELD, Major (Temporary Lieut.-Colonel), Gloucestershire Regt.
BECHER, LANCELOT EDWARD, Capt., Royal Engineers.
BECKETT, WILLIAM THOMAS CLIFFORD, Lieut.-Colonel, North Lancashire Regt., Territorial Force.
BEECROFT, CHARLES THOMAS COOK, Temporary Major, Army Service Corps.
BELLAMY, HUGH MAURICE, M.C., Capt., Lincolnshire Regt.
BENZIE, ROBERT, Temporary Major (Acting Lieut.-Colonel), South Wales Borderers.
BEYTS, JULIAN FALVEY, Temporary Lieut.-Col., Durham Light Infantry.
BIDDER, HAROLD FRANCIS, Major (Temporary Lieut.-Colonel), Royal Sussex Regt., Special Reserve, attached Machine Gun Corps.
BIGGS, GEORGE TRAVERS, Capt. and Brevet Major (Acting Major), Royal Engineers.
BINGHAM, DAVID ANDERSON, Capt. (Acting Major), Liverpool Regt., attached.
BIRCH, ALEXANDER HARRY COLVIN, Lieut.-Colonel, Retired Pay, Royal Artillery.
BIRD, REV. RICHARD, Temporary Chaplain to the Forces, Fourth Class, Army Chaplains' Department.
BIRKBECK, BENEDICT, M.C., Temporary Capt. (Acting Major), Coldstream Guards.
BIRLEY, NORMAN PELLEW, M.C., Capt., South Staffordshire Regt., Special Reserve.
BIRTWISTLE, ARTHUR, C.M.G., Lieut.-Colonel, Royal Field Artillery.
BISHOP, CHARLES GAMBLE, Capt. (Temporary Major), Royal Engineers.
BLACKBURNE, REV. HARRY WILLIAM, M.C., M.A., Chaplain to the Forces, Third Class, Army Chaplains' Department.
BLACKER, FREDERICK ST. JOHN, Capt. (Temporary Lieut.-Col.), Rifle Brigade, Special Reserve.
BLOMFIELD, RICHARD GRAHAM, Second Lieut. (Temporary Major), Guards and Royal Flying Corps.
BLORE, HERBERT RICHARD, Lieut.-Colonel, King's Royal Rifle Corps.

BLOUNT, GEORGE PERCY COSMO, Major (Temporary Lieut.-Colonel), Royal Artillery.
BOARD, ANDREW GEORGE, Major (Temporary Lieut.-Colonel), South Wales Borderers and Royal Flying Corps.
BOND, EDWARD LESLIE, Major (Acting Lieut.-Colonel), Royal Garrison Artillery.
BORTHWICK, FRANCIS HENRY, Lieut.-Colonel, Royal Welsh Fusiliers.
BORWICK, MALCOLM, Capt., Dragoons.
BOTELER, FRANCIS WILFORD, Lieut.-Colonel and Brevet Colonel, Retired Pay, Royal Artillery.
BOUCHIER, RAYMOND WALTER HARRY, Major (Acting Lieut.-Colonel), Royal Field Artillery.
BOWDEN, AUBREY HENRY, Temporary Major, Machine Gun Corps.
BOYD-MOSS, LIONEL BOYD, C.M.G., Major and Brevet Lieut.-Colonel (Temporary Brigadier-General), South Staffordshire Regt.
BOYLE, CHARLES ROGER CAVENDISH, Capt. (Temporary Lieut.-Colonel), Oxfordshire and Buckinghamshire Light Infantry.
BRADISH, FRANCIS LYNDON, Capt. (Temporary Lieut.-Colonel), Royal Army Medical Corps.
BRADLEY, FREDERICK HOYSTED, M.B., Capt. (Acting Lieut.-Colonel), Royal Army Medical Corps.
BRADLEY, SAMUEL GLENHOLME LENNOX, M.C., Capt. (Temporary Lieut.-Colonel), London Regt.
BRAITHWAITE, ALBERT NEWBY, M.C., Temporary Second Lieut. (Temporary Capt.), General List.
BRAITHWAITE, FRANCIS POWELL, M.C., Temporary Lieut.-Colonel, Royal Engineers.
BRANSON, DOUGLAS STEPHENSON, M.C., Capt. (Temporary Major, Acting Lieut.-Colonel), York and Lancaster Regt.
BREBNER, CHARLES STUART, M.D., Capt. (Acting Lieut.-Colonel), Royal Army Medical Corps.
BREWIS, GEOFFREY SYDNEY, Capt. (Temporary Lieut.-Colonel), Welsh Regt.
BRIDGEMAN, THE HON. HENRY GEORGE ORLANDO, M.C., Major, Royal Artillery.
BRIDGWATER, HAVARD NOEL, Capt., Norfolk Regt.
BRIGHTON, EDGAR WILLIAM, C.M.G., Lieut.-Colonel, Bedfordshire Regt. (surname corrected to Brighten [London Gazette, 7 Feb. 1918]).
BRINK, GEORGE EDWIN, Temporary Major, South African Force.
BRISCOE, FRANCIS EDWARD, Temporary Major, Yorkshire Regt.
BROCK-WILLIAMS, DYSON, Temporary Major, Welsh Regt.
BROOKE, NEVILE PATTULLO, Major, Leinster Regt.
BROWN, JOHN, Lieut.-Colonel, Northamptonshire Regt.
BROWNE, GEORGE EDWARD ALLENBY, M.C., Temporary Major, Liverpool Regt.
BROWNE, HUGH SWINTON, Capt. (Acting Major), Royal Field Artillery.
BROWNLOW, CHARLES WILLIAM, Colonel, Royal Garrison Artillery.
BRUCE, WILLIAM FOX, M.C., Capt. (Acting Major), Royal Engineers.
BRUCE, THOMAS, Lieut.-Colonel (Temporary Brigadier-General), Royal Artillery.
BRYAN, HERBERT, C.M.G., Capt. and Brevet Lieut.-Colonel (Temporary Lieut.-Colonel), Reserve of Officers, Retired Pay, Manchester Regt.
BUCKNALL, LEONARD CORFIELD, Major, Yeomanry.
BULSTRODE, CHRISTOPHER VICTOR, M.B., Temporary Capt. (Acting Lieut.-Colonel), Royal Army Medical Corps.
BUNBURY, RICHARD SEYMOUR, Major, Royal Garrison Artillery.
BURCHALL, HAROLD, Capt (Temporary Lieut.-Colonel), Royal Flying Corps, Special Reserve.
BURGES-SHORT, HUBERT GEORGE RICHARD, Major (Temporary Lieut.-Colonel), Somersetshire Light Infantry.
BURROWES, ARNOLD ROBINSON, C.M.G., Lieut.-Colonel, Royal Irish Fusiliers.
BUSHELL, CHRISTOPHER, Capt. (Acting Major), Royal West Surrey Regt., Special Reserve.
BUTLER, BERNARD ARNOLD BARRINGTON, Major and Brevet Lieut.-Colonel (Temporary Lieut.-Colonel), Royal Field Artillery.
BUTLER, THE HON. ROBERT THOMAS ROWLEY PROBYN, M.C., Temporary Major, Tank Corps.
BUTLER BOWDEN, WILLIAM ERDESWICK IGNATIUS, Major (Temporary Lieut.-Colonel), Duke of Cornwall's Light Infantry (surname corrected to Butler-Bowdon).
BUZZARD, CHARLES NORMAN, Lieut.-Colonel, Royal Garrison Artillery.
BYE, WALTER RODERICK GRIFFITH, M.C., Temporary Capt., General List.
BYNG, THE HON. ANTONY SCHOMBERG, Temporary Lieut.-Colonel, General List and Royal Flying Corps.
CALDWELL, ALEXANDER FRANCIS SOMERVILLE, Temporary Major (Acting Lieut.-Colonel), North Lancashire Regt.
CALL, FELIX, Major (Acting Lieut.-Colonel), Royal Irish Regt.
CAMERON, EWEN ALLAN, Temporary Lieut.-Colonel, North Lancashire Regt.
CAMPBELL, REV. EDWARD FITZHARDINGE, B.A., Chaplain to the Forces, Third Class (Temporary Chaplain to the Forces, Second Class), Army Chaplains' Department.
CAMPBELL, HECTOR, M.V.O., Major, Indian Army.
CAMPBELL, THE HON. IAN MALCOLM, Major (Acting Lieut.-Colonel), Lovat's Scouts.
CAMPION, WILLIAM ROBERT, M.P., Major (Acting Lieut.-Colonel), Royal Sussex Regt.
CANNOT, FERNAND GUSTAVE EUGENE, C.M.G., Lieut.-Colonel (Temporary Colonel), Army Service Corps.
CARDEN, ALAN DOUGLAS, Major (Temporary Lieut.-Colonel), Royal Engineers and Royal Flying Corps.

The Distinguished Service Order

CARDEN, D'ARCY VANDELEUR, Temporary Lieut. (Acting Major), Royal Field Artillery.
CAREY, REV. DOUGLAS FALKLAND, M.A., Chaplain to the Forces, Third Class (Temporary Chaplain to the Forces, First Class), Army Chaplains' Department.
CARLISLE, JOHN CHARLES DENTON, M.C., Capt., London Regt.
CARLISLE, THOMAS HAMILTON, Temporary Capt. (Acting Major), Royal Engineers.
CARNWATH, THOMAS, M.B., Capt., Royal Army Medical Corps.
CARTWRIGHT, VINCENT HENRY, Temporary Major, Royal Marine Artillery.
CARUS-WILSON, TREVOR, Lieut.-Colonel, Duke of Cornwall's Light Infantry.
CASSELS, FRANK, Temporary Major, Royal Sussex Regt.
CHEETHAM, GEOFFREY, M.C., Capt., Royal Engineers.
CHENEVIX-TRENCH, LAWRENCE, Major, Royal Engineers.
CHRISTIAN, WILLIAM FRANCIS, Major, Royal Garrison Artillery.
CHRISTIE, ARCHIBALD, Capt. (Temporary Lieut.-Colonel), Royal Artillery and Royal Flying Corps.
CHRISTIE, HENRY ROBERT STARK, Major (Acting Lieut.-Colonel), Royal Engineers.
CLARK, HERBERT NICHOLLS, Major (Acting Lieut.-Colonel), Royal Field Artillery.
CLARKE, FREDERICK ARTHUR STANLEY, Major, London Regt.
CLARKE, DENZIL HARWOOD, M.C., Temporary Capt., Durham Light Infantry.
CLARKE, PETER SKINNER, Major (Temporary Lieut.-Colonel), South African Medical Corps (correction, name should have been placed under " South African Force " in this Gazette Notice [London Gazette, 18 Jan. 1918]).
CLARKE, ROBERT, Lieut.-Colonel, Army Service Corps.
CLARKE, REGINALD GRAHAM, Major and Brevet Lieut.-Colonel (Temporary Lieut.-Colonel), Royal West Surrey Regt., and Machine Gun Corps.
CLAYTON, GERALD MALCOLM, Temporary Major, Liverpool Regt.
COBBOLD, FRANCIS ALFRED WORSHIP, Major, Royal Garrison Artillery.
COCHRAN, HERBERT PHILIP GORDON, Major (Acting Lieut.-Colonel), Middlesex Regt.
COCHRANE, EDWARD WEBBER WARREN, M.B., Lieut.-Colonel, Royal Army Medical Corps.
COFFEY, RICHARD, Major (Acting Lieut.-Colonel), Royal Army Medical Corps.
COKE, EDWARD SACHEVERELL D'EWES, C.M.G., Major and Brevet Lieut.-Colonel (Temporary Brigadier-General), King's Own Scottish Borderers.
COLLARD, ALFRED METHVEN, Major (Temporary Lieut.-Colonel), Duke of Cornwall's Light Infantry.
COLLIER, RICHARD HAMILTON, Capt. (Temporary Lieut.-Colonel), Royal Flying Corps, Special Reserve.
COLLINS, REGINALD THOMAS, Major (Temporary Lieut.-Colonel), Royal Army Medical Corps.
COLLINS, WILLIAM ALEXANDER, Temporary Major, Army Service Corps.
COLSON, DOUGLAS FAIRLEY, Major, Royal Engineers.
COMBER, HENRY GORDON, Capt. (Temporary Major), Unattached List.
CONNOR, REV. JOHN MORGAN, M.A., Chaplain to the Forces, Fourth Class (Temporary Chaplain to the Forces, Third Class), Army Chaplains' Department.
COOKES, DUDLEY, Major (Acting Lieut.-Colonel), Royal Field Artillery.
COOP, REV. JAMES OGDEN, M.A., Chaplain to the Forces, First Class, T.F., Army Chaplains' Department.
COOPER, FRANK SANDIFORD, Major (Temporary Lieut.-Colonel), Suffolk Regt.
COOTE-BROWN, WILLIAM, Temporary Lieut.-Colonel, Royal Sussex Regt.
CORBALLIS, EDWARD ROUX LITTLEDALE, Capt., Royal Dublin Fusiliers and Royal Flying Corps.
CODRINGTON, GEOFFREY RONALD, Major, Yeomanry.
COSENS GORDON PHILIP LEWES, Capt. and Brevet Major (Temporary Lieut.-Colonel), Dragoons.
COTTRELL, REGINALD FOULKES, Major, Royal Garrison Artillery.
COURAGE, MILES RAFE FERGUSON, Major (Acting Lieut.-Colonel), Reserve of Officers, Royal Artillery.
COUSENS, ROBERT BAXTER, Major (Temporary Lieut.-Colonel), Royal Artillery.
COWAN, ARTHUR JAMES, Major, Royal Field Artillery.
COYSH, WILLIAM HENRY, Temporary Major (Temporary Lieut.-Colonel), Royal Engineers.
CRAIK, JAMES, Major (Temporary Lieut.-Colonel), Reserve of Officers, Retired Pay, Indian Army Lancers.
CRASTER, GEORGE, Major, Cavalry, Indian Army.
CRAVEN, ARTHUR JULIUS, Major and Brevet Lieut.-Colonel (Temporary Brigadier-General), Royal Engineers.
CRAWFORD, EDWARD WILLIAM, Temporary Major, Royal Inniskilling Fusiliers.
CRAWFORD, WILLIAM LOFTUS, Capt. (Temporary Major), Lancashire Fusiliers.
CRAWHALL, REV. CANON THOMAS EMERSON, Chaplain to the Forces, Second Class, T.F., Army Chaplains' Department.
CRESSINGHAM, HUGH, Quartermaster and Honorary Major, Bedfordshire Regt.
CRIPPS, THE HON. FREDERICK HEYWORTH, Major, Yeomanry.
CROFTON, SIR MORGAN GEORGE, Bart., Major (Temporary Lieut.-Colonel), Reserve of Officers, Life Guards.
CROMBIE, JOHN FRANK, Major (Temporary Lieut.-Colonel), Royal Army Medical Corps.
CRONSHAW, ARTHUR EDWIN, Major (Acting Lieut.-Colonel), Manchester Regt.
CRUDDAS, BERNARD Major (Acting Lieut.-Colonel), Northumberland Fusiliers.

CRUICKSHANK, ARTHUR LUDLAM, Capt. (Acting Major), Royal Garrison Artillery.
CUNNINGHAM, BERTRAM STEPHEN ROWSELL, Temporary Major, Army Service Corps.
CURLING, RICHARD ROBINSON, Capt. (Acting Lieut.-Colonel), Royal Artillery.
CURTIS, HUBERT MONTAGUE COTTON, Capt. (Acting Major), North Staffordshire Regt.
DA COSTA, EVAN CAMPBELL, Major and Brevet Lieut.-Colonel (Temporary Brigadier-General), East Lancashire Regt.
DANIEL, THOMAS WILLIAM, M.C., Temporary Major, Nottinghamshire and Derbyshire Regt.
DANIELL, NEVILLE REAY, Capt. (Temporary Lieut.-Colonel), Duke of Cornwall's Light Infantry.
DANIELL, WILLIAM AUGUSTUS BAMPFYLDE, Major, Royal Horse Artillery.
DAVID, MARKHAM, Capt. (Temporary Major), Royal Monmouthshire, Royal Engineers, Special Reserve.
DAVID, THOMAS JENKINS, Major, Royal Horse Artillery.
DAVIES, ALAN HIER, Major (Acting Lieut.-Colonel), Royal Field Artillery.
DAVIES, JOHN EDWARD HENRY, Temporary Lieut.-Colonel, Royal Army Medical Corps.
DAVIDSON, GILBERT, Temporary Major, Army Service Corps.
STANLEY-DAVIES, OWEN, Capt. (Temporary Major), Royal Engineers.
DAVIES, THOMAS HENRY, M.C., Second Lieut. (Temporary Capt.), Royal Engineers.
DAVIS, WILLIAM HATHAWAY, M.C., Temporary Major, Machine Gun Corps.
DAWES, HUGH FRANK, M.C., Capt., Royal Fusiliers.
DEAR, HAROLD JOHN, Capt. (Acting Lieut.-Colonel), London Regt.
DE FONBLANQUE, PHILIP, Capt., Royal Engineers.
DE HAVILLAND, THOMAS LYTTLETON, Temporary Major, Royal Scots Fusiliers (Major, South African Defence Force).
DE LA PERRELLE, JOHN NATHAEL, M.C., Major (Temporary Lieut.-Colonel, Royal Fusiliers, Special Reserve.
DEMPSTER, JAMES FINLAY, Capt. (Acting Lieut.-Colonel), Reserve of Officers, Manchester Regt.
DE NEUFVILLE, EUSTACE CHARLES, Temporary Capt. Royal Garrison Artillery.
DENISON-PENDER, HENRY DENISON, M.C., Capt. and Brevet Major, Dragoons.
DENT, BERTIE COORE, Lieut.-Colonel, Leicestershire Regt., Cheshire Regt.
DIGGLE, JOHN NESTON, Major, Royal Field Artillery.
DITMAS, FRANCIS IVAN LESLIE, M.C., Lieut. (Temporary Capt.), Reserve of Officers, Durham Light Infantry.
DOIG, PETER, Major, Royal Garrison Artillery.
DOLPHIN, HARRY CECIL, Capt. (Temporary Major) Reserve of Officers, Hampshire Regt.
DONKIN, FREDERICK LANGLOH, Temporary Capt. (Acting Major), Royal Field Artillery.
DORE, ALAN SYDNEY WHITEHORN, Major, Worcestershire Regt. and Royal Flying Corps.
DORLING, FRANCIS HOLLAND, Major, Manchester Regt.
DOYLE, EDWARD CECIL, Capt. (Temporary Major), Army Veterinary Corps.
DRAKE, REGINALD JOHN, Capt. and Brevet Major (Temporary Lieut.-Colonel), Reserve of Officers, North Staffordshire Regt.
DRESSER, HAROLD BRUCE, Major, Royal Field Artillery, Special Reserve.
DREW, CECIL FRANCIS, Capt. (Temporary Lieut.-Colonel), Scottish Rifles.
DREW, GEORGE BARRY, Major (Temporary Lieut.-Colonel), West Yorkshire Regt.
DREW, HORACE ROBERT HAWLEY, Major, Northamptonshire Regt.
DRUMMOND, WILLIAM STUART GORDON, Lieut. (Temporary Major), Army Service Corps, Special Reserve.
DUCKWORTH, RALPH, Major, South Staffordshire Regt.
DUDGEON, ROBERT MAXWELL, M.C., Major (Temporary Lieut.-Colonel), Cameron Highlanders.
DUGDALE, WILLIAM MARSHALL, Major (Honorary Capt. in Army), Royal Welsh Fusiliers.
DUNCAN, DONALD, M.C., Capt., Gloucestershire Regt.
DUNCAN, HORACE ADRIAN, Major (Temporary Lieut.-Colonel), Argyll and Sutherland Highlanders.
DUNKERTON, NORMAN EDWIN, Major (Temporary Lieut.-Colonel), Royal Army Medical Corps.
DUNN, THOMAS SPENCE, Capt., East African Medical Service.
DURNFORD, GUY EDWARD JERVOISE, Major (Acting Lieut.-Colonel), Royal Engineers.
DYER, BERNARD ALFRED SAUNDERS, Major, Army Service Corps.
DYKE, PERCYVALL HART, Major and Brevet Lieut.-Colonel, Baluchis, Indian Army.
DYMOTT, GERALD LANG, Major, Royal Field Artillery.
EDDIS, BRUCE LINDSAY, Capt. (Acting Lieut.-Colonel), Royal Engineers.
EDWARDS, HAROLD WALTER, M.C., Capt., Royal Warwickshire Regt.
EDWARDS, RICHARD PRIOR FERDINAND, Temporary Major, Army Service Corps.
EGAN, WILLIAM, M.B., Capt. (Acting Lieut.-Colonel), Royal Army Medical Corps.
EILOART, HORACE ANSON, M.C., Capt. London Regt.
ELEY, WILLIAM GARDINER, Major, Retired Pay, Reserve of Officers.
ELGOOD, GARRARD, Capt., Reserve of Officers, Royal West Kent Regt.
ELLICE, EDWARD CHARLES, Capt. (Acting Major), (Retired), Grenadier Guards.
ELLIOT, EDWARD HALHED HUGH, Major (Temporary Lieut.-Colonel), Royal Field Artillery.

ELLIOTT, THOMAS RENTON, Temporary Lieut.-Colonel, Royal Army Medical Corps.
ELLWOOD, ARTHUR ADDISON, M.C., Capt. (Temporary Major), Lincolnshire Regt., attached Machine Gun Corps.
ELSTOB, WILFRED, M.C., Temporary Lieut.-Colonel, Manchester Regt.
ELPHINSTONE-DALRYMPLE, SIR FRANCIS NAPIER, Bart., Major (Temporary Lieut.-Colonel), Royal Artillery.
ELTON, CHARLES ADRIAN ASHFORD, Second Lieut. (Temporary Capt.), Royal Warwickshire Regt.
EMMET, ROBERT (Senr.), Major, Yeomanry.
EVANS, CUTHBERT, C.M.G., Lieut.-Colonel, Royal Artillery.
EVANS, WILLIAM HARRY, Major (Acting Lieut.-Colonel), Royal Engineers.
EVANS-GWYNNE, ALFRED HOWELL, Major, Royal Field Artillery.
EVELEGH, ELIOTT NIAL, M.C., Capt. (Acting Major), Royal Engineers.
EVES, THOMAS SWAN, M.B., Capt. (Acting Lieut.-Colonel), Royal Army Medical Corps.
EWART, CHARLES NICHOLSON, Major, Royal Garrison Artillery.
EWING, WILLIAM TURNER, Major, Royal Scots.
EWART, JOHN KNOX, Temporary Major, Army Service Corps.
EYRES, CRESSWELL JOHN, Temporary Major (Acting Lieut.-Colonel), Royal Garrison Artillery (late Rear-Admiral, Retired, R.N.) (corrected from " late Rear-Admiral, Retired, R.N." to Rear-Admiral, Retired, R.N. [London Gazette, 7 Feb. 1918]).
FAGAN, BERNARD JOSEPH, Major (Acting Lieut.-Colonel), Infantry, Indian Army.
FAIRBANK, HAROLD ARTHUR THOMAS, F.R.C.S., Capt., Royal Army Medical Corps.
FAIRCLOUGH, BRERETON, C.M.G., Lieut.-Colonel, South Lancashire Regt.
FALCONER, ARTHUR WELLESLEY, M.D., Capt. (Temporary Major), Royal Army Medical Corps.
FALCONAR-STEWART, RONALD DUNDAS, Temporary Lieut.-Colonel, Argyll and Sutherland Highlanders.
FALWASSER, ARTHUR THOMAS, Capt. (Temporary Lieut.-Colonel), Royal Army Medical Corps.
FARQUHAR, WILLIAM ALEXANDER, Major (Temporary Lieut.-Colonel), Royal Scots Fusiliers.
FARRELL, JOHN ARTHUR JOSEPH, Capt. (Acting Major), Leinster Regt., Special Reserve.
FEARON, PAUL JOHN, Major (Temporary Lieut.-Colonel), Royal West Surrey Regt.
FERNIE, FRANCIS HOOD, Temporary Major, Tank Corps.
FESTING, MAURICE CHRISTIAN, Major, Royal Marine Light Infantry.
FIELD, LINWOOD, M.C., Capt. (Acting Major), Royal Artillery.
FILSELL, HAROLD STUART, Major (Temporary Lieut.-Colonel), Royal Warwickshire Regt.
FINDLAY, JOHN ALEXANDER, Major, Highland Light Infantry.
FINLAYSON, WALTER TAYLOR, Major, Indian Medical Service.
FISHER, DAVID LEONARD, M.B., Major (Acting Lieut.-Colonel), Royal Army Medical Corps.
FISHER, JAMES THACKERAY, Major, Royal Engineers.
FITZGERALD, ARTHUR STANLEY, Temporary Major, Royal Warwickshire Regt.
FITZHERBERT, EDWARD HERBERT, M.C., Capt., Army Service Corps.
FITZHUGH, TERRICK CHARLES, M.V.O., Capt., Reserve of Officers, Royal Irish Regt.
FITZPATRICK, NOEL TREW, M.C., Capt. and Brevet Major, Royal Engineers.
FLEMING, ARCHIBALD NICOL, M.B., F.R.C.S., Lieut.-Colonel, Indian Medical Service.
FLEMING, FRANK, Lieut.-Colonel, Royal Field Artillery.
FLEMING, PERCY BERESFORD, Capt., Army Service Corps.
FOLJAMBE, THE HON. GERALD WILLIAM FREDERICK SAVILE, Capt. (Acting Lieut.-Colonel), Reserve of Officers, late Oxfordshire and Buckinghamshire Light Infantry.
FOOT, RICHARD MILDMAY, C.M.G., Major (Temporary Lieut.-Colonel) (Lieut.-Colonel, Retired, T.F.), Reserve of Officers, Royal Inniskilling Fusiliers.
FOOT, STEPHEN HENRY, Lieut. (Temporary Capt.), Royal Engineers, Special Reserve.
FORTH, NOWELL BARNARD DE LANCEY, M.C., Major (Acting Lieut.-Colonel,) Manchester Regt.
FOSTER, WILLIAM NELSON, Temporary Capt. (Acting Major), Army Service Corps.
FOWLER, CECIL, Major, Royal Field Artillery.
FOX, GEORGE, Temporary Major, General List.
FOX, REV. HENRY WATSON, Temporary Chaplain to the Forces, Fourth Class (Temporary Chaplain to the Forces, Third Class), Army Chaplains' Department.
FRASER, THE HON. ALASTAIR THOMAS JOSEPH, Capt. (Acting Major), Lovat's Scouts (Cameron Highlanders).
FRASER, JOHN ALEXANDER, Lieut. (Temporary Lieut.-Colonel), Dragoon Guards.
FRASER, THOMAS, M.B., Lieut.-Colonel, Royal Army Medical Corps.
FRASER, THE HON. WILLIAM, M.C., Capt. (Acting Lieut.-Colonel), Gordon Highlanders.
FRENCH, THE HON. EDWARD GERALD, Temporary Major, General List.
FREND, JOHN ROBERTS, Capt. (Acting Major), Leinster Regt., Special Reserve.
FULTON. CHARLES GIBSON, Major, Royal Field Artillery.
FURNIVALL, WILLOUGHBY, Lieut.-Colonel, Royal Field Artillery.
FULLER, WILLIAM FLEETWOOD, Major, Yeomanry.
FURZE, EDWARD KEITH BYRNE, M.C., Capt., Royal West Surrey Regt.
GALBRAITH, EDGAR DAVID, Major, Indian Army.
GALLOWAY, AYLMER GEORGE, Major (Temporary Lieut.-Colonel), Army Service Corps.
GALLOWAY, ROBERT LEECH, Major, Royal Field Artillery.
GALWEY, CHARLES EDWARD, Major (Temporary Lieut.-Colonel), Reserve of Officers, late Royal Irish Regt.
GARDNER, WILLIAM ROSS, M.B., Capt. (Acting Lieut.-Colonel), Royal Army Medical Corps, Special Reserve.
GARFORTH, WILLIAM, M.C., Major, Royal Engineers.
GARWORTH, JOHN REGINALD, Major, Royal Engineers.
GARWOOD, HENRY PERCY, Major, Royal Garrison Artillery.
GASCOIGNE, CECIL CLAUD HUGH ORBY, Temporary Lieut.-Colonel, Worcestershire Regt.
GAUNTLETT, ERIC GERALD, M.B., Capt., Royal Army Medical Corps.
GAY, CYRIL HERBERT, Capt., Royal Artillery.
GEDGE, FREDERICK GEORGE PETER, Second Lieut. (Temporary Major), Royal Engineers.
GELL, WILLIAM CHARLES COLEMAN, M.C., Capt. (Acting Lieut.-Colonel), Royal Warwickshire Regt.
GIBBS, ALFRED JOSEPH, M.C., Capt., Royal Field Artillery.
GIBBS, HUGH EDWARD, Major, Army Veterinary Corps.
GIBSON, ALEXANDER JOHN, Capt., Royal Army Medical Corps, Special Reserve.
GIBSON, HAROLD, Capt. (Acting Lieut.-Colonel), Royal Army Medical Corps.
GIBSON, JOSEPH, Temporary Major, Army Service Corps.
GIBSON, LEWIS, Major, Royal Highlanders.
GIBSONE, DONALD HOPE, Temporary Major (Temporary Colonel), Royal Engineers.
GILL, JOHN GALBRAITH, M.C., M.B., Capt., Royal Army Medical Corps.
GILLAM, REYNOLD ALEXANDER, Major (Temporary Lieut.-Colonel), Royal Engineers.
GILMOUR, JOHN (Jun.), Lieut.-Colonel, Highlanders.
GLENDENNING, SYDNEY ELLIOT, Temporary Capt. (Acting Major), Royal Engineers.
GODSELL, KENNETH BRUCE, M.C., Lieut. (Acting Major), Royal Engineers.
GODWIN, CHARLES ALEXANDER CAMPBELL, Major and Brevet Lieut.-Colonel, Cavalry, Indian Army.
GOLDSMITH, GEORGE EDWARD, Major, Army Service Corps.
GOODWIN, WILLIAM RICHARD, Temporary Lieut.-Colonel, Royal Irish Rifles.
GORDON, ALEXANDER ROBERT GISBORNE, Major, Royal Irish Regt.
GORDON, GEORGE HAMILTON, Lieut.-Colonel, Royal Field Artillery.
GORDON, GRANVILLE CECIL DOUGLAS, Major (Acting Lieut.-Colonel), Welsh Guards.
GORDON, RICHARD GLEGG, Major, Lowland Royal Garrison Artillery (Christian name corrected to Reginald Clegg [London Gazette, 8 March, 1918]).
GORDON, WILLIAM, Major, Royal Garrison Artillery.
GORDON-LENNOX, LORD ESME CHARLES, M.V.O., Major and Brevet Lieut.-Colonel (Temporary Brigadier-General), Scots Guards.
GORE-BROWNE, ERIC, Capt. and Brevet Major, London Regt.
GORING-JONES, MICHAEL DERWAS, C.M.G., Lieut.-Colonel (Temporary Brigadier-General), Durham Light Infantry.
GOUDGE, REV. THOMAS SYDNEY, Chaplain to the Forces, Second Class (Temporary Chaplain to the Forces, First Class), Army Chaplains' Department.
GOULD, ARTHUR ERNEST, M.C., Second Lieut. (Acting Major), Royal Engineers.
GOVER, JOHN MAXWELL, M.B., Major (Acting Lieut.-Colonel), Royal Army Medical Corps.
GRAHAM, MALISE, Capt. (Temporary Lieut.-Colonel), Lancers.
GRAHAM, ROLAND CECIL DOUGLAS, Major, Royal Garrison Artillery.
GRANT SUTTIE, HUBERT FRANCIS, M C., Major, Royal Artillery.
GRANVILLE, BERNARD, Major (Temporary Lieut.-Colonel) (Capt., Retired Pay), Yeomanry.
GRATTAN, HENRY WILLIAM, Lieut.-Colonel (Temporary Colonel), Royal Army Medical Corps.
GREEN, STAFFORD HENRY, M.C., Capt. and Brevet Major, West Yorkshire Regt.
GREEN, WILFRITH GERALD KEY, Major (Temporary Lieut.-Colonel), Indian Army.
GREENHOUGH, FREDERICK HARRY, Temporary Major (Temporary Lieut.-Colonel), Royal Engineers.
GREENWELL, WILLIAM BASIL, Major (Temporary Lieut.-Colonel), Durham Light Infantry.
GREENWOOD, CHARLES FRANCIS HILL, Major (Acting Lieut.-Colonel), London Regt.
GREGG, RICHARD HUGO, M.C., Temporary Major, Royal Fusiliers.
GREGG, WILLIAM THORNTON HUBAND, Capt. (Temporary Major), Royal Irish Fusiliers.
GRENFELL, GEORGE PASCOE, Capt. (Temporary Major,) Royal Flying Corps, Special Reserve.
GRIFFIN REV. JOHN WESLEY KNOX, M.A., Chaplain to the Forces, Fourth Class (Temporary Chaplain to the Forces, Second Class), Army Chaplains' Department.
GRIFFITH, EDWARD WALDEGRAVE, Temporary Lieut.-Colonel, Royal Artillery.
GRIGG, EDWARD WILLIAM MACLEAY, M.C., Lieut. (Temporary Capt.), Grenadier Guards, Special Reserve.
GRIMWADE, HUGH NEOL, M.C., Temporary Second Lieut. (Temporary Capt.), General List.
GROGAN, EWART SCOTT, Capt. (Temporary Major), Unattached List, East African Forces.
GRUBB, HERBERT WATKINS, Major and Brevet Lieut.-Col. (Temporary Lieut.-Colonel), Border Regt.
GUARD, FREDERICK HENRY WICKHAM, Temporary Major (Acting Lieut.-Colonel), Royal Scots.

The Distinguished Service Order

GUGGISBERG, FREDERICK GORDON, C.M.G., Lieut.-Colonel (Temporary Brigadier-General), Royal Engineers.
GUINNESS, ERIC CECIL, Lieut. (Temporary Major), Royal Irish Regt.
GUNN, HAMILTON BRUCE LEVERSON GOWER, M.C., Major (Acting Lieut.-Colonel), Royal Garrison Artillery.
HABGOOD, ARTHUR HENRY, Capt. (Acting Lieut.-Colonel), Royal Army Medical Corps, Special Reserve.
HAIGH, BERNARD, Lieut.-Colonel, Army Service Corps.
HALAHAN, FREDERICK CROSBY, M.V.O., Wing Commander Royal Naval Air Service.
HALL, FREDERICK, M.P., Temporary Lieut.-Colonel, Royal Field Artillery.
HAMILTON, ROBERT SYDNEY, C.M.G., Lieut.-Colonel (Temporary Colonel), Army Ordnance Department.
HAMMONDS, DENYS HUNTINGFORD, M.C., Capt. (Acting Major), Royal Engineers, Special Reserve.
HANCOCK, CLAUDE, Temporary Major, Gloucestershire Regt.
HAIG, JOHN, Major, Yeomanry.
HANCOCK, MORTIMER PAWSON, Major (Acting Lieut.-Colonel), Royal Fusiliers.
HAND, WILLIAM CHARLES, M.C., Temporary Capt., Royal Garrison Artillery.
HANKEY, EDWARD BARNARD, Major and Brevet Lieut.-Colonel, Worcestershire Regt., attached Tank Corps.
HANLEY, HUBERT ARTHUR OLDFIELD, Capt. (Acting Major), Middlesex Regt.
HANNAY, CATHCART CHRISTIAN, Lieut.-Colonel, Dorsetshire Regt.
HANSON, FRANK STEPHEN, M.C., Capt. (Acting Lieut.-Colonel), Royal Warwickshire Regt.
HARDIE, CECIL CLAUD ALEXANDER, Temporary Major, Royal Engineers.
HARDING, GEORGE RICHARDSON, Temporary Capt. (Acting Lieut.-Colonel), Royal Engineers.
HARKER, THOMAS HUBERT, Capt. (Temporary Lieut.-Colonel), King's Royal Rifle Corps, Special Reserve.
HART, CHARLES HARRY, M.C., Capt. (Temporary Major), Army Service Corps.
HART, OWEN, Temporary Capt. (Acting Major), Royal Field Artillery.
HARVEY, CHARLES DARBY, Major (Temporary Lieut.-Colonel), Nottinghamshire and Derbyshire Regt.
HARVEY, COSMO GEORGE SINCLAIR, Major, Royal Field Artillery.
HARVEY, GARDINER HASSELL, Major (Temporary Lieut.-Colonel), Army Service Corps.
HARVEY, JOHN, Capt. and Honorary Major (Temporary Lieut.-Colonel), Reserve of Officers, Retired, Special Reserve.
HASLAM, PERCY LOVELL CLARE, Capt. (Temporary Major), Hussars, attached Tank Corps.
HAWKSLEY, RANDAL PLUNKETT TAYLOR, Major (Temporary Brigadier-General), Royal Engineers.
HAY, JAMES GEORGE, Capt., Retired Pay, late Gordon Highlanders.
HAYES, GEOFFREY, Capt. (Temporary Major, Acting Lieut.-Colonel), Durham Light Infantry.
HAYLEY, WILLIAM BURRELL, Major, Royal Horse Artillery.
HAYWARD, GEORGE WILLIAM, Temporary Lieut.-Colonel, Royal Field Artillery (Riding Master and Honorary Major, Retired).
HAWKINS, EUSTACE FELLOWES SINCLAIR, Lieut. (Temporary Major), Army Service Corps, Special Reserve.
HAZELRIGG, THOMAS, Major (Temporary Lieut.-Colonel), Army Service Corps.
HEADLAM, CUTHBERT MORLEY, Capt., Bedfordshire Yeomanry.
HEARLE, ARTHUR, BASSET, Major, Royal Garrison Artillery.
HEATH, GEORGE NOAH, Major, Cheshire Regt.
HEATH, JOSEPH THOMAS, M.C., Capt. (Acting Major), Royal Engineers.
HEATHER, VINCENT JAMES, Major, Royal Artillery.
HEBBLETHWAITE, ALFRED GEORGE, Capt., Royal Army Medical Corps.
HEELAS, PERCIVAL JOHN BERESFORD, Major, Royal Field Artillery
HENDERSON, HARRY DALTON, Lieut.-Colonel, Army Service Corps.
HEPPER, LIONEL LEES, Lieut.-Colonel, Royal Garrison Artillery.
HESSEY, WILLIAM FRANCIS, Major and Brevet Lieut.-Colonel (Temporary Brigadier-General), Royal Inniskilling Fusiliers, Reserve of Officers.
HEWITT, CHARLES CAULFIELD, M.C., Capt. (Temporary Major, Acting Lieut.-Colonel), Royal Inniskilling Fusiliers and Machine Gun Corps.
HEYGATE, GERALD, Major, Royal Field Artillery.
HEYWOOD, SIR GRAHAM PERCIVAL, Bart., Lieut.-Colonel, 1st Staffordshire Yeomanry.
HILL, HERBERT JOHN, Temporary Lieut. (Acting Capt.), Royal Engineers.
HILL, ROWLAND CLEMENT RIDLEY, Major (Temporary Lieut.-Colonel), Royal Engineers.
HILLS, FRANCIS BARRETT, Major, Royal Garrison Artillery.
HINGE, HARRY ALEXANDER, C.M.G., Lieut.-Colonel (Temporary Colonel), Royal Army Medical Corps.
HITCHINS CHARLES FAUNCE, Capt. and Temporary Major (Temporary Lieut.-Colonel), Royal West Kent Regt., Special Reserve (description changed to Major (Temporary Lieut.-Colonel), Royal West Kent Regt. Special Reserve, attached North Lancashire Regt. [London Gazette, 26 July, 1918]).
HOARE, REGINALD, Colonel (Temporary Brigadier-General), 4th Hussars.
HOBSON, HARRY ROY, Temporary Major, Army Service Corps.
HODGINS, ADAM, Capt. (Temporary Major), Army Veterinary Corps.
HUNT, WILLIAM HOLDSWORTH HOLDSWORTH, Lieut.-Colonel, Royal Garrison Artillery.
HOLLOND, HENRY ARTHUR, Lieut. (Temporary Capt.), Royal Garrison Artillery.
HOOD, FRANCIS JOHN COURTENAY, Temporary Major (Acting Lieut.-Colonel), York and Lancaster Regt.

HOOPER, JOHN CHARLES, Major, Shropshire Light Infantry.
HORN, ROBERT VICTOR GALBRAITH, M.C., Capt. and Brevet Major, Royal Scots Fusiliers.
HOUGHTON, GEORGE JOHN, Major (Temporary Lieut.-Colonel), Royal Army Medical Corps.
HOUGHTON, JOHN WILLIAM HOBART, M.B., Lieut.-Colonel (Temporary Colonel), Royal Army Medical Corps.
HOWARD-BURY, CHARLES KENNETH, Capt. (Temporary Major and Acting Lieut.-Colonel), King's Royal Rifles Corps, Special Reserve.
HOWEL-JONES, WALTER, Lieut.-Colonel, Royal Garrison Artillery.
HUDSON, JAMES THOMAS HAROLD, Quartermaster and Hon. Major, Middlesex Regt.
HUDSPETH, HENRY MOORE, M.C., Temporary Capt. (Acting Major), Royal Engineers.
HUGHES, BASIL, M.B., F.R.C.S., Capt., Royal Army Medical Corps.
HUGHES, EDWARD WILLIAM, M.C., Major, London Regt.
HUGHES, WILLIAM, M.C., Major (Acting Lieut.-Colonel), London Regt.
HULTON, HENRY HORNE, Major, Royal Field Artillery.
HUME, WALTER VERNON, Major, South Lancashire Fusiliers.
HUMPHREYS, GEORGE NOEL, Major (Temporary Lieut.-Colonel), Army Service Corps.
HUNT, ROCHFORD NOEL, M.B., Major (Temporary Lieut.-Colonel), Royal Army Medical Corps.
HUNT, REGINALD SEAGER, Major (Temporary Lieut.-Colonel), Dragoon Guards.
HUNTER, CECIL STUART, Capt. (Temporary Major), Retired Pay, Reserve of Officers, Royal Artillery.
HUNTER, HUGH BLACKBURN, Temporary Major, Army Service Corps.
HUNTER, HENRY NOEL ALEXANDER, Major, Royal West Surrey Regt.
HURST, ARTHUR REGINALD, Temporary Lieut.-Colonel, Royal Field Artillery.
HUSEY, RALPH HAMER, M.C., Major (Acting Lieut.-Colonel), London Regt.
HUTCHISON, COLIN ROSS MARSHALL, M.C., Capt. (Acting Major), Royal Field Artillery.
IBBS, THOMAS CHARLES, Quartermaster and Hon. Major, London Regt.
ILES, HENRY WILSON, Lieut.-Colonel, Royal Garrison Artillery.
IM THURN, BERNHARDT BASIL VON BRUMSY, M.C., Capt., Hampshire Regt.
INGLIS, CHARLES ELLIOTT, Major (Acting Lieut.-Colonel), Royal Garrison Artillery.
INGLIS, RICHARD, Temporary Major (Acting Lieut.-Colonel), King's Royal Rifle Corps.
INGLIS, THOMAS STEWART, Major, Royal Field Artillery.
IRONS, ARTHUR INNES, Temporary Lieut.-Colonel, Middlesex Regt.
IRWIN, NOEL MACKINTOSH STUART, M.C., Capt. (Acting Lieut.-Colonel), Essex Regt.
IZAT, WILLIAM RENNIE, Major, Royal Engineers.
JACKSON, EDWARD DARBY, Capt. (Acting Lieut.-Colonel), King's Own Scottish Borderers.
JACKSON, FRANK WHITFORD, Temporary Major, Army Service Corps.
JACKSON, HERBERT WILLIAM, Major and Brevet Lieut.-Colonel, Indian Army.
JACKSON, RICHARD ROLT BRASH, Major (Acting Lieut.-Colonel), Army Service Corps.
JACOB, ARTHUR LAWRANCE BALDWIN, Major (Acting Lieut.-Colonel), Royal Garrison Artillery.
JAMES, ARCHIBALD HUGH Temporary Major (Acting Lieut.-Colonel), Northumberland Fusiliers, West Yorkshire Regt.
JAMES, RALPH ERNEST HAWEIS, C.M.G., Major and Brevet Lieut.-Col., North Lancashire Regt.
JARRETT, CYRIL, Major, Middlesex Regt.
JAYNE, ARTHUR ALFRED, M.C., Temporary Capt. (Acting Major), Royal Engineers.
JEFFREYS, RICHARD GRIFFITH BASSETT, Major (Temporary Lieut.-Colonel), Royal Dublin Fusiliers.
JENKINS, LEOLINE, M.C., Major, Dorset Royal Garrison Artillery and Royal Flying Corps.
JENNER, SIR WALTER KENTISH WILLIAM, Bart., Major (Temporary Lieut.-Colonel), Reserve of Officers, Retired Pay, late 9th Lancers.
JENOUR, ARTHUR STAWELL, C.M.G., Lieut.-Colonel (Temporary Brigadier-General), Royal Garrison Artillery.
JOHNSON, ARTHUR BAYNES, Major (Temporary Lieut.-Colonel), Lincolnshire Regt.
JOHNSON, ALLEN VICTOR, Lieut.-Colonel, Royal Fusiliers, King's Royal Rifle Corps.
JOHNSON, BENJAMIN SANDFORD, Temporary Major (Acting Lieut.-Colonel), Army Service Corps.
JOHNSON, VICTOR NEVILLE, Major, Gloucestershire Regt.
JOHNSTON, FREDERICK CAMPBELL, Temporary Lieut.-Colonel, Royal Artillery.
JOHNSON, GEORGE BERNARD, Major, Royal Field Artillery.
JOHNSTON, WILLIAM HAMILTON HALL, M.C., Temporary Lieut.-Colonel, Middlesex Regt.
JOLL, HARRY HAWEIS, M.C., Major, Royal Artillery.
JONES, ARCHIBALD NELSON GAVIN, Major, Indian Army.
JOSSELYN, JOHN, Lieut.-Colonel, Suffolk Regt.
KAVANAGH, EDWARD JAMES, M.C., M.B., Capt. (Acting Lieut.-Colonel) Royal Army Medical Corps.
KAY, THOMAS, M.B., Major (Temporary Lieut.-Colonel), Royal Army Medical Corps.
KEMPTHORNE, GERARD AINSLIE, Major (Temporary Lieut.-Colonel), Royal Army Medical Corps.

A 5

KENDRICK, EDWARD HOLT, Capt. and Brevet Major (Temporary Lieut.-Colonel), Royal Dublin Fusiliers.
KENNEDY, WILLIAM, Major, East African Veterinary Corps.
KENT, ALBERT EDMUND, M.C., Lieut. (Temporary Major), Leicestershire Regt., Special Reserve.
KENT, JOHN, Major, Royal Field Artillery.
KENYON, HERBERT EDWARD, Major, Royal Garrison Artillery.
KERSHAW, JOHN VICTOR, Temporary Major, East Lancashire Regt.
KERSHAW, SIDNEY HARDINGE, Major (Temporary Lieut.-Colonel), Northumberland Fusiliers.
KINDELL, FRANCIS PERCY, M.C., Lieut. (Acting Major), Royal Artillery.
KILNER, CHARLES HAROLD, Major (Temporary Lieut.-Colonel), Royal Field Artillery, Reserve of Officers.
KILVERT, ROBERT EDGAR, Major, Royal Marine Artillery.
KING, CHARLES FRANCIS, M.C., Temporary Capt. (Acting Major), Cheshire Regt.
KING, FRANK, Capt. (Temporary Major), 4th Hussars.
KING, JOHN RUSSELL, Temporary Major, Army Service Corps.
KING-HARMAN, WENTWORTH ALEXANDER, Temporary Major, Retired List, late Royal Irish Rifles.
KINGSFORD, GUY THORNHILL, Major, Royal Engineers.
KINNEAR, JOHN LAWSON, M.C., Capt. (Temporary Major), Liverpool Regt. and Royal Flying Corps.
KIRKNESS, LEWIS HAWKER, Temporary Lieut.-Colonel, Special List.
KIRKPATRICK, HARRY FEARNLEY, Major (Acting Lieut.-Colonel), Reserve of Officers, East Kent Regt.
KNAPMAN, LEONARD, Temporary Major, Army Service Corps.
KNYVETT, CHARLES LEYCESTER, M.C., Major, Royal Field Artillery.
KYLE, ROBERT, Temporary Lieut.-Colonel, Highland Light Infantry.
KYNGDON, WILLIAM FREDERICK ROBERT, Major (Acting Lieut.-Colonel), Royal Garrison Artillery.
LAING, RODERICK, M.C., Major (Acting Lieut.-Colonel), Seaforth Highlanders.
LAIRD, JAMES, Major (Acting Lieut.-Colonel), Royal Field Artillery.
LAKE, RONALD DEWE, Capt., Northamptonshire Regt.
LAMOTTE, GEORGE MOORSOM LAGIER, Temporary Major, Royal Engineers, Special Reserve.
LANGRISHE, JOHN DU PLESSIS, M.B., Capt. (Acting Lieut.-Colonel), Royal Army Medical Corps.
LANGTON, JOHN HENRY, Major, Royal Welsh Fusiliers.
LANGWORTHY-PARRY, PERCY EDWARD, Major, Retired Pay (Lieut.-Colonel), London Regt. (description corrected to Lieut.-Colonel, London Regt. (Major, Territorial Force, Retired) [London Gazette, 21 May, 1918]).
LARCOM, SIR THOMAS PERCEVAL, Bart., Major, Royal Artillery.
LARGE, STANLEY DERMOTT, M.C., Capt., Royal Army Medical Corps.
LASCELLES, THE HON. EDWARD CECIL, M.C., Capt., Rifle Brigade, Special Reserve.
LAWRENCE, CHARLES TREVOR, Major, Royal Field Artillery.
LAWRENCE, GEOFFREY, Major, Royal Field Artillery.
LAWRENCE, HERVEY MAJOR, Major (Acting Lieut.-Colonel), Scottish Rifles
LAYTON, ARTHUR BERTRAM, Capt. (Temporary Lieut.-Colonel), South Lancashire Regt.
LE BUTT, RALPH, Temporary Major, Machine Gun Corps.
LECKIE, VICTOR CARMICHAEL, Capt. (Temporary Major), Army Veterinary Corps.
LEE, GUY, M.C., Major, East Kent Regt.
LEE, GEORGE MACONCHY, M.C., Capt., Reserve of Officers, Retired Pay, Royal Fusiliers.
LEE, HARRY ROMER, Major, Reserve of Officers, 20th Hussars.
LEES, EDWARD FREDERICK WILLIAM, Major (Acting Lieut.-Colonel), Royal Engineers.
LEGGAT, ALEXANDER, M.B., Major (Acting Lieut.-Colonel), Royal Army Medical Corps.
LEMBCKE, CHARLES EDWARD, Capt. (Temporary Lieut.-Colonel), Northumberland Fusiliers.
LEMON, FREDERICK JOSEPH, Major, West Yorkshire Regt.
LEWIS, DUDLEY, M.C., Temporary Major, York and Lancaster Regt.
LEWIS, PHILIP EDWARD, Lieut.-Colonel, Royal Artillery.
LINDSELL, WILFRED GORDON, M.C., Capt., Royal Artillery.
LING, CHRISTOPHER GEORGE, M.C., Capt., Royal Engineers.
LINGS, HAROLD CRONSHAW, Major, Manchester Regt.
LITTLETON, THE HON. CHARLES CHRISTOPHER JOSCELINE, Temporary Lieut. (Temporary Capt.), Middlesex Regt.
LIVENS, WILLIAM HOWARD, M.C., Lieut. (Temporary Capt.), Royal Engineers, Special Reserve.
LLEWELLYN, EVAN HENRY, Major (Temporary Brigadier-General), Reserve of Officers, King's African Rifles.
LLOYD, EVAN COLCLOUGH, Major (Acting Lieut.-Colonel), Royal Irish Regt.
LOGGIE, ORMOND MAXWELL, M.C., Lieut. (Acting Major), Royal Garrison Artillery.
LOMAS, KENNETH THURSTON, Temporary Capt. (Acting Major), Royal Engineers.
LONGBOTTOM, THOMAS, Major, West Yorkshire Regt.
LONGCROFT, CHARLES ALEXANDER HOLCOMBE, Capt. and Brevet Lieut.-Colonel (Temporary Brigadier-General), Welsh Regt.
LONGMAN, HENRY KERR, M.C., Capt., Reserve of Officers, late Gordon Highlanders.
LORING, WILLIAM, Lieut.-Colonel, Royal Garrison Artillery.
LOVE, STUART GILKINSON, M.C., Second Lieut. (Temporary Major) (name and description corrected to Stuart Gilkison Love, M.C., Second Lieut. (Temp. Major), Royal Engineers [London Gazette, 8 March, 1918]).

LOWNDES, JOHN GORDON, Major, Reserve of Officers, late North Lancashire Regt.
LOYD, HENRY CHARLES, M.C., Capt., Coldstream Guards.
LUARD, LOWES DALBIAC, Temporary Major, Army Service Corps.
LUDGATE, WILLIAM, Major, Army Veterinary Corps.
LUDLOW-HEWITT, EDGAR RAINEY, M.C., Capt. and Brevet Major (Temporary Lieut.-Colonel), Royal Irish Rifles.
LYNCH, CECIL ST. JOHN, Major, Royal Engineers.
LYNCH, JASPER BEVERLEY, Capt., late 12th Cavalry, Indian Army.
LYSTER, FRANK SANDERSON, Local Major, Special List.
MACCONNELL, ARCHIBALD LAIRD, Major, Argyll and Sutherland Highlanders.
MACDONALD, HAROLD SYMES, M.C., Capt. (Acting Major), Royal Field Artillery.
MACDONALD, JAMES LESLIE AULD, Temporary Major, Royal Scots.
MACDONALD, REGINALD JAMES, Lieut.-Colonel, Royal Garrison Artillery.
MACFARLAN, JOHN BUCHANAN, Major (Acting Lieut.-Colonel), Royal Field Artillery.
MACFARLANE, FANE ANDREW JAMES, Lieut. (Temporary Capt.), London Regt.
MACFARLANE, WALTER, Major, Glasgow Yeomanry.
MACKENZIE, FRANCIS BURNETT, M.C., Capt. (Temporary Major), Royal Scots.
MACKESY, PIERSE JOSEPH, M.C., Major, Royal Engineers.
MACKINTOSH, WILLIAM ALEXANDER ONSLOW CHURCHILL, Capt. and Brevet Major, Royal Artillery.
MACLEAN, CHARLES ALEXANDER HUGH, Major and Brevet Lieut.-Colonel, Argyll and Sutherland Highlanders.
MACLEAN, CHARLES WILBERFORCE, Major, Cameron Highlanders.
MACLEOD, ADAM GORDON, Temporary Major, Army Service Corps.
MACLEOD, DONALD, M.C., Capt. (Temporary Lieut.-Colonel), North Staffordshire Regt., Special Reserve.
MACLEOD, MALCOLM NEYNOE, M.C., Major, Royal Engineers.
MACLEOD, MINDEN WHYTE MELVILLE, Lieut. (Acting Major), Royal Garrison Artillery.
McCANDLISH, PATRICK DALMAHOY, Capt. and Brevet Major (Temporary Lieut.-Colonel), Reserve of Officers, Argyll and Sutherland Highlanders.
McCALL, WILLIAM, M.B., Major (Acting Lieut.-Colonel), Royal Army Medical Corps.
McCLINTOCK, ROBERT SINGLETON, Major, Royal Engineers.
McCLURE, IVOR HERBERT, Temporary Capt., Intelligence Corps.
McCOMBIE, HAMILTON, M.C., Lieut. (Temporary Capt.), Worcestershire Regt.
McCULLAGH, WILLIAM McKIM HERBERT, M.C., M.B., Capt., Royal Army Medical Corps, Special Reserve.
McDIARMID, JAMES INNIS AIKIN, Capt. and Brevet Major, Royal Garrison Artillery.
McLARTY, GORDON ARCHIBALD, M.B., Temporary Capt., Royal Army Medical Corps.
McLEOD, NORMAN MACDONALD, M.C., Major, Royal Field Artillery.
McMASTER, HUGH, M.C., Capt. (Acting Major), Royal Artillery (rank corrected from Capt. (Acting Major) to Major [London Gazette, 21 May, 1918]).
McMULLEN, DONALD JAY, Capt. (Temporary Major), Royal Engineers.
McNEE, JOHN WILLIAM, M.B., Capt., Royal Army Medical Corps, Special Reserve.
MAITLAND-EDWARDS, GEORGE, Temporary Capt. (Temporary Lieut.-Colonel), Royal Engineers.
MALCOLM, GEORGE ALEXANDER, Lieut.-Colonel, Territorial Force Reserve, attached London Regt.
MALLINSON, STUART SYDNEY, M.C., Temporary Capt. (Temporary Lieut.-Colonel), Royal Engineers.
MANIFOLD, JOHN ALEXANDER, M.B., Capt. (Acting Lieut.-Colonel), Royal Army Medical Corps.
MANTON, LIONEL, Capt. (Temporary Lieut.-Colonel), Royal Engineers.
MARINDIN, ARTHUR HENRY, Major and Brevet Lieut.-Colonel (Temporary Brigadier-General), Royal Highlanders.
MARINDIN, CECIL COLVILE, Major and Brevet Lieut.-Colonel (Acting Lieut.-Colonel), Royal Garrison Artillery.
MARRINER, BRYAN LISTER, Capt. (Acting Major), Royal Field Artillery.
MARSH, JOHN FRANCIS HARRISON, Capt. (Acting Lieut.-Colonel), Hampshire Regt.
MARSHALL, ALFRED RUSSEL, M.C., Capt. (Acting Major), Royal Engineers, Special Reserve.
MARSHALL, CHARLES FREDERICK KELK, M.C., Capt. (Acting Major), Royal Field Artillery.
MARSHALL, HENRY ALFRED, Honorary Major (Temporary Honorary Lieut.-Colonel,) Army Ordnance Department.
MARTIN, ERNEST BRASEWHITE, Temporary Major (Temporary Lieut.-Colonel), Royal Engineers.
MASON, DANIEL JOHNSTONE, Major, Royal Field Artillery.
MASON, MALCOLM FORTY, Major (Temporary Lieut.-Colonel), Suffolk Regt.
MASSY, CHARLES WALTER, M.C., Capt. (Acting Major), Royal Field Artillery.
MATTHEWS, REGINALD COSWAY, Major, Army Veterinary Corps.
MATTHEWS, WILLIAM RIDDELL, Temporary Lieut.-Colonel, Royal Army Medical Corps.
MAULE, HUGH PATRICK GUARIN, M.C., Lieut. (Temporary Capt.), Honourable Artillery Company.
MAULE, WILLIAM JAMES, Temporary Major, Special List.
MAYNE, HERBERT BLAIR, Lieut.-Colonel, Royal Garrison Artillery.
MAXWELL, JOHN, M.C., Capt. (Temporary Major), Rifle Brigade.

MAXWELL, JAMES McCALL, C.B., Lieut.-Colonel, Royal Field Artillery.
MAXWELL, ROBERT DAVID PERCIVAL, Temporary Lieut.-Colonel, Royal Irish Rifles.
MEADOWS, SYDNEY MANVERS WOOLNER, Major (Temporary Lieut.-Colonel), Royal Army Medical Corps.
MEARES, CYRIL FRANKLAND, Major (Temporary Lieut.-Colonel), Royal Irish Fusiliers.
MELVILL, TEIGNMOUTH PHILIP, Major (Acting Lieut.-Colonel), Lancers.
MICHIE, DAVID KINLOCH, Temporary Major, Highland Light Infantry.
MILLER, GEORGE WATERSTON, Capt., Royal Army Medical Corps (rank corrected to Major [London Gazette, 7 Feb, 1918]).
MILLER, HUBERT GARRETT BLAIR, M.C., Major (Temporary Lieut.-Colonel), Royal Scots Fusiliers.
MILLER, REV. WILLIAM HERBERT LATIMER, B.A., Chaplain to the Forces, Fourth Class (Temporary Chaplain to the Forces, Second Class), Army Chaplains' Department.
MILLIGAN, JOHN WILLIAMSON, Major, East African Supply Corps.
MILLNER, GEORGE ERNEST, M.C., Capt. (Acting Lieut.-Colonel), London Regt.
MILNER-WHITE, REV. ERIC MILNER, Temporary Chaplain to the Forces, Fourth Class (Temporary Chaplain to the Forces, Third Class), Army Chaplains' Department.
MILSOM, CECIL FRANCIS, Major, Army Service Corps.
MINSHALL, THOMAS HERBERT, Temporary Colonel, General List.
MITCHELL, ARTHUR, Major (Acting Lieut.-Colonel), Royal Garrison Artillery.
MITCHELL, ARCHIBALD MACLAINE, Major, Royal Scots.
MITCHELL, CHARLES, Capt. (Temporary Major), Grenadier Guards.
MITCHELL, WILLIAM GORE SUTHERLAND, M.C. (Capt. Temporary Lieut.-Colonel), Highland Light Infantry.
MONTGOMERY, THOMAS HASSARD, Temporary Major, Army Service Corps.
MOORE, EDWARD DUKE, Major, East Riding Yeomanry.
MOORE, EDWARD HENRY MILNER, Major, Royal Army Medical Corps.
MOORE, GEORGE ABRAHAM, C.M.G., Lieut.-Colonel (Temporary Colonel), Royal Army Medical Corps.
MORGAN, CHARLES ROBERT FAULCONER, Major (Temporary Lieut.-Colonel), Army Service Corps.
MORIARTY, THOMAS BETTESWORTH, Major (Acting Lieut.-Colonel), Royal Army Medical Corps.
MORRIS, EDWARD N. GROVES, Lieut.-Commander, Royal Naval Volunteer Reserve, attached Royal Naval Air Service.
MORRIS, JOHN HUGH, Major (Temporary Lieut.-Colonel), Army Service Corps.
MORRISON, FREDERICK LANSDOWNE, C.B., Lieut.-Colonel and Brevet Colonel, Highland Light Infantry.
MORRISON-SCOTT, ROBERT CHARLES STUART, Temporary Capt. (Acting Major), Royal Marine Artillery.
MORTER, SIDNEY PELHAM, Lieut.-Colonel, Royal Field Artillery.
MOSSOP, ALBERT ISAAC, Temporary Major, attached Oxfordshire and Buckinghamshire Light Infantry.
MOULTRIE, HUGH CRAWFORD, Lieut.-Colonel, Royal Artillery.
MOXON, CHARLES CARTER, C.M.G., Lieut.-Colonel, Yorkshire Light Infantry.
MURIEL, JOHN CARR, Temporary Major, Royal Inniskilling Fusiliers.
MUSSON, EDWARD LIONEL, M.C., Capt. (Temporary Lieut.-Colonel), Manchester Regt.
NAPER, LENOX ARTHUR DUTTON, Major (Temporary Lieut.-Colonel), Royal Field Artillery.
NASH, HENRY EDMUND PALMER, Major (Temporary Lieut.-Colonel), Royal Scots.
NEEDHAM, RODERICK MACAULAY BERNARD, Major, Suffolk Regt.
NEILL, DUNCAN FERGUSON DEMPSTER Capt. (Temporary Colonel), Reserve of Officers, Royal Engineers.
NEILL, REDMOND BARRY, Capt. (Acting Lieut.-Colonel), Reserve of Officers, Royal Irish Fusiliers.
NEVILL, RICHARD AUSTIN, Lieut.-Colonel, Royal Engineers.
NEVILE, GERVYS CHARLES, Major, Royal Field Artillery.
NEWBOLD, THOMAS CLIFFORD, Major, Nottinghamshire and Derbyshire Regt.
NICHOLSON, EDWARD HILLS, Major (Acting Lieut.-Colonel), Royal Fusiliers.
NICHOLSON, HUGH BLOMFIELD, Capt. (Acting Major), Reserve of Officers, King's Royal Rifle Corps.
NICKALLS, CECIL PATERSON, Major, Royal Field Artillery.
NIMMO, JOHN SCOTT, Major, Army Veterinary Corps.
NORMAND, SAMUEL RICHARD, Major, Royal Garrison Artillery.
NORTON, ARTHUR ERNEST, Major (Temporary Lieut.-Colonel), West India Regt.
NOTLEY, WILLIAM KILMINSTER, Temporary Lieut.-Colonel (corrected to Temporary Lieut.-Colonel, Unattached List, East African Forces [London Gazette, 4 Sept. 1918]) (name Kilminster corrected to Kilmister).
NUTT, ALLAN VAUGHAN, Temporary Major, York and Lancaster Regt.
NUTT, NORMAN HENRY, Temporary Major, Tank Corps.
OATES, WILLIAM COOPE, Lieut.-Colonel, Nottinghamshire and Derbyshire Regt.
O'BRIEN, HENRY EOGHAM, Temporary Lieut.-Colonel (Temporary Colonel), Royal Engineers.
ODAM, WILLIAM TASKER, Lieut.-Colonel, Reserve of Officers, Royal Field Artillery.
O'DONOGHUE, RICHARD JOHN LANFORD, Temporary Major, Army Service Corps.
OGILBY, ROBERT JAMES LESLIE, Lieut.-Colonel (Temporary), Reserve of Officers, London Regt.
OGILVY, DAVID, Major (Acting Lieut.-Colonel), Royal Engineers.

O'GORMAN, BERNARDINE, Temporary Major, General List (Christian name corrected to Bernard [London Gazette, 18 Feb. 1918]).
ORR, GERALD MAXWELL, Major and Brevet Lieut.-Colonel (Temporary Colonel), Lancers.
OSBORN, LEWIS JAMES, Lieut.-Colonel, Royal Artillery (T.F.), attached 47th Brigade Royal Field Artillery (as corrected).
OVERTON, GEORGE CECIL RUDALL, Capt. (Temporary Lieut.-Colonel), Reserve of Officers, Royal Fusiliers.
OWEN, LINDSAY CUNLIFFE, Capt. (Temporary Lieut.-Colonel), Royal Engineers.
OXENHAM, NORMAN HENRY, Temporary Major, Machine Gun Corps.
PAGET, BERNARD CHARLES TOLVER, M.C., Capt. and Brevet Major, Oxfordshire and Buckinghamshire Light Infantry.
PALMER, REV. REGINALD, M.C., Temporary Chaplain to the Forces, Fourth Class (Temporary Chaplain to the Forces, Third Class), Army Chaplains' Department.
PARDOE, THOMAS KENYON, Major, Worcestershire Regt.
PARK, JAMES DOVE, Major, Royal Engineers.
PARKER, ALBERT CHEVALLIER, Temporary Capt. (Local Lieut.-Colonel), Special List.
PARKINSON, GEORGE SINGLETON, Capt., Royal Army Medical Corps.
PATESHALL, HENRY EVAN, Major, Retired Pay, Reserve of Officers, Herefordshire Regt.
PAUNCEFORT-DUNCOMBE, SIR EVERARD PHILIP DIGBY, Bart., Major, Buckinghamshire Yeomanry.
PAYNE, DENYS WHITMORE, M.C., Major, Royal Garrison Artillery.
PAYNE, HERBERT GERALD, Temporary Capt., General List.
PEARSON, HUGH DRUMMOND, Major (Temporary Lieut.-Colonel), Royal Engineers.
PEARSON, THOMAS WILLIAM, Major (Acting Lieut.-Colonel), Royal Field Artillery.
PEEBLES, WILLIAM CARMICHAEL, Lieut.-Colonel, Royal Scots.
PEEL, HOME, M.C., Capt., London Regt.
PEEL, WILLOUGHBY EWART, Local Major, Camel Transport Corps.
PELLING, ALBERT JAMES, M.C., Temporary Capt., Royal Engineers.
PELLY, REV. DOUGLAS RAYMOND, Temporary Chaplain to the Forces, Fourth Class (Temporary Chaplain to the Forces, Third Class), Army Chaplains' Department.
PENN, BERTIE HOWARD, Honorary Lieut. (Honorary Major), Army Ordnance Department.
PENNY, FREDERICK SEPTIMUS, C.M.G., M.B., Lieut.-Colonel (Temporary Colonel), Royal Army Medical Corps.
PETTY, WILLIAM, Temporary Major (Acting Lieut.-Colonel), Seaforth Highlanders.
PHELAN, ERNEST CYRIL, M.C., M.B., Capt. (Acting Lieut.-Colonel), Royal Army Medical Corps.
PHIPPS, HENRY RAMSAY, Lieut.-Colonel, Royal Field Artillery.
PHYTHIAN-ADAMS, WILLIAM JOHN, M.C., Temporary Major, Royal Fusiliers.
PICKARD, JOCELYN ARTHUR ADAIR, Capt. (Acting Major), Royal Engineers, Special Reserve.
PILE, FREDERICK ALFRED, M.C., Major, Royal Artillery.
PINSENT, JOHN RYLAND, Capt. (Acting Major), Royal Engineers.
PINWILL, WILLIAM RICHARD, Major and Brevet Lieut.-Colonel (Temporary Lieut.-Colonel), Liverpool Regt.
PLANCK, OSWALD BERTRAM FISHER, Temporary Major, Army Service Corps.
PLAYFAIR, IAN STANLEY ORD, M.C., Lieut. (Temporary Capt.), Royal Engineers.
PLUMMER, THOMAS HERMAN, Major, Royal Garrison Artillery, Special Reserve.
PLUNKETT, JAMES FREDERICK, M.C., Lieut. (Temporary Major), Royal Irish Regt.
POLLARD, ALEXANDER MORTON, Capt. (Acting Lieut.-Colonel), Royal Army Medical Corps.
POLLOK, ROBERT VALENTINE, Capt. (Acting Lieut.-Colonel), Irish Guards.
PORTER, CYRIL LACHLAN, Major and Brevet Lieut.-Colonel (Temporary Brigadier-General), East Kent Regt.
PORTER, JAMES HERBERT, Capt. (Acting Lieut.-Colonel), North Staffordshire Regt.
POTTINGER, EDWARD CHARLES, Major (Temporary Lieut.-Colonel), Reserve of Officers, Royal Artillery (Christian name corrected to Eldred Charles).
POWELL, EDEN BERNARD, Major, Rifle Brigade.
POWELL, EDGAR ELKIN, Lieut.-Colonel, Royal Army Medical Corps.
POWELL, RANDOLPH MACHATTIE, Temporary Major, Royal Garrison Artillery.
POWER, THOMAS, Major, M.L.B.
POWNALL, HENRY ROYDS, M.C., Major, Royal Field Artillery.
PRESCOTT, ALBERT ERNEST, Temporary Major (Temporary Lieut.-Colonel), Royal Engineers.
PRESTON, CLASSON O'DRISCOLL, Major, Royal Field Artillery.
PRICHARD, WALTER CLAVEL HERBERT, Major (Temporary Lieut.-Colonel), Royal Engineers.
PRINCE, PEREGRINE, Major (Temporary Lieut.-Colonel), Shropshire Light Infantry.
PRIOR, EDWARD ROBERT SEYMOUR, M.C., Temporary Major (Acting Lieut.-Colonel), South Lancashire Regt.
PROCKTER, PERCY WILLIAM, Lieut. (Temporary Major), Army Service Corps.
PUDSEY, DENISON, Major, Reserve of Officers, Royal Field Artillery.
PUREY-CUST, RICHARD BROWNLOW, M.C., Capt. (Acting Major), Royal Field Artillery.

RADICE, ALFRED HUTTON, Major (Temporary Lieut.-Colonel), Gloucestershire Regt., South Wales Borderers.
RAIT KERR, ROWAN SCROPE, M.C., Capt. (Acting Major), Royal Engineers.
RAMBAUT, GERARD MARLAND, Capt., Royal Field Artillery.
RAMSAY, JAMES GORDON, Major, Cameron Highlanders.
RANSOME, ALGERNON LEE, M.C., Capt. and Brevet Major (Temporary Lieut.-Colonel), Dorsetshire Regt.
RAWLING, CECIL GODFREY, C.M.G., C.I.E., Major and Brevet Lieut.-Colonel (Temporary Brigadier-General), Somersetshire Light Infantry.
REA, JOHN GEORGE GREY, Capt., Yeomanry.
REEVES, ROBERT CLANMALIER, Major, Royal Field Artillery.
REID, CHARLES SAVILE, Major, Royal Engineers.
RENDELL, HENRY THOMAS, Lieut. (Temporary Major), Army Service Corps, Special Reserve.
REVELL, JOHN WALTER, Temporary Major, Royal Engineers.
RHODES, JOHN PHILLIP, Capt. (Acting Major), Royal Engineers.
RICH, ERNEST EVELYN, Major, Royal Horse Artillery.
RICHARDS, JOHN FREDERICK GWYTHER, M.B., Temporary Capt., Royal Army Medical Corps.
RICKARDS, GERALD ARTHUR, M.C., Major, Royal Artillery.
RICHARDSON, GEORGE CARR, M.C., Major, Royal Artillery.
RIDDELL, ROBERT BUCHANAN, Lieut.-Colonel, Royal Garrison Artillery.
RITCHIE, THE HON. HAROLD, Temporary Major, Scottish Rifles.
ROBERTSON, COLIN McLEOD, Lieut.-Colonel, Royal Garrison Artillery, Royal Field Artillery.
ROBERTSON, FRANK MANSFIELD BOILEAU, Major, Royal Highlanders.
ROBERTSON, WILLIAM CAIRNES, Major, Royal Garrison Artillery.
ROBERTSON-EUSTACE, ROBERT WILLIAM BARRINGTON, Capt., East African Forces.
ROBINSON, ANNESLEY CRAVEN, Major (Temporary Lieut.-Colonel), Army Service Corps.
ROBINSON, JOHN ARMSTRONG PUREFOY, Major (Acting Lieut.-Colonel), Royal Garrison Artillery.
ROBINSON, THOMAS CHAMBERS, Major (Temporary Lieut.-Colonel), East Lancashire Regt.
ROCKE, CYRIL EDMUND ALAN SPENCER, Major, Irish Guards.
ROFFEY, HAROLD BOWYER, Major (Acting Lieut.-Colonel), Lancashire Fusiliers.
ROFFEY, MYLES HERBERT, Temporary Major, Welsh Regt.
ROGERS, WALTER LACY YEA, Major, Royal Horse Artillery.
ROLLS, NORMAN THOMAS, Temporary Major (Acting Lieut.-Colonel), Royal West Surrey Regt.
ROME, CLAUDE STUART, Major and Brevet Lieut.-Colonel (Temporary Brigadier-General), 11th Hussars.
ROOKE, EVERARD HOWE, Major (Acting Lieut.-Colonel), Royal Engineers.
ROPER, EDWARD RIDGILL, M.C., Capt. (Acting Major), Royal Field Artillery.
ROSS, ROBERT KNOX, M.C., Capt., Royal West Surrey Regt.
ROTHWELL, WILLIAM EDWARD, Major (Temporary Lieut.-Colonel), Royal Inniskilling Fusiliers.
ROWE, WILFRED BARTON, Major, Royal Garrison Artillery.
ROWLEY, FRANK GEORGE MATHIAS, C.M.G., Lieut.-Colonel (Temporary Brigadier-General), Middlesex Regt.
RUSSELL, ALBERT, Lieut. (Temporary Major), Royal Engineers.
RUSSELL, BRUCE BREMNER, Colonel, Retired Pay, Reserve of Officers.
RUSSELL, NOEL HUNSLEY CAMPBELL, Major, Retired Pay, Leinster Regt., Special Reserve, and Worcestershire Yeomanry.
RUSSELL, WILLIAM MALCOLM, Temporary Major (Honorary Lieut. in Army), General List.
RUST, WILLIAM THOMAS CUTLER, Major, Army Service Corps.
RYAN, HUGH THOMAS, Major, Army Veterinary Corps.
RYCROFT, JULIAN NEIL OSCAR, M.C., Capt., Royal Highlanders.
SALT, HAROLD FRANCIS, Major (Temporary Lieut.-Colonel), Royal Artillery.
SARSON, EDWARD VIPAN, Major (Acting Lieut.-Colonel), Royal Field Artillery.
SCHUSTER, LIONEL ROBERT, Major, Liverpool Regt.
SCOTHERN, ALBERT EDWARD, Temporary Major (Acting Lieut.-Colonel), Nottinghamshire and Derbyshire Regt.
SCOTT, JOHN DAVIE, Capt. (Acting Major), Royal Irish Regt.
SCOTT, JOHN WALTER LENNOX, Capt. (Acting Lieut.-Colonel), Royal Army Medical Corps.
SCOTT-ELLIOT, WILLIAM, Major (Temporary Lieut.-Colonel), Army Service Corps.
SEARIGHT, HUGH FORDE, Major, 1st Dragoon Guards, Reserve of Officers, Retired Pay.
SEARLE, FRANK, Temporary Major (Temporary Lieut.-Colonel), Tank Corps.
SELLAR, THOMAS BYRNE, C.M.G., Major (Temporary Lieut.-Colonel), late Reserve of Officers, King's Own Scottish Borderers.
SETH-SMITH, HUGH GARDEN, Capt. (Temporary Major), Army Service Corps.
SETTLE, REGINALD HENRY NAPIER, M.C., Capt. (Temporary Major), 19th Hussars.
SEYMOUR, EVELYN FRANCIS EDWARD, Major (Acting Lieut.-Colonel), Royal Dublin Fusiliers.
SEYS, ROGER CECIL, Major, Royal Artillery.
SHAKESPEAR, ARTHUR TALBOT, M.C., Capt. (Acting Major), Royal Engineers.
SHAKESPEAR, GEORGE FREDERICK CORTLAND, M.C., Capt. and Brevet Major, Indian Army.
SHARPE, CHARLES SCHMIDT, Major (Temporary Lieut.-Colonel), York and Lancaster Regt.
SHAW, WILLIAM, Temporary Major, Army Service Corps.

SHEA, HENRY FRANCIS, M.B., Major (Temporary Lieut.-Colonel), Royal Army Medical Corps.
SHEARMAN, CHARLES EDWARD GOWRAN, M.C., Capt., Bedfordshire Regt.
SHEBBEARE, ROBERT AUSTIN, Temporary Major, Army Service Corps.
SHERSTON, JOHN REGINALD VIVIAN, M.C., Capt., Cavalry, Indian Army.
SHORTHOSE, WILLIAM JOHN TOWNSEND, Capt. (Temporary Major), South Staffordshire Regt. and King's African Rifles.
SIMONDS, CECIL BARROW, Major (Temporary Lieut.-Colonel), Reserve of Officers, Royal Garrison Artillery.
SIMPSON, WILLIAM ARTHUR JOHN, M.C., Capt. (Acting Major), Royal Field Artillery.
SIMSON, JAMES ROBERT, Major (Temporary Lieut.-Colonel), Highland Light Infantry.
SINCLAIR, REV. PATRICK, M.A., Chaplain to the Forces, Second Class, Army Chaplains' Department.
SKINNER, ALEXANDER BAIRD, Major, Cavalry, Indian Army.
SKINNER, EDMUND WILLIAM, Quartermaster and Honorary Major, Lincolnshire Regt.
SLAYTER, EDWARD WHEELER, C.M.G., Lieut.-Colonel (Temporary Colonel), Royal Army Medical Corps.
SLOGGETT, ARTHUR JOHN HENRY, Major (Acting Lieut.-Colonel), Rifle Brigade.
SMEATHMAN, LOVELL FRANCIS, M.C., Capt. (Temporary Lieut.-Colonel), Hertfordshire Regt.
SMITH, ARTHUR FRANCIS, M.C., Capt., Coldstream Guards.
SMITH, ISHAM PERCY, Capt. (Acting Major), Royal Garrison Artillery.
SMITH, WILLIAM SELWYN, Capt., Royal Field Artillery.
SMYTH, GERALD JAMES WATT, Major (Temporary Lieut.-Colonel), Royal Engineers.
SMYTH, HENRY, Lieut.-Colonel, Cheshire Regt.
SMYTH, GEORGE ABRAHAM, Lieut.-Colonel, Royal Field Artillery.
SMYTHE, RUPERT CÆSAR, Major (Temporary Lieut.-Colonel), Royal Inniskilling Fusiliers.
SOMERVAIL, WILLIAM FULTON, M.C., Lieut. (Acting Lieut.-Colonel), Scottish Rifles.
SOTHEBY, HERBERT GEORGE, Capt., Argyll and Sutherland Highlanders, Special Reserve.
SPENCER, CHARLES LOUIS, Lieut.-Colonel, Royal Engineers.
SPENS, HUGH BAIRD, Capt. (Acting Lieut.-Colonel), Scottish Rifles.
SPEYER, ALFRED WILLIAM, Temporary Capt., General List, late West Yorkshire Regt., Special Reserve.
STALLARD, SIDNEY, Capt. (Temporary Lieut.-Colonel), London Regt.
STAMFORD, ALFRED RICHARD, Honorary Capt. (Acting Honorary Major), Army Ordnance Department.
STANLEY, THE HON. OLIVER HUGH, Major (Acting Lieut.-Colonel), Reserve of Officers, Royal Artillery.
STANLEY, WILLIAM ALAN, Temporary Major, Machine Gun Corps.
STANLEY-CLARKE, ARTHUR CHRISTOPHER LANCELOT, Capt. (Temporary Lieut.-Colonel), Scottish Rifles.
ST. CLAIR, WILLIAM LOCKHART, Major, Royal Field Artillery.
STEELE, WILLIAM JONES, Temporary Major, Royal Engineers.
STEPHENSON, ARTHUR, M.C., Temporary Lieut.-Colonel, Royal Scots.
STEPHENSON, HENRY KENYON, Lieut.-Colonel, Royal Field Artillery.
STEWARD, CHARLES KNOWLES, M.C., Capt., South Wales Borderers.
STEWART, ALBERT LEWIS, Temporary Major, Machine Gun Corps.
STEWART, WILLIAM MURRAY, Major (Temporary Lieut.-Colonel), Cameron Highlanders.
STEWART, WALTER ROBERT, M.C., Capt. and Brevet Major (Temporary Lieut.-Colonel), Rifle Brigade.
STIRLING, ALEXANDER DICKSON, M.B., Capt., Royal Army Medical Corps.
STIRLING, COLIN ROBERT, HOSTE, M.C., Capt., Scottish Rifles.
STIRLING, WALTER ANDREW, M.C., Major, Royal Artillery.
ST. JOHN, WILLIAM EUSTACE, Major, Yeomanry.
ST. HILL, ASHTON ALEXANDER, Major (Temporary Lieut.-Colonel), West Riding Regt.
STOBART, HUGH MORTON, Capt. (Hon. Lieut.-Colonel) (Temporary Lieut.-Colonel), Yeomanry.
STOKES, ADRIAN, M.D., F.R.C.S., Temporary Capt., Royal Army Medical Corps.
STONEY, HENRY HOWARD, Capt. (Acting Lieut.-Colonel), North Staffordshire Regt.
STROVER, MARTYN ROGERS, Major, Royal Garrison Artillery.
STRUTT, EDWARD LISLE, Major (Temporary Lieut.-Colonel), Royal Scots, Special Reserve.
STUDD, FRANCIS CYRIL RUPERT, Major (Temporary Lieut.-Colonel), East Kent Regt.
STURT, MONTAGUE ALFRED SLINEY, Temporary Major, Army Service Corps.
SWINTON, CHARLES WILLIAM, Lieut.-Colonel, Royal Garrison Artillery.
SYMONDS, WILLIAM FREDERICK JOHN, Major (Acting Lieut.-Colonel), London Regt.
SWANN, HENRY LESLIE ALDERSEY, Temporary Major, Army Service Corps.
TAGG, ERNEST JOHN BOCART, Capt., Royal Marine Light Infantry.
TAYLOR, BRUCE MITCHELL, M.C., Temporary Second Lieut. (Acting Capt.), Duke of Cornwall's Light Infantry.
TAYLOR, CHARLES LANCASTER, Major (Acting Lieut.-Colonel), South Wales Borderers.
TAYLOR, GENLEIGH JOHN SCHILL, Major (Acting Lieut.-Colonel), Royal Field Artillery.
TAYLOR, GEORGE PRITCHARD, M.C., M.B., Capt. (Acting Lieut.-Colonel), Royal Army Medical Corps.

The Distinguished Service Order

TAYLOR, HENRY JEFFREYS, Major (Temporary Lieut.-Colonel), Durham Light Infantry.
TEALL, GEORGE HARRIS, Capt., Lincolnshire Regt.
TEMPLE, RICHARD DURAND, Capt. and Brevet Major (Temporary Lieut.-Colonel), Worcestershire Regt., Special Reserve.
THOMAS, JAMES HUGH, M.B., Capt., Royal Army Medical Corps.
THOMAS, HENRY MELVILLE, C.M.G., Lieut.-Colonel, Royal Artillery.
THOMAS, BASIL, Temporary Major, Gloucestershire Regt.
THOMPSON, ALBERT CHARLES, Temporary Lieut.-Colonel, Royal Dublin Fusiliers.
THOMPSON, CLAUDE ERNEST, M.C., Temporary Lieut. (Temporary Capt.), South Lancashire Regt.
THOMPSON, CYRIL HENRY FARRER, Major, London Regt. (Christian name corrected to Cecil Henry Farrer [London Gazette, 8 March, 1918]).
THOMPSON, JAMES GEORGE COULTHERED, Major, Royal Field Artillery (Christian name Coulthered corrected to Coultherd [London Gazette, 18 Feb. 1918]).
THOMPSON, WILLIAM IRWIN, M.B., Capt. (Temporary Lieut.-Colonel), Royal Army Medical Corps.
THOMSON, GEORGE, M.C., Capt. (Acting Major), Yorkshire Light Infantry.
THORNEYCROFT, GEORGE EDWARD MERVYN, Major, Royal Artillery.
THORNHILL, CUDBERT JOHN MASSEY, Major, Indian Army.
THORP, ARTHUR HUGH, Lieut.-Colonel, Royal Garrison Artillery.
THORP, JOHN CLAUDE, Lieut.-Colonel, Reserve of Officers, Army Ordnance Department.
TILLETT, ALEXANDER, M.C., Lieut. (Acting Lieut.-Colonel), Devonshire Regt.
TOMES, CLEMENT THURSTAN, M.C., Major, Royal Warwickshire Regt.
TOMLIN, JULIAN LATHAM, Capt. (Acting Major), Royal Engineers.
TOWSEY, FRANCIS WILLIAM, C.M.G., Lieut.-Colonel (Temporary Brigadier-General), West Yorkshire Regt.
TRAILL, EDMUND FRANCIS TARLTON, Major (Temporary Lieut.-Colonel), Army Service Corps.
TRIMBLE, JOHN BRERETON OWST, M.C., Major (Acting Lieut.-Colonel), Yorkshire Regt.
TROBRIDGE, FREDERICK GEORGE, Temporary Major, General List.
TUCK, GERALD LOUIS JOHNSON, Capt. (Temporary Major), Unattached List, attached Suffolk Regt.
TULLOCH, DONALD FIDDES, Lieut.-Colonel, Royal Artillery.
TURNER, CANNING, Major (Temporary Lieut.-Colonel), Leicestershire Regt., Special Reserve (Christian name corrected to Charles [London Gazette, 8 March, 1918]).
TURNER, REGINALD AUBREY, M.C., Capt. (Acting Major), Royal Engineers.
TWISS, CLIFFORD CHARLES HORACE, Temporary Capt. (Acting Major), East Yorkshire Regt
TYNDALE, WENTWORTH FRANCIS, C.M.G., M.D., Major (Acting Lieut.-Colonel), Royal Army Medical Corps.
TYRRELL, WILLIAM, M.C., M.B., Capt. (Acting Lieut.-Colonel), Royal Army Medical Corps, Special Reserve.
UBSDELL, THURLO RICHARDSON, Major, Reserve of Officers, late Royal Artillery.
UNTHANK, JOHN SALUSBURY, Major (Temporary Lieut.-Colonel), Durham Light Infantry.
URQUHART, JAMES ALASTAIR BERRY, Lieut. (Temporary Capt.), Royal Garrison Artillery.
VALLINGS, REV. GEORGE ROSS, Temporary Chaplain to the Forces, Fourth Class (Temporary Chaplain to the Forces, Third Class), Army Chaplains' Department.
VERNEY, SIR HARRY CALVERT WILLIAMS, Bart., Temporary Capt. Temporary Lieut.-Colonel), General List.
VERNEY, LEONARD MORRIS, F.R.C.V.S., Major, Army Veterinary Corps.
VICKERS, GEORGE EDWARD, Quartermaster and Honorary Major, Manchester Regt.
VILLIERS, OLIVER G. G., Lieut., Royal Naval Volunteer Reserve, attached Royal Naval Air Service.
VILLIERS-STUART, PATRICK, Major (Acting Lieut.-Colonel), Royal Fusiliers (rank corrected to Temporary Lieut.-Colonel [London Gazette, 8 March, 1918]).
WAGGETT, ERNEST BLECHYNDEN, M.B., Major, Royal Army Medical Corps.
WAINEWRIGHT, ARTHUR REGINALD, Lieut.-Colonel, Royal Artillery.
WAITHMAN, ROLAND HENRY, Major (Acting Lieut.-Colonel), Royal Sussex Regt.
WALKER, GEORGE GOOLD, M.C., Temporary Capt. (Acting Major), Royal Garrison Artillery.
WALLACE, CHARLES JOHN, M.C., Capt. and Brevet Major, Highland Light Infantry.
WALLER, JAMES HARDRESS DE WARRENNE, Temporary Capt., Royal Engineers.
WALTERS, HUBERT DE LANSEY, Major (Temporary Lieut.-Colonel), Royal Garrison Artillery.
WARD, HAROLD MATHIAS ARTHUR, Major, Royal Garrison Artillery.
WARD, JOSEPH, Major (Acting Lieut.-Colonel), Royal Army Medical Corps.
WARE, GEORGE WILLIAM WEBB, M.B., Major, Royal Army Medical Corps.
WARING, HENRY ARCHIBALD, Major (Acting Lieut.-Colonel), Royal West Kent Regt.
WARREN, LIONEL EDWARD, Major (Acting Lieut.-Colonel), Royal Field Artillery.
WARRENS, EDWARD ROBERT CABELL, Major, Royal Field Artillery.
WARWICK, PHILIP HUSKINSON, Major, Yeomanry.
WAY, JAMES, M.C., Major, Royal Artillery.
WAYMAN, HARRY REGINALD BLAND, Temporary Major (Acting Lieut.-Colonel), Northumberland Fusiliers.
WAYTE, ADRIAN BARCLAY, Major, Nottinghamshire and Derbyshire Regt.

WEBB, WALTER EDWARD, Quartermaster and Honorary Major, London Regt.
WEEKS, RONALD MORCE, M.C., Capt., South Lancashire Regt.
WELLS, BARRINGTON CLEMENT, Major (Acting Lieut.-Colonel), Essex Regt.
WEST, RICHARD ANNESLEY, Capt., Yeomanry.
WESTROPP, FREDERICK MALCOLM, Lieut.-Colonel, Royal Engineers.
WHALLEY, FREDERICK, M.B., Major (Temporary Lieut.-Colonel), Royal Army Medical Corps.
WHELDON, WYNN POWELL, Temporary Major, Royal Welsh Fusiliers.
WHETHERLY, WILLIAM STOBART, Major, Hussars.
WHITAKER, ARTHUR PERCY DUNCOMBE, Capt. (Temporary Major), Army Service Corps.
WHITE, CHARLES RICHARDSON, M.B., Major (Temporary Lieut.-Colonel), Royal Army Medical Corps.
WHITE, FRANK AUGUSTIN KINDER, Major and Brevet Lieut.-Colonel, Royal Engineers.
WHITE, NOEL BLANCO, M.C., Temporary Lieut. (Acting Capt.), General List.
WHITE, THE HONOURABLE ROBERT, C.M.G., Major and Brevet Lieut.-Colonel (Temporary Brigadier-General), Reserve of Officers.
WHITEHEAD, EDMUND L'ESTRANGE, Lieut.-Colonel, Royal Artillery.
WHITEHEAD, HECTOR FRASER, Temporary Major (Acting Lieut.-Colonel), East Lancashire Regt.
WHITLEY, EDWARD NATHAN, C.M.G., Lieut.-Colonel (Temporary Brigadier-General), Royal Artillery.
WHITTING, EVERARD LE GRICE, M.C., Major, Royal Artillery.
WHITTINGTON, ALAN RODERICK, Temporary Major, Army Service Corps.
WHYTE, WILLIAM HENRY, Lieut. (Temporary Major, Acting Lieut.-Colonel), Reserve of Officers, Royal Dublin Fusiliers.
WILBERFORCE, HAROLD HARTLEY, Capt. (Temporary Lieut.-Colonel), Army Service Corps.
WILDBLOOD, EDWARD HAROLD, Major (Acting Lieut.-Colonel), Leinster Regt.
WILKINS, CYRIL FRANCIS, M.C., Lieut., Royal Irish Rifles.
WILKINSON, HARRIS VAUGHAN, Temporary Major, Machine Gun Corps.
WILLCOCKS, JAMES LUGARD, M.C., Capt., Royal Highlanders.
WILLCOX, HENRY BERESFORD DENNITTS, M.C., Capt., Nottinghamshire and Derbyshire Regt.
WILLIAMS, GEORGE ARTHUR SECCOMBE, Major, South Staffordshire Regt. (Special Reserve).
WILLIAMS, HERBERT MAINWARING, Major, Army Veterinary Corps.
WILLIAMS, REV. RONALD CHARLES LAMBERT, Chaplain to the Forces, Third Class, Army Chaplains' Department.
WILLOCK, FREDERICK GEORGE, Lieut.-Colonel, Royal Field Artillery.
WILSON, ALBERT EDWARD JACOB, Major, Somersetshire Light Infantry.
WILSON, DONALD CLITHEROE, Major, Royal Field Artillery.
WILSON, DOUGLAS HAMILTON, Temporary Capt. (Temporary Lieut.-Colonel), General List.
WINDER, JAMES HERBERT ROCHE, M.D., Major (Acting Lieut.-Colonel), Royal Army Medical Corps.
WINCH, GORDON BLUETT, Capt. (Temporary Major), Royal Field Artillery.
WINGATE, GODFREY HAROLD FENTON, Major and Brevet Lieut.-Colonel (Temporary Lieut.-Colonel), Royal Scots.
WINTER, ERNEST ARTHUR, M.C., Temporary Lieut.-Colonel, Royal Fusiliers.
WITHYCOMBE, WILLIAM MAUNDER, C.M.G., Lieut.-Colonel (Temporary Brigadier-General), Yorkshire Light Infantry.
WOOD, JAMES, Major (Temporary Lieut.-Colonel), Royal Army Medical Corps.
WOODCOCK, WILFRED JAMES, Capt. (Temporary Lieut.-Colonel), Lancashire Fusiliers, Special Reserve (Capt., Reserve of Officers, late Lancashire Fusiliers).
WOODS, WILLIAM TALBOT, M.C., Capt., Manchester Regt.
WORDSWORTH, ROBERT JAMES, Major, Nottinghamshire and Derbyshire Regt.
WORRALL, PERCY REGINALD, M.C., Major (Acting Lieut.-Colonel), Devonshire Regt.
WORRALL, STEPHEN HENRY, Major (Acting Lieut.-Colonel), Border Regt.
WRIGHT, ANDREW RAE, M.B., Capt. (Acting Lieut.-Colonel), Royal Army Medical Corps.
WRIGHT, HUBERT HOWARD, Major, Army Service Corps.
WRIGHT, WALLACE DUFFIELD, V.C., C.M.G., Major and Brevet Lieut.-Colonel, Royal West Surrey Regt.
WRIGHT, WILLIAM OSWALD, Major, Royal Lancashire Regt.
WROUGHTON, ARTHUR OLIVER BIRD, Lieut.-Colonel, Royal Army Medical Corps.
WYLD, JASPER WILLIAM GEORGE, M.C., Capt., Oxfordshire and Buckinghamshire Light Infantry.
WYLLY, GUY GEORGE EGERTON, V.C., Major, Indian Army.
WYNNE-EYTON, CHARLES SANDFORD, Temporary Major, General List and Royal Flying Corps.
YATES, CECIL McGRIGOR, Major, Royal Artillery.
YATES, ROBERT JAMES BURTON, Cavalry, Indian Army.
YORK, RICHARD LISTER, Major, Royal Field Artillery.
YOUNGER, ARTHUR ALLAN SHAKESPEAR, Major (Acting Lieut.-Colonel), Royal Field Artillery.

AUSTRALIAN FORCE.

BARTON, ALAN SINCLAIR DURVALL, Major, Army Medical Corps (Christian name Durvall corrected to Darvall [London Gazette, 7 Feb. 1918]).
BIRD, THOMAS HAROLD, Major, Light Horse Regt.
BLACK, JAMES JAMISON, Lieut.-Colonel, Army Medical Corps.
BRAZENOR, WILLIAM, Lieut.-Colonel, Infantry.

BRIDGES, WILLIAM FRANCIS NOEL, Major, Infantry.
BURSTON, SAMUEL ROY, Lieut.-Colonel, Army Medical Corps.
CADE, DAVID DUNCAN, Major, Army Medical Corps.
CARTER, HERBERT GORDON, Lieut.-Colonel, Pioneer Battalion.
CASEY, RICHARD GARDINER, M.C., Major, Infantry.
CHAPMAN, CLEMENT LORNE, Major, Army Medical Corps.
CHISHOLM, ALEXANDER, Major, Light Horse Regt.
CHURCHUS, WALTER, Major, Field Artillery.
CONNELLY, ERIC WINFIELD, Major, Infantry.
CORLETTE, JAMES MONTAGUE CHRISTIAN, Temporary Lieut.-Colonel, Engineers.
CORRIGAN, JOHN JOSEPH, Major, Infantry.
DAVID, TANNATT WILLIAM EDGEWORTH, C.M.G., Major, Engineers.
DAVIDSON, WILLIAM JOHN STEVENS, Lieut.-Colonel, Field Artillery.
DOWNEY, MICHAEL HENRY, Lieut.-Colonel, Army Medical Corps.
DOWSE, RICHARD, Lieut.-Colonel, Staff.
BROCKMAN, EDMUND ALFRED DRAKE, C.M.G., Lieut.-Colonel, Infantry.
DUGGAN, BERNARD OSCAR CHARLES, Lieut.-Colonel, Infantry.
EDWARDS, PERCY MALCOLM, Major (Temporary Lieut.-Colonel), Field Artillery.
FARQUHAR, WILLIAM GORDON, Major, Engineers.
FORD, HUBERT CEDRIC, Major, Infantry.
FFRENCH, WILLIAM REGINALD ROGERS, M.C., Major, Machine Gun Corps.
GATLIFF, VIVIAN HAROLD, Major, Field Artillery.
GEE, RICHARD STEWART, Major, Field Artillery.
GLOVER, HENRY JAMES HILL, Capt. (Temporary Major), Field Artillery.
GODDARD, HENRY ARTHUR, Lieut.-Colonel, Infantry.
HARDIE, JOHN LESLIE, Major, General List.
HENRY, JAMES DOUGLAS, Major, Engineers.
HERROD, ERNEST EDWARD, Lieut.-Colonel, Infantry.
HENDERSON, WILLIAM ALEXANDER, Lieut.-Colonel, Pioneer Battn.
HENRY, MAX, Major, Army Veterinary Corps.
HOLMES, BASIL, Major, Infantry.
JOBSON, ALEXANDER, Colonel, Infantry.
KERR, ROBERT, Major, Provost Corps.
KING, WILLIAM SELWYN, Major, Army Service Corps.
KING, GIFFARD HAMILTON MACARTHUR, C.M.G., Lieut.-Colonel, Field Artillery.
JACKSON, ROBERT EDWARD. Major (Temporary Lieut.-Colonel), Infantry (rank corrected from Major (Temporary Lieut.-Colonel) to Lieut.-Colonel [London Gazette, 7 Feb. 1918]).
LAVARACK, JOHN DUDLEY, Lieut.-Colonel, Artillery.
LAWSON, FREDERICK WASHINGTON, Major, Engineers.
MACARTNEY, HENRY DUNDAS KEITH, Lieut.-Colonel, Field Artillery.
McCORMACK, PATRICK JOHN, Major, Field Artillery.
McGREGOR, ROY STANLEY, Major, Army Medical Corps.
McKENZIE, LOUIS EVANDER, Major, Army Veterinary Corps.
MINAGALL, CHARLES FRANCIS, Quartermaster and Honorary Major, Infantry.
MITCHELL, JOHN WESLEY, Lieut.-Colonel, Infantry.
MOORE, DAVID HENRY, Major (Temporary Lieut.-Colonel), Field Artillery.
MOSELEY, ARTHUR HENRY, Lieut.-Colonel, Army Medical Corps.
MULLIGAN, EDRIC NOEL, Australian Engineers.
NEWLAND, HENRY SIMPSON, Lieut.-Colonel, Army Medical Corps.
NORRIE, EDWARD CREER, Lieut.-Colonel, Infantry.
OLDING, EDWIN ANDREW, Major, Field Artillery.
POWER, JOHN JOSEPH, Major, Army Medical Corps.
RALPH, EDGAR MAURICE, Lieut.-Colonel, General List.
READ, GEORGE ARTHUR, Lieut.-Colonel, Infantry.
RICHARDSON, JOHN DALYELL, Major, Light Horse Regt.
RIGGALL, HAROLD WILLIAM, Major (Temporary Lieut.-Colonel), Field Artillery.
ROWE, SEPTIMUS GODOLPHIN, Major, Field Artillery.
SCOTT, EDWARD IRVINE CHARLES, Major, Pioneer Battn. (Christian name Irvine corrected to Irwin [London Gazette, 7 Feb. 1918]).
SHANNON, HERBERT JAMES, Major, Light Horse Regt.
SHELLSHEAR, JOSEPH LEXDEN, Lieut.-Colonel, Field Artillery.
SLANE, JAMES CHARLES FRANCIS, Lieut.-Colonel, Infantry.
SMITH, DUDLEY WALLACE ARABIN, Major, Light Horse Regt.
SMITH, WILLIAM, Major (Temporary Lieut.-Colonel), Provost Corps.
STANSFIELD, WILLIAM, Lieut.-Colonel, Army Service Corps.
STEWART, JOHN MITCHELL YOUNG, Lieut.-Colonel, Army Medical Corps.
TAYLOR, HAROLD BOURNE, Major, Field Artillery.
THWAITES, ALEXANDER HOPKINS, Lieut.-Colonel, Army Medical Service.
TOZER, CLAUDE JOHN, Major, Army Medical Corps.
VERNON, HUGH VENABLES, Lieut.-Colonel, Field Artillery.
WASSELL, CHARLES ERNEST, Temporary Lieut.-Colonel, Army Medical Corps (rank corrected from Temporary Lieut.-Colonel to Lieut.-Colonel [London Gazette, 7 Feb, 1918]).
WILLIAMS, ERNEST MORGAN, Lieut.-Colonel, Light Horse Regt.
WILLIAMS, HENRY JAMES, Major, Army Medical Corps.
WILTON, ERIC ARUNDEL, Major, Machine Gun Corps.
WOODS, PERCY WILLIAM, M.C., Lieut.-Colonel, Infantry.
WOOLCOCK, ARTHUR RAFF, Lieut.-Colonel, Infantry.

CANADIAN FORCE.

ALDERSON, FREDERICK JACKSON, Major, Field Artillery.
ALLEN, CARLETON WOODFORD, Lieut.-Colonel, Pioneer Battn.
ANDERSON, ALEXANDER ALDERSON, Major, Engineers.
ANDERSON, THOMAS VICTOR, Major (Acting Lieut.-Colonel), Engineers.
BAZIN, ALFRED TURNER, Major (Acting Lieut.-Colonel), Army Medical Corps.
BELL, PERCY GEORGE, Major (Acting Lieut.-Colonel), Army Medical Corps.
BENNETT, CHARLES CORBISHLEY, Major, Infantry.
BICKEADIKE, ROBERT, Major, Infantry.
BUTTENSHAW, ALFRED SIDNEY, Major, Ordnance Corps.
CAMPBELL, GLEN, Lieut.-Colonel, Pioneer Battn.
CLARK, ROBERT PERCY, M.C., Lieut.-Colonel, Infantry.
CLARKE, FREDERICK FIELDHOUSE, Lieut.-Colonel, Railway Troops.
CLINE, GEORGE ALTON, Major, Engineers.
COGHLAN, FREDERICK THOMAS, Major (Acting Lieut.-Colonel), Field Artillery.
CORNWALL, JAMES KENNEDY, Lieut.-Colonel, Railway Troops.
CRAWFORD, IAN LAURICE, Major, Infantry (Christian name corrected to Ian Laurie).
DAVEY, JAMES EDGAR, Lieut.-Colonel, Army Medical Corps.
DICKSON, CHARLES HAROLD, Lieut.-Colonel, Army Medical Corps.
DONALDSON, ROBERT LOGGIE MASTERSON, Major, Ordnance Corps.
DONNELLY, JOHN BADENOCH, Lieut.-Colonel, Forestry Corps.
ELKINS, WILLIAM HENRY PFERINGER, Lieut.-Colonel, Horse Artillery.
ELMITT, THOMAS FRANCIS, Major, Infantry.
EWING, ROYAL LINDSAY HAMILTON, M.C., Temporary Major, Infantry.
FRASER, JAMES JOHNSTON, Major (Acting Lieut.-Colonel), Army Medical Corps.
GIBSON, THOMAS, Major, Labour Battn.
GOLDIE, EDWARD CROSBY, Major, Army Service Corps (regiment corrected to Engineers [London Gazette, 22 June, 1918]).
GRIFFIN, ATHOLL EDWIN, Lieut.-Colonel, Railway Troops.
GROSVENOR, THE HONOURABLE FRANCIS EGERTON, M.C., Temporary Major, Infantry.
HANSON, EDWIN GERALD, Lieut.-Colonel, Field Artillery.
HARRIS, EDWARD MONTGOMERY, Major, Army Service Corps.
HARRISON, WILLIAM HENRY, Lieut.-Colonel, Field Artillery.
HATCH, HARRY CECIL, Major, Infantry.
HERTZBERG, HALFDAN FENTON HARHOE, M.C., Major, Engineers.
HERVEY, CHILION LONGLEY, Lieut.-Colonel, Railway Troops.
HILL, CHARLES RAPELJE, Lieut.-Colonel, Infantry.
HYDE, WALTER COURT, Major, Field Artillery.
JOHNSTON, GEORGE CHALMERS, M.C., Lieut.-Colonel, Mounted Rifles.
KILLAM, GEORGE KNIGHT, Major, Infantry.
KING, CHARLES ERNEST, Major, Infantry.
LEASK, THOMAS McCRAE, Temporary Lieut.-Colonel, Army Medical Corps.
LINDSAY, WILLIAM BETHUNE, C.M.G., Lieut.-Colonel (Temporary Brigadier-General), Engineers.
LYNN, EDISON FRANKLIN, M.C., Major, Engineers.
McTAGGART, WILLIAM BRODER, Major, Field Artillery.
MACDONALD, DONALD JOHN, M.C., Major, Cavalry.
MACDONALD, JAMES BRODIE LAUDER, Lieut.-Colonel, Railway Troops.
McKEAN, FREDERICK THOMAS, Major, Army Service Corps.
MACKENDRICK, WILLIAM GORDON, Capt. (Acting Lieut.-Colonel), Engineers.
McPARLAND, JAMES FREDERICK, Major, Field Artillery.
MARTIN, CHARLES KIRWAN CRAWFORD, Lieut. (Temporary Capt.), Field Artillery (Christian name Crawford corrected to Craufurd [London Gazette, 8 March, 1918]).
MARTIN, LAWRENCE THOMAS, Lieut.-Colonel, Railway Troops.
MASSIE, ROBERT FRANK, Major, Field Artillery.
MAUND, ARTHUR CLINTON, Lieut. (Acting Major), Infantry and Royal Flying Corps.
MILLEN, LIONEL HERBERT, Lieut.-Colonel, Infantry.
MINCHIN, FREDERICK FRANK, M.C., Lieut. (Temporary Major), Infantry, attached Royal Flying Corps, Special Reserve.
MONTAGUE, PERCIVAL JOHN, M.C., Major (Temporary Lieut.-Colonel), Infantry.
MOODIE, WALTER HILL, Lieut.-Colonel, Railway Troops.
MORPHY, JOHN AUBREY, Major, Pioneer Battn.
MOTHERSILL, GEORGE SIDNEY, Major, Army Medical Corps.
MURPHY, THOMAS JOSEPH FRANCIS, Lieut.-Colonel, Army Medical Corps.
NEELAND, ROBERT HENRY, Temporary Capt. (Acting Lieut.-Colonel), Labour Corps.
O'DONAHOE DANIEL JEROME, Major, Infantry.
ORD, GARNET LEHRLE, Capt. (Acting Major), Pioneer Battn.
PARKINSON, RICHARD FRANCIS, Major, Infantry.
PEPLER, ERIC, Major, Engineers.
PETERS, CHARLES AYRE, Lieut.-Colonel (Temporary Colonel), Army Medical Corps.
PITMAN, JOHN DOWNEY, Capt. (Acting Major), Ordnance Corps.
POWELL, ALAN TORRENCE, Major, Infantry.
RAMSAY, KENNETH ALAN, Lieut. (Acting Lieut.-Colonel), Railway Troops (rank corrected to Captain (acting Lieut.-Colonel) [London Gazette, 8 March, 1918]).
RANKIN, JAMES SABISTON, Major, Infantry.

The Distinguished Service Order

REASON, CLIFFORD HAMILTON, Major (Temporary Lieut.-Colonel), Army Medical Corps.
REIRDON, WILLIAM ROY, Major, Field Artillery
RIPLEY, BLAIR, Lieut.-Colonel, Railway Troops.
RISPIN, DONALD EDWARD ALLAN, Major, Infantry.
ROGERS, ROBERT PERCY, Major, Engineers.
SCLATER, JAMES, Lieut.-Colonel, Infantry.
SCOTT, MORRIS ALEXANDER, Capt. (Temporary Major), Machine Gun Corps.
SHARPE, SAMUEL SIMPSON, Lieut.-Colonel, Infantry.
SILLS, JOHN HAM, Major, Infantry.
SMITH, HENRY DENNE ST. ALBAN, Major, Engineers.
STAYNER, RICHARD WINSLOW, M.C., Capt., Mounted Rifles.
STEWART, HENRY ARTHUR, Major, Army Service Corps.
STOCKWELL, CECIL VALENTINE, Major, Field Artillery.
SYER, JOSEPH MURRAY, Major, Field Artillery.
TAMBLYN, DAVID SOBEY, Capt. (Temporary Lieut.-Colonel), Army Veterinary Corps.
TROTTER, HAROLD LYNDRIDGE, Major, Engineers.
WHITE, JOHN BURTON, Lieut.-Colonel (Temporary Colonel), Forestry Corps.
WOODS, THE REV. ALBERT WILLIAM, Honorary Lieut.-Colonel, Chaplains' Service.

NEW ZEALAND FORCE.

ALLEN, STEPHEN SHEPHERD, Lieut.-Colonel, Infantry.
CAMERON, FREDERICK, M.B., Major, New Zealand Medical Corps.
CHARTERS, ALEXANDER BURNET, C.M.G., Lieut.-Colonel, Infantry.
ENNIS, WILLIAM OLIVER, Major, Pioneers.
GIBBS, DAVID JOHN, Major, Engineers.
GLENDINING, HALBERT CECIL, Major (Temporary Lieut.-Colonel), Field Artillery.
HULBERT, EDWARD JAMES, Major, Mounted Rifle Brigade.
McCARROLL, JAMES NEIL, Lieut.-Colonel, Mounted Rifles.
McCARE, JOHN, Major, Infantry (surname corrected to McCrae [London Gazette, 7 Feb, 1918]).
MITCHELL, GEORGE, Lieut.-Colonel, Infantry.
MURCHISON, DONALD SINCLAIR, Major, Mounted Rifles.
NEWMAN, CLARENCE NATHANIEL, Major, Field Artillery.
NEWTON, CHARLES TREWEEKI HAND, M.D., F.R.C.S., Lieut.-Colonel, New Zealand Medical Corps.
PUTTICK, EDWARD, Major (Temporary Lieut.-Colonel), Rifle Brigade.
RICHARDSON, HARRY McKELLOR WHITE, M.C., Temporary Major, Rifle Brigade.
RICHMOND, JAMES MACDONALD, M.C., Major, Field Artillery.
ROW, ROBERT AMOS, Lieut.-Colonel, Infantry.
STAFFORD, JAMES, Major, New Zealand Veterinary Corps.
STITT, ALAN DUNCAN, M.C., Major, Infantry.
VICKERMAN, HUGH, Major, Engineers.
WESTON, CLAUDE HORACE, Lieut.-Colonel, Infantry.

SOUTH AFRICAN FORCE.

BLEW, THOMAS HARRY, Temporary Lieut.-Colonel, Heavy Artillery.
CHRISTIAN, EWAN, Lieut.-Colonel, Infantry.
COLLINS, FRANCIS RICHARD, Temporary Lieut.-Colonel, Engineers.
HASELDEN, FRED, Major, Infantry.
LIEFELDT, THEOPHILUS EDWARD, Major, Native Labour Corps.
MULVEY, JOHN JAMES, Major, Pioneer Battn.
OWEN, HUGH BRINDLEY, M.B., Temporary Capt., Uganda Medical Service.
TANNER, WILLIAM ERNEST COLLINS, C.M.G., Brigadier-General, Infantry (rank corrected to Lieut.-Colonel [London Gazette, 8 March, 1918]).
TOMORY, DAVID MORRIS, Major, South African Medical Corps.
VINEY, CHARLES FREDERICK BERNARD, Capt. (Temporary Major), Mounted Rifles.
WARD, ARTHUR BLACKWOOD, M.B., Lieut.-Colonel, South African Medical Corps.
WILLIAMS, GILBERT NEVILLE, Temporary Lieut.-Colonel, South African Forces.

London Gazette, 1 Jan. 1918.—" Admiralty, 1 Jan. 1918. The King has been graciously pleased to give orders for the appointment of the undermentioned Officers to be Companions of the Distinguished Service Order, in recognition of their services in the prosecution of the war."

LE MARCHANT, EVELYN ROBERT, Vice-Admiral.
ALLENBY, REGINALD ARTHUR, M.V.O., Rear-Admiral.
TOWER, CYRIL EVERARD, Rear-Admiral.
FYLER, HERBERT ARTHUR STEVENSON, C.B., Rear-Admiral.
FELLOWES, PEREGRINE FORBES MORANT, Wing Commander, R.N.
RUNDLE, MARK, Engineer Commander, R.N.
MILLER, HUGH, Staff Paymaster (Acting Fleet Paymaster), R.N.
COOPER, HENRY, B.A., Staff Surgeon, R.N.
REDHEAD, CHARLES MAHON, R.D., Lieut.-Commander (Acting Capt.), Royal Naval Reserve.
SHOOK, ALEXANDER MACDONALD, Fleet Commander, D.S.C., Royal Naval Air Service.

To receive a Bar to the Distinguished Service Order:
MARSHALL, WILLIAM, D.S.O., R.D., Commander (Acting Capt.), Royal Naval Reserve.

London Gazette, 9 Jan. 1918.—" War Office, 9 Jan. 1918. With reference to the awards conferred as announced in the London Gazette, dated 26 Sept. 1917, the following are the statements of service for which the decorations were conferred. Awarded a Second Bar to the Distinguished Service Order."
HILL, GERALD VICTOR WILMOT, D.S.O., Capt. and Brevet Major (Temporary Lieut.-Colonel), Royal Irish Fusiliers. For conspicuous gallantry and devotion to duty when in command of his battalion in support. Seeing that the troops in front were held up, he at once decided to attack the enemy, in co-operation with another battalion, in order to gain high ground that was of great tactical importance. It was mainly owing to his personal gallantry and leadership that the attack of his battalion, which had to be conducted without the help of artillery, was successful, and the position gained.
(D.S.O. gazetted 14 Jan. 1916.)
(1st Bar gazetted 17 April, 1917.)

Awarded a Bar to the Distinguished Service Order:
BISHOP, WILLIAM AVERY, V.C., D.S.O., M.C., Lieut. (Temporary Capt.), Canadian Cavalry and Royal Flying Corps. For conspicuous gallantry and devotion to duty when engaging hostile aircraft. His consistent dash and great fearlessness have set a magnificent example to the pilots of his squadron. He has destroyed no less than 45 hostile machines within the past five months, frequently attacking enemy formations single-handed, and on all occasions displaying a fighting spirit and determination to get to close quarters with his opponents which have earned the admiration of all in contact with him.
(D.S.O. gazetted 18 June, 1917.)
BRAND, THE HONOURABLE ROGER, D.S.O., Capt. and Brevet Major (Acting Lieut.-Colonel), Rifle Brigade, Special Reserve. For conspicuous gallantry and devotion to duty. Finding that most of his Officers and N.C.O.'s had become casualties he went to the front line, and by his personal example and resolute bearing held his battalion together throughout the day in spite of shortage of ammunition and strong hostile counter-attacks. Although slightly wounded early in the day, he kept his grip on the fighting with tireless energy, and inspired all ranks by his courage and disregard of danger.
(D.S.O. gazetted 3 June, 1916.)
CLAY, BERTIE GORDON, D.S.O., Major and Brevet Lieut.-Colonel (Temporary Lieut.-Colonel), Dragoon Guards. For conspicuous gallantry and devotion to duty when commanding his battalion in support of an attack. Seeing that the leading troops were held up, and had not gained the important position which was their objective, he at once decided to co-operate with another battalion and attack the enemy. By this prompt and decisive action at a critical moment high ground of the greatest tactical importance was won, and the success of the attack (which had to be conducted without the aid of artillery) was mainly due to the personal gallantry and ability with which Lieut.-Colonel Clay led his battalion.
(D.S.O. gazetted 20 Oct. 1916.)
CORFE, ARTHUR CECIL, D.S.O., Major (Temporary Lieut.-Colonel), South African Defence Force. For conspicuous gallantry and devotion to duty when in command of his battalion. By the prompt and skilful measures which he took on encountering serious opposition, he was able to attain his objective, and by his personal example and cheerfulness the moral of his men was maintained during a very trying period and under most adverse weather conditions.
(D.S.O. gazetted 4 June, 1917.)
DAUBENY, GILES BULTEEL, D.S.O., Major, Royal Garrison Artillery. For conspicuous gallantry and devotion to duty. During an extremely critical period when the situation was by no means clear, he kept up continual fire with his battery and rendered invaluable support to the infantry, although his brigade was exposed to constant and heavy fire and suffering many casualties for two days. His behaviour during this period was beyond praise, and it was in a great measure due to his coolness, courage and personality that fire was kept up.
(D.S.O. gazetted 14 Nov. 1916.)
DENNIS, MICHAEL FREDERICK BEAUCHAMP, D.S.O., Temporary Major (Acting Lieut.-Colonel), King's Own Scottish Borderers. For conspicuous gallantry and devotion to duty. Although wounded in the back by shrapnel, he refused to leave the battlefield, but continued to lead his battalion with the utmost gallantry and disregard of danger, rallying men who had been driven back by hostile counter-attacks and setting a personal example which enabled his battalion to hold their line.
(D.S.O. gazetted 4 Nov. 1915.)
FINCH, LIONEL HUGH KNIGHTLEY, D.S.O., Capt. (Temporary Lieut.-Colonel), Cheshire Regt. For conspicuous gallantry and devotion to duty. Prior to an assault his battalion sustained considerable casualties. Undeterred by these losses, however, he drew up and rehearsed his plans for assembly with the greatest care. During the assault the battalion sustained further heavy casualties, but this officer led the survivors with brilliant initiative and the utmost gallantry in an attack upon an enemy strong point, which he captured, killing or taking prisoners all the garrison. He then pushed his outpost line out and got into touch with the battalions on his flank, making complete dispositions for his advance. He was badly wounded at the end of the day, having set a personal example of fearlessness and fine leadership to which the excellent performance of his battalion was largely due.
(D.S.O. gazetted 1 Jan. 1917.)
GORT, VISCOUNT, JOHN STANDISH SURTEES PRENDERGAST, M.V.O., D.S.O., M.C., Capt. and Brevet Major (Acting Lieut.-Colonel), Grenadier Guards. For conspicuous gallantry and devotion to duty. Although hit in two places in the shoulder by the bursting of a shell early in the day and in great pain, he refused to leave his battalion, and personally superintended the consolidation subsequent to a successful attack. He remained with them until five p.m. on the following day, when he was ordered to come out and have his wounds dressed. His conduct set a very fine example of self-sacrifice, and was of great value in maintaining the high morale and offensive spirit of his battalion.
(D.S.O. gazetted 4 June, 1917.)
HANBURY-SPARROW, ARTHUR ALAN HANBURY, D.S.O., M.C., Capt. (Acting Lieut.-Colonel), Royal Berkshire Regt. For conspicuous gallantry and devotion to duty in an action. When the objective was reached he personally superintended the consolidation of the front line. He continued to hold his line with a force of mixed units until his flank became exposed and he was compelled to withdraw. He rallied his men, organized a new defensive line, and held on until relieved. Throughout the day he set a splendid example to all ranks of self-sacrifice and resolute determination, and by his soldier-like bearing encouraged everyone. He exposed himself fearlessly, and it was due to his magnificent courage that the enemy counter-attacks were driven off.
(D.S.O. gazetted 1 Dec. 1914.)
HINDLE, RALPH, D.S.O., Lieut.-Colonel, North Lancashire Regt. For conspicuous gallantry and devotion to duty whilst commanding his battalion during an advance. He showed the finest leadership throughout, and under his direction his battalion captured all its objectives and inflicted heavy loss on the enemy. His men were greatly inspired by his coolness and personal example.
(D.S.O. gazetted 4 June, 1917.)

INGPEN, PERCY LEIGH, D.S.O., Major (Temporary Lieut.-Colonel), West Yorkshire Regt. For conspicuous gallantry and devotion to duty. During an action his battalion headquarters were demolished by shell fire, and he was only extricated with great difficulty. Though ordered to hand over his command, he went to the front-line trenches on hearing that the enemy was counter-attacking. He remained there until dangerously wounded, restoring confidence by his example at a most critical period.
(D.S.O. gazetted 3 June, 1916.)

MACDONALD, CHARLES LESLIE, D.S.O., Temporary Lieut.-Colonel, Manchester Regt. For conspicuous gallantry and devotion to duty at a moment when a party of his own battalion and other units were held up by an enemy strong point. He pushed forward and organized a bombing attack, but the officer leading it was killed and it failed. Seeing a tank approach, he ran out under fire and got into it, directing the tank towards the strong point. As soon as he had given instructions, he got out again and rejoined his party in the trench under a storm of machine-gun fire. He has on all occasions set a fine example of coolness and contempt of danger.
(D.S.O. gazetted 1 Jan. 1917.)

MORIARTY, OLIVER NASH, D.S.O., Capt. (Acting Major), Royal Garrison Artillery, Special Reserve. For conspicuous gallantry and devotion to duty. During a prolonged and very accurate bombardment of his battery by the enemy he organized a party to put out a fire which had broken out amongst his ammunition He afterwards showed great promptness in taking his party from the heavily shelled area to the B.C. post, where he remained until he was shelled out of it. Subsequently, when the line between the battery and headquarters was broken, he and another officer went out under heavy fire and restored communication. His presence of mind and fearlessness under very trying conditions were beyond all praise.
(D.S.O. gazetted 25 Aug. 1916.)

PEIRS, HUGH JOHN CHEVALLIER, D.S.O., Temporary Major, Royal West Surrey Regt. For conspicuous gallantry and devotion to duty whilst in command of his battalion. It was entirely due to his energy and splendid personal example that his part of the line was consolidated when the officers of the leading companies had suffered heavy casualties. He continually passed through a heavy barrage with utter disregard of personal danger in order to visit his advanced posts, and in spite of unforeseen difficulties which arose during the attack, it was carried out without a hitch owing to his remarkable foresight and fine leadership.
(D.S.O. gazetted 3 June, 1916.)

PETERSON, ARTHUR JAMES, D.S.O., Temporary Capt. (Acting Major), Royal Field Artillery. For conspicuous gallantry and devotion to duty whilst withdrawing his guns from a badly shelled position. Having completed his work he was skirting a heavily shelled corner when the gun of another battery was overturned by a shell which killed a horse and threw the team into confusion. Although shells were dropping six a minute on the corner, he and another officer rushed up and cut the team free, saving three drivers and five horses. At least eight heavy shells dropped within a few yards of them whilst so engaged. He performed this gallant act after a particularly trying three weeks, during which he had only been away 24 hours from his post.
(D.S.O. gazetted 25 Aug. 1916.)

REYNOLDS, LEWIS LESLIE CLAYTON, D.S.O., Major (Temporary Lieut.-Colonel), Oxfordshire and Buckinghamshire Light Infantry. For conspicuous gallantry and devotion to duty. Owing to heavy officer casualties three of his companies became disorganized in an attack. He moved forward at once to the front line, and by his personal gallantry and determination rapidly organized his men and drove off the enemy's counter-attack, inflicting heavy casualties on the enemy. The situation was most critical and had it not been for his splendid example the enemy's counter-attack would have succeeded.
(D.S.O. gazetted 14 Nov. 1916.)

RIDDELL, EDWARD PIUS ARTHUR, D.S.O., Major (Temporary Lieut.-Colonel), Rifle Brigade. For conspicuous gallantry and devotion to duty when in command of a battalion in reserve during an attack. He threw in a counter-attack at a counter stroke by the enemy, and held on to an eminence of the highest tactical importance throughout the afternoon. His dispositions not only allowed the brigade to fall back in order before superior numbers, but materially reduced the enemy's strength, as he held off three counter-attacks and inflicted crushing casualties on the enemy. He eventually assumed command and reorganized two other units of the brigade, and passed four times through a heavy hostile barrage to his brigade headquarters to report on the situation. He handled a most difficult situation with consummate skill, and his utter disregard of danger not only encouraged the men to further effort but was a magnificent example of courage and determination.
(D.S.O. gazetted 11 Dec. 1916.)

ROGERS, JAMES SAMUEL YEAMAN, D.S.O., Major, Royal Army Medical Corps. For conspicuous gallantry and devotion to duty. Throughout several days' operations he attended to the wounded in the open under continuous heavy fire. Though all his stretcher-bearers were casualties, with utter disregard of danger he bound up the wounded and superintended their removal. His gallantry was most marked.
(D.S.O. gazetted 14 Jan. 1916.)

SAMUEL, FREDERICK DUDLEY, D.S.O., Lieut.-Colonel, London Regt. For conspicuous gallantry and devotion to duty. He organized and personally carried out the re-establishment of some posts which had been lost. The ground was quite strange to his men, and it was entirely due to his efforts that the posts were re-established. Later, when all communications except by runner were broken during the operations, it was mainly due to his energy and fearlessness that information was forwarded.
(D.S.O. gazetted 1 Jan. 1917.)

WIENHOLT, WILLIAM HUMPHREY MEYRICK, D.S.O., Temporary Major, North Lancashire Regt. For conspicuous gallantry and devotion to duty when in temporary command of his battalion. In spite of heavy casualties previous to the attack he made careful assembly arrangements, thereby ensuring the complete success of his battalion. They killed a great number of the enemy and dug themselves in with such rapidity that when enemy counter-attacks commenced they were able to deal with every hostile effort and maintain all their positions until relieved. This officer remained cool and collected throughout, in spite of having to frequently change his battalion headquarters, and his conduct throughout was marked by common sense, gallantry and great initiative.
(D.S.O. gazetted 4 June, 1917.)

WOOD, EDWARD ALLAN, D.S.O., Temporary Lieut.-Colonel, Shropshire Light Infantry. For conspicuous gallantry and devotion to duty. His personal example and leading were largely responsible for the dash and grit shown by his battalion during two days' severe fighting. He personally supervised the forming up of his battalion under heavy hostile barrage; leading them to the line of deployment, he deployed them punctually and without confusion four hundred yards from the final objective. During the ensuing three days his personal influence and skill kept his battalion secure against frequent counter-attacks, although his flanks were in a precarious situation owing to the neighbouring troops having been driven back.
(D.S.O. gazetted 1 Jan. 1917.)

Awarded the Distinguished Service Order:

ALEXANDER, THE HONOURABLE WILLIAM SIGISMUND PATRICK, Lieut. (Acting Capt.), Irish Guards. For conspicuous gallantry and devotion to duty. Whilst leading his company in an attack he came under heavy machine-gun fire from a concrete emplacement. He immediately led a successful attack through a gap in our barrage, and outflanked three gun positions, capturing three machine guns and 14 men. He then continued the attack, and seized his objective within the scheduled time, in spite of having to pass through our own barrage as well as that of the enemy. He set a splendid example of fearlessness and resource.

ALLEN, LIONEL RAYMOND, Lieut., Nottinghamshire and Derbyshire Regt., Special Reserve. For conspicuous gallantry and devotion to duty when acting as Battalion Intelligence Officer. He behaved with the utmost fearlessness under an intense bombardment, continually making journeys through very heavy barrage in order to obtain information of the tactical situation. His reports were invaluable. The following evening he made a most gallant and successful reconnaissance of the new enemy line, in the course of which he swam a river and remained half an hour in the water; during this time he was subjected to artillery, rifle and machine-gun fire, but, in spite of this, he returned with very valuable information, having displayed throughout a splendid example of coolness and fearless devotion to duty.

ARCHER, HARRY, Lieut. (Acting Capt.), Devonshire Regt., Special Reserve. For conspicuous gallantry and devotion to duty. After his Commanding Officer had been killed he handled the battalion with marked skill and determination during two days of the attack, and it was due to his fearless example and fine leadership that his battalion succeeded in reaching all the objectives, and holding them in the face of repeated and determined counter-attacks.

BELLEW, FROUDE DILLON, M.C., Major, Somersetshire Light Infantry. For conspicuous gallantry and devotion to duty while in command of his battalion during several days of intense fighting. He continually visited the front line when movement was very difficult owing to hostile fire, and inspired all ranks by his courage and contempt of danger. Later, he commanded all the troops in the right section of the brigade front, and by his skill and enterprise organized a defence that withstood repeated hostile counter-attacks. He displayed fine leadership and great power of command.

BENNETT, THOMAS EDWIN, Major (Temporary Lieut.-Colonel), Army Service Corps. For conspicuous gallantry and devotion to duty. He rendered invaluable assistance at a very critical time to brigade transport, which was taking up ammunition, food and material to the front line, and suffering heavy casualties in doing so. He personally reconnoitred the ground and led the mules over the most dangerous and difficult parts of the track, at times wading thigh deep in water, and removing pack saddles from mules which had fallen into shell holes. He set a splendid example of coolness and devotion to duty.

BETHELL, HUGH KEPPEL, Capt. and Brevet Lieut.-Colonel (Temporary Brigadier-General), Hussars. For conspicuous gallantry and devotion to duty whilst commanding an attack upon a hostile position. It was a very hard fight, and it was due to his fine leadership that the attack was a complete success. By his energy and personal example he very greatly inspired all ranks of his brigade.

BOWELL, ROBERT HENRY, Second Lieut., Leicestershire Regt. For conspicuous gallantry and devotion to duty when in command of two platoons in the outpost line. Owing to the death of his Company Commander and the Company Serjeant-Major, he was not relieved for four days, during which he remained on his line of posts without food or water and unable to get into touch with any other troops. He successfully repelled several raids by the enemy, and finally, when nearly surrounded, and with all his men completely exhausted, he decided to withdraw, and accomplished this successfully without any casualties. His courage and endurance during this exceptionally trying time were beyond all praise.

BOWIE, JOHN DARLING, M.B., Capt. (Acting Lieut.-Colonel), Royal Army Medical Corps. For conspicuous gallantry and devotion to duty. He worked continuously for 36 hours under heavy shell fire, supervising the removal of the wounded from the front line, and by his energetic example and personal assistance all casualties were cleared within a short time after the operations were completed. His disregard of danger and untiring devotion to duty had a splendid effect upon his men.

BRADSHAW, WILLIAM PAT. ARTHUR, Lieut. (Acting Capt.), Scots Guards. For conspicuous gallantry and devotion to duty during an attack upon an enemy position. Hearing that the officers of the company on his left had suffered severely, he went over and reorganized it, so as to make sure that its attack would succeed. He then returned to his own company and took command of the whole battalion frontage and consolidated the position when the objective was reached. He set a splendid example to the two companies under him by his own personal courage and cheerfulness under extremely heavy fire.

BRYCE, EDWARD DANIEL, Capt. (Temporary Major), Tank Corps. For conspicuous gallantry and devotion to duty. His company on the way to the position of deployment came under heavy hostile barrage, by which a number of tank officers and others were wounded and gassed. Major Bryce, although gassed and twice knocked over by shells which burst alongside him, continued to take charge, and walking in front guided his tanks to their positions. Two days afterwards, although still suffering from the effects of gas and partially blinded, he commanded his company in action, and at great personal risk went forward to collect information. His pluck and devotion to duty cannot be too highly praised.

BUCKLEY, ALBERT, Capt. (Temporary Major), North Lancashire Regt. For conspicuous gallantry and devotion to duty. He commanded his battalion in action, and captured all his objectives as well as several points beyond those allotted to him, and during the three days following he continually visited the positions, encouraging the men and organizing the defence under very heavy shell fire. His personal example was of the highest value in maintaining the spirits of officers and men during the very trying time which followed the capture of the position.

CADE, ARTHUR GORDON, M.C., Capt. (Acting Major), Middlesex Regt. For conspicuous gallantry and devotion to duty when in command of his battalion. Hearing that the left flank of his battalion was held up, he at once went forward with as many men and machine guns as he could collect, and throughout the whole day, under intense hostile fire, reorganized his battalion with the utmost disregard of personal safety in full view of the enemy. He strengthened an exposed flank, and held on in the face of determined counter-attacks. His courage and coolness were beyond all praise, and it was solely due to his personal efforts that he kept his battalion in good morale throughout the day.

COKE, THE HONOURABLE EDWARD, M.C., Capt. (Acting Lieut.-Colonel), Rifle Brigade. For conspicuous gallantry and devotion to duty. During the attack and during the five following days while holding the captured position, by his personality, absolute fearlessness, and cheerful example he kept up the spirits of his battalion under very adverse conditions and continuous heavy shelling. The success of the battalion was mainly due to his able leadership.

CONINGHAM, ARTHUR, M.C., Second Lieut. (Temporary Capt.), Royal Flying Corps, Special Reserve. For conspicuous gallantry and devotion to duty. With three other pilots he attacked an enemy machine which was protected by ten others, shot it down, and destroyed another one the same evening. Shortly afterwards he and two others attacked five of the enemy, and although wounded and rendered unconscious for the moment, he succeeded in driving down two of the enemy. In spite of being much exhausted by loss of blood he continued his patrol until he was sure that no more enemy machines were in the vicinity, setting a splendid example of pluck and determination.

DAVENPORT, FRED, M.C., Capt. (Temporary Major), Royal Field Artillery. For conspicuous gallantry and devotion to duty. Under an intensely concentrated and accurate hostile bombardment of his battery position he superintended the withdrawal of his men to their dug-outs, but on his way back was buried by a shell which destroyed the mess in which he had been compelled to take refuge. The instant he was extricated he reorganized his battery and answered two S.O.S. calls before taking part in an offensive barrage. He conducted the latter with complete success under very difficult conditions, the original orders having been destroyed. It was entirely due to his gallantry and invariable cheerfulness under fire that the fire of his battery was available during the whole of this critical and important period.

DAVIDGE, GUY MORTIMER COLERIDGE, Major (Acting Lieut.-Colonel), Worcestershire Regt. For conspicuous gallantry and devotion to duty. When the right flank of his brigade had become exposed he was ordered to form a defensive flank with his battalion. This he did with the utmost skill and success, thereby enabling the troops on his left to maintain the ground they had gained. He visited the position taken by the battalion under very heavy machine-gun and shell fire, displaying splendid coolness and disregard of personal safety.

EATON, THE HONOURABLE FRANCIS ORMOND HENRY, Lieut. (Acting Capt.), Grenadier Guards. For conspicuous gallantry and devotion to duty. At a very critical moment during an attack he deployed his company and went to the assistance of another unit which had suffered such heavy casualties that they were unable to occupy their frontage. It was entirely due to his initiative and leadership that the objective was captured and consolidated up to scheduled time.

EDWARDS, CHRISTOPHER VAUGHAN, Major (Acting Lieut.-Colonel), Yorkshire Regt. For conspicuous gallantry and devotion to duty in going forward under shell and rifle fire and making a daring personal reconnaissance in order to clear up an obscure situation. By his action he not only managed to ascertain the actual situation and to take the necessary measures, but also set a fine example of coolness, and greatly encouraged both officers and men. He has previously displayed great judgment and gallantry under fire.

EDWARDS, CYRIL GEORGE, Second Lieut., West Yorkshire Regt. For conspicuous gallantry and devotion to duty. Having gone out with a N.C.O. to reconnoitre the enemy's wire, they were attacked by bombs. The first one he seized before it exploded and threw it back, and, when the second fell, realizing that they could not both escape unharmed, he threw his legs over it to smother the explosion, and thus protected the N.C.O. By this splendid act of gallantry and self-sacrifice he saved the life of his comrade at the risk of his own. The N.C.O. was able to drag him back to our lines, where he showed great pluck in reporting the information which he had gained by his daring reconnaissance.

FORSTER, HAROLD THOMAS, M.C., Lieut., Royal Berkshire Regt. For conspicuous gallantry and devotion to duty. He took over command of his battalion when his colonel had become a casualty, and led them with great skill to their objective, twice changing direction in order to avoid hostile barrage. He then made a personal reconnaissance and ascertained the position of the enemy, after which he formed a defensive flank, and was able to re-establish his line when it had been driven back by determined hostile counter-attacks. He remained perfectly cheerful throughout, showing a fine example of fearlessness and contempt for danger.

FOULKES, JOHN SIMPSON, Temporary Major, Manchester Regt. For conspicuous gallantry and devotion to duty. During an attack on the enemy trenches he personally closed with a party of the enemy and inflicted severe losses on them, and although wounded in the back by a bomb, continued to control the operation until its conclusion. He set a magnificent example to his men.

FURNESS, CHARLES CLIFFORD, Major, Royal Field Artillery. For conspicuous gallantry and devotion to duty. By his daring and exceptionally fearless personal reconnaissances of the positions which his brigade were about to occupy, he gained and brought back information which was invaluable to the operations, and, although under heavy shell fire and machine-gun fire, displayed a coolness and determination to report accurately upon the situations which were of inestimable value to the subsequent moves and action of his brigade.

GEDDES, GODFREY POWER, Temporary Lieut., Gordon Highlanders. For conspicuous gallantry and devotion to duty. Although dazed and much shaken by the explosion of a shell, he, as Adjutant, took command of the front line when all the other officers had become casualties, and coolly and energetically directed the work of consolidation and organization. He also repulsed an enemy counter-attack by his able handling of the battalion's Lewis guns. On the following day, when very heavily counter-attacked, he directed a short retirement to a stronger defence line, from which he held up the enemy, and eventually drove them back when reinforced, personally leading the attack. Although wounded in the hand, he behaved for three days with the utmost courage and ability, filling a responsible position under very trying conditions and practically unaided, by his fine personal example inspiring all ranks to most untiring efforts in attack and defence.

GLOVER, WILLIAM REID, Major (Acting Lieut.-Colonel), London Regt. For conspicuous gallantry and devotion to duty. He commanded his battalion with great ability and fearlessness under very heavy fire. His example tended to maintain the morale of his men under the most adverse conditions, and it was mainly due to his personal efforts that his battalion was reorganized after being compelled to fall back, and the system of defence re-established.

GORDON, LORD DUDLEY GLADSTONE, Temporary Major, Gordon Highlanders. For conspicuous gallantry and devotion to duty in personally supervising the construction of two artillery tracks over newly-captured ground. Throughout the day he set a splendid example of gallantry and coolness, personally carrying out reconnaissances under heavy fire from rifles and machine guns, and it was due to his fearlessness and disregard of danger that the track was successfully completed.

GOUGH, HORACE FREDERICK, Second Lieut., North Staffordshire Regt. For conspicuous gallantry and devotion to duty. He rallied part of a neighbouring battalion that had lost all its officers and had been forced back from a most important position. He personally led a counter-attack, and retook the position at the point of the bayonet, inflicting heavy casualties on the enemy. He then consolidated the captured position, and remained in command until relieved. By his gallantry, individuality and resource he undoubtedly enabled the troops on his flank to regain a highly important position.

GUINNESS, THE HONOURABLE WALTER EDWARD, Major, Yeomanry. For conspicuous gallantry and devotion to duty as Brigade Major. Previous to an attack his reconnaissance and arrangements for the assault were excellent, and during the action itself he went forward and made a complete and thorough personal reconnaissance regardless of enemy shelling and rifle fire. He remained on an exposed position for two days, keeping in close touch with the situation under continuous shell fire, and by his prompt action on his own initiative staved off at least one counter-attack.

HAMMILL, LONSDALE, M.C., Capt., South Lancashire Regt. For conspicuous gallantry and devotion to duty. During a reconnaissance he saw the enemy advancing to attack an important advanced post. He got to the post under heavy rifle fire, organized the defence, and drove off the enemy. He then saw that the enemy were working round the flank of a company of another battalion which was likely to become surrounded. He immediately organized a counter-attack, formed a defensive flank, and saved what might have been a disastrous situation. Later he captured an enemy sniper. Throughout the operations he displayed great initiative and good leadership, and set a magnificent example to all ranks.

HANNAY, GEORGE MARTIN, Capt. (Temporary Lieut.-Colonel), Reserve of Officers, late King's Own Scottish Borderers. For conspicuous gallantry and devotion to duty. At a critical moment when the battalion in his front was driven in by counter-attacks, he stopped all rearward movement by his personal courage and example, and organized defensive measures which checked the counter-attack. On the following day he again set a splendid example whilst commanding his battalion, and under severe fire stopped a gap in the line with his headquarters details and machine gun and beat off another counter-attack.

HARVEY, ALBERT, Second Lieut., Liverpool Regt. For conspicuous gallantry and devotion to duty. Having led his company to their objective, he noticed that a farm, some 500 yards ahead, was holding up the attack on the left. He at once organized a small party, with which he worked round the flank and rushed the farm, capturing three machine guns and killing and capturing a number of the enemy. By this prompt and plucky action he saved the brigade many casualties. His initiative and enterprise in action are at all times admirable.

HENDERSON-ROE, CHRISTOPHER GORDON, Capt., Royal West Kent Regt., Special Reserve. For conspicuous gallantry and devotion to duty during an attack upon an enemy trench. He continued to lead and direct his men until he was blown down and almost completely buried. He remained in this position for ten hours, eventually extricating himself. On his way back to our lines he bandaged some of our wounded, collected and placed them into shell holes. He then crawled back to the post held by his battalion, and remained there throughout the action, after which he led the stretcher-bearers to the wounded whom he had collected, and personally carried a badly wounded corporal back to our lines. His gallantry throughout the operation was most marked.

HORSFIELD, RICHARD MARSHALL, Major, Royal Field Artillery. For conspicuous gallantry and devotion to duty Amidst intense hostile shelling and exploding ammunition, he went to his battery and cut away the camouflage which had been set on fire by enemy shell fire. But for his gallantry and determination to stay the progress of the fire, the whole battery would undoubtedly have been put out of action.

HUNKIN, SAMUEL LLEWELLYN, Temporary Major, Royal Welsh Fusiliers. For conspicuous gallantry and devotion to duty in commanding his battalion with skill and judgment during an attack. Having reached his objective, his fine example had a decided effect on his men, keeping them cheerful under trying circumstances, and enabling them to carry out the duties assigned to them.

HUTCHESON, JOHN, M.C., Capt., Gordon Highlanders. For conspicuous gallantry and devotion to duty Having led his company to its objective, he commenced to consolidate under observation, at a very low altitude, from enemy aeroplanes. When these had departed, he immediately moved his front line forward about 100 yards, and his support line back about the same distance. Shortly afterwards the enemy commenced to shell his original position heavily, but, thanks to his skilful leadership and admirable foresight, the consolidation was completed on the new line with very few casualties. The absolute confidence with which he inspired his men on this and all other occasions is a guarantee of success in any operation which he is ordered to undertake.

IRWIN, NORMAN LESLIE CROZIER, Temporary Capt., Royal Welsh Fusiliers. For conspicuous gallantry and devotion to duty. He was informed that a company of the attacking battalion to whom he was in support was in danger of being surrounded by the enemy. He immediately reconnoitred the position, organized a skilful attack, and drove out the enemy. His gallantry and grasp of the situation undoubtedly saved the company from being cut off, and probably saved the whole situation at a critical moment.

JEFFERIES, HUGH ST. JOHN, Major (Acting Lieut.-Colonel), Worcestershire Regt. For conspicuous gallantry and devotion to duty. He led his battalion in an exceedingly able manner, securing all the objectives. He made an exceedingly valuable reconnaissance of the situation in the most advanced posts, freely exposing himself to severe machine-gun and shell fire. Later, when both flanks of his battalion became exposed and a withdrawal was necessary, he very skilfully supervised the movement. The counter-attacks of the enemy were checked and heavy losses were inflicted on them. He maintained a high moral standard throughout the operations.

JONES, REGINALD REES, Second Lieut., Welsh Guards. For conspicuous gallantry and devotion to duty during an advance. When the leading waves were temporarily held up by fire from a blockhouse he pushed up to the obstacle and fired his rifle through the slits, regardless of the danger which confronted him He then entered the blockhouse himself, dealt with the occupants, and enabled the advance to be continued. He was later badly wounded in the head, having acted throughout the operation with great gallantry and initiative.

KEWLEY, EDWARD RIGBY, M.C., Capt. (Acting Lieut.-Colonel), Rifle Brigade. For conspicuous gallantry and devotion to duty. Under intense shell and machine-gun fire he made a personal reconnnissance of the forward position held by his battalion, and returned to Brigade Headquarters to report the situation. He again went out to his forward posts and personally superintended the consolidation under heavy shell and machine-gun fire, behaving with the utmost coolness and gallantry through continual heavy fighting.

LANCE, EDWIN CHRISTOPHER, Second Lieut. (Temporary Capt.), Somersetshire Light Infantry. For conspicuous gallantry and devotion to duty. He was the only officer left of his battalion when the final objective was reached. Both flanks of his battalion were exposed, and they were almost surrounded by the enemy. Thereupon he skilfully withdrew his men from a difficult position to a strong one 200 yards in rear, checked the advance of the enemy, and held on under intense artillery fire until relieved two days later. The sound tactics, cool judgment, and the daring example which he set his men undoubtedly secured a very important position.

LEECH, WILLIAM FREDERICK, Temporary Second Lieut., General List and Royal Flying Corps. For conspicuous gallantry and devotion to duty. He carried out a number of valuable reconnaissances under difficult conditions, bringing back information which was invariably correct. When the situation was very obscure during an attack he correctly reported on it during the morning, and in doing so was wounded in the arm. In spite of this he went out again in the afternoon and was severely wounded.

LEES, DAVID, M.B., Temporary Capt., Royal Army Medical Corps. For conspicuous gallantry and devotion to duty. He passed through an intense barrage in order to attend to the wounded who were lying exposed to heavy fire of every description. Single-handed and under heavy shelling, he dressed the wounds of an officer, a sergeant, and a private, and carried each of them in turn to a place of comparative safety. To do this he had to pass through the enemy's barrage no less than four times, but with complete disregard for his personal safety he went forward a fifth time to attend to others, inspiring all ranks by his own splendid example of fearlessness and devotion.

LE PREVOST, ALFRED PAUL HARRISON, Temporary Major (Acting Lieut.-Colonel), Nottinghamshire and Derbyshire Regt. For conspicuous gallantry and devotion to duty. During an attack and during the five following days, while holding his line under very adverse conditions and continuous shelling, by his own personality, fearlessness and cheerful example he kept up the spirits of his battalion. His battalion captured its objectives, reformed quickly, and carried stores of all kinds to the forward dumps, and then without any rest held the line until relieved. The success of the battalion was mainly due to his able leadership.

LEVEY, JOSEPH HENRY, Capt. (Temporary Lieut.-Colonel), Gordon Highlanders. For conspicuous gallantry and devotion to duty. In the assembly for the attack by good judgment he almost entirely avoided casualties. He launched his battalion into the attack with ability, and commanded it throughout the action with judgment, coolness and gallantry. He gained all his objectives, and personally supervised the consolidation of the captured position. Whilst holding the captured position during the following days under continuous heavy artillery fire he displayed coolness, courage and determination, and by his cheerfulness he kept those under him in good heart. His personal example was an incentive to all, and he organized and trained his battalion for the attack with great ability.

LLOYD, ERNEST GUY RICHARDS, Temporary Lieut. (Acting Capt.), Shropshire Light Infantry. For conspicuous gallantry and devotion to duty. When commanding a supporting company during an attack he was suddenly ordered to take over command of the two assaulting companies—an extremely difficult task owing to the extension and uncertainty of our line, which ran through a wood. By his personal example and exceptional ability he succeeded in thoroughly organizing the two front lines and establishing a continuous line of posts through the wood. Throughout the action he maintained connection with his front and flanks, and, in spite of the very heavy casualties in the two companies under his command, carried out a successful operation, with only two young officers (one of them wounded) to assist him. His coolness and masterly dealing with a difficult situation deserve the greatest praise.

LOWCOCK, REGINALD JOHN, M.C., Lieut. (Temporary Capt.), Nottinghamshire and Derbyshire Regt. and Royal Flying Corps. For conspicuous gallantry and devotion to duty in carrying out artillery observation with great skill and success, in spite of very unfavourable weather and strong hostile opposition. On one occasion, although attacked by five hostile machines, he carried on with his work until his machine was riddled with bullets and he was wounded in the leg. He then succeeded in landing in safety, having destroyed one of the hostile machines. He has also done some exceptionally fine contact patrol work.

LYCETT, TIMOTHY, Second Lieut. (Temporary Capt.), King's Royal Rifle Corps. For conspicuous gallantry and devotion to duty. While advancing to its point of deployment for an attack on the final objective his battalion suffered such severe casualties from machine-gun fire that he found himself in command. He at once led them forward, captured the final objective, and by his promptness and skill in handling his reserve was able to stop a determined hostile counter-attack which had forced back his left flank. Throughout the ensuing three days his cheerful and vigorous personality inspired all under his command with confidence.

MACLEAN, IVAN CLARKSON, M.C., Temporary Capt., Royal Army Medical Corps. For conspicuous gallantry and devotion to duty in clearing the wounded. He took his stretcher-bearers well in advance of our forward positions and behaved with the most exemplary courage and devotion throughout, sparing no efforts to collect the wounded men. After his battalion was relieved he continued to work under the heaviest fire for another twenty-four hours, and was severely wounded on his way back after all the cases had been cleared. He set a splendid example of energy and contempt of danger.

MACROBERTS, NOEL DE PUTRON, M.C., Temporary Lieut. (Acting Capt.), Royal Sussex Regt. For conspicuous gallantry and devotion to duty. Although wounded early in the day, he gallantly led his company under heavy shell and machine-gun fire to its objective—a village—which he captured, together with over 200 prisoners, four field guns and two machine guns. He then remained at duty in spite of his wounds, until he had reorganized his company and consolidated his position, greatly inspiring all ranks by his magnificent courage and gallantry.

MAIR, BRODIE VALENTINE, M.C., Capt., Manchester Regt. For conspicuous gallantry and devotion to duty. He superintended the forming up of his brigade in the open all through the night under considerable shell fire, and on the following day, immediately the objective had been captured, he made a very skilful reconnaissance, by which he was able to clear up the dispositions of the units on their final objectives.

MAITLAND, WILLIAM BARCLAY, Second Lieut., Gordon Highlanders. For conspicuous gallantry and devotion to duty under very trying circumstances. When his company was held up by a machine gun he went forward alone, jumping from shell hole to shell hole until he was within a few feet, when he ran forward, killed the whole gun team and captured the gun single-handed.

MARTIN, BERNARD WILLIAM JOHN HANKINS, Second Lieut., Royal Field Artillery, Special Reserve. For conspicuous gallantry and devotion to duty. His battery was very heavily shelled, two of the guns being destroyed, two damaged and two buried. When the bombardment slackened he took command, the battery commander having been wounded, and had the two buried guns dug out and brought into action. Later, when the battery was in action during an attack and one of his two remaining guns was damaged by an enemy shell, he carried out his complete programme by doubling the rate of fire from the only remaining gun. He showed great courage and leadership, and set a splendid example of devotion to duty to his men.

MARTIN, EDWARD CUTHBERT DE RENZY, M.C., Capt. (Temporary-Lieut.-Colonel), Yorkshire Light Infantry. For conspicuous gallantry and devotion to duty. Previous to an assault, in spite of considerable enemy shelling, he had commanded his battalion with such good judgment and determination that on the morning of the assault they had driven strong points into the enemy's line in several places. The result of this was that the left flank of the brigade was thoroughly protected by rifle, machine and Lewis-gun fire during the assault. He successfully and promptly dealt with all enemy attempts to counter-attack, and on one occasion it was due to his initiative that an enemy battalion was caught whilst deploying for an assault, and wiped out. The success of the whole operation was largely due to his skilful leadership.

MAY, HARRY, Second Lieut. (Temporary Lieut. and Acting Capt.), Royal Field Artillery. For conspicuous gallantry and devotion to duty in connection with gas operations with Stokes mortars. He discharged a record number of shells against the enemy position, which involved exceptional hard work undermost unfavourable conditions owing to the exposed nature of his gun position. He reconnoitred positions and organized and superintended carrying parties with the greatest skill and energy, by his personal leadership setting a splendid example to all ranks.

McCARTHY-O'LEARY, HEFFERNAN WILLIAM DENIS, M.C., Capt. (Acting Lieut.-Colonel), Royal Irish Fusiliers. For conspicuous gallantry and devotion to duty. During a heavy hostile counter-attack, which had driven in his advance post and recaptured part of the position, he went forward with one runner, rallied his men and led them forward again, driving the enemy back and restoring the situation. He remained encouraging his men until he was himself severely wounded half an hour later, but he did not leave the field until he had reported the situation to his brigadier.

MONTGOMERY-SMITH, EDWIN CHARLES, Major (Temporary Lieut.-Colonel), Royal Army Medical Corps. For conspicuous gallantry and devotion to duty in the supervision of the arrangements for the evacuation of the wounded. By a systematic study of the ground, clever selection of aid and relay posts and routes, he evacuated a large number of casualties during the operations. He worked untiringly, regardless of his personal safety, visiting all the advanced aid posts. His work was invaluable.

NORTH, PIERS WILLIAM, Lieut.-Colonel, Reserve of Officers, Royal Berkshire Regt. For conspicuous gallantry and devotion to duty. He led his men to the attack with utter disregard of danger under heavy fire, and the dash with which his battalion went forward in the attack and secured a considerable number of prisoners was largely due to his fine personal example. He was shortly afterwards severely wounded in the chest and back.

ORR, JOHN BOYD, M.C., M.B., Temporary Capt., Royal Army Medical Corps. For conspicuous gallantry and devotion to duty. He worked unceasingly for forty-eight hours without an aid post, and under an almost continuous barrage, attending to the wounded of three units of his brigade. He found time to visit the front line twice and attended to numerous cases under machine-gun and shell fire, and, although twice buried and rendered unconscious for two or three hours, he remained at duty until his brigade was relieved, displaying devotion and personal courage which were worthy of the highest praise. His gallant conduct has been brought to notice on more than one occasion by officers commanding units to whose wounded he had attended.

PALLANT, HUBERT ARNOLD, M.C., Temporary Capt., Royal Army Medical Corps. For conspicuous gallantry and devotion to duty. Hearing that a number of men belonging to another battalion were on the enemy bank of a river, and unable to cross it owing to the bridge being destroyed, and to their being apparently unable to swim, he hurried to the scene, swam the river fully clothed, and induced the men to enter the water and cross with the aid of a rope. The most exhausted one he personally conveyed across. During this time the enemy were continually shelling both the river and the banks. He set a splendid example of energy and devotion to duty.

PEGLER, SIDNEY JAMES, Temporary Second Lieut., Rifle Brigade. For conspicuous gallantry and devotion to duty during an attack in leading bombing parties and consolidating a line of shell holes under heavy machine-gun fire and sniping. He on two occasions displayed the utmost fearlessness in personally attacking hostile bombing parties which were attempting to force their way past his flank, and driving them back with Lewis gun and bombs. His dash and initiative were magnificent, and it was chiefly owing to his example that all the objectives gained were held.

PENNELL, RICHARD, Lieut. (Temporary Major), King's Royal Rifle Corps. For conspicuous gallantry and devotion to duty at a critical moment when a hostile counter-attack had driven our troops back in a village. With the greatest promptitude and presence of mind he burnt all his papers, turned out his headquarters, and advanced under machine-gun and rifle fire, picking up all the stray men he met. He then passed down the whole of the brigade front, giving orders to his own battalion and another for an immediate counter-attack, during which he displayed great courage and coolness, and it was due to his gallant conduct that the counter-attack was successful.

PETRIE, DAVID PARKER, Lieut., Scottish Rifles, Special Reserve. For conspicuous gallantry and devotion to duty. He led his company gallantly to the attack, and when held up by machine-gun fire and snipers he quickly rallied his men and personally led a vigorous assault on the enemy's position. He accounted for more than one of the enemy himself, captured a machine gun and a number of the enemy, after which he led what remained of his company to the next objective under very heavy machine-gun and rifle fire, in spite of which he captured another machine gun and the entire team. Later in the day, by his energy and forethought, he repulsed several hostile counter-attacks, and throughout the operation his coolness and gallantry set a splendid example to his men.

POTTER, COLIN KYNASTON, M.C., Major (Acting Lieut.-Colonel), North Lancashire Regt. For conspicuous gallantry and devotion to duty. He commanded his battalion in an attack, captured all his objectives, and personally directed the consolidation of a position, which he held against hostile counter-attacks even after the division on his right had given way. This was largely due to his excellent dispositions and his very gallant personal example.

PRIESTMAN, JOHN HEDLEY THORNTON, Capt., Lincolnshire Regt. For conspicuous gallantry and devotion to duty in making a valuable and daring reconnaissance under very heavy shell fire, during which he was wounded. His information was so precise and accurate that it enabled our barrage to break up hostile counter-attacks. A fortnight later, he made a similar reconnaissance in the same area with equally good results, and, in addition, finding the situation critical on our left flank, he ordered up a battalion on his own initiative in support, and thus enabled the line to be restored.

ROBINSON, ALBERT CHARLES HENRY, Temporary Second Lieut., attached Yorkshire Light Infantry. For conspicuous gallantry and devotion to duty. He led his company in an advance over difficult ground, and although checked by very heavy gun fire from a concrete fort, succeeded in capturing the fort and gaining his objective. He successfully consolidated and held the second objective line through a very trying period of 36 hours, during which his men were continuously and heavily shelled and fired at from aeroplanes. Throughout the whole operation he displayed the utmost courage and the finest leadership and devotion to duty.

SARGEAUNT, PERCY RICHARD, Capt. (Acting Major), Royal Garrison Artillery. For conspicuous gallantry and devotion to duty. His battery was very heavily shelled for three days, in the course of which he continually went about exposed to heavy fire, seeing to the safety of his men, with utter disregard of danger. His fearlessness and calm disregard of his own safety set the finest possible example to the officers and men of the battery.

SHARLAND, ALAN ABBOTT, Capt. (Temporary Major) (Acting Lieut.-Colonel), East Lancashire Regt. For conspicuous gallantry and devotion to duty. Under his successful handling his battalion captured and held its objective in spite of heavy counter-attacks, and of the fact that its right flank was for some time exposed to very heavy machine-gun fire. He visited the position gained, and at once organized a defensive flank.

SHERBROOKE, ROBERT LOWE, Capt. and Brevet Major (Temporary Lieut.-Colonel), Nottinghamshire and Derbyshire Regt. For conspicuous gallantry and devotion to duty. Under his skilful handling his battalion captured and held all its objectives though repeatedly counter-attacked. He visited the position under heavy machine-gun and shell fire, and although slightly gassed before the action he remained with his battalion throughout. The dash of his men in the attack, and their tenacity in holding their position, were very largely due to his personal influence and training.

SLADE, HAROLD ARTHUR, M.C., Temporary Capt., Rifle Brigade. For conspicuous gallantry and devotion to duty during two days' exceptionally heavy fighting, which included the forcing of a river. He dug in with his company under heavy machine-gun fire, and maintained his position in spite of a determined hostile counter-attack. He held his ground until the morning of the second day, inflicting heavy casualties on the enemy, and afterwards, when fresh troops had passed through his line, successfully accomplished the task of mopping up a strong point with only one casualty, killing and capturing many of the enemy. Throughout these operations he sent back valuable information to Headquarters, and displayed courage and coolness of the very highest order.

STEWART, ALEXANDER JOHN, Capt., Royal Highlanders. For conspicuous gallantry and devotion to duty in leading his company in an attack in which he displayed great fearlessness and exceptional skill. He moved up through heavy shelling and hostile machine-gun fire and seized his objective. He then suddenly found himself not only exposed to very severe and accurate machine-gun and sniper fire from three sides, but with his platoon commanders wounded. By his complete grasp of the situation, cool and intrepid behaviour, and magnificent personal example of utter disregard of danger, he inspired his men with complete confidence, and undoubtedly saved a very critical situation.

STRANGE, JOHN STANLEY, M.C., Temporary Capt., Welsh Regt. For conspicuous gallantry and devotion to duty. Having led his company with great ability and determination to its final objective, he took over command of the front line, and held it for three days until relieved. He personally reconnoitred his whole front, and sent back very valuable information, setting a very fine example throughout to all ranks under most trying circumstances.

SUTHERLAND, THOMAS DOUGLAS, M.C., Temporary Capt., Lincolnshire Regt. For conspicuous gallantry and devotion to duty. He led his company with great gallantry in the attack, but on reaching his objective found his flank exposed owing to the troops on his right having been unable to advance. He immediately went back, rallied a company which had lost heavily in officers and senior N.C.O.'s, and led them forward to their objective. He then organized a defensive flank and made the position secure. He showed the greatest courage and leadership, and it was entirely owing to his initiative and determination that the advance of his battalion was successfully carried out.

SUTTON, BESTINE ENTWISLE, M.C., Second Lieut. (Temporary Capt.), Yeomanry and Royal Flying Corps. For conspicuous gallantry and devotion to duty. On very many occasions he carried out extensive and valuable reconnaissances and contact patrols at low altitudes, attacking infantry and transport with his machine gun and taking photographs which proved of the greatest value in subsequent operations. By his energy, skill, and courage he set a magnificent example to his squadron.

SYMON, JAMES ALEXANDER, Lieut. (Acting Capt.), Cameron Highlanders. For conspicuous gallantry and devotion to duty. When commanding his company in the reserve line, he led them out of their trenches and charged a successful hostile counter-attack, driving the enemy back and establishing our original front line. By his coolness and absolute disregard of personal danger, he saved the situation, and, afterwards finding that we were suffering from the fire of snipers, went out himself and shot several of the enemy before he was finally wounded.

THOMAS, ALAN ERNEST WENTWORTH, Second Lieut. (Temporary Capt.) Royal West Kent Regt. For conspicuous gallantry and devotion to duty. Although wounded, he led his company to its objective with great skill and success: afterwards when the troops on his right and left had withdrawn, he held his ground with only six men, two of whom were shortly afterwards wounded. He, however, held on for seventeen hours, and saved the situation, for it was entirely due to his pluck and determination that the attack in the evening was successfully carried out. He set a splendid example of courage and resource in a very trying position.

THOMAS, GWILYM IVOR, M.C., Capt. (Acting Major), Royal Field Artillery. For conspicuous gallantry and devotion to duty. When his battery was being relieved the position was shelled by an intense bombardment, which lasted for over two hours and caused many casualties in both batteries. The pits and ammunition of one section caught fire, and he succeeded in extinguishing this. Later, the telephone pit and mess shelter were wrecked, and he immediately led the way to the rescue of wounded men inside. The camouflage nets of three more guns were then set alight, and the ammunition began to catch fire. This he also saved by tearing down the burning camouflage and smothering the smouldering ammunition, some of which had already begun to explode. Not until all the fires had been extinguished, and he had seen every man, both wounded and unwounded, clear of the position, did he seek cover for himself. His great gallantry and exceptional coolness throughout the whole of this time were worthy of the highest praise.

TRELOAR, GEORGE DEVINE, Lieut. (Acting Capt.), Coldstream Guards, Special Reserve. For conspicuous gallantry and devotion to duty on two successive occasions. He led his company across a canal under very heavy barrage, and, finding the only available bridge was broken, he personally secured a mat from the original line, and laid it down for his company to cross, thereby saving great congestion and countless lives. Later, when the regiment on his left was held up by machine gun-fire, he immediately grasped the situation, and pressed forward with another company, finally capturing the position. By his great presence of mind and personal example of gallantry and cheerfulness he kept his company going under the most adverse circumstances.

TYSON, ERIC JAMES, M.C., Temporary Major, General List and Royal Flying Corps. For conspicuous gallantry and devotion to duty on many occasions. He has displayed the utmost fearlessness in carrying out photographic reconnaissances and artillery registration at extremely low altitudes, being continually under fire, but invaribaly doing excellent work and obtaining most valuable information by his great skill and daring.

WARMAN, CLIVE WILSON, M.C., Second Lieut., General List and Royal Flying Corps. For conspicuous gallantry and devotion to duty. During two days, whilst operating under very difficult conditions in high wind and against strong hostile opposition, he destroyed three enemy machines and a balloon. He displayed the greatest dash and fearlessness in attacking an enemy aerodrome, and on one occasion, when separated from his patrol, and surrounded by 20 hostile machines, he fought his way through, although his machine gun was useless, by attacking them with his "Very" pistol; eventually regaining his own aerodrome with his machine much shot about. His wonderful coolness and courage have on all occasions been beyond praise.

WATKINS, GWILYM DAVID, Temporary Capt., Royal Army Medica Corps. For conspicuous gallantry and devotion to duty. When cries for help were heard coming from a tank which had been abandoned in an isolated position in the outpost line, he went 200 yards through a heavy barrage and rescued a badly-wounded man from the tank. He dressed his wounds and carried him under heavy fire towards safety, until, being completely exhausted, he was compelled to put the man in a shell-hole and go for assistance. He returned with another officer, and, still under heavy fire, brought the man to safety. Throughout six days he displayed the same indomitable courage and extraordinary devotion to duty, constantly going into the open tending the wounded day and night. He undoubtedly saved many lives.

WATSON, CAMPBELL N., Temporary Major, Liverpool Regt. For conspicuous gallantry and devotion to duty at a critical moment. Whilst commanding his battalion in an advance, he suddenly came under heavy artillery and machine-gun fire, but he promptly deployed, attacked the enemy, and gained possession of a commanding position. This he not only held gallantly for four days, but was indefatigable in his endeavours to improve upon his success, and his courage and cheerful bearing had a marked effect in enabling his men to hold their own under most adverse weather conditions and continuous hostile shelling.

WHALLEY, PERCY ROGER, Major (Acting Lieut.-Colonel), Worcestershire Regt. For conspicuous gallantry and devotion to duty. He took charge of a difficult and dangerous situation which had arisen owing to the right flanks of his division being exposed. Quickly grasping the state of affairs, he made excellent dispositions, and refused reinforcements, although they were offered to him, acting with such determination and good judgment that from the moment he took over this sector there was never any doubt that the position would be maintained.

WHEAL, SAMUEL, Second Lieut., East Lancashire Regt. For conspicuous gallantry and devotion to duty. He led the first wave of the attack to its objective, which he captured and cleared, and then led his men forward and captured an enemy strong point, inflicting heavy casualties on the enemy. Later, when he observed a party of the enemy forming up for an attack on his front, he immediately organized a party and skilfully outflanked the enemy, capturing 35 prisoners. Throughout the operations he led his platoon with the greatest gallantry and dash.

WHITE, JOHN DONALD, Capt., Middlesex Regt. For conspicuous gallantry and devotion to duty. He led his men with great gallantry, and consolidated his position with conspicuous ability. When the troops on his flanks were compelled to withdraw, leaving his position isolated and untenable, he nevertheless held on for a considerable time, and when forced to withdraw conducted the retirement with great coolness. He showed utter disregard of danger, continually moving about under heavy shell fire, encouraging and directing his men.

WILLIAMS, JESSE, Temporary Major, Royal Welsh Fusiliers. For conspicuous gallantry and devotion to duty under exceptionally trying conditions. When a counter-attack was expected he took out a patrol and established the fact that there was no attack being made. He then rallied his men and did much to restore the situation by his fine personal example.

WILSON, PERCY NORTON WHITESTONE, M.C., Capt., Royal Fusiliers. For conspicuous gallantry and devotion to duty. It was largely due to his skill in forming up his brigade for an attack that the movement was successfully accomplished, in spite of darkness, rain and swampy ground, rendered nearly impassable by shell-holes. After the attack had proved successful he made a thorough and long personal reconnaissance of the captured line under constant and heavy shell fire, and brought back very valuable information to his brigadier.

YOUNG, KENNETH, Temporary Second Lieut., Lincolnshire Regt. For conspicuous gallantry and devotion to duty under very trying circumstances. He took over command of his battalion on his own initiative when the commanding officer and adjutant were wounded, quickly grasped the situation, and continued to handle the battalion with such success that three counter-attacks were driven off. It was largely due to his energy and resource that the battalion was able to maintain its position, as its right wing was exposed to the enemy's machine-gun fire.

CANADIAN FORCE.

McKINERY, JOHN WILLIAM HERBERT, Lieut.-Colonel, Labour Battn. For conspicuous gallantry and devotion to duty during a very heavy hostile bombardment of the light railway system for which he was responsible. He repeatedly made journeys over the whole of the shelled area, organizing repairs and leading working parties into position. His fine example of fearlessness and energy kept the men together and was instrumental in the work being rapidly and successfully carried out.

PATERSON, ROBERT WALTER, Lieut.-Colonel, Cavalry. For conspicuous gallantry and devotion to duty. By his daring reconnaissances and careful organization he ensured the success of a raid against four lines of enemy defences. He personally reconnoitred the point of attack with an utter disregard of his personal safety.

RALSTON, JAMES LAYTON, Major, Infantry. For conspicuous gallantry and devotion to duty during operations which included the capture of a village. He displayed untiring energy and great personal courage throughout, as well as a very high order of military skill, in supervising the attack and consolidating captured positions, and although wounded and ordered off the field he returned to the line after his wound was dressed, knowing that his battalion was badly depleted of officers. He set a splendid example of pluck and devotion to duty.

London Gazette, 18 Jan. 1918.—"War Office, 18 Jan. 1918. His Majesty the King has been pleased to confer the undermentioned rewards for gallantry and distinguished service in the field. The acts of gallantry for which the decorations have been awarded will be announced in the London Gazette as early as practicable. Awarded a Second Bar to the Distinguished Service Order."

ASQUITH, ARTHUR MELLAND, D.S.O., Temporary Lieut.-Commander (Acting Commander), Royal Naval Volunteer Reserve.
(D.S.O. gazetted 17 April, 1917.)
(1st Bar gazetted 18 July, 1917.)

Awarded a Bar to the Distinguished Service Order:

DUNCAN, KENNETH, D.S.O., Major, Royal Field Artillery.
(D.S.O. gazetted 3 June, 1916.)

JACKSON, GEORGE SCOTT, D.S.O., Major (Temporary Lieut.-Colonel), Northumberland Fusiliers.
(D.S.O. gazetted 3 June, 1916.)

McCRACKEN, WILLIAM JAMES, D.S.O., M.C., M.B., Temporary Surgeon, Royal Navy.
(D.S.O. gazetted 18 July, 1917.)

SEWELL, HORACE SOMERVILLE, D.S.O., Major (Acting Lieut.-Colonel), Dragoon Guards.
(D.S.O. gazetted 23 June, 1915.)

AUSTRALIAN IMPERIAL FORCE.

GRANT, WILLIAM, D.S.O., Lieut.-Colonel (Temporary Brigadier-General), Australian Light Horse.
(D.S.O. gazetted 1 Jan. 1917.)

CANADIAN FORCE.

COSGRAVE, LAWRENCE VINCENT MOORE, D.S.O., Major, Canadian Artillery.
(D.S.O. gazetted 25 Nov. 1916.)
FOSTER, WILLIAM WASBROUGH, D.S.O., Lieut.-Colonel, Canadian Infantry.
(D.S.O. gazetted 25 Nov. 1916.)
MACLEOD, GEORGE WATERS, D.S.O., Major, Canadian Infantry.
(D.S.O. gazetted 14 Nov. 1916.)
NIVEN, HUGH WILDERSPIN, D.S.O., M.C., Major, Canadian Infantry.
(D.S.O. gazetted 19 Aug. 1916.)

Awarded the Distinguished Service Order:
ANDERSON, ARCHIBALD STIRLING KENNEDY, M.C., M.B., Temporary Capt., Royal Army Medical Corps.
ANDERSON-MORSHEAD, RUPERT HENRY, Capt. (Acting Lieut.-Colonel), Devonshire Regt.
BAILLIE, DUNCAN GUS, Lieut.-Colonel, Yeomanry.
BARSTOW, WALTER AGAR THOMAS, M.C., Major, Royal Field Artillery.
BIRKETT, RICHARD MAUL, Major (Temporary Lieut.-Colonel), Royal Sussex Regt., attached Royal West Surrey Regt.
BOWMAN, JAMES THORNELY, M.D., Temporary Capt., Royal Army Medical Corps.
BRACE, HENRY FERGUSSON, Capt., Hussars.
BROMLEY, JOHN EDOUARD MARSDEN, Temporary Capt. (Acting Major), Royal Field Artillery.
CAMERON, JOHN JACKSON, Temporary Capt. (Acting Lieut.-Colonel), South Staffordshire Regt., attached Lancashire Regt.
FRASER-TYTLER, JAMES FRANCIS, Major, Yeomanry, attached Cameron Highlanders.
GRAHAM, HOWARD BOYD, M.B., Temporary Capt., Royal Army Medical Corps.
HENDERSON, CHARLES ERNEST, Second Lieut., London Regt.
HILTON-GREEN, HENRY FRANCIS LEONARD, M.C., Capt. and Brevet Major (Acting Major), Gloucestershire Regt., attached Army Cyclists' Corps.
KNIGHTLEY, PERCY FRANK, Lieut. (Temporary Capt.), Royal Welsh Fusiliers.
McDOUGALL, ARTHUR, Capt., Yeomanry.
NEPEAN, HERBERT DRYDEN HOME YORKE, Lieut. (Acting Capt.), Indian Army.
REES, JOHN GORDON, Major, Yeomanry, attached Royal Welsh Fusiliers (Capt., Reserve of Officers).
ROBERTSON, ROBERT THIN CRAIG, M.B., Capt. (Acting Lieut.-Colonel), Royal Army Medical Corps, Special Reserve.
ROCHFORT, RICHARD ADAIR, M.C., Capt., Royal Warwickshire Regt., attached Royal Berkshire Regt.
RODGERSON, ALAN PATRICK, Capt., Indian Army.
STEDALL, LEIGH PEMBERTON, Major, Yeomanry.
THATCHER, GERALD GANE, Major (Acting Lieut.-Colonel), Royal Garrison Artillery, attached Royal Field Artillery.
UNIACKE, GERALD LAWRENCE, Capt. and Brevet Major (Temporary Lieut.-Colonel), Reserve of Officers, Royal Lancashire Regt.

AUSTRALIAN IMPERIAL FORCE.

A'BECKETT, MALWYN HAYLEY, Major, Infantry.
BOURCHIER, MURRAY WILLIAM JAMES, Lieut.-Colonel, Light Horse Regt.
CAMERON, DONALD, Temporary Lieut.-Colonel, Light Horse Regt.
DAVIES, GEORGE VERNON, Capt., Army Medical Corps.
DIXON, ROBERT DERWENT, Capt., Australian Infantry.
FETHERSTONHAUGH, CUTHBERT MURCHISON, Major, Light Horse Regt.
FRANKLIN, REGINALD NORRIS, Major, Light Horse Regt.
HENDERSON, ROBERT OSWALD, Lieut.-Colonel, Infantry.
HYMAN, ERIC MONTAGUE, Major, Light Horse Regt.
LAWSON, JAMES, Major, Light Horse Regt.
PAYNE, LESLIE HERBERT, Major, Infantry.
SELMES, JEREMIAH CHARLES, Major, Field Artillery.
THOMPSON, ROY MELDRUM, M.C., Major, Field Artillery.

CANADIAN FORCE.

AIKINS, GORDON HAROLD, Major, Mounted Rifles.
BURGESS, WALTER HARTLEY, Lieut., Infantry.
CAMERON, JOHN ANGUS, Lieut., Infantry.
JAMIESON, WILLIAM FRANCIS, Lieut., Infantry.
KENNEDY, HECTOR, Lieut., Infantry.
LAWLESS, WILLIAM THEWLES, Major, Infantry.
MACNAGHTEN, RONALD FREDERICK, Lieut., Infantry.
PEARSON, RONALD WILFRED, M.C., Capt., Infantry.
SAVAGE, HAROLD MURCHINSON, Major, Field Artillery.
WALKER, WILLIAM KEATING, M.C., Capt. (Acting Major), Machine Gun Corps.
WILSON WILLIAM DOUGLAS, Major, Field Artillery.
YOUNG, HARVEY GORDON, Temporary Capt., Canadian Army Medical Corps.

London Gazette, 4 Feb. 1918.—" War Office, 4 Feb. 1918. His Majesty the King has been pleased to confer the undermentioned rewards for gallantry and distinguished service in the field. The acts of gallantry for which the decorations have been awarded will be announced in the London Gazette as early as practicable. Awarded a Bar to the Distinguished Service Order."

BARTON, BAPTIST JOHNSON, D.S.O., Major (Acting Lieut.-Colonel), Reserve of Officers, Yorkshire Light Infantry.
(D.S.O. gazetted 18 Feb. 1915.)
BEATTY, GUY ARCHIBALD HASTINGS, D.S.O., Lieut.-Colonel, Indian Cavalry.
(D.S.O. gazetted 4 June, 1917.)
BOYALL, ALFRED MOREY, D.S.O., Major (Acting Lieut.-Colonel), West Yorkshire Regt.
(D.S.O. gazetted 27 Sept. 1901.)
GRAY-CHEAPE, HUGH ANNESLEY, D.S.O., Major (Temporary Lieut.-Colonel), Yeomanry.
(D.S.O. gazetted 1 Jan. 1917.)
HARDRESS-LLOYD, JOHN, D.S.O., Major (Temporary Colonel), Tank Corps.
(D.S.O. gazetted 1 Jan. 1917.)
HOARE, CHARLES HERVEY, D.S.O., Capt. (Acting Lieut.-Colonel), Yeomanry.
(D.S.O. gazetted 4 June, 1917.)
JACKSON, EDWARD DARBY, D.S.O., Capt. (Acting Lieut.-Colonel), King's Own Scottish Borderers.
(D.S.O. gazetted 1 Jan. 1918.)
JAMES, CHARLES KENNETH, D.S.O., Temporary Major (Acting Lieut.-Colonel), Border Regt.
(D.S.O. gazetted 14 Nov. 1916.)
KNOWLES, GEORGE, D.S.O., Major, Indian Cavalry.
(D.S.O. gazetted Sept. 1902.)
LITTLE, ARTHUR CAMPDEN, D.S.O., Major, Hussars.
(D.S.O. gazetted 18 Feb. 1915.)
MILLS, ARTHUR MORDAUNT, D.S.O., Major, Indian Cavalry.
(D.S.O. gazetted 1 Jan. 1917.)
OSBURN, ARTHUR CARR, D.S.O., Major (Temporary Lieut.-Colonel), Royal Army Medical Corps.
(D.S.O. gazetted 3 June, 1916.)
PLUNKETT, JAMES FREDERICK, D.S.O., M.C., D.C.M., Lieut. (Temporary Lieut.-Colonel), Royal Irish Regt. Reserve.
(D.S.O. gazetted 1 Jan. 1918.)
RAIKES, GEOFFREY TAUNTON, D.S.O., Capt. (Acting Lieut.-Colonel) South Wales Borderers.
(D.S.O. gazetted 22 Sept. 1916.)

CANADIAN FORCE.

DRAPER, DENIS COLBURN, D.S.O., Lieut.-Colonel, Mounted Rifle Battn.
(D.S.O. gazetted 19 Aug. 1916.)

Awarded the Distinguished Service Order:
ALLARDYCE, JAMES, M.M., Second Lieut., London Regt.
BIBBY, ARTHUR HAROLD, Major, Royal Field Artillery.
BOOTH, PATRICK DICK, M.C., Temporary Capt., Royal Field Artillery.
BROWN, AUSTIN HANBURY, M.C., Capt. and Brevet Major (Acting Major), Royal Engineers.
BROWNING, FREDERICK ARTHUR MONTAGUE, Lieut., Grenadier Guards.
CARR-HARRIS, FERGUSON FITTON, M.D., Temporary Capt., Royal Army Medical Corps.
CASTLE, JOSEPH PERCY, Second Lieut., West Riding Regt.
CONLAN, VERNON DOUGLAS ROBERT, Temporary Major, Army Service Corps.
COURAGE, ANTHONY, M.C., Major (Temporary Colonel), Hussars.
DENDY, MURRAY HEATHFIELD, M.C., Major, Royal Artillery.
DUTHIE, ANDREW MAY, Lieut. (Acting Capt.), London Regt.
EVANS, WILLIAM MAURICE, Lieut., South Wales Borderers, Special Reserve.
GERARD, CHARLES ROBERT, Capt., Grenadier Guards.
GLASIER, PHILIP MANNOCK, Capt. (Acting Lieut.-Colonel), London Regt.
GOODALL, TOM, Lieut. (Acting Capt.), West Riding Regt.
HALLSMITH, GUTHRIE, Second Lieut., Suffolk Regt.
HAMILTON, JOHN STEVEN, Lieut., West Yorkshire Regt.
HANCOCK, JOHN ELIOT, Temporary Lieut., Norfolk Regt.
HARTER, JAMES FRANCIS, M.C., Capt., Royal Fusiliers.
HOLCROFT, CYRIL WALTER, Lieut. (Acting Capt.), Worcestershire Regt.
JACKSON, HERBERT SELWYN, Capt., West Riding Regt.
JAMES, WILLIAM GEORGE, Temporary Second Lieut., Yorkshire Light Infantry.
JOFFE, WILLIAM, Second Lieut., Yorkshire Light Infantry.
JOHNSTON, KENNETH ALFRED, Capt. (Acting Lieut.-Colonel), Hampshire Regt.
KNIGHT, EDWARD SPURIN, Second Lieut., London Regt.
LUCAS, CHARLES ROBERT, Temporary Capt., Royal Lancashire Regt.
LYNN, ALFRED CECIL, Lieut. (Acting Capt.), Yorkshire Light Infantry.
MAGINN, JOHN FRANCIS, Second Lieut., London Regt.
MATHIAS, FRANCIS MORGAN, Temporary Capt., Welsh Regt.
McCUDDEN, JAMES THOMAS BYFORD, M.C., Second Lieut. (Temporary Capt.), General List and Royal Flying Corps.
McKEEVER, ANDREW EDWARD, M.C., Second Lieut. (Acting Capt.), Royal Flying Corps, Special Reserve.
MORGAN, DAVID WATTS, Temporary Major, Labour Corps.
MORGAN-GRENVILLE-GAVIN, THE HONOURABLE THOMAS GEORGE BREADALBANE, M.C., Capt. and Brevet Major, Rifle Brigade.
MOXON, CHARLES STONE, Lieut. (Acting Capt.), West Riding Regt.
NIXON, SIR CHRISTOPHER WILLIAM, Bart., Major, Royal Artillery.
NOTMAN, JAMES PARTRIDGE, Second Lieut., Seaforth Highlanders.
O'BRIEN, GERALD, Second Lieut., Royal Munster Fusiliers, Special Reserve.

The Distinguished Service Order

PANK, CECIL HENRY, Major (Acting Lieut.-Colonel), Middlesex Regt.
PAUL, WILLIAM, M.C., Second Lieut. (Acting Capt.), West Yorkshire Regt.
PEEL, JAMES, M.M., Second Lieut., Royal Fusiliers.
POOLE, GILBERT SANDFORD, Major, Yeomanry.
POWER, ROWLAND EDWARD, Major (Acting Lieut.-Colonel), East Kent Regt.
ROSHER, JOHN BRENCHLEY, M.C., Temporary Major (Acting Lieut.-Colonel), Durham Light Infantry.
RUNDALL, CHARLES FRANK, Major (Acting Lieut.-Colonel), Royal Engineers.
RUSSELL, GEORGE GRAY, Lieut.-Colonel, King Edward's Horse, Special Reserve.
SPENCE-JONES, CECIL JOHN HERBERT, Lieut.-Colonel, Yeomanry (surname changed from Spence-Jones to Spence-Colby [London Gazette, 14 May, 1920]).
STIDSON, CHARLES ARTHUR ALGERNON, M.D., Major (Temporary Lieut.-Colonel), Royal Army Medical Corps (surname corrected to Stidston)
STIRLING, JOHN ALEXANDER, M.C., Capt. and Brevet Major, Scots Guards, Special Reserve.
STORR, LEYCESTER PENRHYN, Temporary Major, Liverpool Regt.
STUART, GERALD FITZGERALD, Lieut., West Yorkshire Regt.
TILLOTSON, JOHN EDWIN, Temporary Second Lieut., West Yorkshire Regt.
TUCKEY, ELLIOT CLARKE, Second Lieut., Royal Field Artillery, Special Reserve.
UPTON, WILLIAM ARTHUR, Temporary Second Lieut., Wiltshire Regt.
WARDEN, HERBERT LAWTON, Temporary Lieut.-Colonel, East Surrey Regt.
WESTMACOTT, GUY RANDOLPH, Lieut., Grenadier Guards.
WILSON, BEVIL THOMSON, Capt. and Brevet Major (Acting Major), Royal Engineers.

CANADIAN FORCE.

BIRDS, SAMUEL BUTTREY, M.C., Capt. (Acting Major), Infantry.
BORDEN, ALLISON HART, Lieut.-Colonel, Infantry.
GRANT, ALEXANDER, Major, Infantry.
McEWAN, JOHN ALEXANDER, Major, Infantry.
McNAUGHTON, ANDREW GEORGE LATTA, Lieut.-Colonel, Field Artillery.

NEWFOUNDLAND FORCE.

BUTLER, BERTRAM, M.C., Capt., Newfoundland Regt.

London Gazette, 7 Feb. 1918.—" War Office, 7 Feb. 1918. His Majesty the King has been graciously pleased to approve of the undermentioned rewards for distinguished services rendered in connection with military operations in Mesopotamia. Dated 1 Jan. 1918. Awarded a Bar to the Distinguished Service Order."

MACRAE, JOHN NICOLSON, D.S.O., Capt. and Brevet Major, Seaforth Highlanders.
(D.S.O. gazetted 15 April, 1916.)

Awarded the Distinguished Service Order:
AGAR, JOHN ARNOLD SHELTON, Temporary Major, Royal Warwickshire Regt.
BAGSHAWE, EDWARD LEONARD, C.I.E., Temporary Major (Acting Lieut.-Colonel), Indian Telegraphic Department, attached Royal Engineers.
BARRON, ROBERT MACPHERSON, Major (Temporary Lieut.-Colonel), Indian Medical Service.
BEAZELEY, GEORGE ADAM, Major, Royal Engineers.
BERESFORD-PEIRSE, NOEL MONSON DE LA POER, Capt. (Acting Major), Royal Field Artillery.
BERNARD, RONALD PLAYFAIR ST. VINCENT, M.C., Capt. (Acting Major), Infantry, Indian Army.
BLAKER (late REICHWALD), WILLIAM FREDERICK, Major, Royal Field Artillery.
BLISS, JAMES ARTHUR, M.V.O., Lieut.-Colonel, Infantry, Indian Army.
BLOCK, ADAM, Major, Royal Field Artillery.
BURNE, SAMBROOKE FRANK, Major, Royal Field Artillery.
CASSELS, ROBERT ARCHIBALD, Major and Brevet Colonel (Temporary Brigadier-General), Cavalry, Indian Army.
CONINGHAM, FRANK EVELYN, Lieut.-Colonel, Infantry, Indian Army.
CONNOR, FRANK POWELL, F.R.C.S., Major (Temporary Lieut.-Colonel), Indian Medical Service.
CORFIELD, GERALD FREDERICK CONYNGHAM, Temporary Major, Royal Engineers.
COX, CHARLES EDWARD, Major (Temporary Lieut.-Colonel), Army Service Corps.
CRAKE, RALPH HAMILTON, Major, King's Own Scottish Borderers.
DICK, ROBERT NICHOLAS, Major and Brevet Lieut.-Colonel (Temporary Brigadier-General), Royal Sussex Regt.
EASTON, FREDERICK ARTHUR, Lieut.-Colonel, Royal Garrison Artillery.
FAIRWEATHER, HERBERT, Temporary Major (Lieut.-Commander, Royal Naval Reserve), Royal Engineers.
FRANKLAND, ERNEST ROBERT, Temporary Capt., General List.
GIDLEY, COURTENAY DE BLOIS, Major (Acting Lieut.-Colonel), Royal Field Artillery.
GOURLAY, CHARLES AIKMAN, M.D., Major (Acting Lieut.-Colonel), Indian Medical Service.
GREENSHIELDS, DAVID JOHN, M.C., Major, Royal Field Artillery.
GUNNING, GEORGE HAMILTON, Major, Cavalry, Indian Army.
HALDANE, CHARLES LEVENAX, C.M.G., Lieut.-Colonel, Infantry, Indian Army.
HANMER, LAMBERT ALFRED GRAHAM, Lieut.-Colonel, Cavalry, Indian Army.
HARRISON, JOHN SANDBACH NOEL, Major (Temporary Lieut.-Colonel), Somersetshire Light Infantry, attached North Lancashire Regt.
HART, ERIC GEORGE, Major (Temporary Lieut.-Colonel), Supply and Transport Corps, Indian Army.
HASLAM, BERNARD JOHN, Major, Royal Engineers.
HAUGHTON, EDWARD JUXON HENRY, Major, Infantry, Indian Army.
HEWETT, MURRAY SELWOOD, Major (Temporary Lieut.-Colonel), Supply and Transport Corps, Indian Army.
HICKEY, PATRICK FRANCIS BOURKE, Lieut. (Temporary Capt.), Indian Army, Reserve of Officers.
HUMPHREY, THE REV. FREDERICK JAMES HARRY, Assistant Principal Chaplain and Temporary Chaplain to the Forces, Third Class, Army Chaplains' Department.
INGRAM, CHARLES ROBERT, Major, Royal West Kent Regt.
IZOD, PERCY, Temporary Major (Acting Lieut.-Colonel), Army Service Corps.
JACKSON, FREEMAN ASTLEY, Major, Cavalry, Indian Army.
JAMES, WILLIAM HENRY, Temporary Capt., Army Veterinary Corps.
JOHNS, HAROLD WOOLISCROFT, Temporary Major, Royal Engineers.
JOHNSTONE, GRANVILLE HENRY, Capt. (Acting Major), Royal Field Artillery.
KELLY, THOMAS BERNARD, F.R.C.S., Lieut.-Colonel, Indian Medical Service.
KEMMIS, ARTHUR WILLIAM MARSH, Major, Lancers, Indian Army.
MACFARLANE, THE REV. ANDREW, Temporary Chaplain to the Forces, Third Class, Army Chaplains' Department.
McCUDDEN, JOHN HUGH, M.C., Major, Cavalry, Indian Army.
MEDILL, PERCY MONTGOMERY, Major, Royal Garrison Artillery.
MUSGRAVE, ARTHUR DAVID, Lieut.-Colonel and Brevet Colonel (Temporary Brigadier-General), Royal Field Artillery.
PEEK, SIR WILFRID, Bart., Capt., Yeomanry.
PELLY, EDMUND GODFREY, M.C., Temporary Capt. (Acting Major), Army Service Corps.
PITKEATHLY, JAMES SCOTT, C.V.O., Temporary Major, Special List.
POCOCK, MALCOLM ROBERTSON, Major (Acting Lieut.-Colonel), Infantry, Indian Army.
PRIDGEON, ALEXANDER FLETCHER, Quartermaster and Honorary Major (Temporary Major), Hussars.
PRYOR, THOMAS, Lieut. (Temporary Major), Indian Army, Reserve of Officers.
RATSEY, HAROLD EDWARD, Temporary Major (Temporary Lieut.-Colonel), Royal Engineers.
RAWLENCE, MAURICE, Capt., Royal Engineers.
ROBERTS, EDMUND ARTHUR, Major, Indian Medical Service.
SMITH, LIONEL ABEL, Lieut.-Colonel (Temporary Brigadier-General), Royal Artillery.
SYKES, ARTHUR CLIFTON, Capt., Royal Engineers.
TANDY, MAURICE O'CONNOR, Major, Royal Engineers.
WALKER, CHARLES WILLIAM GARNE, Capt., Infantry, Indian Army.
WHELAN, JOSEPH FRANCIS, M.B., Major (Acting Lieut.-Colonel), Royal Army Medical Corps.

London Gazette, 18 Feb. 1918.—" War Office, 18 Feb. 1918. His Majesty the King has been pleased to confer the undermentioned rewards for gallantry and distinguished service in the field. The acts of gallantry for which the decorations have been awarded will be announced in the London Gazette as early as practicable. Awarded a Second Bar to the Distinguished Service Order."

McDONALD, SAMUEL, D.S.O., Major (Acting Lieut.-Colonel), Gordon Highlanders.
(D.S.O. gazetted 14 Jan. 1916.)
(Bar to D.S.O. gazetted 1 Jan. 1918.)

Awarded a Bar to the Distinguished Service Order:
BENZIE, ROBERT, D.S.O., Temporary Lieut.-Colonel, South Wales Borderers.
(D.S.O. gazetted 1 Jan. 1918.)
BOYLE, CHARLES ROGER CAVENDISH, D.S.O., Capt. (Temporary Lieut.-Colonel), Oxfordshire and Buckinghamshire Light Infantry.
(D.S.O. gazetted 1 Jan. 1918.)
BRYCE, EDWARD DANIEL, D.S.O., Temporary Major (Acting Lieut.-Colonel), Tank Corps.
(D.S.O. gazetted 26 Sept. 1917.)
CROSSE, RICHARD BANASTRE, D.S.O., Capt. and Brevet Major (Temporary Lieut.-Colonel), Oxfordshire and Buckinghamshire Light Infantry.
(D.S.O. gazetted 1 Dec. 1914.)
HOTBLACK, FREDERICK ELLIOTT, D.S.O., M.C., Second Lieut. (Temporary Capt.), Norfolk Regt., attached Tank Corps.
(D.S.O. gazetted 10 Jan. 1917.)
JAMES, ARCHIBALD HUGH, D.S.O., Temporary Major (Acting Lieut.-Colonel), Northumberland Fusiliers.
(D.S.O. gazetted 1 Jan. 1918.)
JANSON, JAMES THEODORE, D.S.O., Temporary Major (Acting Lieut.-Colonel), Yorkshire Light Infantry.
(D.S.O. gazetted 4 June. 1917.)
KNOX, ROBERT SINCLAIR, D.S.O., Temporary Major, Royal Inniskilling Fusiliers.
(D.S.O. gazetted 1 Jan. 1917.)
McCUDDEN, JAMES THOMAS BYFORD, D.S.O., M.C., Second Lieut. (Temporary Capt.), General List and Royal Flying Corps.
(D.S.O. gazetted 4 Feb. 1918.)
McKAIGH, JOHN BICKERTON, D.S.O., Capt. (Acting Lieut.-Colonel), Liverpool Regt.
(D.S.O. gazetted 4 June, 1917.)
NASH, HENRY EDMUND PALMER, D.S.O., Major (Temporary Lieut.-Colonel), Royal Scots.
(D.S.O. gazetted 1 Jan. 1918.)
NELSON, HERBERT, D.S.O., Major (Temporary Brigadier-General), Border Regt.
(D.S.O. gazetted 2 Feb. 1916.)
ROSHER, JOHN BRENCHLEY, D.S.O., M.C., Temporary Lieut.-Colonel, Durham Light Infantry.
(D.S.O. gazetted 4 Feb. 1918.)

STIRLING, COLIN ROBERT HOSTE, D.S.O., M.C., Capt. (Acting Lieut.-Colonel), Scottish Rifles.
(D.S.O. gazetted 1 Jan. 1918.)
THORNE, AUGUSTUS FRANCIS ANDREW NICOL, D.S.O., Major (Acting Lieut.-Colonel), Grenadier Guards.
(D.S.O. gazetted 14 Jan. 1916.)
WATSON, HUGH WHARTON MYDDLETON, D.S.O., Major (Acting Lieut.-Colonel), King's Royal Rifle Corps.
(D.S.O. gazetted 14 Jan. 1916.)
WELCH, HAROLD ECHALAG, D.S.O., Temporary Major (Acting Lieut.-Colonel), Shropshire Light Infantry.
(D.S.O. gazetted 19 Nov. 1917.)
WESTON, SPENCER VAUGHAN PERCY, D.S.O., M.C., Temporary Capt. (Temporary Lieut.-Colonel), Royal Berkshire Regt.
(D.S.O. gazetted 17 April, 1917.)
WIGGIN, WILLIAM HENRY, D.S.O., Major, Yeomanry.
(D.S.O. gazetted 23 Nov. 1916.)

CANADIAN FORCE.
McLAUGHLIN, LORNE TALBOT, D.S.O., Lieut.-Colonel, Infantry.
(D.S.O. gazetted 14 Nov. 1916.)

Awarded the Distinguished Service Order:
BARKER, WILLIAM GEORGE, M.C., Temporary Capt., General List and Royal Flying Corps.
BELCHER, RAYMOND DOUGLAS, M.C., Temporary Capt. (Acting Major), Royal Field Artillery.
BION, WILFRED RUPRECHT, Temporary Second Lieut., Tank Corps.
BONNYMAN, EDWARD WILLIAM, Temporary Capt., Argyll and Sutherland Highlanders.
BROOME, RALPH HOWARD, M.C., Capt. and Brevet Major (Acting Major), Wiltshire Regt. and Tank Corps.
BULTEEL, JOHN CROCKER, M.C., Capt., Yeomanry.
CARRINGTON, CHARLES WORRELL, Second Lieut., Grenadier Guards, Special Reserve.
CHEAPE, GEORGE RONALD HAMILTON, M.C., Capt. (Temporary Brigadier-General), Dragoon Guards.
CRAWFORD, JOHN, Temporary Second Lieut., Rifle Brigade.
CROUCH, THOMAS ALFRED, Lieut. (Acting Capt.), Royal Irish Fusiliers, Special Reserve, attached Tank Corps.
DAMMERS, GEORGE MURRAY, M.C., Capt., Yeomanry.
DAWES, GEORGE, M.C., Capt. and Brevet Major, South Staffordshire Regt.
DIGBY-WINGFIELD-DIGBY, FREDERICK JAMES BOSWORTH, Major, Yeomanry.
DURRANT, ARTHUR WILLIAM, Lieut. (Acting Capt.), London Regt.
ELEY, EDWARD HENRY, C.M.G., Lieut.-Colonel, Royal Field Artillery.
FROST, JOHN MEADOWS, Major, Royal Field Artillery.
GEE, ERNEST EDWARD, M.C., Lieut. (Temporary Major), Royal Garrison Artillery.
GERRARD, WALTER DOUGLAS, Lieut. (Acting Capt.), Yeomanry and Tank Corps.
GILLILAN, EDWARD GIBSON, Capt., Coldstream Guards, Special Reserve.
GROUNDS, GEORGE AMBROSE, Temporary Lieut. (Acting Capt.), Tank Corps.
HARCOURT, ALEXANDER CLARENCE, Lieut. (Acting Capt.), Royal Berkshire Regt. and Tank Corps.
HENSHALL, LOUIS SYDNEY, Capt. (Acting Major), South Lancashire Regt., attached Tank Corps.
HEZLET, CHARLES OWEN, Lieut. (Acting Major), Royal Garrison Artillery, Special Reserve.
HUBBARD, REV. HAROLD EVELYN, Temporary Chaplain to the Forces, Fourth Class, Army Chaplains' Department.
HUNT, GERALD PONSONBY SNEYD, C.M.G., Major (Acting Lieut.-Colonel), Royal Berkshire Regt.
LATCH, ARTHUR RONALD, Temporary Second Lieut., Tank Corps.
LONGDEN, ALFRED APPLEBY, Major, Royal Garrison Artillery.
MAURICE-JONES, KENNETH WYN, Second Lieut., Royal Field Artillery.
McELROY, FREDERICK WILLIAM, Temporary Second Lieut., Tank Corps.
MENZIES, ALASTAIR FORBES, Temporary Lieut., Royal Fusiliers.
MURPHY, WILLIAM HENRY, Major, London Regt.
MURRAY-LYON, DAVID MURRAY, M.C., Capt. (Acting Lieut.-Colonel), Highland Light Infantry.
NICOLLS, EDWARD HUGH JASPER, M.C., Capt. (Acting Lieut.-Colonel), East Surrey Regt.
PEARSON, ALGERNON GEORGE, Capt. (Temporary Major), Royal Berkshire Regt., Special Reserve and Tank Corps.
PRATT, DOUGLAS HENRY, M.C., Capt. (Temporary Major), Royal Irish Regt. and Tank Corps.
RAIKES, DAVID TAUNTON, M.C., Lieut. (Temporary Capt.), South Wales Borderers, Special Reserve, attached Tank Corps.
RICE-JONES, ARTHUR PHILIP, Temporary Lieut. (Acting Capt.), Royal Engineers.
ROBINSON, LAWRENCE, Lieut. (Acting Major), Royal Engineers.
ROSS-SKINNER, HARRY, M.C., Capt. Highland Light Infantry.
SCARLETT, HENRY ASHLEY, Capt. (Temporary Major), Reserve of Officers, Royal Fusiliers.
SCOTT, WILLIAM, M.C., Capt., Royal Irish Fusiliers, Special Reserve.
SKEY, CYRIL OSCAR, M.C., Temporary Capt., Royal Fusiliers.
SMELTZER, ARTHUR SIDNEY, M.C., Second Lieut. (Temporary Lieut.-Colonel), East Kent Regt.
SOMERSET, HENRY ROBERT SOMERS FITZROY DE VERE, Lieut., Coldstream Guards.
STIRKE, HENRY RICHARD, Temporary Major, Royal Dublin Fusiliers.
VAN SOMEREN, WILLIAM VERNON LOGAN, M.C., Temporary Major, Royal Fusiliers.

VINCE, WILLIAM BERNARD, M.C., Capt. (Acting Major), London Regt.
WALSH, JAMES, Lieut. (Acting Major), Royal Inniskilling Fusiliers.
WILLIAMS, FRANCIS SEYMOUR, Lieut., Royal Engineers.
WOODWARD, LESLIE COLLINS, Temporary Capt. (Acting Major), Royal Field Artillery.

AUSTRALIAN FORCE.
DIXON, ERNEST WILLIAM, Lieut., Anzac Imperial Camel Corps.
WILLSALLEN, THOMAS LESLIE, Major, Light Horse Regt.

CANADIAN FORCE.
BROWN, ARCHIE FAIRBURN, Capt. (Acting Major), Infantry.
CARTER, ALBERT DESBRISAY, Major, Infantry and Royal Flying Corps.
CRAWFORD, JOHN KNOX, Capt., Infantry.
MACPHERSON, JOHN ROSS, Temporary Capt., Infantry.

SOUTH AFRICAN FORCE.
HARTIGAN, MARCUS MICHAEL, Major, South African Defence Corps.
(A Bar was substituted for this award [London Gazette, 22 Aug. 1918.])

London Gazette, 22 Feb. 1918.—"Admiralty, 22 Feb. 1918.—Honours for Services in Action with Enemy Submarines. The King has been graciously pleased to approve of the award of the following honours for services in action with enemy submarines. To be Companions of the Distinguished Service Order.'
ROLFE, CLIVE NEVILLE, Lieut.-Commander, R.N.
DOLPHIN, EDGAR HIPPISLEY, Lieut., R.N.
BIRNIE, HARRY CHARLES, Lieut.-Commander, Royal Naval Reserve.
WRIGHTSON, EDMUND GILCHRIST, Lieut. (Acting Lieut.-Commander), Royal Naval Reserve.
ROBINSON, FREDERICK WILLIAM, Lieut. (Acting Lieut.-Commander), Royal Naval Reserve.
FLORENCE, WILLIAM ALEXANDER, Acting Lieut., Royal Naval Reserve.

To receive a Bar to the Distinguished Service Order:
SIMPSON, SALISBURY HAMILTON, D.S.O., Lieut.-Commander, R.N.

To receive a Second Bar to the Distinguished Service Order:
NAYLOR, CEDRIC, D.S.O., D.S.C., Lieut., R.N.

"Honours for Miscellaneous Services.—The King has been graciously pleased to approve of the award of the following honours to the undermentioned Officers. To be Companions of the Distinguished Service Order."
TRIMMER, PHILIP HENRY, Commander, R.N. In recognition of the good work and arduous service performed by him in command of the Rufigi River Transport Service between Dec. 1916, and July, 1917. He carried out the task of transporting motor-boats overland from Dar-es-Salaam to the river near Kibambawe in spite of almost insurmountable difficulties and often under shell fire. The presence of the motor-boats on the upper Rufigi River was of the very greatest assistance to the military operations.
GORE-LANGTON, THE HONOURABLE EVELYN ARTHUR GRENVILLE, Lieut.-Commander (Acting Commander), R.N.
POLLARD, WILLIAM FAULKNER, R.D., Lieut.-Commander (Acting Commander), Royal Naval Reserve. In recognition of their services in mine-sweeping operations abroad during the period June, 1916, to June, 1917.

"Honours for the Royal Naval Air Service.—The King has been graciously pleased to approve of the award of the following honours to Officers of the Royal Naval Air Service. To be a Companion of the Distinguished Service Order."
BOWHILL, FREDERICK WILLIAM, Wing Commander, R.N. In recognition of his invaluable services as Commanding Officer of the Royal Naval Air Service, employed in connection with military operations in East Africa. It is due to his experience and unceasing labour that this small unit of the Royal Naval Air Service has been of such assistance to the military operations. He has instilled a high sense of discipline into those under his orders.

"Honours to the Mercantile Marine.—The King has been graciously pleased to approve of the award of honours to the undermentioned Officer of the British Mercantile Marine in recognition of zeal and devotion to duty shown in carrying on the trade of the country during the war. To be a Companion of the Distinguished Service Order."
POPE, ALFRED THOMPSON, Capt. (Lieut., Royal Naval Reserve).

London Gazette, 4 March, 1918.—"War Office, 4 March, 1918. His Majesty the King has been pleased to confer the undermentioned rewards for gallantry and distinguished service in the field. The acts of gallantry for which the decorations have been awarded will be announced in the London Gazette as early as practicable. Awarded a Bar to the Distinguished Service Order."

BAKER, SIR RANDOLPH LITTLEHALES, D.S.O., Lieut.-Colonel, Yeomanry.
(D.S.O. gazetted 1 Jan. 1918.)
CRIPPS, THE HONOURABLE FREDERICK HAYWOOD, D.S.O., Major (Acting Lieut.-Colonel), Yeomanry (Christian name Haywood corrected to Heyworth).
(D.S.O. gazetted 1 Jan. 1918.)
GILMOUR, JOHN, Junr., D.S.O., Lieut.-Colonel, Yeomanry.
(D.S.O. gazetted 1 Jan. 1918.)
GODWIN, CHARLES ALEXANDER CAMPBELL, D.S.O., Major and Brevet Lieut.-Colonel (Temporary Brigadier-General), Cavalry, Indian Army.
(D.S.O. gazetted 1 Jan. 1918.)
MOORE, LANCELOT GEOFFREY, D.S.O., Capt. and Brevet Major (Acting Lieut.-Colonel), King's Royal Rifle Corps.
(D.S.O. gazetted 1 Jan. 1917.)
ST. JOHN, WILLIAM EUSTACE, D.S.O., Major (Temporary Lieut.-Colonel), Yeomanry.
(D.S.O. gazetted 1 Jan. 1918.)
SEGRAVE, WILLIAM HENRY ERIK, D.S.O., Major (Acting Lieut.-Colonel), Highland Light Infantry.
(D.S.O. gazetted 7 March, 1899.)

NEW ZEALAND FORCE.
McCARROLL, JAMES NEIL, D.S.O., Lieut.-Colonel, Mounted Rifles.

Awarded the Distinguished Service Order :

BAKER, BRIAN EDMUND, M.C., Temporary Second Lieut. (Temporary Capt.), General List and Royal Flying Corps.

BATTERSHILL, LIONEL WARMINGTON, M.C., Temporary Lieut., Machine Gun Corps.

BLACKWOOD, ALBEMARLE PRICE, Major (Acting Lieut.-Colonel), Border Regt.

BUCKLE, ARCHIBALD WALTER, Temporary Lieut.-Commander, Royal Naval Volunteer Reserve.

DONALDSON, HERBERT, Temporary Sub-Lieut., Royal Naval Volunteer Reserve.

FREW, MATTHEW BROWN, M.C., Temporary Capt., General List and Royal Flying Corps.

HARRIS, WALTER KILROY, M.C., Temporary Lieut., Royal Naval Volunteer Reserve.

LLOYD, LEMUEL, Temporary Major, Suffolk Regt.

MARSHALL, FREDERIC ADRIAN JOSEPH EVANS, M.C., Lieut. (Acting Capt.), East Kent Regt.

MORGAN-OWEN, MORGAN MADDOX, Capt. (Acting Lieut.-Colonel), Essex Regt.

PECK, ARTHUR HICKS, M.C., Temporary Capt., General List and Royal Flying Corps.

POLLOCK, HENRY BRODHURST, Temporary Commander, Royal Naval Volunteer Reserve.

READY, JOHN MILNER, M.C., Second Lieut. (Temporary Capt.), Royal Berkshire Regt., Special Reserve.

SALKELD, HAROLD YORKE, Major, Cavalry, Indian Army.

London Gazette, 7 March, 1918.—" War Office, 7 March, 1918. With reference to the awards conferred as announced in the London Gazette dated 18 Oct. 1917, the following are the statements of service for which the decorations were conferred. Awarded a Bar to the Distinguished Service Order."

ORMOND, DANIEL MAWAT, D.S.O., Lieut.-Colonel, Canadian Infantry. For conspicuous gallantry and devotion to duty. He handled his battalion with exceptional ability and success during two days of the fiercest and most bitter fighting ever experienced by his brigade. In spite of the determined resistance by superior numbers of the best troops of the enemy, he captured all his objectives and maintained the organization of his battalion. Although 60 per cent. of his attacking force became casualties, it did not deter him from attacking and routing a hostile force of more than three times their number. During this operation 20 machine guns were captured. Lieut.-Colonel Ormond also displayed the greatest ability and gallantry in repulsing with the remains of his gallant battalion several determined hostile counter-attacks, during which very heavy casualties were inflicted on the enemy. No praise can be too great for the sound judgment and great skill with which he handled his battalion. (D.S.O. gazetted 4 June, 1917.)

Awarded the Distinguished Service Order :

BENSON, CONSTANTINE EVELYN, Second Lieut., Grenadier Guards, Special Reserve. For conspicuous gallantry and devotion to duty. On his own initiative he pushed forward with a small patrol to make a reconnaissance, with the intention of locating the actual line held by the enemy. In doing so, he came under heavy fire from the enemy machine guns, and some of his party were killed. Realizing the great importance of immediately securing certain high ground which had been temporarily evacuated by the enemy, he went back, despite the heavy machine-gun fire, and brought up his platoon to a point where a commanding position was occupied and consolidated. By his quick appreciation of the situation, and his own personal disregard of all danger, a position of considerable tactical importance was secured.

CAMERON, JAMES FREDERICK CAMPBELL, M.C., Temporary Lieut., Argyll and Sutherland Highlanders. For conspicuous gallantry and devotion to duty. During an attack on the enemy lines all the company officers became casualties. He went out from headquarters, collected troops, and organized a line of defence, in spite of close-range sniping, which eventually held back an enemy counter-attack. He remained at this post until the battalion was relieved.

CRAIG, ARCHIBALD HAY, M.C., Temporary Capt., Royal Scots. For conspicuous gallantry and devotion to duty. On three different occasions he went to the forward posts and steadied the men and organized the line after heavy casualties and in full view of the snipers. On the third occasion the men were threatening to come back on part of the line. He led them back to their positions and thus secured the line. It was due to his efforts that a serious situation was averted.

DE MONTMORENCY, HERVEY FRANCIS, Temporary Major, Royal Field Artillery. For conspicuous gallantry and devotion to duty in rallying his men after his battery had been heavily shelled for seven hours and his guns buried, and in getting three into action again. His men were driven back from the guns several times ; but he worked himself to restore confidence. During this time he was practically crippled, having seriously twisted his knee by falling into a shell-hole.

GILL, JOHN HENRY, Temporary Major, West Yorkshire Regt. For conspicuous gallantry and devotion to duty during an enemy attack. After being ordered to form a block, on his own initiative he collected scattered men and worked forward up the trench. On finding a block lightly held, he consolidated it and formed two blocks behind, taking charge of the position until ordered to retire. His personal courage helped greatly to rally the men and to stop the further advance of the enemy at a time when the situation was critical, and in spite of the fact that he himself was wounded.

HARDY, THE REV. THEODORE BAYLEY, Army Chaplains' Department. For conspicuous gallantry and devotion to duty in volunteering to go with a rescue party for some men who had been left stuck in the mud the previous night between the enemy's outpost line and our own. All the men except one were brought in. He then organized a party for the rescue of this man, and remained with it all night, though under rifle fire at close range, which killed one of the party. With his left arm in splints, owing to a broken wrist, and under the worst weather conditions, he crawled out with patrols to within seventy yards of the enemy and remained with wounded men under heavy fire.

KENNEDY, ARTHUR JULIUS RANN, Major, Royal Field Artillery. For conspicuous gallantry and devotion to duty when in charge of a party salving ammunition from a vacated gun position. The position was heavily shelled, and one shell fell near a pit containing a large number of rounds of ammunition, setting fire to the pit. He immediately ran to the pit, which was a sheet of flame by the time he arrived. After a great deal of work by this officer and a party under his supervision the fire was extinguished and the ammunition saved. The position was being shelled continuously during this time. It was entirely due to his prompt and energetic action that the ammunition was saved, and he set a magnificent example of devotion to duty.

MINET, ERNEST CHARLES TEMPLE, M.C., Temporary Lieut. (Acting Capt.), Machine Gun Corps. For conspicuous gallantry and devotion to duty when in command of his company. At a most critical period, when the attack was held up, he took charge of all the troops in the vicinity and established a defensive flank. He rushed up two of his guns into a strong point and dispersed enemy parties as they were forming for attack. He moved about the front line all day controlling fire, encouraging all ranks to greater efforts. His great coolness and courage were an example to all ranks.

MOBERLY, WALTER HAMILTON, Second Lieut., Oxfordshire and Buckinghamshire Light Infantry. For conspicuous gallantry and devotion to duty. In an advance against enemy positions three companies reached their objectives and consolidated. The commanders of all three companies were killed, and he thereupon assumed command of the advanced line. The position was extremely difficult, as the troops on both flanks had failed to reach their objectives, and the enemy were consequently holding positions at and slightly behind his flanks. Communication with battalion headquarters failed, as runners were unable to get through the machine-gun and snipers' fire from the front and flanks. In these circumstances this officer determined to hold on to the advanced line at all costs. He took steps to defend his flanks, and organized an effective resistance to counter-attacks. By his prompt and decisive action and complete disregard of danger he inspired his men with confidence ; and if it had not been for this plucky decision and courageous determination on his part the whole of the objectives gained would have had to be abandoned.

MUIR, JOHN BALDERSTONE, Major (Temporary Lieut.-Colonel), Royal Highlanders. For conspicuous gallantry and devotion to duty during an attack. When the position became one of considerable danger he promptly and personally dealt with the emergency, thus enabling the ground gained to be held and the line maintained. He personally organized the line, and by his example and energy infused such spirit into the defence that a very difficult and dangerous situation was saved. Had it not been for his daring and gallantry it is doubtful if his flank could have been maintained in its position, and subsequent operations would have been rendered extremely difficult.

PARR, VICTOR HENRY, M.C., Temporary Capt., Royal Inniskilling Fusiliers. For conspicuous gallantry and devotion to duty when in command of an advanced battalion headquarters. On his way there he mopped up three machine guns and 50 prisoners. On the battalion being forced back, through both its flanks being exposed, he was responsible for its orderly retreat. Practically all the officers were killed, wounded, or missing, and the casualties by this time were about 60 per cent. He himself was wounded, but by his resolute action the advance of the enemy was delayed and the troops in rear given time to take up covering positions.

REDMOND, WILLIAM ARCHER, Capt., Irish Guards, Special Reserve. For conspicuous gallantry and devotion to duty when in command of a company holding a line of posts. When, following a heavy barrage, the enemy attacked in strength and a bomb fell in his post, knocking out half the occupants, he immediately led the survivors out and drove the enemy back, which enabled him to establish a new defensive line and to hold it against repeated attacks until day broke.

STORRIE, WILLIAM, Second Lieut., Highland Light Infantry, Special Reserve. For conspicuous gallantry and devotion to duty when in command of a reconnoitring patrol. Under heavy fire he went forward in daylight and located two enemy posts and returned to his own lines. He again went out with two men at night and attacked an enemy post of twelve men. Again at daylight he entered an enemy tunnel, blew it up, causing serious damage. His courage, resource and daring are beyond all praise.

VIVIAN, THE HONOURABLE ODO RICHARD, M.V.O., Major, Yeomanry. For conspicuous gallantry and devotion to duty when commanding his battalion. At a most critical period of an attack he rallied his men and led an advance on an enemy strong-point, which was taken and held. He organized the defence of the ground gained, exposing himself under heavy fire for some hours, with an utter disregard of personal safety. Had it not been for his initiative at a difficult time no ground would have been gained at this point.

WENYON, HERBERT JOHN, Temporary Capt., Royal West Kent Regt. For conspicuous gallantry and devotion to duty. He collected a party, and led them through heavy shell fire in a counter-attack upon one of our posts which had been captured by the enemy, and although the position was exceptionally strong, it was retaken at the first attempt. This was entirely due to Capt. Wenyon's prompt action and the determined energy which he displayed at a critical moment.

WETHERALL, HARRY EDWARD DE ROBILLARD, M.C., Capt. (Temporary Lieut.-Colonel), Gloucestershire Regt. For conspicuous gallantry and devotion to duty during an attack. A strong-point held out, and the enemy succeeded in breaking our line and endangering the advance. He immediately organized two attacks on this point, which he captured, thus saving the situation and enabling the line to be straightened and advanced. Next day this point was again seized by the enemy, who were promptly ejected by another attack organized by this officer. By his promptitude and ability many lives were saved and the general situation re-established.

WILSON, GAVIN LAURIE, M.C., Temporary Major, Argyll and Sutherland Highlanders. For conspicuous gallantry and devotion to duty when in command of his battalion. The officers having become casualties, and his men held up by machine-gun fire during an advance, he at once set out from headquarters and personally reorganized his front during a critical time as the enemy were taking the offensive.

CANADIAN FORCE.

BAILEY, CHARLES EDWARD, M.C., Lieut. (Acting Capt.), Infantry. For conspicuous gallantry and devotion to duty. At a critical moment, when an attack was held up by strong enemy posts, he brought up reinforcements and attacked under heavy machine-gun fire, which resulted in heavy casualties to his party. It was only by the skilful leadership and determination of this officer that the enemy strong points were captured, a matter of vital importance in order to hold the line which was being consolidated. He maintained the position with complete success against no less than six counter-attacks, during which he accounted for 17 of the enemy himself.

BROWN, WALTER RICHARD, Major (Acting Lieut.-Colonel), Infantry. For conspicuous gallantry and devotion to duty when temporarily in command of his battalion. He made preparations for attack with great thoroughness. During the attack he handled his battalion with marked ability. By his leadership and coolness in trying circumstances he repelled several counter-attacks, with great loss to the enemy. His conduct throughout the whole operations was most inspiring.

BURNHAM, SYDNEY SMITH, Major, Infantry. For conspicuous gallantry and devotion to duty. Previous to an attack he displayed exceptional initiative and forethought in personally supervising the placing of observation posts in the forward area, thus ensuring that at no time during the battle was there any lack of communication from front to rear. On at least two occasions he made daring personal reconnaissances under very heavy machine-gun and shell fire, and brought back very valuable information. His cheerfulness and coolness throughout this period were a wonderful example to the men in the front line.

COCKERAM, ALAN, Lieut., Infantry. For conspicuous gallantry and devotion to duty in leading his platoon in an attack. On reaching his objective he came under heavy fire from a machine gun. Taking two men with him, he immediately rushed forward, personally killed the gun crew, and then, noticing that a booby trap was attached to the gun, he threw it backwards, on which the trap exploded. He then brought in the gun. During this operation he was wounded, but refused to leave his platoon, and later in the day, while on a reconnaissance with two N.C.O.'s, he met a party of the enemy, all of whom were killed. On the following morning this officer led his platoon in the open against a strong enemy counter-attack, and, after heavy hand-to-hand fighting, in which he personally accounted for several of the enemy, and was severely wounded, the attack was repulsed. His fearlessness throughout was most marked.

GILSON, WILLIAM FORBES, Capt. (Acting Lieut.-Colonel), Infantry. For conspicuous gallantry and devotion to duty. He displayed great initiative and forethought in organizing and preparing his battalion for an assault, and after the final objective had been reached, made a personal reconnaissance of the forward area and brought back very valuable information. Throughout the whole operation he displayed gallantry and devotion to duty of a high order.

JONES, LOUIS ELGIN, Major (Acting Lieut.-Colonel), Infantry. For conspicuous gallantry and devotion to duty in handling his battalion in an attack, and in resisting numerous counter-attacks made by the enemy, in which he displayed marked skill and initiative. Upon one occasion, the enemy having forced an entrance into his position, he made a well-organized counter-attack, which was entirely successful and resulted in regaining all the lost ground, capturing a considerable number of prisoners, and killing a great many of the enemy. Throughout the operations this officer displayed unusual coolness and sound judgment in critical conditions and was a splendid personal example to all ranks.

McEACHERN, NORMAN ANGUS, Lieut., Infantry. For conspicuous gallantry and devotion to duty when in command of his platoon. He captured all the objectives allotted to him. When his company commander was severely wounded he took control of the situation, and the following day led his company on the right flank of the battalion and captured the objective. Finding that the unit on the right had not come up, he personally placed a post on the extreme point of the captured area. Three times this post was annihilated with the exception of one man. On each occasion he personally re-established it. Though he had only six men left on the right flank, he beat off two counter-attacks. He also carried out two most daring reconnaissances in view of the enemy.

MILLER, ALBERT PETER, M.C., Capt. (Acting Major), Infantry. For conspicuous gallantry and devotion to duty. On his battalion's objective being gained this officer took charge, organized, and garrisoned the front and support lines. On two occasions the enemy counter-attacked, driving our men out and occupying the front line. In both cases this officer rallied the men and personally led them against the enemy, driving them back and re-establishing the positions, himself accounting for a number of the enemy with his revolver. His coolness and initiative inspired his men with confidence, and under his direction they charged the enemy with much enthusiasm and splendid spirit. This officer's example has at all times been most outstanding.

MILLS, ARTHUR SAMUEL, Lieut. (Acting Major), Infantry. For conspicuous gallantry and devotion to duty. He commanded his battalion with great distinction during five days' heavy fighting, gaining all his objectives and making several daring personal reconnaissances. His reports on the situation were clear and concise, and it was due to his inspiring personal example that no less than six determined counter-attacks were successfully repulsed with heavy loss to the enemy in the course of one day.

SOUTH AFRICAN FORCE.

DURHAM, CORNEY GEORGE, Major, South African Force. For conspicuous gallantry and devotion to duty when in command of his battalion. At a time when the unit on his right had been forced to give ground owing to a strong counter-attack, he rallied them, and with the reserves of his battalion ordered a bayonet charge, which resulted in the capture of a machine gun and the inflicting of heavy casualties on the enemy.

London Gazette, 8 March, 1918.—" War Office, 8 March, 1918. His Majesty the King has been graciously pleased to approve of the undermentioned rewards for distinguished service in the field. Dated 1 Jan. 1918. Awarded a Bar to the Distinguished Service Order."

BALDWIN, RAYMOND HENRY, D.S.O., Major (Temporary Lieut.-Colonel), East Surrey Regt.
(D.S.O. awarded Gazette 25 Aug. 1916.)

BROOKE, ALAN FRANCIS, D.S.O., Major, Royal Field Artillery.
(D.S.O. awarded Gazette 1 Jan. 1917.)

Awarded the Distinguished Service Order:

ADAMS, REV. JOHN ESSLEMONT, M.C., Assistant Principal Chaplain and Temporary Chaplain to the Forces, First Class, Army Chaplains' Department.

ANDERSON, EDWARD DARNLEY, Capt. (Temporary Major), North Staffordshire Regt.

CHAYTOR, JOHN CLERVAUX, M.C., Capt. and Brevet Major (Temporary Lieut.-Colonel), South Staffordshire Regt.

EVANS, REV. THEODORE HUGH WALBANK, Temporary Chaplain to the Forces, Third Class, Army Chaplains' Department.

FULTON, HENRY, Major (Acting Lieut.-Colonel), Royal Army Medical Corps

GILL, REV. HENRY VINCENT, M.C., Temporary Chaplain to the Forces, Third Class, Army Chaplains' Department.

HESKETH-PRICHARD, HESKETH VERNON, M.C., Temporary Major, General List.

HOLLAND, JOHN EDMUND DAVID, M.C., Capt., Dragoon Guards.

KINLOCH, GRAHAM, Temporary Major, Artillery.

LETCHER, REV. OWEN JAMSON, Temporary Chaplain to the Forces, Second Class, Army Chaplains' Department.

MURRAY, JAMES, Temporary Capt., Royal Scots.

NOBLET, REV. JOHN JAMES, Temporary Chaplain to the Forces, Second Class, Army Chaplains' Department.

NOSWORTHY, FRANCIS POITIER, M.C., Capt. and Brevet Major, Royal Engineers.

PEPYS, WALTER, Major and Honorary Lieut.-Colonel, Yeomanry, Reserve of Officers, late Hussars.

PERKINS, GEORGE FORDER, Capt. and Brevet Major, Hampshire Regt.

ROBINSON, REV. G. LEONARD, Temporary Chaplain to the Forces, Third Class, Army Chaplains' Department.

SAYE, KENNETH NOEL, Temporary Capt. (Acting Major), Royal Engineers.

SCULLY, REV. VINCENT JOSEPH, Temporary Chaplain to the Forces, Third Class, Army Chaplains' Department.

STANDING, REV. GEORGE, M.C., Assistant Principal Chaplain and Temporary Chaplain to the Forces, First Class, Army Chaplains' Department.

TANCRED, THOMAS ANGUS, C.B., C.M.G., Lieut.-Colonel and Brevet Colonel (Temporary Brigadier-General), Royal Artillery.

UZIELLI, THEODORE JOHN, M.C., Capt. and Brevet Major (Temporary Lieut.-Colonel), Royal Lancashire Regt., attached Tank Corps.

WATERHOUSE, THOMAS FRANCIS, Lieut.-Colonel, Reserve.

WHEELER, REV. FRANK HARRIS, Temporary Chaplain to the Forces, Second Class, Army Chaplains' Department.

WHITFIELD, REV. JOSEPH LOUIS, Temporary Chaplain to the Forces, Third Class, Army Chaplains' Department.

WILKS, GEOFFREY LOVELL, Temporary Capt. (Temporary Major), Royal Marine Artillery, attached Tank Corps.

CANADIAN FORCE.

COOKE, WILLIAM FORREST, Temporary Major, Forestry Corps.

McDOUGALL, KENNETH HAMILTON, Temporary Major, Forestry Corps.

STRONG, GARNET MATTHEW, Temporary Major, Forestry Corps.

RUSH, FREDERICK CHARLES, Major, North Brunswick Regt.

London Gazette, 8 March, 1918.—" Admiralty, 8 March, 1918.—Honours for Services in Destroyer and Torpedo Boat Flotillas. The King has been graciously pleased to approve of the award of the following honours for services in destroyer and torpedo boat flotillas during the period ending 31 Dec. 1917. To be Companions of the Distinguished Service Order."

HORNELL, ROBERT ARTHUR, Capt., R.N.

PARNELL, GERALD LANGTON, Commander, R.N.

MACKWORTH, GEOFFREY, Commander, R.N.

MOIR, DASHWOOD FOWLER, Commander, R.N.

HAMOND, ROBERT GERALD, Commander, R.N.

LANG, GEORGE HOLBROW, Commander, R.N.

GOFF, REGINALD STANNUS, Commander, R.N.

KING, RICHARD MATTHEW, Commander, R.N.

CREAGH, JAMES VANDELEUR, Commander, R.N.

KNOWLES, GEORGE HERBERT, Commander, R.N.

ENGLAND, RICHARD BRUCE, Commander, R.N.

SAUNDERS, ALFRED, Engineer-Commander, R.N.

HELYAR, PERCY JOHN, Lieut.-Commander, R.N.

HARRIS-ST. JOHN, RAYMOND JOCELYN, Lieut.-Commander, R.N.

WHITWORTH, WILLIAM JOCK, Lieut.-Commander, R.N.

RIDLEY, JOHN JACKSON CUTHBERT, Lieut.-Commander, R.N.

BROADLEY, EDWARD OSBORNE, Lieut.-Commander, R.N.

BUTLER, VERNON SAUMAREZ, Lieut.-Commander, R.N.

PENDER, EDWARD PENDER USTICKE, Lieut.-Commander, R.N.

LYONS, ALGERNON EDMUND PENRICE, Lieut.-Commander, R.N.

STANISTREET, HENRY DAWSON CRAWFORD, Lieut.-Commander, R.N.

SANDERS, GEORGE HENRY SAMPSON, Engineer Lieut.-Commander, R.N.

JOHNSON, HARRY CYRIL RODNEY, Engineer Lieut.-Commander, R.N.

CAMPBELL, GEORGE DUNCAN, Engineer Lieut.-Commander, R.N.

GRAY, COLIN JOHN, Engineer Lieut.-Commander, R.N.

EDWARDS, CYRIL, Lieut.-Commander, Royal Naval Reserve.

ALEXANDER, ROBERT LOVE, Lieut. (Acting Lieut.-Commander), Royal Naval Reserve.

To receive a Bar to the Distinguished Service Order:

STRONG, FREDERICK EDWARD KETELBEY, D.S.O., Commander, R.N.

London Gazette, 16 March, 1918.—" Admiralty, 16 March, 1918.—Honours for Services in Action with Enemy Submarines. The King has been graciously pleased to approve of the award of the following honours to the undermentioned Officers for services in action with enemy submarines. To be Companions of the Distinguished Service Order."

WHITE, STEPHEN PHILIP ROBEY, D.S.C., Lieut., Royal Naval Reserve.

ASHTON, WILLIAM RICHARD, D.S.C., Staff Paymaster, Royal Naval Reserve.

" Honours for the Royal Naval Air Service.—The King has been graciously pleased to approve of the award of the following honours to Officers of the Royal Naval Air Service. To receive a Bar to the Distinguished Service Order."

MOON, EDWIN ROWLAND, D.S.O., Squadron Commander, Royal Naval Air Service. In recognition of the resource and gallantry displayed by him in the following circumstances: On 6 Jan. 1917, whilst on a reconnaissance flight over the Rufigi Delta with Commander The Honourable Richard O. B. Bridgeman, D.S.O., R.N., as observer, he was obliged by engine trouble to descend in one of the creeks, where it became necessary to destroy the seaplane to avoid the possibility of its being captured. For three whole days the two officers wandered about the delta in their efforts to avoid capture and to rejoin their ship. During this time they had little or nothing to eat, and were continually obliged to swim across the creeks, the bush on the banks being impenetrable. On the morning of 7 Jan. they constructed a raft of three spars and some latticed window-frames. After paddling and drifting on this for the whole of 7 and 8 Jan., they were finally carried out to sea on the morning of the 9th, when Commander Bridgeman, who was not a strong swimmer, died of exhaustion and exposure. In the late afternoon Flight Commander Moon managed to reach the shore, and was taken prisoner by the Germans. He was released from captivity on 21 Nov. 1917. He displayed the greatest gallantry in attempting to save the life of his companion.

" Honours for Miscellaneous Services.—The King has been graciously pleased to approve of the award of the following decoration to the undermentioned Officer. For services with the Royal Naval Transport Service in France. To be a Companion of the Distinguished Service Order."

WARDEN, ST. LEGER STANLEY, Commander R.N.

London Gazette, 18 March, 1918.—"War Office, 18 March, 1918. With reference to the awards conferred as announced in the London Gazette dated 27 Oct. 1917, the following are the statements of services for which the decorations were conferred. Awarded a Bar to the Distinguished Service Order."

DAVIDSON, NORMAN RANDALL, D.S.O., Major and Brevet Lieut.-Colonel, Royal Field Artillery. For conspicuous gallantry and devotion to duty. He showed great courage and determination in superintending the preparation of battery positions. He was constantly under fire, and the success of the undertaking was largely due to his ability and fearlessness. He also carried out a very important reconnaissance.

PRESTON, THE HONOURABLE RICHARD MARTIN PETER, D.S.O., Major, Royal Horse Artillery (formerly Honourable Artillery Company). For conspicuous gallantry and devotion to duty. When on reconnaissance duty, he, with a small patrol, was suddenly attacked and fired upon at close range by a superior number of hostile cavalry. On his patrol retiring, the horse of one of his troopers fell. He immediately rode back, placed the trooper on his own horse, and carried him one and a half miles to safety, being pursued the whole way. At the moment of this gallant rescue the enemy were less than 100 yards away.

ROBINSON, HARRY ABRAHALL, Temporary Major, D.S.O., Royal Fusiliers. For conspicuous gallantry and devotion to duty during a heavy enemy counter-attack, when our line had been broken. With the help of a private, he drove off a party of the enemy who were attacking from the rear, killing several of them and thereby saving the situation. His extreme gallantry and coolness throughout the action were most inspiring.

Awarded the Distinguished Service Order:

DAVIDSON, THOMAS, Major, Royal Field Artillery. For conspicuous gallantry and devotion to duty. He commanded his battery with brilliant success during the operations under very difficult conditions. He went forward on a reconnaissance after an attack, and obtained information as to the dispositions of the infantry which was very valuable to his brigade, and established an observation post from which he was able to bring a withering fire on the enemy during several counter-attacks. He has continually shown great ability and fearless devotion to duty.

DERVICHE-JONES, ARTHUR DANIEL, M.C., Capt. (Acting Lieut.-Colonel), Royal Lancashire Regt. For conspicuous gallantry and devotion to duty. His skilful handling of his battalion resulted in all their objectives being captured and the ground held subsequently against repeated counter-attacks. The success of the battalion was mainly due to his total disregard of danger, splendid example and bold initiative.

DRUMGOLD, ARTHUR, Second Lieut., Royal West Kent Regt., Special Reserve. For conspicuous gallantry and devotion to duty in an attack. He led his company forward and gained his objectives in the face of heavy machine-gun and rifle fire from enemy strong points. With eight men he remained in an isolated position without food or water for thirty-six hours under very heavy artillery fire, holding his position until relieved. He set a splendid example throughout the engagement.

FOORD, ALEXANDER GUNNING, Major (Acting Lieut.-Colonel), Manchester Regt. For conspicuous gallantry and devotion to duty in capturing all the battalion objectives and holding them against counter-attacks. His battalion had a most difficult task to perform, and it was due to his power of command that they so ably carried it out.

GRELLET, REGINALD CHARLES, Temporary Major, Yorkshire Regt. For conspicuous gallantry and devotion to duty. He led his battalion through heavy shell fire, and assisted both in the capture and defence of the furthest objective. By the determination which he inspired at all times, and by his energy, coolness and judgment he raised the highest enthusiasm among his men. As a result of his organization the battalion within a short period took over and maintained with the highest spirit a new portion of the line under most difficult conditions.

HART, REGINALD SETON, Major (Acting Lieut.-Colonel), Nottinghamshire and Derbyshire Regt. For conspicuous gallantry and devotion to duty. When in command of the battalion, by his personal intervention at critical moments, by the energy and courage which he inspired, and by his excellent arrangements and determination the hostile defence was broken and the position captured and maintained against counter-attacks. Owing to his fine skill and organizing powers his battalion was after a short period ready to take over a portion of the line well beyond the original objective.

HENDERSON, GEORGE DUNNETT, M.C., Temporary Capt., Royal West Kent Regt. For conspicuous gallantry and devotion to duty in an attack. When his commanding officer was wounded soon after the advance started he took command of the battalion and directed the operations with marked ability and resource. When the enemy counter-attacked he rallied his men, regained the position, and saved a critical situation. He was largely responsible for the success of the attack, and set a splendid example of coolness and resource in the face of great difficulties.

HUDSON, HERBERT HENRY, M.C., Temporary Major, West Yorkshire Regt. For conspicuous gallantry and devotion to duty. When in command of his battalion he displayed exceptional coolness, judgment and power of command. All ranks were inspired by his courageous example. He in person supervised the consolidation of the captured position under heavy shell and machine-gun fire, freely exposing himself to ensure that his men were well supplied and the position safe.

HUMPHRYS, HERBERT JOHN, M.C., Capt. (Acting Major), Royal Highlanders. The enemy having broken into our protective tunnelling system, he at once grasped the situation and extended another branch of the tunnel into an old crater, thence driving a shaft down on to the captured tunnel. The mine was charged, tamped and fired, the resultant crater effectually blocking the tunnel at a good distance from our front line. Major Humphrys undertook and supervised this work throughout, carrying it out in the open within a few yards of the enemy front line, and by this action the enemy were undoubtedly prevented from blowing up a considerable portion of our front line.

LETHBRIDGE, FRANCIS WASHINGTON, Temporary Major (Acting Lieut.-Colonel), West Riding Regt. For conspicuous gallantry and devotion to duty. He was successful in leading his battalion through heavy fire to attack, capture and hold the furthest objective. By his presence in the front line, both during the attack and subsequent counter-attacks, the position was maintained and consolidated. His fine example imbued all ranks with enthusiasm.

MASON, HAROLD LYALL, M.C., Lieut. (Acting Capt.), Royal Field Artillery, Special Reserve. For conspicuous gallantry and devotion to duty. The battery was continuously shelled, and several dug-outs and the telephone pit were blown up by direct hits. He remained in the open directing his fire and keeping his guns in action, and, in spite of heavy and continuous shelling, carried out his entire bombardment programme. He set a splendid example of coolness and determined leadership.

MILLWARD, WILLIAM COLSEY, Temporary Major (Acting Lieut.-Colonel), Royal Sussex Regt. For conspicuous gallantry and devotion to duty. He assembled his battalion for the attack under artillery fire with only slight losses, and showed splendid leadership and ability in launching the attack. He personally superintended the consolidation of the captured position under heavy fire. Whilst holding the captured position during the two following days, under heavy artillery fire, he displayed great coolness, courage and determination, and, though badly shaken by the explosion of a shell, he remained in command until his battalion was relieved. His personal example was an incentive to all ranks.

RHYS-DAVIDS, ARTHUR PERCIVAL FOLEY, M.C., Second Lieut., Royal Flying Corps, Special Reserve. For conspicuous gallantry and devotion to duty in bringing down nine enemy aircraft in nine weeks. He is a magnificent fighter, never failing to locate enemy aircraft and invariably attacking regardless of the numbers against him.

RITSON, JOHN ANTHONY SYDNEY, M.C., Capt. (Temporary Lieut.-Colonel), Durham Light Infantry. For conspicuous gallantry and devotion to duty. When the attack was held up by machine-gun fire, he went forward to reconnoitre, reorganized the attack, and led it forward successfully. His initiative and gallantry saved what might have been a serious situation.

SALE, JOHN CARUTHERS, M.C., Temporary Capt., Royal Army Medical Corps. For conspicuous gallantry and devotion to duty during an attack. He collected the wounded over a large tract of country exposed to heavy fire, and continuously went out by night in advance of the front line searching for the wounded, many of whom he brought back over most difficult ground and under heavy fire. His coolness and determination were a splendid example to his stretcher-bearers.

STEWART, PATRICK DOUGLAS, Capt. (Acting Lieut.-Colonel), Dragoon Guards. For conspicuous gallantry and devotion to duty. He led his battalion with great skill in an attack, capturing all the objectives and holding them against several counter-attacks. By his example and training he inspired all ranks in his battalion with a very fine fighting spirit.

CANADIAN FORCE.

COLLIER, ERNEST VICTOR, Major, Infantry. For conspicuous gallantry and devotion to duty when in command of a company in a raid on the enemy's position. He led his company with great skill and courage, and was the first to enter the enemy trenches. He was at once wounded by machine-gun fire, but continued to lead his men. When the objective had been reached and the enemy's works had been destroyed, the enemy launched a counter-attack, which he broke up completely. His splendid leadership contributed largely to the success of the enterprise.

KING, WILLIAM HOPE, Lieut., Infantry. For conspicuous gallantry and devotion to duty in a raid on the enemy's trenches. During the advance his Company Commander was killed and he was severely wounded, but he at once took command of the company, and led it into the enemy trench, where heavy fighting took place, and he was again wounded. He continued to direct his company until the entire enemy garrison had been killed or captured and the dug-outs and machine-gun emplacements destroyed. He then directed the withdrawal with the greatest skill and coolness, being the last to leave the enemy trenches, and carried in a wounded serjeant under heavy machine-gun fire. Before having his wounds attended to he personally made a report to his Commanding Officer. His magnificent courage and determination were an inspiring example to all ranks.

McCORMICK, JAMES, Lieut., Infantry. For conspicuous gallantry and devotion to duty. He led his men through a very heavy barrage to the attack. When held up by an enemy machine gun, he led a bombing party and captured the gun and killed the crew after a hand-to-hand fight lasting ten minutes. He finally reached the objective, where he took command of the remainder of another company, consolidated the position, and beat off four counter-attacks. His cheerfulness and courage inspired all his men.

AUSTRALIAN IMPERIAL FORCE.

ELLER, JOSEPH HENRY PETER, Major, Infantry. For conspicuous gallantry and devotion to duty in an attack. He led his company under heavy fire with great skill and complete contempt of danger. When he came under heavy machine-gun fire from a pill-box, he bombed the enemy machine gunners and put the gun out of action single-handed, thus preventing many casualties. He captured and consolidated his objective. His courage and leadership contributed largely to the success of the operations.

ERREY, LEONARD GEORGE PRENTICE, M.C., Lieut., Infantry. For conspicuous gallantry and devotion to duty. After the objective had been captured, an enemy strong point caused many casualties. With four men he rushed through the barrage and attacked it under heavy machine-gun fire, and captured the position, with five officers, 60 other prisoners and two machine guns. His courageous and determined action undoubtedly saved many lives and restored a critical situation.

McCLEAN, FREDERICK STEPHEN, Major, Pioneer Battn. For conspicuous gallantry and devotion to duty while engaged on road construction. The road was subjected to concentrated shell fire every night while his party was at work, but he carried out the work successfully, showing great courage and determination as well as ability in handling the transport units bringing up material. On one occasion, when a building, against which a large quantity of 9.2 shells had been dumped, was set on fire by enemy shelling, he at once organized a party and prevented an explosion by removing all the shells under heavy fire.

London Gazette, 22 March, 1918.—"War Office, 22 March, 1918. With reference to the awards conferred as announced in the London Gazette dated 19 Nov. 1917, the following are the statements of services for which the decorations were conferred. Awarded a Second Bar to the Distinguished Service Order."

CORFE, ARTHUR CECIL, D.S.O., Major (Temporary Lieut.-Colonel), South African Defence Force and Royal West Kent Regt. For conspicuous gallantry and devotion to duty when in command of his battalion during an attack. The assaulting troops in front were checked by heavy rifle fire from a strong point. He at once went forward, and by his inspiring presence and personal leadership reduced the strong point and killed the occupants. He was severely wounded, but continued to advance until exhausted from loss of blood. His splendid example was of the highest value at a critical moment.

Awarded a Bar to the Distinguished Service Order:

CLARK, WILLIAM CHARLES, D.S.O., Temporary Lieut.-Colonel, Royal Fusiliers. For conspicuous gallantry and devotion to duty. When he was the only commanding officer remaining in action in his brigade, he personally led forward the leading waves of the brigade in a most gallant and fearless manner. His personal conduct, coolness and example during the most critical moments secured the eventual success of the attack after a very stubborn fight. During the two days following the attack he rendered most valuable service in organizing the defence of the captured position, though frequently exposed to very heavy shell fire.

CLEMSON, WILLIAM FLETCHER, C.M.G., D.S.O., Lieut.-Colonel (Temporary Brigadier-General), York and Lancaster Regt. For conspicuous gallantry and devotion to duty. When his brigade appeared likely to be held up in an attack owing to hostile machine-gun fire, he proceeded to the front of the attack, and, rallying the leading troops, he led them successfully to their objectives. By his personal example and contempt of danger he instilled new energy into the attack during a very critical period.

JARVIS, TALBOT McLEAVY, D.S.O., Temporary Lieut.-Colonel, King's Royal Rifle Corps (formerly Royal West Surrey Regt.). For conspicuous gallantry and devotion to duty. The enemy opened a very heavy machine-gun fire on his battalion as it was launching its assault. He rallied his men and led them successfully to the attack, although wounded five times. By his gallant conduct and determination he set a magnificent example to his men.

PENNELL, RICHARD, D.S.O., Lieut. (Temporary Lieut.-Colonel), King's Royal Rifle Corps. For conspicuous gallantry and devotion to duty. When the attacking troops on the right of his battalion were driven back, he organized a party of officers and men from his headquarters, and by prompt action saved a most dangerous situation. During the whole five days his battalion was in action he was ill with malaria and suffering from the effects of an old wound, but refused to leave the field until his battalion was relieved.

AUSTRALIAN IMPERIAL FORCE.

STEWART, JAMES CAMPBELL, D.S.O., Lieut.-Colonel, Infantry. For conspicuous gallantry and devotion to duty. When his battalion was ordered to fill a gap in the line caused by an enemy attack, he personally reconnoitred the position in advance of his battalion under an intense enemy barrage. Though the enemy were pressing forward fresh troops and machine guns, by his courageous leadership and example he succeeded in filling the gap with his battalion, consolidated the position in spite of very heavy fire, and held it until relieved. The loyal support which he rendered to other battalions was in a great measure the cause of the success of the operations. On previous occasions he has been largely responsible for the success achieved by his brigade.

Awarded the Distinguished Service Order:

ARMSTRONG, GORDON WILSON, Temporary Capt., Royal Army Medical Corps. For conspicuous gallantry and devotion to duty. He worked in the open under continuous and heavy shell fire, and dressed and evacuated 117 stretcher cases from his aid post in 27 hours. Later on, while the shelling was very severe, he volunteered to go in aid of an officer and an orderly, carrying them to the aid post one after another on his back. Though wounded during the second journey, he refused to leave his post, remaining with his battalion until it was relieved.

BORROW, EDWARD, Temporary Major, Durham Light Infantry. For conspicuous gallantry and devotion to duty in an attack. When the leading troops were suffering severe casualties, he kept the men together by his splendid leadership. Though twice wounded, he led his men to the final objective, and stuck to his post until he collapsed from the effects of his wounds. His courage and example were an inspiration to all ranks.

BOURNE, DENNIS KEMP, Temporary Lieut. (Acting Capt.), Welsh Regt. For conspicuous gallantry and devotion to duty. He took command of his battalion and led them with conspicuous ability and fearlessness to the attack on an enemy position, and captured and held it under very heavy machine-gun fire. His leadership and initiative while in command of the battalion were of the greatest value during a most critical period.

CHRISTIE, MURRAY INGLIS, Temporary Second Lieut., attached Royal Fusiliers. For conspicuous gallantry and devotion to duty. When the leading battalion in an attack was held up by machine-gun fire, he led his company through them and captured the enemy position at a time when the success of the whole operation was endangered. Having captured the first objective, he led his men with great gallantry and determination to the second objective, which he captured and consolidated under heavy fire. His skilful leadership and determination at a critical moment were largely instrumental in securing the flank of the main operation.

DENNISS, CYRIL EDMUND BARTLEY, Major, Royal Field Artillery. For conspicuous gallantry and devotion to duty. He rallied and reformed parties of men who had been driven back under heavy shell fire. He then went to Brigade H.Q. to report on the situation, and returned with a relief to the front line. Though wounded by a shell, he went to Brigade H.Q. to report on the situation before having his wound attended to.

EVANS, IVOR THOMAS, M.C., Temporary Capt., South Wales Borderers. For conspicuous gallantry and devotion to duty. He led his company in the attack with great determination under very heavy machine-gun fire. Though twice severely wounded, he consolidated and held the captured position. Afterwards he went personally to report on the situation under heavy fire, though suffering greatly from his wounds. His fearlessness and devotion to duty were beyond all praise.

GALLIE, OSCAR EUGENE, M.C., Lieut., Royal Field Artillery, Special Reserve. For conspicuous gallantry and devotion to duty. His battery was very heavily shelled while in action, four guns were destroyed, and ammunition dumps were set on fire. He set the battery a splendid example by walking up and down in the open, encouraging the remaining detachments and putting out fires. Later, the battery was again heavily shelled when firing in reply to an S.O.S. signal, and he again behaved with the utmost gallantry, encouraging the men, putting out fires and keeping his guns firing. He set a magnificent example of courage and devotion to duty throughout the operations.

GAYER, AUBREY VIVIAN ARTHUR, Temporary Major (Acting Lieut.-Colonel), Middlesex Regt. For conspicuous gallantry and devotion to duty. He led his battalion in an attack on a strongly held nest of concrete posts. Though wounded during the operations, he continued to command his battalion with great ability for four days until it was relieved, and by his devotion to duty set a magnificent example to all ranks.

GRAY, EDWARD, M.C., Second Lieut. (Temporary Capt.), Durham Light Infantry. For conspicuous gallantry and devotion to duty. During an attack he led his men with great initiative and determination on several enemy strong points, inflicting heavy casualties on the enemy and killing ten himself. During the consolidation of the captured position and subsequent enemy counter-attacks he walked up and down his line under fire with absolute disregard of danger, and kept his commanding officer well in touch with the situation. On another occasion he personally led an attack against an enemy strong point, capturing a machine gun and ten prisoners. Throughout the operations he set a magnificent example of courage and devotion to duty.

HOWITT, THOMAS CECIL, Temporary Major, Leicestershire Regt. For conspicuous gallantry and devotion to duty when in command of his battalion during an enemy counter-attack. He displayed conspicuous ability in handling his battalion and in reorganizing the defences of the front line. He went forward through a very heavy enemy barrage to make a personal reconnaissance, and his coolness and decision contributed very largely to the defence of the line.

JACKSON, DENNYS BRIAN MARRIOTT, Second Lieut. (Acting Capt.), Seaforth Highlanders. For conspicuous gallantry and devotion to duty. Although wounded early in the attack, after having his wound dressed he rejoined his company and assumed command of it, and also of another company. He led them forward to their final objective, and commenced consolidating. He also carried out a personal reconnaissance, in which he was responsible for knocking out an enemy post of six men.

HARDY, CLIVE, Capt., London Regt. For conspicuous gallantry and devotion to duty in an attack. He led his company with great ability to the capture of their objectives. With two or three men he attacked a concrete machine-gun post, which he captured with two machine guns and some 30 prisoners. Though wounded, he remained at duty for 48 hours until his company was relieved. He showed the greatest initiative and determination.

MAXWELL, ALLEN, Temporary Capt. (Acting Major), Royal Fusiliers. For conspicuous gallantry and devotion to duty. He took command of his battalion during an attack when his commanding officer became a casualty, and with great energy and determination led his men forward under heavy and continuous fire. Throughout the attack and during the enemy counter-attacks which followed the capture of the position he set a magnificent example to all by his courage and devotion to duty.

McKIMM, DAVID SIDNEY ALEXANDER, M.C., Temporary Capt., Shropshire Light Infantry. For conspicuous gallantry and devotion to duty in an attack. In spite of an enemy counter-attack being then in full progress and certain of the assaulting troops being diverted to meet the new situation, he launched his attack with the greatest skill and determination. He directed the assaulting parties, and personally held up with Lewis gun fire enemy bombers who were checking the advance. As he advanced he collected a mixed detachment of men of various units and established a forward line, getting into touch with the troops on his right. He showed magnificent leadership, courage and resource throughout.

MOFFAT, FRANCIS JOHN CAMPBELL, Temporary Capt., Gordon Highlanders. For conspicuous gallantry and devotion to duty in an attack. He was in command of the right attacking company, which was opposed to a very powerful system of the enemy's defences. He led his company forward with the greatest courage and determination under heavy fire, but they were eventually held up by a machine-gun firing from a concrete emplacement. This he attacked single-handed, putting all the team out of action. He was badly wounded during this encounter, but, inspiring his men to further efforts, he led them several hundred yards further before he fell exhausted. His splendid courage and determination were undoubtedly responsible for the success of the attack.

MUNRO, ALEXANDER, Second Lieut., Seaforth Highlanders. For conspicuous gallantry and devotion to duty. Although wounded early in the morning, and the only surviving officer in the company, he was mainly responsible for overcoming the very strong resistance of the enemy. He continued in command of the company, and was again wounded, but refused to leave until the situation was cleared.

PRIOR-WANDESFORDE, FERDINAND CHARLES RICHARD, Second Lieut., Royal Field Artillery, Special Reserve. For conspicuous gallantry and devotion to duty. When his battery was in action under heavy enemy shell fire a bomb store close to one of the guns exploded, killing the battery commander and causing other casualties. Seeing that the gun and its detachment were in great danger, he rushed to the bomb store and extinguished the fire at great personal risk. He then assumed command of the battery and kept it in action under very difficult conditions. On several previous occasions he behaved with great gallantry, and set a magnificent example to his men.

ROWBOTHAM, JAMES, M.C., Capt. (Acting Lieut.-Colonel), Highland Light Infantry. For conspicuous gallantry and devotion to duty. During an enemy counter-attack the front line became somewhat disorganized owing to a shortage of ammunition. He personally issued fresh supplies, and by his total disregard for safety and brilliant leadership succeeded in restoring a very difficult situation.

WALKER, FREDERICK WILLIAM, Second Lieut., London Regt. For conspicuous gallantry and devotion to duty. During an attack he saw that the left of his battalion was being held up by an enemy strong point. He immediately collected six men, worked round the enemy's rear, and captured the strong point, together with two machine guns and 20 prisoners.

WARNER, THOMAS LOVELL, Temporary Major, Leicestershire Regt. For conspicuous gallantry and devotion to duty. He was in command of a company in the front line, and held his position with very small numbers against two enemy counter-attacks of great strength. In spite of his right flank being exposed, and in imminent danger of being turned, he remained in his position and inflicted great loss on the enemy, finally handing over his line intact. He set a brilliant example of courage and leadership.

WELCH, HAROLD ECHALEZ, Temporary Major (Acting Lieut.-Colonel), Shropshire Light Infantry. For conspicuous gallantry and devotion to duty. His battalion was in immediate support to an attack which was held up by machine-gun fire from concrete posts, and it was found impossible to continue the advance without further artillery preparation. His battalion meanwhile was held up in a most exposed position. During the hours which elapsed before the advance could continue he moved about under fire regardless of danger, reconnoitring the situation, visiting his companies, and issuing orders. Owing to his efforts his battalion was eventually able to continue the advance successfully. His leadership and courage set a magnificent example to all ranks.

WILLIAMS, REES JOHN, Temporary Second Lieut. (Acting Capt.), Welsh Regt. For conspicuous gallantry and devotion to duty. During an attack on an enemy position he took command of the whole front line. Regardless of danger, under the heaviest machine-gun fire, he passed from place to place collecting his men, organizing the defence, and clearing up the situation for his commanding officer. He went under heavy fire to report on the situation personally, and subsequently reorganized the whole line. His cheerful courage set an excellent example to all ranks.

CANADIAN FORCE.

THOMPSON, WILLIAM WINFRED, Lieut. (Acting Capt.), Infantry. For conspicuous gallantry and devotion to duty. He led his company with great gallantry to the final objective in an attack, and on arriving there took command of the whole situation in the front line, consolidated the position with great skill, and sent in very valuable reports. On the following day, when the battalion attacked again, he was put in command of three companies, and led them with great success in the attack, though the troops on his right were held up, and his flank became badly exposed. He captured the position, which was held by an enemy force of more than double his numbers and 20 machine guns. He consolidated the position and held it with very few men against four determined counter-attacks by the enemy. His gallantry, coolness and exceptional handling of the situation were beyond all praise.

AUSTRALIAN IMPERIAL FORCE.

APPLEYARD, SYDNEY VERE, Major, Army Medical Corps. For conspicuous gallantry and devotion to duty. He established a forward dressing station immediately in rear of the front line during an attack, and attended continuously to the wounded, frequently going out and dressing cases in the open under heavy shell fire. His dressing station was hit by a shell, and, though he was badly shaken, he continued his work with great determination and devotion to duty. His fearlessness was an inspiration to all, and was the means of saving many lives.

BACHTOLD, HENRY, M.C., Major, Engineers. For conspicuous gallantry and devotion to duty. In daylight, under fire and under direct observation by the enemy, he marked out the assembly positions for the attack by his brigade. During the attack he personally reconnoitred the whole brigade position and organized the work of consolidation. His personal courage and his skill in grasping the situation were of the highest order.

FREEMAN, NEIL McKENZIE, Major, Infantry. For conspicuous gallantry and devotion to duty when his battalion was attacked by the enemy after a preliminary bombardment of great intensity. Though his right flank was exposed by the enemy attack, he held his position with the greatest determination and repulsed the enemy, inflicting heavy casualties. When reinforcements arrived he personally directed their dispositions under a very heavy enemy barrage, and continued to send clear and encouraging reports upon the situation. He was able eventually to cover the gap on his flank and to consolidate the position. On a subsequent occasion he rendered great assistance in supporting an attack and in consolidating a captured position. His courage and devotion to duty were beyond all praise.

JOHNSTON, WILLIAM WALLACE STEWART, M.C., Major, Army Medical Corps. For conspicuous gallantry and devotion to duty. While the enemy were shelling very heavily the positions where assaulting troops were assembled he went out into the open with an absolute disregard of personal safety and attended to the wounded where they lay. After the attack was launched he continued to work for several hours under a very heavy enemy barrage until severely wounded. On many previous occasions his fearlessness and devotion to duty while acting as regimental M.O. have been most conspicuous.

MARSHALL, NORMAN, M.C., Lieut.-Colonel, Infantry. For conspicuous gallantry and devotion to duty. When ordered to fill a gap in the line caused by an enemy attack he personally led his battalion through a heavy enemy barrage to its position. He rendered valuable service in arranging the assembly positions for two other battalions which were ordered to join in an attack at very short notice, and in guiding those battalions under fire to their positions with only two casualties. During the attack, when the troops on the right of the brigade were held up, the flank of the brigade seemed likely to become exposed, but by skilful dispositions he succeeded in keeping this flank covered as the advance progressed and consolidated the position under heavy fire. He subsequently led his battalion to the capture of an enemy position of great tactical importance, and afterwards captured several enemy concrete posts with a number of prisoners. His fine leadership and gallantry were largely responsible for the success of the operations.

MASON, CHARLES CONWAY, Lieut.-Colonel, Infantry. For conspicuous gallantry and devotion to duty. He carried out a successful attack on an enemy position with great skill, although the plan of operations had to be altered at very short notice. Though blown up and severely shaken during the attack, he continued in command and consolidated the position, capturing ten machine guns and inflicting heavy casualties on the enemy. The success of the operations was largely due to his courage, determination and devotion to duty.

TOLLEY, HOWARD GEORGE, Major, Engineers. For conspicuous gallantry and devotion to duty. He personally reconnoitred forward routes under a hostile machine-gun and artillery barrage. During the attack he reconnoitred for mines all the concrete posts and dug-outs in the area captured by the brigade, and also assisted in consolidating the captured position under heavy fire. He successfully organized the getting up of engineer stores and the laying out of communication routes, and supervised this work under continuous shell fire. He has at all times set a fine example of cheerfulness and courage under the most adverse conditions.

London Gazette, 26 March, 1918.—" War Office, 26 March, 1918. His Majesty the King has been pleased to confer the undermentioned rewards for gallantry and distinguished service in the field. The acts of gallantry for which the decorations have been awarded will be announced in the London Gazette as early as practicable. Awarded a Bar to the Distinguished Service Order."

ANDERSON, JAMES, C.M.G., D.S.O., Lieut.-Colonel, Highland Light Infantry. (D.S.O. gazetted 2 Feb. 1916.)

FORTH, NOWELL BARNARD DE LANCEY, D.S.O., Major (Acting Lieut.-Colonel), Manchester Regt. (D.S.O. gazetted 1 Jan. 1918.)

FARQUHAR, JAMES, D.S.O., Lieut.-Colonel, Royal Field Artillery. (D.S.O. gazetted 3 June, 1916.)

FORBES-ROBERTSON, JAMES, D.S.O., M.C., Capt. (Acting Lieut.-Colonel), Border Regt. (D.S.O. gazetted 18 June, 1917.)

REES, JOHN GORDON, D.S.O., Major, Yeomanry. (D.S.O. gazetted 18 Jan. 1918.)

ROMANES, JAMES GERALD PAGET, D.S.O., Capt. (Acting Lieut.-Colonel), Royal Scots. (D.S.O. gazetted 25 Nov. 1916.)

Awarded the Distinguished Service Order :

BARBER, THOMAS PHILIP, Major, Yeomanry.

BOWMAN, GEOFFREY HILTON, M.C., Lieut. (Temporary Capt.), Royal Warwickshire Regt., Special Reserve and Royal Flying Corps.

BRAND, DAVID ERNEST, Major, Highland Light Infantry.

CANTRELL-HUBBERSTY, GEORGE ALBERT JESSOP, Major.

CHANNER, GEORGE KENDALL, Major (Acting Lieut.-Colonel), Gurkha Rifles, Indian Army.

COOK, JOHN BLAIR, M.C., Major (Acting Lieut.-Colonel), Royal Scots Fusiliers.

CREWE-READ, RANDULF O. Capt., South Wales Borderers, Special Reserve.

DEAKIN, ERNEST BETTON, Capt., Essex Regt.

DRUMMOND, ROY MAXWELL, M.C., Capt., Royal Flying Corps.

GLAZEBROOK, PHILIP KIRKLAND, Major, Yeomanry.

HAWKINS, EDWARD BRIAN BARKLEY, Capt. (Temporary Major), West Yorkshire Regt. and King's African Rifles.

HAY, ARCHIBALD ASHWORTH BAILIE, M.C., Lieut. (Acting Major), Royal Field Artillery, Special Reserve.

HIND, HUGH WILLIAM, M.C., Lieut. (Acting Capt.), London Regt.

HUNT, DOUGLAS ALEXIS, Temporary Capt., King's African Rifles.

INNES, WILLIAM KEDIE, Capt., King's Own Scottish Borderers.

LANDSBERG, HERBERT VALENTINE, Capt. (Acting Major), Royal Horse Artillery.

LINDSAY, ERIC LAWRENCE, Temporary Capt., King's African Rifles.

NOEL, HAROLD ERNEST, Capt. (Acting Major), Royal Horse Artillery.

SMITH, RONALD KING, M.C., Lieut. (Acting Capt.), Wiltshire Regt., Special Reserve.

URWICK, FRANK DAVIDSON, Major, Somersetshire Light Infantry.

WRAY, EDWARD MILLARD GRUBB, Second Lieut., Essex Regt.

CANADIAN FORCE.

BOWIE, DOUGLAS BAIN, Major, Royal Canadian Dragoons.

PRICE, EDWARD EVAN, M.C., Lieut., Royal Canadian Dragoons.

SOUTH AFRICAN FORCE.

LORCH, ARTHUR EDWARD, Major, South African Field Artillery.

London Gazette, 26 March, 1918.—" War Office, 26 March, 1918. His Majesty the King has been graciously pleased to approve of the undermentioned rewards for distinguished service in the field. Dated 1 Jan. 1918. Awarded the Distinguished Service Order."

BIGNELL, R. L., Major, Indian Army. (Substituted for notification on page 12555, London Gazette, dated 22 Dec. 1916.)

SCOTT, J., M.B., Capt., Indian Medical Service.

London Gazette, 6 April, 1918.—" War Office, 6 April, 1918. With reference to the awards conferred as announced in the London Gazette dated 26 Nov. 1917, the following are the statements of service for which the decorations were conferred. Awarded a Bar to the Distinguished Service Order."

BEAUMAN, ARCHIBALD BENTLEY, D.S.O., Capt. and Brevet Major (Acting Lieut.-Colonel), South Staffordshire Regt. For conspicuous gallantry and devotion to duty. When the troops on the right were in difficulties, and communications with Brigade Headquarters broken down, he made dispositions with his own battalion and other troops which ensured the security of the Divisional front. He proved himself to be a leader of exceptional ability.

HANAFIN, PATRICK JOHN, D.S.O., Major (Temporary Lieut.-Colonel), Royal Army Medical Corps. For conspicuous gallantry and devotion to duty. For nine days he was continuously under heavy shell fire while supervising the evacuation of the wounded in the most adverse circumstances. Finally, although wounded in passing through a heavy barrage, he continued on duty until the last man had been brought in. The successful evacuation of the wounded was largely due to his gallant conduct.

HILL, ROBERT McCOWAN, D.S.O., M.B., Temporary Capt., Royal Army Medical Corps. For conspicuous gallantry and devotion to duty. While on the way to battalion headquarters his party was caught in an enemy barrage and four of them were wounded. He at once dressed their wounds on the spot in a most exposed position and under heavy fire. On arriving at the aid post he was informed that a whole machine-gun team were casualties in an advanced position. No stretcher-bearers were available, and he at once went forward and attended to them on the spot under heavy fire. He then returned and worked at his aid post under intense shelling, often attending to cases in the trench outside when the aid post was full. Casualties were being caused all round him, and he was wounded himself, but, though suffering severely, he remained at duty for 16 hours until the battalion was relieved. He set a most inspiring example of courage and devotion to duty to all ranks.

HUDSON, CHARLES EDWARD, D.S.O., M.C., Temporary Major, Nottinghamshire and Derbyshire Regt. For conspicuous gallantry and devotion to duty. He was in command of a sector of the front line for several days during an action, and organized and carried out the defence of the position under continuous and violent enemy shelling. It was entirely due to his organization and personal supervision of the work that the line was able to resist heavy enemy counter-attacks. He showed splendid leadership and great energy and courage.

JAMES, CECIL POLGLASE, D.S.O., Major (Temporary Lieut.-Colonel), Argyll and Sutherland Highlanders. For conspicuous gallantry and devotion to duty in commanding his battalion during the attack and capture of a position, and in holding it against very severe counter-attacks. He personally superintended the work of consolidation, and showed marked ability and untiring energy in the very difficult work of reorganizing his own and other battalions.

KEARSLEY, EDWARD REGINALD, D.S.O., Capt., Royal Welsh Fusiliers. For conspicuous gallantry and devotion to duty. He took command of his battalion at short notice, and organized and launched an attack which was completely successful, capturing the final objective. He showed great initiative and skill throughout.

LE PREVOST, ALFRED PAUL HARRISON, D.S.O., Temporary Major (Acting Lieut.-Colonel), Nottinghamshire and Derbyshire Regt. For conspicuous gallantry and devotion to duty when in command of a battalion in an attack. Though the battalion on his left was held up, he captured his objectives and also a series of strong points which was holding up the battalion on his left, and formed a defensive flank on a frontage of 600 yards. He personally directed this difficult operation under heavy machine-gun fire. He showed a complete disregard of danger, continually visiting his companies throughout the day, and it was due to his magnificent example and cool leadership that the position was secured and the battalion on his left was eventually enabled to advance.

LINTON, CHARLES STRANGWAY, D.S.O., M.C., Major (Acting Lieut.-Colonel), Worcestershire Regt. For conspicuous gallantry and devotion to duty. In the initial arrangements for an attack, which resulted in the capture of the first two objectives, as well as during the action and the consolidation after, he displayed marked ability and leadership as well as fearlessness in exposing himself when necessary.

SOMERVILLE, WILLIAM ARTHUR TENNISON BELLINGHAM, D.S.O., Major (Acting Lieut.-Colonel), Royal Lancaster Regt. For conspicuous gallantry and devotion to duty in handling his battalion during two attacks. It was largely owing to his courage and ability that a defensive flank was successfully formed on both occasions. His conduct was beyond all praise.

AUSTRALIAN IMPERIAL FORCE.

TOLL, FREDERICK WILLIAM, D.S.O., Lieut.-Colonel, Infantry. For conspicuous gallantry and devotion to duty. He was ordered at very short notice to take part in an attack with his battalion on the following morning. Notwithstanding the limited time available, he made all the necessary arrangements and led his battalion through a heavy barrage to the assembly position. During the attack the unit on his right was held up, his flank became exposed, and heavy casualties were caused by enemy machine guns in numerous strong points. He organized an attack on the strong points in a most able manner, capturing or killing the entire garrison, and taking 14 enemy machine guns. By his prompt and gallant action the advance was continued and the final objective was captured.

Awarded the Distinguished Service Order:

ALDERSON, CHRISTOPHER, Major, Lancashire Fusiliers. For conspicuous gallantry and devotion to duty when in charge of the front line. He organized the men of all units of the brigade, who were mixed together, with energy and skill. He held on in the face of a heavy and accurate barrage.

BAILEY, HERBERT, Capt. (Acting Major), East Lancashire Regt. For conspicuous gallantry and devotion to duty. Owing to the heavy going the two rear battalions were late arriving on the starting tapes. Shortly before zero hour he, whose battalion was only covering the right half of the brigade front, grasped the situation and deployed across the whole front just in time to follow the leading battalion behind the barrage. When severely wounded later, he showed a high example of courage when in great pain.

BEST, ALFRED JOHN, Second Lieut., Royal Engineers. For conspicuous gallantry and devotion to duty. Whilst carrying out a road reconnaissance during an action he saw a large party of men, without officers, who had been driven from their position. He at once rallied the party, led them forward, and succeeded in re-establishing the position. By his example and good leadership he restored a critical situation.

BRIGHTEN, GEORGE STANLEY, Lieut. (Acting Lieut.-Colonel), Liverpool Regt. For conspicuous gallantry and devotion to duty. When his battalion could advance no further owing to intense machine-gun fire, he went forward and personally reorganized it and established a strong defensive line. Later, when this hostile fire slackened, he at once initiated an advance which gained a considerable amount of ground. Throughout, his admirable reports were of the greatest assistance. His ability, coolness, and grasp of the situation had a marked effect on all ranks.

LAYTON, MUIRHEAD COLLINS, Major, Cambridgeshire Regt. For conspicuous gallantry and devotion to duty. He marked out the assembly position for the battalion under very heavy shell and machine-gun fire, and afterwards conducted the relief and assembly for the attack. He carried out a daring reconnaissance of the battalion front in daylight under rifle, machine-gun, and shell fire, and showed the greatest gallantry throughout the operations.

DANE, JAMES AUCHINLECK, Major, Royal Field Artillery, Special Reserve. For conspicuous gallantry and devotion to duty. His battery came under a heavy enemy barrage, during which an ammunition dump was exploded, destroying two gun pits, burying an officer, and killing several men. He at once went through the barrage, and after half an hour's work, with the help of three others, succeeded in rescuing the officer. During this time the barrage was so intense that no other help could reach the position. He set a magnificent example of courage and contempt of danger to his battery.

DAVIES, CHARLES STEWART, Lieut.-Colonel, Leicestershire Regt. For conspicuous gallantry and devotion to duty. He was in command of a battalion which took over an extended line of shell-hole positions after an attack, and by his skilful reorganization of the system of defence he avoided heavy casualties from the enemy's bombardment. On two occasions when his position was heavily counter-attacked by the enemy he kept his line intact and inflicted heavy losses on the enemy. His soldierly spirit and cheerful demeanour under continuous and heavy shell fire were a fine example to his officers and men throughout the operations.

DREW, FRANCIS WILLIAM MASSY, Major (Acting Lieut.-Colonel), South Lancashire Regt. For conspicuous gallantry and devotion to duty. He commanded his battalion in the attack with great gallantry, and took command of the whole of the left sector during the consolidation of the position. He showed great ability and untiring energy in the difficult work of reorganizing different units and allotting them sections of the defence.

DUNN, JAMES CHURCHILL, M.C., M.D., Temporary Capt., Royal Army Medical Corps. For conspicuous gallantry and devotion to duty during an attack. He worked with untiring energy in the open in the front line, searching for and dressing the wounded and constantly exposing himself to machine-gun and rifle fire. His medical orderlies were both wounded, and the greater portion of his work was done without any assistance. He set a magnificent example to all of courage and devotion to duty under continuous heavy fire and enemy counter-attacks.

FULLARD, PHILIP FLETCHER, M.C., Temporary Capt., General List and Royal Flying Corps. For conspicuous gallantry and devotion to duty. As a patrol leader and scout pilot he is without equal. The moral effect of his presence in a patrol is most marked. He has now accounted for fourteen machines destroyed and eighteen driven down out of control in a little over four months.

FURBER, CECIL TIDSWELL, Capt. (Acting Lieut.-Colonel), King's Own Scottish Borderers. For conspicuous gallantry and devotion to duty. When his right attacking company was driven back, this officer left his battalion headquarters, rallied the company, and he himself led the counter-attack, regaining the ground that had been lost. His dash and personal example undoubtedly saved a critical situation.

GARNSWORTHY, RANDALL, Second Lieut., attached Devon Regt. For conspicuous gallantry and devotion to duty. He attacked a strong enemy position, consisting of several concrete dug-outs, with his platoon. In spite of heavy casualties from machine-gun and rifle fire, he rushed one of the dug-outs, killed an enemy officer, and captured the position. He then pushed on to a further objective, showing great coolness throughout the operation.

GELSTHORPE, ALFRED MORRIS, Temporary Lieut. (Acting Capt.), Durham Light Infantry, attached Machine Gun Corps. For conspicuous gallantry and devotion to duty. While he was completing most elaborate arrangements in an advanced position for a machine-gun barrage on the following morning, the enemy attacked during the night under a most intense barrage. He immediately got all his guns into action with great effect, and made a personal reconnaissance forward to see if he could use them to better advantage. His teams suffered heavy casualties during this attack, but he carried out his full barrage programme on the following morning under a heavy bombardment. He showed qualities of leadership and initiative of the highest order, and his example of courage and contempt of danger had the most inspiring influence on his men.

GOGARTY, HENRY EDWARD, Lieut.-Colonel, Worcestershire Regt. For conspicuous gallantry and devotion to duty when in command of his battalion. He was wounded early in the operations, and though he was suffering much pain he refused to leave his post, and remained in command during three days of heavy fighting. He showed great courage and resolution, and largely contributed to the successful defence of the sector against repeated enemy counter-attacks.

GRIFFIN, ERNEST HARRISON, M.C., M.D., Temporary Capt., Royal Army Medical Corps. For conspicuous gallantry and devotion to duty. He established his dressing station well forward during an attack, and went up to the front line through a storm of artillery and machine-gun fire utterly regardless of personal safety. He moved about in the open for 36 hours without food or rest, attending to the wounded, often leading parties of bearers through heavy barrages until every wounded man had been carried back. He remained behind after the battalion was relieved, still searching for wounded, under heavy fire, though he was several times badly shaken by the explosion of shells. He set a most inspiring example of courage and devotion to duty.

HASSELL, LADAS LEWIS, M.C., Lieut. (Acting Capt.), South Staffordshire Regt. For conspicuous gallantry and devotion to duty in leading his company forward through a heavy barrage. In spite of severe casualties, the relief was very little delayed. He pressed home an attack with great ability, captured his objective, and formed a defensive flank when troops on the right were giving way. Though buried by a shell for ten minutes, he continued in command of two companies in the front line till relieved 24 hours later.

HEATH, EDWARD CHARLES, Lieut.-Colonel, Liverpool Regt. For conspicuous gallantry and devotion to duty. When his battalion was checked in front of its objective by heavy enfilade machine-gun fire, he pushed forward reinforcements and secured the position. He himself at once went forward, reorganized his battalion and established a strong defensive line. He also initiated an action which later resulted in the capture of another position. Throughout the fighting he showed great coolness and grasp of the situation, and was a fine example to his men.

HESELTON, JOHN LISTER, Capt. (Acting Lieut.-Colonel), West Yorkshire Regt. For conspicuous gallantry and devotion to duty. The battalion had suffered heavily, and seeing an enemy counter-attack starting he collected 100 men of various units and rushed them up through the enemy barrage to reinforce the front line. With the help of these men those of the enemy who got through our barrage were driven off.

HOBBINS, WILFRED ALSTON, Capt. (Acting Lieut.-Colonel), Lancashire Fusiliers. For conspicuous gallantry and devotion to duty. By skilful leading he brought his battalion into action at a most opportune time. He behaved with the utmost resource against counter-attacks, and rallied the remnants of the front line when, being unsupported, he was compelled to withdraw.

JOHNSTON, HOWARD RICHMOND, Temporary Second Lieut., attached Royal Lancaster Regt. For conspicuous gallantry and devotion to duty. This officer executed a very useful reconnaissance of a stream in front of our lines and of the enemy strong points. When held up during an attack by a strong point, he himself worked forward round it, rushed the door, shot the officer in charge, and compelled the surrender of the garrison. Later, when twice wounded, he had himself brought to battalion headquarters, and gave a clear account of the state of affairs in the firing line.

KING, HENRY JOHN, Temporary Lieut.-Colonel, Yorkshire Light Infantry. For conspicuous gallantry and devotion to duty. He led his battalion with great zeal and determination in the attack. He was untiring in his efforts to keep touch with all the troops under his command, frequently passing through the enemy barrage to encourage and direct his men. The success of his battalion was largely due to his able leadership.

LACON, SIR GEORGE HAWORTH USSHER, Bart., Capt. (Acting Lieut.-Colonel), Royal Warwickshire Regt., Special Reserve. For conspicuous gallantry and devotion to duty. When his battalion was held up by machine-gun fire his skilful handling restored the situation. He made a personal reconnaissance of the front to clear up the situation. On another occasion his skilful handling of his battalion resulted in their gaining their objective, in spite of the mud and the fact that the right of the line was held up.

LIKEMAN, JOHN LONGHURST, Temporary Capt. (Acting Lieut.-Colonel), Gloucestershire Regt. For conspicuous gallantry and devotion to duty. He commanded his battalion with great dash and skill. It was largely owing to his personal leadership on two occasions that they gained all their objectives and beat off heavy enemy counter-attacks.

LINFOOT, HAROLD ANYON, M.C., Lieut. (Acting Capt.), Cheshire Regt. For conspicuous gallantry and devotion to duty. He was acting second-in-command of his battalion and followed the attack with the rear companies. On arriving at the first objective while fighting was still in progress, he rushed a dug-out containing four machine-guns, capturing the guns and teams. He then moved along the line, under continuous shell fire and sniping, organizing the first objective and the further advance. Throughout the action he sent back full and accurate information, and his example and leadership were of the greatest service.

McFEELY, CECIL MICHAEL, M.C., Lieut. (Acting Capt.), Royal Dublin Fusiliers. For conspicuous gallantry and devotion to duty during an attack, which ultimately proved successful. He greatly encouraged his men by his example of audacious courage, and himself accounted for three of the enemy.

MILLAR, JAMES WILLIAM JOSEPH, Second Lieut. (Temporary Lieut. and Acting Capt.), Nottinghamshire and Derbyshire Regt. For conspicuous gallantry and devotion to duty during an attack. Though held up at several points during the advance, he was mainly responsible for the capture and consolidation of the enemy's position under very heavy machine-gun and rifle fire. Later in the day, on seeing the enemy concentrating for a counter-attack, he personally broke up the concentration with a Lewis gun, inflicting heavy casualties on the enemy. Afterwards he led his company to reinforce the front line, and sent in valuable information as to the situation during a threatened enemy counter-attack. He showed splendid courage and judgment.

MORSHEAD, OWEN FREDERICK, M.C., Temporary Capt., Royal Engineers. For conspicuous gallantry and devotion to duty in making his way forward with a supply of pigeons to clear up a situation, and sending back clear information. He also conveyed important orders to the leading battalions. It is impossible to speak too highly of his conduct.

NADEN, FRANK, M.C., Second Lieut. (Temporary Lieut.), Cheshire Regt. For conspicuous gallantry and devotion to duty when in temporary command of his battalion during an action. When the situation was obscure owing to the unit on his left having been held up, he made a thorough reconnaissance at great risk, and obtained valuable information. He then directed the attack of his battalion, capturing all his objectives. Throughout the day and the following days he went about under heavy shell and machine-gun fire, encouraging his men and directing the consolidation. The skilful manner in which he handled a most difficult situation was a great factor in the success achieved.

PANTON, HENRY FORBES, M.C., M.B., Capt. and Brevet Major, Royal Army Medical Corps. For conspicuous gallantry and devotion to duty. The evacuation of casualties, amounting to 60 officers and 1,100 men, after an advance of 3,000 yards was most successfully carried out, chiefly owing to the initiative and sound judgment displayed by him. He spent 24 hours in the forward area, visiting every regimental aid post and sending back hourly reports until the battlefield was completely cleared of wounded.

PEDDIE, TOM ANDERSON, Second Lieut. (Temporary Major), Lincolnshire Regt. For conspicuous gallantry and devotion to duty. He commanded his battalion throughout the operations with great success. His bearing, coolness, and courage were beyond all praise, and the notable success of his battalion was largely due to his example and ability as a leader.

PORTAL, WYNDHAM RAYMOND, Capt. (Temporary Lieut.-Colonel), Life Guards, Special Reserve. For conspicuous gallantry and devotion to duty. When, during an attack, a village in the rear of the attacking troops was discovered to be still occupied by the enemy, he successfully organized a defensive flank, and personally led forward a company, who had lost most of their officers, to fill a gap. The splendid behaviour of his battalion, which suffered heavily in a critical position was largely due to his personality.

PRESTON, JAMES, Second Lieut., Scottish Rifles, Special Reserve. For conspicuous gallantry and devotion to duty in an attack. He led his men with great skill and determination under heavy fire to the capture of a concrete emplacement which was holding up the advance, taking two officers and 22 other ranks prisoners, and inflicting heavy casualties on the enemy. His prompt and fearless action enabled the advance to continue to the final objective.

RADFORD, NORMAN HAROLD, M.C., Temporary Lieut. (Acting Capt.), Royal Welsh Fusiliers. For conspicuous gallantry and devotion to duty. On two occasions he took command of his battalion when the commanding officers became casualties, and displayed the greatest ability and courage under heavy fire throughout the operations. He contributed largely to the success achieved.

ROBINSON, ERNEST HAROLD, M.C., Temporary Capt., Shropshire Light Infantry. For conspicuous gallantry and devotion to duty. He led his company in an attack until further advance was impossible. He then reorganized them, and collecting all men available of other companies, successfully repelled two counter-attacks, although the troops on either flank fell back. His skilful leadership and resolute bearing were a magnificent example to the remainder of the battalion.

SPRING, TREVOR COLERIDGE, Major (Acting Lieut.-Colonel), Hampshire Regt. For conspicuous gallantry and devotion to duty. During the advance of his battalion to a counter-attack between two assaulting battalions he showed an admirable grasp of the situation, filling up the gaps on the flank and reinforcing the front when necessary. Being at short notice ordered to undertake a minor operation, he himself passed through a heavy barrage, in which several of his men had already been killed, to convey the orders to his subordinate officers about the attack, which was a complete success.

STUDDERT, ROBERT HALLAM, M.C., Capt. and Brevet Major (Acting Major), Royal Field Artillery. For conspicuous gallantry and devotion to duty. On two occasions when gun-pits were struck by shells and the camouflage and ammunition set on fire he personally, with the help of two N.C.O.'s, extinguished the fire with water from a shell-hole. It was largely due to his fine example that the morale of the battery, which was suffering heavy casualties, was maintained at a very high standard.

TRON, REV. MAZZINI, M.C., Army Chaplains' Department. For conspicuous gallantry and devotion to duty. His cheerful demeanour had a great influence in keeping up the spirits of all ranks whilst assembling for an attack. He went forward with the attack and exposed himself fearlessly in attending to the wounded, regardless of his own safety. His unceasing efforts under heavy fire and the most adverse conditions are worthy of the highest praise.

WEBSTER, JOHN RYIE, M.C., Temporary Capt. (Acting Major), Nottinghamshire and Derbyshire Regt. For conspicuous gallantry and devotion to duty when in command of a battalion in an attack. When a strong point, manned by four machine guns, had been passed over by the leading troops in the attack, he promptly organized a party and led it to the capture of the strong point. He then led his battalion forward in the advance and, in spite of serious opposition, took all his objectives and held them against three enemy counter-attacks. The remarkable dash and determination of his battalion during the operations was mainly due to his splendid example and leadership.

WILDE, REGINALD COLERIDGE, M.C., Second Lieut. (Acting Capt.), Liverpool Regt. For conspicuous gallantry and devotion to duty. During an attack his party met with very strong resistance from an enemy strong point consisting of ten concrete dug-outs. When he found that he had not sufficient men to capture the position he went back under heavy fire and brought up a party of 40, and after a preliminary bombardment with rifle grenades he led an attack which was entirely successful. Two enemy officers and 20 other ranks were killed and more than 40 prisoners were taken, and also four machine guns. He at once directed the consolidation of the position and showed the greatest coolness, energy, and resource under heavy fire, remaining at duty though he was blown up by a shell.

CANADIAN FORCE

(Corrected to New Zealand Force [London Gazette, 17 April, 1918]).

BLAIR, DUNCAN BARRIE, M.C., Lieut.-Colonel, Infantry. For conspicuous gallantry and devotion to duty during an action. He repeatedly went through the enemy barrage, steadying and encouraging his men, and directing the consolidation of the captured position. His courage and coolness did much to inspire all ranks, and the success of the operations was largely due to his personal efforts.

COCKERELL, ALLAN RICHMOND, Second Lieut., Infantry. For conspicuous gallantry and devotion to duty. While he was endeavouring to fill a gap on his left flank during an attack his platoon came under heavy fire from some pill-boxes and an enemy trench. He at once led his men to the attack, captured the garrison of the trench, and eventually, by a skilful manœuvre, put the pill-boxes out of action. He was cut off from his company and all his platoon had become casualties, but he took command of a few men near him and held his position when the rest of the advance was held up. Later, he rejoined his company, took command, and consolidated the new position. He showed the greatest gallantry, coolness, and leadership throughout.

COLQUHOUN, DUNCAN, Lieut.-Colonel, Infantry. For conspicuous gallantry and devotion to duty. During heavy fighting, when the situation was obscure, he went forward at a critical time through heavy shell fire and made a most valuable personal reconnaissance of the position. He showed courage and ability of a high order during the subsequent operations.

MACCORMICK, KENNETH, Major, Medical Corps. For conspicuous gallantry and devotion to duty when in charge of the evacuation of the wounded during an action. He remained at duty for 48 hours without rest, visiting the advanced posts, searching shell-holes, and bringing in many wounded. When one of his bearer posts was heavily shelled, with great coolness he got all the wounded away, staying behind himself until the last had left. He set a splendid example of courage and untiring energy.

AUSTRALIAN IMPERIAL FORCE.

CRAIG, WILLIAM BANNERMAN, Major, Army Medical Corps. For conspicuous gallantry and devotion to duty during an attack. After the aid post had been blown up he attended the wounded and organized bearer parties in the open. Though wounded he persisted in his work until disabled by another wound.

HAILES, WILLIAM ALLAN, Major, Australian Army Medical Corps. For conspicuous gallantry and devotion to duty in attending to four wounded men in the open under heavy fire and conveying them to cover. His example stimulated the stretcher-bearers to great efforts under most trying circumstances.

LEE, HARRIE BERTIE, M.C., Major, Army Medical Corps. For conspicuous gallantry and devotion to duty. He was in charge of the organization of bearer reliefs during an action, and hearing that the officer in charge of the forward bearer parties had been killed he at once went forward under heavy fire and took charge. He located the new regimental aid posts forward of the former front line, and with absolute disregard of danger arranged for the evacuation of the wounded from these new posts through a heavy barrage. His quick grasp of the situation and prompt and courageous action were of inestimable value.

McMASTER, ROBERT MAXWELL, Major, Army Medical Corps. For conspicuous gallantry and devotion to duty in tending the wounded continuously for ten hours under shell fire. Several of his bearers were killed and wounded, and it was only with the greatest difficulty that he was able to save the wounded from being killed or buried alive.

PURSER, MUIR, Lieut.-Colonel, Infantry. For conspicuous gallantry and devotion to duty. He was ordered at very short notice to take part in an attack with his battalion on the following morning. Notwithstanding the limited time available he made all the necessary arrangements, and led his battalion through a heavy barrage to the assembly position. In the attack he overcame all resistance by assaulting numerous strong points and capturing large numbers of prisoners. After the final objective was captured he was instrumental in repulsing with heavy loss several enemy counter-attacks. He set a splendid example of courage and determination to his battalion.

ROBERTS, PERCIVAL THOMAS, Capt., Infantry. For conspicuous gallantry and devotion to duty. He took command of his battalion in an attack when his commanding officer became a casualty. As soon as the objective was reached he personally reconnoitred the whole front, laid out the line of defence and saw that communication was well established with both flanks. During the four days in the line he displayed great qualities of leadership and organization, and set a most inspiring example to all ranks under his command.

SCALES, JOSEPH LINDLEY, Lieut., Infantry. For conspicuous gallantry and devotion to duty in capturing a strong point 150 yards in front of our line. This he did single-handed. By the effective use of his rifle he killed four of the enemy in the post and two more as they tried to escape. He rushed the post from a distance of 50 yards and captured the machine gun. His devotion and courage inspired his men to further efforts, including the capture of five prisoners.

SLATER, HENRY ERNEST, Lieut., Infantry. For conspicuous gallantry and devotion to duty. After the battalion had reached its objective with few casualties an enemy strong point with several machine guns inflicted severe casualties on the right flank, and threatened the junction with the unit on the right. With a serjeant and two men he attacked the strong point, put the machine-gun crew out of action, and captured the position with 30 prisoners. By his prompt and courageous action he saved many casualties. In the later stages of the fight by his courage and example he inspired his men to withstand and beat off a counter-attack.

TRAILL, JOHN CHARLES MERRIMAN, M.C., Capt., Infantry. For conspicuous gallantry and devotion to duty in an attack. He took command of the whole line when another company commander became a casualty during the advance, and encouraged and inspired his men throughout the attack by his splendid personal example. When the whole line was held up by direct fire from an enemy field gun he worked his way to a flank under heavy machine-gun fire and attacked it single-handed, killing five of the crew with his revolver and capturing the gun, thus allowing the advance to continue. His splendid action not only saved many lives but relieved a very critical situation, and the success of the operations was undoubtedly largely due to his magnificent example.

SOUTH AFRICAN FORCE.

BROWNE, AMBROSE ROBIN INNES, Capt. (Temporary Major and Acting Lieut.-Colonel), South African Defence Force. For conspicuous gallantry and devotion to duty. He was in command of a support battalion during an attack, and on going forward to reconnoitre he found that the advance was completely held up by flanking machine-gun fire from a pill-box. He at once organized an attack upon it, captured it and several other enemy strong points, and was able to establish a definite line, which he held until relieved. He displayed exceptional qualities of leadership and resource at a very critical time.

FORBES, ERNEST CRESPIN, Lieut., Infantry. For conspicuous gallantry and devotion to duty in an attack. He was with the support company, but, hearing that all the senior officers were casualties, he at once went forward and took command of the three leading companies and led them to the final objective. He then superintended the placing of outposts and the defence of the position, sending in clear and concise reports. Though wounded during the advance, he remained with his men under very heavy fire until he was again severely wounded. His gallant behaviour and cool confidence had a splendid effect on all ranks.

SPRENGER, LESLIE FRANCIS, M.C., Capt., Infantry. For conspicuous gallantry and devotion to duty in an attack. When the advance was held up by a cluster of concrete strong points he collected every available man and organized and led the attack on the position, which he captured under very heavy fire. He showed great courage and high qualities of initiative and leadership, and his prompt handling of a critical situation enabled the advance to continue.

London Gazette, 6 April, 1918.—" Admiralty, 6 April, 1918.—Honours for Service in the Auxiliary Patrol. The King has been graciously pleased to approve of the award of the following honours to the undermentioned Officers, in recognition of their services in vessels of the Auxiliary Patrol between 1 Jan. and 31 Dec. 1917. To be Companions of the Distinguished Service Order."

ROLLESTON, JOHN PHILIP, Capt., R.N.R. (Rear-Admiral, retired).

SAUNDERS, WALTER JOHN TITE, Commander, R.N.

FORBES, WYNDHAM, Commander, R.N.

HAMBLY, ANDREW, Commander, R.N.

DE KANTZOW, ARTHUR HENRY, Commander, R.N.

BLACKLIN, RICHARD WILLIAM BROUGHTON, Commander (Acting Capt.), R.D., R.N.R.

SMITH, WILLIAM ERASMUS, Commander (Acting Capt.), R.D., R.N.R.

BROOKS, CECIL, Lieut.-Commander, R.D., R.N.R.

" Honours for Service in Vessels Employed on Patrol and Escort Duty.—The King has been graciously pleased to approve of the award of the following honours to the undermentioned Officers, for services in vessels of the Royal Navy employed on patrol and escort duty during the period 1 Jan. to 31 Dec. 1917. To be Companions of the Distinguished Service Order."

WOODWARD, WALTER EGERTON, Capt., R.N.

DARWALL, WILLIAM HENRY, Commander, R.N.

WILLIAMSON, JAMES DANIEL, Engineer-Commander, R.N.R.

RICHARDSON, REGINALD CARWITHEN, Lieut.-Commander, R.N.

OPPEN, HANS, Lieut.-Commander, R.D., R.N.R.

BENNETT, THOMAS WILLIAM, Lieut.-Commander (Acting Commander), R.D., R.N.R.
EVANS, WILLIAM POWLETT, Lieut., R.N.R.
SIMMONS, CHARLES DOUGLAS, Lieut. (Acting Lieut.-Commander), R.N.R.

"Honours for Services in Action with Enemy Submarines.—The King has been graciously pleased to approve of the award of the following honours to the undermentioned Officers, for services in action with enemy submarines. To be Companions of the Distinguished Service Order."

HARTNOLL, HENRY JAMES, Lieut., R.N.
MELSOM, ARTHUR PERCY, Lieut. (Acting Lieut.-Commander), R.N.R.

"Honours for Miscellaneous Services.—The King has been graciously pleased to approve of the award of the following honour to the undermentioned Officer. To be a Companion of the Distinguished Service Order."

SALMON, REGINALD, Lieut.-Commander (Acting Commander), R.N.R. For services in connection with the recovery of a German mine, which had fouled the wire of H.M. Trawler Manx King, on 12 Dec. 1917. By the measures ordered and personally superintended by him the mine was eventually rendered innocuous. He set an excellent example to all on board by his coolness and courage in a dangerous situation.

"Honours to the Mercantile Marine.—The King has been graciously pleased to approve of the award of the following award to the undermentioned Officer of the British Mercantile Marine, in recognition of zeal and devotion to duty shown in carrying on the trade of the country during the war. To be a Companion of the Distinguished Service Order."

EVANS, EVAN, Capt. (Lieut., R.N.R.).

London Gazette, 11 April, 1918.—" War Office, 11 April, 1918. His Majesty the King has been graciously pleased to approve of the undermentioned rewards for distinguished services in the field in connection with military operations, culminating in the capture of Jerusalem. Dated 1 Jan. 1918. Awarded the Distinguished Service Order."

ABRAHAM, JAMES JOHNSTON, M.D., F.R.C.S., Temporary Major, Royal Army Medical Corps.
ANGWIN, ARTHUR STANLEY, M.C., Capt. (Acting Major), Royal Engineers.
BRAY, GEORGE ARTHUR THEODORE, Lieut.-Colonel (Temporary Colonel), Royal Army Medical Corps.
BURNETT, CHARLES STUART, Capt. (Temporary Lieut.-Colonel), Reserve of Officers.
BURNEY, ARTHUR EDWARD CAVE, M.C., Major, Royal Artillery.
BEAUMONT, KENNETH MACDONALD, Temporary Major, Army Service Corps.
BROWN, JAMES CROSS, Temporary Major (Temporary Lieut.-Colonel), Army Service Corps.
CAHILL, ROBERT JOHN, M.B., Major (Temporary Lieut.-Colonel), Royal Army Medical Corps.
DOWSETT, ERNEST BLAIR, Lieut.-Colonel (Temporary Colonel), Royal Army Medical Corps.
DUNNING, MATTHEW, M.B., Major (Temporary Lieut.-Colonel), Royal Army Medical Corps.
EGERTON-WARBURTON, GEOFFREY, Capt. (Temporary Major), Yeomanry and Machine Gun Corps.
EUSTACE, FREDERICK ROBERT HARRINGTON, Major (Temporary Lieut.-Colonel), Royal Engineers.
EVATT, EVELYN JOHN ROBERT, M.B., Colonel, Royal Army Medical Corps.
FINDLAY, JAMES MARSHALL, Lieut.-Colonel, Scottish Rifles.
FINLAY, DAVID, Temporary Major, Special List.
FRANCIS, JOHN, Major, Royal Engineers.
GARSIA, WILLOUGHBY CLIVE, M.C., Major (Temporary Lieut.-Colonel), Hampshire Regt.
HARBORD, CYRIL RODNEY, Major (Temporary Brigadier-General), Indian Army.
HARRISON, CECIL PRYCE, M.C., Capt. (Acting Major), Royal Horse Artillery.
HORTON, CHARLES WOODRUFFE, Major and Brevet Lieut.-Colonel, Army Service Corps.
JEFFERSON, HAROLD ARTHUR, Major, Royal Welsh Fusiliers.
JOHNSON, FRANK WILLIAM EVANS, Major (Temporary Lieut.-Colonel), Royal Irish Fusiliers.
LAMBKIN, ERNEST CHARLES, M.B., Capt. (Acting Lieut.-Colonel), Royal Army Medical Corps.
LIND, ALEXANDER GORDON, Major (Temporary Lieut.-Colonel), Indian Army.
LUCAS, WALTER RANDOLPH, Lieut. (Acting Major), Army Service Corps.
MACALPINE-LENY, ROBERT LENY, Major (Temporary Lieut.-Colonel), Lancers.
MACFARLANE, HARRY ERSKINE, M.C., Capt.
MACKINTOSH, JOHN KYLE, Major, Army Service Corps.
ORPEN-PALMER, HAROLD BLAND HERBERT, Major and Brevet Lieut.-Colonel (Temporary Brigadier-General), Royal Irish Fusiliers.
PAXTON, ALEXANDER NORMAN, M.C., Major (Acting Lieut.-Colonel), Royal Engineers.
POLLOK-McCALL, JOHN BUCHANAN, C.M.G., Lieut.-Colonel (Temporary Brigadier-General), Retired Pay, Reserve of Officers, late Royal Highlanders.
RADCLIFFE, SAMUEL ROBERTS, Major, Royal Field Artillery.
RICHARDSON, HUGH, M.D., Major (Temporary Colonel), Royal Army Medical Corps.
SCOTT, FREDERICK WILLIAM AGNEW, Lieut.-Colonel, Dorsetshire Regt.
SHEKLETON, ALEXANDER, Capt. (Temporary Lieut.-Colonel), Royal Munster Fusiliers and Royal Flying Corps.
SPENCER, JOHN ALMERIC WALTER, Major (Temporary Lieut.-Colonel), Rifle Brigade.
STEWART-RICHARDSON, NEIL GRAHAM, Major (Acting Lieut.-Colonel), Irish Horse.
STOKES, ALEYN WHITLEY, M.C., Major (Temporary Lieut.-Colonel), Royal Engineers.
THOMSON, CHRISTOPHER BIRDWOOD, Major (Acting Lieut.-Colonel), Royal Engineers.
WADE, HENRY, M.D., F.R.C.S., Temporary Lieut.-Colonel, Royal Army Medical Corps.
WALKER, JAMES WORKMAN, Lieut.-Colonel (Temporary Brigadier-General), Royal Field Artillery.
WATSON, ARTHUR CAMPBELL, Capt. (Acting Major), Hussars.
WEBB, MAURICE EVERETT, M.C., Temporary Capt. (Acting Major), Royal Engineers.
WELLS, LIONEL FORTESCUE, Major (Acting Lieut.-Colonel), Royal Engineers.
WILMER, GRAHAM HORACE, M.C., Major and Brevet Lieut.-Colonel, Essex Regt.
WYATT, GEORGE NEVILLE, Major (Acting Lieut.-Colonel), Royal Field Artillery.

AUSTRALIAN FORCE.

FARR, WALTER PERCY, Lieut.-Colonel, Australian General List.
HUDSON, ERNEST ALFRED KNIGHT, Major, Australian Light Horse.
PARSONS, HARRY MESHACH, Major, Australian Light Horse.
RANKIN, GEORGE JAMES, Major, Australian Light Horse.

NEW ZEALAND FORCE.

HARPER, ROBERT PAUL, M.C., D.C.M., Capt., Machine Gun Squadron.

London Gazette, 17 April, 1918.—" Admiralty, 17 April, 1918.—Honours for Service in Mine-Sweeping Operations. The King has been graciously pleased to approve of the award of the following honours to the undermentioned Officers, in recognition of their services in mine-sweeping operations between the 1st April and 31st Dec. 1917. To be Companions of the Distinguished Service Order."

HAMILTON, ALEXANDER GIBSON, Commander, R.N.
BAILLIE-GROHMAN, HAROLD TOM, Lieut.-Commander, R.N.

"Honours for the Submarine Service.—The King has been graciously pleased to approve of the award of the following honours to the undermentioned Officers, in recognition of their services in submarines. To be Companions of the Distinguished Service Order."

SOMMERVILLE, FREDERICK AVENEL, Commander, R.N.
LAYTON, GEOFFREY, Commander, R.N.
LIMPENNY, CHARLES JOHN, Engineer Lieut.-Commander, R.N.

"Honours for Services in Action with Enemy Submarines.—The King has been graciously pleased to approve of the award of the following honour for services in action with enemy submarines. To be a Companion of the Distinguished Service Order."

SMITHWICK, ALGERNON ROBERT, Lieut.-Commander, R.N.

London Gazette, 22 April, 1918.—" War Office, 22 April, 1918. His Majesty the King has been graciously pleased to approve of the following awards to the undermentioned Officers, in recognition of their gallantry and devotion to duty in the field. Awarded a Third Bar to the Distinguished Service Order."

LUMSDEN, FREDERICK WILLIAM, V.C., D.S.O., Lieut.-Colonel (Temporary Brigadier-General), Royal Marine Artillery. For conspicuous gallantry and devotion to duty. During a large raid on the enemy's lines, in which a portion of his brigade formed the left of the attack, he first superintended the assembly in our advanced line, and then advanced to each successive objective, encouraging the men. At the final objective, where, owing to heavy machine-gun and rifle fire and the exhaustion of the troops, there was some slight hesitation, he led the assault on a group of seven " pill-boxes," and after their capture made a valuable reconnaissance of the enemy's position. He then supervised the withdrawal, forming a covering party, with which he himself withdrew, being the last to leave the enemy's position. Such coolness, determination to succeed, and absolute disregard of danger not only ensured the success of the operation but afforded a magnificent example to all ranks, the value of which can hardly be exaggerated.
(D.S.O. gazetted 1 Jan. 1917.)
(First Bar gazetted 11 May, 1917.)
(Second Bar gazetted 11 May, 1917.)

Awarded a Bar to the Distinguished Service Order :

BLOCK, ADAM, D.S.O., Major, Royal Field Artillery. For conspicuous gallantry and devotion to duty. In order to direct the fire of his battery during an action he exposed himself fearlessly, standing up on the parapet until he was wounded. His courage and skill greatly contributed to the effective shooting of his battery. On a previous occasion he skilfully got his battery into action 1,100 yards from the enemy's trenches, and brought such an accurate and rapid fire to bear that the enemy abandoned his trenches and retired.
(D.S.O. gazetted 7 Feb. 1918.)

DEAR, HAROLD JOHN, D.S.O., Capt. (Temporary Lieut.-Colonel), London Regt. For conspicuous gallantry and devotion to duty. During an action he commanded his battalion in the most gallant and determined manner, rushed the crossing of a stream, and captured many prisoners. It was largely due to his personality and gallantry that this operation proved a success.
(D.S.O. gazetted 1 Jan. 1918.)

EWING, WILLIAM TURNER, D.S.O., Major, Royal Scots. For conspicuous gallantry and devotion to duty. He went forward to the front line companies during an attack to clear up the situation, and set a magnificent example of courage and skill, which had a marked effect on the attacking troops.
(D.S.O. gazetted 1 Jan. 1918.)

FRASER, JOHN ALEXANDER, D.S.O., D.C.M., Lieut. (Temporary Lieut.-Colonel), Dragoon Guards. For conspicuous gallantry and devotion to duty. As officer commanding a raid he personally supervised the forming up of all the parties, and constantly moved up and down the advancing lines encouraging the men. Having paid most careful attention to the maintenance of touch between the various parties, he supervised the reorganization at the final objective and himself withdrew the last covering party. Throughout the operation he displayed magnificent gallantry and the greatest energy and devotion to duty.
(D.S.O. gazetted 1 Jan. 1918.)

GRANVILLE, BERNARD, D.S.O., Major (Acting Lieut.-Colonel), Yeomanry. For conspicuous gallantry and devotion to duty. With half a company and without any reserves, he maintained his position for 24 hours against a vastly superior enemy force, during which period he was continually under heavy fire of all kinds. It was largely owing to his coolness, presence of mind, and the example which he set to his men that the enemy was held back and a critical situation averted.
(D.S.O. gazetted 1 Jan. 1918.)

HEATH, GEORGE NOAH, D.S.O., Major, Cheshire Regt. For conspicuous gallantry and devotion to duty. He went forward to obtain information as to

the situation during an attack. Though wounded he succeeded in reaching the attacking battalion, crossing an extended zone swept by heavy machine-gun and shell fire. He obtained accurate information at a critical time and showed great courage and initiative.
(D.S.O. gazetted 1 Jan. 1918.)

MITCHELL, ARCHIBALD MACLAINE, D.S.O., Major (Acting Lieut.-Colonel), Royal Scots. For conspicuous gallantry and devotion to duty in an attack. He led his battalion with great skill and courage, capturing and holding all his objectives under intense fire. He set a magnificent example to his men.
(D.S.O. gazetted 1 Jan. 1918.)

Awarded the Distinguished Service Order:

FARRINGTON, WYNDHAM BROOKES, Lieut. (Temporary Capt.), Nottinghamshire and Derbyshire Regt., Special Reserve and Royal Flying Corps. For conspicuous gallantry and devotion to duty. On five occasions during a period of three months he has led formations on long-distance bombing raids, in which, despite bad weather conditions, he has found and bombed his objectives with the most excellent results. All the operations in which he has taken part have proved highly successful, and his capabilities have stood out most prominently. He is a keen and most efficient pilot, and by his courage and determination has set a splendid example to his squadron.

LAMB, HARRY LIVINGSTONE, Lieut. (Acting Capt.), London Regt. For conspicuous gallantry and devotion to duty. After three companies had attempted and failed to dislodge the enemy from a dominating ridge, he personally led an outflanking party under heavy machine-gun fire, and succeeded in getting in rear of the enemy's position, with the result that 60 prisoners with six machine guns fell into our hands. Thanks to the gallant dash and enterprise of this officer a ridge affording excellent powers of observation was successfully captured.

SNOW, WILFRED RIPPON, M.C., Lieut. (Temporary Major), Royal Flying Corps, Special Reserve. For conspicuous gallantry and devotion to duty. During a flight lasting three hours and 40 minutes, he successfully registered two siege batteries on a hostile battery, and observed 100 and 150 rounds respectively. On one occasion he made four trips and dropped twelve 112lb. bombs on two aerodrome objectives. He has carried out a large number of successful counter battery and trench registration shoots under exceedingly unfavourable weather conditions, and has at all times carried out his duties in a thoroughly keen and able manner, displaying a magnificent spirit of dash and energy.

TATTERSALL, EDMUND HARRY, Lieut., Dragoon Guards. For conspicuous gallantry and devotion to duty. For 17 consecutive nights prior to a raid on the enemy trenches he was out on patrol along the enemy wire. On the night of the raid he first took out a reconnoitring patrol to ascertain if an enemy post was held. He then returned to take charge of the Bangalore torpedo party, and after the first torpedo had exploded satisfactorily, and while the second torpedo was being placed under the wire, two machine guns opened fire on the party at a range of 20 yards. As there was some difficulty in getting the torpedo through the wire, he, with total disregard of all danger and with magnificent coolness, stood up, and with the light of his electric torch placed the torpedo in the right position. His remarkable courage and presence of mind proved most inspiring to all ranks.

London Gazette, 22 April, 1918.—War Office, 22 April, 1918.

MACDONALD, ANGUS MACGILLIVRAY, Lieut. (Acting Capt.), Seaforth Highlanders. The award of the Military Cross, announced in the London Gazette of 22 March, 1918 (corrected to 19 Nov. 1917), is cancelled, the award of the Distinguished Service Order being substituted. The details of the deed for which the Military Cross was awarded, as given in London Gazette, 22 March, 1918, were as follows: For conspicuous gallantry and devotion to duty. When the enemy counter-attack was meeting with great success he gathered a small party together and boldly attacked the enemy, who was advancing in large numbers. His prompt action retrieved the day, causing the enemy to retreat into our barrage.

London Gazette, 23 April, 1918.—"War Office, 23 April, 1918. With reference to the awards conferred as announced in the London Gazette dated 17 Dec. 1917, the following are the statements of service for which the decorations were conferred. Awarded a Bar to the Distinguished Service Order."

PRETORIUS, PHILIP JACOBUS, D.S.O., Major, East Africa Protectorate Forces, attached Intelligence Department. For conspicuous gallantry and devotion to duty. He remained continuously behind the enemy's lines, and made valuable use of the services of the enemy's natives. He burned several of the enemy's food depots, causing considerable havoc among their supply arrangements, and killed or captured several of the enemy. His personal courage and initiative were quite exceptional.

PYE-SMITH, CHARLES DERWENT, D.S.O., M.C., M.B., F.R.C.S., Temporary Capt. (Temporary Lieut.-Colonel), Royal Army Medical Corps. For conspicuous gallantry and devotion to duty when in command of the three field ambulances of the division during ten days' operations. Though the weather conditions were abnormally bad and a large number of the wounded of another division had not been evacuated, owing to his constant presence and influence all the wounded were got away promptly and without assistance from the Infantry.

ROBINSON, HUGH THOMAS KAY, D.S.O., Temporary Major (Acting Lieut.-Colonel, Royal Sussex Regt. For conspicuous gallantry and devotion to duty when in command of his battalion during three days' operations. In the assembly of his troops, in launching them for the attack, in the attack itself, and in holding the position, he displayed high qualities of leadership and courage.

SUGDEN, RICHARD EDGAR, D.S.O., Lieut.-Colonel, West Riding Regt. For conspicuous gallantry and devotion to duty when in command of his battalion. On several occasions he made personal reconnaissances of the new front under heavy fire. His reports did much to clear up the situation.

WORSLEY, FRANK PICKFORD, D.S.O., Capt. and Brevet Major (Temporary Lieut.-Colonel), Reserve of Officers, West Yorkshire Regt. For conspicuous gallantry and devotion to duty in laying out the tape, on which his battalion was to form up, under intense fire. It was owing to his gallantry and energy that touch was kept with his flanks and command so well maintained in his battalion, though all his company officers became casualties.

AUSTRALIAN IMPERIAL FORCE.

IMLAY, ALEXANDER PETER, D.S.O., Lieut.-Colonel, Infantry. For conspicuous gallantry and devotion to duty when in command of his battalion. The attack, in atrocious weather conditions, was successful. But owing to the retirement of troops on the left, his men were ordered to withdraw. He personally controlled the retiring troops and skilfully overcame a critical situation, being wounded in the effort.

LEANE, RAYMOND LIONEL, D.S.O., M.C., Lieut.-Colonel, Infantry. For conspicuous gallantry and devotion to duty in commanding his battalion in an attack, when he was suffering severely from neuritis. After his battalion had been forced to retire owing to a counter-attack on the flank, he collected stragglers and parties of men who were retiring past their original line and sent them forward again. Though badly wounded he remained at his post till the enemy were checked and the defence was assured.

Awarded the Distinguished Service Order:

ANDERSON, FRANCIS, M.C., Capt., Royal Highlanders. For conspicuous gallantry and devotion to duty as brigade major during seven days' operations. He made a most valuable reconnaissance of the hostile position, besides regularly passing through a heavily shelled area in full view of the enemy's snipers to pay visits to the units in the front line.

BOSANQUET, WILLIAM SYDNEY BENCE, Capt., Coldstream Guards, Special Reserve. For conspicuous gallantry and devotion to duty. On reaching the objective he found he was held up by an enemy strong point which was causing heavy casualties. He organized an attack, which failed. Being reinforced, though under a heavy fire, he organized another attack, which was entirely successful, capturing the strong point with one machine gun and 40 prisoners. The enemy made a determined counter-attack, which was completely wiped out. He set an unparalleled example of coolness, initiative and courage.

CLARK, PHILIP LINDSAY, Temporary Second Lieut. (Acting Capt.), Royal Sussex Regt. For conspicuous gallantry and devotion to duty when in command of the left flank company of the battalion. When the enemy broke through on his left he organized a defensive flank. Finding a gap on his left he filled and held it with some of his own men and of the unit on his left. He personally led a charge against the advancing enemy and dispersed them, and later repelled another attack. He was wounded by a piece of shrapnel in the head, but though dazed continued in command of his company for two days until relieved.

CRAIG, DAVID, Second Lieut., Grenadier Guards, Special Reserve. For conspicuous gallantry and devotion to duty. Though blown up by a shell, stunned and slightly wounded he went forward and established his sub-section of machine guns in the second objective, when he was again wounded in the leg. Hearing that the officer in charge of another sub-section of guns had been killed he took these guns forward to their position in rear of the final objective. He did not come back to the dressing station until ordered to do so. By this time, thanks to his efforts, the position on the right of the brigade was secure against counter-attack.

CRICHTON, ANDREW GAVIN MAITLAND MAKGILL, M.C., Temporary Capt. (Acting Lieut.-Colonel), Cameron Highlanders. For conspicuous gallantry and devotion to duty when in command of his battalion. The attack having been held up he made a personal reconnaissance, crawling from shell-hole to shell-hole in front of his advanced posts under heavy machine-gun fire and active sniping. He brought back most valuable information.

ELIOTT, RICHARD HEYMAN, Major, Royal Field Artillery. For conspicuous gallantry and devotion to duty in getting his battery forward during an attack over almost impassable roads and tracks. He commanded his battery all through the operations in spite of very heavy casualties and great discomfort in a manner worthy of the highest praise.

HADOW, RONALD WALTER, Major (Acting Lieut.-Colonel), Reserve of Officers, Royal Highlanders. For conspicuous gallantry and devotion to duty in personally reconnoitring the ground and forming up his battalion in the correct alignment after the taping party and guides had become casualties. He handled his battalion skilfully in the attack and rendered most useful reports on the situation.

JOHNSTONE, BEDE, Major (Acting Lieut.-Colonel), Royal West Kent Regt. For conspicuous gallantry and devotion to duty. When the attack was held up he immediately grasped the situation and rallied all the men he could from scattered parties of different regiments and sent them forward with his adjutant to form a defensive line. Regardless of danger he continued to reorganize scattered parties of men and to lead them up to the line. By his gallantry and personal example he saved a very dangerous situation.

LAITHWAITE, ALLAN, Second Lieut., London Regt. For conspicuous gallantry and devotion to duty. In spite of being wounded during the advance towards his objective he continued to lead his men, and was wounded again on six different occasions, but refused to give in, and again pressed on with a view to gaining more ground. While so advancing he was wounded for the eighth time, this time in the leg, which rendered it impossible for him to proceed further. By his magnificent endurance and example he was able to lead his men across extremely difficult ground.

LISTER, WILLIAM HOWARD, M.C., Temporary Capt., Royal Army Medical Corps. For conspicuous gallantry and devotion to duty as bearer officer, taking parties to the regimental aid posts, though they suffered heavy casualties on the way. When a regimental medical officer was wounded, he attended to the wounded of his battalion, searching our lines and "No Man's Land" from midday to dark for wounded, and then returned to his field ambulance for another 12 hours' work until relieved.

LOVEDAY, FRANCIS WILLIAM, Major, Royal Garrison Artillery. For conspicuous gallantry and devotion to duty in getting his guns forward along a narrow and broken planked road under heavy shell fire. After several attempts to use horse teams he had to resort to man power.

MARTYN, MICHAEL CLEEVE, M.C., Major (Acting Lieut.-Colonel), Nottinghamshire and Derbyshire Regt. For conspicuous gallantry and devotion to duty in rallying and reorganizing his men at the furthest objectives when men of other units besides his own were wavering under a heavy barrage and enemy preparations for counter-attack, and so averting a serious situation.

MASKELL, WILLIAM CHARLES, M.C., Lieut. (Acting Major), Royal Field Artillery. For conspicuous gallantry and devotion to duty. A few minutes before zero hour his telephone dug-out was blown in by a shell and he himself was buried and badly shaken. In spite of this he continued to command his battery for the next two days, withdrawing them under heavy fire at the end of that time.

OAKMAN, WALTER GEORGE, Lieut., Coldstream Guards, Special Reserve. For conspicuous gallantry and devotion to duty when in command of the left company of an attacking wave, and of both companies, after the company on his right had lost all their officers. Though checked by a group of concrete block-houses, he made dispositions to outflank them, and finally reached the second objective. He had been wounded in the shoulder a few days previously, and was suffering great pain throughout the operations.

OSWALD, KENNETH ALLAN, Major (Acting Lieut.-Colonel), Royal West Surrey Regt. For conspicuous gallantry and devotion to duty when in command of his battalion in action. He not only reconnoitred the assembly position close to and in full view of the enemy in daylight, but entered the enemy's lines after dark. Owing to his enthusiasm the opposition, encountered before the first objective was gained, was overcome with comparatively small loss.

PEMBERTON, GEOFFREY HARRIS, Lieut., Lancashire Fusiliers. For conspicuous gallantry and devotion to duty when in command of the battalion for 24 hours after the commanding officer and senior officers had become casualties. He moved his headquarters to within 300 yards of the front line, and personally supervised the consolidation. During the relief he went out under heavy fire to the advanced posts collecting the men.

PLACE, CHARLES GODFREY MORRIS, M.C., Temporary Capt. (Acting Major), East Surrey Regt. For conspicuous gallantry and devotion to duty when in command of an assaulting company. Being unable, owing to the chaotic state of the ground and heavy shelling, to reconnoitre in daylight, he went up and down his company all night to get them in a position to attack at dawn. He was wounded while organizing attacks on machine-gun positions which were holding up the line, but did not go back until quite certain that the attack could not get on any further.

RUSSELL, BERTIE ANGUS, Temporary Capt., Gloucestershire Regt. For conspicuous gallantry and devotion to duty. He led his company to the assault, though wounded six hours previously, with great courage and endurance, and, in spite of stiff resistance, his company was the first to reach its objective. At a moment when his flank was exposed, he regained touch with the troops on his right by a skilful redistribution of his own men. His reports on the situation were of the utmost value.

STEELE, ROBERT CRAWFORD, Second Lieut., Royal Flying Corps, Special Reserve. For conspicuous gallantry and devotion to duty. He has done consistent good work in aerial fighting during eight months. On one occasion he brought down within our lines an enemy scout of the latest type, and, landing alongside it, made the enemy pilot a prisoner before he could destroy his machine.

TABERER, TRAVERS CHARLES MELVILLE, Second Lieut., Hampshire Regt., Special Reserve. For conspicuous gallantry and devotion to duty when in command of his company after the company commander had been killed. Seeing, however, that part of the company detailed for the final objective had become disorganized owing to heavy casualties, on his own initiative he led forward his own company and captured and consolidated the final objective.

TETLEY, CHARLES HAROLD, Lieut.-Colonel, West Yorkshire Regt. For conspicuous gallantry and devotion to duty when in command of his battalion in an attack, being very successful under most trying conditions and under very heavy artillery and rifle fire.

THOMPSON, HENRY CEDRIC ST. JOHN, Lieut. (Acting Capt.), Coldstream Guards. For conspicuous gallantry and devotion to duty in command of the leading company in the attack on the first objective. At zero he and his company swept across 300 yards to a stream which they plunged into waist deep, discarding mats and bridges, and carried the far bank and a line of block-houses. Ten minutes after the attack began there were 95 prisoners back at Battalion Headquarters and several machine guns were captured. By his initiative and skill he contributed largely to the success of the attack.

WISTANCE, WILLIAM ALLSOP, M.C., Capt. (Temporary Major and Acting Lieut.-Colonel), South Staffordshire Regt. For conspicuous gallantry and devotion to duty when in command of his battalion during an attack. He maintained complete control of the situation under extraordinarily difficult conditions.

AUSTRALIAN IMPERIAL FORCE.

CHRISTIE, ROBERT, Major (Temporary Lieut.-Colonel), Infantry. For conspicuous gallantry and devotion to duty when in command of his battalion. Owing to his excellent arrangements the approach march and deployment were carried out without casualties. He went forward with the battalion in the attack, and established his headquarters close to the final objective. His tactical handling of the battalion reflected great credit upon him.

COLLINS, WILLIAM HENRY, Capt., Army Medical Corps. For conspicuous gallantry and devotion to duty. Finding that his regimental stretcher-bearers were unable to find a regimental aid post which he had established in a German "pill-box," he personally led the first party of them through an intense artillery and machine-gun fire barrage. Although knocked down by a bursting shell, he immediately resumed the dressing of the wounded. Although, owing to casualties, he had only two men to help him, he courageously persevered with his work and himself helped to excavate a dug-out for the wounded under heavy shell fire, during which several of the wounded were killed. He remained on duty for sixty hours and refused to leave his post till the last wounded man had been evacuated. By his constant cheerfulness under the most adverse conditions, and by his utter disregard for his own safety, he kept up the spirits of the wounded and stimulated his surviving helpers to their utmost effort.

FRASER, WILLIAM ARTHUR, Second Lieut., Infantry. For conspicuous gallantry and devotion to duty. When his platoon was checked by a machine gun, he located it and, accompanied only by his runner, attacked the dug-out from the rear, killed ten men and captured 20 others, together with the machine gun.

HURRY, GEOFFRY, Major, Infantry. For conspicuous gallantry and devotion to duty when in command of his battalion in action. He showed a fine example to all ranks, and fought his battalion with great skill, contributing largely towards the success of the operations.

HUTCHINSON, ERIC LLOYD, Major, Army Medical Corps. For conspicuous gallantry and devotion to duty when in charge of the evacuation of wounded from the forward area. He led a relief of stretcher-bearers over a track knee deep in mud, and at times over his waist in water. Another time he led a party through an intense barrage, thus relieving a temporary congestion of the wounded. He had very little rest during the whole four days.

JAMES, TRISTRAM BERNARD WORDSWORTH, Major, Field Artillery. For conspicuous gallantry and devotion to duty. After the men had been ordered to safety owing to heavy shelling, when a gun-pit caught fire he extinguished it single-handed. By his efforts his personnel were rendered safe and his guns were all maintained in action.

MANTON, RUSSELL FULTON, Major, Field Artillery. For conspicuous gallantry and devotion to duty. When his battery was being heavily shelled, the Infantry sent back an S.O.S. call on the battery sector; he personally led the detachments to the guns, attended to the wounded and kept every gun in action. By his determination and personal disregard of danger he set a magnificent example. On several occasions he showed the greatest gallantry and ability when in command of his battery.

MAPLESTONE, PHILIP ALAN, Major, Army Medical Corps. For conspicuous gallantry and devotion to duty. When in charge of all stretcher-bearers and forward posts he showed the utmost coolness under very heavy fire, during which several shelters were hit. By his example he prevented any panic and prevented serious casualties from gas shells. Although gassed himself, he remained on duty till the forenoon of the following day, having been on duty for over 30 hours. Even then he refused to be treated as a casualty, but after a short rest he returned to the advanced dressing station and carried on his duties.

NEW ZEALAND FORCE.

WICKENS, ROBERT CHARLES, Major, Field Artillery. For conspicuous gallantry and devotion to duty. When a gun-pit was set on fire, causing an explosion which killed one man, he set to work personally to localize the fire. As men arrived he organized them into a fire party, and eventually succeeded in extinguishing the fire, thereby saving the other gun and ammunition and probable loss of life.

SOUTH AFRICAN FORCE.

HEAL, FRANK HENRY, Lieut.-Colonel, Infantry. For conspicuous gallantry and devotion to duty. When all his company commanders were casualties and the advance appeared not to be progressing satisfactorily, he went up to his battalion on the first objective and accompanied it in the advance to the second objective, which was gained, two counter-attacks being repulsed.

London Gazette, 24 April, 1918.—"War Office, 24 April, 1918. His Majesty the King has been graciously pleased to approve of the undermentioned rewards for distinguished services rendered in connection with military operations in Mesopotamia. Dated 26 March, 1918. Awarded the Distinguished Service Order."

EWART, ROBERT FREDERICK, Major (Temporary Lieut.-Colonel), Supply and Transport Corps, Indian Army.

HOSKYN, JOHN CUNNINGHAM MOORE, Major (Temporary Lieut.-Colonel), Infantry, Indian Army.

London Gazette, 25 April, 1918.—"War Office, 25 April, 1918. With reference to the awards conferred, as announced in the London Gazette dated 18 Jan. 1918, the following are the statements of service for which the decorations were conferred. Awarded a Second Bar to the Distinguished Service Order."

ASQUITH, ARTHUR MELLAND, D.S.O., Temporary Lieut.-Commander (Acting Commander), Royal Naval Volunteer Reserve. For conspicuous gallantry and devotion to duty during two days' operations. He went through a heavy barrage and made a successful reconnaissance of an advanced position. Later, in bright moonlight, he reconnoitred some buildings which were reported to be occupied by the enemy. His advance was observed, and the enemy opened fire, but he entered one of the buildings and found it occupied by an exhausted British garrison. He returned, under heavy fire, and brought up three platoons to relieve them. He showed great determination and resource.

Awarded a Bar to the Distinguished Service Order:

DUNCAN, KENNETH, D.S.O., Major, Royal Field Artillery. For conspicuous gallantry and devotion to duty in controlling his battery under heavy enemy barrages on five different occasions, and attending to the wounded. On the last occasion he had a gun knocked out, and was forced to evacuate his position. Yet on an S.O.S. signal being sent up he led his men back, in spite of casualties, and started firing again. He showed great determination and resource.

JACKSON, GEORGE SCOTT, D.S.O., Major (Temporary Lieut.-Colonel), Northumberland Fusiliers. For conspicuous gallantry and devotion to duty. He successfully assembled his battalion under very heavy fire. At a critical stage he made a personal reconnaissance under heavy fire, and by judicious use of his reserves gained the battalion's objective.

McCRACKEN, WILLIAM JAMES, D.S.O., M.C., M.B., Temporary Surgeon, Royal Navy. For conspicuous gallantry and devotion to duty in tending and evacuating the wounded in the open under heavy shelling. Hearing that there were many wounded lying in mud and water in shell-holes, he led up two platoons with stretchers. When they were fired on he made them take cover and himself advanced through the enemy's fire, bearing a Red Cross flag on his walking stick. This the enemy eventually respected, and so he was able to clear the area of wounded. By his courageous action he saved many lives.

SEWELL, HORACE SOMERVILLE, D.S.O., Major (Acting Lieut.-Colonel), Dragoon Guards. For conspicuous gallantry and devotion to duty when in command of the advance regiment of his division. By his personal reconnaissance under fire he materially assisted in the destruction of an enemy ammunition column, a raid on an enemy headquarters and the capture of 50 prisoners and two machine guns.

CANADIAN FORCE.

COSGRAVE, LAWRENCE VINCENT MOORE, D.S.O., Major, Artillery. For conspicuous gallantry and devotion to duty. When a lorry in the middle of an ammunition convoy was blown up, and six casualties occurred, he supervised the removal of the wounded under heavy shell-fire. By having the lorries nearest to the burning one removed he minimized the effects of the second explosion when two more lorries blew up. He showed great courage and resource.

FOSTER, WILLIAM WASBROUGH, D.S.O., Lieut.-Colonel, Infantry. For conspicuous gallantry and devotion to duty. When in command of the supporting battalion he personally led two companies of his unit in a flanking attack on some concrete strong points, containing several hostile machine guns. Owing to his personal example of gallantry, his tactical ability and effective leadership, the whole objective was gained with but small loss, and a critical situation was retrieved.

MACLEOD, GEORGE WATERS, D.S.O., Major, Infantry. For conspicuous gallantry and devotion to duty. He displayed the greatest initiative in supervising the assault and accurately reporting the position of the attacking troops. He was untiring in his efforts to strengthen the captured position and contributed largely to the success of the operations. He set a splendid example of coolness and courage.

NIVEN, HUGH WILDERSPIN, D.S.O., M.C., Major, Infantry. For conspicuous gallantry and devotion to duty. He did excellent work in going to the front line during the operations and reorganizing scattered units. He personally carried away the wounded and saw to their evacuation in the face of great difficulties and dangers. His grasp of the situation in the captured position was of a high order.

AUSTRALIAN IMPERIAL FORCE.

GRANT, WILLIAM, D.S.O., Lieut.-Colonel (Temporary Brigadier-General), Australian Light Horse Regt. For conspicuous gallantry and devotion to duty in an attack on a town. He quickly grasped the situation and ordered the attack on the enemy's position. Owing to his promptness the town was occupied and a large number of prisoners were captured.

Awarded the Distinguished Service Order:

ANDERSON, ARCHIBALD STIRLING KENNEDY, M.C., M.B., Temporary Capt., Royal Army Medical Corps. For conspicuous gallantry and devotion to duty. Under heavy shell fire he led forward a party of stretcher-bearers and collected 25 wounded men who were lying within 50 yards of the enemy line. He set a splendid example of courage and self-sacrifice.

ANDERSON-MORSHEAD, RUPERT HENRY, Capt. (Acting Lieut.-Colonel), Devonshire Regt. For conspicuous gallantry and devotion to duty when in command of his battalion in an attack. Though the troops on his left were held up his battalion captured and held an important tactical point. He showed great initiative and skill.

BAILLIE, DUNCAN GUS, Lieut.-Colonel, Yeomanry. For conspicuous gallantry and devotion to duty. He handled his battalion with great skill and determination during a night advance and showed great coolness and courage in an assault on a village. He set a splendid example of pluck and initiative to which the success of the operation was largely due.

BARSTOW, WALTER AGAR THOMAS, M.C., Major, Royal Field Artillery. For conspicuous gallantry and devotion to duty. When his battery was heavily shelled and gassed, five men being killed and several wounded and gassed, though himself gassed he proceeded to get the wounded out of the dug-outs and clear of the shelled area. The control post with all the orders for next morning's barrage being completely destroyed, he sat in a shell hole working out fresh orders while the shelling continued. It was solely due to his having personally registered his guns from the front line that an enemy counter-attack was dispersed. He showed splendid skill and determination.

BIRKETT, RICHARD MAUL, Major (Temporary Lieut.-Colonel), Royal Sussex Regt. For conspicuous gallantry and devotion to duty. When the advance was held up by machine-gun fire, and considerable confusion arose, he went forward to the front line and reorganized units, collecting stragglers and selecting positions for defence. He was under heavy machine-gun and shell fire the whole time, and set a splendid example of contempt of danger.

BOWMAN, JAMES THORNLEY, M.D., Temporary Capt., Royal Army Medical Corps. For conspicuous gallantry and devotion to duty. During an attack he attended to the wounded for five hours in the open under heavy fire. He showed the greatest coolness and courage throughout the day.

BRACE, HENRY FERGUSSON, Capt., Hussars. For conspicuous gallantry and devotion to duty. When in command of a company sent up to reinforce the front line, he displayed the greatest courage and ability in leading and organizing his men. By his personal example of coolness and gallantry he was in a great measure responsible for the successful defence of a locality, which at a very critical time was being continually harassed by snipers and machine guns, and subjected to frequent counter-attacks.

BROMLEY, JOHN EDOUARD MARSDEN, Temporary Capt. (Acting Major), Royal Field Artillery. For conspicuous gallantry and devotion to duty. He assisted in getting wounded out of a dug-out which had been blown in, under intense shell fire, and helped them to the dressing station. When an ammunition dump was set on fire, he put it out under heavy shell fire. When a dug-out, containing 15 men, was blown in, though himself wounded, he worked for an hour and a half rescuing them under intense shelling. He showed splendid courage and coolness.

CAMERON, JOHN JACKSON, Temporary Capt. (Acting Lieut.-Colonel), South Staffordshire Regt. For conspicuous gallantry and devotion to duty. He made a thorough reconnaissance of the ground on which his battalion were to assemble and advance in support of an attack. He guided his battalion to the position, which he found was being heavily shelled, and he assembled them successfully in another position. He showed the greatest ability and skill throughout.

FRASER-TYTLER, JAMES FRANCIS, Major, Yeomanry. For conspicuous gallantry and devotion to duty when in command of two companies in an attack on a village. He led his men through the enemy's outpost line, penetrated into the village, and formed up close to the enemy without being observed. By brilliant and determined leading he then surprised and captured the majority of the garrison.

GRAHAM, HOWARD BOYD, M.B., Temporary Capt., Royal Army Medical Corps. For conspicuous gallantry and devotion to duty. During a heavy barrage he personally reconnoitred the advanced aid posts with the result that many cases were evacuated the moment the barrage lifted. This action undoubtedly saved many lives. On another occasion he went out and brought in two officers and four other ranks who were lying out unattended. Later, hearing that an officer had become a casualty, he went forward and brought him back single-handed to a point whence he was evacuated. His coolness, fearlessness and devotion to duty were beyond praise.

HENDERSON, CHARLES ERNEST, Second Lieut., London Regt. For conspicuous gallantry and devotion to duty in leading a patrol through the enemy outposts to a position in the enemy's main line of resistance which was over 900 yards from our line. His patrol of 20 captured 23 unwounded prisoners and killed or wounded another 25 of the enemy. Though the rifles and Lewis gun jammed owing to mud, he succeeded in covering the withdrawal of the patrol, every man returning safely. He showed magnificent courage and resource.

HILTON-GREEN, HENRY FRANCIS LEONARD, M.C., Capt. and Brevet Major (Acting Major), Gloucestershire Regt., attached Army Cyclists Corps. For conspicuous gallantry and devotion to duty in an attack on a village. He advanced across most difficult country, overcoming considerable opposition, and, though part of his column was delayed, he attacked and cleared the village. He led his men with the greatest determination, and by his courageous leadership defeated a force of over double his own strength.

KNIGHTLEY, PERCY FRANK, Lieut. (Temporary Capt.), Royal Welsh Fusiliers. For conspicuous gallantry and devotion to duty. He took charge of the front line of the attack at a critical moment when, owing to heavy casualties from the enemy's fire, it appeared impossible to advance. He reorganized and rallied the men and led them with great dash to the capture of the objective, afterwards assuming command of the whole battalion front. He showed splendid courage and leadership.

McDOUGALL, ARTHUR, Capt., Yeomanry. For conspicuous gallantry and devotion to duty when a strong enemy force attacked his position, which he had been ordered to hold at all costs. The enemy advanced to within 40 yards of his line and opened machine-gun fire, but he held his position and inflicted heavy casualties on the enemy. He showed great courage and determination.

NEPEAN, HERBERT DRYDEN HOME YORKE, Lieut. (Acting Capt.), Indian Army. For conspicuous gallantry and devotion to duty. He led his men under a withering fire to the capture of a ridge, and organized a strong defensive line on the position. Though wounded, he refused to leave his post for some hours. His fearless bearing was the greatest encouragement to his men.

REES, JOHN GORDON, Major, Yeomanry. For conspicuous gallantry and devotion to duty. When the right of his battalion was held up by artillery and machine-gun fire, he at once made his way up to the front, rallied and reorganized the company, and led them in the assault. His complete indifference to danger and gallant bearing had a most inspiring effect on all ranks.

ROBERTSON, ROBERT THIN CRAIG, M.B., Capt. (Acting Lieut.-Colonel), Royal Army Medical Corps, Special Reserve. For conspicuous gallantry and devotion to duty. When two ammunition lorries were hit by enemy shells he went forward at great risk to where several men had been killed or wounded, dressed their wounds and had them evacuated. He displayed great initiative and coolness.

ROCHFORT, RICHARD ADAIR, M.C., Capt., Royal Warwickshire Regt. For conspicuous gallantry and devotion to duty. When the battalion, on its way up to the line, was heavily bombarded with gas and other shells and was in danger of losing its way in gas masks in the darkness, he placed himself at the head and guided it to its forming-up place in time. Although severely wounded the following day while leading his men, he remained with them for nearly two hours, until forced to desist through sheer exhaustion. He showed splendid determination and resource.

RODGERSON, ALAN PATRICK, Capt., Indian Army. For conspicuous gallantry and devotion to duty in an attack. He led the assaulting companies, on his own initiative, to the capture of a bridge under heavy fire, thereby cutting off the enemy's retreat. Though severely wounded, he refused to go back till he had reported on the situation, and sent in information which was of the greatest value. His conduct throughout was worthy of the highest praise.

STEDALL, LEIGH PEMBERTON, Major, Yeomanry. For conspicuous gallantry and devotion to duty in a counter-attack. He led forward three troops and galloped them across 500 yards of open country, under heavy rifle and machine-gun fire. Though wounded in two places, he led the charge on the enemy's position with the greatest success. He showed splendid leadership and resource.

THATCHER, GERALD GANE, Major (Acting Lieut.-Colonel), Royal Garrison Artillery. For conspicuous gallantry and devotion to duty. He commanded his artillery group with great skill and judgment during the operations. The success of the bombardment was chiefly due to the daring reconnaissances which he had previously made.

UNIACKE, GERALD LAWRENCE, Capt. and Brevet Major (Temporary Lieut.-Colonel), Reserve of Officers, Royal Lancaster Regt. For conspicuous gallantry and devotion to duty. He showed great coolness and skill when in command of his battalion during an enemy attack, and saved a critical situation when the enemy were pressing forward their attack on an exposed portion of his line. His courage was a fine example to all.

CANADIAN FORCE.

AIKINS, GORDON HAROLD, Major, Mounted Rifles. For conspicuous gallantry and devotion to duty as staff captain to an infantry brigade. He constantly visited the battalions in the front line, on several occasions passing through heavy barrages, and organized and supervised the carrying up of ammunition and supplies under the most difficult circumstances. On the afternoon of the attack he supervised the collection of wounded on the battlefield. His initiative and untiring energy contributed largely to the success of the operations, and his courage and example were an inspiration to all ranks.

BURGESS, WALTER HARTLEY, Lieut., Infantry. For conspicuous gallantry and devotion to duty. He took command of his company, which was in support during an engagement. When part of the front line began to be driven back by the enemy, he at once went forward, took command, and by his example and influence succeeded in holding the position. He exposed himself fearlessly to an intense artillery and machine-gun barrage to steady the men and keep them in their position, and he reorganized and established the line, and handed it over intact when relieved. His courageous action undoubtedly saved a critical situation.

CAMERON, JOHN ANGUS, Lieut., Infantry. For conspicuous gallantry and devotion to duty. On the attack being held up by a strong enemy bombing post, he rushed forward, ahead of his platoon, and charged the post single-handed, bayonetting one of the enemy and compelling the other twelve to surrender. Though he had been wounded, he remained with his men, showing a fine example of leadership, until he was again wounded, so severely that his evacuation was necessary.

JAMIESON, WILLIAM FRANCIS, Lieut., Infantry. For conspicuous gallantry and devotion to duty. When the original attack broke down, despite heavy losses, he moved his company forward and held his ground under severe fire until a second attack was made. When this succeeded, he again led his company forward and captured his objective ahead of him with numerous prisoners and machine-guns. He showed great courage and skill.

KENNEDY, HECTOR, Lieut., Infantry. For conspicuous gallantry and devotion to duty. In the attack he led his company in the most determined and courageous manner, through heavy enemy fire, and successfully gained his objective. It was then reported that the company, which had passed through his own to a further objective, was held up by two "pill-boxes." Appreciating the situation, he immediately went forward, and, despite heavy enemy machine-gun fire, accompanied by another officer, he rushed these enemy posts, forcing the garrisons to surrender, taking six officers and five other ranks prisoners. His courage and gallantry, together with his determination and prompt action, cleared up a critical situation, and enabled the final objective to be successfully carried.

LAWLESS, WILLIAM THEWLES, Major, Infantry. For conspicuous gallantry and devotion to duty. When, owing to heavy fire, the original attack failed, he at once advanced to the support company, and reorganized the line. He then went ahead under very heavy fire to select a position from which a further advance could be made. Although wounded by a sniper he remained with the company until he could explain the situation personally to his commanding officer. He displayed great skill and courage.

MACNAGHTEN, RONALD FREDERICK, Lieut., Infantry. For conspicuous gallantry and devotion to duty. This officer was in charge of his platoon, when a machine-gun opened fire, causing several casualties. He very gallantly rushed forward, shot two of the enemy, his platoon killing and bayonetting the others, and capturing two machine guns. His splendid example inspired all ranks.

PEARSON, RONALD WILFRED, M.C., Capt., Infantry. For conspicuous gallantry and devotion to duty. When in command of a company, during an attack on a strong enemy position, he led his men with splendid skill and courage under intense fire. When the success of the attack at one time seemed to be threatened by enemy snipers and machine-gun fire, he seized a machine gun, and moving forward close under the barrage, subdued the enemy fire. His prompt action enabled the attack to proceed without delay, and secured for his men the protection of the barrage. Throughout the operations his courage was outstanding, and his example was an inspiration to his officers and men.

SAVAGE, HAROLD MURCHISON, Major, Field Artillery. For conspicuous gallantry and devotion to duty. When a shell struck a large pile of ammunition, causing a terrific explosion and many casualties, and setting fire to more ammunition, he led five men in among the bursting shells and dragged out six severely wounded men with their clothes on fire. He remained at work with great determination till the last man living had been taken out. A few seconds later another big explosion occurred.

WALKER, WILLIAM KEATING, M.C., Capt. (Acting Major), Machine Gun Corps. For conspicuous gallantry and devotion to duty in building bridges under severe and accurate machine-gun and rifle fire. Though two officers and 18 men became casualties, he persisted until his work was completed. He set a splendid example of coolness and courage.

WILSON, WILLIAM DOUGLAS, Major, Field Artillery. For conspicuous gallantry and devotion to duty. He advanced his guns to a very forward position under most difficult conditions, some of them being two days on the road, though he worked continuously night and day. Though at different times 11 guns were put out of action, he always succeeded in repairing them or bringing up new guns, so that in each of three attacks there were six guns in action when the engagement began. He showed splendid determination and skill.

YOUNG, HARVEY GORDON, Temporary Capt., Army Medical Corps. For conspicuous gallantry and devotion to duty in an attack. He went forward with a stretcher squad through a heavy barrage and established an advanced aid post. For two days he was untiring in his work of attending to the wounded and getting them in from advanced areas with complete disregard of danger. By his skilful organization and untiring energy he attended to and evacuated over 400 cases in two days.

AUSTRALIAN IMPERIAL FORCE.

A'BECKETT, MALWYN HAYLEY, Major, Infantry. For conspicuous gallantry and devotion to duty when in charge of a battalion which relieved the attacking troops. He personally carried out a most valuable reconnaissance under most dangerous conditions, clearing up an obscure situation, and then established a very strong system of posts as a front line of defence. He set a splendid example of courage and resource.

BOURCHIER, MURRAY WILLIAM JAMES, Lieut.-Colonel, Light Horse Regt. For conspicuous gallantry and devotion to duty. As commanding officer, he led his regiment into action in the most gallant and capable manner. By his skilful handling of the regiment and by his magnificent example of courage and determination he was very largely instrumental in the success of the attack and the capture of the objective.

CAMERON, DONALD, Lieut.-Colonel, Light Horse Regt. For conspicuous gallantry and devotion to duty. He directed the attack of his regiment in an extraordinarily able and determined manner. In conjunction with another unit, he was responsible for the marked success of the action, which led to the capture of an important objective, many field guns, machine guns and several hundred prisoners.

DAVIES, GEORGE VERNON, Capt., Army Medical Corps. For conspicuous gallantry and devotion to duty in going forward through an intense barrage and establishing a regiment aid post in an advanced position, remaining on duty continuously for 54 hours, often working in the open under heavy fire. When the aid post was hit by a shell he extricated a man who was buried, and continued his work. He remained for 15 hours after the battalion was relieved till the last man was carried back to safety and set a magnificent example to all.

DIXON, ROBERT DERWENT, Capt., Infantry. For conspicuous gallantry and devotion to duty when in command of the centre company of his battalion in an attack. When held up by a nest of machine guns, with a small party he rushed the position and succeeded in capturing four machine guns and 30 prisoners. He did excellent work during the whole day, and set a splendid example of courage and initiative.

FETHERSTONHAUGH, CUTHBERT MURCHISON, Major, Light Horse Regt. For conspicuous gallantry and devotion to duty. This officer, during the attack, was with his squadron in support when the enemy from his main defences, which were obstructing the attack, opened up a very heavy machine-gun and rifle fire. Quickly appreciating the situation, he led his squadron with great gallantry in a charge on the enemy's trenches, overcame their resistance and enabled the assault to be carried on successfully to the final objective.

FRANKLIN, REGINALD NORRIS, Major, Light Horse Regt. For conspicuous gallantry and devotion to duty. He displayed great coolness and determination in handling his squadron under heavy fire. At a critical period, when the commanding officer of the regiment had become a casualty, he took command, and though twice wounded he continued to lead his men, and set a magnificent example of courage and resource.

HENDERSON, ROBERT OSWALD, Lieut.-Colonel, Infantry. For conspicuous gallantry and devotion to duty. When his battalion had reached its objective he personally supervised the digging-in and remained in the shell-holes with his men. On another occasion, when his battalion was brought up from reserve to replace casualties, he did excellent work in reorganizing the various units under heavy fire, after many officers had become casualties. He set a splendid example to his men.

HYMAN, ERIC MONTAGUE, Major, Light Horse Regt. For conspicuous gallantry and devotion to duty. This officer led his squadron at full gallop against an enemy redoubt, strongly manned with machine guns and rifles. Though the hostile fire was very heavy, yet the charge was so vigorous and determined that the enemy was overrun and his fire silenced, thus enabling the regiment to continue the assault and complete the capture of the objective.

LAWSON, JAMES, Major, Light Horse Regt. For conspicuous gallantry and devotion to duty. During an attack on the enemy trenches he led his squadron at the gallop, under heavy machine-gun and rifle fire, across the first enemy trenches, dismounting immediately a few yards in front of the second line, in which all the enemy were either killed or captured and a machine gun was taken. He then led his squadron with great determination and skill against a very strong trench, heavily garrisoned with machine guns and infantry. The trench was rushed and a hundred of the enemy were either killed or captured.

PAYNE, LESLIE HERBERT, Major, Infantry. For conspicuous gallantry and devotion to duty. He supervised the preparation of the attack, reconnoitring the forward area and organizing the assembly of the battalion under heavy shell fire. He set a splendid example of coolness and skill.

SELMES, JEREMIAH CHARLES, Major, Field Artillery. For conspicuous gallantry and devotion to duty. When all the officers and all but eight men of two batteries were reported to have been gassed he went forward a distance of 300 yards, through a heavy barrage, with complete disregard of danger, had them evacuated and arranged for the manning of the battery until the reliefs could arrive.

THOMPSON, ROY MELDRUM, M.C., Major, Field Artillery. For conspicuous gallantry and devotion to duty. When his battery suffered heavy casualties from high explosive and gas shells he personally got one wounded man away and fetched the medical officer to another, and although gassed himself did not leave till all men were away safely. On the following day when suffering from gas poisoning and ordered to the dressing-station, seeing his battery being shelled, he returned and in attempting to extinguish exploding ammunition was seriously wounded. He showed great courage and determination.

London Gazette, 26 April, 1918.—" Admiralty, 26 April, 1918.—Honours for Miscellaneous Services. The King has been graciously pleased to approve of the award of the following honours to the undermentioned Officers. (i).—Evacuation of Thermi Aerodrome. To be a Companion of the Distinguished Service Order."

CHICHESTER, CECIL GEORGE, Commander, R.N. In recognition of the energy, good judgment and coolness under fire with which he organized and executed the evacuation of the Aerodrome at Thermi, Mityleni, on the 9th to 15th Oct. 1917. The evacuation of the Aerodrome was carried out under continuous bombardment by the enemy, and was effected entirely without casualties and without loss of stores.

(ii).—Operations on the Belgian Coast.

To be Companions of the Distinguished Service Order:

COLLARD, BERNARD ST. GEORGE, Capt., R.N.

MORETON, JOHN ALFRED, Capt., R.N.

HAMMOND-CHAMBERS, ROBERT HERBERT BORGNIS, Lieut.-Commander (Acting Commander), R.N.

PERCIVAL, PERCY RALPH PASSAWER, Lieut.-Commander, R.N.

BAKER, HENRY, Engineer Lieut.-Commander, R.N.R.

" Honours for the Royal Naval Air Service.—(1).—Dunkirk. The King has been graciously pleased to approve of the award of the following honours to Officers of the Royal Naval Air Service, in recognition of their services at Dunkirk. To be Companions of the Distinguished Service Order."

CLARK-HALL, ROBERT HAMILTON, Wing Capt., R.N.

CAVE-BROWN-CAVE, HENRY MEYRICK, Wing Commander, R.N.

DALLAS, RODERIC STANLEY, D.S.C., Squadron Commander, Royal Naval Air Service.

To receive a Bar to the Distinguished Service Order:

MULOCK, REDFORD HENRY, D.S.O., Wing Commander, Royal Naval Air Service.

(2).—Miscellaneous.

To be a Companion of the Distinguished Service Order:

DIGBY, FRANK THOMAS, D.S.C., Flight Commander, Royal Naval Air Service. For the consistent determination, gallantry and skill displayed by him on long-distance bombing raids, particularly on the night of the 24th–25th March, 1918. On that date, in spite of mist, which made the journey most difficult, he eventually reached his objective, which he bombed with good results.

London Gazette, 1 May, 1918.—" Amendment.—The announcement of the award of the Military Cross on page 2162 of the London Gazette of the 18th Feb. 1918, to Lieut. (Temporary Capt.) Alexander Witham, Royal Field Artillery, is cancelled, and the following substituted. Awarded the Distinguished Service Order."

WITHAM, ALEXANDER, Lieut. (Temporary Capt.), Royal Field Artillery.

London Gazette, 1 May, 1918.—" Admiralty, 1 May, 1918.—Honours for the Royal Naval Air Service. The King has been graciously pleased to approve of the award of the following honours to Officers of the Royal Naval Air Service for zeal and devotion to duty during the period from 1 July to 31 Dec. 1917. To be Companions of the Distinguished Service Order."

NOYES, CHARLES ROBERT FINCH, Squadron Commander, R.N.

NICHOLL, VINCENT, D.S.C., Squadron Commander, Royal Naval Air Service.

London Gazette, 13 May, 1918.—" War Office, 13 May, 1918. His Majesty the King has been graciously pleased to approve of the following awards to the undermentioned Officers, in recognition of their gallantry and devotion to duty in the field. Awarded a Second Bar to the Distinguished Service Order."

JACKSON, ARNOLD NUGENT STRODE, D.S.O., Capt. (Temporary Lieut.-Colonel), North Lancashire Regt., attached King's Royal Rifle Corps. For conspicuous gallantry and devotion to duty. His battalion was subjected to an intense bombardment throughout a whole day, which caused many casualties and cut off all communication by wire with the front-line companies. He handled the situation with such skill and initiative that when the enemy attacked towards evening the casualties caused by the bombardment had been evacuated and replaced by reinforcements and communication with the front line had been re-established. It was entirely due to his powers of command and the splendid spirit with which he inspired his men that the attack on the greater part of his front was repulsed, and that the enemy, though they penetrated into parts of the front line, were counter-attacked and held at bay until the arrival of reinforcements. By his skilful dispositions he materially assisted the counter-attack which drove the enemy back with heavy losses and completely re-restablished the position.
(D.S.O. gazetted 4 June, 1917.)
(First Bar gazetted 18 July, 1917.)

Awarded a Bar to the Distinguished Service Order:

FRASER-TYTLER, NEIL, D.S.O., Major, Royal Horse Artillery, attached Royal Field Artillery. For conspicuous gallantry and devotion to duty. When several batteries suffered heavy casualties from a prolonged enemy bombardment of gas and high explosive shells, he showed great courage and coolness. He inspired the men with confidence by his splendid example, and enabled them to carry on their duties under the most difficult conditions.
(D.S.O. gazetted 26 Sept. 1916.)

CANADIAN FORCE.

JONES, ELMER WATSON, D.S.O., Lieut.-Colonel, Canadian Infantry, East Ontario Regt. For conspicuous gallantry and devotion to duty. When a large enemy raiding party, using flammenwerfer, entered his trenches under cover of an intense barrage, he at once went forward under heavy fire and directed a counter-attack which re-established the line without the enemy having gained an identification. Later, under his direction, a raiding party entered the enemy's lines, captured some prisoners, and inflicted severe losses on the enemy. He displayed great resource and initiative.
(D.S.O. gazetted 1 Jan. 1917.)

Awarded the Distinguished Service Order:

BAMBRIDGE, RUPERT CHARLES, M.C., M.M., Temporary Lieut. (Acting Capt.), Royal Fusiliers. For conspicuous gallantry and devotion to duty. He was ordered to lead his company in a counter-attack against the enemy who had gained a footing in part of the front line. The night was very dark, and the exact position of the enemy was unknown, but he led his men to the best position of assembly, and after a personal reconnaissance launched a counter-attack. This attack being only partially successful, he quickly organized another which drove the enemy back a considerable distance. At dawn he launched a third attack, drove the enemy out, and completely re-established the original position. The success of the operation was largely due to his splendid leadership, skill and energy.

BODDINGTON, HUMPHREY WEST, Lieut. (Acting Major), Yeomanry, attached Yorkshire Light Infantry. For conspicuous gallantry and devotion to duty. He was ordered at very short notice to carry out a counter-attack, and re-establish a position which had been captured by the enemy. He organized the operation with great skill and initiative, issued clear orders, and led two

The Distinguished Service Order

companies to the assembly position under heavy fire. His disregard of danger inspired all ranks, with the result that the enemy was driven back, and the position was completely re-established.

HANNAH, ROBERT WILLIAM, M.C., Lieut. (Acting Major), Royal Field Artillery, Special Reserve. For conspicuous gallantry and devotion to duty during an engagement. He maintained the ammunition supply and conducted the advance of his battery with the greatest skill and resource. He kept in touch with the infantry in spite of the difficult state of the ground and intense enemy shelling, and though wounded he remained at duty. He set an example of courage and initiative which had a splendid effect on his men.

HASSELL, JACOB, M.C., Lieut. (Acting Capt.), Yorkshire Light Infantry. For conspicuous gallantry and devotion to duty. When the enemy had gained a footing in part of the outpost line he led his company in a counter-attack at very short notice. In spite of the difficulties of assembling the company for the attack and the intensity of the enemy's machine-gun and shell fire, he carried out the operation with the greatest success, drove the enemy out, and completely re-established the position. He showed magnificent leadership and resource.

WATERS, JOHN DALLAS, Temporary Major (Acting Lieut.-Colonel), Royal Fusiliers. For conspicuous gallantry and devotion to duty. When the enemy, after a heavy bombardment, had gained a footing in the front-line trenches, he skilfully organized a counter-attack which drove them out with heavy losses. He arranged the supply of bombs and ammunition, kept open communications when all the wires were cut, and directed the whole operation with the greatest determination and initiative.

London Gazette, 17 May, 1918.—"Admiralty, 17 May, 1918.—Honours for Services in Action with Enemy Submarines. The King has been graciously pleased to approve of the award of the following honour to the undermentioned Officer. To be a Companion of the Distinguished Service Order."

LECKIE, ROBERT, D.S.C., Flight Commander, Royal Naval Air Service.

"Honours for the Naval Armoured Car Squadron.—The King has been graciously pleased to approve of the award of the following honours to the undermentioned Officers, in recognition of their services with the Naval Armoured Car Squadron during the Russian retreat from Galicia in July–Aug. 1917."

To be a Companion of the Distinguished Service Order:

WELLS-HOOD, WILLIAM, Lieut.-Commander, R.N.V.R. This officer joined the Armoured Cars at the outset of war, and served with them in Belgium, South-West Africa, France, the Caucasus, Armenia, the Dobrudja, and Galicia. Throughout the Galician retreat he fought day and night, under every sort of difficulty, always cheerful and ready, and inflicted very heavy casualties on the enemy. His last fights round Gusiatyn were very severe, and drew the praise of the Russian General in command. In the last day's fight he brought down an enemy aeroplane

To receive a Bar to the Distinguished Service Order:

SMILES, WALTER DORLING, D.S.O., Lieut.-Commander, Royal Naval Volunteer Reserve. When the road to Brzezany was blocked in the attack of 1 July, 1917, this officer called for volunteers to destroy the obstruction, and succeeded in removing it in the face of the fiercest fire by taking cover in the adjoining ditch, and rushing out during lulls to tear down wire and sandbags. Later on during the retreat he fought with characteristic courage until all his cars were lost in action, with the exception of a light-armoured Ford. He then improvised an armoured car by taking the armour off an old car and concealing it round a lorry. With this car and a heavy armoured car borrowed from another squadron he kept the enemy at bay beyond the frontier in Austria for six hours, until all troops had crossed the river. These cars passed over the river five minutes before the last bridge was blown up, and were the last thing on wheels to leave Austrian territory.

"Honours for Miscellaneous Services.—The King has been graciously pleased to approve of the award of the following honours to the undermentioned Officers."

(1).—Action in the Heligoland Bight on the 17th Nov. 1917.

To be a Companion of the Distinguished Service Order:

WILSON, MAURICE FIENNES FITZGERALD, Lieut.-Commander, R.N. On recovering consciousness after being wounded, he returned to duty, and for some time aided the officer who assumed command after the captain had been mortally wounded.

(2).—Services on the Mediterranean Station.

To be Companions of the Distinguished Service Order:

THOROWGOOD, ARTHUR PENTON NAPIER, Commander, R.N.
WARREN, WILLIAM HENRY FARRINGTON, Commander, R.A.N. (since died).
ROBERTS, CYRIL ARTHUR GRAEME, R.D., Commander, R.N.R.
STONE, REGINALD GUY, Lieut.-Commander, R.N.
PAGE, GEORGE FRANCIS LYON LABOUVERIE, Lieut.-Commander, R.N.
BAKER, ARTHUR BANNATYNE ARNOLD, Lieut.-Commander, R.N.
WORSLEY, HUGH BARRINGTON, Lieut.-Commander, R.N.
WILMOT, TREVOR EARDLEY, Lieut.-Commander, R.N.
WODEHOUSE, PHILIP GEORGE, Lieut.-Commander, R.N.
FINNIS, FREDERICK COBB, Lieut.-Commander, R.N.
SMYTH, ARTHUR DRU DRURY, Lieut.-Commander, R.N.
GREENHILL, JOSEPH WILLIAM, Lieut.-Commander (Acting Commander), R.N.R.

(3).—Miscellaneous.

To be Companions of the Distinguished Service Order:

PLUNKETT-ERNLE-ERLE-DRAX, THE HONOURABLE REGINALD AYLMER, RANFURLY, Capt., R.N.
GORDON, ALASTAIR, Lieut.-Commander, R.N.

To receive a Bar to the Distinguished Service Order:

BEST, THE HONOURABLE MATTHEW ROBERT, M.V.O., D.S.O., Capt., Royal Navy.

London Gazette, 31 May, 1918.—"War Office, 31 May, 1918. His Majesty the King has been graciously pleased to approve the following award for gallant services rendered on the occasion of a hostile air raid. To be a Companion of the Distinguished Service Order."

BRAND, CHRISTOPHER JOSEPH QUINTON, M.C., Lieut. (Temporary Capt.), Royal Air Force. For conspicuous gallantry. While on patrol at night he encountered an enemy aeroplane at a height of 8,700 feet. He at once attacked the enemy, firing two bursts of 20 rounds each, which put the enemy's right engine out of action. Closing to a range of 25 yards he fired a further three bursts of 25 rounds each, and as a result the enemy machine caught fire and fell in flames to the ground. Capt. Brand showed great courage and skill in manoeuvring his machine during the encounter, and when the enemy aeroplane burst into flames he was so close that the flames enveloped his machine, scorching his face. This officer has shown great determination and perseverance during the past nine months when on anti-aeroplane patrols at night, and his example of unassuming gallantry and skill has raised his squadron to a very high state of efficiency.

London Gazette, 3 June, 1918.—"War Office, 3 June, 1918. His Majesty the King has been graciously pleased, on the occasion of His Majesty's Birthday, to approve of the undermentioned rewards for distinguished service in connection with military operations in France and Flanders. Dated 3 June, 1918. Awarded a Bar to the Distinguished Service Order."

ACKLOM, SPENCER, D.S.O., M.C., Major (Temporary Lieut.-Colonel), Highland Light Infantry, attached Northumberland Fusiliers.
(D.S.O. gazetted 1 Jan. 1917.)

CAMPBELL, THE HONOURABLE ERIC OCTAVIUS, D.S.O., Capt. and Brevet Major (Temporary Lieut.-Colonel), Seaforth Highlanders.
(D.S.O. gazetted 18 Feb. 1917.)

HAMOND, PHILIP, D.S.O., M.C., Temporary Major (Capt., Reserve of Officers), Tank Corps (late Coldstream Guards) (description corrected to Temporary Major (Capt., Reserve of Officers), Retired Pay, attached Lincolnshire Regt. [London Gazette, 4 Sept. 1918]).
(D.S.O. gazetted 31 Oct. 1902.)

HART-SYNNOT, ARTHUR HENRY SETON, D.S.O., Lieut.-Colonel, East Surrey Regt.
(D.S.O. gazetted 19 April, 1901.)

HEWITT, THE HONOURABLE EVELYN JAMES, D.S.O., Major (Temporary Lieut.-Colonel), Dorset Regt., attached Duke of Cornwall's Light Infantry.
(D.S.O. gazetted 3 June, 1916.)

*HILL, FRANCIS ROWLEY, D.S.O., Temporary Major, Middlesex Regt.

*LUMSDEN, WILLIAM VERNON, D.S.O., M.C., Capt. (Acting Lieut.-Colonel), Argyll and Sutherland Highlanders, attached Scottish Rifles.

*PITTS, ARTHUR THOMAS, D.S.O., Capt. (Temporary Lieut.-Colonel), Royal Army Medical Corps.

RIGG, EDWARD HARRISON, D.S.O., Major (Temporary Lieut.-Colonel), King's Own Yorkshire Light Infantry, attached Royal Inniskilling Fusiliers.
(D.S.O. gazetted 3 June, 1916.)

*STILLWELL, WILLIAM DIGBY, D.S.O., Major (Acting Lieut.-Colonel), Royal Field Artillery.

*TORTISE, HERBERT JAMES, D.S.O., Temporary Capt. (Acting Major), Royal West Surrey Regt.

*WALKER, JAMES, D.S.O., Major (Acting Lieut.-Colonel), West Riding Regt.

CANADIAN FORCE.

EDWARDS, CAMERON MACPHERSON, D.S.O., Lieut.-Colonel, Infantry.
(D.S.O. gazetted 10 Jan. 1917.)

HILLIAM, EDWARD, D.S.O., Lieut.-Colonel (Temporary Brigadier-General), Nova Scotia Regt.
(D.S.O. gazetted 14 Jan. 1916.)

KIRKCALDY, JAMES, D.S.O., Lieut.-Colonel, Infantry.
(D.S.O. gazetted 1 Jan. 1917.)

LATTA, WILLIAM SMITH, D.S.O., Lieut.-Colonel, Infantry.
(D.S.O. gazetted 4 June, 1917.)

PAGE, LIONEL FRANK, D.S.O., Lieut.-Colonel, Infantry.
(D.S.O. gazetted 1 Jan. 1917.)

*NOTE.—In the cases marked by an asterisk the announcements of awards of the D.S.O. have not yet been published in the London Gazette; these rewards will be published in due course.

Awarded the Distinguished Service Order:

ADAMS, FRANCIS, Lieut.-Colonel, Indian Cavalry.
ALLEN, WILLIAM JAMES, Temporary Major, Royal Irish Rifles.
ALTHAM, HARRY SURTEES, M.C., Capt. (Temporary Major), King's Royal Rifle Corps.
ATKIN-BERRY, HERBERT COURTENAY, M.C., Temporary Lieut. (Temporary Capt.), General List.
AYLWARD, RICHARD NUNN, M.C., Temporary Capt. (Acting Major), Royal Engineers.
BAKER, BERNARD GRANVILLE, Temporary Major (Temporary Lieut.-Colonel), Yorkshire Regt.
BALFOUR, GEORGE BOYD, Major (Acting Lieut.-Colonel), Royal Lancaster Regt.
BALL, CHARLES JAMES PRIOR, M.C., Lieut. (Acting Major), Royal Artillery, attached Royal Horse Artillery.
BARKER, AUGUSTINE, M.C., Temporary Capt. (Acting Major), Royal Field Artillery.
BARRON, THOMAS ASHLEY, Major, Royal Army Medical Corps.
BARTER, HERBERT, Capt. (Acting Major), Royal Horse Artillery.
BARTON, RICHARD LIONEL, Major (Acting Lieut.-Colonel), Royal Garrison Artillery.
BATCHELOR, WILLIAM MAJOR, M.C., Temporary Capt. (Acting Major), Royal Engineers.
BATTEN, HERBERT COPELAND CARY, Major (Honorary Colonel, Special Reserve), Dorsetshire Regt.
BAYLEY, LIONEL SETON, Major and Brevet Lieut.-Colonel (Acting Lieut.-Colonel), Royal Garrison Artillery.
BAYNHAM, CUTHBERT THEODORE, Capt. (Temporary Major), Royal Field Artillery.
BENSON, REGINALD LINDSAY, M.C., Capt., Lancers.
BINGHAM, SAMUEL, Temporary Lieut.-Colonel, Liverpool Regt.
BIRCH, JULIUS GUTHLAC, Temporary Lieut.-Colonel, King's Royal Rifle Corps.
BIRCH, PERCY YATES, Capt. (Acting Major), Royal Garrison Artillery.

BIRD, THOMAS GRIFFIN, Temporary Capt. (Acting Major), Royal Engineers.
BIRKETT, GERALD HALSEY, Major, South Wales Borderers.
BISHOP, WILLIAM SAMUEL GEORGE, Deputy Commissary of Ordnance and Honorary Major, Army Ordnance Department.
BLACKWOOD, WILLIAM, M.B., Capt. (Acting Lieut.-Colonel), Royal Army Medical Corps.
BLAKEWAY, THOMAS WOOTTON, Temporary Major, Army Service Corps.
BONHAM-CARTER, ALGERNON LOTHIAN, Capt., King's Royal Rifle Corps.
BOURNE, ALAN GEORGE BARWYS, M.V.O., Major, Royal Marine Artillery.
BOWEN, WILLIAM ALLAN, Temporary Major (Acting Lieut.-Colonel) (Capt., Reserve of Officers), Royal Lancaster Regt.
BRADY, GERALD CHARLES JERVIS, Major, Royal Field Artillery.
BRECKON, JOHN, Lieut. (Temporary Major), Rifle Brigade.
BREMNER, GEORGE, M.C., Temporary Capt. (Acting Major), Royal Engineers.
BRIGGS, RAWDON, M.C., Temporary Lieut. (Acting Major), Royal Engineers.
BRIND, VICTOR CHARLES, Lieut. (Acting Major), Royal Field Artillery.
BRITTON, EDWIN JOHN JAMES, I.O.M., 1st Class, and Honorary Major, Army Ordnance Department.
BROCKBANK, JOHN GRAHAME, Capt. (Temporary Major) (Acting Lieut.-Colonel), Army Service Corps, seconded to Tank Corps.
BROOKE, ROBERT WESTON, M.C., Capt., Yeomanry.
BROWN, HERBERT DEVENISH LENNON, Major, Royal Garrison Artillery.
BROWNE, ALFRED PERCY, Lieut.-Colonel, Indian Cavalry.
BRUCE, GERALD TREVOR, Lieut.-Colonel, Yeomanry, Lincolnshire Regt.
BUCHANAN, EDGAR JAMES BERNARD, Capt. (Acting Major), Royal Engineers.
BUCKLEY, JOHN, M.C., Temporary Capt., General List.
BULLOCK-MARSHAM, FRANCIS WILLIAM, M.C., Capt., Hussars.
CAMPBELL, DUNCAN ELIDOR, Major, Yeomanry.
CARBERY, MURTOUGH, M.C., Temporary Capt., Royal Field Artillery.
CECIL, REGINALD EDWARD, Major, Lancers.
CHAPMAN, MELROSE THOMAS, Capt. (Temporary Major), Army Service Corps.
CHAPMAN, WILLIAM ADAM, Temporary Capt. (Acting Major), Royal Engineers.
CHARLES, WILLIAM GWYTHER, Major and Brevet Lieut.-Colonel (Temporary Lieut.-Colonel), Essex Regt.
CHENEVIX-TRENCH, JULIUS FRANCIS, Capt. and Brevet Major, Northumberland Fusiliers.
CHURCHILL, JOHN STRANGE SPENCER, Major, Yeomanry.
CLARKE, COLIN, M.B., F.R.C.S., Capt. (Acting Lieut.-Colonel), Royal Army Medical Corps.
CLAYTON, GEOFFREY SHAW, Temporary Major, Liverpool Regt.
CLAYTON, WILLIAM BOYER, Major, Army Service Corps.
CLEGG, NORMAN BENSON, Temporary Major, Army Service Corps.
CLEMENTS, STUCKBURGH UPTON LUCAS, Major (Acting Lieut.-Colonel), Royal Irish Fusiliers.
COCHRANE, CHARLES WILLIAM, Lieut.-Colonel, Army Service Corps.
COLES, WILLIAM HEWETT, Temporary Major, Middlesex Regt.
COLLETT, GILBERT FARADAY, Major (Acting Lieut.-Colonel), Gloucestershire Regt.
COLLINS, WILLIAM FELLOWES, Lieut.-Colonel, Dragoons.
COMYN, EDWARD WALTER, Lieut.-Colonel, Royal Garrison Artillery.
CONWAY, JAMES ALPHONSUS, M.C., M.D., Temporary Capt., Royal Army Medical Corps.
COPELAND, RUPERT RAMSAY, Capt. (Acting Lieut.-Colonel), Royal Field Artillery.
CORBETT, CECIL UVEDALE, Major (Lieut., Retired Pay, Temporary Major, Royal Field Artillery), Yeomanry.
CORBETT, GARNET ROBERT DE LA COUR, Major, Royal Garrison Artillery.
CORBETT, GEOFFREY ROBERT JOSCELINE, Lieut., Coldstream Guards.
COUCHMAN, HAROLD JOHN, M.C., Major (Temporary Lieut.-Colonel), Royal Engineers.
COULSON, JOHN, Lieut.-Colonel, Army Service Corps.
COWELL, ERNEST MARSHALL, M.B., F.R.C.S., Capt., Royal Army Medical Corps.
CRANSTON, WILLIAM JAMES, Capt. and Brevet Major (Temporary Lieut.-Colonel), North Staffordshire Regt.
CRAUFURD, ROBERT QUENTIN, Major (Temporary Lieut.-Colonel), Royal Scots Fusiliers.
CROCKER, BERTRAM EDWARD, Lieut.-Colonel, Welsh Regt.
CROPPER, CECIL HOWE, M.C., Temporary Major, Royal Engineers.
CROSS, EDWARD GUY KYNASTON, Capt. (Acting Lieut.-Colonel), Hussars.
CROSSE, WHITWORTH CHARLES, Major (Temporary Lieut.-Colonel), Army Service Corps.
CROSTHWAITE, JOHN DURNFORD, M.C., Capt. (Acting Lieut.-Colonel), London Regt., Norfolk Regt.
CUNNINGHAM, ALAN GORDON, M.C., Major, Royal Field Artillery.
CUNNINGHAM, FRANCIS WILLIAM MURRAY, M.D., Capt. (Temporary Lieut.-Colonel), Royal Army Medical Corps.
CURRAN, EDWARD, M.C., Lieut. (Acting Major), Royal Field Artillery.
DALY, JAMES FAIRLY, Major, Highland Light Infantry, Gloucestershire Regt.
DAVIDSON, CHARLES GEORGE FRANCIS, M.C., Major (Acting Lieut.-Colonel), Royal Garrison Artillery.
DAVIDSON, PAUL VICTOR, Capt. (Temporary Lieut.-Colonel), Royal Warwickshire Regt.
DAVIES, JOHN WHARTON LLOYD, M.C., Temporary Capt. (Acting Major), Royal Engineers.
DAVIES, RICHARD HOWELL, Temporary Capt. (Acting Major), Royal Engineers.
DEAN, HENRY GORDON, Major, Lincolnshire Regt.

DE LAESSOE, HAROLD HENRY, M.C., Temporary Capt., General List.
DELPHIN, LEONCE, M.C., Temporary Capt. (Acting Lieut.-Colonel), Royal Engineers.
DENIS DE VITRE, PERCY THEODOSIUS, Lieut.-Colonel, Royal Engineers.
DE PENTHENY O'KELLY, EDGAR JOHN, Major (Temporary Lieut.-Colonel), Royal Welsh Fusiliers.
DIXON, WILLIAM CHESTER, Major (Acting Lieut.-Colonel), Leicestershire Regt. (description corrected to Major(Acting Lieut.-Colonel), Leicestershire Regt., attached A.O.D. [London Gazette, 7 Nov. 1918]).
DOAKE, SAMUEL HENRY, Capt. (Acting Major), Royal Field Artillery.
DOBIE, JAMES JARDINE, Capt., Hussars.
DOONER, JOHN GRAHAM, Lieut.-Colonel, Royal Field Artillery.
DOUGLAS, MALCOLM GORDON, M.C., Major, Honourable Artillery Company.
DOWDING, CHARLES CHILD, M.C., Temporary Major, Welsh Regt.
DRAKE-BROCKMAN, RALPH EVELYN, Temporary Capt. (Acting Lieut.-Colonel), Royal Army Medical Corps.
DU BOULAY, ARTHUR HOUSSEMAYNE, Major and Brevet Lieut.-Colonel, Royal Engineers.
DUKE, AUGUSTUS CECIL, Major, Reserve of Officers, late Royal Garrison Artillery.
DUKE, ROBERT NORMAN, M.C., Temporary Capt., General List.
DURIE, THOMAS EDWIN, M.C., Major, Royal Field Artillery.
EDMEADES, WILLIAM ALLAIRE, Major (Acting Lieut.-Colonel), Royal Garrison Artillery.
EELES, CECIL AUBREY, Major, Royal Field Artillery.
EGERTON, CHARLES HERTEL, M.C., Capt., Royal Engineers.
ELWES, HENRY CECIL, M.V.O., Capt. (Temporary Lieut.-Colonel), Scots Guards, attached Royal Irish Rifles.
ENGLAND, ABRAHAM, Lieut.-Colonel, Army Service Corps.
FARNHAM, ARTHUR KENLIS, LORD, Major (Acting Lieut.-Colonel), North Irish Horse, attached Royal Inniskilling Fusiliers.
FAWCUS, ARTHUR EDWARD FLYNN, M.C., Major (Temporary Lieut.-Colonel), Manchester Regt., attached North Staffordshire Regt.
FENN, ARTHUR ALSTON, Capt., and Brevet Major, Royal Fusiliers and Intelligence Corps.
FERGUSON, FRANCIS AUGUSTUS, Major, Royal Engineers.
FESTING, HUBERT WOGAN, Major (Temporary Lieut.-Colonel), Durham Light Infantry, attached Yorkshire Light Infantry.
FOGGIE, WILLIAM EDWARD, M.D., Lieut.-Colonel, Royal Army Medical Corps.
FORD, VINCENT TENNYSON RANDLE, Capt. (Temporary Lieut.-Colonel), York and Lancaster Regt., employed Northumberland Fusiliers.
FOSTER, RICHARD FOSTER CARTER, Major and Brevet Lieut.-Colonel (Temporary Lieut.-Colonel), Royal Marine Artillery.
FRANKAU, CLAUDE HOWARD STANLEY, M.B., F.R.C.S., Capt. and Brevet Major (Acting Lieut.-Colonel), Royal Army Medical Corps.
FRANKLYN, HAROLD EDMUND, M.C., Capt. and Brevet Major (Temporary Lieut.-Colonel), Yorkshire Regt.
GADD, HARRY READ, M.C., Capt. (Acting Lieut.-Colonel), Suffolk Regt., attached Nottinghamshire and Derbyshire Regt.
GARDEN, JAMES WILLIAM, Lieut.-Colonel, Royal Field Artillery.
GAVIN, FREDERICK CHARLES, Temporary Capt. (Temporary Major), Army Veterinary Corps.
GERMAN, GEORGE, Major (Acting Lieut.-Colonel), Leicestershire Regt.
GETTINS, JOSEPH HOLMES, Capt. (Acting Major), Army Service Corps.
GIBSON, WILLIE ROLAND, Major, Army Service Corps.
GILLATT, JOHN MAXWELL, Major (Acting Lieut.-Colonel), Royal Scots.
GILLIGAN, GEOFFREY GOYER, Major (Acting Lieut.-Colonel), Argyll and Sutherland Highlanders, attached Nottinghamshire and Derbyshire Regt.
GLASCODINE, RICHARD KENNETH, M.C., Lieut., London Regt., seconded to Trench Mortar Battery.
GLOVER, GUY DE COURCY, M.C., Capt. and Brevet Major, South Staffordshire Regt.
GODSAL, WALTER HUGH, M.C., Major, Durham Light Infantry.
GOODWIN, GEORGE JOSEPH POWER, Major (Acting Lieut.-Colonel), Royal Engineers.
GOULD, GEORGE, Major, Indian Cavalry.
GRAY, WILLIAM, Capt. (Acting Lieut.-Colonel), Army Service Corps.
GREAVES, SAMUEL SOWRAY, M.C., Temporary Capt., Royal Army Medical Corps.
HAIG, WOLSELEY DE HAGA, Capt. and Brevet Major, Royal Engineers.
HALLOWES, RICHARD COLLIS, M.B., Major (Temporary Lieut.-Colonel), Royal Army Medical Corps.
HAMERSLEY, HUGH ST. GEORGE, Major (Acting Lieut.-Colonel), Royal Garrison Artillery.
HAMILTON, GERARD MONTAGUE, Capt. (Acting Major), Royal Field Artillery.
HANKEY, SANDFORD RAYMOND ALERS, Major (Temporary Colonel), South Irish Horse.
HARDY, FRANCIS KYLE, Capt. (Acting Major), York and Lancaster Regt.
HARRIS-ST. JOHN, WILFRED, Major, Royal Welsh Fusiliers.
HART, LEONARD HERBERT POCOCK, Major, Lincolnshire Regt., attached York and Lancaster Regt.
HAWKINS, CHARLES FRANCIS, M.C., Temporary Major, Tank Corps.
HAWKINS, ROWLAND CHARLES, Capt. (Acting Lieut.-Colonel), Honourable Artillery Company.
HAY, RONALD BRUCE, Temporary Capt. (Acting Major), Royal Garrison Artillery.
HEATHCOTE, ROBERT EVELYN MANNERS, Capt. (Temporary Lieut.-Colonel), Royal Scots.
HEDDLE, MALCOLM, Temporary Lieut. (Acting Major), Royal Garrison Artillery.

The Distinguished Service Order

HEMPHILL, ROBERT, Capt. (Acting Lieut.-Colonel), Royal Army Medical Corps.
HENDERSON, JOHN ACHESON, Honorary Major, Honorary Major in Army, Reserve of Officers, Hussars (rank corrected to Major (Honorary Major in Army), Reserve of Officers, Hussars [London Gazette, 22 July, 1918]).
HETHERINGTON, CHARLES GWYNN, Major, Royal Garrison Artillery.
HEWSON, FRANCES BLAND, M.C., Capt., York and Lancaster Regt.
HEXT, FRANCIS JOHN, M.C., Capt. (Acting Major), Royal Field Artillery.
HILL, EUSTACE, Major, Yeomanry.
HILL, GEOFFREY NOEL, Major, Royal Garrison Artillery.
HOBDAY, HERBERT, M.C., Lieut. (Acting Major), Royal Field Artillery.
HODGSON, ERNEST CHARLES, Major (Temporary Lieut.-Colonel), Indian Medical Service.
HOLME, RICHARD CARLYLE, Major, Royal Garrison Artillery.
HOLNESS, HAROLD JAMES, Major, Army Veterinary Corps.
HOPE, JOHN URMSON, Major, Royal Garrison Artillery.
HORTON, THOMAS, Lieut. (Acting Major), Royal Garrison Artillery.
HUNTER, ALAN JOHN, M.C., Major and Brevet Lieut.-Colonel (Temporary Brigadier-General), King's Royal Rifle Corps.
HUNTER, RICHARD DEVAS, Capt. (Acting Major), Scottish Rifles.
HUTCHINSON, EDWARD MAITLAND, Major, Royal Field Artillery.
IRWIN, ARNOLD, Lieut.-Colonel, Northumberland Fusiliers.
IRWIN, REGINALD STRUTT, Capt. (Temporary Major, Acting Lieut.-Colonel), Royal Highlanders, attached Border Regt.
IVEY, THOMAS, Capt. (Acting Major), Royal Irish Rifles.
JAMES, ALBERT JOHN STANLEY, M.C., Temporary Major (Acting Lieut.-Colonel), Royal Welsh Fusiliers, now Entraining Battn.
JENKINS, MONTAGU IRVINE GEDOIN, Major, Devonshire Regt.
JOHNSON, HARRY, Major (Acting Lieut.-Colonel), North Staffordshire Regt.
JOHNSON, SAMUEL GORDON, M.C., Capt. (Acting Major), South Staffordshire Regt., attached Royal Engineers.
JONES, ALBERT, M.C., Temporary Capt. (Acting Lieut.-Colonel), Royal Army Medical Corps.
JONES, CEDRIC LA TOUCHE TURNER, M.C., Capt., Royal Engineers.
JONES, DOUGLAS CHAMPION, Major (Acting Lieut.-Colonel), Royal Engineers.
KEATINGE, OSCAR JOHN FORRESTALL, Major, North Staffordshire Regt.
KELLETT, JOHN PHILIP, M.C., Capt. (Acting Lieut.-Colonel), London Regt.
KNOX, FRANK PERY, Temporary Major, Army Service Corps.
LANGDON, FRANCIS JOHN, Major, Reserve of Officers, Liverpool Regt.
LASCELLES, VISCOUNT, HENRY GEORGE CHARLES, Capt. (Acting Major), Reserve of Officers, Grenadier Guards.
LEA, HAROLD FUTVOYE, Major (Temporary Lieut.-Colonel), Reserve of Officers, Yorkshire Regt.
LEATHER, FRANCIS HOLDSWORTH, Lieut.-Colonel, Army Service Corps.
LEVY, WALTER HENRY, Temporary Major, Army Service Corps.
LEWIS, ROWLAND PHILIP, Major (Acting Lieut.-Colonel), Royal Army Medical Corps.
LINDSAY, CREIGHTON HUTCHINSON, C.M.G., Major (Temporary Colonel), Royal Army Medical Corps.
LLOYD, EDWARD PRINCE, Capt. and Brevet Major (Temporary Lieut.-Colonel), Lincolnshire Regt., attached Northumberland Fusiliers.
LLOYD, REGINAL GEORGE ALBERT, Major, Reserve of Officers, South Lancashire Regt.
LOCKWOOD, AMBROSE LORNE, M.C., Capt., Royal Army Medical Corps.
LONG, ALBERT DE LANDE, Capt. and Brevet Major (Acting Lieut.-Colonel), Gordon Highlanders.
LOWRY, THOMAS MARTIN, M.C., Capt. (Acting Major), Duke of Cornwall's Light Infantry, attached Royal Engineers.
LUMLEY-SMITH, THOMAS GABRIEL LUMLEY, Capt. (Temporary Major), Lancers.
McCRACKEN, WILLIAM, Major, Argyll and Sutherland Highlanders.
MACDONALD, JAMES ALEXANDER, Lieut. (Acting Major), Royal Field Artillery.
MACDONALD, THOMAS WILSON, Capt., Border Regt.
MACFIE, CLAUD, Major, Seaforth Highlanders.
MACLEOD, RAOUL DONALD CARNEGY, Major Lancers, Indian Army.
MACPHERSON, ALAN DAVID, M.C., Capt. (Acting Major), Royal Field Artillery.
McNEILL, ARTHUR NORMAN ROY, Capt. (Acting Lieut.-Colonel), Royal Army Medical Corps.
MACREADY, GORDON NEVIL, M.C., Capt. and Brevet Major (Temporary Lieut.-Colonel), Royal Engineers.
MAITLAND, GEORGE RAMSAY, Major (Temporary Lieut.-Colonel), Indian Cavalry.
MARCHANT, THOMAS HARRY SAUNDERS, Major (Temporary Lieut.-Colonel), Hussars.
MARR, FRANCIS ALLEYNE, M.C., Capt., Cambridgeshire Regt.
MARTIN, ARCHIBALD VICTOR POWELL, Major (Acting Lieut.-Colonel), Wiltshire Regt.
MARTIN, EDWYN SANDYS DAWES, M.C., Capt., Dragoon Guards.
MARTIN, JAMES HALL, M.C., Capt. (Temporary Lieut.-Colonel), Royal Lancaster Regt.
MATTHEWS, ERNEST ALBERT CHURCHWARD, Major, Indian Medical Service.
MATURIN, JOHN WILLIAM HENRY, Major (Temporary Lieut.-Colonel), Army Service Corps.
MEAD, STEPHEN, Major, Royal Garrison Artillery.
MEDLICOTT, HENRY EDWARD, Major (Temporary Lieut.-Colonel), Indian Cavalry.
MIDDLETON, FRANK, Lieut.-Colonel, Royal Field Artillery.
MILFORD, KENNETH EUGENE, Major, Royal Artillery.

MILLER, SINCLAIR, M.C., Capt. (Acting Lieut.-Colonel), Royal Army Medical Corps.
MITCHELL, PERCY REYNOLDS, Major, Royal Garrison Artillery.
MOIR, MALCOLM EDWARD, Capt. (Acting Major), Royal Field Artillery.
MORTON, HARRY, M.C., Temporary Capt. (Acting Major), Nottinghamshire and Derbyshire Regt.
MOULTON-BARRETT, ALTHAM LEONARD, Major (Temporary Lieut.-Colonel), Dorsetshire Regt.
MUIRHEAD, JOHN SPENCER, M.C., Lieut. (Acting Major), Royal Engineers.
MUNBY, ALDWIN MONTGOMERY, Major, Border Regt.
MURRAY, CYRIL ALEXANDER GEORGE OCTAVIUS, Capt. (Acting Lieut.-Colonel), King's Own Scottish Borderers.
NALL, JOSEPH, Major, Royal Field Artillery.
NEWNHAM, CHARLES COWAN, Lieut.-Colonel, Indian Cavalry.
NEWTON, THOMAS COCHRANE, Major (Acting Lieut.-Colonel), Royal Field Artillery.
NICHOLSON, ST. JOHN RICHARDSON, Major, Royal Garrison Artillery.
NIXON, FERGUS BRINSLEY, Major, Royal Inniskilling Fusiliers (Regt. corrected to 6th Inniskilling Dragoons).
NOCKOLDS, HUMPHREY, Temporary Honorary Capt., Royal Army Medical Corps.
NORCOCK, HENRY LOWCAY, Temporary Major, Army Service Corps.
NUNN, REGINALD LEWIS, Temporary Capt. (Acting Major), Royal Engineers.
ODDIE, WILLIAM, Lieut.-Colonel, West Yorkshire Regt.
O'REILLY-BLACKWOOD, EDWIN HERBERT, M.C., Major, Royal Garrison Artillery.
O'RORKE, JOHN MARCUS WILLIAM, Capt., Cavalry, Indian Army.
PACE, THOMAS GEORGE, Temporary Major, Army Service Corps.
PALMER, HENRY WELLINGTON TUTHILL, Capt. (Acting Major), Royal Engineers.
PALMER, HUGH ROBERT, Lieut.-Colonel, Royal Garrison Artillery.
PARSONS, JOHN STANLEY, Lieut. (Temporary Major), Royal Engineers.
PATERSON, ARTHUR ALEXANDER ADAM, M.C., Temporary Capt. (Acting Major), Royal Field Artillery.
PECK, CECIL HERBERT, M.C., Temporary Capt. (Acting Major), Royal Field Artillery.
PERY-KNOX-GORE, IVAN COCKAYNE, M.C., Major, Royal Field Artillery.
POWELL, EDWARD DARLEY, M.C., Temporary Capt., Royal Engineers.
POWELL, JOHN, M.B., Lieut.-Colonel, Royal Army Medical Corps.
PREESTON, NOEL PERCIVAL RICHARD, Major (Acting Lieut.-Colonel), Royal Field Artillery.
PRIDEAUX, HUMPHREY HOLLOND, M.C., Capt (Temporary Major), Northumberland Fusiliers.
RADCLYFFE, CHARLES RAYMOND, Temporary Major, Army Service Corps, attached Tank Corps.
RASHLEIGH, PHILIP, Major, Royal Garrison Artillery.
RAY, ROBERT AMYATT, Major (Temporary Lieut.-Colonel), Royal Lancaster Regt.
REDFERN, JOHN GUILDFORD, Capt., East Yorkshire Regt.
REES, EVAN THOMAS, M.C., Temporary Major (Acting Lieut.-Colonel), South Wales Borderers.
RIDOUT, JULIAN YORKE HAYTER, Major (Acting Lieut.-Colonel), Royal Field Artillery.
RIVIS, THOMAS CHARLES LOCKHART, Major (Acting Lieut.-Colonel), Army Service Corps.
ROBERTSON, GORDON McMAHON, Capt. (Acting Lieut.-Colonel), North Staffordshire Regt., attached Royal Dublin Fusiliers.
ROBINSON, FREDERICK WILFRED, M.C., Temporary Lieut. (Acting Capt.), Machine Gun Corps.
ROGERS, ARTHUR LESLIE, Temporary Capt. (Acting Major), Royal Field Artillery.
ROYLE, REGINALD GEORGE, Temporary Capt. (Acting Major), Yorkshire Light Infantry.
RUNGE, CHARLES HERMANN SCHMETTAU, M.C., Temporary Capt., General List.
RYAN, CURTEIS FRASER MAXWELL NORWOOD, M.C., Capt., Royal Engineers.
RYAN, RUPERT SUMNER, Major (Temporary Lieut.-Colonel), Royal Field Artillery.
SANDEMAN, GERALD ROBERT, M.C., Capt., Border Regt.
SANDERS, REGINALD ERNEST, Temporary Major (Acting Lieut.-Colonel), Army Service Corps.
SAVAGE, ARTHUR JOHNSON, Major (Acting Lieut.-Colonel), Royal Engineers.
SHEA, ARTHUR WILSON, Surgeon-Major, Nottinghamshire and Derbyshire Regt.
SIMPSON, WILLIAM GEORGE, C.M.G., Lieut.-Colonel (Temporary Colonel), London Regt.
SPAIGHT, THOMAS HENRY LIMERICK, Major, Royal Engineers.
SPEIR, KENNETH ROBERT NAPIER, Temporary Lieut.-Colonel, Royal Engineers.
SPROT, ALEXANDER WILLIAM RAMSAY, Major (Acting Lieut.-Colonel), Argyll and Sutherland Highlanders, seconded Tank Corps.
STEEL, MATTHEW REGINALD, M.C., Temporary Capt., Northumberland Fusiliers.
STEEVENSON, JOHN ROBERT, Major, Army Veterinary Corps.
STEPHENS, HENRY FRENCH, M.C., Temporary Capt. (Acting Major), Royal Field Artillery.
STOKES, HAROLD WILLIAM PUZEY, Major (Acting Lieut.-Colonel), Army Service Corps.
STONE, CHRISTOPHER REYNOLDS, M.C., Temporary Major, late Royal Fusiliers.

STONE, JOHN HARTRICK, Major (Temporary Lieut.-Colonel), Army Ordnance Department.
STREET, ARTHUR HUBERT, Temporary Capt. (Acting Major), Royal Garrison Artillery.
SYDENHAM, EDWARD VERRINDER, Major, Royal Warwickshire Regt.
TAYLOR, LYSTER ROBERT EDWARD WATERS, Major, Royal Garrison Artillery.
TENNANT, JAMES, Capt. (Temporary Major), South Lancashire Regt., attached Army Cyclists Corps.
THOMPSON, JAMES GILBERT, M.C., Capt., Liverpool Regt.
THOMSON, VIVIAN HOME, M.C., Capt. (Acting Major), Royal Field Artillery.
THORNTON, NOEL SHIPLEY, Second Lieut. (Temporary Major), Rifle Brigade.
TOWNSEND, MEREDITH DENISON, Capt. (Acting Major), Royal Field Artillery.
TRACY, GEORGE COURTENAY, Major (Temporary Lieut.-Colonel), Duke of Cornwall's Light Infantry.
TROUP, ALAN GORDON, Lieut.-Colonel, Army Service Corps.
TURNER, ALAN CHARLES, Major, Royal Army Medical Corps.
TYLDEN-WRIGHT, WARRINGTON ROYDS, Capt., Hussars.
VICCARS, JOHN ELLIS, Major, Leicestershire Regt.
VIVIAN, LORD, GEORGE CRESPIGNY BRABAZON, Major, Yeomanry, Territorial Force.
WADDY, RICHARD HENRY, Capt. (Acting Lieut.-Colonel), Somersetshire Light Infantry.
WADE, ERNEST WENTWORTH, M.B., Capt. (Acting Lieut.-Colonel), Royal Army Medical Corps.
WAITE, CLEMENT WILLIAM, Temporary Major, East Yorkshire Regt.
WALKER, ARTHUR DUNBAR, Major (Acting Lieut.-Colonel), Royal Engineers.
WALKER, BERTRAM JAMES, Temporary Lieut.-Colonel, Royal Sussex Regt.
WATERS, ARNOLD HORACE SANTO, M.C., Temporary Capt. (Acting Major), Royal Engineers.
WATSON, DOUGLAS PERCIVAL, M.B., Major, Royal Army Medical Corps.
WATSON, THOMAS HOVENDEN, M.C., Capt. (Acting Lieut.-Colonel), Worcestershire Regt., attached Nottinghamshire and Derbyshire Regt.
WHITE, CHARLES RAMSAY, Major (Temporary Lieut.-Colonel), Yorkshire Regt.
WIGHTMAN, JAMES, M.C., Temporary Major, East Surrey Regt.
WILLIAMS, GERARD WILLIAM, M.C., Temporary Capt. (Acting Major), Royal Engineers.
WILLIAMS-FREEMAN, ARTHUR PEERE, Major (Acting Lieut.-Colonel), Duke of Cornwall's Light Infantry (corrected to Duke of Cornwall's Light Infantry, attached A.O.D. [London Gazette, 7 Nov. 1918]).
WILLIAMSON, ALFRED JOHN, Capt. (Acting Lieut.-Colonel), Royal Army Medical Corps.
WILLSON, EDWARD, Capt. (Acting Major), Royal Garrison Artillery.
WINTERSCALE, CYRIL FRANCIS BARONNEAU, Major (Temporary Lieut.-Colonel), Shropshire Light Infantry.
WITHERS, RUPERT BRYSON, Capt. (Acting Major), Royal Garrison Artillery (Christian name corrected to Robert Bryson [London Gazette, 22 July, 1918]).
WOODCOCK, FREDERICK ARTHUR, Temporary Capt. (Acting Lieut.-Colonel), Royal Field Artillery.
WRIGHT, ERNEST TREVOR LANGEBEAR, Temporary Major (Acting Lieut.-Colonel), Army Service Corps (late Capt., Hussars).
WRIGHT, GEOFFREY MACHEL HUNGERFORD, M.C., Capt., Royal Irish Fusiliers.
WRIGHT, SYDNEY CAMPBELL, Capt. (Acting Major), Royal Field Artillery.
YALLAND, ROBERT RENNIE, Capt. (Temporary Major, Acting Lieut.-Colonel), Leicestershire Regt.
YOOL, GEORGE ALEXANDER, Major (Acting Lieut.-Colonel), South Staffordshire Regt., attached Leicestershire Regt. (corrected to attached Lincolnshire Regt.).
YOUNG, JAMES MACLAREN, Major, Royal Lancaster Regt.

CANADIAN FORCE.

BOYCE, GEORGE JOSEPH, Lieut.-Colonel, Army Medical Corps.
BULL, JEFFREY HARPER, Major, Infantry.
CAMERON, GEORGE LYNCH, Major, Infantry.
CHANDLER, WILLIAM KELLMAN, Major, Infantry.
CHATTELL, ARTHUR PAUL, Capt. (Acting Major), Infantry.
CLEARY, EDWARD JOHN, Major, Army Service Corps.
COLE, FREDERICK MINDEN, Lieut.-Colonel, Garrison Artillery.
CRAIG, JOHN CORMACK, Major, Railway Troops.
CUTCLIFFE, ASHTON BLUETT, Major (Temporary Lieut.-Colonel), Army Veterinary Corps.
DONALDSON, ANSON SCOTT, Lieut.-Colonel, Army Medical Corps.
DUGUID, ARCHER FORTESCUE, Major, Field Artillery.
EARCHMAN, ARCHIBALD, Lieut.-Colonel, Railway Troops.
EDGETT, CHARLES EDGAR, Major (Temporary Lieut.-Colonel), Army Veterinary Corps.
ELLIS, DOUGLAS STEWART, Major, Engineers.
FLINT, CHARLES, Major, Railway Construction Corps.
FRENCH, REV. FRANCIS LAURENCE, Honorary Capt. (Acting Lieut.-Colonel), Chaplains' Service.
GENTLES, NORMAN, Major, Infantry.
GIBSON, GEORGE HERBERT RAE, Major, Army Medical Corps.
GILDAY, ARCHIBALD LORNE CAMPBELL, Lieut.-Colonel, Army Medical Corps.
GILLMORE, EDWARD THEODORE BARCLAY, Lieut.-Colonel, Field Artillery.
GREER, WILLIAM DAVID, Major (Acting Lieut.-Colonel), Army Service Corps.

GUNN, JOHN NISBET, Lieut.-Colonel, Army Medical Corps.
HARBOTTLE, COLIN CLARK, Lieut.-Colonel, Infantry.
HAYES, JOSEPH, Lieut.-Colonel, Army Medical Corps.
HEASLEY, HUGH JAMES, Major, Army Service Corps.
HILLMAN, DANIEL, Major, Engineers.
HUMPHREY, ALBERT ERNEST, Major, Cyclist Corps.
HURDMAN, WILLIAM GEORGE, Lieut.-Colonel, Field Artillery.
KAPPELE, DANIEL PAUL, Lieut.-Colonel, Army Medical Corps.
KINGSMILL, WALTER BERNARD, Lieut.-Colonel, Pioneers.
LEIGHTON, GORDON ERNEST, Major, Infantry.
LEONARD, IBBOTSON, Lieut.-Colonel, Cavalry.
LOMER, THEODORE ADOLF, Major, Army Medical Corps.
MACKAY, ATWOOD TALBOT, Major, Field Artillery.
MACKENZIE, ROBERT CARLYLE, Major, Infantry.
MACLEAN, NEIL BRUCE, Major, Garrison Artillery (corrected to Heavy and Siege Artillery).
MAXFIELD, WALTER EDWARD, Major, Mounted Rifles.
MILLER, LAWRENCE WALTER, Major, Mounted Rifles.
MORDY, ARNOTT GRIER, Major, Infantry.
NEILSON, WILLIAM, Major, Infantry.
NELLES, LAFAYETTE HARRY, Lieut.-Colonel, Infantry.
PATERSON, ALEXANDER THOMAS, Major, Field Artillery.
PENHALE, JOHN JENKIN, Lieut.-Colonel, Field Artillery.
PENSE, HENRY EDWARD, Major, Infantry.
PERRY, NORMAN DUNDAS, Major, Central Ontario Regt.
PETERSON, WILLIAM GORDON, Major, Quebec Regt.
PIERCEY, JOHN GEORGE, Lieut.-Colonel, Field Artillery.
RADDALL, THOMAS HEAD, Major, Infantry.
RHOADES, WILLIAM, M.C., Major, Mounted Rifles.
ROBERTSON, NORMAN ROY, Major, Engineers.
RUSSELL, CECIL BELL, Major, Engineers.
SAUNDERS, CHARLES GREATLEY, Major, Army Veterinary Corps.
SEMMENS, JOHN NELSON, Major, Infantry.
SHARPE, WALLACE JAMES, Major, Cavalry.
SHEARER, GEORGE WYMAN, Major, Field Artillery.
STEWART, JAMES CROSSLEY, Lieut.-Colonel, Field Artillery.
TAYLOR, ALLAN ELSWORTH, Major, Infantry.
THACKER, HERBERT CYRIL, C.M.G., Brigadier-General, Field Artillery.
THOMPSON, JOHN THOMAS CONNELLY, Lieut.-Colonel, Infantry.
WALKEM, HUGH CRAWFORD, Lieut.-Colonel, Pioneers.
WALKER, ARTHUR LESLIE, M.C., Major, Infantry.
WHITE, DONALD ALEXANDER, Major, Field Artillery.
WILCOX, EDWARD ALEXANDER CUMBERLAND, Major, Infantry.

AUSTRALIAN FORCE.

BEAVIS, LESLIE ELLIS, Major, Field Artillery Brigade.
BERRY, WILLIAM HENRY, Major, Army Service Corps.
BIGNELL, FRANCIS LAWRENCE, Major, Army Medical Corps.
BLACKLOW, ARCHIBALD CLIFFORD, Major (Temporary Lieut.-Colonel), Machine Gun Corps.
BRAZENOR, JOHN ALEXANDER, Major, Army Service Corps.
BRENNAN, EDWARD THOMAS, M.C., Lieut.-Colonel, Army Medical Corps.
BROWN, ARTHUR BALFOUR DOUGLAS, Major, Provost Corps.
BURRETT, ATHOL FREDERICK, Major, Infantry.
BYRNE, HERBERT RICHARD, Major, Field Artillery.
CLARK, JAMES PURCELL, Lieut.-Colonel, Infantry.
CLAYTON, ARTHUR ROSS, Major, Army Medical Corps.
CLOWES, NORMAN, M.C., Major, Field Artillery.
CRAIG, FREDERICK WILLIAM, Quartermaster and Honorary Major, Infantry.
CRISP, ALAN PERCY, Major, Field Artillery.
DE LOW, HAROLD CHARLES, Major, Field Artillery.
DONALDSON, ROBERT JOHNSTONE, Major, Engineers.
DREYER, NORMAN LOCKHART, Major, Field Artillery.
DUNLOP, ALBERT TANGE, Major, Army Medical Corps.
EVANS, ALEXANDER ARTHUR, M.C., Major, Field Artillery.
EVANS, THOMAS CHARLES CANN, Major, Army Medical Corps.
GIBLIN, LYNDHURST FALKINER, Major, Infantry.
HALLARD, HUGH REGINALD, Major, Field Artillery.
HAMILTON, JOHN, Major, Army Service Corps.
HANCOX, SAMUEL HERBERT, Major, Engineers.
HESLOP, GEORGE GORDON, Major, Army Veterinary Corps.
HINDHAUGH, STANLEY GEORGE ALLEN, Lieut.-Colonel, Light Horse.
HOLMES, MERVYN JOHN, Capt., Army Medical Corps.
HORE, ROBERT WILLIAM, Capt. (Temporary Major), Field Artillery.
JAMES, WILLIAM EDWARD, Lieut.-Colonel, Infantry.
KAY, WILLIAM ELPHINSTONE, Lieut.-Colonel, Army Medical Corps.
LEGGE, REGINALD GEORGE, M.C., Major, Infantry.
MACKENZIE, DONALD STUART, Major, Army Medical Corps.
MAGUIRE, FREDERICK ARTHUR, Lieut.-Colonel (Temporary Colonel), Army Medical Corps.
MARKS, DOUGLAS GRAY, M.C., Major (Temporary Lieut.-Colonel), Infantry.
MARTIN, ERNEST EDWARD, Lieut.-Colonel, Infantry.
MASSIE, ROBERT JOHN ALLWRIGHT, Major, Infantry.
NEWMAN, JOHN, Major, Infantry.
ORDISH, HAROLD, Major, Machine Gun Corps.

The Distinguished Service Order

PAINE, DOUGLAS DUKE, Major, Australian Army Service Corps.
QUICK, BALCOMBE, Lieut.-Colonel, Australian Army Medical Corps.
RANDALL, EDWARD ALFRED HALL, Major, Artillery.
ROSENTHAL, CHARLES, C.B., C.M.G., Colonel (Temporary Brigadier-General), Imperial Force.
SANDFORD, ARTHUR BRUCE, Major, Field Artillery.
SANDO, LESLIE CYRIL, Major, Army Service Corps.
SCANLAN, JOHN JOSEPH, Major (Temporary Lieut.-Colonel), Infantry.
SHEPHERD, ARTHUR EDMUND, Lieut.-Colonel (Temporary Colonel), Army Medical Corps.
STACK, WALTER JAQUES, Major, Army Medical Corps.
STANLEY, RAYMOND AUGUSTUS, Major, Engineers.
VASEY, GEORGE ALAN, Major, Artillery.
VICKERS, WILFRED, Major, Army Medical Corps.
WALKER, SYDNEY JAMES, Major, Field Artillery.
WARK, BLAIR ANDERSON, Major, Infantry.
WATSON, HERBERT FRAZER, M.C., Capt., Infantry.
WILTSHIRE, AUBREY ROY LIDDON, M.C., Lieut.-Colonel, Infantry.
WYNTER, HENRY DOUGLAS, Lieut.-Colonel, General List.
YOUDEN, HERBERT ALEXANDER, Major, Infantry.

NEW ZEALAND FORCE.

GARDNER, DUNCAN ERIC, Major, Field Artillery.
WHYTE, JAMES BINNIE, Major, Army Service Corps.
WIDDOWSON, ERIC ARTHUR, M.C., Major.
WILDING, HENRY GORDON, Major, Field Artillery.

SOUTH AFRICAN CONTINGENT.

BENNETT, GEORGE MELVILLE, Major, Heavy Artillery.
COCHRAN, FRANK EARDLEY, Major, Infantry.
DAWSON, FREDERICK STUART, C.M.G., A.D.C., Lieut.-Colonel (Temporary Brigadier-General), Infantry (description corrected to Lieut.-Colonel (Temporary Brigadier-General) Frederick Stuart Dawson, C.M.G., D.S.O., A.D.C., 1st Battalion South African Infantry [London Gazette, 5 March, 1920]).
EDWARDS, SYDNEY BERNARD, Lieut. (Acting Major), Heavy Artillery.
HARVEY, FRANCIS GEORGE, Lieut.-Colonel, Defence Force.
HEENAN, CLAUDE RIGBY, Major, Infantry.
HEMMING, HERBERT SIDNEY LAMOND, Major, Infantry.
MURRAY, CHARLES MOLTENO, M.C., Major.

London Gazette, 3 June, 1918.—" War Office, 3 June, 1918. His Majesty the King has been graciously pleased, on the occasion of His Majesty's Birthday, to approve of the undermentioned rewards for distinguished service in connection with military operations in Egypt. Dated 3 June, 1918. Awarded a Bar to the Distinguished Service Order."

ELLIOT, EDWARD HALHED HUGH, D.S.O., Lieut.-Colonel, Royal Field Artillery.
(D.S.O. gazetted 1 Jan. 1918.)
PEEBLES, WILLIAM CARMICHAEL, D.S.O., Lieut.-Colonel, Royal Scots.
(D.S.O. gazetted 1 Jan. 1918.)
WILDBLOOD, EDWARD HAROLD, D.S.O., Major (Acting Lieut.-Colonel), Leinster Regt.
(D.S.O. gazetted 1 Jan. 1918.)

Awarded the Distinguished Service Order:

ADAMS, ALEXANDER, Major (Temporary Lieut.-Colonel), Reserve of Officers, Royal Engineers.
ARMSTRONG, ALLAN, Lieut.-Colonel, Wiltshire Regt. (Capt., Retired Pay, Reserve of Officers).
ASHTON, FREDERIC ELLIS, Major (Temporary Lieut.-Colonel), York and Lancaster Regt.
BAYNE-JARDINE, THOMAS EDWARD, Temporary Second Lieut. (Local Major), Special List, attached Camel Transport Corps.
BIDDULPH, HOPE, Lieut.-Colonel, Royal Field Artillery.
BUTCHART, HENRY JACKSON, Major, Yeomanry.
CAMPBELL, GEOFFREY ALEXANDER, Capt. and Brevet Major (Acting Lieut.-Colonel), Army Service Corps.
CAMPBELL, JAMES DONALD, Major, Royal Engineers.
CARSON, HERBERT WILLIAM, M.B., Capt. (Acting Lieut.-Colonel), Royal Army Medical Corps.
CASH, REV. WILLIAM WILSON, Temporary Chaplain to the Forces, 4th Class (Temporary Chaplain to the Forces, 2nd Class), Army Chaplains' Department.
CHAWORTH-MUSTERS, JOHN NEVILE, Major, Yeomanry.
COLVILE, ARTHUR MONTAGU, Major, Royal Garrison Artillery.
COOKE-HURLE, EDWARD FORBES, Lieut.-Colonel, Somersetshire Light Infantry (Major, Retired Pay, Reserve of Officers).
CRAWLEY-BOEVEY, MARTIN, M.C., Capt. and Brevet Major, Duke of Cornwall's Light Infantry.
DALMENY, LORD, ALBERT EDWARD HARRY MEYER ARCHIBALD, M.C., Lieut. (Temporary Lieut.-Colonel), Reserve of Officers, Grenadier Guards.
FAULKNER, GEORGE AUBREY, Temporary Capt. (Acting Major), Royal Field Artillery.
FISHER, CHARLES ALEXANDER, Lieut.-Colonel (Ordnance Officer, 2nd Class) (Acting Colonel and Ordnance Officer, 1st Class), Army Ordnance Department.
GORDON, ANNESLEY DE RINZY, Temporary Capt. (Local Major), Special List, attached Camel Corps.
GLEN, ARCHIBALD, M.C., Temporary Capt. (Temporary Major), Royal Engineers, Special Reserve.
HAMMOND, FREDERIC SNOWDEN, Capt. (Acting Major), London Regt.
HAY, JAMES, Temporary Capt. (Local and Temporary Lieut.-Colonel), Special List.

HENDERSON, ROBERT WYNNE, Major, Indian Cavalry.
HICKLEY, CHARLES MARTIN, Temporary Capt. (Temporary Lieut.-Colonel), Royal Engineers.
HILL, CHARLES WOOD, Major (Temporary Lieut.-Colonel), West India Regt.
HULTON, JOHN MEREDITH, Major (Acting Lieut.-Colonel), Royal Sussex Regt.
JELLICOE, RICHARD CAREY, Major and Brevet Lieut.-Colonel (Temporary Brigadier-General), Army Service Corps.
JOYCE, PIERCE CHARLES, Major and Brevet Lieut.-Colonel, Connaught Rangers.
KEMPSON, GEORGE CHESTER DOUGLAS, Major (Temporary Ordnance Officer, 3rd Class), East Lancashire Regt., attached Army Ordnance Department.
KINNEAR, WILLIAM, Lieut.-Colonel, Royal Field Artillery.
LANDON, JAMES WILLIAM BAINBRIDGE, Capt. (Temporary Major, Acting Lieut.-Colonel), Army Service Corps.
LAYTON, THOMAS BRAMLEY, M.D., Capt. (Acting Lieut.-Colonel), Royal Army Medical Crops.
LEITCH, JOHN WILSON, M.B., Major (Acting Lieut.-Colonel), Royal Army Medical Corps.
LIGHTBODY, JAMES, Lieut.-Colonel, Royal Field Artillery.
McCALL, HUGH WILLIAM, Major and Brevet Lieut.-Colonel, Yorkshire Regt.
McNEILL, ANGUS JOHN, Lieut.-Colonel (Temporary Brigadier-General), Yeomanry.
MAUDE, CHRISTIAN GEORGE, M.C., Capt. and Brevet Major (Temporary Lieut.-Colonel), Royal Fusiliers.
MEEKE, REV. HUGH CRAIG, M.A., Chaplain to the Forces, 2nd Class, Army Chaplains' Department.
NASH, REV. ROBERT HENRY, Chaplain to the Forces, 2nd Class, Army Chaplains' Department.
NEEDHAM, JOSEPH GEORGE, Lieut.-Colonel, Army Service Corps.
OSBORNE, REX HAMILTON, M.C., Capt. and Brevet Major (Temporary Lieut.-Colonel), Hussars.
PEARSON, VERE LORRAINE NUTHALL, Major and Brevet Lieut.-Colonel (Temporary Brigadier-General), Middlesex Regt.
PEEL, EDWARD TOWNLEY, M.C., Temporary Lieut. (Temporary Lieut.-Colonel), Wiltshire Regt.
PORTAL, MAURICE, Temporary Major, Remount Service.
POWELL, HARRY EDWIN, Capt. (Temporary Major), Army Veterinary Corps.
SIMPSON, PERCY JAMES, F.R.C.V.S., Capt. (Temporary Lieut.-Colonel), Army Veterinary Corps.
TEICHMANN, OSKAR, M.C., Capt., Royal Army Medical Corps.
THOMAS, ARTHUR FELIX, Major, Manchester Regt.
THOMSON, HUGH WRIGHT, M.D., Lieut.-Colonel, Royal Army Medical Corps.
TORKINGTON, OLIVER MILES, Major (Acting Lieut.-Colonel), Scottish Rifles.
WILLIAMS, SIDNEY JOSEPH, Capt. (Acting Major), Army Veterinary Corps.
WILSON, HAROLD RENÉ, Major, Royal Field Artillery.
WILSON, SIR MATHEW RICHARD HENRY, Bart., C.S.I., Lieut.-Colonel, Yeomanry (Major, Retired Pay, Reserve of Officers).
WOOLMER, EDWARD, M.C., Major, Lancashire Fusiliers.

AUSTRALIAN FORCES.

BAILEY, PERCIVAL JOHN, Major, Light Horse Regt.
DALY, THOMAS JOSEPH, Major, Light Horse Regt.
DAWSON, ARTHUR LACY, Lieut.-Colonel, Army Medical Corps.
WHITE, HAROLD ALBERT DUCKETT, Major (Temporary Lieut.-Colonel), Light Horse Regt.

NEW ZEALAND FORCES.

HERCUS, CHARLES ERNEST, Major, Medical Corps.
NICHOLLS, STEPHEN CHARLES PHILLIPS, Major, Staff Corps.

London Gazette, 3 June, 1918.—" War Office, 3 June, 1918. His Majesty the King has been graciously pleased, on the occasion of His Majesty's Birthday, to approve of the undermentioned rewards for distinguished service in connection with military operations in Italy. Dated 3 June, 1918. Awarded a Bar to the Distinguished Service Order."

BARNES, ANTHONY CHARLES, D.S.O., Temporary Major, Yorkshire Regt.
(D.S.O. gazetted 14 Nov. 1916.)

Awarded the Distinguished Service Order:

ABBEY, JAMES, M.C., Temporary Capt. (Acting Major), Royal Field Artillery.
ACLAND, ARTHUR NUGENT, M.C., Capt. and Brevet Major, Duke of Cornwall's Light Infantry.
ADAM, RONALD FORBES, Major, Royal Horse Artillery.
ADAM, WILLIAM, Major (Acting Lieut.-Colonel), Worcestershire Regt.
ALPINE, WILLIAM MOORE, Temporary Major, King's Royal Rifle Corps.
ARBUTHNOT, SIR DALRYMPLE, Bart., C.M.G., Lieut.-Colonel and Brevet Colonel (Temporary Brigadier-General), Royal Artillery.
BAKER, ARTHUR BARWICK LLOYD, Major, Oxfordshire and Buckinghamshire Light Infantry.
BLOUNT-DINWIDDIE, JOHN, Capt, and Brevet Major, Army Service Corps.
BONHAM, CHARLES BARNARD, Major (Acting Lieut.-Colonel), Royal Engineers.
BRIDGE, CHARLES EDWARD DUNSCOMB, M.C., Major, Royal Artillery.
BUCHAN, DAVID ADYE, Capt. (Acting Major), Royal Field Artillery.
BURMANN, ROBERT MOYLE, M.C., Capt., East Lancashire Regt.
BURNYEAT, RICHARD WHITESIDE, Major, Royal Field Artillery.
BURT, CHARLES SIDNEY, Capt. (Acting Lieut.-Colonel), South Staffordshire Regt.
CHICHESTER, THE HONOURABLE ARTHUR CLAUDE SPENCER, Major, Irish Guards.
CLARE, JAMES WILLIAM SABBEN, Temporary Major, Army Service Corps.

COATS, STEWART, Major (Acting Lieut.-Colonel), Argyll and Sutherland Highlanders.
CRAWSHAY, HENRY, Major, Reserve of Officers, Worcestershire Regt.
CROLY, WILLIAM CHAPMAN, Lieut.-Colonel, Royal Army Medical Corps.
CUTTING, RAYMOND HOWARTH, M.C., Lieut. (Temporary Major), Devonshire Regt., attached Machine Gun Corps.
DARBY, HAROLD, Capt. (Temporary Major), Army Service Corps.
EBERLE, GEORGE STRACHAN JOHN FULLER, Major, Royal Engineers.
FRASER, ALFRED JAMES, Temporary Major, Army Service Corps.
GALE, HENRY JOHN GORDON, Major, Royal Garrison Artillery.
GRANET, GUY EDWARD AUGUSTUS, M.C., Major, Royal Field Artillery.
GREEN, THOMAS ARTHUR, M.D., Capt. (Temporary Major, Acting Lieut.-Colonel), Royal Army Medical Corps.
HAWES, LEONARD ARTHUR, M.C., Capt., Royal Artillery.
HENNIKER-GOTLEY, GEORGE RAINALD, Temporary Major, Machine Gun Corps.
HYNES, ERNEST THOMAS, Quartermaster and Honorary Major, Special List.
KITSON, THE HONOURABLE RONALD DUDLEY, M.C., Capt., West Yorkshire Regt.
LONGHURST, THOMAS LESLIE, Temporary Capt. (Temporary Major), Army Service Corps.
MACLACHLAN, WILLIAM KEITH, Temporary Major, Northumberland Fusiliers.
McNAUGHTON, FORBES LANKESTER, Capt. (Acting Major), Royal Field Artillery.
MAKGILL-CRICHTON-MAITLAND, FREDERICK LEWIS, Major (Acting Lieut.-Colonel), Gordon Highlanders.
MATHESON, JOHN CAMPBELL MACINTYRE, Capt. (Temporary Major), Cameron Highlanders, attached Machine Gun Corps.
MEREDITH, JOHN CAREW, Capt. (Acting Major), Royal Garrison Artillery.
MILLER, GEORGE SWINEY, Capt. (Temporary Lieut.-Colonel), Royal Warwickshire Regt.
MINOGUE, MARTIN JOSEPH, M.C., Major (Acting Lieut.-Colonel), East Surrey Regt.
NICKALLS, PATTESON WORMERSLEY, Major, Yeomanry.
OLDFIELD, RICHARD WILLIAM, M.C., Capt., Royal Field Artillery.
PEARSON, WILFRED JOHN, M.C., M.B., Temporary Capt., Royal Army Medical Corps.
PERSSE, RICHARD, M.C., Capt. (Temporary Major), South Staffordshire Regt.
PIDSLEY, WILFRID GOULD, Capt., London Regt.
POUNTNEY, FREDERICK SPENCER, Capt. (Acting Lieut.-Colonel), London Regt.
PRATT, OSCAR STANLEY, Temporary Major, Middlesex Regt.
SCHOMBERG, HAROLD ST. GEORGE, Capt. and Brevet Major (Acting Lieut.-Colonel), East Surrey Regt.
SEBAG-MONTEFIORE, THOMAS HENRY, M.C., Major, Royal Horse Artillery.
SHEPPARD, WILLIAM THOMSON, Major (Temporary Lieut.-Colonel), Army Ordnance Department.
SNAPE, JOSEPH, M.C., Lieut. (Acting Major), South Staffordshire Regt., attached Honourable Artillery Company.
SNOWDON, HAROLD SMURTHWAITE KEMPLAY, Major, Royal Garrison Artillery.
STREVENS, HARRY, M.C., Capt. (Acting Lieut.-Colonel), Royal Warwickshire Regt., employed Devonshire Regt.
TALBOT, DOUGLAS HERVEY, M.C., Capt. (Temporary Major), Lancers.
THOMPSON, ARNOLD JOHN, M.C., Lieut. (Temporary Capt.), Scots Guards.
VEREY, HENRY EDWARD, Temporary Lieut. (Acting Major), General List.
WALLACE, JOHN THORNHILL, M.C., Major, Royal Artillery.
WALLER, HARDRESS WILLIAM LUCUIS, M.C., Major, Royal Artillery.
WHITE, ERIC STUART, Capt. and Brevet Major, Army Service Corps.
WILLANS, HARRY, M.C., Lieut. (Temporary Capt.), Bedfordshire Regt.

London Gazette, 3 June, 1918.—" War Office, 3 June, 1918. His Majesty the King has been graciously pleased, on the occasion of His Majesty's Birthday, to approve of the undermentioned rewards for distinguished service in connection with military operations in Salonika. Dated 3 June, 1918. Awarded the Distinguished Service Order."

BARBER, RICHARD FULLER, Inspector of Ordnance Machinery, 2nd Class, and Honorary Major (Temporary Chief Inspector and Honorary Lieut.-Colonel), Army Ordnance Department.
BARRINGTON, THE HONOURABLE RUPERT EDWARD SELBORNE, Capt. (Acting Major), Yeomanry.
BURGES, DANIEL, Major (Acting Lieut.-Colonel), Gloucestershire Regt.
BURT, AUBREY ERNEST, Temporary Major, Oxfordshire and Buckinghamshire Light Infantry.
BYRNE, HUGH FREDERICK, Major (Temporary Lieut.-Colonel), Army Ordnance Department.
CAIRNES, JAMES ELLIOT, Temporary Major, Royal Field Artillery.
CHURCH, LESLIE HUMPHREYS, Major, Army Service Corps.
COBBE, IVOR STAVELEY, Major (Acting Lieut.-Colonel), Royal Garrison Artillery.
COOKE-COLLIS, WILLIAM JAMES NORMAN, Major and Brevet Lieut.-Colonel (Temporary Brigadier-General), Royal Irish Rifles,
DICKSON, MAURICE RHYND, Temporary Major, Royal Scots Fusiliers.
DIPPIE, HERBERT, Temporary Major (Acting Major), Worcestershire Regt.
DITCHAM, HARRY GEORGE, Temporary Major, General List.
ERSKINE, JOHN DAVID BEVERIDGE, Major (Temporary Lieut.-Colonel), Reserve of Officers, Manchester Regt.
FANE, JULIAN, Major and Brevet Lieut.-Colonel (Temporary Lieut.-Colonel), Gloucestershire Regt.
FINCH, GEORGE FORBES CARPENTER, Major, Royal Garrison Artillery.
FINDLAY, JAMES LEMPRIERE ORMIDALE BARCAPLE, Chaplain to the Forces, 2nd Class, Army Chaplains' Department.
FRANKLIN, WILLIAM VEASEY, Temporary Major, South Wales Borderers.
GARLAND, FREDERICK JOSEPH, M.B., Major (Acting Lieut.-Colonel), Royal Army Medical Corps.
HALL, EDWARD CHASE, Major, Royal Field Artillery.
HEILBRON, ISIDOR MORRIS, Capt. (Acting Major), Army Service Corps.
HOLLINS, CHARLES ERNEST, Major and Brevet Lieut.-Colonel (Temporary Lieut.-Colonel), Lincolnshire Regt.
JOHNSON, BENJAMIN, M.B., Capt. and Brevet Major (Acting Lieut.-Colonel), Royal Army Medical Corps.
JONES, CHARLES GODFREY, Temporary Major (Acting Lieut.-Colonel), Welsh Regt.
KIRBY, HORACE AUGUSTUS, M.C., Major, Royal Garrison Artillery.
LEVERSON, GEORGE RILAND FRANCIS, Capt. and Brevet Major (Temporary Lieut.-Colonel), Northumberland Fusiliers.
LOWSLEY, MONTAGU MARMION, Lieut.-Colonel, Royal Army Medical Corps.
MACKENZIE, HECTOR GRAHAM GORDON, M.B., Capt. (Temporary Lieut.-Colonel), Royal Army Medical Corps.
MACKENZIE, JOHN MUNRO, Capt. (Acting Lieut.-Colonel), Royal Scots.
MILLER, WILLIAM, Major and Brevet Lieut.-Colonel (Temporary Lieut.-Colonel), Middlesex Regt.
PHILLIMORE, REGINALD HENRY, Major, Royal Engineers.
PONSONBY, HENRY CHAMBRE, M.C., Major (Acting Lieut.-Colonel), King's Royal Rifle Corps.
RAE, JOHN, Capt. (Acting Major), Army Veterinary Corps, Special Reserve.
REA, CHARLES PERCIVAL, Temporary Capt. (Acting Major), Royal Scots Fusiliers.
SCOTT, OSWALD ARTHUR, Temporary Major, Hampshire Regt.
SOAMES, ALLEN ALDWIN, Major (Acting Lieut.-Colonel), King's Royal Rifle Corps.
VICARY, ALEXANDER CRAVEN, M.C., Capt. and Brevet Major (Acting Lieut.-Colonel), Gloucestershire Regt.
WARD, GUY BERNARD CAMPBELL, Major (Acting Lieut.-Colonel), South Wales Borderers.
WEBB-BOWEN, HILDRED EDWARD, Capt. (Temporary Colonel in Army), Royal Engineers.
WHAIT, JOHN ROBERT, M.B., Lieut.-Colonel, Royal Army Medical Corps.
WHITE, RALPH KOPER, Major, Royal Army Medical Corps.
WILKINSON, GEORGE HAMILTON, Major, Supply and Transport Corps, Indian Army.
WILTSHIRE, HAROLD WATERLOW, M.D., Temporary Major, Royal Army Medical Corps.
WITTS, EDWARD FRANCIS BROOME, Temporary Major, Gloucestershire Regt.
WORTHAM, HAROLD CHARLES WEBSTER HALE, Major and Brevet Lieut.-Colonel (Temporary Lieut.-Colonel), Royal Irish Fusiliers.
WRIGHT, CLIFTON VINCENT REYNOLDS, Major (Temporary Lieut.-Colonel), Reserve of Officers, South Wales Borderers.
YONGE, PHILIP CAYNTON, Major, Essex Regt.

London Gazette, 3 June, 1918.—" War Office, 3 June, 1918. His Majesty the King has been graciously pleased, on the occasion of His Majesty's Birthday, to approve of the undermentioned rewards for distinguished services rendered in connection with military operations on the Indian Frontier. Dated 1 Jan. 1918. Awarded the Distinguished Service Order."

CORNISH, ARTHUR WILLIAM DAUNCEY, M.C., Major, Gurkha Rifles, Indian Army.
TWISS, HORACE WILLIAM FRANCIS, Major, Indian Army.
MONEY, ERNEST DOUGLAS, C.I.E., Lieut.-Colonel, Gurkha Rifles, Indian Army.
JOHNSON, FRANK WILLIAM FREDERICK, Lieut.-Colonel, Royal Sussex Regt.

" His Majesty the King has been graciously pleased, on the occasion of His Majesty's Birthday, to approve of the undermentioned reward for distinguished services rendered with the British Forces on the Mediterranean Line of Communications. Dated 3 June 1918. Awarded the Distinguished Service Order."

LLOYD, THOMAS WILLIAMS, Capt. (Acting Major), Liverpool Regt., Special Reserve, Employed Royal Engineers.

" His Majesty the King has been graciously pleased, on the occasion of His Majesty's Birthday, to approve of the undermentioned reward for distinguished services rendered in connection with military operations in Russia. Dated 3 June, 1918. Awarded the Distinguished Service Order."

BATTINE, REGINALD ST. CLAIR, Lieut.-Colonel, Indian Cavalry.

London Gazette, 3 June, 1918.—" Air Ministry, 3 June, 1918. The King has been graciously pleased, on the occasion of His Majesty's Birthday, to confer the undermentioned rewards for distinguished service.—Royal Air Force. Awarded the Distinguished Service Order."

BALDWIN, JOHN EUSTACE ARTHUR, Major (Temporary Lieut.-Colonel).
BODDAM-WHETHAM, ARTHUR COURTNEY, Major (Temporary Lieut.-Colonel).
HAMILTON, BENJAMIN HENRY NOEL HANS, Capt. (Temporary Major).
HOLT, ALWYN VESEY, Major.
WRIGHT, WARWICK, Capt. (Temporary Major).

London Gazette, 3 June, 1918.—" Admiralty, 3 June, 1918. The King has been graciously pleased to give orders for the appointment of the undermentioned Officers to be Companions of the Distinguished Service Order, in recognition of their services in the prosecution of the war."

HENDERSON, FRANK HANNAN, C.M.G., Vice-Admiral.
HIBBERT, HUGH THOMAS, Rear-Admiral.
YOUNG, GEORGE BENNETT WESTON, Capt., R.N.
HEATHCOTE, ARCHER NAPIER, Capt., R.N. (Christian name corrected to Arthur Napier [London Gazette, 7 June, 1918]).
ROLFE, HERBERT NEVILLE, Capt., R.N.
WALKER, THOMAS PHILIP, Capt., R.N.R. (Admiral, Retired).

OWEN, WILLIAM HENRY, Commander (Acting Capt.), R.N.R.
JONES, THOMAS ALBAN, R.D., Commander (Acting Capt.), R.N.R.
McCOWEN, RANDAL BOROUGH, Commander, R.N.
PALLOT, ELIAS GEORGE, Engineer-Commander, R.N.
TORRANCE, WILLIAM SYMINGTON, Engineer-Commander, R.N.
BARRY, OSWALD CHARLES MERRIMAN, Commander, R.N.
POË, WILLIAM SKEFFINGTON, Major, R.M.A.
LOCKER-LAMPSON, OLIVER, C.M.G., M.P., Lieut.-Commander (Acting Commander), Royal Naval Volunteer Reserve.
SCOTT, ARTHUR AVISON, Lieut.-Commander, R.N.
SWITHINBANK, CUTHBERT WINTHROP, Lieut.-Commander, R.. N
WOOD, CHRISTOPHER JOHN FREDERICK, Lieut.-Commander, R.N.

London Gazette, 7 June, 1918.—" Admiralty, 7 June, 1918.—Honours for Services in Action with Enemy Submarines. The King has been graciously pleased to approve of the award of the following honours to the undermentioned Officers. To be Companions of the Distinguished Service Order."
HILL, SIDNEY ARTHUR GEARY, Commander, R.N.
COOMBS, HENRY MAURICE, Lieut.-Commander, R.N.
PEAT, PERCY SUTCLIFFE, Lieut., R.N.R.

" Honours for Miscellaneous Services.—The King has been graciously pleased to approve of the award of the following honours to the undermentioned Officers. To be Companions of the Distinguished Service Order."
WILLIAMS, HENRY PROSSER, Staff Paymaster, R.N. For services with the Royal Naval Siege Guns on shore in Flanders from July, 1917, to Feb. 1918. He has shown personal bravery, sound judgment, and great devotion to duty, and in addition to his regular duties has performed executive officers' work, which required technical skill and judgment.
LEIGHTON, JOHN ALBERT, Commander, R.N.R. In recognition of his services in connection with the transfer of British ships from the Baltic. He displayed the greatest tact and determination in carrying out this task in the face of great difficulties and opposition.
ADAMS, JAMIESON BOYD, Lieut.-Commander (Acting Commander), R.N.R. For services with the Royal Naval Siege Guns on shore in Flanders from Aug. 1916, to March, 1918. He has on many occasions displayed the greatest gallantry and devotion to duty, and set a high example of cheerfulness, thoroughness and keenness.

To receive a Bar to the Distinguished Service Order :
HEATON, GERVASE WILLIAM HEATON, D.S.O., Lieut.-Commander (Acting Commander), R.N. For skill and bravery shown by him in recovering enemy mines.

London Gazette, 21 June, 1918.—" Admiralty, 21 June, 1918.—Honours for Services in the Action with Enemy Destroyers off the Belgian Coast on the 21st March, 1918. The King has been graciously pleased to approve of the award of the following honours to the undermentioned Officers. To be a Companion to the Distinguished Service Order."
REDE, ROGER L'ESTRANGE MURRAY, Commander, R.N., Commanding H.M.S. Botha. He took his ship through a heavy barrage of gun-fire, and, without waiting to ascertain that the rest of his division were following, proceeded to engage the enemy with ram, torpedo and gun-fire. He rammed and cut in two an enemy torpedo boat. The success of the action was undoubtedly due to his gallant leadership and initiative.

To receive a Bar to the Distinguished Service Order :
PERCIVAL, PERCY RALPH PASSAWER, D.S.O., Lieut.-Commander, Royal Navy, Commanding H.M.S. Morris. For the great initiative and promptitude shown by him. Kept good station during the first stage of the action, opening fire with Botha. On the latter being disabled, showed great initiative in continuing and pressing home the action, torpedoing and sinking an enemy torpedo boat. Showed great promptitude in taking Botha in tow and brought her safely into harbour.

" Honours for Services in Action with Enemy Submarines.—The King has been graciously pleased to approve of the award of the following honours to the undermentioned Officers. To be Companions of the Distinguished Service Order."
HAYES, BERTRAM FOX, C.M.G., R.D., Capt., Royal Naval Reserve.
GODDARD, PHILIP LESLIE, Lieut.-Commander (Acting Commander), R.N.
BARRY, CLAUD BARRINGTON, Lieut., R.N.

" Honours for Service in Patrol Cruisers.—The King has been graciously pleased to give orders for the award of the following honour, decorations and medals for services in the Patrol Cruisers under the command of Vice-Admiral Sir Reginald G. O. Tupper, K.C.B., C.V.O., and Vice-Admiral Sir Montague E. Browning, K.C.B., M.V.O., during the period 1 Jan. to 31 Dec. 1917. (Included in award). To be a Companion of the Distinguished Service Order."
BENNETT, HARRY THRING, Lieut.-Commander, R.N.

" Honours for Miscellaneous Services.—The King has been graciously pleased to approve of the award of the following honours to the undermentioned Officers. To be Companions of the Distinguished Service Order."
GAIMES, JOHN AUSTIN, Lieut.-Commander, R.N. In recognition of his services in submarines.
ATKINSON, EDWARD LEICESTER, Surgeon (Acting Staff-Surgeon), R.N. In recognition of his services as Senior Medical Officer of the R.M.A. Howitzer Brigade since the 26th May, 1916. He has carried out his duties with the greatest zeal and energy, and has shown an excellent example by his fearlessness and devotion to duty. He has been twice wounded, and would have been relieved but for his strong desire to remain at his post.
BRADBURY, WILLIAM, M.B., Surgeon (Acting Staff-Surgeon), Royal Navy. In recognition of his services with the Royal Naval Division in Gallipoli and France. As Medical Officer of the Hawke Battalion, Royal Naval Division, in Gallipoli, he did exceptionally good work, often under the most trying circumstances.

London Gazette, 22 June, 1918.—" War Office, 22 June, 1918. His Majesty the King has been graciously pleased to approve of the following awards to the undermentioned Officers, in recognition of their gallantry and devotion to duty in the field. Awarded a Second Bar to the Distinguished Service Order."
DAWSON, WILLIAM ROBERT AUFRERE, D.S.O., Capt. (Temporary Lieut.-Colonel), Royal West Kent Regt. For conspicuous gallantry and devotion to duty. When a party of the enemy had broken through the brigade front, he led the personnel of his headquarters as a fighting formation, and, co-operating with the counter-attacking battalion, inflicted heavy losses on the enemy and captured two machine guns and some prisoners. On the following day, when the enemy attacked in force, he organized and led a counter-attack with two companies. He repulsed the enemy and re-established and advanced the line. Later, when the enemy attacked some advanced posts, he counter-attacked and drove the enemy off with loss. By his capable leadership, promptness of action and courageous example, he was largely responsible for the position held by his battalion being maintained intact.
(D.S.O. gazetted 15 April, 1916.)
(Bar gazetted 18 July, 1917.)

Awarded a Bar to the Distinguished Service Order :
BURNE, ALFRED HIGGINS, D.S.O., Major, Royal Horse Artillery. For conspicuous gallantry and devotion to duty. During the enemy attack, his battery was subjected to heavy shell fire, two of the guns being buried and one destroyed. He continued fighting his guns over open sights until the enemy were within 600 yards of the position, when he succeeded in withdrawing his five guns. On the same day he rendered great assistance to a neighbouring battery, the guns of which he succeeded in withdrawing. During a period of 12 days, in which his battery inflicted heavy losses on the enemy, his information has been of incalculable value, and his devotion to duty most marked.
(D.S.O. gazetted 9 Nov. 1914.)
HUSEY, RALPH HAMER, D.S.O., M.C., Major (Acting Lieut.-Colonel), London Regt. For conspicuous gallantry and devotion to duty during an enemy attack. When the enemy approached close to his battalion headquarters he held the forward end of a communication trench with the personnel of his headquarters and a few other men, and largely assisted in breaking up the enemy's attack. He used a rifle himself at close range, and inflicted many casualties on the enemy. He then conducted an obstinate withdrawal to the next line of defence, where the enemy were finally held up. He set a magnificent example of courage and determination.
(D.S.O. gazetted 1 Jan. 1918.)
PATERSON, EWING, D.S.O., Lieut.-Colonel, Dragoons. For conspicuous gallantry and devotion to duty. Owing to the neighbouring troops being driven back, his flank became exposed and a gap was made in the line. Though he had very few men, he at once extended his flank and maintained a most gallant and determined resistance for an hour against largely superior numbers, closing the gap at a most critical moment until other troops were able to advance and restore the line. His tactical handling of the brigade during successive withdrawals, often with one or both flanks exposed, was magnificent.
(D.S.O. gazetted 27 Sept. 1901.)
VAN STRAUBENZEE, ALEXANDER WILLIAM, D.S.O., Major, Royal Horse Artillery. For conspicuous gallantry and devotion to duty. On his battery being heavily shelled for a period of five hours, he succeeded in withdrawing all his guns after firing on the advancing enemy with open sights at very close range. His services have been of the greatest value, his personal reconnaissances of our retiring line of inestimable importance, and thanks to his personal example and devotion to duty his battery, after 12 days' continuous and heavy fighting, remained in a high state of discipline and efficiency.
(D.S.O. gazetted 4 June, 1917.)

CANADIAN FORCE.

MACDONALD, DONALD JOHN, D.S.O., M.C., Lieut.-Colonel, Cavalry. For conspicuous gallantry and devotion to duty. In the attack launched by a cavalry brigade he led the reserve squadron of the regiment to the attack. Though suffering acute pain from a wound in the ankle, he continued to direct operations and led his men forward until the position was finally secured. But for his outstanding courage, skill and dash the position could not have been held.
(D.S.O. gazetted 1 Jan. 1918.)

NEW ZEALAND FORCE.

ALLEN, STEPHEN SHEPHERD, D.S.O., Lieut.-Colonel, Auckland Regt. For conspicuous gallantry and devotion to duty. He supervised the assembly of his battalion for an attack in a difficult position. When part of one of the companies was held up during the attack he at once went to the spot, and by skilful leadership enabled the advance to continue. The success of the operation was largely due to his courageous example under intense machine-gun fire, which was an inspiration to all ranks.
(D.S.O. gazetted 1 Jan. 1918.)

Awarded the Distinguished Service Order :
CARLISLE, THOMAS HARTLEY, M.C., Major, Royal Horse Artillery. For conspicuous gallantry and devotion to duty. On two occasions, during a period of ten days' heavy and continuous fighting, he withdrew his battery when it was under a heavy close range fire from the enemy, upon whom his guns inflicted great losses. At all times he has afforded to all ranks of his battery a most inspiring example of courage and confidence.
COWIE, WALTER NICHOLAS, M.C., Temporary Lieut. (Acting Capt.), Royal Field Artillery. For conspicuous gallantry and devotion to duty. He took command of his battery when the battery commander was wounded during an enemy attack. The enemy infantry approached within 500 yards of the batteries of his brigade and opened fire with a machine gun. He kept his battery in action under intense shell and machine-gun fire, covering the withdrawal of the other batteries and continued to fire his guns until another battery was in position further back. Though twice wounded he remained in command, showing the greatest courage and coolness. He finally withdrew his battery with great skill, and though he had suffered heavy casualties, he brought all the guns of his battery into action again within twenty minutes of ceasing fire. It was mainly due to his gallant leadership and example that this was accomplished.
DUNLOP, JOHN, Second Lieut., Royal Field Artillery, Special Reserve. For conspicuous gallantry and devotion to duty. On information being received that the forward section of the battery was being gassed and shelled, and that the officer in charge and the majority of the personnel had become casualties, he voluntarily went forward to the section under an intense barrage, assisted the wounded and brought the guns into action again, firing all the remaining ammunition. Being at this period under machine-gun fire he withdrew the guns to safety. His courage, determination and ability were of the highest order and set a high standard of efficiency which all ranks maintained.
FITZGERALD, EDWARD GALBRAITH AUGUSTINE, Lieut., Grenadier Guards. For conspicuous gallantry and devotion to duty. The enemy launched a heavy attack on the point of junction of his company and the battalion on the right and succeeded in capturing some front line posts. He at once got into touch with the battalion on the right and organized counter-attacks by this battalion and his own company. He led his company under heavy machine-gun fire with such dash and determination that the enemy were ejected and driven well beyond the line of posts. The success of the operation was entirely due to his courage and resource.

JOHNSON, FRANCIS SHAND BYAM, Major (Acting Lieut.-Colonel), Reserve of Officers, Royal Lancaster Regt. For conspicuous gallantry and devotion to duty. When his battalion became isolated during an enemy attack and both flanks were exposed, by his courage and skill he succeeded in withdrawing his battalion without serious loss. The successful withdrawal was entirely due to his splendid leadership and determination.

LEGARD, D'ARCY, Lieut.-Colonel (Temporary Brigadier-General), Lancers. For conspicuous gallantry and devotion to duty. When in command of a brigade during the recent operations he on one occasion obtained valuable information as to the flanks, and undoubtedly saved a critical situation. During a period of 12 days he has handled his troops in a masterly manner, inspiring all ranks by his energy, coolness and cheerfulness.

MORT, GUY MACAULAY, Lieut.-Colonel, Hussars. For conspicuous gallantry and devotion to duty. On it being reported that the enemy had broken through and were about to attack his line in rear, he immediately organized and carried through a counter-attack, which succeeded in recapturing a vital point and thus saving a critical situation. Throughout the day and on subsequent occasions he has displayed cool courage, initiative and fine determination.

PHILLIPS, FRANCIS ASHLEY, Capt. (Acting Major), Yeomany. For conspicuous gallantry and devotion to duty. He was the senior officer in the front line system when the enemy attacked. During the preliminary bombardment he kept battalion headquarters informed as to the situation, and when the enemy launched their attack he organized the defence with the greatest courage and energy. He maintained a determined resistance against heavy odds for over four hours, although he was completely outflanked and attacked from the rear. He led a counter-attack over the open and killed or drove out the enemy who were holding a trench behind his headquarters. When the position became quite untenable he organized a skilful withdrawal. He set a splendid example of determination and resource to his men.

PRICE, ROBERT BERNARD, M.B., Capt. (Acting Lieut.-Colonel), Royal Army Medical Corps. For conspicuous gallantry and devotion to duty. Prior to the division going into action he took over the duties of Assistant Director of Medical Services at half-an-hour's notice. When on one occasion all casualty clearing stations in the neighbourhood of the division were withdrawn, his improvization on the previous night of an emergency casualty clearing station further to the rear proved of such inestimable value, that a large number of casualties were able to be dealt with and all the wounded evacuated with the utmost despatch. Owing to his resource, forethought and exceptional powers of organization the smooth and successful evacuation of all wounded was carried out during the period of 12 days' heavy and continuous fighting in which the division was engaged.

QUIGLEY, FRANK GRANGER, M.C., Temporary Capt., Royal Flying Corps. For conspicuous gallantry and devotion to duty. While leading an offensive patrol he attacked a very large number of enemy aeroplanes, destroyed one of them and drove another down out of control. On the following day, while on a low-flying patrol, he was attacked by several enemy scouts, one of which dived at him. He out-manœuvred this machine and fired on it at very close range. He followed it down to 500 feet, firing on it, and it spiralled very steeply to the ground in a cloud of black smoke. During the three following days, while employed on low-flying work, he showed the greatest skill and determination. He fired over 3,000 rounds and dropped 30 bombs during this period, inflicting heavy casualties on enemy infantry, artillery and transport.

SMITH, ARNOLD EDWARD, M.C., Lieut. (Acting Major), Royal Field Artillery. For conspicuous gallantry and devotion to duty when in command of a brigade of artillery. When a withdrawal became necessary he carried out a reconnaissance of the route and then skilfully withdrew the brigade under very heavy fire. It was due to his courage, tenacity and resource that the operation was successfully carried out.

STEIN, OSWALD FRANKLIN, Lieut. (Acting Capt.), Grenadier Guards, Special Reserve. For conspicuous gallantry and devotion to duty. During a strong enemy attack a party of 50 of the enemy effected an entry into part of the front line trench held by his company. He at once organized a counter-attack, and sending a party to make an outflanking movement and cut the enemy's line of retreat, he personally led a bombing attack. Owing to his splendid leadership and his example of courage and energy the enemy were at once driven out with heavy losses. It was largely due to his quick grasp of the situation and prompt and determined action that the counter-attack was successful.

STONE, ARTHUR, Temporary Major, Lancashire Fusiliers. For conspicuous gallantry and devotion to duty. When in charge of a raiding party, portions of which were unable to force a gap through the enemy wire, he proceeded under heavy machine-gun and rifle fire up to the enemy's wire, and having satisfied himself that it was impassable, ordered the parties held up to withdraw. It was entirely due to his coolness and command of the situation that the withdrawal of the parties and the evacuation of the wounded were successfully effected. Throughout the whole of the raid he displayed the most supreme contempt for danger, and inspired all ranks by his magnificent example.

THOMSON, GEORGE EDWIN, M.C., Lieut. (Temporary Capt.), General List and Royal Flying Corps. For conspicuous gallantry and devotion to duty. On one occasion, encountering a number of enemy two-seater 'planes, he dived on one of these and sent it down in flames. On returning to our lines, he dived on to another enemy machine, the observer of which was seen to collapse in his cockpit, the hostile machine going down, completely out of control. On the following day, observing a hostile two-seater machine, he dived on it, engaging it at 100 yards' range. On the hostile 'plane going down in a slow spin, he followed it to within 2,500 feet, but was compelled to withdraw owing to heavy machine-gun fire from the ground. He has, in all, accounted for 21 enemy machines, and has at all times during recent operations displayed the most marked skill and gallantry.

WHETHAM, PAUL, Temporary Major (Acting Lieut.-Colonel), Manchester Regt. For conspicuous gallantry and devotion to duty. His battalion was continuously in action for four days during an enemy advance, and was successful in repulsing all the enemy's attacks. On two occasions his promptness and skill in organizing and leading counter-attacks resulted in the line being restored. His courageous example and cheerful bearing under most difficult conditions not only maintained but increased the fighting spirit of his men.

WHITWORTH, JOHN HAWARTH, M.C., Capt. (Acting Major), Manchester Regt. For conspicuous gallantry and devotion to duty when temporarily in command of his battalion. He continued to hold his position under intense shelling, and in the face of heavy enemy attacks, although the positions on each of his flanks had been captured by the enemy. After being eventually forced to withdraw, he led the remnants of his battalion and some men of another unit in a counter-attack, recaptured the position, and held it against two attacks until forced to withdraw. It was due to his courage and determined leadership that an important tactical point was held until orders were issued for a withdrawal.

CANADIAN FORCE.

BURBANK, MAURICE AUGUSTUS, Major, Railway Troops. For conspicuous gallantry and devotion to duty. During an enemy advance he superintended the construction of light railway bridges. He completed two bridges in the course of ten hours under heavy enemy shelling and bombing, and in the face of great difficulties, and superintended the withdrawal of a large quantity of light railway material and rolling-stock across a river from the battle area. He showed magnificent courage, skill and resource in a most difficult situation.

MOYER, LESLIE CLARE, Major, Railway Troops. For conspicuous gallantry and devotion to duty. He showed great skill and judgment in handling his company at their work under intense shell fire during an engagement. During later operations he kept his lines open for traffic throughout under very heavy fire until ordered to withdraw, and then succeeded in bringing back all his light railway rolling-stock and stores. His splendid example of courage was an inspiration to his men.

STEVENSON, HERBERT IRVING, Lieut.-Colonel, Cavalry. For conspicuous gallantry and devotion to duty. When our line was temporarily pierced, he led a charge with great skill and dash, by which the enemy were driven back and a new line established. He succeeded in establishing communication with the troops on his right flank, and though heavily outnumbered maintained this line until relieved by fresh infantry units. His prompt action and cool leadership were the means of allowing two battalions of infantry, who were in danger of being cut off, to withdraw safely to our line.

NEW ZEALAND FORCE.

DUTHIE, NORMAN ALEXANDER, Major, Auckland Regt. For conspicuous gallantry and devotion to duty. He led his company into action immediately after a long march in perfect order, and took charge of the left flank of an attack. When the advance was held up by machine-gun fire he led his men with great skill, and it was largely owing to his efforts that the battalion captured the objective. Though wounded early in the attack he remained with his men showing the greatest courage and determination.

ORR, ERIC HAMILTON, Major, Auckland Regt. For conspicuous gallantry and devotion to duty during an attack. He showed great determination and skill during an advance of one and a half miles. On two occasions when the enemy pierced the line of the battalion on the left he led forward a party under intense shell and machine-gun fire, closed the gap and restored the situation.

London Gazette, 22 June, 1918.—War Office, 22 June, 1918. Correction.—The award of the Military Cross which was announced in the London Gazette, dated 4 May, 1917, to the undermentioned officer, is cancelled, the award of the D.S.O. being substituted,

ANDERSON, ROY D., Captain, Congo Carrier Section, East African Transport Corps.

London Gazette, 5 July, 1918.—" War Office, 5 July, 1918. With reference to the awards conferred as announced in the London Gazette dated 4 Feb. 1918, the following are the statements of service for which the decorations were conferred. Awarded a Bar to the Distinguished Service Order."

BARTON, BAPTIST JOHNSON, D.S.O., Major (Acting Lieut.-Colonel), Reserve of Officers, Yorkshire Light Infantry. For conspicuous gallantry and devotion to duty when in command of his battalion during eight days' operations. When his battalion suffered heavy casualties and was forced to withdraw out of a village he rallied his men with great skill and determination, and held the high ground on a ridge against counter-attacks.

BEATTY, GUY ARCHIBALD HASTINGS, D.S.O., Lieut.-Colonel, Indian Cavalry. For conspicuous gallantry and devotion to duty. When a regiment to which he was in support was held up in an attack he led his regiment forward at the gallop under heavy machine-gun and rifle fire and occupied an important position, the capture of which enabled the other regiment to advance and take their objective. His quick decision and skilful handling of his men resulted in an important success.

BOYALL, ALFRED MOREY, D.S.O., Major (Acting Lieut.-Colonel), West Yorkshire Regt. For conspicuous gallantry and devotion to duty. When in command of an advanced guard battalion he pushed forward, after the capture of the first objective, and occupied a more advanced position, which was one of great importance, on his own initiative. His appreciation of the situation and display of bold initiative had considerable bearing on the success of the whole operations.

GRAY-CHEAPE, HUGH ANNESLEY, D.S.O., Major (Temporary Lieut.-Colonel), Yeomanry. For conspicuous gallantry and devotion to duty. He led a charge against the enemy's guns with the utmost gallantry and determination. The enemy's gunners were firing at point-blank range, but the guns were captured and the gunners put out of action.

HARDRESS-LLOYD, JOHN, D.S.O., Major (Temporary Colonel), Tank Corps. For conspicuous gallantry and devotion to duty. He organized the advance of his Tanks with great skill, and made several personal reconnaissances of the whole area to be covered.

HOARE, CHARLES HERVEY, D.S.O., Capt. (Acting Lieut.-Colonel), Yeomanry. For conspicuous gallantry and devotion to duty. When his battalion was twice outflanked and driven back after sharp fighting, on both occasions he led counter-attacks and recaptured the position. Though he was wounded he remained with his men, showing the greatest courage and determination.

JACKSON, EDWARD DARBY, D.S.O., Capt. (Acting Lieut.-Colonel), King's Own Scottish Borderers. For conspicuous gallantry and devotion to duty. After his battalion had gained its first objective in the face of strong and prolonged opposition, it was repeatedly and heavily counter-attacked, suffering heavy casualties. By his courage, energy and personal example he succeeded in reorganizing his battalion and in holding on to the trench system which he had gained. Later, when his battalion was very heavily attacked, his sound dispositions, prompt counter-attack, and fine leadership undoubtedly saved the situation, enabling the extreme flank of the line to be held against the enemy attack.

JAMES, CHARLES KENNETH, D.S.O., Temporary Major (Acting Lieut.-Colonel), Border Regt. For conspicuous gallantry and devotion to duty when in command of his battalion in support of an attacking brigade. The prominent part played by the battalion in the day's operations was mainly due to his leadership and to the information which he had obtained by personal reconnaissance.

KNOWLES, GEORGE, D.S.O., Major, Indian Cavalry. For conspicuous gallantry and devotion to duty. He took command of his regiment when his commanding officer became a casualty, and remained in command though he was wounded. He made most skilful dispositions and clung to his position with the greatest determination, though surrounded on all sides, until he was relieved. He showed great ability and courage.

LITTLE, ARTHUR CAMPDEN, D.S.O., Major, Hussars. For conspicuous gallantry and devotion to duty. When in a dismounted attack his right flank was left exposed, he organized several bodies of scattered infantry to protect it, and thus enabled the objective to be seized. Later, when a large gap occurred between his regiment and the next, he led three companies to fill it, and so enabled the position to be held. He showed great skill and resource.

MILLS, ARTHUR MORDAUNT, D.S.O., Major, Indian Cavalry. For conspicuous gallantry and devotion to duty when in command of his squadron in an attack. Though, owing to heavy casualties, they were at first forced to withdraw a short distance, he reorganized, led them forward with great skill and determination, and captured his objective.

OSBURN, ARTHUR CARR, D.S.O., Major (Temporary Lieut.-Colonel), Royal Army Medical Corps. For conspicuous gallantry and devotion to duty. On seeing the enemy approaching close to his dressing station, he carried out the evacuation of the wounded under heavy shell and rifle fire in the coolest and most gallant manner. Having cleared away all cases by ambulance train and cars, he re-established his dressing station further in rear. As officer commanding bearer divisions, he constantly inspected his line of bearer posts and forward dressing stations under heavy fire. The successful evacuation of the wounded from the divisional front was due to his careful organization and fearless supervision under the most trying conditions. His was an example of gallantry, courage, and resource worthy of the highest praise.

PLUNKETT, JAMES FREDERICK, D.S.O., M.C., D.C.M., Lieut. (Temporary Lieut.-Colonel), Royal Irish Regt. For conspicuous gallantry and devotion to duty during 60 hours' hand-to-hand fighting. When our line was pressed back by a counter-attack and the men began to waver on the right, he reorganized them and succeeded in re-establishing our old line. When reinforcements arrived he organized and led a successful counter-attack. He carried out in person many daring reconnaissances, and undoubtedly saved the situation at many critical moments by his prompt action.

RAIKES, GEOFFREY TAUNTON, D.S.O., Capt. (Acting Lieut.-Colonel), South Wales Borderers. For conspicuous gallantry and devotion to duty. Under very difficult conditions he organized the defence of his line against a strong enemy counter-attack. On a later occasion he led his battalion headquarters to the attack, and thereby checked the advance of the enemy, averting what might have become a very serious situation. Throughout the operations he ceaselessly exposed himself to heavy shell and machine-gun fire, and by his example of fearlessness and energy did much to stimulate the morale of his men.

CANADIAN FORCES.

DRAPER, DENIS COLBURN, D.S.O., Lieut.-Colonel, Mounted Rifles. For conspicuous gallantry and devotion to duty in several engagements. In an attack, when elements of his battalion reached the line of their final objective and held their position though both flanks were in the air, with the aid of two companies of another brigade he formed a defensive flank 500 yards long, and with great skill and coolness secured the left of the ground gained. He afterwards remained in the forward area until the evacuation of all his wounded had been organized.

Awarded the Distinguished Service Order :

ALLARDYCE, JAMES, M.M., Second Lieut., London Regt. For conspicuous gallantry and devotion to duty. The enemy made a violent attack which penetrated the line of the battalion on his flank and threatened to cut off his men entirely, since his other flank was already exposed. He immediately collected a few men, charged the enemy across the open, and drove them into a communication trench, at the end of which he succeeded in forming a block. Despite the very superior numbers of the enemy, and though nearly all his party had become casualties, he held this block against repeated attacks, throwing bombs continuously for three hours. He displayed the greatest dash and initiative under very heavy fire, and it was entirely due to his action that the battalion was not completely cut off.

BIBBY, ARTHUR HAROLD, Major, Royal Field Artillery. For conspicuous gallantry and devotion to duty. When the enemy attacked and advanced towards his battery, he walked up and down behind his guns under heavy fire encouraging his men. Though the enemy continued to advance, he kept his guns in action till the arrival of the limbers, controlling his fire with the greatest coolness. His example was an inspiration to all.

BOOTH, PATRICK DICK, M.C., Temporary Capt., Royal Field Artillery. For conspicuous gallantry and devotion to duty. Having rallied a party of divisional machine-gunners, who were retiring, he, with one machine-gunner, succeeded in holding a ridge against the advancing enemy until an organized defence could be arranged. Later he took command of a party of infantry in order to clear a village just occupied by the enemy. Having captured five of the enemy and cleared the north end of the village, he encountered a party of 20 of the enemy, armed with bombs. Though he was wounded in the subsequent fight, the enemy was driven back, thanks to his courageous efforts and those of the officer accompanying him. It was entirely due to the gallantry displayed by these two officers that an advanced dressing station was recaptured.

BROWN, AUSTIN HANBURY, M.C., Capt. and Brevet Major (Acting Major), Royal Engineers. For conspicuous gallantry and devotion to duty when in charge of the construction of tracks in preparation for the operations. By his splendid example and determination he completed the work in time, in spite of heavy shell fire, and by skilful organization reduced his casualties to a comparatively small number.

BROWNING, FREDERICK ARTHUR MONTAGUE, Lieut., Grenadier Guards. For conspicuous gallantry and devotion to duty. He took command of three companies whose officers had all become casualties, reorganized them, and proceeded to consolidate. Exposing himself to very heavy machine-gun and rifle fire, in two hours he had placed the front line in a strong state of defence. The conduct of this officer, both in the assault and more especially afterwards, was beyond all praise, and the successful handing over of the front to the relieving unit as an entrenched and strongly fortified position was entirely due to his energy and skill.

CARR-HARRIS, FERGUSON FITTON, M.D., Temporary Capt., Royal Army Medical Corps. For conspicuous gallantry and devotion to duty. Hearing that ten men of another battalion were lying wounded in front of the position, he volunteered on completion of the relief to go to their rescue. He was out for eight hours of the night, found nine of the men alive, took two of them back to headquarters, and organized the rescue of the remainder. He showed great coolness and self-sacrifice.

CASTLE, JOSEPH PERCY, Second Lieut., West Riding Regt. For conspicuous gallantry and devotion to duty when in command of a company. He established communication on both flanks under heavy fire. He cleverly cut off and captured an officer and two men from the rear of an enemy company, and scattered the whole company with a Lewis gun. The next day he rushed through heavy machine-gun fire to redirect the fire of the Tanks. Though twice wounded, he remained with his company, setting them a splendid example of courage and determination.

CONLAN, VERNON DOUGLAS ROBERT, Temporary Major, Army Service Corps. For conspicuous gallantry and devotion to duty. Coming up to a captured village in his car, and finding that ammunition had run out, he returned to the dump and brought some in his car under heavy machine-gun fire. He then returned and brought up Lewis gun drums, afterwards advancing with the attacking party. He showed great initiative throughout.

COURAGE, ANTHONY, M.C., Major (Temporary Colonel), Hussars. For conspicuous gallantry and devotion to duty in successfully organizing Tanks in their assembly position and making dispositions which were mainly responsible for their successful attack. He showed splendid skill and resource.

DENDY, MURRAY HEATHFIELD, M.C., Major, Royal Artillery. For conspicuous gallantry and devotion to duty. He reconnoitred sites for batteries and got the batteries to their positions before an attack. Later he showed great coolness and initiative during a counter-attack.

DUTHIE, ANDREW MAY, Lieut. (Acting Capt.), London Regt. For conspicuous gallantry and devotion to duty. He led his company with marked success, and it was largely due to his excellent leadership that the attack was pushed to its final objective. When this had been reached he took out a patrol, and put out of action an enemy machine gun, which was holding up the attack on the flank. Before withdrawing his patrol he was able to have four badly wounded men brought in, whilst on their return the men of his patrol surprised two other hostile machine guns, the crews of which were killed, and the guns were brought in. It was largely due to this officer's splendid example and fine leadership that the attack was carried to a successful end.

EDWARDS, WILLIAM ACE, Second Lieut., Nottinghamshire and Derbyshire Regt., Special Reserve. For conspicuous gallantry and devotion to duty in leading his platoon in an attack. He went forward 100 yards ahead of his men to ensure direction. Finding some machine guns enfilading them which had not been effectively dealt with by the Tanks, he rushed to the emplacement with great determination, covered the crews with his revolver, and enabled his men to surround the enemy. One officer and 14 other ranks and two machine guns were captured.

EVANS, WILLIAM MAURICE, Lieut., South Wales Borderers, Special Reserve. For conspicuous gallantry and devotion to duty when sent up to reorganize the battalion after almost all the other officers had become casualties. Finding that the left flank had been driven back, he rallied the men and led a counter-attack which regained some high ground, which he afterwards held against numerous counter-attacks. He showed great skill and resource.

GERARD, CHARLES ROBERT, Capt., Grenadier Guards. For conspicuous gallantry and devotion to duty. When the flank of the battalion became exposed during an attack on a village and the enemy penetrated between the attacking and the reserve companies, he volunteered to go forward and reconnoitre the situation. He reached the village and made his way round a large portion of it, though it was still held by the enemy, obtained most valuable information, and cleared up a most obscure situation. He afterwards collected some men of various units, led them up to the firing line in the face of very heavy fire, and by his skilful fire orders and his grasp of the situation inflicted heavy casualties on the enemy. He displayed the greatest coolness and initiative.

GLASIER, PHILIP MANNOCK, Capt. (Acting Lieut.-Colonel), London Regt. For conspicuous gallantry and devotion to duty. By his personal energy and leadership he succeeded in assembling his battalion in a shallow trench very close to the enemy. The subsequent attack was most successful, resulting in the capture of more than 70 of the enemy, three machine guns and a trench mortar. Prior to the attack he had, with persistence and resource, organized a series of most successful offensive patrols, in which prisoners were taken and serious losses inflicted on the enemy.

GOODALL, TOM, Lieut. (Acting Capt.), West Riding Regt. For conspicuous gallantry and devotion to duty. When an attack was held up by heavy machine-gun and rifle fire, the commanding officer being killed and heavy casualties sustained, and there was grave danger of disorganization, he went forward amid a hail of bullets to locate the enemy, and signalled back to a platoon of his company to attack. With one man he dashed into a strong point, killing several of the enemy, and this enabled the platoon to capture an officer and 58 other ranks and two machine guns, and to rescue an officer and a N.C.O. who were prisoners in the hands of the enemy. He showed magnificent courage and determination.

HALLSMITH, GUTHRIE, Second Lieut., Suffolk Regt. For conspicuous gallantry and devotion to duty. He attacked a strong point which was held in force by the enemy and captured two machine guns and ten prisoners, and then led his men to the objective. He was eventually forced to withdraw by counter-attacks on both flanks, but hearing that an officer had been wounded and left on the field, he went forward alone to search for him. Later, during the night he led forward patrols to search for the wounded.

HAMILTON, JOHN STEVEN, Lieut., West Yorkshire Regt. For conspicuous gallantry and devotion to duty. He led his company in an attack and captured all his objectives. He then, with one officer and two men, went forward, selected a position commanding the whole front, and remained there till a line of posts could be established. When some troops on his flank fell back during a counter-attack, seeing that they were without officers, he took command, reorganized them, and re-established them in their old position. He set a splendid example of determination and courage.

HANCOCK, JOHN ELIOT, Temporary Lieut., Norfolk Regt. For conspicuous gallantry and devotion to duty. Owing to his company commander being seriously wounded, he took command of the left company in an attack. When they came under heavy machine-gun fire he organized a frontal attack while he, with two N.C.O.'s, rushed across the open from a flank, killed or wounded all the gun teams, and put the guns out of action. He himself killed six men. In the subsequent fighting he showed great initiative in clearing the houses in a village and directing the advance.

HARTER, JAMES FRANCIS, M.C., Capt., Royal Fusiliers. For conspicuous gallantry and devotion to duty. Being sent forward to establish a new headquarters, after the capture of the first objective, he found some troops held up by enemy fire. Having reorganized them, he planned an attack and cleared a wood of the enemy, a prompt action which had an important effect on the progress of the operations. On several later occasions he obtained, by personal reconnaissance, most valuable information, and under difficult situations has been of the greatest assistance to battalion commanders. He has always displayed initiative, gallantry and a soldierly instinct.

HOLCROFT, CYRIL WALTER, Lieut. (Acting Capt.), Worcestershire Regt. For conspicuous gallantry and devotion to duty. When the enemy attacked and broke through the line on the right of his company, he at once formed a defensive flank and prevented the enemy from getting in rear of the front line. Later, when he was again attacked, he fought for several hours at close quarters against greatly superior forces, and finally drove the enemy back and maintained his position. His coolness and courage held up the enemy's attack and saved a most difficult situation.

JACKSON, HERBERT SELWYN, Capt., West Riding Regt. For conspicuous gallantry and devotion to duty in assuming command of the battalion when the commanding officer had been killed and heavy casualties were being incurred and there was grave danger of disorganization. He moved about in the open under a hail of bullets, rallied the men and organized a most successful attack, all the objectives being captured. The following day, when the battalion was engaged in severe fighting, he personally conducted a Tank to the place where the fighting was fiercest, and so enabled the battalion to capture this sector of the enemy trenches. He showed magnificent courage and resource.

JAMES, WILLIAM GEORGE, Temporary Second Lieut., Yorkshire Light Infantry. For conspicuous gallantry and devotion to duty. He crept through the enemy wire right up to their trenches, located and marked existing gaps and cut other gaps. In the attack he led his platoon across about 300 yards of open ground into the enemy trenches, and with two men killed 18 of the enemy. Later, he took command of the battalion owing to heavy officer casualties, and with both flanks exposed he held the enemy in check until reinforcements could reach him. He showed splendid courage and initiative.

JOFFE, WILLIAM, Second Lieut., Yorkshire Light Infantry. For conspicuous gallantry and devotion to duty. Before reaching the final objective, which his company had been detailed to capture, his company commander becoming a casualty, he immediately organized a party, consisting of an N.C.O. and 12 men, and in the face of extremely heavy machine-gun and rifle grenade fire and point-blank fire from an enemy field gun rushed the position and captured the gun. Though wounded, he showed great courage and determination, and the successful capture of the final objective was entirely due to his fine leadership and quick initiative.

JOHNSTON, KENNETH ALFRED, Capt. (Acting Lieut.-Colonel), Hampshire Regt. For conspicuous gallantry and devotion to duty. Finding that the bridge which he had been ordered to cross was broken, he led his battalion over by another bridge exposed to heavy fire. During the night he dealt with a critical situation, and disposed his battalion so as to establish securely the right flank of the brigade.

KNIGHT, EDWARD SPURIN, Second Lieut., London Regt. For conspicuous gallantry and devotion to duty. During the enemy's first rush, which overran our forward bombing blocks, this officer engaged the attacking bombers at our second block, and by the accuracy and determination of his bombing drove the enemy back to the first blocks, thereby enabling our original position to be re-established. His courage and coolness undoubtedly saved the situation.

LUCAS, CHARLES ROBERT, Temporary Capt., Royal Lancaster Regt. For conspicuous gallantry and devotion to duty. After his senior officers had become casualties he took command of the remnants of the brigade and two companies belonging to another brigade. Though unsupported by artillery or machine guns he established a line which was made the basis of a further advance when machine-gun support was available. Here he repulsed two separate counter-attacks.

LYNN, ALFRED CECIL, Lieut. (Acting Capt.), Yorkshire Light Infantry. For conspicuous gallantry and devotion to duty. He led his company forward to the attack with great determination across 350 yards of open ground under heavy enfilade fire, dashing out in front, and being the first to enter the enemy trenches, himself killing four of the enemy and forcing eight others to surrender.

MAGINN, JOHN FRANCIS, Second Lieut., London Regt. For conspicuous gallantry and devotion to duty. When an officer of another regiment was very severely wounded and was unable to move he rushed forward with two stretcher-bearers under heavy machine-gun and sniper's fire and sniped the enemy for 15 minutes, covering the stretcher-bearers, who were thus able to bring the wounded officer back. He showed splendid courage and resource.

MATHIAS, FRANCIS MORGAN, Temporary Capt., Welsh Regt. For conspicuous gallantry and devotion to duty. He took command of the battalion after the commanding officer and second-in-command became casualties. He displayed a thorough grasp of the situation, keeping in close touch with the brigade headquarters and continually readjusted the line under heavy fire. He was wounded early in the action, but continued to carry out his duties with the greatest courage and determination.

McCUDDEN, JAMES BYFORD, M.C., M.M., Second Lieut. (Temporary Capt.), General List and Royal Flying Corps. For conspicuous gallantry and devotion to duty. He attacked and brought down an enemy two-seater machine inside our lines, both the occupants being taken prisoner. On another occasion he encountered an enemy two-seater machine at 2,000 feet. He continued the fight down to a height of 100 feet in very bad weather conditions and destroyed the enemy machine. He came down to within a few feet of the ground on the enemy's side of the lines, and finally crossed the lines at a very low altitude. He has recently destroyed seven enemy machines, two of which fell within our lines, and has set a splendid example of pluck and determination to his squadron.

McKEEVER, ANDREW EDWARD, M.C., Second Lieut. (Temporary Capt.), Royal Flying Corps, Special Reserve. For conspicuous gallantry and devotion to duty. While on patrol by himself over the enemy's lines in very bad weather he encountered two enemy two-seater machines and seven scouts. By skilful manœuvring he engaged one and destroyed it. As he turned to get back to the lines five of the enemy dived on his tail and his observer engaged and destroyed two of them. After an indecisive combat with two others he attacked and destroyed one of the enemy which had overshot him. He continued the fight with the remainder until he was within 20 feet of the ground, when the enemy machines climbed and left him. He has recently destroyed ten enemy machines and has shown great courage and initiative.

MORGAN, DAVID WATTS, Temporary Major, Labour Corps. For conspicuous gallantry and devotion to duty. When his camp was heavily shelled with a few N.C.O.'s and men he turned some dug-outs into a temporary dressing station and assisted the wounded in the vicinity. When shelling rendered his position untenable he brought back his men in good order. He displayed great coolness and resource.

MORGAN-GRENVILLE-GAVIN, THE HONOURABLE THOMAS GEORGE BREADALBANE, M.C., Capt. and Brevet Major, Rifle Brigade. For conspicuous gallantry and devotion to duty. He carried out valuable reconnaissances, readjusted sections of the line, and arranged the assembly positions for subsequent attacks. He showed the greatest courage under difficult conditions.

MOXON, CHARLES STONE, Lieut. (Acting Capt.), West Riding Regt. For conspicuous gallantry and devotion to duty in leading his company in an attack. When held up by an enemy strong point, he entered a Tank and directed it to the spot, but it became ditched. He got out, and single-handed, under heavy rifle fire and a shower of bombs, attacked the strong point, killing several of the enemy and enabling a platoon of his company to capture the strong point and five prisoners. He set a magnificent example of courage and determination.

NIXON, SIR CHRISTOPHER WILLIAM, Bart., Major, Royal Artillery. For conspicuous gallantry and devotion to duty. He continued to command his battery after being wounded in two places. The accurate shooting of the battery was instrumental in repulsing an enemy counter-attack, inflicting heavy casualties on the enemy.

NOTMAN, JAMES PARTRIDGE, Second Lieut., Seaforth Highlanders. For conspicuous gallantry and devotion to duty. When some enemy machine guns were enfilading the battalion during an advance and causing heavy casualties, he rushed well ahead of his platoon and attacked the machine gunners. When they showed fight he shot two and the remainder surrendered. He returned through intense machine-gun fire, carrying a captured machine gun. He afterwards entered a house from which an enemy machine gun was firing, and captured the gun and team. He showed splendid initiative and courage.

O'BRIEN, GERALD, Second Lieut., Royal Munster Fusiliers, Special Reserve. For conspicuous gallantry and devotion to duty. When the centre of the line was held up by machine-gun fire, he rushed forward alone regardless of danger, shot the enemy gunner, and captured the gun. This prompt and gallant action not only saved many lives, but also enabled the advance to continue without loss of time, which was of great importance.

PANK, CECIL HENRY, Major (Acting Lieut.-Colonel), Middlesex Regt. For conspicuous gallantry and devotion to duty. The enemy in overwhelming numbers succeeded in forcing the blocks in our trenches and temporarily cut off communications with headquarters on the flank. He immediately organized a counter-attack, and so infused his men, disorganized by heavy losses, with fresh fighting spirit that he succeeded in re-establishing touch on the flank, and with the help of another unit driving back the enemy and reforming the blocks. Though wounded he showed great personal courage, coolness and resourceful determination, which contributed largely to the success of the counter-attack.

PAUL, WILLIAM, M.C., Second Lieut. (Acting Capt.), West Yorkshire Regt. For conspicuous gallantry and devotion to duty. When the enemy was seen from the battalion transport lines to be advancing about 400 yards away, he at once collected all battalion details, held back the enemy at close range, and held the position for four hours until relieved, thus enabling the units in rear to reform. He was severely wounded, but refused to withdraw until relieved. He showed splendid courage and determination.

PEEL, JAMES, M.M., Second Lieut., Royal Fusiliers. For conspicuous gallantry and devotion to duty. His platoon being held up and suffering many casualties from two machine guns, which were firing from a church, he rushed forward alone and captured the first gun from the flank, killing four and wounding the remainder of the team. Some of his men having by this time caught up with him, he at once rushed them towards the rear of the second gun, which they captured, killing or wounding the whole team. His splendid courage, dashing gallantry and bold initiative were beyond all praise.

POOLE, GILBERT SANDFORD, Major, Yeomanry. For conspicuous gallantry and devotion to duty when in command of his battalion in an attack. He handled his battalion with great skill, and his courage and judgment contributed largely to the success of the operation.

POWER, ROWLAND EDWARD, Major (Acting Lieut.-Colonel), East Kent Regt. For conspicuous gallantry and devotion to duty. After his battalion had suffered heavy casualties in an attack he went forward, reorganized it, and drove the enemy from their position. He showed the greatest initiative and resource throughout the operation.

ROSHER, JOHN BRENCHLEY, M.C., Temporary Major (Acting Lieut.-Colonel), Durham Light Infantry. For conspicuous gallantry and devotion to duty. On our cavalry being temporarily held up, and whilst the reinforcing infantry were still some way in the rear, he immediately despatched two companies to the assistance of the cavalry, and himself led up a third company as reinforcements. His prompt action immediately resulted in the capture of the objective with slight casualties.

RUNDALL, CHARLES FRANK, Major (Acting Lieut.-Colonel), Royal Engineers. For conspicuous gallantry and devotion to duty. He had under his command two companies, and in addition collected a mixed force of two field companies and other details of several different units. Some of these being greatly disorganized, he rapidly reorganized them and formed a defensive line, on which he repelled a small local attack, and shortly after dispersed a considerable body of the enemy which was forming up for an attack. He rendered invaluable assistance in directing a counter-attack and in reconnoitring a front of 7,000 yards under heavy fire.

RUSSELL, GEORGE GRAY, Lieut.-Colonel, King Edward's Horse, Special Reserve. For conspicuous gallantry and devotion to duty when in command of two squadrons attached to an infantry brigade during an advance. He frequently moved about in the foremost line directing reconnaissance work under heavy machine-gun fire, and when the right flank of the brigade was dangerously exposed he conducted a valuable reconnaissance with great skill and resource and cleared up the situation.

SPENCE-JONES, CECIL JOHN HERBERT, Lieut.-Colonel, Yeomanry. For conspicuous gallantry and devotion to duty during an enemy counter-attack. He went forward into the firing line and remained with his men, and by his presence and example under heavy fire encouraged them to hold on to a very difficult and exposed position.

STIDSTON, CHARLES ALGERNON, M.D., Major (Temporary Lieut.-Colonel), Royal Army Medical Corps. For conspicuous gallantry and devotion to duty when his dressing-station was very heavily shelled throughout a whole day and received several direct hits. It was impossible to remove the wounded, and throughout the day he moved about continuously, arranging for their safety with utter disregard of danger. It was owing to his fearless example and splendid organization that all the wounded were finally removed without further casualties.

STIRLING, JOHN ALEXANDER, M.C., Capt. and Brevet Major, Scots Guards, Special Reserve. For conspicuous gallantry and devotion to duty. Orders having been received that the battalion was to retake certain high ground, he, both before the attack, when he made a careful reconnaissance, and after, was continuously up and down the line under heavy machine-gun fire. His initiative was to a great degree the reason for a difficult situation being cleared up successfully, while his courage and contempt of danger inspired all ranks with the greatest confidence.

STORR, LEYCESTER PENRHYN, Temporary Major, Liverpool Regt. For conspicuous gallantry and devotion to duty. When in command of the battalion, on both company commanders of the leading companies becoming casualties, he personally led on the men under heavy fire to the capture of the first objective. Having reorganized the battalion, he led it on to the second objective, which was successfully taken. By his coolness, courage and ability he set a splendid example to all ranks, and the success of the operations was due to his good leadership and initiative during a critical period.

STUART, GERALD FITZGERALD, Lieut., West Yorkshire Regt. For conspicuous gallantry and devotion to duty. When his battalion was counter-attacked and in great danger of being out-flanked he was sent with a party of headquarter details to defend the right flank, which was entirely in the air. With less than 30 men he succeeded in arresting the advance of about two companies of the enemy, and remained exposed to heavy fire at close range for three hours, showing splendid courage and determination.

TILLOTSON, JOHN EDWIN, Temporary Second Lieut., West Yorkshire Regt. For conspicuous gallantry and devotion to duty. He led men of his own and other battalions forward in the face of heavy machine-gun and rifle fire, and was entirely responsible for the capture of the company's objective. When other troops who were passing through his company were held up by a strong point 300 yards forward and suffering heavy casualties, he dashed forward in the face of direct fire from three machine guns and attacked them with the bayonet. He killed 12 of the enemy, put all three guns out of action, and captured two trench mortars. He set a magnificent example of courage and determination.

TUCKEY, ELLIOT CLARKE, Second Lieut., Royal Field Artillery, Special Reserve. For conspicuous gallantry and devotion to duty. He kept his gun in action until ordered to withdraw. When the detachments had been withdrawn he went forward by himself across 50 yards of open ground under heavy fire to attend to a wounded officer. He returned for water, and finally carried the man back under very heavy fire. He showed splendid courage and self-sacrifice.

UPTON, WILLIAM ARTHUR, Temporary Second Lieut., Wiltshire Regt. For conspicuous gallantry and devotion to duty in an attack. He captured an enemy trench and three machine guns. He held on to the position, though subjected to fire from all sides, and inflicted heavy casualties on the enemy. When ordered to withdraw at dusk he covered the withdrawal with rifle grenades. His courage and contempt of danger were magnificent.

WARDEN, HERBERT LAWTON, Temporary Lieut.-Colonel, East Surrey Regt. For conspicuous gallantry and devotion to duty. He took command of the advanced troops in an attack, and maintained his headquarters in a forward position under heavy fire. He drove off three enemy counter-attacks, and handled his reserve with such skill as to be able to withdraw without loss. He then maintained a position where he was able to keep in touch with three companies of another battalion which were under his command. He showed splendid initiative and skill.

WESTMACOTT, GUY RANDOLPH, Lieut., Grenadier Guards. For conspicuous gallantry and devotion to duty. His flank was completely exposed, both during the attack and after reaching the objective, and he had to form a defensive flank with his company throughout the whole action. On the enemy delivering a heavy counter-attack on this exposed flank he formed his company to the right, and shattered it with steady and admirably controlled fire. On reaching the objective he consolidated, covering the flank of the battalion by digging a very strong line, and also providing further protection for the flank of the division by means of several machine guns. The complete success of the attack and the immediate defeat of the hostile counter-attack were largely due to his resource and prompt action.

WILSON, BEVIL THOMSON, Capt. and Brevet Major (Acting Major), Royal Engineers. For conspicuous gallantry and devotion to duty. He reached some canal bridges with the leading waves of infantry, and destroyed the charges of explosives before the bridges could be blown up. During an enemy counter-attack he collected what men he could and drove the enemy back, spending the rest of the day and night in organizing a defensive flank under heavy fire. During the withdrawal across the canal he remained behind until orders were received for the destruction of the bridges. He showed splendid courage and initiative.

CANADIAN FORCES.

BIRDS, SAMUEL BUTTREY, M.C., Capt. (Acting Major), Infantry. For conspicuous gallantry and devotion to duty. He was in support during an attack, and when the leading companies were held up he advanced straight to the position and captured it, together with three machine guns and a large number of prisoners. He reconnoitred the whole position and sent in most accurate sketches and reports. He showed great courage and skill.

BORDEN, ALLISON HART, Lieut.-Colonel, Infantry. For conspicuous gallantry and devotion to duty. By his personal reconnaissance prior to the attack, in the face of great danger from machine-gun and rifle fire, he obtained sufficient information to modify his plans so as to deal with the unexpected situation caused by the enemy's counter-attack. With complete disregard for his own safety, he made a tour of the line, making the necessary adjustments in dispositions to ensure its being held. His example to his battalion was magnificent, and his determination, courageous conduct, and skilful leadership inspired all ranks to hold on to their objective, even though their losses were very heavy.

GRANT, ALEXANDER, Major, Infantry. For conspicuous gallantry and devotion to duty. He led his company to the final objective and organized the defence. When his company was in support and a counter-attack was imminent, he led his company forward through heavy shell fire, established it immediately behind the front line, and took charge of the situation. He set a splendid example to his men.

McEWAN, JOHN ALEXANDER, Major, Infantry. For conspicuous gallantry and devotion to duty in an attack. When all the other officers of his company became casualties, he placed himself in front of his company, under heavy fire, and led them with the greatest skill and determination to their final objective. Though three times buried by shells, he continued to hold the line for four days.

McNAUGHTON, ANDREW GEORGE LATTA, Lieut.-Colonel, Artillery. For conspicuous gallantry and devotion to duty as counter-battery staff officer. He carried out daring reconnaissances, and observed the enemy's batteries from an exposed position under very heavy fire. On one occasion he crossed the enemy's lines in low-flying aeroplane, obtaining valuable information as to the enemy's batteries. He rendered most valuable service during a long period.

NEWFOUNDLAND FORCES.

BUTLER, BERTRAM, M.C., Capt., Infantry. For conspicuous gallantry and devotion to duty. When two attacks had been held up, on his own initiative he organized and led another attack and captured the position. He set a magnificent example of courage and determination.

London Gazette, 18 July, 1918.—" War Office, 18 July, 1918. With reference to the awards conferred as announced in the London Gazette dated 18 Feb. 1918, the following are the statements of service for which the decorations were conferred. Awarded a Second Bar to the Distinguished Service Order."

McDONALD, SAMUEL, D.S.O., Major (Acting Lieut.-Colonel), Gordon Highlanders. For conspicuous gallantry and devotion to duty during an attack. When nearly all the officers had become casualties, and the attack was held up, he not only made a dangerous reconnaissance alone, but subsequently, on three separate occasions during the day, reorganized parties of his battalion, and led them forward in spite of heavy fire and severe losses. He showed magnificent courage and coolness.

Awarded a Bar to the Distinguished Service Order:

BENZIE, ROBERT, D.S.O., Temporary Lieut.-Colonel, South Wales Borderers. For conspicuous gallantry and devotion to duty during lengthy operations. He constantly forced back the enemy and readjusted his line under heavy fire. After nearly all the officers of the brigade had become casualties, he organized the remnants into a unit, which he personally led, with the greatest courage, in a counter-attack, remaining in command of the advanced elements until relieved by another division.

BOYLE, CHARLES ROGER CAVENDISH, D.S.O., Capt. (Temporary Lieut.-Colonel), Oxfordshire and Buckinghamshire Light Infantry. For conspicuous gallantry and devotion to duty during lengthy operations. He led his battalion to an attack, placing himself so that all his men could see him, and, despite the heaviest fire, broke through all opposition. Later, he was ordered to counter-attack over a large area which was swept by severe shell and machine-gun fire. He initiated the advance by section rushes, and then walked calmly forward with his battalion. His personal courage and resource were magnificent.

BRYCE, EDWARD DANIEL, D.S.O., Temporary Major (Acting Lieut.-Colonel), Tank Corps. For conspicuous gallantry and devotion to duty when in command of tanks in an attack. After the capture of the first objective he collected and reorganized his command and carried out a further attack. On the following day he led some of his tanks in an attack on a village, which he captured, inflicting heavy losses on the enemy. His coolness and courage were an inspiration to all, and his judgment and ability contributed largely to the success of the operations.

CROSSE, RICHARD BANASTRE, D.S.O., Capt. and Brevet Major (Temporary Lieut.-Colonel), Oxfordshire and Buckinghamshire Light Infantry. For conspicuous gallantry and devotion to duty during lengthy operations. He displayed great ability in grasping the possibilities of the situation, and in improving the defensive and offensive properties of the line. He personally reconnoitred positions close to the enemy posts, which he caused to be occupied. His indifference to personal danger was most marked.

HOTBLACK, FREDERICK ELLIOTT, D.S.O., M.C., Second Lieut. (Temporary Capt.), Norfolk Regt. and Tank Corps. For conspicuous gallantry and devotion to duty during an attack. He reorganized the infantry whose officers had become casualties, collected tanks, and succeeded in launching a fresh attack under heavy fire. He set a splendid example of courage and initiative on this and many other occasions.

JAMES, ARCHIBALD HUGH, D.S.O., Temporary Major (Acting Lieut.-Colonel), Northumberland Fusiliers. For conspicuous gallantry and devotion to duty in handling the troops under his command during lengthy operations. After severe fighting, he had forced his way forward, only to be driven back by a heavy enemy attack, but by his courage and energy he regained his position. Later, the situation becoming critical, he made a personal reconnaissance under intense fire, cleared up an obscure situation, and, on his own initiative, led his battalion forward again to their objective. He gave a fine example of courage and initiative to all ranks.

JANSON, JAMES THEODORE, D.S.O., Temporary Major (Acting Lieut.-Colonel), Yorkshire Light Infantry. For conspicuous gallantry and devotion to duty. He was in command of a battalion which was in reserve during an enemy attack, and collected and led a large number of men of various units with the greatest coolness and skill. He carried out a reconnaissance of the position, got the situation well in hand, and by his fine example forestalled every attempt of the enemy to break through.

KNOX, ROBERT SINCLAIR, D.S.O., Temporary Major, Royal Inniskilling Fusiliers. For conspicuous gallantry and devotion when in command of a battalion. Owing to previous hostile attacks, the position of the line his battalion took over was very uncertain. By a personal night reconnaissance he was able to adjust the line, and later, when the enemy commenced a bombing attack, he again went forward to reconnoitre the position, which was very critical, and then organized a successful attack, driving back the enemy and taking prisoners. His courage throughout was magnificent.

McCUDDEN, JAMES BYFORD, D.S.O., M.C., Second Lieut. (Temporary Capt.), General List and Royal Flying Corps. For conspicuous gallantry and devotion to duty. He attacked enemy formations, both when leading his patrol and single-handed. By his fearlessness and clever manœuvring he has brought down 31 enemy machines, ten of which have fallen in our lines. His pluck and determination have had a marked effect on the efficiency of the squadron.

McKAIG, JOHN BICKERTON, D.S.O., Capt. (Acting Lieut.-Colonel), Liverpool Regt. For conspicuous gallantry and devotion to duty during a strong enemy attack. When the enemy penetrated the front of the unit on his left, and his flank thereby became exposed, he supervised the redistribution of his battalion and the formation of a defensive flank under intense fire. By his disregard of danger, and the confidence with which he inspired his men by his splendid example, he enabled his battalion to hold their ground against frontal and flank attacks during a most critical period, when a break-through would have had very serious consequences to the whole line.

NASH, HENRY EDMUND PALMER, D.S.O., Major (Temporary Lieut.-Colonel), Royal Scots. For conspicuous gallantry and devotion to duty during an advance. Owing to the troops on his right having failed to gain their objective, he was obliged to detach two companies to safeguard his flank. When this was secure he led them forward, reorganized his battalion, which had been held up by heavy fire, and succeeded in capturing his objective. Throughout the day he showed great contempt of danger, moving freely under the heaviest fire of all kinds, and his splendid example gave great encouragement to the troops under his command.

NELSON, HERBERT, D.S.O., Major (Temporary Brigadier-General), Border Regt. For conspicuous gallantry and devotion to duty. In spite of having no support from tanks or artillery, he led his brigade forward in face of heavy opposition and captured all his objectives. Subsequently, when the brigade was in reserve, and the enemy had made a considerable advance, he at once counter-attacked, driving them back with heavy losses over two miles, again without the assistance of artillery. His personal conduct was most gallant throughout.

ROSHER, JOHN BRENCHLEY, D.S.O., M.C., Temporary Lieut.-Colonel), Durham Light Infantry. For conspicuous gallantry and devotion to duty. When the enemy attacked in great force positions held by his battalion he displayed the greatest courage and ability, inspiring his men to beat off three attacks. When finally pressed back by superior numbers he reorganized the remnants of the battalion, and advancing, reoccupied the trenches from which he had been temporarily ejected.

STIRLING, COLIN ROBERT HOSTE, D.S.O., M.C., Capt. (Acting Lieut.-Colonel), Scottish Rifles. For conspicuous gallantry and devotion to duty. He reorganized his company under most difficult conditions and led them forward to the assembly position. He carried out a personal reconnaissance of our position, getting close to the enemy line and sending in valuable information. He showed splendid initiative and resource.

THORNE, AUGUSTUS FRANCIS ANDREW NICOL, D.S.O., Major (Acting Lieut.-Colonel), Grenadier Guards. For conspicuous gallantry and devotion to duty. When his battalion had captured its objective in an attack he organized the consolidation of the position and supervised the placing of strong points under very heavy fire. It was mainly through his excellent dispositions that the battalion maintained its position against heavy counter-attacks. He showed great coolness and ability.

WATSON, HUGH WHARTON MYDDLETON, D.S.O., Major (Acting Lieut.-Colonel), King's Royal Rifle Corps. For conspicuous gallantry and devotion to duty. He held his position against continued heavy enemy attacks. His battalion was subjected to intense shell fire throughout, but, regardless of danger, he moved about continually among his men, organizing the defence and encouraging all ranks by his fearless example, and proved himself a magnificent leader. On the previous day he had carried out a successful operation against the enemy, capturing and consolidating an important area.

WELCH, HAROLD ECHALAG, D.S.O., Temporary Major (Acting Lieut.-Colonel), Shropshire Light Infantry. For conspicuous gallantry and devotion to duty. He was ordered to capture an enemy position situated on high ground. He led his battalion forward with the greatest determination and skill, under heavy machine-gun and rifle fire, and succeeded in establishing his position on the reverse slopes of the ridge. He inflicted heavy casualties on the enemy, and maintained his position against superior numbers until the whole ridge was captured on the following day. His successful attack contributed largely to the success of the whole operation.

WESTON, SPENCER VAUGHAN PERCY, D.S.O., M.C., Temporary Capt. (Temporary Lieut.-Colonel), Royal Berkshire Regt. For conspicuous gallantry and devotion to duty. When the enemy launched a heavy attack on his position he moved up his reserves and organized the defence with such skill that, though the enemy attacked continually for six hours, his battalion withstood all the enemy's attempts to break through and inflicted very heavy casualties. His tactical skill, coolness, and example were mainly responsible for the successful resistance offered by his battalion.

WIGGIN, WILLIAM HENRY, D.S.O., Major, Yeomanry. For conspicuous gallantry and devotion to duty in leading a charge on the enemy's position. His fearless leadership and example inspired all ranks and were largely responsible for the success of the charge, which swept over an enemy battery firing at point-blank range.

CANADIAN FORCE.

McLAUGHLIN, LORNE TALBOT, D.S.O., Lieut.-Colonel, Infantry. For conspicuous gallantry and devotion to duty. He deployed his battalion for the attack under very difficult conditions and heavy fire, captured all his objectives, and consolidated the position. His conduct was an inspiration to all under his command.

Awarded the Distinguished Service Order :

BARKER, WILLIAM GEORGE, M.C., Temporary Capt., General List and Royal Flying Corps. For conspicuous gallantry and devotion to duty. When on scouting and patrol work he has on five different occasions brought down and destroyed five enemy aeroplanes and two balloons, though on two of these occasions he was attacked by superior numbers. On each occasion the hostile machines were observed to crash to earth, the wreckage bursting into flames. His splendid example of fearlessness and magnificent leadership have been of inestimable value to his squadron.

BELCHER, RAYMOND DOUGLAS, M.C., Temporary Capt. (Acting Major), Royal Field Artillery. For conspicuous gallantry and devotion to duty. On the enemy threatening the front and flank of the battery he continued to move about among his guns, encouraging the men and supervising the laying of the guns. In spite of losses he continued to keep up the fire of his guns, repelling all attempts of the enemy to break through. Although dangerously wounded, he continued to command the battery until he was carried away. The splendid work accomplished by the battery was in a great measure due to his skilful command, determination and fine example.

BION, WILFRED RUPRECHT, Temporary Second Lieut., Tank Corps. For conspicuous gallantry and devotion to duty. When in command of his tank in an attack he engaged a large number of enemy machine guns in strong positions, thus assisting the infantry to advance. When his tank was put out of action by a direct hit he occupied a section of trench with his men and machine guns, and opened fire on the enemy. He moved about in the open, giving directions to other tanks when they arrived, and at one period fired a Lewis gun with great effect from the top of his tank. He also got a captured machine gun into action against the enemy, and when reinforcements arrived he took command of a company of infantry whose commander was killed. He showed magnificent courage and initiative in a most difficult situation.

BONNYMAN, EDWARD WILLIAM, Temporary Capt., Argyll and Sutherland Highlanders. For conspicuous gallantry and devotion to duty. The enemy attacked after a heavy bombardment, and gained a footing in the trenches on both flanks of his company's position. Though his company suffered heavy losses he kept the situation well in hand by his coolness and magnificent example and finally succeeded in driving the enemy out of his trenches, and inflicting heavy casualties on them.

BROOME, RALPH HOWARD, M.C., Capt. and Brevet Major (Acting Major), Wiltshire Regt. and Tank Corps. For conspicuous gallantry and devotion to duty. He commanded 30 tanks during the operations, and handled them with the greatest courage and ability. His tanks cleared the way for the infantry to a most important enemy position, and enabled the infantry to consolidate it. He set a splendid example of pluck and determination throughout.

BULTEEL, JOHN CROCKER, M.C., Capt., Yeomanry. For conspicuous gallantry and devotion to duty. During an attack he was in command of the leading squadron, charged the enemy line and in spite of heavy enfilade fire, organized the consolidation of the position against greatly superior forces. He displayed great courage and admirable resource.

CARRINGTON, CHARLES WORRELL, Second Lieut., Grenadier Guards, Special Reserve. For conspicuous gallantry and devotion to duty. When part of the advance was held up by two enemy machine guns firing from a house he at once organized and led a bayonet charge and captured the house and its occupants. He then led a successful attack on the second objective, and having captured it, beat off a counter-attack. Later, when his flank became exposed, and the enemy attacked him from the rear, he fought his way back, and brought his men out in good order. He set a magnificent example of courage and initiative.

CHEAPE, GEORGE RONALD HAMILTON, M.C., Capt. (Temporary Brigadier-General), Dragoon Guards. For conspicuous gallantry and devotion to duty. He led his brigade with great courage and ability, and captured all his objectives. Subsequently when the enemy had broken through on the flank of his position he repelled 12 heavy attacks in spite of greatly reduced numbers. This splendid performance was mainly due to his magnificent example of courage and determination.

CRAWFORD, JOHN, Temporary Second Lieut., Rifle Brigade. For conspicuous gallantry and devotion to duty. After the enemy had broken through the front line he led his platoon, and a few men from other units, to a forward position of a new line protecting the guns. Although twice driven out by shell-fire he rallied his men on each occasion and attacked again, holding his position long enough to enable the gunners to dismantle their guns and wireless station, and to save important documents. He showed splendid courage and resource.

CROUCH, THOMAS ALFRED, Lieut. (Acting Capt.), Royal Irish Fusiliers, Special Reserve, attached Tank Corps. For conspicuous gallantry and devotion to duty. He showed the greatest judgment and initiative in leading his tanks in an attack. He led them forward to a village in the enemy's lines and, moving about on foot under heavy fire, succeeded in getting them all through the village. Though he had no infantry support he overcame the enemy's resistance and held a most important position.

DAMMERS, GEORGE MURRAY, M.C., Capt., Yeomanry. For conspicuous gallantry and devotion to duty. He handled his squadron with courage and ability when he was the only officer with the squadron. He charged the enemy's position at the gallop under heavy rifle and machine-gun fire. He succeeded in holding the flank against heavy enfilade fire, thereby enabling the rest of the regiment to advance.

DAWES, GEORGE, M.C., Capt. and Brevet Major, South Staffordshire Regt. For conspicuous gallantry and devotion to duty during lengthy operations. He took over an important line and established a strong position. He rendered prompt assistance to a battalion on his left in a successful attack. Later, he organized and directed the withdrawal of the battalion with such skill that hardly any casualties were suffered, and all ammunition and tools were moved back. His courage and cheerfulness never failed, though he was constantly under heavy fire, and was suffering from gas.

DIGBY-WINGFIELD-DIGBY, FREDERICK JAMES BOSWORTH, Major, Yeomanry. For conspicuous gallantry and devotion to duty. He led his squadron in a charge, in which more than 100 prisoners together with a field gun were captured. He handled his squadron with great courage and ability, and the success of the operation was entirely due to the quickness with which he dismounted his men, bringing rifle fire to bear on the enemy's guns, and putting one team out of action.

DURRANT, ARTHUR WILLIAM, Lieut. (Acting Capt.), London Regt. For conspicuous gallantry and devotion to duty when in charge of an advanced post. He was repeatedly attacked by large numbers of the enemy. More than once portions of the post were lost, and he was in danger of being surrounded, but with splendid courage he organized repeated counter-attacks, personally disposing of many of the enemy in hand-to-hand fighting, and withdrew in good order, when his ammunition was exhausted.

ELEY, EDWARD HENRY, C.M.G., Lieut.-Colonel, Royal Field Artillery. For conspicuous gallantry and devotion to duty. When in command of the brigade, he displayed marked courage and ability, and materially assisted in checking the enemy at a most critical moment. He handled the batteries with the greatest skill, and succeeded in keeping himself in touch with the situation on both flanks.

FROST, JOHN MEADOWS, Major, Royal Field Artillery. For conspicuous gallantry and devotion to duty. During a long and continuous advance of the enemy against our positions, he, quickly appreciating the situation, split his battery into sections, and ultimately materially assisted in staying the advance. Later, though men and horses were tired with continuous marching, he achieved a masterly performance in moving his battery in the dark over difficult, mountainous and unreconnoitred country for some considerable distance, so that he succeeded in arriving in time to take part in the bombardment of an important objective.

GEE, ERNEST EDWARD, M.C., Lieut. (Temporary Major), Royal Garrison Artillery. For conspicuous gallantry and devotion to duty. He salved the guns of his battery which were lying in "No Man's Land" close to the enemy's lines. He reconnoitred the position, and found that the enemy had completed preparations to blow up the guns, and having removed the detonators and disconnected the fuses, he directed the withdrawl of the guns. Though Very lights were sent up continually, and the position and the track leading from it were subjected to continual shell fire, he dug the guns out and got them safely to our lines with only one casualty. He showed magnificent coolness and courage at his difficult task and rendered great service by saving four valuable guns.

GERRARD, WALTER DOUGLAS, Lieut. (Acting Capt.), Yeomanry and Tank Corps. For conspicuous gallantry and devotion to duty. When the tank in which he was going forward became ditched he withdrew his crew from the tank, and, finding it impossible to extricate the tank, formed his men into a Lewis gun section and led them forward into action. He organized the crews of three other disabled tanks as Lewis gunners, and also brought a captured machine gun into action with great effect. He showed great initiative and determination.

GILLILAN, EDWARD GIBSON, Capt., Coldstream Guards, Special Reserve. For conspicuous gallantry and devotion to duty in an attack. Though nearly all the officers and platoon serjeants of his company became casualties early in the advance, he organized and led a successful attack on a strong enemy position, inflicting heavy casualties and capturing 200 prisoners. He then led his company to the final objective under very heavy fire, and when in danger of being surrounded owing to the flanks of the position being exposed, he withdrew and established a strong defensive position and beat off an enemy attack. He showed magnificent courage and ability.

GROUNDS, GEORGE AMBROSE, Temporary Lieut. (Acting Capt.), Tank Corps. For conspicuous gallantry and devotion to duty. When three of his tanks were disabled he formed his men into Lewis gun sections and led them into action to assist in repelling the enemy's attack. While going along a trench he met a party of the enemy, and by using enemy bombs he disorganized and held up the party single-handed. He got forward another tank in conjunction with a party of infantry, cleared about 200 yards of enemy trench, capturing 15 machine guns and a large number of prisoners. He showed the greatest initiative and coolness and good leadership, which resulted in a successful advance being carried out.

HARCOURT, ALEXANDER CLARENCE, Lieut. (Acting Capt.), Royal Berkshire Regt., Tank Corps. For conspicuous gallantry and devotion to duty. When tanks were required to assist the infantry who had been held up in an attack on a village he at once went forward on his own initiative with two tanks. They overcame all enemy resistance and held the village until the infantry arrived. The capture of the village was due to his promptness and initiative.

HENSHALL, LOUIS SYDNEY, Capt. (Acting Major), South Lancashire Regt., Tank Corps. For conspicuous gallantry and devotion to duty. He followed his tanks closely on foot in the attack, and, having captured the first objective, collected his tanks and led them forward against a village, which he captured and held. He showed great ability and set a magnificent example of contempt of danger, moving about in the open in full view of the enemy under heavy sniping and machine-gun fire.

HEZLET, CHARLES OWEN, Lieut. (Acting Major), Royal Garrison Artillery, Special Reserve. For conspicuous gallantry and devotion to duty during an enemy attack. He kept his guns firing and encouraged his men until the enemy were within 300 yards of the battery. He remained at his post though the enemy's barrage had passed beyond the battery, and the machine-gun fire was very severe. Every round in the battery was fired. He gave a very fine example of coolness, courage and efficiency.

HUBBARD, REV. HAROLD EVELYN, Army Chaplains' Department. For conspicuous gallantry and devotion to duty. When several men had been killed by a sniper in attempting to rescue a wounded man from a derelict tank, he went out, regardless of danger, and brought the man in. His gallantry and courage were an inspiration to the men throughout the operations.

HUNT, GERALD PONSONBY SNEYD, C.M.G., Major (Acting Lieut.-Colonel), Royal Berkshire Regt. For conspicuous gallantry and devotion to duty. He established and organized the line after an attack by siting a series of posts on commanding ground. During an enemy attack he held his position against repeated thrusts by the enemy, although his right flank was exposed, and when touch was lost with the brigade on his right he re-established communication. He showed splendid leadership and courage.

LATCH, ARTHUR RONALD, Temporary Second Lieut., Tank Corps. For conspicuous gallantry and devotion to duty. He took his tank into action and by his courage and determination saved an infantry battalion from a desperate situation. He drove the enemy from some strong points which were threatening the flank of the infantry. When darkness came on he was surrounded by the enemy, who climbed on to the top of his tank and seized hold of his machine guns, but with great presence of mind and courage he succeeded in driving them off and inflicted heavy casualties upon them. He then dispersed the enemy who were assembling for a counter-attack. He handled his tank in a most able manner under very difficult conditions, and the assistance which he rendered was of the greatest value.

LONGDEN, ALFRED APPLEBY, Major, Royal Garrison Artillery. For conspicuous gallantry and devotion to duty. When the enemy broke through on the left of his position he went forward under heavy fire close to the enemy and reconnoitred the situation. He rallied his men, and, after a counter-attack, got his battery into position very rapidly and opened fire. He rendered valuable assistance to the infantry in the neighbourhood, and kept his guns in action under most difficult conditions and heavy and continuous fire.

MAURICE-JONES, KENNETH WYN, Second Lieut., Royal Field Artillery. For conspicuous gallantry and devotion to duty. When his battery received an S.O.S. call while it was being heavily bombarded with gas and high explosive shells he got all the guns into action within 30 seconds. He moved about regardless of danger, encouraging his men while two ammunition dumps were blown up close beside him. As soon as the battery ceased fire he carried a wounded man to safety, discarding his gas helmet, and though suffering from the effects of gas, continued to encourage his men and assist the wounded until he collapsed. Later, when an ammunition dump was set alight by enemy shell-fire he at once attempted to extinguish it, and continued his efforts until the dump exploded. He set a magnificent example of courage and intiative.

McELROY, FREDERICK WILLIAM, Temporary Second Lieut., Tank Corps. For conspicuous gallantry and devotion to duty in attack. He drove the enemy back and captured two strongly-held craters. When his tank caught fire and had to be evacuated he remained inside in spite of the fumes firing his Lewis gun, and held the enemy back single-handed when they attempted to capture his tank, inflicting heavy casualties on them. When his crew, many of whom were wounded, were surrounded in a shell-hole he killed eight of the enemy with his revolver, and it was owing to his great courage and coolness that the tank and the crew were saved.

MENZIES, ALASTAIR FORBES, Temporary Lieut., Royal Fusiliers. For conspicuous gallantry and devotion to duty. He held his ground during an enemy attack in a communication trench leading towards the enemy's lines and brought heavy enfilade fire to bear on the enemy as they passed his position. His determined action gained time, which was of vital importance to the reorganization of the main line of defence. He organized a bombing attack, regained 200 yards of trench, and established a block. The enemy made five most determined attacks on his position and suffered great loss without gaining any ground. By his courage, coolness and leadership he saved the situation and assisted in inflicting a severe defeat on the enemy.

MURPHY, WILLIAM HENRY, Major, London Regt. For conspicuous gallantry and devotion to duty. Whilst in command of the battalion he reconnoitred the whole of the position and was continually in the front line, where his unfailing cheerfulness was an inspiration to all ranks. On the occasion of an attack he successfully led his battalion in support at very short notice and in darkness. Later, he directed the withdrawal with remarkable skill, and on another occasion, when the outpost line held by his battalion was attacked in large force by the enemy, and eventually pressed back, he re-established the line of posts and organized them into a defensive position, maintaining them until relieved. He displayed magnificent courage, leadership and ability.

MURRAY-LYON, DAVID MURRAY, M.C., Capt. (Acting Lieut.-Colonel), Highland Light Infantry. For conspicuous gallantry and devotion to duty. When the enemy attacked and penetrated the line after intense fighting and continual bombing attacks, by his courage and personal example he succeeded in driving them out and held his position against further heavy attacks with splendid coolness and determination.

NICOLLS, EDWARD HUGH JASPER, M.C., Capt. (Acting Lieut.-Colonel), East Surrey Regt. For conspicuous gallantry and devotion to duty in an attack. When his right company met with strong resistance from the enemy he went to the position and by his courageous example encouraged his men to hold on until reinforcements arrived. His prompt action at an important period of the operation resulted in the whole of his objective being eventually captured and consolidated. He proved himself a gallant and capable leader.

PEARSON, ALGERNON GEORGE, Capt. (Temporary Major), Royal Berkshire Regt., Special Reserve and Tank Corps. For conspicuous gallantry and devotion to duty. He launched a successful attack with his tanks at very short notice, captured a village in the enemy's lines, held it until the infantry established themselves in the position, and brought his tanks safely out of action. He showed the greatest ability and courage in a most difficult operation. He again led his tanks into action two days later with excellent results.

PRATT, DOUGLAS HENRY, M.C., Capt. (Temporary Major), Royal Irish Regt. and Tank Corps. For conspicuous gallantry and devotion to duty in an attack. It was largely owing to his careful preparations and excellent leadership and organization that his tanks were successful in reaching all their objectives. He directed the operations on foot, going forward in front of the infantry and in the face of strong opposition. He never spared himself, and showed the greatest courage and contempt of danger.

RAIKES, DAVID TAUNTON, M.C., Lieut. (Temporary Capt.), South Wales Borderers, Special Reserve, attached Tank Corps. For conspicuous gallantry and devotion to duty. He directed his tanks in an attack with utter disregard of danger, continually going about on foot giving orders in full view of the enemy and exposed to heavy fire. On the following day he directed nine other tanks in addition to his own in the attack, and set a magnificent example of courage and contempt of danger throughout.

RICE-JONES, ARTHUR PHILIP, Temporary Lieut. (Acting Capt.), Royal Engineers. For conspicuous gallantry and devotion to duty. When in charge of the construction of forward lines necessary for the operations he worked under shell fire during the whole of one night and completed the work. On the next night he re-established communication when one of the cables was cut by shell fire a short time before the attack. Later, during an enemy attack, he collected a party of about 100 men, organized the defence, and held up the enemy's advance for about four hours, at a most critical time, until reinforced. He set a splendid example of courage and initiative.

ROBINSON, LAWRENCE, Lieut. (Acting Major), Royal Engineers. For conspicuous gallantry and devotion to duty. During an enemy attack he led his company forward to assist the infantry and established a defensive line. The gallant defence which he made materially checked the enemy's advance and was of the greatest importance in facilitating the recapture of the position later in the day. He showed great initiative and determination.

ROSS-SKINNER, HARRY, M.C., Capt., Highland Light Infantry. For conspicuous gallantry and devotion to duty. He held his position for two days against repeated enemy attacks and succeeded in recapturing some ground which had been lost. He carried out a very difficult relief with great skill, in spite of the close proximity of the enemy, and showed splendid leadership and resource throughout the operations.

ASHLEY-SCARLETT, HENRY, Capt. (Temporary Major), Reserve of Officers, Royal Fusiliers. For conspicuous gallantry and devotion to duty during two heavy enemy counter-attacks. He reorganized troops, who had been driven back, exposing himself freely in face of severe machine-gun and rifle fire, and displaying the greatest determination and coolness. In the second attack he showed splendid courage and resource in rallying and encouraging the men, and although blown out of a trench by a shell and badly shaken, he remained at his post until the battalion was relieved.

SCOTT, WILLIAM, M.C., Capt., Royal Irish Fusiliers, Special Reserve. For conspicuous gallantry and devotion to duty. When a strong point on the way to the assembly position was found to be still in the possession of the enemy he took command of the battalion, the commanding officer being wounded, and led them to the capture of the position with the greatest gallantry. His coolness, courage and leadership, under heavy fire at a critical moment were of the greatest value.

SKEY, CYRIL OSCAR, M.C., Temporary Capt., Royal Fusiliers. For conspicuous gallantry and devotion to duty in action. When left with one officer only, he reorganized the remnants of the battalion and by his good example and leadership succeeded in rallying the men, who had been much shaken, and holding on to his position for 48 hours.

SMELTZER, ARTHUR SIDNEY, M.C., Second Lieut. (Temporary Lieut.-Colonel), East Kent Regt. For conspicuous gallantry and devotion to duty. On the enemy attacking, he led a counter-attack and succeeded in clearing the enemy from a strong point, which he held until forced to withdraw. This withdrawal he effected with great skill, inflicting considerable losses on the enemy. Later, he took command of a composite battalion, and having checked the hostile advance for three hours, during which time he was heavily engaged, established a sound defensive flank, maintaining the line until relieved. He showed great coolness and disregard of danger, and inspired his men by his example of fearlessness and determination.

SOMERSET, HENRY ROBERT SOMERS FITZROY DE VERE, Lieut., Coldstream Guards. For conspicuous gallantry and devotion to duty. He led his men with great dash and determination in an attack, and, having captured the final objective, he organized and led an attack on a strong point, which he captured. He was driven out by heavy shell fire, but at once led another attack and regained and held the position and captured a field gun. He set a magnificent example of courage, initiative and leadership.

STIRKE, HENRY RICHARD, Temporary Major, Royal Dublin Fusiliers. For conspicuous gallantry and devotion to duty in an attack. He established an advanced headquarters when the objective was captured, superintended the consolidation of the position, and sent in most valuable reports. He showed untiring energy and initiative.

VAN SOMEREN, WILLIAM VERNON LOGAN, M.C., Temporary Major, Royal Fusiliers. For conspicuous gallantry and devotion to duty whilst in command of his battalion. He displayed the greatest courage in rallying the men of his own and other units, who had been heavily attacked. He showed great contempt of danger, and his behaviour amidst heavy shell and machine-gun fire, to which he was constantly exposed in reorganizing his battalion, undoubtedly put fresh heart into the men and enabled the position to be held.

VINCE, WILLIAM BERNARD, M.C., Capt. (Acting Major), London Regt. For conspicuous gallantry and devotion to duty in action. He led his battalion with great courage and skill in a counter-attack, which ejected the enemy from their trenches and resulted in the capture of many prisoners and eight machine guns.

WALSH, JAMES, Lieut. (Acting Major), Royal Inniskilling Fusiliers. For conspicuous gallantry and devotion to duty when in command of a battalion. During continual and heavy hostile attacks he visited all portions of his line, regardless of personal danger, and it was owing to his courage and ability in dealing with critical and constantly changing situations that his line was held. He set a splendid example of fearlessness and devotion to duty to all under him.

WILLIAMS, FRANCIS SEYMOUR, Lieut., Royal Engineers. For conspicuous gallantry and devotion to duty during an enemy attack. When the enemy were surrounding his position he withdrew his section gradually a short distance. Having collected a few stragglers and a small party of infantry he led them forward to the attack, drove the enemy back, and recaptured a battery which had been lost. Though again forced to withdraw he succeeded in establishing a defensive position, which he held with the greatest courage and determination.

WITHAM, ALEXANDER, Lieut. (Temporary Capt.), Royal Field Artillery. For conspicuous gallantry and devotion to duty. During an enemy attack he maintained the fire of his battery throughout the day in close support of the infantry, and finally man-handled his guns for 400 yards to a position whence the teams could hook in and saved all the guns. He showed the greatest coolness and resource.

WOODWARD, LESLIE COLLINS, Temporary Capt. (Acting Major), Royal Field Artillery. For conspicuous gallantry and devotion to duty when in command of a brigade. Hearing that the enemy had broken through on his right, he brought up three guns on to a crest, and for several hours fought his battery under heavy artillery, machine-gun and rifle fire, only stopping it when it was no longer possible to see. Throughout the day he displayed the greatest coolness and courage, and the work performed by his battery was invaluable at a critical time.

CANADIAN FORCE.

BROWN, ARCHIE FAIRBURN, Capt. (Acting Major), Infantry. For conspicuous gallantry and devotion to duty in an attack. He led his men over very difficult ground to the capture of the first objective and, when two other company commanders were wounded, he took command of all the assaulting troops and led a successful attack on the final objective. Though he was severely wounded, he remained at the captured position until it was consolidated. His courage and ability were instrumental in securing the success of the attack.

CARTER, ALBERT DESBRISAY, Major, Infantry and Royal Flying Corps. For conspicuous gallantry and devotion to duty. He destroyed two enemy aeroplanes, drove down several others out of control, and on two occasions attacked enemy troops from a low altitude. He showed great keenness and dash as a patrol leader.

CRAWFORD, JOHN KNOX, Capt., Infantry. For conspicuous gallantry and devotion to duty. He commanded two companies in an attack, and when the advance was held up and the situation became critical he rallied his men and led them successfully to the objective, capturing 59 prisoners and five machine guns. His initiative and determination were alone responsible for the success of the operation.

MACPHERSON, JOHN ROSS, Temporary Capt., Infantry. For conspicuous gallantry and devotion to duty. After a personal reconnaissance he led his company forward and surrounded and captured an enemy strong point together with its garrison, in spite of determined resistance and intense shell fire. His energy and initiative were entirely responsible for the success of the operation which straightened out the line for a further successful attack on the following day.

AUSTRALIAN IMPERIAL FORCE.

DIXON, ERNEST WILLIAM, Lieut., Imperial Camel Corps. For conspicuous gallantry and devotion to duty. During an attack, the enemy in turn counter-attacked on the flank of the battalion. He at once grasped the situation, took command of more than 200 men of various units, and held on to a portion of rising ground which was vital to the whole position. Having driven off the attack, he remained in command of the hill for two days, the retention of which vital point was almost entirely due to his personal example and courage.

WILLSALLEN, THOMAS LESLIE, Major, Light Horse Regt. For conspicuous gallantry and devotion to duty. With his squadron he encountered at night a party of the enemy who opened fire on his men. He called upon the enemy to surrender and succeeded in capturing the whole party of 230 of the enemy. He showed the greatest coolness and courage.

SOUTH AFRICAN FORCE.

HARTIGAN, MARCUS MICHAEL, Major, Defence Corps. For conspicuous gallantry and devotion to duty in an attack. He led the assaulting companies with great fearlessness, and was the first to enter the enemy's trench. He showed splendid powers of organization in directing the consolidation of the captured position, and inspired all ranks by his fine example.
(These became details of Bar, London Gazette, 22 Aug. 1918.)

London Gazette, 23 July, 1918.—"Admiralty, 23 July, 1918.—Honours for Services in the Operations against Zeebrugge and Ostend on the Night of the 22nd–23rd April, 1918. The King has been graciously pleased to give orders for the appointment of the undermentioned Officers to be Companions of the Distinguished Service Order."

OSBORNE, EDWARD OLIVER BRUDENELL SEYMOUR, Commander, R.N. Gunnery Officer on Staff of Vice-Admiral Dover. Was responsible for the fitting out of Vindictive with howitzers, mortars, pompom and machine guns. During the action displayed an exceptional combination of knowledge, skill, courage and devotion to duty in circumstances of great difficulty and danger.

GODSAL, ALFRED EDMUND, Commander, R.N. (Since killed in action). This officer in Brilliant led the Ostend blockships and stood in to the shore in the face of a tremendous barrage from the shore batteries, the wind having shifted and driven back the smoke screen at a critical moment. His spirit and bearing were those of a very gallant officer; he at once volunteered on hearing that another operation was in contemplation.

HELYAR, KENNETH CARY, Lieut.-Commander, R.N. (North Star). While his vessel was lying totally disabled and under heavy fire from shore batteries off Zeebrugge, displayed the greatest bravery and devotion to duty. He refused to leave his ship until she was sinking under his feet. Showed throughout an admirable example to those under him.

BODDIE, RONALD CHARLES, Engineer Lieut.-Commander, R.N. (Thetis). When both engines of Thetis had been disabled and the order to clear the engine-room given, the ship being in a sinking condition, this officer returned to the engine-room. He got the starboard engine going ahead, thereby enabling the ship to be turned into the fairway before she was sunk.

HOARE, KEITH ROBIN, D.S.C., Lieut. (Acting Lieut.-Commander), Royal Naval Volunteer Reserve. When Sirius was sinking he went alongside in his motor-launch under very heavy fire and took off 50 of the crew; then proceeding to Brilliant he took on board 16 men, and afterwards returning to Sirius took off remainder of officers and crew. He showed the utmost coolness and judgment in handling his vessel throughout.

CAMPBELL, HAROLD GEORGE, Lieut., R.N. (Daffodil). Handled his ship magnificently under extremely heavy and unceasing fire; but for his skill and devotion the storming parties from Vindictive could neither have landed, nor, having been landed, recovered. During the greater part of the time he was suffering from a wound in the eyes.

BONHAM-CARTER, STUART SUMNER, Lieut., R.N. (Intrepid). Handled his ship with great skill and coolness in a position of considerable danger under heavy fire. Great credit is due to him for his success in sinking Intrepid in the Bruges Canal.

DICKINSON, CECIL COURTENAY, Lieut., R.N. Was in command of the demolition party, displaying able leadership, and did splendid work on the mole. Was of the greatest assistance in securing Vindictive alongside and in facilitating the retirement from the mole. His work after the ship had left the mole was invaluable.

HENDERSON, OSCAR, Lieut., R.N. (Iris II.). When a shell carried away the port side of the bridge of his ship and caused a serious fire amongst the ammunition and bombs, he led a volunteer fire party with a hose on to the upper deck to quench the fire. Took over the command of the ship after Commander Gibbs had been mortally wounded.

WELMAN, ARTHUR ERIC POLE, D.S.C., Lieut., Royal Navy. During the action the units of the coastal motor-boat flotilla under his command were handled in a masterly manner, rendering the greatest service in screening and rescue work. He, himself, was in a coastal motor-boat, and was always in the most exposed positions across the harbour entrance covering Vindictive, Iris II. and Daffodil by smoke screen.

ANNESLEY, JOHN CAMPBELL, Lieut., R.N. In command of a coastal motor-boat showed great bravery when under heavy machine-gun and battery fire at short range. He continued to make smoke screens, and only withdrew when he and all his crew had been wounded.

BILLYARD-LEAKE, EDWARD WHALEY, Lieut., R.N. (Iphigenia). Exhibited the greatest bravery, and is deserving of much credit for placing his ship by calculated manœuvring under heavy fire exactly where he wanted to place her to block the canal, before blowing his charges and leaving the ship.

POCOCK, FRANK PEARCE, M.C., Surgeon, Royal Navy (Iris II.). By his devotion to duty, he undoubtedly saved many lives. When Iris II. was hit he at once commenced tending the wounded, and as all the sick-berth staff were killed, had all the work to do alone. After the dynamo was damaged, he had to work by candle and torchlight.

HOWELL-PRICE, JOHN, D.S.C., Lieut., Royal Naval Reserve (H.M. Submarine C3). His assistance in placing Submarine C3 between the piles of the viaduct before the fuse was lighted and she was abandoned was invaluable. His behaviour in a position of extreme danger was exemplary.

BOURKE, ROLAND, Lieut., R.N.V.R. Throughout the action showed the greatest coolness and skill in handling his motor-launch. Repeatedly went alongside Brilliant under very heavy fire and took off 38 officers and men. Took in tow and brought back to harbour another motor-launch which was damaged.

LITTLETON, HUGH ALEXANDER, Lieut., R.N.V.R. Handled his motor-launch in a magnificent manner. Embarked over 60 officers and men from Thetis under heavy machine-gun fire at close range. It was solely due to his courage and daring that his boat succeeded in making good her escape with the survivors of the Thetis.

CHATER, ARTHUR REGINALD, Capt., R.M.L.I. Was of the greatest assistance in keeping up communication between the various units of the battalion, and carried out his duties in a calm manner, which greatly contributed to the success of the operations. Gave great assistance in the preparation of the plan for the assault.

BROOKS, REGINALD ALEXANDER DALLAS, Lieut. (Acting Capt.), R.M.A. (Vindictive). He imbued his men with the highest degree of devotion to duty. The manner in which the howitzer, in its exposed position on the quarter deck, was used under his personal direction was very fine.

PESHALL, REV. CHARLES JOHN EYRE, B.A., Chaplain, Royal Navy (Vindictive). His cheerful encouragement and assistance to the wounded, calm demeanour during the din of battle, strength of character, and splendid comradeship were most conspicuous to all with whom he came in contact. Showed great physical strength, and did almost superhuman work in carrying wounded from the mole over the brows into Vindictive.

COOKE, THEODORE FREDERIC VERNON, Lieut., R.M.L.I. By his personal bravery under fire set a magnificent example to his men, and led them forward with the greatest courage and dash in spite of being wounded. He was wounded a second time whilst endeavouring to carry a wounded man back to the ship.

To receive a Bar to the Distinguished Service Order:

HARRISON, FRANCIS CHARLES, D.S.O., Lieut., Royal Navy. Was in charge of a coastal motor-boat division operating off Ostend. Led his division with conspicuous ability and resource, and carried out the whole programme up to the last moment. Laid out the calcium flares to mark the pier ends in a most efficient manner under a heavy fire from both shore batteries and machine guns.

London Gazette, 26 July, 1918.—"War Office, 26 July, 1918. His Majesty the King has been graciously pleased to approve of the following awards to the undermentioned Officers, in recognition of their gallantry and devotion to duty in the field. Awarded a Second Bar to the Distinguished Service Order."

CROFT, WILLIAM DENMAN, D.S.O., Major and Brevet Lieut.-Colonel (Temporary Brigadier-General), Scottish Rifles. For conspicuous gallantry and devotion to duty. He constantly showed the greatest courage and skill during many days' operations in command of a brigade. His H.Q. were placed close behind the firing line, as he rightly judged that the situation required his closest supervision. Owing to the movements of troops on his flank, it was necessary for the brigade, already weakened by many casualties, to hold a much-extended front. Without resolution of the highest order, and constantly exposing himself to machine-gun and rifle fire, it would have been impossible to hold the line so long and withdraw as a fighting organization.
(D.S.O. gazetted 1 Jan. 1917.)
(First Bar gazetted 10 Jan. 1917.)

GOSCHEN, ARTHUR ALEC, D.S.O., Major and Brevet Lieut.-Colonel, Royal Field Artillery. For conspicuous gallantry and devotion to duty during a retreat lasting for several days. He handled his brigade throughout with the greatest courage and efficiency, and it was mainly due to his personal efforts that after repeatedly inflicting heavy losses on the enemy, it came through these very difficult operations without losing a gun, and with comparatively small casualties.
(D.S.O. gazetted 22 Sept. 1901.)
(First Bar gazetted 26 Sept. 1917.)

HAIG, ROLAND, D.S.O., Major and Brevet Lieut.-Colonel (Temporary Brigadier-General), Rifle Brigade. For conspicuous gallantry and devotion to duty during a long period of active operations. On one occasion, when there was danger of a line giving way, he rode forward, regardless of personal danger, and re-established it. His great courage and untiring energy set a splendid example to all officers and men.
(D.S.O. gazetted 18 Feb. 1915.)
(First Bar gazetted 18 June, 1917.)

OGILVIE, SHOLTO STUART, D.S.O., Temporary Lieut. (Acting Lieut.-Colonel), Wiltshire Regt. For conspicuous gallantry and devotion to duty. When in command of his battalion, being hard pressed, he frequently went out into the open under heavy artillery and machine-gun fire, collecting stragglers from various units and organized them into fighting forces, which he then employed. It was mainly due to his supervision, and to the fact that he personally reorganized his battalion three or four times, that the withdrawal was able to be carried out in an orderly manner.
(D.S.O. gazetted 25 Aug. 1916.)
(First Bar gazetted 1 Jan. 1918.)

RIDDELL, EDWARD PIUS ARTHUR, D.S.O., Major and Brevet Lieut.-Colonel (Temporary Brigadier-General), Rifle Brigade. For conspicuous gallantry and devotion to duty during several days of severe fighting in rear-guard actions, when he repeatedly organized counter-attacks, and personally led two of them. After the whole of his staff had become casualties, and two of his commanding officers had been hit, his magnificent example, and total disregard of danger had the greatest effect in steadying his command.
(D.S.O. gazetted 11 Dec. 1916.)
(First Bar gazetted 26 Sept. 1917.)

SEAGRAVE, WILLIAM HENRY ERIK, D.S.O., Major (Acting Lieut.-Colonel), Highland Light Infantry. For conspicuous gallantry and devotion to duty. When the enemy developed a strong attack on an exposed flank, this officer, collecting H.Q. details, led two counter-attacks, restoring the situation. He then made a personal reconnaissance under heavy machine-gun fire, and re-organized the defence. His energy and resource throughout frequent attacks encouraged his men in keeping the line unbroken.
(D.S.O. gazetted 7 March, 1899.)
(First Bar gazetted 4 March, 1918.)

WESTON, SPENCER VAUGHAN PERCY, D.S.O., M.C., Capt. (Temporary Lieut.-Colonel), Royal Berkshire Regt. For conspicuous gallantry and devotion to duty during the trying period of a retreat. Despite heavy losses, he withdrew the battalion in good order, inflicting severe casualties on the enemy, and it was largely due to his coolness and personal courage that the retirement was so well carried out. He invariably displayed fine powers of leadership, and his splendid example was of the greatest encouragement to all ranks.
(D.S.O. gazetted 17 April, 1917.)
(First Bar gazetted 18 Feb. 1918.)

Awarded a Bar to the Distinguished Service Order:

ARMITAGE, CHARLES CLEMENT, D.S.O., Major and Brevet Lieut.-Colonel (Temporary Lieut.-Colonel), Royal Artillery. For conspicuous gallantry and devotion to duty during long operations, when he made several invaluable reconnaissances, on one occasion riding about the front in full view of the enemy, and under heavy fire, and rallying those who were inclined to fall back. Finally, when the battalion retired, he organized it on a new position, which was held until a further withdrawal was ordered.
(D.S.O. gazetted 3 June, 1916.)

BEASLEY, ROBERT LONGFIELD, D.S.O., Major (Temporary Lieut.-Colonel), Gloucestershire Regt. For conspicuous gallantry and devotion to duty in action. While visiting front-line posts he saw a hostile party creeping forward to rush the posts. By his prompt and energetic action the enemy were driven in towards our lines and several prisoners taken. He himself disposed of several of the enemy, and his great courage and utter disregard of personal danger inspired his men with his own fine spirit.
(D.S.O. gazetted 1 Jan. 1918.)

BIRT, CHARLES WILLIAM HOWARD, D.S.O., Temporary Major (Acting Lieut.-Colonel), Border Regt. For conspicuous gallantry and devotion to duty while handling his battalion in recent operations. He organized in one day three successful counter-attacks, which re-established the line. His personal gallantry and able leadership enabled his battalion to hold the corps line for 24 hours, until ordered to withdraw.
(D.S.O. gazetted 25 Aug. 1917.)

BORTHWICK, FRANCIS HENRY, D.S.O., Lieut.-Colonel, Royal Welsh Fusiliers. For conspicuous gallantry and devotion to duty. Under very heavy machine-gun and rifle fire he deployed his battalion with great coolness and rapidity and led them to the assault. The quick and clever handling of his men saved many casualties, while his bearing did much to encourage the men under heavy fire.
(D.S.O. gazetted 1 Jan. 1918.)

BREWIS, GEOFFREY SYDNEY, D.S.O., Capt. (Acting Lieut.-Colonel), Welsh Regt. For conspicuous gallantry and devotion to duty. When commanding a battalion during a withdrawal he inspired great confidence by his skilfulness and contempt for personal danger.
(D.S.O. gazetted 1 Jan. 1918.)

BROOKE, GEOFFRY FRANCIS HEREMON, D.S.O., M.C., Capt. and Brevet Major (Temporary Lieut.-Colonel), Lancers. For conspicuous gallantry and devotion to duty. During recent operations he showed exceptional gallantry and devotion to duty in conducting the operations of his regiment. The example he set under heavy shell and machine-gun fire had an excellent effect, and largely contributed to the success of the operations. He was of the greatest assistance, and his gallant services merited highest praise.
(D.S.O. gazetted 1 Jan. 1917.)

BROWNE, GEORGE EDWARD ALLENBY, D.S.O., M.C., Temporary Lieut.-Colonel, Liverpool Regt., Duke of Cornwall's Light Infantry. For conspicuous gallantry and devotion to duty. When in command of a battalion which had had little infantry training, he so efficiently handled his men as to materially assist in the successful withdrawal of the division, a detached platoon of his destroying a party of the enemy with the bayonet. His fine leading and skilful handling converted his slightly trained men into a highly competent infantry battalion.
(D.S.O. gazetted 1 Jan. 1918.)

BUCKLE, ARCHIBALD WALTER, D.S.O., Temporary Lieut.-Commander, Royal Naval Division, Royal Naval Volunteer Reserve. For conspicuous gallantry and devotion to duty when in command of a battalion. He repelled the enemy's attack, organized a counter-attack, and drove the enemy completely out of the menaced area. It was largely due to his courage, initiative and leadership that this important success was obtained.
(D.S.O. gazetted 4 March, 1918.)

BURT, ALFRED, D.S.O., Major and Brevet Lieut.-Colonel, Dragoon Guards. For conspicuous gallantry and devotion to duty during a hostile attack, when, although his left flank was exposed, and the enemy well in his rear, by his personal courage and example he so cheered and inspired his men, that he was able to keep his portion of the defence intact, and inflict severe casualties on the enemy.
(D.S.O. gazetted 18 June, 1917.)

CASEMENT, FRANCIS, D.S.O., Capt. (Acting Lieut.-Colonel), Royal Army Medical Corps. For conspicuous gallantry and devotion to duty when he evacuated all the wounded and salved a large quantity of surgical material, blankets and stretchers during a long retirement. His courage, coolness and resource were most marked during the whole of this trying period.
(D.S.O. gazetted 4 June, 1917.)

CHILD-VILLIERS, THE HONOURABLE ARTHUR GEORGE, D.S.O., Major, Yeomanry. For conspicuous gallantry and devotion to duty. He led his squadron dismounted in a counter-attack with remarkable skill and daring. Although wounded in the leg he refused to be evacuated to the dressing station, but continued to lead his men, and sent back valuable information as to the situation, although in great pain. He set a splendid example of coolness and endurance.
(D.S.O. gazetted 18 July, 1917.)

COFFIN, CLIFFORD, V.C., D.S.O., Lieut.-Colonel and Brevet Colonel (Temporary Brigadier-General), Royal Engineers. For conspicuous gallantry and devotion to duty during a long period of active operations, when he handled his brigade with great skill, especially when covering the withdrawal of the remainder of the division. On one occasion he commanded for a time the infantry of the division with marked success, and his personal courage and example at all times inspired all ranks with him.
(D.S.O. gazetted 1 Jan. 1917.)

COLQUHOUN, SIR IAN, Bart., D.S.O., Capt. and Brevet Major (Temporary Lieut.-Colonel), Scots Guards. For conspicuous gallantry and devotion to duty. He commanded his battalion in a most capable manner throughout six days' critical fighting. When reconnoitring in front of a village with six men, he met an enemy patrol, three of whom he killed with his revolver, being slightly wounded himself.
(D.S.O. gazetted 20 Oct. 1916.)

COLLINS, DUDLEY STUART, D.S.O., Major (Acting Lieut.-Colonel), Royal Engineers. For conspicuous gallantry and devotion to duty. During recent operations he rendered most valuable services in collecting details and organizing defences. Finding the main dressing station closed, he reopened it and kept it working until the arrival of the Cavalry Field Ambulance. He was always on the spot and throughout the operations showed great initiative and presence of mind.
(D.S.O. gazetted 3 June, 1916.)

CRAIGIE-HALKETT, HUGH MARJORIEBANKS, D.S.O., Major and Brevet Lieut.-Colonel (Temporary Lieut.-Colonel), Highland Light Infantry. For conspicuous gallantry and devotion to duty in command of his battalion during lengthy operations, and in the most desperate fighting. At one time he led the battalion forward to reinforce the corps' line, and it was entirely due to his splendid courage and example that the battalion, although much reduced in numbers, was able to hold back the enemy, and inflict very heavy casualties.
(D.S.O. gazetted 1 Jan. 1918.)

CRELLIN, WILLIAM ANDERSON WATSON, D.S.O., Capt. (Acting Lieut.-Colonel), Nottinghamshire and Derbyshire Regt. For conspicuous gallantry and devotion to duty. He organized and led a counter-attack, which restored the situation. He held the position until ordered to withdraw, by which time two companies had almost ceased to exist. With the remainder he carried on continuous fighting until he took over command of the brigade. Throughout the operations he showed great skill and unfailing cheerfulness, and was always on the spot whenever the situation became critical.
(D.S.O. gazetted 4 June, 1917.)

CROFTON, MALBY, D.S.O., Major (Acting Lieut.-Colonel), Royal Field Artillery. For conspicuous gallantry and devotion to duty. Whilst he was in close proximity to the batteries of another brigade during a withdrawal, a party of the enemy suddenly appeared in view on the crest near by, whereupon he immediately ordered the guns to be brought into action. The guns, however, were involved in very bad ground, and despite his personal efforts to attempt to man-handle each gun in turn into action, they all became bogged in shell-holes. He then proceeded towards the enemy in order to discover the exact nature of the situation, after which he himself withdrew, having satisfied himself that each gun had been rendered useless. During the whole day his skilful dispositions, imperturbable bearing, and personal efforts and encouragement inspired all ranks in the highest degree.
(D.S.O. gazetted 14 Jan. 1916.)

CURTIS, HUBERT MONTAGUE COTTON, D.S.O., Capt. (Acting Major), North Staffordshire Regt. For conspicuous gallantry and devotion to duty. In recent operations he rendered invaluable services. Hearing that the enemy had attacked he at once collected all details at the transport lines and brought them up to brigade headquarters. His timely arrival enabled a dangerous gap to be filled and the enemy's advance checked. On another occasion, after his detachment had been relieved and withdrawn to a reserve line, he rallied other troops who were falling back. Reorganizing the line he beat off three attacks on his flank. A splendid example of quick initiative and courage.
(D.S.O. gazetted 1 Jan. 1918.)

DANN, WILLIAM ROWLAND HARRIS, D.S.O., Major (Temporary Lieut.-Colonel), Bedfordshire Regt. For conspicuous gallantry and devotion to duty in action. Although vastly outnumbered by more than six to one, he held up the enemy for many hours until ordered to withdraw, which he did with great skill and in splendid order. He was untiring in his efforts, and by his gallantry and example stimulated the defence to the utmost. He was a tower of strength to the brigade.
(D.S.O. gazetted 18 July, 1917.)

DAVIDSON, HUGH ALLAN, D.S.O., M.B., Major (Temporary Lieut.-Colonel), Royal Army Medical Corps. For conspicuous gallantry and devotion to duty. When in command of his unit he maintained the advanced dressing station in spite of heavy shelling by the enemy, only withdrawing when ordered to do so. He visited the regimental aid posts under heavy shelling, and by his example and energy many casualties were evacuated which might otherwise have been lost.
(D.S.O. gazetted 1 Jan. 1917.)

DAWES, GEORGES, D.S.O., M.C., Capt. and Brevet Major (Acting Lieut.-Colonel), South Staffordshire Regt. For conspicuous gallantry and devotion to duty. With his battalion and some other troops he covered the retirement of the division, maintaining his ground for eight hours, until nearly surrounded, when he fought his way out. On another occasion, when the enemy outflanked his left, he saved the situation, reorganizing the line under heavy machine-gun fire.
(D.S.O. gazetted 18 Feb. 1918.)

DERVICHE-JONES, ARTHUR DANIEL, D.S.O., M.C., Capt., (Temporary Lieut.-Colonel), Royal Lancaster Regt. For conspicuous gallantry and devotion to duty in operations, when he maintained a splendid defence of a position, although outflanked to a depth of more than a mile, and it was mainly due to his courage and fine example that the position was held for hours, with a small force against great numbers of the enemy, to the last possible moment.
(D.S.O. gazetted 27 Oct. 1917.)

DRUMMOND, ROY MAXWELL, D.S.O., M.C., Temporary Capt., Royal Flying Corps. For conspicuous gallantry and devotion to duty. He attacked single-handed a formation of six enemy scouts, and brought down one, which was wrecked on striking the ground. He was then attacked by the remainder, and succeeded in bringing down one out of control before he himself, owing to engine trouble, was forced to land. He got the engine going again, and though stopped by engine trouble on four occasions, he managed to get back to his own lines, thus evading his pursuers. His performance was a gallant and successful one.
(D.S.O. gazetted 26 March, 1918.)

DUMBELL, CHARLES HAROLD, D.S.O., Major (Temporary Lieut.-Colonel), Nottinghamshire and Derbyshire Regt. For conspicuous gallantry and devotion to duty. When in command of a section of the reserve line, although gassed, he went up three times under intense artillery and machine-gun barrage, rallying men of various units who were falling back. Later, he organized a fresh defence line 400 yards from the attacking enemy, and then went out to bring in a wounded man who was lying 150 yards from the enemy.
(D.S.O. gazetted 1 Jan. 1917.)

EVES, THOMAS SWAN, D.S.O., M.B., Capt. (Acting Lieut.-Colonel), Royal Army Medical Corps. For conspicuous gallantry and devotion to duty. He was in charge of an advanced dressing station which was being heavily shelled by the enemy, and he personally and thoroughly carried out a complete change of organization. Later, he was superintending the loading of ambulance cars near a railway bridge which was a special target for the enemy's guns, and though twice thrown over and bruised by bursting shells he stuck to his post till all the wounded had been dressed and evacuated. His fine performance under continuous shell fire till the enemy were close upon him was a splendid example to all.
(D.S.O. gazetted 1 Jan. 1918.)

FAGAN, EDWARD ARTHUR, C.M.G., D.S.O., Lieut.-Colonel (Temporary Brigadier-General), Indian Army. For conspicuous gallantry and devotion to duty. When his front battalion was being overwhelmed he personally directed the action to be taken by other battalions, with the utmost disregard for his personal safety. He inspired all ranks with enthusiasm, and the success of the defence was largely due to his fine example.

(D.S.O. gazetted 1 Jan. 1917.)

FISHER, BERTIE DREW, D.S.O., Major and Brevet Lieut.-Colonel, Lancers. For conspicuous gallantry and devotion to duty while commanding his battalion. The battalion on his right had been penetrated, and he was outflanked by the enemy. He withdrew his men with great skill under very heavy shell fire to a fresh position, which he held throughout the day and handed over practically intact to another division next morning. The importance of this position was great, and by holding it as he did he rendered fine service.

(D.S.O. gazetted 18 Feb. 1915.)

FITZGERALD, FITZGERALD GABBETT, D.S.O., Lieut.-Colonel, Royal Army Medical Corps. For conspicuous gallantry and devotion to duty. When his casualty clearing station was heavily shelled he not only evacuated his patients to places of safety, but salved practically all the stores of his unit. This action was performed twice over, and on both occasions his courage and ability were pre-eminent.

(D.S.O. gazetted 1 Jan. 1917.)

FOORD, WILLIAM PERCY STILLES, D.S.O., Major (Temporary Lieut.-Colonel), Gloucestershire Regt. For conspicuous gallantry and devotion to duty when in command of a battalion in action. For two days he maintained his position, fighting continuously, and with his flanks several times dangerously exposed. It was due to his leadership and fine qualities that the defence was maintained and heavy losses inflicted on the enemy.

(D.S.O. gazetted 1 Jan. 1917.)

GOODERSON, VALENTINE EDGAR, D.S.O., Temporary Major, Highland Light Infantry. For conspicuous gallantry and devotion to duty. When the enemy attacked and drove in the left of the line, he reorganized the battalion a short distance behind and then gallantly leading it forward, restored the position. By his timely action he saved the left flank of the brigade from being turned. Later, when in charge of the rear-guard, he handled his men with great ability and kept back the enemy until the other brigades had been withdrawn.

(D.S.O. gazetted 1 Jan. 1917.)

GROGAN, GEORGE WILLIAM ST. GEORGE, C.M.G., D.S.O., Major and Brevet Lieut.-Colonel (Temporary Brigadier-General), Worcestershire Regt. For conspicuous gallantry and devotion during a long period of active operations. On one occasion, when in command of the left of the division, it was mainly due to his personal efforts that the line was maintained and extended when troops on the left were withdrawn. Whenever the position became critical he went forward himself to restore the situation, and his splendid example of courage and endurance greatly inspired all ranks.

(D.S.O. gazetted 11 May, 1917.)

GUINNESS, THE HONOURABLE WALTER EDWARD, D.S.O., Major, Yeomanry. For conspicuous gallantry and devotion to duty as brigade major throughout operations and during a subsequent retirement. He carried out continual reconnaissances under heavy shell fire and with an absolute disregard of danger, and on one occasion he personally assisted to re-establish the line, leading forward men who had fallen back. His fine example and untiring energy and his reports throughout were invaluable.

(D.S.O. gazetted 26 Sept. 1917.)

GURNEY, CLEMENT HENDERSON, D.S.O., Temporary Lieut.-Colonel, East Yorkshire Regt. For conspicuous gallantry and devotion to duty. When his right flank was exposed owing to the troops on that flank giving way, he restored the situation, capturing several prisoners. He personally superintended and successfully carried out a very difficult withdrawal by night, and throughout the fighting visited all parts of the firing line, encouraging the defence by his splendid example.

(D.S.O. gazetted 14 Jan. 1916 [correct date 1 Jan. 1917]).

HALLIDAY, WILLIAM JOHN FREDERICK, D.S.O., Major, Royal Field Artillery. For conspicuous gallantry and devotion to duty. While bringing his battery back from taking part in a raid, the enemy commenced to shell heavily the road along which it was necessary for the battery to pass. He personally supervised the passing of every man and carriage through the danger zone. When the guns and teams had been got away, he remained with a wounded driver, sheltering him with his body from splinters, until the arrival of the ambulance. He set a most inspiring example of coolness and resource.

(D.S.O. gazetted 16 Aug. 1917.)

HUNT, JOHN PATRICK, D.S.O., Temporary Capt. (Acting Lieut.-Colonel), Royal Dublin Fusiliers. For conspicuous gallantry and devotion to duty. He formed at short notice an improvised force, comprised of troops from several different units, and handled it with great skill. He contributed largely towards the success of a counter-attack, when he rallied his men at a very critical period and drove the enemy back out of a village. Again, later, by his fearless example, he restored the situation, when the enemy were on the point of breaking through the line.

(D.S.O. gazetted 20 Oct. 1916.)

IMPEY, GEORGE HASTINGS, D.S.O., Major (Temporary Lieut.-Colonel), Royal Sussex Regt. For conspicuous gallantry and devotion to duty in action. When his battalion was attacked and cut in two, causing it to fall back, he promptly turned out his battalion headquarters and a few men who had become lost in its neighbourhood, organized them into a garrison, and held the position with great courage and skill against all attacks for several hours, thus saving a most critical situation and allowing time for the battalion to reform, counter-attack, and regain their line.

(D.S.O. gazetted 1 Jan. 1917.)

KELLY, HARRY BEATTY D.S.O. M.B., Major (Temporary Lieut.-Colonel), Royal Army Medical Corps. For conspicuous gallantry and devotion to duty. When the camp, in which over 40 stretcher cases were collected, was heavily shelled, he collected the bearers and removed the wounded to a position of safety. Again, when the infantry were being withdrawn, he collected casualties with the bearers and carried them through a heavy barrage to the ambulance cars, thus saving several lives and setting a fine example to his men.

(D.S.O. gazetted 1 Jan. 1917.)

KENNEDY, JOHN, D.S.O., Major and Brevet Lieut.-Colonel (Temporary Brigadier-General), Argyll and Sutherland Highlanders. For conspicuous gallantry and devotion to duty. When the situation required the closest handling of the brigades, he commanded his in a most skilful and fearless manner during a daylight retirement, having his horse shot under him by rifle fire. His brigade rendered conspicuous service and came out of a severe battle with its morale undiminished, for which his example and leadership were much responsible.

(D.S.O. gazetted 14 Jan. 1916.)

KIRKPATRICK, HARRY FEARNLEY, D.S.O., Major (Acting Lieut.-Colonel), Reserve of Officers, East Kent Regt. For conspicuous gallantry and devotion to duty while in command of his battalion. The enemy attacked and drove in the troops of another division which caused the left flank of his battalion to become much exposed. By his magnificent courage and leadership he succeeded in restoring the situation.

(D.S.O. gazetted 1 Jan. 1918.)

LAING, RODERIC, D.S.O., M.C., Major (Acting Lieut.-Colonel), Seaforth Highlanders. For conspicuous gallantry and devotion to duty during a hostile attack, when he made a personal reconnaissance under very heavy artillery fire and brought back most valuable information to brigade headquarters. The success with which the attack was driven off, and over 100 prisoners taken, was greatly due to his splendid courage and skill. Throughout all operations his invaluable services have maintained the finest discipline and morale in his battalion.

(D.S.O. gazetted 1 Jan. 1918.)

LAWRENSON, REGINALD ROBERT, D.S.O., Major (Temporary Lieut.-Colonel), West India Regt. For conspicuous gallantry and devotion to duty when in command of his battalion during constant attacks. It was owing to his indomitable spirit, personal example and fine leadership that the battalion maintained its position throughout the operations. One night he went to brigade headquarters to report personally, and was then much exhausted, but with characteristic pluck returned to his battalion and handled it in a most efficient manner during the retirement.

(D.S.O. gazetted 4 June, 1917.)

LITTLE, WILLIAM BENJAMIN, D.S.O., M.C., Capt. (Acting Lieut.-Colonel), East Lancashire Regt. For conspicuous gallantry and devotion to duty during several days of severe fighting when in command of a composite battalion. His force was constantly depleted by casualties and augmented by stragglers. During the whole period, by energy, courage and force of character, he held his men together under enemy attacks, and led them in several counter-attacks. Owing to his magnificent example his men, who were in no way organized and very exhausted, behaved with praiseworthy steadiness.

(D.S.O. gazetted 4 June, 1917.)

LLOYD, EVAN COLCLOUGH, D.S.O., Major (Acting Lieut.-Colonel), Royal Irish Regt. For conspicuous gallantry and devotion to duty in command of his battalion in action. In spite of very heavy enemy attacks, preceded by gas and accompanied by a dense bombardment, he succeeded in maintaining his position, although nearly surrounded. A subsequent counter-attack enabled him to withdraw the battalion, inflicting casualties on the enemy in doing so. His courage and tenacity gained valuable time to reorganize the defence in the rear of the battle zone. Later he was severely wounded.

(D.S.O. gazetted 1 Jan. 1918.)

McCLINTOCK, STANLEY ROBERT, D.S.O., Major (Acting Lieut.-Colonel), Gordon Highlanders. For conspicuous gallantry and devotion to duty. While in command of his battalion this officer, when the enemy had broken through the front, support and reserve lines, took up a defensive position with his battalion headquarter details, and held up the attack. Later, while in command of the remnants of his battalion, he showed great tenacity in holding on to the last during the various stages of the withdrawal.

(D.S.O. gazetted 4 June, 1917.)

MELLOR, ABEL, D.S.O., Major (Temporary Lieut.-Colonel), Royal Horse Artillery. For conspicuous gallantry and devotion to duty. When the enemy was shelling canal bridges with salvos of 4.2 shells, causing great confusion to the stream of traffic, this officer, regardless of danger, stood on the bridge for over an hour regulating the transport, and it was entirely due to his single-handed efforts that order was restored.

(D.S.O. gazetted 3 June, 1916.)

METCALFE, FRANCIS EDWARD, C.M.G., D.S.O., Temporary Lieut.-Colonel, Lincolnshire Regt. For conspicuous gallantry and devotion to duty in the defence of a position. By his skilful leadership and ability, his battalion succeeded in beating off six determined attacks by the enemy. He personally directed his battalion during the operation, when his courage and cheerfulness were the greatest inspiration to the entire garrison.

(D.S.O. gazetted 3 June, 1916.)

MOULTON-BARRETT, EDWARD MORRIS, D.S.O., Major and Brevet Lieut.-Colonel (Temporary Lieut.-Colonel), Northumberland Fusiliers. For conspicuous gallantry and devotion to duty. Throughout two days' fighting his courage and resource were an example to all. On receipt of orders he cleverly withdrew his battalion from close contact with the enemy, without a casualty. Some days after he was wounded while holding his headquarters in the support line against heavy hostile attacks, using a rifle himself.

(D.S.O. gazetted 23 June, 1915.)

NORTON, GILBERT PAUL, D.S.O., Lieut.-Colonel, West Riding Regt. For conspicuous gallantry and devotion to duty during lengthy operations, during which he displayed the greatest courage and skill, firstly, in defending a position, and later in organizing and leading a counter-attack. His complete grasp of the situation and fine personal example inspired all ranks with confidence, and greatly contributed in maintaining good order.

(D.S.O. gazetted 14 Jan. 1916.)

PIPON, ROBERT HENRY, D.S.O., M.C., Major (Temporary Lieut.-Colonel), Royal Fusiliers. For conspicuous gallantry and devotion to duty. When the enemy unexpectedly appeared in the rear of the brigade he attacked them with his battalion headquarters personnel, and held them while he brought back his two support companies and elements of other units. With the line thus formed he covered the withdrawal of the rest of the brigade next day under the heaviest fire. He twice assumed command of the brigade at critical moments and conducted the operations with skill and judgment.

(D.S.O. gazetted 26 July, 1917.)

PORTAL, CHARLES FREDERICK ALGERNON, D.S.O., Temporary Lieut., (Temporary Major), Royal Engineers, Special Reserve and Royal Air Force. For conspicuous gallantry and devotion to duty. During a period of four months, chiefly under adverse weather conditions, he repeatedly carried out successful raids by day and night, his ingenuity and daring enabling him to drop many tons of bombs on important enemy posts. One night he crossed the lines five times, only landing between each flight to replenish with bombs. Another day he took on single-handed five enemy machines, and drove down three of them— a most gallant and splendid feat. On another day, despite thick mist, he registered one of our batteries on an enemy battery, causing the destruction of one pit and obtaining one fire and two explosions; and another day, flying for 5½ hours, he carried out two very successful counter-battery shoots, observing 350 rounds. He has always set a most magnificent example to the squadron under his command.

(D.S.O. gazetted 18 July, 1917.)

POWELL, JOHN, D.S.O., M.B., Lieut.-Colonel, Royal Army Medical Corps. For conspicuous gallantry and devotion to duty during a long period of active operations. Owing to the great number of extemporised formations from the divisions, which increased continually from day to day, the task of providing adequate medical facilities was one of extreme difficulty. By his indefatigable energy and powers of organization he successfully met all demands, and completed the evacuation of all wounded with splendid efficiency. On one occasion, hearing some wounded had been left behind, he went himself, under heavy and

continual shell and machine-gun fire, with three ambulances, and brought them in. Throughout, his conduct was beyond all praise.
(D.S.O. gazetted 3 June, 1918.)

PRIDEAUX-BRUNE, DENYS EDWARD, D.S.O., Capt. and Brevet Major (Temporary Lieut.-Colonel), Rifle Brigade. For conspicuous gallantry and devotion to duty. He commanded his battalion and elements of other units with consummate skill, gallantry and disregard of personal danger. He stubbornly defended positions one after another, then skilfully extricated his men and organized fresh ones. He showed great presence of mind, initiative, and resource at all times.
(D.S.O. gazetted 18 July, 1917.)

PRIOR, BERNARD HENRY LEATHES, D.S.O., Lieut.-Colonel, Norfolk Regt. For conspicuous gallantry and devotion to duty. Throughout two days of an enemy advance, and until wounded, he set a splendid example of coolness and courage under most trying conditions, personally supervising the readjustments which had to be made to meet the enemy attacks, and the gallant resistance offered by his battalion was largely due to his magnificent example of fearless determination.
(D.S.O. gazetted 4 June, 1917.)

REVELL, JOHN WALTER, D.S.O., Temporary Major, Royal Engineers. For conspicuous gallantry and devotion during long operations in command of a field company attached to an infantry brigade. When the brigade was in lack of men, and the enemy was pressing its withdrawal, he, with great coolness and courage, covered with his company the right flank, and maintained his position until the brigade had been withdrawn. He then destroyed all huts and blew up the water-mains, thereby depriving the enemy of a billeting area and water supply.
(D.S.O. gazetted 1 Jan. 1918.)

RITSON, JOHN ANTHONY SYDNEY, D.S.O., M.C., Capt. (Temporary Lieut.-Colonel), Durham Light Infantry. For conspicuous gallantry and devotion to duty in command of his battalion in a series of rearguard actions lasting for several days. During this period he displayed exceptional courage and judgment in a series of withdrawals to fresh positions and repelling attacks, causing the enemy heavy casualties. He held on to his last position, repelling all attacks with severe enemy losses until ordered to withdraw, which he succeeded in doing under exceptional difficulties and heavy fire.
(D.S.O. gazetted 27 Oct. 1917.)

ROLLO, GEORGE, D.S.O., Temporary Lieut., Liverpool Regt. For conspicuous gallantry and devotion to duty. In a most admirable manner he collected men from other divisions and organized the defence. He was not at that time in command of his battalion. He subsequently took command of his battalion, and handled them with magnificent skill and coolness during the rearguard action that followed. His splendid courage was an example to all.
(D.S.O. gazetted 1 Jan. 1917.)

ROWBOTHAM, JAMES, D.S.O., M.C., Capt. (Acting Lieut.-Colonel), Highland Light Infantry. For conspicuous gallantry and devotion to duty. He continually visited the front line of his battalion, which was under heavy shell fire and gas, and brought in valuable information. On one occasion, finding the enemy were making progress on his left by bombing and using flammenwerfer, he rallied the men and restored the situation. Subsequently, while directing the defence in a very exposed position, he was severely wounded.
(D.S.O. gazetted 19 Nov. 1917.)

SHAW, LAWRENCE DREW, D.S.O., M.B., Temporary Capt. (Acting Lieut.-Colonel), Royal Army Medical Corps. For conspicuous gallantry and devotion to duty. He was placed in charge of the forward division of the combined field ambulances. Although constantly exposed to heavy shell and machine-gun fire, he organized the system of evacuation and extended it to neighbouring divisional units. By his inspiring example and disregard of danger he ensured a complete and successful evacuation of the wounded.
(D.S.O. gazetted 4 June, 1917.)

SMITH, HERBERT CHARLES HYDE, D.S.O., Major (Acting Lieut.-Colonel) Scottish Rifles. For conspicuous gallantry and devotion to duty. During a ten days' withdrawal he handled his battalion with great gallantry, and repeatedly organized lines of resistance. By his personal example he induced men to defend positions in a most stubborn way, although very much outnumbered, and more than once, thanks to his cool intrepidity, his battalion beat off very heavy attacks and inflicted great loss on the enemy.
(D.S.O. gazetted 4 June, 1917.)

SPOONER, ARTHUR HARDWICKE, C.M.G., D.S.O., Major and Brevet Lieut.-Colonel (Temporary Brigadier-General), Lancashire Fusiliers. For conspicuous gallantry and devotion to duty. He commanded his brigade in very difficult positions with consummate coolness and skill, and on every occasion displayed great initiative and resource. The clever handling of his brigade bettered the situation on the front of two divisions.
(D.S.O. gazetted 18 Feb. 1915.)

STAFFORD, RONALD SEMPILL HOWARD, D.S.O., Lieut. (Acting Lieut.-Colonel), King's Royal Rifle Corps, Special Reserve. For conspicuous gallantry and devotion to duty. During a rearguard action lasting over a period of five days he behaved with consistent coolness and courage. On one occasion, the left flank of his battalion having been driven in and the battalion ordered to establish a defensive flank, he carried out a personal reconnaissance under direct machine-gun fire, gaining valuable information as to the dispositions on his right flank, and personally placed each company in its position. During this time the enemy was fast approaching in massed formation, and artillery fire was opened on his battalion at point-blank range. His total disregard of danger and quickness of decision saved the situation on this and other occasions.
(D.S.O. gazetted 20 Oct. 1916.)

STANLEY-CLARKE, ARTHUR CHRISTOPHER LANCELOT, D.S.O., Capt. (Temporary Lieut.-Colonel), Scottish Rifles. For conspicuous gallantry and devotion to duty when in command of his battalion. The enemy had driven in the troops on his right, and, seeing the danger of the situation, he went forward, and after a personal reconnaissance organized a counter-attack, which was very successful, and which prevented the enemy from advancing further that day. Throughout the operations he set a fine example of initiative and courage.
(D.S.O. gazetted 1 Jan. 1918.)

THOMSON, GEORGE, D.S.O., M.C., Capt. (Temporary Lieut.-Colonel), Yorkshire Light Infantry. For conspicuous gallantry and devotion to duty in action. Although his battalion was used up to reinforce the whole line, he displayed the greatest courage and energy in his efforts to clear up the situation and encourage the defence. He personally visited the left flank when it became outflanked, and disposed the men for its safety, setting a magnificent example, by a total disregard of danger, until finally he was wounded.
(D.S.O. gazetted 1 Jan. 1918.)

TOMKINSON, HENRY ARCHDALE, D.S.O., Major (Acting Lieut.-Colonel), Dragoons. For conspicuous gallantry and devotion to duty in action. When the enemy had penetrated a line, and the infantry were retiring in some disorder, by his quick decision and selection of fire positions he succeeded in holding up the attack in spite of the heavy machine-gun fire. Finally, when the line was re-established, he walked up and down in the open, fully exposed to heavy fire, encouraging the men, until he was badly wounded. His splendid example and leadership saved a most critical situation.
(D.S.O. gazetted 4 June, 1917.)

TORRENS, GEORGE LESLIE, D.S.O., Capt. (Temporary Lieut.-Colonel), Lancashire Fusiliers. For conspicuous gallantry and devotion to duty in handling his battalion with the utmost skill in the defence of the line, and also when in command of the rearguard, and being closely pressed by the enemy, in covering the withdrawal of the brigade. In subsequent actions he always had his battalion well in hand, and displayed splendid leadership and courage.
(D.S.O. gazetted 3 June, 1916.)

TYRRELL, WILLIAM, D.S.O., M.C., M.B., Capt. (Acting Lieut.-Colonel), Royal Army Medical Corps, Special Reserve. For conspicuous gallantry and devotion to duty when in charge of a line of evacuation. He worked continuously for six days, and it was due to his gallantry, organization, and energy that touch was maintained so efficiently with the brigades, and so many casualties evacuated. He displayed great courage and coolness throughout, and inspired those under him by his fine example.
(D.S.O. gazetted 1 Jan. 1918.)

WATSON, CAMPBELL NEWELL, D.S.O., Temporary Major (Acting Lieut.-Colonel), Liverpool Regt. For conspicuous gallantry and devotion to duty while in command of his battalion during lengthy operations. His courage, cheerfulness, and resource at all times set a splendid example to his officers and all ranks under him, and his tenacity during several rearguard actions undoubtedly inflicted severe casualties on the enemy, and delayed his progress.
(D.S.O. gazetted 26 Sept. 1917.)

WHITEHEAD, HECTOR FRASER, D.S.O., Temporary Major (Acting Lieut.-Colonel), Northumberland Fusiliers. For conspicuous gallantry and devotion to duty in operations, when by his gallantry, energy, and marked ability he was able to keep his battalion in a high state of offensive spirit. Later, when his men were really tired out after ten days' continuous fighting and marching, his splendid example encouraged them to hold on, and even to counter-attack under heavy artillery and machine-gun fire.
(D.S.O. gazetted 1 Jan. 1918.)

WILKINSON, WILLIAM THORNTON, D.S.O., Major and Brevet Lieut.-Colonel, King's Own Scottish Borderers. For conspicuous gallantry and devotion to duty. Under difficult circumstances he extricated his battalion in good order, holding two rearguard positions to cover the withdrawal. On another occasion, with two battalions, he held on to some high ground from 9 a.m. to 5 p.m., although his right flank was in the air. Exposed to heavy machine-gun fire, he went up and down the line encouraging his men, being subsequently wounded in the head.
(D.S.O. gazetted 27 Sept. 1901.)

WINSER, CHARLES RUPERT PETER, D.S.O., Capt. (Temporary Brigadier-General), Reserve of Officers, South Lancashire Regt. For conspicuous gallantry and devotion to duty during the progress of repeated enemy attacks. He displayed the utmost skill, coolness, and gallantry whilst in command of his brigade, rallying the men, reforming the line, and inspiring all those about him with confidence by his complete disregard of personal danger.
(D.S.O. gazetted 25 Aug. 1916.)

WINTER, ERNEST ARTHUR, D.S.O., M.C., Temporary Lieut.-Colonel, Royal Fusiliers. For conspicuous gallantry and devotion to duty. When his battalion received orders to withdraw from the line they had been holding since the previous evening he, though suffering severely from the effects of gas, successfully withdrew his battalion and organized his headquarter runners and servants into a rearguard, being himself the last to leave. On another occasion, though completely under enemy observation, he successfully withdrew his transport, his cool courage causing the men to successfully carry out the dispositions made by him.
(D.S.O. gazetted 1 Jan. 1918.)

CANADIAN FORCE.

CLARKE, FREDERICK FIELDHOUSE, D.S.O., Lieut.-Colonel, Canadian Railway Troops. For conspicuous gallantry and devotion to duty during a hostile attack lasting for four days. He organized from his battalion 16 Lewis gun teams, and made all arrangements for ammunition and supplies to be brought up to the front line by his own lorries. Except for the higher direction of the defence, the unit was entirely self-contained. The promptitude and alacrity with which this unit responded for volunteers, the splendid manner with which the defence was organized, the coolness and sustained enthusiasm displayed by all ranks under his command, were largely due to the courage, inspiring example, and fine leadership of the commanding officer.
(D.S.O. gazetted 1 Jan. 1918.)

Awarded the Distinguished Service Order:

ANDERSON, GEORGE HENRY GARSTIN, M.C., Second Lieut. (Acting Capt.), Rifle Brigade. For conspicuous gallantry and devotion to duty during ten days of continuous fighting, when he carried out the duties of adjutant with exceptional skill under almost impossible conditions. By his splendid example of courage and cheerfulness under the hottest fire, he was mainly instrumental in keeping the battalion well in hand, when it might otherwise have become demoralized, and in every withdrawal he was always the last to leave. When any stand was made he moved about, regardless of personal danger, encouraging the men, and although frequently without food or drink, and exhausted from lack of sleep, his exertions for the good of the battalion never failed. No praise can be too high for his devotion to duty.

ANDERSON, HORACE, M.C., Capt. (Acting Major), Royal Irish Regt., Special Reserve. For conspicuous gallantry and devotion to duty. He was sent to take a hill with two companies. In advancing they were exposed to heavy machine-gun fire, causing some wavering. He showed complete disregard of danger, and by his fine example encouraged his men and took his objective.

ANDERSON, PATRICK CAMPBELL, M.C., Capt. (Temporary Major), Seaforth Highlanders. For conspicuous gallantry and devotion to duty during seven critical days of a withdrawal, when he commanded his battalion with the greatest courage and skill under most trying conditions. Again and again he rallied his men, and, on his own initiative, held on to vital points, keeping his men steady by his magnificent example. When relieved, noticing that some of the troops then in the line were slightly unsteady, he remained with them for several hours, helping to keep the situation in hand. His able leadership and constant courage were of inestimable value during these critical days.

ARMSTRONG, WILLIAM FORTESCUE, M.C., Capt. (Acting Major), Royal Garrison Artillery. For conspicuous gallantry and devotion to duty during a period of withdrawals. He used his guns to the very last moment in covering the infantry, and had to run them back under machine-gun fire.

ARTHUR, BECKHAM, Major, Machine Gun Corps. For conspicuous gallantry and devotion to duty when handling his motor machine-gun battery during a defence, and the subsequent withdrawal. It was largely due to his action that two battalions of infantry were enabled to carry out a successful retirement, for his guns inflicted heavy losses on the enemy and materially held up their advance.

ATKINSON, JOSEPH DEAN, Temporary Major, Liverpool Regt. For conspicuous gallantry and devotion to duty. By skilful disposition of Lewis guns during the withdrawal of a brigade, he prevented the enemy from occupying a ridge, thereby enabling the move to be carried out without a casualty. Later, he assisted in a withdrawal from a very difficult position, with the enemy on three sides, successfully accomplishing it without loss, and bringing back all the wounded.

BALL, KENNETH MOORE, Major, Royal Field Artillery. For conspicuous gallantry and devotion to duty during an attack, when, although wounded at the commencement of the bombardment, he remained in command of his battery throughout the day and rendered most valuable assistance in driving off repeated attacks. His courage and skill throughout the operations were most marked.

BATES, CHARLES, Second Lieut., South Staffordshire Regt., Special Reserve. For conspicuous gallantry and devotion to duty. He went forward, through a heavy barrage, to a commanding position, and lay there, under fire, for three hours, sending back valuable information. Then, returning to his platoon, he altered his dispositions and held up the enemy, in spite of repeated efforts to attack and turn his flank. Although twice wounded, he stayed with his command, which he withdrew the following day, when he again stopped the enemy's advance by getting a Lewis gun into position on a railway embankment and firing it himself until all ammunition was exhausted. He then was able to withdraw.

BATTEN-POOLL, JOHN ALEXANDER, M.C., Capt., Lancers. For conspicuous gallantry and devotion to duty in reconnoitring under heavy fire and personally driving the enemy back with bombs over a canal. Later, when the enemy had entered the trenches on his flank, he organized a counter-attack and restored the situation. Though wounded, he continued to direct his squadron, until he was wounded a second time.

BAUDAINS, GEORGE LA CROIX, M.C., Lieut. (Temporary Capt.), London Regt. For conspicuous gallantry and devotion to duty in action. When in command of the right front company of his battalion, a heavy enemy attack drove back the battalion on his right, leaving his flank exposed. In spite of this, he held his support line position against greatly superior numbers, and inflicted heavy losses on the enemy. Subsequently he was entirely cut off, but continued to hold on until he judged that the troops in his rear had had time to take up a new position, when he fought his way out, being wounded while so doing. By his splendid courage and coolness he set a fine example to all with him.

BEAK, DANIEL MARCUS WILLIAM, M.C., Temporary Commander, Royal Naval Division, Royal Naval Volunteer Reserve. For conspicuous gallantry and devotion to duty. During a night attack by the enemy the right flank of his division was left in a dangerous position. He arranged for a flank to be formed in that direction, and subsequently covered the retirement of two brigades with a composite rear-guard which he organized and commanded. His initiative and presence of mind greatly assisted in extricating these brigades from a very difficult situation. Throughout, the skilful handling of his battalion was particularly noticeable.

BIRD, MALCOLM GELLING, Major, Lancashire Fusiliers. For conspicuous gallantry and devotion to duty when, although wounded, he continued to command his battalion, until severely wounded a second time, at a very critical moment, when his gallantry and resource were of valuable service.

BIRNIE, EDWARD D'ARCY, M.C., Temporary Lieut. (Acting Capt.), Border Regt. For conspicuous gallantry and devotion to duty. When hard pressed by the enemy he led several counter-attacks against their bombing parties, and for hours kept large forces of the enemy at bay. At one time he took up a position on the parapet, and (being a marksman) accounted for many of them with a rifle. Finally, when his position became untenable, he successfully withdrew his men. He displayed exceptional skill and courage in the face of great odds.

BOWYER, CHARLES HASTINGS, Temporary Capt., Royal Fusiliers (Lieut., South African Defence Force). For conspicuous gallantry and devotion to duty. By his promptitude in forming a defensive flank he was instrumental in breaking up the enemy's attack, and more than once he saved his battalion from an awkward situation. When the officer commanding his battalion was missing, he assumed command and displayed fine courage and efficiency.

BLACKBURN, ERIC DEANE, M.C., Temporary Capt. (Acting Major), Tank Corps. For conspicuous gallantry and devotion to duty when in command of a company of tanks in a counter-attack. He personally led the tanks on foot under heavy machine-gun fire. Again, hearing that the enemy were advancing on a village, he rushed a Lewis gun party up on a lorry, riding forward to reconnoitre, and denied the village to the enemy, on whom he inflicted heavy casualties and took about 20 prisoners. He was responsible for rallying the infantry in the vicinity, and throughout the whole action showed the greatest determination and total disregard for his own safety.

BROOK, FRANK, M.C., Lieut. (Acting Major), Yorkshire Light Infantry. For conspicuous gallantry and devotion to duty. During an enemy attack on his battalion he showed great coolness under heavy machine-gun and rifle fire at close range, and greatly assisted a successful withdrawal. The same night, when owing to a misunderstanding an unauthorized withdrawal was taking place, he rallied the men, pushed forward with tanks, and restored the line. At various times, by his fine personal example, he maintained the moral of the troops.

CALDER, ARCHIBALD, Temporary Second Lieut., Tank Corps. For conspicuous gallantry and devotion to duty when in charge of eight Lewis guns. On five consecutive days the enemy made heavy attacks, forcing our troops to retire. Second Lieut. Calder invariably displayed the greatest gallantry and coolness in rallying retiring men, leading them back to their original positions, and in bringing his guns into action in support of the defence, holding up the attacks, and causing very heavy enemy casualties. In stopping one attack he three times expended all his ammunition. He set a splendid example of courage and determination.

CAMPBELL, AUBONE CHARLES, Major, Royal Scots (Capt., King's Own Scottish Borderers). For conspicuous gallantry and devotion to duty, when for six days he handled his battalion in a series of rearguard actions, and was seriously wounded. At a critical moment he personally commanded the battalion rearguard, and once succeeded in slipping away when the enemy was right round his flank.

CAPE, HERBERT ANDERSON, Major (Temporary Lieut.-Colonel), Lancers. For conspicuous gallantry and devotion to duty. At a critical time he displayed remarkable coolness and skill in organizing defences. His fine example stimulated all ranks.

CHAMPION, CHARLES COVERLEY, Temporary Major (Acting Lieut.-Colonel), South Lancashire Regt. For conspicuous gallantry and devotion to duty. When the troops on the left flank began to retire, he went forward and took command of two companies. The only line of withdrawal was through a river staked with barbed wire, and it was largely due to his coolness and organization of covering fire that part of the companies succeeded in getting back. He then reformed scattered troops of different units and led them forward, thus enabling a battery to get its guns away. Later, he displayed great courage in a counter-attack.

CHART, STEPHEN, Major (Temporary Lieut.-Colonel), London Regt. For conspicuous gallantry and devotion to duty. His battalion was sent up to reinforce the brigade. His dispositions were excellent, and he handled the situation with great skill and courage. He maintained his position until ordered to conform to the new situation. Never sparing himself, he set a splendid example of coolness and confidence, and greatly inspired all ranks under him.

CLARK, DONALD GORDON, M.C., Capt., Gordon Highlanders. For conspicuous gallantry and devotion to duty. When the line was exposed on the left flank and taken in rear, this officer organized his company in a communication trench and held on till 1.30 a.m. the following day. He was twice bombed out of the position, and each time took up another, inflicting severe casualties on the enemy. Subsequently he showed fine leadership in occupying successive rearguard positions.

CLEGHORN, GEORGE MATTHEW, Temporary Major, Highland Light Infantry. For conspicuous gallantry and devotion to duty. He was in charge of the consolidation of a position, when he found that the enemy was still in possession of the northern side of a village. He organized a storming party, and, with great dash, cleared the village. He afterwards reorganized the line in depth in daylight and in full view of the enemy. His example was worthy of the highest traditions of the service.

CLUTTERBUCK, NOEL STANLEY, Major (Acting Lieut.-Colonel), Royal Marine Light Infantry. For conspicuous gallantry and devotion to duty when he handled his battalion in a most skilful manner during a successful counter-attack, when the whole of the lost ground was regained. He personally led the attack, which was organized with great promptitude.

COCKBURN, WILLIAM, M.C., Lieut. (Temporary Capt.), Yeomanry. For conspicuous gallantry and devotion to duty. On several occasions he displayed qualities of leadership of an exceptional nature. He covered the withdrawal of his battalion by night, fought a brilliant rearguard action, and, by his dash and absolute disregard of his own safety, gained the vigorous cheers of his men.

COLES, JAMES HUGH, Capt. (Acting Major), East Yorkshire Regt. For conspicuous gallantry and devotion while commanding his battalion during several days of severe fighting. By his remarkable coolness and courage in face of the most difficult circumstances, he was enabled to extricate his battalion on at least two occasions when practically surrounded. His fine qualities of leadership and devotion to duty greatly inspired all ranks under him.

COLLINS, REGINALD FRANK, Temporary Capt., Royal Fusiliers. For conspicuous gallantry and devotion to duty. When his battalion was heavily attacked and forced from its position in a wood, he, as the senior officer on the spot, took hold of the situation with vigour and judgment. He moved the battalion, now reduced to less than 200 men, and extending, advanced the whole line against the attacking enemy, who were in vastly larger numbers, and drove them out of the wood, capturing a machine gun himself. His bold handling of a few troops restored a dangerous break in the line. Throughout the operations he has set an inspiring example to all ranks.

COPE, ARTHUR HAWTAYNE, Capt. (Acting Lieut.-Colonel), Devonshire Regt. For conspicuous gallantry and devotion to duty during a long period of active operations when in command of his battalion. Notably he held river crossings in face of fierce attacks, counter-attacking at times, when the enemy had broken through a line, and restoring the situation, and finally, though nearly surrounded, withdrawing the battalion as a formed body. The splendid record of his battalion was due to his great courage and fine leadership throughout.

COX, JOHN ALONZO, Major, Highland Light Infantry. For conspicuous gallantry and devotion to duty when the enemy raided our outposts with mounted patrols and cyclists. During the confusion he, with another officer and a few men, put up a desperate hand-to-hand combat with the raiders and so allowed time for the company to rally and show a united front. His quickness of perception and courage have been of the greatest assistance to his C.O. on many critical occasions.

CROCKER, JOHN TREDINNICK, M.C., Temporary Second Lieut., Machine Gun Corps. For conspicuous gallantry and devotion to duty. When in charge of four machine guns he broke down two strong enemy attacks, holding on from 10 a.m. till dusk, when infantry and reinforcements arrived. The following day he maintained his position till outflanked, when he stood up between two of his guns and directed their fire on the enemy, who were within 30 yards, then covered the withdrawal with bombs and rifle fire, killing many himself at close range. Took up a fresh position until almost surrounded again, when he again went out with bombs. His example throughout was magnificent.

CUBBON, JOHN FREDERICK, M.C., Temporary Capt. (Acting Major), Royal Engineers. For conspicuous gallantry and devotion to duty when in command of a field company during a retreat lasting many days and under most trying conditions. He manœuvred his company with great skill from position to position, covering the retirement of artillery and transport. Later, he was suddenly placed in command of an infantry brigade and ordered to cover a position. This he did in a most able manner at great odds and under heavy machine-gun and rifle fire. Finally, it was owing to his skill and courage that the retirement of a division was successfully conducted.

DEANE, LANCELOT COLIN WILLIAM, M.C., Temporary Capt. (Acting Major), South Wales Borderers. For conspicuous gallantry and devotion to duty. He went up to the front line in every operation, displaying an entire disregard of personal safety and a very quick appreciation of the ever-changing tactical situation. At a most critical period he organized a counter-attack, which he led himself, thereby checking the enemy's advance.

DELAHAYE, JAMES VINER, M.C., Capt. (Acting Major), Royal Field Artillery. For conspicuous gallantry and devotion to duty during the retirement of a brigade. It was largely due to the manner in which he led and inspired his artillery that it was possible to extricate the bulk of the infantry from a serious situation. He constantly remained with the rearmost gun, firing into the enemy at the shortest range. He fought his guns with a coolness of nerve and light-hearted gallantry beyond praise.

DE PASS, GUY ELIOT, Second Lieut., Dragoon Guards. For conspicuous gallantry and devotion to duty on many occasions during lengthy operations, notably carrying out a most difficult and valuable reconnaissance, and when in command of an advance troop establishing posts in a position abandoned earlier by our troops, rallying stragglers, and with them and his own men engaging the advancing enemy, thus enabling a counter-attack to develop, being subjected the whole time to severe artillery and machine-gun fire. His one desire has been to engage the enemy, and by his courage and skill he has invariably been able to do so with success.

DIXON, ROBERT SPEIR, Capt. (Temporary Major), Highland Light Infantry. For conspicuous gallantry and devotion to duty. He conducted a daring reconnaissance, clearing up a difficult situation, and afterwards was of great assistance in organizing and rallying men of other divisions during the battle. When his commanding officer fell he took command, continued the counter-attack, and drove the enemy out of the area. Later, he led his men with great determination and courage against vastly superior numbers, thereby materially assisting the retirement of the whole division.

DREW, CHARLES DOUGLAS, Major, Middlesex Regt. For conspicuous gallantry and devotion to duty throughout ten days of severe fighting. In command of a very small party of battalion headquarter details he, on two occasions, attacked large enemy parties advancing to attack, driving them back, and materially assisting in the successful defence of a bridge, and subsequently on the withdrawal of the battalion. His fine example of courage and energetic initiative was an inspiration to all ranks with him.

DYER, HYDE RIDGWAY, Major (Acting Lieut.-Colonel), Indian Cavalry. For conspicuous gallantry and devotion to duty. In the face of heavy fire he led his men in successful charges with great dash and ability. He twice had his horse shot under him. He proved himself a very able and gallant leader.

FLETCHER, EDWARD KEELING, Major (Acting Lieut.-Colonel), Royal Marine Light Infantry. For conspicuous gallantry and devotion to duty when, by a personal reconnaissance, which proved to be invaluable, he discovered that a gap had been made on the right flank of his battalion, and he dealt with the situation promptly; and again, on the following morning, when he led a successful counter-attack, which regained all the lost ground.

FREER, NIGEL WILLIAM WYNN, M.C., Capt. (Acting Major), Royal Field Artillery. For conspicuous gallantry and devotion to duty. His promptness in running up howitzers into the open enabled fire to be opened on hostile infantry who unexpectedly appeared on a flank. His arrangements and personal supervision of the withdrawal of his guns enabled the move to be carried out without a casualty.

FURSE, RALPH DOLIGNON, Major, King Edward's Horse. For conspicuous gallantry and devotion to duty during a hostile attack when he held, for over five hours, 900 yards of a system with 100 men and a weak company of infantry, ultimately withdrawing in good order in spite of hand-to-hand fighting in the trenches. His skill and courage were most marked.

GELL, EDWARD ANTHONY SYDNEY, M.C., Temporary Lieut. (Acting Lieut.-Colonel), Royal Fusiliers. For conspicuous gallantry and devotion to duty. He had just arrived on leave in England when he heard his division was engaged. He hurried back, and after much difficulty got to them. Within half an hour of arrival he collected about 100 stragglers and attached them to the remnants of his own battalion, his vigour and fearlessness putting fresh life into the defence. Next day, when the line was being driven back, he led a counter-attack with splendid dash under very heavy machine-gun fire.

GRACEY, ROBERT LLOYD, Capt. (Acting Major), Royal Engineers. For conspicuous gallantry and devotion to duty when in command of defensive positions. By his courage, skill, and tenacity he greatly delayed the hostile advance causing heavy enemy losses. For several days he and his men were subjected to a very heavy bombardment, and only his personal example of gallantry and coolness checked the retirement of disorganized bodies of men and maintained the defence.

GRAY, HENRY PHILIP TWELLS, Capt., Seaforth Highlanders. For conspicuous gallantry and devotion to duty. When in command of a battalion holding 800 yards of line he beat off three attacks made by the enemy in greatly superior numbers. He held the line intact all day, arranging for supply of ammunition and sending back valuable information to brigade headquarters. The following day, although both flanks were exposed and the enemy were 2,500 yards behind his line, he held on till 3 p.m., when he extricated the battalion, supervising the withdrawal, although wounded in the face.

GREENWOOD, HARRY, M.C., Temporary Major, Yorkshire Light Infantry. For conspicuous gallantry and devotion to duty during two heavy attacks, made under cover of mist. They were repulsed, but a hostile machine-gun detachment, which succeeded in getting within 50 yards of the line, suffered severely, and an officer and two men ran back to cover. The battalion being very short of machine gunners owing to casualties, he, with a N.C.O., rushed out with the greatest daring, found the officer and men hiding in a hollow with a heavy machine gun, and made them carry it back, being all the time under intense fire. The gun was used later on the enemy with great effect.

GREGORY, FREDERICK CHARLES, Major, Cheshire Regt. For conspicuous gallantry and devotion to duty. By the skilful handling of the battalion under his command he kept the line intact throughout the whole action, and successfully supported the line on his left. On two occasions he organized counter-attacks and drove off the enemy with severe loss. Throughout the action he displayed leadership of a high order.

GRIFFIN, JOHN ARNOLD ATKINSON, Capt. (Acting Major), Lincolnshire Regt. For conspicuous gallantry and devotion to duty. When his C.O. was wounded he took command, and displayed the greatest courage and skill in operations lasting several days, in maintaining positions, leading counter-attacks at every opportunity, and by his splendid personal example encouraging all ranks to do their utmost during a most critical period.

GROVER, ALBERT, M.C., Lieut. (Acting Major), Bedfordshire Regt. For conspicuous gallantry and devotion to duty. He displayed great courage and skill in collecting stragglers and organizing them into a fighting force to enable him to hold a most important line, which was subsequently repeatedly and unsuccessfully attacked. When at length ordered to withdraw he conducted a most skilful rearguard action, personally collecting machine guns and directing their fire until the remainder of his force had taken up their next position. Finally, when severely wounded, he continued to direct operations from a stretcher, refusing to be evacuated until he had explained the situation to another senior officer.

HARCOURT, HARRY GLADWYN, M.C., Second Lieut. (Temporary Lieut. and Acting Major), Royal Dublin Fusiliers. For conspicuous gallantry and devotion to duty during two days of intense fighting, when he visited and located all the machine guns under his command, under heavy artillery and machine-gun fire, and then on horseback led a limber down the line, dropping ammunition and water at each gun. Later he organized defensive points, which he held to the last possible moment, covering troops withdrawing. His actions had incalculable results: firstly, the timely supply of ammunition to the guns; secondly, the defeat of the enemy's attempt to cut off certain valuable positions; and thirdly, successfully covering troop withdrawals.

HARVEY, MARTIN MORNEMONT, M.C., Temporary Capt., Nottinghamshire and Derbyshire Regt. For conspicuous gallantry and devotion to duty during a withdrawal, when his company was on the left flank of the battalion, which was "en l'air." The enemy, perceiving the advantage, established machine guns and snipers on a ridge and enfiladed the whole battalion with great accuracy. He at once appreciated the situation, organized and led a party which drove the enemy off the ridge, and saved the situation. By his initiative and courage he set a wonderful example to all ranks.

HENDERSON, ERNEST JAMES, M.C., Temporary Lieut. (Acting Capt.), East Lancashire Regt. For conspicuous gallantry and devotion to duty. When his C.O. was wounded he took command of the battalion, and handled it with great judgment and success. He invariably displayed the utmost courage and disregard for personal danger, although frequently exposed to heavy machine-gun and rifle fire, and his fine example inspired all ranks with him. Ultimately he was wounded.

HIGGINS, EDWARD LAWRENCE, M.C., Capt., London Regt. For conspicuous gallantry and devotion to duty. He was on leave in England when he heard his division was engaged and promptly rejoined them after considerable difficulty. He then went straight into the fight with a composite company whom he so cheered by his fine spirit that they more than once successfully counter-attacked and inflicted heavy losses on the enemy.

HILDITCH, VICTOR CADIFOR, M.C., Temporary Lieut. (Acting Major), Royal Field Artillery. For conspicuous gallantry and devotion to duty. This officer engaged the enemy with his battery over open sights, under rifle and shell fire, holding them up long enough to enable the infantry to take up fresh positions. He then brought up teams, and got the guns away safely, covering their withdrawal with his own Lewis guns. He was indefatigable in keeping up touch with the infantry.

HODGE, ARTHUR, M.C., Lieut. (Acting Capt.), Manchester Regt. For conspicuous gallantry and devotion to duty when in command of his support company. Troops of other units in a front line withdrew, as also did those on each flank of his company. In spite of this, he maintained his isolated position under heavy shell and machine-gun fire until ordered to withdraw 12 hours later. His gallantry and example were such that not one of his own men joined the shaken troops from the front line, who passed through his position to the rear.

HOWITT, HAROLD GIBSON, M.C., Capt., Yorkshire Regt. For conspicuous gallantry and devotion to duty in action. On many occasions he rallied troops when they were falling back. He displayed complete fearlessness in moving about in the open, under heavy fire, in order to clear up obscure situations. When trying to re-establish the front line, he was once taken prisoner, but after a few hours made good his escape. His leadership and example were of the greatest value.

HUMBY, HOLGATE JOHN BRITTNELL, Second Lieut., Royal Garrison Artillery, Special Reserve. For conspicuous gallantry and devotion to duty at forward observation posts during long hours, and in maintaining communications and despatching invaluable reports under intense shell and machine-gun fire. When the observation post was attacked by low-flying aeroplanes, he drove them off successfully by rifle fire. On one occasion, when communications failed, he went through a heavy barrage alone with a signalling lamp and established visual communication. Though often engaged in the most daring and enterprising undertakings, he always emerged successful. His services throughout the operations were beyond praise, and his courage a splendid example to all.

ILLINGWORTH, ROBERT LESLIE, M.C., Temporary Capt. (Acting Major), Nottinghamshire and Derbyshire Regt. For conspicuous gallantry and devotion to duty. He took over command of a partly-trained composite battalion from a wounded officer. With great skill he maintained the line, organized local counter-attacks, and drove the enemy back. It was in great measure due to his good leadership and courage that the battalion, which was in the heat of the fight, rendered such a good account of itself, both then and again on a subsequent occasion.

INGLIS, JOHN, Major (Acting Lieut.-Colonel), Highland Light Infantry. For conspicuous gallantry and devotion to duty when he ably handled his battalion at a very critical moment. Under heavy fire he made many personal reconnaissances, and was always thoroughly in touch with the situation, sending back most valuable information. His leadership enabled difficult rearguard actions to be fought successfully for seven days.

JACK, JAMES CHARLES, M.C., Lieut. (Acting Major), Royal Field Artillery, Special Reserve. For conspicuous gallantry and devotion to duty. While his battery was being heavily gas shelled he superintended the removal of his guns to higher ground clear of the cloud of gas, and continued to fire heavily throughout the bombardment. Another day, when the enemy got close to the guns, he withdrew his guns without losing one. His fine courage and initiative throughout were a splendid example to the men.

JAGO, HENRY HARRIS, M.C., Second Lieut. (Acting Capt.), Devonshire Regt. For conspicuous gallantry and devotion to duty when leading the first wave of his battalion, through heavy machine-gun fire, in a counter-attack and assisting to press the attack home. Having reached the objective, he was largely responsible for the rapid re-forming of companies and consolidation of the line. His courage and fine example greatly inspired all ranks with him.

JAMES, ERNEST, M.C., Capt. (Acting Lieut.-Colonel), Lincolnshire Regt. For conspicuous gallantry and devotion to duty when the force he was with was heavily attacked and forced to retire in some confusion. He ably summed up the situation, organized a rearguard with part of his battalion, enabling the remainder to get into position, and only withdrew the rearguard when almost surrounded.

JEFFRIES, WILLIAM FRANCIS, Capt. (Acting Major), Royal Dublin Fusiliers, Special Reserve. For conspicuous gallantry and devotion to duty. Although suffering from the effects of gas poisoning at a time when a portion of the line was penetrated, he mustered all scattered troops, and with skilful leadership led them forward and restored the line. His example of courage and contempt of danger had the most inspiring influence on the men.

JEWELS, CHARLES EDGAR, M.C., Temporary Major. For conspicuous gallantry and devotion to duty when commanding a battalion during an enemy attack. His personal example and excellent leadership enabled the battalion to hold on, with both flanks in the air, and in a subsequent counter-attack to inflict severe losses on the enemy. Throughout the operations he displayed great ability and courage.

LABOUCHERE, ARTHUR MAXWELL, Temporary Major, Oxfordshire and Buckinghamshire Light Infantry. For conspicuous gallantry and devotion to duty while commanding his battalion. At a time when a retirement was in progress he showed marked ability and coolness, and it was due to his fine handling of his men that the enemy were checked. His cheerfulness and disregard of danger did much to inspire his men.

LATHAM, STEPHEN GREY, M.C., Capt. (Acting Lieut.-Colonel), Northamptonshire Regt. For conspicuous gallantry and devotion to duty during a long period of active operations. He handled his battalion with great skill and forethought, and by his total disregard of personal danger he set a splendid example to all under his command. It was greatly due to his courage and untiring energy that severe losses were caused to the enemy, and that his battalion was cleared from difficult situations with the minimum casualties.

LAWRENCE, THOMPSON BROOK, M.C., D.C.M., Lieut. (Acting Lieut.-Colonel), Gordon Highlanders. For conspicuous gallantry and devotion to duty in skilfully withdrawing his battalion, when ordered, without a casualty from close contact with the enemy. Also for gallant defence of his H.Q.'s in the support line, when he personally shot a number of the enemy.

LAWSON, ARTHUR BERTRAM, Capt. and Brevet Major (Acting Lieut.-Colonel), Hussars. For conspicuous gallantry and devotion to duty when in command of his battalion in action. On several occasions he handled his men with marked ability, and largely contributed to successful defence, when most heavily attacked by very superior forces. Throughout the operations, he showed great initiative and courage.

LORD, ARTHUR JOSIAH, M.C., Lieut. (Acting Capt.), Royal Fusiliers, Special Reserve. For conspicuous gallantry and devotion to duty. He led his company forward in perfect order during a heavy barrage from the reserve to the support line, personally directing his men to the most advantageous positions. Later, he was personally responsible for an orderly withdrawal, his company being the last to leave the line. The same night he established a line in old trenches and shell holes, closing a gap left by the brigade on his flank.

LOWE, WILLIAM DOUGLAS, M.C., Temporary Major, West Yorkshire Regt. For conspicuous gallantry and devotion to duty. He was indefatigable under all conditions throughout heavy fighting. After the Brigadier and Brigade Major were casualties, and the brigade was without communication to the rear, he shouldered the whole responsibility until touch was regained.

LOWRY, AURIOL ERNEST ERIC, M.C., Capt. (Acting Lieut.-Colonel), West Yorkshire Regt. For conspicuous gallantry and devotion to duty during many days of very fierce fighting, when he led counter-attacks against overwhelming odds, and restored situations after the enemy had broken through; and finally, when surrounded on all sides, he cut his way out, being personally the last to cover the withdrawal. He was overpowered and captured, but during the night escaped from his escort, and made his way back across many miles at the greatest personal risk. His fortitude and indomitable courage throughout a memorable 12 days were beyond all praise.

LUMSDEN, WILLIAM VERNON, M.C., Capt. (Temporary Lieut.-Colonel), Argyll and Sutherland Highlanders. For conspicuous gallantry and devotion to duty. During recent operations he handled his battalion with great skill. His personal example and coolness under heavy fire contributed largely to the stout defence put up by his battalion.

MABEN, HERBERT CARTEIGHE, M.C., Temporary Capt., Worcestershire Regt. For conspicuous gallantry and devotion to duty in action. His commanding officer being wounded, he took charge at a most critical time during a hostile attack, reorganizing and allocating new positions under heavy rifle and machine-gun fire, and by his personal gallantry and coolness so encouraging all ranks that the enemy advance was checked, until he was ordered to withdraw, which, owing to his skill, he successfully accomplished with few further casualties.

MACDONALD, DONALD RAMSAY, M.C., Major, Royal Field Artillery. For conspicuous gallantry and devotion to duty. On various occasions he was the last to withdraw his battery, and his handling of a sub-group placed under his command enabled the infantry to prolong the defence by many hours. His courage and skill were admirable.

MACKENZIE, KENNETH WILLIAM, M.C., M.B., Temporary Capt. (Acting Lieut.-Colonel), Royal Army Medical Corps (late Capt., Indian Medical Service). For conspicuous gallantry and devotion to duty when in charge of the forward evacuation, when he kept in touch with the retiring infantry, continually searching for and collecting the wounded. It was largely due to his great energy, skill and foresight that so many of our casualties were so successfully evacuated.

MARCHMENT, ALAN FREDERICK, M.C., Major (Temporary Lieut.-Colonel), London Regt. For conspicuous gallantry and devotion to duty when commanding his battalion. He directed the operations from the top of his dug-out, and though under heavy artillery, machine-gun and rifle fire during the day he continued to organize and direct his men with the utmost coolness, in spite of many direct hits. On more than one occasion he organized battalion headquarter details for counter-attack. He set a fine example of fearlessness and soldier-like qualities.

McCULLOCH, ANDREW JAMESON, D.C.M., Capt. and Brevet Lieut.-Colonel, Dragoon Guards. For conspicuous gallantry and devotion to duty throughout many days of severe fighting. His courage, energy and unfailing cheerfulness contributed in a most marked manner to the various successful withdrawals of the battalion, and were a magnificent example to his men, whose confidence he gained in the highest degree. Later, in command of a mixed force, his skill and coolness in difficult operations were worthy of the highest praise.

McKENZIE, CYRIL, Temporary Lieut. (Acting Capt.), East Lancashire Regt. For conspicuous gallantry and devotion to duty in leading his company from position to position with uniform success. Five times attacked, he maintained his position until the end. He three times counter-attacked and gained his objective.

MITCHELL, JOHN DOUGLAS, Temporary Major, Durham Light Infantry. For conspicuous gallantry and devotion to duty during long operations, when by his great personal courage and powers of leadership he assisted to hold the battalion together under most trying conditions. After the C.O. had been wounded early in the operations, he assumed command of the battalion, and the success and praise it earned were to a great extent due to the splendid example of energy and devotion set by him.

MOORE, ROBERT FRANK, M.C., Temporary Lieut. (Acting Lieut.-Colonel), Nottinghamshire and Derbyshire Regt. For conspicuous gallantry and devotion to duty during lengthy operations. After his C.O. had been killed, he took command of the battalion, which he handled with great skill and judgment, beating off several determined attacks, and when finally compelled to withdraw, doing so in a masterly manner, and with a minimum of casualties. His conduct throughout the operations set a fine example of courage and leadership, and was of great value in maintaining the high morale of the battalion.

MORLEY, FRANCIS JOSEPH, M.C., Capt. (Acting Major), Dorsetshire Regt. For conspicuous gallantry and devotion to duty. When in command of a company in the front line, he inflicted heavy losses on the advancing enemy, and obtained information of great value to a subsequent operation. Later, he took command of the battalion, and conducted a retirement with great skill, showing much coolness and gallantry, and being wounded when retiring with the last line.

MOSBY, JOHN EDWARD GEORGE, Temporary Lieut., Royal Air Force. For conspicuous gallantry and devotion to duty whilst on an artillery patrol. He was attacked by the enemy machines, two from the front and one from the rear. He engaged and drove off the latter but was hit in the abdomen, and when he turned to engage the others his pilot was hit and instantly killed. Although his machine fell out of control from 3,000 feet to 1,000 feet, he continued to engage them, and was again hit in the abdomen. But he succeeded in driving them off, and though his machine again became out of control he righted it and safely landed it at his aerodrome. He showed indomitable pluck, both during an unequal contest and in determining to land his machine without injury, although nearly unconscious from loss of blood.

NEILSON, DONALD FRANCIS, M.C., Lieut. (Acting Capt.), Lincolnshire Regt. For conspicuous gallantry and devotion to duty. When in charge of a company he met an enemy break-through by forming a defensive flank, and checked it. With much cheerfulness and courage he organized several bombing attacks, and held his original trenches intact. Subsequently, during the retirement, he was conspicuous for good leadership, carrying out difficult operations with complete disregard for personal danger. Later, he held an exposed forward position completely isolated from his brigade, and the stubborn resistance he made was of incalculable value to the success of the operation.

NORTON, EDWARD FELIX, M.C., Major, Royal Horse Artillery. For conspicuous gallantry and devotion to duty. He has earned distinction on many occasions, and invariably handled his battery under heavy fire with great skill; on one occasion fighting a rearguard action with remarkable ability and coolness.

O'KELLEY, ANDREW NOLAN, Major (Acting Lieut.-Colonel), King Edward's Horse, seconded Tank Corps. For conspicuous gallantry and devotion to duty. Owing to his skill and foresight his Tanks rendered the most valuable assistance to the infantry in carrying out local counter-attacks and covering their withdrawal. When his Tanks became derelict, and his men were organized into Lewis gun groups, he held the line against repeated attacks, showing splendid energy, and inflicting severe casualties on the enemy.

ORR, NORMAN CHARLES, Major, Seaforth Highlanders. For conspicuous gallantry and devotion to duty while in command of his battalion during an enemy attack, when he displayed initiative, coolness, and power of command of a high order. He exposed himself fearlessly during personal reconnaissances, and the extrication of the battalion from a critical situation, with both flanks exposed and a river behind, was mainly due to his courage and skill.

PAGE, CHARLES ALEXANDER SHAW, M.C., Major (Acting Lieut.-Colonel), Middlesex Regt. For conspicuous gallantry and devotion to duty during many days of intense fighting, in which, by his high standard of military leadership, he kept his battalion together under the most difficult circumstances. He held river crossings in face of furious attacks, and although on one occasion his flank was turned he offered a desperate resistance against great odds, and finally withdrew, under orders, as a forward body, in spite of heavy losses. Throughout the operations he exposed himself fearlessly, and his magnificent example maintained to the end the high morale and fine spirit of his battalion.

PAGE, CHARLES HENRY, Temporary Major, Nottinghamshire and Derbyshire Regt. For conspicuous gallantry and devotion to duty when, with good leadership, he commanded the rearguard of his battalion during a retirement, and enabled the battalion to get away with few casualties, whilst it inflicted heavy ones on the enemy. Also for making many personal reconnaissances of doubtful spots, and obtaining valuable information.

PARISH, FRANCIS WOODBINE, M.C., Capt. (Acting Lieut.-Colonel), King's Royal Rifle Corps. For conspicuous gallantry and devotion to duty. When the line was forced back this officer, collecting all the available men, led three counter-attacks, restoring the situation, and then, moving about exposed to intense fire, calmly reorganized the battalion.

PERY, THE HONOURABLE EDMUND COLQUHOUN, Major, Yeomanry. For conspicuous gallantry and devotion to duty. This officer went forward and assisted an infantry regiment in a very difficult withdrawal. He then went and brought in a T.M.B. and a M.G. Coy., who had not received orders to withdraw. He then went and assisted the O.C. of an Infantry Regiment to withdraw. All this took place under very heavy fire, and in close contact with the enemy. His conduct and courage throughout the operations has been magnificent.

PITTS, ARTHUR THOMAS, Capt. (Acting Lieut.-Colonel), Royal Army Medical Corps, Special Reserve. For conspicuous gallantry and devotion to duty. He established a dressing station in a forward and very exposed position. During two days and two nights he remained under continuous and terrific shell fire, dressing wounded and evacuating them. His courage and endurance under most trying conditions saved many valuable lives.

POOLE, LEOPOLD THOMAS, M.C., M.B., Capt. (Acting Lieut.-Colonel), Royal Army Medical Corps. For conspicuous gallantry and devotion to duty during a hostile attack. Hearing that a large number of wounded were uncollected, owing to normal communications having been cut by the attack, he proceeded at once to the area, which was subjected to a sustained bombardment, and organized stretcher parties, sending up all his available cars. It was owing to his fine courage and promptitude that upwards of 300 casualties were not left unattended.

RAMSDEN, VINCENT BASIL, M.C., Capt. (Acting Lieut.-Colonel), South Wales Borderers. For conspicuous gallantry and devotion to duty when leading his battalion in an attack. Having reached the final objective, and finding that many of the enemy had been passed over and were firing from the rear, he went back and brought forward his reserve company, which mopped them all up. He killed several of the enemy himself, and forced others to surrender. This success at a critical period was largely due to his personal courage and intrepid enthusiasm.

READ, HERBERT EDWARD, M.C., Temporary Lieut. (Acting Capt.), Yorkshire Regt. For conspicuous gallantry and devotion to duty. When his commanding officer was wounded, he took command and successfully held his position for some time, surrounded by the enemy. He then organized the remnants of the battalion, and fought a brilliant rearguard action. His behaviour at a most critical period of the battle was worthy of the highest praise.

READE, ARTHUR, M.C., Temporary Major, South Lancashire Regt. For conspicuous gallantry and devotion to duty while in command of a composite battalion when the enemy broke through a portion of the line. Calling on 30 men to follow, he led a counter-attack, driving the enemy back, capturing 20 prisoners and seven machine guns and killing about 60, with a loss of four killed and six wounded. He handed over the position intact when relieved on the third night.

REID, DENNIS WHITEHORN, M.C., Temporary Capt., Seaforth Highlanders. For conspicuous gallantry and devotion to duty. He led his company with great dash in the face of machine-gun fire, and on entering the outskirts of a village captured single-handed 14 enemy, and assisted in the taking of five machine guns. On the following day he consolidated and held a position with a mixed body of troops, short of officers and N.C.O.'s. He always set an example of coolness and courage and was to the fore in all the actions in which his battalion took part.

ROME, CHARLES LESLIE, Capt. (Acting Major), Hussars. For conspicuous gallantry and devotion to duty on many occasions in action, and notably when he constantly visited a front line during an intense bombardment, supervising the defences, and by his courage and example encouraging the men. On the occasion of a hostile attack, he personally disposed of three of the enemy, including an officer who was in a car with important documents, and was instrumental in capturing several prisoners. His splendid example has been most inspiring to both officers and other ranks.

RUSSELL, VALENTINE CUBITT, M.C., Lieut. (Acting Capt.), Suffolk Regt. For conspicuous gallantry and devotion to duty. At a period when the situation was critical, the front having been forced in and the flank in the air, he took charge as the parties fell back and organized a fresh defence line, under heavy fire, which he held for several hours. Later, when forced again to withdraw, he was the last to leave, and then only when the enemy were within 40 yards

SHINER, HERBERT, M.C., Lieut. (Acting Major). For conspicuous gallantry and devotion to duty. His battery, in an advanced position, was subjected throughout the day to heavy shelling, and at times to bombing from low-flying aeroplanes, but he kept it in action the whole time, and finally brought out his six guns intact. On another occasion one of his guns got badly ditched, but he took back some men and extricated it. When an ammunition waggon, loaded with shells, was set on fire he, with the assistance of a N.C.O., extinguished the flames.

SIME, ARCHIBALD WILLIAM HEPBURN, M.C., Temporary Second Lieut., Machine Gun Corps. For conspicuous gallantry and devotion to duty, while in charge of four Vickers' machine guns. One night he suspected the close proximity of an enemy party, organized a patrol, and destroyed them. Next day he caught a prisoner with maps showing enemy's objective, and worked his guns so ably during the day that he greatly hampered the enemy's advance. He showed great courage and ability.

STEVENSON, DONALD FASKERN, M.C., Lieut. (Temporary Capt.), Yeomanry and Royal Air Force. For conspicuous gallantry and devotion to duty when carrying out low-flying reconnaissances and contact patrols, under very heavy machine-gun, rifle, and anti-aircraft fire. In his patrols, often lasting many hours, and in bad weather conditions, he attacked enemy infantry, transport and batteries from a low level, using his machine gun and dropping bombs, frequently returning with his machine riddled with bullets, and the information he obtained was quite invaluable. His cheerful spirit, consistent dash, and fearlessness, and his magnificent work have set a splendid example to all in his squadron, and greatly encouraged them at a time when the casualties in it were extremely heavy.

STEWART, FREDERICK NAYLOR, M.C., M.D., Temporary Capt., Royal Army Medical Corps. For conspicuous gallantry and devotion to duty. He collected and dressed cases under the most intense shell fire, and on two occasions, by remaining behind after the order to withdraw had been given, succeeded in evacuating all the stretcher cases. He set a high example of courage and self-sacrifice. He was wounded in the face and thigh.

STEWART, JAMES LENNOX, M.C., M.B., Temporary Capt., Royal Army Medical Corps. For conspicuous gallantry and devotion to duty. Although his aid post was in the open, a few yards behind the front line, he remained there, caring for the wounded, and through his efforts they were all dressed and evacuated. He was the only Medical Officer of the Brigade left.

STILLWELL, WILLIAM DIGBY, Major (Acting Lieut.-Colonel), Royal Field Artillery. For conspicuous gallantry and devotion to duty. When the brigade was under heavy fire all day, and two battery commanders out of three became casualties, he reconnoitred new positions and superintended the withdrawal of his batteries, his signal officer being killed beside him. He was the last to leave the battery positions. The reports which he sent back enabled prompt and effective action to be taken.

STRINGER, CHARLES HERBERT, Capt. (Acting Lieut.-Colonel), Royal Army Medical Corps. For conspicuous gallantry and devotion to duty when in charge of an advanced dressing station. Owing to the whole force retiring, the collection and evacuation of large numbers of wounded, who were lying in thick woods, was a task of extreme difficulty in view of the rapid advance of the enemy. Although subjected to heavy fire, he remained behind till the enemy were almost up to his position, and by skilful organization he succeeded in evacuating practically all the wounded. His magnificent courage and devotion saved many wounded from falling into the enemy's hands.

SUTCLIFFE, RICHARD DOUGLAS, Capt. (Acting Major), London Regt. For conspicuous gallantry and devotion to duty during operations, when he led his company under heavy shell fire, and expelled the enemy from an imporatnt position. Later, after his Colonel had been wounded, he assumed command of the battalion, holding on to the position until forced to fall back owing to the flank being turned. Throughout the five days of operations his gallant leadership inspired all ranks with confidence, and was worthy of the highest praise.

SUTTON, GEORGE WILLIAM, Capt., Lancashire Fusiliers. For conspicuous gallantry and devotion to duty when his commanding officer being wounded he commanded the battalion, and led a most successful counter-attack. His behaviour throughout the day was most gallant.

SWIFT, NEVILLE CROPLEY, M.C., Lieut. (Acting Major), East Lancashire Regt. For conspicuous gallantry and devotion to duty in leading his battalion in a counter-attack, which was completely successful. He continued to set a splendid example until severely wounded.

TAYLOR, JOHN ALEXANDER CHISHOLM, Capt., Manchester Regt. For conspicuous gallantry and devotion to duty. He was in command of the company on the right flank, to which he added some 300 men collected from other divisions. By a prompt counter-attack he defeated the enemy's attempt to envelop the right flank. His coolness, promptitude and personal gallantry were a great incentive to his men.

UTTERSON-KELSO, JOHN EDWARD, M.C., Capt. (Acting Lieut.-Colonel), Royal Scots Fusiliers. For conspicuous gallantry and devotion to duty. Organized counter-attacks, leading his men with great skill and daring throughout prolonged fighting. Though twice buried by shell bursts and badly concussed, he remained at duty, setting a fine example, until his battalion was relieved.

VANNER, JAMES CHARLES, M.C., Temporary Capt., Leicestershire Regt. For conspicuous gallantry and devotion to duty while in command of two companies during a withdrawal. He made a block in a railway cutting and caused the demolition of two bridges over the railway while the enemy were crossing. His was fine conduct throughout.

WALKER, JAMES, Major (Acting Lieut.-Colonel), West Riding Regt. For conspicuous gallantry and devotion to duty. He commanded his battalion with great skill and coolness, and conducted counter-attacks against the enemy successfully when the situation was precarious. At one time he procured the services of a Tank to help in holding the line. All through the operations he set an example of coolness and resource.

WARD, JOSEPH HUGH, M.C., M.B., Capt. (Acting Lieut.-Colonel), Royal Army Medical Corps, Special Reserve. For conspicuous gallantry and devotion to duty while in command of a cavalry field ambulance. During two days of intense fighting, in spite of the enforced moves of his unit, he continued to keep an A.D.S. open until the last possible moment to deal with large numbers of wounded, only retiring when all had been evacuated and when ordered to do so. Throughout this period he showed an example of pluck and determination beyond all praise.

WARDLE, MARK KINGSLEY, M.C., Capt., Leicestershire Regt. For conspicuous gallantry and devotion to duty. By a daring reconnaissance during a withdrawal he located the exact extent of a gap between our troops, and ascertained the position, strength and movement of the enemy. His report was of the utmost value to the brigade commander and to the Higher Command. All through the operations he displayed great courage and enthusiasm.

WATKINS, JAMES WILLIAM, M.C., Temporary Lieut. (Acting Lieut.-Colonel), Lancashire Fusiliers. For conspicuous gallantry and devotion to duty in commanding his battalion and repelling an attack. His personal example of courage and cheerfulness, and his attention to all the details of the measures for assisting the defence, were undoubtedly responsible for the very fine fight made by his battalion at a very critical period, and for the ultimate success of the defence.

WATSON, FRANCIS SHULDHAM, Major, Royal Garrison Artillery. For conspicuous gallantry and devotion to duty. He moved his battery under very trying conditions with great skill. At one time the enemy were within rifle fire of the position, and the roads were being shelled, but he withdrew his guns and all his stores successfully, and then came into action again. On previous occasions and in subsequent operations he has proved himself a very capable battery commander with judgment and resource.

WEDGWOOD, GILBERT HENRY, Major (Acting Lieut.-Colonel), Yorkshire and Lancashire Regt. For conspicuous gallantry and devotion to duty when in command of his battalion. He denied an important locality to the enemy by the promptitude and rapidity of his movements. For three days he beat off heavy attacks, without losing a yard of ground, and the fighting spirit shown by him was a fine example to his men.

WHITWILL, MARK, M.C., Lieut. (Acting Major), Royal Engineers. For conspicuous gallantry and devotion to duty. When his telephone lines were cut, he repeatedly passed through a heavy barrage, in order to keep in touch with the brigade headquarters. He made personal reconnaissances to the posts in front, and on one occasion assumed command of some troops, organized defences, and held the posts until relieved. He constantly exposed himself to heavy fire, and by his coolness and example kept troops together when there was serious danger of their becoming disorganized.

WILLIAMS, EVELYN HUGH WATKIN, Major, Hussars. For conspicuous gallantry and devotion to duty. He led a mounted charge along the hostile line, after the infantry line had broken back, taking the line in flank, and in the face of the heaviest machine-gun fire he carried out the manœuvre successfully, sabring nearly 100 of the enemy, and taking 100 prisoners, although his own troop was only 150. His fine action rallied the infantry, who advanced, and recovered over 3,000 yards in depth of the whole line.

WILLIAMS, ROGER LLEWELLYN, M.C., Temporary Capt., Royal Army Medical Corps. For conspicuous gallantry and devotion to duty during operations, when, with the C.O. and Adjutant, he was the last to withdraw. Shortly after the C.O. was severely wounded, but, with the assistance of another officer, he carried him away for over half a mile under intense machine-gun and rifle fire at close range. Afterwards he continued to dress the wounded, including the Adjutant, under the most intense fire, and throughout the withdrawal he showed the utmost energy and devotion to duty.

WILLIS, HERBERT GEORGE, M.B., M.C., Temporary Capt. (Acting Major), Royal Army Medical Corps. For conspicuous gallantry and devotion to duty. When in command of a bearer division of the Field Ambulance throughout ten days' fighting, he kept all in order by visiting the R.A.P.'s and Ambulance Relay Posts, and when the trolley line was destroyed by shell fire he reorganized the system of evacuation, going round the posts and making the necessary arrangements at great personal risk. By his action he ensured the clearance of the wounded.

WILSON, PERCY PHILLIPS, Major, Durham Light Infantry. For conspicuous gallantry and devotion to duty during recent operations. He showed great coolness and skill while commanding the battalion, particularly on one occasion when the brigade on his right was forced back. Also he stayed in the trenches for four days after being wounded in the foot. He was a fine example to his men.

WOLFE-MURRAY, ROBERT ALEXANDER, M.C., Capt. (Acting Lieut.-Colonel), Gordon Highlanders. For conspicuous gallantry and devotion to duty. When it became necessary to occupy a new shell-hole line, to prevent the enemy massing within striking distance, this officer led two companies across the open under heavy shell and machine-gun fire, and organized the line.

WOOD, JOHN BRUCE, M.C., Temporary Capt., Gordon Highlanders. For conspicuous gallantry and devotion to duty during a hostile attack. When the front line was lost, he organized a line of defence, and by his courage in face of heavy artillery and machine-gun fire he so inspired his men that he was able to hold up the enemy for a considerable time. Later, when his battalion had taken up a fresh position, he displayed the greatest coolness and courage under most trying conditions, and it was largely owing to his untiring efforts that the enemy was prevented from forcing the line.

CANADIAN FORCE.

BENSON, FREDERICK MERRETT, Major, Royal Canadian Horse Artillery. For conspicuous gallantry and devotion to duty throughout a long period of intense fighting, when he commanded his battery with the greatest courage and skill. Although the battery was constantly subjected to heavy machine-gun fire, and from as many as seven low-flying aeroplanes at once, he continually kept up a heavy fire, covering the retirement of the infantry and the remaining batteries of the group. His magnificent example to his men was of the greatest value.

NICHOLSON, WILLIAM CEDRIC, M.C., Capt., Canadian Machine Gun Corps. For conspicuous gallantry and devotion to duty. This officer, with his motor machine gunners, was successful time after time in holding up large masses of the rapidly advancing enemy. He personally tended to wounded men, and sent them back in his motor transport. Later, he had his right arm taken off, and while waiting to be evacuated cheered his men by his courage and grit.

REID, JOHN GARNER, Lieut.-Colonel, Canadian Overseas Railway Construction Corps. For conspicuous gallantry and devotion to duty. Without awaiting orders he arranged to maintain the railway and operate signals. Again he organized parties to maintain railways when labour companies were removed without notice, and also organized demolition parties and a service of runners. By example he encouraged both officers and men under heavy shell fire, and the satisfactory results obtained were largely due to his skill and untiring endeavour.

AUSTRALIAN IMPERIAL FORCE.

ADAMS, WILLIAM GEORGE, M.C., Capt. For conspicuous gallantry and devotion to duty on several occasions. When his battalion was moving up to support the front line, through a heavy barrage, his control and leadership averted many casualties. After digging in, he went forward and found another company being surrounded by the enemy; he extricated them, and held a position further back for two hours against heavy odds. His courage and judgment throughout the operations were beyond praise.

AHRENS, CHARLES, M.C., Capt. For conspicuous gallantry and devotion to duty. He moved his company forward by night, established contact with the enemy and dug in, supervising the siting and construction of the posts under constant sniping and machine-gun fire. The next night, after a daring reconnaissance, he manœuvred his company to within 30 yards of a strong enemy post, compelling them to withdraw. On another occasion he led his company against a strongly-held crest line, capturing 73 prisoners and four machine guns. On several other occasions his splendid handling of his company caused heavy losses to the enemy at small cost.

COLLINS, ARCHIBALD JOHN, M.C., Major, Australian Army Medical Corps. For conspicuous gallantry and devotion to duty when in charge of the evacuation of wounded during intense fighting. Although the A.D.S. in which he was located was subjected to heavy enemy artillery fire, by his splendid energy, coolness and courage, he was enabled to evacuate safely several hundred casualties. His magnificent example inspired all who came in contact with him, and stimulated junior officers and exhausted stretcher-bearers to further efforts.

DUNCAN, WALTER JOHN CLARE, M.C., Capt., Infantry. For conspicuous gallantry and devotion to duty while commanding a company. Troops on his left were being pressed back, but his fine dash and accurate fire caused the enemy to withdraw, leaving him in an excellent defensive position. Later in the day, he led his company in a counter-attack in conjunction with the cavalry, and again drove the enemy back, inflicting heavy casualties. Early next morning, his company made an advance of 600 yards, and materially improved the position. He kept headquarters constantly informed with useful information.

TAYLOR, HARRY, Lieut., Infantry. For conspicuous gallantry and devotion to duty. When at dawn a large party of the enemy were seen approaching, this officer went out alone with a Lewis gun and dispersed them, killing many. When the enemy attack developed in overwhelming force, he worked along the whole of his sector, bombing, sniping, and using captured machine guns; for 3½ hours not a single enemy could get within 10 yards of his line.

YOUNG, CHARLES EUSTON, Capt., Infantry. For conspicuous gallantry and devotion to duty. When two divisions attacked our front line in force, with field guns at close range, this officer's company, under his supervision, held on for 3½ hours, saving the situation. Field guns at 250 yards opened fire on his headquarters, but he sniped the gunners. Later, he crawled out and knocked out a machine gun with rifle grenades. Throughout attack and defence he kept his company well in hand.

NEW ZEALAND FORCE.

MILES, REGINALD, M.C., Major, New Zealand Field Artillery. For conspicuous gallantry and devotion to duty. He fought his battery until the enemy were within 500 yards and his ammunition exhausted, at the same time rallying infantry stragglers and manning a fire trench. Then made a reconnaissance into a wood, sending back valuable information. He was finally wounded by rifle fire at close range.

VERCOE, HENRY RAY, Capt., Auckland Regt. For conspicuous gallantry and devotion to duty. When his company commander was wounded he took command and led the company successfully under very heavy machine-gun fire. Next day he carried a wounded man into safety under heavy fire, and the following day, when some of his men were buried by a minenwerfer he went to the spot and saved the lives of two by digging them out with his bare hands. This officer was a fine example of courage and determination.

London Gazette, 27 July, 1918.—" War Office, 27 July, 1918. His Majesty the King has been graciously pleased to approve of the undermentioned rewards for distinguished service in connection with military operations in East Africa. Dated 3 June, 1918. Awarded a Bar to the Distinguished Service Order."

HOY, CHARLES NORMAN, D.S.O., Major, Cape Corps.

ROSE, RICHARD AUBREY DE BURGH, D.S.O., Major and Brevet Lieut.-Colonel (Temporary Colonel), Worcestershire Regt., attached Gold Coast Regt., West African Field Force.

Awarded the Distinguished Service Order :

ADDERLEY, ARTHUR CHARLES, Lieut.-Colonel, Royal Army Medical Corps.

BADHAM, JOHN FREDERICK, Major and Brevet Lieut.-Colonel, Worcestershire Regt., attached Nigeria Regt., West African Field Force.

BALL, LIONEL PLOMER, Major, Light Infantry, Indian Army.

CHOLMLEY, ROBERT STRICKLAND, Capt. (Temporary Major), West Riding Regt. and King's African Rifles.

COOPER, ALAN LESLIE, Temporary Major, Royal Engineers (late Imperial Light Horse).

CRICHTON, THE HONOURABLE JAMES ARCHIBALD, Capt., Reserve of Officers, Rifle Brigade, and West African Field Force.

DOONER, HUGH BRANDON, M.C., Temporary Capt., General List (Capt.), East African Intelligence Department.

HARDIMAN, EDGAR HENRY MALACHI, M.C., Temporary Capt., General List (Capt., South African Forces).

HAY, WESTWOOD NORMAN, C.I.E., Lieut.-Colonel, Baluchis, Indian Army.

LA FONTAINE, SIDNEY HUBERT, M.C., Temporary Capt., General List (East African Force.)

LAW, JOHN PRESCOTT, Lieut.-Colonel, Devonshire Regt., late Commanding West India Regt.

LEONARD, THOMAS MALCOLM RUSSELL, Temporary Major (Acting Lieut.-Colonel), Special List, West African Medical Service, West African Field Force.

MAHON, ALFRED ERNEST, Major, Rifles, Indian Army.

MARTIN, OWEN, Temporary Lieut. (Temporary Capt.), Special List, attached King's African Rifles.

SYMES-THOMPSON, ARTHUR HOWARD, Major, Royal Field Artillery, attached Kilwa Battery.

TYTLER, HARRY CHRISTOPHER, Colonel, Indian Army.

VAN VELDEN, DIRK OVERGAAUW, Temporary Lieut.-Colonel, General List, Lieut.-Colonel, South African Defence Force.

WALLACE, EDWARD CHARLES LLOYD, Major, Punjabis, Indian Army.

WHITRIDGE, MATTHEW WILLIAM, Temporary Major (Acting Lieut.-Colonel), King's African Rifles.

WILKINSON, JOHN SHANN, M.C., Capt. (Temporary Lieut.-Colonel), Nottinghamshire and Derby Regt. and King's African Rifles.

SOUTH AFRICAN FORCES.

BREYTENBACH, JOHAN HENDRIK, Lieut.-Colonel (Temporary Colonel), South African Infantry.

COCK, WILLIAM CHARLES, Capt. (Acting Major), South African Signalling Company.

COHEN, LIONEL, M.C., Temporary Capt., South African Defence Force (East African Intelligence Department).

COWELL, WILLIAM RALPH, Major, Cape Corps.

GORDON-GRAY, GORDON, M.C., Capt., South African Field Ambulance.

GREEN, ALEXANDER McWATT, Capt. (Acting Major), South African Medical Corps.

SMYTH, TEMPLE, Lieut.-Colonel, South African Medical Corps.

London Gazette, 3 Aug. 1918.—" Air Ministry, 3 Aug. 1918. His Majesty the King has been graciously pleased to confer the undermentioned rewards on Officers of the Royal Air Force, in recognition of gallantry in flying operations against the enemy. Awarded a Second Bar to the Distinguished Service Order."

MANNOCK, EDWARD, D.S.O., M.C., Lieut. (Temporary Capt.) (formerly Royal Engineers). This officer has now accounted for 48 enemy machines. His success is due to wonderful shooting and a determination to get to close quarters; to attain this he displays most skilful leadership and unfailing courage. These characteristics were markedly shown on a recent occasion when he attacked six hostile scouts, three of which he brought down. Later on the same day he attacked a two-seater, which crashed into a tree.

(The announcement of award of Distinguished Service Order, and First Bar thereto, will be published in a later Gazette.)

Awarded the Distinguished Service Order :

GILMOUR, JOHN, M.C., Lieut. (Temporary Capt.) (formerly Argyll and Sutherland Highlanders). He is a most inspiriting patrol leader who has destroyed 23 enemy aircraft, and shot down eight others out of control. While leading an offensive patrol he shot down one enemy biplane in flames and drove down a second. A short time afterwards he, with four others, attacked about 40 enemy scouts. He himself destroyed one in the air, drove another out of control and a third in flames, successfully accounting for five enemy machines in one day.

McCALL, FRED ROBERT, M.C., D.F.C., Lieut., (formerly Alberta Regt.). A brilliant and gallant officer who has accounted for 14 enemy machines. On a recent date he destroyed four during a patrol in the morning, and another in the evening, in each case closing to point-blank range with his opponent. His courage and offensive spirit has inspired all who serve with him.

Awarded the Distinguished Service Order for gallantry and distinguished service in operations in Mesopotamia :

TENNANT, JOHN EDWARD, M.C., Major and Temporary Lieut.-Colonel (formerly Brevet Major, Scots Guards).

London Gazette, 7 Aug. 1918.—" Admiralty, S.W., 7 Aug. 1918.—Honours for Services in Action with Enemy Light Cruisers which attacked Norwegian Convoy on 17 Oct. 1917. The King has been graciously pleased to approve of the award of the following honour, decoration and medals to the undermentioned Officers and men in recognition of their gallantry in the action between H.M. Torpedo-Boat Destroyers Mary Rose and Strongbow and three German light cruisers which attacked a convoy on 17 Oct. 1917." Included in award : To be a Companion of the Distinguished Service Order :

BROOKE, EDWARD, Lieut.-Commander, R.N. In command of H.M.S. Strongbow, fought a gallant action against overwhelming odds in endeavouring to protect a convoy. He was severely wounded during the engagement.

" Honours for Services in Action with Enemy Submarines.—The King has been graciously pleased to approve of the award of the following honours to the undermentioned Officers. To be Companions of the Distinguished Service Order."

PULLEYNE, RICHARD IVOR, D.S.C., Lieut., Royal Navy.

TOTTENHAM, CHARLES LOFTUS, Lieut., Royal Naval Reserve.

" Honours for Services in Mesopotamia and the Persian Gulf.—The King has been graciously pleased to approve of the award of the following honour to the undermentioned Officer. To be a Companion of the Distinguished Service Order."

SUTER, ROY NEVILLE, Lieut.-Commander (Acting Commander), R.N. In recognition of the zeal and ability displayed by him as Flag Commander to the Rear-Admiral, Persian Gulf and Mesopotamia, from June, 1917, to May, 1918. Lieut.-Commander Suter has served in the trying climate of this station for five years, and took part in many actions whilst in command of H.M.S. Lawrence.

" Honours for Miscellaneous Services.—The King has been graciously pleased to approve of the award of the following honour to the undermentioned Officer. To be a Companion of the Distinguished Service Order."

BENSON, CYRIL HERBERT GORDON, Commander, R.N. In recognition of great gallantry displayed in carrying out specially dangerous mine-sweeping operations.

London Gazette, 16 Aug. 1918.—" War Office, 16 Aug. 1918. With reference to the awards conferred as announced in the London Gazette dated 4 March, 1918, the following are the statements of service for which the decorations were conferred. Awarded a Bar to the Distinguished Service Order."

BAKER, SIR RANDOLPH LITTLEHALES, D.S.O., Bart., Major (Temporary Lieut.-Colonel), Yeomanry. For conspicuous gallantry and devotion to duty. He handled his regiment with great skill and intrepidity under shell and rifle fire, which resulted in a strong enemy counter-attack on the flank being repulsed and the position secured.

CRIPPS, THE HONOURABLE FREDERICK HAYWOOD, D.S.O. (name Haywood corrected to Heyworth), Major (Acting Lieut.-Colonel), Yeomanry. For conspicuous gallantry and devotion to duty. He displayed much skill in a reconnaissance, previous to charging the enemy's position, during which he led his regiment, afterwards returning to direct the rear squadron over bad ground, under heavy shell and rifle fire.

GILMOUR, JOHN, Jun., D.S.O., Lieut.-Colonel, Yeomanry. For conspicuous gallantry and devotion to duty when in command of his battalion in an attack. He led his battalion with great skill, and his courage and example contributed largely to the success achieved.

GODWIN, CHARLES ALEXANDER CAMPBELL, D.S.O., Major and Brevet Lieut.-Colonel (Temporary Brigadier-General), Cavalry, Indian Army. For conspicuous gallantry and devotion to duty. He attacked and captured an enemy position in the face of heavy shell, machine-gun and rifle fire. Later, he directed the attack by his brigade on a strong enemy position, and by his skill and determination contributed largely to the success of the operation.

MOORE, LANCELOT GEOFFREY, D.S.O., Capt. and Brevet Major (Acting Lieut.-Colonel), King's Royal Rifle Corps. For conspicuous gallantry and devotion to duty. At a time when the situation was very obscure, he led his battalion under heavy fire of all kinds with great skill and courage to its objective. His able disposition of his companies and quick grasp of the situation enabled a dangerous gap in the line to be closed, and prevented the village from falling into the hands of the enemy. He held his position against repeated attacks for over 48 hours under very heavy shell fire, himself remaining the whole time in the front line. His personal courage and example were of the greatest value in keeping the line intact.

ST. JOHN, WILLIAM EUSTACE, D.S.O., Major (Temporary Lieut.-Colonel), Yeomanry. For conspicuous gallantry and devotion to duty. He was ordered to relieve another unit, which at the time was heavily engaged with the enemy. By his able handling of the situation the relief was successfully accomplished and the fight carried on. During the following days the enemy made repeated attempts to capture the high ground held by his battalion, but they were driven back on every occasion. His gallantry and example were undoubtedly responsible for the determined resistance made by his battalion.

SEGRAVE, WILLIAM HENRY ERIK, D.S.O., Major (Acting Lieut.-Colonel), Highland Light Infantry. For conspicuous gallantry and devotion to duty. When the troops on his flank were pressed back, a gap in the line occurred, and the enemy were on the point of breaking through owing to the heavy casualties of his battalion. He therefore collected all the personnel of his headquarters, and personally led them against the enemy, and succeeded in forming a defensive flank. By his fine example of coolness and total disregard of personal danger, when under intense fire, he restored complete confidence, and undoubtedly saved a very critical situation.

NEW ZEALAND FORCE.

McCARROLL, JAMES NEIL, D.S.O., Lieut.-Colonel, Mounted Rifles. For conspicuous gallantry and devotion to duty. He carried out an attack on the flank of the enemy's position with great skill. When heavily counter-attacked he showed splendid ability in meeting the enemy's attack, altering his dispositions several times to meet the changing circumstances, and drove back the enemy with heavy loss. He set a fine example to his men.

Awarded the Distinguished Service Order:

BAKER, BRIAN EDMUND, M.C., Temporary Second Lieut. (Temporary Capt.), General List and Royal Flying Corps. For conspicuous gallantry and devotion to duty. Whilst on patrol he engaged nine Albatross scouts, five of these being driven down, two of which he accounted for. On another occasion, whilst leading his flight on an offensive patrol, he dived alone on a formation of six enemy scouts, driving one down out of control. During the course of his patrol work he has brought down 10 enemy machines, and his work on all occasions has been magnificent. He is a dashing patrol leader, and inspires all with the greatest keenness.

BATTERSHILL, LIONEL WARMINGTON, M.C., Temporary Lieut., Machine Gun Corps. For conspicuous gallantry and devotion to duty. He, realizing the critical situation, brought up two machine guns to the reserve line under an intense enemy barrage. Owing to the heavy casualties amongst his gun crews, he worked one gun himself, and although four times wounded, continued to fire, inflicting heavy casualties upon the enemy, until he was in a fainting condition and unable to carry the gun away. His courage and determination were of the highest order.

BLACKWOOD, ALBEMARLE PRICE, Major (Acting Lieut.-Colonel), Border Regt. For conspicuous gallantry and devotion to duty. He conducted a most successful raid on a village in the enemy's lines, which resulted in the capture of 55 prisoners and heavy casualties to the enemy. The success of the enterprise was due to his forethought and skilful handling of his command.

BUCKLE, ARCHIBALD WALTER, Temporary Lieut.-Commander, Royal Naval Volunteer Reserve. For conspicuous gallantry and devotion to duty. When in command of a battalion detailed to counter-attack, he carried out a daring reconnaissance, under extremely heavy artillery fire, enabling him to form sound dispositions, which resulted in the recapture of an important position. Throughout the day his coolness and example inspired all ranks.

DONALDSON, HERBERT, Temporary Sub-Lieut., Royal Naval Volunteer Reserve. For conspicuous gallantry and devotion to duty. He was in charge of a company in the front line which was subjected to several intense bombardments, after which the enemy attacked six times. They were driven off on each occasion, and the position was held intact, although one flank was in the air. He worked continually, getting the shattered line into a state of defence, and set his men a magnificent example of courage and determination. When the enemy attacked with liquid flame and forced back his flank a short distance, he led a counter-attack which re-established the position and inflicted heavy losses on the enemy.

FREW, MATTHEW BROWN, M.C., Temporary Capt., General List and Royal Flying Corps. For conspicuous gallantry and devotion to duty. On one occasion when leader of a patrol he shot down an enemy aeroplane, two others being also accounted for in the same fight. On a later occasion he destroyed three enemy machines in one combat, all of which were seen to crash to the ground. Immediately after this combat he had to switch off his engine and make an attempt to glide towards our lines five miles away on account of his machine having received a direct hit. Owing to the great skill and courage he displayed in the handling of his damaged machine, he succeeded in bringing it safely to our lines. He has destroyed 22 enemy machines up to date.

HARRIS, WALTER KILROY, M.C., Temporary Lieut., Royal Naval Volunteer Reserve. For conspicuous gallantry and devotion to duty. When the enemy attacked under an intense bombardment and captured his trench, he directed repeated bombing attacks until he had regained half the trench and established block, which was hotly contested all day. Towards evening he led a bombing attack along both sides of the trench, which regained the whole position and resulted in the capture of five enemy machine guns. Throughout the day he led his company with great courage and determination under heavy fire, and set them a magnificent example. It was entirely due to his efforts that the position was re-established.

LLOYD, LEMUEL, Temporary Major, Suffolk Regt. For conspicuous gallantry and devotion to duty. When the enemy, after a heavy bombardment, succeeded in penetrating the front line, he at once went to the scene of the fight and organized a successful counter-attack. During the following days, when the enemy again succeeded in entering our positions, on two occasions, under heavy gas-shell bombardments and supported by liquid flame, he organized counter-attacks, which each time drove the enemy out, and completely restored the position. He showed magnificent determination and skill, and his courage and energy were of the greatest value during a period of stubborn and difficult fighting.

MARSHALL, FREDERIC ADRIAN JOSEPH EVANS, M.C., Lieut. (Acting Capt.), East Kent Regt. For conspicuous gallantry and devotion to duty. When the enemy attacked and broke through the front line he at once grasped the situation and led his company, which was in reserve, to form a defensive line under heavy fire. He collected men of other units, organized the defence, and held up the enemy. He then led his men in a counter-attack, recaptured part of the lost ground, and inflicted heavy casualties on the enemy. By his courage and resource he undoubtedly saved a critical situation.

MORGAN-OWEN, MORGAN MADDOX, Capt. (Acting Lieut.-Colonel), Essex Regt. For conspicuous gallantry and devotion to duty. On the occasion of the enemy attack, when his battalion was in reserve, he moved it up to resist the attack, and held on to the position for two days, though the troops on his flank were pressed back. His steadfast determination to hold his ground against repeated attacks and under heavy fire largely contributed to restoring and keeping in hand the critical situation which had arisen.

PECK, ARTHUR HICKS, M.C., Temporary Capt., General List and Roya Flying Corps. For conspicuous gallantry and devotion to duty. During two months aerial fighting he has never hesitated to attack the enemy when they were in superior numbers. On one occasion, when piloting a scout, he engaged a hostile formation consisting of four scouts and two two-seaters, completely dispersing them and driving one down out of control. His dash, resourcefulness and skill have been most marked.

POLLOCK, HENRY BRODHURST, Temporary Commander, Royal Nava Volunteer Reserve. For conspicuous gallantry and devotion to duty. He displayed great fearlessness and ability in handling his battalion in a most difficult situation during an attack. Under very heavy shell fire he personally superintended the reorganization of his line, and inspired his men by his example of coolness and gallantry.

READY, JOHN MILNER, M.C., Second Lieut. (Temporary Capt.), Royal Berkshire Regt., Special Reserve. For conspicuous gallantry and devotion to duty. When the enemy attacked he was holding the line on the extreme flank of the division. Realizing that the safety of the battalion depended on holding on until the last possible moment, he organized and led bombing sections against the enemy, holding them up for three hours, in spite of their superior numbers. When ordered to withdraw, he conducted a very successful withdrawal, which enabled him to hold a very important portion of the defence system for two days until relieved.

SALKELD, HAROLD YORKE, Major, Lancers, Indian Army. For conspicuous gallantry and devotion to duty. He led his squadron forward with great skill under heavy fire, and seized a commanding position. He then led a dismounted attack on a further enemy position, which he captured and held against the enemy, although surrounded on three sides. He set a splendid example to his men.

London Gazette, 22 Aug. 1918.—" War Office, 22 Aug. 1918. His Majesty the King has been graciously pleased to approve of the award of the Distinguished Service Order to the undermentioned Officers for distinguished service in the field, and in connection with the Campaign in German South-West Africa, 1914–15. To date 1 Jan. 1916."

STAFF.

BADENHORST, LOURENS PETRUS JOHANNES, Major (Temporary Colonel Commandant), 2nd Mounted Brigade, Permanent Force.

BERRANGE, CHRISTIAN ANTONY LAWSON, C.M.G., Lieut.-Colonel and Brevet Colonel (Temporary Brigadier-General), Permanent Force (S.A.M.R.).

BOUWER, BAREND DANIEL, Lieut.-Colonel, Permanent Force (Staff).

BRINK, ARENDE, Major, 4th Mounted Brigade (10th Dismounted Rifles).

CHEADLE, HARRY, M.C., Lieut. (Temporary Major) (S.A.E.C.).

COLLINS, WILLIAM RICHARD, Colonel Commandant, 2nd Mounted Brigade.

COLLYER, JOHN JOHNSTON, C.B., C.M.G., Lieut.-Colonel (Temporary Brigadier-General), Permanent Force (Staff).

CULLINAN, SIR THOMAS, Major (Supernumerary List).

DE JAGER, MATTHYS JOHAN, Lieut.-Colonel, Permanent Force (Staff).

DE LA REY, PIETER, Colonel Commandant, 1st Mounted Brigade.

DE WAAL, DANIEL, Lieut.-Colonel (Supernumerary List).

HARTIGAN, MARCUS MICHAEL, Lieut.-Colonel, 10th Mounted Brigade (Hartigan's Horse).

(The award of a Bar to the D.S.O. is substituted for the award of a D.S.O. to this Officer, published in London Gazette dated 18 Feb. 1918.)

HIRSCH, HARRY ALPHONSE, Major, Permanent Force (Staff).

HOLLENBACH, JOHAN GEORGE, Capt. (Temporary Major), 3rd Mounted Brigade (S.A.S.C.).

HURST, GODFREY THOMAS, V.D., Major, 8th Mounted Brigade (3rd Mounted Rifles).

JORDAAN, JACOBUS FRANCIS, Lieut.-Colonel (Temporary Colonel Commandant), 3rd Mounted Brigade (13th Mounted Regt.).

LEIPOLDT, JOHANN GOTLIEB WILHELM, Major, Permanent Force (Staff).

MARE, TROSKIE, Major, 5th Mounted Brigade (Supernumerary List).

MACKENZIE, SIR DUNCAN, K.C.M.G., C.B., V.D., Brigadier-General, Retired List, late Natal Militia Force.

MEYER, IZAK JOHANNES, Major (Temporary Lieut.-Colonel) (12th Mounted Rifles).

MULLER, FRED, Major (S.A.E.C.).

MURRAY, DONALD DAVID COGHILL, Major, 5th Mounted Brigade (Supernumerary List).

NUSSEY, WILFRED JOAH, Major, 4th Mounted Brigade (Supernumerary List).

PERROTT, ROBERT ROSS, Capt. (Temporary Major) (Railway Regt.).

PIJPER, SCHALK WILLEM, Colonel Commandant, 5th Mounted Brigade.

PRETTEJOHN, NICHOLAS KINGSWELL, Major (Supernumerary List).

PRETORIUS, HENDRIK STEPHANUS, Major, 4th Mounted Brigade, Supernumerary List.

TANNER, RICHARD MORRISON, Major, 7th Mounted Brigade (1st Mounted Rifles).

VAN DE VENTER, DIRK JACOB CARL BEKKER, Colonel, 4th Mounted Brigade (10th Dismounted Rifles).

WYLIE, JAMES SCOTT, M.V.O., V.D., Lieut.-Colonel (Temporary Colonel), 4th Infantry Brigade (1st Infantry).

ARTILLERY.

WOLMARANS, JAN FRANCOIS, Capt. (Temporary Major), 4th Permanent Battery (S.A.M.R.).

DIVINE, CHARLES HENRY FINERAN, V.D., Major, 6th Citizen Battery.

EDWARDS, GEORGE RICHARD OWEN, Major, 12th Citizen Battery.

(The award of a Bar to the D.S.O. is substituted for the award of a D.S.O. to this Officer, published in London Gazette dated 1 Jan. 1917.)

HEAVY ARTILLERY.

BEGBIE, RONALD PHILLIPS GLYNN, M.C., Capt. (Temporary Major), Royal Garrison Artillery.

PERMANENT FORCE.

CURTIS, GEORGE, Major (Temporary Lieut.-Colonel) (South African Mounted Riflemen), 1st Regt.

RUSH, WILLIAM WELCH, Major (Temporary Lieut.-Colonel), 5th Regt.

MOUNTED RIFLES.

WOODS, JOHN PHILLIPS SYMONDS, Lieut.-Colonel (Active Citizen Force), 2nd Mounted Rifles (Natal Carbineers).
HARBER, AUGUSTUS FREDERICK, Major, 3rd Mounted Rifles (Natal Mounted Rifles).
CARTER, SAMUEL, Lieut.-Colonel, 4th Mounted Rifles (Umvoti Mounted Rifles).
LIGERTWOOD, CHARLES EDWARD, Lieut.-Colonel, 5th Mounted Rifles (Imperial Light Horse).
(The award of a Bar to the D.S.O. is substituted for the award of a D.S.O. to this Officer, published in the London Gazette dated 1 Jan. 1917.)
GREATHED, PERCY, Major (Reserve of Officers), attached 2nd Imperial Light Horse.
COLLETT, EWART JAMES, Lieut.-Colonel, 8th Mounted Rifles (Midlandse Ruiters).
GRIMBECK, JOHAN DANIEL ETZARD, Major (Temporary Lieut.-Colonel), 11th Mounted Rifles (Potchefstroom Ruiters).
ROUX, PETRUS DANIEL ALBERTUS, Lieut.-Colonel, 12th Mounted Rifles (Krugersdorp Ruiters).
VAN DER WESTHUIZEN, PETRUS BENJAMIN, Lieut.-Colonel, 17th Mounted Rifles (Western Province Rifles).
VAN ZYL, JAN STEPHANUS, Lieut.-Colonel, 20th Mounted Rifles (Graaf Reinet Ruiters).

Commandos.

SWEMMER, IVAN VICTOR, Lieut.-Colonel, Botha's Hogevald Ruiters.
BOTHA, THEUNIS, Lieut.-Colonel, Botha's Natal Horse.
DE VILLIERS, JACOBUS, Lieut.-Colonel, Bethel Commando.
BEZUIDENHOUT, JOHANNES JACOBUS, Lieut.-Colonel, Bloemhof Commando.
BREEDT, JOHANNES MARTHINUS NICOLAS, Major, Britstown Commando.
BRONKHURST, JOHANNES GERHARDUS STEPHANUS, Major, Calvinia-Kenhardt Commando.
VERMAAS, PIETER ARNOLDUS, Major, Calvinia-Kenhardt Commando.
VAN ZYL, KARL JOHANNES, Major, Carnarvon Commando.
FOURIE, JOACHIM, Lieut.-Colonel, Carolina Commando.
GRIMBRECK, ADOLF SEIGFREID, Major, Clanwilliam Commando.
DU PLESSIS, PHILLIPUS LODEWICUS, Major, Cradock Commando.
CULLINAN, ARTHUR WILLIAM, Major, Cullinan's Horse.
CLOETE, CORNELIS WILLIAM, Major, Enslin's Horse.
STEENKAMP, WILLEM, Major, Ermelo " B " Commando.
MALAN, GERT STEPHANUS GONS, Major, Hanover Commando.
GREYLING, ANDRIES JACOBUS, Lieut.-Colonel, Heidelberg " A " Commando.
HUNT, EDWIN WATKIN, M.C., Major, Hunt's Scouts.
VAN ZYL, JACOBUS ALBERTUS, Lieut.-Colonel (Temporary Colonel Commandant), Kalahari Horse.
VORSTER, PIETER WILLEM, Lieut.-Colonel, Krugersdorp Commando.
WESSEL, JOHANNES ALBERTUS, Capt., Lichtenburg Commando.
MAREE, CORNELIUS JOHANNES, Major, Lydenburg Commando.
VAN NIEKERK, LOURENZ, Lieut.-Colonel, Marico Commando.
HAMMAN, JAKOB LETTERSTEDT, Major, Middelburg " A " Commando.
MOUTON, WILLEM JOHANNES, Lieut.-Colonel, Middelburg " B " Commando.
BERGEEST, JOHAN WILLEM, Major, Murraysburg Commando.
COUROY, ANDREW MEINTJES, Major, Philiptown Commando.
MOLLER, PIET WILLEM, Lieut.-Colonel, Pietersburg Commando.
DE JAGER, PETRUS LAPAS, Lieut.-Colonel, Piet Retief Commando.
HOLL, GEORGE WILLEM, Lieut.-Colonel, Potchefstroom " A " Commando.
VISSER, PIETER FRANCOIS, Lieut.-Colonel, Potchefstroom " B " Commando.
BOTHA, THEUNIS, Major, Pretoria Commando (Botha's Mounted Rifles).
ROUSSOUW, PIERRE JACQUES, Major, Rustenburg Commando (Van Tonder's Horse).
VAN TONDER, ROELOF JACOBUS PETRUS, Colonel Commandant, Rustenburg Commando (Van Tonder's Horse).
LENS, DAVID, Lieut.-Colonel, Utrecht Commando.
THRING, ALFRED LESTER, Lieut.-Colonel, Vrijstaatse Schutters (1st Regt.).
DE NECKER, JOHAN ADERIAAN, Lieut.-Colonel, Vrijstaatse Schutters (2nd Regt.).
JOUBERT, CHRISTIAN, Major, Vrijstaatse Schutters (5th Regt.).
DU PREEZ, CORNELIUS JOHANNES, Lieut.-Colonel, Vrijstaatse Schutters (6th Regt.).
KRUGER, JOHANNES ANDRIES, Major, Vryheid Commando (Christian name corrected to Jacobus Andries and rank to Lieut.-Colonel [London Gazette, 27 Sept. 1920]).
DE BEER, MARTIN JOHN, Major, Wakkerstroom Commando.
GEYSER, ANDRIES HERMANUS, Major, Waterburg Commando.
PRETORIUS, NICOLAAS JACOBUS, Lieut.-Colonel, Western Transvaal Ruiters.
VAN RENSBURG, MARTHINUS JACOB JANSE, Lieut.-Colonel, Wolmaranstad Commando.

DISMOUNTED RIFLES.

KIRSTEN, JOHAN ROBERT FRANCOIS, Lieut.-Colonel, 6th Dismounted Rifles (Midlandse Schutters).
STEYN, WILLEM HERBERT, Major (Temporary Lieut.-Colonel), 14th Dismounted Rifles (Karroo Schutters).

INFANTRY.

WOODHEAD, BERTRAM MAYNARD, Capt., 2nd nfantry (Duke of Edinburgh's Own Rifles).
BURKE, HERBERT FRANCIS LARDNER, M.C., Capt., 7th Infantry (Kimberley Regt.).
DAWSON-SQUIBB, JOHN, Lieut.-Colonel, 8th Infantry (Transvaal Scottish).
FOX, GEORGE CHARLES, Major, 2nd Transvaal Scottish.
YOUNG, BENJAMIN, Major, 10th Infantry (Witwatersrand Rifles).
MORTON, FRANK WILLOUGHBY, Major, 12th Infantry (Pretoria Regt.).
CRESSWELL, FREDERIC HUGH PAGE, Lieut.-Colonel, Rand Rifles.
CARR, JOSEPH WILSON, Major, Railway Regt.
HEALD, BEN CYRIL, Major, Railway Regt. (Supernumerary List.)

ADMINISTRATIVE SERVICES.

South African Service Corps.

ANDERSON, JAMES DALGLEISH, Major (Transport and Remounts).
KENNARD, DAVID HUGH, Major (Supplies).
KING, CHARLES EDWARD STEWART, Major (Transport and Remounts).
KIRWAN, JOHN THOMAS, Capt. (Temporary Major) (Supplies).

South African Medical Service.

DE KOEK, SERVASE MEYER, Lieut.-Colonel.
HAYDON, LEONARD GUSCOTE, Major.
KNAPP, GEORGE HARVEY, Lieut.-Colonel.
MOFFAT, GEORGE BAIRD, Capt. (description corrected to Captain, South African Medical Corps [London Gazette, 15 Oct. 1918]).

South African Veterinary Corps.

BUSH, JOSEPH GEORGE, Major.
LEE, GEORGE WILLIAM, Major.

Chaplains.

JONES, THE REV. THOMAS HENRY, Chaplain Capt.

Ordnance.

HUMPHREY, MORLEY, Capt. (Temporary Major).

South African Field Post and Telegraph Corps.

McARTHUR, ROBERT TAYLOR, Capt. (Temporary Major).
POOLE, ROBERT, M.C., Major.
VENNING, JAMES ALFRED, Major.

London Gazette, 23 Aug. 1918.—" War Office, 23 Aug. 1918. His Majesty the King has been graciously pleased to approve of the undermentioned rewards for distinguished service in connection with military operations in Mesopotamia, dated 23 Aug. 1918, unless otherwise stated. Awarded the Distinguished Service Order."

GRIER, HARRY DIXON, C.B., Colonel (Temporary Brigadier-General), Royal Artillery.
MATHIAS, LEONARD WILLIAM HENRY, Capt., Pioneers, Indian Army.
MORLAND, WALTER EDWARD THOMSON, M.C., Capt., Oxfordshire and Buckinghamshire Light Infantry.
POCOCK, PHILIP FREDERICK, Lieut.-Colonel, Infantry, Indian Army.

London Gazette, 24 Aug. 1918.—" War Office, 24 Aug. 1918. With reference to the awards conferred as announced in the London Gazette dated 26 March, 1918, the following are the statements of service for which the decorations were conferred. Awarded a Bar to the Distinguished Service Order."

ANDERSON, JAMES, C.M.G., D.S.O., Lieut.-Colonel, Highland Light Infantry. For conspicuous gallantry and devotion to duty. Knowing that reliable information regarding a ford was urgently required, he, accompanied by another officer, proceeded on his own initiative to this point. Though the ford was guarded by three hostile machine guns in a trench 100 yards from the water, they swam out to sea, and turning parallel to the shore, attempted to cross the mouth of the river. Finding themselves on their own side of the river mouth, they made a second attempt, and finally succeeded in reaching the enemy's side of the river mouth. There they ascertained both the depth and breadth of the ford, information which proved to be of inestimable value to subsequent operations. The success of this reconnaissance was due to their coolness and resource.
FORTH, NOWELL BARNARD DE LANCEY, D.S.O., M.C., Major (Acting Lieut.-Colonel), Manchester Regt. For conspicuous gallantry and devotion to duty. By his personal courage and example he inspired the greatest confidence in all ranks. Though his position was most difficult and subject to an intense frontal and enfilade machine-gun fire, he continually moved from position to position, cheering his men. It was largely owing to his fine leadership and great gallantry that this critical position was held all day.
FARQUHAR, JAMES, D.S.O., Lieut.-Colonel, Royal Field Artillery. For conspicuous gallantry and devotion to duty when supporting an infantry attack. He led a section of one of his batteries across the open and got it into action close behind the firing line. His gallant conduct was an inspiration to all.
FORBES-ROBERTSON, JAMES, D.S.O., M.C., Capt. (Acting Lieut.-Colonel), Border Regt. For conspicuous gallantry and devotion to duty. He led his battalion with great dash and determination in a successful attack. Later, during continual enemy attacks, though he was wounded in the eye and unable to see, he was led about by an orderly among his men in the front line, encouraging and inspiring them by his magnificent example of courage and determination.
REES, JOHN GORDON, D.S.O., Major, Yeomanry. For conspicuous gallantry and devotion to duty. With a company barely 100 strong he surrounded and captured a village at dawn, where he found an enemy force of between 500 and 600 strong. Owing to heavy machine-gun fire he was unable to send back the whole of the enemy force as prisoners, but succeeded in sending back 300 of them. Subsequently, on being counter-attacked, it was owing to his able leading and daring gallantry that he was able to withdraw his company under heavy fire, though it was practically surrounded.
ROMANES, JAMES GERALD PAGET, D.S.O., Capt. (Acting Lieut.-Colonel), Royal Scots. For conspicuous gallantry and devotion to duty. He commanded his battalion with great skill and courage in a night attack. Under his leadership the battalion captured all its objectives without a check, inflicted heavy casualties on the enemy, captured over 50 prisoners, and consolidated all the ground won under intense shell fire.

Awarded the Distinguished Service Order :

BARBER, THOMAS PHILIP, Major, Yeomanry. For conspicuous gallantry and devotion to duty. He, seeing that the enemy were taking up a position, rushed to the front, shot two of the enemy with his revolver, and leading his men forward compelled the hostile force to withdraw over the ridge. Further, when he noticed that the enemy were still wavering, he led his men forward again,

The Distinguished Service Order

and drove the enemy back on to another ridge in rear. Throughout the day he showed the greatest contempt of all danger, and set a magnificent example to his men.

BOWMAN, GEOFFREY HILTON, M.C., Lieut. (Temporary Capt.), Royal Warwickshire Regt., Special Reserve, and Royal Flying Corps. For conspicuous gallantry and devotion to duty. He has recently destroyed six enemy aeroplanes and driven down others out of control. He has at all times shown splendid courage and determination, and by his leadership and good example has contributed largely to the success of his squadron.

BRAND, DAVID ERNEST, Major, Highland Light Infantry. For conspicuous gallantry and devotion to duty. He led his company in a bayonet charge on an enemy position in the dark without a previous reconnaissance. He captured the position which dominated the crossing of a river, and thereby secured the crossing for the remainder of the troops. After holding his ground during the night, he captured a further enemy position on the following morning. He showed splendid leadership and skill.

CANTRELL-HUBBERSTY, GEORGE ALBERT JESSOP, Major, Yeomanry. For conspicuous gallantry and devotion to duty. By the gallant and rapid manner in which he led his men and charged the advancing enemy he stopped the hostile attack and thus prevented the flank of the whole line from being turned. His dash and initiative were most meritorious.

CHANNER, GEORGE KENDALL, Major (Acting Lieut.-Colonel), Indian Army. For conspicuous gallantry and devotion to duty. During the defence of the ridge his position was subjected to heavy artillery bombardment and repeated and determined enemy attacks, which had as their object the envelopment of his left flank. These attacks were only frustrated by heavy counter-attacks, led by himself, and although he was wounded on two successive days he continued to command his battalion, personally directing and organizing the defence. By his total indifference to danger, cheerfulness and splendid example he maintained the spirits of his men and enabled them to hold out.

COOK, JOHN BLAIR, M.C., Major (Acting Lieut.-Colonel), Royal Scots Fusiliers. For conspicuous gallantry and devotion to duty. He led his battalion with great determination in an attack. He continually pushed forward, and eventually gained his objective, and consolidated a captured village with great skill. His coolness and courage were most marked.

CREWE-READ, RANDULF O., Capt., South Wales Borderers, Special Reserve. For conspicuous gallantry and devotion to duty. By bold and skilful handling of his company he gained a position in rear of the enemy, and captured two field guns and a number of prisoners. On another occasion he manœuvred his company to a flank, under heavy fire, and captured a position from which the enemy was enfilading the advance. He showed splendid initiative and skill.

DEAKIN, ERNEST BETTON, M.C., Capt., Essex Regt. For conspicuous gallantry and devotion to duty. His company having for its objective a certain redoubt, he found that through an error this redoubt was being attacked by another company, which should have attacked a strongly defended field work. He immediately changed his objective, and attacked and captured this work. He showed remarkable decision and presence of mind, and by his resource and initiative saved what would undoubtedly have been a very serious situation.

DRUMMOND, ROY MAXWELL, M.C., Capt., Royal Flying Corps. For conspicuous gallantry and devotion to duty. While escorting a reconnaissance, on three hostile 'planes being encountered he at once attacked and drove down one of these, although he was being himself attacked in the rear by the remaining two. Drawing these latter away from the reconnaissance machine, he turned, attacked and followed one of these down to a lower altitude, despite heavy anti-aircraft fire. This machine was then seen to strike the ground and turn over. He then attacked the third machine, and, after a long burst of fire at close range, both wings of the enemy 'plane were observed to collapse in the air. The whole action was characterized by the great skill and daring of this officer.

GLAZEBROOK, PHILIP KIRKLAND, Major, Yeomanry. For conspicuous gallantry and devotion to duty. When, by the capture of a neighbouring height, the enemy had rendered the position of two companies most precarious, owing to the fact that they now came under concentrated machine-gun fire from their left rear, he immediately went to the most threatened spot, and by his courageous bearing and great coolness was responsible for the safe withdrawal of these companies. The unfailing energy and resolution shown by this officer were most noticeable.

HAWKINS, EDWARD BRIAN BARKLEY, Capt. (Temporary Major), West Yorkshire Regt. For conspicuous gallantry and devotion to duty. Boldly attacking a superior enemy force, he inflicted severe casualties on them, thus diverting them from their objective, and being instrumental in causing their subsequent surrender. He has at all times shown the greatest courage and initiative, and has afforded a most inspiring example to the troops under him.

HAY, ARCHIBALD ASHWORTH BAILIE, M.C., Lieut. (Acting Major), Royal Field Artillery, Special Reserve. For conspicuous gallantry and devotion to duty in connection with a raid on the enemy's trenches. By his accurate judgment and observation and his skilful preparation he contributed largely to the success of the raid.

HIND, HUGH WILLIAM, M.C., Lieut. (Acting Capt.), London Regt. For conspicuous gallantry and devotion to duty. Having conducted a reconnaissance at great personal risk, he returned to battalion headquarters to find that his commanding officer had been killed. Taking command of the battalion, then heavily engaged, he led it through the remainder of the action, displaying a marked grip of every situation, and inspiring all ranks by his coolness and self-confidence under very trying circumstances.

HUNT, DOUGLAS ALEXIS, Temporary Capt., King's African Rifles. For conspicuous gallantry and devotion to duty. When in command of the firing line, through his personal courage and example he was largely instrumental in repelling several enemy counter-attacks, which were launched against him by very superior forces. On these occasions of danger and difficulty his courage, coolness and determination were of the highest order, only equalled by his courageous conduct on all other previous occasions.

INNES, WILLIAM KEDIE, Capt., King's Own Scottish Borderers. For conspicuous gallantry and devotion to duty. When the enemy attacked and penetrated into a village in our lines he at once organized and led a bombing party, killed and captured several of the enemy and forced them back. He then organized more parties and quickly cleared the enemy from the village. His prompt and determined action saved a critical situation.

LANDSBERG, HERBERT VALENTINE, Capt. (Acting Major), Royal Horse Artillery. For conspicuous gallantry and devotion to duty. When observing fire from a position in the open, he and his battery came under prolonged and heavy shell fire, several casualties being inflicted on men and horses, which necessitated the withdrawal of the teams and the man-handling of the guns to the rear. He, however, remained in his position in the open and brought effective fire to bear on the enemy, rendering great assistance in the capture of the ridge. His courage and devotion to duty were most commendable.

LINDSAY, ERIC LAWRENCE, Temporary Capt., King's African Rifles. For conspicuous gallantry and devotion to duty. With forty men he succeeded in repelling an enemy attack made with greatly superior forces and in inflicting severe casualties on them. Later, when surrounded, he extricated his party with the greatest skill and determination, himself accounting for twelve of the enemy, and succeeded later in joining up with his main body. His conduct in action has always been characterized by courage and resource.

NOEL, HAROLD ERNEST, Capt. (Acting Major), Royal Horse Artillery. For conspicuous gallantry and devotion to duty. His personal example inspired and encouraged his men on what seemed an impossible task, that of making a pathway for the guns under the most difficult and dangerous conditions. Having got his battery in action in time to render material aid in repelling an enemy attack, he remained in the open with a section, which was being subjected to heavy shell and machine-gun fire, displaying marked gallantry, and by his contempt of danger did much to inspire his men with confidence.

SMITH, RONALD KING, M.C., Lieut. (Acting Capt.), Wiltshire Regt., Special Reserve. For conspicuous gallantry and devotion to duty. During a raid on the enemy's positions he led the raiding party on a long march by compass bearing over very difficult country. When he encountered a redoubt strongly held by the enemy, he led the charge which captured the position, inflicting heavy casualties upon the enemy. He showed marked courage and resource.

URWICK, FRANK DAVIDSON, Major, Somersetshire Light Infantry. For conspicuous gallantry and devotion to duty. After the capture of the village by his battalion, on the enemy putting down an intense artillery and machine-gun barrage, he moved his headquarters from a position of cover over this shell-swept zone and, keeping his signallers with him, established in the village the sole means of communication between the two advanced battalions and brigade headquarters. On reaching the village, where he found that the enemy were developing a strong counter-attack against his right flank, he immediately collected a miscellaneous party of men, organized the defence, and succeeded in repulsing the hostile attack. Throughout he displayed the utmost indifference to danger, and set a magnificent example to his men.

WRAY, EDWARD MILLARD GRUBB, Second Lieut., Essex Regt. For conspicuous gallantry and devotion to duty. Although in the second wave of the attack, noticing that his company commander had become a casualty, he at once went forward and took command, leading the attack which cleared the trenches of the enemy. Having vigorously supervised the consolidation, he volunteered to return and report the situation to his commanding officer. Finding on his way his company commander, who was unable to move, he brought him under cover despite a heavy fire. Later, he volunteered to get in touch with the battalion on the flank, and succeeded in establishing communication with it. His conduct throughout was exceptional, and by his utter disregard of danger and by his cheerfulness he did much to encourage his company.

CANADIAN FORCE.

BOWIE, DOUGLAS BAIN, Major, Dragoons. For conspicuous gallantry and devotion to duty when in command of a raid on the enemy's trenches. He led his party with great coolness and courage and cleared three lines of the enemy's trenches on a wide front, killing or capturing the whole enemy garrison in that area.

PRICE, EVAN EDWARD, M.C., Lieut., Dragoons. For conspicuous gallantry and devotion to duty. He led forward parties and blew gaps in two belts of the enemy's wire before a raid. His accurate reconnaissances on the three previous nights, and his splendid courage and initiative on the night of the raid, contributed largely to the success of the enterprise.

SOUTH AFRICAN FORCE.

LORCH, ARTHUR EDWARD, Major, Field Artillery. For conspicuous gallantry and devotion to duty. He showed great courage in boldly reconnoitring forward positions for his battery, whereby he was able to bring his battery into effective action very rapidly. He afforded a splendid example of indifference to danger throughout this reconnaissance, which was carried out under heavy rifle fire.

London Gazette, 26 Aug. 1918.—" War Office, 26 Aug. 1918. His Majesty the King has been graciously pleased to approve of the undermentioned rewards for distinguished service in connection military operations in Mesopotamia. Dated 3 June, 1918, unless otherwise stated. Awarded the Distinguished Service Order."

ALEXANDER, HENRY STIRLING, Lieut.-Colonel, Infantry, Indian Army.
BECHER, GEORGE ARTHUR, Lieut.-Colonel, Cavalry, Indian Army.
BELGRAVE, HEW DACRES, Major and Brevet Lieut.-Colonel, Royal West Kent Regt.
BERNARD, JOSEPH FRANCIS, C.M.G., Ordnance Officer, Second Class, and Lieut.-Colonel, Army Ordnance Department.
BOWEN, HERBERT WALTER, Lieut.-Colonel (Temporary Colonel), Royal Artillery, Indian Ordnance Department.
BROWNE, HARRY HOSKING GORDON, Major (Temporary Lieut.-Colonel), Somersetshire Light Infantry.
BROWN, ROBERT GEOFFREY, Major, Manchester Regt.
BUCKLAND, GUY NEVILLE, Major, Royal Garrison Artillery.
CAMPBELL, CHARLES ROSS, Temporary Major (Temporary Lieut.-Colonel) (Lieut.-Commander, Royal Indian Marine), Royal Engineers.
COPPINGER, WALTER VALENTINE, M.D., F.R.C.S.I., Major, Indian Medical Service.
CROWDY, JAMES DUNSCOMB, Major, Gurkha Rifles, Indian Army.
CUMING, ROBERT JOHN, Major and Brevet Lieut.-Colonel, Pioneers, Indian Army.
DAYRELL, WILFRED STUART, Major, Punjabis, Indian Army.
DEANE, DENNIS, Major and Brevet Lieut.-Colonel, Cavalry, Indian Army.
ETHERIDGE, FRANK, Major, Rajputs, Indian Army.
HEMSLEY, CHARLES, Capt., Pioneers, Indian Army.
HESKETH, WALTER, Major (Acting Lieut.-Colonel), Cavalry, Indian Army.
JENKIN, FREDERICK CHARLES, Major and Brevet Lieut.-Colonel, Royal Artillery, Indian Ordnance Department.
JOHNSTON, PERCY DOUGLAS CAMPBELL, Major, Rajputs, Indian Army.
MACDONALD, HARRY, Capt. and Brevet Major, Cavalry, Indian Army.
MANLEY, EDWARD NORMAN, Major, Royal Engineers.
MARR, CHARLES WILLIAM CLANAN, M.C., Major, Australian Engineers.
MITCHELL, THOMAS JOHN, M.B., Capt. and Brevet Major, Royal Army Medical Corps.

MORE, JAMES CARMICHAEL, Major, Sikhs, Indian Army.
NASH, ERNEST JAMES MARTYN, Temporary Major, Army Service Corps.
NICHOLSON, FRANCIS LOTHIAN, M.C., Capt. (Acting Lieut.-Colonel), Dogras, Indian Army.
NORRIE, CHARLES MATTHEW, Temporary Capt. (Acting Major), Royal Engineers.
PARKER, WALTER MANSEL, C.M.G., Major (Acting Lieut.-Colonel), Army Service Corps.
PEARSON, HENRY LAURENCE, Temporary Major (Temporary Colonel), Royal Engineers.
PRINCE, PAUL ERNEST, Major, Royal Engineers, Sappers and Miners, Indian Army.
PROCTOR, ALFRED HENRY, M.D., Major (Temporary Lieut.-Colonel), Indian Medical Service.
RALPH, ALFRED COLYER, Lieut.-Colonel, Rajputs, Indian Army.
RICE, BRINSLEY ALEXANDER McHENRY, Major (Acting Lieut.-Colonel), Gurkha Rifles, Indian Army.
RICE, GERALD DOMINICK, Major, Supply and Transport Corps.
ROBERTS, WILLIAM HENRY, M.C., Major (Acting Lieut.-Colonel), Royal Engineers.
RODD, WILLIAM JAMES PAOLO, M.I.M.E., I.O.M., First Class, Major, Army Ordnance Department.
SENIOR, HENRY WILLIAM RICHARD, Lieut.-Colonel, late Gurkha Rifles, Indian Army.
SNEPP, ERIC, Temporary Major (Acting Lieut.-Colonel), Army Service Corps.
TURNER, JOHN FISHER, Major (Acting Lieut.-Colonel), Royal Engineers.
TYLDEN-PATTENSON, EDWIN COOKE, Major and Brevet Lieut.-Colonel, Royal Engineers.
WERNICKE, FRANK PHILLIPS, M.B., Major, Indian Medical Service.
WILLIAMS, AUGUSTUS JOHN, F.R.C.V.S., Major (Acting Lieut.-Colonel), Army Veterinary Corps.
WILSON, ROGER COCHRANE, M.C., Major and Brevet Lieut.-Colonel, 114th Mahrattas, Indian Army.
YATES, JAMES AINSWORTH, C.I.E., Major, 103rd Mahrattas, Indian Army.

London Gazette, 28 Aug. 1918.—" Admiralty, 28 Aug. 1918. The following despatch has been received from Vice-Admiral Sir Roger J. B. Keyes, K.C.B., C.M.G., C.V.O., D.S.O., Commanding the Dover Patrol :—
" Fleet House, Dover,
" 24 July, 1918.
" SIR,—With reference to my Despatch No. 2305/003 of 15 June, 1918 (*not published*), I have the honour to bring to the notice of the Lords Commissioners of the Admiralty the names of the following Officers . . . who performed distinguished service in the second blocking operation against Ostend on the night of 9/10 May, 1918.
" 2.—Aerial photographs taken prior to the operation clearly showed that the enemy had made special preparations in anticipation of a renewed attack.
" 3.—The operation was carried out in mined waters in the face of a tremendous fire, and the greatest credit is due to those who so readily volunteered for hazardous service in the Vindictive and in motor boats detailed for rescue work, and to the crews of the numerous craft which covered and screened the approach of the Vindictive, led her to her objective, and rescued the survivors of her crew after she had been blown up between the piers of Ostend Harbour.
" The following Officers . . . performed specially distinguished service in action on the night of 9/10 May, 1918."
ALLEYNE, SIR JOHN M., Bart., D.S.C., Lieut., R.N. Volunteered from a monitor of the Dover Patrol for service in the Vindictive. He rendered valuable service in refitting navigational arrangements which were destroyed in Vindictive on 23 April, and on the actual night of the operation was invaluable on account of his local knowledge. He showed great coolness under a very heavy fire, and most skilfully navigated the Vindictive to the entrance of Ostend harbour. He was severely wounded and rendered unconscious when his captain was killed.
BURY, WILLIAM A., Engineer-Commander, R.N. This gallant officer greatly distinguished himself in Vindictive on 23 April, and as soon as he knew another operation was contemplated, volunteered, begging to be allowed to remain in charge of the engine-room department of that vessel. He worked most energetically to fit her out for further service, and on the night of 9/10 May he again rendered invaluable service, setting a fine example to his men. He remained in the engine-room until the last possible moment, and when everyone was clear he blew the bottom out of the ship by firing the main and auxiliary after charges. He was very severely wounded.
PARRY, REGINALD ST. P., Commander, R.N. Commander Parry commanded a destroyer, and handled his vessel with skill and decision, performing a most valuable service under difficult conditions.
WELMAN, ARTHUR E. P., D.S.O., D.S.C., Lieut., R.N. The part played by the coastal motor boats during the operation was all-important. Lieut. Welman organized and led them in a coastal motor-boat in a most spirited manner. He encountered an enemy torpedo boat near the entrance to Ostend, which switched on searchlights and opened fire. He at once closed with her, and engaged her with Lewis guns to such good effect that she withdrew and left the channel clear for the approach of the blockships.
HOARE, KEITH R., D.S.O., D.S.C., Lieut. (Acting Lieut.-Commander), A.M., Royal Naval Volunteer Reserve. Volunteered for rescue work at Ostend in command of M.L. 283. He was ordered to follow astern and assist two other motor launches which were detailed for rescue work. He remained at the Stroom Bank Buoy position until Vindictive had passed and then followed her, patrolling east and west within a quarter of a mile of the shore under heavy pom-pom and machine-gun fire, searching for survivors until 3.20 a.m., when all hope of finding anyone had passed.
WATSON, WILLIAM W., Commander, Royal Naval Volunteer Reserve. Was in command of M.L. 105, and was of the greatest assistance to Capt. Benn in arranging and supervising the smoke screen. This involved going from end to end of the line and taking his vessel close inshore several times, when he came under heavy barrage fire. He showed great courage and coolness throughout the operation.
SAUNDERS, RAPHAEL, Lieut.-Commander, Royal Naval Volunteer Reserve This officer volunteered for rescue work at Ostend in command of M.L. 128. In company with M.L. 283 he went in after Vindictive to look for survivors. When near the shore he came under heavy fire—his signalman was killed and Lieut. Brayfield and one of the crew wounded. This officer showed great coolness, setting a fine example to his men throughout, and was of the greatest assistance in organizing the smoke screen.
DAYRELL-REED, ARCHIBALD, D.S.C., Lieut., Royal Naval Reserve. Was in command of a coastal motor-boat, and carried out a successful attack on the pier ends, afterwards laying and maintaining good smoke screens close inshore throughout the remainder of the operation under a heavy fire.
MIEVILLE, JEAN S., Lieut.-Commander, Royal Naval Volunteer Reserve. Was in command of M.L. 280 and leader of a smoke-screen unit. He led his unit with skill and judgment in a very exposed position, and it was largely due to him that the screen was so extremely successful in his section.
WATTS, ARTHUR G., Lieut.-Commander, Royal Naval Volunteer Reserve. This officer was in command of M.L. 239 and leader of a smoke-screen unit. He led his unit with skill and judgment in a very exposed position, and it was largely due to him that the screen was so extremely successful in his section.

" Admiralty, 28 Aug. 1918. The King has been graciously pleased to approve of the award of honours to the undermentioned Officers, in recognition of the distinguished services mentioned in the foregoing despatch. To be Companions of the Distinguished Service Order."
PARRY, REGINALD ST. PIERRE, Commander, R.N.
WATSON, WILLIAM WORDIE, Commander, Royal Naval Volunteer Reserve.
BURY, WILLIAM ARCHIBALD, Engineer-Commander, R.N.
MIÉVILLE, JEAN LOUIS, Lieut.-Commander, Royal Naval Volunteer Reserve.
WATTS, ARTHUR GEORGE, Lieut.-Commander, Royal Naval Volunteer Reserve.
SAUNDERS, RAPHAEL, Lieut.-Commander, Royal Naval Volunteer Reserve.
ALLEYNE, SIR JOHN MEYNELL, Bart., D.S.C., Lieut., Royal Navy.

To receive a Bar to the Distinguished Service Order :
HOARE, KEITH ROBIN, D.S.O., D.S.C., Lieut.-Commander, A.M., Royal Naval Volunteer Reserve.
WELMAN, ARTHUR ERIC POLE, D.S.O., D.S.C., Lieut., Royal Navy.
DAYRELL-REED, ARCHIBALD, D.S.O., Lieut., Royal Naval Reserve.

London Gazette, 4 Sept. 1918.—" War Office, 4 Sept. 1918. The King has been graciously pleased to approve of the undermentioned rewards, dated 3 June, 1918, for distinguished services in connection with military operations. Awarded the Distinguished Service Order."

OPERATIONS IN FRANCE AND FLANDERS.
HARRISON, G. A., M.C., Temporary Capt. (Acting Major), Royal Engineers, Canadian Forces.
WEBB, R. H., M.C., Lieut.-Colonel, West Ontario Regt.

OPERATIONS IN EGYPT AND HEDJAZ.
BASSETT, J. R., Major (Temporary Lieut.-Colonel), Royal Berkshire Regt.
DAVENPORT, W. A., M.C., Capt., West Yorkshire Regt.
McCONAGHY, W., Major, Royal Army Medical Corps.
AMIN, MOHAMMED BEY, El Kaim (Lieut.-Colonel), Egyptian Army.
YEHYA, MOHAMMED BEY SADEK, El Mir (Colonel), Egyptian Army.
FERID, ABD EL MAJID BEY, El Kaim (Lieut.-Colonel), Local Mir (Colonel), Egyptian Army.

OPERATIONS IN EAST AFRICA.
KENNEDY, R. S., M.C., M.B., Major, Indian Medical Service.

OPERATIONS AT ADEN.
BOAL, R., Lieut. (Acting Capt.), Royal Engineers.
HOLME, H. L., Major, Royal Garrison Artillery.
NEWTON, P. I., Capt., Royal Garrison Artillery.
PARKIN, J. F., Major, Indian Army.

OPERATIONS IN RUSSIA AND RUMANIA.
ROWLANDSON, M. G. D., Major and Brevet Lieut.-Colonel, Infantry, Indian Army.

London Gazette, 6 Sept. 1918.—" War Office, 5 Sept. 1918. The King has been graciously pleased to approve of the following awards for distinguished and gallant services rendered on the occasion of the destruction or damage by enemy action of hospital ships, transports and storeships. Dated 3 June, 1918. Awarded the Distinguished Service Order."
GIPPS, ALEXANDER GEORGE PEMBERTON, F.R.C.S., Temporary Lieut.-Colonel, Royal Army Medical Corps.
HOLMES, THE REV. CECIL FREDERICK JOY, Temporary Chaplain to the Forces, Third Class, Army Chaplains' Department, Territorial Force.
PURVES, ROBERT BLACK, M.B., F.R.C.S., Major, Royal Army Medical Corps, Territorial Force.

London Gazette, 14 Sept. 1918.—" Admiralty, S.W., 14 Sept. 1918.—Honours for Services in Action with Enemy Submarines. The King has been graciously pleased to approve of the award of the following honours to the undermentioned Officers for services in action with enemy submarines. To be Companions of the Distinguished Service Order."
NORTH, OLIVER, Lieut., R.N.
BARNISH, GEOFFREY HOWARD, Lieut., Royal Naval Reserve.

To receive a Bar to the Distinguished Service Order :
D'OYLY-HUGHES, GUY, D.S.O., D.S.C., Lieut., R.N.

" Honours for Services in Action with the Goeben and Breslau in Jan. 1918.— The King has been graciously pleased to approve of the award of the following honours to the undermentioned Officers in recognition of their services on the occasion of the sortie of the Goeben and Breslau from the Dardanelles on 20 Jan. 1918. To be Companions of the Distinguished Service Order."
NEWILL, JOSEPH BERNARD, Lieut.-Commander, R.N. (H.M.S. Tigress). For the great skill and gallantry displayed by him in handling his ship in the presence of a greatly superior enemy force and under heavy fire. He performed most efficiently his main duty of shadowing the enemy and reporting his movements. He proceeded into the mine-field to engage a superior force of enemy destroyers and drove them back to their base. He again entered the mine-field at great risk to his ship, and gallantly rescued 162 survivors of the Breslau whilst still being fired on from shore batteries.

OHLENSCHLAGER, NORMAN ALBERT GUSTAVE, Lieut., R.N. (H.M.S. Lizard). He showed great skill and gallantry in handling his ship in the presence of a greatly superior enemy force and under very heavy fire. He performed most efficiently his main duty of shadowing the enemy and reporting his movements. He proceeded into the mine-field to engage a superior force of enemy destroyers and drove them back to their base. He again entered the mine-field at great risk to his ship, and gallantly rescued 162 survivors of the Breslau whilst still being fired on from shore batteries.

" Honours for Miscellaneous Services.—The King has been graciously pleased to approve of the award of the following honour to the undermentioned Officer. To be a Companion of the Distinguished Service Order."

ROSE, JOHN MARKHAM, Lieut.-Colonel, Royal Marine Artillery. For the manner in which he organized and commanded the Royal Marine Artillery unit in German South-West Africa during 1914.

London Gazette, 16 Sept. 1918.—" War Office, 16 Sept. 1918. His Majesty the King has been graciously pleased to approve of the following awards to the undermentioned Officers in recognition of their gallantry and devotion to duty in the field. Awarded a Second Bar to the Distinguished Service Order."

BIRT, CHARLES WILLIAM HOWARD, D.S.O., Temporary Major (Acting Lieut.-Colonel), Border Regt. For conspicuous gallantry and devotion to duty. During six days' hard fighting by his great personal courage and the fine example he set his men he repeatedly saved the situation at very critical times. During most of the time he was present in the front line, and being on the spot he was able to keep hold of his men and control the situation in his part of the line, so that any movement that became necessary was carried out in the best manner possible under the circumstances. On one occasion, in particular, when our flanks had been forced back, he covered their withdrawal and then skilfully extricated his battalion from an untenable position, and re-established it in a position in rear.
(D.S.O. gazetted 25 Aug. 1917.)
(1st Bar gazetted 26 July, 1918.)

GREEN, WILLIAM, D.S.O., Major (Temporary Lieut.-Colonel), Royal Highlanders, attached Royal Scots. For conspicuous gallantry and devotion to duty when in command of a battalion during ten days' heavy fighting. His successful withdrawal of his battalion was a brilliant performance. During a counter-attack, and subsequently in defence, he rendered most valuable services, setting a fine example and showing a complete disregard of personal safety.
(D.S.O. gazetted 14 Jan. 1916.)
(1st Bar gazetted 1 Jan. 1918.)

HALLIDAY, WILLIAM JOHN FREDERICK, D.S.O., Major, Royal Field Artillery. For conspicuous gallantry and devotion to duty. He kept his battery in action till the enemy were within 800 yards, getting his guns away under rifle and machine-gun fire, and bringing them into action again in another position under very heavy fire from hostile field guns. He went forward and brought back valuable information, and subsequently covered the retirement of other troops. He commanded his battery with remarkable coolness and ability.
(D.S.O. gazetted 16 Aug. 1917.)
(1st Bar gazetted 26 July, 1918.)

KNOX, ROBERT SINCLAIR, D.S.O., Temporary Major, Royal Inniskilling Fusiliers. For conspicuous gallantry and devotion to duty. He held a position against superior enemy forces until relieved, and made dispositions which held up the enemy for a considerable time. He handled his men under heavy machine-gun fire with coolness and skill, setting a fine example to all under him, and inspiring them with confidence.
(D.S.O. gazetted 1 Jan. 1917.)
(1st Bar gazetted 18 Feb. 1918.)

PEIRS, HUGH JOHN CHEVALLIER, D.S.O., Temporary Major (Acting Lieut.-Colonel), Royal West Surrey Regt. For conspicuous gallantry and devotion to duty in defence of a village, when he fought until surrounded, and then made his way back under cover of a fog. It was entirely due to his great courage and fine leadership that the enemy offensive was delayed for nearly two days.
(D.S.O. gazetted 3 June. 1916.)
(1st Bar gazetted 26 Sept. 1917.)

RAIKES, GEOFFREY TAUNTON, D.S.O., Capt. and Brevet Major (Acting Lieut.-Colonel), South Wales Borderers. For conspicuous gallantry and devotion to duty when in command of the remnants of two brigades, formed as one battalion. Though both flanks had gone he held on, encouraging his men, and repelling frequent enemy attacks. When the situation was critical he inspired his men by his brilliant example, and it was due to his absolute disregard of danger, capacity for command, and powers of organization that the line held to the last.
(D.S.O. gazetted 22 Sept. 1916.)
(1st Bar gazetted 4 Feb. 1918.)

ROBINSON, HUGH THOMAS KAY, D.S.O., Temporary Lieut.-Colonel, Royal Sussex Regt. For conspicuous gallantry and devotion to duty while commanding a composite battalion. He handled his battalion in such a way as to prevent the enemy entering a gap in the line, and so turning the right flank of the division. Later, when in command of another battalion, he, by skilful leadership and courageous example, caused the enemy's advance to be checked at a critical moment with heavy loss.
(D.S.O. gazetted 4 June, 1917.)
(1st Bar gazetted 17 Dec. 1917.)

WOOD, EDWARD ALLAN, D.S.O., Temporary Lieut.-Colonel (Temporary Brigadier-General), Shropshire Light Infantry. For conspicuous gallantry and devotion to duty. When ordered to withdraw he handled his brigade with marked ability and successfully covered the withdrawal; he next day organized a counter-attack, which inflicted severe losses on the enemy. A fortnight later, when his men were being forced back by superior numbers of the enemy, he personally directed the collection and reorganization of his troops on the battle-field under very heavy rifle and machine-gun fire. He then formed his men up, and in conjunction with another division delivered a successful counter-attack, which he personally led. This counter-attack regained a portion of the ground lost in the morning, and he remained on the recaptured ground with the remnants of his brigade until relieved next morning. He did splendid work, and set a fine example to all under most difficult circumstances.
(D.S.O. gazetted 1 Jan. 1917.)
(1st Bar gazetted 26 Sept. 1917.)

Awarded a Bar to the Distinguished Service Order:

ALLARDYCE, JOHN GRAHAME BUCHANAN, D.S.O., Major (Temporary Lieut.-Colonel), Royal Horse Artillery. For conspicuous gallantry and devotion to duty. During an evening attack, and subsequent forced retirement this, officer commanded his brigade with great ability under most difficult circumstances. Under continuous shell fire and gas he remained in a forward headquarter, covering the initial withdrawal of the infantry. It was largely owing to the way in which he handled his brigade on this and other occasions that the enemy advance was delayed and heavy losses inflicted.
(D.S.O. gazetted 1 Jan. 1917.)

BALFOUR, GEORGE BOYD, D.S.O., Major (Acting Lieut.-Colonel), Royal Lancashire Regt. For conspicuous gallantry and devotion to duty. When the enemy entered his trenches he ejected them with heavy losses, and completely restored the line. This occurred after his battalion had suffered from a long and heavy bombardment. His courage and ability inspired his men.
(D.S.O. gazetted 3 June, 1918.)

BARKER, AUGUSTINE, D.S.O., M.C., Temporary Capt. (Acting Major), Royal Field Artillery. For conspicuous gallantry and devotion to duty. For four hours before attacking the enemy tried by gas and high explosive shell to destroy this officer's battery. One officer being killed and another wounded, he was during the worst two hours alone with the guns. He was himself wounded in the leg, but limped about encouraging the men. As stragglers came back he collected them and got them into action. When the enemy got within 500 yards it was decided to withdraw the guns, three being got away without loss, the fourth having all six horses hit. He got the three guns into action about 1,000 yards in the rear. He was then put on a horse and rode up to the front collecting information and rallying infantry. In the evening, having reorganized his battery and salved two guns of another battery, he again rode up to the front to encourage the men, being unable to get off his horse.
(D.S.O. gazetted 3 June, 1918.)

BASTARD, REGINALD, D.S.O., Major (Temporary Lieut.-Colonel), Lincolnshire Regt. For conspicuous gallantry and devotion to duty in leading his battalion throughout a week's fighting with untiring energy and skill. On the first night he reoccupied a village after a sharp struggle with the enemy, and for the five following days his battalion beat off all attacks on the trench line and established a complete superiority over the enemy in " No Man's Land." On the last day, when his battalion was in brigade reserve, he delivered a counter-attack at very short notice and reached the first objective.
(D.S.O. gazetted 28 April, 1915.)

BATEMAN, CHARLES MALCOLM, D.S.O., Lieut.-Colonel, West Riding Regt. For conspicuous gallantry and devotion to duty whilst commanding his battalion during a heavy enemy attack. His fine example of courage and his skilful handling of his men resulted in the total repulse of the attack.
(D.S.O. gazetted 14 Jan. 1916.)

BENFIELD, KARL VERE BARKER, D.S.O., M.C., Capt. (Acting Major), Royal Garrison Artillery. For conspicuous gallantry and devotion to duty, especially on three occasions: (1) He continued firing with his battery under machine-gun fire until the enemy came in view, when he personally supervised the withdrawal of his guns. (2) He kept his battery in action till the last moment while the infantry were retiring through his position. (3) When his battery came under heavy fire with direct observation he continued firing on the advancing enemy with open sights until his ammunition was expended, and then successfully withdrew his guns.
(D.S.O. gazetted 14 Nov. 1916.)

BLACKWOOD, WILLIAM, D.S.O., M.B., Capt. (Acting Lieut.-Colonel), Royal Army Medical Corps. For conspicuous gallantry and devotion to duty while in charge of the evacuation of casualties from the Divisional front during an enemy attack. When communication with the advanced dressing-station was cut by enemy barrage he re-established communication and personally visited the posts under his administration. Throughout the fighting he visited the forward area daily, and his indefatigable energy and exceptional organizing ability were invaluable to the division.
(D.S.O. gazetted 3 June, 1918.)

BRANSON, DOUGLAS STEPHENSON, D.S.O., M.C., Capt. (Acting Lieut.-Colonel), York and Lancaster Regt. For conspicuous gallantry and devotion to duty. He showed great skill and courage while commanding his battalion, and it was largely owing to his personal influence that his battalion did so well. When wounded he reorganized his battalion and other troops in a new position, personally reporting his dispositions at brigade headquarters.
(D.S.O. gazetted 1 Jan. 1918.)

BRIGHTEN, GEORGE STANLEY, D.S.O., Lieut. (Acting Lieut.-Colonel), Liverpool Regt., attached Lancashire Fusiliers. For conspicuous gallantry and devotion to duty during an enemy attack. He was commanding the battalion in reserve, and employed it with such advantage that the attack was held up and the enemy repulsed with heavy loss, many prisoners being taken. His clever disposal of his forces and his fine example of coolness did much to restore the position.
(D.S.O. gazetted 26 Nov. 1917.)

BUCKLEY, ALBERT, D.S.O., Major (Acting Lieut.-Colonel), Liverpool Regt. For conspicuous gallantry and devotion to duty in command of his battalion throughout a week's fighting. At the commencement of the fighting his battalion was holding the front line and was heavily attacked when its left flank was in the air. He continually visited the posts, and made personal reconnaissances, keeping his men in good heart. He organized and carried out two successful counter-attacks, and it was greatly due to his leadership that the line was maintained when the enemy broke through on the left.
(D.S.O. gazetted 26 Sept. 1917.)

BUTLER, BERNARD ARNOLD BARRINGTON, D.S.O., Major and Brevet Lieut.-Colonel (Temporary Lieut.-Colonel), Royal Field Artillery. For conspicuous gallantry and devotion to duty. When the enemy appeared unexpectedly within a few hundred yards of the guns, this officer with his staff opened rifle fire on them. He afterwards turned one of the guns on to some enemy who had got round, driving them back. The following night he organized the withdrawal of guns which had been left in " No Man's Land," and got in all except two, which were in the enemy's hands. By his coolness and initiative he established a new front firing line.
(D.S.O. gazetted 1 Jan. 1918.)

CLARE, OLIVER CECIL, D.S.O., M.C., Temporary Lieut.-Colonel, East Lancashire Regt. For conspicuous gallantry and devotion to duty during an enemy attack. He promptly counter-attacked with his battalion and caused a position to be held. Throughout he showed fine leadership and coolness under heavy machine-gun and shell fire.
(D.S.O. gazetted 4 June, 1917.)

CLARKE, BOWCHER CAMPBELL SENHOUSE, D.S.O., Major (Temporary Lieut.-Colonel), Worcestershire Regt. For conspicuous gallantry and devotion to duty. He commanded his battalion with great skill and energy throughout ten days' operations under very heavy shell fire. He personally went forward and reorganized the troops on his flank under very heavy fire. It was due to his continual supervision that a most difficult situation was kept in hand.
(D.S.O. gazetted 3 June, 1917.)

COX, CHARLES HENRY FORTNOM, D.S.O., Major (Acting Lieut.-Colonel), Royal Field Artillery. For conspicuous gallantry and devotion to duty. This officer commanded his brigade throughout nearly a month's critical operations.

On all occasions he handled it with ability, especially during an enemy attack on an important village, when his headquarters received a direct hit, causing many casualties.
(D.S.O. gazetted 1 Jan. 1917.)

CRAWFORD, EDWARD WILLIAM, D.S.O., Temporary Major, Royal Inniskilling Fusiliers. For conspicuous gallantry and devotion to duty. During a week's heavy fighting he did fine work. He twice led successful counter-attacks, and repeatedly rallied his men and took up defensive positions. His courage and energy set a fine example to all.
(D.S.O. gazetted 1 Jan. 1918.)

DAVIDSON, THOMAS, D.S.O., Major, Royal Field Artillery. For conspicuous gallantry and devotion to duty. The Colonel of the brigade, having been captured, this officer took command, and after succeeding in withdrawing two battalions, he came into action with one gun of his own battery in defence of an important bridge over a canal. Although within 300 yards of the bridge, and in full view of the enemy, he held on for about an hour under heavy rifle and machine-gun fire until reinforcements arrived.
(D.S.O. gazetted 27 Oct. 1917.)

DEANE-DRUMMOND, JOHN DRUMMOND, D.S.O., M.C., Major (Temporary Lieut.-Colonel), Machine Gun Corps. For conspicuous gallantry and devotion to duty. He led machine gunners, armed with rifles, in a counter-attack, and coming on an enemy machine gun, he managed to put gun and team out of action with his rifle, being wounded in so doing. He showed fine courage and determination.
(D.S.O. gazetted 17 Sept. 1917.)

EVANS, LEWIS PUGH, V.C., D.S.O., Major (Acting Lieut.-Colonel), Royal Highlanders. For conspicuous gallantry and devotion to duty in a three-days' battle. On the first day he was moving about everywhere in his forward area directing operations, the next day he personally conducted a reconnaissance for a counter-attack, which was carried out on the third day. It was largely due to his untiring energy and method that the enemy were checked and finally driven out of our forward system.
(D.S.O. gazetted 24 July, 1917.)

FISHER, HERBERT GEORGE, D.S.O., Major (Acting Lieut.-Colonel), Royal Field Artillery. For conspicuous ga lantry and devotion to duty in handling his brigade. He conducted a retirement with masterly calm and determination, and on several occasions, by his prompt movement of batteries and by his reconnaissances and selection of positions, he inflicted heavy casualties on the enemy. Throughout the entire operations he set a magnificent example of cheerful optimism combined with a dogged and determined courage.
(D.S.O. gazetted 1 Jan. 1917.)

FORSTER, HAROLD THOMAS, D.S.O., M.C., Lieut. (Acting Major), Royal Berkshire Regt., attached Northamptonshire Regt. For conspicuous gallantry and devotion to duty. He assumed command of his battalion when his colonel was killed, and by his coolness and skill extricated it from a critical situation and formed a defensive flank of the utmost importance. For three days and nights, by his pluck and energy, he set an example to his men of inestimable value under adverse conditions of continuous and heavy shell fire.
(D.S.O. gazetted 26 Sept. 1917.)

FRIZELL, CHARLES WILLIAM, D.S.O., M.C., Capt. (Temporary Lieut.-Colonel), Royal Berkshire Regt., attached Essex Regt. For conspicuous gallantry and devotion to duty during recent operations, and especially when the battalion under his command took part in a very successful counter-attack. The success of the operations was chiefly due to the skilful dispositions and fine leadership of this officer. Throughout the operations he rendered very valuable services.
(D.S.O. gazetted 4 June, 1917.)

GAYER, AUBREY VIVIAN ARTHUR, D.S.O., Temporary Lieut.-Colonel, Durham Light Infantry. For conspicuous gallantry and devotion to duty while commanding his battalion during an enemy attack. Six times in one morning, owing to his fine example, the battalion repulsed enemy attacks with heavy loss. Next evening, when ordered to withdraw, he did so skilfully, with few casualties. He did fine work.
(D.S.O. gazetted 19 Nov. 1917.)

GREENE, JOHN, D.S.O., Capt. (Temporary Lieut.-Colonel), Dragoon Guards, attached Middlesex Regt. For conspicuous gallantry and devotion to duty while commanding his battalion. During a withdrawal his arrangements and dispositions were so cleverly carried out that he was able to give most valuable assistance to another battalion, and enable it by covering fire to withdraw from a very critical position. Throughout a most trying period he set a fine example of cheerfulness and gallantry.
(D.S.O. gazetted 4 June, 1917.)

HARTY, THOMAS ERNEST, D.S.O., Major (Temporary Lieut.-Colonel), Royal Army Medical Corps. For conspicuous gallantry and devotion to duty. For nearly a month this officer was in charge of the evacuations of the wounded on the front of a whole division. His initiative, courage and resource during much heavy fighting resulted in the successful clearing of all wounded in the forward area, which he frequently visited during heavy shelling to see that his orders were being executed properly, and also to inspire confidence. He never spared himself in his efforts to arrange for the wounded.
(D.S.O. gazetted 1 Jan. 1917.)

HEELAS, PERCIVAL JOHN BERESFORD, D.S.O. Major (Acting Lieut.-Colonel), Royal Field Artillery. For conspicuous gallantry and devotion to duty. This officer commanded his brigade through over three weeks' heavy fighting, showing great skill in withdrawing when positions became untenable, with only those losses which were caused by hostile shell fire, and keeping his control so firm that fresh positions were easily organized and heavy losses inflicted. He always held on until the last moment, going round his command under heavy fire and inspiring those under him by his example.
(D.S.O. gazetted 1 Jan. 1918.)

HESSEY, WILLIAM FRANCIS, D.S.O., Major and Brevet Lieut.-Colonel (Temporary Brigadier-General), Reserve of Officers. For conspicuous gallantry and devotion to duty. For 24 hours he remained in the firing line, rallying and organizing men and checking the enemy, and then conducted a withdrawal with great skill. He personally led a counter-attack, and temporarily regained 1,000 yards of ground. Two days later, after maintaining his position for 36 hours, he withdrew without leaving a wounded man behind. He set a fine example of energy and good leadership.
(D.S.O. gazetted 1 Jan. 1918.)

HIGGINSON, HAROLD WHITLA, D.S.O., Major and Brevet Colonel (Temporary Brigadier-General), Royal Dublin Fusiliers. For conspicuous gallantry and devotion to duty while commanding his brigade. In 14 days' fighting the losses of the brigade exceeded 70 per cent., but owing to his able leadership and the fine example set by him their fighting spirit was in no way impaired. The courageous stands made by them were of great assistance to other brigades.
(D.S.O. gazetted 14 Jan. 1916.)

HILL, MURRAY VICTOR BURROW, D.S.O., M.C., Capt. (Temporary Lieut.-Colonel), Royal Fusiliers, attached Royal Sussex Regt. For conspicuous gallantry and devotion to duty during enemy attacks. He organized and personally led a counter-attack against a body of the enemy who were threatening to envelop the right flank of the brigade, and forced them to withdraw. He set a high example of cheerfulness, determination and good leadership.
(D.S.O. gazetted 25 Aug. 1917.)

HOPKINSON, JOHN OLIVER, D.S.O., M.C., Major (Acting Lieut.-Colonel), Seaforth Highlanders. For conspicuous gallantry and devotion to duty in command of his battalion when ordered to fill a gap which was known to exist in the front line. He carried out his orders with great ability, and in spite of continuous and severe shelling maintained his positions until relieved. By his leadership and courage throughout the operations he inspired the utmost confidence in all ranks.
(D.S.O. gazetted 22 Sept. 1916.)

HOWLETT, REGINALD, D.S.O., MC., Major (Acting Lieut.-Colonel), Royal Fusiliers. For conspicuous gallantry and devotion to duty throughout a week's fighting. On the first night he led his battalion, which was very short of officers, to a position on the enemy side of a village, driving back enemy posts on the way and successfully establishing his line. The next day, by quickly moving up a reserve company to a threatened flank, he maintained his position. It was not until the end of the week that he was forced to give way, when practically surrounded and severely wounded himself.
(D.S.O. gazetted 1 Jan. 1917.)

IRONS, ARTHUR INNES, D.S.O., Temporary Lieut.-Colonel, Middlesex Regt. For conspicuous gallantry and devotion to duty. Under very heavy rifle and machine-gun fire he collected and rallied men and reinforced the line. By his personal example of coolness he encouraged his men to hold their positions and inflict heavy casualties on the enemy.
(D.S.O. gazetted 1 Jan. 1918.)

KEMP-WELCH, MARTIN, D.S.O., M.C., Capt. (Acting Lieut.-Colonel), Royal West Surrey Regt. For conspicuous gallantry and devotion to duty. With his battalion he repulsed four enemy attacks on a village. The battalion suffered heavy casualties, but, thanks to his skilful dispositions, courage, and untiring energy, they successfully held the position.
(D.S.O. gazetted 20 Oct. 1916.)

KEWLEY, EDWARD RIGBY, D.S.O., M.C., Capt. (Acting Lieut.-Colonel), Rifle Brigade. For conspicuous gallantry and devotion to duty and fine leadership in repelling the initial hostile attacks, and subsequently during the withdrawal. His battalion fought to the last moment prior to each withdrawal, and it was entirely due to his magnificent personal example and great courage that these engagements were successful.
(D.S.O. gazetted 26 Sept. 1917.)

KING, CHARLES FRANCIS, D.S.O., M.C., Temporary Major (Temporary Lieut.-Colonel), Cheshire Regt. For conspicuous gallantry and devotion to duty when in command of a battalion. He organized the defence of a village, held it against heavy attacks, and over and over again led forward his small reserve to drive out bodies of the enemy who had obtained a temporary foothold. Throughout the subsequent withdrawal he was the life and soul of the defence, and his example and complete disregard of danger instilled the greatest confidence in his men.
(D.S.O. gazetted 1 Jan. 1918.)

LATHAM, FRANCIS, D.S.O., Capt. and Brevet Major (Acting Lieut.-Colonel), Leicestershire Regt. For conspicuous gallantry and devotion to duty. This officer set a fine example of coolness and fearlessness to all ranks under his command, and encouraged and steadied his men under heavy fire. The splendid defence made by his battalion was to a great extent inspired by his fine example of personal courage.
(D.S.O. gazetted 14 Jan. 1916.)

LAWSON, ARTHUR BERTRAM, D.S.O., Capt. and Brevet Major (Acting Lieut.-Colonel), Hussars, attached Gloucestershire Regt. For conspicuous gallantry and devotion to duty. His battalion attacked a village and captured 120 prisoners and nine machine guns. The position was consolidated in spite of a heavy bombardment, and the next morning the enemy launched a determined counter-attack, which was completely repulsed and another 80 prisoners taken. He superintended the whole of the operation, fearlessly exposing himself to all kinds of fire, and its success was largely due to his courage and ability.
(D.S.O. gazetted 26 July, 1918.)

LLOYD, LEMUEL, D.S.O., Temporary Major (Acting Lieut.-Colonel), Suffolk Regt. For conspicuous gallantry and devotion to duty. He handled his battalion with great skill and initiative, and his was the leading battalion in a most successful counter-attack. This success, which was largely due to his fine leadership and fighting qualities, drove the enemy back 2,000 yards and restored a critical situation.
(D.S.O. gazetted 4 March, 1918.)

LOVE, STUART GILKISON, D.S.O., M.C., Lieut. (Acting Major), Royal Engineers. For conspicuous gallantry and devotion to duty while commanding remnants of three field companies during a withdrawal. He displayed tactical ability of a high order, and considerably delayed the enemy's advance. Throughout the operations he showed extraordinary energy, great skill in placing his men, and utter disregard of personal safety.
(D.S.O. gazetted 1 Jan. 1918.)

MACCLELLAN, GORDON PONSONBY, D.S.O., Major (Acting Lieut.-Colonel), Royal Garrison Artillery, attached Royal Field Artillery. For conspicuous gallantry and devotion to duty during an enemy advance. He maintained his batteries until the enemy were within 300 yards, and then withdrew them singly without loss of guns. He gave close support to the infantry and assisted them in holding the line. His tactical skill and personal courage under heavy fire were of a high order.
(D.S.O. gazetted 1 Jan. 1917.)

MANNOCK, EDWARD, D.S.O., Temporary Second Lieut. (Temporary Capt.), Royal Engineers and Royal Air Force. For conspicuous gallantry and devotion to duty. In company with one other scout this officer attacked eight enemy aeroplanes, shooting down one in flames. The next day, when leading his flight, he engaged eight enemy aeroplanes, destroying three himself. The same week he led his patrol against six enemy aeroplanes, shooting down the rear machine, which broke in pieces in the air. The following day he shot down an Albatross two-seater in flames, but later, meeting five scouts, had great difficulty in getting back, his machine being much shot about, but he destroyed one. Two days later, he shot down another two-seater in flames. Eight machines in five days—a fine feat of marksmanship and determination to get to close quarters. As a patrol leader he is unequalled.
(D.S.O. gazetted in this Gazette.)

MARTIN, CUTHBERT THOMAS, D.S.O., Major and Brevet Lieut.-Colonel (Temporary Brigadier-General), Highland Light Infantry. For conspicuous gallantry and devotion to duty. This officer commanded his brigade with great energy and ability through four days' fighting against vastly superior numbers

of the enemy on a very extended front. Largely by his personal example the fighting value of the brigade was maintained when they had had very heavy casualties and were very tired.
(D.S.O. gazetted 4 June, 1917.)

McCARTHY-O'LEARY, HEFFERNAN WILLIAM DENIS, D.S.O., M.C., Capt. (Acting Lieut.-Colonel), Royal Irish Fusiliers. For conspicuous gallantry and devotion to duty. He was wounded, but refused to be evacuated, and during the severe fighting which ensued he remained in action in command of his battalion until again severely wounded. He displayed marked ability in encouraging and handling his troops, and showed great cheerfulness and total disregard for his own personal safety.
(D.S.O. gazetted 26 Sept. 1917.)

McCULLOCH, ANDREW JAMESON, D.S.O., D.C.M., Capt. and Brevet Lieut.-Colonel (Temporary Lieut.-Colonel), Dragoon Guards, attached Yorkshire Light Infantry. For conspicuous gallantry and devotion to duty. At a most critical time he handled his battalion with great skill and gallantry, and blocked the enemy's advance. While making a valuable reconnaissance he was gassed and wounded, but continued his command of the battalion for another two days until the situation was righted. He showed fine leadership and determination.
(D.S.O. gazetted 26 July, 1918.)

MENZIES, ALEXANDER HENRY, D.S.O., Major (Acting Lieut.-Colonel), Highland Light Infantry. For conspicuous gallantry and devotion to duty when commanding a battalion. Throughout six days' fighting he set a marked example of coolness and courage, and by so doing greatly stimulated all ranks under his command in their determination to hold out in spite of the fact that other troops were falling back.
(D.S.O. gazetted 1 Jan. 1917.)

METCALFE, HERBERT CHARLES, D.S.O., Major (Acting Lieut.-Colonel), Northamptonshire Regt., attached Middlesex Regt. For conspicuous gallantry and devotion to duty, whereby the ground was stoutly held against enemy attacks. Under very heavy machine-gun fire he set a splendid example to his men and inspired all with confidence till eventually severely wounded.
(D.S.O. gazetted in this Gazette.)

NADEN, FRANK, D.S.O., M.C., Lieut. (Acting Major), Cheshire Regt., attached Royal Highlanders. For conspicuous gallantry and devotion to duty. For three days he successfully kept the enemy out of a village, twice organizing counter-attacks after losing ground under constant and intense bombardments. It was largely owing to his personal gallantry and coolness that the village remained in our hands at the end of the enemy attacks.
(D.S.O. gazetted 26 Nov. 1917.)

NOSWORTHY, FRANCIS POITIER, D.S.O., M.C., Capt. and Brevet Major (Temporary Lieut.-Colonel), Royal Engineers. For conspicuous gallantry and devotion to duty during an enemy attack. He constantly visited every part of the fighting line, and was of great assistance to regimental officers, brigade commanders, and Divisional headquarters. He organized the defence of a new line, on which the division fell back. He set a high example of energy and courage.
(D.S.O. gazetted 8 March, 1918.)

ODDIE, WILLIAM, D.S.O., Lieut.-Colonel, West Yorkshire Regt. For conspicuous gallantry and devotion to duty when commanding his battalion. When the enemy had got between his front line and battalion headquarters he fought his way back to the support and reserve lines with his headquarters, and covered by his fire the headquarters of another battalion by refusing his flank. He held on to his reserve line long after his right flank had been turned. Next day he kept a large body of the enemy back, inflicting heavy casualties on them with only his headquarters and a few other men he had collected. He did fine service.
(D.S.O. gazetted 3 June, 1918.)

PEEL, EDWARD JOHN RUSSELL, C.M.G., D.S.O., Lieut.-Colonel, Royal Field Artillery. For conspicuous gallantry and devotion to duty. This officer was in command of the brigade during ten days' operations. Although the enemy were close up to him in a village he kept his batteries in action under a ridge, handling them with consummate skill. It was owing to his personal influence with the brigade that the guns were saved, being withdrawn from under the nose of the enemy one by one as opportunity occurred by night. Throughout the operations he kept the men together and cheerful, and they fought splendidly.
(D.S.O. gazetted 18 Feb. 1915.)

PEEL, WILLIAM RALPH, D.S.O., Temporary Major (Acting Lieut.-Colonel), Yorkshire Regt., attached Manchester Regt. For conspicuous gallantry and devotion to duty. Throughout two days' very hard fighting he displayed great courage and marked ability in dealing with situations of considerable difficulty, going out under extremely heavy fire of all descriptions to select sites for machine guns and to assist advanced posts of the companies of his battalion. On receiving orders to withdraw he directed the operation with great ability, remaining himself in the front line until the last of the troops had retired and all the wounded were evacuated. Throughout the operations his cheerful disregard of all considerations of personal safety was an example to his men, which inspired them with confidence and resolution.
(D.S.O. gazetted 4 June, 1917.)

PILKINGTON, WILLIAM NORMAN, D.S.O., Major, South Lancashire Regt. For conspicuous gallantry and devotion to duty. This officer was in command of two companies, and showed such marked ability and grasp of the situation that he was put in command of the whole of the defence system manned by three companies. He was most energetic in visiting the line and organizing the defence of posts by day and night under heavy fire. He arranged and led a counter-attack which resulted in the capture of 21 prisoners and two machine guns. The positions he held included a defensive flank, and were of great tactical importance.
(D.S.O. gazetted 3 June, 1916.)

PORTER, JAMES HERBERT, D.S.O., Capt. (Acting Lieut.-Colonel), North Staffordshire Regt., Territorial Force. For conspicuous gallantry and devotion to duty. When the enemy had succeeded in reaching his front line, which was on high ground, this officer at once personally led forward his two support companies to counter-attack through heavy shell and machine-gun fire. The attack was perfectly successful, and the posts were then pushed forward again.
(D.S.O. gazetted 1 Jan. 1918.)

POTTER, COLIN KYNASTON, D.S.O., M.C., Major (Acting Lieut.-Colonel), North Lancashire Regt., attached Liverpool Regt. For conspicuous gallantry and devotion to duty in command of his battalion during a week's fighting. At the commencement of the fighting his battalion was in the front line, where it maintained its positions, being stimulated by his frequent visits under heavy fire. He organized and carried out a successful counter-attack, followed shortly after by another one, in which several hundred prisoners were captured.
(D.S.O. gazetted 26 Sept. 1917.)

PRIOR, JOHN HARVEY, D.S.O., Major, Royal Engineers, Special Reserve. For conspicuous gallantry and devotion to duty in action, when he volunteered to attach himself and his company to a battalion which was threatened by an outflanking movement. By his personal courage and excellent handling of his company he was successful in holding the enemy and in assisting the battalion to withdraw at a very critical moment.
(D.S.O. gazetted 27 Sept. 1901.)

RANSOME, ALGERNON LEE, D.S.O., M.C., Capt. and Brevet Major (Temporary Lieut.-Colonel), Dorsetshire Regt., attached East Kent Regt. For conspicuous gallantry and devotion to duty during recent operations. He displayed great skill and courage in defending positions, and handled his battalion with great ability under most difficult circumstances. His sound judgment, combined with his cheerful confidence and personal gallantry, inspired all ranks in the brigade.
(D.S.O. gazetted 1 Jan. 1918.)

RICHARDSON, GEORGE CARR, D.S.O., M.C., Major, Royal Field Artillery. For conspicuous gallantry and devotion to duty. During a fortnight's operations he was constantly in the forward area, and throughout one night he went from battery to battery, bringing them to positions where they could cover a gap that had been made in the line. His work has been of an exceptionally high standard.
(D.S.O. gazetted 1 Jan. 1918.)

RICKMAN, ARTHUR WILMOT, D.S.O., Major (Temporary Lieut.-Colonel), Northumberland Fusiliers, attached East Lancashire Regt. For conspicuous gallantry and devotion to duty. This officer commanded his battalion, covering the retirement of the brigade to a new position after both flanks had been turned. He displayed great courage and judgment. The following day he held an extended front against three determined attacks, and when the troops on his right flank were driven in he rallied them under close fire, and formed a defensive flank with them.
(D.S.O. gazetted 1 Jan. 1917.)

ROBINSON, FRANCIS, D.S.O., Capt. (Acting Lieut.-Colonel), Royal Inniskilling Fusiliers, attached Northumberland Fusiliers. For conspicuous gallantry and devotion to duty in command of a battalion in a successful counter-attack at a critical moment, and on another occasion, after the line on his left had been broken, he countered with such energy and determination that he drove the enemy back 1,500 yards, capturing two machine guns and 50 prisoners. He was wounded during this attack.
(D.S.O. gazetted 4 June, 1917.)

RUSSELL, ALBERT, D.S.O., Lieut. (Acting Major), Royal Engineers. For conspicuous gallantry and devotion to duty during an enemy attack. Under a series of heavy bombardments lasting over several days he handled the men under his command with great ability and successfully repulsed all attacks. He set a fine example of courage and leadership.
(D.S.O. gazetted 1 Jan. 1918.)

SADLEIR-JACKSON, LIONEL WARREN DE VERE, C.M.G., D.S.O., Major and Brevet Lieut.-Colonel (Temporary Brigadier-General), Lancers. For conspicuous gallantry and devotion to duty. Throughout recent operations he proved himself a bold leader of men, and under all conditions full of energy and fine fighting spirit. He personally organized and led most successful counter-attacks, in one of which he recaptured a village and took 150 prisoners and eleven machine guns. He did splendid work under very difficult conditions.
(D.S.O. gazetted 27 Sept. 1901.)

ST. JOHN, EDMUND FARQUHAR, D.S.O., Major (Acting Lieut.-Colonel), Royal Field Artillery. For conspicuous gallantry and devotion to duty. During 14 days the brigade under his command fought with great effect. None of their guns had to be abandoned, nor were any captured. It is not too much to say that his example of courage and his skill were in a very great measure responsible for this fine result. Under heavy enemy shell-fire he kept all his batteries in action, affording all the support possible to the infantry.
(D.S.O. gazetted 1 Jan. 1917.)

SANDFORD, DANIEL ARTHUR, D.S.O., Major, Royal Garrison Artillery. For conspicuous gallantry and devotion to duty during the enemy offensive, especially on the first day, when he succeeded in bringing successfully out of action his three widely-separated sections, and later in the afternoon, under shell and machine-gun fire, he kept his battery at work until 7.30 p.m., when the enemy were within 1,000 yards of his position. On the following day, after sending his battery back, he went forward into a village and stayed there till noon, bringing back valuable information.
(D.S.O. gazetted 2 Feb. 1916.)

SPENS, HUGH BAIRD, D.S.C., Capt. (Acting Lieut.-Colonel), Scottish Rifles. For conspicuous gallantry and devotion to duty. When the enemy had penetrated the line, this officer, at short notice, was ordered to counter-attack and retake the position. This involved an advance of nearly four miles in artillery formation over very difficult ground, in full view of the enemy, with a change of direction in the final stages of the attack. Although there was little time for reconnaissance, and the final advance was under heavy barrage, the counter-attack was quite successful, the enemy declining to await the troops advancing with the bayonet. The success was largely due to his leadership.
(D.S.O. gazetted 1 Jan. 1918.)

SPILLER, DUNCAN WILFRED LAMBERT, D.S.O., Major (Temporary Lieut.-Colonel), Royal Field Artillery. For conspicuous gallantry and devotion to duty while commanding a group throughout operations extending over a fortnight. He was always in front carrying out personal reconnaissances, visiting the infantry, and helping his batteries. His contempt of all personal danger, combined with his capable handling of his guns, was an invaluable example to all near him.
(D.S.O. gazetted 26 July, 1917.)

STOCKLEY, ERNEST NORMAN, D.S.O., Major and Brevet Lieut.-Colonel (Temporary Lieut.-Colonel, Royal Engineers. For conspicuous gallantry and devotion to duty. When the situation was critical, owing to a gap between two divisions, this officer led the three companies under his command, who were at work on a rear line, up to the threatened point, taking up a defensive position in touch with the troops on right and left. This position was held under heavy shell and machine-gun fire, and against repeated attacks, until he finally withdrew according to instructions, bringing his men out in good order.
(D.S.O. gazetted 1 Jan. 1917.)

TUCK, GERALD LOUIS JOHNSON, D.S.O., Temporary Major (Acting Lieut.-Colonel), Suffolk Regt. For conspicuous gallantry and devotion to duty. He commanded his battalion during an enemy attack, and his reports from personal observation were invaluable. When the situation was critical he restored it. By his personal example of coolness and energy he retained positions against largely superior enemy forces.
(D.S.O. gazetted 1 Jan. 1918.)

TWEEDIE, JOHN LANNOY FORBES, D.S.O., Major, (Temporary Lieut.-Colonel), Gloucestershire Regt. For conspicuous gallantry and devotion to duty. His battalion was heavily attacked in front and flank, the enemy penetrating the line in several places and also working round the flank. By the effective counter-measures which this officer took, he restored the situation completely. His cheerfulness and confidence throughout an anxious day were largely responsible for the fine defence put up by his battalion.
(D.S.O. gazetted 1 Jan. 1917.)

VIGNOLES, WALTER ADOLPH, D.S.O., Temporary Lieut.-Colonel, Northumberland Fusiliers. For conspicuous gallantry and devotion to duty during a heavy enemy attack. He organized and led a successful counter-attack at a point threatened by the enemy. Thanks to his promptitude and his gallantry under heavy bombardment, a serious situation was rectified and the line re-established.
(D.S.O. gazetted 18 July, 1917.)

WARDEN, HERBERT LAWTON, D.S.O., Temporary Lieut.-Colonel, East Surrey Regt. For conspicuous gallantry and devotion to duty. Throughout several days' fighting this officer, in command of a battalion, by his personal example several times restored the situation. One morning early, when the enemy had broken through a village, he was ordered to attack. As it did not get on fast enough, he went forward himself and cleared the village. For three days the enemy made continuous efforts to get by another village, but largely owing to his leadership and example they were all frustrated.
(D.S.O. gazetted 4 Feb. 1918.)

WENYON, HERBERT JOHN, D.S.O., Temporary Major (Acting Lieut.-Colonel), Royal West Kent Regt. For conspicuous gallantry and devotion to duty. He organized defences against heavy enemy attacks and held vastly superior numbers of the enemy at bay, inflicting heavy losses on them. He set a very fine example of courage and good leadership.
(D.S.O. gazetted 18 Oct. 1917.)

WHITTALL, PERCIVAL FREDERICK, D.S.O., Temporary Major, Royal Engineers (Capt., Reserve of Officers). For conspicuous gallantry and devotion to duty. During a retirement through a village, he showed great resource in occupying the houses and walls on the front edge, delaying the enemy's advance considerably. He eventually retired fighting at close quarters, under heavy artillery and machine-gun fire, his company being the last to withdraw. He showed great coolness and complete unconcern for his personal safety, moving about the village and disposing his men to the best advantage, though the enemy's fire was severe. On another occasion, at the crossing of a river, he was of most valuable assistance to our troops, owing to the manner in which he was able to retard the enemy's advance by his dispositions.
(D.S.O. gazetted 4 June, 1917.)

WILSON, PERCY NORTON WHITESTONE, D.S.O., M.C., Capt. (Acting Lieut.-Colonel), Royal Fusiliers. For conspicuous gallantry and devotion to duty during an enemy attack. Seeing men wavering on the right flank, he ran 400 yards through heavy machine-gun fire, rallied the men, and re-established the line. This act of gallantry was of great value at a critical moment.
(D.S.O. gazetted 26 Sept. 1917.)

WYNNE, RICHARD OWEN, D.S.O., Capt. (Acting Lieut.-Colonel), Bedford Regt., Special Reserve. For conspicuous gallantry and devotion to duty. He personally led an attack against some enemy machine guns and succeeded in driving them off, himself killing the officer leading the enemy. At all times he commanded his men with great skill and courage and showed complete disregard of his own safety.
(D.S.O. gazetted 1 Jan. 1917.)

CANADIAN FORCE.

CARTER, ALBERT DESBRISAY, D.S.O., Major, New Brunswick Regt. and Royal Air Force. For conspicuous gallantry and devotion to duty as a fighting pilot. In three and a half months he destroyed 13 enemy machines. He showed the utmost determination, keenness and dash, and his various successful encounters, often against odds, make up a splendid record.
(D.S.O. gazetted 18 Feb. 1918.)

ROSS, ALEXANDER, D.S.O., Lieut.-Colonel, Canadian Infantry. For conspicuous gallantry and devotion to duty in commanding his battalion, when he carried out a most successful operation, resulting in the capture of a number of prisoners, five machine guns, and a trench mortar, and inflicting heavy casualties on the enemy. He planned every detail and supervised the withdrawal, which was carried out with difficulty and under a heavy barrage. His personal courage and able leadership were largely responsible for the success of the undertaking.
(D.S.O. gazetted 18 July, 1917.)

AUSTRALIAN IMPERIAL FORCE.

CHRISTIE, ROBERT, D.S.O., Major (Temporary Lieut.-Colonel), Australian Infantry. For conspicuous gallantry and devotion to duty. This officer commanded his battalion in a difficult night operation. The battalion, having already marched six miles, was ordered to counter-attack and recover a village. The ground was strange to everyone, and there was no time for reconnaissance, but the approach march and deployment was carried out without a hitch, and the attack was a brilliant success. He moved about amongst the troops encouraging them, and finally established his headquarters in an open trench under heavy shell fire, from which he could see and control his battalion to the best advantage.
(D.S.O. gazetted 17 Dec. 1917.)

LAYH, HERBERT THOMAS CHRISTOLPH, D.S.O., Lieut.-Colonel, Australian Infantry. For conspicuous gallantry and devotion to duty. This officer commanded his battalion in a counter-attack. At the last moment the orders on which he had based his plans were altered, and he had to make entirely fresh arrangements, which he explained so clearly to his officers that the movement was successful. When he found that the task allotted to other units was not proceeding satisfactorily he detached a portion of his battalion to assist, which proved the turning point, and resulted in the capture of several hundreds of the enemy, 120 machine guns, six trench mortars, and four minenwerfers. Whilst consolidating the position, he pushed out patrols in the most energetic manner, getting into touch with other units.
(D.S.O. gazetted 1 Jan. 1917) (Christian name Christolph corrected to Christoph [London Gazette, 15 Oct. 1918]).

MARSHALL, NORMAN, D.S.O., M.C., Lieut.-Colonel, Australian Infantry. For conspicuous gallantry and devotion to duty. This officer commanded his battalion in a night counter-attack on a village, which was completely successful. At an early stage in the advance in the dark the column lost direction, owing partly to the ground being soaked by enemy gas, necessitating a detour, and to sunken roads and copses, but owing to his personal exertions he got on the move again in the right direction. As soon as the battalion had reached the final objective he supervised its consolidation, and then organized an attack on some strong posts on the left of his line, capturing seven machine guns.
(D.S.O. gazetted 19 Nov. 1917.)

MURPHY, GEORGE FRANCIS, C.M.G., D.S.O., Lieut.-Colonel, Australian Infantry. For conspicuous gallantry and devotion to duty during an attack. He received information that the objective had been gained, but that all but one of the officers in his left company were casualties, and that the position on the left of the brigade sector was doubtful. He went forward in company with one N.C.O., and, noticing that an enemy machine-gun post with seven men had been left undestroyed, he and the N.C.O. rushed this post across 100 yards of open country and captured it entirely. He then went along the whole of the new front and assisted in the consolidation. His fine courage and cheerfulness under heavy rifle and machine-gun fire were a great example to all ranks.
(D.S.O. gazetted 4 June, 1917.)

SALISBURY, ALFRED GEORGE, D.S.O., Lieut.-Colonel, Australian Infantry. For conspicuous gallantry and devotion to duty. This officer commanded his battalion in a difficult night operation with great ability. The battalion, having already marched six miles, was ordered to counter-attack and retake a village. The ground was strange to everyone, and there was no time for reconnaissance, but the approach march and deployment were carried out without a hitch, and the attack was a brilliant success. This officer moved about amongst the men, encouraging and directing them, and finally established his headquarters in an open trench well forward, which was heavily shelled, but from which he was able to see and control his battalion.
(D.S.O. gazetted 4 June. 1917.)

SCANLAN, JOHN JOSEPH, D.S.O., Major (Temporary Lieut.-Colonel), Australian Infantry. For conspicuous gallantry and devotion to duty. This officer commanded a battalion in a counter-attack on a village. The battalion formed the right of the attack on the first and second objectives, and the village, being strongly held, it was necessary to mask the advance of the troops between the two objectives by facing part of them to the right. They had thus to advance into a pocket in which they were enclosed on three sides by the enemy. When the troops were checked by heavy machine gun fire, he urged them forward in an irresistible rush, gaining the second objective with few casualties, but inflicting heavy losses on the enemy. The masking movement was ably carried out, and enabled another unit to pass through to the third objective.
(D.S.O. gazetted 3 June, 1918.)

Awarded the Distinguished Service Order:

ALDWORTH, WILLIAM, Capt. (Acting Major), Essex Regt. For conspicuous gallantry and devotion to duty in clearing a village of a strong force of the enemy. He himself led an attack on a group of houses strongly held by the enemy, who were supported by machine-gun fire. He had only 17 men, and the operation was successful, resulting in the capture of 60 of the enemy and three machine guns. It was entirely due to his great skill and gallantry and splendid courage that the village was cleared.

ALLSOPP, JEROME BOILEAU, Major (Temporary Lieut.-Colonel), South Lancashire Regt. For conspicuous gallantry and devotion to duty. By skilful organization and cool handling of his battalion he restored the situation on more than one occasion when the troops on his flanks had been driven in. On one occasion the gallant stand made by his battalion, for which his courage and example were largely responsible, materially helped to save the situation by giving time for the reorganization of the line.

ANDERSON, CHARLES, M.C., Temporary Major, Royal Scots. For conspicuous gallantry and devotion to duty. He, on his own initiative, constructed a pontoon bridge across a river, enabling guns to be saved from falling into the enemy's hands. He showed an utter disregard of danger at all times, and set a fine example to all.

AUBIN, JEHU FOSBROOKE GERRARD, M.C., Lieut. (Acting Capt.), Durham Light Infantry. For conspicuous gallantry and devotion to duty. The battalion was holding a village, covering the retirement of another unit, when it was attacked by the enemy, and withdrew, leaving one company as rearguard under this officer. He remained with his rear platoon under machine-gun fire and sniping, and beat off the attack while the rest withdrew. Later, three companies were ambushed in the marshes, and he collected almost all the men, organizing a rearguard, so that each company in turn could cross by a bridge, he himself being the last to cross. A few days later his company was in support, when the three forward companies began to fall back. He went up under intense fire, rallied them, and re-established the front line. His grasp of the situation saved the battalion from what might have been annihilation.

BAINES, JOHN CECIL, Capt. (Acting Lieut.-Colonel), Leicestershire Regt. For conspicuous gallantry and devotion to duty. This officer commanded the battalion during a week's fighting with great skill in difficult circumstances, having only joined it the day before. He was constantly in touch with them all, and kept the brigade well informed of the situation, besides filling up gaps with his reserve companies. On one occasion when the line was bent back he counter-attacked at once, restoring the situation. Owing to his close liaison with other units the relief of the brigade was much facilitated.

BARE, ALFRED RAYMOND, M.C., Capt., North Lancashire Regt. For conspicuous gallantry and devotion to duty. Under cover of a heavy barrage the enemy attacked, very quickly surrounding a strong point, where this officer had his company headquarters and one platoon. In face of superior numbers, he put up a stout resistance until forced to retire on to another strong point, where the position was very critical, the officer in charge having been killed. He took command, and after a stiff fight, drove back the enemy. He was twice wounded during the fight.

BELL, JOHN JOSEPH JAMES, M.C., Lieut. (Acting Major), Royal Field Artillery. For conspicuous gallantry and devotion to duty during about a week's operations, especially on one occasion when he kept his battery in action until the enemy was within 600 yards, and then skilfully extricated the whole battery. Throughout the fighting this officer has set a splendid example to all, and has time after time withdrawn his guns under rifle and machine-gun fire.

BICKMORE, DAVID FRANCIS, Lieut. (Acting Lieut.-Colonel), Norfolk Regt., attached Gordon Highlanders. For conspicuous gallantry and devotion to duty in commanding his battalion during an enemy attack. When portions of the line showed signs of wavering, he rallied the men, and in spite of an intense fire, restored the situation. Later, during a critical period, before his battalion was required to attack, he went forward and made a reconnaissance, returning under heavy shell fire, with a valuable report and a clear plan of action. He showed great courage and leadership throughout the operations.

BLIGH, THE HONOURABLE NOEL GERVASE, Capt. (Temporary Major and Acting Lieut.-Colonel), Rifle Brigade, Special Reserve. For conspicuous gallantry and devotion to duty. This officer was in command of his battalion when it was heavily attacked. He went along the front line under intense artillery barrage, encouraging his men by his fine example. When the troops on his right were forced back, he led up a support company in full view of the enemy and formed a defensive flank. When forced to retire he kept his battalion well in hand, and contested every inch of the way.

BOSTOCK, LANCELOT, Temporary Lieut. (Acting Capt.), Northamptonshire Regt. For conspicuous gallantry and devotion to duty during enemy attacks. He commanded his company with great skill and ability under very heavy and machine-gun fire, inflicting heavy losses on the enemy and temporarily checking his advance. His brilliant leadership and fine courage were an example to all.

BOYLAN, EDWARD THOMAS ARTHUR G., M.C., Capt., Royal Horse Artillery. For conspicuous gallantry and devotion to duty. When directing the fire of his battery from a railway truck he was seen by the enemy and heavily shelled for over an hour. Though he was knocked off the truck, and the truck itself was hit several times, he continued to direct the fire, and by his fearlessness took a heavy toll of the enemy. Later, a haystack from which he was directing the fire was hit repeatedly and he was knocked off it and badly shaken, but he continued to fire into the enemy until the infantry retired past the guns. His gallantry and coolness were beyond all praise.

BOYS, STANLEY, Lieut. (Acting Capt.), Durham Light Infantry. For conspicuous gallantry and devotion to duty during a week of fighting, especially when in command of the left flank company, which was attacked by dense masses of the enemy. This officer organized his company and various units of other brigades and formed a defensive flank, working unceasingly along his company front and driving off an enemy attack in eight waves with loss. At night he withdrew across difficult country, and took up another defensive position. The following day he was enveloped, but by maintaining control of his men, and collecting stragglers of other units, he extricated them, being the last to withdraw. It was due to his energy and zeal that the retirement was successfully conducted.

BRATTON, ALLEN BASIL, M.C., Capt., North Lancashire Regt. For conspicuous gallantry and devotion to duty. When the two companies in the front line had suffered heavy casualties from enemy bombardment and attack this officer in command of the support company organized and led counter-attacks. Although outnumbered by the enemy in both men and machine guns he succeeded in driving them back 500 yards and reoccupying the main line of resistance. He then with one man bombed down a trench for 300 yards, and joined up with the next company. His splendid example enabled very good work to be done by very few men.

BRERETON, DAVID LLOYD, Major (Acting Lieut.-Colonel), Durham Light Infantry. For conspicuous gallantry and devotion to duty while commanding his battalion. He personally assisted in a bombing attack and established a block, driving the enemy back and capturing four machine guns. Throughout the operations he set a fine example to his battalion.

BRODIE, PATRICK TAIT, M.C., Temporary Capt., King's African Rifles. For conspicuous gallantry and devotion to duty. He was told to take a hill with a platoon. When he got within 50 yards of the top he was fired on by a Maxim and some 30 rifles. Only two of his men stood fast, and with them he bombed the enemy off the hill. By his dash and gallantry in taking this hill he deprived the enemy of a most advantageous point from which to deliver destructive fire on his men. He did very fine work.

BROWN, GEORGE LANGFORD, Capt. (Acting Lieut.-Colonel), Middlesex Regt. For conspicuous gallantry and devotion to duty while in command of his battalion. He held up the enemy's advance all night, and next morning only withdrew with the last company when surrounded. He showed splendid grit and determination against heavy odds.

BROWN, WILLIAM ERNEST, M.C., Temporary Major (Acting Lieut.-Colonel), South Wales Borderers. For conspicuous gallantry and devotion to duty while commanding his battalion. He held a position successfully with very few men. His fine example of courage and cheerfulness under heavy fire was mainly responsible for the retention of the ground.

BROWNE, LORD ALFRED EDEN, Major (Temporary Lieut.-Colonel), Reserve of Officers, Royal Field Artillery. For conspicuous gallantry and devotion to duty. During successive withdrawals under orders, this officer displayed great skill in artillery rearguard actions, remaining in action until the last moment, running it very fine on three occasions, and then withdrawing by batteries or sections at a time. He was always cool, and showed great power in keeping in touch with both the infantry and the C.R.A. of the division.

BRUCE, GEORGE JAMES, M.C., Temporary Capt., General List. For conspicuous gallantry and devotion to duty during an enemy attack. He rallied a company and rode in front as it once more advanced and took a village. Next day he galloped to two companies under heavy fire, and directed them. When the brigade withdrew he was the last to leave, and covered the withdrawal with Lewis gun sections under his personal supervision. Throughout he displayed high qualities as a Staff Captain, with total disregard for personal safety.

CARPENTER, PETER, M.C., Temporary Capt., Royal Air Force. For conspicuous gallantry and devotion to duty. He has destroyed nine enemy machines, and driven three down out of control. He has led 46 offensive patrols. On one occasion 12 enemy aircraft were attacked, and on another he led two other machines against 19 of the enemy, destroying six of them. He has at all times shown a magnificent example.

CHADWICK, FRANK, M.C., Lieut. (Acting Major), King's Royal Rifle Corps, Special Reserve. For conspicuous gallantry and devotion to duty. This officer was placed in command of the battalion on the death of the Commanding Officer. He led it with great skill throughout the operations, especially in a counter-attack on a village, into which he penetrated, inflicting heavy losses on the enemy and capturing a number of prisoners. Taken in rear by enemy machine guns, he was wounded in the act of withdrawing his battalion.

CHAPMAN, GORDON PATRICK, Second Lieut., Royal Field Artillery, Special Reserve. For conspicuous gallantry and devotion to duty. He was in charge of a forward gun, and under heavy shelling of high explosive and gas, continued to defend his front with gun fire until all his ammunition was exhausted. He then man-handled his gun back to the battery position and sent his detachment for a team to withdraw it, meanwhile holding off the enemy by himself with a machine gun. He showed great courage and resource.

CRUMP, JOHN ARTHUR, Major (Acting Lieut.-Colonel), North Lancashire Regt. For conspicuous gallantry and devotion to duty. Where the enemy penetrated our line and his headquarters were under continuous shell fire, and at one time attacked with bombs, this officer directed the fight with great coolness, which resulted in the enemy being driven off with loss, many prisoners being taken, and the line in his battalion sector completely restored. He set a fine example to all ranks.

DANBY, SILAS, M.C., Temporary Major (Acting Lieut.-Colonel), West Riding Regt., attached Manchester Regt. For conspicuous gallantry and devotion to duty in beating off continuous enemy attacks. He displayed fine courage and skill in commanding his battalion and inflicted severe casualties on the enemy.

DEBENHAM, GERALD ANTHONY, M.C., Second Lieut. (Temporary Capt.), Norfolk Regt. and King's African Rifles. For conspicuous gallantry and devotion to duty in command of a patrol. With great ability and dash he personally led the charge against an enemy company capturing their two machine guns, ammunition, and baggage, and completely dispersing them.

DENNY, ERNEST WRIOTHESLEY, Major, Hussars (Reserve of Officers). For conspicuous gallantry and devotion to duty. During a week's fighting this officer was acting as brigade major to the brigade. When it was difficult to obtain definite information, he visited every company in the front line held by the brigade, in spite of shell and machine-gun fire, sending in a comprehensive report as to the situation. His personality did much to encourage the young soldiers during a trying time for officers and men who had only just been sent to the division, and the majority of whom had not been under fire before.

DE QUETTEVILLE, ROBERT GEORGE, M.C., Temporary Capt., Yorkshire Regt. For conspicuous gallantry and devotion to duty. In advancing to recapture part of a trench from which the enemy had driven some of our troops,

he had to lead his men over some 700 yards of open ground swept by artillery and machine-gun and rifle fire. His skilful dispositions enabled the object to be obtained with fewer casualties than might have occurred. During the night the troops on his flanks having been withdrawn, he found himself almost surrounded by the enemy, as orders for his own retirement had not reached him. However, with great resource and most energetic leadership he withdrew from the trench he had captured and extricated his company from a difficult position and led them eventually back to the battalion, taking three of the enemy prisoners on the way. Throughout the operations his initiative and skill were not less conspicuous than his great courage, and his good leadership saved many casualties.

DESPARD, CHARLES BEAUCLERK, M.C., Temporary Capt., Dragoons. For conspicuous gallantry and devotion to duty. During five days of retirement, while as second in command of the battalion, he throughout displayed very high qualities as a leader. While in command of the rearguard the gallantry and determination with which he disputed the ground was largely responsible for the safe withdrawal of the rest of the main body.

DUFF, HUGH JOHN, M.C., Lieut. (Acting Major), Yeomanry, attached Liverpool Regt. For conspicuous gallantry and devotion to duty during an enemy attack. He commanded his company with marked ability, and at a critical time sent back valuable information to battalion headquarters. He showed courage and cheerfulness under heavy fire.

ELLIOTT, ARTHUR, M.C., Temporary Second Lieut., Lancashire Fusiliers. For conspicuous gallantry and devotion to duty. He ran over under heavy machine-gun fire and rallied men on the right flank who were being driven in, inflicting very heavy losses on the enemy by firing a Lewis gun himself. He covered the withdrawal of his party with nine or ten men, later ordering the main body of his men back and with one man covering their withdrawal. The right flank being again driven in he nevertheless held on to his line for three more hours, practically surrounded and under heavy enfilade fire. He then made a dash with his men for our lines, attached himself to another unit and continued to fight for the rest of the day. His action is worthy of the highest praise.

ELLIS, LYLE FULLAM, Second Lieut., Royal Field Artillery, Special Reserve. For conspicuous gallantry and devotion to duty while in charge of a sector during an enemy attack. He kept his guns firing to the last possible moment, inflicting heavy losses on the enemy, and scattering one of their batteries altogether. He showed great coolness and determination under heavy fire.

EMINSON, RALPH FRANKLIN, Temporary Capt., Royal Army Medical Corps. For conspicuous gallantry and devotion to duty. When two companies who had made a counter-attack and reached a village, were obliged to fall back 150 yards, suffering heavy casualties, whom it was impossible to rescue owing to the accurate machine-gun and rifle fire from the village, this officer went himself, regardless of fire, and in full view of the enemy, across "No Man's Land" many times, and carried and assisted back the wounded, who would otherwise have been left.

ENTWISLE, FRANK, M.C., Capt., London Regt. For conspicuous gallantry and devotion to duty. Having led his company through an intense machine-gun barrage, he established himself on a hill, which became practically isolated owing to all approaches being commanded by the enemy. For three days and two nights he fearlessly exposed himself, organizing the position, which was of vital importance, and encouraging his men, who were continuously under heavy shell and machine-gun fire. After three most determined counter-attacks had been driven off, he was the only unwounded officer of the two half battalions. Assuming command, he rallied the men and beat off a fourth attack. Then clinging to the lower slopes of the hill until dusk, he withdrew with all the wounded and every Lewis gun, having first destroyed any material which had to be abandoned.

ETCHELLS, THOMAS, M.C., Major, Royal Fusiliers. For conspicuous gallantry and devotion to duty. He took over the battalion after the Officer Commanding had been badly wounded, and greatly added to its efficiency by his energy and leadership. He organized a series of patrols under difficult circumstances, and gained valuable information of enemy movement.

FAILES, GERALD WATSON, M.C., Temporary Capt., Norfolk Regt. For conspicuous gallantry and devotion to duty. He showed good initiative in promptly moving all his Lewis guns to meet the direction of an enemy attack, breaking their attack up. He also led a bombing squad successfully, rallied and reorganized stragglers, and by his fine example greatly conduced to the splendid resistance made by his men.

FEARY, STEPHEN, Temporary Lieut. (Acting Capt.), Royal Engineers. For conspicuous gallantry and devotion to duty. With two sections he attacked and captured a farm strongly held by the enemy, killing thirty and capturing eighteen, as well as three machine guns. An enemy officer broke his arm with a revolver bullet; he shot the officer and then established his position. He displayed fine courage and determination.

FIELD, EDWARD, Temporary Second Lieut., Machine Gun Corps. For conspicuous gallantry and devotion to duty when in charge of a section of guns during repeated enemy attacks. For eight hours he fired his guns with great judgment under heavy machine-gun and artillery fire. The enemy poured out of a valley in large numbers, and the guns fired with terrific effect. The enemy was held for seven hours. Then, reinforced, they advanced to within 100 yards of the guns and bombed the positions from the right rear. He ordered his guns to cut their way to new positions while he helped their retirement by throwing the remainder of the bombs. In getting back he was shot through the body. His determination and fearlessness were magnetic. Throughout the day he fought magnificently.

FRASER, HERBERT CECIL, Capt, (Acting Lieut.-Colonel), Yorkshire Light Infantry. For conspicuous gallantry and devotion to duty in leading his men when heavily attacked by the enemy. By his skill in handling his battalion he greatly helped in the holding of a village and in repulsing subsequent enemy attacks.

FULTON, GEORGE KOBERWEIN, Temporary Capt. (Acting Lieut.-Colonel), Cheshire Regt. For conspicuous gallantry and devotion to duty in handling his battalion in a most skilful manner. He set a splendid example of courage and disregard of danger, and was indefatigable in arranging the battalion dispositions, and personally supervising its movements. At all times when the situation was critical he was up in the front line encouraging the men and taking part in the fighting.

FYSH, CHARLES EDWARD, M.C., Lieut. (Acting Major), Seaforth Highlanders. For conspicuous gallantry and devotion to duty in command of his battalion in action. He displayed great capabilities for organization, rallying men of other units and leading them forward through heavy fire to posts, from which they were able to inflict severe loss on the enemy. He made repeated reconnaissances to the front and flanks, regardless of his own safety, and on one occasion it was mainly due to his good work that the enemy failed to effect a crossing over a canal.

GARTHWAITE, ALEN, M.C., Temporary Capt., Wiltshire Regt. For conspicuous gallantry and devotion to duty. Though twice wounded, he refused to leave. He assumed command of his battalion, and remained with it until it was withdrawn. He showed a magnificent spirit, and his work in reorganizing scattered units was of the greatest value. His great gallantry and complete disregard for his own personal safety were a fine example to his men.

GILES, ARTHUR HARRY ASHFIELD, M.C., Temporary Lieut. (Acting Capt.), Nottinghamshire and Derbyshire Regt. For conspicuous gallantry and devotion to duty while commanding a company. He showed great coolness under heavy fire, led a successful counter-attack, and held his position against heavy odds. Later, when he took over command of his battalion, he showed ability and great determination, setting a fine example to all.

GODBY, CHARLES, C.B., C.M.G., Colonel (Temporary Brigadier-General), Royal Engineers. For conspicuous gallantry and devotion to duty. A large ammunition dump was blown up by hostile shell fire, and considerable casualties occurred. He at once went to the dump and personally organized parties to remove the wounded. With the assistance of another officer he succeeded in extricating two officers who were buried under fallen debris, although the adjacent stock of ammunition was on fire and explosions taking place. During the whole time he was at the dump ammunition was still exploding. His courage and determination in the face of considerable danger resulted in the saving of several lives.

GREEN, WILLIAM WYNDHAM, M.C., Major, Royal Field Artillery. For conspicuous gallantry and devotion to duty. Under cover of a heavy morning mist, the enemy came up unperceived close to the battery of which this officer was in command. He armed the Lewis gunners of the battery with rifles, and by skilful dispositions held off the enemy until the guns had been blown up and the detachments withdrawn. On another occasion he helped to cover the removal of a heavy howitzer battery, delaying the advance of the enemy with the fire of his Lewis guns and rifles and inflicting heavy casualties. He fought all day on foot, until the line had been established. His behaviour throughout was marked by great coolness under difficult circumstances and unconcerned courage.

GRICE-HUTCHINSON, CLAUDE BROUGHTON, Major, Royal Field Artillery. For conspicuous gallantry and devotion to duty. This officer commanded his battery with great skill, handling it and controlling it so as to obtain the maximum fire effect on the enemy, then, when absolutely necessary, withdrawing to another well-selected position. His reports and messages were of great use both to the infantry and his brigade. All this work was carried out under fire of every description.

HALL, CECIL CHARLES HATFIELD, Temporary Capt. (Acting Major), Durham Light Infantry. For conspicuous gallantry and devotion to duty. When a call was made by a neighbouring unit for reinforcement, he got together some 20 men, with a Lewis gun and machine gun, and led them forward over an embankment and across a road which was being badly sniped and machine-gunned. He subsequently brought forward more men, and conveyed an important message from Brigade Headquarters. His cool and brilliant example at a very critical time inspired all with confidence.

HANSEN, PERCY HOWARD, V.C., M.C., Capt. (Temporary Major), Lincolnshire Regt. For conspicuous gallantry and devotion to duty. He volunteered to carry out a reconnaissance, and brought back valuable information obtained under heavy artillery and machine-gun fire, which had been unprocurable from other sources. Throughout he did fine work.

HAYBITTEL, LESLIE McGOWAN, Temporary Capt., Royal Field Artillery. For conspicuous gallantry and devotion to duty. He showed great coolness and determination during a heavy enemy attack. He did great execution with his gun, holding off and destroying numbers of the enemy and capturing a machine gun and four prisoners.

HAYLEY-BELL, FRANCIS, Temporary Major (Acting Lieut.-Colonel), West Surrey Regt. For conspicuous gallantry and devotion to duty in assisting to repulse several enemy assaults. He repeatedly went out from his Battalion Headquarters through artillery barrage to visit and encourage the companies in the front line. In the afternoon he was hit in the jaw by a sniper, but carried on until orders were received in the evening for his battalion to withdraw. His personal efforts and presence amongst the men largely contributed to the successful defence.

HAYNE, SYDNEY SPENCER, Major (Acting Lieut.-Colonel), Northamptonshire Regt. For conspicuous gallantry and devotion to duty. He commanded his battalion with marked ability and skill, and when surrounded by the enemy he led a successful counter-attack, thereby relieving the pressure on other troops. He set an example of courage and cheerfulness under most trying conditions.

HESLOP, THOMAS BERNARD, Capt. (Acting Major), Durham Light Infantry. For conspicuous gallantry and devotion to duty. While commanding a battalion holding an outpost line, all the officers except three subalterns and himself were killed or wounded by shell fire. It was entirely due to the personal hold which he had over his men that, with their left flank enveloped, they stood their ground fighting to the last.

HILL, FRANCIS ROWLEY, Temporary Major, Middlesex Regt. For conspicuous gallantry and devotion to duty. During a determined enemy attack on our line this officer saw some of our troops withdrawing. With prompt initiative he rallied the men and reorganized them under heavy fire, and led them back to their original positions, which they held. A very critical situation was thus restored. Throughout the engagement his untiring energy and his devotion to duty were a fine example to all ranks, and his coolness and fine courage worthy of the highest praise.

HODSON, WILLIAM, M.C., Temporary Major (Acting Lieut.-Colonel), Cheshire Regt. For conspicuous gallantry and devotion to duty while in command of his battalion. His coolness under heavy fire and his skilful disposition of his men greatly assisted in checking the enemy's advance.

HOLDEN, VERNON, M.C., Temporary Capt., Royal West Kent Regt. For conspicuous gallantry and devotion to duty during an enemy advance. When his battalion was surrounded he withdrew his company with marked skill through the enveloping enemy, and collected men near him and formed a new line of defence. Throughout his fine leadership and coolness under most difficult circumstances were of a high order.

HOUSE, HARRY WILFRED, M.C., Temporary Major, Wiltshire Regt. For conspicuous gallantry and devotion to duty. This officer, originally in charge of a company, had to take command of the battalion on the second day of the fighting, owing to casualties amongst the senior ranks. He commanded it for a weekof heavy fighting with marked success. His energy and disregard of danger hroughout were an inspiration to his men, especially when he hung on to the front line with a small party of the regiment until completely surrounded, only getting out by his pluck and judgment after dark.

HUSKISSON, GEOFFREY, M.C., Temporary Capt. (Acting Major), Royal Field Artillery. For conspicuous gallantry and devotion to duty. On reaching his observation post through a very heavy barrage of high-explosive and gas shells he proceeded to mend the wire to his battery, which had been cut, sending back valuable information to group headquarters at a time when there was no other means of communication available. When the enemy had advanced nearly up to his observation post he fought them with a Lewis gun, and, when this jammed, with a rifle, until he was nearly cut off, all the while under very heavy fire of all descriptions, being himself wounded in the cheek. He afterwards collected some parties of infantry, and, organizing a defence, held a position of importance for nearly two hours. During seven days' severe fighting he commanded his battery with conspicuous success, and his courage under fire and cheerfulness under all circumstances were a fine example to his men.

HUTCHISON, GRAHAM SETON, M.C., Capt. (Temporary Lieut.-Colonel), Argyll and Sutherland Highlanders, attached Machine Gun Corps. For conspicuous gallantry and devotion to duty while in command of three companies of machine gunners. He drove off four heavy enemy attacks with great slaughter. He handled his guns excellently, and displayed great determination and initiative under the hottest fire.

HUXTABLE, CHARLES HUBERT ANTONY, M.C., Temporary Capt. (Acting Major), Royal Field Artillery. For conspicuous gallantry and devotion to duty during the whole of three weeks' operations. On one occasion, when his battery was in the thick of a heavy barrage, he kept his gun firing despite casualties. He directed the evacuation of the wounded and himself worked one gun single-handed. He kept touch with Brigade Headquarters during the whole time, and found a new position, less exposed, where he swiftly moved his guns during a lull.

IRONSIDE, WILLIAM STEWART, M.C., Lieut. (Acting Major), Royal Field Artillery. For conspicuous gallantry and devotion to duty. For seven days of continuous fighting he kept his battery together splendidly, in spite of heavy casualties. Throughout these trying days and sleepless nights, he set throughout the finest example to his battery in getting up thousands of rounds of ammunition to his guns in action, as well as getting all his own wounded, and several wounded of other units, safely away.

JACK, FREDERICK CHATER, M.C., Lieut. (Acting Major), Royal Field Artillery. For conspicuous gallantry and devotion to duty. After withdrawing his battery across a canal under close-range fire, this officer brought his last gun into action in full view of the enemy, who had rushed the bridge, and occupied a house, by his accurate fire compelling them to evacuate it, and recross the bridge, where they were kept in check for an hour.

JACKSON, ERNEST, M.C., Lieut. (Acting Major), Royal Engineers. For conspicuous gallantry and devotion to duty. When the enemy broke into a village he organized and led a completely successful counter-attack. Although wounded he remained at his post, and when again the enemy broke into the village he continued to direct his company with the utmost courage under intense fire until severely wounded a second time. It was largely due to his courage, coolness and devotion to duty that this important point remained in our hands.

JAMES, LIONEL, Lieut.-Colonel, King Edward's Horse. For conspicuous gallantry and devotion to duty during an enemy attack. He rallied and reorganized troops and put them in position with great skill, showing indifference to heavy machine-gun and artillery fire. His brilliant handling of his men checked the enemy's advance.

JOYCE, JOSEPH, M.C., Temporary Major, Machine Gun Corps. For conspicuous gallantry and devotion to duty when in command of a machine-gun company. It was due in a great degree to his magnificent example and great courage that a position was enabled to be held for so long. Later, he collected a party of stragglers, and, with two of his guns and two trench mortars, he held up a hostile advance. During this defence he was severely wounded, but refused to leave his post, and it was not until the enemy had almost surrounded him that he withdrew to a fresh position, being himself the last to leave. His courage and ability throughout were deserving of the highest praise.

KEET, HUBERT GORDON, M.C., Capt. (Acting Major), Liverpool Regt. For conspicuous gallantry and devotion to duty. This officer did good work as second in command during four days' operations. He was continually round the lines cheering officers and men, keeping touch with the situation and superintending the maintenance of supplies. One afternoon, hearing that a village in the line had fallen into the hands of the enemy, he organized and led a counter-attack, recapturing the position under heavy fire. His fine fighting spirit was an example to the men.

KERMODE, EDGAR MARSDEN, M.C., D.C.M., Second Lieut., West Yorkshire Regt. For conspicuous gallantry and devotion to duty in carrying out several daring reconnaissances under heavy fire. On one occasion he led his party forward with the greatest courage, and gained a hostile outpost, capturing many prisoners and a machine gun. Before withdrawing, he entirely destroyed the position by placing boxes of the enemy bombs in the entrance and igniting them. His courage and fine leadership inspired his men with the utmost confidence, and enabled his operations to be entirely successful.

KETTLEWELL, EDWARD ALEXANDER, Lieut.-Colonel (Brevet Colonel), Indian Army. For conspicuous gallantry and devotion to duty. He was in command of reinforcement camps, and was ordered to fill a gap in our line with such forces as he could collect. Realizing the emergency, he had already reorganized the reinforcements and such stragglers as he could collect into a battalion, and at an hour's notice personally led them forward to a section of the line which he held for two days until relieved. During this period he beat off several attacks, and by his personal example inspired his men with confidence and assurance.

KIRKUP, PHILIP, M.C., Capt. (Acting Major), Durham Light Infantry. For conspicuous gallantry and devotion to duty. While in command of his battalion, holding two bridgeheads, was attacked six times by the enemy in mass. It was due to his courage, tireless energy and initiative in organizing counter-attacks in the face of enormously superior numbers that time was allowed for reserves to come up and prevent a break in the line.

LAMBERTON, JOHN ROBERTSON, M.C., Capt., Highland Light Infantry. For conspicuous gallantry and devotion to duty. As second in command of his battalion he was constantly on the move organizing local counter-attacks. When placed in command of a composite battalion, he held up the enemy advance with great skill, withdrawing his men when ordered to a new line, which he then commanded and held against successive enemy attacks.

LAWLESS, FRANCIS, Temporary Capt., Liverpool Regt. For conspicuous gallantry and devotion to duty. When his commanding officer became a casualty he took command of the battalion and remained as such during the whole of the ensuing week's operations. He fought his battalion magnificently, and his conduct was the admiration of the troops adjoining. His cheerfulness and coolness had a wonderful effect on his men, and his efforts undoubtedly on several occasions caused heavy losses to be inflicted on the enemy and retarded his progress.

LEWIS, LEWIS HEWITT, M.C., Temporary Major, East Lancashire Regt. For conspicuous gallantry and devotion to duty. On many occasions, while in command of the rearguard during two days' hard fighting, the conspicuous services of this officer were of the utmost value. His organization of patrols undoubtedly saved a very difficult situation. On one occasion the non-commissioned officer and two runners who were with him having become casualties, he was left alone, but, with great determination, he was able to carry out the orders given to him. Later on, under heavy machine-gun fire, he was able by his energy and fine example to arrest a retirement that might have assumed serious proportions, but with great courage, in spite of difficulties, he rallied the men, and, collecting the stragglers, he put them into good positions, which he consolidated, and thus restored a very critical situation.

LOW, WALTER ROBERT, M.C., Temporary Capt., King's Royal Rifle Corps. For conspicuous gallantry and devotion to duty throughout the operations in which his battalion took part, especially on the following occasions : (1) He directed flanking rifle fire and established a forward Lewis-gun post, which caused the enemy severe casualties. (2) When the troops on his left had been disorganized by a hostile attack he organized some scattered details and counter-attacked, covering the withdrawal of his battalion. (3) He took command of the battalion when the commanding officer was killed, leading counter-attacks on three separate occasions under heavy fire and re-establishing the line.

MANNOCK, EDWARD, M.C., Temporary Second Lieut. (Temporary Capt.), Royal Engineers, attached Royal Air Force. For conspicuous gallantry and devotion to duty during recent operations. In seven days, while leading patrols and in general engagements, he destroyed seven enemy machines, bringing his total in all to 30. His leadership, dash and courage were of the highest order.

MASTERS, GODFREY, Major (Acting Lieut.-Colonel), Royal Field Artillery. For conspicuous gallantry and devotion to duty. Owing to his quick grasp of the situation and prompt action at a critical time, often under shell fire, the infantry brigade, covered by his guns, was enabled to hold its part of the battle zone until ordered to withdraw. He handled his brigade with skill, coolness and courage throughout the retirement.

MATHESON, WILLIAM MURRAY, M.C., Lieut. (Acting Major), Royal Field Artillery. For conspicuous gallantry and devotion to duty. This officer brought his battery into action in the open in front of a railway embankment during a sudden retirement, and remained until the infantry formed up behind him. His timely assistance was of great value to the infantry, who were exhausted and short of officers. A fortnight later, while his battery was firing a protective barrage, it suddenly came under very heavy and accurate fire, so he cleared the detachments to a flank, and, with thirty volunteers, two of whom have since died of wounds, kept two guns in action to maintain the barrage.

McLACHLAN, THOMAS, M.C., Temporary Capt. (Acting Major), Northumberland Fusiliers. For conspicuous gallantry and devotion to duty. When his commanding officer became a casualty he brought the remnants of the battalion out of action after two and a half days' continuous fighting. Through his untiring energy and good leadership, both in counter-attacking and organizing successive lines of defence, very heavy losses were inflicted upon the enemy, and their advance was materially checked.

METCALFE, HERBERT CHARLES, Temporary Major (Acting Lieut.-Colonel), Northamptonshire Regt., attached Middlesex Regt. For conspicuous gallantry and devotion to duty. At a critical moment this officer was ordered to take a portion of the army line. Advancing with his battalion, he was just in time to repel a formidable counter-attack by the enemy. He remained in the firing line throughout the day and during the next two days and the night he repelled furious attacks made on our positions. He personally led many counter-attacks, and his complete disregard of danger was a most inspiriting example to his men, and his able leadership imbued all ranks with great confidence and a firm determination to hold up the enemy and save the line.

MILLER, ALBERT BASIL, Temporary Lieut., South Staffordshire Regt. For conspicuous gallantry and devotion to duty during an attack. After his senior officers had become casualties he led the battalion with great dash and determination, killing a large number of the enemy and taking 70 prisoners. When withdrawal became necessary, he got his men back to the front line in perfect order. His courage and leadership were of a high order, and he turned a doubtful situation into a brilliant success.

MILLER, JOHN ALEXANDER, Lieut. (Acting Major), London Regt. For conspicuous gallantry and devotion to duty. The line on his left flank having been penetrated, he handled his battalion with great skill, selecting defensive positions, rallying his men, and by his fearless behaviour and inspiriting presence saving an awkward situation. He, later, reconnoitred the line to his left, linked up, and got the various parties into touch with each other, and took the whole situation in hand. His example and skill were an outstanding feature during the operations, and encouraged all with whom he came in contact.

MODERA, FREDERICK STEWART, M.C., Capt. (Acting Lieut.-Colonel), Royal Fusiliers, attached Lancashire Fusiliers. For conspicuous gallantry and devotion to duty. He did fine work in reorganizing lines of resistance during a withdrawal, and in counter-attacking. He showed marked ability and disregard for danger.

MOIR, ROBERT GIFFORD, M.C., Capt. (Temporary Major), Argyll and Sutherland Highlanders. For conspicuous gallantry and devotion to duty when in temporary command of a battalion. Both in attack and defence he has done consistently well, and kept his battalion up to a high standard of fighting spirit, so that they have not lost a position.

MOODIE, PETER ALEXANDER, Lieut., Highland Light Infantry. For conspicuous gallantry and devotion to duty when sent with his company to support another unit. He rallied men who were being driven in, and although wounded held on, stopping the enemy advance. Later, when outflanked and enfiladed, although wounded or the second time, he organized an orderly withdrawal. He made another stand, and received his third wound. Although weak from loss of blood, he waited till all was quiet, and handed over his company. His conduct throughout was magnificent, and preserved the line from being broken through.

MOORE, HENRY, M.C., Temporary Capt. (Acting Major), Royal Army Medical Corps. For conspicuous gallantry and devotion to duty. He went through heavy machine-gun and rifle fire to a dressing station which was being evacuated, and cleared a large number of wounded. He also took cars to battery positions which were being shelled, and removed the wounded to safety. At the dressing-stations during enemy bombardment he remained to the last, and saved many lives by his courage and devotion to duty.

MORGAN, HAROLD DE RIEMER, Capt. (Acting Major), East Kent Regt. For conspicuous gallantry and devotion to duty. This officer commanded his battalion with ability and energy during a trying time. Against heavy odds he stubbornly maintained positions, and showed fine leadership.

MORLIDGE, ARTHUR, Capt., Northumberland Fusiliers. For conspicuous gallantry and devotion to duty. This officer set a magnificent example of leadership under very heavy bombardment and in the face of a powerful enemy attack. When the enemy had penetrated the line on his right, capturing battalion headquarters, he assumed command of the battalion, collected detached parties, and maintained a stubborn resistance, inflicting heavy casualties, until compelled to withdraw, which he did in good order, reorganizing his command at each successive position.

MOSS, WILLIAM, Temporary Capt., Lincolnshire Regt. For conspicuous gallantry and devotion to duty. In an attack on a trench this officer organized and directed the whole of the mopping up. On reaching the second objective, he directed operations skilfully and with coolness under heavy fire, maintaining communications with the rear. Although counter-attacked more than once, he held on until his supply of bombs gave out and his rifles were clogged with mud, when he carried out the withdrawal in a very able manner. Over 100 prisoners and three machine guns were brought back, 22 machine guns being destroyed, and no fewer than 80 dead being counted in one trench. He did splendid work.

MULQUEEN, FREDERICK JAMES, M.C., Temporary Major, Royal Engineers. For conspicuous gallantry and devotion to duty. He was sent up with his company to reinforce the line at a very difficult time. He was of the greatest assistance to the defence. His fearless bearing and gallantry stimulated all ranks and enabled the positions to be held for a long time, though repeatedly attacked by overwhelming numbers.

MUNRO, DAVID CAMPBELL DUNCAN, M.C., D.C.M., Capt. (Temporary Major), Gordon Highlanders, attached Liverpool Regt. For conspicuous gallantry and devotion to duty. This officer commanded his battalion most efficiently throughout a week's operations. At a time when his men were suffering heavily from the bombardment, he was constantly among them encouraging them. It was due to his initiative that an important unoccupied post was seized, and later every attempt to retake it was frustrated. Another of his companies, after being shelled for two days, recaptured in a dashing manner a post of great importance.

MURDOCH, CLIVE, Capt. (Temporary Lieut.-Colonel), Yeomanry, attached Hampshire Regt. For conspicuous gallantry and devotion to duty. He handled his battalion with the greatest skill and coolness while withdrawing; he held on to positions as long as possible, and inflicted heavy loss on the enemy.

NICHOLLS, ERNEST PULESTON, Major, Royal Field Artillery. For conspicuous gallantry and devotion to duty while commanding his battery during an enemy attack. Under most difficult circumstances he fought off the enemy all day, and in the evening withdrew his battery with the loss of only one gun, which had been destroyed by shell fire. He showed great ability in command.

OAKDEN, THOMAS HENRY, Temporary Second Lieut., Border Regt. For conspicuous gallantry and devotion to duty. He led attack after attack against enemy bombers with such success that his unit was able to maintain its position against great odds for over five hours, after the right flank had become enveloped. Subsequently he went forward with another officer to regain touch with troops on his right. When the officer with him was wounded he took charge of the party and successfully withdrew them to another line. Although given orders to withdraw as soon as relieved, he, without food or water, maintained his position for 36 hours, refusing to withdraw until relieved. He was wounded in the foot. His example of courage was exceptionally high.

OSBORNE, LEONARD ALFRED, M.C., Second Lieut. (Acting Capt.), Somersetshire Light Infantry. For conspicuous gallantry and devotion to duty. This officer commanded a support company in the attack. Seeing that the leading companies were held up by machine-gun fire he led forward two of his platoons, and started section rushes, carrying the whole line forward by his example. He was the first to reach the objective, and the companies being then very mixed he took command of the whole, organizing and consolidating the defence. Later, his skilful dispositions enabled a counter-attack to be broken.

PARK, GODFREY WILLIAM ALAN, Temporary Capt., East Yorkshire Regt. For conspicuous gallantry and devotion to duty. This officer was in charge of the left forward flank of the line, where he displayed the greatest ability in reorganizing the details and stragglers from other divisions, which were being absorbed as they came along by the composite battalion with which he was serving. Under most difficult circumstances, his tireless energy and cheerful courage were an invaluable example to all ranks of his command, exhausted as they were with prolonged fighting. At a critical moment, though twice wounded, he rallied his men, and led them forward to restore the front after a personal reconnaissance under heavy shell fire, and he remained directing his command until relieved on the following morning. His courage and resource under most trying conditions were admirable.

PARKIN, FRANK LESLIE, Major (Temporary Lieut.-Colonel), Yorkshire Light Infantry, attached West Riding Regt. For conspicuous gallantry and devotion to duty while in command of a rearguard action. He showed exceptional ability in withdrawing his command under difficult conditions, with very small loss under intense shelling and machine-gun fire.

PEARD, CLIFFORD JAMES, Capt., Somersetshire Light Infantry. For conspicuous gallantry and devotion to duty. This officer led his company in an attack in a wood, which was a mass of broken branches and tangled wire. He captured his first and second objectives, taking many prisoners and killing large numbers. Counter-attacked on his second objective, he for a long time made a determined resistance, but realizing the position was becoming untenable, withdrew, reorganized, and again forced his way forward by bombing attacks. His dash and skill throughout had a great effect on the men.

PEARSON, JOHN HESKETH, M.C., Temporary Major, Nottinghamshire and Derbyshire Regt. For conspicuous gallantry and devotion to duty during an enemy attack. At a critical period he led a successful counter-attack, driving back the enemy and capturing four machine guns and some prisoners. By his prompt action and gallant leadership he restored the situation.

PEARSON, NOEL GERVIS, M.C., Temporary Major, South Wales Borderers. For conspicuous gallantry and devotion to duty in organizing several minor counter-attacks and in carrying out many daring reconnaissances by night, when he invariably brought back valuable information. His cheerful spirit and courageous example inspired great confidence in all on many critical occasions.

PERCIVAL, ARTHUR ERNEST, M.C., Capt. (Temporary Lieut.-Colonel), Essex Regt., attached Bedfordshire Regt. For conspicuous gallantry and devotion to duty during recent operations. He handled his battalion cleverly, showing power of command and knowledge of tactics. He set a fine example during several critical periods.

POWELL, GEORGE, Second Lieut., Nottinghamshire and Derbyshire Regt. For conspicuous gallantry and devotion to duty. This officer in command of a company fought a skilful rearguard action, enabling the battalion to take up a fresh position. On several occasions he went out to reconnoitre, gaining important information, and once, when out with only three men, brought back four prisoners. A few days later, when all other officers had become casualties, he led the battalion in a brilliant attack, gaining the objective, and inflicting heavy losses on the enemy. His example throughout ten days' fighting was of inestimable service.

PRICE-WILLIAMS, HAROLD, M.C., Capt. (Acting Major), Royal Field Artillery. For conspicuous gallantry and devotion to duty. At a critical period he went forward under intense fire of high-explosive and gas shell to ascertain the situation, and then returned to encourage his men to deal with the charging enemy with open sights. He showed fine courage and leadership.

PRITCHARD, RALPH BROOMFIELD, M.C., Temporary Capt., Northumberland Fusiliers. For conspicuous gallantry and devotion to duty. When the battalion was ordered to fill a gap in the front line, this officer, in charge of the advanced guard, acted with such dash that it was mainly through his fine work that the battalion was able to do so. Later, he again advanced and occupied the old line, getting into touch with the flanks, and capturing three men of an enemy patrol. He held the line for the next four days under heavy fire, and finally was severely wounded when leading his company in a counter-attack as it gained its first objective.

PUGH, MERVYN PHIPPEN, M.C., Temporary Lieut. (Acting Capt.), Royal Berkshire Regt. For conspicuous gallantry and devotion to duty. When his Commanding Officer was killed, this officer assumed command of the battalion, and in difficult and intricate situations withdrew from position to position, always keeping it intact and ready for further fighting. When, after four days, the battalion was relieved, he personally reorganized the four companies, nearly all the officers having become casualties. His determination and leadership carried the battalion safely through several critical phases.

RAIMES, ALWYN LESLIE, Major, Durham Light Infantry. For conspicuous gallantry and devotion to duty. This officer organized and led a counter-attack, and, although wounded by a rifle bullet in the thigh, he continued to carry on, holding the enemy up for some hours. Until the success of the attack was assured, and the line re-established, he refused to leave his battalion. While in command of the battalion his example to the men had a great effect.

REID, CHARLES, Capt. (Temporary Major), Gordon Highlanders. For conspicuous gallantry and devotion to duty. While commanding a battalion in the outpost line, during a heavy bombardment with gas shells, although affected by the gas, remained in command, and reorganized the line under shell and machine-gun fire. During prolonged fighting, though practically without sleep, his confident bearing and disregard of danger gave encouragement to all under his command.

REID, HORACE ARTHUR, M.C., Temporary Major, Royal Engineers. For conspicuous gallantry and devotion to duty when commanding his company. He held his position against heavy odds until ammunition was practically exhausted. Seeing a wounded officer lying in a shell-hole in front of the line, he went forward, and, with the assistance of a N.C.O., brought him in under heavy rifle and machine-gun fire. He showed fine courage and determination.

ROBERTS, JOHN PRICE, M.C., Temporary Capt. (Acting Major), Machine Gun Corps. For conspicuous gallantry and devotion to duty. He several times reconnoitred enemy positions under heavy shell and machine-gun fire. By his gallantry, determination and unflagging energy he encouraged all ranks.

ROBERTSON, GEORGE RAYMOND GILDEA, Major, Royal Field Artillery. For conspicuous gallantry and devotion to duty. This officer fought his battery under an exceedingly heavy and continuous barrage to the last ; the two remaining serviceable guns were then put out of action, and the remaining cartridges burnt. He then withdrew his men and reported to the infantry. His coolness and cheerfulness throughout the day encouraged the men to carry out their arduous duties successfully.

SAINT, EDWARD TWELFTREE, Major (Temporary Lieut.-Colonel), Cambridgeshire Regt. For conspicuous gallantry and devotion to duty covering a period of ten days' operations, during the first seven of which he showed marked initiative in organizing lines of defence, especially in front of a town, where he held up the enemy advance, enabling the guns to be withdrawn. When the officer commanding another battalion became a casualty, he assumed command of both battalions. Later, when the officer commanding brigade became a casualty, he took command of the brigade, organizing a counter-attack at a critical time, and reoccupying the line. He kept the men splendidly together when nearly all the officers and non-commissioned officers had become casualties.

SANDERSON, AYMOR EDEN, Capt. and Brevet Major, Oxfordshire and Buckinghamshire Light Infantry. For conspicuous gallantry and devotion to duty. This officer has repeatedly galloped forward from brigade headquarters to the front line rallying and organizing men of various battalions. On one occasion, when the necessity for a counter-attack was pressing, he galloped forward with orders to two battalion commanders, enabling the attack to take place at the right time. Both going and returning, and while delivering the orders, he was under heavy shell and machine-gun fire.

SCRIMGEOUR, GEOFFERY CAMERON, M.C., Lieut. (Acting Capt.), Royal Field Artillery. For conspicuous gallantry and devotion to duty. After a heavy enemy bombardment of gas and high-explosive shell had knocked out all his guns, together with two officers and eight non-commissioned officers, he collected all remaining personnel and manned the trench in front of his battery. With Lewis guns and rifles he held this position till nightfall. He showed fine courage, and set a splendid example to his battery.

SHARP, ROBERT RICH, M.C., Second Lieut. (Acting Capt.), Royal Field Artillery, Special Reserve. For conspicuous gallantry and devotion to duty. He remained in command of his trench mortars till all ammunition was expended, then he organized a party of men and took up a defensive position. Although under continuous short-range fire, he so organized the defence and encouraged his men, that in spite of repeated enemy attacks the position was still holding out six hours later. His timely and gallant action prevented the enemy from pushing a wedge into our lines. Subsequently he carried out a very long and arduous reconnaissance under very severe fire, sending back very valuable information. His good work was conspicuous, and his personal courage and energy were alike remarkable.

SHARPE, ALFRED GERALD MEREDITH, Capt. and Brevet Major, Royal Berkshire Regt. For conspicuous gallantry and devotion to duty during a week's operations. When the enemy had launched a heavy attack, and driven back the brigade on the right, laying open the right flank, this officer went forward under heavy fire to clear up the situation, selected positions, and led up reserve companies to form a defensive flank. He also rallied leaderless men of other units and led them forward into the line. He gave a clear and accurate report of the situation on his return to brigade headquarters.

SIMMONS, JOHN AYNSCOUGH, M.C., Temporary Major, Cheshire Regt. For conspicuous gallantry and devotion to duty during an attack. He led his battalion with fine dash and leadership, and gained his objective. Owing to both flanks being in the air, he was obliged to order a withdrawal, which he covered, together with 20 men. He eventually personally got in touch with his flanks and organized a defensive position. He displayed courage of a high order, and set a splendid example to all.

SLATER, HARRY ANDREW, Temporary Lieut., Nottinghamshire and Derbyshire Regt. For conspicuous gallantry and devotion to duty during an enemy attack. With a few men he protected two light trench mortars, and enabled them to inflict heavy casualties on the enemy. He led successful counter-attacks with great gallantry. In the evening he reconnoitred the enemy's position, which enabled him to lead another successful counter-attack and bring back two enemy trench mortars. He set a fine example to all.

SMITH, ROBERT ARTHUR, M.C., Temporary Lieut.-Colonel, Royal Fusiliers. For conspicuous gallantry and devotion to duty when in command of a battalion. When his right flank was exposed, with a few men he had collected and the personnel of his own battalion headquarters, he formed a defensive flank which successfully held up the enemy's advance. Under heavy fire he personally superintended another successful operation, in which his men had to fight their way back through a village. His indomitable courage and personality at a critical moment saved a very difficult situation. His calmness and absolute disregard of danger under fire were an example to all ranks.

SMYTH, GEORGE OSBERT STIRLING, M.C., Capt. (Acting Major), Royal Field Artillery. For conspicuous gallantry and devotion to duty. Under heavy shelling he went along the battery and helped to put out ammunition that had been set on fire, and with three remaining guns fired on the approaching enemy with open sights, inflicting heavy casualties. Next day, by collecting men near him and machine guns, he held up the enemy for hours.

SPENCER, FRANCIS ELMHIRST, M.C., Major, Royal Garrison Artillery. For conspicuous gallantry and devotion to duty. Under heavy shell and machine-gun fire he used his guns with great effect, destroying numbers of the enemy and materially assisting the infantry. He showed fine dash and leadership.

SPURRELL, WILLIAM JAMES, M.C., Temporary Major, Norfolk Regt. For conspicuous gallantry and devotion to duty. He personally made a reconnaissance of the ground for a counter-attack, giving orders for the disposition of the men under very heavy shell and machine-gun fire. Although wounded, he insisted on carrying on, and gathering every man from battalion headquarters, until he received a second wound. Throughout the whole time he commanded the battalion his example and gallantry were of a very fine order.

STEPHENSON, MARMADUKE BASIL, M.C., Lieut. (Acting Capt.), East Yorkshire Regt., Special Reserve. For conspicuous gallantry and devotion to duty in maintaining an isolated position with his company against several attacks by the enemy in superior numbers. By his determined courage and resolution he inspired his men to hold their line for four days until relieved.

STITT, WILLIAM HEWITT, M.C., Temporary Capt., Royal Irish Fusiliers, attached Royal Dublin Fusiliers. For conspicuous gallantry and devotion to duty. When the battalion was entirely surrounded by the enemy, this officer carried out a personal reconnaissance of the bridge-heads, which were both occupied by the enemy. He ascertained the enemy's password and dispositions, and then led the column over the bridge, killing one of the sentries himself. Further, on finding the enemy in possession of a village, he again reconnoitred, and ascertained their dispositions, getting his column safely through and rejoining our line, bringing with him some 10 officers and 350 other ranks.

STONE, WILLIAM ALFRED COLLIS, M.C., Temporary Capt. (Acting Major), Royal Field Artillery. For conspicuous gallantry and devotion to duty. Suddenly called upon to command the brigade owing to casualties, he did so with complete efficiency during a withdrawal. At a critical period he displayed courage and leadership which inspired confidence in all ranks of the brigade.

STONEY, GERALD JOHNSTON LIPYEATT, M.C., Capt. (Acting Lieut.-Colonel), Worcestershire Regt. For conspicuous gallantry and devotion to duty. He maintained his battalion headquarters in a village for many hours after the greater portion of that village had fallen into enemy hands. By doing so he undoubtedly delayed the enemy's subsequent advance, and inflicted heavy casualties on him. His brilliant example of gallantry and tenacity had a special value in greatly stimulating the courage of all ranks.

TEMPERLEY, ERIC, Major (Acting Lieut.-Colonel), Northumberland Fusiliers. For conspicuous gallantry and devotion to duty. Commanded his battalion throughout four days' continuous fighting, both in attack and defence. By his skilful handling broke up all enemy attacks, inflicting heavy losses, and set a fine example of courage and determination.

THOMPSON, WILLIAM DOUGLAS BAIRD, M.C., Lieut., Durham Light Infantry. For conspicuous gallantry and devotion to duty. Showed great courage and determination in holding the line, which was the left flank of the battalion, and not in touch with any other unit, beating back every attempt of the enemy to advance. After dusk, when the flank was temporarily driven back, he restored the situation by his energy and fearlessness.

THOMPSON, THOMAS ALEXANDER LACY, M.C., Lieut. (Acting Capt.), Northumberland Fusiliers. For conspicuous gallantry and devotion to duty. This officer commanded the battalion for a week, after his commanding officer had been wounded. When the enemy had captured a village on his flank, he led his men in a house-to-house counter-attack, clearing the greater part of the village and re-establishing the line. The following day, in spite of two gunshot wounds in the thigh, after the units on the flank had been driven back, he held on for over an hour until a counter-attack restored the situation.

THOMSON, JAMES ALBERT RAYMOND, Capt. (Acting Lieut.-Colonel), Yorkshire Regt. For conspicuous gallantry and devotion to duty. Throughout ten days' fighting this officer has rendered splendid service, inspiring the brigade by his example of cheerfulness and leadership. When the enemy captured a village he established his battalion on some high ground above it, holding on from 9 a.m. to 5 p.m., although his right was in the air, and he had neither orders nor information. On a later occasion, after encouraging his men throughout a day of intense shelling, he led a counter-attack in the evening to cover the withdrawal of another division. This was successful, as also was his rearguard action afterwards.

TILLIE, WILLIAM KINGSLEY, M.C., Temporary Lieut.-Colonel, Machine Gun Corps. For conspicuous gallantry and devotion to duty. The personal reconnaissances made by him under very heavy fire were of the utmost value. His energy and fearlessness in going amongst his men at critical periods at great personal risk set a fine example and inspired great confidence. The determination with which he handled his machine guns was largely responsible for defeating many hostile attacks.

TOD, DAVID, Temporary Lieut. (Acting Capt.), Mounted Machine Gun Corps. For conspicuous gallantry and devotion to duty. This officer handled his battery with great skill during five days' operations, inflicting many casualties and capturing many prisoners. With marked boldness he rescued two officers from the enemy at a point nearly 50 miles from the nearest supporting troops.

TONG, THOMAS BARLOW, Temporary Lieut. (Acting Capt.), Welsh Regt. For conspicuous gallantry and devotion to duty. He personally led a fighting patrol against a number of snipers and machine guns established in a village. In the face of heavy fire he thrust his way to the far edge of the village and established a strong post there. He then returned and brought up reinforcements, and repeated this operation several times. It was very largely due to him that the enemy was prevented from getting possession of the village.

TONSON-RYE, HUBERT BERNARD, Major, Royal Munster Fusiliers. For conspicuous gallantry and devotion to duty. When the troops on his flanks were withdrawn, and his battalion completely cut off, he held on till dark, counter-attacking and driving the enemy from his flank with machine-gun and rifle fire. During the night he succeeded in leading the remainder of his battalion through the enemy's outpost line, and rejoined his brigade. On another occasion, when the troops in the front line were overwhelmed, he led a counter-attack, driving back the enemy, and reoccupying the trenches.

TORTISE, HERBERT JAMES, Temporary Capt. (Acting Major), Royal West Surrey Regt. For conspicuous gallantry and devotion to duty during enemy attacks. When his commanding officer was wounded he assumed command of the battalion, rallied and reorganized other troops with them, and led them in attack. He showed fine courage and powers of command.

TRAILL, ROBERT FRANCIS, Major, Worcestershire Regt. For conspicuous gallantry and devotion to duty in commanding his battalion, when he counter-attacked, and after capturing his objective was compelled to withdraw, owing to the failure of the attack on the left flank. He executed the retirement with great skill and judgment. Later, he organized a counter-attack and drove the enemy from the line.

TYSOE, WILLIAM, Temporary Second Lieut., Bedfordshire Regt. For conspicuous gallantry and devotion to duty. He showed great skill and ability as the only company officer left, in organizing and consolidating the line after a successful counter-attack; and when next day the enemy again attacked he drove them back, inflicting heavy casualties on them. He showed fine dash and leadership.

WALKER, ARTHUR, Capt. and Brevet Major, Royal Army Medical Corps. For conspicuous gallantry and devotion to duty in establishing forward dressing stations and continuing to work in them until forced to move by the immediate proximity of the enemy. He was repeatedly working in the open under heavy fire, no protection being available. He undoubtedly saved many lives which would have been lost but for his courage and initiative.

WESTMORLAND, HERBERT CAMPBELL, Capt. (Temporary Lieut.-Colonel), Hampshire Regt. For conspicuous gallantry and devotion to duty. He showed an absolute disregard of danger and great skill and energy in supervising his battle front under heavy artillery and machine-gun fire and during many withdrawals. He personally rallied and reorganized men, and under heavy fire re-established the line at a time when the situation was very critical.

WILL, ROBERT ROSS, Capt. (Acting Major), Royal Field Artillery. For conspicuous gallantry and devotion to duty. In addition to commanding his battery throughout six days' fighting, he showed great resource as brigade commander in arranging nine successive withdrawals, without losing any guns or ammunition. He broke up, by the fire of his brigade, heavy enemy outflanking attacks on the left, for four hours on end directing and controlling fire on the enemy in the open.

WILLIAMS, HUGH LLOYD, M.C., Temporary Major, Royal Welsh Fusiliers. For conspicuous gallantry and devotion to duty when in temporary command of a battalion. His flank being exposed, with a quick grasp of the situation he threw back a short defensive flank and then, collecting troops of various units, personally led three counter-attacks against the advancing enemy. His gallant action checked the enemy and allowed his own troops to form a new line. His complete disregard of personal danger set a fine example and inspired the men with the greatest confidence.

WILLIAMS, WALTER ELLIS, Capt. (Acting Lieut.-Colonel), Middlesex Regt., attached Cheshire Regt. For conspicuous gallantry and devotion to duty. Under very heavy artillery and machine-gun fire he reorganized his battalion, got into touch with troops on either side, and successfully held his position.

WOODRUFFE, JOHN SHELDON, Major (Temporary Lieut.-Colonel), Royal Sussex Regt. For conspicuous gallantry and devotion to duty in commanding his battalion in a very difficult situation, and under heavy fire during ten days' operations. On one occasion he personally rallied and reformed troops under heavy shell fire, and led them to the attack, re-establishing the line at a very critical moment. He showed great gallantry in handling his command.

WOOLLETT, HENRY WINSLOW, M.C., Temporary Capt., General List, attached Royal Air Force. For conspicuous gallantry and devotion to duty during recent operations. In two days during three patrols he destroyed eight enemy machines, making his total 22. His leadership, dash and courage were of the highest order.

WRATHALL, WILLIAM PARKER, M.C., Capt., Royal Highlanders. For conspicuous gallantry and devotion to duty. This officer took over temporary command of the brigade at a time when it was much depleted after 48 hours' fighting, and consisted of small parties of various battalions, holding a line of over 5,000 yards, covering two battalions of another division who were digging. For the best part of three days he was untiring in his efforts, collecting scattered parties and organizing the hastily occupied and extended line. In particular when Brigade Headquarters had been rushed by the enemy and nearly surrounded, it was due to his energy that the personnel was extricated with little loss. His personal reconnaissances and unfailing resource in dealing with difficulties were the mainstay of the line.

YOUNG, JOHN ALLEN, M.C., Temporary Major, Royal Field Artillery. For conspicuous gallantry and devotion to duty. Under heavy enemy bombardment he kept his battery under control and firing. When the observation post was cut off, he went under heavy machine-gun fire to a neighbouring ridge and thence directed fire till the enemy were close upon him. He then returned to the battery, put up a most spirited resistance till dusk, and then safely got all his guns away. He set a very fine example to all.

CANADIAN FORCE.

BARBER, HORACE GREELY, Major, Canadian Railway Troops. For conspicuous gallantry and devotion to duty while supervising light railways. Under his supervision valuable stocks of light railway material and coal were salved, maintenance work was carried out, and railway lines patrolled up to the last possible moment. The good work performed by his men was largely due to his coolness, perseverance and inspiring example while frequently under fire night and day.

BLACKBURN, REGINALD VERNON, M.C., Capt., Canadian Infantry. For conspicuous gallantry and devotion to duty. He successfully led his company in a raid under heavy fire. During the operation he rushed a machine-gun post single-handed, and killed two and captured three of the enemy and the gun. A splendid performance.

MUSGROVE, GEORGE HENRY, Major, Canadian Infantry. For conspicuous gallantry and devotion to duty in action. In the preparatory stages of a raid on the enemy defence, he, by his personal courage and example, inspired all ranks, and was able to develop an intensity of observation and a patrol reconnaissance, which was largely responsible for the clear appreciation of the ground gained. Later, under the handicap of only one arm, the other having been lost in previous operations, he personally supervised the forming up of assaulting parties under heavy fire, and returned to his post, keeping the battalion headquarters fully informed as to each stage of the fighting. His keen sense of duty, fearless conduct in the open, and great energy in all preparations contributed in a large measure to the success of the operations.

PULLEN, ERNEST FLEETWOOD, Major, Canadian Railway Troops. For conspicuous gallantry and devotion to duty. The energy and devotion to duty which this officer has displayed while commanding his company throughout the operations have been a conspicuous example to all his men, whom he has led, and whose work he has organized in the forward area. On two different occasions he rallied considerable numbers of stragglers from other units, and, leading them back to the front, placed them again under their officers and warrant officers, and their services, when badly wanted, were instrumental in defeating the enemy. His complete disregard of personal safety had a most inspiring effect on his men, and his intelligent dispositions, often under heavy fire, enabled him to keep his line open as long as it was required, and much material was saved.

TIMMIS, REGINALD SYMMONDS, Major, Canadian Cavalry. For conspicuous gallantry and devotion to duty in successfully leading a counter-attack at a critical moment, giving sufficient time for the withdrawal of other troops who were surrounded. Later, he conducted a most able rearguard action. Thanks to his energetic and prompt action, a successful withdrawal in face of strong bodies of the enemy was accomplished.

AUSTRALIAN IMPERIAL FORCE.

BURDUS, STANLEY GEORGE, Lieut., Australian Infantry. For conspicuous gallantry and devotion to duty. When sent forward with his company to secure the ground held by another company which had suffered heavy casualties, he showed excellent leadership. He reorganized the details of this company and established a good line of posts. Seeing two machine guns which were causing him heavy casualties he single-handed rushed them and shot the crews with his revolver at point-blank range and captured the guns, thus enabling his men to advance.

EDGERTON, ERIC HENRY DRUMMOND, M.M., Lieut., Australian Infantry. For conspicuous gallantry and devotion to duty. Before dawn on the morning of an attack this officer with two men reconnoitred the track from the assembly point to a bridge over the river, across which he had to lead his platoon at zero. Early in the attack he mopped up a post by bombing. Pushing on, he and another man rushed a machine gun, shooting two men with his revolver and capturing the remainder. After clearing several dug-outs, he established a post on his objective, dispersing an enemy attack. In the afternoon he outflanked a machine-gun post, and followed it up by shooting five men with his revolver and capturing one officer and one man. He then bombed a third machine gun, killing the crew. His energy was an inspiration to all.

MATTHEWS, LESLIE WILLIAM, Major, Australian Infantry. For conspicuous gallantry and devotion to duty. This officer commanded his battalion in an attack, previous to which he had reconnoitred the jumping-off ground, and thought out all the arrangements and dispositions. During the attack he moved about under heavy fire, keeping in touch with the situation, directing and controlling the men, and by prompt action in altering dispositions, minimized the losses from shell fire.

METCALFE, JAMES BEVERLEY, M.C., Major, Australian Army Medical Corps. For conspicuous gallantry and devotion to duty. In a village under heavy bombardment of gas and high explosives, this officer, with practically no protection, tended the wounded for four and a half hours. When the advanced dressing-station had been moved to a new site, he remained with four men evacuating odd cases which continued to come in until two shells came right into the dressing-room, severely wounding him. His cheerfulness and coolness throughout encouraged all around him.

RONALD, HARRY, Capt., Australian Infantry. For conspicuous gallantry and devotion to duty. This officer was in command of a company on the left of the line, when the enemy, who had broken through a gap on the right, attacked it from front and rear, effecting a lodgment after severe fighting in his trench. He promptly organized a strong counter-attack, dislodging the enemy, killing about sixty, and taking about fifty prisoners. His quick initiative did much towards the success of the operation.

RYRIE, HAROLD STEWART, Capt. (Temporary Major), Australian Light Horse Regt. For conspicuous gallantry and devotion to duty while commanding his squadron during an attack. Although the enemy was in a strong position, with a great number of well-concealed machine guns, and were threatening to envelop his flank, he led his men forward with the utmost courage. Under a terrific machine-gun fire, he handled his squadron to the best advantage, and set a splendid example of coolness, until he was himself severely wounded.

SMITH, PHILLIP JAMES, Second Lieut., Australian Infantry. For conspicuous gallantry and devotion to duty. This officer was in charge of a party for mopping up, after the capture of a village, and had to swim two creeks to reach his objective, coming under direct fire of an enemy strong post. Without a moment's hesitation, he rushed it, capturing one officer and 11 men. He then rescued one of his men who was lying wounded under fire in the street, then, closing his party round another strong post, he shot one man, and overpowered an officer with his fists, the rest surrendering. Though greatly exhausted, he concluded by dashing across 70 yards of open ground by himself and capturing a party of nine of the enemy.

TASSIE, LESLIE GEMMEL, Major, Australian Army Medical Corps. For conspicuous gallantry and devotion to duty. This officer set a fine example of coolness in going about amongst his stretcher-bearers directing and encouraging them. Day and night he visited the regimental aid post and loading posts, rearranging bearer relays, and supervising the evacuation of wounded. Hearing there were several wounded in a village which was being heavily shelled, he organized parties and cleared the village.

WHITHAM, JOHN LAWRENCE, C.M.G., Lieut.-Colonel, Australian Infantry. For conspicuous gallantry and devotion to duty. This officer commanded his battalion in a difficult night operation with great ability. Following an enemy advance, in which a village was lost, the battalion, which had already marched six miles, took part in a counter-attack. The ground was strange, and there was no time for reconnaissance, but the approach march and deployment was carried out without a hitch, and the attack was a brilliant success. He moved about encouraging and directing his troops, and established his headquarters well forward in an open trench, from which, though under heavy fire, he was able to control his battalion.

WILES, HAROLD JOSEPH, Lieut., Australian Infantry. For conspicuous gallantry and devotion to duty, especially in leading fighting patrols to gain information. On one occasion, when within striking distance of the enemy, he engaged a party and killed five; then, as machine-gun fire and Very lights held up his men, he crawled forward and brought back the required information himself. On another occasion, with a fighting patrol, he rushed an enemy standing patrol, killing one, and chasing another man to within 30 yards of his post, when he took him prisoner and brought him back under heavy fire. The man had his rifle and bayonet, while this officer only had an empty revolver.

NEW ZEALAND FORCE.

MASSEY, FRANK GEORGE, M.C., Lieut. (Acting Major), New Zealand Rifle Brigade, attached Lancashire Fusiliers. For conspicuous gallantry and devotion to duty. During two days' hard fighting, until severely wounded, commanded the battalion in a most efficient manner, inflicting heavy losses on the enemy, at small cost, largely owing to his resource and grasp of the situation.

SOUTH AFRICAN FORCE.

GREENE, LOVELL, M.C., Temporary Capt., South African Infantry. For conspicuous gallantry and devotion to duty. This officer led his company in a counter-attack, securing his first objective, including a strong point, and organizing and consolidating under heavy fire. The next morning, his Commanding Officer becoming a casualty, he took command of the battalion. During heavy enemy attacks our troops were forced back. He immediately went forward, rallying and encouraging them, and, thanks to his efforts, the enemy was beaten back. His work, both as company and battalion commander, was splendid.

London Gazette, 20 Sept. 1918.—" Admiralty, S.W., 20 Sept. 1918.—Honours for Services in the Auxiliary Patrol, Minesweeping and Coastal Motor Boats, between 1 Jan. and 30 June, 1918. The King has been graciously pleased to approve of the award of the following honours to the undermentioned Officers. To be Companions of the Distinguished Service Order."

BURLEIGH, CECIL WILLIS, R.D., Commander, Royal Naval Reserve.
DILLON, STAFFORD HARRY, Lieut.-Commander, R.N.
WEBB, THOMAS PAUL, Lieut.-Commander, Royal Naval Reserve.

" Honours for Services in Monitors and Destroyers of the Dover Patrol, between 1 Jan. and 30 June, 1918.—The King has been graciously pleased to approve of the award of the following honours to the undermentioned Officers. To be Companions of the Distinguished Service Order."

GORE-LANGTON, HUBERT EDWIN, Commander, R.N.
JACKSON, WILLIAM LINDSAY, Lieut.-Commander, R.N.
RAMPLING, ROBIN, Engineer Lieut.-Commander, R.N.

" Honours for Services in Destroyers of the Harwich Force between 1 Jan. and 30 June, 1918.—The King has been graciously pleased to approve of the award of the following honour to the undermentioned Officer. To be a Companion of the Distinguished Service Order."

ASHTON, JAMES, Engineer Lieut.-Commander, R.N.

" Honours for Services in Vessels employed on Escort, Convoy, and Patrol Duties between 1 Jan. and 30 June, 1918.—The King has been graciously pleased to approve of the award of the following honours to the undermentioned Officers. To be Companions of the Distinguished Service Order."

DENNY, HERBERT MAYNARD, Lieut.-Commander (Acting Commander), R.N.
KENNEDY, MICHAEL KAVANAGH HORSLEY, Lieut.-Commander, R.N.

" Honours for Services in Submarines between 1 Jan. and 30 June, 1918.—The King has been graciously pleased to approve of the award of the following honour to the undermentioned Officer. To be a Companion of the Distinguished Service Order."

POLAND, ALLAN, Lieut.-Commander, R.N.

" Honours for Services in Action with Enemy Submarines.—The King has been graciously pleased to approve of the award of the following honour for services in action with enemy submarines. To be a Companion of the Distinguished Service Order."

BENSON, ARTHUR WINNIFRED, Commander, R.N.

" Honours for Miscellaneous Services.—The King has been graciously pleased to approve of the award of the following honour to the undermentioned Officer. To be a Companion of the Distinguished Service Order."

DORLING, HENRY TAPRELL, Commander, R.N.

London Gazette, 21 Sept. 1918.—" Air Ministry, 21 Sept. 1918. His Majesty the King has been graciously pleased to confer the undermentioned rewards on Officers of the Royal Air Force, in recognition of gallantry in flying operations against the enemy. Awarded a Bar to the Distinguished Service Order."

COLLISHAW, RAYMOND, D.S.O., D.S.C., D.F.C., Lieut. (Temporary Major) (late Royal Naval Air Service). A brilliant squadron leader of exceptional daring, who has destroyed 51 enemy machines. Early one morning he, with another pilot, attacked an enemy aerodrome. Seeing three machines brought out of a burning hangar he dived five times, firing bursts at these from a very low altitude, and dropped bombs on the living quarters. He then saw an enemy aeroplane descending over the aerodrome ; he attacked it and drove it down in flames. Later, when returning from a reconnaissance of the damaged hangars, he was attacked by three Albatross scouts, who pursued him to our lines, when he turned and attacked one, which fell out of control and crashed.
(D.S.O. gazetted 11 Aug. 1917 ; D.S.C. gazetted 20 July, 1917 ; D.F.C. gazetted 3 Aug. 1918.)

SMART, BERNARD ARTHUR, D.S.O., Lieut. (Hon. Capt.) (Sea Patrol). Led his flight for 160 miles over sea and land, and destroyed by bombs an important enemy airship shed. This service was carried out under exceptionally difficult circumstances, requiring great skill, and was most creditably performed.
(D.S.O. gazetted 2 Nov. 1917.)

Awarded the Distinguished Service Order.

DICKSON, WILLIAM FORSTER, Lieut. (Honorary Capt.) (Sea Patrol). Displayed great skill and gallantry on the occasion of a long-distance bombing raid. He succeeded in dropping bombs on an airship station from a low altitude with destructive effect, and although subjected to severe fire from the enemy obtained valuable information.

STODART, DAVID EDMUND, D.F.C., Capt. (Temporary Major). Whilst commanding a flight of the Royal Air Force the whole of the flying officers had become incapacitated through sickness or wounds, and their duties were then performed by himself, in addition to his administrative work as commanding officer. During this period Major Stodart dropped 115 bombs on the enemy's position, exposed 326 negatives over enemy territory, and acted as observer for 163 rounds of our heavy artillery. In a period of 21 days this officer was 37 hours in the air, performing all the duties of an entire flight, a record which it would be difficult to surpass.

London Gazette, 24 Sept. 1918.—" War Office, 24 Sept. 1918. His Majesty the King has been graciously pleased to approve of the following awards to the undermentioned Officers, in recognition of their gallantry and devotion to duty in the field. Awarded a Bar to the Distinguished Service Order."

BARTLETT, ALFRED JAMES NAPIER, D.S.O., Capt. and Brevet Major (Acting Lieut.-Colonel), Oxfordshire and Buckinghamshire Light Infantry. For conspicuous gallantry and devotion to duty during an enemy attack. By his skilful handling of his battalion he maintained his position in spite of the line being penetrated on both flanks, thereby checking the enemy's advance, and enabling the line to be completely re-established by counter-attack. By his courage and coolness he set a splendid example to all ranks.
(D.S.O. gazetted 1 Jan. 1918.)

DAVIDGE, GUY MORTIMER COLERIDGE, D.S.O., Major (Acting Lieut.-Colonel), Worcestershire Regt. For conspicuous gallantry and devotion to duty in action. He handled his battalion in a remarkably cool and resourceful way, and frequently anticipated orders according to the exigencies of the situation in difficult conditions. Again, later, he did particularly gallant and soldierly work, freely exposing himself to heavy fire and maintaining a close grip of the situation. It was due to his fine behaviour that his portion of the line remained intact.
(D.S.O. gazetted 26 Sept. 1917.)

HOBDAY, RUPERT EDMUND, D.S.O., Lieut. (Temporary Capt.), West Yorkshire Regt. For conspicuous gallantry and devotion to duty in command of a raiding party of four officers and 120 men. Thanks to his previous reconnaissance, careful organization for the attack, and his gallant leadership during the raid, the operation successfully resulted in the capture of an officer and 41 men. He himself shot four of the enemy, and dashed single-handed at a machine gun, personally carrying in the gun. He brought his party back entire with only one casualty. He set a fine example of courage and determination.
(D.S.O. gazetted 25 Nov. 1916.)

IRWIN, NOEL MACKINTOSH STUART, D.S.O., M.C., Capt. (Acting Lieut.-Colonel), Essex Regt. For conspicuous gallantry and devotion to duty. When the whole of his battalion front was heavily attacked and all communications with his forward companies were cut, this officer personally organized his headquarters and stragglers, and formed a defensive flank so as to obtain touch with the brigade on the right. This flank he held for eight hours against all attacks, organizing two counter-attacks against the enemy during this period, thus averting a critical situation. It was greatly due to his able conduct that the holding of their battle position by his brigade was possible throughout the day. His courage, energy and quick decision inspired the greatest confidence in his men.
(D.S.O. gazetted 1 Jan. 1918.)

JARDINE, COLIN ARTHUR, D.S.O., M.C., Capt. (Acting Major), Royal Field Artillery. For conspicuous gallantry and devotion to duty. When the enemy broke through a gap in the direction of his battery, he promptly gave orders for his guns to be dragged out into the open, while he himself took forward a party of his battery to defend the gap while the guns were being moved. His party succeeded in holding back the enemy sufficiently long, and then his guns opened at point-blank range with such effect that the enemy's attack in this part was entirely shattered. His prompt action was decisive in averting a dangerous situation ; and throughout the day he showed splendid leadership, and his spirit was an inspiration to all about him of whatever rank or arm.
(D.S.O. gazetted 11 Nov. 1914.)

KING, GILBERT EAST, D.S.O., Temporary Lieut.-Colonel, East Yorkshire Regt. For conspicuous gallantry and devotion to duty during a raid made by two battalions into the enemy's lines. His utter disregard of personal danger, skill and cheerfulness throughout, inspired all under his command and proved him to be a leader of a high order. Throughout the raid he remained exposed to enemy fire in an advanced position which would enable him to control the operations, which he did extremely well. It was due to his indomitable example that his battalion was imbued with a fighting spirit which nothing could daunt.
(D.S.O. gazetted 1 Jan. 1917.)

KIRKUP, PHILIP, D.S.O., M.C., Capt. (Acting Lieut.-Colonel), Durham Light Infantry. For conspicuous gallantry and devotion to duty. On the night before a battle opened this officer was sent to the Field Ambulance with a temperature of 103 degrees, but on hearing the barrage he left and attempted to rejoin his unit, which was impossible, so he collected all the men he could and organized a defensive position, which he held on to as long as possible. During the next two days he several times assisted in rallying men and holding up the enemy advance, and when ammunition had almost run out, he rode back and brought up small arms ammunition, riding practically into the front line with it. Throughout the whole period he did much to organize stragglers and keep them in the fighting line, being without sleep, and having little food for five days.
(D.S.O. gazetted 16 Sept. 1918.)

KNOX, JAMES MELDRUM, D.S.O., Major and Brevet Lieut.-Colonel (Acting Lieut.-Colonel), Royal Warwickshire Regt. For conspicuous gallantry and devotion to duty in command of his battalion. He kept touch with the situation till ordered by the division to counter-attack when the enemy had broken through. Thanks to his splendid handling of his battalion, this counter-attack was decisive, the enemy were at once held up, and after heavy fighting were driven back with severe losses, several hundred prisoners being captured and the front line restored.
(D.S.O. gazetted 1 Jan. 1917.)

SAWYER, GUY HENRY, D.S.O., Major (Acting Lieut.-Colonel), Royal Berkshire Regt. For conspicuous gallantry and devotion to duty while in command of a battalion of details of his brigade. At an early period in the day his left flank was completely turned, but by fine leadership and a skilful use of a small reserve, he held his line intact till orders were issued for a withdrawal. Throughout the day, though communications were particularly difficult and the situation obscure, he kept his brigade informed of his position and repelled all attacks of the enemy on his left flank and front. At night, on receipt of orders to withdraw, he successfully extricated his men from a very difficult position, in close touch with the enemy.
(D.S.O. gazetted 3 June, 1916.)

AUSTRALIAN IMPERIAL FORCE.

BRAZENOR, WILLIAM, D.S.O., Lieut.-Colonel, Infantry. For conspicuous gallantry and devotion to duty during an attack. He led his battalion successfully, and supervised, under constant machine-gun and rifle fire, the consolidation of the captured ground. Next day he led a patrol into " No Man's Land " and made a reconnaissance, with the result that the line was pushed forward another 200 yards. Throughout the operation he did fine work.
(D.S.O. gazetted 1 Jan. 1918.)

Awarded the Distinguished Service Order :

BLACK, ALEXANDER MACGREGOR, Temporary Major, Northumberland Fusiliers. For conspicuous gallantry and devotion to duty in rallying broken groups of men in action and posting them in fresh defensive positions. By his personal example and efforts this officer gave the greatest encouragement to his men, and inspired them to a further determined resistance until a withdrawal was ordered.

BRETT, GEORGE ALBERT, M.C., Capt., London Regt. For conspicuous gallantry and devotion to duty when in charge of the right flank of the battalion. He repulsed several strong enemy attacks, organized a counter-attack, and drove the enemy out of a portion of the front in which he had gained a footing. When the troops on his right were forced back he formed a defensive flank and held the position till ordered to withdraw. He remained with the rearguard and covered the withdrawal of the battalion in a masterly manner. His coolness and ability greatly helped in saving a critical situation and inflicting heavy losses on the enemy.

CAREY, JOHN LIONEL ROMILLY, Major, Royal Garrison Artillery. For conspicuous gallantry and devotion to duty. By his example and skilful work he kept his battery in action whilst heavily shelled and gassed. He sent back much invaluable information of the progress of the enemy attack.

CHARLES, ERIC EDMONSTONE, Major, Royal Garrison Artillery. For conspicuous gallantry and devotion to duty. He kept his battery in action throughout the day in spite of constant and heavy shell fire. He was out of communication with brigade headquarters for practically the entire day, and the valuable work done by his battery was entirely due to his initiative.

CLARK, CHARLES ALFRED, M.C., Lieut. (Temporary Major), East Surrey Regt. For conspicuous gallantry and devotion to duty during five days whilst commanding his battalion. He fought his battalion most gallantly against great odds till the great majority were killed and the remainder captured. He was himself severely wounded.

COOTE, COLIN REITH, M.P., Lieut. (Acting Capt.), Gloucestershire Regt. For conspicuous gallantry and devotion to duty during an enemy attack. By his personal example and coolness he held his men together during a critical period and personally led two counter-attacks, inflicting considerable casualties and thus staying the enemy's advance and enabling the situation to be reorganized. He did very fine service.

CORSAN, REGINALD ARTHUR, M.C., Capt. (Acting Major), Royal Field Artillery. For conspicuous gallantry and devotion to duty when the enemy broke through and advanced on the flank of the battery position. He withdrew the personnel, covering the retirement with rifle fire, and from a new position held up the enemy till driven out by close machine-gun fire. He then assisted to get the guns of another battery into action. The whole of the time, some 14 hours, he was under machine-gun and rifle fire at close range, in addition to a heavy gas and high explosive bombardment. His courage and leadership at a most critical period were splendid.

CUNNINGHAME, WILLIAM WALLACE SMITH, Capt. (Temporary Major and Acting Lieut.-Colonel), Life Guards, attached Cheshire Regt. For conspicuous gallantry and devotion to duty. When the left flank of the battalion was badly enfiladed and driven off the plateau, he rode into the valley in face of heavy artillery and machine-gun fire and rallied the men. Then, with the assistance of two other companies, he personally led an assault and inflicted heavy casualties on the enemy, while his horse was shot under him, and he continued to lead on foot. Owing, however, to weakness in numbers, the battalion made no headway, whereupon he again reorganized and led a counter-attack, which was quite successful, and enabled his men to dig in on the top of the plateau. He was shortly after wounded, but his courage and capabilities undoubtedly saved the situation.

DAVIS, FRANK, Second Lieut., South Staffordshire Regt. For conspicuous gallantry and devotion to duty. When the left flank of the battalion was in the air, with the enemy working round in great strength, he kept his men steady, and by his coolness enabled an orderly withdrawal to be effected. Shortly afterwards, when the battalion was almost surrounded, he formed a rearguard with the remaining men of his company, and by skilful leadership of his men enabled the remainder of the battalion to withdraw successfully. Next day he hung on to an important position with great ability and resolution, though losing many men from heavy shell fire and being wounded himself. Throughout these two days' fighting his personal courage was most marked, and his skilful handling of his men saved the battalion on two occasions.

GOATER, WILLIAM HENRY GEORGE, M.C., Temporary Major, Yorkshire Regt. For conspicuous gallantry and devotion to duty in command of two companies during an enemy attack. He personally led two platoons forward and checked the enemy working round his left flank, and later, when overwhelmed, withdrew his companies most skilfully. Next day he went forward alone under heavy fire and reconnoitred a position, and then returned and led forward a Lewis gun section to a position from which they could check the enemy's advance. He showed throughout great coolness, and set a fine example to his men.

GUSH, HENRY WOOD, M.C., Temporary Major (Acting Lieut.-Colonel), Northumberland Fusiliers. For conspicuous gallantry and devotion to duty. His battalion was in reserve at the commencement of operations, and was moved up early in the morning to support the line. This line was maintained till the evening, when it was practically surrounded; he then withdrew his command with the utmost skill and coolness from a difficult position. Next day he covered the withdrawal of the brigade, maintaining his position for several hours under heavy shell and machine-gun fire. The steadiness of the men and the tenacity with which they held their positions were largely due to the splendid personal example of this officer, and the stand made by his battalion was of the utmost importance.

HENCHLEY, ALBERT RICHARD, Major (Temporary Lieut.-Colonel), Royal Army Medical Corps. For conspicuous gallantry and devotion to duty during an enemy attack. In two days he succeeded in evacuating some 1,500 patients. He got away his personnel and lorries under shell and machine-gun fire, and proceeded to a hospital elsewhere from which he evacuated 300 wounded by ambulance trains. His unit was the last to leave the town. His coolness and resource were the means of saving a large number of wounded from falling into the hands of the enemy.

KERBY, ALBERT MAURICE, M.C., Lieut., Royal Field Artillery, Special Reserve. For conspicuous gallantry and devotion to duty. While his battery was being heavily shelled with gas, shrapnel and high explosives he constantly exposed himself, moving from gun to gun and encouraging the detachments. He then went to the observation post to make a report. Whilst visiting the advanced wagon lines he was severely wounded. It was mainly due to his gallantry and fine example that the battery maintained its rate of fire.

McGIVENEY, PHILIP, Second Lieut., Lancashire Fusiliers. For conspicuous gallantry and devotion to duty during an attack. He captured the first objective with his platoon. His company was subsequently ejected by a counter-attack. He, with a handful of men, returned to the attack and retook the objective. He was wounded in the face, but went on single-handed and bombed and took prisoners the occupants of three posts. Later, arranging another bombing party, and advancing again, he was badly wounded in the spine and had to be taken away. It was due to his splendid courage and dash that his company recovered from its reverse and succeeded in re-engaging and inflicting severe casualties on the enemy.

MILLIS, CHARLES HOWARD GOULDEN, M.C., Lieut. (Temporary Capt.), Nottinghamshire and Derbyshire Regt. For conspicuous gallantry and devotion to duty during an enemy attack. He rode up and down the firing line under heavy fire organizing the defence, distributing ammunition and encouraging the men to hold the line at all costs, until, as was inevitable, he was severely wounded. His fine example of courage inspired those around him, and contributed greatly to the holding of the line.

PICKFORD, PERCIVAL, M.C., Capt. (Acting Major), Oxfordshire and Buckinghamshire Light Infantry. For conspicuous gallantry and devotion to duty during an enemy attack. Throughout the fight he continually moved between battalion headquarters and the front line, and when the situation was critical he personally took a handful of men and placed them exactly where they were required, But for his courageous example and quick initiative the battalion might several times have been surrounded.

POPE, EDWARD BENJAMIN, Lieut. (Temporary Capt.), Gloucestershire Regt. For conspicuous gallantry and devotion to duty when an important tactical position was in grave danger. He succeeded in rallying the line and led forward in face of heavy rifle and machine-gun fire. Heavy casualties were inflicted on the enemy, and the line was re-established in its former position. Throughout he showed the greatest courage and resource.

RAMSDEN, ARTHUR GEOFFREY FRANCIS, Capt. (Acting Major), Royal Field Artillery (Special Reserve). For conspicuous gallantry and devotion to duty. While his battery was subjected to an extremely heavy bombardment he kept all his guns in action, firing his programme and S.O.S. Finally, with only one gun left, he ran it out of the pit, engaged the advancing enemy over open sights, assisted by rifle fire of his detachment, so holding the enemy off. He managed to get his gun on to a trolley and got it away, and eventually withdrew the survivors of his detachment, after inflicting heavy casualties on the enemy.

RAPSON, GEORGE FREDERICK EDWIN, Capt. (Acting Lieut.-Colonel), Wiltshire Regt. For conspicuous gallantry and devotion to duty in a counter-attack. He first carried out a personal reconnaissance of the ground under heavy machine-gun fire, and then led his men to the attack in a most gallant manner. Several times the attack was driven back by heavy machine-gun fire, which caused many casualties, but he gained and held his objective. His courage and fine leadership set a splendid example.

RHODES, STEPHEN, Capt. (Acting Lieut.-Colonel), York and Lancaster Regt. For conspicuous gallantry and devotion to duty when, in command of his battalion, he organized and successfully carried out a counter-attack. Throughout the whole operations he handled his men with great skill, and set a fine example of courage and endurance. The success of local operations was largely due to him.

SUMPTER, GEORGE, M.C., Capt. (Acting Major), Royal Field Artillery. For conspicuous gallantry and devotion to duty in action. In the first position he took on the enemy with observed fire coming across the open, causing them very heavy casualties and checking their advance for three hours. During this time, by blowing it up twice, he prevented the enemy building a bridge. Four days later he took on with open sights the advancing enemy infantry and two 7.7.cm. guns. He knocked the first gun out with ten rounds, and soon after knocked the other out. Two days later again he took on an enemy battery in the open and knocked out the four guns. He did splendid service.

WOOD, HENRY GEORGE WESTMORLAND, Capt., Worcestershire Regt. For conspicuous gallantry and devotion to duty during an enemy attack. Though originally detailed as a support company, he saw that the company he was supporting was held up, and immediately went forward and delivered three organized attacks on the enemy, leading his men with the greatest gallantry. He harassed the enemy continuously during the night, and when the successful advance took place early next morning he cleared a large portion of the front line and consolidated quickly. His company captured 100 prisoners and six machine guns.

CANADIAN FORCE.

DOUGHTY, EDWARD SPENCER, Lieut.-Colonel, Infantry. For conspicuous gallantry and devotion to duty in command of a battalion detailed to carry out a raid. A skilful reconnaissance was first made by him, regardless of personal danger; and chiefly owing to his instructions and careful training of each party, the raid was a complete success, many of the enemy being killed and 21 prisoners, three machine guns, and a trench mortar taken. His enthusiasm and energy inspired all ranks to do their utmost. He has previously done fine work.

AUSTRALIAN IMPERIAL FORCE.

CORNISH, CYRIL RICHARD, Lieut., Infantry. For conspicuous gallantry and devotion to duty. In command of a platoon during an attack he rushed two enemy machine guns, killing or capturing the crews, and using the guns in defence of his new position. In a counter-attack by the enemy he led his men in hand-to-hand fighting, and repulsed the attack. Later, the same evening, he led his platoon against an enemy strong point in "No Man's Land," killing many of the enemy and capturing several prisoners and three machine guns. He did splendid service, and set a magnificent example of courage and devotion to duty to his men.

CROMIE, GEORGE LENDRUM, Lieut., Infantry. For conspicuous gallantry and devotion to duty. This officer was severely wounded at the beginning of an attack, but carried on, and when his platoon was held up by machine-gun fire at about 80 yards' range, he rushed straight at the gun, killing all the crew and putting it out of action. He then took charge of the company, the commander having been hit, and worked hard at consolidating the position during the night, being again slightly wounded. Fearing a counter-attack, he refused to go to the regimental aid post, and remained on duty for 30 hours after being first hit.

CROUGHAN, JOHN PHILIP, Lieut., Artillery. For conspicuous gallantry and devotion to duty in an attack. He was artillery forward observer, and went forward with the first wave of the infantry to the final objective, where he gave great assistance in reorganizing the infantry and consolidating the position. He also sent valuable information back to his headquarters, and throughout the day did valuable work in directing the supporting artillery fire. His courage, energy and ability were of great service.

DARNELL, AUBREY HUGH, Major, Infantry. For conspicuous gallantry and devotion to duty. He led the advance to the first objective and sent back important information regarding the progress of the attack. By his skilful handling of his company the position in his sector was gained with slight loss, and many prisoners taken.

ELLIOTT, LESLIE WILLIAM, Capt., Infantry. For conspicuous gallantry and devotion to duty. His company was detailed to form the right flank and get touch with the brigade. This was an enterprise of great importance and danger, and he was exposed to attack on three sides during the movement. Although slightly wounded early in the operations, he led his company with great dash and gallantry, and consolidated and held his position. Next day he successfully led part of his company against enemy positions, and at night linked up with the brigade. By his courage and initiative he successfully accomplished his difficult task.

GLASGOW, ROBERT, M.C., Capt., Infantry. For conspicuous gallantry and devotion to duty in an attack. He was early wounded, but led his men with great dash and ability, reached the first objective, and pushed on. During the consolidation of the ground captured he was of great service; and throughout he showed tactical ability, coolness and determination of a high order.

HARRIS, NORMAN CHARLES, M.C., Major, Engineers. For conspicuous gallantry and devotion to duty during operations which resulted in the capture of a village. Under his direction and supervision four bridges were made and thrown over a river under heavy shell fire. This largely contributed to the success of the attack. The coolness and determination of this officer were most marked.

MARPER, GEORGE, Capt., Infantry. For conspicuous gallantry and devotion to duty in an attack. He led his company with great ability, and headed a rush on an enemy machine gun, shooting three of the enemy himself. He was wounded through the chest and arm, but remained to see the trench mopped up and his company advancing before handing over to his next in command. He showed fine courage and leadership.

REED, ALFRED EFFINGHAM, Major, Infantry. For conspicuous gallantry and devotion to duty in command of his battalion during an attack. After winning his objective he crawled out into No Man's Land, reconnoitred the ground, and pushed his line forward again. Next day he personally directed the mopping up of an enemy post, and under close range machine-gun fire supervised the consolidation of newly-won posts. He set a fine example to his command.

London Gazette, 5 Oct. 1918.—" Admiralty, 5 Oct. 1918.—Honours for Services in the Destroyer Action in the Adriatic on the Night of the 22nd–23rd April, 1918. The King has been graciously pleased to approve of the award of the following honours to the undermentioned Officers. To be Companions of the Distinguished Service Order."

ROBERTS, ARTHUR MILLINGTON, Lieut.-Commander, R.N. In command of one of H.M. Destroyers, engaged a very superior force of the enemy and put it to flight. He handled his ship with skill during a running fight lasting for nearly three hours.

PERSSE, DUDLEY FRANCIS, Lieut., R.N. In command of one of H.M. Destroyers, engaged the enemy, and after his ship had been heavily hit, and though he was himself severely wounded, only relinquished the command after bringing his ship safely into harbour.

" Honours for Services in Action with Enemy Submarines.—The King has been graciously pleased to approve of the award of the following honours to the undermentioned Officers. To be Companions of the Distinguished Service Order."

HARTFORD, GEORGE BIBBY, Commander, R.N.

MACCABE, JOHN FRANCIS, Lieut., R.N.V.R.

" Honours for Miscellaneous Services."

(1.)

" The King has been graciously pleased to approve of the award of the following honours to the undermentioned Officers. To be Companions of the Distinguished Service Order."

LOW, ERNEST EDWARD, Engineer-Commander, R.N.R.

SCOTT, ROBERT ALEXANDER, R.D., Engineer Lieut.-Commander (Acting Engineer-Commander), Royal Naval Reserve.

(2.)

" The King has been graciously pleased to approve of the award of the following honour to the undermentioned Officer. To be a Companion of the Distinguished Service Order."

LE PAGE, GEORGE WILFRED, Engineer Lieut.-Commander (Acting Engineer-Commander), R.N. In recognition of the valuable services rendered by him to the Allied cause in Russia since 1914.

" Additional Awards for Services in the Battle of Jutland on the 31st May, 1916.—The King has been graciously pleased to approve of the following further award in addition to those announced in the London Gazette of the 15th Sept. 1916. To be a Companion of the Distinguished Service Order."

WHITFIELD, PAUL, Lieut.-Commander (now Commander), R.N. (Prisoner of War interned in a neutral country). In command of H.M.S. Nomad, gallantly supported Nestor and Nicator in an attack on the enemy battle-cruisers. Nomad was badly hit and disabled during this attack, but later succeeded in sinking a disabled German destroyer, and finally fired all her torpedoes at the High Sea Fleet, waiting for the last moment before doing so, though the Nomad was sinking at the time.

London Gazette, 15 Oct. 1918.—" War Office, 15 Oct. 1918. His Majesty the King has been graciously pleased to approve of the following awards to the undermentioned Officers and Warrant Officers, in recognition of their gallantry and devotion to duty in the field. Awarded a Second Bar to the Distinguished Service Order."

MACDONALD, DONALD JOHN, D.S.O., M.C., Lieut.-Colonel, Canadian Cavalry. For conspicuous gallantry and devotion to duty. This officer commanded the advance guard regiment of his brigade in an attack. He led his regiment with the greatest determination and with absolutely no regard for his own safety. It was largely due to his splendid leadership that the operation, which resulted in the capture of several miles of enemy territory and large numbers of prisoners and material, was entirely successful.
(D.S.O. gazetted 1 Jan. 1918.)
(Bar gazetted 22 June, 1918.)

Awarded a Bar to the Distinguished Service Order:

BARTON, CHARLES WALTER, C.M.G., D.S.O., Major (Temporary Lieut.-Colonel), Northamptonshire Regt. and King's African Rifles. For conspicuous gallantry in leading his column and bold offensive against the enemy, whereby after a desperate fight at close quarters the enemy were beaten off with heavy casualties. In this action this officer was severely wounded for the third time in this campaign. His courage and coolness in action have always been a splendid example to the young native soldier.
(D.S.O. gazetted 27 Sept. 1901.)

COMBE, HERBERT, D.S.O., Major (Acting Lieut.-Colonel), Hussars. For conspicuous gallantry and fine leadership in an attack. This officer commanded the leading regiment of the brigade and handled it all day with marked courage, ability and dash. It was due to his quick grasp of the situation and determined action that the final objective was successfully reached by the brigade, despite the fact that the regiment was under considerable shell and machine-gun fire from both flanks. He did splendid service.
(D.S.O. gazetted 12 Feb. 1915.)

FURBER, CECIL TIDSWELL, D.S.O., Capt. (Acting Lieut.-Colonel), King's Own Scottish Borderers. For conspicuous gallantry and devot on to duty. The untiring efforts and great ability with which this officer made his preparations for an attack largely contributed to the success of the operation. His gallantry and devotion to duty during the engagement were conspicuous, and when the objective had been gained he supervised the difficult work of consolidation, under heavy fire, with perfect coolness and disregard of danger, setting a fine example which greatly encouraged all ranks of his battalion.
(D.S.O. gazetted 26 April, 1917.)

GRIFFITHS, ALEXANDER HARCOURT, D.S.O., Capt. (Temporary Lieut.-Colonel), Duke of Cornwall's Light Infantry and King's African Rifles. For most gallant and able leadership of his column. By his bold and prompt action when interposing his small force between the enemy rearguard and the main body he inflicted very heavy losses to the enemy in personnel and material.
(D.S.O. gazetted 26 April, 1917.)

ING, GEORGE HAROLD ABSELL, D.S.O., Major (Acting Lieut.-Colonel), Dragoon Guards. For conspicuous gallantry and devotion to duty. During recent operations this officer was in command of the advance guard of the brigade. By riding close up to the attacking infantry and tanks he put himself well in touch with every phase of the advance, and was able to seize the exact moment when to pass through and beyond the infantry, to assist them and to exploit their success. He subsequently led his regiment most gallantly in their attack, capturing several hundred prisoners and many machine guns. He did splendid service.
(D.S.O. gazetted 3 July, 1915.)

MENZIES, JOHN, D.S.O., Lieut.-Colonel, Highland Light Infantry. For conspicuous gallantry and ability as a battalion commander. The success gained by his battalion was largely due to his fine courage and leadership. In several instances, when the situation appeared to demand it, he went forward and personally encouraged his men to further advance.
(D.S.O. gazetted 4 June, 1917.)

MILLER GEORGE SWINEY, D.S.O., Capt. (Temporary Lieut.-Colonel), Royal Warwickshire Regt., Special Reserve. For conspicuous gallantry and devotion to duty. The skill with which he made his plans, and his untiring devotion to duty in reconnoitring the position and training his men preparatory to an attack largely contributed to the success of the operation. When the objective was gained, his gallantry and admirable leadership, which had been conspicuous during the engagement, greatly cheered and encouraged his men during the difficult work of consolidation under heavy shell and machine-gun fire.
(D.S.O. gazetted 3 June, 1918.)

NUTT, ALLAN VAUGHAN, D.S.O., Temporary Major (Acting Lieut.-Colonel), York and Lancaster Regt. For conspicuous gallantry and devotion to duty. He showed great skill and resource in making the arrangements preparatory to an attack, and displayed fine courage and leadership during the engagement. When the objectives had been won, with heavy losses to the enemy, he supervised the dispositions against a counter-attack and the consolidation of the captured positions with ability and conspicuous coolness under heavy fire, inspiring his men with great confidence by his example.
(D.S.O. gazetted 1 Jan. 1918.)

TERROT, CHARLES RUSSELL, D.S.O., Major (Acting Lieut.-Colonel), Inniskilling Dragoons. For conspicuous gallantry during an attack. When sent forward to exploit the infantry success, he led his regiment rapidly through the attacking waves and beyond the final objective. When checked by heavy machine-gun fire from a village, and unable to manœuvre on account of wire, he dismounted and fought his way forward with two squadrons, so enabling his flank squadron to gallop round and operate to the rear of the village. Many enemy were killed, five guns and 700 prisoners captured, and the success of the operation was entirely due to the daring and splendid leadership of this officer.
(D.S.O. gazetted 4 June, 1917.)

YOUNG, HERBERT NUGENT, D.S.O., Major, Royal Inniskilling Fusiliers. For conspicuous gallantry and devotion to duty during an enemy attack. When the enemy, assisted by intense bombardment, had penetrated part of the defences, he went round the front line, found out the situation, and established liaison with other troops, which greatly assisted in the organization of the counter-attack. Shortly after, when his Commanding Officer was wounded, he took command and handled the battalion with great skill. His fine personal courage animated all ranks, and as all communication was broken, the battle was fought by the battalion on its own, Major Young having all the responsibility on his shoulders. He performed splendidly.
(D.S.O. gazetted 1 Jan. 1917.)

AUSTRALIAN IMPERIAL FORCE.

McSHARRY, TERENCE PATRICK, C.M.G., D.S.O., M.C., Lieut.-Colonel, Infantry. For great gallantry and decisive action during an attack. When the battalion was held up by an enemy strong point, which the artillery and tanks had missed, the situation for a time was critical, as the barrage was gradually moving onwards and the battalion was subjected to heavy machine-gun fire. He at once pushed on to the leading company, where his presence and prompt actions resulted in the capture of the position. When the final objective was gained he supervised the consolidation and reorganization under heavy machine-gun fire.
(D.S.O. gazetted 4 June, 1917.)

Awarded the Distinguished Service Order:

BANKS, THOMAS MACDONALD, M.C., Temporary Major (Acting Lieut.-Colonel), Essex Regt. For conspicuous gallantry and good leadership. He led his battalion some 5,000 yards through thick fog and against heavy opposition to the final objective, withdrawing most skilfully to the first objective when almost surrounded by the enemy, and consolidating it. Two days later, when adjacent troops were finding difficulties in consolidating their positions, he personally led their outposts some 400 yards forward, and under heavy fire supervised consolidation. Throughout he set a fine example of cool courage to all ranks.

BINGHAM, THE HONOURABLE JOHN DENIS YELVERTON, Capt. (Temporary Lieut.-Colonel), Hussars, attached Tank Corps. For conspicuous gallantry and perseverance in supervising the assembly of tanks, which he successfully launched in an attack. He had previously reconnoitred the ground over which the tanks were going to operate, being out daily under all conditions of hostile shelling. He showed the utmost devotion to duty in an enterprise which was particularly successful.

BORTHWICK, EDWARD KERR, M.C., Temporary Capt., King's African Rifles. For most conspicuous gallantry in action. When an enemy maxim had been brought into action at 40 yards' range he seized the opportunity of a temporary stoppage of the gun, went out alone, shot the N.C.O. in charge, drove off the team, and captured the gun. Earlier in the day he had most gallantly assisted in an attack on the enemy's camp, and most skilfully covered the retirement when the enemy counter-attacked in superior numbers. He showed courage, determination and leadership of a high order.

BROWNING, CHARLES ERIC, Temporary Major, South Wales Borderers. For conspicuous gallantry in the field. In command of a raiding party he showed great coolness and initiative while directing the wire-cutting under heavy fire, and in plain view of the enemy, owing to their Very lights. He successfully took and occupied the enemy position, while another party went on to carry out a further operation, and finally covered the withdrawal of the latter with great skill. After being the last to leave the captured position, he returned some distance at great personal risk to search for some missing men. Throughout the operation his judgment, gallantry and resource were most marked.

CHAPPEL, WICKHAM FRITH, Major, Dragoon Guards. For conspicuous gallantry and skilled leadership during an attack. He galloped his squadron and captured a wood, taking one officer and 24 other ranks prisoners, and capturing two heavy guns and four machine guns. The success of this masterly action greatly facilitated the further advance of squadrons on his left.

COBB, WILLIAM GRAHAME, M.B., Temporary Capt., Royal Army Medical Corps, attached King's African Rifles. For conspicuous gallantry and devotion to duty in action. For six hours, in the middle of a desperate fight at close quarters, he maintained his dressing station and attended the many wounded. Enemy's fire was coming from three directions, and the only cover was two ant-heaps. He frequently went forward to the firing line and brought in wounded at great personal risk. He undoubtedly saved many lives by his perseverance and determination, all the wounded being safely evacuated under the greatest difficulties.

FLEISCHER, SPENCER RICHARD, M.C., Lieut. (Temporary Capt.), East Lancashire Regt., Special Reserve. For conspicuous gallantry and devotion to duty. He led his company against a strongly fortified position, which he captured in spite of determined resistance, inflicting severe casualties on the enemy, taking field guns, trench mortars, and large numbers of heavy and light machine guns. He personally rushed one of the guns that was delaying our advance. His capture of this important position undoubtedly made subsequent success possible.

FORDE, GORDON MILLER, M.C., Temporary Major (Acting Lieut.-Colonel), Royal Inniskilling Fusiliers. For conspicuous gallantry and devotion to duty. In company with another officer he crawled out about 400 yards from the front line under full observation from the enemy lines, and remained out about seven hours, making a most daring reconnaissance of the enemy's position, and gaining most valuable information, from which he organized a successful raid on the enemy's position. By his personal courage and coolness he set a splendid example to his battalion.

GARTSIDE, LIONEL, Capt. (Acting Lieut.-Colonel), Highland Light Infantry. For conspicuous gallantry and ability to command. For two days he kept up continuous fire on enemy positions in a wood, finally establishing a formed line with his battalion and thereby enabling the right of the brigade to advance. Later, he most ably organized the defences of a new position, and as a result repelled a strong enemy attack. Throughout operations his untiring energy and fine leadership inspired all.

GILL, ROBERT HAWAR, Temporary Major, Northumberland Fusiliers. For conspicuous gallantry and devotion to duty during an enemy attack. He was in command of his battalion, which was continuously attacked throughout the day. When the enemy penetrated the division on his left, he not only organized a defensive flank extending over 600 yards, but he was the means of enabling other troops to capture a large body of the enemy by cutting off their retreat. It was greatly due to his energy and splendid disregard of personal danger that his line was held intact.

GREENE, JOHN, M.C., Temporary Capt. (Acting Major), Royal Army Medical Corps. For conspicuous gallantry and devotion to duty during an enemy attack. Although his advanced dressing station was heavily shelled and gassed he continued at duty, encouraging all by his courage and resourcefulness. He worked continuously for 30 hours, visiting his bearers' posts under heavy shell fire, and only rested when all wounded had been evacuated. His magnificent devotion to duty saved many lives.

HARDYMAN, JOHN HAY MAITLAND, M.C., Temporary Lieut.-Colonel, Somersetshire Light Infantry. For conspicuous gallantry and devotion to duty. After the enemy had penetrated the line in three places he went forward through a heavy barrage to the forward posts, rallied the garrison, and encouraged them by his coolness and absolute disregard of personal danger to successfully repel repeated enemy attacks extending over two days and three nights. Thanks to his gallant leadership and endurance, the position, which was of great tactical importance, was maintained.

HARTLEY, DONALD REGINALD CAVENDISH, Temporary Capt. (Acting Major), Royal Field Artillery. For conspicuous gallantry and devotion to duty during an enemy attack. He first shot two of the enemy who tried to plant a flag on high ground in front of his battery position. Then withdrawing his detachments to the high ground behind, he and two other officers and four men took up a position with rifles, and kept up a steady fire for five hours on the enemy, who were on the high ground in front of the battery. By this action he materially helped to check the enemy's advance and prevented them from entering his battery position. He showed fine courage, initiative and resource, and retained all his guns undamaged.

HORSLEY, BERNARD HILL, M.C., Temporary Capt., King's Own Yorkshire Light Infantry. For conspicuous gallantry and devotion to duty and dashing leadership. During a counter-attack by his company he led a bombing party along the trench, killing many of the enemy and bombing them in dug-outs with such determination that they soon began to surrender. He eventually cleared 300 yards of trench and joined up with other troops. His company altogether captured over 100 prisoners, including six officers, and took six machine guns, three of which were immediately put in action against the enemy. It was greatly owing to his perfect handling of his company throughout that the counter-attack was a complete success. He performed magnificent service.

HUNTER, JAMES WILLIAM, Temporary Capt., Northumberland Fusiliers. For conspicuous gallantry and devotion to duty during an enemy attack. He was in command of a company and held his trench, though his left flank was absolutely exposed, against all attacks throughout the day. Both during the preliminary enemy bombardment and in the hand-to-hand fighting he set a very fine example of courage and coolness to his company.

JAMESON, FRANK ROBERT WORDSWORTH, M.C., Temporary Lieut., Royal Engineers. For conspicuous gallantry and devotion to duty when in command of the brigade signal section during an enemy attack. Under heavy shell fire he superintended the placing under cover of the equipment and personnel. He then went out with his linesmen to repair communications with both front-line battalions. All day long he kept going round his various lines under heavy fire, and it was entirely due to his courage and energy that communication was maintained for certain periods.

JOHNSON, HENRY HOWARD, Capt. (Temporary Major), Royal Sussex Regt., attached Tank Corps. For conspicuous gallantry and devotion to duty. During a long and arduous day's fighting he followed the tanks, of which he was in command, on foot, running from one to the other, directing their operations with the greatest success. He was indefatigable in his efforts, and by his personal reconnaissance of different points was enabled to manœuvre his tanks in such a manner as to break down the resistance of machine guns which were holding up the infantry advance. During the whole day he was exposed to the heavy fire of artillery and machine guns, and his devotion to duty was the admiration of all who saw him.

KAY, JACK KILBOURNE, Capt. (Acting Major), Royal West Kent Regt. For conspicuous gallantry and devotion to duty. He was commanding the battalion, previous to and during an important attack by our troops, and the skill and ability with which he made the preparatory arrangements were no less marked than his gallantry and soldierly bearing during the engagement. When the objectives had been gained, hearing that the two senior officers and a large number of men of his left company had become casualties, he immediately went to the spot, and by his coolness and cheerful example of courage inspired the men with his own resolution

McMILLAN, ANGUS, M.C. (surname corrected to Macmillan), Lieut., Seaforth Highlanders. For conspicuous gallantry and devotion to duty during an attack. He led his company with great dash, and personally cleared up many obstacles. When the objective was gained he organized parties to deal with machine-gun nests in the houses, and surrounded a château, capturing two officers and 100 men before being forced to withdraw. Later, in order to extricate his garrison from a tight place, he went forward and shot the leading gunner of an enemy machine gun and scattered the remainder of the team with bombs. His courage and skill throughout were an inspiration to all ranks.

MILLAR, JOHN, M.C., Capt. (Acting Lieut.-Colonel), Royal Highlanders. For conspicuous gallantry and devotion to duty, and ability as a battalion commander during an attack. Learning that there was a gap between his battalion and the brigade on his right, he went forward and personally diverted one of his companies to fill this in. By this manœuvre he succeeded in capturing a large number of the enemy. The success of the battalion was largely due to his fine example of gallantry and good leadership.

MORRISON, WILLIAM, M.C., D.C.M., Capt. (Acting Major), Gordon Highlanders. For conspicuous gallantry and devotion to duty, and fine leadership, particularly on two occasions when he commanded his battalion with marked ability, enabling them to hold their objective in face of heavy shell-fire. Throughout the operations he showed himself to be a most able and determined commander.

PALMER, RICHARD LODGE, M.C., Major, Royal Artillery. During an attack this officer was in close touch with the brigade commander throughout the operations and manœuvred his battery with the greatest skill. The assistance rendered by his battery to the movements of the brigade were invaluable. Two enemy counter-attacks were stopped, largely as a result of his handling. His quickness in action and clear appreciation of further movement were excellent.

PRIDIE, ERIC DENHOLM, Temporary Capt., Royal Lancaster Regt. For conspicuous gallantry and devotion to duty, and initiative in action. When an attack was held up by a machine gun at close range he led forward a party of men across the open, under heavy fire, and by his most gallant action succeeded in capturing an officer, 12 men and the machine gun. Later, with a revolver in each hand, he again advanced and killed and wounded several of the enemy, causing others to surrender. He behaved magnificently.

ROBINSON, DAVID LUBBOCK, Temporary Capt., Tank Corps (Lieut., Royal Marines). For conspicuous gallantry and devotion to duty. This officer was in charge of two sections of Tanks, which he manœuvred on foot during a long and arduous day's fighting, with the greatest effect and success. He was quite regardless of his own safety, always well ahead of the infantry, though exposed to the heaviest artillery and machine-gun fire. He undoubtedly saved the infantry many casualties by the way he directed his Tanks to the destruction of machine-gun groups, and his example throughout the day was the admiration of all who saw him.

SMITH, HENRY, Lieut., East Yorkshire Regt. For conspicuous gallantry and devotion to duty. He advanced his company in daylight, and without artillery preparation, some 500 yards, capturing a new line and taking prisoner one officer, 60 other ranks and four machine guns. He assisted in the capture of strong points and sent back under heavy shell and machine-gun fire most accurate information, which enabled close liaison to be maintained with the flanks. Through his resolution and ability the operation was completely successful, with unusually few casualties.

SPARROW, RICHARD, C.M.G., Lieut.-Colonel, Dragoon Guards. For conspicuous gallantry during an advance. Throughout the day he showed the greatest dash and initiative in leading his regiment. His quick appreciation of the situation and the realization of the tactical requirements contributed largely to the success of the operations. Under heavy fire his decisions were masterly and decisive, and showed the qualities of a brilliant leader.

STERLING, GEORGE POMEROY, M.C., Temporary Capt., Northumberland Fusiliers. For conspicuous gallantry and devotion to duty during an enemy attack. He was in command of a company, and held his trenches against all attacks throughout the day. On one occasion when the enemy momentarily entered a part of his trenches he led a party and immediately drove them out, killing seven and capturing four. By his courage and coolness he set a very fine example to his company.

TARLETON, FRANCIS ROYLAND, Major (Acting Lieut.-Colonel), Royal Highlanders. For conspicuous gallantry, resource and skill as a battalion commander. On more than one occasion when the situation appeared to be uncertain and the advance threatened he personally went forward and led his battalion on. The success of his battalion was largely due to his bold and capable leadership.

WALKER, THOMAS MATHEWSON, Major, Royal Field Artillery. For conspicuous gallantry and devotion to duty. He fought his battery magnificently through an intense bombardment of seven or eight hours. He had two guns knocked out and had 12 casualties among his detachments. Though the battery position was heavily gassed he kept his guns shooting all day. When at the Observation Post he sent in most valuable information, which was of the greatest assistance. He behaved splendidly.

WAUHOPE, GEORGE BOOTHBY, Major (Temporary Lieut.-Colonel), York and Lancaster Regt. For conspicuous gallantry and devotion to duty. He was in command of his battalion when making a surprise night attack, the successful result of which was due to the skill and resource with which this officer supervised every detail of preparation. The objectives were captured exactly according to programme, and the casualties of the enemy were heavy, both in men and guns. He supervised the process of consolidation with great coolness and disregard of danger under heavy fire, and his example throughout had a fine and inspiring effect on his men.

WIENHOLT, ARNOLD, M.C., Capt., East African Force. For continuous gallant conduct and endurance under most trying circumstances during a period of six months in the bush. He performed a most arduous march, during which his party were more than once attacked by superior enemy forces, through the unknown country which he had to reconnoitre and report on; and finally succeeded in gaining touch with a column as ordered. He performed many other successful reconnaissances during which he had several encounters with the enemy, and furnished valuable information with regard to their movements. Throughout he showed great courage and endurance, and rendered most valuable service.

WINTERBOTTOM, ARCHIBALD DICKSON, Capt., Dragoon Guards. For conspicuous gallantry and dash in an attack. This officer led his squadron over a most difficult country with the greatest skill and ability. He judged the pace for a four-mile gallop to a nicety, disregarded all rifle and machine-gun fire, made straight for his objective, and rode over several hundred of the enemy, killing a good number and subsequently making the rest prisoners. Later in the day, he took command of the regiment when his commanding officer was wounded, and carried out his duties most successfully. He did brilliantly.

CANADIAN FORCE.

PYMAN, COLIN KEITH LEE, Major, Infantry. For conspicuous gallantry and devotion to duty. This officer was in charge of a raiding party of considerable importance, and the success of the operation was largely due to the thorough manner in which he had thought out and supervised every detail beforehand. He directed the operations with a courage and complete disregard of danger that inspired the greatest confidence in the officers and men under his command.

TORRANCE, PERCIVAL VICTOR, Major, Cavalry. For conspicuous gallantry and devotion to duty. He commanded the advanced squadron of the regiment during an attack. His great dash and determination enabled the regiment to capture more than 180 prisoners, several guns, and many machine guns, and to attain its objective. His conduct throughout the day was splendid, and his gallant leadership greatly inspired those under him.

AUSTRALIAN IMPERIAL FORCE.

DAWSON, FORBES CAMPBELL, M.C., Capt., Infantry. For conspicuous gallantry and a fine display of tactical skill during an attack over difficult ground covered with undergrowth and deep shell-holes, many of which the enemy had turned into machine-gun posts. He mopped up each post and secured his objective, accounting for 50 killed, 30 prisoners and 10 machine guns. Though wounded he remained at duty for 46 hours. All the captured guns were at once mounted, turned on the enemy, and kept in action during the fight, materially assisting in repelling enemy counter-attacks.

LYNAS, WILLIAM JAMES DALTON, M.C., Capt., Infantry. For remarkable courage and leadership during an attack. He supervised the placing of the men on the "jumping off" line, and though wounded in two places just after zero, he nevertheless led his company to the assault. He was then again wounded, but refused to go back until the position was taken. Of seven machine guns and four trench mortars captured by his company, he took several himself, and personally inflicted many casualties on the enemy.

McLEISH, ROY STANLEY, Major, Mounted Regt. For conspicuous gallantry and devotion to duty. He displayed great courage and initiative in carrying out the difficult task of reconnoitring in front of the infantry and holding a forward position until relieved. In this and subsequent operations his fine leadership and sound judgment were conspicuous.

MINCHIN, JAMES BASIL, M.C., Lieut., Infantry. For conspicuously gallant conduct during an attack. He led his platoon on the first enemy positions and personally killed one officer and several other men, capturing in all one officer, 20 other ranks, one machine gun and one heavy minenwerfer. In his advance he next rushed a machine-gun nest, killing six of the enemy (two of whom he accounted for personally), and capturing the balance of the crews and the guns. Then, discovering his company commander had been killed, he assumed command and brilliantly completed the task assigned to the company.

London Gazette, 29 Oct. 1918.—"War Office, 29 Oct. 1918. His Majesty the King has been graciously pleased to approve of the undermentioned rewards for distinguished service in connection with military operations in Egypt and the Sudan. Dated 3 June, 1918. Awarded the Distinguished Service Order."

BUTLER, THE HONOURABLE THEOBALD PATRICK PROBYN, Major, Royal Artillery, employed Egyptian Army.

GRAHAM, CLAUDE, Major, Northamptonshire Regt., attached Egyptian Army

MARSHALL, CLAUD COLTART, Major, Royal Lancaster Regt., employed Egyptian Army.

PATTISSON, JOHN HILL, Major (Temporary Lieut.-Colonel), Essex Regt., employed Egyptian Army.

STUART, WILLIAM, Lieut., Yeomanry and Machine Gun Corps.

London Gazette, 29 Oct. 1918.—"Admiralty, 29 Oct. 1918.—Honours for Services in Submarines. The King has been graciously pleased to approve of the award of the following honours to the undermentioned Officers. To be Companions of the Distinguished Service Order."

LAYARD, BROWNLOW VILLIERS, Lieut.-Commander, R.N.

DARKE, REGINALD BURNARD, Lieut.-Commander, R.N.

BOWER, JOHN GRAHAM, Lieut.-Commander, R.N.

"Honours for Services in Action with Enemy Submarines.—The King has been graciously pleased to approve of the award of the following honour to the undermentioned Officer. To be a Companion of the Distinguished Service Order."

NOAKES, CYRIL JOHN LANGHAM, Lieut.-Commander, R.N.

London Gazette, 2 Nov. 1918.—"Air Ministry, 2 Nov. 1918. His Majesty the King has been graciously pleased to confer the undermentioned rewards on Officers of the Royal Air Force, in recognition of gallantry in flying operations against the enemy. Awarded a Bar to the Distinguished Service Order."

BARKER, WILLIAM GEORGE, D.S.O., M.C., Capt. (Temporary Major). A highly distinguished patrol leader whose courage, resource and determination has set a fine example to those around him. Up to the 20th July, 1918, he had destroyed 33 enemy aircraft—21 of these since the date of the last award (Second Bar to the Military Cross) was conferred on him. Major Barker has frequently led formations against greatly superior numbers of the enemy with conspicuous success.
(D.S.O. gazetted 18 Feb. 1918.)
(M.C. gazetted 10 Jan. 1917.)
(First Bar gazetted 18 July, 1917.)
(Second Bar gazetted 16 Sept. 1918.)

Awarded the Distinguished Service Order:

PROCTOR, ANDREW WEATHERBY BEAUCHAMP, M.C., D.F.C., Lieut. (Temporary Capt.). A fighting pilot of great skill, and a splendid leader. He rendered brilliant service on the 22nd Aug., when his Flight was detailed to neutralize hostile balloons. Having shot down one balloon in flames, he attacked the occupants of five others in succession with machine-gun fire, compelling the occupants in each case to take to parachutes. He then drove down another balloon to within 50 feet of the ground, when it burst into flames. In all he has accounted for 33 enemy machines and seven balloons.
(M.C. gazetted 22 June, 1918.)
(Bar to M.C. gazetted 16 Sept. 1918.)
(D.F.C. gazetted 2 July, 1918.)

BURDEN, HENRY JOHN, D.F.C., Lieut. (Temporary Capt.) (Canadian Forestry Corps). Since joining his squadron in charge this officer has accounted for 17 enemy machines—12 crashed, two driven down out of control and three destroyed in flames on the ground during an attack on an aerodrome. On the morning of the 10th Aug. he led his patrol in three attacks, and himself destroyed three enemy machines. In the evening of the same day he destroyed two more. Two days later he attacked a large number of Fokkers, seven of which were destroyed, accounting for three himself. In this encounter Capt. Burden led his patrol with exceptional skill and daring.
(The award of D.F.C. is also announced in this Gazette.)

CLAXTON, WILLIAM GORDON, D.F.C., Lieut. Between 4 July and 12 Aug. this officer destroyed ten enemy aeroplanes and one kite balloon, making in all 30 machines and one kite balloon to his credit. Untiring in attack in the air or on the ground, this officer has rendered brilliant service.
(D.F.C. gazetted 3 Aug. 1918.)
(Bar to D.F.C. gazetted 21 Sept. 1918.)

COBBY, ARTHUR HENRY, D.F.C., Lieut. (Temporary Capt.) (Australian Flying Corps). On the 16th Aug. this officer led an organized raid on an enemy aerodrome. At 200 feet altitude he obtained direct hits with his bombs, and set on fire two hangars; he then opened fire on a machine which was standing out on the aerodrome. The machine caught fire. Afterwards he attacked with machine-gun fire parties of troops and mechanics, inflicting a number of casualties. On the following day he led another important raid on an aerodrome, setting fire to two hangars and effectively bombing gun detachments, anti-aircraft batteries, etc. The success of these two raids was largely due to the determined and skilful leadership of this officer.
(D.F.C. gazetted 3 Aug. 1918.)
(First and Second Bars gazetted 21 Sept. 1918.)

CULLEY, STUART DOUGLAS, Lieut. (Sea Patrol). Ascended to a height of 19,000 feet, at which altitude he attacked an enemy airship, and brought it down in flames completely destroyed. This was a most difficult undertaking, involving great personal risk, and the highest praise is due to Lieut. Culley for the gallantry and skill which he displayed.

DODWELL, THOMAS BRIERLEY, Second Lieut. On a recent occasion this officer, when acting as Observer, performed a very gallant and meritorious action. In diving to the assistance of another machine, his own machine commenced to fall out of control. Despite this he continued to engage three enemy machines that were attacking him, and eventually drove them off, an operation that called for great coolness and skill, as the shooting platform was most unsteady. Realizing that the machine was out of control, owing to the loss of lift in the tail plane, half of this being shot away, he left his cockpit, and climbing along the wing, lay down along the cowling, in front of the pilot, enabling the latter to obtain partial control of the machine and head for home. When nearing the ground he climbed back into his cockpit, to allow the nose to rise, and the pilot succeeded in safely landing. The presence of mind and cool courage of this officer undoubtedly saved the machine, and deserves the highest praise.

HOWELL, CEDRIC ERNEST, M.C., D.F.C., Lieut. (Temporary Capt.). This officer recently attacked, in company with one other machine, an enemy formation of 15 aeroplanes, and succeeded in destroying four of them and bringing one down out of control. Two days afterwards he destroyed another enemy machine, which fell in our lines, and on the following day he led three machines against 16 enemy scouts, destroying two of them. Capt. Howell is a very gallant and determined fighter, who takes no account of the enemy's superior number in his battles.
(M.C. gazetted 16 Sept. 1918.)
(D.F.C. gazetted 21 Sept. 1918.)

JONES, JAMES IRA THOMAS, M.C., D.F.C., M.M., Lieut. (Temporary Capt.). Since joining his present brigade in May last, this officer has destroyed 28 enemy machines. He combines skilful tactics and marksmanship with high courage. While engaged on wireless interception duty he followed a patrol of nine Fokker biplanes, and succeeded in joining their formation unobserved. After a while two Fokkers left the formation to attack one of our artillery observation machines. Following them, Capt. Jones engaged the higher of the two, which fell on its companion, and both machines fell interlocked in flames.
(M.C. gazetted 16 Sept. 1918.)
(D.F.C. gazetted 3 Aug. 1918.)
(Bar to D.F.C. gazetted 21 Sept. 1918.)
(M.M. gazetted 10 Aug. 1916.)

WHISTLER, ALFRED HAROLD, D.F.C., Capt., Dorset Regt. During recent operations this officer has rendered exceptionally brilliant service in attacking enemy aircraft and troops on the ground. On 9 Aug. he dropped four bombs on a hostile battery, engaged and threw into confusion a body of troops, and drove down a hostile balloon, returning to his aerodrome after a patrol of one and a half hours' duration with a most valuable report. He has in all destroyed ten aircraft and driven down five others out of control.
(D.F.C. gazetted 2 July, 1918.)

London Gazette, 7 Nov. 1918.—"War Office, 7 Nov. 1918. His Majesty the King has been graciously pleased to approve of the following awards to the undermentioned Officers, in recognition of their gallantry and devotion to duty in the field. Awarded a Bar to the Distinguished Service Order."

BENSON, CHARLES BINGLEY, D.S.O., Temporary Lieut.-Colonel, London Regt. (Major, Reserve of Officers, Oxfordshire and Buckinghamshire Light Infantry). For conspicuous gallantry and good leadership. When his battalion was held up by heavy machine-gun fire, he led them with great skill and ability, and reached the objective in spite of the enemy's resistance. Though wounded, he remained in the front line until the position had been consolidated. He rejoined the battalion after having had his wound dressed, remaining with them until relieved. He set a fine example of devotion to duty and endurance.
(D.S.O. gazetted 31 Oct. 1902.)

FINDLAY, JAMES MARSHALL, D.S.O., Lieut.-Colonel, Scottish Rifles. For conspicuous gallantry and skill in handling his battalion during an attack. He took charge of the firing line, which was composed of other units besides his own, and constantly moved up and down, under heavy artillery and machine-gun fire. It was largely due to his inspiring example that the advance was kept going.
(D.S.O. gazetted 11 April, 1918.)

HART, LEONARD HERBERT POCOCK, D.S.O., Major (Acting Lieut.-Colonel), Lincolnshire Regt. For conspicuous gallantry and good leadership. He planned and supervised all the preliminary details of an attack. Under great difficulties of darkness and the intricacies of a thick forest he brought up his battalion to the exact position from which the advance was to be made, though at first he was led to the wrong spot. During the engagement that ensued he set a splendid example to all ranks by his coolness and composure under heavy fire.
(D.S.O. gazetted 3 June, 1918.)

KING, DENNIS MALCOLM, D.S.O., M.C., Capt. (Acting Lieut.-Colonel), Liverpool Regt. For conspicuous gallantry and good leadership in organizing three successful raids and compelling the enemy to withdraw from an outpost line overlooking our front line. Valuable identifications were obtained, 22 prisoners were taken, and many of the enemy killed. He showed the greatest energy and ability in preparing these raids, and in the raids themselves set a splendid example of courage and determination.
(D.S.O. gazetted 1 Jan. 1917.)

LAWRENCE, HERVEY MAJOR, D.S.O., Major (Acting Lieut.-Colonel), Scottish Rifles. He set a magnificent example of leadership and courage in an attack. When both his flanks were held up and he was suffering from wounds in the side and arm, he led his battalion forward in the face of heavy rifle and machine-gun fire and advanced the line 1,000 yards. He held the captured position against great odds. His personal influence had the most inspiring effect on officers and men.
(D.S.O. gazetted 1 Jan. 1918.)

McQUEEN, NORMAN, D.S.O., Capt. (Temporary Major), Argyll and Sutherland Highlanders (Special Reserve). For conspicuous gallantry and devotion to duty during an advance. When checked by heavy fire he, by his quick initiative and fearless leading, enabled the advance to continue. Throughout the operations he was always where he was most needed, and his untiring energy, cheerfulness, and personal courage had a most inspiring effect on the battalion.
(D.S.O. gazetted 4 June, 1917.)

OGILBY, ROBERT JAMES LESLIE, D.S.O., Temporary Lieut.-Colonel, Reserve of Officers, attached London Regt. For conspicuous gallantry and ability during an advance. He set a particularly fine example of energy and fearlessness to his men at a critical time. During consolidation, when the situation on the right was obscure, he made a valuable personal reconnaissance, causing him to alter his dispositions and effectually withstand all counter-attacks. He did very fine work.
(D.S.O. gazetted 1 Jan. 1918.)

SMELTZER, ARTHUR SIDNEY, D.S.O., M.C., Lieut. (Temporary Lieut.-Colonel), East Kent Regt. For conspicuous gallantry and good leadership in an attack. Hearing that the operation was postponed, he personally went forward and skilfully withdrew two of his companies, who had already engaged the enemy, to assembly positions from which they attacked successfully later in the day. On the objectives being reached he superintended consolidation, taking command at a critical period of one company who had lost all their officers. It was due to his energy, courage, and inspiring example that the premature advance did not prevent the success of the attack.
(D.S.O. gazetted 18 Feb. 1918.)

TAYLOR, GEORGE PRITCHARD, D.S.O., M.C., M.B., Capt. (Acting Lieut.-Colonel), Royal Army Medical Corps. For conspicuous gallantry and devotion to duty in arranging for clearing the wounded in the forward area during an attack. He personally reconnoitred the whole area and arranged relay posts for the bearers, freely exposing himself in the front line to heavy fire while searching for wounded. Throughout the operations the wounded, thanks to his splendid zeal and devotion to duty, were cleared with remarkable rapidity.
(D.S.O. gazetted 1 Jan. 1918.)

WEST, RICHARD ANNESLEY, D.S.O., M.C., Capt. (Acting Lieut.-Colonel), North Irish Horse (Special Reserve), attached Tank Corps. For conspicuous gallantry during an attack. In addition to directing his Tanks, he rallied and led forward small bodies of infantry lost in the mist, showing throughout a splendid example of leadership and a total disregard of personal safety, and materially contributed to the success of the operations. He commanded the battalion most of the time, his C.O. being early killed.
(D.S.O. gazetted 1 Jan. 1918.)

CANADIAN FORCE.

CAREY, ALFRED BLAKE, D.S.O., Lieut.-Colonel, Central Ontario Regt. For conspicuous gallantry and fine leadership. When his battalion was held up by intense machine-gun fire in front of a village, he organized a party from his reserve company and, under cover of the smoke from a derelict tank that was on fire, he personally led the party and rushed a wood, capturing 16 machine guns, and routed the enemy, who retired on a broad front. He then pushed on his battalion and took the village with a rush. His example of personal gallantry, and his quick appreciation of the situation and rapid action, enabled this important result to be so successfully obtained.
(D.S.O. gazetted 16 Aug. 1917.)

CRAWFORD, IAN LAURIE, D.S.O., Major, Infantry. For conspicuous gallantry and fine leadership during an attack. He personally reconnoitred the whole area the battalion was taking up before launching the attack, making his dispositions most skilfully. In the attack he led his battalion with great gallantry, and his fine example of courage and cheerfulness did much to ensure the success of the operation.
(D.S.O. gazetted 1 Jan. 1918.)

GILSON, WILLIAM FORBES, D.S.O., Lieut.-Colonel, Infantry. For conspicuous gallantry and initiative. He was in command of his battalion in an attack, during which he pushed forward with great determination, though the situation with regard to support was somewhat involved. His skill in directing the operations, and his fine example of courage and resource largely contributed to the success with which the battalion reached the objective.
(D.S.O. gazetted 18 Oct. 1917.)

HARBOTTLE, COLIN CLARK, D.S.O., Lieut.-Colonel, Central Ontario Regt. For conspicuous gallantry and fine leadership. When the advance of the battalion was held up by heavy machine-gun fire, he went to the front at once, and, working forward himself, carried on some of his flank company with him. Eventually these were forced to the ground by the intense fire of the enemy, but he continued to gain ground, by rolling forward, his men following his example till they got sufficiently close to rush the guns. On his signal this was accomplished with complete success, and the enemy wavered, and our advance continued along the whole line. The fine example of personal gallantry and determination displayed by Lieut.-Colonel Harbottle at a critical time enabled this most successful result to be obtained.
(D.S.O. gazetted 3 June, 1918.)

MACDONALD, ERIC WHIDDEN, D.S.O., M.C., Major (Acting Lieut.-Colonel), Infantry. For conspicuous gallantry and resource. He commanded his battalion in an advance, pressing his attack with skill and determination over a considerable amount of open ground, to the capture of isolated woods, the edges of which were full of concealed machine guns. The ability with which he made his dispositions undoubtedly saved many casualties. He set a very fine example to his men which greatly helped in the success obtained.
(D.S.O. gazetted 1 Jan. 1917.)

McCUAIG, GEORGE ERIC, C.M.G., D.S.O., Lieut.-Colonel, Infantry. For conspicuous gallantry and fine leadership during an attack. Through heavy mist he led his battalion nearly three miles to the final objective. He showed great courage and ability, personally leading and directing the assault and capturing a large number of prisoners and guns. He did splendid work.
(D.S.O. gazetted 1 Jan. 1917.)

WALKER, WILLIAM KEATING, D.S.O., M.C., Lieut.-Colonel, Machine Gun Corps. For conspicuous gallantry and skill. He commanded a mixed force composed of motor machine guns, a company of cyclists and a trench mortar detachment, which he handled with boldness and ability, destroying several machine-gun nests and capturing strong points. He inspired his men by his example of personal courage and daring, and contributed to the success of the advance.
(D.S.O. gazetted 18 Jan. 1918.)

AUSTRALIAN IMPERIAL FORCE.

McARTHUR, JOHN, D.S.O., Lieut.-Colonel, Infantry. For conspicuous gallantry while commanding his battalion during an attack. He preceded the battalion to the jumping-off line, and under very heavy fire issued final instructions to the companies. When the advance was temporarily checked he went forward and personally conducted operations, being severely wounded while doing so. It was largely due to his splendid leadership and fine initiative that the battalion reached all its objectives.
(D.S.O. gazetted in this Gazette.)

WILDER-NELIGAN, MAURICE, C.M.G., D.S.O., D.C.M., Lieut.-Colonel, Infantry. For conspicuous gallantry in a night attack on a village. Owing to his skill and courage, the plan of enveloping the village was successfully carried out, resulting in the capture of 200 prisoners and 30 machine guns. The attacking force suffered less than 20 casualties.
(D.S.O. gazetted 25 Aug. 1916.)

To be Companions of the Distinguished Service Order :

ATKINSON, GEORGE PRESTAGE, M.C., Capt., North Lancashire Regt. For conspicuous gallantry and fine leadership in action. When the commanding officer was killed, he rallied and led forward the battalion, until hostile barrages and a vigorous counter-attack forced him to withdraw. Later, he headed an assault and captured an important hill, where, in spite of being wounded through the leg, he remained at duty supervising the consolidation, never leaving the extreme front line until the whole position was safe. Throughout operations his courage in the very front of the battle ensured the success of the battalion.

BASTOW, HAROLD VERMUDEN, Major (Temporary Lieut.-Colonel), Yorkshire Regt. For conspicuous gallantry and devotion to duty. He commanded his battalion, which was new to the particular conditions of warfare they encountered, in a successful attack, which was brilliantly carried through to the objective under heavy machine-gun fire, in spite of the flank being entirely exposed. The spirit and fighting quality shown by all ranks of the battalion was largely due to the fine example he has always shown of personal courage and able leadership.

CAMPBELL, EDWARD FITZGERALD, Capt. (Acting Major), King's Royal Rifle Corps. For conspicuous gallantry and ability. Having only just taken over the line, he reorganized the defence and defeated a strong counter-attack. Though severely wounded in the bombardment that preceded the enemy's advance, he continued to direct operations for five hours until the line was secure, and it was largely owing to his able dispositions and the valuable information he transmitted to brigade headquarters that the position was maintained. His courage and endurance were conspicuous examples to all ranks throughout the engagement.

CHAYTOR, CLERVAUX ALEXANDER, Major (Acting Lieut.-Colonel), Yorkshire Light Infantry. For conspicuous gallantry and able leadership. He commanded his battalion with great success during prolonged operations, though he had very few company commanders, and the country, which there was little time to reconnoitre, was most intricate. He was constantly up among his men, supervising the dispositions under heavy machine-gun and shell fire with a courage and composure that inspired great confidence.

COCKHILL, JOHN BATES, M.C., Lieut. (Acting Capt.), West Riding Regt. For conspicuous gallantry and good leadership. He cleared the flank of a wood with his company, in spite of the strongest opposition, capturing three successive positions that were held with determination, and securing over 100 prisoners and 20 machine guns. On reaching the final objective he was cut off by the enemy, but fought his way back with great skill and determination. He set a splendid example to his men throughout the engagement.

COLT, HENRY ARCHER, M.C., Temporary Major (Acting Lieut.-Colonel), Gloucestershire Regt. For conspicuous gallantry and fine leadership. He commanded his battalion during three days' severe fighting, including the capture of an important village, with very great ability and courage. In spite of heavy casualties he pushed forward to his successive objectives with great determination, being himself severely wounded when leading the final assault on the village. His example greatly inspired his men.

COMBE, HENRY CHRISTIAN SEYMOUR, Capt. (Acting Major), Royal Horse Guards, attached Tank Corps. For conspicuous gallantry while in command of a company of 14 tanks. He carried out an operation which was extremely difficult owing to the nature of the ground, deployed his tanks and supervised their movements under very heavy shell fire. Throughout the engagement he kept in the closest touch with his tanks, his coolness and judgment being the direct means of enabling the infantry with whom he was working to reach their objectives with very few casualties.

COULSON, RICHARD NIVEN, Major (Acting Lieut.-Colonel), Scottish Rifles. For conspicuous gallantry and determination while commanding his battalion during an attack, when there was great difficulty in maintaining direction owing to fog and smoke barrage. On the advance being checked he went forward and reorganized his own firing line and that of units on his flank. Continuously under heavy fire, his personal example had a marked effect on the men.

CRAGG, WILLIAM GILLIAT, Temporary Major, North Lancashire Regt. For conspicuous gallantry and ability when in command of a company. He handled his men with great dash under heavy fire, and by his skilful dispositions enabled two guns and two machine guns to be captured with trifling loss. He pushed forward the attack with determined courage, and rapidly obtained all objectives.

DAWSON, FRED, M.C., Lieut. (Acting Capt.), Tank Corps. For conspicuous gallantry and initiative in handling a section of four tanks, with which he crossed two miles of open country under heavy fire. He directed operations during the clearing of a village, and when the right flank was exposed he took one tank and a platoon of infantry and captured the village.

ENGLAND, NORMAN AYRTON, Capt. (Acting Lieut.-Colonel), West Riding Regt. For conspicuous gallantry and devotion to duty. This officer has commanded his battalion with marked success during severe fighting, which culminated in the brilliant assault and capture of an important enemy position. The spirit and dash shown by all ranks of the battalion has been largely due to the fine example he has continually set them.

FORBES, ROBERT, M.C., Lieut. (Temporary Capt.), Royal Highlandres. For conspicuous gallantry during an attack. He rallied and directed men in thick fog under heavy fire, encouraging them by his personal example ; and on reaching the final objective he obtained valuable information by a daring reconnaissance. When it became necessary to evacuate the objective he displayed great courage and skill in getting the men away under heavy fire. He behaved splendidly throughout.

HAMPSON, GEOFFRY, Temporary Capt. (Acting Major), Tank Corps. For conspicuous gallantry and fine leadership with his tanks in action. He was of the utmost assistance to the infantry and when the cavalry were held up at a wood he cleared it of the enemy and pushed on. He went from tank to tank giving orders and showed an entire disregard for his own safety.

HAYFIELD, CYRIL DUDENEY, M.C., Temporary Capt., East Kent Regt. For conspicuous gallantry and good leadership during an attack. He was lent to another battalion to form them up for attack, and did so with the greatest ability. Later, when the officer commanding was killed, he led them most gallantly to the final objective and consolidated his position. His courage and initiative greatly inspired his men.

HONYWILL, ALBERT JOHN, M.C., Second Lieut. (Acting Capt.), Devonshire Regt. For conspicuous gallantry, skill and ability. He handled his company with great skill in face of heavy machine-gun fire, and captured two machine guns which were holding up our advance. Later in the day he advanced with considerable tactical ability and captured 200 prisoners. He was later wounded in the capture of a village, in which he materially assisted. Throughout the action his coolness and good judgment were remarkable and worthy of great praise.

JOHNSTON, CHARLES EVELYN, M.C., Capt. (Acting Lieut.-Colonel), London Regt. For conspicuous gallantry in action. Under heavy machine-gun fire he personally reorganized his own battalion and stragglers from other units, and when all his officers had become casualties he went forward himself and dealt with the remaining nests of enemy machine guns. He displayed great coolness and composure under intense fire and his example had an excellent effect on his men.

JOHNS, WHITFIELD GLANVILLE, Temporary Major, King' Royal Rifles Corps. For conspicuous gallantry and good leadership while commanding the battalion during an attack after the C.O. had been wounded. Having consolidated the positions gained he carried out a valuable reconnaissance under heavy fire. The information thus gained was largely responsible for the further advance undertaken and the ultimate capture of an important position.

LAMBTON, CLAUD, Capt., Yeomanry, attached Royal Scots Fusiliers. For conspicuous gallantry during an attack. He led his company forward with the greatest dash, taking all objectives together with 23 prisoners and six machine guns. Throughout he showed complete disregard for his personal safety, and by his example inspired his men to accomplish a task which upset the enemy's plans.

MOIR, HOWARD LAWNDES, Major (Acting Lieut.-Colonel), Cheshire Regt. For great gallantry and skill in handling his battalion under the most trying circumstances. On one occasion, although wounded in the side, he remained in command and was continuously under heavy fire, encouraging his men and supervising their movements. Later, he contributed largely to the success of operations by his courageous leadership.

MOSTYN-OWEN, ROGER ARTHUR, Capt. (Acting Lieut.-Colonel), Rifle Brigade. For conspicuous gallantry and good leadership during operations. After capturing and consolidating the objective he went forward and made a personal reconnaissance under heavy shell and machine-gun fire. He then led his battalion with great dash and captured the line of the railway. Later, it was largely owing to his determined and skilful handling of the battalion in an out-flanking movement that a village was successfully occupied.

PARGITER, LAWRENCE LEWIN, Capt. (Temporary Major and Acting Lieut.-Colonel), Middlesex Regt. For conspicuous courage and able leadership during operations. The brilliant way in which he handled his battalion during an attack under trying circumstances resulted in the capture of the objective. The quick consolidation and reorganization of his force enabled a vigorous counter-attack to be repulsed and a defensive flank to be formed at a critical period.

RYCROFT, ALFRED RICHARD HUGH, Major, Yeomanry, attached Tank Corps. For conspicuous gallantry and ability. He led the company of Tanks, of which he was in command, on horseback, and was responsible for the capture of several batteries of artillery. He showed great ability as a leader, and by the example of his personal courage did much to ensure the success gained by his company.

TURNER, JOHN ROBERT, Major, Royal Scots Fusiliers. For conspicuous gallantry and skill. He commanded his battalion in an attack on an important village, which was captured with a minimum of casualties. This result was due largely to his admirable preliminary arrangements and to the ability and coolness with which he directed the operations from a forward position, under heavy fire. He set a splendid example of courage and composure to all ranks of the battalion.

CANADIAN FORCE.

CHRISTIE, WILLIAM DAVIDSON CAIRNS, Lieut., Infantry. For conspicuous gallantry and initiative when his company was held up by machine-gun fire. He got a Lewis gun and some 15 men from company headquarters, and led a charge, resulting in the capture of two machine guns and 40 prisoners. Again, later, he twice cleared machine-gun posts, capturing as many as seven guns. His dash and courage were splendid, and the brilliant service rendered by his small party was due to his magnificent example.

JENNINGS, DOUGLAS CECIL, Major, Infantry. For conspicuous gallantry during an attack. He accompanied the leading Tank of a section to guide the section to its final objective. Later, he went forward and located the positions of enemy machine guns which were causing heavy casualties. Throughout the battle he displayed great courage and devotion to duty.

SAUNDERS, ALEC LAWRENCE, M.C., Capt. (Acting Major), Infantry, Manitoba Regt. For conspicuous gallantry and fine leadership. He assumed command of the battalion under difficult circumstances, the commanding officer being killed and the battalion having suffered heavy casualties in officers and men. In spite of adverse conditions he pushed forward, in the face of heavy machine-gun and rifle fire, and captured and consolidated the objective. His personal courage and cheerful determination were splendid examples to his men, and largely contributed to the success of the operation.

SCOTT, REV. CANON FREDERICK GEORGE, C.M.G. (Honorary Lieut.-Colonel), Canadian Chaplains' Service. For conspicuous gallantry and devotion to duty. He attended to the wounded under heavy fire, and by his cool and confident manner was a source of encouragement to the men when they were suffering heavy casualties. He behaved nobly, and helped to save many lives.

AUSTRALIAN IMPERIAL FORCE.

BURKE, FRANCIS JOSEPH, Lieut., Infantry. For conspicuous gallantry during an attack. He led his platoon with great dash, single-handed rushing a minenwerfer and killing the crew. With a party of six he then took a machine-gun post, capturing the gun and the garrison of eight men. Next, with his platoon, he rushed and captured two field guns, killing four of the crew and capturing 12. After reaching the final objective he went forward with one man and killed four of the enemy. Throughout the operation his courage, determination and leadership were a magnificent example to all.

CHALMERS, FREDERICK ROYDEN, Lieut.-Colonel, Infantry. For conspicuous gallantry during an attack. He filled a dangerous gap between his flank and the next battalion by organizing and leading forward his staff of signallers and runners, capturing several prisoners, of whom he himself took three. Under very heavy fire he then pushed on ahead of the objective, and seized a most advantageous position, from which he made a valuable reconnaissance of nearly a mile of the newly-captured front. His initiative and personal courage were a splendid inspiration to his battalion.

DAVIS, CLAPTON EDGINTON, M.C., Lieut., Infantry. For conspicuous gallantry during an attack. He led his own company and another with splendid dash, and took a position of great importance to the advance. His devotion to duty and absolute fearlessness won the admiration of all ranks, and his brilliant work and example materially assisted in the success of the operation.

LE MESSURIER, FREDERICK NEILL, Major, Army Medical Corps. For conspicuous gallantry and devotion to duty. He was continuously in the front line during both stages of an attack, assisting in collecting and arranging for the prompt disposal of the wounded to the rear. He behaved splendidly, and by his untiring efforts and a complete disregard of his own safety he greatly assisted the brigade throughout.

McARTHUR, JOHN, Lieut.-Colonel, Infantry. For conspicuous gallantry and able leadership. Having personally supervised all preliminary arrangements, he carried out a night attack on the enemy's well-organized trench lines, which was entirely successful. He remained at work for 48 hours, showing a splendid example of courage and devotion to duty which inspired all ranks of the battalion.

PERRY, STANLEY LLEWELLYN, M.C., Lieut.-Colonel, Infantry. For conspicuous gallantry and devotion to duty during an advance. Though early wounded, he refused to leave, and successfully commanded and controlled the capture of the final objective, afterwards directing consolidation and placing the line in a defensive condition. His gallant conduct inspired all ranks.

WILSON, ARTHUR MITCHELL, Lieut.-Colonel, Army Medical Corps. For conspicuous gallantry and devotion to duty during an attack, while in charge of bearer divisions. He followed close on the heels of the infantry into captured villages, establishing bearer posts, and effected the evacuation of the wounded with remarkable rapidity. He worked splendidly throughout, and by his untiring devotion to duty saved a number of lives.

NEW ZEALAND FORCE.

FARR, THOMAS, M.C., Major, Field Artillery. For conspicuous gallantry in action. Under the very heavy shell fire that the enemy were directing on his battery, he walked up and down behind the guns, encouraging his men and directing their fire with the greatest coolness and composure. He set a splendid example which greatly helped the excellent discipline of his men.

HARGEST, JAMES, M.C., Major, Otago Regt. For conspicuous gallantry and devotion to duty during an advance. He commanded his battalion with marked ability. His tactical dispositions were excellent, and he secured and forwarded valuable information. Constantly in the front trenches he inspired all ranks with the keenest offensive spirit, and the uninterrupted success of the battalion operations was largely due to his fine personal leadership.

London Gazette, 29 Nov. 1918.—" Admiralty, 29 Nov. 1918.—Honours for Services in Action with Enemy Submarines. The King has been graciously pleased to approve of the award of the following honours to Officers for services in action with enemy submarines. To be Companions of the Distinguished Service Order."

NASH, GEOFFREY STEWART FLEETWOOD, Lieut.-Commander (now Commander), R.N.

WHITE, CHARLES EVARARD HUGHES, Lieut.-Commander, R.N.

CAMERON, GORDON McLEOD, Lieut.-Commander, R.N.

PLATT, FRANCIS CUTHBERT, Lieut.-Commander, R.N.

To receive a Bar to the Distinguished Service Order:

PAGE, GEORGE FRANCIS LYON LABOUVERIE, D.S.O., Lieut.-Commander, Royal Navy.

PHILLIPS, PHILIP ESMONDE, D.S.O., Lieut.-Commander, Royal Navy.

" Honours for Operations off Terschelling on the 11th Aug. 1918.—The King has been graciously pleased to approve of the award of the following honour . . . to the undermentioned Officers of Coastal Motor Boats, in recognition of their gallantry during a reconnaissance of the West Frisian coast on the 11th Aug. 1918. (Included in award) To be a Companion of the Distinguished Service Order."

COKE, ANTHONY LAUNCELOT HENRY DEAN, Lieut.-Commander, R.N. During the course of the operation the Coastal Motor Boats were attacked by hostile aircraft, and, although greatly outnumbered, succeeded in bringing down two enemy aircraft. Lieut.-Commander Coke, who was Senior Officer of the flotilla, showed great determination, gallantry and courage in continuing his reconnaissance in spite of the presence of the enemy. The Coastal Motor Boats led by Lieut.-Commander Coke fought a very gallant action against superior odds, and continued to do so until all their ammunition was expended or their Lewis guns rendered useless by jambing.

" Additional Award for Services in the Action in the Heligoland Bight on the 17th Nov. 1917.—The King has been graciously pleased to approve of the following award in addition to those announced in the London Gazette of the 17th May, 1918. To be a Companion of the Distinguished Service Order."

CLARKE, HENRY CECIL COURTNEY, Lieut., R.N. In recognition of his services in command of H.M.S. Calypso in action after the Captain had been mortally wounded.

London Gazette, 2 Dec. 1918.—" War Office, 2 Dec. 1918. His Majesty the King has been graciously pleased to approve of the following awards to the undermentioned Officers, in recognition of their gallantry and devotion to duty in the field. Awarded a Third Bar to the Distinguished Service Order."

JACKSON, ARNOLD NUGENT STRODE, D.S.O. (name changed to Arnold Nugent Strode Strode-Jackson), Capt. (Temporary Lieut.-Colonel), North Lancashire Regt., attached 13th Battn. King's Royal Rifle Corps. For conspicuous gallantry and brilliant leadership. During an attack by our troops Lieut.-Colonel Jackson advanced with the leading wave of his battalion, and was among the first to reach the railway embankment. The machine-gun fire against them was intense, but the gallant leading of this officer gave such impetus to the assault that the enemy's main line of resistance was broken. He was subsequently wounded during the work of consolidation.

(D.S.O. gazetted 4 June, 1917.)
(First Bar gazetted 18 July, 1917.)
(Second Bar gazetted 13 May, 1918.)

Awarded a Second Bar to the Distinguished Service Order :

ANDERSON, JAMES, C.M.G., D.S.O., Lieut.-Colonel, 1/6th Battn., Highland Light Infantry, Territorial Force. For conspicuous gallantry in action and fine leadership. When the battalion of which he was in command was held up in their attack on a very strongly fortified position by an intense fire of artillery and machine guns, he walked about the firing line with complete composure and disregard of his own safety, rallying and leading his men forward. He was severely wounded, but remained in the firing line until quite exhausted directing and commanding his men until he had to be carried to a dressing station. His splendid example did much to inspire his men during a time of severe test.
(D.S.O. gazetted 2 Feb. 1916.)
(First Bar gazetted 26 March, 1918.)

JACKSON, EDWARD DARBY, D.S.O., Capt. (Temporary Lieut.-Colonel), King's Own Scottish Borderers, attached 14th Battn. London Regt. For conspicuous gallantry and brilliant leadership. During two days' severe fighting Lieut.-Colonel Jackson greatly contributed to the success obtained by his battalion by his example of personal courage and by his determined leadership in the face of strong resistance which led to hand-to-hand fighting, when on more than one occasion he was obliged to use his pistol. His ready grasp of the situation and his reports to brigade headquarters were also very valuable.
(D.S.O. gazetted 1 Jan. 1918.)
(First Bar gazetted 4 Feb. 1918.)

PLUNKETT, JAMES FREDRICK, D.S.O., M.C., D.C.M., Capt. (Temporary Lieut.-Colonel), Royal Dublin Fusiliers, attached 13th Battn. Royal Inniskilling Fusiliers. For conspicuous gallantry and devotion to duty during an attack. When the line on the right was held up by machine-gun fire he led two companies forward, and through his absolute contempt of danger established and consolidated a line of posts, capturing seven machine guns. Throughout the operation his determination and fine personal example inspired the attacking troops, and was the chief cause of its success.
(D.S.O. gazetted 1 Jan. 1918.)
(First Bar gazetted 4 Feb. 1918.)

THORNE, AUGUSTUS FRANCIS ANDREW NICOL, D.S.O., Major (Acting Lieut.-Colonel), 3rd Battn. Grenadier Guards. When his two leading companies lost direction owing to the fog, he stopped them to reorganize, and personally directed the two supporting companies on to their objective under heavy artillery and machine-gun fire. Throughout three days' operations he displayed most marked powers of leadership, and his courage in organizing the captured objectives under heavy fire was a splendid example to the whole battalion.
(D.S.O. gazetted 14 Jan. 1916.)
(First Bar gazetted 18 Feb. 1918.)

CANADIAN FORCE.

CLARK, JOHN ARTHUR, D.S.O., Lieut.-Colonel, 72nd Battn. Canadian Infantry, British Columbia Regt. For conspicuous gallantry and resourceful leadership. When one of his companies was held up by machine-gun fire from a wood, he led his men forward and by skilful tactics captured the machine guns with their crews. Two days later, when his men were again checked in front of a village, he dashed to the front, and led them to their objective, saving many casualties by his skill and fearlessness.
(D.S.O. gazetted 4 June, 1917.)
(First Bar gazetted 16 Aug. 1917.)

FOSTER, WILLIAM WASBROUGH, D.S.O., Lieut.-Colonel, 52nd Canadian Infantry Battn. Manitoba Regt. For conspicuous gallantry and splendid leadership. After two unsuccessful attacks on a village he made a daring reconnaissance to locate enemy machine guns ; and then having organized two raiding parties he led one of them personally, while the other made a feint attack on a flank. With his own party he accounted for several machine guns, and the eventual result of this third attack was the capture of the village, the defeat of an enemy counter-attack, and the capture of 250 prisoners by his battalion. In the evening he handed over his advanced line to a relieving battalion. He rendered most valuable service.
(D.S.O. gazetted 25 Nov. 1916.)
(First Bar gazetted 18 Jan. 1918.)

KIRKCALDY, JAMES, D.S.O., Lieut.-Colonel, 78th Battn. Canadian Infantry, Manitoba Regt. For conspicuous gallantry and resourceful leadership. When one of his companies was held up by machine-gun fire, he took charge and overcame the opposition. Later, by aggressive fighting, he got his battalion well forward, and formed a defensive flank, using a rifle himself and directing machine-gun and trench-mortar fire, and drove the enemy from their positions. His courage and fighting spirit were an inspiration to all.
(D.S.O. gazetted 1 Jan. 1917.)
(First Bar gazetted 3 June, 1918.)

LATTA, WILLIAM SMITH, D.S.O., Lieut.-Colonel, 29th Battn. Canadian Infantry, British Columbia Regt. For conspicuous gallantry and able leading throughout three days' fighting. He led his battalion in an attack against a village, outstripping the troops on his left, as well as the guns and tanks. In this difficult situation he handled his battalion with such skill that he reached his final objective with comparatively small loss. He has at all times displayed fine leadership in action until severely wounded.
(D.S.O. gazetted 4 June, 1917.)
(First Bar gazetted 3 June, 1918.)

PAGE, LIONEL FRANK, D.S.O., Lieut.-Colonel, 50th Canadian Battn., Alberta Regt. For conspicuous gallantry and devotion to duty. He led his battalion with great ability and determination in the attack and capture of a strongly-held enemy position. Later, during an enemy counter-attack, he made a reconnaissance of the greatest value, and although both his flanks were in the air he skilfully disposed his men so that they were protected and the counter-attack driven off with heavy loss to the enemy.
(D.S.O. gazetted 1 Jan. 1917.)
(First Bar gazetted 3 June, 1918.)

Awarded a Bar to the Distinguished Service Order :

BAINES, CUTHBERT SAVILE, D.S.O., Capt. (Temporary Lieut.-Colonel), Oxfordshire and Buckinghamshire Light Infantry, attached 2/7th Battn. Liverpool Regt., Territorial Force. For conspicuous gallantry and devotion to duty during the capture of a village. The successful attack and consolidation of the objectives, in addition to the taking of 600 prisoners and over 40 machine guns with slight casualties, were entirely due to the fighting spirit infused into as ranks by this officer, whose good leadership and invaluable personal reconnaissances, both before and after the attack, ensured the success of the operations.
(D.S.O. gazetted 1 Dec. 1914.)

BROOKE, GEORGE FRANK, D.S.O., Capt. (Temporary Lieut.-Colonel), Reserve of Officers, 14th Battn. Welsh Regt. For conspicuous gallantry and good leadership. During eight days' very severe fighting he commanded his battalion with great skill and tactical ability, displaying great personal courage and coolness under very difficult conditions. He led his battalion in a successfu attack on a strong position which they had failed to capture two days beforel and this result was largely due to his grasp of the situation and good organization
(D.S.O. gazetted 4 June, 1917.)

COLERIDGE, JOHN FRANCIS STANHOPE DUKE, C.M.G., D.S.O., Major and Brevet Lieut.-Colonel (Temporary Brigadier-General), 8th Gurkha Rifles, Indian Army, Commanding 188th Infantry Brigade. For conspicuous gallantry and fine leadership during an attack. When his battalions were held up by heavy machine-gun fire he walked round his entire line and personally gave instructions to all units for reorganization and pushing on to their objectives. His splendid leadership enabled the brigade to take a deep objective, and was the principal factor in the success of an important operation.
(D.S.O. gazetted 3 June, 1916.)

GREENWOOD, HARRY, D.S.O., M.C., Temporary Major (Acting Lieut.-Colonel), 9th Battn. Yorkshire Light Infantry. For conspicuous gallantry during an attack. Although ill he refused to leave his battalion, and led the first line to the attack, and after being injured by the bursting of a shell captured the first objective. On reaching the second objective he organized his battalion and another, and took up a defensive position from which he beat off two enemy counter-attacks and held his ground until relieved. Next day, when the advance was held up by very heavy machine-gun fire, he made a daring reconnaissance, with the result that he succeeded in getting round the enemy's flank. Throughout he set a splendid example of pluck and devotion to duty to all ranks.
(D.S.O. gazetted 26 July, 1918.)

KENNEDY, JAMES, D.S.O., M.C., D.C.M., Capt. (Temporary Lieut.-Colonel), Royal Highlanders, attached 13th Battn. Welsh Regt. For conspicuous gallantry and able leadership. He reorganized and co-ordinated the efforts of two battalions in spite of very difficult conditions, and subsequently led his battalion in a successful attack on a strong position which they had failed to capture two days before. This result, so soon after the first attempt, was largely due to his grasp of the situation and good organization, and fine example of personal courage.
(D.S.O. gazetted 4 June, 1917.)

LAMBERT, WALTER JOHN, D.S.O., Major, Lancers, Indian Army (Egypt). For conspicuous gallantry and devotion to duty. He led his regiment in a mounted attack with great dash. In front of a bridgehead his leadership and resource were mainly responsible for three mounted attacks converging at the same moment.
(D.S.O. gazetted 1 Jan. 1917.)

MARSHALL, CHARLES FREDERICK KELK, D.S.O., M.C., Capt. (Acting Major), C/78th Brigade, Royal Field Artillery. For conspicuous gallantry and devotion to duty during an attack. He personally brought one of the guns of the battery into action on the line of the leading infantry under direct machine-gun fire, and put out of action the enemy machine guns, thereby enabling the advance to continue. Later, with this gun he materially assisted the infantry to repel a counter-attack. Next day he again brought one of his guns into action in the open in close support of the battalion he was covering. His courage, energy and determination inspired all ranks.
(D.S.O. gazetted 1 Jan. 1918.)

PAYNTER, GEORGE CAMBORNE BEAUCLERK, D.S.O., Major and Brevet Lieut.-Colonel (Temporary Brigadier-General), Scots Guards, General Officer Commanding, 172nd Infantry Brigade. For fine leadership and gallantry while commanding his brigade in an attack, which involved a wheel to the right, to cover the flank of the direct attack of another division. Under heavy fire he personally reconnoitred the position of his troops during the operation, and reported the result when his final objective was attained. Throughout he displayed great courage and initiative.
(D.S.O. gazetted 1 Dec. 1914.)

SANDERS, ARTHUR RICHARD CARELESS, C.M.G., D.S.O., Major and Brevet Lieut.-Colonel, Royal Engineers, attached 1st Battn. Essex Regt. For conspicuous gallantry and devotion to duty. He led his battalion with great courage and determination in an attack, capturing and consolidating all his objectives, in spite of heavy fire. It was due to his initiative that a battery of enemy guns in front of the objective was captured. His personal influence anp good leadership were largely responsible for the success achieved by the battalion.
(D.S.O. gazetted 3 June, 1916.)

SEYMOUR, LORD HENRY CHARLES, D.S.O., Major and Brevet Lieut.-Colonel, Grenadier Guards, attached 9th Battn. Liverpool Regt., Territorial Force. For conspicuous gallantry in action. Realizing that his battalion was losing direction owing to intense machine-gun fire, he went forward and re-directed the leading companies on to their objective. Later, whilst collecting some parties of other units that had lost direction he was seriously wounded. He set a magnificent example by his coolness under very heavy fire.
(D.S.O. gazetted 3 June, 1916.)

CANADIAN FORCE.

DAVIES, REGINALD DANBURY, D.S.O., Lieut.-Colonel, 44th Canadian Infantry Battn., Manitoba Regt. For conspicuous gallantry during an attack. Realizing the importance of the capture of a village when the advance had been held up by wire and very heavy machine-gun fire, he collected all men available and led a dashing assault and overcame the enemy resistance. He personally led a tank through the village, and after completing its capture he pushed out and consolidated a line beyond, and he led it for two days, when he succeeded in joining up with the battalion on his right. By his splendid example and leadership he contributed greatly to the success of the operation.
(D.S.O. gazetted 17 April, 1917.)

DAWSON, HERBERT JOHN, D.S.O., Lieut.-Colonel, 46th Canadian Infantry Battn., Saskatchewan Regt. For conspicuous gallantry and ability during an attack. Thanks to his perfect organization and control his battalion secured their objectives, making an advance of some 2,500 yards. Later, when an enemy counter-attack was developing, he made a daring reconnaissance, and transmitted his report to brigade headquarters. As a consequence of this report it was possible to make such disposition as subsequently entirely defeated the purpose of the enemy. Throughout he showed great coolness and initiative.
(D.S.O. gazetted 4 June, 1917.)

DOUGHTY, EDWARD SPENCER, D.S.O., Lieut.-Colonel, 31st Battn. Canadian Infantry, Alberta Regt. For conspicuous gallantry and devotion to duty. In an attack on a village, when neither tanks nor guns were in a position to assist, he successfully occupied it. After which, observing a counter-attack in course of preparation, he collected two companies, and meeting the enemy as they advanced, beat them off with heavy casualties. His energy and cheerfulness were a great asset to his men.
(D.S.O. gazetted 24 Sept. 1918.)

GROSVENOR, THE HONOURABLE FRANCIS EGERTON, D.S.O., M.C., Major, 29th Battn. Canadian Infantry, British Columbia Regt. (Brigade Major Headquarters, 6th Canadian Infantry Brigade). For conspicuous gallantry and devotion to duty throughout three days' fighting. He first made a valuable reconnaissance on horseback under heavy fire, enabling the brigade to take up an advantageous position. Subsequently, after the capture of a village, he rode all along the line, assisting the commanders to consolidate, and bringing in valuable information of the situation. It was largely due to his energy that the brigade carried out the whole operation without a hitch.
(D.S.O. gazetted 1 Jan. 1918.)

MACBRIEN, JAMES HOWDEN, C.M.G., D.S.O., Major and Brevet Lieut.-Colonel (Temporary Brigadier-General), Royal Canadian Dragoons, General Officer Commanding, 12th Canadian Infantry Brigade. For conspicuous gallantry and fine leadership in an attack. He successfully captured the whole of his first objective, and under heavy machine-gun fire reconnoitred his line and directed further operations, thereby assisting very materially the advance of the flanking units. He has at all times by his courage and ability given to his brigade a wonderful inspiration of determination and aggressiveness.
(D.S.O. gazetted 23 June, 1915.)

MASON, DOUGLAS HERBERT CAMPBELL, D.S.O., Major, 3rd Battn. Canadian Infantry, 1st Central Ontario Regt. For conspicuous gallantry and leadership. This officer in command of an attack against a village cleared the enemy out, and advanced to some high ground east of it, reconnoitring and taking up a commanding position. His handling of the situation was responsible for the success of the operation.
(D.S.O. gazetted 19 Aug. 1916.)

NELLES, LAFAYETTE HENRY, D.S.O., M.C., Lieut.-Colonel, 4th Battn. Canadian Infantry, 1st Central Ontario Regt. For conspicuous gallantry and devotion to duty. This officer led his battalion in an attack on two villages, moving across open ground under heavy fire. Although wounded in the leg by machine-gun fire, he continued in command until the close of the fight, encouraging and inspiring his men.
(D.S.O. gazetted 3 June, 1918.)

ODLUM, VICTOR WENTWORTH, C.B., C.M.G., D.S.O., Lieut.-Colonel (Temporary Brigadier-General), 7th Canadian Infantry Battn., British Columbia Regt., General Officer Commanding, 11th Canadian Infantry Brigade. For conspicuous gallantry and ability during an advance. He personally superintended and carried out a difficult operation under heavy shell fire, inspiring his battalion by his continual resource and intrepid leadership. When his advance was temporarily held up, he organized the details of the successful final attack. He has always shown marked gallantry and initiative.
(D.S.O. gazetted 23 Dec. 1915.)

ROGERS, JOSEPH BARTLETT, D.S.O., M.C., Lieut.-Colonel, 3rd Battn. Canadian Infantry, 1st Central Ontario Regt. For conspicuous gallantry and devotion to duty. While directing the attack of his battalion, a heavy mist obscured the operations, and he suddenly found his party confronted by about 60 of the enemy, who had been passed by. He promptly collected the details and led them across the open against the enemy. His conduct in face of an awkward situation was an example to all.
(D.S.O. gazetted 18 July, 1917.)

SPARLING, ALBERT WALTER, D.S.O., Lieut.-Colonel, 1st Battn. Canadian Infantry, Western Ontario Regt. For conspicuous gallantry and devotion to duty. This officer personally directed his battalion in the attack on two villages, and advancing boldly across open ground under heavy machine-gun fire, encouraged and inspired all ranks in the performance of their duty.
(D.S.O. gazetted 26 July, 1917.)

STOCKWELL, CECIL VALENTINE, D.S.O., Major, 3rd Battery, 1st Brigade, Canadian Field Artillery. For conspicuous gallantry and devotion to duty during an attack. He went forward with the infantry and established an observation post in a village when the enemy were still in it. From this point he directed the fire of 400 rounds from his battery into the retreating enemy with excellent effect. He continued to observe and control fire, although his post was subjected to heavy bombardment and received direct hits. By his daring the advance of the infantry was greatly facilitated.
(D.S.O. gazetted 1 Jan. 1918.)

NEW ZEALAND FORCE.

WILDING, HENRY GORDON, D.S.O., Major, 7th Battery, New Zealand Field Artillery. For conspicuous gallantry and initiative. During a strong counter-attack by the enemy some of our infantry fell back on this officer's battery. He immediately rallied the infantry and, running one of his guns forward, fired over open sights and held the position until reinforcements arrived. His promptitude and courage saved a critical situation.
(D.S.O. gazetted 3 June, 1918.)

Awarded the Distinguished Service Order:

ANDERSON, WILLIAM MENZIES, M.C., Capt. (Acting Major), 1/6th Battn. Highland Light Infantry (Territorial Force). For conspicuous gallantry and ability in commanding his battalion during an attack. In the early stages he showed great determination in getting his battalion through the enemy wire under heavy fire, and, later, with his right flank exposed, he held the enemy off and maintained his position. Throughout the day he showed total disregard for his safety, and by his fine example greatly encouraged his men.

AWDRY, CHARLES SELWYN, Major, Royal Wiltshire Yeomanry, attached 6th Battn. Wiltshire Regt. For conspicuous gallantry and devotion to duty. He showed the greatest coolness and contempt of danger in conducting the retirement of the remnants of his battalion, and though greatly exhausted organized a new line of defence during the night. Next day, by his fine example he did much to steady the men of many scattered units.

BISSETT, GEORGE, M.C., Lieut. (Acting Lieut.-Colonel), 1st Battn. Royal Scots Fusiliers. For conspicuous gallantry and able handling of his battalion during an advance. Under most difficult circumstances, and in thick mist, he personally ensured that the correct line of advance was maintained to the first objective. Under very heavy fire he captured all objectives and held them. It was largely due to his courage and fine leadership that the battalion completely fulfilled its mission.

BLAKE, TERENCE JOSEPH EDWARD, Temporary Major, 13th Battn. Royal Fusiliers. For conspicuous gallantry and ability while in temporary command of his battalion. Though wounded he remained at duty and gained the confidence of his men. He carried out a minor operation with complete success, gaining his objectives and capturing a number of prisoners and machine guns; and later, by his fine leadership, he captured an enemy post with its garrison of nine men and two machine guns. He did splendid work.

BONN, WALTER BASIL LOUIS, M.C., Lieut. (Acting Capt.), 1st Battn. Welsh Guards. For conspicuous gallantry in action. When his C.O. was wounded he took command of the battalion, and fought it with great ability. On one occasion, when troops on the flank lost touch, he went forward through the enemy barrage to readjust the line. In doing so he was cut off by a party of the enemy, but worked his way through and rejoined the battalion. It was due to his courage and initiative that the battalion suffered so few casualties during the operations.

BRAITHWAITE, JOHN CROSBY, M.C., Temporary Second Lieut., 10th Battn. West Yorkshire Regt. For conspicuous gallantry and courage in an attack. He led his company through our barrage to a position 200 yards beyond the final objective and in rear of the enemy's position, and when the barrage lifted he attacked the enemy in rear in conjunction with a frontal attack by other companies. By his bold action he completely demoralized a much larger force than his own, and enabled the battalion to capture 250 prisoners and 21 machine guns. Later, when the enemy counter-attacked he held his position until the remainder of the brigade had taken up a new position, and so saved the flank of the brigade.

BRAND, JOHN CHARLES, M.C., Capt. (Acting Lieut.-Colonel), 1st Battn. Coldstream Guards. For conspicuous gallantry and fine leadership. After his battalion had captured the objective he organized the new line under very heavy shell fire, and it was largely due to his skilful dispositions that a determined enemy counter-attack was repulsed. Two days later, having made a personal reconnaissance under heavy fire, he led his battalion over the railway and through an intense barrage towards the objective.

BROCKMAN, WILLIAM JAMES, Temporary Lieut. (Acting Capt.), 15th Battn. Lancashire Fusiliers. For conspicuous gallantry during an attack. He led his platoon through thick belts of wire to the gun emplacements of four enemy field guns which were in action firing over open sights, and captured the guns, killing the battery commander. It was entirely due to his determined courage that the guns were captured and numerous casualties avoided.

BUSFEILD, JOHNSON ATKINSON, Major (Acting Lieut.-Colonel), Reserve of Officers, 1st Battn. Cheshire Regt., attached 6th Battn. Wiltshire Regt. For conspicuous gallantry and initiative in an attack. He led his company to the final objective without artillery support in the face of intense machine-gun fire, and inflicted heavy losses on the enemy. Though the enemy at once counter-attacked and completely outflanked his position, he held his ground with the greatest determination and skill.

CHICK, FREDERICK, Temporary Lieut., 2nd Battn. Royal Welsh Fusiliers. For conspicuous gallantry while commanding his company. After successful patrolling he faced the crossing of a river in the face of determined opposition. The post commanding the crossing was captured, and he established command of a bridgehead, killing and capturing a number of the enemy and taking four machine guns. Later, in an attack, he led his company with great courage and resource, clearing up the whole of his objectives and capturing many prisoners.

COLLIER, BERTRAM WILLIAM, Major (Temporary Lieut.-Colonel), South Wales Borderers, attached 14th Battn. Royal Welsh Fusiliers. For conspicuous gallantry and devotion to duty during an advance. He repeatedly organized the front line of his battalion and helped to get it forward under heavy machine-gun and artillery fire. It was by his personal efforts and fine leadership that his battalion advanced some 500 yards beyond the flanking units and were successful in beating off a counter-attack.

COOPER, ALFRED DUFF, Second Lieut., Irish Guards, Special Reserve, attached 3rd Battn. For conspicuous gallantry during an attack. Although the remainder of his company lost direction he led his platoon on to the objective and captured part of it. When supports arrived he led two sections against a machine-gun post, the four men immediately behind him were shot, but he went on alone and compelled the surrender of 18 men and two machine guns. Later, with a patrol of six men he succeeded in capturing 89 prisoners. He showed splendid courage and devotion to duty.

COURTENAY, HUGH, M.C., Capt. and Brevet Major (Acting Lieut.-Colonel), 1st Battn. Bedfordshire Regt. For conspicuous gallantry and resource in action. While directing the advance of his battalion one company became slightly disorganized owing to heavy fire. He rushed forward and led the men on. He then went to the left of the attack, where it was held up by wire, and encouraged short rushes, himself setting the example. Finally, he led the first wave himself until the last objective was reached. During the consolidation he was wounded.

DAVIDSON, JAMES EADIE, Temporary Capt. (Acting Major), 19th Siege Battery, Royal Garrison Artillery. For conspicuous gallantry and brilliant leadership in an attack. He reconnoitred a very forward position for his battery, and finally brought up his guns to a point within 1,500 yards of the front line from which he could reach all his objectives. He was here under continuous machine-gun fire, and for 12 hours his was the most forward battery in the sector. Thanks to his courage, initiative and energy the battery rendered valuable aid to the advance.

DAVIES, ARTHUR ROWLAND, M.C., Temporary Major, 226th Field Company, Royal Engineers. For conspicuous gallantry and devotion to duty during an advance. He made a reconnaissance of the forward roads under constant shell fire and made them fit for the volume of traffic which followed up the successful advance. He also entered villages as soon as captured to reconnoitre the water supply. He rendered very valuable service.

DAVIES, CHARLES EDWARD, Major (Temporary Lieut.-Colonel), Royal Warwickshire Regt., attached 16th Battn. Royal Welsh Fusiliers. For conspicuous gallantry during an attack. When his battalion was held up by machine-gun fire he went up to the front line and personally endeavoured to get the companies forward, and then returned to headquarters and procured support from artillery and additional infantry enabling him to capture the enemy machine guns. Throughout the operation his coolness under heavy fire and disregard of danger inspired all ranks with confidence.

DEAKIN, GRAHAME, Temporary Lieut.-Colonel, 16th Battn. Royal Warwickshire Regt. For conspicuous gallantry and initiative in an attack. He personally went forward and, under heavy machine-gun fire, organized one of his companies and some other scattered units which had become mixed owing to the dense fog. He led them forward and captured his final objective, together with an enemy battery, and later, when both his flanks were exposed, he held his ground in spite of heavy counter-attacks until he had organized an orderly withdrawal. He set a splendid example of courage and good leadership.

FALCONER, JOHN FATTES, M.C., Lieut., Indian Army Reserve of Officers, attached 29th Lancers, Indian Army (Egypt). For conspicuous gallantry and devotion to duty in charge of a machine-gun section. Being given a free hand he found that the best position for his section was held by the enemy, so he at once charged and drove them out, bringing his guns into action at 50 yards' range on the retiring enemy, and also silencing a nest of their machine guns. He showed exceptional initiative.

GATHORNE-HARDY, THE HONOURABLE NIGEL CHARLES, Major (Acting Lieut.-Colonel), Rifle Brigade, attached 2/6th Battn. Liverpool Regt., Territorial Force. For conspicuous gallantry in command of his battalion during an attack on a village. It was due to his supervision and personal reconnaissance previous to and after the capture of the village, that the operation was carried out successfully over open country with but few casualties. Numerous machine guns and over 160 prisoners were taken.

GELL, PHILIP FRANCIS, Major, 14th Lancers, Indian Army (Egypt). For conspicuous gallantry and devotion to duty. This officer led a turning movement in front of a bridgehead, which rolled up the enemy. He sabred three of the enemy and dismounted others with the hilt of his sword. He displayed exceptional ability as a cavalry leader.

GIBSON, WILLIAM, M.C., Temporary Major, South Staffordshire Regt., attached 10th Battn. West Yorkshire Regt. For conspicuous gallantry and initiative when in command of his battalion during five days' operations. He reorganized the battalion after an attack with great skill, pursued the retreating enemy, and assisted in the capture of further important enemy positions. His coolness and determination inspired his men throughout and contributed largely to the success of the operations.

GOODMAN, GODFREY DAVENPORT, C.M.G., Lieut.-Colonel (Temporary Brigadier-General), 6th Battn. Nottinghamshire and Derbyshire Regt., Commanding 21st Infantry Brigade. For conspicuous gallantry and devotion to duty. Two of his commanding officers being wounded, this officer on two occasions took over and, by his energy and drive, succeeded in taking the enemy position. On both these occasions he showed the greatest gallantry, moving about freely in the open under heavy fire of all arms. Though wounded he remained at duty until his brigade was relieved.

GREENWOOD, WILLIAM FOSTER, M.C., Temporary Capt., 9th Battn. Yorkshire Regt. (Italy). For conspicuous gallantry and devotion to duty when in charge of a raiding party. The main body losing direction he penetrated the enemy's position with two men. He cleared out a number of dug-outs and shelters, killing all who resisted, and eventually returned with 12 prisoners. By his personal initiative and daring he prevented the raid being a failure, and achieved a partial success.

GROOM, HAROLD LESTER ROBERT JOSEPH, M.C., Lieut. (Acting Capt.), 1/5th Battn. Royal Warwick Regt. (Territorial Force). (Italy). For conspicuous gallantry during a raid. He led his company right up under our barrage and got into a railway cutting before the enemy had time to ma his machine guns. In spite of the severe fighting in the cutting he personally examined sheds and shelters and gained valuable information. During the withdrawal he collected his men and got his wounded away with great skill. Throughout he showed determined leadership and courage.

GROVES, EDWARD JULIAN, M.C., Lieut. (Acting Capt.), 1st Battn. Cheshire Regt. For conspicuous gallantry and initiative in an attack. He led his company to the final objective without artillery support in the face of intense machine-gun fire, inflicted heavy losses on the enemy, and captured a large number of field guns. When the enemy counter-attacked and broke through on both his flanks he carried out a skilful withdrawal and collected and reorganized scattered parties of other units under heavy machine-gun fire.

GUY, OSWALD VERNON, M.C., Temporary Capt. (Acting Major), 7th Battn. Tank Corps. For conspicuous gallantry and ability in command of his company during a fortnight's fighting. He cleared a strong enemy position in the fog and organized attacks at extremely short notice with such complete detail that the success was great, and the infantry greatly assisted in their advance. His energy and co-operation with the infantry staffs gave them detailed information earlier than from any other source.

HELME, ERNEST, Major, Glamorganshire Yeomanry, attached 15th Battn. Welsh Regt. For conspicuous gallantry and ability. He organized and carried out the crossing of a river by his battalion with great foresight and skill, and during the subsequent advance and operations lasting several days his example of personal courage, and his power of organization and command enabled his men successfully to accomplish all the tasks they were called on to perform.

HOBBS, HOWARD FREDERICK, M.C., Temporary Major, 13th Battn. Welsh Regt. For conspicuous gallantry and skill in command of his battalion in an advanced guard. Under heavy shell fire and gassing he kept his men well in hand ; and, later, fought his way forward successfully through strong machine-gun opposition. Thanks to his gallant and noble leadership during three days' strenuous fighting his battalion was completely successful in its duties.

HOGG, SAMUEL ROLLESTON, M.C., Temporary Lieut. (Acting Capt.), 26th Battn. Royal Fusiliers, attached Headquarters, 122nd Infantry Brigade. For conspicuous gallantry and devotion to duty when acting as brigade-major. He organized and directed operations with supreme skill. When the situation was obscure, he went forward in broad daylight, exposed to constant fire, and linked up the forward posts that formed the front line. He then conducted with great daring the operations for new dispositions. As a result, the line was advanced at dusk 500 yards along the brigade front. Throughout difficult operations, he showed fine courage and initative.

HUMPHRIES, CECIL FREDERICK GEORGE, M.C., D.C.M., Temporary Capt. (Acting Lieut.-Colonel), 1st Battn. Duke of Cornwall's Light Infantry, attached 1st Battn. Norfolk Regt. For conspicuous gallantry and fine leadership. Having taken his objective, he reorganized his battalion, and, on hearing that the attack on the final objective was held up, he went forward under heavy fire and reconnoitred the whole position, after which he returned and led the battalion forward. Later, he personally controlled his men during a very determined counter-attack by the enemy under the heaviest machine-gun fire. His courage inspired great confidence throughout the operations.

JAMIESON, JOHN PERCIVAL, Second Lieut. (Acting Capt.), Middlesex Regt., Special Reserve, attached 4th Battn. For conspicuous gallantry and devotion to duty. When the advance of his company was held up by an enemy machine-gun and trench-mortar post, he, with two of his runners, rushed this post, capturing two machine guns, two trench mortars and two prisoners. Although slightly wounded he led his company to the final objective, which he consolidated. Later, with a few runners, he captured a gun team, wounding three of the enemy and taking two prisoners ; and throughout the operations he inspired his men by his wonderful example and total disregard of personal danger.

JOHNSTON, CHARLES ERNEST, Major, 1/6th Battn. Seaforth Highlanders, Territorial Force. For conspicuous gallantry and devotion to duty in command of his battalion. He encouraged his men by his great coolness under very heavy fire, and when the enemy broke through on the left, he organized a defensive flank, subsequently conducting the withdrawal with great skill. It was due to his splendid example that the battalion put up such an excellent defence and inflicted such heavy casualties on the enemy. He was finally wounded.

MOLONY, WILLIAM BERESFORD, Temporary Lieut.-Colonel, 9th Battn. Royal Lancaster Regt., attached 4th Battn. Middlesex Regt. For conspicuous gallantry and good leadership during an attack. When, owing to thick mist and enemy smoke and gas shell, many of the companies were losing direction, he personally rallied them, under very heavy fire, and directed them to their objective. Later, he went forward, and under heavy shell fire, led parties of men who had lost their platoons in the mist. Throughout he set a splendid example to all ranks.

MURRAY, ERIC MACKAY, M.C., Capt., Queen Victoria's Own Corps of Guides, Indian Army, and Royal Flying Corps (Mesopotamia). For conspicuous gallantry and devotion to duty during three months' operations. He persistently showed courage and ability of a high order throughout. He was three times in action against enemy aircraft, and on the last occasion returned with 20 bullet holes in his machine, after his passenger had emptied 1½ drums of ammunition from a Lewis gun at the adversary.

PERKINS, HUGH RICHARDSON, M.C., Temporary Capt., 13th Battn. Welsh Regt. For conspicuous gallantry and devotion to duty. He took command of another battalion when many of the officers had become casualties during an attack and reorganized it under heavy enemy fire. Later, he led the battalion in another attack in the face of intense shell and machine-gun fire, and by his courage and initiative was largely responsible for the capture of the enemy's position with many prisoners.

PAYNE, JOHN EDWARD LENNARD, M.C., Temporary Capt., 10th Battn. West Riding Regt. (Italy). For conspicuous gallantry and fine leadership when in charge of a large raiding party. Although the objective was continuously swept by enfilade machine-gun fire, he carried out the operation successfully and withdrew his party in perfect order, capturing a large number of prisoners. He exhibited great coolness and ability to command.

POPHAM, FRANCIS JAMES, Temporary Major (Acting Lieut.-Colonel), North Lancashire Regt., attached 2/5th Battn. Royal Lancaster Regt. (Territorial Force). For conspicuous gallantry and skill in an attack. He led his battalion in an advance of two miles through the enemy's lines and captured a village, in spite of strong opposition. He showed great initiative and determination both in the attack and in a withdrawal which later became necessary owing to his position being isolated.

POWELL, DAVID WATSON, Major (Acting Lieut.-Colonel), Northamptonshire Regt., attached 1st Battn. Royal Berkshire Regt. For conspicuous gallantry and fine leadership during an attack. When both the company commanders on the right of his battalion were wounded, he went up at once, under heavy machine-gun fire, and personally rushed the attack through to its objective. Later, when the line was temporarily disorganized, he immediately went and, under heavy machine-gun fire, reorganized it. He showed the highest qualities of command under difficult conditions.

ROSSI-ASHTON, CYRIL GEORGE, Temporary Capt. and Brevet Major (Acting Major), 7th Battn. Tank Corps. For conspicuous gallantry and ability during a fortnight's fighting. He commanded his company with skill and judgment, reorganizing his company and achieving with composite crews results with their shooting which gained the appreciation and confidence of the infantry, and thereby combined attainment of his objective on every occasion.

SHAW, ARCHIBALD DOUGLAS McINNES, Temporary Capt., 1st Battn. Royal Scots Fusiliers. For conspicuous gallantry and fine leadership in an attack. In thick fog he led the leading company successfully through to the final objective. When his company was held up by machine-gun fire from a trench, he personally led a bayonet charge and captured the trench, with 20 prisoners. He then pushed on and captured 120 prisoners, besides killing many of the enemy. The success of the operation was largely due to his marked courage and determination.

SHAW, DONALD PATRICK, Temporary Major, 6th Battn. Dorsetshire Regt. For conspicuous gallantry during an attack. He commanded his company with so great enterprise and dash that in one afternoon eight machine guns and 20 prisoners were taken by them. He personally accounted for many of the enemy, and the result of his determined action and initiative was the weakening of an enemy position preparatory to an attack carried out successfully against it that night. Later, in command of his battalion, he showed marked ability and fighting spirit.

SLATER, JOHN MOWAT, Capt. (Acting Major), 1/4th Battn. Royal Scots (Territorial Force). For conspicuous gallantry and skill while commanding his battalion in an attack. By his personal example and leadership he inspired his men with such dash and determination that all objectives were taken, and over 400 prisoners and 40 machine guns were captured. His conduct was magnificent throughout.

SMITHARD, RICHARD GLASSE, M.C., Capt. (Temporary Lieut.-Colonel), 7th Battn. Shropshire Light Infantry. For conspicuous gallantry and skilful handling of his battalion in the capture of a position. After personally reconnoitring the line of advance, he got his battalion round a heavily-gassed area, and in spite of thick fog successfully gained his objective, thereby materially assisting the advance of the battalion on his right. Two days later, he made a further advance and consolidated his position. It was due to his fine example and fine leadership that the battalion successfully fulfilled its mission.

TENNANT, MICHAEL FRANCIS, Lieut., Scots Guards, Special Reserve, attached 1st Battn. For conspicuous gallantry and devotion to duty. He led his men forward with great dash, and captured an officer and 12 men himself. In an attack on a village he led two platoons, and made such good use of ground that they suffered few casualties, in spite of very heavy fire. The village was full of the enemy, by whom at one time he was surrounded, but by the skilful use of his Lewis guns he reached the final objective, killing or capturing the majority of the enemy.

THWAYTES, HARRY DELAMERE, Capt. (Acting Lieut.-Colonel), 1st Battn. Dorsetshire Regt. For conspicuous gallantry and ability during an attack on an enemy position. The battalion commanded by him successfully forced their way through strong wire defences, in face of heavy machine-gun fire, and under his direction successfully maintained and consolidated the position won, though subjected to repeated enemy attempts to recover it.

THOMAS, WILLIAM EDGAR, M.C., Temporary Major, 7th Battn. East Yorkshire Regt. He commanded two companies in an outflanking movement to capture a village which was strongly held by the enemy. By his able dispositions and fearless leading he succeeded, with only two casualties, in taking four machine guns and 50 prisoners. The advance was then continued, and the whole village finally captured. His fine example of courage and leadership inspired all ranks.

WARD, ROBERT, M.C., Lieut. (Temporary Capt.), 9th Battn. Manchester Regt., Territorial Force, attached 1st Battn. Liverpool Regt. For conspicuous gallantry and devotion to duty. After 30 hours' unceasing work under heavy shelling, he volunteered to lead the remnants of two companies in the advance against a village. He cheered the men on in face of intense machine-gun fire until he fell wounded, and by his splendid example and personal courage the long extended line was carried right on to the objective.

WALSH, RUPERT SHARPE, M.M., Lieut., 4th Battn. Gordon Highlanders, Territorial Force, seconded 11th Battn. Tank Corps. For conspicuous gallantry and devotion to duty. During a long and trying day, when he covered some 20 miles and fought several actions, his energy and cheerful courage were a fine example to his men. When the machinery broke down on one occasion, and the enemy made his tank untenable by the fumes of phosphorus bombs, he evacuated the crew, but remained behind himself, with one man, and eventually got the engines started again, and walking along between the front horns of the tank, surrounded by the enemy, who were firing at them with their revolvers, he managed at last to bring the tank back into safety.

WHITEHEAD, TEBBUTT HILL, M.C., Temporary Capt., 13th Battn. Royal Fusiliers. For conspicuous gallantry and resource in an attack. When the attack seemed likely to be held up by intense enemy fire, by his skilful and determined leadership under the most difficult conditions he enabled the advance to continue, with the result that a very strong enemy position was captured, with 500 prisoners. His personal example and initiative contributed largely to the success of the operation.

CANADIAN FORCE.

BASEVI, JAMES, Major, 2nd Battn. Canadian Machine Gun Corps. For conspicuous gallantry and devotion to duty. He commanded four machine-gun batteries in conjunction with the infantry advance. When the entire brigade staff were either killed or wounded by a shell burst, he took charge and carried on until the arrival of a fresh staff. His initiative in meeting the emergency, and the way he managed the fire power of his batteries, were of the greatest value.

GORDON, REV. ALEXANDER MACLENNAN, M.C., Canadian Chaplains' Service, attached 4th Canadian Division. For conspicuous gallantry and devotion to duty. During heavy fighting in the advance he was continually exposed to great danger while attending the wounded in the firing line. While performing his duty he was severely wounded by a machine-gun bullet.

HOPE, JOHN ANDREW, M.C., Major, 46th Canadian Infantry Battn., Saskatchewan Regt. For conspicuous gallantry and resource. After a strong enemy counter-attack he carried out a most valuable reconnaissance under heavy fire, reorganized the line, established touch with the enemy along his whole front, and cleared up a difficult situation. He showed marked initiative and disregard of danger.

KEEGAN, HERBERT LEO, Lieut.-Colonel, 47th Canadian Infantry Battn., West Ontario Regt. For conspicuous gallantry and devotion to duty during an attack. In conjunction with another battalion he stormed and successfully captured enemy positions through uncut wire. Throughout the engagement, fought with his right flank exposed, he displayed marked courage and cheerfulness, and in face of the greatest difficulties advanced and held ground gained for three days.

KILBORN, ARTHUR RUBIN, M.C., M.M., Lieut., 78th Battn. Canadian Infantry, Manitoba Regt. For conspicuous gallantry and devotion to duty as scout officer during four days' operations. Under heavy fire he maintained liaison between the companies and battalion headquarters, his accurate information enabling the positions to be readjusted in the face of obstinate resistance. When the left of the attack was threatened he collected some details, and fearlessly exposing himself, shot two officers at close quarters and restored the situation.

KIPPEN, WILLIAM HAROLD, M.C., Capt. (Acting Major), 3rd Battn. Canadian Infantry, 1st Central Ontario Regt. For conspicuous gallantry and devotion to duty. During an attack, after the second-in-command had been wounded, this officer twice saved a critical situation, first by seizing a trench, and later by clearing out a nest of four machine guns in a sunken road. On reaching his objective he skilfully arranged for its consolidation. His energy and determination were responsible for the success of the operation.

MARTYN, DONALD BRUCE, M.C., Major, 44th Canadian Infantry Battn., New Brunswick Regt. For conspicuous gallantry and devotion to duty during a bombing attack. Noticing that one of the attacking parties of another battalion had taken the wrong trench turning, he immediately went forward and, finding the senior officer had been wounded, took charge and led the party into the correct trench against large numbers of the enemy, of whom he mowed down a company and captured over 40. He remained with the party for over ten hours, during which time he withstood two violent counter-attacks and consolidated the positions captured. He showed marked ccurage and able leadership.

MATHESON, GUY McLEAN, M.C., M.M., Capt. (Acting Major), 25th Battn. Canadian Infantry, Nova Scotia Regt. For conspicuous gallantry and devotion to duty. This officer led his company in the attack, and later, when his C.O. was severely wounded, took command of the battalion and skilfully consolidated the position gained. The following day, in directing the advance of the front line, he was severely wounded, but continued on duty for 24 hours. His courage and coolness set a fine example.

McKECHNIE, DAVID WILLIAM, Capt., No. 6 Field Ambulance, Canadian Army Medical Corps. For conspicuous gallantry and devotion to duty. While preparing an advanced dressing station in a village, it was subjected to an intense bombardment, but he remained at his post dressing the wounded, and refused to take underground cover.

McMURTRY, ALEXANDER OGILVIE, Major, 4th Battery, 1st Brigade, Canadian Field Artillery. For conspicuous gallantry during an attack. When the infantry were held up by machine-gun nests he went forward with a section of his battery and took up a position in the open, and though subjected to machine-gun fire, he was able, by using open sights, to disperse the enemy, thus clearing the way for the infantry advance. His coolness and resource throughout the operations were most marked.

MOORE, ROGER STEVENSON, Capt., 29th Canadian Infantry Battn., British Columbia Regt. For conspicuous gallantry and fine leadership during an attack. He led his company splendidly through heavy fire and captured 16 machine guns and an enemy strong point. His fearless example carried his company forward against all odds and was successful in helping his flanks to advance.

ROSS, STANLEY GRAHAM, M.C., Major, 6th Field Ambulance, Canadian Army Medical Corps. For conspicuous gallantry and devotion to duty. On three successive days this officer was in charge of collecting posts and advanced dressing stations. He accompanied the stretcher-bearers in the advance, to see that proper touch was maintained. His coolness and disregard of danger under heavy fire had an excellent effect on the work of the bearer parties.

SIFTON, CLIFFORD, Jun., Major, 4th Brigade, Canadian Field Artillery. For conspicuous gallantry and determination in command of a composite battery, supporting the infantry advance. By making forward reconnaissances he succeeded in bringing his battery into action at close range against machine guns, tank guns and enemy strong points. His enterprise largely contributed to the success of the attack. Although shot through the wrist he remained at duty.

SIMPSON, ARTHUR FREDERIC, Capt., 28th Canadian Infantry Battn., Saskatchewan Regt. For conspicuous gallantry and devotion to duty while in command of a support company during an attack. Seeing that the attack was likely to become disorganized he led his company in face of heavy fire through the attacking line, reorganized the other units and carried the whole line forward. His bold and skilful leadership enabled other units who were held up to come on. He showed marked courage throughout the operations.

SIMPSON, ROBERT MILLS, Colonel, Canadian Army Medical Corps, Assistant Director of Medical Services, 2nd Canadian Division. For conspicuous gallantry and devotion to duty in establishing, often under heavy fire, his advanced dressing stations and collecting posts, and personally superintending the evacuation of the wounded. When a sudden attack resulted in the capture of a village, he went up under fire and personally dressed the wounds of his men on the field, evacuating all by the evening. His tireless work undoubtedly saved many lives.

WHITAKER, HECTOR CHILD, Lieut., 72nd Battn. Canadian Infantry, British Columbia Regt. For conspicuous gallantry and devotion to duty during four days' operations, when he was in command of the battalion scouts, obtaining and sending back excellent information as to the enemy strong points, thereby saving many casualties. He beat back the enemy outposts, and on one occasion captured a machine gun and crew. Subsequently he rushed a machine gun and crew single-handed, putting it out of action, although wounded in the face. His judgment and dash were most praiseworthy.

WISE, JOHN, M.C., Lieut.-Colonel, 25th Battn. Canadian Infantry, Nova Scotia Regt. For conspicuous gallantry and devotion to duty in leading his battalion and gaining all its objectives. During the attack he was severely wounded in the back, but his determination and indomitable spirit were responsible for the successes of his unit.

AUSTRALIAN IMPERIAL FORCE.

CAMPBELL, ALEXANDER GEORGE, Capt., 8th Battn. Australian Infantry. For conspicuous gallantry and resource. He led his company in an attack against a strong enemy position, captured and consolidated all his objectives, and by his skilful leadership enabled the battalion on his flank to continue the advance when they were held up by the enemy. In a later attack, though he was badly wounded, he continued to lead his men until he collapsed. He set a splendid example of courage and determination.

COX, CHARLES FREDERICK, C.B., C.M.G., Colonel (Temporary Brigadier-General), Commanding 1st Australian Light Horse Brigade (Egypt). For conspicuous gallantry and devotion to duty. His quickness in realizing the situation, and organizing a counter-attack, resulted in the recapture of a position before the enemy had time to consolidate. He also captured about 150 prisoners who were attacking a small post in a neighbouring bluff, and then readjusted his line before supports could arrive to support the enemy storm troops.

DICK, ARCHIE, Major, 3rd Australian Light Horse Regt. (Egypt). For conspicuous gallantry and devotion to duty. When the enemy attacked in overwhelming force his tenacity in holding on to two posts under his command was largely responsible for their repulse with heavy casualties. The exact information which he sent back enabled the batteries to bring accurate fire on the enemy.

WEIR, FRANK VALENTINE, Major, 1st Australian Light Horse Regt. (Egypt). For conspicuous gallantry and devotion to duty. With great dash he worked his squadron in a counter-attack, driving the enemy back and forcing them under fire of the machine guns. This led to the whole of the enemy who had entered the position being captured.

NEW ZEALAND FORCE.

BELL, PETER HARVEY, Lieut.-Colonel, 3rd Battn. New Zealand Rifle Brigade. For conspicuous gallantry and ability. During an attack he found that troops on his flank had been unable to reach their objective owing to the loss of many officers. He immediately rearranged his place of operations and reorganized his men under most difficult circumstances and personally directed the advance of his companies under heavy fire. It was mainly due to his energy and initiative and entire disregard of personal safety that our advance was continued and all objectives were taken.

McCLELLAND, CHARLES HAROLD, Major, 2nd Battn. Auckland Regt. For conspicuous gallantry and devotion to duty. When his battalion commander became a casualty he assumed command and handled his men with remarkable coolness and skill. At the commencement of an attack he was shot in the arm and leg, but refused to leave his command, even to have his wounds dressed, until the battalion was relieved three days later. His example of unfailing courage and endurance inspired all under his command during a very trying time.

SINEL, WILFRED COURTNEY, Major, 2nd Battn. Auckland Regt. For conspicuous gallantry and devotion to duty. When the advance of the battalion of which he was in command was held up by an intense fire of artillery and machine guns he went forward to the front line, and by skilful leadership pushed on the attack. While doing this he was wounded. During the work of consolidation he repelled three determined counter-attacks. Throughout the operations his courage and ability inspired the greatest confidence in his men.

TURNBULL, FRANK KINGDON, M.C., Major, 1st Battn. Wellington Regt. For conspicuous gallantry and devotion to duty. He was in command of his battalion, which he handled with great ability during four days' severe fighting. He was continually with the advance guard while the enemy were retreating, and his accurate reports to brigade headquarters greatly contributed to the success of the operations. He repelled several determined counter-attacks, and during the whole time his unfailing cheerfulness and example of personal courage greatly encouraged his officers and men.

London Gazette, 3 Dec. 1918.—" Air Ministry, 3 Dec. 1918. His Majesty the King has been graciously pleased to confer the undermentioned rewards on Officers and other ranks of the Royal Air Force, in recognition of gallantry in flying operations against the enemy. (Included in award) Awarded the Distinguished Service Order."

McCLAUGHRY, EDGAR JAMES, D.F.C., Capt. (Australian Flying Corps). (France). A bold and fearless officer, who has performed many gallant deeds of daring, notably on 24 Sept., when, attacking a train at 250 feet altitude, he obtained a direct hit, cutting it in two, the rear portion being derailed. He then fired a number of rounds at the fore portion, which pulled up. Sighting a hostile two-seater he engaged it and drove it down. Proceeding home he observed seven Fokker biplanes ; although he had expended the greater part of his ammunition, Capt. McClaughry never hesitated, but engaged the leader. During the combat that ensued he was severely wounded by fire from a scout that attacked him from behind ; turning, he drove this machine off badly damaged. His ammunition being now expended he endeavoured to drive off two hostile scouts by firing Very lights at them. Exhausted by his exertions, he temporarily lost consciousness, but recovered sufficiently to land his machine safely. This officer has destroyed 14 machines and four balloons, and has repeatedly displayed an utter disregard for danger in attacking ground targets.

(D.F.C. gazetted 21 Sept. 1918 ; Bar to D.F.C. same date.)

London Gazette, 11 Dec. 1918.—" Admiralty, 11 Dec. 1918.—Honours for Services in Grand Fleet Destroyers between the 1st Jan. and 30th June, 1918. The King has been graciously pleased to approve of the award of the following honours to the undermentioned Officers. To be Companions of the Distinguished Service Order."

FREMANTLE, CHARLES ALBERT, Commander, R.N.

MACKINNON, EDMOND JULIUS GORDON, Commander, R.N.

LECKY, ARTHUR MACAULAY, Commander, R.N.

BARRON, JOHN OUCHTERLONY, Commander, R.N.

SEARS, HAROLD BAKER, Engineer Lieut.-Commander, R.N.

" Honours for Services in the Auxiliary Patrol and Minesweeping between the 1st Jan. and 30 June, 1918.—The King has been graciously pleased to approve of the award of the following honour to the undermentioned Officer. To be a Companion of the Distinguished Service Order."

LYNE, THOMAS JAMES SPENCE, Commander (Acting Capt.), R.N.

" Honour for Services in Minesweeping Operations.—The King has been graciously pleased to approve of the award of the following honour to the undermentioned Officer. To receive a Bar to the Distinguished Service Order."

SEYMOUR, HUGH, D.S.O., Commander, Royal Navy. For the gallant and able manner in which he conducted continuous and difficult clearances of mines.

The Distinguished Service Order

"Honours for Services on the Mediterranean Station between the 1st Jan. and 30th June, 1918 (Adriatic).—The King has been gracioulsy pleased to approve of the award of the following honours to the undermentioned officers and men. To be Companions of the Distinguished Service Order."
SOMERVILLE, HUGH GAULTIER COGHILL, Capt., R.N.
TURLE, CHARLES EDWARD, Commander, R.N.
FARQUHARSON, JOHN PHELIPS, Lieut.-Commander, R.N.
GRIFFITHS, CYRIL VERITY, Surgeon Lieut.-Commander, R.N.

London Gazette, 12 Dec. 1918.—"Admiralty, 12 Dec. 1918.—Honours for Services in White Sea Operations, 1918.—Modyugski Island, at the sea end of the channels leading to Archangel, was captured on 1 Aug. 1918, after the batteries had been silenced by the Allied warships, and the town of Archangel was occupied on the 2nd Aug., the Bolshevik Forces being quickly and efficiently overcome and driven out of the vicinity. Following these operations, a River Expeditionary Force was organized with local craft, armed and manned by Allied crews, and this expedition succeeded, in co-operation with the military forces, in clearing the River Dwina and the River Vaga of hostile draft up to the time when Allied ships had to be withdrawn to avoid the ice, several of the principal enemy vessels being destroyed.
"The King has been graciously pleased to approve of the award of the following honours to the undermentioned Officers, in recognition of their services during these operations. To be appointed Companions of the Distinguished Service Order."
LYON, FRANCIS HOWARD, Engineer-Commander, R.N., H.M.S. Attentive. He was mainly responsible for the rapidity with which the shps and motor launches were armed, and the engines of the latter put into working order for the Dwina operations. His energy and tireless devotion to duty are deserving of the highest praise.
GREEN, SEBALD WALTER BLUETT, Lieut.-Commander, R.N., Commanding H.M.S. M 25. For the capable handling of his ship, untiring devotion to duty, cheerful and inspiring leadership of officers and men, and utter disregard of personal danger under heavy fire when in charge of the landing party at Tchamova during the Dwina operations.
RENDALL, HENRY EDWARD, Lieut.-Commander, R.N. As gunnery and control officer of H.M.S. Attentive he was largely responsible for the silencing of the battery on Modyugski Island, which disputed the Allied entry to Archangel, on the 1st Aug. 1918. He also landed in command of a naval detachment, and secured the railway to Bakaritsa against Bolshevik attack.
DOBSON, JOHN GREENLAW, M.B., Surgeon-Lieut., Royal Navy, H.M.S. M 25. Though wounded by the explosion of a shell, he carried out all operations that could be effected on the wounded, working continuously from 7 p.m. till 10 p.m., when he collapsed. Throughout this time Surgeon-Lieut. Dobson went about his work as if nothing had happened.

London Gazette, 19 Dec. 1918.—"War Office, 19 Dec. 1918.—Amendment.—The appointment to be an Officer of the Most Excellent Order of the British Empire of Major Stanley Thomas Grigg, M.C., West Yorkshire Regt., published in London Gazette dated 18 Nov. 1918, is cancelled, and the following substituted:—Awarded the Distinguished Service Order."
GRIGG, STANLEY THOMAS, M.C., Major, West Yorkshire Regt.

London Gazette, 1 Jan. 1919.—"War Office, 1 Jan. 1919. His Majesty the King has been graciously pleased to approve of the undermentioned rewards for distinguished service in connection with military operations in France and Flanders. Dated 1 Jan. 1919. Awarded a Bar to the Distinguished Service Order."
AKERMAN, WILLIAM PHILIP JOPP, D.S.O., M.C., Capt. (Acting Major), Royal Field Artillery, attached "A" Battery, 295th (North Midland) Brigade, Royal Field Artillery (Territorial Force).
(D.S.O. gazetted 1 Jan. 1918.)
BATCHELOR, VIVIAN ALLAN, D.S.O., Major (Acting Lieut.-Colonel), Royal Field Artillery.
(D.S.O. gazetted 17 Sept. 1917.)
BOWEN, WILLIAM ALLAN, D.S.O., Temporary Major (Acting Lieut.-Colonel) (Capt., Reserve of Officers), 10th Battn. Worcestershire Regt., Commanding 1/4th Battn. Shropshire Light Infantry, Territorial Force.
(D.S.O. gazetted 3 June, 1918.)
*CHIPP, WILKINS FITZWILLIAM, D.S.O., M.C., Lieut. (Acting Major), 1/1st Battn. Herefordshire Regt.
DAKEYNE, HENRY WOLRYCHE, D.S.O., Capt. (Temporary Lieut.-Colonel), Royal Warwickshire Regt., attached 8th Battn. North Staffordshire Regt.
(D.S.O. gazetted 1 Jan. 1917.)
*DENT, JOHN RALPH CONGREVE, D.S.O., M.C., Capt. (Acting Lieut.-Colonel), 1st Battn. Royal Inniskilling Fusiliers.
*HACKING, ALFRED, D.S.O., M.C., Lieut. (Acting Lieut.-Colonel), 1/8th Battn., attached 1/5th Battn., Nottinghamshire and Derbyshire Regt. (Territorial Force).
KANE, ROMNEY ROBERT GODRED, D.S.O., Capt. (Acting Lieut.-Colonel), 1st Battn. Royal Munster Fusiliers.
(D.S.O. gazetted 8 Nov. 1915.)
*LISTER, CECIL, D.S.O., M.C., Capt. (Acting Lieut.-Colonel), Northampton Regt., attached 6th Battn. South Staffordshire Regt. (Territorial Force).
*SMITH, WILFRID CABOURN, D.S.O., M.C., Lieut. (Acting Lieut.-Colonel), 6th Battn. King's Royal Rifle Corps, attached 17th Battn. Royal Fusiliers
SOLE, DENIS MAVISYN ANSLOW, D.S.O., Capt. and Brevet Major (Temporary Lieut.-Colonel), Border Regt., attached 10th Battn. Worcestershire Regt.
(D.S.O. gazetted 1 Jan. 1917.)

CANADIAN FORCE.
CONNOLLY, CHARLES EDWARD, D.S.O., Major, Lord Strathcona's Horse, Canadian Cavalry.
*TUXFORD, GEORGE STUART, C.B., C.M.G., D.S.O., Brigadier-General, Saskatchewan Regt., Commanding Canadian Infantry Brigade.
NOTE.—In the cases marked by an asterisk the announcements of awards of the Distinguished Service Order have not yet been published in the London Gazette. These awards will be published in due course.

Awarded the Distinguished Service Order:
ADAMS, ROBERT JACKSON, Major (Acting Lieut.-Colonel), Royal Horse and Royal Field Artillery, attached 331st (East Lancashire) Brigade, Royal Field Artillery (Territorial Force).

AGNEW, JAMES, Major (Acting Lieut.-Colonel), 1/5th Battn. Argyll and Sutherland Highlanders (Territorial Force).
ALLAN, ALEXANDER CLAUD, M.C., Capt. (Temporary Lieut.-Colonel), Cameron Highlanders.
ALLEN, ALBERT GEORGE, M.C., Temporary Capt., General List
ALLEN, REGINALD SEYMOUR, Major and Brevet Lieut.-Colonel (Temporary Lieut.-Colonel), Hampshire Regt.
ANGELL, JOHN, M.C., Capt. (Acting Lieut.-Colonel), Dorsetshire Regt. and Machine Gun Corps.
ANSTEY, EDGAR CARNEGIE, Major and Brevet Lieut.-Colonel (Temporary Lieut.-Colonel), Royal Artillery.
ASHCROFT, ALEC HUTCHINSON, Temporary Major, 7th Battn. South Staffordshire Regt.
BAGGALLAY, RICHARD ROMER CLAUDE, M.C., Capt. (Acting Lieut.-Colonel), 1st Battn. Irish Guards.
BAGNALL, CHARLES LANE, M.C., Capt. (Acting Major), 9th Battn. Durham Light Infantry (Territorial Force), attached 50th Division, Signal Company, Royal Engineers.
BALDWIN, JAMES YESCOMBE, Temporary Major, Army Cyclists' Corps.
BALSTON, GEORGE RICHARD, Major (Acting Lieut.-Colonel), Royal Field Artillery, attached 92nd Brigade, Royal Field Artillery (Territorial Force).
BARKLEY, JAMES, Capt. (Temporary Lieut.-Colonel), Royal Army Medical Corps (Territorial Force), attached 2/3rd (Home Counties) Field Ambulance, Royal Army Medical Corps (Territorial Force).
BARRINGTON, JOHN FREDERICK, Major (Acting Lieut.-Colonel), Royal Garrison Artillery, attached Headquarters, 71st Brigade, Royal Garrison Artillery.
BAYLEY, ARTHUR FREDERICK, Major (Acting Lieut.-Colonel), Royal Artillery, attached 307th (South Midland) Brigade, Royal Field Artillery (Territorial Force).
BENNEWITH, JAMES ARTHUR, Temporary Capt. (Acting Major), 8th Battn. Tank Corps.
BINGAY, HUBERT LYLE, Major (Acting Lieut.-Colonel), Royal Engineers.
BISSETT, FREDERIC WILLIAM LYON, M.C., Capt. and Brevet Major, Duke of Cornwall's Light Infantry.
BOARD, ARCHIE VYVYAN, M.C., Lieut. (Temporary Major), Essex Regt. (Special Reserve) and Machine Gun Corps.
BOLTON, HERBERT WILLIAM, Capt. (Temporary Lieut.-Colonel), Royal West Surrey Regt.
BRADLEY, EDWARD DE WINTON HERBERT, M.C., Capt. (Acting Major), 2nd Battn. Yorkshire Light Infantry
BRADLEY-WILLIAMS, WILLIAM PICTON, Capt. (Acting Lieut.-Colonel), 2nd Battn. Yorkshire Light Infantry, attached 5th Battn. Border Regt.
BRADSTOCK, GEORGE, M.C., Temporary Capt. (Acting Major), 407th Battery, 96th Brigade, Royal Field Artillery.
BRANCKER, HENRY RUSSELL, Major (Acting Lieut.-Colonel), 87th Brigade, Royal Garrison Artillery.
BUDDLE, GEOFFREY ARMSTRONG, M.C., Temporary Major, 86th Field Company, Royal Engineers.
BUNKER, SIDNEY WATERFIELD, M.C., Capt. (Acting Lieut.-Colonel), Royal Fusiliers (Special Reserve), employed Special Brigade, Royal Engineers.
BURDETT, JAMES CHARLES, M.C., Temporary Major (Acting Lieut.-Colonel), 6th Battn. Leicestershire Regt.
BURGESS, ROBERT, M.C., Capt. (Acting Lieut.-Colonel), Royal Army Medical Corps (Territorial Force), attached 24th (1/1st Wessex) Field Ambulance.
BUTLER, WILLIAM MAHONY, Major, King Edward's Horse and 12th Battn. Tank Corps.
CALLAM, ALEXANDER, M.B., Major (Acting Lieut.-Colonel), Royal Army Medical Corps (Territorial Force), attached 1/1st (East Lancashire) Field Ambulance.
CAMPBELL, JAMES OLPHERTS, M.C., Capt. (Acting Major), B/88th Brigade, Royal Field Artillery.
CARR, ALFRED EDWARD, M.C., Temporary Major, 1st Field Company, Tank Corps.
CARR, BERTRAM ABBOTT, Capt. (Acting Major), Royal Garrison Artillery (Territorial Force), attached 170th Siege Battery, Royal Garrison Artillery.
CARTER, CYRIL RODNEY, Capt. (Acting Lieut.-Colonel), 1st Battn. Royal Lancaster Regt.
CHALMER, FRANCIS GEORGE, M.C., Capt. and Brevet Major (Temporary Lieut.-Colonel), Royal Highlanders, attached 9th Battn. Machine Gun Corps.
CHELL, RANDOLPH ARTHUR, M.C., Temporary Capt., General List.
CHEVALLIER, PETER TEMPLE, M.C., Temporary Capt., General List.
CHURCH, JAMES ARCHIBALD, M.C., Temporary Capt. (Acting Major), 251st Tunnelling Company, Royal Engineers.
CLARK, CHARLES WILLOUGHBY, M.C., Temporary Capt. (Acting Major), Tank Corps.
CLARK, PERCY WILLIAM, M.C., Temporary Capt. (Acting Major), Royal Engineers.
CLARKSON, WILFRID BAIRSTOW, Temporary Lieut. (Acting Major), 141st Siege Battery, Royal Garrison Artillery.
CLENDINING, HAMILTON, Temporary Major, 10th Battn., attached 22nd Battn., Royal Irish Rifles.
CLIFFORD, ERIC CHARLES, M.C., Capt. (Temporary Major), Royal Field Artillery (Territorial Force), attached C/150th Battery, Royal Field Artillery.
CLOWES, HUGH MURCHISON, Capt. (Temporary Major), 14th Battn. London Regt.
COGAN, LEE DANBY BUXTON, Capt. (Acting Lieut.-Colonel), 88th Field Ambulance, Royal Army Medical Corps (Territorial Force).
CONGREVE, FRANCIS LANE, M.C., Major (Acting Lieut.-Colonel), Royal Field Artillery, Headquarters, 155th Artillery Brigade, Royal Field Artillery.
COOK, FREDERICK CHARLES, M.C., Temporary Capt. (Acting Major), 209th Field Company, Royal Engineers.
COOKE, JOHN CAMPBELL, M.C., Temporary Capt. (Temporary Major), General List.
COOMBS, ARTHUR GEORGE, Temporary Lieut. (Acting Major), 113th Siege Battery, Royal Garrison Artillery.

CORRIE, WILLIAM FRANCIS TAYLOR, Lieut.-Colonel, Royal Garrison Artillery, Headquarters, 69th Brigade.

COUSSMAKER, LANNOY JOHN, M.C., Major (Acting Lieut.-Colonel), Royal Engineers (Territorial Force).

COX, EDWARD HARVIE, M.B., Major (Acting Lieut.-Colonel), 2/3rd (East Lancashire) Field Ambulance, Royal Army Medical Corps (Territorial Force).

COWAN, IAN CAIRNS, M.C., Temporary Capt., General List.

CRANSTOUN, CHARLES JOSEPH EDMONSTOUNE, Major, 1/1st Lanark Yeomanry, attached 6th Battn. Gordon Highlanders (Territorial Force).

CRIPPS, FREDERICK WILLIAM BERESFORD, Major, Gloucestershire Hussars Yeomanry.

CROFT, DESMOND WARWICK, M.C., Temporary Major, South Wales Borderers, late 5th Battn.

CROOKENDEN, ARTHUR, Major and Brevet Lieut.-Colonel, Cheshire Regt.

DALY, DENIS, M.C. Major, Royal Garrison Artillery, attached 17th Brigade, Royal Field Artillery.

DANSEY, HENRY WILLIAM GIFFORD, Temporary Major, General List.

DAVIDSON, FRANCIS HENRY NORMAN, M.C., Capt. (Acting Major), Royal Field Artillery.

DELAP, JAMES ONSLOW KINGSMILL, Lieut. (Acting Major), Royal Garrison Artillery (Territorial Force), attached 303rd Siege Battery, Royal Garrison Artillery.

DEW, JOHN FINLAY, M.C., Capt. (Temporary Major), Scottish Rifles (Special Reserve).

DICKSON, VINCENT HAMILTON, Major, C/330th Brigade (East Lancashire), Royal Field Artillery (Territorial Force).

DIGGLE, WADHAM HEATHCOTE, M.C., Capt. (Temporary Lieut.-Colonel), Coldstream Guards (correction, for Coldstream Guards read Grenadier Guards [London Gazette, 22 March, 1919]).

DIGGLES, JOHN MARSH, M.C., Capt. (Temporary Major), 6th Battn. Cheshire Regt. (Territorial. Force).

DOBSON, FRANCIS GEORGE, M.B., Capt. (Acting Lieut.-Colonel), Royal Army Medical Corps (Territorial Force), attached 1/2nd (West Riding) Field Ambulance.

DRURY, ROBERT COOPER, Temporary Lieut.-Colonel, Royal Field Artillery, attached 50th (Northumbrian) D.A.C., Royal Field Artillery (Territorial Force).

DUGDALE, ARTHUR, C.M.G., Lieut.-Colonel, Oxford Hussars Yeomanry.

DUGUID-McCOMBIE, WILLIAM McCOMBIE, Major (Acting Lieut.-Colonel), 2nd Dragoons.

DUKE, JESSE PEVENSEY, M.C., Capt. and Brevet Major, Royal Warwickshire Regt.

DUN, THOMAS INGRAM, M.C., M.B., Capt. (Acting Major), Royal Army Medical Corps.

DUNCAN, WILLIAM EDMONSTONE, M.C., Capt. and Brevet Major (Acting Major), Royal Field Artillery.

EAMES, CHARLES WILLIAM, M.D., Capt. (Temporary Lieut.-Colonel), Royal Army Medical Corps (Territorial Force), attached 2/2nd (West Riding) Field Ambulance.

EDMUNDS, CLIVE THORNLEY, Major (Acting Lieut.-Colonel), 57th Field Ambulance, Royal Army Medical Corps.

EDWARDS, CYRIL ERNEST, M.C., Temporary Major, 26th Battn. Royal Fusiliers.

ELDRIDGE, WILLIAM JOHN, M.C., Lieut. (Acting Capt.), 90th Siege Battery, Royal Garrison Artillery.

EVANS, JOHN, Lieut.-Colonel, 1/2nd Battn. Monmouthshire Regt.

EVERARD, CHARLES JULIUS, Major, 60th Siege Battery, Royal Garrison Artillery.

FAIRBANK, HENRY NEVILL, M.C., Major, A/174th Brigade, Royal Field Artillery.

FIELDING, ARTHUR EDWARD BRUCE, Temporary Major, 63rd Field Company, Royal Engineers.

FINN, EDWIN, Temporary Major, 21st Battn. West Yorkshire Regt.

FORBES, JOHN LACHLAN, M.C., Major, 16th Siege Battery, Royal Garrison Artillery.

FORSYTH, WILLIAM HENRY, M.B., Major (Acting Lieut.-Colonel), 38th Field Ambulance, Royal Army Medical Corps.

GARTLAN, GERALD IAN, M.C., Capt. and Brevet Major, Royal Irish Rifles.

GASCOIGNE, LIONEL, Major, B/170th Brigade, Royal Field Artillery.

GENT, GERARD EDWARD JAMES, M.C., Capt. (Acting Major), 3rd Battn. Duke of Cornwall's Light Infantry, attached 1st Battn.

GRANT, EWEN, Major (Temporary Lieut.-Colonel), Lovat's Scouts Yeomanry.

GRAY, CHARLES LLOYD RASHLEIGH, Lieut.-Colonel, 63rd Brigade, Royal Garrison Artillery.

GRAY, WILLIAM EDMUND, M.C., Capt. (Acting Lieut.-Colonel), Rifle Brigade and Machine Gun Corps.

GREGORY, MANCHA, M.C., Major, Royal Field Artillery.

GRIFFIN, CYRIL JAMES ANTHONY, M.B., Capt. (Acting Lieut.-Colonel), Royal Army Medical Corps (Special Reserve), attached 5th Cavalry Field Ambulance.

GÜTERBOCK, PAUL GOTTLIEB JULIUS, M.C., Capt., 4th Battn. Gloucestershire Regt. (Territorial Force).

HARMAN, ARTHUR LESLIE, M.C., Capt. (Acting Major), " B " Battery, 110th Brigade, Royal Field Artillery.

HARTLEY, JOHN CABOURN, Temporary Major (Acting Lieut.-Colonel), 4th Battn. Royal Fusiliers.

HATTERSLEY-SMITH, WILFRED PERCY ASHBY, Major, 288th Siege Battery, Royal Garrison Artillery.

HAWKINS, HUGH DOUGLAS, Lieut. (Acting Major), Royal Garrison Artillery (Special Reserve), attached 431st Siege Battery.

HEALING, NORMAN CANNING, M.C., Major, Royal Garrison Artillery.

HELM, CYRIL, M.C., Capt. (Acting Lieut.-Colonel), 42nd Field Ambulance, Royal Army Medical Corps.

HENDERSON, NEVILLE GEORGE BOILEAU, Major, Royal Highlanders.

HERMON, JOHN VICTOR, Capt., Cheshire Yeomanry, attached 6th Dragoon Guards.

HEYWOOD-LONSDALE, HENRY HEYWOOD, Lieut.-Colonel, Shropshire Yeomanry.

HEYWOOD-LONSDALE, JOHN PEMBERTON HEYWOOD, Major, Shropshire Yeomanry, attached 10th Battn Shropshire Light Infantry.

HICKS, WILLIAM EDWARD, M.C., Lieut. (Acting Major), 152nd Heavy Battery, Royal Garrison Artillery.

HICKSON, LIONEL HENRY, Major (Acting Lieut.-Colonel), Royal West Kent Regt.

HILL, ROWLEY RICHARD, Major (Acting Lieut.-Colonel), 58th Artillery Brigade, Royal Garrison Artillery.

HITCHINS, EDWARD NORMAN FORTESCUE, M.C., Capt. and Brevet Major, West Riding Regt., attached 41st Division, Signal Company, Royal Engineers.

HOBART, JAMES WILFRED LANG STANLEY, M.C., Capt. and Brevet Major, North Staffordshire Regt.

HOGGART, JOHN WILLIAM, M.C., Lieut. (Acting Major), C/50th Brigade, Royal Field Artillery.

HOLLAND, HUGH MORITZ, Temporary Major, Royal Garrison Artillery, attached Headquarters, III. Corps.

HOLMPATRICK, LORD HANS WELLESLEY, M.C., Capt., 16th Lancers (Special Reserve).

HOMER, ERNEST ERIC FERRIS, M.C., Temporary Major (Acting Lieut.-Colonel), Royal Engineers.

HONE, PERCY FREDERICK, M.C., Temporary Capt. (Acting Lieut.-Colonel), General List, attached 21st Battn. Middlesex Regt.

HOUSE, MAURICE HENRY NEVILLE, Major, " C " Battery, 56th Brigade, Royal Field Artillery (Territorial Force).

HOWES, SIDNEY, M.C., Capt. (Temporary Major), 21st Lancers.

HUBBACK, ARTHUR BENNISON, C.M.G., Lieut.-Colonel (Temporary Brigadier-General), 20th Battn. London Regt.

HUNNYBUN, KENNETH, Major, Army Cyclists' Corps (Territorial Force), attached 7th Battn. Somersetshire Light Infantry.

INGLEBY, CECIL JORDAN, Major, 4th Battn. East Yorkshire Regt. (Territorial Force).

IRWIN, JOSEPH BOYD, M.C., Temporary Lieut. (Acting Capt.), 1st Battn. Royal Lancaster Regt., attached 12th Trench Mortar Battery.

JACKSON, REGINALD NEVILLE, Capt., General List, attached British Mission, French General Headquarters.

JARVIS, FREDERICK WILLIAM, Lieut.-Colonel, Suffolk Yeomanry.

JOHNSTON, GEORGE FRANCIS, M.C., Temporary Capt. (Acting Major), 180th Tunnelling Company, Royal Engineers.

KAY, D'ARCY HEMSWORTH, Temporary Lieut.-Colonel, 21st Battn. Machine Gun Corps.

KEIR, DAVID ROBERT, Capt. (Acting Major), 7th Battn. Royal Highlanders (Territorial Force).

KELSALL, HARRY JOSEPH, Lieut.-Colonel, Royal Garrison Artillery, 12th Brigade.

KEMBLE, HENRY MAULE, Major, 45th Siege Battery, Royal Garrison Artillery.

KINDERSLEY, JAMES BENJAMIN, M.C., Lieut. (Acting Major), A/63rd Brigade, Royal Field Artillery.

KING, WALTER DIARMID VERE OLDHAM, Temporary Lieut.-Colonel, 17th Battn. Northumberland Fusiliers.

KNIGHT, ALEXANDER EDMOND, M.C., M.B., Temporary Capt. (Acting Major), Royal Army Medical Corps.

KNIGHT, REGINALD COLDHAM, M.C., Temporary Lieut. (Temporary Capt.), 5th Brigade Headquarters, Tank Corps.

LAING, NEVILLE OGILVIE, Capt. (Acting Lieut.-Colonel), 4th Hussars.

LAMOND, JAMES, M.C., Lieut. (Acting Lieut.-Colonel), 2nd Battn. Royal Scots, attached 1/5th Battn. South Staffordshire Regt. (Territorial Force).

LANDER, CHARLES LLEWELLYN, M.C., M.B., Capt. (Acting Lieut.-Colonel), Royal Army Medical Corps (Territorial Force), attached 2/3rd (S.M.) Field Ambulance, Royal Army Medical Corps (Territorial Force).

LEAHY, THOMAS JOSEPH, M.C., Capt. and Brevet Major, Royal Dublin Fusiliers.

LE PELLEY, EDWARD CAREY, Lieut.-Colonel, Royal Garrison Artillery.

LESLIE, JOHN, M.C., Lieut. (Acting Major), 12th Lancers, attached 6th Battn. Tank Corps.

LIDDELL, HUGH, M.C., Capt. (Acting Lieut.-Colonel), 1/7th Battn. Northumberland Fusiliers (Territorial Force).

LING, ROBERT WALTON, M.C., Major, Royal Horse and Royal Field Artillery.

LOCH, GRANVILLE GEORGE, C.M.G., Major and Brevet Lieut.-Colonel (Temporary Brigadier-General), Royal Scots (correction, for Brevet Lieut.-Colonel read Brevet Colonel [London Gazette, 22 March, 1919]).

LOCKHART, JOHN FLEMING KING, Major, Royal Field Artillery, attached 312th (West Riding) Brigade, Royal Field Artillery (Territorial Force).

McALLUM, STUART GERALD, M.D., Major (Acting Lieut.-Colonel), Royal Army Medical Corps (Special Reserve), attached 140th Field Ambulance.

McCULLAGH, HERBERT ROCHFORT, Capt. (Temporary Major, Acting Lieut.-Colonel), 2nd Battn. Durham Light Infantry, attached 19th Battn.

MACDOUGALL, ALASTAIR IAN, M.C., Capt. and Brevet Major, 5th Lancers.

McIVER, KENNETH IAN, M.C., Capt. (Acting Major), 135th Siege Battery, Royal Garrison Artillery.

MACKAY, DANIEL, M.C., Temporary Capt. (Acting Major), C/165th Brigade, Royal Field Artillery.

MACKENZIE, LIONEL DE AMAREL, M.C., Capt. and Brevet Major, Gordon Highlanders.

MACKENZIE, ROBERT HARMAN, M.C., Major (Acting Lieut.-Colonel), Royal Engineers (Territorial Force).

McLENNAN, FARQUHAR, M.B., Lieut.-Colonel (Temporary Colonel), Royal Army Medical Corps.

MACMILLAN, JOHN, M.C., M.B., Capt. (Acting Lieut.-Colonel), Royal Army Medical Corps, attached 5th (London) Field Ambulance, Royal Army Medical Corps (Territorial Force).

MACWATT, STUART LOGAN, M.C., Capt. (Acting Major), 163rd Siege Battery, Royal Garrison Artillery.

The Distinguished Service Order

MARCH, BERNARD OSWALD, M.C., Capt. (Acting Major), Royal Field Artillery (Special Reserve), attached 158th Artillery Brigade.
MARSTON, GORDON SPENCER, M.C., Capt. (Acting Major), Royal Engineers (Special Reserve), attached 234th Field Company, Royal Engineers.
MARSTON, JEFFERY EARDLEY, M.C., Major, Royal Artillery.
MARTIN, CHARLES ROSWELL, Temporary Lieut.-Colonel, 20th (Service) Battn. King's Royal Rifle Corps (Pioneers).
MARTIN, JAMES GODFREY, M.C., Temporary Major, 8th Battn. North Staffordshire Regt.
MEARES, HERBERT MARSH SIMS, M.C., Temporary Capt. (Acting Major), 55th Field Company, Royal Engineers.
MELLONIE, LESLIE WOODFIELD, M.C., Temporary Capt. (Acting Major), 116th Heavy Battery, Royal Garrison Artillery.
MEREDITH, WILLIAM RICE, Major, Royal Inniskilling Fusiliers.
MERRICK, THOMAS, M.C., Lieut. (Acting Major), A/87th Brigade, Royal Field Artillery.
MICKLEM, CHARLES, Temporary Major, Royal Marine Artillery, No. 2 Royal Marine Artillery Howitzer.
MILLER, GEORGE RALPH, Major (Acting Lieut.-Colonel), 123rd Brigade, Royal Field Artillery.
MITCHELL, CHRISTOPHER CARROLL, M.C., Capt. (Acting Major), B/47th Brigade, Royal Field Artillery.
MOKE NORRIE, CHARLES WILLOUGHBY, M.C., Capt., 11th Hussars.
MONIER-WILLIAMS, CRAWFORD VICTOR, M.C., Capt. and Brevet Major (Acting Lieut.-Colonel), York and Lancaster Regt., Seconded Royal Engineers' Signal Service.
MURRAY, ARCHIBALD DIGBY, Major (Acting Lieut.-Colonel), Royal Garrison Artillery.
MYBURGH, PHILIP STAFFORD, M.C., Capt. (Acting Major), "A" Battery, 152nd Brigade, Royal Field Artillery.
NANSON, GEOFFREY GAY, M.C., Temporary Capt. (Acting Major), 3rd Siege Battery, Royal Garrison Artillery.
NUGEE, GEORGE TRAVERS, M.C., Capt. (Acting Major), 88th Battery, 14th Brigade, Royal Field Artillery.
ORMROD, MAURICE SARSFIELD, Capt. (Temporary Major), 11th Battn. King's Royal Rifle Corps.
PAGE, CHARLES MAX, M.B., F.R.C.S., Capt. (Acting Lieut.-Colonel), Royal Army Medical Corps (Special Reserve), attached 90th Field Ambulance.
PATON, MONTGOMERY PATERSON, M.C., M.B., Temporary Capt. (Acting Major), Royal Army Medical Corps.
PAUL, JOHN WILLIAM BALFOUR, Temporary Major (Temporary Lieut.-Colonel), 18th Group Headquarters, Labour Corps.
PEAL, WILFRID EVELYN, Lieut.-Colonel, Royal Field Artillery (Territorial Force), attached 123rd Brigade, Royal Field Artillery.
PERRY, BERTRAM HARRIS HILL, M.C., Capt. (Acting Lieut.-Colonel), Royal Scots, attached 8th Battn. Royal Lancaster Regt.
PHILLIPS, ARTHUR EDWARD, Temporary Major, 7th (Service) Battn. Royal West Kent Regt.
PHILLIPS, FRANK, M.C., Temporary Capt. (Temporary Major), General List.
PHILLIPS, WILLIAM ERIC, M.C., Capt. (Acting Lieut.-Colonel), Leinster Regt., attached 2/6th Battn. Royal Warwickshire Regt. (Territorial Force).
PHIPPS CONSTANTINE JAMES, M.C., Lieut. (Acting Major), Liverpool Regt., attached Army Signalling Service.
PIPER, STEPHEN HARVEY, Second Lieut. (Temporary Major), 9th Battn. Nottinghamshire and Derbyshire Regt.
POLLOCK, WILLIAM, Temporary Major, 465th Battery, 65th Brigade, Royal Field Artillery.
PRESTON, SIR EDWARD HULTON, Bart., M.C., Capt. and Brevet Major, Royal Sussex Regt.
REEVE, JOHN TALBOT WENTWORTH, Capt. (Temporary Lieut.-Colonel), Rifle Brigade and Machine Gun Corps.
REID-KELLETT, ALAN, M.C., Temporary Major, South Wales Borderers, attached 6th Battn.
RIDDICK, JOHN GALLOWAY, Major (Acting Lieut.-Colonel), Royal Engineers (Territorial Force).
ROBERTSON, JAMES ROBERT, Capt. (Acting Lieut.-Colonel), Bedfordshire Regt.
ROBINSON, THOMAS TREVOR HULL, M.B., Major (Acting Lieut.-Colonel), Royal Army Medical Corps, No. 5 Field Ambulance
ROBSON, JOHN COWLEY, Major, Royal Field Artillery (Territorial Force), attached "D" Battery, 52nd Artillery Brigade.
ROGERS, VIVIAN BARRY, M.C., Temporary Capt., General List.
RONEY-DOUGAL, ALISTAIR RICHARD, M.C., Major, Royal Artillery.
ROTHSCHILD, GEORGE FRANCIS, M.C., Temporary Major, 12th Battn. Royal Sussex Regt., attached 2/10th Battn. London Regt. (correction, for 12th Battalion R.S.R, read 13th Battalion R.S.R. [London Gazette, 22 March, 1919]).
ROWE, RICHARD HERBERT, M.C., Major, Royal Garrison Artillery.
ROWLAND, REGINALD HERBERT, Temporary Major, 8th (Service) Battn. Royal West Surrey Regt.
SAYER, HUMPHREY, M.C., Capt., Sussex Yeomanry.
SCAIFE, ANGUS JAMES PERCY, Major, Royal Garrison Artillery (Territorial Force), 187th Siege Battery.
SCOTT, ALEXANDER, M.C., Capt., 1/7th Battn. Argyll and Sutherland Highlanders (Territorial Force).
SEAGRIM, ALBERT HAROLD, Major (Temporary Lieut.-Colonel), Leinster Regt., attached 19th Battn. Highland Light Infantry.
SHAW, RAYMOND MORTON, M.C., Major, Royal Field Artillery (Territorial Force), A/246th (West Riding) Brigade.
SMART, GEORGE EDWARD, Major, Royal Garrison Artillery, 351st Siege Battery.
SPEEDING, JAMES HABERSHAM, Major, Royal Garrison Artillery, attached 283rd Siege Battery.
SPENCER-SMITH, MICHAEL, M.C., Temporary Capt., General List, attached Canadian Corps Horse Artillery.
SPENDER, WILFRID BLISS, M.C., Major and Brevet Lieut.-Colonel (Temporary Lieut.-Colonel), Royal Garrison Artillery.

STEPHEN, JOHN HECTOR, Major (Acting Lieut.-Colonel), 89th (Highland) 1/1st Field Ambulance, Royal Army Medical Corps (Territorial Force).
STEPHENSON-FETHERSTONHAUGH, ALEXANDER JOHN, M.C., Capt. (Temporary Major), Worcestershire Regt. (Special Reserve).
STIRLING-COOKSON, CHARLES SELBY, M.C., Capt., King's Own Scottish Borderers.
STOCKINGS, GEORGE MOORE, Temporary Major (Acting Lieut.-Colonel), 12th Battn. Yorkshire Light Infantry.
STUDD, MALDEN AUGUSTUS, M.C., Major, B/156th Brigade, Royal Field Artillery.
SUTTON, WILLIAM MOXHAY, M.C., Capt. and Brevet Major (Temporary Lieut.-Colonel), Somersetshire Light Infantry.
SUTTON-NELTHORPE, OLIVER, M.C., Capt. and Brevet Major (Temporary Lieut.-Colonel), Rifle Brigade.
SVENSSON, ROBERT, M.C., M.B., Temporary Capt. (Acting Lieut.-Colonel), Royal Army Medical Corps, 102nd Field Ambulance.
TATE, ARTHUR WIGNALL, Capt. (Temporary Major) (Acting Lieut.-Colonel), Royal Highlanders (Special Reserve), attached 41st Battn. Machine Gun Corps.
TELFER-SMOLLETT, ALEXANDER PATRICK DRUMMOND, M.C., Capt. and Brevet Major, Highland Light Infantry.
THIN, EDWARD GORDON, Lieut.-Colonel, 10th Battn. Liverpool Regt. (Territorial Force).
THOMAS, ROBERT HENRY, Major (Temporary Lieut.-Colonel), Royal Engineers.
THOMAS, STANLEY FORD, Temporary Major (Acting Lieut.-Colonel), 6th Battn. Shropshire Light Infantry.
THOMSON, ALAN CHICHESTER, Temporary Capt. (Acting Lieut.-Colonel), Royal Engineers.
THOMSON, GEORGE, Temporary Major, 12th Battn. Royal Irish Rifles.
TROLLOPE, HUGH CHARLES NAPIER, M.C., Capt., 2nd Battn. Suffolk Regt.
VAUGHAN, ARTHUR OWEN, Major (Temporary Lieut.-Colonel), Labour Corps.
WALLACE, FREDERIC CAMPBELL, Lieut. (Temporary Capt.), Royal Irish Rifles (Special Reserve).
WAKEFIELD, NEVILLE, Temporary Lieut. (Acting Major), Royal Field Artillery, attached "G" A.-A. Battery.
WARBURTON, ALSAGER, M.C., Lieut. (Temporary Capt.), 1/6th Battn. Liverpool Regt. (Territorial Force).
WELSH, WILLIAM MILES MOSS O'DONNELL, M.C., Major, C/106th Brigade, Royal Field Artillery.
WILSON, HAROLD GRAHAM, Major (Acting Lieut.-Colonel), 1/5th Battn. Lincolnshire Regt. (Territorial Force).
WILSON-FITZGERALD, FRANCIS WILLIAM, M.C., Capt., 1st Royal Dragoons.
WINTER, WILFRID ORMONDE, Capt. (Acting Major), No. 5 Railway Surveying and Reconnoitring Section, Royal Engineers.
WOODS, ARTHUR GRAHAM, M.C., Temporary Capt., 2nd Brigade, Tank Corps.
YORKE, PHILIP GERALD, Major, Royal Artillery.
YOUNG, JAMES, M.B., Capt. (Acting Lieut.-Colonel), 1/3rd (Lowland) Field Ambulance, Royal Army Medical Corps (Territorial Force).

CANADIAN FORCE.

ARNOLD, FLORENT GEORGES, Major, Canadian Army Service Corps.
BAILEY, JOHN BESWICK, Major, 54th Battn. Canadian Infantry.
BELL-IRVING, RODERICK OGLE, M.C., Major, 16th Battn. Canadian Infantry.
BICK, ARTHUR HARDIE, Major, Canadian Field Artillery.
BROWNE, BEVERLY W., M.C., Major, 16th Battn. Canadian Infantry.
BURNS, WILLIAM JAMES GORDON, Major, 32nd Battery, 8th Brigade, Canadian Field Artillery.
BURRITT, ROYAL, Colonel, Manitoba Regt.
CORRIGALL, DAVID JAMES, M.C., Major, 1st Central Ontario Regt.
CURRIE, SELKIRK GEORGE, M.C., Capt. (Acting Major), Princess Patricia's Canadian Light Infantry.
DE BALINHARD, JOHN CARNEGY, Major, Saskatchewan Regt.
DOBBIE, WALLACE HUGH, Major, 1st Siege Battery, Canadian Garrison Artillery.
DODDS, WILLIAM OKELL HOLDEN, C.M.G., Brigadier-General, Canadian Field Artillery.
DONALD, ALEXANDER STUART, Major, 20th Battery, 5th Brigade, Canadian Field Artillery.
DUNCANSON, ANDREW EASTMAN, Major, 123rd Battn. Canadian Infantry.
EARNSHAW, PHILIP, M.C., Major, 1st Canadian Divisional Signal Company, Canadian Engineers.
FLEXMAN, ERNEST, Major, D/22nd Battery, 6th Brigade, Canadian Field Artillery.
FOULKES, JOHN FORTESCUE, Major, Canadian General List.
FRASER, DANIEL WILLIAM, Major, 6th Battn. Canadian Railway Troops.
GARNER, ALBERT COLEMAN, Lieut.-Colonel, 12th Battn. Canadian Railway Troops.
GREENE, ELLIOT ANSON, Major, 61st Battery, 14th Brigade, Canadian Field Artillery.
HARKNESS, ROBERT DICKSON, M.C., Major, 1st, Mounted Machine Gun Brigade, Machine Gun Corps.
HENNESSY, PATRICK, M.C., Major, Canadian Army Service Corps.
HIBBERT, ARTHUR, M.C., Major, 3rd Canadian Tunnelling Company, Canadian Engineers.
HOULISTON, JOHN, Lieut.-Colonel, Canadian Engineers.
MACAULAY, NORMAN HOLLIDAY, Major, Canadian Field Artillery.
McCONNELL, WALTER ADAM, Lieut.-Colonel, 10th Battn. Canadian Railway Troops.
McEWAN, CUTHBERT FINNIE, Major, Canadian Light Horse.
MOORHOUSE, WALTER NORWOOD, Lieut.-Colonel, 3rd Battn. Canadian Machine Gun Corps.

McINTOSH, JOHN ALEXANDER, Major, 18th Battn. Canadian Infantry.
McSLOY, JAMES IVAN, Major, 4th Brigade, Canadian Field Artillery.
MAGEE, ALLAN ANGUS, Temporary Lieut.-Colonel, Quebec Regt.
MEURLING, HARRY FREDERICK VICTOR, M.C., Major (Acting Lieut.-Colonel), 2nd Mounted Machine Gun Brigade, Canadian Machine Gun Corps.
MORRIS, ERNEST RUSSELL, Major, 1st Battn. Canadian Machine Gun Corps.
MUNRO, WILLIAM AIRD, Lieut.-Colonel, 11th Battn. Canadian Railway Troops.
OLIVER, EDWARD ALBERT, Quartermaster and Major, 38th Battn. Canadian Infantry.
OUTERBRIDGE, LEONARD CECIL, Major, 75th Battn. Canadian Infantry.
PHELAN, FREDERICK ROSS, M.C., Major, 87th Battn. Canadian Infantry.
ROBERTSON, FRANCIS ARTHUR, Major, 12th Siege Battery, Canadian Garrison Artillery.
SAUNDERS, ROBERT PORTEOUS, M.C., Major, 19th Battn. Canadian Infantry.
STUART, KENNETH, M.C., Major, 7th Battn. Canadian Engineers.
SWAN, WILLIAM GEORGE, Temporary Major, 2nd Battn. Canadian Railway Troops.
THOMPSON, EDWARD VIVIAN, Major, 33rd Battery, 9th Brigade, Canadian Field Artillery.
VIPOND, CHARLES WALTER, Temporary Lieut.-Colonel, 9th Field Ambulance, Canadian Army Medical Corps.
WEDD, WILLIAM BASIL, M.C., Major, 1st Central Ontario Regt.
WILLIS-O'CONNOR, HENRY, Major, East Ontario Regt.
WOOD, JAMES HENRY, Major (Acting Lieut.-Colonel), 2nd Field Ambulance, Canadian Army Medical Corps.
WEIR, JAMES GORDON, M.C., Lieut.-Colonel, 2nd Battn. Canadian Machine Gun Corps.

AUSTRALIAN FORCE.

ALDERMAN, WALTER WILLIAM, C.M.G., Lieut.-Colonel, Australian Imperial Force, attached 1st Battn. Auckland Regt., New Zealand Force (correction, for Australian Imperial Force read Australian Commonwealth Forces [London Gazette, 22 March, 1919]).
ANDERSON, JAMES SINCLAIR STANDISH, M.C., Major, 58th Battn., seconded 3rd Australian Infantry Brigade Headquarters (correction, for 58th Battalion read 56th Battalion).
BERRYMAN, FRANK HERTON, Major, 5th Artillery Brigade, Australian Field Artillery.
BUNDOCK, HARRY CHARLES, Major, 36th Australian H.A.B.
CAMERON, HENRY GERVAIS LOVETT, M.C., Major, 56th Battn. Australian Imperial Force.
CAMPBELL, ERIC, Major, 12th Artillery Brigade, Australian Field Artillery.
CARR, REGINALD BLAKENEY, Major, 13th Field Company, Australian Engineers.
CHAMBERS, ROY WILLIAM, Lieut.-Colonel, 11th Field Ambulance, Australian Army Medical Corps.
CLOWES, CYRIL ALBERT, M.C., Major, Australian Field Artillery.
CONNELL, HUGH JOHN, M.C., Major, 35th Battn. Australian Imperial Force.
CROWTHER, WILLIAM EDWARD LODEWYK HAMILTON, Lieut.-Colonel, 5th Field Ambulance, Australian Army Medical Corps.
DIBDIN, EDWARD JOHN, Major, 42nd Battn. Australian Imperial Force.
FARRELL, JOHN, Lieut.-Colonel, 43rd Battn. Australian Imperial Force.
HUTCHIN, ARTHUR WILLIAM, Major, General List.
IRWIN, JOHN MORPHETT, Major, 7th Brigade, Australian Field Artillery.
LEE, JOSEPH EDWARD, M.C., Major, 45th Battn. Australian Imperial Force.
LIND, EDMUND FRANK, Major (Temporary Lieut.-Colonel), 2nd Field Ambulance, Australian Army Medical Corps.
LISTER, EYRL GEORGE, Major, 13th Brigade, Australian Field Artillery.
LITTLE, ROBERT ARTHUR, Major, 1st Brigade, Australian Field Artillery.
MACARTNEY, GEORGE WILLIAM, Lieut.-Colonel, 10th Field Ambulance, Australian Army Medical Corps.
McCALL, JOHN JAMES LAWTON, Major, 20th Battn. Australian Imperial Force.
MACCALLUM, WALTER PATON, M.C., Major, 20th Battn. Australian Imperial Force.
McKILLOP, ARCHIBALD, Major, 1st Field Ambulance, Australian Army Medical Corps
MIDDLETON, SYDNEY ALBERT, Major, 19th Battn. Australian Imperial Force.
MILFORD, EDWARD JAMES, Major, 4th Brigade, Australian Field Artillery.
MORLET, CLAUDE, Major, 13th Field Ambulance, Australian Army Medical Corps.
MORTON, WILLIAM ALEXANDER, Major, Australian Army Medical Corps, attached 3rd Brigade, Australian Field Artillery.
MURDOCH, THOMAS, Lieut.-Colonel, 1st Pioneer Battn. Australian Imperial Force.
PAGE HAROLD HILLIS, M.C., Major, 25th Battn. Australian Imperial Force.
PAIN, JOHN HENRY FRANCIS, M.C., Major, 2nd Battn. Australian Imperial Force.
PARKER, HUBERT STANLEY WYBORN, Major, 6th Artillery Brigade, Australian Field Artillery.
REID, ROBERT STEWART, Major, 5th Field Company, Australian Engineers.
SAMPSON, BURFORD, Major, 15th Battn. Australian Imperial Force.
SANDAY, WILLIAM HENRY, M.C., Lieut.-Colonel, 3rd Pioneer Battn. Australian Imperial Force.
SANDERSON, ALEXANDER, M.C., Major, 3rd Tunnelling Company, Australian Engineers.
SAVAGE, VINCENT WELLESLEY, Major, 3rd Field Ambulance, Australian Army Medical Corps.
SAWERS, WILLIAM CAMPBELL, Major, 14th Field Ambulance, Australian Army Medical Corps.
SLANEY, THOMAS BROWNE, Major, 8th Brigade, Australian Field Artillery.
STEVENSON, GEORGE INGRAM, C.M.G., Lieut.-Colonel, Australian Field Artillery.
STREET, FREDERICK, Major (Temporary Lieut.-Colonel), 30th Battn. Australian Imperial Force.
THORNTHWAITE, FRANCIS, M.C., Major, 5th D.A.C., Australian Field Artillery.
TOVELL, RAYMOND WALTER, Major, 4th Pioneer Battn. Australian Imperial Force.
WATSON, CHARLES VINCENT Lieut.-Colonel, 58th Battn. Australian Imperial Force.
WATSON, STANLEY HOLM, M.C., Major, 2nd Artillery Divisional, Signal Company, Australian Engineers.
WISDOM, FRANK ALAN, M.C., Capt., 30th Battn. Australian Imperial Force.

NEW ZEALAND FORCE.

CRAIG, GEORGE, Lieut.-Colonel, No. 1 New Zealand Field Ambulance, New Zealand Medical Corps.
FALCONER, ALEXANDER SMITH, M.C., Capt., Otago Regt.
JENNINGS, WILLIAM IVAN KIRKE, Major, Machine Gun Corps.
MILLIGAN, ROBERT GRACIE, Major, 15th Battery, 1st Brigade, New Zealand Field Artillery.
SHEPHERD, NORMAN FRANCIS, Lieut.-Colonel, New Zealand Rifle Brigade.
SOMMERVILLE, CLIVE, Major, 12th Battery, 3rd Brigade, New Zealand Field Artillery.
WILSON, NEWMAN ROBERT, M.C., Major, 2nd Battn. Canterbury Regt.
WILSON, ROBERT ADAMS, Major, 6th Battn. 2nd Artillery Brigade, New Zealand Field Artillery (attached from Royal Garrison Artillery).

SOUTH AFRICAN FORCE.

HANDS, PHILIP ALBERT MYBURGH, M.C., Temporary Capt. (Acting Major), South African Horse Artillery, attached 162nd Siege Battery, Royal Garrison Artillery.
JENKINS, HERBERT HAROLD, Major (Temporary Lieut.-Colonel), 1st South African Infantry.
MAASDORP, LIONEL HERBERT, Temporary Major, 75th Siege Battery, South African Horse Artillery.

London Gazette, 1 Jan. 1919.—" War Office, 1 Jan. 1919. His Majesty the King has been graciously pleased to approve of the undermentioned rewards for distinguished service in connection with military operations in Egypt. Dated 1 Jan. 1919. Awarded a Bar to the Distinguished Service Order."

MOIR, HOWARD LOWNDES, D.S.O., Major (Acting Lieut.-Colonel), 1/7th Battn. Cheshire Regt. (Territorial Force).
(D.S.O. gazetted 7 Nov. 1918.)

Awarded the Distinguished Service Order:

ALEXANDER, JOHN HOWARD, M.C., Temporary Capt. (Temporary Major), Royal Engineers.
AUSTEN, ERNEST EDWARD, Major, 28th (City of London) Battn. London Regt., attached Royal Army Medical Corps.
AVERY, LEONARD AVERY, Major, Royal Army Medical Corps (Territorial Force), attached 1/1st Royal Buckinghamshire Hussars, Yeomanry.
BAGNALL, HAROLD GORDON, Major, Royal Garrison Artillery.
BEEMAN, STANLEY WELCH, Major, Liverpool Regt., attached 2/5th Battn. Hampshire Regt.
BENSLY, WILLIAM JAMES, Temporary Major, 1st Battn. British West India Regt.
BROUGHTON, LEIGH HARLEY DELVES, Major (Temporary Lieut.-Colonel), Royal Field Artillery (Reserve of Officers).
CASSELS, GILBERT ROBERT, Lieut.-Colonel, 1st Battn. 123rd Outram's Rifles, Indian Army.
COCHRANE, THOMAS GEORGE FREDERICK, Capt. (Acting Major), Royal Highlanders (Special Reserve), attached 2nd Battn.
CRADDOCK, WALTER MERRY, M.C., Capt. (Acting Major), 2/20th (City of London) Battn. London Regt., attached 2/19th Battn.
DAVY, JOHN EVELYN, Major, Royal Field Artillery (Territorial Force).
DOWNES, JOHN WILLIAM, M.C., Lieut. (Acting Lieut.-Colonel), Shropshire Yeomanry, attached 1/4th Battn. Welsh Regt.
DUNDAS, WALTER LESLIE, Major (Acting Lieut.-Colonel), 4th Battn. 11th Gurkha Rifles, Indian Army (late 2/3rd Gurkha Rifles).
EASTMEAD, CHARLES SIDNEY, Lieut.-Colonel, 2nd Battn. 3rd Gurkha Rifles, Indian Army.
ELLIOTT, NEWLYN MASON, Capt. (Acting Major), Royal Horse Artillery (Territorial Force), attached " B " Battery, Honourable Artillery Company.
EVANS, JOHN, M.D., Major (Acting Lieut.-Colonel), Royal Army Medical Corps (Territorial Force).
FRASER-MACKENZIE, EVELYN ROBERT LEOPOLD, M.C., Capt. (Acting Major), Royal Horse Artillery (Territorial Force), attached Nottinghamshire Battery.
FRENCH, BERNARD RUSSELL, Capt. (Temporary Major), Royal Munster Fusiliers, attached 5th Battn. Royal Irish Fusiliers.
GARDINER, RICHARD, Major (Acting Lieut.-Colonel), 53rd Sikhs (Field Force), Indian Army.
GLYNTON, GERARD MAXWELL, Major, 3rd Gurkha Rifles, Indian Army.
HAMPTON, LORD, HERBERT STUART, Major, 1/1st Worcestershire Yeomanry (late Rifle Brigade).
HOLDEN, HYLA NAPIER, Major and Brevet Lieut.-Colonel, 5th Cavalry, Indian Army.
JERVOIS, JAMES ARTHUR, M.C., Capt. (Acting Lieut.-Colonel), Yorkshire Light Infantry, attached 2/22nd Battn. London Regt.
KIDD, BERTRAM GRAHAM BALFOUR, Major, 1/125th Napier's Rifles, Indian Army, attached 1st Battn. 123rd Outram's Rifles.
LAIRD, HAROLD GORDON CANNY, Capt., 1st Battn. 101st Grenadiers, Indian Army.
McENROY, PATRICK, M.C., Capt., 1st Battn. Leinster Regt.

The Distinguished Service Order

MAYNARD, PERCY GUY WOLFE, Major, Royal Irish Rifles, attached Egyptian Army.
MURRAY, SHADWELL JOHN, Lieut.-Colonel and Brevet Colonel, Connaught Rangers
PHILLIPS, ESTRICKE SIDNEY, Major, 195th Heavy Battery, Royal Garrison Artillery.
ROBINS, THOMAS ELLIS, Major, City of London Yeomanry.
SHAW, HAROLD MIDDLETON DRURY, Major (Acting Lieut.-Colonel), 1st Battn. Gurkha Rifles, attached 3rd Battn. 3rd Gurkha Rifles, Indian Army.
SLADEN, DOUGLAS BROOKE CHARLES, Major, Royal Garrison Artillery, attached 378th Siege Battery.
SMITH, GEORGE EDWARD STANLEY, Lieut.-Colonel, 1/4th Battn. Duke of Cornwall's Light Infantry (Territorial Force).
SMITH, IAN MACKINTOSH, M.C., Major, Somersetshire Light Infantry.
STANLEY, FRANCIS EDMOND CRAWSHAY, Major, Royal Field Artillery (Territorial Force).
VERNON, ANTHONY JOHN, M.C., Lieut. (Acting Lieut.-Colonel), 2nd Battn. Royal Irish Fusiliers.
WALKER, THOMAS HENRY, Major (Acting Lieut.-Colonel), Royal Field Artillery (Territorial Force).
WEISBERG, HARRY, Major (Acting Lieut.-Colonel), City of London Yeomanry, attached Machine Gun Corps (surname changed to Whitehill).
YOUNG, JOHN HAY, M.C., Capt. (Temporary Major, Acting Lieut.-Colonel), Argyll and Sutherland Highlanders, attached 2/16th Battn. London Regt.

AUSTRALIAN FORCE.

ANDERSON, WARREN MELVILLE, Major, 6th Australian Light Horse Regt.
BRUXNER, MICHAEL FREDERICK, Major (Temporary Lieut.-Colonel), 6th Australian Light Horse Regt.
DUNNINGHAM, PERCY, Major (Temporary Lieut.-Colonel), Australian Army Service Corps.
MAUNDER, HAROLD ARTHUR, Major (Temporary Lieut.-Colonel), Australian Army Service Corps.
TOOTH, STUART ARCHIBALD, Major, 6th Australian Light Horse Regt.
WILSON, LACHLAN CHISHOLM, C.M.G., Colonel (Temporary Brigadier-General), 5th Australian Light Horse Regt.

London Gazette, 1 Jan. 1919.—" War Office, 1 Jan. 1919. His Majesty the King has been graciously pleased to approve of the undermentioned rewards for distinguished service in connection with military operations in Italy. Dated 1 Jan. 1919. Awarded a Bar to the Distinguished Service Order."

*CARLTON, HERBERT DUDLEY, Major (Acting Lieut.-Colonel), Royal Scots, attached 2nd Battn. Royal West Surrey Regt.
*LOMAX, CYRIL ERNEST NAPIER, M.C., Capt. (Temporary Lieut.-Colonel), Welsh Regt., attached 21st Battn. Manchester Regt.
*STEELE, JULIAN McCARTY, C.B., C.M.G., Lieut.-Colonel and Brevet Colonel (Temporary Brigadier-General), Coldstream Guards.

NOTE.—In the cases marked by an asterisk the announcements of awards of the Distinguished Service Order have not yet been published in the London Gazette. These awards will be published in due course.

Awarded the Distinguished Service Order:
ABELL, ROBERT LLOYD, M.C., Temporary Capt. (Acting Major), 104th Battery, 22nd Brigade, Royal Field Artillery.
AGNEW, KENNETH MORLAND, M.C., Major, Royal Field Artillery.
BARNARDISTON, ERNALD, Major (Acting Lieut.-Colonel), Royal Engineers.
BATE, JOHN PERCIVAL, M.C., Capt. (Acting Major), 1/8th Battn. Worcestershire Regt., Territorial Force.
BOWSER, HOWARD ARTHUR, Temporary Major, 171st Siege Battery, Royal Garrison Artillery.
BRODERICK, RALPH ALEXANDER, M.C., M.B., Capt. (Acting Lieut.-Colonel), 1/2nd Battn., South Middlesex Brigade, Field Ambulance, Royal Army Medical Corps, Territorial Force.
COMBS, HUGH VIVIAN, M.C., Capt. (Acting Major), Buckinghamshire Battn. Oxfordshire and Buckinghamshire Light Infantry, Territorial Force, attached 23rd Machine Gun Battn.
GREENWOOD, LEONARD MONTAGUE, M.C., Temporary Capt., 13th (Service) Battn. Durham Light Infantry.
HALL, PHILIP ASHLEY, M.C., Capt. (Acting Major), Buckinghamshire Battn. Oxfordshire and Buckinghamshire Light Infantry, Territorial Force.
JACOB, WALTER HENRY BELL, Lieut.-Colonel, Royal Garrison Artillery, Headquarters 104th Brigade, Royal Garrison Artillery.
LUBY, MAURICE, M.C., Capt. (Acting Major), 128th Field Company, Royal Engineers.
MACKENZIE, WILLIAM, M.B., Temporary Capt., Royal Army Medical Corps, attached 9th Battn. South Staffordshire Regt.
MACLEOD, RODERICK, M.C., Capt. (Acting Major), Royal Field Artillery, attached 241st Brigade, Royal Field Artillery, Territorial Force.
MURRAY, DONALD, Temporary Capt., Manchester Regt., attached 21st Battn.
SHARPE, WILLIAM McCORMICK, Temporary Major, 197th Siege Battery, Royal Garrison Artillery.
WALKER, JAMES THOMAS, M.C., Temporary Major, 317th Siege Battery, Royal Garrison Artillery.
WATSON, REGINALD HENRY MONTAGU, Major (Acting Lieut.-Colonel), Royal Garrison Artillery, Headquarters 15th Brigade, Royal Garrison Artillery.

London Gazette, 1 Jan. 1919.—" War Office, 1 Jan. 1919. His Majesty the King has been graciously pleased to approve of the undermentioned rewards for distinguished service in connection with military operations in Salonika. Dated 1 Jan. 1919. Awarded a Bar to the Distinguished Service Order."

NICHOLSON, EDWARD HILLS, D.S.O., Major (Acting Lieut.-Colonel).
(D.S.O. gazetted 1 June, 1918.)

Awarded the Distinguished Service Order:
COWLAND, WALTER STOREY, Temporary Major, 12th Battn. Hampshire Regt.

COX, IVOR RICHARD, Temporary Major, Royal Garrison Artillery.
DUNSTERVILLE, KNIGHTLEY FLETCHER, Major, Royal Garrison Artillery.
EDMOND, JAMES HECTOR, Major, Royal Garrison Artillery.
FAIRTLOUGH, ERIC VICTOR HOWARD, M.C., Major, Royal Artillery.
HARVEY, SYDNEY LANCELOT, M.C., Major, Royal Engineers, Territorial Force.
HOLDEN WILLIAM CORSON, M.C., Capt. (Acting Major), Royal Garrison Artillery.
HOSSIE, DAVID NIEL, Temporary Major, Royal Field Artillery.
JOICEY, THE HONOURABLE HUGH EDWARD, Major and Brevet Lieut.-Colonel (Temporary Lieut.-Colonel), 14th Hussars.
McNAUGHT, GEORGE STANLEY, Capt. (Acting Lieut.-Colonel), Cheshire Regt.
MORRELL, JAMES FREDERICK BAKER, M.V.O., Capt. and Brevet Major (Temporary Lieut.-Colonel), Royal Lancaster Regt.
NEILSON, WILLIAM, Major and Brevet Lieut.-Colonel (Temporary Lieut.-Colonel), 4th Hussars.
SPAN, HENRY JOHN BARTLET, Lieut.-Colonel, 1st Battn. Welsh Regt.
TAYLOR, CLAUDE WATERHOUSE HEARN, Capt. and Brevet Major (Temporary Major), 3rd Battn. Royal West Kent Regt.
TRIST, LESLIE HAMILTON, M.C., Capt. (Acting Lieut.-Colonel), Lincolnshire Regt. (Special Reserve).
WALLACE, CHARLES HENRY, Major (Acting Lieut.-Colonel), Royal Field Artillery.
YATMAN, ARTHUR HAMILTON, Major and Brevet Lieut.-Colonel (Temporary Lieut.-Colonel), Somersetshire Light Infantry.

London Gazette, 1 Jan. 1919.—" War Office, 1 Jan. 1919. His Majesty the King has been graciously pleased to approve of the undermentioned reward for distinguished service in connection with military operations in North Russia. Dated 1 Jan. 1919. Awarded the Distinguished Service Order."

MARSH, FRANK GRAHAM, C.M.G., Major and Brevet Lieut.-Colonel, Indian Army.

London Gazette, 1 Jan. 1919.—" Air Ministry, 1 Jan. 1919. His Majesty the King has been graciously pleased to approve of the undermentioned rewards to Officers and other ranks of the Royal Air Force, in recognition of distinguished service. Awarded the Distinguished Service Order."

CUNNINGHAM, JACK ARMAND, D.F.C., Major (Acting Lieut.-Colonel).
FEENEY, FRANCIS JOSEPH EDWARD, Capt. (Acting Major).
HEWLETT, FRANCIS ESME THEODORE, O.B.E., Lieut.-Colonel.
JACOB, ARTHUR FREDERICK FOY, Capt. (Acting Major).
LONGMORE, ARTHUR MURRAY, Lieut.-Colonel (Acting Colonel).
MALLORY, TRAFFORD LEIGH, Major.
MEYLER, HUGH MOWBRAY, M.C., Lieut.-Colonel.
PITCHER, DUNCAN LE GEYT, C.M.G., Colonel (Acting Brigadier-General)
REID, GEORGE RONALD MACFARLANE, M.C., Major.
VAN RYNEVELD, HELPERUS ANDRIAS, M.C., Lieut.-Colonel.

London Gazette, 1 Jan. 1919.—" Admiralty, 1 Jan. 1919. The King has been graciously pleased to give orders for the appointment of the undermentioned Officers to be Companions of the Distinguished Service Order, in recognition of their services in the prosecution of the war."

MUNDY, GODFREY HARRY BRYDGES, C.B., M.V.O., Vice-Admiral.
KEIGHLY-PEACH, CHARLES WILLIAM, Rear-Admiral.
GIFFARD, FREDERIC, Commander, Royal Navy.
COWAN, CHARLES FREDERIC ROY, Commander, Royal Navy.
GERVERS, CHARLES TIEDMANN, Lieut.-Commander (Acting Commander), Royal Navy.
GOOLDEN, CYRIL, Lieut.-Commander (Acting Commander), Royal Navy.
POPE, ROWLAND KYRLE CECIL, Lieut.-Commander, Royal Navy.
DRENNAN, HENRY DENNIS, M.B., B.A., Surgeon Lieut.-Commander, Royal Navy.

London Gazette, 11 Jan. 1919.—" War Office, 11 Jan. 1919. His Majesty the King has been graciously pleased to approve of the following awards to the undermentioned Officers and Warrant Officers, in recognition of their gallantry and devotion to duty in the field. Awarded a Second Bar to the Distinguished Service Order."

BUCKLE, ARCHIBALD WALTER, D.S.O., Temporary Commander, Anson Battn. Royal Naval Division, Royal Naval Volunteer Reserve. For conspicuous gallantry and devotion to duty. When the progress of the brigade at a critical moment was checked by machine-gun fire, he went forward himself with his battalion staff, reorganized his battalion and led it forward on to commanding ground, seriously threatening the enemy's retreat. The success of the operation was largely due to his courage and fine leadership.
(D.S.O. gazetted 4 March, 1918.)
(First Bar gazetted 26 July, 1918.)

DAWES, GEORGE, D.S.O., M.C., Capt. and Brevet Major (Acting Lieut.-Colonel), 2nd Battn. South Staffordshire Regt., Commanding 21st Battn. London Regt. For conspicuous gallantry and able leadership. When the enemy attacked the flank of the battalion, which had been uncovered owing to the retirement of other troops, and there appeared to be imminent danger of their breaking through at this spot, which was the key of the position, Colonel Dawes went up under an intense fire, and rallied the men by his splendid example of courage and saved the line by his able and determined leadership.
(D.S.O. gazetted 18 Feb. 1918.)
(First Bar gazetted 26 July, 1918.)

GORT, VISCOUNT, JOHN STANDISH SURTEES PRENDERGAST VEREKER, V.C., D.S.O., M.V.O., M.C., Capt. and Brevet Major (Acting Lieut.-Colonel), 1st Battn. Grenadier Guards. For conspicuous gallantry and devotion to duty in command of his battalion. He led his men up by night to relieve a battalion which had attacked and failed to reach its objective. Regardless of danger he personally reconnoitred the line ahead of his troops, and got them on to the objective before dawn. During the three following days he again made forward reconnoissances, and leading his battalion gradually on, advanced the line 800 yards and gained a canal bank. It is impossible to speak too highly of this officer's initiative.
(D.S.O. gazetted 4 June, 1917.)
(First Bar gazetted 26 Sept. 1917.)

IRWIN, NOEL MACKINTOSH STUART, D.S.O., M.C., Capt. (Acting Lieut.-Colonel), Essex Regt., attached 1st Battn. Lincolnshire Regt. For conspicuous gallantry and devotion to duty. This officer, realizing that the battalion was very short of officers, and that many of the men were inexperienced in trench-to-trench fighting, led it himself in the attack, keeping close up with the barrage, with the result that all objectives were gained, and machine guns put out of action before they could open fire. He personally superintended the consolidation, and by his able dispositions minimized casualties.
(D.S.O. gazetted 1 Jan. 1918.)
(First Bar gazetted 24 Sept. 1918.)

McCULLOCH, ANDREW JAMESON, D.S.O., D.C.M., Capt. and Brevet Lieut.-Colonel (Temporary Brigadier-General), 7th Dragoon Guards, Commanding 64th Infantry Brigade. For conspicuous gallantry and ability to command. On a pitch dark night he penetrated 4,500 yards into the enemy's lines, occupied his objective, and captured between 300 and 400 prisoners and two guns, as well as a village. The advance was over the worst country, and the right flank of the brigade was entirely uncovered throughout. Success was entirely due to his magnificent leadership, moving at the head of this brigade.
(D.S.O. gazetted 26 July, 1918.)
(First Bar gazetted 16 Sept. 1918.)

Awarded a Bar to the Distinguished Service Order :

BAILEY, THE HONOURABLE WILFRED RUSSELL, D.S.O., Capt. (Acting Major), 1st Battn. Grenadier Guards. For conspicuous gallantry and outstanding leadership. It was necessary to capture some high ground overlooking a village before dark. This officer in command of the battalion commenced the advance at 3.15 p.m. By 5.45 p.m. all objectives had been taken. In carrying out this task the battalion advanced on a frontage of 1,000 yards with both flanks in the air, penetrated the enemy's lines for a distance of 4,000 yards and captured 197 prisoners, 15 machine guns and many trench mortars. The success of this manœuvre was certainly due to the brilliant leadership of this officer.
(D.S.O. gazetted 14 Nov. 1916.)

DANIEL, THOMAS WILLIAM, D.S.O., M.C., Temporary Major (Acting Lieut-Colonel), 10th Battn. Nottinghamshire and Derbyshire Regt. For conspicuous gallantry and devotion to duty. This officer was in command of his battalion in an attack, where it had to pass through two brigades and advance on a third objective. He controlled and directed this advance with great skill, capturing his objective without delay, although troops on his left had been held up. Later in the day, when the enemy made a partially successful counter-attack, he personally led his men and re-established the line. Throughout the day his example and courage had a great influence on his men.
(D.S.O. gazetted 1 Jan. 1918.)

FLETCHER, EDWARD KEELING, D.S.O., Major (Acting Lieut.-Colonel), Royal Marine Light Infantry, attached 1st Battn. For conspicuous gallantry and able leadership. When the enemy counter-attacked heavily, forcing in a portion of our line, this officer rallied the troops with great gallantry and re-organized them, and, leading them forward personally, restored the situation. Although severely wounded, he remained on the spot and declined to leave until he was able to report that the enemy had been repulsed. His courage and endurance inspired his men to most determined efforts.
(D.S.O. gazetted 26 July, 1918.)

GWYNN, KINGSMILL DOUGLAS HOSEASON, D.S.O., Temporary Major (Acting Lieut.-Colonel), 11th Battn. Royal Fusiliers. For conspicuous gallantry and able leadership. He commanded his battalion in the difficult operation of crossing a river in the face of determined opposition from the enemy, who were holding the opposite bank in strength. All bridges were broken, and the enemy had inundated a great portion of the valley by damming the stream. He himself was suffering from severe gassing, but he overcame all difficulties and, inspiring his men with his own determination and fine example of courage, he effected the crossing and established the battalion on the opposite bank. He rendered most valuable service.
(D.S.O. gazetted 4 Nov. 1915.)

HERBERT, WILLIAM NORMAN, D.S.O., Major and Brevet Lieut.-Colonel (Acting Lieut.-Colonel), 1st Battn. Northumberland Fusiliers. He commanded his battalion with marked ability and skill, and when one of his advanced posts had been captured he organized and led a counter-attack, after a personal reconnaissance, whereby the position was recaptured, together with 59 prisoners. Later, after an assaulting battalion had been held up by heavy machine-gun fire and his battalion was in reserve, he was ordered to clear the situation, which, after a close reconnaissance under heavy machine-gun fire, he did with complete success and slight casualties.
(D.S.O. gazetted 1 Jan. 1917.)

JOHNSON, DUDLEY GRAHAM, D.S.O., M.C., Capt. (Acting Lieut.-Colonel), South Wales Borderers, attached 2nd Battn. Royal Sussex Regt. For conspicuous gallantry and devotion to duty in command of his battalion in the attack. The ground over which his battalion advanced was very difficult, but thanks to his careful dispositions, was successfully negotiated. He personally superintended the reorganization after the objective was reached, and subsequently carried out a night attack, advancing some thousand yards in the face of strenuous opposition. His skilful arrangements and conduct throughout inspired the men under him with a splendid fighting spirit.
(D.S.O. gazetted 16 March, 1915.)

LEAH, THOMAS COULSON, D.S.O., Major, Royal Garrison Artillery, attached A/93rd Brigade, Royal Field Artillery. For conspicuous gallantry and devotion to duty while firing a barrage from an advanced enemy position. When intense enemy fire was put down on his battery he, by his coolness and organization, kept all guns in action and caused the rate of fire to be maintained. Twice during the operation, when ammunition dumps were hit and set alight, he was the first to assist in extinguishing the fire. He afterwards saw to the dressing and evacuation of the wounded.
(D.S.O. gazetted 4 June, 1917.)

LLOYD, EDWARD PRINCE, D.S.O., Capt, and Brevet Major (Acting Lieut.-Colonel), 2nd Battn. Lincolnshire Regt. For conspicuous gallantry and devotion to duty. This officer commanding his battalion gained all objectives on a wide front, his furthest point being 500 yards beyond that of the other battalions. When the situation on the right flank was uncertain he made a personal reconnaissance under heavy machine-gun fire, and sent back a clear report. He superintended the forming up and consolidation of the companies, and by unflagging energy, care and forethought succeeded in the operation with a minimum of casualties.
(D.S.O. gazetted 3 June, 1918.)

ROBERTSON, GORDON McMAHON, D.S.O., Capt. (Acting Lieut.-Colonel), 2nd Battn. North Staffordshire Regt., attached 2nd Battn. Manchester Regt. For conspicuous gallantry and able leadership during an attack. Hearing that the leading battalions had lost both commanding officers he went forward to the front line under heavy artillery and machine-gun fire, ascertained the situation, sent for reinforcements, and returned with valuable information. During the night he supervised the consolidation of the line, and next day handled his battalion most efficiently in support of a brigade.
(D.S.O. gazetted 3 June, 1918.)

SCHOMBERG, REGINALD CHARLES FRANCIS, D.S.O., Major (Acting Lieut.-Colonel), 1st Battn. Seaforth Highlanders (Mesopotamia). For conspicuous gallantry and devotion to duty. He commanded his battalion with great dash and determination in an attack. Though early wounded, he continued to command during the subsequent assault on the enemy's position, and afterwards superintended consolidation and reorganization in the dark, and remained with his battalion in the trenches until morning.
(D.S.O. gazetted 22 Dec. 1916.)

SYKES, FRANCIS BERNARD, D.S.O., Major (Temporary Lieut.-Colonel), Royal Field Artillery, attached 223rd (Home Counties) Brigade, Royal Field Artillery, Territorial Force. For conspicuous gallantry and able leadership. He went forward through a heavy gas barrage on two occasions to deal with an obscure situation and, though severely gassed, continued to direct operations. He utilised four artillery brigades with great ability to crush counter-attacks, and on one occasion, in the absence of linesmen, he personally carried a wire forward under intense machine-gun fire and, thus getting into telephonic communication with batteries, scattered with great losses the enemy whom he had observed to be massing for an advance. His courage, endurance and skill were admirable.
(D.S.O. gazetted 8 Nov. 1915.)

THORNHILL, CUDBERT JOHN MASSY, D.S.O., Major (Temporary Lieut.-Colonel), Indian Army (Northern Russia). For conspicuous gallantry and ability in command of the " Onega " force. With a small detachment he made a most dashing attack on the enemy, who were in far superior numbers, and by the vigour of his attack was successful in detaching a large force of the enemy, who would otherwise have opposed us at Archangel. Throughout all operations the marked courage displayed by Colonel Thornhill inspired all ranks serving under his command.
(D.S.O. gazetted 1 Jan. 1918.)

VICARY, ALEXANDER CRAVEN, D.S.O., M.C., Capt. and Brevet Major (Acting Lieut.-Colonel), 2nd Battn. Gloucestershire Regt. (Salonika). For conspicuous gallantry and devotion to duty during an attack. He set a fine example to all ranks of coolness and courage under heavy shell fire. The manner in which his battalion carried through the operation and consolidated and retained the position under subsequent intense bombardment was undoubtedly due to his personal gallantry and marked ability to command.
(D.S.O. gazetted 3 June, 1918.)

CANADIAN FORCE.

BENT, CHARLES EDWARD, C.M.G., D.S.O., Lieut.-Colonel, 15th Battn. Canadian Infantry, 1st Central Ontario Regt. For gallantry and skill in directing his battalion in an attack. He, under difficulties of mist, led his battalion in close reserve to the three attacking battalions of this brigade, consequently, under the conditions of the day, he was engaged in personal leadership and fighting, helping to clear up the places where the enemy were still holding out. Next day, during another attack, he was severely wounded.
(D.S.O. gazetted 1 Jan. 1917.)

CLARK-KENNEDY, WILLIAM HEW, C.M.G., D.S.O., Lieut.-Colonel, 24th Battn. Canadian Infantry, Quebec Regt. For great gallantry in action during which the battalion under his command reached the objectives allotted to it. On several occasions, at great risk, he personally directed the capture of strong points obstinately defended by the enemy. The success which his battalion obtained in these actions was due in no small degree to the example, courage and resourcefulness of its commander.
(D.S.O. gazetted 14 Jan. 1916.)

DONALDSON, ANSON SCOTT, D.S.O., Lieut.-Colonel, 3rd Field Ambulance, Canadian Army Medical Corps. For conspicuous gallantry and devotion to duty. This officer was in charge of the evacuation of the forward area, and showed great initiative in establishing dressing stations and collecting posts directly in rear of the advancing infantry. He kept in touch with the battalion and succeeded in evacuating the casualties almost as soon as they occurred, in spite of heavy machine-gun and shell fire.
(D.S.O. gazetted 3 June, 1918.)

DUBUC, ARTHUR EDOUARD, D.S.O., Major, 22nd Battn. Canadian Infantry, Quebec Regt. For conspicuous gallantry and determined leadership. This officer commanded his battalion in an attack on an important village. Twice during the morning the advance was checked by very heavy machine-gun fire, causing serious casualties. On both occasions he went forward and personally led the leading waves during these critical moments. He was severely wounded before the battalion reached its objective, and it was greatly due to his fearless leadership that the attack was successful.
(D.S.O. gazetted 1 Jan 1917.)

JONES, LOUIS ELGIN, D.S.O., Lieut.-Colonel, 18th Battn. Canadian Infantry, Western Ontario Regt. He commanded his battalion with marked skill in connection with an attack on a strongly-held position, during which his flanks were threatened. His initiative and personal direction led to the success of the attack and permitted of the advance of his own and neighbouring units. He personally supervised the work of consolidation of the objective gained, and throughout, under exceptionally adverse conditions, he set a splendid example to his officers and men.
(D.S.O. gazetted 18 Oct. 1917.)

JOHNSTON, GEORGE CHALMERS, D.S.O., M.C., Lieut.-Colonel, 2nd Canadian Mounted Rifle Battn., 1st Central Ontario Regt. The day previous to an attack he was ordered to make on a strong enemy position, he made a personal reconnaissance of the ground in the face of heavy machine-gun fire. It was owing to this officer's high qualities of leadership and his knowledge of the ground that the attack was a complete success, and that his battalion suffered a minimum of casualties.
(D.S.O. gazetted 1 Jan. 1918.)

MACFARLANE, ROBERT ALEXANDER, D.S.O., Lieut.-Colonel, 58th Battn. Canadian Infantry, 2nd Central Ontario Regt. His battalion was required to make an advance of nearly 5,000 yards during an attack in which his battalion became involved in very heavy fighting at one point where he personally led forward supporting companies to clear one village and push on to another, which was the final objective. He performed this task with great skill and daring, personally killing two of the enemy. During a subsequent operation he made a reconnaissance forward of his battalion, in which he surprised an enemy machine-gun post ; he killed one of the crew and took four other prisoners. Throughout these operations he showed sound judgment, courage and skill.
(D.S.O. gazetted 4 June, 1917.)

McKENZIE, ARCHIBALD ERNEST GRAHAM, D.S.O., Lieut.-Colonel, 26th Battn. Canadian Infantry, New Brunswick Regt. For conspicuous skill in handling his battalion during the capture and consolidation of the objectives allotted to his command. His coolness and fine example inspired all ranks.

The success which crowned the operations of this unit was in a large measure due to leadership and courage of its C.O.
(D.S.O. gazetted 1 Jan. 1917.)

MILLEN, LIONEL HERBERT, D.S.O., Lieut.-Colonel, 19th Battn. Canadian Infantry, 1st Central Ontario Regt. In connection with an attack on three strongly-held enemy positions he commanded his battalion with such skill and intrepidity that each position was taken in succession, and the final objective was gained. In a subsequent operation he organized and directed a successful attack on a village which resulted in our line being advanced 1,200 yards and the capture of many prisoners and machine guns. His marked ability in handling difficult situations and his courage and example contributed largely to the success of both operations.
(D.S.O. gazetted 1 Jan. 1918.)

MURPHY, THOMAS JOSEPH FRANCIS, D.S.O., Lieut.-Colonel, 6th Field Ambulance, Canadian Army Medical Corps. During an attack there were several wounded cases whose evacuation was being held up by the intense enemy barrage. This officer then brought up two motor ambulances, which he left some distance in rear, and came up with his runner to the village and searched for the regimental aid post, which he found after much difficulty, all the time exposed to heavy fire himself, as he passed several times through the enemy barrage and machine-gun fire. It was through his utter disregard of personal danger that the wounded were safely cleared and many lives saved.
(D.S.O. gazetted 1 Jan. 1918.)

PATERSON, ALEXANDER THOMAS, D.S.O., Major, D/23rd Battery, 5th Brigade, Canadian Field Artillery. For conspicuous gallantry and devotion to duty. When one of the ammunition wagons of his battery was hit by a shell and the ammunition set on fire, he at once ordered the men to a distance while he himself went and opened the door and removed the charges. But for his gallant action a serious disaster might have occurred.
(D.S.O. gazetted 3 June, 1918.)

PECK, CYRUS WESLEY, D.S.O., Lieut.-Colonel, 16th Battn. Canadian Infantry, Manitoba Regt. During an attack he showed fine courage and leadership. He led his battalion, under difficulties caused by heavy mist, to its final objective, nearly three miles, after severe fighting. He personally led his men in an attack on nests of machine guns protecting the enemy's guns, which he captured. Some of the guns were of 8-inch calibre.
(D.S.O. gazetted 4 June, 1917.)

RHOADES, WILLIAM, D.S.O., M.C., Lieut.-Colonel, 5th Battn. Canadian Infantry, Quebec Regt. When the battalion was ordered to move forward and capture a strong position held by enemy machine guns and flanked by strong points, he made personal reconnaissances and guided the attack of his battalion with great skilfulness and determination, and was with the front line when the objectives were taken. It was due to his quick appreciation of the situation and skilful disposition of his troops that the attack was a complete success. His resourcefulness and courage were an inspiration to all ranks.
(D.S.O. gazetted 3 June, 1918.)

RILEY, HAROLD JAMES, D.S.O., Lieut.-Colonel, 27th Battn. Canadian Infantry, Manitoba Regt. For conspicuous gallantry and able leadership. During four days' hard fighting, when his battalion was continuously making attacks at short intervals, his gallantry and indomitable energy inspired his men to their utmost efforts. His personal direction in the advanced lines ensured the success of difficult operations, and on one occasion the attack was made at the end of a hard day's fighting without artillery support, and resulted in the capture of a number of machine guns and prisoners. Throughout the operations his example and leading were splendid.
(D.S.O. gazetted 18 July, 1917.)

STEWART, CHARLES JAMES TOWNSHEND, D.S.O., Lieut.-Colonel, Princess Patricia's Canadian Light Infantry, East Ontario Regt. He, by his extreme energy and resourcefulness, his sound tactical knowledge and ability, overcame great odds in leading his battalion against strongly organized enemy defences in the face of heavy machine-gun and rifle fire, thereby ensuring the attainment of all objectives for the brigade. His consistent cheerfulness, his complete disregard of danger, and his personal example were undoubtedly instrumental in the successes of his battalion.
(D.S.O. gazetted 14 Nov. 1916.)

URQUHART, HUGH MACINTYRE, D.S.O., M.C., Lieut.-Colonel, 43rd Battn. Canadian Infantry, Manitoba Regt. For distinguished services and gallantry on several occasions. He had the difficult task of taking the formidable positions of three woods, all of which he captured at the right time. He showed leadership and skilful handling of the highest order, and out-manœuvred the enemy. On subsequent occasions he made daring personal reconnaissances which resulted in complete defeat of the enemy. On the last enterprise he was severely wounded.
(D.S.O. gazetted 18 July, 1917.)

Awarded the Distinguished Service Order:

BEDDY, PERCY LANGDON, Major and Brevet Lieut.-Colonel, 51st Sikhs (Mesopotamia). For conspicuous gallantry and good leadership. It was largely due to the skill and initiative with which he handled his battalion in the attack following on a night march of twenty miles that the enemy were driven back in a running fight extending over six miles, and by early next morning were turned out of two strongly-prepared positions two miles apart.

BLATHERWICK, THOMAS, M.C., Major (Acting Lieut.-Colonel), 1/6th Battn. Manchester Regt., Territorial Force. He displayed the greatest courage and skill when personally supervising the crossing of a river in face of a position strongly held by the enemy. Later, his battalion was ordered to relieve another battalion at short notice in an attack on positions which had not been previously reconnoitred. He went forward and made a personal reconnaissance, amidst heavy shell bursts and machine-gun fire, and returning led the battalion successfully forward under extremely difficult circumstances.

BRUDENELL-BRUCE, ROBERT HANBURY, Major, Norfolk Regt. For conspicuous gallantry and devotion to duty. During severe fighting for two days he rendered very valuable service by reconnoitring under difficult and dangerous conditions, when situations arose requiring personal reports, as communications were broken. He displayed great coolness and complete disregard of danger in carrying out his dangerous mission, and throughout the operations his conduct was marked by great gallantry and presence of mind.

CARR, GRAHAM, M.C., Temporary Capt., Machine Gun Corps (Motor) (Mesopotamia). For conspicuous gallantry and devotion to duty when in command of a motor battery in the pursuit. His was the first party to enter an enemy town where, in spite of the resistance offered, he captured a number of prisoners. Later, he carried out a daring raid into the enemy's country, and took several prisoners 73 miles from his starting point.

CLARKE, ALFRED DAVID CONRAD, M.C., Lieut. (Acting Major), Royal Field Artillery (Special Reserve), attached C/122nd Brigade. For conspicuous gallantry and devotion to duty on many occasions throughout a ten days' advance. He carried out most daring reconnaissances under heavy shell and machine-gun fire of routes and positions up to within 300 yards of the enemy. When the enemy were retiring he maintained observation from advanced observation posts, and they were frequently cut up by our fire. He kept his battery in close support of the infantry, coming into action with amazing rapidity under very heavy fire. His energy and coolness were invaluable.

CLARKE, JOSEPH, M.C., Temporary Lieut., Drake Battn. Royal Naval Volunteer Reserve. For conspicuous gallantry and devotion to duty during an attack. He led forward the scouts, and it was largely due to his energy and pluck that the correct direction of the battalion was maintained under heavy fire. He and his party were responsible for the capture of several machine guns, one of which he put out of action single-handed. His services throughout were of the greatest value, while his energy and courage were most marked.

COCKBURN, JOHN BRYDGES, Major and Brevet Lieut.-Colonel (Temporary Lieut.-Colonel), 2nd Battn. Royal Welsh Fusiliers. For conspicuous gallantry and devotion to duty. This officer, while commanding his battalion in mopping up a wide area infested by machine guns, was wounded at point-blank range by a machine gun. He kept on superintending the work until the whole area was cleared, more than 500 prisoners and 50 machine guns being captured. His courage and endurance were a splendid example to his men.

COMBE, SYDNEY BOYCE, M.C., Major and Brevet Lieut.-Colonel, 47th Sikhs (Mesopotamia). For conspicuous gallantry and devotion to duty. He carried out a reconnaissance of the enemy's position under heavy fire, pushed back the enemy picquets, and assaulted and carried the whole of his objective, three lines of the enemy trenches. Later, though having suffered heavy casualties in officers and men, he successfully beat off a counter-attack. He has shown great judgment and ability in command on all occasions.

COTTON, RONALD EGERTON, Temporary Major (Acting Lieut.-Colonel), 7th Battn. Yorkshire Regt., attached 10th Battn. Lancashire Fusiliers. For conspicuous gallantry and devotion to duty. When a counter-attack by the enemy threatened to envelop the right flank of two battalions, he went forward and restored the situation. This was the second occasion of his defeating a counter-attack, as he had previously, while reconnoitring in the front line, discovered the enemy concentrating, and by promptly organizing battalion headquarters and a machine-gun section, dispersed them. His energy and courage on these two occasions, both under heavy fire of all descriptions, were a fine example to his men.

DANIEL, JAMES ARTHUR, M.C. (Christian name corrected to James Alfred), Capt., Welsh Regt., attached 15th Battn. (temporarily attached 14th Battn.). For conspicuous gallantry during an attack. He organized a patrol and advanced covering party, who established a bridgehead and covered the crossing over the river of the remainder of the battalion, enabling them to start the attack punctually. He subsequently dealt with some enemy machine guns, and brought on the rear companies to the final objective. It was largely due to his personal influence and power of command that the advance was so successful.

DEWAR, RONALD, Second Lieut., Manchester Regt., Special Reserve, attached 12th Battn. For conspicuous gallantry and good leadership. This officer took command of a company after the second day of the attack, and received the main shock of an enemy counter-attack. He was twice taken prisoner and escaped, but was driven from his position, and had to reform the remnants of his company to form a defensive flank, preventing the enemy from surrounding the battalion. He held his position until relieved, again beating off a third counter-attack at 6 p.m. His skill and determined courage were admirable.

DICK, HAROLD WATSON, M.C., Temporary Lieut. (Acting Capt.), attached West Yorkshire Regt., attached 1/5th Battn. East Lancashire Regt., Territorial Force. During an attack he commanded an assaulting company, which at one time was held up by enfilade fire. Taking three men with him, he rushed the enemy post, personally killing the officer in charge, whilst his men caused other casualties. The remainder of the garrison, 40 in number, then surrendered to him. His fearless leadership and clever tactical handling of his command were an inspiring example to all.

ELLIS, CHARLES GEORGE HOWSON, Lieut. (Acting Capt.), 5th Battn. West Riding Regt., Territorial Force. During an attack he was in command of a company considerably in advance of the troops on his right, when a determined hostile counter-attack at one time pierced the line. With great courage and ability, he at once led his reserves into the gap, threw the enemy back, and restored the position at a most critical time. Later, in command of two companies, he attacked a strongly-fortified system of trenches under heavy shell fire, and by his complete disregard of danger and inspiring example was largely responsible for the success of the attack.

FARRELL, VALENTINE JOSEPH, M.C., Capt., Leinster Regt., Special Reserve, attached 2nd Battn. For conspicuous gallantry and fine leadership in an attack. In command of a company in reserve, he rushed forward at a time when the advance was held up and cleared up several enemy machine-gun positions on the flank, thereby enabling the whole line to move forward and reach the final objective. Afterwards he reorganized the whole line and sent back valuable information regarding the situation. He did splendid work.

GELDARD, NICHOLAS, M.C., Capt., 6th Battn. (attached 2/4th Battn.) West Riding Regt., Territorial Force. For conspicuous gallantry during an attack, when he continually went along the front line, showing the highest courage and skill in directing operations and in keeping in touch with the situation. Although meeting with strong opposition, the operations were successful, and over 150 prisoners taken. His leadership throughout was splendid, and his example kept the morale of his men in a very high state. He was severely wounded.

GOODLAND, HERBERT THOMAS, Temporary Major (Acting Lieut.-Colonel), Royal Berkshire Regt., Commanding 5th Battn. For conspicuous gallantry, coolness and devotion to duty. He led his battalion, which had been in reserve, through a heavy enemy barrage, to reinforce the firing line, and by so doing filled up a dangerous gap and stopped the advance of the enemy. He then personally supervised the consolidation of a vital position under direct fire from machine guns and field guns firing with open sights.

GORDON, JOHN KEILY, Major, "S" Battery, Royal Horse Artillery (Mesopotamia). For conspicuous gallantry and devotion to duty. He commanded his battery with marked skill and ability when subjected to heavy enemy shelling. The good shooting of his battery, and its steadiness in action, were largely due to his coolness and personal influence.

GRAHAM, CHARLES JAMES, M.C., Lieut. (Temporary Capt.), 2/4th Battn. London Regt. For conspicuous gallantry and devotion to duty. During two days' hard fighting he was untiring in his efforts in reconnoitring the front of two brigades, and the information he was able to procure of the absence of the enemy in certain strong points was of the greatest value. He was continually exposed to heavy machine-gun and sniping fire, and his coolness and presence of mind were admirable.

HARRIS, JOSEPH ORLANDO, Temporary Sub-Lieut., Hawke Battn. Royal Naval Volunteer Reserve, Royal Naval Division. For conspicuous gallantry and devotion to duty during an attack. When the advance was checked by heavy machine-gun fire he led his men forward, successfully capturing the machine-gun post and enabling the other companies to advance. Later, he led a party against a bridgehead and captured it, himself charging two machine-gun positions and killing the crews. He set a splendid example of courage and determined leadership.

HOLROYD-SMYTH, CHARLES EDWARD RIDLEY, M.C., Capt. (Temporary Lieut.-Colonel), Reserve of Officers, 3rd Dragoon Guards, Commanding 15th Battn. Durham Light Infantry. For conspicuous gallantry and fine leadership while commanding the battalion in an attack. When the situation was doubtful he went forward to the advanced posts under heavy fire to ascertain the position. Previously he had taken charge of the brigade, and, although surrounded, the brigade overcame the enemy resistance, and was largely instrumental in the capture of a village, together with a number of prisoners and a quantity of stores.

HUTTENBACH, NORMAN HUGH, M.C., Capt. (Acting Major), 120th Battery, 27th Brigade, Royal Field Artillery. For conspicuous gallantry and able leadership. During a fortnight's hard fighting he led the artillery brigade of which he was temporarily in command with great courage and remarkable skill, affording much support to the infantry, whose success was in no small way due to the effective fire of his guns, which he brought into action in an unusually short time after advances of often some miles.

KELLY, GEORGE CHARLES, Major and Brevet Lieut.-Colonel (Temporary Brigadier-General), King's Royal Rifle Corps, Commanding 2nd Infantry Brigade. For conspicuous gallantry and devotion to duty. When his brigade met with unexpected resistance he promptly made a personal reconnaissance, and, by handling his brigade in a masterly way under very heavy fire, gained his objective and repulsed several counter-attacks. His powers of command and brilliant example were admirable.

LAKE, BASIL CHARLES, Capt., King's Own Scottish Borderers (Brigade Major, 13th Infantry Brigade). For conspicuous gallantry while commanding a battalion during an attack. Learning that, through casualties, one company was without orders, he immediately went forward and gave the orders personally and led the company and battalion forward. Though early wounded, he continued to lead the battalion until shot a second time, his leg being then broken. Even then he refused to be carried away until certain that the attack had succeeded. He showed marked courage and devotion to duty.

LAMONBY, LAWRENCE, Major, Border Regt., attached 1/4th Battn. Dorsetshire Regt., Territorial Force (Mesopotamia). For conspicuous gallantry and devotion to duty. He commanded his battalion with great coolness and ability under heavy fire. His initiative and dash enabled the attack to be carried through to a successful conclusion.

LAMONT, GEOFFREY SIMPSON, Second Lieut., Grenadier Guards, Special Reserve, attached 1st Battn. For three days of continuous fighting he showed a supreme contempt of danger, and infused courage in all around him. Throughout an attack he commanded the leading wave, and despite heavy machine-gun fire and thick belts of wire, he never allowed the pace to be checked. Undoubtedly the speed of the advance enabled a commanding position to be captured, with nearly 200 prisoners and 15 machine guns, and at small loss. Later, when with seven men he was surrounded by large numbers of the enemy, he maintained his position for several hours against repeated attacks, and finally effected his escape and joined in a further advance.

LEE, CHARLES HECTOR, M.C., Lieut. (Acting Capt.), Gordon Highlanders, Special Reserve, attached 1st Battn. It was owing to his courage and skill that during two days of severe fighting his company was enabled to capture 12 machine guns and 80 prisoners. On another occasion he carried out a daring reconnaissance under continuously heavy fire over most exposed country, and sent in very valuable information. His company was on an exposed flank for five days, and his gallantry and fine leadership were of the greatest value to the brigade.

LOWCOCK, ALFRED, M.C., Lieut. (Acting Major), Royal Field Artillery, attached B/223rd (Home Counties) Brigade, Royal Field Artillery, Territorial Force. For conspicuous gallantry and devotion to duty. During operations lasting eight days he rendered valuable and conspicuous services by the manner in which he kept his battery continually in close support of the infantry. On one occasion, when the enemy were counter-attacking with determination, he went forward and directed the fire of the whole brigade with great effect, and broke up the attack. Later on he was hit by a machine-gun bullet, but returned to brigade headquarters and remained at duty. He set a very fine example of fortitude and endurance throughout.

LUXMOORE-BALL, RICHARD EDMUND CORYNDON, Lieut. (Acting Major), Welsh Guards, Special Reserve, attached 1st Battn. When in command of his battalion during several days of severe fighting, he was invariably in the front line, superintending operations, without the slightest regard for personal danger. On one occasion, prior to an assault, he walked about in the open, in spite of heavy hostile fire, placing the men in their assembly positions, and the great success achieved by the battalion was mainly due to the splendid example set by him.

McCREADY, THOMAS ROBERT, M.C., Temporary Lieut.-Colonel, Commanding 63rd Battn. Machine Gun Corps, Temporary Major, Royal Marines. For conspicuous gallantry and fine leadership during an advance. In addition to carrying out several reconnaissances he commanded his machine-gun battalion most ably. When the infantry were checked by machine-gun fire he brought his companies into action, and directed fire on the points of resistance so successfully that the infantry were enabled to advance, and by capturing a ridge ensure the success of the operation.

MITCHELL, WILFRID JAMES, Lieut.-Colonel, 2/124th Baluchistan Infantry (Mesopotamia). For conspicuous gallantry and devotion to duty. He handled his battalion most skilfully in the attack, and in spite of heavy casualties from a strong point on his flank, succeeded in capturing his objective. His courage and perseverance on this occasion were most marked.

NAGLE, WILLIAM JOHN, M.C., Temporary Second Lieut. (Acting Capt.), 2nd Battn. Suffolk Regt. When ordered, during operations, to clear a trench area infested with machine guns and holding up an advance, he displayed the greatest courage and determination in leading his company. He cleared over a mile of trench line and sunken roads, and was responsible for the capture of over 200 prisoners and many machine guns. His utter disregard of danger and fine example were primarily responsible for the success of the operation.

NEWSTEAD, BASIL RALPH, Lieut., 1st Battn. Northumberland Fusiliers. His company having been ordered to attack a very strong position which had held up the attacking battalion all day, he made a gallant personal reconnaissance, whereby he was able to dispose his company in so favourable a position that not only were all the objectives gained, and many prisoners and machine guns taken, but patrols were pushed out, enabling the whole original objectives of the brigade to be occupied without further loss. His courage and inspiring example were of a very high order.

NOAKES, SYDNEY MAPLESDEN, Major, C/178th Brigade, Royal Field Artillery. For conspicuous gallantry and devotion to duty during an advance. He made a daring reconnaissance by day to locate our advanced posts, and also a concealed enemy machine-gun nest. He drew the fire of the nest and then returned and turned his battery on it, knocking out the position and establishing and consolidating the line of posts. He did fine work

NORTHCOTE, RICHARD, Temporary Second Lieut., 17th Battn. Machine Gun Corps. For conspicuous gallantry and initiative. This officer with his section was attached to the left leading battalion of the division. On the objective being gained, the enemy counter-attacked in large numbers, and made a gap; the forward troops were being rapidly surrounded, and this officer undoubtedly saved the situation by keeping his guns firing to the front, flank and rear, and in addition manning six Lewis guns and one captured enemy gun. His coolness in keeping the section steady and controlling the fire enabled the infantry to re-form.

PETER, FRED HORRIS, M.C., Lieut. (Acting Lieut.-Colonel), Royal Welsh Fusiliers, attached 5th Battn. Yorkshire Light Infantry, Territorial Force. During operations lasting several days orders could be received at very short notice, and consequently great responsibility and initiative had to be left to commanding officers. Throughout these operations he was untiring in his efforts to arrange all details and plans, especially on one occasion, when he had to proceed through a heavy barrage, including gas, which affected him, to settle details for immediate operations which, mainly owing to his ability and courage, were successful.

POWELL, HENRY LLOYD, Lieut.-Colonel, 215th Brigade, Royal Field Artillery, Territorial Force (Mesopotamia). For conspicuous gallantry and devotion to duty. He commanded his brigade in a bold and intrepid manner in spite of heavy hostile shelling, and conformed to an ever-changing situation with skill and rapidity.

ROBERTSON, DOUGLAS WILLIAM, M.C., Temporary Second Lieut., 1st Battn. King's Royal Rifle Corps. For conspicuous gallantry and devotion to duty. This officer advanced alone to reconnoitre the line of advance for his platoon under intense machine-gun fire, then returned and led his men forward section by section, being wounded in the face while doing so. He refused to leave, but led his men forward to the first objective. He was then hit through the chest and lungs, but continued to hobble forward, disposing his men well in advance of their objective. By this time 11 out of 20 men were wounded, but he had so cowed the enemy by his determination that they began to stream forward with their hands up. The capture of this position was the key to the enemy's defence. He was primarily responsible for the capture of at least 90 prisoners and some 20 machine guns.

SAGAR, ARNOLD LESLIE, Temporary Lieut. (Acting Capt.), 8th Battn. East Lancashire Regt., attached 13th Battn. King's Royal Rifle Corps. For conspicuous gallantry and devotion to duty. This officer got his company into position for the attack despite heavy shelling, then, leading the front wave, he gained his objective. When held up at a strong point, he crawled out with a Lewis gun and one man to a flank, enfilading it with such success that 40 prisoners, two machine guns and one trench mortar were captured. During the ensuing 36 hours his company beat off three determined counter-attacks with heavy loss. He also led a bombing party, clearing a trench and killing or capturing the whole of the enemy. He showed exceptional qualities as a leader.

SCOTT, THOMAS HENRY, M.C., Capt. (Acting Lieut.-Colonel), 14th Field Ambulance, Royal Army Medical Corps. For conspicuous gallantry and devotion to duty. When the vicinity of his advanced dressing station was being heavily shelled, it was due to his coolness and able management that a number of stretcher and walking cases were evacuated quickly and smoothly. His foresight and organization were mainly responsible for the very large numbers of officers and men successfully evacuated during this period under most difficult conditions.

SIMMONDS, TOM, M.C., D.C.M., Temporary Sub-Lieut., Drake Battn. Royal Naval Volunteer Reserve. For conspicuous gallantry and devotion to duty during an attack. He rallied his company under heavy fire and rushed a machine-gun nest, capturing many prisoners and machine guns. After taking his final objective he pushed on and captured a convoy consisting of two large field guns, ammunition limbers and an ambulance wagon, together with many prisoners. He also captured the whole of a party of one officer and 70 men, with transport. Throughout two days' operations he was continually performing gallant acts, and his courage and cheerfulness were a splendid example to his men.

SPENCER, GEORGE ERNEST, Temporary Second Lieut., Yorkshire Light Infantry, attached 2/4th Battn. Territorial Force. When his battalion, moving to positions prior to an attack, was located by low-flying aeroplanes, the courage and skill he displayed in handling the leading company enabled the battalion to take cover with comparatively light casualties. Later, when the battalion was held up by machine-gun fire and subjected to heavy shelling, the advanced posts being driven in, he called up a Lewis gun section, which promptly got into action, and, shouting for his company to follow, he charged the enemy. His fine example was followed by other companies, the enemy driven back with heavy casualties, and a critical situation restored.

SPICER, LANCELOT DYKES, M.C., Temporary Capt., General List (Brigade Major, 64th Infantry Brigade). For conspicuous gallantry and devotion to duty while acting as brigade major during an advance. When the commanding officer was wounded he carried on the immediate reorganization of the brigade and consolidation of the position. His arrangements were very instrumental in causing the defeat of repeated counter-attacks. Later, when the force was entirely surrounded, he crawled out and brought back a report of the situation which enabled arrangements to be made for the relief of the brigade.

ST. AUBYN, EDWARD GEOFFREY, Capt. (Acting Lieut.-Colonel), King's Royal Rifle Corps (Special Reserve), attached 2nd Battn. For conspicuous gallantry and devotion to duty. Although wounded early in the day, he refused to leave his battalion until the fighting died down in the evening. He handled his battalion throughout with marked ability, and superintended the reorganization of his dispositions after the objective had been obtained. The success of the attack was largely due to his determination and to the fighting spirit with which his example inspired the battalion.

STURROCK, WILLIAM DUNCAN, M.D., Capt. (Temporary Major), Royal Army Medical Corps, Territorial Force (Salonika). For conspicuous gallantry and devotion to duty, when the main surgical ward and operating tent of a field ambulance were wrecked by shell fire, one officer and two other ranks being wounded. He very quickly put matters right, and owing to the excellent arrangements made by him throughout the operations the wounded, in spite of difficult country and lack of roads, were very rapidly collected and evacuated.

SWEET, FRED, Temporary Major, Royal Welsh Fusiliers, attached 13th Battn. For conspicuous gallantry and devotion to duty. Throughout a month's operations he commanded his battalion with unvarying success, including four separate attacks. On each occasion his careful arrangements and personal reconnaissances under heavy shell and machine-gun fire ensured the comparatively safe progress of the attack. Throughout the whole operations he set a splendid example to his men.

SYKES, ALEXANDER RICHARD, M.C., Temporary Major, Liverpool Regt., attached 14th Battn. and 10th Battn. South Wales Borderers. For conspicuous gallantry and devotion to duty. After reaching the objective, in command of his battalion, he made a personal reconnaissance under heavy fire and found that the ground in front was only lightly held. This enabled him to advance his battalion to some high ground with very few casualties. Some days later when in support, he handled two companies on the right flank of the brigade with such dash that 40 prisoners, with machine guns, were captured, and the flank secured. He showed great initiative and total disregard of danger.

TABUTEAU, GEORGE GRANT, Major (Acting Lieut.-Colonel), No. 1 Field Ambulance, Royal Army Medical Corps. For conspicuous gallantry and devotion to duty in supervising the evacuation of casualties during three days' operations under heavy shell fire. He maintained a chain of medical posts in close touch with the battalions of his brigade, and the rapid removal of the wounded was due to his coolness and untiring energy, which inspired his officers and men with confidence.

TAYLOR, THOMAS EDGAR HUGH, M.C., Capt. and Brevet Major (Temporary Lieut.-Colonel), Royal Irish Regt., attached 10th Battn. Hampshire Regt. (Salonika). For conspicuous gallantry during an attack. When under a very heavy barrage the enemy almost effected a lodgment in a portion of his most advanced position, he personally organized a counter-attack with such troops as were available, with the result that the enemy was driven out and the position maintained intact. Throughout the whole operation he set a fine example of courage and determination to all ranks.

THOMSON, ARTHUR LUMLEY, Capt. (Acting Lieut.-Colonel), Royal Sussex Regt., Commanding 7th Battn. For conspicuous gallantry and good leadership while commanding his battalion during an intricate relief. He personally saw every company into position under heavy and continuous shell fire. Throughout the operations the success achieved by his battalion was largely due to his courage, energy and power of command. He was slightly wounded, but remained at duty.

TONKIN, FREDERICK CUTHBERT, M.C., Temporary Lieut. (Temporary Capt.), East Yorkshire Regt., attached 7th Battn. For conspicuous gallantry and devotion to duty during an attack. He led his men with great skill and determination, and personally under heavy machine-gun fire reconnoitred the only crossing across a canal, after which he led his company across and covered the crossing for the remainder of the battalion. Throughout the whole of the operations he displayed great initiative and energy.

TWISLETON-WYKEHAM-FIENNES, NATHANIEL IVO EDWARD, Major, 66th Battery, 4th Brigade, Royal Field Artillery (Mesopotamia). For conspicuous gallantry and devotion to duty. Although exposed to heavy and accurate fire throughout the day he handled his battery with marked coolness and courage, pushing his guns well forward and inflicting heavy casualties on the enemy.

WALBY, HERBERT CHARLES, M.C., Lieut. (Acting Capt.), 4th Battn. North Staffordshire Regt., attached 9th Battn. Yorkshire Light Infantry. For conspicuous gallantry during an attack. He led the support company and eventually came up with the leading waves and took the objective, where he reorganized his men under very heavy fire. In a second attack later in the day his fine example inspired those under him, and when the enemy counter-attacked he personally led forward two platoons to a position from which he could bring fire to bear on them.

WALSH, THEOBALD ALFRED, Major, Somersetshire Light Infantry, attached 9th Battn. Yorkshire Light Infantry. For conspicuous gallantry and ability while carrying out two attacks in command of his battalion. After the first attack he went forward under heavy shell fire and personally reorganized the leading companies ; and finding his left flank exposed he crawled out with a N.C.O. across the open under heavy machine-gun fire, got in touch with troops on the left, and then returned and sent forward a platoon to deal with counter-attacks on the flank. His example and courage enabled his battalion to reach its objectives, and when forced to withdraw later he did so most skilfully. Though twice wounded he remained at duty until his battalion was relieved on the following night.

WELCH, ROBERT HALL, Lieut., Royal Lancaster Regt., attached 127th Light Trench Mortar Battery. For conspicuous gallantry, devotion and fine leadership in command of two Stokes gun detachments. Under heavy shell and machine-gun fire he directed and controlled his guns, obtaining many direct hits and causing heavy enemy casualties, and finally leading his men forward he captured several machine guns. After all his ammunition had been expended he rallied the men and, dumping the guns, led them forward with the battalions on either flank and helped to drive back the enemy until the objectives were reached and consolidated.

WILLIAMS, RICHARD DAVID, Temporary Major, 13th Battn. Welsh Regt. For conspicuous gallantry and devotion to duty. This officer commanded the leading companies in the attack, gaining the final objectives in spite of stiff opposition, and supervising the consolidation under heavy machine-gun fire. He made a personal reconnaissance of the left flank, and, finding it exposed, made dispositions for its defence, which proved their soundness when the enemy were beaten off in several attacks. For two days he maintained his position in spite of one successful attempt to penetrate his line, which was immediately rectified.

WOODHOUSE, JAMES DUGALD FORBES, Capt. (Acting Major), 14th Hussars (Mesopotamia). For conspicuous gallantry and devotion to duty. He commanded his squadron with skill, and by his personal ability and coolness under fire materially assisted in beating off the enemy's attack. Later, when his commanding officer became a casualty, he took command of three squadrons, reorganized the line, and made preparations to meet any further attack, being compelled to expose himself to fire at close range in doing so.

WYNNE-EDWARDS, ROBERT MEREDYDD, M.C., Temporary Capt., 13th Battn. Royal Welsh Fusiliers. For conspicuous gallantry and devotion to duty. This officer, while in command of his company in the front line, found another company in difficulties, so, after making a personal reconnaissance, he reorganized it, and got it on to its objective. Later, with his own company of only 35 men, he retook a hostile strong-point of three fortified mounds with deep dug-outs, which the enemy had rushed in the morning. His personal reconnaissance, under machine-gun and rifle fire entirely cleared up an obscure situation.

CANADIAN FORCE.

BELL, JAMES STARK, M.C., Major, 18th Battn. Canadian Infantry, Western Ontario Regt. For conspicuous gallantry and devotion to duty. When the officer commanding had become a casualty he took command of the battalion and handled it in critical circumstances with great ability. His fine example of personal courage under heavy fire and his energy encouraged his men and inspired them with great confidence.

BLISS, ROBERT HAMILTON, Capt. (Acting Major), 19th Battn. Canadian Infantry, 1st Central Ontario Regt. For conspicuous gallantry and cool courage. This officer was given charge of all the attacking troops of his battalion. Shortly after crossing the enemy front line he received word that his left was held up. He at once organized the troops in the vicinity, leading them personally in the attack against a strong point under heavy machine-gun fire, overcame the opposition, killing all the garrison, and enabling the attack to steadily advance He rushed with a few men the village, taking numerous prisoners. Later, with only three others, he captured a senior commander and his staff, in all 35, from one building. He then established and organized a line about half a mile in advance. Throughout a heavy mist made his task the more difficult.

BRADBROOKE, GEORGE HOWARD, M.C., Major, 1st Battn. Canadian Mounted Rifles, Saskatchewan Regt. This officer showed great initiative and gallantry in leading his company. During an attack, by his personal handling of the troops under his command, he captured all the objectives without a single casualty. Again, two days afterwards, in an attack on a strong enemy position, he led his company with an utter disregard for his own safety and captured the objective with few casualties. He set a fine example to all ranks.

CARMICHAEL, DOUGALL, M.C., Major, 58th Battn. Canadian Infantry, 2nd Central Ontario Regt. For conspicuous gallantry and good leadership. During an attack on a village, the battalion being temporarily held up at a sunken road, he quickly made an appreciation of the situation and manœuvred the attacking companies in such a manner as to overpower the whole of the enemy's front-line positions. At the final objective of the battalion he took a small party forward and captured an enemy regimental headquarters, including 60 prisoners and much valuable information.

CHARLTON, BARTHOLOMEW, Capt. (Acting Major), 43rd Battn. Canadian Infantry, Manitoba Regt. During an attack he was in command of a company. A few minutes after zero the enemy placed a heavy barrage upon the assembly area. By his personal example he rallied his men and led them forward. On arriving at his objective it was found that the Tanks had not come up and that the enemy was holding a wood with machine guns and trench mortars. He again led the attack forward, capturing the wood and taking 153 prisoners, 20 trench mortars and numerous machine guns. He set a splendid example to his men, and largely contributed to the success of the operation.

GRAHAM, CHARLES MILTON RICHARDSON, Major, 18th Battn. Canadian Infantry, Western Ontario Regt. For conspicuous gallantry and devotion to duty. When his company was ordered to attack a village he went forward and made a personal reconnaissance which enabled him to plan and carry out the assault with very few casualties, although it had to be made through a heavy barrage. He then supervised the organization of the line some 500 yards in front of the village, which greatly facilitated the advance on the right. His courage and initiative were great factors in the success of the operations.

HOOPER, BERTRAM OSMER, M.C., Major (Acting Lieut.-Colonel), 20th Battn. Canadian Infantry, 1st Central Ontario Regt. For conspicuous gallantry and devotion to duty. He commanded his battalion with great skill during a successful attack, leading some of the units of his command personally under very heavy fire at critical moments. When his men were held up the next day by the stubborn resistance of the enemy, he promptly went to a most forward position and made able dispositions to repel the counter-attack which developed soon afterwards. His presence at points of danger and his fine example had the most encouraging effect on his men.

McCAGHEY, NORMAN FRASER, M.C., Major, 52nd Battn. Canadian Infantry, Manitoba Regt. For conspicuous gallantry and devotion in a successful attack, when his fine courage and initiative were the outstanding features of the occasion. During the enemy counter-attack, when his company was greatly outnumbered, he exposed himself fearlessly in steadying the line, during which time he was severely wounded, and his splendid example largely accounted for the enemy's complete defeat.

PEARKES, GEORGE RANDOLPH, V.C., M.C., Lieut.-Colonel, 116th Battn. Canadian Infantry, 2nd Central Ontario Regt. This officer handled his battalion in a masterly manner, and, with an enveloping movement, completely baffled and overcame the enemy, who were in a very strong position. He then captured a wood, the final objective, which was about 5,000 yards from the start. Before this, however, the men were becoming exhausted, on observing which he at once went into the attack himself, and, by his splendid and fearless example, put new life into the whole attack, which went forward with a rush and captured 16 enemy guns of all calibres up to 8 inches.

SIFTON, WILFRED VICTOR, Major, 4th Battn. Canadian Mounted Rifles, 1st Central Ontario Regt. Owing to his initiative, and as the result of a personal reconnaissance, he was able to save his company from heavy casualties by taking his men to a new jumping-off place. During an advance of four kilometres under heavy fire he directed the attack of three companies, two company commanders having become casualties, and then organized the battalion outpost line. Throughout the entire action he sent back valuable information to his C.O., and by personal reconnaissance established communications with the flanking units. He set a splendid example to all ranks.

SUTHERLAND, JOHN, Major, 116th Battn. Canadian Infantry, 2nd Central Ontario Regt. During an attack he showed conspicuous gallantry and ability in handling three companies, completely outflanking the enemy, holding the high ground, and succeeding in getting behind them and capturing a wood, taking 12 guns, including a battery of 5.9 howitzers. Throughout he set a fine example of coolness and skill. He rapidly consolidated the position he had won, and prevented the enemy from making a successful counter-attack.

TAYLOR, FREDERICK ARTHUR, Lieut., Canadian Light Horse. For conspicuous gallantry and devotion to duty. With a patrol of four men he cut off an enemy convoy of four ammunition wagons and 35 men under an officer. The enemy machine guns and infantry prevented him bringing the convoy back to our lines, but he disabled the convoy and it was taken possession of next morning when our line advanced. He displayed great courage and presence of mind in peculiarly difficult circumstances.

TOPP, CHARLES BERESFORD, M.C., Capt. (Acting Major), 42nd Battn. Canadian Infantry, Quebec Regt. This officer, acting as second-in-command of the battalion, was in charge of operations in which the battalion bombed its way through a complicated trench system for a distance of a mile, encountering very stiff opposition. When the objective was reached the enemy repeatedly counter-attacked, and was driven off with heavy casualties. The success of the operation was largely due to his great skill, initiative and personal courage, on numerous occasions making reconnaissances of the situation in person.

VANIER, GEORGE PHILIAS, M.C., Capt. (Acting Major), 22nd Battn. Canadian Infantry, Quebec Regt. For conspicuous gallantry and devotion to duty. As second-in-command he led a portion of the battalion to the attack and capture of a village. The O.C. the battalion being then called to the command of brigade, this officer took charge of the battalion and led it with great skill to the attack and capture of a large village. His courage, example and will to conquer imbued all under him with the finest fighting spirit.

WORRALL, RICHARD, M.C., Lieut.-Colonel, 14th Battn. Canadian Infantry, Quebec Regt. Under difficulty of mist he personally led and directed his battalion in the attack and capture of the front-line system of enemy positions, including the guns. He displayed great skill and courage in directing the operations on this and other occasions during which the battalion had lost 23 officer casualties.

AUSTRALIAN IMPERIAL FORCE.

CAMPBELL, JOHN CHARLES, Major, 7th Field Ambulance, Australian Army Medical Corps. For conspicuous gallantry and devotion to duty. This officer was in charge of stretcher-bearers, evacuating all wounded from the right sector of the advance throughout five days' fighting. He kept close behind the infantry and kept in touch with the various medical officers under constant heavy fire. One night a direct hit completely demolished his aid post, but he got his men to a place of safety and continued the evacuation of the wounded. He superintended the work for five days continuously with great courage and persistence, setting a fine example to all under him.

NORMAN, REGINALD HAVILL, M.C., Major, 48th Battn. Australian Imperial Force, attached 12th Australian Infantry Brigade Headquarters. For conspicuous gallantry and devotion to duty under heavy artillery and machine-gun fire; this officer went forward and got into touch with advanced troops, ascertaining their position and establishing liaison between units. He was untiring in his efforts to promote the success of the operation.

PHILLIPS, HERBERT PETER, M.C., Major, 3rd Australian Pioneer Battn. For conspicuous gallantry and devotion to duty. This officer carried out reconnaissances immediately behind the infantry advance, reporting on damaged bridges, etc., and within 24 hours after zero had collected the necessary information for putting the work in hand. He was engaged in this work for three days under heavy shell fire, completing his task under most trying circumstances.

SHORROCK, JAMES, Second Lieut., 28th Battn. Australian Imperial Force. For conspicuous gallantry and devotion to duty. This officer led his platoon in the attack with the greatest dash. On one occasion, well ahead of his men, he jumped into a trench, and single-handed captured 20 men and two machine guns. A few days later, when the advance was held up by a strong point, he worked round to a flank, and again single-handed captured ten men and two machine guns. These most daring actions saved the situation, and enabled the advance to continue.

NEW ZEALAND FORCE.

KENNEDY, DONALD, M.C., Lieut., 2nd Battn. New Zealand Rifle Brigade. For conspicuous gallantry and devotion to duty. Prior to the attack ths officer gained valuable information by a reconnaissance, and in the attack he guided his company through a wood, which was partly held by the enemy, and seized the ridge beyond. Although both his flanks were exposed, he beat off a counter-attack. During the following days, with little sleep, continually exposed to shell and machine-gun fire, and in an area deluged by gas, he was in the thick of the fighting, encouraging his men in every way.

London Gazette, 17 Jan. 1919.—" Admiralty, S.W., 17 Jan. 1919.—Honours for Miscellaneous Services. The King has been graciously pleased to approve of the award of the following honours to the undermentioned Officers. To be Companions of the Distinguished Service Order."

RATHBORNE, CHARLES EDWARD HARRY, Wing-Commander, Royal Naval Air Service (Capt., Royal Marine Light Infantry, now Lieut.-Colonel, Royal Air Force.). In recognition of his gallantry and devotion to duty during the course of a long-distance air raid in which he acted as pilot of a fighting machine which formed part of the escort. Wing-Commander Rathborne was brought down whilst protecting the bombing machines, his engine having been put out of action. It was owing to the gallantry and self-sacrifice of this officer and those of the other fighting machines that all the bombing machines returned safely from the raid.

YOUNG, EDWARD HILTON, D.S.C., M.P., Lieut.-Commander, Royal Naval Volunteer Reserve. In recognition of his services in command of an armoured train during the operations on the Archangel-Vologda Railway on the 14th, 15th and 16th Oct. 1918. This officer displayed great initiative, gallantry and dash, invariably pushing forward as far as possible and causing the enemy armoured train to retire by direct fire.

" Honours for the Mercantile Marine.—The King has been graciously pleased to approve of the award of the following honour to the undermentioned Officer of the Mercantile Marine, in recognition of zeal and devotion to duty shown in carrying on the trade of the country during the war. To be a Companion of the Distinguished Service Order."

MOFFAT, GEORGE DICKINSON, Capt. (Lieut., Royal Naval Reserve).

London Gazette, 1 Feb. 1919.—" War Office, 1 Feb. 1919. His Majesty the King has been graciously pleased to approve of the following awards to the undermentioned Officers, in recognition of their gallantry and devotion to duty in the field. Awarded a Second Bar to the Distinguished Service Order."

BRYCE, EDWARD DANIEL, D.S.O., Temporary Lieut.-Colonel, 2nd Battn. Tank Corps (Capt., East Lancashire Regt.). For conspicuous gallantry in command of battalion of Tanks on 8 Aug. 1918, near Villers-Bretonneux. He followed his Tanks on foot, and went with them under heavy artillery and machine-gun fire to the final objective, a distance of some 10,000 yards. It was owing to his personal direction that his Tank companies were instrumental in capturing all objectives. Throughout the day he showed complete disregard for his personal safety, and set a splendid example of leadership.
(D.S.O. gazetted 26 Sept. 1917.)
(First Bar gazetted 18 Feb. 1918.)

LUMSDEN, WILLIAM VERNON, D.S.O., M.C., Capt. (Temporary Lieut.-Colonel), Argyll and Sutherland Highlanders, Commanding 9th Battn. Scottish Rifles. For conspicuous gallantry and devotion to duty during the 9½ miles' advance east of Ypres from 28 Sept. to 5 Oct. 1918. The first day his battalion was one of the leading assault battalions, and advanced five miles on to the southern end of the Passchendaele Ridge, capturing 11 guns and 250 prisoners. He was in the thick of the fighting, although suffering from malaria at the time. The following day the battalion again advanced under his leadership against frontal and enfilade machine-gun fire, and in the evening, when he found that Dadizeele could not be reached by troops on his right, he deflected his advance, and along with other troops captured it.
(D.S.O. gazetted 26 July, 1918.)
(First Bar gazetted 3 June, 1918.)

PETERSON, ARTHUR JAMES, D.S.O., Temporary Major, A/86th Brigade, Royal Field Artillery. For conspicuous gallantry on the night of 29 Aug. 1918, near Maricourt, while selecting a new forward position. The enemy suddenly opened a heavy burst of shelling on the new position which his battery was approaching, and he rushed out of cover to haul the teams away from the shelling, being severely wounded in doing so. Notwithstanding his wound, he selected another position, brought his guns into action, and laid out the lines of fire. He then personally reported to headquarters, giving the location of his battery position before being taken to the dressing station.
(D.S.O. gazetted 25 Aug. 1916.)
(First Bar gazetted 26 Sept. 1917.)

RIGG, EDWARD HARRISON, D.S.O., Major (Acting Lieut.-Colonel), 1st Battn. Yorkshire Light Infantry, attached 10th Battn. East Yorkshire Regt. For conspicuous gallantry and able leadership on 29 and 30 Sept. 1918. When the attack south through Ploegsteert Wood was held up, he reconnoitred the front under heavy machine-gun and shell fire, and located the positions of the posts. It was due to his fine work that the wood was cleared of the enemy and the line advanced to the Warnave River. All his company commanders were casualties, and the battalion had suffered heavy casualties, but he showed absolute disregard of danger, personally leading his patrols forward.
(D.S.O. gazetted 3 June, 1916.)
(First Bar gazetted 3 June, 1918.)

CANADIAN FORCE.

GILSON, WILLIAM FORBES, D.S.O., Lieut.-Colonel, 7th Battn. Canadian Infantry, British Columbia Regt. For conspicuous gallantry and ability to command. He captured with his battalion, on 2 Sept. 1918, the Drocourt-Quéant line, together with 600 prisoners, his bold and able leadership in face of heavy machine-gun fire overcoming all opposition with minimum losses. Later in the day, under heavy artillery and machine fire, he went forward and personally established his new line.
(D.S.O. gazetted 18 Oct. 1917.)
Bar gazetted 7 Nov. 1918.)

MACDONALD, ERIC WHIDDEN, D.S.O., M.C., Lieut.-Colonel, 10th Battn. Canadian Infantry, Alberta Regt. For conspicuous gallantry and devotion to duty. Before Arras on 2 Sept. 1918, the battalion commanded by him captured three villages, a switch trench line, and reached the west bank of a canal. Early in the day, before the attack, and again in the afternoon, he made personal reconnaissances over fire-swept ground, gaining first-hand information which enabled him to handle his men and direct the fire of his guns with remarkable success. His fine leadership, coolness, and disregard of danger, carried his men along with him.
(D.S.O. gazetted 1 Jan. 1917.)
(Bar gazetted 7 Nov. 1918.)

McLAUGHLIN, LORNE TALBOT, D.S.O., Lieut.-Colonel, 2nd Battn. Canadian Infantry, East Ontario Regt. For conspicuous gallantry and devotion to duty. On the morning of the 30th Aug. 1918, between Hendecourt and Vis-en-Artois, while reconnoitring a position which had just been gained, he observed the development of a counter-attack by the enemy, which caused some retirements and confusion in our ranks. He at once organized a counter-stroke, first checking, and finally driving the enemy back in confusion. His energetic personality, coupled with gallant leading, encouraged all ranks, and was entirely responsible for the reconstitution of the line.
(D.S.O. gazetted 14 Nov. 1916.)
(First Bar gazetted 18 Feb. 1918.)

SPARLING, ALBERT WALTER, D.S.O., Lieut.-Colonel, 1st Battn. Canadian Infantry, Western Ontario Regt. For conspicuous gallantry and devotion to duty north of Hendecourt on 30 Aug 1918, and in the neighbourhood of Cagnicourt on 2 and 3 Sept. This officer was the only surviving Lieutenant-Colonel, all other senior field officers having become casualties. He was twice ordered to deal with serious situations on the brigade front, first, in the case of an enemy counter-attack, and a few days later when there was some confusion and loss of direction of our troops. In dealing with these matters he had to cross open ground and appreciate the situation under heavy fire. His conduct and example inspired all ranks to a successful completion of their tasks.
(D.S.O. gazetted 26 July, 1917.)
(First Bar gazetted 2 Dec. 1918.)

AUSTRALIAN IMPERIAL FORCE.

MARSHALL, NORMAN, D.S.O., M.C., Lieut.-Colonel, 54th Battn. Australian Imperial Force. For conspicuous gallantry in the handling of his battalion. Between 1 and 3 Sept. 1918, he captured the greater part of Peronne, after fierce enemy opposition, personally organizing the attack on the ramparts and the mopping-up of the town. Through his splendid energy and example to his men the town was held, and three guns and about 600 prisoners captured by his battalion.
(D.S.O. gazetted 19 Nov. 1917.)
(Bar gazetted 16 Sept. 1918.)

Awarded a Bar to the Distinguished Service Order:

AHERN, DAVID, D.S.O., Major (Temporary Lieut.-Colonel), No. 11 Field Ambulance, Royal Army Medical Corps. For conspicuous gallantry and devotion to duty from 30 Aug. to 3 Sept. 1918, during operations on the Arras front. He was responsible for the clearing of casualties from the divisional front. He showed great forethought in selecting sites for his forward posts, especially in establishing one post in a village which proved of the utmost value as an A.D.S. later on. He was wounded while at his work, but refused to leave until the conclusion of operations. His energy and resource were instrumental in the prompt evacuation of the wounded.
(D.S.O. gazetted 4 June, 1917.)

BACKHOUSE, MILES REGINALD CHARLES, D.S.O., Major (Temporary Lieut.-Colonel), Northumberland Hussars, Commanding 8th Battn. Yorkshire Regt. (Italy). For conspicuous gallantry and leadership. Near the Piave river during the period 27-29 Oct. 1918, he commanded his battalion with great ability and success. He led his battalion across the Piave under heavy machine-gun fire and reached his final objective at the correct hour, capturing many prisoners and many guns. On the 28th he pushed forward and made a long advance. On the 29th he forced a passage of the Monticana river against strong resistance from greatly superior numbers, and during the day took over 600 prisoners. Throughout the three days' fighting he showed courage and leadership of a high order.
(D.S.O. gazetted 31 Oct. 1902.)

BARTON, PATTERSON, D.S.O., Lieut.-Colonel, Headquarters 41st Brigade, Royal Field Artillery. For conspicuous gallantry and skill in handling his battalion near Rumilly in the action of 8 Oct. 1918. On the previous day he had reconnoitred a forward position close to the front line. In the morning, after the opening barrage, he led his batteries forward with such skill that, although the whole route, including the bridges over the canal, was being heavily shelled, the whole brigade was in action again within an hour. He was wounded while organizing the forward position.
(D.S.O. gazetted 23 June, 1915.)

BROOK, FRANK, D.S.O., M.C., Capt. (Acting Lieut.-Colonel), 4th Battn. Yorkshire Light Infantry, Territorial Force, Commanding 2/4th Battn. Hampshire Regt., Territorial Force. For conspicuous gallantry and able leadership at Marcoing on 28 Sept. 1918, in command of one of two battalions detailed to take Marcoing and the bridge beyond. Owing to an order miscarrying, the other battalion (detailed to take the first objective) did not jump off in turn. Whereupon, after rapidly issuing fresh orders, he took both the village and the bridge beyond, thus preventing delay in the attack. On 30 Sept., when the enemy had gained a footing in our front line, he organized two local bombing attacks successfully with absolute disregard of danger.
(D.S.O. gazetted 26 July, 1918.)

BULLOCK, LAWRENCE NEWSAM BEVERLEY, D.S.O., Temporary Major, 9th Battn. South Staffordshire Regt. (Italy). For conspicuous gallantry and devotion to duty. Prior to the operations on the River Piave, from 23 to 27

Oct. 1918, he was entrusted with arrangements for transfer of troops from the right bank to the Island of Grave de Papadopoli, maintenance of the passage, and control of the crossing of futher men and material. His duties were most ably carried out under difficult conditions and considerable shell fire. The success of the division was to a great extent due to his resource and untiring energy.
(D.S.O. gazetted 15 Feb. 1917.)

BURNYEAT, RICHARD WHITESIDE, D.S.O., Major, " A " Battery, 102nd Brigade, Royal Field Artillery, Territorial Force (Italy). During the period from 26 Oct. to 2 Nov. 1918, including the passage of the Piave, when his battery came under heavy shell-fire and the bridge was broken by enemy bombs, he showed great judgment and coolness in getting his battery across with few casualties. Later, in support of the infantry, he always went forward himself at the earliest moment, selecting O.P.'s and carrying out his tasks very often under heavy machine-gun fire. His gallantry was most marked when the infantry were held up at Sacile village.
(D.S.O. gazetted 3 June, 1918.)

CAMPBELL, JAMES ALEXANDER, D.S.O., Capt. and Brevet Major (Acting Lieut.-Colonel), Suffolk Regt., attached East Lancashire Regt. (Salonika). For conspicuous gallantry in the field. He led his battalion in an attack on enemy trenches in Jackson's Ravine on 19 Sept. 1918. While doing so he was wounded, but continued in command. After the first attempt failed he re-organized the battalion and again attacked, but was severely wounded in the advance. Finding his flanks open, and being exposed on all sides to heavy machine-gun fire, he ordered a withdrawal, continuing in command until he was no longer capable of action. He set a fine example of courage and initiative to all under his command.
(D.S.O. gazetted 1 Jan. 1917.)

CARDEW, GEORGE AMBROSE, C.M.G., D.S.O., Lieut.-Colonel, Headquarters 190th Brigade, Royal Field Artillery. For conspicuous gallantry and devotion to duty on 28 Sept. 1918, south of Ypres, when on reconnaissance after the initial attack with a view to the guns of his brigade advancing. Although knocked down, much shaken, and slightly wounded by a bursting shell, he not only continued his reconnaissance, but by his example during the day, and succeeding days, inspired all ranks under his command, and contributed largely to the success of the operations.
(D.S.O. gazetted 1 Jan. 1917.)

CHEAPE, GEORGE RONALD HAMILTON, D.S.O., M.C., Major and Brevet Lieut.-Colonel (Temporary Brigadier-General), 1st Dragoon Guards, Commanding 86th Infantry Brigade. During operations near Gheluvelt, on the 28th Sept. 1918, his personal gallantry inspired all ranks of the brigade. He was always to be found with the leading troops, directing and encouraging them. The success of the operations of his brigade was largely due to his leadership and courage.
(D.S.O. gazetted 18 Feb. 1918.)

DOBBS, RICHARD CONWAY, D.S.O., Major (Temporary Lieut.-Colonel), Royal Irish Fusiliers, attached South Wales Borderers (Salonika). For conspicuous gallantry in the attack on Visoka Cuka on 25 Sept. 1918, in command of the right column of the attack. After reforming his command, which was heavily shelled at the start, he succeeded in reaching a point more than three-quarters of the way up the mountain, where he held on for 24 hours unsupported under rifle and Lewis-gun fire. It was owing to his personal example and determined leadership that the operations were greatly facilitated and the hill eventually taken with little opposition.
(D.S.O. gazetted 4 June, 1917.)

FESTING, HAROLD ENGLAND, D.S.O., Capt. (Acting Lieut.-Colonel), 1st Battn. Border Regt. For conspicuous gallantry and devotion to duty. He was the first commanding officer to reach the high ground west of Gheluvelt on 28 Sept. 1918, at once reorganizing his battalion and selecting a good defensive position. On the 30th he led a rapid advance of about a mile under cross machine-gun fire, without artillery help, and then personally went forward to reconnoitre. He maintained his position until relieved, and showed fine tactical capacity.
(D.S.O. gazetted 2 May, 1916.)

FRASER, ALEXANDER DONALD, D.S.O., M.C., Capt. (Acting Lieut.-Colonel), No. 9 Field Ambulance, Royal Army Medical Corps. For conspicuous gallantry and devotion to duty. He was in charge of bearer divisions during the operations in the neighbourhood of Moyenneville—Ervillers—St. Leger from 21 to 28 Aug. 1918, and was continually among the leading troops under heavy shell and machine-gun fire directing the evacuation of wounded from R.A.P.'s. He managed to get ambulance cars close up to the firing line, which greatly accelerated the clearing of casualties to the rear. He was untiring throughout the whole period, and set a fine example to those under him.
(D.S.O. gazetted 4 June, 1917.)

FREYBERG, BERNARD CYRIL, V.C., D.S.O., Capt. and Brevet Lieut.-Colonel (Temporary Brigadier-General), Royal West Surrey Regt., Commanding 88th Infantry Brigade. He showed himself a fearless and resourceful commander. The success of the operations of his brigade near Gheluvelt on the 28th Sept. and the following days was largely owing to his inspiring example. Wherever the fighting was hardest he was always to be found encouraging and directing his troops.
(D.S.O. gazetted 3 June, 1915.)

GOODWIN, WILLIAM RICHARD, D.S.O., Temporary Lieut.-Colonel, 12th Battn. Royal Irish Rifles. For conspicuous gallantry and devotion to duty near Dadizeele on 30 Sept. 1918. He went forward to rally his reserve company, which was being held up by machine-gun fire, and led them on, capturing Twig Farm, 25 prisoners and several machine guns. He then reorganized and drove the enemy out of a wood near the farm, capturing more machine guns. He then returned for more men, and while he was away the enemy counter-attacked in force. The confidence with which he inspired his men was largely responsible for this success.
(D.S.O. gazetted 1 Jan. 1918.)

GRAEME, JAMES ARCHIBALD, D.S.O., Major (Acting Lieut.-Colonel), Royal Engineers (Commanding Royal Engineers, 63rd Division). For conspicuous gallantry and devotion to duty on the night of 28-29 Sept. 1918, near Cantaing. He selected a site and supervised the erection of a pontoon bridge over the Canal de L'Escaut, and a footbridge across the Escaut River, which was infordable. The approaches to the banks of the canal and river were at the time swept by machine-gun fire, and the construction of these bridges made the subsequent operations possible.
(D.S.O. gazetted 1 Jan. 1917.)

GROUNDS, GEORGE AMBROSE, D.S.O., Temporary Capt. (Acting Major), 8th Battn. Tank Corps. On the night of 10-11 Aug. 1918, during the operations near Prozart, for conspicuous gallantry in charge of two sections of Tanks co-operating with the infantry. When some confusion was caused among the latter by heavy machine-gun fire in the darkness he went forward with complete disregard of danger, and reorganized the column, keeping the leading Tanks in action for an hour and a half after the infantry had withdrawn. He remained out alone for some time after the last Tank had withdrawn to ensure getting accurate touch with the situation.
(D.S.O. gazetted 18 Feb. 1918.)

HARMAN, CHARLES, D.S.O., Major and Brevet Lieut.-Colonel (Temporary Lieut.-Colonel), Leinster Regt., attached 4th Battn. Bedfordshire Regt. For conspicuous gallantry and fine leadership in the attack on Canal du Nord on 27 Sept. 1918, resulting in the capture of 700 prisoners, five guns and many machine guns. When the right half of the battalion was held up by heavy machine-gun fire, and the left half, which had advanced, exposed to reverse fire from a strong point, he led battalion headquarters against it, capturing two officers, 95 men and five machine guns. He showed fine determination and fighting qualities in the subsequent consolidation under heavy fire.
(D.S.O. gazetted 10 Jan. 1917.)

HOLFORD, JAMES HENRY EDWARD, D.S.O., Major (Temporary Lieut.-Colonel), Nottinghamshire Yeomanry, attached 12th Battn. Durham Light Infantry (Italy). For conspicuous gallantry and devotion to duty in command of a battalion during the operations on the Piave from 27 to 30 Oct. 1918. Under heavy machine-gun fire he frequently reorganized his battalion and led them forward to their next objective, showing a total disregard for his own safety. His courage and able leadership were most marked.
(D.S.O. gazetted 15 Jan. 1901.)

IRVINE, ALFRED ERNEST, C.M.G., D.S.O., Major and Brevet Lieut.-Colonel (Temporary Brigadier-General), Durham Light Infantry, Commanding 112th Infantry Brigade. For conspicuous gallantry and devotion to duty on 8 and 9 Sept. 1918, near Havrincourt. The plans for attack on the village necessitated the possession of a slag heap known to be held by the enemy. Pushing out patrols to locate the exact position of the enemy, he went out himself, and with his intelligence officer, made a personal reconnaissance about 200 yards in front of the outposts to the top of the slag heap, and as he was not fired on ordered the patrols to push on there. The next morning he again went up to the outpost line, and reconnoitred some 250 yards beyond under constant sniping. The knowledge he gained enabled him to capture a post and light field gun, and his personal determination cleared up the situation.
(D.S.O. gazetted 31 May, 1916.)

JACKSON, GEORGE HANBURY NOBLE, C.M.G., D.S.O., Major and Brevet Lieut.-Colonel (Temporary Brigadier-General), Border Regt., Commanding 87th Infantry Brigade. For great gallantry and resource in the operations near Gheluvelt on the 28th Sept. 1918, and the following days. Whenever circumstances were in the least difficult he was always to be found with the leading troops fearlessly exposing himself and inspiring all ranks by his example.
(D.S.O. gazetted 27 Sept. 1901.)

KELLETT, JOHN PHILIP, D.S.O., M.C., Capt. (Acting Lieut.-Colonel), 1/2nd Battn. London Regt. For conspicuous gallantry and able leading of his battalion on 27 Sept. 1918, at the crossing of the Canal du Nord during the attack near Oisy-le-Verger. The villages and enclosed ground were occupied by a large number of machine-gun posts, which threatened to hold up a rather thin attack. By quick and skilful manœuvring he reduced the centres of resistance one after the other, capturing a number of prisoners well in excess of his own losses.
(D.S.O. gazetted 3 June, 1918.)

MORRIS, CHARLES READE MUNROE, D.S.O., M.B., Major (Acting Lieut.-Colonel), 99th Field Ambulance, Royal Army Medical Corps. For exceptional gallantry and devotion to duty on 20 to 24 Sept. south-west of Villers Guislain, in working continually for five days under heavy shell fire, supervising and co-ordinating the work of the Medical Officers while at work at night in the advanced dressing station. It was twice blown in by shell burst. He carried out important surgical work, and by his pluck and endurance set a fine example to all around him.
(D.S.O. gazetted 4 June, 1917.)

O'CONNOR, RICHARD NUGENT, D.S.O., M.C., Capt. and Brevet Major (Acting Lieut.-Colonel), Scottish Rifles, attached 2nd Battn. Honourable Artillery Company (Italy). He was entrusted with the command of the troops detailed to capture the Island of Papadopoli on 24 Oct. 1918. By his personal careful reconnaissance and plans for attack the whole island was captured, together with some 600 prisoners, with small loss to his battalion. The operations were carried out at night in two phases under most difficult conditions ; in the second phase he, with a few of his battalion headquarters, came across an enemy point manned by some 60 men and two officers, and immediately charged them and caused the whole garrison to surrender. By his most gallant and able leadership in these operations, the crossing of troops for the main attack was carried out without loss.
(D.S.O. gazetted 16 Aug. 1917.)

PETER, FRED HARRIS, D.S.O., M.C., Capt. (Acting Lieut.-Colonel), Royal Fusiliers, attached 5th Battn. Yorkshire Light Infantry, Territorial Force. For conspicuous gallantry and ability in command of his battalion at Havrincourt, 12-14 Sept. 1918. It was chiefly owing to his arrangements that, in spite of heavy fire, the battalion reached its objective with few casualties. After a heavy counter-attack he successfully cleared the village and took over a 500 yards' frontage facing a different way. After a second counter-attack, when units were mixed, he reorganized the line under heavy bombardment and held it
(D.S.O. gazetted 11 Jan. 1919.)

RITCHIE, THE HONOURABLE HAROLD, D.S.O., Temporary Major, 11th Battn. Scottish Rifles, attached 1st Battn. For conspicuous gallantry and devotion to duty during an attack south of Villers Guislain on 21 Sept. 1918. When he heard that his men were held up by uncut wire and a machine-gun barrage, nearly all the officers being casualties, he went forward and led the attack. In doing so he was wounded, and after he had had the wound dressed again went forward and directed his men in repelling a counter-attack, until he had to be sent to the dressing station. His grit and endurance were a fine example.
(D.S.O. gazetted 1 Jan. 1918.)

ROME, CHARLES LESLIE, D.S.O., Capt. (Temporary Lieut.-Colonel), 11th Hussars, attached 3rd Dragoon Guards. For conspicuous gallantry and fine leadership of his regiment when ordered to capture Honnechy and the high ground east of it on 18 Oct. His quick appreciation and dash enabled the regiment to seize its objective in spite of extreme shelling and enfilade machine-gun fire. Shortly afterwards he was wounded and rendered unconscious when organizing a further advance. On regaining consciousness he insisted on remaining to give the brigadier a clear report of the situation, and only went to the dressing station when ordered to do so. The capture of Honnechy, which was entirely due to his initiative, had a most important bearing on subsequent operations.
(D.S.O. gazetted 26 July, 1918.)

UTTERSON KELSO, JOHN EDWARD, D.S.O., M.C., Capt. (Acting Lieut.-Colonel), 2nd Battn. Royal Scots Fusiliers. For conspicuous gallantry and devotion to duty during the 9½ miles' advance east of Ypres from 28 Sept. to 5 Oct. 1918. His battalion was one of the leading assault battalions in a five miles' advance on to the southern end of Passhendaele Ridge. Although he was knocked down by a shell and severely shaken, he continued in command, refusing to leave. The battalion captured several guns and 200 prisoners. The next day, at a critical period when the front line was held up, he pushed forward his battalion, which was then in support, and relieved the situation.
(D.S.O. gazetted 26 July, 1918.)

WALSH, THEOBALD ALFRED, D.S.O., Major, Somersetshire Light Infantry attached 9th Battn. Yorkshire Light Infantry. For conspicuous gallantry and able leadership at Villers Guislain on 19 Sept. 1918. The battalion which he commanded captured the whole of its final objective. When the enemy counter-attacked the troops on his left, driving them back, he collected 25 men of his Headquarters company and, with a cheer, led them straight into the enemy's flank, driving them back in disorder. He was hit in the leg, but waved the men on as he lay on the ground, and saved a critical situation.
(D.S.O. gazetted 11 Jan. 1919.)

WEST, ALEXANDER HENRY DELAP, D.S.O., Major and Brevet Lieut.-Colonel (Temporary Lieut.-Colonel), 5th Army Brigade, Royal Horse Artillery. For conspicuous gallantry and ability on 25 and 26 Aug. 1918, in handling two brigades of artillery during the operations south of the Somme which resulted in the capture of Château Wood and Olymona Wood, an advance of some 3,000 yards. In spite of a very heavy barrage, he personally handled his brigade, and in a difficult operation contributed largely to the success of the infantry. He showed marked courage and ability to command.
(D.S.O. gazetted 1 Jan. 1917.)

CANADIAN FORCE.

EWING, ROYAL LINDSAY HAMILTON, D.S.O., M.C., Major, 42nd Battn. Canadian Infantry, Quebec Regt. For conspicuous gallantry and devotion to duty while in command of his battalion throughout the operations south of the Scarpe, which resulted in the capture of Jigsaw Wood, 26 to 28 Aug. 1918. His gallantry and able leadership ensured the attainment of objectives upon which rested the success of the brigade. He showed marked initiative and an absolute disregard of personal danger.
(D.S.O. gazetted 1 Jan. 1918.)

McDONALD, JOHN ANGUS, D.S.O., Lieut.-Colonel, 3rd Brigade, Canadian Field Artillery. For conspicuous gallantry on 2 Sept. during the attack east of Arras. He went forward with his brigade in close support of the advancing infantry. He reconnoitred positions for his batteries under heavy shell and machine-gun fire, and set a splendid example by his personal disregard of danger and determination to push forward. The batteries went forward with great dash, and effective fire was brought to bear on many targets, including enemy strong points and hostile batteries. His skilful leadership and the work of his brigade gave the greatest confidence to the attacking infantry.
(D.S.O. gazetted 1 Jan. 1917.)

McEACHERN, NORMAN ANGUS, D.S.O., Lieut., 10th Battn. Canadian Infantry, Alberta Regt. For conspicuous gallantry at Villers-les-Cagnicourt, Bury Switch and the Canal-du-Nord from 2 to 4 Sept. 1918. He led his own company, and at times two others, brilliantly, pushing ahead in face of heavy fire, and beating down all opposition. After making a daring reconnaissance at the head of a patrol, he led his company first to the final objective, where a line was established. Shortly afterwards he was severely wounded. He set a fine example of courage and leadership to all.
(D.S.O. gazetted 18 Oct. 1917.)

PYMAN, COLIN KEITH LEE, D.S.O., Major, 5th Canadian Battn., Saskatchewan Regt. For great skill and gallantry while acting as second-in-command of the battalion between the 7th and 9th Aug. 1918, during the advance on Aubercourt. When the line became much weakened through casualties, he collected men together, and, after a vigorous fight, placed them in the gaps. He was instrumental in capturing a field gun and a number of prisoners, and on another occasion in throwing out a protecting flank, thus enabling the advance to continue. He was wounded on the 9th within 50 yards of the final objective.
(D.S.O. gazetted 15 Oct. 1918.)

RANKIN, JAMES SABISTON, D.S.O., Major, 46th Battn. Canadian Infantry, Saskatchewan Regt. In front of Dury, on 2 Sept., he was in command of the battalion during the successful capture of the village. Later, the enemy launched a heavy counter-attack against the posts to the east of the village, causing them and the adjoining posts to withdraw, and gaining a footing in the position immediately to the east and threatening the village. He showed splendid resource and courage, and went forward, under heavy machine-gun fire, to investigate the situation. He successfully organized and launched a counter-attack from the companies in support of his battalion, and succeeded in restoring the situation.
(D.S.O. gazetted 1 Jan. 1918.)

SHEARER, GEORGE WYMAN, D.S.O., Major, 11th Battery, 3rd Brigade, Canadian Field Artillery. For conspicuous gallantry and determination whilst in support of the attacking infantry after the capture of the Drocourt-Quéant Line on 2 Sept. 1918. He pushed his battery forward and established his observation post south of the windmill on Mount Dury, which was under intense shelling and machine-gun fire. Although wounded, he directed his battery with skill and courage throughout, dealing effectively with hostile machine guns, batteries and enemy troops in the open, remaining on Mount Dury for 18 hours after he was wounded.
(D.S.O. gazetted 3 June, 1918.)

TUDOR, LORN PAULET OWEN, D.S.O., Lieut.-Colonel, 5th Battn. Canadian Infantry, Saskatchewan Regt. On 1 Sept. 1918, for conspicuous gallantry and ability to command. When the enemy had penetrated several hundred yards of the newly-won positions east of the Hendecourt-Dury Road, this officer launched his battalion in a successful counter-attack, regaining previous positions, killing numbers of the enemy and capturing 200 prisoners. He then maintained his position under heavy fire and against repeated enemy attacks until zero hour. His personal example of fearlessness did much to hearten his battalion in the fine work they accomplished.
(D.S.O. gazetted 18 July, 1917.)

WORRALL, RICHARD, D.S.O., M.C., Lieut.-Colonel, 14th Battn. Canadian Infantry, Quebec Regt. On 1 Sept. 1918, for conspicuous gallantry during the attack on the Crow's Nest and Hendecourt Château Woods while in command of his battalion. He advanced his line half a mile, and under heavy fire maintained his position all day. The following day, though his left was exposed to withering machine-gun and artillery fire, he captured a village, taking prisoners a whole battalion. Still pushing on, he took the final objective, and established his position, having advanced some 5,000 yards from the jumping-off line. He displayed fine courage and leadership.
(D.S.O. gazetted 11 Jan. 1919.)

AUSTRALIAN IMPERIAL FORCE.

DUNCAN, WALTER JOHN CLARE, D.S.O., M.C., Capt., 33rd Battn. Australian Imperial Force. For conspicuous gallantry throughout the operations south-west of Bouchavesnes on 31 Aug. 1918. He commanded his company brilliantly, and in face of strong opposition and heavy fire captured some 200 prisoners, 10 machine-guns, and four trench mortars. Throughout the whole operation he displayed wonderful dash and courage, and by his fine leadership succeeded against seemingly overwhelming odds.
(D.S.O. gazetted 26 July, 1918.)

MITCHELL, JOHN WESLEY, D.S.O., Lieut.-Colonel, 8th Battn. Australian Imperial Force. For conspicuous gallantry during the taking of Rosières Station and the village of Lihons on the 9th and 11th Aug. 1918. When his battalion had suffered heavy casualties he personally went forward, and, under heavy fire, reorganized his line. Again, after his battalion had taken Lihons, where the situation was obscure, he again went forward, and did the same under withering machine-gun fire. His fine leadership and coolness under fire were largely responsible for the success achieved by his battalion.
(D.S.O. gazetted 1 Jan, 1918.)

SASSE, CECIL DUNCAN, D.S.O., Major (Temporary Lieut.-Colonel), 4th Battn. Australian Imperial Force. For conspicuous gallantry in the attack on Chuignolles and Chuignes on 23 Aug. 1918. In face of exceedingly heavy fire he brought his battalion through to the final objective with extraordinarily few casualties, and succeeded in capturing several hundred prisoners and some field guns. He then advanced an additional mile, captured Fontaine les Cappy, and skilfully protected his new position. The brilliant success of his battalion was due to his splendid leadership.
(D.S.O. gazetted 29 Oct. 1915.)

STACY, BERTIE VANDELEUR, D.S.O., Lieut.-Colonel, 1st Battn. Australian Imperial Force. For conspicuous gallantry in the attack on Chuignolles and Chuignes on 23 Aug. 1918. He established his headquarters close behind the fighting troops, and in spite of heavy shell fire exercised valuable control during the progress of the fight. By personal reconnaissance he was able to direct the fire of the heavy artillery upon numerous field guns and machine guns, which were causing casualties. Also, by organizing the fire of Vickers and Lewis guns upon enemy machine-guns he was able to send on the attack. Upon gaining the set objective he pushed out patrols, which brought back valuable information, enabling the gain to be further exploited. Owing to his splendid leadership his battalion made an advance of nearly three miles, and captured several hundred prisoners and some machine guns.
(D.S.O. gazetted 4 June, 1917.)

ULRICH, THEODORE FREDERICK, D.S.O., Major (Temporary Lieut.-Colonel), 6th Battn. Australian Infantry. For conspicuous gallantry and leadership in command of his battalion near Herleville Wood on 23 Aug. 1918. He kept in close touch with the attack, and controlled their movements under heavy artillery and machine-gun fire. He made the most of his opportunities, quickly grasping the situation, and set a fine example to his men.
(D.S.O. gazetted 1 Jan. 1917.)

WOODS, PERCY WILLIAM, D.S O., M.C., Lieut.-Colonel, 55th Battn. Australian Imperial Force. For conspicuous gallantry and able handling of his battalion on 1 and 2 Sept. 1918, north of Peronne. The position being obscure after an attack, he went forward personally and consolidated the line under heavy shell and machine-gun fire. The two officers and a runner with him were killed, but he continued his work, and completed consolidation. His courage and devotion to duty greatly inspired his men.
(D.S.O. gazetted 1 Jan. 1918.)

Awarded the Distinguished Service Order :

ARMSTRONG, CYRIL LIONEL, M.C., Temporary Major, 11th Battn. West Yorkshire Regt. (Italy). Near Lido on the nights, 24-26 Oct. 1918, he acted as beachmaster and superintended the embarkation of very large numbers of troops of two divisions under persistent shell fire. His coolness and untiring energy were instrumental in getting them across the first stream of the Piave with no disorganization and few casualties. On 29 Oct. near Soffratu, he handled his battalion brilliantly in the fight for the crossings of the Monticuna river, forcing a crossing against superior numbers of the enemy strongly entrenched, and made a considerable advance, taking over 800 prisoners. He showed courage and leadership of a high order.

BARBER, PHILIP STANLEY, M.C., Temporary Capt., General List (Brigade Major, 50th Infantry Brigade). For conspicuous gallantry and devotion to duty at Martinpuich on 25th Aug. 1918. When a gap was reported on the right of the Divisional front, he rode forward in the face of intense fire to investigate, and righted what, at the time, was a very critical situation. Two days later, when the Brigade was somewhat disorganized by an enemy counter-attack, he again went through heavy machine-gun fire and re-established the positions, gaining the confidence of all ranks by his coolness and disregard of danger.

BEAVAN, FRANK ELLIOT, Lieut. (Acting Capt.), Welsh Horse Yeomanry, attached 25th Battn. Royal Welsh Fusiliers. On the 21st Sept. 1918, a hostile barrage on the battalion, which was waiting to attack, caused heavy losses and confusion. He dashed forward, and, by his magnificent fearlessness and example, at once steadied the battalion, which, owing to all the senior officers having become casualties, he led to the first objective. Only a few junior officers then remaining, he reorganized and led the battalion to the second objective, which he captured. His numbers were by this time reduced to a mere handful of men, and, being unable to withstand a determined enemy attack, he skilfully withdrew, bringing back most of the wounded against odds of twenty to one. His courage, coolness, and splendid example turned a temporary reverse into a moral victory.

BERRELL, JACK SYLVESTER THOMAS, Second Lieut. (Acting Capt.), 7th Battn. London Regt., attached 2/10th Battn. On 9 Aug. 1918, when in command of a support company, the battalion was suffering heavy casualties, and their advance held up by direct machine-gun fire from Chipilly Spur, and enfilade fire down the valley. He worked his company forward, and seeing the nest of enemy machine guns which was causing most of the casualties, with a handful of men rushed through the village, which had not been cleared, under heavy shell and direct fire at close range, capturing eight guns and over 50 prisoners. He then signalled to the assaulting troops, and leading the remainder of his party over the spur, established himself in the final objective. His daring lead, quickness and total disregard of danger were mainly responsible for the capture of the ridge.

BLAND, CHARLES FRANK, Capt., 8th Battn. Essex Regt. (Territorial Force), attached 10th Battn. For conspicuous gallantry and devotion to duty during the action near Becourt on 23 Aug. 1918. With the assistance of one N.C.O., he personally rushed three machine guns in succession, which were holding up the advance, and killed no less than five gunners himself. On reaching the objective he organized his own and other companies in depth under heavy shell and machine-gun fire, handling his men with skill and resource.

BRUNTON, JOSEPH, M.C., Temporary Major, 12/13th Battn. Northumberland Fusiliers. For conspicuous gallantry and devotion to duty in the operations near Walincourt on 8 Oct. 1918. When the battalion was held up west of the wood he led them forward under machine-gun fire and shelling at close range, and captured the wood. Although wounded and considerably shaken by a shell which burst close to him, he returned to battalion headquarters to report. While he was away the battalion was driven out of the wood, so he again went up and restored the situation. The success of the advance under heavy fire without a barrage was due to his energy and resource.

CAVE, WILLIAM STURMY, Capt., 2/4th Battn. Hampshire Regt., Territorial Force. For fine leadership and gallantry during operations at Havrincourt, 12 and 13 Sept. 1918, especially while in command of the leading company in an attack on the village. Hearing that the attack was held up by an enemy machine gun, he at once went forward with a few men, personally shooting the gunner and capturing the gun with four prisoners. Later, he again displayed great courage with a small party of men, and was responsible for the capture of two heavy machine guns, two officers and 16 men.

CHADWICK, ROBERT NEPAUL, Temporary Second Lieut., 10th Battn. Welsh Regt., attached 2nd Battn. For conspicuous gallantry near Bethecourt, on 15 Sept. 1918, when ordered to clear a wood with his platoon. Making clever use of covering fire from his Lewis guns and getting his rifle sections round the flanks he led the attack and single-handed captured a machine gun and crew of six. Although wounded, he advanced again, and with four men rushed a second machine gun, killing two of the crew with his revolver and capturing the gun. He was severely wounded this time, but refused to leave until he had reorganized his platoon and handed over the command to his serjeant. He showed magnificent courage and marked ability to command.

COWLING, HAROLD EDWARD, M.C., Temporary Lieut., 11th Battn. Northumberland Fusiliers (Italy). During the attack on the enemy's lines on the north bank of the Piave on 27 Oct. 1918, this officer was adjutant of his battalion, and after his C.O. and Second-in-Command had become casualties he took command. He reorganized the much depleted force, and but for his most gallant and able leadership the third objective could scarcely have been captured. In addition, ascertaining that his left on the first objective was under enfilade fire from C. Touon, he personally collected some men and captured the two enemy machine guns in this position. He did fine work.

DIGBY, THE HONOURABLE EDWARD KENELM, M.C., Capt. (Acting Major), 1st Battn. Coldstream Guards. For conspicuous gallantry and initiative on and previous to 27 Sept. 1918, during the operations across the Canal du Nord while commanding the battalion. The objective was the Hindenburg support line east of the Canal, which had to be crossed. The battalion was in the front line prior to the attack, so all preparations had to be made while in the forward zone. He thought out everything carefully, and despite heavy opposition from the start, all went smoothly. Although wounded in the leg, he remained at duty until relieved.

FETHERSTON, GUY, M.C., Temporary Capt. (Acting Major), 162nd Brigade, Royal Field Artillery. For conspicuous gallantry as Brigade Commander near Gouzeaucourt on 18 Sept. 1918. He was wounded while making a forward reconnaissance, but continued at duty during the next twelve days, keeping in constant touch with an ever-changing situation, and, under heavy shelling, gaining information of great advantage. He showed great pluck and devotion to duty while suffering from his wound, and his great personal influence contributed much to the success of the brigade.

FISHER, THOMAS DOUGLAS, M.C., Second Lieut., 5th Battn. Lancashire Fusiliers, Territorial Force, attached 2/4th Battn. York and Lancaster Regt., Territorial Force. For conspicuous gallantry and initiative on 2 Sept. 1918, in command of a company in front of Vaulx Vrancourt. He led his men through a hostile barrage to their objective. His other officer was almost immediately wounded, but he encouraged his men in the advance in face of intense machine-gun fire and point-blank fire from three field guns, which were subsequently captured. Later, he held his ground against a strong counter-attack. About midday he and one other officer were the only two left with the battalion, and he reorganized the men of all companies, advanced and consolidated. His behaviour when suddenly saddled with responsibility was magnificent.

GILL, FREDERICK GORDON, Capt. (Acting Major), 1/24th Battn. London Regt. For conspicuous gallantry, leadership and ability during operations on the 30th Aug. 1918, east of Maurepas. After the attack had been successfully carried out, under particularly heavy shell fire, he personally reconnoitred the position gained, under severe shell, machine-gun and rifle fire, to superintend its consolidation. The result of the operations was the capture of over 200 prisoners, three 77 mm. guns and a large number of machine guns.

GOLDTHORP, ROBERT HEWARD, Capt. (Acting Lieut.-Colonel), 4th Battn., attached 2/10th Battn. West Riding Regt. (Territorial Force) (temporarily attached 1/28th Battn. London Regt.). For conspicuous gallantry and devotion to duty on 27 Sept. 1918, in the attack on the spur running south-west from Bourlon Wood and east of Mœuvres. When the leading companies were held up by machine-gun fire, suffering heavy casualties, he went forward collecting personnel and reorganizing the attack, which resulted in the capture of the objective. He showed a fine offensive spirit, which encouraged his men at a critical period.

GREENWOOD, GEOFFREY BRYDE, Second Lieut., 6th Battn. Nottinghamshire and Derbyshire Regt., Territorial Force, attached 10th Battn. For conspicuous gallantry and able leadership round Gauche Wood on 18 Sept. 1918. In a counter-attack delivered by the enemy, the battalion on his left was driven in, and the left company of his battalion was beginning to give way. Quickly grasping the situation, he led his platoon over the open, under heavy machine-gun fire, and recaptured the whole of the lost ground, killing 25 of the enemy and taking six machine guns. He shot five himself with a revolver, and although wounded remained until fresh troops arrived. He did splendid work.

HALL, DOUGLAS MONTGOMERY BERNARD, Capt. (Acting Lieut.-Colonel), Coldstream Guards, attached 4th Battn. North Staffordshire Regt. For conspicuous gallantry and devotion to duty in command of a battalion in the attack near Zandvoorde, on 29 Sept. 1918. When the attack lost direction over difficult ground, he went forward himself and succeeded in changing the direction, in face of heavy machine-gun fire. His coolness and powers of leadership had an inspiring effect on the men of the battalion.

HARRISON, MICHAEL CHARLES COOPER, M.C., Capt. (Acting Lieut.-Colonel), 2nd Battn. Royal Irish Regt. For conspicuous gallantry and devotion to duty on 27 Sept. 1918, in command of the supporting battalion in the attack on Graincourt and Anneux. Throughout the day, under constant artillery and machine-gun fire, he kept in close touch with the front, despatching reinforcements when and where required. On the following days, near Cambrai, he never relaxed his efforts in encouraging all ranks by his courageous bearing.

HERRICK, ROBERT LYSLE WARREN, Lieut., Indian Army Reserve of Officers, attached 29th Lancers, Indian Army (Egypt). For conspicuous gallantry, on 21 Aug. 1918, in the vicinity of Wadi Nimrin, east of Ghoraniyeh bridgehead defences, in charge of a patrol of six. Observing two enemy behind a bush, who opened fire, he went forward to reconnoitre and saw an enemy party of about 20. Detaching the N.C.O. and one man to work round the flank, he charged with his remaining four men, in face of heavy fire, and captured the lot. He then took his prisoners safely back over two miles of open country, under heavy machine-gun and shell fire. He showed fine courage and leadership.

JONES, RICHARD HODKINSON, M.C., Temporary Major, Hampshire Regt. (Salonika). For conspicuous gallantry during an attack on an enemy position at White Scar Hill on 18 Sept. 1918. He was in charge of the attacking party, and, owing largely to his courage and determination, the enemy position was taken by assault. Under subsequent heavy shelling he held on to the position, and when ordered withdrew his force in order to our lines. His coolness and disregard for safety were most marked.

KENNINGTON, JOHN, M.C., Temporary Major, Lincolnshire Regt., attached 1st Battn. Royal Warwickshire Regt. For conspicuous gallantry and devotion to duty east of Arras on 30 Aug. 1918. When his battalion was assembling for the attack it was heavily shelled, and he was wounded in three places and badly shaken. In spite of this he carried on, launching the attack under most trying conditions, and, owing to his careful organization and attention to details, bringing it to a successful conclusion. His determination and courage had a stimulating effect on his men.

KERRICH, WALTER ALLAN FITZGERALD, M.C., Capt. (Acting Lieut.-Colonel), Royal Engineers (Commanding Royal Engineers, 7th Division) (Italy). For conspicuous gallantry and resource. In connection with operations on the Piave it was of vital importance to throw a bridge, and, up to midnight, 24-25 Oct. 1918, every effort to bridge the particular crossing had failed. This officer took the matter in hand, waded the river at various points until he found a possible crossing, and then, under enemy observation, worked unceasingly until the bridge was completed, later maintaining it under heavy shelling and frequent bombs from aeroplanes. Had it not been for his fine work the successful operations on 27 Oct. would have been rendered most difficult.

LAMOTTE, LEWIS, Capt. (Acting Lieut.-Colonel), 2nd Battn. Royal Sussex Regt., attached 2nd Battn. Yorkshire Light Infantry. For conspicuous gallantry and devotion to duty at Herleville during the fighting of 23 Aug. 1918. Thanks to his personal supervision his companies reached their objectives without serious loss, after destroying several machine-gun nests through the village. Throughout the day he was constantly among his men, suggesting improvements and preparing against counter-attacks. The success of the operation was largely due to his energy and judgment.

LEES, SIR JOHN VICTOR ELLIOT, Bart., M.C., Capt. (Acting Major), King's Royal Rifle Corps, attached 18th Battn. For conspicuous gallantry and devotion to duty on 1 and 2 Oct. 1918. The first day, near Villers Farm, he was constantly with the furthest advanced troops, supervising their progress and overcoming difficulties. On the following day, during the attack south-west of Gheluives, he supervised the forming up of two companies, and was constantly under heavy shell fire, while consolidating the captured position, and also during a counter-attack. He did not spare himself for several days in his efforts to ensure success.

LINDESAY, GEORGE WILLIAM GUY, Major (Acting Lieut.-Colonel), retired Indian Army, attached Royal Scots Fusiliers (Salonika). For conspicuous gallantry and fearless leadership of his battalion on 19 Sept. 1918. Though badly wounded he established his headquarters in the Tongue, and continued to command his battalion which had consolidated itself in this position. By his cheerful bearing under intense machine-gun fire and bombardment he encouraged his battalion to hold on to the position for many hours, though both flanks were exposed to enfilade fire.

LINDSEY-RENTON, REGINALD HERBERT, Major, 9th Battn. London Regt. North of the Somme, 2 Aug.–15 Sept. 1918, he commanded his battalion with great gallantry and success throughout lengthy operations. In two successive attacks he gained and held the objectives in spite of most determined resistance on the part of the enemy. The results achieved were largely due to his fine leadership.

LLOYD, WILLIAM JOSEPH, Second Lieut., 7th Battn. Lancashire Fusiliers, Territorial Force, attached 5th Battn. West Riding Regt., Territorial Force. For very gallant leadership at Havrincourt, 12 to 15 Sept. 1918, while in charge of a bombing attack over a sunken road, where six of his men and an officer were killed in attempting to cross. He rallied his party, crossed and recrossed the gap himself several times, and finally captured the objective, taking 20 prisoners and a machine gun. In spite of determined enemy attacks from all sides, he held the position throughout the day, and thereby gave great assistance to his battalion in its advance.

LOWE, THOMAS ALFRED, M.C., Lieut. (Temporary Capt. and Acting Lieut.-Colonel), Royal Irish Regt., attached 1st Battn. Royal Irish Fusiliers. For conspicuous gallantry and devotion to duty on 1 Oct 1918, near Dadizeele. He was visiting his forward posts when the enemy suddenly attacked under cover of shell and machine-gun fire, inflicting numerous casualties. He went round encouraging his men, collecting ammunition from the dead, and inspiring such confidence that the attack was beaten off, and the line properly reorganized.

MACINTYRE, HUGH ROSS, M.C., M.D., Temporary Capt. (Acting Major), Royal Army Medical Corps, attached 69th Field Ambulance (Italy). For conspicuous gallantry and devotion to duty during operations on the Piave between 27 and 29 Oct. 1918, especially on the morning of the 27th when in charge of stretcher-bearers. He crossed to the right bank of the Piave immediately behind the infantry under very heavy fire, and supervised the collection and evacuation of the wounded under great difficulties, having to ford the river several times. He set a very fine example to all under him by his untiring energy and total disregard for his own safety.

McCLEVERTY, GUY MASSY, M.C., Capt., 1/2nd Gurkha Rifles, Indian Army (Mesopotamia). For conspicuous gallantry and devotion to duty at Resht, Persia, on 20 July, 1918. He was in command of a relief party sent to extricate a force besieged in a building. He displayed great courage and initiative, and it was mainly due to his resource and daring leadership that the relief was successfully accomplished. His work throughout the operations was of a very high order.

MUIR, JAMES, Lieut. (Acting Capt.), 5th Battn. Royal Scots, attached 5/6th Battn. Territorial Force. For conspicuous gallantry near Brie on 5 Sept. 1918, while in command of a company. After supervising the reconnaissance he forced the crossing of a river under heavy shell and machine-gun fire concentrated on the bridge. He next located and led a party against an enemy machine gun, capturing or killing the team and securing the gun. His cool courage and determined leadership had a very inspiring effect on all under him.

MUNDY, PIERREPONT RODNEY MILLER, M.C., Capt., 2nd Battn. South Wales Borderers (Salonika). For conspicuous gallantry in command of the leading company in the assault on Grand Couronne on 18 Sept. 1918. Though wounded in the thigh he continued to lead his men to the final assault of the enemy position, and on the readjustment of our line he, with the one other remaining officer, rallied the remnants of the battalion, and organized a new position on the Tonque, beating off an enemy counter-attack. Finally, with only 15 men left, he withdrew them in an orderly manner to our lines. His courage and leadership throughout inspired all ranks.

MURRAY, TERENCE DESMOND, M.C., Capt., 1st Battn. Leinster Regt. (Egypt). For conspicuous gallantry during the raid on Ghurabeh Ridge on night of 12–13 Aug. 1918. He led two companies against the east end of Ghurabeh Ridge. By his skilful leadership and fine example of courage he was responsible for the capture of 110 prisoners and five machine guns. He subsequently organized and carried out with conspicuous success the withdrawal of these two companies from a very extended and difficult position.

NEELY, GEORGE HENRY, M.C., Capt. (Acting Lieut.-Colonel), 6th Battn. London Regt., attached 1/18th Battn. On the evening of the 5th Sept. 1918, he personally led his men, with conspicuous coolness and gallantry, in an assault, and succeeded in clearing out many nests of hostile machine guns, which had been holding up the attack all day. During the night he reorganized his own unit, and assisted others, and completed the work of disposing of further enemy machine-gun posts, finally continuing the advance on Lieramont, driving the enemy from the village, and establishing himself on the high ground to the east. Throughout his magnificent example inspired all in contact with him with the greatest confidence.

PARKER, WILLIAM ALEXANDER, Capt., 5th Battn. attached 9th Battn., Scottish Rifles, Territorial Force. For conspicuous gallantry and devotion to duty during the nine miles' advance east of Ypres, from 28 Sept. to 9 Oct. 1918. He was primarily responsible for maintaining the direction of the advance, and overcame many obstacles in the form of machine-gun nests and concrete emplacements, keeping well up with the barrage, and consequently with light casualties. His company captured a large number of prisoners.

RICHMOND, LEONARD, Temporary Second Lieut., 12th Battn. Cheshire Regt. (Salonika). For conspicuous gallantry and devotion to duty as battalion intelligence officer. He carried out many valuable reconnaissances before the attack on the " P " Ridge on 18 Sept. 1918. He taped out the assembly positions of the leading battalion in Jackson's Ravine, and carried out his duties generally with such skill that the assembly of the brigade proceeded in perfect order. After the attack had developed he assumed command of a company which had lost its leaders and rallied them under intense fire. Later, under very heavy fire, he remained with his commanding officer, who had been mortally wounded. He showed marked courage throughout.

ROBERTON, JAMES BASIL WILKIE, Temporary Capt., 11th Battn. Northumberland Fusiliers (Italy). For conspicuous gallantry and ability during attacks on the enemy's lines on the north bank of the Piave on 27 and 29 Oct. 1918. He led his company brilliantly and captured a large number of machine guns and prisoners, setting a very fine example to his men throughout the operations. On 27 Oct., when the senior officers had become casualties, the battalion under his command captured all objectives.

ROSS, DAVID, M.C., Lieut. (Acting Capt.), 2nd Battn. Argyll and Sutherland Highlanders. For conspicuous gallantry and devotion to duty on 23 Sept. 1918, near Villers Guislain. The night on which he took over a newly-captured trench with his company, he worked past a block on his right and established a new one 200 yards down the trench. The following day he fought up and down the trench with varying results, killing and wounding many of the enemy and taking five prisoners. Day and night for four days he was attacking and counter-attacking with great dash, on one occasion taking 43 prisoners. He inspired the men with fine fighting spirit.

SANDARS, SAMUEL EDGAR, M.C., Capt. (Acting Lieut.-Colonel), Royal Fusiliers (Special Reserve), attached 3rd Battn. London Regt. For remarkable gallantry during operations near Chipilly, 8 to 10 Aug. 1918. In a heavy mist, when companies were apt to lost direction, he pushed forward with his battalion headquarters and led an attack on Malard Wood, capturing large parties of prisoners. Then, in spite of being wounded, he rushed a quarry and captured four machine guns and 70 prisoners. Later he led the line forward under heavy fire to the final objective, where he took charge of elements of the brigade and Allied troops, and established a line of posts. He displayed the greatest courage and was most severely wounded.

SANDERS, HARRY JAMES, M.C., Lieut. (Acting Capt.), 1/24th Battn. London Regt. At Le Forêt and St. Pierre Vaast Wood, 30 Aug. and 2 Sept. 1918, this officer led his company in the attack, and succeeded in capturing the objectives and 60 prisoners, seven machine guns, and two 77mm. guns. When the position on Hill 150, near Rancourt, was obscure, he went forward several times under very heavy shell and machine-gun fire to clear up the situation. Throughout the operations he displayed great courage and ability.

SANDILANDS, PRESCOTT, Major (Acting Lieut.-Colonel), 1st Royal Marine Light Infantry Battn. For conspicuous gallantry and devotion to duty. On 27 Sept. 1918, at Anneux, after the capture of the village, most of the subordinate officers having become casualties, he went up to the forward posts under heavy machine-gun fire and supervised the reorganization, reconnoitring the front, and ensuring that touch was gained with the flanks. That night he was conspicuous in repelling a counter-attack. The next day, by his influence and determination, he worked the battalion forward in the face of strong opposition, and despite heavy casualties.

SAVILL, SYDNEY ROWLAND, M.C., Capt. (Acting Lieut.-Colonel), 1/16th Battn. London Regt. For conspicuous gallantry and devotion to duty on 27 Sept. 1918, during the attack near Oisy-le-Verger. He controlled the passing of his battalion over the Canal du Nord in face of strong opposition, and, pushing forward parties, cleared the other side, capturing over 50. This enabled his battalion to form up for the main attack, which he skilfully conducted. Over 400 prisoners were captured during the day by the Brigade.

SENIOR, EDWARD, Major, 5th Battn. West Riding Regt., Territorial Force. For great gallantry during the crossing of the Escault Canal on 28 Sept. When the attack was proceeding, and the situation obscure, he went forward to clear up the situation. As all companies had to cross in single file at two crossings, a great deal of confusion existed, and his coolness at a critical time, directing the consolidation under very heavy fire, largely contributed to the success of the operations. He then went forward and made daring reconnaissance of the enemy line, bringing back valuable detailed information, on which the evening's attack on the enemy's positions was based. Throughout the operations he did excellent work.

SHEARMAN, THOMAS, Capt. (Acting Major), 5th Battn. Yorkshire Light Infantry, Territorial Force. For conspicuous gallantry and devotion to duty as second-in-command of the battalion, when he exercised splendid control throughout operations. On one occasion during a hostile counter-attack he stuck to his post when others had moved back, and from where he was ascertained the situation, and dealt with it immediately. It was due to his sound judgment that the line, where penetrated, was restored at once. Later, his shelter was blown in and he was imprisoned for two hours, but, in spite of being badly shaken, he displayed great initiative in collecting available troops and driving the enemy back.

SHERINGHAM, CHARLES JOHN DE BUNSEN, M.C., Temporary Capt. (Acting Lieut.-Colonel), General List, attached 8th Battn. Somersetshire Light Infantry. For conspicuous gallantry and able leadership in command of his battalion hear Havrincourt Wood on 9 and 10 Sept. 1918. When the leading troops were checked by a hostile barrage, he went forward to steady and encourage the men, getting them on over open ground to the north of the wood. On both days he handled his battalion with skill and judgment, which kept the casualties down, despite the heavy shelling.

SKEIL, ALEXANDER PATRICK, M.C., Capt. (Temporary Major), Royal Scots Fusiliers (Russia). For conspicuous gallantry and good leadership in Northern Russia during Sept. 1918. He was detached to Ossinova on 11 Sept., and during the next few days captured Preluki, Rapolka, Korovla, and Rostovskaya. By 16 Sept. he advanced on Konitzgorie, but learning that his advance was known to the enemy, he changed his objective, and aimed at Kourgomev, thus undertaking a surprise march of 15 kilometres with a force which had exhausted its rations and had had no rest for 25 kilometres over forest tracks and swamps. In spite of this he arrived with every man, and so lowered the morale of the enemy that they evacuated the strongly fortified positions at Troitska and Gorka, so that Selmsnga, 25 miles up river from Pless, was occupied without opposition. He rendered valuable service.

TANNER, ARCHIBALD GERARD, M.C., Temporary Capt. (Acting Lieut.-Colonel), Royal Fusiliers, attached 10th Battn. For conspicuous gallantry and good leadership at Bihucourt on 23 Aug 1918. After the battalion had gained its objective, he found that the units on either flank had been held up, so making a reconnaissance under heavy artillery and machine-gun fire, he threw back defensive flanks, securing his position. His personal direction and initiative inspired his men with confidence.

TUFFLEY, VICTOR EVELYN, Lieut., 2/10th Battn. London Regt. For conspicuous gallantry and devotion to duty during an attack at Sailly-Laurette on 8 Aug. 1918. When his company officer was killed, he took command, and captured a village leading one party after another against machine-gun nests posted in different parts of it. He took eight machine guns, and was largely responsible for the capture of about 200 prisoners, subsequently consolidating on the further side of the village. His leaadership both at the time and in later operations was full of daring and initiative.

VICKERS, STANSFIELD, Major, Royal Field Artillery, Territorial Force, attached D/82nd Brigade, Royal Field Artillery. He displayed exceptional gallantry and thrust in reconnoitring forward positions for his guns to support the advancing infantry. While out in front of the firing line, he was temporarily held up and shot at by a hostile machine gun at a hundred yards' range, but he noted the position, and on returning to his battery bombarded it with such effect that the occupants, 19 in number, put up the white flag and surrendered. He went down and brought the prisoners in himself.

WHITEHEAD, CLAUDE MAGUIRE, M.C., Temporary Capt., Royal Lancaster Regt. (Salonika). For conspicuous gallantry on 19 Sept. 1918. The commanding officer and adjutant being wounded, he took command of the battalion and personally led them through an attack on the Doiran Front. Though wounded in the first phase of the attack, he continued to lead them on. By his fine example of determined courage he enabled the battalion to reach their second objective ; and when forced to withdraw he supervised the withdrawal, though again wounded, and was the last to leave.

WHITMARSH, ARTHUR JOHN, Temporary Capt., attached East Kent Regt. (7th Battn.). For conspicuous gallantry and fine leadership in command of a company on 22 Aug. 1918, near Albert. He led his men through the town, which had been barely mopped up, under heavy fire without a casualty to their assembly post. He then worked his men forward 500 yards under intense machine-gun fire, and maintained his important position till dark, with the loss of all his officers and 60 per cent. of his men. On the 25th and 26th, with only one officer, two serjeants and 80 men, he fought his way forward, capturing 50 prisoners and inflicting heavy casualties. His energy and determination were an inspiration to all ranks.

WILBERFORCE, WILLIAM, M.C., Capt. (Acting Lieut.-Colonel), 1st Battn. Royal West Kent Regt., attached 14th Battn. Royal Warwickshire Regt. For conspicuous gallantry and devotion to duty near Gouzeaucourt on 27 Sept. 1918, in the attack on the trench system up to Dunraven Trench, and then the formation of a defensive flank to the right. He successfully controlled a very difficult advance diagonally across three parallel lines of trenches. When the enemy counter-attacked with fresh troops and specially trained bombers, driving back his battalion and another, it was largely due to his efforts that a new line of defence was formed and held.

WOODHOUSE, PHILIP RANDAL, M.C., M.B., Temporary Capt. (Acting Major), 9th Field Ambulance, Royal Army Medical Corps. For conspicuous gallantry and devotion to duty in command of a bearer division. On 27 Sept. 1918, at Maison Rouge, when loading wounded on an ambulance wagon, it was damaged, and an ammunition dump close by set on fire by heavy shelling. He at once got the fire out, and evacuated the wounded to safety. On two other occasions he did good work under heavy shell fire, clearing a road which was blocked by a tree blown across it, and also in evacuating wounded when his A.D.S. was hit by a shell.

WORSLEY, SIDNEY JOHN, M.C., Capt., 4th Battn. North Staffordshire Regt. For conspicuous gallantry and devotion to duty near Verbrandenmolen on 28 Sept. 1918. He led his company to the allotted objective, capturing a field gun. The following day, at Zandoovre, he again led his company in the face of very heavy machine-gun fire, and was wounded in the chest while doing so.

YOUNG, JOHN DOUGLAS STARFORTH, M.C., Temporary Lieut., 10th Battn. Argyll and Sutherland Highlanders. For conspicuous gallantry and fine leadership on 10 Sept. 1918, near Attilly. Having assembled his company under peculiarly adverse circumstances, he launched an attack at dawn and captured an important and commanding position, which he held throughout the day in spite of danger to his flanks, which were exposed by the failure of supporting troops to reach their objective. He withstood several attacks and finally routed the enemy by a successful counter-attack, and when relieved at dawn the next day he handed over the line intact. Throughout the operations he displayed exceptional dash in attack and skill in handling his troops in the defence of an important position.

CANADIAN FORCE.

ANDERSON, WILLIAM HAROLD KERR, Lieut.-Colonel, 13th Field Ambulance, Canadian Army Medical Corps. During the operations before Arras, 2–5 Sept., he was in charge of the evacuation of wounded. He succeeded in keeping in close touch with the infantry during the whole of the battle, so that the wounded were evacuated almost as soon as they became casualties. His duties were often performed under enemy artillery fire, which caused many casualties, but by his courage and personal example he kept his men at their splendid work until all casualties were carried out.

BAULD, WILLIAM ALFRED GORDON, Major (Acting Lieut.-Colonel), No. 7 Canadian Cavalry Field Ambulance, Canadian Army Medical Corps. For conspicuous gallantry and devotion to duty during mounted operations from 8 to 11 Oct. 1918. He was in command of the advanced cavalry field ambulances. On the night of the 9th–10th Oct., when ordered to search and clear the wounded from three villages, which were being heavily shelled, and the approaches badly damaged by craters, he organized the evacuation of the wounded, making certain that all were found and removed. He showed great coolness and energy.

BAYNES-REED, REV. WILLIAM LEONARD, Canadian Chaplains' Service, attached 75th Battn. Canadian Infantry, 1st Central Ontario Regt. For conspicuous gallantry and devotion to duty on 8–9 Aug. at the capture of the village of Lequesnel. He was constantly in the forward area, attending to the wounded and ministering to the dying under intense fire of all descriptions. His unselfish devotion to duty and his courage were splendid examples, and his services earned for him the respect and affection of all those among whom he worked.

BLACKSTOCK, GEORGE GRANT, Major, 4th Battn. Canadian Infantry, 1st Central Ontario Regt. For conspicuous gallantry and fine leadership in the attack on the Canal du Nord on 2 to 4 Sept. 1918. He commanded the battalion during this operation with great ability and judgment, and his example of coolness and gallantry under heavy fire in the front line, where he was continually present, had a most inspiriting and encouraging effect on officers and men, and was largely responsible for the determined dash with which the attack was pushed home. He personally made daring reconnaissances under heavy machine-gun fire, which enabled him to make skilful dispositions for further advances.

BRADFIELD, REGINALD HENDERSON, M.C., Capt., 75th Battn. Canadian Infantry, 1st Central Ontario Regt. For conspicuous gallantry and devotion to duty. In command of a company during the attack on 2 Sept. 1918, east of the Drocourt-Quéant line, he rallied his men under very heavy fire, and led them forward over some 500 yards of open ground, capturing a strong position and about 150 prisoners and 18 machine guns. He then led what remained of his company forward and established posts in advance and brought fire to bear on the enemy's flank. He showed determined courage and leadership.

BRITTON, JAMES CAPELL, Major, 4th Battn. Canadian Machine Gun Corps. In front of Dury, 2 Sept., for most conspicuous gallantry. When in command of a machine-gun company he pushed forward his batteries through heavy fire to most advanced positions, enabling them to inflict heavy casualties on the enemy. Later, when the whole situation was in doubt and communication forward temporarily cut, he went forward and made a daring reconnaissance. He was subjected to the heaviest shelling and machine-gun fire, but completed the reconnaissance and returned to headquarters with a valuable report.

BROOKS, ALLAN, Major, 7th Battn. Canadian Infantry, British Columbia Regt., attached 11th Canadian Infantry Brigade. For conspicuous gallantry in the operations of 2 and 3 Sept. in front of Arras. As brigade observing officer he showed great daring and initiative, pushing forward at all times with the most advanced troops under the heaviest fire. Taking a wire with him, he kept brigade headquarters well informed of the situation, and enabled the commander to make decisions which saved many lives. When the enemy were retiring he pushed forward over 500 yards in front of the infantry and telephoned back information from a long distance in front of our advance. During the two days he personally killed 20 of the enemy by sniping shots.

BROWN, ROBERT, Capt., 46th Battn. Canadian Infantry, Saskatchewan Regt. For conspicuous gallantry and good leadership at Dury and Ecourt, St. Quentin, 2 to 4 Sept. 1918. He commanded the right support company, and, finding the assault company held up by very heavy fire and his expected tank broken down, he made a daring reconnaissance forward and then led the assault through the village. By his prompt courage and initiative he was responsible for his company breaking up the southern defences of the village.

COOK, GEORGE HAROLD, Major, 9th Battery, 3rd Brigade, Canadian Field Artillery. For conspicuous gallantry and devotion to duty during the capture of the Drocourt-Quéant line on 2 Sept. 1918. He made a daring reconnaissance and established his battery in a forward position and his observation post on Mount Dury near the windmill. He remained at his post all day under intense shelling, and did admirable work on enemy batteries and strong points. His coolness and ability were most marked.

EWART, CECIL, Major, 8th Battn. Canadian Railway Troops. Near Ypres, between 28 Sept. and 5 Oct. 1918, for conspicuous gallantry and efficiency in reconstructing railway track during the advance. He repaired lines through a cutting under continuous shell fire, and as a result of his determination and courage a line was put into operation by which hundreds of wounded were evacuated to places of safety, and also guns, ammunition and supplies carried forward to the advancing troops. His organization was splendid.

GIRVAN, JOHN POLLANDS, M.C., Major (Acting Lieut.-Colonel), 15th Battn. Canadian Infantry, 1st Central Ontario Regt. For conspicuous gallantry opposite Cherisy on 1 Sept. 1918. He commanded his battalion with the greatest skill and ability, pushing resolutely forward in face of extreme machine-gun fire, and after a personal reconnaissance continuing his advance and capturing and consolidating a position some 6,000 yards in front of the jumping-off line. His courage and leadership were admirable.

GRAHAM, REV. EDWIN ERNEST, M.C., Canadian Chaplains' Service, attached 13th Battn. Canadian Infantry, Quebec Regt. For conspicuous gallantry and devotion to duty on 29 Aug. 1918, in front of the Ulster Trench east of Arras. He went out in broad daylight in full view of the enemy to their wire and brought in wounded men. During the succeeding days he was tireless in his efforts to succour the wounded and dying under heavy fire, and when the battalion attacked the Drocourt-Quéant system on 2 Sept. he was continuously in the forward area, exposing himself regardless of danger, and it was largely due to his personal efforts that all wounded were evacuated during the day. He set a splendid example to all.

GRAHAM, GORDON, Lieut. (Acting Capt.), 10th Battn. Canadian Infantry, Alberta Regt. For conspicuous gallantry at Villers-les-Cagnicourt on 2 Sept. 1918. His company commander having early become a casualty, he assumed command, and handled the company as well as two others for a time with exceptional ability, his tactics and fearless leadership being greatly responsible for the capture of the final objective on his portion of the front. At one period of the advance he personally engaged an enemy field battery with a Lewis gun, with the result that the crew were killed or driven off and the gun captured. He did excellent work.

HALL, GEORGE WILLIAM, Major, 12th Field Ambulance, Canadian Army Medical Corps. For conspicuous gallantry and devotion to duty. During the action in front of Arras, from 2–6 Sept. he was in charge of the evacuation of wounded. Time and time again he went through heavy enemy shell and machine-gun fire to direct the clearing of the wounded. On the afternoon of 2 Sept. he succeeded in clearing a number of wounded who were being shelled with gas shell to a place of safety, and dressed many wounded under heavy fire. His work throughout the battle was admirable.

HANSON, HAROLD STUART, Lieut., 43rd Battn. Canadian Infantry, Manitoba Regt. For conspicuous gallantry and devotion to duty on 27 Aug. 1918, in the capture of Swarty Ridge and four field guns by his company. With his left flank 2,000 yards in the air, and only 30 men, he held the village throughout the night, beating off five enemy fighting patrols. The next day he again led his company in the attack, and with only 8 men left cleared the Remy Bridgehead and held it till relieved. His determination and energy made up for his lack of men.

JUCKSCH, ARNOLD HOMER, M.C., Capt. (Acting Major), 58th Battn. Canadian Infantry, 2nd Central Ontario Regt. For conspicuous gallantry and devotion to duty on 27 Aug. 1918, during the attack on Bois du Sart. He directed the assembly of the battalion under heavy fire, and started all the units off. He then took command of a company which had lost all its officers and led a counter-attack. He next took a patrol into Hatchet Wood and cleared it of the enemy, bringing back all his wounded and about 50 prisoners. His work in reorganization and able tactics enabled the battalion to score several successes.

KILPATRICK, REV. GEORGE GORDON DINWIDDIE, Canadian Chaplains' Service, attached 42nd Battn. Canadian Infantry, Quebec Regt. For conspicuous gallantry and devotion to duty on 8 Aug. 1918, during the capture of Hill 102, east of Domart. Immediately behind the front line, exposed to heavy fire of all descriptions, he dressed and attended to the wounded and ministered to the dying without regard to his own safety, and with an untiring and unselfish devotion to duty that was an inspiration and a splendid example to all.

KIRKPATRICK, GUY HAMILTON, Lieut.-Colonel, 72nd Battn. Canadian Infantry, British Columbia Regt. For conspicuous gallantry and devotion to duty during the operations against the Drocourt-Quéant line, near Dury, on 1 and 2 Sept. 1918. He personally supervised all preparations for the action, and the success of the operations was in a large measure due to his grasp of the situation and organizing ability. On 1 Sept., during an enemy counter-attack, his personal example in the face of the enemy was excellent, and did much to steady all ranks. He also assisted in organizing a counter-attack to meet the enemy. Later he went forward with the attack, reconnoitred captured enemy positions and reorganized preparatory to a new advance. His courage at all times was most marked.

MADDEN, REV. AMBROSE, M.C., Canadian Chaplains' Service, attached 7th Battn. Canadian Infantry, British Columbia Regt. For conspicuous gallantry and devotion to duty on 8 Aug. 1918, in the attack on Caix. He went forward on his own initiative with the attacking troops and assisted the medical officer in attending to the wounded in the open under heavy artillery and machine-gun fire until he himself was severely wounded in three places by shrapnel. The calmness of his demeanour, his disregard of his own safety, and his unflagging efforts were a very fine example to all.

PARRY, JAMES LEWIS ROWAN, Major, 50th Battn. Canadian Infantry, Alberta Regt. For great gallantry and initiative in front of Dury during the operations from 1 to 4 Sept. 1918. He went ahead on a reconnaissance of the assembly positions and took the battalion to its position in darkness under heavy enemy fire, his work being largely responsible for the success of the operations. On 2 Sept. he volunteered to go forward and make a reconnaissance after the objectives had been captured. He did this in face of heavy enemy artillery fire, bringing back valuable information. Later he personally directed the advance of the battalion over a piece of ground badly enfiladed by enemy artillery, and got the battalion into its new position with slight casualties.

PAWLETT, FRANCIS, Lieut.-Colonel, Saskatchewan Regt., seconded 2nd Battn. West Riding Regt. For conspicuous gallantry and devotion to duty during the operations east of Arras from 28 Aug. to 3 Sept. 1918. He commanded the battalion throughout a week's operations, constantly going forward and making personal reconnaissances, which enabled him to send in good information and to issue clear and concise orders to his company commanders. He organized the sending up of reinforcements and stores, which never failed, and helped all ranks to do their best under very heavy strain. His leadership and quick appreciation of the situation were largely instrumental in the success of the operations.

PRATT, ARTHUR WILLIAM, Major, 116th Battn. Canadian Infantry, 2nd Central Ontario Regt. For conspicuous gallantry and devotion to duty in command of the leading company in the attack on Boing village on 28 Aug. 1918. In spite of heavy casualties from gas he got his men to the first objective, where he took over command of the battalion on his C.O. being killed. During the night he beat off two counter-attacks, and in the morning continued the advance, capturing and consolidating the village. His enthusiasm in reorganizing and encouraging exhausted men was admirable.

ROLSTON, JOHN MITCHELL, Major (Acting Lieut.-Colonel), 2nd Battn. Canadian Engineers. For conspicuous gallantry during the attack on the Drocourt-Quéant trench system on 2 Sept. 1918. He made a reconnaissance under heavy fire prior to the attack, and obtained information which enabled him to make the best disposition of his companies for the ensuing operation. During the attack he went forward with the infantry and personally superintended the work of his companies in the removal of road mines and the repair of roads under shell fire, thus facilitating the advance of the artillery in support of the infantry. By his fearless energy he produced the best work from those under him.

SLADE, ARTHUR JOSEPH, Capt., 50th Battn. Canadian Infantry, Alberta Regt. For great gallantry and devotion to duty while in command of a company in front of Dury during the operations 2–4 Sept. 1918. He gained his objective with the greatest dash, capturing close on 400 prisoners and about 20 machine guns. Twice during the attack he personally rushed enemy machine guns, once with six men and the other time with a batman. His work throughout the operations was of the highest order.

SMYTHE, ROLSA ERIC, M.C., Major, 58th Battn. Canadian Infantry, 2nd Central Ontario Regt. For conspicuous gallantry and devotion to duty durine the operations about Bois du Sart, Boiry and Artillery Hill between 27 and 29 Aug. 1918. He commanded his battalion from the jumping off, throughout the heavy fighting at the above places, and his handling of the men when very tired was most skilful, resulting in the repulse of several counter-attacks, and the successful consolidation of the captured positions.

SUTHERLAND, DONALD MATHESON, Lieut.-Colonel, West Ontario Regt., attached 52nd Battn. Canadian Infantry, Manitoba Regt. For conspicuous gallantry in action near Bois-de-Vert, 27–28 Aug. 1918, when he handled his battalion with great tactical ability. His personal courage and leadership were largely responsible for the success of the operations, at a time when casualties were severe and enemy opposition was most stubborn.

TURNER, ROYES LIONEL, Major, Canadian Infantry, Manitoba Regt. (Russia). During the entire operations from 4 Aug. on the Archangel-Vologda Railway, he has done most valuable work and has shown great devotion to duty. He has taken part in every operation, and his reconnaissance work and liaison work with the attacking infantry has always helped our advance to an enormous extent. He has shown great courage under fire, and his influence has always had a great effect over all the Allied infantry.

TWEED, LORNE TRELEAVEN, Major, 1st Battn. Canadian Engineers. For conspicuous gallantry and devotion to duty during an attack on the Drocourt-Quéant line on 2 Sept. 1918. He established a report centre in an open trench, which, owing to a check in the advance, was subjected to heavy machine-gun and artillery fire. Despite this, he got into touch with the engineering companies working on the forward roads, collecting information as to the work, and reporting to Battalion Headquarters. The same afternoon, when the position was obscure, he again worked forward and ascertained what further work was required. His initiative and resource were a great asset.

WEAVER, CHARLES YARDLEY, Major (Acting Lieut.-Colonel), 49th Battn. Canadian Infantry, Alberta Regt. For conspicuous gallantry in command of his battalion during operations south of the Scarpe between 26 and 28 Aug. 1918. His constant presence in the forefront of the battle under severe shelling and machine-gun fire, and his complete grasp of the tactical situation, were responsible for the marked success of his battalion throughout three days' operations.

AUSTRALIAN IMPERIAL FORCE.

ANTHON, DANIEL HERBERT, M.C., Lieut., 20th Battn. Australian Imperial Force. On the 30th Aug. 1918, near Clery-sur-Somme, he advanced at the head of a few men against a strongly-held machine-gun post, which, after bombing, he charged alone, capturing seven men and the gun. He then, by a flanking movement, captured a trench, taking 54 prisoners, besides killing and wounding several others. This gallant action allowed the battalion, which had been held up for a long time, to advance

BRODZIAK, CEDRIC ERROL MEYER, Major, 3rd Battn. Australian Machine Gun Corps. For conspicuous gallantry near Bray-sur-Somme on 22 Aug. 1918. He commanded the flank company of the division in the attack, and in face of strong opposition secured and consolidated his objectives. When the right flank of the division on his left was held up he made good the gaps that occurred, capturing the southern portion of Happy Valley and the Chalk Pit, and thus assuring the advance of the division on his flank. During the afternoon the enemy broke through, and his left flank was in the air, and the enemy behind him, but he held his position and formed a defensive flank. By his fine initiative and determination he enabled the divisional line to be maintained, and inflicted such casualties that the enemy was forced to withdraw.

BROWN, WILLIAM JOHN, Major, 2nd Australian Light Horse Regt. (Egypt). For conspicuous gallantry and devotion to duty on 14 July, 1918, in command of a post near Mussulabeh, which was heavily shelled. The enemy attacked it in strength, but were repulsed. Major Brown, leaving sufficient of his garrison to protect his front, directed the bulk of his machine-gun and rifle fire on to an enemy concentration in Wahi Dhib, and also took their parties attacking Abu Talbut right in reverse, inflicting heavy casualties and demoralizing the enemy. Thereby he materially assisted the counter-attack by another cavalry regiment later in the morning. Throughout the operations he handled his command with great coolness and judgment.

COUTTS, DONALD DUNBAR, Major, Australian Army Medical Corps, attached 24th Battn. Australian Imperial Force. On the 1st Sept. 1918, during the attack at Mont St. Quentin, although the R.A.P. was consistently shelled, he attended the wounded almost continuously for 52 hours, during five of which he was forced to wear his gas respirator, displaying throughout the greatest courage and devotion to duty. On the day prior to the attack a shell burst on a dug-out, wounding several men and pressing one down, severely wounded, blocking the entrance. He immediately went forward, regardless of intense shell fire, and succeeded in extricating the man and removing him, over exposed ground, to the rear.

FERRES, HAROLD DUNSTAN GORDON, M.C., Major, 58th Battn. Australian Imperial Force. For conspicuous gallantry in taking the eastern side of Peronne on 2 Sept. 1918. He had to advance to the attack along a narrow causeway swept by enemy fire, and, while personally leading his battalion, was early severely wounded by shell fire. Though suffering much pain from his wound, he reorganized the battalion, which had suffered severe casualties, and launched the attack. The clearing of the enemy from the ramparts and outskirts of Peronne was entirely due to his resolute leadership and courage. A large number of prisoners and 50 machine guns were captured during this action.

FLETCHER, JAMES LIONEL, M.C., Capt., 25th Battn. Australian Imperial Force. During an attack near Mont St. Quentin, on the 2nd Sept. 1918, an enemy strong point held up the advance. After a daring personal reconnaissance, during which he captured a machine-gun post with three guns, he surrounded and took the strong point, which contained 17 machine guns and two trench mortars. He then reorganized his company and led the attack on the objective. When the acting commanding officer of the battalion was wounded, he took command of the whole front line, and his fine gallantry and untiring efforts set a wonderful example to all.

HOSKING, WILLIAM STANLEY, M.C., Capt., 27th Battn. Australian Imperial Force. In command of a support company during operations on the 2nd Sept. 1918, at Allaines, north-east of Peronne, he displayed conspicuous gallantry and resource in attacking a hostile trench which was holding up the advance, capturing it and taking 60 prisoners. After all the company officers except himself and one other had become casualties, he collected the remnants of the companies and advanced with only 28 other ranks against 600 enemy infantry and a direct-firing hostile battery. This prevented the enemy reorganizing for a counter-attack. His courage and fine leadership were most marked.

HUNT, RALPH ALEC, Lieut., 12th Field Company, Australian Engineers. For conspicuous gallantry on 8 Aug. 1918, near Cherisy. With a small party he reconnoitred and, under machine-gun fire, crossed bridges to the enemy's side. While examining one of the bridges the sapper whom he took with him was wounded, and he carried this man for 200 yards under fire to a place of safety. After getting his pontoons up to the water side under heavy fire, he furnished an accurate report on the state of the roads and bridges in the neighbourhood to his officer commanding. His coolness and excellent work under trying circumstances were most praiseworthy.

LANE, JOHN BAYLEY, Capt., 18th Battn. Australian Imperial Force. For conspicuous gallantry during the attack on 8 Aug. 1918, east of Villers Bretonneux, near Amiens. Single-handed he attacked an enemy strong point held by 17 enemy with a machine gun, killing three of the occupants and capturing the remainder. The following day, near Framerville, after being wounded, he continued to lead his company, and, after gaining his objective, was again wounded, but refused to leave until the position had been made secure. He set a splendid example of courage and devotion to duty.

LOWTHER, GEORGE FREDERICK, M.C., Capt., 18th Battn. Australian Imperial Force. For conspicuous gallantry as company commander in the advance east of Amiens on 8 and 11 Aug. 1918. In spite of thick fog and hidden defences, he gained the final objective. The following day he, with a few men, rushed a machine-gun post, and further captured and consolidated fresh ground. On the 11th he, to conform with the advance of another battalion, established posts forming a defensive flank, and, while doing so, rushed, with four men, another enemy post. On being finally ordered to withdraw, he extricated his company from a difficult position with very few casualties, being himself the last to leave. Throughout he showed fine courage and leadership.

MARFELL, WILLIAM LESLIE, Major, 7th Brigade, Australian Field Artillery. For conspicuous gallantry and devotion to duty on 30 Aug. 1918, east of Clery. During the whole day, under extremely heavy shell and machine-gun fire, he personally directed the fire of his battery from the front line, rendering great assistance to the infantry. His tireless energy and cheerfulness during a week's continuous fighting have set a splendid example to his men.

McCANN, WILLIAM FRANCIS JAMES, M.C., Capt. (Temporary Major), 10th Battn. Australian Imperial Force. For conspicuous gallantry and devotion to duty near Lihous on 10 Aug. 1918. After the attack had failed at Crepey Wood, he successfully captured the position with his company in face of very heavy fire ; and, when the enemy, in greatly superior numbers, counter-attacked, he held them off, personally killing many of the enemy and exposing himself freely until reinforcements enabled him to drive off the enemy and re-establish his original line. His courage and fine leadership prevented an important position alling into the hands of the enemy.

McDONALD, JOHN HINWOOD, M.C., Major, 20th Battn. Australian Imperial Force. On the 31st Aug. 1918, during the attack on Mont St. Quentin, he advanced alone against an enemy machine-gun nest, silencing two guns which were causing casualties and capturing the crews. On arrival at the objective, he rapidly reorganized and consolidated, reconnoitring the whole battalion front under heavy fire. Later, he personally directed a withdrawal in a most skilful manner and under very severe enemy fire, establishing himself in an admirable position with few casualties. Throughout he showed conspicuous gallantry and powers of leadership.

MURRAY, JOHN JOSEPH, M.C., Major, 53rd Battn. Australian Imperial Force. For conspicuous gallantry near Peronne on 1 Sept. 1918. He led his company with great skill and initiative, and cleared the assembly position, thus allowing the remainder of the battalion to take up its position in time for the attack. Later, while advancing under heavy artillery and machine-gun fire, he led his company through two unbroken belts of wire. Finally, under heavy fire, he supervised consolidation of the ground won, and throughout set a fine example of courage and energy to his men.

NOEDL, LEWIS, M.C., Capt., 7th Field Company, Australian Engineers. For very conspicuous gallantry and devotion under exceptionally heavy fire from the 30th Aug. to 1 Sept. 1918, during reconnaissances for a construction of bridges across the Somme Canal. By dint of his example and inspiring spirit in face of every kind of difficulty and opposition, and although time after time driven off by heavy shell and machine-gun fire with severe casualties, he carried out his work, and the ultimate success of the operations was greatly due to his coolness, courage and unflagging energy.

O'SHEA, PATRICK JOSEPH FRANCIS, M.C., Capt., Australian Army Medical Corps, attached 8th Battn. Australian Infantry. For conspicuous gallantry and devotion to duty near Chuignes on 23 Aug. 1918. Keeping up with the advance, he was always in the hottest part of the line, dressing wounded and organizing stretcher-bearers. Realizing that an R.A.P. could not cope with the casualties, he dressed them where they lay and made prisoners carry them back. In many cases he carried men back himself under heavy fire of all descriptions, and working in gas-drenched areas. He had no rest for three days and nights, and did another medical officer's work as well as his own.

TOWL, PERCY GILCHRIST, Capt., 37th Battn. Australian Imperial Force. For conspicuous gallantry and devotion to duty on the night of the 29th–30th Aug. 1918, at Clery. In charge of his company of only 28 men with 25 prisoners, he was attacked by some 150 of the enemy, who had at first surrendered. He was surrounded practically, and by fire from front and flanks his party, before he was reinforced by other troops at 3 p.m. next day, was reduced to 12 men. His performance was a splendid one, and it was due to his determined courage and able leadership that his company, besides holding out, retained their prisoners.

WEBB, ERIC NORMAN, M.C., Major, 7th Field Company, Australian Engineers. During operations near Peronne from the 29th to 31st Aug. 1918, he displayed the greatest courage, skill, and powers of leadership and organization in constructing and repairing bridges for crossing the Somme, under continuous shell and machine-gun fire. He also carried out valuable reconnaissances on water supply and roads up to the front line to assist the advance, and throughout this period his untiring efforts and determination contributed in a large measure to the success of the operations.

WILLIAMS, THOMAS, Major, 4th Australian Light Horse Regt., XXII. Corps, Mounted Regt. For conspicuous gallantry during a period up to 12 Sept. 1918, on the Somme. He worked his patrols in a daring and able manner, keeping divisional headquarters supplied with reliable information. By personal reconnaissances he was able to direct the artillery on to splendid targets with excellent results. His work right through the operations was of a very high order.

NEW ZEALAND FORCE.

BARROWCLOUGH, HAROLD ERIC, M.C., Capt. (Temporary Major), 1st Battn. New Zealand Rifle Brigade. For conspicuous gallantry and able leadership near Havrincourt Wood from 8 to 13 Sept. 1918. He was in command of a battalion up against a strong position stoutly defended by the enemy. He gained good information from personal reconnaissances, during one of which the enemy counter-attacked. He rallied his men, and, leading them forward, drove back the enemy with bomb and bayonet.

JARDINE, LEONARD HANDFORTH, M.C., Lieut.-Colonel, 2nd Battn. New Zealand Rifle Brigade. For conspicuous gallantry and good leadership at Gouzeaucourt from 8 to 13 Sept. 1918. His battalion was engaged in very heavy fighting against strong enemy positions held by picked troops. He constantly reconnoitred the front, having to pass through gas and enemy barrage, and by keeping in the closest touch with the situation he was able to cope with several enemy counter-attacks. It was owing to his skilful leadership that the operation was a success, and his courage and coolness under heavy fire inspired all ranks.

MITCHELL, GORDON ROSS, Major, Otago Mounted Rifles, XXII. Corps, Mounted Troops. For conspicuous gallantry during operations on the Somme from 22 Aug. to 18 Sept. 1918. This officer with his squadron was attached to the division on the left flank, and during the whole time, owing to his splendid leadership, his squadron obtained information of the utmost value. On the 24th Aug., in the vicinity of La Boiselle, when the position was obscure, he personally went forward under heavy machine-gun and shell fire and brought back most valuable information to divisional headquarters. Several times during the operations he made personal reconnaissances and obtained most reliable information.

NEIL, JAMES HARDIE, Lieut.-Colonel, No. 3 Field Ambulance, New Zealand Army Medical Corps. For conspicuous gallantry and devotion to duty during operations near Bapaume and Bancourt from 23 Aug. to 3 Sept. 1918. He was in command of the ambulance, and constantly visited the forward R.A.P. under heavy shell fire, and selected positions for the bearer relay posts. During the action round Bancourt he went forward with two light ambulance cars to within a few hundred yards of the front line and supervised the evacuation. It was owing to his gallantry and personal supervision that the evacuation of the wounded was so successfully carried out.

London Gazette, 7 Feb. 1919.—" War Office, 7 Feb. 1919. His Majesty the King has been graciously pleased to approve of the undermentioned rewards for distinguished service in connection with military operations in East Africa. Dated 1 Jan. 1919. Awarded the Distinguished Service Order."

LILLEY, HARRY ARTHUR, Capt. (Temporary Lieut.-Colonel), Yorkshire Regt. and King's African Rifles.

MILES, ARTHUR TREMAYNE, M.C., Temporary Major, King's African Rifles.

POMEROY, EDMUND JOHN, Major, West India Regt.

WILSON, ROBERT GERALD HAMILTON, M.C., Temporary Major, King's African Rifles.

SOUTH AFRICAN FORCE.

BRADSTOCK, FREDERICK EDGAR, M.C., Temporary Major, Cape Corps, attached King's African Rifles.

London Gazette, 8 Feb. 1919.—"Air Ministry, 8 Feb. 1919. His Majesty the King has been graciously pleased to confer the undermentioned rewards on Officers of the Royal Air Force, in recognition of gallantry in flying operations against the enemy. Awarded a Bar to the Distinguished Service Order."

FELLOWES, PEREGRINE FORBES MORANT, D.S.O., Lieut.-Colonel (Sea Patrol, Flanders). On 28 May, 1918, Lieut.-Colonel Fellowes, Commanding 61st Wing, undertook the task of attacking the lock gate at Zeebrugge, the damaging of which was at that time of great importance. He flew a DH-4, and by very skilful airmanship he succeeded in dropping a 230 lb. bomb from a height of only 200 feet right on the lock gate in question. It has since been ascertained that the effect was considerable, and involved much dislocation of the enemy's plans for many days.
(D.S.O. gazetted 1 Jan. 1918.)

Awarded the Distinguished Service Order :

DARWIN, CHARLES JOHN WHARTON, Capt. (Acting Major) (France). This officer has proved himself an exceptionally skilful and gallant patrol leader, conspicuous for utter fearlessness and disregard of danger. On a recent occasion, in company with one other machine, he attacked a formation of 14 Fokker biplanes, one of which was shot down and crashed. He has accounted for three hostile aircraft.

GOODE, HARRY KING, D.F.C., Second Lieut. (Acting Capt.) (Italy). During the recent operations this officer has displayed magnificent courage and determination in attacking enemy aerodromes, kite balloons and retreating columns, inflicting very heavy loss. On 29 Oct. he led two other machines in a bombing raid against an enemy aerodrome ; he completely destroyed with a bomb one hostile machine on the ground, and, attacking the hangars and workshops with machine-gun fire, he caused many casualties amongst the mechanics. Later on in the same day he returned alone to attack the same aerodrome, and found the enemy about to evacuate it. Flying at a very low altitude—at times his wheels almost touched the ground—he destroyed one machine with a bomb and set fire to another with machine-gun fire. The enemy personnel were driven back into the village by the vigour of his attack. Capt. Goode's utter disregard of personal danger inspired all who served with him.
(D.F.C. gazetted 3 Dec. 1918.)

HAZELL, TOM FALCON, M.C., D.F.C., Capt. (Acting Major) (France). A brilliant fighter, distinguished for his bold determination and rare courage, he has accounted for 29 enemy machines, 20 being destroyed and nine driven down out of control ; he has also destroyed 10 balloons. On 4 Sept. he rendered exceptionally valuable service in leading his flight to attack hostile balloons that were making a certain road impassable. Within an hour three of these balloons were destroyed, Major Hazell accounting for two.
(M.C. gazetted 26 July, 1917.)
(D.F.C. gazetted 2 Nov. 1918.)
(Bar to D.F.C. gazetted 2 Nov. 1918.)

LOVEMORE, ROBERT BAILLIE, Lieut. (France). On 28 Oct. this officer, attacked by two Fokkers, was driven down and compelled to land on marshy ground the enemy side of a river. Having extricated himself from his machine, he saw another of our machines land a short distance away, the pilot being thrown out ; proceeding to the spot, Lieut. Lovemore found the pilot insensible, his head and shoulders under water, and the fuselage over his legs. Releasing him from the fuselage, he dragged him out of the water, and in a few minutes the pilot recovered his senses. Lieut. Lovemore then proceeded towards the river, and seeing a corporal of ours on the other side he directed him to go and get help, he himself returning to the pilot, whom he carried to the river bank. On arriving there he saw an Infantry Officer on the opposite bank, who swam across to join him, and between them they carried the pilot down to the river and swam across, holding him up. The enemy by this time had brought up machine guns, so that they were under fire when swimming across ; they, however, got across in safety, and a stretcher party arriving, the pilot was carried back to our lines. The cool courage and disregard of danger displayed by Lieut. Lovemore is deserving of very high praise.

McCLOUGHRY, WILFRED ASHTON, M.C., D.F.C., Major (Australian Flying Corps) (France). The record of this officer's squadron, when equipped with Sopwith Camels, was unique, not only in the number of aircraft destroyed with almost insignificant loss to ourselves, but also in the persistence with which they carried out innumerable raids at the lowest altitude. The high morale and individual enterprise of the members of this squadron must be largely attributed to the personality and influence of their leader, Major McCloughry. When the squadron was re-armed with Sopwith Snipes the change in type necessitated a complete reversal of their aerial experience. By his careful and untiring leadership he succeeded in so training his squadron that in a series of raids on three successive days they accounted for upwards of 30 hostile aeroplanes.
(M.C. gazetted 18 July, 1917.)
(D.F.C. gazetted 2 Nov. 1918.)

MACLAREN, DONALD RODERICK, M.C., D.F.C., Lieut. (Acting Capt.) (France). Bold in attack and skilful in manœuvre, Capt. MacLaren is conspicuous for his success in aerial combats. On 24 Sept. he and his patrol of three machines attacked a formation of six enemy scouts, although the latter were protected by 16 other enemy aircraft at a higher altitude. Firing a burst at point-blank range, this officer shot down one in flames. In all he has accounted for 48 enemy machines and six kite balloons.
(M.C. gazetted 22 June, 1918.)
(Bar to M.C. gazetted 16 Sept. 1918.)
(D.F.C. gazetted 21 Sept. 1918.)

NETHERSOLE, MICHAEL HENRY BRADDON, Major (France). A squadron commander of exceptional merit, who, by his enthusiasm and fine example has revolutionized the tactics of his squadron. Formerly accustomed to bombing from a high altitude, the members have descended to low altitudes, thus ensuring greater accuracy of aim. On 30 Oct. he led his squadron on a low bombing raid against an aerodrome. The raid was most successful, he himself destroying two hangars. On the return journey he kept his machines so well together that, though they were attacked by large numbers of hostile scouts, they succeeded in destroying five of them with no loss on our side. The engagement continued during the whole of the return journey, but the squadron succeeded in causing considerable damage to hostile troops on the ground in addition to the casualties in the air as noted above.

STRANGE, LOUIS ARBON, M.C., D.F.C., Lieut.-Colonel (France). For his exceptional services in organizing his wing and his brilliant leadership on low bombing raids this officer was awarded the Distinguished Flying Cross not long ago. Since then, by his fine example and inspiring personal influence, he has raised his wing to still higher efficiency and morale, the enthusiasm displayed by the various squadrons for low-flying raids being most marked. On 30 Oct. he accompanied one of these raids against an aerodrome ; watching the work of his machines, he waited until they had finished and then dropped his bombs from 100 feet altitude on hangars that were undamaged ; he then attacked troops and transport in the vicinity of the aerodrome. While thus engaged he saw eight Fokkers flying above him ; at once he climbed and attacked them single-handed ; having driven one down out of control he was fiercely engaged by the other seven, but he maintained the combat until rescued by a patrol of our scouts.
(M.C. gazetted 27 March, 1915.)
(D.F.C. gazetted 2 Nov. 1918.)

London Gazette, 15 Feb. 1919.—"Admiralty, S.W., 15 Feb. 1919.—Honours for Services in Action with Enemy Submarines. The King has been graciously pleased to approve of the award of the following honours to the undermentioned Officers for services in action with enemy submarines. To be Companions of the Distinguished Service Order."

BEST, HUMPHREY WILLIE, Commander, Royal Navy.

MARK-WARDLAW, WILLIAM PENROSE, Lieut. (now Lieut.-Commander), Royal Navy.
(The award of the Distinguished Service Cross to this Officer, which was announced in Gazette of the 13th Sept. 1915, has been cancelled.)

LAKE, HENRY NEVILLE, D.S.C., Lieut., Royal Navy.

To receive a Bar to the Distinguished Service Order :

OLPHERT, WYBRANTS, D.S.O., D.S.C., Lieut.-Commander, Royal Naval Reserve.

"Honours for Services in Minesweeping Operations.—The King has been graciously pleased to approve of the award of the following honours to the undermentioned Officers, in recognition of their services in minesweeping operations off the Belgian Coast, including the minefields off the ports of Ostend and Zeebrugge, between the 18th Oct. and 8th Nov. 1918. To be a Companion of the Distinguished Service Order."

BUCKLAND, ARTHUR EDGAR, D.S.C., Lieut., Royal Navy. In recognition of the courageous and efficient manner in which he controlled and carried out the minesweeping operations off the Belgian coast, including the minefields off Ostend and Zeebrugge, which presented some particularly dangerous and difficult features.

To receive a Bar to the Distinguished Service Order :

CAYLEY, HENRY FRANCIS, D.S.O., Commander (Acting Capt.), Royal Navy. For the gallant manner in which he personally conducted difficult minesweeping operations, rendering invaluable advice.

"Honours for Services in Monitors off the Belgian Coast between the 1st July and 11th Nov. 1918.—The King has been graciously pleased to approve of the award of the following honours to the undermentioned Officers. To be Companions of the Distinguished Service Order."

PARKER, PATRICK EDWARD, Commander (now Capt.), Royal Navy.

MOORE, NORMAN CAMERON, Lieut.-Commander, Royal Navy.

STUDD, RONALD GRANVILLE, Lieut.-Commander, Royal Navy.

"Honours for Miscellaneous Services.—The King has been graciously pleased to approve of the award of the following honour to the undermentioned Officer. To be a Companion of the Distinguished Service Order."

IREMONGER, HAROLD WILLIAM, Major, Royal Marine Artillery. For services with the Royal Marine Artillery Siege Gun Detachment in Flanders. Organized a group of six 7.5 in. guns in February, 1918, and has brought it to a very high gunnery standard. Has established and maintained extremely good and intimate liaison with the Belgian Artillery Authorities.

London Gazette, 15 Feb. 1919.—"War Office, 15 Feb. 1919. His Majesty the King has been graciously pleased to approve of the following awards to the undermentioned Officers, in recognition of their gallantry and devotion to duty in the field. The acts of gallantry for which the decorations have been awarded will be announced in the London Gazette as early as practicable. Awarded a Third Bar to the Distinguished Service Order."

CROFT, WILLIAM DENMAN, D.S.O., Major and Brevet Lieut.-Colonel (Temporary Brigadier-General), Scottish Rifles, General Officer Commanding, 27th Infantry Brigade.
(D.S.O. gazetted 1 Jan. 1917.)
(First Bar gazetted 10 Jan. 1917.)
(Second Bar gazetted 26 July, 1918.)

Awarded a Second Bar to the Distinguished Service Order :

BROOKE, GEORGE FRANK, D.S.O., Temporary Lieut.-Colonel, Reserve of Officers, attached 14th Battn. Welsh Regt.
(D.S.O. gazetted 4 June, 1917.)
(First Bar gazetted 2 Dec. 1918.)

IRWIN, ALFRED PERCY BULTEEL, D.S.O., Capt. and Brevet Major (Temporary Lieut.-Colonel), East Surrey Regt., Commanding 8th Battn.
(D.S.O. gazetted 20 Oct. 1916.)
(First Bar gazetted 26 July, 1917.)

LLOYD, LEMUEL, D.S.O., Temporary Lieut.-Colonel, 12th Battn. Suffolk Regt.
(D.S.O. gazetted 4 March, 1918.)
(First Bar gazetted 16 Sept. 1918.)

REES, JOHN GORDON, D.S.O., Major (Acting Lieut.-Colonel), Welsh Horse Yeomanry, attached 25th Battn. Royal Welsh Fusiliers.
(D.S.O. gazetted 18 Jan. 1918.)
(First Bar gazetted 26 March, 1918.)

ROBERTSON, GORDON McMAHON, D.S.O., Capt. (Acting Lieut.-Colonel), 2nd Battn. North Staffordshire Regt., attached 2nd Battn. Manchester Regt.
(D.S.O. gazetted 3 June, 1918.)
(First Bar gazetted 11 Jan. 1919.)

CANADIAN FORCE.

EDWARDS, CAMERON MACPHERSON, D.S.O., Lieut.-Colonel, 38th Battn. Canadian Infantry.
(D.S.O. gazetted 10 Jan. 1917.)
(First Bar gazetted 3 June, 1918.)

Awarded a Bar to the Distinguished Service Order :

ADLERCRON, RODOLPH LADEVEZE, C.M.G., D.S.O., Major and Brevet Lieut.-Colonel (Temporary Brigadier-General), Cameron Highlanders (General Officer Commanding, 124th Infantry Brigade).
(D.S.O. gazetted 14 Jan. 1916.)

ALBAN, CLIFTON EDWARD RAWDON GRANT, D.S.O., Capt. and Brevet Major (Acting Lieut.-Colonel), Liverpool Regt., attached 15th Battn. Lancashire Fusiliers.
(D.S.O. gazetted 18 July, 1917.)

CAMPBELL, SIR JOHN BRUCE STEWART, Bart., D.S.O., Temporary Lieut.-Colonel, 11th Battn. Royal Scots.
(D.S.O. gazetted 26 July, 1917.)
DANBY, SILAS, D.S.O., M.C., Major (Temporary Lieut.-Colonel), 12th Battn. Manchester Regt.
(D.S.O. gazetted 16 Sept. 1918.)
DEMPSTER, JAMES FINLAY, D.S.O., Temporary Major (Acting Lieut.-Colonel), Manchester Regt., attached 1/8th Battn. Nottinghamshire and Derbyshire Regt. (Capt., Reserve of Officers).
(D.S.O. gazetted 1 Jan. 1918.)
CAMERON, EWEN ALLAN, D.S.O., Temporary Lieut.-Colonel, 10th Battn. North Lancashire Regt., Commanding 9th Battn. East Surrey Regt.
(D.S.O. gazetted 1 Jan. 1918.)
FITZJOHN, TUDOR, D.S.O., Major (Acting Lieut.-Colonel), 1st Battn. Worcestershire Regt., attached 4th Battn.
(D.S.O. gazetted 1 Jan. 1917.)
FLETCHER, JAMES HENRY, D.S.O., M.C., Capt. (Acting Lieut.-Colonel), Royal Army Medical Corps, Commanding 36th Field Ambulance.
(D.S.O. gazetted 18 July, 1917.)
FORD, VINCENT TENNYSON RANDLE, D.S.O., Capt. (Temporary Lieut.-Colonel), 1st Battn. York and Lancaster Regt., attached 8th Battn. Northumberland Fusiliers.
(D.S.O. gazetted 3 June, 1918.)
HELME, ERNEST, D.S.O., Major, Glamorganshire Yeomanry, attached 15th Battn. Welsh Regt.
(D.S.O. gazetted 2 Dec. 1918.)
HOGGART, JOHN WILLIAM, D.S.O., M.C., Lieut. (Acting Major), C/50th Brigade, Royal Field Artillery.
(D.S.O. gazetted 1 Jan. 1919.)
HOWARD, CHARLES ALFRED, D.S.O., Major and Brevet Lieut.-Colonel, 1st Battn. King's Royal Rifle Corps.
(D.S.O. gazetted 1 Jan. 1917.)
MODERA, FREDERICK STEWART, D.S.O., M.C., Capt. (Temporary Major and Lieut.-Colonel), Royal Fusiliers, attached 1st Battn. Lancashire Fusiliers.
(D.S.O. gazetted 16 Sept. 1918.)
SAMPSON, FRANCIS CORNELIUS, D.S.O., M.B., Major (Temporary Lieut.-Colonel), 91st Field Ambulance, Royal Army Medical Corps.
(D.S.O. gazetted 14 Jan. 1916.)
SMITH, ROBERT ARTHUR, D.S.O., M.C., Temporary Lieut.-Colonel, 13th Battn. Royal Fusiliers.
(D.S.O. gazetted 16 Sept. 1918.)
STORY, PHILIP FRANCIS, D.S.O., Temporary Major (Acting Lieut.-Colonel), Royal Engineers (Commanding Royal Engineers, 30th Division).
(D.S.O. gazetted 1 Jan. 1918.)
THORPE, GERVASE, C.M.G., D.S.O., Major and Brevet Lieut.-Colonel (Temporary Brigadier-General), Argyll and Sutherland Highlanders (General Officer Commanding, 17th Infantry Brigade).
(D.S.O. gazetted 18 Feb. 1915.)
TONSON-RYE, HUBERT BERNARD, D.S.O., Major (Acting Lieut.-Colonel), 2nd Battn. Royal Munster Fusiliers.
(D.S.O. gazetted 16 Sept. 1918.)
TURNER, REGINALD, D.S.O., Capt. (Temporary Lieut.-Colonel), Dragoon Guards, Special Reserve, attached 6th Battn. Northampton Regt.
(D.S.O. gazetted 19 April, 1901.)
WESTMORLAND, HERBERT CAMPBELL, D.S.O., Capt. (Acting Lieut.-Colonel), 2nd Battn. Hampshire Regt.
(D.S.O. gazetted 16 Sept. 1918.)

CANADIAN FORCE.

BICKERDIKE, ROBERT, D.S.O., Major, 87th Battn. Canadian Infantry, Quebec Regt.
(D.S.O. gazetted 1 Jan. 1918.)
ELKINS, WILLIAM HENRY PFERINGER, D.S.O., Lieut.-Colonel, Royal Canadian Horse Artillery.
(D.S.O. gazetted 1 Jan. 1918.)
LINDSEY, CHARLES BETHUNE, D.S.O., Major, 19th Battn. Canadian Infantry, 1st Central Ontario Regt. (Brigade Major, 11th Canadian Infantry Brigade, A./G.S.O. II., 4th Canadian Division).
(D.S.O. gazetted 4 June, 1917.)
PERRY, KENNETH MEIKLE, D.S.O., Lieut.-Colonel, 87th Battn. Canadian Infantry, Quebec Regt.
(D.S.O. gazetted 19 Aug. 1916.)
RALSTON, JAMES LAYTON, D.S.O., Lieut.-Colonel, 85th Battn. Canadian Infantry, Nova Scotia Regt.
(D.S.O. gazetted 26 Sept. 1917.)
ROSS, MALCOLM NUGENT, D.S.O., Lieut.-Colonel, 4th Brigade, Canadian Field Artillery.
(D.S.O. gazetted 26 July, 1917.)
STEVENSON, HERBERT IRVING, D.S.O., Lieut.-Colonel, Fort Garry Horse.
(D.S.O. gazetted 22 June, 1918.)

Awarded the Distinguished Service Order:
ADLERCRON, GEORGE ROTHE LADEVEZE, Capt., 8th Hussars.
ALDOUS, FREDERIC CLEMENT, Major (Acting Lieut.-Colonel), 6th Battn. Manchester Regt., Territorial Force, attached 32nd Battn. Machine Gun Corps.
ANGUS, ALEXANDER WILLIAM, Temporary Major (Acting Lieut.-Colonel), 5th Battn. Cameron Highlanders.
ASHMORE, EDWIN JAMES CALDWELL, M.C., Capt. (Acting Major), 10th Gurkha Rifles, attached 2/3rd Gurkha Rifles (Egypt).
BAKER, EUSTON EDWARD FRANCIS, M.C., Capt. (Acting Lieut.-Colonel), Middlesex Regt., Special Reserve, attached 2nd Battn.
BAULD, ROBERT STERLING, M.C., Second Lieut., 5th Battn. Lancashire Fusiliers, Territorial Force, attached 18th Battn.
BUXTON, ROBERT VERE, Capt. (Acting Lieut.-Colonel), Royal West Kent Yeomanry, Commanding 2nd Battn. I.C.C. (Egypt).
BYRNE, LOUIS CAMPBELL, M.C., Lieut. (Acting Major), 2nd Battn. Royal Dublin Fusiliers.
CARTER, WILLIAM, M.C., Lieut. (Temporary Major), Royal Lancaster Regt., G.S.O. II., H.Q. XIII. Corps.
CARTWRIGHT, CHARLES, M.C., Temporary Major (Acting Lieut.-Colonel), 6th Battn. York and Lancaster Regt.

CLOUGH, JOHN, M.C., Temporary Major, 16th Battn. Tank Corps.
COLQUHOUN, ARCHIBALD GORDON CAMPBELL, Capt. (Acting Major), 2nd Battn. Argyll and Sutherland Highlanders.
COOK, FRANCIS ALFRED, M.C., Lieut., 4th Battn. York and Lancaster Regt., Territorial Force, attached 6th Battn.
DAVISON, DOUGLAS STEWART, Capt., 2nd Lancers, Indian Army (Egypt).
DE HOGHTON, GUY, M.C., Capt. (Acting Major), 1st Battn. Yorkshire Light Infantry.
DUNN, PIERS DUNCAN WILLIAMS, M.C., Lieut. (Temporary Capt.), 1st Battn. Lancashire Fusiliers.
FRANKS, KENDAL FERGUSON, Capt. (Temporary Major), 1st Battn. 117th Mahrattas, Indian Army (India).
FREEMAN, CECIL RAYNER, M.C., Capt. (Acting Major), 2nd Battn. Northumberland Fusiliers.
FRENCH, WILLIAM, M.C., Temporary Major (Acting Lieut.-Colonel), 8th Battn. Royal Highlanders.
GAIN, RICHARD SPENCER, Lieut. (Acting Capt.), 11th, attached 1/20th, Battn. London Regt.
GOOCH, HAROLD, M.C., Temporary Major, 121st Field Company, Royal Engineers.
HACKING, ALFRED, M.C., Lieut. (Acting Lieut.-Colonel), 1/8th, attached 1/5th, Battn. Nottinghamshire and Derbyshire Regt., Territorial Force.
HARRISON, GEORGE LEE, Capt. (Acting Lieut.-Colonel), Royal West Surrey Regt., Commanding 7th Battn.
HINGLEY, ALFRED NORMAN, M.C., Major (Temporary Lieut.-Colonel), 13th Battn. Middlesex Regt.
HITCH, ARTHUR TYLER, Temporary Capt. (Acting Lieut.-Colonel), 6th Battn. Bedfordshire Regt., attached 8th Battn. Lincolnshire Regt.
HODGSON, HAROLD JOHN, Capt. (Acting Lieut.-Colonel), Cheshire Regt., attached 7th Battn. Wiltshire Regt.
HOOD, JOHN WEMYSS, M.C., Temporary Capt., attached Border Regt. (1st Battn.).
HOWELL-EVANS, HUGH JOHN, Major (Acting Lieut.-Colonel), Denbigh Yeomanry, attached 10th Battn. Shropshire Light Infantry.
ISAAC, AUBERON GODFREY FAULKNER, M.C., Capt. and Brevet Major (Acting Lieut.-Colonel), 2nd Battn. Royal Berkshire Regt.
JACKSON, RICHARD DINGWALL, M.C., Capt. (Acting Lieut.-Colonel), Royal Engineers (Commanding Royal Engineers, 37th Division).
JERVIS, NICHOLAS GORDON MAINWARING, Major (Acting Lieut.-Colonel), Royal Field Artillery, attached Headquarters 231st (N.M.) Brigade, Royal Field Artillery, Territorial Force.
JOHNSON, WALTER RUSSELL, Lieut.-Colonel, 7th Battn. Essex Regt., Territorial Force, attached 9th Battn.
JONES, JAMES, M.C., Lieut. (Temporary Major and Acting Lieut.-Colonel), 2nd Battn. Durham Light Infantry, attached 17th Battn. Lancashire Fusiliers.
KEEP, LESLIE HOWARD, M.C., Temporary Major, 7th Battn. Bedfordshire Regt., attached 2nd Battn.
KELLY, THOMAS JOSEPH, M.C., Temporary Major, 18th Battn. Manchester Regt., attached 1/6th Battn. Territorial Force.
KING, CECIL HANKEY DICKSON, M.C., Lieut. (Temporary Capt.), King's Royal Rifle Corps, Special Reserve, attached 7th Battn.
KIRKBY, WILLIAM WYNN, Capt., 2nd Battn. Royal Welsh Fusiliers.
KNIGHT, CHARLES FRASER, M.B., Temporary Major, 123rd Field Ambulance, Royal Army Medical Corps.
MARDON, ARTHUR CLAUDE, Lieut.-Colonel, Royal North Devonshire Yeomanry, attached 16th Battn. Devonshire Regt.
MIERS, HANMER JAMES, Capt. (Acting Major), 2nd Battn. Monmouthshire Regt., attached East Lancashire Regt.
MURPHY, JOSEPH LEO, Major, Manchester Regt., Special Reserve, attached 2nd Battn.
MURRAY, JOHN, Major (Acting Lieut.-Colonel), Scottish Horse Yeomanry, attached 12th Battn. Royal Scots.
PETRIE, PAUL CUTHBERT, M.C., Major, D./245th West Riding Brigade, Royal Field Artillery, Territorial Force.
POLLOCK, JOHN ALSAGER, Major (Acting Lieut.-Colonel), Oxfordshire and Buckinghamshire Light Infantry, attached 3rd Battn. London Regt.
PRENTIS, WALTER SLADEN, Lieut.-Colonel, 72nd Punjabis (Egypt).
PRIOR, GEORGE EDWARD REDVERS, M.C., Capt. and Brevet Major (Acting Lieut.-Colonel), 2nd Battn. Devonshire Regt.
REES, THOMAS WYNFORD, M.C., Lieut. (Acting Capt.), 73rd Carnatic Infantry, attached 125th Napier's Rifles, Indian Army (Egypt).
ROBERTS, HARRY, M.C., Lieut. (Acting Capt.), 2nd Battn. Royal Sussex Regt.
SHORLAND, JAMES WILLIAM Temporary Second Lieut., Hampshire Regt., attached 2/4th Battn. Territorial Force.
SMITH, ALBERT JOSEPH, D.C.M., Second Lieut., 1st Battn. Border Regt.
SMITH, BERTRAM ABEL, Major (Temporary Lieut.-Colonel), South Nottinghamshire Hussars, Commanding 23rd Battn. Middlesex Regt.
SMITH, WILFRID CABOURN, M.C., Lieut. (Acting Lieut.-Colonel), King's Royal Rifle Corps, Special Reserve, attached 17th Battn. Royal Fusiliers.
STRUDWICK, SPENCER GORDON, M.C., Lieut. (Acting Major), Royal Field Artillery, Special Reserve, attached B/78th Brigade.
TAPP, JAMES HANSON WILLIAM, Major (Temporary Lieut.-Colonel), Reserve of Officers, attached Headquarters 230th (N.M.) Brigade, Royal Field Artillery, Territorial Force
THOMAS-EVELYN, ROWLAND, Temporary Second Lieut., attached Manchester Regt. (12th Battn.).
VARLEY, OSWALD, M.C., Temporary Capt., 7th Battn. East Yorkshire Regt.
WELDON, HENRY WALTER, Major (Acting Lieut.-Colonel), 2nd Battn. Leinster Regt.
WILLIAMS, AUBREY ELLIS, M.C., Capt. and Brevet Major, South Wales Borderers, G.S.O. II., 30th Division.
WILSON, WILLIAM THOMAS, M.C., Temporary Capt. (Acting Major), 256th Tunnelling Company, Royal Engineers.
WOODS, HUGH KENNEDY, Major and Brevet Lieut.-Colonel (Temporary Lieut.-Colonel), South Lancashire Regt., seconded 9th Battn. Tank Corps.

The Distinguished Service Order

YOUNG, THOMAS FORBES, M.C., Temporary Capt. (Acting Major), 64th Field Company, Royal Engineers.
YOUNGER, JAMES, Lieut.-Colonel, 14th Battn. Royal Highlanders, Territorial Force.

CANADIAN FORCE.

BAKER, EDWIN GODFREY PHIPPS, M.C., Major, 47th Battn. Canadian Infantry, West Ontario Regt.
DAVIS, WILLIAM EDGAR, Major, 11th Battn. Canadian Railway Troops.
DUNWOODY, JAMES MOORE, D.C.M., Lieut. Fort Garry Horse.
ELLIOTT, ORVIL ARD, Major, Canadian Army Dentistry Corps, attached 5th Canadian Field Ambulance.
INGLES, CHARLES JAMES, Major, 20th Battn. Canadian Infantry, 1st Central Ontario Regt.
LOUGH, JOHN ROBERTSON STEWART, M.C., Capt., 72nd Canadian Infantry, British Columbia Regt.
MIDDLEMAST, EDWARD LIDDELL, Major, Fort Garry Horse.
OGILVIE, ALEXANDER THOMAS, Lieut.-Colonel, 14th Brigade, Canadian Field Artillery.
PAULIN, STANLEY, Lieut.-Colonel, 11th Field Ambulance, Canadian Army Medical Corps.
PEARCE, LESLIE FRANK, M.C., Major, 4th Battn. Canadian Machine Gun Corps.
PRESTON, EBENEZER MENZIES, M.M., Lieut., 87th Battn. Canadian Infantry, Quebec Regt.
RYAN, EDUARD JOHN WILSON, Major, 102nd Battn. Canadian Infantry, 2nd Central Ontario Regt.
STAIRS, PHILIP BOYD, Lieut., Canadian Field Artillery, attached Trench Mortar Battery, 5th Canadian Divisional Artillery.

AUSTRALIAN IMPERIAL FORCE.

BAKER, HENRY SEYMOUR, Lieut., 13th Battn. Australian Infantry.
BENNETT, WILLIAM STANLEY, M.C., Lieut., 10th Battn. Australian Infantry.
MACKENZIE, ALEXANDER KENNETH, M.C., Major (Temporary Lieut.-Colonel), 1st Battn. Australian Infantry.
MAY, LEONARD, M.C., Major, Australian Army Medical Corps, attached 11th Battn. Australian Infantry.
McLEAN, JOHN, M.C., Lieut., 42nd Battn. Australian Infantry.
WADSWORTH, WILLIAM ROBERT, M.C., Major, 14th Battn. Australian Infantry.

NEW ZEALAND FORCE.

ARDAGH, PATRICK AUGUSTINE, M.C., Capt., New Zealand Medical Corps, attached 1st Battn. Auckland Regt.

London Gazette, 20 Feb. 1919.—" Admiralty, S.W., 20 Feb. 1919.—Honours for Services in Submarines between the 1st July and 11th Nov. 1918. The King has been graciously pleased to approve of the award of the following honours to the undermentioned Officers. To be Companions of the Distinguished Service Order."
CALVERT, THOMAS FREDERICK PARKER, Commander, Royal Navy.
DERING, CLAUD LACY YEA, Lieut.-Commander, Royal Navy.
HINE, ALFRED GORDON, Lieut.-Commander, Royal Navy.

" Honours for Services in Destroyers of the Harwich Force between the 1st July and 11th Nov. 1918.—The King has been graciously pleased to approve of the following honour to the undermentioned Officer. To be a Companion of the Distinguished Service Order."
KIRKBY, ERNEST WALTER, Lieut.-Commander, Royal Navy.

" Honours for Services in Destroyers of the Dover Patrol between the 1st July and 11th Nov. 1918.—The King has been graciously pleased to approve of the award of the following honours to the undermentioned Officers. To be a Companion of the Distinguished Service Order."
STOKES, OLIVER MAURICE FITZGERALD, Commander, Royal Navy.

To receive a Bar to the Distinguished Service Order :
CUNNINGHAM, ANDREW BROWNE, D.S.O., Commander, Royal Navy.

" Honours for Palestine Operations (Oct.–Dec. 1917).—The King has been graciously pleased to approve of the award of the following honours to the undermentioned Officers, in recognition of their services during naval operations carried out in conjunction with military operations in Palestine from Oct. to Dec. 1917. To be Companions of the Distinguished Service Order."
NARES, JOHN DODD, Commander, Royal Navy, H.M.S. Enterprise. Did most useful service prior to the operations in fixing positions north of Gaza, thus enabling a map to be drawn up. Rendered every assistance to R.A. Egypt from the 6th to 12th Nov. 1917, when the Rear-Admiral's flag was flown in Enterprise.
CROCKER, CECIL JAMES, Commander, Royal Navy, H.M. Monitor M.31. Was senior officer of the M. class Monitors. After the capture of the Sheikh Hassan position, in the early morning of the 2nd Nov. 1917, the monitors and destroyers operated to cover this position whilst it was being consolidated. When the enemy made a strong and determined counter-attack, lasting from about 3 to 4.30 p.m., Commander Crocker closed his squadron inshore and maintained a heavy fire upon the enemy, which went far to break up the attack. He displayed great tact and resource, and maintained close relations with the military on the sea flank of the Expeditionary Force, and it was largely due to his personality that the naval co-operation was so successful.
STANLEY, EDMOND ALAN BERNERS, M.V.O., Commander, Royal Navy, H.M.S. Staunch. Senior officer of destroyers employed guarding the flank of the Army during the Gaza operations, and rendered valuable service during the enemy's counter-attacks upon Sheikh Hassan.
HASELFOOT, FRANCIS EDMUND BLECHYNDEN, Lieut.-Commander (now Commander), Royal Navy, H.M.S. Grafton. This officer's previous experience, coupled with his energy and originality, was of the greatest value. He prepared observation posts and arranged communications from them to the signal stations, designed and constructed spotting clocks, placed landmarks and fixed them by triangulation, produced special squared maps for naval bombarding purposes, and assisted in the survey north of Gaza. During the operations he was attached to the XXIst Corps as Liaison Officer, in which capacity he did excellent work.

LUARD, TRANT BRAMSTON, Major and Brevet Lieut.-Colonel (Temporary Lieut.-Colonel), Royal Marine Light Infantry, H.M.S. Hannibal. Was employed with Lieut.-Commander Haselfoot to establish observation posts before Gaza for naval use. He was in charge of the spotting officers and men, and rendered valuable services in authorizing fire. The accuracy and success of the sea bombardment was largely due to Major Luard's organization.
GREGORY, GEORGE, O.B.E., R.D., Commander, Royal Naval Reserve. Was Naval Transport Officer in charge of the landing of stores and ammunition on the coast. The victualling of the Army and the supply of ammunition was largely dependent on the landing of stores upon an open coast under unfavourable conditions ; it reflected great credit on Commander Gregory and his staff that this work was so well performed, and that such excellent results were obtained from the Egyptian labourers employed on it.
HANNING-LEE, VAUGHAN ALEXANDER EDWARD, Lieut.-Commander (Acting Commander), Royal Navy, H.M.S. Ladybird. Senior officer of river gunboats. These vessels replaced the destroyers on flank guard when the latter were absent fuelling, and were also employed cutting wire defences before the attack upon Sheikh Hassan, and in firing on trenches and observation posts. The Ladybird's fire upon Askelon, about 3.30 p.m. on the 8th Nov. 1917, disorganized the enemy's spotting arrangements and reduced the casualties of our troops.

London Gazette, 3 March, 1919.—" War Office, 3 March, 1919. His Majesty the King has been graciously pleased to approve of the undermentioned awards for distinguished service in connection with military operations in Mesopotamia. Dated 1 Jan. 1919. Awarded a Bar to the Distinguished Service Order."
LYNCH-STAUNTON, REGINALD KIRKPATRICK, D.S.O., Major and Brevet Lieut.-Colonel, Royal Field Artillery.
(D.S.O. gazetted 23 June, 1915.)
McCORMICK, HAROLD BARRY, D.S.O., Temporary Lieut.-Colonel, Reserve of Officers, East Lancashire Regt., Special Reserve.
(D.S.O. gazetted 29 July, 1902.)

Awarded the Distinguished Service Order :
GEOGHEGAN, NORMAN MEREDITH, Major and Brevet Lieut.-Colonel, 89th Punjabis, Indian Army.
GOLDBERG, REUBEN, Temporary Capt., 6th Light Armoured Motor Battery, Machine Gun Corps (Motor)
MATTHEWS, CLAUD LEONARD, Major and Brevet Lieut.-Colonel, Durham Light Infantry, attached Hampshire Regt.

London Gazette, 8 March, 1919.—" War Office, 8 March, 1919. His Majesty the King has been graciously pleased to approve of the following awards to the undermentioned Officers, in recognition of their gallantry and devotion to duty in the field.
" The acts of gallantry for which the decorations have been awarded will be announced in the London Gazette as early as practicable."

Awarded a Third Bar to the Distinguished Service Order :
BUCKLE, ARCHIBALD WALTER, D.S.O., Temporary Commander, Anson Battn., Royal Naval Division, Royal Naval Volunteer Reserve.
(D.S.O. gazetted 4 March, 1918.)
(First Bar gazetted 26 July, 1918.)
(Second Bar gazetted 11 Jan. 1919.)
DAWSON, WILLIAM ROBERT AUFRERE, D.S.O., Capt. and Brevet Major (Temporary Lieut.-Colonel), Commanding 6th Battn. Royal West Kent Regt.
(D.S.O. gazetted 15 April, 1916.)
(First Bar gazetted 18 July, 1917.)
(Second Bar gazetted 22 June, 1918.)
KNOX, ROBERT SINCLAIR, D.S.O., Temporary Major (Acting Lieut.-Colonel), 10th Battn. Royal Inniskilling Fusiliers, attached 9th Battn.
(D.S.O. gazetted 1 Jan. 1917.)
(First Bar gazetted 18 Feb. 1918.)
(Second Bar gazetted 16 Sept. 1918.)

Awarded a Second Bar to the Distinguished Service Order :
BEASLEY, ROBERT LONGFIELD, D.S.O., Major (Temporary Lieut.-Colonel), 2nd Battn. Gloucestershire Regt., attached 17th Battn. Royal Welsh Fusiliers.
(D.S.O. gazetted 1 Jan. 1918.)
(First Bar gazetted 27 July, 1918.)
CURTIS, HUBERT MONTAGU COTTON, D.S.O., Capt. (Acting Lieut.-Colonel), 6th Battn. North Staffordshire Regt., Territorial Force, Commanding 7th Battn. East Kent Regt.
(D.S.O. gazetted 1 Jan. 1918.)
(First Bar gazetted 26 July, 1918.)
DUMBELL, CHARLES HAROLD, D.S.O., Major (Temporary Lieut.-Colonel), Nottinghamshire and Derbyshire Regt., attached 11th Battn. Essex Regt.
(D.S.O. gazetted 1 Jan. 1917.)
(First Bar gazetted 26 July, 1918.)
FRASER, JOHN ALEXANDER, D.S.O., D.C.M., Lieut. (Temporary Lieut.-Colonel), 7th Dragoon Guards, attached 5/6th Battn. Royal Scots, Territorial Force.
(D.S.O. gazetted 1 Jan. 1918.)
(First Bar gazetted 22 April, 1918.)
FREYBERG, BERNARD CYRIL, V.C., D.S.O., Capt. and Brevet Lieut.-Colonel (Temporary Brigadier-General), Royal West Surrey Regt. (G.O.C., 88th Infantry Brigade).
(D.S.O. gazetted 3 June, 1915.)
(First Bar gazetted 1 Feb. 1919.)
LAMBERT, WALTER JOHN, D.S.O., Major, 29th Lancers, Indian Army, attached Mysore Imperial Service Lancers (Egypt).
(D.S.O. gazetted 1 Jan. 1917.)
(First Bar gazetted 2 Dec. 1918.)
MILLS, ARTHUR MORDAUNT, D.S.O., Major, 18th Lancers, Indian Army (Egypt).
(D.S.O. gazetted 1 Jan. 1917.)
(First Bar gazetted 4 Feb. 1918.)
NADEN, FRANK, D.S.O., M.C., Lieut. (Acting Lieut.-Colonel), 1/6th Battn. Cheshire Regt., Territorial Force, attached 7th Battn. Royal Irish Regt.
(D.S.O. gazetted 26 Nov. 1917.)
(First Bar gazetted 16 Sept. 1918.)

CANADIAN FORCE.

MACFARLANE, ROBERT ALEXANDER, D.S.O., Lieut.-Colonel, 58th Infantry Battn., 2nd Central Ontario Regt.
(D.S.O. gazetted 4 June, 1917.)
(First Bar gazetted 11 Jan. 1919.)

RILEY, HAROLD JAMES, D.S.O., Lieut.-Colonel, 27th Infantry Battn., Manitoba Regt.
(D.S.O. gazetted 18 July, 1917.)
(First Bar gazetted 11 Jan. 1919.)

Awarded a First Bar to the Distinguished Service Order:

ANDERSON, FRANCIS, D.S.O., M.C., Capt. (Acting Lieut.-Colonel), 1st Battn. Royal Highlanders.
(D.S.O. gazetted 17 Dec. 1917.)

CLEGHORN, GEORGE MATTHEW, D.S.O., Temporary Major, 15th Battn. Highland Light Infantry.
(D.S.O. gazetted 26 July, 1918.)

CURRIN, RICHARD WILLIAM, D.S.O., Temporary Major (Acting Lieut.-Colonel), York and Lancaster Regt., attached 1/8th Battn. Nottinghamshire and Derbyshire Regt., Territorial Force.
(D.S.O. gazetted 25 Aug. 1916.)

DOWDING, CHARLES CHILD, D.S.O., M.C., Temporary Major (Acting Lieut.-Colonel), Royal Lancaster Regt., attached 1/6th Battn. North Staffordshire Regt., Territorial Force.
(D.S.O. gazetted 3 June, 1918.)

DRAGE, GODFREY, D.S.O., Major (Acting Lieut.-Colonel) (Reserve of Officers), Oxfordshire and Buckinghamshire Light Infantry, attached 1/4th Battn. Cheshire Regt., Territorial Force.
(D.S.O. gazetted 1 Jan. 1917.)

FURSE, RALPH DOLIGNON, D.S.O., Major, King Edward's Horse.
(D.S.O. gazetted 26 July, 1918.)

GARDNER, WILLIAM ROSS, D.S.O., Capt. (Acting Lieut.-Colonel), Royal Army Medical Corps (Special Reserve), attached 138th Field Ambulance.
(D.S.O. gazetted 1 Jan. 1918.)

HART, REGINALD SETON, D.S.O., Major (Temporary Lieut.-Colonel), Nottinghamshire and Derbyshire Regt., attached 9th Battn. Yorkshire Regt.
(D.S.O. gazetted 27 Oct. 1917.)

HOHLER, ARTHUR PRESTON, D.S.O., Major (Acting Lieut.-Colonel), 2/10th Battn. Middlesex Regt., Territorial Force, Commanding 4/5th Battn. Welsh Regt., Territorial Force (Egypt).
(D.S.O. gazetted 16 Aug. 1917.)

HOLDEN, HYLA NAPIER, D.S.O., Lieut.-Colonel, 5th Cavalry, Indian Army, Senior Special Service Officer, employed Jodhpur Imperial Service Lancers (Egypt).
(D.S.O. gazetted 1 Jan. 1919.)

HUDSON, NOEL BARING, D.S.O., M.C., Temporary Lieut.-Colonel, 8th Battn. Royal Berkshire Regt.
(D.S.O. gazetted in this Gazette.)

HUTCHISON, COLIN ROSS MARSHALL, D.S.O., M.C., Capt. (Acting Major), 113th Brigade, Royal Field Artillery, attached 29th Divisional Artillery.
(D.S.O. gazetted 1 Jan. 1918.)

JEWELS, CHARLES EDGAR, D.S.O., M.C., Temporary Lieut.-Colonel, 18th Battn. Lancashire Fusiliers.
(D.S.O. gazetted 26 July, 1918.)

JONES, BRYAN JOHN, D.S.O., Major (Acting Lieut.-Colonel), Leinster Regt., attached 15th Battn. Royal Irish Rifles.
(D.S.O. gazetted 14 Jan. 1916.)

LAURIE, JOHN EMILIUS, D.S.O., Capt. (Acting Lieut.-Colonel), 1st Battn. Seaforth Highlanders, attached 6th Battn. Territorial Force.
(D.S.O. gazetted 22 Sept. 1916.)

LEWIS, DUDLEY, D.S.O., M.C., Temporary Major (Acting Lieut.-Colonel), York and Lancaster Regt., Commanding 1/5th Battn. Gloucestershire Regt., Territorial Force.
(D.S.O. gazetted 1 Jan. 1918.)

MASON, GLYN KEITH MURRAY, D.S.O., Capt. (Acting Lieut.-Colonel), 14th Hussars, Commanding 1/1st Dorset Yeomanry (Egypt).
(D.S.O. gazetted 3 June, 1916.)

MUIRHEAD, MURRAY, D.S.O., Major (Acting Lieut.-Colonel), Headquarters, 51st Brigade, Royal Field Artillery.
(D.S.O. gazetted 18 Feb. 1915.)

POLLOCK, HENRY BRODHURST, D.S.O., Temporary Commander, Hood Battn. Royal Naval Division, Royal Naval Volunteer Reserve.
(D.S.O. gazetted 4 March, 1918.)

RATCLIFFE, WILLIAM CHARLES, D.S.O., Capt. (Temporary Major), Northampton Regt., attached 9th Battn. Yorkshire Light Infantry.
(D.S.O. gazetted in this Gazette.)

SANKEY, CROFTON EDWARD PYM, D.S.O., Major and Brevet Lieut.-Colonel (Acting Lieut.-Colonel), Commanding Royal Engineers, 1st Division, Royal Engineers.
(D.S.O. gazetted 23 June, 1915.)

STOREY, HENRY INNES, D.S.O., Major (Temporary Lieut.-Colonel), Commanding 9th Battn. Devonshire Regt.
(D.S.O. gazetted 15 Feb. 1917.)

STIRLING, WALTER FRANCIS, D.S.O., M.C., Major, Reserve of Officers, Royal Dublin Fusiliers (Egypt).
(D.S.O. gazetted 28 Jan. 1902.)

WEIR, DONALD LORD, D.S.O., M.C., Capt. (Acting Lieut.-Colonel), Leicestershire Regt., attached 1st Battn. West Yorkshire Regt.
(D.S.O. gazetted 15 April, 1916.)

WHEATLEY, LEONARD LANE, C.M.G., D.S.O., Major and Brevet Lieut.-Colonel (Temporary Brigadier-General), Argyll and Sutherland Highlanders, Commanding 1st Infantry Brigade.
(D.S.O. gazetted 20 May, 1898.)

CANADIAN FORCE.

CARMICHAEL, DOUGALL, D.S.O., M.C., Major, 58th, attached 116th, Infantry Battn., 2nd Central Ontario Regt.
(D.S.O. gazetted 11 Jan. 1919.)

CONSTANTINE, CHARLES FRANCIS, D.S.O., Lieut.-Colonel, 5th Brigade, Canadian Field Artillery.
(D.S.O. gazetted 1 Jan. 1917.)

ELLIOTT, ORVIL ARD, D.S.O., Major, Canadian Army Dental Corps, attached 5th Field Ambulance, Canadian Army Medical Corps.
(D.S.O. gazetted 15 Feb. 1919.)

GIRVAN, JOHN POLLANDS, D.S.O., M.C., Major (Acting Lieut.-Colonel), 15th Infantry Battn., 1st Central Ontario Regt.
(D.S.O. gazetted 1 Feb. 1919.)

KAPPELE, DANIEL PAUL, D.S.O., Lieut.-Colonel, 5th Field Ambulance Canadian Army Medical Corps.
(D.S.O. gazetted 3 June, 1918.)

LEASK, THOMAS McCRAE, D.S.O., Lieut.-Colonel, 10th Field Ambulance, Canadian Army Medical Corps.
(D.S.O. gazetted 1 Jan. 1918.)

PHILPOT, DAVID, D.S.O., Major, 7th Infantry Battn. British Columbia Regt.
(D.S.O. gazetted 18 July, 1917.)

AUSTRALIAN IMPERIAL FORCE.

CAMERON, DONALD, D.S.O., Lieut.-Colonel, 12th Australian Light Horse Regt. (Egypt).
(D.S.O. gazetted 18 Jan. 1918.)

CORRIGAN, JOHN JOSEPH, D.S.O., Major (Temporary Lieut.-Colonel), 46th Battn. Australian Imperial Force.
(D.S.O. gazetted 1 Jan. 1918.)

DENEHY, CHARLES ALOYSIUS, D.S.O., Lieut.-Colonel, 57th Battn. Australian Imperial Force.
(D.S.O. gazetted 18 July, 1917.)

McCLEAN, FREDERICK STEPHEN, D.S.O., Major (Temporary Lieut.-Colonel), 5th Pioneer Battn., Australian Infantry.
(D.S.O. gazetted 27 Oct. 1917.)

RANKIN, GEORGE JAMES, D.S.O., Major, 4th Australian Light Horse Regt. (Egypt).
(D.S.O. gazetted 11 April, 1918.)

SCOTT, WILLIAM HENRY, C.M.G., D.S.O., Lieut.-Colonel, 9th Australian Light Horse Regt. (Egypt).
(D.S.O. gazetted 16 May, 1916.)

NEW ZEALAND FORCE.

JARDINE, LEONARD HANDFORTH, D.S.O., M.C., Lieut.-Colonel, 2nd Battn. New Zealand Rifle Brigade.
(D.S.O. gazetted 1 Feb. 1919.)

Awarded the Distinguished Service Order:

ANDREW, WILLIAM CULLEN, M.C., Temporary Major, 33rd Battn, Machine Gun Corps.

ANDREWS, STEPHEN ARTHUR, M.C., Temporary Lieut. (Acting Capt.), 7th Battn. Royal Sussex Regt.

APSLEY, LORD, ALLEN ALGERNON, M.C., Capt., 1/1st Gloucestershire Yeomanry (Egypt).

ARNOLD, CLEMENT BROOMHALL, Temporary Lieut., 6th Battn. Tank Corps.

BAILEY, WALTER GEORGE, M.C., Temporary Second Lieut., 2nd Battn. Suffolk Regt.

BALL, GEORGE HERBERT, Lieut. (Acting Capt.), 1/5th Battn. South Staffordshire Regt., Territorial Force.

BARLTROP, ERNEST WILLIAM, Lieut. (Temporary Capt.), Essex Regt., Special Reserve, attached 9th Battn.

BENNETT, JOHN, M.C., Lieut. (Acting Capt.), 1/9th Battn. Highland Light Infantry, Territorial Force.

BLANDE, ALFRED, Temporary Second Lieut., 24th Battn. Royal Fusiliers.

BOARDMAN, HENRY, M.C., Second Lieut., 1st Battn. Liverpool Regt., attached 4th Battn.

BODINGTON, JOHN REDNER, M.C., Lieut. (Acting Capt.), 2/5th Battn. Lancashire Regt., Territorial Force.

BOSWELL, HAROLD EDWARD, M.C., Temporary Second Lieut., 2nd Battn. Worcestershire Regt.

BOWEN, ARTHUR LLEWELLYN, Major (Acting Lieut.-Colonel), 4th Battn. Welsh Regt., Territorial Force, attached 10th Battn. South Wales Borderers.

BOYCE, WILLIAM WALLACE, Capt. (Acting Lieut.-Colonel), No. 2 Field Ambulance, Royal Army Medical Corps.

BRADY, IRVINE GORDON CAMPBELL, M.C., Temporary Major, 9th Battn. Northumberland Fusiliers.

CALLOW, GRAHAM, M.C., Second Lieut. (Temporary Capt.), Nottinghamshire and Derbyshire Regt., attached 15th Battn.

CAMPBELL, RONALD, Temporary Major, 15th, formerly 12th, Battn. Tank Corps.

CHARLTON, ARTHUR HUMPHREY, Lieut. (Acting Capt.), 1/6th Battn. North Staffordshire Regt., Territorial Force.

CLOUSTON, JAMES, M.M., Temporary Second Lieut., B/107th Brigade, Royal Field Artillery.

COOK, JAMES, M.C., Lieut. (Acting Capt.), 2nd Battn. West Riding Regt.

CASS, EDWARD EARNSHAW EDEN, Lieut. (Acting Capt.), 2nd Battn. Yorkshire Light Infantry.

CHIPP, WILKINS FITZWILLIAM, M.C., Lieut. (Acting Major), 1/1st Battn. Hereford Regt., Territorial Force.

MILLER, GEOFFREY CHRISTIE, M.C., Capt. (Acting Lieut.-Colonel), Buckinghamshire Battn. Oxfordshire and Buckinghamshire Light Infantry, attached 2/5th Battn. Gloucestershire Regt.

CLARKE, HUBERT THOMAS, Major (Acting Lieut.-Colonel) 1/8th Battn. Worcestershire Regt., Territorial Force.

CRAWSHAW, CHARLES HERBERT, M.C., Capt. (Acting Major), 1st Battn. King's Own Scottish Borderers.

DE MIREMONT, GUY EGON RENÉDE, M.C., Capt. (Acting Major), 2nd Battn. Royal Welsh Fusiliers.

DENT, JOHN RALPH CONGRAVE, M.C., Capt. (Acting Lieut.-Colonel), 1st Battn. Royal Inniskilling Fusiliers.

DOAKE, RICHARD LIONEL VERE, M.C., Temporary Capt., 7th Battn. Bedfordshire Regt., attached 2nd Battn.

DUGGAN, HAROLD JOSEPH GEORGE, M.C., Temporary Capt. (Acting Major), North Lancashire Regt., attached 1/4th Battn. Territorial Force.

The Distinguished Service Order

DUNCAN, CHARLES MAITLAND, Temporary Capt., C/110th Brigade, Royal Field Artillery.
EDINBOROUGH, SAMUEL BERNARD, M.C., Second Lieut. (Acting Capt.), 3rd Battn. Lincolnshire Regt., attached 1st Battn.
EDWARDS, JOHN, Temporary Major, Royal Welsh Fusiliers, attached 1st Battn. Nottinghamshire and Derbyshire Regt.
EVANS, THOMAS RICHARD, Temporary Major (Acting Lieut.-Colonel), Royal Welsh Fusiliers, attached 1/6th Battn. North Staffordshire Regt., Territorial Force.
FRISBY, LIONEL CLAUD, M.C., Capt. (Acting Lieut.-Colonel), 6th Battn. Welsh Regt.
GARDEN, JAMES WINTON, M.C., Temporary Capt. (Acting Major), 8th Battn. Machine Gun Corps.
GARROD, EDGAR SAMUEL, M.C., D.C.M., Temporary Second Lieut. (Acting Capt.), 10th Battn. Tank Corps.
GARSTIN, DENIS, Capt., 10th Royal Hussars.
GEMMELL, JOHN SALISBURY, M.C., Temporary Major, 20th Battn. Manchester Regt.
GRAHAM, FERGUS REGINALD WINSFORD, M.C., Capt. and Brevet Major (Acting Lieut.-Colonel), Royal Irish Rifles, attached 10th Battn. London Regt. (Egypt)
GRAY, JOHN EDWARD BOWLES, Temporary Capt., 7th Battn. Rifle Brigade, attached 33rd Battn. London Regt.
GREAVES, HARRY, M.C., Lieut., 3rd Battn. Nottinghamshire and Derbyshire Regt., attached 1st Battn.
GREVILLE, GUY GEORGE FREDERICK FULKE, Capt. (Acting Major), Leinster Regt., attached 6th Battn. Royal Inniskilling Fusiliers.
GRIFFITHS, JAMES LLEWELLYN, Major, 1/5th Battn. Leicestershire Regt., Territorial Force.
GUILD, JOHN ROYES, Capt. (Acting Major), 1st Battn. Gloucestershire Regt.
HARRAGIN, ALFRED ERNEST ALBERT, Temporary Major, 1st Battn. West Indian Regt. (Capt., Trinidad Local Forces) (Egypt).
HOLBECH, LAURENCE, M.C., Lieut., Grenadier Guards (Special Reserve), attached 2nd Battn.
HOPE, PERCY ALBERT, Temporary Lieut. (Acting Capt.), 11th Battn. Royal Fusiliers.
HUDSON, NOEL BARING, M.C., Temporary Lieut.-Colonel, 8th Battn. Royal Berkshire Regt.
JACKSON, MANSEL HALKET, M.C., Capt., 29th Lancers, Indian Army (Egypt).
KER, ROBERT FORDYCE, M.C., Temporary Major (Acting Lieut.-Colonel), 6th Battn. King's Own Scottish Borderers.
KING, GEORGE WILLIAM, M.C., Temporary Capt. (Acting Major), C/160th Brigade, Royal Field Artillery.
LAWSON, EDWARD FREDERICK, M.C., Capt. (Acting Lieut.-Colonel), 1/1st Buckinghamshire Yeomanry, Commanding 1st County of London Yeomanry (Egypt).
LISTER, CECIL, M.C., Capt. (Acting Lieut.-Colonel), Northamptonshire Regt., attached 1/6th Battn. South Staffordshire Regt., Territorial Force.
LOMAX, CYRIL ERNEST NAPIER, M.C., Capt. (Temporary Lieut.-Colonel), Welsh Regt., Commanding 21st Battn. Manchester Regt.
MACDERMOTT, GEORGE ANTHONY, M.C., Capt. (Acting Major), 4th Battn. Highland Light Infantry, seconded 9th Battn. Machine Gun Corps.
MANDLEBERG, LEONARD CHARLES, M.C., Temporary Major, 15th Battn. Lancashire Fusiliers.
MAY, ERNEST RICHARD HALLAM, Temporary Major, Royal Irish Rifles, attached 1st Battn.
McCARTHY, WILLIAM HILGROVE LESLIE, M.C., Capt. (Acting Lieut.-Colonel), Royal Army Medical Corps (Special Reserve), attached 19th Field Ambulance.
McLELLAN, JAMES, M.C., Lieut. (Acting Major), 446th (Northumbrian) Field Company, Royal Engineers, Territorial Force
McNEILE, DONALD HUGH, Lieut.-Colonel, 19th Lancers, Indian Army (Egypt).
METHUEN, HENRY CHARLES, M.C., Capt. (Acting Lieut.-Colonel), 1st Battn. Cameron Highlanders.
MORGAN, CLIFFORD WILLIAM, M.C., Lieut. (Acting Capt.), 5th, attached 4/5th, Battn. Welsh Regt. Territorial Force (Egypt).
MORRIS, CHARLES HENRY, M.C., Capt. (Acting Major), Middlesex Regt., attached 1st Battn. Dorset Regt.
OWEN, WALTER LLEWELLYN, M.C., Capt. and Brevet Major (Temporary Lieut.-Colonel), 5th Battn. Liverpool Regt., Territorial Force, Commanding 11th Battn. Royal West Surrey Regt.
PAIGE, CHARLES JOHN MURRAY, M.C., Temporary Second Lieut. (Acting Capt.), 11th Battn. Royal West Surrey Regt.
PANNALL, CHARLIE, M.C., Lieut. (Temporary Major and Acting Lieut.-Colonel), Royal West Surrey Regt., attached 20th Battn. Durham Light Infantry.
PARKES, WALTER, M.C., Temporary Major (Acting Lieut.-Colonel), 8th Battn. Gloucestershire Regt.
PATERSON, GEORGE ROBERT STEEL, M.C., Temporary Major, Highland Light Infantry, attached 1/5th Battn. King's Own Scottish Borderers, Territorial Force.
PEARSE, REGINALD GUY, M.C., Lieut. (Acting Capt.), 3rd Battn. Nottinghamshire and Derbyshire Regt., attached 1st Battn.
PEBERDY, CHARLES EDWARD VERNON KINGSBURY, M.C., Lieut. (Acting Capt.), 4th Battn. West Yorkshire Regt., attached 1st Battn.
PIGG, NORMAN BATEY, M.C., Temporary Lieut. (Acting Capt.), 1st Battn. Northumberland Fusiliers.
POTTER, J. WATTS, Lieut. (Acting Capt.), 1/5th Battn., attached 1/6th Battn., Nottinghamshire and Derbyshire Regt., Territorial Force.
PRING, BERNARD VINCENT, M.C., Second Lieut. (Acting Capt.), Yorkshire Light Infantry, attached 2nd Battn.
RATCLIFFE, WILLIAM CHARLES, Capt. (Temporary Major), Northamptonshire Regt., attached 9th Battn. Yorkshire Light Infantry.
RAWLINSON, ALFRED, C.M.G., Temporary Lieut.-Colonel, Royal Garrison Artillery (Mesopotamia)

RIDLEY, BASIL WHITE, M.C., Temporary Major (Acting Lieut.-Colonel), 29th Durham Light Infantry (formerly East Lancashire Regt.).
ROBERTS, GEORGE, M.C., Temporary Capt. (Acting Major), A/123rd Brigade, Royal Field Artillery.
ROBINSON, GUY ST. GEORGE, M.C., Capt. (Acting Lieut.-Colonel), 1st Battn. Northamptonshire Regt.
ROGERS, CLAUDE RUPERT DE WARRENNE, Capt., 1st Battn. Leinster Regt., attached 1/5th Battn. Gloucestershire Regt., Territorial Force.
RUSTON, ALPRES HAROLD, Temporary Major, Motor Machine Gun Corps (Mesopotamia).
SCULLY, VINCENT MARCUS BARRON, O.B.E., Capt. (Temporary Lieut.-Colonel), Border Regt., attached 5th Battn. Connaught Rangers.
SHEDDEN, JAMES ALEXANDER, M.C., Lieut. (Acting Major), 7th Battn. Scottish Rifles, Territorial Force, attached 1/6th Battn. Nottinghamshire and Derbyshire Regt., Territorial Force.
SHELDON, JOSEPH, M.C., Lieut., 2nd Battn. Nottinghamshire and Derbyshire Regt.
SIMMONS, WILLIAM GORDON, M.C., Temporary Capt., 7th Battn. Royal West Surrey Regt.
SLADDEN, CYRIL EDGAR, M.C., Temporary Major, 9th Battn. Worcestershire Regt. (Mesopotamia)
STALLARD, CHARLES FRAMPTON, M.C., Temporary Major, 23rd Battn. Middlesex Regt., attached 15th Battn. Hampshire Regt.
SUTCLIFFE, ARTHUR WINDLE, M.C., Capt. (Acting Major), Border Regt., attached 5th Battn. Connaught Rangers.
TAYLER, FRANCIS LIONEL, Major, Deoli Regt., Indian Army (Egypt).
THOMPSON, REGINALD, Major (Acting Lieut.-Colonel), 1/1st Yorkshire Dragoons.
TOMBAZIS, JAMES LYELL, M.C., Second Lieut., 2nd Battn. Nottinghamshire and Derbyshire Rregt.
TRESTRAIL, ALFRED ERNEST YATES, Temporary Major, Cheshire Regt., attached 15th Battn.
TURNER, ROBERT VILLIERS, Major (Acting Lieut.-Colonel), 2nd Battn. Durham Light Infantry.
VIGORS, MERVYN DOYNE, M.C., Major, 9th Hodson's Horse, Indian Army (Egypt).
WALKER, JAMES McCAIG, Temporary Second Lieut., Royal Highlanders, attached 1/6th Battn. Territorial Force.
WALKER, VERNON DUDLEY, M.M., Temporary Second Lieut., 34th Battn. Machine Gun Corps.
WEBSTER, JAMES ALEXANDER, Capt. and Brevet Major, 8th Battn. London Regt., attached Headquarters, 53rd Infantry Brigade.
WELLS, GEORGE KERSLAKE, M.C., Lieut., 4th Battn. King's Royal Rifle Corps.
WHITE, ARTHUR, Capt. (Acting Lieut.-Colonel), 4th Battn. East Surrey Regt., attached 1/5th Battn. South Staffordshire Regt., Territorial Force (christian name corrected to Alfred [London Gazette, 12 July, 1920]).
WHITE, WILLIAM, M.C., Temporary Major, 15th Battn. Highland Light Infantry.
WILLISON, ARTHUR CECIL, M.C., Lieut., 1st Battn. Nottinghamshire and Derbyshire Regt., attached Headquarters, 24th Infantry Brigade.
WILSON, ALEXANDER ROBERT GRAHAM, Capt. (Acting Lieut.-Colonel), 1st Battn. Argyll and Sutherland Highlanders, attached 1/5th Battn. Territorial Force.
WRIGHT, ARTHUR, M.C., Lieut. (Acting Capt.), 2/2nd Battn. London Regt.
YOUNG, CLARENCE RANDOLPH, M.C., Temporary Capt., Royal Army Medical Corps, attached 1st Battn. Shropshire Light Infantry.
YOUNG, HUBERT WINTHROP, Capt. (Temporary Major), 116th Mahratta Light Infantry, Indian Army (Egypt).

CANADIAN FORCE.

ALLEN, EVELYN PRESTWOOD SEYMOUR, Capt., 116th Infantry Battn. 2nd Central Ontario Regt.
BOND, GEORGE FREDERICK DANIELS, M.C., Major, 28th Infantry Battn. Saskatchewan Regt.
BONNER, ARTHUR BERNARD, M.M., Lieut., 116th Infantry, 2nd Central Ontario Regt.
BOWERBANK, GEORGE SCOTT STANTON, M.C., Major, 21st Infantry Battn. East Ontario Regt.
CHARLES, JOHN LESLIE, Major, 13th Battn. Canadian Railway Service.
CHASSE, HENRI, M.C., Major, 22nd Infantry Battn. Quebec Regt.
COSGROVE, JOHN ROBERT, M.C., Major, 8th Battn. Canadian Railway Troops.
HERRIDGE, WILLIAM DUNCAN, M.C., Capt., Canadian Cyclist Corps (Brigade Major, 2nd Canadian Infantry Brigade Headquarters).
ISBESTER, COLIN JOHN FRASER, Major, 10th Battn. Canadian Railway Troops.
JOHNSTON, HUGH ALSTON, M.C., Capt., 13th Infantry Battn. Quebec Regt.
MERSEREAU, CHALVERS JACK, Major, 25th Infantry Battn. Nova Scotia Regt.
MILLER, THOMAS EASSON, M.M., Lieut., 8th Infantry Battn. Manitoba Regt.
PRICE, CHARLES BASIL, D.C.M., Major, 14th Infantry Battn. Quebec Regt.
RITCHIE, CHARLES FREDERICK, M.C., Lieut.-Colonel, 24th Infantry Battn. Quebec Regt.
SINCLAIR, IAN MACINTOSH ROE, M.C., Major, 13th Infantry Battn. Quebec Regt.
SPENCER, NELSON, Major, 31st Infantry Battn. Alberta Regt.
TOBIN HENRY SEYMOUR, Lieut.-Colonel, 29th Infantry Battn. British Columbia Regt.
TUXFORD, GEORGE STUART, C.B., C.M.G., Brigadier-General, Saskatchewan Regt., Commanding 3rd Canadian Infantry Brigade.
WALKER, PHILIP, Major, Manitoba Regt., attached 10th Infantry Battn. Alberta Regt.
WHITE, WILLIAM JAMES, M.C., Capt., 28th Infantry Battn. Saskatchewan Regt.

AUSTRALIAN IMPERIAL FORCE.

ANDERSON, ALEXANDER MILNE, Capt., 48th Battn. Australian Imperial Force.
CAMPBELL, ARCHIE ERIC GORDON, M.C., Major, 14th Australian Light Horse Regt. (Egypt).
CHANTER, JOHN COURTENAY, Major, 4th Australian Light Horse Regt. (Egypt).
CHEESEMAN, WILLIAM JOSEPH ROBERT, M.C., Lieut.-Colonel, 53rd Battn. Australian Imperial Force.
COSTELLO, EDWARD, Major, 11th Australian Light Horse Regt. (Egypt).
COUCHMAN, FRANK MUNGEAM, Major, 46th Battn. Australian Imperial Force.
CRAIG, ROBERT FULTON, Major, 15th Field Ambulance, Australian Army Medical Corps.
DALGLEISH, NORMAN, Lieut., 58th Battn. Australian Imperial Force.
DENSON, HERBERT REGINALD, Major, 14th Australian Light Horse Regt. (Egypt).
DODD, ARTHUR WILLIAM, M.C., Major, 6th Battery, 2nd Brigade, Australian Field Artillery.
HAMLIN, HERBERT BOWEN, Major, 10th Australian Light Horse Regt. (Egypt).
HILL, REGINALD VALENTINE, Lieut., 53rd Battn. Australian Imperial Force.
LANGLEY, GEORGE FURNER, Lieut.-Colonel, Commanding 14th Australian Light Horse Regt. (Egypt).
LEITH, ERIC ALLAN, Lieut., 46th Battn. Australian Imperial Force.
LOYNES, JAMES, Major, 11th Australian Light Horse Regt. (Egypt).
MACPHERSON, LACHLAN ALFRED WILLIAM, M.C., Major, 8th Australian Light Horse Regt. (Egypt).
OLDEN, ARTHUR CHARLES NIVUET, Major, 10th Australian Light Horse Regt. (Egypt).
SAVIGE, STANLEY GEORGE, M.C., Capt., Australian Imperial Force. (Mesopotamia).
YEOMANS, JULIAN CLYDE, Lieut., 30th Battn. Australian Imperial Force.

NEW ZEALAND FORCE.

HERROLD, JOHN HENRY, Major, Auckland Mounted Rifle Regt. (Egypt).
HOLMES, JOHN DUDLEY, Capt., New Zealand Tunnelling Company, New Zealand Engineers.
WILDER, ALAN STANDISH, M.C., Major, Wellington Mounted Rifle Regt. (Egypt).

SOUTH AFRICAN FORCE.

JACOBS, LOUIS MASTERMAN, Temporary Capt., 2nd Battn. South African Infantry.

London Gazette, 17 March, 1919.—" Admiralty, S.W., 17 March, 1919.—Honours for Services in Action with Enemy Submarines. The King has been graciously pleased to approve of the following honour to the undermentioned Officer for services in action with enemy submarines. To be a Companion of the Distinguished Service Order."

BROOK, JAMES KENNETH, Lieut., Royal Naval Reserve.

" Honours for Services in Destroyers of the Grand Fleet Flotillas between the 1st July and the 11th Nov. 1918.—The King has been graciously pleased to approve of the award of the following honours to the undermentioned Officers. To be Companions of the Distinguished Service Order."

MONEY, BRIEN MICHAEL, Capt., Royal Navy.
LEVESON-GOWER, THE HONOURABLE WILLIAM SPENCER, Capt., Royal Navy.
RUTHERFORD, EDWARD MILLER CORRIE, Commander, Royal Navy.
ALLSUP, CLAUD FINLINSON, Commander, Royal Navy.
CRABBE, LEWIS GONNE EYRE, Commander, Royal Navy.
LAWRIE, EDWARD McCONNELL WYNDHAM, Commander, Royal Navy.
GREEN, EDWARD CLARKE, Engineer Commander, Royal Navy.
BROWN, RICHARD JOHN, Engineer Lieut.-Commander, Royal Navy.

" Honours for Miscellaneous Services.—The King has been graciously pleased to approve of the following honours to the undermentioned Officers. To be Companions of the Distinguished Service Order."

HOPE, HERBERT WILLIS WEBLEY, C.B., Capt., Royal Navy. For his services in command of H.M.S. Dartmouth at the bombardment of Durazzo on the 2nd Oct. 1918.
MITFORD, THE HONOURABLE BERTRAM THOMAS CARLYLE OGILVY FREEMAN, Capt., Royal Navy. For his services in command of H.M.S. Lowestoft at the bombardment of Durazzo on the 2nd Oct. 1918.
CRAVEN, FRANCIS WORTHINGTON, Lieut., Royal Navy. In recognition of his services when H.M.S. Otranto was wrecked on the 6th Oct. 1918. H.M.S. Otranto was damaged in collision with the S.S. Kashmir whilst carrying a large number of American troops. Lieut. Craven displayed magnificent courage and seamanship in placing H.M.S. Mounsey alongside H.M.S. Otranto, in spite of the fact that the conditions of wind, weather and sea were exceptionally severe. After going alongside and embarking a certain number of men, it was reported that the Mounsey had sustained considerable damage, and that there was a large quantity of water in the engine-room. Lieut. Craven, therefore, left the Otranto, but on finding the damage was not so serious as had been reported, he again went alongside, though he had previously experienced great difficulty in getting away. His action resulted in the saving of over 600 lives which would certainly otherwise have been lost. His performance was a remarkable one, and in personal courage, coolness and seamanship ranks in the very highest order.

London Gazette, 22 March, 1919.—" War Office, 22 March, 1919. His Majesty the King has been graciously pleased to approve of the undermentioned awards for distinguished service in connection with military operations in the field. Dated 1 Jan. 1919. Awarded the Distinguished Service Order."

BOIS, JOHN, M.C., Major and Brevet Lieut.-Colonel (Temporary Lieut.-Colonel), Royal Lancashire Regt.
FIELD, CHARLES DOUGLAS, Lieut.-Colonel, 75th Carnatic Infantry, Indian Army.
LANDON, CHARLES RICHARD HENRY PALMER, Major (Acting Lieut.-Colonel), 35th Scinde Horse, Indian Army.
WILLIAMS, VIVIAN PERICLES BARROW, Major (Temporary Lieut.-Colonel), 4th Cavalry, Indian Army.

London Gazette, 24 March, 1919.—" Admiralty, S.W., 24 March, 1919.—Honours for Services in Minelaying Operations between the 1st July and 11th Nov. 1918. The King has been graciously pleased to approve of the award of the following honours to the undermentioned Officers. To be Companions of the Distinguished Service Order."

BEATTIE, KENNETH ADAIR, Commander, Royal Navy.
BOWLES, GUY PERCIVAL, Lieut.-Commander, Royal Navy.
KNOWLES, CHARLES HINTON, Lieut.-Commander, Royal Navy.

" Honours for Services in Minesweeping Operations between the 1st July and 31st Dec. 1918.—The King has been graciously pleased to approve of the award of the following honours to the undermentioned Officers. To be a Companion of the Distinguished Service Order."

AGLIONBY, CHARLES EDWARD, Lieut.-Commander (Acting Commander), Royal Navy.

To receive a Bar to the Distinguished Service Order:

BENSON, CYRIL HERBERT GORDON, D.S.O., Commander, Royal Navy.
FISHER, LESLIE DREW, D.S.O., Lieut.-Commander (Acting Commander), Royal Navy.

London Gazette, 1 April, 1919.—" Admiralty, 1 April, 1919. The King has been graciously pleased to give orders for the appointment of the undermentioned Officers to be Companions of the Distinguished Service Order."

BARROW, BENJAMIN WINGATE, Commander, Royal Navy. For valuable services on the occasion of the sinking of Submarine U 8 off Dover on the 4th March, 1915.
RICHARDSON, ROBERT WISE, Lieut.-Commander (Acting Commander), Royal Navy. For valuable services on the occasion of the sinking of Submarine U 8 off Dover on the 4th March, 1915.

London Gazette, 2 April, 1919.—" War Office, 2 April, 1919. His Majesty the King has been graciously pleased to approve of the following awards to the undermentioned Officers, in recognition of their gallantry and devotion to duty in the field. The acts of gallantry for which the decorations have been awarded will be announced in the London Gazette as early as possible. Awarded a Second Bar to the Distinguished Service Order."

ALBAN, CLIFTON EDWARD RAWDON GRANT, D.S.O., Capt. and Brevet Major (Acting Lieut.-Colonel), Liverpool Regt., attached 15th Battn. Lancashire Fusiliers.
  (D.S.O. gazetted 18 July, 1917.)
  (First Bar gazetted 15 Feb. 1919.)
BRANSON, DOUGLAS STEPHENSON, D.S.O., M.C., Capt. (Acting Lieut.-Colonel), 1/4th Battn. York and Lancaster Regt., Territorial Force.
  (D.S.O. gazetted 1 Jan. 1918.)
  (First Bar gazetted 16 Sept. 1918.)
DUNCAN, KENNETH, D.S.O., Lieut.-Colonel, D/246th (West Riding) Brigade, Royal Field Artillery, Territorial Force.
  (D.S.O. gazetted 3 June, 1916.)
  (First Bar gazetted 18 Jan. 1918.)
PEEL, WILLIAM RALPH, D.S.O., Temporary Major (Acting Lieut.-Colonel), 6th Battn. Yorkshire Regt., attached 1/10th Battn. Manchester Regt.
  (D.S.O. gazetted 4 June, 1917.)
  (First Bar gazetted 16 Sept. 1918.)
POLLITT, GEORGE PATON, D.S.O., Major (Acting Lieut.-Colonel), Royal Engineers, attached 11th Battn. Lancashire Fusiliers.
  (D.S.O. gazetted 1 Jan. 1917.)
  (First Bar gazetted 18 July, 1917.)

CANADIAN FORCE.

DAVIES, REGINALD DANBURY, D.S.O., Lieut.-Colonel, 44th Battn. Canadian Infantry, New Brunswick Regt.
  (D.S.O. gazetted 17 April, 1917.)
  (First Bar gazetted 2 Dec. 1918.)
MACKENZIE, JOHN PERCIVAL, D.S.O., Lieut.-Colonel, 1st Brigade, Canadian Engineers.
  (D.S.O. gazetted 1 Jan. 1917.)
  (First Bar gazetted 26 July, 1917.)

Awarded a Bar to the Distinguished Service Order:

BATE, JOHN PERCIVAL, D.S.O., M.C., Capt. (Acting Major), 1/8th Battn. Worcestershire Regt., Territorial Force.
  (D.S.O. gazetted 1 Jan. 1919.)
BROMILOW, DAVID GEORGE, D.S.O., Major, 14th Murray's Jat Lancers, Indian Army (Mesopotamia).
  (D.S.O. gazetted 25 Aug. 1917.)
CARTER, WILLIAM HENRY, D.S.O., M.C., Capt. and Brevet Major (Temporary Lieut.-Colonel), Royal Warwickshire Regt., attached 7th Battn. South Staffordshire Regt.
  (D.S.O. gazetted 20 Oct. 1916.)
CHAPPELL, WICKHAM FRITH, D.S.O., Major, 7th Dragoon Guards.
  (D.S.O. gazetted 15 Oct. 1918.)
CLARKE, HUBERT THOMAS, D.S.O., Major (Acting Lieut.-Colonel), 1/8th Battn. Worcestershire Regt., Territorial Force.
  (D.S.O. gazetted 8 March, 1919.)
CRIPPS, CHARLES WILLIAM, D.S.O., Major, 3rd Battery, 45th Brigade, Royal Field Artillery.
  (D.S.O. gazetted 4 June, 1917.)
FORBES, ROBERT, D.S.O., M.C., Lieut. (Temporary Major and Acting Lieut.-Colonel), 5th Battn. Royal Highlanders, Territorial Force, attached 10th Battn. Essex Regt.
  (D.S.O. gazetted 7 Nov. 1918.)
HONE, PERCY FREDERICK, D.S.O., M.C., Temporary Lieut.-Colonel, General List, attached 13th Battn. Durham Light Infantry.
  (D.S.O. gazetted 1 Jan. 1919.)
HORE-RUTHVEN, THE HONOURABLE ALEXANDER GORE ARKWRIGHT, V.C., C.M.G., D.S.O., Lieut.-Colonel (Temporary Brigadier-General).
  (D.S.O. gazetted 2 May, 1916.)

The Distinguished Service Order

HUNTER, RICHARD DEVAS, D.S.O., Capt. (Acting Lieut.-Colonel), Scottish Rifles, attached 1/8th Battn. Territorial Force.
(D.S.O. gazetted 3 June, 1918.)

JACK, JAMES LOCHHEAD, D.S.O., Major and Brevet Lieut.-Colonel (Temporary Brigadier-General), Scottish Rifles (G.O.C. 28th Infantry Brigade).
(D.S.O. gazetted 18 June, 1917.)

LASCELLES, VISCOUNT, HENRY GEORGE CHARLES, D.S.O., Capt. (Acting Lieut.-Colonel), Grenadier Guards (Reserve of Officers), attached 3rd Battn.
(D.S.O. gazetted 3 June, 1918.)

McGRATH, ARTHUR THOMAS, D.S.O., Major and Brevet Lieut.-Colonel (Acting Lieut.-Colonel), Royal Field Artillery, Commanding 88th Brigade.
(D.S.O. gazetted 1 Jan. 1917.)

MORRELL, JOHN FREDERIC BAKER, M.V.O., Capt. and Brevet Major (Temporary Lieut.-Colonel), Royal Lancaster Regt., attached 9th Battn. Manchester Regt.
(D.S.O. gazetted 1 Jan. 1919.)

MURPHY, JOSEPH LEO, D.S.O., Major, Manchester Regt., Special Reserve, attached 2nd Battn.
(D.S.O. gazetted 15 Feb. 1919.)

MURRAY, DONALD, D.S.O., Temporary Major, Manchester Regt., attached 21st Battn.
(D.S.O. gazetted 1 Jan. 1919.)

PELLY, RAYMOND THEODORE, D.S.O., Major and Brevet Lieut.-Colonel (Temporary Brigadier-General), North Lancashire Regt. (G.O.C. 81st Infantry Brigade) (Italy).
(D.S.O. gazetted 14 Jan. 1916.)

RAMSBOTTOM, GORDON OPENSHAW, D.S.O., Temporary Lieut.-Colonel, 22nd Battn. Manchester Regt. (Italy).
(D.S.O. gazetted 4 June, 1917.)

RAMSDEN, VINCENT BASIL, D.S.O., M.C., Capt. (Acting Major and Temporary Lieut.-Colonel), 1st Battn. South Wales Borderers, attached 15th Battn Highland Light Infantry.
(D.S.O. gazetted 26 July, 1918.)

RICHARDSON, JAMES JARDINE, D.S.O., Lieut.-Colonel, 13th Hussars (Mesopotamia).
(D.S.O. gazetted 25 Aug. 1917.)

SUTHERLAND, THOMAS DOUGLAS, D.S.O., M.C., Temporary Major, 6th Battn. Lincolnshire Regt.
(D.S.O. gazetted 26 Sept. 1917.)

THWAYTES, HARRY DELAMERE, D.S.O., Capt. (Acting Lieut.-Colonel), 1st Battn. Dorsetshire Regt.
(D.S.O. gazetted 2 Dec. 1918.)

VICKERY, CHARLES EDWIN, D.S.O., Major (Brevet Lieut.-Colonel), Royal Field Artillery, Headquarters 74th Brigade.
(D.S.O. gazetted 31 Oct. 1902.)

WORTHINGTON, CLAUDE SWANWICK, D.S.O., Lieut.-Colonel, 6th Battn. Manchester Regt., Territorial Force, attached 5th Battn. Dorsetshire Regt.
(D.S.O. gazetted 2 Feb. 1916.)

CANADIAN FORCE.

BROWN, WALTER RICHARD, D.S.O., Lieut.-Colonel, 26th Battn. Canadian Infantry, New Brunswick Regt.
(D.S.O. gazetted 18 Oct. 1917.)

GRIESBACH, WILLIAM ANTROBUS, C.B., C.M.G., D.S.O., Brigadier-General, Alberta Regt. (G.O.C. 1st Canadian Infantry Brigade).
(D.S.O. gazetted 24 June, 1916.)

JONES, TERENCE PERCIVAL, D.S.O., Major, 4th Battn. Canadian Infantry, 1st Central Ontario Regt. (Brigade Major, 12th Canadian Infantry Brigade).
(D.S.O. gazetted 1 Jan. 1917.)

LOOMIS, FREDERICK OSCAR WARREN, C.B., C.M.G., D.S.O., Major-General, Quebec Regt. (G.O.C. 2nd Canadian Infantry Brigade).
(D.S.O. gazetted 23 June, 1915.)

AUSTRALIAN IMPERIAL FORCE.

ANNAND, FREDERICK WILLIAM GADSBY, D.S.O., Lieut.-Colonel, 2nd Pioneer Battn., Australian Imperial Force.
(D.S.O. gazetted 1 Jan. 1917.)

DUGGAN, BERNARD OSCAR CHARLES, D.S.O., Lieut.-Colonel, 21st Battn. Australian Infantry.
(D.S.O. gazetted 1 Jan. 1918.)

JAMES, WILLIAM EDWARD, D.S.O., Lieut.-Colonel, 24th Battn. Australian Infantry.
(D.S.O. gazetted 3 June, 1918.)

WATSON, CHARLES VINCENT, D.S.O., Lieut.-Colonel, 58th Battn. Australian Infantry.
(D.S.O. gazetted 1 Jan. 1919.)

NEW ZEALAND FORCE.

ALLEN, ROBERT CANDLISH, D.S.O., Lieut.-Colonel, Auckland Regt., attached 1st Battn. New Zealand Rifle Brigade.
(D.S.O. gazetted 16 Aug. 1917.)

Awarded the Distinguished Service Order:

ALLEN, WILLIAM BARNSLEY, V.C., M.C., M.B., Capt. (Acting Major), Royal Army Medical Corps, attached 1/3rd (West Riding) Field Ambulance, Royal Army Medical Corps, Territorial Force.

ALSTON, LLEWELYN ARTHUR AUGUSTUS, M.C., Capt. (Acting Major), 1st Battn. Royal Welsh Fusiliers (Italy).

AMY, ARCHIBALD CRAIG, M.D., Major, Royal Army Medical Corps, attached 2/1st (Highland) Field Ambulance, Royal Army Medical Corps, Territorial Force.

ATKIN, BENJAMIN GEORGE, M.C., Capt. (Temporary Major), 1st Battn. Manchester Regt., attached 22nd Battn. (Italy).

BAYLISS, HERBERT VICTOR, M.C., Capt. (Acting Major), East Surrey Regt., attached 7th Battn. Wiltshire Regt.

BENYON, HUGH SAM, M.C., Capt., Northamptonshire Yeomanry (Italy).

BOMFORD, LESLIE RAYMOND, M.C., Lieut. (Acting Capt.), 1/8th Battn. Worcestershire Regt., Territorial Force.

BRIERLY, SIDNEY CLIFFORD, Major (Acting Lieut.-Colonel), 5th Battn. West Riding Regt., attached 1/4th Battn. Yorkshire Light Infantry, Territorial Force.

CAMPBELL, KEIR ARTHUR, Lieut., 3rd Battn. Grenadier Guards (Special Reserve).

CARLTON, HERBERT DUDLEY, Major (Acting Lieut.-Colonel), Royal Scots, attached Royal West Surrey Regt. (Italy).

CLARKSON, ALFRED BAIRSTOW, M.C., Major, 1/6th Battn. West Riding Regt., Territorial Force.

COLAM, STANLEY D'EYNCOURT, M.C., Capt., Gordon Highlanders, Special Reserve (Brigade Major, 145th Infantry Brigade) (Italy).

COOKE, RONALD CAMPBELL, M.C., Temporary Capt. (Acting Major), 134th Field Ambulance, Royal Army Medical Corps.

CRAMPTON, JAMES, M.C., Temporary Major, 8th Battn. York and Lancaster Regt., attached 9th Battn. (Italy).

CROW, PERCY, M.C., Temporary Capt. (Acting Major), A/161st Brigade, Royal Field Artillery.

CURELL, WILLIAM BROWN, Major, 2nd Battn. Lancashire Fusiliers.

DALE, FRANCIS RICHARD, M.C., Temporary Capt. (Acting Major), 19th Battn. Welsh Regt., attached 16th Battn. Royal Welsh Fusiliers.

DRIVER, ARTHUR, M.C., Lieut. (Temporary Major and Acting Lieut.-Colonel), 6th Battn. West Riding Regt., Territorial Force, attached 9th Battn.

DUDLEY-WARD, CHARLES HUMBLE, M.C., Lieut. (Acting Major), 1st Battn. Welsh Guards.

DUNN, JOHN BRUCE, M.C., Temporary Capt., 15th Battn. Highland Light Infantry.

EDDOWES, HUGH MORTIMER, Temporary Lieut., 185th Tunnelling Company, Royal Engineers.

ELLIS, LIONEL FREDERIC, M.C., Lieut. (Acting Capt.), Welsh Guards, Special Reserve, attached 1st Battn.

ENGLISH-MURPHY, WILLIAM RICHARD, M.C., Lieut. (Acting Lieut.-Colonel), 1st Battn. South Staffordshire Regt. (Italy).

FAWKES, ROWLAND BEATTIE, M.C., Temporary Capt., 6th Battn. Northamptonshire Regt.

FYERS, HARRY AMELIUS BEAUCLERK, Temporary Lieut., 179th Tunnelling Company, Royal Engineers.

GARRARD, FREDERICK BLAKE, Lieut. (Acting Capt.), 2nd Battn. Honourable Artillery Company (Italy).

GIBBONS, CHARLES, M.C., D.C.M., Lieut. (Temporary Capt.), Durham Light Infantry, attached 12th Battn. (Italy).

GRIERSON, KENNETH MACIVER, M.C., Second Lieut. (Temporary Lieut. and Acting Capt.), Manchester Regt., attached 22nd Battn. (Italy).

GRIFFITH-WILLIAMS, ERIC LLEWELLYN GRIFFITH, M.C., Capt. (Acting Major), 135th Battery, 32nd Brigade, Royal Field Artillery.

HEDLEY, JOHN CYPRIAN, M.C., Second Lieut. (Acting Capt.), Royal West Surrey Regt., attached 11th Battn.

HENNESSY, RICHARD GEORGE, M.C., Lieut. (Acting Capt.), 2nd Battn. Border Regt. (Italy).

HODNETT, HARRY, Temporary Second Lieut., Liverpool Regt., attached 1/5th Battn., Territorial Force.

HOGAN, GUY STEWART, Temporary Second Lieut., 16th Battn. King's Royal Rifle Corps.

HOLT, GEOFFREY WILSON, M.C., Lieut. (Acting Major), A/74th Brigade, Royal Field Artillery.

HOWATSON, GEORGE, Temporary Lieut. (Acting Capt.), 185th Tunnelling Company, Royal Engineers.

KAY, WILLIAM, M.C., Second Lieut. (Acting Capt.), Manchester Regt. Special Reserve, attached 2nd Battn.

KEMBLE, ALAN EDWARD, Capt., 2nd Battn. Yorkshire Light Infantry.

KENDRICK, FREDERICK ARTHUR, M.C., Lieut. (Acting Capt.), 1st Battn. South Staffordshire Regt. (Italy).

LAWSON, LIONEL HALL, M.C., Temporary Capt., 11th Battn. West Yorkshire Regt. (Italy).

LEACHMAN, GERARD EVELYN, C.I.E., Major and Brevet Lieut.-Colonel, Royal Sussex Regt., attached Political Department (Mesopotamia).

LEMAN, JOHN FREDERICK, Capt. (Temporary Lieut.-Colonel), Worcestershire Regt., attached 13th Battn. Royal Welsh Fusiliers.

LENNON, JOHN ALFRED, M.C., Lieut. (Acting Capt.), West Riding Regt., Special Reserve, attached 2nd Battn.

LLOYD, RODERICK CROIL, M.C., Capt. (Acting Major), 1/1st Denbigh Yeomanry, attached 24th Battn. Royal Welsh Fusiliers.

LOWTHER, JOHN GEORGE, M.C., Capt., 11th Hussars, attached Northamptonshire Yeomanry (Italy).

MACILWAINE, ALFRED HERBERT, M.C., Capt. (Acting Major), "W" Battery, Royal Horse Artillery (Mesopotamia).

MACMILLAN, ROBERT JAMES ALAN, Major, Royal Garrison Artillery Territorial Force, attached 337th Siege Battery, Royal Garrison Artillery.

MAITLAND, ARTHUR EDWARD, M.C., Capt. (Acting Lieut.-Colonel), 2nd Battn. Essex Regt.

MARTIN, GEORGE NOEL CHADWICK, M.C., Capt. (Acting Major), B/74th Brigade, Royal Field Artillery.

MATHESON, NEAL WILLIAM, M.C., Lieut. (Acting Capt.), Royal Engineers, Territorial Force, attached 54th Field Company, Royal Engineers (Italy).

MOIR, JOHN HAY, M.C., M.D., Temporary Capt., Royal Army Medical Corps, attached 17th Battn. Royal Fusiliers.

MOWAT, ALFRED LAW, M.C., Capt. (Acting Lieut-Colonel), 1/4th Battn. West Riding Regt., Territorial Force.

MUIR, ARTHUR WILLIAM, M.C., Temporary Capt. (Acting Major), 2nd Battn. Northumberland Fusiliers.

NICHOLLS, FRANK, M.C., Temporary Capt., 20th Battn. Manchester Regt.

PAGET-TOMLINSON, WILLIAM, Capt. (Acting Major), 7th Hussars (Mesopotamia).

PARSONS, BERNARD EDWARD THOMAS, Major, 2/4th Battn. Hampshire Regt., Territorial Force.

PEPYS, CHRISTOPHER, M.C., Lieut. (Temporary Major), Devonshire Regt., attached 8th Battn.

RICHARDS, FREDERICK WILLIAM, M.C., Temporary Capt. (Acting Major), 105th Field Company, Royal Engineers.

RODERICK, WILLIAM DAVID, M.C., Temporary Second Lieut. (Acting Capt.), 14th Battn. Royal Welsh Fusiliers.
ROWLANDS, HUGH, M.C., Lieut. (Acting Capt.), 2nd Battn. London Regt.
SALE, GEORGE GEOFFREY, M.C., Temporary Lieut. (Acting Capt.), 179th Tunnelling Company, Royal Engineers.
SHAW, JOSEPH TAYLOR, Temporary Lieut. (Acting Capt.), Yorkshire Regt., attached 8th Battn. (Italy).
SLINGSBY, THOMAS WILLIAM, Major, 22nd Cavalry, Indian Army (Mesopotamia).
SMITH, WILLIAM GEORGE, M.C., Lieut. (Acting Major), 23rd Field Company, Royal Engineers.
SOMERSET, THE HONOURABLE NIGEL FITZROY, M.C., Lieut. (Temporary Capt.), Gloucestershire Regt. and Mounted Machine Gun Corps (Mesopotamia).
SPENCER, JOHN, M.M., Temporary Second Lieut. (Acting Capt.), 17th Battn. Royal Fusiliers.
SPICER, FRANK FITZROY FANE, Lieut. (Acting Capt.), 12th Lancers.
STEELE, JULIAN McCARTY, C.B., C.M.G., C.G., Lieut.-Colonel and Brevet Colonel (Temporary Brigadier-General), G.O.C. 2nd Infantry Brigade (Italy).
STICKNEY, JOSEPH EDWARD DANTHORPE, M.C., Capt. (Acting Major), 2/4th Battn. York and Lancaster Regt., Territorial Force.
TANNER, GILBERT, Major, 1/7th Battn. West Riding Regt., Territorial Force.
TEMPEST, EWART VINCENT, M.C., Lieut., 1/6th Battn. West Yorkshire Regt., Territorial Force (Intelligence Officer, 146th Infantry Brigade).
WEDGBURY, EDMUND, M.C., D.C.M., M.M., Temporary Second Lieut.-Gloucestershire Regt., attached 1/8th Battn. Worcestershire Regt.
WETHERILT, WILLIAM ALFRED, Temporary Second Lieut., Royal Berkshire Regt., attached 1/4th Battn. Territorial Force (Italy).
WHITEHOUSE, PHILIP HENRY, Lieut.-Colonel, 1/8th Battn. Royal Warwickshire Regt., Territorial Force.
WILLIAMS, CHARLES REGINALD, M.C., Capt. (Acting Major), 2nd Battn. Royal Munster Fusiliers.
WILSON, NEIL YOUNG, M.C., Temporary Capt., 11th Battn. Northumberland Fusiliers (Italy).
WRIGHTON, EDWARD, Lieut., 4th Battn. Northumberland Fusiliers, Territorial Force, attached 10th Battn. (Italy).
YOUNG, JAMES HAROLD BERMINGHAM, M.C., Temporary Lieut. (Acting Capt.), 10th Battn. Cheshire Regt., attached 9th Battn.

CANADIAN FORCE.

BLAIR, JOHN FREEMAN, Major, Canadian Army Dental Corps, attached 4th Field Ambulance, Canadian Army Medical Corps.
GYLES, RICHARD WALTER, M.C., Capt., 46th Battn. Canadian Infantry, Saskatchewan Regt.
KELLY, BURNET ELMER, Major, 9th Field Ambulance, Canadian Army Medical Corps.
KEMP, FREDERICK GARFIELD, Lieut. (Acting Capt.), 4th Battn. Canadian Infantry, 1st Central Ontario Regt.
MACLEOD, JOHN PHEE GORDON, Lieut., 46th Battn. Canadian Infantry, Saskatchewan Regt.
McLEAN, CHARLES HENRY, Major, 4th Canadian Mounted Rifle Battn., 1st Central Ontario Regt. (christian name corrected to Charles Herbert [London Gazette, 27 Sept. 1920]).
MILLAR, JOHN MACINTOSH, M.C., Major, 85th Battn. Canadian Infantry, Nova Scotia Regt.
PLUMMER, MAURICE VERNON, Major, 51st (Howitzer) Battery, 13th Brigade, Canadian Field Artillery.
PURVIS, EDSON RUSSELL, Major, 47th Battn. Canadian Infantry, Western Ontario Regt.
TRELEAVEN, GEORGE WILLARD, M.C., Major, 4th Field Ambulance, Canadian Army Medical Corps.

AUSTRALIAN IMPERIAL FORCE.

HOUGHTON, SYDNEY ROBERT, M.C., Capt., 12th Battn. Australian Infantry.
HYNES, JOHN THOMAS, M.M., Capt., 15th Battn. Australian Infantry.

London Gazette, 2 April, 1919.—" War Office, 2 April, 1919. Awarded the Military Cross," but this was cancelled in London Gazette 27 June, 1919, and the Distinguished Service Order awarded in substitution.
PEMBERTON, HAROLD CHARLES, Temporary Capt., 20th Battn. Lancashire Fusiliers, attached 16th Battn. (For description of service see London Gazette, 10 Dec. 1919.)

London Gazette, 5 April, 1919.—" Admiralty, S.W., 5 April, 1919. The King has been graciously pleased to approve of the award of the following honours to the undermentioned Officers. To be Companions of the Distinguished Service Order."
BAILEY, SIDNEY ROBERT, Commander (now Capt.), Royal Navy.
STEVENS, PERCY RICHARD, Commander, Royal Navy.
In recognition of their ability and unremitting work on the Staff of Admiral Sir David Beatty, G.C.B., G.C.V.O., D.S.O., Commander-in-Chief, Grand Fleet.

London Gazette, 5 April, 1919.—" Air Ministry, 5 April, 1919. His Majesty the King has been graciously pleased to confer the undermentioned rewards on Officers of the Royal Air Force, in recognition of gallantry in flying operations against the enemy (including): Awarded the Distinguished Service Order."
ROBINSON, F. L., Squadron Commander, R.N.A.S. (Mesopotamia). A very gallant and able Squadron Commander, who, by his fine leadership and personal example, has raised high the morale of his command. By his untiring energy he has rendered most valuable service on reconnaissance duty and bombing raids.
(M.C. gazetted 6 Sept. 1918).

London Gazette, 11 April, 1919.—" Admiralty, S.W., 11 April, 1919.—Honours for Palestine Operations (September–November, 1918). The King has been graciously pleased to approve of the award of the following honours to the undermentioned Officers, in recognition of their services during naval operations carried out in conjunction with military operations in Palestine from September to November. 1918. To be Companions of the Distinguished Service Order."
DOWN, RICHARD THORNTON, Commander, Royal Navy, H.M.S. Forester, In recognition of the valuable assistance rendered to the Army during the advance along the coast on the 19th Sept. 1918, and the occupation of Haifa on the 28th Sept. 1918.

UNSWORTH, GEOFFREY, D.S.C., Lieut.-Commander (Acting Commander), Royal Naval Reserve. Was in charge of minesweeping operations on the coasts of Palestine and Syria during the advance of the Army. Cleared a channel and anchorage off Haifa with great rapidity, thus enabling the first transport to enter with valuable stores 24 hours earlier than had been anticipated. As mines were laid only seven feet below the surface, it is highly creditable to Lieut.-Commander Unsworth that he succeeded in clearing a large minefield without mishap.

" Honours for Services in the Auxiliary Patrol between the 1st July and 11th Nov. 1918.—The King has been graciously pleased to approve of the award of the following honour to the undermentioned Officer."
(a).—Services in Drifters, Trawlers and Yachts.
To be a Companion of the Distinguished Service Order :
LOVEGROVE, ALFRED VICTOR ROBERTSON, R.D., Commander, Royal Naval Reserve.

" Honours for Services in Destroyers employed on Convoy, Escort and Patrol Duties between the 1st July and 11th Nov. 1918.—The King has been graciously pleased to approve of the award of the following honours to the undermentioned Officers. To be Companions of the Distinguished Service Order."
REINOLD, BASIL EDWARD, Commander, Royal Navy.
PLOWDEN, RICHARD ANTHONY ASTON, Commander, Royal Navy.
BARNE, MICHAEL, Commander, Royal Navy.
KIRBY, RICHARD EVAN WILLIAMS, Commander, Royal Navy.
DENISON, CONYNGHAM CHARLES, Lieut.-Commander (now Commander), Royal Navy.
COLVILE, MANSELL BRABAZON FIENNES, Lieut.-Commander, Royal Navy.

" Honours for Services in Local Defence Flotillas between the 1st July and 11th Nov. 1918.—The King has been graciously pleased to approve of the award of the following honour to the undermentioned Officer. To be a Companion of the Distinguished Service Order."
CRUTCHLEY, ARTHUR FELTON, Lieut.-Commander, Royal Navy.

London Gazette, 22 April, 1919.—" Admiralty, S.W., 22 April, 1919.—Honours for Services in Action with Enemy Submarines. The King has been graciously pleased to approve of the award of the following honour to the undermentioned Officer for services in action with enemy submarines. To be a Companion of the Distinguished Service Order."
HEWETT, GEORGE OSBORNE, Lieut.-Commander (now Commander), Royal Navy.

" Honours for Services on the Mediterranean Station between the 1st July and 11th Nov. 1918.—III. GIBRALTAR. The King has been graciously pleased to approve of the award of the following honour to the undermentioned Officer. To be a Companion of the Distinguished Service Order."
BUCHANAN, ROBERT JAMES, Lieut.-Commander (Acting Commander), Royal Navy.

" Honours for Miscellaneous Services.—The King has been graciously pleased to approve of the award of the following honours to the undermentioned Officers. To be Companions of the Distinguished Service Order."
MACDONALD, WILLIAM BALFOUR, Commander (Acting Capt.), Royal Navy. In recognition of his services whilst attached to the Staff of the Eastern Force in Egypt and Palestine.
MURRAY, JAMES WOLFE, Commander (now Acting Capt.), Royal Navy. Between the 14th and 28th Aug. 1918, displayed great resource in bringing H.M.S. Suffolk's 12-pounder guns rapidly into action, and showed an excellent example of coolness and bravery under fire during the battles in the Ussuri District.
SCOTT, JOHN WILFRED, Commander, Royal Navy. For valuable services in command of the units landed from H.M.S. Cochrane for the defence of Pechenga from the 3rd May, 1918, to the 29th Sept. 1918. During this period the force was frequently attacked by the enemy.
STOKER, HENRY HUGH GORDON DACRES, Lieut.-Commander, Royal Navy. In recognition of his gallantry in making the passage of the Dardanelles in command of H.M. Australian Submarine A.E. 2, on the 25th April, 1915.
ALLEN, CHARLES HENRY, Lieut., Royal Navy. In recognition of his services as Commanding Officer of H.M. Submarine E. 42, which carried out a successful attack on the German battle cruiser Moltke on the 25th April, 1918.

London Gazette, 24 May, 1919.—" Admiralty, S.W., 24 May, 1919.—Honours for Miscellaneous Services. The King has been graciously pleased to approve of the award of the following honours to the undermentioned Officers. To be Companions of the Distinguished Service Order."
EDWARDS, PATRICK HARRINGTON, Commander, Royal Naval Volunteer Reserve. In recognition of his valuable services as Commanding Officer of the Allied Naval Brigade in North Russia between Aug. 1918, and Feb. 1919, when he did very good work under very difficult circumstances.
BUTT, PERCY LOVEL, Engineer Lieut.-Commander (now Engineer-Commander), Royal Navy. For gallant conduct in action on board H.M.S. Partridge on the 12th Dec. 1917. H.M.S. Partridge, while screening a Scandinavian convoy, was attacked by a superior enemy force and put out of action. Engineer Lieut.-Commander Butt, in order to make sure that the ship would sink and not fall into the enemy's hands, went three times into the engine room, which was full of steam, and remained there until there was no doubt that the vessel would sink.

" Honours for the Mercantile Marine.—The King has been graciously pleased to approve of the award of the following honour to the undermentioned Officer of the Mercantile Marine, in recognition of zeal and devotion to duty shown in carrying on the trade of the country during the war. To be a Companion of the Distinguished Service Order."
McNISH, ROWLAND LEONARD HASTINGS, Chief Officer (Lieut., Royal Naval Reserve).

London Gazette, 26 May, 1919.—" War Office, 26 May, 1919. His Majesty the King has been graciously pleased to approve of the following awards to the undermentioned Officers, in recognition of their gallantry and devotion to duty in the field. Awarded a Bar to the Distinguished Service Order."
HARKER, THOMAS HUBERT, D.S.O., Capt. (Temporary Lieut.-Colonel), King's Royal Rifle Corps, Special Reserve, Commanding 1/7th Battn. Royal Welsh Fusiliers, Territorial Force (Egypt). For conspicuous gallantry and able

leadership on the night 19–20 Sept. 1918. He led his battalion ten miles over difficult country, and surprised and captured a strong enemy position, taking over 200 prisoners, 15 machine guns, and a battery of 4.2 in. guns. It was entirely due to his bold and clever leadership that this extremely difficult night operation met with such complete success.
(D.S.O. gazetted 1 Jan. 1918.)

Awarded the Distinguished Service Order :

ALDWORTH, THOMAS PRESTON, Capt., Roya West Kent Regt., Special Reserve, attached 2nd Battn. (Mesopotamia). For conspicuous gallantry and devotion to duty near Sharqat on 28 Oct. 1918. During an attack he encountered an enemy strong point. He collected some 12 men, and by skilful manœuvring and dashing leadership rushed the position, capturing over 100 prisoners and six machine guns. He showed fine courage and leadership, and his splendid action greatly assisted in the success of the advance.

BERRYMAN, EDWARD ROLLESTON PALMER, Capt. and Brevet Major, 2/39th Garwhal Rifles, Indian Army (Brigade Major, 34th Infantry Brigade) (Mesopotamia). For most conspicuous gallantry and devotion to duty throughout the operations at Mushaq and Sharqat, 26–30 Oct. 1918. He displayed the utmost zeal and determination, and, though early wounded, continued to carry out his duties most ably under heavy fire. Weakened by fever and his wounds, he nevertheless remained at duty for four days and rendered invaluable assistance to the brigade.

CATTELL, GILBERT LANDALE, Lieut.-Colonel, 1/7th Gurkha Rifles, Indian Army (Mesopotamia). For conspicuous gallantry and devotion to duty at the Lesser Zab 25 Oct. 1918. In command of an advanced guard he most skilfully reconnoitred, and then forced the Zab under heavy fire, finally seizing the enemy's position on the high ground on the high bank. His able dispositions and bold leadership enabled the objective to be taken with a minimum of losses.

CHANNER, GUY, Major, 14th Sikhs, Indian Army (Mesopotamia). For conspicuous gallantry and devotion to duty at Mushaq on 25 Oct. 1918, and at Sharqat 29 Oct. He was wounded whilst commanding his battalion, but refused to be evacuated until the battalion was drawn back to the reserve. It was largely due to his energy, courage and resource that a determined enemy counter-attack was successfully repulsed.

CURSETJEE, HEERAJEE JEHANGIR MANOCKJEE, M.B., Capt., Indian Medical Service (attached 14th Sikhs) (Mesopotamia). For conspicuous gallantry and devotion to duty at Mushaq 26–27 Oct. 1918, and at Sharqat 29 Oct. Throughout the operations he displayed the greatest zeal and disregard for danger while tending the wounded under heavy fire, working unceasingly for 48 hours. He has previously rendered excellent service, and once was severely wounded.

MARTIN, HUGH GRAY, Major, 337th Brigade, 341st Battery, Royal Field Artillery. For conspicuous gallantry and devotion to duty north of Sharqat on 28 Oct. 1918. He showed marked ability in selecting positions for his guns under continuous and heavy fire, and organized a well-directed enfilading artillery support for the column with which he was operating. He exposed himself freely in the open until communications were established.

SARGON, ARTHUR IRONS, Capt., Indian Army Reserve of Officers, attached 114th Mahrattas (Mesopotamia). For conspicuous gallantry and devotion to duty in command of two companies at Mushaq on 26 Oct. 1918. Although early wounded and exposed to heavy fire, which caused many casualties, he maintained his position for a whole day and night. The excellent service rendered by his companies was in great measure due to his grit and determination.

THOMAS, WILLIAM LLEWELLYN, M.C., Temporary Major, 2nd Battn. British West India Regt. (Egypt). For conspicuous gallantry and devotion to duty on 22 Sept. 1918, at Mafid Joseh. On learning that an officer's patrol was fighting a rearguard action against vastly superior numbers, he took up a platoon and kept the enemy in check until the remainder of the battalion had arrived as reinforcements. The enemy were driven back. He displayed great initiative in the subsequent attack, which resulted in the capture of Mafid Joseh and 40 prisoners.

VILLIERS, ERIC HYDE, Temporary Capt., 1st Battn. Highland Light Infantry (Mesopotamia). For conspicuous gallantry and devotion to duty. His company, acting as advanced guard at night near Mushaq on 25 Oct. 1918, came under heavy fire at close range. He quickly rallied his men, and, with another company, charged through a double line of high wire and captured the enemy trench, with some prisoners. He penetrated and captured part of the enemy's second line. He displayed great dash and courage, and was instrumental in retrieving a critical situation.

WILLIAMS, JAMES HUBERT, Capt., 1/10th Gurkha Rifles, Indian Army (Mesopotamia). For conspicuous gallantry and devotion to duty at Mushaq on 26 Oct. 1918, and at Sharqat on 29 Oct. On two separate occasions he led his company over 2,000 yards of open and exceedingly difficult country to attack the enemy's position. By his courage and fine leadership he forced his way under heavy fire to within 400 yards of the position on the first occasion, and 300 yards on the second. His rapid advance greatly helped operations in other parts of the field.

WINTLE, CHARLES EDMUND HUNTER, Lieut.-Colonel, 114th Mahrattas (Mesopotamia). For conspicuous gallantry and devotion to duty at Sharqat 29 Oct. 1918. He boldly led his battalion into action, and repelled a strong counter-attack. He was then left rather in the air, as the enemy had driven a salient into our line. In spite of this, and having sustained heavy casualties, he held his ground throughout the night, and reorganized his command under heavy fire in a most able manner.

WOULFE-FLANAGAN, RICHARD JOHN, Lieut.-Colonel, 2nd Battn. Royal West Kent Regt. (Mesopotamia). For conspicuous gallantry and devotion to duty near Sharqat 28 Oct. 1918. Throughout the action he commanded his battalion with great judgment, quickly selecting the salient points of attack. Although his numbers were considerably reduced, he, by making use of some machine gunners and a company of another regiment, eventually gained a complete sweep over the enemy, capturing 180 prisoners and nine machine guns. He did fine work.

London Gazette, 27 May, 1919.—" War Office, 27 May, 1919. His Majesty the King has been graciously pleased to approve of the following immediate awards for conspicuous gallantry and devotion to duty in North Russia, conferred by Major-General C. C. M. Maynard, C.B., C.M.G., D.S.O., in pursuance of the powers vested in him by His Majesty. Awarded the Distinguished Service Order."

CANADIAN FORCE.

EASTHAM, ALFRED, M.C., Capt., Canadian Machine Gun Corps, attached Malmoot Company. For conspicuous gallantry in command of the attacking party at Nadvoista 19 Feb. 1919. His dispositions were such that none of the enemy escaped, all being killed or captured. He displayed great courage in the hand-to-hand fighting in the village. He later with his force captured Station 22 and the whole of the garrison of the post at the Onda. Throughout he displayed unfailing energy.

MACKENZIE, LAWRENCE HOWARD, Major, Nova Scotia Regt., attached Malmoot Company. For conspicuous gallantry and devotion to duty when in charge of the party which took Segeja 19 Feb. 1919. The success was due to his arrangements for transport and attack. A distance of 176 versts had to be travelled, and the weather was intensely cold. He took Segeja with slight loss, and the success of the whole operations was largely due to his marked ability for organization, his sound judgment and his courage.

" His Majesty the King has been graciously pleased to approve of the following immediate awards for conspicuous gallantry and devotion to duty in North Russia, conferred by Major-General W. E. Ironside, C.M.G., D.S.O., in pursuance of the powers vested in him by His Majesty. Awarded a Bar to the Distinguished Service Order."

CANADIAN FORCE.

ARNOLDI, FRANK FAUQUIER, D.S.O., Major, Canadian Field Artillery. He has handled his battery on all occasions with marked determination and skill. His work in connection with the retirement from Seltyo, and the battle of Toulgas on 11 Nov. 1918, was of a very high order. He has many times made difficult reconnaissances, and to him is largely due the splendid technical fitness and offensive spirit of the battery.
(D.S.O. gazetted 1 Jan. 1917.)

Awarded the Distinguished Service Order :

GILMORE, GEORGE HENRY, M.C., Temporary Capt. (Acting Major), Royal Sussex Regt., attached 2/10th Battn. Royal Scots. For conspicuous gallantry and good leadership in command of the left wing of the Seletskoe Detachment during operations from 25 Jan. to 10 Feb. 1919. Thanks to his ability and presence of mind the retreat was carried out successfully. On 1 and on 7 Feb. he took personal command of important reconnaissances, and directed operations which enabled the force to extricate itself from a difficult situation.

London Gazette, 27 May, 1919.—" Admiralty, 27 May, 1919. The King has been graciously pleased to approve of the award of the following honours to the undermentioned Officers. To be Companions of the Distinguished Service Order."

CASEMENT, JOHN, Commander (now Capt.), Royal Navy. For distinguished services as Executive Officer of H.M.S. Highflyer on the occasion of the sinking of the German Auxiliary Cruiser Kaiser Wilhelm der Grosse on the 26th Aug. 1914.

BROUNGER, KENNETH, Commander, Royal Navy. For gallantry whilst in command of landing parties on the Syrian coast during 1914 and 1915.

HALLOWELL-CAREW, ROBERT RAYMOND, Lieut.-Commander, Royal Navy. For gallantry whilst in command of H.M.S. Arabis in an engagement with greatly superior enemy forces on the night of the 10th–11th Feb. 1916.

London Gazette, 3 June, 1919.—" War Office, 3 June, 1919. The King has been graciously pleased, on the occasion of His Majesty's Birthday, to approve of the undermentioned rewards for distinguished service in connection with military operations in France and Flanders. Dated 3 June, 1919. Awarded a Bar to the Distinguished Service Order."

FRANKLIN, WILLIAM VEASEY, D.S.O., Temporary Major (Acting Lieut.-Colonel), South Wales Borderers, attached 1st Battn. Worcestershire Regt.
(D.S.O. gazetted 3 June, 1918.)

MURRAY, JOHN, D.S.O., Lieut.-Colonel (Acting Lieut.-Colonel), Scottish Horse Yeomanry, attached 12th Battn. Royal Scots.
(D.S.O. gazetted 15 Feb. 1919.)

CANADIAN FORCE.

SAVAGE, HAROLD MURCHISON, D.S.O., Major, 24th Battery, 8th Brigade, Canadian Field Artillery.
(D.S.O. gazetted 18 Jan. 1918.)

Awarded the Distinguished Service Order :

ALLEN, DOUGLAS CHARLES, Temporary Major, 15th Battn. Tank Corps.

ALLEN, HENRY ADAIR, Capt. and Brevet Major, Royal Inniskilling Fusiliers, Commanding 17th Cyclist Battn.

ANDERSON, FEARNLEY, M.C., Major (Temporary Lieut.-Colonel), Seaforth Highlanders, Commanding 8th Battn.

ARNOLD, WILLIAM, Temporary Major (Temporary Lieut.-Colonel), 2nd Brigade, Tank Corps.

ARTHY, WALTER, Lieut.-Colonel, 56th Brigade, Royal Garrison Artillery.

ASH, ERNEST ARTHUR, Capt. (Acting Lieut.-Colonel), Middlesex Regt., Special Reserve, Commanding 2/6th Battn. Durham Light Infantry, Territorial Force.

BADDELEY, WALTER HUBERT, M.C., Temporary Major (Acting Lieut.-Colonel), 8th Battn. East Surrey Regt.

BADHAM, BASIL HUME, Capt. (Temporary Lieut.-Colonel), Royal Scots Fusiliers, Commanding 49th Battn. Machine Gun Corps.

BAKER, COLIN WILLOUGHBY, M.C., Lieut. (Temporary Major), Leicestershire Regt.

BALLARD, JOHN ARTHUR, Major (Acting Lieut.-Colonel), Headquarters, 5th Brigade, Royal Field Artillery.

BANKIER, ALBERT METHUEN, M.C., Capt., 2nd Battn. Argyll and Sutherland Highlanders.

BARRY, ARTHUR GORDON, M.C., Capt. (Temporary Lieut.-Colonel), Manchester Regt., Commanding 11th Battn. Machine Gun Corps.

BARSTOW, JOHN NELSON, M.C., Capt., Royal Field Artillery, Territorial Force, attached Headquarters, 52nd Infantry Brigade.

BEEVOR, MILES, Major (Temporary Lieut.-Colonel), East Kent Regt., attached 1/7th Battn. Middlesex Regt., Territorial Force.

BENKE, AUGUSTUS CHARLES HERBERT, M.C., Capt. (Acting Major), 2/15th Battn. London Regt.

BERRIDGE, FRED ROLAND, M.C., Temporary Capt., Northampton Regt.

BEWSHER, FREDERICK WILLIAM, M.C., Capt. (Temporary Major), 5th Battn. London Regt.

BICKERDIKE, ROBERT BRYAN, Major, Royal Field Artillery, Territorial Force, attached D/149th Brigade, Royal Field Artillery.

BIGG-WITHER, HUGH GEORGE, Temporary Major, 10th Battn. Duke of Cornwall's Light Infantry.

BIRTWISTLE, WILLIAM, Major, 210th (East Lancashire) Brigade, Royal Field Artillery, Territorial Force.

BLACKER, NORMAN VALENTINE, M.C., Capt. (Temporary Lieut.-Colonel), East Yorkshire Regt., attached 35th Battn. Machine Gun Corps.
BLAIR, PATRICK JAMES, Capt. (Acting Lieut.-Colonel), 9th Battn. Royal Scots, Territorial Force, attached 13th Battn. Royal Highlanders, Territorial Force.
BOLITHO, EDWARD HOBLYN WARREN, Major (Acting Lieut.-Colonel), Headquarters, 170th Brigade, Royal Field Artillery.
BOSHELL, FRANCIS SYDNEY, M.C., Quartermaster and Capt., 1st Battn. Royal Berkshire Regt.
BOYLE, HENRY KIRK, Capt. (Temporary Major), 8th Battn. West Yorkshire Regt., Territorial Force, attached 39th Battn. Machine Gun Corps.
BRASSEY, EDWIN PERCIVAL, M.C., Capt. (Acting Lieut.-Colonel), Coldstream Guards, Special Reserve, attached 2nd Battn.
BROCKLEBANK, RICHARD HUGH ROYDS, Capt. (Acting Lieut.-Colonel), 9th Lancers.
BROWN, DONALD, Major, 211th (East Lancashire) Brigade, Royal Field Artillery, Territorial Force.
BROWNING, HERBERT COMPTON, M.C., Temporary Capt., 2nd Battn. Bedfordshire Regt.
BUCHANAN, JOHN NEVILE, M.C., Lieut. (Temporary Capt.), Grenadier Guards, Special Reserve.
BULLEN, STEPHEN DARLE, Lieut.-Colonel, 34th Brigade, Royal Garrison Artillery.
BURKE, JOHN, M.C., D.C.M., Quartermaster and Major, 2nd Battn. Royal Dublin Fusiliers.
BURNELL, CHARLES DESBOROUGH, Capt. (Acting Lieut.-Colonel), 1/5th Battn. London Regt.
BURNETT, RICHARD PARRY, M.C., Temporary Major (Acting Lieut.-Colonel), 8th Battn. South Staffordshire Regt., attached 7th Battn. Royal Fusiliers.
BURRELL, STANILAUS, Major, 1/1st Northumberland Hussars Yeomanry.
BURROUGHES, HENRY NEVILLE, M.B., Capt. (Acting Lieut.-Colonel), 2/2nd (South Midland) Field Ambulance, Royal Army Medical Corps, Territorial Force.
BUXTON, IVOR, Major, Norfolk Yeomanry.
CAMERON, AYLMER LOCHIEL, M.C., Lieut. (Acting Major), B/58th Brigade, Royal Field Artillery.
CARPENTER, GERALD GOODWIN, Capt. (Acting Lieut.-Colonel), 2nd Battn. Suffolk Regt.
CARWITHEN, SYDNEY, Major, 6th Division, Headquarters, Royal Artillery.
CHRISTIE, JAMES REID, Lieut. (Acting Capt.), 1/6th Battn. Gordon Highlanders, Territorial Force.
CLAPHAM, DOUGLAS, O.B.E., Major (Acting Lieut.-Colonel), 59th Brigade, Royal Garrison Artillery.
CLARK, FREDERICK WILLIAM, M.C., Temporary Capt. (Acting Major), 229th Field Company, Royal Engineers.
CLEGG, HUMPHREY NICHOLS MAVESYN, Lieut.-Colonel, 1/1st Denbighshire Yeomanry, Commanding 24th Battn. Royal Welsh Fusiliers (Capt., Reserve of Officers).
COLDWELL, WILLIAM GEORGE ALEXANDER, Capt. (Temporary Lieut.-Colonel), Northamptonshire Regt., Commanding 12th Battn. Machine Gun Corps.
CONNOLLY, LOUIS ANDREW, M.C., Capt. (Acting Major), A/33th Brigade, Royal Field Artillery.
COOKE, EDWARD DOUGLAS MONTAGUE HUNTER, Major (Acting Lieut.-Colonel), Royal Field Artillery, attached 46th Divisional Artillery.
COOPER, WILLIAM MIDDLESHIP, M.C., Capt. (Acting Major), 255th Siege Battery, Royal Garrison Artillery.
COWAN-DOUGLAS, JOHN ROBERT, M.C., Capt., Highland Light Infantry.
COWLEY, VICTOR LEOPOLD SPENCER, M.C., Capt. (Temporary Lieut.-Colonel), Royal Irish Rifles, attached 31st Battn. Machine Gun Corps.
CRAM, PETER McFARLAND, Capt. (Temporary Major), 4th Battn. Cameron Highlanders, Territorial Force, attached 6th Battn.
CROSSMAN, FRANCIS LINDISFARNE MORLEY, M.C., Major, Royal Field Artillery.
CURRIE, IVOR BERTRAM FENDALL, Lieut.-Colonel, Headquarters, 99th Brigade, Royal Garrison Artillery.
CURTIS, HENRY OSBORNE, M.C., Capt. and Brevet Major, King's Royal Rifle Corps.
D'ARCY, JOSEPH ISIDORE, Major (Acting Lieut.-Colonel), 113th Brigade, Royal Field Artillery.
DAVIES-EVANS, DELMÉ WILLIAM CAMPBELL, Major (Acting Lieut.-Colonel), Pembroke Yeomanry, attached 2/8th Battn. Worcestershire Regt., Territorial Force.
DAWSON, GUY DE HOGHTON, Temporary Capt., Royal Army Medical Corps.
DAY, FRANCIS REGINALD, Major (Acting Lieut.-Colonel), Norfolk Regt., attached 9th Battn.
DAY, NOEL ARTHUR LACY, Major, Royal Artillery.
DEACON, WILLIAM JOHN, Lieut. (Acting Major), B/181st Brigade, Royal Field Artillery.
DENHAM, HAROLD ARTHUR, Major, East Riding Royal Garrison Artillery. Territorial Force, attached 329th Siege Battery, Royal Garrison Artillery.
DE PREE, HUGO DOUGLAS, C.B., C.M.G., Lieut.-Colonel and Brevet Colonel (Temporary Brigadier-General), Royal Artillery, Commanding 115th Infantry Brigade.
DODGE, JOHN BIGELOW, D.S.C., Temporary Major (Acting Lieut.-Colonel), Suffolk Regt., attached 16th Battn. Sussex Regt. (formerly Machine Gun Corps).
DREW, CHARLES MILLIGAN, M.B., Major (Acting Lieut.-Colonel), 134th Field Ambulance, Royal Army Medical Corps.
DUCAT, ARTHUR DAVID, M.B., Lieut.-Colonel, 2/3rd (London) Field Ambulance, Royal Army Medical Corps.
DUDLEY, GEORGE VERNON, M.C., Temporary Capt. (Acting Major), 185th Siege Battery, Royal Garrison Artillery.
DUNSDON, GILBERT EWART, Major, Royal Garrison Artillery, Territorial Force, attached 224th Siege Battery Royal Garrison Artillery.
DYER, GEORGE NOWERS, Major, Royal West Surrey Regt., attached Headquarters, 17th Division.

EASTWOOD, THOMAS RALPH, M.C., Capt. and Brevet Major (Acting Lieut.-Colonel), 2nd Battn. Rifle Brigade.
EDWARDS, GUY JANION, M.C., Capt. (Acting Lieut.-Colonel), 4th Battn. Coldstream Guards.
EDWARDS, HERBERT IVOR POWELL, Major (Temporary Lieut.-Colonel), Sussex Yeomanry, attached 16th Battn. Royal Sussex Regt.
EDYE, JOHN HENRY MURRAY, M.C., Capt., York and Lancaster Regt.
FALKNER, ARTHUR HENRY, Major, Royal Army Medical Corps, Territorial Force, attached 8th Battn. Liverpool Regt.
FERRAND, STAFFORD HUBERT, M.C., Capt. (Temporary Lieut.-Colonel), King's Royal Rifle Corps, attached 11th Battn. East Yorkshire Regt.
FISHER, JOHN MALCOLM, M.C., Capt. (Temporary Major), 1/5th Battn. York and Lancaster Regt., Territorial Force.
FORESTER, TOM, Temporary Major, 15th Battn. Machine Gun Corps.
FORMAN, DOUGLAS EVANS, C.M.G., Lieut.-Colonel, Royal Horse Artillery, attached Headquarters, 33rd Brigade, Royal Field Artillery.
FOSTER, JOHN RAFFRAY, Major (Temporary Lieut.-Colonel), Royal Artillery.
FOSTER, THOMAS, Temporary Major, 9th Battn. Royal Sussex Regt.
FOXTON, JOHN ALEXANDER, Capt. (Acting Lieut.-Colonel), 1/5th Battn. West Yorkshire Regt., Territorial Force, attached 1/7th Battn.
FRANKLYN, GEOFFREY ERNEST WARREN, M.C., Capt. and Brevet Major, Royal Artillery.
FRASER, FRANCIS HUGH, M.C., Lieut. (Temporary Capt.), West Riding Regt.
FRASER, JOHN HENRY PEARSON, M.C., Capt. (Acting Lieut.-Colonel), Royal Army Medical Corps, Territorial Force, attached 53rd Field Ambulance Royal Army Medical Corps.
FRERE, JASPER GRAY, M.C., Lieut. (Temporary Capt. and Acting Major) Suffolk Regt., attached Machine Gun Corps.
GALE, HENRY DAVIS, M.C., Major, Royal Artillery.
GALLOWAY, RUDOLF WILLIAM, M.B., Capt. (Acting Lieut.-Colonel), 2nd Cavalry Field Ambulance, Royal Army Medical Corps.
GIBBS, LANCELOT MERIVALE, M.C., Capt., Coldstream Guards.
GIFFIN, WILLIAM CHARLES DISRAELI, M.C., Lieut., Royal Irish Regt., Special Reserve, attached 2nd Battn.
GLENDINNING, HALBERT JAMES, Capt. and Brevet Major (Acting Major), D/180th Brigade, Royal Field Artillery.
GOFF, THOMAS CROSBIE, Major, 113th Heavy Battery, Royal Garrison Artillery.
GORDON, ALAN DOUGLAS, M.C., Capt. (Temporary Major and Acting Lieut.-Colonel), Royal Berkshire Regt., attached 62nd Battn. Machine Gun Corps.
GORE-LANGTON, GERALD WENTWORTH, M.C., Capt., 18th Hussars.
GOTTO, CHRISTOPHER HUGH, M.C., Capt., 1st Battn. Devonshire Regt.
GOURLAY, KENNETH IAN, M.C., Capt. (Acting Major), 79th Field Company, Royal Engineers.
GRASETT, ARTHUR EDWARD, M.C., Capt. and Brevet Major, Royal Engineers.
GRAYSTONE, FREDERICK RUSS, M.C., Temporary Capt. (Temporary Major), Royal Artillery.
GREIG, JAMES McGAVIN, Temporary Lieut.-Colonel, West Yorkshire Regt., attached 18th Battn. York and Lancaster Regt.
GRIBBLE, HOWARD CHARLES, Major, Royal Field Artillery, Territorial Force, attached 523rd Siege Battery, Royal Garrison Artillery.
GRINLING, EDWARD JOHNS, M.C., Capt., 1/4th Battn. Lincolnshire Regt., Territorial Force.
GUILD, ARTHUR MARJORIBANKS, Major, Highland Cyclists' Battn. attached 1/19th Battn. London Regt.
GUNTER, ATHELSTANE CLAUD, Major, 488th Siege Battery, Royal Garrison Artillery.
HALL, HENRY RONALD, M.C., Capt. (Acting Major), A/47th Brigade, Royal Field Artillery.
HALL, JOHN HATHORN, M.C., Temporary Capt., General List.
HALL, PHILIP DE HAVILLAND, M.C., Major (Acting Lieut.-Colonel), Royal Engineers, Territorial Force.
HARKNESS, ROBERT BRUCE, Temporary Major, Welsh Regt.
HART, ERNEST ALBERT EDWARD, M.C., Lieut. (Acting Major), A/46th Brigade, Royal Field Artillery.
HAWKES, GEORGE WHITE, M.C., Temporary Lieut.-Colonel, 5th Battn. Royal Irish Regt.
HAYWARD, CECIL RICHARD, Capt. (Acting Lieut.-Colonel), West Somerset Yeomanry, Commanding 12th Battn. Somersetshire Light Infantry, Territorial Force.
HAYWOOD, ALFRED NOBLE, Quartermaster and Major, 6th Dragoon Guards.
HEBBERT, HENRY ERIC, M.C., Capt. (Acting Major), 21st Divisional Signalling Company, Royal Engineers.
HEFFERNAN, JAMES GERALD PATRICK, M.C., Temporary Major, 1st Battn. Royal Dublin Fusiliers.
HEMSLEY, HENRY NORRIS, M.C., Temporary Lieut. (Temporary Major), General List.
HENRI, PERCIVAL ROBERT, M.C., Lieut. (Acting Major), 3rd, attached 1st, Battn. London Regt.
HERMON-HODGE, ROBERT EDWARD UDNY, Major, Oxfordshire Yeomanry.
HILL, LAURENCE CARR, M.C., Temporary Major, 177th Tunnelling Company, Royal Engineers.
HOARE, EDWARD GODFREY, Capt. (Acting Lieut.-Colonel), Yorkshire Light Infantry, attached 1/5th Battn. Royal Lancashire Regt., Territorial Force.
HOLLAND, RUPERT THURSTAN, M.C., Major, Royal Artillery.
HORNE, ERNEST WILLIAM, Lieut. (Acting Major), 2nd Battn. Devonshire Regt.
HORNSBY-WRIGHT, GUY JEFFERYS, Lieut.-Colonel, 15th Battn. Essex Regt., Territorial Force.
HOWARD, ALLEN CRAWFORD, M.C., Lieut. (Acting Lieut.-Colonel), Royal Engineers, Territorial Force, attached Royal Engineers.
HOWARD, WILLIAM JAMES HOLDSWORTH, Capt. (Temporary Major and Acting Lieut.-Colonel), Liverpool Regt., attached 13th Battn.

The Distinguished Service Order

HUDLESTON, IVOR ROBERT, Capt. (Acting Lieut.-Colonel), 136th Field Ambulance, Royal Army Medical Corps.

HULL, HUBERT CHARLES EDWARD, Capt. and Brevet Major, Royal West Surrey Regt.

HUNT, ARTHUR FREDERICK, Temporary Major, General List.

INGRAM, JOHN MARKHAM, Major (Acting Lieut.-Colonel), 56th Brigade, Royal Field Artillery.

ISAAC, THOMAS WILLIAM TALBOT, Major (Temporary Lieut.-Colonel), Gloucestershire Regt., attached 15th Battn. Yorkshire Light Infantry.

JACKSON, CLAUD HUGH IRVING, Major (Temporary Colonel), Royal Scots Fusiliers, attached Machine Gun Corps.

KANE, ARTHUR HYDE, Lieut.-Colonel, Headquarters, 72nd Brigade, Royal Garrison Artillery.

KAY, PETER CHRICHTON, M.C., Lieut. (Acting Major), 1/7th Battn. Middlesex Regt., Territorial Force.

KELLY, JOHN DUNBAR, Lieut. (Acting Major), Royal Army Service Corps, attached 24th Divisional Mechanical Transport Company.

KEYS, PERCY HUBERT, M.C., Temporary Capt. (Acting Major), 228th Field Company, Royal Engineers.

KEYSER, ALBERT GEORGE, Temporary Major, 9th Battn. Machine Gun Corps.

KING, MILES HENRY, M.C., Capt. (Temporary Major), 4th Battn. West Riding Regt., Territorial Force.

KINGSFORD, GEOFFRY NEVILLE, M.C., Temporary Capt. (Acting Major), 67th Field Company, Royal Engineers.

KINGSTONE, JAMES JOSEPH, M.C., Capt., 2nd Dragoon Guards.

KITCHIN, CYRIL, Major, Middlesex Regt.

LEDGARD, GEORGE, M.C., Temporary Capt. (Acting Major), 80th Field Company, Royal Engineers.

LEWIS, JOHN EVAN, Temporary Major, 16th Battn. Tank Corps (Capt., Territorial Force Reserve).

LEYLAND, FREDERICK BEADLE, M.V.O., Major, 7th Hussars.

LLOYD, OWEN FITZSTEPHEN, Major (Acting Lieut.-Colonel), Connaught Rangers, seconded Tank Corps.

LOCKWOOD, EDWARD MARSTON, Temporary Lieut.-Commander, Hawke Battn. Royal Naval Division, Royal Naval Volunteer Reserve.

LONGBOTTOM, WILLIAM, Lieut.-Colonel, 1/12th Battn. North Lancashire Regt., Territorial Force.

LOWE, CHARLES EDWARD BERKELEY, M.C., Lieut. (Acting Major), Royal Garrison Artillery, Territorial Force, attached 94th Siege Battery, Royal Garrison Artillery.

LYON, PHILIP, Major (Temporary Lieut.-Colonel), North Staffordshire Regt., attached 13th Battn. Tank Corps.

LYTTELTON, ARCHER GEOFFREY, Capt. and Brevet Major (Temporary Lieut.-Colonel), Welsh Regt., Commanding 38th Battn. Machine Gun Corps.

MACKINNON, LACHLAN, Major (Temporary Lieut.-Colonel), 4th Battn. Gordon Highlanders, Territorial Force, attached 14 Battn. Argyll and Sutherland Highlanders.

MACLEOD, JAMES STRACHAN, Lieut.-Colonel, 8th Battn. Durham Light Infantry, Territorial Force, attached 1/8th Battn. Lancashire Fusiliers, Territorial Force.

MAHAR, THOMAS BERTRAM JOSEPH, M.C., Temporary Lieut. (Temporary Capt.), General List.

MARRYATT, RICHARD HERBERT, Lieut. (Acting Major), Worcestershire Regt. (Special Reserve), attached 4th Battn.

MARTIN, JAMES EVAN BAILLIE, C.V.O., Capt. and Honorary Major, Retired Pay, late King's Royal Rifle Corps.

MATHEWS, FRANK ARNOLD VIVANTI DEWAR, M.C., Lieut. (Acting Major), 455th Field Company, Royal Engineers, Territorial Force.

MAUDE, RALPH WALTER, Temporary Major, Special List.

MAURICE, GODFREY KINDERSLEY, Capt. (Acting Lieut.-Colonel), Royal Army Medical Corps, Territorial Force, attached 8th Field Ambulance.

McCLURE, WILLIAM, Major (Acting Lieut.-Colonel), Commanding 2/4th Battn. South Lancashire Regt., Territorial Force.

McCULLAGH, ARTHUR CECIL HAYS, M.B., Capt. (Acting Lieut.-Colonel), 2/2nd (Northumbrian) Field Ambulance, Royal Army Medical Corps, Territorial Force.

McGHEE, ARTHUR SYDNEY PONSONBY, Major (Acting Lieut.-Colonel), Royal Garrison Artillery, attached Headquarters, 10th Brigade.

McMICKING, NEIL, M.C., Capt. (Temporary Major), Royal Highlanders.

MEIKLE, JOHN HAMILTON, Lieut.-Colonel, 256th (Highland) Brigade, Royal Field Artillery, Territorial Force.

MENZIES, JOHN McKENZIE, M.C., Temporary Capt. (Acting Major), D/76th Army Brigade, Royal Field Artillery.

MICHELMORE, WILLIAM GODWIN, M.C., Lieut. (Acting Major), Royal Engineers, Territorial Force, attached 19th Divisional Signalling Company, Royal Engineers.

MILLER, GERARD WILLIAM, M.C., Lieut. (Acting Capt.), 1st Battn. Liverpool Regt., attached 18th Battn. Lancashire Fusiliers.

MILLER, JOHN, M.C., Capt. (Acting Lieut.-Colonel), 1/2nd (N.M.) Field Ambulance, Royal Army Medical Corps, Territorial Force.

MONTGOMERY, RALPH NOEL VERNON, Major, D/88th Brigade, Royal Field Artillery.

MOORE, FREDERICK WILLIAM, M.C., Temporary Capt. (Acting Major), 12th Field Company, Royal Engineers.

MOORE, HAROLD EDWARD, M.C., Capt. (Temporary Major), No. 1 Siege Company (Royal Monmouthshire), Royal Engineers (Special Reserve).

MOORE-GWYN, HOWEL GWYN, M.C., Capt., Rifle Brigade.

MORGAN, WILLIAM DUTHIE, M.C., Capt. (Acting Major), D/15th Brigade, Royal Field Artillery.

MORRIS, ERIC WELLS, Capt. (Acting Major), 1st Battn. Connaught Rangers, attached 1/4th Battn. Cheshire Regt., Territorial Force.

MOSS, DAVID WILLIAM, M.C., Lieut. (Acting Major), 174th Siege Battery, Royal Garrison Artillery.

MUDIE, THOMAS COUPER, Major and Brevet Lieut.-Colonel (Temporary Lieut.-Colonel), Royal Scots.

MULLER, JOHN, M.C., Capt. (Temporary Major and Acting Lieut.-Colonel), Welsh Regt., Commanding 36th Battn. Machine Gun Corps.

MURRAY, WILLIAM, M.C., Temporary Major (Acting Lieut.-Colonel), 18th Battn. Highland Light Infantry, attached 17th Battn. Royal Scots.

MURRAY, WILLIAM HUGH, Temporary Major (Acting Lieut.-Colonel), 10th Battn. Scottish Rifles.

NASMITH, REGINALD, M.C., Capt. (Temporary Lieut.-Colonel), Highland Light Infantry, Commanding 15th Battn. Machine Gun Corps.

NAYLOR, ROBERT FRANCIS BRYDGES, M.C., Capt. and Brevet Major (Acting Lieut.-Colonel), South Staffordshire Regt.

NEWELL, FREDERICK WILLIAM MONK, Temporary Lieut.-Colonel, Royal Engineers.

NEWTH, ARTHUR LESLIE WALTER, M.C., Capt. (Acting Lieut.-Colonel), 4th Battn. Gloucestershire Regt., Territorial Force, attached 2/23rd Battn. London Regt.

NICHOLSON, RANDOLPH, M C , Lieut. (Acting Major), A/70th Brigade, Royal Field Artillery.

NISBET, DUDLEY, M.C., Capt. (Acting Major), 1/5th Battn. South Lancashire Regt., Territorial Force.

O'GRADY, DONALD DE COURCEY, Major (Acting Lieut.-Colonel), Royal Army Medical Corps.

O'REILLY, HERBERT JOSEPH MARY, M.C., Lieut. (Acting Major), Royal Irish Regt. (Special Reserve), attached 2nd Battn.

OSTROROG, STANISLAUS JULIAN, Temporary Lieut.-Colonel, Royal Artillery.

PARKER, HAROLD, Major, 1/4th Battn. North Lancashire Regt., Territorial Force.

PATERSON, DAVID, Major, 3rd Highland Brigade, Royal Field Artillery, Territorial Force.

PEIRSON, GEOFFREY, M.C., Temporary Capt., General List.

PEPLOE, HAROLD, Capt. (Temporary Lieut.-Colonel), Royal West Kent Regt., Commanding 6th Battn.

PHILLIPS, EDWARD, M.C., M.B., Capt. (Acting Lieut.-Colonel), 106th Field Ambulance, Royal Army Medical Corps.

PIERSON, CHARLES EDWARD, Major, A/307th (S.M.) Brigade, Royal Field Artillery, Territorial Force.

POLLARD, JAMES HAWKINS-WITSHED, C.B., C.M.G., Lieut.-Colonel and Brevet Colonel (Temporary Brigadier-General), Royal Scots Fusiliers, Commanding 106th Infantry Brigade .

POLLOCK, HUGH ALEXANDER, Major, 5th Battn., attached 12th Battn., Royal Scots Fusiliers, Territorial Force.

POOLE, GERALD ROBERT, C.M.G., Lieut.-Colonel, Royal Marine Artillery.

PORTEOUS, NORMAN, M.C., Temporary Capt. (Acting Major), Royal Engineers, Commanding 47th (London) Divisional Signalling Company, Royal Engineers.

QUILLER-COUCH, BRIAN BEVIL, M.C., Capt. (Acting Major), Royal Field Artillery (Special Reserve), attached 9th Battery.

RAE, GEORGE BANTHAM LEATHART, Major, 10th Battn. Liverpool Regt., Territorial Force, attached 17th Battn. Manchester Regt., Territorial Force.

RAIKES, WILFRED TAUNTON, M.C., Capt. (Temporary Lieut.-Colonel), South Wales Borderers (Special Reserve), Commanding 25th Battn. Machine Gun Corps.

RAYNSFORD, RICHARD MONTAGUE, Major, Leinster Regt., attached 6th Battn. Connaught Rangers.

READ, HUGH STANLEY, M.C., Lieut. (Acting Major), 1/20th Battn. London Regt.

REID, ALEXANDER KIRKWOOD, M.C., Major, 9th Battn. Highland Light Infantry, Territorial Force.

REID, NORMAN, M.C., Lieut. (Acting Capt.), Royal Field Artillery (Special Reserve), attached 30th Divisional Trench Mortar Battery (corrected from 30th to 40th Divisional Trench Mortar Battery [London Gazette, 8 August, 1919]).

RENNIE, WILLIAM BROWN, M.C., Temporary Major (Temporary Lieut.-Colonel), Special List.

REYNOLDS, ALAN BOYD, Major (Temporary Lieut.-Colonel), 12th Lancers, Commanding 1/1st Northumberland Hussars Yeomanry.

REYNOLDS, CYRIL HERBERT, M.C., Major, Royal Garrison Artillery.

RICHARDS, COLLEN EDWARD MELVILLE, M.C., Capt. (Acting Lieut.-Colonel), East Lancashire Regt., attached 20th Battn. Middlesex Regt.

RICHARDSON, ADOLPHUS NOAH, M.C., Temporary Major, 39th Battn. Machine Gun Corps.

RICHEY, FREDERICK WILLIAM, Major (Acting Lieut.-Colonel), Royal Garrison Artillery, attached 72nd Army Brigade, Royal Field Artillery.

RIDGWAY, THOMAS, M.C., Capt. (Acting Lieut.-Colonel), 1/4th Battn. South Lancashire Regt., Territorial Force.

RIDLER, REGINALD HARDAY, Capt., 25th Battn. London Regt., attached 11th Battn. Somersetshire Light Infantry, Territorial Force.

RITZEMA, THOMAS PURVIS, Temporary Lieut.-Colonel, Royal Field Artillery, attached 66th (East Lancashire) Divisional Ammunition Column, Royal Field Artillery, Territorial Force.

ROBERTSON, BRIAN HUBERT, M.C., Capt., Royal Engineers.

RODDICK, JAMES ALBERT, M.C., Lieut. (Acting Major), 1/10th Battn. Liverpool Regt., Territorial Force, attached 13th Battn. West Riding Regt.

ROGERS, HARRY PERCIVAL, Temporary Major (Acting Lieut.-Colonel), 23rd Battn. Royal Fusiliers.

ROTHERFORD, ROBSON WILSON, M.C., Temporary Capt., General List.

ROWAN, GILBERT, M.C., Lieut. (Acting Major), 1/7th Battn. Royal Highlanders, Territorial Force, attached 254th Tunnelling Company, Royal Engineers.

SANDERS, WILLIAM ORPEN SKOTTOWE, Major, 324th Siege Battery, Royal Garrison Artillery.

SANFORD, GILBERT AYSHFORD, Major, 20th Hussars.

SAYER, ALFRED CARLISLE, M.C., Major, Sussex Yeomanry, attached 16th Battn. Royal Sussex Regt.

SCOTT, JOHN, Major, Royal Field Artillery, attached 256th (Highland) Brigade, Royal Field Artillery, Territorial Force.

SHARPE, GEOFREY LYNTON, Capt. (Acting Major), 5th Battn. West Riding Regt., Territorial Force, attached Army Cyclists' Corps.

SHAW, ARTHUR LLEWELLYN BANCROFT, Major, 1/8th Battn. Lancashire Fusiliers, Territorial Force.
SHEPPARD, JOHN JAMES, M.C., Lieut. (Acting Major), 1/19th Battn. London Regt.
SMITH, SYDNEY, M.C., Capt. (Acting Major), C/276th (West Lancashire Brigade), Royal Field Artillery, Territorial Force.
SMYTH, WILLIAM, M.C., Temporary Capt. (Acting Major), 122nd Field Company, Royal Engineers.
SOMERS, LORD, ARTHUR HERBERT TENNYSON, M.C., Capt. (Acting Lieut.-Colonel), 1st Life Guards, Commanding 6th Battn. Tank Corps.
SOMERVILLE-SMITH, HERBERT, M.C., Temporary Lieut. (Acting Major), D/113th Army Brigade, Royal Field Artillery.
SOPPER, ERNEST, M.C., Capt. (Temporary Major), 17th Lancers, attached 6th Battn. Leicestershire Regt.
SPONG, CECIL ALLEYN THOMAS, Capt. (Acting Major), 27th Siege Battery, Royal Garrison Artillery.
STANFORD, ARTHUR WARNER, M.C., Lieut. (Acting Major), Royal Field Artillery (Special Reserve), attached 92nd Battery, 17th Brigade.
STEVENSON, WILLIAM SCOTT, M.C., Temporary Major, General List.
STONE, ROBERT GRAHAM WILLIAM HAWKINS, M.C., Capt., Royal Engineers, attached Headquarters, 32nd Infantry Brigade.
STRANGE, FRANCIS GERALD, Major, 1/1st Berkshire Yeomanry, attached 101st Battn. Machine Gun Corps.
STRONGE, HUMPHREY CECIL TRAVELL, M.C., Capt. (Acting Lieut.-Colonel), East Kent Regt., Commanding 7th Battn.
STUART, BILL, Lieut. (Acting Major), D/77th Brigade, Royal Field Artillery.
STUBBS, JOHN WILLIAM COTTER, M.C., M.B., Capt. (Acting Lieut.-Colonel), 16th Field Ambulance, Royal Army Medical Corps.
SUMMERS, FREDERICK, M.C., Temporary Major (Acting Lieut.-Colonel), Royal Engineers.
SUTHERLAND, HECTOR WILLIAM, Temporary Major, 7/8th Battn. King's Own Scottish Borderers.
TAYLOR, GEORGE VERE, M.C., Temporary Major, 16th Battn. Rifle Brigade.
TAYLOR, LEONARD MAINWARING, M.C., Major, 4th Battn. Yorkshire Light Infantry, Territorial Force.
THESIGER, THE HONOURABLE ERIC RICHARD, Major (Temporary Lieut.-Colonel), Surrey Yeomanry, Commanding 10th Battn. Royal West Kent Regt.
THOMSON, DAVID, M.C., Capt. (Acting Major), Royal Field Artillery, attached 93rd Battery, 280th (London) Brigade, Royal Field Artillery.
THOMSON, EDWARD LIONEL, Major (Acting Lieut.-Colonel), York and Lancaster Regt. (Special Reserve), attached 9th Battn. Northumberland Fusiliers (Lieut., Retired Pay, late Norfolk Regt.).
THOMSON, JAMES NOEL, M.C., Major, Royal Field Artillery.
THOMSON, JOHN FERGUSON, Major (Acting Lieut.-Colonel), North Staffordshire Regt., attached 36th Battn. Northumberland Fusiliers.
THORBURN, WILLIAM, Lieut.-Colonel, 1/8th Battn. Royal Scots, Territorial Force.
TILLY, JUSTICE CROSLAND, M.C., Capt. (Acting Lieut.-Colonel), West Yorkshire Regt., Commanding 10th Battn. Tank Corps.
TOLERTON, ROBERT HILL, M.C., Capt. (Acting Lieut.-Colonel), 1/23rd Battn. London Regt.
TOLLEMACHE, THE HONOURABLE DENIS PLANTAGENET, Capt. (Temporary Major), 7th Hussars.
TOLLEMACHE, EDWARD DEVEREUX HAMILTON, M.C., Capt. and Brevet Major (Temporary Major), Coldstream Guards.
TOLLWORTHY, FREDERICK GEORGE, M.C., Lieut. (Acting Major), 1st Battn. London Regt., attached 2/2nd Battn.
TRENT, GEORGE ALEXANDER, C.M.G., Lieut.-Colonel, Northamptonshire Regt., Commanding 5th Battn.
TROUSDELL, ALEXANDER JAMES, M.C., Capt., Royal Irish Fusiliers (Special Reserve).
TURNER, GEORGE FREDERIC BROWN, Major, A./186th Brigade, Royal Field Artillery.
VINEN, HAROLD NORTHCOTE, Major (Acting Lieut.-Colonel), Gloucestershire Regt., Commanding 5th Battn. Border Regt., Territorial Force.
WALKER, MONTAGU GEORGE EDWARD, Capt., Royal Artillery, Headquarters, VIIIth Corps, Horse Artillery.
WALMESLEY, CHARLES TALBOT JOSEPH GERARD, M.C., Major, Berkshire Yeomanry.
WALSH, CHARLES HERBERT, M.C., Capt. (Acting Lieut.-Colonel), Connaught Rangers, attached Signalling Service, Royal Engineers.
WARD, EVAN BERNARD, Major (Acting Lieut.-Colonel), Duke of Cornwall's Light Infantry, attached 1/5th Battn. Territorial Force.
WARD, ROBERT OGIER, Capt. (Acting Major), Honourable Artillery Company, attached C/298th Army Brigade, Royal Field Artillery, Territorial Force.
WARNER, KENNETH CHARLES HARMAN, Major, 2/1st Kent Cyclists' Battn., Territorial Force, attached 7th Battn. York and Lancaster Regt.
WATSON, AUBREY WENTWORTH HARRISON, M.C., Temporary Capt., General List (late 9th Battn. King's Royal Rifle Corps).
WATSON, ROBERT ALBERT, M.C., Capt. (Acting Major), 14th Heavy Battery, Royal Garrison Artillery.
WATSON, WILLIAM HENRY LOWE, D.C.M., Temporary Major, 4th Tank Carrier Company, Tank Corps.
WAY, LESLIE FERGUSON KENNEDY, Capt. (Acting Lieut.-Colonel), 101st Field Ambulance, Royal Army Medical Corps.
WELDON, ERNEST STEUART, Major, 6th Battn. Dorsetshire Regt.
WHATTON, STEWART MONTAGU DE HERIZ, M.C., Capt. (Acting Major), C/23rd Brigade, Royal Field Artillery.
WHITE, HERBERT, M.C., Temporary Lieut. (Acting Capt.), 7th Battn. Royal Irish Regt.
WHYTE, ROBERT, M.C., Capt. (Acting Lieut.-Colonel), 2/14th Battn. London Regt.
WILLIAMS, THOMAS GLYNDWR, M.C., Lieut. (Acting Lieut.-Colonel), 7th Battn. Liverpool Regt., Territorial Force, attached 1/4th Battn. North Lancashire Regt., Territorial Force.

WILSON, EDWARD BERNARD, Temporary Major (Acting Lieut.-Colonel), 6th Battn. Yorkshire Light Infantry, attached 34th Battn. London Regt.
WILSON, THOMAS NEEDHAM FURNIVAL, M.C., Capt., 1st Battn. King's Royal Rifle Corps.
WITTS, FRANK HOLE, M.C., Capt., Irish Guards.
WOODCOCK, JOHN BURRELL HOLME, Major, Pembroke Yeomanry, attached 24th Battn. Welsh Regt., Territorial Force.
WRIGHT, ARTHUR JAMES, M.C., Lieut. (Temporary Capt.), 1/4th Battn. Northamptonshire Regt., Territorial Force.
YATES, ROBERT, M.C., Temporary Capt. (Acting Major), 183rd Tunnelling Company, Royal Engineers.

CANADIAN FORCE.

ARMOUR, STUART DOUGLAS, Major, British Columbia Regt.
BARKER, LOUIS WILLIAM, Major, 4th Siege Battery, Canadian Garrison Artillery.
BELL, WALKER, Lieut.-Colonel, Royal Canadian Dragoons, attached 3rd Battn. Tank Corps.
BLUE, WALTER EDWARD, Major, 58th (Howitzer) Battery, 14th Brigade, Canadian Field Artillery, attached Headquarters, 5th Canadian Divisional Ammunition Column.
BOGART, JOHN LAURANCE HASLETT, Lieut.-Colonel, 7th Battn. Canadian Engineers.
BOND, FRANK LORN CAMPBELL, Major, 10th Battn. Canadian Railway Troops.
BROCK, FREDERICK FREER, Major, Canadian Heavy Artillery, attached 456th Siege Battery, Royal Garrison Artillery.
BROWNE, GEORGE SACKVILLE, Major, 53rd Battery, 13th Brigade, Canadian Field Artillery.
CAMERON, ALEXANDER DOUGLAS, M.C., Lieut.-Colonel, Lord Strathcona's Horse, attached 38th Battn. Canadian Infantry, East Ontario Regt.
CARTER, ROBERT STEWART, Major, 13th Battn. Canadian Railway Troops.
CHARLES, ALLEN HUGHES, Major, Quebec Regt.
CHIVERS, CYRIL WILLIAM UPTON, M.C., Major, Headquarters, 3rd Brigade, Canadian Engineers.
CHURCHILL, CLIFFORD EARL, Major, 10th Battery, 3rd Brigade, Canadian Field Artillery.
COLMAN, PERCY EDWARD, M.C., Major (Acting Lieut.-Colonel), 1st Battn. Canadian Mounted Rifles, Saskatchewan Regt.
COSTIGAN, RICHARD, Lieut.-Colonel, 5th Division, Ammunition Column, Canadian Field Artillery.
COX, HENRY WILLIAM DARLING, Major (Acting Lieut.-Colonel), Alberta Regt., attached 13th Battn. East Lancashire Regt.
CRAIG, CHARLES STUART, M.C., Major, 30th Battery, 8th Brigade, Canadian Field Artillery.
DE GRAVES, WILLIAM ALEXANDER, Major, 3rd Divisional Train, Canadian Army Service Corps.
DESROSIERS, MARIE JOSEPH ROMEO HENRI, Lieut.-Colonel, 22nd Battn. Canadian Infantry, Quebec Regt.
DURKEE, ADELBERT AUGUSTUS, Major, 38th Battery, 10th Brigade, Canadian Field Artillery.
EVELEIGH, WESLEY JOHN, Temporary Major, 50th Battn. Canadian Infantry, Alberta Regt.
FISKE, ROBERT WALTER, Major, 8th Battn. Canadian Infantry, Manitoba Regt.
GIBSON, JOHN McINTYRE, Major, 2nd Battn. Canadian Railway Troops.
GORDON, BEAUMONT ANDREW, Major, 11th Battn. Canadian Engineers.
HAHN, JAMES EMANUEL, M.C., Major, 1st Battn. Canadian Infantry, West Ontario Regt.
HALL, PATTERSON LINDSAY, M.C., Major, 24th Battn. Canadian Infantry, Quebec Regt.
HARDING, RALPH PRICE, M.C., Major, 5th Battery, 2nd Brigade, Canadian Field Artillery.
HARDISTY, RICHARD HENRY MOORE, M.C., Major (Acting Lieut.-Colonel), 6th Field Ambulance, Canadian Army Medical Corps.
HUGHES, HENRY THORESBY, C.M.G., Colonel, Canadian Engineers.
INCHES, CYRUS FISKE, M.C., Major, 1st Heavy Battery, Canadian Garrison Artillery.
KEMP, JAMES COLIN, M.C., Major, 5th Battn. Canadian Mounted Rifles, Quebec Regt.
KETTERSON, ANDREW ROBERT, Major, 1st Battn. Canadian Railway Troops.
LEADER, CHARLES CLINTON, Major, 5th Battn. Canadian Railway Troops.
MACDONALD, RONALD HUGH, M.C., Lieut.-Colonel, 4th Field Ambulance Canadian Army Medical Corps.
MACPHERSON, KENNETH PLUMB, Major, 7th Battn. Canadian Engineers.
MAITLAND, OLIVER MOWAT, Major, Saskatchewan Regt., attached Canadian Engineers, 8th Corps.
MATHEWSON, FRANK STANTON, Major, 13th Battn. Canadian Infantry, Quebec Regt.
McCORKELL, JOSEPH EDWARD, Major, 2nd Battn. Canadian Machine Gun Corps.
McGREGOR, JAMES, Major, 3rd Battn. Canadian Railway Troops.
MIEVILLE, ARTHUR LEONARD, M.C., Major (Acting Lieut.-Colonel), 6th Battn. Canadian Engineers.
REDMOND, RENE MARTIN, Major, 87th Battn. Canadian Infantry, Quebec Regt.
ROBSON, SAMUEL, Major, 19th Battery, 4th Brigade, Canadian Field Artillery, attached 5th Canadian Divisional Artillery.
RYDER, THOMAS ESCOTT, M.C., Major, 7th Siege Battery, Canadian Garrison Artillery.
SCROGGIE, JAMES AUSTIN, M.C., Major, 16th Battn. Canadian Infantry, Manitoba Regt.
SELBY, ERNEST RAYMOND, Major (Acting Lieut.-Colonel), 8th Field Ambulance, Canadian Army Medical Corps.

The Distinguished Service Order

SILCOX, LEONARD ERNEST, Major, 11th Battn. Canadian Railway Troops.
SMITH, SANFORD FLEMING, Lieut.-Colonel, Canadian Light Horse.
WALLIS, HUGH MACDONALD, Capt., Quebec Regt., seconded to 4th Canadian Infantry Brigade.
WHITE, JAMES ALEXANDER GORDON, M.C., Major, Headquarters, 2nd Brigade, Canadian Engineers.
WILLCOCK, RALPH, M.C., Capt. (Acting Major), 42nd Battn. Canadian Infantry, Quebec Regt.
YOUNG, JOHN DOUGLAS, M.C., Major, 52nd Battn. Canadian Infantry, Manitoba Regt.
YOUNGER, LEWIS, M.C., Capt., Alberta Regt.

AUSTRALIAN IMPERIAL FORCE.

ARRELL, WILLIAM LLEWELLYN, Lieut.-Colonel, 14th Battn. Australian Infantry.
AUDSLEY, WILLIAM ALAN, Major, 8th Brigade, Australian Field Artillery.
BEITH, DUNCAN, Major, 23rd Battn. Australian Infantry.
BENNETT, HENRY GORDON, C.B., C.M.G., Colonel (Temporary Brigadier-General), Australian General List, Commanding 3rd Australian Infantry Brigade.
CANNAN, JAMES HAROLD, C.B., C.M.G., Colonel (Temporary Brigadier-General), Commanding 11th Australian Infantry Brigade.
CHAPMAN, JOHN AUSTIN, Major, 30th Battn. Australian Infantry.
DUFFY, JOHN, Quartermaster and Honorary Major, 13th Australian Light Horse Regt., formerly 4th Light Horse.
GOLLAN, HERBERT ROY, M.C., Capt., 56th Battn. Australian Infantry.
GRANT, FRANCIS GEORGE, Major, 31th Battn. Australian Infantry.
HURST, JOHN HERBERT, Lieut.-Colonel, Headquarters, 36th Australian Heavy Artillery Brigade.
LEWERS, HUGH BENNETT, O.B.E., Lieut.-Colonel, 11th Field Ambulance Australian Army Medical Corps.
MITCHELL, ALEXANDER, Major, 13th Australian Light Horse Regt.
MORRIS, BASIL MOORHOUSE, Major, 14th Brigade, Australian Field Artillery.
MUIRHEAD, JOHN ROBB, Major (Temporary Lieut.-Colonel), 5th Field Ambulance, Australian Army Medical Corps.
PARKS, EDWARD JOSEPH, M.C., Major (Temporary Lieut.-Colonel), 16th Battn. Australian Infantry.
PATERSON, ALEXANDER THOMAS, M.C., Lieut.-Colonel, 39th Battn. Australian Infantry.
SADLER, RUPERT MARKHAM, M.C., Lieut.-Colonel, 17th Battn. Australian Infantry.
SMART, EDWARD KENNETH, M.C., Major, 10th Brigade, Australian Field Artillery.
SOUTHEY, MARCUS VICARS, Major, 1st Field Ambulance, Australian Army Medical Corps.
THOMPSON, CLIVE WENTWORTH, Lieut.-Colonel, 14th Field Ambulance, Australian Army Medical Corps.
TOMKINSON, WILLIAM, Major, 10th Brigade, Australian Field Artillery, attached Headquarters, 4th Australian Divisional Artillery Brigade.
WOOSTER, FRANK COUPER, Lieut.-Colonel, 13th Field Ambulance, Australian Army Medical Corps.

NEW ZEALAND FORCE.

BEERE, RAWDON ST. JOHN, Lieut.-Colonel, 4th Battn. New Zealand Rifle Brigade.
JORY, PHILIP JOHN, M.B., Major (Temporary Lieut.-Colonel), 2nd Field Ambulance, New Zealand Army Medical Corps.
MACNAB, ALEXANDER ALLAN, Major, 3rd New Zealand Rifle Brigade.
McQUARRIE, ROBERT STIRRAT, M.C., Lieut.-Colonel, Headquarters, 3rd Brigade, New Zealand Field Artillery.
MEAD, OWEN HERBERT, Lieut.-Colonel, 2nd Battn. Canterbury Regt.
NORTHCROFT, ERIMA HARVEY, Major, 1st Battery, 1st Brigade, New Zealand Field Artillery.
WILLIAMS, ALAN BERNARD, Major, 5th Battery, 2nd Brigade, New Zealand Field Artillery.

SOUTH AFRICAN FORCE.

WARD, CLIFFORD PERCY, Major, 72nd Siege Battery, South African Horse Artillery, attached Royal Garrison Artillery.

London Gazette, 3 June, 1919.—"War Office, 3 June, 1919. The King has been graciously pleased, on the occasion of His Majesty's Birthday, to approve of the undermentioned rewards for distinguished service in connection with military operations in Egypt. Dated 3 June, 1919. Awarded the Distinguished Service Order."

ABBOTT, SAMUEL HERBERT LEE, M.B., Major (Acting Lieut.-Colonel), Indian Medical Service, attached 14th Cavalry Brigade Field Ambulance.
BARNWELL, JOHN, M.C., Capt. (Temporary Major), Leinster Regt. and 10th Battn. Machine Gun Corps.
BISDEE, THOMAS EDWARD, M.C., Capt. (Acting Lieut.-Colonel), Duke of Cornwall's Light Infantry, Commanding 2/13th Battn. London Regt.
BITTLESTON, KENNETH GEORGE, Major, Royal Field Artillery, Commanding 389th Battery.
BOGLE, JOHN SAVILE, Major (Acting Lieut.-Colonel), Indian Army, Commanding 2nd Battn. Corps of Guides, Indian Army.
CALDECOTT, ANDREW HERBERT, Capt. and Brevet Major (Acting Lieut.-Colonel), Royal Irish Regt., Commanding 2nd Battn. Royal Irish Fusiliers.
CAMPBELL, GEORGE FERGUSON, Capt. (Acting Major), Royal Garrison Artillery, attached 10th Mountain Battery.
CAMPBELL, WILLIAM MACLEOD, Major (Acting Lieut.-Colonel), Suffolk Regt., Commanding 1/5th Battn. Suffolk Regt., Territorial Force.
CARNEGY, UGHTRED ELLIOTT CARNEGY, M.C., Capt. (Temporary Major), 3rd Dragoon Guards.
CARTER, EDWARD GEORGE WEBB, Major, Royal Garrison Artillery, attached 11th Mountain Battery.
CLEMSON, WILLIAM, Major, 2nd Battn. Dorset Regt.
COOPER, WILLIAM GEORGE, Lieut.-Colonel, Indian Army, Commanding 34th Poona Horse, Indian Army.
CROSSON, WILLIAM FREDERICK, Capt. (Acting Major), 5th Battn. Hampshire Regt., Territorial Force, attached 1/4th Battn. Wiltshire Regt., Territorial Force.
CUNINGHAME, EDWARD WILLIAM MONTGOMERY, Lieut.-Colonel Royal Field Artillery, Commanding 301st Brigade, Royal Field Artillery.
CUNNINGHAM, CUTHBERT COLPOYS, Major (Acting Lieut.-Colonel), 12th Pioneers, Indian Army, Commanding 2/107th Pioneers, Indian Army.
DAVIES, WARBURTON EDWARD, C.M.G., Major and Brevet Lieut.-Colonel (Temporary Lieut.-Colonel), Rifle Brigade.
DAVSON, HAROLD JOHN HUNTER, Major (Acting Lieut.-Colonel), 82nd Punjabis, Indian Army, Commanding 3/154th Infantry, Indian Army.
DOBBIN, ARTHUR WILLIAM, Major, Royal Garrison Artillery, Commanding Anti-Aircraft Group.
FLINT, ERIC CHARLES MONTAGU, Capt. (Temporary Major), Suffolk Yeomanry, Commanding 19th Squadron, Machine Gun Corps.
FORD-YOUNG, ARCHIBALD, Temporary Major, Royal Engineers, attached 2nd Field Squadron, Australian Engineers.
FORREST, THOMAS BROWN, Capt. (Acting Major), 8th Battn. Highland Light Infantry, Territorial Force, attached 53rd Battn. Machine Gun Corps.
GASKELL, GEOFFREY WHITTAL, Major, Royal Field Artillery, Commanding "A" Battery, 267th Brigade.
GOURLIE, JAMES, Major, 38th Central India Horse, Indian Army.
GWATKIN, FREDERICK, M.C., Major, 18th Lancers, Indian Army.
HAWES, CLAUDE MACKINNON, Major, 20th Punjabis, Indian Army.
HEDLEY, WALTER, Major, Royal Garrison Artillery, Territorial Force, Commanding 300th Siege Battery, Royal Garrison Artillery.
HILL, ERNEST FREDERICK JOHN, M.C., Major and Brevet Lieut.-Colonel (Acting Lieut.-Colonel), Royal Engineers.
HODGSON, WALTER THORNTON, M.C., Major and Brevet Lieut.-Colonel (Temporary Lieut.-Colonel), 1st Royal Dragoons.
HOLDERNESS, HARDWICKE, Major, 1st Gurkha Rifles, Indian Army, attached 1/50th Kumaon Rifles, Indian Army.
IMBERT-TERRY, HENRY BOUHIER, M.C., Major, Royal Artillery.
JARVIS, CECIL, M.C., Major, 20th Deccan Horse, Indian Army.
KEELAN, HENRY PERCIVAL, Lieut.-Colonel, 121st Pioneers, Indian Army.
KEIGHLEY, VERNON AUBREY SCOTT, M.V.O., Lieut.-Colonel, Indian Army, Commanding 18th Lancers, Indian Army.
KENSINGTON, EDGAR CLAUDE, M.C., Major and Brevet Lieut.-Colonel (Acting Lieut.-Colonel), 130th Baluchis, Indian Army, Commanding 91st Punjabis, Indian Army.
KILLICK, ALEXANDER HERBERT, M.C., Lieut. (Temporary Capt. and Acting Major), South Lancashire Regt. and 10th Battn. Machine Gun Corps.
LANE, ROWLAND HILL, Major, Royal Field Artillery, Territorial Force, Commanding "B" Battery, 263rd Brigade, Royal Field Artillery.
LATHAM, ALAN, Major, 1st Gurkha Rifles, Indian Army, attached 1/50th Kumaon Rifles, Indian Army.
LONGDEN, ARTHUR BERRIDGE, Lieut.-Colonel, 38th Dogras, Indian Army.
MACKINTOSH, JOHN BURN, Lieut.-Colonel, Royal Garrison Artillery, Commanding 103rd Brigade.
MARR, JAMES HEPPELL, Temporary Capt. (Acting Major), 65th Field Company, Royal Engineers.
MARRYAT, JOHN RUDOLPH, M.C., Capt. and Brevet Major (Temporary Lieut.-Colonel), Royal Engineers.
MARTIN, JASPER, M.C., Major (Acting Major), 94th Russell's Infantry, Indian Army, Commanding 2/97th Infantry, Indian Army.
McLAREN, HENRY, M.C., Capt. (Acting Major), Royal Engineers, Territorial Force, Commanding General Headquarters, Signalling Company, Royal Engineers.
McPHERSON, JOHN, Major, Royal Field Artillery, Territorial Force, Commanding 372nd Battery, 8th Brigade, Royal Field Artillery.
MELHUISH, HERBERT MICHAEL HENRY, Major and Brevet Lieut.-Colonel (Acting Lieut.-Colonel), Indian Medical Service, Commanding 111th Combined Field Ambulance.
MURRAY, WALTER GODFREY PATRICK, Lieut.-Colonel, Indian Army Commanding 1/21st Punjabis, Indian Army.
NEILL, ELIEZER SHEPHERD, Temporary Major, 38th Battn. Royal Fusiliers.
NORTHAMPTON, THE MARQUIS OF, WILLIAM BINGHAM, Capt. (Acting Major), Royal Horse Guards, Commanding 5th Signalling Squadron, Royal Engineers.
O'HARA, ERRIL ROBERT, C.M.G., Major and Brevet Lieut.-Colonel (Temporary Lieut.-Colonel), Royal Army Service Corps.
PENTON, BERTIE CYRIL, Major (Acting Lieut.-Colonel), 25th Punjabis, Indian Army, Commanding 1/152nd Punjabis, Indian Army.
POË, JOHN HUGH LOVETT, Major (Temporary Lieut.-Colonel), West India Regt., Commanding 2nd British West Indies Regt.
READ, RICHARD VALENTINE, M.C., Capt. (Temporary Major), Essex Regt.
ROWCROFT, CLAUDE HAROLD, Lieut.-Colonel, Indian Army, Commanding 9th Hodson's Horse, Indian Army.
RUCK, OLIVER LAURENCE, Major, 1/54th Sikhs, Indian Army.
SAMUEL, HENRY THOMAS, Major (Acting Lieut.-Colonel), Royal Army Medical Corps, Territorial Force, Commanding 170th Indian Combined Field Ambulance.
SCOTT, GILBERT, Major (Temporary Lieut.-Colonel), 6th Battn. Lancashire Fusiliers, Territorial Force, Commanding 75th Battn. Machine Gun Corps.
SMYTH, VILLIERS GORDON, Capt. (Acting Major), Royal Garrison Artillery, Commanding 16th Mountain Battery.
SOMERVILLE, JAMES AUBREY HENRY BELLINGHAM, Major, Royal Garrison Artillery, Commanding 29th Indian Mountain Battery.
STEWART, JOHN, Major and Brevet Lieut.-Colonel (Acting Lieut.-Colonel), Reserve of Officers, Royal Highlanders, Commanding 2nd Battn. (rank corrected to Major (acting Lieut.-Colonel) [London Gazette, 8 Aug. 1919]).
TREHARNE, DAVID ERIC, Capt. (Acting Major), Royal Field Artillery Territorial Force, attached 265th Brigade, Royal Field Artillery.

WALLER, ROBERT DE WARRENNE, Major, 108th Infantry, Indian Army, attached 58th Rifles, Indian Army.
WATSON, DOUGLAS STRATHAM, Major, 1/5th Battn. Somersetshire Light Infantry, Territorial Force.
WATSON, ERIC VICTOR, Major, Royal Garrison Artillery, Commanding 428th Battery, Royal Field Artillery.
WILKINSON, CHARLES ROBERT, Major (Acting Lieut.-Colonel), 52nd Sikhs, Indian Army, Commanding 2/152nd Punjabis, Indian Army.

AUSTRALIAN IMPERIAL FORCE.

HOWELL-PRICE, FREDERICK PHILLIMORE, Major, Australian Army Service Crops.
NEWTON, FRANK GRAHAM, C.B.E., Lieut.-Colonel, Australian General List.
SINGLE, CLIVE VALLACK, Major (Temporary Lieut.-Colonel), Australian Army Medical Corps, Commanding 4th Light Horse Field Ambulance.
STUART, GERALD EUGENE MACDONALD, Lieut.-Colonel, Australian Army Medical Corps, Commanding 3rd Light Horse Field Ambulance.

London Gazette, 3 June, 1919.—" War Office, 3 June, 1919. The King has been graciously pleased, on the occasion of His Majesty's Birthday, to approve of the undermentioned rewards for distinguished service in connection with military operations in Italy. Dated 3 June, 1919. Awarded a Bar to the Distinguished Service Order."

GELL, WILLIAM CHARLES COLEMAN, D.S.O., M.C., Capt. and Brevet Major (Acting Lieut.-Colonel), 1/5th Battn. Royal Warwickshire Regt., Territorial Force.
(D.S.O. gazetted 1 Jan. 1918.)
PRYOR, WALTER MARLBOROUGH, D.S.O., Capt. and Brevet Major (Acting Lieut.-Colonel), Hertfordshire Regt., attached 1/6th Battn. Royal Warwickshire Regt., Territorial Force.
(D.S.O. gazetted 18 June, 1917.)

Awarded the Distinguished Service Order:
BARNE, WILLIAM BRADLEY GOSSET, Major (Temporary Lieut.-Colonel), Royal Garrison Artillery.
BROOKS, HENRY JAMES, M.C., Temporary Major, General List.
CRAWFORD, JOHN RISDON MURDOCH, M.C., Capt. (Acting Major), 475th (South Midland) Field Company, Royal Engineers, Territorial Force.
GARRATT, LAWRENCE FRANCIS, M.C., Capt. (Acting Major), 105th Siege Battery, Royal Garrison Artillery.
GORDON, WILLIAM, M.C., Capt. (Acting Lieut.-Colonel), 2nd Battn. Gordon Highlanders.
HOARE, ALBERT, M.C., Lieut. (Acting Major), 155th Heavy Battery, Royal Garrison Artillery.
LAWRENCE, EDWARD LAFONE GRAHAM, M.C., Capt. and Brevet Major (Temporary Major), Worcestershire Regt.
LINCOLN, PHILIP LIONEL, M.C., Temporary Major, 10th Battn. Northumberland Fusiliers.
LINDSAY, GEORGE HUMPHREY MAURICE, Capt. and Brevet Major, King's Own Scottish Borderers, Brigade Major, 143rd Infantry Brigade.
MOSLEY, WILFRID HUMPHREY, M.C., Major, 2nd Battn. Wiltshire Regt., attached 11th Battn. Northumberland Fusiliers.
O'REILLY, CHARLES JOSEPH, M.C., M.D., Capt. (Temporary Major), 70th Field Ambulance, Royal Army Medical Corps.
SIMPSON, JAMES GRAY, M.C., Capt. (Temporary Major), Cameron Highlanders.
THOMPSON, ALLEN EDGAR, M.C., M.D., Temporary Capt., Royal Army Medical Corps, attached 8th Battn. York and Lancaster Regt.
VAUGHAN, EDMUND WAYNE, M.C., M.B., Capt. (Acting Lieut.-Colonel), 23rd Field Ambulance, Royal Army Medical Corps.
VINER, EDWARD, Temporary Major, 24th Battn. Manchester Regt.
WRIGHT, PHILIP LOWNDES, M.C., Capt. (Acting Major), Buckinghamshire Battn. Oxfordshire and Buckinghamshire Light Infantry, Territorial Force.
WILSON, CHARLES STUART, C.B., C.M.G., Colonel (Temporary Major-General), late Royal Engineers.

London Gazette, 3 June, 1919.—" War Office, 3 June, 1919. The King has been graciously pleased, on the occasion of His Majesty's Birthday, to approve of the undermentioned rewards for distinguished service in connection with military operations in the Balkans. Dated 3 June, 1919. Awarded the Distinguished Service Order."

BARKER, EVELYN HUGH, M.C., Capt., King's Royal Rifle Corps.
HERRING, EDMUND FRANCIS, M.C., Temporary Lieut. (Acting Major), Royal Field Artillery.
JACKSON, BASIL ARCHER, M.C., Temporary Major, 8th Battn. Shropshire Light Infantry, attached 9th Battn. Royal Lancaster Regt.
KNOLLYS, DENIS ERSKINE, Major (Acting Lieut.-Colonel), Indian Army.
KREYER, JOHN ARTHUR CLAUDE, Major, 28th Light Cavalry, Indian Army.
MASON, HUMPHREY FRANCIS, Temporary Major, Royal Garrison Artillery
PELTZER, ANTON, Temporary Major (Acting Lieut.-Colonel), 9th Battn. East Lancashire Regt.
RICKWOOD, HAROLD GEORGE, M.C., Temporary Major (Acting Lieut.-Colonel), 9th Battn. South Lancashire Regt.
ROGERS-TILLSTONE, ERNEST MONKHOUSE, M.C., Lieut. (Acting Major), Royal Field Artillery, Special Reserve.
SHAW, FRANK VINCENT, M.C., Temporary Major, Royal Field Artillery.
TOMLINSON, PERCY STANLEY, Capt. and Brevet Major (Acting Lieut. Colonel), Royal Army Medical Corps.
WATSON, STANLEY, M.C., Capt. (Temporary Major and Acting Lieut.-Colonel), Cheshire Regt., attached 12th Battn.

London Gazette, 3 June, 1919.—" War Office, 3 June, 1919. The King has been graciously pleased, on the occasion of His Majesty's Birthday, to approve of the undermentioned rewards for distinguished services rendered in connection with military operations in Mesopotamia. Dated 3 June, 1919. Awarded the Distinguished Service Order."

FRAZER, FREDERICK ARTHUR, Lieut.-Colonel, 1/5th Battn. Royal West Kent Regt., Territorial Force.

NOEL, EDWARD WILLIAM CHARLES, C.I.E., Capt., Indian Army, attached Political Department.
SHUTTLEWORTH, DIGBY INGLIS, Major and Brevet Lieut.-Colonel (Temporary Lieut.-Colonel), 3rd Gurkha Rifles, Indian Army.
STOKES, CLAUDE BAYFIELD, C.I.E., Major and Brevet Lieut.-Colonel, 3rd Skinner's Horse, Indian Army.

London Gazette, 3 June, 1919.—" War Office, 3 June, 1919. The King has been graciously pleased, on the occasion of His Majesty's Birthday, to approve of the undermentioned rewards for distinguished service in connection with military operations in East Africa. Dated 3 June, 1919. Awarded the Distinguished Service Order."

BEVAN, EDWARD BECKFORD, Capt. (Temporary Major) (Acting Lieut.-Colonel), Norfolk Regt. and 1/2nd King's African Rifles.
MASTERS, ALEXANDER CHARLES, M.C., Capt. (Temporary Major), South Wales Borderers and 1/1st Battn. King's African Rifles.
PHILLIPS, CHARLES GEORGE, M.C., Capt. (Temporary Lieut.-Colonel), West Yorkshire Regt. and 3/2nd King's African Rifles.

London Gazette, 3 June, 1919.—" War Office, 3 June, 1919. The King has been graciously pleased, on the occasion of His Majesty's Birthday, to approve of the undermentioned rewards for distinguished services rendered in connection with military operations in Eastern Russia. Dated 3 June, 1919. Awarded the Distinguished Service Order."

DUNLOP, CHARLES, O.B.E., Temporary Lieut. (Temporary Major), Scottish Rifles.

CANADIAN FORCES.

BOYLE, JAMES WHITESIDE, Lieut.-Colonel, Canadian Militia (Christian name corrected to Joseph Whiteside).

London Gazette, 3 June, 1919—" Air Ministry, Strand, London, W.C. 2., 3 June, 1919. His Majesty the King has been graciously pleased to approve of the undermentioned rewards to Officers of the Royal Air Force, in recognition of distinguished services rendered during the war. Awarded a Bar to the Distinguished Service Order."

BOWHILL, FREDERICK WILLIAM, D.S.O., Lieut.-Colonel (Mediterranean).
(D.S.O. gazetted 22 Feb. 1918.)

Awarded the Distinguished Service Order:
BIRCH, WYNDHAM LINDSAY, M.B.E., Capt. (Acting Major) (West Yorkshire Regt.) (Egypt).
GOSSAGE, ERNEST LESLIE, M.C., Lieut.-Colonel (Royal Artillery) (France).
KING, ROY, D.F.C., Capt. (Australian Flying Corps) (France).
MACLEAN, CUTHBERT TRELAWDER, M.C., Lieut.-Colonel (Royal Scots Fusiliers) (France).
PATTINSON, LAURENCE ARTHUR, M.C., D.F.C., Major (Acting Lieut.-Colonel) (Royal Fusiliers), I. Force (France).
RISK, CHARLES ERSKINE, Lieut.-Colonel (Royal Marine Light Infantry) (Mediterranean).
RUSSELL, JOHN CANNON, Major (Royal Engineers, Territorial Force) (France).

London Gazette, 11 June, 1919.—" Admiralty, 11 June, 1919. The King has been graciously pleased to approve of the award of the following honours to the undermentioned Officers. To be Companions of the Distinguished Service Order."

HOMAN, EDWIN ANDERSON, Commander, Royal Navy. For distinguished services in command of Torpedo Boat Destroyers throughout the war.
ISGAR, REGINALD CHARLES, DUDLEY Lieut.-Commander (now Commander), Royal Naval Volunteer Reserve. For distinguished services in the prosecution of the war.
HUTCHINGS, JOHN FENWICK, Lieut.-Commander, Royal Navy. For distinguished services in command of submarines throughout the war.

London Gazette, 21 June, 1919.—" Admiralty, 21 June, 1919. The King has been graciously pleased to approve of the award of the following honours to the undermentioned Officers. To be Companions of the Distinguished Service Order."

NICOLSON, THE HONOURABLE ERSKINE ARTHUR, Commander, Royal Navy. For distinguished services as War Staff Officer in the Light Cruiser Squadrons.
ARBUTHNOT, GEOFFRY SCHOMBERG, Commander, Royal Navy. For distinguished services as Executive and Gunnery Officer of H.M.S. Inconstant in the 1st Light Cruiser Squadron (Christian name Geoffry Schomberg corrected to Geoffrey Schomberg [London Gazette, 27 June, 1919]).
BARKER, CECIL, Engineer Commander, Royal Navy. For distinguished services as Engineer Officer of H.M.S. Canterbury in the Harwich Force.
DAVIES, THOMAS GEORGE REES, Engineer Commander, Royal Navy. For distinguished services as Engineer Officer of H.M. Ships Crusader, Nimrod and Dublin.
BADCOCK, KENNETH EDGAR, D.S.C., Paymaster Commander, Royal Navy. For distinguished services as Secretary to Rear-Admiral Sir Reginald Y. Tyrwhitt, K.C.B., D.S.O., throughout the war.
BROUNGER, THOMAS MACLEAN, Lieut.-Commander, Royal Navy. For distinguished services as Navigating Officer of H.M.S. Inconstant in the 1st Light Cruiser Squadron.
BROOKS, ARTHUR WILLIAM, Lieut.-Commander, Royal Navy. For distinguished services as Gunnery Officer of H.M.S. Nottingham and later of H.M.S. Birmingham, Flagship of the 2nd Light Cruiser Squadron.
HENSMAN, MELVILL, Lieut.-Commander, Royal Navy. For distinguished services as Navigating Officer of H.M. Ships Undaunted and Coventry in the Harwich Force.
GELL, WILLIAM HOPE, Lieut.-Commander, Royal Navy. For distinguished services as Navigating Officer of H.M. Ships Penelope and Centaur in the Harwich Force.
SPOONER, ERNEST JOHN, Lieut. (now Lieut.-Commander), Royal Navy. For distinguished services as Navigating Officer of H.M. Ships Constance and Calliope.

" Honours for the Mercantile Marine.—The King has been graciously pleased to approve of the award of the following honour to the undermentioned Officer of the Mercantile Marine, in recognition of zeal and devotion to duty shown in carrying on the trade of the country during the war. To be a Companion of the Distinguished Service Order."

SOLA, PERCY, Capt. (Lieut., Royal Naval Reserve).

London Gazette, 27 June, 1919.—"War Office, 27 June, 1919. His Majesty the King has been graciously pleased to approve of the following awards to the undermentioned Officers, in recognition of their gallantry and devotion to duty in the field. Awarded a Second Bar to the Distinguished Service Order."

BOYALL, ALFRED MOREY, D.S.O., Major and Brevet Lieut.-Colonel, 1st Battn. West Yorkshire Regt. On 21 March, 1918, when the whole of the front line had gone and the reserve to the right of the battalion had been taken by the enemy, he continued to control the situation with the greatest coolness and gallantry, and by his fine example inspired the remaining garrison of the front-line trenches to hold out till dusk. This resistance in the front-line system was most valuable in delaying the enemy's advance on the corps front.
(D.S.O. gazetted 27 Sept. 1901.)
(First Bar gazetted 4 Feb. 1918.)

Awarded a Bar to the Distinguished Service Order:

BUZZARD, FRANK ANSTIE, D.S.O., Lieut.-Colonel, Royal Artillery (Mesopotamia). For conspicuous gallantry and devotion to duty during operations at Sherqat 24–30 Oct. 1918. On night of 26–27 Oct, 1918, and again on night of 29–30 Oct. 1918, he got his brigade on the move and into action with the greatest celerity after a march, on the latter occasion, of 26 miles in 7 hours. It was largely due to his promptness of action that the operation, which resulted in the capture of large numbers of prisoners, was entirely successful.
(D.S.O. gazetted 1 Jan. 1917.)

DEACON, HENRY ROBERT GORDON, D.S.O., Lieut.-Colonel, Connaught Rangers, attached Highland Light Infantry (Mesopotamia). For conspicuous gallantry and devotion to duty during operations at Sherqat 24–30 Oct, 1918. On the 24th Oct. 1918, his battalion, during a night advance, suddenly came under heavy fire at close range from a wired redoubt, which he rushed and captured. It was mainly due to his coolness and the discipline which he had instilled into his battalion that he was able to keep his men together at this critical moment. On the 29th Oct. 1918, he also displayed initiative and gallant leadership.
(D.S.O. gazetted 14 Jan. 1916.)

HAWES, CHARLES HOWARD, D.S.O., M.V.O., Lieut.-Colonel, 23rd Cavalry, Indian Army (Mesopotamia). For conspicuous gallantry and ability to command during operations at Sherqat 24–30 Oct. 1918. He handled his regiment both in attack and defence against vastly superior numbers of the enemy most efficiently, and the success gained was largely due to his gallant example and bold leadership.
(D.S.O. gazetted 22 Dec. 1916.)

McVEAN, DONALD ARCHIBALD DUGALD, D.S.O., Lieut.-Colonel, 45th Sikhs, Indian Army (Mesopotamia). For conspicuous gallantry and devotion to duty and ability as a battalion commander during operations at Sherqat 24–30 Oct. 1918. He led his regiment into action after a series of most trying and arduous marches over difficult country, covering over 60 miles in 70 hours, and in the end through a heavy artillery and machine-gun barrage. He displayed courage, determination and leadership of a high order.
(D.S.O. gazetted 2 Sept. 1902.)

Awarded the Distinguished Service Order:

BODKIN, LEO FRANCIS, Major, 1st Battn. 112th Infantry, Indian Army (Mesopotamia). For conspicuous gallantry and devotion to duty during an attack at Sherqat on 29–30 Oct. 1918. Although wounded in the knee, he made light of the pain and gallantly carried on with great determination and initiative all night, till the enemy surrendered at dawn. He was then unable to move and was evacuated to hospital. His fine example had an inspiriting effect on his men.

COLE-HAMILTON, HUGH ARTHUR WILLOUGHBY, Capt. (Acting Major), York and Lancaster Regt., attached 1st Battn. West Yorkshire Regt. On 21 March, 1918, east of Monchies, in command of two companies, successfully protected the exposed flank of the battalion throughout the day under very heavy fire. During this defence he crawled out some 60 yards in face of point-blank fire and dragged another officer back to safety. Throughout he showed conspicuous courage and devotion to duty, and his determined defence was of great value.

CROSSING, WALTER LEONARD, D.S.C., Temporary Capt., Mounted Machine Gun Corps (Mesopotamia). For conspicuous gallantry and devotion to duty at Kisiliar on 15 Oct. 1918. He drove his armoured car up to the enemy's lines, bringing such a heavy and accurate enfilade fire to bear on the enemy that they were forced to withdraw. His car was eventually struck by a shell, which killed three of the crew and wounded him and another man. In spite of his wounds he carried the man back under heavy fire to our own lines. He has on all occasions displayed great coolness in action.

EDWARDES, JOHN GRAHAME, Lieut.-Colonel, 1st Battn. 3rd Gurkha Rifles, Indian Army (Mesopotamia). For conspicuous gallantry and skilful leadership during operations at Sherqat 24–30 Oct. 1918, and especially on 28 Oct, 1918, when he led his battalion with great skill down to the edge of the river, thereby preventing the enemy from crossing. The success of this bold enterprise, carried out under heavy fire, greatly increased the number of prisoners captured.

HARTLAND-MAHON, MARCUS JAMES, Lieut.-Colonel, Royal Artillery (Mesopotamia). For conspicuous gallantry and ability to command during operations at Sherqat 24–30 Oct. 1918. Owing to his courage, initiative and untiring energy his batteries were always in action at the time and place required by the situation. He never spared himself, and fought his batteries magnificently throughout, greatly facilitating the further advance of the troops engaged.

HILL, GEORGE ALEXANDER, M.C., Capt., 4th Battn. Manchester Regt. and Royal Flying Corps (Northern Russia). He has since early December, 1917, been constantly working between the north of Russia and Roumania and Southern Russia. He has attended Bolshevik meetings at night when street fighting was at its height, passing back and forth through the Bolshevik fighting lines, and has been almost daily under fire without protection. He has conducted himself with courage and coolness and rendered valuable service.

LONG, HOWARD OAKEY, Lieut., No. 3 Squadron, Royal Flying Corps, now Royal Air Force. For most conspicuous gallantry and ability during June and July, 1916. He initiated low-flying attacks on troops, transport and trains far beyond the enemy lines. He also brought down several enemy aeroplanes. These flights were carried out alone and unescorted. He did splendid work.

LUMB, FREDERICK GEORGE EDWARD, M.C., Major (Acting Lieut.-Colonel), 1st Battn. 30th Garhwal Rifles, Indian Army (Mesopotamia). For conspicuous gallantry and determination during operations at Sherqat 24–30 Oct. 1918. After a 33-mile march he crossed a river in support of a cavalry brigade, which was being hard pressed, and by his skilful and bold handling of his battalion inflicted heavy loss on the enemy, and was largely responsible for their surrendering. His quick and clear appreciation of the situation was invaluable.

SHOUBRIDGE, CHARLES ALBAN GREVIS, Major (Acting Lieut.-Colonel), 1st Battn. 112th Infantry, Indian Army (Mesopotamia). For conspicuous gallantry and devotion to duty and ability to command throughout the operations 24–30 Oct. 1918, and especially at Sherqat on 29 Oct. 1918, in which action he displayed marked good judgment and coolness, and by his untiring energy and fine leadership inspired all ranks with confidence. The very high state of efficiency of his battalions was borne out by their steadiness in battle.

STEWART, ARCHIBALD CAMPBELL, Lieut.-Colonel, Corps of Guides, Indian Army (Mesopotamia). For conspicuous gallantry and devotion to duty during operations 21–30 Oct. 1918, at Sherqat. By his personal influence and gallant and cheerful leadership all determined efforts on the part of the enemy to break the right centre of our line during 28 Oct. and night of 28–29 Oct. 1918, were successfully repulsed. His regiment, encouraged by his fine example, displayed conspicuous endurance and staunchness throughout the operations.

WALKER, PHILIP LIONEL EDWARD, Capt. (Acting Lieut.-Colonel), 7th Hussars, attached 1st Battn. East Lancashire Regt. For conspicuous gallantry and devotion to duty during an attempt to cross the River Rhonella, near Marcsches, on 27 Oct. 1918. Hearing that the leading company had crossed a tributary in mistake for the river itself, he took two runners and went forward to reconnoitre the banks. The far bank was strongly held by enemy machine guns and riflemen, and he and his patrol came under their fire at close range, and he was severely wounded.

CANADIAN FORCE.

JOHNSON, WALTER WALLACE, M.C., Lieut. (Acting Capt.), 58th Battn. 2nd Central Ontario Regt. For most conspicuous gallantry and devotion to duty during the attack on Marcoing line 28–29 Sept., and on Pont D'Aire 1 Oct. 1918. He went forward under heavy machine-gun fire, located gaps in the enemy wire, and afterwards led a night attack, progressing some 1,200 yards. He then led parties to clear up isolated posts, himself capturing a light trench mortar crew. Next day he did good work placing his Lewis guns, thereby assisting the advance on the right. On 1 Oct. he and his serjeant-major went forward to make a reconnaissance, during which they rushed a machine-gun post, killing the crew. He showed splendid courage, and his example inspired all ranks.

London Gazette, 27 June, 1919.—"War Office, 27 June, 1919. Amendment. The notification of the award of the Military Cross to the undermentioned Officer, which was published in the London Gazette dated 2 April, 1919, is cancelled, and the award of the D.S.O. is substituted."

PEMBERTON, HAROLD CHARLES, Temporary Captain, 20th Battn., attached 16th Battn. Lancashire Fusiliers.

London Gazette, 27 June, 1919.—"Admiralty, 27 June, 1919. The King has been graciously pleased to approve of the award of the following honours, in recognition of the services of the undermentioned Officers during the war. To be Companions of the Distinguished Service Order."

FRASER, RONALD MOUNTSTEVENS, Commander, Royal Navy. For distinguished services in H.M.S. Galatea, 1st Light Cruiser Squadron, during minelaying operations and in action with the enemy.

JOHNSON, HARRY HERBERT, Engineer Commander, Royal Navy. For distinguished services as Engineer Officer, H.M.S. Caledon, 1st Light Cruiser Squadron.

SHRUBSOLE, PERCY JOSEPH, Engineer Commander, Royal Navy. For distinguished services as Engineer Officer of H.M.S. Calypso, 6th Light Cruiser Squadron.

JOHNSON, CECIL HARVEY, Engineer Commander, Royal Navy. For distinguished services as Engineer Officer of H.M.S. Cassandra, 6th Light Cruiser Squadron.

NICHOLSON, JAMES BELL, Engineer Commander, Royal Navy. For distinguished services as Engineer Officer, H.M.S. Royalist, 1st Light Cruiser Squadron.

COOMBER, THOMAS GEORGE, Engineer Commander, Royal Navy. For distinguished services as Engineer Officer, H.M.S. Galatea, 1st Light Cruiser Squadron.

POWELL, JAMES, Lieut.-Commander, Royal Navy. For distinguished services as Navigating Officer, H.M.S. Royalist, 1st Light Cruiser Squadron, whilst employed in minelaying operations in the North Sea.

LEGGE, THE HONOURABLE HUMPHRY, Lieut.-Commander, Royal Navy. For distinguished services as Flag Lieut. to Rear-Admiral Sir Edwyn S. Alexander-Sinclair, K.C.B., M.V.O., in the 1st and 6th Light Cruiser Squadrons.

LYSTER, ARTHUR LUMLEY ST. GEORGE, Lieut.-Commander, Royal Navy. For distinguished services as Gunnery Officer of H.M.S. Cassandra, 6th Light Cruiser Squadron.

MEIKLEJOHN, NORMAN SINCLAIR, Surgeon Lieut.-Commander, Royal Navy. For distinguished services in H.M.S. Caledon, as Senior Medical Officer, 1st Light Cruiser Squadron.

DE DENNE, CECIL HUGH, Paymaster Lieut.-Commander, Royal Navy. For distinguished services as Secretary to Rear-Admiral Sir Walter H. Cowan, K.C.B., D.S.O., M.V.O., Commanding 1st Light Cruiser Squadron.

WEBSTER, JOHN THOMAS VICTOR, Paymaster Lieut.-Commander, Royal Navy. For valuable services as Secretary to Rear-Admiral Sir Edwyn S. Alexander-Sinclair, K.C.B., M.V.O., in the 1st and 6th Light Cruiser Squadrons.

MORGAN, CHARLES ERIC, Lieut., Royal Navy. For distinguished services as Navigating Officer, H.M.S. Caledon, 1st Light Cruiser Squadron.

London Gazette, 10 July, 1919.—"Admiralty, 10 July, 1919. The King has been graciously pleased to approve of the award of the following honour to the undermentioned Officer. To be a Companion of the Distinguished Service Order."

TOVEY, JOHN CROMYN, Lieut.-Commander (now Commander), Royal Navy. For distinguished services in command of H.M.S. Onslow.

London Gazette, 12 July, 1919.—"Admiralty, S.W., 12 July, 1919. The King has been graciously pleased to approve of the award of the following honours to the undermentioned officers. To be Companions of the Distinguished Service Order."

BOISSIER, MARTIN EDWARD SCOBELL, Commander, Royal Navy. For distinguished services as Flag Commander to Admiral Sir T. H. Martyn Jerram, K.C.B., K.C.M.G., when Vice-Admiral Commanding Second Battle Squadron.

USSHER, RICHARD, Lieut.-Commander, Royal Navy. For distinguished services as Gunnery Officer of H.M.S. Hyacinth, Flagship of the Commander-in-Chief, Cape Station.

BUSH, ATHELSTAN PAUL, Lieut., Royal Navy. For distinguished services during the war.

TUDWAY, LIONEL CHARLES PAUL, D.S.C., Lieut., Royal Navy. For distinguished services in command of H.M. Gunboat Sumana during the Siege of Kut-al-Amarah from the 5th Dec. 1915, to the 29th April, 1916.

London Gazette, 15 July, 1919.—"War Office, 15 July, 1919. His Majesty the King has been graciously pleased to approve of the following immediate awards for conspicuous gallantry and devotion to duty in North Russia, conferred by Major-General C. C. M. Maynard, C.B., C.M.G., D.S.O., in pursuance of the powers vested in him by His ajesty. Awarded the Distinguished Service Order."

CANADIAN FORCE.

ANDERSON, PETER, Major, Alberta Regt., attached Malamute Company. Knowing that the enemy were preparing another attack from Ourosozero, he rapidly replaced a bridge without their knowledge, and attacked them early on 11 April, 1919, with an armoured train, killing and capturing a number, together with two field guns and one machine gun. He showed marked gallantry and nitiative throughout.

"His Majesty the King has been graciously pleased to approve of the following immediate awards for conspicuous gallantry and devotion to duty in North Russia, conferred by Major-General W. E. Ironside, C.M.G., D.S.O., in pursuance of the powers vested in him by His Majesty. Awarded the Distinguished Service Order."

BODY, OLIVER GUY, Capt. (Acting Major), Royal Field Artillery. For conspicuous gallantry and ability in action. During the operations near Kodish on 7 Feb. 1919, he displayed great coolness and courage. The situation having demanded that his guns should be advanced, he personally went forward under heavy machine-gun and rifle fire to reconnoitre, after which he enabled the infantry to withdraw under cover of barrage fire. His work with this force has at all times been excellent.

CARROLL, JOHN WILLIAM VINCENT, C.M.G., Lieut.-Colonel, Norfolk Regt. He commanded the Russian forces at Morjegorskaia during the heavy enemy attacks on 14 and 17 March, 1919. It was due to his fine leadership and personal gallantry that the young Russian troops stood firm and turned a critical situation into a decisive success. His energy and coolness were beyond praise.

HENDERSON, ARCHIE DOUGLAS, Temporary Capt. (Temporary Major), Norfolk Regt. He commanded at Vistafka during enemy attacks, 28 Feb. to 4 March, 1919. Regardless of personal danger, he was the chief source of strength to the garrison, and by his untiring work and devotion to duty held Vistafka for the column, and thus saved the column from a forced withdrawal.

PALMER, ALGEY, Lieut. (Temporary Capt.), 6th Battn. Northumberland Fusiliers, Territorial Force. He showed great courage and ability during the attacks on Vistafka, 28 Feb.–4 March, 1919. During very heavy shelling and machine-gun fire he stood on the roof of a house observing our artillery fire, and by his accurate and prompt reports rendered invaluable services. His whole work during a month's unrelieved service in the front line has been very fine.

WATSON, HENRY NEVILLE GRYLLS, Capt. (Temporary Major), Royal Army Service Corps. For conspicuous ability and coolness during the operations against Zemstova, 24-29 March, 1919. He was responsible for the organization of all transport operating over a very large area during the operations 20 Feb. to 4 April, Pinega Area. He personally took charge of the transport column in the most forward area, and it was owing to him that its withdrawal under fire was uniformly successful.

London Gazette, 17 July, 1919.—"Admiralty, 17 July, 1919. The King has been graciously pleased to approve of the award of the following honour to the undermentioned Officer. To be a Companion of the Distinguished Service Order."

WROTTESLEY, FRANCIS ROBERT, Commander, Royal Navy. For distinguished services in command of No. 14 Kite Balloon Section in Mesopotamia from Aug. 1916, to Feb. 1917.

London Gazette, 30 July, 1919.—"War Office, 30 July, 1919. With reference to the awards conferred as announced in the London Gazette dated 15 Feb. 1919, the following are the statements of services for which the decorations were conferred. Awarded a Third Bar to the Distinguished Service Order."

CROFT, WILLIAM DENMAN, D.S.O., Major and Brevet Lieut.-Colonel (Temporary Brigadier-General), Scottish Rifles, General Officer Commanding 27th Infantry Brigade. From 28 Sept. 1918, onwards he displayed the utmost energy, skill and gallantry in the command of his brigade, notably on 1 Oct., when his right flank was exposed and heavily counter-attacked at Ledeghem. His handling of his brigade on 15 Oct. resulted in his overcoming all opposition and reaching the line of the Lys, and thus attaining all his objectives. On the occasion of the crossing of the Lys on the night 16–17 Oct., which necessitated his crossing in daylight under heavy machine-gun fire at close range to visit his battalions on the eastern bank, his example and confidence inspired his troops, who, though strongly counter-attacked and heavily shelled, maintained their position until relieved.
(D.S.O. gazetted 1 Jan. 1917.)
(1st Bar gazetted 10 Jan. 1917.)
(2nd Bar gazetted 26 July, 1918.)

Awarded a Second Bar to the Distinguished Service Order:

BROOKE, GEORGE FRANK, D.S.O., Temporary Lieut.-Colonel, Reserve of Officers, attached 14th Battn. Welsh Regt. For gallant and skilful leading of his battalion near Villers Outreaux, 8 Oct. 1918. Owing to another brigade having been checked in their attack on the front enemy trenches, his battalion had to delay their advance for some time while suffering heavily from artillery barrage. By his personal efforts, skill and determination the battalion, which had been thrown into some confusion, was rallied and assembled for the further advance, eventually reaching the final objective, which included the capture of Malincourt en route. It was almost entirely due to his gallant leading that the advance was enabled to continue after the check experienced.
(D.S.O. gazetted 4 June, 1917.)
(Bar gazetted 2 Dec. 1918.)

IRWIN, ALFRED PERCY BULTEEL, D.S.O., Capt. and Brevet Major (Temporary Lieut.-Colonel), East Surrey Regt., commanding 8th Battn. For conspicuous gallantry and devotion to duty at Ronssoy, 18 Sept. 1918, in command of his battalion. He kept his troops close behind the attacking unit, and when the latter was held up he went forward with two runners in face of heavy fire and made a rapid reconnaissance. When suddenly attacked by nine of the enemy he and his runners killed them all, afterwards taking many prisoners in the village. He then returned and led his two assaulting companies to their first objective. After reorganizing with reinforcements under intense fire he led the attack on the final objective. Throughout the day his behaviour was splendid, and the great fight put up by his battalion was due to his bold and able leadership.
(D.S.O. gazetted 20 Oct. 1916.)
(Bar gazetted 26 July, 1917.)

LLOYD, LEMUEL, D.S.O., Temporary Lieut.-Colonel, 12th Battn. Suffolk Regt. He displayed the greatest coolness and skill in carrying out the attack on 28 Sept. 1918. The chief objective was the "Bluff," which was the key for the capture of the whole of the country to the south. By his personal direction of the operations he assailed the "Bluff" in flank and rear, thereby taking the enemy by surprise and ensuring its capture. After the capture of both objectives he worked unceasingly till he personally saw his line was secure.
(D.S.O. gazetted 4 March, 1918.)
(1st Bar gazetted 16 Sept. 1918.)

REES, JOHN GORDON, D.S.O., Major (Acting Lieut.-Colonel), Welsh Horse Yeomanry, attached 25th Battn. Royal Welsh Fusiliers (Capt., Reserve of Officers). For conspicuous gallantry and able leadership during the attack on Gillemont Farm and the Cat Post, 21 Sept. 1918. Finding the enemy had reoccupied Cat Post he at once organized his signallers, runners, etc., about eight in all, attacked the post and captured a machine gun. When his party was reduced to three he withdrew, bringing back the wounded. He did fine work.
(D.S.O. gazetted 18 Jan. 1918.)
(Bar gazetted 26 March, 1918.)

ROBERTSON, GORDON McMAHON, D.S.O., Capt. (Acting Lieut.-Colonel), 2nd Battn. North Staffordshire Regt., attached 2nd Battn. Manchester Regt. For the magnificent way in which he handled his battalion during the operations on the Hindenburg Line, and in the attack on the Fonsomme Line, 29 Sept. to 2 Oct. 1918. It was owing to his fine example of courage and endurance under heavy artillery and machine-gun fire that the frequent hostile counter-attacks were driven off and the captured line retained when both flanks were turned by the enemy.
(D.S.O. gazetted 3 June, 1918.)
(1st Bar gazetted 11 Jan. 1919.)

CANADIAN FORCE.

EDWARDS, CAMERON MACPHERSON, D.S.O., Lieut.-Colonel, 38th Battn. Canadian Infantry. On 2 Sept. 1918, during the Drocourt-Quéant battle, he displayed fine leadership and gallantry. He carried out several reconnaissances under very heavy fire, and the information he gained was most valuable in directing artillery fire into points of resistance and enemy movements. His cool courage was an example to all who came in contact with him, but particularly to his battalion, which gained all their objectives in time, thereby creating the desired gap in the Drocourt-Quéant system of trenches.
(D.S.O. gazetted 10 Jan. 1917.)
(1st Bar gazetted 3 June, 1918.)

Awarded a Bar to the Distinguished Service Order:

ADLERCRON, RODOLPH LADEVEZE, C.M.G., D.S.O., Major and Brevet Lieut.-Colonel (Temporary Brigadier-General), Cameron Highlanders (General Officer Commanding 124th Infantry Brigade). During operations 28 Sept.–2 Oct. 1918, between Hollebeke and Comines he commanded a brigade. He handled his troops with skill and dash, personally directing operations in the field. It was due to his gallantry and fine example under machine-gun fire on the 28th that the advance continued without further stop and the capture of Kortwillde was effected that evening.
(D.S.O. gazetted 14 Jan. 1916.)

ALBAN, CLIFTON EDWARD RAWDON GRANT, D.S.O., Capt. and Brevet Major (Acting Lieut.-Colonel), Liverpool Regt., attached 15th Battn. Lancashire Fusiliers. For the gallant way in which he led his battalion in the attack and capture of the village of Joncourt on 3 Oct. 1918, under extremely heavy artillery and machine-gun fire. Although only partially successful the first time, he reorganized his battalion under fire and launched a second and successful attack. He did splendid work.
(D.S.O. gazetted 18 July, 1917.)

CAMPBELL, SIR JOHN BRUCE STEWART, Bart., D.S.O., Temporary Lieut.-Colonel, 11th Battn. Royal Scots. On 28 Sept. 1918, while reconnoitring the line in front of Becelaere he was fired at from 200 yards by an enemy field gun. He immediately got a machine gun into action, and with a few men, under machine-gun fire and the direct fire of the gun, surrounded the field gun, the battery teams running away. It was entirely due to his gallantry and quick action that the battery was captured, thus saving many casualties.
(D.S.O. gazetted 26 July. 1917.)

DANBY, SILAS, D.S.O., M.C., Major (Temporary Lieut.-Colonel), 12th Battn. Manchester Regt. For conspicuous gallantry and initiative at Neuville on 12 Oct. 1918. Owing to his skilful dispositions and the wonderful dash of his men the operation was completely successful with slight casualties, and the objective gained and consolidated under his direction. Later, when in charge of the combined attack to clear the ground north-east of Neuville, he was forced by overwhelming odds to withdraw to a bank east of the river whence he pushed forward patrols to the railway. His courage and determination inspired all under him.
(D.S.O. gazetted 16 Sept. 1918.)

DEMPSTER, JAMES FINLAY, D.S.O., Temporary Major (Acting Lieut. Colonel), Manchester Regt., attached 1/8th Battn. Nottinghamshire and Derbyshire Regt. (Capt., Reserve of Officers). For conspicuous courage and ability in leading his battalion near Bellenglise on 29 Sept. 1918. He immediately followed up the battalion of the brigade which crossed the canal and stormed the Hindenburg Line. He assisted in the clearing up of Bellenglise, and during this operation and the advance to his final objective some hundreds of the enemy and many machine guns and trench mortars were captured. He did splendid work.
(D.S.O. gazetted 1 Jan. 1918.)

CAMERON, EWEN ALLAN, D.S.O., Temporary Lieut.-Colonel, 10th Battn. North Lancashire Regt., commanding 9th Battn. East Surrey Regt. For conspicuous gallantry and brilliant leadership. He organized, on the afternoon of 15 Oct. 1918, and carried out, practically without previous reconnaissance at dawn on 16 Oct., the capture of the village of Haussy, together with about 300 prisoners, and many machine guns and trench mortars. Later, when the enemy counter-attacked under an exceptionally heavy bombardment and forced our troops back, he rallied all the men within reach, and organized fresh resistance, inflicting many casualties on the enemy. He did splendid work.
(D.S.O. gazetted 1 Jan. 1918.)

FITZJOHN, TUDOR, D.S.O., Major (Acting Lieut.-Colonel), 1st Battn. Worcestershire Regt., attached 4th Battn. He displayed great dash and initiative during the period 28 Sept. to 3 Oct. 1918. In the operation which led to the capture of Gheluvelt and Kruiseecke, it was due to his quickness that the important high ground was captured before the enemy had time to reorganize his defences. He displayed great gallantry and devotion to duty throughout the whole operations.
(D.S.O. gazetted 1 Jan. 1917.)

FLETCHER, JAMES HENRY, D.S.O., M.C., Capt. (Acting Lieut.-Colonel), Royal Army Medical Corps, commanding 36th Field Ambulance. For most conspicuous gallantry and devotion to duty near Mametz, on 26 Aug. 1918,

when in command of bearers. With another officer he crawled out under heavy machine-gun fire into "No Man's Land," dragged back two wounded bearers to a more sheltered spot, and after dressing them crawled back for assistance, organized two squads of bearers and brought the wounded men in under heavy fire; also two more wounded men found lying out. He set a splendid example to all serving under him.
(D.S.O. gazetted 18 July, 1917.)

FORD, VINCENT TENNYSON RANDLE, D.S.O., Capt. (Temporary Lieut.-Colonel), 1st Battn. York and Lancaster Regt., attached 8th Battn. Northumberland Fusiliers. In the operations of 27 Sept. 1918, at Oisy le Verger, he commanded his battalion with marked courage and ability. When the battalion which was assaulting the first objective lost direction, he quickly grasped the situation and led his battalion on to the final objective with great dash. By his rapid and determined advance a position of great strength was captured with light casualties. His conduct throughout the day set a fine example to all ranks.
(D.S.O. gazetted 3 June, 1918.)

HELME, ERNEST, D.S.O., Major, Glamorganshire Yeomanry, attached 15th Battn. Welsh Regt. For gallant and skilful leading of his battalion near Villers Outreaux on 8 Oct. 1918. Owing to another brigade having been checked in their attack on the front enemy trenches his battalion had to delay their advance for some time while suffering heavily from artillery barrage. By his personal efforts, skill and determination the battalion, which had been thrown into some confusion, was rallied and assembled for the further advance, eventually reaching a further final objective. It was almost entirely due to his gallant leading that the advance was enabled to continue after the check experienced.
(D.S.O. gazetted 2 Dec. 1918.)

HOGGART, JOHN WILLIAM, D.S.O., M.C., Lieut. (Acting Major), commanding 50th Brigade, Royal Field Artillery. For exceptional gallantry and devotion to duty on 14 Oct. 1918, at Steenbeek. When our infantry was held up by machine-gun fire he brought his battery into action in the open at 800 yards range from the enemy and engaged each machine-gun emplacement in turn and put them out of action, thus enabling our infantry to advance. Later in the day he brought his battery into action in the front line and engaged the machine guns in the houses of Steenbeek, silencing them. He had two gun teams killed by shell and machine-gun fire. He did splendid work.
(D.S.O. gazetted 1 Jan. 1919.)

HOWARD, CHARLES ALFRED, D.S.O., Major and Brevet Lieut.-Colonel, 1st Battn. King's Royal Rifle Corps. For conspicuous gallantry and devotion to duty while in command of his battalion during the operations from 28 Sept. to 8 Oct. 1918. On 28 Sept. he personally organized the line near Noyelles, preventing the enemy from destroying bridges over the Scheldt and the St. Quentin Canal; he also organized the fording of the river crossings, and the consolidation of defences under heavy fire after his battalion had taken their objective. On 8 Oct., when the enemy counter-attacked his battalion with tanks, he showed great gallantry, and though slightly wounded rallied disorganized troops and by his personal example restored the position.
(D.S.O. gazetted 1 Jan. 1917.)

MODERA, FREDERICK STEWART, D.S.O., M.C., Capt. (Temporary Major and Acting Lieut.-Colonel), Royal Fusiliers, attached 1st Battn. Lancashire Fusiliers. East of Ypres on 28 Sept. 1918, and subsequent days he led and commanded his battalion with marked courage and skill. Although wounded in the hand and face in "No Man's Land" when leading his battalion shortly after zero on 28 Sept., he remained on duty for the next five days. His dispositions for both attack and defence were always right, and he proved himself a born leader of men. He personally led his battalion in the attack.
(D.S.O. gazetted 16 Sept. 1918.)

SAMPSON, FRANCIS CORNELIUS, D.S.O., M.B., Major (Temporary Lieut.-Colonel), 91st Field Ambulance, Royal Army Medical Corps. For exemplary devotion to duty on the night of 3–4 Oct. 1918, at Le Baraque (north of St. Quentin) when this area was heavily bombed. This officer, regardless of personal danger, by his initiative and personal influence, organized and accompanied relief parties and was instrumental in the rapid evacuation of the wounded. The bombing was very severe and the casualties heavy, there being 13 amongst the Royal Army Medical Corps bearers alone; the actual number of killed exceeded 40.
(D.S.O. gazetted 14 Jan. 1916.)

SMITH, ROBERT ARTHUR, D.S.O., M.C., Temporary Lieut.-Colonel, 13th Battn. Royal Fusiliers. On 10 Oct. 1918, when his battalion was held up on the outskirts of Caudry he went forward to find out the situation himself, and in spite of machine-gun fire and sniping gained information enabling him to form up his battalion for attack the following night in assembly positions from which the town could be outflanked from the south. Throughout the operations his fearless reconnoitring and gallant leading were a fine example to all, and materially helped the success of the brigade.
(D.S.O. gazetted 16 Sept. 1918).

STORY, PHILIP FRANCIS, D.S.O., Temporary Major (Acting Lieut.-Colonel), Royal Engineers (Commanding Royal Engineers, 30th Division). At Menin, on 14 Oct. 1918, he made a skilful reconnaissance of the river crossings under considerable shell and machine-gun fire, thus enabling a bridge to be thrown across at the earliest opportunity. Again, at Helchin, on 21 Oct., his energy and fearlessness under similar conditions were instrumental in getting a pontoon bridge across the Scheldt under close infantry fire.
(D.S.O. gazetted 1 Jan. 1917.)

THORPE, GERVASE, C.M.G., D.S.O., Major and Brevet Lieut.-Colonel (Temporary Brigadier-General), Argyll and Sutherland Highlanders (General Officer Commanding 17th Infantry Brigade). Near Rieux, east of Cambrai, on 11 Oct. 1918, he showed the greatest gallantry and devotion to duty in rallying troops who had been counter-attacked and temporarily forced to vacate their position. Though exposed to heavy machine-gun fire he galloped up to the front line and by his strong personal example put new heart into the troops and restored the situation. His behaviour was most gallant.
(D.S.O. gazetted 18 Feb. 1915.)

TONSON-RYE, HUBERT BERNARD, D.S.O., Major (Acting Lieut.-Colonel), 2nd Battn. Royal Munster Fusiliers. For conspicuous gallantry on 5 Oct. 1918, during an attack on Le Catelet and the high ground north of it. He got through with his reserve company to the final objective, and by his personal example and courage he held on to this position all day, though the battalion on his flank was held up, suffering many casualties from shell and machine-gun fire. By his action he enabled his brigadier to organize another attack on his flank on the enemy, which was successful, all objectives being gained.
(D.S.O. gazetted 16 Sept. 1918.)

TURNER, REGINALD, D.S.O., Capt. (Temporary Lieut.-Colonel), Dragoon Guards, Special Reserve, attached 6th Battn. Northamptonshire Regt. For conspicuous gallantry and devotion to duty at Ronssoy on 18 Sept. 1918. He got his battalion on the jumping-off line under very difficult conditions and finally led them on under very heavy machine-gun fire, capturing several machine guns and killing the gunners. He personally conducted a great deal of the work of his battalion, and his courage and initiative were most marked.
(D S.O. gazetted 19 April, 1901.)

WESTMORLAND, HERBERT CAMPBELL, D.S.O., Capt. (Acting Lieut.-Colonel), 2nd Battn. Hampshire Regt. This officer displayed the greatest energy and ability in reorganizing and directing his battalion throughout the operations which led up to the capture of Gheluvelt and part ot Gheluwe, from 28 Sept. to 3 Oct. 1918. During these attacks he displayed great gallantry and devotion to duty, and it was mainly due to his efforts that a number of his men were prevented from being captured in Gheluwe on the afternoon of the 3rd.
(D.S.O. gazetted 16 September, 1918.)

CANADIAN FORCE.

BICKERDIKE, ROBERT, D.S.O., Major, 87th Battn. Canadian Infantry, Quebec Regt. For great gallantry and devotion to duty at Bourlon, Blecourt, Cambrai Sector, from 27 Sept. to 1 Oct. 1918. During the night attack made by the battalion east of Bourlon Wood on 27 Sept. he went forward and under heavy fire he gallantly organized the line and held the objective till relieved by troops passing through. On 30 Sept., when troops were driven back, he reorganized the line out of elements of several battalions, and held the front line against counter-attacks till his battalion was withdrawn for reorganization in the evening. On the morning of 1 Oct. he took signallers and scouts forward and established a report centre at the farthest point reached by our advanced troops. The skill and daring displayed by him throughout the whole operations were admirable.
(D.S.O. gazetted 1 Jan. 1918.)

ELKINS, WILLIAM HENRY PFERINGER, D.S.O., Lieut.-Colonel, Royal Canadian Horse Artillery. He commanded a group consisting of Royal Canadian Horse Artillery Brigade and a battery of 4.5 inch howitzers during the operations of 9 Oct. He showed exceptional skill and daring in the handling of his guns under heavy fire, and was largely responsible for the success of the operations. On 10 Oct. he commanded five batteries working in a very advanced position in support of the infantry attack on Neuville. Finding that his communication was cut between himself and the 4.5 inch howitzer battery, he went forward under very heavy shell fire to ascertain the situation: and superintended from a very exposed position the shooting of this battery when he had been ordered to cover a portion of the infantry advance.
(D.S.O. gazetted 1 Jan. 1918.)

LINDSEY, CHARLES BETHUNE, D.S.O., Major, 19th Battn. Canadian Infantry, 1st Central Ontario Regt. (Brigade Major 11th Canadian Infantry Brigade, Acting G.S.O. II., 4th Canadian Division). For great gallantry during the operations of 2, 3 and 4 Sept. 1918, before Arras. He repeatedly made reconnaissances under very heavy shell fire and machine-gun fire and maintained close touch with all forward units under exceedingly trying conditions. The information which he obtained was most valuable.
(D.S.O. gazetted 4 June, 1917.)

PERRY, KENNETH MEIKLE, D.S.O., Lieut.-Colonel, 87th Battn. Canadian Infantry, Quebec Regt. For conspicuous courage and leadership at Bourlon Wood and north of Cambrai from 27 Sept. to 1 Oct. His work was accomplished with dash and precision, although at the cost of heavy casualties. On 30 Sept. the battalion again lost heavy casualties, but, when asked to attack once more the next morning, he, with only 160 men, carried the attack to the very outskirts of Eswars, in spite of the desperate opposition of heavily massed enemy, and in conjunction with the battalion on his left he maintained an advanced position.
(D.S.O. gazetted 19 Aug. 1916.)

RALSTON, JAMES LAYTON, D.S.O., Lieut.-Colonel, 85th Battn. Canadian Infantry, Nova Scotia Regt. For conspicuous gallantry and outstanding leadership in operations before Cambrai, 27 Sept.–2 Oct. 1918. He handled his battalion with great skill and successfully accomplished the allotted tasks in face of very heavy enemy resistance, after making frequent reconnaissances of the most forward positions under heavy machine-gun fire. When the enemy counter-attacked, his tactical skill saved a very critical situation. Though wounded in the face on the third day of the battle he refused to be relieved, and continued at duty until his battalion was withdrawn.
(D.S.O. gazetted 26 Sept. 1917.)

ROSS, MALCOLM NUGENT, D.S.O., Lieut.-Colonel, 4th Brigade Canadian Field Artillery. For conspicuous gallantry on 2 and 3 Sept. 1918, during the attack on the Quéant-Drocourt line and on Saudemont, Ecourt St. Quentin, and Rumaucourt. He went forward with his brigade in the support of the infantry, and throughout the operation showed marked dash and courage. He pushed his batteries well forward after close personal reconnaissance under heavy fire, and engaged enemy positions over open sights. His initiative, quick action, and daring offensive methods materially assisted the advance.
(D.S.O. gazetted 26 July, 1917.)

STEVENSON, HERBERT IRVING, D.S.O., Lieut.-Colonel, Fort Garry Horse. He led his regiment with great gallantry and determination during the advance from Mametz to Le Cateau on 9 Oct. 1918. He directed the operations from most advanced positions under heavy shell and machine-gun fire and showed a total disregard for all danger. The capture of the Bois de Gattigny was entirely due to this officer's initiative, fine leading, and had a most important bearing on the subsequent advance. His conduct throughout the operations was splendid, and he set an inspiring example to his regiment.
(D.S.O. gazetted 22 June, 1918.)

Awarded the Distinguished Service Order:

ADLERCRON, GEORGE ROTHE LADEVEZE, Capt., 8th Hussars. On the night of 21–22 March, 1918, he was sent with his squadron to relieve the infantry holding the important redoubts on the ridge above Hesbecourt. This section of the line was very heavily attacked early in the morning of 22 March, and he was severely wounded in the mouth and jaw about 8 a.m., but, though suffering great pain from the damage to his jaw and teeth, together with the loss of blood, he refused to leave his post. Again, at about 9 a.m., he was shot through the side, but still remained in command of his squadron and held his ground, although the line on both sides gave way and 50 per cent. of his squadron had become casualties. In spite of this, this very gallant officer refused to give up command of his squadron, though he knew fully well that he had already done more than seemed humanly possible, and that he ought to allow himself to be evacuated to have his wounds dressed. At 12 noon he was forced to retire, and conducted the retirement in a most efficient manner; while doing so, he was again severely wounded through the leg, and he still refused to leave the trench until all his men had gone, and would allow no one to remain to help him back, though he fully realized that the danger of his being captured by the advancing enemy was great, and was determined not to allow any of his men to run the same risk as himself. His magnificent courage and devotion to duty at an intensely critical time was an inspiring example to all ranks.

ALDOUS, FREDERIC CLEMENT, Major (Acting Lieut.-Colonel), 6th Battn. Manchester Regt., Territorial Force, attached 32nd Battn. Machine Gun Corps.

On 29 Sept. 1918, near Bellenglise, he displayed the greatest gallantry and ability in the handling of his battalion. The rapid advance of his machine guns across the canal was carried out under his own personal supervision under heavy shell fire at close range, and was of vital consequence to the successful issue of the attack. On 2 Oct. he carried out daring personal reconnaissances of machine-gun positions under heavy shell fire and made dispositions that had far-reaching results on the events of the operation.

ANGUS, ALEXANDER WILLIAM, Temporary Major (Acting Lieut.-Colonel), 5th Battn. Cameron Highlanders. For marked gallantry and initiative, from 28 Sept. to 14 Oct. 1918, and for skilful leading near Rolleghem Capelle on the latter date. He took one of his own companies and led it through troops who had been held up. His prompt action enabled the whole line to advance. Throughout the operations he did excellent work.

ASHMORE, EDWIN JAMES CALDWELL, M.C., Capt. (Acting Major), 10th Gurkha Rifles, attached 2/3rd Gurkha Rifles (Egypt). For conspicuous gallantry on 19 Sept. 1918. With the greatest dash, he personally led his battalion forward during the original attack on the Tabsor Defences when, owing to the dense smoke of our own and the enemy barrage, it had lost direction and formation. The rapidity of the advance of his battalion, and the very heavy losses both in men and material inflicted on the enemy, was in a large measure due to his personal leadership. His example was an inspiration to all ranks.

BAKER, EUSTON EDWARD FRANCIS, M.C., Capt. (Acting Lieut.-Colonel), Middlesex Regt., Special Reserve, attached 2nd Battn. For conspicuous gallantry and able leadership. In particular, in the successful attacks on the Fresnes-Rouvroy line on 7 Oct. and Drocourt-Quéant line on 11 Oct. 1918, resulting in the capture of many prisoners and much material, his resourcefulness and gallantry under fire were most marked. He personally exploited successes, and by his grasp of the situation in the afternoon was instrumental in seizing a most important tactical point which was holding up the corps on the right.

BAULD, ROBERT STERLING, M.C., 2nd Lieut., 5th Battn. Lancashire Fusiliers, Territorial Force, attached 18th Battn. During the attack south-east of Ypres on Hill 60, and the Caterpillar on 28 Sept. 1918, and subsequent operations, he displayed fine courage and initiative. He led his men splendidly, knocking out machine guns in his stride, and pushing well forward of his objective rushed a pill-box, capturing the two machine guns and killing the garrison. On his company commander becoming a casualty, he led the company with marked gallantry and coolness, and at Wervicq encouraged his men under most difficult conditions. On the night of 1–2 Oct., he rushed forward with some 30 men and occupied a pillbox behind the enemy's line, holding on to an isolated position for 48 hours until relieved. He set a magnificent example to his men.

BUXTON, ROBERT VERE, Capt. (Acting Lieut.-Colonel), Royal West Kent Yeomanry, Commanding 2nd Battn. Imperial Camel Corps (Egypt). For gallant and successful services when in command of a flying column of Imperial Camel Corps operating in the Northern Hejaz. On 8 Aug. 1918, this column delivered a surprise attack on the strong Turkish post at Mudawara on the Hejaz Railway, 60 miles south of Maan. As a result the station was captured and destroyed, 35 Turks being killed and 150 prisoners captured. This operation—the success of which was largely due to Colonel Buxton's personal leadership and excellent dispositions—had the effect of completing the isolation of Medina and the Southern Hejaz garrisons from communication with the north.

BYRNE, LOUIS CAMPBELL, M.C., Lieut. (Acting Major), 2nd Battn. Royal Dublin Fusiliers. After being knocked senseless by the explosion of a shell on the night of 6 Oct. 1918, near Vauxhall Quarry, north-east of Gouy, he refused to go to the dressing-station, remained in command of his unit, and personally conducted successful operations against the Masnieres-Beaurevoir line. The success of the operation was largely due to his courage, resolution and personal example.

CARTER, WILLIAM, M.C., Lieut. (Temporary Major), Royal Lancaster Regt., G.S.O.2, H.Q., XIII. Corps. On 4 Oct. 1918, when sent forward to ascertain the situation, he found the attack held up by heavy machine-gun fire and the infantry somewhat disorganized. He collected two tanks, reorganized two companies of infantry, and restarted the advance which had been checked. On 8 Oct., when detailed to report on the progress of the attack, he found that most of Serain was still in the hands of the enemy. He returned, collected more troops, led them into the village, and organized the systematic mopping up of the area. He showed great gallantry, enterprise and determination.

CARTWRIGHT, CHARLES, M.C., Temporary Major (Acting Lieut.-Colonel), 6th Battn. York and Lancaster Regt. At Epinoy, on 1 Oct. 1918, he showed conspicuous gallantry and devotion to duty during a whole day's fighting in which his battalion took part. He remained in a certain position which was continuously shelled both with gas and high-explosive throughout the day, in order that he might better control his battalion. His action had a marked effect towards the success of the operations. His cheerfulness and coolness throughout a very trying time inspired all under his command and was largely responsible for the splendid behaviour of his men.

CLOUGH, JOHN, M.C., Temporary Major, 16th Battn. Tank Corps. For conspicuous gallantry and excellent leadership on 29 Sept. 1918, near Guillemont Farm. When the attack had miscarried and it was found necessary to organize a fresh attack, he went forward in face of heavy machine-gun and shell fire, and showed the tanks where to go and gave his orders. All his section and tank commanders were either killed or wounded during this operation. Again, on the night of 4–5 Oct. at Montbrehain he led his tanks splendidly. By his strenuous efforts and fine example through the night under shell fire he got all his tanks up to the start line, and thereby materially assisted in the capture of Montbrehain.

COLQUHOUN, ARCHIBALD GORDON CAMPBELL, Capt. (Acting Major), 2nd Battn. Argyll and Sutherland Highlanders. For conspicuous gallantry and exemplary leadership of his battalion near Neuvilly on 10 Oct. 1918. He was in temporary command and personally led what remained of his battalion in the second attack made against very strong enemy positions east of the River Selle, succeeding, in spite of violent opposition, in establishing a series of posts on the east side of the river. On the following day, exposed to intense machine-gun and snipers' fire, he personally visited these forward and isolated posts, having to traverse the ground in full view of the enemy in order to do so. He set a fine example of courage and determination to his battalion, which had suffered heavy casualties.

COOK, FRANCIS ALFRED, M.C., Lieut., 4th Battn. York and Lancaster Regt., Territorial Force, attached 6th Battn. On 27 Sept. 1918, near Epinoy, he was responsible for driving off an enemy machine gun from a bridgehead which was holding up the advance of the division. He pressed on to the bank of the Canal du Nord with his men under heavy machine-gun and rifle fire, crossed the canal and drove the enemy into the wood, where they were captured. On 1 Oct. he led his men to the final objective across two belts of wire in face of heavy opposition. Later, when isolated and surrounded by large numbers of the enemy, he inflicted many casualties, himself accounting for a number. He was wounded in the thigh, his leg being badly broken, and throughout the whole operations set a splendid example of gallantry and determination.

DAVISON, DOUGLAS STEWART, Capt., 2nd Lancers, Indian Army (Egypt). For conspicuous skill and gallantry and fine work. Between Lejjun and Afule on 20 Sept. 1918, the 2nd Lancers and one sub-section of the 17th Machine Gun Squadron and 11th Light Armoured Motor Battery were ordered to advance on Afule. Capt. Davison was placed in command of this force. About two miles from Lejjun, the force met with some 500 enemy and three machine guns, who endeavoured to bar the road. A well-planned charge, rapidly executed, resulted in the total destruction of this enemy force, some 47 of them being killed and wounded and 470 taken prisoners. The regiment was very quickly reorganized, and the rapidity and skill with which the final approach to Afule was made resulted in a further capture of prisoners who would otherwise have escaped.

DE HOGHTON, GUY, M.C., Capt. (Acting Major), 1st Battn. Yorkshire Light Infantry. For most conspicuous gallantry and good leadership in command of his battalion during the attack on Le Catelet on 3 Oct. 1918. This officer, five minutes before zero, had to move up his battalion to take the place of another. He doubled his men up to the barrage, and the battalion went forward with great dash, captured their objective, over 300 prisoners, and several machine guns. He was wounded early in the attack, but continued to command.

DUNN, PIERS DUNCAN WILLIAM, M.C., Lieut. (Temporary Capt.), 1st Battn. Lancashire Fusiliers. For most conspicuous gallantry and devotion to duty at Ledeghem on 14 Oct. 1918. He was detailed with his company to mop up the village, and went over with the first wave. With one N.C.O. and two men, and under heavy shell fire and gas, he proceeded down the main street and captured 40 of the enemy out of a pill-box ; and later took another 26 prisoners. In all, he and his little party accounted for 74 prisoners. The dense fog made his conduct all the more praiseworthy. He did splendid work.

FRANKS, KENDAL FERGUSON, Capt. (Temporary Major), 1st Battn. 117th Mahrattas (India). In operations at Zardes on 30 Oct.–1 Nov. 1918, he commanded a small column which became separated from the main column and was surrounded by the enemy. Being unable to bring away his wounded, he took up a defensive position and held it until relieved the following day, being all the time under fire from surrounding hills. He acted with great resourcefulness, skill and courage throughout, and the success of the operations was mainly due to the troops under his command.

FREEMAN, CECIL RAYNER, M.C., Capt. (Acting Major), 2nd Battn. Northumberland Fusiliers. For conspicuous gallantry and skill when commanding a battalion at Le Catelet on 5 Oct. 1918. He encountered a strong enemy post among the ruins in the north of the village. After making a very difficult reconnaissance he led two companies to the attack. By fine courage and leadership he overcame strong opposition, capturing 250 enemy, with five heavy machine guns, 13 light machine guns and two trench mortars, besides inflicting very heavy casualties. He did splendid work.

FRENCH, WILLIAM, M.C., Temporary Major (Acting Lieut.-Colonel), 8th Battn. Royal Highlanders. For conspicuous gallantry and continuous good services during operations in Flanders from 28 Sept.–4 Oct. 1918. During the whole of this period he set a high standard of leadership. He handled his battalion with marked ability, and always kept in a position from whence he could take advantage of opportunities to advance his line. During the attack on 1 Oct. his battalion formed the defensive flank on the left of the brigade, and it was due to his quick, skilful dispositions, which could only have been effected by personal observations and reconnaissance, that the attack against our left flank was beaten off. Subsequently he was of the greatest assistance in re-organizing the line after the attack had come to a standstill.

GAIN, RICHARD SPENCER, Lieut. (Acting Capt.), 11th, attached 1/20th, Battn. London Regt. On 1 Sept. 1918, during operations near Bouchavesnes, he showed most conspicuous gallantry and resource. Though his company was held up on several occasions by machine-gun nests, he organized local attacks on each, and himself alone rushed one nest of seven guns and five gunners, all firing, capturing the whole and so allowing his company to advance. Finally, when the objective was reached on the outskirts of Moislans Wood, he took command of the elements of four companies which had reached the objective and consolidated the position, though being fired on over open sights by two 77 mm. guns, and shot the gunners, thus enabling the consolidation to be continued. He behaved splendidly.

GOOCH, HAROLD, M.C., Temporary Major, 121st Field Coy., Royal Engineers. For courage and great devotion to duty on the night of 19 20 Oct. 1918, when under heavy shell and direct machine-gun fire during the bridging of the River Lys, south of Oyghem. In spite of many casualties, he successfully handled his company and ferried and later bridged the river, enabling the attacking infantry to cross it exactly to time. He conducted the whole operation in the most cool and masterly manner.

HACKING, ALFRED, M.C., Lieut. (Acting Lieut.-Colonel), 1/8th Battn., attached 1/5th Battn., Nottinghamshire and Derbyshire Regt., Territorial Force. For conspicuous gallantry and good leadership whilst leading his battalion to the final objective near Bellenglise on 29 Sept. 1918. During the advance, between 350 and 400 enemy were captured and many killed. Le Haucourt was also cleared up and about 40 guns captured by his battalion. He himself, with his orderly, captured a large number of prisoners. Again, on 30 Sept., owing to the good dispositions made by him, a large number of enemy, who were retiring from in front of the troops on his right, were shot. He did splendid work.

HARRISON, GEORGE LEE, Capt. (Acting Lieut.-Colonel), Royal West Surrey Regt., Commanding 7th Battn. For conspicuous gallantry and good leadership when in command of his battalion on 18 Sept. 1918, during the attack on Ronssoy. He formed his battalion up for the attack on the village with great skill, and proceeded with them when they advanced, sharing with the men in the hand-to-hand fighting that took place. Throughout the operations he showed a great personal example to the men, and skill in handling his battalion, which fought extremely well in the face of heavy enemy opposition.

HINGLEY, ALFRED NORMAN, M.C., Major (Temporary Lieut.-Colonel), 13th Battn. Middlesex Regt. For great gallantry on 10 Oct. 1918, near Rieux. When the advance met with heavy machine-gun and shell fire, and the leading companies had lost many officers, he personally led the battalion to its final objective. Again, on 11 Oct., near Avesnes-les-Aubert, under an intense enemy barrage, it was due to his personal courage and leadership that the ground gained by the battalion was maintained. He set a very fine example to all.

HITCH, ARTHUR TYLER, Temporary Capt. (Acting Lieut.-Colonel), 6th Battn. Bedfordshire Regt., attached 8th Battn. Lincolnshire Regt. For conspicuous gallantry and good leadership in the operations about Havrincourt Wood on 9–10 Sept. 1918. He personally supervised the pushing forward of the line north of the wood over ground which was under very heavy shell fire. Throughout the operations he handled his battalion with great skill, courage and judgment. His good leadership and personal disregard of danger during a difficult phase of wood fighting contributed largely to the rapid retreat of the enemy and the complete success of the day's operations.

HODGSON, HAROLD JOHN, Capt. (Acting Lieut.-Colonel), Cheshire Regt., attached 7th Battn. Wiltshire Regt. For conspicuous gallantry on 5 Oct. 1918, near Le Catelet, when, by his initiative and skill, he attacked and captured the northern slopes of Prospect Hill, which was strongly defended, without a barrage, all the time under heavy shell and machine-gun fire ; and by his action gained a position of great tactical importance. He showed most able leadership and rendered very valuable service.

HOOD, JOHN WEMYSS, M.C., Temporary Capt., attached Border Regt. (1st Battn.). At Hooge, on 28 Sept. 1918, he commanded his company with marked skill and ability. He led an attack on an enemy strong point, personally shot three of a machine-gun crew, and captured the gun and 53 prisoners. On 30 Sept. at Ghelume, he led forward his company without artillery support, and in face of very heavy fire captured his objective, being the first to arrive. Throughout five days' operations he showed fine courage and leadership, and his splendid example inspired all under him.

HOWELL-EVANS, HUGH JOHN, Major (Acting Lieut.-Colonel), Denbighshire Yeomanry, attached 10th Battn. Shropshire Light Infantry. For conspicuous gallantry, initiative and good leadership. During the attack on the Cat Post quadrilateral on 21 Sept. 1918, he fought his battalion with great dash, and when they were held up by machine-gun fire, made a daring reconnaissance and then caused them to take up a position in shell-holes and hold out throughout the day. During the night, with the remains of his battalion, he made a further attack, which was completely successful, killing some 80 of the enemy and capturing 200 prisoners and 30 machine guns in a very strong position. He did splendid work.

ISAAC, AUBERON GODFREY FAULKNER, M.C., Capt. and Brevet Major (Acting Lieut.-Colonel), 2nd Battn. Royal Berkshire Regt. For conspicuous gallantry and determined leadership during the attack on Drocourt-Quéant Line on 11 Oct. 1918. It was due to his fearless leadership and energy that the villages of Izel-les-Esquerchin, Quiery la Motte, Esquerchin, Petit Cuincy and Cuincy were captured during the day. He handled his battalion throughout in a masterly manner, taking advantage of every opportunity to advance his line and giving the enemy no respite.

JACKSON, RICHARD DINGWALL, M.C., Capt. (Acting Lieut.-Colonel), Royal Engineers, Commanding Royal Engineers, 37th Division. For conspicuous gallantry and devotion to duty between Le Bosquet and Vaucelles, 3–6 Oct. 1918. He made several daring reconnaissances of the canal and River d'Escaut to select sites for bridges. The information he obtained enabled him to throw bridges over both, in spite of heavy enemy fire. It was largely due to his ability and inspiring gallantry that the canal and river were successfully bridged.

JERVIS, NICHOLAS GORDON MAINWARING, Major (Acting Lieut.-Colonel), Royal Field Artillery, attached Headquarters 231st (N.M.) Brigade, Royal Field Artillery, Territorial Force. This officer commanded a field artillery group during the operations of the 46th Division on 19 Dec. 1918, near Bellenglise, with great distinction. He also commanded his brigade during the operations on 3 Oct. During this period he made several most valuable reconnaissances. He only received orders to move his batteries forward for the latter operations at 5.30 p.m. on 2 Oct., but by his great energy and a very skilful and fearless reconnaissance he made all his arrangements and moved his batteries a distance of about two miles to forward positions, and was able to take part in the barrage at 6.5 a.m. on 3 Oct. Throughout the operations he did gallant and excellent work.

JOHNSON, WALTER RUSSELL, Lieut.-Colonel, 7th Battn. Essex Regt., Territorial Force, attached 9th Battn. For conspicuous gallantry and good leadership during the attack on Epehy on 18 Sept. 1918. When the companies of his battalion had lost direction owing to the darkness and smoke he reorganized and moved them to a flank while the enemy were still in Epehy. Later, he rallied two companies of another battalion which had become disorganized owing to one of our tanks, which had lost its bearings, firing on them. Throughout he has shown great energy and ability to command.

JONES, JAMES, M.C., Lieut. (Temporary Major and Acting Lieut.-Colonel), 2nd Battn. Durham Light Infantry, attached 17th Battn. Lancashire Fusiliers. He commanded his battalion with conspicuous success during a most difficult operation, involving the capture of Zandvoorde on 28 Sept. 1918. By his behaviour under heavy machine-gun fire at close range, he set a splendid example to the officers and men of his battalion at a very critical period of the attack. All ranks were unanimous in praising his coolness and courage.

KEEP, LESLIE HOWARD, M.C., Temporary Major, 7th Battn. Bedfordshire Regt., attached 2nd Battn. At Ronssoy on 21 Sept. 1918, he commanded the 2nd Battn. Bedfordshire Regt. with marked success. His skill, energy and determination enabled his battalion to hold the ground they won under great difficulties, and to improve their position during the following night. He made personal reconnaissance of the ground under constant machine-gun fire, resulting in the clearing up of a very involved situation.

KELLY, THOMAS JOSEPH, M.C., Temporary Major, 18th Battn. Manchester Regt., attached 1/6th Battn. Territorial Force. For fine leadership, gallantry and ability during the operations east of Trescault on 27 Sept. 1918. He was placed in command of a battalion at a few hours' notice, and the battalion was placed at the disposal of another brigade to carry forward its line to the final objective. He carried out all his plans for the assembly and the attack with such skill and energy that it met with complete success. The whole of the objective was captured and held, and six field guns, two howitzers, and over 250 prisoners taken.

KING, CECIL HANKEY DICKSON, M.C., Lieut. (Temporary Capt.), King's Royal Rifle Corps, Special Reserve, attached 7th Battn. For conspicuous gallantry and devotion to duty on 21 March, 1918. He was in command of his company holding a strong point. The other three companies of the battalion had been wiped out by the enemy. He put up a very fine resistance, killing many of the enemy, and when eventually forced to retire into the village of Benay he effected the retirement with the minimum amount of loss. In Benay he succeeded in holding the enemy off a field ambulance, which passed out between the ranks of his company. Being again outnumbered he retired, firing an 18-pounder gun himself with open sights and killing many of the enemy. He showed most determined courage throughout.

KIRKBY, WILLIAM WYNN, Capt., 2nd Battn. Royal Welsh Fusiliers. For very gallant leadership at Villers Outreaux on the morning of 8 Oct. 1918. His company was ordered to follow two tanks and break the line. This he succeeded in doing in face of heavy machine-gun and artillery fire, and in spite of the fact that both the tanks were "knocked out." His most gallant and determined leadership enabled a footing to be established in the village, and eventually the village was cleared and nearly 200 prisoners taken.

KNIGHT, CHARLES FRASER, M.B., Temporary Major, 133rd Field Ambulance, Royal Army Medical Corps. For conspicuous gallantry and devotion to duty in personally supervising the collection of wounded and visiting forward posts regularly under heavy shell fire. It was largely due to his energy and disregard of danger that the large number of wounded in his sector were successfully cleared. This was during the operation against the Hindenburg Line, east of Ronssoy, on 27, 28 and 29 Sept. 1918.

MARDON, ARTHUR CLAUDE, Lieut.-Colonel, Royal Navy, Devonshire Yeomanry, attached 16th Battn. Devonshire Regt. For conspicuous gallantry and able leadership. During the operations 18–25 Sept. 1918, his battalion suffered heavy casualties. They were called upon to reinforce another infantry brigade, and shortly after the attack on Ronssoy started were completely cut off from their objective by a heavy enemy barrage. He himself promptly led the advance round the barrage and directed his battalion on their objective from a new alignment, thus at the right moment saving a critical situation.

MIERS, HANMER JAMES, Capt. (Acting Major), 2nd Battn. Monmouthshire Regt., attached East Lancashire Regt. For conspicuous gallantry and devotion to duty during the attack on Douai Prison on 14 Oct. 1918. He personally conducted the operation under heavy machine-gun and artillery fire, and it was due to his quick grasp of the situation and tactical handling of his force that this strong position was captured with comparatively few casualties. Throughout the day his exceptional coolness and disregard for personal safety had a magnificent effect on the men.

MURPHY, JOSEPH LEO, Major, Manchester Regt. (Special Reserve), attached 2nd Battn. After the battalion had attacked and broken through the Fonsomme and Beaurevoir Line on 1 Oct. 1918, he was in command of the right wing which was entirely in the air and unsupported by other troops. During the night the right flank was heavily counter-attacked three times, but owing to the clever handling of his men, his own gallant conduct and the confidence with which he inspired the troops the attacks were repulsed and the line gained was retained throughout a very critical period and in spite of heavy casualties.

MURRAY, JOHN, Major (Acting Lieut.-Colonel), Scottish Horse Yeomanry, attached 12th Battn. Royal Scots. On 1 Oct. 1918, during the attack on Ledeghem, the flanks of the battalion under his command became exposed and very heavy casualties were suffered by enfilade machine-gun fire. Colonel Murray, realizing that the dispositions of his battalion needed immediate alteration, went forward and carried this out under close-range rifle and machine-gun fire. His fearless disregard for danger, which was evident to all ranks, and the splendid example which he showed, undoubtedly renewed the confidence of his men during a very critical period.

PETRIE, PAUL CUTHBERT, M.C., Major, D/245th (West Riding) Brigade, Royal Field Artillery, Territorial Force. During an attack on the morning of 11 Oct. 1918, near Iwuy, he displayed remarkable initiative, especially when the enemy launched a heavy counter-attack supported by tanks. He succeeded in bringing into action a section of guns in a forward position and engaged the tanks at close range over open sights and forced them to withdraw. The enemy then showing signs of wavering, he encouraged our infantry to again attack. During the afternoon he again visited the front line on horseback, and by his initiative and utter disregard of personal safety and the successful manner in which he handled the situation showed marked ability as a fighting soldier.

POLLOCK, JOHN ALSAGER, Major (Acting Lieut.-Colonel), Oxfordshire and Buckinghamshire Light Infantry, attached 3rd Battn. London Regt. For conspicuous gallantry and initiative during the attack on Peizière on 18 Sept. 1918. In mopping up the village the battalion encountered considerable opposition from strong points. He promptly went forward accompanied only by his intelligence officer and four runners. He led this small party in face of heavy fire against Proctor's Post, capturing it together with three officers and 47 other ranks. He did splendid work.

PRENTIS, WALTER SLADEN, Lieut.-Colonel, 72nd Punjabis (Egypt). For conspicuous gallantry and initiative in command of his battalion on 19 Sept. 1918. When the 232nd Infantry Brigade was held up in front of El Tireh, and an officer commanding another unit became a casualty, he assumed command of the whole of the right of the attack. His clear and concise reports on the situation, written under the most difficult circumstances and under heavy fire, were of inestimable value to the brigade commander, and enabled him to direct the attack of his battalion to the best advantage.

PRIOR, GEORGE EDWARD REDVERS, M.C., Capt. and Brevet Major (Acting Lieut.-Colonel), 2nd Battn. Devonshire Regt. For gallant and resourceful leadership of his battalion. In particular during the successful attacks at Arleux on 26–27 Sept. 1918, against Fresnes on 7 Oct. and against the Drocourt-Quéant Line on 11 Oct. he made several valuable reconnaissances under heavy fire, and materially facilitated the early and rapid successes gained by the brigade. He rendered very valuable service.

REES, THOMAS WYNFORD, M.C., Lieut. (Acting Capt.), 73rd Carnatic Infantry, attached 125th Napier's Rifles (Egypt). For conspicuous gallantry throughout the day on 19 Sept. 1918, during the attack on the Turkish position about Tabsor, and especially after passing through the last objective into open country. Collecting various details of four different units up to a total of about 80 men, he organized them into parties, charged in face of strong opposition, and took two trenches, capturing about 50 prisoners and two field guns. Subsequently, when mounted on a captured pony, he saw a third field gun escaping, whereupon he galloped after it and, single-handed, captured the gun and team complete. He set a magnificent example to all units by his initiative and utter disregard of danger.

ROBERTS, HARRY, M.C., Lieut. (Acting Capt.), 2nd Battn. Royal Sussex Regt. During the operations north of Gricourt on 24 Sept. 1918, he commanded the right front company of the battalion in the attack. After reaching the final objective and whilst the company was still somewhat disorganized from the attack, the enemy launched a counter-attack with about 400 men against the position occupied by this company. He was out in front of the position when the counter-attack was first seen. He returned to his company and ordered the men to fire on the advancing enemy. As soon as he first saw the first wave of the enemy wavering he again blew his whistle and ordered the whole of the men in that area to fix bayonets and advance against the advancing enemy. The total number of men at his disposal did not exceed 80. By this action he completely routed the counter-attacking enemy and captured many prisoners. Throughout this operation he was walking about fully exposed, and by his calm handling of the situation and skill in selecting the moment to dash out against the enemy with the bayonet, was responsible for the thorough routing of a strong counter-attack and enabling the ground gained in the initial attack to be retained. During this advance he was severely wounded in the arm by a bullet fired at point-blank range, but in spite of this he remained with his company reorganizing his men in defensive position and before being evacuated gave a full report of the situation to the battalion commander.

SHORLAND, JAMES WILLIAM, Temporary Second Lieut., Hampshire Regt., attached 2/4th Battn. Territorial Force. For most determined courage and splendid dash on 30 Sept. and 1 Oct. near Rumilly. A strong pocket of the enemy with numerous machine guns was holding out, and he led his platoon across the open in face of intense machine-gun fire and succeeded in entering the enemy trench. Finally, being forced to withdraw, he was the last to cross the barrier. On the following morning he volunteered to lead a mopping-up party down the same trench after another unit had gone through. Immediately the first wave passed he led the dash, was first over the enemy barrier, and bombed his way along. Twenty-one machine guns were captured altogether, 22 enemy dead counted, and 70 prisoners taken.

SMITH, ALBERT JOSEPH, D.C.M., Second Lieut., 1st Battn. Border Regt. For fine courage and leadership on 28 Sept. 1918, at Hooge. With the greatest dash he led forward his platoon to attack the enemy strong point—Jasper Dug-outs—bayonetting an enemy machine gunner there and capturing the gun. He then bombed the dug-out, killing and wounding several of the enemy. He then went down and brought up as prisoners three officers and over 100 enemy N.C.O.'s and men. He afterwards led on and rushed an enemy machine gun, bayonetting one of the crew himself. On his company commander becoming a casualty he took command and carried on for four days under difficult circumstances with marked success and ability. He did magnificent work.

SMITH, BERTRAM ABEL, M.C., Major (Temporary Lieut.-Colonel), South Nottinghamshire Hussars, commanding 23rd Battn. Middlesex Regt. As battalion commander at Houthem, on 29 Sept. 1918, he showed great gallantry and power of command. When the left flank of his battalion had been left in the air, he overcame a difficult situation by very able handling of his command. Again, near Gheluwe, on 1 Oct. 1918, he led his battalion to the attack with great gallantry through very heavy machine-gun and shell fire, though suffering from the effects of gas. His leadership and personal example maintained a fine fighting spirit in his battalion.

SMITH, WILFRID CABOURN, M.C., Lieut. (Acting Lieut.-Colonel), King's Royal Rifle Corps, Special Reserve, attached 17th Battn. Royal Fusiliers. Near Noyelles, on 28–29 Sept. 1918, during the crossing of the Canal St. Quentin, he commanded his battalion with marked gallantry and skill. The passage of the canal and formation of a bridgehead was conducted under heavy shelling and machine-gun fire. Throughout the period he showed great coolness and ability. Later, when his battalion was suddenly ordered to attack Forenville, thanks to his energy and personal supervision all objectives were gained and many prisoners and guns captured.

STRUDWICK, SPENCER GORDON, M.C., Lieut. (Acting Major), Royal Field Artillery, Special Reserve, attached B/78th Brigade. During operations at Caullery on 9 Oct. 1918, he personally led a gun forward in close support of the advancing infantry, and engaged enemy machine guns successfully over open sights. He continued firing until his gun was disabled by hostile artillery fire. His very gallant action effectually silenced the enemy machine guns and enabled our infantry to advance. Later, he again brought a gun into action within 750 yards of enemy machine gun and destroyed it. He has previously shown marked gallantry and ability.

TAPP, JAMES HANSON WILLIAM, Major (Temporary Lieut.-Colonel), Reserve of Officers, attached Headquarters 230th (N.M.) Brigade, Royal Field Artillery, Territorial Force. During operations on 29 Sept. and 3 Oct. 1918, near Bellenglise, he commanded a Field Artillery Group with great distinction. The time available for preliminary preparation before each of these operations was very short, and it was only by his fearless reconnaissance work and tireless energy that the work was accomplished. On the occasion of the latter operations he only received his orders at 5.30 p.m. on 2 Oct., his batteries then being some distance west of the Canal. He made a very skilful and daring reconnaissance, and by his excellent arrangement he was able to move his batteries to positions two miles east of the canal, and took part in the opening barrage at 6.5 a.m. on 3 Oct. During the whole period of these operations the work of this officer was extremely good.

THOMAS-EVELYN, ROWLAND, Temporary Second Lieut., attached Manchester Regt. (12th Battn.). On 12 Oct., near Neuvilly, in command of the platoon specially detailed to deal with the enemy machine-gun post which had held up every previous attack, he successfully attacked the post, killed the enemy there and captured the two guns, enabling the battalion to set forward. He showed great dash and courage, and was in front during the whole time. Later, as the only officer left with the four companies, he did excellent work in rallying the men after the counter-attack and throughout set a fine example to all.

VARLEY, OSWALD, M.C., Temporary Capt., 7th Battn. East Yorkshire Regt. During the attack on the high ground north-west of Neuvilly on 10 Oct. 1918, he commanded his company with great skill and initiative. Finding no bridges, he led his men across the river under heavy fire, captured 40 prisoners, killed many of the enemy, and destroyed five machine guns, reaching his objective and establishing posts on both flanks. His marked gallantry, sound leadership and cheerfulness inspired his command.

WELDON, HENRY WALTER, Major (Acting Lieut.-Colonel), 2nd Battn. Leinster Regt. For great devotion to duty and gallantry during the attack which led up to the capture of Gheluvelt and Gheluwe on 28 Sept. 1918. He personally led his battalion throughout the operation and showed great skill and gallantry throughout the period from 28 Sept. to 4 Oct. 1918. The success of the operation was largely due to this officer's energy and gallantry.

WILLIAMS, AUBREY ELLIS, M.C., Capt. and Brevet Major, South Wales Borderers, G.S.O.2, 30th Division. At Menin, on 14 Oct. 1918, he made a very bold reconnaissance of the river crossings in face of considerable shell and machine-gun fire and forward of all our infantry posts, thus enabling a bridge to be thrown over at the earliest opportunity. Though badly concussed by a 5.9 inch bursting within a few feet of him, he still continued at duty. His fearlessness at all times was a fine example to all ranks.

WILSON, WILLIAM THOMAS, M.C., Temporary Capt. (Acting Major), 256th Tunnelling Coy., Royal Engineers. For conspicuous devotion to duty at Bellenglise on 30 Sept. 1918, when he supervised the removal of mines and traps from the Bellenglise-Magny Tunnel. With great foresight he arranged for the return of the German engineer to start the lighting plant and forced him to disclose the locations of the mines and firing circuit. When these had been discovered and rendered harmless, he cleared the tunnel, and, at great personal risk, forced the driver to start the engine, despite protests that there might be other mines connected to it. By his coolness and disregard of danger he set a fine example to his men.

WOODS, HUGH KENNEDY, Major and Brevet Lieut.-Colonel (Temporary Lieut.-Colonel), South Lancashire Regt., seconded 9th Battn. Tank Corps. For conspicuous gallantry and devotion to duty north of St. Quentin on 29 Sept. 1918. He personaly deployed his tanks and directed them on to their objectives. It was largely due to his personal gallantry and efforts that the tank attack was successfully launched and obtained such excellent results. He has fought his battalion in previous actions and during the operations in question with conspicuous success.

YOUNG, THOMAS FORBES, M.C., Temporary Capt. (Acting Major), 64th Field Coy., Royal Engineers. On the River Lys at Cuerne, on the night of 16–17 Oct. 1918, for conspicuous gallantry and devotion to duty. He commanded the field company which was entrusted with the task of throwing bridges across the river to enable an infantry brigade to cross and secure a bridgehead. He first made a reconnaissance of the river bank, and later, despite heavy shelling, brought up his equipment and constructed two bridges. Again, on the night of the 19th–20th, thanks to his coolness and ability, a bridge and two ferries were constructed under heavy trench mortar and machine-gun fire, and the brigade enabled to cross.

YOUNGER, JAMES, Lieut.-Colonel, 14th Battn. Royal Highlanders, Territorial Force. For conspicuous gallantry and devotion to duty. During the operations at Moislains on 2 Sept. 1918, when a strong enemy counter-attack was developed and a heavy barrage put down by them, he at once went forward through the barrage and steadied and reorganized the battalion. He was severely wounded in doing so, but continued to command until relieved. He behaved most gallantly.

CANADIAN FORCE.

BAKER, EDWIN GODFREY PHIPPS, M.C., Major, 47th Battn. Canadian Infantry, Western Ontario Regt. For conspicuous gallantry in front of Inchy-en-Artois during the operations 27–29 Sept. 1918. He commanded his battalion in heavy fighting on two successive days, and by his personal example and splendid leadership inspired the officers and men of his command. In particular, on the night of 28 Sept., when it was necessary to again use his battalion in restoring the situation, he led his unit in the attack, defeating the enemy and restoring our line in advance of the position previously held. Throughout the operations his work was of the highest order.

DAVIS, WILLIAM EDGAR, Major, 11th Battn. Canadian Railway Troops. For conspicuous gallantry and devotion to duty on 21 Aug. 1918, whilst in charge of a detachment near Bucquoy. He made reconnaissances of the lines in forward areas to be reconstructed under shell and machine-gun fire, and carried out this work under very difficult conditions. Prior to the operations he superintended the reconstruction of the main light railway line through to Bucquoy, after making skilful surveys almost up to the front-line trenches. He rendered most valuable service, and at all times has shown complete disregard for personal safety.

DUNWOODY, JAMES MOORE, D.C.M., Lieut., Fort Garry Horse. In the action at the Bois de Gattigny on 9 Oct. 1918, he was sent with his troop to ride down enemy machine guns on the right flank of the position at P.25a. In order to draw their fire and if possible to capture their machine guns, thus enabling the right flank of the enemy's position to be turned, he rode with his troops over 2,000 yards constantly under machine-gun fire, and while he and a number of his troop became casualties, he succeeded in driving the enemy from the guns, of which about 15 were captured. This officer's great gallantry and determination prevented heavy casualties, and by silencing the machine guns at this point made a continuation of the advance possible.

ELLIOTT, ORVIL ARD, Major, Canadian Army Dental Corps, attached 5th Canadian Field Ambulance. At Neuville Vitasse, Wancourt, Cherisy, from 26 to 29 Aug. 1918. For marked gallantry and devotion to duty. As the infantry advanced, he followed up closely and although many times he was forced to pass through heavy enemy barrages he kept in close touch with the battalions and kept establishing collecting posts as far forward as possible. He was the direct means of saving many lives, and throughout the operations his untiring efforts and disregard for his personal safety were a constant source of inspiration to those about him.

INGLES, CHARLES JAMES, Major, 20th Battn. Canadian Infantry, 1st Central Ontario Regt. For conspicuous gallantry and determined leadership. On the morning of 26 Aug. he handled his company with great skill and daring, working forward under heavy machine-gun and artillery fire and taking his objective. On two occasions he organized parties to clean out enemy machine-gun nests that were impeding the advance. He was wounded in the arm, but insisted in remaining with his company during the afternoon and night, defending a portion of the line subject to counter-attack. His example was an inspiration to all ranks.

LOUGH, JOHN ROBERTSON STEWART, M.C., Capt., 72nd Battn. Canadian Infantry, British Columbia Regt. For conspicuous gallantry and determined leadership during operations before Cambrai from 27 Sept. to 1 Oct. 1918. He was in charge of a company only numbering 60 during the attack on Sancourt and Blecourt. He mopped up the village and sent to the rear over 200 prisoners out of Sancourt alone; and captured an additional 80 prisoners in Blecourt. Later, he organized his men in defensive posts and reported to battalion headquarters the position, not only of his own posts but also that of the company on his left. His reports throughout were remarkably clear and of the greatest value.

MIDDLEMAST, EDWARD LIDDELL, Major, Fort Garry Horse. On the morning of 9 Oct. 1918, he was in charge of advanced guard squadron of the regiment, and located the enemy with many machine guns in the Bois-du-Mont Aux-Villes and Bois-de-Gattigny. After successfully sizing up the situation and timing himself with the advancing infantry, he charged the wood with the sword around the enemy's right flank, killing large numbers and capturing approximately 200 prisoners and 20 machine guns. Although wounded in this charge, he, after having his wound dressed, resumed command of his squadron and did valuable work during the remainder of the day. He did splendid work.

OGILVIE, ALEXANDER THOMAS, Lieut.-Colonel, 14th Brigade, Canadian Field Artillery. For conspicuous gallantry and ability on 2 Sept. 1918, near Vis-en-Artois. He manœuvred his brigade from the extreme left of the corps front line into a forward position in support of the centre. He made a rapid reconnaissance of the new situation under heavy shell fire, and was in a position to cover the infantry with all his batteries before the former were in position to commence the attack. He was able, through his own reconnaissance and that of his forward observing officer's to give the infantry brigadier much useful information, and throughout the day rendered very valuable support to the infantry.

PAULIN, STANLEY, Lieut.-Colonel, 11th Field Ambulance, Canadian Army Medical Corps. He was in charge of the evacuation of the brigade wounded in the operations about Cambrai. For the five days of that battle he worked day and night with very little rest. He was always leading and directing his men, and by his splendid example was responsible for the wonderful work done by those under him. His work under heavy shell and machine-gun fire was admirable.

PEARCE, LESLIE FRANK, M.C., Major, 4th Battn. Canadian Machine Gun Corps. For conspicuous gallantry and ability to command at Bourlon and north of Cambrai, from 27 Sept.–1 Oct. 1918. Throughout the operation he displayed marked skill in handling his batteries, particularly on 1 Oct., when he was sent forward with instructions to ensure the machine-gun defence of the ground which had been gained. He made personal reconnaissance under heavy fire and rapidly arranged excellent dispositions. That the brigade held its ground was as much due to his skill in handling his machine guns as to the stubbornness of the infantry defence.

PRESTON, EBENEZER MENZIES, M.M., Lieut., 87th Battn. Canadian Infantry, Quebec Regt. For most conspicuous gallantry at Bourlon, 27 Sept. 1918, Cambrai sector. He commanded one of the leading platoons of his company, and as they approached the railway embankment they came under heavy machine-gun fire. He at once called for volunteers, and with two men crawled up to within bombing distance, and then bombed and rushed the post. He killed two of the crew who had escaped the bombs and sent a third out as prisoner. In all, eight of the enemy were accounted for. His fine action enabled his company to continue the advance.

RYAN, EDUARD JOHN WILSON, Major, 102nd Battn. Canadian Infantry, 2nd Central Ontario Regt. For conspicuous gallantry and able leadership in command of his battalion during the whole of the operation from 2–5 Sept. 1918, betwen Dury and the Canal du Nord. He led the battalion from the assembly point to the jumping-off place under a continuous barrage of shell and machine-gun fire, and when on arrival it was found that the battalions through which this unit was to pass had been held up, he withdrew his men into immediate support; and afterwards carried out the relief in pitch darkness over an unknown area, going forward and personally directing the operation. On the following morning he advanced the battalion four miles to the west bank of the Canal du Nord, and finally cleared the enemy out of their last stronghold, a wood on the western bank.

STAIRS, PHILIP BOYD, Lieut., Canadian Field Artillery, attached Trench Mortar Battery, 5th Canadian Divisional Artillery. For conspicuous gallantry and devotion to duty near Villers-les-Cagnicourt on 2 Sept. 1918. He brought his mortar into action mounted upon a lorry, and engaged at short range enemy who were massing for a counter-attack. The whole of his crew being wounded and his mortar being subject to heavy fire from enemy guns firing over open sights, he kept it in action himself until a direct hit put it out and set the lorry on fire. Though he was wounded and there was ammunition on the burning lorry, he then climbed back, rescued his wounded crew, and attempted to extinguish the fire. During this time he was again wounded, but carried on until the ammunition exploded, destroying the lorry. He behaved most gallantly.

AUSTRALIAN IMPERIAL FORCE.

BAKER, HENRY SEYMOUR, Lieut., 13th Battn. Australian Imperial Force. During the advance on 18 Sept. 1918, near Le Verguier, north of St. Quentin, he acted as right guide to his battalion, and despite the great difficulties caused by fog and uncut wire and heavy machine-gun and artillery fire, carried out his duties in a most gallant and skilful manner. On reaching the first objective he went ahead to reconnoitre, and located a large party of the enemy. He threw bombs at them and 20 surrendered. These he brought back with him, and then got together a party of men and again attacked the enemy, taking further prisoners. At the first objective he had received a painful wound in the leg, but carried on right to the final objective. He behaved splendidly.

BENNETT, WILLIAM STANLEY, M.C., Lieut., 10th Battn. Australian Infantry. For most conspicuous gallantry near Villeret on 18 Sept. 1918. Whilst leading his platoon with the first wave he observed a nest of machine guns firing through our barrage and holding up our advance. He ran out ahead of his men into the barrage, worked his way round to the rear of the nest and shot five of the enemy with his revolver, made 30 men surrender and captured their five guns. Thanks to this fine action, which was accomplished single-handed under a hail of bullets, the advance was enabled to continue.

MACKENZIE, ALEXANDER KENNETH, M.C., Major (Temporary Lieut.-Colonel), 1st Battn. Australian Infantry. In the attack on Hargicourt and subsequent operations, 18-21 Sept. 1918, in command of a battalion he showed great skill and gallantry in preparing the attack and during the advance. The attack was in every way successful and resulted in the capture of several hundred prisoners and some field guns. During the difficult period of holding the line he showed ability in disposing his troops, and his work was of the greatest value to the brigade during a delicate situation.

MAY, LEONARD, M.C., Major, Australian Army Medical Corps, attached 11th Battn. Australian Infantry. During the attack near Villeret on 18 Sept. 1918, he displayed great gallantry and devotion to duty whilst attending to the wounded. In consequence of his excellent organization for clearing the wounded he was able to keep in touch with the advance, constantly moving his aid-post forward with the barrage, and maintaining liaison with the attacking companies throughout. He showed great disregard of danger under heavy artillery and machine-gun fire, and by his skill saved many lives.

McLEAN, JOHN, M.C., Lieut., 42nd Battn. Australian Infantry. On 11–12 Aug. 1918, during operations on the Somme, he, with a Lewis gun section, attacked an enemy strong point north of Rosieres which was holding up the advance of a flank company, whose success meant the success of the line. With extraordinary gallantry he accounted for five enemy machine guns, two by himself, cleared the strong point, and enabled the flank company to continue their advance. Just before reaching his final objective he was wounded, but continued to control his platoon until the capture of the final position, and then superintended consolidation. His magnificent example of courageous conduct produced a great moral effect on the whole of the attacking troops and did much to ensure his company's success. He did most splendid work.

WADSWORTH, WILLIAM ROBERT, M.C., Major, 14th Battn. Australian Infantry. For conspicuous gallantry and valuable services near Ascension Wood north of St. Quentin, on 18 Sept. 1918. He led his company with the greatest dash until the whole battalion was held up by intense machine-gun fire on the wire of the Hindenburg outpost line. At this stage he took charge of the battalion and displayed great tactical skill in manœuvring the men to take the position on a flank. He constantly moved up and down the line supervising the action of the companies and showed a complete disregard for his own personal safety. Having successfully reorganized the battalion he, by a series of skilfully planned bombing attacks, succeeded in carrying the enemy line on a frontage of 1,400 yards.

NEW ZEALAND FORCE.

ARDAGH, PATRICK AUGUSTINE, M.C., Capt., New Zealand Medical Corps, attached 1st Battn. Auckland Regt. For conspicuous gallantry and devotion to duty during an attack east of Masnieres. Being forced to place his dressing station in a spot constantly shelled by the enemy for 36 hours, he continued to dress wounded while shells fell on the station. He attended, not only his own battalion wounded, but men of three other battalions, and worked continuously without sleep all the time. He displayed high courage and resource and was the means of saving many lives.

London Gazette, 31 July, 1919.—" Admiralty, S.W., 31 July, 1919. The King has been graciously pleased to approve of the award of the following honours to the undermentioned Officers. To be Companions of the Distinguished Service Order."

ADAMS, BRYAN FULLERTON, Commander, Royal Navy. For distinguished services during the war.

ROSOMAN, ROBERT REYNOLDS, Commander, Royal Navy. For distinguished services during the war.

CHAPPELL, LIONEL SHEARD, D.S.C., Lieut.-Commander, Royal Naval Volunteer Reserve. For distinguished services during the war.

" Honours for Services in Action with an Enemy Submarine.—The King has been graciously pleased to approve of the award of the following honour to the undermentioned Officer. To receive a Bar to the Distinguished Service Order."

HERBERT, GODFREY, D.S.O., Commander, Royal Navy.

London Gazette, 8 Aug. 1919.—" War Office, 8 Aug. 1919. His Majesty the King has been graciously pleased to approve of the following awards to the undermentioned Officers in recognition of their gallantry and devotion to duty in the field. Awarded a Bar to the Distinguished Service Order."

SOUTH AFRICAN FORCE.

DAWSON, FREDERICK STUART, C.M.G., D.S.O. (Christian name corrected to Frederick Stewart [London Gazette, 5 March, 1920]), Lieut.-Colonel (Temporary Brigadier-General), 1st Battn. South African Infantry. He displayed gallantry of the highest degree during the fighting about Chapel Hill, Revelon Farm and Sorel on 21–22 March, 1918. On the afternoon of the 22nd he skilfully withdrew his brigade north to the Green Line. He and the members of his staff, after personally keeping the enemy from entering Sorel for some time, retired through Sorel, fighting under heavy rifle fire at close range. On the 24th, when his brigade only mustered 470 bayonets, they held 1,200 yards of front against overwhelming numbers until 4.30 in the afternoon, when ammunition was expended. He and his brigade did splendidly, and rendered most valuable service.

(D.S.O. gazetted 3 June, 1918.)

Awarded the Distinguished Service Order:

AARONSOHN, ALEXANDER, Local Lieut. (Egypt). For gallant conduct and daring on 2 Sept. 1918, in penetrating the enemy's lines and carrying out a reconnaissance which resulted in obtaining information which proved invaluable in subsequent operations.

AUSTRALIAN IMPERIAL FORCE.

BOASE, LEONARD CHARLES, M.C., Lieut., 52nd Battn. Australian Infantry. On 4 April, 1918, he commanded a platoon of a battalion holding the line from Buire to Dernancourt. On the 5th the enemy launched a strong attack between Dernancourt and Meaulte, which was broken up by the fire of his platoon. Though wounded he continued to lead his men splendidly, and inflicted very heavy casualties on the enemy, holding up their attack for at least two hours. He showed marked gallantry and ability to command, and rendered valuable service.

SOUTH AFRICAN FORCE.

BUNCE, HARRY, Temporary Lieut. (Acting Capt.), 4th Battn. South African Infantry. On the afternoon of 21 March, 1918, when the enemy obtained a footing on Chapel Hill, his company carried out a counter-attack which retook the whole of the hill and re-established the situation. On the 22nd, when his senior officers were casualties, he took command of the battalion, and finally successfully withdrew the remnants, some 140 strong. He commanded the battalion during the fighting of the 23rd and 24th, and on the latter day distinguished himself in a most marked manner. Owing to his courage and leadership a stubborn resistance was maintained.

ORMISTON, THOMAS, Temporary Major, 1st Battn. South African Infantry. He displayed marked courage and leadership during the enemy attack on 24 March, 1918. When the enemy attempted to bring a field gun into action within 100 yards' range, he brought Lewis-gun fire to bear on it, causing the gun to be abandoned. Later, when a second gun was brought up, the fire opened under his direction killed the team, and caused the gun to be overturned. When the left flank of his battalion was enveloped, he organized a defensive flank. He did excellent work.

London Gazette, 11 Aug. 1919.—" Admiralty, 11 Aug. 1919. The King has been graciously pleased to approve of the award of the following honour to the undermentioned Officer. To be a Companion of the Distinguished Service Order."

HUNT, ROBERT GREGORY MAZE DURRANT, Lieut.-Commander, Roya Navy. For distinguished services during the war.

London Gazette, 12 Sept. 1919.—" War Office, 12 Sept. 1919. The King has been graciously pleased to approve of the undermentioned rewards for distinguished services rendered in connection with military operations on the North-West Frontier, India, in Persia and Trans-Caspia. Dated 3 June, 1919. Awarded the Distinguished Service Order."

FRASER, WILLIAM ARCHIBALD KINNETH, M.C., Capt. and Brevet Major, 39th Central Indian Horse, Indian Army.

HARVEY-KELLY, CHARLES HAMILTON GRANT HUME, Capt. and Brevet Major (Acting Major), 127th Baluchistan Light Infantry, Indian Army

HAWLEY, WILLIAM GEORGE BROUGHTON ISCHIA, Major, 28th Light Cavalry, Indian Army.

HOLBROOKE, BERNARD FREDERICK ROPER, Major (Acting Lieut.-Colonel), 3/124th Baluchistan Infantry, Indian Army.

LUCAS, MALCOLM HUGH, Major, 37th Lancers, Indian Army.

MASTERS, JOHN, Major, 16th Rajputs, Indian Army.

VANRENEN, GEORGE RAINER, Lieut.-Colonel, 16th Rajputs, Indian Army.

London Gazette, 16 Sept. 1919.—" Admiralty, S.W., 16 Sept. 1919. The King has been graciously pleased to approve of the award of the following honour to the undermentioned Officer. To be a Companion of the Distinguished Service Order."

BINNEY, THOMAS HUGH, Commander, Royal Navy. For distinguished services during the war.

" Honours for Services in Action with an Enemy Submarine.—The King has been graciously pleased to approve of the award of the following honour to the undermentioned Officer. To be a Companion of the Distinguished Service Order."

BLACKMAN, CHARLES MAURICE, Lieut.-Commander, Royal Navy.

London Gazette, 3 Oct. 1919.—" War Office, 3 Oct. 1919. His Majesty the King has been graciously pleased to approve of the following immediate awards for conspicuous gallantry and devotion to duty in North Russia conferred by Major-General W. E. Ironside, K.C.B., C.M.G., D.S.O., in pursuance of the powers vested in him by His Majesty.—Archangel Command. Awarded the Distinguished Service Order."

LAVIE, HENRY ERNEST, Major (Temporary Lieut.-Colonel), Durham Light Infantry, attached 13th Battn. Yorkshire Regt. For inspiring leadership and devotion to duty when in command of the Seletskoe Detachment. No exertion on his part has been too great in ensuring that proper defensive measures were being taken, and the entire lack of success of enemy attacks made on his front during April, 1919, can be attributed in great measure to the change of morale in the defending troops owing to his personality and power of command.

MONTFORD, IVAN CLAUDE, Capt. (Temporary Lieut.-Colonel), Rifle Brigade, Special Reserve. He conducted a very daring reconnaissance five miles behind the enemy's front, arriving within 1,000 yards of a strong enemy position The information he received was most valuable. He has for five months commanded the troops on both banks of the Dvina River, and by his personal courage and tact has pulled his troops of mixed nationalities through a difficult period.

SOUTH AFRICAN FORCE.

MACFIE, THOMAS GIRDWOOD, M.C., Capt., 4th Battn. South African Infantry. On 2 June, 1919, he was near the 18-pounder position on his way to the observation post. He collected and organized some infantry at this point. He then went back to Priluk, rallying and encouraging Russian infantry who were disorganized, and himself led a counter-attack against Priluk, which was recaptured together with all the guns. This success was due to his marked gallantry and ability to command.

London Gazette, 4 Oct. 1919.—" War Office, 4 Oct. 1919. With reference to the awards conferred as announced in the London Gazette dated 8 March, 1919, the following are the statements of services for which the decorations were conferred. Awarded a Third Bar to the Distinguished Service Order."

BUCKLE, ARCHIBALD WALTER, D.S.O., Temporary Commander, Anson Battn. Royal Naval Division, Royal Naval Volunteer Reserve. During the fighting round Niergnies on 8 Oct. 1918, he showed great courage and powers of leadership. After the enemy had counter-attacked and succeeded in entering our lines, he seized an enemy anti-tank rifle and engaged three hostile tanks with it and drove them off. He then rallied men of various units in his neighbourhood and led them forward to the positions whence they had been forced. Throughout he did excellent work.
(D.S.O. gazetted 4 March, 1918.)
(1st Bar gazetted 26 July, 1918.)
(2nd Bar gazetted 11 Jan. 1919.)

DAWSON, WILLIAM ROBERT AUFRERE, D.S.O., Capt. and Brevet Major (Temporary Lieut.-Colonel), Royal West Kent Regt., Commanding 6th Battn. For conspicuous gallantry and good leadership of his battalion from 18 to 29 Sept. 1918, near Epehy and Vendhuille. During the period they took part in three assaults successfully. On the 21st–22nd and 28th–29th he was continually in the front line, superintending operations and encouraging his men. The success of his battalion on these occasions was largely due to his fine leadership and personal example.
(D.S.O. gazetted 15 April, 1916.)
(1st Bar gazetted 18 July, 1917.)
(2nd Bar gazetted 22 June, 1918.)

KNOX, ROBERT SINCLAIR, D.S.O., Temporary Major (Acting Lieut.-Colonel), 10th Battn. Royal Inniskilling Fusiliers, attached 9th Battn. On the night of 19–20 Oct. 1918, he succeeded in crossing the Lys under the most difficult circumstances, and established a bridgehead which enabled another battalion to cross, and eventually the brigade. He cleared all the ground north of Beveren, captured his objective, and at dawn continued the attack successfully. He was short of officers, and showed marked ability, gallantry and energy.
(D.S.O. gazetted 1 Jan. 1917.)
(1st Bar gazetted 18 Feb. 1918.)
(2nd Bar gazetted 16 Sept. 1918.)

Awarded a Second Bar to the Distinguished Service Order:

BEASLEY, ROBERT LONGFIELD, D.S.O., Major (Temporary Lieut.-Colonel), 2nd Battn. Gloucestershire Regt., attached 17th Battn. Royal Welsh Fusiliers. On 8 Oct. 1918, he led the battalion through the Beaurevoir line to the objective at Villers Outreux and reached the final objective. Throughout this advance he was always at the head of his men, encouraging them and setting them a splendid example. At Englefontaine, on 27 Oct., he was successful, under sniping at close range, in bringing a wounded officer in on his back, undoubtedly saving his life. Throughout he showed great gallantry.
(D.S.O. gazetted 1 Jan. 1918.)
(1st Bar gazetted 27 July, 1918.)

CURTIS, HUBERT MONTAGU COTTON, D.S.O., Capt. (Acting Lieut.-Colonel), 6th Battn. North Staffordshire Regt., Territorial Force, Commanding 7th Battn. East Kent Regt. In the operations around Bousies on 23–26 Oct. 1918, he, in command of his battalion, displayed great gallantry, and by his good leadership ensured the success of an operation that at one time was likely to be held up. When enemy machine guns held up the attack he made a personal reconnaissance and was thus enabled to handle his command to the best advantage.
(D.S.O. gazetted 1 Jan. 1918.)
(1st Bar gazetted 26 July, 1918.)

DUMBELL, CHARLES HAROLD, D.S.O., Major (Temporary Lieut.-Colonel), Nottinghamshire and Derbyshire Regt., attached 11th Battn. Essex Regt. During the operations near Holnon on 24 Sept. 1918, the left of the brigade front was unable to reach its objective owing to the exposed nature of the ground. Towards dusk he went down to the front line, and it was by his own personal effort and leadership that the objective was in all cases gained and the tape laid in time for the troops to assemble. He showed great coolness and gallantry under heavy fire.
(D.S.O. gazetted 1 Jan. 1917.)
(1st Bar gazetted 26 July, 1918.)

FRASER, JOHN ALEXANDER, D.S.O., D.C.M., Lieut. (Temporary Lieut.-Colonel), 7th Dragoon Guards, attached 5th–6th Battn. Royal Scots, Territorial Force. For fine and determined leading of his battalion on 1 Oct. and 2 Oct. 1918, at Sequehart. He attacked and captured Sequehart on the 1st, but was shortly afterwards driven out by a counter-attack. With very depleted numbers he recaptured it, personally killing three of the enemy with his revolver, and capturing altogether close on 500 prisoners. After being driven out again, he again recaptured it and held it for 48 hours. He and his battalion did splendid work.
(D.S.O. gazetted 1 Jan. 1918.)
(1st Bar gazetted 22 April, 1918.)

FREYBURG, BERNARD CYRIL, V.C., D.S.O., Capt. and Brevet Lieut.-Colonel (Temporary Brigadier-General), Royal West Surrey Regt. (General Officer Commanding 88th Infantry Brigade). For marked gallantry and initiative on 11 Nov. 1918, at Lessines. He personally led the cavalry, and though at the time he had only nine men with him, he rushed the town, capturing 100 of the enemy and preventing the blowing up of the important road bridges over the Dendre.
(D.S.O. gazetted 3 June, 1915.)
(1st Bar gazetted 1 Feb. 1919.)

LAMBERT, WALTER JOHN, D.S.O., Major, 29th Lancers, Indian Army, attached Mysore Imperial Service Lancers (Egypt). On 23 Sept. 1918, during the attack on Haifa, Major Lambert commanded the advanced guard of the 15th Imperial Service Cavalry Brigade. He pushed forward and occupied all tactical points close to the enemy's position and led the Mysore Lancers in the attack with great gallantry.
(D.S.O. gazetted 1 Jan. 1917.)
(1st Bar gazetted 2 Dec. 1918.)

MILLS, ARTHUR MORDAUNT, D.S.O., Major, 18th Lancers, Indian Army (Egypt). On the night of 21–22 Sept. 1918, during the attack on Nazareth, he organized and led a counter-attack, which he carried through with 29 Indian other ranks in the face of rifle and machine-gun fire against 300 of the enemy. This counter-attack was completely successful, several of the enemy being killed and 100 prisoners captured. He did fine work.
(D.S.O. gazetted 1 Jan. 1917.)
(1st Bar gazetted 4 Feb. 1918.)

NADEN, FRANK, D.S.O., M.C., Lieut. (Acting Lieut.-Colonel), 1/6th Battn. Cheshire Regt., Territorial Force, attached 7th Battn. Royal Irish Regt. Near Neuve Eglise, on 1 Sept. 1918, he had launched his battalion to attack the village, when he received orders to change direction from south to east. This was done, but the leading companies moved too far to the right. Seeing this, he personally led the right company on to its proper objective in the face of considerable machine-gun and trench-mortar fire. He was shortly afterwards wounded. But on this and the previous day he showed an absolute disregard of danger, and by his fine example and leadership inspired all ranks.
(D.S.O. gazetted 26 Nov. 1917.)
(1st Bar gazetted 16 Sept. 1918.)

CANADIAN FORCE.

MACFARLANE, ROBERT ALEXANDER, D.S.O., Lieut.-Colonel, 58th Infantry Battn. 2nd Central Ontario Regt. Before Cambrai, 27 Sept. to 1 Oct. 1918. On 28 Sept. he led his battalion in the attack on the Marcoing Line, and captured it in spite of most heavy opposition. Altogether this battalion captured over 2,500 yards of the Marcoing Line and 50 enemy machine guns, in addition to killing many of the enemy and capturing 120 prisouers. His marked gallantry and ability were an inspiration to all ranks.
(D.S.O. gazetted 4 June, 1917.)
(1st Bar gazetted 11 Jan. 1919.)

RILEY, HAROLD JAMES, D.S.O., Lieut.-Colonel, 27th Infantry Battn. Manitoba Regt. For conspicuous courage and ability in command of his battalion in operations near Cambrai, on 9, 10 and 11 Oct. 1918. In the attack on Iwuy his men were caught in a heavy barrage and showed signs of becoming disorganized. Immediately he went forward, steadied them, and brought them out of the barrage with light casualties. Throughout the operations he set a very fine example to all under him.
(D.S.O. gazetted 18 July, 1917.)
(1st Bar gazetted 11 Jan. 1919.)

Awarded a First Bar to the Distinguished Service Order:

ANDERSON, FRANCIS, D.S.O., M.C., Capt (Acting Lieut.-Colonel), 1st Battn. Royal Highlanders. On 28–29 Sept. 1918, between Bellenglise and Le Tronquoy, and 18–19 Oct. 1918, between Vaux-Andigny and Wassigny, he proved himself a most able and resourceful battalion commander. He personally reconnoitred positions under heavy machine-gun and shell fire, and the successful attack and capture of Wassigny with light casualties was entirely due to his excellent handling of the battalion. He showed marked gallantry and ability throughout.
(D.S.O. gazetted 17 Dec. 1917.)

CLEGHORN, GEORGE MATTHEW, D.S.O., Temporary Major, 15th Battn. Highland Light Infantry. For conspicuous gallantry and skilful leading of his battalion in the attack on Le Tronquoy on 29 Sept. 1918. With an exposed flank on his right he led his battalion to the attack through the front of another division. Owing to his skilful use of ground and cover very few casualties were suffered by his battalion, while taking and holding all his objectives. During the night he consolidated his position and cleared up a network of enemy trenches, capturing about 300 prisoners.
(D.S.O. gazetted 26 July, 1918.)

CURRIN, RICHARD WILLIAM, D.S.O., Temporary Major (Acting Lieut.-Colonel), York and Lancaster Regt., attached 1/8th Battn. Nottinghamshire and Derbyshire Regt., Territorial Force. For conspicuous gallantry and able leadership in command of his battalion in the attack on Regnicourt on 17 Oct. 1918. During the advance he organized and carried out an attack on a strongly defended locality, which had been passed by the leading waves of the attack on account of the thick fog, and from which machine guns were firing into the backs of our advancing troops. By his prompt action the locality was captured, with upwards of 120 prisoners and 20 machine guns.
(D.S.O. gazetted 25 Aug. 1916.)

DOWDING, CHARLES CHILD, D.S.O., M.C., Temporary Major (Acting Lieut.-Colonel), Royal Lancaster Regt., attached 1/6th Battn. North Staffordshire Regt., Territorial Force. Near Sequehart, for conspicuous gallantry and devotion to duty during the operations on 3 Oct. 1918, in the attack on Mannequin Hill. He showed great coolness and power of leadership. Whilst in command of the 1/6th Battn. North Staffordshire Regt. he handled a difficult situation with great skill under heavy shell and machine-gun fire.
(D.S.O. gazetted 3 June, 1918.)

DRAGE, GODFREY, D.S.O., Major (Acting Lieut.-Colonel), Reserve of Officers, Oxfordshire and Buckinghamshire Light Infantry, attached 1/4th Battn. Cheshire Regt., Territorial Force. During the operations near Menin, on 14 Oct. 1918, he showed marked gallantry and able leadership in command of his battalion. He advanced his line over 3,000 yards and captured a great many machine guns and over 150 prisoners. On reaching his objective he rushed patrols right through Menin, and exploited his success to the full. He passed his information back with extraordinary promptness, and throughout the whole operations his conduct was of a very high order.
(D.S.O. gazetted 1 Jan. 1917.)

FURSE, RALPH DOLIGNON, D.S.O., Major, King Edward's Horse. He handled the advance guard of corps mounted troops in a most skilful and dashing manner during the advance from Lille to the Escaut on the 18th and 19th Oct. 1918. Under heavy machine-gun fire he turned the enemy's flanks and drove them out with the loss of one man killed and one wounded. He showed cool courage and able leadership throughout.
(D.S.O. gazetted 26 July, 1918.)

GARDNER, WILLIAM ROSS, D.S.O., Capt. (Acting Lieut.-Colonel), Royal Army Medical Corps (Special Reserve), attached 138th Field Ambulance. He was in charge of all forward medical arrangements of the division for the period 4 Oct. 1918 to 26 Oct. 1918, first in front of Gheluwe, and then both west and east of Courtrai. During the period in question, night and day, he visited the rear aid posts, relay and forward collecting posts, often under heavy shell fire and gassing in order to personally ascertain that the work of evacuation was proceeding satisfactorily. He showed great gallantry and ability, and his devotion to duty saved many lives.
(D.S.O. gazetted 1 Jan. 1918.)

HART, REGINALD SETON, D.S.O., Major (Temporary Lieut.-Colonel), Nottinghamshire and Derbyshire Regt., attached 9th Battn. Yorkshire Regt. For conspicuous gallantry during the attack on Beaurevoir on 5 Oct. 1918, the advance on Honnechy 9 Oct. and the attack and capture of St. Benin on 10 Oct. Throughout the whole operations from 5 to 11 Oct. 1918, he led his battalion with great skill and judgment. On more than one occasion when his battalion was held up by strong enemy resistance, he personally led his men in the attack, and the success of the operations was largely due to his leadership.
(D.S.O. gazetted 27 Oct. 1917.)

HOHLER, ARTHUR PRESTON, D.S.O., Major (Acting Lieut.-Colonel), 2/10th Battn. Middlesex Regt., Territorial Force, Commanding 4/5th Battn. Welsh Regt. Territorial Force (Egypt). At Hindhead, near El Mugheir, and Bidston Hill, near Kh. Abu Felah, on the 18th Sept. 1918, he displayed great gallantry and coolness, handling his battalion with rare skill, capturing all his objectives with very slight casualties, and inflicting heavy losses on the enemy.
(D.S.O. gazetted 16 Aug. 1917.)

HOLDEN, HYLA NAPIER, D.S.O., Lieut.-Colonel, 5th Cavalry, Indian Army, Senior Special Service Officer, employed Jodhpur Imperial Service Lancers (Egypt). For conspicuous gallantry and brilliant leadership at Haifa on the 23rd Sept. 1918. He personally led the Jodhpur Lancers in a mounted attack by which the town was captured. He galloped his regiment through a narrow defile under heavy fire at close range, directing two squadrons upon certain enemy positions and leading the remainder of the regiment straight through the town. He maintained complete control of his men throughout, and proved himself a most dashing and capable cavalry leader.
(D.S.O. gazetted 1 Jan. 1919.)

HUDSON, NOEL BARING, D.S.O., Temporary Lieut.-Colonel, M.C., 8th Battn. Royal Berkshire Regt. In the attack by his battalion by night on the enemy positions on Mount Carmel (east of Le Cateau), on the 26th Oct. 1918, the assaulting troops had owing to the darkness become dispersed, and no information could be obtained of the progress of the attack. He went forward, and under heavy fire located the position of his companies. When his battalion was compelled to withdraw he succeeded in establishing a defensive line west of Mount Carmel. Though wounded in three places by shell fire, he remained at duty until the operation was completed. His gallantry and ability to command were most marked.
(D.S.O. gazetted in this Gazette.)

HUTCHISON, COLIN ROSS MARSHALL, D.S.O., M.C., Capt. (Acting Major), 113th Brigade, Royal Field Artillery, attached 29th Divisional Artillery. For conspicuous gallantry in command of a brigade of Royal Field Artillery near Courtrai, from 20 to 22 Oct. 1918, inclusive. On 20 Oct. he established an observation post right forward and directed the fire of his brigade on to a strong locality, thereby assisting the infantry to capture it. On 22 Oct. he carried out forward reconnaissances under very heavy fire, and brought part of his brigade close behind the infantry to support their further advance. His fine behaviour inspired all ranks under his command.
(D.S.O. gazetted 1 Jan. 1918.)

JEWELS, CHARLES EDGAR, D.S.O., M.C., Temporary Lieut.-Colonel, 18th Battn. Lancashire Fusiliers. He commanded his battalion with conspicuous success on 28 Sept. 1918, at the capture of Hill 60 and the advance on Wervicq on 1 Oct. He personally led his battalion through the attack on 14 Oct. in which all objectives were taken to a depth of 8,000 yards, crossed the River Lys on the night of 18–19 Oct. and took part in the capture of the Kreupel Ridge on the afternoon of 20 Oct. Throughout he set a splendid example of gallant and able leadership to those under him.
(D.S.O. gazetted 26 July, 1918.)

JONES, BRYAN JOHN, D.S.O., Major (Acting Lieut.-Colonel), Leinster Regt., attached 15th Battn. Royal Irish Rifles. For most conspicuous gallantry and devotion to duty on the 14 Oct. 1918, in the Moorseele Sector. When it was impossible to get accurate information as to the location of the troops during the attack, he went forward and organized his battalion whilst fighting in the streets of Moorseele, and personally placed his machine guns in action, causing the village to be soon cleared of the enemy. He personally shot a machine gunner who was holding up the advance. His fine example and leadership were mainly responsible for the great success attained by his battalion.
(D.S.O. gazetted 14 Jan. 1916.)

LAURIE, JOHN EMILIUS, D.S.O., Capt. (Acting Lieut.-Colonel), 1st Battn. Seaforth Highlanders, attached 6th Battn. Territorial Force. For conspicuous gallantry near Avesnes-le-Sec on the 15th Oct. 1918, when one of the companies under his command was driven back by heavy machine-gun and rifle fire, thus exposing a flank. He immediately went forward under heavy fire, reorganized the company in the open, and himself led them forward again to their position in the line. On 25 Oct. near Famars, he made a personal reconnaissance under heavy fire, reorganized the troops on their original front line, and so consolidated the position securely.
(D.S.O. gazetted 22 Sept. 1916.)

LEWIS, DUDLEY, D.S.O., M.C., Temporary Major (Acting Lieut.-Colonel), York and Lancaster Regt., Commanding 1/5th Battn. Gloucestershire Regt., Territorial Force. For gallant leadership and devotion to duty during the period 5–10 Oct. 1918. He was called upon suddenly to organize and carry out the attack on Beaurevoir. This he did with the greatest skill. His battalion took all their objectives splendidly, thereby making the next big attack possible. On the 9th inst. he successfully attacked Maretz, clearing the village and taking about 30 prisoners. Throughout he showed great courage and ability to command.
(D.S.O. gazetted 1 Jan. 1918.)

MASON, GLYN KEITH MURRAY, D.S.O., Capt. (Acting Lieut.-Colonel), 14th Hussars, Commanding 1/1st Dorsetshire Yeomanry (Egypt). For conspicuous gallantry at Er Remte on the 27th Sept. 1918. While his regiment was holding a position west of the village, it was strongly counter-attacked from the south-west end of the village. His advanced firing line was steadily forced back by superior enemy machine-gun fire, but he at the right moment seized the opportunity to mount his retiring firing line and charge the counter-attacking enemy. The latter were entirely surprised and routed. This action was almost entirely responsible for the rapid capitulation of the enemy holding the village.
(D.S.O. gazetted 3 June, 1916.)

MUIRHEAD, MURRAY, D.S.O., Major (Acting Lieut.-Colonel), Headquarters, 51st Brigade, Royal Field Artillery. For conspicuous gallantry and devotion to duty from 28 Sept. to 26 Oct. 1918. During this period, by his fine example, and by his fearless reconnaissances carried out under heavy shell fire and machine-gun fire right up to the front line, he materially contributed to the success of the operations by the division. On 22 Oct. 1918, near Ooteghem he personally took guns up to within a few hundred yards of houses occupied by enemy machine guns, and from there engaged these targets.
(D.S.O. gazetted 18 Feb. 1915.)

POLLOCK, HENRY BRODHURST, D.S.O., Temporary Commander, Hood Battn., Royal Naval Division, Royal Naval Volunteer Reserve. For marked gallantry and devotion to duty at Niergnies on 8 Oct. 1918. His men were temporarily disorganized by enemy counter-attack with tanks, and under heavy machine-gun fire he stopped a withdrawal. He organized a party and rushed a tank crew and then retook Niergnies. Thanks to his fearless and able leadership the final objective was held against enemy counter-attacks.
(D.S.O. gazetted 4 March, 1918.)

RATCLIFFE, WILLIAM CHARLES, D.S.O., Capt. (Temporary Major), Northamptonshire Regt., attached 9th Battn. Yorkshire Light Infantry. On 7 Nov. 1918, whilst in command of his battalion, he was ordered to attack Limont Fontaine. Owing to casualties he assumed control of another battalion in addition to his own. The battalion entered Limont Fontaine with great dash, killing and capturing numerous enemy, led by him. Pushing right on, his battalion proceeded to capture the next village, Eclaibes. He showed great dash and courage, and his powers of organization ensured the success of a difficult operation
(D.S.O. gazetted in this Gazette.)

SANKEY, CROFTON EDWARD PYM, D.S.O., Major and Brevet Lieut.-Colonel (Acting Lieut.-Colonel), Commanding Royal Engineers, 1st Division, Royal Engineers. For great gallantry in making personal reconnaissances of the Sambre-Oise Canal, south of Catillon, during the period 28 Oct.–3 Nov. 1918. Owing to the able way in which he carried out his work the crossings over the canal were negotiated with comparatively few casualties in the face of a large number of machine guns and heavy shell fire. The success of the operation may be very largely credited to the skill and personal gallantry of Lieut.-Colonel Sankey.
(D.S.O. gazetted 23 June, 1915.)

STOREY, HENRY INNES, D.S.O., Major (Temporary Lieut.-Colonel), Commanding 9th Battn. Devonshire Regt. For conspicuous gallantry and ability to command. On 8 Oct. 1918, he captured Ponchaux, strongly held, with his battalion, a village which had held up the advance for several days. It was owing to the high state of discipline and training which he had instilled into his battalion that the enemy's defences were broken and marked success attained, a large number of prisoners and machine guns being taken.
(D.S.O. gazetted 15 Feb. 1917.)

STIRLING, WALTER FRANCIS, D.S.O., M.C., Major, Reserve of Officers, Royal Dublin Fusiliers (Egypt). For gallant service rendered during the operations resulting in the occupation of Damascus by the Arab forces. By his example and personal courage whilst leading the Arabs, he, in conjunction with another officer, was mainly instrumental in securing the successful occupation of the town, and the establishment without grave disorder of the Arab military authorities therein.
(D.S.O. gazetted 28 Jan. 1902.)

WEIR, DONALD LORD, D.S.O., M.C., Capt. (Acting Lieut.-Colonel), Leicestershire Regt., attached 1st Battn. West Yorkshire Regt. During the operations near Holnon on the 24th–25th Sept. 1918, he displayed marked gallantry and initiative in securing his objectives in the neighbourhood of Selency Village and Wood. The success of these operations in the face of determined enemy resistance was largely due to his personal leadership. Again on 8 Oct. near Sequehart, he did splendid work, securing his objective without the aid of artillery, and capturing 250 prisoners and many machine guns.
(D.S.O. gazetted 15 April, 1916.)

WHEATLEY, LEONARD LANE, C.M.G., D.S.O., Major and Brevet Lieut.-Colonel (Temporary Brigadier-General), Argyll and Sutherland Highlanders Commanding 1st Infantry Brigade. He has commanded his brigade in five distinct operations during the last six weeks. His personal gallantry and example have had a most marked effect, and his fine powers of leadership caused the success which has attended all the operations he has been engaged in. Notably, in the forcing of the Sambre Canal, his reconnaissance for previous assembly by night at a point close to the canal bank, and his handling of his brigade throughout the day, were fine achievements.
(D.S.O. gazetted 20 May, 1898.)

CANADIAN FORCE.

CARMICHAEL, DOUGALL, D.S.O., M.C., Major, 58th, attached 116th, Infantry Battn., 2nd Central Ontario Regt. Before Cambrai, 27 Sept.–1 Oct. 1918. For marked gallantry in action. On 28 Sept. he was in command of his battalion when it captured the western portion of St. Olle. Next day he again attacked and cleared the village. Some days later, while leading his battalion, he was badly wounded in the face, but remained on duty and pressed on to Ramillies, the final objective. His fine courage and determined leadership inspired all under him.
(D.S.O. gazetted 11 Jan. 1919.)

CONSTANTINE, CHARLES FRANCIS, D.S.O., Lieut.-Colonel, 5th Brigade, Canadian Field Artillery. For conspicuous gallantry in command of a mobile Field Artillery brigade during operations in the Arras-Cambrai sector, 26 Aug. to 6 Oct. 1918. He made many bold reconnaissances under heavy fire. Severely burned about the head and arms in an explosion caused by hostile shelling, he refused to leave his command until the 6th Oct., when the C.R.A. ordered him to do so. The fearless example set by this officer inspired all serving under him to their greatest efforts.
(D.S.O. gazetted 1 Jan. 1917.)

ELLIOTT, ORVIL ARD, D.S.O., Major, Canadian Army Dental Corps, attached 5th Field Ambulance, Canadian Army Medical Corps. For conspicuous gallantry and devotion to duty in the area forward of Iwuy, north-east of Cambrai, on 11 Oct. 1918. On hearing that there were two wounded men lying in a road in front of our lines, he collected a party of bearers and led them forward under heavy fire. It was through his personal efforts and disregard of danger that the wounded, numbering eight, were successfully evacuated, and he was without doubt the means of saving their lives.
(D.S.O. gazetted 15 Feb. 1919.)

GIRVAN, JOHN POLLANDS, D.S.O., M.C., Major (Acting Lieut.-Colonel), 15th Infantry Battn. 1st Central Ontario Regt. For marked gallantry and ability in the attack on the Canal du Nord on 27 Sept. 1918. Crossing the canal on light bridges, and the River Agache by planks, under heavy machine-gun and sniping fire, he pushed on. He personally attacked and captured an enemy machine gun, shooting the gunner and turning the gun on the enemy. He went on and assisted in capturing Chapel Corner and the village of Marquion, and then gained his final objectives. His courage and dash were a fine example to his command.
(D.S.O. gazetted 1 Feb. 1919.)

KAPPELE, DANIEL PAUL, D.S.O., Lieut.-Colonel, 5th Field Ambulance, Canadian Army Medical Corps. For conspicuous gallantry on 12 Oct. 1918, in the vicinity of Iwuy, north-east of Cambrai. He drove a car to the forward area through shell fire, which wounded him and others. He proceeded to dress the wounds of the others, directing and assisting in their removal to a place of safety. It was not until all were attended to and removed from danger that he allowed himself to be taken away and suffered his own wounds to be dressed. He showed great pluck and devotion to duty.
(D.S.O. gazetted 3 June, 1918.)

LEASK, THOMAS McCRAE, D.S.O., Lieut.-Colonel, 10th Field Ambulance, Canadian Army Medical Corps. During recent operations in front of Cambrai he was given the task of clearing the wounded of a division. For five days on end he worked with untiring energy and absolute disregard for personal danger. On the night of 30 Sept.–1 Oct. 1918, he, with the help of a near-by N.C.O. and one of the wounded drivers, succeeded in rescuing patients from a burning car, and had them immediately evacuated. His conduct throughout was admirable. (D.S.O. gazetted 1 Jan. 1918.)

PHILPOT, DAVID, D.S.O., Major, 7th Infantry Battn. British Columbia Regt. For great gallantry and devotion to duty. During the Bourlon Wood operations, 27 Sept. to 2 Oct. 1918, he commanded a battalion with great success. After the capture of Marquion he withdrew the company committed to its capture, and with his battalion advanced without artillery barrage. During this phase and the subsequent action up to the Blue Line, he showed consummate leadership. When the Blue Line was reached he inspected his foremost positions under heavy fire, so as to prepare most advantageously for a possible counter-attack. Throughout his courage and able leadership inspired those under him. (D.S.O. gazetted 18 July, 1917.)

AUSTRALIAN IMPERIAL FORCE.

CAMERON, DONALD, D.S.O., Lieut.-Colonel, 12th Australian Light Horse Regt. (Egypt). For continuous good work with his regiment from El Kuneitra to Damascus. On the 30th Sept. 1918, when Kaukab was strongly held by the enemy infantry and machine guns, he was ordered to attack the enemy's left flank with his regiment mounted. He led the charge, seized his objectives with great dash, and drove the enemy in disorder towards Damascus. Over 70 prisoners and eight machine guns were captured, in conjunction with the 4th Australian Light Horse Regt. He proved himself a gallant and able leader of troops. (D.S.O. gazetted 18 Jan. 1918.)

CORRIGAN, JOHN JOSEPH, D.S.O., Lieut.-Colonel, 46th Battn. Australian Imperial Force. For conspicuous good work and devotion to duty during the advance west of Bellenglise on 18 Sept. 1918. He commanded his battalion with great skill and courage, and after the second objective had been captured he moved his battalion forward unsupported on his right, and captured the Outpost Line of the Hindenburg System under very heavy fire, capturing 15 officers and 436 other ranks. He showed marked ability to command. (D.S.O. gazetted 1 Jan. 1918.)

DENEHY, CHARLES ALOYSIUS, D.S.O., Lieut.-Colonel, 57th Battn. Australian Imperial Force. For conspicuous gallantry during the attack on the Hindenburg Line near Bellicourt from 29 Sept. to 2 Oct. 1918. On 29 Sept. the task of the brigade was to pass through other troops who had carried out the initial attack. The latter proved unable to consolidate on their objective, and he pushed his battalion forward, and under very heavy fire reorganized other troops as part of his battalion, eventually clearing up the situation. Later in the day he pushed his battalion forward and subsequently consolidated in the Le Catelet system. Throughout the operations his able leadership was most marked. (D.S.O. gazetted 18 July, 1917.)

McCLEAN, FREDERICK STEPHEN, D.S.O., Major (Temporary Lieut.-Colonel), 5th Pioneer Battn. Australian Infantry. Near Bellicourt on 29 Sept. 1918. He was in charge of the work entrusted to this battalion on two roads. He organized the whole of the preliminary details in a most thorough manner, and under continuous shell fire reconnoitred both roads up to the enemy lines, and did not leave the work until he was assured that the roads were through. Throughout he showed great gallantry, and was a great inspiration to all under his command. (D.S.O. gazetted 27 Oct. 1917.)

RANKIN, GEORGE JAMES, D.S.O., Major, 4th Australian Light Horse Regt. (Egypt). For great gallantry, dash and initiative during the operations from El Kuneitra to Damascus. On the 30th Sept. 1918, when his regiment acted as advance guard from Sasa to Kaukab, owing to his rapid movements, they captured 340 prisoners, one field gun and eight machine guns. Kaukab was strongly held by the enemy, and when this officer was ordered to make a frontal attack his leadership was excellent and his regiment seized all objectives, capturing nine officers, over 70 other ranks and eight machine guns. In this action the enemy's cavalry were driven in disorder towards Damascus. On the morning of the 1st Oct. 1918, when ordered to seize the Military Barracks in Damascus, he showed great skill in manœuvring his troops in such a manner that he was largely instrumental in capturing the whole enemy garrison in Damascus, numbering over 11,000. (D.S.O. gazetted 11 April, 1918.)

SCOTT, WILLIAM HENRY, C.M.G., D.S.O., Lieut.-Colonel, 9th Australian Light Horse Regt. (Egypt). On the 2nd Oct. 1918, while the brigade was bivouacked near Duma, a report was received that a large column of enemy was moving across to enter the foothills at Kubbet I Asafi. The brigade was at once ordered out in pursuit. This officer got his regiment away in particularly quick time, and, moving rapidly for six miles, headed the enemy off, and charged and captured the whole column consisting of 1,450 of the enemy, 26 machine guns, one mountain gun, two field guns and 12 automatic rifles. If this advance regiment had been 20 minutes later the enemy could have gained the entrance to the foothills and could easily have kept the brigade off with the machine guns and artillery they had and so escaped. He did splendid work. (D.S.O. gazetted 16 May, 1916.)

NEW ZEALAND FORCE.

JARDINE, LEONARD HANDFORTH, D.S.O., M.C., Lieut.-Colonel, 2nd Battn. New Zealand Rifle Brigade. For conspicuous gallantry and resource at Le Quesnoy on the 4th Nov. 1918. His battalion was detailed to capture the city. The enemy was holding a railway embankment in front of the city from which he brought such heavy machine-gun fire to bear on our troops that the attack was temporarily held up. He promptly used his reserve troops with such skill that he overcame the resistance of the enemy and enabled the advance to be continued. Finally, by his gallant and able leadership he was instrumental in bringing about the fall of the city. (D.S.O. gazetted 1 Feb. 1919.)

Awarded the Distinguished Service Order:

ANDREW, WILLIAM CULLEN, M.C., Temporary Major, 33rd Battn. Machine Gun Corps. For conspicuous gallantry, leadership and devotion to duty on the 24th, 25th, 26th and 27 Oct. 1918, during the attack on Englefontaine. Time after time, when the enemy attempted to work through on the flanks, he reconnoitred their positions in the face of heavy fire, and then, returning to our lines, placed guns in position, inflicting heavy casualties on the enemy, and effectively restoring the situation. On many occasions during these four days he, by his personal example, gallantry and grim determination, enabled our line to be held against all assaults of the enemy.

ANDREWS, STEPHEN ARTHUR, M.C., Temporary Lieut. (Acting Capt.), 7th Battn. Royal Sussex Regt. For conspicuous gallantry and good work near Epehy on 18 Sept. 1918. His company was allotted the task of clearing the railway embankment of the enemy. Although enfiladed by machine-gun nests from the village, and having sustained heavy casualties, he personally led forward the remainder of his company, and was one of very few to reach the objective. He then organized under very heavy fire and held the position until the situation was cleared up.

APSLEY, LORD, ALLEN ALGERNON, M.C., Capt., 1/1st Gloucestershire Yeomanry (Egypt). On the 30th Sept. 1918, near Damascus, he was sent out with a troop of 20 men and a Hotchkiss gun to seize the Kadem wireless station. Near Kadem Station he was held up by a body of the enemy, whose strength was double his own. He charged, killing 12 with his sword, the remainder being put to flight. On arrival at his objective the wireless station was found to have been already destroyed, and the enemy, who had been strongly reinforced, was threatening to cut off his troop. This officer carried out the retirement of the troop in perfect order, and, when attacked by the enemy from a flank, another charge was made, inflicting loss and enabling him to get away intact. Throughout this mission he showed splendid gallantry and marked ability to command.

ARNOLD, CLEMENT BROOMHALL, Temporary Lieut., 6th Battn. Tank Corps. On 8 Aug. 1918, near Harbonieres, he attacked a battery of field guns and put them out of action. On the same day his tank was reported missing, one of the crew was found dead, and he is now reported wounded and a prisoner of war. Round his tank the next day were found the bodies of 40 enemy dead, which testified to this officer's extremely gallant conduct though entirely surrounded by the enemy after his tank was put out of action.

BAILEY, WALTER GEORGE, M.C., Temporary Second Lieut., 2nd Battn. Suffolk Regt. For conspicuous gallantry and able leadership as Battalion Intelligence Officer at Romeries, Escarmain and Beaudignies on 23 Oct. 1918. He went forward and found that a company had become disorganized owing to the loss of all its officers, and was hesitating to go forward. He immediately took command, rallied the men, and succeeded in getting them to their objective under heavy shell fire. Later, he led them in the assault on the final objective. He showed great skill in consolidating the positions gained and in the disposal of his force.

BALL, GEORGE HERBERT, Lieut. (Acting Capt.), 1/5th Battn. South Staffordshire Regt., Territorial Force. On the 27th–28th Sept. 1918, north of Bellenglise, he by a counter-attack ejected the enemy, who had bombed their way into newly-captured trenches. Later, being short of ammunition and bombs, he was forced to fall back, showing great courage and stubbornness, and inflicting heavy casualties on the enemy. Next day he made a reconnaissance with a small patrol, and with two men went forward and captured 16 enemy and two machine guns. He did fine work.

BARLTROP, ERNEST WILLIAM, Lieut. (Temporary Capt.), Essex Regt., Special Reserve, attached 9th Battn. On 4 Sept. 1918, he led his company across the canal east of Manancourt, and in the attack successfully gained his objective. When counter-attacked, the enemy was driven off owing to his organization and personal example. Next morning he led the remnants of three companies under a very heavy machine-gun fire, and took some 100 prisoners and several machine guns. Throughout he displayed marked ability and great skill in leading his men.

BENNETT, JOHN, M.C., Lieut. (Acting Capt.), 1/9th Battn. Highland Light Infantry, Territorial Force. During the advance from the river Selle to Englefontaine, between 22 Oct. and 27 Oct. 1918, his initiative and courage largely helped in the success of the operations and undoubtedly saved many lives. The advance of a unit on the right was held up by a strong point at Paul Jacques Farm. On his own initiative, with a few men and a Lewis gun, he outflanked the position, rushed across the open, killed two of the enemy himself, and captured seven. He took the farm, and his gallantry enabled the advance to proceed. On 26 Oct. he led the attack on Englefontaine. The success of this attack was very largely due to his leadership and example.

BLANDE, ALFRED, Temporary Second Lieut., 24th Battn. Royal Fusiliers. Mt. Sur l'Oeuvre, on the high ground north of Rumilly, had been organized for a determined defence by the enemy, and it had defied several attacks. On 1 Oct. 1918, he led his greatly depleted company against it successfully, capturing in all some 400 prisoners and 40 machine guns. He showed marked courage and ability to command.

BOARDMAN, HENRY, M.C., Second Lieut., 1st Battn. Liverpool Regt., attached 4th Battn. During operations on the Montay-Englefontaine road, 23–26 Oct. 1918, whilst in command of a company, he displayed conspicuous gallantry and initiative. On the 23rd Oct. he led his company to the capture of Caluyaux. Again, on the 25th, he organized an attack on Englefontaine, which helped to capture the village and secure 60 prisoners.

BODINGTON, JOHN REDNER, M.C., Lieut. (Acting Capt.), 2/5th Battn. Lancaster Regt., Territorial Force. For conspicuous gallantry and ability from 17 to 22 Oct. 1918. On 17 Oct. he was in command of the forward companies during the enemy retirement south of Lille. He commanded the advanced guard over a wide stretch of country with such energy and skill that the enemy rearguards were driven from successive positions, in one case in face of artillery at close range, the advance reaching a depth of 17,000 yards in one day.

BOSWELL, HAROLD EDWARD, M.C., Temporary Second Lieut., 2nd Battn. Worcestershire Regt. During the operations 22–23 Oct. 1918, up to the capture of Englefontaine, he led his company with great skill and gallantry. On the night of the assault on the village he led his company and another under heavy machine-gun fire to their final objective, and consolidated his position. During the actual assault he, with his runner, was responsible for the capture of 50 of the enemy, including three serjeant-majors. The success of the enterprise was largely due to the fine example of courage and energy set by him.

BOWEN, ARTHUR LLEWELLYN, Major (Acting Lieut.-Colonel), 4th Battn. Welsh Regt., Territorial Force, attached 10th Battn. South Wales Borderers. On the morning of the 4th Nov. 1918, in the attack against the Forêt de Mormal, his battalion was held up before reaching the edge of the forest by heavy machine-gun fire. Immediately on hearing of the situation he went forward to the leading companies, reorganized the attack, and personally led the advancing troops, who, inspired by his fine example of cool courage under heavy fire, pushed on to their final objective and completely routed the enemy.

BOYCE, WILLIAM WALLACE, Capt. (Acting Lieut.-Colonel), No. 2 Field Ambulance, Royal Army Medical Corps. For great gallantry, initiative and resource in personally supervising the evacuation of casualties during the operations on 4 Nov. 1918, near Petit Cambresis. He effected the rapid removal of wounded across the Sambre Canal under very difficult circumstances and considerable shell and machine-gun fire. On one occasion, when his advanced dressing station was blown in by shell fire, he personally reorganized his stretcher-bearers in a new site, inspired confidence in his officers and men, and undoubtedly saved many wounded under heavy fire.

BRADY, IRVINE GORDON CAMPBELL, M.C., Temporary Major, 9th Battn. Northumberland Fusiliers. For conspicuous gallantry and good leading during the attack on 24 Oct. 1918, on Bermerain. He led his company with great dash and determination against a large village strongly held by many machine guns, which he captured. When troops on the left were checked he assisted to rally them, and he formed a defensive flank. His company reached the objective, and dug in before being ordered to conform to the general line. He showed absolute fearlessness under trying circumstances.

CALLOW GRAHAM, M.C., Second Lieut. (Temporary Capt.), Nottinghamshire and Derbyshire Regt., attached 15th Battn. During operations east of Terhand on the 14th Oct. 1918, he showed great courage and initiative when the battalion was held up by a battery of enemy guns in action about 500 yards away. He organized two parties and led them forward against the guns, putting the guns out of action and shooting down several teams of horses. Pushing forward, he cleared several enemy machine-gun posts and shot down another team of horses retiring with a gun. He did splendid work.

CAMPBELL, RONALD, Temporary Major, 15th, formerly 12th, Battn. Tank Corps. During the operations against Niergnies on 8 Oct. 1918, he was in command of a company of tanks. Previous to the operations he personally reconnoitred the ground, and on the evening of 7 Oct. he led his tanks to their start points under a heavy enemy barrage. His conduct at all times was of a very high order, and his cool courage and ability under fire a fine example to all ranks.

CASS, EDWARD EARNSHAW EDEN, Lieut. (Acting Capt.), 2nd Battn. Yorkshire Light Infantry. For conspicuous gallantry, initiative and general leadership of his company in the operations of 29 Sept. 1918, and the following day. Observing an enemy battery withdrawing their guns, he directed the concentrated fire of his company at the teams, seizing and working a Lewis gun himself under direct fire of another hostile field battery. After which he led forward two platoons of his company and seized the hostile battery, consisting of H.V. and 18-in. howitzers. Later, he led his company right through the village of Levergies, capturing 30 prisoners. He did fine work.

CHARLTON, ARTHUR HUMPHREY, Lieut. (Acting Capt.), 1/6th Battn. North Staffordshire Regt., Territorial Force. For distinguished gallantry. On the 29th Sept. 1918, during the storming of the St. Quentin Canal, north of Bellenglise, he and his company were held up by machine-gun fire from a trench guarding the approach to a bridge. He took forward a party of nine men, captured the gun, killing all the crew by bayonet, and then carried on to the bridge, which he captured, killing a large number of the enemy, and saving the bridge from destruction. He did fine work.

CLOUSTON, JAMES, M.M., Temporary Second Lieut., B/107th Brigade, Royal Field Artillery. North of Maresches, on the 1st Nov. 1918, he was in command of a section of forward 18-pounders. During the morning the enemy counter-attacked, supported by tanks, and reached to within 500 yards of where this officer's guns were in action in the open. Under direct machine-gun fire he kept his guns in action, knocked out one tank and hit another. He showed great courage and determination. He also put out several machine guns in turn at point-blank range.

CHIPP, WILKINS FITZWILLIAM, M.C., Lieut. (Acting Major), 1/1st Battn. Hereford Regt. During the operations near Menin, on 14, 15 and 16 Oct. 1918, he commanded his battalion with great skill and gallantry. With only part of his command he was ordered to take over the whole front and push on—an extremely difficult operation, which he carried out at once under heavy shelling and machine-gun and minenwerfer fire. It was entirely due to his own personal reconnaissance of the country under fire and his perfect control that enabled his men to overcome every obstacle.

MILLER, GEOFFREY CHRISTIE, M.C., Capt. (Acting Lieut.-Colonel), Buckinghamshire Battn. Oxfordshire and Buckinghamshire Light Infantry, Territorial Force, attached 2/5th Battn. Gloucestershire Regt. On 30 Sept. and 1 Oct. 1918, his battalion was engaged in operations south of Fleurbaix. He reconnoitred the ground beforehand, established his headquarters far forward, and maintained it there for two days under continuous shelling. The successful issue of the fighting was due to his personal control and fine example of indifference to danger. He continued to command his battalion after being wounded.

CLARKE, HUBERT THOMAS, Major (Acting Lieut.-Colonel), 1/8th Battn. Worcestershire Regt., Territorial Force. For fine leadership and gallantry during the period 5–10 Oct. 1918. He was called upon suddenly to organize and carry out the attack on Beaurevoir. This he did with the greatest skill, his battalion, in face of heavy opposition, finally gaining all their objectives, and thereby making the next big attack possible. Later, he captured Honnechy, showing skill and ability in doing so. Throughout these operations his grasp of the situation was clear and concise.

COOK, JAMES, M.C., Lieut. (Acting Capt.), 2nd Battn. West Riding Regt. Near Verchain, during the fighting on the 24th Oct. 1918, which resulted in the capture of Mur Copse and Pimple Sunken Road and trench system beyond, he showed fine courage and leadership. On one occasion with two men he attacked a machine-gun nest of two guns which were enfilading his company and holding up the advance. He shot the gunners, putting the guns out of action, afterwards mopping up the remainder of the post and taking about 20 prisoners, thereby enabling the advance to continue. Later, though wounded, he continued to lead his men.

CRAWSHAW, CHARLES HERBERT, M.C., Capt. (Acting Major), 1st Battn. King's Own Scottish Borderers. In command of his battalion on the 15th Oct. 1918, between Salines and Cuerne, he went beyond the final objective and established posts along the Heulebeck, capturing several pill-boxes and many machine guns. Later, he pushed still further forward and established posts on the Lys River, thereby avoiding the necessity for a brigade attack. He handled his force with consummate skill, and it was due to his able and fearless leadership that the Lys was reached. He did fine work.

DE MIREMONT, GUY EGON RENE, M.C., Capt. (Acting Major), 2nd Battn. Royal Welsh Fusiliers. On the morning of 4 Nov. 1918, during the attack on Forêt de Mormal, he, finding that the advance of the battalion he was commanding was being held up early in the attack by a strong post of enemy in a group of houses, organized and led personally a party from battalion headquarters against the houses, and, with the help of a tank, took this post. Later he went forward to the leading troops and personally directed them in the mist to their objective under heavy fire. It was largely due to his prompt action and gallant example that the right objective was taken.

DENT, JOHN RALPH CONGRAVE, M.C., Capt. (Acting Lieut.-Colonel), 1st Battn. Royal Inniskilling Fusiliers. For conspicuous gallantry and good leadership in command of his battalion during operations from 14–16 Oct. 1918, in the Moorseele–Gulleghem–Heule Sector. His skilful leading enabled the battalion to reach its final objective in face of determined resistance and over difficult ground. After making a personal reconnaissance he again led his leading companies, and cleared the ground to the Heule area. He did good work.

DOAKE, RICHARD LIONEL VERE, M.C., Temporary Capt., 7th Battn. Bedfordshire Regt., attached 2nd Battn. During the attack on Preux-au-Bois, on the 4th Nov. 1918, he was in command of one of the leading companies of the assault. He led his company forward when the companies on either flank were held up, and, after killing several enemy himself, reached his final objective. He then sent parties out to either flank to help the other companies forward. This was completely successful, and the whole objective was captured. He showed marked gallantry and ability.

DUGGAN, HAROLD JOSEPH GEORGE, M.C., Temporary Capt. (Acting Major), Loyal North Lancashire Regt., attached 1/4th Battn. Territorial Force. For conspicuous courage and leadership during the fighting in the advance from La Bassée on Tournai between 16 and 22 Oct. 1918. On 16 Oct. 1918, it was largely due to his enterprise that the crossings of the Haute Deule Canal at the Bac de Wavrin were secured, and later, near Tournai, on 22 Oct. 1918, he directed the capture of strong tactical positions. His hard fighting qualities and fine leadership greatly helped the success of these operations.

DUNCAN, CHARLES MAITLAND, Temporary Capt., C/110th Brigade, Royal Field Artillery. On the 18th Sept. 1918, near Ronssoy, he was in command of a section of guns acting in close support of our infantry attack. In the first phase of the attack he took his guns forward with the infantry and engaged parties of the enemy and hostile machine guns with great effect over open sights. He then advanced with the infantry until they were held up by heavy machine-gun fire. Seeing the situation, he led his guns up in face of heavy machine-gun fire, and took up a forward position. For the rest of the day and all the next day he engaged enemy's guns and machine-gun posts, rendering the greatest assistance to the infantry. Throughout the operation he displayed the greatest courage and dash.

EDINBOROUGH, SAMUEL BERNARD, M.C., 2nd Lieut. (Acting Capt.), 3rd Battn. Lincolnshire Regt., attached 1st Battn. For conspicuous gallantry and skill in leading his company during the attack from Ovillers on 23 Oct. 1918. The troops to capture second objective were held up, so he led his company close up to leading troops, assisted in the capture of the second objective, and then pushed on and captured Vendegies. Next day he led his company forward 3,000 yards and captured his objective, overcoming stiff opposition and capturing many prisoners. Throughout he showed marked gallantry and enterprise.

EDWARDS, JOHN, Temporary Major, Royal Welsh Fusiliers, attached 1st Battn. Nottinghamshire and Derbyshire Regt. During the operations from 3–9 Oct. 1918, which resulted in the capture of Oppy Village and the piercing of the Fresnes–Rouvroy line, he was in command of his battalion. By his gallant and determined leadership all objectives were successfully obtained and heavy casualties were inflicted on the enemy. Two officers, two warrant officers and 66 other ranks were taken prisoners, also ten machine guns and two minenwerfers. The battalion did fine work, and he set an example of energy to all ranks.

EVANS, THOMAS RICHARD, Temporary Major (Acting Lieut.-Colonel), Royal Welsh Fusiliers, attached 1/6th Battn. North Staffordshire Regt., Territorial Force. Near Bellenglise, on 29 Sept. 1918, his battalion stormed a most difficult section of the Hindenburg Line, after crossing a wide canal with banks 30 feet in height, and captured over 300 prisoners, with few casualties. By his personal gallantry and energy whilst holding the line and during the attack he was to a large extent responsible for the success which his battalion achieved.

FRISBY, LIONEL CLAUD, M.C., Capt. (Acting Lieut.-Colonel), 6th Battn. Welsh Regt. He distinguished himself during the attack on Maissemy on 15 Sept. 1918, and again on 18 Sept., when he did valuable service by reconnoitring and forming lateral communication across the marshes north of Pontru. On the 24th Sept., when reconnoitring before the attack, he had a bombing encounter with an enemy patrol. His conduct during the operations on 17 and 18 Oct. was of a high order.

GARDEN, JAMES WINTON, M.C., Temporary Capt. (Acting Major), 8th Battn. Machine Gun Corps. For devotion to duty and gallantry on many occasions during the attack on the Fresnes–Rouvroy line on the 7th Oct. 1918, the attack on the Drocourt–Quéant line on the 11th Oct., and in the ensuing fighting up to the crossing of the Haute Deule Canal, while commanding the machine guns of the 23rd Infantry Brigade Group. Throughout this period he organized the work of the machine guns with great efficiency, initiative and judgment. He was untiring in going round his forward positions under heavy fire, and, after inflicting heavy casualties on the enemy, forced them to retire from Hill Metier. His personal example and cheerfulness throughout these operations were a great example to all who came in contact with him.

GARROD, EDGAR SAMUEL, M.C., D.C.M., Temporary Second Lieut. (Acting Capt.), 10th Battn. Tank Corps. For conspicuous gallantry and devotion to duty near Bousies on 23–24 Oct. 1918, in charge of a section of four Tanks. He personally led his Tanks on foot into the village of Bousies and directed their fire on various strong points and machine-gun nests in houses. Throughout the two days' operations he had no rest, and under very heavy machine-gun, rifle and shell fire showed great energy and courage.

GARSTIN, DENIS, Capt., 10th Royal Hussars (North Russia). For conspicuous gallantry and devotion to duty. In a successful attack upon the Seletokoe village, the capture of the village, the enemy's armoured car, and machine gun was due to his very able handling of the men under his command. He always set a splendid example of cheerfulness under trying circumstances and steadiness under fire to the troops of the force, and his intimate knowledge of the language was invaluable. His courage won the admiration of all. He was afterwards killed in a most gallant attempt to force the enemy from his positions.

GEMMELL, JOHN SALISBURY, M.C., Temporary Major, 20th Battn. Manchester Regt. For conspicuous gallantry and initiative in command of the reserve battalion between Pouchaux and Premonton, 8 Oct. 1918. Finding that machine-gun fire was coming from a copse 1,000 yards outside the divisional boundary, he at once formed a defensive flank to safeguard the right flank of the brigade. He then attacked the copse, which contained several machine guns and mortars, and mopped it up. By doing so he greatly assisted the advance.

GRAHAM, FERGUS REGINALD WINSFORD, M.C., Capt. and Brevet Major (Acting Lieut.-Colonel), Royal Irish Rifles, attached 10th Battn. London Regt. (Egypt). For conspicuous gallantry and initiative on the 19th Sept. 1918, at Kefr Kasim. He showed great dash, gallantry, and a quick grasp of the situation in these operations, pressing the attack and subsequent pursuit most resolutely. Throughout he exercised the most inspiriting influence on his troops.

GRAY, JOHN EDWARD BOWLES, Temporary Capt., 7th Battn. Rifle Brigade, attached 33rd Battn. London Regt. For conspicuous gallantry and skilful leadership. Near Helchin on night 4–5 Nov. 1918, he led his company across River Scheldt in face of strong opposition from the enemy, who occupied numerous machine-gun and rifle posts on his side of the river. He himself was the first to cross the centre bridge of three bridges, and succeeded, after great difficulties, in getting a Lewis-gun section across before the bridge broke down. Seventeen enemy were killed and 23 taken prisoner. He also brought up ammunition under heavy shell fire.

GREAVES, HARRY, M.C., Lieut., 3rd Battn. Nottinghamshire and Derbyshire Regt., attached 1st Battn. For most conspicuous gallantry and initiative. On the 6th–7th Oct. 1918, near Oppy, he successfully led his platoon on two occasions in face of very heavy fire and stubborn resistance to their objective, where they captured 23 prisoners and two machine guns. He set a fine example to those under him, and did splendid work.

GREVILLE, GUY GEORGE FREDERICK FULKE, Capt. (Acting Major), Leinster Regt., attached 6th Battn. Royal Inniskilling Fusiliers. For marked gallantry, good leadership and excellent work in command of his battalion in action at Le Catelet on 3 Oct. and near Le Cateau on 17 Oct. 1918. On each occasion he displayed great initiative and dash in face of strong enemy opposition. Owing to his personal example, both operations were successful, and each time his battalion captured over 250 prisoners and many machine guns.

GRIFFITHS, JAMES LLEWELLYN, Major, 1/5th Battn. Leicestershire Regt., Territorial Force. For gallantry and able leadership. On 29 Sept. 1918, he led his battalion by companies through the thick fog from Le Vergier to the assembly position. Afterwards he personally supervised the crossing of the St. Quentin Canal and formed up the battalion on the east side and led the advance toward the final objective. Later, he made a daring reconnaissance, during which he was wounded, before the attack on Doon Hill. He showed cool courage and cheerfulness throughout.

GUILD, JOHN ROYES, Capt. (Acting Major), 1st Battn. Gloucestershire Regt. For gallantry and tactical ability. He displayed great initiative while holding a line east of the village of Mazinghien from 30 Oct.–3 Nov. 1918. His outposts were constantly attacked by the enemy, and in every case he handled the situation with coolness and ability, advancing his line and inflicting heavy casualties. The attack on Catillon took place on 4 Nov., and ended in the capture of that village and the forcing of the canal at that point, many prisoners being taken. This result was largely due to his very able tactical handling of his men and personal example of gallantry.

HARRAGIN, ALFRED ERNEST ALBERT, Temporary Major, 1st Battn. British West India Regt. (Capt., Trinidad Local Forces) (Egypt). For gallantry and successful leadership of his company on the 22nd Sept. 1918, at Damieh bridgehead, Jordan Valley. He and his company took over 100 prisoners and three machine guns, and were responsible for about 50 killed and wounded of the enemy. He did splendid work.

HOLBECH, LAURENCE, M.C., Lieut., Grenadier Guards (Special Reserve), attached 2nd Battn. For conspicuous gallantry and leadership during the night attack between St. Python and Vertain, on 20 Oct. 1918. He was in command of the right leading company of the battalion, and gained his objectives. On one occasion he got round a large part of the enemy, charged them with the bayonet from the rear, and cleared the way for the advance. He showed fearless and able leadership throughout.

HOPE, PERCY ALBERT, Temporary Lieut. (Acting Capt.), 11th Battn. Royal Fusiliers. For marked gallantry and determined leadership on 4 Nov. 1918, near Preux-au-Bois. He commanded a composite company composed of the remains of two companies in the attack. Although held up by machine-gun nests and the breakdown of the tank which was to deal with them at the commencement of the attack, he eventually succeeded in breaking through with some 20 men. Without waiting for the remainder, he at once pushed on with such effect that he succeeded in clearing up the whole area, capturing over 20 machine guns and some 200 prisoners, including five officers. He did fine work.

HUDSON, NOEL BARING, M.C., Temporary Lieut.-Colonel, 8th Battn. Royal Berkshire Regt. For consistent gallantry and able leadership, particularly on 8 Aug. 1918, south of Morlancourt, when h personally led his battalion forward to the attack through heavy fog and intense shell and machine-gun fire. When they were held up by machine guns he pushed forward alone, knocking out one machine gun and getting wounded in doing so. In spite of this, he rushed two other machine guns which were holding up the advance, and continued to lead his battalion forward until he was again seriously wounded by machine-gun fire in three places. He showed splendid courage and determination.

JACKSON, MANSEL HALKET, M.C., Capt., 29th Lancers, Indian Army (Egypt). On the 23rd Sept. 1918, while his brigade was advancing down the right bank of the Jordan from Baisan towards Jisr ed Damie, the advanced guard was held up by a large enemy detachment. After a personal reconnaissance of the enemy formation, Capt. Jackson made a wide outflanking movement round the enemy's left, then charging home, under heavy rifle and machine-gun fire, he succeeded in capturing the position held by about 1,000 infantry, 18 machine guns and 12 automatic rifles. Capt. Jackson led the charge and behaved with most conspicuous personal gallantry, and handled his detachment throughout with great skill and coolness. The captures included a Divisional General.

KER, ROBERT FORDYCE, M.C., Temporary Major (Acting Lieut.-Colonel), 6th Battn. King's Own Scottish Borderers. At Vichte, on 22 Oct. 1918, while commanding his battalion in support of another, he cleared the village of machine gunners and any remaining enemy. Later, he captured Hill 50 with great gallantry and tactical ability. Throughout he displayed great coolness and a thorough grasp of an awkward situation.

KING, GEORGE WILLIAM, M.C., Temporary Capt. (Acting Major), C/160th Brigade, Royal Field Artillery. On 31 Oct. 1918, during the operations near Anseghem, he had a forward section of 18-pounders working in close support of the infantry. He went forward himself and directed the fire of this section on an enemy 7.7 cm. gun which was firing at short range and causing casualties to our infantry. After silencing this gun he turned fire on to enemy machine guns which were firing on our troops. He then made a daring reconnaissance which was of the greatest value in enabling the batteries to be pushed forward as the situation on the left was obscure. He showed great gallantry and initiative.

LAWSON, EDWARD FREDERICK, M.C., Capt. (Acting Lieut.-Colonel), 1/1st Buckinghamshire Yeomanry, Commanding 1st County of London Yeomanry (Egypt). On the 23rd Sept. 1918, the brigade came into contact with a strong flank guard of the 7th Turkish Army, which was covering the crossing of that army over the River Jordan by the ford at Mkt. Fettal es Sufah. He so manœuvred his regiment that it got behind the left rear of the flank guard, which thus left the column exposed to an attack. This attack was promptly pushed home, resulting in the capture of some 3,000 prisoners, eight field guns, two camel guns, and many machine guns, the abandoning of numerous transport vehicles, and the complete disorganization of this Turkish Army as a fighting force. He did magnificent work.

LISTER, CECIL, M.C., Capt. (Acting Lieut.-Colonel), Northamptonshire Regt., attached 1/6th Battn. South Staffordshire Regt., Territorial Force. His battalion was allotted the difficult task of storming the St. Quentin Canal and capturing the village of Bellenglise on the further bank. Amongst the defences he had to attack was a tunnel system. On the 29th Sept. 1918, he achieved a complete success with slight casualties, and this was in great measure due to his careful preparation of the attack and the determination with which he personally inspired all ranks serving under him during the action.

LOMAX, CYRIL ERNEST NAPIER, M.C., Capt. (Temporary Lieut.-Colonel), Welsh Regt., Commanding 21st Battn. Manchester Regt. Throughout the operations extending from 4 to 12 Oct. 1918, he displayed marked gallantry and power of command. He led his battalion in the attack on Ponchaux, when they successfully stormed and captured the second objective. Later, when the attack on Honnechy was held up, he went forward and consulted with the commanding officers of the battalions in front of him, with the result that a fresh attack was successfully launched. He did excellent work throughout.

MACDERMOTT, GEORGE ANTHONY, M.C., Capt. (Acting Major), 4th Battn. Highland Light Infantry, Seconded 9th Battn. Machine Gun Corps. Near Harlebeke, on 17 Oct. 1918, the bridgehead which had been established during the night was heavily counter-attacked, the bridge being destroyed by artillery fire. He swam the river, which was under a heavy machine-gun and artillery barrage, and so managed to reach his two sections which were heavily engaged. His personal example greatly assisted the repulse of the counter-attack. During the operations extending from 29 Sept. to 22 Oct. he has displayed marked ability and coolness in handling his guns at critical periods.

MANDLEBERG, LEONARD CHARLES, M.C., Temporary Major, 15th Battn. Lancashire Fusiliers. For conspicuous gallantry and devotion to duty in the attack on the Fonsomne line on 1–2 Oct. 1918. He rendered valuable aid in personal reconnaissances during the action, and, later, in reorganizing the defence. He took up supports and tried to rush the position when the Tanks failed to reach their final objective. Later, when an enemy counter-attack was developing, he took command of the firing line, and steadied the men, and brought fire to bear on the enemy. His work throughout was excellent.

MAY, ERNEST RICHARD HALLAM, Temporary Major, Royal Irish Rifles, attached 1st Battn. For conspicuous gallantry and good leadership during the attack on Moorseele and Gulleghem on 14–15 Oct. 1918. After zero on the 14th he walked through a heavy artillery barrage to visit his battalion. He organized his companies, and, despite a thick fog, ensured that correct direction was kept. For two days he worked unceasingly during the heavy fighting, and by his clear orders and personal example greatly assisted his battalion to reach its objective.

McCARTHY, WILLIAM HILGROVE LESLIE, M.C., Capt. (Acting Lieut.-Colonel), Royal Army Medical Corps (Special Reserve), attached 19th Field Ambulance. During the operations connected with the crossing of the Sambre, 4 to 8 Nov. 1918, he exhibited marked gallantry and devotion to duty. He was in command of the advanced dressing station and maintained the closest touch with the front-line troops, arranging for the immediate evacuation of casualties as they occurred. He worked continuously for three days and three nights, and his energy, able management and devotion to duty saved many lives.

McLELLAN, JAMES, M.C., Lieut. (Acting Major), 446th (Northumbrian) Field Coy., Royal Engineers, Territorial Force. For great gallantry and devotion to duty in the attack on the enemy positions east of River Selle, south of Le Cateau, on 17 Oct. 1918. For three nights previous to the attack he made valuable reconnaissances of the river in front of our outpost line where the enemy were holding the east bank of the stream. He subsequently organized the bridging of the river, and, on the morning of the 17th, he led his men forward in advance of the infantry and threw his bridges over the stream, thus enabling five battalions of infantry to cross and carry out a most successful operation.

McNEILE, DONALD HUGH, Lieut.-Colonel, 19th Lancers, Indian Army (Egypt). On the 19th–20th Sept. 1918, he, with his regiment, covered a distance of some 90 miles from Selmeh to Jisr Mujamia, within 48 hours, during which he seized and prepared for the demolition of the bridge at Jisr Mujamia by daylight. This performance included two consecutive all-night marches over difficult country, and during the whole period there was practically no rest for man or horse. He did fine work.

METHUEN, HENRY CHARLES, M.C., Capt. (Acting Lieut.-Colonel), 1st Battn. Cameron Highlanders. On 17 Oct. 1918, near La Vallée Moulatre, for conspicuous gallantry and able leadership. When the advance was held up by heavy machine-gun and artillery fire he made a personal reconnaissance and made such dispositions that the leading companies were enabled to advance again after one skilfully handled platoon had outflanked the machine guns. The position eventually taken by his battalion was of exceptional strength, and 60 machine guns were collected on a front of under 1,000 yards, besides many automatic rifles and four field guns.

MORGAN, CLIFFORD WILLIAM, M.C., Lieut. (Acting Capt.), 5th, attached 4/5th, Battn. Welsh Regt., Territorial Force (Egypt). This officer showed the greatest dash and gallantry when the enemy counter-attacked after the capture of Bidston Hill, near Kh. Abu Felah, on the 18th Sept. 1918. He personally led a bayonet charge which broke up the counter-attack and inflicted serious casualties on the enemy. Later, he took a neighbouring hill with 18 prisoners and two machine guns without artillery support, and his courage and personal example had much to do with the success of the operations entrusted to the battalion on the night of 18–19 Sept.

MORRIS, CHARLES HENRY, M.C., Capt. (Acting Major), Middlesex Regt., attached 1st Battn. Dorsetshire Regt. For conspicuous gallantry and skilful leading of his battalion on the 29th Sept. 1918, at Fleche Wood. He led his battalion by short rushes across an open slope under very heavy fire, gained all objectives, and consolidated his new position. The following morning, at 15 minutes' notice, he was ordered to capture the village of Levergies in conjunction with another brigade. He successfully carried out his task up to time. He rendered excellent service.

OWEN, WALTER LLEWELLYN, M.C., Capt. and Brevet Major (Temporary Lieut.-Colonel), 5th Battn. Liverpool Regt., Territorial Force, Commanding 11th Battn. Royal West Surrey Regt. As battalion commander in the advance to l'Escaut on the 25th Oct. 1918, he showed great gallantry and power of command. At a critical time, when his left flank had been left in the air, he overcame a very difficult situation by able handling of his command. Later, during the taking of Heestert Spichestraat, his leadership was again of great value.

PAIGE, CHARLES JOHN MURRAY, M.C., Temporary Second Lieut. (Acting Capt.), 11th Battn. Royal West Surrey Regt. For conspicuous leadership and gallantry on 19 Oct. 1918, at Courtrai. He took his company across the River Lys in an improvised ferry boat under heavy shell fire. In a surprisingly short time he had either captured, killed or driven away the enemy and had advanced on an 800 yards' frontage along the Courtrai–Harlebeke Railway, being an advance to a depth of 1,500 yards. It was largely due to his personal supervision, leadership and dash that the objective was gained, organized and held. His gallant and able leadership contributed materially to the success of the whole operation.

PANNALL, CHARLIE, M.C., Lieut. (Temporary Major and Acting Lieut.-Colonel), Royal West Surrey Regt., attached 20th Battn. Durham Light Infantry. On 14–15 Oct. 1918, near Wevelghem, his great gallantry and fine leadership greatly contributed to the success of the battalion under his command. During the attack on the 14th Oct. he directed the attack on the first line personally through a dense fog, and towards the end of the day placed his men in position on the final objective, exposing himself throughout to heavy shell and machine-gun fire. He has at all times shown gallantry and devotion to duty of a high order.

PARKES, WALTER, M.C., Temporary Major (Acting Lieut.-Colonel), 8th Battn. Gloucestershire Regt. For gallantry and good leadership in operations near Haussy between 20–24 Oct. 1918. His battalion was twice ordered to carry out an attack, on the 20th and 23rd Oct. respectively. He personally led the leading platoons across the Selle River under machine-gun and rifle fire. Throughout he showed great courage and ability to command.

PATERSON, GEORGE ROBERT STEEL, M.C., Temporary Major, Highland Light Infantry, attached 1/5th Battn. King's Own Scottish Borderers, Territorial Force. On 14 Oct. 1918, at Gheluwe, he was in command of his battalion in the left front of the brigade attack, and by his fine leadership ensured the success of the advance. When the battalion's advance was temporarily held up, he personally went round his whole front, collected parties lost in the mist, and attacked Uniform Farm, capturing a battery and three machine guns. Throughout the day he displayed great gallantry, initiative and endurance.

PEARSE, REGINALD GUY, M.C., Lieut. (Acting Capt.), 3rd Battn. Nottinghamshire and Derbyshire Regt., attached 1st Battn. At Oppy, on 6 Oct. 1918, he showed marked gallantry, skill and ability in the handling of his company, capturing an enemy strong point yielding 34 prisoners and six machine guns, and establishing positions in front of it. His coolness and personal courage during the fighting were a splendid example to his men, raising their spirits to a very high pitch of offensive enthusiasm.

PEBERDY, CHARLES EDWARD VERNON KINGSBURY, M.C., Lieut. (Acting Capt.), 4th Battn. West Yorkshire Regt., attached 1st Battn. At Selency, on 24–25 Sept. 1918, the gaining of all the objectives on the right of the battalion, including the village of Selency, was in a very great measure due to his excellent work. After his objectives were gained he made reconnaissances well in front of the captured position, obtaining valuable information as to the whereabouts of the enemy by exposing himself and drawing their fire. Throughout he showed marked gallantry and devotion to duty, and on one occasion with a small party outflanked and captured 20 of the enemy.

PIGG, NORMAN BATEY, M.C., Temporary Lieut. (Acting Capt.), 1st Battn. Northumberland Fusiliers. For most conspicuous gallantry and initiative during the operations east of Solesmes, from 23 to 26 Oct. 1918. He commanded a company which made three assaults during the operations. On one occasion he pushed forward with a small party, and captured a machine gun which had been causing casualties. Later he observed an enemy field battery, which he at once charged and routed the gunners. His fine acts of gallantry undoubtedly saved the battalion many casualties.

POTTER, JOHN WATTS, Lieut. (Acting Capt.), 1/5th Battn., attached 1/6th Battn., Nottinghamshire and Derbyshire Regt., Territorial Force. For marked gallantry and leadership near Montbrehain on 3 Oct. 1918, in command of a company. During the early stages of the attack his company successfully captured several nests of machine guns, and later, pressing on through the village of Montbrehain, they rushed and captured six field guns, killing and capturing some of the gun teams. He made several gallant attempts to lead his men beyond the village under intense fire, and finally, when heavily counter-attacked, he hung on to this position with great determination until his ammunition was almost exhausted. Throughout he showed splendid courage and initiative.

PRING, BERNARD VINCENT, M.C., Second Lieut. (Acting Capt.), Yorkshire Light Infantry, attached 2nd Battn. For marked gallantry and able leadership of his company in the action of the 29th–30th Sept. 1918, against Levergies, which culminated in the capture of that village. Leading his company well in advance, he captured a battery of field guns and several machine guns. Next day he succeeded in entering the outskirts of the village, thus opening the way to the successful capture of the village. He did excellent work.

RATCLIFFE, WILLIAM CHARLES, Capt. (Temporary Major), Northamptonshire Regt., attached 9th Battn. Yorkshire Light Infantry. For marked courage and determined leadership during the operations 23–24 Oct. 1918, at Ovillers and Vendegies. During the advance very heavy enfilade fire was poured into the right flank of the battalion from enemy machine-gun nests. Five of these machine-gun nests were rushed by his company, and in one instance he rushed a machine gun himself, killing some and capturing the rest of the crew. As a result the right flank of the battalion was enabled to get forward and the objectives taken. Throughout these operations, by his fearless and able leadership, he rendered excellent service.

RAWLINSON, ALFRED, C.M.G., Temporary Lieut.-Colonel, Royal Garrison Artillery (Mesopotamia). For conspicuous gallantry and devotion to duty, near Baku, on night of 14 Sept. 1918. With an escort of four men he brought away a steamer loaded with munitions from Baku under fire, in spite of the opposition of the captain and crew, who refused to navigate her. Although fired on heavily from a guardship, which hit the steamer several times, he, by his personal energy and resource, made the crew work, and got the steamer safely to Enzeli. He thus, by his enterprise and determination, saved a valuable cargo.

RIDLEY, BASIL WHITE, M.C., Temporary Major (Acting Lieut.-Colonel), 29th Battn. Durham Light Infantry (formerly East Lancashire Regt.). He showed conspicuous gallantry and ability in personally supervising, under heavy shell and machine-gun fire, the crossing of the Lys River, near Comines, on 14 and 15 Oct. 1918. It was due to him that the situation was controlled and ended in complete success, notwithstanding heavy casualties to the bridging parties and patrols of his battalion, which was the first to cross the river. He visited posts, and by his personal example encouraged men who were much exhausted.

ROBERTS, GEORGE, M.C., Temporary Capt. (Acting Major), A/123rd Brigade, Royal Field Artillery. For marked gallantry and initiative on the morning of 23 Oct. 1918, near Beaurain. He pushed on and selected his battery position under machine-gun and shell fire before the first objective had been consolidated. Returning he was able to give his artillery brigade commander valuable information as to the situation in front. Though gassed while reconnoitring he refused to go to a dressing station and fought his battery ably throughout the day.

ROBINSON, GUY ST. GEORGE, M.C., Capt. (Acting Lieut.-Colonel), 1st Battn. Northamptonshire Regt. For conspicuous gallantry and devotion to duty on the 17th Oct. 1918, during an attack by his battalion near Vaux Andigny. In very dense fog and under very heavy fire he went from company to company and brought his troops on to their correct line of advance, with the result that the village of La Vallée Mulatre was captured. On the 23rd Oct. 1918, near Mazinghien, his excellent dispositions again resulted in his battalion gaining all its objectives with little loss.

ROGERS, CLAUDE RUPERT DE WARRENNE, Capt., 1st Battn. Leinster Regt., attached 1/5th Battn. Gloucestershire Regt., Territorial Force. For conspicuous gallantry and fearless leadership in leading his company during the attacks on Beaurevoir, Maretz, and during the advance on Le Cateau, 5, 6 and 10 Oct. respectively. He led his company splendidly throughout the attack and enabled the battalion on the left to carry their portion of the village, where they had previously been held up. During the advance on Le Cateau, although wounded the day previously, he again led his company forward, and when the leading battalion was held up by heavy machine-gun fire he made a most gallant attempt to assist them by pushing on until both he and all his officers were casualties.

RUSTON, ALPRES HAROLD, Temporary Major, Motor Machine Gun Corps (Mesopotamia). For conspicuous gallantry and devotion to duty near Baku on 26 Aug. 1918. At a critical moment he took command of the infantry when all their officers had become casualties. He reorganized the line under heavy fire and carried out a withdrawal in good order to a position in rear. His ability and coolness saved a critical situation. He was eventually severely wounded.

SCULLY, VINCENT MARCUS BARRON, O.B.E., Capt. (Temporary Lieut.-Colonel), Border Regt., attached 5th Battn. Connaught Rangers. For conspicuous gallantry and devotion to duty at Le Cateau on night 10–11 Oct. 1918. Though wounded, he led his battalion in the attack, and forced his way through the enemy defences of the town to the eastern outskirts. The success of the operation was largely due to his determination, enterprise and personal courage in action.

SHEDDEN, JAMES ALEXANDER, M.C., Lieut. (Acting Major), 7th Battn. Scottish Rifles, Territorial Force, attached 1/6th Battn. Nottinghamshire and Derbyshire Regt., Territorial Force. For conspicuous gallantry and ability in command of a battalion during the attack on Ramicourt and Montbrehain on 3 Oct. 1918. When his commanding officer was killed he took command of his battalion and led it to the final objective in front of Montbrehain. In this large village there was a great deal of fighting, and 1,000 of the enemy were captured. He took complete control and held the village for three hours without support, finally skilfully withdrawing, while inflicting heavy casualties on the enemy.

SHELDON, JOSEPH, M.C., Lieut., 2nd Battn. Nottinghamshire and Derbyshire Regt. On 8 Oct. 1918, near Bohain, when in command of a company, he showed conspicuous gallantry and exceptional ability in leading his men in the advance. When the front line, depleted of officers, came under heavy fire, he, by his personal coolness and disregard of danger, held the line, reorganized, and later put the whole position in a state of defence. Throughout the operations, from the 8th to the 13th, he has had a company in the line. He has been unfailingly cheerful in adverse circumstances, and has himself been directly responsible for the capture of about 200 prisoners and 15 machine guns, located in various strong points.

SIMMONS, WILLIAM GORDON, M.C., Temporary Capt., 7th Battn. Royal West Surrey Regt. On 1 Sept. 1918, during his company's attack on Fregicourt, he rendered most gallant and valuable service. A daring personal reconnaissance gave him the location of the enemy. As he was forming up his company to attack the enemy attacked him, but by clever handling of his company he succeeded in completely mastering them and captured the village with 300 prisoners, several machine guns and four trench mortars. He did fine work.

SLADDEN, CYRIL EDGAR, M.C., Temporary Major, 9th Battn. Worcestershire Regt. (Mesopotamia). For conspicuous gallantry and devotion to duty at Baku on 14 Sept. 1918. He handled his battalion with marked ability and daring throughout the day under most difficult circumstances. When the troops on his left flank had withdrawn he skilfully extricated his command from an awkward position, inflicting heavy losses on the enemy, who greatly outnumbered him. His conduct was admirable.

STALLARD, CHARLES FRAMPTON, M.C. Temporary Major, 23rd Battn. Middlesex Regt., attached 15th Battn. Hampshire Regt. For marked gallantry and leadership during operations east of Courtrai from 20–26 Oct. 1918, whilst temporarily commanding a battalion. When the whole battalion was held up on the canal bank at Knokke on the 21st Oct. by direct and enfilade machine-gun fire from the opposite bank, he personally went forward and reorganized the position, and led his battalion across the canal. After reforming the battalion on the other side of the canal he led the advance up the slope and established a commanding position. Throughout the operations he did excellent work.

SUTCLIFFE, ARTHUR WINDLE, M.C., Capt. (Acting Major), 3rd Battn. Border Regt., attached 1st Battn. On 14–15 Oct. 1918, as Commanding Officer during the fighting from Ledeghem to Cuerne, his untiring energy and fine example of gallantry, together with his marked tactical ability, ensured the success of the operations, and greatly inspired his battalion in carrying out a difficult task under heavy machine-gun fire with their right flank in the air. He did excellent work.

TAYLER, FRANCIS LIONEL, Major, Deoli Regt., Indian Army (Egypt). For conspicuous gallantry on the 20th Sept. 1918, while in command of the leading three companies in the attack on Ras Aish, when, unsupported by artillery fire, he gained his objective after heavy casualties under very heavy shell and machine-gun fire. He personally conducted the attack, being cut off for some time from all communication with battalion headquarters. His splendid devotion to duty inspired all ranks with that fortitude and endurance which eventually enabled them to reach their objective.

THOMPSON, REGINALD, Major (Acting Lieut.-Colonel), 1–1st Yorkshire Dragoons. During the advance to the Lys, after the capture of Steenbeek Hill on 15 Oct. 1918, he handled his command of cyclists and motor machine guns with conspicuous ability. When the left flank of the brigade was dangerously exposed owing to the enemy counter-attack further north, he made it possible for the brigade to gain ground, though under heavy machine-gun fire, and by hustling the enemy broke down their opposition in Cuerne. Throughout he displayed great gallantry and ability.

TOMBAZIS, JAMES LYELL, M.C., Second Lieut., 2nd Battn. Nottinghamshire and Derbyshire Regt. On the morning of 18 Sept. 1918, in front of St. Quentin, while in command of a platoon, he displayed conspicuous gallantry, initiative, and power of leadership, organizing an attack of a hostile strong point and capturing three machine guns. Later, while in command of a patrol on the night of the 28th Sept. 1918, coming upon a hostile patrol in the dark, he rushed forward, seized and brought in a prisoner, at the same time ordering his men to fire. The remainder fled, leaving one dead.

TRESTRAIL, ALFRED ERNEST YATES Temporary Major, Cheshire Regt., attached 15th Battn. During the operations east of Terhand on the 14th Oct. 1918, he led his men to the attack in a most determined way, and when heavy hostile machine-gun fire was encountered from numerous strong points he got his men to surround them, and either killed or captured the occupants. His marked gallantry, cheeriness, and initiative were largely responsible for the objective being carried promptly.

TURNER, ROBERT, VILLIERS, Major (Acting Lieut.-Colonel), 2nd Battn. Durham Light Infantry. For conspicuous gallantry and able leadership. During the operations on 23 Oct. 1918, near Catillon, owing to the enclosed nature of the ground the barrage was lost before the final objective overlooking the canal was reached. All further advance was carried out by means of fighting patrols. The success of the Durham Light Infantry in reaching positions commanding the canal was due to his personal leadership and initiative in the forward area, where he reorganized and personally directed the whole of the operations.

VIGORS, MERVYN DOYNE, M.C., Major, 9th Hodson's Horse, Indian Army (Egypt). On the 30th Sept. 1918, at Kiswe, when vanguard commander, with only one squadron and two machine guns, he attacked a column of 1,500 of the enemy, capturing 650 prisoners and four guns. It was greatly due to his resolution, quick decision, dash and gallantry that the advance of the whole corps was so rapid and successful.

WALKER, JAMES McCAIG, Temporary Second Lieut., Royal Highlanders, attached 1/6th Battn., Territorial Force. On 24 Oct. 1918, near Monchaux, he, on finding that the bridges which he carried were unsuitable for spanning the River Ecaillon, jumped in and swam the river, followed by his platoon, thereby forming a defensive flank to the right and covering crossing of other platoons. He afterwards led his platoon forward, and materially assisted in the capture of the village of Monchaux and the taking of over 50 prisoners. With a few Lewis gunners he outflanked an enemy machine gun, personally killing the gunner. Throughout two days' fighting his gallantry and leadership were most conspicuous.

WALKER, VERNON DUDLEY, M.M., Temporary Second Lieut., 34th Battn. Machine Gun Corps. During the attack near Menin on 14 Oct. 1918, he went forward with the leading wave and, despite heavy artillery and machine-gun fire, pushed boldly forward to his objective. Although isolated from the infantry, he succeeded in capturing a field gun with the officer and personnel. Previously, he entered a trench and caused 27 of the enemy to surrender. For two hours he maintained his position until the infantry came up, and then moved forward with them. Throughout he displayed great courage and initiative.

WEBSTER, JAMES ALEXANDER, Capt. and Brevet Major, 8th Battn. London Regt., attached Headquarters 53rd Infantry Brigade. For conspicuous gallantry and devotion to duty during the operations in the vicinity of Mormal Forest, 23 Oct. to 4 Nov. 1918. He, acting as Brigade Major in both actions, went forward to ascertain the situation, and for many hours remained exposed to heavy fire of all kinds in order to keep his brigade commander informed. On 4 Nov. he again went forward and visited all parts of the line under heavy fire, and sent back valuable information, which enabled the necessary orders to be issued, and thus materially assisted in the capture of the final objective.

WELLS, GEORGE KERSLAKE, M.C., Lieut., 4th Battn. King's Royal Rifle Corps. On 17 Oct. 1918, during the attack on the enemy positions near St. Souplet, he showed conspicuous gallantry and power of leadership. In the early stages of the attack, when the company commanders of the two leading companies became casualties, he assumed command, reformed the line under very heavy machine-gun fire, pushed forward his support company to reinforce the attacking companies and won through to his objective. His excellent work caused the enemy machine gunners to retreat in confusion and secured the capture by the battalion of two field guns, 40 machine guns and 60 prisoners.

WHITE, ARTHUR (corrected to Alfred [London Gazette, 12 July, 1920)], Capt. (Acting Lieut.-Colonel), 4th Battn. East Surrey Regt., attached 4/5th Battn. South Staffordshire Regt., Territorial Force. On the 28th Sept. 1918, his battalion on the day previous to a general attack on the St. Quentin Canal, was heavily attacked by the enemy in our outpost line near Bellenglise. During the succeeding night he reorganized his battalion and completed with three companies preparations for an attack which was organized for four companies. He led his battalion to the attack, and its success was largely due to his forethought in preparation and his coolness in action.

WHITE, WILLIAM, M.C., Temporary Major, 15th Battn. Highland Light Infantry. After the third successful attack on Sequehart on 3 Oct. 1918, information was received of a determined enemy counter-attack in progress. He at once proceeded towards the village, made a personal reconnaissance, and found it only weakly held. He then returned and led forward his battalion, which was in reserve, and re-established our positions on the far side of the village. But for his enterprise and judgment the enemy would have shortly reoccupied the village in strength.

WILLISON, ARTHUR CECIL, M.C., Lieut., 1st Battn. Nottinghamshire and Derbyshire Regt., attached Headquarters 24th Infantry Brigade. For conspicuous gallantry and devotion to duty as brigade intelligence officer during the advance from the Fresnes-Rouvroy to the Escaut River, east of St. Amand (12 to 27 Oct. 1918). Throughout the advance he was employed daily right forward. On 19 Oct. he was the first man to enter Marchiennes. On 23 Oct., when going forward, he came across a patrol who were hotly engaged with the enemy between La Broyere and St. Amand. He at once took charge of the party and attacked. He killed two of the enemy with his own hand and captured four others, together with a machine gun. Throughout these operations he showed fearless dash and initiative.

WILSON, ALEXANDER ROBERT GRAHAM, Capt. (Acting Lieut.-Colonel), 1st Battn. Argyll and Sutherland Highlanders, attached 1/5th Battn., Territorial Force. While commanding his battalion during the advance at Wytschaete on 28–29 Sept. 1918, he showed marked gallantry and ability to command. When one of his companies had been repulsed by a counter-attack he collected them and restarted the attack, reorganizing the men under heavy machine-gun fire. Later, he made a daring reconnaissance, enabling one of his companies to capture an enemy position under heavy enfilade fire. Again, on 14 Oct., near Menin, he showed great gallantry and devotion to duty, personally directing each company on its objective and thereby greatly contributing to the enemy's losses.

WRIGHT, ARTHUR, M.C., Lieut. (Acting Capt.), 2/2nd Battn. London Regt. For conspicuous gallantry during the operations at Peizieres 18–19 Sept. 1918. He succeeded in spite of all opposition of the enemy, and though his right flank was in the air, in reaching his final objective. Whilst in command of remnants of three companies, he personally organized bombing attacks from 8 p.m., 18 Sept., to 7 p.m., 19th Sept., until the final objective was ultimately captured. During the whole of the period the drive and determination of this officer was the main factor in keeping this composite company to maintain their offensive spirit, which culminated in the capture of Poplar Trench.

YOUNG, CLARENCE RANDOLPH, M.C., Temporary Capt., Royal Army Medical Corps, attached 1st Battn. Shropshire Light Infantry. On the 18th Sept. 1918, when the battalion had suffered very heavy casualties, he followed up and remained close behind the front line and in ground swept by the enemy's machine-gun fire, and exposed to artillery fire, spent the whole day tending and clearing the wounded; and on the following morning he went up, and, after spending some hours in No Man's Land, he got in several wounded men. By his gallantry and devotion to duty he undoubtedly saved many lives.

YOUNG, HUBERT WINTHROP, Capt. (Temporary Major), 116th Mahratta Light Infantry, Indian Army (Egypt). For gallantry and coolness under fire in the attack by the Arab forces on Mezerib on 17 Sept. 1918. Having gained the station buildings he organized and personally directed the destruction of the enemy's railway and telegraph communications at that place. He also rendered consistent good service during subsequent engagements in which he acted as adviser to the Arab regular army.

CANADIAN FORCE.

ALLEN, EVELYN PRESTWOOD SEYMOUR, Capt., 116th Infantry Battn. 2nd Central Ontario Regt. During the attack on the village of St. Olle on 29 Sept. 1918, he was acting as adjutant. During the attack two companies were held up. He went back through heavy fire and got in touch with a forward section of the artillery, and with their co-operation the attack was able to move forward. Again, on the 1st Oct., in the attack on Ramillies, when the Commanding Officer was wounded, he led the battalion forward to their objective. He personally reorganized a company, and by skilful manœuvring, worked around a battery of enemy artillery who were firing at them point-blank, killing or capturing the crews, and thus enabling the advance to continue. Throughout these operations he showed conspicuous gallantry and ability.

BOND, GEORGE FREDERICK DANIELS, M.C., Major, 28th Infantry Battn. Saskatchewan Regt. For conspicuous courage and devotion to duty near Iwuy on 10 and 11 Oct. 1918. He was in command of his battalion, which was held up in an attack on Iwuy by machine-gun fire from strong enemy positions on the River Erclin, whereupon he went forward under heavy fire to his most forward troops and made a personal reconnaissance of the situation, afterwards establishing a line from which the village was captured next day. Throughout the operations his work was excellent.

BONNER, ARTHUR BERNARD, M.M., Lieut., 116th Infantry Battn. 2nd Central Ontario Regt. For marked courage and initiative. During our attack on the village of St. Olle, in front of Cambrai, on the 29th Sept. 1918, two companies were caught under intense machine-gun fire coming from a trench in front of the village of St. Olle. Taking two platoons, he, by skilful manœuvring, reached a sunken road to the north-west of the village of St. Olle, where he rushed a machine-gun post and where, with his two platoons, he accounted for 15 machine guns and 94 prisoners altogether. He did splendid work and rendered most valuable service.

BOWERBANK, GEORGE SCOTT STANTON, M.C., Major, 21st Infantry Battn. East Ontario Regt. For conspicuous gallantry and ability north-east of Cambrai, 10–11 Oct. 1918. The success of his battalion in two successive days' operations was largely due to his exercise of control, initiative and determination. Working from an advanced position, he on two occasions carried out daring preliminary reconnaissances, and arranged all details for the pending attacks, exposing himself continually to heavy fire.

CHARLES, JOHN LESLIE, Major, 13th Battn. Canadian Railway Service For gallant and distinguished conduct in carrying out reconnaissances of railways as the advance progressed between 27 Oct. and 11 Nov. 1918. He daily reconnoitred the railways, keeping right up to our outposts from Louvain to Mons under fire. Because of his skill, ability, and energy most valuable information was quickly obtained. This was invaluable for the proper planning of works, and was a large factor in the progress of the railways.

CHASSE, HENRI, M.C., Major, 22nd Infantry Battn. Quebec Regt. For conspicuous gallantry and devotion to duty in operations north of Cambrai, 1–14 Oct. 1918. During the night of 1–2 Oct. his battalion relieved the front line under specially trying conditions, and under heavy machine-gun and artillery fire, without a preliminary reconnaissance. His personal leadership was responsible for the success of the relief. Later, he led his men across the Canal de l'Escaut during a night attack, afterwards reforming them in the dark and leading them to the capture of a village. Throughout these operations his work was excellent.

COSGROVE, JOHN ROBERT, M.C., Major, 8th Battn. Canadian Railway Troops. For conspicuous gallantry and devotion to duty in the reconstruction and maintenance of light railway lines and in the conversion of metre gauge railway into 60 cm. lines from Moorslede to Hulste, and from Beythem southwards towards Ledeghem during the operations commencing on the 14th Oct. 1918. His coolness and example of energy under continuous shell fire resulted in the work being accomplished in record time.

HERRIDGE, WILLIAM DUNCAN, M.C., Capt., Canadian Cyclist Corps (Brigade Major, 2nd Canadian Infantry Brigade Headquarters). For conspicuous gallantry and devotion to duty during the attack east of the Canal du Nord from 27 to 30 Sept. 1918. When the situation was very obscure, he, with great courage, made a reconnaissance through very heavy fire and obtained information of great value in repelling the enemy counter-attack.

ISBESTER, COLIN JOHN FRASER, Major, 10th Battn. Canadian Railway Troops. For distinguished conduct and devotion to duty in the vicinity of Ledeghem in connection with operations which commenced on the 14th Oct. 1918. He was responsible for the repairing of the H.4 light railway line running from Jagerhof to Ledeghem. The success which attended the operations for which he was responsible was very largely due to the excellent arrangements made by him, to his close supervision of every part of the work, and to the splendid example he set his men.

JOHNSTON, HUGH ALSTON, M.C., Capt., 13th Infantry Battn. Quebec Regt. On 27 Sept. 1918, during the attack across the Canal du Nord which led up to the capture of Marquion, he led his company with marked gallantry. He was wounded just as the company attacked, but continued to lead his men through heavy fire to his objective, where he supervised the consolidation of his position after his company had captured prisoners outnumbering their own strength. Though wounded, he remained at duty, and his conduct throughout was splendid.

MERSEREAU, CHALVERS JACK, Major, 25th Infantry Battn. Nova Scotia Regt. For conspicuous gallantry and devotion to duty in operations north of Cambrai during the period 1–14 Oct. 1918. During the night 1–2 Oct. his battalion relieved the front line under heavy artillery and machine-gun fire. During the night 8–9 Oct. they carried out a most successful night operation, crossing a canal under very difficult conditions, afterwards capturing a village and inflicting heavy casualties and taking many prisoners. The success of this operation was largely due to the initiative and gallant behaviour shown by this officer.

MILLER, THOMAS EASSON, M.M., Lieut., 8th Infantry Battn. Manitoba Regt. He personally rushed a group of the enemy and alone captured 22 prisoners. When troops on each flank failed to keep up with him, he reorganized his men and consolidated a line, which repelled three counter-attacks. Though shortly afterwards wounded he remained at duty until the battalion was relieved. His fine courage and determined dash were most inspiring to those with him.

PRICE, CHARLES BASIL, D.C.M., Major, 14th Infantry Battn. Quebec Regt. For sound ability in handling his battalion and great gallantry in the attack on the Canal du Nord on 27 Sept. 1918. He successfully gained all his objectives and captured and cleared up the village of Sains-les-Marquion, and, though wounded, refused to be evacuated until his colonel, arriving opportunely from leave as the barrage started, arrived on the scene and relieved him. He had complete grasp of the situation at all times.

RITCHIE, CHARLES FREDERICK, M.C., Lieut.-Colonel, 24th Infantry Battn. Quebec Regt. For conspicuous gallantry and devotion to duty in operations north of Cambrai 1–14 Oct. 1918. His battalion held the front line for nine days under very trying conditions prior to our attack. Several counter-attacks were completely repulsed, the enemy suffering heavy casualties, and prisoners were made. On the 12th Oct. he led his battalion into action, at very short notice, in a highly satisfactory manner. His work throughout these operations was of a very high order.

SINCLAIR, IAN MACINTOSH ROE, M.C., Major, 13th Infantry Battn. Quebec Regt. For sound tactical judgment and conspicuous gallantry in the handling of his battalion at the Canal du Nord on 27 Sept. 1918. The canal crossing had to be made on a 500-yard front, which was swept by machine-gun fire from Lock 3. Pushing forward, he established his headquarters close to the front-line objective gained by another battalion, and finally, in conjunction with them, succeeded in capturing the village of Marquion and his final objective.

SPENCER, NELSON, Major, 31st Infantry Battn. Alberta Regt. For conspicuous gallantry and devotion to duty near Iwuy on 11 Oct. 1918. He was in command of a battalion detailed to follow the battalion attacking Iwuy, and carry the attack forward. When the advance was checked he went forward with the leading troops, and, by skilful and determined leadership, overcame the resistance of the enemy and cleared the way for a further advance. Throughout three days' fighting he displayed marked courage and resource, and contributed largely to the success of the operations.

TOBIN, HENRY SEYMOUR, Lieut.-Colonel, 29th Infantry Battn. British Columbia Regt. For great gallantry and devotion to duty in operations near Cambrai on 9, 10 and 11 Oct. 1918. He went forward with the advancing troops, directed their movement under heavy fire, and greatly contributed to the success of the operation. Later, when his troops were held up by heavy fire in a swamp, he went forward, reorganized them, and secured valuable information, which materially assisted in the ultimate success of the operation.

TUXFORD, GEORGE STUART, C.B., C.M.G., Brigadier-General, Saskatchewan Regt., Commanding 3rd Canadian Infantry Brigade. For conspicuous gallantry and able leadership whilst commanding his brigade in the attack across the Canal du Nord on the 27th Sept. 1918, and the operations of the following days. His brigade had to attack on a very narrow front across the Canal du Nord, and then to fan out and attack on a wide frontage, including the towns of Sains-les-Marquion and Marquion. The operation was successfully accomplished, thanks to his ability and continuous presence with the forward troops. His work during the last two months' operations has been excellent.

WALKER, PHILIP, Major, Manitoba Regt., attached 10th Infantry Battn. Alberta Regt. For conspicuous gallantry and initiative during operations on 27–28 Sept. 1918, east of Haynecourt. When the advance had been temporarily held up he visited the companies under very heavy machine-gun fire, and successfully superintended the necessary changes that had to be made before the attack could proceed. His work throughout was of a very high order.

WHITE, WILLIAM JAMES, M.C., Capt., 28th Infantry Battn. Saskatchewan Regt. On 11 Oct. 1918, he commanded a company in the attack upon the village of Iwuy, which was strongly held by the enemy. He several times led small groups of men against enemy machine-guns in defended localities, overwhelming by his dash and gallantry the enemy resistance. On one occasion he rushed out and, single-handed, killed or captured the entire post, consisting of eight or ten men, thus ensuring the success of the operation. He showed splendid courage and dash.

AUSTRALIAN IMPERIAL FORCE.

ANDERSON, ALEXANDER MILNE, Capt., 48th Battn. Australian Imperial Force. For most conspicuous gallantry and initiative during the advance near Le Verquier, north-west of St. Quentin, on the 18th Sept. 1918. When his company encountered very strong opposition on the objective he continually exposed himself to gather information, and, by directing his men, he was able to work along trenches and so cut the enemy off, who were defending a very commanding position. In this position he captured 220 of the enemy, a number of machine guns, four minenwerfers, and one 77-mm. gun. He did fine work.

CAMPBELL, ARCHIE ERIC GORDON, M.C., Major, 14th Australian Light Horse Regt. (Egypt). For distinguished leadership and devotion to duty. On the 30th Sept. 1918, at Salahiye (Damascus), he was charged with the work of clearing the gardens to the south of the village, in expectation of the whole force following. In spite of the main body being deflected by another order, this officer pursued a very vigorous course through the gardens, clearing out 150 enemy and many machine guns before reaching the railway line. He also did very valuable work in consolidating the position taken up across the road. Throughout the operation his work was excellent.

CHANTER, JOHN COURTENAY, Major, 4th Australian Light Horse Regt. (Egypt). For conspicuous gallantry, initiative and devotion to duty whilst leading his squadron across the Jordan near El Min, on the 28th Sept. 1918, under heavy fire. By personal reconnaissance he found a way across, was one of the first to get over, and remained under fire assisting and directing his squadron, thereby keeping casualties down to a minimum. Again, on the 1st Oct. 1918, he has in command of the squadron which made the reconnaissance to Meidan Railway Station, and his great dash and determination were the means of securing many thousands of prisoners. Throughout the whole operations he set a fine example to his squadron.

CHEESEMAN, WILLIAM JOSEPH ROBERT, M.C., Lieut.-Colonel, 53rd Battn. Australian Imperial Force. North of Bellicourt, on 1 Oct. 1918, he showed marked gallantry and initiative. His battalion had to attack at dawn, and to reach the start line had to move over a mile and a half of ground intersected by the Hindenburg system in the dark. When dawn broke they came under heavy converging machine-gun fire, and he got his men into artillery columns and personally led them over to the start line and got the attack up in line with the flank troops. Later in the day he made a reconnaissance forward under exceptionally heavy fire, and obtained most valuable information.

COSTELLO, EDWARD, Major, 11th Australian Light Horse Regt. (Egypt). At Semakh, on the 25th Sept. 1918, he was in command of one of the squadrons that charged the enemy's position covering the east and southern part of the town. His dash and energy went a long way to make the attack a success. After going through the enemy's lines they still resisted under covering fire from machine guns placed in the town, but he collected his men—who were under fire at point-blank range of an enemy 12-pounder gun—and dismounted them for a bayonet charge. This gun was subsequently captured, together with a machine gun. After losing two officers and having his horse shot under him, he beat off a counter-attack.

COUCHMAN, FRANK MUNGEAM, Major, 46th Battn. Australian Imperial Force. For great gallantry and leadership during the operations west of Bellenglise, north of St. Quentin, on the 18th Sept. 1918. He was in command of the right company, and when the unit on his left was held up he pushed a party forward, protected his flank, and, under intense machine-gun fire, finally succeeded in reaching a sunken road, where he established his line. Throughout his work was excellent.

CRAIG, ROBERT FULTON, Major, 15th Field Ambulance, Australian Army Medical Corps. For conspicuous gallantry and devotion to duty in charge of the bearer division near Bellicourt, from 29 Sept. to 2 Oct. 1918. During the whole of this period he rendered valuable service, and by his coolness and initiative surmounted all difficulties under most trying conditions. He not only worked the evacuation of wounded from rear aid-posts of his own brigade, but he personally reorganized the evacuation from other brigades under very heavy shell and machine-gun fire.

DALGLEISH, NORMAN, Lieut., 58th Battn. Australian Imperial Force. For most conspicuous gallantry and determination during operations north-east of Bellicourt, between 29 Sept. and 1 Oct. 1918. On the first day, owing to casualties, he found himself in command of a company, and, although wounded, gained his objective for the day. That night he led a patrol forward to reconnoitre a strongly fortified farm. He gained valuable information, which enabled it to be rushed and captured the following morning. Three times wounded in these operations, he showed fine courage and devotion to duty, and rendered valuable service.

DENSON, HERBERT REGINALD, Major, 14th Australian Light Horse Regt. (Egypt). For distinguished gallantry, devotion to duty and marked initiative at Nablus, on the 21st Sept. 1918. He was in charge of the advanced squadron, and by his initiative and dash he cleared the gardens covering the road of machine guns, which resulted in the capture of the town and many hundreds of prisoners. He led the charge through the town in person.

DODD ARTHUR WILLIAM, M.C., Major, 6th Battery, 2nd Brigade, Australian Field Artillery. For conspicuous gallantry and devotion to duty at Nauroy, near Bellicourt, on the night 2–3 Oct. 1918. During heavy enemy bombardment a gas shell fell on the parapet of the trench in which he and two of his officers were working. Although he was badly gassed he remained with his battery, completed his orders for an attack which was to be launched a few hours later, and carried out the task allotted to his battery. He showed courage and determination of a high order throughout.

HAMLIN, HERBERT BOWEN, Major, 10th Australian Light Horse Regt. (Egypt). At Gisr Benat Yakub, on the 27th Sept. 1918, after forcing the ford, he led his squadron in the face of heavy fire and charged against the enemy's position, which he captured after a severe mêlée. He displayed great courage and dash, and throughout set a magnificent example to his command. Fifty enemy, with three machine guns and two field guns, were captured.

HILL, REGINALD VALENTINE, Lieut., 53rd Battn. Australian Imperial Force. During the operations near Bellicourt from 30 Sept. to 2 Oct. 1918, he displayed most conspicuous courage and leadership. He led a charge against an enemy machine-gun strong post, mopped up the garrison of about 20, and captured three machine guns. Shortly after this he and his party of six men came across a double-entrance dug-out, manned with a machine gun at each entrance. Here he personally shot three men with his revolver and accounted for a total of 15, and captured two guns. He did magnificent work.

LANGLEY, GEORGE FURNER, Lieut.-Colonel, Commanding 14th Australian Light Horse Regt. (Egypt). For skilful leadership and conspicuous gallantry in action. At Nablus on the 21st Sept. 1918, he was in command of the advanced guard. At several points the main road was strongly held by enemy machine guns, but, despite the difficult nature of the country, he overcame all opposition and pushed forward with all speed. By his dash and determination he succeeded in capturing a large number of prisoners and a quantity of war material in the town. At Damascus, on the 30th Sept. 1918, he again distinguished himself by his coolness in the face of the enemy, and gained command of an important point on the Damascus-Beirut road, resulting in the capture of about 4,000 prisoners and a large quantity of war material.

LEITH, ERIC ALLAN, Lieut., 46th Battn. Australian Imperial Force. For most conspicuous gallantry and leadership during the attack on the Hindenburg Line on the 18th–19th Sept. 1918, west of Bellenglise, north of St. Quentin. He was in command of the left company, and by his determination and brilliant leadership he got his men across the dense mass of enemy wire. He was severely wounded when rushing the trench, but continued on, captured the trench, and took many prisoners and machine guns. Pushing on to the second trench, he captured the position, taking over 100 prisoners and six machine guns. He showed fine courage and did splendid work.

LOYNES, JAMES, Major, 11th Australian Light Horse Regt. (Egypt). At Semakh, on the morning of the 25th Sept. 1918, he was in command of one of the squadrons that charged the town. His coolness and dash in the charge were a good example to the men, and went a long way towards the success of the operation. He organized a bayonet charge from the west of the town, and by collecting all the men he could, and by his resourcefulness and untiring energy he was able to stop what might have been a repulse, and finally, in the general clearing up of the town, he did great work.

MACPHERSON, LACHLAN ALFRED WILLIAM, M.C., Major, 8th Australian Light Horse Regt. (Egypt). For gallantry and smart leadership at Tiberias on the 25th Sept. 1918. He was sent forward with his squadron in advance of the brigade to reconnoitre, and on finding the place lightly held he made his disposals, quickly capturing the town and a number of prisoners and motor and horse transport. The information sent back enabled the advance to proceed more quickly than was anticipated.

OLDEN, ARTHUR CHARLES NIQUET, Major, 10th Australian Light Horse Regt. (Egypt). He was in charge of his regiment, which formed the advance guard to the Brigade, when the latter was ordered to occupy Jenin on the 20th Sept. 1918. He rapidly cut the roads leading from Jenin north and north-east, covering a distance of 11 miles, and thus took prisoners fugitives who were already several miles from the town. During the ensuing night his regiment covered the Nablus road from the south and captured further prisoners. The total number of prisoners taken in this operation was 8,107 and five guns. He showed great initiative and ability to command.

SAVIGE, STANLEY GEORGE, M.C., Capt., Australian Imperial Force (Mesopotamia). For conspicuous gallantry and devotion to duty during the retirement of refugees from Sain Keleh to Tikkan Tappah, 26–28 July, 1918; also at Chalkaman, 5–6 Aug. In command of a small party sent to protect the rear of the column of refugees, he by his resource and able dispositions kept off the enemy, who were in greatly superior numbers. He hung on to position after position until nearly surrounded, and on each occasion extricated his command most skilfully. His cool determination and fine example inspired his men and put heart into the frightened refugees.

YEOMANS, JULIAN CLYDE, Lieut., 30th Battn. Australian Imperial Force. For most conspicuous gallantry and dash during the operations in the vicinity of Nauroy and Bellicourt on 29 Sept. 1918. He led a patrol of 25 men forward under heavy fire to ascertain the enemy's dispositions in and around Nauroy. Nearing the village he noticed a tank, and with the aid of this tank he attacked the village and the Le Catelet-Nauroy trench immediately in front so successfully that the trench and village were mopped up with heavy losses to the enemy, in addition to 18 prisoners and seven machine guns being captured. He himself rushed a machine gun, personally killing the crew and capturing the gun. He did splendid work, showing great courage and most determined leadership.

NEW ZEALAND FORCE.

HERROLD, JOHN HENRY, Major, Auckland Mounted Rifle Regt. (Egypt). On the night of the 24th–25th Sept. 1918, he took command of a party of 100 men with orders to cut the Amman-Derra railway line north of Amman. He marched by night over roadless country, intersected by innumerable wadis, which made progress very difficult. On reaching the line he found an enemy party at work, but moving further south, he accomplished his object, removing a set of rails from the line, although large numbers of the enemy were continually moving along the road just east of the line.

HOLMES, JOHN DUDLEY, Capt., New Zealand Tunnelling Coy., New Zealand Engineers. For gallantry and devotion to duty during the construction of the bridge over the gap between Hermies and Havrincourt. This bridge was commenced on the evening of the 27th Sept. under shell fire, which demanded great personal discipline to ensure that the preparations went through without a hitch. By his example he made this possible, and all through the construction of the bridge, which was successfully completed, showed absolute disregard for personal safety.

WILDER, ALAN STANDISH, M.C., Major, Wellington Mounted Rifle Regt. (Egypt). For conspicuous gallantry and devotion to duty on the morning of the 25th Sept. 1918. He was in charge of the vanguard during the march on Amman. Though his squadron came under heavy rifle, machine-gun and shell fire he skilfully made dispositions and forced back the enemy. During the attack he made personal reconnaissances, and brilliantly led his squadron in the attack, capturing prisoners and machine guns. His energy, initiative and sound judgment set a magnificent example to all ranks under his command.

SOUTH AFRICAN FORCE.

JACOBS, LOUIS MASTERMAN, Temporary Capt., 2nd Battn. South African Infantry. On the 8th Oct. 1918, east of Beaurevoir, four enemy field guns firing at point-blank range and supported by a number of machine guns were a source of great trouble to the advance. His skilful handling of his company enabled the guns and machine guns to be outflanked, severe casualties being inflicted on the crews and a number of the enemy taken prisoners. In the attack north-east of Le Cateau in a thick mist under heavy fire he did excellent work in supervising the advance and capture of the objective. He showed marked gallantry and initiative during twelve days' operations.

London Gazette, 17 Oct. 1919.—"Admiralty, 17 Oct. 1919.—Honours for services in Russia, 1919. The King has been graciously pleased to approve of the award of the following honours to the undermentioned Officers. To be Companions of the Distinguished Service Order."

HALLILEY, ALAN KERR, McCLINTOCK, Lieut., Royal Navy. As Senior Officer of Tunnel Minesweepers has performed most gallant work day after day, sweeping under fire. On the 24th June, 1919, his ship H.M.S. Sword Dance was mined and sunk, but he continued his duties without intermission, in spite of being wounded. The example set by him to officers and men has been admirable.

McLAUGHLIN, CYRIL EDWARD, Acting Lieut., Royal Navy (since killed). In recognition of the gallantry and devotion to duty displayed by him in sweeping and destroying mines, often under heavy enemy fire.

To receive a Bar to the Distinguished Service Order :

WORSLEY, FRANK ARTHUR, D.S.O., R.D., Lieut.-Commander, Royal Naval Reserve. In recognition of the gallantry displayed by him at Pocha in North Russia between the 2nd and 5th Aug. 1919. This officer formed one of a large patrol which in circumstances of great danger and difficulty penetrated many miles behind the enemy lines, and by his unfailingly cheery leadership he kept up the spirits of all under trying conditions. By his assistance in bridging an unfordable river behind the enemy lines, he greatly helped the success of the enterprise.

"Honours for Services in Minesweeping Operations between the 1st July and 31st Dec. 1918.—The King has been graciously pleased to approve of the award of the following honours to the undermentioned Officers. To be Companions of the Distinguished Service Order."

DAMMERS, CHARLES MONTAGU, Commander, Royal Navy.
LAMOTTE, HAROLD DE GALLYE, Lieut.-Commander, Royal Navy.

"Honours for Services in the Mine Clearance Force between the 1st Jan. and 30th June, 1919.—The King has been graciously pleased to approve of the award of the following honours to the undermentioned Officers. To be Companions of the Distinguished Service Order."

INGLIS, COLIN STUART, Commander, Royal Navy.
BELL, CHARLES COURTENAY, Commander, Royal Navy.
FORTIER, RICHARD LOFTUS, Lieut.-Commander (Acting Commander), Royal Naval Reserve.
GILBERTSON, GEORGE NOEL, Lieut.-Commander, Royal Navy.
BOUCHER, MAITLAND WALTER SABINE, Lieut.-Commander, Royal Navy.
MACQUEEN, JOHN ALEXANDER, Lieut. (Acting Lieut.-Commander), Royal Naval Volunteer Reserve.

London Gazette, 23 Oct. 1919.—"War Office, 23 Oct. 1919. The King has been graciously pleased to approve of the undermentioned rewards for distinguished service in connection with the defence of Kut-al-Amarah. Dated 3 June, 1919. Awarded the Distinguished Service Order."

BAINES, EDGAR FRANCIS EARDLEY, Lieut.-Colonel, Indian Medical Service.
BARBER, CHARLES HARRISON, M.B., Major, Indian Medical Service.
BAYLAY, EDWARD JOHN LAKE, Major, Royal Artillery.
BROWN, WALTER HENRY, C.B., Lieut.-Colonel, 103rd Mahratta Light Infantry, Indian Army.
CANE, ARTHUR SKELDING, O.B.E., M.D., Capt. (Acting Major), Royal Army Medical Corps.
CANE, EDWARD GEOFFREY STAYNE, Capt., Royal Army Medical Corps.
DAVIE, JAMES HENRY MORISON, Lieut.-Colonel, 34th Horse, Indian Army.
DUNN, ERNEST GEORGE, Major, Royal Irish Rifles.
FLOYD, ARTHUR BOWEN, Capt., Reserve of Officers, late Norfolk Regt.
FOOTNER, FOSTER LAKE, Major, Hampshire Regt., Territorial Force.
FORBES, EDWARD ERNEST, Major, Supply and Transport Corps, Indian Army.
GOLDFRAP, HAROLD WYN, M.C., Capt., 103rd Infantry, Indian Army.
GUNN, ALISTAIR DUDLEY, Capt., 110th Infantry, Indian Army.
JOHNSON, MAURICE EUSTACE STANLEY, Major, 48th Pioneers, Indian Army.
LAING, STANLEY VAN BUREN, M.C., Major, 76th Punjabis, Indian Army.
MARTIN, ERSKINE THACKERAY, Major, Royal Artillery.
MILFORD, EDWARD, Major, 76th Punjabis, Indian Army.
POWELL, WILLIAM BOWEN, C.M.G., Lieut.-Colonel, 2/7th Gurkha Rifles, Indian Army.
RAYNOR, CYRIL ARTHUR, M.C., Capt., 48th Pioneers, Indian Army.
SANDES, EDWARD WARREN CAULFEILD, M.C., Major, Royal Engineers.
SMITH, STEPHEN CHRISTOPHER WINFIELD, Capt., East Surrey Regt., Special Reserve, and Royal Air Force.
STEWART, ALEXANDER FREDERICK, Lieut.-Colonel, Supply and Transport Corps, Indian Army (rank corrected to Major [London Gazette, 12 July, 1920]).
STOCKLEY, CHARLES HUGH, M.C., Major, 66th Punjabis, Indian Army.
SUTHERLAND, ARTHUR ORR, Major, 22nd Punjabis, Indian Army.
WALLACE, CHARLES WILLIAM, Major, 22nd Punjabis, Indian Army.

London Gazette, 11 Nov. 1919.—"Admiralty, S.W., 11 Nov. 1919. Honours for Services in Russia, 1919.—The King has been graciously pleased to approve of the award of the following honours to the undermentioned Officers. To be Companions of the Distinguished Service Order."

BRAMBLE, FRANK GEORGE, Commander, Royal Navy. For distinguished services as Chief Staff Officer to the Senior Naval Officer, Archangel River Expedition.

MURRAY, ARTHUR JOHN LAYARD, O.B.E., Lieut.-Commander, Royal Navy. For distinguished services in connection with the recovery and refitting of enemy mines. In carrying out this work Lieut.-Commander Murray was severely injured by a premature explosion.

FAWSSETT, ARTHUR CHARLES, Lieut.-Commander, Royal Navy. For distinguished services in command of H.M.S. M26, and in charge of operations off Onega, 30 July to 2 Aug. 1919, which he carried out with great skill, courage and coolness.

JOHNSTONE, ANDREW, Lieut.-Commander, Royal Navy. For distinguished services in command of H.M.S. Humber. Lieut.-Commander Johnstone fought his ship frequently under heavy fire with great gallantry.

YATES, FRANCIS BERTRAND, Engineer Lieut. (Acting Engineer Lieut.-Commander), Royal Navy. For distinguished services on the occasion of the attack on Kronstadt Harbour on the 18th Aug. 1919.

AGAR, AUGUSTINE WILLINGTON SHELTON, V.C., Lieut., Royal Navy. For distinguished services in command of H.M. Coastal Motor Boat No. 7 in the attack on Kronstadt Harbour on the 18th Aug. 1919. He piloted two other boats into the harbour through the forts under a heavy fire and then patrolled the mouth of the harbour to cover their withdrawal.

McBEAN, RUSSELL HAMILTON, D.S.C., Lieut., Royal Navy. For distinguished services in command of H.M. Coastal Motor Boat No. 31 in the attack on Kronstadt Harbour on the 18th Aug. 1919. Under a very heavy fire he entered the harbour, torpedoed the Bolshevik battleship Andrei Pervozanni, and returned through the fire of the forts and batteries to the open sea.

BODLEY, EDWARD ROLAND, Sub-Lieut. (Acting), Royal Naval Reserve. For distinguished services in command of H.M. Coastal Motor Boat No. 72 in the attack on Kronstadt Harbour, on the 18th Aug. 1919. After passing through the line of forts and reaching the entrance to the middle harbour under heavy fire, he attacked a Bolshevik destroyer. His steering gear, however, broke down, and he withdrew towards the line of forts, where he encountered and took in tow another boat, escorting her safely out of action under fire from all the forts.

"Honours for Services in the Caspian Sea, 1918, 1919.—The King has been graciously pleased to approve of the award of the following honours to the undermentioned Officers. To be Companions of the Distinguished Service Order."

WASHINGTON, BASIL GEORGE, C.M.G., Capt., Royal Navy. For distinguished services in command of Windsor Castle in action off Fort Alexandrovsk on the 21st May, 1919.

GRIEVE, EDWARD LEONARD, Commander, Royal Navy. For distinguished services on the staff of the Senior Naval Officer, Caspian Sea.

GUY, KENNETH ALLAN FERRERS, Commander, Royal Navy. For distinguished services in command of the Emile Nobel in action off Fort Alexandrovsk on the 21st May, 1919.

HARRISON, RICHARD, R.D., Lieut.-Commander (Acting Commander), Royal Naval Reserve. For distinguished services in command of the Venture in action off Fort Alexandrovsk on the 21st May, 1919, and on the occasion of the destruction of the Bolshevik base at Staro Terechnaya.

CHARSLEY, FREDERICK GASCOIGNE, Lieut.-Commander, Royal Navy. For distinguished services in command of the Zoraster in action with Bolshevik ships on the 8th Dec. 1918.

WILSON, ALEXANDER GUY BERNERS, Lieut., Royal Navy. For distinguished services in command of the Asia in action with Bolshevik destroyers on the 19th April, 1919, and off Fort Alexandrovsk on the 21st May, 1919.

PERTWEE, HERBERT GUY, Acting Paymaster Lieut., Royal Navy. For distinguished services as Secretary to Commander David T. Norris, C.B., Senior Naval Officer, Caspian Sea.

"Honours for Services in the Mine Clearance Force subsequent to the 30th June, 1919.—The King has been graciously pleased to approve of the award of the following honour to the undermentioned Officer. To be a Companion of the Distinguished Service Order."

HINDMARSH, JOHN DALGLASH, D.S.C., Lieut. (Acting Lieut.-Commander), Royal Naval Reserve.

"Honours for Miscellaneous Services. (I.)—The King has been graciously pleased to approve of the award of the following honour to the undermentioned Officer. To be a Companion of the Distinguished Service Order."

REED, WILLIAM LOUIS, Engineer Sub-Lieut., Royal Naval Reserve. For gallant and distinguished services as a volunteer in H.M.S. Julnar on the 24th April, 1916, when that vessel attempted to reach Kut-El-Amarah with stores for the besieged garrison.

II.—To receive a Bar to the Distinguished Service Order .

COCHRANE, ARCHIBALD DOUGLAS, D.S.O., Commander, Royal Navy. In recognition of the determination, spirit and resource displayed by him on the occasion of a successful attempt to escape from the prison camp at Yozgad, Aug. 1918.

London Gazette, 18 Nov. 1919.—"Air Ministry, Kingsway, London, W.C.2, 18 Nov. 1919. His Majesty the King has been pleased to approve of the undermentioned rewards, conferred by the General Officer Commanding the North Russian Expeditionary Force. Awarded the Distinguished Service Order."

GREY, ROBIN, Squadron Leader (Acting Wing Commander), Grenadier Guards. Commanded the Royal Air Force, Archangel Area, with great distinction. Owing to the lack of Pilots and Observers during the winter, he carried out personally the most dangerous reconnaissances. On the 8th April, 1919, at Obozerskaya, he carried out a reconnaissance in bad weather, bringing back valuable information. On the 22nd April, 1919, he carried out two most important reconnaissances with success, but met with a bad accident on landing the second time. Although considerably shaken physically, he continued to command the Royal Air Force with marked success until the conclusion of the operations in North Russia.

STEWART-DAWSON, NORMAN GORDON, D.S.C., Flight Lieut. Successfully led several raids with great success during the operations with the Syren Force in North Russia from June to September, 1919, notably in the attack on the enemy at Koikori on the 7th Sept. Flight Lieut. Stewart-Dawson has displayed exceptionally good qualities in leadership during these operations in the air, and equally distinguished services in ground-work organization, where the difficulties were many.

London Gazette, 29 Nov. 1919.—" War Office, 29 Nov. 1919. His Majesty the King has been graciously pleased to approve of the following awards to the undermentioned Officers, in recognition of their gallantry and devotion to duty in the field. Awarded the Distinguished Service Order."

HICKIE, HENRY WHITTEN, Major, 84th Punjabis, Indian Army. By his skilful handling of a tactical situation at Shusha on the 4th June, 1919, he enabled one company of the 84th Punjabis to be interposed, with very slight loss, between considerable forces of Tartars and Armenians engaged in a faction fight. To carry this out he walked under heavy rifle fire from the Armenian trenches to the Tartar positions, showing great coolness and resource.

PRENDERGAST, NORMAN HENRY, Capt., Queen Victoria's Own Corps of Guides, attached North Waziristan Militia, Indian Army. He has led detachments of his corps gallantly on all operations, especially on 27 May, 1919, at Miranshah, and has always shown high soldierly qualities. The fact that practically the whole of his corps has remained loyal is chiefly due to his personal influence and power of command.

London Gazette, 10 Dec. 1919.—" War Office, 10 Dec. 1919. With reference to the awards conferred as announced in the London Gazette dated 2 April, 1919, the following are the statements of services for which the decorations were conferred. Awarded a Second Bar to the Distinguished Service Order."

ALBAN, CLIFTON EDWARD RAWDON GRANT, D.S.O., Capt. and Brevet Major (Acting Lieut.-Colonel), Liverpool Regt., attached 15th Battn. Lancashire Fusiliers. During the operations on the Oise-Sambre Canal, near Ors, during the 2nd, 3rd and 4th Nov. 1918, the way in which he handled his battalion was most praiseworthy. On two occasions during counter-attacks he took up reinforcements under heavy fire and restored the situation. It was due to his gallant leadership and example that the attack on the 4th Nov. was so successful, a battery of high-velocity guns, over 200 prisoners, and many machine guns being captured.
(D.S.O. gazetted 18 July, 1917.)
(1st Bar gazetted 15 Feb. 1919.)

BRANSON, DOUGLAS STEPHENSON, D.S.O., M.C., Capt. (Acting Lieut.-Colonel), 1/4th Battn. York and Lancaster Regt., Territorial Force. For conspicuous gallantry and devotion during the attack on Haspres on 13 Oct. 1918. After his battalion had suffered heavy casualties, all the company officers being wounded, he collected the remnants of the battalion under intense fire, led them forward, and consolidated a position. His personal courage and resource were magnificent.
(D.S.O. gazetted 1 Jan. 1918.)
(1st Bar gazetted 16 Sept. 1918.)

DUNCAN, KENNETH, D.S.O., Lieut.-Colonel, D/246th (West Riding) Brigade, Royal Field Artillery, Territorial Force. For conspicuous gallantry during an attack near Avesnes Le Sec on 13 Oct. 1918. Although the battery suffered very heavy casualties, by his magnificent example and complete disregard for his own safety he kept it in action, and, though so short of men that he was obliged to serve a gun himself, he completed the barrage in support of the attack.
(D.S.O. gazetted 3 June, 1916.)
(1st Bar gazetted 18 Jan. 1918.)

PEEL, WILLIAM RALPH, Temporary Major (Acting Lieut.-Colonel), D.S.O., 6th Battn. Yorkshire Regt., attached 1/10th Battn. Manchester Regt. For conspicuous gallantry and devotion to duty during the operations east of the Forêt de Mormal from 6 to 8 Nov. 1918. He led his battalion for four days in continuous rain without shelter, and captured the town of Hautmont. To accomplish this he had to supervise the construction of a hasty bridge over the Sambre river and cross it while the enemy troops were still in the town.
(D.S.O. gazetted 4 June, 1917.)
(1st Bar gazetted 16 Sept. 1918.)

POLLITT, GEORGE PATON, D.S.O., Major (Acting Lieut.-Colonel), Royal Engineers, attached 11th Battn. Lancashire Fusiliers. For conspicuous gallantry during the fighting on 27 May, 1918, on the Aisne. He had his battalion in repeated local counter-attacks against overwhelming odds, holding up the enemy and inflicting severe casualties. Thanks to his example and leadership his battalion put up a splendid defence when over forty per cent. of them had become casualties and the remainder were almost surrounded.
(D.S.O. gazetted 1 Jan. 1917.)
(1st Bar gazetted 18 July, 1917.)

CANADIAN FORCE.

DAVIES, REGINALD DANBURY, D.S.O., Lieut.-Colonel, 44th Battn. Canadian Infantry, North Brunswick Regt. In front of Inchy-en-Artois, 27 Sept. 1918, for marked gallantry and determination. In command of the battalion, he led a most successful attack against the enemy positions. Again, on 28 Sept., near Raillencourt, notwithstanding most severe casualties, he again led his battalion in the attack and reached his objective, later materially assisting in beating off a strong enemy counter-attack. His reports throughout the operations were most clear and invaluable in determining the situation forward.
(D.S.O. gazetted 17 April, 1917.)
(1st Bar gazetted 2 Dec. 1918.)

MACKENZIE, JOHN PERCIVAL, D.S.O., Lieut.-Colonel, 1st Brigade, Canadian Engineers. During the recent operations he has on several occasions under fire made daylight reconnaissances in order to get the required information for the selection of bridge crossings. During the advance on Cambrai and Douai, Sept. and Oct. 1918, it was due to his quick grasp of the situation and determined action that the infantry, field and heavy artillery, ambulance and ammunition were able to cross all obstacles with the least possible delay.
(D.S.O. gazetted 1 Jan. 1917.)
(1st Bar gazetted 26 July, 1917.)

Awarded a Bar to the Distinguished Service Order:

BATE, JOHN PERCIVAL, D.S.O., M.C., Capt. (Acting Major), 1/8th Battn. Worcestershire Regt., Territorial Force. For marked gallantry and able leadership of his battalion during operations 23–24 Oct. 1918, near Pommereuil. His battalion reached its final objective in front of all flanking troops, thereby greatly facilitating the advance of division on his left. During the day his battalion captured three howitzers and over 200 prisoners. Next day his battalion again did excellent work, taking all their objectives.
(D.S.O. gazetted 1 Jan. 1919.)

BROMILOW, DAVID GEORGE, D.S.O., Major, 14th Murray's Jat Lancers, Indian Army (Mesopotamia). For conspicuous gallantry and devotion to duty north of Shargat on 30 Oct. 1918. When advancing to cut off a body of the enemy, heavy fire was suddenly opened on his squadron. He thereupon immediately attacked the enemy with great daring, causing the surrender of 200, including 25 officers and several machine guns. He did fine work.
(D.S.O. gazetted 25 Aug. 1917.)

CARTER, WILLIAM HENRY, D.S.O., M.C., Capt. and Brevet Major (Temporary Lieut.-Colonel), Royal Warwickshire Regt., attached 7th Battn. South Staffordshire Regt. For skilful leading of his battalion during the operations 8 and 9 Nov. 1918, in the advance from Autreppe to Geognies Chaussée. On 8 Nov. 1918, he by his drive and initiative kept his battalion going forward through heavy enemy opposition and by a personal reconnaissance reported his exact dispositions at the end of the day. He has at all times set a very fine example to those under him.
(D.S.O. gazetted 20 Oct. 1916.)

CHAPPELL, WICKHAM FRITH, D.S.O., Major, 7th Dragoon Guards. For conspicuous gallantry and skill as a Squadron Commander during operations which resulted in the capture of the crossing over the River Dendre at Lessines on 11 Nov. 1918. He organized and led a successful attack under heavy fire, capturing the town of Lessines, with four officers, 102 other ranks, and several machine guns. It was greatly due to his courage, energy and example that the operation was successful.
(D.S.O. gazetted 15 Oct. 1918.)

CLARKE, HUBERT THOMAS, D.S.O., Major (Acting Lieut.-Colonel), 1/8th Battn. Worcestershire Regt., Territorial Force. For gallant leadership and good work during the attack on Landrecies on 4 Nov. 1918. His battalion was allotted the very difficult task of crossing the canal, taking the town, and establishing themselves on the high ground beyond. All of this they did, in spite of the fact that they had to help the two leading battalions in their fight up to the canal. This battalion took nearly 300 prisoners and several guns.
(D.S.O. gazetted 8 March, 1919.)

CRIPPS, CHARLES WILLIAM, D.S.O., Major, 3rd Battery, 45th Brigade, Royal Field Artillery. During the operations between 10 and 23 Oct. 1918, he performed brilliant service, and by his bold and dashing action contributed largely towards the success attained; particularly on 12 Oct., his skilful handling of his battery dislodged the enemy from the Prison Faubourg D'Esquerchin at close range under machine-gun fire. Throughout his work was excellent.
(D.S.O. gazetted 4 June, 1917.)

FORBES, ROBERT, D.S.O., M.C., Lieut. (Temporary Major) (Acting Lieut.-Colonel), 5th Battn. Royal Highlanders, Territorial Force, attached 10th Battn. Essex Regt. For conspicuous gallantry in leading his battalion into action in Mormal Forest on the 4th Nov. 1918. During the whole of the advance, owing to the difficulty of the situation, he personally conducted the action of the foremost troops. It was due to his skilful leadership and example that the attainment of the objective by his battalion was assured.
(D.S.O. gazetted 7 Nov. 1918.)

HONE, PERCY FREDERICK, D.S.O., M.C., Temporary Lieut.-Colonel, General List, attached 13th Battn. Durham Light Infantry. He commanded his battalion during the attack north-east of Le Cateau on 23 and 24 Oct. 1918. He personally led his battalion in the attack south-east of Fontaine au Bois, having previously gone forward to reconnoitre. On the 24th Oct. 1918, when reconnoitring in advance of his battalion, he was wounded. His fine example of courage and determination contributed in a large measure to the success of the operations.
(D.S.O. gazetted 1 Jan. 1919.)

HORE-RUTHVEN, THE HON. ALEXANDER GORE ARKWRIGHT, V.C., C.M.G., D.S.O., Lieut.-Colonel (Temporary Brigadier-General). He commanded his brigade with conspicuous gallantry and judgment throughout the operations east of Ypres from 28 Sept. to 27 Oct. 1918, inclusive. His presence and personal bearing at critical times during the fighting was of decisive value, especially during a strong enemy counter-attack. On 20 Oct. at St. Louis, he went forward among the attacking troops at a critical juncture, and inspired them to the final effort, whereby the high ground of great tactical value was captured.
(D.S.O. gazetted 2 May, 1916.)

HUNTER, RICHARD DEVAS, D.S.O., Capt. (Acting Lieut.-Colonel), Scottish Rifles, attached 1/8th Battn. Territorial Force. Throughout the operations near Anseghem on 31 Oct. and 1 Nov. 1918, he commanded his battalion with conspicuous skill and gallantry. His presence among his men at the critical moments and his personal control of the fight were mainly responsible for the ultimate success of his own battalion, and was of the greatest assistance to the division on the left.
(D.S.O. gazetted 3 June, 1918.)

JACK, JAMES LOCHHEAD, D.S.O., Major and Brevet Lieut.-Colonel (Temporary Brigadier-General), Scottish Rifles (General Officer Commanding 28th Infantry Brigade). He commanded his brigade with great dash and gallantry throughout the operations east of Ypres from 28 Sept. to 28 Oct. 1918. On 2 Oct. the enemy opened a heavy barrage and counter-attacked at Ledeghem. Troops on the immediate left of his brigade gave way. He formed them up in the barrage and personally led them forward again and re-established the front line. He then went across to his own front line under heavy machine-gun fire, and by his energy and example inspired his men to save an awkward situation.
(D.S.O. gazetted 18 June, 1917.)

LASCELLES, VISCOUNT, HENRY GEORGE CHARLES, D.S.O., Capt. (Acting Lieut.-Colonel), Grenadier Guards (Reserve of Officers), attached 3rd Battn. For conspicuous gallantry and skilful leadership. At Villers Pol, on 4 Nov. 1918, when his battalion was checked by heavy machine-gun fire, he went forward and personally organized an attack, which enabled the advance to be continued. On the night of 8–9 Nov. 1918, when his battalion was suddenly ordered to capture Maubeuge, he skilfully directed the advance over a distance of four miles. His energy during the whole operations was splendid.
(D.S.O. gazetted 3 June, 1918.)

McGRATH, ARTHUR THOMAS, D.S.O., Major and Brevet Lieut.-Colonel (Acting Lieut.-Colonel), Royal Field Artillery, Commanding 88th Brigade. For conspicuous gallantry and devotion to duty on 1 Nov. 1918. When his headquarters near Artres were heavily shelled, he was wounded, but, although unable to ride, and obliged to have his wound dressed daily, he personally led with the greatest courage and coolness the forward sections of his brigade during the remainder of the advance, and rendered invaluable help to the infantry by shelling machine-gun nests at short range over open sights.
(D.S.O. gazetted 1 Jan. 1917.)

MORRELL, JOHN FREDERIC BAKER, D.S.O., M.V.O., Capt. and Brevet Major (Temporary Lieut.-Colonel), Royal Lancaster Regt., attached 9th Battn. Manchester Regt. On 8 Oct. 1918, in the action round Serain, under heavy machine-gun fire, he visited all the forward posts on his battalion front, and so kept the closest touch with the situation. Later, when touch had been lost on his flank, he reconnoitred again and obtained touch with the flanking brigade and closed a dangerous gap. Throughout the fighting from 8 to 11 Oct. he showed great courage and ability to command.
(D.S.O. gazetted 1 Jan. 1919.)

MURPHY, JOSEPH LEO, D.S.O., Major, Manchester Regt., Special Reserve, attached 2nd Battn. He handled his battalion with the greatest dash and ability in the forcing of the passage of the Oise-Sambre Canal near Ors on the 4th Nov. 1918. In spite of heavy artillery, rifle and machine-gun fire he got his battalion across the canal and continued to drive back the enemy, capturing a field battery of 5.9 guns and many prisoners and machine guns.
(D.S.O. gazetted 15 Feb. 1919.)

MURRAY, DONALD, D.S.O., Temporary Major, Manchester Regt., attached 21st Battn. In the absence of his commanding officer he commanded his battalion throughout the operations from 22 Oct. to 28 Oct. 1918. In the attack on Pommereuil on 23 Oct., when, owing to darkness and mist, units had lost direction and became intermixed, he went forward and reorganized the attack, which was then entirely successful. He showed great courage and ability to command.
(D.S.O. gazetted 1 Jan. 1919.)

PELLY, RAYMOND THEODORE, D.S.O., Major and Brevet Lieut.-Colonel (Temporary Brigadier-General), North Lancashire Regt. (General Officer Commanding 81st Infantry Brigade) (Italy). For gallantry and conspicuous good service. He handled the left brigade of the 7th Division at the crossing of the Piave, 27 Oct. 1918, with marked success. This brigade particularly distinguished itself, gained all its objectives after stiff fighting, and captured many prisoners. The brigade again distinguished itself on the Monticano, particularly in the capture of Cimetta, when stubborn resistance was encountered. Brigadier-General Pelly showed great judgment and coolness in personally superintending the final capture of this village from the banks of the Monticano, when they were under heavy artillery and machine-gun fire the whole time. Throughout the whole operations he set a fine example to his brigade.
(D.S.O. gazetted 14 Jan. 1916.)

RAMSBOTTOM, GORDON OPENSHAW, D.S.O., Temporary Lieut.-Colonel, 22nd Battn. Manchester Regt. (Italy). In the attack across the Piave on the 27th Oct. 1918, and following days, he showed the greatest skill in leading his men, combined with the highest courage and contempt for danger. When his men were in difficulties owing to the swift current and the wire on the river bank, he led the leading company across and inspired his men with such a splendid spirit and determination that they carried all before them and broke the principal point of the enemy's resistance, capturing hundreds of prisoners and nine guns. Although nearly drowned in the river crossing, nothing could stop this gallant officer, who was indefatigable in pressing the attack.
(D.S.O. gazetted 4 June, 1917.)

RAMSDEN, VINCENT BASIL, D.S.O., M.C., Capt. (Acting Major and Temporary Lieut.-Colonel), 1st Battn. South Wales Borderers, attached 15th Battn. Highland Light Infantry. For conspicuous gallantry and ability in command of his battalion at Ors on the 4th Nov. 1918, when it was detailed for the capture of a second and third position. He carried out the task with marked courage and resource, pushing on in face of heavy opposition well into the night, and securing all objectives by dawn. The work done by the battalion under his leadership has been of a very high order throughout these operations.
(D.S.O. gazetted 26 July, 1918.)

RICHARDSON, JAMES JARDINE, D.S.O., Lieut.-Colonel, 13th Hussars (Mesopotamia). For conspicuous gallantry and devotion to duty at Hadranizah on 29 Oct. 1918. He led his regiment under heavy fire to the successful assault of a bluff. His cool and determined action had a great and far-reaching effect at a critical point of the operations.
(D.S.O. gazetted 25 Aug. 1917.)

SUTHERLAND, THOMAS DOUGLAS, D.S.O., M.C., Temporary Major, 6th Battn. Lincolnshire Regt. For conspicuous gallantry and initiative during operations on the 6th and 7th Nov. 1918, on the east bank of Grande Honnelle River. His battalion was held up in an attack by mist and heavy machine-gun fire, and suffered severe casualties, but by his personal courage, fine example and skilful dispositions, he was able to inspire all ranks with his own splendid fighting spirit, and to hold on at a most critical period for a day, taking the leading companies forward the following day and capturing the position.
(D.S.O. gazetted 26 Sept. 1917.)

THWAYTES, HARRY DELAMERE, D.S.O., Capt. (Acting Lieut.-Colonel), 1st Battn. Dorsetshire Regt. For conspicuous gallantry and ability in handling his battalion at the forcing of the passage of the Sambre Canal, near Ors, on the 4th Nov. 1918. This he effected by a single footbridge, and as soon as his advanced parties had cleared the enemy from the immediate vicinity he succeeded in pushing the whole battalion across without delay. His personal courage and resource under heavy fire were deserving of high praise.
(D.S.O. gazetted 2 Dec. 1918.)

VICKERY, CHARLES, EDWIN, D.S.O., Major and Brevet Lieut.-Colonel, Royal Field Artillery, Headquarters 74th Brigade. For conspicuous gallantry and able leadership. At Les Mottes, on 9 Nov. 1918, the brigade was in close support of the infantry, who were held up by fire from 77 mm. guns and machine guns. He made a daring reconnaissance, and, galloping back, brought his battery into action within 700 yards of the enemy's guns, silencing them, and enabling the advance to be resumed. His cheerfulness and excellent liaison with the infantry were a brilliant example to all.
(D.S.O. gazetted 31 Oct. 1902.)

WORTHINGTON, CLAUDE SWANWICK, D.S.O., Lieut.-Colonel, 6th Battn. Manchester Regt., Territorial Force, attached 5th Battn. Dorsetshire Regt. During the operations at Oisy le Verger, on 27 Sept. 1918, he displayed conspicuous gallantry whilst in command of his battalion. When two companies were held up he went forward in face of heavy fire and cleared up the situation on taking and consolidating his objective. Later, at Epinoy, on 1 Oct. when the battalion was held up by heavy machine-gun fire, he went forward to the companies which were held up and helped them on to the objective. Throughout he set a fine example of determined leadership.
(D.S.O. gazetted 2 Feb. 1916.)

CANADIAN FORCE.

BROWN, WALTER RICHARD, D.S.O., Lieut.-Colonel, 26th Battn. Canadian Infantry, New Brunswick Regt. For conspicuous gallantry and resource in operations north of Cambrai during the night 8–9 Oct. 1918, when he led his battalion in an attack across the Canal d'Escaut with great skill and devotion in most trying conditions and under heavy artillery fire. His personal courage at the bridges while his men were crossing, and the manner in which he afterwards reorganized the battalion in the dark and led them to the capture of a village, displayed fine qualities of leadership and determination.
(D.S.O. gazetted 18 Oct. 1917.)

GRIESBACH, WILLIAM ANTROBUS, C.B., C.M.G., D.S.O., Brigadier-General, Alberta Regt. (General Officer Commanding 1st Canadian Infantry Brigade). For brilliant leadership and great gallantry in the operations of 8 Aug. 1918, south-east of Amiens ; 2 and 3 Sept. 1918, east of Arras, and 27–28 Sept. 1918, west and north-west of Cambrai in the crossing of the Canal du Nord and attack on Bourlon Wood, and during operations 17–21 Oct. He made several personal reconnaissances, and his presence amongst the attacking troops and his coolness under critical conditions were largely responsible for the success that attended the operations.
(D.S.O. gazetted 24 June, 1916.)

JONES, TERENCE PERCIVAL, D.S.O., Major, 4th Battn. Canadian Infantry, 1st Central Ontario Regt. (Brigade Major, 12th Canadian Infantry Brigade). For conspicuous gallantry and devotion in the operations near Valenciennes from the 1st to 6th Nov. 1918. His work as brigade major was of the highest order, and largely contributed to the success of the brigade in the capture of Valenciennes and towns further east. He also made several daring personal reconnaissances under severe fire, and secured exact information which enabled the enemy's disposition to be effectively dealt with and the advance to continue.
(D.S.O. gazetted 1 Jan. 1917.)

LOOMIS, FREDERICK OSCAR WARREN, C.B., C.M.G., D.S.O., Major-General, Quebec Regt. (General Officer Commanding 2nd Canadian Infantry Brigade). For great gallantry and brilliant leadership during the operations south-east of Amiens, 8–9 Aug. 1918, and east of Arras, 2 Sept. 1918. He made reconnaissances under heavy fire, personally superintending the disposition of troops and encouraging all by his coolness and ability. The results achieved by the brigade were of an outstanding nature.
(D.S.O. gazetted 23 June, 1915.)

AUSTRALIAN IMPERIAL FORCE.

ANNAND, FREDERICK WILLIAM GADSBY, D.S.O., Lieut.-Colonel, 2nd Pioneer Battn. Australian Imperial Force. On Montbrehain, east of Peronne, on 5 Oct. 1918, in charge of a pioneer battalion, he succeeded in carrying out a very difficult relief in pitch darkness. A few hours after this he ably carried out a flanking movement to the attack on the town of Montbrehain, driving back the enemy and ensuring a defence which proved to be unbreakable. His reconnaissances had to be carried out under heavy shell fire. He showed rare qualities of leadership.
(D.S.O. gazetted 1 Jan. 1917.)

DUGGAN, BERNARD OSCAR CHARLES, Lieut.-Colonel, D.S.O., 21st Battn. Australian Infantry. At Montbrehain, on 5 Oct. 1918, he having been ordered to attack with his battalion carried out a careful reconnaissance under heavy shell fire of the routes leading to and the jumping-off line for the attack. During the attack he set a fine example of zeal and energy to his command, with the result that the enemy position was taken and held, although the enemy repeatedly attempted to break through and nullify the success.
(D.S.O. gazetted 1 Jan. 1918.)

JAMES, WILLIAM EDWARD, D.S.O., Lieut.-Colonel, 24th Battn. Australian Infantry. At Montbrehain, east of Peronne, on 5 Oct. 1918, he led his battalion in the very successful attack and subsequent retention of the village of Montbrehain. To a large extent the great success of this operation was due to the skilful leadership displayed by him and to his gallant demeanour in the earlier stages of the attack.
(D.S.O. gazetted 3 June, 1918.)

WATSON, CHARLES VINCENT, D.S.O., Lieut.-Colonel, 58th Battn. Australian Infantry. For conspicuous gallantry and good leadership during the attack on Hindenburg Line near Bellicourt, from 28 Sept. to 2 Oct. 1918. The prompt action of this officer under very heavy fire in personally reconnoitring and ascertaining the exact situation at a critical time enabled him to make dispositions restoring the situation. Throughout he commanded his battalion most ably, and captured a number of prisoners and machine guns.
(D.S.O. gazetted 1 Jan. 1919.)

NEW ZEALAND FORCE.

ALLEN, ROBERT CANDLISH, D.S.O., Lieut.-Colonel, Auckland Regt., attached 1st Battn. New Zealand Rifle Brigade. At Le Quesnoy, on the 4th Nov. 1918, he displayed great courage and skill in handling his battalion, and the success of his attack greatly assisted the storming of the town. After being wounded he continued to carry out his duties until all objectives were taken. He has previously done good work.
(D.S.O. gazetted 16 Aug. 1917.)

Awarded the Distinguished Service Order :

ALLEN, WILLIAM BARNSLEY, V.C., M.C., M.B., Capt. (Acting Major), Royal Army Medical Corps, attached 1/3rd (West Riding) Field Ambulance, Royal Army Medical Corps, Territorial Force. For conspicuous gallantry and devotion to duty during the fighting west of Saulzoir for the Selle River line between the 11th and 14th Oct. 1918. He showed a very high degree of fearless initiative in organizing the collection of wounded from ground under continuous hostile shell fire, and by his inspiring example, untiring energy and contempt of danger, he was able to move large numbers of helpless wounded from positions of danger before he was himself gassed.

ALSTON, LLEWELYN ARTHUR AUGUSTUS, Capt. (Acting Major), M.C., 1st Battn. Royal Welsh Fusiliers (Italy). He was in command of the Royal Welsh Fusiliers in the attack on Papadopoli Island on the 23rd Oct. 1918, and showed great coolness and daring under heavy gun, rifle and machine-gun fire. He personally led his men into action, and by skilful handling of his battalion contributed largely to the success. He later on in the night collected a party of men and rounded up a team of enemy machine gunners who had crept up in the dark and were firing at 60 yards' range into the huts in which brigade and battalion headquarters were situated. He did fine work.

AMY, ARCHIBALD CRAIG, M.D., Major, Royal Army Medical Corps, attached 2/1st (Highland) Field Ambulance, Royal Army Medical Corps, Territorial Force. For conspicuous gallantry and devotion to duty on 24 Oct. 1918, at Douchy, when in charge of the advanced dressing station there. The town was shelled with high-velocity guns for four hours, many shells bursting in the vicinity of the advanced dressing station, one shell causing 21 casualties. A large number of wounded were brought in, and by his coolness and energy he prevented any confusion resulting, and cleared his advanced dressing station successfully.

ATKIN, BENJAMIN GEORGE, M.C., Capt. (Temporary Major), 1st Battn. Manchester Regt., attached 22nd Battn. (Italy). During the night advance on Vazzola on the 28th–29th Oct. 1918, in command of a battalion, he carried out an exceedingly difficult operation with conspicuous courage and skill. Owing largely to his leadership the operation was completely successful. The following day his battalion was detailed for flank guard to the brigade in the advance on Cimetta. In very close and difficult country the enemy was found strongly posted on the banks of the Monticana River. The advance guard was held up, but Major Atkin, with admirable dash and skill, led his battalion forward under extremely heavy shell and machine-gun fire and captured the south bank of the river, taking several hundred prisoners and relieving the pressure on the advanced guard, which was then able to effect a crossing. His gallant and fearless bearing throughout the day had a most inspiring effect on all around him.

BAYLISS, HERBERT VICTOR, M.C., Capt. (Acting Major), East Surrey Regt., attached 7th Battn. Wiltshire Regt. He was ordered with his battalion to make good the two crossings of the Grandhelpe on 4 Nov. 1918. Thanks to his gallant and able leadership the crossings were established and the bridges repaired, enabling our troops and two 18-pounders attached to them to continue the advance next day without delay.

BENYON, HUGH SAM, M.C., Capt., Northamptonshire Yeomanry (Italy). For leading his squadron with great gallantry and ability on 29 Oct. 1918, against the enemy on the Monticano River, where, thanks to his dash and good leading, his men overcame the garrison of 500 to 600 strong, and prevented the bridge over the river between Vazzola and Cimetta from being blown up. Again on 30 Oct. 1918, when the corps mounted troops were attacking Sacile and his squadron was sent round the right flank, by his sound leading and his own personal disregard of danger his squadron inflicted severe casualties on the enemy, and when he got orders to retire he brought back one officer and over 100 other ranks prisoners under very difficult circumstances.

BOMFORD, LESLIE RAYMOND, M.C., Lieut. (Acting Capt.), 1/8th Battn. Worcestershire Regt., Territorial Force. In the attack on Landrecies on 4 Nov. 1918, he led his company with marked gallantry and initiative. During the early stage of the advance machine-gun fire was encountered, coming from a house on the flank, and, summoning a tank, he led it personally to attack the house, supported by his company, and captured there four officers and 35 men. Later he made a daring reconnaissance of the bridge over the canal, finally getting his company across and capturing the town. He did splendid work.

BRIERLY, SIDNEY CLIFFORD, Major (Acting Lieut.-Colonel), 5th Battn. West Riding Regt., attached 1/4th Battn. Yorkshire Light Infantry, Territorial Force. For conspicuous gallantry and devotion to duty near Valenciennes on the night of 1 Nov. 1918, when, under circumstances of great difficulty, he relieved a battalion in the front line, and advanced at dawn. The same afternoon his battalion attacked and captured all its objectives. Two days later his battalion again made a successful attack, wheeling to the right during the operation. His skilful leadership was a great asset.

CAMPBELL, KEIR ARTHUR, Lieut., 3rd Battn. Grenadier Guards (Special Reserve). For conspicuous gallantry and devotion to duty at Preux-au-Sart on 4 Nov. 1918. He commanded the right front company, which came under heavy machine-gun fire the moment it advanced. He was continually with his leading sections, directing and controlling the platoons against an organized line of machine guns commanding an open slope. Towards dusk all his officers were lost, and he was wounded, but he remained until consolidation was complete, showing splendid endurance.

CARLTON, HERBERT DUDLEY, Major (Acting Lieut.-Colonel), Royal Scots, attached Royal West Surrey Regt. (Italy). In the attack across the Piave on 27 Oct. 1918, and following days he handled his battalion with remarkable coolness and skill and showed conspicuous gallantry. On 29 Oct. he was in command of the advanced guard of the 91st Brigade, consisting of the 2nd Queen's and a battery of Italian Mountain Artillery. The enemy made a determined stand on the River Monticano, but owing to his able handling of the advanced guard the passage of the river was forced and the village of Cimetta taken. He handled an exceedingly difficult situation with marked skill and courage and showed a soldierly spirit and ability of the highest order.

CLARKSON, ALFRED BAIRSTOW, M.C., Major, 1/6th Battn. West Riding Regt., Territorial Force. For conspicuous gallantry and devotion to duty in command of his battalion near Valenciennes on 1 Nov. 1918. The attack over bare open slopes was partly held up, but by his personal example in visiting every part of his front line, exposed to intense fire, he was largely responsible for its successful accomplishment.

COLAM, STANLEY D'EYNCOURT, M.C., Capt., Gordon Highlanders, Special Reserve (Brigade Major 145th Infantry Brigade) (Italy). For conspicuous gallantry and devotion to duty as brigade major during the attack on enemy positions north of Asiago on 1 and 2 Nov. 1918, and the subsequent advance. At a critical time he was sent forward to clear up the situation, and in spite of very heavy fire worked his way to the most advanced positions reached by our troops and returned with accurate reports of the positions held. This daring reconnaissance proved of the utmost value to his commander, and throughout the whole of the operations he kept in the closest personal touch with the attacking troops, visiting each unit and inspiring all by his courage and example.

COOKE, RONALD CAMPBELL, M.C., Temporary Capt. (Acting Major), 134th Field Ambulance, Royal Army Medical Corps. He was always equal to the occasion when, owing to considerable advances made by our troops, fresh organization and alteration of schemes of evacuation were demanded to meet the conditions, and his unit was short-handed. His skill and fine devotion to duty over a difficult period were admirable.

CRAMPTON, JAMES, M.C., Temporary Major, 8th Battn. York and Lancaster Regt., attached 9th Battn. (Italy). For conspicuous ability and gallantry on 31 Oct. 1918, during the Piave battle in organizing a crossing of the River Livenza into Sacile. After several unsuccessful attempts had been made to improvise a bridge and effect a crossing owing to intense enemy machine-gun fire, he organized a party of pioneers, constructed a bridge, and bringing up six-inch mortars, Stokes mortars and machine guns, succeeded in getting three companies across the river. This result was entirely due to his remarkably clear grip of the situation, and the skilful manner in which he superintended the work. Throughout the bridging, the organization of the mortar and machine-gun fire and the crossing of the infantry, he was moving about exposed to heavy machine-gun and rifle fire from the houses. His determination, resource, and complete disregard of his personal safety were admirable.

CROW, PERCY, M.C., Temporary Capt. (Acting Major), A/161st Brigade, Royal Field Artillery. He was in command of the battery, which closely supported the advance of the infantry on 7 and 8 Nov. 1918, near Avesnes. During these two days he acted with the greatest vigour and determination, kept his guns close up behind the infantry, and fired at many machine guns with open sights. He showed great courage and initiative, and materially assisted the advance.

CURELL, WILLIAM BROWN, Major, 2nd Battn. Lancashire Fusiliers. For gallantry and capable leadership of a battalion during operations east of Verchain, near Artres, on 26 Oct. 1918. At zero hour he followed the support companies to the attack with an orderly, and established a battle headquarter in a château on the outskirts of Artres, from which, under heavy fire, he observed magnificent targets for the artillery, and twice spotted and informed them of an impending counter-attack by the enemy, which was immediately engaged. His excellent dispositions and initiative throughout were greatly responsible for the success obtained.

DALE, FRANCIS RICHARD, M.C., Temporary Capt. (Acting Major), 19th Battn. Welsh Regt., attached 16th Battn. Royal Welsh Fusiliers. For conspicuous gallantry and devotion in command of his battalion at the crossing of the River Selle, near Le Cateau, on the 20th Oct. 1918. The operation was extremely difficult, but, after daring reconnaissances, his orders, combined with his splendid leadership and example, were responsible for the complete success of the operation. On two occasions later he led his battalion through heavy barrages and intricate country, with the greatest courage, gaining the objectives and capturing four .77 guns.

DRIVER, ARTHUR, M.C., Lieut. (Temporary Major and Acting Lieut.-Colonel), 6th Battn. West Riding Regt., Territorial Force, attached 9th Battn. For conspicuous gallantry and able leadership when in command of his battalion during active operations, especially on the 12th Oct. 1918, in the attack on Neuvilly, when he very ably led his battalion, and, although himself wounded, reorganized it under heavy shell and machine-gun fire at a critical stage of the battle. He also distinguished himself on 4 Nov. 1918, at the capture of Futoy.

DUDLEY-WARD, CHARLES HUMBLE, M.C., Lieut. (Acting Major), 1st Battn. Welsh Guards. For conspicuous gallantry and devotion to duty in command of his battalion in the attack south of Bavai, 8 Nov. 1918. By his untiring efforts the battalion advanced, step by step, for nearly two miles with an exposed flank. He took risks at the right place and time, and showed himself to be a real leader of men.

DUNN, JOHN BRUCE, M.C., Temporary Capt., 15th Battn. Highland Light Infantry. In the attack on the Oise-Sambre Canal, on the 4th Nov. 1918, when the Commanding Officer was killed, he took command of the remnants of the battalion. In face of heavy fire, he led them across the canal, causing the enemy heavy casualties, and gaining his objective. It was due to his example of courage and initiative that the battalion succeeded in capturing six field guns, 16 machine guns, and many prisoners.

EDDOWES, HUGH MORTIMER, Temporary Lieut., 185th Tunnelling Coy., Royal Engineers. For conspicuous gallantry and devotion to duty at Flines Station on 20 Nov. 1918. Information having been received from the enemy that a delay action mine had been laid, and was timed to explode five days before, he located and fired it. The work was exceptionally dangerous, as the mine might have exploded at any moment.

ELLIS, LIONEL FREDERIC, M.C., Lieut. (Acting Capt.), Welsh Guards, Special Reserve, attached 1st Battn. For conspicuous gallantry and devotion to duty in the advance south of Bavai on 6 Nov. 1918. When the whole battalion was held up at the railway, he brought his company headquarters up to reinforce his company, and, calling on his men to follow him, rushed across the railway bank, surprising and routing the enemy, whom he followed up a spur, until held up by a fresh machine-gun position. His energy and resource encouraged his men to overcome all difficulties, and resulted in the capture of Prihart Farm. He subsequently reorganized the company on his left, which was in difficulties, and finally brought up and posted a support company, securing the left flank of the division.

ENGLISH-MURPHY, WILLIAM RICHARD, M.C., Lieut. (Acting Lieut.-Colonel), 1st Battn. South Staffordshire Regt. (Italy). In the attack across the Piave on 27 Oct. 1918, and following days, he handled his battalion with conspicuous gallantry and skill. Seeing the leading battalion in difficulties owing to the swiftness of the river and the wire on the river bank, he on his own initiative moved his battalion up on the flank of the leading battalion, and gave most valuable assistance in the capture of the first objective at a somewhat critical period. He then reorganized his battalion and led them rapidly forward, capturing the villages of Smichele Di Piave and Tezze, with hundreds of prisoners and several guns. Throughout the operations he set his men a splendid example of fearlessness and dash, which materially helped to ensure the great success achieved.

FAWKES, ROWLAND BEATTIE, M.C., Temporary Capt., 6th Battn. Northamptonshire Regt. For great gallantry and fine leadership during operations near Preux on 4 Nov. 1918. He commanded the company, taking the first of the battalion's objectives in face of strong enemy opposition. The company won its way by rifle and machine-gun fire and captured a number of machine guns and took over 100 prisoners.

FYERS, HARRY AMELIUS BEAUCLERK, Temporary Lieut., 179th Tunnelling Coy., Royal Engineers. For conspicuous gallantry and good work between 25 Oct. and 17 Nov. 1918, in detecting and removing enemy acid delay action and other mines from the railway. On 12 Nov. he superintended the removal of three mines at Monchecourt Station, himself removing the fuse from one mine, which was reported to be six days overdue and liable to go off at any moment. His section removed over 8,000 lb. of explosives during the above period.

GARRARD, FREDERICK BLAKE, Lieut. (Acting Capt.), 2nd Battn. Honourable Artillery Company (Italy). For conspicuous gallantry during the attack carried out by the battalion on the Grave Di Papadopoli on the night of the 23rd–24th Oct. 1918. He showed the most consummate coolness and skill in collecting and forming up his company under the most intense shell fire. Again, particularly on the night of the 25th–26th Oct., during the attack on the southern portion of the island, he showed fine powers of leadership and complete disregard of danger, and was greatly responsible for the large capture of prisoners. During the final operations, when the enemy was offering a most stubborn resistance, he was severely wounded, but still continued to direct and command his company until the enemy resistance was finally overcome.

GIBBONS, CHARLES, M.C., Lieut. (Temporary Capt.), D.C.M., Durham Light Infantry, attached 12th Battn. (Italy). For most conspicuous gallantry and devotion to duty. At the forcing of the River Piave on 27 Oct. 1918, near the Island of Papadopoli, the battalion, after passing the most northerly stream under very heavy fire, was held up by uncut wire. He with four N.C.O.'s and men ran forward from his own company and through the leading company to cut the wire, which was swept from end to end with shell fire and by machine-gun fire from the front and in enfilade. All the party except himself were killed and he was wounded. In spite of his wound he continued until a lane had been cut, helped only by one other rank, who had already been wounded and who came up to his assistance. But for this act of devoted heroism the attack must have failed and the battalion been repulsed. Suffering from a most painful wound, he continued to lead his company until they had taken the third and final objective.

GRIERSON, KENNETH MACIVER, M.C., Second Lieut. (Temporary Lieut. and Acting Capt.), Manchester Regt., attached 22nd Battn. (Italy). He was in command of one of the leading companies in the attack on the 27th Oct. 1918. He led his men across the Piave in a magnificent manner. When the enemy bank had been reached he crawled forward and helped to cut a gap in the wire to within 15 yards of the enemy; all this time he was under observation and fire from the embankment, which was still held by the enemy. The splendid example he set to his men contributed in a large extent to the successful capture of the first objective. Later, in the taking of all objectives, he showed himself to be a fine leader both in skill and courage. All the houses and strong points were tackled under his direction in a systematic and dashing way.

GRIFFITH-WILLIAMS, ERIC LLEWELLYN GRIFFITH, M.C., Capt. (Acting Major), 135th Battery, 32nd Brigade, Royal Field Artillery. For conspicuous gallantry in action near Villers en Cauchies, on the 13th Oct. 1918. His battalion occupied a very forward and exposed position in support of an attack, and came under heavy shell fire throughout the day. It was owing to the fearless and skilful way in which he handled the battalion and arranged shelter for the men that he was able to keep up an uninterrupted fire with great effect. He also went forward under heavy fire to ascertain the progress of the battle, and later, when ordered to withdraw, displayed the greatest skill and courage in carrying out this difficult manœuvre.

HEDLEY, JOHN CYPRIAN, M.C., Second Lieut. (Acting Capt.), Royal West Surrey Regt., attached 11th Battn. For conspicuous gallantry and devotion on the night of the 8th–9th Nov. 1918, during and after the crossing of the Scheldt at Neersche, when, although opposed by thick belts of wire and water-logged marshes, and finally by a very deep ditch 15 yards wide and full of water, he led his company, under heavy and direct fire, with the greatest courage and determination, and, surmounting all obstacles, forced his way into the village, capturing it with many prisoners and machine guns. The forcing of the river was entirely due to his splendid personal gallantry and energy.

HENNESSY, RICHARD GEORGE, M.C., Lieut. (Acting Capt.), 2nd Battn. Border Regt. (Italy). For conspicuous gallantry and initiative. On the 27th Oct. 1918, he was sent forward to ascertain the situation in front of the battalion on the eastern bank of the Piave, and found a portion of the brigade front held up by machine-gun nests. He quickly had the situation in hand, organizing parties, and led them forward to the final objective. His quick appreciation of the situation and fine display of leadership inspired all ranks. Again, on the 28th Oct., when the battalion was ordered to advance from the " Red dotted line " to the " Blue dotted line," his grip of the situation on the left and the speed with which he got the two left companies going, clearing several machine-gun nests, enabled the advance to the " Blue dotted line " to be carried out.

HODNETT, HARRY, Temporary Second Lieut., Liverpool Regt., attached 1/5th Battn., Territorial Force. For conspicuous gallantry and devotion to duty at Ere on 6 Nov. 1918, when he led his platoon in a silent raid in broad daylight, capturing one officer, 34 men and two machine guns, rushing three posts in succession. The total strength of his platoon was only 18, and after providing covering party, escorts, and allowing for casualties, his final party consisted only of himself and three men, operating some 500 yards in advance of the line. His determination and dash took the enemy by surprise.

HOGAN, GUY STEWART, Temporary Second Lieut., 16th Battn. King's Royal Rifle Corps. For most conspicuous gallantry and devotion to duty on the night 24-25 Sept. 1918. During a minor operation south of Villers Guislain, he was in charge of a platoon detailed to carry out a bombing attack along a trench. After being twice wounded he rallied his platoon, again led them to the attack, and succeeded in gaining the objective. Shortly afterwards he was hit by a bomb, which blew off his right foot, and rendered him unconscious. When he came to, he refused to be taken away, and continued to direct his men until he fainted again. He behaved magnificently.

HOLT, GEOFFREY WILSON, M.C., Lieut. (Acting Major), A/74th Brigade, Royal Field Artillery. For conspicuous gallantry and inspiring leadership at Flaque Farm on 4 Nov. 1918. When the infantry were held up by machine guns and 77 mm. guns, firing at close range, he led a section at full gallop over the crest, down the slope, through a hail of fire, losing several horses, and came into action out of view just west of Preux au Sart, 100 yards behind the advanced infantry posts, sweeping the valley and the reverse slope of the crest. His quick grasp of the situation assisted the infantry to advance.

HOWATSON, GEORGE, Temporary Lieut. (Acting Capt.), 185th Tunnelling Coy., Royal Engineers. For conspicuous gallantry and resource in searching for and removing enemy traps and mines, especially on 12 and 13 of Nov., in removing delay action mines indicated by the enemy. He spent 36 hours in excavating a shaft and gallery approaching the large delay action mine in Douai Station, due to explode on 7 Nov. 1918.

KAY, WILLIAM, M.C. Second Lieut. (Acting Capt.), Manchester Regt., Special Reserve, attached 2nd Battn. On 4 Nov. 1918, during the attack on the Oise-Sambre Canal, he displayed marked courage and able leadership when his battalion was temporarily held up. Under intense machine-gun fire he went back to brigade headquarters and reported the situation. Later, his leadership materially contributed to the success of the day's operations.

KEMBLE, ALAN EDWARD, Capt., 2nd Battn. Yorkshire Light Infantry. For conspicuous gallantry and leadership when suddenly called upon to command the battalion during the advance from the Sambre Canal to the capture of Avesnes from 4 to 8 Nov. 1918. Throughout the whole five days he kept his battalion well in hand, being continuously with the leading platoons, under intense fire, directing and co-ordinating the advance. On 7 Nov. 1918, when the attack on Avesnes was checked, he personally advanced and reconnoitred, clearing up the situation. On 8 Nov. 1918, he led his company through the town, and formed up some two kilometres beyond, after exercising 27 hours' unrelenting pressure. Here he was badly wounded by a sniper, which resulted in the loss of a leg.

KENDRICK, FREDERICK ARTHUR, M.C., Lieut. (Acting Capt.), 1st Battn. South Staffordshire Regt. (Italy). During the operations 27-29 Oct. 1918, he showed the greatest gallantry, coolness and devotion to duty. On the 27th he pushed forward rapidly with his company, and captured the village of Tezze, three field guns and 240 prisoners. Again, on the 28th, his company was first to reach the objective, and he organized the battalion front for defence. On the 29th, at Cimetta, he was given charge of the two front-line companies of the battalion. At the beginning of this operation he had one arm broken by a machine-gun bullet, but continued to lead the attack through very difficult country and under heavy machine-gun fire. Before reaching his objective he was again hit in the other arm, but insisted on continuing to lead the advance, finally clearing the village and capturing a large number of prisoners and machine guns. He only consented to leave after consolidation was complete. By his absolute fearlessness, disregard of his wounds and skilful leadership he ensured the success of a difficult operation and set a splendid example.

LAWSON, LIONEL HALL, M.C., Temporary Capt., 11th Battn. West Yorkshire Regt. (Italy). For most conspicuous gallantry and able leadership. Throughout a most exhausting period of three days on the Island of Lido, from night 23-24 to night 26-27 Oct. 1918, under heavy shelling, he so animated all ranks with his own spirit of determination that under his leadership his company took a most conspicuous share in the operations of 27-29 Oct. On the 27th, after reaching the north bank of the Piave, he found the situation on the extreme right unsatisfactory ; he at once led a small party to this flank and pushed on, himself killing and capturing many of the enemy, until he had obtained touch with the division on the right, and so cleared up the situation. On the 28th, with one platoon, he patrolled forward, and taking Borgo Villa in rear, cleared this large village of a number of the enemy. Later on the same night he captured Soffratta, and thus at small cost brought his line forward over a kilometre. On the 29th, in very difficult country, with a small party he pushed forward after the crossing of the Monticano, and by his personal dash mopped up large bodies of the enemy, and destroyed or captured several machine guns which were holding out.

LEACHMAN, GERARD EVELYN, C.I.E., Major and Brevet Lieut.-Colonel, Royal Sussex Regt., attached Political Department (Mesopotamia). For conspicuous gallantry and devotion to duty at Huwaish on 28 Oct. 1918, and again at Qaiyarah on 30 Oct. 1918. He displayed marked courage in personally reconnoitring in his own unarmoured car, under heavy fire, ground over which the heavier armoured cars could not move. He then returned to guide them to the attack. The success attained by these cars during the operations was largely due to his intimate knowledge of the country and fearless leading over a trackless desert.

LEMAN, JOHN FREDERICK, Capt. (Temporary Lieut.-Colonel), Worcestershire Regt., attached 13th Battn. Royal Welsh Fusiliers. During the operations of the 8th Oct. 1918, at Mortho Wood, he displayed great gallantry and energy in pressing the attack of his battalion on the left of the brigade front. On the 4th Nov., in the Forest of Mormal, he led his battalion under one of the heaviest barrages experienced since the commencement of the advance straight to their objective, and captured four .77 guns and a 5.9 gun. His thoroughness in his work has been largely responsible for the unvarying success obtained by his battalion.

LENNON, JOHN ALFRED, M.C., Lieut. (Acting Capt.), West Riding Regt., Special Reserve, attached 2nd Battn. During the operations on the 24th Oct. 1918, against the high ground east of Verchain, he, owing to casualties amongst the company commanders, took command of two companies, and showed marked courage and determined leadership. He rushed a machine-gun post with his serjeant-major, and although the latter was killed, he completed the work, killing or capturing the whole crew single-handed. He then led his companies on, and captured and consolidated his objective.

LLOYD, RODERICK CROIL, M.C., Capt., (Acting Major) 1/1st Denbighshire Yeomanry, attached 24th Battn. Royal Welsh Fusiliers. During the successful operations of 31 Oct. 1918, in the vicinity of Tieghem, he showed great gallantry and able leadership in command of his battalion. At one period of the operations he went forward to the leading company commander, and with him so effectively reorganized the company under heavy fire that he was able to order it forward to the attack on the second objective. He then found the supporting company, who had lost direction, reorganized it and placed it in position.

LOWTHER, JOHN GEORGE, M.C., Capt., 11th Hussars, attached Northamptonshire Yeomanry (Italy). During the advance of the Corps Mounted Troops on Sacile on 30 Oct. 1918, he led his squadron, which was advance guard, with great gallantry and dash, and by maintaining such a rapid pace of advance in the face of much opposition he prevented the main body from being held up. Later in the day he made a daring attack on Sacile from the north, and when heavily counter-attacked he held on, inflicting very heavy casualties to the enemy until almost surrounded, when by his sound leading he got all his men away under their officers to a position just in rear.

MACILWAINE, ALFRED HERBERT, M.C., Capt. (Acting Major), " W " Battery, Royal Horse Artillery (Mesopotamia). For conspicuous gallantry and devotion to duty at Huwaish 27-29 Oct. 1918. His battery was continuously in action for three days, and during this strenuous time he directed the fire from an advanced outpost in the front line. Under heavy fire he exposed himself fearlessly to obtain good observation, and contributed largely to repelling all enemy attempts to break through. His tactical handling of his own and another battery was admirable, and his coolness and determination inspired all ranks with confidence.

MACMILLAN, ROBERT JAMES ALAN, Major, Royal Garrison Artillery, Territorial Force, attached 337th Siege Battery, Royal Garrison Artillery. For conspicuous gallantry and devotion to duty at Herin on 1 Nov. 1918, in support of an early morning attack by the infantry on Valenciennes. His battery came under heavy fire, and although knocked down by the explosion of a shell and slightly gassed, he refused to leave, and remained in charge until the barrage was completed and Valenciennes captured.

MAITLAND, ARTHUR EDWARD, M.C., Capt. (Acting Lieut.-Colonel), 2nd Battn. Essex Regt. For courage and good leadership whilst in command of a battalion during the operations east of Verchain from 25 to 28 Oct. 1918. His battalion carried out attacks on two successive days, the 25th and 26th, and it was largely due to his personal reconnaissance beforehand, followed by his excellent dispositions, that each attack was successful.

MARTIN, GEORGE NOEL CHADWICK, M.C., Capt. (Acting Major), B/74th Brigade, Royal Field Artillery. For conspicuous gallantry and brilliant leadership at Les Mottes on 8 Nov. 1918. He led a gun at a gallop through the foremost infantry, coming into action at 700 yards, silencing several machine guns which were holding up the advance. He remained in action in the open for several hours, keeping down hostile fire and denying the ridge 600 yards distant to the enemy. He also silenced two 77 mm. guns, which were firing on the troops at about 1,500 yards range. His intrepid behaviour set a fine example.

MATHESON, NEAL WILLIAM, M.C., Lieut. (Acting Capt.), Royal Engineers, Territorial Force, attached 54th Field Coy., Royal Engineers (Italy). At Salettuol throughout the bridging operations of 26-28 Oct. 1918, his services stood out pre-eminently. He took part in the preliminary reconnaissances across channels of unknown depth to determine the site of the bridge, and when this had been done was entrusted with the task of co-ordinating the work of the different units engaged on the work. When shelling and bombing interrupted the work he displayed the greatest coolness and disregard of danger. Though wounded he refused to leave the work. He did much to ensure the success of the operations.

MOIR, JOHN HAY, M.C., M.D., Temporary Capt., Royal Army Medical Corps, attached 17th Battn. Royal Fusiliers. For conspicuous gallantry and devotion to duty on 27, 28 and 29 Sept. 1918, near Noyelles. On the 27th, while a stretcher-party moving to the rear received a direct hit, he rushed out to its assistance and attended to the survivors under intense shell fire, carrying them to a place of safety. On the 28th he worked his aid-post under concentrated fire, dressing the wounded in the open after the cellar was full. He was very badly shaken by a shell burst, but carried on his work into the night, and assisted to pick up wounded in a counter-attack. Although utterly exhausted on the 29th he continued attending the wounded with energy and determination.

MOWAT, ALFRED LAW, M.C., Capt. (Acting Lieut.-Colonel), 1/4th Battn. West Riding Regt., Territorial Force. For conspicuous gallantry and devotion during operations east of Naues, lasting from the 11th to the 17th Oct. 1918. Always regardless of personal danger, he continually moved about his battalion area by day and night during every phase of the action, and on one occasion, when the enemy attacked with tanks and the line withdrew, he rallied the men, and led them forward again. Throughout the whole operations his gallantry and coolness set a magnificent example to all ranks under his command.

MUIR, ARTHUR WILLIAM, M.C., Temporary Capt. (Acting Major), 2nd Battn. Northumberland Fusiliers. During the phase of operations on the 4th, 5th and 6th Nov. 1918, he was in command of his battalion. Throughout the operations he displayed great skill and gallantry in the leading of his men, especially on the evening of the 6th. It was due to his untiring efforts and personal reconnaissances under heavy fire that he was able to report his battalion on their objective that night.

NICHOLLS, FRANK, M.C., Temporary Capt., 20th Battn. Manchester Regt. On the 6th Nov. 1918, the battalion was detailed as advanced guard during the advance from Maroilles to Dompierre ; he was placed in command of the two companies forming the point and vanguard. He carried out his duties in a most masterly and efficient manner, outflanking an enemy position, inflicting casualties, and taking several prisoners. Throughout he did excellent work.

PAGET-TOMLINSON, WILLIAM, Capt. (Acting Major), 7th Hussars (Mesopotamia). For conspicuous gallantry and devotion to duty at Huwaish on 28 Oct. 1918. When his regiment was attacking superior enemy numbers he showed most marked coolness and disregard of danger under fire. Though early wounded he remained at duty, and by his leadership and fine example in a brilliant attack, which caused heavy casualties on the enemy and was only checked within point-blank range of their guns, he inspired all ranks near him. Later, in spite of his wounds, he again went into action. He behaved most pluckily.

PARSONS, BERNARD EDWARD THOMAS, Major, 2/4th Battn. Hampshire Regt., Territorial Force. For conspicuous gallantry and valuable services. On 4 Nov. 1918, near Le Quesnoy, he went forward through the open fire-swept zone to co-ordinate the attack of his battalion, and went forward with the leading waves to the final objectives, capturing 250 prisoners and many machine guns and trench mortars. Again, on 6 Nov. 1918, near Le Timon, when the left flank was in the air and being heavily enfiladed, he went forward and cleared up the situation, reorganizing the attack and enabling the companies to reach their objectives.

PEMBERTON, HAROLD CHARLES, Temporary Capt., 20th Battn. Lancashire Fusiliers, attached 16th Battn. During the attack on the Oise-Sambre Canal on 4 Nov. 1918, he attempted to cross the bridge as soon as it was ready. As he was crossing, the floats at the enemy's end of the bridge broke loose. Under heavy machine-gun fire he succeeded in repairing it, thus enabling one officer and three men to cross before it was again broken by shell fire. In the advance he rendered excellent service.

PEPYS, CHRISTOPHER, M.C., Lieut. (Temporary Major), Devonshire Regt., attached 8th Battn. (Italy). For conspicuous gallantry and devotion to duty in the attack on the left bank of the Piave on 27 Oct. 1918. In command of the battalion, which was in brigade support, he led his troops across the Piave under very heavy fire, and hearing there was a gap between the front-line battalion and troops on the right, he at once pushed forward to fill the gap, and pushed his advance until held up in front of C. Palaclin, a formidable strong point. Hearing that the troops on his left were held up and the commanding officer killed, he went to them under heavy fire, reorganized them, and supervised consolidation until reinforcements arrived. During the further advance next day into villages occupied by the enemy he showed great initiative and courage in directing attacks on strong positions.

RICHARDS, FREDERICK WILLIAM, M.C., Temporary Capt. (Acting Major), 105th Field Coy., Royal Engineers. On the 4th Nov. 1918, during the successful attack on Landrecies, the Field Coy., Royal Engineers, commanded by him, carried out the bridging operations, assisted by a pioneer company. He elaborated the design of a most practical petrol tin bridging equipment. He accompanied the advance, and supervised the bridging operations under fire. He materially assisted the exceptional success of the attack that day.

RODERICK, WILLIAM DAVID, M.C., Temporary Second Lieut. (Acting Capt.), 14th Battn. Royal Welsh Fusiliers. For conspicuous gallantry and devotion to duty in the attack on Mormal Forest on 4 Nov. 1918. Whilst moving his company to the assembly position he was twice wounded by shell fire, and in the attack he was again wounded, but with indomitable pluck he led his men to their final objective. Later on, when all battalion headquarters officers had become casualties, he assumed command of the battalion, and made dispositions for a further advance before handing over and being evacuated to hospital.

ROWLANDS, HUGH, M.C., Lieut. (Acting Capt.), 2nd Battn. London Regt. At the Bois de Beaufort, near Angreau, on 6 Nov. 1918, for determined courage and leadership. Having lost all his platoon commanders and being held up by heavy machine-gun fire, he reorganized his company and the remnants of another company and got his force across a swollen river up to within 500 yards of the first objective, under very heavy fire. Though surrounded on three sides by the enemy, he eventually succeeded in fighting his way back across the river, bringing back with him all his wounded.

SALE, GEORGE GEOFFREY, M.C., Temporary Lieut. (Acting Capt.), 179th Tunnelling Coy., Royal Engineers. For conspicuous gallantry and good work in locating and removing acid-fused delay action and other mines from the railway at Waller's yard and Somain yard between 25 Oct. and 17 Nov. 1918. During this period his section removed eight delay-action and 42 other mines, two of which were due to explode on the day they were removed. He showed remarkable energy and skill.

SHAW, JOSEPH TAYLOR, Temporary Lieut. (Acting Capt.), Yorkshire Regt., attached 8th Battn. (Italy), In the Piave battle, 27–29 Oct. 1918, he commanded his company with great skill and conspicuous gallantry during the entire operations. On the 27th his company led the attack of his battalion, and, in spite of darkness and the difficult crossings of the river, he led his company straight to the battalion objective, and captured it, although out of touch with troops on right and left. On the night of 28th his company was sent forward to seize the bridge over Monticano river. Although unable to reach his objective owing to much superior enemy forces, he established himself just south of the river, capturing two guns and prisoners. His action enabled his battalion to deploy successfully next morning. On the 29th, when sent up to support, his right flank was in the air, and was being enfiladed from the right rear; he, however, held on, and largely assisted in breaking off a counter-attack.

SLINGSBY, THOMAS WILLIAM, Major, 22nd Cavalry, Indian Army (Mesopotamia). For conspicuous gallantry and devotion to duty at Tuz Khurmatli on 29 April, 1918. He boldly led his squadron at a gallop against two guns, which he captured, and, going through them, charged to the top of the ridge and caused the enemy to surrender.

SMITH, WILLIAM GEORGE, M.C., Lieut. (Acting Major), 23rd Field Coy., Royal Engineers. For great gallantry and devotion to duty during the forcing of the Sambre-Oise Canal south of Catillon, on 4 Nov. 1918. He, with his company, was in charge of the bridging operations at the canal bend, including the preparation and assembly of all material; the rapidity of the crossing was largely due to his good organization and example to those under him.

SOMERSET, THE HON. NIGEL FITZROY, M.C., Lieut. (Temporary Capt.), Gloucestershire Regt. and Motor Machine Gun Corps (Mesopotamia). For conspicuous gallantry and devotion to duty near Qaiyarah on 30 Oct. 1918. Owing to the bold and skilful handling of his armoured cars under heavy fire a retreating force of 500 of the enemy, with 10 machine guns, were forced to halt, thus giving an opportunity for a successful attack by a cavalry regiment, to whom he had sent information. As a result of this encounter the entire hostile force was captured. He displayed marked coolness and initiative throughout the operations.

SPENCER, JOHN, M.M., Temporary Second Lieut. (Acting Capt.), 17th Battn. Royal Fusiliers. For conspicuous gallantry and leadership on 28 and 29 Sept. 1918, near Noyelles sur L'Escaut. He was acting adjutant and in charge of a report centre during an attack across the canal. During the night the enemy counter-attacked, and, realizing the situation was critical, he went out under heavy shell fire and rallied the men, being twice wounded, but refusing to leave the line. The next day, when helping to establish the line, he was again twice wounded, and, after having his wounds dressed, reported at battalion headquarters to hand over all the papers.

SPICER, FRANK FITZROY FANE, Lieut. (Acting Capt.), 12th Lancers. On the 9th Nov. 1918, east of the Avesnes-Maubeuge Road, for brilliant and skilful leadership when in command of an advanced squadron. When the infantry had broken down the enemy resistance, he pushed boldly through to a depth of more than eight miles, capturing prisoners, guns and an immense amount of material and rolling stock, and clearing one large town and several villages. He continued pushing on until checked by a strongly held defensive line, which he reconnoitred, sending back an accurate report.

STEELE, JULIAN McCARTY, C.B., C.M.G., Lieut.-Colonel and Brevet Colonel (Temporary Brigadier-General), Coldstream Guards (General Officer Commanding 22nd Infantry Brigade) (Italy). For marked ability and gallantry during the battle of the Piave, 24 Oct. 1918. During the second phase of the capture of Papadopoli Island, he assumed direct command of all troops on the island. He crossed at Lido, under heavy machine-gun fire. On the first attempt his boat was riddled with bullets, and he was wounded in the head. Though suffering from severe concussion, which for a time had rendered him unconscious, he succeeded in reaching the island on his second attempt, and joined his troops. He was present in the front line during the subsequent Austrian counter-attack. Though suffering from his wound he refused to leave his brigade, and remained in command of it until the termination of operations on 4 Nov. He set a fine soldierly example of grit and commanded his brigade throughout with conspicuous success.

STICKNEY, JOSEPH EDWARD DANTHORPE, M.C., Capt. (Acting Major), 2/4th Battn. York and Lancaster Regt., Territorial Force. For conspicuous gallantry and leadership in command of a battalion on 4 Nov. 1918, in front of Fresnoy. After a personal reconnaissance under enemy barrage of the assembly position, he led his battalion up, in spite of fog and smoke barrage. During the attack, when the position was obscure, he controlled the direction under heavy machine-gun fire. Again, on 7 Nov. 1918, he formed his battalion up in the darkness, and successfully launched the attack on Neuf Mesnil, reorganizing and consolidating under intense fire. His energy and close personal supervision greatly encouraged his men.

TANNER, GILBERT, Major, 1/7th Battn. West Riding Regt., Territorial Force. For conspicuous gallantry and resource in command of a unit other than his own east of Naves on 11 Oct. 1918. The success of the operations carried out by the brigade was largely due to his excellent arrangements for the hurried assembly of his battalion, and his courage and energy in leading his men, and reorganizing them, after an enemy counter-attack with tanks, were worthy of high praise.

TEMPEST, EWART VINCENT, M.C., Lieut., 1/6th Battn. West Yorkshire Regt., Territorial Force (Intelligence Officer, 146th Infantry Brigade). During the operations south-east of Iwuy, on 11 and 12 Oct. 1918, this officer carried out his duties as Brigade Intelligence Officer with the utmost zeal and gallantry. He made a daring reconnaissance, sending back valuable information, and, later, when a hostile counter-attack, with tanks, had driven our forces off high ground just captured, he rallied the men, collected stragglers and led them forward through heavy artillery and machine-gun fire, thus restoring the situation at a most critical time.

WEDGBURY, EDMUND, M.C., D.C.M., M.M., Temporary Second Lieut., Gloucestershire Regt., attached 1/8th Battn. Worcestershire Regt. (Territorial Force). For conspicuous gallantry and leadership in command of a company forming a defensive flank along north-west edge of Eveque Wood, on 25 Oct. 1918. He advanced three miles through country held by the enemy, picking up two platoons which had lost direction and reached Tilleuls Farm, two miles in rear of the enemy's main line of resistance. Here, with only 17 men, he charged and captured three 4.2 howitzers, killing the battery commander himself and capturing two other officers and the crews. Thanks to his determination and coolness, the defensive flank was successfully formed, with a total capture of five officers and 156 men.

WETHERILT, WILLIAM ALFRED, Temporary Second Lieut., Royal Berkshire Regt., attached 1/4th Battn., Territorial Force (Italy). For conspicuous gallantry and able leadership as platoon commander during an attack on enemy positions in the neighbourhood of Asiago on 29 Oct. to 1 Nov. 1918. On the 29th he captured the enemy front-line trenches at Sec, and pushed on to the Winter Stelling at Costa, under very heavy machine-gun and shell fire. On 1 Nov. he cleared Costa and led the attack up Mt. Catry, where prisoners and machine guns were captured; he finally forced his way through most difficult country to the final objective on Mt. Mosciach, capturing numerous guns and consolidating his position. Throughout he set a splendid example of fearlessness and determination.

WHITEHOUSE, PHILIP HENRY, Lieut.-Colonel, 1/8th Battn. Royal Warwickshire Regt., Territorial Force. For gallant leadership during the crossing of the Somme-Oise Canal and the capture of Landrecies on 4 Nov. 1918. His battalion fought their way down to and crossed the canal against heavy opposition and helped to take Landrecies, capturing over 200 prisoners, some guns, and many minenwerfer and machine guns. He did fine work.

WILLIAMS, CHARLES REGINALD, M.C., Capt. (Acting Major), 2nd Battn. Royal Munster Fusiliers. For conspicuous gallantry and good leadership near Monceau St. Waast. On 6 Nov. 1918, towards evening, when the advance was held up by heavy fire, he pushed on, and by his personal reconnaissances and sound dispositions was able to establish his battalion on their final objective that evening. Throughout the operations from 4 to 6 Nov. he carried out all tasks allotted to him with marked skill and determination.

WILSON, NEIL YOUNG, M.C., Temporary Capt., 11th Battn. Northumberland Fusiliers (Italy). For most conspicuous gallantry and initiative during the attacks on the enemy's lines on the north bank of the Piave on the 27th and 29th Oct. 1918. He was in command of a company on both days, and by his skilful leadership strong positions of the enemy were captured. During the attack on the 27th his company captured one battery of field guns and two batteries of heavy guns, which were in action during the attack. He was the senior officer of the battalion in the actual attack on the third objective, which he personally led with the greatest gallantry and skill. In the flank attack on the north bank of the Monticano River on 29 Oct. he displayed most brilliant leadership and resource, capturing his objective and a large number of prisoners and machine guns with a minimum of casualties.

WRIGHTON, EDWARD, Lieut., 4th Battn. Northumberland Fusiliers, Territorial Force, attached 10th Battn. (Italy). On the Piave, 27 Oct. 1918, in the initial attack, he was left in command of the company, all other officers being killed or wounded. This company had orders to form a defensive flank, but Lieut. Wrighton, seeing that the attack in front was held up by uncut wire, led his company forward, cut a belt of wire by hand under severe machine-gun fire and assisted in taking the first objective. He personally shot down an enemy machine gunner who was causing many casualties. Ultimately his company formed a defensive flank to the brigade, and though losing over 50 in casualties he maintained and even improved his position by enterprise and patrols. On 29 Oct. he led his company again in an attack over several kilometres, capturing many prisoners and machine guns. Throughout the entire operations he showed exceptional gallantry and marked powers of leadership.

YOUNG, JAMES HAROLD BERMINGHAM, M.C., Temporary Lieut. (Acting Capt.), 10th Battn. Cheshire Regt., attached 9th Battn. For marked gallantry and dashing leadership near Jenlain, on 3 and 4 Nov. 1918. He led his company into a gap against determined opposition, capturing prisoners and securing the safety of his battalion. He then reorganized his company and led them in attack, securing his objective and beyond, capturing prisoners, machine guns, and a field gun, and mopping up Wargnies-le-Grand.

CANADIAN FORCE.

BLAIR, JOHN FREEMAN, Major, Canadian Army Dental Corps, attached 4th Field Ambulance, Canadian Army Medical Corps. For conspicuous gallantry and devotion to duty from 5 to 11 Nov. 1918, in the Valenciennes-Mons area, as liaison officer between regimental aid posts and forward collecting posts. Keeping in close touch with the rapidly advancing infantry, he was continuously under fire, but ensured the rapid evacuation of the wounded. On several occasions he dressed the wounded in the open under fire, remaining to superintend their removal on the arrival of the stretcher-bearers.

GYLES, RICHARD WALTER, M.C., Capt., 46th Battn. Canadian Infantry, Saskatchewan Regt. For conspicuous gallantry and devotion to duty in the attack on Mount Huoy on 1 Nov. 1918, when he successfully led his company, with magnificent courage and determination, against points of resistance held by the enemy in great strength. On reaching an objective, the company was reduced to 15 men, but meeting a party of 50 of the enemy, he at once attacked, killing many and taking the survivors prisoners. In the advance his company captured three field guns, many machine guns, and a trench mortar, besides about 300 prisoners.

KELLY, BURNET ELMER, Major, 9th Field Ambulance, Canadian Army Medical Corps. For conspicuous gallantry and devotion to duty from 22 to 30 Oct. 1918, between Raismes and Bruay. In charge of the evacuation of wounded of the 9th Canadian Infantry Brigade, he personally went over the field, night and day, with his stretcher-bearers, collecting wounded, most of the time under machine-gun and shell fire. His energy was an outstanding example to all ranks.

KEMP, FREDERICK GARFIELD, Lieut. (Acting Capt.), 4th Battn. Canadian Infantry, 1st Central Ontario Regt. For conspicuous gallantry and presence of mind at critical times. During the assault on the Canal du Nord, on 27 Sept. 1918, he did excellent work. Upon reaching the Canal du Nord line his men came under heavy machine-gun fire from the left. He rushed enemy posts in the trench with two men, killing and wounding three or four himself, and scattering the others with a bomb. In the advance he, by fearless leadership, captured two field guns and killed all of the enemy machine gunners holding the emplacements. Throughout these operations he did excellently.

MACLEOD, JOHN PHEE GORDON, Lieut., 46th Battn. Canadian Infantry, Saskatchewan Regt. For conspicuous gallantry and devotion in the attack before Valenciennes on 1 Nov. 1918. He led his platoon forward in face of heavy opposition, and, reaching his objective, he established an advanced post of eight men, taking four more forward. He encountered a large enemy party, and, attacking at once, forced them to surrender. But before they could be disarmed the Bosche officer, realizing the weakness of his opponents, shot the N.C.O. and opened fire. With utter disregard of danger, and in face of enormous odds, Lieut. MacLeod and one man gallantly stood their ground, covering the withdrawal. Later, in face of direct machine-gun fire, he made his way out, and succeeded in carrying the wounded N.C.O. to safety.

McLEAN, CHARLES HENRY (name Henry corrected to Herbert), Major, 4th Canadian Mounted Rifle Battn., 1st Central Ontario Regt. For conspicuous gallantry and devotion to duty near Valenciennes on 1 Nov. 1918. With a view to locating points for bridging the Escaut Canal, he and one man crossed it on an improvised bridge of a plank, raft and boat. Here he was immediately engaged by a machine gun, which he at once attacked, killing one man, and holding the remainder at bay until assistance arrived, when he captured the machine gun and ten men. A post was thus established, which enabled a crossing to be effected on the entire battalion frontage without a casualty.

MILLAR, JOHN MACINTOSH, M.C., Major, 85th Battn. Canadian Infantry, Nova Scotia Regt. For conspicuous gallantry and fine leadership in command of his battalion in the operations near Valenciennes from 24 Oct. to 6 Nov. 1918. In the attempts to cross the Canal de L'Escaut on the 25th and 26th Oct., he displayed the greatest courage and perseverance under intense machine-gun fire in securing information, which ultimately proved of the utmost value in the final crossing on 1 Nov. His work throughout that period was of the highest order, and his pluck and endurance were an inspiration to all ranks.

PLUMMER, MAURICE VERNON, Major, 51st (Howitzer) Battery, 13th Brigade, Canadian Field Artillery. For conspicuous gallantry and devotion to duty at Valenciennes on 2 Nov. 1918, and preceding days, while acting in command of an artillery brigade in support of infantry, when his courage and untiring efforts materially assisted in the capture of the city. By a daring reconnaissance on 1 Nov. he so placed his forward batteries that they were able to engage hostile machine guns so effectually as to enable the infantry to cross the canal with slight casualties.

PURVIS, EDSON RUSSELL, Major, 47th Battn. Canadian Infantry, Western Ontario Regt. For conspicuous gallantry and fine leadership during operations near Valenciennes from the 17th to 21st Oct. 1918, when acting as second in command, and in charge of the advanced headquarters of the battalion. Throughout that period he made several daring reconnaissances, and carried out most valuable liaison work, during much of which he was obliged to cross open ground swept by machine-gun fire and rifle fire from snipers. Later he assumed command of the battalion, and handled the attack with the greatest courage and ability.

TRELEAVEN, GEORGE WILLARD, M.C., Major, 4th Field Ambulance, Canadian Army Medical Corps. For conspicuous gallantry and devotion to duty from 5 to 10 Nov. 1918, in the Valenciennes–Monsana, in charge of the evacuation of casualties from the forward area of the division. For five days he was continuously under fire in the open, selecting aid posts and superintending the evacuation of the wounded. He frequently led stretcher parties forward across open ground fully exposed to enemy fire, and his disregard of danger was a splendid example to all ranks.

AUSTRALIAN IMPERIAL FORCE.

HOUGHTON, SYDNEY ROBERT, M.C., Capt., 12th Battn. Australian Infantry. Near Jeancourt, on 18 Sept. 1918, his company had to advance over 2,500 yards before attaining their objective. His gallant and able leadership resulted in the rapid and successful capture of each point of resistance by successive operations. With 120 rifles he captured more than 130 prisoners and 12 machine guns. He did fine work.

HYNES, JOHN THOMAS, M.M., Capt., 15th Battn. Australian Infantry. During the operations near Jeancourt, north-west of St. Quentin, on 18 Sept. 1918, he led his company with great skill and courage in the attack, gaining his objective at little cost. He captured about 150 prisoners, two field guns and numerous machine guns. He did fine work.

London Gazette, 12 Dec. 1919.—" Admiralty, S.W., 12 Dec. 1919. Honours for Services in Russia, 1918, 1919.—The King has been graciously pleased to approve of the award of the following honours to the undermentioned Officers. To be Companions of the Distinguished Service Order."

ROBINSON, HUGH BEAUMONT, Commander, Royal Navy. For distinguished services on the Staff of the Senior Naval Officer, River Dvina Expedition.

PARKER, GEORGE HOSKINS IRTON, Lieut.-Commander, Royal Navy. For distinguished and gallant services in command of H.M.S. M.27 in Russia.

ST. JOHN, ST. ANDREW OLIVER, Lieut.-Commander, Royal Navy. For distinguished and gallant services in command of H.M.S. M.23 in R ssia.

BACK, FRANCIS LEONARD, Lieut.-Commander, Royal Navy. For distinguished and gallant services in command of H.M.S. M.31 in Russia.

SIMPSON, CECIL, Engineer Lieut.-Commander, Royal Navy. For distinguished services with the River Dvina Force in Russia.

To receive a Bar to the Distinguished Service Order:

GOLDSMITH, MALCOLM LENNON, D.S.O., Capt, Royal Navy. For distinguished and gallant services in command of H.M.S. Montrose, Black Sea.

London Gazette, 12 Dec. 1919.—" War Office, 12 Dec. 1919. The King has been graciously pleased to approve of the undermentioned rewards for distinguished service in connection with military operations in France and Flanders. Dated 3 June, 1919. Awarded a Third Bar to the Distinguished Service Order."

WOOD, EDWARD ALLAN, C.M.G., D.S.O., Temporary Lieut.-Colonel (Temporary Brigadier-General), General List.
(D.S.O. gazetted 1 Jan. 1917.)
(1st Bar gazetted 26 Sept. 1917.)
(2nd Bar gazetted 16 Sept. 1918.)

Awarded a Second Bar to the Distinguished Service Order:

CRAIGIE-HALKETT, HUGH MARJORIBANKS, C.M.G., D.S.O., Major and Brevet Lieut.-Colonel (Temporary Brigadier-General), Highland Light Infantry
(D.S.O. gazetted 16 Aug. 1917.)
(1st Bar gazetted 26 July, 1918.)

Awarded the Distinguished Service Order:

BRETT, RUPERT JOHN, Capt. and Brevet Major (Temporary Lieut.-Colonel), Oxfordshire and Buckinghamshire Light Infantry, attached Royal Berkshire Regt.

DORMAN, EDWARD MUNGO, M.C., Major, 4th Dragoon Guards. (In substitution of Brevet Major notified in London Gazette 3 June, 1919.)

EDWARDS, FRANCIS HYDE, M.C., Capt. and Brevet Major (Acting Lieut.-Colonel), Bedfordshire and Hertfordshire Regt., attached 4th Battn. Leicestershire Regt., Territorial Force.

GORDON, ALAN FRANCIS LINDSAY, M.C., Capt. (Temporary Lieut.-Colonel), Irish Guards.

KERR, CHARLES, M.C., Capt. (Temporary Major), Reserve of Officers, late Royal Horse Guards, attached Machine Gun Corps.

SIMPSON, WILLIAM, M.C., D.C.M., Quartermaster and Capt., King's Own Scottish Borderers.

VIBART, NOEL MEREDITH, M.C., Capt., Royal Engineers

SOUTH AFRICAN FORCES.

CLERK, EDWARD GEORGE, Major, 4th Battn. South African Infantry.

London Gazette, 12 Dec. 1919.—" War Office, 12 Dec. 1919. The King has been graciously pleased to approve of the undermentioned rewards for distinguished service in connection with military operations in Egypt and Palestine. Dated 3 June, 1919. Awarded the Distinguished Service Order."

CAVE-BROWNE, WILLIAM, M.C., Capt. (Acting Major), Royal Engineers, Indian Army.

CHURCHILL, ROSS DEAS, Lieut.-Colonel, 1/19th, attached 2/19th, Punjabis, Indian Army.

CROCKATT, NORMAN RICHARD, M.C., Capt. (Temporary Major), Royal Scots.

DELMÉ-RADCLIFFE, ALFRED, Major (Acting Lieut.-Colonel), 105th Mahratta Light Infantry, Indian Army.

EVANS, WALTER JAMES, Major (Acting Lieut.-Colonel), 1/1st Gurkha Rifles, Indian Army.

FRASER, DAVID, M.C., Major, 1/1st Inverness Battery, Royal Horse Artillery, Territorial Force.

HUTCHINSON, RONALD OLIPHANT, M.C., Major (Acting Lieut.-Colonel), Fife and Forfar Yeomanry and Machine Gun Corps, Commanding 7th Indian Division, Machine Gun Battn.

JAMESON, WILLIAM KENNETH EUSTACE, Lieut.-Colonel, Royal Horse and Royal Field Artillery.

McSWINEY, HERBERT FREDERICK CYRIL, M.C., Capt. (Temporary Major), 2/3rd Gurkha Rifles, Indian Army.

MILNE, THOMAS, Major, 1/55th (Cooke's) Rifles, Indian Army.

TYRRELL, GEORGE GERALD MONTAGUE, Capt. (Acting Lieut.-Colonel), 5th Lancers, Commanding 21st Corps, Cavalry Regt.

WALKER, CECIL EDWARD, M.C., Major, Royal Artillery.

AUSTRALIAN IMPERIAL FORCE.

BEITH, JOHN ROBERT McNEIL, Lieut.-Colonel, Australian Army Medical Corps, attached 1st Light Horse Field Ambulance.

CAVE, MEYLIES WYAMARUS, Lieut.-Colonel, Australian Army Medical Corps, attached 1st Light Horse Field Ambulance.

CLERKE, JAMES MARTYN, Major, 3rd Australian Light Horse Regt.

CROSS, DONALD GORDON, Major, 6th Australian Light Horse Regt.

EASTERBROOK, CLAUDE CADMAN, M.C., Major, 7th Australian Light Horse Regt.

MILLS, ARTHUR JAMES, Lieut.-Colonel, 15th Australian Light Horse Regt.

London Gazette, 12 Dec. 1919—" War Office, 12 Dec. 1919. The King has been graciously pleased on the occasion of His Majesty's Birthday to approve of the undermentioned reward for distinguished service in connection with military operations in Italy. Dated 3 June, 1919. Awarded the Distinguished Service Order."

MAYALL, ROBERT CECIL, M.C., Temporary Capt., 11th Battn. Northumberland Fusiliers.

London Gazette, 12 Dec. 1919—" War Office, 12 Dec. 1919. The King has been graciously pleased to approve of the undermentioned reward for distinguished service in connection with military operations in the Balkans and with the British Army of the Black Sea. Dated 3 June, 1919. Awarded the Distinguished Service Order."

GRACEY, GEORGE FREDERICK HANDEL, Temporary Capt., Special List.

London Gazette, 12 Dec, 1919.—" War Office, 12 Dec. 1919. The King has been graciously pleased to approve of the undermentioned reward for distinguished service in connection with military operations in Mesopotamia. Dated 3 June, 1919. Awarded the Distinguished Service Order."

HILL, HENRY WALTER DUNLOP, Major, 16th Cavalry, Indian Army.

London Gazette, 12 Dec. 1919.—" War Office, 12 Dec. 1919. His Majesty the King has been graciously pleased to approve of the undermentioned rewards for distinguished service in connection with military operations in East Africa, Somaliland and Nigeria. Dated 3 June, 1919. Awarded the Distinguished Service Order."

HOWARD, CHARLES ALFRED LOWRAY, Capt. (Temporary Major), 32nd Lancers, Indian Army.

LOCH, ERIC ERSKINE, Capt., Highland Light Infantry and Machine Gun Corps.

STEVENS, HARRY WHITEHILL, Major, Retired Pay, Reserve of Officers late South Wales Borderers. (In substitution of Brevet Major notified in London Gazette 1 Jan. 1918.)

REYNOLDS, DENYS WALTER, Capt. (Acting Lieut.-Colonel), York and Lancaster Regt., Commanding 2/2nd King's African Rifles.

London Gazette, 16 Dec. 1919.—" Air Ministry, Kingsway, London, W.C.2, 16 Dec. 1919. His Majesty the King has been pleased to approve of recognition being accorded, as indicated below, to Officers of the Royal Air Force, for gallantry whilst prisoners of war in escaping, or attempting to escape, from captivity, or for valuable services rendered in the prison camps of the enemy. Awarded a Bar to the Distinguished Service Order."

BRIGGS, EDWARD FEATHERSTONE, D.S.O., O.B.E., Wing Commander.

RATHBORNE, CHARLES EDWARD HENRY, D.S.O., Wing Commander.

London Gazette, 22 Dec. 1919.—" Air Ministry, Kingsway, London, W.C.2, 22 Dec. 1919. His Majesty the King has been graciously pleased to approve of the undermentioned rewards to Officers of the Royal Air Force, in recognition of distinguished services rendered during the war and since the close of hostilities. Among the rewards is included: Awarded the Distinguished Service Order."

TOMKINSON, LANCELOT, Squadron Leader, Air Force Cross (North Russia).

London Gazette, 15 Jan. 1920.—" War Office, 15 Jan. 1920. His Majesty the King has been graciously pleased to approve of the following awards to the undermentioned Officers, in recognition of their gallantry and devotion to duty in the Field. Awarded a Bar to the Distinguished Service Order."

SOUTH AFRICAN FORCE.

CHRISTIAN, EWAN, D.S.O., M.C., Temporary Lieut.-Colonel, 2nd Battn. South African Infantry (France). He commanded his battalion during the operations 21–24 March, 1918, in a most able and courageous manner. Though very heavily attacked on the 21st and 22nd, he held his ground until ordered to withdraw. On the 22nd, when the enemy were within a few hundred yards of battalion headquarters, he sent back the majority of the brigade staff, and stayed behind to extricate the remains of his battalion, which was pressed very heavily from the front and flank. This he succeeded in doing. On the 24th also he did excellent work.
(D.S.O. gazetted 1 Jan. 1918.)

Awarded the Distinguished Service Order:

FRASER, JAMES DONALD, Capt. (Acting Major), 32nd Lancers, Indian Army (Mesopotamia). For marked gallantry and good leadership when in command of a small force heavily attacked for 24 hours, on 30–31 May, 1919, at Qarah Anjir. He inspired all ranks to greater efforts, and maintained a stout defence until the arrival of reinforcements.

SOUTH AFRICAN FORCE.

BEVERLEY, ROBERT, M.C., Temporary Capt., 2nd Battn. South African Infantry (France). For conspicuous gallantry and devotion to duty when, as acting Brigade Major, on the 22nd March, 1919, he conveyed important orders under heavy fire to all battalion headquarters, and by personal reconnaissance gained valuable information. On the 24th March he again displayed great courage in the performance of his duties under heavy machine-gun and shell fire.

London Gazette, 21 Jan. 1920.—" War Office, 21 Jan. 1920. His Majesty the King has been graciously pleased to approve of the following immediate awards for conspicuous gallantry and devotion to duty in North Russia conferred by Major-General C. C. M. Maynard, K.C.B., C.M.G., D.S.O. in pursuance of the powers vested in him by His Majesty."

MURMANSK COMMAND.

Awarded the Distinguished Service Order:

BLENNERHASSETT, WILLIAM LEWIS ROWLAND PAUL SEBASTIAN, Temporary Capt., Special List, Intelligence Department. For conspicuous gallantry near Siding on 11 June, 1919, when doing intelligence duties. On the advance of the Russian troops being held up he collected three men and led an advance under heavy fire, thereby assisting greatly in re-establishing the situation. As intelligence officer in charge forward area he has rendered invaluable services in controlling an area of some 3,000 square miles.

BURROWS, MONTAGUE BROCAS, Lieut. (Acting Major), 5th Dragoon Guards. For gallant and able leadership of a landing party on the night of the 13th–14th Sept. 1919. He took his party of 120 men across 15 miles of Lake Onega, this part being in the hands of the enemy, landed them near Vate Navolok, 21 versts in rear of the enemy front line, and captured the garrison of this place. He then took his party on to the railway west of Vate Navolok, and by his skilful dispositions greatly assisted the column operating on the railway.

CHURCH, ARCHIBALD GEORGE, M.C., Lieut. (Acting Major), Royal Garrison Artillery, Special Reserve, attached 434th Battery, 6th Brigade, Royal Field Artillery. For conspicuous gallantry and zeal during the operations from Medveja-gora to Unitsa, 8 June to 26 July, 1919. When the Russian infantry were driven back near Perguba he pushed his guns up to the front line and restored the situation by his accurate shooting. At Fedotova, on the 22nd June, under heavy shelling, he kept his guns in action, silencing the enemy and causing them to move their guns.

HAYHURST-FRANCE, GEORGE FREDERICK HAYHURST, Capt., M.C., King's Royal Rifle Corps. He has commanded the Special Service Coy., King's Royal Rifle Corps, with conspicuous success. During the various engagements in which the company took part, especially on 12 May, 12 June, and the 3–6 July, 1919, he carried out daring reconnaissances of the enemy positions, bringing information of great assistance to the column commander in his plan of attack. Many casualties were avoided owing to these reconnaissances.

MATHER, JAMES HENRY (Christian name corrected from James Henry to John Hugh [London Gazette, 5 March, 1920], Temporary Major, Royal Engineers (Lieut.-Commander, Royal Naval Volunteer Reserve). For conspicuous gallantry and devotion to duty, on the 5th June, 1919, before Shunski Bor, Lake Onega. When in command of four motor boats he engaged four enemy steamers, carrying many heavy guns, in order to relieve the Russians who were being heavily attacked. Notwithstanding the disparity in armament he caused the enemy vessels to retire south and so enabled the Russians to counter-attack with success. He showed throughout great courage and devotion to duty and set a fine example to all.

SMALL, EDWARD ALFRED, Temporary Lieut., General List. He, with 37 partisans, gallantly penetrated into the rear of the Bolshevik lines and captured the complete brigade staff, including brigade commander, regimental commander and 50 prisoners, and took away the breech block of a 3 in. gun. On 23 June he penetrated further into the Bolshevik lines and burnt the Suna Bridge. At Suna Station they surprised the guards, capturing two machine guns.

CANADIAN FORCE.

STIBBARD, CLAUDE CHARLES, Lieut. (Temporary Lieut.-Colonel), Canadian Infantry, Manitoba Regt. For valuable service, from 1 Feb. 1919, to 22 July, 1919, as D.A.D. of Railways, Syren Force. During May, June and July his work has been chiefly in the forward area of the Murmansk front, where he has shown untiring energy and a personal disregard of danger in connection with the work of repair of the railway at all possible speed.

ARCHANGEL COMMAND.

Awarded a Bar to the Distinguished Service Order:

GALE, HENRY JOHN GORDON, D.S.O., Major, Royal Artillery. Throughout the operations on the Kodish front between 28 and 30 Aug. 1919, he showed great gallantry. He carried out the duties of F.O.O., and without any regard to his personal safety, remained near the enemy's wire, so as to be able to ensure the accuracy of the artillery fire.
(D.S.O. gazetted 3 June, 1918.)

HARCOURT, HARRY GLADWIN, D.S.O., M.C., Lieut. (Acting Major), Royal Dublin Fusiliers, attached Machine Gun Corps. For great gallantry and good leadership in command of a company on 29 Aug. 1919. His guide led him to the wrong objective, and the company unexpectedly came under heavy fire. He showed great coolness and ability, and finally, with the assistance of another company, took the main battery position. He was wounded early in the action.
(D.S.O. gazetted 26 July, 1918.)

PERCIVAL, ARTHUR ERNEST, D.S.O., M.C., Capt. and Brevet Major, Essex Regt., attached 45th Battn. Royal Fusiliers (Lieut.-Colonel, Bedfordshire Regt.). He commanded the Gorodok column on the 9th–10th Aug. 1919, with great gallantry and skill, and owing to the success of this column the force on the right bank of the Dvina were able to capture all its objectives. During the enemy counter-attack from Selmenga on Gorodok he handled his men excellently. The enemy were repulsed with great loss, leaving 400 prisoners in our hands.
(D.S.O. gazetted 16 Sept. 1918.)

Awarded the Distinguished Service Order:

HEATON, HARRY, M.C., Temporary Capt., 19th Battn. Durham Light Infantry, attached 45th Battn. Royal Fusiliers. On the 10th Aug. 1919, during attacks on Kochamika, Sludka and Lipovets, he was commanding the battalion. He personally led his troops in all these attacks, and showed conspicuous gallantry and efficiency throughout under heavy fire, taking all objectives.

LYLE, WILLIAM JAMES, M.C., Capt., 2nd Battn. Highland Light Infantry. On 31 Aug. 1919, and throughout the operations of the attack on Emtsa, he showed great gallantry. As liaison officer he led his Russian company in the attack on the redoubt system, and set a most inspiring example to his men.

NORTHCOTE, ARTHUR FREDERICK, Major, Devonshire Regt., attached 1st Oxfordshire and Buckinghamshire Light Infantry. For gallant and able leadership in the attack on Ust Vaga, on the 1st Sept. 1919. Although his headquarters were surrounded, he organized the defence, took the offensive and cleared the village of the enemy,. He also did good service in the raid on Ignatovskaya on 26–27 June, 1919.

London Gazette, 22 Jan. 1920.—" Admiralty, S.W., 22 Jan. 1920. The King has been graciously pleased to approve of the award of the following honour to the undermentioned Officer. To be a Companion of the Distinguished Service Order."

JERRAM, ROWLAND CHRISTOPHER, Paymaster-Lieut., Royal Navy. For distinguished services on the Staff of the Commander-in-Chief, Grand Fleet.

" Honours for Services in Russia, 1919.—The King has been graciously pleased to approve of the award of the following honours to the undermentioned Officers. To be Companions of the Distinguished Service Order."

CURTEIS, ROBERT WOODWARD, SUTTON, Commander, Royal Naval Reserve (Commander, Royal Navy, retired). For distinguished services in command of the Allied Lake Flotilla. On several occasions he exhibited great gallantry and devotion to duty during operations on shore.

MORSE, HAROLD EDWARD, Lieut., Royal Navy. For distinguished services under fire on several occasions.

" Honours for Services in Action with an Enemy Submarine.—The King has been graciously pleased to approve of the award of the following honour to the undermentioned Officer. To receive a Bar to the Distinguished Service Order."

WOODWARD, HUGH JOSEPH, D.S.O., Lieut.-Commander, Royal Navy.

" Honours for Services in the Mine Clearance Force (Final).—The King has been graciously pleased to approve of the award of the following honours to the undermentioned Officers. To be a Companion of the Distinguished Service Order."

MORGAN, HORACE LESLIE, Lieut.-Commander, Royal Navy.

To receive a Bar to the Distinguished Service Order:

BROOKE, BASIL RICHARD, D.S.O., Commander, Royal Navy.

London Gazette, 30 Jan. 1920.—" War Office, 30 Jan. 1920. His Majesty the King has been graciously pleased to approve of the undermentioned rewards in recognition of gallant and distinguished services in the field, which have been brought to notice in accordance with the terms of Army Order 193 of 1919. To be dated 5 May, 1919, unless otherwise stated. Awarded a Bar to the Distinguished Service Order."

BOND, REGINALD COPLESTON, D.S.O., Lieut.-Colonel, 2nd Battn. Yorkshire Light Infantry.
(D.S.O. gazetted 27 Sept. 1901.)
COLE-HAMILTON, CLAUD GEORGE, C.M.G., D.S.O., Lieut.-Colonel, Reserve of Officers, late Royal Irish Rifles, Special Reserve.
(D.S.O. gazetted 31 Oct. 1902.)
McTAGGART, MAXWELL FIELDING, D.S.O., Major and Brevet Lieut.-Colonel, 5th Lancers.
(D.S.O. gazetted 14 Jan. 1916.)
SIMNER, PERCY REGINALD OWEN ABEL, D.S.O., Temporary Lieut.-Colonel, 10th Battn. West Yorkshire Regt.
(D.S.O. gazetted 1 Jan. 1917.)

Awarded the Distinguished Service Order:
BAYLY, ABINGDON ROBERT, Lieut.-Colonel, 118th Battery, 1st Brigade, Royal Field Artillery.
BLUHM, QUENTIN MANGUILL, Major, 1/8th Battn. Manchester Regt., Territorial Force.
BOGER, DUDLEY CORYNDON, Lieut.-Colonel, 1st Battn. Cheshire Regt.
CORNWALL, CHARLES ERNEST, Temporary Major, Special List, attached 6th Battn. Gordon Highlanders (Major, South African Defence Force).
CROWDER, WILLIAM HARRISON, Second Lieut., D/256th Brigade, Royal Field Artillery, Territorial Force.
CUNNINGHAM, JOHN CRAWFORD, Temporary Lieut., 6th Battn. Oxfordshire and Buckinghamshire Light Infantry, attached 2/4th Battn. Territorial Force.
DAVIES, HUGH WARBURTON, M.C., Capt., 2/8th Battn. Worcestershire Regt., Territorial Force.
DOUGHTY, ERNEST CHRISTIE, Major, 2nd Battn. Suffolk Regt.
FORBES, IAN ROSE-INNES FOSTER, Major, Royal Scots Fusiliers, Special Reserve, attached 2nd Battn.
FORBES, JAMES FREDERICK, Lieut.-Colonel, 2nd Battn. Wiltshire Regt.
FOSTER, PERCY JOHN, Major, 2nd Battn. Royal Warwickshire Regt.
HARDY, JOCELYN LEE, M.C., Capt., 2nd Battn. Connaught Rangers.
HARRIS, FRANK E., Temporary Lieut., 2nd Battn. Devonshire Regt.
PEVERELL, THOMAS HENRY, M.C., Capt., 1/4th Battn. Seaforth Highlanders.
PHILLIPS, ERIC CHARLES MALCOLM, Major (Acting Lieut.-Colonel), Bedfordshire and Hertfordshire Regt., Territorial Force.
RUDKIN, CHARLES MARK CLEMENT, Temporary Lieut.-Colonel, Royal Field Artillery.
SHORE, JOHN LINTORN, Major, 1st Battn. Cheshire Regt.
SINCLAIR, WILLIAM CARFRAE CRAW, Major, 1/4th Battn. Royal Scots, Territorial Force.
SMITH, ARTHUR GEORGE BAIRD, Lieut.-Colonel, Reserve of Officers, retired pay, late Commanding 2nd Battn. Royal Scots Fusiliers.
STAIR, EARL OF, JOHN JAMES, Major, 2nd Battn. Scots Guards.
STEWART, JOHN, Lieut., Highland Light Infantry, Special Reserve, attached 16th Battn.
STEWART, JOHN HAZELTON, M.C., Temporary Capt., 15th Battn. Royal Irish Rifles.
TOWNSEND, EDWARD NEVILLE, Major, 2nd Battn. West Riding Regt.
VANSITTART, EDEN, Colonel, U.S.L., Indian Army, late Commanding 8th Battn. Royal West Kent Regt.
WILLIAMS-THOMAS, FRANK SILVERS, M.C., Major, Worcestershire Yeomanry.

CANADIAN FORCE.

OSBORNE, J. EWART, Temporary Lieut.-Colonel, 15th Battn. Canadian Infantry.

London Gazette, 30 Jan. 1920.—" War Office, 30 Jan. 1920. His Majesty the King has been graciously pleased to approve of the undermentioned rewards in recognition of gallant conduct and determination displayed in escaping or attempting to escape from captivity, which services have been brought to notice in accordance with the terms of Army Order 193 of 1919. To be dated 5 May, 1919, unless otherwise stated. Awarded a Bar to the Distinguished Service Order."

CANADIAN FORCE.

ANDERSON, PETER, D.S.O., Lieut.-Colonel, 3rd Battn. Canadian Infantry. (To date 31 Dec. 1919.)
(D.S.O. gazetted 15 July, 1919.)

Awarded the Distinguished Service Order:
HALL, CHARLES ROBERT, Major, Royal Munster Fusiliers.
VANDELEUR, CROFTON BURY, Lieut.-Colonel, Scottish Rifles.

London Gazette, 3 Feb. 1920.—" War Office, 3 Feb. 1920. The King has been graciously pleased to approve of the undermentioned rewards, on the recommendation of the General Officer Commanding-in-Chief, Allied Forces, for distinguished service in connection with military operations in Archangel, North Russia. Dated 11 Nov. 1919, unless otherwise stated. Awarded a Bar to the Distinguished Service Order."

EDWARDS, PATRICK HARRINGTON, D.S.O., Lieut.-Colonel, Royal Naval Volunteer Reserve. (Seconded from Royal Naval Volunteer Reserve, Temporary Commander.)
(D.S.O. gazetted 24 May, 1919.)
PATERSON, ADRIAN GORDON, D.S.O., M.C., Capt. and Brevet Major, King's Own Scottish Borderers, attached 45th Battn. Royal Fusiliers.
(D.S.O. gazetted 25 Aug. 1917.)

Awarded the Distinguished Service Order:
BLACKBURN, JOHN CECIL, M.C., Capt. (Acting Major), West Yorkshire Regt., attached 46th Battn. Royal Fusiliers.
BURDON, CYRIL WALMESLEY, Major, Royal Artillery.
CAMPION, DOUGLAS JOHN MONTRION, Major, Royal Garrison Artillery.
CAVENDISH, FREDERICK GEORGE, M.C., Capt. (Acting Major), 1st Battn. Leinster Regt., attached 45th Battn. Royal Fusiliers.
GREEN, LUKE LOT, M.C., Lieut., Rifle Brigade, Special Reserve, attached 46th Battn. Royal Fusiliers.
IRVINE-FORTESCUE, ARCHER, M.B., Major, Royal Army Medical Corps.
WASS, ARTHUR EDWARD, M.C., Lieut. (Acting Capt.), 4th Hussars, attached 46th Battn. Royal Fusiliers.

CANADIAN FORCE.

WHITE, WILFRED ORMONDE, M.C., Major, Eastern Ontario Regt.

London Gazette, 3 Feb. 1920.—" War Office, 3 Feb. 1920. The King has been graciously pleased to approve of the undermentioned rewards, on the recommendation of the General Officer Commanding-in-Chief, Allied Forces, for distinguished service in connection with military operations in Murmansk, North Russia. Dated 11 Nov. 1919. Awarded the Distinguished Service Order."

DRAKE-BROCKMAN, GUY PERCY LUMSDEN, M.C., Capt., Border Regt.
MASON, JOHN, M.C., Temporary Capt., Royal Engineers.
SHEFFIELD, WILLIAM GEORGE FREESE, Capt. (Temporary Major), Middlesex Regt., Special Reserve, and Machine Gun Corps.
STENHOUSE, JOSEPH RUSSELL, D.S.C., Lieut., Royal Naval Reserve.
WATTS, ROBERT ALGERNON BRISCOE PONSONBY, Capt., Somersetshire Light Infantry.

London Gazette, 3 Feb. 1920.—" War Office, 3 Feb. 1920. The King has been graciously pleased to approve of the undermentioned rewards, on the recommendation of the Chief of the British Military Mission, for distinguished service in connection with military operations in Finland and the Baltic States. Dated 11 Nov. 1919. Awarded a Bar to the Distinguished Service Order."

GROVE, THOMAS THACKERAY, C.M.G., D.S.O., Major and Brevet Lieut.-Colonel (Temporary Lieut.-Colonel), Royal Engineers.
(D.S.O. gazetted 1 Jan. 1917.)

Awarded the Distinguished Service Order:
CARSON, ERNEST HOPE, M.C., Temporary Major, Tank Corps.
KEENAN, AUGUSTINE HENRY, O.B.E., M.C., Lieut. (Temporary Major), Royal Highlanders, Territorial Force.
McCROSTIE, HUGH CECIL, Temporary Capt. Tank Corps.

London Gazette, 12 Feb. 1920.—" War Office, 12 Feb. 1920. The King has been graciously pleased to approve of the undermentioned rewards, on the recommendation of the General Officer Commanding-in-Chief, Mesopotamian Expeditionary Force, for distinguished service in Southern and Central Kurdistan. Dated 15 Nov. 1919. Awarded a Bar to the distinguished Service Order."

RYAN, DENIS GEORGE, JOCELYN, D.S.O., Capt. and Brevet Major, 1/6th Gurkha Rifles, Indian Army.
(D.S.O. gazetted 25 Aug. 1915.)

Awarded the Distinguished Service Order:
MORRIS, CHARLES EDWARD, Major (Acting Lieut.-Colonel), Corps of Guides, attached 85th Burman Rifles, Indian Army.
WYNTER, CHARLES PHILIP, Lieut.-Colonel, 52nd Sikhs, Indian Army.

London Gazette, 8 March, 1920.—" Admiralty, S.W., 8 March, 1920. Honours for Services in Siberia, 1919.—The King has been graciously pleased to approve of the award of the following honour to the undermentioned Officer. To be a Companion of the Distinguished Service Order."

JAMESON, THOMAS HENRY, Capt., Royal Marine Light Infantry. For distinguished services in command of the British Naval Detachment manning the river steamers Kent and Suffolk operating on the Kama River.

" Honours for Services in North Russia, 1919.—The King has been graciously pleased to approve of the award of the following honours to the undermentioned Officers. To be Companions of the Distinguished Service Order."

BECK, OLIVER LAURENCE, C.B.E., Capt., Royal Navy. For distinguished services as Divisional Naval Transport Officer, Murmansk.
OHLSON, BASIL JAMES, R.D., Commander, Royal Naval Reserve. For distinguished services as Divisional Naval Transport Officer, North Dwina River.
HODGE, JOHN MACKEY, Paymaster Commander, O.B.E., Royal Navy. For distinguished services in connection with Naval Transport at Archangel and on the Dwina River.
DAWES, HUGH CAMPBELL FREDERICK, O.B.E., Acting Lieut.-Commander, Royal Naval Volunteer Reserve. For distinguished services as Divisional Naval Transport Officer, Archangel.

London Gazette, 8 March, 1920.—" Admiralty, S.W., 8 March, 1920. Honours for Services in the Baltic, 1919.—The King has been graciously pleased to approve of the award of the following honours to the undermentioned Officers. To be Companions of the Distinguished Service Order."

PILCHER, CECIL HORACE, Capt., Royal Navy. For distinguished services in command of H.M.S. Dauntless.
TILLARD, AUBREY THOMAS, Commander, Royal Navy. For distinguished services as Divisional Destroyer Leader.
WINTER, GERALD CHARLES, O.B.E., Commander, Royal Navy. For distinguished services as Senior Officer of H.M. Destroyers operating at Riga.
EYRE, RALPH VINCENT, Commander, Royal Navy. For distinguished services in command of H.M.S. Wryneck.
RAWLINGS, HENRY CLIVE, Commander, Royal Navy. For distinguished services as Senior Officer of advanced patrols in the Baltic.
BATE, CLAUDE LINDESAY, Commander, Royal Navy. For distinguished services in command of the First Destroyer Flotilla.
ALEXANDER, FREDERICK, Engineer Commander, Royal Navy. For distinguished services in H.M.S. Cleopatra.
McGHIE, HENRY BUMSTED, Engineer Commander, Royal Navy. For distinguished services in maintaining the engine-room department of H.M.S. Walker in a high state of efficiency.
HARRISON, JULIAN, Lieut.-Commander, Royal Navy. For distinguished services in H.M.S. Vortigern.
MASTER, ERNALD GILBERT HOSKINS, Lieut.-Commander, Royal Navy. For distinguished services in command of H.M.S. Whitley.
WRIGHT, ARTHUR EDWARD HEXT, Lieut.-Commander, Royal Navy. For distinguished services in the Second Destroyer Flotilla.

The Distinguished Service Order

MAJEE, WILLIAM EDWARD BLACKWOOD, Lieut.-Commander, Royal Navy. For distinguished services in command of H.M.S. Watchman.
FRASER, THE HON. GEORGE, Lieut.-Commander, Royal Navy. For distinguished services in command of H.M.S. Winchester.
ABBAY, AMBROSE THOMAS NORMAN, Lieut.-Commander, Royal Navy. For distinguished services in command of H.M.S. Walker.
STUART, CHARLES GAGE, Lieut.-Commander, D.S.C., Royal Navy. For distinguished services in H.M.S. Voyager.
DANIEL, HENRY MARTIN, Lieut.-Commander, Royal Navy. For distinguished services as Executive and Gunnery Officer of H.M.S. Dauntless.
WILLIS, ALGERNON USBORNE, Lieut.-Commander, Royal Navy. For distinguished services in preserving the efficiency of the Torpedo and Depth Charge Armaments of the First Destroyer Flotilla.
ACLAND, HUBERT GUY DYKE, Lieut.-Commander, Royal Navy. For distinguished services as Gunnery Officer of the First Destroyer Flotilla.
KEATE, HARRY ALEXANDER DYKES, Lieut.-Commander, Royal Navy. For distinguished services on the occasion of the mining of H.M.S. Verulam.
WALES, JOHN, Acting Lieut.-Commander, Royal Naval Reserve. For distinguished services in command of the Eleventh Fleet Sweeping Flotilla.
McMURCHIE, JOHN WELSH, Acting Lieut.-Commander, Royal Naval Volunteer Reserve. For distinguished services in command of the Motor Launch Minesweepers.
GRAHAM-WATSON, CLAUDE BOOTHBY, Lieut., Royal Navy. For distinguished services as Flag Lieut. to Rear-Admiral Sir Walter H. Cowan, K.C.B., D.S.O., M.V.O.
BREMNER, WILLIAM HAMILTON, D.S.C., Lieut., Royal Navy. For distinguished services in command of H.M. Coastal Motor Boat 79A in the attack on Kronstadt Harbour on the 18th Aug. 1919.

To receive a Second Bar to the Distinguished Service Order :
CUNNINGHAM, ANDREW BROWNE, D.S.O., Capt., Royal Navy. For distinguished services in command of H.M.S. Seafire.
HORTON, MAX KENNEDY, D.S.O., Commander, Royal Navy. For distinguished services in command of the Third Submarine Flotilla and as Senior Naval Officer, Reval.

To receive a Bar to the Distinguished Service Order :
HAMOND, ROBERT GERALD, D.S.O., Capt., Royal Navy. For distinguished services in command of the First Destroyer Flotilla.
CLARK, JAMES CONYNGHAM, D.S.O., Commander, Royal Navy. For distinguished services as Second-in-Command of H.M.S. Delhi and on the Staff of the Senior Naval Officer.

"Honours for Services in the Mine Clearance Force.—The King has been graciously pleased to approve of the award of the following honours to the undermentioned Officers. To be a Companion of the Distinguished Service Order."
WILLIAMS, GEORGE DAVIES, Acting Lieut.-Commander, Royal Naval Reserve.

To receive a Bar to the Distinguished Service Order :
ROLFE, CLIVE NEVILLE, D.S.O., Lieut.-Commander, Royal Navy.

London Gazette, 1 April, 1920.—" Air Ministry, Kingsway, London, W.C.2. His Majesty the King has been pleased to approve of the undermentioned rewards being conferred in recognition of gallant and distinguished services."

ROYAL AIR FORCE.
Awarded the Distinguished Service Order :
ANDERSON, WALTER FRASER, Flight-Lieut. (Pilot).
MITCHELL, JOHN, Observer Officer (Observer). " C " Flight, 47th Squadron. On 30 July, 1919, near Cherni Yar (Volga), these officers acted respectively as Pilot and Observer on a D.H.9 machine, which descended to an altitude of 1,000 feet to take oblique photographs of the enemy's positions. A second machine of the same flight, which followed as escort, was completely disabled by machine-gun fire, and forced to land five miles behind the enemy's foremost troops. Parties of hostile cavalry which attempted to capture the pilot and observer of the crashed machine were kept away by the observer's Lewis gun whilst the pilot burnt the machine. Flight Lieut. Anderson, notwithstanding that his petrol tank had been pierced by a machine-gun bullet, landed alongside the wrecked aeroplane, picked up the pilot and observer, and got safely home. The risk involved in attempting this gallant rescue was very great, as had any accident occurred in landing, the fate of all four officers can only be conjectured. The difficult circumstances of the rescue will be fully appreciated when it is remembered that Observer Officer Mitchell had to mount the port plane to stop the holes in the petrol tank with his thumbs for a period of 50 minutes' flying on the return journey.
FROGLEY, GILBERT, D.F.C., Flying Officer, " A " Detachment (3/Royal Berkshire). A fleet of about 40 Bolshevik vessels, armed with all descriptions of guns, having broken through the defences of the Volunteer Army, commenced a bombardment of Tzaritzin. Flying Officer Frogley led a formation of machines on 15 Oct. 1919, and at a height of 1,000 feet dropped his bombs with such effect that the fleet was dispersed, several vessels having been destroyed. During a period of four months this officer has rendered invaluable services in South Russia. (The award of Distinguished Flying Cross is announced in this Gazette.)
KINKEAD, SAMUEL MARCUS, Flying Officer, D.S.C., D.F.C. (late Highland Light Infantry and Royal Naval Air Service), " A " Detachment. On 12 Oct. 1919, near Kotluban, this officer led a formation of Camel machines and attacked the Cavalry Division of Damenko. By skilful tactics in low flying he dispersed this force, which had turned the left flank of the Caucasian Army and threatened to jeopardize the whole defence of Tzaritzin. Flying Officer Kinkead has carried out similar attacks on enemy troops, batteries, camps and transport with great success and at considerable personal risk.
Previous rewards : D.S. Cross, 22 Feb. 1918 ; Bar to D.S. Cross, 26 April, 1918 ; D.F. Cross, 3 Aug. 1918 ; Bar to D.F. Cross, 2 Nov. 1918 (201st Squadron, France).

London Gazette, 20 April, 1920.—" War Office, 20 April, 1920. The King has been graciously pleased to approve of the undermentioned rewards for distinguished service in connection with operations against the Northern Turkana and kindred tribes. Dated 3 June, 1919. Awarded the Distinguished Service Order."

WHITE, RICHARD FINCH, Major, Essex Regt., attached Egyptian Army.

London Gazette, 4 May, 1920.—" Admiralty, 4 May, 1920. The King has been graciously pleased to approve of the award of the following honour to the undermentioned Officer. To be a Companion of the Distinguished Service Order."
NAPIER, LAWRENCE EGERTON SCOTT, Lieut., Royal Navy. For distinguished services in command of H.M. Coastal Motor Boat 24A in the attack on Kronstadt Harbour on the 18th Aug. 1919.

London Gazette, 14 May, 1920.—" Admiralty, S.W., 14 May, 1920. The King has been graciously pleased to approve of the award of the following honours to the undermentioned Officers. To be Companions of the Distinguished Service Order."
TUDOR, EDWARD OWEN, Commander, Royal Navy. For distinguished services as Senior Commander of the 20th Destroyer Flotilla in the Baltic.
DAMANT, WALTER SANCROFT, M.V.O., Engineer Commander, Royal Navy. For distinguished services in maintaining the efficiency of the Motor Launch Minesweepers in the Baltic.

London Gazette, 10 June, 1920.—" War Office, 10 June, 1920. His Majesty the King has been graciously pleased to approve of the undermentioned rewards in recognition of gallant and distinguished services in the field, which have been brought to notice in accordance with the terms of Army Order 193 of 1919. To be dated 5 May, 1919, unless otherwise stated. Awarded the Distinguished Service Order."
BIRLEY, RICHARD ARCHIBALD, Major, 80th Battery, Royal Field Artillery.
JONES, EUSTACE HENRY, Lieut.-Colonel, 37th Battery, Royal Field Artillery.
MOLLOY, HENRY TOWNSEND, Major, 5th Gurkha Rifles, Indian Army.
NUTT, ARTHUR CHARLES ROTHERY, Lieut.-Colonel, 52nd Battery, Royal Field Artillery.

CANADIAN FORCE.
HENDRIE, WILLIAM IAN STRATHEARN, Major, 18th Battery, Canadian Field Artillery.
SANSOM, ERNEST WILLIAM, Lieut.-Colonel, 4th Battn. Canadian Machine Gun Corps.

London Gazette, 12 July, 1920.—" Air Ministry, Kingsway, London, W.C.2, 12 July, 1920. His Majesty the King has been graciously pleased to approve of the undermentioned rewards for gallantry and distinguished services."

ROYAL AIR FORCE.
Awarded the Distinguished Service Order :
GRIGSON, JOHN WILLIAM BOLDERO, Flight Lieut., D.F.C. (South Russia).
LALE, HORACE PERCY, D.F.C., Flying Officer (Waziristan).

London Gazette, 23 July, 1920.—" War Office, 23 July, 1920. His Majesty the King has been graciously pleased to approve of the undermentioned awards, on the recommendation of the Government of India, for distinguished services rendered in connection with military operations in Burma. To be dated 3 June, 1919. Awarded the Distinguished Service Order."
BROOME, WILLIAM GEORGE KING, Capt., 89th Punjabis, Indian Army.
HACKETT, THOMAS DALBY HUTCHISON, Major, Indian Army.

London Gazette, 3 Aug. 1920.—" War Office, 3 Aug. 1920. The King has been graciously pleased to approve of the undermentioned rewards, on the recommendation of the Government of India, for distinguished service in the field in the Afghan War, 1919. To be dated 1 Jan. 1920. Awarded a Bar to the distinguished Service Order."
LEE, STANLAKE SWINTON, D.S.O., Capt. (Temporary Major), Royal Artillery. (D.S.O. gazetted 25 Aug. 1917.)

Awarded the Distinguished Service Order :
BARRETT, ARTHUR LENNARD, Lieut.-Colonel, 2/33rd Punjabis, Indian Army.
COAKER, VERE ARTHUR, Major (Acting Lieut.-Colonel), 3rd Skinner's Horse, Indian Army.
COOPER, WILLIAM ROWLAND FREDERIC, M.C., Capt., 1st Dragoon Guards.
DODD, PERCY CHARLES RUSSELL, Major, 31st Lancers, Indian Army, Commanding Kurram Militia.
DOYLE, ERIC EDWARD, Capt. and Brevet Major (Temporary Major), Indian Medical Service.
FOX, EDWARD VIGOR, Lieut.-Colonel, 2nd Battn. North Staffordshire Regt.
GRIFFITH, LLEWELYN, Major, 107th Pioneers, Indian Army.
HOUSTON, ARTHUR MANSON, Lieut.-Colonel, 1/69th Punjabis, Indian Army.
HUNT, WILLIAM MORGAN, M.C., Major, No. 8 Mountain Battery, No. 1 British Mountain Artillery Brigade, Royal Garrison Artillery.
JOHNSON, ALLEN EDWIN, Major (Acting Lieut.-Colonel), 2/1st, attached 1/11th, Gurkha Rifles, Indian Army.
KEOGH, JOHN HENRY, Lieut.-Colonel, No. 1 British Artillery Brigade, Royal Garrison Artillery.
MEIN, DESBRISAY BLUNDELL, M.C., Capt. (Acting Major), 55th Coke's Rifles, Indian Army.
REILLY, NOEL EDMUND, Major, Chitral Scouts, Indian Army.
ROSS, HARRY, Lieut.-Colonel, 1/103rd Mahratta Light Infantry, Indian Army.
RUSSELL, GUY HAMILTON, Major, 126th Baluchistan Infantry, Indian Army.

London Gazette, 27 Sept. 1920.—" War Office, 27 Sept. 1920. His Majesty the King has been graciously pleased to approve of the undermentioned rewards for distinguished service in the field in South Russia. Awarded the Distinguished Service Order."
McPHERSON, ANGUS, M.C., D.C.M., Lieut. (Temporary Capt.), Argyll and Sutherland Highlanders and Machine Gun Corps. For gallantry and devotion to duty during the fighting round Odessa, at the end of Jan. 1920. Capt.

McPherson particularly distinguished himself by his excellent work with his Machine Gun School Cadets, who would follow him anywhere, and who were used in the defence of the town at the last moment. He set a fine example of courage and devotion to duty.

WILLIAMSON, HUDLESTON NOEL HEDWORTH, M.C., Major, Royal Field Artillery. For gallantry and devotion to duty at Celeschina, on 27 July, 1919, when he assisted a young Russian officer who was fighting an 18-pounder gun against an armoured train at 3,000 yards' range. The fire from the train was heavy, and it was entirely due to Major Williamson's advice and presence that the duel ended in favour of the single 18-pounder.

" His Majesty the King has been graciously pleased to approve of the undermentioned rewards for distinguished service in the field with the Waziristan Force, India. Awarded a Bar to the Distinguished Service Order."

JATAR, NILKANTH SHRIRAM, D.S.O., Capt., Indian Med cal Service, attached 2/76th Punjabis, Indian Army. For gallantry near Kotkai, on 5 Jan. 1920, when, during a withdrawal under heavy fire, he rendered valuable assistance in bringing in wounded, and, whilst doing so, was himself severely wounded. (D.S.O. gazetted 4 June, 1917.)

Awarded the Distinguished Service Order :

CATTERSON-SMITH, THOMAS MERVYN OSBORNE, Capt., 1/12th Pioneers, attached 3/34th Sikh Pioneers, Indian Army. For gallantry at Pioneer Piquet, on 21 Dec. 1919. Owing to the retirement of the covering party, his working party was suddenly attacked in force and surrounded. By his coolness, sound leadership and example, he inspired his men and repulsed five assaults. Though twice wounded he remained in control, and did not withdraw his command till all ammunition had been expended.

EXHAM, HAROLD, O.B.E., Major, 2/7th, attached 2/9th, Gurkha Rifles, Indian Army. For cool courage and fine leadership. On the 14th Jan. 1920, when the Commanding Officer of the 2/5th Gurkha Rifles had been killed and the battalion and the accompanying troops had sustained very heavy casualties, Major Exham was ordered to take over command. By fine leadership and determination he succeeded in holding a position with very few troops against several strongly pressed enemy attacks. Again at Makin, on the 21st Feb. 1920, he commanded the 2/5th Gurkha Rifles, and carried out successfully a difficult operation under heavy fire, and subsequently extricated his advanced companies and a considerable number of wounded by skilful handling of his command.

FAGAN, HERBERT ARCHER, M.C., Lieut. (Temporary Capt.), 2/9th Gurkha Rifles, Indian Army. For gallantry and determination on several occasions, particularly at Sorarogha, on the 18th Jan., and at Makin, on the 19th Feb. 1920. In the first instance he was in charge of a company ordered to establish a piquet in a position which was much exposed and commanded by fire. He set a fine example in beating off attacks and in attempting to establish the piquet. Subsequently he withdrew his company with great skill. In the second instance he again showed gallantry and leadership, when troops on the left were ordered to withdraw.

" His Majesty the King has been graciously pleased to approve of the undermentioned reward for distinguished service in the field in Mesopotamia. Awarded the Distinguished Service Order."

ROBERTSON, DONALD ELPHINSTON, Major and Brevet Lieut.-Colonel, 11th Lancers, Indian Army. For gallantry and skilful leadership near Quirayah, on the 9th June, 1920, when, having been attacked by superior forces, he was forced to retire. His dispositions were most judicious, and he inflicted heavy casualties on the enemy, and, when reinforced, his vigorous offensive was most effective.

London Gazette, 28 Oct. 1920.—" War Office, 28 Oct. 1920. His Majesty the King has been graciously pleased to approve of the undermentioned reward for distinguished services in the field in Mesopotamia." Awarded the Distinguished Service Order."

GORING, CHARLES HUBERT, M.C., Lieut., Royal Fusiliers, attached Motor Machine Gun Corps. For conspicuous gallantry and devotion to duty during an attack on a motor convoy near the Wadi Sefrah on the 12th May, 1920, when about 150 of the enemy opened fire on the convoy at very close range. By the skilful use of his cars and his determination the convoy was able to get through. Subsequently he returned three times and recovered the loads and wounded off four vans that had been destroyed by enemy fire. He set a magnificent example to all.

" His Majesty the King has been graciously pleased to approve of the undermentioned reward for distinguished service in connection with military service with the army in the Black Sea. Awarded the Distinguished Service Order."

LYELL, ALFRED GEORGE, Major, 2/39th Garhwal Rifles, Indian Army For consistent good work in the field as battalion commander in the recent operations against the Nationalist Forces, and, in particular, on the 21st June, 1920, near Beglik Dagh, when, his battalion coming under heavy fire from a concealed enemy, by skilful dispositions he inflicted considerable loss and caused them to retire. The efficient handling of his battalion on the 13th July, 1920, also contributed largely to the success of the action at Gebze.

London Gazette, 29 Nov. 1920.—" War Office, 29 Nov. 1920. His Majesty the King has been graciously pleased, on the recommendation of His Excellency the Governor and Commander-in-Chief, Somaliland Protectorate, to approve of the undermentioned rewards in recognition of distinguished services rendered in connection with military operations in Somaliland. To be dated 1 Oct. 1920. Awarded the Distinguished Service Order."

GIBB, ALLAN, D.C.M., Capt., Tribal Levy, late Somaliland Camel Corps.

ISMAY, HASTINGS LIONEL, Capt. and Brevet Major (Temporary Lieut.-Colonel), 21st Cavalry, Indian Army, attached Somaliland Camel Corps.

LAWRANCE, ARTHUR SALISBURY, Major, Reserve of Officers, retired Territorial Force, late Somaliland Camel Corps.

London Gazette, 14 Jan. 1921.—" Admiralty, S.W., 14 Jan. 1921. The King has been graciously pleased to approve of the following honours to the undermentioned Officers. Honours for Services in Asia Minor, 1920. To be Companions of the Distinguished Service Order."

WELLS, LIONEL VICTOR, Commander, Royal Navy.

HYNES, WILLIAM BAYARD, Lieut.-Commander, Royal Navy.

To receive a Bar to the Distinguished Service Order :

WILLIAMS-FREEMAN, FREDERICK ARTHUR PEERE, D.S.O., Lieut.-Commander, Royal Navy.

London Gazette, 20 Jan. 1921.—" War Office, 20 Jan. 1921. The King has been graciously pleased to approve of the undermentioned reward, on the recommendation of the General Officer Commanding-in-Chief, for distinguished service in the field in Mesopotamia. Awarded the Distinguished Service Order."

MAINWARING, GUY ROWLAND, Major, 1/39th Garhwal Rifles, Indian Army.

London Gazette, 20 Jan. 1921.—" War Office, 20 Jan. 1921. His Majesty the King has been graciously pleased to approve of the undermentioned reward, on the recommendation of the Government of India, in recognition of distinguished service in the field in connection with military operations in South Persia. Awarded the Distinguished Service Order."

MUNN, FREDERICK LEGH RICHMOND, M.C., Capt., 46th Punjabis, Indian Army. For gallantry and good leadership at Tul Ashki on 22 July, 1920, when he fearlessly exposed himself to very heavy fire in order to encourage his command and to restore " moral " after an ambush. As a result, he was able to press home the attack, which ended in complete success.

London Gazette, 15 March, 1921.—" War Office, 15 March, 1921. His Majesty the King has been graciously pleased to approve of the undermentioned award for distinguished services rendered in Palestine. To be dated 15 Dec. 1920. Awarded the Distinguished Service Order."

HUTCHISON, JOHN ROBERT, Major, 38th Central India Horse, Indian Army. On the 24th April, 1920, when Semakh was heavily attacked by Arab tribesmen and Bedouins, Major Hutchison displayed great ability in the organization of the few troops at his disposal for the defence of an extended area. The situation was for some time critical, and the small garrison in danger of being overcome. It was due to this officer's able handling of the situation that the attack was definitely repulsed before reinforcements could reach him.

London Gazette, 21 April, 1921.—" War Office, 21 April, 1921. His Majesty the King has been graciously pleased to approve of the undermentioned reward for distinguished services in the field with the Waziristan Force, India. Awarded the Distinguished Service Order."

JONES, WALTER HENRY CLULEE, Lieut., 2/127th Baluchistan Light Infantry, Indian Army. For conspicuous gallantry and devotion to duty near Sorarogha on the 14th Jan. 1921. When the road protection troops were attacked by Mahsuds, he continued to command his men for over three hours, although three times wounded.

London Gazette, 10 June, 1921.—" War Office, 10 June. 1921. The King has been graciously pleased to approve of the undermentioned rewards, on the recommendation of the Government of India, for distinguished service in the field with the Waziristan Force. To be dated 1 August, 1920. Awarded the Distinguished Service Order."

BIRCH, VALENTINE KINGSTON, Major (Acting Lieut.-Colonel) 29th Lancers, Indian Army.

COLLINGRIDGE, HERBERT FREDERIC, Major (Acting Lieut.-Colonel), 9th Gurkha Rifles, Indian Army.

MOLYNEUX, PHILIP LUCAS, Capt., Indian Army, attached 39th Garhwal Rifles.

WISE, ALAN DOUGLAS, Major, 27th Light Cavalry, Indian Army.

London Gazette, 17 June, 1921.—" War Office, 17 June, 1921. The King has been graciously pleased to approve of the undermentioned reward on the recommendation of the Government of India, for distinguished services rendered in connection with minor military operations within the Indian Empire (or in territories adjacent thereto). To be dated 14 Oct. 1920. Awarded a Bar to the Distinguished Service Order."

FRASER, WILLIAM ARCHIBALD KENNETH, D.S.O., M.C., Capt. and Brevet Major (Acting Lieut.-Colonel), 39th Central Indian Horse, Indian Army. (D.S.O. awarded London Gazette dated 12 Sept. 1919.)

London Gazette, 10 Aug. 1921.—" War Office, 10 Aug. 1921. His Majesty the King has been graciously pleased to approve of the undermentioned rewards for distinguished services in the field in Mesopotamia. Awarded a Bar to the Distinguished Service Order."

GASKELL, HERBERT STUART, D.S.O., Major and Brevet Lieut.-Colonel (Acting Lieut.-Colonel), Royal Engineers. For conspicuous gallantry and devotion to duty whilst commanding a column operating in the Quraitu Qisil Robat area, between the 18th and 28th Aug. 1920. During this period the column relieved two isolated posts, and fought three actions against a determined and numerically superior enemy. Although his troops were mainly young and untrained soldiers, he inflicted heavy casualties on the enemy, and cleared the area effectively. His many successes were mainly due to his rapid appreciation of a situation and his total disregard of danger. (D.S.O. gazetted 14 Jan. 1916.)

SCOTT, HENRY LAWRENCE, D.S.O., M.C., Major and Brevet Lieut.-Colonel, 1/1st (with 1/10th) Gurkha Rifles, Indian Army. For conspicuous gallantry and devotion to duty on the 19th July, 1920, near Rumaitha. On his own initiative he marched his column to the sound of the guns, and brought reinforcements at a critical moment. Later, by his capable handling of the battalion against a very superior enemy, he established a position across the river, and so enabled the whole force to get water which was urgently required. It was owing to his gallant example and bold leadership that the operations throughout the day were successful. (D.S.O. gazetted 25 Aug. 1917.)

Awarded the Distinguished Service Order :

BEALES, WILLIAM LEWIS, Capt., 1/94th Infantry, Indian Army. For conspicuous gallantry and devotion to duty on 19/20 Aug. 1920, at Kifri. He was despatched from camp at night with two sections of his unit to reinforce a platoon which was being attacked by approximately 500 hostile tribesmen. Capt. Beales attempted to enter the village by the main street, but met with such opposition that he was compelled to withdraw. He then endeavoured to force an entrance by another route, and after two hours' heavy fighting reached the platoon. Though under close fire of the enemy, he so inspired his men by his determination and absolute disregard of danger that the insurgents were forced to retire. When the officer commanding the platoon was severely wounded he carried him under fire to a place of safety about 400 yards in rear, and then directed the retirement of his force. Had it not been for his pluck and the skilful handling of his men in face of overwhelming odds, it is doubtful whether the troops engaged would have been extricated.

BRADNEY, EDWARD, Capt. and Brevet Major, Royal Engineers. For conspicuous gallantry and devotion to duty at Tuwariz on the 12th Oct. 1920. whilst in command of a Field Company of Sappers and Miners, during an attempt to save a bridge from destruction by the insurgents, and in the saving of another. This officer, by his daring and coolness under heavy fire at close quarters, inspired his command to a rigid determination, which was rewarded by a success of considerable importance. On all occasions he has set a fine example of fearless leadership.

CAMPBELL, ROY NEIL BOYD, O.B.E., Major, 1/23rd Pioneers (with 3/23rd Infantry), Indian Army. For conspicuous gallantry and devotion to duty on the 11th Nov. 1920, during an attack on Falbah, when his men were becoming disheartened owing to the shortage of ammunition. They were in an unfavourable position, and being heavily counter-attacked at very close quarters. Regardless of danger, Major Campbell sprang out from cover, and, shouting the Sikhs' war cry, led a successful bayonet charge with the most beneficial results. The success of this operation was mainly due to his fine example.

CONNOP, HARRY ERNEST, Major, 35th Scinde Horse, Indian Army. For bold and skilful handling of two squadrons at Kufa, on the 17th Oct. 1920. He led two mounted attacks against the insurgents, sabreing three himself He then seized an important tactical feature, from which considerable loss was inflicted on the enemy, and supported the main advance by machine-gun fire. Throughout his handling of the cavalry he showed marked ability and power of command.

HANNA, ARTHUR LESLIE, Lieut., 11th Lancers, Indian Army. For conspicuous gallantry and devotion to duty on the 11th Aug. 1920, at Shaik-Ibrahim. He was sent up with a troop to reinforce a squadron which was heavily engaged. While passing over the open he saw a dismounted man wave to him. He at once galloped over and found a wounded man who had been stripped of his clothing and equipment by the Arabs. While endeavouring to lift the man on to his horse the enemy opened heavy fire, one bullet passing through his coat. Lieut. Hanna got the man on to his horse and brought him safely in.

HAY, ARTHUR SIDNEY, Major, 31st Lancers, attached 114th Mahrattas, Indian Army. For conspicuous gallantry and devotion to duty during the siege of Samawah, from July to Sept. 1920. The situation was often critical and the conditions under which the troops had to live were most trying, owing to the intense heat and shortage of rations. Major Hay, by his cheerful endurance and unremitting zeal, not only overcame the many difficulties with which he had to contend, but also set a fine example of courage and devotion to duty.

NORBURY, PAUL FITZGERALD, Major, 34th Poona Horse, Indian Army, attached Political Department. For conspicuous gallantry and devotion to duty during the siege of Kufah, from the 20th July to 17th Oct. 1920. On one occasion, when a corner of the defences had been set on fire by the insurgents, Major Norbury and one other officer, with a small party, broke through the defences to discover the place from which the fire was originating. This party was heavily fired on by the enemy, and the other officer was killed, but Major Norbury remained outside until he had obtained the necessary information to enable the garrison to successfully extinguish the fire. Throughout the siege his cheerfulness and disregard of personal danger afforded a fine example to the garrison.

London Gazette, 9 Sept. 1921.—" War Office, 9 Sept. 1921. The King has been graciously pleased to approve of the undermentioned rewards for distinguished service in connection with military operations in Mesopotamia. To be dated 7 Feb. 1921. Awarded the Distinguished Service Order."

BOYLE, CECIL ALEXANDER, Capt. and Brevet Major (Temporary Major), 11th Lancers, Indian Army.

KNIGHT, JOHN HERVEY, Major, Royal Garrison Artillery.

MITCHELL, HAY STEWART, Major, 1/32nd Sikh Pioneers, Indian Army.

London Gazette, 25 Nov. 1921.—" War Office, 25 Nov. 1921. His Majesty the King has been graciously pleased to approve of the undermentioned rewards for distinguished services in the field in Iraq. Awarded the Distinguished Service Order.

LUBBOCK, MERLIN GORDON, M.C., Major, Royal Field Artillery, employed Mesopotamian Railways. For conspicuous gallantry and devotion to duty during the period 30 July, 1920, to the 8th Aug. 1920, during the withdrawal from Diwaniyeh to Hillah. and especially for his daring reconnaissances, firstly, on the 1st Aug. 1920, when he rode ahead of a cavalry screen into Guchan, and having arranged for co-operation with the garrison at that place, returned with very valuable information, and secondly, on the 4th Aug. 1920, near Jerbuiyah, on which occasion he had to be called back owing to the danger of his being cut off by the enemy.

London Gazette, 19 Dec. 1922.—" War Office, 19 Dec. 1922. The King has been graciously pleased to approve of the undermentioned rewards for distinguished service in the field with the Waziristan Force, 1920-1921. To be dated 23 Oct. 1921. Awarded the Distinguished Service Order."

GRANT, JOHN DUNCAN, V.C., Lieut.-Colonel, 13th Rajputs, Indian Army.

HOGG, WILLOUGHBY LUGARD, Major, 3rd Brahmans, Indian Army.

LICKMAN, HARRY SYLVANUS, Capt. (Acting Major), Royal Garrison Artillery.

LOW, GORDON STEWART, Major, Royal Artillery.

MORROGH, WALTER FRANCIS, M.C., Capt. (Acting Major), Leinster Rifles and Machine Gun Corps.

PAIGE, CYRIL PENROSE, C.I.E., Major (Acting Lieut.-Colonel), 109th Infantry, Indian Army.

London Gazette, 3 April, 1923.—" War Office, 3 April, 1923. The King has been graciously pleased to approve of the undermentioned reward for distinguished service rendered in the field with the Waziristan Force, April, 1921, to December, 1921. To be dated 24 May, 1922. Awarded the Distinguished Service Order."

JACKSON, DAVID ROBERT HENRY, Major, 2/16th Gurkha Rifles, Indian Army.

London Gazette, 25 May, 1923.—" War Office, 25 May, 1923. His Majesty the King has been graciously pleased to approve of the undermentioned reward for distinguished service in the field with the Waziristan Force. Awarded the Distinguished Service Order.

PARSONS, ARTHUR EDWARD BROADBENT, O.B.E., Major, 2nd Battn., 12th Frontier Force, Indian Army. As Political Officer he volunteered to fly as a passenger with the Royal Air Force Squadrons in bombing operations against the hostile Mahsuds, whose location in difficult country it was hardly possible to find except under his personal guidance. This he has done on several occasions with complete success, and has shown conspicuous daring and initiative in finding the targets. While guiding the raid on the Jelal Khel on 24th Dec. 1922, he was severely wounded in the arm while flying at a low altitude. His gallantry has been of the greatest value to the Royal Air Force in enabling them to find and deal with their objective.

London Gazette, 12 June, 1923.—" War Office, 12 June, 1923. His Majesty the King has been graciously pleased to approve of the undermentioned reward for distinguished service in the field with the Razmak Force. Awarded the Distinguished Service Order."

DEED, LESLIE CHARLES BERTRAM, Major, Royal Engineers.

EXPLANATORY NOTE TO INDEX

The letters " L. G." mean " The London Gazette." The material extracts from all the Gazettes referred to which have been published since the 1st January, 1916, will be found in the first part of this volume.

A compound surname should be looked for in the different parts of the name, but it is believed that all such names have cross references.

Details are sometimes given in the Index of the deed for which the D.S.O. was awarded. In some cases this has been done because the London Gazette has not recorded it; in others, to give additional information.

The words " served European War " have been omitted from some of the entries, but it may be taken generally that all who were decorated with the D.S.O. after the beginning of the War served in it in some form or other.

Fuller records of the holders of the D.S.O. who have also won the V.C. will be found in the volume " The Victoria Cross," published by the same publishers.

INDEX
TO
COMPANIONS OF THE DISTINGUISHED SERVICE ORDER

Created from 1st January, 1916, to date,

and to Companions previously created who have during this period been awarded Bars to their D.S.O.'s,

WITH INFORMATIVE DETAILS, INCLUDING REFERENCES TO THE GAZETTE NOTICES OF THE AWARDS AND OF THE SERVICES WHICH WON THE DISTINCTIONS

The Gazette Notices form the first part of this volume, and have been arranged chronologically for convenience of reference.

AARONSOHN, A. (D.S.O. L.G. 8.8.19). A Turkish subject whose family headed the British espionage system in Palestine. He himself penetrated the Turkish lines, and his father and a sister, Sarah, paid with their lives for being pro-British. Rifkah, another sister, escaped in an American cruiser. Capt. Aaronsohn's D.S.O. is a unique honour for an enemy subject.

A. Aaronsohn.

ABADIE, R. N. (D.S.O. L.G. 14.1.16), Lt.-Col. K.R.R.C.; Gazetted to K.R.R.C. 10.3.00; Lt. 15.4.01; Capt. 27.10.10; served in S. African War (Queen's Medal with clasp). He was killed in action 10.7.17.

ABBAY, A. T. N. (D.S.O. L.G. 8.3.20), Lt.-Commander, R.N.

ABBEY, J. (D.S.O. L.G. 3.6.18), T/Capt. (A/Major), R.F.A.; M.C.

ABBOTT, S. H. L., M.B. (D.S.O. L.G. 3.6.19); b. 6.9.77; Lt., I.M.S., 29.1.02; Capt. 29.1.05; Major 29.7.13; Despatches.

À BECKETT, M. H. (D.S.O. L.G. 18.1.18), (Details, L.G. 25.4.18), Capt., Aust. Mil. Forces.

ABELL, R. LL. (D.S.O. L.G. 1.1.19), M.C., T/Capt. (A/Major), 104th By. 22nd Bde. R.F.A.

ABERCROMBIE, A. R. (D.S.O. L.G. 15.4.16): b. 14.10.96; s. of Lt.-Col. A. W. Abercrombie, Connaught Rangers; educ. Haileybury; Sandhurst; ent. Queen's Rgt. 1.10.14; M.C. for gallantry at Hill 60; D.S.O. for Hohenzollern Redoubt; served in France from Oct. 1915; commanded escort to Sir D. Haig in 1916; T/Lt.-Col.; captured near Le Cateau commanding his regiment, and died a prisoner of war at Magdeburg 31.12.18 of wounds received on 9 Oct.

ABERCROMBY, SIR G. W., 8th Bart. (D.S.O. L.G. 26.7.17); b. 18.3.86; suc. father, 1895; educ. Sandhurst; ent. S. Gds. 1905; R. Highrs. 1914; T/Lt.-Col. Is Chief of Clan.

ABRAHAM, J. J., M.A., M.D., F.R.C.S. (D.S.O. L.G. 11.4.18); b. 1876; s. of W. Abraham, J.P.; educ. Coleraine Academy; Trinity Coll. Dublin; London Hospital; served Serbia, 1914-15; Egypt, Palestine, 1917-19; Despatches; C.B.E.

ABSON, J., F.R.C.V.S. (D.S.O. L.G. 14.1.16); b. 24.10.88; s. of J. and E. Abson; m. a daughter of J. Elliott; one son (J. F. B. Abson, Capt., K.O.Y.L.I.).

ACLAND, A. N. (D.S.O. L.G. 3.6.18); b. 7.9.85; ent. Army 16.2.07; Lt. 20.3.09; Adjt., D.C.L.I., 11.4.13 to 21.1.15; Capt. 28.2.15; Bt.-Major 3.6.17; Despatches; M.C.

ACLAND, H. G. DYKE (D.S.O. L.G. 8.3.20). Lt.-Comdr. R.N.

ACLAND-TROYTE, G. J. (D.S.O. L.G. 14.1.16); educ. Eton; Trinity Hall, Camb.; ent. K.R.R. 8.2.99; Major 1.9.15; Bt. Lt.-Col. 1.1.19; served S. African War, 1901 (dangerously wounded; Q. Medal, cl.); E. Africa, 1904; Somaliland (Med., cl.).

ACKLOM, S. (D.S.O. L.G. 1.1.17) (Bar, L.G. 3.6.18); b. 1883; s. of Lt.-Col. S. Acklom, late Connaught Rangers; educ. St. Paul's, London; Sandhurst; m. Lucie, d. of M. Spencer; ent. Army, 1901; H.L.I. 1902; Adjt., 1st Battn., 1913; Europ. War, 1914; transferred to Northd. Fus., May. 1916; T/Lt.-Col. 1916; M.C. 1916, for gallantry at Richebourg; won D.S.O. at La Boiselle; Despatches four times; recommended for a brigade. He was killed in action 21.3.18.

ACTON, W. M. (D.S.O. L.G. 3.6.16); b. 15.7.78; m. L. Bell, d. of High Sheriff for Wilts; educ. Oxford Mil. College; 2nd Lt., R. Irish Rgt., 23.12.99; Lt. 8.12.00; Adjt., R. Ir. Rgt., 1903 to 1906, and 1913-15; Capt. 11.8.06; Major 1.9.15; S. African War, 1900-2 (Queen's and King's Medals and 5 clasps); Europ. War from 1914.

ACTON-ADAMS, P. M. (D.S.O. L.G. 4.6.17); b. 13.7.78; s. of W. Acton-Adams; educ. Christ's College, Christchurch, N.Z. Major Acton-Adams served in the Europ. War 16.10.14 to 10.8.19; Despatches.

ACWORTH, B. (D.S.O. L.G. 2.11.17), Cdr., R.N., 30.6.19.

ADAIR, H. S. (D.S.O. L.G. 1.1.1918); b. 13.10.78; 2nd Lt., Ches. R., 18.1.99; Lt. 7.11.00; Capt. 26.6.06; Adjt., Ches. R., 1907-10; Major 1.9.15; S. African War, 1900-2 (Queen's Medal, 3 clasps); Europ. War, 1914-18; Despatches twice.

ADAM, R. F. (D.S.O. L.G. 3.6.18); b. 30.10.85; e. s. of Sir F. F. Adam; m. A. Pitman; ent. R.A. 27.7.05; Lt. 27.7.08; Capt. 30.10.14; Adjt., R.A., 8.7.15; Major 14.11.16; served Europ. War (Egypt); Despatches.

ADAM, W. (D.S.O. L.G. 3.6.18), Major (A/Lt.-Col.), Worcester R.

ADAMS, A. (D.S.O. L.G. 3.6.18); b. 27.5.67; 1st Com. 28.7.88; ret., R.E., 4.9.07; Major, R. of O., 1.8.15. He died in 1921.

ADAMS, B. F. (D.S.O. L.G. 31.7.19), Cdr., R.N., 23.4.18.

ADAMS, F. (D.S.O. L.G. 3.6.18); b. 17.4.74; 2nd Lt., Unatt., 2.6.94; I.S.C. 5.10.95; Lt., I.A., 3.8.97; Capt. 2.6.03; Major 2.6.12; Lt.-Col. 29.7.16; Colonel 9.5.20; Despatches.

ADAMS, H. R. (D.S.O. L.G. 1.1.18); b. 22.7.80; ent. R.A. 17.3.00; Lt. 3.4.01; Capt. 26.4.11; Adjt., R.A., 1915; Major 16.10.15; A/Lt.-Col., R.A., 9.5.18; Despatches.

ADAMS, J. B. (D.S.O. L.G. 7.6.18), b. 1880; s. of G. N. Adams, M.D.; m. Phebe Carnac Thompson Fisher, d. of Bishop Fisher; one s.; one d.; ent. Merchant Service at the age of 13; joined R.N.R. as a Midshipman, and served four years in R.N. as Sub-Lt. and Lt., R.N.R.; Cdr., R.N.R.; was second-in-command of British Antarctic Expedition, 1907-9, and accompanied Shackleton to within 97 miles of the South Pole. On outbreak of war was appointed Flag Lieutenant to Admiral Hood, and took part in the operations off the Belgian coast; awarded D.S.O. for services with R.N. siege guns on shore in Flanders, 1916-18; promoted to Commander; severely wounded (Croix de Guerre).

ADAMS, REV. J. E., B.D. (D.S.O. L.G. 8.3.18), T/Chapl. to the Forces (M.C.).

ADAMS, P. M. ACTON- (see Acton-Adams, P. M.).

ADAMS, R. J. (D.S.O. L.G. 1.1.19); b. 18.9.74; ent. R.A. 5.5.00; Lt. 17.4.01; Capt. 1.4.10; Major 30.10.14; A/Lt.-Col., T.F., 15.12.17; Despatches.

ADAMS, W. A. (D.S.O. L.G. 4.6.17), Major, Australian Pioneer Bn. He was killed in action 15.10.17.

ADAMS, W. G. (D.S.O. L.G. 26.7.18), Capt., A.I.F. (M.C.).

ADAMS, W. J. PHYTHIAN- (see Phythian-Adams, W. J.).

ADAMSON, A. ST. A. M. (D.S.O. L.G. 3.6.16), Capt. 1.3.06; Major, P.P.C.L.I. Canadian Foot Guards.

ADDERLEY, A. C. (D.S.O. L.G. 27.7.18); b. 2.1.73; Capt., R.A.M.C., 30.5.03; Major 30.5.12; Lt.-Col. 15.4.18; Despatches.

ADLER, THE REV. M., B.A. (D.S.O. L.G. 1.1.18); b. 27.7.68; s. of J. and E. Adler; m. Bertha, d. of Mrs. M. Lorie; educ. at Jews' and University Colleges, London; ent. T.F. in 1909, serving in Europ. War from Jan. 1915, to July, 1918; Senior Jewish Minister to the Forces.

ADLERCRON, G. R. L. (D.S.O. L.G. 15.2.19) (Details, L.G. 30.7.19); b. 21.10.84; entered Yorks. L.I. 10.10.03; Lt. 19.7.06; Capt. 4.4.14. He died 10.4.20, at Colobar Hospital, Bombay, aged 35.

G. R. L. Adlercron.

ADLERCRON, R. L. (D.S.O. L.G. 14.1.16) (Bar, L.G. 15.2.19) (Details, L.G. 30.7.19); b. 5.7.73; s. of G. R. L. Adlercron of Moyglare; m. Hester Bancroft; educ. Eton; ent. Cam. Highrs. 2.6.94; Lt. 3.4.97; Capt. 24.11.99; Major, 9.3.13; Bt. Lt.-Col. 1.1.17; T/Brig.-Genl. 8.6.16; Nile Exp. 1898; Battles of Atbara and Khartum (Despatches; Egyptian Medal with 2 clasps; Medal); S. African War, 1899-01; dangerously wounded (Despatches; Queen's Medal, 4 clasps); Europ. War, 1914-18 (C.M.G. 1918).

AGAR, A. W. S., V.C. (D.S.O. L.G. 11.11.19); Lt.-Cdr., R.N., 30.6.20; V.C. (see "The Victoria Cross," by same publishers).

AGAR, J. A. S. (D.S.O. L.G. 7.2.18), T/Major, R. Warwicks. R.

AGER, F. G. (D.S.O. L.G. 1.1.17); Capt., T/Major, R.A.S.C., T.F.

AGG, F. J. G. (D.S.O. L.G. 14.1.16); b. 19.3.79; s. of late Col. W. Agg; m. Mabel Beatrix, d. of late A Cumming; entered Militia, 1898; K.O.Y.L.I. 20.5.99; Lieut. 1899; Capt. 1906; Major, 1915; T/Lt.-Col. 1918-1919; served Europ. War; Despatches 5 times; Légion d'Honneur.

AGLIONBY, C. E. (D.S.O. L.G. 24.3.19), Lieut., R.N., 26.6.03; Commander 11.11.18; retired.

R. L. Adlercron.

AGNEW, J. (D.S.O. L.G. 1.1.19), Major (A/Lt.-Col.), Arg. and Suthd. Highrs. T.F.

AGNEW, K. M. (D.S.O. L.G. 1.1.19); b. 25.5.86; entered Army 28.7.06; Lieut. 25.7.09; Capt. 30.10.14; Major 9.2.17; Brig.-Major, R.A., 7th Div., B.E.F., Italy, 1918; Despatches; M.C.

AHERN, D. (D.S.O. L.G. 4.6.17) (Bar L.G. 1.2.19); b. 2.1.78; m. Eileen Maher; educ. Clongowes; entered R.A.M.C. 31.1.03; Capt. 31.7.06; Major 31.10.14; T/Lt.-Col. 12.7.18; No. 11 Field Ambulance, R.A.M.C.; served Europ. War; Despatches; M.C.

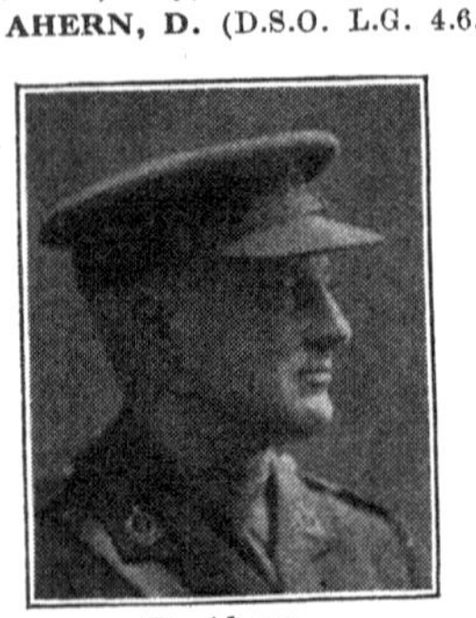
D. Ahern.

AHERNE, REV. D. (D.S.O. L.G. 4.6.17); b. 2.1.71; s. of D. Aherne; educ. Fermoy, Paris and Rome; priest, 1895 (Congregation of the Most Holy Redeemer); served in the Europ. War; Despatches.

AHRENS, C. (D.S.O. L.G. 26.7.18), M.C., Capt., A.I.F.

AIKINS, G. H. (D.S.O. L.G. 18.1.18) (Details, L.G. 25.4.18), Major, Can. Mtd. Rifles.

AINSLIE, C. M. (D.S.O. L.G. 1.1.17); s. of late Capt. E. C. Ainslie, 60th Rifles; m. Sophie, d. of Rev. F. W. Hogan; educ. Campbell College, Ireland; served in S. A. War; 2nd Lieut., Connaught Rangers, 10.11.00; transferred to A.S.C. 1.10.02; Lt. 10.11.03; Major, R.A.S.C., 30.10.14; served in France, 1915; Despatches, Belgian Croix de Guerre.

AINSWORTH, J. (D.S.O. L.G. 1.1.18); b. 16.6.64; s. of J. D. and Margaret Ainsworth; m. Ina Cameron Scott, d. of late J. Scott; Local Colonel; Chief Native Commissioner, E. Africa Protectorate, and Member of the Executive and Legislative Councils, E.A.P.; served Europ. War; C.M.G.

AINSWORTH, R. B. (D.S.O. L.G. 14.1.16); b. 26.9.75; s. of late Capt. W. Ainsworth; educ. St. Paul's School; St. George's Hospital; entered R.N. 1900; resigned, 1902; entered R.A.M.C. 1.9.02; Capt. 1.3.06; Major 1.3.14; Bt. Lt.-Col. 3.6.19; served in France and Russia; Despatches 3 times.

AIREY, R. B. (D.S.O. L.G. 3.6.16); b. 21.9.74; s. of Major R. H. B. Airey, late 24th Rgt.; m. Helen Mabel Hall; educ. Tonbridge, and R.M.C., Sandhurst; gazetted to S.W.B. 9.1.97; A.S.C. 1.1.98; Capt. 1.1.01; Major 1.4.12; served Europ. War, 1914–18; Bt. Lt.-Col. 18.2.15; Despatches; C.M.G.

AITKEN, J. J. (D.S.O., L.G. 3.6.16); b. 7.7.78; entered A.V.C. 13.4.01; Capt. 3.4.06; Major 10.7.15; Bt. Lt.-Col. 1.1.18; S. African War (Queen's and King's Medals and 5 clasps); Europ. War; C.M.G.; Despatches.

AITKEN, N. W. (D.S.O. L.G. 1.1.18); b. 18.12.82; entered R.A. 24.12.02; Lieut. 24.12.05; Capt. 30.10.14; Major 13.7.17; served in France; Brigade Major, Heavy Artillery, Canadian Force; M.C.

AKERMAN, W. P. J. (D.S.O. L.G. 1.1.18) (Bar, L.G. 1.1.19); b. 16.1.88; ent. R.A. 29.7.08; Lieut. 29.7.11; Capt. 30.10.14; Major 22.3.18; A/Lt.-Col. (Terr.), 5.11.18; European War; Despatches; M.C.

ALBAN, C. E. R. G. (D.S.O. L.G. 18.7.17) (1st Bar, 15.2.19) (Details, L.G. 30.7.19) (2nd Bar, 2.4.19) (Details, L.G. 10.12.19); b. 4.12.89; entered Army 20.4.10; Lt. 26.2.13; Capt. 19.8.15; Bt. Major 3.6.18; A/Lt.-Col 3.5.17; Despatches.

ALDAM, W. ST. A. WARDE- (see Warde-Aldam, W. St. A.).

ALDERMAN, W. J. (D.S.O. L.G. 4.6.17), Capt. (A/Lt.-Colonel), The Queen's Own Rgt. He was killed in action 20.11.17.

ALDERMAN, W. W. (D.S.O. L.G. 1.1.19), Capt. (T/Lt.-Col.), Aust. Commonwealth Forces, attached N.Z. Ex. Force; C.M.G.

ALDERSON, C. (D.S.O. L.G. 26.11.17) (Details, L.G. 6.4.18), Major, 1/7th Lancs. Fus.; e. s. of Rev. R. E. Alderson; m. Gladys Florence Pemberton.

ALDERSON, E., M.D. (D.S.O. L.G. 1.1.18); b. 1883; m. Ellen Harley; educ. Liverpool University; Capt. (A/Lt.-Col.), R.A.M.C.; served Europ. War; Despatches.

ALDERSON, F. J. (D.S.O. L.G. 1.1.18); s. of W. E. Alderson, of Winnipeg; Major, Can. Fld. Arty; wounded Europ. War.

ALDOUS, F. C. (D.S.O. L.G. 15.2.19) (Details, L.G. 30.7.19), Major (A/Lt.-Col.), 6th Manchester R., T.F.

ALDWORTH, T. P. (D.S.O. L.G. 23.5.19), Capt., R.W. Kent Regt.

ALDWORTH, W. (D.S.O. L.G. 16.9.18); b. 27.6.78; 2nd Lt. 21.11.14; Lt. 6.5.15; Capt., Essex R., 1.1.17; A/Major 24.10.17.

ALEXANDER, C. T. (D.S.O. L.G. 2.2.16), Major, Lanc. Fus., T.F.

ALEXANDER, F. (D.S.O. L.G. 8.3.20), Engr. Cdr., R.N. (deceased).

ALEXANDER, HON. H. R. L. G. (D.S.O. L.G. 20.10.16, for the Somme); b. 10.12.91; s. of 4th Earl of Caledon; educ. Harrow and Sandhurst; played for Harrow v. Eton, 1910, at Lords, and in running held the record for Harrow Steeplechase, and the record for one mile, and two miles, at Sandhurst; won the Irish Amateur Mile in 4 minutes, 33 seconds, in 1914, and was 2nd in the Mile at Glasgow for Ireland v. England and Scotland; entered the Irish Guards 23.9.11; Lieut. 5.12.12; Capt. 7.2.15; Major 1.8.17; served France (M.C. for Loos; Legion of Honour for Marne) and Russia; commanded Baltic Landwehr (5,000) in the Lettish Army and fought against the Bolsheviks from 25.8.19 to 1.4.20; once wounded in Russia, and received the Order of St. Anne with Swords, 2nd Class; Despatches.

ALEXANDER, H. S. (D.S.O. L.G. 26.8.18); b. 21.4.70; 2nd Lt., Wilts R., 23.3.89; Lieut., I.S.C., 13.11.90; Capt., I.A., 23.3.00; Major 23.3.07; Lt.-Col. 23.3.15.

ALEXANDER J. D., M.B. (D.S.O. L.G. 4.6.17); b. 11.4.67; Capt., R.A.M.C., 30.1.95; Major 30.1.04; Lt.-Col. 31.8.14; Colonel 26.12.17; served Europ. War; C.B.E.

ALEXANDER, J. H., M.C. (D.S.O. L.G. 1.1.19), T/Capt. (T/Major), R.E.

ALEXANDER, J. W. (D.S.O. L.G. 3.6.16), Major (T/Lt.-Col.), W. Yorks R. (T.F.).

ALEXANDER, SIR L. C. W., Bart. (D.S.O. L.G. 14.1.16); b. 23.9.85; s. of 5th Bart.; m. Noorouz Weston, d. of Sir E. Cable; one s.; 2nd Lt., G. Gds., 1.2.07; retired with rank of Lieut.; Capt., 23rd Batt. London R., 1914.

ALEXANDER, R. D. T. (D.S.O. L.G. 25.8.17), Capt. (A/Major), London R.

ALEXANDER, R. L. (D.S.O. L.G. 8.3.18), Lt.-Cdr. (R.D.), R.N.R., 26.11.18.

ALEXANDER, R. O. (D.S.O. L.G. 1.1.17); b. 7.8.88; s. of J. A. Alexander; m. 1917, Gertrude Williams, d. of the Rt. Rev. the Lord Bishop of Quebec; educ. Bedford; entered Canadian Militia, 1908; R. Can. Rgt. 1910; Capt. 1915; Major, 1915; T/Lt.-Col. 1916; served Europ. War; Despatches.

ALEXANDER W. (D.S.O. L.G. 14.1.16); b. 4.5.74; s. of late T. Alexander; m. Beatrice Ritchie; educ. Kelvinside Academy; Glasgow University, and Göttingen; joined T.F. 1889; Capt. 1906; Brig.-Genl. 1918; served Europ. War with 6th Black Watch; C.B.; C.M.G.; Despatches.

ALEXANDER, W. D. (D.S.O. L.G. 1.1.17); b. 5.8.75; 2nd Lt., R.A., 15.6.95; Lt. 15.6.98; Capt. 1.3.01; Major 30.10.14; Despatches.

ALEXANDER, W. N. S. (D.S.O. L.G. 18.2.15) (Bar to D.S.O. L.G. 1.1.18); Major (T/Lt.-Col.), Connaught Rangers (see "The Distinguished Service Order," from its institution to 31.12.15, by same publishers).

ALEXANDER, HON. W. S. P. (D.S.O. L.G. 26.9.17) (Details, L.G. 8.1.18); b. 16.11.95; y. s. of 4th Earl of Caledon; educ. Harrow; Sandhurst; entered, 2nd Lt., Irish Gds. 11.11.14; Lt. 15.7.15; Capt. 22.7.17; A/Major 16.7.18; Europ. War, 1914–17; wounded; Despatches.

ALGIE, W. (D.S.O. L.G. 26.3.17); b. 20.6.88; s. of Peter and Margaret Algie; educ. at the John Neilson Institution, Paisley; gazetted to the Northumberland Fusiliers, June, 1916; Lt., R.F.C.; R.A.F. Feb. 1918; Capt. Sept. 1918; Despatches 9.4.17 and Oct. 1918; awarded Air Force Cross, Nov. 1919, for night flying in London Defences.

ALISON, R. V. (D.S.O. L.G. 15.9.16), Commander, R.N., 31.11.18.

ALLAN, A. C. (D.S.O. L.G. 1.1.19); b. 10.2.88; 2nd Lt., Cam. Hldrs., 9.2.07; Lt. 19.5.11; T/Capt. 22.12.14; Capt. 16.2.15; A/Major 15.3.17; A/Lt.-Col. 20.8.17; Despatches; M.C.

ALLAN, J. G. (D.S.O. L.G. 4.6.17), Capt. (T/Major), R.E.

ALLAN, P. S. (D.S.O. L.G. 1.1.18); b. 11.12.74; entered Army 6.3.95; Major 5.7.13; Bt. Lt.-Col., G. Hldrs., 1.1.17; retired 14.5.19.

ALLAN, W. D. (D.S.O. L.G. 3.6.16), Lt.-Col., 3rd Bn. Can. Inf. He died of wounds 1.10.16.

ALLARDYCE, J. (D.S.O. L.G. 4.2.18) (Details, L.G. 5.7.18) (Bar, L.G. 16.9.18), 2nd Lt., London R.; M.M.

ALLARDYCE, J. G. B. (D.S.O. L.G. 1.1.17) (Bar, L.G. 16.9.18); b. 27.6.78; 2nd Lt., R.A., 23.12.97; Lt. 23.12.00; Capt. 7.2.05; Adjt., R.A., 28.3.05 to 27.3.08; Major 30.10.14; Bt. Lt.-Col. 1.1.18; Lt.-Col. 3.7.18; Despatches; C.M.G.

ALLASON, W. (D.S.O. L.G. 18.2.15) (Bar, L.G. 14.11.16) (see volume "The D.S.O." from its institution to 31 Dec. 1915, by same publishers).

ALLDEN, S. G. (D.S.O. L.G. 1.1.18); b. 14.8.88; entered A.S.C. 19.9.08; Lt. 19.9.11; Capt. 30.10.14; Major, R.A.S.C., 30.11.14; served in Europ. War (Egypt).

ALLDERIDGE, C. D. (D.S.O. L.G. 4.6.17), Capt. (A/Major), R.G.A.

ALLEN, A. G. (D.S.O. L.G. 1.1.19), M.C., T/Capt., Gen. List.

ALLEN, A. S. (D.S.O. L.G. 25.8.17); b. 10.3.94; s. of J. Allen (formerly of Macclesfield), a Govt. Locomotive Inspector in N.S. Wales, another of whose sons also served in the war; 2nd Lt., A.I.F., 19.1.15; Lt., Feb. 1916; Capt. 12.3.16; T/Major 5.7.16; Major 9.9.17; T/Lt.-Col. 9.4.18; noted for Bt. Major on promotion to Capt.

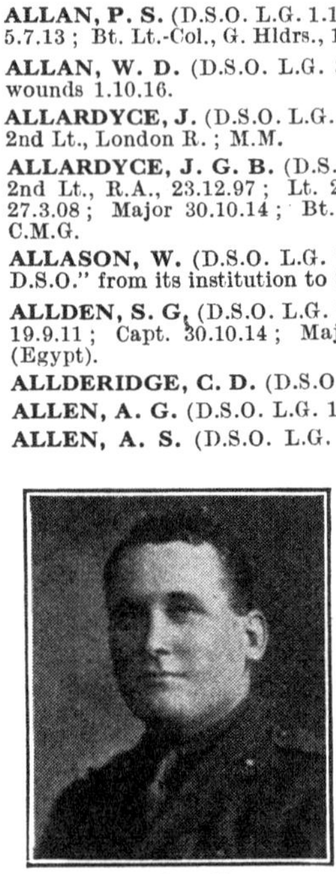
A. S. Allen.

ALLEN, C. (D.S.O. L.G. 1.1.17), Capt. (T/Major), R.F.A.; s. of Col. Sir Charles Allen.

ALLEN, C. H. (D.S.O. L.G. 22.4.19), Lt., R.N., 15.7.13; qualified in submarine duties.

ALLEN, C. W. (D.S.O. L.G. 1.1.18), Lt.-Col., Can. E. F. Pioneer Bn., 12.10.15.

ALLEN, D. C. (D.S.O. L.G. 3.6.19), T/Major, 15th Bn. Tank Corps.

ALLEN, E. P. S. (D.S.O. L.G. 8.3.19) (Details, L.G. 4.10.19), Capt., 116th Inf. Bn. 2nd Cent. Ont. R., Can. Mil. Forces.

ALLEN, H. (D.S.O. L.G. 1.1.17); b. 23.9.81; 2nd Lt., R.A., 18.8.00; Lt. 24.9.02; Capt. 18.8.13; Major 30.12.15; Despatches.

ALLEN, H. A, (D.S.O. L.G. 3.6.19); b. 18.7.93; 2nd Lt., R. Innis. Fus., 4.9.12; Lt. 4.9.14; Capt. 17.11.15; T/Major, Cyclist Corps, 7.6.16; Bt. Major 3.6.18; Despatches.

ALLEN, H. I. (D.S.O. L.G. 25.8.17); b. 18.11.87; s. of G. C. and A. C. Allen; educ. Wellington College; ent. Army 22.4.08; Lt. 8.1.19; Capt. 1.3.15; Bt. Major 3.6.18, N. Staffs. R. He served in France, 1915, with the Indian Corps in Mesopotamia, 1916, to March, 1919; Despatches.

ALLEN, L. A. (D.S.O. L.G. 1.1.18), Lt.-Col., R.A.S.C.

ALLEN, L. R. (D.S.O. L.G. 26.9.17) (Details, L.G. 9.1.18), Lt., Notts and Derby R. (S.R.).

ALLEN, M. V. (D.S.O. L.G. 1.1.17), Major, Br. Columbia Horse, 9.12.11.

ALLEN, R. C. (D.S.O. L.G. 16.8.17) (Bar, L.G. 2.4.19) (Details of Bar, L.G. 10.12.19), Lt.-Col., N.Z. Inf.

ALLEN, R. S. (D.S.O. L.G. 1.1.19); b. 30.1.79; entered Lanc. Fus. 17.2.00; Lt. 30.6.00; Capt. 23.1.05; Hants Rgt. 10.1.08; Major 1.5.15; Bt. Lt.-Col. 1.1.18; Despatches.

ALLEN, S. S. (D.S.O. L.G. 1.1.18) (Bar, L.G. 22.6.18), Lt.-Col., N.Z. Inf.; C.M.G.; b. in N.Z.; s. of late W. S. Allen, M.P. (N.Z.); m. Mary I. H. Foster.

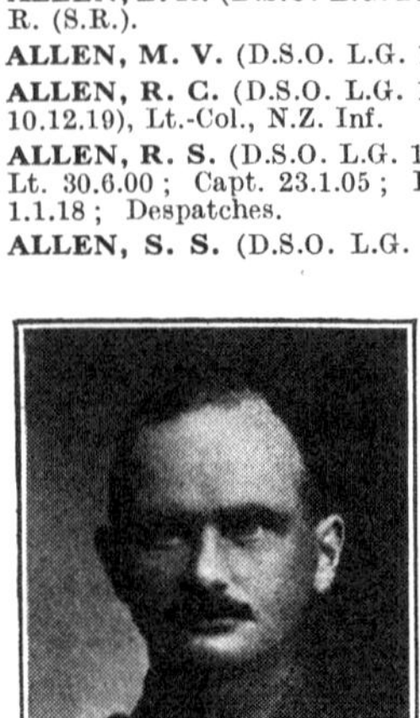
S. S. Allen.

ALLEN, W. B., M.B. (D.S.O. L.G. 2.4.19) (Details, L.G. 10.12.19), Capt., R.A.M.C.; V.C. (see vol. "The Victoria Cross," by same publishers); M.C. and Bar.

ALLEN, W. J. (D.S.O. L.G. 3.6.18); T/Major, R. Irish Rifles.

ALLENBY, R. A. (D.S.O. L.G. 1.1.18); s. of Major R. Allenby, J.P.; m. Nina J., d. of late Major-Genl. H. Shaw, V.C., C.B.; entered H.M.S. Britannia, 1875; Commander, 1897; Capt. 1902; Rear-Admiral, 1913; retired, 1915; M.V.O.; served in Europ. War; Vice-Admiral; retired 1918.

ALLERTON, C. (D.S.O. L.G. 14.11.16), T/Lt., Suffolk R.

ALLETSON, G. C. (D.S.O. L.G. 1.1.17); s. of G. H. Allerton; m. Norah Trevor Roper; one s.; one d.; served in S. African War (Denbighshire Yeom.); then Lt., Prince of Wales' Light Horse; Capt., Remount Service, France, Oct. 1914; Major, May, 1915; Despatches.

ALLEYNE, SIR. J. M., Bart. (D.S.O. L.G. 28.8.18) : b. 11.8.89 ; s. of Reynold Alleyne (e. s. of 3rd Bart.) and Susanna, d. of the late J. Meynell, of Meynell Langley, Derbyshire ; succeeded grandfather, 1912 ; Lt.-Cdr., R.N. ; served Europ. War ; wounded ; D.S.C. 23.5.17.

ALLFREY, E. M. (D.S.O. L.G. 4.6.17) ; b. 13.7.86 ; ent. R. Berks. R., from Militia, 16.2.07 ; Lt. 27.7.10 ; Capt. 6.1.15 ; T/Major, 20.1.16 ; commanded Battalion, A. Cyclist Corps, 23.6.16 ; D.A. Prov. Marshal, N. Command, 6.1.19 ; served Europ. War ; Despatches.

ALLFREY, H. I. R. (D.S.O. L.G. 1.1.18) ; b. 2.2.79 ; ent. Army 4.1.99 ; Lt. 9.3.00 ; Capt. 15.4.04 ; Adjt., Som. L.I., 16.11.07 ; Major 1.9.15 ; Bt. Lt.-Col. 3.6.19 ; served Europ. War, on Staff of 7th A.C. and 5th Army ; M.C. ; C.M.G.

ALLGOOD, W. H. L. (D.S.O. L.G. 4.6.17) ; b. 16.2.68 ; m. Sophia B. S., d. of late Col. J. H. G. Smyth, C.M.G. : ent. K.R.R.C. 17.1.91 ; R. of O. 13.2.14 ; T/Brig.-Genl. 13.4.16 ; Lt.-Col., late K.R.R.C. ; served Burma War, 1891–2 ; S. African War (Despatches, L.G. 8.2.01 and 10.9.01 ; Queen's Medal, 3 clasps) ; Europ. War ; Despatches 4 times ; C.M.G. ; M.C.

ALLHUSEN, F. H. (D.S.O. L.G. 23.11.16) ; b. 24.1.72 ; s. of the late H. C. Allhusen, Stoke Court, Bucks ; m. Enid, d. of Commander H. W. Swithinbank ; three s. ; educ. Cheltenham College ; entered 9th Lancers, 1893 ; served in S. African War (Despatches ; Queen's Medal, 4 clasps) ; Europ. War ; joined Lovat's Scouts, 1914 ; served in Gallipoli, Egypt and France, 1914–19 (Despatches twice ; C.M.G.) ; Lt.-Col., retired pay, 9th Lancers ; won Kadir Cup, Hog Hunters' Cup, 1899.

ALLSOP, W. G. (D.S.O. L.G. 4.6.17), Lt.-Col., Aust. F.A. ; served Europ. War ; C.M.G.

ALLSOPP, J. B. (D.S.O. L.G. 16.9.18), A/Lt.-Col., S. Lan. R. He was killed in action 27.5.18, and an obituary notice appeared in the "Times" of 3.9.18.

ALLSUP, C. F. (D.S.O. L.G. 17.3.19), Commander, R.N., 31.12.14.

ALLSUP, E. S. (D.S.O. L.G. 1.1.17) ; b. 27.11.79 ; s. of late W. J. Allsup ; educ. Monkton Combe School, Bath ; 2nd Lt., R.A., 26.5.00 ; Capt. 26.5.13 ; Major, R.F.A., 18.8.15 ; served N.W.F., India, Mohmand F.F., 1908 (Medal and clasp) ; Europ. War, 1914–18 ; 1914 Star ; Despatches.

ALPINE, W. M. (D.S.O. L.G. 3.6.18), T/Major, K.R.R.C.

ALSTON, LL. A. A. (D.S.O. L.G. 2.4.19) (Details, L.G. 10.12.19) ; b. 21.12.90 ; ent. Army 4.12.12 ; Lt. 10.3.14 ; Capt. 8.10.15 ; served Europ. War ; Despatches ; M.C.

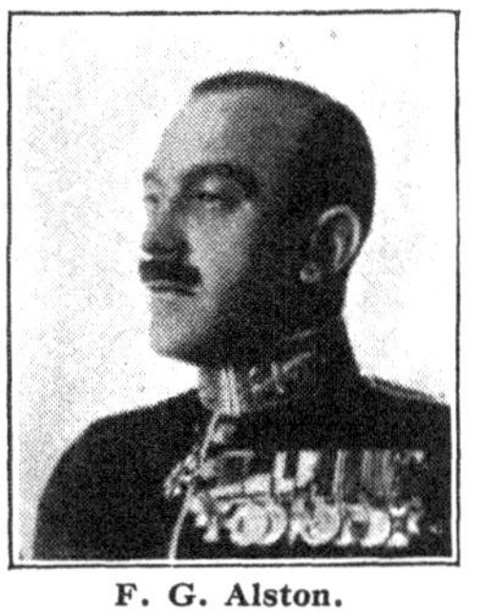

F. G. Alston.

ALSTON, F. G. (D.S.O. L.G. 14.1.16) ; b. 19.7.78 ; s. of the late Sir F. B. Alston, K.C.M.G. ; m. Antoinette, d. of the late J. Tarn ; one s. ; two d. ; educ. at the Rev. E. St. J. Parry's Prep. School, Slough ; at Eton and abroad ; ent. S. Guards 2.6.00 ; Lt. 11.10.02 ; served S. African War, 1900–02 (wounded ; Queen's Medal, 3 clasps ; King's Medal, 2 clasps) ; Capt. 30.2.05 ; Adjt., 2nd Bn. S. Guards, 1.1.06 to 30.6.07 ; Regimental Adjutant, S. Guards, 7.11.09 to 2.2.11 ; went to France 2.4.15, as Brigade Major, 20th Inf. Bde., 7th Divn. ; Major 1.2.15 ; D.A.A. and Q.M.G., Guards Division, B.E.F., 15.8.15 ; A.A. and Q.M.G., Guards Division, B.E.F., 25.12.16, with temp. rank of Lt.-Col. (Despatches 4 times ; Croix de Guerre, Nov. 1917 ; Bt. Lt.-Col. 3.6.18) ; Brig.-Genl. in C. of Administration, London District, 8.12.18 ; holds Coronation Medal (King George V.).

ALTHAM, H. S. (D.S.O. L.G. 3.6.1918) ; b. 30.11.88 ; s. of Lt.-Genl. Sir E. A. Altham, K.C.B., K.C.I.E., C.M.G. ; m. Alision Livingstone-Learmonth ; educ. Repton School ; Trinity College, Oxon. ; joined 60th Rifles, Aug. 1914 ; served Europ. War in France, 1915–19 (M.C. ; Despatches thrice) ; Assistant Master, Winchester College.

ALVES, H. M. J. (D.S.O. L.G. 3.6.16) ; b. 1.4.83 ; s. of the late Col. J. M. Alves R.A. ; m. Beatrice Maud, widow of the late Major H. N. Kelly, 33rd Punjabis, and d. of the late Sir S. Ismay, K.C.S.I. ; one s. ; educ. Edinburgh Academy ; ent. R.A. 24.5.02 ; Capt. 30.10.14 ; Major 28.2.16 ; served Europ. War, 1914–18 ; went to France, Oct. 1914, with I.E.F. ; Despatches ; Belgian Croix de Guerre ; Bt. of Lt.-Col. 3.6.19.

AMBROSE, C. F. N. (D.S.O. L.G. 18.6.17), T/2nd Lt., M.G.C.

AMIN, MOHAMMED BEY, El Kaim, Egyptian Army (D.S.O. L.G. 4.9.18).

AMY, A. C., M.D. (D.S.O. L.G. 2.4.19) (Details, L.G. 10.12.19) ; b. 28.3.82 ; Lt., R.A.M.C., 30.7.06 ; Capt. 30.1.10 ; Major 30.7.18 ; Despatches.

ANDERSON, A. A. (D.S.O. L.G. 1.1.18) ; b. 23.9.89, at Ottawa ; s. of Lt.-Col. W. P. Anderson, C.M.G., and Dorothea S. Anderson ; educ. R.M.C. of Canada, and McGill University ; ent. Can. Mil. Forces 28.11.14 as Lieutenant (having been granted a commission, June, 1909, in R. of O., Can. Engrs.) ; Capt., June, 1916 ; Major, Aug. 1917. Services : 4 years out of Canada ; 2 years, 6 months in France ; returned to R. of O. as Major 29 Aug. 1919, on demobilization.

ANDERSON, A. E. D. (D.S.O. L.G. 1.1.18), Capt., K.O.S.B., S.R. ; M.C.

ANDERSON, A. M. (D.S.O. L.G. 8.3.19) (Details, L.G. 4.10.19), Capt., 48th Bn., A.I.F.

ANDERSON, A. S. K., M.B. (D.S.O. L.G. 18.1.18) (Details, L.G. 25.4.18) ; s. of A. Anderson and C. Anderson (*née* Cockerill) ; educ. Aberdeen University (M.A., M.B.) ; entered R.A.M.C. 1.10.14 ; Capt. 10.10.15 ; Major 4.1.18 ; served with 12th Division, 63rd R.N. Division, and 15th Division ; in last-named Division as D.A.D.M.S. ; Despatches, L.G. June, 1918 ; awarded M.C., L.G. Aug. 1918, and a Bar to the M.C., L.G. March, 1918.

ANDERSON, B. E. (D.S.O. L.G. 22.12.16) ; b. 15.9.81 ; s. of B. Anderson (late Chief Engineer, Madras Railway) and of a daughter of late M. O'Shaughnessy, Q.C. ; ent. Army 8.5.01 ; I.A., Nov. 1902 ; Lieut. 8.8.03 ; Capt. 8.5.10 ; Bt. Major 18.2.15 ; Major, I.A., 8.5.16 ; Despatches.

ANDERSON, CHARLES (D.S.O. L.G. 16.9.18), T/Major, R. Scots ; M.C.

ANDERSON, CHARLES ABBOT (D.S.O. L.G. 1.1.18) ; b. 22.1.75 ; entered Manchester Rgt. 5.5.00 ; Lt. 20.5.01 ; Capt. 7.2.11 ; Major 1.9.15 ; A/Lt.-Col. 24.10.16.

ANDERSON, CHARLES AGNEW (D.S.O. L.G. 1.1.18), T/Major, S. African War Supply Corps.

ANDERSON, C. F. (D.S.O. L.G. 1.1.18) ; b. 23.12.72 ; 2nd Lt., R.E., 22.7.92 ; Lt. 22.7.95 ; Capt. 22.7.03 ; Major 22.7.12 ; Bt. Lt.-Col. 3.6.16 ; Lt.-Col. 1.10.20 ; Despatches. He died 6.3.20.

ANDERSON, E. D. (D.S.O. L.G. 8.3.18), Major (Tp.), N. Staffs R. He died 13.11.17.

ANDERSON, E. P. (D.S.O. L.G. 1.1.17) ; b. 30.3.83 ; 2nd Lt., R.E., 13.1.03 ; Lt. 13.1.04 ; Capt. 13.1.11 ; Major 6.11.16 ; A/Lt.-Col. 22.11.16.

ANDERSON, FEARNLEY (D.S.O. L.G. 3.6.19) ; b. 25.9.83 ; entered Army 22.10.02 ; Lt. 27.6.06 ; Capt. 22.10.14 ; Major, Seaforth Hldrs., 22.10.17 ; T/Lt.-Col. 30.8.17 ; M.C. He was murdered in India 8.4.23.

ANDERSON, FRANCIS (D.S.O. L.G. 17.12.17) (Details. L.G. 23.4.18) (Bar, L.G. 8.3.19) (Details, L.G. 4.10.19) ; b. 15.3.88 ; 2nd Lt., R. Hldrs., 4.5.07 ; Lt. 20.6.10 ; Capt. 29.12.14 ; A/Lt.-Col. 11.6.18 ; Europ. War, 1914–18 ; Despatches ; Bt. Lt.-Col. 3.6.19 ; M.C.

ANDERSON, G. H. G. (D.S.O. L.G. 26.7.18) ; b. 22.4.96 ; s. of J. D. Anderson, I.C.S., and F. L. Anderson ; educ. Cambridge ; entered the R. Bgde. 25.1.18 ; A/Capt. ; Despatches, 1918 ; M.C. and Bar.

ANDERSON, H. (D.S.O. L.G. 26.7.18), Capt. (A/Major), R. Irish Rgt. ; S.R. ; M.C.

ANDERSON, JAMES (D.S.O. L.G. 2.2.16) (Bar, L.G. 26.3.18) (Details, L.G. 24.8.18) (2nd Bar, L.G. 2.12.18), Lt.-Col., H.L.I. ; served Europ. War, 1914–18 ; wounded ; Despatches five times ; C.M.G.

ANDERSON, JOHN (D.S.O. L.G. 1.1.18), T/Capt., R.A.M.C.

ANDERSON, J. D. (D.S.O. L.G. 22.8.18), Lt.-Col., S. African Mil. Forces.

ANDERSON, J. F. H. (D.S.O. L.G. 22.12.16) ; b. 10.12.83 ; 2nd Lt., Unatt., 27.8.02 ; I.A. 16.1.04 ; Lt. 27.11.04 ; Capt. 27.8.11 ; Bt. Major 3.6.17 ; Major, 27.8.17 ; Bt. Lt.-Col. 3.6.18 ; Despatches.

ANDERSON, J. S. S. (D.S.O. L.G. 1.1.19), Major, 56th Bn., Seconded 3rd Aust. Inf. Bgde. Hd. Qrs.

ANDERSON, L., M.B. (D.S.O. L.G. 17.9.17), T/Capt., R.A.M.C. ; born in Jamaica, 1879 ; s. of L. Anderson ; m. Mabel, d. of J. M. Cookes ; educ. Edinburgh University, and King's College, London ; M.B., Ch.M.Edin. ; D.P.H. London ; entered Army as Lt., 1914 ; T/Capt., 1915 ; T/Major, 1918 ; Major, D.A.D.M.S., 32nd Division ; D.A.D.M.S., V. Corps ; Despatches, 1917 ; M.C. ; Croix de Guerre (French) ; D.C.M.S., Ministry of Pensions.

ANDERSON, L. J. G. (D.S.O. L.G. 23.5.17), Commander, R.N., 23.5.17.

ANDERSON, P. (D.S.O. L.G. 15.7.19) (Bar, L.G. 30.1.20), Lt.-Col. Can. Infy.

ANDERSON, P. C. (D.S.O. L.G. 26.7.18) ; b. 16.11.94 ; m. Gladys Erica Abdy ; educ. Harrow School ; entered Seaforth Hldrs. 25.2.14 ; Lt. 28.4.15 ; Capt. 1.1.17 ; Major ; Despatches ; M.C.

ANDERSON, R. D. (D.S.O. L.G. 4.5.17), Capt., Carrier Section, E. African Trans. Corps ; M.C. gazetted 4.5.17 ; afterwards cancelled, and D.S.O. substituted (L.G. 22.6.18).

ANDERSON, S. B. (D.S.O. L.G. 4.6.17), Lt.-Col., 19 Batt. C.F.A. ; C.M.G.

ANDERSON, S. M. (D.S.O. L.G. 1.1.17), Lt.-Col., Aust. Artillery, A.I.F.

ANDERSON, T. G. (D.S.O. L.G. 4.6.17), Major, R.F.A.

ANDERSON, T. V. (D.S.O. L.G. 1.1.18) ; b. Ottawa, 4.7.81 ; s. of Lt.-Col. W. P. Anderson, C.M.G. ; m. Elizabeth Grace, d. of Col. W. D. Gordon, Kingston, Canada ; three d. ; educ. R.M. College, Kingston ; McGill University, Toronto ; entered Canadian Permanent Force (R. Can. Engrs.), 1905 ; in charge of Military Survey of Canada, 1910–14 ; served Europ. War in France, Feb. 1915, to April, 1917 ; C.R.E., 3rd Can. Division, 1916–17 (severely wounded ; Russian Order of St. Anne, 2nd Class with Swords ; Despatches 4 times, 1914–15 Star) ; Commandant, Canadian Engineers' Training Centre, England, from August, 1917.

ANDERSON, W. (D.S.O. L.G. 4.6.17), Lt., T/Capt., Northumberland Fusiliers ; M.C.

ANDERSON, W. B. (D.S.O. L.G. 1.1.17) ; b. 9.9.77 ; s. of Lt.-Col. W. P. Anderson, C.M.G. ; m. Lois Winnifred Taylor ; one s. ; educ. R.M. College, Kingston ; McGill University, Toronto ; first commission in Can. Permanent Force, Captain, 1905 ; Bt. Lt.-Colonel, Director of Military Training, Canada, 1912–13 ; G.S.O., 4th Canadian Div. Montreal, 1913, to outbreak of war ; served on the Staff, Canadian E.F. in France ; C.M.G. ; Bt. Lt.-Col.

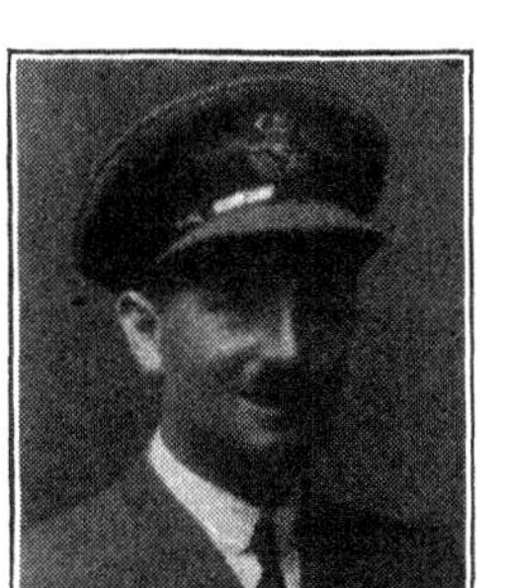

W. F. Anderson.

ANDERSON, W. F. (D.S.O. L.G. 1.4.20), Fl. Lt. (Pilot), R.A.F.

ANDERSON, W. H. K., M.D. (D.S.O. L.G. 1.2.19), Capt., Can. A.M.C., 16.6.12 ; Lt.-Col., 13th Field Amb. Can. A.M.C.

ANDERSON, WARREN MELVILLE (D.S.O. L.G. 1.1.19), Major, 6th Aust. L. Horse R.

ANDERSON, WILLIAM MENZIES (D.S.O. L.G. 2.12.18), Capt. (A/Major), 1/6th Bn. H.L.I., T.F. ; M.C.

ANDERSON-MORSHEAD, R. H. (D.S.O. L.G. 18.1.18) (Details, L.G. 25.4.18), Capt. (A/Lt.-Col.), Devons. R. He was killed in action 27.5.18.

ANDREW, F. A. (D.S.O. L.G. 25.8.17) ; b. 20.5.68 ; entered R.I.R. 23.3.89 ; Capt., I.A., 23.3.00 ; Major 23.3.07 ; Lt.-Col. 23.3.15 ; Bt. Col. 1.1.19 ; T/Brig.-Genl. 15.7.17.

ANDREW, W. C. (D.S.O. L.G. 8.3.19) (Details, L.G. 4.10.19), M.C., T/Major, 33rd Bn. M.G.C.

ANDREWES, F. E. (D.S.O. L.G. 14.1.16) ; b. 8.5.78 ; s. of Rev. Nesfield Andrewes and Katherine Andrewes (*née* Phillips) ; m. Margaret Agnes Malden ; 4 s. ; one d. ; 2nd Lt., R.A., 24.6.98 ; Lt. 16.2.01 ; Capt. 15.2.04 ; Adjt., R.A., 14.11.13 to 1915 ; Major 30.10.14 ; Bt. Lt.-Col. 1.1.19 ; Despatches. Lt.-Col. F. E. Andrewes died 29.3.20.

ANDREWES, W. (D.S.O. L.G. 1.1.17) ; b. 16.10.74 ; s. of the late W. J. Andrewes and G. K. Andrewes (*née* Lockwood) ; m. L. J. Vosburg ; two s. ; two d. ; educ. Beccles, Suffolk, and went to Canada with his parents ; served in S. African War ; Europ. War from 1914 ; Major, Can. Inf.

ANDREWS, G. W. (D.S.O. L.G. 14.1.16), Major, 8th Can. Inf.

ANDREWS, JOHN OLIVER (D.S.O. L.G. 26.7.17) ; b. 20.7.96 ; ent. Army 9.10.14 ; Lt., R. Scots, 1.7.17 ; T/Capt. 30.4.16 ; M.C. ; Despatches.

ANDREWS, JOHN OWEN (D.S.O. L.G. 4.6.17) ; b. 8.5.83 ; ent. Army 3.2.06 ; Capt. 3.2.11 ; T/Major 7.9.15 ; Major, R.A.V.C., 3.2.21 ; served Europ. War ; Despatches.

ANDREWS, R. J. (D.S.O. L.G. 18.7.17), T/2nd Lt. (A/Major), Devon R. (attd. Welsh R.) ; M.C. His D.S.O. was awarded for services in La Vacquerie 3–6th May, 1917. He was accidentally killed in Jan. 1923.

ANDREWS, S. A. (D.S.O. L.G. 8.3.19) (Details, L.G. 4.10.19), T/Lt. (A/Capt.), 7th Bn. R. Sussex R. ; M.C.

ANDROS, R. C. (D.S.O. L.G. 1.1.17) ; b. 7.2.71 ; s. of Capt. E. B. Andros, 95th Rgt. (Imp.) ; m. F. M. L., d. of Capt. Hewett, R.M. ; one s. ; three d. ; educ. Upper Canada College ; served four years in R.N.W.M.P. ; five years in Canadian Militia ; served three years with the B.E.F. in France.

ANGELL, J. (D.S.O. L.G. 1.1.19) ; b. 29.6.90 ; 2nd Lt., S. Lan. R., 5.1.16 ; Lt. 21.1.17 ; Capt., Dorset R., 23.12.17 ; A/Lt.-Col. 8.8.18 ; Despatches ; M.C.

198 The Distinguished Service Order

ANGUS, A. W. (D.S.O. L.G. 15.2.19) (Details, L.G. 30.7.19), T/Major (A/Lt.-Col.), 5th Batt. Cam'n. Hldrs.

ANGWIN, A. S. (D.S.O. L.G. 11.4.18), Capt. and Bt. Major, R.E.; M.C.

ANLEY, W. B. (D.S.O. L.G. 1.1.17); b. 3.5.71; 2nd Lt., R.A., 24.7.91; Lt. 24.7.94; Capt. 8.11.99; Major 7.10.11; T/Brig.-Genl. 8.11.18 to 28.8.19; Lt.-Col. 1.5.17; Despatches.

ANNAND, F. W. G. (D.S.O. L.G. 1.1.17) (Bar, L.G. 2.4.19) (Details, L.G. 10.12.19); b. 7.5.72, at Toowoomba, Queensland; s. of J. Annand and Harriet Annand (*née* Gadsby); educ. High School, Toowoomba; joined Queensland M.I. 4.2.97; Lieut. 28.5.97. His regiment was merged in the Australian Light Horse 1.7.03; Capt. 1.1.04; transferred to a Corps of Australian Engineers 6.1.06; Major 6.2.11; Major, A.I.F., and to command 7th Field Coy., Engineers, 11.11.15; 2nd Pioneer Bn. 1.3.16; Lt.-Col. 12.3.16; served Europ. War, 1916–18; Despatches thrice; Bt. Lt.-Col.; V.D.

ANNESLEY, A. C. (D.S.O. L.G. 15.4.16), Lt.-Col. (Tp.), R. Fus. He died of wounds 8.7.16.

ANNESLEY, C. R. T. (D.S.O. L.G. 3.6.16); b. 4.1.77; entered Norfolk R. 24.3.97; Lt. 31.12.98; Capt. A.S.C. 1.4.03; Major 5.8.14; Bt. Lt.-Col. 1.1.18; Lt.-Col., R.A.S.C., 5.1.21; Despatches.

ANNESLEY, J. C. (D.S.O. L.G. 23.7.18), Lt., R.N.; b. 2.8.95; s. of late William Gore Annesley; m. Cicely Anne Walton, d. of late James Craig; one s.; educ. Eastman's, Southsea; R.N. Colleges; served throughout Europ. War from 1914; wounded; Despatches; Croix de Guerre.

ANNESLEY, W. H. (D.S.O. L.G. 1.1.17); b. 5.5.76; s. of Lt.-Col. R. M. S. Annesley; m. Gertrude A. Reif; Major, R. of O., R.W.Kent R.; served Europ. War, 1915–17; C.M.G.; Brevet Major.

ANSTEY, E. C. (D.S.O. L.G. 1.1.19); b. 11.5.82; 2nd Lt., R.A., 21.12.00; Lt. 21.12.03; Capt. 10.5.13; Major, 18.8.15; Bt. Lt.-Col. 3.6.17; Despatches.

ANSTRUTHER, P. N. (D.S.O. L.G. 20.10.16); b. 2.9.91; s. of Rear-Admiral R. H. Anstruther, C.M.G. (third s. of Sir R. Anstruther, fifth Baronet), and Edith Flora, d. of the late W. F. Peel; educ. Sherborne School; R.M.C., Sandhurst; 2nd Lt., Unatt., 18.1.11; 2nd Lt., I.A., 27.3.12; Lt., I.A., 18.4.13; R.W. Kent R. 16.8.13; Adjt., 7th (S.) Bn.; Capt., R.W. Kent R., 27.3.15, serving with his regiment throughout the war; Despatches twice; M.C. His D.S.O. was awarded for services 13–14 July, 1916, Trônes Wood.

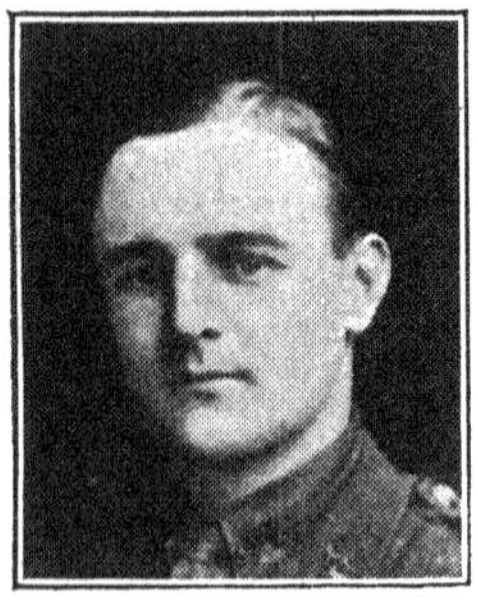

P. N. Anstruther.

ANSTRUTHER, R. A. (D.S.O. L.G. 4.6.17); b. 3.8.79; ent. R.A. 23.6.98; Lieut. 16.2.01; Capt. 24.11.05; Adjt. 5.8.14 to 29.10.14; Major 30.10.14; Despatches.

ANTHON, D. H. (D.S.O. L.G. 1.2.19), Lt., A.I.F.; M.C.

APLIN, H. (D.S.O. L.G. 4.6.17), T/Major, R. Munster Fus.

APPLEYARD, S. V. (D.S.O. L.G. 19.11.17) (Details, L.G. 23.3.18), Capt., A.A.M.C.

APSLEY, LORD (ALLEN ALGERNON) (D.S.O. L.G. 8.3.19) (Details, L.G. 4.10.19); b. 3.8.95; e. s. of 7th Earl Bathurst and Countess Bathurst (Hon. Lilias M. F. Borthwick, d. of Baron Glenesk); educ. Eton; Christ Church, Oxford; served Europ. War, 1915–19; Capt., 1/1st Glos. Hussars Yeom., Egypt; M.C.

APTHORP, S. E. (D.S.O. L.G. 15.3.16); b. 2.1.82; s. of late Col. F. E. Apthorp, R. Inniskilling Fusiliers, and g.s. of late Maj.-Gen. East Apthorp, C.B.; m. Molly Joyce, d. of F. L. Mainwaring; joined 3rd Batt. R. Innis. Fus., 1899; served S. Africa with Imp. Yeom. (Queen's Medal with 5 clasps); ent. R. Irish R. 28.1.03; Lt. 18.4.04; Lt., I.A., 15.7.05; Capt. 22.9.10; served 4th K.A. Rifles, Uganda, 1910–13; Persian Gulf, 1914–15; N.W. Frontier, 1919 (Despatches); Major, 96th Berar Infantry, I.A.

ARBUTHNOT, SIR D. (Bart.), (D.S.O. L.G. 3.6.18); b. 1.4.67; 2nd s. of 3rd Bart. and A. M., d. of Rev. M. C. Tompson; m. Alice Maud, d. of H. Arbuthnot; one s.; 1st commission 17.2.86; Colonel 19.10.17; retired 13.4.19; Hon. Brig.-Gen. 13.4.20; served Europ. War, 1914–18; Despatches; C.M.G.; Bt. Colonel.

ARBUTHNOT, E. K. (D.S.O. L.G. 21.9.17); b. 3.9.76; s. of Major A. E. Arbuthnot, Madras Cavalry; m. 1st, Evie Greene (who died in 1917); 2nd, Gladys, d. of W. B. Mann; educ. H.M.S. Britannia; joined Royal Navy as Cadet, 1890; Lt., R.N., 30.9.98; Commander, retired, 11.11.11; rejoined Navy, 1914; took part in Battle of Heligoland (Despatches); air raid on Cuxhaven; Battle of the Dogger Bank; operations in the North Sea (Despatches; Order of St. Maurice and St. Lazarus); Capture of Baghdad (Despatches; D.S.O.); Commodore of Convoys, 1918–19; Chief Constable, Oxfordshire.

ARBUTHNOT, G. S. (D.S.O. L.G. 21.6.19); b. 1885; e. s. of late Admiral C. Arbuthnot and late Emily Caroline, d. of Rear-Admiral C. F. Schomberg; m. Jessie Marguerite Henderson; two s.; one d.; educ. Summerfields, near Oxford; Stubbington House, Fareham, Hants; joined Britannia, Jan. 1900; served in H.M.S. Amethyst, Staff of Commodore Tyrwhitt. On this ship paying off he was commissioned H.M.S. Inconstant as Gunnery Officer, and remained there till May, 1918. D.S.O. awarded for services as Executive and Gunnery Officer of H.M.S. Inconstant; present at Battle of Jutland and in Bight of Heligoland, 17.11.17; commissioned H.M.S. Danae, June, 1918; served in her as Executive and Gunnery Officer until Dec. 1918; Cdr., R.N., H.M.S. Téméraire; Legion of Honour.

ARCHAMBAULT, J. P. U. (D.S.O. L.G. 18.7.17), Capt. (A/Major), 85th Can. R., 2.1.15; M.C. His D.S.O. was awarded for services on 9th April, 1917, on Vimy Ridge.

ARCHDALE, A. S. (D.S.O. L.G. 4.6.17); b. 8.9.82; ent. R.A. 21.12.01; Lt. 21.12.04; Capt. 30.10.14; Adjt. 28.5.15 to 19.2.17; Major 14.2.16; Despatches.

ARCHER, HARRY (D.S.O. L.G. 26.9.17) (Details, L.G. 9.1.18), Lt. (A/Major), Devonshire R. (S.R.). His D.S.O. was awarded for services on 31st July and 1st August, 1916, at Westhoek. He was killed in action 25.11.17.

ARCHER, HENRY (D.S.O. L.G. 1.1.17); b. 17.4.83; s. of H. C. Archer; m. Sybil Mary Cooke; one d.; educ. Oundle; R.M.A., Woolwich; 2nd Lt., R.A., 24.12.02; Lt. 24.12.05; Capt. 30.10.14; Major 3.5.16; served continuously in France, Aug. 1914–19; Croix de Guerre with Silver Star.

ARCHER, H. E. M. (D.S.O. L.G. 14.7.16); b. Aug. 1879; e. s. of late W. E. Archer, C.B.; m. Millicent Mary, d. of G. J. H. Pearson; one s.; two d.; entered R.N., 1896; served Europ. War from 1914; D.S.O. for mine-sweeping work.

ARCHIBALD, G. K. (D.S.O. L.G. 17.9.17); b. 12.5.85; entered A.S.C. 22.11.05; Lt. 22.11.07; Capt., R.A.S.C., 5.8.14. Major Archibald served Europ. War, 1914–17; Despatches; Bt. of Major.

ARCHIBALD, R. G., M.D. (D.S.O. L.G. 1.1.17); b. 1880; s. of Rev. W. F. Archibald, C.F.; m. Olive Chapman Cant; educ. Dollar Academy; Edinburgh University (M.B., Ch.B.); ent. R.A.M.C., 1906; Major; Director, Wellcome Tropical Research Laboratories, Khartum, since 1920; served Blue Nile operations, 1908 (Despatches); Mediterranean E.F., Dardanelles, 1915; Darfur Exp., Sudan, 1916 (4th Class Medjidieh and D.S.O.).

ARDAGH, P. A., M.B. (D.S.O. L.G. 15.2.19) (Details, L.G. 30.7.19), Capt. N.Z. Med. Corps; M.C.

ARGYLE, E. P. (D.S.O. L.G. 4.6.17); b. 7.9.75; ent. Army 23.1.04; Capt. 23.10.9; Major 10.7.15; A/Lt.-Col. 12.8.17; Bt. Lt.-Col., R.A.V.C., 3.6.19.

ARMITAGE, C. C. (D.S.O. L.G. 3.6.16) (Bar, L.G. 26.7.18); b. 12.12.81; m. Hilda, d. of T. J. Hirst; two s.; one d.; 2nd Lt., R.A., 6.1.00; Lt. 3.4.01; Capt. 14.7.08; Adjt., R.A., 4.11.08 to 26.7.10; Major 30.10.14; Bt. Lt.-Col. 1.1.17; Lt.-Colonel; Despatches 7 times; C.M.G.; Legion of Honour; Officer, Order of Leopold.

ARMITAGE, F. A. W. (D.S.O. L.G. 18.7.17); b. 12.9.83; s. of A. C. and A. B. Armitage; m. Eileen C. R., d. of Rev. E. R. Day, C.M.G., C.B.E., Asst. Chaplain-General, H.M. Forces in France; one daughter; educ. Cheltenham; Sandhurst; ent. W. Yorks. R., 1902; Lt. 6.6.07; Capt. 4.2.11; Major; A/Lt.-Col., Aug. 1916, attd. Hants R.; served on N.W. Frontier of India, 1908 (Medal); Europ. War. His D.S.O. was given for services 9–11.4.17, N. of Fampoux. He was killed in action 22.4.18.

ARMITAGE, F. R., M.B. (D.S.O. L.G. 1.1.17); b. 1883; s. of Dr. A. Armitage; educ. Oundle, and Pembroke College, Cambridge; entered R.A.M.C., 1914; Captain. He was killed in action 30.7.17.

ARMITAGE, T. W. (D.S.O. L.G. 1.1.18), T/Major, S. African Staff Corps.

ARMITAGE, W. A. (D.S.O. L.G. 1.1.18); b. 11.12.79; s. of W. H. Armitage; educ. Charterhouse; Clare College, Cambridge (B.A.); entered Army (Militia), 1906; Lt., 1908; Capt., 1912; T/Major, 1916; served in France, Oct. 1914, to July, 1915 (1914 Star); commanded Light Armoured Motor Brigade, Palestine; previously on Western Desert of Egypt, operating against the Senussi at Baharia and Dakla. D.S.O. awarded for 1st Battle of Gaza, March, 1917.

ARMOUR, S. D. (D.S.O. L.G. 3.6.19), Major, Br. Columbia R., Can. Mil. Forces.

ARMSTRONG, A. (D.S.O. L.G. 3.6.18). He was the eldest and only surviving son of the late J. S. Armstrong, Bengal C.S.; educ. Bedford Grammar School and Sandhurst, and joined the Wilts. R.; served 15 years and retired; became 2nd in command of the Wilts. Co. Territorial Bn.; left for India with Bn. in Oct. 1914, and in 1915 succeeded the Earl of Radnor in the command of the battalion, which he took to Egypt in 1917; was in the action at Gaza and during the advance to Jerusalem (D.S.O.). Lt.-Col. Armstrong died on 19.9.18, aged 43, of wounds received in action.

ARMSTRONG, C. L. (D.S.O. L.G. 1.2.19), T/Major, W. Yorks. R.; M.C.

ARMSTRONG, E. (D.S.O. L.G. 4.6.17); b. 16.1.69; entered H.L.I. 19.10.92; Lt. 1.1.95; Capt. 1.8.00; Bt. Major 22.8.02; Major 4.11.11.; Bt. Lt.-Col. 18.7.19; served N.W.F. of India, 1897–98 (Medal and clasp); S. African War, 1901–02 (Despatches; Queen's Medal and three clasps); Europ. War; C.M.G.

ARMSTRONG, G. W. (D.S.O.L.G. 19.11.17) (Details, L.G. 22.3.18), T/Capt., R.A.M.C.

ARMSTRONG, M. (D.S.O. L.G. 16.2.17); b. 24.4.85; s. of T. and E. Armstrong; m. Gertrude Mary, d. of T. A. McCoy. At the outbreak of war he was Third Officer, R.M.S. Ortega (P.S.N.Co.), which was chased by the German cruiser Dresden, and escaped through Nelson's Straits, a passage near Magellan Straits which had never before been navigated. His D.S.O. was awarded for gallantry on 2.12.16, as Lt., R.N.R.

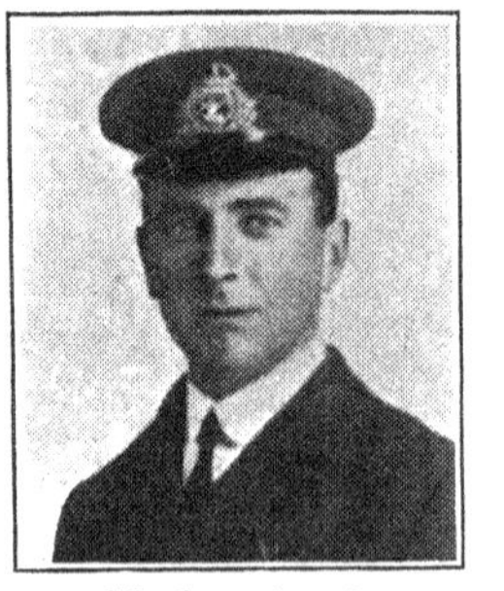

M. Armstrong.

ARMSTRONG, W. F. (D.S.O. L.G. 26.7.18); b. 13.8.85; s. of H. B. Armstrong; educ. Charterhouse, and R.M.A., Woolwich; enlisted R.G.A. 21.12.1904; Lt., Dec. 1907; Capt. 30.10.14; Bt. Major 1.1.19; M.C. and Bar; Despatches 3 times.

ARMYTAGE, SIR G. A., Bart. (D.S.O. L.G. 1.1.17); b. 2.3.72; s. of 6th Bart. and Ellen (who died in 1890), d. of Rev. A. Fawkes, of Farnley Hall, Yorks; succeeded father, 1918; m. Aimée, d. of Sir L. M. Swinnerton-Pilkington, 11th Bart.; two s.; one d.; 2nd Lt., K.R.R.C., 2.6.94; Lt. 21.8.97; Capt. 26.6.10; Adjt., Rif. Depôt, 16.5.03 to 15.5.06; Major, 18.3.12; Bt. Lt.-Col. 1.1.16; Lt.-Col. 18.12.19 (Despatches; C.M.G.); Colonel Commanding, 2nd West Riding Inf. Bde., T.F.

ARNOLD, B. M. (D.S.O. L.G. 1.1.18); b. 4.8.84; s. of B. Arnold and Emilie Arnold; educ. St. Paul's School and Jesus College, Cambridge; ent. Hants R.G.A. 28.2.10; Lt., 1911; Capt. 3.12.13; Major, 1.6.16; served B.E.F., commanding A.A. Bty. 1916–1918.

ARNOLD, C. B. (D.S.O. L.G. 8.3.19) (Details, L.G. 4.10.19), T/Lt., 6th Bn. Tank Corps.

ARNOLD, F. G. (D.S.O. L.G. 1.1.19); Major, Can. A.S.C.

ARNOLD, H. T. (D.S.O L.G. 3.6.16); b. 5.4.67; ent. Wilts. R. 8.6.89; Capt. 20.3.97; transferred to A.P.D. 4.7.01; Major 8.6.09; Bt. Lt.-Col. 3.6.18; C.B.E.

ARNOLD, J. E. (D.S.O. L.G. 1.1.17); b. 1882; s. of P. Arnold, London Manager, Bank of Adelaide; m. Nettie Beatrix Hughes; educ. Lancing College; served 4 years in King's Colonials (Yeomanry); ent. A.S.C., Sept. 1914; served Europ. War; Despatches twice.

ARNOLD, WILLIAM (D.S.O. L.G. 3.6.19), T/Major (T/Lt.-Col.), 2nd Bde., Tank Corps.

ARNOLD-FOSTER, FREDERICK ANSON (Christian names gazetted as Francis Anson (D.S.O. L.G. 1.1.18), Major, R.G.A.

ARNOLDI, F. F. (D.S.O. L.G. 1.1.17) (Bar, L.G. 27.5.19); b. 7.7.89; s. of F. Arnoldi, K.C., and Emily Louisa Arnoldi (*née* Fauquier); educ. Upper Canada College, and Royal Military College, Canada; Subaltern, 15th Battery, Can. F.A., C.E.F., Dec. 1914; served in France, 1915–17 (D.S.O.); N. Russia, 1918–19; Bar to D.S.O., Order of St. Nicholas, Russia.

ARNOTT, K. H. L. (D.S.O. L.G. 1.1.18), Capt. (T/Lt.-Col.), E. Lancs. R., attd. King's Shrops. L.I.; only son of Colonel N. Arnott, late R.E. Lt.-Col. K. H. L. Arnott was killed in action 30.5.18.

ARNOTT, R. (D.S.O. L.G. 1.1.17), Major, R.A.; b. 17.10.81; 2nd Lt., R.A., 2.5.00; Lt. 3.4.01; Capt. 26.11.12; Major 30.12.15; Despatches.

ARRELL, W. L. (D.S.O. L.G. 3.6.19), Lt.-Col., 14th Bn., Aust. Inf.

ARROWSMITH-BROWN, J. A. (D.S.O. L.G. 1.1.18); b. 1882; s. of J. P. Brown, J.P., and Mrs. Brown (*née* Arrowsmith); educ. Clifton College; entered the business of his uncle, the late J. W. Arrowsmith, Printer and Publisher, and after his death became Chairman of Directors of the Company. Many years a Territorial officer, he served at the front in France and elsewhere from 1915, in command of the 48th Signal Co. most of the war, and subsequently as A.D. Signals at Corps H.Q. (Despatches four times). His brother, Major Kenneth Brown, was also awarded the D.S.O.

ARROWSMITH-BROWN, K. (D.S.O. L.G. 17.4.17), Temp. Major, Devons. Regt.

ARTHUR, B. (D.S.O. L.G. 26.7.18), Major, M.G.C.

ARTHUR, L. F. (D.S.O. L.G. 1.1.17); b. 14.3.76; s. of late Edward Jenkins, M.P. for Dundee (Author of "Ginx's Baby"); m. Mona Emilie Hunting; one s.; one d.; educ. St. Paul's; Neuenheim College, Heidelberg; R.M.C., Sandhurst; 2nd Lt., Unatt. List, I.A.; 5.8.96; Lt., I.S.C., 22.10.97; Lt., I.A., 5.11.98; Capt. 5.8.05; Major 5.8.14; Brig. Major, Imp. Service Cav. Bgde., Sept. 1914; Egypt, 1914–16 (Despatches); France (Despatches; D.S.O.); 3rd Afghan War, 1919, G.S.O. (1); Waziristan Force; Despatches.

ARTHY, W. (D.S.O. L.G. 3.6.19); b. 30.3.68; ent. R.A. 17.2.88; Lt. 17.2.91; Capt. 1.7.98; Adjt. 17.7.00; Major 1.9.07; Lt.-Col., R.G.A., 16.10.15; retired 18.6.20.

ARUNDELL, HON. G. V. A. MONCKTON- (see Monckton-Arundell, The Hon. G. V. A.).

ASH, E. A. (D.S.O. L.G. 3.6.19), Capt. (A/Lt.-Col), Middlesex R., S.R.

ASH, W. C. C. (D.S.O. L.G. 14.1.16); s. of W. H. Ash; ent. Middx. R. 28.9.92; Lt. 31.7.95; Capt. 14.3.00; Major 1.4.09; T/Lt.-Col. He died of wounds 29.9.16.

ASHBURNER, H. W. (D.S.O. L.G. 22.12.16); b. 13.12.75; s. of Col. F. J. Ashburner; 2nd Lt., Unatt., 5.8.96; I.S.C. 20.10.97; Lt., I.A., 5.11.98; Capt. 5.8.05; Major 5.8.14; Despatches.

ASHCROFT, A. H. (D.S.O. L.G. 1.1.19); b. 1887; s. of C. W. Ashcroft; m. Bertha Elizabeth Tillard; two s.; educ. Birkenhead School; Gonville and Caius College, Cambridge; served Europ. War, Gallipoli, Egypt and France (Despatches thrice; Order of the Crown of Italy); played Rugby football for England and Cambridge University; Headmaster of Fettes College since 1919.

ASHLEY-SCARLETT, H. (see Scarlett H. Ashley-).

ASHMORE, E. J. C. (D.S.O. L.G. 15.2.19) (Details, L.G. 30.7.19); b. 11.7.93; 2nd Lt., I.A., 9.3.14; Lt. 29.4.15; Capt. 22.1.17; Despatches; C.B.E.; M.C.

ASHTON, C. G. ROSSI- (see Rossi-Ashton, C. G.).

ASHTON, E. J. (D.S.O. L.G. 14.1.16); b. Turnby, Lincs, 18.6.79; s. of E. Ashton, J.P., and Lucy Ashton (*née* Ashton); m. Mary Louise, d. of J. Webster; one s.; two d.; educ. Louth Grammar School; Lt., Light Horse, 1907; Capt. 1909; Major, 1910; served S. African War in Imp. Yeom. (Queen's Medal with 5 clasps); Europ. War, 1914–16; in charge of front line of 10th Batt. Can. Inf. attacks at Festubert on nights of 20–21.5.15; wounded both attacks; Despatches.

ASHTON, F. E. (D.S.O. L.G. 3.6.18); b. 25.11.67; 2nd Lt. York and Lanc. R., 28.6.90; Lt. 27.11.94; Capt. 5.2.01; Major 2.6.09; Despatches.

ASHTON, H. G. G. (D.S.O. L.G. 14.11.16); b. 25.11.69; s. of the late Lt. J. W. Ashton, R.N.; served Europ. War, 1914–19; T/Capt., W. Guards; severely wounded in the Battle of the Somme 16.9.16. His D.S.O. was awarded for services on 9th–11th Sept. 1916, at Ginchy.

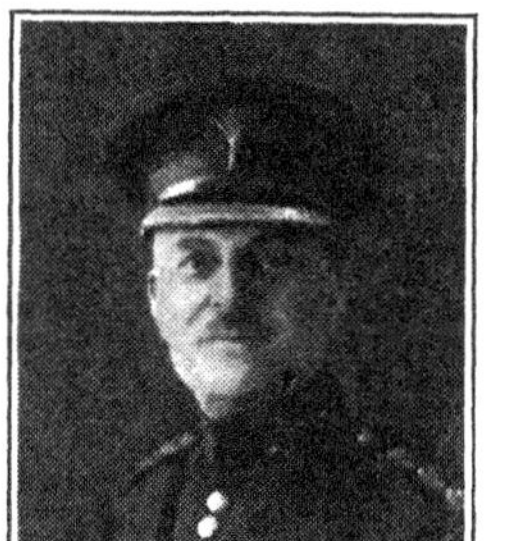

H. G. G. Ashton.

ASHTON, JAMES (D.S.O. L.G. 20.9.18), Eng. Lt.-Cdr., R.N., 1.5.15.

ASHTON, W. R. (D.S.O. L.G. 16.3.18), Paymaster Lt.-Cdr., R.N.R.; D.S.C.

ASHWANDEN, S. W. L. (surname changed from Aschwanden) (D.S.O. L.G. 1.1.18); b. at Watford; s. of W. L. Ashwanden; ent. R.F.A. (T.F.); Lt., 1904; Capt., 1908; Major, 1912; Lt.-Colonel, 1916; was given command of 5th London Brigade, R.F.A.; Despatches thrice; wounded, Aug. 1916.

ASHWELL, A. L. (D.S.O. L.G. 14.1.16); b. 19.1.86; s. of A. T. Ashwell; educ. Lambrook, Bracknell and Winchester College; joined the T.F. in 1911; went to France with the 46th Division 25.2.15; was wounded in May, and again in Oct. 1915; Despatches.

ASPINALL, C. F. (D.S.O. L.G. 4.6.17); b. 8.2.78; s. of H. E. Aspinall; m. Frances Maud, d. of P. Huth; educ. Rugby; 2nd Lt., 4th V. Bn. E. Surrey R., 1898; Lt., 7th Bn. R.F. (Militia), 1899; 2nd Lt., R. Munster Fus., April, 1900; Capt., 1906; Bt. Lt.-Col. 1.1.16; served W. Africa, 1900; op. in Ashanti (Despatches); S. African War, 1901 (Queen's Medal); Europ. War from 1915; Despatches 10 times; C.M.G.; Legion of Honour; also holds Order of White Elephant of Siam, 2nd Class.

ASQUITH, A. M. (D.S.O. L.G. 17.4.17) (1st Bar, L.G. 18.7.17) (2nd Bar, L.G. 18.1.18) (Details of 2nd Bar, L.G. 25.4.18); s. of Rt. Hon. H. H. Asquith, P.C., M.P., and Helen (who died in 1891), d. of F. Melland; m. Hon. Betty Constance Manners, d. of Lord Manners; 2 d.; educ. Winchester; New College, Oxford; joined R.N.V.R. in the beginning of the European War; served with R.N.D. Antwerp and Gallipoli (wounded); France (again wounded; D.S.O.; 2 Bars); retired with hon. rank of Brig.-Genl. His D.S.O. was awarded for services 3–4.2.17, near Beaucourt; First Bar for services on 23.4.17.

ASTON, REV. B. (D.S.O. L.G. 25.8.16); b. 1880; s. of Rev. E. H. Aston, Rector of Codford St. Mary, Wilts; educ. St. John's College, Oxford; served as Chaplain to the Forces, European War, 1915–19; wounded; Despatches twice.

ATKIN, B. G. (D.S.O. L.G. 2.4.19) (Details, L.G. 10.12.19); b. 12.11.84; 2nd Lt., Manch. R., 28.7.09; Lt. 5.3.13; Capt. 10.6.15; Despatches; M.C.

ATKIN-BERRY, H. C. (D.S.O. L.G. 3.6.18), T/Lt. (T/Capt.), Gen. List; M.C.

ATKINSON, E. L. (D.S.O. L.G. 21.6.18), Surgeon (A/Staff Surgeon), R.N.

ATKINSON, F. ST. J. (D.S.O. L.G. 1.1.18), Major, 9th Hodson's Horse. He was killed in action in France on 30.11.18.

ATKINSON, G. M. (D.S.O. L.G. 24.6.16) (Details, L.G. 27.7.16); b. 31.3.82; s. of late Lt.-Col. G. N. Atkinson, Shrops. L.I.; entered the K.R.R.C. 18.1.02; became Lt. 2.2.06; was Adjt., K.R.R.C., 1.2.10 to 30.11.13; Capt. 5.8.14; Major 18.1.17; served S. African War (Queen's Medal and 4 clasps); served Europ. War; Brigade Major, Australian Training Group "E," 21.4.17 to 13.9.18.

ATKINSON, G. P. (D.S.O. L.G. 7.11.18); b. 16.10.85; e. s. of Brig.-Gen. F. G. Atkinson, I.A.; m. Eileen Aylmer, d. of J. G. Wilson; one s.; one d.; educ. Reading School; enlisted 16.10.17 in 1st G. Hldrs.; commissioned 20.4.10 in L.N. Lancs. R.; Lt. 27.11.12; Capt. 9.2.15; E. Africa from 22.1.15 (actions of Bukoba and Mbuyuni); commanded M.I. Coy, and a mixed force near Maktau; present at several actions; attached to 17th Cav., I.A. (action of Wami River); later to 3rd Jammu and Kashmir Rifles, as Special Service Officer (Mgeta River; Behobeho; Kibambawe); mentioned in Gen. Hoskins' Despatch 7.3.18. In May, 1917, he rejoined 2nd Bn. L.N. Lancs. R. in El Arish; Adjt. from 27.2.18; Jaffa, April, 1918; France, May, 1918; 2nd in Command, 2nd L.N. Lancs. R., July, 1918 (Papcy; Tigny; Ouichy-le-Château, 29.7.18); commanded 2nd L.N. Lancs. in actions of Grand Rozoy and Wytschaete; 2nd in command during crossing of the Lys and advance of 34th Div. and 2nd Army to the Scheldt; and subsequently to 4.5.19; Despatches 18.11.18 and 16.3.19; Brevet Major 3.6.19; M.C.; Croix de Guerre, 1st Class.

ATKINSON, J. (D.S.O. L.G. 4.6.17), T/Lt.-Col., A.S.C. (Capt., A.S.C. T.F.); Despatches 4 times; O.B.E.; awarded the 2nd Silver Medal of the Alliance Française for literary services in France.

ATKINSON, J. D. (D.S.O. L.G. 26.7.18), T/Major, Liverpool R.

AUBIN, J. F. G. (D.S.O. L.G. 16.9.18), Capt., 6th Bn. (Territorial) The Durham L.I.; M.C. and Bar. He was killed in action 9.4.18.

AUBREY-FLETCHER, H. L. (D.S.O. L.G. 1.1.18); b. 10.9.87; s. of Sir L. Aubrey-Fletcher, Bart.; m. Mary Augusta, d. of Rev. R. W. Chilton; educ. Eton; New College, Oxford; 2nd Lt., G. Gds. 1.8.10; Lt. 8.11.11; Capt. 8.4.15; Bt. Major 3.6.19; M.V.O.; served in Europ. War (Staff); Despatches; twice wounded.

AUCHINLECK, C. J. E. (D.S.O. L.G. 25.8.17); b. 21.6.84; ent. I.A. 21.1.03; Lt. 21.4.05; Capt. 21.1.12; A/Major 21.2.16; A/Lt.-Col. 24.2.17; Major, I.A., 21.1.18; Bt. Lt.-Col. 15.11.19; served Mesopotamia; Despatches; O.B.E.

AUDSLEY, W. A. (D.S.O. L.G. 3.6.19), 2nd Lt., Aust. F.A.

AUSTEN, E. E. (D.S.O. L.G. 1.1.19); b. 19.10.67; s. of A. Austen; m. Cecile Buchanan; two d.; educ. Rugby and Heidelberg; served S. Africa (Queen's Medal, 4 clasps); Europ. War (Despatches twice); Major, late 28th Bn. London R. (Artists' Rifles); is Assistant Keeper in British Museum (Natural History Department of Entomology; in charge of collection of Diptera).

AUSTEN, W. S. (D.S.O. L.G. 3.6.16), Major, N.Z. Rifle Brigade.

AVERY, H. E. (D.S.O. L.G. 3.6.16), Major, N.Z. Mil. Forces.

AVERY, L. A. (D.S.O. L.G. 1.1.19); b. Queensland, Australia; educ. Queensland; Wadham College, Oxford; St. George's Hospital joined Yeomanry, 1902; became Major; served from outbreak of war, Egypt, Gallipoli, Senussi Campaign and through Palestine; Despatches; Order of the Nile.

AWDRY, C. S. (D.S.O. L.G. 2.12.18), Major, R. Wilts. Yeom., attd. 6th Bn. R. Wilts. R He was killed in action 24.3.18.

AXE, H. J. (D.S.O. L.G. 4.6.17); b. 20.8.63; entered Army 3.2.92; Lt.-Col 10.7.18; retired 20.8.18.

AYLEN, E. V. (D.S.O. L.G. 19.10.16); b. 5.3.77; s. of S. Aylen and A. L., d. of Capt. H. G. Haynes, late R.N.; educ. St. Helen's College, Southsea; London, Hospital (M.B.); entered R.A.M.C. as Lt. 27.6.01; Capt., I.M.S., 27.6.04; Major 27.3.13; served in China, 1901–5; India, 1908–15; Mesopotamia, 1916; Siege of Kut-el-Amara; prisoner of the Turks; Despatches twice.

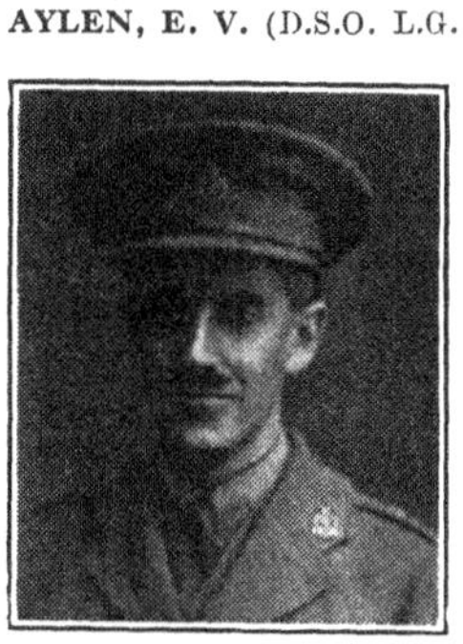

E. V. Aylen.

AYLMER, R. (D.S.O. L.G. 17.5.18), Capt. R.N.

AYLWARD, R. N., M.C. (D.S.O. L.G. 3.6.18); m. Agnes Scott Clarke; Major, R.E. (Spec. Res.).

AYLWIN-FOSTER, E. W. F. (D.S.O. L.G. 1.1.18); b. 25.5.91; s. of Rev. E. C. Aylwin-Foster; m. Dorothy, widow of Col. J. L. Swainson, D.S.O.; entered A.S.C. 14.1.11; Lt. 14.1.14; Capt. 14.1.17; A/Major 13.3.18; served Great War, 1914–18; Despatches.

BABINGTON, M. H. (D.S.O. L.G. 1.1.17), Lt.-Col., R.A.M.C.

BABINGTON, S. C. (D.S.O. L.G. 1.1.18); b. 8.12.66; Lt., R.E., 7.2.86; Capt. 1.3.96; Major 1.9.04; Lt.-Col. 2.11.12; Colonel, 2.11.16; Despatches; C.M.G.

BACCHUS, R. (D.S.O. L.G. 14.3.16), Lt.-Cdr., R.N.; b. 24.4.83; s. of Col. R. Bacchus; m. Gertrude N. Flenberg; ent. H.M.S. Britannia; gazetted Sub-Lt., 1903, and Lieutenant, 1905; Lt.-Cdr., 1913; in command of H.M.S. Grampus he served at Gallipoli, April, 1915, during landing of Exp. Force; also engaged in mine-sweeping in the Dardanelles (Despatches, D.S.O); commanded H.M.S. Napier, 12th Flotilla, Grand Fleet.

BACHTOLD, H. (D.S.O. L.G. 19.11.17) (Details, L.G. 22.3.18), Major, Aust. Engrs.; Despatches; M.C.

BACK, F. L. (D.S.O. L.G. 12.12.19), Lt.-Cdr., R.N.

BACKHOUSE, M. R. C. (D.S.O. L.G. 31.10.02) (Bar to D.S.O., L.G. 1.2.19). For D.S.O. see "The Distinguished Service Order" (from institution to end of 1915) by same publishers.

BADCOCK, G. E. (D.S.O. L.G. 4.6.17); b. 26.8.83; y. s. of the late Gen. Sir A. Badcock; m. Beatrice, y. d. of late J. Badger Clark; one s.; educ. Wellington College; Pembroke College, Cambridge; 2nd Lt., A.S.C., 4.6.04; Lt.; 12.6.06; Capt. 15.12.13; Adjt., A.S.C., 5.8.14 to 16.2.15; Major., R.A.S.C., 15.2.18; Europ. War, 1914–18; Gallipoli, Egypt, Palestine, Syria; Despatches; Bt. Lt.-Col. 3.6.18; C.B.E.

BADCOCK, K. E. (D.S.O. L.G. 21.6.19), Paymr. Cdr., R.N.; D.S.C.

BADDELEY, W. H. (D.S.O. L.G. 3.6.19), T/Major (A/Lt.-Col), 8th Bn., E. Surrey R.; M.C.

BADENHORST, L. P. J. (D.S.O. L.G. 22.8.18), Mounted Brigade, Permanent Force (S. African).

BADHAM, B. H. (D.S.O. L.G. 3.6.19); b. 11.11.84; 2nd Lt., R. Sc. Fus., 4.8.09; Lt. 23.9.11; Capt. 31.1.15; A/Lt.-Col., M.G.C., 28.10.16; Despatches.

BADHAM, J. F. (D.S.O. L.G. 27.7.18); b. 12.8.77; 2nd Lt., Worc. R. 23.4.02 Lt. 17.11.04; Adjt., Worc. R.; Capt. 18.9.14; Major 29.1.17; Bt. Lt.-Col 1.1.18; attd. Nigeria R.W.A.F.F. (Despatches).

BADHAM-THORNHILL, G. (D.S.O. L.G. 1.1.17); b. 25.12.78; 2nd Lt., R.A., 19.1.98; Lt. 19.1.01; Capt. 19.9.03; Major 30.10.14; Bt. Lt.-Col. 1.1.19; Despatches.

BAGGALLAY, R. R. C. (D.S.O. L.G. 1.1.19); b. 4.5.84; 2nd Lt., 11th Hussars, 13.8.04; Lt. 17.3.05; Capt. 2.3.11; Ret. Pay, 3.1.14; Capt. Irish Guards from S.R. 5.10.16; T/Lt.-Col., Irish Guards, 20.6.18; Welsh Guards 14.10.16; Despatches; M.C.

BAGNALL, C. L. (D.S.O. L.G. 1.1.19), Capt. (A/Major), 9th Bn. Durham L.I. (T.F.), attd. 50th Divl. Signal Co., R.E.; M.C.

BAGNALL, H. G. (D.S.O. L.G. 1.1.19); Major, R.G.A.

BAGSHAWE, E. L. (D.S.O. L.G. 7.2.18); b. 15.11.76; 3rd s. of late C. W. Bagshawe; m. Annie Josephine Lambert, y. d. of Lt.-Col. J. Sladen and Lady Sarah Sophia Sladen, y. d. of the 8th Earl of Cavan; educ. St. Cuthbert's College, Ushaw; Dover College; R.I.E. College; ent. Telegraph Service, 1897; served Europ. War (Mesopotamia), attached R.E., 1915–18; T/Major (A/Lt.-Col.); Despatches 7 times; C.I.E.; O.B.E.

BAGSHAWE, H. V. (D.S.O. L.G. 3.6.16); b. 11.8.74; Lt., R.A.M.C., 1.9.02; Capt. 1.3.06; Major 1.9.14; A.D.M.S., G.H.Q., Egyptian Exp. Force, 23.10.16; Despatches; Bt. Lt.-Col. 3.6.18; C.I.E.

BAHR, P. H., M.D. (surname changed to Manson-Bahr) (see Manson-Bahr, P. H.).

BAILEY, C. E. (D.S.O. L.G. 18.10.17) (Details, L.G. 7.3.18), Lt. (A/Capt.), Can. Inf.; M.C.

BAILEY, E. A. H. (D.S.O. L.G. 1.1.18), Major (A/Lt.-Col.), R.F.A.

BAILEY, F. W. (D.S.O. L.G. 20.10.16); b. 1871; s. of Surgeon Colonel F. J. Bailey; educ. Liverpool College; Liverpool University (M.R.C.S. England., L.R.C.P. London, 1894); commissioned in the 3rd W. Lancs., R.F.A., in 1903, and served in the Europ. War, being on active service from Aug. 1914; on foreign service continuously from 1915, and served on the whole of the British front as M.O. in the Field Ambulance Casualty Clearing Station (wounded; Despatches); D.S.O. for services on 12.8.16, at Guillemont, during the Battle of the Somme.

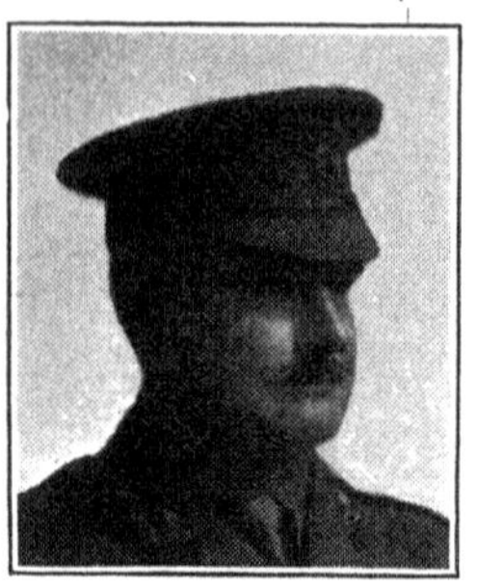
F. W. Bailey.

BAILEY, G. C. (D.S.O. L.G. 3.3.17); b. 15.7.90; son of Dr. Bailey; m. Phyllis, d. of Sir J. Foster Stevens; educ. King Edward VI. School, Stratford-on-Avon, and at Manchester University (B.Sc. Honours); served Europ. War, 1914–18; T/Major, R.A.F.; D.S.O. for services S. of Loos on 10.1.17.

BAILEY, H. (D.S.O. L.G. 26.11.17) (Details, L.G. 6.4.18), Capt. (A/Major), E. Lancs. R.

BAILEY, J. B. (D.S.O. L.G. 1.1.19), Major, 54th Bn. Can. Inf.

BAILEY, J. H. (D.S.O. L.G. 14.1.16) b. 29.1.71; s. of Rev. A. W. Bailey; educ. Oakham; ent. Shrops. L.I. 15.3.93; Lt. 6.4.98; Capt. 11.6.01; Major, 19.8.13; employed in B.E.A. Protectorate 1.3.99, to 14.4.04; with K.A.R. 6.11.05, to 22.9.08.

BAILEY, P. J. (D.S.O. L.G. 3.6.18), Major, Aust. L. Horse Rgt.

BAILEY, S. R. (D.S.O. L.G. 5.4.19), Cdr. (now Capt.), R.N.

BAILEY, V. T. (D.S.O. L.G. 14.1.16); b. 11.12.68; 2nd s. of late J. Bailey; educ. St. Columba's College, Rathfarnham, co. Dublin; King's College, London; ent. 8th The King's Rgt. 17.9.91; Lt. 1.11.93; Capt. 11.11.99; Adjt., L'pool Rgt., 28.3.00 to 31.10.01; Major 17.2.12; Bt. Lt.-Col. 3.6.17; retired Liverpool Rgt.; Hon. Brig.-Gen. 31.7.19; served S. African War, 1901 (Queen's Medal with 4 clasps); European War; Despatches.

BAILEY, W. G. (D.S.O. L.G. 8.3.19) (Details, L.G. 4.10.19), T/2nd Lt., 2nd Bn. Suffolk R.; M.C.

BAILEY, HON. W. R. (D.S.O. 14.11.16) (Bar, 11.1.19); b. 27.6.91; e. s. of 2nd Lord Glanusk; m. Victoria Enid Anne, d. of Lt.-Col. F. Dugdale; 2nd Lt., G. Gds., 4.2.11; Lt. 28.9.12; Capt. 15.7.15; Bt. Major 3.6.19; Lt.-Col.; served Europ. War, 1914–18; Despatches; D.S.O. for services 15.9.16, near Guinchy.

BAILLIE, D. G. (D.S.O. L.G. 18.1.18) (Details, L.G. 25.4.18); b. 1872; m. Mary Evelyn, d. of Capt. B. O. Cochrane, O.B.E.; served with C.T.O.'s, S. African War, 1900; Europ. War, 1914–18; Despatches; C.M.G.; 1919; Lt.-Col. Yeomanry.

BAILLIE-GROHMAN, H. T. (D.S.O. L.G. 17.4.18), Lt.-Cdr., R.N.; s. of Mr. and Mrs. Baillie-Grohman, Boxley Abbey, Maidstone; m. Evelyn, d. of A. S. Taylor, M.D., M.R.C.S., of Kingston-on-Thames. He was in command of a flotilla of mine-sweepers in Northern seas for nearly a year.

BAINES, REV. C. F., M.A. (D.S.O. L.G. 1.1.18); b. 1862; s. of late James Baines, Birmingham; m. 1891, Mary Helen, d. of Richard Carrow; educ. privately; Wadham College, Oxford; Wells Theological College; C.F., 1891–1918; served S. Africa, 1899–1900 (Queen's Medal, 2 clasps); Europ. War, 1914–18; Despatches three times; Rector, St. Ninian's, Castle Douglas, since 1918.

BAINES, C. S. (D.S.O. 1.12.14) (Bar, 2.12.18) (see volume " D.S.O." from its institution to 31.12.1915, by same publishers).

BAINES, E. F. E. (D.S.O. L.G. 23.10.19); b. 2.2.71; Lt., I.M.S., 28.1.97; Capt. 28.1.00; Major 28.1.09; Lt.-Col. 28.1.17; Despatches.

BAINES, J. C. (D.S.O. L.G. 16.9.18), Capt. (A/Lt.-Col), Leic. Regt.

BAKER, A. B. A. (D.S.O. L.G. 17.5.18), Lt.-Cdr., R.N.

BAKER, A. B. LL. (D.S.O. L.G. 3.6.18), Major, Oxf. and Bucks. L.I.

BAKER, B. E. (D.S.O. L.G. 4.3.18) (Details, L.G. 16.8.18), T/2nd Lt. (T/Capt.), Gen. List and R.F.C.; M.C.

BAKER, B. G. (D.S.O. L.G. 3.6.18); b. 23.10.70; s. of M. B. Baker, I.C.S. (Bombay) and Harriet F. Baker; m. Lorina, d. of Rev. A. O. Hartley; educ. Winchester; Military College, Dresden; served with 21st Hussars (India, detached to Q.M.G. Branch, Upper Burma), 1890–94; 9th Prussian Hussars, 1894-1900; Imp. Yeom., S. Africa, 1900–01 (Despatches twice; Queen's Medal and 4 clasps); joined Indian Corps Staff, France, 1914; 2nd in Command, 20th Bn. Midx. R., 1915; Major (T/Lt.-Col.), Yorks. R.; Lt.-Col. Commanding 13th Bn. The Yorks R., 1916; Br. Commissioner for Propaganda in Enemy Countries, Italian and Salonika fronts, 1918; Supreme Economic Council's Mission to Central Europe, 1919; retired Dec. 1919; Despatches twice.

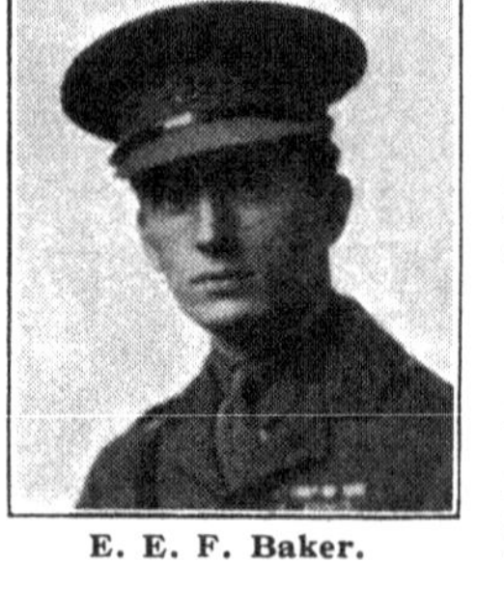
E. E. F. Baker.

BAKER, C. W. (D.S.O. L.G. 3.6.19); b. 11.1.77; 2nd Lt., Leic. Rgt., 13.7.15; Lt. 1.7.17; T/Major 25.2.18 to 11.4.19; M.C.

BAKER, E. E. F. (D.S.O. L.G. 15.2.19) (Details, L.G. 30.7.19); b. 5.4.95; s. of H. R. Baker; m. Mary Helena, d. of T. Sampson; educ. Sherborne; gazetted to 5th Middlesex Rgt. 15.8.14; served in France, 1914–19, continuously; Capt. (A/Lt.-Colonel); commanded 2nd Battalion, Middlesex Rgt. 1918–19; Despatches thrice; M.C. and Bar.

BAKER, E. G. P. (D.S.O. L.G. 15.2.19) (Details, L.G. 30.7.19), Major, 47th Bn. Can. Inf., W. Ontario R.; M.C.

BAKER, E. M. (D.S.O. L.G. 14.1.16); b. 15.1.75; entered the Manchester Rgt. 15.5.97; Lt. 17.8.98; Capt. 5.1.01; Capt., R. Fusiliers, 15.2.08; Major 12.2.13; was empl. with the W. Afr. Frontier Force, 1901–06; 1909–13. He served in the Europ. War; was given the Bt. of Lt.-Col. 3.6.17.

BAKER, HENRY (D.S.O. L.G. 26.4.18), Eng. Lt.-Cdr., R.N.R.

BAKER, H. S. (D.S.O. L.G. 15.2.19) (Details, L.G. 30.7.19), Lt., 13th Bn. Aust. Inf.

BAKER, J. M. (D.S.O. L.G. 3.6.16), T/Major in Army; Major, S. African Defence Force.

BAKER, R. G. (D.S.O. L.G. 17.3.17) (Details, L.G. 26.4.17), Major, Punjabis, I.A. He was killed in action 24.2.17.

BAKER, SIR R. L., Bt. (D.S.O. L.G. 1.1.18) (Bar, L.G. 4.3.18) (Details, L.G. 16.8.18), ; born 20.7.79; s. of 3rd Bt. and Amy, d. of Lt.-Col. Marryat; m. 1920, Elsie, widow of Major Boyd Cunninghame, and d. of the late Robert George Burrell. He served in the European War, 1914–18; Lt.-Col., M.P. (U.), N. Dorset, 1910–18; twice wounded.

BAKER, W. H. G. (D.S.O. L.G. 4.6.17); born 7.12.88; 2nd Lt., Unatt., 20.1.09; I.A. 29.3.10; Lt. 20.4.11; Capt. 1.9.15; Bt. Major 1.1.18; Despatches.

BAKER-CARR, C. D'A. B. S. (D.S.O. L.G. 14.1.16); b. 1878; served Nile Exp., 1898; S. African War, 1899–1902; Major and Comdt., Machine Gun School; Europ. War; C.M.G.

BALD, P. R. (D.S.O. L.G. 1.1.17); b. 27.4.83; 2nd Lt., R.E., 18.4.00; Lt. 18.8.03; Capt. 18.8.10; Major 2.11.16; Bt. Major 3.6.19; Lt.-Colonel; Despatches.

BALDWIN, J. E. A. (D.S.O. L.G. 3.6.18); b. 13.4.92; 2nd Lt., 9th Hussars, 9.9.11; Lt. 2.2.16; employed under Air Ministry 1.4.18; Major (T/Lt.-Col.), R.A.F.; Despatches; O.B.E.

BALDWIN, J. Y. (D.S.O. L.G. 1.1.19), T/Major, Army Cyclists' Corps.

BALDWIN, R. H. (D.S.O. L.G. 25.8.16) (Bar, L.G. 8.3.18) (Details, L.G. 16.8.18); b. 29.3.72; 2nd Lt., E. Surrey Rgt., 2.6.94; Lt. 22.12.96; Capt. 28.4.03; Major 10.5.13; T/Lt.-Colonel from 17.9.14; served in S. Africa, 1904; op. in Somaliland and action at Jidballi (Medal with 2 clasps); European War; Despatches. His Bar was awarded for services 7–8 July, 1916, Ovillers.

BALFOUR, A. M. (D.S.O. L.G. 4.6.17); b. 4.2.62; ent. R.A. 22.2.82; Major 13.12.99; retired 10.12.02; S. African War, 1899-02 (Queen's Medal, 3 clasps; King's Medal, 2 clasps); Europ. War, 1914–17; Despatches twice. His only son, Major J. M. Balfour, M.C., was killed in action in 1917.

BALFOUR, G. B. (D.S.O. L.G. 3.6.18) (Bar, L.G. 16.9.18), Major, A/Lt.-Col., R. Lancs. R.

BALFOUR, P. (D.S.O. L.G. 4.6.17), Major (T/Lt.-Col.), Bedfordshire Rgt. (S.R.). He was killed in action while commanding a battalion of the Worcestershire Rgt. on 12.12.17. A memorial service was held for him at St. Jude's Church, Hampstead.

BALFOUR, W. M. (D.S.O. L.G. 1.1.17), Major, Can. Mtd. Rifle Bn.

BALL, A. (D.S.O. L.G. 26.9.16) (1st Bar, L.G. 26.9.16) (2nd Bar, L.G. 25.11.16), Capt., Sherwood Foresters and R.F.C.; killed in action 7.5.18; Victoria Cross (see " The Victoria Cross," same publishers).

BALL, C. J. P. (D.S.O. L.G. 3.6.18); b. 15.2.93; 2nd Lt., R.A., 7.7.15; Lt. 1.7.15; A/Major, R.A., 24.4.17; Temp. Major 9.10.19; Despatches; M.C.

BALL, G. H. (D.S.O. L.G. 8.3.19) (Details, 4.10.19), Lt. (A/Capt.), 1/5th Bn. S. Staffs. R., T.F.

BALL, J. C. (D.S.O. L.G. 1.1.17), Major, Can. Fld. Arty.

BALL, K. M. (D.S.O. L.G. 26.7.18); b. 22.7.85; 2nd. Lt., R.A., 29.7.04; Lt. 29.7.07; Capt. 30.10.14; Major, R.F.A., 28.8.16; Despatches.

BALL, L. P. (D.S.O. L.G. 27.7.18); b. 22.1.82; 2nd Lt., S. Lanc. R., 23.4.02; I.A. 2.3.03; Lt. 23.7.04; Capt. 23.4.11; Major 23.4.17; A/Lt.-Col., I.A., from 17.7.17.

BALLANTINE-DYKES, F. H. (D.S.O. L.G. 4.6.17); b. 16.9.81; s. of the late L. F. Ballantine-Dykes and Edith Georgina, d. of the late R. Howard Brooke; m. Winifred Mary Miller; educ. Oxford; ent. Scots Guards, 1903; Lt., 1904; Capt. Oct. 1916; retired with rank of Major 1.4.1919; appointed 2nd in Command, 5th Bn. Border Rgt. (T.F.), 1920.

BALLARD, J. A. (D.S.O. L.G. 3.6.19); b. 19.11.79; 2nd Lt., R.A., 9.8.99; Lt. 18.2.01; Capt. 3.3.08; Major 30.10.14; Lt.-Col. 1.1.21; Despatches.

BALLINGALL, H. M. (D.S.O. L.G. 1.1.17); b. 14.4.78; 2nd Lt., R.A., 3.6.99; Lt. 16.2.01; Capt. 21.10.07; Major 30.10.14; Lt.-Col. 1.1.21; Despatches.

BALSTON, G. R. (D.S.O. L.G. 1.1.19); b. 27.2.79; s. of R. J. Balston; m. Edith Marion, d. of the late Lt.-Gen. Hon. B. M. Ward, C.B.; 4 s.; educ. Eton; ent. R.A. 9.8.99; Lt. 16.2.01; Capt. 3.3.08; Major 30.10.14; Lt.-Col. 1.1.21; Despatches.

BAMBERGER, A. P. W. (D.S.O. L.G. 4.6.17), T/Major, A.S.C.

BAMBRIDGE, R. C. (D.S.O. L.G. 13.5.18), T/Lt. (A/Capt., R.F.), M.C.; M.M. He died of wounds 23.5.18.

BAMFIELD, H. J. K. (D.S.O. L.G. 4.6.17); b. 18.9.70; Capt., I.M.S., 28.7.97; Major 28.7.06; Lt.-Col. 28.7.14; Despatches.

BAMFORD, E. (D.S.O. L.G. 15.9.16); V.C. (see " The Victoria Cross," same publishers).

BAMFORD, R. C. (D.S.O. L.G. 1.1.18); s. of R. L. Bamford, J.P.; m. Sybil, d. of late R. Edmonds; Major, W. Yorks. R.; served Europ. War, 1914–18; Despatches.

BANKIER, A. M. (D.S.O. L.G. 3.6.19); b. 2.5.94; 2nd Lt., Arg. and Suth'd. Highrs. 5.9.14; Lt. 20.2.15; Adjt., A. and S. Highrs., 23.9.15 to 22.5.17; Brig. Major, 26th Inf. Bde., Br. Armies in France, 11.5.18 to 13.2.19; Captain; Despatches; M.C.

BANKS, T. M. (D.S.O. L.G. 15.10.18); born 1891; educ. Elizabeth College, Guernsey; Private Secretary to Sir E. Murray, K.C.B., the Secretary to the Post Office; served Europ. War in France, 1915–18; commanded 10th (S.) Bn. Essex R. and 8th (S.) Bn. R. Berks. R.; Lt.-Col.; Despatches twice; M.C.; French Croix de Guerre.

BANNATYNE, E. J. (D.S.O. L.G. 1.1.17); only s. of A. E. Bannatyne, of Glen Bevan, Croom, Co. Limerick; educ. Wellington College, and Caius College, Cambridge; joined 19th Hussars in 1913, and went to France, Aug. 1914, and Egypt, Feb. 1916; as Flight Commander took part in the Darfur Exp. (D.S.O.); was given a squadron at Ismailia. Major Bannatyne was killed in an aeroplane accident at Cirencester 11.9.17.

BANNERMAN, B. (D.S.O. L.G. 2.11.17), Lt.-Cdr., R.N.

BANNERMAN, J. A. M. (D.S.O. L.G. 4.6.17); b. 14.9.81; s. of the late J. M. Bannerman, J.P., D.L.; m. Aline de L. Ryrie; educ. Wellington College; 2nd Lt., R. War. R., 5.1.01; Lt. 8.1.02; Capt. 14.12.12; Bt. Major 18.2.15; Bt. Lt.-Col. 3.6.19; served N.W. Frontier, 1908; in Zakka Khel and Mohmand country (Medal and clasp); served in France on Staff and in command 1st Bn. R. Warwick. Rgt., from 20.8.1914 to end of the War; Despatches 3 times.

BARBER, C. H. (M.B.) (D.S.O. L.G. 23.10.19); b. 10.3.77; Lt., I.M.S., 30.1.04.; Capt. 30.1.07; Lt.-Col. 1.7.15; Despatches; M.C.

BARBER, G. W. (D.S.O. L.G. 1.1.17); b. 20.11.68; s. of C. W. Barber and Isabella Barber; m. Janet Watson Salmond; one s.; three d.; served Europ. War, 1914–18; C.B.; C.M.G.; Despatches; Croix de Guerre avec Etoile; Col. Aust. A.M.C., P.M.O., 5th Military District.

BARBER, H. G. (D.S.O. L.G. 16.9.18), Major, Can. Rly. Troops.

BARBER, P. S. (D.S.O. L.G. 1.2.19), T/Capt., Gen. List; Bde. Major, 50th Inf. Bde.; M.C.

BARBER, R. F. (D.S.O. L.G. 3.6.18); born 23.12.80; Major, R.A.O.D., 1.7.17; Inspector of Ordnance Machinery, 3rd Class, 19.12.03; 2nd Class 19.12.09; 1st Class 19.12.18; Hon. Lt.-Colonel; Despatches.

BARBER, T. P. (D.S.O. L.G. 24.3.18) (Details, L.G. 23.8.18); b. 28.1.76; s. of T. Barber (late Capt., S. Notts Hussars) and Annie Barber; m. Beatrice Mary, d. of Col. Merritt, late of 20th Foot, and of a daughter of General Adams; two s.; three d.; educ. Eton, and Trinity College, Cambridge; rowed in Trial Eights, Cambridge, 1894; stroked winning Clinker Four (3rd Trin.), 1894; stroked 3rd Trin. 1st May Boat, and Light Four, in 1895 and 1896; joined Imperial Yeomanry, Dec. 1892; served in S. African War (Despatches twice; Queen's Medal with 5 clasps); served in European War, Gallipoli (Despatches); Palestine (D.S.O. for services on 28.11.17 at Tahta, Palestine; Despatches). Major Barber holds the T.D. He is an ex-High Sheriff of Notts, and is D.L., Notts.

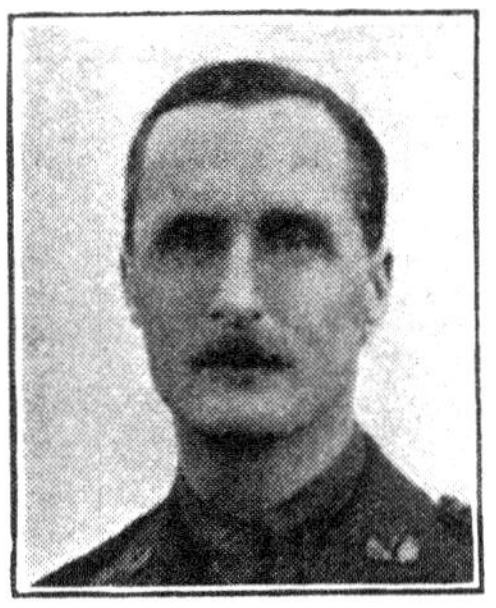

T. P. Barber.

BARE, A. R. (D.S.O. L.G. 16.9.18); b. 26.3.86; Capt., N. Lan. R., 1.7.16) Despatches; M.C.

BARFF, W. H. (D.S.O. L.G. 21.12.16); b. 30.1.77; s. of late William Barff, of Cadogan Mansions, S.W.; m. Nora Isabel, d. of late J. Dickson, J.P.; educ. Charterhouse; Bedford; served Europ. War, 1914–18; T/Major, Ches. R.

BARGE, K. (D.S.O. L.G. 1.1.18); b. 27.5.83; s. of R. H. Barge; m. Debonnaire Eva Ruth, o.c. of Major-Gen. Sir H. Mansfield, K.C.B.; two s.; one d.; educ. Larchfield Academy; Trinity College, Glenalmond; served in S. Africa with 3rd A. and S. Highrs. (Queen's Medal, 2 clasps); 2nd Lt., Sco. Rif., 9.9.03; I.A., 6.1.05; Lt. 9.12.05; Capt. 18.1.12; Major, 18.1.18; Despatches thrice; M.C.; Order of the White Eagle while serving in the Balkans at end of war; Major, 17th Cav., I.A.

BARKER, A. (D.S.O. L.G. 3.6.18) (Bar, L.G. 16.9.18), T/Capt. (A/Major), R.F.A.; M.C.

BARKER, C. (D.S.O. L.G. 21.6.19), Eng.-Cdr., R.N.

BARKER, E. F. W. (D.S.O. L.G. 14.1.16); b. 2.7.77.; e. s. of Col. Sir F. Barker; m. Enid, d. of Colonel Boyce, R.E.; educ. Dover College; 2nd Lt., Yorks. L.I., 16.2.98; served S. Africa (Queen's Medal, 3 clasps; King's Medal, 2 clasps); Lt. 29.3.99; Capt. 16.11.01; Major 3.5.15; was Asst. Signal Officer in Chief, G.H.Q., B.E.F., in 1918; Despatches thrice; Bt. Lt.-Col. 1.1.19.

BARKER, E. H. (D.S.O. L.G. 3.6.19); b. 22.5.94; 2nd Lt., K.R.R.C., 5.2.13; Lt. 27.11.14; Capt. 10.4.16; Despatches; M.C.

BARKER, F. E. LL. (D.S.O. L.G. 1.1.18); b. 7.3.68; 2nd Lt., R.A., 28.6.88; Lt. 28.6.91; Capt. 31.10.98; Div. Adjt., R.A., 26.10.00 to 31.3.01; Adjt., R.A., 1.4.01 to 31.3.04; Major 1.4.04; Lt.-Col. 30.10.14; Colonel 30.10.18; retired 20.8.20 with hon. rank of Brig.-Gen.; Despatches.

BARKER, L. W. (D.S.O. L.G. 3.6.19); Major, 4th Siege By. Can. Garr. Arty.

BARKER, M. G. H. (D.S.O. L.G. 1.1.17) (Bar, L.G. 1.1.18); b. 15.10.84; s. of E. V. P. Barker, of the Priory, Glastonbury; m. Barbara Maud Bentall; one d.; educ. Malvern; served S. African War, 1902 (Queen's Medal, two clasps); 2nd Lt., Linc. R., 4.7.03; Lt. 22.12.05; Adjt., Lincolns. Rgt., 4.5.10 to 3.11.13; Capt. 18.12.13; served Europ. War, 1914–18; Despatches; Bt.-Major 3.6.16; Bt. Lt.-Col. 1.1.19; Legion of Honour.

BARKER, R. B. (D.S.O. L.G. 20.10.16) (Bar, L.G. 26.7.17); b. 1870; e. s. of late Major J. Barnett Barker, 5th Fus.; m. Ellinor Gertrude, d. of R. Hobson, J.P., D.L.; two s.; entered R.W. Fus. 1891. He retired from the Army. He commanded the 22nd Bn. R. Fusiliers when they embarked for France. He served European War, and was four times mentioned in Despatches; awarded a Brevet Majority and gained his D.S.O., "For personal gallantry and marked ability between 1st and 3rd Aug. 1916, in Delville Wood." The Bar to his D.S.O. was awarded for services at Oppy Wood, Arras. He was present in the following actions: Vimy Ridge, 1916; Delville Wood, 1916; Beaumont Hamel, 1916; Ancre advance, and Miraumont Battle, 1917, and Arras, 1917; T/Brig.-Gen., Oct. 1918, and fell at Gueudecourt 24.3.1918, in the Second Battle of the Somme, in command of 99th Brigade.

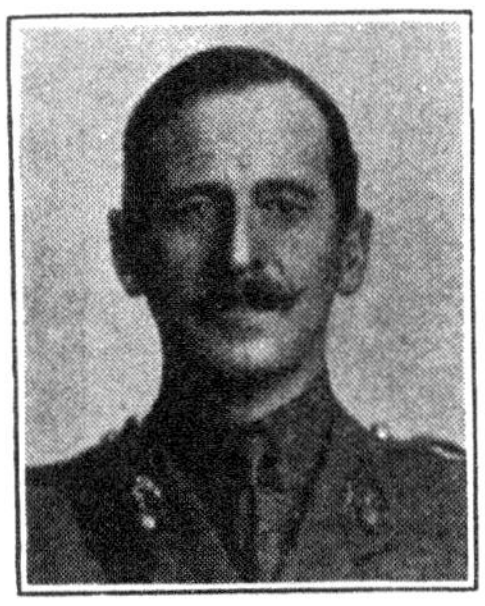

R. B. Barker.

BARKER, W. A. J. (D.S.O. L.G. 30.3.16); b. 1879; s. of Col. Sir. F. W. J. Barker and Jessie, d. of late J. Foster; ent. S. Staffs. R., 1899; served S. Africa, 1900–02 (Queen's Medal with 3 clasps; King's Medal with 2 clasps); resigned 1909; rejoined; served Europ. War, 1914–16; wounded three times; Despatches thrice; Croix de Guerre with Palms; Lt.-Col. commanding 8th S. Staffs R.

BARKER, W. G. (D.S.O. L.G. 18.2.18) (Details, L.G. 18.7.18) (Bar, L.G. 2.11.18); M.C. and 2 Bars, and V.C. (see "The Victoria Cross," by same publishers).

BARKLEY, J. (D.S.O. L.G. 1.1.19), Capt. (T/Lt.-Col.), R.A.M.C. (T.F.).

BARLEY, L. J. (D.S.O. L.G. 1.1.17); b. 7.7.90; s. of A. G. Barley; m. Muriel More Lone; two d.; educ. Taunton School; University College, Southampton; Kiel University and Queen's College Oxford; commissioned Cameronians, June, 1913; served in France from 1914; Lt. 2.2.15; Capt. 19.4.15; commanded Grenadier Company; Army Chemical Adviser, June 1915; Asst. Dir. of Gas Services Italy, Nov. 1917; Superintendent, Anti-Gas Dept. (Ministry of Munitions), 1919; Despatches thrice; Brevet Major; Croix de Guerre; Cavalier Order of St. Maurice and St. Lazarus of Jerusalem; Officer of the Order of the Crown of Italy.

BARLOW, J. E. (D.S.O. L.G. 16.8.17), T/Capt., York. R., S.R.; M.C.

BARLTROP, E. W. (D.S.O. L.G. 8.3.19) (Details, L.G. 4.10.19), Lt. (T/Capt.), Essex R., S.R.

BARNARD, E. (D.S.O. L.G. 25.8.17), T/Capt. (A/Major), Glouc. R.

BARNARD, W. G. F. (D.S.O. L.G. 4.6.17), Capt. (A/Major), E. Kent. R., S.R.

BARNARD, C. D. V. CARY- (see Cary-Barnard, C. D. V.).

BARNARDISTON, E. (D.S.O. L.G. 1.1.19); b. 28.7.71; 2nd Lt., R.E., 13.2.91; Lt. 13.2.94; Capt. 29.12.01; Major 13.2.11; Lt.-Col. 24.9.18; T/Brig.-Gen.; Chief Engr., 14th Army Corps, British Force in Italy, 1918.

BARNE, MICHAEL (D.S.O. L.G. 11.4.19), Cdr., R.N.

BARNE, MILES (D.S.O. L.G. 1.1.17); b. 15.3.74; e. s. of the late Frederick St. John Newdegate Barne and the late Lady Constance Adelaide Seymour, 5th daughter of the fifth Marquess of Hertford; m. Violet Ella, d. of Sir A. Orr-Ewing, 3rd Bart.; three s.; educ. Eton and Sandhurst; gazetted to S. Guards, Aug. 1913; T/Major, S. Guards; served S. African War, 1900–2; served Europ. War, Major, Suffolk Yeom. He died 17.9.17.

BARNE, W. B. G. (D.S.O. L.G. 3.6.19); b. 10.9.80; s. of late Capt. W. C. Barne, 14th R.; m. Dorothy Isabel, d. of Col. Malcolm, C.B., of Poltalloch; four d.; educ. Gore Court, Sittingbourne; Clifton; R.M.A., Woolwich; Staff College, 1910–11; 2nd Lt., R.A., 25.6.99; Lt. 16.2.01; Capt. 28.4.06; Adjt., R.A., 1.5.12 to 4.2.13; Major 30.10.14; served Europ. War from 1914 (Despatches); British Military Mission to Volunteer Army (Despatches); Anatolia, 1920; C.B.E.; Italian Croce di Guerra; Order of St. Vladimir, 6th Class; Staff, Army of the Rhine.

BARNES, A. C. (D.S.O. L.G. 14.11.16) (Bar L.G. 3.6.18); b. 13.10.91; s. of Sir G. S. Barnes, K.C.B., and of Sybil de Gournay Barnes, d. of the late C. Buxton, at one time M.P. for Cobham, Surrey; m. Honor Dorothea, d. of S. V. Coote; educ. Eton; New College, Oxford; T/2nd Lt. Yorks R., Sept. 1914; T/Lt.-Colonel 11.6.18; served in France and Italy, Aug. 1915, to March, 1918; commanded 4th T. Bn. Yorks R., June, 1918, to Oct. 1918, and 15th S. Bn. Durham L.I., Oct. 1918, to April, 1919; Despatches thrice.

BARNES, D T. (D.S.O. L.G. 26.7.17), T/Lt. (A/Capt.), Oxf. and Bucks L.I.

BARNES, F. P. (D.S.O. L.G. 14.1.16); b. 2.10.80; s. of Rev. Canon J. P. Barnes; m. Frances Alice Beck (who died in 1915; one son; educ. Bilton Grange; Rugby; Tonbridge School, and Magdalene College, Cambridge; entered A.S.C. 27.1.01; Lt. 27.1.06; Capt. 21.11.13; Major, R.A.S.C., 30.5.17; served Europ. War from 1914; O.B.E.

BARNETT, G. H. (D.S.O. L.G. 3.6.16); b. 12.11.80; s. of the late F. H. Barnett, of Glympton Park, Woodstock; m. Mary Dorothea, d. of late Rev. R. L. Baker; two s.; three d.; educ. Radley; R.M.C., Sandhurst; ent. Army 25.10.99; Capt. 9.10.07; Major 1.9.15; Bt. Lt.-Col. 1.1.18; served S. Africa, 1901–2 (Queen's Medal and 5 clasps); Somaliland, 1902–03 (Medal and clasp); Europ. War, 1914–18; C.M.G.

BARNETT, W. H. L. (D.S.O. L.G. 14.11.16), Lt. (T/Capt.), Bedf. R., S.R. The D.S.O. was awarded for gallantry on 3.9.16.

BARNISH, G. H. (D.S.O. L.G. 14.9.18), Lt., R.N.R.

BARNWELL, A. S. (D.S.O. L.G. 1.1.18), Major, R.F.A. (Spec. Res.).

BARNWELL, J. (D.S.O. L.G. 3.6.19); b. 29.3.84; 2nd Lt., Leins. R., 6.3.15; Lt. 6.12.15; Capt. 18.3.17; Despatches; M.C.

BARR, E. H. (D.S.O. L.G. 1.1.16); ent. R.M.A. 1.9.97; Lt. 1.7.98; Capt. 1.9.06; Major 15.5.16; ret. 17.3.19.

BARRETT, A. L. (D.S.O. L.G. 3.8.20); b. 9.11.72; 2nd Lt., Unatt., 30.8.93; Lt., I.S.C., 24.1.95; Capt., I.A., 30.8.02; Major 30.8.11; Bt. Lt.-Col. 1.1.18; Lt.-Col. 30.8.19; Despatches.

BARRETT, A. L. MOULTON- (see Moulton-Barrett, A. L.).

BARRETT, E. M. MOULTON- (see Moulton-Barrett, E. M.).

BARRINGTON, J. F. (D.S.O. L.G. 1.1.19); b. 30.8.81; s. of late Col. J. T. Barrington; m. Christine M. S., d. of C. Kuhling; two s.; educ. R.M.A., Woolwich; 2nd Lt., R.A., 22.11.99; Lt. 16.2.01; Capt. 27.4.07; Major, R.G.A., 1.12.14; Despatches; served Somaliland, 1902–04 (Medal with clasp); European War from 1915; Despatches.

BARRINGTON, HON. R. E. S. (D.S.O. L.G. 3.6.18); b. 1877; y. s. of 9th Viscount Barrington; m. Mary Georgina, d. of Lt.-Col. G. A. Ferguson; one s.; served S. African War, 1900–1, in Yeomanry; Europ. War, 1914–18; wounded.

BARRINGTON-WARD, R. M'G. (D.S.O. L.G. 1.1.18); 4th s. of Rev. M. J. Barrington-Ward, D.D.; educ. Westminster; Balliol College, Oxford; B.A.; President Oxford Union Society, 1912; Editorial Secretary "The Times," 1913, and Assistant Editor "The Observer," 1919; served Europ. War, 1914–1919, in France and Belgium; 2nd Lt.; subsequently Capt. and Adjt., 6th D.C.L.I.; served on Gen. Staff., G.H.Q.; Despatches 3 times; M.C.

BARRINGTON-WARD, V. M. (D.S.O. L.G. 20.10.16); 3rd s. of Rev. M. J. Barrington-Ward, D.D.; m. Barbara, d. of T. J. Pilling; educ. Westminster; Edinburgh; B.Sc. (Engineering), Edinburgh; Miller Prizeman, Institute of Civil Engineers; Capt., S. Lancs. R.; transferred to R.E.; Lt.-Col.; Despatches 4 times; Bt. Lt.-Col; Citation, French Army, and Croix de Guerre with Palm; Director Railway Operations, Ministry of Transport, 1919.

BARRON, J. O. (D.S.O. L.G. 11.12.18); b. 5.10.82; y. s. of late Netterville Barron; m. Evelyn Violet, y. d. of late Capt. S. Buckle, R.E.; one s.; educ. H.M.S. Britannia; joined R. Navy, 1895; Commander; served Europ. War, 1914–18; Despatches; M.V.O.

BARRON, N. G. (D.S.O. L.G. 1.1.18); b. 8.12.67; s. of Netterville John Barron, 5th Northd. Fus.; educ. Haileybury; R.M.A., Woolwich; 2nd Lt.; R. Art., 16.2.87; Lt. 16.2.90; Capt. 9.10.97; Major 2.5.05; Lt.-Colonel 30.10.14; Col. 30.10.18; Ret. Pay; Hon. Brig.-Gen. 29.7.20; Europ. War, 1914–18; Despatches; C.M.G.

BARRON, R. MACPHERSON (D.S.O. L.G. 7.2.18); b. 24.3.74); Lt., I.M.S. 29.1.02; Capt. 29.1.05; Major 29.7.13; Bt. Lt.-Col. 1.1.18; Despatches.

BARRON, T. A. (D.S.O. L.G 3.6.18), Major, R.A.M.C.

BARROW, B. W. (D.S.O. L.G. 1.4.19), Cdr. R.N.

BARROW, H. P. W. (D.S.O. L.G. 1.1.18) ; b. 20.6.76 ; Lt., R.A.M.C., 28.1.99 ; Capt. 28.1.02 ; Major 28.1.10 ; Lt.-Col. 1.3.15 ; served S. African War, 1900–2 (both Medals with 5 clasps) ; European War, 1914–18 ; Asst. Dir. of Medical Services, 17th Div. British Armies in France 2.11.16–17.9.18 ; C.M.G. ; O.B.E. ; Ordre de la Couronne Belge.

BARROWCLOUGH, H. E. (D.S.O. L.G. 1.2.19), Capt. (T/Major), 1st Bn. N.Z.R. Bde. ; M.C.

BARRY, A. G., M.C. (D.S.O. L.G. 3.6.19) ; b. 6.9.85 ; temp. commission 12.9.14 ; Capt., Manchester R., 7.5.16 ; T/Lt.-Col. 1917-19 ; Despatches ; M.C.

BARRY, C. B. (D.S.O. L.G. 21.6.18), Lt., R.N.

BARRY, REV. F. R. (D.S.O. L.G. 25.11.16) ; b. 28.1.90 ; e. s. of Rev. G. D. Barry, B.D., and Edith Geraldine Barry (*née* Reid) ; educ. Bradfield and Oriel College, Oxford (Fellow of Oriel) ; T.C.F., Nov. 1915 ; proceeded to Egypt ; served on two fronts, and took part in operations on the Somme (1st Battalion) ; the Ancre, Arras, Passchendaele, etc. ; subsequently S.C.F. of 20th Div. and D.A.C.G., 13th Army Corps. His D.S.O. was awarded for gallantry during the operations at Mouquet Farm, near Thiépval ; Despatches ; Silver Medal for Military Valour from the King of Montenegro.

BARRY, J. H. (D.S.O. L.G. 18.7.17) ; b. 18.4.88 ; 2nd s. of Lt.-Col. Barry, of Inver, Queenstown ; m. 1919, Ruth, y. d. of late A. G. Hanbury ; served Europ. War ; Lt., R.A.M.C., 11.9.14 ; Capt. 11.3.18 to 1.6.18 ; M.C.

BARRY, J. R. (D.S.O. L.G. 18.6.17) ; b. 19.9.89 ; s. of Col. Barry, of Inver, Queenstown ; m. Mary, d. of late Major H. R. F. Anderson, I.A. ; educ. Oratory School ; 2nd Lt., R.A., 23.7.09 ; Lt. 23.7.12 ; Capt. 23.7.15 ; Adjt., R.A., 29.10.19 ; Major, R.F.A. ; Despatches.

BARRY, O. C. M. (D.S.O. L.G. 3.6.18), Cdr., R.N.

BARRY-DREW, G. (see Drew, G. Barry-).

BARSTOW, J. N. (D.S.O. L.G. 3.6.19), Capt. (T/Lt.-Col.), Manchester R. ; commanding 11th Bn. M.G.C. ; M.C.

BARSTOW, W. A. T. (D.S.O. L.G. 18.1.18) (Details, L.G. 25.4.18) ; b. 22.7.86 ; 2nd Lt., R.A., 20.12.05 ; Lt. 20.12.08 ; Capt. 30.10.14 ; Major 19.12.16 ; Brig. Major, British Armies in France, 8.6.18 to 24.11.18 ; Adjt., R.A., 1.2.20 to 5.4.20 ; Despatches ; M.C.

BARTER, H. (D.S.O. L.G. 3.6.18), Capt. (A/Major), R.H.A.

BARTHOLOMEW, W. H. (D.S.O. L.G. 1.1.17) ; b. 16.3.77 ; s. of J. S. Bartholomew ; m. Violet Alice, d. of Major H. E. Penton, I.A. ; one s. ; one d. ; educ. R.M.A., Woolwich ; 2nd Lt., R.A., 23.3.97 ; Lt. 23.3.00 ; Capt. 25.3.02 ; Adjt., R.A., 17.7.06 to 18.2.09 ; Major 16.5.14 ; Bt. Lt.-Col. 1.1.16 ; Lt.-Col. 1.7.17 ; T/Brig.-Gen. ; Bt. Col. 10.8.20 ; Despatches ; C.B. ; C.M.G.

BARTLETT, A. J. N. (D.S.O. L.G. 1.1.18) (Bar, L.G. 24.9.18) ; b. 29.6.84 ; 2nd Lt., Oxf. L.I., 4.11.03 ; Lt., Oxf. and Bucks L.I., 22.1.06 ; Capt. 22.3.14 ; Bt. Major 1.1.17 ; Major 4.11.18 ; T/Lt.-Col. ; Despatches.

BARTLETT, B. S. (D.S.O. L.G. 3.6.16) ; b. 7.9.77 ; Lt., R.A.M.C., 25.4.00 ; Capt. 25.4.03 ; Major 25.1.12 ; Lt.-Col. 26.12.17 ; Despatches.

BARTON, A. S. D. (D.S.O. L.G. 1.1.18) ; y. s. of R. Barton, of Bathurst, N.S.W., Australia ; m. Dorothy, d. of W. J. Duffy, of Inverell, N.S.W. ; Major, A.A.M.C.

BARTON, B. J. (D.S.O. L.G. 18.2.15) (Bar, L.G. 4.2.18) (Details, L.G. 5.7.18) (see also " The Distinguished Service Order," from its institution to 31.12.1915, by same publishers).

BARTON, C. W. (D.S.O. L.G. 27.9.01 (Bar, L.G. 15.10.18) (see also " The Distinguished Service Order," from its institution to 31.12.1915, by same publishers).

BARTON, N. A. D. (D.S.O. L.G. 4.6.17) ; b. 29.11.57 ; 1st commission 16.2.78 ; Major 10.3.97 ; retired Connaught Rangers 29.11.05 ; Lt.-Col., Army, 27.5.19 ; Despatches.

BARTON, P. (D.S.O. L.G. 23.6.15) (Bar, L.G. 1.2.19) (see " The Distinguished Service Order," from its institution to 31.12.15, by same publishers).

BARTON, R. L. (D.S.O. L.G. 3.6.18) ; b. 1.5.75 ; 2nd Lt., R.A. 15.6.95 ; Lt. 15.6.98 ; Capt. 26.11.00 ; Adjt., R.A., 1.4.04 to 31.3.07 ; Major 30.10.14 ; Lt.-Col., R.G.A. ; served S. African War, 1899–1900 (Queen's Medal and 3 clasps) ; Europ. War ; Croix de Guerre.

BARTON, W. H. (D.S.O. L.G. 1.1.17) ; b. 30.5.74 ; e. s. of late Capt. C. R. Barton and Henrietta Martha, d. of H. Mervyn Richardson, D.L. ; m. Ardyn Marion, d. of late Col. H. T. S. Patteson ; one s. ; one d. ; 1st com. 12.12.94 ; Capt., Sc. Rifles, 25.1.00 ; Major 21.11.13 ; retired, R.A.S.C., 1.4.20 with rank of Lt.-Col. in the Army ; Despatches.

BARTTELOT, SIR W. B., Bart. (D.S.O. L.G. 22.12.16) ; b. 22.3.1880 ; s. of 2nd Baronet and Georgina Mary, daughter of G. E. Balfour ; m. Gladys St. Aubyn, youngest d. of W. C. Angove ; two s. ; educ. Eton and Sandhurst ; ent. Dorset R., Dec. 1899 ; C. Guards, Feb. 1901 ; served in S. Africa, 1899–1902 ; Europ. War, Dardanelles ; was Military Attaché, Teheran ; Bt. Lt.-Col. Sir W. Barttelot died 23.10.18.

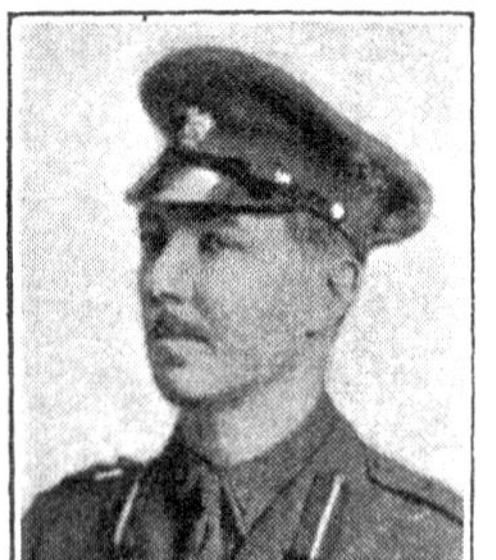

Sir W. B. Barttelot.

BASEVI, J. (D.S.O. L.G. 2.12.18), Major, Can. M.G.C.

BASSETT, J. C. (D.S.O. L.G. 1.1.18) ; b. 18.6.80 ; 2nd Lt., R.A., 7.4.00 ; Lt 3.4.01 ; Capt. 21.8.12 ; Major, R.F.A., 30.12.15 ; Despatches.

BASSETT, J. R. (D.S.O. L.G. 4.9.18) ; b. 27.10.78 ; 2nd Lt., R. Berks R., 1.6.98 ; Lt. 12.12.00 ; Capt. 2.6.09 ; Major 1.9.15 ; retired 1.9.20 with rank of Lt.-Col. in the Army.

BASSETT, T. P. (D.S.O. L.G. 23.11.16) ; b. 4.11.83 ; 2nd Lt., R.E., 31.7.02 ; Lt. 14.1.05 ; Capt. 31.7.13 ; Bt. Major 3.7.15 ; Major 31.7.17.

BASTARD, R. (D.S.O. L.G. 28.4.15) (Bar, L.G. 16.9.18) (see " The Distinguished Service Order," from its institution to 31.12.1915, by same publishers).

BASTOW, H. V. (D.S.O. L.G. 7.11.18) ; b. 2.7.78 ; 2nd Lt., Yorks. R., 20.12.99 ; Lt. 16.1.01 ; Capt. 14.2.08 ; Major 29.12.15 ; Despatches.

BATCHELOR, V. A. (D.S.O. L.G. 17.9.17) (Bar, L.G. 1.1.19) ; b. 24.8.82 ; 2nd Lt., R.A., 21.12.00 ; Lt. 21.12.03 ; Capt. 13.11.13 ; Major 31.8.15 ; Despatches.

BATCHELOR, W. M. (D.S.O. L.G. 3.6.18), T/Capt. (A/Major), R.E. ; M.C.

BATE, C. L. (D.S.O. L.G. 8.3.20), Cdr., R.N.

BATE, J. P. (D.S.O. L.G. 1.1.19) (Bar, L.G. 2.4.19), (Details, L.G. 10.12.19), Capt. (A/Major), Worc. R., T.F. ; M.C.

BATEMAN, C. M. (D.S.O. L.G. 14.1.16) (Bar, L.G. 16.9.18), Lt.-Col. W. Riding R., T.F.

BATEMAN, H. H. (D.S.O. L.G. 1.1.18) ; b. 3.7.88 ; 2nd Lt., R.E., 29.7.08 ; Lt. 18.8.10 ; Capt. 30.10.14 ; Bt. Major 3.6.19 ; Despatches ; M.C.

BATES, A. G. (D.S.O. L.G. 1.1.18) ; b. 19.8.91 ; 6th s. of late Sir E. P. Bates, Bart. ; m. Jean M. C., d. of Col. J. Hunter ; 2nd Lt., R.A., 20.7.11 ; Lt. 20.7.14 ; Capt. 8.8.16 ; Despatches ; M.C.

BATES, CHARLES (D.S.O. L.G. 28.7.18), s. of late Sir E. Bates, Bart. Major Bates m. Hylda, widow of Capt. G. M. James, and d. of Sir James and Lady Heath ; Europ. War. ; M.C.

BATES, C. R. (D.S.O. L.G. 1.1.18), 2nd Lt., R.A., T.F., 6.1.00 ; Lt. 3.4.01; Capt. 6.6.08 ; Major, R. of O., R.F.A. ; M.C.

BATES, F. S. MONTAGUE- (see Montague-Bates, F. S.).

BATESON, J. H. (D.S.O. L.G. 1.1.17) ; b. June, 1880 ; s. of H. Bateson ; m. 1st, Mary Elizabeth, d. of J. Prestwich ; 2nd, Madeline de Vere, d. of late Major-Genl. W. W. Hopton Scott, C.B., XIth Lancers, I.A. ; one s. ; one d. ; educ. privately and Manchester Univ. ; 2nd Lt., R.A., 28.3.00 ; Lt. 3.4.01 ; Capt. 16.3.12 ; Major 30.12.15 ; served N.W. Frontier ; Mohmand Campaign, 1908 ; Europ. War ; Gen. Staff and Staff of the Heavy Artillery ; Bt. Lt.-Col. 3.6.18 ; Despatches ; C.M.G. ; Croix de Guerre.

BATHER, E. J. (D.S.O. L.G. 4.6.17) ; b. 3.8.88 ; 2nd Lt., R.A., 23.7.10 ; Lt. 23.7.13 ; Capt. 23.7.16 ; Despatches.

BATHURST, SIR F. E. W. HERVEY-, Bart. (see Hervey-Bathurst, Sir F. E. W., Bart.).

BATTEN, A. W. CHISHOLM- (see Chisholm-Batten, A. W.).

BATTEN, F. G. (D.S.O. L.G. 1.2.17), Lt. 6.5.85 ; Capt. 6.5.96 ; Major 6.5.03 ; Colonel, I.A., 3.6.15 ; retired 13.9.19 ; Despatches.

BATTEN, H. C. C. (D.S.O. L.G. 3.6.18) ; 2nd s. of Col. H. C. G. Batten, O.B.E., and his first wife, Eleanor Frances, d. of J. Beardmore ; m. Dorothy Lilian Hyde, d. of Rev. E. A. Milner, J.P. ; one d. ; educ. Winchester College ; Trinity Hall, Cambridge ; Europ. War, 1914–18 ; Despatches 5 times ; Major (Hon. Col.), S.R., Dorsets. R.

BATTEN, J. B. (D.S.O. L.G. 1.1.17) ; b. 30.3.83 ; s. of Col. H. C. G. Batten and his first wife, Eleanor F., d. of J. Beardmore ; m. Mary Evelyn, d. of J. Loch ; one s. ; educ. Bilton Grange and Rugby, and at Winchester College ; 1st com. 4.5.01, R. Fus. ; Capt. 9.11.16 ; Major, 1918 ; A/Lt.-Colonel, R.A.F. ; retired 24.8.12 ; served Europ. War ; commanded 24th Bn. Manch. R., 1915–17 ; wounded in battle of Neuve Chapelle ; D.S.O. for Battle of the Somme.

BATTEN-POOLL, J. A. (D.S.O. L.G. 26.7.18) ; b. 5.10.89 ; 2nd Lt., 5th Lancers, 23.2.10 ; Capt. 7.3.17 ; Europ. War ; Despatches ; M.C.

BATTERSHILL, L. W. (D.S.O. L.G. 4.3.18) (Details, L.G. 16.8.18), T/Lt., M.G.C. ; M.C.

BATTINE, R. ST. C. (D.S.O. L.G. 3.6.18) ; b. 4.9.69 ; 2nd Lt., 16th Lancers 23.7.90 ; Lt., 16th Lancers, 23.5.91 ; Lt., I.S.C., 31.7.94 ; Capt., I.A., 10.7.01 ; Major 23.7.08 ; Lt.-Col. 23.7.16 ; retired 14.11.19 ; served in Europ. War from 1914 ; Despatches.

BATTYE, B. C. (D.S.O. L.G. 24.6.16) (Details, L.G. 27.7.16) ; b. 24.9.82 ; s. of Major L. R. Battye, late 5th Gurkhas ; m. Edith Lilian d. of J. W. Cole ; two s. ; two d. ; educ. R.M.A., Woolwich ; ent. R.E., 18.8.00 ; Lt. 18.8.03 ; Capt. 18.8.10 ; served Somaliland, 1903–4 (Medal and clasp) ; Europ. War, 1914–18 ; wounded ; Despatches 7 times ; Bt. Major 3.6.15 ; Bt. Lt.-Col. 1.1.19 ; D.S.O. for services at Vimy Ridge 21–25 May, 1916.

BATTYE, I. U. (D.S.O. L.G. 26.6.16) ; b. 5.3.75 ; 5th s. of late Major L. R. Battye, 5th Gurkha Rifles ; m. Marie, d. of late Col. J. Robertson ; two s. ; two d. ; educ. Combe Down School, Bath ; Sandhurst ; 2nd Lt., Unatt., 16.1.95 ; I.S.C. 1.4.96 ; Lt., I.A., 17.7.97 ; Capt. 16.1.04 ; Major, I.A., 16.1.13 ; served N.W. Frontier of India, 1897–98 (Medal with 2 clasps) ; N.W. Frontier of India, 1915 ; dangerously wounded ; Despatches ; D.S.O. ; again served on N.W. Frontier, 1916–17 ; Mesopotamia, 1917 ; Palestine and Syria, 1918 (Despatches) ; Syria, 1919 ; Despatches ; Bt. of Lt.-Col. 3.6.19, Q.V.O. Corps of Guides, F.F.

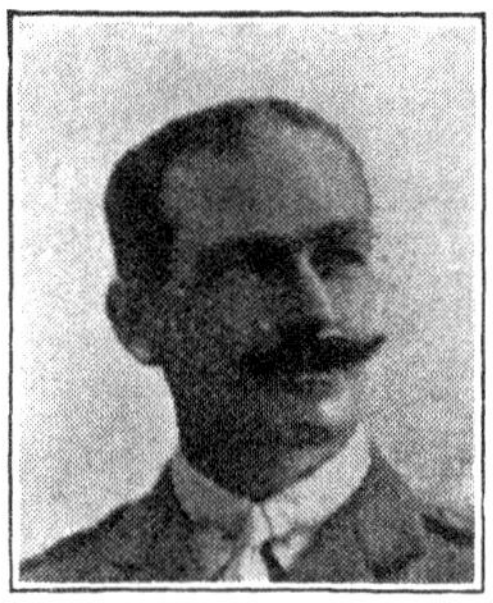

I. U. Battye.

BATTYE, W. R., M.R.C.S., L.R.C.P., M.B., B.S. (D.S.O. L.G. 2.2.16) ; b. 20.1.1874 ; 3rd s. of late Major L. R. Battye, 5th Gurkha Rifles, F.F., and Margaret, e. d. of Major-General Augustus Moffat ; m. Maud St. G., d. of late Lt.-Col. A. O. Molesworth, R.A. ; two s. ; one d. ; educ. privately ; University College, London ; Army Medical School, Netley ; Lt., I.M.S., 27.7.98 ; Capt. 27.7.01 ; Major 28.1.10 ; Lt.-Col. 28.1.18 ; O.C. 108th Indian Field Ambulance, 1914 ; served for three months at Cape Helles with 29th Division, and four and a half months at Anzac, till the evacuation ; Despatches ; Knight of the Legion of Honour.

BAUDAINS, G. LA C. (D.S.O. L.G. 26.7.18) ; y. son of P. A. Baudains ; educ. Modern School, Jersey ; King's College, London ; Capt. 9th Batt. R.F. ; served France from Jan. 1915 ; Despatches ; M.C. ; three times wounded.

BAUGH, G. J. (D.S.O. L.G. 4.6.17) ; b. 1862 ; s. of H. B. Baugh, Col., Bengal S.C. ; m. Grace Geraldine, d. of E. Franks ; two s. ; educ. Westward Ho ! College ; ent. R.I.M., 1882 ; Lt., 1884 ; Cdr., 1894 ; Capt., 1920 ; Temp. Major, 1915, War Office, as D.A.D. of Movements ; served in France as A.D. and D.D., Inland Water Transport, R.E., 1915–17, with rank of Col. ; Despatches twice.

BAUGH, R. S. (D.S.O. L.G. 14.11.16) ; b. 1889 ; s. of R. B. Baugh ; Capt., C. Gds., S.R. ; served Europ. War ; wounded ; Despatches ; D.S.O. for services on 15.9.16 at Les Bœufs.

BAULD, R. S. (D.S.O. L.G. 15.2.19) (Details, L.G. 30.7.19), 2nd Lt., Lancs. Fus., T.F. ; M.C.

BAULD, W. A. G. (D.S.O. L.G. 1.2.19), Major (A/Lt.-Col.), C.A.M.C.

BAUMGARTNER, J. S. J. (see Percy, Sir J. S. J.).

BAWDEN, V. C. (D.S.O. L.G. 1.1.17) ; b. 5.6.86 ; 2nd s. of late H. Bawden ; m. Ada Walton, d. of late T. White ; one s. ; commissioned in 17th Bn. London R., 1909 ; Capt., 1912 ; Major ; has been Adjt., Company Commander and Second-in-Command ; was Brigade Major, April, 1917 ; Despatches twice.

BAXTER, G. L. (D.S.O. L.G. 25.11.16) ; b. 18.1.83 ; s. of E. A. Baxter and Isobel, d. of late W. Scott Elliot ; educ. Eton ; 1st com. 5.4.05 ; Capt. 12.10.14 ; retired as Lt.-Col., Army, 9.10.20 ; served Europ. War, 1914–18 ; T/Lt.-Col., 1st K.A. Rifles, Nyasaland F.F. ; several times mentioned in Despatches. Among other mentions the Govt. Gazette of 11.10.15 says : " Capt. G. L. Baxter displayed conspicuous coolness at Kasoa on 9.9.14, inspiring confidence in the troops by his contempt of danger." An extract from the Nyasaland Govt.

Gazette says of Capt. Baxter: "At the engagement at Malangali on the 24th July, this officer was in command of part of the force which was attacked by the enemy in far superior numbers. He showed great ability in the disposition of his forces, and by his coolness under heavy and accurate maxim and rifle fire, maintained the confidence of his men and repulsed the enemy with considerable losses. He also assisted No. 108 Rifleman A. A. Vial (1st South African Rifles) to bring off 2nd Lieut. McKenzie, who was severely wounded, under a heavy and accurate machine-gun fire."

BAYLAY, A. C. (D.S.O. L.G. 1.1.17); b. 1.9.79; s. of late Col. F. G. Baylay, R.A.; m. Maria Edmondson, d. of late Governor J. B. Groome, of Maryland, U.S.A.; one d.; educ. Cheltenham College; R.M. Academy, Woolwich; 2nd Lt., R.E., 23.12.1898; Lt., 1901; Capt., 1907; Major, 1915; Bt. Lt.-Col., 1918; Lt.-Col. 27.6.19; retired R.E. 27.6.19; Hon. Brig.-Genl. 7.6.19; served Europ. War, 1915–18; Despatches.

BAYLAY, E. J. L. (D.S.O. L.G. 23.10.19); b. 12.12.81; s. of late Col. C. Baylay, Bengal H.A.; m. Violet Mary, d. of Rear-Admiral Hon. R. Bingham; two s.; one d.; educ. Wellington; 1st commission 23.7.01; Major 10.11.15; retired R.A. 1.7.20; served Europ. War (Mesopotamia), 1914–16; Despatches.

BAYLEY, A. F. (D.S.O. L.G. 1.1.19); b. 8.3.78; 2nd Lt., R.A., 2.5.00; Lt. 3.4.21; Capt. 25.9.09; Major 30.10.14; A/Lt.-Col.; Despatches.

BAYLEY, A. G. (D.S.O. L.G. 3.3.16); b. 5.7.78; 2nd Lt., Oxf. L.I., 7.5.98; Lt. 4.11.99; Capt. 3.10.04; Major 1.9.15; served S. African War; Queen's Medal with 3 clasps, and King's Medal with 2 clasps; served Europ. War; Despatches; Bt. Lt.-Col. 3.6.18; C.B.E.

BAYLEY, L. S. (D.S.O. L.G. 3.6.18); b. 2.7.1875; s. of Sir S. C. Bayley, G.C.S.I.; m. Sybil Dora, d. of late Major L. F. Barton, R. Scots; one d.; 2nd Lt., R.A., 15.6.95; Lt. 15.6 98; Capt. 23.1.01; Major 30.10.14; Europ. War, 1914–18; Despatches; Bt. Lt.-Col. 8.11.15; M.C.; Croix de Guerre.

BAYLISS, H. V., M.C. (D.S.O. L.G. 2.4.19) (Details, L.G. 10.12.19): b. 20.3.85; 2nd Lt., E. Surrey Rgt., 24.7.07; Lt. 4.8.09; Adjt., E. Surrey Rgt., 1.11.12 to 17.12.15; Capt. 27.8.14; Despatches.

BAYLY A. R. (D.S.O. L.G. 30.1.20); b. 7.3.71; 2nd Lt., R.A., 14.2.90; Lt. 14.2.93; Capt. 3.2.00; Major 14.10.07; Lt.-Col. 30.10.14; Despatches; O.B.E.

BAYLY, E. A. T. (D.S.O. L.G. 1.1.17); b. 19.6.77; s. of late Col. E. R. Bayly, D.L.; m. Ileene Caroline Ethel Otway, d. of Major Inglefield; educ. Radley College; University College, Oxford; 2nd Lt., R.W.F., 1899; Capt., 1907; Major, 1915; S. Africa, 1899–02; severely wounded; Queen's Medal with 5 clasps; King's Medal with 2 clasps; Sudan, 1908 (Egyptian Medal and clasps); Sudan, 1910 (Sudan Medal with clasp); Sudan, 1916; conquest of Darfur (Despatches; clasp to Sudan Medal; D.S.O.); Sudan, 1917; operations against Lan Miers (in command); Despatches; 3rd Class Order of the Nile and clasp to Sudan Medal; Palestine, 1918.

BAYNE-JARDINE, C. W. (D.S.O. L.G. 26.7.17); b. 25.7.88; 2nd Lt., R.A., 23.7.09; Lt. 23.7.12; Capt. 23.7.15; Major 31.8.18; Despatches; M.C.

BAYNE-JARDINE, T. E. (D.S.O. L.G. 3.6.18), T/2nd Lt., Spec. List.

BAYNES-REED, REV. W. L. (D.S.O. L.G. 1.2.19), Can. Chaplains' Service.

BAYNHAM, C. T. (D.S.O. L.G. 3.6.18); b. 7.1.89; s. of late Rev. J. F. Baynham; m. Elsie Dorothea, d. of late Lt.-Col. C. Conyers, R.I. Fus.; educ. Dover College; Jesus College, Cambridge (B.A.); joined R.A. 20.7.11; Lt. 20.7.14; Capt. 8.8.16; proceeded to France with 4th Division; Brig. Major, R.A., 31st Div. from 12.11.18; Despatches thrice; commanded B Battery, 285th Bde. R.F.A., 57th Division; Capt. R.H.A.

BAZIN, A. T. (D.S.O. L.G. 1.1.18), Major, Can A.M.C.

BAZLEY-WHITE, R. B. L. (D.S.O. L.G. 8.8.17); b. 25.5.86; 2nd Lt., R.W. Kent R., 23.5.06; Lt. 1.3.09; Capt. 28.10.14; Despatches. He was accidentally killed.

BEACH, L. H. F. (D.S.O. L.G. 16.8.17), Capt., 4th Batt. (T.) R.W. Surrey R. D.S.O. awarded for services in Egypt 27.3.17. He died 28.11.18.

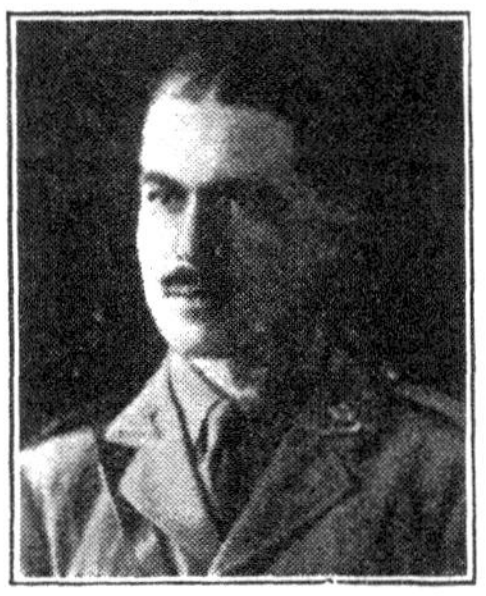

L. H. F. Beach.

BEACH, W. H. (D.S.O. L.G. 23.11.16); b. 7.6.71; s. of Rev. Canon W. R. Beach; m. 1914, Constance M., d. of A. A. Cammell, 14th Hussars; 2nd Lt., R.E., 27.7.89; Lt. 27.7.92; Capt. 28.5.00; Major 27.7.09; Bt. Lt.-Col. 1.1.16; Lt.-Col. 1.7.17; Bt. Col. 3.6.18; C.B.; C.M.G.; Despatches.

BEADON, L. R. (D.S.O. L.G. 1.1.18); b. 11.12.75; y. s. of late Sir Cecil Beadon, K.C.S.I.; m. 1904, Hilda M., e. d. of late Major-Genl. A. C. Roper, C.V.O.; one d.; educ. Winchester and Sandhurst; 2nd Lt., W.I.R., 5.9.96; Lt. 22.12.97; Capt. 5.11.00; Capt., A.S.C., 1.2.02; Adjt. 4.10.07–16.9.10; Major 18.12.13; Lt.-Col. 26.9.18; served W. Africa, 1897–8 (clasp); Sierra Leone, 1898–9 (clasp); Europ. War., 1914–18; C.M.G.; Despatches thrice; Legion of Honour.

BEAK, D. M. W. (D.S.O. L.G. 26.7.18), T/Cdr., R.N.D., R.N.V.R.; V.C. (see "The Victoria Cross," by same publishers).

BEALE, C. O. B. (D.S.O. L.G. 26.5.17), T/2nd Lt., Gen. List.

BEALE-BROWNE, D. J. E. (D.S.O. L.G. 26.6.16); b. 4.7.70; s. of late J. Beale-Browne, J.P., D.L.; m. Ethel Jowers; educ. Eton; Trinity Hall, Cambridge; 2nd Lt., 9th Lancers, 30.5.91; Lt. 1.1.93; Adjt. 13.3.95–19.4.99; Capt. 1.1.01; Bt. Lt.-Col. 3.6.15; Lt.-Col. 15.3.16; T/Brig.-Genl., Oct. 1915; ret. pay, 1920; serv. S. Afr. (Queen's Med., 4 clasps, and King's Med., 2 clasps); Europ. War, 1914–18; Despatches twice.

BEALES, W. L. (D.S.O. L.G. 10.8.21), Capt., Inf., I.A.

BEAMAN, A. A. H. (D.S.O. L.G. 26.6.16); b. 18.8.86; e. s. of Sir Frank Beaman; m. Diana V. C., d. of Sir W. Guise, Bart.; educ. Rugby and Sandhurst; 2nd Lt., Unatt., 5.8.05; Ind. Army 30.9.06; Lt. 5.11.07; Capt. 5.8.14; Capt., 1st Lancers, I.A.; served Zakka Khel Expedition, 1908; Mohmand Frontier, including actions of 18 April, 5 Sept. and 8 Oct. 1915; France, 1917–19; Despatches; Croix de Guerre.

BEAMAN, W. K., M.R.C.S., L.R.C.P. (D.S.O. L.G. 1.1.17); b. 7.11.82; s. of H. H. Beaman and Hannah Beaman (*née* Hanson); educ. Charing Cross Hosp.; R.A.M. College; Lt., R.A.M.C., 28.1.07; Capt. 28.7.10; Major 28.1.19; Lt.-Col., served Crete and Malta, 1909–14; served Europ. War from 1914; Despatches; prisoner of war, Germany, 1914–18.

BEARD, G. J. A. (D.S.O. L.G. 25.11.16); m. E. M. Myers; one s.; one d.; serv. S.A. Rebellion, 11th Mounted Regt., Oct. 1914; German S.W. Africa Campaign; Lt.-Col.; Despatches.

BEARDSMORE, R. H. (D.S.O. L.G. 26.9.16); b. 12.8.72; 2nd s. of W. Beardsmore; m. Ethel Mary Clack; one s.; two d.; educ. Sydney Public High School, and Sydney University (B.A.); 2nd Lt., 1895; Major, Aug. 1915; Lt.-Col. Comdg. 32nd Batt. A.I.F., July, 1916; served with Australian Exp. Force to German New Guinea, Aug. 1914; wounded July, 1915; Despatches.

BEARN, F. A., M.D. (D.S.O. L.G. 1.1.17), Capt., R.A.M.C., S.R.; educ University of Manchester; served Europ. War, 1914–19; in Mesopotamia, 1918; India, 1919; Despatches; M.C.

BEASLEY, J. H. M. (D.S.O. L.G. 4.6.17); b. 4.3.76; 2nd Lt., R.A., 21.3.96; Lt. 21.3.99; Capt. 4.9.01; Adjt. 1912–14; Major 30.10.14; A/Lt.-Col.; Despatches.

BEASLEY, R. L. (D.S.O. L.G. 1.1.18) (1st Bar, 27.7.18) (2nd Bar, 8.3.19) (Details, 4.10.19); b. 16.11.78; 2nd Lt., Gloucs. R., 4.1.99; Lt. 22.2.00; Capt. 25.7.06; Major 1.9.15; Despatches.

BEASLEY, W. H. (D.S.O. L.G. 15.4.16); b. 18.2.91; s. of W. T. Beasley; m. Florence Elizabeth, d. of J. Collyear; one s.; member of Gold Coast Vols. W. Afr., 1910–15; ent. R.E., 1915; Capt., 1916; served Europ., 1915–16; Despatches. D.S.O. awarded for services on 8–9.3.1916, at Cordonnerie.

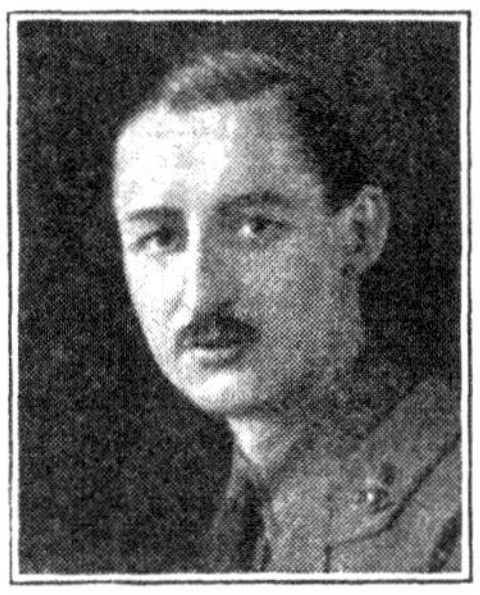

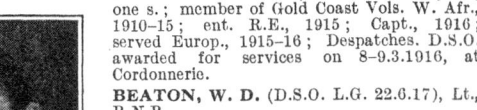

W. H. Beasley.

BEATON, W. D. (D.S.O. L.G. 22.6.17), Lt., R.N.R.

BEATTIE, K. A. (D.S.O. L.G. 24.3.19), Cdr., R.N., 31.12.18.

BEATTIE, M. A. (D.S.O. L.G. 17.9.17); b. 11.4.80; 2nd Lt. 25.6.99; Lt. 16.2.01; Adjt. 16.3.06 to 30.10.08; Capt. 1.4.06; Major 30.10.14; A/Lt.-Col. 6.5.18; Despatches. D.S.O. awarded for services from 3-6.7.1917, near Elverdinghe.

BEATTY, G. A. H. (D.S.O. L.G. 4.6.17) (Bar, L.G. 4.2.18) (Details of Bar, L.G. 5.7.18); b. 22.6.70; s. of Surg.-Gen. T. B. Beatty and Augusta Sarah Beatty (*née* Ellis); one s.; one d.; educ. Newton College; Charterhouse; 2nd Lt., R.I. Regt., 21.12.89; Lt. 29.4.91; Lt., Ind. S.C., 27.5.92; Capt., Ind. Army, 21.12.00; Major 21.12.07 Lt.-Col. 21.12.15; T/Brig.-Gen. 18.12.17 to 4.5.19; C.M.G.; Despatches.

BEATY-POWNALL, G. E. (D.S.O. L.G. 4.6.17), Major (A/Lt.-Col.), Border R. (att. 1st K.O.S.B.). He died of wounds 10.10.18.

BEAUCHAMP-PROCTOR, A. W. (D.S.O. L.G. 2.11.18), Lt. (T/Capt.), R.A.F.; M.C.; Bar to M.C.; D.F.C.; V.C. (see "The Victoria Cross," by same publishers).

BEAUMAN, A. B. (D.S.O. L.G. 6.9.15) (Bar, L.G. 26.11.17) (Details, L.G. 6.4.18) (see "The Distinguished Service Order" from its institution to 31.12.1915, by same publishers).

BEAUMONT, K. MACDONALD (D.S.O. L.G. 11.4.18), T/Major, A.S.C.

BEAVAN, F. E. (D.S.O. L.G. 1.2.19), Lt. (A/Capt.), Welsh Horse Yeomanry.

BEAVIS, L. E. (D.S.O. L.G. 3.6.18), Major, Aust. F.A. Brigade.

BEAZELEY, G. A. (D.S.O. L.G. 7.2.18); b. 7.7.70; 2nd Lt., R.E., 14.2.90; Lt. 14.2.93; Capt. 22.10.00; Major 26.1.10; Lt.-Col. 19.12.17; Despatches.

BECHER, C. M. L. (D.S.O. L.G. 1.1.17); b. 9.7.70; o. s. of late J. P. Becher; m. 1917, Winifred G., o. d. of E. Page, K.C.; educ. Christ's Hospital; 2nd Lt., R.I. Rif., 21.4.00; Lt. 22.3.04; Capt. 22.1.09; Major 1.9.15; served S. Afr. (Queen's Med., 4 clasps); Europ. War, 1914; present at the Battles of Mons, the Marne, and Aisne (twice wounded), 2nd Battle of Ypres (wounded); commanded 6th Battn. R.I. Rif. in Serbia; Macedonia and Palestine, 1916–18; commanded 2nd Battn. R.I. Rif. 6.10.18 to 31.3.19; Despatches twice; Officier de l'Ordre de Léopold et Croix de Guerre (Belge).

BECHER, G. A. (D.S.O. L.G. 26.8.18); b. 15.3.69; 2nd Lt., Norf. R., 27.4.89; Lt. 21.10.91; Lt., Ind. S.C., 14.3.92; Capt., Ind. A., 27.4.00; Major 27.4.07; Lt.-Col. 27.4.15; I.A. retired 8.2.20; Despatches.

BECHER, H. W. (D.S.O. L.G. 4.6.17); b. 27.7.66; 2nd Lt. 8.12.86; Bt. Major 22.8.02; Major 7.10.05; retired 6.2.07; rank of Lt.-Col. in Army 19.1.15; Despatches.

BECHER, L. E. (D.S.O. L.G. 1.1.18); b. 17.9.82; s. of late J. H. Becher; m. Margaret Lucy, d. of late Hon. A. Lyttelton, Bishop of Southampton; two d.; educ. Oundle School; Cooper's Hill; 2nd Lt., R.E., 1.10.04; Lt. 23.6.07; Capt. 30.10.14; Adjt. 1.9.15 to 25.6.16; retired R.E. 1.4.20 with rank of Lt.-Col. in Army; Despatches thrice.

BECK, E. A. (D.S.O. L.G. 14.1.16); b. 16.3.80; o. s. of Col. C. E. Beck; m. 1912, Mary, o. d. of Rt. Rev. H. R. Wakefield, Bishop of Birmingham; two d.; educ. Wellington; Sandhurst; 2nd Lt., R. Sc. Fus., 20.1.00; Lt. 6.4.01; Adjt. 1906–09; Capt. 1.10.10; Major 1.9.15; Bt. Lt.-Col. 3.6.19; served S. Afr. (Queen's Med., 3 clasps; King's Med., 2 clasps); Europ. War, 1914–18; Despatches.

BECK, E. W. T., M.A., LL.B. (D.S.O. L.G. 25.8.16); b. 28.6.86; s. of late A. W. Beck, J.P.; educ. Uppingham; Clare Coll., Cambridge; called to the Bar, Inner Temple, 1909; T/commission in R. Fus., Aug. 1914; Regular Capt. 1.11.16; Despatches 4 times; wounded twice. His D.S.O. was awarded for Ovillers 8.7.16.

BECK, O. L. (D.S.O. L.G. 8.3.20), Capt., R.N.; C.B.E.; D.S.O. awarded for dist. services as Divl. Naval Transport Officer, Murmansk.

BECKE, J. H. W. (D.S.O. L.G. 1.1.17); b. 17.9.79; m. 1915, Annie P. Adamson; two s.; educ. Trinity College, Glenalmond; 2nd Lt., Notts and Derby R. 4.5.01; Lt. 1.4.05; Capt. 28.9.09; Bt. Major 22.6.14; Major 8.5.16; Bt. Lt.-Col. 1.1.18; T/Brig.-Gen. 30.12.16 to 31.3.18; served S. Africa, 1899–02 (Queen's Med., 3 clasps; King's Med. 2 clasps); Europ. War, 1914–18; Despatches seven times; C.M.G., 1918; A.F.C., 1919; Officier Legion of Honour Croix de Guerre.

BECKETT, W. T. C. (D.S.O. L.G. 1.1.18), Lt.-Col., N. Lancs. R., T.F.

BECKLEY, T. H. (D.S.O. L.G. 25.8.17); b. 8.2.86; 2nd Lt., R.A., 23.5.06; Lt. 23.5.09; Capt. 30.10.14; Major 7.1.17; Despatches.

BECKWITH, W. M. (D.S.O. L.G. 3.6.16); b. 20.8.77; o. s. of H. J. Beckwith; m. 1904, Lady Muriel Beatrix Gordon-Lennox, 3rd d. of 7th Duke of Richmond and Gordon; one s.; two d.; educ. Eton; New College, Oxford; ent. C. Gds. 4.1.99; Capt. 3.2.07; retired 21.1.14; Major 17.7.15 (Res. of Off.); served in S. Afr., 1899 (severely wounded); Europ. War in France; Despatches.

BEDDINGTON, E. H. L. (D.S.O. L.G. 4.6.17); b. 7.1.84; m. 1907, Elsie, d. of Raoul H. Foà; three s.; educ. Eton and R.M.C., Sandhurst; 2nd Lt., 16 Lrs., 22.10.02; Lt. 13.8.03; Capt. 5.8.14; Bt. Major 3.6.16; Bt. Lt.-Col. 1.1.18; served Europ. War, 1914–19; Despatches five times; M.C.; C.M.G.; Legion of Honour; Comdr. of the Order of Aviz.

BEDDY, B. L. (D.S.O. L.G. 3.6.16); b. 26.9.78; 2nd Lt., A.S.C., 21.2.00; Lt. 1.4.01; Capt. 18.2.04; Major, R.A.S.C., 7.10.14; Bt. Lt.-Col. 1.1.19; Lt.-Col. 4.2.21; Despatches.

BEDDY, P. L. (D.S.O. L.G. 11.1.19); b. 3.10.76; 2nd Lt., Unatt., 20.1.97; Ind. S.C. 28.3.98; Lt., Ind. A., 20.4.99; Capt. 20.1.06; Major 20.1.15; Bt. Lt.-Col. 3.6.16; Colonel 1.5.20; Despatches; C.M.G.

BEECROFT, C. T. C. (D.S.O. L.G. 1.1.18), T/Major, R.A.S.C.

BEEMAN, S. W. (D.S.O. L.G. 1.1.19); b. 8.12.79; educ. Tonbridge School, Kent, and privately; 2nd Lt., R. Scots, 30.4.02; Ind. Army 12.12.03; Lt. 30.7.04; Capt. 19.10.10; Capt., L'pool R., 29.2.12; Major 28.1.16; served in S. Afr., 1900–2 (Queen's Med., 3 clasps; King's Med., 2 clasps); Zakka Khel Exp. N.W. Frontier, India, 1908 (Med. and clasp); Europ. War, France, 1916; Palestine, 1918; Despatches; Durbar Medal; Royal Humane Society's Award for Life Saving; raised the first battalion for Kitchener's Army, Lord Kitchener becoming its Hon. Colonel.

BEEMAN, W. G. (D.S.O. L.G. 1.1.17); b. 28.6.84; s. of M. I. Beeman, M.B.; educ. R.M.C., Kingston; Lt., R. Can. Art., 1905; Capt., 1910; Major, 1915; Comdg. 1st Can. Siege Bty., B.E.F., France, Jan. 1916.

BEERE, R. ST. J. (D.S.O. L.G. 3.6.19), Major, N.Z. Inf. 21.1.12.

BEEVOR, M. (D.S.O. L.G. 3.6.19); b. 5.12.79; 2nd Lt., E. Kent R., 18.4.00; Lt. 14.10.01; Capt. 10.6.11; Major 1.9.15; Despatches.

BEGBIE, R. P. G. (D.S.O. L.G. 22.8.18); b. 18.7.85; s. of Lt.-Col. A. B. Begbie (Ret., R.E.); m. 1912, Helen G. Dolphin; one s.; one d.; educ. Cheltenham Coll.; R.M.A., Woolwich; 2nd Lt., R.A., 29.7.04; Lt. 29.7.07; Capt. 30.10.14; served under Gen. Botha with the Union Defence Force Heavy Art. in German S.W. Afr., Oct. 1914, to July, 1915 (Despatches); in France and Belgium (Despatches; M.C.; Chevalier Ordre de Couronne and Croix de Guerre with Palm (Belgium).

BEHARRELL, SIR JOHN G., Kt. (D.S.O. L.G. 4.6.17); b. 11.3.73; s. of G. Beharrell; m. Kate, o. d. of Jos. Ripley; three s.; one d.; Asst. General Manager, etc., N.E. Rly.; Assistant Director-General of Transport all theatres of war; rank Lt.-Col; Director-General of Finance and Statistics, Ministry of Transport.

BEITH, D. (D.S.O. L.G. 3.6.19), Major, Aust. Inf., 1.6.18.

BEITH, J. R. McN. (D.S.O. L.G. 12.12.19), Lt.-Col., Aust. A.M.C.

BELCHER, R. D. (D.S.O. L.G. 18.2.18) (Details, L.G. 18.7.18), T/Capt. (A/Major), R.F.A.; M.C. He died of wounds 7.12.17.

BELGRAVE, H. D. (D.S.O. L.G. 26.8.18); b. 14.3.80; e. s. of Lt.-Col. D. T. C. Belgrave; m. 1919, Katharine M., widow of Major G. F. Muller, R.M.L.I.; 2nd Lt., R.W. Kent R., 21.4.00; Lt. 8.2.02; Capt. 11.9.07; Adjt. 1912–14; Major 1.9.15; served S. Africa, 1900–2; Despatches; Queen's Med., 2 clasps; King's Med., 2 clasps); Europ. War (Mesopotamia), 1914–18; Despatches; Bt. Lt.-Col. 3.6.16.

H. D. Belgrave.

BELGRAVE, J. D. (D.S.O. L.G. 14.1.16); b. 10.9.81; e. s. of Colonel D. Belgrave; m. 1910, Gwladys, o. d. of Colonel Newcomen Watts; two s.; educ. Malvern; Woolwich; 2nd Lt., R.A., 6.1.00; Lt. 3.4.01; Capt. 23.5.08; Major 30.10.14; Bt. Lt.-Col. 3.6.19; served S. Afr. (King's Med.; 4 clasps); Europ. War, in France and Egypt; Bt. Lt.-Col.; Despatches five times.

BELL, ARTHUR HENRY (D.S.O. L.G. 1.1.17) Capt., Can. Inf., 1.5.10; Bt. Major 1.7.15; T/Lt.-Col. 4.11.14; T/Brig.-Gen.; C.M.G.

BELL, ARTHUR HUGH (D.S.O. L.G. 3.6.16); b. 16.4.78; 2nd Lt., R.E., 23.3.98; Lt. 14.2.01; Capt. 23.3.07; Major 30.10.14; T/Lt.-Col. 6.5.19 (Despatches); Asst. Dir. of Works, India, 6.5.19.

BELL, BERTRAM CHARLES (D.S.O. L.G. 21.4.17), Flt. Lt. (A/Flt. Cdr.), R.N.A.S.

BELL, C. C. (D.S.O. L.G. 17.10.19), Cdr., R.N., 30.6.17.

BELL, C. F. (D.S.O. L.G. 4.6.17), T/Major, A.S.C.; Lt.-Col. (Ret.); O.B.E.

BELL, G. M. (D.S.O. L.G. 1.1.17), Major, Hants R. He was killed in action 31.7.16.

BELL, J. G., M.B. (D.S.O. L.G. 2.5.16); b. 25.1.75; Lt., R.A.M.C., 31.1.03; Capt. 31.7.06; Major 31.10.14; Bt. Lt.-Col. 1.1.19; Despatches.

BELL, J. J. J. (D.S.O. L.G. 16.9.18); b. 11.10.77; 2nd Lt., R.A., 15.11.14; Lt. 9.6.15; ret. R.A. 17.10.20 with rank of Major; Despatches; M.C.

BELL, J. S. (D.S.O. L.G. 11.1.19), Lt., Can. Inf., 9.10.14; Major, 18th Bn. Can. Inf., W. Ontario R.; M.C.

BELL, M. C. (D.S.O. L.G. 20.10.16); b. 8.6.92; 2nd Lt., R. Fus., 14.2.12; Lt. 19.10.14; Capt. 29.10.15; Despatches; M.C.; D.S.O. awarded for services on 21.8.16, near Guillemont.

BELL, PERCY GEORGE (D.S.O. L.G. 1.1.18), Major (A/Lt.-Col.), Can. A.M.C.

BELL, P. H. (D.S.O. L.G. 2.12.18), Lt.-Col., 3rd Bn. N. Zealand Rif. Bde.

BELL, R. C. (D.S.O. L.G. 1.1.17); b. 21.6.68; s. of Rev. Canon J. S. Bell; m. 1899, Mildred C., d. of Rev. B. C. Davidson-Houston; two d.; educ. Trinity Coll., Stratford-on-Avon; 2nd Lt., S. Lan. R., 18-11-87; Lt. 5.7.89; Ind. S.C. 19.10.91; Capt., Ind. A., 16.11.98; Major 16.11.05; Lt.-Col. 16.11.13; in command 15 Bn. R.W. Fus. 1915–16; served Tirah Expedition, 1897–98 (Med., 3 clasps); Seistan Boundary Commission in Eastern Persia, and Afghanistan, 1904–06; Europ. War; Despatches thrice; O.B.E.

BELL, W. (D.S.O. L.G. 3.6.19), Lt., Can. Cav., 25.11.15; Lt.-Col., R. Can. Dns.

BELL, W. C. H. (D.S.O. L.G. 1.1.17); b. 21.10.75; s. of N. Heward Bell, J.P., D.L.; m. 1903, Violet M., d. of late Capt. D. Bowly, R.E.; one s.; one d.; educ. Westminster; R.M.A., Woolwich; 2nd Lt., R.A., 2.11.95; retired 23.8.11; rejoined 1914; Major (R. of O.), 15.11.15; Lt.-Col., R.F.A.; served S. Afr. (Queen's Medal, 4 clasps); Europ. War, 1914–19; Lt.-Colonel; Despatches twice; cité in orders of French 35th Corps, Oct. 1918; Croix de Guerre; M.P., Devizes Div., since Dec. 1918.

BELL-IRVING, M. McB. (D.S.O. L.G. 22.1.16), Capt., R.F.C., S.R.

BELL-IRVING, R. O. (D.S.O. L.G. 1.1.19), Capt., Can. Inf., 20.10.14; Major, 16th Bn. Can. Inf.; O.B.E.; M.C.; deceased.

BELL-KINGSLEY, H. E. W. (D.S.O. L.G. 25.8.17); b. 23.12.85; 2nd Lt., Unatt., 18.1.05; Ind. Army 16.3.06; Lt. 18.4.07; Capt. 18.1.14; Major 18.1.20; Despatches.

BELLAMY, C. V. (D.S.O. L.G. 4.6.17); b. 5.4.67; s. of G. D. Bellamy, M.Inst. C.E.; m. 1893, Ellen H., d. of S. Spurrell; one d.; educ. Plymouth College; 2nd Lt. (P. of W.), V.B., Devon Regt., 1886; Lt., Ceylon Light Inf. Vols., 1889–95; Capt., Southern Nigeria Vols., 1907; Major, 1909; V.D., 1913; Major, T.F. Reserve, Nov. 1914; Major, R.E., June, 1915; Lt.-Col. 1917; served at Anzac, 1915; Egypt, 1915; Flanders, 1916–18; Rhine Army, 1919; Retired, Aug. 1919; wounded; Despatches twice.

BELLAMY, H. M. (D.S.O. L.G. 1.1.18), Capt., Lincs. R.; M.C.

BELLEW, F. D. (now Trollope-Bellew) (D.S.O. L.G. 26.9.17) (Details, L.G. 9.1.18); b. 22.2.88; s. of late H. B. Bellew; m. 1918, Hon. Nesta Trollope, sister of 3rd Lord Kesteven (d. 1915); 2nd Lt., Som. L. Inf., 21.12.07; Lt. 27.11.09; Capt. 10.6.15; Lt.-Col.; Europ. War, 1914–19; Despatches; M.C.

BELLINGHAM, E. H. C. P. (D.S.O. L.G. 20.10.16); b. 26.1.79; e. s. and heir of Sir Henry Bellingham, 4th Bart; m. 1904, Charlotte Elizabeth, d. of Alfred Payne, and widow of F. Gough; one d.; educ. the Oratory School and Sandhurst; late British Vice-Consul, Guatemala; Royal Scots 29.8.99 to 25.3.04; Resigned 26.3.04; T/Capt. 18.10.14; T/Maj. 1.4.15; T/Lt.-Col. 9.2.16; Major, R. Scots, 21.2.17; T/Brig.-Gen. 3.2.17 to 28.5.18; served S. Africa, 1899–02 (Queen's and King's Medals, 3 clasps); Europ. War, 1914–18; Bt. Lt.-Col. 5.5.19; C.M.G.; Despatches.

BELT, F. W. (D.S.O. L.G. 30.11.17), Lt.-Cdr. (A/Cdr.), R.N.V.R.

BENFIELD, K. V. B. (D.S.O. L.G. 14.11.16) (Bar, L.G. 16.9.18); b. 20.10.92; 2nd Lt., R.A., 18.7.13; Lt. 9.6.15; Capt. 18.7.17; Despatches; M.C.; D.S.O. awarded for services on 16.9.16, Les Bœufs.

BENKE, A. C. H. (D.S.O. L.G. 3.6.19), Capt. (A/Major), London R.; M.C.

BENN, I. H., M.P. (D.S.O. L.G. 20.7.17), Cdr., R.N.R.

BENN, W. W., F.R.G.S. (D.S.O. L.G. 4.6.17); b. 10.5.77; 2nd s. of Sir J. Williams Benn, Bart.; educ. Petit Lycée Condorcet, Paris; University College, London; served with Yeomanry in Egypt and Gallipoli with R.N.A.S. as Observer, 1916, till H.M.S. Ben-my-Chree was sunk by the Turks, Jan. 1917; Seaplane Pilot, 1917; served on Staff Adriatic Barrage, June–Oct. 1917; flying on Piave and Asiago Fronts, Nov. 1917, to Sept. 1918; Capt.; 1914–15 Star; D.S.O. for flying services; Legion of Honour and Croix de Guerre, in connection with defence of Castelorizo; Italian Bronze Valour Medal for flying services; D.F.C. for special night work; Italian War Cross; M.P. He wrote "In the Side Shows."

W. W. Benn.

BENNETT, C. C. (D.S.O. L.G. 1.1.18), Lt.-Col., Can. Inf., 1.7.15.

BENNETT, G. M. (D.S.O. L.G. 3.6.18), Major, S. African Heavy Arty.

BENNETT, H. G. (D.S.O. L.G. 3.6.19), Bt. Lt.-Col. 24.9.17; Col. (T/Brig.-Gen.), Aust. Gen. List., Comdg., 3rd Aust. Inf. Bgde.; C.B., C.M.G.

BENNETT, H. T. (D.S.O. L.G. 21.6.18), Lt.-Cdr., R.N., 30.7.17.

BENNETT, J. (D.S.O. L.G. 8.3.19) (Details, L.G. 4.10.19), Lt. (A/Capt.), H.L.I., T.F.; M.C.

BENNETT, T. E. (D.S.O. L.G. 26.9.17) (Details, L.G. 9.1.18); b. 22.11.81; 2nd Lt., A.S.C., 1.5.02; Capt. 10.11.06; Major, R.A.S.C., 30.10.14; Despatches; O.B.E.; D.S.O. awarded for services on 31.7.1917, Pilckem Ridge.

BENNETT, T. W. (D.S.O. L.G. 6.4.18), Lt.-Cdr. (A/Cdr.), R.N.R.D.

BENNETT, W., M.B. (D.S.O. L.G. 1.1.17); b. 26.7.74; Lt., R.A.M.C., 25.4.00; Capt. 25.4.03; Major 12.1.12; Lt.-Col. 26.12.17; T/Col. 9.4.18 to 7.5.19; Despatches.

BENNETT, W. S. (D.S.O. L.G. 15.2.19) (Details, L.G. 30.7.19), Lt., Aust. Inf.; M.C.

BENNETT, W. STERNDALE- (see Sterndale-Bennett, W.).

BENNEWITH, J. A. (D.S.O. L.G. 1.1.19), T/Capt. (A/Major), Tank Corps.

BENNING, C. S. (D.S.O. L.G. 25.10.16); b. 28.11.84; 2nd s. of Crichton S. Benning; m. 1908, Effie, 2nd d. of R. Byrth Rowson; educ. Dunstable; joined H.M.S. Britannia, 1899; Lieut., 1905; joined submarine service, 1905; appointed E5, 1914; Comdr., 1915; in command of the British submarines in the Mediterranean, 1918; present at the Heligoland Bight; Despatches; Order of the Crown of Italy.

C. S. Benning.

BENSKIN, J. (D.S.O. L.G. 3.6.16); b. 1.4.83; e. sur. s. of late T. Benskin; m. 1919, d. of M. P. Grace, widow of Capt. Hamilton-Grace; educ. Harrow; 2nd Lt., R.E., 17.8.02; Lt. 21.3.05; Capt. 17.8.03; Major 17.8.17; T/Lt.-Col. 15.8.18 to 31.8.19; served European War, 1914–16; Despatches; O.B.E.

BENSLEY, W. J. (D.S.O. L.G. 1.1.19), T/Major, British W. India Rgt.

BENSON, A. W. (D.S.O. L.G. 20.9.18), Cdr., R.N., 30.6.18.

BENSON, C. B. (D.S.O. L.G. 31.10.02) (Bar, L.G. 7.11.18) (see "The Distinguished Service Order" from its institution to 31.12.1915, by same publishers).

BENSON, C. E. (D.S.O. L.G. 18.10.17) (Details, L.G. 7.3.18), 2nd Lt., G. Gds., S.R.

BENSON, C. H. G (D.S.O. L.G. 7.8.18) (Bar, L.G. 24.3.19); s. of James Bourne Benson; m. 1918, May W., d. of late James Boyd; educ. Winchester; H.M.S. Britannia; served Europ. War, 1914–18; Cdr., R.N.; Despatches.

BENSON, F. M. (D.S.O. L.G. 26.7.18), Major, Can. Arty., 22.11.15.

BENSON, R. (D.S.O. L.G. 1.1.17); b. 20.5.81; 2nd Lt., R.A., 19.12.00; Lt. 19.12.03; Capt. 6.1.13; Adjt. 1.1.14–5.4.14; Major 22.7.15; Despatches.

BENSON, R. L. (D.S.O. L.G. 3.6.18); b. 20.8.89; 2nd s. of R. H. Benson and Evelyn Benson (*née* Holford); educ. Eton and Oxford; 2nd Lt., 9th Lrs., 25.5.10; Lt. 2.9.11; Adjt. 8.9.14; Capt. 25.5.15; Despatches; M.C.; Legion of Honour; Croix de Guerre.

BENSON, W., M.A., M.B., B.Ch., B.A.O. (D.S.O. L.G. 1.2.17); b. 14.6.78; Lt., R.A.M.C., 31.7.05; Capt. 31.1.09; Major 15.10.15; Bt. Lt.-Col. 3.6.18; served N.W. Frontier, India, 1908 (Med. and clasp); Europ. War, 1914–17; Despatches.
BENSON, W. A. (D.S.O. L.G. 1.1.17), Lt.-Col., R.A.M.C.
BENT, C. E. (D.S.O. L.G. 1.1.17) (Bar, L.G. 11.1.19), Capt., Can. Inf., 7.9.04; Lt.-Col.; Europ. War, 1914–18; Despatches; C.M.G.
BENT, P. E. (D.S.O. L.G. 4.6.17); V.C.; T/Lt.-Col., Leic. R. He was killed in action 1.10.17 (see "The Victoria Cross," by same publishers).
BENTINCK, LORD C. CAVENDISH (D.S.O. L.G. 2.2.16); b. 8.7.68; h.-bro. 6th Duke of Portland; m. 1897, Cicely M., d. of C. S. Grenfell; educ. Eton; 2nd Lt., 9th Lrs., 8.6.89; Capt. 18.11.00; Bt. Major 29.11.00; Ret. 3.1.06; served S. Afr., 1899–01 (wounded; Despatches); Europ. War, 1914–19 (wounded; Despatches); Bt. Lt.-Col., R. of O., late 9th Lancers.
BENWELL, W. F. (D.S.O. L.G. 4.6.17), Capt., R.N.
BENYON, H. S. (D.S.O. L.G. 2.4.19) (Details, L.G. 10.12.19), Capt., Northants Yeom.; M.C.
BENZIE, R. (D.S.O. L.G. 1.1.18) (Bar, L.G. 18.2.18) (Details of Bar, L.G. 18.7.18), T/Lt.-Col., S.W.B.
BERESFORD, M. J. B. de la POER (D.S.O. L.G. 3.6.16); b. 10.4.68; 2nd Lt. 6.7.89; Major 29.11.07; Ret., S.W.B., 7.7.09; T/Lt.-Col. R. of O.; Comdg. S. Bn., S.W.B.

Lord C. Cavendish Bentinck.

BERESFORD, P. W. (D.S.O. L.G. 18.7.17), Lt.-Col., 3rd Batt. London R. He died of wounds 26.10.17; D.S.O. awarded for services on 13 and 14th May, 1917, at Bullecourt.
BERESFORD-PEIRSE, N. M. de la P. (D.S.O. L.G. 7.2.18); b. 22.12.87; s. of Col. W. J. de la P. Beresford-Peirse; m. 1912, Hazel M., d. of late J. A. Cochrane; 2nd Lt., R.A., 18.12.07; Lt. 18.12.10; Capt. 30.10.14; Major 5.12.17; Adjt., R.A., 9.3.20; Europ. War; Despatches.
BERGEEST, J. W. (D.S.O. L.G. 22.8.18), Major, Murraysburg Commando, for the Campaign in German S.W. Africa.
BERKELEY, R. E. (D.S.O. L.G. 4.6.17); b. 27.11.73; 2nd Lt., N. Lanc. Fus., 7.12.95; Lt. 2.11.98; Capt. 24.12.01; Major 18.8.15; Bt. Lt.-Col. 3.6.18; Lt.-Col., N. Lan. R., 6.10.20; Despatches.
BERKLEY, J. (D.S.O. L.G. 14.1.16); b. 15.1.63; y. s. of Sir Geo. Berkley, K.C.M.G.; m. 1889, Mary A. Hall; educ. Winchester; 2nd Lt. 14.2.83; Major 13.2.00; Ret., R.A., 11.12.07; Major, R. of O., R.A.; served Europ. War, 1914–16; twice wounded; Bt. Lt.-Col. 1.1.18.
BERNARD, D. J. C. K. (D.S.O. L.G. 1.1.17); b. 22.10.82; s. of P. B. Bernard and Mary, d. of Denis Kirwan; educ. Eton and Sandhurst; 2nd Lt., Rif. Brig., 22.10.02; Lt. 21.7.06; Adjt. 17.7.09–16.7.12; Capt. 25.5.12; Major 22.10.17; served in France, Gallipoli, Salonika and Egypt (Despatches); Bt. Major 3.6.16; Bt. Lt.-Col. 3.6.17; Croix de Guerre; C.M.G.
BERNARD, J. F. (D.S.O. L.G. 26.8.18); b. 24.10.71; 2nd Lt., R. Malta Art., 15.7.91; Lt. 15.7.94; Capt. 4.10.96; Adjt. 27.3.97–11.11.99; Major 23.5.07; Lt.-Col. 8.12.14; 3rd Class Medjidie, 1912; served S. Africa, 1900–02 (Queen's Med., 3 clasps; King's Med., 2 clasps); Europ. War, 1914–18; Despatches five times; C.M.G.
BERNARD, R. P. ST. V. (D.S.O. L.G. 7.2.18); b. 25.4.88; 2nd Lt., Unatt., 17.8.07; Ind. Army 11.11.08; Lt. 17.11.09; Capt. 1.9.15; Despatches; M.C.
BERNAYS, L. A. (D.S.O. L.G. 20.7.17), Lt.-Cdr., R.N.; C.M.G.
BERNERS, R. A. (D.S.O. L.G. 4.6.17); b. 14.6.71; 2nd Lt., R.W.F., 29.10.90; Lt. 12.4.93; Capt. 22.2.99; Major 4.7.08; Colonel 31.1.19; Ret. Pay 27.11.20 with rank of Hon. Brig-Genl.; served Hazara Exp. 1891; Medal with clasps; Europ. War.
BERRANGE, C. A. L. (D.S.O. L.G. 22.8.18), Lt.-Col. and Bt. Col. (T/Brig.-Genl.), Permanent Force (S.A.M.R.); C.M.G.
BERRELL, J. S. T. (D.S.O. L.G. 1.2.19), 2nd Lt. (A/Capt.), London R.
BERRIDGE, F. R. (D.S.O. L.G. 3.6.19), T/Capt., Northants R.; M.C.
BERRY, W. H. (D.S.O. L.G. 3.6.18), Major, A.A.S.C., 24.9.13.
BERRYMAN, E. R. P. (D.S.O. L.G. 26.5.19); b. 10.7.83; s. late Rev. C. P. Berryman; m. 1919, Ellen P., 4th d. of J. Fielding; one s.; 2nd Lt., Unatt., 13.8.04; Ind. Army 29.10.05; Lt. 13.11.06; Capt. 13.8.13; Bt. Major 1.1.18; wounded twice; Despatches.
BERRYMAN, F. H. (D.S.O. L.G. 1.1.19), Lt., Aust. Field Arty.
BERTIE, HON. A. M. (D.S.O. L.G. 18.6.17); b. 29.9.86; 2nd s. of 7th Earl of Abingdon; educ. Austria; Balliol College, Oxford; Honorary Attaché, Petrograd Embassy, 1906–7; Major, R. Bgde.; served Europ. War, 1915–18; twice wounded; M.C.; Despatches twice; D.S.O. awarded for services on 4.4.17 at Havrincourt Wood; attd. to British Armistice Commission, Spa, 1918–19; Inter-Allied Military Control Commission, Germany, 1920.
BERTRAM, W. R. (D.S.O. L.G. 1.1.17); b. 1888; s. of late Major W. Bertram; educ. Wellington Coll. and R.M.A., Woolwich; m. 1917, Zoe W. l'Estrange, y. d. of Colonel W. l'Estrange Eames, C.B.; served in Gordon Hgldrs., 1907–11; relinquished commission and went to Canada; served Europ. War, 1914–19; Despatches; C.M.G.; Belgian Croix de Guerre.
BEST, A. J. (D.S.O. L.G. 26.11.17) (Details, L.G. 6.4.18), 2nd Lt., R.E.
BEST, H. W. (D.S.O. L.G. 15.2.19), Cdr., R.N., 31.12.18.
BEST, HON. M. R. (D.S.O. L.G. 15.9.16) (Bar, L.G. 17.5.18); b. 18.6.78; s. of 6th Baron Wynford; m. 1908, Annis E., 2nd d. of F. Wood; one s.; one d.; educ. H.M.S. Britannia; Capt., 1916; served in the Battle of Jutland; Despatches; M.V.O., 1910.
BEST, T. A. D. (D.S.O. L.G. 2.5.16) (Bar, L.G. 1.1.18); b. 12.7.79; 2nd Lt., R. Innis. Fus., 7.2.99; Lt. 20.6.00; Capt. 27.1.04; Major; T/Lt.-Col.; served S. African War, 1899–1902 (Queen's Medal with 5 clasps; King's Medal with 2 clasps). He was killed in action 20.11.17.
BETHELL, H. K. (D.S.O. L.G. 26.9.17) (Details, L.G. 9.1.18); b. 24.9.82; s. of Col. E. H. Bethell; educ. Charterhouse; R.M.A.,

T. A. D. Best.

Woolwich; 2nd Lt., R.A., 24.12.02; Ind. Army 16.6.05; Capt. 24.12.11; Capt., 7th Hus., 14.2.14; Bt. Major 3.6.16; Bt. Lt.- Col. 1.1.17; Bt. Col. 1.1.19; Col. 2.6.19; T/Brig.-Gen. 18.10.16–30.3.18; military attaché, Washington, March, 1919; C.M.G.; C.V.O.; American Distinguished Service Medal; Croix de Guerre avec Palmes; Croce di Guerra; Belgian Croix de Guerre. D.S.O. awarded for services on 16.8.1917, Westhoek Ridge.
BETTS, J. (D.S.O. L.G. 4.6.17); b. 4.12.69; Master at Arms Gym. Staff, 1907–14; Supt. Gym. and Byt. Trng., 1914–17; Supt. of Phys. and Bayt. Trng., 1917–18; Asst. Insp. Phys. and Recreation Trng., 1918–19; Capt. 3.4.17; T/Lt.-Col. 12.4.19.
BETTY, A. KEMMIS (D.S.O. L.G. 23.5.17); b. 11.7.77; s. of late Col. J. F. Kemmis Betty, R.A., and the late Sarah Elizabeth Betty, d. of Sir W. C. Medlycott, Bart.; m. Ethel Beatrix Mary Ellen Agar, d. of A. P. Agar, Commissioner of the Indian Police; one s.; educ. Bedford Grammar School, and at Kearsney, near Dover; ent. R.N., June, 1891; served in H.M.S. Bulwark on the Staff of Admiral Sir Compton Domvile, Commander-in-Chief, Mediterranean; 1st Lt., H.M.S. Euryalus; present at the relief of survivors of Messina Earthquake (granted Messina Medal); qualified for the Naval War Staff at the R.N. College, Portsmouth, 1912; Commander of Torpedo Boats, Patrol Flotilla, Aug. 1914, to Jan. 1915. From Jan. 1915, to June, 1917, Flag-Commander to the Commander-in-Chief, Coast of Scotland. From June, 1917, to the termination of hostilities, Commander on the Staff of Admiral Sir Charles Madden, Second-in-Command, Grand Fleet; Capt. 30.6.18; Despatches; 1914 Star.
BEUTTLER, V. O. (D.S.O. L.G. 1.1.17); b. 4.2.86; 2nd Lt., W. Rid. R., 2.3.07; A.S.C. 1.10.08; Lt. 2.3.10; Capt., R.A.S.C., 7.10.14; Bt. Major 3.6.19; Despatches.
BEVAN, E. B. (D.S.O. L.G. 3.6.19), Capt. (T/Major) (A/Lt.-Col.), Norfolk R. and 1/2nd King's African Rifles.

A. Kemmis Betty.

G. P. Bevan.

BEVAN, G. P. (D.S.O. L.G. 14.3.16); b. 23.6.78; s. of J. F. Bevan; m. Lilian, d. of J. W. Daw; educ. H.M.S. Britannia; was a Commander at the outbreak of war, serving as Naval Secretary to the Ordnance Board at Woolwich. In March, 1915, he was selected to command a flotilla of some 50 trawlers and drifters fitting out for the Dardanelles, and he remained in the Eastern Mediterranean until the evacuation of Gallipoli, when he was awarded the D.S.O., and promoted to Captain, June, 1916. He was then appointed to the Staff of the Governor-General of the Province of Archangel, being in charge of the landing and sending on munitions to the Russian front. For these services he was gazetted Commodore and awarded the C.M.G. He also had the Legion of Honour and the Order of St. Anne of Russia. In Feb. 1918, he was recalled to London and appointed Naval Assistant Director of Transports and Shipping. In Dec. 1918, he went to Germany with the Allied Naval Commission. He held the Albert Medal; was twice mentioned in Despatches, and received the thanks of the Admiralty. Capt. Bevan was a gunnery specialist, and had passed for the rank of Lieutenant with "Firsts" in every subject after only one year's service as Sub-Lieut. He died on 14.1.20 quite suddenly at Aden, when in command of H.M.S. Triad and on his way out to the Persian Gulf to take up his duties as Senior Naval Officer, Persian Gulf.
BEVAN, R. H. L. (D.S.O. L.G. 14.3.16); b. 10.7.85; s. of late Capt. E. B. L. Bevan, R.W. Kent R.; educ. Foster's, Stubbington House; H.M.S. Britannia; Midshipman in Implacable, 1901–4; Sub-Lt. in Drake, 1905–6; Lt., Aboukir, 1907–9; Lt., H.M.S. Balmoral Castle, 1910; in comd. of T.B.D. Express, 1911; Lt., H.M.S. Medina; Flag-Lieut. to Vice-Adm. Sir Rosslyn Wemyss, in Orion, 1912–13; Comdr., 1918; landed at Cape Helles in charge of signal stations during occupation of Gallipoli; present at evacuation of Suvla and Anzac; Order of the Nile, 4th Class, 1917; Legion of Honour, Chevalier, 1918.
BEVERLEY, B. ROBINSON- (see Robinson-Beverley, B.).
BEVERLEY, R. (D.S.O. L.G. 15.1.20), T/Capt., S. Afr. Inf. (France); M.C.
BEWSHER, F. W. (D.S.O. L.G. 3.6.19), Capt. (T/Major), London R.; M.C.
BEWSHER, W. D. (D.S.O. L.G. 15.2.17); b. 27.3.68; s. of Rev. W. B. Bewsher; educ. Clifton College and Sandhurst; 2nd Lt., 2nd Hamps. Regt., 22.8.88; Major 2.8.05; R. of O. 17.7.09; T/Lt.-Col. 10.10.14; in command S. Hamps. Regt.; served India, Aden Hinterland Expedition, 1903; Europ. War; Despatches.
BEYTS, J. F. (D.S.O. L.G. 1.1.18), T/Lt.-Col., Durham L.I. He was killed in action 5.10.17.
BEZUIDENHOUT, J. J. (D.S.O. L.G. 22.8.18), Lt.-Col., Bloemhof Commando, S. A. Military Forces.
BHARUCHA, PHIROZSHAH BYRANJI, F.R.C.S. (D.S.O. L.G. 17.4.16), Capt., I.M.S.
BIBBY, A. H. (D.S.O. L.G. 4.2.18) (Details, L.G. 5.7.18), Lt., R.F.A., T.F., 25.5.10; Major.
BIBBY, J. V. (D.S.O. L.G. 19.8.16), Major, Northd. Fus.; Europ. War, 1914–17; Despatches; D.S.O. awarded for services on 1.7.1916, at La Boisselle.
BICK, A. H. (D.S.O. L.G. 1.1.19), Major, Can. F.A.
BICKERDIKE, R. (Gazetted as Bickeadike) (D.S.O. L.G. 1.1.18) (Bar, L.G. 15.2.19) (Details, L.G. 30.7.19), Major, Can. Inf.
BICKERDIKE, R. (D.S.O. L.G. 3.6.19), Major, R.F.A., T.F.
BICKERTON, R. E., M.B. (D.S.O. L.G. 1.1.17); b. 1870; s. of late T. Bickerton, F.R.C.S.Edin.; m. Constance, d. of late W. H. Livesay; one s.; twin d.; educ. King Edward VI. School, Berkhampstead; University College, Liverpool; Vienna; Berlin; Zurich; Lt., R.A.M.C. (T.), 1909; Capt., 1912; served British Exp. Force, Belgium and France; Medit. Ex. Force, Alexandria; Army of the Black Sea, Turkey and Asia Minor (Despatches twice); Lt.-Col. in command 4th Field Ambulance from Aug. 1916, and att. to 28th Div. throughout; Ophthalmic Specialist, B.S.F., and Acting A.D.M.S. to Army of the Black Sea, 1919.

BICKFORD, B. R. (D.S.O. L.G. 15.9.16), Staff Surgeon, R.N. He was invested with the D.S.O. by the King at sea, June, 1917.

BICKFORD, W. G. H. (D.S.O. L.G. 12.1.16); s. of late Col. Bickford, R.M.A.; Cdr., R.N.; served Europ. War; Despatches.

BICKMORE, D. F. (D.S.O. L.G. 16.9.18), Lt. (A/Lt.-Col.), Norfolk R. He was killed in action 19.7.18.

D. F. Bickmore.

BICKNELL, H. P. F. (D.S.O. L.G. 3.6.16); b. 12.4.79; ent. Army 20.5.99; Lt. 14.3.00; Capt. 23.11.01 (Middx. R.); Adjt. 9.3.05 to 8.3.08; Major 11.12.14; T/Lt.-Col., Middx. R., 27.10.15; served S. African War, 1899–1902; Queen's Medal with 5 clasps; King's Medal with 2 clasps; Europ. War; Despatches.

BIDDER, H. F., M.A., F.S.A. (D.S.O. L.G. 1.1.18); b. 26.12.75; 2nd s. of late G. P. Bidder, Q.C., and Anna, d. of J. R. McClean (sometime President Inst. C.E.); m. Lilias Vivian, d. of H. M. Rush; one s.; educ. St. Paul's School; Trinity College, Cambridge; joined 3rd Bn. R. Sussex R.; served in S. Africa, 1901–2 (Queen's Medal, 5 clasps); called up 4.8.14; att. 1st Bn. S. Staffs. R., Dec. 1914–Feb. 1915; Brigade Machine-Gun Officer, 21st Bgde., May–Sept. 1915 (Loos); T/Lt.-Col. commanding 2nd Bedford R., Oct.–Nov. 1915; commanding 21st M.G. Company, March–Sept. 1915 (Somme); T/Lt.-Col. and Corps M.G. Officer, X. Corps, 1917; commanding 1st Bn., M.G.C., Feb. to May, 1918.

BIDDER, M. MacC. (D.S.O. L.G. 1.1.17), M.Inst.C.E.; b. 1879; s. of G. P. Bidder, Q.C.; m. Elinor Phyllis, d. of E. Ames; three d.; educ. St. Paul's School; R. Indian Engineering College, Cooper's Hill; served Europ. War, 1914–18; R.E.; Despatches; Bt. Lt.-Col.

BIDDLE, F. L. (D.S.O. L.G. 14.11.16); b. 27.10.85; s. of James and Helena Biddle; educ. Hawthorn College, Melbourne; Melbourne University. He joined the Australian F.A. (Militia) in 1904; served with the A.I.F. in the Europ. War; seconded from the Australian Field Artillery; served in Gallipoli, remaining at Anzac until the Peninsula was evacuated; was promoted Major, 1916. His D.S.O. was awarded for gal. on 23–24 July, 1916, at Pozières. He was wounded in action (second time) in Belgium on 16.8.17, and admitted to 32nd Casualty Clearing Station, where he died the following day. He was one of the evacuation officers when the Australian troops left Gallipoli, and was in the last boat to leave Anzac Cove.

BIDDULPH, HARRY (D.S.O. L.G. 1.1.17); b. 1872; m. 1904, Constance Emily, d. of Rowland Smith; 2nd Lt., R.E., 12.7.92; Lt. 22.7.95; Capt. 14.5.03; Major 22.7.12; Bt. Lt.-Col. 1.1.16; Colonel 3.6.19; served Tirah Exp. 1897; Waziristan Exp. 1902 (Medal, two clasps); Europ. War, 1914–17; Despatches; C.M.G.

BIDDULPH, HOPE (D.S.O. L.G. 3.6.18); b. 27.10.66; s. of late Gen. Sir R. Biddulph, G.C.B., G.C.M.G.; m., 1st, Mabel Gordon, d. of Capt. J. Urquhart; 2nd, Mabel Alice, d. of Col. T. Edmonds Holmes; two s.; one d.; educ. Charterhouse; R.M.A., Woolwich; 2nd Lt., R.A., 29.4.85; Captain 1.4.95; Major 7.7.00; Lt.-Colonel, R.F.A., 12.12.13; served China, 1900 (Medal); Europ. War, 1914–18; Despatches.

BIGG-WITHER, H. G. (D.S.O. L.G. 3.6.19), T/Major, 10th Bn. D.C.L.I.

BIGGS, G. T. (D.S.O. L.G. 1.1.18); served overseas from the latter end of 1914; Despatches several times; Capt. and Bt. Major, R.E.

BIGNELL, F. L. (D.S.O. L.G. 3.6.18), Major, Aust. A.M.C.

BIGNELL, R. L. (D.S.O. L.G. 26.3.18); b. 4.6.81; s. of R. A. D'O. Bignell and K. Lowis; m. Sibyl Mitford Boodle; educ. Laleham, Staines; Haileybury College, and Sandhurst; 2nd Lt., Unatt., 20.1.00; Ind. S.C. 27.4.01; Lt., I.A., 20.4.02; Capt. 20.1.09; Major 1.9.15; A/Lt.-Col. 22.8.16; 2nd-in-Command, 141st Dogras; served India, China, Mesopotamia and Palestine; served Abor Exp.; Europ. War; Despatches; Bt. Major; Order of St. Stanislaus; Afghan War.

BIGSWORTH, A. W. (D.S.O. L.G. 13.9.15) (Bar, L.G 1.10.17) (see "The Distinguished Service Order" from its institution to 31.12.1915, by same publishers).

BILLYARD-LEAKE, E. W. (D.S.O. L.G. 23.7.18); b. 13.11.95; s. of C. A. M. and L. S. Billyard-Leake; m. Leila V. D. Traquair; educ. R.N. College, Osborne; R.N. College, Dartmouth; joined the Navy, 1908; Midshipman H.M.A.S. Australia, 1913; Sub-Lt., 1915; H.M.S. Warspite, Aug. 1915; Lt., June, 1917; H.M.S. Canada, Aug. 1917; joined Submarine Service, June, 1918; present at capture of German Pacific Colonies, 1914; Battle of Jutland, H.M.S. Warspite; Zeebrugge operations, as Capt. H.M.S. Iphigenia; Chevalier, Legion of Honour; Croix de Guerre with Palm.

E. W. Billyard-Leake.

BINGAY, H. L. (D.S.O. L.G. 1.1.19); b. 9.12.80; 2nd Lt., R.E., 19.6.99; Lt. 29.12.01; Capt. 19.6.08; Major 7.10.15; Despatches.

BINGHAM, C. H. M. (D.S.O. L.G. 3.6.16); b. 27.12.73; s. of late Col. C. T. Bingham, I.A.; educ. Sandhurst; m. Rose Aylmer, d. of Col. A. S. Cameron, V.C., C.B., Seaf. Highrs. and K.O.S.B.; two s.; one d.; 2nd Lt., L.N. Lan. R., 19.7.93; Lt. 1.7.95; Capt. 1.5.01; Major 3.1.14; Lt.-Col. R.A.S.C., 21.11.18; served S. African War, 1899–01; twice severely wounded, losing his left arm; Despatches; Queen's Medal with 4 clasps; Europ. War, France, 1915–16; Despatches; then Italy to end of war; Despatches twice; C.M.G.

BINGHAM, D. A. (D.S.O. L.G. 1.1.18), Capt. (A/Major), L'pool R.

BINGHAM, THE HON. J. D. Y. (D.S.O. L.G. 15.10.18); b. 11.8.80; 2nd s. of Baron Clanmorris; educ. Harrow and Sandhurst; 2nd Lt., 15 Hrs., 20.1.00; Lt. 30.1.01; Capt. 1.7.08; T/Maj., M.G.C., 30.3.17 to 27.7.17; T/Major, Tank Corps, 28.7.17–26.12.17; T/Lt.-Col., Tank Corps, 27.12.17; Bt. Lt.-Col., Europ. War, 1914–19; Despatches.

BINGHAM, R. C. (D.S.O. L.G. 4.6.17), Capt. (T/Lt.-Col), R. of O., late C. Gds. (M.G.Gds.)

BINGHAM, S. (D.S.O. L.G. 3.6.18), T/Lt.-Col., L'pool R.

BINNEY, E. V. (D.S.O. L.G. 25.8.17); b. 4.3.85; 2nd Lt., R.E., 5.7.03; Lt. 31.12.05; Capt. 15.6.14; Major 5.7.18; Despatches.

BINNIE, T. H. (D.S.O. L.G. 16.9.19), Cdr., R.N., 31.12.16; Naval Assistant to 4th Sea Lord from 1.8.19.

BION, W. R. (D.S.O. L.G. 18.2.18) (Details, L.G. 18.7.18), T/2nd Lt., Tank Corps.

BIRCH, A. G., B.A. (D.S.O. L.G. 14.1.16) (Bar, L.G. 14.11.16); b. 22.1.82; s. of late J. G. Birch, founder of Messrs. John Birch & Co. Ltd., Merchants and Engineers, and Annie Isabella, d. of J. Turnbull; educ. Cordwalles School, Maidenhead; Winchester Coll. and Trinity College, Cambridge, gaining the Mechanical Services Tripos, 1903; he is an Associate Member of the Institute of Civil Engineers; m. 11.9.12, Grace M., d. of F. H. A. Booth; one s.; gazetted 2nd Lt., 4th London Field Coy. (T.F.), 5.8.11; Lt. 27.2.14; Capt. 5.4.15; Major 28.6.15; Comd. 1/3 London Field Coy., R.E., 47th Div. 28.6.15–15.9.16; he subsequently served in the Light Railway Directorate under Director-General of Transportation, and was promoted Lt.-Col., R.E. (T.A.) in Feb. 1920, and C.R.E., 47th (2nd Lond.) Div., T.A.; wounded 15.9.16 on the Somme; Despatches, 30.11.15; 17.11.16 and Dec. 1918; D.S.O. awarded for services on 15.9.16, Bazentin; Managing Director, Light Railways Ltd., London.

A. G. Birch.

BIRCH, A. H. C. (D.S.O. L.G. 1.1.18); b. 5.10.61; Lt., R.A., 27.7.80; Capt. 2.4.89; Bt. Major 20.5.98; Major 5.1.99; Lt.-Col. 28.1.09; Ret., R.A., 28.1.14; Despatches.

BIRCH, J. G. (D.S.O. L.G. 3.6.18), T/Lt.-Col., K.R.R.C.

BIRCH, J. M. (D.S.O. L.G. 25.8.17), A/Major, S. Lan. R.

BIRCH, P. Y. (D.S.O. L.G. 3.6.18); b. 8.11.84; 2nd Lt., R.A., 23.12.03; Lt. 23.12.06; Capt. 30.10.14; Major 11.9.18; Despatches.

BIRCH, V. K. (D.S.O. L.G. 10.6.21); b. 4.7.75; 2nd Lt., Unatt., 16.1.95; Ind., S.C., 29.3.96; Lt., Ind. Army, 16.4.97; Capt. 16.1.04; Major 16.1.13; A/Lt.-Col. 22.5.18; 29th Lrs., I.A.

BIRCH, W. L. (D.S.O. L.G. 3.6.19); b. 22.3.79; s. of Sir A. Birch; m. Susan, d. of 7th Earl of Hardwicke; one s.; educ. Marlborough; served as Private in London Scottish; as Subaltern, W. Yorks. R.; as Observer and Pilot in the R.F.C. and R.A.F., in France, Salonika, Palestine, Syria and Somaliland; Despatches twice; M.B.E.; Croix de Guerre; Prime Warden of the Fishmongers' Company.

BIRCHALL, E. V. D. (D.S.O. L.G. 25.8.16), Capt., Oxf. and Bucks. L.I. His D.S.O. was awarded for services on 23.7.1916, Pozières. He died of wounds 10.8.16.

BIRD, A W. (D.S.O. L.G. 26.5.17); m. 1919, Clarice Mary, d. of late S. B. French, of New York and Virginia, U.S.A., and Mrs. Barton French, of Paris and 3, Albemarle st. W.; served Europ. War, 1914–18; Major, R.A.F.; Despatches; D.S.O. awarded for services on 9.4.17, Givenchy.

A. W. Bird.

BIRD, C. A. (D.S.O. L.G. 1.1.17); b. 5.2.85; s. of Clarence and Clara M. Bird; educ. Cheltenham Coll.; 2nd Lt., R.E., 24.12.04; Lt. 24.6.07; Capt. 30.10.14; Bt. Major 1.1.18. He served in France from Oct. 1914; Despatches thrice; 1914 Star.

BIRD, E. B. (D.S.O. L.G. 1.1.17); b. 24.3.81; s. of G. Beverly Bird, late King's Own Yorks. Light Inf.; educ. Cheltenham College, and Trinity College, Dublin; m. 1909, Hon. Gladys Rice, e. d. of 6th Baron Dynevor; Lt.-Col., 3rd Wessex Field Ambulance, R.A.M.C. (T.F.); served Europ. War, 1914–19; Despatches 4 times; Bt. Lt.-Col.; Croix de Guerre (Français).

BIRD, F. G. (D.S.O. L.G. 12.1.16), Capt., R.N.; Despatches.

BIRD, L. G. (D.S.O. L.G. 21.12.16); b. 1878; s. of late Col. F. V. G. Bird, R.M.L.I.; m. Margaret S., o. d. of Hon. Sir J. A. Cockburn; educ. Felsted; Lt.-Col. late R.W. Surrey R.; served Europ. War, 1915–18, France; Despatches; wounded.

BIRD, L. W. (D.S.O. L.G. 14.1.16); b. 1.9.83; y. s. of A. Bird, J.P.; m. 29.4.16, Hilda, d. of R. A. Lett, B.A., M.D., M.Ch.; one s.; educ. Harrow, and Trinity Coll., Cambridge; 2nd Lt., R. Berk. R., 29.7.03; Lt. 15.12.05; Capt. 3.6.11; Major 26.7.18; Ret. 9.5.19; served Europ. War, France; commanded 1st Bn.; O.B.E.; Despatches twice; wounded twice.

BIRD, M. G. (D.S.O. L.G. 26.7.18); b. 15.6.81; 2nd s. of T. J. Bird; educ. Sedbergh; 2nd Lt., 1909; Lt., 1911; Capt., 1913; Major, 1915; Lan. Fus.; served Europ. War, Egypt, 1914–15; Gallipoli, 1915 (wounded); Sinai Peninsula, 1916; France, 1917–18 (severely wounded); Despatches.

BIRD, REV. R., M.A. (D.S.O. L.G. 1.1.18); b. 1882; s. of T. J. Bird; educ. Trinity College, Dublin; ordained 1905; Rector of Ballyfin, 1907; Chaplain to the Forces, 1915; Rector of St. Kevin's, S.C.R., Dublin, 1919; served Europ. War; prisoner of war, March, 1918; Despatches twice.

BIRD, T. G. (D.S.O. L.G. 3.6.18), T/Capt. (A/Major), R.E.

BIRD, T. H. (D.S.O. L.G. 1.1.18), Lt., Aust. L. Horse R., 1.7.15; Capt. 24.9.17; Major.

BIRDS, S. B. (D.S.O. L.G. 4.2.18) (Details, L.G. 18.7.18), Capt. (A/Major), Can. Inf.; M.C.

BIRKBECK, B. (D.S.O. L.G. 1.1.18), T/Capt. (A/Major), C. Gds.; M.C.

BIRKBECK, G. (D.S.O. L.G. 3.3.17); b. March, 1876; s. of R. E. Birkbeck; of Glenmore, Queensland, Australia; m. Jacintha, d. of J. Antonus; one s.; two d.; commissioned in the Mil. Forces of the Commonwealth of Australia, 1908; commanded A Squadron of the 2nd Light Horse R.; served Europ. War in Gallipoli; wounded twice.

BIRKETT, G. H. (D.S.O. L.G. 3.6.18); b. 17.1.83; 2nd Lt., S. Wales Bord., 4.7.03; Lt. 26.4.06; Adjt. 5.2.12 to 3.2.15; Capt. 9.6.15; Major 4.12.17; Despatches three times; D.S.O. awarded for services on 3.12.16, Magdwaha. His brother, Capt. J. G. G. Birkett, R.G.A., is well known in International football.

BIRKETT, M. B. (D.S.O. L.G. 4.6.17), Cdr., R.N. 30.6.16.

BIRKETT, R. M. (D.S.O. L.G. 18.1.18); b. 2.1.82; 2nd Lt., R. Suss. R., 18.1.02; Lt. 17.12.04; Adjt. 5.10.10–4.10.13; Capt. 2.2.11; Maj. 18.1.17; Bt. Lt.-Col. 1.1.19; Despatches.

BIRLEY, B. L. (D.S.O. L.G. 25.8.17) ; b. 19.9.84 ; s. of H. L. Birley and Amy Birley (*née* Chichester) ; m. Eleanor Mary Cordeaux ; one s. ; one d. ; educ. Winchester ; 2nd Lt., S. Lan. R., 5.12.06 ; Lt. 15.2.08 ; Adjt. 11.8.14 to 10.8.15 ; Capt. 23.2.15 ; Brevet of Major 3.6.18 ; Actg. Lt.-Col., comdg. 6 Bn. R. Lanc. R., 11.2.19 ; Europ. War, Gallipoli and Mesopotamia, 1915–19 ; Despatches twice ; Brevet Major.

BIRLEY, N. P. (D.S.O. L.G. 1.1.18) ; b. 29.4.91 ; s. of Rev. H. H. Birley ; m. Eileen A. Morgan ; educ. Hamilton House, Lansdown, Bath ; Repton School, and New College, Oxford ; History Master, Gresham's School, Holt, 1919 ; left Oxford, 1914 ; enlisted in Public Schools Battalion (22nd R.F.) ; commissioned 3rd Bn. S. Staffs. R., 27.10.14 ; went to France 13.5.15 ; posted to 1st Bn. Sherwood Foresters till Dec. 1916 (Adjt., July–Dec. 1916) ; Bde. Major, 25th Inf. Bde, 25.2.17 ; Bde. Major, 27th (Res.) Inf. Bde., Londonderry, Aug. 1918 ; wounded 27.3.18 ; Despatches twice ; M.C.

BIRLEY, R. A. (D.S.O. L.G. 10.6.20) ; b. 4.8.73 ; 2nd Lt., R.A., 1.4.94 ; Major, R.F.A., 1.2.11 ; Ret. 18.1.19 ; Despatches.

BIRNEY, C. F. (D.S.O. L.G. 4.6.17) ; b. 24.12.78 ; s. of late Col. J. Birney, R. (Bengal) E. ; m. 1910, Rachael, D. D., d. of late Lt.-Col. J. T. W. Leslie, C.I.E., I.M.S. ; 2 sons ; educ. St. David's, Reigate, and Marlborough College ; 2nd Lt., R.E., 23.6.98 ; Lt. 18.2.01 ; Capt. 23.6.07 ; Major 30.10.14 ; Bt. Lt.-Col. 3.6.18 ; T/Brig.-Gen. 3.4.19 ; served in Tibet, 1903–04 (Med., clasp) ; Europ. War, 1914–19 ; Despatches 5 times, Jan. 1916 and 1917 ; May, 1917 ; Dec. 1917 ; May, 1918 ; Croix de Chevalier, Legion of Honour.

BIRNIE, E. D'A. (D.S.O. L.G. 26.7.18), T/Lt. (A/Capt.), Border R. He died of wounds 22.3.18 ; M.C.

BIRNIE, H. C. (D.S.O. L.G. 22.2.18), Lt.-Cdr., R.N.R.

BIRT, C. W. H. (D.S.O. L.G. 25.8.17) (1st Bar, L.G. 26.7.18) (2nd Bar, L.G. 16.9.18) ; m. Rosalind L., e. d. of W. O. Blott ; served Europ. War (Border R.), 1914–18 ; wounded thrice ; Despatches twice.

BIRTWISLE, A. (D.S.O. L.G. 1.1.18) ; b. 29.5.77 ; s. of W. Birtwisle ; m. Alice, d. of W. Hillmen ; served Europ. War (Dardanelles), 1914–15 ; (France), 1915–18 (Despatches twice ; C.M.G. ; D.S.O.) ; C.B., 1919 ; T.D. ; Colonel ; Brig.-Gen. 1.12.17 ; J.P., Lancaster.

BIRTWISLE, W. (D.S.O. L.G. 3.6.19), Major, 210th (E. Lancs.) Bde. R.F.A., T.F.

BISDEE, T. E. (D.S.O. L.G. 3.6.19) ; b. 11.6.88 ; 2nd Lt., D. of Corn. L.I., 22.5.99 ; Lt. 1.4.11 ; Adjt. 19.9.14–30.3.16 ; Capt. 12.4.15 ; Despatches ; M.C.

BISHOP, C. G. (D.S.O. L.G. 1.1.18), Capt. (T/Major), R.E. He was killed in action on 30.10.17.

BISHOP, W. A. (D.S.O. L.G. 18.6.17) (Bar, L.G. 26.9.17) (Details, L.G. 9.1.18), Lt. (T/Capt.), Can. Cav. and R.F.C. ; M.C. ; V.C. (see " The Victoria Cross," by same publishers).

BISHOP, W. S. G. (D.S.O. L.G. 3.6.18) ; b. 6.2.63 ; Asst. Comy. of Ord. 4.6.02 ; Depy. Comy. of Ord. 26.2.12 ; Comy. of Ord. 14.2.18 ; Major 1.1.17 ; Retired 1.12.19 ; Despatches.

BISSETT, F. W. L. (D.S.O. L.G. 1.1.19) ; b. 4.6.88 ; 2nd Lt., Duke of Corn. L.I., 6.2.09 ; Lt. 1.4.11 ; Capt. 12.4.15 ; Despatches ; Bt. Major 1.1.18 ; Adjt., D.C.L.I., 25.1.21 ; M.C.

BISSETT, G. (D.S.O. L.G. 2.12.18), Lt. (A/Major), 1st Bn. R. Scots Fus. ; M.C. ; died of wounds 18.10.18.

BITTLESTON, K. G. (D.S.O. L.G. 3.6.19) ; b. 10.5.84 ; s. of Col. G. H. Bittleston, R.A. ; m. Alice Katharine, d. of late Hon. J. Dundas ; one s. ; one d. ; educ. Westminster ; R.M.A., Woolwich ; 2nd Lt., R.F.A., 1902 ; Lt., 1905 ; Remount Staff, S Africa, 1907–11 ; Capt., R.F.A., 1914 ; Major 16.11.16 ; served Europ. War in France and Flanders with 4th Division, 1914–15, and with 34th Div. 1916 ; Egyptian Exp. Force, 1917–18 ; Despatches three times ; D.S.O.

BLACK, A McG. (D.S.O. L.G. 24.9.18), T/Major, Northd. Fus. ; m. May, widow of S. D. Simonds.

BLACK, C. H. G. (D.S.O. L.G. 1.1.17) ; b. 29.5.81 ; s. of Rev. J. Black ; educ. Cheltenham College, and Sandhurst ; m. 1913, Augusta S., d. of T. J. Shipton-Green ; two s. ; 2nd Lt., Unatt., 20.1.00 ; Ind. S.C., 20.4.01 ; Lt., Ind. Army, 20.4.02 ; Capt. 20.1.09 ; Capt., 12 Lrs., 4.9.14 ; Bt. Major 3.6.17 ; Bt. Lt.-Col. 3.6.19 ; served Europ. War in France, and in Army of Occupation in Germany, on the British Delegation and Peace Conference in Paris, and on the Allied Military Committee of Versailles ; Despatches

BLACK, J. J. (D.S.O. L.G. 1.1.18), Lt.-Col. Aust. A.M.C. ; Capt. 8.5.11 ; Hon. Lt.-Col. 20.11.16 ; M.O., 63rd Bgde. A.I.F., 1.7.13. ; Despatches

BLACK, P. (D.S.O. L.G. 14.11.16), Major, Aust. Inf.

BLACK, R. B., M.B. (D.S.O. L.G. 1.1.17) ; b. 26.10.76 ; ent. R.A.M.C. 14.10.00 ; Major 14.8.12 ; Despatches.

BLACKBURN, C. C. (D.S.O. L.G. 3.6.16) ; b. 18.6.67 ; s. of H. C. Blackburn ; educ. Repton ; 2nd Lt. 11.2.88 ; Capt. 10.2.98 ; Ret. Norf. R. 1.4.03 ; Bt. Maj. (R. of O.) 3.6.18 ; Ret. 9.4.19 with rank of Lt.-Col. ; served in S. Afr. 1899–02 (Despatches ; Queen's Med., 3 clasps ; King's Med., 2 clasps) ; served in Natal Rebellion, 1906 ; Lt., Royston's Horse (Med.) ; Europ. War, in Gallipoli and in France ; as A.D., Ordnance Services, Mediterranean L. of C., 1917 ; A.D. Ordnance Services, 5th Corps, 1918 ; as Chief Ordnance Officer, Rouen Base, 1918.

BLACKBURN, E. D. (D.S.O. L.G. 26.7.18), T/Capt. (A/Major), Tank Corps ; M.C.

BLACKBURN, J. C. (D.S.O. L.G. 3.2.20) ; b. 14.4.91 ; 2nd Lt., W. York. R., 5.10.10 ; Lt. 10.10.12 ; Capt. 21.12.14 ; Despatches ; M.C.

BLACKBURN, R. V. (D.S.O. L.G. 16.9.18), Capt., Can. Inf. ; M.C.

BLACKBURNE, REV. H. W., M.A. (D.S.O. L.G. 1.1.18) ; b. 25.1.78 ; s. of late C. E. Blackburne ; m. 1904, Haidee F., d. of Major-Gen. Creagh, Ind. A. ; educ. Tonbridge ; Clare College, Cambridge ; Chaplain 4th Class 15.10.03–14.2.04 ; Chaplain 3rd Class 14.2.14 ; 2nd Class 14.2.19 ; 1st Class 3.6.19 ; Chaplain to H.M. The King, 1920, and R.M.C., Sandhurst ; served as Trooper, West Kent I.Y., 1900 ; Queen's Med. ; Europ. War ; Despatches seven times ; M.C., 1915.

BLACKER, F. ST. J. (D.S.O. L.G. 1.1.18) ; b. 6.3.81 ; 2nd Lt. 23.12.99 ; Capt. 1.7.05 ; Ret. Rif. Brig. 8.10.10 ; served in Europ. War ; T/Lt.-Col. ; Despatches.

BLACKER, N. V. (D.S.O. L.G. 3.6.19) ; b. 15.5.89 ; 2nd Lt., E. York. R., 11.12.09 ; Lt. 12.12.13 ; Capt. 23.5.15 ; M.C. ; Despatches.

BLACKER, S. W. W., D.L. (D.S.O. L.G. 1.1.17) ; b. 4.7.65 ; s. of late Canon R. S. C. Blacker ; educ. R.M.A., Woolwich ; m. 1903, Eva L. M. St. J., d. of Col. E. A. Fitzroy ; 2nd Lt., R.A., 1885 ; Capt., 1895 ; Major, 1900 ; Ret. 1903 ; raised and commanded 9th Res. Batt. R. Ir. Fus. ; commanded 20th Res. Batt. R. Ir. Fus. ; served N.W.F., 1897 (severely wounded ; Despatches) ; S. African War, 1899–1900 ; Europ. War ; Despatches thrice ; Bt. Lt.-Col. ; Officier of Legion of Honour.

BLACKHAM, R. J., M.D., M.R.C.P.E., D.P.H.Lond. (D.S.O. L.G. 1.1.17) ; b. 15.9.68 ; Lt., R.A.M.C., 29.7.95 ; Capt. 29.7.98 ; Major 29.1.07 ; Lt.-Col. 1.3.15 ; Col. 26.12.17 ; served with No. 3 British Gen. Hosp., Tirah F.F., 1897–98 ; with the Khyber Brigade, 1898–99 ; C.I.E. ; Europ. War, 1914–19 ; C.B. ; C.M.G. ; Despatches 5 times ; 1914–15 Star ; General Service and Victory Medals ; Croix de Guerre with Palm and Star, 1918.

BLACKLIN, R W B (D.S.O. L.G. 6.4.18) ; 2nd s. of late Capt. R. J. Blacklin ; Cdr. (A/Capt.), R.D., R.N.R.

BLACKLOCK, C. A. (D.S.O. L.G. 3.6.16) (Bar, L.G. 14.11.16) ; Major-Gen., comdg. 10th Batt K.R.R.C. ; served Europ. War ; Despatches ; C.B. ; C.M.G. The Bar to his D.S.O. was awarded for services on 3.9.16 at Guillemont.

BLACKLOW, A. C. (D.S.O. L.G. 3.6.18), Capt., A.I.F., 16.8.13 ; Major (T/Lt.-Col.), Aust. M.G.C. ; Despatches.

BLACKMAN, C. M. (D.S.O. L.G. 16.9.19) ; b. 7.3.90 ; s. of late C. Blackman ; m. Brenda Olive, d. of late L. Hargrave ; educ. Stubbington House, Farnham ; H.M.S. Britannia ; Lt., R.N., 1910 ; Lt.-Cdr. ; Europ. War, 1914–18 ; Baltic operations, 1919–20.

BLACKSTOCK, G. G. (D.S.O. L.G. 1.2.19), Major, 4th Bn. Can. Inf.

BLACKWALL, J. E. (D.S.O. L.G. 1.1.17) ; b. 27.9.73 ; e. s. of late J. Blackwall ; m. 1905, Elinor S., y. d. of W. Statham ; three s. ; two d. ; educ. Cambridge ; Lt.-Col. Comdg. 4th Batt. Leics. Regt. ; served S. Afr., 1900–2 ; Europ. War, 1914 18.

BLACKWELL, S. F. B. (D.S.O. L.G. 25.11.16), 2nd Lt., Norf. R.

BLACKWOOD, A. P. (D.S.O. L.G. 4.3.18) (Details, L.G. 16.8.18) ; b. 4.11.81 ; s. of Major P. F. Blackwood ; educ. Eton and Sandhurst ; m. 1920, Kyra, d. of late A. L. Hughes ; 2nd Lt., Unatt., 8.1.01 ; Border R. 9.3.01 ; Lt. 7.1.03 ; Capt. 20.10.12 ; Major 8.1.16 ; Bt. Lt.-Col. 3.6.18 ; T/Brig.-Gen. 18.2.19 ; served S. Afr. 1901–2 ; Europ. War, 1914–18 ; 2nd Class Vladimir, Star of Roumania ; Despatches.

BLACKWOOD, M. B. R. (D.S.O. L.G. 17.11.17), Cdr., R.N. ; was with Commander Smiles in Q Boat adventure.

BLACKWOOD, W., M.B. (D.S.O. L.G. 3.6.18) (Bar, 16.9.18), Capt. (A/Lt.-Col., R.A.M.C.). When in practice at Camborne, Col. Blackwood was in charge of the local company of the 2nd Wessex Field Ambulance (T.). He served in France from 1914 ; Mons Star.

BLACKWOOD, E. H. O'REILLY- (see O'Reilly-Blackwood, E. H.).

BLAIR, D. B. (D.S.O. L.G. 26.11.17) (Details, L.G. 6.4.18), Lt.-Col., N.Z. Inf. ; Despatches ; M.C.

BLAIR, J. F. (D.S.O. L.G. 2.4.19) (Details, L.G. 10.12.19.), Major, Can. Army Dental Corps Despatches.

BLAIR, J. M. (D.S.O. L.G. 24.1.17) ; b. 15.7.80 ; s. of C. Blair, J.P., and Amy F., d. of Sir G. Molesworth ; m. 20.4.09, Lilian L. A., d. of Col. O. R. A. Julian, C.B., C.M.G. ; educ. Winchester College, and Magdalen College, Oxford ; rowed in Magdalen Coll. Eight in 1900 ; Head of the River ; 2nd Lt., R. Highrs., 26.6.01 ; Lt. 21.10.05 ; Adjt. 21.4.07–30.9.09 ; Capt., G. Highrs., 12.8.11 ; Major 18.1.17 ; Bt. Lt.-Col. 3.6.18 ; T/Brig.-Gen. 6.1.19–10.8.20 ; served S. Afr. (Queen's Med., 5 clasps) ; N.W.F., 1908 (Med.) ; Europ. War ; 4th Class Order of St. Vladimir with Swords ; 2nd Class Order of St. Stanislas ; C.M.G. ; Despatches.

BLAIR, P. J. (D.S.O. L.G. 3.6.19), Capt. (A/Lt.-Col.), R. Scots, T.F.

BLAKE, C. P. (D.S.O. L.G. 15.9.16) ; b. 2.1.85 ; o. s. of Sir Patrick Blake ; m. 1916, Florence W., d. of Eng.-Capt. W. R. Apps ; one d. ; Lt.-Comdr., R.N. ; served Europ. War, including Battle of Jutland ; Order of St. Anne (Russia) ; Despatches.

BLAKE, G (D.S.O. L.G. 15.9.16), Cdr., R.N. ; b. 1882 ; s. of T. N. Blake ; m. Jean St. J., d. of Sir W. St. J. Carr ; served Europ. War, including Battle of Jutland ; Order of St. Anne (Russia) ; Despatches.

BLAKE, T. J. E. (D.S.O. L.G. 2.12.18) ; b. 1886 ; m. 1910, Ethel M. Moore ; 2 sons ; educ. Owen's School ; joined 2/1st Queen's Westminster Rifles ; commissioned Dec. 1914, in 13th R. Fus. ; Lt.-Col. ; served Europ. War, 1914–19 ; wounded thrice ; Despatches thrice.

BLAKER, W. F. (D.S.O. L.G. 7.2.18) ; b. 9.4.77 ; 2nd Lt., R.A., 21.4.98 ; Lt. 16.2.01 ; Capt. 14.11.05 ; Major, R.F.A., 30.10.14 ; Lt.-Col. 24.7.18 ; O.B.E. ; Despatches.

BLAKEWAY, T. W. (D.S.O. L.G. 3.6.18), T/Major, A.S.C.

BLAKISTON-HOUSTON, J. (D.S.O. L.G. 1.1.17) ; b. 18.4.81 ; s. of late Blakiston-Houston ; m. 1910, Louisa Henrietta, d. of M.'le Conte, of Port St. Ouen, France ; 2nd Lt., 11 Hrs., 15.2.02 ; Lt. 21.9.04 ; Capt. 16.9.09 ; Adjt., 1915–16 ; T/Lt.-Col. 18.1.18 ; served S. Africa, 1901–2 (Queen's Med., 5 clasps) ; Europ. War, 1914–18 ; wounded ; Despatches.

BLAMEY, E. H. (D.S.O. L.G. 14.1.16) ; b. 20.11.77 ; 2nd Lt., A.S.C., 16.8.02 ; Lt. 13.2.04 ; Capt. 1.1.11 ; Major, R.A.S.C., 30.10.14 ; Bt. Lt.-Col. 1.1.18.

BLAMEY, T. A. (D.S.O. L.G. 1.1.17), Major, A.I.F., 1.7.14 ; Bt. Lt.-Col. 24.9.17 ; Europ. War, 1914–17 ; C.B. ; C.M.G. ; Despatches.

BLAND, C. F. (D.S.O. L.G. 1.2.19), Capt., Essex R., T.F.

BLANDE, A. (D.S.O. L.G. 8.3.19) (Details, L.G. 4.10.19), T/2nd Lt., R.F.

BLANEY, J. A. H. (D.S.O. L.G. 1.2.17), Capt., Permanent Forces, S. Africa.

BLATHERWICK, T. (D.S.O. L.G. 11.1.19), Major, Manchester R., T.F. ; M.C.

BLENCOWE, E. P. (D.S.O. L.G. 14.1.16) ; b. 9.6.77 ; s. of Rev. A. J. Blencowe ; Residentiary Canon of Chester Cathedral ; m. 1919, Irene Sybil, d. of late Rev. W. Maude-Roxby ; educ. Marlborough ; Oxford University ; 2nd Lt., Hamps. R., 17.2.00 ; Lt. 20.12.01 ; 2nd Lt., A.S.C., 1.1.02 ; Lt. 1.1.03 ; Capt. 1.5.07 ; Major 30.10.14 ; Bt. Lt.-Col. 3.6.19 ; served S. Africa, 1900–01 Queen's Med., 3 clasps) ; Europ. War, 1914–18 ; Despatches.

BLENNERHASSETT, W. L. R. P. S. (D.S.O. L.G. 21.1.20), T/Capt., Spec. List.

BLEW, T. H. (D.S.O. L.G. 1.1.18), T/Lt.-Col., S. African Heavy Artillery ; Despatches.

BLEWITT, G. (D.S.O. L.G. 4.6.17) ; b. 5.12.84 ; e. s. of Maj.-Gen. W. E. Blewitt, C.B., C.M.G. ; m. 1917, Audrey Ethel, d. of Capt. C. H. Fenwick, late 60th Rifles ; one d. ; educ. Harrow ; 2nd Lt., Oxf. L. Inf., 28.1.05 ; Lt. 6.4.07 ; Capt. 18.4.14 ; Bt. Major 3.6.16 ; T/Lt.-Col. 29.6.18 ; Europ. War ; M.C. ; Despatches five times.

BLIGH, THE HON. N. G. (D.S.O. L.G. 16.9.18) ; b. 1888 ; s. of Earl of Darnley ; m. 1912, Mary Jack, d. of late Capt. G. A. Frost, R.A. ; two d. ; late R. Bde. ; Lt.-Col., R. of O. ; Europ. War, 1914–18 ; Despatches.

BLISS, E. W., M.R.C.S.Eng., L.R.C.P.Lond. (D.S.O. L.G. 1.1.17) ; b. 19.9.69 ; s. of late Rev. W. B. Bliss ; m. Florence Ruth, d. of late T. Greves ; educ. Dudley Grammar School ; Queen's College ; Queen's and General Hospital, Birmingham ; Lt., R.A.M.C., 28.1.97 ; Capt. 16.11.98 ; Major 29.10.07 ; Bt. Lt.-Col. 18.2.15 ; Col. 26.12.17 ; served in Soudan ; Battles of Atbara and Omdurman ; Despatches twice ; Europ. War ; C.M.G. ; Officier Légion d'Honneur ; Croix de Guerre with Palm ; Despatches five times.

BLISS, J. A. (D.S.O. L.G. 7.2.18); b. 15.2.70; s. of late Sir Henry Bliss, K.C.I.E.; m. 1913, Anna Lucy, d. of late H. Thomas: 2nd Lt., Middx. R., 3.5.90; Lt., Ind. S.C., 4.12.91; Adjt., Impl. Yeo., 24.3.01–22.1.02; Capt., Ind. Army, 3.5.01; Major 3.5.08; Lt.-Col. 3.5.16; served Burma, 1892–93 (Med. with clasp); N.W.F., 1897–98 (Med., 2 clasps); Tirah, 1897–98 (clasp); S. Africa, 1901–2 (Queen's Med., 5 clasps); Tibet, 1903–4 (Medal); Europ. War, 1914–17; M.V.O., 1912; Despatches.

BLISS, R. H. (D.S.O. L.G. 11.1.19), Capt., Can. Inf.

BLOCK, A. (D.S.O. L.G. 7.2.18) (Bar, L.G. 22.4.18); b. 17.8.83; 2nd Lt., R.A., 24.12.02; Lt. 24.12.05; Capt. 30.10.14; Major, R.F.A., 8.8.16.

BLOIS, A. O. (D.S.O. L.G. 18.7.17); Capt., Can. Inf., 16.6.13.

BLOIS, D. G. (D.S.O. L.G. 14.1.16); b. 12.2.75; s. of late Sir John Blois (8th Bart.) and Dowager Lady Blois; m. 1914, Georgina Isabella Frances, 2nd d. of Admiral Sir Compton Domvile, G.C.B., G.C.V.O.; one son; one d.; educ. Wellington; 2nd Lt., R.A., 1894; Major 17.11.11; served S. Africa (Despatches; Queen's Med., 4 clasps; King's Med., 2 clasps); Europ. War, 1914–16, serving in all parts of the British line; was present at 2nd Battle of Ypres, taking part in actions at Hill 60; advance on the Somme 14.7.16. Lt.-Col. Blois fell in action. The following is an extract from a letter from his General, under date July, 1916: "I had the greatest reliance on his courage, coolness and judgment. His Brigade had done extremely well in the recent operations, and the General Commanding the Infantry Brigade with which he has always been affiliated had particularly asked me to say that both he and all his Brigade feel they have lost a friend and an Artillery Commander in whom they had the greatest confidence. . . . We all respected him; he was a gallant soldier and died doing his duty."

D. G. Blois.

BLOMFIELD, R. G. (D.S.O. L.G. 1.1.18); b. 7.12.90; Mobd. Terr. F. to 8.5.16; 2nd Lt., 5 D.G., 31.3 16–9.5.16 (R.F.C. 9.5.16–31.3.18); Lt., 5 D.G., 1.10.17; T/Lt.-Col. 30.10.17–31.3.18; Despatches.

BLORE, H. R. (D.S.O. L.G. 1.1.18); b. 5.5.71; 2nd Lt., K.R.R.C., 29.10.90; Lt. 22.2.93; Capt. 14.9.98; Adjt. 11.3.99–2.9.02; Bt. Major 29.11.00; Major 21.10.07; Lt.-Col. 20.8.16; Despatches.

G. R. B. Blount.

BLOUNT, G. P. C. (D.S.O. L.G. 1.1.18); b. 29.11.73; 2nd Lt., R.A., 17.11.94; Lt. 17.11.97; Capt. 1.7.00; Adjt. 25.1.06–12.11.06, and 30.11.10 to 3.6.12; Major 30.10.14; Bt. Lt.-Col. 3.6.19; Despatches.

BLOUNT, G. R. B. (D.S.O. L.G. 23.5.17), Capt., R.N.

BLOUNT, H. (D.S.O. L.G. 1.1.17); b. 11.10.81; 2nd Lt., R.M.A., 1.9.98; Lt. 1.7.99; Capt. 1.9.09; Major 10.1.17; Despatches.

BLOUNT-DINWIDDIE, J. (D.S.O. L.G. 3.6.18); b. 23.6.86; 2nd Lt., A.S.C., 24.1.06; Lt. 24.1.08; Capt., R.A.S.C., 5.8.14; Bt. Major 3.6.15; Despatches.

BLUE, W. E. (D.S.O. L.G. 3.6.19), Major, Can. F.A.

BLUHM, Q. M. (D.S.O. L.G. 30.1.20), Manch. R., T.F.

BLUNDELL, F. B. MOSS- (see Moss-Blundell, F. B.).

Q. M. Bluhm.

BLUNT, C. E. G. (D.S.O. L.G. 1.1.17); b. 21.2.68; e. s. of late Major-Gen. Grant Blunt, R.E.; m. 1900 (1st), Aimée (who died, 1918), d. of Col. A. Stragham, C.B.; one s.; one d.; m. (2ndly) Beatrice, w. of F. Fullajer; 2nd Lt. 23.3.89; Major 24.8.01; Bt. Major 16.11.98; served Dongola Expedition, 1896 (Despatches, 4th Class Medjidie); Nile Expedition, 1898 (Despatches); Europ. War, 1915–19; Despatches; C.B.E., 1919; 3rd Class Osmanieh; 2nd Class Order of the Nile.

BLUNT, D. H. (D.S.O. L.G. 14.11.16); b. May, 1878; s. of late C. H. Blunt; 2nd Lt., Devon R., Jan. 1899; Capt. 1903; Major, 1915; T/Lt.-Col., 1916; served S. Africa (Queen's and King's Medals, 5 clasps); Europ. War; Despatches. He died of wounds 3.10.17.

BLUNT, G. C. G. (D.S.O. L.G. 3.6.16); b. 10.6.83; s. of G. H. Blunt; educ. Sedbergh, and Sandhurst; 2nd Lt., A.S.C., 23.8.02; Lt. 18.2.04; Capt. 1.1.11; Major, R.A.S.C., 30.10.14; served Europ. War; commanded 1st Indian Cavalry Supply Column, 1914–16; joined Indian Cavalry Div. on their arrival at the front in Nov. 1914; commanded XI. Corps Amm. Park, H.Q., Aug. to Sept. 1916; comdg. R.A.S.C. Base Mech. Transport Depôt (Northern) from Sept. 1916; Despatches twice; O.B.E., 1919.

BOAK, H. E. (D.S.O. L.G. 1.1.17); b. 26.12.84; s. of H. W. C. Boak; educ. R.M. College, Canada; ent. Can. F.A., 1905; R. Can. H.A., 1905; Bt. Capt., 1910; Capt., R. Can. H.A., 1911; Major, R.H.A., Canadians, 1915; T/Lt.-Col., 9.5.17; Lt.-Colonel; Adjt., R. Can. H.A., 1911–16, then on Staff from 1916; A.A. and Q.M.G., 2nd Can. Div., 11.5.17.

BOAL, R. (D.S.O. L.G. 4.9.18); b. 14.2.74; Lt., R.E., 23.7.16; Capt. 24.3.18; Europ. War; Despatches.

BOARD, A. G. (D.S.O. L.G. 1.1.18); b. 11.5.78; 2nd Lt., S.W.B., 18.4.00; Lt. 20.5.03; Capt. 9.6.09; Major 1.9.15; Group Captain, R.A.F., Europ. War, 1914–18; Despatches; C.M.G.

BOARD, A. V. (D.S.O. L.G. 1.1.19), Lt. (T/Major), Essex R.; M.C.

BOARDMAN, H. (D.S.O. L.G. 8.3.19) (Details, L.G. 4.10.19); b. 26.9.95; 2nd Lt., L'pool R., 25.8.17; Lt. 25.2.19; Despatches; M.C.

BOARDMAN, T. H. (D.S.O. L.G. 1.1.17); educ. Huish Grammar School, Taunton; Christ's Hospital O.T.C.; was for a long time in the auxiliary forces; Lt.-Colonel commanding S. Bn. of the R. Inniskillings from Sept. 1916; died of wounds 5.8.17.

BOASE, L. C. (D.S.O. L.G. 8.8.19), Lt., Aust. Inf.; M.C.

BODDAM-WHETHAM, A. C. (D.S.O. L.G. 3.6.18); served S. African War, 1901–2; Queen's Medal with 2 clasps; T/Lt.-Col., A. and S. Highrs.; att. R.A.F. He was killed 22.6.18.

BODDAM-WHETHAM, E. K. (D.S.O. L.G. 14.9.17); s. of late J. W. Boddam-Whetham, of Kirklington Hall, Notts; m. Elizabeth Margaret, widow of Gordon Ayres; educ. Sandroyd; H.M.S. Britannia; Commander, R.N.

BODDAM-WHETHAM, S. A. (D.S.O. L.G. 1.1.17); b. 4.5.85; s. of late J. W. Boddam-Whetham and Harriet Adelaide Boddam-Whetham, d. of John Manning, of Sydney, N.S.W.; m. Edith Sybil, d. of J. L. Brinkley; educ. Oundle; R.M.A., Woolwich; ent. R.A. 23.12.03; Lt. 23.12.06; Adjt., R.A., 10.10.13 to 1915; Capt. 30.10.14; Major 30.7.16; served Europ. War continuously with 7th Div. in Belgium, France and Italy, then transferred to a Corps; Despatches six times; M.C.; Belgian Croix de Guerre.

BODDIE, R. C. (D.S.O. L.G. 23.7.18), Engr. Lt.-Cdr., R.N.

BODDINGTON, H. W. (D.S.O. L.G. 13.5.18), Lt. (A/Major), Yeom., att. Yorks. L.I.

BODINGTON, J. R. (D.S.O. L.G. 8.3.19) (Details, L.G. 4.10.19), Lt. (A/Capt.), Lanc. R., T.F.; M.C.

BODKIN, L. F. (D.S.O. L.G. 27.6.19), Major, Inf. I.A.

BODLEY, E. R. (D.S.O. L.G. 11.11.19), A/Sub Lt., R.N.R.

BODWELL, HOWARD LIONEL (D.S.O. L.G. 14.11.16); b. 13.10.81; s. of E. G. and E. Bodwell; educ. Ingersoll Collegiate Institute; R.M.C., Canada; Lieut., R. of O., Canadian Engineers, 24.6.1913; served in the Europ. War; Lt. in the 72nd Regiment, Seaforth Highrs. of Canada, 14.10.14; transferred to the 47th Bn. Can. Infantry, with the rank of Major, March, 1915; Maj. and 2nd-in-Command, the 2nd Bn. Can. Pnrs.; Lt.-Col.; landed in France in March, 1916; was wounded on the 10th April, and returned to duty on the 1st July; Despatches; C.M.G. His D.S.O. was awarded for gallantry at Courcelette 16.9.16. Lt.-Col. Bodwell has since died.

BODY, JOHN (D.S.O. L.G. 22.12.16) (Bar, L.G. 17.3.17); b. 27.8.75; s. of J. Body, J.P., and Mary Body; m. Mabel, d. of late T. Kenwood, J.P.; educ. Tonbridge School; ent. Army, Jan. 1894; Lt.-Col., 1/5th The Buffs; served four years in Mesopotamia; commanded his battalion, which was the first to enter and occupy Baghdad on 10.3.17; then June to August, 1919, was in command of a column (known as Body's Column) against Sheik Mahmud's followers in Southern Kurdistan; Despatches. After the Armistice was Master of the Tigris Vale Foxhounds in Mesopotamia.

BODY, O. G. (D.S.O. L.G. 15.7.19); b. 5.11.90; s. of late R. B. Body, of Hyde End, Shinfield, Berks; 2nd Lt., R.A., 23.12.10; Lt. 23.12.13; Adjt., R.A., 5.8.15 to 31.10.15; Capt. 8.8.16; Despatches.

BOEVEY, M. CRAWLEY- (see Crawley-Boevey, M.).

BOGART, J. L. H. (D.S.O. L.G. 3.6.19), Lt.-Col., 7th Bn. Can. Engrs.

BOGER, D. C. (D.S.O. L.G. 30.1.20), Lt.-Col., 1st Bn. Cheshire Regt.

BOGLE, J. S. (D.S.O. L.G. 3.6.19), Major (A/Lt.-Col.), I.A.

BOIS, J. (D.S.O. L.G. 22.3.19); b. 24.10.81; 2nd Lt., Unatt., 8.1.01; R. Lanc. R. 9.3.01; Lt. 26.4.02; Capt. 20.11.07; Major 8.1.16; Bt. Lt.-Col. 3.6.17; Despatches; M.C.

BOISSIER, M. E. S. (D.S.O. L.G. 12.7.19), Cdr., R.N.

BOLINGBROKE, A. G. (D.S.O. L.G. 16.8.17), Major, Aust. Mil. Forces.

BOLITHO, E. H. W. (D.S.O. L.G. 3.6.19); b. 20.4.82; 1st com. 21.12.00; Lt. 21.12.03; Adjt., R.A., 29.10.12; Major 13.9.15; retired R.A. 13.4.19 with rank of Lt.-Col. in the Army.

BOLSTER, T. C. C. (D.S.O. L.G. 23.5.17), Lt.-Cdr., R.N.

BOLTON, A. H. (see Boulton, A. H.).

BOLTON, H. W. (D.S.O. L.G. 1.1.19); b. 19.12.31; 2nd Lt., R.W. Surrey R., 26.9.14; Lt. 7.4.15; Capt. 5.5.17; Despatches.

BOLTON, R. E. C. (D.S.O. L.G. 1.2.17), Eng. R.I. Marine.

BOMFORD, L. R. (D.S.O. L.G. 2.4.19) (Details, L.G. 10.12.19), Lt. (A/Capt.), Worc. R., T.F.; M.C.

BOND, E. L. (D.S.O. L.G. 1.1.18); b. 19.9.78; 2nd Lt., R.A., 4.3.99; Lt. 16.2.01; Capt. 1.2.08; Major 30.10.14; Bt. Lt.-Col. 3.6.19; served N.E. Frontier of India, 1902; op. against the Darwesh Khel Waziris.

BOND, F. L. C. (D.S.O. L.G. 3.6.19), Major, Can. Rly. Troops.

BOND, G. F. D. (D.S.O. L.G. 8.3.19) (Details, L.G. 4.10.19), Major, Can. Inf.; M.C.

BOND, G. M. (D.S.O. L.G. 4.6.17); born 11.6.80; 2nd Lt., Yorks. L.I., 24.7.01; Lt. 14.1.05; Capt. 22.1.14; Major 8.5.16; employed with K.A. Rifles 25.6.05 to 15.3.08; served S. African War, 1900–1; Europ. War.

BOND, G. W. (D.S.O. L.G. 22.12.16); b. 10.6.73; s. of G. M. Bond, J.P.; m. Elsie Gertrude, d. of Lt. C. Eastmead; one s.; educ. Brighton College, and Clare College, Cambridge; enlisted in 1st Bn. York. and Lanc. R., 28.3.96; commissioned R. War. R. 11.4.00; Capt. 11.4.09; Capt., I.A., 7.10.09; Major 1.9.15; served Abor Exp. 1911–12 (Despatches; Medal with clasp); Europ. War, France and Belgium, 1914–15 (Despatches); Mesopotamia, 1916; Despatches.

BOND, H. H. (D.S.O. L.G. 1.1.17), e. s. of late Major-Gen. H. Bond, R.A.; Bt. Colonel, late R.A.; was T/Brig.-Gen.; served S. African War, 1902 (Queen's Medal, 4 clasps). He died in Dublin, aged 46 years.

BOND, J. H. R. (D.S.O. L.G. 25.8.17); b. 21.7.71; Lt., R.A.M.C., 27.7.99; Capt. 27.7.02; Major 27.7.11; Lt.-Col. 1.3.15; served S. African War, 1899–1902; Queen's Medal with 6 clasps; King's Medal with 2 clasps.

BOND, L. W. (D.S.O. L.G. 18.7.17), Major, Aust. A.M.C.

BOND, R. C. (D.S.O. L.G. 27.9.01) (Bar, L.G. 30.1.20), Lt.-Col., Yorks. L.I. (see "The Distinguished Service Order," from its institution to 31.12.15), by same publishers.

T. A. Bond.

BOND, T. A. (D.S.O. L.G. 11.1.16); b. 1872; educ. Brisbane; joined Australian Naval Forces, 1898; Lt.-Commander; went to New Guinea in command Naval Reserve Company, which captured Bita Paka Wireless Station, 1914 (Despatches twice); was at landing at Suvla, Aug. 1915; took part in Battle of Chocolate Hill 21.8.15, having command of a company 1st R.A.N.B.T.; stayed on Gallipoli until evacuation; Despatches twice.

BONE, R. J. (D.S.O. L.G. 7.4.16), Lt., R.N.; Fl.-Cdr., R.N.A.S.

BONHAM, C. B. (D.S.O. L.G. 3.6.18); b. 12.11.71; m. Camille Claire, sister of the 6th Marquis Testaferrata Olivier; three s.; two d.; 2nd Lt., R.E., 13.2.91; Lt. 13.2.94; Capt. 29.10.01; Major 13.2.11; Lt.-Col. 24.9.18; Despatches.

BONHAM-CARTER, A. L. (D.S.O. L.G. 3.6.18) ; b. 1.1.88 ; 2nd Lt., K.R.R.C., 9.10.07 ; Lt. 4.5.10 ; Capt. 4.3.15 ; Bt. Major 3.6.19 ; Despatches.

BONHAM-CARTER, C. (D.S.O. L.G. 1.1.17) ; b. 25.2.76 ; s. of late H. Bonham-Carter, 5 Hyde Park Square, W., and Sibella Charlotte, d. of late G. W. Norman ; m. 1st, Gladys Beryl, d. of Lt.-Col. A. B. Coddington, R.E. ; two s. ; 2nd, Gabrielle Madge Jeannette, d. of Capt. E. Fisher ; one s. ; educ. Clifton College ; R.M.C., Sandhurst ; Staff College ; 2nd Lt., R.W. Kent R., 29.2.96 ; Lt. 16.7.98 ; Adjt., 1901 ; Capt., R. War. R., 16.11.01 ; Capt., R.W. Kent R., 18.12.07 ; Major 28.10.14 ; Bt. Lt.-Col. 1.1.16 ; Bt. Col. 1.1.18 ; T/Brig.-Genl. 12.4.17 ; served S. African War, 1900–1 ; Queen's Medal, 4 clasps ; Europ. War, 1914–18 ; Despatches ; Officier, Légion d'Honneur ; American Distinguished Service Medal ; C.M.G., 1919.

BONHAM-CARTER, S. S. (D.S.O. L.G. 23.7.18), Lt., R.N.

BONN, W. B. L. (D.S.O. L.G. 2.12.18) ; b. 27.2.85 ; s. of Leo Bonn ; educ. Eton ; New College, Oxford ; served Europ. War, 1914–18, with Leic. Yeom. and W. Gds. ; Despatches ; Mons Star ; M.C. ; Major, Leic. Yeom.

BONNER, A. B. (D.S.O. L.G. 8.3.19) (Details, L.G. 4.10.19.), Lt.,Can. Inf.; M.M.

BONNYMAN, E. W. (D.S.O. L.G. 18.2.18) (Details, L.G. 18.7.18) ; s. of late Col. Bonnyman, R.A.M.C. ; educ. Beaumont College, Old Windsor, and passed for Woolwich, 1906, but failed in the medical examination owing to his eyesight ; was gazetted to A. and S. Highrs., Sept. 1914 ; went out to France, May, 1915, and saw more or less continuous service except for 6 months on sick leave ; T/Capt. ; M.C. He died of wounds 11.8.18.

BOONE, H. G. (D.S.O. L.G. 3.6.16) ; b. 16.11.80 ; ent. R.A. 6.1.00 ; Lt. 3.4.01 ; Capt. 12.10.09 ; Major ; served in Tibet, 1903–4 ; op. in and around Gyantse ; Medal and clasp. Major Boone died of wounds received in action 5.9.17.

BOOTH, E. B. (D.S.O. L.G. 14.1.16) ; b. 23.7.79 ; s. of late B. S. Booth, M.D. ; m. Margaret Agnes, widow of Capt. L. J. S. Allen, Hants R., and d. of J. Currie ; ent. R.A.M.C. 31.1.05 ; Capt. 31.7.08 ; Major 15.10.15 ; Europ. War, 1914–18 ; A.D.M.S., Cameroons Exp. Force, 13.8.15 to 8.3.16 ; Despatches.

BOOTH, P. D. (D.S.O. L.G. 4.2.18) (Details, L.G. 5.7.18) ; s. of P. Booth, Aligarh, Liberton, Midlothian ; T/Capt., R.F.A. (Div. T. M. Officer) ; M.C. He died of wounds 2.12.17.

BOOTH, T. M. (D.S.O. L.G. 3.6.16) (Bar, L.G. 10.1.17) ; b. 10.4.74 ; e. s. of the Rt. Hon. Charles Booth, P.C., and Mary, d. of the late Charles Zachary Macaulay, youngest brother of Lord Macaulay, the historian ; m. Elizabeth Alice, d. of late Capt. W. Powell ; educ. Harrow ; Trinity College, Cambridge ; entered G. Highrs., May, 1895 ; Lieutenant 18.5.98 ; Captain 31.12.00 ; served in the South African War, 1900–02 (Queen's Medal with three clasps) ; Adjutant, Volunteers (London Scottish), 10.3.05 to 14.1.08 ; Brigade Major, Seaforth Cameron Infantry Brigade, Scottish Command, 12.8.11 to 4.8.14 ; served Europ. War, 1915–18 ; Brigade Major from 5.8.14 ; Major 11.12.14 ; T/Lt.-Col., commanding the 1/7th Gordon Highrs.

BOOTHBY, E. L. B. (D.S.O. L.G. 14.7.16), Cdr., R.N.

BORDEN, A. H. (D.S.O. L.G. 14.2.18) (Details, L.G. 5.7.18), Lt.-Col., Can. Infy.

BORLAND, J. McI. (D.S.O. L.G. 23.5.17), Cdr., R.N.R., R.D.

BORRETT, O. C. (D.S.O. L.G. 3.6.15) (Bar, L.G. 18.7.17) (see " The Distinguished Service Order," from its institution to 31.12.15, by same publishers.

BORROW, E. (D.S.O. L.G. 19.11.17) (Details, L.G. 22.3.18) ; served Europ. War, 13th Durham L.I., and att. W. Riding R. 1914–17 ; Despatches ; Major Borrow was British Delegate, I.A.T.C., Vienna, 1919 ; employed Klagenfurt Plebiscite Commission, 1920.

E. K. Borthwick

BORTHWICK, E. K. (D.S.O. L.G. 15.10.18), T/Capt., K.A.R. ; M.C.

BORTHWICK, F. H. (D.S.O. L.G. 1.1.18) (Bar, L.G. 26.7.18) ; s. of A. Borthwick, of Colwyn Bay ; Lt.-Col., R.W.F. He went out to Gallipoli in charge of the Colwyn Bay Company of the Fusiliers ; Lt.-Col. commanding a battalion, R.W.F.

BORTON, A. D. (D.S.O. L.G. 31.5.16). He was awarded the Victoria Cross (see " The Victoria Cross," by same publishers).

BORWICK, G. O. (D.S.O. L.G. 4.6.17) ; b. 1879 ; s. of J. C. Borwick ; m. Hon. Mary Cavendish, e. d. of Baron Waterpark ; educ. Harrow and Trinity College, Oxford ; ent Surrey Yeom., 1901 ; served with them in France, Jan.–Nov. 1915, and in Salonika till the Armistice ; Despatches thrice. Major Borwick is a Director, George Borwick and Sons ; M.P. (C.U.), North Croydon, from Dec. 1918.

BORWICK, M. (D.S.O. L.G. 1.1.18) ; b. 25.6.82 ; 2nd Lt., 2 Dns., 11.6.02 ; Lt. 15.6.07 ; Capt. 6.10.11 ; served S. African War, 1901 ; Europ. War ; Bt. Major 1.1.19 ; Chief Instructor, Equitation Wing, Cavalry School, Netheravon.

BORWICK, T. F. (D.S.O. L.G. 4.6.17) ; b. 1890 ; s. of H. B. Borwick, Melbourne ; m. Elsa, d. of Edoardo and Fanny de Ambrosis, of Florence ; one d. ; educ. Melbourne University ; served Europ. War, 1915–17 ; twice wounded ; Despatches.

BOSANQUET, W. S. B. (D.S.O. L.G. 17.12.17) (Details, L.G. 23.4.18) ; b. 1893 ; s. of Sir Albert Bosanquet and Philippa Frances, d. of W. Bence Jones ; m. Esther, d. of the late Grover Cleveland, President of U.S.A. ; two d. ; educ. Eton ; King's College, Cambridge ; served Europ. War ; Capt., C. Gds., S.R.

BOSCAWEN, HON. M. T. (D.S.O. L.G. 20.10.16) b. 5.2.92 ; fourth s. of seventh Viscount Falmouth and Kathleen, d. of second Lord Penrhyn ; educ. Cambridge (B.A.) ; b. 5.2.92 ; 2nd Lt., R. Brig., 21.1.13 ; Lt. 10.11.14 ; Capt. 25.10.15 ; A/Lt.-Col., S. Bn., Rif. Brig., 9.5.18 ; served Europ. War, 1914–18 ; Despatches ; M.C. ; D.S.O. awarded for services at Guillemont 12–21.8.1916.

BOSHELL, F. S. (D.S.O. L.G. 3.6.19) ; b. 2.5.69 ; Capt. R. Berks R. 6.9.15 ; Despatches ; M.C. He is a son-in-law of Mr. H. Barrow, of Wynberg.

BOSTOCK, L. (D.S.O. L.G. 16.9.18), T/Lt. (A/Capt.), Northants R.

BOSWELL, H. E. (D.S.O. L.G. 8.3.19) (Details, L.G. 4.10.19), T/2nd Lt., Worc. R. ; M.C.

BOTELER, F. W. (D.S.O. L.G. 1.1.18) ; b. 16.12.54 ; 1st com. 12.2.74 ; Lt.-Col. 13.2.00 ; Bt. Col. 10.2.04 ; retired with the rank of Colonel 3.6.05 ; Despatches.

BOTHA, P. S. G. (D.S.O. L.G. 1.2.17), Lt.-Col., S. African Horse.

BOTHA, THEUNIS (D.S.O. L.G. 22.8.18). Lt.-Col. Theunis Botha is the only surviving brother of General Botha. Mrs. Botha is the daughter of Mrs. Caroline Mon and the late Mr. Mon, of Roodepoort, Utrecht district, Natal. Lieut.-Colonel Botha received the D.S.O. for his services during the Rebellion and South-West campaign, and raised the regiment Botha's Natal Horse.

BOTHA, THEUNIS (D.S.O. L.G. 22.8.18.), Major, Pretoria Command (Botha's Mounted Rifles), S. African Forces.

BOUCHER, M. W. S. (D.S.O. L.G. 17.10.19), Lt. Cdr., R.N.

BOULTON, A. H. (D.S.O. L.G. 1.1.17) ; b. 14.1.82 ; s. of F. J. Boulton ; m. Violet Catherine, d. of G. W. Richardson ; one s. ; educ. May Place, Malvern Wells ; Hereford Cathedral School, 1899 ; Capt. 1906 ; att. Can. Militia, 1910 ; rejoined 1st Bn. Herefords, 1914 ; sent as Adjt. to New Army 7.1.15, and posted 13th (S.) Bn. Glos. R., as Adjt., ; Major 7.1.15 ; appointed 2nd-in-Command, June, 1915 ; appointed to command and given temp. rank of Lt.-Col. 14.8.15 ; went overseas in command ; slightly wounded.

BOURCHIER, M. W. J. (D.S.O. L.G. 18.1.18) (Details, L.G. 25.4.18), Lt.-Col., Aust. L.H. Rgt.

BOURCHIER, R. W. H. (gazetted as Bouchier, R. W. H.) (D.S.O. L.G. 1.1.18) ; b. 26.2.80 ; 2nd Lt., R.A., 23.12.98 ; Lt. 16.2.01 ; Capt. 8.6.07 ; Adjt., R.A., 4.3.08 to 3.3.11 ; Major 30.10.14 ; served S. African War, 1900–2 (Queen's Medal with 3 clasps ; King's Medal with 2 clasps) ; Europ. War ; Bt. Lt.-Col. 1.1.19.

BOURDILLON, L. G. (D.S.O. L.G. 22.9.16), T/Capt., R.A.M.C. ; D.S.O. awarded for services on 19–20 July, 1916, N.E. of Pozières.

BOURKE, E. A. (D.S.O. L.G. 3.6.16) ; b. 25.3.70 ; s. of the late Edward Bourke ; m. Rachel, d. of R. Waters ; two s. ; educ. Wesley College, and R. College of Surgeons, Dublin ; ent. R.A.M.C. 28.1.98 ; Capt. 28.1.01 ; Major 28.10.09 ; Lt.-Col. 1.3.15 ; retired pay, 17.3.21 ; O.C. No. X. Stationary Hospital, 1914–18 ; Despatches twice.

BOURKE, R. (D.S.O. L.G. 23.7.18), Lt., R.N.V.R.

BOURNE, A. G. B. (D.S.O. L.G. 3.6.18) ; b. 25.7.82 ; s. of Rev. C. W. Bourne ; m. Lilian M. P., d. of late Col. P. Gabbett, R.A.M.C. ; one d. ; 2nd Lt., R.M.A., 1.9.99 ; Lt. 1.7.00 ; Capt. 1.9.10 ; Major 6.6.17 ; T/Lt.-Col. 14.6.18 ; served on H.M.S. Renown, 1905–6, on occasion of visit of Prince and Princess of Wales to India ; M.V.O., 1909 ; Capt., 1910 ; Major. 1917 ; served on board H.M.S. Balmoral Castle during the visit of the Duke and Duchess of Connaught to S. Africa, 1910 ; served Europ. War ; Cavalier, Order of St. Maurice and St. Lazarus ; Military Medal for Valour (Italian).

BOURNE, D. K. (D.S.O. L.G. 19.11.17) (Details, L.G. 22.3.18), T/Lt., A/Capt., Welsh R.

BOURNE, G. H. (D.S.O. L.G. 20.10.16) ; b. 21.11.81 ; s. of J. S. P. Bourne and of Mrs. J. E. Bourne, d. of late A. J. Hocking ; educ. at Brisbane Grammar School ; In 1905 he joined the Commonwealth Military Forces ; Major in March, 1914. He served in Gallipoli and throughout the Sinai-Palestine Campaign to the Armistice ; Despatches ; D.S.O. awarded for services on 3–4.8.16, Romani, Egypt ; promoted to Lt.-Col., Commanding the 2nd Light Horse Brigade ; Honorary Extra A.D.C. to the Governor-General of Australia. Lt.-Col. Bourne is Manager of the Bank of New South Wales, Mackay, North Queensland.

BOUSFIELD, H. D. (D.S.O. L.G. 14.1.16) ; b. 3.3.72 ; s. of C. E. Bousfield ; m. Mary Ethel, d. of C. S. Close ; educ. Leeds Grammar School ; Queen's College, Oxford (B.A.) ; served S. African War. 1900–01 (Queen's Medal with 4 clasps) ; went to France with 49th Div., April, 1915, and remained until wounded 9.10.17 ; returned to France 6.2.18 ; commanded 1/5th W. Yorks. R. 2.7.16 to 9.10.17 ; taken prisoner 25.4.18 with the French on Kemmel Hill ; Lt.-Colonel ; C.M.G. ; Belgian Croix de Guerre ; French Croix de Guerre.

BOUVERIE, THE HON. S. PLEYDELL- (see Pleydell-Bouverie, The Hon.S.).

BOUWER, B. D. (D.S.O. L.G. 22.8.18), Lt.-Col., S. African Permanent Force (Staff) ; D.S.O. for services German S.W. Africa.

BOWDEN, A. H. (D.S.O. L.G. 1.1.18) ; s. of H. W. Bowden ; m. Helen, d. of H. G. Modera ; one s. ; educ. King's College, Wimbledon ; Hove ; commissioned 11th (S.) Bn. R. War. R. ; Major, M.G.C. ; Instructor, M.G.C. Instructional Staff, Grantham.

BOWDLER, B. W. B. (D.S.O. L.G. 14.1.16) ; b 30.3.73 ; s. of late Col. C. W. B. Bowdler, C.B. He m. Helen Dalrymple, d. of the late Captain R. B.W. Copland-Crawford, 60th Rifles ; educ. at Bedford Grammar School ; ent. R.E. 22.7.92 ; Lt. 22.7.95 ; Capt. 26.5.03 ; Major 22.7.12. He served in the European War ; Despatches 5 times ; Brevet of Lt.-Col. ; Officer, Legion of Honour ; Order of St. Stanislaus ; Belgian Croix de Guerre.

BOWDON, W. E. I. BUTLER- (see Butler-Bowdon, W. E. I.).

BOWELL, R. H. WAKE- (see Wake-Bowell, R. H.).

BOWEN, A. J. HAMILTON- (see Hamilton-Bowen, A. J.).

BOWEN, A. LL. (D.S.O. L.G. 8.3.19) (Details, L.G. 4.10.19), Major (A/Lt.-Col.), Welsh R., T.F.

BOWEN, A. W. N., L.R.C.S. and P. (Ireland) (D.S.O. L.G. 4.6.17), was born on 13.1.73 ; y. s. of the late Mr. G. E. and Mrs. Bowen, of Portaferry, co. Down, Ireland ; m. Edith, d. of S. A. Hickson. He was educated at Derry and Dublin ; Lt., R.A.M.C., 28.7.97 ; Captain 28.7.00 ; Major 28.4.09 ; Lt.-Col. 1.3.15, and T/Col. in France (A.D.M.S., 16th Division) ; served in the Europ. War, France, from Aug. 1914 till Feb. 1919 (with the exception of 7 months on sick list) ; C.B.E. ; five times mentioned in Despatches ; wounded June, 1917.

BOWEN, F. O. (D.S.O. L.G. 1.1.17) ; b. 8.10.77 ; 2nd Lt., R. Garr. R., 27.8.09 ; Lt., R. Garr. R., 25.3.03 ; R. Ir. Rgt., 4.10.05 ; Capt. 26.1.10 ; Major 24.10.16 ; Despatches.

BOWEN, H. E. WEBB- (see Webb-Bowen, H. E.).

BOWEN, H. R. (D.S.O. L.G. 2.5.16) ; b. 10.9.80 ; s. of late Lt.-Col. H. G. Bowen, Conn. Rangers ; educ. Wellington College ; commissioned Essex R. 18.4.00 ; Lt. 12.11.00 ; Capt. 25.8.10 ; Major 1.9.15 ; served S. African War, 1900–2 ; Queen's Medal with 3 clasps ; King's Medal with 2 clasps ; Europ. War, 1914–18 ; 3 times wounded ; Despatches 4 times ; Croix de Guerre.

BOWEN, H. W. (D.S.O. L.G. 26.8.18) ; b. 18.9.70 ; 2nd Lt., R.A., 25.7.90 ; Lt. 25.7.93 ; Capt. 14.10.99 ; Major 30.5.11 ; Bt. Lt.-Col. 1.1.17 ; Lt.-Col., R.A., 1.5.17.

BOWEN, W. A. (D.S.O. L.G. 3.6.18) (Bar, L.G. 1.1.19), Major (A/Lt.-Col.), R. of O., R. Lanc. R.

BOWEN, W. J. WEBB- (see Webb-Bowen, W. J.).

BOWER, C. E. S. (D.S.O. L.G. 1.1.17) ; b. 23.5.81 ; 2nd Lt., R.A., 17.3.00 ; Lt. 3.4.01 ; Capt. 16.10.08 ; Adjt. 7.7.11 to 5.7.14 ; Major 30.10.14 ; Bt. Lt.-Col. 3.6.19.

BOWER, J. G. (D.S.O. L.G. 29.10.18), Cdr., R.N.

BOWERBANK, G. S. S. (D.S.O. L.G. 8.3.19) (Details, L.G. 4.10.19), Major, Can. Inf. ; M.C.

BOWES, W. (D.S.O. L.G. 1.1.17) ; b. 29.9.65 ; 1st com. 17.1.00 ; rank of Lt.-Colonel 3.6.18 ; retired 1.9.19 ; Lan. Fus.

BOWHILL, F. W. (D.S.O. L.G. 22.2.18) (Bar, L.G. 3.6.19), Lt.-Col., R.A.F.

BOWIE, D. B. (D.S.O. L.G. 26.3.18) (Details, L.G. 24.8.18), Major, R. Can. Dns.

BOWIE, J. D., M.B. (D.S.O. L.G. 26.9.17) (Details, L.G. 9.1.18), Capt. (A/Lt.-Col.), R.A.M.C. ; b. 20.2.83 ; Lt., R.A.M.C., 29.7.10 ; Capt. 29.1.14 ; Major 3.6.19.

BOWLES, G. P. (D.S.O. L.G. 24.3.19); s. of G. Bowles; b. 1885; Lt.-Cdr., R.N.; Commander, Light Cruiser Platoon since 1921; served Europ. War, 1914–19; Despatches.

BOWLES, J. de V. (D.S.O. L.G. 3.6.16); b. 19.3.77; 2nd Lt., R.A., 28.3.00; Lt. 3.4.01; Capt. 22.2.09; Major 30.10.14; Bt. Lt.-Col. 3.6.18; Despatches.

BOWMAN, G. H. (D.S.O. L.G. 26.3.18) (Details, L.G. 24.8.18); b. Old Trafford, 2.5.91; s. of G. Bowman, M.D.; educ. Haileybury,; Trinity College, Cambridge; joined 3rd R. Warwicks. R. as 2nd Lt. 15.8.14; went to France twice in infantry (wounded); joined R.F.C. 20.3.16; went to France to a Scout Squadron 5.7.16; returned 17.12.16; joined 56th Squadron, B.E.F. (Capt., Ball's V.C. Squadron), 11.5.17 as a Flight Commander; M.C.; Bar to M.C.; promoted Squadron Commander; D.F.C.; Belgian Croix de Guerre; Major; Squadron Leader, R.A.F.

BOWMAN, J. T., M.D. (D.S.O. L.G. 18.1.18), T/Capt., R.A.M.C.

BOWRING, H. W. (D.S.O. L.G. 12.1.16), Capt., R.N.

BOWSER, H. A. (D.S.O. L.G. 1.1.19), T/Major, 171st Siege By., R.G.A.

BOWYER, C. H. (D.S.O. L.G. 26.7.18), T/Capt., R.W.F.; Lt., S. African Defence Force. He died of wounds 24.3.18.

BOYALL, A. M. (D.S.O. L.G. 27.9.01) (1st Bar, L.G. 4.2.18) (Details, L.G. 5.7.18) (2nd Bar, L.G. 27.6.19) (see "The Distinguished Service Order," from its institution to 31.12.1915, by same publishers).

BOYCE, C. E. (D.S.O. L.G. 1.1.17); b. 28.11.82; educ. Haileybury College; R.M. Academy, Woolwich; 2nd Lt., R.A., 23.7.01; Lt. 25.7.04; Capt. 25.7.14; Major 7.11.15; Bt. Lt.-Colonel 3.6.19; Despatches.

BOYCE, G. J. (D.S.O. L.G. 3.6.18), Lt.-Col., Can. A.M.C.

BOYCE, H. A. (D.S.O. L.G. 1.1.17); b. 30.11.70; 2nd Lt., R.A., 25.7.90; Lt. 25.7.93; Capt. 13.2.00; Major 6.3.08; Lt.-Col. 23.1.15.

BOYCE, W. W. (D.S.O. L.G. 8.3.19) (Details, L.G. 4.10.19); b. 5.2.83; Lt., R.A.M.C., 30.7.06; Capt. 30.1.10; Major 28.1.19.

BOYD, H. A., B A. (D.S.O. L.G. 3.6.16); b. Dublin, 11.7.77; s. of the late Sir Walter Boyd, Bart., and Annie, d. of Matthew Anderson, LL.D., Dublin; m. Moya Shaw, d. of J. S. Exham; one s. and one d.; educ. at Trinity Coll., Dublin. He played for the University at Rugby football, and has won the Open Irish Golf Championship once, and the Closed Championship three times; ent. R.A. 28.3.00; served in 1901 and 1902 in South Africa (Queen's Medal with 5 clasps); Capt. 26.2.09; Major 31.10.14; served continuously in France from Sept. 1914, to the conclusion of the war; Brigade-Major, 24th Brigade, R.F.A., Third Canadian Division, from June, 1916, to June, 1917; C.M.G.; Croix de Chevalier of the Legion of Honour; 1914 Star; Despatches four times.

BOYD, J. DOPPING (D.S.O. L.G. 1.1.15) (Bar, L.G. 1.1.18) (see "The Distinguished Service Order," from its institution to 31.12.1915, by same publishers).

BOYD, S. (D.S.O. L.G. 25.8.17); b. 11.9.81; 2nd Lt., R.E. 18.8.00; Capt. 18.0.03; Major 18.8.10; Lt.-Col. 2.11.16.

BOYD-MOSS, L. B. (D.S.O. L.G. 1.1.18); b. 20.7.73; 2nd Lt., S. Staffs. R., 6.6.96; Major 26.12.01; Bt. Major 22.8.02; Bt. Lt.-Col. 17.8.15; Bt. Col. 1.1.19; T/Brig.-Gen. 10.11.15; Despatches; C.M.G.

BOYD-ROCHFORT, H. (D.S.O. L.G. 4.6.17); b. 18.7.81; ent. 21st Lancers 5.1.01; Lt. 7.5.02; Capt. 4.4.12; Bt. Lt.-Col. 6.8.20; retired 21st Lancers 5.8.20; Despatches; M.C.

BOYD-SHANNON, W. (see Shannon, W. Boyd-).

BOYLAN, E. T. A. G. (D.S.O. L.G. 16.9.18); b. 23.2.94; educ. The Oratory School, Edgbaston; R.M.A., Woolwich; posted R.F.A. 19.12.13; Lt. 9.6.15; Capt. 3.11.17; Adjt., R.A., 1.2.17 to 12.11.17, and 23.6.19; Despatches; M.C.

BOYLE, C. A. (D.S.O. L.G. 9.9.21); b. 28.3.88; 2nd Lt., Unatt., 19.1.07; I.A. 13.3.08; Lt. 13.4.09; Capt. 1.9.10; Bt. Major 3.6.19; Despatches.

BOYLE, C. R. C. (D.S.O. L.G. 1.1.18) (Bar, L.G. 18.2.18) (Details, L.G. 18.7.18); b. 16.8.86; 2nd Lt., Oxf. and Bucks. L.I.; Lt. 7.4.09; Capt. 17.5.15; T/Lt.-Col.; Despatches.

BOYLE, E. C. P. (D.S.O. L.G. 1.1.17), Lt.-Col., H.A.C. (T.F.). He was killed in action 7.2.17.

BOYLE, H. K. (D.S.O. L.G. 3.6.19), Capt., T/Major, W. Yorks. R., T.F.

BOYLE, THE HON. J. D. (D.S.O. L.G. 4.6.17); b. 8.7.84; s. of 7th Earl of Glasgow; m. Ethel, d. of Sir H. A. Hodges, Judge of the Supreme Court, Victoria, Australia; educ. Winchester; ent. 2nd R. Brig. 16.5.06; Lt. 23.3.10; Capt. 5.8.14; Bt. Major 3.6.19; Despatches; C.B.E.

L. S. Bracegirdle.

W. Bradbury.

BOYLE, J. W. (D.S.O. L.G. 3.6.19), Lt.-Col., Can. Militia.

BOYS, S. (D.S.O. L.G. 16.9.18), Capt., 5th Bn. Durham L.I., T.F.

BRACE, H. F. (D.S.O. L.G. 18.1.18) (Details, L.G. 25.4.18); b. 10.10.18; s. of late F. A. Brace, J.P. and Annie Isobel, d. of late H. Fergusson; m. Beatrice Ida, d. of Sir W. H. Feilden, Bart.; one s.; 2nd Lt., 15 Hrs., 8.2.08; Lt. 22.9.11; Adjt., 15 Hrs., 6.8.14 to 31.12.14; Capt. 25.3.15; Major 1.7.20; M.C.; Despatches twice; wounded twice.

BRACEGIRDLE, L. S. (D.S.O. L.G. 3.6.16); b. 31.5.81; 4th s. of late Capt. F. Bracegirdle and Mrs. Bracegirdle, of Kaikoura, E. Balmain, Sydney; m. 1910, Lilian Annie, 2nd d. of Paterson Saunders; two s.; educ. Sydney High School; joined N.S.W. Naval Forces as Naval Cadet, 1898; Midshipman, 1900; Lieut., S. African Irregular Forces, 1901–02; Sub. Lieut. in Australian Naval Forces, 1902; Lieut., R. Aust. N., 1911; Acting Lt.-Comdr.; Comd. 1st Royal Aust. Naval Bridging Train abroad, 1915–17; District Naval Officer, S. Australia; served as Midshipman with Naval Brigade in China (Boxer Campaign)), 1900–01 (China Medal); S. Africa, 1901–02 (Queen's Medal, 3 clasps); European War, German New Guinea, Sept. 1914; Suvla Bay, Gallipoli, Suez Canal and Palestine; Despatches thrice; promoted Commander.

BRACKLEY, H. G. (D.S.O. L.G. 22.6.17), Fl. Lt., R.N.A.S., D.S.C.

BRADBROOKE, G. H. (D.S.O. L.G. 11.1.19), Capt., Can. Cav., 26.1.12; Major, Can. Mtd. Rif.; Despatches; M.C.

BRADBURY, W., M.B. (D.S.O. L.G. 21.6.18); b. 22.12.84; s. of S. and E. Bradbury; m. Norah Michael, d. of G. M. Williams; two s.; one d.; Surgeon, R.N., Nov. 1908; Surg. Lt.-Cdr., Nov. 1916; Staff Surgeon; served in China during Chinese Revolution, 1913; was notified of the "satisfaction of the Admiralty" for services rendered to the Chinese wounded; Chinese Medal for same services; Medical Officer, H.M.S. Circe (mine-sweeper), Aug. 1914, to Dec. 1914; with R.N. Div. from Dec. 1914, to Jan. 1917 (Gallipoli and France); with Harwich Light Cruiser Force from Jan. 1917, to Feb. 1919; wounded in Gallipoli; Despatches.

BRADFIELD, R. H. (D.S.O. L.G. 1.2.19); Capt., 75th Bn. Can. Inf., 1st Can. Ontario Regt. (Toronto); Capt. 18.5.16; Despatches; M.C.

BRADFORD, E. A. (D.S.O. L.G. 1.1.17); b. 8.12.79; y. s. of late Col. Sir Ed. R. C. Bradford, Bart., G.C.B., G.C.S.I.; m. 1908, Margaret, d. of late H. C. Hardy; one s.; three d.; educ. Evelyn's; Eton; R.M.A., Woolwich; 2nd Lt., K.R.R.C., 25.10.99; Lt. 13.1.01; Capt. 4.6.07; Major 1.9.15; served S. Afr., 1899–02 (Queen's Med.; King's Med., 8 clasps; Despatches); Europ. War, 1914–19; Despatches twice; Bt. Lt.-Col. 1.1.19.

BRADFORD, T. A. (D.S.O. L.G. 14.1.16); b. 23.3.96; e. s. of G. Bradford, of Milbanke, Darlington; m. 1915, Honor R., d. of Col. W. C. Blackett; one s.; educ. Royal Naval School, Kent; 2nd Lt., Durham L. Inf., 1906; Capt. 8.2.10; later York and Lancaster Regt.; served Europ. War, 1914–16; Despatches twice. He played cricket and Rugby football for Durham county for several years. Two of his brothers won the Victoria Cross.

BRADISH, F. L. (D.S.O. L.G. 1.1.18); b. 15.8.79; Lt., R.A.M.C., 30.7.06; Capt. 30.1.10; Major 30.7.18; Despatches.

BRADLEY, C. G., M.I.M.E., A.M.I.C.E. (D.S.O. L.G. 14.1.16); b. 1880; m. 1906, Annie, y. d. of Caleb Thornton; educ. Birmingham University; France, Germany; S. African War, 1902 (Queen's Medal and two clasps); Europ. War, 1914–17; Lt.-Col., Yorks L.I., T.F.; Despatches thrice.

BRADLEY, E. de W. H. (D.S.O. L.G. 1.1.19); b. 7.7.89; 2nd Lt., Yorks. L. Inf., 6.2.09; Lt. 9.4.13; Capt. 6.2.15; Despatches; Bt. Major 3.6.19; M.C.

BRADLEY, F. H., M.B. (D.S.O. L.G. 1.1.18); b. 22.11.83; y. s. of late Rev. Canon Bradley, Rector of Monaghan; Lt., R.A.M.C., 4.2.08; Capt. 4.8.11 (A/Lt.-Col., R.A.M.C.). He was killed in action 29.9.18.

BRADLEY, S. G. L. (D.S.O. L.G. 1.1.18), Capt. (T/Lt.-Col.), London R.; M.C.

BRADLEY W. (D.S.O. L.G. 27.6.17), Lt.-Cdr. (A/Cdr.), R.N.R., R.D.

BRADLEY-WILLIAMS, W. P. (D.S.O. L.G. 1.1.19); b. 9.10.90; 2nd Lt., Yorks. L.I., 22.5.12; Lt. 1.9.14; Capt. 1.10.15; A/Lt.-Col., Yorks. L.I., att. 5th Bn. Border R.; Despatches.

BRADNEY, E. (D.S.O. L.G. 10.8.21; b. 20.6.89; 2nd Lt., R.E., 20.9.19; Lt. 23.1.12; Capt. 20.9.15; Bt. Major 3.6.18; Despatches.

BRADSHAW, F. E. (D.S.O. L.G. 1 ..17); b. 1865; s. of Surg.-Maj.-Gen. Sir A. F. Bradshaw; m. 1894, Gwendolen, d. of late R. C. L. Bevan; Lt., 1st Batt. Royal Irish Rifles, 1884; joined 15th Sikhs, 1886; Assistant Commissioner, Punjab, 1890; later served as Deputy Commissioner and District Magistrate of the Muzaffargarh, Jullundur and Delhi Districts; Capt., 1895; Major 6.2.02; retired 15.12.04; rejoined (R. of O.), 1914; Hon. Lt.-Col., R. of O., 12.3.18; served Europ. War, 1914–18; Rifle Brigade, Norfolk Regt., Sherwood Foresters and Welsh Regt.; twice wounded; Despatches.

BRADSHAW, G. F. (D.S.O. L.G. 12.5.17), Lt., R.N.

BRADSHAW, W. P. A. (D.S.O. L.G. 26.9.17) (Details, L.G. 9.1.18); b. 8.3.97; 2nd Lt., S. Gds., 16.12.14; Lt. 2.1.15; Capt. 9.4.18; Despatches; D.S.O. awarded for services on 31.7.17 near Boisinghe.

BRADSTOCK, F. E. (D.S.O. L.G. 7.2.19), T/Major, Cape Corps, att. K.A. Rifles.

BRADSTOCK, G. (D.S.O. L.G. 1.1.19), 90th, Brig. R.F.A., T.F.; Major 21.2.20; M.C.

BRADY, G. C. J. (D.S.O. L.G. 3.6.18), Major, R.F.A.

BRADY, I. G. C. (D.S.O. L.G. 8.3.19) (Details, L.G. 4.10.19), T/Major, 9th Bn. North'd. Fus.; M.C.

BRADY, J. B. (D.S.O. L.G. 4.6.17), Capt., K.R.R.C., S.R.

BRAINE, H. E. R. R. (D.S.O. L.G. 14.1.16); b. 1.7.76; s. of late E. F. Braine, Ind. Army; educ. Dulwich College; 2nd Lt., R. Muns. Fus., 21.4.00; Lt. 1.4.02; Capt. 1.3.10; Major 11.8.15; served S. Africa, 1900–2 (Despatches; Queen's Medal, 4 clasps); N.W. Frontier of India, 1908 (Despatches; Medal and clasp; Europ. War, 1914–18; Despatches seven times; Bt. Major 24.7.15; Bt. Lt.-Col. 1.1.17; C.M.G.

BRAITHWAITE, A. N. (D.S.O. L.G. 1.1.18), T/2nd Lt. (T/Capt.), Gen. List; Lt., Yorks. Hus. 25.5.21; M.C.

BRAITHWAITE, F. P. (D.S.O. L.G. 1.1.18), T/Lt.-Col., R.E.; M.C.

BRAITHWAITE, J. (D.S.O. L.G. 4.6.17), T/Major, Graves Registration Section, Gen. List.

BRAITHWAITE, J. C. (D.S.O. L.G. 2.12.18), T/2nd Lt., W. Yorks. R.; M.C.

BRAMBLE, F. G. (D.S.O. L.G. 11.11.19), Cdr., R.N.

BRAMLEY, A. W. JENNINGS- (see Jennings-Bramley, A. W.).

BRANCKER, H. R. (D.S.O. L.G. 1.1.19); b. 19.1.79; 2nd Lt., R.A., 23.6.98; Lt. 16.2.01; Capt. 30.1.04; Major 30.10.14 (R.G.A.); Despatches.

BRANCKER, J. D. D. (D.S.O. L.G. 4.6.17); b. 7.1.78; 2nd Lt., R.A., 29.8.00; Lt. 11.10.02; Capt. 29.8.13; Major. He was killed in action 1.5.17.

BRAND, SIR C. J. Q. (D.S.O. L.G. 31.5.18); s. of E. C. J. Brand, nephew of the late Sir John Brand; m. 1920, Marie, d. of Mr. and Mrs. Vaughan; educ. Marist Brothers, Johannesburg; served Europ. War, 1914–19; Lt. (T/Capt.), R.A.F.; destroyed a Gotha in the last air raid on England; flew from London to Capt Town, 1920; K.B.E.; M.C.; D.F.C.; Despatches.

BRAND, D. E. (D.S.O. L.G. 26.3.18) (Details, L.G. 24.8.18); s. of late Adam Brand; m. 1918, Mary Chrisabel, y. d. of Capt. W. B. Billinghurst; Lt.-Col., 5th Bn. (T.) H.L.I., 16.2.20.

BRAND, J. C. (D.S.O. L.G. 2.12.18); b. 24.11.85; s. of late Hon. Charles Brand, 4th s. of 1st Viscount Hampden and Alice, d. of late Jean Sylvain Van de Weyer; m. 1916, Lady Rosabelle Millicent, d. of 5th Earl of Rosslyn and widow of D. C. Bingham; one s.; educ. Eton; R.M.C., Sandhurst; 2nd Lt., C. Gds., 16.8.05; Lt. 3.9.08; Adjt., C. Gds., 30.4.10 to 29.4.13; Capt. 29.4.15; Major 21.4.20; served Europ. War, 1914–19, in Gallipoli, as Staff Capt. and Brig. Major, 29th Div., and as Lt.-Col., Batt. Coldstream Guards, France; Despatches four times; M.C.; Chevalier, Legion of Honour.

BRAND, THE HON. R. (D.S.O. L.G. 3.6.16) (Bar, L.G. 26.9.17) (Details, L.G. 9.1.18); b. 23.11.80; 5th s. of 2nd Viscount Hampden; m. 1913, Muriel H. L., d. of H. B. Montgomery; 2nd Lt., R. Bde., 24.11.00; Lt. 22.1.02; retired 9.3.10; served S. Africa, 1900–2 (two medals, 5 clasps); Europ. War; Bt. Major, S.R.; C.M.G.; Hon. Brig.-Gen. late R. Brig.; Chevalier, Légion d'Honneur; Despatches.

The Distinguished Service Order

BRANDON, A. de B. (D.S.O. L.G. 4.10.16); b. 21.7.83; s. of Alfred de B. Brandon; educ. Wellington College, New Zealand, and Trinity College, Cambridge; 2nd Lt., R.F.C. (Special Reserve), 8.12.15; Major; served Europ. War; M.C., 1916; Despatches three times.

BRANDON, O. G. (D.S.O. L.G. 14.1.16); b. 1876; m. 1903, Margaret Irene, e. d. of C. M. Mathews; one s.; two d.; 2nd Lt., R.E., 1896; Capt. 1905; Major 30.10.14; Public Works Dept., Railways in India, 1899–03; Adjt., S. Midland R.E., 1911–14; served Europ. War; wounded; Despatches; Bt. Lt.-Col. 1.1.18; C.M.G.

BRANSON, D. S. (D.S.O. L.G. 1.1.18) (1st Bar, L.G. 16.9.18) (2nd Bar, L.G. 2.4.19) (Details, L.G. 10.12.19), Capt. (A/Lt.-Col.), 1/4th Bn. York. and Lan. R., T.F.; Lt.-Col. 16.2.20; Despatches; M.C.

BRASH, J. (D.S.O. L.G. 26.7.17), 2nd Lt., Sea. Highrs., S.R.; M.C. He died of wounds 9.11.18.

BRASSEY, E. P. (D.S.O. L.G. 3.6.19); b. 2.10.82; 2nd Lt. 18.1.02; Capt. 26.6.11; ret., 7 Hrs., 21.3.14; served Europ. War (Capt., Spec. Cav. Res.) (T/Lt.-Col., C. Gds.); Despatches; M.C.

BRATTON, A. B. (D.S.O. L.G. 16.9.18), Capt., N. Lancs. R.; M.C.

BRAY, G. A. T. (D.S.O. L.G. 11.4.18); b. 27.4.64; Lt., R.A.M.C., 29.7.90; Major 29.7.02; Lt.-Col. 13.11.12; Asst. Dir. of Med. Services 27.4.19; Despatches.

BRAY, R. N. (D.S.O. L.G. 1.1.17); b. 7.12.72; s. of Major-Gen. G. F. C. Bray. m. 1907, Ruth Ellinor Boys; two s.; educ. United Services College, Westward Ho; 2nd Lt., West Riding R. 12.12.94; Lt. 15.9.97; Capt. 22.2.01; Adjt., W. Rid. R., 29.1.03 to 8.3.06; Major 6.4.11; T/Brig.-Gen.; served in China, 1900; present at the Relief of Pekin; Europ. War, in France; Bt. Lt.-Col. 3.6.17; C.M.G.; Despatches.

BRAZENOR, J. A. (D.S.O. L.G. 3.6.18), Major, Aust. A.S.C.; Despatches.

BRAZENOR, W. (D.S.O. L.G. 1.1.18) (Bar, L.G. 24.9.18), Bt. Major, Aust. Inf., 24.9.17; Major 16.6.18; Lt.-Col.; Despatches.

BREARLEY, N. (D.S.O. L.G. 10.1.17), 2nd Lt., L'pool R. and R.F.C.; M.C.

BREBNER, C. S., M.D., Ch.B. (D.S.O. L.G. 1.1.18); b. 3.8.76; s. of late D. Brebner; m. 1914, Gertrude, d. of F. Neil, J.P.; one d.; educ. Edinburgh and Liverpool Universities; Barrister-at-law, Gray's Inn, 1918; Medical Officer of Health, Chiswick, W.; Lt., R.A.M.C. (T.F.), 1908; Capt., 1911; T/Major, 1914; A/Lt.-Col., 1916; served Europ. War; O.C., 2/1 London Field Ambulance, 1914–18; Despatches twice.

N. Brearley.

BRECKON, J. (D.S.O. L.G. 3.6.18); b. 2.8.79; in Ranks 16 years, 96 days; 2nd Lt., Rif. Brig. 6.11.15; Lt. 11.2.17; T/Lt.-Col. Comdg. 12 Bn. Rif. Brig. 23.3.18; Despatches.

BREDIN, C. E. A. (D.S.O. L.G. 14.11.16), Capt., Can. Inf.; D.S.O. awarded for gallantry at Courcelette on 15.9.16.

BREEDT, J. M. N. (D.S.O. L.G. 22.8.18), Major, Britstown Commando, S. African Forces.

BREMNER, G. (D.S.O. L.G. 3.6.18), T/Capt. (A/Major), R.E.; M.C. He was killed in action 23.3.18.

C. S. Brebner.

BREMNER, N. F. (D.S.O. L.G. 25.8.17), Lt., Aust. Inf.

BREMNER, W. H. (D.S.O. L.G. 8.3.20), Lt., R.N.; D.S.C.

BRENNAN, E. T. (D.S.O. L.G. 3.6.18), Lt.-Col. Aust. A.M.C.; M.C.; Despatches.

BRENT, E. C. (D.S.O. L.G. 23.5.17), Lt.-Cdr., R.N.

BRERETON, D. LL. (D.S.O. L.G. 16.9.18); b. 11.9.75; s. of late Rev. Prebendary Brereton, of Little Massingham, Norfolk; m. 1915, Marjorie Frances, d. of late Reginald Cadman; two d.; 2nd Lt., Durh. L. Inf., 28.7.97; Lt. 11.11.99; Capt. 12.6.03; Major 1.9.15; O.C., Depot, D.L.I., 22.9.19; served Europ. War, 1914–18, and Brigade Major, S. African Res. Brig., 1916–17; Despatches.

W. G. N. Breton.

BRETON, W. G. N. (D.S.O. L.G. 4.6.17); b. 8.1.88; s. of E. W. Breton; Deputy Chief Constable, Stafford; educ. Earl of Macclesfield's Grammar School, Leek, and Leek High School; 2nd Lt., R.G.A., T.F., 21.9.14; Lt., Jan. 1915; Adjt., R.G.A., 1915; Capt. 13.10.15; Major 29.11.16; Despatches twice. He was killed in action 14.9.17.

BRETT, G. A. (D.S.O. L.G. 24.9.18); e. s. of T. Brett; m. 1919, Lilian Edith, e. d. of G. C. Grant; served Europ. War, 1914–18; Capt., 23rd London R.; Despatches; M.C.

BRETT, R. J. (D.S.O. L.G. 12.12.19); b. 14.11.90; 2nd Lt., Oxf. and Bucks. L. Inf., 5.10.10; Lt. 25.10.13; Capt. 18.10.15; Despatches; Bt. Major 1.1.19.

BRETTINGHAM-MOORE, H. M. (D.S.O. L.G. 14.11.16), Hon. Capt., Aust. Commonwealth Forces; R. of O., 10.7.16; D.S.O. awarded for gallantry at Pozières 8–9.8.1916.

BREWILL, A. W. (D.S.O. L.G. 3.6.16); b. 17.5.61; s. of late W. R. Brewill; m. Clementine K. Thornley; three s.; two d.; educ. University School; private tutor; F.R.I.B.A., and for 20 years Surveyor to the Diocese of Southwell; Lt. in the Robin Hoods,

A. W. Brewill.

1881 (now the 7th Batt. Sherwood Foresters); commanded the Batt. at Hooge 31.7.15; commanded the Batt. in the attack on Hohenzollern Redoubt 13.10.15; Despatches; Major and Hon. Lt.-Col., Notts and Derby. R., T.F. He died 18.2.23.

BREWIS, G. S. (D.S.O. L.G. 1.1.18) (Bar, L.G. 26.7.18), Capt., Welsh R., 26.4.15; was A/Lt.-Col.

BREYTENBACH, J. H. (D.S.O. L.G. 27.7.18), Lt.-Col. (T/Col.), S. Afr. Inf.

BRICKWOOD, R. (D.S.O. L.G. 25.8.16); b. 25.2.88; s. of late R. J. Brickwood and Elizabeth, d. of S. Elston; educ. Brighton Municipal School; Private, 1st C. Gds., 1907; at the outbreak of Europ. War, Reg. Sergt.-Major at Shoreham; Lt., R. War. R., 1915; T/Capt., R. Brig., 1915; went to France as Company Commander (wounded); Capt.

BRIDCUTT, J. H. (D.S.O. L.G. 4.6.17), Capt. (A/Lt.-Col.), R. Irish Rifles. He was killed in action 1.10.18.

BRIDGE, C. E. D. (D.S.O. L.G. 3.6.18); b. 22.2.88; s. of Brig.-Gen. Sir C. H. Bridge, K.C.M.G., C.B.; m. Georgena, d. of the late J. Wesley-Hall, Melbourne, Australia; one s.; one d.; educ. Parkfield; Haywards Heath; Bradfield College; R.M.A., Woolwich; 1st commission, R.F.A., 21.12.1904; Lt. 21.12.07; R.H.A., 1909; Capt. 30.10.14; Major 21.10.16; Gen. Staff, 1915; Temp. Lt.-Col. 1918; M.C.; Order of Leopold, and French, Belgian and Italian Croix de Guerre.

BRIDGE, R. E. A. (D.S.O. L.G. 25.8.17); b. 13.4.82; 2nd Lt., R.A., 4.6.04; Lt. 4.6.07; Ind. Army 26.9.07; Capt. 4.6.13; Major 4.6.19; Despatches.

BRIDGE, W. B. C. (D.S.O. L.G. 1.1.17); b. 24.9.74; e. s. of late Col. W. A. Bridge, R. Scots Fus.; m. Ariana Violet, d. of the late G. B. Charleton; educ. Wellington College; joined the H.L.I. Militia, 1894; H.L.I. 24.3.97; Capt. 23.1.1907; ret. H.L.I. 5.4.11; Lt.-Col., R. of O., 1.10.21; served N.W.F. of India, 1897–8 (Medal and 2 clasps); S. African War, 1901–2 (Medal and 6 clasps); Europ. War, Dardanelles and France; Despatches three times; Remount Officer, Scottish Command, No. 6 District.

BRIDGEMAN, HON. H. G. O. (D.S.O. L.G. 1.1.18); b. 15.8.82; s. of 4th Earl of Bradford; educ. Harrow; R.M.A., Woolwich; ent. R.F.A. 23.7.1901; Lt. 23.7.04; Capt. 1914; Major 7.11.1915; retired 18.5.19, with rank of Lt.-Col., Army; commanded a Battery of Field Artillery in France, Sept. 1914, to Jan. 1917, when posted as Brig.-Major, 47th Div. Art.; commanded Brigade, R.F.A., Oct. 1918, to end of war; Despatches five times; M.C.; Order of Danilo of Montenegro.

BRIDGEMAN, THE HON. R. O. B. (D.S.O. L.G. 14.7.16); b. Feb. 1879; 2nd son of the 4th Earl of Bradford and Lady Ida Anabella Frances Lumley, 2nd d. of the 9th Earl of Scarbrough; Lieutenant, R.N., 1900; Commander in 1912. Just before the war he was serving in the light cruiser Hyacinth. He was with the squadron that took part in the operations that led to the destruction of the German cruiser Königsberg. Vice-Admiral Sir Herbert G. King Hall mentioned Commander Bridgeman in his illuminative Despatch published in the London Gazette on 8 Dec. quoted in the Gazette of Commander Bridgeman's decoration. Commander Bridgeman was First Lieutenant of the Medina during the voyage of the King and Queen to India (Nov. 1911, to Feb. 1912), and was promoted Commander from the date of the ship's paying off on 15.2.1912. He was killed in action on 6.1.17.

Hon. R. O. B. Bridgeman.

BRIDGES, A. H. (D.S.O. L.G. 4.6.17); b. 21.4.71; 2nd Lt., Durham L.I., 25.3.91; Lt., I.S.C., 8.7.92; Capt., I.A., 10.7.01; Major 25.3.09; Lt.-Col. 25.3.17; served S. African War, 1899–1900; Despatches twice; Bt. Major 11.7.01; served Europ. War; Despatches; Bt. Lt.-Col. 1.1.17; C.I.E.

BRIDGES, E. C. P. (D.S.O. L.G. 2.2.16); b. 11.4.70; 1st com. 3.5.90; Lt. 15.7.91; Capt. 30.11.99; ret. S. Staffs. R. 6.12.05; Lt.-Col., R. of O. 23.2.18.

BRIDGES, H. D. (D.S.O. L.G. 14.7.16), Cdr., R.N.

BRIDGES, J. V. (D.S.O. L.G. 18.7.17); b. 28.7.87; 2nd Lt., Worc. R., 11.12.07; Lt. 23.1.11; Capt. 15.3.15; T/Major; Despatches.

BRIDGES, R. H. (D.S.O. L.G. 4.6.17); b. 7.2.79; s. of late Lt.-Col. R. H. Bridges, B.S.C.; educ. at Clevedon; Blundell's School, and St. Thomas's Hospital, where he took his degrees in 1902, joining the R.A.M.C. 31.1.03, and becoming Capt. 31.7.06 and Major 31.10.14. He served five years in India; returned to England in 1909, and at the outbreak of war took command of training camps at Hounslow and Eastbourne, afterwards going in the yacht Liberty on a six months' tour of inspection to the Dardanelles and Mediterranean. He subsequently went to Egypt on the Headquarters Staff, and in Sept. 1917, became Commandant of the Military Hospital, Helouan; accompanied the Duke of Connaught as M.O. up the Nile and to Palestine; at his own request was transferred to a unit at the front, and was commanding a combined Indian field ambulance when he was drowned while bathing at Jaffa, in Palestine, 22.8.18. He was twice mentioned in Despatches.

BRIDGES, W. F. N. (D.S.O. L.G. 1.1.18), Major, Aust. Inf.

BRIDGWATER, H. N., M.A. (D.S.O. L.G. 1.1.18); b. in 1878; s. of late T. Bridgwater, M.B., LL.D., J.P., of Harrow-on-the-Hill, and Uckfield, Sussex; m. Mary Holly, d. of late Col. H. Wood, C.B., Rif Brig.; one d.; educ. Harrow; Trinity Hall, Cambridge; served Europ. War, 1914–18; Major, late Norfolk R., T.F.; Despatches; O.B.E.; holds the T.D.

BRIERLEY, E. C. (D.S.O. L.G. 1.1.17); b. 14.1.72; s. of Rev. Prebendary J. H. Brierley; m. Dorothy Frances, d. of Major-Gen. J. Talbot Coke; one s.; two d.; educ. Rossall; gazetted to 1st Lanc. Fus. 19.7.93; Lt. 14.9.96; Capt. 7.10.99; retired Lan. Fus. 4.3.11; Lt.-Col., R. of O. 26.4.19; served S. African War, 1899–02; Europ. War, A.P.M. to 27th Div., B.E.F., 1914–15; Despatches; A.P.M. to 3rd Army Corps, B.E.F., 1915–18; Despatches; Croix de Guerre; Order de l'Etoile Noire (official); Deputy P.M., 5th Army, 1918–19; Despatches; O.B.E.

BRIERLY, S. C. (D.S.O. L.G. 2.4.19) (Details, L.G. 10.12.19), Major, 5th Bn. W. Riding R. (T.F.), 1.6.16.

BRIGGS, E. (D.S.O. L.G. 4.6.17), Capt. (T/Major), R.E.; Lt.-Col., Divl. Engr., 48th (S. Midland), R.E., T.F., 16.2.20.

BRIGGS, E. F. (D.S.O. L.G. 1.1.15) (Bar, L.G. 16.12.19), Wing Cdr., R.A.F.; O.B.E. (see "The Distinguished Service Order," from its institution to 31.12.15, by same publishers).

BRIGGS, F. C. C. (D.S.O. L.G. 25.8.17); b. 26.11.89; educ. Bedford School; 2nd Lt., L'pool R., 3.11.09; Lt. 29.6.10; Capt. 12.1.15; Despatches.

BRIGGS, H. G. (D.S.O. L.G. 23.5.17); b. 4.5.83; s. of J. Briggs, of Barbados, W.I.; m. May, y. d. of late John Hopkins; one s.; educ. H.M.S. Britannia; Midshipman, 1899; Sub-Lt., 1902; Lt., 1905; Cdr., 1916; served in H.M.S.Endymion on China Station, 1899–1901; was landed during Boxer Rebellion; Medal and clasp for Taku Forts; Bronze Medal of R. Humane Society while serving in H.M.S. Vulture, 1912; D.S.O. for services with Destroyer Patrol Flotillas.

BRIGGS, R. (D.S.O. L.G. 3.6.18), Capt., R.E., 5.2.21; M.C.

BRIGHTEN, E. W. (D.S.O. L.G. 1.1.18); b. 18.5.80; s. of W. G. Brighten, Solicitor, late Capt., H.A.C.; m. Sarah Hirell, d. of late Dr. A. J. Biggleswade; two s.; one d.; educ. Fauconberg School, Beccles; Christ's College, Blackheath; 2nd Lt., 3rd Vol. Batt. Bedford R., 1898; served S. African War; Capt., 1902; transferred to 5th Bedford R. on creation of T.F.; Major, 1912; Lt.-Col. in command, 1915; Major, Bedford and Herts R. (from T.F.), 21.2.17; served Europ. War; Despatches; C.M.G.; Bt. Lt.-Col. 3.6.19; Solicitor; Freeman of City of London.

BRIGHTEN, G. S. (D.S.O. L.G. 26.11.17) (Details, L.G. 6.4.18) (Bar, L.G. 16.9.18); b. 14.5.90; s. of W. G. and F. E. Brighten; m. Sisselle Vivien (who died in 1918), o. c. of late G. C. Wray; educ. Pilmuir, Falmouth; Haileybury; Solicitor; Lt.-Col., 2/5th Lanc. Fus., 1917; Despatches thrice; Chevalier, Order of the Crown of Belgium; Croix de Guerre; 1914–15 Star; two Medals; Lt.-Col., T.F. Reserve, 1919.

BRIGHTON, E. W. (see Brighten, E. W.).

BRIMS, R. W. (D.S.O. L.G. 4.6.17); b. 1.11.87; s. of late D. N. Brims; educ. Sedbergh; served Europ. War, 1914–18; commanded 87th (Field) Coy., R.E., 1916-18; T/Major, R.E.; wounded and gassed; Despatches three times; M.C.; is a Civil Engineer.

BRIND, V. C. (D.S.O. L.G. 3.6.18); b. 6.8.84; 2nd Lt., R.A., 17.9.14; Lt. 9.6.15; Capt., R.F.A., 22.3.18; Despatches.

BRINDLEY, J. (D.S.O. L.G. 14.11.16); b. 21.12.79; s. of George and Mary Brindley, of Manchester (both deceased); commissioned E. Yorks. R. 1.10.14; Lt. 6.2.15 and Capt. 12.12.16; joined as Private, E. York. R., 21.11.98; mentioned in South African Army Orders dated 8.1.02 as having rendered good service at Kaffir Spruit on 19.12.01; promoted Sergeant for "Distinguished gallantry" in the field; Despatches, 8.1.02; Queen's S.A. Medal, 3 clasps; King's S.A. Medal, 2 clasps. He was wounded thrice: Hooge, 9.8.15; Flers 15.9.16; Grandecourt 26.9.16; Bronze Star, 1914; Adjutant, Regimental Depôt, 26.6.17; awarded M.C.; D.S.O. for gallantry at Guillemont on 26.9.16.

J. Brindley.

BRINK, A. (D.S.O. L.G. 22.8.18), Major, 4th S. African Mtd. Bde (10th Dismounted Rifles), Staff. For German S.W. Africa.

BRINK, A. J. E. (D.S.O. L.G. 1.2.17), Major and Bt. Lt.-Col. (T/Colonel), Permanent Forces, S. Africa.

BRINK, C. (D.S.O. L.G. 1.2.17), Major (T/Lt.-Col.), S. African Defence Force.

BRINK, G. E. (D.S.O. L.G. 1.1.18), T/Major, S. African Force.

BRINSON, H. N. (D.S.O. L.G. 25.8.16), T/2nd Lt. (T/Capt.), L'pool R.

BRISCOE, F. E. (D.S.O. L.G. 1.1.18), T/Major, Yorks. R.

BRISCOE, G. S. (D.S.O. L.G. 26.9.16); b. 30.3.82; s. of late J. G. Briscoe, J.P.; m. Margaret Feilding, d. of Rev. R. N. Kane, J.P.; educ. Mostyn House School, Parkgate, Cheshire; Brighton College; on the Continent; ent. E. Surrey Militia, 1900; served S. African War, 1901–2; Queen's Medal, 4 clasps; 2nd Lt., Worc. R., 28.1.03; Lt. 22.9.06; Capt. 20.9.14; Major 28.1.18; served S. African War, 1901–2; Queen's Medal, 4 clasps; Europ. War, in France from Feb. 1915; present at Neuve Chapelle, Festubert, Loos, Vimy Ridge; operations on the Somme, July and Aug. 1916; wounded; Despatches.

BRISCOE, J. E. (D.S.O. L.G. 13.2.17), Major, S. African Medical Corps.

BRITTAN, R. H. (D.S.O. L.G. 1.1.17), Lt.-Col., Can. F.A. He was killed in action 1917.

BRITTON, A. H. D. (D.S.O. L.G. 1.1.17); b. 19.10.75; y. s. of Henry William Britton; m. (1st), 1900, Mary Maud, 3rd d. of late E. A. Greenslade (d. 1905); (2nd), 1907, Ellen Gertrude, y. d. of C. A. Carlyon, B.A.; educ. Llantrissant House, Clifton, Bristol; Glous. V.A., 1892; 1st V.B. Royal Fus., 1893; 3rd Batt. Royal Fus. 1893–96; 3rd Batt. Royal Inniskilling Fus. 1896–99; 2nd Batt. R. Dublin Fus., 1899–1907; 5th Batt. R. Dublin Fus., 1907–11; retired with rank of Major; took part in the operations in the Lagos Hinterland, 1898 (W. African Medal, and clasp); served in S. Africa (Queen's Medal, 5 clasps, and King's Medal, 2 clasps; Despatches twice); Europ. War; operations in the Somme sector; Despatches.

A. H. D. Britton.

BRITTON, E. J. J. (D.S.O. L.G. 3.6.18), Lt.-Col., R.A.O.D., 23.5.15.

BRITTON, J. C. (D.S.O. L.G. 1.2.19), Major, Can. M.G.C.

BRITTON, R. H. (D.S.O. L.G. 1.1.17), Lt.-Col., Can. F.A. He was killed in action 2.5.17.

BROAD, C. N. F. (D.S.O.. L.G. 4.6.17); b. 29.12.82; 2nd Lt., R.A., 17.5.05; Lt. 7.5.08; Capt. 30.10.14; Bt. Major 3.6.16; Major 9.11.16; Despatches.

BROADBENT, E. N. (D.S.O. L.G. 23.11.16); b. 5.5.75; s. of Col. J. E. Broadbent, C.B.; m. 1911, Florence Anna, 2nd d. of C. Kay, J.P., D.L.; educ. Sedbergh; Sandhurst; 2nd Lt., K.O.S.B., 28.9.95; Lt. 26.10.97; Capt. 18.5.01; Major 1.9.14; Bt. Lt.-Col. 3.6.15 (T/Brig.-Gen. 2.5.17 to 20.8.19); Lt.-Col. 9.6.21; saw active service (attached to Rifle Bgde.) in the Tochi Valley Expedition (Indian Frontier Medal and clasp); Tirah Expedition, 1897–98 (clasp to Indian Medal inscribed Tirah); S. African War (Queen's and King's Medals with 5 clasps); service with Egyptian Army, 1905; served in Camel Corps and commanded 10th Sudanese Regt., Tagoi Mountain Expedition (Medal and clasp; Despatches; Order of the Osmanieh, 4th Class); commanded the British Camel Corps at Cairo; served Europ. War, G.O.C., Palestine Lines of Communications; C.B., 1919; C.M.G., 1918; Despatches five times; Order of the White Eagle of Serbia, 4th Class; Officer of the Legion of Honour; 3rd Class of the Order of the Sacred Treasure (Japan); Order of the Nile, 3rd Class.

BROADLEY, E. O. (D.S.O. L.G. 8.3.18), Lt.-Cdr., R.N.

E. O. Broadley.

BROCK, F. F. (D.S.O. L.G. 3.6.19), Lt., Can. Force, 17.12.15; Major, Can. Heavy Arty.

BROCK, H. J. (D.S.O. L.G. 1.1.17); b. 17.4.70; s. of late Capt. O. de B. Brock, R.N.; educ. Haileybury College; R.M.A., Woolwich; 2nd Lt., R.A., 15.2.89; Lt. 15.2.92; Capt. 17.3.99; Div. Adjt., R.A., 23.10.00 to 9.12.01; Adjt., R.A., 12.4.04 to 31.8.04; Major 19.8.04; Lt.-Col. 30.10.14; (T/Brig.-Gen. 10.11.15 to 16.12.18); Col. 30.10.18; commanding Welsh Bord. Inf. Bgde., T.F.; served S. Africa, 1900–2 (wounded; Queen's Medal, three clasps; King's Medal, two clasps; Europ. War, 1914–18; C.B.; C.M.G.; Despatches.

BROCK, H. LE M. (D.S.O. L.G. 14.1.16); b. 5.5.89; s. of late Rev. H. W. Brock; Rector of St. Peter-in-the-Wood, Guernsey; m. 1917, Daphne Fanshawe, e. d. of C. A. Carey; educ. Elizabeth College, Guernsey; 2nd. Lt., R. War. R., 11.12.09; Lt. 16.11.12; Capt. 31.12.14; R.F.C., 1913; Flight Comdr., 1914; Squad. Comdr., 1915; Wing Comdr. and Lt.-Col., 1916; served Europ. War 1914–19; Despatches five times; He distinguished himself in rifle shooting at school and in the Militia, twice captaining his school team in the Ashburton Shield, and twice representing Guernsey in the Kolapore Cup at Bisley. In 1908 he was top in the 1st Stage of the King's Prize, winning the Bronze Medal; and both in 1908 and 1909 was in the King's Hundred, finishing 7th in 1909.

BROCK-WILLIAMS, D. (D.S.O. L.G. 1.1.18). Colonel Brock-Williams, formerly of the Welch R., was a member of a prominent Swansea family. He won his D.S.O. for gallantry when in command of his regiment. He was much interested in sport, a keen Rugby player, and an exceptionally good cricketer. He played for the Glamorgan County Cricket Club, and was in their team that played against the Australians. He died 18.4.22.

BROCKBANK, J. G. (D.S.O. L.G. 3.6.18); b. 20.11.83; s. of J. B. Brockbank, M.A., of Chappels, St. Bees, Cumberland; m. Eirène Marguerite, d. of Lionel G. Robinson, J.P., of Old Buckenham Hall, Attleborough, Norfolk; one d.; educ. Cranleigh; King's College; served Europ. War from 1914, S.R. of Officers; Colonel; Despatches; C.B.E.; last post held, Chief Engineer, Tank Corps.

BROCKLEBANK, R. H. R. (D.S.O. L.G. 3.6.19); b. 3.1.81; 2nd Lt., 9 Lrs., 5.1.01; Lt. 1.5.04; Adjt., 9 Lrs., 13.1.10 to 31.10.12; Capt. 11.5.10; Major 11.3.19; served S. African War, 1901–2; Queen's Medal with 3 clasps; King's Medal with 2 clasps; served European War.

BROCKMAN, E. A. DRAKE- (see Drake-Brockman, E. A.).

BROCKMAN, G. P. L. DRAKE- (see Drake-Brockman, G. P. L.).

BROCKMAN, R. E. DRAKE- (see Drake-Brockman, R.E.).

BROCKMAN, W. J. (D.S.O. L.G. 2.12.18), T/Lt. (A/Capt.), 15th Bn. Lancs. Fus.; Capt., The Devon Regt., 7.7.21; Despatches.

BRODERICK, R. A., M.B. (D.S.O. L.G. 1.1.19), Lt.-Col., R.A.M.C., T.F., 16.2.20; M.C.

BRODIE, P. T. (D.S.O. L.G. 16.9.18), T/Capt., K.A.R.; M.C.

BRODZIAK, C. E. M. (D.S.O. L.G. 1.2.19), Major, 3rd Bn. Aust. M.G.C.

BROKE-SMITH, H. (see Smith, H. Broke-).

BROKE-SMITH, P. W. L. (D.S.O. L.G. 22.12.16); b. 27.8.82; s. of Surg.-Major-Gen. P. Broke-Smith, A.M.S.; m. Dorothy Margaret, d. of Vice-Admiral G. O. Twiss, R.N.; educ. Cheltenham College; R.M.A., Woolwich; 2nd Lt., R.E., 18.8.00; Lt. 18.8.03; Capt. 18.8.10; Major 2.11.16; T/Lt.-Col. 8.5.19; Adjutant and Instructor, Balloon School, R.F.C. (Squadron Commander), 1912; Airship Pilot, 1910–12; Aeroplane Pilot, 1912; D.A.D.Aviation (subsequently A.D. Aviation), Mesopotamia Exp. Force, in charge of formation and administration of Flying Services, Mesopotamia, 1915–16; Military Works, N.W. Frontier of India, 1906–10, 1913–15 and 1916–19, including Mohmand Blockade (Field Engineer in technical charge of blockade line), 1916–17; Afghan War, 1919 (A.D. Works, N.W.F. Force); A.D. Works, Army Headquarters, India, since 1919; T/Lt.-Col.

BROMET, G. R. (D.S.O. L.G. 12.5.17); b. 28.8.91; s. of G. A. and E. I. Bromet; m. Ida Margaret, d. of Major R. Ratliffe, Worc. R.; educ. Bradfield College and R.N. Colleges of Osborne and Dartmouth; Midshipman, Jan. 1909; Sub-Lt., 1912; Lt., May, 1914; Flight Lt., July, 1914; Fl. Cdr., May, 1915; Sqn. Cdr., Dec. 1916; Wing Cdr., Dec. 1917; Lt.-Col., R.A.F., 1.4.18; granted a permanent commission in the R.A.F. 1.8.19, with the rank of Sqn. Leader; Despatches for services Dardanelles, 1915; France, 1917; Legion of Honour.

BROMILOW, D. G. (D.S.O. L.G. 25.8.17) (Bar, L.G. 2.4.19) (Details, L.G. 10.12.19); b. 8.2.84; 2nd Lt., Unatt., 21.1.03; I.A. 10.4.04; Lt. 8.1.06; Capt. 21.1.12; Major, 14th Murray's Jat Lrs., I.A., 21.1.18; Despatches.

BROMLEY, F. W. (D.S.O. L.G. 14.9.17), Eng. Lt.-Cdr., R.N.

BROMLEY, J. E. M. (D.S.O. L.G. 18.1.18) (Details, L.G. 25.4.18), T/Capt. (A/Major), R.F.A. He was killed in action 7.6.18.

BRONKHORST, J. G. (D.S.O. L.G. 22.8.18), Major, Calvinia-Kenhardt Command, S. African Military Forces.

BROOK, F. (D.S.O. L.G. 26.7.18) (Bar, L.G. 1.2.19), Lt. (A/Major), Yorks. L.I.; M.C.

BROOK, J. K. (D.S.O. L.G. 17.3.19), Lt., R.N.R.

BROOK, R. J. (D.S.O. L.G. 3.6.16); b. 1885 s. of A. Brook; m. Eleanor Dartington; one s.; one d.; educ. Uppingham; Capt., Can. Forces, 21.3.15; Lt.-Col., R. Can. R.; served Europ. War, 1914–18; in Russia, 1918–19; Despatches; C.B.E.; A.A. and Q.M.G., M.D.2 Canada.

BROOKE, A. C. (D.S.O. L.G. 25.8.17); b. 26.9.86; 2nd Lt., R.A., 23.7.07; Lt. 23.7.10; Capt. 30.10.14; Major 21.7.17; Despatches.

BROOKE, A. F. (D.S.O. L.G. 1.1.17) (Bar, L.G. 8.3.18); b. 23.7.83; s. of the late Sir Victor Brooke, Bart., and Alice, d. of Sir Alan Bellingham, Bart.; m. Jane Mary, d. of Col. Richardson; one s.; one d.; ent. R.F.A. 24.12.02; Lt. 24.12.05; posted to R.H.A., N By., 1909; Capt. 30.10.14; Adjt., R.A., 1.4.15 to 20.11.15; Major 24.4.16; proceeded to the war in France with the Secunderabad Cavalry Brigade, Sept. 1914, in command of a R.H.A. ammunition column; Adjt., 2nd

A. F. Brooke.

Indian R.H.A. Brigade, Feb. 1915; Brigade Major, 18th Div. Art., Nov. 1915; was G.S.O.2, R.A. Can. Corps, Feb. 1917, and G.S.O.1, R.A., 1st Army, July, 1918; Staff College, Camberley, March, 1919; Despatches six times; Bt. Lt.-Col. 1.1.19.

BROOKE, B. R. (D.S.O. L.G. 2.7.17) (Bar, L.G. 22.1.20); b. 1882; s. of late J. J. Brooke and Lady Wilhelmine Brooke; educ. Arnold House, Llandulas; H.M.S. Britannia; Naval Cadet, 1898; Midshipman, 1898; Sub-Lt., 1901; Lt., 1903; Lt.-Cdr., 1911; Cdr., 1916; Europ. War, 1914–17; Despatches; Chevalier, Legion of Honour.

BROOKE, C. B. (D.S.O. L.G. 14.1.16); only s. of C. B. Brooke; educ. Bilton Grange, near Rugby, and at Bradfield College, and gazetted to 3rd Suffolk R., Dec. 1914. He went to France, attached to the 1st Queen's, and was promoted to Captain; was seriously wounded while leading his company in the attack on 25.9.1915, and was mentioned in Despatches. He was given a commission in the Regular Army, being gazetted to the Yorks. R. Captain Brooke was killed in action 1.7.16, while leading his company into action.

BROOKE, E. (D.S.O. L.G. 7.8.18); only s. of Mrs. E. L. Malsey; Lt.-Cdr., R.N.; died in London 10.2.19.

BROOKE, E. W. (D.S.O. L.G. 3.6.16); b. 2.2.70; s. of Lt.-Col. R. W. Brooke, 60th Rifles, and Elizabeth Joanna, d. of Gen. Sir Duncan McGregor, K.C.B.; m. Beatrice Anna, d. of C. Lloyd; one s.; educ. Monckton Combe School; Trinity College, Cambridge; R.M.C., Sandhurst; gazetted to 1st Bn. K.R.R.C., 9.11.92; Lt. 15.5.95; Lt., A.S.C., 1.10.95; Capt. 1.4.00; Major 22.5.07; Lt.-Col. 30.10.14; served Chitral; taking of Malakand Pass; action at Khar; served S. African War, 1899–02; was Staff Officer, Transport, to General Walter Kitchener's Force throughout its existence. The first Colonial V.C. was won by Trooper (Lt.-Col.) Bisdee for carrying Capt. Brooke out of action at Warm Baths when wounded. On the same occasion Lt. (Major) Wylly won the same decoration. Capt. Brooke was their commanding officer. Lt.-Col. Brooke served in the Europ. War with the B.E.F.; Despatches three times.

Eardley Wilmot Brooke.

BROOKE, E. W. S. (D.S.O. L.G. 1.1.17); b. 25.3.73; s. of late Col. William S. Brooke, Bengal Army, and grandson of the late Rev. E. P. Brooke, Precentor and Canon of Dromore Cathedral, and Rector of Maralin; 2nd Lt., R.A., 11 8.92; Lt. 11.8.96; Capt. 29.6.00; Adjt., R.A., 21.11.07 to 30.6.09; Major 28.5.10; Europ. War, 1914–18; Despatches; Bt. Lt.-Col. 18.2.15; C.M.G.

BROOKE, G. F. (D.S.O. L.G. 4.6.17) (1st Bar, L.G. 2.12.18) (2nd Bar, L.G., 15.2.19) (Details, L.G. 30.7.19); b. 30.10.78; 2nd Lt., Conn. Rangers, 1.12.97; Lt. 9.10.99; Capt., R. of O., late Conn. Rangers; T/Lt.-Col., Welsh R.

BROOKE, G. F. H. (D.S.O. L.G. 1.1.17) (Bar, L.G. 26.7.18); b. 14.6.84; 2nd Lt., 16 Lrs., 22.7.03; Lt. 6.9.08; Capt. 10.10.14; Bt. Lt.-Col. 3.6.19; Despatches; M.C.

BROOKE, N. P. (D.S.O. L.G. 1.1.18); b. 26.7.77; 2nd Lt., Leins. R., 24.1.00; Lt. 20.11.01; Capt. 3.5.09; Major 1.9.15; Despatches.

BROOKE, R. W. (D.S.O. L.G. 3.6.18); s. of J. A. Brooke, of Fenay Hall, Huddersfield; ent. Queen's Own Yorks. Dragoons (Yeomanry), 1904; mobilized with them when the war broke out, serving in England for about a year before going to the front. Later he was attached to the staff of a division, and was awarded the M.C.

BROOKS, A. (D.S.O. L.G. 1.2.19), Major, 7th Bn. Can. Inf. Br., Columbia Rgt.

BROOKS, A. W. (D.S.O. L.G. 21.6.19), Lt.-Cdr., R.N.

BROOKS, C. (D.S.O. L.G. 6.4.18), Lt.-Cdr., R.D., R.N.R.

BROOKS, H. J. (D.S.O. L.G. 3.6.19), Capt., 4th Bn. (T.), Hants R. 23.7.20 Despatches; M.C.

BROOKS, J. J. (D.S.O. L.G. 3.3.17), Major, Aust. L.H.

BROOKS, R. A. D. (D.S.O. L.G. 23.7.18), Lt. (A/Capt.), R.M.A., Vindictive.

BROOME, R. H. (D.S.O. L.G. 18.2.18) (Details, L.G. 18.7.18); b. 5.8.89; s. of late Maj.-Genl. R. C. Broome, C.I.E.; m. Muriel, d. of late Major J. C. Ambrose; one d.; educ. Wellington College; 2nd Lt., Wilts Regt., 18.9.09; Lt. 25.1.11; Capt. 11.12.14; Bt. Major 3.6.17; joined Tank Corps 28.8.17; served Europ. War, 1914–18; M.C.; Despatches.

BROOME, W. G. K. (D.S.O. L.G. 23.7.20); b. 17.12.84; s. of late Major-Gen. R. C. Broome, C.I.E.; m. Muriel, d. of late Major J. C. Ambrose; one d.; educ. Wellington College; 2nd Lt., Unatt., 18.1.05; 2nd Lt., Ind. Army, 9.3.06; Lt. 18.4.07; Capt. 18.1.14; Major 18.1.20.

BROUGHTON, L. H. D. (D.S.O. L.G. 1.1.19); b. 28.10.73; 2nd Lt., R.A., 6.4.93; Major 1.4.10; retired R.A. 28.5.10; Lt.-Col. (R. of O.), 9.5.19; served S. Africa, 1900–02; Queen's Medal, 5 clasps; King's Medal, 2 clasps; Europ. War; Despatches.

BROUGHTON, N. W., M.B. (D.S.O. L.G. 26.9.16), T/Capt., R.A.M.C. His D.S.O. was awarded for services on 25.8.16, between Mametz Wood and Bazentin-le-Petit. He was killed in action 10.9.16.

BROUNGER, R. (D.S.O. L.G. 27.5.17), Cdr., R.N.

BROUNGER, T. MacL. (D.S.O. L.G. 21.6.19), Lt.-Cdr., R.N.

BROUSSON, F. (D.S.O. L.G. 1.1.17); b. 5.9.76; 2nd Lt., R.A. 28.3.00; Lt. 3.4.01; Capt. 15.2.09; Adjt., R.A., 11.4.13 to 29.10.14; Major 30.10.14; served S. Africa, 1901–2 (Queen's Medal, 5 clasps); Europ. War; Croix de Guerre with Silver Star; Despatches.

BROWN, A. (D.S.O. L.G. 18.7.17), Capt. (T/Major), Aust. Inf., M.C.

BROWN, A. B. D. (D.S.O. L.G. 3.6.18), Major, Aust. Provost Corps.

BROWN, A. F. (D.S.O. L.G. 18.2.18), (Details L.G. 18.7.17); Capt. (A/Major), Can. Infy

BROWN, A. H. (D.S.O. L.G. 4.2.18) (Details L.G. 5.7.18); 2nd s. of Sir Robert Hanbury Brown; m. Charity Hampton, e. d. of late Arthur Weekes, J.P., B.C.S.; Capt. and Bt. Major (A/Major), R.E.; M.C. He was killed in action 27.3.18.

F. Brousson.

BROWN, A. J. (D.S.O. L.G. 2.11.16); b. 26.5.84; s. of late Arthur John and Emma Russell Brown; m. 1916, Beatrice, d. of late J. P. Fitzgerald; educ. Woolstone College, Hants, and University College, Southampton and London Hospital; joined R.A.M.C. (S.R.) 30.4.12; Capt. 1.4.15; served Europ. War, in France, from Aug. 1914; took part in the Retreat from Mons, and whilst staying behind at Landrecies to tend the wounded, was captured by the Germans, but was released in July, 1915; he served with the Cameroons Exp. Force; D.S.O. awarded for services at Gardelegen Prisoners of War Camp, Germany; Gold Medal of the Order of St. John of Jerusalem; 1914 Star.

BROWN, A. M. YEATS- (see Yeats-Brown, A. M.).

BROWN, A. R. HAIG- (see Haig-Brown, A. R.).

A. J. Brown.

BROWN, C. RUSSELL- (see Russell-Brown, C.).

BROWN, C. T. (D.S.O. L.G. 1.1.17), Major, R.E.; Lt.-Col., R.E., 16.2.20; Despatches.

BROWN, D. (D.S.O. L.G. 3.6.19); b. 27.8.96; 2nd Lt. (Spec. Res.), R.A., 27.8.15; Lt. 4.3.18; A/Major 25.10.18; Major, R.F.A., T.F.

BROWN, REV. F. E. (D.S.O. L.G. 4.6.17), T/Chapl. to the Forces, A/Chapl. Dept.

BROWN, F. L. (D.S.O. L.G. 4.6.17), T/Major, S. African Staff Corps.

BROWN, G. H. J., M.B. (D.S.O. L.G. 14.1.16); b. 20.5.75; Lt., R.A.M.C., 31.1.03; Capt. 31.7.06; Major 1.9.14.

BROWN, G. L. (D.S.O. L.G. 16.9.18); b. 3.4.86; 2nd Lt., Middx. R., 29.8.06; Lt. 26.8.09; Capt. 8.12.14; Bt. Major 3.6.19.

BROWN, H. D. L. (D.S.O. L.G. 3.6.18); b. 22.3.83; 2nd Lt. 31.7.02; Lt. 31.7.05; Capt. 30.10.14; Major 1.5.17; Adjt., R.G.A., 10.3.20; Despatches.

BROWN, H. R. (D.S.O. L.G. 14.1.16) (Bar, L.G. 26.7.17); b. 8.7.71; s. of R. Brown (late Capt., 16th Regt.); m. 1898, Miriam, d. of late W. T. Dewe; 2 sons; educ. Harrow; 2nd Lt. 8.9.92; Capt. 15.11.98; Bt. Major 22.8.02; ret. Cam Highrs. 17.5.05; Lt.-Col. 14.2.19; served Nile Expedition, 1898, in Battle of Khartoum (Egyptian Medal with clasp; Medal); S. Africa, 1900–2 (Despatches, L.G. 10.9.01 and 29.7.02; Queen's Medal, 4 clasps; King's Medal, 2 clasps); Europ. War.

BROWN, J. A. ARROWSMITH- (see Arrowsmith.Brown, J. A.).

BROWN, JOHN (D.S.O. L.G. 1.1.18), Lt.-Col., Northants R., 15.10.16.

BROWN, J. C. (D.S.O. L.G. 11.4.18), Major (T/Lt.-Col.), A.S.C.

BROWN, J. H. I. (D.S.O. L.G. 11.5.17), Major, Can. Inf.

BROWN, J. N. (D.S.O. L.G. 23.11.16), Bt. Major, Manchester R. (T.F.); Lt.-Col. 31.10.20; Despatches.

BROWN, J. P., M.A., M.B. (D.S.O. L.G. 14.1.16), s. of late T. Brown, of Ardmore, Campbeltown; served S. Africa, 1899–01; Despatches; Queen's Medal, 4 clasps; T.D.

BROWN, J. S. (D.S.O. L.G. 14.1.16); b. 28.6.81; s. of late F. A. Brown and A. MacI. Brown (née Horne); m. 27.6.16, Clare Temple, d. of late T. Corsan; one son; educ. Simcoe Grammar School; Toronto University; joined 39th Regt. Canadian Militia, Sept. 1895; commissioned (at the age of fourteen) in Royal Canadian Regt., Permanent Forces, 25.6.06; Capt. 11.2.11; passed Staff College, Camberley, 1914; Major 16.9.14; Lt.-Col. 8.6.18; Director of Organization, Militia H.Q., Ottawa, 9.1.19; served Europ. War, 1914–18, in France; on the Somme, Vimy, Arleux and Fresnoy; Hill 70 and Passchendaele; Despatches, June, 1918, and Jan. 1919; C.M.G., 1918; Director of Organization, Militia H.Q., Ottawa.

BROWN, JAMES HARDY (gazetted as James Henry Brown) (D.S.O. L.G. 11.5.17) (Details, L.G. 18.7.17); T/Sub-Lt., R.N.V.R.

BROWN, K. ARROWSMITH- (see Arrowsmith-Brown, K.).

BROWN, L. N. F: (D.S.O. L.G. 4.6.17); b. 25.12.91; 2nd Lt., R.A., 23.12.11; Lt. 23.12.14; Capt. 8.8.16.

BROWN, O. (D.S.O. L.G. 1.1.17); b. 8.11.64; 4th s. of T. Dixon Brown; m. 1889, Alice, d. of W. Rice Stevenson; five s.; one d.; educ. Glebe House School, Woolwich; Engineer Apprentice, Woolwich Arsenal; Whitworth Exhibition £100, and Bronze Medal; Lieut. for Inspection of Ordnance Machinery, R.A., 1891; Capt., A.O.D., 11.11.97; Major, 1909; Lt.-Col. 20.2.17; Chief Inspector of Ordnance Machinery; served in India, Ceylon, China and France; Despatches twice.

BROWN, O. H. (D.S.O. L.G. 25.8.16), s. of A. Robert Brown; educ. Peter Symond's School; Winchester, and Pembroke College, Cambridge; joined Rifle Bgde., Sept. 1914; 2nd Lt., Suff. R.; M.C. He was killed in action 2.11.16, aged 24.

BROWN, P. W. (D.S.O. L.G. 14.1.16); b. 12.10.76; s. of late Thomas Brown; educ. Uppingham; Sandhurst; 2nd Lt., G. Hldrs., 4.11.96; Lt. 17.12.98; Capt. 16.6.01; Major 11.12.14; Lt.-Col. 10.5.20; served S. Africa, 1899–02 (Despatches, Queen's Medal, 4 clasps, and King's Medal 2 clasps); Europ. War, 1914–18; Despatches; C.M.G.; Bt. Lt.-Col. 1.1.18.

BROWN, R. (D.S.O. L.G. 1.2.19), Capt., 46th Bn. Can. Inf., Sask. R.

BROWN, R. G. (D.S.O. L.G. 26.8.18), Major, Manch. R.

BROWN, R. J. (D.S.O. L.G. 17.3.19), Engineer Lt.-Comdr., R.N.

BROWN, R. T., M.D. (D.S.O. L.G. 26.6.16); b. 26.6.73; s. of Surg. Lt.-Col. R. Ross-Brown, L.R.C.P., etc., V.D., J.P.; m. 1904, Pauline, d. of F. Normandy; Barrister-at-Law; educ. King's School, Rochester; Guy's Hospital, London; Durham University Medical School (M.B., B.S.); 1st Kent Art. Vol. 1894–1900; Lt., R.A.M.C., 1900; Lt.-Col. 26.12.17; served in E. Africa, 1914–15; D.A.D.M.S., G.H.Q., 1916; A.D.M.S., 1917–19; Despatches thrice; C.M.G., 1918; O.C., Royal Herbert Hospital, Woolwich.

BROWN, T. (D.S.O. L.G. 3.6.16), Capt., Aust. A.M.C.

BROWN, W. C. (D.S.O. L.G. 1.1.18), T/Lt.-Col., R. Sussex R.

BROWN, W. E. (D.S.O. L.G. 16.9.18), T/Major (A/Lt.-Col.), S.W.B.; M.C.

BROWN, W. H. (D.S.O. L.G. 23.10.19); b. 27.1.67; s. of Major Francis Brown, Carabineers; m. Edith, d. of late Col. D. Stewart; three d.; educ. Lancing College, and R.M.C., Sandhurst; Lt., R.W. Kent R., 25.8.86; 2 Lt., Ind. S.C., 17.10.87; Lt. 2.12.89; Capt. 25.8.97; Major, Ind. S. 8.8.04; Lt.-Col. 10.5.12; retired 1920; served Europ. War, 1914–18, Mesopotamia; Despatches; C.B.

BROWN, W. J. (D.S.O. L.G. 1.2.19), Major, 2nd Aust. L.H. Rgt.

BROWN, WALTER RICHARD (D.S.O. L.G. 18.10.17) (Details, L.G. 7.3.18) (Bar, L.G. 2.4.19) (Details, L.G. 10.12.19); Lt., Can. Inf., 31.8.14; Major (A/Lt.-Col.); Despatches.

BROWN, WILLIAM REID (D.S.O. L.G. 4.6.17); Capt. (T/Major), R.A.

BROWNE, A. D. M. (D.S.O. L.G. 1.1.17); b. 17.9.78; 2nd Lt., R. Lanc. R., 20.5.99; Lt. 24.2.00; Capt. 14.9.04; Adjt., R. Lanc. R., 15.7.08 to 14.7.11; Major 1.9.15; Bt. Lt.-Col. 1.1.18; served S. African War, 1899–1902 (Queen's Medal, 3 clasps; King's Medal, 2 clasps); Europ. War, 1914–18; Despatches.

BROWNE, LORD A. E. (D.S.O. L.G. 16.9.18); b. 30.11.78; s. of the 5th Marquess of Sligo; Capt., R.A., 1905; Major (T/Lt.-Col.), R. of O., R.F.A. He was killed in action 27.8.18.

BROWNE, A. P. (D.S.O. L.G. 3.6.18); b. 15.1.68; s. of late General Sir Samuel Browne, V.C., G.C.B., K.C.S.I.; m. Winifred Marie, e. d. of Lt.-Col. J. E. Rhodes, late K.R. Rifles; one d.; 2nd Lt., 6 D.G., 5.2.87; Lt., Ind. C.S., 10.5.88; Capt., Ind. A., 5.2.98; Major 5.2.05; Lt.-Col. 5.2.13; served N.W. Frontier of India, operations in the Kurram Valley, 1897–8 (Medal, 2 clasps); Tirah, 1897–8; operations against the Khani Khel Chamkanis (clasp); China, 1900; Relief of Pekin; Actions Peitsang and Yangtsun (Despatches, L.G. 14.5.01; Medal and clasp); Europ. War.

BROWNE, A. R. I. (D.S.O. L.G. 26.11.17) (Details, L.G. 6.4.18), T/Major and A/Lt.-Col.), S. African Defence Force.

BROWNE, B. W. (D.S.O. L.G. 1.1.19), Capt., Can. Inf., 21.10.14; Major; Despatches; M.C.

BROWNE, E. GORE- (see Gore-Browne, E.).

BROWNE, E. MONTEAGLE- (see Monteagle-Browne, E.).

BROWNE, G. B. (D.S.O. L.G. 1.1.17); s. of George Buckston Browne, of Wimpole Street, W; m. a daughter of late Major-Gen. Sir John Dartnell, K.C.B., C.M.G.; one s.; 2nd Lt., Ceylon Mounted Rifles; Lt., 1902; Capt. and Adjt., 4th S. Midland Bgde. R.F.A.; Lt.-Col., Nov. 1914; served S. African War; Queen's Medal with 3 clasps; Europ. War, 1914. Died at Doncaster.

BROWNE, G. E. A. (D.S.O. L.G. 1.1.18) (Bar, L.G. 26.7.18), T/Major, L'pool R.; M.C.

BROWNE, G. S. (D.S.O. L.G. 3.6.19), Major, Can. Field Artillery, 9.11.17; Despatches.

BROWNE, H. H. G. (D.S.O. L.G. 26.8.18), Major (T/Lt.-Col., Som. L.I.).

BROWNE, H. S. (D.S.O. L.G. 1.1.18), 2nd Lt., R.A., 23.7.09; Lt. 23.7.12; Capt., R.F.A., 23.7.15 (A/Major); Despatches.

BROWNE, JAMES CLENDINNING (D.S.O. L.G. 14.1.16); b. 20.7.78; s. of Major James Browne, late Devon Regt.; educ. U.S. College, Dublin; 2nd Lt., W. India R., 25.1.99; 2nd Lt., A.S.C., 12.2.00; Lt. 12.2.01; Capt. 15.10.02; Adjt., A.S.C., 16.10.13 to 4.8.14; Major., R.A.S.C., 5.8.14; Bt. Lt.-Col. 1.1.18; Lt.-Col. 1.1.18; served S. Africa, 1900–02 (Queen's Medal, three clasps; King's Medal, 2 clasps); Europ. War, 1914–16; Despatches five times; C.M.G., 1919.

BROWNE, JOHN GILBERT (D.S.O. L.G. 1.1.17); b. 26.7.78; educ. Wellington College; 2nd Lt., 14 Hrs., 4.11.99; Lt. 4.7.00; Capt. 30.5.06; Major 3.5.12; Bt. Lt.-Col. 3.6.17; served S. African War, 1900–02 (Queen's and King's Medals with 9 clasps); N. Nigeria, 1906 (Medal and clasp); Europ. War, 1914–18; Despatches; C.M.G., 1918.

BROWNE, R. G. (D.S.O. L.G. 22.8.18), 2nd Lt., Manch. R., 19.10.01; Lt. 5.10.03; served S. African War, 1901; Medal with 2 clasps; Europ. War. Major Browne died 1.11.18.

BROWNE, S. GORE- (see Gore-Browne, S.).

BROWNE, W. CAVE- (see Cave-Browne, W.).

BROWNE, W. T. R. (D.S.O. L.G. 1.1.17); b. 27.11.80; 2nd Lt., Leins. Regt., 4.5.01; 2nd Lt., A.S.C., 4.5.02; Lt. 18.2.04; Capt. 18.11.10; Major, R.A.S.C., 30.10.14; Bt. Lt.-Col. 3.6.18; served S. African War, 1899–02; both Medals with 5 clasps; served Europ. War, going to France with the first Exp. Force; Order of the Crown of Italy (Officer).

BROWNE-CAVE, H. M. CAVE- (see Cave-Browne-Cave, H. M.).

BROWNE-CLAYTON, R. C. (D.S.O. L.G. 20.10.16); b. 24.2.70; 2nd Lt. 24.12.90; Major 2.11.07; retired, 5 Lrs., 22.5.09; served S. African War; Despatches thrice; Bt. Major; both Medals with 7 clasps; Europ. War; D.S.O. for services on 20.7.16, near Trônes Wood; Bt. Lt.-Col., R. of Off., 1.1.17.

BROWNE-MASON, H. O. B. (D.S.O. L.G. 19.10.16); b. 29.11.72; s. of John and Jessie Browne-Mason; m. Leonie Sophie Brooke, d. of Michael J. Jamieson; one d.; educ. Sherborne School; Lt., R.A.M.C., 28.1.98; Capt. 28.1.01; Major 28.7.09; Lt.-Col. 1.3.15; served Europ. War, 6th Poona War Division, and in Mesopotamia from Nov. 1914, to the fall of Kut-el-Amara, and was a prisoner of war till exchanged in 1916.

BROWNELL, H. P. (D.S.O. L.G. 18.7.17), Major, A.A.M.C.

BROWNING, C. E. (D.S.O. L.G. 15.10.18), T/Major, S.W.B.

BROWNING, F. A. M. (D.S.O. L.G. 4.2.18) (Details, L.G. 5.7.18); b. 20.12.96; 2nd Lt., G. Gds., 16.6.15; Lt. 15.7.15; Adjt. 4.11.18; Capt. 24.11.20; Despatches.

BROWNING, H. C. (D.S.O. L.G. 3.6.19), T/Capt., Beds. R.; M.C.

BROWNLOW, C. A. L. (D.S.O. L.G. 4.6.17); b. 31.1.89; s. of Col. C. C. Brownlow, C.B., and Rosalie, d. of late Rev. J. R. Munn; m. Ninie, d. of J. Robinson; one d.; educ. Clifton College, and R.M.A., Woolwich; 2nd Lt., R.F.A., 23.7.09 (Tombs Scholarship, 1909); Lt. 23.7.12; Capt. 23.7.15; Major 21.8.18; served in France, Aug. 1914, to June, 1917; Adjt., R.A., 27.4.20; Despatches.

BROWNLOW, C. W. (D.S.O. L.G. 1.1.18); b. 3.10.62; Lt., R.A., 1.10.82; Capt. 4.11.91; Major 10.10.00; Lt.-Col. 26.4.11; Col. 15.12.14; retired R.A. 2.3.19; served Zhob Valley Exp., 1890; Burma, 1891–2 (Medal with clasp); N.W.F. of India, 1897–8; Malakand; operations in Bajaur, Mohmand (Medal with clasp); Tirah, 1897–8; Capture of the Sampagha and Arhanga Passes; operations in the Bazar Valley 25–30.12.97; Clasp.

BROWNLOW, G. J. (D.S.O. L.G. 1.1.17); b. 26.12.83; 2nd Lt., R. Brig., 13.8.04; Lt. 2.4.08; Capt. 4.10.13; Bt. Major 18.2.15; Despatches.

BROWNRIGG, H. J. S. (D.S.O. L.G. 15.9.16); b. 3.9.82; s. of Lt. H. S. Brownrigg, late Rifle Brigade; m. Lilian Amy Norah, d. of G. P. Kinahan; one s.; one d.; educ. Littlejohn's, Greenwich; ent. Britannia 4.9.97; Captain, R.N.; Despatches, Sept. 1900; China Medal, Relief of Pekin; Europ. War; Despatches.

BROWNRIGG, W. D. S. (gazetted as Brownrigg, W. D.) (D.S.O. L.G. 22.12.16); b. 21.4.86; s. of late Gen. J. S. Brownrigg (formerly G. Gds.); m. Mona Editha Jeffreys, d. of Major-Gen. H. B. Jeffreys; 2nd Lt., Notts. and Derby R., 28.1.05; Lt. 16.2.07; Adjt., Notts. and Derby. R., 1.2.10 to 30.7.13; Capt. 21.1.13; Bt. Major 1.1.16; Bt. Lt.-Col. 1.1.18; Despatches.

BROWSE, G., M.D. (D.S.O. L.G. 25.8.17); b. 4.4.74; s. of late G. W. H. Browse; m. Catherine Mary, d. of late Staff Paymaster H. A. Haswell, R.N.; educ. Clare College, Cambridge; St. Bartholomew's Hospital; Lt., I.M.S., 27.1.00; Capt. 27.1.03; Major 27.7.11; Lt.-Col. 27.7.19; Despatches; served Europ. War; Bt. Lt.-Col. 1.1.16.

BRUCE, A. C. (D.S.O. L.G. 23.5.17); b. 19.1.73; s. of Cdr. J. Bruce, R.N. (who died 1880) and Annie Marie Bruce (*née* Boyes); educ. Cheltenham College; Silligs, Bellerive, Vevey, Switzerland, and Burney's Royal Naval Academy, Gosport; ent. H.M.S. Britannia 15.7.86; Midshipman, H.M.S. Monarch 14.9.88; Sub-Lt. 14.9.92; Lt., Sept. 1894; Commander, June, 1905; in command of War Colleges, Chatham and Devonport from Aug. 1912, to Dec. 1913; promoted Captain 30.6.13. He was appointed War Staff Officer (without qualifying course) 1.1.13; D.S.O. was awarded for service as Captain "D" in command of the 7th and 9th Destroyer Flotillas employed on the East coast of England during the war. French Croix de Guerre with Palm. "Est cité à l'ordre de l'Armée: Le 16 décembre, 1914, lors du bombardement de Hartlepool par les croiseurs de bataille allemands, a fait preuve de courage et de qualités de marin en manœuvrant sous un feu violent de l'ennemi." Mention in Despatches of June, 1918, was for "good services as Capt. 'D,' of 7th Destroyer Flotilla in 1917." C.B. was awarded for service as S.N.O., Archangel, from May to Oct. 1919. Official account (13.12.1919) states: "For valuable services as Senior Naval Officer at Archangel and as Chief of the Staff and the Senior Naval Officer, White Sea (Rear-Admiral John F. E. Green, C.B.)."

A. C. Bruce.

BRUCE, G. D. (D.S.O. L.G. 14.1.16); b. 7.10.72; 2nd Lt., R. Fus., 20.5.93 Lt., I.S.C., 27.2.97; Capt., I.A., 20.5.02; Major, 61st K.G.O. Pnrs., 20.5.11; Lt.-Col. 13.8.18; Col. 8.6.20; Bt. Lt.-Col. 1.1.17; Despatches.

BRUCE, G. J. (D.S.O. L.G. 16.9.18); b. 3.6.81; educ. Winchester and Oxford; gazetted T/Capt., 13th Royal Irish Rifles, 36th Div., Sept. 1914; served all the time in France with Ulster Div. with the exception of three months when Brigade Major to 147th Bde.; M.C. He was killed in action 2.10.18.

BRUCE, G. T. (D.S.O. L.G. 3.6.18), Lt.-Col., Yeom., Lincs. R.

BRUCE, K. H. (D.S.O. L.G. 1.1.17); b. 26.5.79; s. of A. C. Bruce and Helen Bruce (*née* Fletcher); m. Lorna, d. of T. M. Burn-Murdoch, M.D., M.R.C.P.E.; 2 s.; 3 d.; educ. Trinity College, Oxford; joined 2nd Bn. G. Highrs., 1900; served S. African War (Medal and 3 clasps); India; Mohmand Exp., 1908 (Medal and clasp); Europ. War from 1914; wounded at Ypres; Palestine; from 3.6.19, A.A.G., G.H.Q., British Army of the Rhine; Bt. Lt.-Col.

BRUCE, K. M. (D.S.O. L.G. 1.1.16); s. of J. M. Bruce, M.A., M.D., Hon. LL.D., F.R.C.P., Hon. F.R.C.P.I.; m. Madeleine, d. of H. W. Birks; two s.; Lt.-Cdr., R.N.; served Europ. War from 1914; Chevalier, Order of St. Maurice and St. Lazarus; Commander, Crown of Italy.

K. M. Bruce.

BRUCE, P. R. (D.S.O. L.G. 3.6.16); b. 1872; s. of Sir H. J. L. Bruce, 4th Bart.; m. 1st, Aletheia Georgina (who died in 1904), d. of the Rt. Hon. Sir R. H. Paget, Bart; and 2nd, Evelyn Mary Amelia, d. of Major T. Leith; one s.; served Europ. War, 1914–18; C.M.G.

BRUCE, R. (D.S.O. L.G. 1.1.17), T/Lt.-Col., G. Highrs.

BRUCE, T. (D.S.O. L.G. 1.1.18); b. 11.8.71; 2nd Lt., R.A., 13.2.91; Lt. 13.2.94; Capt. 13.2.00; Adjt., R.A., 20.4.07 to 11.9.08; Major 12.9.08; Lt.-Col. 1.4.15; Col. 1.4.20; T/Brig.-Gen. 1.4.20; Despatches; Bts. of Lt.-Col. 18.2.15 and Col. 3.6.18; C.M.G.

BRUCE, W. F. (D.S.O. L.G. 1.1.18); b. 7.8.83; s. of Hon. W. N. Bruce, C.B.; educ. New Coll., Oxford; Capt. (A/Major), R.E.; Major, Royal Corps of Signals, T.F.; Europ. War, 1914–18; wounded; Despatches thrice; M.C.; R. Humane Society's Bronze Medal.

BRUCE-GARDYNE, E. (D.S.O. L.G. 20.7.17), Lt.-Cdr., R.N.

BRUDENELL-BRUCE, R. H. (D.S.O. L.G. 11.1.19); b. 24.10.81; 2nd Lt., Norf. R., 18.4.00; Lt. 25.12.01; Capt. 7.1.09; Bt. Major 18.2.15; Major 1.9.15; Despatches.

BRUGGY, S. (D.S.O. L.G. 1.1.17), Major, Commonwealth Military Forces.

BRUNE, D. E. PRIDEAUX- (see Prideaux-Brune, D. E.).

BRUNGER, R. (D.S.O. L.G. 24.6.16); b. 25.5.93; s. of W. T. Brunger, Secretary to the Governors, Framlingham College; educ. Framlingham College; Capt., Suffolk R., T.F.; served Europ. War; went to France for first time Jan. 1915; invalided to England, May, 1915; returned to France, Oct. 1915; wounded once; Despatches; D.S.O. awarded for commanding a company in a light raid on the German trenches at the Brecstacks, Givenchy, in France on 15.5.16; wounded. He was killed in action 8.10.18.

BRUNSKILL, J. H., B.A., M.B., B.Ch., B.A.O., D.P.H. (D.S.O. L.G. 1.1.17); b. 17.4.75; s. of late T. R. Brunskill; m. Elizabeth Mabel, d. of late A. Robinson; one s.; two d.; educ. Trin. Coll., Dublin; joined R.A.M.C., 1900; Capt. 1903; Major, 1912; Lt.-Col., 1918; Europ. War from Aug. 1914, with B.E.F.; Despatches 4 times; O.B.E.; S.M.O., Dunsterforce, N. Persia, 1918; A.D.M.S., Norperforce, 1918.

BRUNTON, J. (D.S.O. L.G. 1.2.19), T/Major, Northd. Fus.; M.C.

BRUTINEL, R. (D.S.O. L.G. 3.6.16); b. 1882; served Europ. War; Lt.-Col., Can. M.M.G. Bde.; Brig.-Gen.; C.B. and C.M.G.

BRUXNER, M. F. (D.S.O. L.G. 1.1.19), Major (T/Lt.-Col.), 6th Aust. L.H. Rgt.

BRYAN, C. C. (D.S.O. L.G. 14.1.16), Major, R.E., T.F. He volunteered for service at the beginning of the war, and served with great distinction. He was killed in action 11.8.17.

BRYAN, H. (D.S.O. L.G. 1.1.18); b. 13.6.65; s. of the Rev. H. Bryan and Mary Emily Bryan (*née* Leigh); m. Christobel, d. of C. A. Wetenhall; educ. Oakham School; ent. 7th Hussars, 1885; 2nd Lt., Linc. R., 18.6.92; served W. Africa, 1897–98 (Despatches; Medal and 2 clasps); Capt., Manchester R., Nov. 1899; served Nigeria, 1900 (Despatches; clasp); Ashanti, 1900 (Despatches twice; Medal; Bt. Major); retired Manch. R. 17.2.04; Bt. Lt.-Col., R. of O., Ret. Pay; Europ. War; Despatches; Bt. Lt.-Col. 3.6.16; Bt. Col. 3.6.19; C.M.G.

H. Bryan.

BRYANT, A. (D.S.O. L.G. 1.1.17); b. 10.4.69; s. of G. R. Bryant; m. Millicent, d. of late Sir G. Morice, Pasha, K.C.M.G.; one s.; one d.; educ. Marlborough; Cassel, and Sandhurst; 2nd Lt., Glouc. R., 29.3.90; Lt. 1.7.91; Capt. 24.2.00; Major 25.10.11; T/Lt.-Col.; served in France from 1915, and was commanding a Battalion of the Northd. Fus. when he was killed in action 17.10.17.

BRYANT, C. E. (D.S.O. L.G. 18.2.15) (Bar, L.G. 18.7.17) (see " The Distinguished Service Order," from its institution to 31.12.15, by same publishers).

BRYANT, F. C. (D.S.O. L.G. 4.6.17); b. 10.12.79; s. of late T. H. Bryant; m. Rosamond, d. of P. Beresford Hope; educ. Harrow, and R.M.A., Woolwich; ent. Army, 1898; Capt., 1907; Adjt., 1909–10; Major, 1914; employed with W.A.F.F., 1910–15; commanded Togoland F.F., 1914; served with B.E.F., France, 1915–18 (Despatches; C.M.G.; Bt. Lt.-Col.); Officer, Legion of Honour.

BRYCE, E. D. (D.S.O. L.G. 26.9.17) (Details, L.G. 9.1.18) (1st Bar, L.G. 18.2.18) (Details, L.G. 18.7.18) (2nd Bar, L.G. 1.2.19); b. 22.4.79; s. of J. P. Bryce, J.P., D.L., and Mercedes Bryce; m. Vera, d. of Sir David Salomons, Bart., and Laura, d. of Baron de Stern; educ. at Harrow, and afterwards at a tutor's (Colonel Fox, of Camberley). In 1903 he explored in the Amazon Valley in Peru, and from 1905 to 1914 was a rubber planter in Johore; commissioned in the Devons. R., he went to France with the 2nd Devons early in 1915; was promoted to Capt. end of 1915 in 1st Bn. N. Lancs. R., and a year later joined the Tank Corps. He became Lt.-Colonel, and was five times mentioned in Despatches.

E. D. Bryce.

BRYDEN, R. A. (D.S.O. L.G. 1.1.17); b. 30.8.82; Lt., R.A.M.C., 31.7.05; Major 15.10.15.

BRYDON, W. (D.S.O. L.G. 1.1.17), T/Major, S. African Heavy Artillery.

BUCHAN, D. A. (D.S.O. L.G. 3.6.18); b. 7.9.90; 2nd Lt., R.A., 23.7.10; Lt. 23.7.13; Capt. 23.7.16; Adjt. 17.3.21; Despatches.

BUCHANAN, E. J. B. (D.S.O. L.G. 3.6.18); b. 16.2.92; 2nd Lt., R.E., 23.12.11; Lt. 6.12.14; Capt. 26.6.17; Despatches.

BUCHANAN, J. N., B.A., LL.B. (D.S.O. L.G. 3.6.19); s. of Hon. Sir J. Buchanan; m. Nancy Isabel, d. of D. A. and Hon. Dame Maud Bevan; two s.; one d.; educ. Charterhouse; Trinity College, Cambridge; Cambridge Cricket XI., 1906–9; Capt., 1909; Tennis, Cambridge v. Oxford, 1908; S.R. Coldstream Gds., Aug. 1914, to March, 1920; M.C.

BUCHANAN, K. G. (D.S.O. L.G. 14.1.16); b. 25.1.80; m. Muriel Kate, d. of T. F. Cumming; one daughter; educ. Harrow; R.M.C., Sandhurst; 2nd Lt., Sea. Hldrs., 20.1.00; Lt. 21.1.01; Capt. 24.3.06; Adjt., Sea. Hldrs., 1906 to 1909; Major 1.9.15; played polo for the team in the Indian Infantry Tournament in 1904, and golf for the Regimental side that won the Army Gold Cup in 1913; served N.W.F., India, 1908; op. in the Zakka Khel country; Despaches; Medal with clasp; Europ. War; Bt. Lt.-Col. 1.1.17; Despatches; C.M.G.

BUCHANAN, R. J. (D.S.O. L.G. 22.8.19), Lt.-Cdr. (A/Cdr.), R.N.

BUCHANAN, V. C. (D.S.O. L.G. 3.6.16); b. at Montreal, 26.9.69; s. of late W. O. Buchanan; educ. Montreal High School; Capt., Can. Mil. Forces, 1905; Major in 1st Can. Contigent, 1914; commanded his old regiment from 1916; Lt.-Col. V. C. Buchanan was killed in action 3.6.16.

BUCK, P. H. (D.S.O. L.G. 4.6.17), Major, N.Z. Pioneer Bn.

BUCKLAND, A. E. (D.S.O. L G. 15.2.19) (Details, L.G. 30.7.19), Lt., R.N.; D.S.C.

BUCKLAND, G. N. (D.S.O. L.G. 26.8.18); b. 7.10.84; 2nd Lt., R.A., 23.12.03; Lt. 23.12.06; Capt. 30.10.14; Major 13.4.18; Despatches.

BUCKLE, A. W. (D.S.O. L.G. 4.3.18) (1st Bar, L.G. 26.7.18) (Details, L.G. 16.8.18) (2nd Bar, L.G. 11.1.19) (3rd Bar, L.G. 8.3.19) (Details, L.G. 4.10.19); served Europ. War, Cdr., R.N.V.R.; Despatches 5 times; Director, King's Canadian Camp School.

BUCKLE, C. G. (D.S.O. L.G. 11.5.17); b. 15.3.88; 2nd Lt., Northants R., 9.10.07; Lt. 30.6.09; employed with W.A.F.F. 10.1.12; Capt. (A/Lt.-Col.), Northants R.; M.C. He was killed in action 27.5.18.

BUCKLEY, A. (D.S.O. L.G. 26.9.17) (Details, L.G. 9.1.18) (Bar, L.G. 16.9.18); b. 10.4.77; s. of late W. Buckley, J.P.; m. Elsie Juanita, d. of J. E. Fisher; one s.; educ. Aldenham School, Herts; served S.African War, 1901–2, Lt., Vol. Coy. King's L'pool R.; Queen's Medal, 3 clasps; Europ. War, 1914–18, Lt.-Col., L'pool R.; Despatches twice; D.S.O. awarded for services 31.7.–3.8.1917, nr. Ypres; M.P., Waterloo Division of Lancs, from Dec. 1918; Parliamentary Private Secretary to Mr. F. G. Kellaway, M.P., Dept. of Overseas Trade; Junior Unionist Whip, 1921.

G. A. M. Buckley.

BUCKLEY, G. A. M., F.R.G.S. (D.S.O. L.G. 14.11.16); b. 25.10.66; s. of late G. Buckley, Esq.; m. Mabel Gertrude Warren; one s.; two d.; educ. Christ's College, Christchurch, N.Z.; Cheltenham College; ent. Army, 1897; served in E. Lancs. and Hants. R., and N.Z. Defence Force till 1900; Capt., 12th Bn. Hants. R., 1914; Europ. War, 1914–17; commanded 7th Leins. R., 47th Brig., 16th (Irish) Div., 1915 (Despatches 3 times); invalided from France, 1918; C.B.E., 1919; member of exploring party, Patagonia, 1897; Shackleton's British Antarctic Expedition, 1908. His D.S.O. was awarded for services on 3.9.16 at Guillemont.

BUCKLEY, J. (D.S.O. L.G. 3.6.18), T/Capt., Gen. List; M.C.

BUCKNALL, L. C. (D.S.O. L.G. 1.1.18), Major, Yeom.

BUDDEN, E. F. (D.S.O. L.G. 4.6.17); b. 15.4.86; 2nd Lt., R.A., 29.6.06; Lt. 29.6.09; Capt. 30.10.14; Major 17.1.17; Despatches.

BUDDLE, G. A. (D.S.O. L.G. 1.1.19), T/Major, R.E.; M.C.

BUDGE, P. P. (D.S.O. L.G. 14.1.16); b. 14.9.82; s. of the late Sir P. E. L. Budge, of Poole, Dorset; m. Evelyn Prideaux, d. of the late J. W. Gibson-Watt; 2nd Lt., R.A., 21.4.00; Lt. 10.12.03; Capt. 26.8.12; Major; served in France from Feb. 1915; was given command of a brigade; several times mentioned in Despatches; Bt. Lt.-Col. He was severely wounded. He died 11.9.18 of wounds received in action (" Times " 24.9.18).

BUDGEN, W. N. (D.S.O. L.G. 1.1.17); b. 30.12.79; s. of Col. W. T. Budgen, D.S.O., R.A.; m. Alice Emily Carey, d. of Dr. and Mrs. Aikman; one s.; one d.; educ. Cheltenham College; R.M.A., Woolwich; 2nd Lt., R.A., 23.12.98; Lt. 16.2.01; Capt. 5.7.04; Adjt., R.A., 25.4.07 to 25.5.11; Major 30.10.14; served S. African War, 1900–2 (Medal with 3 clasps); Europ. War, Dardanelles; Suvla Bay, Oct.–Nov. 1915, and on the Suez Canal 15 Dec.–March, 1916; in France, April, 1916, to Nov. 1918; Despatches thrice; Bt. Lt.-Col. 1.1.19.

BULL, G. (D.S.O. L.G. 3.6.16); b. 10.5.77; s. of R. G. Bull, late Resident Magistrate, Newry, Ireland; 2nd Lt., R. Garr. R., 9.12.03; Leins. R. 7.6.05; Lt., R. Ir. Fus., 3.2.07; Capt. 3.8.12; served S. Africa, 1900–2; Queen's Medal with 4 clasps; King's Medal with 2 clasps. At the outbreak of the Europ. War he went to the front; was twice mentioned in Despatches by Sir J. French, and once by Sir D. Haig, and was given the Bt. of Major; was slightly wounded in 1915; was given command of a Batt. of the R.I. Rifles; subsequently commanded a brigade; Brig.-Gen. Bull died 11.12.16 of wounds received in action 3.7.16, after 28 months in the trenches.

G. Bull.

BULL, H. S. (D.S.O. L.G. 25.8.17); s. of late C. P. Bull, P.W.D., India; educ. Eastbourne College, and St. Paul's School. In Calcutta when war broke out, but left for England on 8.8.14, being commissioned in the E. Lanc. R. within a month of landing; served Gallipoli campaign; Suvla Bay landing, and final evacuation (Despatches twice); Serbian Order of the White Eagle for services on another front. He was slightly and again dangerously wounded. Major Bull died in hospital abroad on 30.7.18.

BULL, J. H. (D.S.O. L.G. 3.6.18), Major, Can. Inf.

BULL, P. C. (D.S.O. L.G. 20.10.16), T/Capt., Suffolk R. His D.S.O. was awarded for services on 19.7.16 at Longueval Wood.

BULLEN, S. D. (D.S.O. L.G. 3.6.19); b. 30.4.70; 2nd Lt., R.A., 14.2.90; Lt. 14.2.93; Capt. 9.10.99; Adjt., R.A., 1900; Major 17.3.11; Lt.-Col. 1.5.17.

BULLER, F. A. W. (D.S.O. L.G. 4.6.17); b. 1879; s. of late Sir Alexander Buller, G.C.B.; m. Mary Caroline, d. of Stephen Hammick; Capt., R.N., 31.12.17; Europ. War, 1914–17; Despatches.

BULLER, J. D. (D.S.O. L.G. 1.1.17); b. 17.8.78; s. of Col. J. H. Buller, late Body-Guard, and Emily Augusta Dashwood; m. Sybil Collier; educ. Eton; 2nd Lt., Worc. R., 8.9.97; A.S.C. 2.10.99; Lt. 2.10.00; Capt. 1.4.02; Major 5.8.14; Lt.-Col., R.A.S.C., 26.11.20; served S. African War, 1900–2; Queen's Medal with 3 clasps; King's Medal with 2 clasps; Europ. War; Despatches; C.M.G.

BULLER, J. H. G. (D.S.O. L.G. 26.7.17); b. 16.8.81; 2nd Lt., Unatt., 8.1.01; Conn. Rangers 9.3.01; Lt., I.A., 16.11.03; Capt. 8.1.10; Major 8.1.16; served in S. African War, 1901–2; Queen's Medal with 4 clasps; Despatches.

BULLOCH, R. A. (D.S.O. L.G. 1.1.17); b. 19.12.79; 2nd Lt., R. Highrs., 18.10.99; Lt. 13.11.00; Capt. 7.5.06; Major 1.9.15; Bt. Lt.-Col. 3.6.19; S. African War, 1899–1902; Queen's Medal with 4 clasps; King's Medal with 2 clasps; Europ. War; Despatches.

BULLOCK, C. J. TROYTE- (see Troyte-Bullock, C. J.).

BULLOCK, L. N. B. (D.S.O. L.G. 15.2.17) (Bar, L.G. 1.2.19); served in European War as Capt. (T/Major), Can. Engrs., later T/Major, S. Staffs R.

BULLOCK, R. L. (D.S.O. L.G. 14.1.16); b. 8.4.71; s. of the late Rev. Canon Bullock, Vicar of Shurdington, Cheltenham, Prebendary of Lincoln; educ. King's School, Canterbury; served 20 years in 1st W.R. Brig., R.F.A.; retired Aug. 1914; rejoined Aug. 1914; served European War; Despatches; holds T.D.; Major, T.F. Reserve.

BULLOCK-MARSHAM, F. W. (D.S.O. L.G. 3.6.18); b. 14.7.83; 2nd Lt., 19th Hrs., 25.5.10; Adjt., 19 Hrs., 14.7.10 to 13.7.13; Capt. 25.6.14; Major, 3rd D. Gds., 26.8.19; Despatches; M.C.

BULLOUGH, C. B. (D.S.O. L.G. 4.6.17); b. 31.12.76; s. of late J. Bullough, J.P.; educ. at Marlborough; 2nd Lt., R.A., 5.5.00; Lt., June, 1901; Capt. 5.5.13; Major 20.4.16. He served in France from Feb. 1915; was present at Neuve Chapelle, Festubert, Richebourg, St. Vaast, Loos, the Somme, Bullecourt, Passchendaele, Sanctuary Wood, Ypres, Bois de Buie and other engagements. His battery was selected and visited by H.M. the King during one of his tours in France. He formed the 117th Siege By. and commanded it for two years. He was twice mentioned in Despatches, and was killed in action on 25.4.18, at Reningsheist.

C. B. Bullough.

BULSTRODE, C. V., M.D. (D.S.O. L.G. 1.1.18), Major, R.A.M.C., T.A., 10.2.18; T.D.

BULTEEL, J. C. (D.S.O. L.G. 18.2.18) (Details, L.G. 18.7.18); b. 1890; s. of J. G. Bulteel and Mariquita Masini, d. of late Pascoe du Pre Grenfell, of Wilton Park, Bucks; m. 1919, widow of Major Douglas Reynolds, V.C.; one d.; served Europ. War, Yeomanry; M.C.

BUNBURY, R. S. (D.S.O. L.G. 1.1.18); b. 19.9.80; 2nd Lt., R.A., 6.1.00; Lt. 3.4.01; Capt. 2.1.11; Major, R.G.A., 18.8.15; Despatches.

BUNCE, H. (D.S.O. L.G. 8.8.19), T/Lt. (A/Capt.), 4th Bn. S. African Inf.

BUNDOCK, H. C. (D.S.O. L.G. 1.1.19), Major, 36th Aust. H.A.B.

BUNKER, S. W. (D.S.O. L.G. 1.1.19), Capt. (A/Lt.-Col.), R. Fus. (S.R.); R.E.; M.C.

BURBANK, M. A. (D.S.O. L.G. 22.6.18), Major, Can. Rly. Troops.

BURCHALL, H. (D.S.O. L.G. 1.1.18), Capt. (T/Lt.-Col.), R.F.C., S.R.

BURDEN, H. J. (D.S.O. L.G. 29.10.18), Lt. (T/Capt.), Can. Forestry Corps; D.F.C.

BURDETT, A. B. (D.S.O. L.G. 1.1.17); b. 12.6.79; 2nd Lt., York. and Lanc. R., 3.8.98; Lt. 27.6.00; Capt. 1.1.06; Adjt., York and Lanc. R., 2.12.13 to 29.6.14; Major 25.7.15; Bt. Lt.-Col. 1.1.18; served in Europ. War, York. and Lanc. R., and R.F.C.; Despatches.

BURDETT, J. C. (D.S.O. L.G. 1.1.19), T/Major (A/Lt.-Col.), Leic. R.; M.C.

BURDON, C. W. (D.S.O. L.G. 3.2.20); b. 13.9.82; 2nd Lt., R.A., 18.8.00; Lt. 18.8.03; Capt. 30.8.11; Major 23.12.14.

BURDUS, S. G. (D.S.O. L.G. 16.9.18), Lt., Aust. Inf., Aust. Imp. Force.

BURGES, D. (D.S.O. L.G. 3.6.18), Lt.-Col., Glouc. R.; V.C. (see "The Victoria Cross," by same publishers).

BURGES-SHORT, H. G. R. (D.S.O. L.G. 1.1.18); b. 14.2.75; s. of late Major G. Burges-Short; 2nd Lt., Som. L.I., 23.2.98; Lt. 29.1.00; Capt. 12.6.06; Major 1.9.15; T/Lt.-Col.; served S. African War, 1899–1902; Queen's Medal with 5 clasps; King's Medal with 2 clasps; Europ. War. He was reported killed in action on Palm Sunday, 24.3.18, whilst commanding his Battalion, but was subsequently reported a prisoner of war.

BURGESS, A. (D.S.O. L.G. 12.3.17), 2nd Lt., R. Berks. R. His D.S.O. was awarded for services on 4–5.2.1917, at Courcelette.

BURGESS, C. R. (D.S.O. L.G. 1.2.17), Capt. and Bt. Major (T/Lt.-Col.), Permanent Forces, S. Africa.

BURGESS, R. (D.S.O. L.G. 1.1.19); m. Marjorie Constance Fetherstonhaugh; late Lt.-Col., R.A.M.C., T.F.; M.C.

BURGESS, W. H. (D.S.O. L.G. 18.1.18) (Details, L.G. 25.4.18), Lt., Can. Inf.

BURGESS, W. L. H. (D.S.O. L.G. 14.1.16); b. 1880; s. of Rev. G. Burgess; m. Flora Macdonald Pembroke, d. of Mrs. Cecil King; served Europ. War, 1914–18, on N.Z. Staff; transferred to Commonwealth Forces; Major, Aust. Art.; T/Brig.-Gen.; Lt.-Col.; Despatches 6 times; C.B.; C.M.G.; Officer, Legion of Honour.

BURKE, B. B. (D.S.O. L.G. 14.1.16); b. 7.1.76; s. of late James Burke, M.I.C.E., and of Jane Burke; m. Anna, daughter of Surgeon-Gen. Sir A. S. Reid, K.C.B.; one d.; educ. High School, Dublin, and at the Royal College of Surgeons, Ireland; ent. R.A.M.C. 21.2.06; Major 21.12.11; Lt.-Col. 26.12.17; Europ. War, 1914–18; Despatches four times; C.B.E.

BURKE, E. T., M.B., Ch.B., F.R.I.P.H., F.R.G.S. (D.S.O. L.G. 25.8.17); b. 18.4.88; s. of W. M. Burke, J.P., F.S.A. Scotland, City Chamberlain, Dundee; m. Mina, d. of the late C. S. Craigie; one s.; educ. Perth Academy; Glasgow Univ.; original member of Glasgow University O.T.C.; in S.R. 23.2.13; mobilized R.A.M.C. from S.R. to 31.3.19—4 yrs., 216 days; Capt., R.A.M.C., 28.2.18, and Lt.-Col.; Despatches; served Gallipoli; Despatches; Mesopotamia; Despatches; Serbian Order of the White Eagle with Swords; A.D.M.S., N. Persian Force, 1918; Caucasus, 1918–19; S.M.O., Baku,; Despatches; commanded 40th British F. Amb., 13th Div., 1915–19.

BURKE, F. J. (D.S.O. L.G. 7.11.18), Lt., Aust. Inf.

BURKE, H. F. LARDNER- (see Lardner-Burke, H. F.).

BURKE, J. (D.S.O. L.G. 3.6.19); Q.M. and Major, R. Dublin Fus.; M.C. D.C.M.

BURKE, T. F. (D.S.O. L.G. 18.7.17); served in Europ. War, Sc. Rif. and M.G.C.; Lt., 6th Bn. (T.) Sc. Rifles, 2.4.18; Despatches.

BURKHARDT, V. R. (D.S.O. L.G. 4.6.17); b. 21.12.84; 2nd Lt., R.A., 23.12.03; Lt. 23.12.06; Capt. 30.10.14; Major 22.7.16; Despatches.

BURLEIGH, C. W. (D.S.O. L.G. 20.9.18); R.D.; Cdr., R.N.R.

BURMANN, R. M. (D.S.O. L.G. 3.6.18), Capt., E. Lancs. R.; M.C. He was killed in action 27.10.18.

BURNAND, N. G. (D.S.O. L.G. 4.6.17); b. 4.10.76; 2nd Lt. 9.12.99; Lt. 14.3.01; Capt. 20.3.09; Adjt., Leinster Rgt., 3.5.09 to 2.5.12; Major 1.9.15; S. African War, 1902; slightly wounded; Queen's Medal with 3 clasps; Europ. War.

BURNE, A. H. (D.S.O. L.G. 9.11.14) (Bar, L.G. 22.6.18) (see "The Distinguished Service Order," from its institution to 31.12.1915, by same publishers).

BURNE, E. R. (D.S.O. L.G. 14.1.16); b. 14.8.76; 2nd Lt., R.A., 21.9.96; Lt. 21.9.99; Capt. 4.2.02; Major 12.9.13; served in S. African War, 1901; Despatches; Queen's Medal with 4 clasps; Europ. War. Lt.-Col. Burne was killed in action 1.10.18.

BURNE, N. H. M. (D.S.O. L.G. 14.11.16); b. 21.7.72; s. of F. N. and L. M. Burne; m. Hillian Ross Blakeway; four s.; joined Cape M.R., 1890; 1st comm., 1897; served Matabeleland, 1893–4; Langeburg (S.A.), 1897; S. African War, 1899–1902; G.S.W. Africa, 1914–15 (Despatches; Croix de Guerre); G. E. Africa, 1916–17 (Despatches twice; D.S.O. for gallantry at Koadoa, Irangi, on 9–10 May, 1916); Europ. War, with 55th Div., Festubert-Givenchy-La Bassée Canal Sector, June–Aug. 1918, and with 3rd Div. during final operations, Sept. to Nov. 1918; Army of Occupation; Despatches twice; C.M.G.

BURNE, S. F. (D.S.O. L.G. 7.2.18); b. 4.2.85; 2nd Lt., R.A., 21.12.04; Lt. 21.12.07; Capt. 30.10.14; Major, R.F.A., 1.10.16; served Europ. War in France.

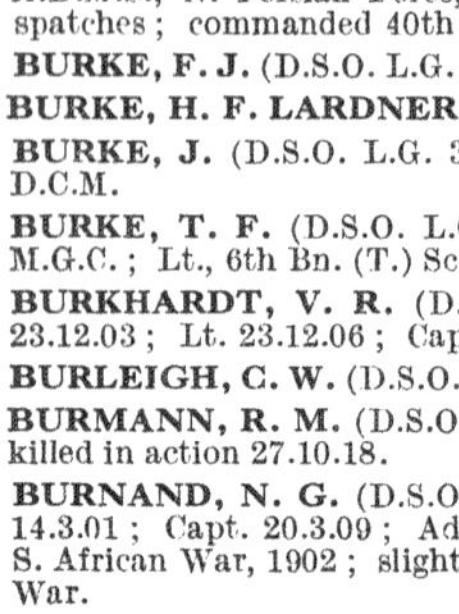

F. H. Burnell-Nugent.

BURNELL, C. D. (D.S.O. L.G. 3.6.19), Major, London R.; T/Lt.-Colonel; Despatches.

BURNELL-NUGENT, F. H. (D.S.O. L.G. 14.1.16); b. 5.9.80; s. of late A. Nugent; m. Ellen Mary, d. of T. Coke Burnell, of St. Cross Grange, Winchester; one s.; educ. Horris Hill; Winchester College; R.M. College, Camberley; entered R. Brig. 11.11.99; Lt. 18.12.00; Captain 8.3.05; Major 1.9.15; T/Brig.-Genl. 5.2.16; served S. African War, 1899–1901; dangerously wounded; Queen's Medal with 3 clasps; Europ. War, 1914–17; Le Cateau; Retreat from Mons (wounded); Battles of Marne and of Aisne (wounded); commanded 2nd Bn. R. Brig., 1915–16, and 167th and 182nd Inf. Brigades (Despatches); served with 1st Batt. R.Brig. during suppression of Arab rebellion in Mesopotamia, 1921; Bt. Lt.-Col. 3.6.16; O.B.E.

BURNETT, A. H. (D.S.O. L.G. 25.8.17); b. 9.6.84; 2nd Lt., Border R., 28.1.03; I.A. 20.8.04; Lt. 28.4.05; Capt. 28.1.12; Major, 28.1.18; S. African War, 1902; served in Mediterranean; Medal; Europ. War.

BURNETT, C. S. (D.S.O. L.G. 11.4.18); b. 1882; s. of J. A. Burnett; m. Sybil Bell; one d.; served S. African War, 1900–01; Medal and 3 clasps; N. Nigeria, 1904–5 (Despatches; Medal and 3 clasps); Europ. War, 1914–18; Group Captain, R.A.F.; Despatches; C.B.E.; 3rd Class Order of the Nile.

BURNETT, J. L. G. (D.S.O. L.G. 18.2.15) (Bar, L.G. 17.9.17), Major and Bt. Lt.-Col., G. Highrs. (see "The Distinguished Service Order," from its institution to 31.12.1915).

BURNETT, P. (D.S.O. L.G. 11.12.16), Major, Can. A.M.C.

BURNETT, R. P. (D.S.O. L.G. 3.6.19), T/Major (A./Lt-Col.), S. Staffs R.; M.C.

BURNETT, WILLIAM (D.S.O. L.G. 3.6.16), Lt.-Col., N. Staffs R. (Territorial). He died of wounds 3.7.16.

BURNETT-STUART, G. R. (D.S.O. L.G. 17.9.17); b. 2.3.85; 1st commission 23.12.03; Lt. 23.12.06; retired R.A. 2.11.12; Lt., retired pay (employed 5.8.14) 24.5.16; Major, R.F.A., S.R.

BURNEY, A. E. C. (D.S.O. L.G. 11.4.18); b. 15.3.83; s. of A. G. Burney; m. Dorothy, d. of late Lt.-Col. G. F. A. Norton, R.A.; two s.; one d.; educ. Haileybury College; R.M.A., Woolwich; 2nd Lt. 23.7.01; Lt. 11.5.04; Capt. 23.7.14; Major, R.G.A., 1.5.17; Europ. War (Gallipoli and Palestine), 1914–18; Despatches; Bt. Lt.-Col. 3.6.19; M.C.

BURNHAM, S. S. (D.S.O. L.G. 18.10.17) (Details, L.G. 7.3.18), Major, Can. Inf.

BURNS, W. J. G. (D.S.O. L.G. 1.1.19), Major, Can. F.A.

BURNSIDE, F. R. (D.S.O. L.G. 1.1.17); b. 25.6.76; s. of Sir B. T. Burnside and Mary Elizabeth Burnside; m. Mary Geraldine, d. of Lt.-Col. Fitzgerald, I.A.; educ. Sherborne, and Bradfield College; Lt., C.I.V., 1.1.00; 2nd Lt., 3rd Hussars, 5.5.00; Lt. 12.4.01; Capt. 18.7.08; Major 13.9.19; served S. African War, with C.I.V. and 3rd K.O. Hussars, 1900–01; Queen's Medal, 5 clasps; Somaliland (clasp); German S.W. African Campaign, 1914; Western Front, 1915–19; Bt. Major 1.1.18; Bt. Lt.-Col. 3.6.19; Despatches 4 times.

BURNYEAT, R. W. (D.S.O. L.G. 3.6.18) (Bar, L.G. 1.2.19), Major, R.F.A., T.F., 1.6.16; T.D.; Despatches.

BURRELL, S. (D.S.O. L.G. 3.6.19), Major, Northd. Hussars, Yeom.

BURRETT, A. F. (D.S.O. L.G. 3.6.18), Major, Aust. Inf.

BURRITT, R. (D.S.O. L.G. 1.1.19), Col., Can. Forces 24.5.16.

BURROUGHES, H. N., M.B. (D.S.O. L.G. 3.6.19), Capt. (A/Lt.-Col.), R.A.M.C., T.F.

BURROWES, A. R. (D.S.O. L.G. 1.1.18); b. 29.3.67; m. Lilian Emma, d. of late Rev. R. Pigott, J.P.; 2nd Lt., R. Ir. Fus., 11.2.88; Lt. 31.7.89; Adjt., R.I. Fus., 16.9.91 to 15.9.95; Capt. 1.6.97; Major 10.11.06; Lt.-Col. 14.9.14; Col. 14.9.18; Brig.-General retired, 1920; Hazara Exp., 1891 (Medal with clasp); S. African War, 1899–1902 (Queen's Medal with 4 clasps; King's Medal with 2 clasps); Europ. War; Despatches 4 times; C.M.G.; Croix de Guerre.

BURROWS, M. B. (D.S.O. L.G. 21.1.20), Capt., 5th Dr. Gds., 1.5.20.

BURSTON, S. R. (D.S.O. L.G. 1.1.18), Lt.-Col., Aust. A.M.C.

BURT, A. (D.S.O. L.G. 18.6.17) (Bar, L.G. 26.7.18); b. 18.4.75; s. of F. J. Burt; educ. Oundle; Heidelberg; Artist Volunteers, 1894; 3rd Bn. R. Warwicks. R., 1895–6; 2nd Lt., 3 D.G., 6.6.96; Lt. 30.1.99; Adjt. 3 D.G., 22.9.99 to 9.7.04; Capt. 9.12.00; Major 10.5.11; Lt.-Col. 2.7.16; retired with rank of Brig.-Gen., 1920; S. African War, 1899–1902; Despatches; Queen's Medal with 5 clasps; King's Medal with 2 clasps; Bt. of Major 22.8.02; Europ. War, 1915–19, commanding 3rd Dn. Gds. till 1918, when commanded 7th Cav. Brig.; Despatches 5 times; Albert Medal; Legion of Honour; Chief of Military Mission to Latvia and Lithuania, June, 1919–Feb. 1920; Despatches; C.B.

BURT, A. E. (D.S.O. L.G. 3.6.18), T/Major, Oxf. and Bucks. L.I

BURT, C. S. (D.S.O. L.G. 3.6.18); b. 9.7.87; 2nd Lt., S. Staffs. R., 27.1.12; Lt. 6.5.14; Capt. 12.8.15; A/Lt.-Col., S. Staffs R., 10.10.17; Despatches.

BURTON, C. (D.S.O. L.G. 1.1.17); b. 3.7.83; m. Gladys Astley, d. of Major, L. L. Astley-Cooper; one s.; two d.; educ. Marlborough College; 2nd Lt. R. War. R., 30.4.02; A.S.C. 9.10.05; Lt. 9.10.06; Capt. 6.5.12; Major 15.10.15; S. African War, 1900–02; Queen's Medal with 4 clasps; Europ. War, 1914–18; Despatches; Bt. Lt.-Col. 1.1.19.

BURY, C. K. HOWARD- (see Howard-Bury, C. K.).

BURY, W. A. (D.S.O. L.G. 28.8.18); m.; one s.; served Europ. War, 1914–18; Engineer-Cdr., R.N.; Engineer Officer of H.M.S. Vindictive, Zeebrugge Raid, 23.4.18; Despatches; Engineer Officer of H.M.S. Vindictive, sunk at Ostend entrance, 10.5.18; Despatches; seriously wounded. His D.S.O. was awarded for services in this connection.

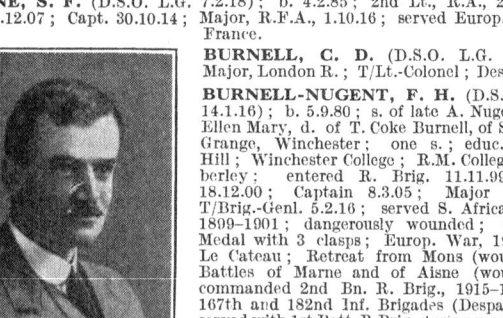

W. A. Bury.

BUSFEILD, J. A. (D.S.O. L.G. 2.12.18); b. 3.12.77; 2nd Lt., Ches. R., 4.1.99; Lt. 1.8.00; Capt. 26.5.06; S. African War, 1900–02; Queen's Medal with 3 clasps; King's Medal with 2 clasps; Europ. War; Major (A/Lt.-Col.), R. of O., 1st Bn. Ches. R.

BUSH, A. P. (D.S.O. L.G. 12.7.19), Lt., R.N.

BUSH, C. G. (D.S.O. L.G. 4.6.17), y. s. of Mrs. Bush, of Normandy Lodge, Blackheath. He served in the European War, as T/Major, R.A.S.C., and died on 25.11.18, in France.

BUSH, H. F. (D.S.O. L.G. 1.1.17), T/Major, R.A.S.C.

BUSH, J. G. (D.S.O. L.G. 22.8.18), Major, S. Afr. Vety. Corps.

BUSHELL, C. (D.S.O. L.G. 1.1.18), Capt. (A/Major), R. W. Surrey R., S.R.; V.C. He was killed in action 8.8.18 (see "The Victoria Cross," by same publishers).

BUTCHART, H. J. (D.S.O. L.G. 3.6.18); b. 18.4.82; s. of J. S. Butchart; m. Catherine, d. of A. Johnston, of Aberdeen; educ. Aberdeen Grammar School; Universities of Aberdeen and Edinburgh; ent. 1st V.B. G. Highrs., 1907; transferred to Scottish Horse, 1908; Capt. 1913; Major, 1916; served Europ. War, 1914–18; Despatches; Secretary of the University of Aberdeen since 1919.

BUTCHART, J. A. (D.S.O. L.G. 1.1.17); b. 4.10.77; 2nd Lt., R.A., 26.5.00; Lt. 13.3.02; Capt. 23.2.11; Major 30.10.14; A/Lt.-Col., R.A., 29.12.17; A.D.C. to Governor of Madras, 1906 and 1912–14; European War, 1914–18; Despatches.

BUTCHER, H. C. (D.S.O. L.G. 26.9.16); b. 3.5.90; s. of G. Butcher; m. Hester Katherine, d. of D. MacLeod; educ. St. Paul's School; Lt.-Col., late K.O.Y.L.I.; Despatches four times; wounded four times.

BUTLER, B. (D.S.O. L.G. 4.2.18) (Details, L.G. 5.7.18), Capt., Infantry, Newfoundland Forces; M.C.

BUTLER, B. A. B. (D.S.O. L.G. 1.1.18) (Bar, L.G. 16.9.18); b. 6.5.78; 2nd Lt., R.A., 23.12.97; Lt. 23.12.00; Capt. 23.1.05; Major; Europ. War.; Bt. Lt.-Col.; T/Lt.-Col., R.F.A. (156 Bde.). He died of wounds 23.10.18.

BUTLER, C. H. (D.S.O. L.G. 20.7.17) (Bar, L.G. 11.8.17), Sq.-Cdr., R.N.A.S.; D.S.C. He had single-handed combats with a number of powerful enemy machines twice on one day. Over the Thames estuary he attacked six raiders, and later at Ostend he fought two. In each combat he brought down one enemy plane.

BUTLER, C. P. (D.S.O. L.G. 4.6.17); b. 1880; s. of Hon. Sir R. Butler and Helena Kate, d. of E. W. Lagton, of Sydney; m. Bertha Smeaton Hawkins; educ. St. Peter's College, Adelaide; served S. Africa, 1901–2; Queen's Medal, 5 clasps; Europ. War, 1915–17; Major, T/Lt.-Col. A.I.F.; Despatches.

BUTLER, H. N. (D.S.O. L.G. 4.6.17) Lt.-Col., Aust. A.M.C.

BUTLER, J. F. P. (D.S.O. L.G. 26.6.16), Capt., K.R.R.C.; V.C. He was killed in action 4.9.16. (See "The Victoria Cross," by same publishers.)

BUTLER, HON. L. J. P. (D.S.O. L.G. 14.1.16); b. 22.4.76; s. of the 25th Baron Dunboyne; educ. Winchester, and New College, Oxford; 2nd Lt., Durham L.I., 28.3.00; I. Gds. 20.2.01; Lt. 1.1.02; Adjt., I. Gds., 1.1.07 to 31.12.07; Capt. 27.3.09; Major 14.7.13; Lt.-Col. 15.7.15; Colonel 18.2.19; T/Brig.-Gen. 5.5.16 to 30.3.19; S. African War, 1899–1902; Queen's Medal with clasp; Europ. War; Despatches six times; C.M.G.; Bt. Lt.-Col. 18.2.15.

BUTLER, P. R. (D.S.O. L.G. 1.1.17); b. 7.11.80; s. of late Lt.-Gen. Sir Wm. Butler, G.C.B., and Lady Elizabeth Butler; educ. Stonyhurst; Weybridge; 2nd Lt., R.I. Rgt., 7.5.02; Lt. 1.4.04; Capt. 18.9.09; Major 21.10.16; S. African War, 1901–2; served in Mediterranean; Medal; Europ. War from 1914; A.D.C. to late Major-Gen. Sir T. Capper; was in the retreat from Ghent to Ypres and through the First Battle of Ypres (severely wounded); last part of Second Battle of Ypres and in France, and later in Salonika; in France again July, 1918, and served throughout the offensive; Despatches 3 times; Bt. Lt.-Col. 3.6.19.

BUTLER, THE HON. R. T. R. P. (D.S.O. L.G. 1.1.18); b. 8.10.82; 3rd s. of 25th Baron Dunboyne; m. Grace Theodosia Farquhar, d. of G. Kinloch; served Europ. War, 1915–18; Capt., R.E., 1.7.20; T/Major, Tank Corps, 1.1.21; Despatches; M.C.

BUTLER, S. S. (D.S.O. L.G. 4.6.17); b. 6.10.80; s. of Rev. G. H. Butler; m. Phyllis, d. of Capt. H. Critchley-Salmonson; one s.; educ. Winchester; joined 3rd Northd. Fus., 1897; 2nd Lt., R. War. R., 20.5.99; Lt. 1.4.00; Capt., R. War. R., 18.1.08; Capt., S. Staffs. R., 20.5.08; Major 12.8.15; Lt.-Col. 2.1.21; served S. African War, 1899–1901 (Queen's Medal with 5 clasps); B.E. Africa, Nandi Exp., 1906, and Embu Exp., 1907 (African G.S. Medal and 2 clasps); Sudan, Tagoi Patrol, 1911 (Sudan Medal and clasp); Europ. War, Egyptian Exp. Force, 1914–15; Dardanelles, 1915–16; France from Feb. 1916; promoted Colonel on Staff, 1918; Despatches three times; 1914–15 Star; Bt. Lt.-Col. 3.6.18; Croix de Guerre with Palm; Order of the Nile, 4th Class; Sacred Treasure, 3rd Class.

BUTLER, HON. T. P. P. (D.S.O. L.G. 29.10.18); b. 3.7.84; 2nd Lt., R.A., 23.12.03; Lt. 23.12.06; Capt. 30.10.14; Major 22.7.16; employed Egyptian Army; Europ. War; Despatches.

BUTLER, V. S. (D.S.O. L.G. 8.3.18), Lt.-Cdr., R.N.; Cdr. 31.12.18.

BUTLER, W. M. (D.S.O. L.G. 1.1.19), Major, King Edward's Horse, and Tank Corps.

BUTLER-BOWDON, W. E. I. (D.S.O. L.G. 1.1.18) (surname gazetted as Butler-Bowden); b. 16.1.80; s. of Col. J. E. Butler-Bowdon and the Hon. Monica Mary, d. of 12th Lord Petre; m. Gertrude Mary, d. of late A. de Trafford; two s.; educ. Oratory School, Edgbaston; R.M.C., Sandhurst; 2nd Lt., D.C.L.I., 12.8.99; Lt. 15.12.00; Capt. 12.1.05; Major 1.9.15; T/Lt.-Col. 9.5.17; S. African War, 1899–1902; Despatches; Queen's Medal with 4 clasps; King's Medal with 2 clasps; Europ. War, 1914–18; Despatches.

BUTT, P. L. (D.S.O. L.G. 24.5.19), Eng. Lt.-Cdr. R.N.

BUTTENSHAW, A. S. (D.S.O. L.G. 1.1.18), Inspector, 2nd Class, R.A.O.D., with rank of Capt. 20.7.21.

BUTTERFIELD, E. (D.S.O. L.G. 17.4.16); b. 9.4.80; 2nd Lt., Unatt., 20.1.00; I.S.C. 18.4.01; Lt., I.A., 20.4.02; Capt. 20.1.09; Major, I.A., 1.9.15.

BUTTERWORTH, R. F. A. (D.S.O. L.G. 3.6.16) (Bar, L.G. 26.7.17); b. 4.1.76; s. of R. W. Butterworth; m. Margaret Elaine, d. of late J. W. Morison; one s.; one d.; educ. Eton; 2nd Lt., R.E., 6.8.95; Lt. 8.8.98; Capt. 6.8.04; Major 30.10.14; served in France from July, 1915; Lt.-Col., R.F.A., 2.12.21; Despatches 5 times; Bt. Lt.-Col. 1.1.18; C.M.G.

BUXTON, A. (D.S.O. L.G. 3.6.16); b. 2.9.81; s. of E. N. Buxton, J.P., D.L., and of a daughter of Hon. and Rev. R. H. Digby; educ. Harrow; Trinity College, Cambridge; graduated Natural Science Tripos, 1904; played in the Harrow Eleven, 1900–01; joined Essex Yeomanry, 1902; promoted Major, June, 1912. On 13.5.1915, at Potijze, the regiment suffered very heavy casualties. All Officers present and senior to himself being killed, wounded or missing, Major Buxton was left in temporary command, and was recommended by Divisional Headquarter Staff "for showing conspicuous ability in rallying those who survived after the regiment had suffered heavy casualties at Potijze;" attached 10th R. Hussars, 1918–19; Despatches thrice; appointed Secretary, Headquarters, League of Nations.

A. Buxton.

BUXTON, B. (D.S.O. L.G. 21.9.17); b. 21.10.82; s. of G. F. Buxton, C.B.; m. Lady Hermione Grimston, d. of 3rd Earl of Verulam; three s.; one d.; educ. Cheam School; H.M.S. Britannia, Mediterranean (Crete), 1908; Naval Staff College, 1913; North Sea, 1914 and 1915; Mesopotamia, 1916 and 1917; Admiralty, 1918; Staff College, Camberley, 1921.

BUXTON, I. (D.S.O. L.G. 3.6.19); b. 28.8.84; s. of G. F. Buxton, C.B., Director of Barclay & Co. Ltd., Bankers; m. Phyllis Dorothy Johnson, d. of H. G. Barclay, M.V.O., V.D., J.P., late Vice-Chairman, Barclay & Co. Ltd.; one d.; educ. Cheam; Eton; Trinity College, Cambridge; Major, Norfolk Yeom.

BUXTON, J. L. (D.S.O. L.G. 3.6.16); b. 1.12.77; s. of F. W. Buxton and the Hon. Mrs. F. W. Buxton; m. Evelyne, d. of late Rev. J. W. Rynd; educ. Eton; University College, Oxford; 2nd Lt., R. Bde., 11.3.99; Lt. 24.4.00; Capt. 14.5.04; Major, R. Bde., 16.3.15; S. African War, 1899–1900–02; severely wounded at Pieter's Hill; Despatches thrice; Queen's Medal with 5 clasps; King's Medal with clasp; Europ. War, 1914–18; Bt. Lt.-Col. 1.1.18; C.M.G.

BUXTON, R. V. (D.S.O. L.G. 15.2.19) (Details, L.G. 30.7.19), Capt. (A/Lt.-Col.), R.W. Kent Yeom.

BUZZARD, C. N. (D.S.O. L.G. 1.1.18); b. 29.4.73; 2nd Lt., R.A., 15.8.99; Lt. 18.8.95; Capt. 1.2.00; Divl. Adjt., R.A., 1901–3; Adjt., R.A., 1903–05, and 1909–12; Major 6.1.14; Bt. Lt.-Col. 1.1.17; Lt.-Col. 16.6.17.

BUZZARD, F. A. (D.S.O. L.G. 1.1.17) (Bar, L.G. 27.6.19); s. of late T. Buzzard, M.D.; m. Joan, d. of Hon. John Collier; two s.; one d. b. 9.11.75; 2nd Lt., R.A., 2.11.95; Lt. 2.11.98; Capt. 13.6.01; Major 15.2.12; Lt.-Col., R.F.A., 9.8.16; T/Brig.-Gen. 20.3.19; Europ. War, 1914–18, including Mesopotamia; Despatches.

BYE, W. R. G. (D.S.O. L.G. 1.1.18), T/Capt., Gen. List.; M.C.

BYL, J. VAN DER (see Van der Byl, J.).

BYNG, HON. A. S. (D.S.O. L.G. 1.1.18); b. 31.3.76; 5th s. of 5th Earl of Strafford; m. Lucy Margaret, d. of E. H. Greenly; one s.; one d.; T/Major, R.F.C., and Commander, Kite Balloon Squadron; served Europ. War; Legion of Honour, Croix d'Officier.

BYRNE, G.C. (D.S.O. L.G. 4.6.17), T/Major, Aust. A.M.C.

BYRNE, H. F. (D.S.O. L.G. 3.6.18); b. 25.3.75; 2nd Lt., York. and Lanc. R., 7.12.95; Lt. 18.6.99; Capt. 16.6.02; Major 22.7.15; now R.A.O.C.; served E. Africa, 1901–4; op. in Somaliland; action at Jidballi; Despatches; Medal with 3 clasps; Europ. War.

BYRNE, H. R. (D.S.O. L.G. 3.6.18.), Major, Aust. F.A.

BYRNE, J. D. (D.S.O. L.G. 1.1.17); b. 9.11.75; s. of late W. H. Byrne; m. Lena, widow of Capt. C. J. C. Barrett, R. Scots Fus.; educ. Beaumont College, Windsor; 2nd Lt., R.A., 10.1.00; Lt. 3.4.01; Capt. 23.1.11; Major 16.10.15; Bt. Lt.-Col. 3.6.19; Lt.-Col.; served N.W. Frontier of India, 1908; operations in the Mohmand country; Medal with clasp; served in France from 1914; Neuve Chapelle, Aubers Ridge, Festubert, Loos, Somme, and Passchendaele; op. in Egypt, 1915, and Palestine, 1918 (wounded at Festubert, Loos and Ypres); Despatches three times; Bt. Lt.-Col. Russian Order of St. Stanilas with Swords.

BYRNE, L. C. (D.S.O. L.G. 15.2.19) (Details, L.G. 30.7.19); s. of Dr. R. Byrne; educ. Mount St. Mary's College, Chesterfield; Sandhurst; served with 2nd Battn. R. Dublin Fus. in France, May, 1915, until cessation of hostilities; Lt. 26.1.16; Despatches; M.C. and Bar.

BYRNE, P. A. LANGAN- (see Langan-Byrne, P. A.).

BYRON, THE HON. J. J. (D.S.O. L.G. 1.2.17); s. of late J. Byron; m. Mary, d. of late W. M. Alderson; joined Australian Military Forces, 1885; commanded the Queensland Rgt., R.A.A., from 1895 to 1899; attaché with the United States Army in the Philippines War of 1899; served in the S. African War, and was present at Belmont, Graspan, Modder River, and Magersfontein (severely wounded); was A.D.C. to Lord Roberts at the Battles of Paardeberg, Poplar Grove, Dreifontein (Despatches twice); was an extra A.D.C. to the Duke of Cornwall during his Colonial tour in 1901; A.A.G. for Artillery Headquarters Staff, Commonwealth Military Forces, 1902; in German S.W. African Campaign of 1914–15 he commanded a mixed brigade, and was wounded; in the East Central African Campaigns he commanded the 5th S.A.I., 1st E.A. Brigade and Sayea Column (three wound stripes; Despatches 4 times); served in Flanders, and as 2nd-in-Command, Dunsterforce, N.W. Persia; C.M.G.; Order of S. Stanislaus; Légion d'Honneur; Brig.-Gen.; Member Legislative Assembly.

CADDY, H. O. (D.S.O. L.G. 4.6.17); b. 1882; Bt. Major, Aust. F.A., 24.9.17; Major 16.6.18; served Europ. War; C.M.G., 1919; Croix de Guerre; Despatches.

CADE, A. G. (D.S.O. L.G. 26.9.17) (Details, L.G. 9.1.18); s. of the late E. A. Cade; m. M. A. Ellen, d. of J. D. Young; served in the European War, and was awarded the Military Cross; Lt.-Col., 2nd Bn. Middlesex R. He was killed in action near Mount Kemmel 26.4.18, while commanding the 1st Bn. Wilts. R., aged 26 years.

CADE, D. D. (D.S.O. L.G. 1.1.18), Aust. A. Med. C., att. 19th Light Horse served Europ. War; Despatches.

CADELL, J. G. (D.S.O. L.G. 4.6.17); b. 7.3.79; 2nd Lt. 27.7.98; 2nd Lt., Ind. S.C., 2.11.99; Lt. 27.10.00; Capt. 27.7.07; Major 1.9.15; Brig. Maj., 2 E. Af. Brig., E. Af. Force, 1.2.16; Despatches.

CADMAN, E. C. (D.S.O. L.G. 4.6.17); b. 1876; s. of the late Ed. Cadman, of Clifton Holme, York; educ. at Repton; ent. Terr. 1899; Lt.-Col., 5 Bn. Terr., R. Lancaster R. He was killed in action 27.5.18.

CAHILL, R. J. (D.S.O. L.G. 11.4.18); b. 20.10.81; s. of late Dr. M. Cahill, of Dublin; Lt., R.A.M.C., 30.1.04; Capt. 30.7.07; Major 1.7.15; Lt.-Col. 13.2.16; att. 1st Norfolk Regt.; taken prisoner of war during the Retreat from Mons, 1914; exchanged, and served in Dardanelles and Egypt; Despatches.

CAHUSAC, C. F. (D.S.O. L.G. 17.9.17); b. 6.9.85; m. Alice Marion, d. of Genl. G. H. Bamfield, I.S.C., and widow of Lt.-Col. J. Sherston, D.S.O., R. Bde.; educ. Wellington; ent. S.W. Bord. 24.1.06; 2nd Lt., Ind. Army, 19.9.07; Lt. 24.4.08; Capt. 24.1 15; Major 24.1.21; served Europ. War. 1914–17; Despatches.

CAIRNES, J. E. (D.S.O. L.G. 3.6.18), T/Major, R.F.A.

CAIRNES, T. A. E. (D.S.O. L.G. 1.1.17); b. 7.6.88; 2nd Lt., 7 D.G., 29.8.06; Lt. 25.12.07; Capt. 22.4.11; R.F. Corps 16.11.15 to 31.3.18; Bt. Major 3.6.19; Major 12.5.20; served Europ. War; Despatches.

CALDECOTT, A. H. (D.S.O. L.G. 3.6.19); b. 15.11.13; 2nd Lt., R. Ir. Regt., 4.6.04; Lt. 21.11.06; Capt. 1.6.12; Adjt. 1.6.12; Bt. Major 3.6.17; served Europ. War.

CALDECOTT, E. L. (D.S.O. L.G. 3.6.16); b. 31.8.74; s. of the late H. Caldecott; educ. Barham House, St. Leonards-on-Sea; Rugby and Oriel College; Cricket, Rugby XXII. and Oriel College XI.; Rugby football, House XV. and Oriel XV.; also played for Hampshire; rode winner of jumping championship of Burma; 2nd Lt., R.A., 9.5.00; Lt. 30.4.01; Capt. 9.5.13; Major 30.12.15; Adjt., R.A., 20.1.20; was A.D.C. to Sir Herbert Thirkell White, K.C.I.E., Lt.-Governor of Burma, 1907–10; Private Secretary to Sir H. Adamson, K.C.S.I.; Lt.-Governor of Burma, 1910–12; went out with Exp. Force to France 17.8.14, as Capt., 35th Heavy Battery, R.G.A.; C.O., 19th Heavy By., R.G.A., Oct. 1915; C.O., 4th Hy. Artillery Group, Nov. 1916; was A/Lt.-Col., R.A., 28.9.18 to 22.6.19.

E. L. Caldecott.

CALDER, A. (D.S.O. L.G. 26.7.18), T/2nd Lt., Tank Corps.

CALDER, H. M., M.B. (D.S.O. L.G. 1.1.17) ent. R.A.M.C.; Lt.; Capt. 1.4.15.

CALDWELL, A. F. S. (D.S.O. L.G. 1.1.18), T/Major (A/Lt.-Col.), N. Lanc. R.

CALL, F. (D.S.O. L.G. 1.1.18); b. 29.3.83; ent. Army 8.5.01; R.I. Regt.; Lt. 9.12.03; Capt. 3.8.09; Maj. 8.5.16; A/Lt.-Col.; served in W. Af., 1907–10; Europ. War; Despatches.

CALLAGHAN, M. A. (D.S.O. L.G. 25.8.16); b. 29.12.88, at Rathmore; 3rd s. of John Callaghan (ex-Head Constable, R. Ir. Constabulary) and the late Katie Callaghan (*née* O'Regan), of Dunmore House, Rosscarbery, co. Cork; educ. Christian Brothers' Schools, Cork; held a commission in the Irish National Volunteers, Cork City Regt.; was gazetted 2nd Lt., 11 S. Bn. Lancs. Fus., 25.2.15; Lt., 1916; Capt., 1919; att. to British War Mission in N. America, Montreal, Canada, 1918–19; served Europ. War; Despatches; twice wounded; D.S.O. for services on 16.7.16, east of Ovilliers.

CALLAM, A., M.B. (D.S.O. L.G. 1.1.19), Lt.-Col., R.A.M.C., 16.2.20.

CALLOW, G. (D.S.O. L.G. 8.3.19) (Details, L.G. 4.10.19); b. 13.3.94; ent. Terr. Forces, 1916; 2nd Lt., Notts and Derbys.; Lieut. 25.2.19; Despatches; M.C.

CALVERLEY, G. W. (D.S.O. L.G. 25.8.16); b. 1896; s. of late W. Calverley; Lt., R.I. Rifles (att. R.F.C.); D.S.O. awarded for services 7-16.7.16, La Boisselle; killed in an aeroplane accident 7.1.18.

CALVERT, T. F. P. (D.S.O. L.G. 20.2.19); Comm., R.N., 30.6.16.

CAMERON, A. D. (D.S.O. L.G. 3.6.19), Strathcona's Horse (Can. E.F.); Capt. 19.11.17; Lt.-Col.; Despatches; M.C.

CAMERON, A. G. (D.S.O. L.G. 3.6.16); ent. Army, 5th Regt., R.H. of Canada; Capt. 1.10.13; Despatches.

CAMERON, A. L. (D.S.O. L.G. 3.6.19); b. 2.11.98; ent. R.A. 8.8.14; Lt. 12.2.17; A/Major; M.C.; Despatches.

CAMERON, C. A. (D.S.O. L.G. 1.1.17); b. 11.9.83; 2nd Lt., R.A., 21.12.01; Lt. 21.12.04; Major 6.2.16; served in Europ. War, and with Staff Mission to Russia, 1918–19; Despatches; C.B.E.

CAMERON, D. (D.S.O. L.G. 18.1.18) (Details, L.G. 25.4.18) (Bar, L.G. 8.3.19) (Details, L.G. 4.10.19); Lt.-Col., 12th Aust. Light Horse Regt.; Egypt.

CAMERON, D. C. (D.S.O. L.G. 16.8.17), Aust. (Res. of Off.) Unattached List; Capt. 20.9.09; Major; Despatches.

CAMERON, E. A. (D.S.O. L.G. 1.1.18) (Bar, L.G. 15.2.19) (Details, L.G. 30.7.19); T/Lt.-Col., 10th Bn. N. Lancs. R.; Comdg., 9th Bn. E. Surrey Regt.; C.M.G.

CAMERON, F., M.B. (D.S.O. L.G 1.1.18), Capt., New Zea. Med. Corps, 28.7.14; Despatches.

CAMERON, G. L. (D.S.O. L.G. 3.6.18), Can. 27th Cav. Capt. 5.2.12; Despatches.

CAMERON, G. McL. (D.S.O. L.G. 29.11.18), Lt.-Cdr., R.N.

CAMERON, H. G. L. (D.S.O. L.G. 1.1.19), Major, Australian Mil. Forces; M.C.

CAMERON, J. A. (D.S.O. L.G. 18.1.18) (Details, L.G. 25.4.18), Major, 5th Dns. (Can.), 16.3.12; served Europ. War; Despatches. He was killed in action 17.2.18.

CAMERON, J. B., M.A., LL.B. (D.S.O. L.G. 4.6.17); b. 1882; s. of J. Cameron, Keeper of H.M. Register of Deeds, Edinburgh; m. Helen Rhenius, d. of F. Coles, Antiquarian; one d.; educ. George Watson's College, Edinburgh; Edinburgh Univ.; served Europ. War, 1914–18, in command of City of Edinburgh Heavy Battery, and of various brigades of R.G.A.; Despatches; Lt.-Col., R.G.A., T.A., 1.4.20; commanding 2nd (Lowland) Medium Brigade, R.G.A., T.D.

CAMERON, J. F. C. (D.S.O. L.G. 18.10.17) (Details L.G. 7.3.18); twin s. of A. G. Cameron; 2nd Lt., Arg. and Suth. Hldrs., Oct. 1914; served Europ. War; M.C.; Despatches.

CAMERON, J. J. (D.S.O. L.G. 18.1.18) (Details, L.G. 25.4.18), S. Staff. R.

CAMERON, J. S. (D.S.O. L.G. 14.1.16); b. 22.1.74; s. of J. D. Cameron; m. Gladys Isabel, d. of Rev. W. J. Bradford; 2nd Lt., R. Sussex R., 29.5.95; Lt. 7.10.97; Capt. 21.3.03; Major 12.8.15; Bt. Lt.-Col. 3.6.18; served in S. Africa (Queen's Medal, 3 clasps; King's Medal, 2 clasps); Europ. War; on Staff in France; Despatches.

CAMERON, O. S. (D.S.O. L.G. 4.6.17); b. 23.5.78; 2nd Lt., R.A., 23.12.07; ret. 2.4.12; Major (Res. of Off.), 30.10.14; Bt. Lt.-Col. 1.1.19; Europ. War; Despatches.

CAMPBELL, A. (D.S.O. L.G. 24.6.16) (Details, L.G. 27.7.16); b. 14.3.81; s. of A. G. Campbell; educ. Edinburgh Academy, and R.M.A., Woolwich; ent. R.E. 6.1.00; Lieut. 6.1.03; Capt. 6.1.09; Adj. 19.3.15; Maj. 24.10.16; served S. Af. (Queen's Medal, 5 clasps); N.W. Frontier of India, 1908 (Medal, 1 clasp); Europ. War; C.M.G., 1919; Despatches six times.

CAMPBELL, A. C. (D.S.O. L.G. 26.7.18), Capt., K.O.S.B. He died of wounds 3.4.18 at Doulens.

CAMPBELL, A. E. G. (D.S.O. L.G. 8.3.19) (Details, L.G. 4.10.19), Major, 14th Aust. L.H. Regt. (Egypt); M.C.

CAMPBELL, A. G. (D.S.O. L.G. 2.12.18), Capt., Aust. Inf.

CAMPBELL, A. J. (D.S.O. L.G. 17.10.17); b. 10.5.65; m. M. G. M., d. of late Col. A. S. Grove, D.S.O.; 2nd Lt., E. Lancs., 9.5.85; Ind. Army (S.C.), 11.1.89; Capt. 9.5.96; Major 9.5.03; Lt.-Col. 9.5.11; Col. 1.1.17; T/Brig.-Gen. 5.1.18; served in Burma, 1889–91–92; 1893–94; Europ. War (dangerously wounded nr. Aden); commanded 55th Inf. Bde.; Despatches.

CAMPBELL, A. V. (D.S.O. L.G. 11.4.17); ent. R.N., 1887; Lt., 1894; Cdr., 1905; Capt., 1913; M.V.O., 1910; served Dardanelles, 1915; Despatches.

CAMPBELL, C. R. (D.S.O. L.G. 26.8.18); s. of Capt. A. Campbell, R.I.M.; m. H. R., d. of Col. Grant, Bengal Staff Corps; one son; one d.; educ. Bedford Gram. School; H.M.S. Conway; ent. R.I.M., 1898; Lieut., 1902; Lt.-Comm., 1910; Comm., 1917; trans. to R.E., as Maj., 1916; Lt.-Col., 1917; rejoined R.I.M., 1919; granted rank of Lt.-Col., R.E., 1919; served in Persian Gulf, 1912–13 (N.G.S. Med. and clasp), and Mesopotamia, 1915–19; Despatches five times.

CAMPBELL, D. E. (D.S.O. L.G. 3.6.18), e. s. of Capt. Hon. A. F. H. Campbell, s. of 3rd Earl Cawdor; m. Florence Evelyne, d. of F. Willey; two s.; educ. Wellington College; served Europ. War, with 1/1 North'd Hussars, in France and Belgium, 1914–15; afterwards on Staff in France.

CAMPBELL, E. (D.S.O. L.G. 1.1.19), Major, Aust. F.A.

CAMPBELL, E. FITZ-G. (D.S.O. L.G. 7.11.18); b. 7.10.93; 2nd Lt., K.R.R., 17.9.13; Lt. 28.12.14; Capt. 30.4.16; Adjt. 11.12.16; served Europ. War; Despatches.

CAMPBELL, REV. E. FITZ-H. (D.S.O. L.G. 1.1.18); b. 17.1.80; e. s. of Rev. E. F. Campbell, M.A.; m. 1917, Edith Mary, d. of the late E. Dunk; one d.; educ. Trinity College, Dublin (B.A.); Curate of St. Mary's, Dublin, 1904; C.F., 4th Class, 1906; Chaplain, 3rd Class, 1916, and Deputy Assist. Chaplain-General, 1917; served S. Africa; Europ. War, 1914; Despatches thrice.

The Hon. E. O. Campbell.

CAMPBELL, THE HON. E. O. (D.S.O. L.G. 18.2.15) (Bar, L.G. 3.6.18), Major (T/Lt.-Col.), Seaf. Highrs. (see "The Distinguished Service Order," from its institution to 31 Dec. 1915, same publishers).

CAMPBELL, ERIC (D.S.O. L.G. 1.1.19), Lt., Aust. F.A., 1.7.15; Major.

CAMPBELL, GLEN (D.S.O. L.G. 1.1.18), Lt.-Col., Can. Pioneer Bn. (deceased).

CAMPBELL, G. (D.S.O. L.G. 31.5.16) (1st Bar, L.G. 20.7.17) (2nd Bar, L.G. 2.11.17), Capt., R.N.; V.C. (see "The Victoria Cross," by same publishers).

CAMPBELL, G. A. (D.S.O. L.G. 3.6.18); b. 30.6.87; 2nd Lt., A.S.C. (from Mil.), 20.5.05; Lieut., R.A.S.C., 20.5.07; Capt. 5.8.14; Bt. Maj. 1.1.17; Maj. 21.11.18; Despatches.

CAMPBELL, G. F. (D.S.O. L.G. 3.6.19); b. 5.8.90; 2nd Lt., R.A., 23.7.10; Lt. 23.7.13; Capt., R.G.A., 23.7.16; served Europ. War; Despatches.

CAMPBELL, G. D. (D.S.O. L.G. 8.3.18), Lt.-Cdr., R.N.

CAMPBELL, HECTOR (D.S.O. L.G. 1.1.18); b. 24.10.17; s. of Major-Gen. R. B. P. P. Campbell and Ada, d. of late L. G. A. Campbell; educ. Haileybury College, and R.M.C., Sandhurst; 2nd Lt. (unatt.) 20.1.97; 2nd Lt., Ind. S.C., 31.3.98; Lt., Ind. Army, 9.10.99; Capt. 20.1.06; Major, 1915; Lt.-Col. 1.2.21; served in Tirah Expedition (att. 1st. Gordon Hldrs.), 1897–98; in the actions of Chagru Kotal and Dargai, and capture of Sampagha and Arhanga Passes; operations in the Waran Valley and Bara Valley (Medal and 2 clasps); China Expeditionary Force, 1900 (Medal); M.V.O., 1906; was in winning team, Indian Championship Polo Tournament, 1909–10; Europ. War.

CAMPBELL, HUGH (D.S.O. L.G. 18.6.17), Lt.-Col., London Regt., 13.8.15 served Europ. War; O.B.E.; Despatches.

CAMPBELL, H. G. (D.S.O. L.G. 23.7.18), Lt., R.N.; served Europ. War, commanding Daffodil at Zeebrugge; wounded; Despatches.

CAMPBELL, H. La T. (D.S.O. L.G. 14.1.16), Major, R.E., T.F.

CAMPBELL, THE HON. I. M., M.A. (D.S.O. L.G. 1.1.18); b. 17.11.83; 5th s. of 3rd Earl of Cawdor and the Dowager Countess of Cawdor; educ. Eton, and Trinity College, Cambridge; 2nd Lt., 2nd Lovat's Scouts (Yeom.), May, 1906; Capt., Feb. 1914; Major 24.2.16; was mobilized with Lovat's Scouts at outbreak of war; served abroad from Sept. 1915; in Gallipoli and Egypt; attached 8th E. Lanc. R. in France from Aug. 1916; in command from April, 1917, to Feb. 1918, when the battalion was disbanded; May, 1918, to April, 1919, in command of 2nd Bn. A. and S. Highrs; Despatches; Fellow and Director of Agricultural Studies, Trinity Hall, Cambridge, since 1919.

CAMPBELL, J. A. (D.S.O. L.G. 1.1.17) (Bar, L.G. 1.2.19); b. 3.12.86; s. of late J. Campbell; ent. Suff. Regt. 29.8.06; Lt. 2.8.09; Capt. 11.11.14; Adj. 24.10.15; Brev. Maj. 1.1.18; served Europ. War (wounded); Despatches thrice.

CAMPBELL, SIR J. B. S. (D.S.O. L.G. 26.7.17) (1st Bar, L.G. 15.2.19) (Details, L.G. 30.7.19); b. 3.1.77; s. of 9th Bart.; m. 1902, Jessie, d. of J. Hiller; one son; T/Major, R. Scots; served S. Afr. War (Medals, clasps); Europ. War (wounded); Despatches.

CAMPBELL, J. C. (D.S.O. L.G. 11.1.19), Capt., Aust. A.M.C., 1.12 14; Major; Despatches.

CAMPBELL, J. D. (D.S.O. L.G. 3.6.18); b. 3.5.84; s. of late A. D. Campbell, Surgeon, and Isabella Leslie Campbell (*née* Tweedie); 2nd Lt., R.E., 21.12.01; Lt. 1.4.04; Capt. 21.12.12; Major 21.12.16; served in Europ. War, 1914–18; Despatches.

CAMPBELL, J. H., M.B., B.Ch. (D.S.O. L.G. 14.1.16); b. 8.6.79; s. of late Wm. Campbell; m. 1916, Mary, d. of Alfred Williams; educ. Belfast University; Lt., R.A.M.C., 30.7.04; Capt. 30.1.08; Maj. 1.7.15; retired R.A.M.C., 1920; served Europ. War, 1914–18.

CAMPBELL, J. O. (D.S.O. L.G. 1.1.19); b. 18.7.91; ent. R.A., 20.7.11 Lieut. 20.7.14; Capt. 8.8.16; Despatches; M.C.

CAMPBELL, K. A. (D.S.O. L.G. 2.4.19) (Details, L.G. 10.12.19), Lt., 3rd Batt. Grenadier Gds. (Spec. Res.).

CAMPBELL, K. G. (D.S.O. L.G. 3.6.16); b. 29.10.76; s. of Col. W. M. Campbell, late R.A.; m. Marjorie, d. of E. R. Syfret; one son; educ. Dulwich College; R.M.A., Woolwich; 1st com., 1896; served op. ag. Ogaden Somalis, Jubaland, 1901 (Medal with clasp); Europ. War, Defence of Suez Canal, Feb. 1915; Gallipoli; Mesopotamia; Despatches; Commandant, 26th Jacob's Mountain Battery.

CAMPBELL, L. G. B. A. (D.S.O. L.G. 14.3.16); m. 1906, Norah, d. of Rev. Robert Hereford; entered Navy, 1897; Commdr., 1915; served Europ. War, 1915–16; Despatches.

CAMPBELL, N. ST. C. (D.S.O. L.G. 3.6.16); 2nd Lt., R.A., 23.3.97; Lt. 28.3.00; Capt. 3.2.04; Maj. 16.9.14; Bt. Lt.-Col. 3.6.17; Europ. War; C.M.G.; Despatches.

CAMPBELL, ROBERT (D.S.O. L.G. 1.1.17) (Bar, L.G. 26.7.17); b. 23.1.78; 2nd Lt., Cameron Highldrs., 8.3.99; Lt. 5.3.00; Adjt. 21.11.04; Capt. 23.10.05; Major 1.9.15; served Europ. War, 1914–17; Despatches.

CAMPBELL, RONALD (D.S.O. L.G. 8.3.19) (Details, L.G. 4.10.19), T/Major, Tank Corps; M.C.

CAMPBELL, R. B. (D.S.O. L.G. 1.1.17); b. 14.9.78; 2nd Lt., D.C.L.I., 19.5.00; Lt. 12.8.02; Lt., Gordon Hldrs., 20.5.08; Capt. 22.2.09; Major 1.9.15; Bt. Lt.-Col. 3.6.17; served in S. Africa, 1900–01 (Queen's Medal, 5 clasps); Europ. War; Despatches.

CAMPBELL, R. D. (D.S.O. L.G. 3.6.16); ent. Aust. A.M.C.; Capt. 31.7.13; T/Major; served Europ. War; Despatches.

CAMPBELL, R. N. B. (D.S.O. L.G. 10.8.21), Major, 1/23rd Pnrs., I.A.; O.B.E.

CAMPBELL, R. O. (D.S.O. L.G. 4.6.17), T/Lt.-Col., R.W. Fus.

CAMPBELL, R. W. (D.S.O. L.G. 14.1.16); b. 24.10.65; s. of J. S. Campbell; m. Amy L. Young; educ. Edinburgh Academy, and Dulwich College; 2nd Lt., R. Scots; retired 1906, with rank of Lt.-Col. (in 3rd Cameronians S.R. of Officers, retiring 1910); rejoined R. Scots, 1914; served S. Africa, 1899–1902 (Queen's Medal, 3 clasps; King's Medal, 2 clasps); Europ. War, 1914–18; Despatches; 1914–15 Star and a French Decoration.

CAMPBELL, V. L. A. (D.S.O. L.G. 3.6.15) (Bar, L.G. 22.6.17), Cdr., R.N.; O.B.E. (see "The Distinguished Service Order," from its institution to 31.12.15, by same publishers).

The Distinguished Service Order 219

CAMPBELL, W. (D.S.O. L.G. 23.11.16); b. 19.1.79; s. of Capt. A. Campbell, C.I.E., D.S.O., R.I.M.; m. Dorothy Este Lyne; one s.; one d.; educ. Bedford Grammar School, and King's College, London; joined Cape Mounted Rifles, 1897; 2nd Lt., High. L. Inf., 4.9.01; 2nd Lt., Ind. Army, 29.10.02; Lt. 14.12.03; Capt. 24.3.10; Major, Ind. Army (Supply and Transport Corps), 24.3.16; served S. Africa, 1899–1901 (severely wounded; Queen's Medal and 4 clasps); Tibet, 1903–4 (Medal); Indian Exp. Force "A" in France (Despatches); Indian Exp. Force "D," Mespotamia; Despatches.

CAMPBELL, W. C. (D.S.O. L.G. 17.9.17), 2nd Lt. (T/Capt.), R.F.C. (Spec. Res.); M.C.

CAMPBELL, W. K., M.B. (D.S.O. L.G. 22.9.16); b. 12.11.89; entered (Spec. Res.) R.A.M.C., 1915; Lieut. 1.1.17; Capt. 6.8.18; A/Major 4.1.18; served Europ. War; M.C.; Despatches. His D.S.O. was awarded for services on 14.7.16 at Longueval.

CAMPBELL, W. M. (D.S.O. L.G. 3.6.19); b. 30.5.79; ent. ranks, 1899; 2nd Lt., Suff. Regt., 30.4.02; Lt. 15.3.05; Capt. 24.2.14; Major 11.5.16; Adjt. 11.6.20; served Europ. War; Despatches; M.C.

CAMPBELL, W. N. (D.S.O. L.G. 22.12.16); s. of late James Campbell; m. Beatrice, e. d. of Col. Foord; educ. Edinburgh Academy, and R.M.C., Sandhurst; 2nd Lt. (Munster Fus.), 1884; Ind. Army, 1885; Major 6.2.02; retired 13.2.07; rejoined Beds. Regt., 1914; transferred to 3rd Echelon, Rouen; Lt.-Col., May–Sept. 1917; Brig.-Gen.; served Burmese Expedition, 1886–87 (Despatches, L.G. 8.9.87; Medal with clasp); Europ. War, in France and Mesopotamia; C.M.G., 1917; C.S.I., 1918; Despatches.

CAMPION, D. J. M. (D.S.O. L.G. 3.2.20); b. 14.12.83; 2nd Lt., R.A., 24.12.02; Lt. 24.12.05; Major, R.G.A., 2.9.17; served Europ. War.

CAMPION, W. R. (D.S.O. L.G. 1.1.18); b. 3.7.70; e. s. of Col. W. H. Campion; m. 1894, Katharine Mary, 3rd d. of Rev. Hon. William Bryon; educ. Eton, and New College, Oxford; M.P. (C.), Mid-Sussex Division, since 1910; Lt.-Col., R. Suss. Regt., 26.3.17; served Europ. War; Despatches.

CANE, A. S., M.D. (D.S.O. L.G. 23.10.19); b. 3.6.85; Lt., R.A.M.C., 31.7.09; Capt. 31.1.13; Major, R.A.M.C., 31.7.21; served Europ. War; O.B.E.; Despatches.

CANE, E. G. S., M.B. (D.S.O. L.G. 23.10.19); b. 2.5.86; Lt., R.A.M.C., 27.1.11; Capt. 27.7.14; served Europ. War; Despatches.

CANGLEY, F. G. (D.S.O. L.G. 14.11.16), T/2nd Lt., Liverpool Regt. His D.S.O. was awarded for services on 16.9.16, at Les Bœufs.

CANNAN, H. J. (D.S.O. L.G. 22.9.16), T/Capt., R.F.A. His D.S.O. was awarded for services on 15th July and 6th Aug. 1916, at High Wood and Delville Wood. He died of wounds on 2.11.16.

CANNAN, J. H. (D.S.O. L.G. 3.6.19); b. 29.8.82; s. of John Kenney and Bessie Constance Cannan; m. Eileen Clare Ranken; educ. Brisbane State School, and Grammar School; Lt., 1st Queenslanders (Infantry), 1903; merged into 9th Inf. Commonwealth; Adjt. of that battalion for five years; Capt., 1907; Major, 1910; transferred as 2nd-in-command of 8th Inf. Bn.; Lt.-Col. and commanded this battalion, 1914; served Europ. War, 1914–15 (Dardanelles); Despatches; C.B.; Col. and T/Brig.-Gen. 30.8.16; commanded 11th Inf. Bde.; C.M.G.; Despatches seven times.

CANNOT, F. G. E. (D.S.O. L.G. 1.1.18); b. 1.2.73; m. Mildred G., d. of late W. Barker, J.P.; educ. Jesuits' College, Canterbury; King's College; ent. S. Staffs. R., '92; A.S.C., '95; Capt., '00; Maj., '07; Lt.-Col., '14; Brig.-Genl.; served S. Af., '99–00 (Queen's Med., 3 clasps); Europ. War, '14–18; C.B.; C.M.G.; an Hon. Associate of St. John of Jerusalem; Off. Order of Leopold, Belgium; Off. St. Maurice and St. Lazarus, Italy; Belgian Croix de Guerre; Order of Military Merit (Spain); Off. de Instruction Publique (France).

CANTLIE, G. S. (D.S.O. L.G. 1.1.17), Lt.-Col., Can. Inf., 15.8.06; served Europ. War; Despatches.

CANTRELL-HUBBERSTY, G. A. J. (D.S.O. L.G. 26.3.18) (Details, L.G. 24.8.18), Major (S. Notts Hussars), Yeom., 1.6.16; Despatches.

CAPE, E. G. M. (D.S.O. L.G. 4.6.17), Can. Art.

CAPE, H. A. (D.S.O. L.G. 26.7.18); b. 18.7.72; s. of late G. A. Cape; m. Edith, d. of late W. Sopper, J.P.; 2 d.; educ. Charterhouse; 2nd Lt., 18 Hrs., 12.12.94; Lt. 28.10.99; Adjt. 20.9.02 to 19.3.06; Capt. 28.9.04; Major, 5th Lancers, 6.11.07; Lt.-Col. 30.7.19; served S. African War, 1899–00 (wounded; Queen's Medal, with clasp); Europ. War; Despatches twice.

CAPPER, A. S. (D.S.O. L.G. 25.8.17); b. 2.3.71; 2nd Lt., R.A., 24.7.91; Lt., Ind. S.C., 12.8.93; Capt., Ind. A., 10.7.01; Major 24.7.09; Lt.-Col. 15.2.17; served Tirah, 1897–8 (Medal with clasp); Europ. War, Mesopotamia; Despatches.

CARBERY, M. (D.S.O. L.G. 3.6.18), T/Capt., R.F.A.; served Europ. War; M.C.

CARDEN, A. D. (D.S.O. L.G. 1.1.18); b. 15.7.74; ent. R.E. 12.12.94; Lt. 12.12.97; Capt. 1.4.04; R.F.C. 13.5.12; Maj., R.E., 30.10.14; Lt.-Col. 1.7.21; served Europ. War; Despatches.

CARDEN, D'A. V. (D.S.O. L.G. 1.1.18), T/Lt. (A/Major), R.F.A.

CARDEW, G. A. (D.S.O. L.G. 1.1.17) (Bar, L.G. 1.2.19); b. 22.6.65; s. of Hon. E. J. Cardew; m. 1895, L. Sirley; one s.; one d.; educ. Wellington College; R.M.A., Woolwich; King's Messenger (Temp.); Lt., R.A., 29.4.85; Capt. 1.4.95; Major 10.7.00; Lt.-Col. 18.5.12; served Eurp. War, 1914–18; C.M.G., 1918.

CAREW, R. R. HALLOWELL- (see Hallowell-Carew, R. R.).

CAREY, ALFRED BLAKE (D.S.O. L.G. 16.8.17) (Bar, L.G. 7.11.18), Lieut. 31.7.15, 50th Can. Inf.; Lt.-Col.

CAREY, ARTHUR BASIL (D.S.O. L.G. 4.6.17); b. 3.3.72; 2nd Lt., R.E., 24.7.91; Lt. 24.7.94; Capt. 24.7.02; Major 24.7.11; T/Lt.-Col., R. Mar. 21.8.14; Bt. Lt.-Col. 3.6.16; Lt.-Col. 24.9.18; Bt. Col. 7.2.21; T/Brig.-Gen. 23.10.18 (Despatches); served Europ. War., R.N. Div., Dardanelles; Despatches; C.M.G.; Director of Military and Public Works, 1920.

CAREY, THE REV. D. F., M.A. (D.S.O. L.G. 1.1.18); b. 10.1.76; C.F., 4th Class, 12.2.02; 3rd Class 22.2.13; 2nd Class 22.2.18; 1st Class 3.6.19. A newspaper says: "Genl. Sir Ian Hamilton inspected a parade of local ex-service men at Eltham, where the fifth anniversary of the landing of the 29th Division in Gallipoli was observed by a solemn requiem at Holy Trinity Church. The Rev. D. F. Carey, D.S.O., preached."

CAREY, H. E. (D.S.O. L.G. 1.1.17); s. of late Major-Genl. W. D. Carey; m. Elsie, d. of F. Hughes; one s.; two d.; educ. United Services College, Westward Ho!; Lt., R.A., 6.4.96; Capt. 16.6.00; Adjt., R.A., 24.6.02; Major 1.4.10; Lt.-Col. 24.11.15; T/Brig.-Genl. 3.7.18; Col. 3.6.19; half-pay 14.11.20; served S. African War; Queen's Medal with 4 clasps; King's Medal with 2 clasps; served Europ. War in 3rd Div., France, from 17.8.14; Salonika; C.M.G.

CAREY, J. L. R. (D.S.O. L.G. 24.9.18); b. 3.5.82; ent. R.A. 23.7.01; Lt. 15.4.04; Capt. 23.7.14; Major 24.9.16; Adjt., Channel I. Militia, 24.9.16.

J. L. R. Carey.

CAREY, W. L. de M. (D.S.O. L.G. 1.1.17); b. 4.7.81; s. of Rev. D. Carey, late Capt., Madras L.I. (s. of Sir Octavius Carey, of Guernsey), and Jane Charlotte Leathes, of Herringfleet Hall, nr. Lowestoft. He m. Constance, d. of J. Meagher; two s.; educ. Cheltenham College; R.M.A., Woolwich; ent. R.E. 22.11.99; Lt. 24.7.02; Capt. 22.11.08; T/Major 6.2.16; Major 25.7.16; Europ. War in France, 1914–18; Bt. Lt.-Col. 1.1.19; Legion of Honour.

CARLETON, H. A. (D.S.O. L.G. 25.8.17); b. 12.9.68; 2nd Lt., W. Rid. R., 24.4.98; Hants R. 16.10.89; Lt. 3.5.91; I.S.C. 22.7.91; Capt., I.A., 24.4.00; Major 24.4.07; Bt. Lt.-Col. 24.4.15; Despatches.

CARLISLE, J. C. D. (D.S.O. L.G. 1.1.18), Capt., London R.; M.C.

CARLISLE, THOMAS HAMILTON (D.S.O. L.G. 1.1.18), T/Capt. (A/Major), R.E.

CARLISLE, THOMAS HARTLEY (D.S.O. L.G. 22.6.18); b. 26.9.82; 2nd Lt., R.A., 21.12.01; Lt. 21.12.04; Capt. 30.10.14; Adjt. 24.3.15; Major 22.1.16 Despatches; M.C.

CARLISLE, T. R. M. (D.S.O. L.G. 19.10.16); b. 10.10.83; educ. Wellington Col., and R.M.A., Woolwich; ent. R.A. 21.12.01; Lieut. 21.12.04; Adj. 18.6.08; Capt. 30.10.14; Maj. 17.1.16; with Gen. Townshend in Mesopotamia; prisoner of war to Turks from Kut-el-Amarah; Despatches.

CARLTON, H. D. (D.S.O. L.G. 2.4.19) (Details, L.G. 10.12.19) (Bar, L.G. 1.1.19); b. 10.6.78; 1st com. 27.10.00; Lt., R. Scots, 14.3.03; Adjt. 9.10.06; Capt. 18.10.09; Major 27.10.15; Bt. Lt.-Col. 3.6.19; Medit. Force (Staff).

CARLYON, T. (D.S.O. L.G. 14.1.16); b. 4.8.77; s. of A. K. Carlyon; m. 1918, Aileen, d. of late Sir E. H. Hudson-Kinahan, 1st Bart.; one d.; educ. Harrow and Oxford; ent. R.A. 22.8.00; Lt. 22.8.03; Capt. 20.2.12; Major 13.2.15; serv. in Salonika; Brig. Maj., 10th Div.; Despatches; Bt. Lt.-Col. 1.1.18.

CARMICHAEL, D. (D.S.O. L.G. 11.1.19) (Bar, L.G. 8.3.19) (Details, L.G. 4.10.19), Major Can. Inf.; M.C.

CARMICHAEL, THE REV. I., M.A. (D.S.O. L.G. 26.9.16); educ. Appin, Argyllshire; George Watson's School, and Glasgow University; T/2nd Lt., March, 1915; H.L.I.; D.S.O. awarded for 22–23.8.1916, Calonne; M.C.; wounded; licensed as a probationer of the Church of Scotland, May, 1914; ordained whilst serving in the A. and S. Highrs., Nov. 1914.

CARMICHAEL, J. (D.S.O. L.G. 1.1.16); Eng. Cdr., R N.R.

CARNEGY, G. P. O. (D.S.O. L.G. 22.12.16); b. 25.11.73; ent. S. Staff. R. 7.12.95; Ind. S.C. 24.10.97; Lt. 7.3.98; Capt. 7.12.04; Maj. 7.12.12; Lt.-Col. 15.3.18; Despatches.

CARNEGY, U. E. C. (D.S.O. L.G. 3.6.19); b. 13.6.86; 2nd Lt., 3 Dr. Gds., 2.2.07; Lt. 6.9.09; Capt. 8.11.14; Major 1.1.21; Despatches; M.C.

CARNWATH, T., B.A., M.B., D.P.H. (D.S.O. L.G. 1.1.18); b. 1878; s. of late J. Carnwath; m. Margaret Ethel, d. of A. M'Kee; two s.; educ. Foyle College, Derry; Queen's College, Belfast; University of Berlin; Medical Officer, Ministry of Health; Capt., R.A.M.C. (T.F.), att. H.A.C.; served Europ. War, 1914–18; Despatches; 1914 Star.

CARPENTER, C. M. (D.S.O. L.G. 3.6.16); b. 18.8.70; ent. R.E. 25.7.90; Lt. 25.7.93; Capt. 17.4.01; Maj. 25.7.10; Lt.-Col. 1.9.18; T/Brig.-Gen. 8.4.18; Chf. Eng., 4th Army Corps, Brit. Arm. in France, 8.4.18 to 2.2.19; served in China, 1900 (Medal with clasp); Bt. Lt.-Col. 3.6.17; C.M.G.; Despatches.

CARPENTER, G. G. (D.S.O. L.G. 3.6.19), b. 20.12.91; 2nd Lt., Suffolk R., 20.9.11; Lt. 2.3.14; Capt. 12.9.15; Despatches.

CARPENTER, P. (D.S.O. L.G. 16.9.18), T/Capt., R.A.F.; M.C. and Bar.

CARR, A. E. (D.S.O. L.G. 1.1.19), T/Major, Tank Corps; M.C.

CARR, B. A. (D.S.O. L.G. 1.1.19), Capt. (A/Major), R.G.A., T.F.

CARR, C. C. (D.S.O. L.G. 1.1.17); b. 2.6.65; ent. R. Fus. 30.1.86; Lt.-Col. 23.10.17 (Res. of Off.); Despatches; O.B.E.

CARR, G. (D.S.O. L.G. 11.1.19), T/Capt., M.G.C. (Motor) (Mesopotamia); M.C.

CARR, G. A. B. (D.S.O. L.G. 1.1.17), Lt.-Col., T.F. Res. (Lond. T.F.A.) (Hon.).

CARR, H. A. (D.S.O. L.G. 2.5.16); b. 2.9.72; e. s. of late Col. E. Carr, 36th Regt.; m. in 1913, Elsie P., d. of Sir Thomas Putman; one s.; one d.; educ. Haileybury and Sandhurst; ent. Worc. R. 21.10.93; Lt. 14.12.96; Capt. 17.2.00; Adjt., Worc. R., 6.3.03–5.9.06; Major 11.6.10; Lt.-Col. 2.3.19; served S. Af. 1899–1902; Asst. Prov.-Marshal, graded S. Capt., 1.9.00–26.6.02; (Queen's Med., 3 clasps; King's Med., 2 clasps); Europ. War, Dardanelles; wounded; Comdt. (Off. Suptg. Instn. at Offrs'. Conval. Hosptl. 1.1.19–30.3.19); Despatches twice; Brev. Lt.-Col. 1.1.18; Lt.-Col. 2.3.19; retired 23.11.21.

CARR, H. G. (D.S.O. L.G. 1.1.17); b. 12.2.77; s. of late Dep. Surg.-Genl. J. K. Carr, M.D.; m. 1918, Madeleine, d. of Col. Dening; R.A. 21.9.96; Lt. 21.9.99; Capt. 24.12.01; Adjt. 25.5.14–29.10.14; Major 30.10.14; Lt.-Col. 1.5.21; empld. with Burma Mil. Police 15.8.02–24.5.09; served N.W. Frontier of India 1901–02 (Med., 6 clasps); Despatches.

CARR, J. W. (D.S.O. L.G. 22.8.18), Major, S. African Rly. Rgt.

CARR, L. (D.S.O. L.G. 1.1.17); b. 14.4.86; ent. Gord. Hrs. 9.8.04; Lieut. 13.2.09; Capt. 11.12.14; Adj., G. Highrs., 24.7.15; Brev. Maj. 3.6.16; served Europ. War, France (Staff); Despatches; O.B.E.

CARR, R. B. (D.S.O. L.G. 1.1.19); b. 1887; s. of Edward Carr; Major, Aust. Engrs.; served Europ. War from 1915; Despatches.

CARR-HARRIS, F. F., M.D. (D.S.O. L.G. 4.2.18) (Details, L.G. 5.7.18) T/Capt., R.A.M.C.

CARRINGTON, C. R. B. (D.S.O. L.G. 3.6.16); b. 7.4.80; s. of C. Carrington; m. Violet M., d. of H. Herbert Smith; educ. Eton; ent. R.A., 5.5.01; Lt. 3.6.01; Capt. 1.4.10; Maj. 30.10.14; Brev. Lt.-Col. 3.6.18. He went to France with the original B.E.F.; was all through the Retreat from Mons; was in the Battle of the Aisne, the Marne, Loos, the Somme, etc.; Despatches five times. He has won many Point-to-Points, including the New Forest Light Weight, 1906; Duke of Beaufort's, 1907, and many steeplechases besides.

CARRINGTON, C. W. (D.S.O. L.G. 18.2.18) (Details, L.G. 18.7.18), 2nd Lt., G. Gds.

CARRINGTON, J. W. (D.S.O. L.G. 15.9.16); b. 5.1.79; s. of Sir John Carrington, C.M.G., Chief Justice of Hong-Kong; m. 1918, Mary E., d. of Rear-Ad. C. J. Eyres, D.S.O.; one d.; educ. King's School, Canterbury; H.M.S.

Britannia; Midshipman, Nov. 1894; Sub.-Lt., May, 1898; Lt., Oct. 1900; Lt.-Comdr., Oct., 1908; Comdr., Oct. 1912; Capt. 31.12.17; was present at the action off Falkland Is. and Dardanelles, 1915, in H.M.S. Inflexible, and Battle of Jutland in H.M.S. King George V.

CARRINGTON, R. H. (D.S.O. L.G. 14.1.16); b. 7.11.82; educ. Winchester Col.; ent. R.A. 16.11.01; Lieut. 16.11.04; Capt. 16.9.14; Maj. 16.11.15; served in S. Afr. 1901–02 (Queen's Med., 5 clasps); was Bgde. Maj., R.A., 57th Div., Home F., Br. Armies in France, 13.3.16–30.10.18; G.S.O.2, 7th Army Corps, B.A., in France, 31.10.18–18.1.19; G.S.O.2, 8th Army Corps, in France, 19.1.19; Despatches; Bt. Lt.-Col. 3.6.18.

CARROLL, F. F., M.B., B.Ch., B.A.O. (D.S.O. L.G. 1.1.17); b. 27.11.74; s. of F. M. Carroll, J.P.; m. Evelyn, d. of Col. E. E. Bernard; educ. Dublin Univ.; Bonn; Vienna; Lt., R.A.M.C., 28.1.98; Capt. 28.1.01; Major 28.10.09; Lt.-Col. 1.3.15; Col. 23.3.22, late R.A.M.C.; served Aden, 1903–4; Sudan, 1914–17 (Despatches); Officer in Charge, Netley Hospital.

CARROLL, J. W. V. (D.S.O. L.G. 15.7.19); b. 12.7.69; s. of the late F. W. Carroll; m. Barbara, d. of late J. T. Woodroffe, C.S.I.; two s.; one d.; educ. Woburn; Oratory School; ent. Norfolk R. 10.10.91; Lt. 13.6.94; Capt. 14.5.00; Bt. Major 19.9.00; Major 2.9.11; Lt.-Col. 1.9.16; T/Brig.-Gen. 25.9.15; retired Norf. Rgt. 20.9.19, with hon. rank of Brig.-Genl.; served W. Africa, N. Nigeria, 1895–99; 2 Medals, 6 clasps; S. African War; Queen's Medal with 3 clasps; Bt. Major; Europ. War, in France; commanded Batt. Norf. R. 19.8.14; T/Brig.-Gen., commanding 17th Inf. Brig.; in Russia, 1919; C.M.G. His D.S.O. was awarded for services when in command of the Russian Force at Morjegorskaia, March, 1919.

CARSCALLEN, H. G. (D.S.O. L.G. 1.1.17); b. 4.4.73; s. of late Henry Carscallen, K.C.; m. 1907, Marion Myles; one s.; one d.; Maj. 15.9.09; Colonel, Can. Arty; served Europ. War, 1914–18; Despatches thrice.

CARSON, E. H. (D.S.O. L.G. 3.2.20), T/Major, Tank Corps; M.C.

CARSON, H. W., M.B. (D.S.O. L.G. 3.6.18), Capt. (A/Major), R.A.M.C. He died 12.10.18.

CARTER, A. D. (D.S.O. L.G. 18.2.18) (Details, L.G. 18.7.18) (Bar, L.G. 16.9.18), Lieut. 18.4.12, 74th Can. Inf. (the Brunswick Rangers), later Can. R. Air Force. He was killed whilst flying near Lancing College.

CARTER, A. L. BONHAM- (see Bonham-Carter, A. L.).

CARTER, C. BONHAM- (see Bonham-Carter, C.).

CARTER, C. R. (D.S.O. L.G. 1.1.19); b. 22.1.88; ent. R. Lancs. Regt. 4.5.07 Lt. 30.12.09; Capt. 2.3.15; Despatches.

CARTER, E. G. W. (D.S.O. L.G. 3.6.19); b. 30.10.82; ent. Army 18.8.00; Lieut. 5.7.02; Capt. 18.8.13; Major, R.G.A., 30.12.15.

CARTER, H. G. (D.S.O. L.G. 1.1.18), Lt.-Col., Aust. Pnr. Bn.

CARTER, L. A. L. (D.S.O. L.G. 1.1.17); b. 20.10.86; ent. R.A.S.C. 29.10.06; Lieut. 2.8.09; Capt. 5.8.14; Despatches.

CARTER, L. J. (D.S.O. L.G. 22.12.16); b. 2.8.72; ent. Oxf. and Bucks L. Inf. 4.1.93; Lieut. 1.3.96; Capt. 27.2.00; Major 23.1.13; ret. Oxf. and Bucks L.I. 4.1.20; Despatches.

CARTER, R. S. (D.S.O. L.G. 3.6.19); Lt., 103rd Can. Inf. (Calgary), 1.12.15; Major, Can. Rly. Troops; Despatches.

CARTER, S. (D.S.O. L.G. 22.8.18), Lt.-Col., 4th Mtd. Rif. (Imp. L.H.), S. African Forces.

CARTER, S. S. BONHAM- (see Bonham-Carter, S. S.).

CARTER, T. H. H. (D.S.O. L.G. 22.9.16), Capt. (T), R. War. R. D.S.O. awarded for services at Mauquissart.

CARTER, W. (D.S.O. L.G. 15.2.19) (Details, L.G. 30.7.19); b. 3.11.78; 2nd Lt., R. Lancs. R., 7.11.14; Lt. 11.5.15; Capt., Wilts, 25.10.18; Despatches; M.C.

CARTER, W. H. (D.S.O. L.G. 20.10.16) (Bar, L.G. 2.4.19) (Details, L.G. 10.12.19); b. 20.3.80; s. of W. J. Carter; 2nd Lt., S. Staff. R., 4.1.15; Lt. 18.6.15; Capt., R. War. R., 11.12.16; Lt.-Col. Commdg. S. Staff. R. 14.11.17; served Europ. War., Brev. Major, 3.6.18; D.S.O. awarded for gallantry at Guillemont on 6.8.16; M.C. and Bar; Despatches.

CARTWRIGHT, C. (D.S.O. L.G. 15.2.19) (Details, L.G. 30.7.19); T/Major (A/Lt.-Col.), York and Lanc. R.; M.C.

CARTWRIGHT, F. J. W. (D.S.O. L.G. 13.2.17); b. 9.9.75; s. of late T. B. Cartwright; ent. Royal Marines 1.2.94; Lt. 1.1.95; Capt. 20.9.00; Major 11.9.12; T/Lt.-Col. His D.S.O. was awarded for services on 13–15.11.16, near the Ancre. He died of wounds 30.4.17.

CARTWRIGHT, J. R. (D.S.O. L.G. 4.6.17); b. 6.1.82; 2nd Lt., Devons. R., 26.8.03; Lt. 22.1.07; Capt. 14.2.15; Bt. Major 1.1.16; Major 24.1.18; served Europ. War, Salonika, Egypt; Despatches.

CARTWRIGHT, V. H. (D.S.O. L.G. 1.1.18); s. of W. T. Cartwright; T/Major, R.M.A., 5.6.17.

CARUS-WILSON, T. (D.S.O. L.G. 1.1.18),; b. 1869; s. of late E. S. Carus-Wilson and g.s. of the Rev. W. Carus-Wilson, founder of the Casterton Clergy-Daughters' School; m. 1905, Dorothy Selina, d. of the late Capt. E. Carter; served S. African War (Queen's Medal with 5 clasps). He went to India on the outbreak of the Europ. War with the 1/4th D.C.L.I.; served in France from May, 1916, and commanded a battalion of the same regiment from Dec. 1916; was three times mentioned in Despatches. He died on 27.3.18, of wounds received in action. He held the Territorial Decoration.

CARVER, E. C. (D.S.O. L.G. 4.6.17); b. 20.9.73; s. of H. C. Carver; m., 1915, Alison, d. of Col. E. W. Creswell, R.E.; two s.; ent. R.N., 1886; Lieut., 1894; Cdr., 1904; ret. Capt. 30.6.12; R.F.C., 1918; served Europ. War, R.N. and R.F.C.; Despatches.

CARWITHEN, S. (D.S.O. L.G. 3.6.19); b. 13.3.75; ent. Army (from local S. Af. forces) 23.5.00; Lt. 1.10.01; Capt. 23.5.13; Major 30.12.15; Brig. Major, 28th Div. Salonika, and 6th Div. France; Despatches.

CARY, THE HON. B. P. (D.S.O. L.G. 2.11.17); Lt.-Cdr., R.N. (since killed).

CARY-BARNARD, C. D. V. (D.S.O. L.G. 1.1.15 (Bar, L.G. 25.8.17); Major (T/Lt.-Col.), Wilts. R. (see "The Distinguished Service Order," from its institution to 31.12.15, by same publishers).

CASE, H. A. (D.S.O. L.G. 25.8.17); b. 23.4.79; 2nd Lt., Dorset R., 17.2.00; Lt. 13.6.01; Capt. 1.4.09; Major 1.9.15; Brev. Lt.-Col. 3.6.16; empld. with King's African Rif. 8.6.06–7.6.11; Adjt., Ind. Vols., 28.4.14; Despatches.

CASEMENT, F., M.B. (D.S.O. L.G. 4.6.17) (Bar, 26.7.18); b. 29.10.81; Lt., R.A.M.C., 28.1.07; Capt. 28.7.10; Major 28.1.19; Despatches

CASEMENT, J. (D.S.O. L.G. 27.5.19); Capt., R.N., 31.12.18; Despatches.

CASEY, R. G. (D.S.O. L.G. 1.1.18); Major, Aust. Inf.; M.C.

CASH, REV. W. W. (D.S.O. L.G. 3.6.18); C.F. 4th Class.

CASS, E. E. E. (D.S.O. L.G. 8.3.19 (Details, L.G. 4.10.19); b. 3.3.98; ent. Yorks. L. Inf. 27.10.16; Lt. 27.4.18 (A/Capt.); M.C.; Despatches.

CASSELS, F. (D.S.O. L.G. 1.1.18); T/Major, R. Sussex R. He died of wounds 27.3.18.

CASSELS, G. R. (D.S.O. L.G. 1.1.19); b. 4.4.70; 2nd Lt., Worc. R., 24.4.89; Lt. 18.2.91; I.A. 20.2.92; Capt. 4.4.00; Major 24.4.07; Lt.-Col. (123rd Outram's Rifles, I.A.), 24.4.15; Col. 27.7.19; T/Col. Comdt.; served Europ. War, Ind. Exp. Force "D"; Despatches.

CASSELS, R. A. (D.S.O. L.G. 7.2.18); b. 15.3.76; ent. Army 22.1.96; Ind. S.C. 30.3.97; Lieut., Ind. Army, 22.4.98; Capt. 22.1.05; Major 22.1.14; Brev. Lt.-Col. 3.6.16; Brev. Col. 10.3.17; Major-Gen. 1.1.19; D.A.A.G. India; Ind. Ex. Fce. "D" and Mesopotamia; C.B.; Despatches; C.S.I. 1920.

CASSON, W. F. S. (D.S.O. L.G. 14.1.16); b. 4.10.77; e. s. of Lt.-Col. B. T. Casson; m. Ethel Philippa, d. of Brig.-Gen. H. S. Fitzgerald C.B., C.M.G.; one d.; educ. St. Edmund's, Ware; R.M. College, Sandhurst, and Staff College, Camberley; 2nd Lt. (Unatt.) 4.8.97; Lt., 27th Light Cavalry, I.A., 8.11.98; Lt. 4.11.99; Capt. 4.8.06; Major 4.8.15; Staff Off., Havre, 1916; D.A.Q.M.G., Havre, 1916; G.S.O., Meerut Div., 1916; Brigade Major, Garhwal Brigade, 1916; Despatches three times; 1914 Star; Bt. Lt.-Col. 1.1.18.

CASTLE, J. P. (D.S.O. L.G. 4.2.18) (Details, L.G. 5.7.18); b. 17.3.95; s. of T. Castle, Cloth Designer; educ. Norristhorpe Board School, Heckmondwike, and Dewsbury Technical School; ent. Army 2.9.14, as a Private, 1/4th West Riding R.; served Europ. War, joining the B.E.F. on 14.4.15; promoted L.-Corpl. 30.10.15, for "valuable military drawings executed"; L.-Sergt. 15.1.16; Sergt. 30.9.16; commissioned 4th W. Riding R.; rejoined B.E.F. in 2/4th W. Riding R., May, 1917; promoted to Lt., 2/35th Sikhs, I.A., 28.12.18.

J. P. Castle.

CASTLE, R. W. (D.S.O. L.G. 1.1.17); b. 14.7.74; s. of late E. J. Castle, K.C.; educ. Westminster School and R.M.A., Woolwich; ent. R.A. 17.11.94; Lt. 17.11.97; Capt. 10.10.00; Adj. 22.8.12 to 29.10.14; Major 30.10.14; Lt.-Col. 6.3.21; Despatches twice; C.M.G.

CATTELL, G. L. (D.S.O. L.G. 26.5.19); b. 23.10.71; 2nd Lt., Middlesex R., 27.1.92; Lt. 18.9.93; I.S.C. 4.8.96; Capt., I.A., 10.7.01; Major 27.1.10; Lt.-Col., Gurkha Rif., I.A., 27.1.18; Despatches.

CATTERSON-SMITH, T. M. O. (D.S.O. L.G. 27.9.20); b. 1.6.88; ent. Army 4.9.08; Lt. 9.12.10; Capt., 12th Pioneers, I.A., 1.9.15. He was wounded at Pioneer Picquet, Waziristan, 21.12.19, and died at Rawal Pindi Hospital, 10.2.20.

CATTY, T. C. (D.S.O. L.G. 25.8.17); b. 6.11.79; ent. W. Yorks. R. 12.8.99; I.A. 6.7.01; Lt. 12.11.01; Capt. 12.11.08; Major 1.9.15; served Europ. War, Mesopotamia; Despatches; Bt. Lt.-Col. 3.6.18; C.M.G.

CAVE, M. W. (D.S.O. L.G. 12.12.19); Lt.-Col., Aust. A.M.C.

CAVE, W. STURMY (D.S.O. L.G. 1.2.19); b. 1897; s. of Sir T. Sturmy Cave, K.C.B., and Beatrice Maria, d. of E. Carlile and sister of Prebendary Carlile, of the Church Army; m. Lorna R., d. of Col. Wishart; Major, 5th Bn. Queen's R. (W. Surrey) R., 16.7.21; Despatches.

W. Sturmy Cave.

CAVE-BROWNE, W. (D.S.O. L.G. 12.12.19); b. 18.9.84; 2nd Lt., R.E., 17.9.05; Lt. 23.3.08; Capt. 30.10.14; Adjt. 24.11.16 to 28.1.18; M.C.

CAVE-BROWNE-CAVE, H. M. (D.S.O. L.G. 26.4.18); Wing Cdr., R.A.F.; b. 1.2.87; s. of Sir T. Cave-Browne-Cave and Blanche M. M. A., d. of the late Sir J. Milton; served Europ. War, 1914–18; D.S.O. for services at Dunkirk; also D.F.C., 1918.

CAVENDISH, F. G. (D.S.O. L.G. 3.2.20); b. 2.11.91; 2nd Lt., Leins. R., 4.3.11; Lt., Leins. R., 21.9.12; Capt. 1.10.15; Despatches; M.C.

CAVENDISH, F. W. L. S. H. (D.S.O. L.G. 14.1.16); b. 11.9.77; s. of W. T. Cavendish; educ. Wellington College and R.M.C., Sandhurst; m. Enid, e. d. of Charles Lindeman, and widow of Robert Cameron; ent. 9th Lancers 8.9.97; Lt. 8.6.00; Capt. 1.5.04; Major 29.8.14; Brev. Lt.-Col. 3.6.16; T/Brig.-Gen. 16.9.18; served in S. Africa (Queen's and King's Medals, 9 clasps); was att. French General H.Q. as G.S.O. 1st Grade, 12.2.16 to 15.9.18; C.M.G., 1918; Despatches.

CAVENDISH-BENTINCK, LORD C. (see Bentinck, Lord C. Cavendish-).

CAYLEY, H. F. (D.S.O. L.G. 27.6.17) (Bar, L.G. 15.2.19); Lt., R.N., 31.12.94; ret. Cdr. 3.7.13; Capt. 11.11.18.

CAZALET, C. H. L. (D.S.O. L.G. 4.6.17); s. of late W. C. Cazalet; m. Gertrude Violet Langston Cazalet; educ. Rugby School; Trinity College, Cambridge; was Single and Double Lawn Tennis Champion of Cambridge University. Major Cazalet served in the European War, 1914–19; Despatches.

CAZALET, G. L. (D.S.O. L.G. 26.9.16); b. 31.3.89; Capt., R. Fus., 15.8.16; Brig.-Major, 47th Inf. Bde., Br. Armies in France, 26.10.17 to 8.1.20; Despatches; M.C. His D.S.O. was awarded for services on 4.8.16, near Pozières.

CECIL, R. E. (D.S.O. L.G. 3.6.18); 2nd Lt., Hrs., 18.1.99; 2nd Lt., 21st Lrs., 13.10.99; Lt. 2.3.00; Capt. 26.6.01; Adjt. 6.7.04 to 5.7.07; Major 10.12.13; ret., 21st Lrs., 19.3.21, with rank of Lt.-Col. in the Army; Despatches.

CHADWICK, F. (D.S.O. L.G. 16.9.18); Lt. (A/Major), K.R.R.C., Spec. Res.; M.C.

CHADWICK, J. H. (corr. to J. H. H.) (D.S.O. L.G. 4.6.17); T/Lt.-Col., Manch. R. He was killed in action 4.5.17.

CHADWICK, R. N. (D.S.O. L.G. 1.2.19); T/2nd Lt., Welsh R.

CHALLENOR, E. L. (gazetted as Challinor) (D.S.O. L.G. 21.12.16); b. 10.3.73; m. Edith, d. of W. E. Sampson; 2nd Lt., Leic. Regt., 19.7.93; Lt. 1.7.96; Capt. 26.10.01; Major 20.6.12; Bt. Lt.-Col. 3.6.16; T/Brig.-Gen. 16.3.17; Lt.-Col. 3.8.19; served S. Africa, 1899–1902 (Queen's Medal with 4 clasps; King's Medal with 2 clasps); Europ. War; C.B. 1919; C.M.G. 1918.

CHALLINOR, W. F. (D.S.O. L.G. 3.6.16); b. 20.6.82; s. of William E. and Catherine Challinor; m. 1917, Florence Bertha, e. d. of C. C. Ellis; educ. Rugby; Trinity College, Cambridge; joined 1st Vol. Bn. N. Staffs. Regt. 1901; Major, to command 3rd Staffs. Battery R.F.A. 1908 (embodied Aug. 1914); T/Lt.-Col. while commanding 46th Div. Amm. Column; served Europ. War, 1914–16; Despatches.

CHALMER, F. G. (D.S.O. L.G. 1.1.19); b. 28.11.84; 2nd Lt., R. Highrs., 14.5.04; Lt. 2.1.07; Capt. 26.9.14; Bt. Major 1.1.17 (att. Machine Gun Corps); served Europ. War; M.C.

CHALMERS, F. R. (D.S.O. L.G. 7.11.18); Lt.-Col., Aust. Infy.

CHAMBERLAYNE, E. T. (D.S.O. L.G. 3.6.16); Major, Warw. Yeo., 11.12.14; served Europ. War; Despatches.

CHAMBERS, P. R. (D.S.O. L.G. 18.8.16); b. 1.1.81; s. of Col. C. J. O. Chambers (Ind. Army); m. Edith Mary, widow of W. Blackburne-Maze; educ. Cheltenham; R.M.C., Sandhurst; 2nd Lt., Ind. S.C., 18.4.01; Lt., Ind. Army, 17.4.02; Capt. 17.1.09; Major 1.9.15; Bt. Major 3.6.16; Bt. Lt.-Col. 1.1.19; served Europ. War in France, Gallipoli, Salonika, Suez Canal and Senussi.

CHAMBERS, R. H. HAMMOND- (see Hammond-Chambers, R. H.).

CHAMBERS, R. W. (D.S.O. L.G. 1.1.19); Lt.-Col., Aust. A.M.C.

CHAMIER, J. A. (D.S.O. L.G. 1.1.17); b. 26.12.83; s. of Major-Gen. F. E. A. Chamier; educ. St. Paul's School; R.M.C. Sandhurst; 2nd Lt. (Unatt.) 27.8.02; 2nd Lt., Ind. Army, 11.1.04; Lt. 27.11.04; Capt. 27.8.11; Major 27.8.17; employed under Air Ministry 1.4.18; Group Capt.; served Somaliland, 1904; Europ. War, 1914–17; C.M.G.; O.B.E.; Despatches.

CHAMPION, C. C. (D.S.O. L.G. 26.7.18); T/Major; A/Lt.-Col., S. Lancs. R.

CHAMPION, J. P. (D.S.O. L.G. 15.9.16); Cdr. R.N.; Despatches (Sir John Jellicoe's) 23.8.16.

CHAMPION DE CRESPIGNY, C. R. (D.S.O. L.G. 14.1.16); b. 19.9.76; s. of Sir Claude Champion de Crespigny, 4th Bart.; m. 1913, Vere, d. of late Charles P. Sykes; 2nd Lt., G. Gds., 17.1.00; Lt. 1.4.03; Capt. 14.2.08; Major 30.1.15; Bt. Lt.-Col. 3.6.17; T/Brig.-Gen. 22.9.17; retired, G. Gds., 1920, with hon. rank of Brig.-Gen.; served S. Africa, 1901–2 (Queen's Medal, 4 clasps); Europ. War, 1914–18; Despatches four times; C.B.; C.M.G.; Montenegrin Cross.

CHAMPION DE CRESPIGNY, C. T. (D.S.O. L.G. 4.6.17), Lt.-Col. (T/Col.), Aust. A.M.C.

CHANCE, G. H. DE P. (D.S.O. L.G. 14.3.16); Lt.-Cdr., R.N.

CHANCE, K. M. (D.S.O. L.G. 4.6.17); T/Major, Border R.

CHANCE, O. K. (D.S.O. L.G. 14.1.16); b. 1.11.80; s. of William E. Chance; m. 1909, Fanny Isabel, 2nd d. of Sir G. W. Agnew, Bart.; one s.; one d.; educ. Eton; 2nd Lt., 5th Lcrs., 18.10.99; Lt. 3.10.00; Capt. 22.4.05; Adjt. 22.5.07–21.5.10; Major 16.1.13; Bt. Lt.-Col. 1.1.17; T/Brig.-Gen. 1.4.18–14.9.19; ret. 10.2.20, with hon. rank of Brig.-Gen.; served in S. Africa (Queen's Medal, 5 clasps; King's Medal, 2 clasps); Europ. War; C.M.G. 1919; 1914 Star; Despatches four times.

CHANDLER, W. K. (D.S.O. L.G. 3.6.18); b. 1883; s. of His Honour Sir W. K. Chandler, C.M.G., LL.D., and Ella Delisle, d. of Hon. J. T. Jones, of Barbados; m. Eileen, s. d. of E. O. Denison; educ. Trinity Hall, Cambridge, LL.B.; Bar, Inner Temple, 1906; served Europ. War, 1915–18; Lt.-Col., Can. Inf.; Despatches; Croix de Guerre.

CHANNER, GUY (D.S.O. L.G. 26.5.19); b. 12.11.84; 2nd Lt. (Unatt.), 21.1.03; Ind. Army, 8.4.04; Lt. 21.4.05; Capt. 21.1.12; Major 21.1.18; 14th K.G.O. Sikhs, I.A.; served Europ. War, Mesopotamia; Despatches.

CHANNER, G. K. (D.S.O. L.G. 26.3.18); b. 5.10.73; e. s. of late General G. N. Channer, V.C., C.B.; m. 1900, Gertrude Susan Hood, y. d. of late Robert Linzee; one s.; one d.; educ. Shrewsbury; R.M.C., Sandhurst; 2nd Lt. (Unatt.), 16.1.95; Ind. S.C. 3.4.96; Ind. Army, 16.4.97; Capt. 16.1.04; Major 16.1.13; Lt.-Col.; awarded the Royal Humane Society's Bronze Medal for saving life at sea, 1894; with clasp, 1901 (for saving native from drowning in India); awarded the Indian General Service Medal of 1895; with clasps for Punjab Frontier, 1897–98; Samana and in the Kurram Valley, 1897; Tirah, 1897–98; Waziristan, 1901–2 (wounded; Despatches); Delhi Durbar Medal; Indian Frontier, 1916; Egyptian Expeditionary Force, 1916–17; Palestine and Gaza and operations in the capture of Jerusalem, 1917; raised the 3rd Bn. 3rd Gurkhas in Egypt, 3.2.17; wounded five times; Despatches; the Order of the Crown of Italy (Officer).

G. K. Channer.

CHANTER, J. C. (D.S.O. L.G. 8.3.19) Details, L.G. 4.10.19); Major, Aust. L.H. Regt. (Egypt).

CHAPMAN, C. L. (D.S.O. L.G. 1.1.18); Aust. A.M.C.

CHAPMAN, G. A. E. (D.S.O. L.G. 1.1.17); b. 13.8.81; 2nd Lt., E. Kent R., 4.5.01; Lt. 9.12.04; ret. 25.6.10; S. African War, 1899–1902 (Queen's Medal with 3 clasps; King's Medal with 2 clasps); served Europ. War; Despatches.

CHAPMAN, G. P. (D.S.O. L.G. 16.9.18); 2nd Lt., R.A.; Spec. Res.

CHAPMAN, J. A. (D.S.O. L.G. 3.6.19); Major, Aust. Inf.

CHAPMAN, M. T. (D.S.O. L.G. 3.6.18); b. 25.6.88; 2nd s. of Major J. T. Chapman, R.A.; m. 1919, Hilda Emily, o. d. of A. W. Warde; 2nd Lt., A.S.C., 4.10.13; Lt. 4.10.14; Capt., R.A.S.C., 5.9.17; served Europ. War, 1914–18; Despatches.

CHAPMAN, R. (D.S.O. L.G. 14.1.16); b. 1880; m. 1909, Hélène Paris, d. of James George MacGowan; educ. High School, S. Shields; Major, 4th Durham Battery R.F.A. (T.F.); Lt.-Col. 1.6.16; served Europ. War, 1914–18; wounded; Despatches four times; C.M.G., 1918; Legion of Honour.

CHAPMAN, W. A. (D.S.O. L.G. 3.6.18); T/Capt. (A/Major), R.E.

CHAPPELL, L. S. (D.S.O. L.G. 31.7.19); Lt.-Cdr., R.N.V.R.; D.S.C.

CHAPPELL, W. F. (surname gazetted Chappel) (D.S.O. L.G. 15.10.18) (Bar, L.G. 2.4.19) (Details, L.G. 10.12.19); b. 15.5.75; 2nd Lt., 7th D.G., 7.5.98; Lt. 3.6.99; Capt. 1.5.03; Major, att. 3rd D.G., 24.12.14; served S. African War (Queen's Medal with 5 clasps; King's Medal with 2 clasps); served Europ. War.

CHAPPLE, F. J. (D.S.O. L.G. 14.1.16); b. 10.11.89; 2nd Lt. 13.8.18; Capt. (T/Major), R.G.A. (T.F.); M.C.

CHARGE, J. A. WILSON- (see Wilson-Charge, J. A.).

CHARLES, A. H. (D.S.O. L.G. 3.6.19); Major, Quebec R.

CHARLES, E. E. (D.S.O. L.G. 23.9.18); b. 21.2.83; 2nd Lt., R.A., 23.6.01; Lt. 17.3.04; Capt. 23.7.14; Adjt. 9.5.15–22.12.15; Major 17.7.16.

CHARLES, E. M. S. (D.S.O. L.G. 1.1.17); b. 22.2.78; s. of late T. E. Charles, M.D.; m. Lola Beatrice, d. of late W. F. Powell; one d.; educ. Winchester; 2nd Lt., R.E., 1.1.98; Lt. 1.1.01; Capt. 1.1.07; Adjt. 9.11.07–8.11.10; Major 30.10.14; served S. African War, 1900–2 (Queen's Medal with 3 clasps; King's Medal with 2 clasps); served Europ. War; Despatches five times; C.M.G.; Bt. Lt.-Col. 1.1.18.

E. M. S. Charles.

CHARLES, F. W. (D.S.O. L.G. 12.5.17); Lt., R.N.R.

CHARLES, J. L. (D.S.O. L.G. 8.3.19) (Details, L.G. 4.10.19); Major, Can. Rly. Service.

CHARLES, W. G. (D.S.O. L.G. 3.6.18); b. 14.6.80; 2nd Lt., Essex R., 20.1.00; Lt. 8.9.00; Adjt., Essex R., 2.9.06 to 1.9.09; Capt. 6.3.10; Major 1.9.15; served S. African War, 1901–2 (Queen's Medal with 5 clasps); Europ. War; Bt. Lt.-Col. 1.1.18; Despatches; C.M.G.

CHARLTON, A. H. (D.S.O. L.G. 8.3.19) (Details, L.G. 4.10.19); Lt. (A/Capt.), 1/6th Bn. N. Staffs. R., T.F.

CHARLTON, B. (D.S.O. L.G. 11.1.19); Lt., 79th Cameron Highrs., Canada, 15.7.15; M.C.

CHARLTON, C. E. C. G. (D.S.O. L.G. 1.1.17); b. 25.8.71; s. of late Lt.-Col. R. G. Charlton; m. Gwendoline, d. of A. Whitaker; one s.; one d.; educ. privately; R.M. Academy, Woolwich; 2nd Lt., R.A., 24.7.91; Lt. 24.7.94; Capt. 13.2.00; Major 19.4.09; Lt.-Col. 9.5.15; T/Brig.-Gen. 4.11.16–24.4.19; commanding Artillery, 16th Division; op. on N.W. Frontier of India, 1897–98; Tirah Exp. Force; op. in the Bara Valley (Medal and 2 clasps); Sudan, 1900–2 (Egyptian Medal and clasp); Europ. War; Despatches four times; Bt.-Col. 1.1.18; C.M.G.; Belgian Croix de Guerre; Osmanieh, 3rd Class; Medjidie, 4th Class; King's Coronation Medal.

CHARLTON, F. H. (D.S.O. L.G. 17.3.17); b. 29.9.82; y. s. of late W. A. Charlton and M. G. Charlton; m. 1913, Mary M., d. of H. A. Scott; 2nd Lt., Northd. Fus., 7.5.02; Lt. 17.1.06; Capt., S. Lancs., 7.4.14; Major 7.5.17; Bt. Major, April, 1917; Bt. Lt.-Col. 3.6.18; served S. Africa 1901 (Queen's Medal with 4 clasps); Europ. War; Gallipoli and Mesopotamia; Order of St. Stanislaus with Swords; Despatches three times.

CHARRINGTON, S. H. (D.S.O. L.G. 1.1.17); b. 1.12.78; educ. Eton; 2nd Lt., 15th (The King's) Hussars, 1899; Capt. and Adjt. 1906–10; resigned commission, 1912; Lt.-Col., R. of O., 15th Hussars, 1919; played in 15th Hussars' polo team, 1904–11; served Europ. War; E. Africa, 1914; Suvla Bay, 1915; Southern Force, Egypt, 1916; Major, Northants. R., France, May–Oct. 1916; Lt.-Col. 17.10.16; Brig.-Gen. 2.11.18; C.M.G.; Croix de Guerre avec Palme.

CHARSLEY, F. G. (D.S.O. L.G. 11.11.19); Lt.-Cdr., R.N., 30.6.16.

CHART, S. (D.S.O. L.G. 26.7.18); Major, London R.

CHARTERIS, N. K. (D.S.O. L.G. 1.1.17); b. 10.3.78; s. of Capt. Hon. F. W. Charteris, R.N., s. of 9th Earl of Wemyss and Lady Louisa Keppel, d. of 6th Earl of Albemarle; m. Katherine Margaret, d. of Sir J. Buchanan Riddell, Bart.; two s.; two d.; educ. Winchester; Christ Church, Oxford; joined Militia, 1897; commissioned 1st R. Scots, 1899; served S. African War, 1899–1902 (Despatches twice; both medals and clasps); Lt. 4.7.01; Adjt. 20.2.02–23.11.03; Capt. 25.9.07; Major 1.9.15; served Europ. War, 1914–18; Medit. Exp. Force, 1915; Egyptian Exp. Force, 1916; B.E.F., France, 1918; Despatches thrice; Bt. Lt.-Col. 1.1.18; C.M.G.

CHARTERS, A. B. (D.S.O. L.G. 1.1.18); Lt.-Col., N.Z. Inf.; C.M.G.

CHASE, A. A. (D.S.O. L.G. 14.1.16); b. 16.9.84; 3rd s. of late W. H. Chase and P. J. Chase; educ. Modern School, Bedford, and R.M.A., Woolwich; m. 1910, Gladys M., d. of Crichton Waller; one d.; one s.; ent. R.E. 29.7.04; Lt. 23.3.07; Capt. 30.10.14; Bt. Major at Thiepval; Lt.-Col. O.C. R. Sussex Pioneers; Despatches three times. He fell "mortally wounded by a shell at Irles about 5 p.m. on the 10th March, 1917, when carrying out a reconnaissance with Col. Henderson, R.E. Henderson was killed on the spot, and Chase succumbed the same evening, shortly after reaching hospital, and so died a hero of heroes. He was buried on the 11th in the military cemetery at Aveluy, a small village two miles from Albert" (extract from letter of Brig.-Gen. Richard P. Lee, R.E.). The funeral service was conducted by the Chaplain to the Forces—the 8th Royal Sussex Pioneers—the Rev. R. Douglas Canadine, who wrote that he had laid to rest a "very gallant soldier and gentleman." The Commander of the Division with which Col. Chase was associated, Sir Ivor Maxse, also wrote: "I used to look upon Chase as the very best type of British officer in every respect. He was a real leader of men as well as a thoughtful and most capable Staff officer. . . . He possessed that quality which endeared him to all true soldiers, and did much for the division to which he was attached." Col. Chase was recommended for decoration by Col. Evans, and his grandfather, curiously, was decorated by Queen Isabella of Spain on the recommendation of an officer also named Evans.

A. A. Chase.

CHASSE, H. (D.S.O. L.G. 8.3.19) (Details, L.G. 4.10.19); Major, 22nd Can. Inf. Bn.; M.C.

CHATER, A. R. (D.S.O. L.G. 26.7.18); b. 7.2.96; 2nd Lt., R. Mar., 1.10.13; Lt. 19.9.14; Capt. 17.9.17; Bt. Major 23.4.18; Adjt. 12.7.18 to 14.7.21; Despatches.

CHATTELL, A. P. (D.S.O. L.G. 3.6.18); Lt. (Can.), 5.1.15; Capt. (A/Major), Can. Inf.

CHATTERTON, G. D. L. (D.S.O. L.G. 18.8.16); b. 22.12.67; 2nd Lt., Shrops. L. Inf., 8.12.88; Lt., I.S.C., 13.3.90; Capt., I.A., 8.12.99; Major 8.12.06; Lt.-Col. 1.6.14; served Waziristan Exp. 1894–95; Egyptian Medal; Medal; N.W. Frontier of India, 1897–98, Tochi (Medal with clasp); China, 1900, Relief of Pekin (Medal with clasp); served Europ. War.

CHAWORTH-MUSTERS, J. N. (D.S.O. L.G. 3.6.18); b. 1890; e. s. of J. P. Chaworth-Musters, of Annesley Park, Notts; m. Daphne, d. of Capt. H. Wilberforce Bell; one s.; one d.; educ. Stubbington House; Osborne; Major, S. Notts Hussars, 27.10.17.

CHAYTOR, C. A. (D.S.O. L.G. 7.11.18); b. 8.9.81; 2nd Lt., Yorks. L. Inf., 5.1.01; Lt. 22.3.02; Capt. 12.1.10; Major 5.1.16; Bt. Lt.-Col. 3.6.19; West Africa (N. Nigeria), 1906 (Medal and clasp); wounded; Despatches and clasp; served Europ. War; retired Yorks. L.I. 1.9.21.

CHAYTOR, J. C. (D.S.O. L.G. 8.3.18); b. 20.11.88; s. of Lt.-Col. R. J. Chaytor and Frances Thomasina Chaytor; m. Agnes Mary, widow of J. H. Jaques and d. of Rt. Rev. J. Macarthur, D.D., Bishop of Southampton; one s.; 2nd Lt., S. Staff. R., 22.2.08; Lt. 5.5.09; Adjt. 1.3.12–28.2.15; Capt. 20.4.15; Bt. Major 3.6.16; Europ. War, 1914–18; Despatches; Legion of Honour, 5th Class; Bt. Major 3.6.16; M.C.

CHEADLE, H. (D.S.O. L.G. 22.8.18); Lt. (T/Major), S.A.E.C.; M.C.

CHEAPE, G. R. H. (D.S.O. L.G. 18.2.18) (Details, L.G. 18.7.18) (Bar, L.G. 1.2.19); b. 20.2.81; s. of late Lt.-Col. G. C. Cheape; m. Margaret Bruce, d. of J. Bruce Ismay; three s.; 2nd Lt., 1st D.G. (from I.Y. and from Militia), 21.12.01; Lt. 1.4.05; Capt. 1.1.08; Bt. Lt.-Col. 15.6.18; Lt.-Col. 2.3.19; Brig.-Gen. retired from Army, 1.4.19; served with Imp. Yeom. in S. Africa, 1900–2 (Queen's Medal and 3 clasps); Europ. War, 1914–19; Despatches six times; C.M.G.; M.C.

CHEAPE, H. A. GRAY- (see Gray-Cheape, H. A.).

CHEESEMAN, W. J. R. (D.S.O. L.G. 8.3.19) (Details, L.G. 4.10.19); Lt., Aust. Mil. Forces, 1.7.15; Lt.-Col.; M.C.

CHEESEWRIGHT, W. F. (D.S.O. L.G. 1.1.17); Lt.-Col., R.E.

CHEETHAM, G. (D.S.O. L.G. 1.1.18); b. 24.6.91; 2nd Lt., R.E., 20.7.11; Lt. 31.7.13; Capt. 26.6.17; Major 19.9.17; Staff Capt., British Mil. Mission, Portuguese Contgt., 16.8.17–18.9.17; M.C.

CHEETHAM, H. C. V. B. (D.S.O. L.G. 1.1.17); Cdr., R.N.R.; R.D.

CHELL, R. A. (D.S.O. L.G. 1.1.19); b. 1893; m. Lucy Ashworth, B.A., d. of E. J. Stafford; one s.; served Europ. War, 1914–18; was Brig. Major, 55th Inf. Bgde.; Despatches; M.C. and Bar.

CHENEVIX-TRENCH, J. F. (D.S.O. L.G. 3.6.18); b. 2.11.85; s. of Major-Gen. F. Chenevix-Trench, C.M.G., 20th Hussars, and Blanche, d. of late Capt. C. Mulville, 3rd Dn. Gds.; educ. Wellington College; R.M.C., Sandhurst; 2nd Lt., Northd. Fus., 3.2.06; Lt. 4.3.11; Adjt. 17.9.14–31.12.15; Capt. 8.1.15; served Europ. War, 1914–18; Despatches four times; Bt. Major 3.6.17.

CHENEVIX-TRENCH, L. (D.S.O. L.G. 1.1.18); b. 24.3.83; 2nd Lt., R.E., 21.12.01; Lt. 8.8.04; Capt. 21.12.12; Major 21.12.16; Europ. War, 1914–18; wounded; Despatches; C.M.G.; Legion of Honour.

CHESNEY, C. H. R. (D.S.O. L.G. 3.6.16); b. 23.7.83; s. of Col. H. F. Chesney; educ. Blundell's School, Tiverton, and Woolwich; ent. R.E. 21.12.01; Lt. 1.4.04; Capt. 21.12.12; Major 21.12.16; served Europ. War, 1914–18.

C. H. R. Chesney.

CHESSE, H. (D.S.O. L.G. 8.3.19) (Details, L.G. 4.10.19); Major, Quebec R.; M.C.

CHESTER-MASTER, R. C. (D.S.O L.G. 4.6.17) (Bar, L.G. 16.8.17); b. 29.8.70; e. s. of Col. T. W. Chester-Master and Georgina Emily, d. of J. E. W. Rolls; m. Geraldine Mary Rose, d. of the late J. H. Arkwright; educ. Cornish's Schools, Clevedon; Harrow; and Christ Church, Oxford; joined K.R.R.C. 9.8.93; Lt. 1.1.96; Capt. 13.1.01; retired, K.R.R.C., as Major, 18.5.10; served S. Africa, 1899–1902 (Despatches); Bt. of Major 14.1.01; Queen's Medal with 6 clasps; King's Medal with 2 clasps. Lt.-Col. Chester-Master, who was Chief Constable of Gloucestershire, was killed in action 30.8.17.

CHEVALLIER, P. T. (D.S.O. L.G. 1.1.19); T/Capt., Gen. List; M.C.

CHICHESTER, HON. A. C. S. (D.S.O. L.G. 3.6.18); b. 12.9.80; e. s. of 3rd Baron Templemore and Evelyn (who died in 1883), d. of late Rev. W. J. Stracey-Clitherow; m. Hon. Clare Meriel Wingfield, d. of 7th Viscount Powerscourt; three s.; educ. Harrow; Sandhurst; served S. Africa, 1902 (Queen's Medal, 4 clasps); Tibet, 1904, including march to Lhassa (Medal and clasp); Europ. War; 1914 Star; O.B.E.; Italian Croce di Guerra; Major, Irish Guards, 18.1.16; late Capt. R.F.

CHICHESTER, C. G. (D.S.O. L.G. 26.4.18); b. 25.9.75; s. of late Gen. H. Chichester, R.A.; m. Katherine Elizabeth Cottrell-Dormer; two s.; one d.; educ. H.M.S. Britannia; Dartmouth; Midshipman, 1892–95; present at raising of H.M.S. Howe; Sub-Lt. 1895–98; Lt. 1898–1908; Cdr. 1908; qualified as Gunnery Lt. 1901; commanded H.M.T.B.D. Hornet, 1913–15; H.M.S. Forward (L.C.), 1915–18; served in Harwich Flotilla and Ægean Squadron, Europ. War; present at Battle of Dogger Bank; Despatches; Legion of Honour; Order of the Redeemer; received R. Humane Society's Medal, 1915.

CHICHESTER-CONSTABLE, R. C. J. (D.S.O. L.G. 14.1.16); b. 21.12.90; e. s. of W. G. C. Chichester-Constable, J.P., D.L., and of Edith, d. of J. H. Smyth-Pigott; m. Gladys Consuelo, d. of E. Hanly; 2nd Lt., R. Brig. S.R., 22.5.12; Lt. 5.8.14; Adjt., R. Brig., 1915–16; Capt. 2.10.15; served in Europ. War in France; Despatches; Bt. Major 1.1.19.

CHICK, F. (D.S.O. L.G. 2.12.18); b. 30.1.90; ent. Army 9.1.17; T/Lt., R.W.F.; ret. 20.9.17.

CHILD, SIR SMITH HILL, Bart. (D.S.O. L.G. 3.6.16); b. 19.9.80; s. of J. G. Child and Helen, d. of the Rev. G. Mather, Prebendary of Lichfield; educ. at Eton College and Christ Church, Oxford; ent. 3rd Bn. R. Scots, Oct. 1899; served in S. Africa, 1900 (Queen's Medal with 2 clasps); ent. 1st Bn. Irish Guards, July, 1901; M.V.O. 1910; gazetted Lt.-Col. commdg. 2nd North Midland Brigade, R.F.A., Feb. 1910; commanded this unit in France, Feb. 1915–March, 1918; Brig.-Gen., R.A., 46th North Midland Divn., March, 1918–April, 1919; Despatches four times; C.B.; C.M.G.; is Col. commdg. R.A. 46th North Midland Div. (T.F.); M.P. for Stone (Staffordshire) since 1918.

CHILD-VILLIERS, HON. A. G. (D.S.O. L.G. 18.7.17) (Bar, L.G. 26.7.18); b. 24.11.83; 2nd s. of 7th Earl of Jersey; educ. Eton; Oxford; joined Oxfordsh. Yeomanry; served Europ. War, 1914–18; Croix de Guerre; Managing Director of Baring Brothers and Co. since 1919.

CHILES-EVANS, D. B., M.R.C.S., L.R.C.P.Lond. (D.S.O. L.G. 3.6.16); educ. University Colleges of London and Cardiff; was a well-known practitioner in Swansea; was in the Special Reserve. On the outbreak of war he volunteered for active service; Lt.-Col. Chiles-Evans died on 23.4.17, of wounds received in action.

CHIPP, W. F. (D.S.O., L.G. 8.3.19) (Details L.G. 4.10.19) (Bar, L.G. 1.1.19); Lt. (A/Major), Hereford R., T.F.; M.C.

CHISHOLM, A. (D.S.O. L.G. 1.1.18); Major, Aust. L.H. Rgt.

CHISHOLM-BATTEN, A. W. (D.S.O. L.G. 4.6.17); b. 28.9.51; s. of E. Chisholm-Batten; m. Brittie Ellen Wood; one s.; two d.; educ. Eagle House; joined R.N. 1865; member War Office Committees, Coast Defence; employed suppression slave trade; protection British interests Lorenzo Marques; present Bangkok during French Blockade; Ordnance Dept., Admiralty; A.D.C. to the King, 1905; retired 1907; served afloat as Capt., R.N.R., 1915–17; M.V.O.

CHIVERS, C. W. U. (D.S.O. L.G. 3.6.19); Lt., Can. Mil. Forces, 1.6.12; Major, H.Q. 3rd Bde. Can. Engrs., 1.6.12; M.C.

CHOLMLEY, R. S. (D.S.O. L.G. 27.7.18); b. 16.5.87; 2nd Lt., W. Riding R., 4.5.07; Lt. 10.4.09; Capt. 19.4.15; Adjt., W. Riding R., 28.10.19; employed with K.A.R. 1914–19; Despatches.

CHRISTIAN, E. (D.S.O. L.G. 1.1.18) (Bar, L.G. 15.1.20); T/Lt.-Col. S. African Infantry (France); M.C.

CHRISTIAN, W. F. (D.S.O. L.G. 1.1.18); b. 4.9.79; s. of late Major G. A. Christian, Ches. R.; m. Marguerite Annie Hornby; three s.; three d.; educ. Clongowes Wood College; 2nd Lt., R.A., 5.5.00; Lt. 3.4.01; Capt. 5.5.01; Major 30.12.15; served Europ. War at the Siege of Tsing Tau, and in France and Belgium; Chevalier, Order of Leopold; Croix de Guerre; Despatches thrice.

CHRISTIE, A. (D.S.O. L.G. 1.1.18); b. 1889; s. of A. Christie, I.C.S., and Ellen Ruth Christie (*née* Coates); m. Agatha, d. of F. Miller; one d.; educ. Clifton College; R.M. Academy, Woolwich; ent. R.F.A. 1909; transferred to R.F.C. 1913, having become a qualified pilot, 1912; served in France, Aug. 1914–Sept. 1918, with R.F.C. and R.A.F.; C.M.G.; Order of St. Stanislaus, 3rd Class with Swords; Despatches five times. Col. Christie resigned his commission June, 1919.

CHRISTIE, H. R. S. (D.S.O. L.G. 1.1.18); b. 29.10.68; 2nd Lt. 13.2.90; Lt. 13.2.93; Capt. 24.9.00; Major 22.1.10; Major 23.11.17; T/Brig.-Gen. 18.12.17–16.2.18.

CHRISTIE, J. R. (D.S.O. L.G. 3.6.19); Lt. (A/Capt.), G. Highrs., T.F.

CHRISTIE, M. G. (D.S.O. L.G. 24.1.17); 3rd s. of J. A. Christie; educ. Leamington Preparatory School; the University, Aix-la-Chapelle; joined R.F.C. on outbreak of war; became Lt.-Col.; Wing Cdr., R.A.F., and Commandant of No. 2 School of Bombing and Aerial Navigation, R.A.F., Andover; C.M.G.; M.C.

CHRISTIE, M. I. (D.S.O. L.G. 19.11.17) (Details, L.G. 22.3.18); s. of G. W. Christie; joined H.A.C., and commissioned and att. R. Fus.; T/Lt. (A/Capt.). The General of his division wrote, after the fighting at Tower Hamlets Ridge, Sept. 1917, that he wished to place on record his appreciation of Capt. Christie's bravery and courage on that occasion. He died of wounds 24.3.18.

CHRISTIE, R. (D.S.O. L.G. 17.12.17) (Details, L.G. 23.4.18) (Bar, L.G. 16.9.18); Lt.-Col., Aust. Inf.

CHRISTIE, W. D. C. (D.S.O. L.G. 7.11.18); Lt., Can. Inf.

W. D. C. Christie.

CHRISTIE, W. E. TOLFREY (D.S.O. L.G. 1.2.17); b. 10.11.77; 2nd Lt., R. Mar., 1.9.96; Lt. 1.7.97; Capt., A.S.C., 2.10.02; Major 5.8.14; Bt. Lt.-Col., R.A.S.C.; C.M.G. He died 22.10.18.

CHRISTIE-MILLER, G. (D.S.O. L.G. 8.3.19) (Details, L.G. 4.10.19); Capt. (A/Lt.-Col.), Oxf. and Bucks. L.I.; M.C.

CHURCH, A. G. (D.S.O. L.G. 21.1.20); Lt. (A/Major), R.G.A.; M.C.

CHURCH, D. R. (D.S.O. L.G. 16.8.17); 2nd Lt. (T/Capt.), Northants. R.

CHURCH, J. A. (D.S.O. L.G. 1.1.19); T/Capt. (A/Major), R.E.; M.C.

CHURCH, L. H. (D.S.O. L.G. 3.6.18); Major, A.S.C.

CHURCHILL, C. E. (D.S.O. L.G. 3.6.19); Major, Can. F.A.

CHURCHILL, G. R. D. (gazetted as Churchill, R. D.) (D.S.O. L.G. 12.12.19); b. 2.7.70; s. of the late J. F. Churchill, D.P.W., Ceylon; 2nd Lt., E.Surrey R., 25.7.91; Lt. 23.4.93; Lt., I.S.C., 9.2.96; Capt. 10.7.01; Major 25.7.09; served in op. in Chitral, 1895 (Medal and clasp); Europ. War; Despatches. Lt.-Col. Churchill, O.C. 2/19th Punjabis, was killed in action in Waziristan.

W. E. Tolfrey Christie.

CHURCHILL, J. S. S. (D.S.O. L.G. 3.6.18); Major, Oxf. Yeo.; served S. African War, 1900 (Queen's Medal with 5 clasps); Europ. War.

CHURCHUS, W. (D.S.O. L.G. 1.1.18); Major, Aust. F.A. He died 1.4.18.

CHURTON, W. A. V. (D.S.O. L.G. 1.1.17); Capt. (T/Major), Ches. R.

CLAPHAM, D. (D.S.O. L.G. 3.6.19); b. 19.1.76; 2nd Lt., R.A., 2.11.95; Lt. 2.11.98; Capt. 1.4.01; Major 30.10.14; Lt.-Col. 1.5.21; served S. Afr. War. 1899–1900 (Queen's Medal with clasp; China Medal); Despatches; O.B.E.

CLARE, E. T. NEWTON- (see Newton-Clare, E. T.).

CLARE, J. W. S. (D.S.O. L.G. 3.6.18); T/Major, A.S.C.

CLARE, O. C. (D.S.O. L.G. 4.6.17) (Bar, L.G. 16.9.18); b. 18.3.81; e. s. of George Clare; m. Gladys Emily, e. d. of Alfred J. Sewell, M.R.C.V.S.; two s.; served S. African War; Europ. War, 1914–17; Lt.-Col.; Despatches; M.C.

CLARK, A. N. (D.S.O. L.G. 21.12.16); Capt., Durham L. Inf. 2.10.14.

CLARK, C. A. (D.S.O. L.G. 24.9.18); b. 9.12.78; 2nd Lt., E. Surr. R., 7.1.16; Lt. 7.7.17; M.C.

L. H. Church.

CLARK, C. A. G. (D.S.O. L.G. 1.1.17); b. 2.3.64; 2nd Lt. 23.8.84; Major 14.8.01; ret. K.R.R.C., 2.8.05; served S. African War, 1899–1902 (Queen's Medal with 4 clasps); Europ. War, including Egypt and capture of Jerusalem; C.M.G., 1918; Despatches.

CLARK, C. H. (D.S.O. L.G. 3.6.16); b. 24.10.80; s. of late W. S. Clark; educ. Harrow; 2nd Lt., R.A., 18.10.99; Lt. 16.2.01; Capt. 4.3.08; Adjt. 11.11.08 to 31.10.11; Major 30.10.14; Bt. Lt.-Col. 3.6.19; Lt.-Col. 3.1.21; served S. Africa, 1900–1 (Queen's Medal, 3 clasps); Despatches; India, 1901–13; Europ. War; Egypt; Gallipoli, 1915, and France, 1916–19.

CLARK, C. W. (D.S.O. L.G. 1.1.19), T/Capt. (A/Major) Tank Corps; M.C.

CLARK, D. G. (D.S.O. L.G. 26.7.18); Capt., 6th (Banff and Donside) Bn. (T.) Gordon Highlanders; M.C. He died of wounds, 13.4.18.

CLARK, E. G. (D.S.O. L.G. 12.12.19); Major, 4th Bn. S. African Inf.

CLARK, F. W. (D.S.O. L.G. 3.6.19); T/Capt. (A/Major), R.E.; M.C.

CLARK, H. N. (D.S.O. L.G. 1.1.18); Major, R.F.A. (T.F.), 1.4.08; Hon. Col., R.F.A. (Lt.-Col. ret., T.F.), 3.11.21.

CLARK, J. A. (D.S.O. L.G. 4.6.17) (1st Bar, L.G. 16.8.17) (2nd Bar, L.G. 2.12.18); Lt.-Col., Can. Infy.

CLARK, J. L. C. (D.S.O. L.G. 14.3.16) (Bar, L.G. 8.3.20) (Christian name Lenox omitted from gazette of Bar); b. Sept. 1884; s. of Col. J. J. Clark, H.M. Lieutenant for co. Londonderry, and Mary, e. d. of late Sir W. F. Lenox Conyngham, K.C.B.; m. Marion, d. of the late Lt.-Col. Chichester, D.L., M.P.; educ. Royal Navy; joined H.M. Navy, 1899; Lt., 1906; Lt.-Cdr., 1914; Cdr., 1917; served in H.M.S. Mosquito in Red Sea and at Dardanelles; then H.M.S. Turbulent in North Sea.

CLARK, J. P. (D.S.O. L.G. 3.6.18); Capt., Aust. Mil. Forces, 23.2.13.

CLARK, J. W. (D.S.O. L.G. 1.1.17); b. 7.9.77, at Newcastle, N.S.W.; s. of J. B. Clark; m. 1902, Dora, d. of T. L. Hood; one s.; one d.; educ. Maitland High School, N.S.W.; Lt., 4th Aust. Inf. R., 1897; Lt.-Col. comdg. 8th Inf. Bgde. A.I.F., 1915; served Europ. War; Despatches.

CLARK, P. L. (D.S.O. L.G. 17.12.17) (Details, L.G. 23.4.18); T/2nd Lt. (A/Capt.), R. Sussex R.

CLARK, P. W. (D.S.O. L.G. 1.1.19); b. 1888; s. of James Clark, R.I., A.R.B.C.; educ. St. Mark's, Chelsea; London University; Associate Member of the Institute of Civil Engineers; given a commission, Sept. 1914; Major in command of the 61st Div. Sig. Div.; served three and a half years in France; M.C.

CLARK, R. P. (D.S.O. L.G. 1.1.18); Adjt. (Can.), 2.1.14; M.C.

CLARK, W. C. (D.S.O. L.G. 25.8.17) (Bar, L.G. 19.11.17) (Details, L.G. 22.3.18; b. 8.5.77; s. of W. S. Clark and Mary Ann Ford Clark (*née* Nevitt); m. Kathleen Mary Jordan, d. of Major Bell, R.F.; one s.; educ. Harrow (Sixth Form); Oxford (Trinity); B.A., Honours, June, 1898; entered Old Army Militia, March, 1900; Line, Jan. 1902; New Army, 30.10.14 (from India); became Lt.-Col.; served S. African War, 1901–2; in Belgium, France and Italy, two and a quarter years in the trenches, except when slightly wounded.

CLARK-HALL, R. H. (D.S.O. L.G. 26.4.18); m. Lilias, d. of Col. R. Eliott Lockhart; served Europ. War, 1915–18; Lt.-Col. R.A.F.; Despatches.

CLARK-KENNEDY, W. H. (D.S.O. L.G. 14.1.16) (Bar, L.G. 11.1.19); V.C.; C.M.G.; Lt.-Col., late Can. E.F (see "The Victoria Cross," same publishers).

CLARKE, A. C. (D.S.O. L.G. 4.6.17); b. 9.8.48; m. 1895, Margaret Macgregor, d. of J. L. Adams, U.S.A.; ent. R.N., 1861; Lt., 1872; Comdr., 1883; Capt., 1891; Rr.-Admiral, 1904; retired, 1903; Vice-Admiral, 1908; served Abyssinia, 1868 (Medal); China, 1901 (Medal; C.M.G., 1902); Europ. War; Officer of Legion of Honour; C.M.G., C.B.E.

CLARKE, A. D. C. (D.S.O. L.G. 11.1.19); Lt. (A/Major), R.F.A. (Spec. Res.); M.C.

CLARKE, A. C. L. STANLEY- (see Stanley-Clarke, A. C. L.).

CLARKE, A. E. STANLEY (D.S.O. L.G. 4.6.17); b. 1879; o. s. of the late Major-Gen. S. de A. C. Clarke; m. 1907, Evelyn, e. d. of Sir Alexander Baird (1st Bart.); two s.; educ. Eton and Sandhurst; Page of Honour to Queen Victoria; Conservative candidate for S.W. Norfolk; Scots Gds., 1898 to 1910; Bt. Major (R. of Off.); served S. Africa (at Belmont, Graspan, Modder River and Magersfontein); in the Macedonian Gendarmerie, 1904–7; Private Secretary to Sir John French, 1907–10; M.V.O.; Europ. War, 1914–18.

CLARKE, A. L. C. (D.S.O. L.G. 14.1.16); b. 30.8.74; 2nd s. of J. Crisp Clarke; m. 1910, Mary Frances, d. of Sir Alexander Bradshaw, K.C.B.; educ. Rugby School; 2nd Lt., 1st A. and S. Highrs., 6.6.96; Lt. 4.5.98; Capt. 27.8.04; Lt.-Col., R. of O., 6.6.20; ret. pay, 6.6.20; served S. Africa (Despatches; Queen's Medal, 5 clasps); Europ. War, 1914–19, in France and Macedonia; Bt. Lt.-Col. 3.6.18; Despatches.

CLARKE, B. C. S. (D.S.O. L.G. 4.6.17) (Bar, L.G. 16.9.18); b. 19.4.82; 2nd Lt., Worc. R., 28.1.03; Lt. 1.4.12; Capt. 18.9.14; Bt. Major 18.2.15; Major 7.5.17; Despatches.

CLARKE, COLIN, M.B. (D.S.O. L.G. 3.6.18); b. 29.6.81; Lt., R.A.M.C., 1.8.08; Capt. 1.2.12; Major 1.8.20; Despatches.

CLARKE, COLIN (D.S.O. L.G. 4.6.17), Major S. African Engrs.

CLARKE, C. J. (D.S.O. L.G. 4.6.17); b. 3.6.75; 2nd Lt., R.E., 27.2.94; Lt. 27.2.97; Capt. 1.4.04; Major 27.2.14; Lt.-Col. 1.1.21; Despatches.

CLARKE, D. H. (D.S.O. L.G. 1.1.18); M.C.; T/Capt. Durham L.I.

CLARKE, SIR E. H. ST. L., Bart. (D.S.O. L.G. 1.1.17); b. 17.4.57; s. of late Rev. J. W. Clarke; m. 1884, Susan Douglas (d. 1913), d. of Charles Langton; one d.; Major (late Worc. R.) 23.10.90; Bt. Lt.-Col. (R. of Off.) 29.10.90; served Europ. War, 1914–18; C.M.G.

CLARKE, E. P. (D.S.O. L.G. 1.1.17); Capt. (T/Major), Suff. R. (T.F.); Major, Suff. R., 16.2.20.

CLARKE, F. A. S. (D.S.O. L.G. 1.1.18); Major, London R.

CLARKE, F. F. (D.S.O. L.G. 1.1.18) (Bar, L.G. 26.7.18); Major, Can. Force, 6.5.14.

CLARKE, H. C. C. (D.S.O. L.G. 29.11.18); Lt.-Cdr., R.N., 15.2.19.

CLARKE, H. T. (D.S.O. L.G. 8.3.19) (Details, L.G. 4.10.19) (Bar, L.G. 2.4.19) (Details, L.G. 10.12.19); Major (A/Lt.-Col.), Worc. R., T.F.

CLARKE, J. (D.S.O. L.G. 11.1.19); T/Lt., Drake Bn. R.N.V.R.; M.C.

CLARKE, M. F. (D.S.O. L.G. 1.1.17); b. 3.2.76; 4th s. of late Marshal N. Clarke; m. 1910, Olive, d. of Canon L. Garnett, Rector of Christleton, Ches.; one s.; two d.; educ. Eton; Trinity College, Oxford; 2nd Lt., Ches. R., 28.5.98; Lt. 17.8.99; Capt. 15.4.05; Major 1.9.15; retired Cheshire R. 19.10.21, with rank of Lt.-Col., Army; served S. African War, 1900–2; Europ. War, France, 1914–18; Despatches.

CLARKE, M. O. (D.S.O. L.G. 1.1.17); b. 22.12.78; 2nd Lt., R. Fus., 3.8.98; Lt. 27.9.99; Capt. 12.2.04; Major 1.9.15; Bt. Lt.-Col. 3.6.19; Despatches.

CLARKE, P. S. (D.S.O. L.G. 1.1.18); Major (T/Lt.-Col.), S. African Med. Corps; M.C.

CLARKE, R. (D.S.O. L.G. 1.1.18), Lt.-Col. 1.6.16., 52nd (Lowland) Bn. R.A.S.C., T.A.; T.D.

CLARKE, R. G. (D.S.O. L.G. 1.1.18); b. 21.8.79; 2nd Lt., R.W. Surr. R., 18.10.99; Lt. 22.1.02; Capt. 22.1.11; Major, 1.9.15; Bt. Lt.-Col. 1.1.17; served S. African War, 1899–1902 (Despatches; Queen's Medal with 5 clasps; King's Medal with 2 clasps); Europ. War; Despatches; C.M.G.

CLARKE, R. J. (D.S.O. L.G. 14.11.16); Lt.-Col., R. Berks. R.; served in S. African War, 1900–1 (Queen's Medal with 4 clasps); Europ. War.; D.S.O. awarded for gallantry on 25.7.16 near Ovillers.

CLARKE, W. H. (D.S.O. L.G. 6.9.16), R.N.; Eng.-Cdr., R.N., 1.4.18.

CLARKSON, A. B. (D.S.O. L.G. 2.4.19) (Details, L.G. 10.12.19), Major, West Rid. R. (T.F.), 1.6.16; M.C.

CLARKSON, B. ST. J. (D.S.O. L.G. 25.8.17); b. 8.11.68; s. of late T. H. Clarkson; m. 1898, Constance Mary, e. d. of late Rt. Hon. Sir J. E. Gorst; 2nd Lt., North'd Fus., 3.4.89; 2nd Lt., Dorset R., 14.8.89; Lt., Dorset R. 5.7.90; Capt. 14.6.97; Major 23.1.07; Lt.-Col. 25.10.14; retired 17.8.19; commanding 3rd Bn. Dorset R.; served Tirah, 1897–98 (Despatches; Medal; 2 clasps); Europ. War, 1914–18; C.M.G., 1916.

CLARKSON, W. B. (D.S.O. L.G. 1.1.19), T/Lt. (A/Major), R.G.A.

CLAUDET, G. F. (D.S.O. L.G. 17.9.17), Lt. (A/Capt.), R.F.A.

CLAVERING, N. W. NAPIER- (see Napier-Clavering, N. W.).

CLAXTON, W. G. (D.S.O. L.G. 2.11.18), Lt., R.A.F., D.F.C. and Bar.

CLAY, B. G. (D.S.O. L.G. 20.10.16) (Bar, L.G. 26.9.17) (Details, L.G. 9.1.18); b. 15.5.74; 2nd Lt., 5 D.G., 21.10.93; Lt. 11.9.95; Capt. 1.2.01; Adjt. 16.6.03 to 15.7.06; Major 6.3.07; Major, 7th D.G., 6.2.09; T/Brig.-Gen. 22.8.17 to 16.4.19; Lt.-Col., 7 D.G., 24.12.18; served in S. Africa, 1899–02; (Queen's Medal with 4 clasps; King's Medal with 2 clasps); Europ. War, 1914–18; C.B., 1919; C.M.G., 1918; Despatches; Bt. Lt.-Col. 3.6.17; D.S.O. awarded for services 25 June to 21 July, Somme.

CLAYTON, A. R. (D.S.O. L.G. 3.6.18), Major, Aust. A.M.C.

CLAYTON, E. R. (D.S.O. L.G. 14.1.16); b. 13.9.77; 2nd Lt., Oxf. and Bucks. L. Inf., 20.2.97; Lt. 3.3.98; Capt. 11.9.02; Adjt. 1.3.04–28.2.07; Major 1.9.15; Lt.-Col. 15.2.20; served N.W. Frontier of India, 1897–98; with Mohmand Field and Tirah Exped. Forces (Medal, 2 clasps); Europ. War; Despatches; Bt. Lt.-Col. 3.6.18.

CLAYTON, G. M. (D.S.O. L.G. 1.1.18), T/Major, L'pool R.

CLAYTON, G. S. (D.S.O. L.G. 3.6.18), T/Major, Liverpool R.; Lt. (North'd Yeo.), 24.4.01; served S. African War, 1900–1; Queen's Medal, 4 clasps.

CLAYTON, M. C. (D.S.O. L.G. 26.11.17) (Details, L.G. 6.4.18), Major, Cambs. Regt.

CLAYTON, R. C. BROWNE- (see Browne-Clayton, R.C.).

CLAYTON, W. B. (D.S.O. L.G. 3.6.18), Major, A.S.C.

CLEARY, E. J. (D.S.O. L.G. 3.6.18), Major (Can.), A.S.C.

CLEAVER, D. W. (D.S.O. L.G. 4.6.17); 2nd s. of W. B. Cleaver; T/Lt. (A/Major), R.G.A.

CLEAVER, F. H. (D.S.O. L.G. 1.1.17), T/Major, Spec. List and R.F.C.

CLEGG, H. N. M. (D.S.O. L.G. 3.6.19), Lt.-Col., Denbighshire Yeo.

CLEGG, N. B. (D.S.O. L.G. 3.6.18), T/Major, A.S.C.

CLEGG-HILL, THE HON. A. R. (D.S.O. L.G. 4.6.17); b. 1877; 4th s. of late Viscount Hill; bro. of the present Peer; educ. Radley College; Hon. Lt., Ches. R., 5.10.02; Major, Cheshire Regt., 1915; T/Lt.-Col., 1916; served S. Africa (Queen's Medal, 3 clasps). He volunteered for the European War, rejoining his old regiment, and was in command of the Cheshire Rgt. for 2½ years. He was several times mentioned in Despatches, and was killed in action 18.9.18.

CLEGHORN, G. M. (D.S.O. L.G. 26.7.18) (Bar, L.G. 8.3.19) (Details, L.G. 4.10.19); b. 1889; s. of William Cleghorn; m. 1919, Winifred, d. of Francis Stevenson; educ. Clifton College; T/Major, High. Light Inf.; served Europ. War, 1914–18; Despatches and Croix de Guerre.

CLEMENTS, R. W., M.B. (D.S.O. L.G. 1.1.17); b. 7.4.70; educ. Queen's College, Galway; Edinburgh; Diploma of Tropical Medicine, Liverpool; Lt., R.A.M.C., 29.7.96; Capt. 29.7.99; Major 29.1.08; Lt.-Col. 1.3.15; Col. 26.12.17; served Europ. War, 1914–18; Despatches five times; C.M.G., 1918.

CLEMENTS, S. U. L. (D.S.O. L.G. 3.6.18), Major, R. Ir. Fus.; served S. African War, 1901–02; Queen's Medal with 4 clasps.

CLEMINSON, C. R. D. (D.S.O. L.G. 14.11.16), T/Capt., Liverpool Regt.; served S. African War, 1901; Europ. War. His D.S.O. was awarded for services on 3.9.16, at Guillemont.

CLEMSON, A. W. (D.S.O. L.G. 21.4.17), Lt.-Cdr., R.N.A.S.

CLEMSON, W. (D.S.O. L.G. 3.6.19); b. 29.6.84; 2nd Lt., Dorset Regt., 10.10.03; Lt. 19.3.06; Capt. 26.5.10; Major 10.10.18; Adjt. 6.9.19 to 5.9.21; Despatches.

CLEMSON, W. F. (D.S.O. L.G. 23.6.15) (Bar, L.G. 19.11.17) (Details, L.G. 22.3.18) (see "The Distinguished Service Order," from its institution to 31.12.15, by same publishers).

CLENDINING, H. (D.S.O. L.G. 1.1.19), T/Major, R. Ir. Rifles.

CLERK, A. G. (D.S.O. L.G. 26.1.17), Capt., Herts Regt.; M.C. His D.S.O. was awarded for gallantry on 14.11.16, at Hansaline.

CLERK, E. G. (D.S.O. L.G. 12.12.19); b. 30.5.74, at Wanganui, N.Z.; s. of the late Edward George Charles Clerk and the late Annie Clerk; m. Celia Blanche Daisy Buchanan; one s.; became Captain, S. African Scottish, 1.9.14; Major; served S. African War, 1899–1902, as an officer in the Queensland Forces; Capt. Royston's Horse during Zulu Rebellion of 1906; severely wounded; lost use of left arm; Despatches; assisted Brig.-Gen. Royston to raise Natal Light Horse in Aug. 1914; commanded A Squadron during the operations on Orange River; raised special service squadron for services with 4th Mounted Rifles in German S.W. Africa; took part in actions of Keimos, Katrama, Keis Drift and Gibeon during 1914–15; on conclusion of German West Campaign formed Natal Company for South African Scottish; landed in England with South African Brigade, Oct. 1915; wounded at Bernagay Wood 11.7.16; at Fampoux, Scarpe River, 12.4.17; slightly gassed Quentin Redoubt 14.3.18; severely gassed Revelon Farm 21.3.18; severely wounded Le Cateau 17.10.18. He is a very well known horseman.

CLERKE, J. M. (D.S.O. L.G. 12.12.19), Major, 3rd Aust. L.H. Regt.

CLIFFORD, E. C. (D.S.O. L.G. 1.1.19), Major, R.F.A. (T.F.); M.C.

CLIFFORD, R. C. (D.S.O. L.G. 19.10.16; b. 17.9.84; 2nd Lt., Ind. Med. Serv., 30.6.10; Capt. 30.7.13; served Europ. War; Despatches; was prisoner of war in Turkey.

CLIFTON, P. J. (D.S.O. L.G. 1.1.17), Capt., R.A. He died of wounds 26.8.18.

CLIFTON, P. R. (see Bruce, P. R.; name changed from Bruce to Clifton).

CLINE, G. A. (D.S.O. L.G. 1.1.18), Major, Can. Engrs.

CLISSOLD, H. (D.S.O. L.G. 3.6.16); e. s. of W. G. Clissold, J.P., C.C., of Nailsworth, Glos.; educ. Clifton College, and Trinity College, Cambridge; Assistant Physics Master at Marlborough College, 1893–94, and a master at Clifton College, 1894–1914; commanded the Cadet Corps, 1906–12; House Master, 1912; served European War from 1914, in R.E.; twice mentioned in Despatches. Major Clissold was killed in action 26.9.17, in France.

CLOETE, C. W. (D.S.O. L.G. 22.8.18), Major, Enslin's Horse, S. African Military Forces.

CLOUGH, J. (D.S.O. L.G. 15.2.19) (Details, L.G. 30.7.19), T/Major, Tank Corps; M.C.

CLOUSTON, J. (D.S.O. L.G. 8.3.19) (Details, L.G. 4.10.19), T/2nd Lt., R.F.A.; M.M.

CLOWES, C. A. (D.S.O. L.G. 1.1.19), Major, Aust. F.A.; M.C.

CLOWES, G. C. K. (D.S.O. L.G. 1.1.17), Capt. (T/Major), Lond. Regt.

CLOWES, H. M. (D.S.O. L.G. 1.1.19); b. 27.4.85; m. Diana Violet, d. of R. W. Pretor-Pinney; educ. Eton; Christ Church, Oxford; served Europ. War from 1914; Despatches; Major, London R.

CLOWES, N. (D.S.O. L.G. 3.6.18); m. Vera Elizabeth Ingleby Pengilly; Major, Permanent Australian Forces; M.C.

CLUTTERBUCK, F. A. (D.S.O. L.G. 23.5.17); b. 28.1.78; s. of Alexander and Adelaide Clutterbuck; m. Evelyn Marguerite, d. of late Rev. G. S. Barrow; three s.; two d.; educ. Mannamead School, Plymouth; ent. R.N., Jan. 1892; Captain 30.6.18; served S. African War; Despatches; Queen's Medal with 5 clasps; Europ. War; Despatches, July, 1918, for valuable services as Second-in-Command of the 20th Destroyer Mine-laying Flotilla.

CLUTTERBUCK, N. S. (D.S.O. L.G. 26.7.18); b. 5.5.79; 2nd Lt., R.M.L.I., 1.1.98; Lt. 1.3.99; Capt. 10.2.06; Maj. 1.6.16; served S. African War, 1900; Europ. War; Despatches.

COAKER, V. A. (D.S.O. L.G. 3.8.20); b. 4.1.78; 2nd Lt., Unatt., 22.1.98; 2nd Lt., Ind. S.C., 30.3.99; Lt., Ind. A., 6.5.01; Capt. 22.1.07; Maj. 1.9.05; A/Lt.-Col; Despatches.

COATES, F. G. C. (D.S.O. L.G. 23.5.17); s. of Rev. G. Coates; ent. R.N.; Lt.-Cdr. 1.10.08.

COATES, P. L. (D.S.O. L.G. 1.1.17), Major (T/Lt.-Col.), Glouc. R.

COATES, W. H. (D.S.O. L.G. 23.5.17), Cdr., R.N.R., R.D.

COATS, S. (D.S.O. L.G. 3.6.18), Major (A/Lt.-Col), A. and S. Highrs.

COBB, E. C. (D.S.O. L.G. 19.8.16); b. Darwin, Falkland Is., 4.9.91; s. of late G. A. Cobb; m. Gladys Ryder, d. of H. J. King; one d.; educ. St. Paul's School, and Sandhurst; 2nd Lt., North'n Regt., 25.3.11; Lt. 27.5.12; Capt. 10.5.15; Adjt., North'd Fus., 16.9.15–22.2.17; served with W. African Regt., 1914; joined Cameroons Ex. Force, Sept. 1914; wounded; Adjt., 26th Northumberland Fusiliers, Sept. 1915; wounded 1 July, 1916; Despatches.

COBB, W. G., M.B. (D.S.O. L.G. 15.10.18), T/Capt., R.A.M.C., att. K.A.R.

COBBE, I. S. (D.S.O. L.G. 3.6.18); b. 1.12.76; 2nd Lt., R.A., 21.3.96; Lt. 21.3.99; Capt. 9.11.01; Major 30.10.14.

COBBOLD, F. A. W. (D.S.O. L.G. 1.1.18), Major, R.G.A.

COBBOLD, R. P. (D.S.O. L.G. 1.1.17); s. of late J. P. Cobbold, M.P., of Ipswich; m. Minnie Diana, widow of Hermann Eckstein; one s.; Lt.-Col. late 60th Rifles; served Burma; N.E. Frontier; S. Africa, 1900 (Despatches; Medal and 5 clasps); Somaliland (Despatches, Medal and clasp); Europ. War, 1915–17; has Star of Ethiopia, 2nd Class.

COBBY, A. H. (D.S.O. L.G. 2.11.18), Lt. (T/Capt.), Aust. F.C., D.F.C. and 2 Bars.

COBHAM, H. W. (D.S.O. L.G. 1.1.17); s. of late T. Cobham; m. 1902, Edith A., d. of late Colonel A. Locke Nicholson, late 107th Regt.; one s.; one d.; 2nd Lt., R. Fus. (Mil.), 1886; 2nd Lt., 1st Worcs. Regt., 1888 (transferred to Indian Cavalry); Capt., 1899; Major 9.5.06; ret. 27.10.10; rejoined; Bt. Lt.-Col. 3.6.17; Lt.-Col.; Brig.-Gen. 10.5.19; served in Bechuanaland Exp., 1884–85; N.W. Frontier of India, Tirah, 1897–98 (Medal, two clasps); Europ. War; Despatches five times; C.M.G., 1919.

COCHRAN, F. E. (D.S.O. L.G. 3.6.18), Major, S. African Infantry.

COCHRAN, G. W. (D.S.O. L.G. 18.8.16); b. 13.1.82; s. of late J. T. Cochran; m. Gertrude Somerville, d. of J. Bacchus; 2nd Lt., Unatt., 8.5.01; Lt., I.A., 3.11.02; Capt. 8.8.03; Major 8.5.10; served Europ. War, 1914–18; Despatches; Bt. Lt.-Col. 3.6.18.

COCHRAN, H. P. G. (D.S.O. L.G. 1.1.18); b. 6.4.77; 2nd Lt., Middlesex R., 5.7.99; Lt. 14.3.00; Capt. 24.9.02; Major (A/Lt.-Col.); served in the S. African War, 1902; Queen's Medal with 2 clasps. He was killed in action 24.3.18.

COCHRAN-PATRICK, W. J. C. KENNEDY- (D.S.O. L.G. 17.9.17); b. 25.5.96; s. of Capt. N. K. Cochran-Patrick, R.S.F.; m. Ella Gross; educ. Wellington College; Sandhurst; went to Trinity College, Cambridge; on outbreak of war transferred to Sandhurst; commissioned in R.B. 4.2.15; att. R.F.C.; Major; Squadron Commander, R.A.F.; landed in France 24.12.15; Despatches; M.C. and Bar.

COCHRANE, THE HON. A. D. (D.S.O. L.G. 13.9.15) (Bar, L.G. 11.11.19), Cdr., R.N. (see "The Distinguished Service Order," from its institution to 31.12.15, by same publishers).

COCHRANE, C. W. (D.S.O. L.G. 3.6.18), Lt.-Col., A.S.C.

COCHRANE, E. W. W., M.B. (D.S.O. L.G. 1.1.18); b. 2.5.72; Lt., R.A.M.C., 29.7.96; Capt. 29.7.99; Major 29.1.08; Lt.-Col. 1.3.15; T/Col. 29.9.17 to 16.3.19; Despatches.

COCHRANE, M. E. (D.S.O. L.G. 14.7.16); b. 1879; y. s. of late J. H. Cochrane; m. 1908, Charlotte, d. of Col. W. H. Newton, R.A.; one s.; three d.; ent. R.N., 1893; Lt., 1900; A/Comdr., 1916; Cdr., 1919; serv. in China, 1900 (Medal and clasp); Somaliland, 1903–04 (Medal and clasp); Europ., 1914; Chevalier St. Maurice and St. Lazarus; Comp. of the Order of the White Eagle, 4th Class, with Swords.

J. B. Cockburn.

COCHRANE, HON. T. G. F., B.A. (D.S.O. L.G. 1.1.19); b. 19.3.83; e. s. of 1st Baron Cochrane and Lady Gertrude Boyle, d. of 6th Earl of Glasgow; m. Hon. Elin Douglas-Pennant, d. of 2nd Baron Penrhyn; educ. Eton; Christ Church, Oxford; served Europ. War, 1914–19; Major, Black Watch, S.R.; wounded thrice; Despatches thrice.

COCK, W. C. (D.S.O. L.G. 27.7.18), S. African Sig. Serv.

COCKBURN, G. E. G. (D.S.O. L.G. 17.9.17); b. 6.4.94; 2nd Lt., R.I. Fus., 3.9.13; Lt. 17.9.14; Capt. 7.8.16; Despatches; M.C.

COCKBURN, J. B. (D.S.O. L.G. 11.1.19); b. 23.12.70; y. s. of Sir Ed. Cockburn, 8th Bart; m. 1919, Isabel Hunter, y. d. of late J. McQueen; educ. Cheltenham Coll.; 2nd Lt., R.W. Fus., 23.12.93; Lt. 8.5.96; Capt. 6.10.00; Maj. 12.5.12; Bt. Lt.-Col. 3.6.15; Lt.-Col. 31.1.19, comdg. R.W. Fus.; serv. in Lagos Hinterland, 1898 (Med., cl.); Munshi Exp., 1900 (clasp; Despatches); S. Afr., 1901–2, including operations in Transvaal and O.R.C. (Med., 5 cl.); Nigeria, 1906, action against Sokoto Rebels (Med. and cl.); in Cameroon Campaign, 1914–16 (Despatches and Bt. Lt.-Col.); France, 1916–18 (Despatches twice); twice severely wounded; Officer, Légion d'Honneur; 1914–15 Star; awarded Silver Medal Royal Humane Society.

COCKBURN, W. (D.S.O. L.G. 26.7.18), Lt. (T/Capt.), N. Som. Yeo.; M.C.

COCKCRAFT, L. W. LA T. (D.S.O. L.G. 3.6.16); b. 20.6.80; s. of late Col. La T. Cockcraft, R.M.A.; m. V. H. Case-Morriss; 2nd Lt., R.A., 22.11.99; Lt. 16.3.01; Capt. 2.12.08; Major 30.10.14; served S. Afr., 1900–2 (Despatches; Q.'s. Med., 3 cl., and K.'s Med., 2 cl.); Europ. War, Suez Canal, Cape Helles, Gallipoli, France; Despatches; Bt. Lt.-Col. 1.1.19; Belgian Croix de Guerre.

COCKERAM, A. (D.S.O. L.G. 18.10.17) (Details, L.G. 7.3.18), Lt., Can. Inf.

COCKERELL, A. R. (D.S.O. L.G. 26.11.17) (Details, L.G. 6.4.18), 2nd Lt., N.Z. Inf., 25.1.17.

COCKHILL, J. B. (D.S.O. L.G. 7.11.18), Lt. (A/Capt.), West Riding R.; M.C.

COCKRAM, F. S. (D.S.O. L.G. 1.1.17), Capt., Middlesex R.

COCKRELL, L. C. (D.S.O. L.G. 27.6.17), Lt. (A/Lt.-Cdr.), R.N.R.

CODRINGTON, G. R. (D.S.O. L.G. 1.1.18), Major, Yeom.

COFFEY, R. (D.S.O. L.G. 1.1.18), Major (A/Lt.-Col.), R.A.M.C., T.F., 18.10.14.

COFFIN, C. (D.S.O. L.G. 1.1.17) (Bar, L.G. 26.7.18); V.C.; C.B., Col. (T/Col.-Comdt.), R.E. (see "The Victoria Cross," by same publishers).

COGAN, L. D. B. (D.S.O. L.G. 1.1.19), Capt. (A/Lt.-Col.), R.A.M.C., T.F.

COGHLAN, F. T. (D.S.O. L.G. 1.1.18), Major (A/Lt.-Col.), Can. F. Arty.

COHEN, H. E. (D.S.O. L.G. 1.1.17); s. of M. Cohen; educ. St. Xavier's College, Kew, Melbourne; Lt.-Col. 15.3.09, Aust. Artillery; served Europ. War; Despatches; C.M.G., 1918.

COHEN, J. W. (D.S.O. L.G. 3.6.16); b. 1874; s. of late N. L. Cohen; m. Katherine, d. of late Rt. Hon. A. Cohen, K.C.; one s.; one d.; educ. Clifton College; Merton College, Oxford; joined Queen's Westminster Rifle Volunteers, 1893; served S. African War, 1900, with C.I.V.; Despatches; Medal and 4 clasps. Lt.Col. Cohen served in the Europ. War with Queen's Westminster Rifles and Army Signals, 1914–19; Despatches; C.M.G.; promoted Lt.-Col. 17.9.17; Croix de Guerre, France.

COHEN, L. (D.S.O. L.G. 27.7.18), T/Capt., S. African Defence Force; M.C.

COKE, A. L. H. D. (D.S.O. L.G. 29.11.18), Cdr., R.N., 31.12.18.

COKE, THE HON. E. (D.S.O. L.G. 26.9.17) (Details, L.G. 9.1.18); b. 17.10.79; 6th s. of 2nd Earl of Leicester and his 2nd wife, Hon. Georgina Caroline Cavendish, d. of 2nd Baron Chesham; served Europ. War; Capt., 5th Bn. R. Bgde.; Despatches; M.C.

COKE, E. S. D'E. (D.S.O. L.G. 1.1.18); b. 31.12.72; m. Maud, d. of late J. A. Deane; two s.; two d.; 2nd Lt., K.O.S.Bord., 10.10.94; Lt. 29.7.97; Capt. 31.3.01; Adjt. 28.3.04–30.3.05; Capt. 10.11.13; Bt. Lt.-Col. 1.1.16; Lt.-Col. 28.4.19; T/Brig.-Gen. 5.2.16; Colonel 7.6.20; served Chitral, 1895; severely wounded; Medal with clasp; N.W.F. of India, 1897–98; two clasps; Europ. War, 1914–18; Despatches; Bt. Lt.-Col. 1.1.19; C.M.G.; Legion of Honour.

COKER, H. O. (D.S.O. L.G. 4.6.17), Major, Rhodesia R.

COLAM, S. D'E. (D.S.O. L.G. 2.4.19) (Details, L.G. 10.12.19), Capt., G. Hldrs., S.R.; M.C.

COLAN, H. N. (D.S.O. L.G. 17.4.16); b. 15.6.80; 2nd Lt., Manch. R., 27.7.01; Lt. 10.11.02; Lt., Ind. A., 3.3.03; Capt. 27.7.10; Maj. 27.7.16; served in S. Afr. (Queen's Med., 3 cl.; King's Med., 2 cl.); Despatches.

COLAN, W. R. B. (D.S.O. L.G. 25.8.17); b. 25.5.70; 2nd Lt., W. York. R., 3.5.90; Lt., Ind. S.C., 14.12.91; Capt., Ind. A., 3.5.01; Maj. 3.5.08; Lt.-Col. 3.5.16; retired 22.11.21; Despatches.

COLBECK, B. B. (D.S.O. L.G. 14.1.16); b. 17.6.79; 3rd s. of Dr. T. W. Colbeck, L.R.C.P. and M.R.C.S.; educ. Dover College and Woolwich; ent. R.A. 14.9.98; 2nd Lt. 16.2.01; Capt. 25.2.04; Adjt., R.A., 11.7.04–30.5.06; Adjt. 4.11.12–29.10.14; Major 30.10.14; serv. in S. Afr.; Queen's Med., 3 clasps; King's Med., 2 clasps; Despatches; Bt. Lt.-Col. 3.6.19; Greek Military Cross.

COLBY, C. J. H. SPENCE- (see Spence-Colby, C. J. H.).

COLDWELL, W. G. A. (D.S.O. L.G. 3.6.19); b. 21.10.92; 2nd Lt., North'n R., 14.2.12; Lt. 19.2.13; Capt. 1.10.15; T/Lt.-Col.; Despatches.

COLE, F. M. (D.S.O. L.G. 3.6.18), Lt.-Col., Can. Arty., 22.4.92.

COLE, G. E. (D.S.O. L.G. 4.6.17), Major, Aust. A.M.C.

COLE-HAMILTON, C. G. (D.S.O. L.G. 31.10.02) (Bar, L.G. 30.1.20), Lt.-Col., R. of O., late R. Ir. Rifles; C.M.G. (see "The Distinguished Service Order," from its institution to 31.12.15, by same publishers).

COLE-HAMILTON, H. A. W. (D.S.O. L.G. 27.6.19); b. 10.10.87; s. of J. Cole-Hamilton; educ. Charterhouse; 2nd Lt., York and Lanc. R., 16.12.08; Lt. 1.4.11; Capt. 25.4.15; served Europ. War in France, 1914–18; prisone of war, 1918; Despatches thrice.

COLEMAN, G. B. (D.S.O. L.G. 1.1.17); b. 19.8.77; 2nd Lt., R. Garr. R., 5.11.02; Lt. 11.5.04; 2nd Lt., A.S.C., 1.10.06; Lt., A.S.C., 1.10.07; Capt. 9.6.12; Major, R.A.S.C., 1.1.16; Lt.-Col. 8.9.19; served Europ. War; Despatches; Bt. Lt.-Col. 1.1.18.

COLEMAN, P. G. (D.S.O. L.G. 26.7.17), 2nd Lt. (T/Lt., N. Staffs. R.).

COLEMAN, T. R. (D.S.O. L.G. 18.7.17), T/Major, Can. Inf.; M.C.

J. F. S. D. Coleridge.

COLERIDGE, J. F. S. D. (D.S.O. L.G. 3.6.16) (Bar, L.G. 2.12.18); b. 25.4.78; s. of Lt. and Adjt. P. D. Coleridge, R.M.L.I.; m. Marjorie M. Kemball-Cook; two d.; educ. Wellington and Sandhurst; 2nd Lt., Unatt., 20.7.98; 2nd Lt., I.S.C., 16.4.00; Lt., Ind. A., 20.5.01; Capt. 20.7.07; Maj 1.9.15; Temp. Brig.-Gen. 31.10.17–27.11.18; Col. 30.6.20; served in Tibet, 1903–4 (Med. and cl.); N.E. Frontier of India, 1911–12; Medal and clasp; Despatches; Europ. War, Egypt, Gallipoli and France; Despatches thrice; Bt. Lt.-Col. 1.1.17; Bt. Col. 1.1.19; C.B.; C.M.G.

COLES, G. A. (D.S.O. L.G. 15.9.16), Cdr., R.N., 31.12.16; served Europ. War, 1914–19, including Jutland Bank.

COLES, J. H. (D.S.O. L.G. 26.7.18), Capt. (A/Lt.-Col.), 1st Bn. E. Yorks. R. He was killed in action near Wytschaete, Belgium, 24.4.18.

COLES, W. H. (D.S.O. L.G. 3.6.18); T. Major Middlx. R.

COLLACOTT, J. R. (D.S.O. L.G. 1.1.17); b. 21.10.67; Lt., R.A., 18.5.92; Insp. of Ord. Mach., 3rd Class, 1.4.96; 2nd Class, 18.5.98; 1st Class, 18.5.07; Chf. Insp. 28.11.17; Lt.-Col. 20.7.17; Despatches.

COLLARD, A. M. (D.S.O. L.G. 1.1.18); b. 6.5.77; 2nd Lt., D. of Corn. L. Inf., 23.12.96; Lt. 23.12.98; Capt. 19.2.04; Major 1.9.15; served in op. on N.W. Frontier of India, 1897–98, with Tirah Exp. Force; Medal with 2 clasps; Europ. War; Lt.-Col. 12.1.21; Despatches; Bt. Lt.-Col. 1.1.19.

COLLARD, B. ST. G. (D.S.O. L.G. 26.4.18); b. 27.2.76; s. of late Rev. Canon J. M. Collard; m. Rosamond, d. of J. F. Starkey; one s.; one d.; educ. Clifton College; entered Britannia, 1890; Capt. 1915; served (including Europ. War) Naval Staff Intelligence Division, 1912–15; Assistant Beach Master, "W" Beach, Gallipoli, 1915; invalided home; commanded Monitor Lord Clive in the Dover Patrol, 1915–18.

COLLAS, W. J. J. (D.S.O. L.G. 25.8.17); b. 15.4.79; 2nd Lt., S. Staff. R., 21.4.00; Lt. 23.10.01; Capt. 28.12.08; Maj. 1.9.15; Despatches; Bt. Lt.-Col. 3.6.19.

COLLETT, E. J. (D.S.O. L.G. 22.8.18), Lt.-Col., 8th Mtd. Rifles, S. African Military Forces.

COLLETT, G. F. (D.S.O. L.G. 3.6.18), Major (T/Lt.-Col.), Glouc. R.

COLLETT, H. B. (D.S.O. L.G. 1.1.17); b. 12.11.77; 2nd s. of late F. A. E. Collett; m. Annie, d. of T. E. Whitfield; two s.; educ. Perth Grammar School, W. Australia; ent. the Jubilee Service, 1891; Volunteer Force, 1894; comd. 11th Aus. Inf. Regt., 1908–15; raised and comd. 20th Bn. Colonel Collett served in Egypt, Gallipoli and France; C.M.G., 1919; Despatches.

COLLEY, F. (D.S.O. L.G. 22.9.16) (Bar, L.G. 16.8.17), T/Capt., York and Lanc. R. D.S.O. awarded for services near Ovillers.

COLLIER, B. W. (D.S.O. L.G. 2.12.18); b. 18.3.74; 2nd Lt., S. Wales Bord., 7.12.95; Lt. 14.4.97; Capt. 26.4.06; Maj. 10.8.15; served S. African War, 1900–2 (Queen's Medal with 3 clasps; King's Medal with 2 clasps); retired 17.2.20, with rank of Lt.-Col., Army.

COLLIER, E. V. (D.S.O. L.G. 27.10.17) (Details, L.G. 18.3.18); b. 12.9.78; s. of late Capt. E. R. Collier, of H.M. Indian Marine, and Margaret Collett (*née* Jeffrey); educ. Falmouth Grammar School, and private tuition; served Europ. War with Can. Ex. Force, Infantry, Vimy and Hill 70; wounded, Despatches; with Can. Engineers, Amiens, Arras and Cambrai Battles; Capt., 1916; Major, 1916; Lt.-Col., 1919.

COLLIER, R. H. (D.S.O. L.G. 1.1.18), Capt. (T/Lt.-Col.), R.F.C., S.R.

COLLINGRIDGE, H. F. (D.S.O. L.G. 10.6.21); b. 24.7.81; 2nd Lt., R. Scots, 5.1.01; Ind. Army 19.12.02; Lt. 5.4.03; Capt. 2.3.09; Major 1.9.15; served S. African War, 1900; Queen's Medal with clasp; Europ. War; Despatches.

COLLINGS-WELLS, J. S. (D.S.O. L.G. 18.7.17), Capt. (A/Lt.-Col.), Bedfords. R.; V.C. He was killed in action 27.3.18. (See "The Victoria Cross," by same publishers.)

COLLINGS-WELLS, R. P. (D.S.O. L.G. 3.3.17); b. Nov. 1882; s. of A. Collings-Wells, of Brands House, Hughenden, Bucks; educ. Harrow; Sandhurst; entered 15th The King's Hussars, 1902; served in India and S. Africa; Europ. War (severely wounded at Mons); with Duke of Westminster's armoured cars in Egypt; took part in the whole campaign against the Sennussi (slightly wounded); Despatches twice; Médaille Khédiviale; O.B.E., 1919.

R. P. Collings-Wells.

COLLINGWOOD, C. W. (D.S.O. L.G. 14.1.16); b. 29.4.73; s. of late Maj.-Genl. Clennell Collingwood, R.A.; m. 1906, N. P., o. d. of H. Pollock; one s.; educ. Halifax, N.S., and R.M.A., Woolwich; ent. R.A. 22.7.92; Lt. 22.7.95; Capt. 1.2.00; Adjt. 16.1.01–31.3.03; Adjt. 1.4.03–30.12.04; Maj. 1.1.14; Bt. Lt.-Col. 1.1.17; Bt. Col. 1.1.19; Col. 8.9.20; Temp. Brig.-Gen. from 9.5.17; C.M.G., 1918; A.D. of Ordnance from 1920; Despatches three times.

COLLINS, A. J. (D.S.O. L.G. 26.7.18), Major, Aust. A.M.C.; M.C.

COLLINS, C. B. (D.S.O. L.G. 26.6.16); ent. R.E.; Lt. 18.2.86; Capt. 7.10.96; Maj. 4.11.04; Lt.-Col. (T/Col.); C.M.G. He died 1.3.17.

COLLINS, D. S. (D.S.O. L.G. 3.6.16) (Bar, L.G. 26.7.18); b. 14.1.81; s. of H. M. Collins (late Manager in Australasia of Reuter's) and Isabella M. Collins; m. Edith Lakeman, d. of F. Collins; educ. St. Michael's, Westgate-on-Sea, and Haileybury College; R.M.A., Woolwich; ent. R.E. 22.11.19; Lt. 27.8.02; Capt. 22.11.08; Maj. 12.8.16; Bt. Lt.-Col. 1.1.19; serv. S. Afr., 1901–2; in Sept. 1914, took command of 71st Fd. Coy. R.E.; disembarked with it at Helles (Gallipoli) on 5.7.15; was wounded on 12th July; rejoined company at Anzac in Sept. 1915; moved to Suvla with it, and remained there till evacuation at end of December (mentioned in Despatches and D.S.O.); invalided from Mudros in Jan. to England; took command of 224th Fd. Coy. in May, 1916, in England; landed in France 2.6.16; appointed Bde. Major of 121st Inf. Bde. 13.9.16 (mentioned in Despatches 1.1.17); appointed C.R.E. of a division 7.5.17; Despatches twice.

COLLINS, F. R. (D.S.O. L.G. 1.1.18); b. 11.5.73; s. of late Rev. R. Collins, M.A., C.M.S.; m. Alicia Eleanor, d. of late J. E. H. A. Wright; one s.; one d.; Lt.-Colonel, S. Afr. Engrs.; served S.W. Africa, 1914–15; France, 1916–19; Despatches; Officier, Légion d'Honneur.

COLLINS, H. S. (D.S.O. L.G. 3.6.16); b. 7.10.87; 2nd Lt., Shrops. L. Inf., 6.10.06; Lt. 29.3.09; Capt. 10.6.15; retired 7.8.20 with rank of Major in the Army; Despatches.

COLLINS, P. R. M. (D.S.O. L.G. 4.6.17); b. 16.7.90; 2nd Lt., R.A., 23.12.10; Lt. 23.12.13; Capt., A/Major, R.G.A. He died of wounds 25.6.17.

COLLINS, R. F. (D.S.O. L.G. 26.7.18), T/Capt., R. Fus.

COLLINS, R. J. (D.S.O. L.G. 3.6.16); b. 22.8.80; y. s. of late H. Collins; m. Violet Hill, widow of Capt. E. S. Hill, and d. of Alex. Monro, C.I.E.; educ. Marlborough Coll.; ent. R. Berks. Regt. 2.8.99; Lt. 12.12.00; Capt. 2.6.00; Major 1.9.15; T/Brig.-Gen. 16.7.18–23.3.19; serv. S. Afr., 1899–02 (Queen's Med., 3 cl., and King's Med., 2 cl.); Egyptian Army, 1904–11 (A.D.C., Sirdar, 23.8.05–30.9.08); Europ. War, 1914–19; Bt. Major 8.6.15; Bt. Lt.-Col. 1.1.17; C.M.G.; Despatches nine times; 4th Class Medjidie; Chevalier Legion of Honour; Croix de Guerre.

COLLINS, R. T. (D.S.O. L.G. 1.1.18); o. s. of Dr. and Mrs. Wolfenden Collins; Major (T/Lt.-Col.), R.A.M.C.; served European War (attached 17th F.A.); Croix de Guerre. He was killed in action 18.9.18.

COLLINS, W. A. (D.S.O. L.G. 1.1.18); b. 26.3.73; e. s. of late A. G. Collins; m. Grace, d. of W. Brander; three s.; one d.; educ. Temple Grove; Harrow; joined R.A.S.C., Feb. 1915; became Lt.-Col.; served in France, May, 1915–July, 1919; appointed A.D. of Supply and Transport, 1918; Despatches; Ordem Militar de Airs (Portuguese), 1919; Chairman and Managing Director, William Collins, Sons & Co. Ltd., the publishers.

COLLINS, W. F. (D.S.O. L.G. 3.6.18); b. 17.9.65; s. of late Rev. W. Collins, and Jane, d. of late Rev. T. Collins; m. Lady Evelyn Innes-Ker, d. of the 7th Duke of Roxburghe; educ. Charterhouse; University College, Oxford; 1st com. 6.2.89; Col. 19.8.19, formerly 2nd Dragoons; retired 18.1.20; served S. African War; Queen's Medal with 3 clasps; Europ. War; Despatches.

COLLINS, W. H. (D.S.O. L.G. 17.12.17), (Details, L.G.23.4.18); Aust. A.M.C.

COLLINS, W. R. (D.S.O. L.G. 22.8.18), Col. Commandant, Mounted Brig., S. African Mil. Forces.

COLLINSON, H., M.B., F.R.C.S. (D.S.O. L.G. 1.1.17); b. 19.8.76; s. of late J. W. Collinson; m. Alice Maude, d. of late J. B. Pickford; served Europ. War, 1914–18; Lt.-Col., R.A.M.C., T.F.; Despatches; C.B.; C.M.G.; is Chevalier, Légion d'Honneur.

COLLISHAW, R. (D.S.O. L.G. 11.8.17) (Bar, L.G. 21.9.18), Lt. (T/Major, late R.N.A.S.), R.A.F.; D.S.C.; D.F.C.

COLLISON, C. S. (D.S.O. L.G. 3.6.16); b. 23.4.71; 2nd s. of late C. S. Collison; m. 1904, Geraldine, o. d. Col. J. G. White, C.M.G., D.L.; educ. Charterhouse; ent. the 57th (Mdx.) Regt. 19.10.92; Adjt., W. India Regt., 1902–3; Adjt., 1st (Vol.) Bn. Devon R., 1904–8; transferred to the Duke of Wellington's West Riding Regt., 1906; retired 5.4.11; joined the 5th (Reserve) Bn. Middlx. Regt.; Major (R. of O.), 1.9.15; Lt.-Col., 1912; served S. Africa (Queen's Med., 4 cl.; Europ. War; Despatches; Bt. Col. (R. of O.), Duke of Wellington's Regt., 3.6.18; Col. (R. of O.), L.G. 1.1.19.

COLLUM, H. W. A. (D.S.O. L.G. 1.1.17); b. 28.9.75; 2nd Lt., A.S.C., 21.2.00; Lt. 1.4.01; Capt. 7.1.03; Major, R.A.S.C., 5.8.14; Bt. Lt.-Col. 1.1.19; Lt.-Col., R.A.S.C., 5.1.21; S. African War, 1900–2; Queen's Medal with 3 clasps; King's Medal with 2 clasps; Sudan, 1908; Egyptian Medal; Sudan, 1910; Medal with clasp; Europ. War; Despatches; Bt. Lt.-Col. 1.1.19.

COLLUM, J. A. (D.S.O. L.G. 17.10.17); b. 3.8.84; 2nd Lt. (Unatt.), 13.8.04; 2nd Lt., Ind. A., 3.11.05; Lt. 13.11.06; Capt. 13.8.13; Major 13.8.19; Despatches.

COLLYER, J. J. (D.S.O. L.G. 22.8.18); b. 21.9.70; e. s. of J. M. Collyer; m. Hilda, d. of M. H. Quinn; served European War, 1915–18; C.B.; C.M.G.; Brig.-Gen., late Chief of the General Staff, S. African Military Forces.

COLMAN, P. E. (D.S.O. L.G. 3.6.19), Major (A/Lt.-Col.), Can. Mtd. Rif.; M.C.

COLQUHOUN, A. G. C. (D.S.O. L.G. 15.2.19) (Details, L.G. 30.7.19); b. 26.1.87; 2nd Lt., A. and S. Highrs., 4.5.07; Lt. 28.4.09; Capt. 12.12.14; served Europ. War; Bt. Major 1.1.19; Despatches.

COLQUHOUN, D. (D.S.O. L.G. 26.11.17) (Details, L.G.6.4.18); Lt.-Col., N.Z.Inf.

COLQUHOUN, SIR I. (D.S.O. L.G. 20.10.16) (Bar, L.G. 26.7.18); b. 20.6.87; s. of 13th Bart. and Justine, d. of John Kennedy; 14th Bart., of Colquhoun and Luss; Chief of Clan; m. 1915, Geraldine Bryde, d. of Francis Tennant; 2 s.; 2 d.; 2nd Lt., S. Gds., 1.8.10; Lt. 1.4.12; Capt. 30.1.15; Europ. War, 1914–18; Despatches; Bt. Major 1.1.18; wounded. D.S.O. awarded for gallantry at Les Bœufs 5.9.16.

COLQUHOUN, J. C. (D.S.O. L.G. 1.1.17); b. 31.12.70; s. of W. C. Colquhoun and Charlotte Emily Julian, d. of Rev. L. Shafto Orde; Major, R. of O., Leins. R.; served S. African War, 1902; Queen's Medal, 4 clasps; Europ. War, 1914–18.

COLQUHOUN, M. A. (D.S.O. L.G. 14.1.16), Major, 38th Can. Rgt., 19.6.15 served in Europ. War; Lt.-Col., 4th Can. Inf. Bn.; C.M.G.

COLSON, D. F. (D.S.O. L.G. 1.1.18); e. s. of the late A. Colson, M.I.C.E., M.I.E.E.; ent. R.E.; Major, T.F.; 20 years' service in Volunteers and Territorial Forces; served in S. Afr. (Queen's Med., 2 cl.); served Europ. War, Gallipoli, France, Salonika, Egypt and through the whole of the Palestine Campaign under Sir E. Allenby; Despatches twice. He died 3.2.19, at Mersina, Asia Minor.

COLSTON, THE HON. E. M. (L.G. 26.6.16); b. 31.12.80; e. s. of 1st Baron Roundway; educ. Eton; m. 1904, Blanche Gladys, d. of G. Duddell; one d.; ent. G. Gds. 21.2.00; Lt. 23.8.03; Capt. 12.5.08; Maj. 13.3.15; Lt.-Col., Nov. 1919 (T/Brig.-Gen.) 25.5.17; served S. Africa (wounded; Queen's Med., 3 cl.); Europ. War; was present throughout the Retreat from Mons, also at the battles of the Marne, the Aisne, etc.; was wounded and invalided home; was subsequently sent to Egypt with the rank of T/Lt.-Colonel to form a School of Technical Instruction for the whole army in Egypt, termed the Imperial School of Instruction; Despatches six times; Bt. Lt.-Col. 3.6.17; C.M.G., 1918; M.V.O., 1908; Order of the Nile; Order of White Eagle of Serbia.

COLT, H. A. (D.S.O. L.G. 7.11.18), T/Major (A/Lt.-Col.), Glos. R.; M.C.

COLVILE, A. M. (D.S.O. L.G. 3.6.18); b. 12.4.76; 2nd Lt., R.A., 21.3.96; Lt. 21.3.99; Capt. 24.8.01; Adjt. 4.5.03–21.1.06; Major 30.10.14; Lt.-Col. 1.5.21; Despatches.

COLVILE, M. B. F. (D.S.O. L.G. 11.4.19), Lt.-Cdr., R.N.

COLVIN, G. L. (D.S.O. L.G. 1.1.17); b. 27.3.78; e. s. of late C. S. Colvin, C.S.I., Secretary for Public Works, India Office, London; m. Katherine Isabella Mylne; one s.; one d.; educ. Westminster; served in the Army in France and Italy during the Europ. War, and from 1918 to termination of war was Director-General Transportation, B.E.F., Italy; Despatches five times; C.B.; C.M.G.; Hon. Brig.-Gen. in the Army; Director of Plans, Ministry of Transport.

COMBE, H. (D.S.O. L.G. 12.2.15) (Bar L.G. 15.10.18), Major, Hussars (see "The Distinguished Service Order," from its institution to 31.12.1915, by same publishers).

COMBE, H. C. S. (D.S.O. L.G. 7.11.18); b. 28.2.90; 2nd Lt., R.H.G., 15.9.09; Lt. 7.10.11; Capt. 13.5.15; Tank Corps 5.1.18 to 7.8.19; Major 26.8.20; Despatches.

COMBE, S. B. (D.S.O. L.G. 11.1.19); b. 13.6.78; y. s. of General B. Combe, C.B.; m. Grace, 2nd d. of G. B. Behrens; 2nd Lt., Unatt., 22.1.98; 2nd Lt., Ind. S.C., 23.3.99; Lt., Ind. Army, 22.4.00; Capt. 22.1.07; Maj. 1.9.15; Bt. Lt.-Col. 3.6.17; M.C.; retired 22.1.21.

COMBER, H. G. (D.S.O. L.G. 1.1.18), Capt. (T/Major), Unatt. List.

COMBS, H. V. (D.S.O. L.G. 1.1.19), Capt. (A/Major), Oxf. and Bucks. L.I.; M.C.

COMMINGS, P. R. C. (D.S.O. L.G. 14.1.16); b. 9.7.80; ent. S. Staffs. Regt. 2.7.00; Lt. 25.2.03; Adjt. 14.8.07–13.8.10; Capt. 19.10.09; Maj. 1.9.15; serv. S. Africa, 1899–1902 (Queen's Med., 3 cl., and King's Med., 2 cl.); Europ. War, 1914–18; Despatches; Bt. Lt.-Col. 3.6.17; C.M.G.

COMMON, L. A. (D.S.O. L.G. 4.6.17), Lt. (T/Major), R.F.A.

COMPTON, W. B. (D.S.O. L.G. 23.5.17); m. Madeleine, d. of the late J. Pyman; one s.; ent. R.N., 1890; Lt., 1899; Capt. 30.6.17; M.V.O., 1905; served Europ. War, 1914–17.

COMPTON-SMITH, G. L. (D.S.O. L.G. 18.7.17); b. 19.8.89; 2nd Lt., York. R., 20.4.10; Lt. 19.7.11; Capt., R.W. Fus., 10.6.15; Bt. Major 3.6.17; A/Lt.-Col.; Despatches. He served in Ireland, and sent the following message to his wife: " I am to be shot in an hour's time. Dearest, your hubby will die with your name on his lips, your face before his eyes, and he will die like an Englishman and a soldier." The gallant officer was murdered by Sinn Feiners after being held captive for a month.

COMYN, E. W. (D.S.O. L.G. 3.6.18); b. 2.8.68; s. of late S. E. Comyn, M.D.; m., 1st, Elinor, d. of J. Fall; 2nd, Margaret, widow of late Lt. G. S. Taylor, R.A.S.C., M.C.; educ. Oxford Military College; R.M.A., Woolwich; 2nd Lt., R.A., 16.2.87; Lt. 16.2.90; Capt. 9.10.97; Maj. 11.4.09; Lt.-Col. 30.10.14; served on Western Front, 1915–18; Despatches four times; C.M.G.; Croix de Guerre.

COMYN, L. J. (D.S.O. L.G. 14.1.16); b. 13.3.72; s. of A. N. Comyn; m. Mary Esther, d. of Mr. de Courcey Duff; one s.; one d.; educ. Clongowes Wood Coll. and Dublin University; 2nd Lt., Conn. Rangers, 20.5.99; Lt. 6.11.09; Capt. 27.1.08; Adjt. 1.4.08–31.3.11; Maj. 1.9.15.; Despatches; Bt. Lt.-Col. 1.1.17; C.M.G., 1918.

CONDER, G. (D.S.O. L.G. 3.6.16); b. 25.3.73; s. of late Rev. A. Conder, Rector of Middleton, Sussex; educ. Middleton School, Bognor; Capt., A.V.C., 5.10.03; Maj. 6.7.13; served S. Africa, 1899–02 (Queen's Med., 3 clasps and King's Med., 2 clasps); slightly wounded; Europ. War, 1914–18; Despatches twice.

CONGREVE, F. L. (D.S.O. L.G. 1.1.19); b. 21.3.81; 2nd Lt., R.A., 19.12.00; Lt. 19.12.03; Capt. 6.1.13; Adjt., R.A., 5.1.15–19.7.15; Maj. 20.7.15; Despatches; M.C.

CONGREVE, W. LA T. (D.S.O. L.G. 16.5.16), Major, R. Bgde.; V.C.; M.C. He was killed in action 20.7.16. (See " The Victoria Cross," by same publishers).

CONINGHAM, A. (D.S.O. L.G. 26.9.17) (Details, L.G. 9.1.18), 2nd Lt. (T/Capt.) R.F.C. Spec. Res.; M.C.

CONINGHAM, F. E. (D.S.O. L.G. 7.2.18); b. 6.6.70; 2nd Lt., Border R., 8.10.90; Lt. 10.7.01; Major 8.10.08; Lt.-Col., Ind. I.A.; 8.10.16; Col. 17.5.20; C.B.; C.M.G.; Despatches.

CONLAN, V. D. R. (D.S.O. L.G. 4.2.18) (Details, L.G. 5.7.18), T/Major, A.S.C.

CONNELL, H. J. (D.S.O. L.G. 1.1.19), Major, Aust. Mil. Forces; M.C.

CONNELLY, E. W. (D.S.O. L.G. 1.1.18), Major, Aust. Inf.

CONNOLLY, C. E. (D.S.O. L.G. 17.9.17) (Bar, L.G. 1.1.19), Major, Lord Strathcona's Horse, Can. Cav. His D.S.O. was awarded for gallantry from 4 to 12.6.17, S.W. of Lens.

CONNOLLY, L. A. (D.S.O. L.G. 3.6.19), Capt. (A/Major), R.F.A.; M.C.

CONNOP, H. E. (D.S.O. L.G. 10.8.21), Major, 35th Scinde Horse, Indian Army.

CONNOR, F. P., F.R.C.S. (D.S.O. L.G. 7.2.18); s. of late J. Connor; b. 5.10.77; m. Grace Ellen, d. of R. O. Lees; educ. St. Bartholomew's Hospital; Lt., I.M.S., 1.9.02; Capt. 1.9.05; Major 1.3.14; left India with Indian Exp. Force, Sept. 1914; served in France, England and Mesopotamia; Despatches four times; 1914 Star; Bt. Lt.-Col. 3.6.19.

CONNOR, REV. J. M., M.A. (D.S.O. L.G. 1.1.19); b. 27.1.72; T/Ch. to the Forces, 3rd Class, 1.1.21; served Europ. War; Despatches.

CONRAN, W. D. B. (D.S.O. L.G. 25.8.17); b. 4.12.81; 2nd Lt., R.E., 2.5.00; Lt. 2.5.03; Capt. 2.5.10; Major 2.11.16; Despatches.

CONRICK, H. V. P. (D.S.O. L.G. 18.7.17), Major, Aust. A.M.C.

CONSTANTINE, C. F. (D.S.O. L.G. 1.1.17) (Bar, L.G. 8.3.19) (Details, L.G. 4.10.19); b. 21.10.83; s. of C. Constantine, late Superintendent, R.N.W. Mounted Police, and Henrietta A. Constantine, d. of E. Armstrong, Esq.; m. Marie Gladys, d. of John Bell and Elizabeth Bell (née Carruthers); one d.; educ. Upper Canada College, Toronto, and R.M.C., Kingston, Canada; commissioned R. Can. Arty.; Lt. 22.6.05; Capt., 1909; Major 22.2.15; Lt.-Col. 3.5.17; Brig. Major, 1st Can. Div. Arty., 22.9.14, and served on the Western Front with them until June, 1915; from then until August he commanded 7th By. Can. F.A.; Aug. 1915, to Feb. 1917, Brigade Major, 2nd Can. Div. Arty.; G.S.O.2, Can. Div., Feb. to May, 1917; Lt.-Col. commanding 5th Can. F.A. Brigade, 3.5.17 to 23.4.19; Despatches four times; 1914–15 Star; Legion of Honour; Professor of Artillery, R.M. College, Canada; holds King George's Coronation Medal.

CONWAY, A. S. (D.S.O. L.G. 14.1.16); b. Oct. 1877; 7th s. of late J. Conway and Helen R. Conway; educ. Haileybury and Sandhurst; entered N. Staffs. R., Feb. 1898; Capt., April, 1906; Major; S. African War (Queen's and King's Medals and 5 clasps); Europ. War from Sept. 1914; Despatches. He was killed in action 17.6.17. Brigadier-General W. F. Sweny wrote to Mrs. Conway: " Not knowing your address I was not able to tell you before how deeply all at Brigade Headquarters felt the loss of your very gallant son : he was a great loss both to his Regiment, which he so loyally served, and to us, his friends. The only consolation that I know of is that he died commanding his Battalion, which he had so gallantly rejoined after his very severe wounds. I had so hoped that he might have held this command permanently."

CONWAY, J. A., M.D. (D.S.O. L.G. 3.6.18), T/Capt., R.A.M.C.; M.C.

CONWAY, J. M. H., F.R.C.S.I. (D.S.O. L.G. 1.1.17); b. 19.12.74; s. of Rev. T. R. Conway; m. Helena Margaret, d. of J. Erskine; one s.; two d.; educ. Corrig School, and School of Surgery, Dublin; served in the R.N., 1900–2 (Civil Surg. 313 days); Surg., R.N., 1 yr., 259 days); Lt., R.A.M.C., 1.9.02; Capt. 1.3.06; Major, June, 1914; served in France, 1915–16; in Palestine from Aug. 1917; Bt. Lt.-Col. 3.6.19; Despatches.

CONYNGHAM, H. M. LENOX- (see Lenox-Conyngham, H. M.).

COODE, C. P. R. (D.S.O. L.G. 1.1.16), Capt., R.N.

COOK, C. C. (D.S.O. L.G. 18.8.16); b. 22.8.66; s. of Surg.-Gen. H. Cook, M.D., F.R.C.P., F.R.C.S.; m. Harriet Mary, d. of H. B. Goad; one s.; one d.; educ. Eton (King's Scholar); passed 1st into R.M.C., Sandhurst, 1885; direct commission in R.A. 18.2.86; Lt., Ind. S.C., 30.3.88; Capt., Ind. Army, 18.2.97; Maj. 18.2.04; Lt.-Col. 18.2.12; Colonel 18.4.17; ret. 1.3.20; commanded 7th Hariana Rgt. in Mesopotamia, 1915–16; Despatches three times; Order of the White Eagle, Serbia.

COOK, C. F. D. (D.S.O. L.G. 4.6.17), Lt.-Col., N.Z. Inf. Rgt.

COOK, F. A. (D.S.O. L.G. 15.2.19) (Details, L.G. 30.7.19), Lt., York and Lanc. R., T.F.; M.C.

COOK, F. C. (D.S.O. L.G. 1.1.19), T/Capt. (A/Major), R.E.; M.C.

COOK, G. H. (D.S.O. L.G. 1.2.19), Lt., Can. F. Arty., 6.5.14; Capt. 1.5.09; Major.

COOK, J. (D.S.O. L.G. 8.3.19) (Details, L.G. 4.10.19), Lt. (A/Capt.), W.R. Rgt.; M.C.

COOK, J. B. (D.S.O. L.G. 26.3.18) (Details, L.G. 24.8.18), Lt.-Col., 5th Bn. R. Scots Fus., T.F.; M.C. He was killed in action 24.11.17.

COOKE, B. H. H. (D.S.O. L.G. 3.6.16); b. 3.7.74; s. of late J. E. Cooke, R.N.; m. Mary Henrietta, d. of T. H. Cardwell; two s.; one d.; educ. Eton; Sandhurst; 2nd Lt., Rif. Brig., 22.5.95; Lt. 28.7.97; Capt. 20.2.01; Maj. 15.10.13; Temp. Brig.-Gen. 3.6.16–31.3.18; Lt.-Col. 1.1.17; Despatches; served Nile Exp., 1898; Battle of Omdurman; Queen's Medal and Khedive's Medal and clasp; S. African War, 1901–2, with M.I.; wounded; Queen's Medal and 5 clasps; Europ. War, 1914–18; severely wounded, Battle of the Marne; Despatches five times; Bt. Lt.-Col. 3.6.15; C.M.G.; C.B.E.; 1914 Star; Order of St. Stanislas, 3rd Class, with Swords (Russia); Belgian Croix de Guerre; Commandeur, Ordre du Mérite Agricole (France); served with R.A.F., 1918–19, as Brig.-Gen. in charge of Administration, and in Command of Midland Area.

COOKE, E. D. M. H. (D.S.O. L.G. 3.6.19); b. 6.7.77; 2nd Lt., R. Art., 14.6.99; Lt. 1.2.01; Capt. 12.11.07; Major 30.10.14; A/Lt.-Col., R. Art. (T.F.), 28.1.19; retired R.A. 22.4.21; served Europ. War, att 46th Can. Div. Art.; Despatches.

COOKE, G. S. C. (D.S.O. L.G. 1.1.17); b. 29.6.78; 2nd Lt., R.E., 23.3.98; Lt. 14.2.01; Capt. 23.3.07; Maj. 30.10.14; served S. African War, 1899–1902; Queen's Medal with 2 clasps; King's Medal with 2 clasps; Europ. War; Despatches.

COOKE, H. F. (D.S.O. L.G. 1.1.17); b. 13.11.71; s. of Col. W. S. Cooke, late 22nd Foot; m. Nancy Emelyn (who died in 1919), d. of C. de J. Andrewes; one s.; one d.; educ. All Hallows School, Honiton; R.M.C., Sandhurst; 2nd Lt., Ches. R., 7.1.92; Lt., I.S.C., 24.11.93; Capt. 10.7.01; Major 27.1.10; Bt. Lt.-Col. 10.7.12; Lt.-Col. 3.6.16; Col. 5.9.17; Major-Genl. 31.1.21; served Chitral, 1895; Medal and 1 clasp; Tirah, 1897; 2 clasps; Waziristan, 1902; clasp; Tibet Exp., 1904; Medal and 1 clasp; Despatches five times; Bt. Col. 3.6.17; C.B.; C.S.I.

COOKE, J. C. (D.S.O. L.G. 1.1.19), T/Capt. (T/Major), Gen. List.; M.C.

COOKE, R. C. (D.S.O. L.G. 2.4.19) (Details, L.G. 10.12.19), T/Capt (A/Major), R.A.M.C.; M.C.

COOKE, T. F. V. (D.S.O. L.G. 23.7.18); b. 22.6.96; 2nd Lt., R. Mar., 22.8.14; Lt. 27.3.15; Capt. 7.5.18; Bt. Major 7.5.18; Despatches.

COOKE, W. F. (D.S.O. L.G. 8.3.18), T/Major, Can. Forestry Corps.

COOKE-COLLIS, W. J. N. (D.S.O. L.G. 3.6.18); b. 7.5.76; 2nd Lt., R. Ir. Rifles, 24.2.00; Lt. 10.12.02; Capt. 28.6.08; Major 1.9.15; Bt. Lt.-Col. 3.6.16; T/Brig.-Genl. 25.8.17 to 12.8.20; Despatches; C.B.; C.M.G.

COOKE-HURLE, E. F. (D.S.O. L.G. 3.6.18); b. 3.6.66; s. of late J. Cooke-Hurle; m., 1st, Grace (who died in 1908), d. of late T. Davey; one d.; 2nd, Muriel Penelope, d. of Major Maitland; one s.; 2nd Lt. 5.2.87; Maj. 30.10.07; retired Som. L.I. 26.6.09; Burma, 1892–93; severely wounded; Medal with clasp; N.W. Frontier of India, 1897–98; Mohmand; Medal with clasp; Europ. War, 1914–18; Despatches.

COOKES, D. (D.S.O. L.G. 1.1.18); b. 1882; s. of T. S. Cookes, Average Adjuster of Lloyd's; Capt., H.A.C., Horse Artillery; served with R.F.A. in France as Lt.-Col., 1914–19; Despatches thrice; Belgian Croix de Guerre; Average Adjuster of Lloyd's.

COOKSON, C. S. STIRLING- (see Stirling-Cookson, C. S.).

COOMBER, T. G. (D.S.O. L.G. 27.6.19), Eng.-Cdr., R.N., 21.4.17.

COOMBS, A. G. (D.S.O. L.G. 1.1.19), T/Lt. (A/Major), R.G.A.

COOMBS, H. M. (D.S.O. L.G. 7.6.18), Lt.-Cdr., R.N., 30.6.16.

COOP, THE REV. J. O. (D.S.O. L.G. 1.1.18); b. 1869; s. of J. H. and Sarah Coop; m. Ethel, d. of late C. J. Wolstenholme; five d.; educ. Manchester Grammar School; Exeter College, Oxford (3rd Class Modern History); Chaplain, 1st Class, T.F., 1913; Senior Chaplain, C.E., 55th Division, 1914–19; Despatches twice; holds T.D.; Hon. Canon of Liverpool Cathedral.

COOPER, A. DUFF (D.S.O. L.G. 2.12.18); b. 1890; s. of late Sir A. Cooper, F.R.C.S., and Lady Agnes Duff, sister of 1st Duke of Fife; m. 1919, Lady Diana Manners, y. d. of 8th Duke of Rutland; educ. Eton; New College, Oxford (Honours, Modern History); served Europ. War, 1914–19; Despatches.

COOPER, A. L. (D.S.O. L.G. 27.7.18); b. 10.8.75; s. of William Marsh; m. Elizabeth Sarah, d. of late C. H. A. Russell, C.B.; one d.; educ. Haileybury College; served S. Africa, 1899–02; Despatches; Queen's Medal, 5 clasps; King's Medal, 2 clasps; Europ. War; Major, R. of O., R.E.

COOPER, A. R. (D.S.O. L.G. 26.7.17), T/Capt.; serv. Bn. Worc. R.

COOPER, C. G. A. (D.S.O. L.G. 4.6.17); b. 13.7.81; s. of Major L. L. Astley-Cooper; m. Ida Mary, d. of late H. L. Forbes; one s.; educ. R.M.A., Woolwich; ent. R.A. 18.8.00; Lt. 18.8.03; Capt. 5.2.12; Major 12.2.15; served S. African War, 1901–2; Queen's Medal with 3 clasps; Europ. War; Despatches

COOPER, F. S. (D.S.O. L.G. 1.1.18); b. 26.8.73; 2nd Lt., Suff. R., 3.5.99; Lt. 18.8.00 (C.R.I. 21.3.01–26.5.04); Capt. 21.10.05; Adjt. 30.12.10–30.12.13;

Maj. 11.12.14; Bt. Lt.-Col. 3.6.19; T/Col. 11.6.18; served W. Africa, 1897–98, Lagos; employed in Hinterland Borgu; Medal with clasp; Europ. War; Despatches.

COOPER, G. S. (D.S.O. L.G. 4.6.17); b. 30.5.81; 2nd Lt., R. Art., 4.12.01; Lt. 4.12.04; Adjt. 3.9.13; Capt. 16.9.14; Maj. 23.11.15; Despatches.

COOPER, H., B.A. (D.S.O. L.G. 1.1.18), Staff Surgeon, R.N.

COOPER, J. (D.S.O. L.G. 23.11.16), T/Major, A.S.C.

COOPER, L. N. (D.S.O. L.G. 4.6.17), T/Capt. (T/Lt.-Col.), R.E.

COOPER, N. B. ELLIOTT- (see Elliott-Cooper, N. B.).

COOPER, R. A. (D.S.O. L.G. 4.6.17), Lt. (T/Major), Yeom. and R.F.C. (late Capt., D. Gds.).

COOPER, V. M. (D.S.O. L.G. 2.11.17), Lt.-Cdr., R.N.

COOPER, V. S. (D.S.O. L.G. 22.9.16); b. 2.4.92; s. of P. E. S. Cooper and E. L. Cooper; m. Nessie S. A. Lankester, d. of H. J. King; she was for five years in charge of Y.M.C.A. hut at Southampton; educ. Brisbane Grammar School, and Matriculated University of Queensland, 1910; Qualified Licensed Surveyor Brisbane, Oct. 1919; joined A.I.F., March, 1915; L.-Sergt., June, 1915; Lt., July, 1916; Capt., Feb. 1917; M.C. 2.9.18; Despatches; three times wounded. D.S.O. awarded for services 6–7 Aug. 1916, at Pozières.

V. S. Cooper.

COOPER, W. G. (D.S.O. L.G. 3.6.19); b. 31.12.68; 2nd Lt., Leic. R., 22.8.88; Lt. 21.3.90; Ind. S.C. 9.4.90; Capt., I.A., 29.8.99; Major 22.8.06; Lt.-Col. 22.8.14; served China, 1900; Medal; Europ. War; Despatches.

COOPER, W. M. (D.S.O. L.G. 3.6.19); b. 22.2.79; 2nd Lt. 15.11.14; Lt. 9.6.15; Capt. 3.11.17; A/Major, R.G.A.; Despatches; M.C.

COOPER, W. R. F. (D.S.O. L.G. 3.8.20); b. 1.6.83; 2nd Lt., Lan. Fus., 15.8.03; Lt., 1st Dn. Guards, 23.3.07; Capt. 14.6.14; Adjt., 1st D.G., 5.9.14–19.2.17; Major 21.9.20; M.C.; Despatches.

COOPER-KEY, A. D. C. (D.S.O. L.G. 23.5.17); b. 30.12.83; s. of Admiral the Rt. Honble. Sir Astley Cooper-Key, G.C.B., and Evelyn, d. of Signor Bartolucci; m. Pauline, d. of the Hon. L. O'B. Furlong, of St. John's, Newfoundland; one son; educ. at Stanmore Park, and on H.M.S. Britannia; entered R.N., Midshipman, May, 1900; Sub-Lt. 15.5.03; Lt. 31.12.05; Lt.-Cdr. 31.12.13; Cdr. 31.12.18.

COOTE, C. R., M.P. (D.S.O. L.G. 24.9.18), Lt. (A/Capt.), Glouc. R.

COOTE-BROWN, W. (D.S.O. L.G. 1.1.18), T/Lt.-Col., R. Sussex R.

COPE, A. H. (D.S.O. L.G. 26.7.18); b. 7.10.92; s. of Sir Arthur Cope; 2nd Lt., Devon R., 20.9.11; Lt. 15.3.15; Capt. 3.2.17; Despatches.

COPE, T. G. (D.S.O. L.G. 15.4.16) (Bar, L.G. 10.1.17); b. 10.2.84; e. s. of Sir T. Cope, Bart., and Alice Kate (who died in 1916), d. of G. Walker; educ. Eton, and Trinity College, Cambridge; 2nd Lt., R. Fus., 13.1.06; Lt. 28.9.08; Capt. 13.11.14; Bt. Major 1.1.16; Bt. Lt.-Col. 1.1.18. He was Adjt., 8th Bn. R. Fus., from Aug. 1914; proceeded to France, May, 1915; Second-in-Command 8th Bn. R. Fus., June, 1915; wounded, March, 1916; T/Lt.-Col., April, 1916; in command 6th Bn. The Buffs; wounded Oct. 1916; T/Brig.-Gen., June, 1917; Despatches; C.M.G. His D.S.O. was awarded for services at Hohenzollern Redoubt on 2.3.16.

T. G. Cope.

COPELAND, R. R. (D.S.O. L.G. 3.6.18); b. 13.12.92; 2nd Lt., R. Art., 18.7.13; Lt. 9.6.15; Capt. 18.7.17; M.C. He was killed in action in Mesopotamia 24.9.20.

COPEMAN, H. C. (D.S.O. L.G. 14.1.16); b. 19.1.62; s. of G. Copeman; educ. Haileybury and Sandhurst; 2nd Lt. 22.10.81; Maj. 23.3.00; ret. Essex R. 27.2.04 (Lt.-Col., late Terr. Force Bn. Suff. R.); Despatches; served S. African War, 1899–1902; Queen's Medal with 5 clasps; King's Medal with 2 clasps; Europ. War; Despatches; C.M.G.; Order of St. Stanislas, 3rd Class.

COPLANS, M., M.D. (D.S.O. L.G. 1.1.17), Capt., R.A.M.C.

COPPINGER, W. V., M.D., F.R.C.S.I. (D.S.O. L.G. 26.8.18); b. 1.3.75; Lt., Ind. Med. Serv., 28.6.00; Capt. 28.6.03; Maj. 28.12.11; Lt.-Col. 28.12.19; Despatches.

CORBALLIS, E. R. L. (D.S.O. L.G. 1.1.18); b. 24.9.90; 2nd Lt., R. Dub. Fus., 20.4.10; Lt. 1.3.12; R.F. Corps 13.9.13–31.3.18; Capt. 28.4.15.

CORBETT, C. U. (D.S.O. L.G. 3.6.18), Major (Lt., Ret. Pay; T/Major, R.F.A.), Yeo.

CORBETT, G. R. DE LA C. (D.S.O. L.G. 3.6.18); b. 16.9.82; 2nd Lt., R. Art., 21.12.01; Lt. 21.12.04; Capt. 30.10.14; Maj. R.G.A., 1.5.17.

CORBETT, G. R. J. (D.S.O. L.G. 3.6.18), Lt., C. Guards.

CORBETT, R. G. (D.S.O. L.G. 22.6.16); b. 1872; s. of J. E. Corbett; m. Phyllis Dorothy, d. of A. H. Chanter; educ. Leamington College, and Burney's, Gosport; entered R.N., 1885; promoted to Captain, 1912; received the thanks of the U.S. Govt. on two occasions, for services on the coast of Mexico in 1914, when Senior Naval Officer on W. Coast of America; served Europ. War from 1914.

CORFE, A. C. (D.S.O. L.G. 4.6.17) (1st Bar, L.G. 26.9.17) (Details, L.G. 9.1.18) (2nd Bar, L.G. 19.11.17) (Details, L.G. 22.3.18), Major (T/Lt.-Col.), S. African Defence Force and R.W. Kent Rgt.

CORFIELD, F. A. (D.S.O. L.G. 1.1.17); b. 10.11.84; 2nd Lt., A.S.C., 27.1.04; Lt. 6.5.07; Capt. 5.8.14; Major 22.10.18; Despatches; O.B.E.

CORFIELD, G. F. C. (D.S.O. L.G. 7.2.18), T/Major, R.E.

CORLETTE, J. M. C. (D.S.O. L.G. 1.1.18), T/Lt.-Col., Aust. Engrs.

CORNISH, A. W. D. (D.S.O. L.G. 3.6.18); b. 24.4.84; 2nd Lt., E. York. R., 22.10.02; Ind. Army 7.3.04; Lt., Ind. Army, 22.1.05; Capt. 22.10.11; Maj. 22.10.17; Despatches; M.C.

CORNISH, C. R. (D.S.O. L.G. 24.9.18), Lt., Aust. Inf.

CORNWALL, C. E. (D.S.O. L.G. 30.1.20), T/Major, Spec. List.

CORNWALL, J. H. M. (D.S.O. L.G. 4.6.17); b. 27.5.87; s. of J. Cornwall, I.C.S., retired (late Postmaster-General, U.P., of Agra and Oudh); educ. Edinburgh Academy, 1896–98; at Cargilfield, 1898–1901; Rugby, 1901–5; R.M.A., 1905–7; 2nd Lt., R. Art., 23.7.07; Lt. 23.7.10; Capt. 30.10.14; Bt. Maj. 3.6.16; Maj. 9.7.17; Bt. Lt.-Col. 3.6.18; Adjt., R.A., 19.1.20 to 15.2.21; served Europ. War; went to France with B.E.F., Aug. 1914; Despatches (L.G. 19.10.14); M.C.; C.B.E.

CORNWALL, J. K. (D.S.O. L.G. 1.1.18), Lt.-Col. Can. Rly. Troops.

CORNWALLIS, K. (D.S.O. L.G. 8.8.17), T/Major, Spec. List.

CORRIE, W. F. T. (D.S.O. L.G. 1.1.19); b. 4.4.69; 2nd Lt., R.A., 17.2.88; Lt. 17.2.91; Capt. 17.8.98; Major 20.6.08; Lt.-Col., R.G.A., 9.12.15; retired 9.12.20; Despatches; served Tirah, 1897–98; Medal with 2 clasps; S. African War, 1900–2; Queen's Medal with 3 clasps; King's Medal with 2 clasps; Europ. War; Despatches.

CORRIGALL, D. J. (D.S.O. L.G. 1.1.19), 2nd Lt., Can. Inf., 8.9.14; Major, Can. Mil. Forces; M.C.

CORRIGAN, C. A. (D.S.O. L.G. 1.1.17), 2nd Lt., Can. Inf., 18.3.11; T/Major, Can. A.S.C.

CORRIGAN, J. J. (D.S.O. L.G. 1.1.18) (Bar, L.G. 8.3.19) (Details, L.G. 4.10.19), Lt.-Col., Aust. Mil. Forces.

CORSAN, R. A. (D.S.O. L.G. 24.9.18), Capt. (A/Major), R.F.A.; M.C.

CORSAR, J. K. (D.S.O. L.G. 15.9.16), Engr. Lt.-Cdr., R.N., 17.6.15; served in Battle of Jutland; Despatches.

COSENS, G. P. L. (D.S.O. L.G. 1.1.18); b. 14.10.84; 2nd Lt., 1 Dns., 3.12.04; Lt. 19.3.08; Capt. 4.4.14; Bt. Maj. 3.6.15; Lt.-Col., Army, 14.8.20; retired 1st Dns. 14.8.20; Despatches.

COSGRAVE, L. V. M. (D.S.O. L.G. 25.11.16) (Bar, L.G. 18.1.18) (Details, L.G. 25.4.18), Lt., Can. Cav. 20.6.12; Major, Can. F.A. D.S.O. awarded for gallantry on 15–17.9.16, Somme.

COSGROVE, J. R. (D.S.O. L.G. 8.3.19) (Details, L.G. 4.10.19), Major, Can. Rly. Troops; M.C.

COSSART, A. R. B. (D.S.O. L.G. 20.10.16); b. 27.8.77; s. of Charles John Cossart, of Quinta da Levada, Funchal, Madeira; m. Evelyn Mary, d. of Rev. G. Carter, M.A.; two d.; educ. at Bloxham; Wren's, and Maguire's, and ent. Militia, 1896, and R.A. 22.12.98; Lt. 16.2.01; Capt. 21.9.06; Adjt., R.A., 16.5.07 to 30.6.09, and 24.9.09 to 23.9.10; Major 30.10.14; Lt.-Col. 1.1.21; served in S. African War; Queen's Medal with 3 clasps; King's Medal with 2 clasps; European War, in command 242nd Bgde, R.F.A., B.E.F., and later as Counter Battery Staff Officer, XI. Corps; Despatches four times; Bt. Lt.-Col. 3.6.18; Order of the Crown of Italy. His D.S.O. was awarded for gallantry 21–28 July and 13–29 Aug. 1916, at Ovillers.

COSTELLO, E. (D.S.O. L.G. 8.3.19) (Details, L.G.4.10.19), Major, 11st Aust. L.H. Rgt. (Egypt).

COSTELLO, E. W. (D.S.O. L.G. 25.8.17), Col., I.A., 29.3.20; V.C.; C.M.G.; C.V.O. (see "The Victoria Cross," by same publishers).

COSTIGAN, R. (D.S.O. L.G. 3.6.19), Lt.-Col., Can. Arty., 14.10.14.

COSTIN, E. B. (D.S.O. L.G. 4.6.17); b. 2.8.89; Capt. (from Can. Mil. Forces), W. Yorks. R., 11.9.15; Bt. Major 3.6.19; Despatches.

COTGRAVE, T. S. (D.S.O. L.G. 4.6.17); b. 12.9.82; 2nd Lt., A.S.C., 4.7.03; Lt. 31.3.05; Capt. 16.12.11; Major, R.A.S.C., 30.10.14; Bt. Lt.-Col. 1.1.19; Despatches; served S. African War, 1902; Queen's Medal with 2 clasps; Europ. War, 1914; Despatches (L.G. 19.10.14).

COTTEE, H. (D.S.O. L.G. 4.6.17); b. 19.10.80; 1st com. 9.4.15; Lt. 9.4.17; retired R.A. 17.10.20; rank of Major 18.11.20.

COTTER, E. B. (D.S.O. L.G. 4.6.17); b. 11.3.79; 2nd Lt., R.A., 26.2.98; Lt. 16.2.01; Capt. 2.9.03; Major, R.G.A., 30.10.14; served N.W. Frontier of India, Waziristan, 1901–2; Medal with clasp; Europ. War; Despatches.

COTTER, H. J. (D.S.O. L.G. 17.4.16); b. 10.9.71; s. of Major J. Cotter, The Buffs; m. Alice Elizabeth, d. of Rev. G. Armitage; one s.; educ. Kelly College, Tavistock; R.M.A., Woolwich; 2nd Lt., R.A., 25.7.90; Lt. 25.7.93; Capt. 9.10.99; Maj. 1.4.11; Lt.-Col. 1.5.17; served Isazai Exp., 1892; Chitral, 1895, with the Relief Force (Medal and clasp); China, 1900 (Medal); Europ. War; Despatches; C.I.E.; Serbian Order of the White Eagle, 4th Class. He died in July, 1921.

COTTON, A. E. (D.S.O. L.G. 1.1.17); b. 1876; 3rd (twin) son of late C. C. Cotton; m. Beryl Marie, d. of late H. J. Cumming; three d.; Lt.-Col., late R. Bgde. from 1914; served throughout Europ. War, R. Brig.; wounded twice; Despatches thrice; 1914–15 Star.

COTTON, H. T. (D.S.O. L.G. 3.6.16), Lt.-Col., S. Lanc. R.; served S. African War, 1902; Queen's Medal with 4 clasps; Europ. War. He was killed in action on 3.9.16.

COTTON, R. E. (D.S.O. L.G. 11.1.19); b. 8.3.76; 2nd (twin) s. of late C. C. Cotton and Kate Cotton (*née* de la Rue); m. Hilda, d. of late Capt. C. D. Inglis, R.N.; one d.; educ. Stubbington; served with Imp. Yeom. in S. African War, 1900–1 (Queen's Medal and 3 clasps); with Yorks. R. (Service Bn.) in Europ. War from 1914; T/Major (A/Lt.-Col.); 3½ years' active service in France and Flanders; commanded 10th Bn. Lancs. Fus. in France, June–Nov. 1918, and 25th Recruit Distribution Bn. in England, Dec. 1918–June, 1919.

COTTRELL, A. F. B. (D.S.O. L.G. 4.6.17); b. 4.4.91; 2nd Lt., R.A., 20.7.11; Lt. 20.7.14; Capt. 8.8.16; A/Major, R.F.A.; Despatches.

COTTRELL, J. (D.S.O. L.G. 14.1.16); b. 10.10.70; ent. Army 10.10.14; Lt. 31.1.15; ret. R.W. Fus. with rank of Capt. 14.11.18; served S. African War, 1899–1902; Queen's Medal with 5 clasps; King's Medal with 2 clasps; D.C.M.; Europ. War; Despatches.

COTTRELL, R. F. (D.S.O. L.G. 1.1.18); b. 23.4.85; s. of Major W. F. Cottrell, R.E.; m. Margaret (who died in 1921), d. of late R. English; educ. privately; R.M.A., Woolwich; ent. R.A. 15.7.03; retired 5.1.07; rejoined Army 5.8.14; Major, R.G.A., 8.8.16; served Europ. War, 1914–18; Despatches twice; Bt. Lt.-Col. 1.1.19; Mons Star; Order of the Redeemer; Greek Medal for Military Merit; Asst. Director, W.O., 1919–21.

COUCH, B. B. QUILLER- (see Quiller-Couch, B. B.).

COUCHMAN, F. M. (D.S.O. L.G. 8.3.19) (Details, L.G. 4.10.19), Major, Aust. Mil. Forces.

COUCHMAN, H. J. (D.S.O. L.G. 3.6.18); b. 29.7.82; 2nd Lt., R.E., 18.8.00; Lt. 18.8.03; Capt. 18.8.10; Adjt., R.E., 19.11.14 to 14.1.16; Maj. 2.11.16; M.C.

COULSON, J. (D.S.O. L.G. 3.6.18); b. 30.9.73; 1st com. 20.5.93; Lt.-Col. 24.2.15; ret. pay (late R.A.S.C.), 8.9.20; Despatches.

COULSON, R. N. (D.S.O. L.G. 7.11.18), Major (A/Lt.-Col.), Sc. Rifles.

COULTER, G. (D.S.O. L.G. 1.1.17), Lt.-Col., Aust. Mil. Forces.

COULTER, L. J. (D.S.O. L.G. 26.9.16), Major, Aust. Eng. D.S.O. awarded for gallantry on 15 and 16 July, 1916, at Ferme-des-Bois.

COURAGE, A. (D.S.O. L.G. 4.2.18) (Details, L.G. 5.7.18); b. 22.10.75; s. of late H. Courage; m. May, d. of Sir J. Hewett, G.C.S.I.; two s.; two d.; educ. Rugby; 2nd Lt., 15 Hrs., 9.12.96; Lt. 23.3.98; Adjt. 15.12.01–16.12.04; Capt. 10.10.03; Maj. 10.10.15; Lt.-Col., Tank Corps, 1.8.19; ret. Tank Corps with hon. rank of Brig.-Gen. 2.2.21; served in France, Cambrai, 1917; commanded 5th Tank Brigade (att. Australian Corps), Hamel, Montdidier, Villers Bretonneux, Amiens, Hindenburg Line; appointed to command Group of two Tank Brigades; Despatches six times; Bt. Lt.-Col. 1.1.18; sailed with 15th Hussars in original Exp. Force, through Retreat from Mons, Battles of Marne, Aisne, First, Second, Third Battles of Ypres, Messines, Cambrai; wounded Second Battle of Ypres; employed on Staff, G.H.Q., France, 1916; commanded 2nd Tank Brigade, Messines; 3rd, Ypres; Bt.-Col. 3.6.19; M.C.; Croix de Guerre avec Palme.

COURAGE, M. R. F. (D.S.O. L.G. 1.1.18); served S. African War, 1900–1; Despatches; Bt. of Major; Queen's Medal with 3 clasps; Europ. War; Major, R. of O., R.A.; Major, H.A.C. (R.H.A.).

COUROY, A. M. (D.S.O. L.G. 22.8.18), Major, Philiptown Commando, S. African Mil. Forces.

COURT, R. E. HOLMES À (see Holmes à Court, R. E.).

COURTENAY, H. (D.S.O. L.G. 2.12.18), Bt. Major (A/Lt.-Col.), 1st Bn. Bedfords. R.; M.C. He died of wounds 23.8.18.

COURTICE, J. G. (D.S.O. L.G. 14.1.16); b. 18.5.70; s. of G. Courtice; m. Olivia Marion Sandeman; two s.; two d.; 2nd Lt., R.A., 6.5.00; Lt. 18.11.01; Capt. 30.1.12; Maj. 8.12.14; retired R.A.O.C. with rank of Colonel in the Army 16.7.20; served Europ. War; Despatches thrice; Bt. Lt.-Col. 3.6.18.

COURTNEY, C. LL. (D.S.O. L.G. 30.11.17); b. 27.6.90; y. s. of W. L. Courtney, M.A., LL.D.; educ. Bradfield College, Berks; ent. H.M.S. Britannia as Naval Cadet, 1905; Midshipman, R.N., 1906; Sub-Lt. 1909; Lt. 1911; joined R.N.A.S., as Flying Officer, 1912; Fl. Cdr., 1912; Sqn. Cdr., 1914; Wing Cdr., 1917; Lt.-Col., R.A.F.; A/Col., R.A.F., 1918; A/Brig.-Gen., R.A.F., 1918; Despatches; Legion of Honour; C.B.E.

COURTNEY, F. H. (D.S.O. L.G. 1.1.17); b. 31.10.75; 6th s. of late Rt. Rev. F. Courtney, Lord Bishop of Nova Scotia; m. Mary Elsie, d. of S. Davis; one s.; educ. St. Paul's School, Concord, New Hampshire, U.S.A.; R.M. College, Kingston, Canada; 2nd Lt., R.A., 5.9.97; Lt. 15.9.00; Capt. 29.3.02; Maj., R.G.A., 30.10.14; T/Lt.-Col.; served with B.E.F., 1914, in France to 1917; wounded four times.

COUSENS, R. B. (D.S.O. L.G. 1.1.18); b. 26.3.80; 2nd Lt., R.A., 6 May, 1900; Lt. 24.12.02; Adjt., R.A., 15.7.07 to 14.7.10; Capt. 25.4.11; Major 30.10.14; Bt. Lt.-Col. 1.1.19; Despatches.

COUSSMAKER, L. J. (D.S.O. L.G. 1.1.19), Major (A/Lt.-Col.), R.E., T.F.; M.C.

COUTTS, D. D. (D.S.O. L.G. 1.2.19), Major, Aust. A.M.C.

COWAN, A. J. (D.S.O. L.G. 1.1.18), Major, R.F.A.

COWAN, C. F. R. (D.S.O. L.G. 1.1.19), Cdr., R.N.

COWAN, I. C. (D.S.O. L.G. 1.1.19); s. of R. L. Cowan, of Hallguards, Ecclefechan; m. Bessie Cuthbertson, d. of ex-Provost Anderson, of Renfrew; Capt., late H.L.I.; served in Europ. War; acted as Brigade Major; Despatches; M.C.

COWAN, S. H. (D.S.O. L.G. 14.1.16); b. 21.4.78; s. of Rev. C. J. Cowan, B.D.; m. Jean Mildred, d. of late W. H. Hore; one s.; one d.; educ. Edinburgh Academy, and R.M.A., Woolwich; 2nd Lt., R.E., 21.7.97; Lt. 21.7.00; Capt. 21.7.06; Major 30.10.14; served Europ. War, 1914–18; Despatches three times.

COWAN-DOUGLAS, J. R. (D.S.O. L.G. 3.6.19); b. 29.5.93; 2nd Lt., High. L. Inf., 3.9.13; Lt. 14.11.14; Capt. 3.3.16; Despatches; M.C.

COWELL, E. M., M.D., F.R.C.S. (D.S.O. L.G. 3.6.18); Lt.-Col., R.A.M.C., T.A.

COWELL, W. R. (D.S.O. L.G. 27.7.18), Major, Cape Corps, S. African Forces. He was killed in action in Palestine 18.9.18.

COWIE, W. N. (D.S.O. L.G. 22.6.18), T/Lt. (A/Capt.), R.F.A.; M.C.

COWLAND, W. S. (D.S.O. L.G. 1.1.19), T/Major, Hants R.

COWLEY, V. L. S. (D.S.O. L.G. 3.6.19); b. 7.6.89; 2nd Lt., R. Ir. Rifles, 6.11.09; Lt. 24.1.14; Capt. 1.10.15; Despatches; M.C.

COWLING, H. E. (D.S.O. L.G. 1.2.19), T/Lt., serv. Bn. North'd Fus.; M.C.

COWPER, M. G. (D.S.O. L.G. 1.1.17); b. 16.11.77; 3rd s. of late J. Cowper and of Margaret Caroline, d. of G. G. Emmott; m. Margaret Farrer, d. of H. Tunstill; three s.; one d.; 2nd Lt., E. Yorks R., 20.5.99; Lt. 26.5.00; Capt. 28.3.12; Maj. 1.9.15; ret. E. Yorks R. 20.5.20, with rank of Lt.-Col. Army; served Europ. War, 1914–18; Despatches.

COX, C. E. (D.S.O. L.G. 7.2.18); b. 30.1.81; 2nd Lt., A.S.C., 21.2.00; Lt. 1.4.01; Capt. 1.8.05; Major, R.A.S.C., 30.10.14; served S. African War, 1901–2; Queen's Medal with 5 clasps; Sudan, 1912; Sudan Medal with clasp; Europ. War; Despatches; Bt. Lt.-Col. 3.6.19.

COX, C. F. (D.S.O. L.G. 2.12.18); b. 2.5.63; s. of F. C. Cox, of Carlingford; m. Minnie, d. of W. K. Gibbens; one d.; served S. Africa, 1899–1902; Despatches; Queen's Medal with 6 clasps; King's Medal with 2 clasps; Europ. War, 1914–18; Col. (T/Brig.-Gen., Commanding 1st Aust. L.H. Brig.); Despatches; C.B.; C.M.G.; holds Queen's Jubilee Medal; King's Coronation Medal.

COX, C. H. F. (D.S.O. L.G. 1.1.17) (Bar, L.G. 16.9.18); b. 3.4.80; s. of S. H. Cox, Emeritus Professor of Mining, Royal School of Mines, S. Kensington, S.W., and Amy Gertrude, d. of Charles Thomas Batkin; m. Edith, y. d. of R. L. Michell, C.M.G.; educ. Rugby; R.M.A.; 2nd Lt., R.F.A., 6.1.00; Lt., April, 1902; Capt., March, 1908; Major, Oct. 1914; Lt.-Col. 1.7.21; served S. African War, 1901–2; Queen's Medal with 5 clasps; Europ. War, with 88th and 89th Brigades, R.F.A., in France, July, 1915, to November, 1916; Member of Military Mission to the Hedjaz, Dec. 1916, to Feb. 1917; in France from Sept. 1917; commanded 86th Army Brigade, R.F.A., from 18.10.17 to March, 1919; Despatches three times; Bt. Lt.-Col. 1.1.19.

COX, E. H., M.B. (D.S.O. L.G. 1.1.19), Major (A/Lt.-Col.), R.A.M.C., T.F.

COX, F. T. (D.S.O. L.G. 4.6.17); s. of W. Cox; m. Irene, d. of H. Taylor; Lt.-Col., T.F.; served Europ. War, 1914–19; Despatches; Bt. Major.

COX, H. W. D. (D.S.O. L.G. 3.6.19), Lt., Can. Cav., 16.4.15.

COX, J. A. (D.S.O. L.G. 26.7.18), Major, The Highland Cyclist Bn. He was killed in action 29.9.18.

COX, I. R. (D.S.O. L.G. 1.1.19), T/Major, R.G.A.

COX, P. G. A. (D.S.O. L.G. 1.1.17); b. 10.10.72; ent. Army 21.2.94; Lt.-Col. (Res. of Off.), 19.10.19; retired R. Brig. 15.2.11; served S. African War, 1899–1902; Bt. of Major 22.8.02; Queen's Medal with 4 clasps; King's Medal with 2 clasps; Europ. War.

COX, W. T. (D.S.O. L.G. 4.6.17), Lt.-Col., R.F.A.

COX-TAYLOR, H. J. (D.S.O. L.G. 1.1.17), Lt.-Col., Aust. Arty.

COXEN, W. A. (D.S.O. L.G. 1.1.17), Lt.-Col., Aust. I.F., 14.8.14; Bt.-Col. 24.9.17; Col.; Hon. Brig.-Gen.; A.D.C. to the King; served Europ. War from 1914; Despatches; C.B.; C.M.G.; Croix de Guerre.

COYSH, W. H. (D.S.O. L.G. 1.1.18), T/Major (T/Lt.-Col.), R.E.

L. G. E. Crabbe.

C. S. Craig.

D. Craig.

CRABBE, L. G. E. (D.S.O. L.G. 17.3.19), Cdr., R.N.

CRACROFT, H. (D.S.O. L.G. 3.6.16); b. 23.8.73; 2nd Lt., R. Ir. Fus., 7.3.94; Lt. 15.12.96; Capt., R. Ir. Fus., 19.4.00; A.S. Corps 1.2.02; Major 15.12.13; Lt.-Col., R.A.S.C., 3.6.18. He served in the S. African War, 1899–1902; Despatches; Queen's Medal with 6 clasps; King's Medal with 2 clasps; N.W. Frontier of India, 1908; Medal with clasp; Europ. War; Despatches (L.G. 19.10.14).

CRADDOCK, W. M. (D.S.O. L.G. 1.1.19), Capt. (A/Major), London R.; M.C.

CRAGG, W. G. (D.S.O. L.G. 7.11.18); b. 1883; s. of W. A. Cragg, J.P.; m. Violet Emily, d. of L. W. Andrews, J.P.; two s.; two d.; educ. Shrewsbury; R.M.C., Sandhurst; 2nd Lt., 1st L.N. Lanc. Rgt., 1903; served Europ. War (Major, L.N. Lanc. R.); Despatches; 1914-15 Star.

CRAIG, A. H. (D.S.O. 18.10.17) (Details, 7.3.18); b. 28.9.86; s. of late A. Craig, M.D.; m. Lilian, d. of late J. Armstrong; one s.; educ. George Watson's College, and University, Edinburgh; enlisted in 14th Company of London Bn. London Scottish, Jan. 1913; went to France with Battalion, Sept. 1914; wounded; T/2nd Lt., 13th Bn. R. Scots, 1915; T/Capt. In France again from Oct. 1915, till wounded 22.7.18; Despatches; M.C.; A/Adjt., 13th (S.) Bn. The R. Scots.

CRAIG, C. S. (D.S.O. L.G. 3.6.19), Major, Can. F.A.; M.C.; comes from Cobourg in Canada; is a First Contingent man, and was awarded the M.C. in the summer of 1915, thus being one of the first Canadian officers to win the decoration. He has the French Croix de Guerre.

CRAIG, D. (D.S.O. L.G. 17.12.17) (Details, L.G. 23.4.18); s. of D. Craig, cloth inspector, Arbroath, and before the war played football for St. Johnstone, Perth. At the outbreak of war he was a lance-corporal in a Yeomanry regiment. He fought right through the Gallipoli campaign, and afterwards went to another front. For services rendered in Gallipoli he was granted a commission in the Grenadier Guards in June, 1917.

CRAIG, F. W. (D.S.O. L.G. 3.6.18), Q.M. and Hon. Major, Aust. Inf.

CRAIG, G. (D.S.O. L.G. 1.1.19), Capt., New Zea. Med. Corps.

CRAIG, J. C. (D.S.O. L.G. 3.6.18), Lt., Can. Art., 5.5.14; Major, Can. Rly. Troops.

CRAIG, N. L. (D.S.O. L.G. 4.6.17); b. 11.11.84; 2nd Lt. 19.1.06; Lt., A.S.C., 27.1.10; Capt., R.A.S.C., 7.10.14; T/Lt.-Col. 6.12.18; Despatches; O.B.E.

CRAIG, R. F. (D.S.O. L.G. 8.3.19) (Details, L.G. 4.10.19), Capt., A.A.M.C., 1.6.15; Major.

CRAIG, W. B. (D.S.O. L.G. 26.11.17) (Details, L.G. 6.4.18), Major, Aust. A.M.C.

CRAIGIE-McFEELY, C. M. (gazetted as McFeely, C. M.) (D.S.O. L.G. 26.11.17) (Details, L.G. 6.4.18); b. 31.1.95, at Allingham Lodge, Bundoran, Co. Donegal, Ireland; s. of J. D. McFeely, M.D., F.R.C.S.I., L.R.C.P., etc., and of Sarah McFeely (*née* Craig), of Belfast; educ. Ushaw College, Durham; London and Liverpool Universities, and Sandhurst, Surrey; joined the Army 2.2.15; commissioned R. Dublin Fusiliers 14.7.16; Lt. 24.7.15; A/Captain 17.8.16 to 13.11.16, and from Jan. 1917; served European War in the "incomparable 29th Division" from May, 1916, being allowed six months on substitution at home in Oct. 1917; was present Somme, 1916–17; Arras, April, 1917; 3rd Battle of Ypres, July, 1917; Lys Valley, Sept. 1918; 4th Battle of Ypres, Sept. 1918; Battle of Cambrai, Oct. 1918; Despatches; M.C. and Bar.

CRAIGIE-HALKETT, H. M. (D.S.O. L.G. 16.8.17) (1st Bar, L.G. 26.7.18) (2nd Bar, L.G. 12.12.19); b. 28.9.80; 2nd Lt., H.L.I., 18.4.00; Lt. 27.3.01; Capt. 11.5.10; Major 1.9.15; served S. African War; Queen's Medal with 2 clasps; King's medal with 2 clasps; E. Africa, 1904; Op. in Somaliland; Medal with clasp; Nandi Exp., 1905–6 (clasp); Sudan, 1912 (Medal with clasp); Europ. War, 1914–18; Despatches; Bt. Lt.-Col. 1.1.18; C.M.G.

CRAIK, J. (D.S.O. L.G. 1.1.18), Major (T/Lt.-Col.), R. of O., Ret. Pay, Lrs., I. Army.

CRAKE, R. H. (D.S.O. L.G. 7.2.18); b. 13.4.82; s. of W. P. and E. N. Crake; m. Marjorie Noel, d. of late Major P. Marrow, K.D.G.; educ. Harrow; Harrow Cricket XI.; with F. B. Wilson the first pair to beat Eton at fives at Eton; 2nd Lt., K.O. Sc. Bord., 11.5.01; Adjt. 25.7.08–24.7.11; Capt. 10.11.08; Maj. 11.5.16; served S. African War, 1901–2; Queen's Medal; served Europ. War, 1914–18; Despatches twice; 1915–18, Mesopotamia; 1914–15 Star.

CRAM, P. McF. (D.S.O. L.G. 3.6.19), Capt. (T/Major), Cam. Highrs., T.F.

CRAMPTON, D. B. (D.S.O. L.G. 14.7.16); b. 14.6.73; s. of late J. G. Crampton; m. Evangeline Beatrice, d. of Col. E. Dickinson, R.E.; educ. Stubbington House, and H.M.S. Britannia; ent. R.N., 1884; Commander, 1904; Captain 22.6.11; Lt. of the Thrush, Bear River Exp., 1895 (General African Medal, Brass River clasp); present at bombardment of Sultan of Zanzibar's Palace, 1896; served in Yacht Victoria and Albert, 1907–11; holds 2nd Class Russian

The Distinguished Service Order 229

Order of Stanislaus; 2nd Class Order of Dannebrog; Grecian Order of Redeemer; M.V.O.; C.B.E.

CRAMPTON, J. (D.S.O. L.G. 2.4.19) (Details, L.G. 10.12.19); b. 11.6.96; Lt., York. and Lanc. R., 7.10.18; T/Major, York and Lanc. R. (Italy); M.C.

CRANSTON, W. J. (D.S.O. L.G. 3.6.18); b. 10.2.77; 2nd Lt., R. Sc. Fus., 25.7.15; Lt. 29.12.16; Capt., N. Staff. R., 23.12.17; Bt. Maj. 24.12.17; T/Lt.-Col., Mach. Gun Corps, 27.12.17.

CRANSTOUN, C. J. E. (D.S.O. L.G. 1.1.19), Major, Lanark Yeom.

CRASTER, G. (D.S.O. L.G. 1.1.18); b. 27.12.78; 2nd Lt., Unatt., 20.7.98; Ind. S.C. 16.10.99; Lt., Ind. Army, 20.10.00; Capt. 20.7.07; Major 1.9.15; Despatches; O.B.E.

CRAUFURD, R. Q. (D.S.O. L.G. 3.6.18); b. 9.3.80; e. s. of Capt. H. R. Craufurd, and a cousin of Sir C. Craufurd, 4th Bart.; 2nd Lt., R. Sc. Fus. 23.8.99; Lt. 28.2.00; Capt. 14.6.05; Maj. 1.9.15; Bt. Lt.-Col. 3.6.19; served S. African War, 1899–1902; Queen's Medal with 5 clasps; King's Medal with 2 clasps; Europ. War; Despatches; Croix de Guerre.

CRAVEN, A. J. (D.S.O. L.G. 1.1.18); b. 11.12.67; m. Edith Maude, d. of late A. Smallwood; 2nd Lt., R.Eng., 23.11.89; Lt. 23.11.92; Capt. 12.8.00; Lt. Col. 1.10.17 (T/Brig.Gen. 3.5.17–11.6.18); T/Col. 31.8.18; served S. African War, 1899–02; Despatches; Bt. of Major 26.6.02; Queen's Medal with 5 clasps; King's Medal with 2 clasps; Europ. War; Despatches; Bt. Lt.-Col. 3.6.16.

CRAVEN, F. W. (D.S.O. L.G. 17.3.19), Lt.-Cdr., R.N., 1.7.19; D.S.O. awarded for remarkable courage and seamanship when H.M.S. Otranto was damaged in collison with the S.S. Kashmir 5.10.18.

CRAVEN, W. S. D. (D.S.O. L.G. 1.1.17); b. 8.8.80; s. of Rev. Dacre Craven, St. Andrew's Rectory, Holborn; m. daughter of late Sir F. Mirrielees, and granddaughter of late Sir Donald Currie; 2nd Lt., R.A., 23.12.98; Lt. 16.2.01; Capt. 5.12.06; Major 30.10.14; Bt. Lt.-Col. 3.6.18; ret. R.A. with rank of Lt.-Col. in the Army 24.12.20; served S. African War, 1899–1902; Despatches twice; Queen's Medal with 6 clasps; King's Medal with 2 clasps; Europ. War; Despatches; Bt. Lt.-Col. 3.6.16. Lt.-Col. Craven is the well-known Blackheath footballer, and is also a boxer of more than average merit, having won the Navy and Army Heavyweight title in 1905.

W. S. D. Craven.

CRAWFORD, E. W. (D.S.O. L.G. 1.1.18) (Bar, L.G. 16.9.18): b. 18.5.79; T/Major, R. Innis. Fus.; Lt.-Col., C.M.A., 19.11.19; Col. 19.11.20; Despatches.

CRAWFORD, I. L. (D.S.O. L.G. 1.1.18) (Bar, L.G. 7.11.18), Major, Can. Inf.

CRAWFORD, J. (D.S.O. L.G. 18.2.18) (Details, L.G. 18.7.18), T/2nd Lt., R. Bde.

CRAWFORD, J. D. (D.S.O. L.G. 17.9.17); b. 21.1.85; 2nd Lt., Unatt., 9.1.05; Ind. Army 11.3.05; Lt. Ind. A. 4.6.06; Capt. 9.1.13; Bt. Major 1.1.18; Major 9.1.19; Despatches; M.C.

CRAWFORD, J. K. (D.S.O. L.G. 18.2.18) (Details, L.G. 18.7.18), Lt., Can. Inf., 10.8.14.

CRAWFORD, J. N. (D.S.O. L.G. 14.1.16); b. 10.7.74; 2nd Lt., R. Innis. Fus., 7.12.95; Lt. 13.4.98; Capt. 1.8.01; Major 28.5.15; Lt.-Col. 10.1.19; served S. African War, 1899–1902; Despatches; Queen's Medal with 5 clasps; King's Medal with 2 clasps; Europ. War; Despatches.

CRAWFORD, J. R. M. (D.S.O. L.G. 3.6.19), Capt. (A/Major), 475th (S. Midand) Field Co., R.E., T.F.; M.C.

CRAWFORD, R. D. (D.S.O. L.G. 14.1.16); b. 16.9.80; m. Gertrude Margaret, d. of C. A. Tomes; one d.; 2nd Lt., R.A., 23.6.99; Lt. 16.2.01; Capt. 1.4.06; Adjt. 13.2.09–12.2.12; Maj. 30.10.14; served S. African War, 1901–2; Queen's Medal with 5 clasps; Europ. War; Despatches; Bt. Lt.-Col. 3.6.18.

CRAWFORD, W. L. (D.S.O. L.G. 1.1.18), Capt. (T/Major), Lanc. Fus.

CRAWFURD, R. B. J. (D.S.O. L.G. 3.6.16); b. 27.11.80; o. s. of C. W. Jervis Crawfurd, of Brocksford Hall, Derby; m. Eileen, d. of Sir G. Pigot, Bart; educ. Eton and Sandhurst; ent. C. Guards 12.8.99; Lt., 1901; Capt. 27.3.09; Regimental Adjt., C. Gds. 1914; Major 17.7.15; T/Lt.-Col., C. Gds., 1.5.14; ret. with rank of Lt.-Col., Army, 15.1.20; served S. African War, 1899–1902; Queen's Medal with 5 clasps; King's Medal with 2 clasps; served in Europ. War, 1915–16, in command Res. Bn., C. Gds., 27.10.17; Despatches.

CRAWHALL, REV. CANON T. E. (D.S.O. L.G. 1.1.18); s. of T. E. Crawhall and Margaret Elizabeth Crawhall (*née* Wooler); m. Louisa Helen Cruddas, d. of Rev. Canon G. Cruddas; four s.; educ. Wellington College, Berks, and Trinity College, Cambridge, and served in the Territorial Force in the Europ. War; Despatches twice. He holds the Territorial Decoration; is Hon. Canon of Newcastle.

CRAWLEY, R. P. (D.S.O. L.G. 1.1.17); b. 10.7.76; s. of late Rev. W. P. Crawley; m. Alice Vida Mary, d. of Rev. D. C. Cochrane; one s.; two d.; 2nd Lt., S. Wales Bord., 20.2.97; Lt. 26.7.98; Capt., A.S.C., 20.2.03; Maj., R.A.S.C., 5.8.14; Lt.-Col., R.A.C.S., 1915; served S. African War, 1900–1; Despatches twice; Queen's Medal with 4 clasps; served Europ. War; was D.D.T., Italy, 1917–18; D.D.S.T., Archangel, 1918–19; Despatches seven times; Bt. Lt.-Col. 1.1.18; O.B.E.; M.V.O. (1902).

CRAWLEY-BOEVEY, M., B.A. (D.S.O. L.G. 3.6.18); b. 17.9.83; s. of late A. W. Crawley-Boevey; m. Elizabeth Adela, widow of Lt.-Col. N. R. Daniell, D.S.O., D.C.L.I., and d. of late Capt. Roger Hall, D.L.; one s.; educ. Winchester; Trin. Coll., Oxford; 2nd Lt., Duke of Corn. L. Inf., 10.8.04; Lt. 4.2.07; Capt. 14.9.14; Bt. Maj. 3.1.17; retired 12.3.21, with rank of Major in the Army; served Somaliland, 1908–10 (Medal and clasp); Europ. War, 1914–18; Despatches; M.C.

C. H. R. Crawshay.

CRAWSHAW, C. H. (D.S.O. L.G. 8.3.19) (Details, L.G. 4.10.19), Capt. (A/Major), 1st Bn. K.O.S.B.; M.C.

CRAWSHAY, C. H. R. (D.S.O. L.G. 1.1.17); b. 29.10.82; s. of Rev. E. H. Crawshay, of Llanfair Rectory, Abergavenny, and of Emily Howard, d. of J. Cartland; m. Leonie Mabel, d. of Sir W. Nelson, Bart.; one s.; two d.; 2nd Lt., R. W. Fus., 27.7.01; Lt. 3.11.04; Capt. 23.11.11; Major 11.5.16; retired 16.7.20, with rank of Lt.-Col., Army; served S. African War; Queen's Medal, 2 clasps; Europ. War, 1914–17.

CRAWSHAY, H. (D.S.O. L.G. 3.6.18); b. 10.10.73; 1st com. 19.9.94; Capt. 20.6.00; retired Worc. R. 24.11.09; Major, R. of O., Worc. R.; served S. African War, 1900–1; Despatches; Queen's Medal with 3 clasps; Europ. War; Despatches.

CREAGH, J. V. (D.S.O. L.G. 8.3.18); b. 1883; s. of the late Charles Vandeleur Creagh, C.M.G., of Cahirbane, co. Clare; m. Adela May, d. of P. C. Cork; one s.; one d.; Cdr., R.N., 30.6.16; served Europ. War, 1914–18; Despatches; Croix de Guerre; invested with the D.S.O. by the King at Harwich 26.2.18.

CREELMAN, J. J. (D.S.O. L.G. 1.1.17); b. 14.2.81, at Toronto, Canada; s. of A. R. Creelman, K.C.; m. 1st, Katharine Mélanie Weekes (who died in 1918); one s.; one d.; m. 2nd, Maud Hamilton Baker; educ. Upper Canada College, Toronto ("Head Boy," 1900); University of Toronto (B.A., 1904); McGill University (B.C.L., 1907); University of Grenoble, France (Diploma); admitted to the Bar of Province of Quebec; Lecturer in Railway Economics, McGill University; Member of Council of Can. Artillery Association; Lt.-Col., 6th Montreal Brigade, Can. F.A., 1912; Member of Canadian Coronation Contingent, 1911; served Europ. War, O.C., 2nd Can. F.A. Brigade, B.E.F., Aug. 1914–March, 1917; wounded; Despatches twice; Russian Order of St. Stanislas, 3rd Class with Swords; Col. Commandant, 2nd Montreal R. Can. Arty., 1920.

J. J. Creelman.

CRELLIN, W. A. W. (D.S.O. L.G. 4.6.17) (Bar, L.G. 26.7.18); b. 10.12.92; third s. of the late J. C. Crellin, J.P., C.P., of Ballachurry, Andreas, Isle of Man; m. Valerie, only child of His Honour the Deemster and Mrs. La Motte, Isle of Man; 2nd Lt., Notts and Derby R., 14.2.12; Capt. (T/Lt.-Col.), The Sherwood Foresters. He died on 8.10.18 of wounds received in action.

CRERAR, H. D. G. (D.S.O. L.G. 4.6.17), Major, Can. Field Arty.

CRESSINGHAM, H. (D.S.O. L.G. 1.1.18); b. 31.3.63; 1st com. 14.2.03; Lt.-Col. 3.1.19; retired 15.4.20; Bedf. and Herts R.; served S. African War, 1900-2; Queen's Medal with 2 clasps; King's Medal with 2 clasps; D.C.M.

CRESSWELL, F. H. P. (D.S.O. L.G. 22.8.18), Lt.-Col., Rand Rifles, S. African Mil. Forces.

CRESWELL, E. F. (D.S.O. L.G. 3.6.16); b. 17.12.76; s. of Col. E. W. Creswell, R.E.; m. Anne Richards, d. of C. W. Carver; educ. Wellington College; R.M.A., Woolwich; 2nd Lt., R.A., 21.3.96; Lt. 21.3.99; Capt. 11.9.01; Maj. 30.10.14; Lt.-Col. 1.5.21; served N.W.F. of India, Waziristan. 1901–2; Medal with clasp; Europ. War; Despatches; in Belgium and France 1914–18; Bt. Lt.-Col. 1.1.18.

CREWE-READ, R. O. (D.S.O. L.G. 26.3.18) (Details, L.G. 24.8.18), Capt., S.W.B., Spec. Res.

CRICHTON, A. G. MAITLAND-MAKGILL- (D.S.O. L.G. 17.12.17) (Details, L.G. 23.4.18); s. of A. G. Maitland-Makgill-Crichton, 19, Cumberland Place, London, and a cousin of the late Major C. M. Makgill-Crichton, of Lathrisk, and Largo, in Fife; while he is a grandson of Mr. D. M. N. Crichton, of Rankeilour. Two of his brothers entered the Navy, and two the Army, one being well known in Inverness as a former Adjutant of the 4th Camerons (T.). A. G. Maitland-Makgill-Crichton was commissioned in the Camerons only three years before, as a Capt. and T/Lieut.-Colonel, he won his D.S.O.; M.C.

CRICHTON, H. C. MAITLAND-MAKGILL- (see Maitland-Makgill-Crichton H. C.).

CRICHTON, HON. J. A. (D.S.O. L.G. 27.7.18); served S. African War, 1902; Queen's Medal with 3 clasps; served Europ. War, Capt., R. of O., R. Brig. and African Field Force.

CRIPPS, C. W. (D.S.O. L.G. 4.6.17) (Bar, L.G. 2.4.19) (Details, L.G. 10.12.19); b. 19.11.81; 2nd Lt., R.A., 23.7.01; Lt. 23.7.04; Capt. 23.7.14; Major 27.10.15; R.F.A.; Despatches.

CRIPPS, THE HON. F. H. (D.S.O. L.G. 1.1.18) (Bar L.G. 4.3.18) (Details, L.G. 16.8.18); b. 4.7.85; s. of Lord Parmoor, P.C., K.C.V.O.; educ. Winchester and New College, Oxford; Master of the Drag Hounds, and President of the Bullingdon Club, Oxford; played polo for Oxford in 1906; served Europ. War; was in command of the Bucks Hussars during the Palestine Campaign; severely wounded at Gallipoli, Aug. 1915.

CRIPPS, F. W. B. (D.S.O. L.G. 1.1.19), Major, Glouc. Hussars Yeom.

CRIPPS, H. H. (D.S.O. L.G. 2.5.16; b. 19.6.87; s. of W. Harrison Cripps, F.R.C.S.; m. Hilda Barbour, d. of H. G. Pring; 2nd Lt., R. Fus., 4.5.07; Lt. 29.1.10; Capt. 24.12.14; Adjt., R. Fus., 2.5.15–17.11.15; Adjt., R. Fus., 6.1.19; He landed with the 29th Div. at Cape Helles, Gallipoli, 25.4.15, and took part in the evacuation of Suvla and Helles; wounded; Despatches thrice; Bt. of Major 3.6.16; subsequently served in France; Despatches; again wounded.

CRISP, A. P. (D.S.O. L.G. 3.6.18), Lt., Unatt. List, 7.3.10; Major, Aust. F.A.

CRITCHLEY, A. C. (D.S.O. L.G. 3.6.16); b. 1890, at Calgary, Canada; s. of Capt. O. A. Critchley; m. 1916, Marion, d. of J. Galt, President of the Union Bank of Canada; one s.; one d.; educ. St. Bees School, Cumberland; Lt. 21.6.10; Bt. Capt. 21.6.15; Adjt. of Strathcona's Horse, 1915–18; Lt.-Colonel 3.11.16; seconded to R.F.C. from Canadian Forces, Feb. 1918; as Brig.-Gen., R.A.F., April, 1918; Brig.-Genl. Critchley went to Reserve of Officers, Can. Forces, Jan. 1919; Despatches; C.M.G. He played polo in the Regimental team which won Western Canadian Championship for two years.

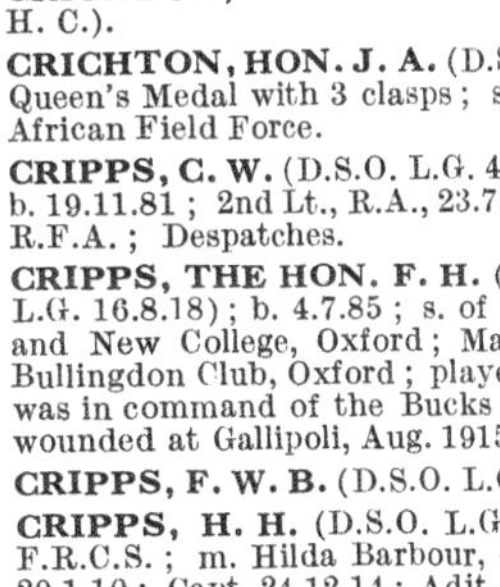

A. C. Critchley.

CRITCHLEY, W. R. (D.S.O. L.G. 26.7.17); Major, Can. Infy.

CROCKATT, N. R. (D.S.O. L.G. 12.12.19); b. 12.4.94; 2nd Lt. R. Scots, 17.9.13; Lt. 25.11.14 (A/Cyclists Corps 18.12.14–15); Capt. 17.8.16; M.C.; Despatches.

CROCKER, B. E. (D.S.O. L.G. 3.6.18); b. 30.10.65; 2nd Lt., R.I. Fus., 23.7.90; Lt. 25.6.97; Capt., Lan. Fus., 5.4.99; Maj., Welsh R., 9.1.09; Lt.-Col. 30.12.16; in command of the 52nd Bn. W.R. 3.11.18–29.3.19; Lt.-Col. retired 13.8.20; served S. African War, 1901–2; Queen's Medal with 5 clasps.

CROCKER, C. J. (D.S.O. L.G. 20.2.19), Commander, R.N.

CROCKER, H. E. (D.S.O. L.G. 2.2.16); b. 10.9.77; s. of H. J. Crocker and Blanche Crocker (*née* Greenhill); m. Gladys Mary, d. of Commander and Mrs. Edye; educ. St. Michael's School, Westgate-on-Sea, and at Shrewsbury School; 2nd Lt., Essex R., 5.5.00; Lt. 21.11.01; Capt. 4.1.11.; Major 1.9.15; served S. African War; wounded; Queen's Medal and 6 clasps; served in Gallipoli in command of 13th Signal Co.; wounded twice; Despatches four times; Bt. Lt.-Col. 3.6.17; C.M.G.

H. E. Crocker.

CROCKER, J. T. (D.S.O. L.G. 26.7.18); b. 3.1.96; T/2nd Lt., M.G.C.; Lt., Middlesex R., 26.6.19; M.C.

CROCKETT, B. E. (D.S.O. L.G. 1.1.17), T/Lt.-Col., Hants R.

CROFT, D. W. (D.S.O. L.G. 1.1.19), T/Major, S.W.B.; M.C.

CROFT, W. D. (D.S.O. L.G. 1.1.17) (1st Bar, L.G. 10.1.17) (2nd Bar, L.G. 26.7.18) (3rd Bar, L.G. 15.2.19) (Details, L.G. 30.7.19); b. 5.3.79; s. of Sir H. A. Croft, 9th Bart.; m. Esmé, d. of Sir A. E. Sutton, 7th Bart.; three children; educ. Oxford Military College; 2nd Lt., Sco. Rif., 7.3.00; Lt. 9.5.03; Capt. 12.3.12; Maj. 1.9.15; Bt. Lt.-Col. 1.1.18; Temp. Brig.-Gen. 14.9.17–17.3.19; Lt.-Col. Tank Corps, 30.4.20; seconded with Nigerian R., W.A.F.F., 1904–7; severely wounded by poisoned arrows, 1907; in France 2.11.14; Adjt., Sco. Rif.; commanded 11th R. Scots 4.12.15; commanding Lowland Brig. 14.9.17 to end of war; Despatches ten times; C.M.G.; Légion d'Honneur; Croix d'Officier. He has written "Three Years with the 9th Division."

CROFTON, M. (D.S.O. L.G. 14.1.16) (Bar, L.G. 26.7.18); b. 19.3.81; 2nd Lt., R.A., 25.6.99; Lt. 15.3.01; Capt. 19.12.07; Adjt. 10.8.08–10.8.11; Maj. 30.10.14; Bt. Lt.-Col. 3.6.19; Lt.-Col. 1.1.21; served S. African War, 1901–2; Queen's Medal with 5 clasps; Europ. War; Despatches.

CROFTON, SIR M. G., Bart (D.S.O. L.G. 1.1.18); b. 27.11.79; s. of late Capt. E. H. Crofton, Rifle Brigade; educ. Rugby; m. 1st, 1905, Maud, d. of late Col. H. Irley; one s.; 2nd, 1919, Adele, d. of Sir Geo. Donaldson; 2nd Lt., Lancs. Fus., 20.5.99; trans. I. Gds., 1901; 2nd L.G., 1903; Maj. (Res. of Off.), 12.7.15; serv. S. Afr., 1899–1901 (severely wounded in Relief of Ladysmith); Queen's Medal with 2 clasps; ret. 2nd L. Gds. 25.7.14; Lt.-Col., R. of O., 4.5.20; Europ. War; Legion of Honour; Despatches twice.

CROFTON, M. R. H. (D.S.O. L.G. 22.12.16) (Bar, L.G. 17.3.17) (Details, L.G. 17.4.17); b. 18.9.81; e. s. of Sir Malby Crofton, Bart.; m. 1918, Katharine Beatrix, o. d. of late G. S. Pollard, J.P.; educ. Aysgarth, Winchester; R.M.A., Woolwich; 2nd Lt., R.A., 18.8.00; Lt. 18.8.03; Capt. 23.8.11; Maj. 18.12.14; Comdg. 86th Batt. R.F.A.; served Africa and India. Major Crofton landed in France, October, 1914, with the Indian Army Corps; proceeded to Mesopotamia in December, 1915; severely wounded and invalided home February, 1917; returned to France, January, 1918; was four times wounded; Despatches twice and the Mons 1914 Star; served in N. Russia, 1919.

CROFTS, L. M. (D.S.O. L.G. 1.1.17); b. 16.12.67; s. of late Major E. Crofts, R.W.F.; m. Margaret, d. of late Col. W. A. Spence; one s.; one d.; educ. St. Edward's, Oxford, and Sandhurst; 2nd Lt., E. Lancs R., 6.3.89; R.W. Surrey R. 23.3.89; Lt. 8.12.90; Capt. 28.8.07; Maj. 17.2.12; Lt.-Col. 2.10.16; ret. pay, R. W. Surrey R., 18.5.21; served S. African War, 1899–02; Queen's Medal with 5 clasps; King's Medal with 2 clasps; Europ. War, 1914–18; Despatches thrice; wounded thrice; Chevalier de l'Ordre de Léopold.

CROLY, W. C. (D.S.O. L.G. 3.6.18); b. 3.4.74; Lt., R.A.M.C., 4.12.99; Capt. 4.12.02; Major 4.12.11; Lt.-Col. 26.12.17; served S. African War, 1900–2; Queen's Medal with 3 clasps; King's Medal with 2 clasps; Europ. War; Despatches.

CROMBIE, J. F. (D.S.O. L.G. 1.1.18); s. of J. L. Crombie, M.D.; m. Evelyn Mina, widow of Major A. B. King, 7th A. and S. Highrs.; served in Europ. War; Major; T/Lt.-Col., R.A.M.C. (T.).

CROMIE, F. N. A. (D.S.O. L.G. 31.5.16); b. at Duncannon Fort, Ireland, 30.1.82; s. of late Capt. F. C. Cromie, Hants R., Consul General at Dakar; educ. at Haverfordwest Grammar School, and in H.M.S. Britannia (where he became a cadet in May, 1898); he joined H.M.S. Repulse on passing out, and as Midshipman of H.M.S. Barfleur he took part in Seymour's Expedition to China in June, 1900; Despatches; China Medal with Peking clasp; Lieutenant, 1901, and two years later obtained four "firsts" on his promotion to lieutenant. In the same year he entered the submarine service. While serving in submarine A 3 at Spithead he tried to save a man who was washed overboard, and was awarded the bronze medal of the Royal Humane Society. In 1911–12 he commanded H.M.S. Onyx and a flotilla of submarines at Devonport, and in 1913–14 H.M.S. Rosario and the China submarine flotilla. In August, 1915, he commissioned Submarine E 19, and in the following month forced a passage into the Baltic, where he entirely suspended German traffic for a week (Russian Orders of St. Vladimir and St. Anne; 4th class with swords). On 7.11.1915 he sank the German cruiser Undine (D.S.O.); promoted Commander; St. George's Cross. Capt. Cromie was murdered in Russia while defending the British Embassy in Petrograd 31.8.18. He was awarded a posthumous C.B. "In recognition of his distinguished service in the Allied cause in Russia, and of the devotion to duty which he displayed in remaining at his post as British Naval Attaché in Russia, when the British Embassy was withdrawn. This devotion to duty cost him his life." The King received Capt. Cromie's widow at Buckingham Palace, and handed to her the D.S.O. and the C.B.

CROMIE, G. L. (D.S.O. L.G. 24.9.18), Lt., Aust. Inf.

CRONSHAW, A. E. (D.S.O. L.G. 1.1.18), Major (A/Lt.-Col.), Manch. R.; served S. African War, 1901–2; Queen's Medal with 4 clasps; Europ. War; Despatches.

CROOK, F. J. F. (D.S.O. L.G. 20.10.16); s. of Col. H. T. Crook, V.D., D.L.; m. Katherine May, d. of late J. Porter; Lt.-Col. Crook served in the Europ. War, and won the D.S.O. as T/Major, Lanc. Fus. He commanded the 5th Res. Bn. Lan. Fus. in France. His D.S.O. was awarded for gallantry at Le Falfemont Farm on 25.8.16.

CROOKENDEN, A. (D.S.O. L.G. 1.1.19); b. 4.1.77; 2nd Lt., Ches. R., 20.2.97; Lt. 28.12.98; Capt. 19.2.02; Adjt. 22.1.04–21.1.07; Maj. 7.5.15; Bt. Lt.-Col. 3.6.17; served S. African War, 1902; Queen's Medal with 4 clasps; Europ. War; Despatches.

CROOKENDEN, J. (D.S.O. L.G. 26.6.16), Major, The Buffs, 8.1.16.

CROOKSHANK, S. D'A. (D.S.O. L.G. 3.6.16); b. 3.6.70; s. of late Col. A. C. W. Crookshank, C.B., I.A.; m. Beryl Mary, d. of late Cdr. W. Still, R.N.; 2nd Lt., R. Eng., 27.7.89; Lt. 27.7.92; Capt. 6.5.00; Major 27.7.09; Lt.-Col. 22.6.17; Bt. Col. 1.1.18; Temp. Maj.-Gen. 19.1.18–31.5.19; Lt.-Col. 2.6.19; Hon. Col.; T/Major-Gen. 19.1.18; served with Chitral Relief Force, 1895 (Medal with clasp); Europ. War in France and Flanders; Despatches; Bt. Col. 1.1.18; K.C.M.G.; C.B.; C.I.E.; M.V.O.; Knight of Grace, Order of St. John of Jerusalem; Commander, Legion of Honour and Croix de Guerre; Commander, Order of Leopold and Croix de Guerre; Grand Officer, Ordre d'Aviz; American D.S.M.

CROPPER, C. H. (D.S.O. L.G. 3.6.18); m. May, d. of J. T. Salveson; Major, late R.E.; served Europ. War, 1914–18; Despatches; M.C.

CROSBIE, J. D. (D.S.O. L.G. 1.1.17); b. 19.8.65; s. of Col. J. Crosbie, J.P., D.L., and of Mrs. Crosbie, daughter of Sir J. Lister-Kaye; m. Maria Caroline Leith, d. of late Major J. Leith, V.C.; one d.; educ. Harrow; Sandhurst; joined 2nd Bn. 23rd R.W.F., Aug. 1885; retired as Lieut., Jan. 1893; rejoined the Army 19.8.14; Major 8.10.14; Lt.-Col. 15.2.15; Brig.-Gen. 5.6.16; Lt.-Col. 13.1.17; Colonel 13.11.18; Brig.-Gen. 26.5.19; demobilized as Hon. Brig.-Gen. 17.10.19; Commanded 11th Bn. Lan. Fus. 15.2.15 to 4.6.16; 12th Inf. Brig. 5.6.16 to 12.1.17; 16th Queen's Rgt. 16.3.17 to 12.11.18; Base, Archangel, 13.11.18 to 6.10.19; C.M.G.; St. Vladimir, Class IV. with bow and swords; St. Anne, Class II. with swords; Despatches; France, July, 1916; Jan. 1917; Home, May, 1918; Russia, June, 1918; Feb. 1920.

CROSBIE, J. P. G. (D.S.O. L.G. 4.6.17); b. 17.3.81; 2nd Lt., Unatt., 8.1.01; R. Brig. 9.3.01; Lt. 15.12.04; Capt. 14.6.11; Major 18.5.16; Bt. Lt.-Col. 3.6.19; served S. African War, 1901–2; Queen's Medal with clasp; Europ. War; Despatches; Bt. Lt.-Col. 3.6.19.

CROSBIE, W. McC. (D.S.O. L.G. 14.11.16); b. 28.9.78; m. Honor Alice, d. of Very Rev. L. H. O'Brien; 2nd Lt., R. Muns. Fus., 19.9.00; Lt. 3.10.03; Adjt. 18.5.06–17.5.09; Capt. 1.4.19; Major 1.9.15; served S. African War, 1902; Queen's Medal with 3 clasps; Europ. War, 1914–16; wounded; Despatches; D.S.O. awarded for gallantry on 3.9.16 at Guillemont.

CROSFIELD, G. R. (D.S.O. L.G. 30.3.16); b. 29.4.77; s. of John Crosfield, Soap and Chemical Manufacturer, of Warrington, and Elizabeth Crosfield (*née* Dickson); and brother of Sir A. Crosfield; educ. Harrow; ent. Army 8.7.96; Lt.-Col., T.F. Res., S. Lanc. R.; commanded 77th Co. I.Y. in S. African War (Queen's Medal, 5 clasps); worked for 10 years for the National Service League; crossed to France, Feb. 1915, as Second-in-Command to 1/4th S. Lancs.; subsequently commanded 2nd Suffolks and 10th R.W.F. in the field; leg amputated as result of wound at St. Eloi, March, 1916. His D.S.O. was awarded for a personal reconnaissance prior to the Battle of the Bluff 2.3.16. He has the Czecho-Slovak Croix de Guerre. After the Armistice he gave up his time and energies to the British Legion.

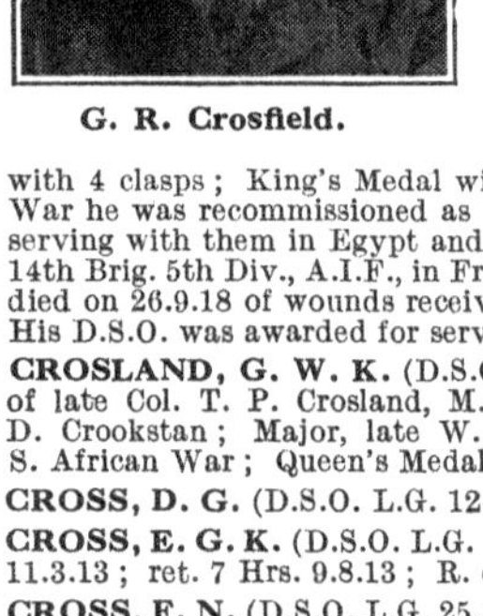

G. R. Crosfield.

CROSHAW, O. M. (D.S.O. L.G. 26.9.16); b. 11.3.79; s. of late George Croshaw and of Ellen Mary Croshaw; educ. at Harrow; commissioned 19th Hussars, 1899; served S. African War, 1899–1902; Queen's Medal with 4 clasps; King's Medal with 2 clasps. On the outbreak of the European War he was recommissioned as Second-in-Command City of London Yeomanry, serving with them in Egypt and Gallipoli, Aug. 1916; Lt.-Col. of the 53rd Batt. 14th Brig. 5th Div., A.I.F., in France; Despatches three times. Lt.-Col. Croshaw died on 26.9.18 of wounds received in the attack on Polygon Wood on that day. His D.S.O. was awarded for services 19–20.7.1916, at Petilon.

CROSLAND, G. W. K. (D.S.O. L.G. 3.6.16); s. of late G. W. Crosland; g.s. of late Col. T. P. Crosland, M.P., Huddersfield; m. Ann Frances, d. of late D. Crookstan; Major, late W. Riding R., T.F.; served as Civil Surgeon in S. African War; Queen's Medal with 3 clasps; Europ. War; Despatches.

CROSS, D. G. (D.S.O. L.G. 12.12.19), Major, Aust. L.H. Rgt.

CROSS, E. G. K. (D.S.O. L.G. 3.6.18); b. 23.11.84; ent. Army 4.11.03; Capt. 11.3.13; ret. 7 Hrs. 9.8.13; R. of O.

CROSS, F. N. (D.S.O. L.G. 25.11.16); b. 15.5.95; s. of F. R. Cross; m. Eileen Mary, d. of late G. S. Bleasdale; T/2nd Lt. 22.9.14 to 1915; T/Lt., 1915 to 1918 (Liverpool R.); Lt., Army, 22.6.16; I.A. 5.4.18; Capt. 22.6.19; Despatches; D.S.O. awarded for gallantry on 13–14th Sept. 1916.

CROSS, J. A. (D.S.O. L.G. 4.6.17), Lt.-Colonel J. A. Cross, M.L.A., of the Can. Inf., commanded the 15th Res. Bn. at Bramshott.

CROSSE, REV. E. C., M.A. (D.S.O. L.G. 1.1.17); b. 18.3.87; educ. Clifton College; Balliol College, Oxford; Asst. Master, Marlborough College, 1911–14 and 1919; Deacon, 1913; Priest, 1914; Headmaster of Christ College Grammar Schools, Christchurch, N.Z., 1920; T/Chaplain to the Forces from 1915; att. 8th Devons; Senior Chaplain, C.E., 7th Div., 1917; Croce di Guerra. He has written "The Place and Work of a Chaplain with Fighting Troops" (1917) and other books.

CROSSE, R. B. (D.S.O. L.G. 1.12.14) (Bar, L.G. 18.2.18) (Details, L.G. 18.7.18), Major, Oxf. and Bucks. L.I. (see "The Distinguished Service Order," from its institution to 31.12.1915, by same publishers).

CROSSE, W. C. (D.S.O. L.G. 3.6.18); b. 23.6.79; 2nd Lt., W.I.R., 12.8.99; A.S.C. 12.2.00; Lt. 12.2.01; Capt. 15.10.02; Major, R.A.S.C., 5.8.14; Lt.-Col. 5.1.21; Temp. Lt.-Col. 22.6.16; served S. African War, 1900–02; Queen's Medal with 5 clasps; Europ. War; Despatches.

CROSSING, W. L. (D.S.O. L.G. 27.6.19), T/Capt., Mtd. M.G.C. (Mesopotamia); D.S.C.

CROSSMAN, F. L. M. (D.S.O. L.G. 3.6.19); b. 16.8.88; s. of late L. M. Crossman; m. Ruth, d. of Capt. V. Gartside Tippings; one d.; educ. Wellington College; R.M.A., Woolwich; 2nd Lt., R. Art., 18.12.07; Lt. 18.12.10; Adjt. 12.10.11–5.3.15; Capt. 30.10.14; Major, R.F.A., 26.11.17; Despatches five times; M.C.

CROSSON, W. F. (D.S.O. L.G. 3.6.19), Capt. (A/Major), Hants R., T.F.

CROSTHWAITE, J. D. (D.S.O. L.G. 3.6.18); b. 1891; m. Claire Trollope; two s.; educ. Uppingham; Neuchatel University; Capt., London Rgt.; served in European War; was A/Lt.-Col.

CROUCH, E. (D.S.O. L.G. 4.6.17), 2nd Lt. (A/Major (Durham L.I.).

CROUCH, T. A. (D.S.O. L.G. 18.2.18) (Details, L.G. 18.7.18), 2nd Lt. (A/Capt.), R.I. Fus. S.R., attd. Tank Corps

CROUGHAM, J. P. (D.S.O. L.G. 24.9.18), Lt., Aust. Arty.

CROW, P. (D.S.O. L.G. 2.4.19) (Details, L.G. 10.12.19), T/Capt. (A/Major), R.F.A.

CROWDER, W. H. (D.S.O. L.G. 30.1.20), 2nd Lt., R.F.A., T.F.

CROWDY, J. D. (D.S.O. L.G. 26.8.18); b. 11.1.81; 2nd Lt., R.A., 6.1.00; Lt. 3.4.00; Ind. Army 7.3.05; Capt. 6.6.09; Major 1.9.15.

CROWTHER, H. A., M.A. (D.S.O. L.G. 26.4.17); b. 29.7.87, at Brighton, Victoria, Australia; s. of Dr. George Henry Crowther, M.A., LL.D. (Headmaster of Brighton Grammar School), and of A. E. Crowther; educ. Brighton Grammar School, and Trinity College, University of Melbourne; College Colours, Rowing,

The Distinguished Service Order 231

Football; joined Australian Exp. Force 5.5.15; became Lt.-Col. commanding 14th Bn. A.I.F.; served at Anzac, Gallipoli, to December; was a member of the final "C" party at evacuation; was leader of volunteer stokers when H.M.T. Southland was torpedoed off Lemnos; served on Sinai Peninsula, 1916; at Armentières, Pozières, Ypres, 1916; Grevillers and other engagements, Ypres, all engagements, 1917; Hébuterne, Villers Bretonneux, Schor Farm, Morcourt and elsewhere, 1918; Member of Australian Mission to U.S.A. troops, Heidelberg Line, Oct. 1918; Despatches.

CROWTHER, W. E. L. H. (D.S.O. L.G. 1.1.19), Lt.-Col., Aust. A.M.C.

CROZIER, F. P. (D.S.O. L.G. 1.1.17), T/Lt.-Col. (T. Brig.-Gen.), R. Ir. Rifles.

CRUDDAS, B. (D.S.O. L.G. 1.1.18); b. 1.1.82; 2nd Lt., North'd Fus., 11.8.00; Lt. 11.12.01; Capt. 12.9.09; Major 1.9.15; Despatches.

CRUICKSHANK, A. J. (D.S.O. L.G. 25.8.17); b. 11.3.91; 2nd Lt., R. Eng., 23.12.10; Lt. 21.12.12; Capt. 23.12.16; Despatches.

CRUICKSHANK, A. L. (D.S.O. L.G. 1.1.18); b. 30.8.83; 2nd Lt., R.A., 15.7.03; Lt. 15.7.06; Capt. 30.10.14; Adjt., R.A., 10.5.15 to 4.8.16; Major, R.G.A., 1.10.17; Despatches.

CRUMP, J. A. (D.S.O. L.G. 16.9.18); s. of Rev. J. Crump, of Arnside, Westmorland; m. Elspeth Beryl, only daughter of the late Col. F. R. Thackeray, R.A.; Lt.-Col., L.N. Lancs. R.

CRUTCHLEY, A. F. (D.S.O. L.G. 11.4.19), Lt.-Cdr., R.N.

CUBBON, J. F. (D.S.O. L.G. 26.7.18), T/Capt., R.E.; M.C.

CUFFE, J. A. F. (D.S.O. L.G. 14.1.16); b. 1876; s. of late L. Cuffe, J.P., of Clonskeagh, co. Dublin, and Rathnew, co. Wicklow; m. Gertrude Ella Mary, d. of late Sir J. Jackson; one d.; 2nd Lt., R. Marines, 1.1.96; Lt. 1.1.97; Capt. 29.4.03; Major, R. Munster Fus., 24.1.15; Lt.-Col. 23.5.19; served with K.A. Rifles, Nandi Exp., 1905–6; served in France from 24.1.15; Despatches; Bt. Lt.-Col. 1.1.18; C.M.G.; Legion of Honour; Ordre de la Couronne and Belgian Croix de Guerre.

CULLEY, S. D. (D.S.O. L.G. 2.11.18), Lt. (Sea Patrol), R.A.F.

CULLINAN, A. W. (D.S.O. L.G. 22.8.18), Major, Cullinan's Horse, S. African Mil. Forces.

CULLINAN, SIR T. (D.S.O. L.G. 22.8.18); b. Elands Post, 1862; m. Miss Harding; nine children; educ. Aliwal North, C.P.; Discoverer and Chairman of the Premier Diamond Mine; advocated responsible Government for Transvaal and Free State, and represented Pretoria North in the first Transvaal Parliament, and same constituency in first Union Parliament; Chairman for S.A. Party for the W. W. Rand; Chairman and Director of the New Eland Diamonds Ltd.; Director of several Gold Mining Companies; owner of the Consolidated Rand Brick, Pottery and Lime Co. Ltd.; served in Europ. War as Major, Supernumerary List, S. African Military Forces.

CUMBERLEGE, G. F. J. (D.S.O. L.G. 17.4.17), T/Capt., R. Fus.

CUMINE, G. J. G. G. (D.S.O. L.G. 14.1.16), Capt., G. Highrs. Serv. Bn.; served S. African War, 1901–2 (Queen's Medal with 3 clasps); Europ. War.

CUMING, R. J. (D.S.O. L.G. 26.8.18); b. 28.8.72; 2nd Lt., Suff. R., 7.3.94; Lt. 8.8.96; Ind. Army, 2.8.97; Capt. 7.3.03; Major 7.3.12; Lt.-Col. 24.6.18; Col. 8.9.20; served China, 1900 (Medal); Europ. War; Despatches; Bt. Lt.-Col. 3.6.17; O.B.E.

CUMING, R. S. D. (D.S.O. L.G. 2.7.17), Admiral (T/Capt. R.N.R.).

CUMMING, H. R. (D.S.O. L.G. 4.6.17); b. 9.10.67; 2nd Lt., Durh. L. Inf., 8.6.89; Lt. 28.7.91; Capt. 24.11.97; Lt.-Col. 29.3.16–22.9.19; T/Brig.-Gen. 23.11.16–26.5.17–16.3.18 to April, 1919; served S. African War, 1899–1901 (Despatches; Bt. of Major, 29.11.00; Queen's Medal with 4 clasps); Europ. War; Despatches; Bt.-Col. 1.1.19. He was killed in Ireland 6.3.21.

CUMMINS, C. E. (D.S.O. L.G. 1.1.17), T/Major, Durham L.I.

CUMMINS, E. J. (D.S.O. L.G. 3.6.16); b. 18.4.79; 2nd Lt., R.A., 26.5.00; Lt. 28.9.02; Capt. 13.5.13; Major 26.5.13; Adjt. 1.10.13–29.12.15; Major 30.12.15; Bt. Lt.-Col. 1.1.19.

CUNINGHAME, E. W. M. (D.S.O. L.G. 3.6.19); b. 30.5.78; 2nd Lt., R.A., 19.1.98; Lt. 19.1.01; Capt. 1.5.05; Adjt., R.A., 1907–9; Major, 30.10.14; Lt.-Col., R.F.A., 3.7.18; served S. African War, 1899–1902 (Despatches twice; Queen's Medal with 7 clasps; King's Medal with 2 clasps); Europ. War; Despatches.

CUNNINGHAM, ANDREW BROWNE (D.S.O. L.G. 14.1.16; Bar, L.G. 20.2.19; 2nd Bar, L.G. 8.3.20), Capt., R.N.

CUNNINGHAM, AYLMER BASIL (D.S.O. L.G. 14.1.16;) b. 5.1.79; 2nd Lt., R.E., 16.3.98; Lt. 14.2.01; Capt. 16.3.07; Major, 30.10.14; Bt. Lt.-Col. 3.6.17.

CUNNINGHAM, A. G. (D.S.O. L.G. 3.6.18); b. 1.5.87; 2nd Lt., R.A., 20.12.06; Lt. 20.12.09; Capt. 30.10.14; Major, 13.6.17; Despatches; M.C.

CUNNINGHAM, B. S. R (D.S.O. L.G. 1.1.18), T/Major, A.S.C.

CUNNINGHAM, C. C. (D.S.O. L.G. 3.6.19); b. 13.10.81; s. of late J. K. Cunningham, of See Tor, Axminster; 2nd Lt., Unattd., 28.7.00; Ind. Army, 11.10.01; Lt. 26.1.03; Capt. 28.7.09; Major, 2/107th Pioneers, I.A., 1.9.15; served in Europ. War; was a prisoner of war at Antwerp, but escaped; Despatches. His brother, Major J. F. Cunningham, who served in France from 1915, was awarded the O.B.E.

CUNNINGHAM, F. W. M. (D.S.O. L.G. 3.6.18), Capt. (T/Lt.-Col.), M.D., R.A.M.C.

CUNNINGHAM, H. T. (D.S.O. L.G. 14.1.16); b. 24.7.80; 2nd Lt., R.A., 26.6.99; Lt. 18.2.01; Capt. 22.4.04; Major, R.A. and I.R.A.O.D., 30.10.14; Lt.-Col., R. of O., 22.2.19; retired 25.8.21; served in China, 1900 (Medal); Europ. War; was a Q.M.G., G.H.Q., British Armies in France, 20.2.18; Despatches: Bt. Lt.-Col. 1.1.19.

CUNNINGHAM, J. A. (D.S.O. L.G. 1.1.19), Major (A/Lt.-Col.), R.A.F., D.F.C.

CUNNINGHAM, J. C. (D.S.O. L.G. 30.1.20), T/Lt., Oxf. and Bucks. L.I.

CUNNINGHAM, J. S. (D.S.O. L.G. 4.6.17); b. 6.12.76; 2nd Lt., Middlesex R., 5.5.00; Lt. 29.3.01; Capt. 11.3.05; Adjt., Middlesex R., 28.11.05 to 27.11.08; Major, 1.9.15; ret., Middx. R., 5.11.21; Lt.-Col., R. of O., 5.11.21; served S. African War, 1902; served in St. Helena, March to 31.5.02; Europ. War; served with Medit. Exp. Force and in Egypt and Palestine; Despatches; Bt. Lt.-Col. 1.1.19.

CUNNINGHAM, T. L. (D.S.O. L.G. 3.6.16), T/Major, Cam. Hldrs., Service Battn.

CUNNINGHAM, W. H. (D.S.O. L.G. 1.1.17), Lt.-Col., N.Z. Military Forces.

CUNNINGHAM-CUNNINGHAM, T. (D.S.O. L.G. 1.1.17); b. 7.8.77; 2nd Lt., RA., 26.5.00; Lt. 31.1.02; Capt. 26.5.13; Adjt. 21.1.14–30.11.14; Major, 30.12.15; served S. African War, 1900; Europ. War; Despatches.

CUNNINGHAME, W. W. SMITH (D.S.O. L.G. 24.9.18); b. 18.5.89; 2nd Lt., 2nd Life Guards, 19.9.08; Lt. 6.1.09; Capt. 24.5.12; Major 23.1.20; served Europ. War; Despatches.

CURELL, W. B. (D.S.O. L.G. 2.4.19) (Details, L.G. 10.12.19); b. 21.8.82; 2nd Lt., Lan. Fus., 8.5.01; Lt. 15.7.04; Capt. 6.7.14; Major 8.5.16; ret. Lan. Fus., 6.11.19; Despatches.

CURLING, R. R. (D.S.O. L.G. 1.1.18); b. 2.1.84; 2nd Lt., R. Art., 2.9.05; Lt. 2.9.08; Capt. 30.10.14; Bt. Major, 3.1.19; Despatches.

CURRAN, E. (D.S.O. L.G. 3.6.18), Lt. (A/Major), M.C., R.F.A.

CURREY, H. S. (D.S.O. L.G. 15.9.16); e. s. of late Lt.-Col. C. H. Currey, 4th D. Gds.; m. Cecil, d. of late Lt. R. Fulford, R.N.; Capt., R.N. He helped to save the "Marlborough" after she was torpedoed.

CURRIE, I. B. F. (D.S.O. L.G. 3.6.19), Lt.-Col., R.G.A.; b. 2.8.72; 1st Com. 1.4.92; Lt.-Col. 1.5.17; ret., R.A., 1.11.21.

CURRIE, JOHN, (D.S.O. L.G. 26.3.17), 2nd Lt., S. African Arty.; D.S.O. awarded for gallantry on 17.2.17, near Grandcourt.

CURRIE, P. (D.S.O. L.G. 26.9.16), Major, Aust. Inf.

CURRIE, R. A. M. (D.S.O. L.G. 14.1.16); b. 18.6.75; s. of late Lt.-Col. F. A. Currie, Norfolk R.; m. Ida Melville, d. of J. H. Hatchell, M.D.; educ. Wellington College; ent. Som. L.I. 6.6.96; Lt. 14.12.98; Capt. 1.1.04; Major, 1.9.15; T/Brig.-Gen.; served on N.W. Frontier of India, 1897–8 (Medal with clasp); Europ. War; Despatches 6 times; Bt. Major, 18.2.15; Bt. Lt.-Col. 1.1.17; Bt. Col. 1.1.18; C.M.G. He died at Danzig, E. Prussia, 30.3.20.

CURRIE, S. G. (D.S.O. L.G. 1.1.19), Capt. (A/Major), P.P. Can. L.I.; M.C.

CURRIN, R. W. (D.S.O. L.G. 25.8.16) (Bar, L.G. 8.3.19) (Details, L.G. 4.10.19); b. 1872; s. of late R. Currin and E. J. Currin; m. Ethel Cawood, d. of W. and J. Glass, and g.d. of late Sir T. Cawood; educ. at Kleinmonde, S. Africa; took part in the Jameson Raid; served in Bechuanaland, 1897, with the Kaffrarian Rifles; S. African War, 1899–1902; in Europ. War, in German S.W. Africa, commanding a company, reverted to 2nd Lt., and was sent to England by the Imperial Government, 1915, and posted to the 13th Yorks. and Lancs. Regt. He went to Egypt, Dec. 1915, and to France, 1916. He was promoted Capt. 1915 and Major, 1916; Lt.-Col. 28.11.17. D.S.O. awarded for gallantry at Serre, 1.7.16; Despatches 5 times.

CURRY, W. H. (D.S.O. L.G. 26.5.17), 2nd Lt. (A/Capt.), S. Staffs. R., Spec. Res. He was killed in action, 25.10.17. His D.S.O. was awarded for gallantry on 25.3.17, at Croiselles.

CURSETJEE, H. J. M., M.B. (D.S.O. L.G. 26.5.19), Capt., I.M.S.

CURTEIS, C. S. S. (D.S.O. L.G. 3.6.16; b. 15.3.74; Major, R.A., 30.10.14 (previous full pay service, 15.11.94 to 16.11.09; ret. pay, 1909; R. of O., recalled); Bt. Lt.-Col. 3.6.18; Despatches; C.M.G.

CURTEIS, R. W. S. (D.S.O. L.G. 22.1.20); Cdr., R.N.R. (Cdr. R.N. retired) (for Russia).

CURTIS, B. (D.S.O. L.G. 23.5.17) (Bar, L.G. 1.10.17); Capt., R.N.

CURTIS, G. (D.S.O. L.G. 22.8.18); b. 10.2.80; Major (T/Lt.-Col.), S. African Mtd. Riflemen, 1st Regt.

CURTIS, H. M. C. (D.S.O. L.G. 1.1.18) (1st Bar, L.G. 27.7.18) (2nd Bar, L.G. 8.3.19) (Details, L.G. 4.10.19), Capt. (A/Lt.-Col.), N. Staffs. R., T.F.; served S. African War, 1900, in I.Y. (Queen's Medal with 3 clasps); Europ. War; Despatches.

CURTIS, H. O. (D.S.O. L.G. 3.6.19); b. Nov. 1888; 2nd Lt., K.R.R.C., 14.10.08; Lt. 7.9.11; Capt. 10.5.15; Bt. Major, 3.6.18; Major; Despatches; M.C.

CUST, R. B. PUREY (see Purey Cust, R. B.).

CUSTANCE, F. H. M. (D.S.O. L.G. 27.6.17); s. of a former vicar of Colwell; m. a dau. of late F. R. Jarrett, of Bourton-on-the-Hill; Cdr., R.N.R., R.D. He died 3.1.21.

CUTBILL, R. H. L. (D.S.O. L.G. 1.1.17); b. 28.4.78; 2nd Lt., A.S.C., 21.2.00; Lt. 1.4.01; Capt. 18.2.04; Major, R.A.S.C., 5.8.14; Lt.-Col. 5.1.21; served S. African War, 1899–1902 (Queen's Medal with 3 clasps; King's Medal with 2 clasps); served Europ. War; Despatches; Bt. Lt.-Col. 3.6.18; C.M.G.; Legion of Honour, 5th Class.

R. H. L. Cutbill.

CUTCLIFFE, A. B. (D.S.O. L.G. 3.6.18), Lt., Can. A.V.C., 6.4.12; Major (T/Lt.-Col.).

CUTTING, R. H. (D.S.O. L.G. 3.6.18), Lt. (T/Major), Devons. R., attd. M.G.C.; M.C.

DA COSTA, E. C. (D.S.O. L.G. 1.1.18); b. 10.10.71; y. s. of late D. C. Da Costa; m. Jean, e. d. of late William Milne; one s.; educ. Harrow; R.M.C., Sandhurst; 2nd Lt., R. Lan. R., 13.7.92; Lt. 1.1.94; Capt. 4.6.00; Adjt. 29.10.02 to 25.5.06; Major, 12.3.13; Bt. Lt.-Col. 3.6.18; Bt. Col. 1.1.19; Col. 13.4.20; served Chitral Relief Expedition, 1895 (Medal, clasp); served S. African War, 1900–02 (Queen's Medal and 3 clasps; King's Medal, two clasps); Europ. War, 1914–18; Despatches; C.M.G.; 3rd Class Order of the Nile.

DAKEYNE, H. W. (D.S.O. L.G. 1.1.17) (Bar, L.G. 1.1.19); b. 24.11.86; s. of late Lt.-Col. Henry Fitzroy Dakeyne, Indian Army; educ. Wellington College; Blundell's College; R.M.C., Sandhurst; 2nd Lt., R. War. R., 4.1.08; Lt. 17.9.09; Capt. 14.9.14; commanded 10th Batt. R. War. R., July, 1916; commanding 8th Battn. North Staffs. Regt.; commanded 6th (Pioneers) Battn. S. Wales Borderers, 1919; served S. Africa; N.W. Frontier of India, 1908 (Medal with clasp); Cameroon Expeditionary Force, 1914; Europ. War, 1916; Despatches.

DALBIAC, J. H. (D.S.O. L.G. 22.6.16), Lt. R.M.A.

DALBY, T. G. (D.S.O. L.G. 1.1.17); b. 13.6.80; 2nd K. R. Rif. C. 5.4.99; Lt. 17.3.00; Capt. 22.1.06; Major, 1.9.15; Bt. Lt.-Col. 1.1.19; served S. African War, 1901–2 (Queen's Medal with 3 clasps; Despatches); E. Africa, 1904; operations in Somaliland (Medal with clasp); Europ. War; Bt. Lt.-Col. 1.1.19.

DALE, F. R. (D.S.O. L.G. 2.4.19) (Details, L.G. 10.12.19), T/Capt. (A/Major), 19th Bn. Welsh R., T.F.; b. 7.3.83; s. of J. F. Dale; m. 1909, Mary, d. of E. J. M. Phillips; two s.; two d.; educ. Oundle; Trinity College, Cambridge; Classical VIth Form Master, Leeds Grammar School, 1906–15; head master of Plymouth College since 1920; served Europ. War, 1916–19, in R.W.F., T.F.; T/Capt. (A/Major), 19th Bn., attd. 16th Bn.; M.C.

DALGETY, R. W. (D.S.O. L.G. 2.7.17), Cdr. R.N.

DALGLEISH, N. (D.S.O. L.G. 8.3.19) (Details, L.G. 4.10.19), Lt., Aust. Mil. Forces.

DALLAS, R. S. (D.S.O. L.G. 26.4.18), Sqdn.-Cdr., R.N.A.S.; Major, R.A.F.; D.S.C.

DALMENY (A. E. H.), LORD (D.S.O. L.G. 3.6.18); b. 8.1.82; e. s. of 5th Earl of Rosebery; m. 1909, Dorothy, y. d. of late Lord Henry Grosvenor; 2ndly, Dora Nina, e. d. of James A. Erskine Wemyss; one s.; one d.; educ. Eton; M.P. (L.), Midlothian, 1906–10; Lt. (T/Lt.-Col.), R. of O., G. Gds., ; served Europ. War, 1914–18; wounded; M.C. His D.S.O. was awarded for service under Gen. Allenby in Palestine, where his brother, the Hon. N. Primrose, was killed some months previously.

DALTON, D. GRANT- (see Grant-Dalton, D.).

DALTON, S. GRANT- (see Grant-Dalton, S.).

DALTRY, H. J. (D.S.O. L.G. 4.6.17), Fld. Arty., N.Z. Major Daltry, Live Stock Commissioner for Yorkshire, was temporarily loaned to the Supreme Economic Council at Paris.

DALY, C. W. D. (D.S.O. L.G. 1.1.17), Major, Aust. I. Force.

DALY, D. (D.S.O. L.G. 1.1.19); b. 19.8.83; 2nd Lt., R.A., 24.12.02; Lt. 24.12.05; Capt. 30.10.14; Major, 16.9.17; served Europ. War; M.C.

DALY, J. F. (D.S.O. L.G. 3.6.18), Major, 6th Batt. H.L.I.

DALY, L. D. (D.S.O. L.G. 14.1.16); b. 5.8.85; s. of Maurice Dominic Daly; educ. Downside School, near Bath; served with 4th Royal Muns. Fus. (Kerry Militia), 1905–07; 2nd Lt., Leins. R., 11.12.07; Lt. 1.4.10; Capt. 16.5.15; Bt. Major, 1.1.18; served Europ. War. 1914–18, France and Belgium; Despatches thrice; slightly wounded.

DALY, T. J. (D.S.O. L.G. 3.6.18), Lt., Aust. Lt. Horse.

DAMANT, W. S. (D.S.O. L.G. 14.5.20), Engr.-Cdr. R.N.; M.V.O.

DAMMERS, C. M. (D.S.O. L.G. 17.10.19), Cdr. R.N.

DAMMERS, G. M. (D.S.O. L.G. 18.2.18; Details, L.G. 18.7.18), Capt., Yeomanry; M.C.

DANBY, S. (D.S.O. L.G. 16.9.18) (Bar, L.G. 15.2.19) (Details, L.G. 30.7.19), Major (T/Lt.-Col.), Manch. R.; M.C.

DANE, J. A. (D.S.O. L.G. 26.11.17) (Details, L.G. 6.4.18); b. 18.5.83; s. of late Judge Richard Martin Dane, K.C., former M.P. for N. Fermanagh; m. 1909, Elgiva Mary Kathorn Wentworth Fitzwilliam, d. of late Hon. Thomas Wentworth Fitzwilliam; two s., one d.; educ. Portora Royal School, Enniskillen; Trinity College, Dublin; and R.M.A.; 2nd Lt., R.A., 29.12.02; Lt. 15.7.06, retiring 1910 (Spec. Res.); Capt. 24.12.12; rejoining 1914; Major, R.F.A., 16.11.15; T/Lt.-Col. 24.4.15 to 15.7.16; served in Europ. War, 1914–18; wounded; Despatches thrice.

J. A. Dane.

DANFORD, B. W. Y. (D.S.O. L.G. 3.6.16); b. 6.6.75; ent. R.E. 17.8.94; Lt. 17.8.97; Capt. 1.4.04; Adjt., R.E., 5.8.14 to 18.3.15; Asst. Inspector of Mines, G.H.Q., Br. Armies in France, from 4.4.18; Despatches; Bt. Lt.-Col. 1.1.18.

DANIEL, H. M. (D.S.O. L.G. 8.3.20), Lt.-Comdr., R.N.

DANIEL, J. A. (D.S.O. L.G. 11.1.19), Capt., Welsh Regt.; M.C.

DANIEL, T. W. (D.S.O. L.G. 1.1.18) (Bar, L.G. 11.1.19); b. 30.9.95; T/2nd Lt. 28.11.14; T/Lt. 18.7.15; T/Capt. 8.7.16; T/Major, 24.4.17; A/Lt.-Col., 10th Bn. Notts. and Derbys. Regt., 2.9.18; Capt., 7th Hrs., 1.1.21; M.C.; Despatches.

DANIELL, F. W. (D.S.O. L.G. 1.1.17), Major (T/Lt.-Col), North'd Fus.

DANIELL, N. R. (D.S.O. L.G. 1.1.18), Capt. (T/Lt.-Col.), D.C.L.I., attd. K.O.Y.L.I. He was killed in action at Polygon Wood on 4.10.17.

DANIELL, W. A. B. (D.S.O. L.G. 1.1.18), Major, R.H.A.; served S. African War, 1901; Europ. War; Despatches.

DANIELSEN, F. G. (D.S.O. L.G. 1.1.17), Major (T/Lt.-Col.) R. War. R.

DANIELSEN, J. W. (D.S.O. L.G. 4.6.17); m.; one s. and one d.; Lt.-Col., R.E. (T.F.).

DANN, W. R. H. (D.S.O. L.G. 18.7.17) (Bar, L.G. 26.7.18); b. 20.10 76; 2nd Lt., Manch. R., 12.5.00; Lt. 1.7.01; Lt., Bedf. R., 8.2.08; Capt. 5.1.10; Bt. Major, 3.6.15; Bt. Lt.-Col. 3.6.18; Brig.-Gen. 14.6.18; served S. African War, 1899–02 (Queen's Medal with 5 clasps); E. Africa (Somaliland), 1908–10 (Medal with clasp); Europ. War; Despatches.

DANNREUTHER, H. E. (D.S.O. L.G. 15.9.16); b. 12.12.80; y. s. of late Professor Edward Dannreuhter; m. 1916, Janie, y. d. of J. Hay Thornburn; one s.; educ. privately; joined H.M.S. Britannia, 1895; Chief Cadet Capt., 1896; Lieut., 1902; Gunnery Lieut. of Exmouth, flagship of Mediterranean Fleet, 1911–12; Comdr., 1914; Captain, 1920; served Europ. War in action of the Heligoland Bight, 28.8.14; Battle of Falkland Islands, 8.12.14; Battle of Jutland, 31.5.16; Despatches; Croix de Guerre avec Palme; Order of St. Anne, 3rd Class, with Swords.

DANSEY, F. H. (D.S.O. L.G. 14.1.16); b. 31.5.78; s. of late Sir R. D. Green-Price, 2nd Bt.; m. Nora Fitzgerald, 2nd d. of Capt. J. F. Tuthill; one s.; educ. Cheltenham College; R.M.C., Sandhurst; 2nd Lt., Wilts. R., 16.2.98; Lt. 14.11.99; Capt. 24.8.04; Adjt. 5.10.09 to 4.10.12; Major, 25.1.15; Bt. Lt.-Col. 3.6.17; served Europ. War; Despatches; C.M.G., 1918; Chevalier Légion d'Honneur, 1918; Comendador of the Order of Aviz (Portugal).

DANSEY, H. W. G. (D.S.O. L.G. 1.1.19), T/Major, Gen. List.

DARBY, H. (D.S.O. L.G. 3.6.18), Capt. (T/Major), A.S.C. (for Italy).

D'ARCY, J. I. (D.S.O. L.G. 3.6.19), Major (A/Lt.-Col.), 113th Bde. R.F.A.

D'ARCY, S. H. A. (D.S.O. L.G. 26.7.17), 2nd Lt., R.F.C., S.R.; killed whilst flying, on active service, 8.6.18; aged 19.

DARE, C. M. M. (D.S.O. L.G. 3.6.16); b. 27.5.88; s. of Montague Charles Dare; m. 1916, D. V. Moss; educ. Carlton College, Victoria; Melbourne Church of England Grammar School; 2nd Lt., 5th Squad. 10th Aust. L. Horse, 1907; transferred to Victorian Rifles, 1908; Lt. 1909; Capt. 1912; Militia Adjt. 1912; Major, 1914; Lt.-Col. 1915; served Europ. War, in Gallipoli.

DARELL, H. F. (D.S.O. L.G. 14.11.16); b. 18.8.72; only s. of late Edward Tierney Gilchrist Darell; m. 1915, Florence, d. of late Henry M. Leavitt, New York; educ. Eton; R.M.C., Sandhurst; 2nd Lt., Rifle Brigade; Lt.-Col. (R. of O.); served Tochi Expedition, 1897–98 (Medal with clasp); Europ. War, 1914–17; Despatches. His D.S.O. was awarded for gallantry on 3.9.16, at Hamel.

DARELL, SIR L. E. H. M., Bart. (D.S.O. L.G. 4.6.17); b. 2.5.76; s. of 5th Bart. and Helen Frances, o. c. of late Edward Marsland; m. 1903, Eleanor, d. of Capt. J. H. Edwards-Heathcote; two d.; educ. Eton; Christ Church, Oxford; 2nd Lt., 1st L.G., 22.3.99; Lt. 7.3.00; Capt. 16.9.05; Major, 21.10.14; served Europ. War, 1914–17; wounded; Despatches twice. Sir L. E. H. M. Darell was for a time Adjt. of the Gloucestershire Hussars.

DARKE, R. B. (D.S.O. L.G. 29.10.18), Lt.-Comdr., R.N.

DARLEY, C. G. (D.S.O. L.G. 25.8.17); b. 20.6.85; 2nd Lt., 14th Hrs., 16.1.07; Lt. 22.8.08; Capt. 8.7.16; Major, 14.5.20; Despatches.

DARLEY, J. R. (D.S.O. L.G. 18.8.16); b. 3.1.68; y. s. of B. G. Darley, M.D.; m. 1904, Hester Guinevère, o.d. of late J. B. Sandford, Barrister-at-Law, Dublin; educ. privately; Trinity College, Dublin; 2nd Lt., Glouc. R., 6.8.89; transferred to Lt. Ind. S.C. 20.12.90; Capt. Ind. Army, 6.8.00; Major, 6.8.07; Lt.-Col. 6.7.15; commanded 1/119th Infantry from April, 1915, to April, 1920; served Europ. War; six times mentioned in Despatcehs; C.I.E. 1917; very severely wounded, 22.11.15, at Ctesiphon.

DARLING, J. C. (D.S.O. L.G. 3.6.16); b. 15.6.87; o. s. of Rt. Hon. Sir C. J. Darling (Mr. Justice Darling); m. 1918, Joan, e. d. of Martin Powell; one s.; educ. St. Neots; Eton College; R.M.C., Sandhurst; 2nd Lt., 20th Hussars, 29.8.06; Lt. 22.1.08; Capt. 14.6.13; Major, 20th Hrs., 13.1.21; Major, 14th Hrs., 23.11.21; served Europ. War, 1914–16; Despatches.

DARLING, J. M., M.B., F.R.C.S. (D.S.O. L.G. 3.6.16); b. 1878; s. of late William Darling; m. Jean, d. of late Neil Clark, J.P.; one s.; educ. Royal High School, University, Edinburgh (M.A.); surgeon to Eye, Ear and Throat Infirmary, Edinburgh; Major, R.A.M.C. (S.R.).

DARLINGTON, A. J. (D.S.O. L.G. 4.6.17); b. 7.2.82; s. of E. Darlington; m. 1912, Mabel Jean Grant, d. of Major-General A. G. Dallas; one s., one d.; 2nd Lt., R.E., 23.7.01; Lt. 1.4.04; Capt. 23.1.12; Adjt. 5.8.14–31.5.16; Major, 2.11.16; served Europ. War, 1914–18; Despatches.

DARNELL, A. H. (D.S.O. L.G. 24.9.18); b. May, 1886; s. of late Rev. F. A. Darnell, Senior Chaplain to the Forces in Ireland; Major, Australian Military Forces; served Europ. War; died of wounds, 24.9.18.

DARWALL, R. H. (D.S.O. L.G. 1.1.17); b. 3.10.79; s. of R. C. Darwall; educ. Stubbington House, Fareham; Dover College; 2nd Lt., R. Mar., 1.1.98; Lt. 1.1.99; Adjt. 18.8.05 to 17.8.10; Capt. 1.2.07; Major, 8.6.16; Bt. Lt.-Col. 3.6.19; attd. Egyptian Army, commanding 14th Sudanese; served Europ. War; C.B.E.; Despatches.

DARWALL, W. H. (D.S.O. L.G. 6.4.18), Cdr., R.N.

DARWIN, C. J. W. (D.S.O. L.G. 8.2.19); b. 12.12.94; e. s. of Col. Charles Waring Darwin, C.B.; 2nd Lt., C. Gds., 25.2.14; Lt., C. Gds., 17.7.15; R. F. Corps, 11.5.16 to 31.3.16; T/Capt., R.F.C., 30.7.16 to 15.9.16; Capt., C. Gds., 16.9.16; T/Major, C. Gds., attd. R.A.F.; commanded the 87th squadron R.A.F.; Despatches; wounded, 1915.

DAUBENY, G. B. (D.S.O. L.G. 14.11.16) (Bar, L.G. 26.9.17) (Details, L.G. 9.1.18); b. 19.12.82; s. of late Giles Andrew Daubeny, Capt. 82nd Foot; educ. Kelly College, Tavistock, and R.M.A., Woolwich; 2nd Lt., R.A., 2.5.00; Lt. 3.5.01; Capt. 22.11.12; Major, 30.12.15; Lt.-Col. August, 1917; retired with rank of Lt.-Col. August, 1920; served Europ. War; Despatches, 3 times; severely wounded; Croix de Guerre avec Palme, for services with the 10th French Army, August, 1918. His D.S.O. was awarded for gallantry on 15.9.16, at Martinpuich.

DAVENPORT, F. (D.S.O. L.G. 26.9.17) (Details, L.G. 9.1.18), Major, R.F.A.; served Europ. War; M.C. Major Davenport was killed in action 28.9.17. He was chairman of Messrs. Wardell and Davenport Limited, Silk Manufacturers, Leek.

DAVENPORT, S. (D.S.O. L.G. 3.6.16), Lt.-Col., Glos. Regt.

DAVENPORT, W. A. (D.S.O. L.G. 4.9.18); b. 22.10.81; 2nd Lt., W. York. R., 22.5.03; Lt. 14.7.08; Capt. 22.1.14; Major, 22.5.18; M.C.; Despatches.

DAVEY, J. E. (D.S.O. L.G. 1.1.18), Major, Can. A.M.C., 10.8.11; served Europ. War; Despatches.

DAVID, M. (D.S.O. L.G. 1.1.18), Capt. (T/Major), R. Monmouthshire R.E., Spec. Res.

DAVID, T. J. (D.S.O. L.G. 1.1.18); b. 1881; s. of late Lt.-Col. D. R. David, J.P.; m. 1912, Nita, d. of late Pendrill Charles; one s., one d.; educ. Malvern; Christ College, Brecon; admitted (solicitor), 1904; retired, 1919; 2nd Lt., 2nd Vol. Battn. Welsh Regt.; Capt.. R.H.A.; Lt.-Col., commanding 1st Welsh Brigade, R.G.A.; served Europ. War, 1914–18; Despatches; Territorial Decoration.

DAVID, T. W. E. (D.S.O. L.G. 1.1.18), Major, Aust. Engrs.; C.M.G.

DAVIDGE, G. M. C. (D.S.O. L.G. 26.9.17) (Details, L.G. 9.1.18) (Bar, L.G. 20.9.18); b. 2.3.78; 2nd Lt., Worc. R., 16.2.98; Lt. 10.1.00; Capt. 21.12.01; Major, 2.3.15; served S. African War, 1899–1902 (Queen's Medal with 3 clasps; King's Medal with 2 clasps); Europ. War; Despatches. D.S.O. awarded for gallantry on 31.7.17, east of Ypres.

DAVIDS, A. P. F. RHYS- (see Rhys-Davids, A. P. F.).

DAVIDSON, A. E. (D.S.O. L.G. 14.1.16); b. 15.8.80; s. of late Colonel John Davidson, C.B.; m. Janie, d. of late C. McColl; educ. Blackheath School; R.M.A., Woolwich; 2nd Lt., R.E., 22.11.99; Lt. 24.7.02; Capt. 22.11.08; Major, 5.8.16; Bt. Lt.-Col. 3.6.18; served S. African War, 1902 (Queen's Medal, 3 clasps); Europ. War; Despatches.

DAVIDSON, A. N. (D.S.O. L.G. 24.6.16 and 27.7.16) (Details, L.G. 19.8.16); o. s. of William Davidson, of Hillpark, Wormit, Fife; m. 1918, Hilda Blanche, o. d. of F. L. M'Kinnon; Capt., G. Hldrs. His D.S.O. was awarded for gallantry on 1.7.16, at Mametz; killed in action.

DAVIDSON, A. P. (D.S.O. L.G. 14.3.16), Capt., R.N.; in charge of Suvla covering force.

DAVIDSON, C. G. F. (D.S.O. L.G. 3.6.18); b. 5.1.84; 2nd Lt., R.A., 15.7.03; Lt. 15.7.06; Capt. 30.10.14; Major, 22.11.17; M.C.

DAVIDSON, F. H. N. (D.S.O. L.G. 1.1.19); b. 1.4.92; e. s. of L. F. Davidson; 2nd Lt., R.A., 23.12.11; Capt. 23.12.14; Capt. 8.8.16; served Europ. War; Despatches; M.C.

DAVIDSON, G. (D.S.O. L.G. 1.1.18), T/Major, A.S.C.

DAVIDSON, H. A., M.B. (D.S.O. L.G. 1.1.17) (Bar, L.G. 26.7.18); b. 25.5.75; Lt., R.A.M.C., 29.11.00; Lt.-Col. 13.9.18; retired, 29.5.20.

DAVIDSON, J. E. (D.S.O. L.G. 2.12.18), T/Capt. (A/Major), R.G.A. He died of wounds 16.10.18.

DAVIDSON, N. R. (D.S.O. L.G 14.1.16) (Bar, L.G. 27.10.17) (Details, L.G. 18.3.18), Major and Bt. Lt.-Col., R.F.A.; served S. African War, 1899–1902 (Despatches; Queen's Medal with 3 clasps; King's Medal with 2 clasps); Europ. War; Despatches. He died of wounds 5.10.17.

DAVIDSON, P. V. (D.S.O. L.G. 3.6.18); b. 20.6.86; 2nd Lt., R. War. R., 24.6.06; Lt. 18.6.09; Capt. 12.9.14; Despatches.

DAVIDSON, T., (D.S.O. L.G. 27.10.17) (Details, L.G. 18.3.18) (Bar, L.G. 16.9.18), Major, R.F.A.

DAVIDSON, W. J. S. (D.S.O. L.G. 1.1.18), Lt.-Col., Aust. F. Arty.

DAVIE, J. H. M. (D.S.O. L.G. 23.10.19); b. 13.8.70; 2nd Lt., R. Scots, 7.11.91; Lt. 17.4.95; Capt. 22.4.99; Adjt., R. Scots, 1.11.99 to 8.10.03; Capt., Ind. Army, 13.1.07; Major, 7.11.09; Lt.-Col. 7.11.17; Col. 9.3.20; served S. African War, 1902 (Queen's Medal, 3 clasps); Europ. War; Despatches; Bt. Lt.-Col. 3.6.16.

DAVIE, K. M. (D.S.O. L.G. 4.6.17); b. 14.7.68; 2nd Lt., Glouc. R., 14.9.87; Col. 11.5.19; served S. African War, 1900 (Despatches; Queen's Medal, 4 clasps); Europ. War; Despatches.

DAVIES, A. H. (D.S.O. L.G. 1.1.18); b. 29.12.71; s. of E. F. and E. A. Davies; educ. Lewisham House School, Weston-super-Mare; 1st com., 1899; Lt.-Col., R.F.A.; served Europ. War, France, Egypt, Palestine, 1914–18, and afterwards to 1919; commanded 263rd Bde. R.F.A. from Sept. 1917.

A. H. Davies.

DAVIES, A. R. (D.S.O. L.G. 2.12.18), T/Major, R.E.; Europ. War; M.C.

DAVIES, C. E. (D.S.O. L.G. 2.12.18); b. 8.5.81; 2nd Lt., R. War. R., 29.1.02; Lt. 23.9.06; Capt. 14.4.14; Major, 29.1.17; served N.W. Frontier of India, 1908; operations in Zakka Khel Country (Medal with clasp); Europ. War; Despatches.

DAVIES, C. S. (D.S.O. L.G. 26.11.17; Details, L.G. 6.4.18); b. 7.9.80; 2nd Lt., Leic. R., 16.5.00; Lt. 1.4.02 (W. Afr. R. 2.3.07 to 25.10.11); Capt. 4.8.08; Major, 1.9.15; Bt. Lt.-Col. 3.6.19; served S. African War, 1899–1901 (Queen's Medal, 3 clasps; King's Medal, 2 clasps); Europ. War; Despatches; Bt. Lt.-Col. 3.6.19.

DAVIES, E. VAUGHAN (D.S.O. L.G. 23.3.17), Lt., R.N.R.

DAVIES, G. V. (D.S.O. L.G. 18.1.18) (Details, L.G. 25.4.18), Capt., Aust. A.M.C.

DAVIES, H. W. (D.S.O. L.G. 30.1.20), Capt., 2/8th Bn. Worc. R., T.F.; M.C.

DAVIES, J. E. H. (D.S.O. L.G. 1.1.18), T/Lt.-Col., R.A.M.C. He commanded the 130th St. John Field Ambulance in France.

DAVIES, J. W. LL. (D.S.O. L.G. 3.6.18), T/Capt. (A/Major), R.E.; M.C.

DAVIES, O. S. (D.S.O. L.G. 1.1.18), Capt. (T/Major), R.E.

DAVIES, P. M. (D.S.O. L.G. 1.1.17); b. 13.6.73; 2nd Lt., R. W. Kent R., 21.1.93; Lt. 10.9.94; Lt., A.S.C., 1.4.95; Capt. 19.2.00; Major 20.3.07; Lt.-Col., R.A.S.C.

DAVIES, R. D. (D.S.O. L.G. 17.4.17) (1st Bar, L.G. 2.12.18) (2nd Bar, L.G. 2.4.19) (Details, L.G. 10.12.19), Lt.-Col., Can. Inf.

DAVIES, R. H. (D.S.O. L.G. 3.6.18), T/Capt. (A/Major), R.E.; Assoc.M.Inst. C.E.; served Europ. War, 1914–18; Despatches; Officier de l'Ordre de la Couronne.

DAVIES, T. G. R. (D.S.O. L.G. 21.6.19), Eng.-Cdr., R.N.

DAVIES, T. H. (D.S.O. L.G. 1.1.18), 2nd Lt., R.E.

DAVIES, W. E. (D.S.O. L.G. 3.6.19); b. 14.7.79; s. of Byam Davies; educ. Eton; Sandhurst; 2nd Lt., Rif. Brig., 4.2.99; Lt. 7.4.00; Capt. 29.4.04; Major, 30.12.14; Bt. Lt.-Col. 1.1.16; Lt.-Col. 28.9.19; served S. African War, 1899–1902 (Despatches; Queen's Medal, 3 clasps; King's Medal, 2 Clasps); Europ. War, 1914–18, in France, Flanders and Palestine; Despatches thrice; C.M.G. 1917; Order of the Crown of Italy; Order of the Sacred Treasure; Order of the Nile.

DAVIES, W. P. L. (D.S.O. L.G. 14.1.16); b. 14.1.71; 2nd s. of Rev. W. P. Davies; 2nd Lt., R.A., 1.2.93; Lt. 1.2.96; Capt. 21.5.00; Major, 13.2.10; Lt.-Col. 7.11.15; T/Brig.-Gen. 11.12.16 to 31.12.20; Bt. Col. 10.3.17; Col. 10.8.20; T/Col. Comdt. 14.10.21; served S. African War, 1900–02 (Despatches; Queen's Medal, 5 clasps; King's Medal, 2 clasps); Europ. War, 1914–18, with Indian Exp. Force (Despatches twice); Mesopotamia (Despatches thrice); C.M.G. 1919; Croix de Guerre.

DAVIES-EVANS, D. W. C. (D.S.O. L.G. 3.6.19), Major (A/Lt.-Col.), Pembrokeshire Yeom., attd. 2/8th Bn. Worc. R., T.F.

DAVIS, A. H. (D.S.O. L.G. 3.6.16); b. 15.3.86; s. of R. T. H. Davis; educ. Loughborough Grammar School; University College, London; called to Bar, Middle Temple, 1920; joined A.S.C. 1914; T/Major; served Europ. War, 1914–19.

DAVIS, A. W. (D.S.O. L.G. 15.2.17), T/Major, Can. Eng.

DAVIS, C. E. (D.S.O. L.G. 7.11.18), Lt., Aust. Inf.; M.C.

DAVIS, C. H. (D.S.O. L.G. 4.6.17), Lt.-Col., Aust. Mil. Forces, 9.2.16; C.B.E.; Despatches.

DAVIS, F. (D.S.O. L.G. 24.9.18), 2nd Lt., S. Staffs. R.; served in S. African War; Europ. War; wounded five times.

DAVIS, G. J. (D.S.O. L.G. 3.6.16); b. 9.11.69; s. of late Major-Gen. Gronow Davis, V.C., R.A.; m. Evelyn Mary, d. of W. C. Beloe, J.P.; three s.; one d.; educ. Clifton College; R.M.C., Sandhurst; 2nd Lt., Scot. Rif., 1.3.90; Lt., Ind. S.C., 15.2.92; Capt., Ind. Army, 1.3.01; Major, 1.3.08; Lt.-Col. Comdg. 9th K.R.R.C.; served N.W. Frontier of India, 1897–8 (Medal, 2 clasps); Tirah, 1897–8 (Clasp); N.W. Frontier, 1898–9; E. Africa, operations in Somaliland, 1902–4 (Medal, 2 clasps); Europ. War; Despatches, Jan. 1916, June, 1916; died, 20.6.19.

DAVIS, H. J. N. (D.S.O. L.G. 26.5.17); b. 15.3.82; s. of late Surg.-Lt.-Col. J. Norman Davis; m. 1915, Margaret Georgiana, d. of Capt. S. Hyde-Smith, late 12th R. Lancers; two s.; one d.; educ. King's School, Warwick, and R.M.C., Sandhurst; 2nd Lt., Conn. Rang., 11.8.00; Lt. 12.4.02; Capt. 8.5.09; Bt. Major, 18.2.15; Major, 1.9.15; in command 15th Battn. High. Light Inf., and 47th and 9th Battns. Mach. G. Corps; served S. African War, 1900–02, (Queen's Medal, 4 clasps); Europ. War; Despatches, 5 times; C.M.G. 1919.

DAVIS, S. A. (D.S.O. L.G. 22.9.16), T/2nd Lt. (T/Lt.), Gen. List. D.S.O. awarded for gallantry at Bazentin-le-Petit Wood.

DAVIS, W. E. (D.S.O. L.G. 15.2.19; Details, L.G. 30.7.19), Lt., Can. Inf., 7.3.15; Major, 11th Bn. Can. Rly. Troops; Despatches.

DAVIS, W. H. (D.S.O. L.G. 1.1.18), T/Major, M.G. Corps; M.C.

DAVISON, D. S. (D.S.O. L.G. 15.2.19; Details, L.G. 30.7.19); b. 17.2.88; 2nd Lt. (Unatt.), 17.8.07; 2nd Lt., Ind. Army, 12.11.08; Lt. 17.11.09; Major, 1.9.15; Despatches.

DAVSON, H. J. H. (D.S.O. L.G. 3.6.19); b. 15.1.80; educ. Dartmouth; 2nd Lt., R. Mar., 1.9.98; Lt. 1.7.99; 2nd Lt., Unatt., 24.10.01; Lt., Ind. Army, 27.11.02; Capt. 18.1.09; Major, 1.9.15, 82nd Punjabis, I.A.; served Europ. War; D.S.O. awarded for services in Egypt and Palestine; also served in France and Mesopotamia; Despatches.

H. J. H. Davson

DAVSON, H. M. (D.S.O. L.G. 4.6.17); b. 4.6.72; s. of late Sir Henry Davson; m. 1910, Violet St. Clair, d. of 15th Baron Sinclair; one s.; 2nd Lt., R.A., 12.2.92; Lt. 12.2.95; Capt. 5.1.07; Major, 13.6.09; Lt.-Col. 8.7.15; served S. African War, 1899–1900 (Despatches; Queen's Medal, 3 clasps); Europ. War, 1914–19; Despatches; C.M.G. 1919.

DAVY, J. E. (D.S.O. L.G. 1.1.19), Major R.F.A., T.F. He died 9.12.18.

DAWES, G. (D.S.O. L.G. 18.2.18; Details, L.G. 18.7.18) (1st Bar, L.G. 26.7.18; 2nd Bar, L.G. 11.1.19); b. 21.2.90; 2nd Lt. S. Staff. R., 18.9.09; Lt. 15.11.11; Capt. 26.5.15; Bt. Major, 1.1.17; Despatches; M.C.

DAWES, G. W. P. (D.S.O. L.G. 1.1.17); b. 8.4.80; 2nd Lt., R. Berks. R., 27.7.01; Lt., May, 1904; Capt. 30.4.11 (Air Bn. R. Eng. 10.4.12 to 12.5.12; R.F.C. 13.5.12 to 31.3.18); Major, R. Berks. Regt., 14.9.16; Bt. Lt.-Col. 3.6.17 (Tank Corps, 14.7.20); served S. African War, 1900–2 (Queen's Medal with 3 clasps; King's Medal with 2 clasps); served Europ. War; Despatches; Croix d'Officier of the Legion of Honour; Croix de Guerre (French); Cross of Commander of the Order of the Redeemer (Greece); A.F.C.

DAWES, H. C. F. (D.S.O. L.G. 8.3.20), A/Lt.-Cdr., R.N.V.R.; O.B.E.

DAWES, H. F. (D.S.O. L.G. 1.1.18); b. 24.6.84; 2nd Lt., R. Fus., 23.5.06; Lt. 26.4.09; Capt. 12.12.14; served Europ. War, 1914–18; Despatches; M.C.

DAWNAY, A. G. C. (D.S.O. L.G. 1.1.17); b. 24.3.88; 2nd Lt., C. Gds., 6.3.09; Lt. 18.5.10; Adjt., C. Gds., 6.6.13 to 15.3.15; Capt. 17.7.15; Bt. Major, 3.6.17; Major, 1.10.20; served Europ. War; Despatches.

DAWSON, A. L. (D.S.O. L.G. 3.6.18), Bt. Major, Aust. A.M.C., 24.9.17; Lt.-Col.; Despatches.

DAWSON, F. (D.S.O. L.G. 7.11.18), Lt. (A/Capt.), Tank Corps; M.C.

DAWSON, F. C. (D.S.O. L.G. 15.10.18), Capt., Aust. Inf.; M.C.

DAWSON, F. E. M. (D.S.O. L.G. 2.7.17), Capt., R.N.

DAWSON, F. S. (D.S.O. L.G. 3.6.18) (Bar, L.G. 8.8.19), T/Brig.-Gen., S. African Defence Force; A.D.C. to H.M. 3.6.17; served Europ. War, 1914–18; Bt.-Col.; Despatches; C.M.G. 1916.

DAWSON, G. DE H. (D.S.O. L.G. 3.6.19), T/Capt., R.A.M.C.

DAWSON, H. J. (D.S.O. L.G. 4.6.17) (Bar, L.G. 2.12.18), Lt.-Col., 48th Can. Inf.; served Europ. War, 1915–18; Despatches twice; C.M.G. 1919; Croix de Guerre.

DAWSON, H. K., M.D. (D.S.O. L.G. 4.6.17); s. of J. Dawson; m. 1905, Mabel Mary, 3rd d. of Rev. R. Piggott; educ. Durham University; Capt. R.A.M.C.; served as Surgeon, S. African War (Queen's Medal with 3 clasps); Europ. War, 1914–18; Despatches twice.

DAWSON, N. G. STEWART- (see Stewart-Dawson, N. G.).

DAWSON, W., M.B. (D.S.O. L.G. 24.6.16; Details, L.G. 27.7.16), T/Capt. R.A.M.C.

DAWSON, W. R. A. (D.S.O. L.G. 15.4.16) (1st Bar, L.G. 18.7.17) (2nd Bar, L.G. 22.6.18) (3rd Bar, L.G. 8.3.19) (Details, L.G. 4.10.19); b. 23.6.91; s. of William Dawson, M.A. Oxford, and Mrs. Dawson, d. of late Capt. Henry Hill Dawson, 19th Regt. of Foot; educ. Hildersham House, St. Peter's, Kent; Bradfield College; Oriel College, Oxford; 2nd Lt., Queen's Own R.W. Kent R. 9.6.14; Capt. (T/Lt.-Col.), commanding 6th Bn. R.W. Kent R.; served Europ. War; Despatches; Bt. Major; wounded twice in 1916. He died of wounds 3.12.18. His D.S.O. was awarded for gallantry on 7th–8th and 8th–9th March, 1916, in the craters.

W. R. A. Dawson.

DAWSON-SQUIBB, J. (D.S.O. L.G. 22.8.16), Lt.-Col., S. African Mil. Forces.

DAY, F. R. (D.S.O. L.G. 3.6.19); b. 1.1.78; 2nd Lt., Norf. R., 16.2.98; Lt. 1.5.99; Capt. 29.3.05; Major, 1.9.15; Lt.-Col. 16.3.21; served S. African War, 1900–2 (Queen's Medal with 3 clasps; King's Medal with 2 clasps); Europ. War; Despatches.

DAY, THE REV. JAMES (D.S.O. L.G. 1.2.19), Chaplain to the Forces, 3rd Class.

DAY, JOHN (D.S.O. L.G. 1.1.17); b. 20.7.82; 2nd Lt., R.E., 18.8.00; Lt. 18.8.03; Capt. 18.8.10; Major, 2.11.16; Bt. Lt.-Col. 3.6.19; Despatches.

DAY, N. A. L. (D.S.O. L.G. 3.6.19); b. 8.12 82; 2nd Lt., R.A., 21.12.01; Lt. 21.12.04; Capt. 30.10.14; Major, 12.2.16; Despatches.

DAY, R. W. (D.S.O. L.G. 4.6.17), T/Major, Gen. List, late A.S.C.

DAY, S. M. (D.S.O. L.G. 22.6.17), Capt., R.D., R.N.R.

DAYRELL, W. S. (D.S.O. L.G. 26.8.18); b. 28.12.82; 2nd Lt., Gord. Highrs., 8.5.01; Lt., Ind. Army, 11.2.04; Capt. 8.5.10; Major, 8.5.16; retired, 13.11.19; served S. African War, 1901–2 (Queen's Medal with 2 clasps); Despatches.

DAYRELL-REED, A. (D.S.O. L.G. 12.5.17) (Bar, L. G. 28.8.18), Lt., R.N.R.; Despatches, 26.8.18.

DEACON, H. R. G. (D.S.O. L.G. 14.1.16) (Bar, L.G. 27.6.19); b. 11.10.71; s. of Rev. J. H. Deacon, B.A., Vicar of Trinity Church, Belfast; m. 1898, Kathleen, 4th d. of Col. W. Long, C.M.G.; one d.; educ. Belfast Academy; Sherborne School; R.M.C., Sandhurst; 2nd Lt., Conn. Rangers, 7.11.91; Lt. 14.8.93; Capt. 9.4.00; Adjt. 18.2.09 to 8.3.11; Major, 4.3.11; Bt. Lt.-Col. 3.6.16; Lt.-Col. 11.12.18; retired, 4.2.21; served N.W. Frontier of India, 1897–8, operations on the Samana (Medal, 2 clasps); S. African War, 1901–2 (Queen's Medal, 4 clasps); Europ. War, in France, Belgium and Mesopotamia; Despatches; Legion of Honour (Croix de Chevalier).

DEACON, W. J. (D.S.O. L.G. 3.6.19); b. 13.6.82; 2nd Lt., R.F.A., 17.8.15; Lt. 1.7.17 (retired pay, 8.12.20); Despatches.

DEAKIN, E. B. (D.S.O. L.G. 26.3.18) (Bar, L.G. 22.8.18); b. 23.9.89; s. of Betton Deakin; m. 1918, Gertrude Mary, d. of John Davies; educ. Warwick School; 2nd Lt., 1/5th Essex Regt., Aug. 1913; Lt., Nov. 1914; Capt., June, 1916; A/Major, March, 1917; served Europ. War, at Suvla Bay, Egypt and Palestine; M.C.; Despatches.

DEAKIN, F. F. (D.S.O. L.G. 1.1.17), Yorkshire Hussars; m. 1918, Marjorie, e. d. of Hon. Geoffrey Dawnay; Lt.-Col. (retired pay), 2nd Dragoon Guards; served S. African War, 1899–1902 (Despatches; wounded twice; Queen's Medal, 4 clasps; King's Medal, 2 clasps); Europ. War, 1914–18; Despatches; wounded.

DEAKIN, G. (D.S.O. L.G. 2.12.18), T/Lt.-Col. R. Warwicks. R.

DEALY, J. A. (D.S.O. L.G. 1.2.17); b. 21.3.65; Lt., R.E., 15.2.84; Capt. 25.5.92; Major, 1.10.00; Lt.-Col. 27.10.09; Col. 2.6.13; T/Brig.-Gen. 7.12.15–to 31.12.20 (T/Col. on Staff, 1.1.21); served Burma, 1885 (Medal with clasp); Waziristan, 1901–02 (Medal with clasp); Europ. War, 1914–18; C.M.G.; C.I.E.; Despatches.

DEAN, A. C. H. (D.S.O. L.G. 1.1.17); b. 1.2.78; s. of Charles Percy Dean; m. 1901, Elizabeth Rybot; one d.; educ. Bishop's College School, Province of Quebec; R.M.C., Kingston; Chief Instructor in Map Reading and Field Sketching, R.M.A., Woolwich; 2nd Lt., R.A., 26.2.98; Lt. 16.2.01; Capt. 16.1.04; Major, 30.10.14; served Bermuda, 1900; Halifax, 1901–2; Malta, 1909–10; Europ. War; Despatches; O.B.E.

DEAN, E. T. (D.S.O. L.G. 16.8.17); b. 1884; s. of Col. G. H. Dean; Major, Aust. Arty.; served Europ. War, 1914–18; Despatches; Chevalier Legion of Honour.

DEAN, H. G. (D.S.O. L.G. 3.6.18), Major, Linc. Regt.

DEANE, D. (D.S.O. L.G. 26.8.18); b. 14.9.74; 2nd Lt., R.A., 14.9.93; Lt., R.A., 14.9.96; Lt., Ind. Army, 22.9.97; Capt. 14.9.02; Major, 14.9.11; Bt. Lt.-Col. 1.1.17; Lt.-Col. 3.4.19; Col. 8.6.20 (T/Brig.-Gen. 2.9.17); served Tirah, 1897–8 (Medal, 2 clasps); S. African War, 1901–2 (Queen's Medal, 5 clasps); Europ. War; Despatches.

DEANE, L. C. W. (D.S.O. L.G. 26.7.18), T/Capt. (A/Major), S. Wales Borderers; M.C. He was killed in action 29.5.18.

DEANE-DRUMMOND, J. D. (D.S.O. L.G. 17.9.17) (Bar, L.G. 16.9.18), T/Major, Ches. R.

DEAR, H. J. (D.S.O. L.G. 1.1.18) (Bar, L.G. 22.4.18), Capt. (T/Lt.-Col.), London R.

DEARDEN, J. F. (D.S.O. L.G. 17.4.17), Lt. (T/Capt.), R.F.; M.C.

DE BALINHARD, J. C. (D.S.O. L.G. 1.1.19), Major, Can. Mil. Forces, Sask. R.

DE BEER, M. J. (D.S.O. L.G. 22.8.18), Major, Wakkerstroom Commando, S. African Mil. Forces.

DEBENHAM, G. A. (D.S.O. L.G. 16.9.18); b. 18.10 94; 2nd Lt., Norf. R., 7.7.16; Lt. 7.1.18; T/Capt. 22.1.17; Despatches; M.C.

DE BURGH, C. (D.S.O. L.G. 2.11.17), Lt.-Comdr., R.N.

DE BURGH, E. (D.S.O. L.G. 3.6.16); b. 10.5.81; 2nd Lt., Manch. R., 28.1.03; Ind. Army, 28.7.04; Lt. 28.4.05; Capt. 21.6.11; Bt. Major, 3.6.16; Major, 21.6.17; Bt. Lt.-Col. 3.6.19; served S. African War, 1902 (Queen's Medal, 4 clasps); Europ. War; Despatches.

DE BURGH, H. H. (D.S.O. L.G. 14.9.17); e. s. of Col. T. J. de Burgh and Emily, e. d. of Baron de Robeck; m. 1917, Margory, d. of late A. D. Buchan; one s.; educ. St. Mark's, Windsor; H.M.S. Britannia, Dartmouth; joined H.M.S. Ramillies, Flagship Mediterranean, 1895; Sub-Lieut. 1898; Lt. 1901; Comdr. 1916; served in following ships: H.M.S. Renown, 1901–3; H.M.S. Britannia, 1903–5; H.M.S. Renown, 1905–6; H.M.S. Stag, 1906–8; H.M.S. Queen, 1908–10; H.M.S. Niobe, 1910–12; H.M.S. Southampton, 1912–13; H.M.S. Queen Mary, 1913–15; H.M.S. Melpomene, 1915–17; H.M.S. Satyr, 1917–19; H.M.S. Speedy, 1919–20; H.M.S. Surprise, 1920; served Europ. War; Légion d'Honneur, 1917; Despatches twice; Letter of Commendation from Lords Commissioners of the Admiralty.

DE BUTTS, F. C. (D.S.O. L.G. 15.2.17); b. 6.11.88; s. of Capt. F. R. McC. De Butts, R.A. (killed in Tirah Campaign), s. of Major-Gen. De Butts, R.E., s. of Major-Gen. Sir Augustus De Butts, K.B., R.E.; m. 1915, 1st—K. P. M. (d. 1916), d. of O. O'Donnell; one s.; 2nd—1920, Sybil Katherine, d. of late Canon H. W. Beauchamp, of Copdock, Suffolk; educ. Wellington College; R.M.C., Sandhurst; 2nd Lt., Unatt., 17.8.07; Ind. Army 27.10.07; Lt. 17.10.09; Capt. 1.9.15; served Europ. War; Despatches twice; wounded; M.C.

DE CALRY, V. A. MAGAWLY CERATI (see Magawly Cerati de Calry, V. A.).

DECIE, C. PRESCOTT- (see Prescott-Decie, C.).

DE COURCY, THE HON. M. W. R. (D.S.O. L.G. 25.8.17); b. 26.9.82; o. s. of 33rd Baron of Kingsale; m. 1906, Constance Mary Rance, d. of Major-Gen. Sir T. P. Woodhouse; one s.; three d.; educ. Dulwich College; Kelly College, Tavistock; Sandhurst; 2nd Lt., Conn. Rang., 22.10.02; Ind. Army, 29.7.04; Lt. 22.1.05; Capt. 22.10.11; Major, 22.10.17; served Tibet, 1904; Abor Expedition, 1911–12 (Despatches); Europ. War, 1915–18 (Despatches three times); Marri operations, 1918 (Despatches); N.W.F. Force against Afghans, 1919; Despatches.

DE CRESPIGNY, C. R. CHAMPION (see Champion de Crespigny, C. R.).

DE CRESPIGNY, C. T. CHAMPION (see Champion de Crespigny, C. T.).

DE DENNE, C. H. (D.S.O. L.G. 27.6.19), Paymaster Lt.-Cdr., R.N.

DEED, L. C. B. (D.S.O. L.G. 12.6.23), Major, R.E.

DEEDES, SIR W. H., Kt. (D.S.O. L.G. 2.5.16); b. 10.3.83; Civil Secretary to the Administration, Palestine, since 1920; 2nd Lt., K.R.R.C., 14.9.01; Lt. 22.1.06; Capt. 5.8.14; Major, 14.9.16; Bt. Lt.-Col. 3.6.17; T/Brig.-Gen. 17.11.18 to 7.10.19; served S. African War, 1901–2 (Queen's Medal, 5 clasps); Europ. War; C.M.G.

DE FONBLANQUE, P. (D.S.O. L.G. 1.1.18); b. 16.11.85; e. s. of L. R. de Fonblanque; m. 1916, Stella Mary Augusta, e. d. of Sir F. H. May, G.C.M.G.; one d.; educ. Rugby; R.M.A., Woolwich; 2nd Lt., R.E., 21.3.05; Lt. 23.12.07; Adjt., R.E., 21.11.14 to 6.7.16; Capt. 30.10.14; G.S.O. 3rd Grade since 1921; Europ. War, 1914–18, in France and Italy; Despatches; Order of Crown of Italy.

DE GRAVES, W. A. (D.S.O. L.G. 3.6.19), Major, 3rd Div. Train, Can. A.S.C.

DE GREY, HON. G. (D.S.O. L.G. 15.3.16); b. 9.5.84; e. s. of 7th Baron Walsingham; m. 1919, Hyacinth, o. d. of late Lt.-Col. L. H. Bouwens, R.A.; educ. Eton; R.M.C., Sandhurst; 2nd Lt., Norf. R., 6.1.04; Lt. 16.1.06; Capt. 1.9.12; Adjt., Norf. R., 28.11.13 to 1.2.17; Bt. Lt.-Col. 3.6.17; served Europ. War, in Mesopotamia and France; wounded thrice; Despatches five times.

DE HAVILLAND, H. (D.S.O. L.G. 17.3.17; Details, L.G. 26.5.17), Capt. (T/Major), R.F.C., S.R. His D.S.O. was awarded for distinguished service in the field in Mesopotamia.

DE HAVILLAND, T. L. (D.S.O. L.G. 1.1.18), T/Major, R. Sco. Fus., S. Afr. Def. Force.

DE HOGHTON, G. (D.S.O. L.G. 15.2.19; Details, L.G. 30.7.19); b. 21.11.86; 2nd Lt., Yorks. L.I., 6.10.06; Lt. 1.4.11; Capt. 28.12.14; G.S.O., 3rd Bgde., H.Q., India, 12.1.21; M.C.; Despatches.

DE JAGER, M. J. (D.S.O. L.G. 22.8.18), Lt.-Col. S. African Permanent Force.

DE JAGER, P. L. (D.S.O. L.G. 22.8.18), Lt.-Col. Piet Relief Commando, S. African Military Forces.

DE KANTZOW, A. H. (D.S.O. L.G. 6.4.18); b. 20.7.77; s. of Capt. Walter Sidney de Kantzow and Eleanor Agnes de Kantzow; m. 1910, Sybil Dorothy, d. of Rev. and Mrs. Sprigg; three d.; educ. Summerfield; H.M.S. Britannia; entered H.M.S. Britannia, Jan. 1891; Lt. Oct. 1899; invalided, 1905; rejoined R.N. Aug. 1914; Comdr. 1917; retired; Political Dept. S. Nigerian Civil Service, 1906–13; served Europ. War; Croix de Guerre.

DE KOEK, S. M. (D.S.O. L.G. 22.8.18), Lt.-Col., S. African Med. Serv.

DELACOMBE, A. (D.S.O. L.G. 3.6.16); b. 19.11.65; s. of late Lt.-Col. W. A. Delacombe, R.M.L.I., for many years Military Governor of the San Juan Islands; m. 1896, Emma Louise Mary, o. d. of late J. S. Leland, M.D.; one s.; one d.; educ. Anglo-French College, Finchley; 2nd Lt., Conn. Rang., 6.6.94; Lt. 10.9.98; Capt., R. War. R., 22.8.00; Major, 27.1.11; Lt.-Col. 1.5.18; served S. African War (Queen's Medal, 3 clasps); Europ. War, 1915–19, with Intelligence Branch, General Staff, in the Dardanelles, Egypt and Palestine.

DE LAESSOE, H. H. (D.S.O. L.G. 3.6.18), T/Capt. Gen. List; M.C.

DE LA FONTAINE, H. V. M. (D.S.O. L.G. 1.1.17); b. 2.12.72; s. of Colonel Mottet de la Fontaine, Madras Army; 2nd Lt., E. Surrey R., 25.2.93; Lt. 8.2.95; Capt. 9.12.01; Major, 21.6.11; Lt.-Col.; served S. African War (Queen's Medal, 4 clasps; King's Medal, 2 clasps; Despatches; wounded); Europ. War. He was killed in action 5.8.17.

H. V. M. de la Fontaine.

DELAHAYE, J. V. (D.S.O. L.G. 26.7.18); b. 14.12.90; 2nd Lt., R.A., 23.12.10; Lt. 23.12.13; Capt. 8.8.16; Bt. Major, 3.6.19; Despatches; M.C.

DE LA MOTTE, R.B. (D.S.O. L.G. 22.12.16); b. 19.8.78; 2nd Lt., A.S. Corps, 16.8.02; Lt., A.S.C., 18.2.04; 2nd Lt., Unatt., 31.12.05; Lt. Ind. Army,, 21.12.05; Capt. 28.3.10; Major, 28.3.16; Despatches.

DELAP, J. O. K. (D.S.O. L.G. 1.1.19), Lt. (A/Major), R.G.A., T.F.

DE LA PERRELLE, J. N. (D.S.O. L.G. 1.1.18), Major (T/Lt.-Col.), R. Fus., Spec. Res.; M.C.

DE LA POER BERESFORD, M. J. (see Beresford, M. J. de la Poer).

DE LA PRYME, P. C. (D.S.O. L.G. 4.6.17); b. 24.9.75; m. 1909, Kathleen Lucy Mary, e. d. of E. A. Mangin; educ. private tutor; Dover College; University of Edinburgh; M.A.; nominated for commission in Regular Army by the University; 2nd Lt., A.S.C., 22.5.00; Lt. 1.6.01; Capt. 1.10.04; Adjt. 5.8.14; Major, R.A.S.C., 30.10.14; Bt. Lt.-Col. 1.1.19; Lt.-Col. 15.7.21; served S. African War (Queen's Medal, 5 clasps); Europ. War, 1914–18; Despatches.

DE LA REY, P. (D.S.O. L.G. 22.8.18), Col. Commandant, 1st Mtd. Brigade, S. African Mil. Forces.

DELMÉ-MURRAY, G. A. (D.S.O. L.G. 4.6.17); b. 23.1.79; date of first commission, 15.11.99; Major, 1.8.15; retired, Shrops. L. Inf., 27.5.20; Despatches.

DELMÉ-RADCLIFFE, A. (D.S.O. L.G. 12.12.19); b. 14.6.79; 2nd Lt., S. Lan. R., 3.8.98; Lt. 26.5.00; Lt., Ind. Army, 8.8.00; Capt. 3.8.07; Major, 1.9.15; Lt.-Col. 25.3.19; retired, 31.1.21; Despatches.

DE LOW, H. C. (D.S.O. L.G. 3.6.18), Capt., Aust. F.A., 1.6.14; Despatches.

DELPHIN, L. (D.S.O. L.G. 3.6.18), T/Capt. (A/Lt.-Col.), R.E.

DE MIREMONT, G. E. R. (D.S.O. L.G. 8.3.19; Details, L.G. 4.10.19); b. 3.6.88; 2nd Lt., R.W. Fus., 4.5.07; Lt. 3.5.11; Capt. 25.10.14; Adjt. 18.2.20; Despatches; M.C.

DE MONTMORENCY, H. F. (D.S.O. L.G. 18.10.17) (Details, L.G. 7.3.18), T/Major, R.F.A.

DEMPSTER, J. F. (D.S.O. L.G. 1.1.18) (Bar, L.G. 15.2.19) (Details, L.G. 30.7.19), Capt. (A/Lt.-Col.), R. of O., Manch. R.

DENDY, M. H. (D.S.O. L.G. 4.2.18; Details, L.G. 5.7.18); b. 12.11.85; e. s. of Charles Dendy; m. 1919, Lettice, y. d. of late Charles Van Neck and Mrs. Van Neck; 2nd Lt., R.A., 21.12.04; Lt. 21.12.07; Capt. 30.10.14; Major, 30.9.16; served Europ. War, 1914–18; Despatches; M.C.; Legion of Honour.

DENE, A. P. (D.S.O. L.G. 26.7.17); b. 11.5.78; m. Elsie Beatrice Yvonne (d. 1918), y. d. of Maj.-Gen. F. W. B. Koe; one s.; one d.; 2nd Lt., D. of Corn. L.I., 24.6.99; Lt. 1.8.00; Capt. 4.10.04; Major 1.9.15; Bt. Lt.-Col. 1.1.17; served Europ. War, 1914–18; Despatches; C.M.G., 1919; Officer Legion of Honour.

DENE, H. (D.S.O. L.G. 27.7.16), Capt., Welsh Guards, 28.9.15; Acting Lt.-Colonel, Welsh Guards, 27.2.18; Despatches; Bt. of Major 1.1.17.

DE NECKER, J. A. (D.S.O. L.G. 22.8.18), Lt.-Col., Vrijstaatse Schutters, S. African Mil. Forces.

DENEHY, C. A. (D.S.O. L.G. 18.7.17) (Bar, L.G. 8.3.19) (Details, L.G.4.10.19), Lt.-Col., Aust. Mil. Force.

DE NEUFVILLE, E. C. (D.S.O. L.G. 1.1.18), T/Capt., R.G.A.

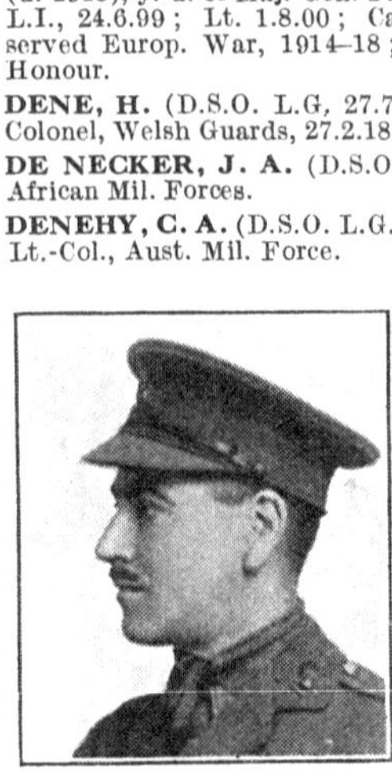

E. C. De Neufville.

DENHAM, H. A. (D.S.O. L.G. 3.6.19); b. 20.3.78; s. of Arthur Denham; m. Phyllis Janet, d. of John Tyrrell; two d.; educ. St. John's College, Cambridge (M.A.); Foundation Scholar and Prizeman, 1st Class, Nat. Sci. Trip., 1901; Senior Science Master, High School, S. Shields, 1903–5; Headmaster of the Harvey Grammar School, Folkestone, 1920; commissioned in E. Riding of Yorkshire Volunteer R.G.A., 1907; East Riding R.G.A. (T.F.), 1908; Captain, 1912; Major, 1916; served Europ. War, 1914–18; Despatches; died July, 1921.

DENHAM, H. K. (D.S.O. L.G. 4.6.17), Lt.-Col., A.I.F., 2.12.16.

DENIS DE VITRÉ, P. T. (D.S.O. L.G. 3.6.18); b. 5.7.70; 2nd Lt., R.E., 27.7.89; Lt. 27.7.92; Capt. 1.4.00; Major 22.1.09; Lt.-Col. 1.6.17; Despatches.

DENISON, C. C. (D.S.O. L.G. 11.4.19), Lt.-Comdr. (now Comdr.), R.N.

DENISON, E. B. (D.S.O. L.G. 20.10.16); b. 25.9.80; e. s. of Colonel H. Denison, C.B.; educ. Eton; 2nd Lt., K.R.R.C., 6.1.01; Lt. 20.12.01; Capt. 17.7.12; Major 5.1.16; T/Lt.-Col. to 31.1.16; commanded 2nd Batt., R. Welsh Fus., 7 Jan. to 31 Jan. 1916; commanded 21st Royal Fusiliers till disbanded; served Europ. War, taking part in the Retreat from Mons, Marne, Aisne, First Battle Ypres, Loos and Somme; Despatches thrice; slightly wounded at Loos; M.C.

DENISON, G. W. (D.S.O. L.G. 23.11.16); b. 8.9.76; s. of Lt.-Col. G. T. Denison; m. 1906, Agnes Keating, of Toronto; two s.; educ. Upper Canada College, Toronto, and R.M.C., Kingston; 2nd Lt., R.E., 1.8.98; Lt. 21.5.01; Capt. 1.9.07; Major 28.4.15; Bt. Lt.-Col. 3.6.18; served W. Africa, 1903 (Medal and clasp); African General Service Medal; Delhi Durbar Medal, 1911; Europ. War in Egypt; Gallipoli; France; Despatches.

DENISON, H. (D.S.O. L.G. 3.6.16); b. 12.4.82; 2nd s. of Brig.-Gen. and Mrs. Denison; educ. Eton; R.M.A., Woolwich; 2nd Lt., R.A., 21.12.00; Lt. 21.12.03; Capt.; Major 11.9.15; served Europ. War in Gallipoli; Despatches. On 27.8.1917 he was wounded and died on the following day. He was a good, all-round sportsman, and as a boy held the "record" for bowling, taking on one occasion nine wickets for one run, and five in one over.

DENISON, JOHN (D.S.O. L.G. 4.6.17), T/Capt., R.N.R.

DENISON, W. W. (D.S.O. L.G. 19.8.16); b. 27.8.79; s. of Lt.-Col. C. A. Denison; educ. Upper Canada College, and the R.M.C. Law School of Upper Canada; called to the Bar, 1906, and practised in Toronto and the North; Lieutenant in the Governor-General of Canada's Body Guard (Militia), 1899; Captain, 1901; Major, 1908; Lt.-Col. comdg. the Regiment, 1921; joined Nov. 1914, the 4th Canadian Mounted Rifles; C.E.F.; served Europ. War in France.

DENISON-PENDER, H. D. (D.S.O. L.G. 1.1.18), Capt. and Bt. Major, Dragoons; M.C.

DENNIS, M. F. B. (D.S.O. L.G. 4.11.15) (Bar, L.G. 26.9.17) (Details, L.G. 9.1.18) T/Major (A/Lt.-Col.), K.O.S.B. (see "The Distinguished Service Order," from its institution to 31.12.15, by same publishers).

C. E. B. Denniss.

DENNISS, C. E. B. (D.S.O. L.G. 19.11.17) (Details, L.G. 22.3.18); s. of Mr. Bartley Denniss, M.P.; Major, R.A.F.

DENNISTOUN, G. H. (D.S.O. L.G. 24.2.16); b. 23.9.84; 2nd s. of G. J. Dennistoun, of New Zealand; m. 1914, Ethel Beatrix, 2nd d. of late F. H. Pyne; one s.; one d.; educ. Wanganui, N.Z.; Stubbington House, Fareham; joined H.M.S. Britannia, 1899; Midshipman, H.M.S. Glory, flagship of Adm. Sir Cyprian Bridge, G.C.B.; China Squadron, 1900–3; Sub-Lt., 1903; Lieut., 1906; Lieut., H.M.S. Hindustan; Channel Fleet, 1907–9; H.M.S. Pioneer, 1909–10; 1st Lieut., 1910–12; H.M.S. Pyramus, 1912–14 (Member of New Hebrides Mixed Naval Commission); H.M.S. Psyche at occupation of Samoa, Aug. 1914; Naval Transport Officer with 1st New Zealand Force, 1914; Senior Naval Officer, Lake Nyasa, and 1st Officer, Marine Transport Dept., Nyasaland Protectorate, 1915–18; Comdr. 30.12.18; Despatches; Medal, Royal Humane Society for saving life 29.9.14.

DENNISTOUN, J. G. (D.S.O. L.G. 1.1.17); b. 24.5.71; o. s. of late J. W. Dennistoun, of Dennistoun, Renfrewshire, and Caroline Joanna, d. of Henry Gore Booth; m. 1910, Clara, y. d. of late Maj.-Gen. Rhodes-Morgan, Ind. Army; Master of the Ootacamund Hounds since 1920; 1st commission 27.7.91; Lt.-Col., R.A., 10.5.15; Retired List 18.12.19; served S. African War, 1902 (Queen's Medal, 2 clasps); Europ. War, 1914–17; Despatches.

DENNY, E. W. (D.S.O. L.G. 16.9.18); b. 15.2.72; s. of T. Anthony Denny; m. 1906, Lois Marjorie, d. of late Lt.-Col. Hon. E. H. Legge, C. Gds.; four s.; two d.; educ. Wellington College; New College, Oxford; J.P. for Norfolk; 2nd Lt., 13 Hrs., 30.1.93; Adjt. 1901–4; Bt. Major 22.8.02; Major 3.10.06; exchanged into 19th Hussars, 1907 (retired pay, 1910); rejoined 5.8.14; in command of South Cavalry Depot, 1915–17; served S. African War (Despatches thrice); Europ. War in France, with Inf. Div., and on Staff; Despatches twice.

DENNY, H. M. (D.S.O. L.G. 20.9.18); b. 9.4.76; s. of Rev. William Henry Denny, M.A., Vicar of St. James', Fulham; m. 1903, Frances Jane Edwards; one s.; educ. Stubbington House, Fareham; H.M.S. Britannia, Naval Cadet, 1890; Midshipman, 1893; Sub-Lieut., 1896; Lieut., 1899; Lt. Comdr., 1907; Comdr. (retired), 1920; Capt. Supt. of the Clyde Training Ship since 1920; served E. African Coast, 1895; M'Wele; S. African War, 1900–1; Europ. War, Patrol Flotillas, 1914–15; command of Monitor M.16, Gallipoli, 1915–16; command of Destroyers and Convoys, E. Coast and North Sea, 1917–19; Despatches.

DENSON, H. R. (D.S.O. L.G. 8.3.19) (Details, L.G. 4.10.19), Major, 14th Aust. L.H.R. (Egypt).

DENT, B. C. (D.S.O. L.G. 1.1.18); b. 22.3.72; 2nd Lt., Leic. R., 18.6.92; Lt. 1.1.94; Capt. 24.6.00; Major 11.12.09; Bt. Lt.-Col. 3.6.15; Col. 3.6.19; T/Brig.-Gen. 8.5.16; T/Comdt. 1.1.21; C.M.G.; Despatches.

DENT, J. R. C. (D.S.O. L.G. 8.3.19) (Details, L.G. 4.10.19) (Bar, L.G. 1.1.19); b. 25.2.84; m. 1920, Margaret Honor, yr. d. of late A. T. Keen and Mrs. Keen, Harborne Park, near Birmingham; educ. Bromsgrove School; R.M.C., Sandhurst; 2nd Lt., Manch. R., 10.10.03; Lt., R. Innis. Fus., 4.5.07; Capt. 22.9.14; A/Lt.-Col.; served Europ. War, 1914–19; M.C.; Croix de Guerre Française.

DENT, W. (D.S.O. L.G. 17.4.16); b. 11.6.82; 2nd Lt., Unatt., 27.8.02; Ind. Army 19.1.04; Lt. 3.4.05; Capt. 27.8.11; Major 27.8.17; Bt. Lt.-Col. 1.1.18; served Europ. War; C.B.E.; Despatches.

DE PASS, G. E. (D.S.O. L.G. 26.7.18); b. 30.10.98; 2nd Lt., Dr. Gds., 27.10.16; Lt. 27.4.18; Despatches.

DE PENTHENY O'KELLY, E. J. (D.S.O. L.G. 3.6.18); b. 23.6.78; 2nd Lt., R. War. R., 20.5.99; Lt. 1.4.00; Capt. 28.8.07; Capt., R.W.F., 15.2.08; Major 1.9.15; Despatches.

DE PREE, H. D. (D.S.O. L.G. 3.6.19); b. 25.12.70; s. of Col. G. C. De Pree and Mary, d. of John Haig, of Fife; m. Diones, d. of F. E. Thornhill, J.P.; three s.; one d.; educ. Eton; R.M.A., Woolwich; 2nd Lt., R.A., 25.7.90; Lt. 25.7.93; Capt. 3.2.00; Div. Adjt. 11.4.00 to 18.4.01; Major 19.1.08; Lt.-Col. 11.1.15 to 10.1.20; T/Brig.-Gen. 5.3.16 to 26.4.19; Bt. Col. 1.1.17; T/Brig.-Gen. 2.12.19–31.12.20; Col. 11.1.19; Col. Comdt. 1.1.21; served N.W. Frontier, India, 1897–98 (Medal, 2 clasps); British E. Africa, 1901 (Medal, clasp); S. Africa, 1901–2 (Queen's Medal, 5 clasps); Europ. War, 1914–18; Despatches five times; C.B., 1918; C.M.G., 1916.

DE QUETTEVILLE, R. G. (D.S.O. L.G. 16.9.18); b. 5.3.96; o. s. of W. F. L. de Quetteville, Registrar of the Probate Division; m. 1919, Molly, o. d. of late James Austen-Cartmell, Barrister; educ. Eton; T/Capt., Yorks R.; served Europ. War, 1914–18; Despatches; M.C.; Prisoner of War.

DERHAM, F. P. (D.S.O. L.G. 1.1.17); b. 15.5.85; s. of Thomas P. Derham, Barrister and Solicitor, Melbourne; m. 1909, Adeline Matilda, d. of John C. Bowden, of Melbourne; educ. Camberwell Grammar School, Melbourne; Melbourne University; practised as Barrister and Solicitor at Melbourne; Major, Aust. F.A., 1.1.15; served Europ. War in France, in command of the 11th Battery, Aust. F.A.; Despatches.

DERING, C. L. Y. (D.S.O. L.G. 20.2.19), Lt.-Cdr., R.N.

DERVICHE-JONES, A. D. (D.S.O. L.G. 27.10.17) (Details, L.G. 18.3.18) (Bar, L.G. 26.7.18); b. 4.4.73; 1st commission 4.11.16; Capt. 4.11.16; Lt.-Col. 15.5.20; retired R. Lanc. R. 15.5.20; Despatches; M.C.

DE SATGÉ, H. V. B. (D.S.O. L.G. 3.6.16); b. 1874; s. of late H. de Satgé, of Dorset; m. 1897, Lorna Mary, d. of Sir Gerald Smith, K.C.M.G., Governor of W. Australia; one s.; educ. Eton; called to the Bar, 1906; A.D.C. to the Governor of W. Australia, 1896–97; was in Dorset and East Surrey Militia, S.R.; commanded 6th Staffordshire Battery, 3rd N. Midland Brigade, R.F.A., 1911; Lt.-Col., 1916; served Europ. War, 1915–17; Despatches; C.M.G.

DE SMIDT, G. E. O. (D.S.O. L.G. 25.8.17), T/Capt., R.E.

DESPARD, C. B. (D.S.O. L.G. 16.9.18), T/Capt., 6th (Inniskilling) Dragoons, att. R. Ir. Fus.; M.C. He was killed in action at Kemmel 18.4.18.

DESROSIERS, M. J. R. H. (D.S.O. L.G. 3.6.19), Lt.-Col., 22nd Batt. Can. Inf., Quebec R.

D'ESTERRE, P. O. E. (D.S.O. L.G. 1.1.17); b. 7.5.82; 2nd Lt., Unatt., 8.1.01; 2nd Lt., E. Lan. R., 9.3.01; Lt. 9.4.04; Capt. 1.4.08; Major 8.1.16; Despatches.

DEVAS, THE REV. F. C. (D.S.O. L.G. 1.1.17), Army Chaplain Dept.; b. 3.4.77; e. s. of Charles Stanton Devas; educ. Beaumont College, Old Windsor; and abroad; entered the Society of Jesus, 1895; Priest, 1909; commission as Chapl. of Forces 14.11.14; served in Europ. War in Gallipoli and France.

DE VILLIERS, J. (D.S.O. L.G. 22.8.18), Lt.-Col., Bethel Commando, S. African Mil. Forces.

DE VITRÉ, P. T. DENIS (see Denis de Vitré, P. T.).

DEVONSHIRE, W. P. (D.S.O. L.G. 26.9.16), Lt., 78th Aust. Inf., 1.7.15; Capt., Aust. Inf.

DEW, J. F. (D.S.O. L.G. 1.1.19), T/Major, Sc. Rifles (S.R.).; M.C.

DE WAAL, D. (D.S.O. L.G. 22.8.18), Lt.-Col., Supernumerary List, S. African Mil. Forces.

DEWAR, R. (D.S.O. L.G. 11.1.19), 2nd Lt., Manch R. (S.R.).

DEWES, H. F. (D.S.O. L.G. 1.1.18), Capt., R. Fus.; M.C.

DEWING, R. E. (D.S.O. L.G. 25.8.16), Capt. (A/Lt.-Col.), R.E. He was killed in action 4.4.18.

DEWING, R. H. (D.S.O. L.G. 25.8.17); b. 15.1.91; s. of the Rev. R. S. Dewing, of Stowlangtoft, Bury St. Edmunds; m. Helen, e. d. of Lt.-Col. Wogan Browne, late 33rd (Q.V.O.) Cavalry; 2nd Lt., R.E., 20.7.11; Lt. 31.7.13; Capt. 26.7.17; Bt. Major 15.11.19; A/Lt.-Col. 16.5.18; served Europ. War; Despatches; M.C.

DE WINTON, R. S. (D.S.O. L.G. 1.1.17); b. 17.12.69; 1st commission 27.7.89; Lt.-Col. 23.8.16; retired R.A. 24.3.21; Despatches.

DEXTER, THE REV. W. E., M.A. (D.S.O. L.G. 14.1.16), Chaplain, 4th Class, Aust. Mil. Forces.

DEY, REV. J. (D.S.O. L.G. 1.2.17), Chaplain to the Forces.

DIBDIN, E. J. (D.S.O. L.G. 1.1.19), Capt., Aust. Mil. Forces, 16,6,18; Major, Aust. Mil. Forces.

DICK, A. (D.S.O. L.G. 2.12.18), Major, 3rd Aust., L.H.R.

DICK, H. W. (D.S.O. L.G. 11.1.19), T/Lt. (A/Capt.), att. W. Yorks. R.; M.C.

DICK, R. N. (D.S.O. L.G. 7.2.18); b. 16.8.79; s. of late Sir James N. Dick, K.C.B.; m. 1919, Mary Dorothea, o. d. of late Robert Melvil Barry, of Otter-Barry; one s.; 2nd Lt., R. Suss. R., 11.2.99; Lt. 13.12.99; Adjt., R. Suss. R., 4.9.03 to 3.9.06; Capt. 5.10.07; Major 1.9.15; Bt. Lt.-Col. 3.6.16; T/Brig.-Gen. 14.11.17 to 6.4.19; served Somaliland 1908–10 (Despatches; Medal and clasp); Europ. War, 1914–18; C.M.G.; Despatches.

DICK, T. S. (D.S.O. L.G. 4.6.17), T/Major, M.G.C.

DICKENSON, THE REV. L. G. (D.S.O. L.G. 4.6.17); b. 20.11.64; y. s. of late F. B. Newton Dickenson, J.P., D.L., of Syston Court, Glos., and Harriett Elizabeth, co-heiress of Fiennes Trotman; m. 1894, Sybil Frances, d. of late T. J. Evans, J.P.; three s.; one d. His first son, Edward Newton, is a Lt. in the K.R.R.C.; his second son, Aubrey Greville Newton (Lt., K.R.R.C.), was killed at Loos, 30.6.16; his youngest son, Bernard Lenthall Newton, is Lt., 1st Bn. R. W. Fus.; educ. Sherborne School; Selwyn College, Cambridge (B.A. 1892, M.A. 1899); curate of Brecon, 1892–6; Eton, 1896–9; Rector of Brome, Suffolk, 1899–1910; Vicar of Downton, Salisbury, 1910–16; Chaplain to the Forces, 7.7.15; Senior Chaplain to 25th Division, B.E.F., 1916–17; Senior Chaplain, Winchester District, 1919; assumed by Royal Licence the additional name and arms of Trotman, 1920; Despatches twice.

DICKIE, D., F.R.C.S. (D.S.O. L.G. 1.1.17); b. 1880; s. of Rev. David Dickie; m. 1915, Sheen, d. of James MacEwen, of Glasgow; educ. High School and University, Glasgow; Royal College of Surgeons, Edinburgh; Surgeon to Out-patients, Western Infirmary, Glasgow; Surgeon to Out-patients, Royal Hospital for Sick Children, Glasgow; Capt., R.A.M.C.; served Europ. War, 1914–17.

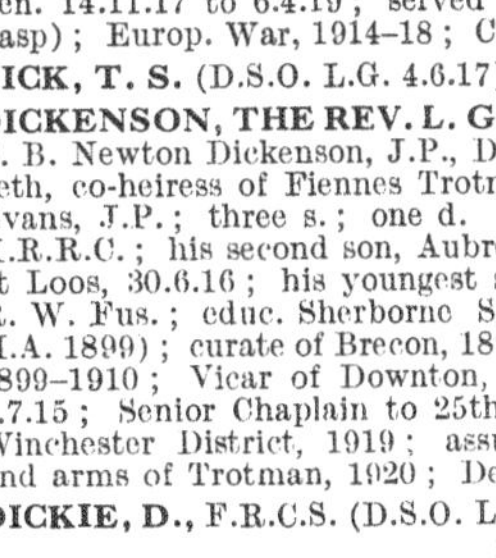
D. Dickie.

DICKINS, V. W. F. (D.S.O. L.G. 14.1.16); b. 15.9.67; s. of late Lt.-Col. Henry Francis Dickins, V.D., and Lucy Catherine Dickins; m. 1901, Mary Sydney, e. d. of Sidney Wilson; one s.; Director of Dickins and Jones Ltd. and other companies; joined the 1st Middx. Victoria Rifles, 3.12.84; 2nd Lt. 10.5.90; Lt. 5.3.92; Capt. 22.11.99; Major, 9th Lond. Regt., 11.12.12; Lt.-Col. 13.7.15; Col. 1919; served Europ. War, 1914–17; Despatches four times, 1.1.16, 13.6.16, 4.6.17, and on a subsequent occasion; holds Volunteer Officers' Decoration.

DICKINSON, C. C. (D.S.O. L.G. 23.7.18), Lt., R.N.

DICKINSON, D. P. (D.S.O. L.G. 4.6.17); b. 6.11.86; 2nd Lt., Welsh R., 6.10.06; Lt. 25.7.08; Capt. 15.9.14; Bt. Major, 1.1.19; M.C.

DICKINSON, G. F. (D.S.O. L.G. 4.6.17), Lt., Aust. 12th Inf., 1.7.15; Major, A.I.F.; Despatches.

DICKINSON, R. S. W. (D.S.O. L.G. 22.6.16); b. 15.1.97; s. of the Rt. Hon. Sir W. H. Dickinson, P.C., K.B.E., and Lady Dickinson, d. of Gen. Sir Richard Meade, K.C.S.I., C.I.E.; educ. Summerfield, Oxford, and Eton; Sub-Lt., R.N.A.S., 12.7.15; invalided out; joined C. Gds. Feb. 1917; served Europ. War; Despatches; Croix de Guerre avec Palme.

DICKSON, C. H., M.D. (D.S.O. L.G. 1.1.18), Capt., Can. A.M.C., 8.6.13; Lt.-Col., Despatches.

DICKSON, M. R. (D.S.O. L.G. 3.6.18), T/Major, R. Scots. Fus.

DICKSON, V. H. (D.S.O. L.G. 1.1.19), Major, R.F.A. (T.F.).

DICKSON, W. F. (D.S.O. L.G. 21.9.18), Lt. (Hon. Capt.) (Sea Patrol), R.A.F.

DIGBY (E. K.), LORD (D.S.O. L.G. 1.2.19); b. 1.8.94; e. s. of Lord and Lady Digby; m. Hon. Pamela Bruce, d. of Lord and Lady Aberdare; one d.; educ. Eton and Sandhurst; 2nd Lt., C. Gds., 15.8.14; Lt. 17.7.15; Adjt., C. Gds. 30.9.15 to 15.1.18; Capt. 1.1.17; A/Major 17.1.18; served Europ. War; Despatches twice; French Despatches once; 1914-15 Star; M.C. and Bar; Croix de Guerre.

DIGBY, F. T. (D.S.O. L.G. 26.4.18), Fl.-Cdr., R.N.A.S.; D.S.C.

DIGBY-SMITH, A. (D.S.O. L.G. 16.8.17), Major, N.Z. Inf.

DIGBY-WINGFIELD-DIGBY, F. J. B. (D.S.O. L.G. 18.2.18) (Details, L.G. 18.7.18); b. 22.8.85; s. of late J. K. Digby-Wingfield-Digby, J.P., M.P., and 1st wife, Hon. Georgiana Rosamond, 5th d. of 4th Viscount Lifford; m. 1909, Gwendolen Marjory, d. of G. Hamilton Fletcher; two s.; two d.; educ. Harrow; Trinity Hall, Cambridge; Major, Yeomanry; J.P.; served Europ. War, 1914–18.

DIGGLE, J. N. (D.S.O. L.G. 1.1.18); b. 21.1.84; 1st commission, 21.12.01; Major, R.F.A., 6.2.16; retired, R.A., 6.9.19; Despatches.

DIGGLE, W. H. (D.S.O. L.G. 1.1.19); b. 4.6.85; 3rd s. of Wadham N. Diggle; m. 1919, Nancy, e. d. of Henry Conran; served Royal Navy, 1899–1905; 2nd Lt., G. Gds., 1.2.07; Lt. 10.3.08; Adjt., G. Gds., 15.9.10 to 14.8.12; Capt. 22.8.14; G.S.O., 2nd Grade, 1920; Egyptian Army, 1912–14; served Europ. War, 1914–19; Despatches; M.C.; Legion of Honour; Croix de Guerre (France).

DIGGLES, J. M. (D.S.O. L.G. 1.1.19), T/Major, Ches. R., T.F.; M.C.

DILLON, S. H. (D.S.O. L.G. 20.9.18), Lt.-Cdr., R.N.

DINWIDDIE, J. BLOUNT- (see Blount-Dinwiddie, J.).

DINWIDDIE, M. (D.S.O. L.G. 4.6.17); b. 18.7.92; 2nd s. of Rev. J. L. Dinwiddie, of Ruthwell; m. 1920, Arna, e. d. of Alexander Guild; Lt., G. Hldrs., 11.12.14; Capt. 1.1.17; T/Major, 22.10.17 to 2.10.19; served Europ. War, 1914–18; Despatches; O.B.E.; M.C.

DIPPIE, H. (D.S.O. L.G. 3.6.18), T/Major (A/Major), Worc. R.

DITCHAM, H. G. (D.S.O. L.G. 3.6.18), T/Major, Gen. List.

DITMAS, F. I. L. (D.S.O. L.G. 1.1.18); b. 12.8.76; o. s. of Col. F. F. Ditmas, late R.A., and Isabel, e. d. of Rear-Admiral John Adams, R.N.; m. 1906, Alice Sarah Louise, o. d. of late Major Arthur Nevill Hayne, 88th Regt. (Con. Rangers); two s.; educ. privately; Germany and France; F.G.S., M.I.M.E., A.I.E.E.; Consulting Railway and Mining Engineer; Engineer with E. Indian Ry. Co., Calcutta; R. of Officers, 1902; Lt.-Col., R. of O., Durh. L. Inf.; Technical Adviser to Reparation Commission, Paris; Germany; was present at Peace Conference, Versailles; served S. African War (Medal, 2 clasps); Europ. War, 1914–18; Despatches thrice; M.C.; Croix d'Officier de la Légion d'Honneur; French Croix de Guerre avec Palme; Croix l'Officier de l'Ordre de Léopold.

DIVE, G. H. (D.S.O. L.G. 1.1.17); b. 29.5.82; 3rd s. of W. E. Dive, J.P.; educ. Wanganui College; University of Otago; St. Bartholomew's Hospital; Junior School, University of N. Zealand, 1900; House Physician, West London Hospital, 1907; Prizeman Military Surgery, R.A.M. College, 1909; Clinical Assistant to Professor of Tropical Medicine, Military Hospital, Millbank, 1910–12; Lt., R.A.M.C., 31.7.09; Capt. 31.1.13; Bt. Major, 1.1.18; Major, 31.7.21; served Europ. War; B.E.F., Tsingtau, 1914 (Despatches); B.E.F., Belgium and France, 1915–19 (Despatches three times); Médaille d'Honneur des Epidémies; French Army Orders; Croix de Guerre.

F. A. Dixon.

R. S. Dixon.

DIVINE, C. F. (D.S.O. L.G. 22.8.18), V.D. Major, 6th Citizen Battery.

DIX, C. C. (D.S.O. L.G. 14.3.16), Cdr., R.N.

DIXON, E. W. (D.S.O. L.G. 18.2.18) (Details, L.G. 18.7.18), Lt., Imperial Camel Corps, Aust. Mil. Forces.

DIXON, F. A. (D.S.O. L.G. 1.1.17); b. 27.3.80; s. of late John Picken Dixon, J.P., and Mrs. Dixon, of The Mount, Marton, Lancs; m. 29.4.08, Ethel Howard, o. d. of late James Coulston, of Preston; one s.; three d.; educ. Rossall; Commissioned Lancs. Vol. Artillery, 1900; Tipperary Militia Artillery, 1900; R.H. and R.F.A., 1901; Capt. about Oct. 1914; Lt.-Col. 18.2.15; raised and commanded 150th Army Bde., R.H.A., Feb. 1915; served Europ. War; Despatches (April 30 and Nov. 13, 1916; Christmas, 1917; June, 1918); C.M.G.

DIXON, O. F. (D.S.O. L.G. 4.6.17), Capt. (T/Major), Aust. Artillery.

DIXON, R. D. (D.S.O. L.G. 18.1.18), Lt., 35th Aust. Inf., 1.8.15; Capt.; Despatches.

DIXON, R. S. (D.S.O. L.G. 26.7.18); b. 5.1.94; s. of A. J. Dixon; 2nd Lt., High. L.I., 25.2.14; Lt. 22.12.14; Capt. 25.8.16; served Europ. War in France; Despatches; M.C.

DIXON, T. F. HOMER (D.S.O. L.G. 1.1.17); b. 6.12.71; e. s. of Benjamin Homer-Dixon, K.N.L., of Toronto, Consul-General of the Netherlands; m. 1909, Evelyn Anne, d. of Sir Douglas Cameron; three d.; educ. Upper Canada College, Toronto; Uppingham; Lt.-Col., Lord Strathcona's Horse (Royal Canadians), 1915; formerly in 17th Lancers; 5th Dragoon Guards; served N.W. Frontier of India, 1897–8 (Medal, 2 clasps); S. African War, 1899–1902 (wounded; Queen's Medal, 5 clasps; King's Medal, 2 clasps); W. African Frontier Force, N. Ashanti, 1902–3; Europ. War, 1914–18; Despatches.

DIXON, W. C. (D.S.O. L.G. 3.6.18); b. 5.3.78; 2nd Lt., R. Garr. R., 10.9.02; Lt. 4.4.03; Lt., Leic. R., 8.9.05; Capt. 17.10.08; Adjt., Leic. R., 30.1.11 to 13.10.12; Major, 22.10.17; O.B.E.; Despatches.

DIXON-NUTTALL, W. F. (D.S.O. L.G. 3.6.16); e. s. of F. R. Dixon-Nuttall, J.P.; m. 1917, Gladys Lena, o. d. of W. Henry Gregory; Capt. (T/Major), R.E., T.F.; Despatches; O.B.E.

DOAKE, R. L. V. (D.S.O. L.G. 8.3.19) (Details, 4.10.19.), T/Capt. Bedf., Regt.; M.C.

DOAKE, S. H. (D.S.O. L.G. 3.6.18), Capt. (A/Major), R.F.A. He was killed in action 30.3.18.

DOBBIE, W. G. S. (D.S.O. L.G. 14.1.16); b. 12.7.79; s. of W. H. Dobbie, C.I.E., late Accountant-General, Madras, and of Margaret Dobbie, d. of Col. Dobbie, Ind. Army; m. 1904, Sybil, y. d. of Capt. Orde-Browne, R.A.; two s.; one d.; educ. Charterhouse; R.M.A., Woolwich; passed through School of Military Engineering, Chatham; 2nd Lt., R.E., 6.8.99; Lt. 1.4.02; Capt. 6.8.08; Major, 1.4.16; Lt.-Col. 1.1.17; G.S.O., 1st Grade; served S. African War (Medal, 5 clasps); Europ. War, 1914–18; Despatches seven times; Legion of Honour; C.M.G. 1919; Officier d' Ordre Léopold; Croix de Guerre (Belgian); Croix de Guerre avec Palme (French).

DOBBIE, W. H. (D.S.O. L.G. 1.1.19), Lt., Can. G.A., 30.10.14; Major; Despatches.

DOBBIN, A. W. (D.S.O. L.G. 3.6.19); b. 24.3.83; 2nd Lt., R.A., 24.12.02; Lt. 24.12.05; Capt. 30.10.14; Major, 14.6.17; Despatches; M.C.

DOBBIN, H. T. (D.S.O. L.G. 20.10.16) (for services at Ovillers, 17.7.16); b. 27.5.78; s. of Lt.-Col. G. M. Dobbin; educ. Bedford; privately; 2nd Lt., D. of Corn. L. Inf., 18.1.99; Lt. 9.5.00; Capt. 8.7.04; Major, 1.9.15; Bt. Lt.-Col. 3.6.19; T/Lt.-Col. 2.10.20; T/Brig.-Gen. 9.2.18 to 16.4.19; served Europ. War; Despatches.

DOBBIN, L. G. W. (D.S.O. L.G. 14.1.16); b. 1.3.71; 2nd Lt., North'n. R., 23.5.91; Lt. 29.11.93; Capt. 8.3.02; Major, 8.11.12; Lt.-Col. North'n. R., 30.3.19; served on the N.W. Frontier of India, 1897–8; operations on the Samana (Medal, 2 clasps); served at Tirah, 1897–8 (Clasp); S. African War, 1902 (Queen's Medal, 2 clasps); Europ. War; Despatches.

DOBBS, C. F. (D.S.O. L.G. 1.2.17); b. 1.7.72; e. s. of late Col. A. F. Dobbs, Ind. Army; m. Margaret Eleanor Jopp; one s.; two d.; educ. Bedford School; R.M.C., Sandhurst; 2nd Lt., Lan. Fus., 18.6.92; Lt. 14.6.93; Lt., Ind. S.C., 11.10.94; Capt., Ind. Army, 10.7.01; Major, 18.6.10; Bt. Lt.-Col. 1.1.16; Lt.-Col. 4.2.17; served Europ. War, 1914–17; in E. Africa; 3rd Class, Order of St. Anne (Russian); Despatches three times; Southern Persia, 1918–19; (Despatches); C.I.E. 1920; Afghan War, 1919 (Despatches); C.B.E. 1919; Mesopotamia, 1920.

DOBBS, R. C. (D.S.O. L.G. 4.6.17) (Bar, L.G. 1.2.19); b. 21.11.78; 2nd Lt., R. Irish Fus., 21.4.00; Lt. 12.3.02; Capt. 11.6.10; Major, 1.9.15; Bt. Lt.-Col. 1.1.19; Despatches.

DOBIE, J. J. (D.S.O. L.G. 3.6.18), Capt., 3rd K.O. Hussars; M.C. He was killed in action 30.9.18.

DOBSON, A. C. (D.S.O. L.G. 1.1.17); b. 8.9.79; s. of Lt. A. E. Dobson, R.E.; m. 1907, Susanna, d. of H. S. Oppenheim, J.P.; one s.; educ. Dulwich College; R.M.A., Woolwich; 2nd Lt., R.E., 23.3.99; Lt. 1.10.01; Capt. 23.3.08; Major, 1.10.15; Bt. Lt.-Col. 1.1.19; served in Gibraltar and Singapore; Europ. War, 1914–19; Despatches four times; Croix de Guerre avec Palme (French).

DOBSON, F. G., M.B. (D.S.O. L.G. 1.1.19), Capt. (A/Lt.-Col.), R.A.M.C., T.F.

DOBSON, J. G., M.B. (D.S.O. L.G. 12.12.18), Surg.-Lt., R.N., H.M.S. M.25.

DOBSON, J. H. (D.S.O. L.G. 13.2.17), Major, S. African Pioneers.

DOCHERTY, M. (D.S.O. L.G. 3.6.16), Major, Lord Strathcona's Horse, Can. Force.

DODD, A. W. (D.S.O. L.G. 8.3.19; Details, L.G. 4.10.19), Lt., Aust. F.A., 1.7.15; Major, 6th Bn., 2nd Brig., Aust. F.A.; M.C.

DODD, P. C. R. (D.S.O. L.G. 3.8.20); b. 15.11.85; 2nd Lt., Unatt., 9.1.04; 2nd Lt., Ind. Army, 2.9.05; Lt. 9.4.06; Capt. 9.1.13; Major, 31st Lrs., I.A., 9.1.19, commanding Kurram Militia; Despatches.

DODD, W. T. (D.S.O. L.G. 3.6.16); s. of W. H. Dodd, Liverpool; m.; one s.; educ. St. Francis Xavier's College, Liverpool; Capt. (T/Major), R.E., T.F.; served Europ. War; Despatches; M.C.

DODDS, W. O. H. (D.S.O. L.G. 1.1.19); b. 3.7.67; s. of Charles Dodds; m. 1910, Jean Hamilton Holt, d. of Robert Tyre, Montreal; educ. Yarmouth Academy, Nova Scotia; connected with Canadian Militia for 25 years; Lt.-Col., Can. Art., 1915; Brig.-Gen. Oct. 1916; O.C. 5th Can. Div. Art.; served Europ. War, 1915–18, in France; Despatches; C.M.G. 1916.

DODGE, J. B. (D.S.O. L.G. 3.6.19), T/Major (A/Lt.-Col.), Suff. R., attd. 16th Bn. Sussex R. (formerly M.G.C.); D.S.C.

DODGSON, R. C. (D.S.O. L.G. 2.2.16); b. 11.12.82; 2nd Lt., R.A., 4.5.01; Major, 6.10.15; Bt. Lt.-Col. 1.1.19; retired, 5.1.19; Despatches.

DODS, J. E., M.B. (D.S.O. L.G. 1.1.17); b. 29.6.74; s. of R. S. Dods; m. Anna Ruth, d. of late J. W. Walker, Melbourne; two s.; one d.; educ. Brisbane Grammar School; Switzerland; Edinburgh University, M.B.; Government Medical Officer, Brisbane; Major, Aust. A.M.C.; served S. African War, 1899–1900 (Queen's Medal, 4 clasps); Europ. War, 1914–17; Despatches twice; M.C.

DODWELL, T. B. (D.S.O. L.G. 2.11.18), Lt., R.A.F.

DOIG, C. P. (D.S.O. L.G. 14.1.16); b. 11.2.74; 2nd Lt., Seaf. Highrs., 10.10.94; Lt. 29.4.96; Capt. 2.2.01; Major 27.3.11; Lt.-Col. 24.4.19; retired 24.4.19; served during operations in Chitral, 1895 (Medal, clasp); Nile Expedition, 1898; Battle of Khartoum; South African War, 1899–1902 (Queen's Medal, 3 clasps and King's Medal, 2 clasps); Europ. War; Despatches; O.B.E.

DOIG, P. (D.S.O. L.G. 1.1.18), Major, R.G.A.

DOLPHIN, E. H. (D.S.O. L.G. 22.2.18); m. Evelyn (d. 1918), o. c. of H. B. Tidswell; Lieut., R.N.; retired 1921. His D.S.O. was awarded for work against enemy submarines.

DOLPHIN, E. J. (D.S.O. L.G. 4.6.17), Capt., London R.

DOLPHIN, H. C. (D.S.O. L.G. 1.1.18); b. 21.8.76; Capt. (T/Major), R. of O., Hants R.); retired 3.12.13 (Res. of Off., recalled to 2.6.19); A/Lt.-Col. and Ord. Off., 2nd Class, 4.5.18 to 5.12.19; A/Ord. Off., 3rd Cl., 6.12.19; Major 28.1.16; Despatches.

DON, J. A. (D.S.O. L.G. 1.1.17); b. 21.4.83; 2nd Lt., R.A., 31.7.02; Lt. 31.7.05; Capt. 30.10.14; Major 14.3.16; Despatches.

DONALD, A. S. (D.S.O. L.G. 1.1.19), Lt., Can. F.A., 2.4.10; Major, Can. F.A.; Despatches.

DONALDSON, A. S., M.D. (D.S.O. L.G. 3.6.18) (Bar, L.G. 11.1.19), Capt., Can. A.M.C., 8.8.15; Lt.-Col.

DONALDSON, H. (D.S.O. L.G. 4.3.18) (Details, L.G. 16.8.18), T/Sub-Lt., R.N.V.R.

DONALDSON, R. J. (D.S.O. L.G. 3.6.18), Major, Aust. Engrs.

DONALDSON, R. L. M. (D.S.O. L.G. 1.1.18), Lt., Can. Ord. Corps, 1.10.07 ; Hon. Major 1.10.17 ; Despatches.

DONALDSON-HUDSON, R. C. (D.S.O. L.G. 1.1.17), Capt. (T/Lt.-Col.), T.F.; Res. and R.F.C.

DONE, H. R. (D.S.O. L.G. 18.2.15) (Bar, L.G. 20.10.16), Bt. Lt.-Col. (T/Brig.-Gen.), Norf. R. (see " The Distinguished Service Order," from its institution to 31.12.15, by same publishers).

DONE, R. J. (D.S.O. L.G. 4.6.17) ; b. 10.4.74 ; s. of Richard Henry Done, of Salterswell, near Tarporley, Cheshire ; m. 1915, Marjorie, d. of James Broadfoot ; educ. Harrow ; R.M.A., Woolwich ; served two years at S.M.E., Chatham ; 2nd Lt., R.E., 27.2.94 ; Lt. 27.2.97 ; Capt. 1.4.04 ; Major 27.2.14 ; Bt. Lt.-Col. 1.1.19 ; Lt.-Col. 8.2.21 ; employed with Egyptian Army, 1898 to 1909 (Dongola Medal, clasp) ; Sudan, 1899 ; Mejidieh, 4th Class ; rejoined British Army, 1909 ; served Europ. War ; Légion d'Honneur ; Croix de Chevalier ; Croix de Guerre avec Palme ; 1914–15 Star ; Despatches five times ; wounded.

DONKIN, F. L. (D.S.O. L.G. 1.1.18), T/Capt. (A/Major), R.F.A.

DONNELLY, J. B. (D.S.O. L.G. 1.1.18), Major, Can. Forestry Corps ; Lt., Can. Inf., 11.9.14 ; Despatches.

DONNELLY, J. F. (D.S.O. L.G. 4.6.17), Major, Aust. Inf.

DONNELLY, T. (D.S.O. L.G. 4.6.17) ; b. 4.4.83 ; 2nd Lt., R.A., 21.12 01 ; Lt. 16.8.04 ; Capt. 30.10.14 ; Major 1.5.17 ; Bt. Lt.-Col. 3.6.19 ; Despatches.

DONOVAN, C. O., M.B. (D.S.O. L.G. 3.3.17), T/Capt., R.A.M.C., att. N. Lancs. R.

DONOVAN, S. J. (D.S.O. L.G. 4.6.17) ; b. 1.4.76 ; y. surv. s. of late Rev. R. H. Donovan, Chaplain, R.N. ; m. 1919, Helen, widow of Lt.-Col. Carrington-Smith, and y. d. of late C. C. Redfern, Barrister-at-Law, Inner Temple ; 2nd Lt., A.S.C., 22.5.00 ; Lt. 1.6.01 ; Capt. 1.10.04 ; Major 30.10.14 ; Lt.-Col., R.A.S.C., 19.9.21 ; served S. African War, 1901–2 (Queen's Medal, 5 clasps) ; Europ. War, 1914–17 ; Despatches.

DOONER, H. BRANDON (D.S.O. L.G. 27.7.18), T/Capt., Gen. List (Capt., E. African Intelligence Dept.) ; M.C.

DOONER, J. G. (D.S.O. L.G. 3.6.18), Lt.-Col., R.F.A. He was killed in action 31.7.18.

DOPPING-BOYD, J. (see Boyd, J. Dopping-).

DOPPING-HEPENSTAL, M. E. (D.S.O. L.G. 24.6.16) (Details, L.G. 27.6.16) ; b. 7.3.72 ; 3rd s. of late Col. R. A. Dopping-Hepenstal, D.L. ; educ. King William's College, Isle-of-Man ; R.M.C., Sandhurst ; 2nd Lt., Worc. R., 18.6.92 ; Lt. 9.10.93 ; Lt., Ind. S.C., 25.7.96 ; Capt., Ind. Army, 10.7.01 ; Major 18.6.10 ; Lt.-Col. 11.3.18 ; served Tirah Expedition, 1897–98 (Medal, clasp) ; Waziristan, 1901–2 (clasp) ; Europ. War ; Afghan War, 1919 ; C.B.E.

DORAN, J. C. M. (D.S.O. L.G. 14.1.16) ; b. 23.8.80 ; s. of late Rev. J. W. Doran, M.A., Rector of Souldern, Oxon ; m. 1917, Hester Maude, y. d. of Edward Field, of Blackdon Hill, Leamington ; educ. St. Edward's School, Summerton, Oxford ; 2nd Lt., A.S.C., 26.11.02 ; Lt. 15.11.04 ; Capt. 9.6.11 ; Major, R.A.S.C., 30.10.15 ; Bt. Lt.-Col. 3.6.18 ; served S. African War, 1901–2, with Militia (Queen's Medal, 5 clasps) ; Europ. War ; Despatches twice ; C.B.E.

DORE, A. S. W. (D.S.O. L.G. 1.1.18) ; b. 16.9.82 ; s. of late S. L. Dore, of Pinner Hill, Pinner ; m. 1918, Miéle, d. of E. A. Maund ; two d. ; educ. Mill Hill School ; Jesus College, Cambridge ; Manager for Baldwins Ltd., Iron and Steel Manufacturers ; commissioned Territorials, 1905 ; Lt.-Col., late R.A.F. ; served Europ. War in France ; wounded, April, 1915 ; Despatches twice.

DORLING, F. H. (D.S.O. L.G. 1.1.18) ; b. 11.4.77 ; 2nd Lt., Manch. R., 8.9.97 ; Lt. 17.8.98 ; Capt. 5.1.01 ; Major 10.3.15 ; Bt. Lt.-Col. 3.6.18 ; Lt.-Col. 1.9.20 ; served S. African War, 1900–2, on Staff (Queen's Medal, 3 clasps ; King's Medal, 2 clasps) ; Europ. War, 1914 ; Despatches.

DORLING, H. T. (D.S.O. L.G. 20.9.18) ; 2nd s. of Col. Francis Dorling, late Sussex Regt., of Farnborough, Hants ; m. 1909, Evelyne, d. of late Roderick MacDonald, of Kew, Surrey ; one s. ; educ. H.M.S. Britannia, 1897 ; Cdr., R.N. ; served S. Africa and China, including Relief of Pekin, 1900 ; Europ. War, 1914–18 ; Gold Medal from Swedish Government for saving life at sea, 1917.

DORMAN, E. M. (D.S.O. L.G. 12.12.19), Major, 4th Dr. Gds. ; M.C.

DORMAN, L. C. (D.S.O. L.G. 4.6.17) ; b. 20.7.79 ; 2nd Lt., Worc. R., 12.8.99 ; Lt. 20.6.00 ; Capt. 22.3.03 ; Major 11.8.15 ; T/Lt.-Col., 7th Bn., 21.4.16 to 28.10.17 ; served S. African War (Despatches ; Queen's Medal, 3 clasps ; King's Medal, 2 clasps) ; Europ. War, 1914 ; Despatches.

DORMAN, T. S. L. (D.S.O. L.G. 6.9.16), Lt.-Cdr., R.N. Killed in action 5.5.17.

DOUGHTY, E. C. (D.S.O. L.G. 30.1.20) ; b. 6.8.68 ; 1st commission 20.10.90 ; Major 8.7.11 ; retired Suff. Regt. 26.12.19 ; Despatches.

DOUGHTY, E. S. (D.S.O. L.G. 24.9.18) (Bar, L.G. 2.12.18), Lt.-Col., 31st. Bn. Can. Inf.

DOUGLAS, J. R. COWAN- (see Cowan-Douglas, J. R.).

DOUGLAS, J. W. (D.S.O. L.G. 21.12.16), T/Major, R.E.

DOUGLAS, M. G. (D.S.O. L.G. 3.6.18), Major, H.A.C. ; M.C.

DOUGLAS-JONES, S. D. (D.S.O. L.G. 4.6.17) ; b. 19.11.85 ; 2nd Lt. 7.12.04 ; Lt. 17.12.07 ; Capt. 30.10.14 ; Bt. Major 1.1.19 ; M.C. ; Despatches.

DOWDEN, C. H. (D.S.O. L.G. 18.2.15) (Bar, L.G. 1.1.18), Major, retired, K.R.R.C. ; M.C. (see " The Distinguished Service Order," from its institution to 31 Dec. 1915, same publishers).

DOWDING, C. C. (D.S.O. L.G. 3.6.18) (Bar, L.G. 8.3.19) (Details, L.G. 4.10.19), T/Major (A/Lt.-Col.), R. Lanc. R., att. 1/6th Bn. N. Staff R., T.F.

DOWN, R. T. (D.S.O. L.G. 11.4.19), Cdr., R.N., H.M.S. Forester. D.S.O. awarded for Palestine Operations.

DOWNES, J. W. (D.S.O. L.G. 1.1.19), Lt. (A/Lt.-Col.), Shrops. Yeomanry, att. Welsh R. ; M.C.

DOWNEY, J. A. (D.S.O. L.G. 4.6.17), T/Major, Durham Light Inf.

DOWNEY, M. H. (D.S.O. L.G. 1.1.18), Lt.-Col., Aust. A.M.C., 1.1.15 ; Despatches.

DOWNIE, J., M.B. (D.S.O. L.G. 14.1.16), Capt., R.A.M.C. (T.F.).

DOWSE, R. (D.S.O. L.G. 1.1.18), Bt. Lt.-Col., Aust. Mil. Forces, 24.9.17 ; C.M.G. ; Despatches.

DOWSETT, E. B. (D.S.O. L.G. 11.4.18), Lt.-Col. (T/Col.), R.A.M.C.

DOYLE, E. C. (D.S.O. L.G. 1.1.18) ; b. 11.7.86 ; Lt A.V.C., 3.9.10 ; Capt. 3.9.15 ; Despatches.

DOYLE, E. E. (D.S.O. L.G. 3.8.20) ; b. 18.8.86 ; Lt., Ind. Med. Serv., 29.7.11 ; Capt. 29.7.14 ; Bt. Major, 3.6.19 ; Despatches.

DOYLE, J. F. I. H. (D.S.O. L.G. 14.1.16) ; b. 31.3.73 ; s. of late Charles Altamont Doyle, of Edinburgh, and bro. of Sir Arthur Conan Doyle ; educ. Richmond, Yorkshire ; R.M.A., Woolwich ; 2nd Lt., R.A., April, 1893 ; Capt. 6.6.00 ; Major 30.3.10 ; Lt.-Col. 14.11.15 ; Bt. Col. 1.1.19 ; served in China, 1900 (Medal) ; S. African War (Queen's Medal, 4 clasps) ; Europ. War ; Despatches five times ; C.M.G.

D'OYLEY-HUGHES, G. (D.S.O. L.G. 8.10.15) (Bar, L.G. 14.9.18), Lieut., R.N. ; D.S.C. (see " The Distinguished Service Order," from its institution to 31.12.15, by same publishers).

DRAFFEN, F. G. W. (D.S.O. L.G. 1.1.17) ; b. 21.2.80 ; e. s. of F. J. Draffen, of Royal Crescent, W. ; educ. St. Paul's School ; 1st commission 18.10.99 ; Major 1.9.15 ; Lt.-Col. 23.3.21 ; retired Sco. Rif. 23.3.21 ; served S. African War (wounded in action at Spion Kop ; Queen's Medal, 4 clasps) ; Europ. War, as Adjt., 6th Scottish Rifles (wounded, 15.6.15) ; commanded 13th Batt. R. Sussex Regt. ; later in command of 1st Batt. The Cameronians (wounded twice) ; Despatches.

DRAGE, GILBERT (D.S.O. L.G. 1.1.17) ; 1st commission 1.9.90 ; Major 1.10.08 ; retired R. Marines 1.10.13 ; T/Lt.-Col., 1st Bn. Hereford R.

DRAGE, GODFREY, J.P. (D.S.O. L.G. 1.1.17) (Bar, L.G. 8.3.19) (Details, L.G. 4.10.19) ; b. 19.6.68 ; e. s. of Major W. H. Drage, late 52nd and 85th Light Inf. Regts. ; m. Dorothy, d. of J. E. Greaves, Lord Lt. ; two d. ; educ. Christ's Hospital ; Blundell's School, Tiverton ; R.M.C., Sandhurst ; gazetted 2nd Batt. Oxf. Light Inf. 1889 ; served in the 90th Punjabis, Burma Military Police, Burma Civil Service, and Political Dept. till 1907 ; retired ; served till 1912 in Vols. and Territorial Batts. R.W.F. ; gazetted to the Royal Muns. Fus., Sept. 1914 ; commanded Service Batt. R. Muns. Fus., 1915–18 ; served Chin Hills and Lushai Hills Expedition, 1891–92 and 1895–96 (Indian Frontier Medal) ; served Europ. War as Major (A/Lt.-Col.), R. of O., Oxf. and Bucks L.I., attd. 1/4th Bn. Ches. R., T.F., in Suvla, Serbia, Bulgaria, Macedonia, Egypt, Palestine, France, Flanders, Rhine ; Despatches thrice ; Légion d'Honneur ; Serbian White Eagle.

DRAKE, R. J. (D.S.O. L.G. 1.1.18) ; b. 2.2.76 ; s. of late Reginald Drake, I.S.C. (U.) ; m. 1911, Lilian, d. of T. Martin, of Plympton, S. Devon ; educ. Haileybury ; R.M.C., Sandhurst ; 1st commission 14.2.90 ; Lt.-Col., R. of Off., 11.10.19 ; Bt. Lt.-Col. 3.6.19 ; retired N. Staffs. Regt. 17.4.12 ; served S. African War, 1900–2 (Queen's Medal, 3 clasps ; King's Medal, 2 clasps) ; Europ. War, 1914–19 ; Despatches ; Officer, Légion d'Honneur ; Croix de Guerre.

DRAKE-BROCKMAN, E. A. (D.S.O. L.G. 1.1.18), Lt.-Col., 11th Batt. A.I.F., 11.5.16 ; commanded 16th Batt. A.I.F. 1916–18 ; served Europ. War, 1914–18, in the Dardanelles, France ; Despatches ; C.M.G., 1915 ; Order of Danilo, 4th Class.

R. E. Drake-Brockman.

DRAKE-BROCKMAN, G. P. L. (D.S.O. L.G. 3.2.20), Capt., Border Regt. ; M.C.

DRAKE-BROCKMAN, R. E. (D.S.O. L.G. 3.6.18) ; b. 1.10.75 ; 7th s. of late William Drake-Brockman, of Bournemouth ; m. 1917, Helen Maud, 2nd d. of Major Sir Henry Pilkington ; one son ; educ. Dulwich College ; St. George's Hospital ; M.R.C.S.Eng., L.R.C.P. Lond. ; Deputy Commissioner of Medical Services, Ministry of Pensions ; Capt., R.A.M.C., 1916 ; Lt.-Col., 1917 ; O.C., 150th and 95th Field Ambulances ; retired with rank of Lt.-Col., March, 1919 ; served S. African War, 1899–1900 (Queen's Medal, 2 clasps) ; Medical Officer, Foreign Office, Uganda, and B.E. Africa Protectorates, 1900–3 ; Nandi and Suk-Turkana Expeditions (G.A.S. Medal and clasp) ; Medical Officer, Colonial Office, 1904–15 ; Somaliland Protectorate Expeditions against Mullah, 1908–10 and 1914–15 (2 clasps ; G.A.S. Medal) ; Europ. War ; Despatches twice.

DRAPER, D. C. (D.S.O. L.G. 19.8.16) (Bar, L.G. 4.2.18) (Details, L.G. 5.7.18), Capt., Can. Cav. 1.9.12 ; T/Brig.-Gen. ; Despatches. His D.S.O. was awarded for gallantry at Maple Copse 2–3.6.1916.

DRENNAN, H. D., M.B., B.A. (D.S.O. L.G. 1.1.19), Surg. Lt.-Cdr.

DRAX, THE HON. R. A. R. PLUNKETT-ERNLE-ERLE- (see Plunkett-Ernle-Erle Drax, R. A. R.).

DRESSER, H. B. (D.S.O. L.G. 1.1.18) ; b. 1875 ; m. 1895, Guillerma Justa Norton ; Major, R.F.A., S.R. ; served Europ. War, 1914–19 ; Despatches ; wounded ; 1914 Star.

DRESSER, P. B. (D.S.O. L.G. 4.6.17) ; b. 9.3.86 ; 2nd Lt., R.A., 20.12.05 ; Lt. 4.5.09 ; Capt. 30.10.14 ; Major 3.1.17 ; A/Lt.-Col. 19.2.17 to 9.3.17 ; Adjt., R.A., 1.2.20 ; Despatches.

DREW, C. D. (D.S.O. L.G. 26.7.18) ; b. 4.5.83 ; 1st commission 18.1.02 ; Major 18.1.17 ; Bt. Lt.-Col. 11.11.19 ; retired Middx. Regt. 9.3.20 ; Despatches.

DREW, C. F. (D.S.O. L.G. 1.1.18) ; b. 16.11.90 ; 2nd Sco. Rif. 5.10.10 ; Lt. 19.2.13 ; Capt. 11.3.15 ; Despatches.

DREW, C. M., M.B. (D.S.O. L.G. 3.6.19) ; b. 22.4.80 ; Lt., R.A.M.C., 30.1.06 ; Capt. 30.7.09 ; Major 30.1.18 ; Despatches.

DREW, F. W. M. (D.S.O. L.G. 26.11.17) (Details, L.G. 6.4.18) ; b. 3.10.81 ; 2nd Lt., R. Garr. R., 22.11.02 ; Lt. R. Garr. R., 30.5.04 ; Lt., S. Lan. R., 8.7.05 ; Adjt., S. Lan. R., 24.9.10 to 23.9.13 ; Capt. 27.5.14 ; Major 18.1.17 ; Adjt., S. Lan. R., 1.10.19 to 30.9.21 ; T/Lt.-Col., 9th Bn. L'pool R., 4.1.18 to 8.7.19 ; Despatches.

DREW, G. BARRY- (D.S.O. L.G. 1.1.18) ; b. 14.6.68 ; s. of Maj.-Gen. F. Barry-Drew, C.B., and A. E. Barry-Drew (*née* Tyrwhitt-Drake) m. Violet Gwendoline, d. of Col. A. Fryer two d. ; educ. Wellington College ; R.M.C., Sandhurst ; 2nd Lt., W. Yorks. Rgt., 22.8.88 ; Lt. 24.9.90 ; Capt. 20.2.95 ; Adjt., 1900–3 ; Major 23.2.08 ; Lt.-Col. 7.3.18 ; wounded ; Despatches ; holds Royal Humane Society Medal.

DREW, G. L. (D.S.O. L.G. 10.1.17), Lt., Can. F.A., 1.11.14 ; Despatches.

DREW, H. R. H. (D.S.O. L.G. 1.1.18) ; b. 25.9.71 ; 1st commission 23.12.93 ; Lt.-Col. 2.6.19 ; retired Northants R. 27.4.21 ; served N.W. Frontier of India, 1897–98 (Medal and 3 clasps) ; Europ. War, 1914–18 (wounded ; Despatches).

DREW, J. S. (D.S.O. L.G. 4.6.17) ; b. 1.9.83 ; s. of T. A. Drew ; m. 1918, Victoria, y. d. of W. Herries Maxwell, of Munches ; one s. ; educ. Harrow ; 2nd Lt., Cam'n Highrs., 18.1.02 ; Lt. 26.4.05 ; Adjt., Cam'n Highrs., 5th Bn. 29.8.14 to 29.1.16 ; Capt. 27.9.14 ; Bt. Major 3.6.16 ; served Europ. War, 1914–18 ; Despatches ; M.C.

DREYER, J. T. (D.S.O. L.G. 14.1.16) ; b. 24.12.76 ; e. s. of J. L. E. Dreyer ; m. 1914, Penelope Aylmer, d. of A. R. Holme ; two s. ; educ. Royal School, Armagh ; R.M.A., Woolwich ; Assistant Director of Artillery, War Office ; 2nd Lt., R.A., 23.3.97 ; Lt. 23.3.00 ; Capt. 6.2.02 ; Major 30.10.14 ; Bt. Lt.-Col. 1.1.17 ; Bt. Col. 1.1.19 ; Col. 8.9.20 ; served S. African War, 1901–2 (Queen's Medal, 5 clasps) ; Europ. War, 1914–18 ; Despatches ; C.B. ; Chevalier of the Legion of Honour ; Officier of the Order of Leopold ; Belgian Croix de Guerre ; Lefroy Gold Medal of the R.A. Institute, 1914.

DREYER, N. L. (D.S.O. L.G. 3.6.18), Major, Aust. F.A.

DRIVER, A. (D.S.O. L.G. 2.4.19) (Details, L.G. 10.12.19), T/Major (A/Lt.-Col.), 6th Bn. W. Riding R., T.F., att. 9th Bn.; M.C.

DRIVER, H. (D.S.O. L.G. 31.5.16); b. 29.5.87; s. of Joseph Briggs Driver; educ. Lady Berkeley's School, Wotton, Glos.; T/2nd Lt., 7th Bn. Bedf. R., 1915; Capt. 4.5.17; served Europ. War; Despatches; five times wounded; M.C.; killed in action 10.8.19.

DRUMGOLD, A. (D.S.O. L.G. 27.10.17) (Details, L.G. 18.3.18), 2nd Lt., R.W. Kent R.

DRUMMOND, THE HON. M. C. A. (D.S.O. L.G. 14.1.16); b. 30.11.77; 3rd s. of the 10th Viscount Strathallan, late Major, 11th Hussars; m. Ida Mary, 3rd d. of late George Drummond, of Swaylands, Penshurst, Kent, and Drummond's Bank; one s.; two d.; educ. Eton; 2nd Lt., R. Highrs., 20.5.99; Lt. 5.8.00; Adjt., R. Highrs., 21.4.04 to 20.4.07; Capt. 1.9.15; Bt. Lt.-Col. 1.1.18; served S. African War (severely wounded at Magersfontein); Despatches; Queen's Medal, 3 clasps; King's Medal, 2 clasps); Europ. War, 1914–18; Despatches several times; wounded Battle of Marne; Chevalier, Legion of Honour; C.M.G.

DRUMMOND, R. M. (D.S.O. L.G. 26.3.18) (Details, L.G. 24.8.18) (Bar, L.G. 26.7.18), Capt., R.F.C.; M.C.

DRUMMOND, W. S. G. (D.S.O. L.G. 1.1.18), Lt. (T/Major), A.S.C., S.R.

DRURY, R. C. F. (D.S.O. L.G. 1.1.19), T/Lt.-Col., R.F.A.

DRURY-LOWE, W. D. (D.S.O. L.G. 3.6.16); e. s. of late William D. N. Drury-Lowe and Lady Lucy Drury-Lowe; m. The Hon. Hylda Harriet Marianne Sugden, d. of the 2nd Lord St. Leonards; educ. Eton; 2nd Lt., Grenadier Gds., 1900; retired Aug. 1908, with rank of Captain; the same month was given a commission as Major, commanding 2nd Derbyshire Battery, 4th N. Midland (Howitzer) Brigade, R.F.A.; commanded this battery for over seven years, and accompanied it to France, Feb. 1915; appointed to command the 4th North Midland (Howitzer) Brigade; rejoined the Grenadier Gds., 1916; T/Lt.-Col.; served S. African War, 1901–2 (Queen's Medal, 3 clasps); Europ. War; Despatches. He was killed in action 25.9.16.

DRYNAN, W. B. (D.S.O. L.G. 16.8.17), T/Major, York and Lan. R.

DRYSDALE, A. E. (D.S.O. L.G. 22.12.16); b. 7.5.89; Lt., Unatt., 8.9.09; 2nd Lt., Ind. Army, 3.11.10; Lt. 8.12.11; Capt. 1.9.15; served Europ. War; M.C.; Despatches.

DU BOULAY, A. H. (D.S.O. L.G. 3.6.18); b. 18.6.80; 2nd Lt., R.E., 22.11.99; Lt. 22.11.02; Capt. 22.11.08; Major and Bt. Lt.-Col.; Despatches. He died 25.10.18.

DUBUC, A. E. (D.S.O. L.G. 1.1.17) (Bar, L.G. 11.1.19); b. Montreal 18.5.80; s. of Arthur Dubac and Angeline Racicot; educ. Mount St. Louis Institute and Ecole Polytechnique, Laval University, Montreal; Civil Engineer and B.Sc., 1901; Member Engineering Inst. of Canada; Lieut., Corps of Guides, Canadian Militia, 1908; Capt. 27.10.14; Major, 1915; Second-in-Command, 22nd French Canadian Inf. Batt. 24.1.16, later commanding the Batt.; served Europ. War, 1915–18 (wounded thrice); Chevalier de la Légion d'Honneur, 1917.

DUCAT, A. B., M.B. (D.S.O. L.G. 3.6.19), Lt.-Col., 2/3rd London F. Amb., R.A.M.C.

DUCK, F. P. (D.S.O. L.G. 2.2.16); b. 4.10.86; o. s. of Sir Francis Duck; educ. Beaumont; Capt., S. Staff. R., 29.12.15; T/Major 1.11.18 to 31.12.18; served Europ. War, 1914–16 (Despatches; see L.G. Gazette); T/Capt. (T/Major), 6th (S.) Bn. Linc. Regt.

DUCKETT, J. S. (D.S.O. L.G. 1.1.17), T/Capt. (T/Major), Lancs. R. of O.

DUCKWORTH, R. (D.S.O. L.G. 1.1.18); b. 13.11.76; 1st commission 9.12.90 Major 1.9.15; Bt. Lt.-Col. 3.6.19; retired S. Staff. R. 9.11.19; Despatches.

DUDGEON, R. M. (D.S.O. L.G. 1.1.18); b. 20.2.81; s. of Col. R. F. Dudgeon, C.B., Lord Lieut. of Kirkcudbrightshire, and Margaret Dudgeon (*née* Maxwell); m. Kathleen J. M., d. of the late A. Taylor; educ. Uppingham and Loretto; 1st commission 5.1.01; Bt. Lt.-Col. 3.6.19; Lt.-Col. (Res. of Off.) 29.1.21; served S. African War; Queen's Medal, 5 clasps; Europ. War; M.C.; Despatches four times; Legion of Honour.

R. M. Dudgeon.

DUDLEY, G. V. (D.S.O. L.G. 3.6.19), T/Capt. (A/Major), 185th Siege By. R.G.A.; M.C.

DUDLEY-WARD, C. H. (D.S.O. L.G. 2.4.19) (Details, L.G. 10.12.19); b. 5.12.97; 2nd Lt., W. Gds., 16.9.15; Lt. 10.1.17; M.C.; Despatches.

DUFF, G. B. (D.S.O. L.G. 14.1.16); b. 6.12.79; s. of Garden A. Duff, J.P.; m. 1913, Doris, d. of Lindsay Eric Smith; 2nd Lt., Cam'n Highrs., 16.8.99; Lt. 9.3.01; Capt. 3.4.10; Major 1.9.15; Bt. Lt.-Col. 1.1.17; retired 1.1.17; Despatches three times.

DUFF, H. J. (D.S.O. L.G. 16.9.18), Lt. (A/Major), Yeom.; M.C. Killed in action 6.9.18.

DUFF-COOPER, A. (see Cooper, A. Duff-).

DUFF-DUNBAR, K. J. (D.S.O. L.G. 10.1.16), Lt.-Cdr., R.N. Killed in action 22.8.16.

DUFFY, J. A. (D.S.O. L.G. 3.6.19), Qr. Mr. and Hon. Major, 13th Aust. L.H.R., formerly 4th L.H.

DUGDALE, A. (D.S.O. L.G. 1.1.19); b. 1869; s. of late James Dugdale, of Sezincote, Moreton-in-Marsh; m. 1904, Ethel Innes, e. d. of late Col. John Sherston, D.S.O., Rifle Brigade; one s.; educ. Winchester College; Christ Church, Oxford (M.A.); Lt.-Col. commanding Q.O. Oxfordshire Hussars; served Europ. War; C.M.G.

DUGDALE, W. M. (D.S.O. L.G. 1.1.18), Major (Hon. Capt. in Army), R.W. Fus.

DUGGAN, B. O. C. (D.S.O. L.G. 1.1.18) (Bar, L.G. 2.4.19) (Details, L.G. 10.12.19), Lt.-Col., Aust. Inf.

DUGGAN, H. J. G. (D.S.O. L.G. 8.3.19) (Details, L.G. 4.10.19), T/Capt. (A/Major), N. Lancs. R., att. 1/4th Bn. T.F.; M.C.

DUGUID, A. F. (D.S.O. L.G. 3.6.18); b. 1887; y. s. of late Peter Duguid, of Bourtie, Aberdeenshire; m. (1st), 1916, Naomi (d. 1920), e. d. of Edward Pelham Winslow, of Winnipeg; one s.; (2nd), 1921, Frances, d. of Edward Pelham Winslow; educ. Fettes College, Edinburgh; McGill University, Montreal; Major, Can. F.A.; served Europ. War, 1914–18 (wounded); Despatches.

DUGUID, C. F. (D.S.O. L.G. 11.5.17), Capt., Manch. R.; M.C. He was killed in action 13.5.17.

DUGUID-McCOMBIE, W. McC. (D.S.O. L.G. 1.1.19); b. 2.4.74; 2nd Lt., 2 Dns., 6.12.99; Lt. 3.10.00; Capt. 23.6.09; Major 19.8.15; Bt. Lt.-Col. 3.6.19; Lt.-Col. 19.8.19; served S. African War (Despatches 28.7.02; Queen's Medal, 3 clasps; King's Medal, 2 clasps); Europ. War; Despatches.

DUIGAN, J. E. (D.S.O. L.G. 4.6.17), Major, New Zea. (Staff Corps).

DUKE, A. C. H. (gazetted as Duke, A. C.) (D.S.O. L.G. 3.6.18); b. 12.5.79; 1st commission 26.5.00; Lt.-Col. (R. of Off.), 13.3.19; retired R.A. 25.10.13; C.M.G.; Despatches.

DUKE, B. L. (D.S.O. L.G. 1.1.17); b. 2.11.82; 2nd Lt., R.A., 21.12.01; Lt. 21.12.04; Capt. 30.10.14; Adjt., R.A., 25.3.15; Major 25.12.15; O.B.E.; Despatches.

DUKE, J. P. (D.S.O. L.G. 1.1.19); b. 10.6.90; 2nd Lt., R. War. R., 9.3.10; Lt. 22.11.12; Capt. 31.12.14; Bt. Major 3.6.17; Adjt., R. War R. 8.4.20; Despatches; M.C.

DUKE, R. M. (D.S.O. L.G. 3.6.18), T/Capt., Gen. List.; M.C.

DUMBELL, C. H. (D.S.O. L.G. 1.1.17) (1st Bar, L.G. 26.7.18) (2nd Bar, L.G. 8.3.19) (Details, L.G. 4.10.19); b. 1.5.78; 2nd Lt., Notts and Derby R., 26.6.01; Lt. 22.11.05; Capt. 9.7.10; Major 26.6.16; Bt. Lt.-Col. 3.6.19; served S. African War, 1899–1901 (Despatches 10.9.01; Queen's Medal, clasp); Europ. War; Despatches.

DUN, T. I., M.B. (D.S.O. L.G. 1.1.19), Capt. (A/Major), R.A.M.C.; M.C.

DUNBAR, B. H. V., M.D. (D.S.O. L.G. 4.6.17); b. 19.9.78; Lt., R.A.M.C., 31.1.03; Capt. 31.7.06; Major 31.10.14; Despatches.

DUNBAR, J. C. (D.S.O. L.G. 3.6.18); b. 20.8.79; o. s. of J. C. Dunbar, late of Ceylon; m Miss Temple-Layton, of Brampton Grange, Huntingdon; one d.; educ. Downside Abbey, near Bath; 2nd Lt., R.A., 17.3.00; Lt. 3.4.01; Capt. 21.10.08; Major 30.10.14; served W. Africa; S. Africa (Medal, 4 clasps); Europ. War, in France, Gallipoli (Suvla Bay); Despatches twice.

DUNCAN, C. M. (D.S.O. L.G. 8.3.19) (Details, L.G. 4.10.19); b. 22.1.96; 2nd Lt., R.A., 18.9.14; Lt. 9.6.15; Capt. 13.2.18; Despatches; M.C.

DUNCAN, D. (D.S.O. L.G. 1.1.18), Capt., Glouc. R.; M.C.

DUNCAN, H. A. (D.S.O. L.G. 1.1.18); b. 13.11.75; 2nd Lt., A. and S. Highrs., 21.4.00; Lt. 27.8.04; Capt. 25.5.12; Major 17.7.16; Despatches.

DUNCAN, J. F. (D.S.O. L.G. 4.6.17), T/Lt.-Col., R.A. (Capt., T.F.); served Europ. War, 1914–17; Despatches.

DUNCAN, K. (D.S.O. L.G. 3.6.16) (1st Bar, L.G. 18.1.18) (Details, L.G. 25.4.18) (2nd Bar, L.G. 2.4.19) (Details, L.G. 10.12.19); b. 12.4.84; s. of T. Arthur Duncan, J.P., of Westbourne, Otley; m. 1913, Evelyn Barker; two d.; educ. Sedbergh; served Europ. War, in command of 10th W.R. (How.) Battery, R.F.A., in France; Despatches.

DUNCAN, W. E. (D.S.O. L.G. 1.1.19); b. 19.3.90; 2nd Lt., R.A., 23.12.10; Lt. 23.12.13; Capt. 8.8.16; Bt.-Major 1.1.18; Despatches; M.C.

DUNCAN, W. J. C. (D.S.O. L.G. 26.7.18) (Bar, L.G. 1.2.19), Lt. (from Aust. Mil. Forces) 1.10.17; Lt., Ind. Army, 12.1.19; Capt. 1.10.20; Despatches; M.C.

DUNCANSON, A. E. (D.S.O. L.G. 1.1.19), Major, 123rd Battn. Can Inf.

DUNCOMBE, SIR E. P. D. PAUNCEFORT- (see Pauncefort-Duncombe, Sir E. P. D.).

DUNDAS, F. C. (D.S.O. L.G. 1.1.17); b. 16.1.68; s. of late Comdr. Frederick George Dundas, R.N.; m. Elizabeth Drummond, e. d. of James Thomson, of Glenpark, Midlothian; educ. Westminster; Sandhurst; 2nd Lt., Arg. and Suth. Highrs., 23.3.89; Capt., 1899; Major, 1911; Bt. Lt.-Col. 18.2.15; Lt.-Col. 1.1.17; h.p. late Arg. and Suth. Highrs., 29.6.19; served Europ. War; Despatches.

DUNDAS, J. C. (D.S.O. L.G. 4.6.17); b. 6.1.83; 2nd Lt., R.A., 21.12.00; Lt. 21.12.03; Capt. 27.8.13; Adjt. 15.3.14 to 29.5.15; Major 29.8.15; Bt. Lt.-Col. 1.1.19; Despatches.

DUNDAS, W. L. (D.S.O. L.G. 1.1.19); b. 22.3.72; 2nd Lt., Unatt., 14.8.95; Ind. S.C. 13.12.96; Lt., Ind. Army, 14.11.97; Capt. 14.8.04; Major 14.8.13; Lt.-Col. 28.2.20; served N.W. Frontier of India, 1897–98, Tochi (Medal with clasp); Europ. War; Despatches.

DUNFORD, R. C. (D.S.O. L.G. 14.11.16); b. 7.6.81; e. s. of C. G. Dunford and Barbara Jane Craig, his wife, of Kirkcudbright; m. 1911, Helen Walker, y. d. of E. Chalmers; educ. Richmond (Yorkshire) Grammar School; on leaving school, was articled to Messrs. J. M. Winter and Sons, Chartered Accountants; in 1904, after qualifying, commenced practice on his own account at St. Nicholas Chambers, Newcastle-on-Tyne; an old Volunteer, he was given a commission in the 6th North'd Fus.; became Capt.; served in France (slightly wounded Sept. 1915); returned to France 8.1.16; recommended for the Victoria Cross; fatally wounded and died 10.11.16. His Adjutant, in writing, Oct. 10, congratulating him, said: "I had the extreme pleasure to read aloud to Assembly at Battalion Headquarters the announcement of your award (D.S.O.). Dawson is now dictating the award to appear in Orders. Our hero! the man the 6th are proud of, not only because of his decoration, but because of his sterling qualities as a man and soldier."

R. C. Dunford.

DUNKERTON, N. E. (D.S.O. L.G. 1.1.18); b. 17.11.79; Lt., R.A.M.C., 31.8.03; Capt. 28.2.07; Major, 28.2.15; Despatches.

DUNLOP, A. T. (D.S.O. L.G. 3.6.18), Major, Can. A.M.C.

DUNLOP, C. (D.S.O. L.G. 3.6.19), T/Lt. (T/Major), Sc. Rif.; O.B.E.

DUNLOP, F. P. (D.S.O. L.G. 1.1.17); b. 3.9.77; 2nd Lt., Worc. R., 5.5.00; Lt. 2.1.01; Capt. 17.11.04; Major, 1.9.15; Bt. Lt.-Col. 3.6.19; in command 20th Bn. Middlx. R. 14.3.16 to 6.10.17; served S. African War, 1899–1902 (Queen's Medal, 2 clasps; King's Medal, 2 clasps); Europ. War (wounded); Despatches.

DUNLOP, J. (D.S.O. L.G. 22.6.18), 2nd Lt., R.F.A.

DUNLOP, R. W. L. (D.S.O. L.G. 4.6.17); b. 19.8.69; s. of late Robert Vetch Dunlop, Vicar of Holy Trinity, Scarborough; m. 1919, Irene Lois, widow of Capt. Keith Forbes Robertson, Rifle Brigade; educ. Repton; Col., Bombay Volunteer Rifles; T/Lt.-Col., R.F.A.; Hon. A.D.C. to Governor of Bombay; Additional Member, Bombay Legislative Council; Solicitor to Government of India; served Europ. War, 1914–17; Despatches.

DUNLOP, W. B. (D.S.O. L.G. 26.6.16); b. 2.11.77; s. of A. J, Dunlop, C.I.E.; m. 1918, Evelyn, yr. d. of late P. Brennan, Birn, Ireland; educ. Sedbergh; 2nd Lt., Unatt., 22.1.98; 2nd Lt., Ind. S.C., 5.3.99; Lt., Ind. Army, 26.5.00; Capt. 22.1.07; Major, 1.9.15; Bt. Lt.-Col. 1.1.18; served in Tibet, 1903–4 (Despatches, L.G. 13.12.04; Medal); operations in the Abor country, 1911–12 (Despatches, L.G. 16.7.12; Medal with clasp); Europ. War, 1914–18, with E. African Exp. Force; Despatches; 1914–15 Star, General Service and Victory Medals; Afghan War, 1919; Despatches; O.B.E.; Clasp (Afghanistan, 1919) to Indian General Service Medal.

DUNMORE, EARL OF (A. E.) (D.S.O. L.G. 1.1.17); V.C.; M.V.O. (see "The Victoria Cross," same publishers).

DUNN, E. G. (D.S.O. L.G. 23.10.19); b. 31.5.77; 2nd Lt., R. Ir. R., 8.9.97; Lt. 18.1.99; Capt. 16.6.04; Major, 17.4.15; Despatches.

DUNN, HENRY NASON, B.A., M.B. (corrected from Dunn, Henry Mason) (D.S.O. L.G. 1.1.17); b. 7.9.64; s. of Dr. G. N. Dunn, of Kinsale; m. Maud, 3rd d. of late W. Grosvenor-Jennings, of Beamhurst Hall, Uttoxeter; one s., one d.; educ. Trinity College, Dublin; late Senior Resident Medical Officer, N.W. Hospital, London; 1st commission, 3.1.95; Col. 15.4.18; retired from Staff, 26.3.21; seconded Egyptian Army, 1896; served Dongola, 1896 (Despatches; Medal, clasp); Nile, 1897–8–9 (Despatches twice, 4 clasps; Medal; 3rd Class Medjidie; 4th Class Osmanieh); served with Abyssinian Exp. Force, Somaliland, 1903–4 (Medal, clasp); N.W. Frontier, India, 1908 (Medal, clasp); Europ. War, 1914–18; Despatches four times; severely wounded; C.M.G. 1918.

DUNN, J. B. (D.S.O. L.G. 2.4.19) (Details, L.G. 10.12.19), T/Capt., 15th Bn. H. L. Inf.; M.C.

DUNN, J. C., M.D. (D.S.O. L.G. 26.11.17) (Details, L.G. 6.4.18), T/Capt., R.A.M.C.; M.C.

DUNN, P. D. W. (D.S.O. L.G. 15.2.19) (Details, L.G. 30.7.19); b. 3.10.96; 2nd Lt., Lan. Fus., 1.10.14; Lt. 6.5.15; Capt., Bord. R., 2.11.21; Despatches; M.C.

DUNN, T. S. (D.S.O. L.G. 1.1.18), Capt., E. African Medical Service.

DUNNING, M., M.B. (D.S.O. L.G. 11.4.18), Major (T/Lt.-Col.), R.A.M.C.

DUNNINGHAM, P. (D.S.O. L.G. 1.1.19), Lt., Aust. A.S.C., 1.7.15; Despatches.

DUNNINGTON-JEFFERSON, J. A. (D.S.O. L.G. 4.6.17); b. 10.4.84; 2nd Lt., R. Fus., 2.3.04; Lt. 9.12.05; Adjt. 1.10.11 to 4.8.14; Capt. 4.9.12; Bt. Major, 1.1.16; Lt.-Col. 8.11.19; retired R. Fus. 8.11.19; Despatches.

DUNSDON, G. E. (D.S.O. L.G. 3.6.19), Major, R.G.A.

DUNSFORD, F. P. S. (D.S.O. L.G. 25.8.17); b. 20.10.66; 2nd Lt., Durh. L.I., 16.11.87; Lt., Ind. S.C., 11.12.88; Capt., Ind. Army, 16.11.09; Major, 16.11.05; Lt.-Col. 16.11.13; T/Brig.-Gen.; retired, 9.11.20; Despatches.

DUNSTERVILLE, K. F. (D.S.O. L.G. 1.1.19); b. 24.6.83; 2nd Lt., R.A., 31.7.02; Lt. 31.7.05; Capt. 30.10.14; Major, 1.5.17; A/Lt.-Col. 24.2.19 to 25.3.19; Despatches.

DUNWOODY, J. M. (D.S.O. L.G. 15.2.19) (Details, L.G. 30.7.19), Lt., Fort Garry Horse, 16.2.17; D.C.M.

DU PLESSIS, P. L. (D.S.O. L.G. 22.8.18), Major, Cradock Commando, S. African Mil. Forces.

DU PORT, O. C. (D.S.O. L.G. 4.6.17); b. 9.7.75; 1st commission, 2.11.95; Lt.-Col. (Res. of Off.), 2.5.19; Bt. Lt.-Col. 3.6.19; retired R.A. 26.2.13; Despatches.

DU PRE, F. J. (D.S.O. L.G. 1.1.17); b. 3.2.81; 3rd s. of late James Du Pre and Selina, d. of late Richard Stokoe, M.D.; m. 1904, Dorothy Margaret, o. d. of E. J. Kitts, I.C.S.; one s.; educ. Eton; Sandhurst; 2nd Lt., 3rd Hrs., 12.8.99; Lt. 9.11.00; Adjt. 12.7.04 to 11.7.07; Capt. 16.1.08; Major, 3rd Hrs., 2.4.17 (Tank Corps, 5.7.20); served S. Africa, 1902 (Queen's Medal, 3 clasps); Europ. War, 1914–17; Despatches twice.

DU PREEZ, C. J. (D.S.O. L.G. 22.8.18), Lt.-Col., Vrijstaatse Schutters (6th Regt.), S. African Mil. Forces.

DURHAM, C. G. (D.S.O. L.G. 18.10.17), Major.

DURIE, T. E. (D.S.O. L.G. 3.6.18); b. 28.8.84; 2nd Lt., R.A., 29.7.04; Lt. 29.7.07; Capt. 30.10.14; Major, 9.9.16; Despatches; M.C.

DURKEE, A. A. (D.S.O. L.G. 3.6.19), Major, 38th By., 10th Bde., Can. F.A.; Adjt. 31.3.14; Despatches.

DURNFORD, G. E. J. (D.S.O. L.G. 1.1.18); b. 29.5.76; s. of late Colonel Arthur George Durnford, R.E.; m. 1901, Bessie Muriel, y. d. of Lt.-Col. John Ford, R.A.; one s.; one d.; educ. Uppingham (Scholar); R.M.A., Woolwich; 2nd Lt., R.E., 3.8.95; Lt. 3.8.98; Capt. 3.8.04, Major, 30.10.14, Bt. Lt.-Col. 1.1.19, Lt.-Col. 9.11.21; served Europ. War; Despatches.

DURNFORD, R. C. (D.S.O. L.G. 17.3.17) (Details, L.G. 18.6.17); Hants Regt. Capt. Durnford was killed in action 21.6.18.

DURRANT, A. W. (D.S.O. L.G. 18.2.18) (Details, L.G. 18.7.18), Lt. (A/Capt.), London Regt.

DURRANT, J. M. A. (D.S.O. L.G. 1.1.17); b. 17.3.85; s. of Jonathan William Durrant and Margaret Elizabeth Durrant, of Adelaide; m. 1911, Clara Ellen, d. of Henry Birk, of Westmead, N.S.W.; educ. privately; Adelaide University; joined the Permanent Staff, Aust. Mil. Forces, 1907; Lt. 1910; Capt. and Adjt., 13th Batt. A.I.F., 1.7.14; Bt. Major, 1.12.15; Lt.-Col., to command 12th Batt. A.I.F., 1916; served Europ. War in Gallipoli, Egypt and France; Order of the White Eagle of Serbia, 4th Class with swords; Despatches.

DUTHIE, ANDREW MAY (D.S.O. L.G. 4.2.18) (Details, L.G. 5.7.18), Lt. (A/Capt.), London Regt.

DUTHIE, ARTHUR MURRAY (D.S.O. L.G. 14.1.16); b. 12.6.81; s. of John Firminger Duthie, Director of botanical Survey, N. India; m. 1917, Yseult, d. of late Edmond de la Poer, of Gurteen le Poer, Ireland; educ. Marlborough; R.M.A., Woolwich; 2nd Lt., R.A., 22.11.99; Lt. 16.2.01 (Impl. Yeo. 13.2.02 to 30.11.02); Capt. 1.4.08; Major 30.10.14; Lt.-Col. 11.6.21; Commandant Artillery School, Quetta, since 1921; served S. African War, 1902 (Queen's Medal, 2 clasps); Europ. War, 1914–18; Despatches five times; O.B.E. 1919; Chevalier of the Legion of Honour; served with Baluchistan Force, Afghanistan War, 1919.

DUTHIE, N. A. (D.S.O. L.G. 22.6.18), Major, Auckland R., N.Z. Mil. Forces.

DUTTON, R. B. (D.S.O. L.G. 4.6.17), Major (T/Lt.-Col.), R.E.

DWYER, A. J. (D.S.O. L.G. 1.1.17), Capt., A.I.F., 1.8.12; Despatches.

Arthur Murray Duthie.

DWYER, J. J. (D.S.O. L.G. 4.6.17), Capt., R.A.M.C. He died 19.2.19.

DWYER-HAMPTON, B. C. (surname corrected from Dwyer) (D.S.O. L.G. 1.1.17); b. 12.7.72; 1st commission 1.11.72; Lt.-Col. 11.11.18; Bt. Lt.-Col. 29.11.15; retired Leic. R. 21.12.19; Despatches.

DYER, B. A. S. (D.S.O. L.G. 1.1.18); b. 8.5.83; 2nd Lt., R. Fus., 30.4.02; Lt., R. Fus., 25.3.05; 2nd Lt., A.S.C., 9.10.05; Lt., A.S.C., 9.10.06; Capt. 24.5.12; Major, R.A.S.C., 1.1.16; Despatches.

DYER, G. N. (D.S.O. L.G. 3.6.19); b. 21.5.81; 3rd s. of Frederick Dyer, J.P., The Pentlands, Croydon; m. 1913, Dorothy Graham, 4th. d. of Charles Dyer, 8, Craven Hill Gardens, W.2; one s.; two d.; educ. Rugby; R.M.C., Sandhurst; 2nd Lt., R.W. Surr. R., 11.8.00; Lt. 1.1.03; Capt. 29.8.11; Adjt. 22.1.12 to 7.10.13; Major, 1.9.15; served Europ. War, 1914–19; Despatches twice; Croix de Guerre.

DYER, H. M. (D.S.O. L.G. 14.1.16) (Bar, L.G. 26.7.17), Major, 5th Can. Inf. Brig., 22.3.07; served Europ. War; C.B.; C.M.G.; Despatches.

DYER, H. R. (D.S.O. L.G. 26.7.18); b. 29.6.80; 2nd Lt., 3rd D. Gds., 10.11.00; Lt., 3rd D. Gds., 1.4.01; Lt., Ind. Army, 7.10.02; Capt. 15.1.09; Major, 1.9.15 (A/Lt.-Col., Ind. Army) 2.4.18; Despatches.

DYER, R. J. (D.S.O. L.G. 1.1.17); b. Sydney, N.S.W., 8.12.93; s. of F. H. Dyer, Blackheath, England; educ. Sydney Church of England Grammar School, N. Sydney; joined Aust. R.E. 1912; Capt. 1915; Major, 1915; commanded 1st Field Coy. Aust. Eng.; served Europ. War, in Gallipoli and France; Croix de Chevalier; Despatches twice.

DYKE, P. HART (D.S.O. L.G. 1.1.18); b. 24.8.72; 2nd Lt., R. Worc. R., 18.5.92; Lt., R. Worc. R., 11.8.93; Lt., Ind. S.C., 4.8.96; Capt., Ind. Army, 10.7.01; Major, 18.5.10; Bt. Lt.-Col. 1.1.17; Lt.-Col. 18.5.18; Col., Ind. Army, 1.8.21; served Uganda, 1897–8 (Despatches; Medal, 2 clasps); N.W. Frontier of India, 1908 (Despatches; Medal, clasp); Somaliland, 1908–10 (Medal, clasp); Europ. War; Despatches.

DYKES, F. H. BALLANTINE- (see Ballantine-Dykes, F. H.).

DYMOTT, G. L. (D.S.O. L.G. 1.1.18), Major, R.F.A.

DYSON, L. M. (D.S.O. L.G. 4.6.17); b. 30.3.73; 1st commission, 12.12.94; Major, 1.8.11; retired R.A. 17.2.12; Lt.-Col., R.F.A. (T.F.); served S. African War (Despatches, L.G. 20.8.01; Queen's Medal, 5 clasps; King's Medal, 2 clasps); Europ. War; Despatches.

EADIE, J. I. (D.S.O. L.G. 25.8.17); b. 6.6.83; 2nd Lt., Unatt., 13.1.02; Ind. Army, 6.4.03; Lt. 18.4.04; Capt. 18.1.11; Major, 18.1.17; Despatches.

EAGLES, C. E. C. (D.S.O. L.G. 1.1.17); b. 16.11.83; s. of C. F. Eagles, M.A., B.N.C., Oxford, Vicar of Congleton, Warwickshire, Rural Dean and Hon. Canon of Coventry, and Susan Nicholls Eagles (who died in 1915); m. Esmé Beatrice, d. of Col. C. Field, R.M.L.I.; one s.; educ. at Marlborough; ent. R.M.L.I. 1.9.01; Lt. 1.7.02; Capt. 1.9.12. Major Eagles served in Gallipoli, in France (mentioned 2.1.16), and was killed in action at the landing at Zeebrugge, April, 1918.

EAMES, C. W., M.D. (D.S.O. L.G. 1.1.19); s. of late Dr. J. D. Eames, of Leeds. Some years before the war he raised a contingent of the R.A.M.C. at Shipley, and he was on active service from the outbreak of hostilities; Capt. (T/Lt.-Col.), R.A.M.C.; Despatches twice.

EARCHMAN, A. (D.S.O. L.G. 3.6.18), Capt., Can. Inf., 10.7.05; T/Lt.-Col. 6.3.16; O.B.E.

C. E. C. Eagles.

EARDLEY-WILMOT, THEODORE (D.S.O. L.G. 1.1.17); b. 15.12.79; s. of Robert Eardley-Wilmot, J.P., of Petworth, Sussex; m. Mildred Clare, d. of W. F. Reynolds; one s.; one d.; educ. Tonbridge and Sandhurst; 2nd Lt., E. Surrey R., 12.8.99; Lt., E. Surrey R., 9.1.01; Ind. Army, 20.6.01; Capt., Ind. Army, 12.8.08; York and Lanc. R., 16.3.09; Major (T/Lt.-Col.). He was severely wounded at the 2nd Battle of Ypres, and returned to the front in 1916 with a service battalion of the Suffolk R., in command of which he was killed in action on 22.3.18. He had been mentioned in Despatches.

EARDLEY-WILMOT, TREVOR (D.S.O. L.G.17.5.18); was promoted to Commander for war services, 11.11.18.

EARLE, F. W. (D.S.O. L.G. 16.8.17); b. 1.7.81; s. of late Thomas Earle; m. Blanche Marie, d. of Bertram L. Stivens, M.D.; one s.; 2nd Lt.. Hamps. R., 4.5.01; Lt. 22.1.04; Capt. 21.3.09; Major, 8.1.16; Bt. Lt.-Col. 3.6.19; in command 15th Bn. Hamps. R., 2.4.17–2.6.19; served S. Africa, 1900–2 (Queen's Medal, 3 clasps; King's Medal, 2 clasps); Europ. War, 1914–17; Despatches.

EARNSHAW, P. (D.S.O. L.G. 1.1.19), Major, Can. Eng., 19.8.14; M.C.

EASTERBROOK, C. C. (D.S.O. L.G. 12.12.19), Major, 7th Aust. L. H. Regt.; M.C.

EASTHAM, A. (D.S.O. L.G. 27.5.19), Lt. Can. Infy. 6.1.15; M.C.

EASTMEAD, C. S. (D.S.O. L.G. 1.1.19); b. 30.9.69; 2nd Lt., Manch. R., 11.2.88; Lt. Ind. S.C., 18.7.89; Capt., Ind. Army, 11.2.99; Major, 11.2.06; Lt.-Col. 11.2.14; Despatches.

EASTON, F. A. (D.S.O. L.G. 7.2.18); b. 2.5.71; 2nd Lt. 25.7.90; Lt.-Col., R.G.A., 1.5.21; Brig.-Gen. (hon.), 1.11.21; Despatches.

EASTON, P. G. (D.S.O. L.G. 14.1.16); b. 15.12.78, y. s. of the late John Easton, M.D.; m. 1913, Winifred, y. d. of Philip Witham; educ. Lancing; St. Mary's Hospital; Lt., Ind. Med. Serv., 1.9.02; Capt. 1.9.05; R.A.M.C. 28.11.18; Major, 1.3.14; served Europ. War, 1914–16; C.B.E.; Despatches twice.

EASTWOOD, T. R. (D.S.O. L.G. 3.6.19); b. 1.5.90; Lt., Rif. Brig., 9.3.10; Lt. 11.11.11; Capt. 30.12.14; Bt. Major, 1.1.18; M.C.

EATON, A. E. (D.S.O. L.G. 22.1.16); b. 24.12.84; 2nd s. of John Eaton; m. 1907, Dorothy Florence Isbell; educ. Wyggeston School, Leicester; 2nd Lt., 7th Leics., March, 1915; transferred to R.E.; Capt., Feb. 1916; Lt.-Col. 1918; Col. 1919; served Europ. War; Despatches twice; mentioned in French Army Orders; Légion d'Honneur; Croix de Guerre with Palms. He made on foot a most daring reconnaissance Jan. 1916, remaining nearly seven hours behind the German lines.

A. E. Eaton.

EATON, THE HON. F. O. H. (D.S.O. L.G. 26.9.17) (Details, L.G. 9.1.18); b. 19.6.93; e. s. of 3rd Baron Cheylesmore; m. 1916, Nora Mary, d. of Erskine Parker, Tasmania; educ. Eton; Trinity College, Cambridge; R.M.C., Sandhurst; 2nd Lt., G. Gds., 16.12.14; Lt. 30.6.15; Capt., 3rd Batt. G. Gds.; served Europ. War. His D.S.O. was awarded for gallantry on July 31st, 1917, Boisinghe, Pilckem; Despatches.

EAVES, F. (D.S.O. L.G. 3.6.16), Capt. (T/Lt.-Col.), R. Lancs. R., T.F.

EBERLE, G. S. J. F. (D.S.O. L.G. 3.6.18), Major, R.E.

EDDIS, B. L. (D.S.O. L.G. 1.1.18); b. 17.8.83; 2nd Lt., R. Eng., 31.1.03; Lt. 21.9.05; Capt. 31.1.14; Major, 31.1.18; Bt. Lt.-Col. 3.6.19; Despatches.

EDDOWES, H. M. (D.S.O. L.G. 2.4.19) (Details, L.G. 10.12.19), T/Lt., 185th Tunnelling Coy., R.E.

EDEN, A. J. F. (D.S.O. L.G. 3.6.16); b. 20.1.72; s. of late Lt.-Col. A. D. Eden, Cameronians; m. 1903, Isabella Anne, d. of late Rev. E. M. Weir, Rector of Tydavnet, co. Monaghan; one d.; educ. Haileybury College; R.M.C., Sandhurst; 2nd Lt., Oxf. and Bucks. Light Inf., 18.6.92; Lt. 17.3.94; Capt. 24.2.00; Bt. Major, 29.11.00; Bt. Lt.-Col. 3.6.15; Lt.-Col. 18.9.15; Col. 3.6.19; employed with W. African Field Force, 1898–1901; served Niger Hinterland, 1898 (Medal, with clasp); Ashanti Expedition, 1900 (Despatches; Medal with clasp); S. African War, 1901–2 (Medal with 5 clasps); Europ. War; Despatches; C.M.G.

EDEN, S. H. (D.S.O. L.G. 1.1.17); b. 18.3.73; s. of late Henley Eden, and Amy Frances, d. of late Lord Charles Lennox Kerr; 2nd Lt., R. Highrs., 24.3.97; Lt. 12.12.99; Capt. 13.6.03; Major, 17.2.15; served S. African War, 1901–2 (Queen's Medal, 4 clasps); Europ. War, 1914–18; Despatches; Bt. Lt.-Col. 1.1.18; C.M.G.; Legion of Honour.

EDGAR, D. K. (D.S.O. L.G. 17.9.17); b. 29.11 79; 2nd Lt., R. Eng., 19.6.02; Lt. 24.9.04; Capt. 19.6.13; Major, 19.6.17; Lt.-Col. 3.6.19; Despatches.

EDGERTON, E. H. D. (D.S.O. L.G. 16.9.18), Lt., Aust. Inf.; M.M.

EDGETT, C. E. (D.S.O. L.G. 3.6.18), Lt., Can. A.V.C., 9.8.13; Major (T/Lt.-Col.).

EDGEWORTH, K. E. (D.S.O. L.G. 4.6.17); b. 26.2.89; s. of Thomas N. Edgeworth; m. Isabel Mary, widow of A. F. Eves, Resident Engineer, Cawnpore; educ. Marlborough; 2nd Lt., R. Eng., 3.12.98; Lt. 3.7.01; Capt. 26.1.08; Major, 12.8.15; Lt.-Col., R.C. of Sigs., 28.6.20; served S. African War (Queen's Medal, 2 clasps; King's Medal, 2 clasps); E. Africa, 1903–4, in Somaliland (Medal with clasp); Soudan, 1908 (Egyptian Medal with clasp); Europ. War; Despatches three times; M.C.

EDGLEY, J. M. (D.S.O. L.G. 4.6.17), Lt., Aust. Mil. Forces, 1.3.10; Major.

EDINBOROUGH, S. B. (D.S.O. L.G. 8.3.19) (Details, L.G. 4.10.19), 2nd Lt. (A/Capt.), 3rd Bn. Lincs. R., attd. 1st Battn.; M.C.

EDLMANN, F. J. F. (D.S.O. L.G. 1.1.17), T/Major, North'd. Fus.

EDMEADES, W. A. (D.S.O. L.G. 3.6.18), Major (A/Lt.-Col.), R.G.A.

EDMOND, J. H. (D.S.O. L.G. 1.1.19); b. 11.10.82; 2nd Lt., R. Art., 21.12.00; Lt. 7.9.03; Capt. 21.12.13; Major, 30.12.15; A/Lt.-Col. 3.11.18 to 16.11.18; served N.W. Frontier of India, 1908, operations in the Mohmand country (Medal, clasp); Europ. War; Despatches.

EDMUNDS, C. T. (D.S.O. L.G. 1.1.19); b. 9.11.80; Lt., R.A.M.C., 30.1.06; Capt. 30.7.09; Major, 30.1.18; A/Lt.-Col. 12.5.18 to 13.5.19; served N.W. Frontier of India, 1908, operations in Mohmand country (Medal with clasp); Europ. War; Despatches.

EDWARDES, J. G. (D.S.O. L.G. 27.6.19); b. 9.9.69; 2nd Lt., R. Ir. R., 29.11.90; Lt. 24.11.91; Lt., Ind. S.C., 10.8.92; Capt., Ind. A., 10.7.01; Major, 29.11.08; Lt.-Col., 3rd Gurkha Rif., I.A., 29.11.16; Despatches.

EDWARDS, C. (D.S.O. L.G. 8.3.18), Lt.-Comdr., R.N.R.

EDWARDS, C. E. (D.S.O. L.G. 1.1.19), T/Major, 26th Battn. R. Fus.; M.C.

EDWARDS, C. G. (D.S.O. L.G. 26.9.17) (Details, L.G. 9.1.18), 2nd Lt., W. Yorks R. His D.S.O. was awarded for gallantry on 27.7.17, at Rancourt.

EDWARDS, C. M. (D.S.O. L.G. 10.1.17) (1st Bar, L.G. 3.6.18; 2nd Bar, L.G. 15.2.19) (Details, L.G. 30.7.19); b. 28.9.81; s. of John Cameron Edwards; m. 1913, Agnes, d. of late W. Wallace Watson, of Montreal; one s.; educ. Ottawa Public School; Collegiate Institute; McGill University, Montreal; fifteen years an officer in the Canadian Militia; Lt.-Col. Comdg. 38th Ottawa Batt., C.E.F., 1915; A.D.C. to the Governor-General of Canada, June, 1919; served Europ. War in France, 1914–19; in France, at Ypres, Somme and Vimy Ridge, etc.; wounded, 1917, on Vimy Ridge.

EDWARDS, C. V. (D.S.O. L.G. 26.9.17) (Details, L.G. 9.1.18), 2nd Lt., York. R., 28.9.95; Lt. 23.11.97; Capt. 9.5.04; Major, 28.3.11; Bt. Lt.-Col. 3.6.18; Lt.-Col. 1.1.19; T/Brig.-Gen. 26.8.18 to 29.3.19; served Tirah, 1897–8 (Medal, 2 clasps); S. African War, 1899–1900 (Queen's Medal, 2 clasps); E. Africa, 1904 (Medal, 2 clasps). His D.S.O. was awarded for gallantry on 31.7.17, east of Ypres; Europ. War; Despatches; C.M.G.

EDWARDS, C. W. (D.S.O. L.G. 3.6.16); b. 18.10.84; 2nd Lt., A.S.C., 10.10.03; Lt. 31.3.05; Capt. 12.9.12; Major, R.A.S.C., 9.6.16; Despatches.

EDWARDS, E. H. (D.S.O. L.G. 23.5.17), Capt., R.N.

EDWARDS, F. H. (D.S.O. L.G. 12.12.19); b. 29.9.73; 2nd Lt., Lan. Fus., 26.6.01; Lt. 20.7.04 (W. Afr. R. 29.5.09–25.10.13); Capt., Bedf. and Herts R. 7.5.13; Bt. Major, 3.6.16; Major, E. Lan. R., 1.6.20; served S. African War, 1899–1902 (Queen's Medal, 2 clasps; King's Medal, 2 clasps); Europ. War; Despatches; M.C.

EDWARDS, G. B. (D.S.O. L.G. 1.1.17); b. 2.7.81; o. s. of late Paymaster-in-Chief E. G. Edwards, R.N.; m. 1906, o. d. of late E. A. Price, A.K.C.; one s.; one d.; educ. Mannamead College, Plymouth; London Hospital; Lt., R.A.M.C., 30.1.06; Capt. 30.7.09; Major, 30.1.18; served Europ. War; Despatches twice.

G. B. Edwards.

EDWARDS, G. E. (D.S.O. L.G. 13.2.17), 2nd Lt. (A/Capt.) Seaforth Highrs. He was killed in action, 20.11.17.

EDWARDS, G. J. (D.S.O. L.G. 3.6.19); b. 11.5.81; 2nd Lt., C. Gds., 18.6.04; Lt. 22.1.07; Adjt., C. Gds., 6.6.10 to 5.6.13; Capt. 24.1.14; Major, 20.11.19; Despatches; M.C.

EDWARDS, G. MAITLAND, (D.S.O. L.G. 1.1.18); b. 13.12.82; m. 1919, Josephine, d. of E. A. Mitchell Innes, K.C.; educ. privately; Aspatria, Cumberland; Mining Engineer and Assoc.M.Inst.M.M.; 2nd Lt., R.G.A., 1914; Lt., R.F.A., 22nd Div.; Capt., R.E., 1915; Lt.-Col. Oct. 1917; on special mission to Washington, June to Sept. 1918; served Europ. War, Gallipoli, France and Russia; Croix de Guerre with Palms; Third and Fourth Class Order of St. Vladimir with Swords; Third Class St. Anne with Swords; Officer of Order of Star of Rumania with Swords.

EDWARDS, G. R. O. (D.S.O. L.G. 22.8.18) (Bar, L.G. 1.1.17); s. of late H. O. Edwards and of Mrs. Edwards, of Durban, Natal; saw service in S. Africa from Oct. 1899 to Aug. 1915, during which time he served in the Natal Mounted Rifles, the Natal Field Artillery, the Durban Garrison Artillery and the Field Artillery; for the S. African War he received the Queen's Medal and clasps, and for service during the native rebellion, 1906–7–8, he received the Medal and bar. He commanded a field battery during operations in German S.W. Africa, and was mentioned in Despatches for services in the action at Gibeon 29.4.15. Major Edwards came to England after that campaign to take up his appointment as Major in the R.F.A. He was killed in action 17.6.17.

EDWARDS, H. I. POWELL (D.S.O. L.G. 3.6.19), Major (T/Lt.-Col.), Sussex Yeom., attd. 16th Bn. R. Sussex R.

EDWARDS, H. M. (D.S.O. L.G. 4.6.17); b. 6.10.83; s. of Rev. H. M. Edwards; educ. R.M.A., Woolwich; 2nd Lt., R. Eng., 27.8.03; Lt. 21.7.06; Capt. 27.8.14; Bt. Major, 8.11.15; A/Lt.-Col. 8.4.18–31.3.19; served Europ. War, 1914–17; Despatches.

H. M. Edwards.

EDWARDS, H. W. (D.S.O. L.G. 1.1.18); b. 1887; s. of Councillor S. E. Edwards; m. Celia, d. of A. A. Smith; educ. March Grammar School; Christ's College, Cambridge; four years' active service with R. Warwickshire Regt. and on the Staff; Lt.-Col.; Despatches twice; D.S.O.; M.C.; Croix de Guerre (French).

EDWARDS, JOHN (D.S.O. L.G. 8.3.19) (Details, L.G. 4.10.19); b. 1882; s. of Rev. James Edwards, M.P. (Co.-L.) Aberavon Division of Glamorganshire; educ. British and Intermediate Schools, Neath; University College of Wales; London University (B.A.); served in ranks to Lt.-Col., R.W.F.; Despatches; has written "The Call of the Sea," "The Broken Reed," etc.

EDWARDS, P. H. (D.S.O. L.G. 24.5.19) (Bar, L.G. 3.2.20), Lt.-Col. (T/Comdr.), R.N.V.R.

EDWARDS, P. M. (D.S.O. L.G. 1.1.18), Major (T/Lt.-Col.), Aust. F. Art.; D.C.M.

EDWARDS, R. M. WYNNE- (see Wynne-Edwards, R. M.).

EDWARDS, R. P. F. (D.S.O. L.G. 1.1.18), T/Major, A.S.C.

EDWARDS, S. B. (D.S.O. L.G. 3.6.18), Lt. (A/Major), S. Afri. Heavy Artillery

EDWARDS, W. A. (D.S.O. L.G. 4.2.18) (Details, L.G. 5.7.18), 2nd Lt., Notts. and Derby. R.

EDYE, J. M. (D.S.O. L.G. 3.6.19); b. 9.10.94; 2nd Lt., York and Lancs. R., 25.2.14; Lt. 10.3.15; Capt. 2.10.16; M.C.

EELES, C. A. (D.S.O. L.G. 3.6.18); b. 22.3.85; 2nd Lt., R. Art., 27.7.05; Lt. 27.7.08; Capt. 30.10.14; Major, R.F.A., 20.11.16; Despatches.

EGAN, W., M.B. (D.S.O. L.G. 1.1.18); b. 20.9.81; educ. St. Vincent's College, Castleknock; Royal University of Ireland; Lt., R.A.M.C., 30.1.06; Capt. 30.7.09; Major, 30.1.18; served Europ. War, 1914–18; Despatches.

EGERTON, C. H. (D.S.O. L.G. 3.6.18); b. 22.9.84; 2nd Lt., R.E., 23.12.03; Lt. 27.8.06; Capt. 30.10.14; Adjt. 19.12.14–2.8.15; Adjt. 4.8.15–15.3.16; M.C.

EGERTON, W. DE M. (D.S.O. L.G. 4.6.17); b. 1879; e. s. of Sir C. C. Egerton; m. 1913, Anita Adolphine, o. d. of A. R. David; one s.; one d.; Capt., R.N.; served in the Harwich Force, Europ. War, 1914–17; Despatches twice; Deputy-Director of Torpedoes and Mining since 1921.

EGERTON, W. M. LE C. (D.S.O. L.G. 6.9.16); b. 28.10.83; s. of Admiral Sir G. Le C. Egerton, K.C.B., and Frances, d. of the late M. Gladstone; m. Dollie, d. of late H. C. Paxton and widow of Capt. A. C. Graham; educ. Wellington College; a member of the firm of Ogilvy, Gillandar and Co. from 1906; entered R.N.D. 1.10.14; Cdr. R.N.V.R.; went to the Dardanelles, Feb. 1915; was wounded 6.5.15, but was present till the evacuation. He proceeded to France, 1916; was wounded there 21.1.17; Despatches.

EGERTON-WARBURTON, G. (D.S.O. L.G. 11.4.18), Capt. (T/Major), Yeomanry and Machine Gun Corps.

EILOART, H. A. (D.S.O. L.G. 1.1.18), Capt., London Regt.; M.C. He died 20.6.20.

ELDRIDGE, W. J. (D.S.O. L.G. 1.1.19); b. 2.8.98; 2nd Lt., R. Art., 27.10.15; Lt., R.G.A., 1.7.17; Despatches; M.C.

ELEY, D. R. A. (D.S.O. L.G. 3.3.17); b. 2.2.91; 2nd Lt., Suff. R., 5.10.10; Lt. 20.9.11; Capt. 17.2.15; Despatches. His D.S.O. was awarded for gallantry 15th to 19th Nov. 1916, Ancre.

ELEY, E. H. (D.S.O. L.G. 18.2.18) (Details, L.G. 18.7.18), Lt.-Col. R.F.A.; Col. 8th London Brigade (T.F.); served Europ. War, 1914–18; C.M.G.; Despatches. He holds the T.D.

ELEY, W. G. (D.S.O. L.G. 1.1.18); b. 26.8.67; 2nd Lt., 14th Hrs., 10.11.88; Major 23.5.03; Lt.-Col. (R. of Off.) 30.9.18; served Europ. War, 1914–18.

ELGOOD, G. (D.S.O. L.G. 1.1.18); b. 4.9.79; 2nd Lt., R. W. Kent R., 4.1.99; Major (R. of Off.) 1.9.15; served S. Africa, 1900–2 (Queen's Medal, 3 clasps; King's Medal, 2 clasps); Europ. War.

J. F. Elkington.

ELIOTT, R. H. (D.S.O. L.G. 17.12.17) (Details, L.G. 23.4.18); b. 18.2.83; 2nd Lt., R.A., 21.12.01; Lt. 21.12.04; Capt. 30.10.14; Major 12.2.16; A/Lt.-Col. 20.10.18 to 16.11.18.

ELKINGTON, C. G. (D.S.O. L.G. 26.1.17), T/Capt. Glos. Regt.

ELKINGTON, J. F. (D.S.O. L.G. 28.10.16); b. 3.2.66; e. s. of Lt.-Gen. J. H. F. Elkington, C.B.; m. 1908, Mary, d. of late J. Rew; two s.; one d.; educ. Sandhurst; 2nd Lt., R. Worcs. R., 30.1.86; Capt. 25.1.93; Major 10.4.01; Lt.-Col. 6.4.10; served S. African War, 1899–1901 (Queen's Medal, 4 clasps); Europ. War, with the Foreign Legion, with the French Army; severely wounded in

Battle of Champagne; mentioned in French Army Orders; Médaille Militaire; Croix de Guerre avec Palme.

ELKINGTON, R. J. G. (D.S.O. L.G. 4.6.17); b. 28.8.67; 2nd s. of late Lt.-Gen. J. F. Elkington, C.B.; m. 1917, Eileen, o. d. of Claude Marzetti; educ. Elizabeth College, Guernsey; 2nd Lt., R.A., 17.2.86; Capt. 1896; Major 1901; Lt.-Col. 1913; Col. 12.9.17 (Brig.-Gen.); served N.W. Frontier, India, 1897–8 (Despatches; Medal with clasp); Europ. War, 1914–17; Despatches; C.B.; C.M.G.

ELKINS, W. H. P. (D.S.O. L.G. 1.1.18) (Bar, L.G. 15.2.19) (Details, L.G. 30.7.19), Lt.-Col. Can. Horse Arty.

ELLER, J. H. P. (D.S.O. L.G. 27.10.17) (Details, L.G. 18.3.18); Lt., Aust. Inf., 1.7.15; Major, 20.10.16.

ELLES, H. J. (D.S.O. L.G. 3.6.16); b. 27.4.80; y. s. of Lt.-Gen. Sir E. R. Elles, G.C.I.E., K.C.B., and Clare Gertrude (who died in 1904), d. of the late Gen. Rothney, C.B., C.S.I.; m. Geraldine, d. of Lt.-Gen. Sir Gerald Morton, K.C.I.E., C.B., C.V.O.; educ. Clifton College; R.M.A., Woolwich; ent. R.E. 25.6.99; Lt. 31.12.01; Capt. 25.6.08; Adjt. 10.4.09–9.10.12; Major 22.11.15; Col. 2.6.19; T/Major-Gen. from 16.4.18; Bt. Major 12.2.15; Bt. Lt.-Col. 3.6.18; Col.; C.B. 1917; K.C.M.G.; Officier de la Légion d'Honneur, 1917; Commandeur de la Couronne, 1917.

ELLICE, E. C. (D.S.O. L.G. 1.1.18); b. 1.1.58; s. of late Robert Ellice (secretary to Sir George Grey), and of a d. of Gen. Balfour, of Balbirnie; m. 1889, Margaret Georgiana, d. of Freeman F. Thomas; two s.; four d.; educ. Harrow; Sandhurst; joined Grenadier Guards, 1876; Capt. 1886; retired, 1892; served S. Africa with Lovat's Scouts; rejoined G. Gds. 1914; Major, 1915; commanding Guards Entrenching Batt. in France; retired, 1918; late M.P. for the St. Andrews Burghs. Major Ellice lost three sons in the war.

ELLIOT, E. H. H. (D.S.O. L.G. 1.1.18) (Bar, L.G. 3.6.18); b. 18.12.76; 2nd Lt., R.A., 1.9.96; Lt. 21.9.99; Capt. 7.3.02; Major 23.11.13; Lt.-Col. 24.6.17.

ELLIOT, W. SCOTT- (see Scott-Elliot, W.).

ELLIOTT, A. (D.S.O. L.G. 16.9.18), T/2nd Lt. Lanc. Fus.; M.C.

ELLIOTT, C. A. (D.S.O. L.G. 1.1.17), Major (T/Lt.-Col.) R.E.

ELLIOTT, C. H. (D.S.O. L.G. 1.1.17) (Bar, L.G. 18.6.17); b. 19.8.82; s. of late R. Elliott; educ. Friends' High School, Hobart; m. 20.12.17, Alice Gordon King, a sister of the Aust. Army Nursing Service; commissioned in 93rd (Derwent) Aust. Infy., 1907; Capt., 1911; Lt.-Col.; was Coy.-Comdr. 12th Batt. A.I.F. 1914; served in Gallipoli and France; C.M.G. 3.6.18; Legion of Honour (Croix de Chevalier 7.3.18); wounded three times; Despatches four times.

ELLIOTT, G. C. E. (D.S.O. L.G. 23.11.16); b. 1872; s. of Dr. G. Elliott; educ. Clifton College; served in Western Canada, later under Canadian Government in Eastern Canada; was serving in Australia under Aust. Government when war broke out, and came over as C.R.E.; subsequently transferred to 2nd, and later to 4th, Australian Division; Lt.-Col., C.R.E., 5th Divn.; Despatches; C.M.G.

ELLIOTT, H. E., LL.B. (D.S.O. L.G. 18.7.17); b. 19.6.87, at W. Charlton, Victoria; s. of late T. Elliott; educ. Ballarat College; Ormond College; Melbourne University; m. 1906, Catherine Fraser, d. of late Alex. Campbell; joined Melbourne University Officers' Corps; served in Rhodesia, Transvaal, Orange Free State and Cape Colony with Victorian Imperial Bushmen (Despatches; D.C.M.); received commission with 2nd Battn. R. Berks. R., but remained with Australians as A/Adjt. (mentioned in Col. Henniker's Column Orders); joined Border Scouts (Queen's Medal, 4 clasps; King's Medal, 2 clasps); commission in 5th A.I.R. (Commonwealth Militia), 1904; Capt. 1908; Major, 1909; Lt.-Col. Comdg. 53rd Battn. (C.M.F.) and 7th Battn. A.I.F. Aug. 1914; Bt. Col.; Col.; served in Europ. War, in Egypt, Gallipoli (engagement of Lone Pine); wounded; Despatches; in France, engagements near Fromelles and on the Somme (Cross of St. Anne of Russia, 2nd Class and with Swords; Despatches; C.M.G.); present at engagements at Bapaume, Fremincourt, Beugny, Delsaux Farm, Beaumetz, Bullecourt, Polygon Wood, Brocdoenele, Messines, Villers-Bretonneux, Amiens, Péronne, etc.; Despatches; wounded; C.B.; Croix de Guerre, France.

ELLIOTT, L. W. (D.S.O. L.G. 24.9.18), Capt. Aust. Infy.

ELLIOTT, N. M. (D.S.O. L.G. 1.1.19), Capt. (A/Major), R.H.A. (T.F.), attd. B By. H.A.C.

ELLIOTT, O. A. (D.S.O. L.G. 15.2.19) (Details, L.G. 30.7.19) (Bar, L.G. 8.3.19) (Details, L.G. 4.10.19), Major, Can. Army Medical Corps, attd. 5th Fld. Amb. Can. Army Med. Corps.

ELLIOTT, T. R., F.R.S. (D.S.O. L.G. 1.1.18); m. Martha, d. of late A. K. McCosh; T/Lt.-Col. R.A.M.C.; C.B.E.

ELLIOTT, W. (D.S.O. L.G. 4.6.17); b. 14.3.79; 2nd Lt., A.S.C., 23.10.01; Lt. 1.1.03; Capt. 10.11.06; Major, R.A.S.C., 30.10.14; Bt.Lt.-Col. 1.1.19; T/Col. 6.8.17; Despatches; C.B.E.

ELLIOTT-COOPER, N. B. (D.S.O. L.G. 18.7.17); V.C.; M.C.; died of wounds 11.2.18 (in German hands) (see "The Victoria Cross," same publishers).

ELLIS, A. J. (D.S.O. L.G. 22.9.16) (Bar, L.G. 1.1.18); b. 18.5.81; 2nd Lt., Bord. R., 5.1.01; Lt. 21.9.02; Capt. 24.2.12; Adjt. 1.10.13; Major 1.9.15; T/Lt.-Col. 1.1.19. D.S.O. awarded for gallantry near Beaumont Hamel 1.7.16.

ELLIS, B. H. (D.S.O. L.G. 26.1.17), T/Lt.-Cdr., R.N.V.R. He died of wounds 21.4.18.

ELLIS, C. G. H. (D.S.O. L.G. 11.1.19), Lt. (A/Capt.), 5th Bn. W. Riding R.

ELLIS, D. S. (D.S.O. L.G. 3.6.18), Capt., Can. Engrs., 1.11.15; Major.

ELLIS, LIONEL FREDERIC (D.S.O. L.G. 2.4.19) (Details, L.G. 10.12.19), Lt. (A/Capt.), Welsh Gds. S.R., attd. 1st Bat.; M.C.

ELLIS, LYLE FULLAM (D.S.O. L.G. 16.9.18), 2nd Lt., R.F.A., S.R.

ELLIS, S. G. VENN (D.S.O. L.G. 4.6.17); b. 20.2.80; 2nd Lt., W. India Rgt., 20.5.99; Lt. 25.7.00; Capt. Indian Army, 20.5.08; Major 1.9.15; T/Lt.-Col. 1.9.18 to 23.10.18; Despatches.

ELLWOOD, A. A. (D.S.O. L.G. 1.1.18), Capt. (T/Major), Linc. R., attd. M.G.C.; M.C.

ELMITT, T. F. (D.S.O. L.G. 1.1.18), Capt., Can. Inf. 31.3.10; Major.

ELMSLEY, J. H. (D.S.O. L.G. 3.6.16); b. 1878; s. of late R. Elmsley and Nina Elmsley (*née* Bradshaw); m. Florence A. G. Boulton; one s.; one d.; educ. Oratory School, Edgbaston; Lt., Canadian Militia, 1898; Capt. 1905; Major 1907; served S. African War (dangerously wounded; Queen's Medal, 5 clasps; King's Medal, 2 clasps); left Canada with 1st Can. Contingent as Second-in-Command; Major, R. Can. Dns.; Lt.-Col., Staff, 1st Can. Div., 1915; commanded Can. Cav. Corps; commanded 8th Can. Inf. Brig. 1916–18; was Major-Gen. in command B.E.F. to Siberia, Sept. 1918; C.B.; C.M.G.

ELPHINSTONE DALRYMPLE, SIR F. W., Bart. (D.S.O. L.G. 1.1.18); b. 17.7.82; 2nd Lt., R.A., 23.7.01; Lt. 16.4.04; Capt. 23.7.14; Major 29.9.16; Bt. Lt.-Col. 3.6.19.

ELSNER, O. W. A. (D.S.O. L.G. 1.1.17); b. 4.6.71, in Stillorgan; educ. Galway Grammar School; R. College of Surgeons, Ireland; Lt., R.A.M.C., 27.7.99; Capt. 27.7.02; Major 27.7.11; Lt.-Col. 1.3.15; Despatches; C.B.E.; Belgian Croix de Guerre.

ELSTOB, W. (D.S.O. L.G. 1.1.18), Lt.-Col., Manchester R., V.C., M.C.; killed in action 21.3.18 (see "The Victoria Cross," by same publishers).

ELTON, C. A. A. (D.S.O. L.G. 1.1.18), 2nd Lt. (T/Capt.), R. War. R.

ELTON, G. D. G. (D.S.O. L.G. 4.6.17); b. 31.12.88; o. s. of Lt.-Col. A. G. G. Elton, commanding 7th (R.) R. War. R., and grandson of Col. Gordon Young, late Punjab Commission; m. Doris, d. of R. Miller; educ. Rev. Henry Wilson's, Surbiton; Wellington College, and Sandhurst; 2nd Lt., R. Ir. Fus., 6.11.09; Lt. 21.10.11; Capt.; A.D.C. to Divisional Commander, 15.4.14 to 15.10.14; resigned appointment to accompany his regiment to France; Orderly Officer to Brigade Commander; awarded M.C.; severely wounded May, 1915; sent to Gallipoli as Brigade Major; present at evacuation; went to Egypt, and thence to another front; G.S.O. to a division; four times mentioned in Despatches He was killed in action on 5.11.17.

ELVERY, P. G. M. (D.S.O. L.G. 4.6.17); b. 29.1.85; e. s. of W. Elvery; m. 1920, Dorothy, d. of late J. Bradford; Lt., R.A.M.C., 30.1.09; Capt. 30.7.12; A/Lt.-Col.; served Europ. War, 1914–17; Despatches; M.C.

ELWES, H. C. (D.S.O. L.G. 3.6.18); b. 25.8.74; s. of H. J. Elwes; m. Muriel, d. of J. Hargreaves, of Leckhampton Court; one s.; three d.; 1st com. 6.3.95; Capt. 14.12.01; Scots Guards; retired 2.11.04; Major, Glouc. Yeom.; M.V.O.; T/Lt.-Col., Scots Guards, Spec. Res.; served S. African War, 1899–1900; advance on Kimberley, including actions at Belmont, Enslin and Modder River (seriously wounded; Queen's Medal with 2 clasps; M.V.O.); served Europ. War; Despatches.

EMERSON, H. H. A., M.B. (D.S.O. L.G. 1.1.17); b. 18.9.81; Lt., R.A.M.C., 31.7.05; Capt. 31.1.09; Major 15.10.15; A/Lt.-Col. 5.12.16–11.3.19.

EMINSON, R. F., M.B. (D.S.O., L.G. 16.9.18), T/Capt., R.A.M.C.

EMMET, R. (Senr.), (D.S.O. L.G. 1.1.18), Major, Yeom.

ENGLAND, A. (D.S.O. L.G. 3.6.18), Lt.-Col., A.S.C.

ENGLAND, N. A. (D.S.O. L.G. 7.11.18), Capt. (A/Lt.-Col.), W. Riding R.

ENGLAND, R. B. (D.S.O. L.G. 8.3.18), Cdr., R.N.

ENGLISH, E. R. M. (D.S.O. L.G. 4.6.17); b. 2.12.74; 2nd s. of late Major-General F. English, C.B., 53rd Rgt., and Ellen Sophia, d. of late Cdr. R. S. Maling, R.N.; m. Mabel Ianthe, d. of W. G. Lardner; one d.; educ. Wellington College; R.M.C., Sandhurst; 2nd Lt., Shrops. L.I., 28.9.95; Lt. 24.6.99; Capt. 19.8.05; Major 1.9.15; retired 20.11.19.; served S. African War, 1899–1902 (wounded; Queen's Medal, 4 clasps; King's Medal, 2 clasps); Europ. War, 1914–18 (wounded; Croix de Guerre; Despatches twice); Secretary, The London Flying Club, Hendon.

ENGLISH-MURPHY, W. R. (D.S.O. L.G. 2.4.19) (Details, L.G. 10.12.19), Lt. (A/Capt.), 1st Bn. S. Staffs. R.; M.C.

ENNIS, W. O. (D.S.O. L.G. 1.1.18), Major, New Zea. Pioneers.

ENSLIN, B. G. L. (D.S.O. L.G. 1.2.17); b. 6.6.79; s. of Commandant G. F. Enslin; m. S. J., d. of D. J. J. Oothnizen, of Colesberg; one d.; one s.; educ. Potchefstroom, and Grey College, Bloemfontein; took part in Anglo-Boer War as Lieutenant of Theron's Scouts; seriously wounded and captured at Jagersfontein Road; sent as prisoner of war to Bermuda; on declaration of peace visited America, England and Europe; in 1906 proceeded with General Botha to the Imperial Conference, England, as Joint Private Secretary; proceeded to German West Front on outbreak of European War, as Chief Staff Officer to the O.C., Southern Force; commanded Enslin's Horse and Botha's Hogeveld Ruiters Regiments, 1914; Wing Commander of the 4th Mounted Brigade, German West Africa, 1915; O.C., 4th Mounted Brigade with rank of Colonel, 1915 (Legion of Honour, Croix d'Officier); Acting Director of Transport and Remounts for purpose of reorganizing Department; O.C., 2nd Mounted Brigade, German E. Africa, with rank of Brig.-Genl., 1917 (D.S.O.); Chief of the Sheep and Wool Division of the Agricultural Dept. since 1912.

ENTWISLE, F. (D.S.O. L.G. 16.9.18), Capt., London R.; M.C. He died 25.11.21.

ERREY, L. G. P. (D.S.O. L.G. 27.10.17) (Details, L.G. 18.3.18); Lt., Aust. Infy.; M.C. He died of wounds 4.10.17.

ERSKINE, A. E. (D.S.O. L.G. 3.6.16); b. 1881; s. of Sir H. David Erskine, K.C.V.O., and Lady Horatia (*née* Seymour), d. of 5th Marquess of Hertford; educ. R.M.A., Woolwich; 2nd Lt., R.A., 6.1.00; Lt. 3.4.01; Capt. 14.7.08; Adjt. 1.9.12–29.10.14; Major 30.10.14; served in S. Africa; served Europ. War, 1914–18; Despatches; Bt. Lt.-Col. 1.1.18; an Equerry in Ordinary to the King, 1919.

ERSKINE, J. D. B. (D.S.O. L.G. 3.6.18); b. 3.4.74; ent. Army 6.6.96; Major 5.1.16; Bt. Lt.-Col. 1.1.19 (R. of O., Manch. R.); commanded a battalion of the Shropshires from Feb. 1915; D.S.O. awarded for service in Salonika.

ERSKINE, SIR T. W. H. J., Bart (D.S.O. L.G. 3.6.16); b. 27.5.80; s. of 3rd Baronet (who died in 1912), and Grace, d. of T. Hargreaves; m. Magdalen Janet, d. of Sir R. W. Anstruther, Bart., C.B.E., and Mildred Harriet, d. of E. Hussey; 2 sons; 2 d.; educ. at Eton; ent. Army 18.3.00; Major 1.9.15; Lt.-Col. 28.3.19; ret. Cam'n Hldrs. 28.3.19.

ERSKINE-MURRAY, A. (D.S.O. L.G. 3.6.16); b. 9.10.77; s. of A. E. Erskine-Murray, and g.s. of Hon. J. Murray; m. Ena Nelson, d. of Dr. H. Trestrail, F.R.C.S.; one s.; educ. Kelvinside Academy, Glasgow; Glasgow and Edinburgh Universities; 2nd Lt., R.A., 28.3.00; Lt. 3.4.01; Capt. 28.5.11; Adjt., R.A., 1.12.11. to 4.8.14; Major 9.12.15; served S. Africa, 1901–2 (Queen's Medal with 5 clasps); served Dardanelles, 1915 (Despatches), and subsequently in Egypt and France.

ESTRIDGE, C. L. (D.S.O. L.G. 1.1.17), Capt. (T/Lt.-Col.), Yorks. R.

ETCHELLS, T. (D.S.O. L.G. 16.9.18), Major, R. Fus.; M.C.

ETHERIDGE, F. (D.S.O. L.G. 26.8.18); b. 17.8.80; 2nd Lt., Norf. R., 4.5.01; Ind. Army 7.4.03; Lt. 27.8.03; Capt. 4.5.10; Major, Rajputs, 4.5.16.

ETON, E. (D.S.O. L.G. 14.1.16); b. 1884; s. of A. T. Eton; m. Nancy Edith, d. of E. G. Ledger; educ. Woolwich High School; King's College, London; Rouen; served as an Officer in 2nd Kent R.G.A. Volunteers, 1903–8; transferred to London R.F.A., T.F., as Captain, 1908; Major, 1912; Commanding 21st London (Howitzer) Battery, in which capacity went to France, March, 1915 (Despatches twice); Lt.-Col. 1916.

EUGSTER, O. L. (D.S.O. L.G. 3.6.16); b. London, 1880; s. of late Joseph Eugster; m. Edith Mary, d. of late W. R. Howell; one s.; one d.; educ. Feldkirch; King's College, London; commanded A Battery, H.A.C., from May, 1913 (Despatches); Order of the Nile, 3rd Class; Lt.-Col., 20th Bde., R.H.A.

EUSTACE, F. R. H. (D.S.O. L.G. 11.4.18); b. 14.8.95; 2nd Lt., R.E., 8.8.95; Lt. 8.8.98; Capt. 8.8.04; Major 30.10.14; Bt. Lt.-Col. 3.1.19.

EVANS, A. A. (D.S.O. L.G. 3.6.18), Lt., Aust. Mil. Forces, 1.7.15; Major, Aust. F.A.; M.C.

EVANS, A. P. (D.S.O. L.G. 1.1.17); b. 3.10.82; 2nd Lt., K.R.R.C., 4.12.01; Lt. 22.1.06; Capt. 5.8.14; Major 4.12.16.

EVANS, A. WINTER- (see Winter-Evans, A.).

EVANS, C. (D.S.O. L.G. 1.1.18); b. 8.8.71; s. of late Rev. H. J. Evans; educ. Winchester; 2nd Lt., R.A., 24.7.91; Lt. 24.7.94; Capt. 13.2.00; Div. Adjt. 26.10.00–31.3.01; Adjt. 1.4.01–4.12.04; Major 15.2.09; Lt.-Col. 16.4.15; T/Brig.-Gen. 30.3.18; served S. Africa, 1899–1902 (Despatches; Queen's Medal, 3 clasps; King's Medal, 2 clasps); served Europ. War, 1914–18; Despatches; C.B.; C.M.G.; Croix de Guerre; Order of the Crown of Belgium; Order of the Crown of Italy.

EVANS, C. H. D. (D.S.O. L.G. 17.9.17), Major, N. Z. Force. His D.S.O. was awarded for gallantry 5–9.6.1917, near Messines.

EVANS, D. B. CHILES- (see Chiles-Evans, D. B.).

EVANS, D. E. (D.S.O. L.G. 1.1.17); b. 8.5.85; s. of C. H. Evans and Mary Evans (*née* Millard); m. Kathleen Mary Durack; 3 d.; educ. Central and Technical College, Queensland; Engineer Training, Bundaberg Foundry, Queensland; Colonel, Aust. Engineers; Principal, Evans Deakin and Co., Brisbane, Engineering Contractors.

EVANS, D. W. C. DAVIES- (see Davies-Evans, D. W. C.).

EVANS, E. (D.S.O. L.G. 6.4.18), Capt., Mercantile Marine (Lt., R.N.R.).

EVANS, E. G. (D.S.O. L.G. 4.6.17); b. 8.8.72; 2nd Lt., R. Lancs. Regt., 20.5.93; Lt. 10.11.93; Lt., A.S.C., 1.10.96; Capt. 1.1.01; Major 1.1.11; Lt.-Col., R.A.S.C., 1.8.15; Despatches.

EVANS, E. R. G. R. (D.S.O. L.G. 10.5.17); b. 28.10.81; s. of Frank and Eliza Evans; m. (1st), Hilda Beatrice Russell (who died in 1913); and (2ndly), Elsa, d. of R. Andvord; educ. Merchant Taylors' School; Beaumont House, Kenley; H.M. Training Ship Worcester; entered R.N. as Naval Cadet 15.1.97; Midshipman, May, 1897; Sub-Lieutenant, 1900; Lieutenant, 1902; served in S.Y. Morning, relief ship to the "Discovery" Expedition, 1902–4; awarded the Shadwell Prize by the Lords Commissioners of the Admiralty, 1907; Second-in-Command, British Antarctic Expedition, Oct. 1912. After the death of Capt. Scott he took command of the expedition, and brought it home; promoted to Commander, 1912; C.B., 1913; he served in the European War; commanded Mohawk in bombardment of right wing of German Army on the Belgian Coast in 1914; Despatches. D.S.O. awarded for services when in command of H.M.S. Broke, when that ship with H.M.S. Swift engaged and defeated six German destroyers. The Broke sank G85 and G42, besides torpedoing a third.

The following is an extract from the Log Book of Broke, dated "Night of April 20th and 21st, 1917: 0.15—Heard gun fire and saw flashes in direction south eastward. Proceeded S40E, 25 knots. 0.20—Altered course S75E. 0.27—Altered course S.W. 0.34—Altered course W. Reduced to 15 knots. 0.44—Observed Number 3A Buoy bearing N61W. 0.57—South Goodwin Light Vessel N86W. Number 3A Buoy N36E. Altered course S83W. 15 knots. 1.2—Proceeded S80E and as requisite for patrolling after Swift. 1.40—Course S83W. 1.42—Observed enemy gunfire on the port bow. Altered course eight points to port. 27 knots after Swift. 1.45—Course as requisite for action with German torpedo craft. Full speed. Torpedoed No. 2 in the line: G.85. Rammed No. 3 in the line: G.42. Torpedoed No. 4 in the line. 2.20—Silenced G.85 with two 4" rounds and port after torpedo. 2.25—Ceased fire, speed reduced to slow owing to shot in boiler room. 2.30—Stopped—taken in tow by Mentor. Anchored with Mentor alongside anchor bearings Number 2A Buoy, S60W, 4 cables, veered to 6 shackles. 7.10—Slipped cable, tug secured alongside. 7.15—Proceeded in tow. 9.5—Passed through gap. Course as requisite for Dover. 11.45—Secure alongside eastern arm."

Capt. Evans holds the King Edward VII. and King George V. Medals for Antarctic Exploration; is Officer, Legion of Honour; Commander, Order of St. Olaf of Norway; Officer, Order of Leopold of Belgium; Cavalier, Military Order of Savoy, Italy. He holds the Croix de Guerre, France; the Order of the Tower and Sword, Portugal, 2nd Class; Navy Cross, United States; Belgian Médaille Civique for saving life at sea, etc., etc. He is a Gold Medallist of the R. Hungarian and R. Belgian Geographical Societies; was awarded Gold Medals from the city of Paris, the city of Rouen, and from the Geographical Societies of Marseilles, Rouen and Newcastle; is an honorary member of many Geographical Societies.

EVANS, F. E. (D.S.O. L.G. 14.1.16); b. 15.4.86; 2nd s. of Major F. Evans, T.D.; m. Hilda G., 2nd d. of J. C. Hatch, J.P.; educ. Ilford College, and Cranbrook College; joined 15th Mdlx. Vol. Rifle Corps, 1902; commissioned in 17th Batt. Lond. Regt., 1908; Captain, 1912; Major, June, 1916; served Europ. War; present at Givenchy, Festubert, Loos, and other engagements; was severely wounded and gassed at the Battle of Loos; Despatches; seconded for service with Egyptian Army, 1917; attached to Sudan Government for service in the Bahr-el-Gazal Province and Khartoum Province; 1st Class Magistrate.

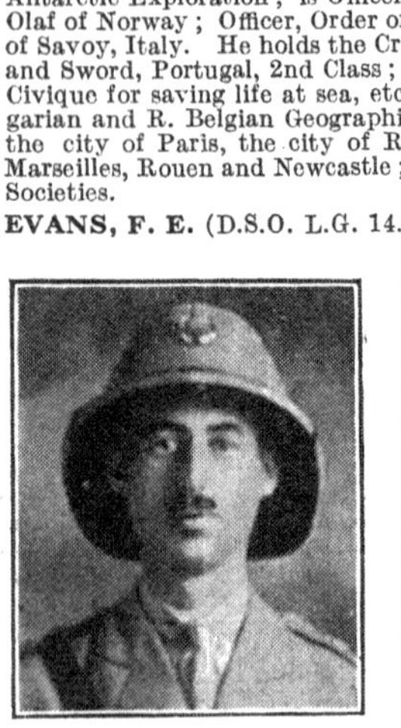

F. E. Evans.

EVANS, F. S. (D.S.O. L.G. 4.6.17), T/Major (A/Lt.-Col.), R.F.A.

EVANS, G. F. (D.S.O. L.G. 1.1.17); b. 15.2.78; s. of H. Farrington Evans, C.S.I.; m. Eleanor, d. of Col. E. Austin, I.A.; 2nd Lt., R.E., 31.12.96; Lt. 31.12.99; Capt. 31.12.05; Major 30.10.14; A/Lt.-Col. 31.10.16; served throughout S. African War (2 Medals, 8 clasps); Europ. War, 1914–18; 1914 Star; wounded; Despatches five times.

EVANS, H. C. (D.S.O. L.G. 22.9.16); b. 1879; s. of late W. H. Evans; educ. Mr. Fendall's, Woodcote House, Windlesham; and Haileybury; joined Alberta Dragoons, 1914; commissioned 1915, 2nd Lt., Gen. List, and att. R.F.C. He was killed in action 3.9.16.

EVANS, H. J. HOWELL- (see Howell-Evans, H. J.).

EVANS, I. T. (D.S.O. L.G. 19.11.17), T/Capt., S.W.B., att. Welsh R.; M.C.

EVANS, JOHN, M.D. (D.S.O. L.G. 1.1.19), Major (A/Lt.-Col.), R.A.M.C., T.F.

EVANS, JOHN (D.S.O. L.G. 1.1.19), Lt.-Col., 1/2nd Bn. Monmouthshire R.

EVANS, LL. (D.S.O. L.G. 1.1.71); b. 6.6.79; s. of late Rev. H. J. Evans; m. Margaret, d. of Lt.-Gen. Sir A. Sloggett; 2nd Lt., R.E., 23.6.98; Lt. 1.2.01; Capt. 23.6.07; Major 30.10.14; retired from the Army, 1920, with rank of Lt.-Colonel; served S. African War, 1900–2 (Despatches; Queen's Medal and 6 clasps; King's Medal and 2 clasps); Europ. War, 1914–18; Despatches; Bt. Lt.-Col. 1.1.18; C.M.G.; Chevalier, Legion of Honour; Chevalier, Order of the Crown of Belgium.

EVANS, L. P. (D.S.O. L.G. 24.7.17) (Bar, L.G. 16.9.18), Major (A/Lt.-Col.), R. Highrs.; V.C. (see "The Victoria Cross," by same publishers).

EVANS, T. C. C. (D.S.O. L.G. 3.6.18); m. Joyce, y. d. of Lt.-Col. C. J. Dennys, I.A. retired; Major, Aust. A. Medical Corps; Europ. War, 1915–18; Despatches.

EVANS, REV. T. H. W. (D.S.O. L.G. 8.3.18), T/Chapl. to the Forces, 3rd Class, A. Chaplains' Dept.

EVANS, T. R. (D.S.O. L.G. 8.3.19) (Details, L.G. 4.10.19), T/Major (A/Lt.-Col.), R.W.F., att. 1/6th Bn. N. Staffs. R. He was killed in action 3.10.18.

EVANS, W. B. (D.S.O. L.G. 4.6.17), Major 1.10.14; Can. Inf.

EVANS, W. H. (D.S.O. L.G. 1.1.18); b. 22.7.76; 2nd Lt., R.E., 21.9.96; Lt. 21.9.99; Capt. 21.9.05; Adjt. 14.11.14–10.9.16; Major 30.10.14; Bt. Lt.-Col. 1.1.19.

EVANS, W. J. (D.S.O. L.G. 12.12.19); b. 3.5.78; 2nd Lt., Unatt., 30.7.98; Ind. S.C. 3.10.99; Lt. 20.10.00; Capt. 20.7.07; Major, 1/1st Gurkha Rif., I.A., 1.9.15; A/Lt.-Col. 1.9.18.

EVANS, W. K. (D.S.O. L.G. 18.2.15) (Bar, L.G. 16.8.17), Major (T/Lt.-Col.), Manch. R. (see "The Distinguished Service Order," from its institution to 31.12.1915, by same publishers).

EVANS, W. M. (D.S.O. L.G. 4.2.18), Lt., S.W.B., S.R.

EVANS, W. P. (D.S.O. L.G. 6.4.18), Lt., R.N.R.

EVANS-GWYNNE, A. H. (D.S.O. L.G. 1.1.18); b. 17.11.82; s. of Rev. G. F. J. G. Evans-Gwynne; m. Phyllis, d. of Lt.-Gen. Sir F. C. Shaw, K.C.B.; two d.; educ. Malvern College; 2nd Lt., R.F.A., 24.12.02; Lt. 24.12.05; Capt. 30.10.14; Major 23.4.16; served in India and U.K. till 1915; Egypt, Macedonia, Serbia, France and Belgium in European War, till wounded Aug. 1918; Despatches; D.S.O.; Brig. Major, R.A., 1st Div., Aldershot, 1920.

EVATT, E. J. R., M.B. (D.S.O. L.G. 11.4.18). He was Professor of Anatomy in the Schools of Surgery attached to the Royal College of Surgeons in Ireland. He served throughout the Gallipoli Campaign, and was later A.D. of Medical Services to the 53rd Division.

EVELEGH, E. N. (D.S.O. L.G. 1.1.18); b. 17.12.90; 2nd Lt., R.E., 23.12.10; Lt. 31.7.13; Capt. 23.12.16; Bt. Lt.-Col. 3.6.19; M.C.

EVELEIGH, W. J. (D.S.O. L.G. 3.6.19), Lt., Can. Cav., 14.5.15; T/Major, 50th Bn. Can. Inf. Alberta R.

EVELYN, R. THOMAS- (see Thomas-Evelyn, R.).

EVERARD, C. J. (D.S.O. L.G. 1.1.19); b. 3.11.80; s. of G. W. Everard; educ. Trinity College, Stratford; R.M.A., Woolwich; 2nd Lt., R.A., 6.1.00; Lt. 3.4.01; Capt. 22.1.08; Adjt. 25.11.08–24.5.12; and 10.2.15–21.4.15; Major 22.4.15; O.C., 32 Pack Battery, India.

EVERETT, M. (D.S.O. L.G. 22.12.16); b. 17.7.87; 2nd Lt., R.E., 20.12.06; Lt. 23.11.08; Capt. 30.10.14; Bt. Lt.-Col. 3.6.18.

EVERINGHAM, A. E. (D.S.O. L.G. 3.6.16); b. 22.6.64; Lt.-Col. 3.6.18.

EVES, T. S., M.B. (D.S.O. L.G. 1.1.18) (Bar, L.G. 26.7.18); b. 31.3.84; Lt., R.A.M.C., 4.2.08; Capt. 4.8.11.

EVILL, C. A. (D.S.O. L.G. 3.6.16) (Lt.-Col.), Mon. R. (T.F.); served Europ. War; Despatches; has T.D.

EWART, C. (D.S.O. L.G. 1.2.19), Major, 8th Bn. Can. Rly. Troops.

EWART, C. N. (D.S.O. L.G. 1.1.18); b. 18.12.72; ent. Army 10.1.93; Major 18.2.14; Lt.-Col. 25.3.19; ret. R.A. 25.3.19.

EWART, J. K. (D.S.O. L.G. 1.1.18), T/Major, A.S.C.

EWART, R. F. (D.S.O. L.G. 24.4.18); b. 8.5.75; 2nd Lt., R.A., 25.7.00; Lt. 25.7.03; Capt. 25.7.09; Ind. Army 2.5.10; Major 1.9.15; S. and T. Corps, I.A.; Bt. Lt.-Col. 3.6.19.

EWER, G. G. (D.S.O. L.G. 16.8.17), Major, Essex R. D.S.O. awarded for services in Egypt 26.3.17.

EWING, R. L. H. (D.S.O. L.G. 1.1.18) (Bar, L.G. 1.2.19), Major, 42nd Bn. Can. Inf.; M.C.

EWING, W. T. (D.S.O. L.G. 1.1.18) (Bar, L.G. 22.4.18); s. of J. L. Ewing, LL.D.; Lt.-Col., R. Scots.

EXHAM, F. S. (D.S.O. L.G. 3.6.16); b. 18.2.75; 2nd Lt., W. Riding R., 7.12.95; Lt. 8.2.99; Capt. 24.7.01; appointed to the A.O.D.; Major 3.9.13; Bt. Lt.-Col. 3.6.18; served in S. African War, 1899–1902 (Queen's Medal with 4 clasps; King's Medal with 2 clasps; Despatches); served in Europ. War in France, 1914–18; Despatches.

EXHAM, H. (D.S.O. L.G. 27.9.20); b. 13.10.84; 2nd Lt., Yorks. and Lancs. R., 10.10.03; Lt. 10.6.06; Ind. Army 23.7.07; Capt. 10.10.12; Major 10.10.18.

EYERS, E. (D.S.O. L.G. 31.5.16), Cdr., R.N.R.

EYRE, M. S. (D.S.O. L.G. 4.6.17); b. 16.5.63; 1st com. 28.7.83; Lt.-Col. 18.5.12; retired R.G.A. 17.10.18.

EYRE, R. V. (D.S.O. L.G. 8.3.20), Cdr., R.N.

EYRES, C. J. (D.S.O. L.G. 1.1.18); b. 1862; 3rd s. of Rev. C. Eyres, Rector of Great Melton, Norfolk; m. Rose, d. of J. Phipps Townsend, of Walpole, Norfolk, and Downfields, Tottenham; three d.; entered R.N. as Cadet, 1874; Commander, 1898; Capt. 1903; Naval Attaché with Russians during Russo-Japanese War, 1904–5; commanded H.M.S. Jupiter, Spartiale and Irresistible; Commodore-in-Charge, Hong-Kong, 1910–12; A.D.C. to the King, 1912–13; commanded H.M.S. Temeraire; Rear-Admiral, 1913; retired to take active service abroad, 1914 (D.S.O.); Temp. Capt., R.N.R.; Temp. Lt.-Col., R.G.A.; retired 1918; Commander, Legion of Honour.

EYTON, C. S. WYNNE- (see Wynne-Eyton, C. S.).

FAGAN, B. J. (D.S.O. L.G. 1.1.18); b. 8.10.74; 2nd Lt., R. Muns. Fus., 6.3.95; Lt. 30.9.97; Ind. Army 23.11.98; Capt. 6.3.04; Major 6.3.13; A/Lt.-Col. 18.8.17–21.12.17.

FAGAN, E. A. (D.S.O. L.G. 1.1.17) (Bar, L.G. 26.7.18); b. 27.11.71; m. Mary Dawbney, d. of Rev. R. E. Follett; 2nd Lt., S. Staffs. R., 2.5.91; R.W. Kent R. 8.2.93; Lt., I.S.C., 3.7.94; Capt. 19.7.01; Major 2.5.09; Lt.-Col. 18.2.16; Col., I.A., 1.1.19; T/Col. Commandant; served Tirah Campaign, 1897–98 (Medal with 2 clasps); Tibet, 1903–4 (Medal); Europ. War, 1914–18; wounded; Despatches twice; C.M.G.; Afghan War, 1920; C.S.I.

FAGAN, H. A. (D.S.O. L.G. 27.9.20), Lt., Army, from T.F. 13.7.18; I.A. 19.5.18; Capt. 13.7.20; Despatches; M.C.

FAHEY, REV. FATHER J. (D.S.O. L.G. 14.1.16); b. 1882, Rossmore, co. Tipperary; educ. Ireland; Genoa; Priest, 1906; went to W. Australia, 1909; ministered at Yarloop and Kalgoorlie; served as C.F. with W. Australian troops, A.I.F., during Europ. War; Despatches.

FAHMI, AHMED (Effendi) (D.S.O. L.G. 1.1.17), El Bimbashi (Major), Egyptian Army.

FAILES, G. W. (D.S.O. L.G. 16.9.18), T/Capt., Norfolk R.; M.C. He was killed in action 15.4.18.

FAIR, CHARLES HENRY (D.S.O. L.G. 4.6.17), Major, Rhodesia Police.

FAIR, CHARLES HERBERT, M.A. (D.S.O. L.G. 1.1.17); b. 20.6.85; son of Rev. R. Fair; m. Marjorie, d. of H. E. Secretan; two d.; educ. Marlborough College; Pembroke College, Cambridge; enlisted in H.A.C., Aug. 1914; T/Capt., 1915; Hon. Major, 1918; Despatches; Assistant Master at Haileybury.

FAIRBANK, H. A. T., F.R.C.S., M.B. (D.S.O. L.G. 1.1.18); b. 28.3.76; s. of late T. Fairbank, M.D.; educ. Epsom College, and Charing Cross Hospital; m. Florence Kathleen, y. d. of late A. G. Ogilvie; one s.; two d.; Major R.A.M.C. (T.), 3rd City of London Field Ambulance; T/Lt.-Col.; Assistant Consulting Surgeon, B.S.F.; served in S. Africa (Queen's Medal, 5 clasps); Europ. War; Despatches thrice; O.B.E.; Lt.-Col., R.A.M.C. (T.) retired; Surgeon to In-Patients, Hospital for Sick Children, Great Ormond Street; Senior Orthopædic Surgeon, King's College Hospital, etc., etc.

FAIRBANK, H. N. (D.S.O. L.G. 1.1.19); b. 14.2.88; s. of W. Fairbank; m. Joyce, d. of J. A. Thomas; one s.; educ. Eton; R.M.A., Woolwich; 2nd Lt., R. Art., 24.12.02; Lt. 24.12.05; Capt. 30.10.14; Major 1.6.16; M.C.; Despatches thrice; Bt. Lt.-Col. 3.6.17.

FAIRCLOUGH, B. (D.S.O. L.G. 1.1.18), Lt.-Col., S. Lancs. R. (T.F.); served S. Afr., 1901–2 (Queen's Medal, 5 clasps); Europ. War, 1914–18; Despatches twice; C.M.G.

FAIRCLOUGH, E. (D.S.O. L.G. 4.6.17); s. of R. T. Fairclough; m. a daughter of R. Hulton; educ. Warrington Grammar School, and Monmouth; Capt. (T/Major), S. Lancs. R. Lt.-Col. B. Fairclough, who also won the D.S.O., is his brother.

FAIRFAX, W. G. A. RAMSAY- (see Ramsay-Fairfax, W. G. A.).

FAIRTLOUGH, E. V. H. (D.S.O. L.G. 1.1.19); b. 6.2.87; 2nd R.A. 23.7.07; Lt. 23.7.10; Capt. 30.10.14; Adjt. 11.8.16–21.8.17; Major 9.7.17; A/Lt.-Col. 19.4.19; M.C.

FAIRWEATHER, C. E. (D.S.O. L.G. 14.11.16), T/Major, Can. Inf.

FAIRWEATHER, H. (D.S.O. L.G. 7.2.18), T/Major (Lt.-Cdr., R.N.R.), R.E.

FALCON, C. G. (D.S.O. L.G. 3.6.16); b. 26.1.70; s. of late C. Falcon; educ. R.M.A., Woolwich; 2nd Lt., R.E., 15.2.89; Lt. 15.2.92; Capt. 15.2.00; Major 1.8.08; Lt.-Col. 6.8.16; retired pay, 1921; serv. S. Africa; Despatches; Bt.-Major 29.11.00; Queen's Medal, 2 clasps (wounded at Spion Kop); Europ. War.

FALCONAR-STEWART, R. D. (D.S.O. L.G. 1.1.18); e. s. of C. Falconar-Stewart, late of Binny, West Lothian, and late Secretary of the Local Government Board for Scotland. At the age of 17 Captain Falconar-Stewart served with the A. and S. Highrs. in the S. African War (Queen's and King's Medals); gazetted in 1901 to the 2nd Bn.; retired 1908. At the outbreak of the Europ. war he returned from Brazil; rejoined the A. and S. H., and assumed command of a battalion, April, 1916, rejoining the Regular Forces, July, 1917. A younger brother, Ian, a Subaltern in the Argylls, died in July, 1916, of wounds received in action. Capt. (T/Lt.-Col.) R. D. Falconar-Stewart was killed in action on 19.9.18, aged 35.

R. D. Falconar-Stewart.

FALCONER, A. S. (D.S.O. L.G. 1.1.19), Capt. Otago R., N.Z. Force; M.C.

FALCONER, A. W., M.D., M.R.C.P.Lond. (D.S.O. L.G. 1.1.18); educ. Aberdeen, London, Berlin and Vienna; M.D. with Honours, 1907; late T/Lt.-Col., R.A.M.C., and Assistant Consulting Physician, Salonika Forces; C.B.E.; Fellow of the R. Society of Medicine; Member of the Association of Physicians of Gt. Britain and Ireland; Professor of Medicine, Cape Town University. Has published numerous papers in various medical journals, chiefly on diseases of the heart and blood vessels, and malaria.

FALCONER, J. F. (D.S.O. L.G. 2.12.18); 2nd s. of W. Falconer; m. 1919, Janet L., d. of Capt. J. L. M'Naughton, M.B.E., V.D.; Capt., 29th Lancers, I.A., R.O.; M.C.

FALKNER, A. H. (D.S.O. L.G. 3.6.19), Major, R.A.M.C., T.F., att. 8th Bn. Liverpool R.

FALKNER, E. F. (D.S.O. L.G. 4.6.17); b. 30.3.80; e. s. of Rev. T. Falkner, D.S.O., M.A.; m. Elaine A., o. d. of Maj.-Gen. Sir W. G. A. Bedford, K.C.M.G., C.B.; one d.; 2nd Lt., Hamps. R., 7.3.00; A.S.C. 19.6.01; Lt. 19.6.02; Capt. 1.5.06; Major, R.A.S.C., 30.10.14; serv. S. Afr. 1900–1 (Queen's medal, 3 clasps); Europ. War; Despatches seven times; Bt. Lt.-Col. 3.6.18; C.M.G. (1919); Order of St. John of Jerusalem (Associate 1918); 1914 Star; Croce di Guerra, 1918; D.A.A. and Q.M.G., Inter-Allied Military Commission of Control of Austria, 1920.

FALLA, N. S. (D.S.O. L.G. 14.1.16); b. 3.5.83; s. of S. Falla; m. 1911, Audrey F., d. of B. Stock; one s.; joined N.Z. Volunteers, 1903; Lt., N.Z.F.A., 1909; Capt. 1911; Major, 1915; Lt.-Col. 1916; served Gallipoli and France; Despatches four times; C.M.G.

FALLE, P. V. Le G. (D.S.O. L.G. 3.6.16); b. 19.3.85; s. of Cmdr. P. J. Falle, R.I.M.; educ. R.N. School, Reading; 2nd Lt., A.S.C., 4.7.03; Lt. 31.3.05; Capt. 27.10.11; Adjt. 1.4.12–4.8.14; Major, R.A.S.C., 30.10.14; serv. E. Africa (Somaliland), 1909–10 (Medal and clasp); commanding R.A.S.C., Sierra Leone, 13.10.14; Europ. War.

FALWASSER, A. T. (D.S.O. L.G. 1.1.18); b. 1873; s. of late Rev. J. Falwasser; m. 1901, Charlotte, o. d. of late W. T. Shiela; educ. Marlborough; R.A.M.C., served Europ. War, 1914–18; Despatches.

FANE, J. (D.S.O. L.G. 3.6.18); b. 19.12.76; 2nd Lt., Glouc. R., 4.5.98; Lt. 24.2.00; Capt. 25.7.06; Major 1.9.15; served S. African War, 1900–2; Queen's Medal with 4 clasps; King's Medal with 2 clasps; W. Africa (S. Nigeria, 1905–6; Medal with clasp); Europ. War; Bt. Lt.-Col. 3.6.17.

FANE, O. E. (D.S.O. L.G. 4.6.17); b. 15.10.86; 2nd Lt., R.A., 20.12.06; Lt. 20.12.09; Capt. 30.10.14; A/Major, R.G.A.; Europ. War; M.C. He died of wounds 18.9.18.

FANNING, R. E. (D.S.O. L.G. 4.6.17), Lt., Aust. Military Forces, 30.10.14; Capt. (T/Major), Aust. Arty.

FANSHAWE, L. A. (D.S.O. L.G. 26.6.16); b. 7.3.74; s. of Sir Arthur U. Fanshawe; m. 1906 Eva Pemberton; one s.; one d.; educ. Dulwich College, and Pembroke Coll., Oxford; 2nd Lt., R.G.A., 26.5.00; Lt. 1.1.02; Capt. 26.5.13; Major 30.12.15; A/Lt.-Col. 1918–20; served Europ. War, in campaign on N.W.F. of India against the Mohmands in 1915, and in Mesopotamia, 1918–20; Despatches twice; O.B.E.

FARFAN, A. J. T. (D.S.O. L.G. 1.2.17); b. 22.9.82; s. of Dr. V. Farfan; educ. Reading School, and R.M.A., Woolwich; 2nd Lt., R.A., 21.12.00; Lt. 27.8.03; Capt. 21.12.13; Major, R.G.A., 30.12.15; Bt. Lt.-Col. 3.6.18; mentioned Gen. Smut's 1st Despatch, E. Afr.; French Croix de Guerre; O.B.E.

FARMER, C. (D.S.O. L.G. 4.6.17); b. October, 1883; s. of late Rev. C. H. Farmer; passed out of Woolwich with the R.A., 1902; Capt. Oct. 1914; A/Major, Dec. 1916. He was Adjutant for three years before the war, in which he was three times mentioned in Despatches, and awarded the M.C. He died on 3.8.17 of wounds received in action on Aug. 2.

FARNHAM (A. K.) LORD (D.S.O. L.G. 3.6.18); b. 2.10.79; s. of 10th Baron and Florence Jane, 5th d. of 3rd Marquess of Headfort; m. Aileen Selina, 2nd d. of late C. P. Coote; one s.; two d.; educ. Harrow; Sandhurst; Irish Representative Peer since 1908; late Lieut., 10th Hussars; Major, North Irish Horse, att. R. Innis. Fus.; served S. Africa, 1900–2 (Queen's Medal with 2 clasps; King's Medal with 2 clasps); Europ. War.

FARQUHAR, J. (D.S.O. L.G. 3.6.16) (Bar, L.G. 26.3.18) (Details, L.G. 24.8.18); b. 1.12.75; e. s. of Lt.-Col. H. R. Farquhar; m. Frances B., o. d. of C. A. Webb; educ. Wellington Coll., and R.M.A., Woolwich; ent. R.A. 21.3.96; Lt. 21.3.99; Capt. 5.1.02; Major 16.8.12; Lt.-Col. 30.11.16; served S. Afr. 1899–1900 (Queen's Medal, 2 clasps); N. Afr. (N. Nigeria, 1902); with the Kontagora Expedition (Medal and clasp), N. Nigeria, 1903; Kano-Sokoto Campaign (slightly wounded; clasp); Europ. War, 1914–18.

FARQUHAR, W. A. (D.S.O. L.G. 1.1.18); b. 14.8.79; 2nd Lt., R. Sc. Fus., 18.4.00; Lt. 6.5.01; Adjt. 8.3.07–31.8.08; Capt. 1.10.10; Major 1.9.15; A/Lt.-Col., Arg. and Suth'd Highrs., 28.5.18–30.5.18.

FARQUHAR, W. G. (D.S.O. L.G. 1.1.18), Major, Aust. Engrs.

FARQUHARSON, J. P. (D.S.O. L.G. 11.12.18); b. 14.6.84; e. s. of Capt. A. J. Farquharson, R.N.; m. Phyllis R., d. of Major E. E. Prescott; one s.; H.M.S. Britannia, Naval Cadet, 1899–1901; Midshipman, 1901–4; Sub-Lieut., 1904–6; Lt. 1906–14; Lt.-Cdr. 1914–18; Cdr. 31.12.18; O.B.E.; Despatches twice; Croix de Guerre.

FARR, T. (D.S.O. L.G. 7.11.18), Major, Otago Rgt., N.Z. Field Arty.; M.C.

FARR, W. P. (D.S.O. L.G. 11.4.18), Lt.-Col., Aust. Gen. List.

FARRAN, G. L. (D.S.O. L.G. 17.10.17); b. 30.1.81; s. of late Sir C. F. Farran; m. Myrtle Keatinge; one s.; one d.; educ. Rugby; Cheltenham; Sandhurst; 2nd Lt., Unatt., 14.2.00; 2nd Lt., I.A., 12.5.01; Lt. 13.7.03; Capt. 14.2.09; Major 1.9.15; Major, 4th Cav. I.A.; served Waziristan operations, 1901–2 (Medal and clasp); Europ. War, France, 1914–15; Egypt, 1915; Mesopotamia, 1915–16; S. Persia, 1916–19; Despatches; O.B.E.; M.C.

FARRANT, C., F.R.C.P. (D.S.O. L.G. 3.6.16); m. Gertrude, e. d. of Col. O. H. Channer; was House Physician and Surgeon, Westminster Hospital; became Surgeon, Taunton Hospital; Lt.-Col., R.A.M.C., T.F.; commd. 26th Stationary Hospital, Ismailia; S.M.O. Ismailia district.

FARRAR, A. D. M. (D.S.O. L.G. 17.3.17) (Details, L.G. 26.4.17), T/Capt., R. Welch Fusiliers.

FARRELL, J. (D.S.O. L.G. 1.1.19), Lt.-Col. 43rd Bn. Australians.

FARRELL, J. A. J. (D.S.O. L.G. 1.1.18), Lt. (from S.R.), Leins. R., 13.3.16; Capt. (A/Major), Leins. R.; M.C.

FARRELL, V. J. (D.S.O. L.G. 11.1.19), Capt., Leins. R., S.R.; M.C.

FARRINGTON, W. B. (D.S.O. L.G. 22.4.18), Lt. (T/Capt.), Notts. and Derby S.R. and R.F.C.

FAULKNER, G. A. (D.S.O. L.G. 3.6.18), T/Capt. (A/Major), R.F.A.

FAVIELL, W. F. O. (D.S.O. L.G. 25.8.17); b. 5.6.82; 2nd Lt. Worc. R., 30.4.02; Lt. 10.12.04; Capt. 18.9.14; Major 29.1.17; T/Lt.-Col. Comdg. Serv. Bn. Worc. R., 24.2.17; served S. African War, 1901–2 (Queen's Medal with 3 clasps).

FAWCETT, H. H. J. (D.S.O. L.G. 25.11.16); b. 29.5.79; s. of Surgeon-Gen. W. J. Fawcett, C.B., R.A.M.C., D.L., J.P., and the late Mary Fawcett; m. Margaret Félicie, d. of late J. S. Burra; educ. Wellington College and Trinity College, Cambridge (B.A.); passed through St. Mary's Hospital, London; Lt., R.A.M.C., 31.8.03; Capt. 28.2.07; Adjt., Oct. 1911; Major 28.2.15; served Europ. War, Gallipoli, Suvla Bay, Egypt and France; at one time tended the wounded continuously for 72 hours; Despatches.

FAWCETT, P. H. (D.S.O. L.G. 4.6.17); b. 11.8.67; 1st com. 24.7.86; Lt.-Col. 1.3.18; retired R.A. 19.1.10; Despatches.

FAWCETT, R. F. M. (D.S.O. L.G. 3.6.16); b. 2.10.73; s. of Col. M. J. Fawcett, R.F., and Alice Grace, d. of Admiral Pennell; m. Lilian Brandish Moore, d. of Llewellyn Rees; one s.; one d.; educ. M'Gill University, Montreal; joined R.A.M.C. 1900; became Major; served S. African War, 1901–2 (Queen's Medal, 4 clasps); Europ. War, with 14th Field Ambulance; retreat from Mons; action at Le Cateau; retreat on Paris; Battles of Marne, Aisne, actions near La Bassée, Oct. 1914; Ypres, 1915; Despatches.

FAWCUS, A. E. F. (D.S.O. L.G. 3.6.18); b. 19.10.86; s. of late W. P. and Bessie L. M. Fawcus, of Keswick, Cumberland; m. Alexandra, 2nd d. of late William James and Mrs. Brinton, of West Dean Park, Chichester; one s.; Lt.-Col., Notts. and Derby R., 20.10.20; served Marakwet Patrol, B.E.A. 1911 (Despatches); Europ. War, 1914–18; Despatches thrice; M.C.; Chevalier, Legion of Honour; holds T.D. His D.S.O. was awarded June, 1918, for commanding a battalion, 1/5th N. Staffs Rgt., and afterwards 1/5th Sherwood Foresters, on the Western Front (France) for 18 months; M.C. awarded for leading a night attack at Cape Helles on 6.8.15; Legion of Honour awarded for bombing work on Gallipoli; served British and German E. Africa 5.8.14 to Feb. 1915, with K.A. Rifles; Egypt, March and April, 1915, with 7th Manchester Rgt.; Gallipoli 2.5.15 to 7.1.16 with 7th Manchester R.; 1/6th Lancs. Fus.; Egypt, Jan. 1916 to July, 1916, with 7th, 8th and 9th Manch. Rgt.; France, July, 1916, to July, 1918, in command of 1/5th N. Staffs. Rgt. and 1/5th Notts. and Derby. Rgt.

A. E. F. Fawcus.

FAWCUS, H. B., M.B. (D.S.O. L.G. 4.6.17); b. 20.5.76; m. Mary H. C., d. of late Major Ross, P.A.S.L.I.; one s.; two d.; Lt., R.A.M.C., 25.4.00; Capt. 25.4.03; Major 27.4.11; Lt.-Col. 1.3.15; served S. African War, 1900–2 (Queen's Medal, 4 clasps; King's Medal, 2 clasps); Europ. War, 1914–18; Despatches thrice; Bt.-Col. 3.6.19; C.M.G.; Croix de Guerre.

FAWKES, R. B. (D.S.O. L.G. 2.4.19) (Details, L.G. 10.12.19), T/Capt., 6th Bn. Northants. R.; M.C.

FAWSSETT, A. C. (D.S.O. L.G. 11.11.19), Lt.-Cdr., R.N.

FEARENSIDE, E. (D.S.O. L.G. 26.9.16); b. 2.6.81; s. of T. C. Fearenside; educ. Ellesmere and Denstone Colleges; Queen's College, Oxford; commissioned Sept. 1914; T/Capt. Dec. 1914; T/Major, April, 1917; A/Lt.-Col. Sept. 1917–Jan. 1918; April, 1918; July, 1919; Comdg. 14th S. Lancs. R. Oct. 1918–July, 1919; demobilized, July, 1919; Despatches twice; O.B.E. (Mil. Div. June, 1919). D.S.O. awarded for gallantry near Pozières on 4.8.11.

FEARMAN, H. D. (D.S.O. L.G. 18.7.17), Lt., Can. Inf., 14.9.14. D.S.O. awarded for gallantry on 9th April, 1917, east of Neuville St. Vaast.

FEARON, P. J. (D.S.O. L.G. 1.1.18); b. 15.2.80; 2nd Lt., R. W. Surr. R., 18.10.99; Lt. 30.10.01; Adjt. 28.5.07–21.5.10; Capt. 15.10.10; Major 1.9.15; Bt. Lt.-Col. 3.6.19; served S. African War, 1899–1902 (Queen's Medal with 4 clasps; King's Medal with 2 clasps).

FEARY, S. (D.S.O. L.G. 16.9.18), T/Lt. (A/Capt.), R.E.

FEENEY, F. J. E. (D.S.O. L.G. 1.1.19), Capt. (A/Major), R.A.F.

FEILDING, R. C. (D.S.O. L.G. 4.6.17); 3rd s. of Rev. Hon. C. W. A. Feilding (4th s. of 7th Earl of Denbigh), and Lucy, d. of J. Grant, of Kilgraston; m. Edith Mary, d. of F. Stapleton-Bretherton; four d.; educ. at Haileybury; Royal School of Mines, Germany; Capt., C. Gds. S.R.; T/Lt.-Col. Comdg. 6th Battn. Connaught Rangers, Sept. 1916–Aug. 1918, and 1st Civil Service Rifles (1–15th London Regt.), Aug. 1918–May, 1919; fought in Matabele Rebellion, 1896, in Gifford's Horse (wounded); was Capt. City of London Yeomanry; transferred (6.4.15) to Special Res. C. Gds. and went to France to the regiment same month. Lt.-Col. Feilding was the last Commanding Officer of the Civil Service Rifles in France (Despatches twice).

FELL, L. F. R. (D.S.O. L.G. 4.6.17), Lt.-Col.; only s. of late Col. W. E. Fell; m. Mary Dolores Maude Walker; served Europ. War, 1914–18; Despatches; O.B.E.

FELLOWES, HON. R. T. (D.S.O. L.G. 18.7.18); b. 7.12.86; e. s. of 1st Baron Ailwyn of Honingham; m. Mildred, d. of Lorraine King; educ. Eton; 2nd Lt., Rif. Brig., 1.6.07; Lt. 1.1.11; Capt. 5.8.14; Bt. Major 3.6.18; Europ. War, 1914–18; Despatches; M.C. D.S.O. awarded for gallantry north of Fampoux, 9 to 16.4.17.

FELLOWS, P. F. M. (D.S.O. L.G. 1.1.18) (Bar, L.G. 8.2.19), Wing-Cdr., R.N.A.S.

FENN, A. A. (D.S.O. L.G. 3.6.18); b. 13.5.87; 2nd Lt., R. Fus., 16.8.05; Lt. 20.8.08; Capt. 30.9.14; Bt. Major 1.1.17.

FENN, H. F. (D.S.O. L.G. 1.1.17), T/Lt.-Col. 1.1.17.

FENNING, E. G. (D.S.O. L.G. 4.5.17); 2nd s. of G. W. Fenning; m. E. Katheleen, d. of G. Ashdown, Surgeon; served Europ. War, 1914–18; Despatches.

FENTON, G. C. V. (D.S.O. L.G. 4.6.17); b. 22.4.83; 2nd Lt., R.E., 21.12.01; Lt. 31.7.04; Capt. 21.12.12; Major 21.12.16.

FERGUSON, F. A. (D.S.O. L.G. 3.6.18); b. 4.3.83; 2nd Lt., R.E., 21.12.01; Lt. 3.8.04; Capt. 21.12.12; Bt. Major 8.11.15; A/Lt.-Col. 8.4.18–31.3.19; Despatches.

FERGUSON, G. A. (D.S.O. L.G. 1.1.17), Lt.-Col. Aust. Mil. Forces; O.C. 3rd Inf. Bdge.

FERGUSON, G. D. (D.S.O. L.G. 14.11.16); b. 2.4.90; graduated M.B., Ch.B.Edin. in 1913; joined R.A.M.C. Aug. 1914; served Europ. War in France and Flanders; Despatches. D.S.O. awarded for gallantry at Delville Wood on 15.9.16. Capt. Ferguson was killed in action, 23.4.17, on Vimy Ridge.

FERGUSON, H. C. (D.S.O. L.G. 26.7.17), Lt. Can. Inf. 20.8.14; A/Capt.

FERGUSON, H. G. DE L. (D.S.O. L.G. 9.1.00) (Bar, L.G. 1.1.18), Bt. Lt.-Col., R. of O. (see "The Distinguished Service Order," from its institution to 31.12.15, same publishers).

FERGUSSON, A. C. (D.S.O. L.G. 17.9.17); b. 2.7.71; 2nd Lt., R.A. 13.2.91; Lt. 13.2.94; Capt. 21.10.99; Major 29.9.11; Bt. Lt.-Col. 1.1.16; Lt.-Col. 1.5.17; served Tirah, 1897–8 (Medal with 2 clasps); N.W. Frontier of India, 1902.

FERGUSSON, V. M. (D.S.O. L.G. 14.1.16); b. 31.8.78; 3rd s. of late J. Fergusson, F.R.C.S.E.; m. 1918, Dulce Alice Mollie D'Ewes, d. of P. W. Allen, I.C.S.; gazetted to R.A. 17.3.00; Lt. 3.4.01; Capt. 29.10.08; Adjt. 3.4.10–18.2.13; Major 30.10.14; Lt.-Col. R.H.A.; Europ. War, 1914–18; was D.A.A.G., R.A., 16th A.C., Medit. Exp. Force; Egyptian Exp. Force, 13.2.16 to 8.5.16; G.S.O.2, 52nd Div., Egyptian Exp. Force, 9.5.16 to 22.10.16; G.S.O.1, No. 2 Section, Canal Defence, Egyptian Exp. Force, 23.10.16 to 30.8.17; Despatches; Bt. Lt.-Col. 3.6.17.

FERID, ABD. EL MAGID BEY (D.S.O. L.G. 4.9.18), El Kaim (Lt.-Col.); Local Mir (Col.), Egyptian Army.

FERNIE, F. H. (D.S.O. L.G. 1.1.18), T/Major, Tank Corps.

FERRAND, J. B. P. (D.S.O. L.G. 1.1.16); b. 29.3.95; o. s. of G. A. Ferrand (*Morning Post* Correspondent and Trooper, I.L.H., killed at Ladysmith, 1900), and Ellen Rose, d. of the late J. Hadden, M.D.; educ. Malvern College; joined R.N.A.S. 1915; Flight-Lt. 1916; Flight-Comdr. 1917; served Europ. War, 1915–17.

FERRAND, S. H. (D.S.O. L.G. 3.6.19); b. 1.3.98; s. of Mr. Ferrand, of St. Ives, Bingley; 2nd Lt., K.R. Rif. C., 19.9.08; Lt. 12.8.11; Capt. 20.4.15; T/Lt.-Col.; commanded 11th E. Yorks. R. in France from Dec. 1916; Despatches; Bt. Major 3.6.19; M.C.; Belgian Officier de l'Ordre de Léopold; French Croix de Guerre.

S. H. Ferrand.

FERRERS-GUY, K. A. (see Guy, K. A. Ferrers-).

FERRERS-GUY, M. C. (D.S.O. L.G. 2.2.16) (Bar, L.G. 1.1.18); b. 1877; s. of late T. Ferrers-Guy; m. 1902, Monica Isabel, d. of A. Boursot; educ. Westminster; Major, Lancs. Fus.; served S. African War, 1900–1; Europ. War; wounded twice; Despatches thrice.

FERRES, H. D. G. (D.S.O. L.G. 1.2.19), Major, 58th Bn. Aust. Mil. Forces; M.C.

FESSENDEN, J. H. (D.S.O. L.G. 4.6.17), b. 29.7.88; 2nd Lt., A.S.C., 21.7.00; Lt. 1.11.01; Capt. 1.2.05; Major, R.A.S.C., 30.10.14; served S. African War, 1902 (Queen's Medal with 2 clasps); Europ. War; Bt. Lt.-Col. 3.6.19; Despatches.

FESTING, H. E. (D.S.O. L.G. 2.5.16) (Bar, L.G. 1.2.19); b. 18.2.86; s. of late Major-Gen. Sir Francis W. Festing, K.C.M.G., C.B., R.M.L.I.; educ. Cheltenham College; R.M.C., Sandhurst; was Page of Honour to Queen Victoria and King Edward VII.; commissioned in the Border Regt. 28.1.05; Lt. 5.12.08; Capt. 13.12.14; Major 8.2.22; served in Europ. War; wounded in Gallipoli; Despatches; French Croix de Guerre; awarded the Royal Humane Society's Medal in India.

FESTING, H. W. (D.S.O. L.G. 3.6.18), Major (T/Lt.-Col.), Durham L.I., attd. 10th Yorks. L.I.; served S. African War, 1901–2 (Queen's Medal with 3 clasps). He was killed in action, 21.3.18.

FESTING, M. C. (D.S.O. L.G. 1.1.18); b. 16.9.79; 2nd Lt., R. Mar., 1.9.98; Lt. 1.7.99; Adjt. 29.1.09–25.12.11; Capt. 31.8.09; served in China, 1900 (Medal); Bt. Major 1.5.16.

FETHERS, W. K. (D.S.O. L.G. 1.1.17); b. 1885; s. of J. Fethers; m. Phyllis Doyne; one s.; educ. Caulfeild Grammar School, Victoria; commissioned in Victoria Vol. Forces, 1905; Capt. in Militia, 1910; Major, 1913; Lt.-Col., May, 1914; Comdg. 5th Battn. 24th Imp. Regt., A.M.F.; served Gallipoli and France.

FETHERSTON, G. (D.S.O. L.G. 1.2.19), T/Capt. (A/Major), 162nd Brig. R.F.A.; M.C.

FETHERSTONHAUGH, A.J. STEPHENSON- (see Stephenson-Fetherstonhaugh, A. J.).

FETHERSTONHAUGH, C. M. (D.S.O. L.G. 18.1.18) (Details, L.G. 25.4.18), Major, Aust. L.H. Regt.

FETHERSTONHAUGH, T. (D.S.O. L.G. 3.6.16); b. 1.1.69; o. s. of late T. Fetherstonhaugh, formerly 13th Hussars, and Hon. Maria Georgiana, d. of 3rd Lord Dorchester; m. 1899, Nancy (died 1917), d. of J. M. Carr-Lloyd; one s.; two d.; ent. Seaforth Highrs. 21.12.89; Major 7.9.07; Bt. Lt.-Col. (R. of O.) 3.6.17; served in the Hazara Exp. 1891 (Medal and clasp), and Isazai Campaign; with the Chitral Campaign in 1895 (Medal with clasp); in S. African War (severely wounded at Magersfontein; Queen's Medal with clasp); retired 23.1.09; served Europ. War; raised 9th Battn. Seaforth Hldrs; Despatches thrice; Bt. Lt.-Col., R. of O., 3.6.17.

FETHERSTONHAUGH, W. A. (D.S.O. L.G. 1.1.17); b. 24.10.76; e. s. of late Lt.-Col. W. A. Fetherstonhaugh; m. Adela Mary, d. of C. Cayley; one s.; one d.; educ. Sandhurst; 2nd Lt., Unatt., 5.8.96; Ind. S.C. 4.11.97; Lt., Ind. Army, 5.11.98; Capt. 5.8.05; Major 5.8.14; Bt. Lt.-Col. 3.6.17; Col.; served Punjab Frontier, 1897–8 (Medal, 2 clasps); Despatches four times; Légion d'Honneur; promoted Bt. Lt.-Col; 1914 Star and clasp; G.S. and Victory Medals; Afghanistan and N.W. Frontier, 1919; Despatches; C.B.E.; Medal and clasp.

FEW, R. J. (D.S.O. L.G. 16.8.17), Major, 5th Bn. R.W. Surrey R.; served S. African War, 1900–1 (Queen's Medal with 3 clasps); Europ. War.

FEWTRELL, A. C. (D.S.O. L.G. 1.1.17), Capt., Aust. Mil. Forces; Bt. Major 24.9.17; Lt.-Col. Invested with Insignia of D.S.O. in Hyde Park, June 2, 1917.

FFRENCH, W. R. R. (D.S.O. L.G. 1.1.18); Major M.G.C., M.C.

FIELD, C. D. (D.S.O. L.G. 22.3.19), Lt.-Col., 75th Carnatic Inf., I.A.

FIELD, E. (D.S.O. L.G. 16.9.18); s. of J. Field; educ. Wheelwright Grammar School, Dewsbury; 2nd Lt., M.G.C.

FIELD, K. D. (D.S.O. L.G. 1.1.17), Major, R.G.A.; served N.W. Frontier of India, Waziristan, 1901–2 (Medal with clasp); N.W. Frontier of India, 1902; Tibet, 1903–4 (Medal); Europ. War; Despatches.

K. D. Field.

FIELD, L. R. (D.S.O. L.G. 1.1.18); s. of G. M. R. Field; Capt. (A/Major), R.A.; M.C. He was killed in action 26.10.17.

FIELDING, A. E. B. (D.S.O. L.G. 1.1.19), T/Major, 63rd Field Co., R.E.

FIENNES, N. I. E. TWISLETON-WYKEHAM- (see Twisleton-Wykeham-Fiennes, N. I. E.).

FIFE, R. B. (D.S.O. L.G. 1.1.17); b. 9.12.69; 2nd Lt., R.A., 27.7.89; Lt. 27.7.92; Capt. 16.9.99; Major 11.9.10; Lt.-Col. 28.7.16.

FIFE, R. D. A. (D.S.O. L.G. 4.6.17); b. 19.3.68; s. of W. H. Fife and Caroline Jane, d. of Sir Thomas Digby Legard, 8th Bt.; educ. Radley; R.M.C., Sandhurst; m. 1st, Alice Louisa (died 1898), d. of A. Duncombe; 2ndly, Margaret, d. of A. Rutson; ent. Army, 1887; Adjt., Yorks. R., 1896–1900; A.D.C. to Governor of Madras, 1901–5; Mil. Secretary to Governor of Cape Colony, 1906–8; served Kachin Expedition, 1893; Tirah Campaign, 1897 (Medal, 2 clasps); Europ. War, 1914–17, Comdg. 7th Yorks. Regt.; Despatches four times; severely wounded, 1917; C.M.G.; Master of Peshawar Vale Hounds, 1898; Master of Ootacamund Hounds, 1901–6.

FIFOOT, E. L. (D.S.O. L.G. 26.9.16); b. 1891; o. s. of E. Fifoot; m. 1919, Signe Johanne Baars, e. d. of Dr. Eriksen, of Vittingfor, Norway; one d.; educ. Berkhamsted (under Dr. Fry); spent several years in Norway and Sweden; interested in paper-making and afforestation; joined Royal Fus. 1914; wounded at Ovillers and Pozières and sight of left eye destroyed; D.S.O. awarded for gallantry on 4.8.16, near Pozières; Despatches; Capt., 9th R.F.

FILSELL, H. S. (D.S.O. L.G. 1.1.18); b. 25.4.82; 2nd Lt., R. War. R., 7.5.02; Lt. 1.10.06; Capt. 13.5.14; Major 29.1.17; T/Lt.-Col. 21.5.19; S. African War, 1901–2; served in Mediterranean (Medal); Europ. War.

FINCH, G. F. C. (D.S.O. L.G. 3.6.18); b. 16.5.74; 2nd Lt., R.A., 17.11.94; Lt. 17.11.97; Capt. 1.6.00; Adjt. 22.3.02–16.4.05; Major, R.G.A., 30.10.14; Lt.-Col. 1.1.21; Despatches.

FINCH, H. W. E. (D.S.O. L.G. 4.6.17); b. 3.8.68; 2nd Lt., Middlesex R., 9.11.89; Lt. 1.10.91; Capt. 25.1.00; Major 22.2.05; Bt. Lt.-Col. 18.2.15; Despatches; C.B.E.

FINCH, L. H. K. (D.S.O. L.G. 1.1.17) (Bar, L.G. 26.9.17) (Details, 9.1.18); b. 18.7.88; o. s. of Mrs. E. H. F. Finch; m. Hildegaard, d. of Mrs. Sepp, of Nijmegen, Holland; educ. Birmingham University; London University; 2nd Lt., R. Sussex R., 7.12.10; Lt. 16.4.13; Capt., Cheshire R., 23.1.15; Bt. Major 1.1.18; Lt.-Col.; served Europ. War; Despatches; O.B.E.

FINDLATER, A., M.D. (D.S.O. L.G. 22.1.16); s. of late J. Findlater, J.P.; educ. Neuwied-on-Rhine; Trinity College, Dublin; m. Emily A., d. of T. Donnelly; joined T.F. March, 1909, and the London Mounted Brigade Field Ambulance, and served with it from Aug. 1914–Feb. 1917; Capt., R.A.M.C., T.F.; in Egypt, Suvla Bay and Salonika.

FINDLAY, J. (D.S.O. L.G. 1.1.17), Lt.-Col., Canterbury Mtd. Rifles, N.Z. Imp. Force; served S. Africa, 1900–1 (Despatches; Queen's Medal, 5 clasps); Europ. War, Dardanelles, 1914–17; Despatches; C.B.

FINDLAY, J. A. (D.S.O. L.G. 1.1.18), Major, 5th (City of Glasgow) Bn. (Territorial) The H.L.I. He was killed in action 8.11.17.

FINDLAY, REV. J. L. O. B. (D.S.O. L.G. 3.6.18); b. Nairn, N.B., 9.5.67; s. of Lt.-Col. Findlay, 3rd W.I. Regt., and A. R. de Ste. Croix; m. Dorothy, d. of Col. Giffard; educ. Dollar Academy; George Watson's College, Edinburgh; University College, Durham; C.F. 1901; attd. 2nd Bn. G. Gds. Boer War (Queen's Medal, 5 clasps); Europ. War, France, 1914; Salonika, 1915–19; Principal Chaplain, Constantinople, 1920; Mons Medal with Star; Order of Redeemer; Croce di Guerra (Italy); Despatches thrice; Senior Chaplain, The Tank Corps.

FINDLAY, J. M. (D.S.O. L.G. 7.4.18) (Bar, L.G. 7.11.18), Lt.-Col., Sc. Rif.

FINDLAY, W. H. DE LA TOUR D'A. (D.S.O. L.G. 1.1.17); b. 3.10.64; e. s. of Lt.-Col. Alex. Findlay, 3rd W.I. Regt., and Alice Rocnel de Ste. Croix; m. 1st, Isabella M., y. d. of Canon Hodgson; two d.; 2ndly, Josephine M., y. d. of T. V. Anthony; educ. Dollar Institution and Edinburgh University; ent. the Royal Sussex Regt.; Major, Can. A.S.C., 1.9.14; Lt.-Col. (Comdg. the 3rd Canadian Divisional Train) 28.1.16; served S. Africa (Medal, 5 clasps; Despatches twice); Europ. War from 1914; Lt.-Col. Can. A.S.C.; Despatches; O.B.E.; Croix de Guerre.

FINLAY, D. (D.S.O. L.G. 11.4.18), T/Major, Spec. List.

FINLAY, R. F. (D.S.O. L.G. 26.6.16); b. 31.1.77; s. of late W. A. Finlay, M.D., F.R.C.S.E.; educ. Cargilfield; Rugby; 2nd Lt., R.A., 22.10.97; Lt. 22.10.00; Ind. Army 7.10.00; Capt. 22.10.06; Major 1.9.15, 58th Rifles, F.F./I.A.; N.W. Frontier of India, Waziristan, 1901–2 (Medal with clasp); N.W. Frontier of India, 1902, operations against the Darwesh Khel Waziris, Tibet, 1903–4 (Medal); N.W. Frontier of India, 1908, operations in the Mohmand country (slightly wounded; Medal and clasp; Europ. War; Afghan War, 1919; Bt. Lt.-Col. 1.1.20.

FINLAYSON, H. W., M.B. (D.S.O. L.G. 15.9.16), Fleet Surgeon, R.N.; served in the Battle of Jutland; Sir J. Jellicoe's Despatches, 23.8.15.

FINLAYSON, W. T., L.R.C.P.(Lond.), M.R.C.S. (D.S.O. L.G. 1.1.18); b. 14.7.77; s. of D. Finlayson; m. 1905, Elizabeth Mary Dorothea, 6th d. of late B. Neville; two d.; educ. Haileybury College; Melbourne University; St. Mary's Hospital, London; entered I.M.S. 3.1.04; Capt. 30.1.07; Major 1.7.15; served Europ. War, 1914–18; Despatches.

FINN, E. (D.S.O. L.G. 1.1.19), T/Major, 21st Bn. W. Yorks. R.

FINNIS, F. C. (D.S.O. L.G. 17.5.18), Lt.-Cdr., R.N.

FIRTH, R. A. (D.S.O. L.G. 2.2.16); b. 17.11.66; s. of late Major-Gen. H. H. Firth, I.A.; m. 1st, 1894, Matilda C. Cox (who died 1895); 2ndly, 1898, Florence Ina Forster; two s.; educ. Bedford Grammar School; ent. E. Yorks. Regt. 8.12.22; Lt., I.C.S., 2.4.91; Capt., Ind. Army, 8.12.99; Major 8.12.06; Lt.-Col. 8.12.14 (Comdg. 2/8th Gurkha Rifles); served in Burma, 1892–3, operations in the Chin Hills (Medal and clasp); Egypt, 1914–15; Dardanelles and Gallipoli, 1915; Despatches.

FISHE, A. F. B. (D.S.O. L.G. 1.1.17); b. 17.5.79; 2nd Lt., R.A., 26.2.08; Lt. 16.2.01; Capt. 9.10.09; Major 30.10.14; A/Lt.-Col. 28.8.17–23.2.19.

FISHER, B. D. (D.S.O. L.G. 18.2.15) (Bar, L.G. 26.7.18), Brig.-Gen., 17th Lancers; C.M.G. (see "The Distinguished Service Order," from its institution to Dec. 31, 1915, same publishers).

FISHER, C. A. (D.S.O. L.G. 3.6.18); b. 8.8.72; 2nd Lt., R.A., 1.2.93; Lt. 1.2.96; Capt. 1.4.08; Major 8.12.14; Lt.-Col. and Ord. Officer, 1st Class, 13.2.21; Despatches.

FISHER, C. J. (D.S.O. L.G. 25.8.17), Capt. (A/Major), Middx. R.

FISHER, D. L., M.B. (D.S.O. L.G. 1.1.18), Lt.-Col., R.A.M.C.; s. of late J. Fisher.

FISHER, D. R. D. (D.S.O. L.G. 26.7.17); b. 5.2.90; s. of late T. A. Fisher; 2nd Lt., R.A., 23.12.10; Lt., R.A., 23.12.12; Capt. 23.12.15; Despatches. D.S.O. awarded for gallantry at Arras 9.4.17.

FISHER, H. G. (D.S.O. L.G. 1.1.17) (Bar, L.G. 16.9.18); b. 24.6.79; 2nd Lt. R.A., 2.5.00; Lt. 3.4.01; Capt. 9.10.09; Major, R.G.A., 30.10.14; served S. African War, 1902 (Queen's Medal with 2 clasps); Europ. War; Despatches.

FISHER, J. M. (D.S.O. L.G. 3.6.19); e. s. of Rev. W. Fisher; m. 1919, Ailie, y. d. of Lady Bell; educ. Westminster School; Capt., 5th Bn. York and Lanc. R., T.F.; served Europ. War, 1914–19; Despatches; M.C.

FISHER, J. T. (D.S.O. L.G. 1.1.18); b. 26.3.83 2nd Lt. R.E. 21.12.01; Lt. 6.8.04; Capt. 21.12.12; Major, 21.12.16; served Europ. War, 1914–18; wounded; Despatches.

FISHER, J. W. (D.S.O. L.G. 30.3.16), T/Capt., 10th Bn. Sher. Foresters; D.S.O. awarded for gallantry on 14.2.16, Iser Canal. He died of wounds 8.7.16.

FISHER, L. D. (D.S.O. L.G. 1.1.17) (Bar, L.G. 24.3.19), Lt.-Cdr. (A/Cdr.) R.N.

FISHER, P. S. (D.S.O. L.G. 17.11.17), A/Fl.-Cdr., R.N.A.S.; D.S.C.

FISHER, T. P. (D.S.O. L.G. 1.2.19), Lancs. Fus., T.F.; M.C.

FISKE, R. W. (D.S.O. L.G. 3.6.19), Capt., Can. Mil. Forces, 19.1.14; Major, 8th Can. Cav.

FITZGERALD, A. S. (D.S.O. L.G. 1.1.18), T/Major, R. War. R.

FITZGERALD, C. R. L. (D.S.O. L.G. 3.6.16); b. 17.5.82; s. of late G. B. Fitzgerald; educ. Harrow; 2nd Lt., North'd Fus., 28.1.03; Lt., Ind. Army, 14.12.05; Capt. 29.1.11; Major, 126th Baluchis, 29.1.17; served in S. Africa, 1900–2 (Queen's Medal, 3 clasps); Europ. War, Dardanelles (Suvla operations) Egypt; Indian Frontier; S. Persia, 1917–18 (Despatches); N. Persia, 1919–20.

FITZGERALD, E. G. A. (D.S.O. L.G. 22.6.18), Lt., G. Gds.

FITZGERALD, FITZG. G., L.R.C.S.I., L.R.C.P.I. (D.S.O. L.G. 1.1.17) (Bar, L.G. 26.7.18); b. 29.5.78; educ. Royal College of Surgeons of Ireland; L.M. Rotunda Hospital, Dublin; Lt., R.A.M.C., 25.4.00; Capt. 25.4.03; Major 25.1.12; Lt.-Col.; was in retreat from Mons; Despatches twice; Bt. Lt.-Col. 1.1.16.

FITZGERALD, F. W. WILSON- (D.S.O. L.G. 1.1.19); b. 8.12.86; s. of H. W. Fitzgerald, D.L., J.P.; educ. Eton; New College, Oxford; gazetted from Oxford University to 1st R. Dns. in India, 1908; S. Africa, 1911–14; Lt. 12.4.10; Capt. 12.9.14; Adjt. 1914–17; Major 9.7.21; served Europ. War in France, 1914–18; Army of Occupation, Rhine, 1918–19; Despatches four times; M.C.; 1914 Star.

M. J. F. FitzGerald.

FITZGERALD, M. J. F. (D.S.O. L.G. 14.1.16); b. 3.4.74; 2nd s. of late Surgeon-Gen. P. G. FitzGerald, Madras Med. Service, and Louisa Charlotte FitzGerald (*née* Garstin); m. 1915, Gertrude C., y. d. of late G. A. F. Baillie; educ. Clifton College; R.M.A., Woolwich; 2nd Lt., R.A., 1.9.94; Lt. 1.9.97; Capt. 23.10.00; Adjt. 24.1.05–28.2.06; Major 11.2.11; Lt.-Col. 13.4.16; served S. Africa, 1899–1901 (Queen's Medal, 6 clasps); Europ. War, 1914–17; Depatches thrice.

FITZGERALD, P. F. (D.S.O. L.G. 1.1.17); b. 22.9.79; e. s. of R. FitzGerald, D.L.; m. Baroness Adrienne de Geer; three s.; educ. Haileybury; R.M.C., Sandhurst; 2nd Lt., Shrops. L.I., 11.2.99; Lt. 9.6.00; Capt. 15.8.06; Major 1.9.15; Lt.-Col., Shrops. L.I., 11.2.22; served S. Africa (wounded; Despatches; Queen's Medal, 7 clasps); Europ. War, 1914–18 (wounded); Despatches; Bt. Lt.-Col. 3.6.18.

P. F. FitzGerald.

FITZGERALD, R. F. (D.S.O. L.G. 3.6.16); b. 23.8.80, at Orange, N.S.W.; educ. Holy Cross College, Ryde, N.S.W.; ent. N.S.W. Irish Rifles R. 1908; Capt. 1912; Major, 1915, Commd. 18th and 20th Battn. A.I.F. at Anzac; Despatches.

FITZGIBBON, F. (D.S.O. L.G. 18.6.17); b. 17.8.83; 2nd Lt., R.A., 24.12.02; Lt. 24.12.05; Capt. 30.10.14; Major 22.5.16; Despatches.

FITZHERBERT, E. H. (D.S.O. L.G. 1.1.18); b. 3.12.85; s. of late Col. E. H. Fitzherbert, K.O.R.L. Regt.; educ. Rossall School; R.M.C., Camberley; 2nd Lt., A.S.C., 16.8.05; Lt. 16.8.07; Capt., R.A.S.C., 5.8.14; T/Major (A/Lt.-Col.) 11.12.17; served Europ. War, 1914–18; Despatches thrice; M.C.

FITZHUGH, T. C. (D.S.O. L.G. 1.1.18); b. 16.11.76; s. of late W. H. FitzHugh; m. Nesta Mary, d. of late W. Richardson; ent. Royal Irish Regt. 1896; Capt. 1903; served N.W. Frontier, India, 1897–8 (Medal, 2 clasps); S. Africa, 1899–1900 (Queen's Medal, 2 clasps); M.V.O. 1903; Europ. War; Despatches.

FITZJOHN, T. (D.S.O. L.G. 1.1.17) (Bar, L.G. 15.2.19) (Details, L.G. 30.7.19); b. 9.7.75; 2nd Lt., Worc. R., 21.4.00; Lt. 8.12.00; Capt. 25.8.06; Major 26.10.15; served S. African War, 1901–2 (Queen's Medal with 3 clasps).

FITZMAURICE, RAYMOND (D.S.O. L.G. 1.1.16); b. 7.8.78; s. of J. G. Fitzmaurice; m. 1912, Evelyn (died 1914), d. of C. Threlfall; ent. R.N. 1892; Lt. 1901; Comdr. 1913; Second-in-Command, H.M.S. Chatham, 1913–16; Capt. 1918; in command H.M.S. Espiègle, 1916–18; A.D. of Naval Intelligence 1918–19; Naval Adviser to Sir R. Tower, High Commissioner of Dantzig, 1919–20.

FITZMAURICE, ROBERT (D.S.O. L.G. 4.6.17); b. 7.1.66; m. Violet Beryl, 2nd d. of C. G. Macpherson, C.S.I.; educ. Royal School, Armagh; Trinity College, Dublin; Lt., R.A., 18.2.86; Capt. 21.12.96; Adjt. 21.3.00–31.10.01; Major, Nov. 1901; Lt.-Col. 5.3.14; T/Brig.-Gen. 25.12.15–13.7.16; Europ. War, 1914–17; Despatches four times.

FITZPATRICK, E. R. (D.S.O. L.G. 1.1.17); b. 12.2.78; e. s. of Rev. N. R. Fitzpatrick, M.A.; m. 1903, Georgina E., y. d. of T. Robinson; one s.; educ. Marlborough; Trinity College, Cambridge; 2nd Lt., N. Lanc. R., 4.10.99; Lt. 31.1.01; Capt. 5.4.06; Major 1.9.15; T/Col. 1.3.19; T/Brig.-Gen. 1916; served S. Africa, 1899–1902 (severely wounded; Queen's Medal, 4 clasps; King's Medal, 2 clasps); Europ. War; Despatches 3 times; C.B.E. 1919; Bt. Major 3.6.15; Bt. Lt.-Col. 1.1.18; Chevalier, Légion d'Honneur.

FITZPATRICK, N. T. (D.S.O. L.G. 1.1.18); b. 24.12.88; 2nd Lt., R.E. 18.12.08; Lt. 21.12.10; Capt. 18.12.14; Bt. Major 1.1.17; Adjt., R.E., 30.4.19; T/Lt.-Col. Comdg. Serv. Battn. S. Wales Bord., 27.10.17–1919; M.C.

FLANAGAN, E. M. WOULFE- (see Woulfe-Flanagan, E. M.).

FLANAGAN, R. J. WOULFE- (see Woulfe-Flanagan, R. J.).

FLEISCHER, S. R. (D.S.O. L.G. 15.10.18); Lt. (T/Capt.), E. Lancs. R., S.R.; M.C.

FLEMING, A. F. (D.S.O. L.G. 6.9.16); b. 1876; s. of Michael and Mary A. Fleming, Youghal, co. Cork; m. Ivy A. Johnson; one s.; educ. Queen's College, Cork; and Clongowes; L.R.C.P. and S.Edin., L.R.F.P.S.Glas.; Surg., R.N., 1903; Surg.-Comm. 1919; served Europ. War; Despatches.

FLEMING, A. N., M.B., F.R.C.S.Edin. (D.S.O. L.G. 1.1.18); b. 9.9.70; Lt., Ind. Med. Serv. (Madras), 29.7.96; Capt. 29.7.99; Major 29.1.08; Lt.-Col. 29.1.16; served N.W.F. of India, 1897–98; Medal with clasp; Tirah, 1897–98 (clasp).

FLEMING, F. (D.S.O. L.G. 1.1.18); b. 6.10.61; Major, R.A., 3.2.09; Lt.-Col., R.F.A.

FLEMING, G. (D.S.O. L.G. 14.1.16); s. of late Col. G. Fleming; C.B., LL.D.; m. Simone, d. of late M. C. P. Gresy; educ. Epsom College, and University College, London; 2nd Lt., Som. L. Inf., 24.7.01; Lt. 29.5.04; Capt. 21.4.14; Adjt. 1912–15; Major 31.10.15; Bt. Lt.-Col. 3.6.17; served S. Afr. 1900–1 (Queen's Medal, 4 clasps); India, 1901–8; Europ. War, 1915–18, in France and Mesopotamia; 3rd Class Order of St. Stanislas with Swords, 1915; Despatches.

J. G. Fleming.

FLEMING, J. G. (D.S.O. L.G. 14.1.16); b. 9.1.80; 2nd s. of late W. J. Fleming; m. Blanche Mabel, d. of late L. A. D. Déglon; one s.; three d.; educ. Haileybury College; R.M.A., Woolwich; 2nd Lt., R.E., 23.12.98; Lt. 25.7.01; Capt. 23.12.07; Adjt., R.E., 1.2.15 to 4.10.15; Major 29.7.15; Bt. Lt.-Col. 1.1.18; served S. African War, 1901–2; Queen's Medal with 5 clasps; Europ. War; Despatches; C.B.E.

FLEMING J. G. G. (D.S.O. L.G. 25.8.17), Lt., Army, 3.9.15; I.A. 25.3.18; Capt., I.A., 3.9.20; Despatches. D.S.O. awarded for gallantry at Infantry Hill, east of Monchy, on 14.6.17.

FLEMING, P. B. (D.S.O. L.G. 1.1.18); b. 19.2.92; 2nd Lt., A.S.C., 4.9.12; Lt. 9.6.15; Capt., R.A.S.C., 5.9.17.

FLEMING, V. (D.S.O. L.G. 4.6.17), Major, Cheshire Yeomanry, T.F.; M.P.; of Pitt House, Hampstead, N.W., and Arnisdale, Glenelg, Inverness-shire. He was killed in action 20.5.17.

FLETCHER, E. K. (D.S.O. L.G. 26.7.18) (Bar, L.G. 11.1.19); b. 10.4.80; 2nd Lt., R.M.L.I., 1.9.98; Lt. 1.7.99; Capt. 3.8.07; Major 22.7.16; served Europ. War; wounded. He died 15.10.21.

FLETCHER, H. L. AUBREY- (see Aubrey-Fletcher, H. L.).

H. P. Fletcher.

FLETCHER, H. P. (D.S.O. L.G. 19.8.16),

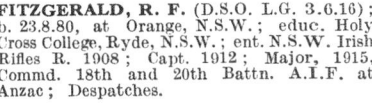

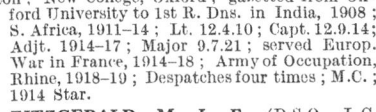

Major, 1st Co. of London Yeomanry; served Europ. War, 1914–18; Despatches. He was killed in a flying accident in Aug. 1917.

FLETCHER, J. H. (D.S.O. L.G. 18.7.17) (Bar, L.G. 15.2.19) (Details, L.G. 30.7.19); b. 23.5.88; e. s. of J. H. Fletcher; m. Irene Stuart, d. of late R. S. Blee, M.R.C.V.S.; Capt., R.A.M.C., 4.3.18; Lt.-Col.; M.C.; D.S.O. awarded for gallantry at Arras on 13.4.17.

FLETCHER, J. L. (D.S.O. L.G. 1.2.19), Capt. 25th Bn. Aust. Mil. Forces; M.C.

FLEXMAN, E. (D.S.O. L.G. 1.1.19), Major, Can. F.A. He was appointed Director of Vocational Training, Dept. of Soldiers' Civil Re-establishment of Canada.

FLINT, C. (D.S.O. L.G. 3.6.18), Lt., Can. Eng., 11.6.15; Rly. Constr. Corps, Can.

FLINT, E. C. M. (D.S.O. L.G. 3.6.19); b. 19.11.83; s. of Brig.-Gen. E. M. Flint, late R.A., and Mildred Salome, d. of the late T. Kekewich; m. Frances Sarah Nancy, d. of C. Hulbert; one s.; one d.; educ. Eton; New College, Oxford; B.A.; called to Bar, Inner Temple, 1907; Fellow, R. Colonial Institute; Major, Suffolk Yeom.; served Europ. War, 1914–19; Gallipoli, with Suffolk Yeom.; with M.G.C. (Cavalry) in Egypt; Palestine and Syria; Despatches.

FLOOD, R. E. SOLLY (see Solly Flood R. E.).

FLORENCE, W. A. (D.S.O. L.G. 22.2.18); s. of W. Florence, of Dundee; educ. Morgan Academy; A/Lt., R.N.R.

FLOWER, H. J. (D.S.O. L.G. 3.6.16); b. 6.4.93; ent. Army 22.10.02; Lt. 19.7.07; Major 22.10.17; retired K.R.R.C. 22.5.18; Despatches.

FLOWER, V. A. (D.S.O. L.G. 1.1.17); s. of late Sir William Flower; Bt. Major; Major (T/Lt.-Col.), 13th (Co. of London) Bn. The London R. (Princess Louise's Kensington Bn.). He was killed in action 15.8.17, aged 40.

FLOYD, A. B. (D.S.O. L.G. 23.10.19), Capt., R. of O., late Norfolk R.

FLUKE, W. G. (D.S.O. L.G. 20.10.16); b. 19.12.96; s. of A. J. Fluke; m. 1919, Dorothy, e. d. of J. Meredith Tompson; educ. King's School, Canterbury; R.M.C., Sandhurst; 2nd Lt., S. Staffs. R., 15.4.15; Lt. 25.9.15; Capt. 22.1.21; employed under Air Ministry 1.4.18–11.5.19. He served in the Europ. War on the Western front from May, 1915, to Sept. 1917, with the 2nd Bn. He then became attached to the R.F.C., and took part in reprisal raids on the Rhine towns. He was shot down and taken prisoner on 24.3.18, after a successful bombing raid on Mannheim. He was mentioned in Despatches. His D.S.O. was awarded for gallantry on 29.7.16 at Delville Wood. He went to Singapore with 1st Bn. S. Staffs R., Oct. 1919.

W. G. Fluke.

FOGGIE, W. E., M.D. (D.S.O. L.G. 3.6.18), Lt.-Col., R.A.M.C.

FOLGER, K. C. (D.S.O. L.G. 1.1.17), Major, Can. Ordnance Corps; C.M.G.

FOLJAMBE, THE HON. G. W. F. S. (D.S.O. L.G. 1.1.18); b. 12.5.78; half-b. of 2nd Earl of Liverpool; m. 1909, Constance I., o. c. of J. Holden; educ. Eton; R.M.C., Sandhurst; ent. Army 16.2.98; ret. Oxf. and Bucks. 19.2.13; Lt.-Col. (R. of Off.), 11.2.19. Col. Foljambe is one of four soldier brothers, three of whom saw active service in the S. African War. While riding his own horse, Francis II., in the Hunters' Steeplechase at Southwell races, he met with a serious accident, and had to have his right foot amputated.

FOLLETT, F. B. (D.S.O. L.G. 18.7.17); b. 24.4.76; s. of Rev. R. F. Follett and Mrs. Follett, of Winscombe Court, Somerset; 2nd Lt., R. War. R., 4.12.01; Lt. 19.7.05; Adjt. 2.7.10–1.7.13; Capt. 14.4.14; Major 4.12.16; served in S. African War (Lumsden's Horse); Queen's Medal with 3 clasps; Europ. War; Despatches; Bt. Lt.-Col. 3.6.19; M.C. His D.S.O. was awarded for gallantry at River Cogeul.

G. B. S. Follett.

FOLLETT, G. B. S. (D.S.O. L.G. 10.1.17); b. 1878; o. s. of J. S. Follett; m. 1904, Lady Mildred, fifth d. of 7th Earl of Dunmore; educ. Eton and Sandhurst; ent. C. Gds. 1899; Major, 1914; Bt. Lt.-Col. Jan. 1918; T/Brig.-Gen.; M.V.O.; served S. Africa (wounded; Queen's Medal, 2 clasps); Europ. War; thrice wounded; Despatches. He was killed in action 27.9.18.

FOLLETT, R. S. (D.S.O. L.G. 14.1.16); b. 19.10.82; s. of W. W. S. Follett and Constance Elizabeth, d. of Sir R. Millar-Mundy; m. 1915, Dorothy, d. of W. Fanning; one d.; educ. Eton; 2nd Lt., Rif Brig., 5.1.01; Lt. 8.2.02; Adjt. 17.7.06–16.7.09; Capt. 15.4.10; Major 1.9.15; served in S. Afr. 1901–2 (Queen's Medal, 5 clasps); Europ. War, in France from 1914; Despatches four times; Bt. Lt.-Col. 3.6.19.

R. S. Follett.

FOLLIT, C. A. R. (D.S.O. L.G. 20.10.16), late T/Capt., R.W.F.; served in Europ. War, 1914–18; Despatches. His D.S.O. was awarded for gallantry on 14.7.16 at Delville Wood. He died of wounds 20.8.16.

FOORD, A. G. (D.S.O. L.G. 27.10.17) (Details, L.G. 18.3.18); b. 14.4.76; 2nd Lt., Manch. R., 5.1.01; Lt. 30.10.01; Adjt. 1.12.06–30.11.09; Capt. 1.12.12; Major 5.1.16; Despatches.

FOORD, W. P. S. (D.S.O. L.G. 1.1.17) (Bar, L.G. 26.7.18); b. 21.11.81; 2nd Lt., Glouc. R., 21.2.03; Lt. 24.1.06; Capt. 22.1.12; Major 3.5.17; T/Brig.-Gen. 25.4.18–14.3.19; Bt. Lt.-Col. 3.6.18; S. African War, 1901–2; Queen's Medal with 5 clasps; Europ. War; Despatches.

FOOT, R. M. (D.S.O. L.G. 1.1.18); b. 8.10.65; s. of the Rev. C. N. Foot; m. 1st, 1891, Frances S., d. of L. H. Daniell, and 2ndly, 1902, Lucy A., d. of Sir Richard P. Cooper, 1st Bart.; one s.; one d.; educ. Sandhurst; R. of Off. (Lt.-Col., retired), R. Innis. Fus.; served Zululand, 1888; S. Africa, 1899–1902 (wounded; Despatches; Queen's Medal, 3 clasps; King's Medal, 2 clasps); Europ. War, 1914–18; wounded; Despatches; C.B., 1919; C.M.G. 1916; Croix de Guerre and Order of Leopold (Belgian); Croix de Guerre (French).

FOOT, S. H. (D.S.O. L.G. 1.1.18), Lt. (T/Capt.), R.E., Spec. Res.

FOOTNER, F. L. (D.S.O. L.G. 23.10.19), Major, Hants. R., T.F.

FORBES, A. M. H. (D.S.O. L.G. 1.1.17); b. 22.7.70; 4th s. of late Major F. M. H. Forbes and Honoria, d. of Rev. W. K. Marshall, Prebendary of Hereford; m. Alice R., d. of late N. C. Tuely, and widow of Major G. A. Keef, R. Scots Fus.; 2nd Lt. 4.3.91; Major 1.7.11; Lt.-Col. 1.6.19; served N.W. Frontier of India, 1897–98 (Medal and clasp); Tirah, 1897–98; clasp; Europ. War; Despatches twice; wounded.

FORBES, A. W. (D.S.O. L.G. 23.5.17), Lt., R.N. He was killed in action in submarine 6.3.18.

FORBES, C. M. (D.S.O. L.G. 15.9.16); b. 22.11.80; s. of J. Forbes, of Colombo, Ceylon, and Mount Grace, Potters Bar; m. a daughter of the late J. A. Ewen, J.P.; educ. Dollar Academy; Eastman's, Southsea; ent. R.N., 1894; Cdr., 1912; served Europ. War from 1914; action at Jutland Bank; Dardanelles operations; Despatches (L.G. 6.7.16); promoted Captain, 1917.

FORBES, HON. D. A. (D.S.O. L.G. 25.8.17); b. 3.9.80; s. of late Earl of Granard; m. Mary Doreen, d. of late A. Lawson and Hon. Mrs. Bethell; 2nd Lt., R.A., 17.3.00; Lt. 3.4.01; Capt. 21.10.08; Major, R.H.A., 30.10.14; served S. African War, 1901–2; Queen's Medal with 5 clasps; M.V.O.; Europ. War; Despatches.

FORBES, E. C. (D.S.O. L.G. 26.11.17) (Details, L.G. 6.4.18), Lt., S. African Infantry.

FORBES, E. E. (D.S.O. L.G. 23.10.19), Major, S. and T. Corps, I.A.; served N.W. Frontier of India, 1897–98; Medal with 2 clasps; Tirah, 1897–98; clasp; Europ. War; Despatches.

FORBES, F. W. D. (D.S.O. L.G. 1.1.17), Lt.-Col., Aust. Mil. Forces. He was invested with the Insignia of the D.S.O. by the King in Hyde Park 2.6.17.

FORBES, I. R. I. J. (D.S.O. L.G. 30.1.20); b. Jacobabad, India, 28.10.75; e. s. of late Col. J. F. Forbes, J.P., D.L., of Rothiemay, and Mary Livesay, d. of late T. Wardle; m. Lady Helen Craven, d. of 3rd Earl of Craven; two s.; four d.; entered Army, 1894; Capt., 1901; Major, 1914; Lt.-Col., 1915; served S. African War, 1899–1900; Queen's Medal, 3 clasps; wounded; Europ. War, 1914–18; wounded; Despatches thrice; 1914 Star.

FORBES, J. (D.S.O. L.G. 25.8.17), 2nd Lt., Seaf. Highrs.

FORBES, J. F. (D.S.O. L.G. 30.1.20), Lt.-Col., 2nd Bn. Wilts R.

FORBES, J. L. (D.S.O. L.G. 1.1.19); b. 15.5.83; s. of late Major Forbes, H.E.I.C., 2nd Bengal Grenadiers and H.M. 31st Rgt.; m. Eleanor Valentine, d. of the late Rev. Canon Glyn, of Brancepeth, Durham; 2nd Lt., R.A., 24.12.02; Lt. 24.12.05; Capt. 30.10.14; Major 2.9.17, R.G.A.; served Europ. War, 1914–18; Despatches; M.C.; Order of Leopold of Belgium; Belgian Croix de Guerre.

FORBES, J. W. (D.S.O. L.G. 1.1.17); b. 28.7.78; s. of E. and S. L. Forbes, of St. John, New Brunswick; m. Lena Louise Rowe; four children; educ. University of Mount Allison, N.B.; entered Can. Militia; Capt., 1912; came overseas with 1st Can. Contingent, 1914; severely wounded at Ypres; rejoined his battalion in France, Jan. 1917; was promoted Major; Second-in-Command, 15th Canadian Bn. (48th Highrs. of Canada).

FORBES, R. (D.S.O. L.G. 7.11.18) (Bar, L.G. 2.4.19) (Details, L.G. 10.12.19), Lt. (T/Major) (A/Lt.-Col.), 5th Bn. R. Highrs., T.F.; M.C.

FORBES, R. F. (D.S.O. L.G. 1.1.17) (Bar, L.G. 1.1.18); s. of Col. J. F. Forbes, of Rothiemay, Banffs., and Mary Livesay, o. d. of T. Wardle; m. Sylvia Mary, o. d. of Lt.-Col. C. R. A. Leslie, G. Highrs (of Balquhain); one s.; Colonel, H.L.I.; served S. Africa, 1900–1 (one Medal and 3 clasps); Europ. War, 1914–18; Despatches six times, O.B.E.

FORBES, R. R. (D.S.O. L.G. 25.11.16); b. 25.4.80; s. of late H. L. Forbes; m. Jessie W. Paton; two s.; educ. Charterhouse; ent. A. and S. Highrs. 18.4.00; Lt. 26.8.03; Capt. 10.9.10; Adjt., A. and S. Highrs., March, 1911, to Jan. 1914; Major 1.9.15; served S. African War, 1899–1900; Queen's Medal with clasp; Europ. War, 1914–18; Despatches; Bt. Lt.-Col. 1.1.18.

FORBES, W. (D.S.O. L.G. 6.4.18), Cdr., R.N.

FORBES-MITCHELL, W. J. (D.S.O. L.G. 4.6.17), Capt. (A/Major), Can. Inf.

FORBES-ROBERTSON, J. (D.S.O. L.G. 18.6.17) (Bar, L.G. 26.3.18) (Details, L.G. 24.8.18); D.S.O. awarded for gallantry on 14.4.17 at Monchy; V.C.; M.C. (see "The Victoria Cross," by same publishers).

FORD, E. (D.S.O. L.G. 3.6.16), Major, 15th Divl. Signal Co., Can. Forces.

FORD, H. C. (D.S.O. L.G. 1.1.18), Major, Aust. Inf.

FORD, J. R. MINSHULL- (see Minshull-Ford, J. R.).

FORD, V. T. R. (D.S.O. L.G. 3.6.18) (Bar, L.G. 15.2.19) (Details, L.G. 30.7.19); b. 24.11.85; 2nd Lt., York. and Lanc. R., 24.1.06; Lt. 27.10.08; Capt. 28.8.14; Bt. Major 3.6.18; Despatches.

FORD-YOUNG, R. (D.S.O. L.G. 3.6.19), T/Major, R.E., att. 2nd Field Squadron, Aust. Engrs.

FORDE, G. M. (D.S.O. L.G. 15.10.18), T/Major (A/Lt.-Col.), R.F.; M.C.

FORESTER, T. (D.S.O. L.G. 3.6.19), T/Major, 15th Bn. M.G.C.

FORESTIER-WALKER, C. E. (D.S.O. L.G. 1.2.17); s. of Gen. E. Forestier-Walker, formerly Governor of Hong-Kong, and cousin of Sir G. Forestier-Walker; ent. Army, 1886; Lt.-Col., R.G.A.; served with Exp. to Dongola, 1896; Egyptian Medal; Europ. War; Despatches.

FORESTIER-WALKER, R. S. (D.S.O. L.G. 14.1.16); b. 30.10.71; s. of Sir G. F. Forestier-Walker, Bart., and the Hon. Mrs. Fanny Henrietta Forestier-Walker (*née* Morgan), d. of the 1st Baron Tredegar; m. Olive, d. of the late R. T. Bassett, whom he divorced in 1917. He joined the Army for service in the S. African War, March, 1900, to Oct. 1901; Queen's Medal with 3 clasps; was commissioned to the Monmouthshire R.E. (S.R.), March, 1906; Lt.-Colonel; served in Europ. War, with B.E.F., from 2.11.16; Despatches twice and D.S.O. for general good work with 2nd and 6th Army Corps.

FORMAN, D. E. (D.S.O. L.G. 3.6.19), Lt.-Col., R.H.A.; C.M.G.; served S. African War, 1902; Queen's Medal with 4 clasps.

FORREST, T. B. (D.S.O. L.G. 3.6.19), Capt. (A/Major), 8th Bn. H.L.I., T.F., att. 53rd Bn., M.G.C.

FORREST, T. H., M.B. (D.S.O. L.G. 3.6.16), Lt.-Col., R.A.M.C.

FORSTER, D. (D.S.O. L.G. 3.6.16); b. 23.1.78; s. of Lt.-Col. W. D. Forster, late R.A.; m. Isabel Frances, d. of Lt.-Gen. H. A. Brownlow, late R.E.; one s.; two d.; educ. St. Paul's School; R.M.A., Woolwich (Pollock Medal); ent. R.E. 23.12.96; Lt. 23.12.99; Capt. 23.12.05; Major 30.10.14; served S. African War (Queen's Medal with 2 clasps); on outbreak of war was appointed Staff Capt., Garhwal Brigade, Meerut Division; served in France through the winter of 1914–15; returned to France, Sept. 1915; Battles of Loos, the Somme, Arras and Third Ypres; twice wounded; four times mentioned in Despatches; Bt. Lt.-Col. 3.6.17; C.M.G.

FORSTER, G. N. B. (D.S.O. L.G. 1.1.17); b. 28.10.72; s. of Lt.-Gen. B. L. Forster, Col.-Comdt., R.A.; m. Margaret Ethel, d. of Brig.-Gen. R. A. Gilchrist, I.A.; educ. U.S. College, Westward Ho!; Sandhurst; gazetted 2nd Lt., R. War. R., 1893; Capt., 1900; Adjt. 1st Bn. 1902–4; Major, 1911; Lt.-Col., 1916; T/Brig.-Gen., 1917. He served in the Nile Exp. of 1898, under Lord Kitchener in the reconquest of the Sudan (Queen's Medal and Khedive's Medal with clasps for Atbara and Khartum); S. Africa, 1899–1902 (Despatches; Queen's Medal with 5 clasps). He went to France with the 7th Bn. of his regiment in the 7th Division, and during part of his time on that front he commanded a battalion; 1914 Star; twice wounded; Despatches several times; C.M.G. He was killed in action 4.4.18.

FORSTER, H. T. (D.S.O. L.G. 26.9.17) (Details, L.G. 9.1.18) (Bar, L.G. 16.9.18), Lt., R. Berks. R.; M.C.

FORSYTH, C. G. (D.S.O. L.G. 14.1.16); b. 4.5.87; 2nd Lt., Yorks. R., 29.8.06; Lt. 12.5.09; Adjt., Yorks. R., 12.4.12 to 31.7.15; Capt. 30.10.14; T/Major from 21.7.15; T/Lt.-Col., Yorks. R., att. 6th Bn. He was killed in action 14.9.16 ("Times," 23.9.16).

FORSYTH, J. A. C. (D.S.O. L.G. 14.1.16); b. 15.6.71; only son of A. Forsyth; m. Ethel Winifred, d. of J. Robin; educ. Haileybury College, and R.M.A., Woolwich; 2nd Lt., R.A., 1.9.97; Lt. 1.9.00; Capt. 5.3.04; Major 30.10.14; Lt.-Col. 25.12.17; served S. African War, 1899–1900; Queen's Medal with 3 clasps; Europ. War, 1914–18; Despatches 4 times; Bt. Lt.-Col. 1.1.18; C.M.G. He died 21.11.22.

FORSYTH, M. H. (D.S.O. L.G. 26.3.17), T/Major, The Cameronians (Scottish Rifles); M.C. He died of wounds 11.3.18.

FORSYTH, W. H., M.B. (D.S.O. L.G. 1.1.19); m. Maisie Prentice; Major (A/Lt.-Col.), 38th Field Amb., R.A.M.C.

FORTESCUE, A. IRVINE- (see Irvine-Fortescue, A.).

FORTESCUE, C. (D.S.O. L.G. 14.11.16), Capt., Aust. Inf. D.S.O. awarded for gallantry on 3.9.16 at Mouquet Farm.

FORTH, N. B. DE L. (D.S.O. L.G. 1.1.18) (Bar, L.G. 26.3.18) (Details, L.G. 24.8.18); b. 22.12.79; 2nd Lt., Manch. R., 19.5.00 (from Queensland Bushmen); Lt. 3.7.01; Capt. 20.7.12; Major 1.9.15; served in S. African War, 1900–1, with Queensland Bushmen (Queen's Medal with four clasps); Sudan, 1908; slightly wounded (Egyptian Medal with clasp); Sudan, 1910; Sudan Medal with clasp; Despatches; M.C.

FORTIER, R. L. (D.S.O. L.G. 17.10.19), Lt.-Cdr. (A/Cdr.) R.N.R. He died 7.3.21.

FORTUNE, V. M. (D.S.O. L.G. 3.6.16); b. 21.8.83; s. of J. Fortune, of Bengaivin, Castle Douglas; m. Eleanor, d. of A. J. Steel-Kirkwood; 2 d.; educ. Winchester; 2nd Lt., R. Highrs., 19.12.03; Lt. 8.11.06; Capt. 17.9.14; Adjt., R. Highrs. 4.12.14 to 10.11.15; Bt. Major 18.2.15; T/Brig.-Gen. 28.6.18; served Europ. War, in France, 1914–18; Despatches; Bt. Lt.-Col. 1.1.19.

FOSTER, A. H. B. (D.S.O. L.G. 3.6.16); b. 27.12.76; s. of C. W. Foster; m. Constance Mary Ethel Lloyd, d. of late Bishop of Swansea; 2nd Lt., R. Lanc. R., 9.12.99; Lt. 3.3.00; Capt. 15.11.06; Major 1.9.15; served S. African War, 1899–1902; Queen's Medal, 4 clasps; King's Medal, 2 clasps; Europ. War; Despatches twice.

FOSTER, E. W. F. AYLWIN- (see Aylwin-Foster, E. W. F.).

FOSTER, F. A. ARNOLD- (see Arnold-Foster, F. A.).

FOSTER, H. W. A., LL.B. (D.S.O. L.G. 12.3.17); b. in Toronto 25.9.82; only son of late W. A. Foster, Q.C., and late J. M. Foster (*née* Bowes); m. Anna H. G., d. of late J. A. Strathy; one s.; educ. in Paris; Dulwich College; Osgoode Hall Law School, Toronto (Bronze Medallist); University, Toronto; enlisted in 36th Peel Rgt., Sept. 1914; Lt. 20th Can. Bn., Nov. 1914; went to France, Sept. 1915; A/Major, Sept. 1916; served in Europ. War, 1915–19; three times wounded; Despatches six times.

FOSTER, J. R. (D.S.O. L.G. 3.6.19), Major (T/Lt.-Col.), R.A.

FOSTER, P. J. (D.S.O. L.G. 30.1.20); b. 26.4.73; 2nd Lt., R. War. R., 24.3.97; Lt. 6.4.98; Capt. 10.12.00; Major 14.9.11; Despatches.

FOSTER, R. F. C. (D.S.O. L.G. 3.6.18); b. 27.1.79; 2nd Lt., R.M.A., 1.9.97; Lt. 1.7.98; Capt. 8.8.04; Major 23.9.15; Bt. Lt.-Col. 3.6.17; Despatches; C.M.G.

FOSTER, R. T. (D.S.O. L.G. 1.1.17); b. 15.11.82; 2nd Lt., Notts. and Derby. R., 11.5.01; Lt. 20.7.05; Capt. 1.4.10; Notts. and Derby. R., 11.5.16.

FOSTER, T. (D.S.O. L.G. 3.6.19), T/Major, 9th Bn. R. Sussex R.

FOSTER, W. J. (D.S.O. L.G. 2.5.16); served Europ. War, including Egypt, 1914–18; Capt., Staff, Aust. Mil. Forces; Major; Despatches; Lt.-Col.; C.B.; C.M.G.; Bt. Major 1.12.15.

FOSTER, W. M. A. (D.S.O. L.G. 25.8.17), Capt., I.A.

FOSTER, W. N. (D.S.O. L.G. 1.1.18), T/Capt. (A/Major), A.S.C.

FOSTER, W. W. (D.S.O. L.G. 25.11.16) (1st Bar, L.G. 18.1.18) (Details, L.G. 25.4.18) (2nd Bar, L.G. 2.12.18); b. 10.1.76, in Gloucestershire, England; s. of W. Foster, of Vancouver, B.A., and Augusta Anne Foster; m. Olive Hewart, of Bristol, England; 4 s.; educ. Wycliffe College; Capt., Victoria Horse, 14.8.14; Capt., 2nd Can. Mtd. Rifles, Nov. 1914; Major, July, 1916; Lt.-Col., 52nd Can. Inf. Bn., July, 1917; served in Europ. War; Despatches five times; French Croix de Guerre with Gold Star; Belgian Croix de Guerre; D.S.O. awarded for gallantry on 16–17.9.16 at Mouquet Farm; Vice-President, Alpine Club, Canada; made first ascent of highest peak in Canada (Mount Robson) with Capt. MacCarthy, U.S.N., and Conrad Kain, July, 1913.

W. W. Foster.

FOULIS, D. A., M.A. (D.S.O. L.G. 16.8.17); b. 24.4.86; y. s. of Thomas Foulis, Librarian, of Edinburgh; educ. Edinburgh University; late 10th Scottish Rifles; served Europ. War, 1914–18; Despatches. D.S.O. awarded for gallantry east of Arras 9.4.17.

FOULKES, J. F. (D.S.O. L.G. 1.1.19), Major, Can. Gen. List.

FOULKES, J. S. (D.S.O. L.G. 26.9.17) (Details, L.G. 9.1.18), T/Major, Manch. R.

FOURIE, J. (D.S.O. L.G. 22.8.18), Lt.-Col., Carolina Commando, S. African Mil. Forces.

FOWLER, C. (D.S.O. L.G. 1.1.18), Major, R.F.A.

FOX, E. V. (D.S.O. L.G. 3.8.20); Lt.-Col. N. Staffs R.

FOX, G. (D.S.O. L.G. 1.1.18), T/Major, Gen. List.

FOX, G. C. (D.S.O. L.G. 22.8.18), Major, 2nd Transvaal Scottish, S. African Infantry.

FOX, REV. H. W. (D.S.O. L.G. 1.1.18), T/Chapl. to the Forces; Despatches.

FOXTON, J. A. (D.S.O. L.G. 3.6.19), Capt. (A/Lt.-Col.), W. Yorks. R., T.F.

FRAME, A. C. (D.S.O. L.G. 27.7.16), 2nd Lt. (T/Capt.), H.L.I., T.F. D.S.O. awarded for gallantry S.W. of Ouchy.

FRANCE, G. F. H. HAYHURST- (see Hayhurst-France, G. F. H.).

FRANCIS, F. H. (D.S.O. L.G. 3.6.16), Major, Aust. A.S.C.

FRANCIS, J. (D.S.O. L.G. 11.4.18); s. of late John Francis. On the outbreak of hostilities he mobilized with the Welsh Field Col, R.E. (T.F.), in which he was a Captain. He served in the Dardanelles, where he gained his majority, and subsequently served in Egypt and Palestine; was mentioned in Despatches, and awarded the D.S.O. for services which culminated in the capture of Jerusalem.

FRANCIS, M. J. (D.S.O. L.G. 16.8.17), Major, Can. Inf. D.S.O. awarded for gallantry at Vimy Ridge in front of Souchez 9.–13.4.1917.

FRANCIS, R. (D.S.O. L.G. 20.10.16); b. 31.12.91 at Hollesley, Suffolk; s. of William Francis; educ. at Hollesley; commissioned in the Norfolk R. 12.12.14; Lt. 31.4.16; Despatches Nov. 1914; Oct. 1916; Jan. 1917; M.C. Nov. 1918. He was wounded twice on the day he won his D.S.O.

FRANCIS, S. G. (D.S.O. L.G. 27.9.01) (Bar, L.G. 1.1.18); Bt.-Col., R. Berks. R. (see "The Distinguished Service Order," from its institutution to 31 Dec. 1915, same publishers).

FRANK, F. A. (D.S.O. L.G. 21.4.17), Lt. (A/Lt.-Cdr.), R.N.R.

FRANKAU, C. H. S., M.B., F.R.C.S. (D.S.O. L.G. 3.6.18); b. 11.2.83; s. of F. J. Frankau; m. Edith Lorne MacDougall, of Rendham; two s.; one d.; educ. Rugby; St. George's Hospital; Capt. and Bt. Major, R.A.M.C. (T.F.); served Europ. War (France), 1915–19, as Surgical Specialist; in command of 2nd London Clearing Station, and for the last part of the war as Consulting Surgeon to 5th Army, B.E.F., with temporary rank of Colonel; Despatches three times; Bt. Majority; C.B.E.; slightly wounded.

FRANKLAND, E. R. (D.S.O. L.G. 7.2.18), T/Capt., Gen. List.

FRANKLIN, C. P. (D.S.O. L.G. 2.7.17), Lt.-Cdr., R.N.

FRANKLIN, H. S. E. (D.S.O. L.G. 14.1.16); b. 25.11.78; s. of late Sir B. Franklin, K.C.I.E., I.M.S.; m. Kathleen Elizabeth, d. of late Surgeon-Major Deane; one d.; educ. Marlborough and Sandhurst; 1st com. 4.8.97; ent. Ind. Army, 1898; Lt., 15th Ludhiana Sikhs, 4.11.99; Capt. 4.8.06; Major 4.8.15; Colonel; served in the Tirah Campaign, 1903–4; Medal with clasp; with Expeditionary Force in China, 1900 (Medal). On outbreak of Europ. War he accompanied the Exp. Force to France, and in Jan. 1916, was sent to Mesopotamia; was appointed Director of Army Signals and Telegraphs, Mesopotamia Exp. Force, with temp. rank of Brig.-Gen. 22.10.17; was several times mentioned in Despatches; C.M.G.; Bt. Lt.-Col. 11.6.16.

FRANKLIN, R. N. (D.S.O. L.G. 18.1.18) (Details, L.G. 25.4.18), Major, 2nd Australian L.H. Rgt., late of the Bank of N.S. Wales; died after an operation. He had been married in the preceding year.

FRANKLIN, W. H. (D.S.O. L.G. 20.10.16), Colonel, Newfoundland Contingent. His D.S.O. was awarded for gallantry near Serre on 1.7.16, when he was severely wounded; Despatches twice; C.B.E. He was subsequently appointed H.M. Trade Commissioner in E. Africa, stationed at Nairobi.

FRANKLIN, W. V. (D.S.O. L.G. 3.6.18) (Bar, L.G. 3.6.19), T/Major (A/Lt.-Col.), S.W.B., att. 1st Bn. Worc. R.

FRANKLYN, G. E. W. (D.S.O. L.G. 3.6.19); b. 26.8.89; 2nd Lt., R.A. 23.12.09; Lt. 23.12.12; Capt. 23.12.15; Bt. Major 3.6.17; Despatches (L.G. 19.10.14); M.C.

FRANKLYN, H. E. (D.S.O. L.G. 3.6.18); b. 28.11.85; 2nd Lt., York. R., 16.8.05; Lt. 16.1.08; Capt. 30.10.14; Bt. Major 3.6.16; Despatches; M.C.

FRANKS, G. D. (D.S.O. L.G. 1.1.17); b. 9.1.73; 2nd Lt., 19th Hussars, 7.3.94; Lt. 27.4.98; Capt. 1.4.03; Major 3.1.08; Lt.-Col.; served in S. African War, 1899–1900; Despatches; Queen's Medal with 4 clasps; Europ. War; Despatches; C.M.G. He was killed in action 8.10.18.

FRANKS, K. F. (D.S.O. L.G. 15.2.19) (Details, L.G. 30.7.19); b. 22.9.86; 2nd Lt., R. War. R., 16.8.05; Lt., Army, 16.11.07; Ind. Army 16.8.14; Major 16.8.20; served on N.W.F. of India, 1908; (p. in the Zakka Khel country; Medal with clasp; Europ. War; Despatches.

FRASER, A. D., M.B. (D.S.O. L.G. 4.6.17) (Bar, L.G. 1.2.19); born 9.6.84; Lt., R.A.M.C., 28.1.07; Capt. 28.7.10; Major 28.1.19; Despatches; M.C.

FRASER, A. I. (D.S.O. L.G. 1.1.17), Capt. (T/Major), Ind. Cavalry. He was killed in action 30.11.17.

FRASER, A. J. (D.S.O. L.G. 3.6.18), T/Major, A.S.C.

FRASER, A. N., M.B., Ch.B. (D.S.O. L.G. 3.6.16); b. March, 1881; s. of A. D. Fraser, M.D.; m. Constance, d. of H. Ogden; educ. Blair Lodge and Edinburgh University, and served in the ranks in S. Africa, 1900–1 (Queen's Medal with 5 clasps); entered R.A.M.C. 30.7.04; Capt. 30.1.08; Major 1.7.15; T/Lt.-Col., R.A.M.C., 23.7.17 to 25.10.17; A/Lt.-Col. 6.12.18; Despatches.

FRASER, HON. A. T. J. (D.S.O. L.G. 1.1.18), Capt. (A/Major), Lovat's Scouts (Cameron Highrs.).

FRASER, A. W. (D.S.O. L.G. 22.9.16), T/2nd Lt., Border R. He died of wounds 6.9.15.

FRASER, DAVID (D.S.O. L.G. 12.12.19), Major, 1/1st Inverness By., R.H.A., T.F.; M.C.

FRASER, REV. DONALD (D.S.O. L.G. 4.6.17), Army Chaplains' Dept. He was accidentally killed on 2.6.18.

FRASER, D. W. (D.S.O. L.G. 1.1.19), Major, 6th Bn. Can. Rly. Troops.

FRASER, F. H. (D.S.O. L.G. 3.6.19); b. 7.7.93; 2nd Lt., W. Riding R., 25.2.14; Lt. 11.12.14; Capt. 20.5.20; Despatches; M.C.

FRASER, HON. G. (D.S.O. L.G. 8.3.20), Lt.-Cdr. R.N.

FRASER, G. I. (D.S.O. L.G. 3.6.16); b. 18.7.76; 2nd Lt., Cam. Highrs., 6.4.98; Lt. 15.12.98; Capt. 22.1.02; Major 1.9.15; served with Nile Exp., 1898 (Battle of Khartum; Medal; Egyptian Medal and clasp); served in France from 30.9.14 to 22.8.15, and in Salonika from 6.9.15; Bt. Lt.-Col. 3.6.17; Despatches several times; C.M.G.

FRASER, H. (D.S.O. L.G. 4.6.17), Major, R.F.A.

FRASER, H. C. (D.S.O. L.G. 16.9.18), Capt. (A/Lt.-Col.), Yorks. L.I.

FRASER, J. A. (D.S.O. L.G. 1.1.18) (1st Bar, L.G. 22.4.18) (2nd Bar, L.G. 8.3.19) (Details, L.G. 4.10.19); b. 14.5.79; 2nd Lt., 7th D.G., 6.12.14; Lt. 15.7.16; Capt., D.C.L.I., 7.11.18; A/Lt.-Col., S.W.B., 28.6.19 to 30.3.20; Despatches; D.C.M.; Bt. Major 3.6.19.

FRASER, J. D. (D.S.O. L.G. 15.1.20); b. 16.1.94; 2nd Lt., Unatt., 15.8.14; Lt. 1.9.15; Capt. 15.8.18; Despatches.

FRASER, J. E. (D.S.O. L.G. 4.6.17), Major, Aust. Engrs.

FRASER, J. H. P. (D.S.O. L.G. 3.6.19), Capt. (A/Lt.-Col.), R.A.M.C., T.F.; M.C.

FRASER, J. J. (D.S.O. L.G. 1.1.18), Major (A/Lt.-Col.), Can. A.M.C.

FRASER, J. S. G. (D.S.O. L.G. 20.7.17), Cdr., R.N.

FRASER, P. B. (D.S.O. L.G. 1.1.17); b. 14.11.81; s. of G. J. Fraser, R.N., and Margaret Butler Fraser; m. Cicely Sanders; one s.; educ. Portsmouth and Sandhurst; commissioned in the Hants R. 11.8.00, and joined in Peshawar, 1900; transferred to A.S.C. 1.1.02; Lt. 1.1.03; Capt. 1.5.07; Major, R.A.S.C., 30.10.14; served Europ. War with 6th Division in original Exp. Force, in France until Dec. 1914; was in the landing at Suvla Bay with 11th Div. on 6.8.15; joined 29th Div. on the Peninsula 1.10.15 as D.A.Q.M.G., and served with them up to the Armistice on Peninsula, Egypt and France; Despatches; O.B.E.

FRASER, R. M. (D.S.O. L.G. 27.6.19), Cdr., R.N.

FRASER, T., M.B. (D.S.O. L.G. 1.1.18), Lt.-Col., R.A.M.C.

FRASER, HON. W. (D.S.O. L.G. 1.1.18); b. 4.7.90; y. s. of 18th Baron Saltoun; m. Pamela Cynthia, widow of Major W. La T. Congreve, V.C., D.S.O., d. of Cyril Maude; one s.; educ. Charterhouse; Sandhurst; ent. Gordon Highlanders 27.7.10; Lt. 22.12.11; Capt. 14.3.15; Bt. Major 3.6.19; served Europ. War, 1914–18; twice wounded; Despatches; M.C.

Hon. W. Fraser.

FRASER, WILLIAM ANGUS (D.S.O. L.G. 4.6.17), Major, Aust. A.M.C.

FRASER, WILLIAM ARTHUR (D.S.O. L.G. 17.12.17) (Details, L.G. 23.4.18), 2nd Lt., Aust. Inf.

FRASER, W. A. K. (D.S.O. L.G. 12.9.19) (Bar, L.G. 17.6.21); b. 19.12.86; 2nd Lt., Unatt., 5.8.05; 2nd Lt., I.A., 7.12.06; Lt. 5.11.07; Capt. 5.8.14; Despatches; Bt. Major 1.1.18; Major, I.A., 5.8.20; M.C.

FRASER-MACKENZIE, E. R. L. (D.S.O. L.G. 1.1.19), Capt. (A/Major), R.H.A. (T.F.), attd. Notts. By.

FRASER-TYTLER, J. F. (D.S.O. L.G. 18.1.18) (Details, L.G. 25.4.18), Major, Yeom., attd. Cam. Highrs.

FRASER-TYTLER, N. (D.S.O. L.G. 26.9.16) (Bar, L.G. 13.5.18); o. s. of the late Lt.-Col. E. G. Fraser-Tytler, of Aldourie Castle, Inverness, and late Edith Adriana Fraser-Tytler (*née* Selwyn); m. Christian Helen Shairp, d. of the late J. Campbell Shairp, Sheriff Substitute of Ayr; educ. Ludgrove; Eton; joined Inverness R.H.A. (T.F.) as 2nd Lt., Oct. 1908; Capt. Aug. 1914; Major, March, 1917; went to France Nov. 1915, in command of a howitzer battery in the 30th Division; Despatches three times; Croix de Guerre with Divisional Citation, Oct. 1916; Army Citation, Nov. 1917; Coronation Medal, King George V.; Mons–1915 Star. His D.S.O. was awarded for services during the Battle of the Somme, observing from Trônes Wood during the ten days after its capture; Bar for bombardment previous to the Battle of Messines, June, 1917.

N. Fraser-Tytler.

FRAZER, F. A. (D.S.O. L.G. 3.6.19), Lt.-Col., 1/5th Bn. R. W. Kent R., T.F.

FRAZER, W. P. B. (D.S.O. L.G. 4.6.17); b. 24.11.83; 2nd Lt., R. Inniskilling Fusiliers, 9.8.05; Lt. 24.10.07; Capt. 12.10.14; S. African War, 1901–2; served in St. Helena (Queen's Medal); Bt. Major 3.6.18; Despatches.

FREELAND, H. F. E. (D.S.O. L.G. 3.6.16); b. 29.12.70; m. Ethel Louise, d. of Col. T. Malcolm Walker R.A.; 2nd Lt., R.E., 13.2.91; Lt. 13.2.94; Capt. 18.1.02; Major 13.2.11; Lt.-Col. 24.9.18; Major-Gen. retired on Indian Pension, 1920; served in Chitral, 1895 (Medal and clasp); with China Exp. Force, 1900–2; M.V.O., 1911; served in France as A.D. of R.T., B.E.F., from 25.11.14; D.D. of R.T. from 6.5.15; Director of Transportation, British Armies in France, from 20.10.16; D.D. of R.T., British Armies in France, from 23.2.17; Despatches twice; Bt. Lt.-Col. 8.6.15; C.B.; Officier, Legion of Honour; K.C.S.I.

FREEMAN, A. P. WILLIAMS- (see Williams-Freeman, A. P.).

FREEMAN, C. R. (D.S.O. L.G. 15.2.19) (Details, L.G. 30.7.19), Capt. (A/Major), 2nd Bn. Northd. Fus.; M.C.

FREEMAN, F. A. P. WILLIAMS- (see Williams-Freeman, F. A. P.).

FREEMAN, N. M. (D.S.O. L.G. 19.11.17) (Details, L.G. 22.3.18), Major, Aust. Infy.

FREEMAN, W. R. (D.S.O. L.G. 23.11.16), Capt. (T/Lt.-Col.), Manch. R. and R.F.C.; Wing Commander R.A.F.; served Europ. War, 1914–18; Despatches; M.C.; Légion d'Honneur.

FREEMAN-MITFORD, THE HON. B. T. C. O. (see Mitford, Hon. B. T. C. O. Freeman-).

FREER, N. W. W. (D.S.O. L.G. 26.7.18); b. 14.12.92; 2nd Lt., R.A., 19.7.12; Lt., June, 1915; Capt. 8.8.16; Despatches; M.C. He died as the result of a hunting accident 26.2.23.

FREESTUN, W. H. M. (D.S.O. L.G. 1.1.17); b. 19.12.78; 2nd Lt., Som. L.I. 20.5.99; Lt. 22.7.00; Capt. 1.3.09; served S. African War, 1899–1902 (Queen's Medal with 5 clasps; King's Medal with 2 clasps); Europ. War; Bt. Major 3.6.15; Major 1.9.15; Bt. Lt.-Col. 3.6.17; Despatches; C.M.G.

FREETH, J. C. (D.S.O. L.G. 31.5.16), Lt.-Col., 7th S. African Infantry, D.S.O. awarded for gallantry 11–12th March, 1916, at Reata Nek.

FREMANTLE, C. A. (D.S.O. L.G. 11.12.18); b. 1878; s. of the late Hon. Sir C. Fremantle, K.C.B.; m. Margaret Griselda (who died in 1918), d. of Sir W. Wedderburn, 4th Bart.; one d.; Capt., R.N.; served Europ. War, 1914–18. He was in command of the Badger on Oct. 25, 1914, when that vessel rammed a German submarine off the Dutch coast. He was commended for his services in the Battle of Jutland, and was made a Chevalier of the Legion of Honour by the French President.

FRENCH, B. R. (D.S.O. L.G. 1.1.19); b. 21.3.84; T/Lt. 4.9.14; T/Capt. 26.11.14; Capt., R. Munster Fusiliers, 1.7.16; Despatches; Bt. Major 11.11.19.

FRENCH, HON. E. G. (D.S.O. L.G. 1.1.18); b. 11.12.83; s. of the Earl of Ypres; m. Leila, d. of R. King; two d.; educ. Wellington College; joined Cape Colonial Forces, 1904; served during Zulu Rebellion, 1906 (Medal); joined British N. Borneo Constabulary, 1910; Adjt., 11th Bn. Yorks. R., 1914; Major, Second-in-Command, 11th Bn. Ches. R., Sept. 1915, and proceeded to France; served Europ. War; Despatches; slightly wounded; reliquished commission, 1920.

FRENCH, REV. F. L. (D.S.O. L.G. 3.6.18), Can. Chapl. Service; Hon. Capt. (A/Lt.-Col.).

FRENCH, J. P. (D.S.O. L.G. 26.7.17), Capt. (A/Major), Mtd. Rifles, 1st C.M.R. Bn., B.E.F.; D.S.O. awarded for gallantry at Vimy Ridge, 9–11.4.17.

FRENCH, W. (D.S.O. L.G. 15.2.19) (Details, L.G. 30.7.19), T/Major (A/Lt.-Col.), 8th Bn. R. Highrs.; M.C.

FREND, J. R. (D.S.O. L.G. 1.1.18), Capt. (A/Major), Leins. R., S.R.

FRERE, J. G. (D.S.O. L.G. 3.6.19); b. 2.1.94; 2nd Lt., Suffolk R., 17.12.14; Lt. 6.5.15; Corps Machine Gun Officer, 5th Army Corps, British Armies in France, 27.8.18; M.C.

FREW, M. B. (D.S.O. L.G. 4.3.18) (Details, L.G. 16.8.18), T/Capt., Gen. List and R.F.C.; M.C.

FREWEN, L. (D.S.O. L.G. 1.1.17), T/Capt. (T/Major), K.R.R.C.

FREYBURG, B. C. (D.S.O. 3.6.15) (Bar, L.G. 1.2.19) (2nd Bar, L.G. 8.3.19) (Details, L.G. 4.10.19), Capt. and Bt. Lt.-Col. (T/Brig.-Gen.), R.W. Surrey Regt.; V.C. (see " Victoria Cross," same publishers).

FRIEND, R. S. I. (D.S.O. L.G. 17.9.17), Major (A/Lt.-Col.), E. Kent R.; served in S. African War, 1902, E. Kent R. (Queen's Medal with 4 clasps); served Europ. War, London R. D.S.O. awarded for gallantry on 10.6.17, near Ypres.

FRISBY, L. C. (D.S.O. L.G. 8.3.19) (Details, L.G. 4.10.19), Capt. (A/Lt.-Col.), 6th Bn. Welsh R.; M.C.

FRITH, G. R. (D.S.O. L.G. 3.6.16); b. 15.9.73; 2nd Lt., R.E., 2.6.95; Lt. 26.6.98; Capt. 26.6.04; Bt. Major 26.11.13; T/Brig.-Gen. 14.3.17 to 2.4.19; served S. African War, 1899–1902 (Despatches; Queen's Medal with 4 clasps; King's Medal with 2 clasps); Assistant Commissioner, Anglo-French Boundary Commission, east of the Niger, 4.10.02 to 5.6.04; served in Kano-Sokoto Campaign (Medal and clasp); Europ. War in France from 12.7.15; Despatches; Bt. Lt.-Col. 3.6.15; Bt. Col. 1.1.17; C.M.G.

FRIZELL, C. W. (D.S.O. L.G. 4.6.17) (Bar, L.G. 16.9.18); b. 7.1.88; 2nd Lt., R. Berks. R., 9.10.07; Lt. 1.8.10; Capt. 11.3.15; T/Brig.-Gen. 1.10.18; Bt. Major 3.6.18; Bt. Lt.-Col. 3.6.19; Despatches; M.C.

FROGLEY, G. (D.S.O. L.G. 1.4.20), Flying Officer, R.A.F.; D.F.C.

FROST, J. M. (D.S.O. L.G. 8.2.18) (Details, L.G. 18.7.18); s. of Sir J. M. Frost; m. Olivia, d. of H. Skelmerdine; one s.; Major, R.F.A.; served in the Europ. War, 1914–18; Despatches.

FROST, R. W. (D.S.O. L.G. 10.1.17), Lt.-Col., Can. Inf.

FRY, A. B., M.B. (D.S.O. L.G. 25.8.17); b. 29.5.73; Lt., I.M.S., 27.7.99; Capt. 27.7.02; Major 28.1.11; Lt.-Col. 28.1.19; served N.W. Frontier of India, Waziristan, 1901–2 (Despatches); N.W. Frontier of India, 1902, operations against the Darwesh Khel Waziris; Tibet, 1903–4 (Medal); Europ. War; Despatches; C.I.E.

FRY, H. K. (D.S.O. L.G. 1.1.17), Major, Aust. A.M.C.

FRY, P. G. (D.S.O. L.G. 14.1.16), Major, 2nd Wessex Field Co., R. Essex T.F.

FULLARD, P. F. (D.S.O. L.G. 26.11.17) (Details, L.G. 6.4.18), T/Capt., Gen. List and R.F.C.; M.C.

FULLER, C. D. (D.S.O. L.G. 1.1.17), Capt. 26th Illawarra L.H., Aust. Mil. Forces.

FULLER, C. G. (D.S.O. L.G. 1.1.17); b. 15.10.74; s. of late G. Fuller, M.I.C.E., D.Sc.; m. Princess Sophie, d. of late Prince Vladimir Shahoffsky; two s.; educ. Beaumont College; R.M.A., Woolwich; 2nd Lt., R.E. 25.7.93; Lt. 25.7.96; Capt. 1.4.04; Major 25.7.13; served in S. African War, 1899–1902 (Despatches; Queen's Medal with 5 clasps; King's Medal with 2 clasps); Europ. War, 1915–18, in Gallipoli, Egypt and France; Despatches; Bts. of Lt.-Col. 1.1.16 and Col. 3.6.18; C.M.G.; Commander, Legion of Honour.

FULLER, C. T. M. (D.S.O. L.G. 28.7.16); b. 1874; s. of late Capt. T. Fuller, 18th Hussars; m. Edith Margaret Connel; ent. R.N. 1887; Lt. 1894; Cdr. 1903; Capt. 1910; Rear-Admiral, 1921; served with Togoland and Cameroons Exp. Forces, 1914–16, as Senior Naval Officer (Despatches); commanded H.M.S. Repulse, 1916; was in command of the Naval Forces in the operations against the Cameroons in 1914; Despatches; C.M.G.; Legion of Honour; Croix de Guerre avec Palme; Order of Crown of Italy; Bronze Medal for saving life; U.S. Naval D.S.M.; Order of Rising Sun; Chief of Staff to Admiral Sir C. Madden in the Atlantic Fleet from 1920.

FULLER, J. F. C. (D.S.O. L.G. 1.1.17); b. 1.9.78; m. Sonia, d. of Dr. M. Karnatzki, of Warsaw; 2nd Lt., Oxf. and Bucks. L.I., 3.8.98; Lt. 24.2.00; Capt. 21.6.05; Major 1.9.15; Col. 31.8.20; served S. African War, 1899–1902 (Queen's Medal and 3 clasps; King's Medal and 2 clasps); Europ. War, 1914–18, Oxf. and Bucks. L.I.; Despatches; Bts. Lt.-Col. 1.1.18 and Col. 1.1.19; Legion of Honour. Col. Fuller wrote " Tanks in the Great War, 1914–18 " (1920).

J. S. Fuller.

FULLER, J. S. (D.S.O. L.G. 14.11.16); b. 1881; s. of C. Fuller; m. Edith Adeline, d. of late F. Griffiths; educ. Hythe and Folkestone; served in the Europ. War in France with the 2nd Bn. Coldstream Guards; promoted Lt. 3.9.16; seriously wounded on the Somme, 15.9.16. D.S.O. awarded for gallantry on 15.9.16 at Ginchy.

FULLER, W. F. (D.S.O. L.G. 1.1.18); b. 17.9.65; 2nd s. of G. P. Fuller, of Neston Park, Corsham; educ. Wellington College; Master N. Bucks. Harriers, 1899–1905; Master (joint) Cattistock Fox Hounds, 1905–10; served Europ. War; Despatches; Lt.-Col., R. Wilts. Yeom.; J.P., Wilts and Dorset.

FULLERTON, J. C. (D.S.O. L.G. 1.1.17); b. 15.8.80; 2nd Lt., R.A., 4.8.01; Lt. 15.6.04; Adjt. R.A., 1.10.11; Capt. 1.4.14; Major 12.10.15; served S. African War, 1900–2 (Queen's Medal with 3 clasps; King's Medal with 2 clasps); Despatches.

FULTON, C. G. (D.S.O. L.G. 1.1.18), Major, R.F.A.

FULTON, G. K. (D.S.O. L.G. 16.9.18), T/Capt. (A/Lt.-Col.), Cheshire R. He was killed in action 14.4.18.

FULTON, H. (D.S.O. L.G. 8.3.18), Major (T/Lt.-Col.), R.A.M.C.

FULTON, HERBERT ANGUS (D.S.O. L.G. 4.6.17; name first incorrectly given as Herbert Albrecht Fuller); b. 3.10.72; 2nd Lt., York. R., 27.1.92; Lt. 14.7.96; Capt., Worc. R., 20.6.00; Adjt., Worc. R., 5.10.00 to 4.10.04; Major 2.3.11; Lt.-Col. 25.8.19; served in Tirah Campaign 1897–8 (Medal with 2 clasps); Europ. War; Despatches.

FUNNELL, HARRY EDWARD (gazetted as Harry Ernest) (D.S.O. L.G. 4.6.17); e. s. of late Harry Funnell; served in Europ. War; T/Lt.-Cdr., R.N.V.R., and later T/Major, M.G.C., attd. G.H.Q. Italy. He died of pneumonia in Italy, 10.12.18, aged 30.

FURBER, C. T. (D.S.O. L.G. 26.11.17) (Details, L.G. 6.4.18) (Bar, L.G. 15.10.18); b. 4.5.83; 2nd Lt., K.O.S.B., 20.5.05; Lt. 3.7.07; Adjt., K.O.S.B., 25.7.11 to 14.5.14; Capt. 19.2.14; Major, 2nd Battn. K.O.S.B.; served S. African War, 1901–2 (Queen's Medal and 3 clasps); Europ. War, 1914–18; Despatches thrice; Bt. Major 3.6.16.

FURBER, R. I (D.S.O. L.G. 25.8.17), Major, Aust. A.M.C.

FURNEAUX, C. H. (D.S.O. L.G. 23.11.16); s. of Rev. H. Furneaux, M.A. Oxford; m. Joyce, only child of Major Calverley, Down Hall, Harlow, Essex; one d.; gazetted to A.S.C., May, 1901; Lt., May, 1902; Capt., May, 1915; Major, R.A.S.C., Oct. 1914; served S. African War, 1899–1902 (Queen's Medal with 3 clasps); Europ. War, 1914–18; A.Q.M.G.; Despatches; 4th Class Serbian Order of White Eagle; Order of Redeemer of Greece.

FURNESS, C. C. (D.S.O. L.G. 26.9.17) (Details, L.G. 9.1.18), Major, R.F.A.

FURNIVALL, W. (D.S.O. L.G. 1.1.18), Lt.-Col., R.F.A.; b. 7.7.76; 2nd Lt. R.A., 21.3.96; Lt. 21.3.99; Capt. 21.12.01; Major 27.7.12; served S. African War, 1899–1901 (Despatches; Queen's Medal with 6 clasps); Europ. War; Despatches.

FURSE, R. D., B.A. (D.S.O. L.G. 26.7.18) (Bar, L.G. 8.3.19) (Details, L.G. 4.10.19); b. 1887; s. of J. H. M. Furse; m. Margaret Cecilia, d. of Sir H. J. Newbolt; one s.; one d.; educ. Eton; Balliol College, Oxford; Major, King Edward's Horse; served Europ. War, 1914–18; Despatches twice; Asst. Private Secretary to Secretary of State for Colonies.

FURZE, E. K. B. (D.S.O. L.G. 1.1.18); b. 26.6.90; 2nd s. of Herbert and Mary Furze, of Avonmore Road, Kensington; educ. at Charterhouse; commissioned in the Queen's Regt. 22.5.12, serving with his regiment in Bermuda and S. Africa until the outbreak of war; Lt. 9.8.14; Adjt., R.W. Surrey R., 1915–16; Capt. 2.10.15. He wet to France with the 7th Division, and was wounded at the First Battle of Ypres; subsequently he took part in the actions of Neuve Chapelle, Festubert, Loos and the Battles of the Somme, and was present at the capture of Messines Ridge, when he was slightly wounded; Despatches three times; M.C.; commanded Bn. Wilts. R.; Bt. Major 3.6.19.

FYERS, H. A. B. (D.S.O. L.G. 2.4.19) (Details, L.G., 10.12.19), T/Lt., 179th Tunnelling Co., R.E.

FYLER, H. A. S. (D.S.O. L.G. 1.1.18); b. 7.1.64; s. of Capt. J. W. T. Fyler; m. Vera M., d. of R. Brett, Barrister-at-Law; one s.; one d.; educ. Stubbington House, Fareham; H.M.S. Britannia; Lt., R.N., 1885 (four First Class Certificates); Capt. 1904; Rear-Admiral retired; served Benin Exp. 1897; present at capture of Benin City (Despatches; Medal and clasp); Torpedo Lt. of Agincourt (Flag), Camperdown, Theseus and Magnificent (Flag); Commander of Gunnery School, Sheerness, and Royal Oak (Flag); in command of the Agamemnon during Europ. War; assisted in the destruction of the outer forts of the Dardanelles 19 and 25 Feb. 1915; present at the action on 18 March in the attempt to force the Narrows; in command of squadron inside the Straits, clearing the mine fields on the great landing on 25 April and following days; Despatches twice; C.B.; Escort Admiral to Atlantic Convoys, May, 1917; Order of the Rising Sun, 2nd Class.

H. A. S. Fyler.

FYSH, C. E. (D.S.O. L.G. 16.9.18), Lt. (A/Major), 6th (Morayshire) Bn. (Territorial) Seaf. Highrs.; M.C. and Bar. He was killed in action 28.7.18.

GADD, H. R. (D.S.O. L.G. 3.6.18); b. 14.12.89; 2nd Lt., Suff. R., 6.11.09; Lt. 1.4.11; Capt. 11.12.14; Bt. Major 3.6.19; Adjt. 28.7.19 to 25.7.20; Despatches; M.C.

GAGE, M. F. (D.S.O. L.G. 14.1.16); b. 12.1.73; y. s. of Lt.-Gen. Hon. Edward Thomas Gage, C.B., and 2nd wife, Ella Henrietta, d. of late James Maxse; m. (1st) 1902, Annie Massie, d. of William Everard Strong, of New York; two s.; (2nd) 1916, Frances, d. of Senator H. F. Lippitt, of Rhode Island; one s.; one d.; educ. Sandhurst; Staff College, Camberley; was Attaché at Washington; 2nd Lt., 7th D.G., 12.3.92; Lt. 15.4.96; Capt. 19.9.99; Major, 7th D.G., 18.3.07; Major, 5th D.G., 6.2.09; Lt.-Col. 31.8.18; Bt. Lt.-Col. 1.1.17; Brig.-Gen., h.p., 5th D.G., 30.6.19; commanded Lucknow Cavalry Brigade, B.E.F.; served Uganda, 1898–9 (Despatches; Medal and clasp; slightly wounded); S. African War, 1899–1902 (Despatches, L.G. 10.9.01; Queen's Medal, 5 clasps; King's Medal, 2 clasps); Europ. War, 1914–18; Despatches twice.

GAILEY, J. H. (D.S.O. L.G. 4.6.17), T/Major, Unatt. List., E. Afri. Pro. Forces.

GAIMES, J. A. (D.S.O. L.G. 21.6.18), Lt.-Cdr., R.N.; died 20.1.21.

GAIN, R. S. (D.S.O. L.G. 15.2.19) (Details, L.G. 30.7.19), Lt. (A/Capt.), 11th, attd. 1/20th, Bn. London Regt.

GAIRDNER, E. D., M.B. (D.S.O. L.G. 3.6.16) (Bar, L.G. 16.8.17); b. 1878; s. of late Sir William Tennant Gairdner, K.C.B., M.D., F.R.S.; educ. St. Ninian's, Moffat; Rossall; Edinburgh and Glasgow Universities; Major, R.A.M.C., (T.F.), attd. 1/5th R. Scots Fus.; served in S. Africa with Scottish Hospital (Medal, 2, clasps); Europ. War in Gallipoli; Despatches; Croix de Guerre avec Palme; Board of Trade Medal for life-saving at sea.

GALBRAITH, E. D. (D.S.O. L.G. 1.1.18); b. 4.2.81; 2nd Lt., E. Lan. R., 19.6.01; Lt., Ind. Army, 9.6.04; Capt. 19.6.10; Major 19.6.16; served N.W. Frontier of India, 1908 (Medal, clasp); Europ. War; Despatches. He was killed in action 27.5.18.

GALBRAITH, J. E. E. (D.S.O. L.G. 4.6.17); b. 23.12.87; 2nd Lt., R. Fus., 9.10.07; Lt. 9.11.10; A/Lt.-Col. 23.5.18 to 15.7.18; Despatches.

GALE, A. W. (D.S.O. L.G. 30.3.16); b. 1.11.74; s. of late Alfred Christopher Gale; educ. Marlborough; joined 1st V.B. Hampshire Regt. 15.8.00; Feb. 1901, 21st Imperial Yeomanry; served S. African War, 1899–1902 (Despatches; Queen's Medal, 5 clasps; King's Medal, 2 clasps); 7th Dragoon Gds., R. of O., 30.9.14; 3rd D.G. (Res. R.), Nov. 1914; was attd. 2nd L. Gds., being later transferred to them. In autumn of 1915 he was lent to the R.F.A. and given command of 3rd Div. Trench Mortars; Despatches; killed in action 10.4.16.

A. W. Gale.

GALE, H. D. (D.S.O. L.G. 3.6.19); b. 1.11.86; 2nd Lt., R.A., 20.12.06; Lt. 20.12.09; Capt. 30.10.14; Major 13.6.17; Despatches.

GALE, H. J. G. (D.S.O. L.G. 3.6.18) (Bar, L.G. 21.1.20), Major, R.A.

GALLAGHER, MAURICE (gazetted as Gallagher, Michael) (D.S.O. L.G. 26.6.16), Hon. Major; Works Manager, Uganda Railway.

GALLAHER, A. (D.S.O. L.G. 1.1.17); b. 14.7.87; educ. R.M.C., Sandhurst; 2nd Lt., 4th D.G., 19.9.08; Lt. 26.2.10; Capt. 5.5.15 (T/Major 15.3.18 to 31.3.18); Aviator's Certificate, 1913; served Europ. War; Despatches thrice; M.C.; Mons Star, 1914; Médaille Sauvetage, 1917; wounded five times.

GALLAUGHER, H. (D.S.O. L.G. 22.9.16); b. Balleighan, Manorcunningham, Co. Donegal; s. of John Gallaugher and Jane Park Gallaugher (*née* Campbell); educ. The Model School, Londonderry; Dr. Moffat's Private Academy, Letterkenny; commissioned in the Donegal and Fermanagh Volunteers 21.9.14; Capt., 11th R. Innis. Fusiliers, 2.7.16; served Europ. War; Despatches twice; recommended for the V.C. and also for the Legion of Honour. He was a Company Commander in the Manorcunningham Ulster Volunteer Force when he volunteered his services on the outbreak of war. He was appointed Battalion Transport Officer. Before the fighting of July, 1916, he volunteered to take part in the attack and was given command of a platoon. The following was written of Capt. H. Gallaugher: "This officer was the only officer of the Battalion to return unwounded of those who went forward in the attack on the German lines at R.19.d. and R.25.b. on 1.7.16. After Captain Sewell was killed he took charge and led the men to their objective—the Crucifix at R.19.d.9.3. On the way at R.19.b.2.1. he noticed Germans firing on our wounded, and got into a shell-hole with Private Toland and shot six German snipers with his orderly's rifle. When at the Crucifix he had only nine men, with which he erected barricades on the right flank. He then went back to the German front line and collected a number of men, some of which he placed under Corporal Porterfield on a barricade, the remainder he brought back again to the Crucifix. In carrying out these details he came in contact with several parties of Germans, which he killed or took prisoners. On arriving at the Crucifix he found Major Gaffikin, 9th Rl. Irish Rifles, in command, and he returned to 'B' line, where his Battalion was. He also carried in, with Lieut. Austin, 10th Rl. Innis. Fus., a wounded officer (2nd Lt. M. Jackson, of a Trench Mortar Battery) from the enemy's wire to our own lines. After the Battalion was relieved from Thiépval Wood and were stationed at Martinsart Wood on the night of 3/4 in July, this officer, along with Captain Moore and 20 men, volunteered to proceed back to the trenches and rescue wounded from 'No Man's Land.' This party rescued 28 wounded men between the hours of 10 p.m. and 2.30 a.m." Capt. Gallaugher was killed in action 7.6.17. His D.S.O. was awarded for gallantry in France on 1.7.16. At the time of Captain Gallaugher's death Lt.-Col. A. C. Pratt, commanding 11th Bn. R. Innis. Fus., wrote to Capt. Gallaugher's father: "It is with heartfelt sympathy that I write to tell you that your son was killed at the head of his company while leading them on to victory on the Messines-Wytschaete ridge. He had been wounded in the shoulder soon after the attack started, but he gamely carried on until he was killed close to our objective. His loss is most keenly felt by us; he was universally beloved and was one of the finest characters I have ever met; he was a true soldier, and a great leader and organiser." The following is an extract from a letter written by Captain Gallaugher to his father in July, 1916: "I am sorry some of our boys are missing. We all expected them to give a good account of themselves. I don't think Ulstermen have betrayed the trust, and I think the Inniskillings led the way. We are all proud of our old 109th Brigade; it was the first Brigade complimented by the Army Commander."

H. Gallaugher.

GALLIE, J. S. (D.S.O. L.G. 3.6.16); b. 20.3.70; Lt., R.A.M.C., 27.7.98; Capt. 27.7.01; Major 27.4.10; Lt.-Col. 1.3.15; Bt. Col. 3.6.19; served Europ. War, 1914–18; Despatches; C.M.G.

GALLIE, O. E. (D.S.O. L.G. 19.11.17) (Details, L. G. 22.3.18), Lt., R.F.A.; S.R.; M.C.

GALLOWAY, A. G. (D.S.O. L.G. 1.1.18); b. 6.4.77; 2nd Lt., Linc. R., 16.2.98; 2nd Lt., A.S.C., 2.10.99; Lt., A.S.C., 2.10.00; Capt. 1.4.02; Major 5.8.14; Lt.-Col., R.A.S.C., 26.11.20; served S. African War, 1900–2 (Queen's Medal, 3 clasps; King's Medal, 2 clasps); Europ. War; Despatches.

GALLOWAY, R. L. (D.S.O. L.G. 1.1.18); b. 22.7.84; y. s. of Colonel and Mrs. Galloway, of Norwood House, Leamington; 2nd Lt., R.A., 15.7.03; Lt. 15.7.06; Capt. 30.10.14; Major 18.7.16; Despatches.

GALLOWAY, R. W., M.B. (D.S.O. L.G. 3.6.19); b. 22.7.91; T/Lt., R.A.M.C., 22.8.14 to 21.8.15; T/Capt. 22.8.15 to 21.2.18; A/Lt.-Col. 16.12.17 to 7.4.19; Capt. 22.2.18; Despatches.

GALPIN, C. J. (D.S.O. L.G. 22.6.17), Flight Lt., R.N.A.S.

GALWEY, C. E. (D.S.O. L.G. 1.1.18), Major (T/Lt.-Col.), R. of O., late R. Irish R.

GAMMELL, J. A. H. (D.S.O. L.G. 26.3.17); b. 26.9.92; e. s. of Sydney J. Gammell, of Countesswells, Aberdeenshire; m. 1919, Gertrude, e. d. of late Gilbert W. Don; one s.; educ. Winchester; Pembroke College, Cambridge (B.A.); 2nd Lt., R.A., 19.12.12; Lt. 9.6.15; Capt. 19.12.16; served Europ. War, 1914–18; Despatches; M.C.; Order of Karageorge, 4th Class with Swords.

GARDEN, JAMES WILLIAM (D.S.O. L.G. 3.6.18), Lt.-Col., R.F.A.

GARDEN, JAMES WINTON (D.S.O. L.G. 8.3.19) (Details, L.G. 4.10.19), T/Capt. (A/Major), 8th Bn. M.G.C.; M.C.

GARDINER, R. (D.S.O. L.G. 1.1.19); b. 31.10.74; 2nd Lt., S. Lan. R., 6.3.95; Lt. 28.10.97; Capt., Ind. A., 6.3.04; Major 6.3.13; Lt.-Col. 10.3.18; Despatches.

GARDNER, D. E. (D.S.O. L.G. 3.6.18), Major, N.Z. Field Artillery.

GARDNER, J. A. (D.S.O. L.G. 4.6.17); b. 17.7.81; 2nd Lt., R.A., 17.3.00; Lt. 3.4.01; Capt. 7.5.11; Major 16.10.15; Despatches.

GARD'NER, M. M. (D.S.O. L.G. 4.6.17), Lt.-Col., N.Z. Field Art.

GARDNER, W. R., M.B. (D.S.O. L.G. 1.1.18) (Bar, L.G. 8.3.19) (Details, L.G. 4.10.19), Capt. (A/Lt.-Col.), R.A.M.C., Spec. Res., attd. 138th Field Amb.

GARDYNE, E. BRUCE- (see Bruce-Gardyne, E.).

GARFORTH, W. (D.S.O. L.G. 1.1.18); b. 20.7.82; 2nd Lt., R.E., 23.7.01; Lt. 1.4.04; Capt. 23.1.12; Major 2.11.16; Despatches; M.C.

GARLAND, F. J., M.B. (D.S.O. L.G. 3.6.18), Major (A/Lt.-Col.), R.A.M.C.

GARNER, A. C. (D.S.O. L.G. 1.1.19), Capt., Can. Inf., 15.11.13; Lt.-Col., 12th Bn. Can. Inf.

GARNETT, W. B. (D.S.O. L.G. 4.6.17); b. 31.7.75; 3rd s. of late Frederick Brooksbank Garnett, C.B.; m. 1915, Eleanor Constance, e. d. of John B. Story; one d.; educ. Charterhouse; 2nd Lt. from C.I.V., R.W. Fus., 3.5.00; Lt. 28.5.03; Capt. 11.4.11; Major 1.9.15; Bt. Lt.-Col. 3.6.18; commanded Public Schools Batt. R. Fus. 1916; Batt. R.W. Fus. 1917–18; Brig.-Gen. commanding 121st Inf. Brigade, May to Sept. 1918; commanded 2nd Battn. The Welsh R., Oct. 1918, to May, 1919; served S. African War, 1900 (Queen's Medal, 4 clasps); Europ. War; Despatches four times.

GARNSWORTHY, R. (D.S.O. L.G. 26.11.17) (Details, L.G. 6.4.18); b. 3.10.96; s. of Thomas Garnsworthy; educ. Hele's School, Exeter; joined 8th Battn. Devon Regt. 24.7.15; 2nd Lt., 1/6th King's Liverpool, 27.6.17; served Europ. War; Despatches.

R. Garnsworthy.

GARRARD, F. B. (D.S.O. L.G. 2.4.19) (Details, L.G. 10.12.19), Lt. (A/Capt.), 2nd Bn. H.A.C. (Italy).

GARRATT, L. F. (D.S.O. L.G. 3.6.19); b. 9.7.93; 2nd Lt., R.A., 18.7.13; Lt. 9.6.15; Adjt., R.A., 17.1.16 to 28.2.17; Capt. 18.7.17; Adjt. 13.8.19; Despatches; M.C.

GARROD, E. S. (D.S.O. L.G. 8.3.19) (Details, L.G. 4.10.19), T/2nd Lt. (A/Capt.), 10th Bn. Tank Corps; M.C.; D.C.M.

GARSIA, W. C. (D.S.O. L.G. 11.4.18); b. 22.2.81; first commission 4.5.01; Lt.-Col. (Res. of Off.) 13.10.20; Bt. Lt.-Col. 3.6.19; retired Hamps. R. 13.10.20; Despatches; M.C.

GARSTIN, D. N. (gazetted as Garstin, D.) (D.S.O. L.G. 8.3.19) (Details, L.G. 4.10.19), T/Lt. (T/Capt.), M.G.C.; Capt., 10th R. Hussars; served in N. Russia. He was killed in action 15.8.18.

GARSTIN, H. E. (D.S.O. L.G. 1.1.17); b. 16.7.72; 2nd Lt., R.A., 1.4.92; Lt. 1.14.95; Capt. 5.4.00; Major 2.10.09; Lt.-Col. 3.9.15; Bt.-Col. 3.6.19; Col. 3.9.20; h.p. 3.9.20; Despatches.

GARTHWAITE, A. (D.S.O. L.G. 16.9.18), T/Capt., Wilts. R.; M.C.

GARTLAN, G. I. (D.S.O. L.G. 1.1.19); b. 24.6.89; 2nd Lt., R. Ir. Rifles, 18.9.09; Lt. 11.7.10; Capt. 27.5.15; Bt. Major 1.1.18; Despatches; M.C.

GARTSIDE, L. (D.S.O. L.G. 15.10.18); b. 13.2.87; 2nd Lt., W. York. R., 14.10.08; Lt. 8.2.10; res'd. 17.4.12; Capt., High. L.I., 16.1.16; Bt. Major 3.6.19; Despatches.

GARWOOD, H. P. (D.S.O. L.G. 1.1.18); b. 13.4.82; 2nd Lt., R.A., 18.4.00; Lt. 28.9.02; Adjt. 1.10.10 to 31.8.12 and 19.10.12 to 27.8.16; Capt. 18.8.13; Major 13.12.15; Bt. Lt.-Col. 1.1.19; Despatches.

GARWOOD, J. R. (D.S.O. L.G. 1.1.18), Major, R.E.

GASCOIGNE, C. C. H. O. (D.S.O. L.G. 1.1.18); b. 31.1.77; y. s. of late Lt.-Col. Clifton Gascoigne, late Grenadier Guards; m. 1904, Eva Marion, e. d. of Sir Hector Munro, Bart., of Foulis; three s.; two d.; educ. Eton; a Freeman of the City of London; entered the Army, 1900; Lt.-Col., Seaforth Highlanders, attd. Worcs. Regt.; served S. Africa, 1900–1 (Queen's Medal, 5 clasps); Europ. War in France; Despatches.

GASCOIGNE, F. A. DE L. (D.S.O. L.G. 1.1.17); educ. Brockville, Ontario; entered the employ of Canadian Pacific Rly. Co., Montreal, P.Q., 1886; Car Accountant, 1904; Supt., Car Service, Eastern Lines, 1911; Lt.-Col. Can. Inf., 1.10.14; raised and commanded the 60th Can. Inf. Battn.; served Europ. War, in France, in the Ypres salient, on the Somme, 1916; Thelus and Vimy Ridge.

GASCOIGNE, L. (D.S.O. L.G. 1.1.19); b. 29.10.80; first commission 6.1.00; Major 26.9.17; retired, R.A., 25.3.19; Despatches.

GASK, G. E., F.R.C.S., L.R.C.P. (D.S.O. L.G. 4.6.17); b. 1.8.75; 4th s. of late Henry Gask; m. 1913, Ada A., d. of Lt.-Col. Alexander Crombie, C.B., M.D., I.M.S.; one s.; educ. Dulwich College; Freiburg-i.-Baden; St. Bartholomew's Hospital; Surgeon and Director of Surgical Unit to St. Bartholomew's Hospital; Major, R.A.M.C.; served Europ. War; C.M.G.

GASKELL, G. W. (D.S.O. L.G. 3.6.19), Major, R.F.A.

GASKELL, H. S. (D.S.O. L.G. 14.1.16) (Bar, L.G. 10.8.21); b. 24.4.82; 2nd Lt., R.E., 18.8.00; Lt. 18.8.03; Capt. 18.8.10; Major 2.11.16; Bt. Lt.-Col. 1.1.19; Despatches.

GATER, G. H. (D.S.O. L.G. 3.6.16) (Bar, L.G. 17.9.17); b. 1886, s. of W. H. Gater, of Winslow House, West End, Southampton; educ. Winchester; New College, Oxford; on the Oxfordshire Educational Committee, 1911–12; Assistant Director of Education, Nottinghamshire, 1912–14; T/Lt.-Col., Notts. and Derbys. R.; Brig.-Gen.; served Europ. War in Gallipoli, Egypt and France; Despatches four times; twice wounded; C.M.G.

GATHORNE-HARDY, HON. N. C. (D.S.O. L.G. 2.12.18); b. 31.3.80; y. s. of 2nd Earl of Cranbrook; m. 1910, Doris Cecilia Featherstone, d. of Hon. Sir Charles Johnstone, M.L.C., of Karori, N. Zealand; one s.; one d.; educ. Radley; A.D.C. to Governor of New Zealand, 1907–10; first commission 7.3.00; Major 15.6.15; Lt.-Col. (Army) 23.11.21; retired, Rifle Brig., 23.11.21; served Europ. War, 1914–18; Despatches four times.

GATLIFF, V. H. (D.S.O. L.G. 1.1.18); Lt., Aust. F.A., 1.7.15; Hon. Capt. 24.9.17; Despatches.

GATTIE, K. F. D. (D.S.O. L.G. 16.8.17); b. 22.4.90; mobd. Terr. Force, 2 years, 221 days; Capt., S. Wales Bord., 14.3.17; Despatches; M.C.

GAUNT, C. R. (D.S.O. L.G. 25.8.17); b. 1.10.63; e. s. of late Judge Gaunt, of Melbourne, Australia; m. 1904, Maud, o. d. of late Major-Gen. C. J. Moorsom, late 30th Regt.; educ. C.E. Grammar School, Melbourne; enlisted in 13th Hussars, 1887; 2nd Lt., 4th Dn. Gds., 27.6.91; Major 10.12.04; Bt. Lt.-Col. (Res. of Off.) 3.6.16; Lt.-Col. 20.4.20; served N.W. Frontier of India, 1897–8; Orderly Officer to Major-Gen. Sir W. Meiklejohn, K.C.B. (Despatches twice; two clasps); S. African War, 1899–1902 (wounded; Despatches; Queen's Medal, 4 clasps; King's Medal, 2 clasps); Europ. War, in Mesopotamia; Despatches four times; O.B.E.; commanded Rawalpindi Area, 1919; Despatches.

GAUNTLETT, E. G., M.B. (D.S.O. L.G. 1.1.18); b. 1885; s. of T. L. Gauntlett, of Putney, S.W.; m. 1919, Hilda Mary Gerrard, R.R.C.; educ. King's College; King's College Hospital; M.B., B.S. (Gold Medal), London; Surgical Registrar and Tutor, King's College Hospital; Assistant Surgeon, Paddington Green Children's Hospital; late Lt.-Col., R.A.M.C. and Consulting Surgeon to Forces, Salonika; served Europ. War in Salonika; Despatches; C.B.E.

GAVIN, F. C. (D.S.O. L.G. 3.6.18), T/Capt. (T/Major), A.V.C.

GAVIN, THE HON. T. G. B. MORGAN-GRENVILLE- (see Morgan-Grenville-Gavin, The Hon. T. G. B.).

GAY, C. H. (D.S.O. L.G. 1.1.18); b. 4.2.84; 2nd Lt., R.A., 17.5.05; Lt. 17.5.08; Adjt. 17.5.08; Capt. 30.10.14; Bt. Major 1.1.19; Bt. Lt.-Col. 1.1.21; Despatches.

GAYER, A. V. A. (D.S.O. L.G. 19.11.17) (Details, L.G. 22.3.18) (Bar, L.G. 16.9.18), T/Lt.-Col., Durham L. Inf.

GEARY, J. A. (D.S.O. L.G. 14.1.16); b. 16.10.77; s. of Lt.-Gen. Sir Henry Le G. Geary; m. 1912, Edeline, e. d. of late Leonard Roberts-West; one s.; one d.; educ. privately; Aide-de-Camp to his father the Governor of Bermuda, 1902–3; 2nd Lt., R.A., 23.3.00; Lt. 3.4.01; Capt. 17.8.12; Major 26.7.15; served Europ. War, from August 14: Despatches four times; He served throughout Mons, Le Cateau and in Flanders and France and Salonika. He was torpedoed once and wounded once; 1914 Star.

J. A. Geary.

GEDDES, G. P. (D.S.O. L.G. 26.9.17) (Details, L.G. 9.1.18); s. of James Geddes, of Culter Mills; T/Lt., G. Highrs.; served Europ. War; Despatches twice.

GEDGE, F. G. P. (D.S.O. L.G. 1.1.18), 2nd Lt. (T/Major), R.E.

GEE, E. E. (D.S.O. L.G. 18.2.18) (Details, L.G. 18.7.18); b. 27.11.88; 2nd Lt., R.A., 13.6.15; Lt. 1.7.17; Despatches; M.C.

GEE, R. S. (D.S.O. L.G. 1.1.18), Lt., A.F.A., 22.7.12; Major; Despatches.

GEHRKE, R. A. (D.S.O. L.G. 25.11.16); b. 11.6.86; e. s. of A. H. Gehrke; educ. Dulwich College; joined Public Schools Battn. as Private 9.9.14; Inns of Court O.T.C. Nov. 1914; 2nd Lt. (S.R.) 3.3.15; Lt. 31.3.16; late Dublin Fus.; served Europ. War in Egypt, Salonika and N. Russia; Despatches; wounded three times.

GEIGER, G. J. P. (D.S.O. L.G. 1.1.17); b. 12.5.76; s. of John Geiger; m. 1901, May, d. of Adm. Sir Francis Powell; educ. Harrow; R.M.C., Sandhurst; first commission, 5.9.96; Major 31.1.15; retired R.W. Fus. 18.6.21; served Europ. War, 1914–18; Despatches; Croix de Guerre; Legion of Honour; O.B.E.

GELDARD, N. (D.S.O. L.G. 11.1.19), Capt., 6th Bn. (attd. 2/4th Bn.) W. Riding R. (T.F.); M.C.

GELL, E. A. S. (D.S.O. L.G. 26.7.18), T/Lt. (A/Lt.-Col.), R.F.; M.C.

GELL, P. F. (D.S.O. L.G. 2.12.18); b. 6.3.80; 2nd Lt., Manch. R., 21.4.00; Lt. 15.2.01; Lt., Ind. Army, 12.4.02; Capt. 21.4.09; Major 1.9.15; retired 1.4.20; T/Lt.-Col. 26.10.18; Despatches.

GELL, W. C. C., M.A., LL.B. (D.S.O. L.G. 1.1.18) (Bar, L.G. 3.6.19); y. s. of W. J. Gell, of Cora Lyn, Solihull; educ. Cambridge; Capt. and Bt. Major (A/Lt.-Col), 1/5th Bn. R. War. R. (T.F.); served Europ. War in France; M.C.

GELL, W. H. (D.S.O. L.G. 21.6.19), Lt.-Cdr., R.N.

GELLIBRAND, SIR JOHN, K.C.B. (D.S.O. L.G. 2.5.16) (Bar, L.G. 18.6.17); b. 5.12.72; first commission, 21.10.93; Capt. 26.5.00; retired Manch. R. 27.5.12; Bt. Major (R. of Off.) 1.1.17; T/Major-Gen., Aust. Impl. Force, 30.6.18; served S. African War, 1899–1900 (Queen's Medal, 2 clasps); Europ. War. 1914–18; Despatches; C.B.

GELSTHORPE, A. M. (D.S.O. L.G. 26.11.17)(Details, 6.4.18), T/Lt. (A/Capt.), Durh. L. Inf., attd. M.G.C.

GEMMELL, J. S. (D.S.O. L.G. 8.3.19) (Details, L.G. 4.10.19), T/Major, 20th Bn. Manch. R.; M.C.

GEMMELL, W. A. S. (D.S.O. L.G. 3.6.16); b. 23.9.74; first commission, 20.9.94; Major 29.3.11; retired North'd Fus. 15.7.20; Despatches; O.B.E.

GENET, H. A. (D.S.O. L.G. 1.1.17); b. 20.2.64; s. of Frederick James Genet, M.R.C.S., L.S.A., and Augusta, d. of John Minney, War Office; m. 1887, Fanny Lucy, d. of John Taylor; two s., both of whom have won the Military Cross; educ. St. Mark's College, Chelsea, London, England; Private, 2nd (South) Middlx. R.V. (Corp. and Sergt.), 1882–7; Lt., 38th Regt. Can. Inf., May, 1897; Lt.-Col. 14.10.14; O.C. 4th Can. Res. Bn. to April, 1918; appointed A.A.G., Mil. Dist. No. 3, Kingston, Ont., 20.5.18; served Europ. War, on the Somme, 1916, Vimy Ridge, Lens, Passchendaele; Despatches, L.G. 1.1.17 and L.G. 1.1.18; holder of Colonial Aux. Forces Long Service Medal and Officers' Decoration.

GENT, G. E. J. (D.S.O. L.G. 1.1.19), Capt. and Bt. Major, 3rd Bn. D.C.L.I., attd. 1st Bn.; M.C.

GENTLES, N. (D.S.O. L.G. 3.6.18), Lt., Can. Inf. 1.8.14; Despatches.

GEOGHEGAN, N. M. (D.S.O. L.G. 3.3.19); b. 7.9.76; 2nd Lt., Unatt., 5.8.96; 2nd Lt., I.S.C., 22.10.97; Lt. 5.11.98; Capt. 5.8.05; Major 5.8.14; Bt. Lt.-Col. 3.6.16; Lt.-Col. 16.5.20; Despatches.

B. W. George.

GEORGE, B. W. (D.S.O. L.G. 2.11.17); b. 10.1.86; s. of Thomas George, Capt. Mercantile Marine, and Margaret, his wife; m. Annie Jane, d. of Capt. John Howard and Elizabeth Howard; one s.; one d.; educ. Fishguard Grammar School; joined Mercantile Marine as an apprentice, Sept. 1891; Capt. Mercantile Marine, in command of S.S. Tredegar Hall, 1917; Lt., R.N.R., 13.7.17; served Europ. War; wounded; Gold Medal and Diploma from the Shipowners' Association of England.

GEPP, E. C. (D.S.O. L.G. 14.1.16) (Bar, L.G. 18.6.17); b. 7.7.79; s. of Rev. H. J. Gepp, for many years Vicar of Adderbury, Oxon; m. Eveline Marion, y. d. of late Lt.-Col. G. Wilbraham Northey, J.P., D.L.,

of Ashley Manor, Box; educ. Marlborough College; entered the Army, 22.5.01; retired 21.10.11; rejoined, 1914; Major, D. of Corn. L. Inf., 10.5.17; Bt. Lt.-Col. 1.1.19; T/Lt.-Col. 26.9.20; 1st Grade, G.S.O., Quetta, since 1920; served S. African War, 1900 (wounded; Queen's Medal, 3 clasps); Somaliland, 1909–10 (Despatches); Europ. War; Despatches twice.

GERARD, C. R. T. M. (gazetted as Gerard C. R.) (D.S.O. L.G. 4.2.18) (Details, 5.7.18); b. 28.2.94; o. s. of Hon. R. Gerard, of Wrightington Hall, Wigan, and cousin of Lord Gerard; m. 1915, Annie, d. of Sir R. T. R. Clarke, 2nd Bart.; one s.; educ. Eton; Sandhurst; Capt. G. Gds.; served Europ. War, 1914–18, in France; Despatches.

GERMAN, G. (D.S.O. L.G. 3.6.18), Major (A/Lt.-Col.), Leic. R.

GERRARD, E. L. (D.S.O. L.G. 22.6.16); b. 14.7.81; s. of T. Gerrard, Crown Solicitor for Carlow, King's County; educ. Warwick School; joined Royal Marines, 1900; Capt. 1911; Bt. Major, 1914; T/Lt.-Col. 1914; Wing-Comdr., R.N.A.S.; served with the first naval airship (Mayfly), 1910; began flying aeroplanes at Eastchurch, 1911; world's record for duration, aviator and passenger, 16.8.11, and British distance cross-country record; British height record, pilot and two passengers, 1914; commanded squadron of naval aeroplanes prior to and during siege of Antwerp; Düsseldorf anti-Zeppelin raids; commanded a Wing in E. Mediterranean; served Europ. War; C.M.G.

GERRARD, W. D. (D.S.O. L.G. 18.2.18) (Details, L.G. 18.7.18), Lt.(A/Capt.)' Yeo. and Tank Corps.

GERVERS, C. T. (D.S.O. L.G. 1.1.19), Lt.-Cdr. (A/Cdr.), R.N.

GETHIN, SIR R. W. ST. L., Bart. (D.S.O. L.G. 1.1.17); b. 16.2.78; s. of Sir Richard Gethin, 8th Bart., and Catherine, d. of F. E. B. Scott, of Ingham Lodge, Cheshire; s. father, 1921; m. 1906, Helen, d. of W. B. Thornhill, of Castle Bellingham, Ireland; educ. Radley College; R.M.A., Woolwich; 2nd Lt., R.F.A., 23.3.07; Lt. 23.3.00; Capt. 19.3.92; Major 1.4.14; Bt. Lt.-Col. 1.1.16; Lt.-Col. 1.7.17; Col. 1.1.20; served S. African War, 1899–1901 (wounded; Queen's Medal, 5 clasps); Europ. War, 1914–18, in France; Despatches; C.M.G.; Légion d'Honneur, Croix de Chevalier, 1918.

GETTINS, J. H. (D.S.O. L.G. 3.6.18), Capt. (A/Major), A.S.C.

GEYSER, A. H. (D.S.O. L.G. 22.8.18), Major, Waterburg Commando, S. African Mil. Forces.

GIBB, A. (D.S.O. L.G. 29.11.20), Capt. Tribal Levy, late Somaliland Camel Corps; D.C.M.

GIBB, A. S. (D.S.O. L.G. 14.7.16); b. 15.5.87; s. of William Gibb, Master Mariner; m. 1905, Louie, d. of John Newman; one s.; educ. Rhodes House School, Manchester; the school ship Conway; Midshipman, R.N.R., 1884; commissioned to H.M.Y. Catania, Sept. 1914; transferred to command H.M.S. Nairn, North Sea Patrol, 1917; served Europ. War; Royal Naval Reserve Decoration; Order of the Russian Crown; the Humane Society's Swimming Medal and twenty-four other prizes and certificates.

GIBBON, J. H. (D.S.O. L.G. 2.5.16); b. 22.7.78; e. s. of late James Houghton Gibbon, Rector of Willersey, Glos.; m. 1916; Jessie Willoughby, 2nd d. of Brabazon Campbell; two s.; two d.; educ. Eton; Trinity College, Cambridge (M.A.); 2nd Lt., R.A., 28.3.00; Lt. 3.4.01; Capt. 2.6.09; Major 30.10.14; Bt. Col. 3.6.19; served W. Africa (Aro Expedition), 1901–2 (Medal, clasp); S. Nigeria, 1904–5; N. Nigeria, 1905–6 and 1907–8; Europ. War, 1914–19, in France, Dardanelles, Egypt; Despatches thrice.

GIBBON, W. D. (D.S.O. L.G. 17.3.17); b. 1880; s. of late Sir W. D. Gibbon and Katherine (died 1916), d. of Andrew Murray, of Allathan, Aberdeen; educ. Dulwich College; Trinity College, Oxford (M.A.); T/Capt. (A/Lt.-Col.), Worc. Regt.; served S. African War, 1900–1; Europ. War, Gallipoli, Mesopotamia; Persia, 1918; Trans-Caucasia; M.C.

GIBBONS, C. (D.S.O. L.G. 2.4.19) (Details, L.G. 10.12.19), Lt. (T/Capt.), Durham Lt. Inf.; M.C.; D.C.M.

GIBBONS, T. (D.S.O. L.G. 3.6.16), Capt. (T/Lt.-Col.), Essex R. (T.F.).

GIBBS, A. J. (D.S.O. L.G. 1.1.18); b. 26.5.87; 2nd Lt., R.A., 18.12.07; Lt. 18.12.10; Capt. 30.10.14; Major 2.12.17; Despatches; M.C.

GIBBS, D. J. (D.S.O. L.G. 1.1.18), Major, N.Z. Corps.

GIBBS, G. L. D. (D.S.O. L.G. 25.7.16); b. 30.7.82; served Europ. War, in command of Crusader in bombardment of German Army left wing from coast, 1915 (Despatches); patrol work, 1916, in H.M.S. Thruster, Harwich Force, 1917 (Despatches); commanded Royal Naval College, Dartmouth, 1919; in command of H.M.S. Bryony since 1921.

GIBBS, H. E. (D.S.O. L.G. 1.1.18); b. 18.1.79; m. Yvonne du Fossé de Bosmelet; one d.; Lt., A.V.C., 16.5.03; Capt. 16.5.08; Major 10.7.15; A/Lt.-Col. 15.6.18 to 25.9.19; Despatches.

GIBBS, J. A. (D.S.O. L.G. 4.6.17); b. 28.9.81; s. of late J. A. Gibbs; m. Susan Gladys, d. of Sir T. and Lady Morel; one s.; educ. Queen's College, Taunton; enlisted in the Glam. Yeomanry 28.9.14; Lt., Welsh Regt., 4.11.14; Capt., Dec. 1914; A/Major 20.6.17; served Europ. War; Despatches, L.G. 24.6.17. He was killed in action 20.9.17.

J. A. Gibbs.

GIBBS, L. M. (D.S.O. L.G. 3.6.19), Capt., Colds. Gds.

GIBLIN, L. F. (D.S.O. L.G. 3.6.18); b. 12.5.72; s. of Thomas Giblin; m. Muriel Gertrude, d. of G. M. Maxwell, of Hobart, Tasmania; Principal Medical Officer, Tasmania, 1903–14; Officer commanding 1st Australian Clearing Hospital, Egypt, 1914; Assistant Director, Medical Service, A.I.F., England, 1915–16; served Europ. War, 1914–16; Despatches; C.B.

GIBSON, A. J. (D.S.O. L.G. 1.1.18); b. 14.3.95; (from Ind. Army Res. of Off.) 2nd Lt. 19.12.18; Capt., R.A.M.C. (S.R.); Despatches; M.C.

GIBSON, B. D. (D.S.O. L.G. 1.1.17); o. s. of Col. W. Gibson, V.D., of Hexham, Northumberland; m. 1907, Margaret Elizabeth, d. of Collingwood Forster Jackson; one s.; one d.; educ. Ushaw College, Durham; admitted Solicitor, 1899, and was in partnership with his father at Hexham; Lt.-Col. North'd. Fus. 1915; served Europ. War; Despatches three times; 1915 Star; Croix de Guerre. He was killed in action 27.5.18.

GIBSON, G. H. R. (D.S.O. L.G. 3.6.18), Capt., Can. A.M.C., 2.7.13; O.C. Canadian Officers' Convalescent Hospital; Major, Can. A.M.C.; Despatches.

GIBSON, H. (D.S.O. L.G. 1.1.18), Capt. (A/Lt.-Col.), R.A.M.C., attd. 17th F.A.; died of wounds 17.10.17.

GIBSON, JOSEPH, M.A. (D.S.O. L.G. 1.1.18); b. 1877; 2nd s. of late H. E. Hollins; assumed name of Gibson on succeeding to Whelprigg estates; m. 1910, Catherine Joan Machell, 2nd d. of J. T. Ware, of York; two s.; one d.; educ. Haileybury; Pembroke College, Cambridge (M.A.); Major, A.S.C.; J.P.; served Europ. War, 1915–18; Despatches twice.

GIBSON, J. McI. (D.S.O. L.G. 3.6.19), Major, 2nd Bn. Can. Rly. Troops.

GIBSON, L. (D.S.O. L.G. 1.1.18); b. 26.1.80; s. of Col. A. Gibson, V.D.; m. 1914, Isabel Macallaster Best; one s.; one d.; educ. Morrison's Academy, Crieff; Edinburgh Institution; Agent, Union Bank of Scotland Ltd., Perth; J.P., Perthshire; went to France as Adjt., 6th Black Watch, April, 1915; Staff Capt., 153rd Brig. Highland Div., June, 1915; Major, Aug. 1915; served Europ. War; Despatches thrice; T.D.; French Croix de Guerre.

L. Gibson.

GIBSON, T. (D.S.O. L.G. 1.1.18); b. 14.6.75; s. of Joseph and Janet Gibson (*née* Buchanan); m. 1903, Clara Annie, d. of F. Sharon; two s.; three d.; educ. Ingersoll Collegiate Institute; Toronto University; Osgoode Hall; Barrister-at-Law; called to Ontario Bar, 1900; practised Law, Ingersoll, 1900–3, etc.; assisted in recruiting; Second-in-Command, 168th Battn. Oxford's Own, C.E.F.; upon this battalion being broken up in England, appointed Senior Major, 4th Pioneer Battn.; Assistant Deputy Minister, Overseas Militia Forces, Canada, London; served Europ. War; C.M.G. 1919; Médaille d'Honneur avec Glaives en Vermeil, 1921.

GIBSON, W. (D.S.O. L.G. 2.12.18), T/Major, S. Staffs, attd. 10th Bn. W. Yorks. R.; M.C.

GIBSON, W. R. (D.S.O. L.G. 3.6.18), Major, A.S.C. (now R.A.S.C.) (T.F.).

GIBSONE, D. H. (D.S.O. L.G. 1.1.18); Harbour Master of Berwick; served for twenty-five years in Royal Indian Marine, and held the rank of Commander till 1914; T/Maj. (T/Col.), R.E.; served Europ. War; Despatches three times.

GIBSONE, W. W. P. (D.S.O. L.G. 1.1.17), Canadian Divisional Headquarters; served Europ. War, 1914–17; Despatches; C.M.G. 1918.

GIDLEY, C. DE B. (D.S.O. L.G. 7.2.18); b. 16.9.76; 2nd Lt., R.A., 16.5.00; Lt. 16.11.01; Capt. 20.12.10; Major 30.10.14; A/Lt.-Col. 19.7.16 to 21.11.19; Despatches.

GIFFARD, F. (D.S.O. L.G. 1.1.19), Cdr., R.N.

GIFFARD, G. J. (D.S.O. L.G. 4.6.17); b. 27.9.86; 2nd Lt., R.W. Surr. R., 24.1.06; Lt. 22.1.11; Capt. 10.2.15; Bt. Major 1.1.18; Bt. Lt.-Col. 1.1.19; Despatches.

GIFFIN, W. C. D. (D.S.O. L.G. 3.6.19); b. 27.1.81; s. of late George Giffin, of Dublin; Lt., R. Ir. R., S.R., attd. 2nd Bn.; served Europ. War; Despatches; wounded; M.C.

GILBERTSON, G. N. (D.S.O. L.G. 17.10.19), Lt.-Cdr., R.N.

GILCHRIST, H. G. (D.S.O. L.G. 4.6.17), T/Capt., R.E.; M.C.

GILDAY, A. L. C. (D.S.O. L.G. 3.6.18), Lt.-Col., A.M.C.

GILES, A. H. A. (D.S.O. L.G. 16.9.18), T/Lt. (A/Capt.), Notts. and Derbys. R.; M.C.

A. H. A. Giles.

GILES, E. D. (D.S.O. L.G. 3.6.16); b. 13.10.79; s. of Edward Giles, C.I.E., and Rose Ethel Louise, e. d. of Gen. Sir J. Schneider, K.C.B.; m. 1915, Eileen Graham, o. c. of late C. G. Dingwall-Fordyce; educ. Marlborough College; R.M.C., Sandhurst; 2nd Lt., Shrops. L.I., 12.8.99; Lt. 1.8.00; Ind. Army, 17.1.01; Capt. 12.8.08; Major 1.9.15; Bt. Lt.-Col. 3.6.18; T/Lt.-Col. 2.4.19 to 31.10.19; served Europ. War in France; Despatches; G.S.O.1 of British Military Mission, Jan. to Nov. 1918; C.M.G.; American D.S.M.

GILES, F. G. (D.S.O. L.G. 4.6.17), Capt., Aust. Inf. 16.1.15; Despatches.

GILES, F. L. N. (D.S.O. L.G. 14.1.16); b. 25.6.79; s. of late Frank Giles, I.C.S.; m. 1916, Elgiva, y. d. of Capt. Ackland Allen, J.P., of St. Hilary Manor, Glamorgan; one s.; one d.; educ. Marlborough; R.M.A., Woolwich; 2nd Lt., R.E., 23.3.99; Lt. 1.10.01; Capt. 23.3.08; Major 27.9.15; A/Lt.-Col. 24.5.17 to 21.9.19; served S. African War, 1902 (Queen's Medal, 3 clasps); Europ. War, 1914–17, including Cameroon Campaign; Despatches.

GILES, S. E. H. (D.S.O. L.G. 1.1.17); b. 28.6.81; 2nd Lt., R. Ir. Rifles, 29.1.02; 2nd Lt., A.S.C., 1.10.03; Lt. 29.1.05; Capt. 22.7.11; Major, R.A.S.C., 30.10.14; served S. African War, 1902 (Queen's Medal, 3 clasps); Soudan, 1910 (Soudan Medal, clasp); Europ. War; Despatches.

GILES, V. (D.S.O. L.G. 1.1.17); b. 12.2.77; 5th s. of Professor H. A. Giles, M.A.Camb., LL.D.Aberd.; m. 1902, Margaret, e. d. of W. L. Mollison, Master of Clare College, Cambridge; one s.; one d.; educ. College, St. Servais, Liége; Coll. Stella Matutina, Feldkirch; Aberdeen University; 2nd Lt., R.E., 22.2.97; Lt. 22.2.00; Capt. 22.2.06; Major 30.10.14; Bt. Lt.-Col. 1.1.18; served Tibet Expedition, 1903–4; Europ. War, 1915–18, in France; Despatches thrice; O.B.E.

GILL, D. H. (D.S.O. L.G. 1.1.17); b. 21.2.77; s. of late Rev. T. Howard Gill, M.A., formerly Chaplain to British Embassy, Paris; m. 1912, Sallie, widow of Woodbury Kane, of New York; educ. Tonbridge School; R.M.A., Woolwich; 2nd Lt., R.A., 23.3.97; Lt. 23.3.00; Capt. 31.3.02; Major 6.6.14; Lt.-Col. 9.7.17; h.p. 9.7.21; served S. African War, 1899–1902, in R.H.A. and R.F.A. batteries (Queen's Medal, 5 clasps; severely wounded); Europ. War; Despatches; C.M.G.; Chevalier Légion d'Honneur.

GILL, F. G. (D.S.O. L.G. 1.2.19), Capt. (A/Major) 1/24th Bn. London Regt.

GILL, G. H. (D.S.O. L.G. 1.1.17); b. 2.4.82; 2nd Lt., R. Muns. Fus., 30.4.02; A.S.C. 9.10.05; Lt. 9.10.06; Capt. 15.10.12; Major, R.A.S.C., 27.10.16; Bt. Lt.-Col. 3.6.18; served Europ. War, 1914–18; Despatches; Order of Aviz of Portugal.

GILL, REV. H. V. (D.S.O. L.G. 8.3.18), T/Ch. to the Forces, 3rd Class, A. Chapl. Dept.; M.C.

GILL, J. G., M.B. (D.S.O. L.G. 1.1.18); b. 7.11.73; Lt., R.A.M.C., 28.1.99; Capt. 28.1.02; Major 28.1.11; Lt.-Col. 1.3.15; A/Col. 4.2.17 to 31.5.17; Despatches; C.B.E.

GILL, JAMES GEOFFREY (D.S.O. L.G. 4.6.17); b. 7.11.73; Lt., R.A.M.C., 28.1.99; Capt. 28.1.02; Major 28.1.11; Lt.-Col. 1.3.15; A/Col. 4.2.17 to 31.5.17; Despatches; O.B.E.

GILL, JOHN GALBRAITH, M.B. (D.S.O. L.G. 1.1.18); b. 6.4.89; Lt., R.A.M.C., 30.1.14; Capt. 30.3.15; A/Lt.-Col. 3.12.17 to 12.2.19; Despatches; O.B.E.; M. C.

GILL, J. H. (D.S.O. L.G. 18.10.17), T/Major, W. Yorks. R.

GILL, R. H. (D.S.O. L.G. 15.10.18), T/Major, North'd Fus.

GILLAM, J. G. (D.S.O. L.G. 4.6.17); b. 22.12.83, y. s. of late George Gillam, of Preston Park; educ. Brighton, Slough and London; Manager of the Birmingham branch of Charles Tennant and Sons and Co. Ltd. since 1912; enlisted in H.A.C. 4.8.14; 2nd Lt., Nov. 1914; Capt., Jan. 1915; Major, A.S.C., May, 1916; served Europ. War, taking part in the original landing on Cape Helles, Gallipoli, also in defence of Masnières and Marcoing; Despatches twice.

GILLAM, R. A. (D.S.O. L.G. 1.1.18); b. 23.10.72; 2nd s. of late F. A. Gillam; m. 1906, Gwladys, d. of T. Lindsay Watson; one s.; one d.; educ. privately; R.M.A., Woolwich; 2nd Lt., R.E., 13.2.91; Lt., R.E., 13.2.94; Capt. 31.12.01; Major 13.2.17; Lt.-Col. 24.9.18; Bt. Col. 3.6.19; T/Brig.-Gen. 1917–18; served Chin Hills, Burma, 1893–6; N.W. Frontier of India, Tirah, 1897–8 (Medal, 2 clasps); S. African War, 1900–2 (Queen's Medal, 2 clasps; King's Medal, 2 clasps); Europ. War, 1914–18; wounded; Despatches three times; C.M.G. 1918; French Croix de Guerre; 1914–15 Star; General Service and Victory Medals.

GILLATT, J. M. (D.S.O. L.G. 3.6.18), Major (A/Lt.-Col.), R. Scots.

GILLESPIE, E. (D.S.O. L.G. 31.3.16); b. 18.6.84; 2nd Lt., R. Mar., 1.8.02; Lt. 1.8.03; Capt. 1.8.13; Bt. Major 1.1.18; Major 1.8.18; Despatches.

GILLESPIE, H. J. (D.S.O. L.G. 1.1.17), T/Major, R.F.A.

GILLESPIE, R. H. (D.S.O. L.G. 1.1.17); b. 12.11.84; 2nd Lt., Leics. R., 18.8.05; Lt. 15.6.07; Capt. 8.3.13; Bt. Major 3.6.16; Despatches.

GILLETT, C. R. (D.S.O. L.G. 1.1.17); b. 24.8.80; s. of Rev. H. H. Gillett and Evelyn Mary Geraldine, sister of 3rd Baron Lyveden; m. 1906, Gwynne Eveline Dykes, d. of Robert Keate; two s.; 2nd Lt., R.A., 6.1.00; Lt. 3.4.01; Capt. 7.12.10; Adjt. 22.1.12 to 1.4.12; Major 25.7.15; Bt. Lt.-Col. 3.6.18; served Europ. War, 1914–18; Despatches.

GILLIBRAND, A. (D.S.O. L.G. 4.6.17), T/Major, A.S.C.

GILLIGAN, G. G. D.S.O. L.G. 3.6.18), Major (A/Lt.-Col.), Arg. and Suth'd Highrs., attd. Notts. and Derbys. R.

GILLILAN, E. G. (D.S.O. L.G. 18.2.18) (Details, L.G. 18.7.18), Capt., C. Gds. (S.R.).

GILLMORE, E. T. B. (D.S.O. L.G. 3.6.18), Lt.-Col., Can. F.A.

GILLSON, R. M. T. (D.S.O. L.G. 26.9.16); b. 5.4.78; 2nd Lt., Wilts. R. 20.8.99; Lt. 24.2.00; Capt. 16.9.05; Major 1.9.15; Bt. Lt.-Col. 1.1.18; Despatches.

R. M. T. Gillson.

GILLUM, W. W. (D.S.O. L.G. 30.3.16); b. 16.8.84; s. of late Rev. Sidney Gillum, then Vicar of Kewstoke, Somerset; m. 1914, Beryl Mary Gordon Jones; one s.; one d.; educ. Horris Hill, Winchester; R.M.A., Woolwich; 2nd Lt., R.A., 23.12.03; Lt. 23.12.06; Capt. 30.10.14; Major 30.7.16; served Europ. War, 1914–16; Despatches twice; wounded twice; D.S.O. awarded for gallantry on 19.2.15.

GILMAN, F. (D.S.O. L.G. 4.6.17), Major, Can. Dns.

GILMORE, G. H. (D.S.O. L.G. 27.5.19), T/Capt. (A/Major), R. Sussex R., att. R. Scots; M.C.

GILMOUR, JOHN (D.S.O. L.G. 3.8.18), Lt. (T/Capt.), formerly Arg. and Suth. Highrs.

GILMOUR, JOHN, Jun. (D.S.O. L.G. 1.1.18) (Bar, L.G. 4.3.18) (Details, L.G. 16.8.18), Lt.-Col., Yeomanry; M.C.

GILSON, W. F. (D.S.O. L.G. 18.10.17) (Details, L.G. 7.3.18.) (Bar, L.G. 7.11.18) (2nd Bar, L.G. 1.2.19), Lt.-Col., 7th Bn. Can. Inf., Br. Columbia R.

W. W. Gillum.

GIMSON, E. C., M.B. (D.S.O. L.G. 19.8.16); b. 2.6.77; s. of William Gimson, of Witham, Essex, Physician and Surgeon; educ. Edinburgh University; M.B., Ch.B., Edinburgh; Lt., R.A.M.C., 10.10.14; Capt.; served Europ. War, 1914–18; Despatches; D.S.O. awarded for gallantry on 1st June, 1916, at Montauban.

GIPPS, A. G. P., F.R.C.S. (D.S.O. L.G. 6.9.18), T/Lt.-Col., R.A.M.C.

GIRDLESTONE, REV. F. S. P. L. (D.S.O. L.G. 4.6.17), T/Ch. to the Forces, 3rd Class, A. Chapl. Dept.

GIRDWOOD, A. C. (D.S.O. L.G. 27.9.01) (Bar, L.G. 18.6.17), Major (T/Lt.-Col.), North'd Fus., attd. Border R. (see the "Distinguished Service Order," from its institution to 31 Dec. 1915, same publishers).

GIRDWOOD, R. L. (D.S.O. L.G. 4.6.17), Lt.-Col., S. African Med. Corps, S. African Mil. Forces.

GIRVAN, J. P. (D.S.O. L.G. 1.2.19) (Bar, L.G. 8.3.19), (Details, L.G. 4.10.19); Major (A/Lt.-Col.), 15th Inf. Bn. 1st Cent. Ontario R.; M.C.

GLASCODINE, R. K. (D.S.O. L.G. 3.6.18), Lt., London R., seconded to French Mortar Battery; M.C.

GLASFURD, A. I. R. (D.S.O. L.G. 3.6.16); b. 4.12.70; s. of Major-Gen. C. L. R. Glasfurd; m. 1894, Mabel, d. of the Rev. E. Hignett; two s.; educ. Fettes College, Edinburgh; R.M.C., Sandhurst; 2nd Lt., N. Lan. R., 29.3.90; Lt., Ind. S.C., 17.6.91; Capt., Ind. Army, 29.3.01; Major 29.3.08; Lt.-Col. 29.3.16; Col. (T/Brig.-Gen.); served Europ. War; Despatches twice; C.M.G.

GLASGOW, A. E. (D.S.O. L.G. 3.6.16); b. 21.6.70; 2nd Lt., R. Suss. R., 4.3.91; Lt. 13.4.92; Adjt. 4.9.95–3.9.99; Capt. 22.3.99; Major 2.2.11; Bt. Lt.-Col. 3.6.17; Bt. Col.3.6.18; A/Lt.-Col. 18.4.19 to 9.7.19; Despatches; C.M.G.

GLASGOW, R. (D.S.O. L.G. 24.9.18), Capt., Aust. Infy.; M.C.

GLASIER, P. M. (D.S.O. L.G. 4.2.18) (Details, L.G. 5.7.18), Capt. (A/Lt.-Col.), London R. (Queen's Westminster Rifles). He was killed in action 2.6.18.

GLAZEBROOK, P. K. (D.S.O. L.G. 26.3.18) (Details, L.G. 24.8.18), Major, Yeom. He was killed in action 7.3.18.

GLEN, A. (D.S.O. L.G. 3.6.18), Major, R.E., 29.11.14; Despatches.

GLEN, G. C. (D.S.O. L.G. 2.7.17); b. 25.3.85; e. s. of late Reginald Cunningham Glen, Barrister-at-Law, M.A., LL.B., V.D., and Margaret Allan, d. of Francis Barrow, Barrister-at-Law, County Court Judge and Recorder of Rochester, Kent; m. 1914, May, d. of Alexander Bennett, of Plymouth; one s.; joined H.M.S. Britannia, 1900; Lt.-Com. 1914; served on Home, Mediterranean and Pacific Stations; served Europ. War, 1914–18; wounded while mine-sweeping, 1917; Despatches.

GLENCROSS, J. B. (D.S.O. L.G. 2.11.17), Lt.-Cdr., R.N.

GLENDENNING, S. E. (D.S.O. L.G. 1.1.18), T/Capt. (A/Major), R.E.

GLENDINNING, H. C. (D.S.O. L.G. 1.1.18), Major (T/Lt.-Col.), New Zea. Fld. Art.

GLENDINNING, H. J. (D.S.O. L.G. 3.6.19); b. 17.3.89; 2nd Lt., R.A., 23.12.09; Lt. 2.12.12; Capt. 23.12.15; Bt. Major 1.1.17; Despatches.

GLENNIE, E. A. (D.S.O. L.G. 25.8.17); b. 18.7.89; 2nd Lt., R.E., 23.7.10; Lt. 21.12.12; Capt. 23.7.16; Despatches.

GLOVER, G. DE C. (D.S.O. L.G. 3.6.18); b. 27.4.87; s. of Col. R. F. B. Glover, D.S.O.; m. 1918, Vera Phœbe, d. of Rev. T. M. Bell-Salter; one s.; educ. Cheltenham and Sandhurst; 2nd Lt., S. Staff. R., 29.8.06; Lt. 30.11.07; Adjt. 14.8.10 to 14.8.13; Capt. 1.11.14; Bt. Major 3.6.17; served Europ. War, 1914–18; Despatches six times; M.C.; 1914 Star; Portuguese Order of Aviz, 2nd Class; Italian Service Medal for Military Valour.

GLOVER, G. W. (D.S.O. L.G. 22.9.16), Lt., Rif. Brig.; D.S.O. awarded for gallantry on 1st July, 1916, south of Serre. He died of wounds 31.8.18.

GLOVER, H. J. H. (D.S.O. L.G. 1.1.18), Capt. (T/Major), F.A.

GLOVER, W. R. (D.S.O. L.G. 26.9.17) (Details, L.G. 9.1.18), Lt.-Col. London Regt.; served Europ. War, 1914–17; Despatches; C.M.G.

GLYN, SIR R. F., Bart. (D.S.O. L.G. 14.1.16); b. 13.5.75; s. of 3rd Bart. and Frances, d. of Major Fitzgerald, of Maperton House, Somerset; s. father, 1918; m. 1906, Edith Hilda, e. d. of W. G. Hamilton-Gordon; two s.; one d.; T/Capt. (R. of O., 1st Dns.), A.S.C.; served S. African War, 1899–1902; Europ. War, 1914–18; Despatches twice; Chevalier, Legion of Honour.

GLYNTON, G. M. (D.S.O. L.G. 1.1.19); b. 18.2.79; s. of late Charles Maxwell Glynton, of Bath; m. Irene Mary, d. of B. J. Hall, of Fieldend, Eastcote, Middlesex; educ. Bath College, Sandhurst; 2nd Lt., Unatt., 25.1.99; Ind. S.C. 16.4.00; Lt. Ind. Army, 25.4.01; Capt. 25.1.08; Major, 1.9.15; served Europ. War in Mesopotamia, Egypt and Palestine; Despatches.

GOATER, W. H. G. (D.S.O. L.G. 24.9.18); b. 17.1.94; 1st appointment, R.W. Kent R. 22.6.15; Lt. 27.12.16; Actg. Major 1.12.18 to 21.3.19; Despatches; M.C.

GOBLE, S. J. (D.S.O. L.G. 16.2.17), Fl.-Lt., R.N.A.S.; D.S.C.

GODBY, C. (D.S.O. L.G. 16.9.18); b. 31.10.63; m. 1895, G. H. S. Hamilton-Jones, of Moneyglas, co. Antrim; one s.; four d.; Lt., R.E., 10.10.82; Capt. 4.5.91; Major 24.1.00; Lt.-Col. 18.1.07 to 17.1.12; Colonel 19.7.11; Temp. Brig.-Gen. 12.4.15; Chief Engineer, 1915–19; served Sudan, 1885 (Medal, 2 clasps; Bronze Star); Sudan, 1889 (clasp, 4th Class Medjidie); Europ. War; C.B.; C.M.G.; Despatches.

GODDARD, C. J. (D.S.O. L.G. 4.6.17), Major, Commanding Supply Co., Aust. Mil. Forces.

GODDARD, G. H. (D.S.O. L.G. 4.6.17); b. 18.1.73; Lt., R.A.M.C., 28.1.99; Capt. 28.1.02; Major 28.7.10; Lt.-Col. 1.3.15; Despatches.

GODDARD, H. A. (D.S.O. L.G. 1.1.18); b. 1871; m. Maud, d. of late E. Marrow; Lt.-Col., Aust. Inf.; J.P.; served Europ. War, 1915–18; Despatches.

GODDARD, P. L. (D.S.O. L.G. 21.6.18), Lt.-Cdr. (A/Cdr.), R.N.

GODFREY, H. R. (D.S.O. L.G. 14.3.16); b. 11.10.75; 5th s. of late Lt.-Colonel C. J. Godfrey, Madras Staff Corps; m. 1911, Mary Caroline Pearl, 2nd d. of W. Barrett-Lennard, of Vancouver; one d.; educ. Stubbington House, Fareham; entered Britannia, 1890; Lieut., 1898; Comdr., 1910; Capt., 1915; Captain commanding a Destroyer Flotilla, Grand Fleet, since March, 1917; served in H.M.S. Daphne, in China during Boxer Rising (China Medal, 1900); served in H.M.S. Porpoise during operations against Mullah, 1903–4 (Somaliland Medal and clasp); served in H.M.S. Beagle, destroyer, during Dardanelles operations, 1914–15; Despatches; C.B.; Royal Humane Society Testimonial, 1903, for saving a man from drowning at Invergordon whilst in H.M.S. Anson.

GODFREY, W. (D.S.O. L.G. 4.6.17), T/Major (A/Lt.-Col.), Welsh Regt.; Despatches.

GODKIN, S. R., F.R.C.S.I. (D.S.O. L.G. 25.8.17); b. 29.8.78; 3rd s. of Samuel Godkin, of Sunrise, Wexford; m. 1919, Beatrice Emily, A.R.R.C., late T.F.N.S., d. of late Rev. Albert Seacome and Mrs. Seacome; one s.; educ. Royal College of Surgeons, Dublin; L. and L.M., R.C.P.I., L.M., R.C.S.I.; studied dentistry at the Dental Hospital, Dublin, 1904–5; held the appointment Specialist in Advanced Operative Surgery in the Poona, Secunderabad and Burma Divisions, 1910–15; Lt., Ind. Med. Serv., 28.6.00; Capt. 28.6.03; Major 28.12.11; Lt.-Col. 28.12.19; Commanding Officer, Indian Station Hospital, Multan; served in Mesopotamia, Feb. 1916, as Medical Officer, 64th Pioneers; appointed to the command of 57th Combined Stationary Hospital at Kurna, Mesopotamia, Aug. 1917; invalided from Mesopotamia, Jan. 1918.

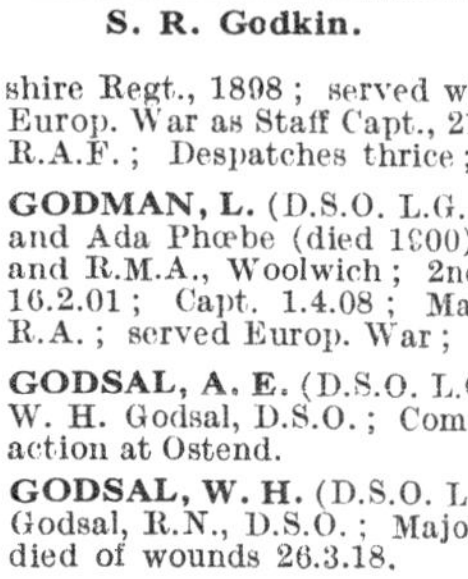

S. R. Godkin.

GODMAN, A. L. (D.S.O. L.G. 4.6.17); b. 1877; e. s. of Colonel A. F. Godman; m. 1908, Ivy Mary, d. of Col. R. Bayard, C.B.; one s.; one d.; educ. Rugby; joined Yorkshire Regt., 1898; served with M.I. in Somaliland Expedition, 1904–5; served Europ. War as Staff Capt., 21st Infantry Brigade, and later on Staff, R.F.C. and R.A.F.; Despatches thrice; C.M.G.

GODMAN, L. (D.S.O. L.G. 14.1.16); b. 4.9.80; y. s. of Colonel A. F. Godman and Ada Phœbe (died 1900), y. d. of Sir Lowthian Bell, Bart.; educ. Rugby, and R.M.A., Woolwich; 2nd Lt., R.A., 22.11.99; transferred to R.H.A.; Lt. 16.2.01; Capt. 1.4.08; Major 30.9.14; Lt.-Col. commanding 46th Brigade, R.A.; served Europ. War; Despatches thrice. He died of wounds 30.9.17.

GODSAL, A. E. (D.S.O. L.G. 23.7.18); s. of Major Godsal; bro. of late Major W. H. Godsal, D.S.O.; Comdr., R.N.; served Europ. War. He was killed in action at Ostend.

GODSAL, W. H. (D.S.O. L.G.3.6.18); s. of Major Godsal; bro. of late Comdr. Godsal, R.N., D.S.O.; Major, Durham Light Inf.; served Europ. War; M.C.; died of wounds 26.3.18.

The Distinguished Service Order 253

GODSELL, K. B. (D.S.O. L.G. 1.1.18); b. 12.5.93; s. of James U. Godsell, of Stratford Court, Stroud, Glos.; m. 1921, Freda Kate, d. of Frederick Fosdick; educ. Harrow; R.M.A., Woolwich; 2nd Lt., R.E., 20.12.12; Lt. 13.11.14; Capt. 3.11.17; Adjt. 5.11.18; Bt. Major 1.1.19; served Europ. War, 1914–18; wounded; Despatches, April, 1915; January, 1918; M.C.; Mons Star.

GODWIN, C. A. C. (D.S.O. L.G. 1.1.18) (Bar, L.G. 4.3.18) (Details, L.G. 16.8.18); b. 28.10.73; 2nd Lt. (Unatt.), Ind. S.C., 16.1.95; Lt., Ind. Army, 16.4.97; Capt. 16.1.04; Major 16.1.13; Bt. Lt.-Col. 3.1.16; Temp. Brig.-Gen. 30.9.17 to 4.2.20; Bt. Col. 3.6.18; Colonel 5.1.20; served Europ. War; C.M.G.

GOFF, R. S. (D.S.O. L.G. 8.3.18); b. 27.2.82; 2nd s. of late Lt.-Col. Trevor Goff; m. 1918, Vera Colville, widow of Colonel A. D. Geddes, The Buffs; entered H.M.S. Britannia, 1896; Midshipman, 1897; Sub-Lt., 1901; Lieut., 1903; Comdr., 1916.

GOFF T. C. (D.S.O. L.G. 3.6.19); b. 19.12.79; 2nd Lt., R.A. 22.11.99; Lt. 16.2.01; Capt. 2.6.06; Major 30.10.14; Despatches.

GOGARTY, H. E. (D.S.O. L.G. 26.11.17) (Details, L.G. 6.4.18); b. 4.4.68; 2nd Lt., R. Sc. Fus., 22.8.88; Lt. 12.1.92; Capt. 1.8.08; Bt. Major 29.11.00; Major, Worc. R., 24.10.08; Bt. Lt.-Col. 21.2.12; Col.; Zhob Valley Expedition, 1890; S. African War, 1899–1901 (Despatches; Queen's Medal, 6 clasps; King's Medal, 2 clasps); Europ. War, 1914–17; Despatches.

GOLD, C. R. (D.S.O. L.G. 18.7.17); o. s. of C. P. Gold, of Beaulieu, Cambridge Park, E. Twickenham; educ. Alleyn Court School, Westcliff-on-Sea; Uppingham; joined the 2nd Battery, H.A.C.; received a commission in the Yeomanry 20.11.15; promoted Captain; served in France (att. Durham L. Inf.). He was killed in action 21.11.17.

GOLD, E., F.R.S., M.A. (D.S.O. L.G. 14.1.16); b. 1881; s. of John Gold, of Lapworth, Warwickshire; m. 1907, Catherine L., d. of late John Harlow, of Edinburgh; one d.; educ. Coleshill Grammar School; Mason's College, Birmingham; St. John's College, Cambridge; Third Wrangler, 1903; Nat. Sci. Tripos, Part. II., 1904; Fellow of St. John's College, Cambridge, 1906; Schuster Reader in Dynamical Meteorology, 1907–10; discovered in 1908 a rational physical explanation of the Isothermal Condition of the Upper Atmosphere of Stratosphere; Supdt. of Statistics, Meteorological Office, London, 1910; Vice-President, Royal Meteorological Society, 1913–15; Asst. Director, Meteorological Office, Air Ministry, 1919; appointed Commandant, Meteorological Section, R.E., G.H.Q., B.E.F.; T/Capt., June, 1915; T/Major, Sept. 1915; T/Lt.-Col. March, 1918; served Europ. War, 1915–19; Despatches.

GOLDBERG, R. (D.S.O. L.G. 3.3.19), T/Capt., 6th Light Armoured Motor By. M.G.C. (Motor).

GOLDFRAP, H. W. (D.S.O. L.G. 23.10.19); b. 8.4.84; 2nd Lt., Unatt., 18.1.05; Ind. Army 8.3.06; Lt. 18.4.07; Capt. 18.1.14; Major 18.1.20; served Europ. War; Despatches; M.C.

GOLDIE, E. C. (D.S.O. L.G. 1.1.18), Major, Can. Engrs.

GOLDING, J. (D.S.O. L.G. 4.6.17), Capt., R.A.M.C.

GOLDSMITH, G. E. (D.S.O. L.G. 1.1.18); b. 15.3.83; 2nd Lt., Ches. R., 4.12.01; A.S.C. 1.10.03; Lt. 4.12.04; Capt. 2.8.11; Major, R.A.S.C., 1.4.15.

GOLDSMITH, H. D. (D.S.O. L.G. 3.3.16); b. 6.5.78; s. of H. St. B. Goldsmith, of Halfway House, near Guildford; m. Grave Apperley, y. d. of late Rev. F. C. Kinglake, of West Monkton, Somerset; educ. Felsted School; 2nd Lt., D. of Corn. L. Inf., 8.9.97; Lt. 21.5.99; Capt. 30.4.04; Bt. Major 3.6.15; Major 1.9.15; Bt. Lt.-Col. 1.1.17; served Tirah Expedition, 1897–98 (Medal, 2 clasps); Egyptian Army, 1904–6; Staff College, 1911–12; Europ. War, 1914–18; Despatches.

GOLDSMITH, M. L. (D.S.O. L.G. 4.6.17) (Bar, L.G. 12.12.19); s. of the late J. P. Goldsmith, a former Mayor of Devonport; Capt., R.N.

GOLDTHORP, R. H. (D.S.O. L.G. 1.2.19); e. s. of the late Guy Goldthorp; Capt. (A/Lt.-Col.), 4th Bn., att. 2/10th Bn., W. Riding R., Temp. att. 1/28th London Regt.

GOLLAN, H. R. (D.S.O. L.G. 3.6.19), Capt., 56th Bn. Aust. Inf.; M.C.

GOOCH, H. (D.S.O. L.G. 15.2.19) (Details, L.G. 30.7.19); b. 7.12.83; Lt. 21.9.16; T/Major, 121st Field Co., R.E.; Despatches; M.C.

GOODALL, T. (D.S.O. L.G. 4.2.18) (Details, L.G. 5.7.18), Lt. (A/Capt.), W. Riding R.

GOODE, H. K. (D.S.O. L.G. 8.2.19), 2nd Lt. (A/Capt.), R.A.F.; D.F.C.

GOODERSON, V. E. (D.S.O. L.G. 1.1.17) (Bar, L.G. 26.7.18), T/Maj., High. Light Inf.

GOODEVE, L. C. (D.S.O. L.G. 14.1.16), Major, 1st Batty. Canadian Arty.

GOODHART, F. H. H. (D.S.O. L.G. 31.5.16); b. 10.7.74; s. of the Vicar of St. Barnabas, Sheffield, later 23 years Rector of Lambourne, Essex; m. 1912, Isabella Turner; two d.; educ. Chigwell Grammar School; H.M.S. Britannia; Lieut., 1905; Comdr., 1915; served in H.M.S. Ramillies, 1900–3; H.M.S. Magnificent and Agamemnon, 1910–11; H.M.S. Maidstone; commanded Submarine E8, Aug. 1914; served Europ. War; Despatches; Order of Vladimir, 4th Class; Order of St. George, 4th Class; Legion of Honour (Chevalier). He was accidentally drowned 31.1.17. (The Insignia were presented to the widow by C.-in-C., Portsmouth.)

GOODLAND, H. T. (D.S.O. L.G. 11.1.19), T/Major (A/Lt.-Col.), R. Berks. R.

GOODMAN, G. D. (D.S.O. L.G. 2.12.18); b. 14.10.68; e. s. of Thomas Davenport Goodman and Emily Jane, d. of Andrew Jukes Worthington, of Leek; m. 1901, Elizabeth Jane Cleland, e. d. of late Major Herbert Buchanan; two s.; two d.; educ. Manchester Grammar School; commanded 6th Batt. Sherwood Foresters, 1914–16, and, 1916–19, the 52nd and 21st Infantry Brigades; T/Brig.-Gen.; served S. African War, 1901; Europ. War, 1915–19; C.M.G.; D.L., co. Derby.

GOODMAN, H. R. (D.S.O. L.G. 17.9.17); b. 18.8.75; e. s. of late J. F. Goodman; 2nd Lt., R. Ir. Rif., 7.3.00; Lt. 28.5.03; Adjt. 1.1.07 to 31.12.09; Capt. 28.6.08; Major 1.9.15; served S. African War, att. A.S.C., 1899–1902 (slightly wounded; Queen's Medal, 4 clasps; King's Medal, 2 clasps); Europ. War, 1914; Despatches.

GOODWIN, F. R. (D.S.O. L.G. 29.8.17), Engr. Cdr., R.N.

GOODWIN, G. J. P. (D.S.O. L.G. 3.6.18); b. 24.2.77; 2nd Lt., R.E., 21.9.96; Lt. 21.9.99; Capt. 21.9.05; Major 30.10.14; Bt. Lt.-Col. 3.6.19; Despatches.

GOODWIN, H. (D.S.O. L.G. 4.6.17); b. 13.8.77; 2nd Lt., Middlesex R., 24.7.01; Lt. 7.4.03; Capt. 21.1.11; Major 24.7.16; Bt. Lt.-Col. 1.1.19; Despatches; Croix de Guerre.

GOODWIN, W. R. (D.S.O. L.G. 1.1.18) (Bar, L.G. 1.2.19), Temp. Lt.-Col., R. Irish Rif.

GOODWIN, W. R. P. (D.S.O. L.G. 1.1.17); b. 25.5.75; 3rd s. of Surgeon-Major John Goodwin, late Army Medical Staff, and Marion Agnes Goodwin; m. 1907, Myrtle, y. d. of Elton Forrest, Indian Forest Service; educ. Newton College, Devon; St. Mary's Hospital, London; Lt. R.A.M.C., 26.11.00; Capt. 29.11.03; Major 29.5.12; Lt.-Col. 27.1.18; Bt. Col. 3.6.19; Europ. War; Despatches.

GOOLDEN, C. (D.S.O. L.G. 1.1.19), Lt.-Cdr. (A/Cdr.), R.N.

GORDON, A. (D.S.O. L.G. 17.5.18), Lt.-Cdr., R.N.

GORDON, A. D. (D.S.O. L.G. 3.6.19); b. 1.11.89; 2nd Lt., R. Berks R., 18.9.09; Lt. 22.6.11; Capt. 10.5.15; A/Lt.-Col., M.G.C., 4.12.16 to 10.1.17 and 24.9.18 to 23.3.19; M.C.; Despatches.

GORDON, A. DE R. (D.S.O. L.G. 3.6.18), T/Capt. (Local Major), Spec. List att. Camel Corps.

GORDON, A. F. L. (D.S.O. L.G. 12.12.19), Capt. (T/Lt.-Col.), Irish Gds.; M.C.

GORDON, REV. A. MacL. (D.S.O. L.G. 2.12.18), Can. Chapl. Service, att. 4th Can. Div.; M.C.

GORDON, A. R. G. (D.S.O. L.G. 1.1.18); b. 28.7.82; 2nd Lt., R. Ir. Regt., 8.5.01; Lt. 29.1.04; Capt. 3.8.09; Adjt. 1.10.09 to 30.9.12; Major 8.5.16; Bt. Lt.-Col. 3.6.19; Despatches.

GORDON, B. A. (D.S.O. L.G. 3.6.19), Major, 11th Bn. Can. Engrs.

GORDON, B. G. R. (D.S.O. L.G. 3.6.16); b. 7.11.80; 2nd Lt., R. War. R., 20.1.00; Lt. 4.8.00; Capt. 18.1.08; Capt., Gordon Highrs., 20.5.08; Major, (T/Lt.-Col.), Gordon Highrs.; Despatches; served S. African War, 1902 (Queen's Medal, clasp); N.W. Frontier of India, 1908 (Medal, clasp); Europ. War; Despatches. He was killed in action 20.7.16.

GORDON, LORD D. G. (D.S.O. L.G. 26.9.17) (Details, L.G. 9.1.18); b. 6.5.83; 2nd s. of 1st Marquis of Aberdeen; m. 1907; Cécile Elizabeth, d. of late George Drummond, of Swaylands, Penshurst, Kent; four s.; one d.; educ. Harrow; served apprenticeship in Hall, Russell Co.'s Shipbuilding Yard, at Aberdeen, and afterwards to W. H. Allen, Son and Co., Engineers, of Bedford; Managing Director of J. and E. Hall, Engineers, of Dartford; Captain, 2nd V.B. Gordon Highrs., 1902–5; served Europ. War, 1914–18.

GORDON, D. H. (D.S.O. L.G. 17.3.17) (Details, L.G. 17.4.17); b. 27.1.95; 2nd Lt. (Unatt.) 14.1.14; Ind. Army 11.10.14; Lt. 1.9.15; Capt. 14.1.18; served Europ. War; Despatches.

GORDON, E. B. (D.S.O. L.G. 3.6.16); b. 6.10.77; s. of late Charles William Gordon, of Wincombe Park, Shaftesbury; m. Martha Florence, d. of late Dr. Wheldon, of Mauritius; educ. Stubbington House, Fareham; 2nd Lt., North'd Fus., 5.5.00; Lt. 18.6.01; Adjt. 1.10.06; Capt. 22.8.07; Bt. Major 18.2.15; Major 1.9.15; Bt. Lt.-Col. 1.1.17; served S. African War, 1900–2 (Queen's Medal, 3 clasps; King's Medal, 2 clasps); N.W. Frontier of India, 1907–8 (Medal, clasp); Europ. War, 1914–18; Despatches five times; C.M.G.

GORDON, E. H. H. (D.S.O. L.G. 3.6.16); b. 8.11.61; s. of Major-General G. H. Gordon, R.E.; educ. Wellington College; Sandhurst; rejoined his old regiment 1914, 9th S. Batt. Gordon Highrs., and was Lt.-Col. commanding; served in Egyptian Campaign, 1884–85 (Medal), and in the Sudan (Medal); Europ. War; Despatches.

GORDON, F. L. R. (D.S.O. L.G. 1.1.17), T/Lt.-Col., R. Ir. Rifles.

GORDON, G. C. D. (D.S.O. L.G. 1.1.18); b. 28.4.83; s. of Lord Granville Armyne Gordon (d. 1907) and Charlotte D'Olier (d. 1900), d. of Henry Roe; n. and heir-pres. of 11th Marquess of Huntly; m. 1907, Violet Ida, o. c. of Gerard and Ida Streatfield; four s.; educ. Eton; 1st commission 14.9.01; Capt. 8.6.12; retired S. Gds. 18.1.13; Lt.-Col., Welsh Gds.; served S. African War, 1901–2; Queen's Medal, 5 clasps; Europ. War, 1914–18; Despatches; Croix de Guerre.

GORDON, G. G. S. (D.S.O. L.G. 1.1.17), Major, Aust. Engrs.

GORDON, G. H. (D.S.O. L.G. 1.1.18); b. 29.3.75; 2nd Lt., R.A., 2.11.95; Lt. 2.11.98; Capt. 2.11.01; Adjt. 8.1.08 to 13.10.10; Major 23.4.12; Lt.-Col., R.F.A.; Despatches.

GORDON, H. D. L. (D.S.O. L.G. 1.1.17); b. 1873; s. of W. H. Lockhart Gordon, Barrister-at-Law; m. Kathleen H., d. of Hon. Sir Walter P. G. Cassels, Chief Justice, Exchequer Court, Ottawa; three s.; two d.; educ. Upper Canada College, Toronto; Royal Military College, Kingston; Lt. (Res. of Off.), Canadian Militia, 1894; Lt. 9th Mississanga Horse, 1901; Capt. 1902; Major, 1904; Lt.-Col. and to command Regt., 1913; reverted to rank of Major to come overseas, and appointed to command A Squadron, 4th C.M.R.R., 13.11.14; appointed Second-in-Command, June, 1915; Lt.-Col. and to command Batt. 7.6.16; served Europ. War; Despatches.

GORDON, H. W. (D.S.O. L.G. 1.1.17); b. 5.2.71; 2nd Lt., R.E., 14.2.90; Lt. 14.2.93; Capt. 14.2.01; Major 14.2.10; Bt. Lt.-Col. 1.1.18; Lt.-Col. 3.4.18; Bt. Col. 1.1.19; Colonel 1.12.21; served S. African War, 1900–2; Queen's Medal, 2 clasps; King's Medal, 2 clasps; Europ. War; Despatches.

GORDON, J. K. (D.S.O. L.G. 11.1.19); b. 31.3.83; 2nd Lt., R.A., 21.12.01; Lieut. 21.12.04; Capt. 30.10.14; Major 27.1.16; Despatches.

GORDON, REGINALD CLEGG (gazetted as Richard Glegg Gordon) (D.S.O. L.G. 1.1.18), Major, Lowland R.G.A. He was killed in action 26.3.18.

GORDON, WILLIAM (D.S.O. L.G. 3.6.19); appointed Adjutant of the 5th (Buchan and Formartine) Battalion Gordon Highlanders. Captain Gordon saw much active service, and rose from the ranks to be Acting Lieutenant-Colonel. He was in charge of the cadre of the 2nd Battalion, Gordon Highlanders on its return home from Italy; served Europ. War; Despatches; M.C.

GORDON, WILLIAM (D.S.O. L.G. 1.1.18); b. 15.7.83; 2nd Lt., R.A., 24.12.02; Lt. 24.12.05; Capt. 30.10.14; Major 9.6.17; Despatches.

GORDON, W. A. (D.S.O. L.G. 2.2.16); b. 9.5.69; s. of Gen. G. H. Gordon, R.E., and Mrs. Gordon; educ. Trinity College, Oxford; late Private Secretary to Governor Cape of Good Hope. He joined the Worcestershire Militia in 1897; Major, 6th Batt. Worcs. Regt. (Res. of Off.); Lt.-Col., March, 1916; Colonel, 1917; Commandant of Amara, Mesopotamia, 1917; served S. African War; Queen's Medal and King's Medal; Europ. War, 1914–19, in Gallipoli and Mesopotamia; C.M.G.; C.I.E.; Despatches.

GORDON, W. F. L. (D.S.O. L.G. 4.6.17); b. 28.5.72; 2nd Lt., Norfolk Regt., 1.7.93; Lt. 5.8.96; Adjt. 20.8.99 to 2.2.01; Capt. 16.2.01; Major 1.9.12; Bt. Lt.-Col. 3.6.16; Lt.-Col. 10.1.18; Europ. War; Despatches; C.M.G.

GORDON-GRAY, G. (D.S.O. L.G. 27.7.18), Capt., S. African Field Ambulance; M.C.

GORDON-HALL, G. C. W. (D.S.O. L.G. 14.1.16); b. 30.4.75; s. of the late Surgeon F. W. Gordon-Hall, Bengal Staff Corps; m. 1901, Ruth, d. of late John Meeson; one d.; educ. privately; R.M.C., Sandhurst; 2nd Lt., Yorks. L. Inf., 10.10.94; Lt. 22.5.98; Capt. 9.6.00; Major 1.9.14; Bt. Lt.-Col. 3.6.17; retired pay, 1921; served N.W. Frontier, India, 1898 (severely wounded; Medal, 2 clasps); S. African War, 1899–1900 (severely wounded; Despatches, L.G. 10.9.01; Queen's Medal, 2 clasps); Europ. War, 1914–18; Despatches five times; C.M.G., 1918.

GORDON-KIDD, A. L. (D.S.O. L.G. 19.8.16), Lt. (T/Capt.), 4th Dr. Gds., att. R.F.C.; died of wounds 27.8.17. His D.S.O. was awarded for gallantry south of Aubigny-au-Bac 1.7.16.

GORDON-LENNOX, LORD E. C. (D.S.O. L.G. 1.1.18); b. 10.2.75; 2nd s. of 7th Duke of Richmond; m. 1909, Hon. Hermione Frances Caroline Fellowes, d. of 2nd Baron de Ramsay; one s.; 2nd Lt., S. Gds., 16.12.96; Lt. 13.4.98; Capt. 3.12.02; Major 25.4.10; Bt. Lt.-Col., 1917; Colonel, S. Gds.; Brig-Gen., 1916; served S. Africa, 1900–2, on Staff (Queen's Medal, 3 clasps; King's Medal, 2 clasps); West Africa, 1903 (Medal and clasp); M.V.O., 1907; European War, 1914–18 (wounded Ypres, 1914; 2nd time, 1918); Italian Order of St. Maurice and St. Lazarus, 1918; C.M.G.

GORE-BROWNE, E. (D.S.O. L.G. 1.1.18); b. 2.10.85; m. 1912, Mary Imogen, d. of late Rt. Hon. Charles Booth, of Gracedieu Manor, Whitwick, Leicestershire; two s.; two d.; educ. Malvern; Worcester College, Oxford; Barrister-at-Law; Secretary of Glyn, Mills, Currie and Co., since 1919; Capt. and Bt. Major, London Regt.; served Europ. War, 1914–18; Despatches; Croix de Guerre.

GORE, A. F. G. PERY-KNOX- (see Pery-Knox-Gore, A. F. G.).

GORE, I. C. PERY-KNOX- (see Pery-Knox-Gore, I. C.).

GORE-BROWNE, S. (D.S.O. L.G. 1.1.17); b. 3.5.83; e. s. of Frank Gore-Browne; educ. Harrow; R.M.A., Woolwich; on Belgian-Anglo Boundary Commission, 1909–11; 2nd Lt., R.A., 21.12.01; Lt. 21.12.04; Capt. 30.10.14; Bt. Lt.-Col.; served Europ. War, 1914–18; Despatches.

GORE-LANGTON, THE HON. E. A. G. TEMPLE- (see Temple-Gore-Langton-, The Hon. E. A. G.).

GORE-LANGTON, G. W. (D.S.O. L.G. 3.6.19); b. 23.8.85; 2nd Lt., 18th Hrs., 2.2.07; Lt., 18th Hrs., 24.12.08; resd. 10.8.10; Lt. (S.R.) 27.10.14; Capt. 14.5.15; Adjt. 19.6.15 to 17.5.16; Despatches; M.C.

GORE-LANGTON, H. E. (D.S.O. L.G. 20.9.18), Comdr., R.N.

GORELL, LORD (D.S.O. L.G. 14.11.16); b. 21.1.82; e. s. of 1st Baron and Mary Humpston, d. of T. Mitchell, of West Arthurlie; s. father, 1913; educ. Winchester; Trinity College, Oxford; Harvard University; Barrister, 1906; Secretary to the President of the Probate, Divorce, and Admiralty Division of the High Court of Justice, 1906–10; to County Courts Committee, 1908–9; to Royal Commission on Divorce and Matrimonial Causes, 1909–1912; Chairman, Kensington Division Red Cross Society; Capt. 18th Battery, 7th London Brigade, R.F.A. (T.F.); T/Major; served Europ. War. He died of wounds 16.1.17.

GORING, C. H. (D.S.O. L.G. 28.10.20); b. 16.2.86; 2nd Lt., R. Fus., 19.11.15; M.G.C. 26.2.16 to 31.12.20; Lieut. 1.7.17; Tank Corps 1.1.21; Despatches; M.C.

GORING-JONES, M. D. (D.S.O. L.G. 1.1.18); entered the Army, 1886; commanded a brigade; Lt.-Col. (T/Brig.-Gen.), Dur. L. Inf.; served Europ. War; C.M.G.

GORSSLINE, R. M. (D.S.O. L.G. 4.6.17), Major, Can. A.M.C.

GORT (J. S. S. P.), VISCOUNT (D.S.O. L.G. 4.6.17) (1st Bar, L.G. 26.9.17) (Details, L.G. 9.1.18) (2nd Bar, L.G. 11.1.19); V.C.; M.V.O.; M.C. (see "The "Victoria Cross," by same publishers).

GOSCHEN, A. A. (D.S.O. L.G. 27.9.01) (1st Bar, L.G. 26.9.16) (2nd Bar, L.G. 26.7.18) (see "The Distinguished Service Order," from its institution to 31.12.15, by same publishers).

GOSLING, S. F. (D.S.O. L.G. 4.6.17); b. 5.9.71; 3rd s. of late Robert Gosling, M.F.H., Essex; late Capt., Essex Imperial Yeomanry, and Lt.-Col. R.F.A.

GOSSAGE, E. L. (D.S.O. L.G. 3.6.19); b. 3.2.91; er. s. of Lt.-Col. E. F. Gossage, of Winwood, Budleigh Salterton, Devon; m. 1917, Eileen Gladys, d. of Brig.-Gen. E. O'Brien; two s.; educ. Rugby School; Trinity College, Cambridge; 2nd Lt., R.F.A., 1912; proceeded to France with XXVth Brigade R.F.A.; seconded for service with R.F.C. 12.5.15; Fl.-Cdr. and T/Capt. 5.9.15; Sq.-Cdr. and T/Major 1.6.16; Wing Cdr. and T/Lt.-Col. 5.12.17; granted a permanent commission in R.A.F.; Sq.-Leader 1.8.19; Wing-Cdr., 1921; served Europ. War; Despatches four times; M.C.

GOSTLING, E. V., M.A., M.R.C.S., L.R.C.P.Lond. (D.S.O. L.G. 2.5.16); b. 6.4.72; m. 1917, Joan Edith, d. of Rev. C. Wilton, of Beverley, Yorks; one s.; educ. Cambridge; St. Thomas's Hospital; late House Physician, Royal Infirmary, Derby, and Senior House Surgeon, Addenbrooke's Hospital, Cambridge; Lt.-Col., R.A.M.C. (T.F.); late A.D.M.S., East Anglian Div., T.A., 1920; Europ. War, 1914–16.

GOTLEY, G. R. HENNIKER- (see Henniker-Gotley, G. R.).

GOTTO, C. H. (D.S.O. L.G. 3.6.19); b. 29.12.86; 2nd Lt. (S.R.), Devon R., 27.5.11; Lt. 19.12.14; Adjt. 20.8.15 to 26.5.16; Capt. 25.8.16; Adjt. 10.10.20; M.C.; Despatches.

GOUDGE, REV. T. S. (D.S.O. L.G. 1.1.18), Ch. to the Forces, 2nd Class; T/Ch. to the Forces, Army Chaplains' Dept.

GOUGH, H. F. (D.S.O. L.G. 26.9.17) (Details, L.G. 9.1.18), 2nd Lt., N. Staffs. Regt. He was killed in action 21.9.17.

GOUGH, R. I. (D.S.O. L.G. 22.9.16); commissioned early in the war; T/Capt., Nov. 1915, R. War. R. He died of wounds 14.10.16.

GOULD, A. E. (D.S.O. L.G. 1.1.18), 2nd Lt. (A/Major), R.E.; M.C.

GOULD, G. (D.S.O. L.G. 3.6.18), Major, Ind. Cav.

GOURLAY, C. A., M.A., M.D. (D.S.O. L.G. 7.2.18); s. of late John Gourlay, C.A., of Thomson, Jackson, Gourlay and Taylor C.A., Glasgow, and Mrs. Gourlay; m. 1908, Elsie, d. of late James Copeland, Civil Engineer, of Glasgow; educ. Kelvinside Academy, Glasgow; Glasgow University; M.B., Ch.B., 1900; entered Indian Medical Service, 1902; appointed to Civil Medical Dept., Bengal, 1905; recalled to military duty, Aug. 1914; returned to Civil Medical Dept.; Lt., Ind. Med. Serv., 26.7.02; Capt. 26.7.05; Major 26.1.14; A/Lt.-Col., Ind. Med. Serv,. 12.9.16 to 24.3.19.

GOURLAY, K. I. (D.S.O. L.G. 3.6.19); b. 24.7.91; 2nd Lt., R.E., 20.7.11; Lt. 23.8.13; Capt. 26.6.17; A/Major 11.7.18 to 24.9.19; Despatches; M.C.

GOURLIE, J. (D.S.O. L.G. 3.6.19), Major, 38th Central India Horse, I.A.

GOVER, C. R. (D.S.O. L.G. 1.1.17); b. 6.3.81; 2nd Lt., R.A., 12.12.00; Lt. 19.12.03; Capt. 4.1.13; Adjt., R.A., 4.4.15 to 14.11.15; Major 8.7.15; A/Lt.-Col. 11.2.18 to 9.6.18; Despatches.

GOVER, J. M., M.B. (D.S.O. L.G. 1.1.18), Major (A/Lt.-Col.), R.A.M.C.

GOW, A. (D.S.O. L.G. 14.11.16), T/Capt., Cam. Highrs. His D.S.O. was awarded for gallantry on 15.9.16 at Martinpuich.

GOW, P. F., M.B. (D.S.O. L.G. 24.6.16) (Details, L.G. 27.7.16); b. 28.6.85; s. of James C. Gow, of Oakbank, Maryfield, Dundee; educ. University College, Dundee; St. Andrews University (M.A., 1905; M.B., Ch.B., 1909; D.P.H., 1910); Lt., Ind. Med. Serv., 27.1.12; served with 16th and 17th Cavalry; appointed Specialist in Prevention of Disease, Allahabad and Fyzabad Brigades, 1913; proceeded with Indian Exp. Force A to France, Sept. 1914; Capt. 27.1.15; joined Indian Exp. Force D in Mesopotamia, Jan. 1916; Special Infectious Diseases Officer on Staff, May to July 1916; Staff-Surgeon, H.Q., 1st Indian Army Corps, Mesopotamia, July, 1916; Despatches twice.

GOW, R. W. (D.S.O. L.G. 2.11.17); only s. of Mr. and Mrs. Gow, of Hoylake, Cheshire; m. Gladys, y. d. of Mr. and Mrs. William Hodgson, of Westwood Hall, Beverley; Observation Lieut., R.N.A.S.; served Europ. War; D.S.C.; Croix de Guerre.

GOWER, P. LEVESON- (see Leveson-Gower, P.).

GOWER, THE HON. W. S. LEVESON- (see Leveson-Gower, the Hon. W. S.).

GOWLLAND, E. L., M.B. (D.S.O. L.G. 4.6.17); b. 14.12.76; s. of late Richard Sankey Gowlland, Chief Secretary, H.M. Office of Works; m. Mary Florence Alexander; twin s.; educ. Christ's Hospital; St. Mary's Hospital; in general practice at Faversham, Kent, 1901–14; Major, R.G.A. (T.F.), commanding the Kent Heavy Battery and Ammunition Column, 1909–15; Member Territorial Association for Kent; Surgical Deputy Commissioner for Medical Services, London Region, Ministry of Pensions; Temporary commission R.A.M.C. 1.2.15.

GRACEY, G. F. H. (D.S.O. L.G. 12.12.19), T/Capt., Spec. List.

GRACEY, R. LL., M.A.Cantab., A.M.I.C.E. (D.S.O. L.G. 26.7.18); b. 15.5.92; s. of R. Gracey and the late Edith Georgina, d. of the late H. C. Lloyd, J.P.; educ. Clifton College; Trinity College, Cambridge (Prizeman); Major, R.E.; served Europ. War, 1914–18; Despatches; White Eagle of Serbia (5th Class, with Swords).

GRAEME, J. A. (D.S.O. L.G. 1.1.17) (Bar, L.G. 1.2.19); b. 2.6.83; e. s. of Col. Frederick James Graeme, late R.A., and Florence Augusta, 2nd d. of Col. W. Bell, C.B.; m. Muriel Beatrice, d. of Dr. Ernest L. Robinson; three s.; educ. Elizabeth College, Guernsey; R.M.A., Woolwich; 2nd Lt., R.E., 1901; Lt. 3.8.04; Capt. 21.12.12; Major 21.12.16; A/Lt.-Col. 9.8.17 to 18.3.19; served Europ. War, 1914–17; Despatches.

GRAHAM, C. (D.S.O. L.G. 29.10.18); b. 5.9.81; 2nd Lt., North'n R., 18.4.00; Lieut. 30.3.03; Capt. 21.8.09; Major 1.9.15; Despatches.

GRAHAM, C. J. (D.S.O. L.G. 11.1.19); b. 28.11.85; s. of J. Graham; m. Winifred Scott, d of J. A. Fairweather; two s.; educ. Clifton College; enlisted in Inns of Court O.T.C., Sept. 1915; 2nd Lt., 4th London R., June, 1916; Captain; fought in France and Flanders from 1916; demobilized, June, 1919; M.C. and Bar; Despatches.

GRAHAM, C. M. R. (D.S.O. L.G. 11.1.19), Major, 18th Battn. Can. Inf.

C. W. Graham.

GRAHAM C. W. (D.S.O. L.G. 24.2.16); b. 12.11.93; son of Charles Knott Graham and Helena Reutt; educ. Merchant Taylors' School. In 1913 he won the private owners' prize and gold medal in the Warwickshire Club's 100-Mile Open Motor Cycle Event; he was at Stuttgart when war broke out, but got home via Switzerland; he took up aviation at Hendon, and taught himself to fly, creating records (see "Flight," April, 1915); commissioned in the R.N.A.S. 12.4.15, and was one of the pioneer pilot scouts at Dunkerque of No. 1 Wing, R.N.A.S., from May, 1915. On 14.12.15, as Pilot of a small land machine, he (with Flight Sub-Lieut Ince) fought and destroyed a large German seaplane off La Panne, Belgium; he fell in the sea upside down, strapped in his machine, and managed not only to extricate himself but also to rescue Ince from drowning; promoted Lieut. 1.1.16; was very dangerously injured at Dunkerque 8.2.16; he was the first Pilot to get himself out of a spinning nose dive (see "In the Royal Naval Air Service," by Harold Rosher). At the age of 23 was accidentally killed on sea patrol duty by bomb explosions off Yarmouth 8.9.16.

Lord D. M. Graham.

GRAHAM, LORD DOUGLAS MALISE (D.S.O. L.G. 4.6.17); b. 14.10.83; 2nd s. of 5th Duke and Duchess of Montrose; m. Hon. Rachael Mary Holland, y. d. of Viscount Knutsford; one s.; educ. Wixenford; Cheltenham, and R.M.A., Woolwich; 2nd Lt., R.A., 21.12.01; Lt. 21.12.04; Capt. 30.10.14; A.D.C. to Gen. Sir Charles Fergusson, 1914; Major 22.1.16; Bt. Lt.-Col. 3.6.19; served Europ. War, 1914–18, taking part in the Battle of Mons; Despatches six times; M.C.

GRAHAM, REV. E. E. (D.S.O. L.G. 1.2.19), Can. Chapl. Service, attached 13th Bn. Can. Inf., Quebec Regt.; M.C.

GRAHAM, F. R. W. (D.S.O. L.G. 8.3.19) (Details, L.G. 4.10.19); b. 26.10.84; 2nd Lt., R. Ir. Rif., 29.10.05; Lt. 5.12.07; Capt. 20.12.14; Bt. Lt.-Col. 3.6.17; A/Lt.-Col., 6th Bn. R. Ir. Rif., 7.10.17 to 11.10.17; A/Lt.-Col., 6 Bn. Leins. R., 24.12.17 to 22.1.18; T/Lt.-Col., 10th Bn. London Regt., 9.7.18 to 15.12.19; Local Lt.-Col. 2.2.22; Despatches; M.C.

GRAHAM, G. (D.S.O. L.G. 1.2.19); b. 27.10.88; s. of Herbert Clement and Annie Graham; educ. Brandon; 2nd Lt. 15.1.15, 10th Batt. Alberta Regt., Canadian Inf.; served Europ. War (wounded in the final advance at Cambrai 27.9.18, and rejoined his regiment only two days before the Armistice). He was in the march to the Rhine 15.11 to 13.12.1918, and was then at the Cologne Bridgehead till 15.1.19; Despatches.

GRAHAM, H. B., M.B. (D.S.O. L.G. 18.1.18) (Details, L.G. 25.4.18), T/Capt., R.A.M.C.

GRAHAM, J. M. A. (D.S.O. L.G. 27.9.01) (Bar, L.G. 1.1.18) (see "The Distinguished Service Order," from its institution to 31.12.15, by same publishers).

GRAHAM, MALISE (D.S.O. L.G. 1.1.18); b. 12.2.84; 2nd s. of Sir R. Graham, 8th Bart.; m. Cecil Lorna, d. of Col. H. G. Barclay; one s.; 2nd Lt., 16th Lrs., 10.10.03; Lt. 23.5.07; Adjt., 16th Lrs., 27.1.09 to 25.1.12; Capt. 10.10.14; Bt. Major 3.6.18; Bt. Lt.-Col. 19.8.20; served Europ. War, 1914–18; G.S.O.1, 1917–19; Despatches five times.

GRAHAM, O. B. (D.S.O. L.G. 4.6.17); b. 8.7.91; s. of O. B. Graham; m. Winifred M. B., d. of Rev. Canon Harford, of Ripon Cathedral; educ. Harrow (Cricket XI.); Trinity College, Oxford; 2nd Lt., Rif. Brig., 19.1.12; Lt. 5.8.14; Capt. 15.9.15; Adjt. 2.9.19; served Europ. War (France), 1914–19; Despatches.

GRAHAM, R. (D.S.O. L.G. 17.11.17); m. Phyllis (Nancy), d. of H. E. Farmer, of Rushall Hall, Walsall; Major, R.A.F.; served Europ. War, 1914–17; Despatches; D.S.C.; D.F.C.; Order of Crown of Belgium.

GRAHAM, R. C. D. (D.S.O. L.G. 1.1.18); b. 14.7.81; 2nd Lt., R.A., 2.5.00; Lt. 3.4.01; Capt. 1.2.13; Major 30.12.15; A/Lt.-Col. 30.10.18 to 9.11.18; Despatches.

The Distinguished Service Order

GRAHAM, SIR R. G., 9th Bart. (D.S.O. L.G. 4.6.17); b. 28.5.78; e. s. of Sir R. H. Graham, 8th Bart (who died in 1920), and Annie Mary (who died in 1917), d. of late T. Shiffner, of Westergate House, Sussex; m. Katharine Noel, d. of F. Stobart; three s.; educ. Eton College; served with 1st Batt. R.B. South Africa, 1899–1902 (severely wounded at Colenso); Queen's Medal, 5 clasps; King's Medal, 2 clasps; Europ. War, 1914–18.

GRAHAM-WATSON, C. B. (D.S.O. L.G. 8.3.20), Lt., R.N.

GRANET, G. E. A. (D.S.O. L.G. 3.6.18); b. 21.9.87; 2nd Lt., R.A., 23.7.07; Lt. 23.7.10; Capt. 30.10.14; Major 10.8.17; Despatches; M.C.

GRANGE, G. R. (D.S.O. L.G. 4.6.17); e. s. of W. D'Oyly Grange, M.D., of 3, Clarence Drive, Harrogate; m. Hope, widow of Ronald Travis Townsend, and y. d. of C. J. MacLean; Capt. (T/Major), R.E.; M.C.

GRANT, A. (D.S.O. L.G. 4.2.18) (Details, L.G. 18.7.18); e. s. of Andrew Grant, of Tomnahurich Lodge, Inverness; educ. The High School, Inverness; his brother, Hugh Mackintosh Grant, Royal Scots, was killed in action at the Dardanelles; Major, Can. Inf.; served S. African War, with the Lovat's Scouts; Europ. War; Despatches. He was killed in action.

GRANT, A. K. (D.S.O. L.G. 3.6.16); b. 23.4.81; 2nd Lt., R. West Kent R., 7.3.00; Lt. 25.10.01; Capt. 23.1.05; Adjt. 14.8.09 to 13.8.12; Major 1.9.15; Bt. Lt.-Col. 3.6.19; served S. African War, 1899–1902; Despatches (L.G. 27.7.02); Queen's Medal, 3 clasps; King's Medal, 2 clasps; Europ. War; Despatches.

GRANT, D. H. F. (D.S.O. L.G. 3.6.16); b. 15.6.72; 2nd Lt., Linc. R., 13.8.92; Lt. 5.5.94; Adjt. (Temp.) 22.11.99 to 5.8.00; Capt. 14.6.02; Major 3.8.12; retired from Linc. R. 11.3.19; served S. African War, 1900–2; Queen's Medal, 2 clasps; King's Medal and clasp; Europ. War; Despatches.

GRANT, E. (D.S.O. L.G. 1.1.19), Major (T/Lt.-Col.), Lovat's Scouts Yeomanry; served S. African War, 1900–2; Queen's Medal, 3 clasps; Europ. War; Despatches.

GRANT, F. G. (D.S.O. L.G. 3.6.19), Major, 34th Bn. Aust. Inf.

GRANT, H. F. L. (D.S.O. L.G. 1.2.17); b. 20.11.79; 2nd Lt., R.A., 20.5.99; Lt. 16.2.01; Capt. 16.4.04; Major 30.10.14; Bt. Lt.-Col. 3.6.18; T/Lt.-Col. 17.11.18 to 19.3.19; Despatches.

GRANT, I. C. (D.S.O. L.G. 22.9.16); b. 28.5.91; s. of J. C. Grant, of Holly Lodge, Barnes, S.W.13; m. Pamela Molony, d. of late R. O'Connor, of Cragganowen, co. Clare; two d.; educ. St. Neots; Eversley; Cheltenham College; R.M.C., Sandhurst; 2nd Lt., Cam. Highrs., 26.10.10; Lt. 14.1.14; Capt. 22.3.15; Bt. Major 3.6.19; served European War as Regimental Officer, and as G.S.O.3, 29th Division, Brig.-Major, 86th Brig, and D.A.A.G., War Office; Staff Captain, War Office; twice wounded; Despatches three times; home service once; Bt. Majority; Chevalier, Order of the Crown of Belgium. His D.S.O. was awarded for gallantry on 17.1.16 at Beaumont-Hamel.

GRANT, J. D. (D.S.O. L.G. 19.12.22), Lt.-Col., 13th Rajputs, I.A.; V.C. (see "The Victoria Cross," same publishers).

GRANT, W. (D.S.O. L.G. 1.1.17) (Bar, L.G. 18.1.18) (Details, L.G. 25.4.18); b. Stawell, Victoria, Australia, 30.9.70; s. of E. C. Grant; m. Eveline, d. of J. S. Westcott; three s.; two d.; educ. Brighton Grammar School; Melbourne University (Bachelor of Civil Engineering); joined Defence Force as Lt., 1901; served continuously in the Darling Downs Light Horse Rgt.; commanded Rgt., 1910 up to joining the A.I.F.; formed the 11th L.H. Rgt. (A.I.F.), March, 1915, and served with it continuously in Gallipoli, Egypt and Sinai; G.O.C., 4th L.H. Brigade, Sept. 1917; took part in the operations, capture of Barsheba, Jerusalem, Tiberias, and Damascus, until the Armistice; was in temp. command of the Australian Mounted Division at the time of the Armistice; C.M.G.; 3rd Class Order of the Nile.

GRANT-DALTON, D. (D.S.O. L.G. 4.6.17); b. 7.3.81; s. of Col. G. Grant-Dalton and E. K. Grant-Dalton; m. Gwavas May, d. of late S. Spry; educ. Felsted School; 2nd Lt., W. Yorks. R., 27.7.01; Lt. 7.12.04; Capt. 11.8.10; Major 4.5.16; T/Lt.-Col., R.E. (T.F.), 24.2.20 to 15.6.20; served S. African War, 1900–2; Queen's Medal and 3 clasps; King's Medal and 2 clasps; Europ. War, in France, 1915, to close of War; Despatches twice; C.M.G.

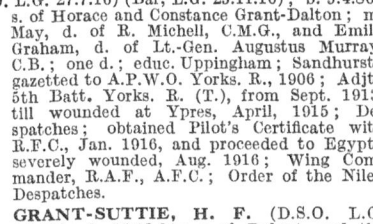

GRANT-DALTON, S. (D.S.O. L.G. 27.7.16) (Bar, L.G. 25.11.16); b. 5.4.86; s. of Horace and Constance Grant-Dalton; m. May, d. of R. Michell, C.M.G., and Emily Graham, d. of Lt.-Gen. Augustus Murray, C.B.; one d.; educ. Uppingham; Sandhurst; gazetted to A.P.W.O. Yorks. R., 1906; Adjt., 5th Batt. Yorks. R. (T.), from Sept. 1913, till wounded at Ypres, April, 1915; Despatches; obtained Pilot's Certificate with R.F.C., Jan. 1916, and proceeded to Egypt; severely wounded, Aug. 1916; Wing Commander, R.A.F., A.F.C.; Order of the Nile; Despatches.

S. Grant-Dalton.

GRANT-SUTTIE, H. F. (D.S.O. L.G. 1.1.18); b. 15.12.84; s. of Robert and the Hon. Mrs. Grant-Suttie; m. Torfrida Alianore, e. d. of Sir Wroth Lethbridge, Bart; 2nd Lt., R.A., 29.7.04; Lt. 29.7.07; A.D.C. to Gov. and Com.-in-Chief, Trinidad and Tobago, 13.11.07 to 19.8.08; Capt. 30.10.14; Major, R.F.A., 22.8.16; served Europ. War; M.C.

GRANT-THOROLD, R. S. (D.S.O. L.G. 4.6.17); b. 1868; s. of late A. W. T. Grant; educ. Eton; Sandhurst; Lt., R.W. Fus. (retired 1891); Major R.W. Fus., 1915; Lt.-Col., commanding 18th Bn. The Welsh Regt., 1916; served S. African War (S.A.L.H.); Despatches; Queen's Medal, 6 clasps; King's Medal, 2 clasps; Europ. War, with 1st Australian Naval and Military Force to New Guinea; wounded; Despatches.

GRANVILLE, B. (D.S.O. L.G. 1.1.18) (Bar, L.G. 22.4.18); s. of Major P. Granville, of Wellesbourne, Warwickshire; m. Edith, d. of Rt. Hon. Sir F. Halsey, Bart., and Mary, d. of late F. O. Wells; educ. Eton; joined 3rd K.O. Hussars, 1896; served S. African War; retired 1908; joined Warwicks. Yeomanry; served Europ. War in Salonika, Egypt, Palestine and France, 1914 to end of war; wounded; retired as Colonel from Warwicks. Yeomanry, 1921; Hon. Sec., Warwickshire Hounds.

GRANVILLE, C. H. (D.S.O. L.G. 3.6.16); b. 26.1.77; m. Louisa Thursa, d. of late A. J. Beveridge, of Dollar Vale, Tunee, N.S.W.; educ. Eagle House, Brook Green; Repton; served S. African War, 1900; Queen's Medal, 2 clasps; Europ. War, 1915–16.

GRASETT, A. E. (D.S.O. L.G. 3.6.19); b. 20.10.88; 2nd Lt., R.E., 24.6.09; Lieut. 4.2.11; Capt. 24.6.15; Bt. Major 1.1.18; Despatches; M.C.

GRASSIE, J. T. (D.S.O. L.G. 22.12.16); b. 14.9.90; s. of J. J. Grassie; m. Jane Menzies M'Gregor; two d.; educ. Borgue Academy, Kirkcudbright; joined 1st Battn. The Black Watch (R.H.), as a Private, 1907; Sergeant, 1914; proceeded to France on the outbreak of hostilities, and took part in the Retreat from Mons, the Battles of the Marne and Aisne; wounded in the head and shoulder 14.9.14; invalided home, and proceeded once more to France in March, 1915 (wounded in the left foot at Richebourg 9.5.15); 2nd Lt., in Black Watch, 18.12.15; Lt. 1.7.17; A/Captain 9.8.17 to 21.2.20; half pay, April, 1921; embarked for Mesopotamia to join 2nd Batt. Black Watch; took part in the attempt to relieve Kut-el-Amara (wounded both arms and right leg; Despatches).

GRASSIE, W. (D.S.O. L.G. 4.6.17), Lt.-Col., Can. Inf.

GRATTAN, E. L. C. (D.S.O. L.G. 14.3.16); b. 24.6.84; s. of late W. H. Colley Grattan, Major in Kildare Rifles, and Emily Alice White West, d. of George White West; m. Stella B. A., d. of Canon J. B. McCaul, and g.d. of Alex. McCaul, D.D.; educ. Dublin; Stubbington House, Fareham; joined Britannia, 1899; joined H.M.S. Diana, 1901; Renown, 1902; Sub-Lt., 1904; obtained "five ones and a two," Glory, 1905; Lt. 1905; Submarines, 1906; Aboukir, 1910; Warrior, 1911; Admiralty, 1913; lent for special service at Gallipoli for Shore Wireless Telegraphy and Signal Stations; Egmont for Wireless Telegraphy Stations at Malta, 1916; Admiralty for W.T. Stations, 1918; Act.-Comdr., July, 1918; Commander.

GRATTAN, H. W. (D.S.O. L.G. 1.1.18); b. 11.4.72; Lt., R.A.M.C., 29.7.95; Capt. 29.7.98; Major 29.1.07; Lt.-Col. (T/Col.); Despatches.

GRAY, C. J. (D.S.O. L.G. 8.3.18), Engr. Lt.-Cdr., R.N.

GRAY, C. LL. R. (D.S.O. L.G. 1.1.19); b. 14.4.71; 2nd Lt., R.A., 14.2.90; Lt. 14.2.93; Capt. 27.9.99; Adjt. 1.5.07 to 30.4.10; Major 2.11.10; Lt.-Col., 63rd Brig., R.G.A.; Despatches.

GRAY, C. O. V. (D.S.O. L.G. 3.6.16); b. 7.7.82; s. of Evelyn Gray, I.C.S., and Violet, d. of General Wilkins, R.E.; m. Vere, d. of Sir Elwin Palmer, K.C.B., K.C.M.G., Governor of the National Bank of Egypt; one s.; one d.; educ. Cheltenham College; Sandhurst; 2nd Lt., Unatt., 8.1.01; 2nd Lt., Sea. Highrs., 8.3.01; Lt. 23.2.05; Capt. 12.10.11; Major, 16th Bn.; Lieut.-Col., 1918; served Frontier Exp. against Mohmands, 1908, when A.D.C. to Sir James Willcocks (dangerously wounded; Medal with clasp); 2nd Batt. Seaf. Highrs. 1911; Adjt., 9th A. and S. Highrs., 1912–15; served Europ. War, 1915, first with them and then attached to A.G.'s office, G.H.Q., April, 1915; Major, 1916 retired Seaf. Highrs.; Despatches six times; Bt. Lt.-Col. 1.1.18; C.M.G.; Chevalier, Légion d'Honneur, March, 1920.

GRAY, D. F. B. (D.S.O. L.G. 3.6.16); b. 9.11.84; s. of Rev. H. B. Gray, D.D.; m. Kathleen St. Clair Mackenzie; educ. Winchester College; 2nd Lt., K.O.S.B., 1904; resigned Commission as Lt., 1909; joined P.P.C.L.I., as Lt.-Capt., March, 1915; Major, June, 1915; served Europ. War; Despatches twice; wounded.

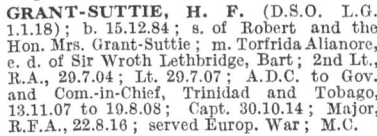

E. Gray.

GRAY, E. (D.S.O. L.G. 19.11.17) (Details, L.G. 22.3.18); b. 6.4.75; 2nd Lt., Durh. L. Inf., 27.8.16; Lieut. 27.2.18; Despatches; M.C.; M.M.

GRAY, F. W. (D.S.O. L.G. 17.11.17), Lt., R.N.R.

GRAY, H. P. T. (D.S.O. L.G. 26.7.18), Capt., Seaf. Highrs.

GRAY, J. A. S. (D.S.O. L.G. 3.6.16), Temp. Lt.-Colonel, Spec. List.

GRAY, J. E. B. (D.S.O. L.G. 8.3.19) (Details, L.G. 4.10.19); b. Cambridge 25.11.95; s. of Rev. E. A. Gray, R.D., and Mrs. Gray, O.B.E., of Lidgate Rectory, Newmarket; m. Florence Ethelwyn, d. of F. J. Clerke; one d.; educ. St. Faith's School, Cambridge; Uppingham School; Matriculated for University College, Oxford, 1914, but did not enter owing to the War; joined 16th (P.S.B.) Batt. Middlesex R. 4.9.14; 2nd Lt., 9th Batt. R. Brig., 29.12.14; Captain; served France and Flanders, 1915–18; wounded thrice. In Alsace and Germany from Nov. 1918; Camp Commandant, British Military Mission, Berlin, 1919–21; with Directorate of Graves Registration and Enquiries (Central Europe), Berlin, from 1921.

GRAY, J. N. (D.S.O. L.G. 1.1.17), Lt. (T/Capt.), Special List.

GRAY, W. (D.S.O. L.G. 3.6.18), Capt. (A/Lt.-Col.), A.S.C., now R.A.S.C.

GRAY, W. E. (D.S.O. L.G. 1.1.19), Capt. (A/Lt.-Col.), R. Brig. and M.G.C.; M.C.

GRAY, W. K. (D.S.O. L.G. 1.1.17), Major (T/Lt.-Col.), R.F.A.

GRAY-CHEAPE, H. A. (D.S.O. L.G. 1.1.17) (Bar, L.G. 4.2.18) (Details, L.G. 5.7.18); e. s. of late Colonel Gray-Cheape, of Wellfield, Fife; Major, T/Lt.-Col., Worc. Yeom.; served S. African War, 1901–2; Europ. War; drowned at sea through enemy action on 27.5.18.

GRAY, G. GORDON- (see Gordon-Gray, G.).

GRAYSTONE, F. R. (D.S.O. L.G. 3.6.19), T/Capt. (T/Major), R.A.; M.C.

GRAZEDBROOK, G. C. (D.S.O. L.G. 14.1.16); b. 4.12.73; 2nd Lt., R. Innis. Fus., 29.5.95; Lt. 6.4.98; Capt. 20.9.01; Major 10.5.15; Bt. Lt.-Col. 3.6.17; Lt.-Col. 13.3.18; Staff Employ. 10.2.20; served N.W. Frontier of India, 1897–98; Medal and clasp; served Tirah, 1897–98; operations in the Bara Valley 7–14.12.97; clasp; S. African War, 1902; Queen's Medal, 3 clasps; Europ. War; Despatches; C.M.G.

GREATHED, P. (D.S.O. L.G. 22.8.18) (Reserve of Officers, S. African M.R.), attached 2nd Imperial Light Horse.

GREATWOOD, F. W. (D.S.O. L.G. 16.8.17), Major (A/Lt.-Col.), Linc. R.

GREAVES, H. (D.S.O. L.G. 8.3.19) (Details, L.G. 4.10.19), Lt., 3rd Bn. Notts. and Derby. R., att. 1st Bn.; M.C.

GREAVES, S. S. (D.S.O. L.G. 3.6.18), T/Capt., R.A.M.C.; M.C.

GRECH, J. (D.S.O. L.G. 3.6.16); b. 22.4.71; Lt., R.A.M.C., 29.7.95; Capt. 29.7.98; Major 29.1.07; Lt.-Col. 1.3.15; served S. African War, 1900–1; Queen's Medal, 4 clasps; Europ. War, as Assist. Dir. of Medical Services in Salonika and France; Despatches.

GREEN, A. F. U. (D.S.O. L.G. 1.1.17); b. 20.8.78; 2nd Lt., R.A., 23.12.97; Lt. 28.12.00; Capt. 29.3.02; Adjt. 3.5.07 to 2.12.08; Major 30.10.14; Bt. Lt.-Col. 3.6.16; T/Brig.-Gen. 13.11.16 to 21.8.19; Bt. Col. 3.6.18; Col. 31.8.20; Local Col. on the Staff 22.6.21; served S. African War, 1899–1902; Queen's Medal, 3 clasps; King's Medal, 2 clasps; Europ. War; C.M.G.

GREEN, A. LL. B. (D.S.O. L.G. 16.8.17), Capt. (T/Major), Herefords. Regt.

GREEN, ALEX. McWATT (D.S.O. L.G. 22.7.18), Capt. (A/Major), South African Medical Corps.

GREEN, C. J. S. (D.S.O. L.G. 4.6.17), Major, London R.; M.C.

GREEN, E. C. (D.S.O. L.G. 17.3.19), Eng. Cdr., R.N.

GREEN, G. W. MURLIS, (D.S.O. L.G. 18.6.17) (Bar, L.G. 18.12.17), T/Capt., Gen. List., R.F.C.; M.C., 2 bars; the Serbian Order, Karageorge.

GREEN, H. C. R. (D.S.O. L.G. 3.6.16); b. 15.5.72; 2nd Lt., K.R.R.C., 18.11.91; Lt. 3.1.95; Adjt., K.R.R.C., 23.10.99 to 5.11.01; Capt. 7.1.00; Major 1.9.08; Bt. Lt.-Col. 1.1.17; Col. 3.6.18; commanding 2nd Batt. K.R.R.C.; served S. African War, 1899–1902; Queen's Medal and 5 clasps; Europ. War, 1914–18; wounded; Despatches; Bt. Lt.-Col.; C.B.; C.M.G.; Belgian Order of the Crown; Croix de Guerre.

GREEN, H. F. L. HILTON- (see Hilton-Green, H. F. L.).

GREEN, H. W. (D.S.O. L.G. 1.1.17); 2nd s. of late Walter James Green and Mrs. Green, 13 Queen's Road, Tunbridge Wells; educ. Charterhouse, and Exeter College, Oxford; Major (Bt./Lt.-Col.), E. Kent R. "He was given a University Commission in the Buffs at the time of the Boer War, and joined the regiment in India, proceeding from there to Hong-Kong, and then to S. Africa. On the outbreak of European War was serving in Nigeria with the West African Forces, and proceeded to Cameroon. Returning home, he held the command of the first Batt. of the 11th Essex R., and afterwards of the 1st Buffs, becoming later Brig.-Gen. in command of the 10th Inf. Brigade, and was commanding the 1st Queen's at the time of his death." He was several times mentioned in Despatches; died 31.12.18 at Rouen.

GREEN, L. L. (D.S.O. L.G. 3.2.20), Lt., R. Brig., S.R., att. 46th Bn. R. Fus.; M.C.

GREEN, S. H. (D.S.O. L.G. 1.1.18); b. 8.9.85; 2nd Lt., Bedf. R., 16.8.05; W. York. R., 16.9.05; Lt. 31.3.09; Adjt. 1.8.10 to 31.7.13; Capt. 22.1.14; Bt. Major 1.1.17; M.C.

GREEN, S. W. B. (D.S.O. L.G. 12.12.18), Lt.-Cdr., R.N.

GREEN, T. A., M.D. (D.S.O. L.G. 3.6.18), Capt. (T/Major), A/Lt.-Col., R.A.M.C.

GREEN, W. (D.S.O. L.G. 14.1.16) (1st Bar, L.G. 1.1.18) (2nd Bar, L.G. 16.9.18); b. 1.8.82; 2nd Lt., R. Highrs., 11.8.00; Lt. 12.11.01; Capt. 9.11.06; Major 1.9.15; Bt. Lt.-Col. 1.1.19; T/Brig.-Gen. 15.4.18 to 1919; served S. African War, 1901–2; Queen's Medal, 4 clasps; Europ. War; Despatches.

GREEN, W. G. K. (D.S.O. L.G. 1.1.18); b. 3.11.72; 2nd Lt., E. Yorks. R., 9.12.95; Ind. S.C. 3.10.97; Lt. 7.3.98; Capt. 7.12.04; Major 7.12.13; Bt. Lt.-Col. 1.1.19; Ind. Army 18.2.20 (Temp. Col. Comdt. 1.1.21); C.M.G.; Despatches.

GREEN, W. W. (D.S.O. L.G. 16.9.18); b. 15.5.87; 2nd Lt., R.A., 18.12.07; Lieut. 18.12.10; Capt. 30.10.14; Adjt., R.A., 15.5.15; Major 2.12.17; Despatches; M.C.

GREEN-WILKINSON, L. F. (D.S.O. L.G. 4.6.17); b. 16.12.65; 1st commission 14.4.86; Major 3.11.03; Bt. Lt.-Col., R. of O., 3.6.16; Bt. Col., R. of O., 1.1.17; T/Brig.-Gen.; served Burmese Expedition, 1886–88; Medal with clasp; Burmese Expedition, 1888–89; clasp; Expedition to Dongola, 1896, with Camel Corps; Despatches (L.G. 3.11.96); 4th Class Medjidie; Egyptian Medal with 2 clasps; Nile Expedition, 1897; clasp to Egyptian Medal; Nile Expedition, 1898; Battle of Khartoum; Despatches (L.G. 30.9.98); 4th Class Osmanieh; clasp to Egyptian Medal; Medal; S. African War, 1899–1902; Despatches (L.G. 8.2.01); Bt. of Major; Queen's Medal, 6 clasps; King's Medal, 2 clasps; Europ. War; Despatches; C.M.G.

GREENE, E. A. (D.S.O. L.G. 1.1.19), Major, 61st By. 14th Brigade, Can. F.A.

GREENE, JOHN (D.S.O. L.G. 4.6.17) (Bar, L.G. 16.9.18); b. 26.5.78; 2nd Lt., 7th Dn. Gds., 15.8.00; Lt. 17.9.03; Capt. 9.11.10; Major, 5.8.19; Bt. Lt.-Col. 6.8.19; served S. African War, 1900–2; Queen's Medal, 3 clasps; King's Medal, 2 clasps; Europ. War; Despatches.

GREENE, JOHN (D.S.O. L.G. 15.10.18), T/Capt. (A/Major), R.A.M.C.; M.C.

GREENE, L. (D.S.O. L.G. 16.9.18), T/Capt., S. African Arty.; M.C.

GREENE, SIR W. RAYMOND (D.S.O. L.G. 14.1.16); b. 1869; e. s. of Sir E. Walter Greene and the late Anne E. Greene, his wife, d. of the Rev. C. Royds, of Haughton Rectory, Prebendary of Lichfield Cathedral; educ. Eton and Oriel College, Oxford; B.A.; has represented North Hackney since 1910; from 1895 to 1905 M.P. for Cambridge; 1906 to 1911 Acting Lt.-Col. Commanding Duke of York's Own Loyal Suffolk Hussars; served S. African War, 1899 to 1900; Queen's Medal, 3 clasps; Europ. War, serving with the 9th Lancers in France, subsequently commanding 2/3rd County of London Yeomanry.

GREENFIELD, T. W. B. (D.S.O. L.G. 1.1.17); b. 20.11.65; s. of W. R. Greenfield, of Haynes Park, Bedford; educ. Eton; Trinity Hall, Cambridge; Major, Irish Guards; served in S. African War, 1899–1900; Despatches; Queen's Medal, 3 clasps; Europ. War, 1914–16; Despatches.

GREENHILL, J. W. (D.S.O. L.G. 17.5.18), Lt.-Cdr. (A/Cdr.), R.N.R.

GREENHOUGH, F. H., M.Inst.C.E. (D.S.O. L.G. 1.1.18); b. 1871; Deputy General Manager, Nigerian Railways; T/Major (T/Lt.-Col.), R.E.; Colonel Greenhough served in European War, 1914–18; Despatches.

GREENLESS, J. R. C. (D.S.O. L.G. 15.4.15) (Bar, L.G. 1.1.18), T/Capt. (A/Lt.-Col.), R.A.M.C. (see "The Distinguished Service Order," from its institution to 31.12.15, by same publishers).

GREENLEY, W. A. (D.S.O. L.G. 4.6.17); b. 1.1.84; s. of J. E. and of Bertha Clara Greenley (*née* Dowson); m. Kathleen Mary, d. of G. H. Grimshaw; one s.; Produce Broker in City of London; entered the Army, Oct. 1914; served continuously in France and Belgium until 23.1.19; commanded 2nd Divisional Train (Horse Transport) 5.2.18–23.1.19; Despatches three times; C.M.G.

GREENSHIELDS, D. J. (D.S.O. L.G. 7.2.18); b. 2.8.85; 2nd Lt., R.A., 20.12.05; Lt. 20.12.08; Capt. 30.10.14; Major 30.12.16; Despatches; M.C.

GREENSHIELDS, D. M. (D.S.O. L.G. 26.7.17), 2nd Lt., H.L.I.

GREENWAY, H. (D.S.O. L.G. 4.6.17), Major, Aust. Engrs.

GREENWAY, T. C. (D.S.O. L.G. 2.5.16); b. 6.11.76; 2nd Lt., S. Wales Borderers, 1.12.97; Capt. 19.6.07; Adjt., S.R., 26.9.08–25.9.12; Major 1.9.15; Bt. Lt.-Col. 1.1.19; Despatches.

GREENWELL, W. B. (D.S.O. L.G. 1.1.18); b. 29.10.81; s. of Alan and Isabella Augusta Greenwell; educ. Durham Grammar School; 2nd Lt., Durh. L. Inf., 4.5.01; Lt. 31.7.03; Adjt. 10.4.13 to 31.5.16; Capt. 7.4.14; Major 4.5.16; Bt. Lt.-Col. 3.6.19; served S. African War, 1901–2; Medal, 3 clasps; Europ. War from 1914.

GREENWOOD, C. F. H. (D.S.O. L.G. 1.1.18), Major (A/Lt.-Col.), London R.

GREENWOOD, G. B. (D.S.O. L.G. 1.2.19), 2nd Lt., 6th Bn. Notts. and Derby. R., T.F., attd. 10th Bn.

GREENWOOD, H. (D.S.O. L.G. 26.7.18) (Bar, L.G. 2.12.18), Lt.-Col., late Yorks. L.I.; V.C.; M.C. (see "The Victoria Cross," by same publishers).

GREENWOOD, L. M. (D.S.O. L.G. 1.1.19), T/Major, 13th (S.) Bn. Durham Light Inf.; M.C. He died 17.10.18.

GREENWOOD, W. F. (D.S.O. L.G. 2.12.18); b. 12.5.95; s. of W. E. Greenwood; m. Sarah Esther, o. c. of Capt. Vernon Lander, of Torquay; Lt., York. R., 2.8.16; T/Capt.; served Europ. War; Despatches three times; M.C.; M.B.E.; Croix de Guerre.

GREER, F. A. (D.S.O. L.G. 4.6.17); b. 20.2.71; 2nd Lt., R. Ir. Fus., 29.10.90; Lt. 1.4.93; Capt. 1.12.99; Major 19.3.10; Lt.-Col. 14.3.17; T/Brig.-Gen. 7.5.17 to 1.5.19; served S. African War, 1902 (Queen's Medal, 2 clasps); Europ. War, 1914–18; Despatches; C.M.G.

GREER, W. D. (D.S.O. L.G. 3.6.18), Major (A/Lt.-Col.), Can. A.S.C.

GREGG, R. H. (D.S.O. L.G. 1.1.18), T/Major, Royal Fusiliers; M.C.

W. T. H. Gregg.

GREGG, W. T. H. (D.S.O. L.G. 1.1.18); b. 12.7.88; s. of H. G. Gregg, J.P.; m. Frances Lyndall, d. of the late Rt. Hon. W. P. Schreiner, P.C., C.M.G., K.C.; educ. Marlborough College; R.M.C., Sandhurst; 2nd Lt., R. Ir. Fus., 29.8.06; Lt. 4.9.06; Captain 7.6.13; seconded to the K.A. Rifles, 1912; served in the operations against the Marehan in B.E.A., 1913–14; African G.S. Medal with Bar; East Africa, 1913–14; served Europ. War with the K.A. Rifles, Aug. 1914 to Nov. 1918, in B.E.A., G.E.A., P.E.A.; Croix de Guerre avec Palmes; Bt. Lt.-Colonel on promotion to Major; Despatches; T/Lt.-Col. commanding 2nd K.A.R.

GREGORIE, H. G. (D.S.O. L.G. 1.1.17); b. 3.8.78; 2nd Lt., R. Ir. Regt., 19.5.00; Lt. 1.4.03; Capt. 3.10.08; Major 1.9.15; Bt. Lt.-Col. 1.1.18; T/Brig.-Gen. 24.11.17 to 24.4.18; served S. African War, 1899–1902; Despatches (L.G. 8.2.01 and 16.4.01); Queen's Medal, 4 clasps; King's Medal, 2 clasps; Europ. War; Despatches.

GREGORY, A. J. R. (D.S.O. L.G. 1.1.17); b. 17.11.82; 2nd Lt., R.A., 21.12.00; Lt. 23.9.03; Adjt. 20.8.07 to 8.1.11; Capt. 21.12.13; Major. He died 4.12.18.

GREGORY, F. C. (D.S.O. L.G. 26.7.18), Major, Ches. Regt.

GREGORY, G. (D.S.O. L.G. 20.2.19); b. 1872; s. of J. S. Gregory; m. Margaret Amy, d. of late G. F. Ross; one s.; educ. H.M.S. School Ship, Conway, River Mersey; earlier sea training in sailing ships; Midshipman, R.N.R., 1888; Captain, R.N.R., retired; Officer, Union and Union Castle SS. Co.; in command R.M.S. Cairo and Heliopolis, of Egyptian Mail S.S. Co.; served in H.M.S. Indefatigable, on N. America and W. Indies Station; Marine Superintendent, Canadian Northern S.S. Co., Avonmouth, Bristol; R. N. Transport Service during war, Aug. 1914, to Sept. 1919; Dardanelles, Egypt, Syria, Palestine; Divisional Naval Transport Officer, Syrian Coast, with General Allenby's Army; Despatches four times; C.B.E.; Order of the Nile; elder brother of Trinity House since 1919.

GREGORY, M. (D.S.O. L.G. 1.1.19); b. 20.8.85; 2nd Lt., R.A., 27.7.05; Lt. 27.7.08; Capt. 30.10.14; Major 9.11.16; Adjt. 9.3.20; Despatches; M.C.

GREGSON, G. K. (D.S.O. L.G. 25.8.17); b. 8.9.81; 2nd Lt., R.A., 2.5.00; Lt. 3.4.01; Capt. 24.12.10; Major 30.10.14; T/Lt.-Col. 24.10.15 to 11.12.15; Despatches.

GREIG, J. McG. (D.S.O. L.G. 3.6.19), T/Lt.-Col., W. Yorks. R., att. 18th Bn. York. and Lanc. R.

GRELLET, R. C. (D.S.O. L.G. 27.10.17) (Details, L.G. 18.3.18), T/Major, Yorks. R.

GRENFELL, A. M. (D.S.O. L.G. 20.10.16); b. 21.10.73; 6th s. of late Pascoe du Pre Grenfell, of Wilton Park, Beaconsfield, and of his cousin, Sophia, d. of Vice-Admiral John Pascoe Grenfell; m. (1st) Lady Victoria Sybil Mary Grey (who died in 1907), d. of 4th Earl Grey; two s.; one d., and (2ndly) Hilda Margaret, 2nd d. of Gen. Rt. Hon. Sir N. G. Lyttelton, P.C., G.C.B., G.C.V.O., and Katharine, d. of Rt. Hon. J. Stuart Wortley; four d.; Major, Bucks. Yeo.; served Europ. War; wounded twice; Despatches thrice. Has the T.D.

GRENFELL, F. H. (D.S.O. L.G. 1.1.17) (Bar, L.G. 23.3.17), Cdr., R.N.

GRENFELL, G. P. (D.S.O. L.G. 1.1.18), Capt. (T/Major), R.F.C., S.R.

GREVILLE, C. H. (D.S.O. L.G. 4.6.17); b. 28.5.89; s. of Col. Hon. A Greville, C.V.O., and Mabel Elizabeth Georgiana, d. of Ernald Smith; m. Gwendolen, d. of Col. Geoffrey Carr Glyn, M.V.O., D.S.O., T.D., and the Hon. Winifred Harbord, d. of 5th Baron Suffield; educ. Eton; ent. Army, 1910; 2nd Lt., G. Gds., 1.8.01; Lt. 27.7.12; Capt. 3.5.15; served Europ. War, 1914–18; Despatches.

GREVILLE, G. G. F. F. (D.S.O. L.G. 8.3.19) (Details, L.G. 4.10.19); b. 19.1.84; 2nd Lt., Leins. R., 2.3.07; Lt. 13.2.09; Capt. 16.2.15; Despatches.

GREY, R. (D.S.O. L.G. 18.11.19); b. 28.6.74; s. of Sir W. Grey, K.C.S.I., late Governor of Bengal and Jamaica; educ. Harrow; Major, 2nd Bn. G. Gds., was A.D.C. to Sir Trevor Plowden in India; served Matabeleland Campaign, 1896; Secretary to Lord Beresford, 1898–1900; served S. African War; seconded for service with R.F.C., 1913; flew to France on outbreak of war as Second-in-Command, 5th Squadron, R.F.C.; Chevalier de la Légion d'Honneur at the end of the Retreat; later taken prisoner; after the Armistice went to Archangel; became C.R.A.F. in N. Russia; Despatches twice.

GREYLING, A. J. (D.S.O. L.G. 22.8.18), Lt.-Col., Heidelberg "A" Commando, S. African Mil. Forces.

GRIBBLE, H. C. (D.S.O. L.G. 3.6.19); b. 16.5.86; s. of E. F. Gribble; m. Augusta Grace, d. of A. W. Gosset, Capt. (retired), Queen's Rgt., and niece of late Major-Gen. Sir M. W. Gosset, K.C.B.; two d.; educ. Bishop's Stortford School; 2nd Lt., R.F.A. (T.F.), 1909; Lt. 1910; Capt. 1916; Major, 1918; served Europ. War in France, 1914–19; Despatches.

GRIBBON, H. H. (D.S.O. L.G. 25.8.17); b. 22.1.80; 2nd Lt., R. Garr. R., 12.8.02; Lt. 21.3.03; Lt., Hamps., 5.9.06; Capt. 1.12.13; Despatches.

GRICE-HUTCHINSON, C. B. (D.S.O. L.G. 16.9.18); b. 28.2.81; 2nd Lt., R.A., 2.5.00; Lt. 3.4.01; Capt. 1.2.10; Major 30.10.14; Despatches.

GRIER, H. D. (D.S.O. L.G. 22.8.18); b. 31.5.63; s. of Capt. A. D. Grier, late 89th Rgt.; m. Jane Bertram, d. of W. Sanderson, J.P.; one s.; two d.; Brigadier-General, late R.A.; served Burma, 1889–91; Medal with clasp; Isazai Exp., 1892; Chitral, 1895; honourably mentioned; Medal and clasp; Tirah, 1897–98; Despatches; Bt. Major; clasp; served Europ. War, 1914–18; one of the garrison of Kut-el-Amara; Despatches five times; twice wounded; C.B.

GRIERSON, K. M. (D.S.O. L.G. 2.4.19) (Details, L.G. 10.12.19); b. 1897; s. of C. MacIver Grierson, R.I., and Ethel, d. of late Cochran Davys, Clerk of the Crown and Peace, Sligo, Ireland; one s.; two d.; educ. Richmond; joined Artists' Rifles, 1915; received temporary commission, Manchester R., Aug. 1916; transferred to Regular Army, Aug. 1917; 2nd Lt., Manchester R., 4.8.17; Lt. 4.2.19; served in France, 1915–17; Italy, 1917–19; M.C.

GRIERSON, W. A. (D.S.O. L.G. 4.6.17), Lt. (A/Major), N. Lanc. R.

GRIESBACH, W. A. (D.S.O. L.G. 24.6.16) (Bar, L.G. 2.4.19) (Details, L.G. 10.12.19); b. Fort Qu'Appelle, N.W. Territories, 3.1.78; s. of late Lt.-Col. A. H. Griesbach, R.N.W. Mounted Police, and Emma Griesbach (*née* Hodgins); m. Janet Scott McDonald Lander; educ. St. John's College, Winnipeg; served S. African War, 1900; Lt., 19th Alberta Dragoons, 1906; seconded from 19th Alberta Dragoons with rank of Major for Divisional Cavalry, 1st Can. Contingent, 1914; commanded 49th Can. Batt. (Edmonton R.), which he raised 1915–17; Brig.-Gen. 12.2.17; commanded 1st Can. Inf. Brig., B.E.F., France; Despatches seven times; C.B.; C.M.G.; M.P., West Edmonton, from 1917; K.C.

W. A. Griesbach.

GRIEVE, E. L. (D.S.O. L.G. 11.11.19), Cdr., R.N.

GRIFFIN, A. E. (D.S.O. L.G. 1.1.18), Lt.-Col., Can. Rly. Troops.

GRIFFIN, C. J., C.M.G. (D.S.O. L.G. 18.2.15) (Bar, L.G. 18.7.17), Major and Bt. Lt.-Col. (T/Lt.-Col.), Lanc. Fus. (see "The Distinguished Service Order," from its institution to 31.12.15, by same publishers).

GRIFFIN, C. J. A., M.B. (D.S.O. L.G. 1.1.19), Capt. (A/Lt.-Col.), R.A.M.C., S.R., att. 5th Can. Field Amb.

GRIFFIN, E. H., M.D. (D.S.O. L.G. 26.11.17) (Details, L.G. 6.4.18); s. of late John Griffin, who established the "Walsall Observer"; educ. Queen Mary's Grammar School, and Cambridge; T/Capt., R.A.M.C. He was a member of the British Red Cross Ambulance which served with the Turkish Forces during the Turko-Italian War in Tripoli; served Europ. War in France; Despatches; M.C. and Bar; wounded on three occasions; was officially reported killed in action, but later prisoner of war in Germany.

GRIFFIN, J. A. A. (D.S.O. L G. 26.7.18); b. 5.10.91; m. a daughter of late W. Palmer; one d.; 2nd Lt., Linc. R., 4.3.11; Lt. 11.5.12; Capt. 2.2.15; Capt. (A/Major), Linc. R.; Europ. War, 1914–18; Despatches.

J. A. A. Griffin.

GRIFFIN, REV. J. W. K., M.A. (D.S.O. L.G. 1.1.18); b. 14.10.80; s. of the Rev. James Griffin, D.D., and the late Maria Griffin; m. 4.7.19, Dorothy Gertrude, only d. of late W. G. Palmer and Mrs. Palmer, of 3, The Chine, Winchmore Hill, London; educ. Trinity College, Dublin; Chaplain to the Forces, 4th Class, 18.4.14; 3rd Class 1.1.21 (Temp. 2nd Class 7.12.16 to 20.3.19; Temp. 1st Class 21.3.19); served Europ. War; Despatches.

GRIFFIN, P. G. (D.S.O. L.G. 4.6.17), Major, R.F.A. (S.R.); Despatches. He died 26.3.21.

GRIFFITH, E. W. (D.S.O. L.G. 1.1.18); b. 1871; s. of late Capt. Wynne Griffith; m. Bertha, d. of late Sir G. Greenall, 1st Bart.; two s.; one d.; educ. Harrow; joined the Cheshire Regt., 1892; Denbighshire Yeom., 1902; Capt., 1910; transferred to R.F.A. in France; served with 2nd Div. till Feb. 1916, and 56th Div., 1918; Lt.-Col., R.F.A., 1916; served Europ. War in France since March, 1915; invalided home, 1918, and was employed to deliver His Majesty's Message to the American Troops, and afterwards commanded Western Command Transfer Centre and Dispersal Units, 1919; Despatches twice; 1914–15 Star; Master of the Flint and Denbigh Hounds since 1912; D.L., Denbighshire.

GRIFFITH, J. J., F.R.C.V.S. (D.S.O. L.G. 3.6.16); b. 26.4.71; 1st appointment, A.V.C., 24.8.98; Capt. 5.8.03; Major 24.8.13; retired with rank of Lt.-Col. 16.3.19; served S. African War, 1900–1 (Queen's Medal, 5 clasps; King's Medal, 2 clasps); Europ. War, 1914–18; Despatches.

GRIFFITH, LL. (D.S.O. L.G. 3.8.20), Major, 107th Pioneers, Ind. Army.

GRIFFITH-WILLIAMS, E. LL. G. (D.S.O. L.G. 2.4.19) (Details, L.G. 10.12.19); b. 2.5.94; 2nd Lt., R.A., 12.8.14; Lt. 9.6.15; Adjt., R.A., 6.11.15 to 17.11.16; Capt. 3.11.17; Despatches; M.C.

GRIFFITHS, A. H. (D.S.O. L.G. 26.4.17) (Bar, L.G. 15.10.18); b. 9.3.84; son of late Col. H. Harcourt Griffiths; educ. Blundell's School, Tiverton; 2nd Lt., D. of Corn. L. Inf., 13.8.04; Lt. 18.1.08; Adjt. 11.4.10 to 10.4.13; Capt. 22.10.14; served Europ. War. He was mentioned in Despatches on 4.8.15. "Captain A. H. Griffiths, Duke of Cornwall's Light Infantry, 1st King's African Rifles, commanded the relieving force at Karonga on 9.9.14, and attacked the enemy with great dash, capturing two Maxims, and routing an enemy about twice the strength of his own force." Again mentioned in Despatches 11.10.17.

GRIFFITHS, C. V. (D.S.O. L.G. 11.12.18), Surg., Lt.-Cdr., R.N.

GRIFFITHS, J. LL. (D.S.O. L.G. 8.3.19) (Details, L.G. 4.10.19), Major, 1/5th Bn. Leic. R., T.F.

GRIFFITHS, SIR J. N. (D.S.O. L.G. 14.1.16); b. 13.7.71; s. of late J. Griffiths; m. Gwladys, d. of late T. Wood; two s.; two d.; Engineer and Public Works Contractor; in command of Scouts in Matabele War, 1896–97; then S. African Field Force, Brabant's (2nd Division), and afterwards as Captain and Adjutant, Lord Roberts's Bodyguard, H.Q. Staff; Despatches thrice; 2 Medals and clasps. Authority to raise 2nd King Edward's Horse, Europ. War, 1914; subsequently attached to Staff of Engineer-in-Chief, G.H.Q., to organize and initiate Tunnelling Companies, R.E.; Despatches thrice; Major; Temp. Lt.-Col.; G.S.O.1 on special mission in connection with corn and oil stores in Roumania, 1916; made Commander, Grand Star of Roumania; Officer, Legion of Honour; Order of St. Vladimir; K.C.B.; M.P., Wednesbury.

GRIFFITHS, T. (D.S.O. L.G. 3.6.16), Hon. Capt., Staff., Aust. Imp. Force.

GRIGG, SIR E. W. M. (D.S.O. L.G. 1.1.18); s. of late H. B. Grigg, C.I.E., I.C.S., and Elizabeth, d. of Sir E. Deas-Thomson, Colonial Secretary of N.S.W.; educ. Winchester (Scholar); New College, Oxford (Scholar); joined editorial staff of "The Times," 1903; Assistant Editor of the "Outlook," 1905–6; travelled 1907–8; rejoined editorial staff of "The Times," 1908; resigned 1913; joined G. Gds., 1914; became G.S.O.1, Guards' Division; Military Secretary to the Prince of Wales, Canada, 1919, Australia and New Zealand; K.C.V.O.; C.M.G.; M.C.

GRIGG, S. T. (D.S.O. L.G. 19.12.18); b. 11.10.82; 2nd Lt., W. Yorks. R., 18.1.02; Lt. 1.11.06; Adjt., W. York. R., 27.8.09 to 26.6.12; Capt. 4.2.11; Major 18.1.17; M.C.; Despatches.

GRIGOR, R. R. (D.S.O. L.G. 3.6.16), Lt.-Col., Otago Mounted Rifle Regt., N.Z. Mil. Forces.

GRIGSON, J. W. B. (D.S.O. L.G. 12.7.20), Fl.-Lt., R.A.F.; D.F.C. D.S.O. awarded for services in S. Russia.

GRIMBECK, J. D. E. (D.S.O. L.G. 22.8.18), Major (T/Lt.-Col.), 11th Mounted Rifles (Potchefstroom Ruiters).

GRIMBRECK, A. S. (D.S.O. L.G. 22.8.18), Major, Clanwilliam Commando, S. African Mil. Forces.

GRIMWADE, H. N. (D.S.O. L.G. 1.1.18), T/2nd Lt. (T/Capt.), Gen. List; M.C.

GRIMWOOD, J. (D.S.O. L.G. 1.1.17); b. 1873; s. of late G. A. Grimwood; m. Amy Mander Allender, widow of Lt. C. E. Fenwick, R.N.; educ. Forest School, Walthamstow; Marburg University; Sandhurst; obtained his commission and served with the 1st Batt. S.W.B. in Egypt; subsequently retired; rejoined the Army, Sept. 1914 (7th S.W.B.), and obtained command of Batt., 1915; Lt.-Col.; Despatches; C.B.; Controller of Cost Accounts, War Office, Jan. 1920 (temp.).

GRIMWOOD, R. F. (D.S.O. L.G. 4.6.17), Capt., London Regt.

GRINLING, E. J. (D.S.O. L.G. 3.6.19), Capt., 1/4th Bn. Linc. R., T.F.; M.C.

GRINLINTON, J. L. (D.S.O. L.G. 26.9.16); b. 25.1.80; 2nd Lt., R.A., 10.1.00; Lt. 3.4.01; Capt. 28.1.11; Major 16.10.15; Despatches. D.S.O. awarded for services 25–31.7.16, near Carnoys.

GRISSELL, B. S. (D.S.O. L.G. 1.1.17); b. 10.10.79; 2nd s. of late Thomas de la Garde Grissell, of Redisham Hall, Beccles, Suffolk; m. Olive, d. of Col. H. Wood, C.B., Rif. Brig.; one s.; two d.; educ. Warren Hill, and Harrow; 2nd Lt., Norf. Regt., 4.1.99; Lt. 14.5.00; Adjt. 28.11.05 to 27.11.07; Capt. 16.1.06; Adjt., S.R., 30.12.13; Maj. (T/Lt.Col.); extra A.D.C. to the King during the Indian Tour of 1911; was Attaché to Army Headquarters, India Q.M.G.'s branch, 1913–14. In 1916 was given command of a battalion of his own regiment; was gazetted D.A.A.G.; served S. African War, 1900–2; Queen's Medal, 3 clasps; King's Medal, 2 clasps; Europ. War; killed in action 19.4.17. His cousin, 2nd Lt. R. de M. Leathes, R.F.A., was killed near Arras 19.4.17, on the same day as Lt.-Col. Grissell was killed near Gaza.

GROGAN, SIR E. I. B., Bart. (D.S.O. L.G. 1.1.17); b. 29.11.73; s. of 1st Bart. and Katherine Charlotte, d. of Sir B. B. McMahon, 2nd Bart.; m. Ellinor, d. of R. Bosworth Smith, and widow of Sir H. Langhorne Thompson, K.C.M.G.; 2nd Lt., Rif. Brig., 19.7.93; Lt. 12.3.98; Capt. 27.6.00; Major 24.3.10; Lt.-Col. 15.6.15; Bt. Col. 3.6.18; Col. 15.6.19; served S. African War, 1899–1900; Despatches; Queen's Medal, 5 clasps; served in Imperial Ottoman Gendarmerie, 1906–8; Military Attaché, S. America, 1911–14; Europ. War, 1914–18; Despatches; C.M.G.

GROGAN, E. S. (D.S.O. L.G. 1.1.18), Capt. (T/Major), Unatt. List., E. African Forces; mentioned in Despatches (Lieut.-General Van Deventer, 21.1.1918).

GROGAN, G. M. (D.S.O. L.G. 1.1.17), T/Lt.-Col.; R. of O.; served S. African War, 1899–1902; Queen's Medal, 3 clasps; King's Medal, 2 clasps; Europ. War; Despatches.

GROGAN, G. W. ST. G. (D.S.O. L.G. 11.5.17) (Bar, L.G. 26.7.18), Brig.-Gen.; V.C.; C.B.; C.M.G. (see "The Victoria Cross," by same publishers).

GROOM, H. L. R. J. (D.S.O. L.G. 2.12.18), Lt. (A/Capt.), 1/5th Bn. R. War. R. (T.F.); M.C.

GROSE, D. C. E. (D.S.O. L.G. 4.6.17); b. 30.3.74; 2nd Lt., Derby. R., 10.10.94; A.S.C. 1.4.96; Lt. 1.4.97; Capt. 1.1.01; Major 27.10.11; Lt.-Col., R.A.S.C., 1.1.16; served S. African War, 1899–1902; Queen's Medal, clasp; King's Medal, 2 clasps; Europ. War; Despatches.

GROSS, R. F. (D.S.O. L.G. 4.6.17); b. 28.6.79; 2nd Lt., S.W.B., 4.1.99; Lt. 4.5.01; Capt. 29.11.07; Major 1.9.15; Bt. Lt.-Col. 3.6.19; served S. African War, 1900–2; Despatches (L.G. 10.9.01); Queen's Medal, 4 clasps; King's Medal, 2 clasps; Europ. War; Despatches.

GROSVENOR, HON. F. E. (D.S.O. L.G. 1.1.18) (Bar, L.G. 2.12.18); b. 8.9.83; s. of 2nd Baron Ebury; m. Mary Adela Glasson; two s.; one d.; educ. Harrow; worked as a Labourer and Pitman in mines in Isle of Man; went to Canada, 1903, and worked as Metallurgical Chemist; Asst. Managing Director, Norton Griffiths Contracting Firm in Western Canada, 1911; employed by late Duke of Sutherland to organize imperial emigration scheme in Canada, 1912; Managing Director of Norton Griffiths' interests in British Columbia, Dec. 1912, until outbreak of war; joined 29th Vancouver Batt. Can. Exp. Force, Nov. 1914 (wounded); A.D.C. to Brig.-Gen. H. D. B. Ketchen, C.E.F., 1916; Staff Capt., 1916; G.S.O.3, 1917; Brigade Major, 1917; G.S.O., 1918, and S.S.O., 1919, 4th Canadian Division; M.C. and Bar; Croix de Guerre with Palms; Despatches four times.

GROUND, T. L. (D.S.O. L.G. 3.3.17); b. 8.4.88; s. of T. Ground; educ. privately; Barton School, Wisbech; enlisted in 10th Batt. R.Fus. on formation of Batt. 29.8.14; commission March, 1916; late Temp. Capt., R. Fusiliers; served Europ. War, 1914–17; Despatches; British Military Mission to America, Oct. 1917.

GROUNDS, G. A. (D.S.O. L.G. 18.2.18) (Bar, L.G. 1.2.19), T/Capt. (A/Major), 8th Bn. Tank Corps.

GROVE, T. T. (D.S.O. L.G. 1.1.17) (Details, L.G. 18.7.18) (Bar, L.G. 3.2.20); b. 1879; 2nd Lt., R.E., 23.6.98; Lt. 1.4.01; Capt. 23.6.07; Major 30.1.15; Bt. Lt.-Col. 1.1.18; served Europ. War, 1914–17; Despatches; Bt. Lt.-Col.; C.M.G.

GROVER, A. (D.S.O. L.G. 26.7.18), Lt. (A/Major), Bedfords. R.; M.C.

GROVES, E. J. (D.S.O. L.G. 2.12.18); b. 23.8.94; 2nd s. of Col. J. E. G. Groves, C.M.G., and Ethel Lloyd Groves, d. of late C. J. Allen; m. Hon. Norah Evelyn McGarel-Hogg, d. of 2nd Baron Magheramorne and his wife, *née* Lady Evelyn Baring; one s.; educ. The Leas School, Hoylake; Uppingham; 2nd Lt., Ches. R., 14.8.14; Lt. 1.12.14; Capt., S. Gds., 16.1.20; served Europ. War, 1914–18; Despatches thrice; twice severely wounded; M.C.; transferred S. Gds., 1920.

GROVES, P. R. C. (D.S.O. L.G. 1.1.17); b. 26.3.78; s. of J. Groves, late P.W.D., India; m. Suzanne, d. of E. Steen; educ. Bedford; joined K.S.L.I., 1899; Capt., 1910; Major, 1915; T/Lt.-Col., 1916; Colonel, 1919; T/Brig.-Gen., 1918; transferred to R.A.F. with rank of Group Captain, 1919; served S. African War; Queen's Medal, 4 clasps; King's Medal, 2 clasps; employed with W. African R., 1903–4; Territorial Adjt., 1909–12; joined R.F.C., 1914; served with Air Services, France, 1914–15; Dardanelles, 1915–16; Middle East, 1916–18; Air Ministry, 1918–19; Observer; Pilot; G.S.O.3; G.S.O.2; G.S.O.1; Wing Commander; Director of Flying Operations, Air Ministry, April, 1918; British Air Representative Peace Conference, Jan. 1919; Despatches thrice; C.B.; C.M.G.; Order of the White Eagle of Serbia, 3rd Class with Swords; Commander of the Legion of Honour; Air Adviser to the British Ambassador, Paris, for Peace Treaties, and British Air Representative on the Permanent Advisory Commission to the League of Nations.

GROVES, R. M. (D.S.O. L.G. 22.6.16); b. 1880; 2nd son of late James Grimble Groves, D.L., J.P.; m. Cecily, d. of Fredk. Platt Higgins; one s.; two d.; educ. Rossall, and R.N. School, Eltham; H.M.S. Britannia; Naval Cadet, 1894; Midshipman, 1896; Sub-Lt., 1899; Lt., 1900; Cdr., 1911; Capt., 1917; entered R.N.A.S. as Wing Cdr., 1914; Wing Capt., 1917; Deputy Chief of Air

Staff; Lt.-Col. (T/Brig.-Gen.), R.A.F.; served Europ. War; Despatches; Officier, Legion of Honour, 1917; A.F.C., 1918; C.B.

GRUBB, H. W. (D.S.O. L.G. 1.1.18); b. 26.12.75; s. of Lt.-Col. Alex. Grubb, J.P. (late R.A.); m. Eva Noel, d. of late Capt. Arthur Mears, Madras Staff Corps; two s.; one d.; educ. Wellington College; 2nd Lt., Bord. R., 9.12.95; Lt. 11.7.00; Adjt. 24.6.03 to 23.6.06; Capt. 4.2.07; Major 18.5.15; Bt. Lt.-Col. 1.1.17; C.M.G.; Mérite Agricole, Grade d'Officier.

GRUTE, J. (D.S.O. L.G. 1.1.17); b. 23.10.67; Lt., R.A., 4.3.93; Insp. O. Mach., 3rd Class, 1.4.96 (attd.); 2nd Class 4.3.99; 1st Class 4.3.08; Major, A.O.D., 4.3.11; Act. Chf. Insp., R.A.O.C., 9.3.17 to July, 1917; Despatches.

GUARD, F. H. W. (D.S.O. L.G. 1.1.18), Lt.-Col., late R. Scots.; served Europ. War, 1914–18; Despatches; C.M.G.

GUBBINS, S. (D.S.O. L.G. 15.4.16); b. 25.6.82; s. of E. H. Gubbins; educ. Church of England Grammar School, Melbourne; 2nd Lt., R. Fus., 23.4.02, from 5th Contingent, Victorian Mounted Rifles; Capt. 24.4.12; Major 7.3.16; Lt.-Colonel, ret. pay, 1921; served S. Africa, 1900–2; Queen's Medal, 5 clasps; was 5 years in the Bush in N. Nigeria; employed with W.A.F.F., 1904–9; served Europ. War from 1914; O.B.E.

CUEST, HON. F. E. (D.S.O. L.G. 4.5.17); b. 14.6.75; s. of 1st Baron Wimborne; m. Amy, d. of H. Phipps; two sons; one daughter; Capt. R. of O., late 1st Life Guards; served Nile Exp., 1899; Despatches; Egyptian Medal with 2 clasps; S. African War, 1901–2; Queen's Medal with 5 clasps; Europ. War from 1914, first as A.D.C. to F.M. Sir John French; in E. Africa, 1916–17; Despatches twice; Chevalier; C.B.E.; was Private Secretary to Mr. Winston Churchill; Treasurer of H.M.'s Household, 1912–15; was made a Privy Councillor.

GUGGISBERG, F. G. (D.S.O. L.G. 1.1.18); b. 20.7.69; e. s. of late F. Guggisberg; m. Lilian Decima Moore, C.B.E.; educ. Burney's, Hampshire; R.M.A., Woolwich; ent. R.E. 15.2.89; Lt. 15.2.92; Capt. 15.2.00; Major 4.10.08; Lt.-Col., 1916; Brig.-General; was Surveyor-General of Nigeria, 1910–14; commanded 94th Field Co., R.E., 1914; C.R.E., 8th Division, 1915; C.R.E., 66th Division, 1916; commanded 170th Inf. Brig., 1917; Asst. Inspector-General of Training, G.H.Q., France, 1918; commanded 100th Inf. Brig., 1919; Despatches 5 times; Bt. Col., 1919; C.M.G.; Chevalier, Legion of Honour; has written "The Shop: the Story of the R.M.A." and other books.

GUILD, A. M. (D.S.O. L.G. 3.6.19), Major, Highland Cyclists' Batt. London R.

GUILD, J. R. (D.S.O. L.G. 8.3.19) (Details, L.G. 4.10.19); b. 25.5.88; 2nd Lt., Glouc. R., 3.2.09; Lt. 12.7.11; Capt. 27.11.14; served Europ. War; Despatches; Bt. Major 3.6.19.

GUINNESS, E. C. (D.S.O. L.G. 1.1.18), Lt. (T/Major), R. Irish Rgt.

GUINNESS, HON. W. E. (D.S.O. L.G. 26.9.17) (Details, L.G. 9.1.18) (Bar, L.G. 26.7.18); b. 1880; s. of 1st Viscount Iveagh; m. Lady Evelyn Erskine, d. of 14th Earl of Buchan; two s.; one d.; educ. Eton; rowed three years in Eton eight, and was Captain of the Boats; Lt.-Colonel, formerly D.Y.O. Loyal Suffolk Hussars; served in S. Africa, as Captain, 44th (Suffolk) Co., Imp. Yeom.; wounded; Despatches; Queen's Medal, 4 clasps; Europ. War, 1914–18, in command of batt. as Brig.-Major and G.S.O.2; Despatches thrice; Officer, Crown of Roumania.

GUNN, A. D. (D.S.O. L.G. 23.10.19); b. 17.4.84; 2nd Lt., Devon. R., 2.3.84; I.A. 11.7.05; Lt. 2.6.06; Capt., 110th Inf., I.A., 2.8.13; Major 2.8.19; Despatches.

GUNN, H. B. L. G. (D.S.O. L.G. 1.1.18); b. 17.10.80; 2nd Lt., R.A., 4.5.01; Lt. 31.1.04; Adjt., R.A., 12.10.11; Capt. 4.5.14; Adjt., R.A., 1.3.15 to 26.4.15; Major 30.12.15; served Europ. War; Bt. Lt.-Col. 3.6.19; Despatches; M.C.

GUNN, J. A. (D.S.O. L.G. 1.1.17), Lt.-Col., Can. Inf.; served Europ. War, 1914–18; Despatches; C.M.G.

GUNN, J. N. (D.S.O. L.G. 3.6.18), Lt.-Col., Can. A.M.C.

GUNNING, G. H. (D.S.O. L.G. 7.2.18); b. 3.11.76; 2nd Lt., Unatt., 20.1.97; I.S.C. 15.3.98; Lt., I.A., 20.4.99; Capt. 20.1.06; Major 20.1.15; Bt. Major 1.1.19; served Tirah, 1897–98; Medal with 2 clasps; N.W. Frontier of India, Waziristan, 1901–2; clasp; N.W. Frontier of India, 1902; operations against the Darwesh Khel Waziris; Europ. War; Despatches.

GUNNING, O. G. (D.S.O. L.G. 17.3.17) (Details, L.G. 11.5.17); b. 31.7.67; s. of Col. J. Gunning; m. Margaret Cecilia, d. of Clinton Dawkins, of the Foreign Office, sometime Consul-General of Venice; one s.; two d.; educ. Haileybury College; 2nd Lt., Manch. R., 22.3.88; 35th Sikhs, I.A., 17.11.94; Capt. 22.8.99; Major 22.8.06; Lt.-Colonel 22.8.14; Bt. Colonel; served Miranzai (2nd) Exp., 1891; Medal with clasp; Exp. to Dongola, 1896; Egyptian Medal; Medal; N.W. Frontier of India, 1897–98, Malakand; operations in Bajaur and in the Mamund country; Utman Khel (severely wounded); Despatches twice; Medal with clasp. On leave in England at outbreak of war, 1914; lent to War Office; posted to 47th Sikhs in France 12.1.14 (entitled to 1914 Star); returned to India, March, 1915; left India for service with 36th Sikhs in Mesopotamia 21.2.16; wounded 1.2.17; invalided home, Aug. 1917; died at Wynberg Hospital, Cape Town, 14.11.17. Brig.-Gen. Gunning was four times mentioned in Despatches during the Europ. War.; C.M.G.; Russian Order of St. Stanislas.

GUNTER, A. C. (D.S.O. L.G. 3.6.19); b. 6.3.81; 2nd Lt., R.A., 2.5.00; Lt. 3.4.01; Capt. 9.11.12; Adjt., R.A., 23.3.14 to 29.12.15; Major, R.G.A., 30.12.15; Despatches.

GUNTER, F. E., M.B. (D.S.O. L.G. 1.2.17); b. 6.3.81; 2nd Lt., R.A., 2.5.00; Lt. 3.4.01; Capt. 9.11.12; Major; Lt.-Col. 1.5.15; retired R.A.M.C. 24.9.19.

GURNEY, C. H. (D.S.O. L.G. 1.1.17) (Bar, L.G. 26.7.18), T/Lt.-Col., E. Yorks. R.

GUSH, H. W. (D.S.O. L.G. 24.9.18), T/Major, (A/Lt.-Col.), North'd Fusiliers; M.C.

GÜTERBOCK, P. G. J. (D.S.O. L.G. 1.1.19), Capt., 4th Bn. Glouc. R., T.F.

O. V. Guy.

GUY, B. J. D. (D.S.O. L.G. 23.5.17), Cdr., R.N.; V.C. (see "The Victoria Cross," by same publishers).

GUY, K. A. FERRERS- (D.S.O. L.G. 11.11.19), Cdr., R.N., 30.6.18.

GUY, O. V. (D.S.O. L.G. 2.12.18); b. 15.12.90; s. of Rev. Canon D. S. Guy and Mary, d. of Rev. H. Owen; m. Ethel Frances, d. of Col. R. K. Teversham, D.S.O., O.B.E.; educ. Preparatory School, Sedbergh; Marlborough (Scholar); Jesus College, Cambridge (1st Class Honours Classical Tripos, Part I., 1913); joined 9th W. Yorks. R., 9.9.14; Lt., Dec. 1914; Capt. 10.8.15; transferred to Tank Corps 22.1.17; Major; served in Gallipoli, 1915; Egypt and France, 1916; France, 1917–18; M.C. awarded for Somme 14.9.16; Bar awarded for Cambrai 20–23.11.17.

GUY, R. F. (D.S.O. L.G. 14.1.16); b. 1878; s. of late R. J. Guy, of Taranaki, N.Z.; m. Mrs. M. A. Dolphin (*née* de Blaquiere); educ. Monkton Combe School, near Bath; joined Wilts. R., in S. Africa, 21.4.00 from the 9th K.R.R.C; Lt. 31.1.01; Adjt., Wilts. R., 7.9.05 to 6.9.08; Capt. 17.10.08; Major 1.9.15; served S. African War, 1899–1902; Queen's Medal with 3 clasps; King's Medal with 2 clasps; Europ. War; Despatches; Bt. Lt.-Col. 3.6.18; C.M.G.

GWATKIN, F. (D.S.O. L.G. 3.6.19); b. 12.4.85; m. Lydia Winifred, d. of late Col. E. C. Stanton, R.E.; 2nd Lt., Unatt., 19.8.03; Indian Army 19.12.04; Lt. 19.11.05; Capt. 19.8.12; Major, 18th Lancers, I.A., 19.8.18; Despatches; M.C.

GWYN, H. G. MOORE- (see Moore-Gwyn, H. G.)

GWYN-THOMAS G. (D.S.O. L.G., 14.11.16); b. 19.7.71; 2nd Lt., Devon R., 4.3.91; Lt., Devon. R., 23.11.94; Lt., I.S.C., 25.5.95; Capt., I.A., 10.7.01; Major 4.3.09; Lt.-Col. 4.3.17; Colonel 19.7.20; T/Col.-Comdt. 1.1.21; Despatches; C.M.G.

R. V. Gwynne.

GWYNN, K. D. H. (D.S.O. L.G. 4.11.15) (Bar, L.G. 11.1.19), T/Major, 11th Batt., R.F. (see "The Distinguished Service Order," from its institution to 31.12.15, by same publishers).

GWYNN, R. S. (D.S.O. L.G. 14.1.16); b. 17.7.80; s. of late H. Gwynn; educ. Clifton College; Sandhurst; 2nd Lt., S.W.B., 20.1.00; Lt. 17.3.02; Capt. 5.7.08; Major 1.9.15; Adjt., 1st S.W.B., 1915; served S. African War, 1899–1902; Queen's Medal with 3 clasps; King's Medal with 2 clasps; served Europ. War; T/Lt.-Col., Sept. 1915, and commanded the Battalion in the Battle of Loos; Despatches; and subsequently served on the Staff; Despatches.

GWYNNE A. H. EVANS- (see Evans-Gwynne, A. H.

GWYNNE, R. V. (D.S.O. L.G. 17.4.17); b. 16.5.82, at 97, Harley Street, London, W.; s. of James Eglinton Anderson Gwynne, of Folkington Manor, Polegate, Sussex (now dead), and Mary Earle Gwynne, of above address (*née* Purvis); educ. privately; Trinity Hall, Cambridge; played polo for Cambridge University, 1902; Barrister, Inner Temple; joined Sussex Yeomanry, April, 1904; Lt., 1906; Capt., 1910; Major, Nov. 1914; served Europ. War, 1914–19, in France and Belgium; attached to 10th Queen's R.W. Surrey Rgt., Oct. 1916, and transferred to the Batt., March, 1917; A/Lt.-Col., June, 1917; wounded 24.2.17; Despatches, May, 1917; very severely wounded 1.8.17. D.S.O. awarded for gallantry on 24.2.17 (Immediate Award).

A. Gwynne-Jones.

GWYNNE-JONES, A. (D.S.O. L.G. 20.10.16), 2nd Lt., E. Surrey Regt., S.R.; later Welsh Guards.

GWYTHER, G. H. (D.S.O. L.G. 1.1.17); b. 30.8.72., 2nd Lt. (from Mil.), R.W.F. 7.3.00; Lt. 4.2.03; Capt. 6.4.11.; Major (T/Lt.-Col.), R.W.F.

GYLES, R. W. (D.S.O. L.G. 2.4.19) Details, L.G. 10.12.19), Capt., 46th Batt. Can. Inf., Saskatchewan R.; M.C.

HABGOOD, A. H., B.A., B.C., M.B., M.R.C.S., L.R.C.P., D.P.H.Eng. (D.S.O. L.G. 1.1.18); b. 23.7.82; s. of Dr. H. Habgood (Surg.-Col. T.F., V.D.) and the late Sarah L. Habgood, d. of the late Dr. G. Mundie; educ. at Dover College; Jesus College, Cambridge, and the London Hospital; R.A.M.C., S.R., as Lt. 23.9.09; Capt., March, 1913; went to France, Aug. 1914, with 3rd Division; Mons 1914 Star, and was in the Retreat from Mons. He served with the division for three and a half years, and was given the command of the 142nd F.A. in Sept. 1916; was mentioned in Despatches, Dec. 1917; severely wounded, Aug. 1918, during the last British offensive.

HACKETT, T. D. H. (D.S.O. L.G. 23.7.20), b. 19.9.81; 2nd Lt., R.A., 19.12.00; Lt. 19.12.03; Capt. 17.9.07; Major, I.A., 19.12.15; served S. African War, 1902, with Imp. Yeom. (Queen's Medal with 2 clasps); Europ. War.

HACKING, A. (D.S.O. L.G. 15.2.19) (Details, L.G. 30.7.19) (Bar, L.G. 1.1.19); b. 1884; son of Ven. Archdeacon Egbert Hacking, M.A., and Margaret, d. of W. Bentham; educ. Marlborough; served in France, 1915–18, commanding 5th Bn. Sherwood Foresters; Despatches three times; M.C.; commanded 19th County of London Bn., 1920–1; Lt.-Col.

HADOW, R. W. (D.S.O. L.G. 17.12.17) (Details, L.G. 23.4.18), Major (A/Lt.-Col.), R. of O., R. Highrs.; served S. African War, 1901–2 (Queen's Medal with 4 clasps); Sudan, 1910 (Sudan Medal with clasp); Europ. War.

HAGARTY, W. G. (D.S.O. L.G. 20.10.16); b. 2.8.85; s. of J. H. G. Hagarty, of Toronto, g. s. of late Sir J. H. Hagarty, Chief Justice of Ontario; m. Florence Taaffe, d. of late Francis Charles Plunkett, M.D.; one d.; educ. Trinity College School, Port Hope, Canada; R.M.C., Canada; commissioned in R. Can. Artillery, 1906; Capt. 1912; Major, R. Can. Horse Artillery, 1916; served Europ. War; Despatches. His D.S.O. was awarded for gallantry on 30.8.16 at Angle Wood.

HAHN, J. E. (D.S.O. L.G. 3.6.19), Major, 1st Battn. Can. Inf., W. Ontario R.; M.C.

HAIG, A. G. (D.S.O. L.G. 14.1.16); b. 12.1.77; s. of late H. A. Haig; m. Mary Astley, d. of late J. Bromwich; three s.; educ. Winchester College; 2nd Lt., R.A., 21.9.96; Lt. 21.9.99; Capt. 23.12.01; Major 30.10.14; Lt.-Col., R.G.A., 1.5.21; served S. African War, 1900–2 (Queen's Medal and 3 clasps; King's Medal and 2 clasps); Europ. War, 1914–19: Despatches; C.M.G.; Bt. Lt.-Col. 1.1.17; commanding Mountain Artillery Brigade, Peshawar.

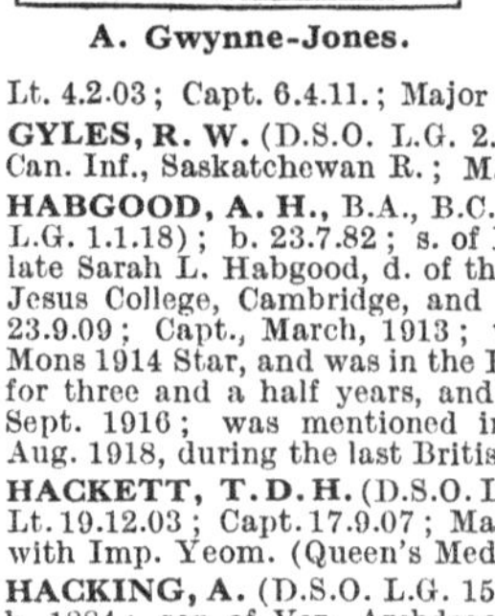

J. Haig.

HAIG, C. H. (D.S.O. L.G. 1.1.17); b. 16.1.74; s. of late H. A. Haig and Agnes Catherine, d. of M. Pollock; m. Mabel, d. of Sir Horatio Davies; educ. Winchester College; 2nd Lt., Leic. R., 7.3.94; Lt. 17.7.97; Capt. 1.4.02; Adjt., Leic. R., 23.3.05 to 22.3.08; Major 11.11.14; Lt.-Col. 5.7.21; served S. African War, 1899–1902 (Queen's Medal, 5 clasps; King's Medal, 2 clasps); Europ. War, 1914–18; Bt. Lt.-Col. 1.1.19.

HAIG, J. (D.S.O. L.G. 1.1.18); b. 1.2.78; s. of H. V. Haig and A. A. Haig, and nephew of F.M. Earl Haig; m. R. D. Wolseley, d. of C. E. Hay; one s.; one d.; educ. Eton; Trinity Hall, Cambridge; 2nd Lt., Fife Light Horse, 1900; Capt.; transferred to Westminster Dragoons Yeomanry, 1910; served Europ.

War; Major, 1.1.14; in Egypt, Sept. 1914; Ind. Exp. Force (Suez Canal), 1915; Salonika, operations round Dorian, 1915–16, commanding Composite Yeomanry Regt.; on the Western Frontier, Egypt, 1916; Sinai and Palestine, 1917–18. D.S.O. for work done in the field whilst commanding Divisional Cavalry Squadron, summer of 1917. He served in France, 1918; Lt.-Col. July, 1918; Despatches three times.

HAIG, R. C. (D.S.O. L.G. 18.2.15) (1st Bar, L.G. 18.6.17) (2nd Bar, L.G. 26.7.18); Bars gazetted as Haig, Roland (see "The Distinguished Service Order," from its institution to 31st Dec. 1915, same publishers).

HAIG, W., M.B. (D.S.O. L.G. 1.1.17); b. 3.12.70; s. of W. Haig and Martha, d. of D. Colville; educ. Edinburgh University and Edinburgh Royal College of Surgeons; M.B. and Master in Surgery; ent. Volunteer Force in 1900; Territorials, 1908; has T.D.; served Europ. War, M.O., with Forth Garrison Artillery and R.E., from Aug. 1914, to April, 1915; went abroad, May, 1915, with 1st Black Watch (R. Highrs.), and served with them till March, 1917; served with 1/3rd Highland Field Amb. from March, 1917, to Oct. 1917; attd. to 34th Amb. Train; subsequently commanded 37th Amb. Train (The Fair Maid of Perth) from its mobilization in Nov. 1917, until its demobilization July, 1919.

HAIG, W. DE H. (D.S.O. L.G. 3.6.18); b. 25.8.84; 2nd Lt., R.E., 15.7.03; Lt. 1.1.06; Capt. 15.7.14; Bt. Major.

HAIG-BROWN, A. R. (D.S.O. L.G. 4.6.17); y. s. of late Rev. Canon Haig-Brown, Master of Charterhouse; m. Le Violet Mary, d. of A. Pope; one s.; two d.; educ. at Charterhouse and Cambridge; represented Pembroke College for running and cricket; he was the author of "Sporting Sonnets," "My Game Book" and "The O.T.C. in the Great War." For nearly nine years he commanded the Lancing College O.T.C. Col. Haig-Brown became Second-in-Command of a service battalion of the Middlesex Regt. He was afterwards promoted to Lt.-Col. of the same battalion. He was killed in action 25.3.18.

HAIGH, B. (D.S.O. L.G. 1.1.18), Lt.-Col., A.S.C.; served S. African War, 1900, Imperial Yeomanry (Queen's Medal with 3 clasps); Europ. War; Despatches.

HAILES, W. A. (D.S.O. L.G. 26.11.17) (Details, L.G. 6.4.18), Major, Aust. A.M.C.

HAINES, L. E. (D.S.O. L.G. 3.6.16), Major, 7th Can. Inf. Bn.

HALAHAN, F. C. (D.S.O. L.G. 1.1.18); s. of late Col. S. H. Halahan; m. Muriel, d. of late J. G. Groves, D.L., J.P. Cheshire; two s.; one d.; educ. Dulwich College; ent. R.N., 1896; Lt. 1900; Wing Capt., R.N.A.S., 1917; T/Col. and Lt.-Col., R.A.F., April, 1918; Air Commodore; M.V.O. 1907; served Europ. War, 1914–18; C.M.G.; promoted Wing Capt.; Legion of Honour.

HALDANE, C. L. (D.S.O. L.G. 7.2.18); b. 23.11.66; 2nd Lt., W. York. R., 10.11.88; Lt., W. York. R., 24.9.90; I.S.C. 21.4.91; Capt., I.A., 10.11.99; Major 10.11.14; Lt.-Col.; served Europ. War; Despatches; C.M.G.; Order of the Nile, 4th Class.

HALDANE, L. A. (D.S.O. L.G. 14.1.16); b. 20.7.83; 2nd Lt., North'n R., 22.4.03; Lt. 20.5.05; Capt. 11.1.11; T/Major, June, 1915; Camp Commandant 3.9.15 to 14.2.16. He was killed in action 2.4.16.

HALES, REV. J. P., M.A. (D.S.O. L.G. 1.1.17); b. 7.10.70; s. of George and Ann Hales; m. Augusta Margaret Cantrell, d. of Col. and Mrs. Cantrell-Hubbersty; one s.; four d.; educ. Winchester; Jesus College, Cambridge; Deacon, 1893; Priest, 1895; Chaplain to 8th Sherwood Foresters, 1913, and to the Sherwood Foresters Territorial Brigade, 1915, on its leaving for service abroad; Divisional Chaplain, 1916; T/Deputy Assistant Chaplain-Gen. 12.2.18; Rector of Cotgrave, Nottingham, since 1897.

HALKETT, H. M. CRAIGIE- (see Craigie-Halkett, H. M.).

HALL, C. C. H. (D.S.O. L.G. 16.9.18), T/Capt. (A/Major), Durham L.I. He was killed in action 27.5.18.

HALL, C. H. T. B. (D.S.O. L.G. 14.1.16), T/Major, M.M.G. Service.

HALL, C. R. (D.S.O. L.G. 30.1.20); b. 5.11.77; 2nd Lt., R. Munster Fus., 4.5.98; Lt. 4.12.99; Capt. 1.9.07; Major 23.5.15; served S. African War, 1899–1902 (Queen's Medal with clasp; King's Medal with 2 clasps); served Europ. War; Despatches.

HALL, D. K. E. (D.S.O. L.G. 4.6.17); b. 7.4.69; e. s. of late Col. Sir Angus W. Hall, K.C.B.; m. Katharine Isabel, d. of T. A. Lewis; one s.; two d.; educ. Cheltenham College; entered Army, Sc. Rifles, 1888; Major, R. of O., 3rd Bn. Dorset R., 20.5.98; Lt.-Col., Retired List; served Ashanti Exp. 1895–6 (Honourably Mentioned; Star); operations in S. Africa, 1896–7 (Despatches; Brevet of Major; Medal and clasp); Staff Capt., Egypt, 1899–1902; Egyptian Army, 1902–6 (Medjidieh, 3rd Class); Europ. War, 1914–18; D.A.Q.M.G. and A.A. and Q.M.G.; Base Commandant, Salonika Exp. Force; G.O.C., Lines of Communication, Army of Black Sea; Bt. Lt.-Col.; T/Major-Gen.; C.M.G.; French Croix de Guerre; Greek Orders of the Redeemer and Military Merit; Serbian Order of the White Eagle.

HALL, D. M. B. (D.S.O. L.G. 1.2.19); b. 30.12.96; s. of Sir D. B. Hall, Bart., and Caroline, d. of T. Y. Montgomery; m. Mary, d. of Capt. W. A. Grant, late 13th Hrs.; one d.; educ. Eton; R.M.C., Sandhurst; 2nd Lt., C. Gds., 9.9.11; Lt. 24.1.14; Capt. 30.9.15; served Europ. War, 1914–19; wounded twice; Despatches thrice.

HALL, E. (D.S.O. L.G. 1.1.17), Major, Notts. and Derby. R.

HALL, E. C. (D.S.O. L.G. 3.6.18), Maj., R.F.A.

HALL, F., M.P. (D.S.O. L.G. 1.1.18), T/Lt.-Col., R.F.A.

HALL, G. W. (D.S.O. L.G. 1.2.19), Major, 12th Field Ambulance, Can. A.M.C.

HALL, H. F. (D.S.O. L.G. 4.6.17), Major, R.F.A., T.D.

HALL, H. R. (D.S.O. L.G. 3.6.19), Capt. (A/Major), A/47th Brig. R.F.A.; M.C.

HALL, H. S. H. (D.S.O. L.G. 22.9.16), Capt., R. Fus.

HALL, JOHN HAMILTON (D.S.O. L.G. 23.9.16) (Bar, L.G. 18.6.17); b. 23.2.71; educ. Fettes College, Edinburgh, and at Sandhurst; passed into the Army in 1891; 2nd Lt., Middx. R., 7.11.91; Lt. 16.9.92; Capt. 14.3.00; Major 17.2.08; Lt.-Col.; 28.9.16; Col. 28.9.20; served in S. African War, 1901–2, on the Staff; operations in Transvaal, June, 1901, to 31.5.02; also in Orange River Colony, March to April, 1902 (Queen's Medal with 4 clasps); served Europ. War; Despatches. D.S.O. for gallantry at Beaumont Hamel on 1.7.16. Bar for gallantry at Heudecourt.

HALL, JOHN HATHORN (D.S.O. L.G. 3.6.19), T Capt. Gen., List; M.C.

HALL, P. A. (D.S.O. L.G. 1.1.19), Capt. (A/Major), Bucks. Bn. Oxf. and Bucks. L.I., T.F.; M.C.

HALL, P. DE H. (D.S.O. L.G. 3.6.19); Major (A/Lt.-Col.), R.E., T.F.; served Europ. War; Despatches; M.C.

HALL, P. L. (D.S.O. L.G. 3.6.19), Major, 24th Bn. Can. Inf., Quebec R.; M.C.

HALL, P. S. (D.S.O. L.G. 20.10.16); b. 12.9.79; s. of Rev. T. G. Sarsfield Hall; m. Maud Elizabeth Glennie; educ. Dover College; Sandhurst; Lt.-Col.; served S. African War with W. Kent. R., 1900–1; Europ. War, 1914–17; Second-in-Command 17th W. Yorks. R. 9.3.15 to 11.7.16; commanding 13th Cheshire R. 11.7.16 to 21.10.16, during the Battle of the Somme (wounded); commanded 15th (S.B.) Cheshire R., from Feb. 1917.

P. S. Hall.

HALL, R. H. CLARK- (see Clark-Hall, R.H.).

HALL G. C. W. GORDON- (see Gordon-Hall, G. C. W.).

HALLARD, H. R. (D.S.O. L.G. 3.6.18), Major, Aust. F.A.

HALLETT, J I. (D.S.O. L.G. 29.8.17), Lt.-Cdr., R.N.

HALLIDAY, W. J. F. (D.S.O. L.G. 16.8.17) (1st Bar, L.G. 26.7.18) (2nd Bar, L.G. 16.9.18); b. 6.8.82; 2nd Lt., R.A., 4.12.01; Lt. 4.12.04; Capt. 1.10.14; Major, R.F.A., 21.12.15; Despatches.

HALLIFAX, O. E. (D.S.O. L.G. 17.11.17) (Details, 23.3.18), Lt.-Cdr., R.N. 15.12.18.

HALLILEY, A. K. McC. (D.S.O. L.G. 17.10.19), Lt., R.N., 30.6.12.

HALLOWELL-CAREW, R. R. (D.S.O. L.G. 27.5.19), Lt.-Cdr., R.N., 1.4.15.

HALLOWES, R. C., M.B. (D.S.O. L.G. 3.6.18), Major (T/Lt.-Col.), R.A.M.C.

HALLSMITH, G. (D.S.O. L.G. 4.2.18) (Details, L.G. 5.7.18), 2nd Lt., Suffolk R.

HALLWARD, B. M. (D.S.O. L.G. 4.6.17), 2nd Lt. (T/Major), R. Brig., S.R.

HALLWRIGHT, W. W. (D.S.O. L.G. 12.5.17); y. s. of Matthew Hallwright, M.R.C.S. and E. Janet Hallwright; Lt.-Cdr. R.N. He was killed in action in command of his ship wnen on special service, 21.4.17.

HAMBLY, A. (D.S.O. L.G. 6.4.18), Cdr., R.N.

HAMER, M. A. (D.S.O. L.G. 22.12.16); b. 11.8.77; 2nd Lt., Unatt., 22.1.98; I.S.C. 29.3.99; Lt. 22.4.00; Capt. 22.1.07; Major 1.9.15; 129th Baluchis, I.A.; Lt.-Col. 1.2.21; Despatches; M.C.

HAMERSLEY, HAROLD ST. G. (D.S.O. L.G. 3.6.16); b. 3.3.82; s. of Lt.-Col. A. St. G. Hamersley, K.C., M.P., and Isabella Maud, d. of Hastings Snow; m. Martha Emily, d. of Rear-Admiral R. Carter; one s.; two d.; educ. R.M.C., Kingston, Canada; 2nd Lt., A.S.C., 6.8.04; Lt. 6.8.06; Capt. 19.12.13; Major, R.A.S.C., 19.4.18; D.A.D. of S. and T. in Salonika, 23.8.17 to 24.12.17; served in Europ. War, 1914–18, in France, taking part in the Retreat from Mons, and the advance over the Marne; Salonika, 1917–19; Despatches twice.

HAMERSLEY, HUGH ST. G. (D.S.O. L.G. 3.6.18); b. 11.11.78; e. s. of Lt.-Col. A. St. G. Hamersley, K.C., M.P., and Isabella Maud, d. of Hastings Snow; m. Marguerite Eveline, d. of late Dr. J. R. H. Sutton, formerly of Dublin; two d.; educ. R.M.C., Kingston, Canada; 2nd Lt., R.A., 1898; Lt. 1901; Capt. 1904; Major, 1914; A/Lt.-Col. 1917; served S. African War, 1900–1 (Queen's Medal with 4 clasps); Europ. War; commanded, 1916, 121st Siege By. Western Front, and, 1917–19, 64th Brig. R.G.A., Western Front; Despatches twice; British War Medal; Victory Medal and Oak Leaf; Officier de Léopold with Palm; Belgian Croix de Guerre; Inter-Allied Commission of Control, Germany, 1919–21.

HAMILTON, A. G. (D.S.O. L.G. 17.4.18), Cdr., R.N.

HAMILTON, B. H. N. H. (D.S.O. L.G. 3.6.18), Capt. (T/Major), R.A.F.

HAMILTON, C. G. COLE- (see Cole-Hamilton, C. G.).

HAMILTON, C. L. C. (D.S.O. L.G. 3.6.16); b. 14.2.74; s. of H. Hamilton; m. Veronica, d. of J. I. Boswell; two s.; one d.; educ. at Haileybury and Woolwich; ent. R.A. 1.4.93; Lt. 1.4.96; Capt. 28.5.00; Adjt. 17 March, 1905, to 31.3.08; Major 30.3.10; Lt.-Col. 14.11.15; served in S. African War, 1902 (Queen's Medal with 3 clasps); served Europ. War, 1914–18; Despatches; C.M.G.

HAMILTON, E. G. (D.S.O. L.G. 24.6.16) (Details, L.G. 27.7.16); b. 20.1.83; s. of late C. G. Hamilton; m. Ethel Marie, d. of late J. M. Frith; two s.; educ. Wellington College; Sandhurst; joined Connaught Rangers, 1902; Capt., 1911; served in France with Exp. Force, Aug. 1914–Feb. 1915; Staff Capt., Feb. 1915; Brig. Major, Sept. 1915; went to Mesopotamia with Indian Corps, Dec. 1915, having served continuously from outbreak of war; Despatches thrice; C.M.G.; Military Cross; promoted.

HAMILTON, G. B. ROWAN- (see Rowan-Hamilton, G. B.).

HAMILTON, G. M. (D.S.O. L.G. 3.6.18), Capt. (A/Major), R.F.A.

HAMILTON, G. T. (D.S.O. L.G. 4.6.17); b. 5.7.81; s. of His Grace the Most Rev. C. Hamilton, D.D., late Archbishop of Ottawa, and Frances, d. of T. H. Thomson; m. Nancy, d. of H. Butler, of Le Houlme, near Rouen; one d.; educ. Trinity College School and R.M. College, Canada; 2nd Lt., R.A., 23.5.00; Lt. 1.2.02; Adjt., R.A., 15.7.10 to 29.5.13; Capt., Jan. 1911; Major 30.10.14; Lt.-Col.

HAMILTON, H. A. W. COLE- (see Cole-Hamilton, H. A. W.).

HAMILTON, H. W. R. (D.S.O. L.G. 25.8.17); b. 13.4.92; 2nd Lt., R.E., 23.12.11; Lt. 24.12.13; Capt. 26.6.17; Despatches; M.C.

HAMILTON, J. (D.S.O. L.G. 3.6.18), s. of Judge Hamilton, of Sydney, N.S. Wales; Major, Australian Military Forces.

HAMILTON, J. A. (D.S.O. L.G. 1.1.17), Major (T/Lt.-Col.), R.A.S.C., late West India Regt.; Tsing Sen, 1914; France, 1915 (command of 20th Divisional Train); 1919, North Russia, 238th Special Brigade; New Year, 1921, Waziristan Force, India. He died on the 19th July, 1921, on Indus, Dera Ismail Khan, of illness contracted on active service and excessive heat.

J. S. Hamilton.

HAMILTON, J. M. (D.S.O. L.G. 3.6.16); b. 4.11.86; s. of L. Hamilton; m. Violet Anne, d. of late Lt.-Col. J. Colquhoun; educ. Winchester and Sandhurst; gazetted to G. Highrs. 1907; Lt. 1910; Capt. 1915; Bt. Major, 1915; G.S.O.2, 1917; Brig.-Major, 31st Inf. Brigade; Despatches three times; Legion of Honour (Officer).

HAMILTON, J. S. (D.S.O. L.G. 4.2.18) (Details, L.G. 5.7.18); 2nd s. of J. B. Hamilton; 2nd Lt., W. Yorks. R. His D.S.O. was awarded for services in the brilliant advance of the W. Yorks. R., which was the subject of high commendation by F.M. Sir D. Haig.

HAMILTON, N. C. (D.S.O. L.G. 2.5.16); b. 2.8.79; 2nd Lt., A.S.C., 25.7.03; Lt. 31.3.05; Capt. 9.3.12; Major 30.10.14, R.A.S.C.; served S. African War, 1900–1; Europ. War; Despatches; O.B.E.

HAMILTON, R. S. (D.S.O. L.G. 1.1.18) b. 5.3.71; s. of late Ven. F. C. Hamilton, Archdeacon of Limerick; m. Mary Eleanor, d. of Sir Alexander Shaw and Eleanor R. Gubbins, d. of late William Gough-Gubbins; ent. R.A. 13.2.91; Lt. 13.2.94; Capt. 18.10.99; Major 12.2.05; Lt.-Col., A.O.D., 5.4.11; Ordnance Officer, 4th Class, 1898–1905; 3rd Class, 1905–11; 2nd Class, 1911; served S. Africa, 1899–1902 (Queen's Medal, 5 clasps; King's Medal, 2 clasps); Europ. War, 1914–18; C.M.G.

HAMILTON, S. W. S. (D.S.O. L.G. 15.4.16) (Bar, L.G. 18.7.17); b. 3.11.82, at Clonmel, co. Tipperary, Ireland; s. of late S. B. Hamilton and Eva Maria Eleanor, d. of Gen. C. A. Benson, I.S.C.; m. Margaret Dowell, d. of S. C. Hester; one s.; educ. at Tonbridge School; St. Columba's College, Ireland; R.M.A., Woolwich; 2nd Lt., R.E., 23.7.01; S.M.E., Chatham, 1901–3 (awarded Haines Memorial Medal); Lt. 1.4.04; Capt. 23.1.12; Major 2.11.16; Bt. Lt.-Col. 1.1.19; joined Survey of India, 1906; temporarily reverted to military employ; served Europ. War, 1914–17; 70th Coy., R.E., 1914–16; Staff, 1916; 90th Field Coy., R.E., 1916–17; D.S.O. awarded for gallantry on 2–3 March, 1916, at Hohenzollern Redoubt; Bar awarded for gallantry east of Arras; Chief Instructor on Staff, Military Engineering, R.M.A., Woolwich, since 1917.

HAMILTON, W. H., F.R.C.S. (D.S.O. L.G. 22.12.16); b. 21.12.80; Lt., I.M.S., 1.2.05; Capt. 1.2.08; Major 15.10.15; Bt. Lt.-Col. 1.1.18; Despatches; C.I.E.; C.B.E.; served in operations in the Abor country, 1911–12 (Medal and clasp).

HAMILTON-BOWEN, A. J. (D.S.O. L.G. 3.7.15) (Bar, L.G. 12.3.17). He was killed in action 20.3.17. (See "The Distinguished Service Order," from its institution to 31.12.15, same publishers.)

HAMILTON-STUBBER, R. (D.S.O. L.G. 3.6.16); b. 28.9.79; m. 1920, Lady Hugh Grosvenor M.B.E. (*née* Lady Mabel Florence Mary Crichton), d. of the 4th Earl of Erne; ent. Army, 25.10.99; Capt., 1st Life Guards, 6.12.06; retired, 1912; Major, Household Cavalry, S.R.; served S. African War, 1901–2 (Queen's Medal and 5 clasps); Europ. War, 1914–18; Despatches; D.L.; J.P., Queen's County.

HAMLIN, H. B. (D.S.O. L.G. 8.3.19) (Details, 4.10.19), Major, 10th Aust. L.H. Regt.

HAMMAN, J. L. (D.S.O. L.G. 22.8.18), Major, Middelburg "A" Commando, S. African Mil. Forces.

HAMMERTON, G. H. L. (D.S.O. L.G. 4.6.17); b. 1875; Lt.-Col., R.A.M.C.; served Europ. War, 1914–18; Despatches twice; C.M.G.

HAMMICK, R. T. (D.S.O. L.G. 1.1.17); b. 10.8.82; 2nd Lt., R.A., 21.12.01; Lt. 21.12.04; Adjt., R.A., 12.10.08 to 11.10.11 and 23.9.14 to 13.11.15; Capt. 30.10.14; Major 12.2.16; Despatches; Bt. Lt.-Col. 3.6.19.

HAMMILL, L. (D.S.O. L.G. 26.9.17)(Details, L.G. 9.1.18), Capt., S. Lanc. R.; M.C.

HAMMOND, F. D. (D.S.O. L.G. 14.1.16); b. 10.11.81; s. of late Col. F. Hammond, 5th Punjab Cavalry; educ. Temple Grove, East Sheen; Eton; 2nd Lt., R.E., 2.5.00; Lt. 2.5.03; Capt. 2.5.10; Major 2.11.16; Lt.-Col.; served in S. African War, 1901–2 (Queen's Medal with 5 clasps); Europ. War, D.A.D. of Rly. Transport, Aug. 1914–June, 1915; A.D. of Rly. Transport, June, 1915 to Nov. 1916; D. of Rlys., Br. Salonika Force, Nov. 1916, to April, 1918; Asst. Inspr.-Gen. of Transportation, April, 1918, to April, 1919; Despatches seven times; Bt. Lt.-Col. 1.1.17; C.B.E.

HAMMOND, F. S. (D.S.O. L.G. 3.6.18), Capt. (A/Major), London R.

HAMMOND, J. M., M.B. (D.S.O. L.G. 17.4.17), T/Lt., R.A.M.C. He died of wounds, 15.3.17.

HAMMOND, R. C. (D.S.O. L.G. 3.6.16); b. 12.4.77; ent. R.E. 31.12.96 Lt. 31.12.99; Capt. 31.12.05; Major 30.10.14.

HAMMOND-CHAMBERS, R. H. B. (D.S.O. L.G. 26.4.18), Lt.-Cdr. (A/Cdr.), R.N.

HAMMONDS, D. H. (D.S.O. L.G. 1.1.18); o. s. of Prebendary Hammonds, of Chichester; educ. King's School, Canterbury, and later graduated B.Sc. with honours at London University. He originally belonged to the S.R., R.E., and returned in 1914 from India, where he was in the Public Works Dept., E.B.S.R., and was afterwards on active service at the front as Capt. (A/Major), R.E. He was killed leading his men on March 30, 1918. He was several times mentioned in Despatches and had the M.C. The Insignia of the D.S.O. were sent to Rev. Prebendary Hammond.

HAMOND, P. (D.S.O. L.G. 31.10.02) (Bar, L.G. 3.6.18), T/Major (Capt., R. of O.), Ret. Pay, attd. Lincs. R.; M.C. (See "The Distinguished Service Order," from its institution to 31.12.15, by same publishers.)

HAMOND, R. G. (D.S.O. L.G. 8.3.18) (Bar, L.G. 8.3.20); b. 1.12.79; s. of Commander R. N. Hamond, R.N., and Janetta, d. of Admiral J. Tacker, of Trematon Castle, Cornwall; educ. H.M.S. Britannia and R.N. College, Greenwich; ent. R.N., Jan. 1894; became Capt.; Despatches, Sept. 1917. D.S.O. awarded (March, 1918) for service in destroyers with the Grand Fleet. Bar to D.S.O. for service on destroyers in the Baltic in 1919.

HAMPSON, G. T. (D.S.O. L.G. 7.11.18), T/Capt. (A/Major), Tank Corps.

HAMPTON, B. C. DWYER- (see Dwyer-Hampton, B. C.).

HAMPTON (H. S.), LORD (D.S.O. L.G. 1.1.19); b. 15.5.83; s. of 3rd Baron Hampton and Evelyn Nina Frances, d. of Sir G. Baker, 3rd Bart.; 4th Baron and a Baronet; educ. Wellington; R.M.C., Sandhurst; was Lt., R. Brig.; later Major, Worc. Yeomanry; D.L., co. of Worcester.

HANAFIN, P. J. (D.S.O. L.G. 14.1.16) (Bar, L.G. 26.11.17) (Details, L.G. 6.4.18); b. 3.6.80; s. of Dr. James Hanafin; m. Margaret Simcocks, d. of J. Simcocks, F.R.C.V.S.; b. 3.6.80; Lt., R.A.M.C., 31.8.03; Capt. 28.2.07; Major 28.2.15; Bt. Lt.-Col. 1.1.19; Despatches.

HANAN, H. F. W. (gazetted as Hanan, F. W.) (D.S.O. L.G. 21.4.17), Cdr., R.N.

HANBURY-SPARROW, A. A. H. (D.S.O. L.G. 1.12.14) (Bar, L.G. 26.9.17) (Details, L.G. 9.1.18), Capt. (A/Lt.-Col.), R. Berks. R.; M.C. (See "The Distinguished Service Order," from its institution to 31.12.15, same publishers.)

HANCE, H. M. (D.S.O. L.G. 22.9.16); b. 18.4.79; s. of E. M. and Mary Amelia Hance; educ. Liverpool College, Upper School; Victoria University; 2nd Lt., Ind. Army, R. of O.; proceeded to France with draft of 1st (K.G.O.) Sappers and Miners, Jan. 1915; seconded to R.E., April, 1915; Lt., May, 1915; Capt., Oct. 1915; Major 1.1.16; served in Palestine, 1918, with 7th Indian Division (Despatches thrice); released from military service, April, 1919; M.C. D.S.O. awarded for gallantry on 1.7.16 at La Boiselle.

HANCOCK, C. (D.S.O. L.G. 1.1.18), T/Major, Glouc. R.

HANCOCK, J. E. (D.S.O. L.G. 4.2.18) (Details, L.G. 5.7.18), T/Capt. Norfolk R. He was killed in action 21.3.18.

HANCOCK, M. P. (D.S.O. L.G. 1.1.18); b. 16.9.70; 2nd Lt., R.E., 10.10.91; Lt. 23.6.93; Capt. 1.4.99; Adjt., R.F., 15.2.02 to 3.5.04; Major 28.11.09; Lt.-Col. 12.11.18; Despatches.

HANCOCK, R. L. (D.S.O. L.G. 25.7.16); b. 4.6.80; m. Millicent, d. of D. T. Stuart, of Wellington, N.Z.; ent. R.N.; became Cdr.; served in Europ. War, when he was engaged on surveying operations. D.S.O. awarded for services set forth in the Despatch of Vice-Admiral Sir R. H. S. Bacon, K.C.B., C.V.O., D.S.O., commanding the Dover Patrol 29.5.16

R. L. Hancock.

HANCOX, S. H. (D.S.O. L.G. 3.6.18), Major, Aust. Engineers.

HAND, W. C. (D.S.O. L.G. 1.1.18), T/Capt., R.G.A.; M.C.

HANDS, P. A. M. (D.S.O. L.G. 1.1.19), Major, S. African Horse Artillery; M.C.

HANKEY, E. B. (D.S.O. L.G. 1.1.18); b. 6.4.75; 2nd Lt., Worc. R., 7.12.95; Lt. 6.3.99; Capt. 1.9.00; Major 20.3.14; Bt. Lt.-Col. 18.2.15; Lt.-Col., Tank Corps, 1.8.19; served S. African War, 1899–1901 (Queen's Medal with 4 clasps); Sudan, 1904 (Egyptian Medal with clasp); Europ. War; Despatches; Bt. Lt.-Col. 1.1.19.

HANKEY, S. R. A. (D.S.O. L.G. 3.6.18), Major (T/Lt.-Col.), S. Irish Horse; served S. African War, 1901–2 (Queen's Medal with 5 clasps); Europ. War; Despatches.

HANLEY, H. A. O. (D.S.O. L.G. 1.1.18); b. 26.10.81; 2nd Lt., Middx. R., 25.5.04; Lt. 27.6.06; Capt. 4.9.14.

HANMER, L. A. G. (D.S.O. L.G. 7.2.18); b. 21.10.68; 2nd Lt., W. Riding R., 23.8.89; Lt., I.S.C., 29.10.90; Capt., I.A., 23.3.00; Major 23.3.07; Lt.-Col., Cav., I.A.; served Waziristan Exp. (Medal with clasp), N.W. Frontier of India, 1897–8, Tochi (Medal with clasp); Europ. War; Despatches. He was killed in action 29.4.18.

HANNA, A. L. (D.S.O. L.G. 10.8.21), Lt., 11th Lrs., I.A.

HANNA, J. C. (D.S.O. L.G. 1.1.17); b. 17.8.71; 2nd Lt., R.A., 1.4.92; Lt. 1.4.95; Div. Adjt., R.A., 1899–1901; Capt. 4.1.00; Major, R.G.A., 6.12.12.

HANNAH, R. W. (D.S.O. L.G. 13.5.18), Lt. (A/Major), R.F.A., Spec. Res.; M.C.

HANNAY, A. G. RAINSFORD- (see Rainsford-Hannay, A. G.).

HANNAY, C. C. (D.S.O. L.G. 1.1.18), b. 16.4.72; 2nd Lt., Dorset. R., 19.11.92; Lt. 5.3.96; Adjt., Dorset. R., 11.1.01 to 31.3.05; Capt. 6.10.01; Major 6.1.12; Lt.-Col.; served Tirah, 1897–8 (Medal with 2 clasps); Europ. War; Despatches.

HANNAY, F. RAINSFORD- (see Rainsford-Hannay, F.).

HANNAY, G. M. (D.S.O. L.G. 26.9.17) (Details, L.G. 9.1.18); b. 12.2.71; first commission, 9.9.93; Capt. 23.6.00; Capt., K.O.S.B.; retired, 17.4.09; Capt. (T/Lt.-Col.), R. of O., late K.O.S.B.; served S. African War, 1900–2 (Queen's Medal with 3 clasps; King's Medal with 2 clasps); Europ. War; Despatches.

HANNAY, J. RAINSFORD- (see Rainsford-Hannay, J.).

HANNING-LEE, V. A. E. (D.S.O. L.G. 20.2.19), Lt.-Cdr., R.N., 31.12.18; O.B.E.

HANSEN, P. H. (D.S.O. L.G. 16.9.18), Capt. (T/Major), Linc. R.; V.C.; M.C. (see "The Victoria Cross," by same publishers).

HANSON, E. G. (D.S.O. L.G. 1.1.18), Lt.-Col., Can. Field Artillery; M.C.

HANSON, F. S. (D.S.O. L.G. 1.1.18), Capt. (A/Lt.-Col.), R. War. R.; M.C.

HANSON, H. E. (D.S.O. L.G. 14.1.16); b. 1873, at Edinburgh; s. of H. H. and Martha Hanson; educ. Cheltenham College and Marlborough College; joined Volunteer Artillery in 1893; was transferred to the Territorial F.A. in 1908; Lt.-Col., 2nd North'd Brig., R.F.A., 1911; awarded the Territorial Long Service Medal, 1912; transferred to T.F. Reserve, 1913; served in the Europ. War as O.C. "A" Battery, 251st Brig., R.F.A., 50th Div. Arty.; D.S.O. awarded for services on the Ypres front; promoted to Substantive Lt.-Col., July, 1918; several times mentioned in Despatches.

H. E. Hanson.

HANSON, H. S. (D.S.O. L.G. 1.2.19), Lt., 43rd Bn. Can. Inf., Manitoba R.

HAPPOLD, F. C. (D.S.O. L.G. 24.6.16); b. 15.2.93; s. of A. C. Happold and Margaret Annie, d. of J. Crossfield; educ. Rydal Mount School, Colwyn Bay, and Peterhouse, Cambridge; ent. 5th K.O.R.L. Regt. 6.9.14; was gazetted to 9th L.N. Lancs. Regt. 18.12.14; Lt.; Despatches; 1915 Star; D.S.O. awarded for services on 9.5.16, on Vimy Ridge; wounded; served on Intelligence Staff, 5th Corps, 5th Army, in France and Belgium; as G.S.O.3, on Instructional Staff of Intelligence School, Harrow, 1914–19; Despatches; Senior History Master, Perse School, Cambridge; Lecturer in History to Cambridge University Extension Syndicate.

HARBER, A. F. (D.S.O. L.G. 22.8.18), Major, 3rd Mounted Rifles (Natal Mounted Rifles).

HARBORD, C. R. (D.S.O. L.G. 11.4.18): b. 2.12.73; 2nd Lt., Unatt., 3.9.92; I.S.C. 26.12.93; Lt. 3.12.94; Capt. 3.9.01; Major 3.9.10; Lt.-Col. 1.9.18; T/Brig.-Gen.; served S. African War, 1899–1902 (Queen's Medal with 3 clasps; King's Medal with 2 clasps); Europ. War; Despatches; C.M.G.

HARBORD, E. W. (D.S.O. L.G. 2.7.17); b. 14.3.79; e. s. of late Hon. Walter Harbord and of his first wife, Lady Eleanor Fitzroy, d. of 7th Duke of Grafton and widow of Herbert Fitzroy Eaton; m. Rose Mary Adeline Dagmar Amelia, d. of Lt.-Col. G. C. K. Johnstone, late G. Gds.; Cdr., R.N.; decorated for mine-sweeping.

HARBORD, H. W. (D.S.O. L.G. 1.1.17), Major, Can. Mtd. Rif.

HARBOTTLE, C. C. (D.S.O. L.G. 3.6.18) (Bar, L.G. 7.11.18); b. 1875; educ. Toronto; qualified at Stanley Barracks, Toronto; Field Officer's Certificates, 1901; Lt.-Col., Central Ontario R.; enlisted with 67th Battn., C.E.F., July, 1915, for overseas, as Adjutant; promoted to Second-in-Command and O.C. 4th Can. Div. Training School, Pernes, France; took command 75th Can. Inf. Bn., April, 1917; returned to Canada with Battn., July, 1919; in France three years, four months; wounded at Drocourt Line, 2.9.18; Despatches thrice; C.M.G.

HARBOTTLE, F. (D.S.O. L.G. 1.1.17); b. 1872; s. of J. Harbottle; m. Olive, d. of Major P. W. Grant Pinnock; one s.; one d.; educ. Christ College, Hobart; joined Volunteer Artillery, 1889; Major, Australian Artillery; Hon.

Sec. to Tasmanian Rifle Association for some years before the war; introduced English and rainbow trout into several mountain lakes in Tasmania; served Europ. War; was in Tasmania from 1914; joined 2nd Australian Division, Field Artillery, Sept. 1915; was in Egypt, Dec. 1915–March, 1916, and in France; gassed at Passchendaele, Nov. 1917.

HARCOURT, A. C. (D.S.O. L.G. 18.2.18) (Details, L.G. 18.7.18); b. 4.8.94; 2nd Lt., R. Berks. R., 25.10.15; Lt. 28.10.16; served also in Tank Corps; employed with W. African Frontier Force 6.4.21; Despatches; M.C.

HARCOURT, H. G. (D.S.O. L.G. 26.7.18) (Bar, L.G. 21.1.20); b. 13.2.95; Lt., R. Dublin Fus., 26.11.17; Adjt., Ind. Aux. Forces, 20.4.21; was A/Major; Despatches; M.C.

HARCOURT-VERNON, G. C. F. (D.S.O. L.G. 14.11.16); b. 30.5.91; s. of E. E. Harcourt-Vernon; educ. Eton; 2nd Lt., G. Guards, 10.8.10; Lt., Aug. 1914; Capt. 15.7.15; A/Major, Aug. 1918; retired Aug. 1919; gazetted Major, R. of O., on the same day; served in the Europ. War; three times wounded—1st, seriously, on 14.9.14, just above Soupir on the Aisne; 2nd, on 15.9.16, in the advance from Ginchy, towards Les Bœufs; 3rd, on 25.9.16, when Les Bœufs was taken; M.C.

HARDCASTLE, E. L. (D.S.O. L.G. 1.1.17); b. 17.4.74; 2nd Lt., R.A., 23.11.93; Lt. 23.11.96; Capt. 1.4.00; Major 7.9.14; Lt.-Col., R.G.A., 23.6.18; Despatches.

HARDEN, G. E. (D.S.O. L.G. 25.10.16); b. 1.8.89; s. of Lt.-Col. G. Harden (late of the R. Sussex R.) and of Mrs. Harden (*née* Angelo); m. Eanswythe, d. of Sir Alexander Wood Renton; one d.; educ. Hillbrow, Rugby; H.M.S. Britannia; Naval Cadet, May, 1904; Midshipman, Sept. 1905; Sub-Lt., Nov. 1908; passed for Lt. with six "firsts" in 1909; promoted to Lt., 1910; Lt.-Cdr. 30.11.17; took part in earlier operations in the Shatt-el-Ara River as navigator in H.M.S. Espiègle, and was present at the actions at Abadan and Zain, and also assisted in the capture of Kurna on the 4th–9th Dec. 1914. In 1915 he was fighting on the Tigris and Euphrates Rivers, and took part in an attack on a Turkish position above Kurna 31.5.15. Subsequent to the attack, he chased the Turkish gunboat Marmaris up the Tigris, and succeeded in sinking it on the night of June 1–2nd, 1915. He assisted in the capture of Amara with a small force under Gen. Townshend, in the river gunboat Comet, and his conduct on this occasion was mentioned in Despatches. His D.S.O. was awarded for gallantry at Guinchy on 15.9.16; appointed to R.N. Staff College, 1919.

HARDIE, C. C. A. (D.S.O. L.G. 1.1.18); b. 28.4.83; s. of Alexander Robertson and Florence Hardie; m. Gladys Mary Reiner; educ. Westminster School; University College, London; Engineer, English Electric Co. Ltd., since 1919; Lt.-Col., late R.E.; served Aug. 1914–Feb. 1919; in France, Oct. 1915–Feb. 1919; Despatches twice.

HARDIE, J. L. (D.S.O. L.G. 1.1.18), Major, Gen. List.

HARDIE, R. D. (D.S.O. L.G. 16.8.17), Major, N.Z. M.G. Corps.

HARDIE, S. J. L., M.A. (D.S.O. L.G. 1.1.17); b. 1885; s. of the late J. Hardie; m. Marie, d. of late D. H. Nicolson; educ. Paisley Grammar School; Glasgow University; served Europ. War, 1914–19, with 6th A. and S. Highrs.; Lt. (T/Capt.) (T/Major); commanded 51st Battn. M.G.C.; Despatches thrice.

HARDIMAN, E. H. M. (D.S.O. L.G. 27.7.18), T/Capt., Gen. List (Capt. S. African Forces); M.C.

HARDING, C. (D.S.O. L.G. 1.1.17); b. 15.8.63; s. of late C. Harding; m. Margaret S. Porter, d. of R. Porter; served in Mashonaland Rebellion, 1896–7 (Despatches twice), first as Galloper to Col. Alderson, Officer Commanding Mashonaland Field Force; then obtained commission in B.S.A. Police, 1896; gazetted as Capt. or Inspector in 1897, and Major, or Chief Inspector, in Nov. 1897, to command Native Police, Mashonaland; proceeded to N. Rhodesia; recruited and equipped force of 500 police for that country, May, 1898; Acting Administrator for Barotseland and Officer Commanding Police in same country, Sept. 1899; District Commission, Northern Territories, Ashanti, 1909; helped to raise 2nd King Edward's Horse, 1915, and served in France; commanded 15th R. Warwicks., 1915 and 1916; Col.; Despatches twice; C.M.G.; Provincial Commissioner, Gold Coast Colony; has published "In Remotest Barotseland."

HARDING, D. L., F.R.C.S.I. (D.S.O. L.G. 14.1.16); b. 13.3.77; Lt., R.A.M.C., 26.4.01; Capt. 26.4.04; Major 26.4.13; served S. African War, 1900–2 (Queen's Medal with 3 clasps); Europ. War; Despatches.

HARDING, G. R. (D.S.O. L.G. 1.1.18), T/Capt. (A/Lt.-Col.), R.E.

HARDING, R. P. (D.S.O. L.G. 3.6.19) Major Can. F. A.; M.C.

HARDINGE, T. S. N. (D.S.O. L.G. 1.1.17); b. 22.9.77; 2nd Lt., R.A., 23.3.97; Lt. 23.3.00; Capt. 24.1.02; Major, R.G.A., 30.10.14; South African War, 1900–2; served in St. Helena (Queen's Medal); Europ. War; Despatches.

HARDISTY, R. H. M. (D.S.O. L.G. 3.6.19), Major (A/Lt.-Col.), 6th Field Ambulance Can. A.M.C.; M.C.

HARDMAN, R. S. (D.S.O. L.G. 1.1.17); b. 15.1.70; s. of Rev. J. W. Hardman, LL.D., of Cadbury House, Yatton, Somerset; m. Mildred Alice Turner, d. of A. J. Thornton; one d.; educ. privately; R.M.A., Woolwich; commissioned in R.A., 1889; Capt., 1899; Major, 1906; Lt.-Col., 1914; retired, 1919; served through S. African War (Queen's and King's Medals with 8 clasps; Despatches); Europ. War, with original Exp. Force, in command of 86th Battery, R.F.A.; on promotion took out the 81st Bde., R.F.A., with the 17th Division; Despatches twice; has published "Stable Management and Horse Mastership."

HARDRESS-LLOYD, J. (D.S.O. L.G. 1.1.17) (Bar, L.G. 4.2.18) (Details, L.G. 5.7.18); b. 14.8.74; s. of J. Lloyd, D.L., of Gloster, King's County, and Susan, d. of R. Colclough, D.L., of Tintern Abbey, co. Wexford; m. Adeline, d. of late Sir Samuel Wilson, M.P.; educ. Wellington; Sandhurst; joined 4th Dragoon Guards; served Tirah, N.W. Frontier, 1897; S. Africa, 1901–2, as A.D.C. to Lt.-Gen. Sir E. L. Elliot; went out with 4th Dn. Gds., Aug. 1914; Gallipoli, May, 1915, to Jan. 1916, with 29th Division; commanded 1st Inniskilling Fusiliers, May, 1916, to Jan. 1917; joined Tank Corps, Jan. 1917; Brig.-Cdr., April, 1917; Despatches six times; Legion of Honour; captained English Polo Team, America, 1911; Irish Team *v.* England on several occasions.

HARDWICK, P. E. (D.S.O. L.G. 14.1.16); b. 21.4.75; 2nd Lt., 1st Dns., 11.8.97; Lt. 1.2.00; Adjt., 1st Dns., 22.12.02 to 21.12.05 Capt. 9.8.05; Major, 15.11.14; served S. African War, 1899–1902 (Queen's Medal with 5 clasps; King's Medal with 2 clasps;) served Europ. War, Belgium, Flanders, France; wounded twice; Despatches; 1914 Star. He died of wounds 9.6.19.

HARDY, C. (Clive) (D.S.O. L.G. 19.11.17) (Details, L.G. 22.3.18), late London Regt., attd. 25th Bn. Liverpool Regt. (The King's); served Europ. War, 1914–17; Despatches.

HARDY, C. H. W. (D.S.O. L.G. 1.1.17), Lt.-Col., A.A.M.C.; V.D.

HARDY, E. B. (D.S.O. L.G. 14.11.16), Lt.-Col., Can. A.M.C.

HARDY, E. J. (D.S.O. L.G. 1.1.17), Capt., 2nd Dns. (R. Scots Greys).

HARDY, F. K. (D.S.O. L.G. 3.6.18), Capt. (A/Major), York and Lancaster R.

HARDY, H. N. M. (D.S.O. L.G. 14.3.16); b. 1.12.84, in London; s. of J. A. Hardy, Hobart, Tasmania, and Sydney, N.S.W.; m. Jessie Fraser, d. of G. K. Mackenzie; two d.: educ. Hillbrow, Eastbourne, and H.M.S. Britannia (in his examination for rank of Lt., he obtained all 1st Class certificates), and entered R.N. 1899; Sub-Lt., 1904; Lt., 1905; Lt.-Cdr., 1913; Cdr., 24.4.18; served in Australian Force, taking over German possessions in N. Guinea and the Pacific; served also in the Dardanelles; awarded Croix de Guerre en Argent by French Government for rescuing wounded under fire in Morto Bay; Despatches; D.S.O. awarded for services in a trawler flotilla, and in H.M.S. Folkestone and H.M.S. Racoon; commanded H.M.S. Sirius in the attempt to block Ostend, April, 1918; especially promoted to Commander for his services on this occasion and awarded a Bar to the Croix de Guerre. He commanded H.M.S. Sappho in the second attack on Ostend.

HARDY, J. L. (D.S.O. L.G. 30.1.20); b. 10.6.94; 2nd Lt., Conn. R., 24.1.14; Lt. 21.9.14, Capt. 1.1.17, Despatches; M.C.

HARDY, THE HON. N. C. GATHORNE- (see Gathorne-Hardy, The Hon. N. C.).

HARDY, S. J. (D.S.O. L.G. 4.6.17); b. 1.7.82; 2nd Lt., Unatt., 8.1.01; 2nd Dns. 9.3.01; Lt. 26.2.02; Capt. 1.8.11; Adjt., 2nd Dns., 1.8.11 to 31.7.14; Major, 25.12.17; served S. African War, 1902 (Queen's Medal with 3 clasps); Europ. War; Despatches.

HARDY, REV. T. B. (D.S.O. L.G. 18.10.17) (Details, L.G. 7.3.18), A. Ch. Dept., attd. 8th Linc. R.; V.C.; M.C. He died of wounds 18.10.18. (See "The Victoria Cross," same publishers.)

HARDYMAN, J. H. M. (D.S.O. L.G. 15.10.18); b. 23.9.94, at Bath; s. of Dr. Hardyman; educ. Fettes College, Edinburgh, 1908–11 (open Scholar, 1909); Edinburgh University, 1911–14 (Arts Course; Students' Representative, Council, 1912–13–14); enlisted 4th Somerset L.I. 20.8.14; R.F.C. Training at Brooklands, Dec. 1914–Jan. 1915; commission in 9th Som. L.I. 5.2.15; Acting Adjt., 7th Som. L.I., Wareham, 1915; att. Brigade Staff, Swanage, 1915; att. Divl. Staff, Acting Brigade Major, 37th Div., 1917–18; Brigade Liaison Officer, 1917; Lt.-Col., May, 1918; M.C. He was killed in action 24.8.18 at Biefvillers. The Divisional General wrote: "His death is indeed a loss to the Division and to the Army. He was a brilliant leader—he did not know what fear was. . . . He was a born soldier, and had he lived would soon have got an infantry brigade, and eventually risen even much higher."

J. H. M. Hardyman.

HARE, J. W. (D.S.O. L.G. 1.1.17); b. 24.8.83; s. of C. E. Hare, of St. Martin's, Lee-on-Solent; m. Irene Victoria, d. of C. Eardley-Wilmot; one s.; 2nd Lt., R.A., 15.7.03; Lt. 15.7.06; Capt. 30.10.14; Adjt., R.A., 29.12.16 to 25.8.17; Major 1.10.17; Adjt., R.G.A., 11.2.20.

HARGEST, J. (D.S.O. L.G. 7.11.18), Major, Otago R., N.Z. Force; M.C.

HARGREAVES, T. C. (D.S.O. L.G. 14.11.16), Major, 23rd (County of London) Bn. The London Regt. His D.S.O. was awarded for gallantry at Starfish, near Flers, on 18.9.16. Major Hargreaves was killed in action 23.3.18.

HARINGTON, W. G. (D.S.O. L.G. 25.11.16); b. 6.5.85; commissioned R.A., Dec. 1904; Lt., Dec. 1907; transferred to I.A., March, 1908; Capt. I.A., Dec. 1913; served in the European War with his regiment, the Gurkha Rifles, and was killed in action 28.9.17.

HARKER, T. H. (D.S.O. L.G. 1.1.18) (Bar, L.G. 26.5.19); s. of late William Harker; was a Capt., K.R.R.C. (Special Reserve); T. Lt.-Col. He had left the Army two years before the European War, having served in the Boer War and been on the Viceroy's Staff in India.

HARKNESS, R. B. (D.S.O. L.G. 3.6.19), T/Major, Welsh R.; M.C.

HARKNESS, R. D. (D.S.O. L.G. 1.1.19), Major, 1st Mounted Machine Gun Brigade, M.G.C.; M.C.

HARLEY, A. B. (D.S.O. L.G. 25.8.17); b. 30.9.81; 2nd Lt., Unatt., 8.1.01; E. Kent R. 9.3.01; Lt. 1.7.04; I.A. 12.4.06; Capt. 8.1.10; Major 8.1.16; served in Aden, 1903–4, operations in the interior; Europ. War; Despatches; Bt. Lt.-Col. 3.6.19.

HARMAN, A. E. W. (D.S.O. L.G. 3.6.16); b. 21.4.72; ent. 3rd D.G. 31.1.94; Lt. 3.4.95; Lt., A.S.C., 1.4.96; Capt. 1.4.00; Capt., 3rd D.G., 29.7.08; Adjt., 3rd D.G., 29.7.08 to 19.9.11; Major, 2nd D.G., 2.9.11; T/Brig.-Gen. 28.5.16; Bt. Major 1.1.17; Bt. Lt.-Col. 3.6.18; Col. 2.6.19; served Europ. War; Despatches; C.B.

HARMAN, A. L. (D.S.O. L.G. 1.1.19); b. 29.8.93; 2nd Lt., R.A., 18.7.13; Lt. 9.6.15; Adjt., R.A., 27.8.15 to 14.5.16; Capt. 18.7.17; Adjt., R.A., 31.8.21; Despatches; M.C.

HARMAN, A. R. (D.S.O. L.G. 20.10.16); b. 1877; s. of late Sir G. B. Harman, K.C.B.; Worc. R., Brig.-Gen.; served Nile Exp., 1888 (Medal and clasp; Khedive's Star); S. African War, 1899–1901 (Despatches; Queen's Medal and 3 clasps); Europ. War, 1914–18; C.M.G. D.S.O. awarded for gallantry on 17–19 July and 20–21st Aug. 1916, Ovillers.

HARMAN, C. C., B.A. (gazetted as Harman, C.) (D.S.O. L.G. 10.1.17) (Bar, L.G. 1.2.19); b. 23.8.77; s. of W. Harman; m. Muriel, d. of P. Huth; one d.; one s.; educ. Coleraine; Trinity College, Dublin University; 2nd Lt., Leins. R., 23.5.00; Lt. 29.6.02; Capt. 3.7.09; Major 1.9.15; Bt. Lt.-Col. 1.1.18; Lt.-Col.; Despatches four times; won 100 yards and quarter-mile championships of Dublin University in 1899 and 1900; quarter-mile amateur championship of Ireland, 1899; 440 yards' championship, Army in Ireland, 1905 and 1906.

HARMAN, F. DE W. (D.S.O. L.G. 2.5.16); b. 31.3.79; s. of late Rev. Canon S. T. Harman, Chancellor of Cork Cathedral; m. Evelyne Mary, d. of Lt.-Col. S. M. Gully; one d.; educ. Trin. Coll., Dublin; ent. Army 24.1.00; Lt. 25.6.01; Capt. 10.10.08; Major 1.9.15; employed with Egyptian Army, 1908–18; served in Sudan, 1910 (Medal with clasp); attd. to 1st R. Inniskilling Fusiliers, Dardanelles F.F., May to July, 1915; Despatches.

HARMAN, H. A. A. F. (D.S.O. L.G. 4.6.17); s. of H. J. Harman, of Cheltenham; Capt. (T/Major), S. Staffs. R., S.R., and Gold Coast R.

HARMAN, W. A. KING- (see King-Harman, W. A.).

HARMAR, C. D'O. (D.S.O. L.G. 23.3.17); b. 2.1.78; 2nd Lt., R. Marines, 1.1.97; Lt. 1.1.98; Capt. 20.10.03; Major 23.9.15; served China, 1900; Europ. War; Despatches.

HAROLD, A. E. (D.S.O. L.G. 22.12.16), Cdr., R.I. Marine.

HARPER, R. P. (D.S.O. L.G. 11.4.18), Capt., Machine Gun Squadron, N.Z. Military Forces; M.C.; D.C.M.

HARPER, R. R. (D.S.O. L.G. 26.9.16), Capt., Aust. Inf. D.S.O. awarded for gallantry near Pozières on 25–26 July, 1916.

HARRAGIN, A. E. A. (D.S.O. L.G. 8.3.19) (Details, L.G. 4.10.19), T/Major, 1st Bn. Br. W. India Regt.; Capt., Trinidad Local Forces (Egypt).

HARRIS, A. (D.S.O. L.G. 1.1.17); b. 3.3.88; s. of A. H. Harris; m. Rosa Alfreda Alderson; one s.; one d.; joined R.G.A. (V.), 1904; first commission, R.F.A., 1910; Capt. 1913; Major, 1914; served Europ. War, 1914–18.

HARRIS, A. E. F. (D.S.O. L.G. 23.6.15) (Bar, L.G. 4.6.17), Major, R. Berks. R. (see "The Distinguished Service Order," from its institution to 31.12.15, by same publishers).

HARRIS, D. R. (D.S.O. L.G. 1.1.17), Major, Aust. Art.

HARRIS, E. M. (D.S.O. L.G. 1.1.18), Major, Can. A.S.C.

HARRIS, E. T., M.B. (D.S.O. L.G. 4.6.17); b. 27.4.78; Lt., I.M.S., 31.8.03; Capt. 31.8.06; Major 28.2.15; Despatches.

HARRIS, F. E. (D.S.O. L.G. 30.1.20), T/Lt., 2nd Bn. Devons. R.

HARRIS, G. A. (D.S.O. L.G. 24.1.17); b. 27.10.79; educ. Trinity College, Dublin; Hon. M.A., University of Dublin; Major, late 12th Middlesex R. and 15th London R.; Despatches twice; O.B.E.; T.D.; late D.A.Q.M.G., Gen. H.Q., Dublin.

HARRIS, J. O. (D.S.O. L.G. 11.1.19), T/Sub-Lt., Hawke Bn., R.N.V.R., R.N.D.; served for nearly three years with the Post Office Rifles; commissioned in June, 1917, in the R.N.D., and died of wounds in France, Oct. 10, 1918.

HARRIS, N. C. (D.S.O. L.G. 24.9.18), Major, Aust. Engrs.; M.C.

HARRIS, T. B. (D.S.O. L.G. 1.1.17); b. 16.12.84; s. of B. F. Harris; m. Phyllis Mary, d. of Mrs. Goode; educ. Marlborough; R.M.A., Woolwich; 2nd Lt., R.E., 26.12.03; Lt. 23.9.06; Capt. 30.10.14; served S. African War, 1899–1902 (Despatches; Queen's Medal with 3 clasps; King's Medal with 2 clasps); Europ. War, 1914–18; wounded; Despatches.

HARRIS, W. K. (D.S.O. L.G. 4.3.18) (Details, L.G. 16.8.18); b. at Mayfield, Newcastle, N.S.W.; s. of H. W. Harris, Publisher, of Newcastle, N.S.W.; educ. Newcastle; commissioned in Australian Command of Legion of Frontiersmen, 1913; Trooper, King Edward's Horse; commissioned R.N. Division, 26.6.15; became Capt.; Lt., R.N.V.R.; active service, Mudros, France, Belgium; wounded slightly, but remained at duty, three occasions; once seriously; Despatches; M.C. and two Bars.

HARRIS-ST. JOHN, R. J. (D.S.O. L.G. 8.3.18), Lt.-Cdr., R.N.

HARRIS-ST. JOHN, W. (D.S.O. L.G. 3.6.18); b. 25.6.78; 2nd Lt., R.W.F., 7.5.98; Lt. 14.4.00; Adjt., R.W.F., 1904–5; Capt. 5.5.06; Major; served S. African War, 1899–1902 (Queen's Medal with 5 clasps; King's Medal with 2 clasps); Europ. War; Despatches.

HARRISON, A. (D.S.O. L.G. 25.8.16), T/2nd Lt., N. Lancs. R. D.S.O. awarded for services on 3–13 July, 1916, Leipzig salient and Ovillers.

HARRISON, A. L. (D.S.O. L.G. 4.6.17), T/Major, M.G.C.

HARRISON, C. P. (D.S.O. L.G. 11.4.18), Capt. (A/Major), Notts. R.H.A.; Hon. Capt. in Army; served S. African War, 1899–1901; Europ. War; Despatches; M.C.

HARRISON, F. C. (D.S.O. L.G. 12.5.17) (Bar, 23.7.18), A/Lt., R.N.

HARRISON, G. A. (D.S.O. L.G. 4.9.18), T/Capt. (A/Major), R.E.; M.C.

HARRISON, G. H. (D.S.O. L.G. 1.1.17); b. 24.9.77; s. of late Capt. G. H. Harrison, the 53rd Regt., and of Mrs. Riley, of Broadhurst, Bedford; 2nd Lt., Border R., 22.3.99; Lt. 23.10.01; Capt. 7.3.10; Major 1.9.15; served S. African War, 1899–1900 (Despatches; Queen's Medal with 3 clasps); Europ. War; Despatches; Bt. Lt.-Col. 1.1.19.

HARRISON, G. L. (D.S.O. L.G. 15.2.19) (Details, L.G. 30.7.19); b. 22.6.84; Capt., R.W. Surrey R., 1.7.16; Despatches.

HARRISON, H. C. (D.S.O. L.G. 25.8.16); b. 26.2.89, at Olton, Warwickshire; s. of E. J. Harrison, of Broad View, Bromley, Kent; educ. at King Edward's School, Birmingham, and R.M.A., Woolwich; 2nd Lt., R. Mar., 1.9.07; Lt. 1.7.08; Capt. 30.1.17; Adjt., R.M.A., 29.4.19 to 21.1.21; commanded S. African Siege Battery, Aug. 1915, to March, 1917; Major Instructor of Gunnery, Lydd and Salisbury, from June, 1917, to July, 1918; Brigade Major, 11th Corps, Heavy Artillery, Oct. 1918, to Feb. 1919; he was gassed on July, 1916; slight shell wound, Oct. 1918; Despatches three times; Bt. Major 1.1.19. D.S.O. awarded for gallantry on 23–24 July, 1916, at Pozières.

H. C. Harrison.

HARRISON, J. (D.S.O. L.G. 8.3.20), Lt.-Cdr., R.N. 15.8.15.

HARRISON, J. M. R. (D.S.O. L.G. 14.1.16); b. 1.10.80; 2nd Lt., R.A., 2.5.00; Lt. 3.4.01; Capt. 31.3.10; Major 30.10.14; Bt. Lt.-Col. 3.6.18.

HARRISON, J. S. N. (D.S.O. L.G. 7.2.18); b. 9.11.77; m. Averil Frances, d. of H. J. S. Stobart; 2nd Lt., Som. L.I., 8.6.98; Lt. 22.2.00; Capt. 1.4.04; Adjt., Som. L.I., 1.1.10 to 31.12.12; Major 1.9.15; Despatches.

HARRISON, M. C. C. (D.S.O. L.G. 1.2.19); b. 22.1.88; s. of R. F. Harrison, K.C.; educ. Bradford; Sandhurst; 2nd Lt., R. Irish R., 7.11.06; Lt. 18.7.08; Adjt., R. Irish Regt. 24.8.14 to 20.10.14; Capt. 24.8.14; was severely wounded and taken prisoner; Despatches. After five attempts to escape from Germany, 1915, succeeded in Sept. 1917, and rejoined his old battalion in France in Dec.; Acting Major and Second-in-Command, Feb. 1918, and T/Lt.-Col., March, 1918; Despatches twice; Bt. Major, 3.6.19; M.C. and Bar; Italian Silver Medal Al Valore Militaire.

N. Harrison.

HARRISON, N., A.M.I.C.E. (D.S.O. L.G. 1.1.17); b. 1873; son of the late Richard Thomas Harrison; m. Marguerite Ethel Dovy, of Jersey; one s. He was educ. in Natal; was Engineer, Postal Telegraphs, Transvaal, 1903–9; Chief Engineer, 1909–10; S. Africa, 1910–14; Director of Army Signals, German S.W. Africa Campaign, 1914–15; A.D., Army Signals, B.E.F., France, 1915–19, and O.C., S. African Signal Units. He is Engineer-in-Chief, Postal Telegraphs, Union of S. Africa. For his services in the Europ. War he was created a C.M.G. in 1919. He was promoted Lt.-Col.

HARRISON, R. (D.S.O. L.G. 11.11.19), Lt. Cdr. (A/Cdr.), R.N.R., R.D.

HARRISON, W. H. (D.S.O. L.G. 1.1.18), Lt.-Col., Can. F.A.

HARRISON, W. R. E. (D.S.O. L.G. 17.3.17) (Details, L.G. 11.5.17); b. 4.6.91; 2nd Lt., R.A., 20.7.11; Lt. 30.7.14; Capt. 8.8.16; Despatches; M.C.

HARRISSON, GEOFFREY HARNETT (name corrected from Harrisson, Geoffrey Harnett, L.G. 1.6.17) (D.S.O. L.G. 1.1.17), T/Lt.-Col., R.M.; General Manager, Entrerios and Argentine North-Eastern Railways; served S. African War, 1901–2; Europ. War, 1914–18; Despatches; C.M.G.; Order of the Crown of Belgium and Croix de Guerre.

HARRISSON, R. D. (D.S.O. L.G. 20.10.16); b. 22.7.81; s. of D. Harrisson, F.R.C.S.E., of Liverpool; m. Hilda Beatrice Corbett Grierson, d. of S. M. Grierson; one s.; one d.; educ. Liverpool College and privately; 2nd Lt., R.A., Dec. 1900; Lt. Dec. 1903; Capt. Aug. 1912; Major, May, 1915; served Europ. War; Despatches. He was killed in action 16.9.17. His D.S.O. was awarded for gallantry at Guillemont 20 July to 2 Aug. 1916.

R. D. Harrisson.

HARSTONE, J. B. (D.S.O. L.G. 14.11.16), Capt. (T/Major), Can. Inf. D.S.O. awarded for gallantry at Courcelette on 15–17 Sept. 1916.

HART, C. H. (D.S.O. L.G. 1.1.18); b. 9.10.83; 2nd Lt., Ches. R., 27.1.04; Lt. 29.3.05; 2nd Lt., A.S.C., 9.10.05; Lt., A.S.C., 27.1.07; Capt. 5.8.14; Major, R.A.S.C., 30.9.18; Despatches; M.C.

HART, E. A. E. (D.S.O. L.G. 3.6.19), Lt. (A/Major), A/46th Bgde., R.F.A.; M.C.

HART, E. G. (D.S.O. L.G. 7.2.18); b. 6.2.78; 2nd Lt., R.A., 1.9.97; Lt. 1.9.00; Capt., Army, 1.9.06; Capt., I.A., 26.2.09; Major 1.9.15; served Europ. War; Despatches; Bt. Major.

HART, G. A. (D.S.O. L.G. 4.6.17); b. 13.9.75; 2nd Lt., R.A., 25.3.15; Lt. 12.2.17; Despatches.

HART, H. P. (D.S.O. L.G. 1.1.17), T/Major, Scottish Borderers.

HART, L. H. P. (D.S.O. L.G. 3.6.18) (Bar, L.G. 7.11.18), Major, Linc. R., attd. York and Lanc. R.

HART, O. (D.S.O. L.G. 1.1.18), T/Capt. (A/Major), R.F.A.

HART, R. S. (D.S.O. L.G. 27.10.17) (Bar, 8.3.19) (Details, L.G. 4.10.19); b. 27.6.82; s. of Gen. Sir R. Hart, V.C., K.C.B.; m. Madeline Stretton, d. of Col. B. C. McCalmont, C.B., C.B.E.; 2nd Lt., Notts. and Derby. R., 8.5.01; Lt. 20.7.05; Capt. 26.7.08; Major 8.5.16; served with 1st King's African Rifles in Somaliland Field Force, 1903–4; action at Jidballi (Medal and 2 clasps); Nandi Field Force, B.E. Africa, 1905–6 (clasp); with Egyptian Army, 1910–17; operations in S. Kordofan (Medal and clasp; 4th Class Order of the Nile); Europ. War, served in France and Flanders, Italy, Gallipoli (wounded), and Suez Canal; Despatches four times; Bt. Lt.-Col. 3.6.19.

HART-SYNNOT, A. H. S. (D.S.O. L.G. 19.4.01) (Bar, L.G. 3.6.18), Brig.-Gen., C.M.G. (see "The Distinguished Service Order," from its institution to 31.12.15, by same publishers).

HARTER, J. F. (D.S.O. L.G. 4.2.18) (Details, L.G. 5.7.18); b. 30.8.88; s. of C. B. Harter; m. Violet Emily, d. of T. C. Garfit, of Kenwick Hall, Louth, Lincs.; one s.; one d.; 2nd Lt., R. Fus., 9.10.07; Lt. 3.6.10; Capt. 16.1.15; Bt. Major 3.6.19; served Europ. War, 1914–18; Despatches five times; M.C. Croix de Guerre.

HARTFORD, G. B. (D.S.O. L.G. 5.10.18); m. Alice Wells (who died, 1920), d. of the late J. Walter, of Yokohama; one s.; one d.; educ. Cliff House School, Southdown; Eastman's R.N. Academy, Northwood Park, Winchester; ent. R.N.; Commander; served Europ. War, 1914–18; Despatches; commanded H.M.S. Kinsha, and Chief Staff Officer to Admiral and Senior Naval Officer, Yangtse.

HARTIGAN, J. A., M.B., B.S. (D.S.O. L.G. 14.1.16); b. 30.11.76; educ. Durham University; Lt., R.A.M.C., 4.12.99; Capt. 4.12.02; Major 4.9.11; Lt.-Col. 26.12.17; Col. 3.6.19; served S. African War, 1900–2 (Queen's Medal with 3 clasps; King's Medal with 2 clasps); served Europ. War; Despatches; Bt. Col. 3.6.19; C.M.G.

HARTIGAN, M. M. (D.S.O. L.G. 22.8.18) (Bar, L.G. 18.2.18) (Details, L.G. 18.7.18); Lt.-Col. 10th Mounted Brigade (Hartigan's Horse), S. African Military Forces. The award of the Bar to the D.S.O. was substituted for the award of a D.S.O. gazetted on 18.2.18.

M. M. Hartigan.

HARTLAND-MAHON, M. C. J. (gazetted as Hartland-Mahon, M. J.) (D.S.O. L.G. 27.6.19), Lt.-Col., R.A.; b. 24.9.76; 2nd Lt., R.A., 23.3.97; Lt. 23.3.00; Capt. 9.4.02; Major 7.9.14; served S. African War (Despatches; both Medals with 5 clasps); Europ. War; Despatches. D.S.O. for Mesopotamia.

HARTLEY, A. F. (D.S.O. L.G. 4.6.17); b. 24.10.82; 2nd Lt., Unatt., 8.1.01; Durham L.I. 9.3.01; Lt., Durham L.I., 5.6.03; Lt., I.A., 10.5.05; rank corrected from Capt. (A/Major) to Major (A/Lt.-Col.), I.A.; Capt. 8.1.10; Major 3.1.16; served S. African War (Queen's Medal with 3 clasps); Europ. War; Despatches.

HARTLEY, D. R. C. (D.S.O. L.G. 15.10.18), T/Capt. (A/Major), R.F.A.

HARTLEY, J. C. (D.S.O. L.G. 1.1.19); b. 15.11.74; s. of E. F. Hartley, of Burnley, Lancashire; m. Violet (who died in 1920), d. of R. C. Darby; educ. Tonbridge; Brasenose College, Oxford; ent. R. Fus., 1898; Major, R. of O., R. Fusiliers; served S. African War (Queen's Medal, 5 clasps; King's Medal, 2 clasps); Despatches; Europ. War, 1914–18, commanding battalions of R. Fusiliers and W. Yorks. Regts.; twice wounded; Despatches thrice; M.C.; M.M.

HARTNOLL, H. J. (D.S.O. L.G. 6.4.18); b. 1890; e. s. of Sir H. S. Hartnoll and Grace, d. of late P. D. Digges La Touche; m. Grace, d. of E. P. Frederick; one s.; Lt., R.N., 30.11.13.

HARTWELL, J. R. (D.S.O. L.G. 23.11.16); b. 7.5.87; 2nd Lt., Unatt., 24.1.06; I.A. 18.3.07; Lt. 24.4.08; Capt. 24.1.15; Major, Gurkha Rifles, 24.1.21; Despatches.

HARTY, T. E. (D.S.O. L.G. 1.1.17) (Bar, L.G. 16.9.18), Major (T/Lt.-Col.), R.A.M.C.

HARVEY, A. (D.S.O. L.G. 26.9.17) (Details, L.G. 9.1.18), 2nd Lt., L'pool R.

HARVEY, C. D. (D.S.O. L.G. 1.1.18); b. 10.2.81; s. of Col. C. L. Harvey, late A.A.G., Lucknow; m. Julia Mary Ridley, d. of Rev. C. R. Carr; one s.; two d.; educ. Haileybury College; R.M.C., Sandhurst; ent. Army 8.1.01, as 2nd Lt., Unattached; 2nd Lt., Notts. and Derby. R., 9.3.01; Lt. 21.2.05; Capt. 15.3.09; Major 8.5.16; Despatches; served S. Africa, 1901–2 (Queen's Medal with 5 clasps); Adjt., 3rd Sherwood Foresters, 1914–15; Second-in-Command, 10th S.W.B., Dec. 1915, for active service in France, in command of same battalion, 1916–18; Despatches twice.

HARVEY, C. G. ST. C. (gazetted as Harvey, C. G. Sinclair) (D.S.O. L.G. 1.1.18); b. 22.6.81; s. of late W. J. Harvey, J.P.; m. Constance Armine, d. of H. B. Sandford, J.P.; two d.; educ. Eton; R.M.A., Woolwich; 2nd Lt., R.A., 2.5.00; Lt. 3.4.01; Capt. 15.3.10; Major, R.F.A., 30.10.14; served in Egypt and India; served Europ. War, 1915–18, in Guards Division; commanded 15th Bde., R.F.A., 5th Division, in last phase of the war; Despatches.

HARVEY, D. (D.S.O. L.G. 22.12.16), Capt., 31st Punjabis, I.A. He was killed in action 10.2.17.

HARVEY, F. G. (D.S.O. L.G. 3.6.18), Lt.-Col., S. African Defence Force.

HARVEY, F. H. (D.S.O. L.G. 1.1.17); b. 9.11.78; 2nd Lt., Border R., 3.8.98; Lt. 20.10.01; I.A. 27.2.03; Capt., I.A., 3.8.07; E. York. R. 4.4.08; Major 15.5.15; Bt. Lt.-Col. 3.6.18; Lt.-Col. 11.11.20; served S. African War, 1899–1901 (Queen's Medal with 3 clasps); Europ. War; Despatches; C.M.G.

HARVEY, G. H. (D.S.O. L.G. 1.1.18); b. 24.10.76; 2nd Lt., A.S.C., 22.5.00; Lt. 1.6.01; Capt. 1.2.05; Major, R.A.S.C., 10.3.22; served S. African War, 1901–2 (Queen's Medal with 5 clasps); Europ. War; Despatches.

HARVEY, J. (D.S.O. L.G. 1.1.18), Capt. and Hon. Major (T/Lt.-Col.), R. of O., retired, S.R.; served S. African War, 1899–1900 (Queen's Medal with 3 clasps); Europ. War; Despatches.

HARVEY, M. M. (D.S.O. L.G. 26.7.18), T/Capt., Notts. and Derby. R.; M.C.

HARVEY, S. L. (D.S.O. L.G. 1.1.19), Major, R.E., T.F.; M.C. He died 9.1.19.

HARVEY, V. V. (D.S.O. L.G. 10.1.17), Major, Can. Inf.

HARVEY, W. J. S. (D.S.O. L.G. 1.1.17); b. 18.5.74; Lt., R.A.M.C., 14.1.02; Capt. 14.1.05; Major 14.1.14; Despatches.

HARVEY-KELLY, C. H. G. H. (D.S.O. L.G. 12.9.19); b. 15.6.85; 2nd Lt., Unatt., 18.1.05; I.A. 10.3.06; Lt. 18.4.07; Capt. 18.1.14; Bt. Major 3.6.17; Major 18.1.20; served E. Africa (Somaliland), 1908–10 (Medal with clasp); Europ. War; Despatches.

HARWOOD, R. (D.S.O. L.G. 14.11.16), Capt., 16th Bn. Aust. Inf.

HASELDEN, F. (D.S.O. L.G. 1.1.18), Major, S. African Inf.; was wounded while fighting Bolsheviks in Central Russia.

HASELDINE, R. H. (D.S.O. L.G. 25.8.17); b. 3.1.78; 2nd Lt., S. Lan. R., 16.12.03; Lt. 11.4.07; Adjt., S. Lan. R., 1.10.08 to 23.9.10; Capt. 4.7.10; Major 1.9.15; served W. Africa (Liberia), 1905 (severely wounded; Medal and clasp); Europ. War; Despatches; Bt. Lt.-Col. 3.6.18.

HASELFOOT, F. E. B. (D.S.O. L.G. 20.2.19), Cdr., R.N., 31.12.18, H.M.S. Grafton.

HASKARD, J. M'D. (D.S.O. L.G. 1.1.17); b. in Florence, 27.11.76; s. of W. T. Haskard; m. Alicia Isabel, d. of S. Newburgh Hutchins; one s.; educ. Blairlodge, Stirlingshire; 2nd Lt., R. Dublin Fusiliers, 1.12.97; Lt. 10.5.99; Capt. 16.7.04; Major 28.4.15; served S. African War (wounded; Despatches; Queen's Medal, 6 clasps; King's Medal, 2 clasps); operations in the Aden Hinterland, 1903; served in the Egyptian A. 1908–11; Europ. War from 1914, serving in France, Salonika and Egypt; amongst other engagements, was present at the Battles of the Somme and Ancre; Ypres, 1917; Cambrai and St. Quentin; Despatches five times; C.M.G.; Bt. Lt.-Col. 1.1.18; G.S.O.1, Staff College, Camberley, 1919–20.

HASLAM, B. J. (D.S.O. L.G. 7.2.18); b. 31.3.75; 2nd Lt., R.E., 1.4.95; Lt. 1.4.98; Capt. 1.4.04; Major; served N.W. Frontier of India, 1897–8 (Medal with 2 clasps); Tirah, 1897–8 (clasp); Europ. War; Despatches. He was killed in action 26.8.18.

HASLAM, P. L. C. (D.S.O. L.G. 1.1.18), Capt. (T/Major), Hrs., attd. Tank Corps.

HASSELL, J. (D.S.O. L.G. 13.5.18), Lt. (A/Capt.), Yorks. L.I.; M.C.

HASSELL, L. L. (D.S.O. L.G. 26.11.17) (Details, L.G. 6.4.18); b. 5.6.94; 2nd Lt., S. Staffs. R., 16.5.15; Lt. 4.1.16; Capt. 6.7.21; Despatches; M.C.

HASTED, J. O. C. (D.S.O. L.G. 25.8.17); b. 20.8.90; s. of late J. E. H. Hasted and F. G. Hasted (*née* Cobbold); m. Phyllis Mary (d. 1921), d. of F.M. Sir A. Barrett; one s.; 2nd Lt., Durham L.I., 20.4.10; Lt. 7.11.13; Capt. 30.4.16; Adjt., Durham L.I., 20.9.17 to 31.10.17

HASTINGS, J. H. (D.S.O. L.G. 8.8.17); b. 1858; s. of William and Anna Hastings; educ. Huddersfield College; served Europ. War; raised the 2/6th W. Yorks. R.; commanded it in France, Jan. to July, 1917; Ancre, Bullecourt (Despatches); resigned; a Town Major, Arras, 1917–18; Town Commandant, 1918–19; O.B.E.; promoted Colonel, 1918; Croix d'Officier, Légion d'Honneur.

HASTINGS, N. F. (D.S.O. L.G. 14.1.16), Major, Wellington Mounted Rifles, N.Z. Mil. Forces.

HASTINGS, W. H. (D.S.O. L.G. 1.1.17); b. 17.3.84; s. of late Cdr. W. C. H. Hastings, R.N.; m. Mary, d. of late R. M. Kennedy, I.C.S.; two s.; educ. United Services College, Westward Ho!; R.M.C., Sandhurst; 2nd Lt., Unatt., 21.1.03; 92nd Punjabis, I.A., 6.4.04; Lt. 21.4.05; Capt. 21.1.12; Major 21.1.18; Despatches; Bt. Major 1.1.16; Bt. Lt.-Col. 3.6.19; proceeded on Field Service, Oct. 1914; present during Turkish attack on Suez Canal, Feb. 1915; Gallipoli, in command of special machine guns for A.N.Z.A. Corps; served with 1st Australian Light Horse Brigade, and on Staff of N.Z. and A. Division till the evacuation (severely wounded 26 June); Bt. Major, 1.1.16; France, with N.Z. Division, 1916–17; Battle of Somme (slightly wounded 15 Sept.; D.S.O.); Mesopotamia 1917, commanding 92nd Punjabis; Egyptian Exp. Force, 1918–19, including attack of 19 Sept., advance through Lebanon to Beyrout and Tripoli, and occupation of Cilicia; Bt. Lt.-Col. 3.6.19; Despatches four times; N.W. Frontier of India, Waziristan, Dec. 1919, to Jan. 1920; Mesopotamia, 1920–21.

HATCH, H. C. (D.S.O. L.G. 1.1.18), Major, Can. Inf.

HATCHER, J. O. (D.S.O. L.G. 14.7.16), Cdr., R.N.

HATFIELD, E. R. (D.S.O. L.G. 14.11.16); b. 1883; s. of R. Hatfield; joined Volunteers, and passed through the ranks of the Westminster Dragoons Yeomanry, leaving as a Sergt. in 1912 to take a commission in the 5th London Brig. R.F.A. (T.F.); Lt., 1913; Capt. 1914; Major, June, 1916; mobilized with the 14th London Battery, and sailed with his unit to France, March, 1915; served with it at Festubert, Loos, Vimy, the Somme, Ypres salient, Messines, Passchendaele and Cambrai, 1917; severely wounded at Havrincourt in the Cambrai battle, 12.12.17; Despatches; 1914–15 Star; commands 9th London Battery, T.A. His D.S.O. was awarded for gallantry on 16 Sept. 1916, Bazentin-le-Grand.

HATTERSLEY-SMITH, W. P. A. (D.S.O. L.G. 1.1.19); b. 8.12.81; s. of Rev. P. Hattersley-Smith; educ. Rugby; Woolwich; 2nd Lt., R.A., 6.1.00; Lt. 3.4.01; Capt. 2.1.11; Major 7.9.15; served Europ. War, 1914–18; Egypt, Salonika and France; Despatches.

HAUGHTON, E. J. H. (D.S.O. L.G. 7.2.18); b. 19.1.83; 2nd Lt., R. War. R., 18.1.02; 2nd Lt., I.A., 13.11.05; Lt. 18.4.04; Capt. 18.1.11; Major.

HAWES, C. H. (D.S.O. L.G. 22.12.16) (Bar, L.G. 27.6.19), Lt.-Col. 23rd Cavalry, I.A. (Mesopotamia); b. 31.8.71; s. of late Major-Gen. W. H. Hawes, Bengal Army; educ. Wellington College; entered W. Yorks. R., 1891; 3rd Punjab Cavalry, F.F. (now 23rd Cavalry, F.F.), 1895; served N.W. Frontier of India, 1897, and Tirah (Medal and 3 clasps); in charge of the King's India Orderly Officers, 1913 (M.V.O.); served Mesopotamia with regiment, May, 1915; Brigade Major. 6th Cavalry Brigade, July, 1915, to Nov. 1916; present at Battles of Ctesiphon, Retreat to Kut, and Ali-el-Gharbi; with Kut Relieving Force, Battles of Shaik Saad, Wadi, Hannah and Dujailah (D.S.O.; Despatches); operations on the Euphrates, 1919 (Despatches); on the Tigris, Battle of Huwaish, 27th–30th Oct. 1918 (Bar to D.S.O.); Afghanistan, 1919; commanding 23rd Cavalry, Frontier Force, Mesopotamia.

HAWES, C. M. (D.S.O. L.G. 3.6.19); b. 20.5.82; 2nd Lt., Unatt., 21.1.03; Lt., I.A., 4.4.04; Capt. 21.4.05; Major 21.1.12; Lt.-Col. 21.1.18; Despatches.

HAWES, G. E. (D.S.O. L.G. 4.6.17); b. 24.3.82; s. of G. C. Hawes, J.P., Combe Park, Bath, Somerset; m. Millicent, Duchess of Sutherland, d. of 4th Earl of Rosslyn; 2nd Lt., Unatt., 8.1.01; R. Fus. 1.10.08 to 30.9.11; Capt. 21.2.10; Major 8.1.16; Lt.-Col; served Europ. War, 1914–17; Despatches; M.C.; Bt. Lt.-Col.; Legion of Honour.

HAWES, L. A. (D.S.O. L.G. 3.6.18); b. 22.7.92; s. of C. A. Hawes; m. Gwendolen Mary, d. of D. H. Grimsdale, J.P.; educ. Bedford; R.M.A., Woolwich; Lt., R.G.A., 1911; Capt., 1916; T/Major, 1917; served Europ. War, 1914–18; wounded; M.C.; Order of Crown of Italy; Despatches.

HAWKES, C. ST. L. G. (D.S.O. L.G. 1.1.17); b. 23.3.71; s. of late C. Hawkes; m. Eleanor Muriel, d. of E. H. Pares; one s.; one d.; 2nd Lt., R.A., 19.8.93; Lt. 19.8.96; Capt. 30.6.00; Adjt., R.A., 22.10.06 to 18.9.07; Major 20.7.10; Lt.-Col., R.F.A., 13.2.16; retired pay, 1921; served S. African War, Nov. 1899, to May, 1901 (Queen's Medal and 6 clasps); Europ. War in France, 1914–19; Despatches four times; C.M.G.; 1914 Star; French Croix de Guerre.

HAWKES, G. W. (D.S.O. L.G. 3.6.19), T/Lt.-Col., 5th Bn. R. Irish Regt.; M.C.

HAWKES, W. C. W. (D.S.O. L.G. 1.1.17); b. 13.6.72; 2nd Lt., Unatt., 23.12.93; I.S.C. 27.3.95; Lt. 23.3.96; Capt., I.A., 23.12.02; Major 23.12.11; T/Lt.-Col.

HAWKINS, C. F. (D.S.O. L.G. 3.6.18), formerly Capt., 1st Can. Machine Gun Brigade, and transferred to the Imperial Army, Sept. 1916; Despatches; M.C.

HAWKINS, E. B. B. (D.S.O. L.G. 26.3.18) (Details, L.G. 24.8.18); b. 9.12.89; 2nd Lt., W. York. R., 18.9.09; Lt. 7.3.10; Capt. 13.11.14; Bt. Major 3.6.19; Despatches.

HAWKINS, E. F. S. (D.S.O. L.G. 1.1.18); s. of late Reginald Hawkins and Marguerite Wilhelmina, d. of Rev. W. C. Lukes; Lt. (T/Major), R.A.S.C., S. Reserve; served Europ. War, 1914–18; Despatches.

HAWKINS, E. M. (D.S.O. L.G. 23.3.17), Lt., R.N.R.

HAWKINS, H. D. (D.S.O. L.G. 1.1.19), Lt. (A/Major), R.G.A. (S.R.), attd. 431st Siege Battery.

HAWKINS, R. C. (D.S.O. L.G. 3.6.18); s. of W. Hawkins; m. Mary, d. of W. Stonard; Capt., H.A.C.

HAWKSLEY, J. P. V. (D.S.O. L.G. 14.1.16); b. 21.12.77; 2nd Lt., R.A., 1.9.97; Lt. 1.9.00; Capt. 14.7.04; Major 30.10.14; served S. African War, 1899–1902 (Despatches; Queen's Medal with 5 clasps; King's Medal with 2 clasps); employed with Egyptian Army, 5.5.05 to 4.5.12; operations in S. Kordofan, 1910 (Sudan Medal and clasp); Europ. War; Despatches. Lt.-Col. Hawksley was killed in action 5.8.16.

HAWKSLEY, R. P. T. (D.S.O. L.G. 1.1.18); b. 1870; s. of late J. T. Hawksley, of Caldy Island, Pembrokeshire; m. Kate Marjorie, d. of late B. P. Woosnam, D.L.; two d.; educ. Harrow; served N.W. Frontier of India, 1897–8 (Medal and clasp); S. African War, 1900–2 (Queen's Medal and 2 clasps; King's Medal and 2 clasps); Europ. War, 1914–18; served in the Army of the Union of S. Africa during the Boer Rebellion of 1914 and the campaign in German S.W. Africa; served in R.E. in the British Isles, India, S. Africa, Gallipoli, Egypt, Palestine, Syria and Asia Minor; Chief Engineer, 21st Corps, 1917–19; Chief Engineer, Palestine, 1919–20; Brig.-Gen.; Despatches; C.M.G.; Order of the White Eagle; Order of the Nile; 1914–15 Star.

HAWLEY, W. G. B. I. (D.S.O. L.G. 12.9.19); b. 16.8.77; 2nd Lt., Unatt., 4.8.97; 2nd Lt., I.S.C., 25.11.98; Lt., I.A., 4.11.99; Capt. 4.8.06; Major, 28th Light Cav., I.A., 4.8.15; Despatches.

HAWTHORN, F., M.D., M.R.C.S., L.R.C.P. (D.S.O. L.G. 1.1.17); s. of late J. Hawthorn, Surgeon; educ. Durham University College of Medicine; Lt.-Col., R.A.M.C., T.F.; commanding the 1st Northumbrian Field Ambulance since 1913; Regimental Medical Officer, R.G.A. (Vols.).

HAWTHORN, G. M. P. (D.S.O. L.G. 2.2.16); b. 16.12.73; 2nd Lt., L'pool R., 7.3.94; Lt. 17.11.97; Capt. 21.3.00; Adjt., L'pool R., 4.7.10 to 3.7.13; commanded 1st Bn. K.A.R.; Brigadier-General; served in W. Africa, 1900 (Medal); E. Africa, 1904 (Medal and 2 clasps); Rhodesia-Nyasaland F.F. from 1.7.18; Despatches; Bt. Major 1.9.15; Bt. Lt.-Col. 1.1.18; Col. 31.8.20.

HAWTREY, H. C. (D.S.O. L.G. 26.6.17); b. 1882; s. of late Rev. H. C. Hawtrey, Vicar of Nursling, near Southampton; m. Emily Mildred. d. of late F. C. Gough; educ. Uppingham; R.M.A., Woolwich; ent. R.E. 1900; Capt., 1910; Lt.-Col., 1921; served Europ. War, 1914–18; Despatches; C.M.G.; Bt. Lt.-Col.; transferred from R.E. into Royal Corps of Signals, 1920; won five-mile race in Olympic Games at Athens, 1906; won ten-mile championship, L.A.C.; equalled mile record.

HAY, A. A. B. (D.S.O. L.G. 26.3.18) (Details, L.G. 24.8.18), Lt. (A/Major), R.F.A., S.R.; M.C.

HAY, A. K. (D.S.O. L.G. 1.1.17); b. 12.5.84; 2nd Lt., R.A., 31.7.02; Lt. 31.7.05; Capt. 30.10.14; Major 27.3.16; Despatches.

HAY, A. S. (D.S.O. L.G. 10.8.21); b. 21.2.79; 2nd Lt., Suffolk R., 3.8.98; Lt. 15.8.00; Capt., I.A., 2.10.00; Capt. 3.8.07; Major 1.9.15; Despatches.

HAY, C. J. B. (D.S.O. L.G. 14.1.16); b. 18.5.77; s. of late Col. C. Hay; m. Agatha, d. of late Rev. J. Mangin, D.D., LL.D.; one d.; educ. Wellington College; R.M.C., Sandhurst; 2nd Lt., Unatt., 4.8.97; I.S.C. 24.11.98; Lt., I.A., 4.11.99; Capt. 4.8.06; Major 4.8.15; Bt. Lt.-Col. 1.1.17; Col. 26.6.20; served N.W. Frontier of India, 1897–8 (Medal with clasp); Tirah, 1897–8 (clasp); N.W. Frontier of India, Waziristan, 1901–2 (Clasp; Despatches); Europ. War, 1914–19; G.S.O.1, H.Q., Aden F.F., 1917; 1st Grade, G.H.Q.,

Mesopotamian Exp. Force, 1917–19; Despatches five times; Brevet of Lt.-Col.; C.M.G.; Third Afghan War, 1919; G.S.O.1, H.Q., N.W.F.F. (Medal with clasp; Despatches); Q.V.O., Corps of Guides, G.S.

HAY, G. H. (D.S.O. L.G. 26.7.17); b. 30.8.93; s. of W. Hope Hay; graduated from R.M.C., Kingston, 1913; 2nd Lt., R. Scots, 26.7.13; Lt. 13.4.14; Capt. 17.4.16; served Europ. War; was in Retreat from Mons; was a prisoner in Russia; Despatches; wounded three times. D.S.O. awarded for gallantry east of Arras 9.4.17.

HAY, G. L. (D.S.O. L.G. 4.6.17); b. 1.2.73; Capt., A.O.D., 3.9.16; Major 18.10.16; Bt. Lt.-Col. 3.6.18; R.A.O.D.; served Europ. War, 1914–18; Despatches; C.B.E.

HAY, J. (D.S.O. L.G. 3.6.18), T/Capt. (Local and T/Lt.-Col.), Spec. List.

HAY, J. G. (D.S.O. L.G. 1.1.18), Capt., retired pay, late G. Highrs.; b. 3.6.78; first commission, 9.12.90; Capt. 22.1.06; ret. pay, 11.4.08; T/Lt.-Col., 7th Bn. G. Highrs.; served S. African War, 1899–1900 (Despatches; Queen's Medal with 3 clasps); Europ. War; Despatches.

HAY, R. B. (D.S.O. L.G. 3.6.18), T/Capt. (A/Major), R.G.A.

HAY, S. (D.S.O. L.G. 2.2.16); b. 28.3.76; s. of late Capt. W. D. O. Hay-Newton; m. Irma Vera Evelyn, d. of late Hon. L. G. Scott; three d.; 2nd Lt., Q.O. Cameron Highrs., 15.5.97; Lt. 2.11.98; Capt. 21.11.01; Major 1.9.15; served S. African War, 1900–2 (Queen's Medal with 3 clasps; King's Medal with 2 clasps); served Europ. War; Despatches; Bt. Lt.-Col. 3.6.17.

HAY, W. N. (D.S.O. L.G. 27.7.18); b. 1871; m. Violet Maud, d. of A. W. Cowdell; two s.; three d.; educ. Haileybury; R.M.A., Woolwich; Col. 129th Baluchis, I.A.; served China, 1900 (Medal); E. Africa, 1917–18 (D.S.O.); Afghanistan, 1919; N.W. Frontier of India, 1919–20; C.I.E.

HAYBITTEL, L. McG. (D.S.O. L.G. 16.9.18), T/Capt., R.F.A.

HAYDON, L. G. (D.S.O. L.G. 22.8.18), Major, S. African Medical Service.

HAYDON, W. P. (D.S.O. L.G. 25.8.17), Lt.-Col., I.A.

HAYES, SIR B. F. (D.S.O. L.G. 21.6.18); served in Europ. War, 1914–18; Capt., R.N.R., retired list, 1921; C.M.G. 1917; K.C.M.G., 1920; R.D. D.S.O. awarded for services in action with enemy submarines.

HAYES, G. (D.S.O. L.G. 1.1.18); b. 30.8.87; 2nd Lt., Durham L.I., 4.5.07; Lt. 4.1.12; Capt. 10.6.15.

HAYES, J. (D.S.O. L.G. 3.6.18), Lt.-Col., Can. A.M.C.

HAYES, J. H. (D.S.O. L.G. 1.1.17), Major (T/Lt.-Col.), Shrops. Yeomanry.

HAYES, W. (D.S.O. L.G. 4.6.17), Capt. (T/Major), The Queen's R.W. Surrey R. He died 20.10.18.

HAYFIELD, C. D. (D.S.O. L.G. 7.11.18), T/Capt., E. Kent R.; M.C.

HAYHURST-FRANCE, G. F. H. (D.S.O. L.G. 21.1.20); b. 3.3.95; 2nd Lt., K.R.R.C., 1.10.14; Lt. 18.5.15; Capt. 1.1.17; Despatches; M.C.

HAYLEY, S. T. (D.S.O. L.G. 1.1.17); b. 20.1.79; 2nd Lt., Devon R., 11.2.99; Lt. 7.1.00; Capt. 1.1.04; Major, Devon R., 1.9.15; permanently appointed to R.A.O.C.; served S. African War, 1899–1902 (Queen's Medal with 2 clasps; King's Medal with 2 clasps); Europ. War; Despatches; O.B.E.

HAYLEY, W. B. (D.S.O. L.G. 1.1.18); b. 17.4.82; 2nd Lt., R.A., 21.12.00; Lt. 21.12.03; Capt. 21.12.13; Major, R.H.A., 9.9.15; Despatches.

HAYLEY-BELL, F. (D.S.O. L.G. 16.9.18), T/Major (A/Lt.-Col.), W. Surrey R.

HAYMAN, W. M. (D.S.O. L.G. 1.1.17); commissioned in the Queen's Regt. in the early months of the war; transferred to the Corps of R. Engineers; became Captain in March, 1915, and Major in the following May. He died of wounds 13.7.17.

HAYNE, S. S. (D.S.O. L.G. 16.9.18); b. 26.1.82; s. of late H. Hayne; m. Agnes, d. of late S. H. Wilkinson; 2nd Lt., Northants. R., 5.1.01; Lt. 21.5.03; Capt. 1.4.10; Major 1.9.15; served S. African War, 1900 (Medal); Europ. War, 1914–18; Despatches.

HAYNES, W. H. (D.S.O. L.G. 18.12.17), T/Capt., R.F.C. D.S.O. awarded for anti-aircraft services.

HAYTER, H. R. (D.S.O. L.G. 3.6.16); b. 13.8.77; s. of R. W. and S. M. Hayter; m. 1st, Lily Temple (deceased), d. of J. Douglas, LL.D.; 2ndly, Elsie Helen Evelyn Winterton, d. of Major Pidcock-Henzell; two s.; three d.; educ. Upper Canada College, Toronto; Queen's Own Rifles (Canadian Militia), 1895–8; R. Fusiliers (5th Bn.); 2nd Lt., A.S.C., 1900; Capt., 1904; Major, 1914; Lt.-Col. 1921; served S. African War, 1901–2 (Queen's Medal, 4 clasps); Europ. War, 1914–18; Despatches; Bt. Lt.-Col.; Lt.-Col., R.A.S.C.

HAYWARD, C. R. (D.S.O. L.G. 3.6.19), Capt. (A/Lt.-Col.), W. Somerset Yeomanry, commanding 12th Battn. Somerset L.I., T.F.

HAYWARD, G. W. (D.S.O. L.G. 1.1.18), T/Col., R.F.A.

HAYWOOD, A. N. (D.S.O. L.G. 3.6.19), Quartermaster and Major, 6th Dragoon Guards; served S. African War, 1899–1902 (Queen's Medal with 4 clasps; King's Medal with 2 clasps); Europ. War; Despatches.

HAZELL, T. F. (D.S.O. L.G. 8.2.19), Capt. (A/Major), R.A.F. (France); M.C.; D.F.C.; Bar to D.F.C.

HAZELRIGG, T. (D.S.O. L.G. 1.1.18); b. 1.6.77; 2nd Lt., A.S.C., 23.11.01; Lt. 1.1.03; Capt. 1.1.11; Major, R.A.S.C., 30.10.14; served S. African War (Queen's Medal with 2 clasps); Europ. War; Despatches.

HEAD, A. E. M. (D.S.O. L.G. 1.1.17); b. 18.6.76; s. of late H. H. Head, J.P.; educ. Charterhouse; R.M.A., Woolwich; joined R.A. in 1896; 2nd Lt. 21.3.96; Lt. 21.3.99; Capt. 22.1.02; Adjt., R.A., 14.8.05 to 15.1.07; Major 4.1.13; Lt.-Col., R.F.A., 1917; retired pay, 1920; served China, 1900 (Medal); Europ. War; Despatches twice.

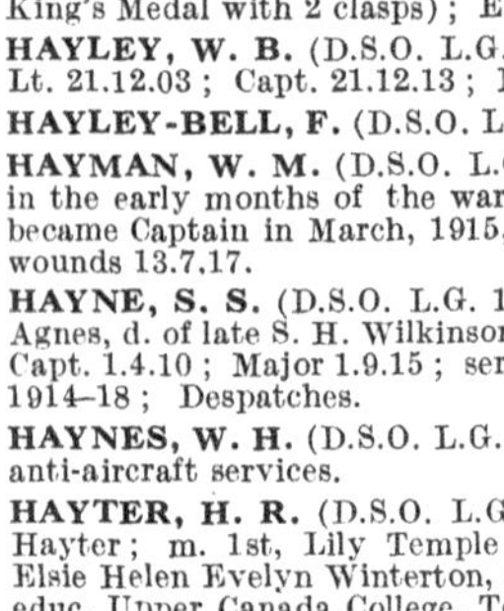

E. J. Headlam.

HEAD, C. O. (D.S.O. L.G. 1.1.17); b. 30.5.69; s. of W. H. Head, D.L., of Derrylaban Park, Birr, Ireland, and I. E. Head (*née* Biddulph); m. Alice Margaret, d. of C. Threlfall, of Tarporley, Cheshire; one s.; two d.; educ. privately; R.M.A., Woolwich; 2nd Lt., R.A., 23.7.87; Major 7.11.02; retired 10.8.10; Lt.-Col., R. of O.; served in India and S. Africa; Boxer Campaign, 1900 (Medal); actively employed since Aug. 1914; France, 1915–18; Despatches three times.

HEADLAM, C. M. (D.S.O. L.G. 1.1.18); b. 27.4.76; s. of late F. J. Headlam; m. Beatrice, d. of late G. B. Crawley, Clerk in Parliament Office, 1897; called to the Bar, Inner Temple, 1906; Clerk of Public Bills in the House of Lords since 1910; joined Bedfords. Yeom. 1910; Capt. 1915; served in France and Belgium; Europ. War, 1915–18; Despatches five times.

HEADLAM, E. J. (D.S.O. L.G. 14.1.16); b. 1.5.73; s. of late M. Headlam; m. Nancey Benyon, widow of A. Hobson; educ. Durham School; H.M.S. Conway; Sub-Lt., R.I.M., 1894; Lt., 1900; Cdr., 1913; Capt.; Deputy Director, R.I. Marine; Marine Survey of India, 1897–1914; Naval Transport Officer, E. African Forces, 1914–17; Principal Naval Transport Officer, S. and E. Africa, 1917–19; Asst. Marine Transport Officer, B.E.F., N. China, 1900–1 (Medal; Despatches); R. Humane Society's Medal; Hon. Member, American Military Order of Dragon; served Europ. War; Despatches four times; C.M.G.; special promotion to Capt., 1914–15; Bronze Star; 1914–15 Star. Has written "History of Sea Service under the Government of India."

HEAL, F. H. (D.S.O. L.G. 17.12.17) (Details, L.G. 23.4.18); s. of Capt. W. H. Heal: educ. Perse School, Cambridge, where he gained his colours in football: Lt.-Col., S. African Inf. Regt.; commissioned in the Yeomanry; promoted to Lt. and made Adjt.; was posted to the Cape Peninsula Rifles, and in Sept. 1915, left with the first S. African Contingent for Egypt, afterwards to another front; was given command of a battalion of S. African infantry, and was mentioned in Despatches. He was wounded twice, and was reported missing and afterwards as killed 21–24.3.18.

HEALD, B. C. (D.S.O. L.G. 22.8.18), Major, S. African Rly. R. (Supernumerary List).

HEALING, N. C. (D.S.O. L.G. 1.1.19); b. 14.1.85; 2nd Lt., R.A., 31.7.02; Lt. 31.7.05; Capt. 30.10.14; Major, R.G.A., 1.5.17; Despatches; M.C.

HEARLE, A. B. (D.S.O. L.G. 1.1.18), Major, R.G.A.; served Europ. War, 1914–18; Despatches.

HEARN, G. R. (D.S.O. L.G. 1.1.17); b. 7.9.71; s. of late Major C. S. Hearn, C.I.E.; Inspector-Gen. of Police, Madras; m. Olive, d. of Lt.-Col. H. Cates, Bombay Political Depot; two s.; educ. Temple Grove, East Sheen; Winchester College (Scholar); Woolwich; commissioned in R.E. 25 July, 1890; Lt. 25.7.93; Capt. 21.7.01; Major 25.7.10; Indian State Railways, 1894; was on active service with the Malakand, Mohmand and Tirah Field Forces, 1897–8 (Medal with 2 clasps); returned to railway service on construction Agra Delhi Chord Railway; has been three times Government Inspector of Railways; returned to England, and commanded a Field company, 1914, afterwards becoming C.R.E. of a division; Despatches four times; Bt. Lt.-Col. 1.1.18. Has published "The Seven Cities of Delhi" (with the late A. G. Watson) and "The Railway Engineer's Field Book."

HEARNE, W. W. (D.S.O. L.G. 4.6.17), Lt.-Col. (T/Col.), Aust. A.M.C.

HEARSON, J. G. (D.S.O. L.G. 14.1.16); b. 5.8.83, at Blackheath; s. of late Professor T. A. Hearson; m. Winifred Maude, d. of G. Shaw, of Syston, Leicestershire; one s.; educ. Marlborough College and R.M.A., Woolwich; 2nd Lt., R.E., 31.7.02; Lt. 22.2.05; Capt. 31.7.13; Major, 1917; Fl.-Cdr., R.F.C., 1915; Wing Cdr., 1916; T/Brig.-Gen. 1.1.17; employed on Cross River, S. Nigeria Boundary Commission, 1905–6; Niger-Chad Boundary Commission, 1906–8; Superintendent of Roads, Gold Coast Colony, 1910–12; served Europ. War, 1914–18; Despatches four times; C.B.; Order of St. Anne, 3rd Class; Bt. Major 1.1.17; Director of Training, R.A.F., Air Ministry, from 1.4.18. His D.S.O. was awarded for work in the air during the summer of 1915 and on the Western Front.

HEASLEY, H. J. (D.S.O. L.G. 3.6.18), Major, Can. A.S.C.

HEATH, C. P. (D.S.O. L.G. 4.6.17); b. 17.9.93; 2nd Lt., R.A., 18.7.13; Lt. 9.6.15; Adjt., R.A., 29.2.16 to 26.11.16; Capt. 18.7.17; Despatches.

HEATH, E. C. (D.S.O. L.G. 26.11.17) (Details, L.G. 6.4.18), Lt.-Col. L'pool R.

HEATH, G. N. (D.S.O. L.G. 1.1.18) (Bar, L.G. 22.4.18); b. 23.6.81; s. of G. H. Heath, J.P., of Macclesfield, and F. L. J. Heath (*née* Wheeler); m. Kate Lisette, d. of W. Smale, J.P., C.C., of Macclesfield; three d.; educ. Macclesfield Grammar School; Uppingham; joined 5th Vol. Battn. Cheshire R., 1900; Major, Cheshire R.; mobilized 4.8.14; served Europ. War, 1914–18, in Gallipoli, Egypt, Sinai Peninsula, Palestine and Syria; Despatches.

HEATH, J. T. (D.S.O. L.G. 1.1.18); b. 18.3.86; 2nd Lt., R.E., 25.7.06; Lt. 22.11.08; Capt. 30.10.14; served in Europ. War; M.C.

HEATHCOTE, ARTHUR NAPIER (Christian name gazetted as "Archer Napier") (D.S.O. L.G. 3.6.18), Capt., R.N.

HEATHCOTE, R. E. M. (D.S.O. L.G. 3.6.18); b. 4.9.84; s. of R. Heathcote, of Lobthorpe and Manton; m. Edith Millicent, d. of W. Walton, of Horsley Priory, Gloucestershire; one s.; one d.; educ. Eton; Lt.-Col., R. Scots; served Europ. War, 1914–18; Despatches four times.

HEATHER, V. J. (D.S.O. L.G. 1.1.18); b. 12.2.76; 2nd Lt. 18.7.00; Lt. 25.2.03; Capt. 28.6.11; Major, R.A.

HEATON, D. R. (D.S.O. L.G. 20.10.16); b. 19.6.93; s. of Beresford R. and Mary Isabel Heaton; m. Isa Marie, d. of F. F. Freeman; two d.; educ. Eton; Trinity College, Cambridge; T/2nd Lt., R.W. Surrey R., Sept. 1914: Lt., March, 1915; Capt., July, 1916; Staff Capt., April, 1918; retired from R.W. Surrey R.; served Europ. War (France), 1914–17; was twice wounded and mentioned in Despatches. His D.S.O. was awarded for gallantry at Montauban Ridge on 1.7.16.

HEATON, G. W. H. (D.S.O. L.G. 1.1.16) (Bar, L.G. 7.6.18); b. 3.3.82; s. of G. W. Heaton (for some time High Sheriff of Vancouver, B.C.) and Annette Hannah, d. of James Gordon Campbell, 9th Bengal Lancers and Indian Civil Service; educ. Ascham House, Bournemouth; H.M.S. Britannia, Dartmouth; Midshipman in the Anson, Gibraltar and Theseus, Mediterranean Station, and saw most of the disturbances in Crete, 1897–9; in the Diadem and Thrasher, Home Waters, 1900–1; Sub-Lt., 1901; Lt., 1903; 1st Lt. in H.M.S. Ganges II, Training Ship, then as a Lt. in H.M.S. Britannia, Battleship, 1907–8; in command of H.M. Destroyers Zebra, Wolfe, Sylvia, 1910–12; Lt.-Cdr., 1911; retired, 1912; A/Commander, R.N., in charge of a Flotilla of Minesweepers; lost left hand in a motor smash 31.12.14; volunteered and left California, Jan. 1915; was put in command of two minesweepers, and later of a division of minesweepers; made A/Commander for Special Service, Aug. 1915; Despatches; Croix de Guerre with Palms, May, 1917.

HEATON, H. (D.S.O. L.G. 21.1.20), T/Capt., 19th Battn. Durham L.I., attd. 45th Battn. R. Fus. (Archangel Command, N. Russia); M.C.

HEBBERT, H. E. (D.S.O. L.G. 3.6.19); b. 30.9.93; 2nd Lt., R.E., 17.7.14; Lt. 9.6.15; Capt. 3.11.17; A/Major, R.E., 24.1.18 to 20.1.19; Capt. (A/Major), 21st Div. Signalling Co., R.E.; M.C.

HEBBLETHWAITE, A. G., M.R.C.S., L.R.C.P. (D.S.O. L.G. 1.1.18); b. 1869; s. of late G. H. Hebblethwaite; m. Annie Blackburn, d. of J. Barnard, C.C., of Owston Ferry, Doncaster; educ. Sedbergh School; Leeds and Victoria University; Lt.-Col., R.A.M.C.; Senior Surgeon, Mobile Unit of B.R.C.S. Field Ambulance, attached to French Cavalry, 1914; Second-in-Command, 2/2nd W.R. Field Ambulance, 1915; appointed D.A.D.M.S., 6th Corps, B.E.F., France; Despatches; Lt.-Col. in command of 2/1st W.R. Field Ambulance, 1918; Deputy Commissioner of Medical Services on H.Q. Staff, Ministry of Pensions, Leeds.

HEDDLE, M., B.Sc., Assoc.M.Inst.C.E. (D.S.O. L.G. 3.6.18); b. 2.3.89; s. of M. Heddle, late County Surveyor, Orkney; m. Elizabeth, d. of R. Scott, of Trenabie; one d.; educ. Edinburgh University; Major; served Europ. War, 1914–18; Despatches.

HEDGES, K. M. F. (D.S.O. L.G. 4.6.17); b. 29.9.90; 2nd Lt., A.S.C., 3.2.11; Lt. 3.2.14; Capt., R.A.S.C., 3.2.17; Despatches.

HEDLEY, J. C. (D.S.O. L.G. 2.4.19) (Details, L.G. 10.12.19), 2nd Lt., R.W. Surrey R.; M.C.

HEDLEY, J. R. (D.S.O. L.G. 3.6.16); b. 21.3.71; s. of J. Hedley; m. Ada Marie, d. of T. H. Bainbridge; educ. privately; Royal Grammar School, Newcastle-on-Tyne; ent. Northumberland Fusiliers, Jan. 1901; Major, 1912; Lt.-Col. 11.11.15. He died of wounds 15.7.16.

HEDLEY, W. (D.S.O. L.G. 3.6.19); b. 25.2.79; s. of J. Hedley, M.D., of Cleveland Lodge, Middlesbrough; educ. Uppingham; King's College, Cambridge (Scholar); called to the Bar, 1904; Recorder of Richmond, Yorks., since 1920; served Europ. War with R.G.A. in France, Salonika and Palestine, 1914–19; Despatches.

HEELAS, P. J. B. (D.S.O. L.G. 1.1.18) (Bar, L.G. 16.9.18); b. 25.4.79; 2nd Lt., R.A., 19.12.00; Lt. 19.12.03; Capt. 16.8.12; Major, R.F.A., 15.6.15.

HEENAN, C. R. (D.S.O. L.G. 3.6.18), Major, S. African Inf.

HEFFERNAN, J. G. P. (D.S.O. L.G. 3.6.19), T/Major, 1st Battn. R. Dublin Fus.; M.C.

HEILBRON, I. M., D.Sc., Ph.D., F.I.C. (D.S.O. L.G. 3.6.18); born 6.11.86; s. of D. Heilbron; educated at the High School, Glasgow; Royal Technical College, Glasgow (Nobel Company Prize, James Young Exhibition for Research); University of Leipzig (Ph.D.); D.Sc. (Glasgow University); Heath Harrison Professor of Organic Chemistry, The University, Liverpool, since 1920; Lt., R.A.S.C., 1910, 52nd Div.; proceeded overseas, 1915; D.A.D.S.T., G.H.Q., Salonika, 1917; Lt.-Col. (A.D. of Supplies), G.H.Q., Salonika, 1918; Despatches thrice; M.C.; Greek Order of the Redeemer; Médaille d'Honneur. Has published "Chemical Theory and Calculations" (with Prof. F. J. Wilson) and "The Identification of Organic Compounds."

HELM, C. (D.S.O. L.G. 1.1.19); b. 7.9.88; Lt., R.A.M.C., 24.1.13; Capt. (A/Lt.-Col.), 42nd Field Ambulance, R.A.M.C.; Europ. War; Despatches, L.G. 19.10.14; M.C.

HELME, E. (D.S.O. L.G. 2.12.18) (Bar, L.G. 15.2.19) (Details, L.G. 30.7.19), Major, Glamorganshire Yeomanry; Lt.-Col., commanding 15th Battn. Welsh R. From Aug. 25 until the signing of the Armistice on Nov. 11. the battalion, under the command of Lt.-Col. E. Helme, D.S.O., took part in every engagement in which the 38th (Welsh) Division was involved, the most important of these being the crossing of the Canal du Nord, Gouzeaucourt, Selle River Crossing and Normal Forest. During this period the casualties amounted to 40 officers and 900 other ranks killed and wounded. The casualties of the battalion, from its landing in France, were approximately as follows: 26 officers killed, 48 wounded; 393 other ranks killed, 1,073 wounded.

HELYAR, K. C. (D.S.O. L.G. 23.7.18), Lt.-Cdr., R.N. (North Star).

HELYAR, P. J. (D.S.O. L.G. 8.3.18), Lt.-Cdr., R.N.

HEMELRYK, E. V. (D.S.O. L.G. 4.6.17); b. 9.9.85; s. of late P. E. J. Hemelryk, O.R.S., K.C.S.G., J.P.; m. Norah Frances Maccabe; one s.; one d.; educ. The Oratory, Edgbaston; Château du Rosay, Rolle; Handelschule, Cologne; Lt., 4th W. Lancs. Arty. Volunteers, 1907; Capt. (T.F.), 1914; Major, R.F.A., Jan. 1916; promoted Lt.-Col. to command the 4th W. Lancs. Mtd. Brig., R.G.A., 1920; mobilized on 4.8.14, and proceeded to France 26.9.15; took part in the Battle of the Somme, Messines, Ypres, Cambrai, and in the holding of Givenchy by the 55th Div.; wounded in France 22.4.18; Despatches; took over command of C/275th Battery, R.F.A., and took part in the advance from Béthune to Ath.

HEMMING, H. S. J. L. (gazetted as Hemming, H. S. L.) (D.S.O. L.G. 3.6.18); b. 28.6.82; s. of Dr. J. Hemming, M.A., and Lily Florence E., d. of Sir W. Jenner; educ. privately; Bedford Grammar School; 2nd Lt., E. Lancs. R., 1900; resigned commission, 1906; Capt. and Adjt., 3rd S. African Infantry, Aug. 1915; Major, 1915; Lt.-Col., 1918, commanding S. African Reserve Battn.; retired, disability pay, 3rd S. African Infantry; served S. African War, 1900–2; Somaliland, 1903; joined S. African Forces, Sept. 1914; Capt. and Adjt., Rand Rifles, Boer Rebellion and German S.W. Africa Campaign; served with S.A. Forces in Egypt, Dec. 1915; lost right arm at Battle of Agagir; France, July, 1916, Battle of Somme (again wounded); gassed Battle of Passchendaele 20.9.17; wounded, Gouzeaucourt, 1918; commanded temporarily 3rd S.A. Inf., Sept.–Oct. 1917, and Dec. 1917–Jan. 1918; Lt.-Col., 1918, commanding S.A. Reserve Battn.; Despatches thrice; Croix de Guerre; served as G.S.O.1. on Gen. Crozier's Mission in Lithuania (Russia), Oct. 1919, to March, 1920, operations against Germans and Bolsheviks; spent nine years exploring and great-game hunting in interior of Africa; served with Portuguese Forces in Machemba and Matuka Expeditions.

HEMPHILL, R., B.A., M.B., B.Ch., B.A.O. (D.S.O. L.G. 3.6.18); b. 28.8.88; educ. Dublin University; Lt., R.A.M.C., 24.1.13; Capt. 30.3.15; served Europ. War. 1914–18; Despatches.

HEMPSON, C. D. (D.S.O. L.G. 17.3.17) (Details, L.G. 26.5.17); s. of late J. Hempson and Mrs. Hempson, of Ipswich; T/Capt., Suffolk R.; attd. K.O.R. Lancaster R. He was killed in action 8.3.17.

HEMSLEY, C. (D.S.O. L.G. 26.8.18); b. 18.2.84; s. of Rev. C. Hemsley, of Thurleigh Vicarage, Bedfordshire; 2nd Lt., Unatt., 19.8.03; Ind. Army 19.12.04; Lt. 19.11.05; Capt. 19.8.12; Major 19.8.18; Europ. War; Despatches.

HEMSLEY, H. N. (D.S.O. L.G. 3.6.19), T/Lt. (T/Major), Gen. List; M.C.

HENCHLEY, A. R., M.D., L.R.C.P., L.R.C.S., etc., etc. (D.S.O. L.G. 24.9.18); b. 1871; s. of J. R. Henchley; educ. North London Collegiate School; Middlesex Hospital; King's College, London; Edinburgh; University of Brussels; Civil Surgeon attached R.A.M.C. during S. African War; raised, trained and commanded a unit of R.A.M.C. (Vols.) at Canterbury, subsequently expanding this into the 2nd Home Counties Field Ambulance, R.A.M.C., on formation of the T.F.; Major, 1908; Lt.-Col., 1910; resigned, June, 1911. He was given command of 2/1st N.M. (59th) C.C.S., Sept. 1915; went to Ireland during Rebellion, 1916, commanding 59th C.C.S., and Princess Patricia of Connaught's Hospital, Bray, co. Wicklow; proceeded to France in command of 59th C.C.S., Feb. 1917; transferred to command of 48th C.C.S. 2.1.18 (Battles of Cambrai and Marne); D.S.O. Immediate Award; Despatches.

HENDERSON, A. D. (D.S.O. L.G. 15.7.19), T/Capt. (T/Major), Norfolk R.

HENDERSON, C. E. (D.S.O. L.G. 18.1.18) (Details, L.G. 25.4.18), 2nd Lt., London R.

HENDERSON, E. J. (D.S.O. L.G. 26.7.18); b. 1891; s. of R. C. Henderson, J.P.; m. Kathleen Helena, d. of R. E. Rocke; one d.; educ. Abbotsholme and abroad; member of Stock Exchange, London, 1913; enlisted Artists' Rifles, Aug. 1914; B.E.F., Oct. 1914; temporary commission, 2nd E. Lancs. R., March, 1915; Capt., late E. Lancs. Regt.; twice severely wounded; Despatches; M.C.

HENDERSON, F. H. (D.S.O. L.G. 3.6.18), Vice-Admiral, R.N.; C.M.G. He died 26.6.18.

HENDERSON, G. D. (D.S.O. L.G. 27.10.17) (Details, L.G. 18.3.18): b. 13.3.96, at Bondi, Sydney, N.S. Wales; s. of Andrew Dunnett and Clari Kate Henderson; educ. Dulwich College (1908–14); enlisted 1st Battn. H.A.C., 8.8.14; B.E.F. Sept. 1914; Lt. 16.9.15; Capt. Queen's Own R.W. Kent R., 9.11.16; Adjt., Queen's Regt., Dec. 1917; served in France, Sept. 1914, to July, 1915; May, 1916, to March, 1917; served in Italy, Nov. 1917, to March, 1918; captured near Bapaume, 23.3.18; wounded in the head, 16.6.15, in Battle of Hooge (Ypres), and in arm 15.9.16, Flers (Somme); Despatches; M.C. awarded for gallantry on Oct. 7., 1916, at Eaucourt l'Abbaye, Somme. D.S.O. 20.9.17, Tower Hamlets, Passchendaele.

HENDERSON, G. S. (D.S.O. L.G. 31.5.16) (Bar, L.G. 25.8.17); b. 5.12.93; ent. Manch. R. 24.1.14; Lt. 9.11.14; Capt. 24.7.16; Bar for services in Mesopotamia; M.C.

HENDERSON, H. D. (D.S.O. L.G. 1.1.18), Lt.-Col., A.S.C.

HENDERSON, H. E. (D.S.O. L.G. 1.1.17); b. 19.3.80; 2nd Lt., R.A., 22.11.99; Lt. 16.2.01; Capt. 23.5.06; Major, R.F.A., 30.10.14; served E. Africa, 1904 (Despatches, L.G. 2.9.04; Medal, 2 clasps); Europ. War; Despatches.

HENDERSON, J. A. (D.S.O. L.G. 3.6.18), Hon. Major in Army, R. of O., Hussars; served S. African War, 1899–1902 (Despatches, L.G. 15.11.01; Queen's Medal, 4 clasps; King's Medal, 2 clasps); Europ. War; Despatches.

HENDERSON, K. (D.S.O. L.G. 3.6.16); b. 4.4.75; ent. Army 14.8.95; 2nd Lt., Unatt.; 2nd Lt., Ind. S.C., 26.10.96; Lt. 14.11.97; Capt. 14.8.04; Major, 39th Garwhal Rifles, 14.8.13; Lt.-Col. 1.7.20; employed with K.A. Rifles, 1900–1; served in Uganda, 1900 (Despatches, L.G. 10.9.01; Medal with 2 clasps); S. African War, 1900–2 (Queen's Medal, 4 clasps); Brig.-Major, 6th Inf. Brig., New Armies, B.E.F., 2.5.16 to 24.9.16; G.S.O., Br. Armies in France, 2.5.16.

HENDERSON, MALCOLM (R. Scots) (D.S.O. L.G. 1.1.17); s. of J. Henderson; educ. Stubbington; Repton; R.M.C., Sandhurst; first commission, 1903; 2nd Lt. 18.11.03; Lt. 25.9.07; Adjt., 2nd R. Scots, 1911–14; Capt. 9.8.14; Bt. Major 3.6.16; Bt. Lt.-Col. 3.6.19; Lt.-Col. The Royal Scots: served in France with 2nd Battn. The Royal Scots 14.8.14; took part in Battles of Mons, Le Cateau, Marne and Aisne (wounded 15.9.14); took part in operation north of Béthune, Oct. 1914 (wounded 15.10.14); took part in Battle of Ypres, May, 1915; Loos 25.9.15; Vimy, May, 1916; Somme, July–Aug. 1916; Arras, April, May and June, 1917 (wounded 7.4.17); served in Italy, Nov. 1917, till March, 1918; engaged in operations, April, 1918; commanded 2nd Bn. The Royal Scots during final offensive from 21 Aug. up to the Armistice; Despatches seven times; Legion of Honour, Croix Chevalier; St. Maurice and St. Lazare, Chevalier.

HENDERSON, MALCOLM (R.A.F.) (D.S.O. L.G. 30.3.16); s. of late L. Henderson; g.s. of late G. Malcolm, of Dundee; m. Elizabeth, d. of F. Craig; one s.; served with 1st Battn. London Scottish in France, Sept. 1914, to Jan. 1915; commissioned Seaforth Highrs., 1915; transferred R.F.C., May. 1915; Capt. 1916; Major, 1918 (R.A.F.); served with R.F.C. in France, Oct. 1915–Feb. 1916; Despatches; French Croix de Guerre; severely wounded while on photographic reconnaissance, south-east of La Bassée, 1916, losing left leg by anti-aircraft gun-fire at height of 8,000 feet.

HENDERSON, N. G. B. (D.S.O. L.G. 1.1.19); b. 2.8.83; 2nd Lt., R. Highrs., 8.1.02; Lt. 1.5.06; Capt. 16.5.14; Major, R. Highrs.; Despatches.

HENDERSON, O. (D.S.O. L.G. 23.7.18); b. 7.10.91; s. of late Sir J. Henderson, D.L., and Lady Henderson, of Oakley House, Belfast; m. Alicia Mary, d. of R. B. Henry, of Belfast; educ. Bradfield College, Berks.; R.N. Colleges, Osborne and Dartmouth; Midshipman, 1909; Lt., 1915; served in Exmouth, Flagship of Mediterranean, 1911; Minotaur, Flagship of China, 1913; Europ. War; China, 1914–Jan. 1915; Gallipoli, 1915–16; Despatches twice; Grand Fleet, 1916–18; Zeebrugge; Despatches; Croix de Guerre; in command of destroyer in Grand Fleet till July, 1919.

HENDERSON, P. H., M.B., Ch.B., D.P.H. (D.S.O. L.G. 3.6.16); b. 17.2.76 s. of late W. Henderson, of Lawton, Perthshire, and Margaret Campbell Henderson; m. Alice Ethel, d. of late Gen. Charles Thompson, of Longparish, Hants, and g.d. of late Admiral J. Thompson; educ. Dollar; Edinburgh University; and in passing out of Netley into R.A.M.C. in 1900, took first place, and after the Senior Officers' Course at the R.A.M. College in 1907, he received six months' accelerated promotion; Lt., R.A.M.C., 21.6.00; Capt. 21.6.03; Major 21.12.11; Bt. Lt.-Col. 3.6.17; From 5.8.14 to 11.12.14 he assisted Surg.-Gen. Donovan, C.B., in the medical arrangements at Southampton for the embarkation of the Expeditionary Force, and the disembarkation and distribution of the casualties from overseas. In Dec. 1914, he proceeded to France as O.C. No. 9., C.C.S. On 4.1.15 he was appointed D.A.D. of Medical Supplies, 7th Division, and served in that capacity till 21.10.15, taking part in the actions at Neuve Chapelle, Rouge Banc, Festubert, Givenchy and Loos. On 21.10.15 he proceeded to Egypt with 28th Div. as D.A.D. of Medical Services of that division. He left Egypt in this capacity in Nov., and arrived at Salonika on 30.11.15, taking part in the various actions in the Struma Valley, 1916–18. He proceeded with this division to S. Russia in Dec. 1918; Despatches four times; Bt. Lt.-Colonel.

P. H. Henderson.

HENDERSON, R. O. (D.S.O. L.G. 18.1.18) (Details, L.G. 25.4.18), Lt.-Col., Aust. Infy.

HENDERSON, R. W. (D.S.O. L.G. 3.6.18), Major, Ind. Cav.

HENDERSON, W. A. (D.S.O. L.G. 1.1.18), Lt.-Col., Aust. Pioneer Battn.

HENDERSON-ROE, C. G. (D.S.O. L.G. 26.9.17) (Details, L.G. 9.1.18), Capt., R.W. Kent R., S.R. D.S.O. awarded for gallantry on 17.7.17, near Monchy-le-Preux.

HENDRIE, W. I. S. (D.S.O. L.G. 10.6.20); Major 18th By. Can. F.A.

HENDRY, W. B. (D.S.O. L.G. 4.6.17), Lt.-Col., Can. A.M.C.

HENEAGE, A. P. (D.S.O. L.G. 4.6.17); b. 11.7.81; s. of late Capt. F. W. Heneage, R.E. (s. of late G. Heneage, M.P. for Lincoln and Grimsby), and Ann, d. of late Major-Gen. E. C. A. Gordon, R.E.; m. Anne, d. of late Brig.-Gen. N. D. Findlay, C.B., R.A.; one s.; two d.; educ. Eton; R.M.A., Woolwich; 2nd Lt., R.A., 18.8.00; Lt. 18.8.03; Capt. 22.1.12; Major, R.F.A., 23.1.15; served Europ. War, 1914–18; on the French and Balkan fronts as Staff Capt., D.A.A.G., R.A., and commanding a Field Artillery Brigade; Despatches thrice; a member of the Military International Commission of Control in Berlin; played polo, 1907, for the regiment in the Inter-Regimental; Master of the R.A. Harriers, 1912–13.

HENEAGE, G. C. W. (D.S.O. L.G. 1.1.17); b. 17.5.68; s. of late Major Heneage, V.C., and Henrietta Letitia Victoria, d. of late J. H. Vivian; m. Dorothy Margaret, d. of late H. A. Helyar and Lady Savile; one s.; educ Eton; ent. Army 29.12.88; Capt. 1898; Major 14.4.04; late G. Gds.; served

S. Africa, 1899–1900, including Belmont, Modder River, Magersfontein (Queen's Medal, 2 clasps); Europ. War, 1914–17; Despatches five times; M.V.O.

HENLEY, HON. A. M. (D.S.O. L.G. 3.6.16); b. 4.8.73; s. of 3rd Baron Henley; m. Sylvia Laura, d. of 4th Baron Sheffield and Mary Katherine, C.B.E., d. of Sir Lowthian Bell, 1st Bart; three d.; educ. Eton; Balliol College, Oxford; Director of Arthur Capel and Co., Shipowners and Coal Exporters; called to Bar, 1897; enlisted I.Y., 1899; served with Scots Greys 23.5.00 to 1907; Capt. 16.11.07; with 5th Lancers, 1907–14; served S. Africa, 1899–1902 (Queen's Medal and 3 clasps; King's Medal and 2 clasps); G.S., 1914–17, commanding 127th Inf. Brig., 1917–19; Despatches; C.M.G.; Bt. Major 3.6.15; Bt. Lt.-Col. 3.6.17; Bt. Col. 1.1.19.

HENLEY, F. LE L. (D.S.O. L.G. 1.1.17), Major, Aust. A.S.C.

HENNESSY, P. (D.S.O. L.G. 1.1.19), Major, Can. A.S.C.; M.C.

HENNESSY, R. G. (D.S.O. L.G. 2.4.19) (Details, L.G. 10.12.19); b. 14.11.97; 2nd Lt., Bord. R., 17.3.15; Lt. 15.8.15; Lt. (A/Capt.), 2nd Battn. Border R. (Italy); Capt. 14.2.21; served Europ. War; Despatches; M.C.

HENNIKER-GOTLEY, G. R. (D.S.O. L.G. 3.6.18); s. of the Vicar of West Ashby; Major, M.G.C. When he was awarded the D.S.O. he had served three years on the Western and Italian Fronts, and had been three times mentioned in Despatches.

HENNING, P. W. B. (D.S.O. L.G. 1.1.17); b. 3.12.70; s. of late Lt.-Gen. S. Henning; m. Henrietta Rose, d. of Col. W. W. Marriott Smith, R.F.A.; two d.; educ. Burney's; Woolwich; 2nd Lt., R.A., 25.7.90; Lt. 25.7.93; Capt. 13.2.00; Major 1.4.08; retired, 1920; Lt.-Col., late R.F.A.; served S. African War, 1899–1900 (Queen's Medal and 3 clasps); went out with Exp. Force to France, Aug. 1914; severely wounded at Le Cateau; commanded 11th Battery, R.F.A.; returned to France, Aug. 1915; Despatches twice; severely wounded at Ypres 1.5.17.

HENRI, P. R. (D.S.O. L.G. 3.6.19), Lt. (A/Major), 3rd, attd. 1st, Battn. London R.; M.C.

HENRY, J. D. (D.S.O. L.G. 1.1.18), Major, Aust. Engrs.

HENRY, M. (D.S.O. L.G. 1.1.18), Major, Aust. A.V.C.

HENSHALL, L. S. (D.S.O. L.G. 18.2.18) (Details, L.G. 18.7.18), S. Lan. R., attd. Tank Corps.

HENSMAN, M. (D.S.O. L.G. 21.6.19), Lt.-Cdr., R.N.

HENVEY, R. (D.S.O. L.G. 4.6.17); b. 3.1.76; 2nd Lt., R.A., 21.3.96; Lt. 21.3.99; Capt. 15.2.02; Bt. Major 6.11.03; Adjt. 27.8.07 to 21.1.10; Major 5.10.12; Bt. Lt.-Col. 1.1.16; Lt.-Col. 3.1.17; Colonel, R.A., 1.1.20; served S. African War, 1899–1900; Despatches; Queen's Medal and 5 clasps; N. Nigeria, 1901–3; Despatches twice; 2 Medals and 2 clasps; Bt. Major; Europ. War, 1914–17; Despatches; C.M.G.

HEPENSTAL, M. E. DOPPING- (see Dopping-Hepenstal, M. E.).

HEPPER, L. L. (D.S.O. L.G. 1.1.18); b. 4.4.71; 2nd Lt. 27.7.89; Lt. 27.7.92; Capt. 20.9.99; Major 20.9.10; Lt.-Col., R.G.A.

HERBERT, A. H. (D.S.O. L.G. 4.6.17), Lt.-Col., A.O.D., now R.A.O.D.

HERBERT, G. (D.S.O. L.G. 13.9.15) (Bar, L.G. 31.7.19), Cdr., R.N. (see "The Distinguished Service Order," from its institution to 31.12.15, by same publishers).

HERBERT, G. M. (D.S.O. L.G. 15.3.16); b. 20.3.77; 2nd Lt., Dorsets. R., 1.12.97; Lt. 20.1.00; Capt. 1.4.05; Adjt., Dorsets. R., 8.6.07 to 7.6.10; Major 1.9.15; T/Lt.-Col., Dorsets. R., 23.11.15 to 31.12.16 served S. African War, 1899–1902; slightly wounded; Queen's Medal with 6 clasps; King's Medal with 2 clasps; Europ. War; Despatches; Bt. Lt.-Col. 1.1.17. D.S.O. awarded for gallantry on 22.11.15 at Ctesiphon.

HERBERT, L. W. (D.S.O. L.G. 3.6.16); b. 9.3.73; ent. Army 7.12.95; Capt. 26.4.02; Major, S. Lancs. Rgt., S.R.; op. in Sierra Leone; Medal with clasp; S. African War of 1899–1902; Queen's Medal with 3 clasps; King's Medal with 2 clasps; Europ. War; Despatches.

HERBERT, P. T. C. (D.S.O. L.G. 22.12.16); b. 15.8.68; 1st com. 17.2.88; Capt. 2.7.98; retired R.A. 25.2.03; Major, R. of O., R.F.A.; operations on N.W.F. of India, 1897–8, with Tirah Exp. Force, as Trans. Officer; Despatches; Medal with clasp; S. African War, 1899–1902; Adjt., Brig., R.F.A.; Despatches; Queen's Medal with 3 clasps; King's Medal with 2 clasps.

HERBERT, W. N. (D.S.O. L.G. 1.1.17) (Bar, L.G. 11.1.19); b. 26.8.80; 2nd Lt., North'd Fus., 11.8.00; Lt. 11.12.01; Capt. 4.1.11; Adjt., North'd Fus., 1.10.12 to 16.6.15; Major 1.9.15; served S. African War, 1901–2; Queen's Medal with 5 clasps; W. Africa (N. Nigeria), 1906; Medal with clasp; Europ. War; Despatches; Bt. Lt.-Col. 1.1.18; T/Brig.-Gen. 27.9.18 to 31.3.19; C.M.G.

HERBERT-STEPNEY, C. C. (D.S.O. L.G. 1.1.17) (Bar, L.G. 1.1.18); b. 3.6.71; s. of Capt. H. Herbert-Stepney; m. Evelyn, d. of the late H. Bowden, D.L., late 78th Highrs.; educ. Rugby School; R.M.C., Sandhurst; ent. Army 25.6.91; Major 1.9.15; Lieut.-Col. R. of O., K.R.R.C.; retired K.R.R.C. 25.7.06; served in Isazai Exp., 1892; in Chitral, 1895; Medal with clasp; served Europ. War; Despatches four times. D.S.O. awarded for capture of St. Pierre Divion by 16th Sherwood Foresters 13.11.16. The German Battalion Commander, 13 officers and 729 other ranks were captured by the Battalion on this occasion. The men fought with the utmost gallantry, and captured the entire position, including the German Battalion H.Q. and the famous tunnel dug-outs. Bar awarded for capture of St. Julien 31.7.17. He was wounded at Hollebeke and left arm amputated as a result.

HERCUS, C. E. (D.S.O. L.G. 3.6.18), Major, N.Z. Medical Corps.

HERD, H. J. (D.S.O. L.G. 24.6.16) (Details, L.G. 27.7.16), 2nd Lt. (T/Lt.), 1/7th Batt. R. Highrs., T.F. D.S.O. awarded for gallantry at Neuville St. Vaast on 3.6.16.

HEREFORD, F. R. (D.S.O. L.G. 20.7.17), A/Lt., R.N.R.; D.S.C. Bar to D.S.C. 2.11.17.

HERKLOTS, A. (D.S.O. L.G. 1.1.17); b. 18.10.79; 2nd Lt., A.S.C., from Imp. Yeo. and Militia, 16.8.02; Lt. 18.2.04; Capt. 10.12.10; Major 30.10.14; served S. African War, 1901–2; Queen's Medal with 5 clasps; Europ. War; Despatches.

HERMON, EDWARD WILLIAM (Christian names gazetted as "Ernest William") (D.S.O. L.G. 4.6.17); b. 10.6.78; 1st com. 9.5.00; Capt. 12.2.10; retired 7th Hussars 22.2.11; Major, retired pay, late Hussars; served S. African War; Capt., retired pay; Major, King Edward's Horse, 1901–2; Queen's Medal with 5 clasps; served Europ. War, as T/Lt.-Col., King Edward's Horse, commanding 24th Northants Fusiliers. He was killed in action 9.4.17.

HERMON, J. V. (D.S.O. L.G. 1.1.19), Capt., Cheshire Yeom., att. 6th Dn. Gds.

HERMON-HODGE, R. E. U. (D.S.O. L.G. 3.6.19), Major, Oxfords. Yeom.

HERMON-HODGE, HON. R. H. (D.S.O. L.G. 4.6.17); b. 10.7.80; e. s. of 1st Baron Wyfold and Frances Caroline, d. of E. Hermon, formerly M.P. for Preston; m. Dorothy, d. of R. Fleming; one s.; four d.; Lt.-Col., G. Gds.; M.V.O.; served S. Africa, 1900–2; Queen's Medal with 5 clasps; King's Meda with 2 clasps; Europ. War from 1914; J.P., Oxfordshire.

HERON, A. R. (D.S.O. L.G. 25.8.17), Major, Aust. Inf.

HERON, G. W., M.R.C.S., L.R.C.P. (D.S.O. L.G. 3.6.16); b. 16.10.80; m. Elsa Burch; one s.; one d.; educ. Rugby; Westminster Hospital; Director of Health, Government of Palestine; ent. R.A.M.C. 31.1.05; Capt. 31.7.08; Major 15.10.15; A/Lt.-Col. 11.6.17; T/Colonel, 1918; seconded for service with Egyptian Government, 1908; lent to E.E.F., 1914; A.D.M.S., G.H.Q., Egyptian Exp. Force, 1916–18; A.D.M.S.; Occupied Enemy Territory Area 22.11.18; O.B.E.; Order of the Nile.

HERON, L. D. (D.S.O. L.G. 14.11.16), Capt., 20th Batt. Can. Inf.; M.C.

HERRICK, H. (D.S.O. L.G. 4.6.17); b. 12.1.72; Lt., R.A.M.C., 27.7.98; Capt. 27.7.01; Major 27.4.10; Lt.-Col. 1.3.15; Colonel; served S. African War, 1902 (Queen's Medal); Europ. War, 1914–17; Despatches; C.M.G.

HERRICK, R. DE S. B. (D.S.O. L.G. 22.12.16); b. 23.12.84; Lt., I.M.S., 30.7.10; Capt., I.M.S., 30.7.13; Despatches.

HERRICK, R. L. W. (D.S.O. L.G. 1.2.19); b. 26.5.95; I.A., R. of O., attd. 29th Lrs., I.A.; Capt., I.A. (from I.A. Res. of Off.), 20.8.19.

HERRIDGE, W. D. (D.S.O. L.G. 8.3.19) (Details, L.G. 4.10.19), Capt., Can. Cyclist Corps (Brigade Major, 2nd Can. Inf. Brig., H.Q.); M.C. and Bar.

HERRING, E. F. (D.S.O. L.G. 3.6.19), T/Lt. (A/Major), R.F.A.; M.C.

HERRING, J. H. (D.S.O. L.G. 3.3.17); b. 1889; s. of H. H. Herring, J.P., Berks; m. Honor Harratt, d. of late Mr. de Saint; educ. Clifton College; Christ's College, Cambridge; served in Europ. War, first in Volunteers and then in R.F.C. and R.A.F.; Major, R.A.F., in France, 1915; Mesopotamia, 1916; Salonika, 1917–18; Despatches several times; M.C.; French Croix de Guerre.

HERRING, S. C. E. (D.S.O. L.G. 1.1.17); b. 8.10.82; s. of late G. E. Herring, of Bracondale, Gladesville, N.S.W.; m. Florence Elizabeth, d. of late T. de M. Murray-Prior, of Marroon, Queensland; one d.; left Australia, Dec. 1914, as Captain in 13th Batt. A.I.F.; Major in Egypt, Jan. 1915; took part in the landing at Gallipoli, April, 1915, and served there continuously until the evacuation, Dec. 1915; Legion of Honour; served in Egypt, Jan.–May, 1916; transferred to 45th Batt., and promoted Lt.-Colonel, March, 1916; landed in France, June, 1916, and served there continuously; Colonel, June, 1918; Brig.-Gen. 30.6.19; commanding 13th Australian Infantry; C.M.G.; Croix de Guerre.

HERROD, E. E. (D.S.O. L.G. 1.1.18); m. Kathleen Elizabeth Ireson, d. of J. K. Rogan, of Parramatta, N.S.W.; Lt.-Col., Australian Infantry; served Europ. War, 1915–18; Despatches; C.M.G.; Serbian Order of White Eagle.

HERROLD, J. H. (D.S.O. L.G. 8.3.19) (Details, L.G. 4.10.19), Major, Auckland Mtd. Rifle R., N.Z. Force (Egypt).

HERTZBERG, H. F. H. (D.S.O. L.G. 1.1.18); b. 3.9.84; s. of late A. L. Hertzberg, Civil Engineer, of Toronto, s. of late Col. P. H. Hertzberg, Norwegian Army, and of d. of late Capt. W. F. McMaster, Toronto Naval Brigade; m. Dorothy Hope, d. of late Ernest Judah, of Montreal; one s.; educ. Upper Canada College; St. Andrew's College; University of Toronto; Lt., 2nd Field Company, Canadian Engineers, 1905; Lt., R. Can. Engrs., 1915; Capt. 1917; Major and Bt. Colonel, 1920; Colonel, commanding R. Canadian Engineers, Military District No. 6, Halifax, Nova Scotia; served in Belgium and France, Feb. 1915, to end of war, with Canadian Engineers in 1st Canadian Division, B.E.F.; Despatches four times; C.M.G.; M.C.

HERVEY, C. L. (D.S.O. L.G. 1.1.18), Lt.-Col., Can. Rly. Troops.

HERVEY-BATHURST, SIR F. E. W. (D.S.O. L.G. 4.6.17); b. 11.2.70; s. of 4th Bart. and Ada, d. of Sir J. Ribton, 4th Bart.; m. 1st, Hon. Moira O'Brien (whom he divorced), 2nd d. of 14th Baron Inchiquin; heir, son, Frederick Peter Methuen; m. 2ndly, 1919, Katherine, d. of late Alex. Dick-Cunyngham, and widow of J. H. Nevill, G. Gds.; educ. Eton; 1st commission 25.7.91; Capt. 12.7.99; retired G. Gds. 29.8.06; served in Egyptian Campaign, 1898; Battle of Khartum; Egyptian Medal with clasp; Medal; also S. African War, 1899–1900; Despatches twice; Queen's Medal with 2 clasps; Europ. War; Despatches three times; Chevalier, Crown of Italy.

HESELTINE, J. E. N. (D.S.O. L.G. 1.1.17); b. 16.12.80; m. Mrs. Noel Edwards; 2nd Lt., K.R.R.C., 17.1.00; Lt. 10.3.01; Capt. 22.1.08; Lt.-Col., late K.R.R.C.; served S. African War, 1899–1900; Queen's Medal with clasp; Europ. War, 1914–18; Despatches; Bt. Lt.-Col.; Legion of Honour; Order of the Crown of Belgium; Croix de Guerre.

HESELTON, J. L. (D.S.O. L.G. 26.11.17) (Details, L.G. 6.4.18); b. 12.4.90; Capt., Worc. R., 10.12.16; M.C.

HESKETH, G. (D.S.O. L.G. 14.1.16); b. 4.4.78; s. of Col. G. Hesketh, V.D., late 2nd V.B. Loyal N. Lancs. R.; m. Muriel, d. of T. B. Bentley; one s.; one d.; educ. All Saints, Banbury; Rossall; Cotton Spinner; joined 2nd V.B. Loyal N. Lancs. Rgt., 1896; Capt., 1900; Major, 1912; Lt.-Col., 1915; late commanding 1/5th L.N. Lancs. Rgt.; served S. Africa, 1900; Queen's Medal, 4 clasps; Despatches.; Europ. War; Despatches thrice; holds Territorial Decoration.

HESKETH, W. (D.S.O. L.G. 26.8.18); b. 1.11.72; 2nd Lt., Unatt., 28.11.94; 2nd Lt., I.S.C., 22.2.96; Lt., I.A., 5.4.97; Capt. 28.11.03; Major 28.11.12; Lt.-Col. 21.6.20; operations in Chitral, 1895; severely wounded; Medal with clasp; N.W. Frontier of India, 1897–8; Malakand; op. in the Mamund country; clasp; Europ. War; Despatches.

HESKETH-PRICHARD, H. V. (D.S.O. L.G. 8.3.18) T/Major, Gen. List; M.C.; b. Nov. 1876; s. of Lt. Hesketh B. Prichard and Kate, d. of Gen. Ryall; m. Lady Elizabeth Grimston, d. of 3rd Earl of Verulam; two s.; one d.; educ. Fettes; travelled and shot big game in Patagonia, Labrador, Canada, Sardinia, Spain, Mexico, Newfoundland, Haiti, etc.; played cricket for Hampshire, 1899–1913, and Gentlemen *v.* Players, 1903–4–5; Major; A.D.C. to Lord Lieutenant of Ireland, 1907; served Europ. War, 1914–18, as T/Major, Gen. List; Despatches twice; Commander of the Military Order of Avis. Major Hesketh-Prichard died on 14th June, 1922. He wrote many books, some of them in collaboration with his mother, the late Mrs. K. Hesketh Prichard. The last of his books published is "Sniping in France."

A. H. Heslop.

HESLOP, A. H., M.B., B.S. (D.S.O. L.G. 3.6.16); b. 3.3.80; s. of late Rev. R. C. Heslop, M.A.; educ. High School, Oxford; Durham University; Newcastle Royal Infirmary; ent. R.A.M.C. 30.7.06; Capt. 30.1.10; Major 30.7.18; served Europ. War, 1914–18; D.A.D.M.S. I. Corps, B.E.F., 1915–16; D.A.D.M.S., G.H.Q., British Armies, France, 1916–19; Despatches five times; O.B.E.

HESLOP, G. G. (D.S.O. L.G. 3.6.18), Major, Australian A.V.C.

HESLOP, T. B. (D.S.O. L.G. 16.9.18); b. 16.3.91; s. of Major J. W. B. Heslop, late Durham L.I.; m. Sybil C., d. of G. Liddell; one d.; educ. Richmond School, Yorks; admitted Solicitor, 1913; 3rd Class Honours, Final, 1913; 2nd Lt., Durham L.I., 1913; Major, late 6th Batt. Durham L.I.; served France, April, 1915, to June, 1918; Despatches twice; commanded 6th Batt. Durham L.I., 1918.

HESSEY, W. F. (D.S.O. L.G. 1.1.18) (Bar, L.G. 16.9.18); b. 31.12.68; 1st com. 29.3.90; Major 27.1.08; retired, R. Innis. Fus. 17.5.13; T/Lt.-Col., in command 11th Batt. R. Innis. Fus.; T/Brig.-Gen., S. African War, 1899–1902; Bt. of Major; Queen's Medal with 5 clasps; King's Medal with 2 clasps; Europ. War; Despatches; Bt. Lt.-Col., R. Innis. Fus., R. of O.

HETHERINGTON, C. G. (D.S.O. L.G. 3.6.18); b. 4.8.83; 2nd Lt., R.A., 21.12.01; Lt. 10.8.04; Adjt., R.A., 5.9.05 to 17.7.06; Capt. 30.10.14; Major, R.G.A., 1.5.17; Despatches.

HEWETSON, H., M.R.C.S., L.R.C.P.Lond., D.P.H. R.C.P.S.Eng. (D.S.O. L.G. 1.1.17); b. 21.7.69; s. of late Rev. J. Hewetson, of Measham; m. Margaret Elizabeth, d. of late H. Buse; educ. Repton; Guy's Hospital; ent. Army 29.7.96; Capt. 29.7.99; Major 29.7.08; Lt.-Col. 1.3.15; was Sanitary Officer, Straits Settlements; served Europ. War, B.E.F., 1914–19; I.E.F., 1918; Despatches thrice; Order of St. Anne, Russia, 2nd Class with Swords; Officer, Crown of Italy.

HEWETT, E. V. O. (D.S.O. L.G. 20.10.16); b. 14.3.67; s. of Lt.-Gen. E. O. Hewett, C.M.G., R.E., and Catherine Frances Hewett, d. of Col. Briscoe, R.E.; m. Brenda, d. of F. P. Higgins, J.P., M.P. N. Salford; one d.; educ. Trinity College School and at the R.M. College, Canada; ent. Queen's Own (R.W. Kent) Rgt. 2.9.85; Capt., March, 1894; Major 27.5.03; retired Jan. 1909, R. of O.; served Sudan, 1885–6 (action of Ginnis); Medal; Bronze Star; N.W. Frontier of India, 1897–8; Despatches; Medal with clasp; Professor of Strategy, Tactics, Military History, Reconnaissance, R.M. College, Canada, 1900–6; Acting Commandant for the last six months; commanded 6th Batt. S.W.B.; Europ. War, 1914–17; Despatches thrice; C.M.G.; O.B.E.; Commanding 3rd S.R. Batt. The Queen's Own (R.W. Kent R.); R. of O.

HEWETT, G. (D.S.O. L.G. 17.4.16); b. 18.3.81; 2nd Lt., Unatt., 20.1.00; 2nd Lt., I.S.C., 30.4.01; Lt., I.A., 20.4.02; Capt., 48th Pioneers, I.A., 20.1.09; Major 1.9.15; served N.W.F. of India, Waziristan, 1901–2; Medal with clasp; Europ. War; Despatches.

HEWETT, G. O. (D.S.O. L.G. 22.4.19), Cdr., R.N., 31.12.18.

HEWETT, M. S. (D.S.O. L.G. 7.2.18); b. 22.11.81; s. of late Gen. W. S. Hewett; m. Grace Enid, d. of E. Mount; 2nd Lt., Unatt., 28.7.00; I.A. 11.10.01; Lt. 13.7.03; Capt. 28.7.09; Major 1.9.15; Colonel, I.A.; served Europ. War, 1914–18; Despatches.

HEWITT, A. S. (D.S.O. L.G. 1.1.17); b. Mackay, Queensland, 5.9.76; s. of late A. Hewitt, J.P., of Lisle Court, Wootton, Isle of Wight; m. Nora, d. of late G. Maclean, and g.d. of Gen. Sir G. Maclean, K.C.B.; educ. Warwick; Christ Church, Oxford (Scholar); played Rugby football for the Harlequins, Hampshire, and Kent, and on occasions for the 'Varsity; Capt. of College Teams for cricket, Rugby football and athletics. On outbreak of S. African War joined R.E. Kent Mounted Rifles, and served with them for fourteen months in S. Africa; Queen's Medal with 5 clasps; commissioned in R.W. Kent R. 14.9.01; Lt. 21.1.04; Capt. 1.9.11; Adjt., 4th R.W. Kent R., 1911–14; Major 14.9.16; T/Lt.-Col. R.W. Kent R.; served with 2nd Queen's, Oct. 1914–March, 1915; Despatches; O.B.E.

HEWITT, C. C. (D.S.O. L.G. 1.1.18); b. 20.3.83; 2nd Lt. R. Innis. Fus. 22.10.02; Lt. 4.11.05; Capt. 19.2.14; Major 22.10.17; served with M.G.C. 1915–21; Despatches; M.C.

C. C. Hewitt.

HEWITT, HON. E. J. (D.S.O. L.G. 3.6.16) Bar L.G. 3.6.18); b. 18.12.80; e. s. of 6th Viscount Lifford and Helen Blanche d. of late C. S. Geach; m. Charlotte Rankine d. of Sir R. Maule and of the late Lady Maule (*née* Janet M'Intosh, who died in 1914), and widow of Capt. E. W. Walker, E. Yorks. R.; educ. Haileybury; Dresden; Geneva; studied with a view to the Diplomatic Service, but obtained commission in Worcestershire Militia, 1900; 2nd Lieut., 1st Dorsets., 26.8.03; Lt. 9.4.05; Capt. 26.5.10; transferred to 5th Dorsets., 1915; Major 22.10.17; Capt., 1910; Major; T/Lt.-Col., Dorset R.; Officer commanding Depot, Dorset R.; served S. Africa, 1902; Queen's Medal, 2 clasps; European War, 1914–16, including Dardanelles (till evacuation), Egypt and France; Despatches.

HEWITT, R. P. (D.S.O. L.G. 4.6.17), T/Major, A.S.C.

HEWITT, R. W. (D.S.O. L.G. 25.8.17); b. March, 1880; only son of Mrs. R. H. Hewitt, of Daneholme, Daventry, and of the late R. H. Hewitt; educ. Charterhouse; commissioned Norfolk R., April, 18.4.00; Lt., Norfolk R., 14.12.01; 14th Hrs. 9.12.03; Capt. 30.4.06; Major, May, 1915; T/Lt.-Col., May, 1916; served S. African War; Queen's and King's Medals and 5 clasps. In Nov. 1915, he accompanied his regiment to the front as its commanding officer, remaining with it until his death, taking part in important and successful operations. He died on 30.9.17 of wounds received in action the previous day.

HEWLETT, E. (D.S.O. L.G. 14.1.16); b. 4.6.79; 2nd Lt., Lan. Fus., 11.2.99; Lt. 2.1.00; Adjt., Lan. Fus., 4.5.02 to 3.5.05; Capt., Lan. Fus., 13.12.02; Major, Devon. R., 20.5.08; Lt.-Col. 1.9.15; T/Brig.-Gen. 10.12.18 to 31.1.20; served Europ. War, 1914–17; Despatches; Bt. Lt.-Col. 1.1.18; C.M.G.

HEWLETT, F. E. T. (D.S.O. L.G. 1.1.19), Lt.-Col., R.A.F.; O.B.E.

HEWSON, F. B. (D.S.O. L.G. 3.6.18), Capt., York. and Lanc. R.; M.C.

HEXT, F. J. (D.S.O. L.G. 3.6.18), Capt. (A/Major), R.F.A.; Croix de Guerre; M.C. and Bar; 1914 Star. Major Hext died 9.5.18, aged 22, of wounds received 12th April, at Locan, near Béthune; M.C.

HEXT, G. T. B. (D.S.O. L.G. 1.2.17); b. 23.4.81; s. of G. H. Hext and Claire, d. of E. M. Perkins; m. Blanche Ellen, d. of late Capt. Stratford; joined R.F.A. 2.5.00; Lt. 3.4.01; Lt., I.A., 1.12.03; Capt., S. and T. Corps, I.A., 2.5.09; Major 1.9.15; served Europ. War, E. African Exp. Force, 1915–17; Despatches.

HEYGATE, G. (D.S.O. L.G. 1.1.18); b. 1.8.82; 2nd Lt., R.A., 23.7.01; Lt. 23.7.04; Capt. 23.7.14; Major, R.F.A., 15.10.15; Despatches.

HEYLAND, H. M. (D.S.O. L.G. 4.6.17); b. 23.1.91; mobilized Spec. Res. to 14.6.21, 6 years, 304 days; Capt. (from Spec. Res.), K.R.R.C., 1.1.21; T/Major, M.G.C., 15.6.21; Capt. (T/Major), K.R.R.C., S.R.

HEYMAN, A. A. I. (D.S.O. L.G. 1.1.17); b. 19.9.64; s. of Major-General H. Heyman, R.A.; educ. Oxford Military College; R.M.C., Sandhurst; joined Sherwood Foresters, 1884; Lt.-Colonel; served Sikkim Exp., 1888; Medal with clasp; Matabele Rebellion, 1896; Medal; S. African War; Medal with clasp. At the outbreak of Europ. War joined Canadian Forces, and came over with the 2nd Canadian Division; served with them in Flanders; Despatches; commanded battalion, H.L.I., 1916.

HEYWOOD, C. P. (D.S.O. L.G. 3.6.16); b. 17.5.80; s. of Sir A. P. Heywood, 3rd Bart. and brother of Sir G. P. Heywood, 4th Bart.; m. Margaret Vere, d. of A. H. Kerr; one s.; one d.; 2nd Lt., C. Gds., 12.8.99; Lt. 9.3.01; Adjt. 6.6.04 to 5.6.07; Capt. 27.3.06; Major 17.7.15; T/Brig.-Gen. 13.7.18 to 5.2.19; Lt.-Colonel, C. Guards; G.S.O.1, 1916–19; served S. African War, 1900–2; wounded; Queen's Medal, 5 clasps; King's Medal, 2 clasps; Sudan, 1908; Egyptian Medal and clasp; Europ. War, 1914–18, in France and Russia; commanded 3rd Guards Brig., 1918; wounded; Despatches seven times; Bt. Major 18.2.15; Bt. Lt.-Col. 1.1.17; C.M.G.

HEYWOOD, SIR G. P., 4th Bart. (D.S.O. L.G. 1.1.18); b. 14.7.78; s. of 3rd Bart. and Margaret Effie, d. of Rt. Rev. G. H. Sumner, Bishop of Guildford; Lt.-Colonel, commanding 1/1st Staffs. Yeom., 1916–18 and 1920; served Europ. War; holds Territorial Decoration; J.P.; D.L.

HEYWOOD, M. B. (D.S.O. L.G. 4.6.17); b. 26.11.86; s. of Lt. de la P. Beresford and Florence Newton Heywood; m. Margaret Constance Curtis-Hayward; one s.; two d.; educ. Eton College; Electric Mining Engineer for five years; Apprentice in Electrical Works in Germany; Stockbroker; volunteered 1914; 2nd Lt. in Northumberland Hussars Yeomanry; T/Captain, France, 1915–17; Italy, 1917–18; Germany, 1918–19; Despatches; M.V.O.; Chevalier, Legion of Honour; Crown of Belgium; Crown of Italy; Croix de Guerre Belge.

HEYWOOD-LONSDALE, H. H. (D.S.O. L.G. 1.1.19); b. 4.1.64; e. s. of late A. P. Heywood-Lonsdale and Frances Elizabeth, d. of D. Neilson; m. Hon. Helena Mabel Hamilton, d. of 1st Baron Hamilton of Dalzell; three s.; educ. Eton; R.M.C., Sandhurst; late Capt., G. Guards; Major, R. of O.; Major, Shrops. Yeom.

HEYWOOD-LONSDALE, J. P. H., B.A. (D.S.O. L.G. 1.1.19); b. 1869; 2nd s. of late A. P. Heywood-Lonsdale; m. Hon. Helen Annesley, d. of 11th Viscount Valentia and Laura Sarah, d. of D. H. Webb, and widow of Sir A. W. Peyton, 4th Bart.; educ. Eton; New College, Oxford; Member of the University Eight, 1889–90–91–92; Master of the Bicester Foxhounds; Sheriff, co. Louth, 1902; Major, Shropshire Yeom.; served Europ. War; Despatches.

HEZLET, C. O. (D.S.O. L.G. 8.2.18) (Details, L.G. 18.7.18); b. 1891; s. of Lt.-Col. R. J. Hezlet, R.A.; m. Anni Maitland, d. of J. S. Somerset; was a pupil at Coleraine Academical Institution; Major, R.G.A., S.R.; served Europ. War, 1914–18; Despatches thrice; Captain, Royal Portrush Golf Club from June, 1915; was runner-up for the Amateur Golf Championship at Sandwich, May, 1914; won Irish Golf Championship, 1920.

HEZLET, R. K. (D.S.O. L.G. 22.12.16); b. at Dungannon, co. Tyrone, 21.12.79; s. of Lt.-Col. R. J. Hezlet, late R.A.; m. Josepha Dorothy Arter; one s.; two d.; educ. Clifton College; R.M. Academy, Woolwich; 2nd Lt., R.A., 23.12.98; Lt. 16.2.01; Capt. 5.12.06; Major 30.10.14; Lt.-Col., R.F.A., 1.1.21; served in France and Mesopotamia, 1915–16; Despatches twice; Bt. Lt.-Col. 1.1.18; C.B.E.; Member Ordnance Committee, 1916; Superintendent External Ballistics, Ordnance Committee, 1920; has published "Nomography," 1913.

HIBBERT, A. (D.S.O. L.G. 1.1.19), Major, 3rd Canadian Tunnelling Company, Canadian Engineers; M.C.

HIBBERT, C. B. (D.S.O. L.G. 3.3.17); b. 4.1.82; 5th s. of C. G. Hibbert, of The Anchorage, Keswick Road, Boscombe; m. 1911, Winifred, d. of Mr. and Mrs. Phillip; 3 d.; educ. Tonbridge School; 2nd Lt., 13th Middl'x, Queen's Westminster Vol. Rifles, 1902–4; 2nd Lt., 60th Rifles, K.R.R.C.; seconded Machine Gun Corps, Nov. 1916 to March, 1918; appointed Second-in-Command 18th Batt. M.G. Coy., March, 1918, to March, 1919; served S. African War, 1901–2; Europ. War; Despatches, 1917; M.C. (L.G. May, 1919).

HIBBERT, H. T. (D.S.O. L.G. 3.6.18); b. 5.8.63; s. of late Col. H. R. Hibbert, Roy. Fusiliers; D.L.; J.P.; m. 1892, Katharini Brownlow, d. of U. A. Butterfield, of Bermuda; one s.; educ. W. Hawtrey's, Slough; Dartmouth; as a Lieutenant, R.N., helped to capture two dhows, Pemba, Zanzibar, 1888; commanded Coastguard, South of Ireland, 1912; Rear-Admiral, R.N.; retired; served European War; C.B.E.

HIBBERT, O. Y. (D.S.O. L.G. 17.4.16); b. 26.1.82; 2nd Lt., R.W. Kent R., 18.1.02; Lt. 19.3.04; Capt. 26.3.13; Major 17.12.16; served S. African War, 1902 (Queen's Medal, 3 clasps); Europ. War; Despatches; M.C.

HICKEY, P. F. B. (D.S.O. L.G. 7.2.18), Lt. (Temp. Capt.), Indian Army, R. of Off.

HICKIE, H. W. (D.S.O. L.G. 29.11.19); b. 18.8.84; 2nd Lt., Unatt., 21.1.03; Ind. Army 7.4.04; Lieut. 21.4.05; Capt. 21.1.12; Major 21.1.18; served Europ. War; Despatches.

HICKLEY, C. M. (D.S.O. L.G. 3.6.18), T/Capt. (T Lt.-Col.), R.E.

HICKLING, C. L. (D.S.O. L.G. 3.6.16); b. 27.5.79; s. of Rev. E. L. Hickling, M.A.; educ. R.M.A., Woolwich; 2nd Lt., R.A., 14.9.98; Lt. 16.2.01; Capt. 22.7.05; Adjt. 13.11.06 to 2.11.09; Major 30.10.14; served S. African War, 1899–1902; Despatches (L.G. 10.9.01); Queen's Medal, 4 clasps; King's Medal, 2 clasps; was with R.A. in Gibraltar, Hong-Kong and Singapore; Europ. War, 1914–19; Despatches; Croix de Guerre.

HICKLING, H. C. B. (D.S.O. L.G. 4.6.17); e. s. of Horace Hickling, of Little Firs, Woking; m. 1917, Katharine, 3rd d. of Fred W. Portal; one d.; Major, R.E.; served Europ. War; M.C.

HICKMAN, C. S. (D.S.O. L.G. 17.4.16), Cdr., R.I.M.

HICKS, W. E. (D.S.O. L.G. 1.1.19), Lt. (A/Major), 152nd H. Battery, R.G.A.; served Europ. War; M.C.

HICKSON, L. H. (D.S.O. L.G. 1.1.19), Major (A/Lt.-Col.), R.W. Kent R.

HIGGINBOTTOM, T. A. (D.S.O. L.G. 4.6.17) (surname corrected from Higginsbotham, L.G. 8.7.17), Lt.-Col., R.F.A.

HIGGINS, C. G. (D.S.O. L.G. 14.1.16) (Bar, L.G. 1.1.18); b. 12.8.79; e. s. of late Capt. C. C. Higgins, 13th Hussars, of Boycott Manor, Buckingham; m. 1909, Algitha, d. of Capt. John Howard; one s.; one d.; educ. Charterhouse; 2nd Lt., Oxf. and Bucks. L. Inf. 21.4.00; Lt. 23.2.03; Capt. 13.2.09; Major 1.9.15; Bt. Lt.-Col. 1.1.17; Brig.-Gen. 21.4.17 to 15.4.19; served S. African War; Queen's Medal, 3 clasps; King's Medal, 2 clasps); Europ. War, 1914–18; wounded; Despatches four times; C.M.G., 1919.

HIGGINS, E. L. (D.S.O. L.G. 26.7.18); o. s. of S. E. Higgins, of Stonehill, E. Sheen; m. 1919, Emilie Beryl, y. d. of Edgar Fifoot; Capt., London Regt.; served Europ. War; M.C.

HIGGINS, H. G. (D.S.O. L.G. 30.11.17), y. s. of H. A. Higgins; m. 1919, Lilian Annie, y. d. of W. G. Leete, of The Chalet, Oxton, Cheshire; Lt.-Cdr., R.N.; served Europ. War, 1914–17; Despatches.

HIGGINSON, A. B. W. (D.S.O. L.G. 27.6.17), Cdr., R.N.

HIGGINSON, H. W. (D.S.O. L.G. 14.1.16) (Bar, 16.9.18); b. 10.11.73; s. of Colonel T. Higginson, C.B., Ind. Army, and of Ada Whitla, of Lisburn, co.

Antrim; m. 1903, Ivy Letitia, 4th d. of the late James Brown, J.P.; one s.; one d.; educ. St. Lawrence College, Ramsgate; R.M.C., Sandhurst; 2nd Lt., R. Dub. Fus., 10.10.94; Lt. 23.10.96; Capt. 16.12.99; Adjt., R. Dub. Fus., 26.5.11 to 24.1.13; Major 25.1.13; Bt. Lt.-Col. 3.6.16; Bt. Col. 1.1.18; Temp. Major-Gen. 26.4.18 to 17.3.19; Temp. Brig.-Gen. 18.3.19 to 31.12.20; Colonel 2.6.19; served W. Africa, 1897–98 (Medal, 2 clasps); S. Africa, 1899–1902 (Queen's Medal, 4 clasps; King's Medal, 2 clasps; Despatches); Aden, operations in the interior, 1903; Blue Nile, 1908 (Khedive's Medal); Europ. War, 1914–18; Despatches; C.B., 1919; Commander, Star of Rumania; Officier, de la Légion d'Honneur.

V. C. Hilditch.

HILDITCH, V. C. (D.S.O. L.G. 26.7.18), T/Capt. (A/Major), London R.; M.C. He died of wounds 11.2.19.

HILDRETH, H. C., F.R.C.S. (D.S.O. L.G. 4.6.17); b. 25.10.76; Lt., R.A.M.C., 31.8.03; Capt. 28.2.07; Major 28.2.15 (Temp. Lt.-Col. 2.6.16 to 1.11.17); served Europ. War; Despatches.

HILDYARD, H. C. T. (D.S.O. L.G. 14.1.16); b. 16.7.72; s. of late Gen. Sir H. Hildyard, G.C.B., and Annette, his wife, d. of the late Admiral J. C. Prevost; m. Selina Constance, d. of late Rev. S. l'Estrange; one s.; one d.; 1st commission 24.11.91; Major 5.6.09; retired, R.A., 4.6.13; Lt.-Col., R. of Off., R.A., 29.2.16; Hon. Brig.-Gen. 27.3.19; served S. African War, 1899–1902 (Despatches; Queen's Medal, 4 clasps; King's Medal, 2 clasps); Europ. War, 1914; Despatches (L.G. 4.12.14); C.M.G.

HILL, THE HON. A. R. CLEGG- (see Clegg-Hill, The Hon. A. R.).

HILL, B. A. (D.S.O. L.G. 1.1.17); b. 23.4.80; s. of Michael and Anne Hill; m. 1907, Edith Marian, d. of late Alexander Thomson, of Edinburgh; educ. Neuenheim College, Heidelberg; 2nd Lt., R.M.A., 1.9.97; Lt. 1.7.98; transferred to A.O.D., 1908; Adjt., A.O.D., 1.12.10 to 9.10.12; Major 8.12.14; Bt. Lt.-Col., R.A.O.C., 1.1.19; served Europ. War with the British and Japanese Forces at the Siege of Tsingtau, Nov. 1914; with the Mediterranean Exped. Force at Gallipoli (Despatches); Egyptian Exp. Force (Despatches).

HILL, C. (D.S.O. L.G. 4.6.17) (Bar, L.G. 1.1.18), Major, E. African Mtd. Rif.

HILL, C. H. (D.S.O. L.G. 19.8.16), Lt.-Col. Can. Inf.; D.S.O. awarded for gallantry at Hooge.

HILL, CHARLES RAPELJE (D.S.O. L.G. 1.1.18), Lt.-Col., Can. Inf.

HILL, CONWAY ROWLAY (D.S.O. L.G. 14.1.16); b. 16.9.81; s. of Lt.-Col. Rowlay Hill; educ. St. Ninian's, Moffat, and Wellington College; 2nd Lt., R.A., 18.8.00; Lt. 18.8.03; Capt. 1.11.11; Major 10.1.15; A/Lt.-Col. 1.5.18 to 5.3.19; served Europ. War; awarded the Fifth Class (Chevalier), Legion of Honour; Despatches.

HILL, C. W. (D.S.O. L.G. 3.6.18); Major (T/Lt.-Col.), W. India Rgt.

HILL, D. J. J. (D.S.O. L.G. 4.6.17); b. 27.6.72; 2nd Lt., N. Staff. R., 4.11.96; Lt. 6.3.99; Capt. A.O.D., 12.2.02; Major 19.2.11; Lt.-Col. 10.8.16; A/Col. 25.5.20; served Europ. War, 1914–18; Despatches; C.M.G., 1918.

HILL, E. (D.S.O. L.G. 3.6.18); b. 30.4.69; 3rd s. of James Duke Hill, of Terlings Park, Harlow, Essex; m. 1913, Barbara le Grand, d. of George J. Gribble, of 34, Eaton Square, S.W.; two s.; two d.; educ. Harrow; Essex Yeomanry, 1901; Lt.-Col. Commanding Essex Yeomanry, May, 1920; served Europ. War, 1914–18; Despatches.

HILL, E. F. J. (D.S.O. L.G. 3.6.19); b. 6.8.79; 2nd Lt., R.E., 23.12.98; Lt. 25.7.01; Capt. 23.12.07; Major 17.6.15; Bt. Lt.-Col. 3.6.17; served N.W. Frontier of India, Waziristan, 1901–2 (Medal with clasp); Tibet, 1903–4; Medal; Europ. War; Despatches; M.C.

HILL, E. R. (D.S.O. L.G. 4.6.17); b. 10.11.68; 2nd Lt., H.L.I., 23.3.89; Capt. 20.1.97; Major 23.2.07; Bt. Lt.-Col. 18.2.15; T/Brig.-Gen.; served at Kandia, 1898; affair of 6th Sept.; Despatches (L.G. 24.1.99); S. African War, 1899–1902 (Queen's Medal, 2 clasps; King's Medal, 2 clasps); Europ. War; Despatches.

HILL, F. G. E. (D.S.O. L.G. 21.9.17), Surgeon, R.N.

HILL, F. R. (D.S.O. L.G. 16.9.18) (Bar, L.G. 3.6.18); b. 1872; s. of late Col. P. E. Hill, C.B.; m. 1917, Eva, d. of Sir Ralph C. Forster, Bart.; one s.; educ. Marlborough College; fourteen years in Banks in Scotland and India; four years a Rubber Planter in Malaya; travelled in E. Indies, Canada, United States, etc.; enlisted in Public Schools' Battalion, Middlesex Regt.; commission, Sept. 1914; served Europ. War, 1914–18; wounded; Despatches twice; prisoner of war, April–Dec. 1918.

HILL, F. W. (D.S.O. L.G. 14.1.16); b. 8.8.66; s. of Andrew Gregory Hill; educ. at Toronto University and Osgoode Hall, Toronto, Ontario; m. Henriette, d. of H. T. Johnson; appointed to command the 1st Can. Battn. 22.9.14, on its formation, and afterwards, in Jan. 1916, promoted to the command of the 9th Canadian Infantry Brigade, 3rd Canadian Division, on formation; served in the Europ. War, and was present at the Second Battle of Ypres, April, 1915; Festubert, May, 1915; Givenchy, June, 1915; Sanctuary Wood, June, 1916; The Somme, Sept. 1916; Vimy Ridge, April, 1917; Passchendaele, Oct. 1917; Arras, April, 1918; Brig.-Gen.; Despatches six times: C.M.G.: C.B.

HILL, G. A. (D.S.O. L.G. 27.6.19), Capt., 4th Battn. Manchester Regt., and Royal Flying Corps (North Russia); M.C.

G. N. Hill.

HILL, G. E. M. (D.S.O. L.G. 14.1.16); b. 21.2.76; 2nd Lt., E. Lancs. R., 5.9.96; Lt. 10.8.98; Capt. 10.3.06; Adjt. 23.12.07 to 22.12.10; Major 14.5.15; Lt.-Col. 22.4.21; served S. African War, 1899–1902 (Queen's Medal, 4 clasps; King's Medal, 2 clasps; Despatches, L.G. 10.9.01); Europ. War; Despatches.

HILL, G. N. (D.S.O. L.G. 3.6.18); b. 6.1.81; 2nd s. of late Major-Gen. C. R. Hill, R.A., and Mrs. Hill; 2nd Lt., R.A., 6.1.00; Lt. 3.4.01; Capt. 2.1.11; Major 5.9.15; served Europ. War, 1914–18; Despatches twice.

HILL, G. V. W. (D.S.O. L.G. 14.1.16) (1st Bar, L.G. 17.4.17) (2nd Bar, L.G. 26.9.17) (Details, L.G. 8.1.18); b. 24.8.87; s. of late Brig.-Gen. Augustus West Hill, C.B., and Alice, d. of Hon. George Vane, C.M.G.; m. 1916, Enid Geraldine O'Bryen Callaghan; educ. United Services College, Westward Ho!; Woolwich; 2nd Lt., R. Ir. Fus., 7.11.06; Lt. 16.1.09; Capt. 7.6.13; Bt. Major 3.6.16; Bt. Lt.- Col. 3.6.18; Europ. War, 1914–19; Despatches.

HILL, SIR H. B., 6th Bart. (D.S.O. L.G. 1.1.17); b. 31.3.67; s. of 4th Bart. and Charlotte Isabella, d. of H. B. Blyth; suc. brother, 1878; m. 1907, Eliza Maud, y. d. of George Bowdler Gipps, of Howletts, Kent; educ. Marlborough; first commission 10.10.88; Capt. 9.2.98; Bt. Major 26.12.98; retired, R. Ir. Fus. 3.6.08; Lt.-Col., 10th Battn. Manchester Regt.; served Soudan, 1898 (4th Class Medjidieh; also 3rd Class Osmanieh); Europ. War, 1914–19; Despatches.

HILL, H. C. (D.S.O. L.G. 19.10.16); b. 17.9.69; s. of Major-Gen. I. T. Hill; m. 1908, Joan, d. of Col. Landon, of Heavitree, Exeter; educ. Honiton, Devon; Lancing College; R.M.C., Sandhurst; 2nd Lt., R. Muns. Fus., 29.10.90; Lt. 3.6.92; Ind S.C. 20.2.93; Capt., Ind. Army, 10.7.01; Major 29.10.08; Lt.-Col., Oct. 1916; served Europ. War with the 6th Poona Div. in Mesopotamia, and was taken prisoner by the Turks with the garrison of Kut-al-Amara.

HILL, H. J. (D.S.O. L.G. 1.1.18), T/Lt. (A/Capt.), R.E.

HILL, H. W. (D.S.O. L.G. 1.1.17); b. 4.2.77; y. s. of Pearson Hill; g. s. of Sir Rowland Hill, K.C.B.; m. 1918, Ellinor Janet Marcia, o. d. of Rowland Percy Walters; educ. Bradfield College; R.M.A., Woolwich; 2nd Lt., R.A., 21.9.96; Lt. 21.9.99; Capt. 25.2.02; Major 1.10.13; Lt.-Col. 22.6.17; Col. 22.6.21; on Experimental Staff, Shoeburyness, 1906–9; Ordnance Committee; served S. African War, 1899–1902 (Despatches, L.G. 10.9.01; Queen's Medal, 3 clasps; King's Medal. 2 clasps); Europ. War; went out with 7th Division, Oct. 1914; wounded at Ypres, 1914; Despatches thrice; C.M.G., 1918; Croix de Guerre; Lefroy Gold Medal.

HILL, H. W. D. (D.S.O. L.G. 12.12.19); b. 2.3.79; 2nd Lt., R. Suss. R. 9.8.99; Lt. 19.2.02; Ind. Army 28.2.02; Capt. 9.8.08; Major 1.9.15 Despatches.

HILL, J. C. H. (D.S.O. L.G. 26.9.16), 2nd Lt. (T/Lt.), Worc. R. He died of wounds 23.12.18.

HILL, L. C. (D.S.O. L.G. 3.6.19); b. 19.6.90; e. and o. surv. s. of late Alexander Hill and Mrs. Hill; m. 1920, Nan Brolochan, e. d. of Dr. R. Russell Ross, of Rio Tinto, Spain; one s.; educ. St. Lawrence College, Ramsgate; Royal School of Mines, S. Kensington; on Staff of Rio Tinto Coy., Spain, since 1912; Major, R.E.; served Europ. War, 1914–19; Despatches; M.C.

HILL, M. V. B. (D.S.O. L.G. 25.8.17) (Bar, L.G. 16.9.18), Capt. (T/Lt.-Col.), R.F., attd. R. Sussex R.; M.C.

R. C. R. Hill.

HILL, R. C. R. (D.S.O. L.G. 1.1.18); b. 3.9.79; s. of Major-Gen. C. R. Hill (nephew of 1st Viscount Hill) and Elizabeth Hill (*née* Ridley); m. Margaret, d. of late P. Vickers; 2nd Lt., R.E., 25.9.99; Lt. 2.4.02; Capt. 25.9.08; Bt. Major 1.1.16; Major 4.7.16; D.S.O. awarded for services whilst commanding a battalion of the Tank Corps during 1917; served in England till March, 1903 (Chatham 25.9.99 to July, 1900; Submarine Mining Company, Plymouth, July, 1900, to March, 1903); proceeded to India, March, 1903; served at Karachi, Aden and Calcutta; in charge submarine and searchlight defences till June, 1906; posted to military works, 1906, and 1st Sappers and Miners' contingent, Feb. 1911, to command a company; service at Aden, 1904, allowed to count as war service for work in Aden Hinterland; sailed with 1st Field Troop, Sappers and Miners, to France from Bombay 2.9.14; commanded Field Troop with Secunderabad Cav. Bde; commanded Field Squadron with 2nd Indian Cav. Div. till 18.12.16; commanded Battn. Tank Corps 18.12.16 to 27.9.17, when ordered back to India; Despatches three times; Bt. Major 1.1.16.

HILL, R. McC., M.B. (D.S.O. L.G. 16.5.16) (Bar, L.G. 26.11.17) (Details, L.G. 6.4.18), T/Capt., R.A.M.C., attd. 2nd Bn. A. and S. Highrs. D.S.O. awarded for gallantry on 23.3.16, near Cuinchy.

HILL, R. R. (D.S.O. L.G. 1.1.19); b. 21.7.76; 2nd Lt., R.A., 21.9.96; Lt. 21.9.99; Capt. 22.1.02; Adjt., R.A., 25.11.05 to 24.11.08; Major 30.10.14; Lt.-Col. 1.5.21; served N.W. Frontier of India, Waziristan, 1901–2 (Despatches, L.G. 8.8.02; Medal with clasp); Europ. War; Despatches.

HILL, R. V. (D.S.O. L.G. 8.3.19) (Details, L.G. 4.10.19), Lt., 53rd Bn. Aust. Imp. Force.

HILL, S. A. G. (D.S.O. L.G. 7.6.18); b. 5.8.81; e. s. of Col. Arthur Hill, R.E.; m. 1912, Gladys Mary, o. d. of late Rev. Edward Child; one s., educ. South Lodge School, Lowestoft; H.M.S. Britannia; Lt., 1903; Cdr., 1917; commanding H.M.S. Endeavour; served in H.M.S. Dido, N. China, Boxer Rebellion, 1900 (China Medal); Europ. War, 1914–18; Despatches; American Distinguished Service Medal.

HILL, W. J. M. (D.S.O. L.G. 1.1.17), Capt., R. of Officers.

HILL, W. P. H. (D.S.O. L.G. 3.6.16); b. 10.6.77; 2nd Lt., R. Fus., 18.10.99; Lt. 19.9.00; Capt. 4.5.07; Adjt. 25.3.10 to 14.1.13; Major 1.9.15; Bt. Lt.-Col. 3.6.17; served S. African War, 1899–1902 (Queen's Medal with 3 clasps; King's Medal with 2 clasps); Europ. War from 1914; C.M.G.

HILLARY, M. J. (D.S.O. L.G. 17.9.17), Lt., Aust. Engrs.

HILLIAM, E. (D.S.O. L.G. 14.1.16) (Bar, L.G. 3.6.18); b. Dec. 1865; s. of Capt. T. Hilliam, Royal South Lincoln Militia; m. Letitia, d. of Arthur Wallace, of London, Ontario; educ. Spalding Grammar School; 17th Lancers, 1883–93; R.N.W.M. Police, Canada, 1893 to 1900; served S. African War, 1900–2; S.A. Constabulary, 1902–5; retired and took up fruit ranching in British Columbia; on the outbreak of war rejoined Army, and went to France as Adjt., 5th Canadian Battn.; served Europ. War, 1914–18; Despatches; C.B., 1919; C.M.G., 1917.

HILLMAN, D. (D.S.O. L.G. 3.6.18), Major, Engineers.

HILLS, F. B. (D.S.O. L.G. 1.1.18), Major, R.G.A.

HILTON-GREEN, H. F. L. (D.S.O. L.G. 18.1.18) (Details, L.G. 25.4.18); b. 23.6.86; 2nd Lt., Glouc. R., 6.10.06; Lt. 7.10.08; Capt. 24.10.14; Bt. Major 3.6.17; (A/Lt.-Col., 10th Bn. Devon R., 11.9.18 to 1.7.19); Despatches; M.C.

HIME, H. C. R., M.B. (D.S.O. L.G. 1.1.17); b. 8.11.77; s. of T. W. Hime, M.D., Ch.B. (Vict. Univ.), D.P.H. Leeds; Lt., R.A.M.C., 4.12.99; Capt. 4.12.02; Major 4.6.11; Lt.-Col. 1.3.15; A/Lt.-Col. 9.11.18 to 18.4.19; served S. African War, 1899–1902 (Queen's Medal, 3 clasps; King's Medal, 2 clasps); Europ War, 1914–18.

HIND, H. W. (D.S.O. L.G. 26.3.18) (Details, L.G. 24.8.18); b. 8.3.99; e. s. of J. E. Hind; m. 1918, Nora, e. d. of George Clinch; one s.; Lt., Army, 29.7.16; Lt., Ind. Army, 18.10.18; Capt., Ind. Army, 29.7.19; served Europ. War, 1914–18; M.C.; Despatches.

The Distinguished Service Order 269

HINDHAUGH, S. G. A. (D.S.O. L.G. 3.6.18), Lt.-Col., Aust. Light Horse.

HINDLE, R. (D.S.O. L.G. 4.6.17) (Bar, L.G. 26.9.17) (Details, L.G. 9.1.18), Lt.-Col., L.N. Lancs. Regt., 4th Bn. (T.). Killed in action 30.11.17.

HINDMARSH, J. D. (D.S.O. L.G. 11.11.19), Lt. (A/Lt.-Cdr.), R.N.R.; D.S.C.

HINE, A. G. (D.S.O. L.G. 20.2.19), Lt.-Cdr., R.N.

HINGE, H. A. (D.S.O. L.G. 1.1.18); b. 18.10.68; Capt., R.A.M.C., 27.7.95 (three years' previous service); Major 26.7.04; Lt.-Col. 19.9.14; Col. 26.12.17; Commandant, R.A.M. College, Grosvenor Road, S.W.1.; served N.W. Frontier, India, 1897–98 (Medal with clasp); S. African War, 1902 (Queen's Medal, 3 clasps); Europ. War, 1914–18; Despatches five times; C.B., 1919; C.M.G., 1916.

HINGLEY, A. N. (D.S.O. L.G. 15.2.19) (Details, L.G. 30.7.19), T/Capt. (A/Lt.-Col.), 13th Bn. Middlesex Regt.; M.C.

HIRSCH, H. A. (D.S.O. L.G. 22.8.18): b. 22.1.75; e. s. of late A. Hirsch, of Port Elizabeth, S. Africa; m. 1915, Gladys, y. d. of late W. E. Paddon, of London; entered Cape Colonial Forces, 1901; served Anglo-Boer War as Lt., in Prince Alfred's Guard Mt. Inf. (Queen's Medal, 3 clasps); Staff Officer, No. 3, Military District, Union Defence Force, 1912; D.A.A.G. Northern Force, German S. West African Campaign; Despatches; served in France, 1916–17.

HITCH, A. T. (D.S.O. L.G. 15.2.19) (Details, L.G. 30.7.19), T/Capt. (A/Lt.-Col.), 6th Bn. Bedf. Regt., attd. 8th Bn. Linc. Regt.

HITCHIN, H. E. (D.S.O. L.G. 26.4.17), T/2nd Lt., Durham L. Inf. D.S.O. awarded for gallantry on 3.3.17, near Rossignol Wood.

HITCHINS, C. F. (D.S.O. L.G. 1.1.18) (see corr. L.G. 26.7.18), General Manager, Agricultural and General Engineers Ltd.; Major (T/Lt.-Col.), R.W. Kent R., S.R., attd. N. Lan. R.; Lt.-Col., R.W. Kent R.; served Europ. War, 1914–18; Despatches.

HITCHINS, E. N. F. (D.S.O. L.G. 1.1.19); b. 16.1.84; 2nd Lt., W. Rid. R., 3.12.04; Lt. 25.9.06; Capt. 18.12.14; R.C. of Sigs. 25.11.20; Bt. Major 1.1.18; R.C. of Sigs. 11.6.21; served Europ. War; Despatches; M.C.

HOARE, A. (D.S.O. L.G. 3.6.19), Lt. (A/Major), 155th Heavy Battery, R.G.A.; M.C.

HOARE, C. H. (D.S.O. L.G. 4.6.17) (Bar, L.G. 4.2.18) (Details, L.G. 5.7.18); b. 16.12.75; s. of Charles Hoare, of 37, Fleet Street, E.C., and Katherine, d. of Lord Arthur Hervey, Bishop of Bath and Wells; m. 1st, Marie Elizabeth (who died in 1917), widow of Sir Lepel Griffin, K.C.S.I.; one d.; 2ndly, a d. of A. Grey, and widow of Viscount Mountgarret; educ. Eton; New College, Oxford (Honours, Natural Science); Master of the Drag, President of the Bullingdon Club and Secretary of the Canning Club; served S. African War (Queen's Medal, 3 clasps); Europ. War, as Staff Capt. to a Yeomanry Brigade; Brigade Major to an Infantry Brigade; Infantry and Machine Gun Battn. Commander in France; Lt.-Col.; Despatches five times; twice wounded.

HOARE, E. G. (D.S.O. L.G. 3.6.19), Capt. (A/Lt.-Col.), Yorks. L.I., attd. 1/5th Battn. R. Lancs. R., T.F.

HOARE, H. N. (D.S.O. L.G. 1.1.17), T/Major, A.S.C.

HOARE, K. R. (D.S.O. L.G. 23.7.18) (Bar, L.G. 28.8.18); b. 1889; s. of C. A. R. Hoare, Hamble, Hants, and Beatrice Hoare (*née* Holme-Sumner); m. Brenda, d. of A. Bardsley; educ. Northwood Park; Loretto, Scotland; joined Navy during Europ. War; promoted to Lt.-Commander for services in action in the operations against Ostend, 22-23 April, 1918; D.S.C.,; Albert Medal.

HOARE, L. L. (D.S.O. L.G. 3.6.16); b. 24.7.81; s. of W. Hoare, of Summerhill, Benenden, Cranbrook, and Laura, d. of Sir John Lennard, Bart.; m. Audrey, d. of Lt.-Col. G. H. Woodard; three d.; educ. Lambrook; Eton; R.M.A., Woolwich; 2nd Lt., R.A., 22.11.99; Lt. 16.2.01; Capt. 1.4.08; Major, A.O.D. (now R.A.O.C.), 8.12.14; transferred to A.O.D., 1906; Lt.-Col.; Ord. Off., 4th Class, 3.5.06; Adjt., A.O.C., 10.10.12; Ord. Off., 3rd Class, 8.12.14; 2nd Class, 1.1.16; served S. African War, 1901–2 (Queen's Medal with 5 clasps); Europ. War from 1914; Despatches twice.

HOARE, R. (D.S.O. L.G. 1.1.18); b. 18.9.65; 7th s. of late T. R. Hoare; m. Violet Eliza Reid, d. of J. Reid Walker; one s.; educ. Eton College; Lt., 4th Hussars, 30.1.86; Capt. 10.5.93; Major 4.2.99; Lt.-Col. 13.5.05; Bt. Col. 13.5.08; Col. 19.6.09; Brig.-Gen.; served S. African War, 1901–2 (Queen's Medal with 5 clasps); Europ. War, 1914–18; wounded; Despatches; C.M.G.

HOARE, W. J. G. (D.S.O. L.G. 20.10.16), T/Capt., 11th Battn. R. Fusiliers. His D.S.O. was awarded for gallantry on 18.7.16, south of Trônes Wood. He was killed in action on 25.10.16.

HOBART, J. W. L. S. (D.S.O. L.G. 1.1.19); b. 28.4.90; 2nd Lt., N. Staffs. R., 18.9.09; Lt. 19.6.12; Adjt., N. Staffs. R., 20.10.14 to Nov. 1915; Capt. 12.5.15; Bt. Major 3.6.17; Despatches; M.C.

HOBART, P. C. S. (D.S.O. L.G. 24.6.16) (Details, L.G. 27.7.16); b. 4.6.85; s. of R. T. Hobart, I.C.S., and Janetta, d. of C. Stanley; educ. Temple Grove; Clifton College; 2nd Lt., R.E., 29.7.04; went to India and joined 1st Sappers and Miners, 1906; Lt. 15.4.07; Capt. 30.10.14; served N.W. Frontier of India, 1908, operations in the Mohmand country (Medal with clasp); Staff, Delhi Durbar, 1911; served Europ. War with 1st Sappers and Miners, in France, 1915; present at Neuve Chapelle (Military Cross); Festubert, May, 1915, and September Offensive, 1915; General Staff, Sept. 1915; Mesopotamia, Jan. 1916; took part in all operations of Kut relief forces; Bt. Major 1.1.18. His D.S.O. was awarded for gallantry on the right bank of the Tigris, April 1916. He was shot down in an aeroplane on the Euphrates in March, 1918, and taken prisoner; rejoined three days later; Palestine, 1918–19; O.B.E.; G.S.O., War Office.

HOBBINS, A. K. (D.S.O. L.G. 19.8.16), Major, Canadian Infantry. D.S.O. awarded for gallantry near Zillebeke on 3.6.16.

C. J. W. Hobbs.

HOBBINS, W. A. (D.S.O. L.G. 26.11.17) (Details, L.G. 6.4.18), Capt. (A/Lt.-Col.), Lanc. Fusiliers.

HOBBS, B. D. (D.S.O. L.G. 20.7.17), Fl.-Lt., R.N.A.S.; D.S.C.

HOBBS, C. J. W. (D.S.O. L.G. 14.1.16); b. 23.1.76; s. of Capt. S. H. Hobbs (late 89th Foot) and Mrs. Hobbs (*née* Bayley); m. Dorothea Jessy, d. of Major A. Bell (48th Northants. R.); two d.; educ. Rossall School and R.M.C. Sandhurst; 2nd Lt., Derby R., 5.9.96; Lt. 5.2.98; Capt. 4.1.01; served Tirah, 1897–8 (Medal with 2 clasps); S. African War, 1901–2 (Despatches; Queen's Medal with 3 clasps); Europ. War; Despatches three times. His D.S.O. was awarded for services while commanding his battalion at Hooge, his Colonel having been wounded on his way up to the attack the night before. Lt.-Col. Hobbs died of wounds on 16.10.16.

HOBBS, H. F. (D.S.O. L.G. 2.12.18), T/Major, 13th Battn. Welsh R.; M.C.

HOBDAY, H. (D.S.O. L.G. 3.6.18), Lt. (A/Major), R.F.A.; M.C.

HOBDAY, R. E. (D.S.O. L.G. 25.11.16) (Bar, L.G. 24.9.18); b. 25.10.94; 2nd Lt., W. Yorks. R., 24.9.15; Lt. 1.7.17; Despatches. D.S.O. awarded for gallantry on 7.10.16 at Le Sens.

HOBKIRK, C. J. (D.S.O. L.G. 3.6.16); b. 16.7.69; s. of late J. Hobkirk and Baroness Farina Firrao; m. Nora Louisa, d. of late A. Bosanquet, I.C.S.; one s.; one d.; educ. Cheltenham College; Sandhurst; 2nd Lt., Essex R., 3.5.90; Lt. 5.4.93; Capt. 23.2.00; Major 27.11.12; Substantive Lt.-Col. Commanding 2nd Battn. Essex R., 1919; retired, 1920, with rank of Brig.-General; served S. African War, 1900–2 (Despatches twice; Queen's Medal with 5 clasps; King's Medal with 2 clasps); (Temp.) Military Attaché, Rome and Berne, 1914; served Europ. War, 1915–16, as T/Lt.-Col. commanding 11th Essex R.; 1916–18, as T/Brig.-Gen. commanding 14th Australian Inf. Brigade and 120th (Highland) Infantry Brigade; Despatches six times; Bt. Lt.-Col.; C.M.G.

HOBSON, A. F. (D.S.O. L.G. 22.9.16); s. of A. J. Hobson, of Esholt, Sheffield, 2nd Lt. (T/Major), R.E. D.S.O. awarded for gallantry on 1st and 9th July; 1916, at Thiépval. He was killed in action 28.8.16.

HOBSON, F. G., M.A., M.B., B.Ch., M.R.C.P., M.R.C.S. (D.S.O. L.G. 25.8.16); b. 6.8.91; s. of T. F. Hobson, J.P.; m. Audrey Gotch; one s.; one d.; educ. Westminster School; New College, Oxford, and St. Thomas's Hospital, London, S.W.; was House Surgeon and House Physician, St. Thomas's Hospital; 2nd Lt., W. Yorks. R., Dec. 1914; Lt., Feb. 1915; Capt., April, 1916; Europ. War from 1914 to June, 1917; Staff Capt., 21st Inf. Brig., 7th Div.; Brigade Major, 21st Inf. Brig., 30th Div., July, 1916; Despatches four times.

HOBSON, H. R. (D.S.O. L.G. 1.1.18), T/Lt.-Col., late A.S.C. (now R.A.S.C.); served Europ. War, 1914–18; Despatches four times; Assistant Secretary of the Sun Insurance Office since 1919.

HOCKLEY, R. R. (D.S.O. L.G. 4.6.17), Major (T/Lt.-Col., Aust. Mil. Forces.

HODDER, A. E., M.A., M.B., B.Ch. (D.S.O. L.G. 1.1.17); b. 10.5.76; s. of C. Hodder, Master Mariner; educ. Bedford School; King's College, Cambridge (Vintner Exhibition); 2nd Class, Natural Science Tripos; St. Mary's Hospital; late Hon. Sec. St. Mary's Hospital Medical Society and House Surgeon, St. Mary's Hospital; served Europ. War, 1914–18; Major, late R.A.M.C.

HODGE, A. (D.S.O. L.G. 26.7.18), Lt. (A/Capt.), Manchester R.; M.C.

HODGE, J. M. (D.S.O. L.G. 8.3.20), Paymaster Commander, R.N., 1.8.19.

HODGE, R. E. U. HERMON- (see Hermon-Hodge, R. E. U.).

HODGE, THE HON. R. H. HERMON- (see Hermon-Hodge, The Hon. R. H.).

HODGENS, S. F. (D.S.O. L.G. 25.8.17), Major, Australian Field Artillery.

HODGINS, A. (D.S.O. L.G. 1.1.18); b. 19.2.85; Lt., A.V.C., 13.2.07; Capt., R.A.V.C., 13.2.12; Major 13.2.22; Despatches.

HODGINS, F. O. (D.S.O. L.G. 1.1.17); b. at Ottawa, 6.10.87; s. of Major-Gen. W. E. Hodgins, C.M.G.; educ. R.M. College of Canada (graduated with Honours, 1907); Lt., R. Can. Engineers, 1907; Major, 1915; went to France with 1st Can. Div., Feb. 1915; Despatches thrice; Bt. Lt.-Col., 1918.

HODGKINS, J. R., F.R.C.V.S. (D.S.O. L.G. 3.6.16); b. 29.9.81; Lt., A.V.C., 26.8.05; Capt., R.A.V.C., 26.8.10; Major 26.8.20; Despatches.

HODGSON, E. C. (D.S.O. L.G. 3.6.18); b. 22.10.78; Lt., I.M.S., 30.1.04; Capt. 30.1.07; Major (T/Lt.-Col.).

HODGSON, H. J. (D.S.O. L.G. 15.2.19) (Details, L.G. 30.7.19), Capt. (A/Lt.-Col.), Cheshire R., attd. 7th Battn. Wilts. R.

HODGSON, J. C. (D.S.O. L.G. 1.1.17), Cdr., R.N., 31.12.14.

HODGSON, P. E. (D.S.O. L.G. 4.6.17); b. 26.9.74; 2nd Lt., R.E., 25.7.93; Lt. 25.7.96; Capt. 1.4.04; Major 25.7.13; Lt.-Col. 1.1.21; served in Tibet, 1903–4 (Medal); Europ. War; Despatches; Bt. Lt.-Col. 1.1.21.

HODGSON, W. T. (D.S.O. L.G. 3.6.19); b. 2.4.80; 2nd Lt., Midd'x R., 4.8.00; Lt. 24.12.01; Lt., 1st Dragoons, 2.8.02; Adjt., 1st Dns., 1905–8; Capt. 27.1.09; Major 1.5.16; Bt. Lt.-Col. 3.6.18; served S. African War, 1900–1 (Queen's Medal with 6 clasps); Despatches; M.C.

HODNETT, H. (D.S.O. L.G. 2.4.19) (Details, L.G. 10.12.19), T/2nd Lt., L'pool R., attd. 1/5th Battn. T.F.

HODSOLL, F. (D.S.O. L.G. 3.6.16), T/Major, A.S.C. (now R.A.S.C.).

HODSON, SIR E. A., Bart. (D.S.O. L.G. 4.6.17); b. 22.3.93; s. of late R.E. Hodson and Margaret, d. of Rev. S. Pemberton; succeeded uncle, 1921; educ. Marlborough; Trinity College, Cambridge; 2nd Lt., Rif. Brig., 23.1.14; Lt. 30.12.14; Capt. 23.7.16; T/Major, M.G.C., 1.1.17 to 27.7.19; served Europ. War, 1914–18; Despatches.

HODSON, G. C. (D.S.O. L.G. 4.6.17), Lt.-Col., Can. Inf.

HODSON, G. L. (D.S.O. L.G. 1.3.16); b. 28.8.83; s. of Rev. T. Hodson, M.A., late Vicar of Oddington, Glos., and Catherine Anne Hodson (*née* Maskew); m. Ethel May, d. of J. D. Hedderwick, LL.D.; two d.; educ. H.M.S. Britannia; went to sea as Midshipman in H.M.S. Terrible, 1899; landed with Naval Brigade, S. African War, 1899–1900 (Despatches, Medal with 2 clasps, and two years' seniority); 1st Lt., H.M.S. Imogene, Constantinople, 1905–7; H.M.S. Fox, Persian Gulf, 1910–12 (Medal); Europ. War, Home Fleet, 1914–15; Mediterranean, 1915–19; Commander, 31.12.18; commanding H.M.S. Bee, China Station.

HODSON, W. (D.S.O. L.G. 16.9.18), T/Major (A/Lt.-Col.), Cheshire R.; M.C.

HOGAN, G. S. (D.S.O. L.G. 2.4.19) (Details, L.G. 10.12.19), T/2nd Lt., 16th Battn. K.R.R.C.

HOGARTH, D. M. (gazetted as Hogarth, D.) (D.S.O. L.G. 4.6.17), Brig.-Gen., Can. A.S.C.; served Europ. War, 1915–18; Despatches; C.M.G.

HOGG, C. M. T. (D.S.O. L.G. 1.1.17); b. 25.1.79; s. of late Col. T. W. Hogg; m. Winifred, d. of late Capt. Dacres, R.N.; two s.; educ. Bedford Grammar School; Sandhurst; 2nd Lt., S. Lanc. R., 3.8.98; Lt., S. Lanc. R., 26.5.00; Lt., 4th Gurkha Rifles, I.A., 23.8.00; Capt. 3.8.07; Major 1.9.15; Lt.-Col. 1.11.21; served Europ. War from Nov. 1914; wounded Neuve Chapelle; on Staff of 31st Div., Sept. 1915–Jan. 1917; on Staff of 3rd Army from May, 1917, to July, 1917; then ordered to India; General Staff, 5th Mhow Div., C.I.; was in school football XV. and cricket XI. for three years; won public schools middle-weight boxing championship at Aldershot in 1897, and middle-weight at Sandhurst, 1898.

HOGG, P. G. H. (D.S.O. L.G. 3.6.16); b. 21.12.78; 2nd Lt., R.E., 27.8.97; Lt. 27.8.00; Capt. 27.8.06; Adjt., R.E., 19.11.14; Major 30.10.14; served S. African War, 1899–1900 (Queen's Medal with 3 clasps); Europ. War, 1914–18; Despatches.

HOGG, S. R. (D.S.O. L.G. 2.12.18); m. Margery, d. of J. A. Walker; Capt., R. Fusiliers; M.C.

HOGG, W. L. (D.S.O. L.G. 19.12.22), Major, 3rd Brahmans, I.A.

HOGGART, J. W. (D.S.O., L.G. 1.1.19) (Bar, L.G. 15.2.19) (Details, L.G. 30.7.19); b. 11.4.73; 2nd Lt., R.A., 15.11.14; Lt. (A/Major), commanding

50th Brig., R.F.A.; served S. African War, 1899–1902 (Queen's Medal with 5 clasps; King's Medal with 2 clasps); Europ. War; Despatches; M.C.

HOHLER, A. P. (gazetted as Hobler, corr. L.G. 25.8.17) (D.S.O. L.G. 16.8.17). (Bar, L.G. 8.3.19) (Details, L.G. 4.10.19); s. of F. S. Hohler; Major (A/Lt.-Col.), 2/10th Battn. Middx. R.; was an officer in the Territorials before 1914; among the first on active service, and served on the Staff both in this country and in Gallipoli, subsequently going to Palestine, where he remained until after the Armistice. In that country he commanded a battalion of the Welsh R., and gained the D.S.O. and Bar. He attained to the rank of Lt.-Col. He died on 7.3.19, of pneumonia, leaving a widow and two sons. Col. Hohler rode Knotting Fox in the National Hunt Steeplechase at Cheltenham in 1915, and finished sixth. On April 7th, 1915, he rode as "Mr. A. Chilton," his racing pseudonym, in the Soldiers' and Sailors' Handicap Steeplechase at Lingfield, and won at 4 to 1, beating Schoolmoney, who started at 11 to 10 on. Next day, April 8th, he won the United Kingdom Hunters' Handicap Steeplechase. Col. Hohler also owned and rode Les Ormes and Sir Halbert. The former won some races for him, but not when he was able to ride himself. Col. Hohler hunted with the South Oxfordshire.

A. P. Hohler.

HOLBECH, L. (D.S.O. L.G. 8.3.19) (Details, L.G. 4.10.19), Lt., G. Gds., S.R.; M.C.

HOLBROOK, A. E. (D.S.O. L.G. 3.6.16); b. 14.4.80; s. of Col. Sir A. R. Holbrook, K.B.E., and Amelia Mary, d. of late Alexander Parks; m. Winifred Evelyn, d. of late Rev. T. H. Edwards; two s.; two d.; educ. Portsmouth; 2nd Lt., Hants. R., 23.4.02; 2nd Lt., A.S.C., 1.4.04; Lt., A.S.C., 23.4.05; Capt. 4.4.12; Major, R.A.S.C., 30.10.14; served S. African War, 1901–2 (Queen's Medal with 5 clasps); Europ. War, 1915–19; Despatches six times; Bt. Lt.-Col. 3.6.18.

HOLBROOKE, B. F. R. (D.S.O. L.G. 12.9.19); b. 7.10.71; 2nd Lt., Unatt., 28.6.93; 2nd Lt., I.S.C., 20.10.94; Lt. 28.9.95; Capt. 28.6.02; Major, 3/124th Baluchistan Inf., I.A., 28.6.11; A/Lt.-Col.; served S. African War, 1901–2 (Queen's Medal with 4 clasps); Europ. War; Despatches.

HOLCROFT, C. W. (D.S.O. L.G. 4.2.18) (Details, L.G. 5.7.18); s. of W. Holcroft, of Sidmouth; m. Jeanie Copley Knight, d. of Arthur Knight; Major, Worcesters. R.

HOLDEN, C. W., L.R.C.P.I. and L.M., L.R.C.S.I. and L.M., D.P.H.R.C.P.S.I. (D.S.O. L.G. 1.1.17); b. 1.2.79; educ. Royal College of Surgeons, Ireland; Diploma of Tropical Medicine and Hygiene, Cambridge; Lt., R.A.M.C., 31.1.03; Capt. 31.7.06; Major 1.9.14; served as a Civil Surgeon in S. African War, 1901–2 (Queen's Medal, 3 clasps); Europ. War, 1914–18; Despatches; C.M.G; Bt. Lt.-Col. 3.6.18.

HOLDEN, H. N. (D.S.O. L.G. 1.1.19) (Bar, L.G. 8.3.19) (Details, L.G. 4.10.19; b. 13.4.71; 2nd Lt., Oxf. L.I., 12.3.92; Lt. 19.7.93; Lt., I.S.C., 18.8.94); Capt. 10.7.01; Major, 5th Cav., I.A., 12.3.10; served N.W. Frontier of India, 1908 (Medal with clasp); Europ. War; Despatches; Bt. Lt.-Col. He was killed in action 26.10.18.

HOLDEN, V. (D.S.O. L.G. 16.9.18), T/Major, The Queen's Own R.W. Kent R., attd. W. Surrey Regt.; M.C. He died of wounds 2.10.18.

HOLDEN, W. C. (D.S.O. L.G. 1.1.19); b. 10.2.93; 2nd Lt., R.A., 10.12.13; Lt. 9.6.15; Adjt., R.A., 1916–17; Capt. 18.7.17; Despatches; M.C.

HOLDERNESS, H. (D.S.O. L.G. 3.6.19); b. 10.1.79; 2nd Lt. (from local Mil. Forces, N. Zealand) Essex R., 11.4.00; Lt., Essex R., 18.10.00; Lt., I.A., 21.11.01; Capt. 11.4.09; Major 1.9.15; served N.W. Frontier of India, Waziristan, 1901–2 (Medal with clasp); Europ. War; Despatches.

HOLDICH, G. W. V. (D.S.O. L.G. 14.1.16); b. 30.9.82; s. of Col. Sir T. H. Holdich, K.C.M.G., K.C.I.E., C.B., and of Ada, his wife; m. Winifred, d. of A. Fraser; educ. Wellington College, Berks., and R.M.A., Woolwich; 2nd Lt. R.G.A., 18.8.00; Lt. 10.6.02; Capt. 18.8.13; Major 28.12.15; Bt. Lt.-Col. 3.6.18; served Europ. War; was present at the repulse of the Turks in the Suez Canal, Jan. 1915; served through the Dardanelles Campaign, including the evacuation, and Salonika. Later, was Chief Intelligence Officer to the E.E.F. in 1916. In 1917 was present at 1st, 2nd and 3rd Battles of Gaza, and went through the campaign, culminating in the capture of Jerusalem, and in the crossing of the River Auja by the 52nd Lowland Division; transferred to France; took part in the great offensive of 1918; was present at the Battles of Arras, Bapaume and Cambrai, and finished up the war on 11.11.18, a couple of miles north of Mons. After the Armistice, joined the General Staff of 5th Army H.Q.; Order of the Nile; Officer of the Crown of Italy; Chevalier of the Legion of Honour. He died 13.4.21.

HOLDICH, H. A. (D.S.O. L.G. 22.12.16); b. 20.3.74; e. s. of Col. Sir T. H. Holdich, K.C.M.G., K.C.I.E., C.B.; m. Gertrude Elizabeth, d. of W. Brooke; one s.; two d.; 2nd Lt., Scottish Rifles, 10.10.94; Lt., Sco. Rif., 19.2.96; Lt., I.A., 9.10.97; Capt. 10.10.03; Major 10.10.12; Col. (T/Col. Comdt.); served Tirah, 1897–8 (Medal with 2 clasps); Europ. War, 1915–18; Despatches; Bt. Lt.-Col. 3.6.15; Bt. Col. 3.6.19.

HOLDSWORTH, A. A. (D.S.O. L.G. 3.6.16); b. at Bendigo, Victoria, Australia; s. of J. Holdsworth, late of Bendigo, who was born in Yorks., and arrived Australia about 1850; Lt.-Col. V.D., commanding 4th Aust. Divl. Train (Aust. A.S.C.); served S. African War, 1899–1901; Lt., with 2nd Victoria Mounted Rifles, attd. Imperial A.S. Corps (Medal, 6 clasps); enlisted A.I.F., Aug. 1914; embarked with 1st Aust. Div., A.D.S.T., H.Q. Staff, Western Frontier Force, Egypt; Despatches.

HOLDSWORTH-HUNT, W. H. (D.S.O. L.G. 1.1.18); b. 16.11.70; 2nd Lt., R.A., 15.2.89; Lt. 15.2.92; Capt. 19.4.19; Adjt. 19.12.05 to 2.7.09; Major 25.5.09; Lt.-Col. 11.4.16; served Europ. War; Despatches.

HOLFORD, J. H. E. (D.S.O. L.G. 15.1.01) (Bar, L.G. 1.2.19), Major (T/Lt.-Col.), Notts. Yeomanry, attd. 12th Battn. D.L.I. (see "The Distinguished Service Order," from its institution to 31.12.15, same publishers).

HOLL, G. W. (D.S.O. L.G. 22.8.18), Lt.-Col. Potchefstroom "A" Commando, S. African Military Forces.

HOLLAND, H. M. (D.S.O. L.G. 1.1.19); b. 20.1.84; s. of Dr. J. F. Holland, of St. Moritz, Switzerland; m. Dorothy, d. of late J. A. F. Bennett; one s.; educ. Tonbridge School; R.M.A., Woolwich; joined R.A., 1903; retired, 1910; served Europ. War, 1914–18, T/Major, R.G.A., attd. H.Q. III. Corps; Despatches.

HOLLAND, H. W. (D.S.O. L.G. 1.1.17), Capt., Special List.

HOLLAND, J. E. D. (D.S.O. L.G. 8.3.18); b. 15.12.79; 2nd Lt. 7th D.G., 23.5.00; Lt. 13.5.01; Capt. 7th D.G., 4.7.08; 5th D.G. 10.6.14; served S. African War 1901–2 (Queen's Medal with 5 clasps); Despatches; M.C.

HOLLAND, R. T. (D.S.O. L.G. 3.6.19); b. 17.10.85; 2nd Lt., R.A., 23.12.03; Lt. 23.12.06; Capt. 30.10.14; Major 25.7.16; Despatches; M.C.

HOLLAND, S. C. (D.S.O. L.G. 1.1.17), Capt. and Bt. Major, R. of O., late Dragoon Guards; served S. African War, 1901–2; Queen's Medal with 5 clasps; served Europ. War.

HOLLAND-PRYOR, P. (D.S.O. L.G. 26.6.16); b. 7.7.66; 2nd Lt., 3rd Dragoon Guards, 16.11.87; Lt., I.S.C., 14.1.91; Capt., I.A., 16.11.98; Major 16.11.05; Lt.-Col. 16.11.13; Col. 15.5.19; Major-General 28.1.21; M.V.O.; served Waziristan Exp., 1894–95; Medal with clasp; N.W. Frontier of India, 1897–98; Mohmand, Medal with clasp; Tirah, 1897–98; Despatches (L.G. 5.4.98); clasp; S. African War, 1899–1902; Despatches twice; Bt. of Major 29.11.00; Queen's Medal with 3 clasps; King's Medal with 2 clasps; Europ. War; Despatches; Bt. Col. 1.1.17; C.B.; C.M.G.; Deputy Adjutant-General in India.

HOLLENBACH, J. G. (D.S.O. L.G. 22.8.18), Capt. (T/Major), 3rd Mounted Brigade, S.A.S.C., S. African Military Forces.

HOLLIDAY, F. P. (D.S.O. L.G. 25.8.17), T/Lt., Gen. List, and R.F.C.

HOLLINS, C. E. (D.S.O. L.G. 3.6.18); b. 14.12.75; 2nd Lt., Linc. R., 26.2.96; Lt. 1.4.99; Capt. 19.11.04; Major 15.3.15; served Nile Exp., 1898; Battles of the Atbara and Khartum; Egyptian Medal with 2 clasps; Medal; Europ. War; Despatches; Bt. Lt.-Col. 1.1.17.

HOLLOND, H. A. (D.S.O. L.G. 1.1.18), Lt. (T/Capt.), R.G.A.

HOLLOND, S. E. (D.S.O. L.G. 14.1.16); b. 19.3.74; s. of late J. R. Hollond; m. 1st, Lula (who died in 1911, d. of C. Pfizer, of New York; one s.; 2nd, Mrs. Hubert Crichton, widow of late Major Hubert Crichton, Irish Guards; educ. Harrow; Cambridge; 2nd Lt., Rif. Brig., 19.6.95; Lt. 13.8.97; Capt. 20.2.01; Major 1.12.13; Bt. Major 1.1.17; T/Brig.-Gen. 15.1.17 to 31.12.20; Major, Rif. Brig., 3.6.19; Colonel 7.4.20; served S. African War, 1899–1900; Despatches; Queen's Medal with 4 clasps; Europ. War, 1914–18; Despatches; Bt. Colonel 1.1.18; T/Col.-Comdt. 17.11.21; C.B.; C.M.G.; Legion of Honour.

HOLME, H. L. (D.S.O. L.G. 4.9.18); b. 20.1.79, at Naples, Italy; s. of R. M. Holme, Banker, and Henrietta Holme (*née* Leupold); m. Iva Cordelia Eveline Basden, d. of F. G. Basden; educ. Bedford Grammar School; 2nd Lt., R.A., 14.9.98; Lt. 6.2.01; Capt. 10.7.05; Major, R.G.A., 30.10.14; Europ. War; Despatches for military operations at Aden during the period from 16.8.17 to 31.1.18.

HOLME, R. C. (D.S.O. L.G. 3.6.18); b. 9.11.77; 2nd Lt., R.A., 6.5.00; Lt. 1.2.02; Capt. 26.5.13; Major, R.G.A., 30.12.15; Despatches.

HOLMES, B. (D.S.O. L.G. 1.1.18), Major, Aust. Inf.

HOLMES, THE REV. C. F. J. (D.S.O. L.G. 6.9.18); b. 1.8.77; m. Gertrude Louise, d. of Rev. Canon Torr; one s.; one d.; educ. Brighton College; Keble College, Oxford; Cuddesdon; Deacon, 1901; Priest, 1903; Charleville Bush Brotherhood, Queensland, 1905–11; Rector of Knipton in the Vale of Belvoir; Chaplain, 1/1st Lincoln Yeomanry, 1914; S.C.F. Yeomanry Mounted Division, 1917; S.C.F., 4th Cavalry Division, 1918; served with E.E.F. in Fayoum, Egypt, Palestine and Syria; was twice mentioned in Despatches, and awarded the Legion of Honour for work in Palestine; was wounded in the battle which took place prior to the fall of Jerusalem.

HOLMES, J. D. (D.S.O. L.G. 8.3.19) (Details, L.G. 4.10.19), Capt., N.Z. Tunnelling Co., N.Z. Engrs.

HOLMES, J. M'A., M.B., Ch.M., B.A.O. (D.S.O. L.G. 15.9.16); b. 28.2.80; s. of late J. Holmes and Isabel E. Holmes (*née* Swan), of Annavale, Island-Magee, co. Antrim; g.g.s. of Rev. W. Holmes, who fought for the King in the Irish Rebellion, 1798; m. Alice J., d. of late J. Poole, of Dunedin, N.Z.; one s.; one d.; educ. Methodist College and Queen's University, Belfast; played Rugby football for Collegians, 1st XV.; joined H.M. Navy; Staff Surgeon, R.N.; served in H.M.S. Sandpiper, China Station, 3½ years, and in Achilles and Castor during Europ. War. D.S.O. for Battle of Jutland. Invested with the Insignia by the King at sea, June, 1917.

HOLMES, M. J. (D.S.O. L.G. 3.6.18), Capt., Aust. A.M.C.

HOLMES, W. G. (D.S.O. L.G. 1.1.17) (Bar, L.G. 18.7.17); b. 20.8.92; 2nd Lt., R.W.F., 1.10.11; Lt. 15.2.14; Capt. 1.10.15; Bt. Major 1.1.18; Bt. Lt.-Col. 1.1.19; Adjt., R.W.F., 1.7.19; Despatches; Bar to D.S.O. awarded for gallantry on 15.5.17 at Bullecourt.

HOLMES, W. J. H. (D.S.O. L.G. 4.6.17), T/Col., Pioneer Batt. Br. Columbia R.

HOLMES à COURT, R. E. (D.S.O. L.G. 1.1.17); b. 6.2.82; s. of Col. Hon. E. A. Holmes à Court and Adelaide Sophie, d. of H. Hamersley; m. Linda, d. of late Rev. Cecil E. Smith; 2nd Lt., Unatt., 8.1.01; 2nd Lt., Shrops. L.I., 9.3.01; Lt. 5.7.05; Capt. 1.4.10; Adjt., Shrops. L.I., 1911–14; Major 8.1.16; Lt.-Col.; served S. African War, 1901–2; Queen's Medal with 3 clasps; Europ. War; Bt. Lt.-Col. 1.1.19; Despatches.

HOLMPATRICK, LORD (H. W. H.) (Christian name gazetted as H. W.) (D.S.O. L.G. 1.1.19); b. 8.8.86; s. of 1st Baron and Lady Victoria Alexandrina, d. of General Lord Charles Wellesley and sister of 4th Duke of Wellington; succeeded father, 1898; Capt., 16th Lancers, S.R.; served European War, 1914–18; wounded; Despatches; M.C.

HOLNESS, H. J. (D.S.O. L.G. 3.6.18); b. 22.9.82; Lt., A.V.C., 6.2.04; Capt. 6.2.09; Major, R.A.V.C., 10.7.15; Despatches.

HOLROYD-SMYTH, C. E. R. (D.S.O. L.G. 11.1.19); s. of late Col. J. H. G. Holroyd-Smyth, of Ballynatray, and of Lady Harriette Gertrude Isabella Holroyd-Smyth, d. of the 5th Earl of Mountcashell. He became a Lieut. in the R. of O. at the beginning of Aug. 1914, joining the Dragoon Guards at the end of that month, and was promoted Temp. Capt. in July, 1915; awarded the M.C., Dec. 1917, and in March, 1918, was given command of a battalion of the Durham L.I. Lt.-Col. Holroyd-Smyth died of wounds on 23.9.18.

HOLT, A. V. (D.S.O. L.G. 3.6.18); b. 21.11.87; 4th s. of Sir Vesey Holt, K.B.E., Senior Partner, Holt and Co., Bankers and Army Agents, and Mabel Mary, d. of late W. Drummond; educ. Eton; Sandhurst; 2nd Lt., R. Highrs., 9.10.07; Lt. 13.9.10; Capt. 30.1.15 (Capt., R.F.C., 22.11.15 to 31.3.18); T/Major 30.1.15; Lt.-Colonel, R.A.F.; served with Black Watch in Europ. War (wounded); att. to R.F.C., 1915; Wing Commander, 1918; Despatches; Officer, Legion of Honour; Officer, Croix de Guerre with Palm Leaves; Belgian Order of the Crown.

A. V. Holt.

HOLT, G. W. (D.S.O. L.G. 2.4.19) (Details, L.G. 10.12.19); b. 28.4.94; 2nd Lt., R.A., 12.6.15; Lt. 1.7.17; A/Major, R.A., 17.9.17; M.C.

HOLT, R. V. (D.S.O. L.G. 20.7.17); b. 1884; 2nd s. of Sir Vesey Holt; m. Evelyn Constance, d. of late Col. R. Day; two s.;

one d.; educ. Eton; H.M.S. Britannia; served as Midshipman in H.M. Ships Jupiter, Goliath, Empress of India; Sub-Lieutenant, 1904; served in H.M. Destroyers Dee and Hart; Lieut., 1906; H.M.S. Magnificent, T.B. 055, and T.B. 85 in command; H.M.S. Rainbow, H.M. Destroyer Doon, in command; Lt.-Commander, 1914; during Europ. War in command of H.M. Destroyer Itchen, T.B.16; from Feb. 1916–May, 1919, with Harwich Forces in command of H.M. Destroyers Mastiff and Redoubt; promoted Commander 31.12.17; in command of H.M.S. Maenad. His brothers, Col. F. V. Holt, C.M.G., and Lt.-Col. A. V. Holt, R.A.F., have both been awarded the D.S.O.

R. V. Holt.

HOMAN, E. A. (D.S.O. L.G. 11.6.19), Cdr., R.N., 30.6.16.

HOME, G. A. S. (D.S.O. L.G. 1.2.17); b. Swinton House, Berwickshire, 25.4.75; s. of late Rev. Robert Home; m. Ethel Margaret, d. of W. P. Lindsay, W.S. Edinburgh; joined 5th Dragoon Gds. 6.6.96; Major 21.3.11; retired 5th D.G. 6.3.12; served S. African War, 1899–1901; Queen's Medal with 2 clasps; King's Medal with 2 clasps; recalled at beginning of war, 1914; appointed Commandant E. African Volunteer Forces; served throughout German E. African Campaign on Staff; promoted Lt.-Col., Oct. 1914; O.B.E.; Belgian Ordre du Couronne.

HOMER, E. E. F. (D.S.O. L.G. 1.1.19), T/Major (A/Lt.-Col.), R.E.; M.C.

HOMER-DIXON, T. F. (see Dixon, T. F. Homer-).

HONE, P. F. (D.S.O. L.G. 1.1.19) (Bar, L.G. 2.4.19) (Details, L.G. 10.12.19), T/Lt.-Col., Gen. List, att. 13th Bn. Durham L.I.; M.C. and two Bars.

HONYWILL, A. J. (D.S.O. L.G. 7.11.18), 2nd Lt. (A/Capt.), Devons. R.; M.C.

HOOD, B. F. (D.S.O. L.G. 14.3.16); b. 20.9.86; s. of the late Rev. J. F. Hood, B.A., and Mrs. C. du Plat Hood (*née* Richardson-Griffiths); educ. St. John's School, Leatherhead; ent. R.N., 1904; Asst. Paymaster, 1907; Paymaster, 1911; Secretary to Admiral of Patrols, 1912–14; Secretary to Vice-Admiral commanding Eastern Mediterranean during Gallipoli Campaign, 1915–16; Despatches twice; specially promoted to Paymaster Lt.-Cdr.; Paymaster Captain (Temp.) and Secretary to Sir John de Robeck.

HOOD, E. T. F. (D.S.O. L.G. 4.6.17); b. 5.5.80; s. of late S. F. Hood; educ. Bradfield, and R.M.A., Woolwich; ent. R.A. 15.11.99; Lt. 16.2.01; Lt., retired R.H.A., 18.1.08, having served in the S. African War, 1902 (Queen's Medal and 2 clasps), and took a commission in Lincolns. Yeomanry, becoming Major, T/Lt.-Colonel. He was a fine horseman and well known in hunting circles, and his experience was of great value to the Remount Department, in which he held an appointment for several years up to the outbreak of war. He was given command of a battery in his old regiment, and went to France in 1915. He fought at Loos and on the Somme, and was several times mentioned in Despatches. In 1917 Lt.-Col. Hood commanded a Field Artillery Brigade, with which he took part in the Battle of Passchendaele. He was decorated on the field with the Croix de Guerre (Silver Star) for the part he played in defeating an enemy attack. A few days later he was hit by a shell, and died in a clearing hospital on 15.5.18. His brother, Lieut.-Cdr. Martin Hood, R.N., has since died, and another brother, the Rev. Ivo Hood, C.F., fell in the war.

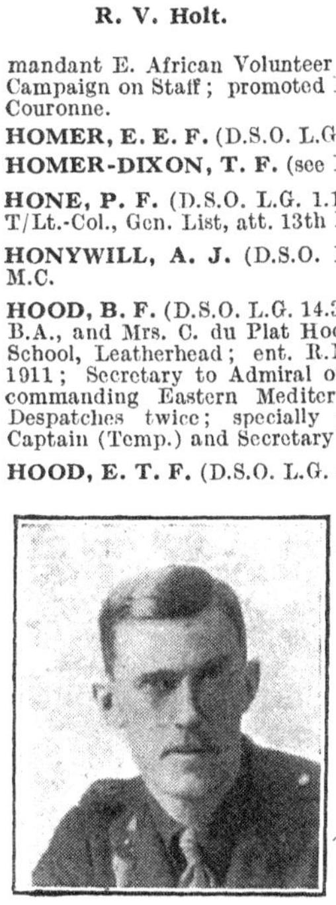

E. T. F. Hood.

HOOD, F. J. C. (D.S.O. L.G. 1.1.18), T/Major (A/Lt.-Col.), York. and Lanc. R.

HOOD, J. W. (D.S.O. L.G. 15.2.19) (Details, L.G. 30.7.19); b. 16.11.90; Lt., Border R., 7.7.17; Despatches; M.C.

HOOD, HON. N. A. (D.S.O. L.G. 1.1.17); b. 4.10.72; 4th s. of 4th Viscount Hood; m. Eveline Mary, d. of H. U. Pender; one s.; three d.; educ. Clifton College; R.M.A., Woolwich; 1st com. 20.10.92; Capt. 1.2.00; R.A., retired 24.9.10; Lt.-Col., R. of O., R.G.A.; served S. African War, 1899–1902; Despatches twice; Queen's Medal with 4 clasps; King's Medal with 2 clasps; Europ. War, 1914–18; Despatches thrice; C.M.G.

HOOD, W. WELLS- (D.S.O. L.G. 17.5.17), Lt.-Cdr., R.N.V.R.

HOOPER, B. O. (D.S.O. L.G. 11.1.19); b. 20.8.79; s. of James and Elizabeth Hooper; m. Nina Louise (now deceased), d. of late Colonel F. Barrow, and ward of Lady Sinclair, of Stevenson; educ. Hamilton Collegiate; Subaltern, 13th Royal Rgt. at outbreak of Europ. War; became Colonel; served 1914–19; Despatches thrice; M.C.; O.C., 20th Canadian Battalion at close of war; O.C., 3rd Canadian M.G. Brigade (Canadian Militia); Director, Board of Trade; Manager, Bank of Hamilton, Hamilton, Ontario, Canada; M.C.

HOOPER, J. C. (D.S.O. L.G. 1.1.18); b. 14.9.78; s. of Capt. C. F. Hooper, late King's Own Lancs. R.; m. Irene, d. of late Dr. William Anderson; one s.; one d.; educated at Charterhouse; 2nd Lt., Shrops. L.I., 18.10.99; Lt. 30.1.01; Capt. 29.3.09; Adjt., Shrops. L.I., 11.1.11 to 11.1.14; Major 1.9.15; served S. African War, 1899–1902; Despatches; Queen's Medal with 6 clasps; King's Medal with 2 clasps; European War; Despatches twice.

HOPE, H. W. W. (D.S.O. L.G. 17.3.19); b. 26.5.78; m. Katherine Kewley, d. of Rev. F. Kewley, M.A.; one s.; two d.; ent. R.N., 1892; Capt. 30.6.15; Lieut. for Experimental Duties, Excellent, 1905–9; Comdr. of Prince of Wales Coronation Review, 1911 (Medal); of King Edward VII., occupation of Scutari, 1913; on Staff of War College, 1913; War Staff Officer, 1914; commanded H.M.S. Dartmouth in the operations in the Adriatic, 1918; Ordnance Committee; C.B.

HOPE, J. A. (D.S.O. L.G. 2.12.18); b. Perth, Ontario, 4.5.90; s. of Peter Hope and Jane L. Hope (*née* Holmes); m. Hilda, d. of W. J. Southcombe; educ. Perth Collegiate Institute; Toronto University; Law School, Osgoode Hall, Toronto; Lt., 42nd Lanark and Renfrew Rgt., 1910; Capt. and Adjt., 59th Batt. Can. E.F.; went to France 20.9.16, joining 46th Batt. Saskatchewan Rgt.; Major; served as Company Commander, Adjt., and Second-in-Command, Battalion; wounded at Passchendaele 27.10.17, and at Drocourt-Quéant 3.9.18; Despatches; M.C.; Second-in-Command, Lanark and Renfrew Rgt., Can. Militia.

HOPE, J. F. R. (D.S.O. L.G. 14.11.16); b. 14.8.83; s. of late H. J. Hope, J.P.; educ. Winchester; R.M.C., Sandhurst; 2nd Lt., K.R.R.C., 22.10.02; Lt. 3.4.07; Capt. 5.9.14; Major 22.10.17; T/Brig.-Gen. 21.9.18; Bt. Lt.-Col. Jan. 1919; wounded three times; Despatches four times.

HOPE, J. U. (D.S.O. L.G. 3.6.18); b. 25.6.81; 2nd Lt., R.A., 6.1.00; Lt. 3.4.01; Capt. 30.11.10; Major, R.G.A., 12.7.15; Despatches.

HOPE, P. A. (D.S.O. L.G. 8.3.19) (Details, L.G. 4.10.19), T/Lt. (A/Capt.), 11th Batt. R. Fus.

HOPKINS, L. E. (D.S.O. L.G. 4.6.17); b. 21.1.73; 2nd Lt., R.E., 22.7.92; Lt. 22.7.96; Capt. 22.7.03; Major 22.7.12; Lt.-Col. 30.9.20; Despatches; O.B.E.

HOPKINS, R. SCOTT (D.S.O. L.G. 21.12.16); b. 28.1.82; educ. Eton and Sandhurst; 2nd Lt., E. York. R., 8.5.01; Lt. 26.3.04; Capt. 18.12.12; served S. African War, 1901–2; Queen's Medal with 5 clasps; Europ. War; Despatches; M.C.

HOPKINSON, J. O. (D.S.O. L.G. 22.9.16) (Bar, L.G. 16.9.18); b. 19.5.77; 2nd Lt., Sea. Highrs., 5.12.00; Lt. 14.3.03; Capt. 3.6.11; Major 5.12.15; A/Lt.-Col. 4th Bn. Seaf. Highrs. 5.4.18 to 8.10.18; served E. Africa, 1904; Medal with 2 clasps; Europ. War; Despatches; M.C. His D.S.O. was awarded for gallantry at Beaumont Hamel on 1.7.16.

HOPLEY, F. J. VAN DER B. (D.S.O. L.G. 20.10.16); b. 28.8.83; s. of late Hon. W. M. Hopley; educ. Harrow; Pembroke College, Cambridge; Lt. (T/Capt.), G. Gds., S.R. (attd. 3rd Bn.); served Europ. War, 1914–18; wounded; Despatches. His D.S.O. was awarded for gallantry at Les Bœufs on 15.9.16.

HOPWOOD, A. H. (D.S.O. L.G. 4.6.17) (Bar, L.G. 26.7.17); b. 16.4.82; 2nd Lt., Linc. R., 30.4.02; Lt. 19.11.04; Capt. 15.8.13; Major 6.9.16; served S. African War, 1901–2; Queen's Medal with 3 clasps; E. Africa (Somaliland), 1908–10; Medal with clasp; Despatches. The Bar to his D.S.O. was awarded for gallantry on 9.4.17, east of Arras.

HORE, R. W. (D.S.O. L.G. 3.6.18), Capt. (T/Major), Aust. F.A.

HORE-RUTHVEN, HON. A. G. A. (D.S.O. L.G. 2.5.16) (1st Bar, L.G. 2.4.19) (Details, L.G. 10.12.19); Col., Welsh Guards; V.C.; C.B.; C.M.G. (see "The Victoria Cross," by same publishers).

HORN, R. (D.S.O. L.G. 4.6.17) (Bar, L.G. 26.7.17); b. 30.5.81; 2nd Lt., Seaf. Highrs., 20.1.00; Lt. 21.1.01; Capt. 21.4.06; Adjt., Seaf. Highrs., 1.5.12; Major (T/Lt.-Col.); served on N.W. Frontier of India, 1908; op. in the Zakka Khel country; op. in the Mohmand country; Medal with clasp; served Europ. War; Despatches; Bar to D.S.O. awarded for gallantry at Arras on 7.4.17; M.C. He was killed in action 23.4.18.

HORN, R. V. G. (D.S.O. L.G. 1.1.18); b. 5.3.86; 2nd Lt., R. Sc. Fus., 2.9.05; Lt. 28.9.10; Adjt., R. Sc. Fus., 22.1.12 to 28.8.15; Capt. 19.10.14; Bt. Major 1.1.17; Despatches; O.B.E.; M.C.

HORNE, E. W. (D.S.O. L.G. 3.6.19); b. 3.4.77; 2nd Lt., Devons. R., 20.12.14; served S. African War, 1899–1902; Queen's Medal with 5 clasps; King's Medal with 2 clasps; Europ. War; A/Major, 2nd Bn. Devons. R.; Despatches.

HORNE, R. (D.S.O. L.G. 15.9.16), Cdr., R.N.; served Europ. War; mentioned in Despatches by Sir J. Jellicoe.

HORNELL, R. A. (D.S.O. L.G. 8.3.18), Capt., R.N.; was appointed Commander, in command of torpedo boat 14 at the outbreak of the war; was subsequently appointed to command of H.M.S. Colossus.

HORNOR, B. F. (D.S.O. L.G. 17.3.17) (Details, L.G. 18.6.17); b. 12.3.89; s. of Francis and Alice Lydia Hornor, of The Lawns, Thorpe Hamlet, Norwich; m. Muriel, d. of S. Wainwright, of Norwich; educ. King Edward VI. School, Norwich; ent. Army, Sept. 1915; did training with 3rd Bn. Norfolk R. at Felixstowe; sailed for Mesopotamia in Sept. 1916, and joined 2nd Bn. Norfolk Rgt.; took part in operations beginning in Dec. 1916; present at recapture of Kut-el-Amara and capture of Baghdad, afterwards taking part in several minor operations on the Persian border. Immediate award of D.S.O. at recapture of Kut-el-Amara. He returned to England on leave Jan. 1919. Demobilized in Feb. 1919.

HORNSBY-WRIGHT, G. J. (D.S.O. L.G. 3.6.19), Lt.-Col., 15th Batt. Essex R., T.F.

HORSFALL, A. G. (D.S.O. L.G. 18.7.17); b. 15.7.76; 2nd Lt., W. Rid. R., 5.9.96; Lt. 14.10.99; Capt. 7.2.02; Major (A/Lt.-Col.). He served in the S. African War, 1902; Queen's Medal with 2 clasps. His D.S.O. was awarded for gallantry near Arras, 9–11.4.17. He was killed in action 9.10.17.

HORSFIELD, R. M. (D.S.O. L.G. 26.9.17) (Details, L.G. 9.1.18), e. s. of late R. M. Horsfield, of Meanwood, near Leeds; m. Stella, d. of A. G. Burchardt-Ashton; Major, R.F.A.; served Europ. War, 1914–17; Despatches; has the Territorial Decoration.

HORSLEY, B. H. (D.S.O. L.G. 15.10.18), T/Capt., K.O.Y.L.I.; M.C.

HORTON, C. W. (D.S.O. L.G. 11.4.18); b. 21.11.77; Hon. Lt., 8th Hussars, 22.4.03; Lt., A.S.C., 9.9.05; Capt. 21.10.09; Major, R.A.S.C., 30.10.14; served N.W. Frontier of India, 1897–98; Medal with clasp; Europ. War; Despatches; Bt. Lt.-Col. 3.6.17.

HORTON, M. K. (D.S.O. L.G. 23.10.14) (Bar, L.G. 2.11.17) (2nd Bar, L.G. 8.3.20), Commander, R.N. (see "The Distinguished Service Order," from its institution to 31.12.15, by same publishers).

HORTON, T. (D.S.O. L.G. 3.6.18); b. 5.12.89; 2nd Lt., R.A., 31.8.15; Lt. 1.7.17; A/Major, R.A., 25.8.17 to 13.8.19; Despatches.

HORWOOD, W. T. F. (D.S.O. L.G. 4.6.17); s. of late C. Horwood, of The Manor House, Broadwater, Sussex; m. eldest daughter of late Lt.-Gen. J. G. Fife; one d.; ent. 5th Lancers, 1888; retired, late 5th Lrs.; Brig.-Gen.; served as Brig. Major to 24th F.A. Brig. 1902–4; was D.A.A.G., War Office, 1914; late Provost-Marshal, G.H.Q., B.E.F., France, from Dec. 1915, until the signing of the Armistice; K.C.B.; Officer, Legion of Honour; Order of Leopold; Croix de Guerre of Belgium; Commander, Order of Dannebrog; 2nd Class Rising Sun (Japan); Despatches seven times; Assistant Commissioner, Metropolitan Police, 1918–20; succeeded Gen. Sir N. Macready as Commissioner, Metropolitan Police, since 1920.

HOSKING, W. S. (D.S.O. L.G. 1.2.19), Capt., Aust. Mil. Forces; M.C.

HOSKYN, J. C. M. (D.S.O. L.G. 24.4.18); b. 20.12.75; 2nd Lt., Unatt., 16.1.95; I.S.C. 27.3.96; Lt. 16.4.97; Capt. 16.1.04; Major 16.1.13; Bt. Lt.-Col. 1.1.19; Lt.-Col., I.A., 15.12.20; Despatches twice; C.B.E.

HOSSIE, D. N. (D.S.O. L.G. 1.1.19), T/Major, R.F.A.

HOTBLACK, F. E. (D.S.O. L.G. 10.1.17) (Bar, L.G. 18.2.18) (Details, L.G. 18.7.18); b. 12.3.87; T/2nd Lt. 9.9.14; 2nd Lt., Norf. R., 9.6.15; Lt. 1.7.17; Capt., Northamptonshire R., 25.10.18 (Tank Corps 22.3.21); Despatches; M.C. D.S.O. awarded for gallantry on 18.11.16, east of Beaumont Hamel.

HOUBLON, R. A. (D.S.O. L.G. 22.9.16); b. 13.10.84; s. of late Col. G. B. Houblon and Lady Alice Francis, d. of the 25th Earl of Crawford and Balcarres; Major, late R.H.A.; served Europ. War, 1914–17. His D.S.O. was awarded for gallantry in July, 1916, near Laventie.

HOUGHTON, G. J. (D.S.O. L.G. 1.1.18); b. 20.9.73; Lt., R.A.M.C., 25.4.00; Capt. 25.4.03; Major 25.1.12; Lt.-Col. 26.12.17; served S. African War, 1901–2; Queen's Medal with 5 clasps; A.D. of Med. Services, 30th Div., Br. Armies in France, 24.4.18 to 13.4.19; Despatches.

HOUGHTON, J. W. H., M.B. (D.S.O. L.G. 1.1.18); b. 17.1.76; m. Agatha Margaret, d. of T. W. Pim; Lt., R.A.M.C., 28.1.99; Capt. 28.1.02; Major 28.10.10; Lt.-Col. 1.3.15; served S. African War, 1899–1902; Queen's Medal with 6 clasps; King's Medal with 2 clasps; Balkan Campaign, 1912–13; British Red Cross Commissioner, attached Greek Army in Macedonia and Epirus; Officer, Order of the Redeemer; Greek War Medal; Europ. War, 1914–18; Despatches.

HOUGHTON, S. R. (D.S.O. L.G. 2.4.19) (Details, L.G. 10.12.19), 12th Batt. Aust. Inf.; M.C.

HOULISTON, J. (D.S.O. L.G. 1.1.19), Lt.-Col., Can. Engrs.

HOUSE, H. W. (D.S.O. L.G. 16.9.18), T/Capt., Wilts. R.; M.C.

HOUSE, M. H. N. (D.S.O. L.G. 1.1.19), Major, "C" Battery, 56th Brig., R.F.A., T.F.

HOUSTON, A. M. (D.S.O. L.G. 3.8.20); b. 16.10.70; 2nd Lt., Manch. R., 5.12.91; Lt. 11.5.95; Capt. 10.7.01; Major 5.12.09; Lt.-Col. 5.12.17; served N.W. Frontier of India, 1897–98, Tochi; Medal with clasp; N.W. Frontier of India, 1908; operations in the Mohmand country; engagement at Kargha; Despatches; Medal with clasp; Europ. War; Despatches.

HOUSTON, J. BLAKISTON- (see Blakiston-Houston, J.).

HOUSTON, J. W., M.B. (D.S.O. L.G. 14.1.16); b. 3.4.81; Lt., R.A.M.C., 4.2.08; Capt. 4.8.11; Major 4.2.20; Despatches.

HOVIL, R. (D.S.O. L.G. 1.1.17); b. 3.2.79; s. of late Capt. R. Hovil; educ. Sherborne School; Jesus College, Cambridge; entered R.A. as 2nd Lt. 6.10.00, as a University Candidate from 3rd Batt. The Buffs (Militia); Lt. 6.10.03; Capt. 26.4.12; Major, R.F.A., 1.5.15; served Europ. War, 1915–18; Despatches.

HOWARD, A. C. (D.S.O. L.G. 3.6.19); b. at Gloucester 21.2.83; educ. King Edward's School, Birmingham; Civil and Mining Engineer; Director, Sociedad Espanola Tratamiento de Minerales per Flotacion; Lt.-Colonel, T.F. (Reserve, March, 1919); served Europ. War in France and Belgium, 1915–19, first in command of 459th (W. Riding) Field Co., R.E., and latterly as Commanding Royal Engineer, 59th and 41st Divisions; Despatches; M.C.

HOWARD, C. A. (D.S.O. L.G. 1.1.17) (Bar, L.G. 15.2.19) (Details, L.G. 30.7.19); b. 29.7.78; s. of Hon. G. T. Howard, s. of 17th Earl of Suffolk and Berkshire, and Lady Audrey Howard, d. of 4th Marquis Townshend (who married 2ndly late Sir Redvers Buller, V.C.); m. Miriam Eleanore, d. of Lt.-Col. E. M. Dansey, 1st Life Gds.; educ. Eton; Sandhurst; 2nd Lt., Shrops. L.I., 3.8.98; Lt. 9.5.00; Lt., K.R.R.C., 19.1.01; Capt. 19.7.07; Major 1.9.15; Lt.-Colonel; served S. African War, 1900; Special Service Officer; A.D.C. to Sir R. Buller, and with S. African L.H.; Queen's Medal with 4 clasps; on Staff, 1912–16; appointed to command 16th K.R.R., 1916; wounded, Aug. 1916; Despatches; Légion d'Honneur.

HOWARD, C. A. L. (D.S.O. L.G. 12.12.19); b. 15.3.86; 2nd Lt., S. Lanc. R., 7.11.06; 2nd Lt., I.A., 24.11.08; Lt. 7.2.09; Capt. 1.9.15; Major 7.11.21 (T/Lt.-Col. 1.4.20); employed with K.A. Rifles 11.4.13; Somaliland Camel Corps 1.4.20; Despatches; M.C.

HOWARD, F. J. L. (D.S.O. L.G. 1.1.17); b. 19.5.70; 2nd Lt., L'pool R., 29.11.90; Lt., L'pool R., 22.9.92; Lt., A.S.C., 1.10.93; Capt. 24.1.98; Major 16.3.07; Lt.-Col., R.A.S.C., 30.10.14; Colonel 30.10.18; Despatches; C.B.E.; served in Exp. to Dongola, 1896; Despatches; Egyptian Medal; Nile Exp., 1897; clasp to Egyptian Medal; Nile Exp., 1898; Despatches; 4th Class Medjidie; clasp to Egyptian Medal; Medal; Nile Exp., 1899; Despatches; 2 clasps to Egyptian Medal; Bt. of Major 14.3.00; Europ. War; Despatches; C.B.E.

HOWARD, H. C. LL. (D.S.O. L.G. 1.1.17)(Bar, L.G. 25.8.17); b. 30.8.82; 2nd Lt., Unatt., 8.1.01; Lt., 16th Lancers, 9.3.01; Capt. 3.9.02; Adjt., 16th Lrs., 1906–9; Capt. 5.8.14; Bt. Major 1.1.16; Major 1.4.18; served S. African War, 1901–2; Queen's Medal with 4 clasps; Bt. Lt.-Col. 3.6.18; Lt.-Col. 18.1.21; Despatches; C.M.G.

HOWARD, L. C. (D.S.O. L.G. 22.1.16), T/Lt.-Col., 8th Batt. Somerset L.I. He was killed in action on 23.12.15 in France.

HOWARD, S. W. (D.S.O. L.G. 31.5.16); b. 24.12.88; s. of Major R.T. Howard and Mrs. Howard, of Annaginny Lodge, Dungannon, co. Tyrone; m. Dorothy Wilberforce Bird, stepdaughter of Col.-Comdt. Gwyn-Thomas, C.M.G., D.S.O.; 2nd Lt., Conn. Rangers, 6.11.09; Lt. 23.1.11; Capt., 1st Connaught Rangers, 19.3.15. He served with the Nigeria Rgt., 1913–14; served Europ. War, with the 4th Connaught Rangers, 1914–15; with the 1st Conn. Rangers, 1915, in France; 1916–18 in Mesopotamia; 1918–19 in Palestine; Despatches; employed with the Egyptian Army from 1919. His D.S.O. was awarded for gallantry on 11.3.16 at Abu Rouman.

HOWARD, T. N. S. M. (D.S.O. L.G. 8.8.17) (Bar, L.G. 26.7.17); b. 15.6.72; 2nd Lt., W. Yorks. R., 17.12.92; Lt. 29.9.94; Capt. 24.11.00; Major 14.3.14; Lt.-Col. 23.2.20; Col. 3.9.20 (T/Brig.-Gen. 9.9.19 to 9.12.19); Despatches; served Uganda, 1900; Nandi Exp.; Medal with clasp; Uganda, 1901; Exp. into the Lango country; severely wounded; clasp; E. Africa, 1902–4; operations in Somaliland; slightly wounded; Despatches twice; Medal with clasp; Europ. War; Despatches; Bt. Lt.-Col. 3.6.15; Bt. Col. 3.6.19.

HOWARD, W. J. H. (D.S.O. L.G. 3.6.19); b. 3.9.89; 2nd Lt., L'pool R., 6.11.09; Lt. 24.4.12; Capt. 11.3.15; Despatches.

HOWARD, W. V. (D.S.O. L.G. 14.7.16); b. 1859; s. of late Rev. W. W. Howard, Chief Inspector of Schools, Devon; m. Violet Angel, d. of late Sir P. H. Scratchley, K.C.M.G., R.E.; educ. Honiton Grammar School; ent. R.N., 1872; Lt. 1882; Cdr., 1897; retired 1905; Capt. 1912; served during the blockade of the Zanzibar Coast; 1st Man-of-War to enter the Chindi River, 1889–90; served Europ. War from 1914; as D.N.T.O., Belfast, commanding H.M.Y. Diane, 1914–15; Captain, Trawler Patrol, 1915–19; Despatches twice.

HOWARD-BURY, C. K. (D.S.O. L.G. 1.1.18); b. 15.8.83; 1st com. 18.5.04; Lt. 13.2.08; retired K.R.R.C. 21.6.13; Capt., 6th Bn. K.R.R.C.; T/Major; A/Lt.-Col., K.R.R.C., S.R. Lt.-Col. Howard-Bury led the Mount Everest Expedition.

HOWATSON, G. (D.S.O. L.G. 2.4.19) (Details, L.G. 10.12.19), T/Lt. (A/Capt.), 185th Tunn. Co., R.E.

HOWEL-JONES, W. (gazetted as Jones, W. Howell) (D.S.O. L.G. 1.1.18); b. 16.4.68; s. of Major-Gen. Howel-Jones, Royal (late Bengal) Artillery; m. Leonie, d. of Admiral Forbes; one d.; educ. Cheltenham College; 2nd Lt., R.A.; Capt. 1.9.97; Adjt. 16.11.04 to 13.2.06; Lt.-Col. R.G.A. 13.10.14; retired R.G.A., 1919; served Miranzai Exp., 1891; Isazai Exp., 1892 (Indian Medal and clasp); Chitral Relief Force, 1895; Mohmand Exp., 1897 (Indian Medal, 1895, and 2 clasps; Europ. War in Belgium and France, 1915–18, in command of an Artillery Brigade, and as Brig.-Gen., 2nd Anzac Heavy Artillery; in Germany with the Army of Occupation until the end of 1919; Despatches four times; 1915 Star; C.M.G.

HOWELL, C. E. (D.S.O. L.G. 2.11.18), Capt., Australian Flying Corps; Lt. (T/Capt.), R.A.F.; M.C.; D.F.C. Capt. Howell and Private Henry Fraser, both of the Australian Flying Corps, lost their lives off the island of Corfu when attempting a flight from England to Australia on a Martinsyde aeroplane constructed at the Woking works. A memorial service for them, conducted by the Rev. Canon Devereux, of Christ Church, Woking, was held at Messrs. Martinsyde's aeroplane factory at Woking.

HOWELL, F. D. G., M.R.C.S., L.R.C.P., D.P.H. (D.S.O. L.G. 1.1.17); b. 30.4.81; s. of late M. G. Howell, of Llanelwedd Hall, Radnorshire; m. Gertrude, d. of J. A. Sinclair; educ. privately; St. Thomas's Hospital, London; Lt., R.A.M.C., 30.1.16; Capt. 30.7.09; Major 30.1.18; served Europ. War, 1914–18; A.D. of Med. Services, 4th Army, Br. Armies in France, 2.4.18 to 7.4.18; A.D.M.S., 2nd Army, Br. Armies in France; A.D.M.S., Br. Army of the Rhine, 8.4.18 to 11.11.19; Despatches five times; Bt. Lt.-Col. 3.6.19; M.C. His brother, Major H. G. Howell won the D.S.O. in 1915.

HOWELL, J. A. (D.S.O. L.G. 16.8.17), T/Major, Cheshire R.; M.C. His D.S.O. was awarded for gallantry at Messines Ridge 7.6.17.

HOWELL-EVANS, H. J. (D.S.O. L.G. 15.2.19) (Details, L.G. 30.7.19); m. Constance Jessie, d. of Hon. A. R. Parker; three d.; educ. Marlborough College; Lt.-Col., Denbighshire Yeom.; served in Egypt, Palestine and France with Denbighshire Yeomanry; subsequently commanded 10th (Shropshire and Cheshire Yeomanry) K.S.L.I. in France until end of hostilities; Despatches.

HOWELL-PRICE, F. P. (D.S.O. L.G. 3.6.19), Major, Aust. A.S.C.

HOWELL-PRICE, J. (D.S.O. L.G. 23.7.18), Lt., R.N.R. (H.M. Submarine C3).

HOWELL-PRICE, O. G. (D.S.O. L.G. 1.1.17); s. of Rev. J. Howell-Price, of Waterloo, formerly of Balmain, Sydney, N.S.W.; Lt.-Col., Aust. Mil. Forces; M.C.

HOWELL-PRICE, P. LL. (D.S.O. L.G. 27.7.16), Major, F. Co. 1st Batt. 1st Aust. Inf. Brig. Landed at Anzac Beach, Gallipoli, remaining till troops were withdrawn. Proceeded to France with 1st Aust. Troops; Brig. Major, 2nd Inf. Brigade (Victorians), France; three times wounded. His D.S.O. was awarded for gallantry on 29–30.6.16, near Sailly.

HOWES, S. (D.S.O. L.G. 1.1.19); b. 4.3.85; 2nd Lt., 21st Lancers, 10.7.09; Lt. 16.1.12; Capt. 31.1.15; Capt., 1st Dragoons, 29.3.22; Despatches; M.C.

HOWITT, H. G. (D.S.O. L.G. 26.7.18), Capt., Yorks. R.; M.C.

HOWITT, T. C., A.R.I.B.A. (D.S.O. L.G. 19.11.17) (Details, L.G. 22.3.18); b. 1889; s. of J. C. Howitt; m. Irene Adelaide, d. of W. Woolley, late of Australia, subsequently of Strawberry Hill, Middlesex; one d.; educ. Nottingham High School; Arch. Assoc., Westminster; travels in Italy, Greece and Germany; Bronze Medallist in Architectural Design, 1911–13; Temp. commission in Leic. R., Oct. 1914; T/Major, Oct. 1916; Major, Leic. R.; T/Lt.-Col., commanding 8th Batt. Leic. R., winter, 1917; Despatches thrice; Légion d'Honneur; commanded Batt., Ypres battles (wounded, 1917). Has published "Measured Drawings of Various Standard Architectural Works," 1910–13.

HOWKINS, C. H., M.R.C.S., L.R.C.P., L.D.S. (D.S.O. L.G. 4.6.17); b. 1876; m. Ann, d. of late H. Shaw; two s.; one d.; educ. Mason College, and Birmingham University; Lt.-Col., R.A.M.C.; served S. African War, 1901–2; Queen's Medal with 4 clasps; commanded Field Ambulance (T.F.), 1910–17; Asst. Director of Medical Services, B.E.F., 1917–19; Despatches three times; C.B.E. 1919; Member Warwicks. County T.F. Association; Fellow of Royal Society of Medicine; Member of British Medical and Dental Associations.

HOWLETT, R. (D.S.O. L.G. 1.1.17) (Bar, L.G. 16.9.18); b. 25.3.82; 2nd Lt., R. Fus., 11.8.00; Lt. 12.2.04; Capt. 16.12.09; Adjt., R. Fus., 1913–15; Major 1.9.15; A/Lt.-Col.; served S. African War, 1901–2; Queen's Medal with 5 clasps; Europ. War; Despatches; M.C.

HOY, C. N. (D.S.O. L.G. 4.6.17) (Bar, L.G. 27.7.18), Major, S. African Military Forces.

HOYSTED, D. M. F. (D.S.O. L.G. 1.1.17); b. 7.8.74; s. of late Surg.-Gen. T. N. Hoysted; m. Sybil, d. of Col. I. Hoysted, of Greta, Sidcup; two s.; two d.; educ. Rugby (W. G. Michell's House); 2nd Lt., R.E., 27.2.94; Lt. 27.2.97; Capt. 1.4.04; Major 27.2.14; Lt.-Colonel 26.2.21; served S. African War, 1899–1902, with Br. Cav. Division, 7th Inf. Div., and Gen. Sir Bruce Hamilton's Columns (Queen's Medal, 3 clasps; King's Medal, 2 clasps); Europ. War in France 8.8.14, with 4th Inf. Div. in command of 9th Field Co., R.E., till Sept. 1915; C.R.E., 22nd Inf. Div., Serbian Exp. Force, Sept. 1915, to Aug. 1917; Chief Instructor, Fortification, R.E. Training Centre, Deganwy, till March, 1918; C.R.E., part of the IInd Army Defence Lines, B.E.F., France, March, 1918; Despatches; Bt. Lt.-Colonel 3.6.15. His D.S.O. was awarded for services during the successful attack by the 22nd Div. on the "Pip" Ridge, Ghevgheli.

HUBBACK, A. B. (D.S.O. L.G. 1.1.19); b. 13.4.71; e. s. of late Joseph Hubback, J.P., of Liverpool; m. 1901, Margaret Rose Frances, 2nd d. of Sir Gordon Blennerhassett Voules, Bart.; one s.; one d.; educ. Fettes College, Edinburgh; Malay States Volunteer Rifles, 1902; Capt. 1902; Major, 1910; Lt.-Col., 1913; Major, London Regt., T.F., Sept. 1914; Lt.-Col.; T/Brig.-Gen.; Despatches six times; wounded; C.M.G.

HUBBARD, REV. H. E. (D.S.O. L.G. 18.2.18) (Details, L.G. 18.7.18); b. 12.2.83; e. s. of Hon. Evelyn Hubbard; educ. Eton; Christ Church, Oxford; Deacon, 1907; Priest, 1908; Curate of S. Hilda's, S. Shields, 1907–10; S. Mary of Eton, Hackney Wick, 1910–11; Skelton-in-Cleveland, Yorks, 1911–14; Chaplain to Forces, 1914–19; Rector of Gisborough-in-Cleveland, Yorks., since 1919; served Europ. War, 1914–18; in France, 1914–15; with Guards' Division, 1916–18; M.C.

HUBBERSTY, G. A. J. CANTRELL- (see Cantrell-Hubbersty, G. A. J.).

HUDDLESTON, H. J. (D.S.O. L.G. 1.1.17) (Bar, L.G. 3.3.17); b. 22.1.80; 2nd Lt., Dorset R., 26.5.00; Lt. 19.11.01; Capt. 1.4.09; Major 1.9.15; Bt. Lt.-Col. 3.6.17; served S. African War, 1899–1902 (Despatches); Queen's Medal, 4 clasps; King's Medal, 2 clasps); Sudan, 1910 (Medal and clasp); Europ. War, 1914–18; Despatches; C.M.G., 1918; M.C.

HUDGELL, G. (D.S.O. L.G. 16.8.17), 2nd Lt. (T/Capt.), Yeom., att. Welsh R.

HUDLESTON, I. R. (D.S.O. L.G. 3.6.19); b. 4.6.86; Lt., R.A.M.C., 28.7.11; Capt. (A/Lt.-Col.), 136th Field Ambulance, R.A.M.C.

HUDLESTON, W. E., M.R.C.S., L.R.C.P.Lond. (D.S.O. L.G. 1.1.17); b. 22.8.72; s. of late Lt.-Col. Wilfred Hudleston, Madras Staff Corps; m. 1908, Alice Maud Mary, d. of late William Ferguson, W.S., of Edinburgh; one s.; one d.; educ. All Saints' School, Bloxham; Middlesex Hospital; late House Surgeon, Middlesex Hospital; House Surgeon, Royal Berkshire Hospital; Lt., R.A.M.C., 28.1.97; Capt. 28.1.00; Major 29.7.08; Lt.-Col.; Colonel, A.D.M.S., 35th Division, in Nov. 1916; Colonel 26.12.17; served Nile, 1898 (2 Medals); Europ. War, 1914–18; Despatches six times; C.M.G.; C.B.E.

HUDSON, A. R. (D.S.O. L.G. 1.1.17); b. 3.1.76; 2nd Lt., R.A., 21.3.96; Lt. 21.3.99; Capt. 5.1.02; Major 5.9.13; Lt.-Col. 1.6.17; served Europ. War; Despatches; C.M.G.

The Distinguished Service Order 273

HUDSON, C. E. (D.S.O. L.G. 16.8.17) (Bar, L.G. 26.11.17) (Details, L.G. 6.4.18), T/Major, Notts. and Derby. R.; V.C., M.C. (see "The Victoria Cross," same publishers).

HUDSON, E. A. K. (D.S.O. L.G. 11.4.18), Major, Aust. Light Horse.

HUDSON, H. H. (D.S.O. L.G. 27.10.17) (Details, L.G. 18.3.18), T/Major, W. Yorks. Regt.; M.C.

HUDSON, J. T. H. (D.S.O. L.G. 1.1.18), Qr.-M. and Hon. Maj., Middlesex Regt.

HUDSON, N. (D.S.O. L.G. 4.6.17); b. 28.7.84; 2nd Lt., R.A., 12.12.03; Lt. 12.12.06; Capt. 30.10.14; Bt. Major 3.6.16; Major, R.A., 4.3.18 (Tank Corps 1.6.20); Lt.-Col. 2.11.20; served Europ. War; Despatches.

HUDSON, N. B. (D.S.O. L.G. 8.3.19) (Details, L.G. 4.10.19) (Bar, L.G. 8.3.19) (Details, L.G. 4.10.19), T/Lt.-Col., 8th Battn. Royal Berkshire Regt.; M.C.

HUDSON, P. (D.S.O. L.G. 14.1.16); b. 10.6.75; educ. Eastbourne College; 2nd Lt., L'pool R., 5.5.00; Lt. 23.5.01; Adjt., Ind. Vols., 25.8.07 to 24.8.13; Capt. 4.7.10; Adjt., L'pool R., 16.9.12 to 27.2.14; Bt. Major 18.2.15; Major 1.9.15; Bt. Lt.-Col. 3.6.17; served S. African War, 1900–2 (Queen's Medal, 3 clasps; King's Medal, 2 clasps); Europ. War, 1914–18; Despatches; C.M.G., 1919.

HUDSON, R. A. (D.S.O. L.G. 14.1.16); b. 16.6.80; 3rd s. of late Robert Hudson; m. Mary Vere, e. d. of Mark Senior, of Ossett; one s.; educ. Giggleswick Grammar School; commissioned in the 3rd V.B., P.W.O., W. Yorks. R., 1898; served Europ. War, with the 1/8th P.W.O. (W. Yorks.) Regt. (Leeds Rifles) T.F.; Major; Despatches. He was killed in action 9.10.17.

HUDSON, R. C. DONALD- (see Donald-Hudson, R. C.).

HUDSPETH, H. M. (D.S.O. L.G. 1.1.18), T/Capt. (A/Major), R.E.; M.C.

HUGGINS, A. (D.S.O. L.G. 1.1.17), Capt. (T/Lt.-Col.), R.F.C., S.R.

HUGHES, G. D'OYLEY- (see D'Oyley-Hughes, G.).

HUGHES, B., M.A., F.R.C.S., B.Sc. (D.S.O. L.G. 1.1.18); b. 1878; s. of John Edward Hughes, late Capt., R.N., and Mary Anne Hughes, of Daresbury Hall, Cheshire; educ. Eastman's R.N. Academy; Cambridge; served Europ. War; published (with Capt. H. Stanley Banks), "War Surgery from Firing Line to Base," 1918.

HUGHES, E. L. (D.S.O. L.G. 3.6.16); b. Feb. 1880; s. of Robert Harry Hughes, M.B., and Laetitia Hughes, of Down House, Whitchurch, Tavistock; m. 1906, Mary, e. d. of W. Tatham Hughes, I.S.O.; one s.; educ. Kelly College, Tavistock; Marlborough College; Clare College, Cambridge; entered Army, 1st Northamptons in India, as a 'Varsity Candidate, 1900; Capt. 1908; Major, 1915; Adjt., 15th Batt. Durh. L. Inf., 1910–13; qualified for Staff College, 1913; served Europ. War, 1914–18; wounded at Battle of the Marne; Officer of the Order of St. Maurice and St. Lazarus.

HUGHES, E. W. (D.S.O. L.G. 1.1.18), Major, London Regt.; M.C.

HUGHES, F. A. (D.S.O. L.G. 1.1.17); b. 9.3.74; s. of Alfred Hughes, of Brisbane; educ. St. Joseph's College, Brisbane; entered the Aust. F.A. Commonwealth Mil. Forces, 1907; Lt. 1908; Capt. 1910; Major, 1913; served in European War in command of the 7th Field Battery, A.I.F., at Gallipoli, till the evacuation, when the 4th Aust. Div. was formed in Egypt, May, 1916; he was promoted Lt.-Col., and given command of the 11st Aust. F.A. Bdge., which afterwards served in France, being in action in Ypres, Armentières, Fleur Baix Somme, etc.

HUGHES, H. B. W. (D.S.O. L.G. 25.8.17); b. 8.5.87; 2nd Lt., R.E., 20.12.06; Lieut. 6.1.09; Capt. 30.10.14; Bt. Major 3.6.19; served Europ. War; Despatches; O.B.E.

HUGHES, H. F. (D.S.O. L.G. 4.6.17), T/Major, A.S.C.

H. Ll. G. Hughes.

HUGHES, H. LL. G., M.R.C.S.Eng., L.R.C.P.Lond. (D.S.O. L.G. 25.8.16) (Bar, L.G. 14.11.16); b. 25.7.92, Ventersburg, O.R.C., S. Africa; son of late H. G. Hughes, M.R.C.S., L.R.C.P., and Mrs. Hughes, d. of Llew. Davies, J.P.; m. 1920, Armorel Anselma Swynford, o. d. of late T. Rought Jones, of East Grinstead; educ. Epsom College; University College Hospital, London (Scholar); Carr Exhibition; Matric. 1st Class; Fellowes Medal for Clinical Medicine, 1914; House Physician, University College Hospital; Assist. Surgeon, Cheltenham Eye, Ear and Throat Hospital; Lieut., R.A.M.C., 1915, att. 1st Battn. Wilts. Regt.; served previously in Artists' Rifles from 1910; served Europ. War, 1914–18; Despatches; M.C., 1918; French Croix de Guerre. His D.S.O. was awarded for gallantry on 4.7.16, Leipzig Salient.

HUGHES, H. T. (D.S.O. L.G. 3.6.19); b. 1873; Col., Can. Engrs.; served Europ. War, 1914–16; Despatches; C.M.G.

HUGHES, R. H. W. (D.S.O. L.G. 1.1.16); b. 1872; m. 1904; Kathleen, d. of J. F. Chapman, of Louth, Lincolnshire; educ. H.M.S.S. Conway; Cdr., R.N.R.; Brig.-Gen., 1917; Director of Inland Water Transport, Mesopotamian Exp. Force; R.D., R.E.; served S. Africa, 1899–1902; S. Nigeria, 1903; Cameroons, 1914–16; Mesopotamia, 1916–18; C.M.G.; C.S.I.; Officier, Legion of Honour.

HUGHES, W. ST. PIERRE (D.S.O. L.G. 1.1.17), Lt.-Col. (T/Brig.-Gen.), Can. Inf.

HUGHES, W. (D.S.O. L.G. 1.1.18), Major (A/Lt.-Col.), Lond. Regt.; M.C.

HULBERT, E. J. (D.S.O. L.G. 1.1.18), Major, N. Zea. Mtd. Rifle Bde.

HULKE, W. B. (D.S.O. L.G. 1.1.17); b. 10.9.72; 1st commission 19.11.92; Capt. 2.1.03; retired Lincs. Regt. 25.2.11; recalled Capt. (T/Lt.-Col.), York. and Lanc. R., R. of O., Linc. R.; Brig.-Gen.; served in the Chinese Regiment of Infantry, also has been suptd. of Army Gymnasia, and Adjt. of the Huntingdonshire Vols. and the Beds. Territorials; commanded a battalion of the York and Lancaster Regt. in Europ. War; Despatches twice.

HULL, C. R. I. (D.S.O. L.G. 1.1.17); b. 22.7.72; 2nd Lt., 19th Hrs., 21.3.00; Lt. 3.10.00; Lt., R. Garr. R., 17.12.02; Adjt., R. Garr. R., 9.12.03; Capt., R. Garr. R., 29.5.04; Capt., 13th Hrs., 19.7.05; Capt., A.S.C., 11.4.06; Major, A.S.C., 30.10.14; served S. African War, 1899–1902 (Queen's Medal, 3 clasps; King's Medal, 2 clasps); Europ. War; Despatches.

HULL, H. C. E. (D.S.O. L.G. 3.6.19), Capt. and Brevet Major, Royal West Surrey Regt.

HULSEBERG, H. (D.S.O. L.G. 14.1.16) (Bar, L.G. 4.6.17); b. 16.10.70; 3rd s. of late Brigade-Surgeon J. W. Hulseberg, A.M.S.; m. 1901, Hilda Mary, d. of late Major C. F. Glass, R.A.; educ. Dulwich College; 2nd Lt., Ches. R., 9.9.91; Lt. 14.5.95; Ind. S.C. 17.6.96; Capt., Ind. Army, 10.7.01; Major 9.9.09; Lt.-Col. 9.9.17; Officer Commanding, 129th (Duke of Connaught's Own) Baluchis; served Uganda, Soudanese Campaign, 1897–99 (Despatches; Medal with clasp); Mekran, 1901–2; Capture of Nodiz Fort (Despatches); Somaliland, 1910 (Medal with clasp); European War, 1914–16; Despatches.

H. H. Hulton.

HULTON, H. H. (D.S.O. L.G. 1.1.18); b. 3.11.82; e. s. of late Rev. William Hulton; m. 1908, Isobel Hope Millicent, y. d. of J. Jackson, J.P., D.L.; one s.; one d.; educ. Eton; 2nd Lt., R.A., 19.12.00; Lt. 19.12.03; Capt. 29.7.12; Adjt. 30.3.14 to 13.5.15; Major 14.5.15 (A/Lt.-Col. 8.9.18 to 24.3.19); served S. African War, 1902; Queen's Medal, 2 clasps; Delhi Durbar and Coronation Medals; Europ. War, in the following actions: Mons, Basse Maroilles, Villers Cotteret, Marne, Aisne, First Ypres, Givenchy, Festubert, Somme, 1916; Vimy Ridge, Hill 70, Third Ypres, Amiens, Villers Bretonneux, Hamel, etc.; Despatches four times; wounded twice; 1914 Star.

HULTON, J. M. (D.S.O. L.G. 3.6.18), Major (A/Lt.-Col.), R. Sussex R.

HUMBLE, BERNARD (gazetted as Hunble, Bernard Maynard) (D.S.O. L.G. 1.1.17), Major, Can. Inf.

HUMBY, H. J. B. (D.S.O. L.G. 26.7.18), 2nd Lt., R.G.A., Spec. Res.

HUME, J. E. (D.S.O. L.G. 4.6.17); b. 1.3.86; 2nd Lt., Conn. Rang., 29.8.06; Lt. 8.5.09; 2nd Lt., A.S.C., 1.10.09; Lt., A.S.C., 1.10.10; Lt., Conn. Rang., 6.4.11; Capt. 11.12.14; T/Major 27.12.15 to 25.6.18; T/Lt.-Col. 8.11.19 to 31.3.21; served Europ. War; Despatches.

HUME, W. V. (D.S.O. L.G. 1.1.18); b. 27.4.75; 2nd Lt., S. Lan. R., 17.3.00; Lt. 12.3.01; Capt. 11.9.06; Major 1.9.15; empld. with W. Afr. Frontier Force 1.5.01 to 16.3.05; served Europ. War; Despatches.

HUME-SPRY, C. A. N. (D.S.O. L.G. 25.8.16); b. 24.8.81; y. s. of late Major F. E. Spry, Indian Staff Corps, and Florence Constance, y. d. of late Surgeon-General William Johnston, H.E.I.C.; m. 1st, 1910, Amy Hammond, y. d. of the Rev. Francis de Gruchy, M.A., Rector of St. Peter's, Jersey; 2nd, 1919, Frances Evelyn, 2nd d. of the Rev. H. R. Howard; one s.; educ. Cheltenham College; R.M.A., Woolwich; 2nd Lt., R.A., 2.5.00; Lt. 3.4.01; Capt. 23.1.13; Major 30.12.15; served with Hankow Mobile Column during Chinese Revolution, 1911; attached R.F.A., 1915; Europ. War in France, 1915–16; Mesopotamia, 1917–18; Despatches. His D.S.O. was awarded for gallantry at Contalmaison on 16.7.16.

HUME-SPRY, W. E. (D.S.O. L.G. 22.12.16); b. 20.7.79; 2nd s. of late Major F. E. Spry, Indian Staff Corps; m. 1902, Violet Ellen, e. d. of Lt.-Col. B. T. M'Creery, R.A.M.C.; two d.; educ. Blundell's School, Tiverton; R.M.C., Sandhurst; 2nd Lt., Unatt., 25.1.99; Ind. S.C. 17.4.00; Lt., Ind. Army, 25.4.01; Capt. 25.1.08; Major 1.9.15; served Europ. War; went to France with the Indian Exp. Force, Aug. 1914; with the Meerut Division to Mesopotamia, Dec. 1915; Despatches.

HUMPHREY, A. E. (D.S.O. L.G. 3.6.18), Major, Cyclist Corps.

HUMPHREY, REV. F. J. H. (D.S.O. L.G. 7.2.18), Assistant Principal Chaplain and T/Chaplain to the Forces.

HUMPHREY, M. (D.S.O. L.G. 22.8.18); b. 17.7.61; s. of G. F. Humphrey; m. 1902, Jessie Helen, only d. of John F. Scott; educ. Osborne House, Margate; Clapham Grammar School; joined the Canadian Mounted Rifles 16.3.92; obtained a commission in the Canadian Mounted Rifles 1.2.90; Capt. (T/Major), S. African Field Post and Telegraph Corps; served in Matabeleland, 1893; S. African War, 1899–1902 (Queen's Medal, 4 clasps; King's Medal, 2 clasps); Europ. War, first as Senior Ordnance Officer in the German South-West African Campaign, under General Botha, from 30.8.14 to 23.9.15; 1914–15 Star.

HUMPHREYS, A. S. (D.S.O. L.G. 14.1.16); b. 13.1.80; 2nd Lt., A.S.C. 23.10.01; Lt. 1.1.03; Capt. 1.11.05; Major 30.10.14; retired 18.11.17; served Europ. War; Despatches.

HUMPHREYS, E. T. (D.S.O. L.G. 14.1.16); b. 5.11.78; m. 1919, Dorothy Grace, y. d. of Captain F. T. Penton, of 43, Portland Place, W.; educ. Charterhouse; R.M.C., Sandhurst; 2nd Lt., Lan. Fus., 7.5.98; Lt. 1.4.99; Capt. 5.10.01; Adjt., Lan. Fus., 15.3.04 to 14.3.07; Major 1.9.15; Bt. Lt.-Col. 1.1.17; Lt.-Col., Leins. Regt., 20.9.19; Bt. Col. 1.1.18 (T/Brig.-Gen. 4.6.20 to 3.12.20); served S. African War, 1899–1902 (Despatches; Queen's Medal, 2 clasps; King's Medal, 2 clasps); Europ. War, 1914–18; Despatches four times; C.M.G., 1919.

HUMPHREYS, G. N. (D.S.O. L.G. 1.1.18); b. 24.12.83; 2nd Lt., A.S.C., 26.11.02; Lt. 1.10.04; Capt. 1.1.11; Major., R.A.S.C., 30.10.14 (A/Lt.-Col. 15.6.15 to 8.5.19); served Europ. War; Despatches.

HUMPHREYS, H. J. (D.S.O. L.G. 27.10.17) (Details, L.G. 18.3.18), Capt. (A/Major), R. Highrs.; M.C.

HUMPHRIES, C. F. G. (D.S.O. L.G. 2.12.18), T/Capt. (A/Lt.-Col.), D.C.L.I., att. 1 Norf. R.; served Europ. War; Despatches; M.C.; D.C.M. He died of wounds 22.8.18.

HUNKIN, S. LL. (D.S.O. L.G. 26.9.17) (Details, L.G. 9.1.18), T/Major, R.W. Fus. D.S.O. awarded for gallantry on 31.7.17, Pilckem.

HUNNYBUN, K. (D.S.O. L.G. 1.1.19), Major, Army Cyclists' Corps (T.F.), att. 7th Battn. Somersetshire Light Inf.

HUNT, A. F. (D.S.O. L.G. 3.6.19), Temp. Major, General List.

HUNT, D. A. (D.S.O. L.G. 26.3.18) (Details, L.G. 24.8.18), T/Capt., K.A. Rifles. He died of wounds 30.11.17.

HUNT, E. W. (D.S.O. L.G. 22.8.18), Major, Hunt's Scouts, S. African Mil. Forces; M.C.

HUNT, G. P. S. (D.S.O. L.G. 18.2.18) (Details, L.G. 18.7.18); b. 24.7.77; 3rd s. of late R. Ponsonby Carew Hunt; m. 1911, Helen Penuel, y. d. of the late Lt.-Col. Arbuthnott, P.B.S., Dunbar, N.B.; one s.; one d.; educ. Harrow; 2nd Lt., R. Berks R., 8.9.97; Lt. 25.5.00; Capt. 11.2.05; T/Major 17.6.15; appointed to command a Territorial Inf. Bde., Dec. 1915; T/Brig.-Gen.; served S. African War, 1899–1902 (Queen's Medal, 3 clasps; King's Medal, 2 clasps); Europ. War; Despatches; C.M.G. He was killed in action 23.3.18.

HUNT, G. V. (D.S.O. L.G. 1.1.17); b. 20.2.75; 2nd Lt., Shrops. L. Inf., 19.9.00; A.S.C. 19.9.01; Lt. 19.9.02; Capt. 1.5.06; Major, R.A.S.C., 30.10.14 (A/Lt.-Col. 11.1.17 to 2.3.20); Despatches.

HUNT, H. R. A. (D.S.O. L.G. 24.6.16) (Details, L.G. 27.7.16); b. 24.7.79; 2nd Lt., Unatt., 25.1.99; 2nd Lt., Ind. S.C., 14.4.00; Lt. 25.4.01; Capt., Ind. Army, 25.1.08; Major 1.9.15; A/Lt., Ind. Army, 19.12.17; served N.W. Frontier of India, 1908; Medal with clasp; Europ. War; Despatches.

HUNT, J. P. (D.S.O. L.G. 20.10.16) (Bar, L.G. 26.7.18); b. 8.3.75; s. of Thomas and Sarah Hunt; m. Bertha Moore; four s.; one d.; educ. Christian Brothers' Schools; joined the Service, 1891; Lt. and Adjt., 1915; Capt., 1916; A/Major, 2nd i/C 2nd R. Dublin Fus., 1917; commanded 9th Royal Dublin Fus., May, 1917; served S. African War; Queen's Medal; King's Medal; served operations Aden Hinterland, 1902–3; Europ. War, including Ginchy; formed and held a defensive flank for ten hours under heavy fire until relieved; C.M.G.; D.C.M.

HUNT, R. A. (D.S.O. L.G. 1.2.19), Lieut., 12th Field Coy., Aust. Engrs.

HUNT, R. G. M. D. (D.S.O. L.G. 11.8.19); b. 26.2.86; s. of Francis Durrant and Ada Jane Hunt; m. Constance Gwendoline Kenrick, d. of late Rev. — Kenrick, of Barnstaple, Devon; educ. Dunchurch Hall, near Rugby; joined Navy, Sept. 1900; commissioned April, 1905; Lt. 1.10.07; Lt.-Cdr. 1.10.15; served European War; twice mentioned in Despatches: (i.) Nov. 1917, for work in command of H.M.S. M.32, on the Bulgarian and Turkish coasts; (ii.) For work in connection with General Allenby's Army at the taking of Gaza and subsequent advance in command of H.M.S. M.32; took part in the Dardanelles Campaign as a Lieutenant in H.M.S. Lord Nelson; was present at the bombardments of the Narrows forts on 11 and 18.3.15, and also at the landing on 25.4.15; in charge of English Quay at Salonika for landing of Army in Oct. 1915; rejoined Lord Nelson for evacuation of Gallipoli Peninsula; returned to Salonika, Feb. 1916, for work on Transport Staff and for Blockade of Greece; appointed in command of H.M.S. M32 in Sept. 1916, and worked from then till the Armistice on Bulgarian, Turkish, Gallipoli and Palestine coasts in conjunction with the Army.

HUNT, R. N., M.B. (D.S.O. L.G. 1.1.18); b. 7.12.72; Lt., R.A.M.C., 29.11.00; Capt. 29.11.03; Major 29.11.12; Despatches.

HUNT, R. S. (D.S.O. L.G. 1.1.18); b. 24.2.74; 2nd Lt., 3rd Hrs., 15.5.97; Lt. 13.9.98; Capt. 26.4.01; Major 14.7.10; D. Gds., 31.3.11; served S. African War, 1902; Queen's Medal, 3 clasps; Europ. War; Despatches.

HUNT, T. E. C. (D.S.O. L.G. 3.6.16); b. 21.11.74; 2nd Lt., R. Berks., 15.5.97; Lt. 10.2.00; Capt. 5.8.04; Major 1.9.15; T/Lt.-Col. 15.4.18 to 16.9.19; served Europ. War; Despatches; O.B.E.

HUNT, W. H. HOLDSWORTH- (see Holdsworth-Hunt, W. H.).

HUNT, W. M. (D.S.O. L.G. 3.8.20); b. 1.11.81; 2nd Lt., R.A., 17.3.00; Lt. 3.4.01; Capt. 25.4.11; Major 23.11.15; served Europ. War; Despatches; M.C.

HUNT, W. W. (D.S.O. L.G. 23.5.17); b. 1893; m. 1911, Sophy Alice, d. of late Adm. Sir G. D. Morant, K.C.B.; one s.; three d.; served S. Africa, 1900–1; Somaliland, 1908–9; Persian Gulf, 1909–10 (Despatches); Europ. War, 1914–18; Despatches; Legion of Honour.

HUNTER, A. J. (D.S.O. L.G. 3.6.18); b. 5.10.81; 2nd Lt., K.R.R.C., 4.5.01; Lt. 22.4.05; Capt. 19.4.13; Major 4.5.16; Bt. Lt.-Col. 1.1.17; T/Brig.-Gen. 17.4.17 to 19.5.19); served S. African War, 1902; Queen's Medal, 2 clasps; Europ. War; C.M.G.; M.C.

HUNTER, C. F. (D.S.O. L.G. 3.6.16); b. 20.1.80; y. s. of James Hunter, of Glenapp, Ayrshire, and Gertrude Leslie Crawford, d. of Lord Ardmillan; m. Nancy Wingrave, d. of Sir William Cobbett; two s.; educ. Repton; 2nd Lt., 4th D. Gds., 11.2.99; Lt. 1.4.00; Capt. 17.5.05; Major 19.10.13; Bt. Lt.-Col. 3.6.17; Lt.-Col. 3.6.19; served Europ. War, 1914–18; Mons till after Aisne; invalided; commanded 4th D. Gds. from March to May, 1915; Staff till May, 1916; appointed A.A.G., 5th Army; polo player; in Winning Team Inter-Regimental, 1911; played in most of the leading tournaments in London during four years before the war, including trial matches for American Team, 1914; Despatches four times; Légion d'Honneur.

HUNTER, C. S. (D.S.O. L.G. 1.1.18); b. 1.3.82; 1st commission 2.5.00; Lt. 3.5.01; retired, R.A. 16.11.12; Major (R. of Off.), 8.6.17; served Europ. War; Despatches; O.B.E.

HUNTER, D. W., M.B. (D.S.O. L.G. 25.8.16) (Details substituted in L.G. 26.9.16 for those in L.G. 25.8.16); educ. Glasgow University; Ch.B.Glasgow; D.P.H.Cambridge; T/Capt., R.A.M.C. (att. 10th W. Yorks Regt.); served Europ. War, 1914; Despatches. He was killed in action 25.3.18. His D.S.O. was awarded for gallantry at Fricourt on 1.7.16.

HUNTER, F. F. (D.S.O. L.G. 17.10.17); b. 7.8.76; 2nd Lt., Unatt., 10.8.98; 2nd Lt., Ind. S.C., 18.11.99; Lt., Ind. Army, 10.11.00; Capt. 10.8.07; Major 1.9.15; T/Lt.-Col. 1.11.16 to 23.7.17; served China, 1900; Medal; Europ. War; Despatches.

HUNTER, H. B. (D.S.O. L.G. 1.1.18); o. s. of late Rev. David Hunter, D.D., of Galashiels, one time minister of Kelso; T/Major, A.S.C.; served Europ. War; Despatches.

HUNTER, H. N. A. (D.S.O. L.G. 1.1.18); b. 14.1.81; m. 1912, Meta, 2nd d. of late A. G. Steel, K.C., and Mrs. Steel, of 12, Cleveland Gdns., W; two s.; one d.; educ. Temple Grove; Haileybury College; 2nd Lt., R.W. Surr. R., 18.4.00; Lt., July, 1902; Capt. 22.1.11; Major 1.9.15; Bt. Lt.-Col. 3.6.19; late G.S.O.1, Northern Command, India; served S. African War, 1899–1902; Queen's Medal, 3 clasps; King's Medal, 2 clasps; Europ. War, 1914–18; Despatches.

HUNTER, J. (D.S.O. L.G. 4.6.17), T/Capt. (A/Major), H.L. Inf.

HUNTER, J. W. (D.S.O. L.G. 15.10.18), T/Capt., North'd Fus.

HUNTER, R. D. (D.S.O. L.G. 3.6.18) (Bar, L.G. 2.4.19) (Details, L.G. 10.12.19); b. 3.7.88; y. s. of Robert Lewin Hunter, of Lincoln's Inn; m. 1918, Constance (Vixen), d. of Harry Lomas; one s.; 2nd Lt., Sco. Rif., 16.12.08; Lt. 1.4.10; Capt. 23.1.15; served Europ. War; Despatches thrice; Ordre de Léopold avec Croix de Guerre.

HUNTINGTON, R. H. (D.S.O. L.G. 22.1.16); b. 9.6.88; s. of late Thomas Huntington, of Liverpool; m. 1918, Irene Alice, e. d. of C. Reginald Johnson; one d.; educ. Ampleforth College, Yorks; interested in Commerce; spent 4½ years in Philippine Islands; enlisted in Rifle Brigade at outbreak of War, 1914; T/Capt., 1914; T/Major, 1915; A/Lt.-Col. 27.10.18; commanded 2/5th Bn. Gloucs. Regt. from Oct. 1918 (during the last few weeks of fighting on the Western Front); served Europ. War, 1915–18; Despatches. His D.S.O. was awarded for gallantry at Messines Rd., 15.12.15.

HURDMAN, W. G. (D.S.O. L.G. 3.6.18), Lt.-Col., Can. Field Arty.

HURLE, E. F. COOKE- (see Cooke-Hurle, E. F.).

HURRY, G. (D.S.O. L.G. 17.12.17) (Details, L.G. 23.4.18), Major, Aust. Inf.

HURST, A. R. (D.S.O. L.G. 1.1.18), T/Lt.-Col., R.F.A.

HURST, G. T. (D.S.O. L.G. 22.8.18), Major, 8th Mtd. Brig. (3rd Mtd. Rif.), . African Mil. Forces; V.D.

HURST, H. C. (D.S.O. L.G. 3.6.16); b. 22.11.84, at Opawa, Christchurch, New Zealand; educ. Opawa School; continuous Military Service since April, 1903; Active Service since 9.8.14; Major, Canterbury Mounted Rifle Regt.; served Europ. War; Despatches five times; wounded four times.

HURST, J. H. (D.S.O. L.G. 3.6.19), Lt.-Col., H.Q., 36th Aust. Heavy Arty. Bde.

HUSBAND, G. S., M.B. (D.S.O. L.G. 3.6.16), Major, I.M.S. He died 21.2.17.

HUSEY, R. H. (D.S.O. L.G. 1.1.18) (Bar, L.G. 22.6.18), Brig.-Gen., 5th (City of London) Batt. The London R. (London Rifle Bde.); served Europ. War; M.C. He died of wounds 30.5.18 (in German hands).

HUSKINSON, G. (D.S.O. L.G. 16.9.18), T/Capt. (A/Major), R.F.A.; M.C.

HUSKISSON, W. G. (D.S.O. L.G. 4.6.17); b. 23.12.77; 2nd Lt., A.S.C., 21.2.00; Lt. 1.4.01; Capt. 18.2.04; Major, R.A.S.C., 5.8.14; T/Lt.-Col. 1.2.19 to 25.8.19; Lt.-Col. 4.11.19; served S. African War, 1900–2; Queen's Medal, 3 clasps; King's Medal, 2 clasps; E. Africa, 1903–4; operations in Somaliland; Europ. War; Despatches; C.B.E.

HUTCHESON, J. (D.S.O. L.G. 26.9.17) (Details, L.G. 9.1.18), Capt., G. Highrs. His D.S.O. was awarded for gallantry in the Third Battle of Ypres; Despatches; M.C.

HUTCHIN, A. W. (D.S.O. L.G. 1.1.19), Major, Gen. List, Aust. Force.

HUTCHINGS, J. F. (D.S.O. L.G. 11.6.19), Lt.-Cdr., R.N. His D.S.O. was awarded for distinguished services in command of Submarines throughout the war.

HUTCHINS, S. (D.S.O. L.G. 4.6.17); b. 30.8.77; 2nd Lt., R. Ir. Regt., 4.5.01; A.S.C. 1.10.02; Lt. 1.5.04; Capt. 21.12.10; Major, R.A.S.C., 30.10.14; Bt. Lt.-Col. 3.6.19; served S. African War, 1900–2 (Queen's Medal, 3 clasps; King's Medal, 2 clasps); Soudan, 1910; operations in Southern Kordofan; Soudan Medal with clasp; Europ. War; Despatches.

HUTCHINSON, C. A. R. (D.S.O. L.G. 14.1.16); b. 31.5.72; y. s. of late Surg.-Gen. J. A. Hutchinson, I.M.S.; m. 1916, Barbara Anne Betsy, 2nd d. of late James Fowler Allan; one d.; educ. Bedford Grammar School; Sandhurst; 2nd Lieut., 18th R. Irish Regt., 7.11.91; Indian Army (3rd Sikhs, Frontier Force); Lt. 7.4.96; 41st Dogras, 1900; Capt. 10.7.01; Major 7.11.09; Bt. Lt.-Colonel 6.6.12; served N.W. Frontier of India, 1897–98; Tochi (Medal and clasp); Samana (clasp); Tirah, 1897–98 (clasp); actions of Dargai, Sampagha Pass, Arhanga Pass; operations against Khani Khel Chamkannis, and in the Bazar Valley, 1897; Abor Expedition, 1911–12 (Despatches; Medal and clasp); Europ. War, 1914; Despatches; very severely wounded.

HUTCHINSON, C. B. GRICE- (see Grice-Hutchinson, C. B.).

HUTCHINSON, E. LLOYD (D.S.O. L.G. 17.12.17) (Details, L.G. 23.4.18), Major, Aust. A.M.C.

HUTCHINSON, E. M. (D.S.O. L.G. 3.6.18); b. 21.11.84; y. s. of Lt.-Col. J. B. Hutchinson, C.S.I.; m. 1915, Phyllis Maud, 4th d. of Andrew Motion; one s.; one d.; educ. Clifton; R.M.A., Woolwich; 2nd Lt., R.A., 23.12.03; Lt. 23.12.06; Capt. 30.10.14; Major 20.7.16; served Egyptian Army, 1912–16; with B.E.F. in France, 1917–19; Despatches.

HUTCHINSON, F. P. (D.S.O. L.G. 14.1.16); b. 19.11.68; 2nd s. of late Rev. C. P. Hutchinson, Rector of Wonston; m. 1898, Edith Mabel, e. d. of late Lewis Brown; one s.; two d.; educ. Lancing College; R.M.A., Woolwich; 2nd Lt., R.A., 17.2.88; Lt. 17.2.91; Capt. 18.4.98; Major 7.5.07; Lt.-Col. 25.7.15; served Europ. War in France and Egypt; Despatches five times; C.M.G.

HUTCHINSON, R. O. (D.S.O. L.G. 12.12.19), Major (A/Lt.-Col.), Fife and Forfar Yeomanry and M.G.C.; M.C.

HUTCHINSON, T. M., M.I.A.E., M.I.Mech.E. (D.S.O. L.G. 1.1.17); b. 14.2.77; s. of Rev. T. W. Hutchinson, M.A., Vicar of Stoke Row, Henley-on-Thames; educ. Cambridge; City and Guilds Institute, London; gazetted 1st E. Surrey Rgt., 2nd Lt. 18.10.99; Lt. 14.1.01; transferred to A.S.C. 1.5.01; Capt. 1.2.05; Major, R.A.S.C., 30.10.14; A/Lt.-Col. 23.6.17 to 29.2.20; served S. African War; Queen's Medal, 4 clasps; King's Medal, 2 clasps; Chief Inspector of Mechanical Transport to B.E.F. in France and Flanders; on Staff of Transport Directorate, 1915–20; Despatches thrice; 1915 Star; O.B.E.; Senior Inspector, Mechanical Transport, R.A.S.C., 1.3.20.

HUTCHISON, A. R. H. (D.S.O. L.G. 13.2.17); b. 2.8.71; s. of late Lt.-Col. F. J. Hutchison, 64th N. Staffs. Rgt.; m. Georgina Courtenay Haswell, d. of late Fleet-Paymaster H. Haswell, R.N.; one s.; one d.; 2nd Lt., R. Mar. 1.2.89; Lt. 28.3.90; Capt. 6.12.97; Major 20.11.07; Bt. Lt.-Col. 20.11.14; Lt.-Col. 11.4.15; Col., 2nd Comdt., 26.11.19; Col. Comdt. 11.4.21; served S. African War, 1900–2 on Staff; Queen's Medal, 3 clasps; King's Medal, 2 clasps; Europ. War, Gallipoli, with R.N.D., 1915–16; Despatches; C.M.G., France, 1916–18; Despatches twice; C.B.; Marine A.D.C. to the King.

A. R. H. Hutchison.

HUTCHISON, C. R. M. (D.S.O. L.G. 1.1.18) (Bar, L.G. 8.3.19) (Details, L.G. 4.10.19); b. 16.1.93; 2nd Lt., R.A., 20.12.12; Lt. 9.6.15; Adjt., R.A., 20.10.15 to 16.3.16; Capt. 20.12.16; Europ. War; Despatches; M.C.

HUTCHISON, G. S. (D.S.O. L.G. 16.9.18); b. 20.1.90; s. of late J. A. Hutchison and Beatrice Jameson, d. of late J. A. Waterlow; m. Emilie Beatrice, d. of C. H. Durham; educ. Bradfield College; R.M.A., Woolwich; ent. K.O.S.B., 1909; R. of O., 1912; Lt., 3rd A. and S. H., 1913; Capt., 1915; T/Major, 1917; Lt.-Col., 1918; served Egypt, Sudan and India; Staff Officer to Durbar Committee, 1911 (Medal); served Europ. War from 1914, 93rd Highrs.; 100th M.G.Coy.; 33rd Batt. M.G.C.; wounded slightly thrice; Despatches four times; 1914 Star and clasp; M.C. He wrote "Memoir of 33rd Batt. Machine Gun Corps," and "History of the 33rd Division."

HUTCHISON, H. (D.S.O. L.G. 26.7.17), Lt. (A/Major), Can. Inf. D.S.O. awarded for gallantry on 3.7.17 at Fresnoy. He died 5.11.17.

HUTCHISON, H. O. (D.S.O. L.G. 18.7.17); b. 3.7.83; 2nd Lt., R.A., 15.7.03; Lt. 15.7.06; Capt. 30.10.14; Major 18.7.16; Europ. War; Despatches; Bt. Lt.-Col. 3.6.19; M.C. His D.S.O. was awarded for gallantry on 26.4.17 in France.

HUTCHISON, J. R. (D.S.O. L.G. 15.3.21); b. 1.2.83; 2nd Lt., R.A., 15.5.01; Lt., I.A., 3.12.03; Capt. 15.5.10; Major, 38th Central India Horse, I.A., 15.5.16; operations in the Abor country, 1911–12; severely wounded; Medal with clasp; Europ. War; Despatches.

HUTSON, H. P. W. (D.S.O. L.G. 17.9.17); b. 22.3.93; 2nd Lt., R.E., 19.12.13; Lt. 9.6.15; Capt. 3.11.17; served Europ. War; Despatches; O.B.E.; M.C.

HUTTENBACH, N. H. (D.S.O. L.G. 11.1.19); b. 16.9.91; 2nd Lt., R.A., 20.7.11; Lt. 20.7.14; Capt. 8.8.16; A/Major, R.A., 26.11.16 to 13.3.17; A/Major, 120th By., 27th Brig., R.F.A., 22.5.18 to 12.2.19; Despatches; M.C.

HUTTON, G. F. (D.S.O. L.G. 2.5.16); b. 6.4.84; s. of late Col. Hutton, of Thorney Hall, Notts.; m. Rose Mairehau, d. of Arthur Rhodes, of Tekoraha, Christchurch, N.Z.; one s.; one d.; 2nd Lt., R.W.F., 26.8.03; Lt. 4.12.06; Capt. 19.10.12; retired; served Europ. War, 1914–18; Despatches.

HUTTON, V. M. (D.S.O. L.G. 1.1.17); b. 29.12.77; s. of late Capt. F. W. Hutton, F.R.S., and Annie, d. of W. Montgomerie, M.D.; m. May Louisa, d. of late Col. W. A. Yule; one s.; served S. African War in N.Z.M.R.; Major, late R.A.S.C.; served Europ. War, 1914–17; Despatches.

HUTTON-SQUIRE, R. H. E. (D.S.O. L.G. 1.1.17); b. 10.10.77, at Holtby Hall, Bedale, Yorks; s. of late Robert Hutton-Squire, late Lt.-Col., 4th Batt. A.P.W.O.-Yorks. R., and Catherine Lucy, his wife (née Prior); m. Violet Isabel Hamilton, d. of J. Warrack; one s.; educ. Charterhouse and the Royal Indian College, Cooper's Hill. On leaving Cooper's Hill he took up an appointment in Madras (1899), but on being offered a commission in the R.A. joined the R.G.A. on 2.5.00. He served in India and Burma; was appointed to a British Mountain Battery, and saw service during the Kelat Expedition in 1908. He went to France, Sept. 1914; served for a time with the R.G.A., but was given command of 85th By. R.F.A., 11th Brigade, in April, 1915, and was present at most of the principal battles from that time, being continually in action, usually with the Australian and Canadian Forces in the neighbourhood of Ypres. For about 10 weeks in the Somme Battle, from early in Aug. 1916. On 7.4.17, after a very heavy close bombardment near Arras to prevent the Germans bringing up supplies on the Vimy Ridge, Major Hutton-Squire and three other officers being together in their hut, a shell burst in their midst, killing one officer instantaneously and mortally wounding Major Hutton-Squire and one other. Both of them died the following day (Easter Day), and all three lie in Barlin Cemetery.

R. H. E. Hutton-Squire.

His Colonel wrote of him: "He was beloved by all. He was such a good friend, and so absolutely indifferent to danger—nothing upset his nerves—and a sound gunner. He had wonderful patience and power of observation, and the reports he sent in were most valuable; he was my right hand and mainstay. We all mourn him as a real warm-hearted friend and most gallant soldier."

He was more than once mentioned in Despatches, and on 4.1.17 by General Sir Douglas (now F.M. Lord) Haig for gallant and distinguished service in the field. He was a keen sportsman and excellent shot, and during his Indian service he made two expeditions to Upper Cashmere and Ladakh in 1905 and 1908, bringing back many fine speciments of markhor, ovis ammon, ibex, etc.

HUXHAM, H. H. (D.S.O. L.G. 14.9.17), Engr. Lt.-Commander, R.N., 1.12.14.

HUXTABLE, C. H. A. (D.S.O. L.G. 16.9.18); s. of late H. A. Huxtable, of Dorchester, Dorset; m. Helen Mary, d. of Rev. P. W. Bates; one s.; educ. Harrow School; served in Royal Dorset Garrison Artillery Territorial, 1906–12; joined R.F.A., April, 1915, and served till the end of the war; T/Capt. (A/Major); Despatches; M.C. with 2 Bars.

HUXTABLE, R. B., M.B., C.M. (D.S.O. L.G. 4.6.17); b. 1867; m. Teresa, d. of M. F. Shine; educ. Otago; Edinburgh University; Lt.-Colonel, Aust. A.M.C.; served Europ. War, 1915–18; Despatches; C.M.G.

HYDE, D. O., M.B. (D.S.O. L.G. 1.1.17); b. 1.12.77; Lt., R.A.M.C., 25.4.00; Capt. 25.4.03; Major 25.1.12; Lt.-Col. 26.12.17; served S. African War, 1901–2; Queen's Medal and 3 clasps; T/Col; served European War, in France; Despatches; C.B.E.

HYDE, W. C. (D.S.O. L.G. 1.1.18), Major, Can. F.A.

HYDE-SMITH, H. C. (see Smith H. C. Hyde-).

HYMAN, E. M. (D.S.O. L.G. 18.1.18) (Details, L.G. 25.4.18), Major, Aust. Light Horse Rgt.

HYNES, E. T. (D.S.O. L.G. 3.6.18); b. 23.9.67; T/Major 15.2.16; Lt.-Colonel 3.6.19; Staff Capt., G.H.Q., Br. Exp. Force; served in France 1915–18.

HYNES, G. B. (D.S.O. L.G. 1.1.17); b. 12.4.87; 2nd Lt., R.A., 20.12.05; Lt. 20.12.08; Capt. 30.10.14; T/Colonel 1.12.17; served Europ. War; Despatches; Bt. Major 3.6.18.

HYNES, J. T. (D.S.O. L.G. 2.4.19) (Details, L.G. 10.12.19), Capt., 15th Batt. Aust. Inf.; M.M.

HYNES, W. B. (D.S.O. L.G. 14.1.21), Lt.-Commander, R.N., 15.7.17.

IBBS, T. C. (D.S.O. L.G. 1.1.18), Hon. Major, London R.

IEVERS, O., M.B., M.R.C.S., L.R.C.P. (D.S.O. L.G. 1.1.17); b. 27.2.19; 3rd s. of Dr. E. Ievers; m. Norah, d. of late P. Ryan; one d.; educ. Tonbridge School; St. Mary's Hospital, London; Lt., R.A.M.C., 31.8.03; Capt. 28.2.07; Major 28.2.15; Bt. Lt.-Col. 3.6.19; went to France, Aug. 1914; Major, 1915; invalided home, Oct. 1916; to Salonika, April, 1917.

ILES, F. A. (D.S.O. L.G. 4.6.17); b. 19.12.74; 2nd Lt., R.E., 25.7.93; Lt. 25.7.96; Capt. 1.4.04; Major 25.7.13; Bt. Lt.-Col. 1.1.19; T/Col. 1.4.21.

ILES, H. W. (D.S.O. L.G. 1.1.18); b. 30.5.65; e. s. of Francis Henry Iles, M.D.; Lt., R.A., 29.4.85; Capt. 1.4.95; Major 28.1.04; Lt.-Col. 31.3.13; served Hazara Expedition, 1888 (Medal with clasp); Burmese Exped., 1889; 2 clasps; Exp. to Manipur, 1891; Despatches (L.G. 14.8.91); clasp; Europ. War; Despatches. He died 28.4.20.

ILLINGWORTH, R. L. (D.S.O. L.G. 26.7.18), T/Capt. (A/Major), Notts. and Derby. Regt.; M.C.

IMBERT-TERRY, C. H. M. (D.S.O. L.G. 14.1.16); b. 31.8.80; 2nd Lt., Devon Regt., 5.1.01; Lt. 25.5.03; Capt. 16.12.11; Major 24.10.15; served S. African War, 1901-2; Queen's Medal, 3 clasps; served Europ. War; Despatches.

IMBERT-TERRY, H. B. (D.S.O. L.G. 3.6.19); b. 10.2.85; e. s. of Sir H. Imbert-Terry, 1st Bart., and Lydia (who died in 1918), d. of late C. G. Roberts; m. Mildred Dorothy, o. d. of Brig.-Gen. E. M. Flint, R.A.; one s.; two d.; educ. Charterhouse; 2nd Lt., R.A., 3.12.04; Lt. 3.12.07; Capt. 30.10.14; Major, R.F.A., 27.9.16; served Europ. War, 1914–18; Despatches; M.C.

IMLAY, A. P. (D.S.O. L.G. 4.6.17) (Bar, L.G. 17.12.17) (Details, L.G. 23.4.18), Lt.-Col., Aust. Imp. Force.; Capt. (from Aust. Mil. Forces), Gordon Highrs., 1.1.21.

IMPEY, G. H. (D.S.O. L.G. 1.1.17) (Bar, L.G. 26.7.18); b. 11.6.82; s. of late Lt.-Col. A. G. Impey, R. Sussex R.; educ. Marlborough College; R.M.C., Sandhurst; 2nd Lt., R. Sussex R., 1902; Lt. 3.2.05; Capt. 14.1.12; Substantive Major, R. Sussex R., 18.1.17; Bt. Lt.-Col. 3.6.19; commanded 12th S. Bn. R. Sussex R.; also 7th (S.) Bn. R. Sussex R., 1917–18; Despatches five times; wounded twice.

IM THURN, B. B. VON B. (D.S.O. L.G. 1.1.18); b. 13.2.87; 2nd Lt., Hamps. R., 29.8.06; Lt. 12.6.09; Capt. 1.11.14; Bt. Major 3.6.19; served Europ. War, 1914; Despatches 19.10.14; M.C.

INCHES, C. F. (D.S.O. L.G. 3.6.19), Major, 1st Hy. By. Can. Garr. Arty.; M.C.

INCHES, E. J. (D.S.O. L.G. 1.1.17), Major, R.F.A.; Despatches.

INCLEDON-WEBBER, A. B. (D.S.O. L.G. 14.1.16); b. 23.1.76; y. s. of late Edward Chichester Incledon-Webber.; 2nd Lt., R. Ir. Fus., 26.6.01; Lt. 21.4.06; Capt. 18.8.10; Adjt., R. Ir. Fus., 5.10.10 to 4.10.13; Major 1.9.15; Bt. Lt.-Col. 1.1.18; served S. African War, 1900–2; Queen's Medal, 3 clasps; King's Medal, 2 clasps; Europ. War; Despatches; C.M.G.

ING, G. H. A. (D.S.O. L.G. 3.7.15) (Bar, L.G. 15.10.18), Major (A/Lt.-Col., D. Gds.) (see "The Distinguished Service Order," from its institution to 31.12.15, by same publishers).

INGHAM, C. ST. M. (D.S.O. L.G. 1.1.17); b. 5.9.73; s. of J. P. Ingham, e. s. of Sir J. T. Ingham and Lady Caroline, d. of 7th Earl of Harrington; m. Phyllis Geraldine, d. of R. B. Betton-Foster; one d.; educ. Eton (Scholar); R.M.A., Woolwich; 2nd Lt., R.A., 17.11.94; Col. 13.4.20; Hon. Brig.-Gen. 1.7.21; went to S. Africa with R.H.A., and served throughout S. African Campaign; Queen's Medal, 6 clasps; King's Medal, 2 clasps; Despatches; went to France with 3rd Division, Aug. 1914; wounded, Dec. 1914; Despatches four times; C.M.G.; retired pay, 1921.

INGHAM, J. G. P. (D.S.O. L.G. 15.9.16); b. 26.3.79; e. s. of His Honour Judge Ingham and Mary, d. of Rev. J. D. Penrose; m. Zelda Raney, d. of late W. Dalrymple; two s.; one d.; educ. Eastman's R.N. Academy, Fareham; joined H.M.S. Britannia, 1893; Lt., 1901; Comdr., 1914; Capt., 1920; served China, 1900 (Medal); Europ. War; D.S.O. for Battle of Jutland; Despatches; 2nd Class St. Stanislaus with Sword.

R. J. Fitz-G. Ingham.

INGHAM, R. J. FITZ-G. (D.S.O. L.G. 14.1.16); b. 15.11.80; 2nd Lt. 22.11.99; Lt. 16.2.01; Capt. 8.5.07; Major 20.3.15; served Tibet, 1903–4; Europ. War; Despatches; died of wounds 1.7.17.

INGLEBY, C. J. (D.S.O. L.G. 1.1.19); b. 5.2.91; s. of late E. W. Ingleby; m. Enid, d. of F. A. Winkley; one d.; educ. The Old College, Windermere; Charterhouse. Gazetted to 4th Bn. E. Yorks. R. (T.F.), 1909; Major; served in France with this battalion; twice wounded; Despatches; invalided from service on account of wounds, March, 1919.

C. J. Ingleby.

INGLES, C. J. (D.S.O. L.G. 15.2.19) (Details, L.G. 30.7.19), Major, 20th Bn. Can. Inf., 1st Cent. Ontario Regt.

INGLES, J. D. (D.S.O. L.G. 1.1.17); b. 18.12.72; s. of late J. C. Ingles, D.I.G., R.N.; 2nd Lt., Devons. R., 12.12.94; Lt. 9.4.98; Capt. 12.11.00; Major 2.10.14; Bt. Lt.-Col. 3.6.15; T/Brig.-Gen. 17.5.16 to 8.6.18; served S. Africa, 1899–1902; Despatches; Queen's Medal, 4 clasps; King's Medal, 2 clasps; Europ. War, 1914–18; Despatches five times; C.M.G.

INGLIS, A. M. (D.S.O. L.G. 20.10.16), Capt., Glouc. Regt., att. "C" Coy., Hy. Sec., M. Gun C.

INGLIS, C. E. ((D.S.O. L.G. 1.1.18); b. 20.5.78; first commission 23.12.97; retired for R.A. with rank of Lt.-Col. 8.7.21; served S. African War, 1902; Queen's Medal, 2 clasps; Europ. War; Despatches.

INGLIS, C. S. (D.S.O. L.G. 17.10.19), Cdr., R.N.

INGLIS H. J. (D.S.O. L.G. 20.10.16); b. 21.6.85; s. of Charles George Inglis; educ. Uppingham; before the Europ. War had been fruit growing in Nelson, British Columbia; Lieut. (Temp. Capt.), S. Wales Borderers; served Europ. War in Gallipoli (wounded, 1915) and France at Loos and in the Somme battles of 1915–1916; Despatches twice; M.C.; invalided home from France 1917, and joined the Tank Corps.

INGLIS, J. (D.S.O. L.G. 26.7.18); b. 28.6.82; s. of J. T. Inglis; m. Helen Jean, d. of late Lt.-Col. C. L. Logan; educ. Winchester; R.M.C., Sandhurst; 2nd Lt., H.L.I., 8.5.00; Lt. 9.6.06; Capt. 12.6.12; Major 8.5.16; Lt.-Col. 17.7.19; Adjt., 1st H.L.I., 1911; served S. African War; Queen's Medal, 3 clasps; served Europ. War; twice wounded; Despatches twice; C.M.G.; commanded 17th H.L.I., July, 1917, to Feb. 1918; 5th Q.O. Cameron Highrs., March, 1918, to Feb. 1919.

INGLIS, R. (D.S.O. L.G. 1.1.18); b. 8.5.82; Assistant Master at St. Dunstan's College, Catford; Temp. Lt. 4.11.14; T/Capt. 2.12.14; T/Major, K.R.R.C., 3.3.16; A/Lt.-Col. 23.11.16; Major from R.A.F., A.E.C., 15.6.20; served Europ. War, 1915–18; Despatches twice.

INGLIS, T. S. (D.S.O. L.G. 1.1.18), Major, R.F.A.

INGPEN, P. L. (D.S.O. L.G. 3.6.16) (Bar, L.G. 26.9.17) (Details, L.G. 9.1.18); b. 28.2.74; 2nd Lt., W. Yorks. R., 10.10.94; Lt. 31.10.95; Capt. 1.3.01; Bt. Major 3.6.15; Bt. Lt.-Col. 1.1.18; served S. African War, 1902; Queen's Medal, 2 clasps; Europ. War; commanded 2nd Batt. in action at Neuve Chapelle; commanded 1/8th Middx. R. actions Loos, Somme, Arras, Ypres (1st and 3rd), Fromelles; twice wounded, once severely; Despatches eight times; Belgian Croix de Guerre; Belgian Order of the Crown (Officier).

INGRAM, C. R. (D.S.O. L.G. 7.2.18); b. 15.1.82; 2nd s. of late Colonel R. Bethune Ingram; 2nd Lt., R.W. Kents., 8.1.01; Lt. 7.1.03; Capt. 25.1.08; Major 8.1.16; T/Lt.-Col. 15.7.19; served Europ. War; Despatches several times; Croix de Chevalier; O.B.E. His D.S.O. was awarded for gallantry in Mesopotamia.

INGRAM, J. M. (D.S.O. L.G. 3.6.19); b. 6.7.81; 2nd Lt., R.A., 6.1.00; Lt. 3.4.01; Capt. 5.8.08; Major 30.10.14; Lt.-Col. 10.8.21; served N.W. Frontier of India, 1908; Medal, with clasp; Europ. War; Despatches.

INGRAM, J. O'D. (D.S.O. L.G. 3.6.16); b. 12.2.70; s. of M. J. T. Ingram; m. Eileen, d. of J. C. Dunbar; educ. privately; Sandhurst; 2nd Lt., 1st Glos. R., 1890; Lt.-Col., late Glos. R.; served S. African War (Medal, 3 clasps); Adjt., 1st Glos. R., 1905–8; accompanied 1st Batt. Glos. R. as Senior Major, when ordered to France with 1st Division of 1st Corps, under Sir Douglas Haig; severely wounded, Nov. 1914, at 1st Battle of Ypres, when in command of the Batt.; Despatches twice; C.B.E.

INGRAM, T. L., M.R.C.S., L.R.C.P., M.A.Cantab. (D.S.O. L.G. 31.5.16); b. 1875; e. s. of T. L. Ingram; m. 1909, Lilian, d. of late Lt.-Col. Donnithorne, Scots Greys; one s.; one d.; educ. Monkton Combe School, nr. Bath; Trinity

College, Cambridge; London Hospital; served with the Middlesex Yeomanry in the S. African War (Queen's Medal, 3 clasps); during Europ. War was T/Capt. R.A.M.C., att. Shropshire Light Inf., Nov. 1914; Despatches; M.C. He was killed in action 16.9.16. His D.S.O. was awarded for gallantry at Morteldje.

INKSON, E. T. (D.S.O. L.G. 1.1.17), Lt.-Col., R.A.M.C.; V.C. (see "The Victoria Cross," by same publishers).

INKSON, N. L. (D.S.O. L.G. 17.3.17), Lt., Ind. Army (R. of O.). His D.S.O. was awarded for gallantry in Mesopotamia.

INNES, S. A. (D.S.O. L.G. 1.1.17) (Bar, L.G. 18.7.17); y. s. of late Alex. Innes, of Raemoir and Cowie; m. Constance Edith, d. of late S. Blain; two s.; one d.; educ. Rugby; 2nd Lt., R. Highrs., 14.9.98; Lt. 16.12.99; Capt. 12.12.03; Major 1.9.15; served S. African War, 1899–1900; Queen's Medal, 3 clasps; Europ. War, 1914–18.

INNES, W. K. (D.S.O. L.G. 26.3.18) (Details, L.G. 24.8.18), Capt., K.O.S.B.

INSKIP, R. D. (D.S.O. L.G. 22.12.16); b. 17.9.85; s. of Rev. O. D. Inskip, Rector of Harleston, Norfolk; m. Evelyn, d. of J. Rickard; one s.; 2nd Lt. Ind. Army, 5.8.05; Lt. 5.11.07; Capt. 5.8.14; Bt. Major 1.1.19; served N.W. Frontier of India, 1908 (Medal and clasp); Europ. War, France, Mesopotamia Palestine, 1914–18; Despatches five times; M.C.

IONIDES, P. D. (D.S.O. L.G. 4.6.17); b. 1876; s. of L. A. Ionides; m. Norah Mary, d. of late J. Addie; educ. Harrow; Lt.-Col.; served Europ. War, 1914–19; very seriously wounded while commanding 10th Batt. D.C.L.I.; Despatches.

IRELAND, G. (D.S.O. L.G. 1.2.17), T/Major, S. African A.S.C.

IREMONGER, H. W. (D.S.O. L.G. 15.2.19); b. 20.9.82; 2nd Lt., R. Mar. Art., 1.1.00; Lt. 1.1.01; Capt. 1.1.11; Major 6.6.17; Bt. Lt.-Col. 1.1.19.

IRONS, A. I. (D.S.O. L.G. 1.1.18) (Bar, L.G. 16.9.18), T/Lt.-Col., Middlx. Regt.; served S. African War, 1900–1; Medal; Europ. War; Despatches.

IRONSIDE, W. S. (D.S.O. L.G. 16.9.18), Lt. (A/Major), R.F.A., 24th Bde.; served Europ. War; Despatches; M.C.; killed in action 2.11.18.

IRVINE, A. E. (D.S.O. L.G. 31.5.16) (Bar, L.G. 1.2.19); b. 28.9.76; s. of late John Irvine and late Rebecca Mary Ann, d. of late Surgeon G. E. Nixon, H.M.E.I.S.; m. Katharine Helen, d. of Brig.-Gen. H. M. C. W. Graham, C.M.G.; one s.; educ. privately; King's College, London; 2nd Lt., Durh. L.I., 24.3.97; Lt. 9.10.99; Capt. 5.6.03; Major 1.9.15; T/Lt.-Col. 7.2.16; Temp. Brig.-Gen. 17.2.16; served Europ. War, 1914–18; Despatches; C.B.; C.M.G.; Bt. Lt.-Col. 1.1.17; Officier, Ordre de Léopold; Croix de Guerre, Belgium.

IRVINE, A. E. S., L.R.C.P.I., L.R.C.S.I., L.M. (D.S.O. L.G. 14.1.16); b. 11.4.80; s. of late Rev. Canon R. Irvine, D.D., R.D., Vicar of St. Stephen's, Belfast, and Frances, d. of R. Stewart, M.D.; m. Sara Evelyn Gertrude, d. of Col. H. Adair-Hall, late Sherwood Foresters and Cheshire Rgts.; one s.; one d.; educ. Campbell College, Belfast; Trinity College, Dublin; Belfast University; College Surgeon, Ireland; Lieut., R.A.M.C., 31.7.05; Capt. 31.1.09; Major 15.10.15; T/Lt.-Col.; was in S. Africa, 1907–12; served Europ. War, 1914–18; joined H.Q. Division, R.E.; 1st Division, 5.8.14; Mons Retreat, Marne, Aisne, 1st Battle of Ypres; Neuve Chapelle, Festubert, Loos; Despatches four times; Officer, Ordre du Mérite Agricole.

IRVINE, G. (D.S.O. L.G. 20.7.17), Lt., R.N.R.

IRVINE, M. McB. BELL- (see Bell-Irvine, M. McB.).

IRVINE, R. A. (D.S.O. L.G. 4.6.17), Lt.-Col. Commanding 3rd Batt. (Res. Lancs. Fus.); served W. Africa, 1897–98; Medal with clasp; W. Africa, 1899–1900; Despatches; Ashanti; Medal; served Europ. War, 1915–18; Bt. Lt.-Col.; C.M.G.

IRVINE, R. O. BELL- (see Bell-Irvine, R. O.).

IRVINE-FORTESCUE, A., M.B. (D.S.O. L.G. 3.2.20); b. 6.7.80; Lt., R.A.M.C., 28.1.07; Capt. 28.7.10; Major 28.1.19; served Europ. War; Despatches.

IRVING, T. C. (D.S.O. L.G. 3.6.16); b. 31.8.79; s. of Thomas Craik Irving, of Toronto, Canada; m. 1916, Jessie, d. of Angus Murray, of Toronto; educ. Toronto; McGill University; was in practice as a Civil Engineer; Major, Canadian Engrs.; Officer Commanding, 1st Canadian Div., B.E.F.; served Europ. War; Despatches.

IRWIN, A. (D.S.O. L.G. 3.6.18), Lt.-Col., North'd. Fus.

IRWIN, A. P. B. (D.S.O. L.G. 20.10.16) (1st Bar, L.G. 26.7.17) (2nd Bar, L.G. 15.2.19) (Details, L.G. 30.7.19); b. 30.9.97; o. s. of late Sir A. Irwin, C.S.I.; m. Eileen, d. of H. N. Holberton, M.D.; one s.; educ. Sedbergh School; Gonville and Caius College, Cambridge; commissioned E. Surrey R., 1909; Adjt., 8th Bn., 1914; was in command of 8th Bn.; Lt.-Col. late E. Surrey R.; wounded thrice; Bt. Major; with N. Russian Relief Force, 1919; retired 1921.

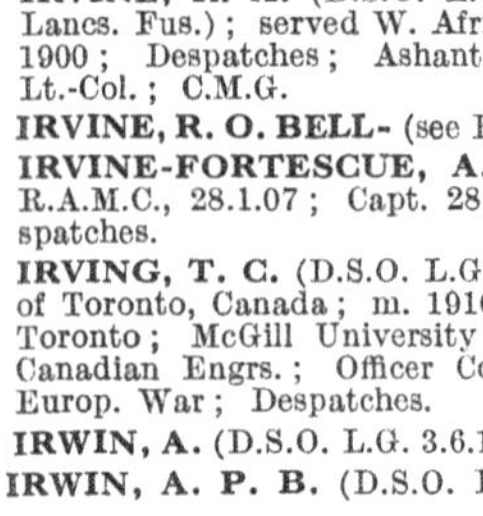

N. M. S. Irwin.

IRWIN, J. B. (D.S.O. L.G. 1.1.19), T/Lt. (A/Capt.), 1st Bn. R. Lancs. R., att. 12th Trench Mortar By.; M.C.

IRWIN, J. M. (D.S.O. L.G. 1.1.19), Major, 7th Brig. Aust. F.A.

IRWIN, N. L. C. (D.S.O. L.G. 26.9.17) (Details, L.G. 9.1.18), T/Capt., R.W. Fus.

IRWIN, N. M. S. (D.S.O. L.G. 1.1.18) (1st Bar, L.G. 24.9.18) (2nd Bar, L.G. 11.1.19); b. 24.12.92; s. of W. S. Irwin; m. Margaret Maud, d. of late B. Bavin, and widow of Lt.-Col. S. G. Mallock, Essex R.; one s.; educ. Marlborough College; R.M.C., Sandhurst; joined the Essex R., 1912; Major; served France with Batt., Aug. 1914; commanded 2nd Linc. R., 1918; 1st Bn. Linc. R., 1918–19; Temp. Col., Sub-District Commandant, Avesnes, Abbeville, May to Dec. 1919; M.C; Croix de Guerre; 1914 Star; Despatches five times; played hockey for Battalion and once for Army; three years Marlborough College Shooting VIII.; one year Captain of Shooting VIII.

Rev. R. J. B. Irwin.

IRWIN, REV. R. J. B. (D.S.O. L.G. 22.12.16); b. 1.8.80; o. s. of late Rev. A. Irwin, of Richmunt, co. Longford, and Alicia, d. of W. D. Dent, J.P.; educ. Winchester; Keble College, Oxford (M.A.); ordained 1905; Chaplain in India, 1909–14; served Europ. War, 1914–18; Despatches; M.C. and Bar; Croix de Guerre; special promotion to Senior Chaplain; was Chaplain-General of 4th Army; Canon of Allahabad Cathedral since 1920.

IRWIN, R. S. (D.S.O. L.G. 3.6.18); b. 3.10.86; Capt. (from Spec. Res. R.), Highrs. 1.7.16; Temp. Lt.-Col. 7.8.16.

ISAAC, A. G. F. (D.S.O. L.G. 15.2.19) (Details, L.G. 30.7.19); b. 26.9.86; 2nd Lt., R. Berks. R., 29.8.06; Lt. 16.2.10; Capt. 19.12.14; Bt. Major 1.1.17; M.C.

ISAAC, T. W. T. (D.S.O. L.G. 3.6.19); b. 25.12.80; 2nd Lt., Lancs. Fus. 18.4.00; Lt. 21.10.00; Capt. 7.11.06; Major, Glos. R., 1.9.15; served S. African War, 1901–2; Queen's Medal, 5 clasps; Europ. War; Despatches.

ISACKE, C. V. (D.S.O. L.G. 15.2.17); b. 20.1.70; 2nd Lt., Conn. R., 1.3.90; Lt. 9.1.93; Capt. 13.3.00; Major 1.3.10; Lt.-Col. 23.5.21.

ISBESTER, C. J. F. (D.S.O. L.G. 8.3.19) (Details, L.G. 4.10.19), Major, 10th Bn. Can. Rly. Troops.

ISGAR, R. C. D. (D.S.O. L.G. 11.6.19), Lt.-Cdr. (now Cdr.), R.N.V.R.

ISMAY, H. L. (D.S.O. L.G. 29.11.20); b. 21.6.87; 2nd Lt. 5.8.05; Lt., Ind. Army, 5.11.07; Capt. 5.8.14; Bt. Major 1.1.18; Major 5.8.20; 21st Cav., Ind. Army, att. Somaliland Camel Corps; served N.W. Frontier of India, 1908 (Medal, with clasp); Europ. War; Despatches.

IVEY, T. (D.S.O. L.G. 3.6.18); b. 20.9.81; 2nd Lt., R. Ir. R., 1.10.14; Lt. 15.3.15; M.G.C., March, 1915, to March, 1916; Capt. 1.1.17.

IZAT, W. R. (D.S.O. L.G. 1.1.18); b. 27.8.77; s. of Alex. Izat, C.I.E., of Balliliesk, Dollar; 2nd Lt., R.E., 31.12.96; Lt. 31.12.99; Capt. 31.12.05; Major 30.10.14; Bt. Lt.-Col. 3.6.19; served Europ. War in Salonika; Despatches twice.

IZOD, P. (D.S.O. L.G. 7.2.18), T/Major (A/Lt.-Col.), A.S.C.

JACK, E. M. (D.S.O. L.G. 1.1.17); b. 31.7.73; s. of late Evan A. Jack; educ. Credition, and Hastings Grammar Schools; R.M.A., Woolwich; commissioned in R.E. 25.7.93; Lt. 25.7.96; Capt. 1.4.04; Major 25.7.13; Lt.-Colonel 1.1.21; served S. African War; went to France, Aug. 1914; Bt. Lt.-Col. 3.6.15; C.M.G.; Belgian Ordre de la Couronne; Belgian Croix de Guerre; French Legion of Honour; American Distinguished Service Medal; Founder's Medal, R. Geographical Society, 1919.

JACK, F. C. (D.S.O. L.G. 16.9.18), Lt. (A/Major), R.F.A.; M.C.

JACK, J. C. (D.S.O. L.G. 26.7.18); b. 22.8.76; e. s. of late Alexander Jack; educ. Merchant Taylors' School, Crosby; passed into Indian Civil Service, 1898; commissioned R.F.A. Spec. Reserve, May, 1915; promoted Capt., and to command of 4 Gun Battery, R.F.A., in the spring of 1916; afterwards Major; Despatches several times; M.C. and Bar. He died on 31.5.18 of wounds received in action near Amiens. A senior officer wrote: "On General Congreve's recommendation his promotion to the rank of Lt.-Col. to command a battalion of infantry was sanctioned, and received at Corps Headquarters on the date of his death, so I regret he never knew this. . . . He was to have been made a Brig.-Gen. as soon as possible."

J. C. Jack.

JACK, J. L. (D.S.O. L.G. 18.6.17) (Bar, L.G. 2.4.19) (Details, L.G. 10.12.19); b. 18.4.80; 2nd Lt., Sco. Rif., 4.9.03; Lt. 14.4.09; Capt. 5.3.13; Major 9.9.18; Bt. Lt.-Col. 10.9.18; retired with rank of Brig.-Gen. 22.4.21. His D.S.O. was awarded for gallantry on 18.14.17 at Villers Gurzlaines; Despatches.

JACKSON, A. H. K. (D.S.O. L.G. 4.6.17); s. of A. Hardie Jackson; educ. J. W. Hawtrey's; Charterhouse; Sandhurst; joined 1st Batt. R. Warwicks. R. 5.2.13; Lt. 25.6.14; Capt. 2.10.15; served Europ. War in France from Aug. 1914; Staff Captain, April, 1916; Brig. Major, Sept. 1916; M.C.

JACKSON, A. N. S. STRODE (see Strode-Jackson, A. N. S.).

JACKSON, B. (D.S.O. L.G. 14.1.16); b. 15.5.81; s. of Francis Henry Jackson; educ. Charterhouse; joined the Territorial Force, 1900; Capt. (T/Major), Yorks. R. (T.F.); served Europ. War from April, 1915 to 1918; Despatches. He died 9.8.20.

JACKSON, B. A. (D.S.O. L.G. 3.6.19), T/Major, 8th Bn. Shrops. L. Inf., att. 9th Bn. R. Lancaster R.; M.C.

JACKSON, C. H. I. (D.S.O. L.G. 3.6.19); b. 4.4.77; 2nd Lt., R. Scots. Fus., 5.1.98; Lt. 9.10.99; Capt. 31.1.02; Major 1.9.15; Temp. Col. 25.3.18; served S. African War, 1901–2; Queen's Medal, 5 clasps; King's Medal, clasp; Europ. War; Despatches.

JACKSON, D. B. M. (D.S.O. L.G. 19.11.17), 2nd Lt. (A/Capt.), Sea. Highrs.

JACKSON, D. R. H. (D.S.O. L.G. 3.4.23), Major, 2/6th Gurkha Rifles, I.A.

JACKSON, E. (D.S.O. L.G. 16.9.18), Lt. (A/Major), R.E. (T.F.); served Europ. War; M.C. He died of wounds 15.4.18.

JACKSON, E. C. (D.S.O. L.G. 22.1.16), T/Capt., 5th Can. Inf. Bn.

JACKSON, E. D. (D.S.O. L.G. 1.1.18) (1st Bar, L.G. 4.2.18) (Details, L.G. 5.7.18) (2nd Bar, L.G. 2.12.18); b. 16.9.84; 2nd Lt., K.O.S.B., 28.1.05; Lt. 13.2.07; Capt. 19.2.14; Bt. Major 1.1.19.

JACKSON, E. S. (D.S.O. L.G. 1.2.17); b. 1872; Capt., R. of O., late Welsh R.; served S. African War, 1900–1; wounded; Queen's Medal and 4 clasps; Europ. War, 1914–18; Despatches; C.M.G.; Bt. Major.

JACKSON, F. A. (D.S.O. L.G. 7.2.18); b. 11.3.74; 2nd Lt., R.W. Kent R., 24.6.96; Lt., Ind. Army, 10.3.99; Capt. 24.6.05; Major 24.6.14; served N. Frontier of India, 1897–98 (Medal with clasp); Nile Expedition, 1898; Medal, Egyptian Medal with clasp; N.W. Frontier of India, 1901–2; clasp; N.W. Frontier of India, 1908; Despatches; Medal with clasp; Europ. War; Despatches.

JACKSON, F. W. (D.S.O. L.G. 1.1.18), T/Major, A.S.C.

JACKSON, F. W. F. (D.S.O. L.G. 1.1.17); b. 3.7.81; s. of Francis W. Jackson, M.A.; m. Ethel, d. of late F. Gray; 2nd Lt., R.A., 17.3.00; Lt. 3.4.01; was seconded under the Colonial Office, 1904; retired from the Army and joined the Special Reserve, 1909; services lent to Imperial Government, 1915; served S. African War, 1900–1 (Despatches; Queen's Medal, 4 clasps); Europ. War in France, 1915; Despatches thrice.

JACKSON, G. H. N. (D.S.O. L.G. 27.9.01) (Bar, L.G. 1.2.19), Major, Bt. Col., Bord. Regt. (see "The Distinguished Service Order," from its institution to 31.12.15, by same publishers).

JACKSON, G. S., M.D. (D.S.O. L.G. 3.6.16) (Bar, L.G. 18.1.18) (Details, L.G. 25.4.18); s. of late D. Jackson, M.D.; m. Maud, d. of late C. Harrison; one s.; two d.; educ. Durham School; Glasgow University; Lt.-Col. Commanding 1/7th Batt. North'd Fus., T.F., since 20.4.15; transferred to R.A.M.C., Jan. 1918, and commanded 30 General Hospital till June, 1919; served Europ.

War, including 2nd Battle of Ypres; Despatches six times; Bt. Lt.-Col.; has played for University at Rugby football; held W. of Scotland and Lanarkshire Championship for tennis for three years.

JACKSON, H. C. (D.S.O. L.G. 14.1.16); b. 12.8.79; s. of H. Jackson, O.M., and Margaret Edith, d. of E. Thornton; m. Dorothy Nina, d. of late General Lord William Seymour; educ. Haileybury; Trinity College, Cambridge; 2nd Lt., 1st Bedfordshire R., 4.1.99; Lt. 23.2.00; Capt. 2.11.06; Adjt. 1903–6; Major 3.2.15; Bt. Lt.-Col. 3.6.17; Bt. Col. 1.1.19; Colonel 2.6.19; T/Col. Commandant 1.1.21; served Europ. War, 1914–18; Despatches eight times; C.B.; Bt. Colonel; C.M.G.

JACKSON, HERBERT SELWYN (D.S.O. L.G. 4.2.18) (Details, L.G. 5.7.18); s. of P. R. Jackson; Capt., W. Riding Regt.

JACKSON, HUGH STANLEY (D.S.O. L.G. 25.8.17), Major, R.A.

JACKSON, H. W. (D.S.O. L.G. 1.1.18); b. 9.6.72; 2nd Lt., Midd'x R., 5.12.91; Lt., I.S.C., 23.8.93; Capt., Ind. Army, 10.7.01; Major 5.12.06; Bt. Lt.-Col. 1.1.17; Lt.-Col. 5.12.17; Bt. Col. 3.6.19; Colonel 3.6.20; T/Brig.-Gen. 30.9.18; T/Col. on Staff 1.1.21; served in Burma, 1895–96; Europ. War; Despatches; C.S.I.

JACKSON, L. C. (D.S.O. L.G. 4.6.17); b. 28.9.75; s. of late H. Jackson; m. Olive Margaret, d. of late Sir Howard Elphinstone, V.C., K.C.B., C.M.G.; two s.; educ. Clifton College; Woolwich; 2nd Lt., R.E., 3.8.95; Lt. 3.8.98; Capt. 3.8.04; Adjt., R.E., 5.8.14 to 2.11.14; Major 30.10.14; Bt. Lt.-Col. 3.6.16; served S. Africa, 1900–2; Queen's Medal with 3 clasps; King's Medal with 2 clasps; C.M.G. in 1908 for Military Survey of O.R. Colony; served Europ. War, 1914–18; Despatches six times; Bt. Lt.-Col.; Order of the Crown of Roumania (Officier), 1914; Star with clasp.

JACKSON, L. W. de V. SADLEIR- (see Sadleir-Jackson, L. W. de V.).

JACKSON, M. H. (D.S.O. L.G. 8.3.19) (Details, L.G. 4.10.19); b. 24.11.82; 2nd Lt., Ind. Army, 19.7.05; Lt. 19.10.07; Capt. 19.7.14; Major 19.7.20; M.C.

JACKSON, R. D. (D.S.O. L.G. 15.2.19) (Details, L.G. 30.7.19); b. 25.4.86; 2nd Lt., R.E., 20.9.04; Lt. 23.6.07; Capt. 30.10.14; M.C.

JACKSON, R. E. (D.S.O. L.G. 1.1.18), Lt.-Col., Aust. Inf.

JACKSON, R. N. (D.S.O. L.G. 1.1.19); b. 23.2.87; s. of Frederic Nevill Jackson; m. Jennie, d. of J. Suggitt, J.P., of W. Hartlepool; one s.; educ. Felsted; London Rifle Brigade Territorials, July, 1914; wounded; commission, 2nd Lt., General List, 27.2.15; Liaison Officer with French Army as Acting Major, April, 1918 (Croix de Guerre with Gold Star; cité 2nd time; Croix de Guerre, cité 3rd time; Croix de Guerre; Despatches); Chevalier, Legion of Honour.

R. N. Jackson.

JACKSON, R. R. B. (D.S.O. L.G. 1.1.18); b. 15.12.74; 2nd Lt., R. Muns. Fus., 28.9.95; Lt. 4.12.97; Capt., A.S.C., 31.12.09; Major 30.10.14; served S. African War, 1899–1902; (Despatches; Queen's Medal, 3 clasps; King's Medal, 2 clasps); Europ. War; Despatches.

JACKSON, SIR T. D., Bart. (D.S.O. L.G. 31.10.02) (Bar, L.G. 1.1.18), Major and Brevet Lt.-Col., R. Lanc. Regt.; M.V.O. (see "The Distinguished Service Order," from its institution to 31.12.15, by same publishers).

JACKSON, V. A. (D.S.O. L.G. 1.1.17); b. 1.9.82; m. D. E. Garthside Spaight, of Derry Castle, Killaloe, co. Clare, Ireland; educ. Wellington College, Berks; 2nd Lt., York. and Lanc. R., 29.1.02; Lt. 12.3.03; Capt. 1.9.11; Major 6.1.17; Bt. Lt.-Col. 1.1.19; served Europ. War; Despatches five times; Belgian Croix de Guerre.

JACKSON, W. L. (D.S.O. L.G. 20.9.18); s. of late W. M. Jackson; m. Evelyn, d. of late W. V. Gilchrist; one d.; educ. H.M.S. Britannia; ent. R.N., 1904; Lt.-Cdr., 1918; served Europ. War on the Belgian Coast from 1915 to the Armistice; commanded the Naval Guard of Honour which received F.M. Lord Haigh and his Generals when they landed at Dover after the Armistice. D.S.O. awarded for services in monitors on the Belgian Coast; Chevalier, Star of Roumania and Belgian Croix de Guerre.

JACOB, A. F. F. (D.S.O. L.G. 1.1.19), Capt. (Acting Major), R.A.F.

JACOB, A. L. B. (D.S.O. L.G. 1.1.18); b. 9.4.74; 2nd Lt., R.A., 4.7.94; Lt. 14.7.97; Capt. 28.5.00; Major 30.10.14; Lt.-Col. 1.1.21.

JACOB, W. H. B. (D.S.O. L.G. 1.1.19); b. 13.6.71; s. of T. W. Jacob (late of War Office) and Louisa, d. of late William Bell; m. Mildred Jessie (who died in 1920), d. of late Capt. Horatio Paul; educ. St. Paul's School; R.M.A., Woolwich; 2nd Lt., R.G.A., 27.7.89; Lt. 27.7.92; Capt. 13.9.99; Major 7.10.99; Lt.-Col. 18.6.96; Lt.-Col.; retired pay 1.7.21; served S. African War; Despatches; Queen's Medal and 2 clasps; Europ. War; Serbian White Eagle with Swords, 4th Class; Italian Croce di Guerra.

JACOBS, L. M. (D.S.O. L.G. 8.3.19) (Details, L.G. 4.10.19), T/Capt., 2nd Bn. S.A. Mil. Forces.

JACQUES, H. M. (D.S.O. L.G. 14.11.16), Lt.-Col., Can. A.M.C. His D.S.O. was awarded for gallantry on 15–18.9.16 at Albert.

JAGO, H. H. (D.S.O. L.G. 26.7.18), 2nd Lt. (A/Capt.), Devons. Regt.; M.C.

JAMES, A. H. (D.S.O. L.G. 1.1.18) (Bar, L.G. 18.2.18) (Details, L.G. 18.7.18); b. 1877; s. of the late W. E. A. James; educ. Clifton College; commissioned in the North'd Fus.; wounded at Gallipoli; and as second-in-command of his battalion took part in the Battle of the Somme from the beginning; later he was promoted to command of a battalion of the W. Yorks. R.; Despatches twice. He was killed in action 26.3.18 at Macquoy, France.

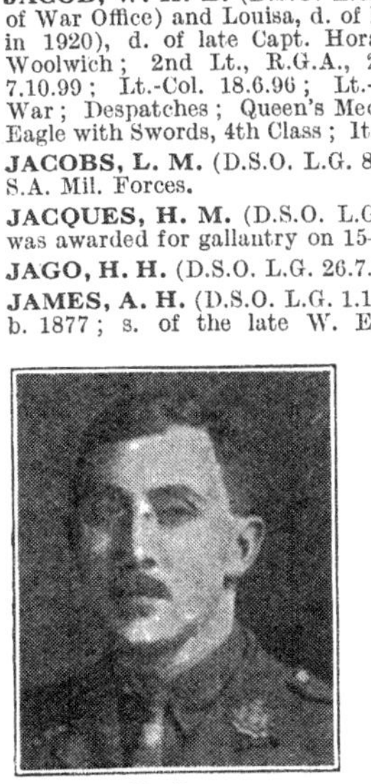

C. K. James.

JAMES, A. J. S. (D.S.O. L.G. 3.6.18), T/Major (A/Lt.-Col.), R.W.F.; served Europ. War; M.C. He was killed in action 28.3.18.

JAMES, B. C. (D.S.O. L.G. 1.1.17), T/Lt.-Col., Devons. R.

JAMES, C. K. (D.S.O. L.G. 14.11.16) (Bar, L.G. 4.2.18) (Details, L.G. 5.7.18), T/Maj. (A/Lt.-Col.), The Border R. He was killed in action 19.5.18.

JAMES, C. P. (D.S.O. L.G. 1.1.17) (Bar, L.G. 26.11.17) (Details, L.G. 6.4.18); b. 5.3.79; 2nd Lt., A. and S. Highrs., 4.7.00; Lt. 20.9.04; Capt. 1.2.13; Major 1.9.15; Bt. Lt.-Col. 1.1.18; served Europ. War; Despatches.

E. G. James.

JAMES, E. (D.S.O. L.G. 26.7.18); b. 21.10.83; 2nd Lt., Linc. R., 4.7.03; Lt. 12.2.06; Capt. (from Spec. Res.), 15.8.16; served Europ. War; Despatches; M.C.

JAMES, E. G. (D.S.O. L.G. 14.11.16); b. 25.8.93; s. of Francis R. James, Solicitor, of Hereford; educ. Cheltenham; 2nd Lt., King's Shrops. L. Inf., 15.8.14; Lt., May, 1915; Capt., Aug. 1915; served Europ. War in France; Despatches (L.G. 30.4.16; L.G. 23.12.15). He died of wounds 15.10.16. His Colonel wrote of him: "The only thing I can say is that if ever a man deserved the D.S.O. Jimmie did." His D.S.O. was awarded for gallantry 15–18.9.16 at Quadrilateral.

JAMES, L. (D.S.O. L.G. 16.9.18); b. 1871; s. of late Lt.-Col. L. H. S. James, R.A.; educ. Cranleigh; Reuter's Special Correspondent in Chitral Campaign, 1894–95; Mohmund, Malakand and Tirah Campaigns, 1897–98; Sudan, 1898; on Staff of "Times," 1899; "Times" Special Correspondent in S. Africa, 1899–1901; America and Macedonia, 1903; Manchuria, 1904; India, 1907; N.W. Frontier, India, 1908; Persia and Turkey, 1908; Balkans, 1909; with the Spanish Army in Morocco, 1909; with the Turkish Army in Albania, 1910; with the French on the march to Fez, 1911; with the Italians in Tripoli, 1911; with the Turks in Thrace, 1912; with the Bulgarians in Thrace, 1913; retired from journalism and the Staff of the "Times," 1913; commanded King Edward's Horse with B.E.F., France and Italy, 1915–18; Despatches twice; Crown of Italy. He has written many books.

JAMES, P. C. (D.S.O. L.G. 1.1.17), Temp. Lt.-Col., Devon Regt.

JAMES, R. E. H. (D.S.O. L.G. 1.1.18); b. 31.10.75; 2nd Lt., N. Lancs. R., 29.5.95; Lt. 2.10.97; Capt. 24.12.01; Bt. Major 29.7.11; Bt. Lt.-Col. 3.6.15; retired with rank of Lt.-Col. 16.11.19; served China, 1900; Medal; Europ. War; Despatches; C.M.G.

JAMES, R. STREATFIELD- (see Streatfield-James, R.).

JAMES, T. B. W. (D.S.O. L.G. 17.12.17) (Details, L.G. 23.4.18), Major, Aust. F.A.

JAMES, W. E. (D.S.O. L.G. 3.6.18) (Bar, L.G. 2.4.19) (Details, L.G. 10.12.19), Lt.-Col., 24th Battn. Aust. Inf.

JAMES, W. G. (D.S.O. L.G. 4.2.18) (Details, L.G. 5.7.18); s. of Tom James, of Rodborough; educ. Rodborough Council School; formerly a Sergt. in S. Western Mounted Brigade Field Ambulance; joined the Army, Feb. 1915; obtained a commission as T/2nd Lt., K.O.Y.L.Inf.; became Captain; served Europ. War in France; Despatches. His elder brother, Sergt. H. E. James, was killed in action in France.

JAMES, W. H., M.R.C.V.S. (D.S.O. L.G. 7.2.18); m. Miss Wall, of Frome, e. d. of late T. Wall; T/Capt., A.V.C. (now R.A.V.C.); promoted Major, and given the staff appointment of Assistant Director of Veterinary Services to the Mesopotamia Field Force. His D.S.O. was awarded for services in Mesopotamia.

JAMESON, E. J. (D.S.O. L.G. 3.6.16); b. 11.6.75; 1st commission 15.5.97; Capt. 27.6.03; retired 23.4.10; Leins. R., Spec. Res.; served S. African War; Despatches; Queen's Medal, 7 clasps; King's Medal, 2 clasps; Europ. War; Despatches. He died of wounds 27.3.17.

JAMESON, F. R. W. (D.S.O. L.G. 15.10.18), T/Lt., R.E.; M.C.

JAMESON, J. H. (D.S.O. L.G. 13.2.17); b. 12.11.89; Lt. (from S.R.) 22.6.16; Capt. 22.6.19, L'pool Regt., S.R.; served Europ. War.

JAMESON, T. H. (D.S.O. L.G. 8.3.20); b. 10.12.94; s. of Robert William Jameson and Catherine Anne; educ. Monkton Combe School, nr. Bath, Somerset; 2nd Lt., R.M.L.I., 1.10.13; Lt. 19.9.14; Capt. 11.11.17; served with Royal Marine Brigade in 1914, Lille and Antwerp; Gallipoli, 1915, in H.M.S. Resolution, 1916–17; H.M.S. Kent, 1918 to 1919; in command of detachment of Royal Marines from H.M.S. Kent, who volunteered to form part of and assist Admiral Kolchak's Russian Naval Flotilla on the River Kama (Russia). "This force proceeded inland from Vladivostok to Perm, and there, in six days, mounted guns and other equipment in two ships, and in company with similar ships manned with Russian crews took part against the Bolsheviks on the Eastern front, successfully engaged the 'Red' Flotilla (sinking three of their ships) and supported the retirement of the Siberian forces until the fall of Perm. Whilst performing this latter rôle, the Flotilla was more than once cut off." Despatches, 1915.

JAMESON, W. K. E. (D.S.O. L.G. 12.12.19); b. 15.5.76; 2nd Lt., R.A., 22.10.97; Capt. 23.1.04; Lt.-Col. 14.6.18; retired 10.3.21; served S. African War, 1899–1900; Queen's Medal with clasp; Europ. War; Despatches.

JAMIESON, J. P. (D.S.O. L.G. 2.12.18), 2nd Lt. (A/Capt.), Middx. Regt., S.R., att 4th Bn.

JAMIESON, W. F. (D.S.O. L.G. 18.1.18) (Details, L.G. 25.4.18), Lt., Can. Inf.

JANION, C. W. J. (D.S.O. L.G. 20.10.16), Temp. 2nd Lt., E. Surr. Regt. His D.S.O. was awarded for services on 1.7.16 at Montauban.

JANSON, J. T. (D.S.O. L.G. 4.6.17) (Bar, L.G. 18.2.18) (Details, L.G. 18.7.18), T/Major (A/Lt.-Col.), Yorks. L. Inf.

JARDINE, C. A. (D.S.O. L.G. 11.11.14) (Bar, L.G. 24.9.18), Capt., R.F.A. (see "The Distinguished Service Order," from its institution to 31.12.15, by same publishers).

JARDINE, C. W. BAYNE- (see Bayne-Jardine, C. W.).

JARDINE, L. H. (D.S.O. L.G. 1.2.19) (Bar, L.G. 8.3.19) (Details, L.G. 4.10.19); m. Agnes Wreford Maud, d. of late E. A. Lewis; Colonel, 3rd Rifle Brigade, N.Z. Forces; M.C.

JARDINE, T. E. BAYNE- (see Bayne-Jardine, T. E.).

JARRETT, C. (D.S.O. L.G. 1.1.18), Major, Midd'x R.; served in S. Africa, 1900; Queen's Medal, 4 clasps; Europ. War; Despatches.

JARVIS, C. (D.S.O. L.G. 3.6.19), Major, 20th Deccan Horse, Ind. Army; M.C.

JARVIS, E. H. (D.S.O. L.G. 3.6.16), Major, 4th R. Innisk. Fus., S.R.; served S. African War, 1899–1901 (Queen's Medal, 2 clasps); Europ. War, 1914–18; Despatches.

JARVIS, F. W. (D.S.O. L.G. 1.1.19), Lt.-Col., Suff. Yeom.

JARVIS, T. McL. (D.S.O. L.G. 4.6.17) (Bar, L.G. 19.11.17) (Details, L.G. 22.3.18); commissioned in Queen's Regt., and went to France as second-in-command of a battalion, which he commanded for some time; commanded a battalion, K.R.R.C.; T/Lt.-Col. 17.10.16; served Europ. War, in the Battle of the Somme; Messines Ridge; wounded.

JATAR, NILKRANTH SKRIRĀM (D.S.O. L.G. 4.6.17) (Bar, L.G. 27.9.20); b. 26.5.87; s. of late Rao Bahadur S. B. Jatar, C.I.E.; m. Bhagirathi, d. of G. R. Moghe, of Sion, Bombay; two d.; educ. Poona High School; G. M. College, Bombay; University College Hospital, London; L.M.S., Bombay University; L.R.C.P. (London); M.R.C.S. (England); commissioned in I.M.S., 1914; Captain; served with Indian Exp. Force, in Mesopotamia, 1915 and 1916; Despatches; Serbian Order of White Eagle, 5th Class with Swords; prisoner of war with the Turks 29.4.16 to 11.11.18; served with Waziristan F.F. 1919–20; Bar to D.S.O.

JAY, C. D. (D.S.O. L.G. 4.6.17); s. of Rev. W. P. Jay; m. Kathleen H., d. of late D. L. Beddington; one s.; T/Major, M.G.C.; served Europ. War; relinquished commission, 1921.

JAYNE, A. A. (D.S.O. L.G. 1.1.18), T/Capt. (A/Major), R.E.; M.C.

JEFFERIES, H. ST. J. (D.S.O. L.G. 26.9.17) (Details, L.G. 9.1.18); b. 24.3.80; 2nd Lt., Worc. R., 24.4.00; Lt. 2.1.01; Capt. 15.5.07; Major 26.10.15; served S. African War, 1899–1902; Queen's Medal, 4 clasps; Europ. War; Despatches. His D.S.O. was awarded for gallantry at Mouquet Farm 13–15.8.16.

JEFFERSON, H. A. F. (gazetted as Jefferson, H. A.) (D.S.O. L.G. 11.4.18); b. 22.2.93; s. of George Arthur Jefferson; educ. King's School, Chester; St. Mary's College, Holywell, N. Wales; at the time of the outbreak of war was farming in Nova Scotia, Canada, and returned to England in command of 300 reservists rejoining the colours; Major, 1/5th Bn. Royal Welch Fusiliers, 12.4.11; A/Lt.-Col., Feb. 1919; att. 158th Bde., H.Q.; A/Bde. Major, 158th Bde., Sept. 1918; served Europ. War, 10.8.15 to 3.12.15, Suvla Bay; Dec. 1915, to Aug. 1916, Western Desert, Egypt; Jan. 1917, Palestine; mentioned in Despatches, Sept. 1918; wounded in attack on Tel-Asur, Palestine, 9.3.18.

H. A. F. Jefferson.

JEFFERSON, J. A. DUNNINGTON- (see Dunnington-Jefferson, J. A.).

JEFFREY, D. G. (D.S.O. L.G. 17.11.17), Lt., R.N.R.

JEFFREYS, J. W. (D.S.O. L.G. 14.1.16); b. 24.9.77; s. of J. Jeffreys; m. Evelyn Katherine, d. of late Major G. Douglas, R.M.A.; two s.; 2nd Lt., Durh. L. Inf., 4.5.98; Lt. 7.2.00; Capt. 31.7.03; Major 1.9.15; Bt. Lt.-Col. 3.6.19; served S. African War, 1899–1902; Queen's Medal, 5 clasps; King's Medal, 2 clasps; served Europ. War, 1914–18; wounded; Despatches; Bt. Lt.-Col.

JEFFREYS, R. G. B. (D.S.O. L.G. 1.1.18); b. 28.3.75; 2nd Lt., R. Dub. Fus., 8.2.99; Lt. 16.12.99; Capt. 28.12.05; Major 1.9.15; S. African War; Despatches; Queen's Medal, 5 clasps; King's Medal, 2 clasps; Europ. War; Despatches.

JEFFRIES, L. W. (D.S.O. L.G. 14.11.16), Major, Aust. A.M.C.

JEFFRIES, W. F. (D.S.O. L.G. 26.7.18), Capt. (A/Major), R. Dub. Fus., S.R.

JELLICOE, R. C., B.A., LL.D. (D.S.O. L.G. 3.6.18); b. 1875; m. Sophia Mary, d. of late Bt. Col. F. Howard, R.A.; one s.; educ. Trinity College, Dublin University; commission in Army, 1900; 2nd Lt., A.S.C., 22.5.00; Lt. 1.6.01; Capt. 1.10.04; Major 30.10.14; Bt. Lt.-Col. 3.6.17; Lt.-Col. 4.7.21; Director of Labour (T/Brig.-Gen.), 1917–20; served S. African War, 1901–2 (Medal and 4 clasps); served with G.H.Q., Mediterranean and Egyptian Exp. Forces during Europ. War; Despatches five times; Bt. Lt.-Col.; C.B.E.; White Eagle of Serbia with Swords; Order of the Nile, 3rd Class.

JELLICOE, R. V. (D.S.O. L.G. 3.6.16), Major (R. of O.), late R.E.

JENKIN, F. C. (D.S.O. L.G. 26.8.18); b. 31.10.79; 2nd Lt., R.A., 12.5.00; Lt. 14.5.01; Capt. 12.5.13; Major 30.12.15; Bt. Lt.-Col. 10.3.17; Europ. War; despatches.

JENKINS, H. H. (D.S.O. L.G. 1.1.19). Lt.-Colonel H. H. Jenkins commanded the 1st S. African Inf. on the Western front, and when the S. African Brigade returned to England, was given command of the 46th Royal Fusiliers in Sadleir Jackson's Brigade, in the North Russian Relief Force. During the offensive against the Bolshevist forces Lt.-Col. Jenkins commanded the forces on the right bank of the Dwina, and the three columns under his command inflicted a severe defeat upon the enemy, capturing over 1,000 prisoners, nine guns, and a large number of machine guns, trench mortars and stores (C.M.G.; Despatches). Lt.-Col. Jenkins was twice wounded on the Western front, and served with the S. African Brigade in Egypt, and the 2nd Kimberley Regiment in German S.W. Africa; 2nd Class Order of St. Anna, and the French Croix de Guerre.

JENKINS, J. S. (D.S.O. L.G. 4.6.17); m. E. Louisa Macleod Mitchell; educ. Loyala College, Montreal; Lt.-Col., Can. A.M.C.; served Europ. War; Despatches thrice.

JENKINS, L. (D.S.O. L.G. 1.1.18), Lt.-Col. Dorset R.G.A. and R.F.C.; served Europ. War; Despatches. He died of pneumonia 20.11.18; M.C.

JENKINS, M. I. G. (D.S.O. L.G. 3.6.18); b. 17.9.81; 2nd Lt., Devon R., 14.9.01; Lt. 2.3.04; Capt. 3.1.13; Major 24.10.15; served S. African War, 1901–2; Queen's Medal, 5 clasps; Europ. War; Despatches.

JENKINS, W. J. G. (D.S.O. L.G. 3.6.18), Major, Devon Regt.

JENNER, L. C. D. (D.S.O. L.G. 3.6.16); b. 24.10.69; 5th s. of Sir William Jenner, 1st Bart.; m. Nora Helen Gertrude, d. of Field-Marshal Sir Donald Stewart, 1st Bart.; educ. Marlborough and Sandhurst; 2nd Lt., K.R.R., 1888; Adjt., 1891–95; Capt., 1896; retired 1904; rejoined Army on mobilization, Aug. 1914; served Egypt, April–July, 1915; Gallipoli, Aug.–Dec. 1915; Despatches; France, June, 1916–April, 1919; Despatches three times; C.M.G.; Officer of the Order of the Crown of Roumania; promoted to Lt.-Col.; won Army Fencing Championship, Royal Military Tournament, 1894–95; Joint Polo Manager, Ranelagh Club, 1904–11, when he resigned; winning teams Roehampton Cup, 1905, 1907–10; Open Cup, Ranelagh, 1908; Champion Cup, 1907; Public Schools Cup, 8 years; selected to play for England v. Ireland, 1907.

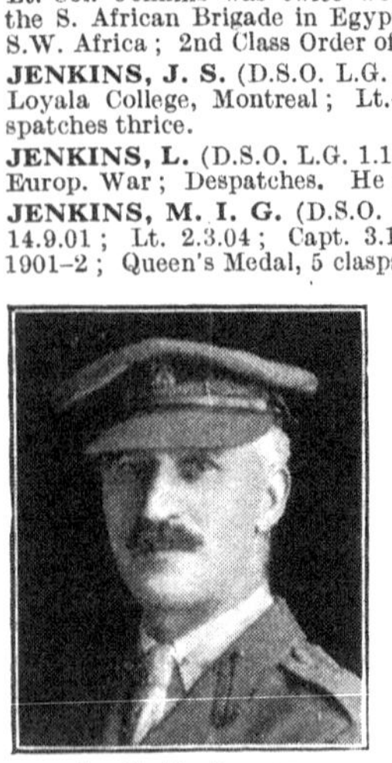

L. C. D. Jenner.

JENNER, SIR W. K. W., Bart. (D.S.O. L.G. 1.1.18); b. 12.10.60; s. of Sir W. Jenner, 1st Bart., Physician, and Adela, d. of S. Adey; m. Flora (who died in 1921), d. of Field-Marshal Sir Donald Stewart, 1st Bart.; one d.; educ. Charterhouse; Sandhurst; Staff College, Camberley; 2nd Lt. 16.10.80; Major 12.3.98; retired 27.9.02; Lt.-Col. 5.12.16; Bt. Lt.-Col. 1.1.19; Lt.-Col. (Retired Pay), late 9th Lancers; rejoined Army, Aug. 1914; Despatches three times.

JENNINGS, D. C. (D.S.O. L.G. 7.11.18); b. 10.3.92, at Canterbury, England; s. of John Adolphus and Anne Mary Jennings; m. a d. of J. J. Magrath; one s.; one d.; Major, Can. Inf.; served Europ. War; Despatches. Major Jennings has done a good deal of big game shooting in British Columbia, and has explored parts of the Mackenzie River District in the far north.

JENNINGS, W. (D.S.O. L.G. 4.6.17); b. 29.6.68; 2nd Lt., R.A., 17.2.88; Lt. 17.2.91; Capt. 18.6.98; Major 1.9.07; Lt.-Col. 17.9.15; retired 7.3.21; served N.W. Frontier of India, 1897–98; Medal with clasp; Europ. War; Despatches.

JENNINGS, W. I. K. (D.S.O. L.G. 1.1.19), Major, N.Z.M.G.C.

JENNINGS-BRAMLEY, A. W. (D.S.O. L.G. 23.11.16); b. 27.3.75; s. of John Robert Jennings-Bramley; m. 7.9.07, Mary Dorothy, d. of H. C. Steel, of Winchester; educ. Winchester College; R.M.C., Sandhurst; 2nd Lt., 2 Dr. Gds., 6.3.95; transferred to 20th Hussars, Nov. 1895; Lt. 5.8.98; Capt. 21.7.06; Major 9.9.11; Lt.-Col. 9.9.14; retired 1.3.17; served S. African War (Queen's Medal, 4 clasps); employed with Egyptian Army; 4th Class Medjidie; Europ. War; Despatches three times; 4th Class Serbian White Eagle with Swords, 1916.

JENOUR, A. S. (D.S.O. L.G. 1.1.18); b. 31.7.67; s. of late A. C. Jenour, M.I.C.E.; m. Emily, d. of late T. J. Beynon, J.P., D.L.; one s.; two d.; educ. private schools; R.M. Academy, Woolwich; Lt., R.A., 17.2.86; Capt. 11.4.96; Major 18.5.04; Col. 18.5.18; retired with hon. rank of Brig.-Gen. 25.3.20; served Europ. War in France, 1915–19; Despatches; C.B.; C.M.G.; French Croix de Guerre with Palm.

JERRAM, C. F. (D.S.O. L.G. 1.1.17); b. 13.11.82; s. of C. S. Jerram, M.A., and M. F., daughter of E. Knight, of Pap Castle, Cumberland; m. Sibyl V. G., d. of Dr. J. G. O'Neill, of Auckland, N.Z.; one s.; two d.; educ. Hillside, Godalming; 2nd Lt., R.M.L.I., 1.9.01; Lt. 1.7.02; Capt. 1.9.12; Major 1.9.17; posted to Plymouth Division; served in H.M.S. Hogue and Suffolk in Mediterranean under Captain (now Admiral) Beatty; H.M.S. Astræa and Flora in China (received thanks of Admiralty for reconnaissance in China); served European War, H.M.S. Euryalus, in North Sea until Nov. 1914; Staff Captain, Royal Marines Brigade, Dec. 1914; Brigade Major, June, 1915; served in action of Kum Kaleh, Feb. 1915; landed Gallipoli 26.4.15, and served during whole campaign with R. Naval Division (Despatches); G.S.O.2, 31st Division, 1917 (Despatches twice); G.S.O.1, 46th Division, 1918; C.M.G.; Despatches.

JERRAM, R. C. (D.S.O. L.G. 22.1.20), Paymaster-Lt., R.N.

JERVIS, B. C. LOCKHART- (see Lockhart-Jervis, B. C.).

JERVIS, E. C. S. (D.S.O. L.G. 18.7.17), Capt. (T/Major), R. of O., and M.G.C.; served S. African War; Queen's Medal, 5 clasps; King's Medal, 2 clasps; Europ. War; Despatches. His D.S.O. was awarded for gallantry 12.4.17 in France.

JERVIS, N. G. M. (D.S.O. L.G. 15.2.19) (Details, L.G. 30.7.19); b. 13.12.81; 2nd Lt., R.A., 6.1.00; Lt. 3.4.01; Capt. 11.8.08; Adjt. 10.11.12 to 29.10.14; Major 30.10.14; served Europ. War; Despatches.

JERVOIS, J. A. (D.S.O. L.G. 1.1.19); b. 25.7.89; 2nd Lt., Yorks. L. Inf., 18.9.09; Lt. 18.1.14; Capt. 6.2.15; Adjutant 10.5.15 to 18.2.17; served Europ. War; M.C.

JESS, C. H. (D.S.O. L.G. 1.1.17), Lt.-Col., Aust. Mil. Forces.

JESSE, J. L. (D.S.O. L.G. 14.1.16); b. 4.4.76; s. of W. Jesse; m. Mary Henrietta, d. of F. Mandy, J.P.; educ. Lancing; Pembroke College, Oxford; 2nd Lt., R.M.L.I., 1.1.97; Lt. 1.1.98; Lt., A.S.C., 1900; Capt. 7.4.02; Adjt. 17.9.10 to 15.10.13; Major 5.8.14; Lt.-Col. 26.11.20; served S. African War, 1901–2; Despatches; Queen's Medal, 2 clasps; Somaliland, 1908–10; Despatches; Medal with clasp; Europ. War, France and Italy, 1914–18; Despatches thrice; C.M.G.

JESSOP, J. DE B. (D.S.O. L.G. 1.1.17); b. 28.8.85; s. of late W. de B. Jessop, of Overton Hall, Derbyshire, and Judith, d. of Sir J. G. N. Alleyne, 3rd Bart.; m. Ethel Joane, d. of Capt. C. H. Hill, late Glouc. R.; one d.; Lt.-Cdr., R.N.; served Europ. War, 1914–18.

JESSUP, W. H. G. (D.S.O. L.G. 26.9.16), T/2nd Lt., D.C.L.I. Hon. Capt. His D.S.O. was awarded for gallantry on 18.3.16 at Delville Wood. He died of wounds 24.12.18.

JEWELS, C. E. (D.S.O. L.G. 26.7.18) (Bar, L.G. 8.3.19) (Details, L.G. 4.10.19), T/Lt.-Col., 18th Bn. Lancs. Fus.; served Europ. War; Despatches; M.C.

JOBSON, ALEX. (D.S.O. L.G. 1.1.18), Col., Aust. Inf.

JOFFE, W. (D.S.O. L.G. 4.2.18) (Details, L.G. 5.7.18), 2nd Lt., Yorks. L. Inf.

JOHNS, H. W. (D.S.O. L.G. 7.2.18), T/Major, R.E.

JOHNS, W. G. (D.S.O. L.G. 7.11.18), T/Major, K.R.R.C.

JOHNSON, A. B. (D.S.O. L.G. 1.1.18); b. 13.5.79; 2nd Lt., Linc. R., 3.8.98; Lt. 7.4.00; Capt. 5.11.05; Major 1.9.15; served S. African War; Queen's Medal, 3 clasps; King's Medal, 2 clasps; Europ. War; Despatches.

JOHNSON, A. E. (D.S.O. L.G. 3.8.20), Maj. (A/Lt.-Col.), Gurkha Rifles.

JOHNSON, A. V. (D.S.O. L.G. 1.1.18); b. 20.8.71; s. of late General Sir Charles Johnson, G.C.B., and Lady Johnson; m. Mrs. Kenna, widow of Brig.-General P. A. Kenna, V.C., D.S.O., A.D.C., and the d. of Hubert Hibbert; 2nd Lt., R. Fus., 4.3.91; Lt. 26.6.92; Capt. 1898; Major 19.12.06; Col. 12.3.20; retired 18.9.20; served in Tibet, 1903–4; Medal with clasp; Europ. War; Despatches.

JOHNSON, A. WEBB- (see Webb-Johnson, A.).

JOHNSON, B., M.B. (D.S.O. L.G. 3.6.18); b. 9.5.83; Lt., R.A.M.C., 30.7.06; Capt. 30.1.10; Bt. Major 3.6.17; Major 30.7.18; served Europ. War; Despatches.

JOHNSON, B. L. (D.S.O. L.G. 2.11.17), Lt.-Cdr., R.N.R.

JOHNSON, B. S. (D.S.O. L.G. 1.1.18); b. Jan. 1881; s. of Dr. H. Sandford Johnson, of Buckfastleigh and Totnes; m. Hope, d. of P. Power; one s.; educ. privately; joined 5th R.I. Fusiliers, 1900; R. Garrison Rgt., 1902; West African and York. and Lancs. Rgt., 1905–8; Capt., R.A.S.C., 1914; Major, 1914; A/Lt.-Col. Sept. 1915, to March, 1920; served S. Africa, 1901; Remount Dept. Operations, Transvaal and Cape Colony; Queen's Medal; 2 clasps; Europ. War, 1914; France, 1915; Italy, 1916; Despatches thrice.

JOHNSON, C. D. (D.S.O. L.G. 12.1.16); b. 1869; s. of Rev. Canon Johnson; ent. R.N., 1882; Lt., 1892; Cdr., 1903; Rear Admiral, 1920; M.V.O., 1912; served Europ. War, 1914–18; Despatches; C.B.; Officer, Legion of Honour; commanded Sixth Destroyer Flotilla.

JOHNSON, C. H. (D.S.O. L.G. 27.6.19), Eng.-Cdr., R.N.

JOHNSON, C. S. (D.S.O. L.G. 15.9.16), Paymaster, R.N.; served Europ. War in the Battle of Jutland, and action at Falkland Islands; mentioned in Despatches.

JOHNSON, D. G. (D.S.O. L.G. 16.3.15) (Bar, L.G. 11.1.19), Capt. (A/Lt.-Col.), S.W.B.; V.C.; M.C. (see " The Victoria Cross," by same publishers, also " The Distinguished Service Order," from its institution to 31.12.15, by same publishers).

JOHNSON, E. P. (D.S.O. L.G. 1.1.17), Captain, R.F.A.; brother of late Major G. B. Johnson, D.S.O., R.F.A.; served Europ. War; Despatches.

JOHNSON, F. E. (D.S.O. L.G. 1.1.17); b. 11.10.74; 2nd Lt., Glos. R., 4.3.00; Lt., A.S.C., 1.1.03; Capt. 1.5.07; Major 30.10.14; Bt. Lt.-Col. 3.6.19; Lt.-Col. 5.4.20; served S. African War, 1900; Queen's Medal, 2 clasps; Europ. War; Despatches.

JOHNSON, F. S. B. (D.S.O. L.G. 22.6.18); b. 23.2.69; 2nd Lt. 19.10. 92; Major 23.11.07; retired N. Lancs. R. 23.4.13; Major (A/Lt.-Col.), R. Sussex R.; served S. African War, 1901–2; Despatches; Queen's Medal, 5 clasps; European War; Despatches.

JOHNSON, F. W. E. (D.S.O. L.G. 11.4.18); b. 15.6.80; 2nd Lt., R. Ir. Fus., 18.4.00; Lt. 26.12.01; Capt. 1.2.10; Major 1.9.15; Bt. Lt.-Col. 3.6.19; served S. African War, 1899–1902; Queen's Medal, 3 clasps; King's Medal, 2 clasps; Europ. War; Despatches.

JOHNSON, F. W. F. (D.S.O. L.G. 3.6.18), Lt.-Col., R. Sussex R.

JOHNSON, G. B. (D.S.O. L.G. 1.1.18); s. of S. H. Johnson; educ. Greenbank School, Liverpool; Sedbergh School; for several years he took a keen interest in the Territorials, and was an Officer in the 1st West Lancashire Regt.; R.F.A.; he went to France at the end of 1915; Major Johnson was through all the fighting at Ypres and in other engagements on the Western front. He was killed in action 18.4.18. His brother, Major E. P. Johnson, also won the D.S.O.

JOHNSON, G. E. A. (D.S.O. L.G. 1.2.17), T/Lt. (Temp. Capt.), A.O.D.

JOHNSON, H. (D.S.O. L.G. 3.6.18), Major (A/Lt.-Col.), N. Staff. R.; served S. African War; Queen's Medal; 4 clasps; Europ. War; Despatches.

JOHNSON, H. A. (D.S.O. L.G. 1.1.17); b. 21.11.73; 2nd Lt., R. Inns. Fus., 29.5.95; Lt. 13.1.98; Capt. 17.6.01; Major, A.S.C., 2.2.14; Bt. Lt.-Col. 1.1.18; Lt.-Col. 15.12.18; served N.W. Frontier of India, 1897–98; Medal, 2 clasps; Europ. War; Despatches.

JOHNSON, H. C. R. (D.S.O. L.G. 8.3.18), Engr. Lt.-Cdr., R.N.

JOHNSON, HARRY HERBERT (D.S.O. L.G. 27.6.19), Eng.-Cdr., R.N.

JOHNSON, HENRY HOWARD (D.S.O. L.G. 15.10.18), Capt. (T/Major), R. Sussex R., att. Tank Corps.

JOHNSON, J. G. T., B.A. (D.S.O. L.G. 1.1.17); b. 29.7.86; s. of J. T. Johnson, of Oak Hurst, Derbyshire; m. Dorothy Babington, d. of late W. de B. Jessop, J.P., of Overton Hall, Derbyshire; two d.; educ. Fonthill; Eton; Trinity Hall, Cambridge; acted as Whipper-in to Cambridge Draghounds, 1908–9, and Whipper-in to F. A. Hurt's Hounds, 1910; 2nd Lt., Derbyshire Yeomanry, 1910; Capt., 1915; served Europ. War in Egypt, Gallipoli and Salonika; Despatches twice; D.S.O.

JOHNSON, J. T., M.D., B.S., B.Hygiene, D.P.H. (D.S.O. L.G. 1.1.17); b. 4.6.78; s. of late J. Johnson, of Newcastle-on-Tyne; m. Mary Heron Reid, of Sydney, Australia; one d.; educ. Durham University; Lt., R.A.M.C., 14.11.00; Captain 14.11.03; Major 14.5.12; Bt. Lt.-Col. 1.1.18; Lt.-Col. 18.1.18; served S. African War, 1900–2; Medal, 2 clasps; China and India; served Europ. War; Bt. Lt.-Col., 1918; Order of St. Sava (Serbian), 1917; Fellow of Royal Society of Tropical Medicine; was appointed Asst. Director of Hygiene, Irish Command.

JOHNSON, M. E. S. (D.S.O. L.G. 23.10.19); b. 21.4.79; 2nd Lt. 27.7.98; Lt., Ind. Army, 27.10.00; Capt. 27.7.07; Major 1.9.15; served N.W. Frontier of India, 1901–2; Medal with clasp; Europ. War; Despatches.

JOHNSON, P. H. (D.S.O. L.G. 4.6.17), T/Capt. (A/Major), M.G.C.

JOHNSON, R. I. B. (D.S.O. L.G. 25.8.17); b. 31.11.74; 2nd Lt., R.W. Fus., 6.6.96; Capt. 10.6.05; retired 3.12.13; Lt.-Col. 7.6.18; served China, 1900; Medal with clasp; Europ. War; Despatches.

JOHNSON, R. M. (D.S.O. L.G. 1.1.17); b. 4.11.73; s. of late Thomas Marr Johnson; m. Gladys, d. of Major-Gen. Sir John Leech, K.C.V.O.; one s.; educ. Fonthill, Radley; R.M.A., Woolwich; 2nd Lt., R.A., 4.3.93; Lt. 4.3.96; Capt. 26.5.00; Major 14.2.10; Bt. Lt.-Col. 3.6.15; Col. 3.6.19; Temp. Brig.-Gen. 12.12.17 to 27.5.19; served China, 1900; Medal; Europ. War, 1914–18; Despatches; C.M.G., 1919; seconded for service with Shanghai Volunteer Corps, 1920.

JOHNSON, S. G. (D.S.O. L.G. 3.6.18); b. 1.1.86; 2nd Lt., S. Staff. R., 29.11.05; Lt. 9.11.07; Capt. 1.1.13; Major 2.1.21; Temp. Lt.-Col. 1.3.20; att. R.E.; served Europ. War; Despatches; M.C.

JOHNSON, T. H. F. (D.S.O. L.G. 1.1.17), T/Major, Dorset R. He was killed in action 12.6.18.

JOHNSON, T. P. (D.S.O. L.G. 1.1.17); b. 16.6.71; 2nd Lt., Bedf. R., 18.5.92; Lt. 3.6.95; Capt., A.S.C., 1.4.00; Major 4.7.09; promoted Lt.-Col.; served during operations in Chitral, 1895; Medal with clasp; Uganda, 1897–98; Medal with clasp; Uganda, 1900; Despatches; Medal with clasp; Europ. War; Despatches.

JOHNSON, V. N. (D.S.O. L.G. 1.1.18); b. 14.8.82; 2nd Lt., R.G.A., 12.8.02; Lt. 21.3.03; Capt., Glouc. R., 8.7.05; Capt. 15.7.11; Bt. Major 3.6.16; Major 18.1.17; Bt. Lt.-Col. 3.6.19; served Europ. War; Despatches.

JOHNSON, W. R. (D.S.O. L.G. 15.2.19) (Details, L.G. 30.7.19), Lt.-Col., 7th Bn. Essex R., T.F., att. 9th Bn.

JOHNSON, W. W. (D.S.O. L.G. 27.6.19), Lt. (A/Capt.), 58th Bn. Ont. Regt., Can. Mil. Forces; served Europ. War; M.C.; Despatches.

W. W. Johnson.

JOHNSTON, A. C. (D.S.O. L.G. 4.6.17) (Bar, L.G. 1.1.18); b. 26.1.85; s. of Colonel Sir D. A. Johnston, K.C.M.G., C.B., C.B.E., and Clare Millicent (who died in 1914), d. of F. H. Mackenzie; m. Esmé Monica, d. of G. J. Cooper; one d.; educ. Winchester College; R.M. College, Sandhurst; 2nd Lt., Worc. R., 4.11.03; Lt. 25.6.07; Capt. 22.9.14; Bt. Major 1.1.16; Major 4.11.18; Lt.-Col., A.E.C., 1.1.21; att. 1st Battn. N. Nigeria R., 1906–10; T/Brig.-Gen., 1917; served Europ. War, 1914–17; Despatches five times; M.C.; French Croix de Guerre; wounded four times; Commandant, Duke of York's Royal Military School, Dover, since 1921; played cricket for Hampshire, 1902–14, and for Gentlemen *v.* Players, 1911 and 1912.

JOHNSTON, C. A., M.B., D.P.H. (D.S.O. L.G. 1.2.17); b. 28.2.67; m. Isabel Mary, d. of late Dr. J. H. Honeyman; one s.; Capt., I.M.S., 31.3.90; Major 31.3.02; Lt.-Col. 31.3.10; Col., 1920; retired; served Manipur, 1891 (Medal with clasp); Burma, 1891–92; Despatches; clasp; China, 1900 (Medal); Europ. War, 1914–18; Despatches twice; C.B.; C.I.E.

JOHNSTON, CHARLES ERNEST (D.S.O. L.G. 2.12.18); 2nd s. of Col. C. T. Johnston and Mrs. Johnston; m. 1919, Irene Storey; three d.; educ. Malvern College; Recruiting Officer for Morayshire, Scotland, 1914; appointed to raise the 3/6th Batt. Seaforths, 1915; Major, Seaforth Highrs.; sent to France as Second-in-Command of 6th Seaforths, 1917; served Europ. War; Despatches twice; was reported missing 23.3.18; officially presumed killed in action on that date 19.2.19.

The following is an account of the deed for which the award of the D.S.O. was given: During the operations east of Bapaume this Officer was in command of his battalion in the Beaumetz-Morchies line, south-east of Beaumetz, on 21–22.3.18, and also in a line behind Beaumetz 23.3.18. Although subjected to a heavy hostile artillery and machine-gun barrage, he moved about, supervising his dispositions and encouraging his men to make a firm stand to the last. When the enemy broke through on the left of the battalion, he, with great skill and daring, organized a defensive flank on the Cambrai road, which prevented the enemy entering Beaumetz. When the battalion received orders to withdraw to a new line behind Beaumetz, this Officer personally organized and supervised the withdrawal and the taking up of the new position. He showed in the highest degree a great devotion to duty, remarkable organizing skill and most consummate bravery. It was largely owing to his splendid example that the battalion put up such an excellent defence and inflicted such heavy casualties on the enemy, and to him must be attributed in no small degree the stand made by this division on the Bapaume–Cambrai road, which did so much to save the situation on this part of the field. He commanded his battalion most gallantly till he fell wounded on 23rd March, when, owing to the proximity of the enemy, it was impossible to bring him back to our lines.

JOHNSTON, CHARLES EVELYN (D.S.O. L.G. 7.11.18); b. 29.5.78; s. of R. E. Johnston; m. Pleasance, d. of Col. W. J. Alt, C.B.; three s.; one d.; educ. Eton; New College, Oxford (M.A.); Director, London Joint City and Midland Bank; Lt.-Col. Commanding 7th London R.; served Europ. War, 1914–18; Despatches; M.C. Colonel Johnston lost his life in a gallant attempt to save his daughter from drowning while bathing at Widemouth Sands, five miles from Bude, Cornwall, Sept. 1922.

JOHNSTON, C. M. (D.S.O. L.G. 4.6.17); s. of the late Judge Johnston, of Melbourne; Major, Aust. A.M.C.; served Europ. War; Despatches; M.C.

JOHNSTON, F. C. (D.S.O. L.G. 1.1.18), Capt., R. of O., R.A., 1.4.92; Egyptian Expedition, 1884; Medal with clasp; Bronze Star; Sudan Expedition, 1885; 2 clasps.

JOHNSTON, F. G. D. (D.S.O. L.G. 3.6.16); Lt.-Col., R.F.A. (T.F.), T.D.; served S. African War, 1900–2; Despatches; Queen's Medal, 3 clasps; Europ. War, 1914–18; Despatches; C.M.G.; Chief Inspector, Sir W. G. Armstrong, Whitworth & Co.

JOHNSTON, G. C. (D.S.O. L.G. 1.1.18) (Bar, L.G. 11.1.19), Lt.-Col., Can. Mtd. Rifles; served Europ. War; Despatches; M.C.

JOHNSTON, G. F. (D.S.O. L.G. 1.1.19), T/Capt. (A/Major), 180th Tunnelling Co., R.E.; M.C.

JOHNSTON, G. N. (D.S.O. L.G. 26.6.16); b. 2.8.68, in Canada; s. of Peter Johnston; m. 1893, Margaret Hilda Stairs; one s.; one d.; educ. R.M. College, Kingston; commissioned R.A., 1888, since then Adjt. five years; Colonel; Gunnery Instructor, Punjab, India, three years; Director of Artillery, N.Z., 1911; when Europ. War broke out organized N.Z. Divisional Artillery, and commanded it throughout Gallipoli Campaign, and in France and Flanders till end of war; commanded N.Z. Division, Cologne, Germany, till demobilization; C.M.G.; Bt.-Col.; Despatches eight times.

JOHNSTON, H. (D.S.O. L.G. 4.6.17) T/Major, Ches. R.

JOHNSTON, H. A. (D.S.O. L.G. 8.3.19) (Details, L.G. 4.10.19), Capt., 13th Inf. Battn. Quebec Regt.; M.C.

JOHNSTON, H. B. H. (D.S.O. L.G. 29.7.21); b. 10.11.76; 2nd Lt., R.A., 21.9.96; Lt. 21.1.99; Capt. 4.1.02; promoted Major; served S. African War, 1899–1901; Queen's Medal, 3 clasps; Europ. War; Despatches. He died of wounds 27.10.16, but his D.S.O. was not gazetted until some years later.

JOHNSTON, H. R. (D.S.O. L.G. 26.11.17) (Details, L.G. 6.4.18); e. s. of W. Johnston; joined the University and Public School Corps, Sept. 1914; T/2nd Lt., att. R. Lanc. R.

JOHNSTON, J. H. (D.S.O. L.G. 1.1.17); b. 30.11.83; s. of late Major W. Johnston, R.A.; m. Mildred Ligonier, d. of Colonel W. E. L. Balfour, of Balfour Castle, Orkney; educ. R.M.A., Woolwich; 2nd Lt., R.G.A., 24.12.02; Lt. 24.12.05; Capt. 30.10.14; Major 13.7.17; served Europ. War in France, May–Dec. 1915, in command of a battery of R.F.A. (Despatches); in Salonika, Aug. 1916, to April, 1918; T/Major, Aug. 1916; Despatches; D.S.O.; in France, 1918; Egypt from 1920.

JOHNSTON, K. A. (D.S.O. L.G. 4.2.18) (Details, L.G. 5.7.18); b. 22.10.92; 2nd Lt., Hants R., 11.10.11; Lt. 5.8.14; Capt. 1.10.15; served Europ. War; Despatches.

JOHNSTON, P. D. C. (D.S.O. L.G. 26.8.18); b. 8.7.82; 2nd Lt., Shrops. L. Inf., 11.8.00; Lt. 23.2.02; Capt., Ind. Army, 11.8.09; Major 1.9.15.

JOHNSTON, ROBERT (D.S.O. L.G. 22.12.16) (see correction L.G. 17.4.17); b. 9.4.79; 2nd Lt. 27.7.98; Lt. 27.10.00; Capt. 27.7.07; Major 1.9.15; served Europ. War, 1914–18; Despatches.

JOHNSTON, T. P. (D.S.O. L.G. 1.1.17), Lt.-Col., A.S.C.

JOHNSTON, W. E. WILSON- (see Wilson-Johnston, W. E.).

JOHNSTON, W. H. H. (D.S.O. L.G. 1.1.18), T/Lt.-Col., Midd'x R.; served Europ. War; Despatches; M.C.

JOHNSTON, W. M. P. (D.S.O. L.G. 26.5.17), 4th s. of Captain W. M. Johnston, late 8th Foot (King's Liverpool); T/Capt. (A/Major), R.F.A.

JOHNSTON, W. W. S. (D.S.O. L.G. 19.11.17) (Details, L.G. 22.3.18), Major, Aust. A.M.C.; served Europ. War; Despatches; M.C.

JOHNSTONE, A. (D.S.O. L.G. 11.11.19), Lt.-Cdr., R.N.

JOHNSTONE, A. C. (D.S.O. L.G. 4.6.17), Capt. and Bt. Major (T/Lt.-Col.), Worc. R.; served Europ. War; Despatches; M.C.

JOHNSTONE, B. (D.S.O. L.G. 17.12.17) (Details, L.G. 23.4.18); b. 16.8.77; 2nd Lt. 26.6.01; Lt. 4.1.04; Capt. 28.3.08; Major 8.5.16; Bt. Lt.-Col. 1.1.19; served S. African War, 1900–2; Queen's Medal, 4 clasps; King's Medal, 2 clasps; Europ. War; Despatches.

JOHNSTONE, G. H. (D.S.O. L.G. 7.2.18); b. 18.12.91; 2nd Lt., R.A., 23.12.11; Lt. 23.12.14; Capt. 8.8.16.

JOICEY, HON. H. E. (D.S.O. L.G. 1.1.19); b. 21.11.81; 2nd s. of Lord Joicey; educ. Harrow; served in the Northumberland Fusiliers Militia, 1899; gazetted to 14th Hussars, 1900; 2nd Lt., Hus., 3.10.00; Capt. 30.4.06; Adjt., 14th Hussars, 1905–8; Bt. Lt.-Col. 3.6.16; Lt.-Colonel, R. of O., 24.10.19; served S. African War, 1900–2; Queen's Medal and 3 clasps; served with 2nd Life Guards in France, 1914–15; commanded 1st Batt. Suffolk R., 1915–18, bringing the 14th Hussars home from Mesopotamia, 1919; has the Order of the Redeemer of Greece, 2nd Class.

JOLL, H. H. (D.S.O. L.G. 1.1.18); b. 5.6.82; 2nd Lt., R.A., 21.12.00; Lt. 21.12.03; Capt. 12.9.13; Major 31.18.15; served N.W. Frontier of India, 1908; Medal with clasp; Europ. War; Despatches; M.C.

JONES, ALBERT (D.S.O. L.G. 3.6.18), T/Capt. (A/Lt.-Col.), R.A.M.C.; M.C.

JONES, A. D. DERVICHE- (see Derviche-Jones, A. D.).

JONES, A. GWYNNE- (see Gwynne-Jones, A.).

JONES, A. N. G. (D.S.O. L.G. 1.1.18); b. 11.11.82; 2nd Lt., R.A., 4.5.01; Lt., Ind. Army, 9.10.03; Capt. 4.5.10; Major 4.5.16; retired with rank of Lt.-Col. 2.3.21.

JONES, A. P. RICE- (see Rice-Jones, A. P.).

JONES, B. J. (D.S.O. L.G. 14.1.16) (Bar, L.G. 8.3.19) (Details, L G. 4.10.19); b. 13.5.74; e. sur. s. of Colonel T. J. Jones, late R.A., of Lisnawilly, Dundalk; educ. privately; 2nd Lt., Leins. R., 12.12.94; Lt. 2.12.96; Capt. 19.12.00; Major, Aug. 1915; att. R. Ir. Rifles; served S. African War, 1900–2; Despatches; Queen's Medal, 3 clasps; King's Medal, 2 clasps; Europ. War; Despatches. He was killed in action 20.10.18.

JONES, B. M. (D.S.O. L.G. 4.6.17), T/Capt., Gen. List.

JONES, C. G. (D.S.O. L.G. 3.6.18), T/Major (A/Lt.-Col.), Welsh R.

JONES, C. H. (D.S.O. L.G. 22.6.17), Lt.-Cdr., R.N.

JONES, C. J. H. SPENCE- (see, changed name, Spence-Colby, C. J. H.).

JONES, C. LA T. (D.S.O. L.G. 3.6.18); b. 3.11.87; 2nd Lt., R.E., 25.7.06; Lt. 25.9.08; Capt., R.E., 30.10.14; served Europ. War, 1914–18; Despatches; M.C.

JONES, C. R. (D.S.O. L.G. 3.6.16); b. 11.8.80; Bt. Lt.-Col., R.A.O.C.; served S. African War, 1899–1902; Queen's Medal, 6 clasps; King's Medal, 2 clasps; Europ. War, 1914–18; Despatches; Bt. Lt.-Col.

JONES, D. A. (D.S.O. L.G. 25.8.16), T/Lt., Lincs. Regt. His D.S.O. was awarded for gallantry on 3.7.16 at Contalmaison.

JONES, D. C. (D.S.O. L.G. 3.6.18); b. 9.6.77; s. of late Lt.-Col. Champion Jones, R. Warwicks. R.; m. Dorothy Helen, d. of Sir M. F. Ommaney, G.C.M.G., and Charlotte (who died in 1913), d. of O. Ommaney; educ. Shrewsbury School; R.M.A., Woolwich; 2nd Lt., R.E., 21.9.96; Lt. 21.9.99; Major, R.E., 30.10.14; served Europ. War, 1914–18; Despatches five times; Legion of Honour.

JONES, E. H. (D.S.O. L.G. 10.6.20); b. 2.10.75; 2nd Lt., R.A., 2.11.95; Lt. 2.11.98; Capt. 23.11.01; Major 19.6.12; Lt.-Col. 11.4.16; served in China, 1900; Medal with clasp; Europ. War; Despatches.

JONES, E. W. (D.S.O. L.G. 1.1.17) (Bar, L.G. 13.5.18), Lt.-Col., Can. Inf.

JONES, G. N. (D.S.O. L.G. 12.5.17), Lt., R.N.R.

JONES, H. LL. (D.S.O. L.G. 1.1.17); b. 10.8.86; 2nd Lt., 13th Hrs.; Lt. 8.10.10; Capt. 1.1.16; Bt. Major 1.1.18; Major 11.11.20.

JONES, H. M. PRYCE- (see Pryce-Jones, H. M.).

JONES, H. P. (D.S.O. L.G. 1.1.17), Capt. (T/Major), R.F.A.

JONES, J. (D.S.O. L.G. 15.2.19) (Details, L.G. 30.7.19), Lt. (T/Major); A/Lt.-Col. 2nd Bn. Durham L. Inf., att. 17th Bn. Lancs. Fus.; served Europ. War; Despatches; M.C. He died of wounds 14.10.18.

JONES, J. H. H. (D.S.O. L.G. 14.1.16); b. 14.4.76; educ. Cheltenham College; ent. R.A., 1896; Capt. 1901; Major, 1914; Bt. Lt.-Col., 1919; Lt.-Col., 1921; commanding 4th Brig., R.G.A.; served Europ. War, 1914–18; Despatches five times; Légion d'Honneur.

JONES, J. I. T. (D.S.O. L.G. 2.11.18), Lt. (T/Capt.), R.A.F.; m. Mrs. O. G. Edmund-Davies; joined Flying Corps, 1915; served Europ. War; M.C.; D.F.C. and Bar; M.M.; Order of St. George; Despatches.

JONES, J. W., M.B. (D.S.O. L.G. 22.9.16), Capt., I.M.S.

JONES, K. W. MAURICE- (see Maurice-Jones, K. W.).

JONES, L. E. (D.S.O. L.G. 18.10.17) (Details, L.G. 7.3.18) (Bar, L.G. 11.1.19), Lt.-Col., 18th Bn. Can. Cav., W. Ont. Regt.

JONES, M. D. GORING- (see Goring-Jones, M. D.).

JONES, R. C. R. (D.S.O. L.G. 14.1.16); b. 31.10.75; e. s. of late Major-Gen. R. R. Jones, R.A.; Major, King's Liverpool R.; served S. African War, 1899–1902; Queen's Medal, 3 clasps; King's Medal, 2 clasps; Europ. War, 1914–18; Despatches.

JONES, R. H. (D.S.O. L.G. 1.2.19), T/Major, Hants Regt.; M.C. His D.S.O. was awarded for services in Salonika.

JONES, R. L. (D.S.O. L.G. 14.3.16), Lt., R.N.R.

JONES, R. R. (D.S.O. L.G. 26.9.17) (Details, L.G. 9.1.18), 2nd Lt., Welsh Guards. His D.S.O. was awarded for services on 31.7.17 at Yser Canal. He died of wounds 25.8.17.

JONES, S. D. DOUGLAS- (see Douglas-Jones, S. D.).

JONES, T. A. (D.S.O. L.G. 3.6.18), Cdr. (A/Capt.), R.N.R., R.D. Capt. T. A. Jones won £69,000 by Humorist's Derby victory (1921). He bought the winning ticket in the great Calcutta Sweep for 14s. Never before had Capt. Jones taken part in a sweepstake, and he has never made a bet. He bought the ticket from his friend, Mr. J. A. Hussey, who held the next numbered ticket.

JONES, REV. T. H., M.A. (D.S.O. L.G. 22.8.18), S. Africans, Chaplains' Dept.

JONES, T. P. (D.S.O. L.G. 1.1.17) (Bar, L.G. 2.4.19) (Details, L.G. 10.12.19), Major 4th Bn. Can. Inf., 1st Cent. Ont. R.; Brig.-Major, 12th Can. Inf. Brig.

JONES, W. A. F. (D.S.O. L.G. 3.6.16), Major, R.A.; b. 16.7.80; 2nd Lt., R.A., 16.7.00; Lt. 4.2.03; Capt. 15.5.11; Major; served S. African War, 1900–1; Queen's Medal with 4 clasps.

JONES, W. HOWEL- (see Howel-Jones, W.).

JONES, W. H. C. (D.S.O. L.G. 21.4.21); b. 17.10.99; 2nd Lt., 31.8.18; Lt. 2/127th Baluchistan L. Inf., Ind. Army.

JOPP, A. H. K. (D.S.O. L.G. 1.1.17); b. 1.5.90; s. of George Keith Jopp, of Brisbane, Queensland; m. Anne Talbot, d. of Mr. Baines, of Westbrook, Horsham, Sussex; educ. Queensland; Lt., R. Aust. Artillery, 1908; Capt., 1914; Major, 1916; served Egypt, 1914–15; Gallipoli Campaign, 1915 (Despatches); seconded to R.F.C., June to Dec. 1915.

JORDAAN, J. F. (D.S.O. L.G. 22.8.18), Lt.-Col. (T/Col. Comdt.), 3rd Mtd. Brig., 13th Mtd. Regt., Staff, S. African Mil. Forces.

JORDAN, W. (D.S.O. L.G. 21.4.17), Eng.-Cdr., R.N.R.

JORY, P. J., M.B. (D.S.O. L.G. 3.6.19), Major (T/Lt.-Col.), 2nd Field Ambulance, N.Z. Army Medical Corps.

JOSEPH, R. H. (D.S.O. L.G. 14.1.16); b. 25.1.86; s. of late Julian Joseph; educ. St. Paul's School; Lt.-Col., R.E. (T.F.); served Europ. War, 1914–18; Despatches; wounded; C.R.E., Independent Forces, with acting rank of Lt.-Col., April, 1918.

JOSSELYN, J. (D.S.O. L.G. 1.1.18); b. 28.10.72; s. of F. Josselyn and Mary Elizabeth, d. of Rev. H. L. Oswell; m. Lilian Bella, d. of Ven. W. W. Elwes, Archdeacon of Madras; one s.; one d.; served in Suffolk Yeomanry, Madras Guards, Madras Artillery Volunteers, and the Suffolk Rgt., T.F.; mobilized, 1914; Brigade Major, 1915; Lt.-Col., 1916; Colonel; commanded 2/5th W. Yorks. in England and France; went to N. Russia, June, 1918; served Murmansk Railway; commanded Dvina River Force, Archangel; President, Claims Commission, N. Russia; T.D.; O.B.E.; C.M.G.; Croix de Guerre and Russian Order, St. Vladimir, 3rd Class with Swords; St. Anne, 2nd Class with Swords; Despatches thrice.

JOUBERT, C. (D.S.O. L.G. 22.8.18), Major, Vrijstaatse Schutters, 5th Regt., S. African Mil. Forces.

JOUBERT DE LA FERTE, P. B. (D.S.O. L.G. 1.1.17); b. 21.5.87; educ Elstree; Harrow; Woolwich; 2nd Lt., R.F.A., 23.7.07; Lt. 23.7.10; seconded Royal Flying Corps 7.3.13; Wing-Cdr., R.A.F.; served in France from Aug. 1914; Egypt, 1916–17; Italy, 1917–18; Despatches six times; C.M.G.; Order of SS. Maurice and Lazarus, Cavaliere; Croce di Guerra.

JOURDIER, M. J. A. (D.S.O. L.G. 1.1.17); b. 4.4.84; 2nd Lt., E. Surrey R., 10.10.03; Lt. 21.4.06; Capt. 19.2.13; Bt. Major 3.6.18; Major 10.10.18.

JOYCE, J. (D.S.O. L.G. 16.9.18), T/Major, M.G.C.; M.C.

JOYCE, P. C. (D.S.O. L.G. 3.6.18); b. 25.6.78; s. of Pierce J. Joyce, D.L.; educ. Beaumont College, Old Windsor; 2nd Lt., 1st Batt. The Connaught Rangers, 21.4.00; Lt. 11.4.02; Capt. 8.5.09; Major 1.9.15; Bt. Lt.-Col. 3.6.17; served S. African War, 1900–2; severely wounded; Queen's Medal with 3 clasps; King's Medal with 2 clasps; att. Egyptian Army, 1907–16; Egyptian Medal with clasp; 4th Class Order of the Medjidie; 4th Class Order of the Nile; served Europ. War, 1915–18; Gallipoli; Egyptian Exp. Force; C.B.E.; Croix d'Officier, Legion of Honour; Arabian Order of the Nahda, 2nd Class.

JUCKSCH, A. H. (D.S.O. L.G. 1.2.19), Capt. (A/Major), 5th Batt. Can. Inf. 2nd Cent. Ont. Regt.

JUKES, A. H. (D.S.O. L.G. 15.3.16); b. 11.11.85; s. of A. Jukes, of Vancouver, B.C.; m. Editha Maud, d. of E. A. Goward; one son; educ. Collegiate School, Victoria, B.C.; R.M. College, Kingston, Ontario; 2nd Lt. 22.6.05; Ind. Army, Lt. 22.9.07; Capt. 22.6.14; Bt. Major 1.1.17; Major 22.6.00; served Europ. War; Despatches.

JUPE, P. W. (D.S.O. L.G. 3.6.16), Major, late H.L.I.; m. Margaret Dora, d. of W. Heyworth; one s.; served Europ. War, 1914–18; wounded; Despatches.

KAMBAL, BESHIR (BEY) (D.S.O. L.G. 1.1.17), El Miralai (Colonel), Egyptian Army; b. 1855; served under Gordon Pasha in 1876; Khartoum, Sennar, Red Sea Coast, Exp. of Darfur, Kassala and Abyssinian frontiers; was in captivity for many years in Omdurman; Inspector Kordofan Arab tribes.

KANE, A. H. (D.S.O. L.G. 3.6.19); b. 6.9.70; 2nd Lt., R.A., 27.7.89; Lt. 27.7.92; Capt. 13.9.99; Adjt., R.A., 30.6.04 to 19.7.07; Major 23.1.10; Lt.-Col. 13.7.16; Despatches.

KANE, R. R. G. (D.S.O. L.G. 8.11.15) (Bar, L.G. 1.1.19), Capt. (A/Lt.-Col.), R. Munster Fus. He died of wounds 1.10.18 (see "The Distinguished Service Order," from its institution to 31.12.15, same publishers).

KAPPELE, D. P. (D.S.O. L.G. 3.6.18) (Bar, L.G. 8.3.19) (Details, 4.10.19), Lt.-Col., Can. A.M.C.

KAVANAGH, E. J., M.B. (D.S.O. L.G. 1.1.18); b. 25.11.81; Lt., R.A.M.C., 30.7.06; Capt. 30.1.10; Major 30.7.18; Despatches; M.C.

KAY, D'A. H. (D.S.O. L.G. 1.1.19), T/Lt.-Col., 21st Batt. M.G.C.

KAY, REV. D. M., D.D. (D.S.O. L.G. 4.6.17); educ. St. Andrew's (double honours; first-class mathematics; second classics); Edinburgh Divinity Hall (Pitt Club Scholarship); Professor of Hebrew and Oriental Languages, University of St. Andrew's; Chaplain on active service abroad, 1915–19; has written "Translation from Syriac and from Greek of the Apology of Aristides in Ante-Nicene Fathers," Vol. IX.; an English version of Dalman's "Die Worte Jesu," and "Susanna" in Oxford Apocrypha.

KAY, J. K. (D.S.O. L.G. 15.10.18); b. 23.8.88; 2nd Lt., R.W. Kent R., 16.12.08; Lt., R.W. Kent Rgt., 22.1.12; Capt. 10.6.15; Europ. War, 1914–18; Despatches.

KAY, P. C. (D.S.O. L.G. 3.6.19); Lt. (A/Major) 1/7 Middx. R., T.F.; M.C.

KAY, T., M.B. (D.S.O. L.G. 1.1.18), Major (T/Lt.-Col.), R.A.M.C.

KAY, W. (D.S.O. L.G. 2.4.19) (Details, L.G. 10.12.19.), 2nd Lt. (A/Capt.), Manch. R.; M.C.

KAY, W. E. (D.S.O. L.G. 3.6.18), Lt.-Col., Aust. A.M.C.

KAY, W. H. (D.S.O. L.G. 14.1.16); b. 2.7.71; educ. Rossall; R.M.A., Woolwich; 2nd Lt., R.A., 13.2.91; Lt. 13.2.94; Capt. 13.2.00; Adjt., R.H.A., 30.3.01 to 22.4.04; Major 17.8.08; Lt.-Col. 29.3.15; Bt.-Col. 1.1.17; T/Brig.-Gen. 25.2.19; served Europ. War, 1914–18, commanding R.A., 1st Division; Despatches; C.B.

KAYE, H. S. (D.S.O. L.G. 3.6.16); b. 9.5.82; s. of J. Watson Kaye; m. Dora Margaret, d. of Sir J. Porter; one s.; two d.; educ. Riber Castle, Matlock; Harrow; Sandhurst; 2nd Lt., Yorks. L.I., 8.5.01; Lt. 28.5.04; Capt. 19.7.10; Major 8.5.16; Lt.-Col.; retired Nov. 1919; commanding 4th K.O.Y.L.I.; Despatches five times; M.C.

H. S. Kaye.

KEANE, G. J., M.D., D.P.H., D.T.M. (D.S.O. L.G. 1.2.17); b. 18.12.80; s. of J. H. Keane, of Liverpool; educ. S. Francis Xavier's College; Mount St. Mary's College, Chesterfield; Liverpool University; Fellow of the Royal Society of Tropical Medicine; ent. Army 4.2.08; Capt., R.A.M.C., 4.8.11; seconded for Special Service, Uganda Government, since 1908; formed African Native Medical Corps; served Europ. War; T/Major, 1914–17; Despatches.

KEANE, SIR J., Bart. (D.S.O. L.G. 14.1.16); b. 3.6.73; s. of 4th Bart. and Adelaide Sydney, d. of J. Vance, M.P.; m. Lady Eleanor Hicks-Beach, d. of 1st Earl St. Aldwyn; one s.;

three d.; educ. R.M.A., Woolwich; ent. Army 17.6.83; Capt., 1900; retired 17.6.08; Major, 1916; Lt.-Col., Army, 17.5.17; R. of O. 17.3.19; served S. Africa, 1899–1902; Despatches; Medal with 3 clasps; Europ. War, 1914–18; Despatches; Legion of Honour; High Sheriff of Waterford, 1911; D.L.

KEARSLEY, E. R. (D.S.O. L.G. 4.11.15) (Bar, L.G. 26.11.17) (Details, L.G. 6.4.18), Major, R.W. Fusiliers (see "The Distinguished Service Order," from its institution to 31.12.15, same publishers).

KEATE, H. A. D. (D.S.O. L.G. 8.3.20), Lt.-Cdr., R.N., 30.7.19.

KEATINGE, O. J. F. (D.S.O. L.G. 3.6.18), Major, N. Staffs Rgt.

KEBLE, A. E. C., L.R.C.S. (D.S.O. L.G. 26.6.16); b. 19.7.69; s. of late Capt. J. A. Keble, E. Surrey Rgt.; m. Violet, d. of late H. C. Miller; one s.; educ. Ennis College, co. Clare; Licentiate R.C.S. and P.Ireland, 1890; D.P.H., R.C.S.London, 1907; ent. Army Medical Staff, 1893; Colonel; served Indian Frontier, 1897–98; Medal and 2 clasps; served Europ. War, 1915–16, as A.D.M.S., Gen. H.Q., Medit. Exp. Force, throughout Gallipoli operations; Despatches four times; elsewhere 1916–18 (C.B.; C.M.G.); D.D.M.S., N. Russian Exp. Force, during the latter half of 1918; Order of White Eagle of Serbia, 3rd Class with Swords, 1916; A.D.M.S., Waziristan Force; Hon. Associate, Order of St. John of Jerusalem, 1917; Hon. Life Member, St. John's Ambulance Association.

KEDDIE, H. W. G. (D.S.O. L.G. 4.6.17); b. 24.7.73; 2nd Lt., R.A., 14.3.94; Lt. 4.3.97; Capt. 9.5.00; Major, A.O.D. (now R.A.O.D.), 13.7.06; Lt.-Col. 8.12.14; served S. African War, 1899–1902; Queen's Medal, 2 clasps; King's Medal, 2 clasps; E. Africa, 1902–3; Medal with clasp; Europ. War; Despatches.

KEEGAN, H. L. (D.S.O. L.G. 2.12.18), Lt.-Col., 47th Can. Inf. Bn. W. Ontario R.

KEELAN, H. P. (D.S.O. L.G. 3.6.19); b. 26.2.72; 2nd Lt., Lan. Fus. 18.6.92; Lt. 14.6.93; Capt., I.A., 10.11.01; Major 18.6.10; Bt. Lt.-Col. 3.6.16; Lt.-Col., 121st Pioneers, I.A., 14.8.16; retired 31.7.21; East Africa, 1902–4; Medal with clasp; served Europ. War; Despatches.

KEEN, F. S. (D.S.O. L.G. 14.1.16); b. 27.6.74; 2nd Lt., Unatt. List, 31.1.94; Lt., Ind. A., 4.11.96; Capt. 31.1.03; Major 1.1.12; Bt. Lt.-Col. 1.1.19; Lt.-Col. 16.11.19; 45th Rattray's Sikhs, I.A., Tirah, 1897–98; Medal, 2 clasps; Somaliland, 1898; Medal with clasp; Uganda, 1898–99, clasp; N.W. Frontier, 1902 and 1908; Despatches; Europ. War; Despatches.

KEEN, S. (D.S.O. L.G. 1.1.17); b. 1868; s. of late J. R. Keen, J.P.; m. Rosalie Augusta Ada, d. of H. Flower; two d.; joined 1st Gloucester Engineer Volunteer Corps, 1881; all ranks to Sergeant; commissioned in 1st Gloucester Engineer Volunteers, 1888 (name changed to 1st Devon and Somerset Engineer Volunteers, 1889); Lt., 1889; Capt., 1892; Major, 1903; Adjt. of the Corps, 1904–6; Lt.-Col., 1908; Colonel; became C.R.E. Wessex Division on formation of the Territorial Force, 1908; volunteered for active service on outbreak of war, and took the 1st Line R.E. of the Wessex Division to France, Dec. 1914, having been appointed C.R.E. to the 27th Division; holds the Territorial Decoration; Despatches three times; Médaille du Roi Albert.

KEENAN, A. H. (D.S.O. L.G. 3.2.20), Lt. (T/Maj.), R. Highrs., T.F.; O.B.E.; M.C.

KEENE, G. G. (D.S.O. L.G. 25.8.17); b. 29.4.87; m. Carol, d. of A. N. Latham; 2 d.; 2nd Lt., R.A., 20.12.06; Lt. 20.12.09; Capt. 30.10.14; Europ. War (Gallipoli and Mesopotamia), 1915–17; Despatches.

KEEP, L. H. (D.S.O. L.G. 15.2.19) (Details, L.G. 30.7.19), T/Major, 7th Batt. Bedfordshire R., att. 2nd Batt.; M.C. He was killed by an avalanche near Pontresina, Switzerland, on 20.1.22.

KEET, H. G. (D.S.O. L.G. 16.9.18); b. 7.7.94; Lt. (from Terr. Army), W. Riding R., 1.7.17; T/Lt.-Col., Defence Force, 11.4.21 to 24.7.21; M.C.

KEIGHLEY, V. A. S. (D.S.O. L.G. 3.6.19); b. 15.12.74; m. Aimée Evelyn, d. of late Sir F. A. Robertson; 2nd Lt., Sco. Rif., 28.12.95; Lt. 22.12.97; Capt., Ind. Army, 28.12.04; Major 28.12.13; Lt.-Col. 2.12.17; N.W. Frontier, 1897–98 (Medal with clasp); commanded Viceroy's Bodyguard at Coronation Durbar; Europ. War, France, 1916–18; Palestine in command of 18th (K.G.O.) Lancers, 1918; Despatches twice; M.V.O., 1912.

KEIGHLY-PEACH, C. W. (D.S.O. L.G. 1.1.19), Rear-Admiral, R.N.

KEILY, F. P. C. (D.S.O. L.G. 15.4.16); b. 25.12.70; s. of E. W. Keily; m. Kathleen, d. of S. F. Keating; educ. Stonyhurst; 2nd Lt., R. Lanc. R., 25.7.91; Lt., Ind. Army, 10.7.01; Capt. 25.7.09; Major 24.9.16; Bt. Lt.-Col. 3.6.19; Colonel 8.5.20; Temp. Brig.-Gen. 3.10.18 to 31.12.20; served E. Africa, 1895–96; Medal; Somaliland, 1902–4; Medal with clasp; Europ. War; wounded four times; C.M.G.; Order of St. Stanislaus, 3rd Class.

KEIR, D. R. (D.S.O. L.G. 1.1.19), Capt. (A/Major), 7th Batt., R. Highrs.

KEITH, G. T. E. (D.S.O. L.G. 4.6.17); 2nd Lt., R. Lanc. R., 28.1.03; Lt. 4.5.07; Capt. 22.10.14; Major 28.1.18; Despatches; O.B.E.; S. Africa, 1902; Queen's Medal; 3 clasps.

KELLETT, A. I. C. REID- (see Reid-Kellett, A. I. C.).

KELLETT, J. P. (D.S.O. L.G. 3.6.18) (Bar, L.G. 1.2.19); b. 28.7.90; mobilized Terr. Force, 5 years, 10 days; T/Capt. and Adjt., Defence Force, 9.4.21 to 7.7.21; Capt. (from Terr. Force), R. Fus., 1.1.21 to 9.7.21; Despatches; M.C.

KELLNER, P. T. R. (D.S.O. L.G. 3.6.16); s. of late E. W. Kellner, C.I.E.; m. d. of Rev. A. Bourne; educ. Giggleswick Grammar School; joined Indian Government Service (Finance Dept.), 1894; Deputy Examiner, 1898; Examiner, 1903; T/Lt.-Col., R.E., on deputation under War Office, 1914.

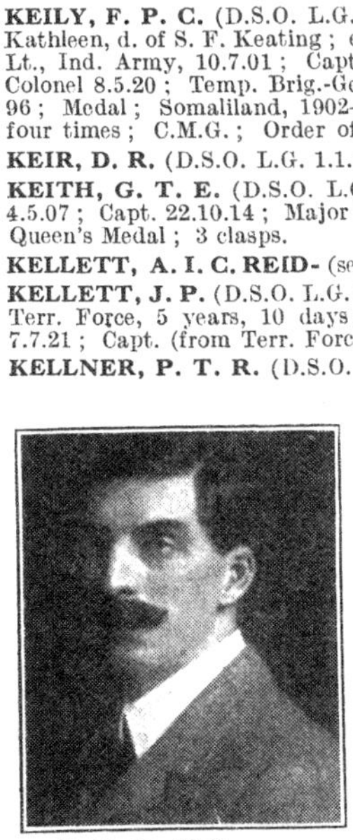

P. T. R. Kellner.

KELLY, B. E. (D.S.O. L.G. 2.4.19) (Details, L.G. 10.12.19), Major, 9th Field Ambulance, Can. Army Corps.

KELLY, C. H. G. H. HARVEY- (see Harvey-Kelly, C. H. G. H.).

KELLY, C. R. (D.S.O. L.G. 4.6.17); b. 20.2.72; s. of late Henry Russell Kelly, of Dungannon, co. Tyrone; educ. Charterhouse; ent. R.A. 18.5.92; Lt. 18.5.95; Capt. 1.2.00; Major 15.7.13; Bt. Lt.-Col. 3.6.16; Lt.-Col. 1.5.17; Col. 3.6.20; Half-pay List 1.5.21; served Somaliland, 1903–4; Medal and clasp; Europ. War, 1914–17; Despatches; Legion of Honour; C.M.G.

KELLY, E. H. (D.S.O. L.G. 20.10.16; b. 26.7.83; s. of Major-Gen. F. H. Kelly, C.B.; m. Helen Beatrice, d. of late P. G. Heyworth, and widow of Major Carson; educ. R.M.A., Woolwich (Sword of Honour); commissioned R.E. 31.7.02; Lt. 22.10.04; Adjt., 1st K.G.O. Sappers and Miners, 1909–12; Capt. 31.7.13; Major 31.7.17; served N.W. Frontier of India, 1908; Mohmand Exp.; Medal and clasp; Europ. War, 1914–18; severely wounded; Despatches seven times; Bt. Lt.-Col. 3.6.19; M.C.

KELLY, E. ROCHE- (see Roche-Kelly, E.).

KELLY, G. C. (D.S.O. L.G. 11.1.19); b. 10.10.80; 2nd Lt., K.R.R.C., 10.11.99; Lt. 19.2.01; Capt. 22.1.08; Brevet Major 18.2.15; Major 1.9.15; Bt. Lt.-Col. 3.6.18; South African War, 1899–1900, 1902; Despatches twice; Queen's Medal, six clasps; East Africa, 1903–4; Medal, 2 clasps; Europ. War; Despatches.

KELLY, H. B., M.B. (D.S.O. L.G. 1.1.17) (Bar, L.G. 26.7.18); b. 24.10.79; s. of W. B. Kelly, Inspector-General of Jails, Burmah; m. H. M. Filby; educ. Dublin University; Lt., R.A.M.C., 31.1.04; Capt. 31.7.17; Major 31.10.14; Lt.-Col. 13.9.15; Europ. War; Despatches.

KELLY, J. D. (D.S.O. L.G. 3.6.19), Lt. (A/Major), R.A.S.C., att. 24th Div. Mech. Transport Co.

KELLY, J. U. (D.S.O. L.G. 22.9.16); b. 18.9.82; s. of R. Kelly, of Summerhill, Enniskerry; m. Eileen Miriam, d. of late H. Adams; one s.; educ. Uppingham; 2nd Lt., Wilts. R., 28.1.03; Lt. 29.10.04; Capt. 26.1.11; Major 28.1.18; Squadron Commander, R.F.C.; served S. Africa, 1900–1; Europ. War, France, 1915–16; Despatches.

KELLY, J. SHERWOOD- (see Sherwood-Kelly, J.).

KELLY, P. J. V. (D.S.O. L.G. 1.1.17); b. 1.9.77; 2nd Lt., 3rd Hrs. 4.5.98; Lt. 17.1.00; Capt. 21.1.03; Major 2.4.13; Bt. Lt.-Col. 1.1.17; served S. Africa, 1901–2; Queen's Medal, 4 clasps; Sudan, 1908–10; 2 Medals, 2 clasps; Europ. War, 1914–18; Despatches; C.M.G.

KELLY, T. B., F.R.C.S. (D.S.O. L.G. 7.2.18); b. 11.3.70; Lt., I.M.S., 28.1.97; Capt. 28.1.00; Major 28.1.09; Lt.-Col. 28.1.17; Tibet, 1903–4; Despatches; Medal with clasp; Europ. War; Despatches.

KELLY, T. J. (D.S.O. L.G. 15.2.19) (Details, L.G. 30.7.19), T/Major, 18th Batt. Manch. R., att. 1/6th Batt. T.F.

KELLY, W. D. C. (D.S.O. L.G. 4.6.17); b. 1.9.77; m. Miss Wolseley; Lt. R.A.M.C., 1.9.02; Capt. 1.3.06; Major 1.6.14; Europ. War; Despatches.

KELLY, WILLIAM HENRY (D.S.O. L.G. 27.6.17), Lt.-Cdr., R.N.R.

KELLY, WILLIAM HYDE (D.S.O. L.G. 3.6.16), Capt., R.E.

KELLY, W. H. F. (D.S.O. L.G. 1.1.17); b. 30.7.76; s. of Col. W. E. R. Kelly, late The Buffs; m. Marjorie Leslie, d. of F. L. Jefferson; two d.; educ. Wellington College; 2nd Lt., 3rd Batt. The Buffs, 1895; 2nd Lt., A.S.C., 21.2.00; Lt. 1.4.01; Capt. 7.1.03; Major 5.8.14; Lt.-Col. 5.1.21; served in S. Africa, 1900–2, with Col. H. B. de Lisle's Column; Despatches; Queen's Medal, 3 clasps; King's Medal, 2 clasps; Europ. War, at Salonika, commanding 28th Divl. Train; Despatches several times; Bt. Lt.-Colonel.

KELSALL, H. J. (D.S.O. L.G. 1.1.19); b. 27.4.67; Lt., R.A., 24.7.86; Capt. 2.6.97; Major 22.11.04; Lt. 30.10.14; retired 30.4.20.

KELSALL, R., M.B. (D.S.O. L.G. 22.12.16); b. 18.10.75; s. of T. Kelsall; m. Margaret Florence, d. of late W. A. Elderton; Lt., I.M.S., 31.8.03; Capt. 31.8.06; Major 28.2.15.

KELSALL, T. E. (D.S.O. L.G. 14.1.16); b. 5.4.73; 2nd Lt., R.E., 10.2.93; Lt. 10.2.96; Capt. 10.2.04; Major 10.2.13; Bt. Lt.-Col. 1.1.18; Lt.-Col. 28.10.20; South African War, 1899–1900; Queen's Medal with clasp.

KELSO, J. E. UTTERSON- (see Utterson-Kelso, J. E.).

KEMBALL, A. H. G. (D.S.O. L.G. 10.1.17); 2nd s. of Maj.-Gen. J. S. Kemball; m. Alvilda Sundt, of Christiania; 2 d.; educ. Wellington College; Sandhurst; 2nd Lt., R. Scots Fus., 1880; Indian Army (5th Gurkhas), 1881; Bt. Lt.-Col., 1905; Col., 1907; retired 11.8.12; Hazara Expedition, 1888 (Medal, clasp) and 1891; Hazai Expedition, 1892; N.W. Frontier of India 1897–98; Despatches; Medal with clasp; Tirah, 1897–98; Despatches; clasp; Bt. of Major; C.B. He was killed in action 1.3.17, while leading his men through the Messines wire.

KEMBLE, A. E. (D.S.O. L.G. 2.4.19) (Details, L.G. 10.12.19); b. 16.5.95; 1st commission 11.11.14; Capt. 12.8.17; Retired Pay, 21.7.20, Yorks. L.I.

KEMBLE, H. H. (D.S.O. L.G. 1.1.17), Lt.-Col. 15th Batt. London R. He died of wounds 7.6.17; M.C.

KEMBLE, H. M. (D.S.O. L.G. 1.1.19); b. 29.6.77; 2nd Lt., R.A., 28.3.00; Lt. 3.4.01; Capt. 16.10.11; Major 9.12.15; retired 10.6.21; Aden operations, 1903–4; Europ. War; Despatches.

KEMMIS, A. W. M. (D.S.O. L.G. 7.2.18); b. 7.7.81; 2nd Lt., R. Ir. Rgt., 20.1.00; Lt. 27.4.01; Capt., I.A., 20.1.09; Major, I.A., 1.9.15; Bt. Lt.-Col. 20.9.20.

KEMMIS-BETTY, A. (see Betty, A. Kemmis-).

KEMP, C. M. (D.S.O. L.G. 18.7.17); s. of W. A. Kemp; educ. Eton College Choristers' School; joined S. African Mounted Police; took part in the campaign in German S.W. Africa; returned to England; received a commission, and at the front was promoted Major, Manchester R. Major Kemp, who was 39 years of age, was leading his battalion when he was killed in action 9.10.17.

KEMP, F. G. (D.S.O. L.G. 2.4.19) (Details, L.G. 10.12.19), Lt. (A/Capt.), 4th Batt. Can. Inf., 1st Cent. Ont. Rgt.

KEMP, J. C. (D.S.O. L.G. 3.6.19), Major, 5th Batt. Can. Mtd. Rif., Quebec R.; M.C.

KEMP, W. F. (D.S.O. L.G. 1.1.17); b. 19.10.84; s. of David Campbell Kemp, Shipowner, of Belfast, and Elizabeth Brownlee Little Kemp; m. Hyacinth Mary, d. of late D. Metcalfe, Barrister-at-Law; educ. Oundle (O.T.C.); Belfast Univ. (O.T.C.); 72nd Seaforth Highdrs. of Canada, 1910–14; commissioned in Canadian Scottish (15th Can. Bn.); Major.

KEMP-WELCH, M. (D.S.O. L.G. 20.10.16) (Bar, L.G. 16.9.18); b. 30.10.85; s. of late C. D. Kemp-Welch, J.P., D.L.; educ. Charterhouse; joined the Queen's Rgt. from Militia, 2.2.07; Lt. 22.1.11; Capt. 10.2.15; Major 9.11.21; Bt. Lt.-Col. 10.11.21; T/Brig.-Gen., 1918; *p.s.c.*; served Europ. War; Despatches five times; M.C.; Belgian and French Croix de Guerre. His D.S.O. was awarded for gallantry on 1.7.16 at Montauban Ridge.

KEMPSON, G. C. D. (D.S.O. L.G. 3.6.18); b. 1.2.79; 2nd Lt., E. Lancs. R., 21.2.00; Lt. 14.10.00; Capt. 14.2.08; Major 12.8.15; R.A.O.C. 10.9.21; South African War, 1899–1902; Queen's Medal, 3 clasps; King's Medal, 2 clasps.

KEMPSTER, I. T. (D.S.O. L.G. 4.6.17), T/Chapl. to the Forces, 3rd Class; A/Chapl. Dept.

KEMPTHORNE, G. A. (D.S.O. L.G. 1.1.18); b. 10.5.76; Lt., R.A.M.C., 31.8.03; Capt. 28.2.07; Major 28.2.15.

KEMPTHORNE, H. N. (D.S.O. L.G. 1.2.17), Capt. (T/Major), Capt., R. of O., late R. Scots Fus., att. R.E.; served N. Nigeria, 1903; Despatches; Medal with clasp.

KENDRICK, E. H. (D.S.O. L.G. 1.1.18); b. 2.12.84; 2nd Lt., R. Munster Fus., 19.9.14; Lt. 18.8.15; Bt. Major 3.6.17.

KENDRICK, F. A. (D.S.O. L.G. 2.4.19) (Details, L.G. 10.12.19), Lt. (A/Capt.), 1st Bn. S. Staffs. R.; served in European War; Despatches; M.C.; Bar to M.C.; Italian Medal for Valour; Italian Bronze Medal for Valour.

KENNARD, D. H. (D.S.O. L.G. 22.8.18), Major, S. African Service Corps.

KENNEDY, A. A. (D.S.O. L.G. 14.1.16); b. 1870; s. of Thomas and Louisa Kennedy (née Arral); joined 1st Lanarkshire Rifle Volunteers, 1890; 2nd Lt., 1896; Lt.-Col. 1916; served (1st Volunteer Co. Scottish Rifles) S. Africa, 1900; volunteered for foreign service, Aug. 1914; served Europ. War from 1914; Despatches; wounded at High Wood; O.B.E.; T.D.

KENNEDY, A. C. (D.S.O. L.G. 25.8.17); b. 5 9.72; 2nd Lt., R.A., 4.11.91; Lt. 4.11.94; Capt. 25.11.99; Major 16.10.11; Lt.-Col., R.G.A., 1.5.17; retired 20.5.21.

KENNEDY, A. J. R. (D.S.O. L.G. 18.10.17) (Details, L.G. 7.3.18); b. 26.2.83; 2nd Lt., R.A., 31.7.02; Lt. 31.7.05; Capt. 30.10.14; Major, R.F.A., 22.3.16.

KENNEDY, D. (D.S.O. L.G. 11.1.19), Lt., N.Z. Rifle Brigade; M.C.

KENNEDY, D. S. (D.S.O. L.G. 1.1.17), T/Major, A.S.C. (now R.A.S.C.).

KENNEDY, H. (D.S.O. L.G. 18.1.18) (Details, L.G. 25.4.18), Lt., Can. Infantry.

KENNEDY, H. B. P. L. (D.S.O. L.G. 3.6.16); s. of late Vice-Admiral J. J. Kennedy, C.B.; m. Ruby, d. of late C. Trelawny, and cousin of the late Sir W. L. S. Trelawny, 10th Bart.; one d.; educ. Eton; 2nd Lt., 60th Rifles, 12.10.98; Lt. 18.12.99; Capt. 8.8.04; Major 1.9.15; Bt. Lt.-Col. 3.6.17; Bt. Col. 1.1.19; Colonel 17.9.20; T/Col. Comdt 1.1.21; S. African War, 1899–1902; Queen's Medal, 4 clasps; King's Medal, 2 clasps; Europ. War; Despatches seven times; C.M.G.; Grand Officer Military Order of Avis; Grand Officer Tower and Sword of Portugal; Croix de Guerre with Palm.

KENNEDY, JAMES (D.S.O. L.G. 4.6.17) (Bar, L.G. 2.12.18); b. 26.12.81; 2nd Lt., R. Highrs., 4.2.14; Lt. 10.5.15; Capt. 25.3.17; served Europ. War; Despatches; Bt. Major 3.6.19; M.C.; D.C.M.

KENNEDY, JOHN (D.S.O. L.G. 14.1.16) (Bar, 26.7.18); b. 20.11.78; m. Mrs. Pawson; 2nd Lt., Arg. and Suth'd Highrs., 16.2.98; Lt. 24.11.99; Capt. 28.4.09; Major 1.9.15; served Europ. War, 1914–18; Despatches; C.M.G.; Bt. Lt.-Col. 3.6.17; Bt.-Col. 3.6.19.

KENNEDY, REV. J. J. (D.S.O. L.G. 26.9.16); b. 1882; s. of J. Kennedy; educ. All-Hallows College, Dublin; Priest, 1905; served Europ. War as Chaplain to Australian Inf. Brigade, 1915–18; Despatches twice.

KENNEDY, M. K. H. (D.S.O. L.G. 20.9.18), Lt.-Cdr., R.N., 31.12.13.

KENNEDY, N. (D.S.O. L.G. 4.6.17), Major, R. Sc. Fusiliers.

KENNEDY, R. S., M.B., B.Ch. (D.S.O. L.G. 4.9.18); b. 8.12.82; s. of J. S. Kennedy; educ. Cork Grammar School; Queen's College, Cork; B.A.O. (with Honours), in Royal University of Ireland, 1905; Lt., I.M.S., 1.2.06; Capt. 1.2.09; Major 1.2.18; served in Abor Exp., 1911–12; E. African Campaign, 1914–17; Despatches thrice; M.C.; Afghan War, 1919; Bt. Lt.-Col. 1.1.20.

KENNEDY, W. (D.S.O. L.G. 1.1.18), Major, E. African Veterinary Corps.

KENNEDY, W. H. CLARK- (see Clark-Kennedy, W. H.).

KENNEDY-COCHRAN-PATRICK, W. J. C. (see Cochran-Patrick, W. J. C. Kennedy-).

KENNINGTON, J. (D.S.O. L.G. 1.2.19), T/Major, Linc. R.; M.C.

KENSINGTON, E. C. (D.S.O. L.G. 3.6.19); b. 2.6.79; 2nd Lt., Unatt., 27.7.98; I.S.C. 15.10.99; Lt., Ind. Army, 27.10.06; Capt. 27.7.07; Major 1.9.15; Bt. Lt.-Col. 3.6.18; 130th Baluchis, I.A.; Colonel 28.11.20; served Aden, 1903–4; Europ. War; Despatches.

KENT, A. E. (D.S.O. L.G. 1.1.18), Lt. (T/Major), Leic. R., S.R.; M.C.

KENT. J. (D.S.O. L.G. 1.1.18), Major, R.F.A.

KENTISH, L. W. (D.S.O. L.G. 4.6.17), Capt., R. Fus., S.R.

KENYON, H. E. (D.S.O. L.G. 1.1.18); b. 2.12.81; s. of Major-Gen. E. R. Kenyon, C.B., C.M.G., and Katharine Mary McCrea, d. of Major-General J. C. De Butts, R.E.; m. Gwendoline Ethel Graham Ommaney; two s.; one d.; educ. Winchester College; R.M.A., Woolwich; 1st commission, R.A., 23.7.01; Lt. 13.5.04; Capt. 23.7.14; Major 1.5.17; commanding Indian Mountain Battery; served with Indian Mountain Artillery, 1907–15; Persian Gulf Exp., 1910; Adjt. 1914–15; Egypt, 1914–15; Gallipoli, 1915, original landing at Anzac and evacuation of Anzac and Helles; G.S.O., Dec. 1915–June, 1916; France, 1916–18; Brig.-Major, 18th Corps Heavy Artillery, 15.1.17 to 22.9.18; Staff Officer, R.A., Second Army and Army of the Rhine, 23.9.18 to 4.4.19; Despatches four times; French Croix de Guerre; Belgian Croix de Guerre; North-West Frontier, 1919; Medal and clasp.

KEOGH, J. B. (D.S.O. L.G. 3.3.17); b. 25.1.71; 2nd Lt., R. Lancs. R., 9.9.91; Lt. 30.12.93; I.S.C. 10.11.95; Capt., I.A., 10.7.01; Major, Lancers, I.A., 9.9.09; Lt.-Col. 23.4.17; Col. 28.1.21; C.I.E.

KEOGH, J. H. (D.S.O. L.G. 3.8.20); b. 16.8.72; 2nd Lt., R.A., 13.5.93; Lt. 13.5.96; Capt. 17.3.00; Major 1.1.14; Lt.-Col. 1.3.18; Europ. War; Despatches; Bt.-Col. 1.8.20.

KER, R. F. (D.S.O. L.G. 8.3.19) (Details, L.G. 4.10.19), T/Major (A/Lt.-Col.), 6th Batt. K.O.S.B.; M.C.

KERANS, E. T. J. (D.S.O. L.G. 4.6.17); b. 26.2.80; 2nd Lt., Worc. R., 28.1.03; Lt. 28.7.06; Capt. 20.9.14; Bt. Major 3.6.16; served S. African War, 1900–2; Queen's Medal, 3 clasps.

KERANS, G. C. L. (D.S.O. L.G. 14.1.16); b. 15.10.77; m. Joyce Fielding (who died in 1921), d. of Major J. Proctor Humphris; one d.; Lt., I.M.S., 27.6.01; Capt. 27.6.04; Major 27.12.12; Lt.-Col. 27.12.20; N.W. Frontier, 1901–2; Medal, clasp.

KERBY, A. M. (D.S.O. L.G. 24.9.18), Lt., R.F.A., S.R.; M.C.

KERMODE, E. M. (D.S.O. L.G. 16.9.18), 2nd Lt., W. Yorks. Rgt.; M.C. and Bar; D.C.M. He was killed in action 28.7.18.

KERR, C. (D.S.O. L.G. 12.12.19), Capt. (T/Major), R. of O., late R.H. Guards, att. M.G.C.; M.C.

KERR, J. C. M. (D.S.O. L.G. 14.1.16), Major, Sc. Signal Co., R.E., T.F.

KERR, R. (D.S.O. L.G. 1.1.18), Major, Aust. Provost Corps.

KERR, R. S. RAIT- (see Rait-Kerr, R. S.).

KERR, W. (D.S.O. L.G. 31.5.16); b. 2.3.77; m., 1st, Ester Isobel Dalton; one child; 2nd, Emily Dalton; educ. St. Patrick's, Carlisle; entered Army, 1895; 2nd Lt., Border Regt., 21.10.14; Lt. 20.12.14; Capt. 19.1.15; S. African War, 1899–1900; Queen's Medal, 7 clasps; Europ. War; was present at the battles of Ypres, Neuve Chapelle, Festubert and Loos, and was wounded at Festubert; Despatches; M.C. He was killed in action 3.5.18. His D.S.O. was awarded for gallantry near Bray, 19–20.4.16.

KERRICH, W. A. F. (D.S.O. L.G. 1.2.19); b. 13.5.90; 2nd Lt., R.E., 23.7.10; Lt. 21.12.12; Capt. 23.7.12; commanded R.E., 7th Division, in Italy; Despatches; M.C.

KERSHAW, J. V. (D.S.O. L.G. 1.1.18), T/Major, E. Lancs. R.

KERSHAW, S. H. (D.S.O. L.G. 1.1.18); b. 20.5.81; m. Marjorie Melville, d. of Capt. Melville Tuke; one s.; one d.; 2nd Lt., North'd Fus., 11.8.00; Lt. 12.10.01; Capt. 1.9.09; Major 1.9.15; Lt.-Col., Northumberland Fusiliers, employed G.S., E. Anglian Div., T.A.; served S. African War, 1901–2; Queen's Medal, 4 clasps; Europ. War, 1914–18; Despatches; Bt. Lt.-Col. 1.1.19; Order of Nile, 3rd Class; White Eagle (Serbia), 4th Class.

KETTERSON, A. R. (D.S.O. L.G. 3.6.19), Major, 1st Batt. Can. Rly. Troops.

KETTLEWELL, E. A. (D.S.O. L.G. 16.9.18), Lt.-Col., I.A., 1.6.04; Bt. Col. 6.6.07; retired pay, 13.8.11; served Burmese Exp. 1885–87; Medal, clasp; N.W.F. of India, 1897–98; Medal, 2 clasps; Tirah, 1897–98; Despatches; clasp; China, 1900; Medal.

KETTLEWELL, L. (D.S.O. L.G. 25.8.17), T/Capt., Wilts R.

KEWLEY, E. R. (D.S.O. L.G. 26.9.17) (Details, L.G. 9.1.18) (Bar, L.G. 16.9.18); b. 27.11.89; 2nd Lt., Rif. Brig., 19.9.11; Lt. 17.4.13; Capt. 15.6.15; Bt. Major 3.6.18; M.C.

KEY, A. D. C. COOPER- (see Cooper-Key, A. D. C.).

KEYES, SIR R. J. B., Bart. (D.S.O. L.G. 3.6.16); b. 1872; s. of the late General Sir Charles Keyes; m. Eva M. Salvin Bowlby, d. of the late Edward Salvin Bowlby, D.L.; two s.; three d.; entered Navy, 1885; Commander, 1900; Capt., 1905; Commodore in charge of Submarine Service, 1912; Vitu, 1890; Medal and clasp; China, 1900; Despatches; promoted Commander; Medal, 2 clasps; M.V.O.; C.B.; Europ. War; C.M.G.; Commander of the Legion of Honour; in command of the operations against Zeebrugge and Ostend 23.4.18; K.C.B.; Croix de Guerre; G.C.V.O., 1918; created a Baronet 1919; appointed to command of the Battle Cruiser Squadron, Atlantic Fleet, 1919.

KEYS, P. H. (D.S.O. L.G. 3.6.19), T/Capt. (A/Major), 228th Field Co., R.E.; M.C.

KEYSER, A. G. (D.S.O. L.G. 3.6.19), T/Major, 9th Batt., M.G.C.

KEYWORTH, R. G. (D.S.O. L.G. 4.6.17); b. 24.1.73; 2nd Lt., R.A., 17.10.92; Lt. 17.10.95; Capt. 11.4.00; Major 20.10.09; Lt.-Col. 17.9.15; Col. 17.9.20; served S. African War, 1902; Queen's Medal and 4 clasps; Europ. War; Despatches; Bt.-Col. 1.1.19.

KIDD, A. L. GORDON- (see Gordon-Kidd, A. L.).

KIDD, B. G. B. (D.S.O. L.G 1.1.19); b 6.12.75; 2nd Lt., Unatt., 16.1.95; 2nd Lt., Ind. S.C. 27.3.96; Lt., I.A., 16.4.97; Capt. 16.1.04; Major 16.1.13; Lt.-Col. 24.9.20; served N.W. Frontier of India, 1901–2; Medal with clasp; Aden, 1903–4; Europ. War; Despatches.

KIDD, G. E. (D.S.O. L.G. 14.11.16), 2nd Lt., R.A., 21.12.01; Lt. 21.12.04. Major Kidd was killed in action 26.9.16.

KILBORN, A. R. (D.S.O. L.G. 2.12.18), Lt., 78th Batt. Can. Inf., Manitoba R.; M.C.; M.M.

KILLAM, G. K. (D.S.O. L.G. 1.1.18), Major, Can. Inf.

KILLICK, A. H. (D.S.O. L.G. 3.6.19); b. 10.2.94; T/Lt. 6.12.14; 2nd Lt., S. Lancs. R., 8.7.15; Lt. 2.7.16; Capt. 26.5.21; M.C.

KILMER, C. E. (D.S.O. L.G. 22.9.16), Capt., Can. Inf. His D.S.O. was awarded for gallantry on 29.7.16, at St. Eloi.

KILNER, C. F. (D.S.O. L.G. 19.2.15) (Bar, L.G. 1.10.17), Sqn.-Cdr., R.N.A.S.; Capt. (T/Major), R.M.L.I. (see "The Distinguished Service Order," from its institution to 31.12.15, same publishers).

KILNER, C. H. (D.S.O. L.G. 1.1.18); b. 15.8.64; 1st commission 5.7.84; Major 15.3.00; R.A., retired 13.1.06; Major (T/Lt.-Col.), R. of O., R.F.A; Lt.-Col., Army, 15.12.15; served S. African War, 1899–1900; Queen's Medal, 4 clasps; Europ. War; Despatches.

KILPATRICK, REV. G. G. D. (D.S.O. L.G. 1.2.19); b. 12.4.88; s. of the Rev. T. B. Kilpatrick, D.D., of Toronto; educ. Aberdeen Grammar School; Winnipeg Collegiate Institute, and Toronto University; C.F., June, 1915; Senior Chaplain, 3rd Can. Division, Nov. 1918.

KILVERT, R. E. (D.S.O. L.G. 1.1.18); b. 20.3.81; 2nd Lt., R.M.A., 1.1.98; Lt. 1.1.99; Capt. 1.9.07; Major 30.6.16.

KINCH, A. G. (D.S.O. L.G. 22.12.16), Lt., R. Ind. Marine.

KINDELL, F. P. (D.S.O. L.G. 1.1.18), Lt. (A/Major), R.A.; served Europ. War, 1914–18; M.C.

KINDERSLEY, D. (D.S.O. L.G. 4.6.17); b. 8.8.73; s. of H. W. S. Kindersley; m. Ivy Maud Tyler; educ. Edinburgh Academy; entered the Army, Aug. 1914; gazetted 2nd Lt., H.L.I. Capt. Kindersley was killed in action 22.6.17.

KINDERSLEY, J. B. (D.S.O. L.G. 1.1.19), T/Lt. (A/Capt.), R.F.A.; M.C. He was in the Oxford Boat in 1914.

KING, C. E. (D.S.O. L.G. 1.1.18), Major, Can. Inf.

KING, C. E. S. (D.S.O. L.G. 22.8.18); s. of late Rev. R. King, of Ballymena; m. Adela, d. of late W. Gihon; Major, late R.A.S.C., and Union Defence Force, S.A.; served German S.W. Africa, 1914–15; Despatches.

KING, C. F. (D.S.O. L.G. 1.1.18) (Bar, L.G. 16.9.18), T/Major (T/Lt.-Col.), Cheshire Rgt.; M.C.

KING, C. H. D. (D.S.O. L.G. 15.2.19) (Details, L.G. 30.7.19); b. 17.8.97; s. of Col. C. D. King, C.B.E., late R.F.A., and Evelyn Marie, d. of late E. A. Hankey; educ. Wellington College; 2nd Lt., K.R.R.C. (from Spec. Res.); Lt. 1.1.17; Capt. 1.4.21; served Europ. War; M.C.

KING, C. T. (D.S.O. L.G. 1.1.18), Major, Can. Inf.

KING, D. M. (D.S.O. L.G. 1.1.17) (Bar, L.G. 7.11.18); b. 25.11.86; 2nd Lt., L'pool R., 6.10.06; Lt. 4.11.08; Capt. 1.10.14; Major 3.6.19; M.C.

KING, F. (D.S.O. L.G. 1.1.18), Capt. (T/Major), 4th Hussars.

KING, G. A. (D.S.O. L.G. 3.6.16) (Bar, L.G. 1.1.18), Lt.-Col., Canterbury Rgt., N.Z. Force.

KING, G. E. (D.S.O. L.G. 1.1.17) (Bar, L.G. 24.9.18), T/Major, E. Yorks. R.

KING, G. H. (D.S.O. L.G. 1.1.17); s. of Hartley and Louisa King, of Stourbridge; b. 28.3.82; educ. Westminster School; R.M.A., Woolwich; 2nd Lt., R.A., 23.7.01; Lt. 23.7.04; Capt. 18.4.14; Major 15.10.15; served Europ. War; Despatches twice.

KING, G. H. M. (D.S.O. L.G. 1.1.18), Lt.-Col., Aust. F.A.; C.M.G.

KING, G. W. (D.S.O. L.G. 8.3.19) (Details, L.G. 4.10.19), T/Capt. (A/Major), C., 160th Brig., R.F.A.; M.C.

KING, H. J. (D.S.O. L.G. 26.11.17) (Details, L.G. 6.4.18), T/Lt.-Col., Yorks L.D.

KING, J. R. (D.S.O. L.G. 1.1.18), T/Major, A.S.C.

KING, M. (D.S.O. L.G. 26.4.17), Lt., C. Gds., S.R.

KING, M. H. (D.S.O. L.G. 3.6.19), Capt. (T/Major), 4th Batt. W. Riding R., T.F.; M.C.

KING, P. W. S. (D.S.O. (L.G. 23.3.17); m. Elvyn Margaret, widow of Gordon Bostock (Lt., R.G.A.), Cdr., R.N., 30.6.19.

KING, R. (D.S.O. L.G. 3.6.19), Capt., Aust. Flying Corps (France), R.A.F.; D.F.C.

KING, R. M. (D.S.O. L.G. 8.3.18), Cdr., R.N., 30.6.16.

KING, W. (D.S.O. L.G. 11.8.17), Lt., R.N.V.R.

KING, W. A. DE C. (D.S.O. L.G. 3.6.16); b. 19.9.74; 2nd Lt., R.E., 1.10.94; Capt. 1.4.04; Major; served S. African War, 1901–2; Queen's Medal, 3 clasps. He was killed in action 27.5.17.

KING, W. D. V. O. (D.S.O. L.G. 1.1.19), T/Lt.-Col., 17th Batt. North'd Fus.

KING, W. H., B.A. (D.S.O. L.G. 27.10.17) (Details, L.G. 18.3.18); b. 10.8.87; s. of W. C. J. King (Branch Manager, Canadian Bank of Commerce) and Zina M. H. King (*née* Horneby); m. Kathleen Ewen, d. of P. W. D. Brodrick and Florence Ada Brodrick; educ. Public High Schools in Ontario and Quebec; University of Toronto; Runner-up, Middle and Heavies (Boxing), University of Toronto, 1909; Runner-up, Middle Weights Boxing, University of Toronto, 1910; Lt., Can. Infantry. The official account of his D.S.O. refers to a raid carried out on 4.9.17 at 12.30 a.m. by A, B and D Companies (Lt. King was attached to A Company) of 52nd Batt. Can. Inf. (C.O., Lt.-Col. W. W. Foster, D.S.O.). Objective was portions of Cinnabar Trench, Nabob's Alley (just north of city of Lens). The raid lasted about 40 minutes, and was successful. Casualties were inflicted on the enemy, prisoners and machine guns taken, and machine-gun emplacements and dug-outs destroyed. Lt. King was in France with 52nd Batt. Can. Inf. from 1.5.17 to 4.9.17; wounded 4.9.17 and invalided to Canada; Despatches.

KING, W. S. (D.S.O. L.G. 1.1.18), Major, Aust. A.S.C.

KING-HARMAN, W. A. (D.S.O. L.G. 1.1.18); b. 3.1.69; s. of late Col. W. H. King-Harman, D.L., R.A.; educ. Marlborough; R.M.C., Sandhurst; joined 1st Batt. R. Ir. Rifles, 1890; took part in Rhodesian Campaign, 1896 (Medal); joined R.I. Rifles Militia, 4th Batt., 1899; Special Reserve, 3rd Batt., 1908; rejoined Army, 1914; Brig.-Major of 7th Reserve Brigade, 1915; proceeded to France, 1916; appointed to Staff of G.H.Q., 3rd Echelon, as D.A.A.G., Nov. 1916.

KINGSFORD, G. N. (D.S.O. L.G. 3.6.19), T/Capt. (A/Major), 67th Field Co., R.E.; M.C.

KINGSFORD, G. T. (D.S.O. L.G. 1.1.18), Major, R.E.

KINGSLEY, H. E. W. BELL- (see Bell-Kingsley, H. E. W.).

KINGSMILL, A. DE P. (D.S.O. L.G. 4.6.17), Capt. (T/Lt.-Col.), R. of O., late G. Guards; M.C.

KINGSMILL, H. F. (D.S.O. L.G. 22.9.16), Major, Aust. Artillery.

KINGSMILL, W. B. (D.S.O. L.G. 3.6.18), Lt.-Col., Can. Pioneers.

KINGSTONE, J. J. (D.S.O. L.G. 3.6.19); b. 26.8.92; 2nd Lt., 2nd D.G., 4.9.12; Lt. 21.1.16; Capt. 22.10.17; M.C.

KININMONTH, J. C. (D.S.O. L.G. 4.6.17), Aust. Ordnance Corps; served Europ. War, 1915–17; Despatches.

KINKEAD, S. M. (D.S.O. L.G. 1.4.20), Flying Officer, R.A.F., late H.L.I., and R.N.A.S.; D.S.C. and Bar; D.F. Cross and Bar.

KINLOCH, G. (D.S.O. L.G. 8.3.18); s. of late R. C. Kinloch; T/Major, R.G.A.

KINNEAR, J. L. (D.S.O. L.G. 1.1.18), Major, L'pool R. and R.F.C.; M.C. He was killed in action 28.4.18.

KINNEAR, W. (D.S.O. L.G. 3.6.18), Lt.-Col., R.F.A.

KIPPEN, W. H. (D.S.O. L.G. 2.12.18), Capt. (A/Major), 3rd Batt. Can. Inf., 1st Central Ontario Rgt.; M.C.

KIRBY, H. (D.S.O. L.G. 4.6.17); b. 25.10.78; Lt., A.V.C., 11.5.04; Capt. 11.5.09; Major, R.A.V.C., 10.7.15.

KIRBY, H. A. (D.S.O. L.G. 3.6.18); b. 18.1.81; 2nd Lt., R.A., 15.5.01; Lt. 2.5.04; Capt. 23.7.14; Major 1.5.17; M.C.

KIRBY, J. T. (D.S.O. L.G. 17.3.17); b. 2.8.80; 2nd Lt., R. War. R., 4.5.01; Lt., I.A., 4.8.03; Capt. 4.5.10; Major 4.5.16; Bt. Lt.-Col. 3.6.18; Europ. War; Despatches.

KIRBY, R. E. W. (D.S.O. L.G. 11.4.19); s. of late R. J. Kirby, of Tokio, Japan; Cdr., R.N., 31.12.17; retired.

KIRBY, W. L. C. (D.S.O. L.G. 4.6.17); b. 23.10.79; 2nd Lt., R.A., 26.5.00; Lt. 14.8.02; Capt., 12th Lancers, 18.9.09; Bt. Major 1.1.19; Major 21.1.21; served S. African War, 1902; Queen's Medal, 2 clasps; Europ. War; Despatches; O.B.E.

KIRK, J. W. C. (D.S.O. L.G. 1.1.17); b. 21.1.78; s. of Sir John Kirk, G.C.M.G., K.C.B., and Helen (who died in 1914), d. of C. Cooke; m. Agnes Maud, d. of Col. F. H. Haynes, A.P.D.; educ. Marlborough; Cambridge University; 2nd Lt, D.C.L.I., 18.10.99; Lt. 16.2.01; Capt. 4.5.07; Major 1.9.15; served S. African War, 1899–1902; Despatches; Queen's Medal, 4 clasps; King's Medal, 2 clasps; Somaliland, 1902–4; Medal, 2 clasps; Europ. War, 1914–18; Despatches; Bt. Lt.-Col. 3.6.19.

KIRKBY, E. W. (D.S.O. L.G. 20.2.19), Cdr., R.N., 30.6.19.

KIRKBY, W. W. (D.S.O. L.G. 15.2.19) (Details, L.G. 30.7.19); b. 30.8.84; Capt. R.W.F., from Spec. Res., 2.10.15.

KIRKCALDY, J. (D.S.O. L.G. 1.1.17) (1st Bar, L.G. 3.6.18) (2nd Bar, L.G. 2.12.18), Lt.-Col., 78th Batt. Can. Inf., Manitoba R.

KIRKE, E. ST. G. (D.S.O. L.G. 1.2.17); b. 27.1.83; s. of Col. St. G. M. Kirke (formerly R.E.); m. Ethel Jessie, d. of Rev. J. Longley, Rector of Tydd St. Mary's, Lincolnshire; two d.; educ. St. Peter's School (Head of School); R.M.A., Woolwich, 1900–2; passed first into R.E. (with the King's and Pollock Gold Medals) 31.7.02; Lt. 24.9.04; Capt. 31.7.13; Major, R.E., 31.7.17; served E. Africa, 1914–17; Despatches; Punjab, N.W.F.P., Officers' Light Weight Boxing Champion, Army and Navy, 1903.

KIRKE, K. ST. G. (D.S.O. L.G. 1.1.17); b. 5.1.75; e. s. of Col. St. G. M. Kirke, R.E; m. Kathleen, d. of S. Perry, J.P., D.L., late 12th Lancers, of Woodrooffe, Clonmel; educ. Clifton College; R.M.A., Woolwich; commissioned R.A. 15.6.95; Lieut. 15.6.98; Capt. 15.4.01; Major 30.9.11; Lt.-Col. 1.6.16; retired pay 19.4.20; served S. African War, 1899–1900; Queen's Medal and clasp; Europ. War, 1914–17.

KIRKE, W. M. ST. G. (D.S.O. L.G. 3.6.16); b. 16.1.77; s. of Col. St. G. M. Kirke, R.E.; m. Lilian Ethel, d. of J. Macliesh; two s.; three d.; educ. Haileybury; R.M. Academy, Woolwich; ent. R.A. 21.1.96; Lt. 21.9.99; Capt. 4.12.01; Bt. Major 21.2.14; Bt. Lt.-Col. 18.2.15; Bt. Col. 1.1.17; Colonel 10.8.20; Waziristan, 1901–2; Medal and clasp; commanded Wellaung Punitive Exp.; S. Chin Hills, 1905–6; served Europ. War, 1914–18; Despatches six times; Bt. Lt.-Col.; Bt. Col.; C.B.; C.M.G.; Order of the Crown of Belgium; Officer, Legion of Honour; French and Belgian Croix de Guerre; White Eagle of Serbia.

KIRKLAND, T. (D.S.O. L.G. 1.1.17); b. 17.7.81; 2nd Lt., R.A., 23.5.00; Lt. 1.2.02; Capt. 22.1.11; Major 30.10.14.

KIRKNESS, L. H. (D.S.O. L.G. 1.1.18), T/Lt.-Col., Spec. List.

KIRKPATRICK, A. R. Y. (D.S.O. L.G. 14.1.16); b. 9.4.68; 2nd Lt., R.A., 17.2.88; Lt. 17.2.91; Capt. 15.10.98; Major 28.11.08; Lt.-Col. 29.12.15; retired 30.10.19; C.M.G.; Europ. War, 1914–18; Despatches; C.M.G.

KIRKPATRICK, G. H. (D.S.O. L.G. 1.2.19), Lt.-Col., 72nd Batt. Can. Inf.; served S. African War, 1901–2; Queen's Medal, 2 clasps.

KIRKPATRICK, H. C. B. (D.S.O. L.G. 4.6.17), Capt., K.O.S.B.; M.C. He was killed in action 1.10.18.

KIRKPATRICK, H. F. (D.S.O. L.G. 1.1.18) (Bar, L.G. 26.7.18), Maj. (A/Lt.-Col.), R. of O., E. Kent Rgt. He died 23.7.18.

KIRKUP, P. (D.S.O. L.G. 16.9.18) (Bar, L.G. 24.9.18), Capt. (A/Lt.-Col.), Durham L.I.; M.C.

KIRKWOOD, J. G. (D.S.O. L.G. 3.6.16), T/Major, S. Batt. Gloucesters. R.

KIRKWOOD, J. H. M. (D.S.O. L.G. 16.8.17); b. 11.5.77; s. of J. M. Kirkwood; m. Gertrude, d. of Sir R. Lyle, Bart.; two s.; one d.; educ. Harrow; was in 7th Dn. Gds.; Capt., R.N. Devon Hussars; T/Major, Household Bn.; served S. Africa, 1899–1901; wounded; Queen's Medal, 3 clasps; King's Medal, 2 clasps; Despatches; served with 4th Dn. Gds., 1914–15 (wounded); with 1st Life Guards and Household Batt. R. Irish Rifles; J.P.; M.P. (C.), S.E. Essex, 1910–12

KIRKWOOD, J. R. N. (D.S.O. L.G. 4.6.17), T.Major, R.E.

KIRSTEN, J. R. F. (D.S.O. L.G. 22.8.18), Lt.-Col., 6th Dismounted Rifles (Midlandse Schutters), S. African Military Forces.

KIRWAN, J. T. (D.S.O. L.G. 22.8.18), Capt. (T/Major) (Supplies), S. African Service Corps.

KISCH, F. H. (D.S.O. L.G. 14.1.16); b. 23.8.88; s. of H. M. Kisch, C.S.I., and Alice Charlotte, d. of late J. L. Elkin; m. Jeanne, d. of P. Colin, of Neuchâtel, Switzerland; educ. Clifton College; R.M.A., Woolwich; 2nd Lt., R.E., 23.7.07; Lt. 1.6.09; Capt. 30.10.14; served Europ. War, France, 1914–15; Mesopotamia, 1916–17; Despatches thrice; wounded thrice; Croix de Guerre; Bt. Major 1.1.18; Bt. Lt.-Col. 3.6.19; C.B.E.

KITCHIN, C. (D.S.O. L.G. 3.6.19); b. 5.1.83; 2nd Lt. 22.10.02; Lt. 8.10.04; Capt. 1.4.12; Major 22.10.17.

KITCHIN, C. E. (D.S.O. L.G. 3.6.16); b. 27.4.77; 2nd Lt., S. Wales Bord.; Capt. 19.6.07; retired 1.9.12; Bt. Lt.-Col. 3.6.18; Lt.-Col. 30.4.19.

KITCHING, C. H. (D.S.O. L.G. 4.6.17); b. 7.5.81; m. Phyllis Dora, d. of late W. Whitworth; 2nd Lt., Worc. R., 8.1.01; Capt. 1.4.10; Retired Pay, 13.7.12.

KITCHING, H. W. (D.S.O. L.G. 15.9.16); b. 12.4.72; s. of Rev. W. Kitching, M.A.; m. Alice, d. of late F. Felkin; educ. Glyngarth School, Cheltenham; Royal Naval Engineering College, Devonport; ent. R.N. as Assistant Engineer, 1893; served in Undaunted in China, 1894–97; Illustrious in Mediterranean, 1898–1901; Destroyers in Home Waters and in Mediterranean, 1902–8; miscellaneous duties in Skipjack and Gibraltar, 1908–12; Engineer-Commander, 1911; Engineer Captain (Retired); served in Warrior, 1912–16; took part in Battle of Jutland 31.5.16; Russian Order of St. Stanislas, 2nd Class.

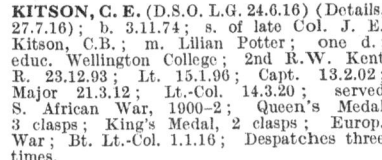

H. W. Kitching.

KITSON, C. E. (D.S.O. L.G. 24.6.16) (Details, 27.7.16); b. 3.11.74; s. of late Col. J. E. Kitson, C.B.; m. Lilian Potter; one d.; educ. Wellington College; 2nd R.W. Kent R. 23.12.93; Lt. 15.1.96; Capt. 13.2.02; Major 21.3.12; Lt.-Col. 14.3.20; served S. African War, 1900–2; Queen's Medal 3 clasps; King's Medal, 2 clasps; Europ. War; Bt. Lt.-Col. 1.1.16; Despatches three times.

KITSON, J. B. (D.S.O. L.G. 15.9.16); b. Dec. 1883; s. of Rev. J. Buller Kitson, Rector of Laureath; m. Hon. Frances Margaret Palmer Howard, e. d. of Baroness Strathcona and Mount Royal; two s.; two d.; educ. Northam Place, Herts; joined R.N., 1898; Lt. 1905; Commander, 1917; served Europ. War, including Jutland Bank; Despatches.

KITSON, HON. R. D., B.A. (D.S.O. L.G. 3.6.18); b. 19.7.82; s. of 1st Lord Airedale; m. Sheila Grace, d. of late F. E. Vandeleur; one s.; one d.; educ. Westminster; Trinity College, Cambridge; Capt., 1/8th West Yorks R.; served Europ. War; M.C.; J.P. West Riding.

KNAPMAN, L. (D.S.O. L.G. 1.1.18); s. of late E. Knapman; educ. Exeter School; T/Major, A.S.C. (now R.A.S.C.), Mounted Section.

KNAPP, E. (D.S.O. L.G. 25.8.17), T/Major (A/Lt.-Col.), S. African Inf.

KNAPP, G. H. (D.S.O. L.G. 22.8.18), Lt.-Col., S. African Medical Service; served Bechuanaland, 1897; Medal with clasp; S. African War, 1899–1902; Queen's Medal, 3 clasps; King's Medal, 2 clasps.

KNAPP, THE REV. S. S. (D.S.O. L.G. 4.6.17); b. 1858; educ. St. Edmund's Catholic College, Ware; O.D.C.; served S. African War; Queen's Medal and 4 clasps; Europ. War; Despatches; M.C. He died of wounds 1.8.17, in Flanders. The Earl of Ypres (then Viscount French) unveiled a stained glass window to his memory in the Carmelite Church, Kensington, subscribed for by officers, non-commissioned officers and men of the Irish Guards. Lord French said: "Father Knapp was a credit to that sacred Order to which he belonged, and indeed to the whole Catholic faith throughout Christendom. He gained the esteem and sincere affection of the soldiers with whom he served."

KNIGHT, A. E., M.B. (D.S.O. L.G. 1.1.19), T/Capt. (A/Major), R.A.M.C.; M.C.

KNIGHT, A. G. (D.S.O. L.G. 11.12.16), 2nd Lt., R.F.C.; M.C. He was killed in action 28.12.16.

KNIGHT, C. F., M.B. (D.S.O. L.G. 15.2.19) (Details, L.G. 30.7.19), T/Major, 133rd Field Ambulance, R.A.M.C.

KNIGHT, C. L. W. M. (D.S.O. L.G. 3.6.16), T/Lt.-Col., late R. of O., R.A.

KNIGHT, E. S. (D.S.O. L.G. 4.2.18) (Details, L.G. 5.7.18); b. 18.11.90; s. of George and Beatrice Emma Knight; educ. Churcher's College, Petersfield; 2nd Lt., 12th London Rgt. (The Rangers); served Europ. War; Despatches. Represented the Inns of Court O.T.C. 1916 Cross Country Races, and won the Championship Cup, 2/12 London Regt., Aug. 1915.

KNIGHT, H. L. (D.S.O. L.G. 4.6.17); b. 24.3.74; 2nd Lt., R. I. Fusiliers, 10.10.94; Lt. 27.1.98; Capt. 1.5.02; Major 21.1.14; Lt.-Col. 14.3.17; Col. 4.8.21; Temp. Brig.-Gen., Jan. 1918–July, 1919; served S. African War, 1899–1900; Despatches; Queen's Medal and 5 clasps; Europ. War, 1914–18; Bt. Lt.-Col.; Bt. Col.; Despatches; C.M.G.

KNIGHT, J. H. (D.S.O. L.G. 9.9.21); b. 30.9.83; s. of late Rev. J. W. Knight, sometime Fellow of Magdalen College, Oxford, and Vicar of Washington, Sussex; 2nd Lt., R.A., 4.6.04; Lt. 4.6.07; Capt. 30.10.14; Bt. Major 3.6.17; Abor, 1911–12; Despatches; Medal with clasp.

KNIGHT, R. C. (D.S.O. L.G. 1.1.19); b. 13.11.91; s. of S. C. Knight; m. Sybil Christine, d. of A. Naylor; one d.; educ. Horsham Grammar School; served Europ. War, 4½ years overseas with 18th Royal Fusiliers, and Brig. Major in Tank Corps; M.C. and Bar; 1914–15 Star; Despatches; Town Clerk of Guildford.

KNIGHTLEY, P. F. (D.S.O. L.G. 18.1.18) (Details, L.G. 25.4.18), Lt. (T/Capt.), R.W.F.

KNOLLES, R. M. (D.S.O. L.G. 1.1.17); b. 8.9.81; m. Ruth Margery, d. of Mrs. Glendinning; Capt. (from Spec. Res.), R.A., 5.8.14; Major 16.11.15; served S. African War, 1902; Queen's Medal and 2 clasps; Europ. War, 1914–17; Despatches.

KNOLLYS, D. E. (D.S.O. L.G. 3.6.19); b. 20.2.84; 2nd Lt. (Unatt.), 19.8.03; 2nd Lt., I.A., 18.12.04; Lt., I.A., 19.11.05; Capt. 19.8.12; Major 19.8.18.

KNOTHE, H. (D.S.O. L.G. 1.1.17), Lt. (T/Major), A.S.C. (now R.A.S.C.), S.R.; M.C.

KNOTT, REV. A. E. (D.S.O. L.G. 25.8.17), T/Chapl. to the Forces, 1st Class.

KNOTT, J. E. (D.S.O. L.G. 24.6.16); s. of H. Knott, J.P., and of Mrs. Knott, d. of the late T. P. Wakefield, of Hall, Moate, co. Westmeath; m. Dorothy, d. of M. Spring Rice Bayly; educ. Leighton Park School, Reading; Trooper, S. Irish Horse, 1914; 2nd Lt., R. Innis. Fus., Nov. 1914; T/Capt. His D.S.O. was awarded for gallantry at "The Kink," 29.4.16.

KNOTT, J. L. (D.S.O. L.G. 3.6.16); b. 1882; s. of Sir James Knott, Bart., a former M.P. for Sunderland; was Deputy Managing Director of the Prince Line of Steamships; served in the European War as T/Major, Service Batt. W. Yorks. R. Major Knott was killed in action 1.7.16.

KNOWLES, C. H. (D.S.O. L.G. 24.3.19), Lt.-Cdr., R.N., 3.6.16.

KNOWLES, G. (D.S.O. L.G. 12.9.02) (Bar, L.G. 4.2.18) (Details, L.G. 5.7.18), Major, Indian Cavalry (see "The Distinguished Service Order," from its institution to 31.12.15).

KNOWLES, G. H. (D.S.O. L.G. 8.3.18), Cdr., R.N., 31.12.15.

KNOX, E. F. (D.S.O. L.G. 22.12.16); b. 27.7.71; 2nd Lt., Norfolk Regt., 29.11.90; Lt. 6.10.93; Capt., Ind. Army, 10.7.01; Maj. 29.11.08; Lt.-Col. 29.11.10; Col. 31.5.20; Tirah, 1897–98; Medal, 2 clasps.

KNOX, F. P. (D.S.O. L.G. 3.6.18), T/Major, A.S.C. (now R.A.S.C.).

KNOX, H. H. S. (D.S.O. L.G. 1.1.17); b. 5.11.73; s. of late V. E. Knox, of Shimnah, Newcastle, co. Down; m. Grace Una, d. of Rev. R. A. Storrs, Rector, Shanklin, I. of Wight; one d.; educ. St. Columbia's College, Rathfarnham, Dublin; 2nd Lt., Northants R., 9.9.93; Lt. 26.8.95; Capt. 1.4.02; Adjt., 1st Batt. Northants R., 1902–5; Major 15.6.13; Lt.-Col. 2.6.19; Col. 7.4.20; served Samana, Tirah and N.W. Frontier, India, 1897–98 (Medal, 3 clasps); Uganda Protectorate with Uganda Rifles, 1900–1; Europ. War; B.E.F., France, 1915–19; Brig.-Gen., G.S., XV. Army Corps, 1917–19; wounded; Despatches seven times; Bt. Lt.-Col. 1.1.16; Bt. Col. 1.1.18; C.B.; Croix de Guerre; Officier, Legion of Honour; Officier, Couronne Belge; A/Major-General, G.S., First Army, 6.2.19–7.3.19.

KNOX, J. M. (D.S.O. L.G. 1.1.17) (Bar, L.G. 24.9.18); b. 10.4.78; s. of James and Elizabeth Knox; the eldest of nine brothers, six of whom served in the European War. One brother was killed in action, and another, Lt. K. Knox, R.E., was the first Nuneaton man to win the Victoria Cross. He m. D. M., d. of Dr. Isles, of Watford; educ. Nuneaton Grammar School; Bedford Modern School; ent. 1/7th R. War. R. (Vol.), 4.11.99; Lt. 1900; Capt., 1904; Major, 1914; served S. African War, 1902; Queen's Medal, 5 clasps; Europ. War; Despatches five times; Bt. Lt.-Col. 1.1.18; served first in France, and was killed in action in Italy in Sept. 1918.

KNOX, R. S. (D.S.O. L.G. 1.1.17) (1st Bar, L.G. 18.2.18) (Details, L.G. 18.7.18) (2nd Bar, L.G. 16.9.18); (3rd Bar, L.G. 8.3.19) (Details, L.G. 4.10.19); b. 2.3.81; s. of late W. J. Knox and Nannie, his wife; m. Ivy, d. of W. D. Lynch, Managing Director, Canadian Vickers Ltd.; educ. Intermediate School, Ballymoney; joined 10th R. Inniskilling Fusiliers 15.9.14; Major, June, 1916; Lt.-Col., April, 1918; commanded 9th R. Inniskilling Fus., April, 1918, until the end of the war; Despatches several times; Croix de Guerre and Gold Star.

KNOX, R. U. E. (D.S.O. L.G. 15.3.16), T/Lt., 8th Batt. The Suffolk R.

KNYVETT, C. L. (D.S.O. L.G. 1.1.18), Maj., R.F.A.; M.C.

KNYVETT, F. B. (D.S.O. L.G. 4.6.17), T/Major, R.F.A.

KOEBEL, F. E. (D.S.O. L.G. 16.8.17); b. 20.9.81; 5th s. of late Oscar Koebel, of Murley Grange, Bishopsteignton, S. Devon; m. Evelyn Annie Whateley; two d.; educ. Stubbington House, Fareham; 2nd Lt., R.A., 17.3.00; Lt., R.A., 3.4.01; Ind. Army 12.1.04; Capt. 17.3.09; Major 1.9.15 (51st Sikhs, F.F., I.A.); served S. African War, 1900; Queen's Medal and clasp; Europ. War, 1914–17; Despatches.

KOEBEL, F. O. (D.S.O. L.G. 26.7.17); b. 25.8.80; s. of late Oscar Koebel; m. Mary, d. of G. F. Gee; educ. Eastbourne College; 2nd Lt., N. Staffs R., from Militia, 5.1.01; Lt. 11.10.02; Capt. 17.3.09; Major 1.9.15; served S. Africa, 1900; Europ. War; Despatches. He was awarded the D.S.O. for services in Macedonia.

KOEN, J. J. (D.S.O. L.G. 1.2.17), Lt.-Col., S. African Horse.

KOSTER, R. H. (D.S.O. L.G. 1.1.17), Capt., R. of O., S. Lanc. R.

KREFT, C. J. (D.S.O. L.G. 4.6.17), Major, S. African Infantry.

KREYER, J. A. C. (D.S.O. L.G. 3.6.19), Major, 28th Light Cavalry, I.A.

KRUGER, J. A. (Jacobus Andries, gazetted as Johannes Andries) (D.S.O. L.G. 22.8.18), Major, Vryheid Commando, S. African Military Forces.

KUHNE, C. H. (D.S.O. L.G. 4.6.17); b. 24.6.91; 2nd Lt. 10.10.14; Capt., R.A.S.C., 8.6.20.

KYLE, R. (D.S.O. L.G. 1.1.18), T/Lt.-Col., H.L.I.

KYNGDON, W. F. R. (D.S.O. L.G. 1.1.18); b. 10.4.81; 2nd Lt., R.A., 24.12.02; Lt. 24.12.05; Capt. 30.10.14; Major 16.6.17.

KYRKE, H. V. V. (D.S.O. L.G. 4.6.17); b. 4.3.81; s. of Col. V. Kyrke; m. Frances Mary Craven, d. of Lt.-Col. Craven Hoyle; one d.; 2nd Lt., R.W. Fus., 18.10.99; Lt. 27.11.02; Capt. 4.12.09; Major 1.9.15; served S. African War, 1899–1902; Despatches; Queen's Medal and 5 clasps; King's Medal and 2 clasps; Europ. War, 1914–18; Despatches; 4th Class Medjidie; 4th Class Nile.

LABOUCHERE, A. M. (D.S.O. L.G. 26.7.18); y. s. of Arthur Labouchere, and nephew of the late Henry Labouchere; educ. Wellington College, and Oriel College, Oxford; served in Europ. War as Temporary Major, Oxford and Bucks L.I.; was wounded and taken prisoner, and died on April 20th, 1918.

LACON, SIR G. H. U., Bart. (D.S.O. L.G. 26.11.17) (Details, L.G. 6.4.18); b. 15.3.81; s. of T. B. U. Lacon and Florence, d. of R. G. Banks, of Toronto; s. brother, 1911; m. Vere Valerie Florence Eleanore (who died in 1916), o. d. of late H. S. H. Lacon, of Ormesby Hall, Norfolk; one s., George Vere Francis; one d.; educ. Eton; Capt. 4th Batt. R. War. Rgt.; served S. African War, 1899–1901 (Queen's Medal, 3 clasps); Europ. War, 1914–18; wounded; Despatches.

LAFLECHE, L. R. (D.S.O. L.G. 4.6.17), Major, Can. Inf.; served Europ. War; Despatches; Legion of Honour.

LA FONTAINE, S. H. (D.S.O. L.G. 27.7.18), T/Capt., Gen. List. E. African Force; M.C.

LAING, N. O. (D.S.O. L.G. 1.1.19); b. 20.3.84; 2nd Lt., 4th Hussars, 10.10.03; Lt. 11.4.08; Capt. 1.3.12; A/Lt.-Col. 4.11.17; Despatches.

LAING, R. (D.S.O. L.G. 1.1.18) (Bar, L.G. 26.7.18); b. 11.11.79; 1st Com. 7.3.00; Major 1.9.15; Lt.-Col., Army, 18.7.19; retired, Seaf. Highrs., 18.7.19; served S. African War, 1900–2; Queen's Medal with 3 clasps; King's Medal with 2 clasps; Europ. War; Despatches; M.C.

LAING, S. VAN B. (D.S.O. L.G. 23.10.19); b. 21.4.84; 2nd Lt., Unatt., 21.4.03; 2nd Lt., I.A., 6.4.04; Lt. 21.4.05; Capt. 21.1.12; Major 21.1.18; served Europ. War (Mesopotamia), 1914–16; Despatches; M.C.

LAIRD, H. G. C. (D.S.O. L.G. 1.1.19); b. 6.1.89; 2nd Lt., Unatt., 9.9.08; Ind. Army, 10.12.09; Lt. 9.12.10; Capt., 1st Batt. 101st Grenadiers, I.A., 1.9.15.

LAIRD, J. (D.S.O. L.G. 1.1.18), Major (A/Lt.-Col.), R.F.A.

LAIRD, K. M. (D.S.O. L.G. 4.6.17); b. 5.4.80; 2nd Lt., A. and S. Highrs., 20.1.00; Lt. 28.12.01; Capt. 25.8.09; Major 1.9.15; served S. African War; Queen's Medal with 3 clasps; King's Medal with 2 clasps; Europ. War; Bt. Lt.-Col. 3.6.18; Despatches.

LAITHWAITE, A. (D.S.O. L.G. 17.12.17) (Details, L.G. 23.4.18), 2nd Lt., London R.

LAKE, B. C. (D.S.O. L.G. 11.1.19); b. 7.4.89; 2nd Lt., K.O.S.B., 24.3.09; Lt. 26.6.12; Capt. 10.6.15; Despatches.

LAKE, B. L. (D.S.O. L.G. 1.1.17); b. 8.9.74; 2nd Lt., A.V.C., 13.4.01; Capt. 13.4.06; Major 10.7.15; A.D. of Vety. Services, 17th Army Corps, British Armies in France, 16.6.17 to 5.10.19; A.D. of Vety. Services, 11.3.21 to 8.4.21; served S. African War, 1900–2; Queen's Medal with 3 clasps; King's Medal with 2 clasps; Europ. War; Despatches; O.B.E.

LAKE, H. N. (D.S.O. L.G. 15.2.19), Lt., R.N., 15.4.15; D.S.C.

LAKE, R. D. (D.S.O. L.G. 1.1.18); b. 9.5.91; s. of E. W. Lake and the late Blanche Frampton Lake; m. Sybella Noel, d. of the late Major-Gen. Noel Harris and Mrs. Noel Harris, of 13, Brechin Place, S.W.; one s.; one d.; educ. Lydgate House, Hunstanton; Twyford School, Winchester; Uppingham; R.M.C., Camberley; 2nd Lt., Northants R., 4.3.11; Lt. 27.5.12; Capt. 28.4.15; served Europ. War as a regimental officer with the B.E.F. from Nov. 1914, to Oct. 1916; Capt. 28.4.15; Staff Capt., 15th Inf. Brig., from Oct. 1916; D.A.Q.M.G., 9th Corps, Feb. 1917; D.A.Q.M.G., Royal Naval Division, 4.8.18; A/Major, 28.2.19.

LALE, H. P. (D.S.O. L.G. 12.7.20), Flight-Lieut., R.A.F.; D.F.C.

LAMB, H. J. (D.S.O. L.G. 25.8.16); b. 6.12.71; s. of R. I. Lamb and Susan Saurin; educ. R.M.C., Canada; joined Can. Exp. Force, Aug. 1914; served Europ. War in France on General Staff, 1st Canadian Division, and subsequently on G.S., 3rd Can. Div., Feb. 1915, to March, 1917; Despatches.

LAMB, H. L. (D.S.O. L.G. 22.4.18), Lt. (A/Capt.), London R.

LAMB, R. M. R. (D.S.O. L.G. 1.1.17); b. 14.9.81; s. of C. B. Lamb, J.P., of W. Riding, Yorks, and Lucy Lamb; m. Ethel Audrey Barker; one s.; educ. Wellington College; joined Militia, 1900; proceeded to S. Africa; 2nd Lt., Northumberland Fusiliers 14.9.01; Lt. 30.5.04; Capt. 27.11.13; Major 8.5.16; Lt.-Col., retired pay, 5th Fusiliers; served in S. Africa, 1900–2; Queen's Medal with 2 clasps; King's Medal with 2 clasps; was in S. Africa till 1903; home, 1908; then India (1st Batt.), where stationed till the Batt. came home from foreign service; India again (2nd Batt.), 1913–14; returned 1914 with Batt., and proceeded to France, Jan. 1915; served Europ. War, 1915–18; Despatches; Chevalier, Legion of Honour; Delhi Durbar Medal.

LAMBART, THE HON. L. J. O. (D.S.O. L.G. 14.3.16); b. 16.7.73, at Wheathampstead House, Herts; s. of the Earl and Countess of Cavan; m. Adelaide Douglas Randolph, d. of late Capt. A. Randolph, 15th Hussars, and the late Mrs. William C. Whitney, of New York, U.S.A.; one d.; educ. Mr. Foster's School, Stubbington House, Fareham, Hants; joined H.M.S. Britannia at Dartmouth, 1886; served Europ. War (Dardanelles), 1914–15; promoted A/Capt., R.N., 31.12.15 in H.M.S. Queen; Staff of Vice-Admiral Sir John de Robeck, Commanding Eastern Mediterranean, 1916; commanded H.M.S. Diamond, 1917; Staff of Admiral Commanding 2nd Battle Squadron, Grand Fleet, 1917–18; promoted Capt., R.N. (retired), 11.11.18; J.P., Dorset.

LAMBE, C. L. (D.S.O. L.G. 12.5.17), Air Commodore, R.A.F., late Captain, R.N.; served Benin Exp., 1897 (Medal and clasp); Europ. War, 1914–18; commanded R.N.A.S. units on the Belgian coast; Despatches; C.M.G.; Order of Leopold of Belgium; Belgian Croix de Guerre; Legion of Honour; Order of the Crown of Belgium; French Croix de Guerre; Director of Equipment, R.A.F., Air Ministry; C.B.

LAMBERT, R. C. K. (D.S.O. L.G. 31.5.16), Capt., R.N., 30.6.15.

LAMBERT, W. J. (D.S.O. L.G. 1.1.17) (1st Bar, L.G. 2.12.18) (2nd Bar, L.G. 8.3.19) (Details, L.G. 4.10.19); b. 2.4.74; s. of late Sir J. Lambert, K.C.I.E.; m. Mabel Janetta, widow of Capt. Sir M. Cholmely, Bart., and d. of M. W. Sibthorp, J.P.; educ. Brighton College; Sherborne School; R.M.C., Sandhurst; 2nd Lt., E. Lanc. R., 7.3.94; Lt., E. Lanc. R., 25.10.97; Lt., I.A., 19.10.97; Capt. 7.3.03; Major 7.3.12; Lt.-Col., 29th Lancers, I.A., 3.7.20; Brig.-Gen. 15.3.19; joined Indian Cavalry in France, March, 1915; commanded a service Batt. 14th King's Liverpool R., Salonika, Sept. 1915; Despatches thrice; joined Egyptian Exp. Force, 1917; commanded a Cavalry Rgt. and Cavalry Brig.

LAMBERTON, J. R. (D.S.O. L.G. 16.9.18), Capt., H.L.I.; M.C.

LAMBKIN, E. C., M.B. (D.S.O. L.G. 11.4.18); b. 9.8.84; Lt., R.A.M.C., 30.1.09; Capt. 30.7.12; Major 30.1.21; Despatches.

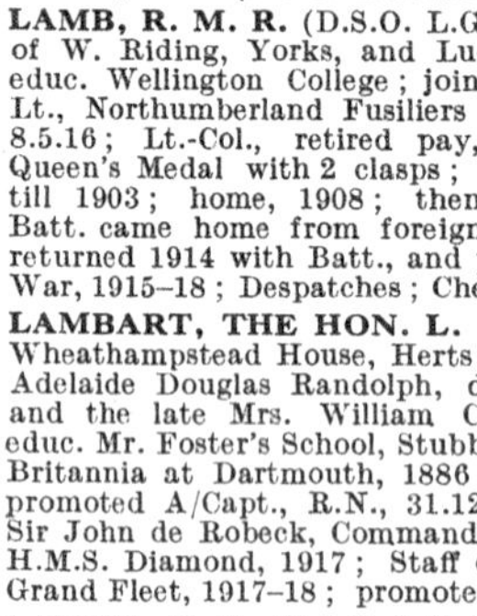

L. Lamonby.

LAMBTON, C. (D.S.O. L.G. 7.11.18); b. 1888; s. of Hon. F. W. Lambton; m. Olive Isabel Eleanor, d. of W. R. P. Lockwood; one d.; Capt., Yeomanry, att. R. Sc. Fusiliers; served Europ. War, 1914–18; wounded.

LAMONBY, I. W. (D.S.O. L.G. 4.6.17), T/Major, R.E.

LAMONBY, L. (D.S.O. L.G. 11.1.19); b. at Penrith, Cumberland, 18.12.83; s. of Tom and Jane Lamonby; educ. Uppingham; joined U.S. Rifle V.C. Corps, 1900–2; 1st V.B. The Border R. 4.7.04; continued in Border R. on introduction of T.F.; Major, 4th Border R.; mobilized 4.8.14; left England for India, Oct. 1914; stationed in Burma; Cable Censor, Rangoon, May and June, 1918; Mesopotamia, arrived Basra, Oct. 1916; att. 1/4th Dorset R. In August, 1917, he was a Captain, commanding a company of the 1/4th Dorsets. In Sept. he found himself commanding the battalion at Baghdad, with operations pending. The attack on Ramadi involved a week's trek and a night advance. This was the first action in which he had been engaged ; Despatches.

LAMOND, J. (D.S.O. L.G. 1.1.19) ; b. 27.5.81 ; 2nd Lt., R. Scots, 1.10.14 ; Lt. 14.4.15 ; T/Lt.-Col. 8.11.18 to 5.3.19 ; Despatches ; M.C.

LAMONT, G. S. (D.S.O. L.G. 11.1.19), 2nd Lt., G. Gds. He was killed in action 5.11.18.

LAMONT, J. W. F. (D.S.O. L.G. 14.1.16) ; b. 11.9.72 ; s. of late C. Lamont, of Crambeth, Kinross-shire, and Agnes, d. of late W. Fraser, of Inverkeithing ; educ. Merchiston Castle School, Edinburgh ; R.M.A., Woolwich ; 2nd Lt., R.A., 1.1.93 ; Lt. 1.1.96 ; Capt. 18.4.00 ; Bt. Major 29.11.00 ; Major 20.12.09 ; Lt.-Col. 6.10.15 ; Bt. Col. 1.1.18 ; Col. 6.10.20 ; T/Brig.-Gen. 1916–19 ; served S. African War with R.H.A., 1899–1902 ; Despatches ; Queen's Medal, 5 clasps ; King's Medal, 2 clasps ; Natal Native Rebellion, 1906 ; Medal with clasp ; Despatches ; C.B. ; Europ. War, in France and Belgium, 1914–18 ; C.M.G. ; Legion of Honour (Officier) ; 1914 Star ; Persian Military Commission, 1920 ; C.R.A., 18th Div., Mesopotamia.

LAMOTTE, G. M. L. (D.S.O. L.G. 1.1.18) ; b. April, 1869 ; s. of Rev. F. L. Lamotte ; educ. Fort Augustus ; Major, R. Monmouthshire R.E. Militia, retired, 1891–1904 ; S. African War, 1901–2 (Queen's Medal, 5 clasps) ; Europ. War, 1915–19 ; T/Major, R.E., S.R.

LAMOTTE, H. DE G. (D.S.O. L.G. 17.10.19), Lt.-Cdr., R.N., 15.1.13.

LAMOTTE, L. (D.S.O. L.G. 1.2.19), Capt. (A/Lt.-Col.), 2nd Batt. R. Sussex R.

LAMPEN, F. H. (D.S.O. L.G. 1.1.17), Major, N.Z. Staff Corps.

LAMPSON, O. LOCKER- (see Locker-Lampson, O.).

LANCE, E. C. (D.S.O. L.G. 26.9.17) (Details, L.G. 9.1.18), 2nd Lt. (T/Capt.), Som. L.I.

LANDEN, A. (D.S.O. L.G. 4.6.17), Qr.-Mr. and Hon. Major, North'd Fusiliers.

LANDER, C. LL., M.B. (D.S.O. L.G. 1.1.19), Capt. (A/Lt.-Col.), R.A.M.C., T.F. ; M.C.

LANDON, C. R. H. P. (D.S.O. L.G. 22.3.19), Major (A/Lt.-Col.), 35th Scinde Horse, I.A. ; b. 6.6.79 ; 2nd Lt., Unatt., 25.1.99 ; I.S.C. 22.3.00 ; Lt., I.A., 7.10.01 ; Capt. 25.1.08 ; Major, 35th Scinde Horse, I.A., 1.9.15 ; Despatches.

LANDON, C. W. (D.S.O. L.G. 4.6.17), T/Major, A.S.C.

LANDON, J. H. A. (D.S.O. L.G. 4.6.17), Major, retired, 4th Bn. Essex R., T.F. (Lt.-Col., R.A.F.).

LANDON, J. W. B. (D.S.O. L.G. 3.6.18), Capt. (A/Lt.-Col.), R.A.S.C., T.F.

LANDSBERG, H. V. (D.S.O. L.G. 26.3.18) (Details, L.G. 24.8.18), Major, H.A.C. ; m. Florence Caroline Rose, d. of late Col. C. Seymour, Royal Hospital, Chelsea ; served Europ. War, 1914–18 ; Despatches.

LANE, J. B. (D.S.O. L.G. 1.2.19), Capt., Aust. Mil. Forces.

LANE, R. H. (D.S.O. L.G. 3.6.19), Major, R.F.A., T.F.

LANG, B. J. (D.S.O. L.G. 3.6.16) ; b. 14.1.78 ; s. of late Basil Lang, Advocate-General, Bombay, and Mrs. Basil Lang, d. of the late Col. T. Haggard, R.A. ; educ. Harrow ; R.M.C., Sandhurst ; joined 1st Batt. A. and S. Highrs. 18.5.98 ; Lt. 11.1.00 ; Capt. 28.4.09 ; Major 1.9.15 ; served S. African War ; Queen's Medal with 5 clasps ; King's Medal with 2 clasps ; went out to France with Exp. Force, 10.8.14 ; served in France to Nov. 1917, and in Italy, Nov. 1917, to end of war ; Despatches six times ; C.B. ; C.M.G. ; Bt. Lt.-Col. 3.6.17 ; 1914 Star ; French Croix de Guerre with Palm ; Italian Croce di Guerra, and Officier Mérite Agricole.

LANG, G. G. (D.S.O. L.G. 14.1.16) ; b. 24.4.67 ; s. of late G. L. Lang, I.C.S., and Louisa Astell ; m. Isabel Frances Emily, d. of late R. P. Ebden, C.B. ; one d. ; educ. Clifton College ; Bedford Grammar School ; Sandhurst ; b. 24.4.67 ; 2nd Lt., W. Yorks. R., 5.2.87 ; Lt. 8.5.89 ; Capt. 13.6.94 ; Major 8.12.07 ; Lt.-Col. 23.2.16 ; Retired Pay, 1921 ; late 2nd Batt. W. Yorks. Rgt. ; served N.W. Frontier of India, 1907 ; Medal with clasp ; Europ. War ; Despatches twice.

LANG, G. H. (D.S.O. L.G. 8.3.18) ; s. of Rev. J. P. Lang, of Stirling, and nephew of Rev. Gavin Lang ; Cdr., R.N., 31.12.14. His D.S.O. was the fifth decoration that Commander Lang received during his service in the Navy, then extending over 20 years.

LANGAN-BYRNE, P. A. (D.S.O. L.G. 14.11.16), 2nd Lt., R.A., and R.F.C. His D.S.O. was awarded for gallantry on 15.9.16, Irles and Thilloy. His death is presumed to have been on about 17.10.16.

LANGDON, F. J. (D.S.O. L.G. 3.6.18) ; b. 18.8.73 ; 1st com. 23.12.93 ; Capt. 21.3.00 ; Retired, L'pool R., 27.4.10 ; Major, R. of O., L'pool R. ; served Nile Exp., 1899 ; Despatches ; Egyptian Medal with 2 clasps ; Europ. War ; Despatches.

LANGDON, J. F. P. (D.S.O. L.G. 1.1.17) ; b. 4.3.66 ; s. of Col. J. Langdon, R.A.M.C. (s. of Rev. J. Langdon, C. of E.), and of Eliza Elizabeth Langdon, d. of Peter Foss, of Devonshire ; educ. Crewkerne ; Chartres ; ent. Army 9.5.88 ; Major 17.8.06 ; retired, R. Sussex R., 13.7.10 ; Lt.-Colonel, May, 1918 ; served N.W. Frontier of India, 1897–98 ; Medal with clasp ; Tirah, 1897–98 ; operations in the Bazar Valley ; clasp ; served Europ. War. His D.S.O. and two mentions in Despatches were for general service at the Battle of Loos, 24–25–26 and 27.9.15, as Company Commander, defence of slag heap at Foss 8, and later the Hohenzollern Redoubt. His Regt. was relieved by the Berkshire Rgt. His Battalion lost 19 officers and over 300 men. At the Battle of the Somme, 17 and 30.8.16. His post on 26 Sept. was at the cross trenches of Big Willy and the Redoubt. His company, mixed with men of other regiments, manned the trench of the Redoubt on either flank. That night the Germans attacked from dusk to dawn. The men were handicapped by want of ammunition, bombs and machine guns, and were without water for three days Bombing attacks were driven off by throwing back German bombs before they burst. He saved the life of a wounded officer by picking up and throwing back a live bomb that rolled near his prostrate body, and shot with his revolver the leader of the German bombers at ten paces. At the Somme, 15 and 30.8.16 he saved his battalion from being surrounded. He shot the record head of chinkara, which he presented to his battalion.

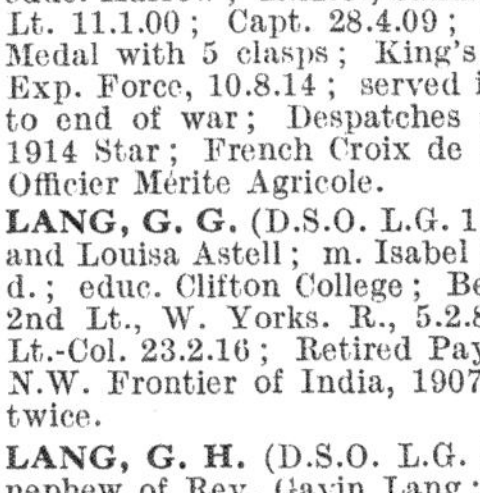

J. F. P. Langdon.

LANGFORD, E. G. (D.S.O. L.G. 4.6.17) ; b. 2.7.81 ; s. of W. T. Langford ; m. Winifred Lettice, d. of J. O. Adair ; one s. ; educ. Harrow ; 2nd Lt., R.A., 5.5.00 ; Lt. 17.6.01 ; Adjt. R.A., 1908–11 ; Capt. 11.6.10 ; Major, R.F.A., 30.10.14 ; T/Lt.-Col., 1916 ; A/Lt.-Col., 1917 ; proceeded to France, Aug. 1914 ; Despatches thrice. His younger brother, Capt. C. C. Langford, R.F.A., was killed in action.

LANGLEY, ARTHUR WYNTON (gazetted as Langley, Arthur Winton) (D.S.O. L.G. 4.6.17) ; b. 30.1.84 ; 2nd Lt., R.A., 15.7.03 ; Lt. 15.7.08 ; Capt. 30.10.14 ; Major, R.G.A., 22.10.17 ; served Europ. War ; Despatches ; M.C.

LANGLEY, G. F. (D.S.O. L.G. 8.3.19) (Details, L.G. 4.10.19) ; served in Europ. War ; Lt.-Col. Commanding 14th Australian Light Horse Rgt. in Egypt.

LANGRISHE, JOHN DU P., M.B. (D.S.O. L.G. 1.1.18) ; s. of R. Langrishe, J.P., of Archersfield, Kilkenny ; b. 11.9.83 ; Lt., R.A.M.C., 28.1.07 ; Capt. 28.7.10 ; Major 28.1.19.

LANGSTAFF, J. W., L.R.C.P.I., L.R.C.S.I. (D.S.O. L.G. 1.1.17) ; b. 19.5.76 ; s. of late H. H. Langstaff, M.D., of Athlone ; m. Dorothy, d. of Sir Ronald Ross ; one s. ; educ. R. College of Surgeons of Ireland ; L.M., Rotunda Hospital, Dublin ; Lt., R.A.M.C., 27.7.99 ; Capt. 27.7.02 ; Major 27.4.11 ; Lt.-Col. 1.3.15 ; served S. African War, 1899–1902 ; 2 Medals, 7 clasps ; Europ. War, 1914–18 ; Despatches thrice ; Officer Commanding British Station Hospital, Balgaum S. India.

LANGTON, A. W. GORE- (see Gore-Langton, A. W.).

LANGTON, HON. E. A. G. TEMPLE-GORE- (see Temple-Gore-Langton, Hon. E. A. G.).

LANGTON, H. E. GORE- (see Gore-Langton, H. E.).

LANGTON, J. H. (D.S.O. L.G. 1.1.18), Major, R.W.F. ; enlisted in Rifle Brigade in 1888 ; later transferred to R.E. ; retired from Army, 1910, with the rank of Sergeant-Major. On outbreak of war he joined the R.W.F., though over military age, and fought in France from 1914 until the Armistice. His D.S.O. was awarded "for conspicuous organizing ability" in connection with the Messines Ridge attack. Twice during the war Col. Langton was recommended for the C.M.G. During the great retreat of 1918 he kept back large numbers of the enemy with a handful of men, and, it is said, saved a regiment from destruction.

LANGWORTHY-PARRY, P. E. (D.S.O. L.G. 1.1.18), Lt.-Col., 9th Batt. London R. ; Major (T.F.) ; retired ; O.B.E. ; T.D.

LANNOWE, B. H. H. MATHEW- (see Mathew-Lannowe, B. H. H.).

LANNOWE, E. B. MATHEW- (see Mathew-Lannowe, E. B.).

LANYON, O. M. (D.S.O. L.G. 3.6.16) ; b. 13.9.82 ; s. of Louis M. Lanyon and Laura, d. of C. V. Phillips ; m. Jeanie, d. of Major P. Jeffcock, J.P. ; educ. Rugby ; Woolwich ; commissioned 21.12.00, R.A. ; Lt. 21.12.03 ; Capt. 10.5.13 ; Major, R.F.A., 18.8.15 ; Lt.-Col. On the outbreak of war he went to France with the 4th Div. as A.D.C. to C.R.A ; from 22 Aug. to March was Staff Capt. to 4th D.A. He took part with the 4th Div. in the Retreat, and advanced from St. Omer to Armentières and Ypres 25th May ; went home as Brig. Major on 1 Aug. to transfer to 30th D.A. ; went out with them on 29.11.15 ; operations at Frise–Somme 1 to 31 July, also 27.9.16 to 18.11.16 ; Despatches five times ; Bt. Lt.-Col. 1.1.19.

LARCOM, SIR T. P., Bart. (D.S.O. L.G. 1.1.18) ; b. in Ireland 5.10.82 ; s. of 2nd Bart. and Jeanie, d. of A. Perceval ; educ. Eton ; ent. R.A., 31.7.02 ; Lt. 31.7.05 ; Capt. 31.10.14 ; Major, R.H.A., 27.3.16 ; served Europ. War, 1914–18 ; Despatches.

LARDNER-BURKE, H. F. (D.S.O. L.G. 22.8.18), Capt., 7th Inf., Kimberley R., S. African Mil. Forces ; M.C.

LARGE, EDWIN RYDER (gazetted Edward for Edwin) (D.S.O. L.G. 12.5.17) ; s. of late A. R. Large ; m. Elsa Marguerite, d. of late Hon T. King ; educ. ; Woolston College, Hants ; ent. Mercantile Marine, 1893 ; Commander, R.N.R. ; commanded steamers of Ellerman and Bucknall S.S. Coy. since 1905 ; Younger Brother of Trinity House, 1913 ; served in Calcutta Naval Volunteers, 1895–96 ; various Gunnery, Torpedo and Signal Courses, and periods of service in H.M. Fleet ; served Europ. War, 1914–19 ; commanded H.M.T. Karroo, including service att. to Gallipoli Exp. (1915–16) from First Landing until Final Evacuation (Despatches) ; successful gunnery actions against enemy submarines (Monetary Awards) ; received presentation Telescope from Admiral Sir Lewis Bayly, Commander-in-Chief, Coast of Ireland ; Address of Appreciation from Ship's Company ; Appreciation of High Commissioner for Australia for services under Australian Government ; Appreciation of Lords Commissioners of Admiralty on three occasions ; General Service and Mercantile Marine War Medals ; Lloyd's Silver Medal for Meritorious Services ; Lloyd's Silver Medal for saving life at sea ; Royal Humane Society's Bronze Medal for jumping overboard from Karroo during a heavy sea, and rescuing an Indian seaman who had fallen overboard ; whilst commanding H.M.T. Karroo acted as Vice-Commodore and Commodore of Convoy ; represented the Mercantile Marine at the Admiralty on Mercantile Marine Awards Committee, Feb. 1918–Feb. 1919 ; O.B.E. for services in connection with inquiries into submarine attacks on British merchant vessels ; F.R.G.S.

LARGE, S. D., L.D.S., L.R.C.P. and S.Edin. (D.S.O. L.G. 1.1.18) ; b. Larne, Ireland, 22.10.89 ; s. of W. H. Large ; m. Violet Muriel Elise, d. of D. Cowan ; one s. ; educ. Royal High School, Edinburgh ; College of Surgeons, Edinburgh ; b. 21.10.89 ; Lt., R.A.M.C., 24.1.13 ; Capt. 30.3.15 ; A/Lt.-Col., 1918 ; served in France throughout the war ; commanded 76th F.A. 2.9.18 to end of war ; M.C. ; Despatches twice.

LARKIN, J. P. (D.S.O. L.G. 4.6.17), T/Capt. (A/Major), K.O.S.B.

LARMOUR, F. G. (D.S.O. L.G. 1.1.17) ; b. 24.12.80 ; 2nd Lt., R.A., 6.1.00 ; Lt. 3.4.01 ; Capt. 1.4.08 ; Major 8.12.14 ; T/Lt.-Col. 22.12.15 ; Ord. Officer, 4th Class, 30.1.05 ; Ord. Officer, 2nd Class (Acting), 25.10.20 ; Despatches.

LASCELLES, HON. E. C. (D.S.O. L.G. 1.1.18) ; b. 28.7.87 ; 2nd s. of 5th Earl of Harewood and Lady Florence Katherine Bridgeman, d. of 3rd Earl of Bradford ; m. Joan Eleanor Campbell, d. of Colonel Eustace Balfour and Lady Frances Balfour, d. of 8th Duke of Argyll ; Capt., R. Brigade, S.R. ; served Europ. War, 1914–18, Rifle Brigade ; resigned commission and joined Special Reserve, 1912 ; Staff Capt., 140th Rifle Brigade, March to Dec. 1915 ; 55th, Dec. 1915 to Aug. 1916 ; Brigade Major, 89th Inf. Bde., Aug. 1916–Nov. 1917 ; G.S.O.2, 55th Div., Nov. 1917–June, 1918 ; G.S.O.2, First Army, June, 1918–1919 ; several times mentioned in Despatches ; Bt. of Major ; M.C.

LASCELLES (H. G. C.), VISCOUNT (D.S.O. L.G. 3.6.18) (Bar, L.G. 2.4.19) (Details, L.G. 10.12.19) ; b. 9.9.82 ; e. s. of 5th Earl of Harewood and Lady Florence Katherine Bridgeman, d. of 3rd Earl of Bradford ; m. H.R.H. The Princess Mary, only daughter of H.M. King George V. and H.M. Queen Mary ; educ. Eton ; late 2nd Lieut., Grenadier Guards ; Capt. (T/Lt.-Col.), R. of O., G. Gds. ; Hon. Attaché, Rome, 1905–7 ; A.D.C. to Governor-General of Canada, 1907–11 ; served Europ. War, 1914–18 ; wounded three times ; French Croix de Guerre ; Member of the Jockey Club.

LASCELLES, R. H. (D.S.O. L.G. 1.1.17) ; o. s. of late Arthur H. Lascelles, of Narberth ; was gazetted to the R.A. 25.6.99 ; 2nd Lt., R.A., 25.6.99 ; Lt. 16.2.01 ; Capt. 21.11.07 ; Major 30.10.14 ; served S. African War, 1899–1900 ; wounded ; Despatches ; Queen's Medal with 2 clasps ; Europ. War ; Despatches ; Legion of Honour. Lt.-Colonel Lascelles died of pneumonia following influenza, at the age of 38.

LAST, A. J. (D.S.O. L.G. 4.6.17) ; b. 24.5.62 ; Inspector of Ordnance Machinery, 1st Class, 6.5.08 ; Lt.-Col. 3.6.18.

LATCH, A. R. (D.S.O. L.G. 18.2.18) (Details, L.G. 18.7.18), T/2nd Lt., Tank Corps.

LATHAM, A. (D.S.O. L.G. 3.6.19); b. 15.2.81; 2nd Lt., Unatt., 28.7.00; 2nd Lt., I.A., 7.10.01; Lt. 28.10.02; Capt. 28.7.09; Major, 1st Gurkha Rifles, I.A., 1.9.15; served N.W. Frontier of India, Waziristan, 1901–2; Medal with clasp; Europ. War; Despatches.

LATHAM, F. (D.S.O. L.G. 14.1.16) (Bar, L.G. 16.9.18); b. 25.8.83; s. of late Col. H. Latham, R.A., and of the late Emily Dallas Latham (*née* Baker); m. Muriel, d. of late J. H. Humphreys, M.D., and of the late Helen Jacquina Humphreys (*née* Harratt); educ. Tonbridge School; 4th Militia Bn. Yorks Rgt., 1901; 2nd Lt., W. India Rgt., 27.1.04; Lt., W.I.R., 19.1.06; Lt., Leic. R. 16.2.07; Capt. 8.3.13; Adjt., Leic. R., 23.3.14 to 28.11.15; Major 31.12.21; served S. Africa, 1902; Queen's Medal with 2 clasps; was subsequently stationed in W. Africa and Jamaica, when, owing to a reduction of the W. India Rgt., he was posted to the 2nd Batt. Leic. Rgt. in India; served Europ. War, in France with Meerut Division, Oct. 1914–June, 1915; in France with 6th British Division, March, 1916; April, 1918; July, 1918; was severely wounded near Richebourg 16.6.15, and again near Ypres 29.4.18; Despatches five times; T/Lt.-Col., 9th Batt. Suffolk R., 1916–18; A/Lt.-Col., 1st Leic. Rgt., 1918–19; Bt. Major 1.1.18; Officier de l'Ordre de la Couronne (Belgian), Jan. 1919.

LATHAM, S. G. (D.S.O. L.G. 26.7.18), Capt. (A/Lt.-Col.), The Northants R. (att. 2nd Batt. Northants R.). He was killed in action on 24.4.18.; M.C.

LATTA, W. S. (D.S.O. L.G. 4.6.17) (1st Bar, L.G. 3.6.18) (2nd Bar, L.G. 2.12.18), Major, Can. Inf.

LAUDER, J. LA F., M.R.C.S., L.R.C.P., M.R.C.P. (D.S.O. L.G. 18.4.16); b. 19.6.89; s. of James Stack and Annie Pierrette La Fayette Lauder; m. Ethel Green; educ. Dulwich College; M.R.C.S., L.R.C.P.London; M.R.C.P. Edinburgh; holds the Gold Medal of St. John of Jerusalem; ent. R.A.M.C. as T/Lt. 8.8.14; T/Capt. 13.11.16 to 29.11.16; A/Major 4.1.18 to 16.4.19; Capt. 8.2.19; severely wounded; Despatches. He was awarded the D.S.O. for distinguished service in the camp at Wittenberg, Germany; Despatches four times; M.C.

LAURENCE, N. F. (D.S.O. L.G. 24.2.16) (Bar, L.G. 1.1.17); s. of F. Laurence; m. Esmé J. Coghlan White; two s.; ent. R.N., 1899; Cdr. 31.12.14; Captain; was in command of Submarine E1; torpedoed two German battleships near Jutland, 1915; Despatches; holds Russian Order of St. George, 4th Class; Chevalier, Legion of Honour; Russian Order of St. Vladimir, 4th Class.

LAURIE, J. E. (D.S.O. L.G. 22.9.16) (Bar, L.G. 8.3.19) (Details, L.G. 4.10.19); b. 12.8.92; s. of William Emilius Laurie and his wife, d. of late J. Stirling; educ. Eton and Sandhurst; 2nd Lt., Seaf. Highrs., 14.2.12; Lt. 30.10.14; Capt. 2.12.15; Adjt., Seaf. Highrs., 7.12.15 to 8.12.16; served Europ. War, 1914–18; Despatches five times; Bt. Major 1.1.19; Chevalier, Legion of Honour. His D.S.O. was awarded for gallantry at Beaumont Hamel on 1.7.16.

LAURIE, P. R. (D.S.O. L.G. 14.1.16); b. 5.11.80; s. of A. Laurie, J.P.; m. Ethel Frances Lawson-Johnston; one s.; one d.; educ. Harrow; 2nd Lt., 2nd Dragoons, 26.3.02; Lt. 11.10.03; Adjt., 1909–1911; Capt. 6.10.11; Major, 6.7.19; Lt.-Colonel; Private Secretary to Chief of Imperial General Staff, 1914; served in Europ. War from 1914; Despatches six times; Bt. Major 1.1.17; Order of Leopold; Order of Crown of Belgium; Croix de Guerre Française avec Palme; Croix de Guerre Belge avec Palme; Mons Star; Deputy Assistant Commissioner, Metropolitan Police, and Chief of the Mounted Branch, Scotland Yard.

LAURIE, R. M. (D.S.O. L.G. 16.8.17); b. 1869; s. of R. P. Laurie, C.B., M.P. for Canterbury and Bath, and Amy, d. of Sir Ranald Martin, C.B.; m. Florence Albreda, d. of Hon. Greville Vernon; one s.; educ. Eton; Christ Church, Oxford; Lt.-Col., Commanding 2nd East Anglian Brigade, R.F.A. (T.F.); served Europ. War in France, Egypt and Palestine from 1914; Despatches; Order of the Nile, 3rd Class.

LAUTH, J. F. R. (D.S.O. L.G. 4.6.17), Major, S. African Infantry.

LAVERACK, J. D. (D.S.O. L.G. 1.1.18), Lt.-Col., Aust. Arty.

LAVIE, H. E. (D.S.O. L.G. 3.10.19); b. 5.8.79; 2nd Lt., Durham L.I., 18.4.00; Lt. 13.7.01; Capt. 26.4.09; Major 7.10.15; Bt. Lt.-Col. 11.11.19.

LAW, F. W. B. (D.S.O. L.G. 3.6.16); b. 12.5.73; s. of W. F. Law; m. Florence Turley, d. of B. S. Parkes; three s.; one d.; educ. Commercial School, Stratford-on-Avon; joined 3rd V.B., S. Staffs R., on outbreak of S. African War, 1899, transferring to the Territorial Force, and took over the command of the Sedgley and Tipton Companies; Lt.-Col., late commanding 1/6th S. Staffs Rgt., T.F.; served Europ. War, 1915–17; Despatches.

LAW, J. P. (D.S.O. L.G. 27.7.18); b. 24.12.68; 2nd Lt., Devon R., 6.7.89; Lt. 15.12.90; Capt. 1.12.98; Major 22.11.08; Lt.-Col. 22.11.16, late commanding W. India R.; served S. African War, 1899–1902; Queen's Medal with 6 clasps; King's Medal with 2 clasps; Europ. War; Despatches.

LAW, W. H. P., B.A. (D.S.O. L.G. 1.1.17); b. 14.2.76; s. of Francis Law, of H.M. War Office, and Julia, d. of Henry Taylor Jones; m. Dorothy, d. of late Sir J. A. Brooke, Bart.; one s.; two d.; educ. Charterhouse and Oriel College, Oxford (Honours, Modern History); 2nd Lt., R. War. Rgt., 21.4.00; A.S. Corps 21.5.00; Lt. 1.6.01; Capt. 1.10.04; Major, R.A.S.C., 30.10.14; Lt.-Col. 30.4.31; served S. African War, 1901–2; Queen's Medal with 5 clasps; Staff Capt., War Office, 1914–15; D.A.A. and Q.M.G., 1915; A.D. of Supplies; Despatches thrice; Bt. Lt.-Col. 1.1.19; Chevalier, Order of Leopold; D.A.D. of Supplies, War Office, since 1920.

LAWFORD, V. A. (D.S.O. L.G. 31.3.16); b. 6.1.71; 9th s. of late J. Lawford; m. Agnes Jane, d. of W. B. Mapplebeck; four s.; one d.; educ. Tottenham and Blackheath; entered R.N. as Assistant Clerk, 1887; became Assistant Paymaster, 1892; Order of Crown of Italy and Messina Medal, 1908; Fleet Paymaster, 1910; Paymaster Captain; served as Secretary to Commodores, Hong Kong, and S.E. Coast of America, to Rear Admiral, 2nd-in-command, Mediterranean, to Admiral Commanding Coastguard and Reserves, to Rear-Admiral Commanding 10th Cruiser Squadron, to Naval Adviser, Foreign Office; Naval Liaison Officer, Foreign Office; Member of British War Mission to U.S.A., 1917; C.M.G.

F. Lawless.

LAWLESS, F. (D.S.O. L.G. 16.9.18), T/Capt., L'pool R.

LAWLESS, W. T. (D.S.O. L.G. 18.1.18) (Details, L.G. 25.4.18), Major, Can. Inf.

LAWRANCE, A. S. (D.S.O. L.G. 29.11.20), Major, R. of O., retired T.F., late Somaliland Camel Corps; served S. African War, 1900–2; Queen's Medal with 3 clasps; King's Medal with 2 clasps; E. Africa (Somaliland, 1908–10); Despatches (L.G. 17.6.10); Medal with clasp.

LAWRANCE, S. N. (D.S.O. L.G. 22.9.16), Capt., Aust. Inf.

LAWRENCE, C. T. (D.S.O. L.G. 1.1.18); b. 29.5.79; 2nd s. of Rt. Hon. Sir A. T. Lawrence, Lord Chief Justice of England, and Jessie Elizabeth, d. of G. Lawrence; 2nd Lt., R.A., 8.9.00; Lt. 8.9.03; Capt. 26.4.12; Major, R.H.A., 12.4.15; served Europ. War, 1914–18; N. Russia, 1918–19; Despatches thrice; St. Anne of Russia, 3rd Class, with Swords.

LAWRENCE, E. L. G. (D.S.O. L.G. 3.6.19); b. 17.10.90; 2nd Lt., Worc. R., 5.10.10; Lt. 8.7.14; Capt. 1.7.15; Bt. Major 1.1.18; Despatches; M.C.

LAWRENCE, G. (D.S.O. L.G. 1.1.18); b. 1880; y. s. of Rt. Hon. Sir A. T. Lawrence, Barrister, Inner Temple, 1906; Lt.-Col., Commanding 86th East Anglian Yeomanry (Herts) Brigade, R.F.A.; served Europ. War; Despatches twice.

LAWRENCE, H. M. (D.S.O. L.G. 1.1.18) (Bar, L.G. 7.11.18); b. 24.2.81; m. (1st), Dorothy Marshall Snelgrove, d. of John and Georgena Snelgrove; two s.; one d.; and (2nd) Kathleen, d. of late J. Galbraith; 1st com. 19.10.01; Major 1.9.15; retired Sc. Rifles 3.5.19 with rank of Lt.-Colonel in the Army; served S. African War, 1900–1 (Queen's Medal, 3 clasps); Europ. War, from 1914; Gallipoli, Aug. to Dec. 1915; Egypt and Palestine, Dec. 1915 to June, 1918; France, June to Sept. 1918; D.S.O. gained at 1st Battle of Gaza, Palestine, while in command of 1/7th Batt. Cheshire Rgt.; Bar to D.S.O.; Legion of Honour and Croix de Guerre avec Palme, while in command of 1/1st Herefordshire Rgt. in the operations south of Soissons, Aug. 1918; wounded; Despatches four times; 1914–15 Star; O.B.E. "The History of Kent Cricket," edited by Lord Harris, says of Col. Lawrence: "He assisted the county on four occasions in 1899, being tried for his fast medium-paced bowling. In all matches in which he took part in that year he obtained 209 wickets at a cost of 1,953 runs. He left England for S. Africa early in 1900, and afterwards proceeded to India, returning home in 1905. In 1906 he was unable to play, owing to a dislocated knee. In the field he was generally short slip."

H. M. Lawrence.

LAWRENCE, T. B. (D.S.O. L.G. 26.7.18); b. 7.4.79; 2nd Lt., G. Highrs., 29.6.16; Lt. 28.12.17 (A/Lt.-Col.); Despatches; M.C.; D.C.M.

LAWRENSON, R. R. (D.S.O. L.G. 4.6.17) (Bar, L.G. 26.7.18); b. 25.12.71; 2nd Lt., W.I. Rgt., 8.6.92; Lt. 1.1.94; Capt. 27.8.98; Major, W. India R.; served W. Coast of Africa, 1893–94; operations against the Sofas; served Europ. War; Major (T/Lt.-Col.), The W. India R. (att. HL.I.). He died of wounds 27.4.18.

E. McC. W. Lawrie.

LAWRIE, E. McC. W. (D.S.O. L.G. 17.3.19), Cdr., R.N., 31.12.16.

LAWRIE, J. (D.S.O. L.G. 11.8.17), Lt., R.N.R.; D.S.C.

LAWS, B. (D.S.O. L.G. 3.3.17); b. 3.3.87, at Prudhoe, Northumberland; s. of J. B. E. Laws and Hannah Laws; m. Elsie Gertrude, d. of late T. Corah; educ. School of Science and Arts, Newcastle-on-Tyne; enlisted in 1898 as a Trooper in the N.W. Mounted Police of Canada, transferring in 1899 to 1st Can. Rifles, and serving with them as a Trooper in the S. African War, 1899–1902; commissioned as Lieut. in Saskatchewan Light Horse, Sept. 1908; Capt. and Adjutant 10.4.10; on 1.12.14 he joined the 1st Can. Mtd. Rifles as Capt. and Adjutant, and served in the Europ. War with this unit in France and Belgium, 1914–19; Major and 2nd-in-Command 2.6.16. In Oct. 1918, he was decorated with the Croix de Guerre by the General Commanding the 47th French Division in the field for good work of the battalion, 8–15.8.18.

LAWSON, A. B. (D.S.O. L.G. 26.7.18) (Bar, L.G. 16.9.18); b. 18.12.82; 2nd Lt., 11th Hussars, 8.5.01; Lt. 27.2.02; Capt. 22.2.09; Adjt., 11th Hrs., 1.3.11 to 31.12.13; A.D.C. to G.O. Commanding-in-Chief the Forces in Ireland, 1.1.14 to 14.6.14; served Europ. War; Capt. and Bt. Major, 11th Hussars, att. 2/5th Glouc. Rgt. He was killed in action 24.6.18.

LAWSON, E. F., B.A. (D.S.O. L.G. 8.3.19) (Details, L.G. 4.10.19); b. 16.6.90; only surviving son of Col. the Hon. W. A. W. Lawson, D.S.O.; m. Enid, d. of H. Scott Robson; one s.; educ. Eton; Balliol College, Oxford; served Europ. War, 1915–19; Lt.-Col., 1/1st Bucks. Yeomanry, Commanding 1st Co. of London Yeom.; Despatches thrice; M.C.

LAWSON, F. W., M.Inst.C.E., M.Inst.M.E. (D.S.O. L.G. 1.1.18); b. Launceston, Tasmania, 12.6.69; m. Christina Vernon; three s.; one d.; Vice-President, Inst. Engineers, Australia; served with Aust. Engineers in France; promoted Major; Despatches; Engineer for Metropolitan Water Supply and Sewerage, Perth, W. Australia.

LAWSON, J. (D.S.O. L.G. 18.1.18) (Details, L.G. 25.4.18); s. of ex-Police-Supt. Lawson, formerly of Todmorden; Major, 4th Aust. L.H. Rgt.; formerly a Clerk at Todmorden for the Manchester and Liverpool Bank. His D.S.O. was awarded for gallantry in the taking of Beersheba 31.10.17.

LAWSON, L. H. (D.S.O. L.G. 2.4.19) (Details, L.G. 10.12.19), T/Capt., 11th Batt. W. Yorks. R.; M.C.

LAYARD, B. V. (D.S.O. L.G. 29.10.18), Cdr., R.N., 31.12.18.

LAYH, H. T. C. (D.S.O. L.G. 1.1.17) (Bar, L.G. 16.9.18); b. 1885; Lt.-Col., Aust. Inf.; served Europ. War, 1914–17; wounded; Despatches; C.M.G.

LAYTON, A. B. (D.S.O. L.G. 1.1.18), Capt. (T/Lt.-Col.), S. Lancs. R., with which regiment he had been associated for over thirteen years when he was awarded the D.S.O. He was twice mentioned in Despatches. Lt.-Col. A. B. Layton is an Electrical Engineer.

LAYTON, E. (D.S.O. L.G. 26.7.17), T/Major, A. and S. Highrs. His D.S.O. was awarded for gallantry in Salonika 8–9.5.17.

LAYTON, G. (D.S.O. L.G. 17.4.18); 4th s. of G. Layton, Solicitor and Notary, of Liverpool; educ. Britannia; Cdr., R.N., 31.12.16. Commander Layton was in command of Submarine E 13 when she grounded on the Danish Island of Saltholm on 19.8.15, and was subsequently shelled by two German destroyers in the presence of Danish destroyers. Commander Layton was interned in Holland, but eventually escaped. His crew were interned on parole, but Com-

The Distinguished Service Order 287

mander Layton refused to promise not to attempt to escape, and accordingly was kept under close surveillance at the naval barracks at Copenhagen. Despite the utmost vigilance he quitted his bed one night, leaving in his place a dummy, and got through the pantry window. From Copenhagen he made his way to Bergen, and thence to Newcastle-on-Tyne.

LAYTON, T. B., F.R.C.S., M.D. (D.S.O. L.G. 3.6.18); b. 8.6.82; s. of T. Layton, Solicitor; m. Edney Eleanor Sampson; one s.; one d.; educ. Bradfield College; Guy's Hospital, 1900–6; Surgical Registrar and Anatomy Demonstrator, Guy's Hospital, 1908–12; travelled for Study in Vienna and Berlin, 1912; Surgeon to the Throat and Ear Dept., Guy's Hospital, since 1912. Major, R.A.M.C. (T.), late Acting Lt.-Col.; O.C. 2/4th London Field Ambulance.

LEA, H. F. (D.S.O. L.G. 3.6.18); b. 19.9.67; 1st commission 14.9.87; Major 29.9.06; retired from York R. 28.10.08; Major (T/Lt.-Col.), R. of O., York. Regt.; served Europ. War; Despatches.

LEA, P. G. P. (D.S.O. L.G. 3.6.16); b. 28.3.75; s. of late Col. Samuel Job Lea, C.B.; m. 1911, Elsie Grant, y. d. of Frederick Spencer, J.P., D.L., of Oakhill, Somerset; entered the 33rd Duke of Wellington's Regt., 1895; transferred to A.S.C., 1899; Capt. 1.1.01; Major 26.9.13; Lt.-Col. 1.2.18; served S. African War, 1899–1902; Despatches; Queen's Medal, 5 clasps; King's Medal, 2 clasps; Europ. War, 1914–18; Despatches four times; C.M.G.

LEACHMAN, G. E. (D.S.O. L.G. 2.4.19) (Details, L.G. 10.12.19); b. 27.7.80; 2nd Lt., R. Suss. R., 20.1.00; Lt. 15.10.02; Capt. 19.3.10; Major and Bt. Lt.-Col., R. Sussex R., att. Political Dept. (Mesopotamia); C.I.E.; served Europ. War; Despatches.

LEADER, C. C. (D.S.O. L.G. 3.6.19), Major, 5th Batt. Can. Rly. Troops.

LEAF, H. M. (D.S.O. L.G. 1.1.16); b. Oct. 1862; s. of late F. H. Leaf, of Burlington Lodge, Streatham, S.W.; m. Anna Maria Elizabeth, d. of late Robert Cust, LL.D., Bengal Civil Service; educ. Marlborough; Trinity College, Cambridge; Captain in London Electrical Engineers in S. African War, 1900; Queen's Medal, 3 clasps; O.C. 1910–14; served as Capt., R.N.D. Transport, 1914 and 1915; joined R.M.A. as Captain, 1915; Major, 1917; served Europ. War; wounded; Despatches.

LEAH, T. C. (D.S.O. L.G. 4.6.17) (Bar, L.G. 11.1.19); b. 3.8.81; 2nd Lt., R.A., 22.11.99; Lt. 16.2.01; Capt. 31.12.07; served S. African War, 1900; Queen's Medal, 2 clasps; Europ. War; Despatches.

LEAHY, T. B. A. (D.S.O. L.G. 1.1.17); b. 13.6.78; 7th s. of late Col. Arthur Leahy, R.E.; m. 1904, Agnes Wentworth, d. of Dr. Mordaunt Stevens, of Palais Victor Hugo, Nice; one s.; one d.; educ. Stubbington House, Fareham; Cheltenham; 2nd Lt., R.M.A., 1896; Captain, 1903; passed Ordnance Course, 1905; transferred to A.O.D., 1913; Lt.-Col., R.A.O.C.; served China, 1900 (on board Flagship H.M.S. Centurion); Europ. War, 1914–18; Despatches; C.M.G.

LEAHY, T. J. (D.S.O. L.G. 1.1.19); b. 12.2.89; 2nd Lt., R. Dub. Fus., 18.9.09; Lt. 22.6.10; Capt. and Bt. Major, R. Dublin Fus.; served Europ. War; Despatches (L.G. 19.10.14); M.C.; Legion of Honour (5th Class).

LEAKE, E. W. BILLYARD- (see Billyard-Leake, E. W.).

LEAKE, F. MARTIN- (D.S.O. L.G. 22.6.17); b. 16.3.69; s. of late Stephen Martin-Leake, J.P., Barrister-at-Law, and Isabel Martin-Leake, of Marshalls, Hertfordshire, and Thorpe Hall, Essex; educ. The Grange, Stevenage, Herts, by the Rev. J. O. Seager; entered R.N., Sept. 1884; Capt. 28.6.11; Coronation Medal, King George V.; served Europ. War; commanded H.M.S. Pathfinder, sunk by German torpedo, N. Sea, 5.9.14; survivor, wounded; Despatches His D.S.O. was awarded for miscellaneous service.

LEAKE, G. E. A. (D.S.O. L.G. 26.7.17), Capt., London Regt. He was awarded the D.S.O. for gallantry at Bullecourt 14–15.5.17. He died of wounds 26.6.17.

LEAN, A. I. (D.S.O. L.G. 1.2.17); b. 11.12.72; 2nd Lt., R.W. Fus., 28.9.92; Lt. 2.4.95; Capt. 21.1.98; Major 11.5.07; Lt.-Col. 11.5.12; Paym., A.P. Dept., 21.1.98 to 10.5.07; 1st Cl. Asst. Acct., A. Accts. Dept., 1.5.05–31.12.09; Staff Paym. 11.5.07; served S. African War, 1900–2; Queen's Medal with clasp; King's Medal, 2 clasps; Europ. War; Despatches.

LEANE, R. L. (D.S.O. L.G. 3.6.16) (Bar, L.G. 17.12.17) (Details, L.G. 23.4.18); b. 12.7.78; m. Edith Louise, d. of T. L. Smith, of Adelaide; one d.; three s.; educ. The Public School, Adelaide; for 15 years in the Australian Volunteer and Citizen forces; Garrison Artillery, W. Australia, 1899; 2nd Lt., Aust. Inf., 1905; Lt., 1900; Capt., 1910; T/Major, 1915; T/Lt.-Col., 1916; served Europ. War at Gallipoli; Despatches; M.C.

LEANING, A. (D.S.O. L.G. 1.1.17); b. 6.5.76; s. of H. Leaning, of Colchester; m. Isabel Mary Agnes, d. of Col. W. F. Kerr, late Commanding 1st Buffs; two d.; educ. Kent College, Canterbury; joined A.V.C., 1901; served South Africa, 1901–2; Medal, 2 clasps; Somaliland, 1903–4; Action Jidballi; Europ. War, in S. Africa, India, France, 2nd Indian Cavalry Division, as V.O., 2/6th Mhow Cavalry Brigade, and afterwards Asst. Director of Veterinary Services, 24th Division, B.E.F.; served on the Western front at Ypres, Loos, Arras.

LEARMOUNT, L. W. (D.S.O. L.G. 18.7.17); s. of R. K. Learmount, of Gosforth; m. 1918, Ada Elizabeth, d. of H. Ball; one s.; Lt. (T/Major), Gen. List, R.F.C., S.R.; served Europ. War (wounded); Despatches; M.C.; Croix de Guerre with Palm. His D.S.O. was awarded for gallantry on 19.5.17, Hindenburg Line.

LEASK, T. Mc.C. (D.S.O. L.G. 1.1.18) (Bar, L.G. 8.3.19) (Details, L.G. 4.10.19), Lt.-Col., 10th Field Ambulance, Can. A.M.C.

LEATHER, F. H. (D.S.O. L.G. 3.6.18); b. 17.10.64; s. of late A. W. D. Leather; m. 1893, Ella Mary, d. of James Smith of Monkton Court, Hereford; one s.; educ. Hereford Cathedral School; articled James and Bodenham, Hereford; admitted Solicitor, 1888, practising Weobley; Clerk to Justices, Guardians and R.D.C.; joined Vols. as a Private, 1883; mobilized 4.8.14; with 53rd (Welsh) Division in command of the Train, afterwards commanding it in France attached to 11th Div.; Lt.-Col., A.S.C.; Coronation Medal, 1911; served Europ. War; Despatches four times.

LE BUTT, R. (D.S.O. L.G. 1.1.18), T/Lt.-Col., M.G.C.

LECKIE, R. (D.S.O. L.G. 17.5.18), Fl.-Cdr., R.N.A.S.; served Europ. War; Despatches; D.S.C.

LECKIE, V. C. (D.S.O. L.G. 1.1.18); b. 25.8.83; Lt., A.V.C., 5.9.06; Capt., R.A.V.C., 5.9.11; Major 5.9.21; served Europ. War; Despatches.

LECKY, A. M. (D.S.O. L.G. 11.12.18), Cdr., R.N.

LECKY, C. S. (D.S.O. L.G. 18.7.17), Major, Aust. Inf. He was awarded the D.S.O. for gallantry on 15.5.17, France.

LECKY, M. D. (D.S.O. L.G. 4.6.17); b. 10.5.83; m.; one s.; 2nd Lt., R.A., 21.12.01; Lt. 27.8.04; Capt. 30.10.14; Adjt. 9.9.15; Major 1.5.17; Adjt., R.A., 29.5.20; served Europ. War, 1914–17; Despatches.

LEDGARD, G. (D.S.O. L.G. 3.6.19), T/Capt. (A/Major), 80th Field Co., R.E.; served Europ. War; Despatches; M.C.

LEDGARD, W. R. (D.S.O. L.G. 1.1.17), T/Capt., R.M.A.; served Europ. War; Despatches. He died 23.7.17.

LEE, A. N. (D.S.O. L.G. 15.2.17), Major, Notts. and Derbys. Regt.; served Europ. War; Despatches; M.C.

LEE, C. H. (D.S.O. L.G. 11.1.19), Lt. (A/Capt.), G. Highrs.; served Europ. War; M.C.

LEE, G. (D.S.O. L.G. 1.1.18); b. 17.11.80; 2nd Lt., E. Kent R., 23.11.01; Lt. 3.11.06; Capt. 26.2.13; Major 11.12.16; served Europ. War; Despatches; M.C.

LEE, G. M. (D.S.O. L.G. 1.1.18); b. 31.8.78; m. 1908, Kathleen Florence, d. of late Col. A. W. Macnaghton; one s.; 2nd Lt., R. Fus., 7.5.98; Lt. 1.4.99; Major (R. of O.), 1.9.15; retired R. Fus. 25.3.14; served Europ. War, 1914–18; Despatches; M.C.

LEE, G. W. (D.S.O. L.G. 22.8.18), Major, S. Afr. Vety. Corps.

LEE, H. B. (D.S.O. L.G. 26.11.17) (Details, L.G. 6.4.18), Major, Aust. A.M.C.; served Europ. War; Despatches; M.C.

LEE, H. H. (D.S.O. L.G. 14.1.16); b. 13.3.77; s. of Capt. W. F. Lee, R.N.; m. 1912, Lilias Robertson (d. 1920), yr. d. of Capt. D. G. Fowler, late Arg. and Suth. Highrs.; one s.; 2nd Lt., Sco. Rif, 4.5.98; Lt. 3.5.99; Capt. 4.11.03; Adjt. 29.10.05 to 6.11.08; Major 1.9.15; served Europ. War, 1914–16; twice wounded; Despatches.

LEE, H. R. (D.S.O. L.G. 1.1.18); b. 21.7.74; 1st commission 20.2.95; Major 17.7.09; retired 20th Hrs. 22.3.11; Major, R. of Off.; served S. African War, 1899–1900–1–2; slightly wounded (Queen's Medal, 6 clasps); Europ. War; Despatches.

LEE, J. (D.S.O. L.G. 4.6.17), T/Capt., Gen. List.

LEE, J. E. (D.S.O. L.G. 1.1.19), Major, 45th Batt. Aust. Mil. Forces; served Europ. War; M.C.

LEE, J. H. (D.S.O. L.G. 14.11.16), T/2nd Lt., King's Royal Rifles. His D.S.O. was awarded for gallantry at Bazentin-le-Grand 9.9.16.

LEE, R. T. (D.S.O. L.G. 1.1.17); b. 2.7.78; m.; one d.; 2nd Lt., W. Surrey R. 4.12.01; Lt. 13.8.04; Capt. 2.3.13; Bt. Major 3.6.16; Major 4.12.16; Bt. Lt.-Col. 3.6.17; served S. African War, 1902; Queen's Medal and 3 clasps; Europ. War, 1914–17; Despatches; C.M.G., 1919; Order of the Crown of Belgium; Croix de Guerre.

LEE, S. S. (D.S.O. L.G. 25.8.17) (Bar, L.G. 3.8.20); b. 18.9.90; 2nd Lt., R.A., 23.7.10; Lt. 23.7.13; Capt. 23.7.16; served Europ. War; Despatches.

LEECH, A. G. (D.S.O. L.G. 14.1.16); b. 17.9.77; e. s. of H. Brougham Leech, LL.D.; m. 1911, Amy Mary, d. of late C. O. Booth, Shooters Hill, Woolwich; educ. St. Columba's College, Rathfarnham, Dublin; Trinity College, Dublin (B.A., 1899; LL.B., 1903; LL.D., 1904); joined R.A., 1900; called to the Bar, 1901; Staff Service A.D.C., 4th Div. 1904–5; Instructor at R.M.A., 1909–14; served Europ. War; D.A.A.G., 1914; Brig.-Major, R.A., 1914–19; G.S.O., 2nd Grade, 1917; 1st Grade, 1918; 2nd Grade, British Army of the Rhine, 1919; in Belgium, France, Balkans and Germany; Despatches.

LEECH, W. F. (D.S.O. L.G. 26.9.17) (Details, L.G. 9.1.18), T/2nd Lt., Gen. List, and R.F.C. He died of wounds 18.8.17.

LEEDS, T. L. (D.S.O. L.G. 23.11.16); b. 25.7.69; 3rd s. of late Edward Montagu Leeds, and Jessie, d. of Thomas Spears; m. 1904, Clara Guion, d. of Col. Kilburn, U.S.A. Army; one d.; educ. Sherborne; 2nd Lt., Derby R., 9.9.91; Lt. 14.12.92; Ind. S.C. 13.7.94; Capt., Ind. Army, 10.7.01; Major 9.9.09; Bt. Lt.-Col. 3.6.15; Lt.-Col. 20.2.17; retired 1921; served China, Zakka Khel and Mohmand Expeditions (Medal and clasp for China, 1900; Zakka and Mohmand Expeditions, 1908); served Europ. War in France and Mesopotamia; Despatches; 3rd Class Order of St. Stanislas.

LEES, D., M.B. (D.S.O. L.G. 26.9.17) (Details, L.G. 9.1.18); s. of late Robert Lees, of Lagg, near Ayr; educ. Ayr Academy and Edinburgh University, where he graduated M.A. and M.B., Ch.B.; Capt., R.A.M.C.; served Europ. War; Despatches. His D.S.O. was awarded for services E. of the Yser Canal on 31.7.17.

LEES, E. F. W. (D.S.O. L.G. 1.1.18); b. 2.6.81; 2nd Lt., R.E., 2.5.00; Lt. 2.5.03; Capt. 10.12.10; Adjt., R.E., 8.2.15 to 24.4.16; Bt. Major 3.6.16; Major 2.11.16; Bt. Lt.-Col. 3.6.19; served Europ. War; Despatches.

LEES, SIR J. V. E., Bart. (D.S.O. L.G. 1.2.19); b. 11.12.87; s. of 1st Bart. and Florence, d. of late Patrick Keith; m. 1915, Madelaine, 2nd d. of Sir Harold Pelly, Bart.; one s.; one d.; s. Brother, 1915; educ. Eton and Sandhurst; 2nd Lt., K.R.R.C., 9.10.07; Lt. 8.5.10; Capt. 24.3.15; Bt. Major 3.6.19; served Europ. War; Despatches; wounded twice; M.C.; Croix de Guerre.

LEESE, N. (D.S.O. L.G. 1.1.17), Temp. Major, R.A.S.C.

LEESE, O. W. H. (D.S.O. L.G. 14.11.16); b. 27.10.94; 2nd Lt., C. Gds., 15.5.15; Lt. 5.9.15; Capt. 1.4.21; served Europ. War; Despatches. His D.S.O. was awarded for gallantry 16.9.16, at Guinchy.

LEESON, A. N. (D.S.O. L.G. 25.8.17); b. 1895; only s. of Edward Leeson and Margaret Leeson; educ. Clifton Bank, St. Andrews; Bengeo School, Hertford, and Rugby, where he was in the Army Class, and a Cadet Officer in the O.T.C. In Aug. 1914, he entered Woolwich, where he was Under-Officer, and was awarded the Tombs Memorial Prize; commissioned in the R.F.A. in Feb. 1915, and joined his battery in Ireland; in July, 1915, he went to the Dardanelles with the 13th Division. He was invalided with scarlet fever to Mudros; rejoined his regiment in Egypt, Feb. 1916, and after several months of active service was transferred to the R.H.A.; in Aug. 1917, became attached as an observer to the R.F.C. He was killed in action 22.10.17.

A. N. Leeson.

LE FEVRE, A. T. (D.S.O. L.G. 4.6.17), Major (T/Lt.-Col.), Rly. Construction Corps; served Europ. War; Despatches.

LEFROY, H. P. T. (D.S.O. L.G. 4.6.17); b. 6.10.80; 2nd Lt., R.E., 22.11.99; Lt. 12.10.02; Capt. 22.11.08; Major 13.8.16; served S. African War, 1901–2; Queen's Medal, 5 clasps; Europ. War; Despatches; M.C.

LEGARD, D'A. (D.S.O. L.G. 22.6.18); b. 5.6.73; s. of Rev. F. Digby Legard, Rector of Stokesley; m. 1908, Lady Edith Foljambe, d. of 4th Earl of Liverpool; three s.; educ. Winchester; New College, Oxon; 2nd Lt., 17th Lrs., 7.12.95; Lt. 4.7.96; Capt. 29.3.00; Major 11.10.05; Lt.-Col. 24.2.15; Temp. Brig.-Gen. 31.10.16 to 23.9.19; Colonel 24.2.19; served S. African War, 1899–1902 (wounded; Despatches; Queen's Medal, 4 clasps; King's Medal, 2 clasps); Europ. War; commanded 17th Lancers, 1915–16; commanded Hussars Brigade, 1916–19; Despatches; C.M.G.

LEGGAT, A., M.B. (D.S.O. L.G. 1.1.18), Major (A/Lt.-Col.), R.A.M.C.

LEGGE, HON. H. (D.S.O. L.G. 27.6.19); b. 1888; yr. s. of 6th Earl of Dartmouth; Comdr., R.N., retired list; served Europ. War, 1914–19; Despatches.

LEGGE, M. G. B. (D.S.O. L.G. 15.9.16); b. 16.12.83; 3rd s. of late Lt.-Col. Hon. Edward Henry Legge; Cdr., R.N.; served Europ. War, 1914–18, including Battle of Jutland; Despatches.

LEGGE, R. F. (D.S.O. L.G. 1.1.17); b. 22.9.73; 4th s. of Heneage S. Legge; m. 1900, Rosalind, o. c. of H.E. the late Selim Faris; three s.; one d.; educ. St. Paul's School; R.M.C., Sandhurst; 2nd Lt., Leins. R., 20.5.93; Lt. 4.9.94; Capt. 5.7.99; Major 12.7.11; Bt. Lt.-Col. 3.6.17; Lt.-Col. 23.5.19; T/Brig.-Gen. 6.12.18; retired pay, 1920; served in Nigeria, West Africa, 1898–99; Medal and 2 clasps; S. Africa, 1900–2; Queen's Medal, 3 clasps; King's Medal, 2 clasps; Europ. War, in France, 1915–17; Despatches thrice; C.B.E., 1919; Croix de Chevalier; Légion d'Honneur.

LEGGE, R. G. (D.S.O. L.G. 3.6.18), Major, Aust. Inf.; served Europ. War; Despatches; M.C.

LEGGE, W. K. (D.S.O. L.G. 1.1.17); b. 13.6.69; s. of the Hon. Charles Gounter Legge, H.M. Inspector of Constabulary, and the Hon. Mary Legge, d. of the Dean of Norwich; m. Constance Adeline, d. of J. D. Palmer; two s.; educ. Bedford Grammar School; 2nd Lt., Essex R., 30.1.89; Lt. 6.7.91; Adjt., Essex R., 2.9.95 to 1.9.99; Capt. 20.1.00; Major 5.1.08; Bt. Lt.-Col. 1.1.16; Lt.-Col. 23.1.16; T/Brig.-Gen. 30.10.16 to 11.4.19; Bt. Col. 1.1.19; Colonel 10.8.20; h.p. 10.1.19; served S. African War, 1899–1902 (Despatches twice); *p.s.c.*, 1905; Dublin, 1906–10; S. Africa, 1912–13; Gibraltar, 1914; Europ. War, as D.A.A.G.; Despatches six times; C.M.G.

LEGGETT, A. H. (D.S.O. L.G. 27.9.01) (Bar, L.G. 12.3.17), Bt. Major (T/Lt.-Col.), R. of O., late R. Scots Fus. (see "The Distinguished Service Order," from its institution to 31.12.15, by same publishers).

LEGGETT, R. A. C. L. (D.S.O. L.G. 1.1.17); b. 8.11.74; 1st commission 24.3.97; Capt. 29.12.00; retired Worc. R. 27.3.12; Capt. (T/Col.), R. of O.; served S. African War, 1899–1902; Despatches (L.G. 29.7.02); Queen's Medal, 3 clasps; King's Medal, 2 clasps; Europ. War; Despatches.

LEIGHTON, G. E. (D.S.O. L.G. 3.6.18); m. 1918, Mary Hoskins, d. of late David Mitchell Robertson; one s.; Major, Can. Inf.; served Europ. War, 1915–18; Despatches.

LEIGHTON, J. A. (D.S.O. L.G. 7.6.18), Cdr., R.N.R.; served Europ. War; Despatches.

LEIPOLDT, J. G. W. (D.S.O. L.G. 22.8.18), Major, S. African Permanent Force; served Europ. War; Despatches. His D.S.O. was awarded for gallantry in campaign in German S.W. Africa.

LEIR, E. W. (D.S.O. L.G. 25.10.16); b. 1883; s. of Rev. C. E. Leir, of Ditcheat, Somerset; m. 1905, Muriel Amyatt, o. d. of Rev. E. Amyatt-Burney; two s.; one d.; educ. King's School, Bruton; entered Navy, 1898; served as Midshipman on China Station, 1899–1902; took part in relief of the Legations in Pekin, 1900; Lieut., 1903; attached to the Submarine Service; in the Bight of Heligoland action, Aug. 1914; served Europ. War; Despatches. His D.S.O. was awarded for services rendered in oversea submarine work.

E. W. Leir.

L. Leith.

LEITCH, J. W., M.B. (D.S.O. L.G. 3.6.18), Major (A/Lt.-Col.), R.A.M.C.; served Europ. War Despatches.

LEITH, E. A. (D.S.O. L.G. 8.3.19) (Details, L.G. 4.10.19), Lieut., 46th Bn. Aust. Imp. Force; served Europ. War; Despatches.

LEITH, L. (D.S.O. L.G. 1.10.17); b. 2.6.76; 2nd s. of late Walter Leith, J.P., of the Manor House, Ashby-de-la-Zouch; m. 1919, Norah, 2nd d. of late James Hewitt Barry; educ. Burney's Royal Naval Academy, Gosport; joined H.M.S. Britannia, 1890; Lieut., 1898; Comdr., 1910; Capt., 1916; served Europ. War; Despatches; C.M.G.

LELAND, F. W. G. (D.S.O. L.G. 17.9.17); b. 20.8.77; 2nd s. of John Leland, of Beltichburne, Drogheda; m. Ellen Adelaide, y. d. of Thomas Payne James; one s.; educ. Drogheda Grammar School; King's School, Warwick; Neuenheim College; Trinity College, Dublin (B.A.); 2nd Lt., A.S.C., 22.5.00; Lt. 1.6.01; Capt. 1.8.05; Major, R.A.S.C., 30.10.14; Bt. Lt.-Col. 3.6.18; served S. African War, 1901–2 (Queen's Medal, 4 clasps); Europ. War, 1914–19; Despatches; C.B.E.

LE MAISTRE, F. W. (D.S.O. L.G. 3.6.16); b. 1882, at St. Kilda, Victoria, Australia; educ. St. Kilda; entered 5th Batt., A.I.F., as Major, Aug. 1914; Lt.-Col., Aug. 1915; served Europ. War, in Egypt, Gallipoli, Sinai Peninsula, France; Despatches.

LEMAN, J. F. (D.S.O. L.G. 2.4.19) (Details, L.G. 10.12.19); b. 11.2.86; 2nd Lt., Worc. R., 9.8.06; Lt. 22.1.09; Capt. 2.1.15; served Europ. War; Despatches.

LE MARCHANT, E. R. (D.S.O. L.G. 1.1.18), Vice-Admiral, R.N. (Retired List); served at the Messina Earthquake, 1909 (Italian Order, St. Maurice and St. Lazarus); Europ. War; Despatches.

LEMBCKE, C. E. (D.S.O. L.G. 1.1.18), Capt. (A/Lt.-Col.), Northd. Fus.

LE MESSURIER, F. N. (D.S.O. L.G. 7.11.18), Major, Aust. A.M.C.; served Europ. War; Despatches.

LEMMON, C. H. (D.S.O. L.G. 1.1.17); b. 25.1.87; o. c. of Colonel T. W. Lemmon, C.B.; m. 1911, Josephine Eliza, 4th d. of Edmund Kimber, of Shooters Hill; two d.; educ. Clifton; privately; R.M.A., Woolwich; 2nd Lt., R.A., 20.12.06; Lt. 20.12.09; Capt. 30.10.14; Major 6.4.17; served Europ. War, during operations on the Western front, including 2nd Battle of Ypres, and the commanded Somme; 5th Durham Battery (T.F.) in final offensive, Western front, June to Nov. 1918; Despatches.

LEMON, F. J. (D.S.O. L.G. 19.1.18); b. 1.8.79; y. s. of Colonel R. S. Lemon, late commanding West Yorkshire Regt., of Rathcarn, Westmeath, Ireland; m. 1910, Laura, y. d. of John Miles Dawson; one s.; educ. Bedford School; R.M.C., Sandhurst; Chief Constable of Leeds since 1919; 2nd Lt., W. York R., 11.2.99; Lt. 28.6.00; Capt. 7.11.08; Major 1.9.15; served S. African War, 1899–1902; Queen's Medal, 5 clasps; King's Medal, 2 clasps; Europ. War (severely wounded); Despatches thrice; 1914 Star; British War Medal; Victory Medal.

LENEY, C. (D.S.O. L.G. 4.6.17), Capt. (T/Major), R.G.A.

LENNON, J. A. (D.S.O. L.G. 2.4.19) (Details, L.G. 10.12.19); b. 26.8.95; Lt., W. Rid. R., 28.8.19; served Europ. War; Despatches; M.C.

LENNOX, LORD E. C. GORDON- (see Gordon-Lennox, Lord E. C.).

LENOX-CONYNGHAM, H. M., F.R.C.V.S. (D.S.O. L.G. 1.1.17); 7th s. of late Col. Sir W. F. Lenox-Conyngham, K.C.B., and Lady Lenox-Conyngham; entered A.V.C., 1896; served in Somaliland, 1902–4, with late Gen. J. E. Gough, V.C.; Europ. War, as A.L.V.S. with 6th Div., Sept. 1914 (Despatches twice, Sir J. French); D.D.V.S., 5th Army, under Sir H. Gough, 1916; served all through the fighting on the Somme and Ancre (Despatches, Sir D. Haig); invalided, May, 1917; later A.D.V.S., W. Command. He died suddenly at Chester, 15.3.18, leaving a widow, son and daughter.

LENS, D. (D.S.O. L.G. 22.8.18), Lt.-Col., Utrecht Commando, S. African Mil. Forces.

LENTAIGNE, E. C. (D.S.O. L.G. 25.8.17); b. 16.6.84; s. of late Sir John Lentaigne, F.R.C.S.I.; m. 1919, Cecilia Mary, d. of late Lt.-Col. C. T. Bunbury, Rifle Brigade, and Lady Harriott Bunbury, of Cotswold House, Winchester; one d.; educ. Stubbington House, Fareham; R.M.C., Sandhurst; 2nd Lt., Linc. R., 2.3.04; Ind. Army 13.8.05; Lt. 2.6.06; Capt. 2.3.13; Major 2.3.19; A.D.C. to Lt.-Governor, Burma, 1909–12; Private Secretary, 1913–14; served on Staff, A.H.Q., India, 1920; present appointment under Political Dept., Govt. of Bombay; served Europ. War in France and Mesopotamia; twice wounded; Despatches; Legion of Honour.

LENY, R. L. MACALPINE- (see Macalpine-Leny, R. L.).

LEONARD, C. F. (D.S.O. L.G. 18.7.17), Capt. (A/-Major), Can. Inf.; served Europ. War; Despatches.

LEONARD, E. W. (D.S.O. L.G. 14.1.16), Major, 12th Battery, Can. Inf.; served Europ. War; Despatches.

LEONARD, I. (D.S.O. L.G. 3.6.18), Lt.-Col., Can. Cav.; served Europ. War; Despatches.

LEONARD, THE REV. M. P. G., M.A. (D.S.O. L.G. 14.11.16); b. 5.7.89; s. of Rev. John Grainge Leonard; educ. Rossall School; Oriel College, Oxford; before and after the war, Assistant Missioner at Rossall School Mission, Manchester; Resident Chaplain to Cheltenham College; served in Territorials for four years; at Rossall School Mission, Scout Master of the 15th Manchester Troop Boy Scouts; Deacon, 1913; Priest, 1914; Chaplain to the Forces, 1914; att. 8th Batt. King's Own Regt.; served Europ. War, 1914–19; Despatches. His D.S.O. was awarded for gallantry near Longueval.

LEONARD, T. M. R. (D.S.O. L.G. 27.7.18); T/Major (A/Lt.-Col.), Spec. List, W. African Medical Service, W.A. Field Force; served Europ. War; Despatches.

LE PAGE, G. W. (D.S.O. L.G. 5.10.18), Engr. Lt.-Cdr., R.N.; served Europ. War; Despatches.

LE PELLEY, E. C. (D.S.O. L.G. 1.1.19); b. 2.11.70; 2nd Lt., R.A., 25.7.90; Lt. 25.7.93; Capt. 9.10.99; Adjt. 27.1.08 to 2.10.10; Major 25.4.11; Lt.-Col., R.G.A.; served Europ. War; Despatches.

LE PREVOST, A. P. H. (D.S.O. L.G. 26.9.17) (Details, L.G. 9.1.18) (Bar, L.G. 26.11.17) (Details, L.G. 6.4.18), T/Major (A/Lt.-Col.), Notts. and Derby. Regt.; served Europ. War; Despatches.

LESLIE, J. (D.S.O. L.G. 1.1.19), Lt. (A/Major), 12th Lancers, att. 6th Batt. Tank Corps; served Europ. War; Despatches; M.C.

LESLIE, W. S. (D.S.O. L.G. 25.8.17); b. 23.3.76; 3rd s. of late Lt.-Col. A. Y. Leslie, of Kinivie, Banffshire; m. 1911, Lora Mary, 2nd d. of late James Corballis, J.P.; educ. R.M.C., Sandhurst; 2nd Lt., R.W. Kent R., 29.2.96; Lt., R.W. Kent R., 9.2.98; Ind. Army 22.9.98; Capt. 1.3.05; Major 1.3.14; Bt. Lt.-Col. 3.6.16; Bt. Col. 3.6.18; Col. 27.4.20; T/Brig.-Gen. 11.10.18; T/Major-Gen. 26.5.20 to 31.3.21; served Malakand and Buner Campaign, 1897–98; Europ. War, 1914–18, in France, Mesopotamia, Palestine; Despatches several times; C.M.G., 1918; Order of the White Eagle; Order of the Nile; commanded the Troops in Cilicia; B.G.G.S., North Force, Syria, 1919; Mahsud Campaign, 1919; commanded the Wana Column operations; against the Waziris, 1920–21; C.B., 1920.

LETCHER, REV. O. J. (D.S.O. L.G. 8.3.18), T/C.F., 2nd Class, A/Chapln. Dept.; served Europ. War; Despatches.

LETHBRIDGE, F. W. (D.S.O. L.G. 27.10.18) (Details, L.G. 18.3.18); b. 3.2.67; e. and o. surv. s. of late Sir Roper Lethbridge, K.C.I.E.; m. 1888, Gertrude Ethel Mary, y. d. of Admiral Henry Croft; one d.; educ. Charterhouse; Exeter College, Oxford; R.M.C., Sandhurst; 2nd Lt., The Buffs, 1887; transferred to Indian Staff Corps, 1888; Lieut., 5th Gurkhas; Capt., 1898; served in Black Mountain Campaign, 1891, and other minor campaigns on N.W. Frontier of India (Medal and clasp); retired 1901; rejoined Army on the outbreak of European War as Capt., 8th Batt. Duke of Wellington's Regt.; commanding a company (severely wounded during operations at Suvla Bay); went to France, 1917; Second-in-Command, 8th Batt. D. of W. Regt.; Major, 1917; Lt.-Col.; commanded 10th Batt. D. of W. Regt., 1917–19; O.C., British Troops, Calais; Officer in Charge of Demobilization, Europe and Near East, 1919–20; retired 1920; served European War; Despatches three times; Italian Silver Medal for Valour; M.C.

LEVENTHORPE, G. S. (D.S.O. L.G. 4.6.17); b. 4.11.90; s. of J. B. Leventhorpe, P.W.D.; m. 1920, Dorothy, widow of G. Lambton, Coldstream Gds.; educ. Marlborough; R.M.A., Woolwich; 2nd Lt., R.A., 23.7.10; Lt. 23.7.13; Capt. 24.7.16; served Europ. War, 1914–18; Despatches.

LEVERSON, G. R. F. (D.S.O. L.G. 3.6.18); b. 21.10.86; 2nd Lt., North'd Fus., 24.1.10; Adjt. 26.6.10 to 25.6.13; Lt. 18.2.11; Capt. 8.1.15; Bt. Major 1.1.17; served Europ. War; Despatches.

LEVESON-GOWER, P. (D.S.O. L.G. 1.1.17); b. 6.2.71; s. of late Hugh Broke Boscawen Leveson Gower and Janet Elizabeth, d. of Rev. H. C. Cherry; m. 1899, Eleanor Marcia, d. of Christopher R. Nugent one s.; one d.; 2nd Lt., Derby R., 9.9.91; Lt. 14.12.92; Capt. 23.4.98; Major 12.5.08; Bt. Lt.-Col. 18.2.15; Lt.-Col., June, 1915; Bt. Col. 1.1.19; Colonel 18.2.19; T/Brig.-Gen. 29.11.15; served N.W. Frontier of India, 1897–98 (Medal, 2 clasps); S. African War, 1899–1901; Despatches; Queen's Medal, 2 clasps; Europ. War, 1914–18; wounded twice; Despatches five times; C.M.G.; Belgian Croix de Guerre.

LEVESON-GOWER, HON. W. S. (D.S.O. L.G. 17.3.19); b. 11.7.80; brother of 3rd Earl Granville; m. 1916, Lady Rose Bowes-Lyon, d. of 14th Earl of Strathmore; one s.; one d.; Captain, R.N.; served Europ. War, 1914–19; Despatches.

LEVEY, J. H. (D.S.O. L.G. 26.9.17) (Details, L.G. 9.1.18), Capt. (T/Lt.-Col.), Gordon Highrs.; served Europ. War; Despatches.

LEVY, W. H. (D.S.O. L.G. 3.6.18), T/Major, A.S.C.; served Europ. War; Despatches.

LEWER, L. W. (D.S.O. L.G. 14.1.16); b. 13.9.81; o. s. of Surgeon-Major A. Lewer, A.M.S. (retired), and Mrs. Lewer; m. 1903, Laura Lord, 2nd d. of late Charles Butler Holmes; two s.; educ. Cheltenham College; R.M.A., Woolwich; 2nd Lt. 6.1.00; Lt. 1.4.01; Capt. 17.8.08; Major 30.10.14; served S. African War; Queen's Medal, 4 clasps; Europ. War, 1914–18, in France, with W.R. Division; Staff Officer (D.A.A.G.), R.A.; Despatches four times.

LEWERS, H. B. (D.S.O. L.G. 3.6.19), Lt.-Col., 11th Fld. Amb. Aust. A.M.C.; served Europ. War; Despatches; O.B.E.

LEWES, C. G. (D.S.O. L.G. 14.1.16); b. 25.8.69; 3rd s. of late Colonel John Lewes, of Llanlear, Cardiganshire; m. 1908, Edith Harriet, d. of H. R. Sperling, of Netherfield Court, Battle; educ. Charterhouse; Sandhurst; 2nd Lt., Essex Regt., 21.9.89; Lt. 23.9.92; Capt., 1900; Major 6.5.10; commanded the Depôt, Essex Regt., 1913–14; he raised and commanded 9th Batt. the Essex Regt., Aug. 1914 to Sept. 1916; since has commanded 147th Brigade; Bt. Lt.-Col. 1.1.16; Bt. Col. 1.1.19 (retired); served N.W. Frontier of India, 1896–97 (Despatches; Medal with clasp); S. African War, 1899–1902 (Queen's Medal, 4 clasps); served Europ. War, 1914–18; wounded three times; Despatches five times; C.M.G.

LEWES, P. K. (D.S.O. L.G. 3.6.16); b. 1870; s. of late Major Price Lewes, late R.A., and Florence, d. of late T. C. Kinnear; m. (1st), Ethel Georgiana Murray Prust; (2nd) Ellen Elizabeth Vezey Jones; one s.; educ. Charterhouse; 2nd Lt., R.A., 14.2.90; Lt. 14.2.93; Capt. 1.10.99; Major 7.12.10; Lt.-Col. 4.2.17; Colonel, 1921; served Europ. War; Despatches; C.M.G.

LEWIN, E. O. (D.S.O. L.G. 14.1.16); b. 7.4.79; 3rd s. of late F. A. Lewin, Barrister; m. 1920, Anne Elizabeth Henderson, e. d. of Robert Slack, of Derwent Hill, Keswick; educ. Winchester; King's College, Cambridge (B.A., with Honours); 2nd Lt., R.A., 26.5.00; Lt., R.A., 9.4.02; Capt. 3.4.11; Adjt., R.A., 3.11.11 to 14.9.13, and 14.7.14 to 19.8.15; Major 30.10.14; Bt. Lt.-Col. 1.1.17; Col. 1.1.21; served 10 years in India with R.H.A.; Europ. War, 1914–18; Despatches four times; C.B., 1920; C.M.G.

LEWIS, D. (D.S.O. L.G. 1.1.18) (Bar, L.G. 8.3.19) (Details, L.G. 4.10.19); m. F. I. E. Pitt Fox; one d.; educ. City of London School; T/Major (A/Lt.-Col.), York. and Lanc. R.; commanding 1/5th Bn. Gloucs. Regt.; served Europ. War, 1914–18; Despatches thrice; wounded; M.C. and Bar.

LEWIS, E. A. (D.S.O. L.G. 3.6.16), Major, R.E. (T.F.); served Europ. War; Despatches.

LEWIS, H. L. (D.S.O. L.G. 14.1.16); b. 5.1.79; 2nd Lt., R.E., 23.12.97; Lt. 23.12.00; Capt. 23.10.06; Major 30.10.14; Bt. Lt.-Col. 3.6.18; served Tibet, 1903–4; Europ. War; Despatches.

LEWIS, H. V. (D.S.O. L.G. 4.6.17); b. 6.9.87; 2nd Lt., Unatt., 9.9.08; Ind. Army 15.11.09; Lt. 9.12.10; Capt. 1.9.15; served Europ. War; Despatches; M.C.

LEWIS, J. E. (D.S.O. L.G. 3.6.19), T/Major, 16th Batt. Tanks Corps (Capt., T.F. Res.); served Europ. War; Despatches.

LEWIS, L. H. (D.S.O. L.G. 16.9.18), T/Major, E. Lancs. R.; served Europ. War; Despatches; M.C.

LEWIS, N. A. (D.S.O. L.G. 26.7.17), T/Capt., R. Fus.; served Europ. War; Despatches; M.C. His D.S.O. was awarded for gallantry on 3.5.17, France.

LEWIS, P. E. (D.S.O. L.G. 1.1.18); b. 23.4.76; 2nd Lt., R.A., 21.3.96; Lt. 21.3.99; Capt. 17.12.01; Major 27.7.12; Bt. Lt.-Col. 29.11.15; Lt.-Colonel 14.9.16; Bt. Col. 1.1.19; served Europ. War; Despatches.

LEWIS, R. P. (D.S.O. L.G. 3.6.18); b. 28.5.82; Lt., R.A.M.C., 31.7.05; Capt. 31.1.09; Major 15.10.15; served Europ. War, 1914–18; Despatches.

LEWIS, W. A. (D.S.O. L.G. 4.6.17), Major, Monmouth R.; served Europ. War; Despatches.

LEWIS, W. H. (D.S.O. L.G. 4.6.17); b. 24.4.84; 2nd Lt., R.A., 15.7.03; Lt. 15.7.06; Capt. 30.10.14; Major 3.10.17; served Europ. War; Despatches; M.C.

LEY, E. M. (D.S.O. L.G. 18.6.17), T/Lt.-Col., K.R.R.C.; served Europ. War; Despatches. His D.S.O. was awarded for gallantry on 4.4.17 at Metz-en-Couture.

LEY, J. W. (D.S.O. L.G. 25.8.17); b. 10.7.77; e. s. of J. V. Ley, of Whitegate, Bushey Heath; educ. Sandhurst; 2nd Lt., N. Staff. R., 20.2.97; Lt. 22.10.99; Capt. 22.11.02; Major 20.12.13; served S. African War, 1900–2; Queen's Medal, 3 clasps; King's Medal, 2 clasps; Europ. War, in Mesopotamia; Despatches. He died 22.10.18.

LEYLAND, F. B. (D.S.O. L.G. 3.6.19); b. 15.4.81; 2nd Lt., 7th Hrs., 12.8.99; Lt. 10.3.00; Capt. 10.2.06; Major 26.6.15; served S. African War, 1901–2 (slightly wounded; Queen's Medal, 5 clasps); Europ. War; Despatches; M.V.O.

LIARDET, C. F. (D.S.O. L.G. 1.1.17); b. 26.9.81; y. s. of Lieut. H. M. Liardet, late H.M.I.N.; m. 1906, Dorothy, y. d. of A. R. Hopper, M.D.; one s.; one d.; educ. Bedford School; 2nd Lt., Volunteer G.A., 1899; Capt., 1905; transferred to Lancs. and Ches. R.G.A. on formation of Territorial Force; Major, 1914; Bt. Lt.-Col., June, 1919; served Europ. War; Despatches five times; Territorial Decoration; King George V. Coronation Decoration.

LICKMAN, H. S. (D.S.O. L.G. 19.12.22), Major, 13th Brahmans, I.A.

LIDBURY, D. J. (D.S.O. L.G. 3.6.16), Major, R.E., Spec. Res.; served Europ. War; Despatches.

LIDDELL, A. R. (D.S.O. L.G. 4.6.17); b. 16.8.72; s. of late Captain John Liddell, R.N.; m. Alice Maud, 3rd d. of Thomas Mills, o Longsdown Lodge, Sandhurst, Berks; 2nd Lt., 4th D.G., 2.6.94; Lt. 31.7.95; Lt., A.S.C., 1.4.96; Capt. 1.4.00; Major 6.10.09; Lt.-Col., R.A.S.C., 24.2.15; served S. African War, 1899–1900; Queen's Medal, 7 clasps; Europ. War, 1914–19; Despatches five times; C.M.G.

LIDDELL, H. (D.S.O. L.G. 1.1.19), Capt. (A/Lt.-Col.), 1/7th Batt. North'd Fus. (T.F.); M.C.

LIDDELL, J. S. (D.S.O. L.G. 14.1.16); b. 11.10.68; s. of late Capt. J. Liddell, R.N.; m. (1st) 1904, Gertrude (d. 1914), d. of E. Morgan; two s.; (2nd) 1916, Theresa, e. d. of Paul Rothenburg, LL.D.; two d.; educ. Haileybury College; R.M.A., Woolwich; 1st commission 23.7.87; Major 31.12.05; retired R. Eng. 14.10.08; T/Lt.-Col., Dec. 1915; served Nile Expedition, 1899; Medal with clasp (4th Class Medjidieh); Europ. War, 1914–16; Despatches; Order of the Nile; C.M.G. He was appointed Inspector-General, Egyptian State Telegraphs, at Cairo, and rendered in this capacity most valuable service, General Sir A. Murray, Commander-in-Chief of the Egyptian Expeditionary Force, writing as follows: "I beg to bring to your notice the services of the Egyptian Telegraph Department, under Lieutenant-Colonel J. S. Liddell, D.S.O., Royal Engineers, and to express my thanks to the Egyptian Telegraph Department and the Telephone Company of Egypt, who have given my Director of Army Signals unceasing valuable help." He was appointed Under-Secretary to the Ministry of Communications, Cairo.

LIEFELDT, T. E. (D.S.O. L.G. 1.1.18), Major, S. African Native Labour Corps

LIGERTWOOD, C. E. (D.S.O. L.G. 22.8.18) (Bar, L.G. 1.1.17), Major (T/Lt.-Col.), R.A.M.C.

LIGHTBODY, J. (D.S.O. L.G. 3.6.18), Lt.-Colonel, R.F.A.

LIGHTSTONE, HERBERT (gazetted as Lightstone, Hyman) (D.S.O. L.G. 4.6.17), Capt., R.A.M.C.; served in S. African War, 1900, in R. Canadian F.A.; Queen's Medal with 3 clasps; Europ. War; Despatches; M.C.

LIKEMAN, J. L. (D.S.O. L.G. 26.11.17) (Details, L.G. 6.4.18); b. 3.2.82; Capt., Suffolk R., 28.10.17; Bt. Major 1.1.19; Despatches.

LILLEY, H. A. (D.S.O. L.G. 7.2.19), Capt. (T/Lt.-Col.), Yorks. R. and K.A.R.

LILLIE, C. McE. ((D.S.O. L.G. 1.1.17), Capt., Aust. Mil. Forces.

LIMPENNY, C. J. (D.S.O. L.G. 17.4.18), Eng.-Cdr., R.N., 1.4.14.

LINCOLN, P. L. (D.S.O. L.G. 3.6.19), T/Major, 10th Batt. North'd Fus.; M.C.

LIND, A. G. (D.S.O. L.G. 11.4.18); b. 15.6.77; 2nd Lt., York. and Lanc. R., 1.12.97; Lt. 4.4.00; Lt., I.A., 16.9.00; Capt. 1.12.06; Major 1.9.15; Lt.-Col. 1.2.21; Despatches.

LIND, E. F. (D.S.O. L.G. 1.1.19), Major (T/Lt.-Col.), 2nd Field Ambulance, A.A.M.C.

LINDEMANN, C. L. (gazetted as Lindermann, C. L.) (D.S.O. L.G. 4.6.17), T/Major, Gen. List.

LINDESAY, G. W. G. (D.S.O. L.G. 1.2.19), Major, I.A., 29.10.08; retired 27.4.10; served Isazai Exp., 1892; Exp. to Dongola, 1896; Egyptian Medal; Medal; N.W.F. of India, 1897–98; Tochi, Malakand; Medal with 2 clasps; Europ. War; Despatches; Bt. Lt.-Col., Service Batt. R. Sc. Fus.

LINDSAY, C. H., M.D., B.Ch., D.P.H. (D.S.O. L.G. 3.6.18); b. 25.4.77; s. of S. Lindsay; m. Margaret Hélène Swenarton; one s.; two d.; educ. Dublin and Edinburgh University; served in Edinburgh City Volunteer Artillery, 1897–1901; Lt., R.A.M.C. (Vol.), 1907; transferred to T.F., 1908; Capt., 1911; Major, 1914; T/Lt.-Col., 1915; T/Col., 1917; Lt.-Col.; Col., A.M.S., Territorial Army; D.A.D.M.S. W. Lancs. Div.; left England in March, 1915, with 29th Div.; was S.M.O. in charge of landing at Y Beach, Gallipoli, on 25.4.15; commanded 87th Field Ambulance after the landing; Despatches eight times; C.M.G.

LINDSAY, C. M. (D.S.O. L.G. 4.6.17), Major, R. Brig.

LINDSAY, E. L. (D.S.O. L.G. 26.3.18) (Details, L.G. 24.8.18), T/Capt., King's African Rifles.

LINDSAY, G. H. M. (D.S.O. L.G. 3.6.19); b. 23.10.88; s. of A. Lindsay; g.s. of Hon. Colin Lindsay; m. Edith Christian Brown Baird; educ. Cheltenham College; R.M.C., Sandhurst; 2nd Lt., K.O.S.B., 6.2.09; Lt. 1.10.11; Capt. 5.6.15; sailed with Exp. Force, 1914; served in France and Italy, 1914–18; Despatches twice; Bt. Major 1.1.18.

LINDSAY, G. M. (D.S.O. L.G. 4.6.17); b. 1880; s. of late Lt.-Col. and Hon. Mrs. Lindsay, of Glasnevin House, Dublin; m. Constance, d. of G. S. Hamilton; one d.; educ. Radley; 2nd Lt., Rif. Brig., 24.1.00; Lt. 22.2.01; Capt. 15.12.06; Major, Sept. 1915; served S. African War, 1900–2; Despatches; Queen's Medal and 4 clasps; King's Medal and 2 clasps; Europ. War from 1914; Despatches; Bt. Lt.-Col. 3.6.18; C.M.G.; Croix de Guerre; Order of Leopold of Belgium.

LINDSAY, J. H., M.A., LL.B. (D.S.O. L.G. 1.1.17); s. of W. A. Lindsay, K.C.; m. Joanna Lucy, d. of T. Gordon Duff; two s.; educ. Malvern College; Trin. Coll., Cambs; called to Bar, 1905; 2nd Lt., London Scottish, 1899; Capt., 1903; Major, 1915; Lt.-Col., 1918; Lt.-Col. T.F. Reserve; Staff Capt., 4th London Inf. Brig., Aug. 1914, to March, 1915; commanded 1st Batt. London Scottish at Loos, and subsequent engagements (Despatches); also commanded the battalion during the Battle of the Somme; wounded in action during that battle.

LINDSAY, M. E. (D.S.O. L.G. 1.1.17); b. 26.3.80; 2nd Lt., 7th D.G., 28.3.00; Lt. 4.4.01; Capt. 6.4.07; Major 24.12.18; served S. African War, 1899–1901, with 1st N. Zealand Contingent; Despatches; slightly wounded; Queen's Medal with 4 clasps; Europ. War; Despatches.

LINDSAY, W. B. (D.S.O. L.G. 1.1.18); b. 3.11.80; s. of late Dr. W. B. Lindsay; educ. R.M.C., Kingston, Canada; joined R. Can. Engrs., 1904; organized, equipped and trained the 1st Can. Div. Engineers, Aug. 1914; came to England with them, Oct. 1914, as Major and O.C., 2nd Field Co., C.E.; to France, Feb. 1915; Lt.-Col. and C.R.E., 1st Can. Div., Sept. 1915; Brig.-Gen. and Chief Engineer, Can. Army Corps, March, 1916; Major-Gen. and G.O.C., Can. Engrs., 1.8.18; Despatches seven times; C.B.; C.M.G.

LINDSELL, W. G. (D.S.O. L.G. 1.1.18); b. 29.9.84; s. of Col. R. F. Lindsell, C.B., Gloucestershire R., and Kathleen Emma, d. of R. Eaton; m. Marjorie Ellis, d. of Admiral Swinton C. Holland; two d.; educ. Birkenhead School; Victoria College, Jersey; R.M.A., Woolwich; 2nd Lt., R.A., 23.12.03; Lt. 23.12.06; Capt. 30.10.14; Major 11.9.18; served Europ. War, 1914–18; Despatches four times; O.B.E.; M.C.; Croix de Guerre Française.

LINDSEY, C. B. (D.S.O. L.G. 4.6.17) (Bar, L.G. 15.2.19) (Details, L.G. 30.7.19), Major, Can. Inf.

LINDSEY-RENTON, R. H. (D.S.O. L.G. 1.2.19), Major, 9th Batt. London R.

LINFOOT, H. A. (D.S.O. L.G. 26.11.17) (Details, L.G. 6.4.18), Lt. (A/Capt.), Ches. R.; M.C.

LING, C. G. (D.S.O. L.G. 1.1.18); b. 6.11.80; 2nd Lt., R.E., 1.10.02; Lt. 25.7.05; Capt. 1.10.13; Major 1.10.17; Despatches; M.C.

LING, R. W. (D.S.O. L.G. 1.1.19); b. 29.3.86; s. of late C. Ling, J.P.; m. Mia Dorothy, d. of T. R. Lane; educ. West Downs, Winchester; Bradford College; R.M.A., Woolwich; Senior Under-Officer; Capt., Cricket and Association Football Elevens; Sword of Honour, 1906; represented Army at Hockey, 1910 and 1911, and at Rugby Football, 1913 and 1914; Hon. Sec., Army Rugby Union; 2nd Lt., R.F.A., 25.7.06; Lt. 25.7.09; Capt. 30.10.14; Major 16.2.17; served Europ. War, 1914–18; wounded twice; M.C.; Chief Artillery Liaison Officer, S. Russia, April, 1919, to July, 1920; C.B.E.; 4th Class Order of Vladimir; 2nd Class Order of St. Stanislas; Military Operations Directorate, War Office, July, 1920.

LINGS, H. C. (D.S.O. L.G. 1.1.18), Major, Manch. R.

LINNELL, H. R. (D.S.O. L.G. 16.8.17), Major, Can. Inf.

LINTON, C. S. (D.S.O. L.G. 26.6.16) (Bar, L.G. 26.11.17) (Details, L.G. 6.4.18); b. 9.8.81; s. of late H. P. Linton, of Llandaff, S. Wales; educ. Wainfleet (Mr. J. H. Wilkinson), and at Winchester; 2nd Lt., Worc. R., 14.9.01; Lt. 16.1.04; Adjt., Worc. R., 23.11.10 to 23.11.13; Capt. 28.6.11; A/Lt.-Colonel; Major, 1916; served S. African War, 1900–2; Queen's Medal with clasp; King's Medal with 2 clasps. He went to France with his regiment in Oct. 1914; was wounded at Neuve Chapelle, and was killed in action on 20.11.17;

Despatches several times; M.C. One of his brothers, Major F. H. Linton, Welsh Rgt., also received the D.S.O., and a third brother, E. G. Linton, who enlisted in the Northants Rgt., was killed early in the war.

LINTON, F. H. (D.S.O. L.G. 16.8.17); b. 3.1.84; 2nd Lt., Welsh R., 4.6.04; Lt. 14.3.08; Capt. 14.8.13; Major 22.2.22; served Europ. War, 1914–17; Despatches; Bt. Major 3.6.19.

LINTOTT, A. L. (D.S.O. L.G. 1.1.17); b. 15.4.81; m. Margaret, d. of F. Campbell Bayard, LL.B., C.C.; one s.; one d.; educ. Mercers' School; London University; joined 1st Batt. L.R.B., Oct. 1897; transferred to M.G.C., Dec. 1915; Major, April, 1916; served S. African War; Queen's Medal; King's Medal with 5 clasps; Europ. War from 1914, in France, Macedonia, Bulgaria, Roumania, Novorrossik, S. Russia, Egypt, Turkey-in-Europe, Greece, Asia Minor, and on the Staff of Admiral de Robeck, C.-in-C., Medit. Fleet. His D.S.O. was awarded for conspicuous gallantry in regaining possession of two machine guns after our troops had been driven back from advanced positions in Delville Wood by heavy counter-attack; Manager, Manchester Branch, London Guarantee and Accident Company, from 1920.

A. L. Lintott.

LISTER, C. (D.S.O. L.G. 8.3.19) (Details, L.G. 4.10.19) (Bar, L.G. 1.1.19); b. 26.8.84; Mobilized T.F. to 14.8.16, 2 years, 10 days; Capt., Northants R., from T.F., 15.8.16; T/Lt.-Col. 11.3.17; Despatches; M.C.

LISTER, E. G. (D.S.O. L.G. 1.1.19), Major, 13th Brig., Aust. F.A.

LISTER, F. (D.S.O. L.G. 17.9.17), Capt. (A/Major), Can. Inf.; M.C.

LISTER, F. H. (D.S.O. L.G. 3.6.16); b. 5.12.80; s. of late Sir T. Villiers Lister, K.C.M.G., and Lady Lister (sister of the 10th Lord Belhaven and Stenton; m. Mrs. G. Sandys, d. of late Duncan Cameron; educ. Radley College, and R.M.A., Woolwich; 2nd Lt., R.A., 6.1.00; Lt. 3.4.01; Capt. 11.1.11; Major 6.10.15; G.S.O.1, Belgian G.H.Q. (1917); R.A. Hd. Qrs., G.H.Q., France (1917). In charge of British Mission, 1st French Army, 1918; Supreme War Council, Versailles, 1918, where he was in charge of the German Delegation at the Peace Conference; Gen. Staff, British Military Mission with Gen. Denikin in S. Russia, 1919; Despatches; Bt. Lt.-Col. 3.6.18.

LISTER, W. H. (D.S.O. L.G. 17.12.17) (Details, L.G. 23.4.18); educ. University College, London; T/Capt., R.A.M.C., att. 21st F.A.; Despatches; M.C. He was killed in action in Italy 9.8.18.

LITCHFIELD-SPEER, F. S. (D.S.O. L.G. 3.6.16); b. 24.3.74; e. s. of F. and G. S. Litchfield; assumed additional name of Speer by Royal Licence, 1915); m. Marianne Frances Cecilia, d. of late E. F. Sandys; five s.; educ. Stubbington House, Fareham; H.M.S. Britannia; ent. R.N., 1887; Commander, 1905; Capt. 1911; in command of Mine-layer Squadron, 1915–17; (Despatches; C.M.G.); Deputy Director of Mining, Admiralty, 1918–19. He died suddenly, aged 49.

LITTLE, A. C. (D.S.O. L.G. 18.2.15) (Bar, L.G. 4.2.18) (Details, L.G. 5.7.18). Lt.-Col., 20th Hussars (see "The Distinguished Service Order," from its institution to 31.12.15, by same publishers).

LITTLE, C. H. (D.S.O. L.G. 1.1.17); b. 7.3.80, in Norfolk Square, London; s. of Col. W. H. Little, late E. Lancs. R., and Amy Powys Little; m. Dorothea Katharine, d. of S. H. Romilly and the late Lady Arabella Romilly; educ. Cheltenham College; ent. Som. L.I. 15.2.99; Lt. 20.6.00; Capt. 30.5.04; Adjt., 2nd Batt. Somerset L.I., Nov. 1904, to Nov. 1907; Major 1.9.15; Bt. Lt.-Col. 3.6.19; served S. African War, 1899–1902; Queen's Medal and 5 clasps; King's Medal and 2 clasps; joined the Egyptian Army, March, 1908; operations in Blue Nile, 1908; Atwot Expedition (Sudan), 1910; Sudan Medal with clasp; Sudan Western Frontier Force, 1916 (Darfur Expedition); present at Battle of Beringia and capture of El Fasher; was on H.Q. Staff of E.A., Oct. 1914, to Oct. 1916; G.S.O.2, British Army, Dec. 1914, to Oct. 1916; subsequently commanded the Eastern Arab Corps, E.A.; Despatches; Bt. Lt.-Col.; Order of the Nile.

LITTLE, ROBERT ALEXANDER (D.S.O. L.G. 11.8.17) (Bar, L.G. 14.9.17); s. of R. Little, of 263 College Street, Melbourne, Capt., R.A.F. (late R.N.A.S.); joined R.N.A.S., Jan. 1916; proceeded on active service on the Belgian coast in June of that year; afterwards with R.N.A.S. Squadrons co-operating with the Army on the Somme; was officially credited with having destroyed 47 enemy machines, and at the time of his death held the "record" among pilots of the R.N.A.S. for enemy machines destroyed. He was killed abroad in an aerial combat at night. An obituary notice appeared in the "Times" of 24.7.18; D.S.C. and Bar; Croix de Guerre.

LITTLE, ROBERT ARTHUR (D.S.O. L.G. 1.1.19), Major, 1st Brig., Aust. F.A.

LITTLE, W. B. (D.S.O. L.G. 4.6.17) (Bar, L.G. 26.7.18); m. Doris Maud, d. of late T. Turner, of Preston Park, Brighton, and Mrs. Vanston, of Brighton; one s.; Capt., E. Lancs. R., 26.8.16; Bt. Major, 2nd Batt. E. Lancs. R.; served Europ. War, 1914–18; Despatches; M.C.; Croix de Guerre.

LITTLEJOHNS, A. S. (D.S.O. L.G. 4.6.17); b. 31.10.79; Lt., R.A.M.C., 30.1.06; Capt. 30.7.09; Major 30.1.18; Despatches.

LITTLER, C. A. (D.S.O. L.G. 3.6.16); b. 26.3.68, at Launceston, Tasmania; s. of Augustus East Littler (Native of Launceston, Tasmania) and Hannah S. Littler (*née* Murray) (born at Evandale, Tasmania); m. at Devonport, W. Tasmania, Helen Cotgrave Thomas, d. of B. W. Thomas and Louisa Caroline Thomas (*née* Ashburner); three s.; educ. Launceston; joined Aust. Mil. Forces 12.9.02; Capt., 3rd Batt. Tasmanian Inf. Rgt.; served in the Europ. War; Despatches. Capt. Littler was killed in action on 3.9.16, at the taking of Mouquet Farm during the Somme Offensive.

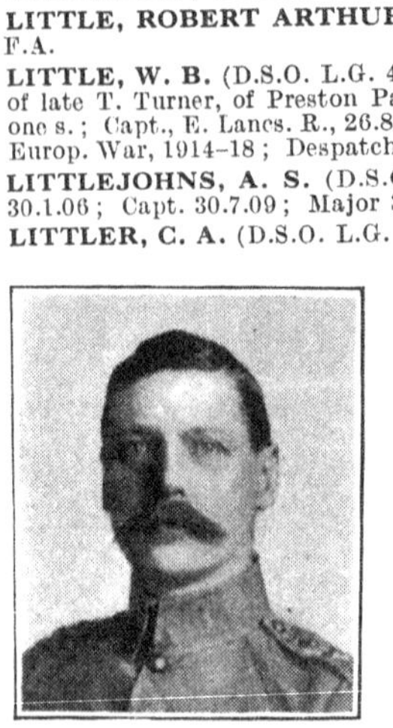
C. A. Littler.

LITTLETON, HON. C. C. J. (D.S.O. L.G. 1.1.18); b. 18.7.72; s. of E. G. P. Littleton, 3rd Baron Hatherton, and Charlotte, Lady Hatherton; m. Aileen Beatrix, d. of the late Sir F. H. Bathurst, of the Grenadier Guards, who died 5.7.19; Lt., 7th Batt. Middlesex R., 15.9.14; became Capt.; T/Lt.-Col. 21.6.19; Despatches three times; awarded 4th Class Order of the Nalda by H.M. the King of the Hedjaz, 1920

LITTLETON, H. A. (D.S.O. L.G. 23.7.18), Lt., R.N.V.R.

LIVENS, W. H. (D.S.O. L.G. 1.1.18), Lt. (T/Capt.), R.E., S.R.; M.C.

LLEWELLYN, E. H. (D.S.O. L.G. 1.1.18); b. 31.7.71; 1st com. 23.5.91; retired R. Innis. Fus. 5.7.11; Major, R. of O., 1.9.15; T/Brig.-Gen., King's African Rifles, 1.1.17.

LLOYD, C. R. (D.S.O. L.G. 25.8.17); b. 7.10.82; 2nd Lt., A.S.C., 1.5.01; Lt., Army, 1.8.03; Ind. Army 22.1.09; Capt. 1.5.10; Major 1.5.16; Bt. Major 3.6.18; Asst. Dir. of Transport, Mes. Exp. Force, 25.1.18; Despatches.

LLOYD, E. C. (D.S.O. L.G. 1.1.18) (Bar, L.G. 26.7.18); b. 4.1.77; s. of J. Lloyd, J.P., D.L., of Gloster, Brosna, King's Co., Ireland, and Susan Lloyd (*née* Colclough), of Tintern Abbey, Co. Wexford; m. Mary, d. of late Sir H. Considine; one s.; educ. Wellington College, Berks; 2nd Lt., R. Irish Rgt., 4.5.98; Lt. 23.10.99; Capt. 29.11.04; Major 25.8.15; served S. African War, 1899–1902; Despatches; Queen's Medal, 5 clasps; King's Medal, 2 clasps; Europ. War; Despatches three times; 1914–15 Star.

LLOYD, E. G. R. (D.S.O. L.G. 26.9.17) (Details, L.G. 9.1.18); b. 1890; s. of Major E. T. Lloyd, late Bengal Civil Service; m. Helen Kynaston, d. of late Lt.-Col. E. W. Greg, C.B., V.D., The Cheshire R.; two d.; Capt., R. of O., K.S.L.I.; served Europ. War, 1914–17; Despatches. His brother, Capt. O. R. Lloyd, K.S.L.I., was awarded the M.C., and another brother, Capt. W. L. Lloyd, the M.C. and Bar.

LLOYD, E. P. (D.S.O. L.G. 3.6.18) (Bar, L.G. 11.1.19); b. 22.7.87; 2nd Lt., Linc. R., 24.1.06; Lt. 28.12.10; Adjt., Linc. R., 16.11.13 to 27.10.15; Capt. 4.8.14; Bt. Major 1.1.16; Adjt., Linc. R., 12.4.20; Despatches.

LLOYD, G. (D.S.O. L.G. 4.6.17); b. 8.10.92; Capt., R.A.V.C. (from Spec. Res.), 10.7.19.

LLOYD, SIR G. A., F.R.G.S. (D.S.O. L.G. 3.3.17); b. 19.9.79; s. of S. S. Lloyd, of The Priory, Warwick, and Dolobrau, Montgomeryshire, Wales; m. Hon. Blanche (late Maid of Honour to Queen Alexandra), d. of Hon. F. C. Lascelles (2nd s. of 4th Earl of Harewood and 1st wife, Elizabeth Joanna, e. d. of 1st Marquess of Clanricarde) and Frederica Maria (who died in 1891), d. of late Hon. Sir A. Liddell, K.C.B.; one s.; educ. Eton; Cambridge; served Europ. War in Egypt, Gallipoli, Mesopotamia and the Hedjaz, 1914–18; Star of the Nile; St. Ann of Russia; Order (Hedjaz); Governor of Bombay since 1918; G.C.I.E.; M.P. for W. Staffs (U.), 1910–18.

LLOYD, H. (D.S.O. L.G. 1.1.17); b. 27.4.82; s. of N. Lloyd and Emily Ann Lloyd, d. of late G. Walmsley; m. Margaret Jessica, d. of late J. Goddard and widow of Major J. B. Aldridge, D.S.O., R.H.A.; one d.; educ. Uppingham School; 2nd Lt., Northants R., 28.1.03; Lt. 7.12.04; Capt. 15.8.10; Adjt., Northants R., 1912; Major 5.9.16; ret. Northants R., 6.6.19; served S. African War, 1899–1900; Queen's Medal with 4 clasps; went to France, Aug. 1914; present at Mons; through the whole retreat, Marne, Aisne (very severely wounded); returned to France on the General Staff of a New Army Division, and took part in various operations, including the Battle of the Somme; Despatches.

LLOYD, J. HARDRESS- (see Hardress-Lloyd, J.).

LLOYD, J. HENRY (D.S.O. L.G. 4.6.17); b. 13.7.72; 1st com. 13.8.92; Capt. 25.1.00; retired R. Lanc. R. 18.12.07; Lt.-Col., Spec. Res.; T/Brig.-Gen. 23.9.16.

LLOYD, L. (D.S.O. L.G. 4.3.18) (Details, L.G. 16.8.18) (1st Bar, L.G. 16.9.18) (2nd Bar, L.G. 15.2.19) (Details, L.G. 30.7.19), Lt.-Col., 12th Batt. Suff. R.

LLOYD, O. F. (D.S.O. L.G. 3.6.19); b. 10.4.79; 2nd Lt., Conn. Rangers, 15.11.99; Lt., 12.5.01; Capt. 21.4.06; Major 1.9.15; Major (A/Lt.-Col.), Conn. Rangers (seconded Tank Corps); served S. African War, 1900–2; Queen's Medal with 5 clasps; King's Medal with 2 clasps; Europ. War; Despatches.

LLOYD, R. A., M.D., M.R.C.S., L.R.C.P. (D.S.O. L.G. 17.9.17); b. 14.4.78; s. of R. H. Lloyd, M.D.; Lt., I.M.S., 26.7.02; m. Ivy Frances Byard, d. of R. B. Clayton; educ. Westminster School; St. Bartholomew's Hospital; Capt. 26.7.05; Major 26.1.14; served N.W. Frontier of India, 1908; operations in the Mohmand country; Medal with clasp; Europ. War; mobilized No. 12 Meerut Indian Hospital, Aug. 1914; commanded same throughout the war; Despatches twice; Bt. Lt.-Col. 3.6.19.

LLOYD, R. C. (D.S.O. L.G. 2.4.19) (Details, L.G. 10.12.19), Capt. (A/Major), 1/1st Denbighshire R., att. 24th Batt. R. Welsh Fus.; M.C.

LLOYD, R. G. A. (D.S.O. L.G. 3.6.18), Capt., R. of O., S. Lancs. R. (Hon.) Capt., R. of O., 5.9.02; Major, R. of O., S. Lancs. R.

LLOYD, R. W. M. (D.S.O. L.G. 30.11.17); b. 14.2.84; s. of Col. E. Lloyd, late Punjab Cav.; m. Gladys, d. of Brig.-Gen. A. C. Painter, C.M.G., and Amy Caroline (who died in 1895), d. of late Thomas Whistler Smith, of Glenrock, Sydney, N.S.W.; one d.; educ. Bedford School; H.M.S. Britannia; served in Mediterranean and China; Sub Lt., 1903; two 1st class certificates; Lt., 1905; Lt.-Cdr. 5.11.13; Commander, 1918; served in Atlantic, Home and China Fleets and Yangtzekiang; commanded expedition up the Han River, China, in H.M.S. Woodlark, in connection with massacres by the Chinese brigand, White Wolf, 1914, and penetrated beyond city of Siang Yang, 85 miles higher up than had been previously reached by steam craft; served in H.M.S. Hampshire, 1914–16; commanded H.M. Ships Nasturtium (mined and sunk), Marguerite and Berberis (in Mediterranean) and Narwhal (North Sea and Atlantic); Despatches; Rugby Football (Blackheath, Kent County and United Services).

LLOYD, T. W. (D.S.O. L.G. 3.6.18); s. of W. E. Lloyd, of Liverpool; Major, late R.E.

LLOYD, W. J. (D.S.O. L.G. 1.2.19), 2nd Lt., 7th Batt. Lanc. Fus., T.F., att. 5th Batt. W. Riding R., T.F.

LLOYD-WILLIAMS, H., B.A. (D.S.O. L.G. 16.9.18) (gazetted under Williams, H. Lloyd); b. 16.10.89; m. Dorothy Marion, d. of the late Major the Hon. F. Le Poer-Trench, 2nd s. of the 3rd Earl of Clancarty; educ. Friars School, Bangor; University of Wales; joined O.T.C., Oct. 1909; was First President of Central S.R.C., University of Wales; was prominent Sprinter, Footballer and Oarsman in University of Wales; served Europ. War; A/Lt.-Col., R. Welsh Fus., 1914–18; Despatches; M.C. awarded for gallantry in the operations around La Boisselle, Contalmaison, High Wood, in July, 1916. His D.S.O. was awarded for gallantry while in command of a battalion on 24.3.18, on the right flank of the 3rd Army near Frémicourt.

H. Lloyd-Williams.

LOCH, A. A. F. (D.S.O. L.G. 30.3.16); b. 27.10.95; s. of F. G. Loch; 2nd Lt., 1st Batt. S.W.B., 1.10.14; Lt. (T/Capt.). He was reported missing on 22.7.16, and afterwards officially presumed to have been killed on that date, aged only twenty years.

LOCH, E. E. (D.S.O. L.G. 12.12.19); b. 9.5.91; 2nd Lt., H.L.I., 5.10.10; Lt. 11.5.13; Capt. 17.5.15; M.G.C. 2.7.18.

LOCH, G. G. (D.S.O. L.G. 1.1.19); b. 22.7.70; 2nd Lt., R. Scots, 3.5.90; Lt. 10.5.93; Capt. 26.6.97; Major 14.8.08; Col. 27.5.21; T/Brig.-Gen. 8.7.20; served Europ. War, 1914–18; Bt. Lt.-Colonel 1.1.17; Bt.-Col. 1.1.18; Despatches; C.M.G.

LOCK, F. R. E. (D.S.O. L.G. 25.8.17); b. 21.4.67; s. of late Col. E. S. Lock, 2nd S. Lancs. R., and Caroline Louisa Lock (*née* Cardew); m. d. of late E. F. Duncanson; one s.; one d.; educ. Warrington Grammar School; Sandhurst; commissioned in 2nd Gloucester Rgt., 1886; transferred to Indian Army, 1889; Colonel 3.5.17; Hon. Brig.-Gen. 19.8.19; transferred to Pension Establishment; served Aden operations in the interior, 1903–4; N.W. Frontier, 1915; Mesopotamia Exp. Force, 1915–18; Despatches three times; G.O.C., Euphrates, L. of C. Defences, Mesopotamia Exp. Force, 1916–18; commanded 112th Inf., I.A., 1911–16.

LOCK, J. M. B. (D.S.O. L.G. 26.7.17), 2nd Lt., Middx. R., S.R. His D.S.O. was awarded for gallantry at Fontaine-les-Croiselles 23.4.17.

LOCKER-LAMPSON, O. (D.S.O. L.G. 3.6.18); b. 1881; s. of F. Locker, the Poet, and Jane Lampson, d. of Sir C. Lampson, 1st Bart.; educ. Cheam Private School; Eton; Trinity College, Cambridge; Winner of Prince Consort's Prize for German, 1898; took Honours Tripos Degree in Modern Languages, 1902, and an Honours Tripos Degree in History, 1903; edited "Granta," 1900; President of Amateur Dramatic Co., 1903; called to the Bar, 1907; assisted various journals, and wrote for leading magazines; Lieut.-Comdr. in R.N.A.S., Dec. 1914; A/Cdr., July, 1915; Cross of Officer of the Order of Leopold, Dec. 1915; Order of St. Vladimir, 1916; St. George, 1917; saw service with armoured cars in France, Belgium, Russia, Turkey, Persia, Roumania and Austria during the Europ. War; Russian representative of Ministry of Information, 1918; Parliamentary Private Secretary to Chancellor of Exchequer, March, 1919; C.M.G.

LOCKHART, J. F. K. (D.S.O. L.G. 1.1.19); b. 27.11.81; 2nd Lt., R.A., 24.5.02; Lt. 24.5.05; Capt. 30.10.14; Major, R.F.A., 7.3.16; Despatches.

LOCKHART, R. N. (D.S.O. L.G. 1.1.17); b. 26.6.73; 2nd Lt., R.A., 16.3.92; Lt. 16.3.95; Capt. 3.1.00; Major 4.10.12; Lt.-Col. 1.5.17; Despatches.

LOCKHART-JERVIS, B. C. (D.S.O. L.G. 4.6.17), T/Capt. (A/Major), R.E.

LOCKWOOD, A. L. (D.S.O. L.G. 3.6.18), Capt., R.A.M.C.; M.C.

LOCKWOOD, E. M. (D.S.O. L.G. 3.6.19); s. of A. C. Lockwood; m. Winifred (who died in 1918), d. of H. L. Mather; educ. Bradfield College; Trinity Hall, Cambridge; A/Cdr., R.N.V.R., of the Hawke Batt. R.N.D.

LOCKYER, E. L. B. (D.S.O. L.G. 1.1.15) (Bar, L.G. 23.3.17), Cdr., R.N. (see "The Distinguished Service Order," from its institution to 31.12.15, by same publishers).

LODGE, A. B. (D.S.O. L.G. 22.9.16); b. 1.8.95; Capt., Aust. Inf.; Lt., Army (from Aust. Imp. Force), 28.1.17; Ind. Army 29.7.18; Capt. 29.1.20; Despatches.

LODGE, F. C. (D.S.O. L.G. 17.4.16); b. 29.11.68; 2nd Lt., Norfolk R., 12.3.92; Lt. 1.1.95; Capt. 6.6.00; Adjt., Norf. R,. 28.11.01 to 27.11.04; Major 15.11.11; Lt.-Col. 12.1.17; Retired Pay, 1921; served S. African War, 1899–1902; Queen's Medal with 3 clasps; King's Medal with 2 clasps; Europ. War (Mesopotamia), 1915–18; Despatches; C.M.G.

LOGAN, D. D., M.D. (D.S.O. L.G. 4.6.17), T/Lt.-Col., R.A.M.C. (retired).

LOGAN, F. D. (D.S.O. L.G. 1.1.17); b. 31.7.75; s. of late D. Logan; m. Alice Maude, d. of late Capt. A. W. Chitty, C.I.E., late Indian Navy; one s.; two d.; educ. Charterhouse; Woolwich; 2nd Lt., R.A., 2.11.95; Lt. 2.11.98; Capt. 23.11.01; Major 19.6.12; Lt.-Col. 11.9.16; Col. 31.8.20; T/Brig.-Gen.; served Omdurman Campaign, 1898; Europ. War; Despatches four times; Bt. Lt.-Col. 1.1.16; Bt. Col. 3.6.19; C.M.G.; Croix d'Officier, Légion d'Honneur.

LOGGIE, O. M. (D.S.O. L.G. 1.1.18), Lt. (A/Major), R.G.A.; M.C.

LOMAS, K. T. (D.S.O. L.G. 1.1.18); b. 4.12.79; s. of J. Lomas and Maria Thurston Lomas; m. Frances Mary, d. of Rev. G. Cotesworth; educ. Bradfield College, Berks; University College, London; Principal Resident Officer, L.C.C. Housing Scheme; 2nd Lt., R.E., 4.9.15; Overseas with Railway Construction Troops 1.10.15; Capt., April, 1916; Major, April, 1917; Lt.-Col., Railway Construction Engineers, June, 1917; Railway Construction Engineer to 4th Army, Coastal Area, June–Nov. 1917; to 2nd Army, Nov. 1917, to March, 1919; reconstructed railways through devastated area and Belgium behind 2nd Army; from Ypres, constructed bridge over Lys and Schelt; Technical Adviser, Railway Sub-Commission, Cologne, March–June, 1917; A.D., General Transport, 25.6.19; demobilized 3.11.19; Despatches twice; Légion d'Honneur; Croix de Guerre (twice). After demobilization was appointed Controller-General of Communications to the Inter-Allied Plebiscite Commission, Allenstein, E. Prussia.

LOMAX, C. E. N. (D.S.O. L.G. 8.3.19) (Details, L.G. 4.10.19) (Bar, L.G. 1.1.19); m. Rene Burgoyne Doyley; one s.; Capt. (T/Lt.-Col.), Welsh R.; served Europ. War, 1914–19; Despatches; M.C.

LOMER, G. (D.S.O. L.G. 4.6.17); s. of late G. Lomer, F.R.G.S.; m. Mavis Mary, d. of Capt. R. Garrett, R.F.A.; one d.; Capt., H.A.C.; Lt., R.F.A.

LOMER, T. A. (D.S.O. L.G. 3.6.18), Major, Can. A.M.C.

LONG, A. DE L. (D.S.O. L.G. 3.6.18); b. 1880; m. Nan, d. of late A. Paterson; educ. Winchester; New College, Oxford; served Europ. War, 1914–18; Despatches thrice; Bt. Major; Major, Gordon Highlanders.

LONG, H. O. (D.S.O. L.G. 27.6.19), Lt., No. 3 Squadron, R.F.C. (now R.A.F.).

LONG, S. H. (D.S.O. L.G. 12.3.17); s. of Maj.-Gen. S. S. Long, C.B., and Augusta Elizabeth, d. of late Col. T. G. Glover, R.E.; educ. Imperial Services College; Sandhurst; 2nd Lt., Durham L.I., 1914; joined R.F.C., 1914; Lt., Durham L.I., 1915; Major, R.A.F.; Despatches five times; M.C. His D.S.O. was awarded for gallantry at Morval.

LONGBOTTOM, T. (D.S.O. L.G. 1.1.18); m. Elsie Keturah Balmforth; Major, W. Yorks. R.

LONGBOTTOM, W. (D.S.O. L.G. 3.6.19); b. 7.6.84; educ. Huddersfield College School; 2nd Lt., L.N. Lancs. R., July, 1918; Lt.-Colonel; served Europ. War, Salonika; Palestine; Despatches.

LONGBOURNE, H. R. (D.S.O. L.G. 25.11.16); s. of late C. R. V. Longbourne and C. E. A. Longbourne; educ. Repton; Capt., The Queen's Rgt.; served in the European War; was present at engagements on the Somme and Ancre; was awarded the D.S.O. for gallantry at Schwaben Redoubt, and was killed in action on 22.5.17, during an attack on Cherisy.

LONGCROFT, C. A. H. (D.S.O. L.G. 1.1.18); b. 13.5.83; s. of C. E. Longcroft and Catharine Alicia Longcroft (*née* Holcombe); m. Marjorie, widow of Capt. W. D. Hepburn, Seaf. Highrs., and d. of J. W. McKerrell-Brown; educ. Charterhouse and Sandhurst; 2nd Lt., Welch R., 2.5.03; Lt. 13.12.06; Capt. 13.8.13; Bt. Major 22.6.14; Major 2.5.18; Bt. Lt.-Col. 1.1.17; T/Major-Gen. 18.10.17; Major; Bt. Lt.-Col., The Welch R.; Air Commodore, R.A.F.; served in India, 1904–6; S. Africa, 1906–9; learnt to fly, Oct. 1911; joined R.F.C. on formation, May, 1912; awarded Britannia Trophy, 1913, for long-distance flight from Montrose to Southampton to Farnborough, non-stop; duration 7 hours, 20 minutes; served Europ. War; 1914 Star; Officier, Légion d'Honneur; Order of St. Stanislas, 3rd Class with Swords; Despatches four times.

LONGDEN, A. A. (D.S.O. L.G. 18.2.18) (Details, L.G. 18.7.18); s. of J. A. Longden and Annie Walker Longden (*née* Morley); m. Betty Marie, d. of P. Sorensen, of Copenhagen; one d.; educ. Durham School; Royal College of Art (Medallist); exhibited in R.A. and other Exhibitions; Director, British Institute of Industrial Art, Board of Trade; Major, R.G.A. (T.); served in R.G.A.; Europ. War; Despatches twice.

LONGDEN, A. B. (D.S.O. L.G. 3.6.19); b. 10.3.68; 2nd Lt., R. War. R., 11.2.88; Lt. 5.7.89; Lt., I.S.C., 25.12.91; Capt. 11.2.99; Major 11.2.06; Lt.-Col., 38th Dogras, I.A., 11.2.14; served op. in Chitral, 1895, with Relief Force; Medal and clasp; N.W. Frontier of India, 1897–98; Mohmand; clasp.

LONGHURST, G. F. (D.S.O. L.G. 15.9.16), Cdr., R.N., 30.6.16; served in the Battle of Jutland; was mentioned in Sir J. Jellicoe's Despatch dated 23.8.16. He died 8.1.21.

LONGHURST, T. L. (D.S.O. L.G. 3.6.18); s. of Rev. T. J. Longhurst, Pastor of the Free Church, Frinton-on-Sea; T/Major, A.S.C. (now R.A.S.C.). His D.S.O. was awarded for service in Italy.

LONGMAN, H. K. (D.S.O. L.G. 1.1.18), e. s. of George Longman, of Messrs. Longmans & Co., Publishers; Capt., R. of O., late G. Highrs.; served Europ. War; Despatches; M.C.

LONGMORE, A. M. (D.S.O. L.G. 1.1.19); m. Marjorie, d. of late W. J. Maitland, C.I.E.; two s.; one d.; Lt.-Cdr., R.N., 30.12.14; Group Captain, R.A.F.

LONGMORE, C. M. (D.S.O. L.G. 1.1.17); b. 14.11.82; 2nd Lt., R.A., 21.12.01; Lt. 2.12.04; Adjt., R.A., 19.1.14 to 26.8.15; Capt. 30.10.14; Major, R.F.A., 18.1.16; Bt. Lt.-Col. 3.6.19; Adjt., R.A., 22.1.21.

LONGSTAFF, R. (D.S.O. L.G. 14.1.16); b. 10.10.78; educ. Winchester; ent. R.A. 9.5.00; Lt. 3.9.01; Capt. 27.7.10; Major 30.10.14; served S. African War, 1901–2; Queen's Medal with 5 clasps; Europ. War from 1914; Despatches; Legion of Honour.

LONGUEVILLE, F. (D.S.O. L.G. 14.11.16); b. 23.12.92; s. of T. Longueville and Mary Frances, d. of A. Robertson, of Balgownie; m. Gertrude, d. of late R. G. Venables; one d.; educ. Oratory School, Edgbaston; R.M.C., Sandhurst; 2nd Lt., Coldstream Guards, 4.9.12; Lt. 27.12.14; Capt. 23.2.16; A/Major, Second-in-Command, 3rd Batt. C. Gds., Sept. 1916, to Oct. 1917; A/Lt.-Col., 3rd Batt. C. Gds., Oct. 1917 to May, 1918; served Europ. War, 1915–18; wounded; Despatches thrice; M.C. His D.S.O. was awarded for gallantry on 15.9.16.

LONSDALE, H. H. HEYWOOD- (see Heywood-Lonsdale, H. H.).

LONSDALE, J. P. H. HEYWOOD- (see Heywood-Lonsdale, J. P. H.).

LOOKER, A. W. (D.S.O. L.G. 25.8.16), 2nd Lt., Cambs. R.

LOOMIS, SIR F. O. W. (D.S.O. L.G. 23.6.15) (Bar, L.G. 2.4.19) (Details, L.G. 10.12.19), Major-Gen., Can. Mil. Forces; K.C.B.; C.M.G. (see "The Distinguished Service Order," from its institution to 31.12.15, by same publishers).

LORAINE, R. (D.S.O. L.G. 4.6.17); b. 14.1.76; s. of late H. Loraine; m. Winifred Lydia, d. of Sir T. Strangman, and Winifred, d. of Capt. W. J. J. Warneford; educ. High School, New Brighton; made first appearance on Stage, 1889; Lt.-Colonel, R.A.F.; served S. African War with machine guns (Queen's Medal with 3 clasps); Europ. War, 1914–18; Despatches six times; dangerously wounded twice; M.C.; made first flight across Irish Sea 11.9.10.

LORCH, A. E. (D.S.O. L.G. 26.3.18) (Details, L.G. 24.8.18), Major, Field Artillery, S. African Military Forces.

LORD, A. J. (D.S.O. L.G. 26.7.18), Lt. (T/Capt.), R. Fus., Spec. Res.; M.C.

LORD, F. B. (D.S.O. L.G. 4.6.17); b. 3.7.76; 2nd Lt., York. and Lanc. R., 25.3.96; 2nd Lt., A.S.C., 1.1.98; Lt. 1.1.99; Capt. 1.1.01; Major 11.9.12; Lt.-Col., R.A.S.C., 1.4.17; served S. African War, 1899–1901; employed with Remounts, afterwards on Staff; Queen's Medal with 6 clasps Europ. War; Despatches.

LORD, J. ERNEST C. (gazetted as Lord, J. Edward C.) (D.S.O. L.G. 4.6.17), Lt.-Col., Aust. Mil. Forces.

LORING, W. (D.S.O. L.G. 1.1.18); b. 4.9.72; s. of late Admiral Sir W. Loring, K.C.B., of Stonelands, Ryde, I.W.; m. Cicely Catherine Schonswar, d. of Vice-Admiral C. Johnstone; two s.; educ. Marlborough College; R.M.A., Woolwich; 2nd Lt., R.A., 21.12.92; Lt. 2.12.95; Capt. 7.2.00; Adjt., R.A., 1.5.06 to 30.4.09; Major 28.1.14; Lt.-Col. 13.7.17; Col., R.G.A., 3.6.19; served Europ. War; commanded 110th Heavy Battery on Western front, Sept. 1914, to April, 1916; commanded Heavy Artillery Groups on Western front, April, 1916, to Feb. 1918; Counter-Battery Staff Officer on Western front, Feb. 1918, to March, 1919; Despatches four times; Bt. Lt.-Col. 3.6.15; C.M.G.; Croix de Guerre Belge.

LOUGH, J. R. S. (D.S.O. L.G. 15.2.19) (Details, L.G. 30.7.19), Capt., 72nd Batt. Can. Inf., Br. Col. Rgt.; M.C.

LOUGH, R. D. H. (D.S.O. L.G. 6.9.16), Capt. (T/Major), R.M.L.I.

LOUTIT, N. M. (D.S.O. L.G. 4.6.17) (Bar, L.G. 18.6.17); b. 8.3.94; s. of T. I. Loutit; ent. Aust. Mil. Forces, Oct. 1913; Capt., Feb. 1916; Major, Oct. 1916; Lt.-Col., 1918; served Gallipoli until evacuation; Despatches six times. He was awarded the D.S.O. for gallantry from 2–4.4.17, at Moreuil.

LOVE, STUART GILKSON (gazetted as Love, Stuart Gilkinson) (D.S.O. L.G. 1.1.18) (Bar, L.G. 16.9.18), Lt. (A/Major), R.E.; M.C.

LOVEDAY, F. W. (D.S.O. L.G. 17.12.17) (Details, L.G. 23.4.18); b. 12.7.79; 2nd Lt., R.A., 23.12.98; Lt. 16.2 01; Capt. 9.3.04; Major, R.G.A., 30.10.14; Bt. Lt.-Col. 1.1.19; Despatches.

LOVEGROVE, A. V. R. (D.S.O. L.G. 11.4.19), Cdr., R.N.R.; R.D.

LOVELACE (L. F. K.), EARL OF (D.S.O. L.G. 1.1.17); b. 16.11.65; s. of 1st Earl of Lovelace and Jane, widow of E. Jenkins, of Bengal; m. Lady Edith Anson, d. of 2nd Earl of Lichfield; one s; three d.; educ. Eton; Sandhurst; formerly Capt. and Adjt., 9th Lancers, he served in the European War, 1915–19, as Temp. Major, North'd Fus. and Gen. List is J.P. and D.L.

LOVELESS, L. S. (D.S.O. L.G. 23.3.17); s. of late S. Loveless, of Cardiff; Eng.-Lt., R.N.R.; D.S.C. and Bar.

LOVEMORE, R. B. (D.S.O. L.G. 8.2.19); e. s. of R. Lovemore, of 'Mbabane, Swaziland, and nephew of R. Raw, of Pretoria; m. Gwendolen Amy, d. of H. C. Edwards; served in Europ. War; Lt., 3rd Batt. London Rgt.; Lt., R.A.F. (late Native Affairs Dept., Johannesburg); as only a boy he "saw service in the Rebellion, when he not only was seriously wounded, but mentioned in Despatches for excellent services rendered. He was also much in evidence in South-West and East Africa. . . . For some particularly smart piece of aviation work he had the D.S.O. bestowed upon him."

R. B. Lovemore.

LOVEROCK, R. C. (D.S.O. L.G. 17.9.17); b. 6.12.79; 2nd Lt., Oxf. and Bucks, L.I., 7.11.14; Lt. 18.8.15; Capt. 1.1.17; Despatches; O.B.E.

LOW, E. E. (D.S.O. L.G. 5.10.18), Eng.-Cdr., R.N.R.

LOW, G. S. (D.S.O. L.G. 19.12.22), Major, R.A.

LOW, N. (D.S.O. L.G. 14.1.16); b. 15.4.79; Lt., R.A.M.C., 30.7.04; Capt. 30.1.08; Major 1.7.15; A/Lt.-Col. 25.3.17; served in Europ. War from 1914; Despatches.

LOW, S. (D.S.O. L.G. 1.1.17); b. 1.12.88; s. of A. Low, J.P., Banker (Grindlay & Co.), and Stephanie Low; m. Lucy Gwen, d. of Hon. Mr. Justice and Lady Atkin; two s.; one d.; educ. Mr. Lynam's Preparatory School, Oxford, and Winchester College; partner in Grindlay & Co. At the outbreak of war was Lt., 2nd London Heavy Battery, R.G.A. (T.F.); Capt., 1915; Major 3.10.16; served in France from March, 1915; commanded a battery from Dec. 1915; Despatches twice.

LOW, W. R. (D.S.O. L.G. 16.9.18), T/Capt., K.R.R.C.; M.C.

LOWCOCK, A. (D.S.O. L.G. 11.1.19), Lt. (A/Major), R.F.A., T.F.; M.C.

LOWCOCK, R. J. (D.S.O. L.G. 26.9.17) (Details, L.G. 9.1.18), Lt. (T/Capt.), Notts. and Derby. R. and R.F.C.; M.C. His D.S.O. was awarded for gallantry on 18.7.17, near Westende.

LOWE, C. E. B. (D.S.O. L.G 3.6.19), Lt. (A/Major), R.G.A., T.F.; M.C.

LOWE, T. A. (D.S.O. L.G. 1.2.19); b. 7.4.88; 2nd Lt., R. Irish Rgt., 17.12.14; Lt. 13.4.15; Adjt., R. Irish Rgt., 6.9.15 to 11.4.17; Capt., Essex R., 21.12.20; Bt. Major 22.12.20; Despatches; M.C.

LOWE, W. D., M.A., D.Litt. Dublin (D.S.O. L.G. 26.7.18); s. of late Rev. Canon Lowe, of Manchester; educ. Shrewsbury School; elected to a Scholarship at Pembroke College, Cambridge, he took a First Class in the Classical Tripos, and rowed for his College. He later studied in Germany. Afterwards was on the Staff of Bradfield College. Nearly 20 years ago he was appointed Classical Lecturer at Durham University, where he coached the Durham University Crews. Shortly after the outbreak of war Dr. Lowe was appointed Capt. and Adjt., 18th Batt. Durham L.I., and went with them to Egypt and France. He ultimately commanded the Batt.; Despatches; M.C. He edited a narrative of the Battalion's services. Dr. Lowe was taken suddenly ill while attending service in chapel, and died within half an hour. He was 43.

LOWE, W. D. DRURY- (see Drury-Lowe, W. D.).

LOWIS, P. S. (D.S.O. L.G. 1.1.17); b. 17.12.70; s. of late Col. N. Lowis; m. Marie, d. of late R. G. Currie, Bengal C.S.; 2nd Lt., R.A., 25.7.90; Lt. 25.7.93; Capt. 9.10.99; Major 15.5.11; Lt.-Col. 1.5.17; Retired R.G.A., 1920; served N.W. Frontier of India, 1897–98 (Medal and clasp); Europ. War, 1914–18; Despatches; C.M.G.; Croix de Guerre.

LOWNDES, J. G. (D.S.O. L.G. 1.1.18); b. 27.9.68; 1st com. 30.7.90; Major, 9.6.09; Retired 4.3.14; Major, R. of O., late N. Lancs. R.; served S. African War, 1899–1902 as Adjt., 2nd Batt. N. Lanc. R.; Despatches three times; Bt. of Major; Queen's Medal with clasp; Europ. War; Despatches.

LOWRY, A. E. E. (D.S.O. L.G. 26.7.18); b. 4.12.92; second and only surviving son of W. B. Lowry; educ. St. Andrew's, Southborough; Cheltenham College (Southwood House); Sandhurst, where he was a Prize Cadet, Corporal of his Company, and at the passing-out examination he won the French Prize; 2nd Lt., W. Yorks R., 5.2.13; Lt. 7.3.14; Adjt., March, 1915; A/Lt.-Colonel commanding battalion for over a year; was slightly wounded; held the 1914 Star; M.C.; Croix de Guerre avec Palme, and was killed in action on 23.9.18, his elder brother, 2nd Lt. W. A. H. Lowry, I.A.R., att. 14th Sikhs, having been killed in Gallipoli on 4.6.15, and his younger brother, Lt. (A/Capt.) C. J. P. Lowry, W. Yorks. R., on 25.3.18.

LOWRY, T. M. (D.S.O. L.G. 3.6.18); s. of late T. S. Lowry, of Bank House, Camborne; educ. at Truro College; Camborne School of Mines; Capt. (A/Major), D.C.L.I., att. R.E.; gained M.C. in Tunnelling Section, R.E.

LOWSLEY, H. de L. POLLARD- (see Pollard-Lowsley, H. de L.).

LOWSLEY, M. M. (D.S.O. L.G. 3.6.18); b. 24.9.72; Lt., R.A.M.C., 28.1.98; Capt. 28.1.01; Major 28.10.09; Lt.-Col. 1.3.15; Despatches.

LOWTHER, SIR C. B., Bart. (D.S.O. L.G. 1.1.17); b. 22.7.80; s. of late G. W. Lowther, e. s. of 3rd Bart., and Mary Frances Alice, d. of late Col. C. Bingham, R.A.; m. Marjory, d. of late T. Fielden, M.P.; one s.; one d.; educ. Winchester; R.M.C., Sandhurst; ent. 8th Hussars 12.8.99; left 1907, as Captain; joined Northants Yeomanry, 1910, as Captain; Lt.-Colonel; served S. African War, 1900–1; Queen's Medal with 5 clasps; Europ. War from 1914; commanded Northants Yeomanry from April, 1917, and the Mounted Troops of the Italian Exp. Force from June, 1918, and during the final offensive against the Austrians; Despatches four times; Master of Pytchley Hunt, 1914–18.

LOWTHER, G. F. (D.S.O. L.G. 1.2.19), Capt., Australian Mil. Forces; M.C.

LOWTHER, J. G. (D.S.O. L.G. 2.4.19) (Details, L.G. 10.12.19); b. 9.8.85; 2nd s. of G. W. Lowther, and brother of Lt.-Col. Sir C. B. Lowther, Bart., D.S.O.; m. Hon. Lilah White, d. of Lord Annaly; one s.; one d.; educ. Winchester; 2nd Lt., 11th Hrs., from I.Y., 29.11.05; Lt. 22.1.09; Capt. 1.8.14; Major, Northants Yeom.; served Europ. War; was severely wounded in the offensive near Arras 10.4.17; won D.S.O. while att. Northants Yeom.; 1914 Star; Despatches twice; M.C. He played polo for the 11th Hussars, 1910–14, and has won many point-to-point races.

LOYD, H. C. (D.S.O. L.G. 1.1.18); b. 21.2.91; s. of Mr. and Hon. Mrs. Loyd, of Langleybury, Herts; m. Lady Moyra Brodrick, d. of the Earl of Midleton; 2nd Lt., C. Gds., 3.9.10; Lt. 1.4.12; Capt. 17.7.15; Major 30.11.21; Despatches; M.C.

LOYNES, J. (D.S.O. L.G. 8.3.19) (Details, L.G. 4.10.19), Major, 11th Aust. L.H. Rgt.

LUARD, L. D. (D.S.O. L.G. 1.1.18), T/Major, A.S.C.; served Europ. War; Despatches; M.C.

LUARD, T. B. (D.S.O. L.G. 20.2.19); b. 3.11.73; s. of late Rev. Bixby Garnham Luard, Rector of Birch, Essex; m. 1920, Helen Ann Frances, widow of late C. J. Cockburn, M.C., Ind. Army; educ. Forest School, Walthamstow; 2nd Lt., R.M., 1.9.93; Lt. 1.7.94; Capt. 1.4.00; Major 5.5.11 Bt. Lt.-Col. 5.5.18; Lt.-Col. 30.11.20; served Europ. War on the Naval Staff in Ceylon, Egypt and Palestine; Despatches.

LUBBOCK, G. (D.S.O. L.G. 23.11.16); b. 9.10.70; s. of Frederic, 6th s. of Sir J. W. Lubbock, 3rd Bart., and bro. of 1st Baron Avebury; m. 1912, Lettice Isabella, 3rd d. of R. H. Mason, J.P.; one s.; educ. Eton; Woolwich; 2nd Lt., R.E., 27.7.89; Lt. 27.7.92; Capt. 1.4.00; Major 5.4.09; served in Burma, 1891–92 (Medal with clasp); operations in Chitral, 1895 (Medal with clasp); S. African War, 1901–2, on Staff; Queen's Medal, clasp; Europ. War; German East Africa, France, Egypt, Mesopotamia; C.M.G., 1917; Chevalier of the Legion of Honour; Serbian Order of the White Eagle with Swords.

LUBBOCK, M. G. (D.S.O. L.G. 25.11.21), Major, R.F.A.; M.C.

LUBY, M. (D.S.O. L.G. 1.1.19); b. 24.3.93; 2nd Lt., R.E., 19.7.12; Lt. 5.8.14 Adjt., R.E., 11.10.15; Capt. 26.6.17.; M.C.

LUCAS, C. H. T. (D.S.O. L.G. 1.1.17); b. 1.3.79; s. of William Tindall Lucas, of Foxholes, Hitchin; m. 1917, Joan, d. of late Arthur F. Holdsworth; two s.; educ. Marlborough; Sandhurst; 2nd Lt., R. Berks. R., 7.5.98; Lt. 1.8.00; Capt. 1.4.09; Bt. Major 18.2.15; Major 1.9.15; T/Brig.-Gen. 15.8.15 to 14.10.18; Bt. Lt.-Col. 8.11.15; T/Major-Gen. 15.10.18 to 17.3.19; Bt. Colonel 1.1.19; T/Brig.-Gen. 18.3.19 to 31.12.20; Colonel 30.10.19; T/Col.-Comdt. 1.1.21; served S. African War, 1899–1902 (Queen's Medal, 3 clasps; King's Medal, 2 clasps); Europ. War, 1914–18; Despatches; C.B., 1921; C.M.G.; Deputy Lieut., Hertfordshire.

LUCAS, C. R. (D.S.O. L.G. 4.2.18) (Details, L.G. 5.7.18), T/Capt., R. Lanc. R.

LUCAS, L. W. (D.S.O. L.G. 20.10.16); b. 14.5.79; 5th son of J. Lucas, J.P., of Birkdale, Branksome Park, Bournemouth; m. 1917, Susie Frances, widow of late Capt. G. B. T. Friend, The Buffs; one s.; educ. Trinity Hall, Cambridge; 2nd Lt., 5th R. Fus., 1898; 2nd Lt., The Buffs, 4.4.00; Lt., Feb. 1901; Capt. 7.2.07; Major 1.9.15; Bt. Lt.-Col. 1.1.19; served operations Aden Hinterland, 1903; Europ. War in France, 1914–17; Despatches four times; M.C. His D.S.O. was awarded for gallantry near Guillemont.

LUCAS, M. H. (D.S.O. L.G. 12.9.19); b. 2.1.82; 2nd Lt., Midd'x Regt., 18.1.02; 2nd Lt., Ind. Army, 22.5.03; Lt. 18.4.04; Capt. 18.1.11; Major, 37th Lancers, Ind. Army.

LUCAS, W. R. (D.S.O. L.G. 11.4.18), Lt. (A/Major), A.S.C.

LUCEY, W. F. (D.S.O. L.G. 3.6.16), Major, R.F.A.

LUCK, B. J. M. (D.S.O. L.G. 4.6.17); b. 6.7.74; 2nd Lt., R.A., 30.3.93; Lt. 30.3.98; Capt. 7.3.00; Adjt. 1.10.10 to 30.9.13; Major 1.4.14; Lt.-Col. 8.9.17; C.M.G.

LUCK, C. M. (D.S.O. L.G. 1.1.17); b. 12.1.72; m. 1920, Joyce Gwendolen, 4th d. of Lt.-Col. A. A. Ruck, late 8th (The King's) Regt.; one d.; educ. Barrow Grammar School; H.M.S. Worcester; 2nd Lt., Royal Indian Marine, 1892; Lt. 1898; Comdr., 1909; retired 1912; granted temp. commission 3.9.14; Comdr., R.N.; was Naval Transport Officer, France, till 18.1.15; T/Major, R.E., War Office; promoted T/Lt.-Col.; Col.; T/Brig.-Gen., 1917; Hon. Brig.-Gen.; Director of Inland Water Transport, France, 1917–19; served Persian Gulf, 1909–11 (Medal and clasp); Europ. War, 1914–19; went to Antwerp for Admiralty (secret mission), Aug. 1914; Despatches six times; C.M.G.; Commandeur de l'Ordre de la Couronne; Belgian Croix de Guerre; Officier de l'Ordre National de la Légion d'Honneur; Knight of Grace of the Order of St. John of Jerusalem in England.

LUDGATE, W. (D.S.O. L.G. 1.1.18); b. 10.3.78; Lt., A.V.C., 16.5.03; Capt. 16.5.08; Major, R.A.V.C., 10.7.15.

LUDLOW-HEWITT, E. R. (D.S.O. L.G. 1.1.18); b. 9.6.86; 2nd Lt., R. Ir. Rif., 16.8.05; Lt. 24.9.07; R.F. Corps 12.9.14 to 31.3.18; Capt., R. Ir. R., 20.12.14; Bt. Major 1.1.17; Temp. Brig.-Gen. 17.10.17 to 31.3.18.; M.C.

LUIS-PALLANT, S. (see Pallant, S. Luis-).

LUMB, F. G. E. (D.S.O. L.G. 27.6.19); b. 10.1.77; s. of late Edward Henry Lumb and Mrs. Lumb; m. 1920, Eva Mary, yr. d. Robert Kennaway Leigh, of Bardon, Washford; educ. Bedford School; R.M.C., Sandhurst; 2nd Lt., Unatt., 4.8.97; Ind. S.C. 21.11.98; Lt. 4.11.99; Capt., Ind. Army, 4.8.06; Major 4.8.15; Bt. Lt.-Col. 15.11.19; Lt.-Col. 1.2.21; served China, 1900–1; Europ. War in France, 1914–19; Egypt, Arabia, Mesopotamia, Kurdistan; Despatches four times; M.C.; Legion of Honour.

LUMLEY-SMITH, T. G. L. (D.S.O. L.G. 3.6.18); b. 27.10.79; only s. of late Sir Lumley-Smith, K.C., Judge of London and Central Criminal Courts, 1901–13; m. 1911, y. d. of Charles Edward Coles, Pasha; two s.; one d.; educ. Eton; Trinity College, Cambridge; 2nd Lt., 21st Lancers, 23.5.00; Capt. 16.1.12; Major 1.4.17; R. of O., 21st Lrs., since 1919; served in Ireland, England, Egypt and India; Adjt., Herts Yeo., 1914; served with that regiment in Egypt (Suez Canal operations) and Gallipoli, 1915; France and Belgium, 1916–19; with 3rd Div. and Cavalry Corps; Despatches twice.

LUMSDEN, A. F. (D.S.O. L.G. 4.6.17); b. 3.6.77; s. of late J. F. Lumsden, of Aberdeen; 2nd Lt., R. Scots, 2.4.00; Lt. 15.3.02; Capt. 5.10.09; served S. African War, 1899–1901; Queen's Medal, 3 clasps; Europ. War; Despatches; wounded, Feb. 1918. He was killed in action 24.6.18.

LUMSDEN, F. W. (D.S.O. L.G. 1.1.17) (1st Bar, L.G. 11.5.17) (2nd Bar, L.G. 11.5.17) (3rd Bar, L.G. 22.4.18), Lt.-Col. (T/Brig.-Gen.), R.M.A.; V.C. (see "The Victoria Cross," by same publishers).

LUMSDEN, W. F. (D.S.O. L.G. 1.1.17); b. 4.9.79; 2nd Lt., R.A., 28.3.00 Lt. 3.4.01; Capt. 24.11.11; Major 30.12.15; T/Lt.-Col. 11.4.19.

LUMSDEN, W. V. (D.S.O. L.G. 26.7.18) (1st Bar, L.G. 3.6.18) (2nd Bar, L.G. 1.2.19); b. 1.1.87; s. of late W. H. Lumsden, of Balmedie; 2nd Lt., Arg. and Suth'd Highrs., 11.12.07; Lt. 20.5.09; Capt. 12.12.14; Bt. Major 3.6.19; Tank Corps 24.12.22.; M.C.

LUND, O. M. (D.S.O. L.G. 4.6.17); b. 28.11.91; o. s. of Capt. and Mrs. Albert Lund; m. Margaret, d. of Frank Harrison, of Bombay; 2nd Lt., R.A., 20.7.11; Lt. 20.7.14; Capt. 8.8.16; Bt. Major 3.6.19; A.D.C. to Commander-in-Chief.

LUNDIE, R. C. (D.S.O. L.G. 4.6.17); s. of Dr. and Mrs. R. A. Lundie, of 55A, Grange Road, Edinburgh; B.A. (Cantab.); A.M.I.C.E.; Lt. (A/Major), R.E., Spec. Res. He was killed in action 14–15.10.18.

LUXMOORE, N. (D.S.O. L.G. 1.1.17); b. 28.12.71; 2nd Lt., Devon R., 12.12.94; Lt. 2.1.98; Capt. 18.4.00; Major 14.2.15; Bt. Lt.-Col. 3.6.19; served S. African War, 1899–1902; Queen's Medal, 5 clasps; Europ. War; Despatches.

LUXMOORE-BALL, R. E. C. (D.S.O. L.G. 11.1.19), Lt. (A/Maj.), Welsh Guards, Spec. Res., att. 11th Bn.; D.C.M.

LUXTON, D. A. (D.S.O. L.G. 1.1.17), Major, Aust. Inf.

LYALL, E. (D.S.O. L.G. 30.3.16), Lt., R.A.M.C. (T.F.). He was killed in action 18.6.17.

LYALL, R. A. (D.S.O. L.G. 1.2.17); b. 20.10.76; 1st commission 5.8.96; Major 5.8.14; Major, Supernumerary List, I.A., att. Imp. Service Rifles; served during operations on N.W. Frontier of India, 1897–98; Medal with clasp; Europ. War; Despatches.

LYCETT, T. (D.S.O. L.G. 26.9.17) (Details, L.G. 9.1.18), 2nd Lt. (T/Capt.), Notts. and Derby. R. and R.F.C. He died of wounds 5.10.18.

LYELL, A. G. (D.S.O. L.G. 28.10.20); b. 20.6.82; 2nd Lt., Unatt., 8.1.01; Ind. Army 8.4.02; Lt. 8.4.03; Capt. 8.1.10; Major 8.1.16.

LYELL, D. (D.S.O. L.G. 4.6.17); b. 1866; 3rd s. of late Alexander Lyell, of Gardyne, Co. Forfar; m. 1909, Kathleen Constance May, d. of late Colonel C. J. Briggs, D.L.I.; two s.; T/Capt. (T/Col.), R.E.; served S. African War, 1900–2; Europ. War, 1914–18; Despatches; C.M.G., 1918; Order of Leopold of Belgium; Legion of Honour; Order of Aviz of Portugal; Croix de Guerre; was Chief Engineer to the British Army in France.

LYLE, H. (D.S.O. L.G. 4.6.17), Capt. (A/Major), Can. Inf.

LYLE, W. J. (D.S.O. L.G. 21.1.20); b. 11.12.88; 2nd Lt., High. L. Inf., 1.10.14; Lieut. 14.3.15; Capt. 1.1.17; M.C.

LYNAS, W. J. D. (D.S.O. L.G. 15.10.18), Capt., Aust. Inf.; M.C.

LYNCH, C. ST. J. (D.S.O. L.G. 1.1.18); b. 27.1.82; 2nd Lt., R.E., 18.8.00; Lt. 18.8.03; Capt. 18.8.10; Major 2.10.16; A/Lt.-Col. 8.12.17 to 24.9.18.

LYNCH, C. W. D. (D.S.O. L.G. 3.6.16), T/Lt.-Col., The King's Own (Yorks. L.I.). He was killed in action 2.7.16.

LYNCH, J. B. (D.S.O. L.G. 1.1.18); b. 11.12.83; 2nd Lt., R. Ir. Fus. 4.12.01; Lt. 14.9.06; Lt., Ind. Army, 20.6.08; Capt. 4.12.10; served S. African War, 1902 (Queen's Medal, 3 clasps); Europ. War; Despatches.

LYNCH-STAUNTON, R. K. (D.S.O. L.G. 23.6.15) (Bar, L.G. 3.3.19), Major and Bt. Lt.-Col., R.F.A. He died of wounds 7.11.18. (See "The Distinguished Service Order," from its institution to 31.12.15, by same publishers).

LYNE, T. J. S. (D.S.O. L.G. 11.12.18); b. 1870; s. of late W. J. Lyne and Janet, d. of late Colin Reid Cromarty; m. Ethel Louise, d. of late Ralph Stobbart; one d.; educ. Beer's Private School, Stoke Damerel, Devon; entered R.N., 1885; Lieut. 26.6.02; Comdr. 28.9.12; Capt. 31.12.18; commanded many of H.M. ships at home and abroad; later in Atlantic Fleet; served S. African War, when, while serving in a torpedo boat on the W. Coast of Cape Colony, he saved his ship from destruction by a brilliant piece of seamanship, and for this he was promoted to Lieutenant (Despatches); later he commanded the gunboat Kinsha, when he was commended by the Admiralty for surveying and other work in connection with the native risings, and his directions for the navigation of the Hau Kiang and other rivers were published as a Blue Book.

T. J. S. Lyne.

LYNN, A. C. (D.S.O. L.G. 4.2.18) (Details, L.G. 5.7.18); b. 7.6.94; o. s. of Jame Lynn, Head Master of the Temple Street Council School, Castleford; educ. Pontefract King's School; 2nd Lt., Yorks. L. Inf., 10.8.15; Lt. 1.7.17; M.C.

LYNN, E. F. (D.S.O. L.G. 1.1.18), Major, Can Engrs.; M.C.

LYNN, G. R., M.B. (D.S.O. L.G. 25.8.17); b. 21.1.85; Lt., Ind. Med. Serv., 31.7.09; Capt. 31.7.12; Major, 31.7.21.

LYON, A. (D.S.O. L.G. 14.1.16); b. 1884; s. of Sir Alexander Lyon; m. 1912; one s.; Capt (T/Major), Gordon Highrs.

LYON, C. A. (D.S.O. L.G. 4.6.17); b. 11.8.80; 2nd Lt., R.A., 25.6.99; Lt. 16.2.01; Capt. 28.4.06; Major 30.10.14; Bt. Lt.-Col. 3.6.19.

LYON, C. D. G. (D.S.O. L.G. 3.6.16); b. 25 1.78; 2nd Lt., R.A., 22.8.00; Lt. 22.8.03; Capt. 1.3.12; Major 19.3.15; Bt. Lt.-Col. 1.1.19; in command 1st (Somerset) Brig., R.A., 17.4.20.

LYON, C. H. (D.S.O. L.G. 14.1.16); b. 18.3.78; 2nd Lt., 21.4.00; Lt. 19.1.01; Capt. 17.3.09; Major 1.9.15; Bt. Lt.-Col. 1.1.17; T/Brig.-Gen. 16.12.17; served S. Africa, 1900–2 (Despatches; Queen's Medal, 3 clasps; King's Medal, 2 clasps); Europ. War, 1914–18; Despatches: C.B.; C.M.G.

LYON, F. H. (D.S.O. L.G. 12.12.18); b. 3.1.75; s. of Comdr. G. F. Lyon, R.N.; educ. Fettes College; entered R.N., Nov. 1897; Eng.-Cdr., R.N.; served in China, 1900; Europ. War in H.M.S. Landrail, Harwich Force, 1914 to 1916; H.M.S. Floste, 13th Flotilla, 1916; in H.M.S. Attentive, Dover Patrol, 1917–18; served in Dwina River Expeditions, 1918 and 1919; awarded the Order of St. Stanislaus, 2nd Class; 1914–15 Star.

LYON, P. (D.S.O. L.G. 3.6.19); b. 23.3.79; 2nd Lt., N. Staff. R., 6.11.01; Lieut. 20.11.05; Capt. 1.9.14; Major 6.5.16; served S. African War, 1901; Queen's Medal, 2 clasps; Europ. War; Despatches.

LYONS, A. E. P. (D.S.O. L.G. 8.3.18); b. 17.8.86; s. of Admiral of the Fleet Sir Algernon McLennan Lyons, G.C.B., and Lady Lyons; m. Isobel Augusta, d. of Ernest Knightley Little, C.B.E.; educ. Shortlands, Eastbourne; joined H.M.S. Britannia 15.9.01; served in Ariadne, Flagship, N. America and West Indies, as Naval Cadet and Midshipman; Commonwealth, Atlantic Squadron, as Midshipman and Acting Sub-Lieut.; Destroyers at Home, as Sub-Lieutenant; Virago and Otter, China Station, as Lieutenant; Indomitable, Home Fleet, Flagship of R.A. Sir Lewis Bailey, 24.7.11 to 20.2.12; Minotaur, Flag China Station, under V.A. Winsloe, 26.5.12 to 28.2.13; V.A. Sir Martin Jerram 29.2.13; was in Minotaur for Jutland; Minotaur and China Squadron attempted to bring German Eastern Squadron to action at outbreak of war, and spent some time in East Indies chasing Emden; destroyed German W/T Station at Yap, in Caroline Is.; conveyed the first large convoy of N.Z. and Australian troops from Wellington, N.Z., to within nine hours of Cocos Is.; in Brisk, 2nd Destroyer Flotilla; Convoy duty; in Command as Lieut. and Lt.-Cdr. 8.6.16 to 13.11.17; in Vega, Paladin, Wakeful, as Lieut.-Comdr.; in command 24.11.17 to Dec. 1919, 13th Flotilla, attached to Battle Cruiser Fleet.

LYONS, D. M. (D.S.O. L.G. 18.2.18), Capt. (A/Lt.-Col.), High. L. Inf.

LYSTER, A. L. ST. G. (D.S.O. L.G. 27.6.19), Lt.-Cdr., R.N., 15.3.15.

LYSTER, F. S. (D.S.O., L.G. 1.1.18), Local Major, Special List.

LYTTELTON, A. G. (D.S.O. L.G. 3.6.19); b. 7.5.84; 2nd Lt., Welsh R., 6.10.06; Lt. 4.7.08; Adjt., Welsh R., 2.6.10 to 1.6.12; Capt. 14.8.13; Bt. Major 3.6.16; Despatches.

LYTTELTON, O. (D.S.O. L.G. 20.10.16); b. 15.3.93; o. s. of the late Rt. Rev. A. Lyttelton, Bishop of Southampton, and Edith Sophy Lyttelton; m. Maureen, d. of Harold Smith; educ. Eton and Trinity College, Cambridge; played Golf for the Varsity, 1913; entered G. Gds., Dec. 1914, being on active service throughout the war; Lt., Adjt., 3rd Batt. 15.10.15; A/Captain; was present at the Battles of Festubert and Loos; Staff Capt., 2nd Guards Brigade, June, 1917; present at Third Battle of Ypres; Brigade Major, 4th Guards Brigade, during German drive in March and in April, 1918, in defence of Hazebrouck; wounded April, 1918; rejoined Sept. 1918, as Brigade Major, 2nd Guards Brigade, and served at final battle and at capture of Maubeuge. His D.S.O. was awarded for gallantry at Les Bœufs.

MAASDORP, L. H. (D.S.O. L.G. 1.1.19), T/Major, S.A.H.A.

MABEN, H. C. (D.S.O. L.G. 26.7.18), Capt., Worc. R.

McALESTER, W. H. S. (D.S.O. L.G. 2.5.16); b. 5.5.71; 2nd Lt., K.O.Sco Bord., 13.7.92; Lt. 23.5.94; Capt. 9.6.00; Maj. 20.7.08; retired pay 6.7.20; Chitral, 1895; Medal, clasp; Tirah, 1897–98; 2 clasps; served Europ. War; Despatches.

McALLISTER, E. J. (D.S.O. L.G. 3.6.16); b. 18.4.79; s. of P. McAllister; m. Ida Mary, d. of A. Square; educ. Belvedere College, Dublin; Royal University of Ireland; 2nd Lt., A.S.C., 22.5.00; Lt. 1.6.01; Capt. 1.10.04; Major 30.10.14; Bt. Lt.-Col., R.A.S.C., 3.6.19; served S. African War; Queen's Medal, 3 clasps; Europ. War; Despatches three times.

McALLUM, S. G., M.D. (D.S.O. L.G. 1.1.19), Major (A/Lt.-Col.), R.A.M.C. (S.R.), att. 140th Field Ambulance. He died 3.6.21.

MACALPINE-LENY, R. L. (D.S.O. L.G. 11.4.18); b. 11.2.70; 2nd Lt., 16th Lrs., 8.10.90; Lt. 17.2.94; Capt. 9.10.99; Maj. 1.4.03; Bt. Lt.-Col. 3.6.19; retired pay 15.8.20; S. African War, 1900–2; Queen's Medal, 5 clasps; King's Medal, 2 clasps; served Europ. War; Despatches.

McARTHUR, J. (D.S.O. L.G. 7.11.18) (Bar, L.G. 7.11.18), Lt.-Col., Aust. Inf.

McARTHUR, R. T. (D.S.O. L.G. 22.8.18), Capt. (T/Major), S. African Field Post and Telegraph Services.

MACARTHUR, W. P., M.D., B.Ch., F.R.C.P. (D.S.O. L.G. 14.1.16); b. 1884; s. of J. P. MacArthur; m. Eugénie Thérèse, d. of late Dr. L. F. Antelme; one s.; educ. Queen's University, Belfast; ent. R.A.M.C. 30.1.09; Capt. 30.7.12; A/Lt.-Col. 24.10.18; served Europ. War, 1914–16; Despatches; Bt. Lt.-Col., R.A.M.C.; O.B.E.

MACARTNEY, G. W. (D.S.O. L.G. 1.1.19), Lt.-Col., Aust. A.M.C.

MACARTNEY, H. D. K. (D.S.O. L.G. 1.1.18); b. 1.2.80; s. of J. A. Macartney, of Ormiston House, Ormiston, near Brisbane, and Annie Flora, d. of A. C. F. W. Dunlop; m. Alexandrina Vans, d. of Stanislaus Zichy Wolnarski; Lt.-Col., Aust. F.A.; served Europ. War, 1916–19; Despatches; C.M.G.

MACAULAY, N. H. (D.S.O. L.G. 1.1.19), Major, Can. F.A.

MACAULAY, R. K. A. (D.S.O. L.G. 2.5.16); b. 26.3.84; commissioned R.E. 17.1.03; Lt. 21.9.05; Capt. 17.1.14; Adjt., R.E., 1.6.14 to 6.6.15; Major 17.1.18; served Europ. War; Despatches; Bt. Major 3.6.16; Bt. Lt.-Col. 3.6.19.

McAVITY, T. M. (D.S.O. L.G. 3.6.16); b. 14.3.89, at St. John, New Brunswick; s. of J. A. McAvity; m. Frances, d. of Sir Douglas Hazen; educ. Rothsay Collegiate School; R.M.C., Canada, 1910; was Brig. Major, 5th Bde., from 16.1.15 to 3.10.16; Major, 26th New Brunswick Cdn. Bn., 2.11.14; Lieut.-Colonel; 13 months' active service with Brigade in the field; promoted G.S.O.2, 2nd Can. Bn., 3.10.16.

McBEAN, R. H. (D.S.O. L.G. 11.11.19), Lt., R.N.; D.S.C.

MACBRIEN, J. H. (D.S.O. L.G. 23.6.15) (Bar, L.G. 2.12.18), Major and Bt. Lt.-Col.; Brig.-Gen., R. Can. Dns. (see "The Distinguished Service Order," from its institution to 31.12.15, by same publishers).

MACCABE, J. F. (D.S.O. L.G. 5.10.18), Lt., R.N.V.R.

McCAGHEY, N. F. (D.S.O. L.G. 11.1.19), Major, 52nd Batt. Can. Inf.; M.C.

McCALL, F. R. (D.S.O. L.G. 3.8.18), Lieut., R.F.A.; M.C.; D.F.C.

McCALL, H. W. (D.S.O. L.G. 3.6.18); b. 28.9.78; 2nd Lt., York. R., 23.5.00; Lt. 11.4.02; Capt. 29.6.06; Maj. 1.9.15; S. African War, 1900–2; Queen's Medal, 5 clasps; Bt. Lt.-Col. 1.1.18; Europ War; Despatches; C.M.G.

McCALL, J. J. L. (D.S.O. L.G. 1.1.19), Lt., Aust. Mil. Forces, 29.6.15.

McCALL, R. L. (D.S.O. L.G. 25.11.16); b. 10.4.84; 2nd Lt., Cam. Highrs., 1.2.04; Lt. 20.8.09; Capt. 30.9.14; Bt. Major 1.1.18; Bt. Lt.-Col. 3.6.18; Despatches; M.C.

McCALL, W., M.B. (D.S.O. L.G. 1.1.18), Major (A/Lt.-Col.), R.A.M.C.

M'CALLUM, E. E. N. (D.S.O. L.G. 19.8.16); b. 25.7.94; s. of the late A. C. O. M'Callum and Mrs. M'Callum, of Fowl Bay, N.B.; educ. Victoria High School; M'Gill University; Capt., The R. Canadian Rgt.; served Europ. War; wounded; Despatches. His D.S.O. was awarded for gallantry at Yeomanry Post.

MACCALLUM, H. (D.S.O. L.G. 18.7.17), T/Capt., Royal Indian Marines.

McCALLUM, J. D. M. (D.S.O. L.G. 22.9.16); b. 2.9.83; s. of late J. McCallum, Financial Secretary, National Education Board, Ireland, and of a daughter of Rev. J. D. Martin; m. Eveleen Lindsay, d. of L. H. Lloyd; educ. R. Academical Institution, Belfast; Queen's College, Belfast; graduated 1906; commissioned in T.F. (Unattached List), 1908, and posted in Belfast University O.T.C.; Capt. 1911; Major; Capt. and Adjt. of 8th R. Irish Rifles, 1914. He proceeded to France 3.10.15. He was present at the Battle of Thiepval 1.7.16, the Battle of Messines 7.7.17, and commanded his battalion at the Third Battle of Ypres 16.8.17, the Battle of Cambrai 21.11.17, and the Retreat at St. Quentin, March, 1918, and as Acting Lieutenant-Colonel, Aug. 1917, commanding the 8th Battalion, the Royal Irish Rifles, and from 8.2.18 to 12.5.18, commanding the 21st Entrenching Battalion. During the final victorious advance in Sept., Oct., Nov. 1918, he commanded temporarily the 2nd Battalion, the Royal Irish Rifles, and the 15th (S.) Battalion, the Royal Irish Rifles, until the latter battalion were withdrawn from the fighting with the 36th (Ulster) Division in the beginning of Nov. He was mentioned in Despatches and awarded the French Croix de Guerre in Dec. 1918; C.B.E.

MACCALLUM, W. P. (D.S.O. L.G. 1.1.19), Lt., 26th Aust. Inf.; M.C.

M'CALMONT, R. C. A. (D.S.O. L.G. 1.1.17); b. 29.8.81; s. of late Col. J. M. M'Calmont (M.P., Antrim E., 1885–1913) and Mary Caroline, d. of late Col. R. Romer; m. Mary Caroline, d. of late A. Skeen, I.M.S., and Lady Prinsep; three d.; educ. Eton; M.P. (U.), Antrim E., 1913–19; 2nd Lt., 6th (M.) Batt. R. Warwicks. R., 1899; 2nd Lt., Irish Guards on formation 15.8.00; Lt. 1.1.01; Capt. 1.1.04; Major 19.11.10; T/Lt.-Col., 1914 (R. Irish Rifles); T/Brig.-Gen., 1917; Lt.-Col., 1916; Colonel 4.2.20; served S. African War, 1900 (Queen's Medal with clasps); formed and commanded 12th (Central Antrim) S.B.R., Irish Rifles (Ulster Division), 1914–15; commanded 1st Batt. Irish Guards, 1915–17; Despatches twice; T/Brig.-Gen. Commanding 3rd Inf. Brig., 1917; Despatches; Colonel commanding Irish Guards from 1919.

McCANDLISH, P. D. (D.S.O. L.G. 1.1.18); b. 6.6.71; 2nd Lt., Arg. and Suthd. Highrs., 2.6.94; Capt. 14.2.00; retired pay 13.12.13; N.W. Frontier, 1897–98 (Medal with clasp); served Europ. War; Lt.-Col., R. of O., 28.5.19; Bt. Lt.-Col. 3.6.18; C.B.E.

McCANN, W. F. J. (D.S.O. L.G. 1.2.19), Capt., Can. Inf.; M.C.

McCARROLL, J. N. (D.S.O. L.G. 1.1.18) (Bar, L.G. 4.3.18) (Details, L.G. 16.8.18), Lt.-Col., N.Z. Mtd. Rifles.

McCARTHY, J. J. (D.S.O. L.G. 4.6.17); m. Dorothy Lilian, d. of late H. Dacre Tonge; one d.; Lt.-Col., N. Rhodesian Police; served European War, 1914–17; Despatches; M.C.; C.B.E.

M'CARTHY, W. H. L., M.A., M.D., M.R.C.P., D.P.H. (D.S.O. L.G. 8.3.19) (Details, L.G. 4.10.19); b. 21.6.85; s. of late R. Hilgrove M'Carthy, J.P.; educ. Trinity College, Dublin; St. Thomas's Hospital; Paris; Vienna; Fellow Royal Society of Medicine; Arnott Gold Medal; Senior Moderator and Gold Medallist in Natural Science; Stewart Medical Scholar; Reid Exhibitioner, Experimental Science; University Medallist in Political Economy and Aesthetics; Physician, Special Medical Board, Ministry of Pensions; J.P. Lt.-Colonel M'Carthy served in the European War (Belgium and France), 1914–19 (thrice wounded); Despatches thrice; M.C. and Bar; Medical Officer, Guards Brigade, 1914–16; commanded Infantry Field Ambulances, 1916–19. He has published "Heredity and Environment in Relation to Crime," and other works.

McCARTHY-O'LEARY, H. W. D. (D.S.O. L.G. 26.9.17) (Details, L.G. 9.1.18) (Bar, L.G. 16.9.18); b. 2.8.85; s. of late Lt.-Col. W. McCarthy-O'Leary; educ. Stonyhurst; 2nd Lt., R. Irish Fusiliers, 16.8.05; Lt. 24.2.07; Adjt., R. Ir. Fus., 1913–16; Capt. 3.8.12; A/Lt.-Col. 12.1.18; served Europ. War; Despatches; M.C.

McCAY, R. C. (D.S.O. L.G. 4.6.17); b. 18.9.95; Lieut., Army (from Aust. Mil. Forces), 17.5.16; Ind. Army 25.3.18; Capt. 20.5.19.

McCLAUGHRY, E. J., B.A. (D.S.O. L.G. 3.12.18); b. 10.9.96; s. of J. K. McClaughry, of N. Adelaide, S. Australia; educ. Trinity College, Cambridge; Adelaide University; Fellow of S. Australian School of Mines and Industries, 1914; ent. Army, 1914; Lt., 1915; Capt., Flying Corps, 1917; Flight Command in the Australian Flying Corps; served Europ. War, 1914–18; Egypt, 1916; D.F.C. and Bar.

McCLEAN, F. S. (D.S.O. L.G. 27.10.17) (Details, L.G. 18.3.18) (Bar, L.G. 8.3.19) (Details, L.G. 4.10.19), Major (T/Lt.-Col.), 5th Pioneer Batt. Aust. Inf.

MACCLELLAN, G. P. (D.S.O. L.G. 1.1.17) (Bar, L.G. 16.9.18; b. 4.2.81; 2nd Lt., R.A., 22.11.99; Lt. 16.2.01; Capt. 19.10.07; Major, R.G.A., 5.4.15; S. Africa 1900–2; Queen's Medal, 2 clasps; King's Medal, 2 clasps; Europ. War; Despatches; Bt. Lt.-Col. 3.6.19.

McCLELLAND, C. H. (D.S.O. L.G. 2.12.18), Major, New Zealand Force.

McCLEVERTY, G. M. (D.S.O. L.G. 1.2.19); b. 17.9.85; s. of Col. J. McCleverty; m. Evelyn, d. of Major-Gen. Sir R. Ewart, K.C.M.G.; educ. Malvern College; Sandhurst; 2nd Lt. W. Yorks. R. 16.8.05; Bedfordshire R. 16.9.05; Lt., Ind. Army, 16.11.07; Capt., 16.8.14; Major, 16.8.20; served in Abor Campaign, 1911–12; went to France with Indian Exp. Force, 1914, and served in Egypt, Mesopotamia and N. Persia; wounded twice; Despatches thrice; M.C.

M'CLINTOCK, A. G. (D.S.O. L.G. 8.8.17); b. 30.4.78; s. of A. G. F. M'Clintock, Public Trustee, Ireland, and Catharine Brownlow, d. of Sir J. M. Stronge, Bart.; m. Susan, d. of late J. Heywood-Collins; five s.; one d.; educ. Farnborough; joined 4th Batt. Oxf. L.I., 1896; 5th Lancers, 15.11.99; Lt. 3.10.00; Capt. 3.7.07; 8th Hussars 23.11.01; Major, 5th Lancers, 16.1.17; T/Lt.-Col., Tank Corps; served S. African War, 1899–1901; Queen's Medal, 3 clasps; Europ. War; Despatches.

McCLINTOCK, J. W. L. (D.S.O. L.G. 14.3.16); b. 1874; s. of late Admiral Sir L. McClintock, K.C.B., and Annette Elizabeth, d. of R. F. Dunlop; m. The Hon. Rose Anne Mary O'Neill, d. of 2nd Baron O'Neill and Lady Louisa K. E. Cochrane, d. of 11th Earl of Dundonald; one d.; ent. R. Navy, 1887; Commander, 1905; Capt., 1912; served European War (Dardanelles) in command H.M.S. Lord Nelson; Dreadnought, King George V. and Conqueror; Commodore of Royal Naval Barracks, Portsmouth, 1920; holds Medal for life-saving, 1907; C.B.; Commander of Order of Crown of Italy; Officer, Légion d'Honneur.

J. W. L. McClintock.

McCLINTOCK, R. S. (D.S.O. L.G. 1.1.18); b. 26.7.76; s. of late Col. W. McClintock, R.A.; m. Jeanie, d. of Sir G. Casson Walker, K.C.S.I.; one s.; 2nd Lt., R. Eng., 3.8.95; Lt. 3.8.98; Capt. 3.8.04; Bt. Major 4.8.04; Lt.-Col. 2.11.21; *p.s.c.*; Ashanti, 1900; Despatches; Medal with clasp; Northern Nigeria, 1900; Medal with clasp; S. Africa, 1901–2; Queen's Medal, clasp; Europ. War; Despatches; Bt. Lt.-Col. 1.1.19; C.M.G.

McCLINTOCK, S. R. (D.S.O. L.G. 4.6.17) (Bar, L.G. 26.7.18); b. 7.5.82; 2nd Lt., Gord. Highrs., 18.1.02; Lt. 18.2.07; Capt. 10.8.11; Major 18.1.17; S. Africa, 1902; Queen's Medal, 4 clasps; Europ. War; Despatches; Bt. Major 3.6.17.

McCLOUGHRY, W. A. (D.S.O. L.G. 8.2.19), Major, Aust. F.C.; M.C.; D.F.C.

McCLURE, I. H. (D.S.O. L.G. 1.1.18), T/Capt., Intelligence Corps.

McCLURE, W. S. (gazetted as McClure, W.) (D.S.O. L.G. 3.6.19), Major (A/Lt.-Col.), 2/4th Bn. S. Lancs. R., T.F.

McCLYMONT, R. A. (D.S.O. L.G. 22.9.16); b. 14.9.74; 2nd Lt., R.A., 26.5.00; Lt. 25.2.02; Capt. 7.2.11; Major, R.F.A., 30.10.14; T/Lt.-Col. 9.3.18; Lt.-Col., retired pay, 14.1.20; employed with K.A.R., 1903–7; Egyptian Army, 1911–13; served S. African War, 1902 (Queen's Medal, four clasps); Somaliland, 1904 (Medal, two clasps); Europ. War, 1914–17; Despatches; C.B.E.

McCOMBE, G. (D.S.O. L.G. 4.6.17); b. 26.3.85; s. of late A. McCombe, M.A., of Trinity College, Dublin; m. Marjorie Orme; one d.; educ. Montreal; served Europ. War, 1915–18; Major, 3rd Can. Rgt., 1.10.14; Commanded Royal Montreal Rgt.; Despatches four times.

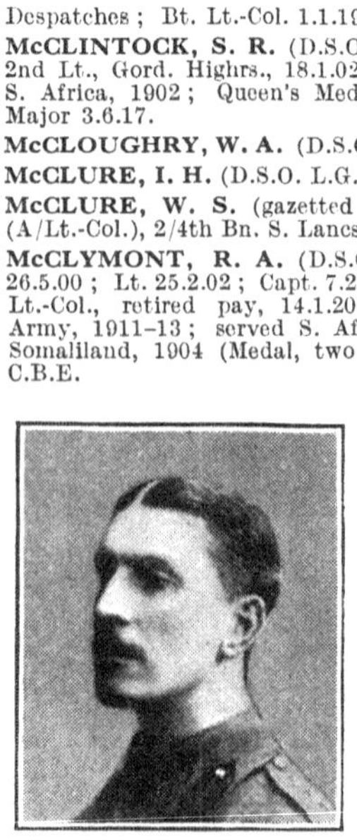

J. S. McCombe.

McCOMBE, J. S., M.B. (D.S.O. L.G. 25.8.17); b. 9.4.85; s. of R. McCombe; m. Doris, d. of late G. Maunsell-Smythe and widow of Capt. F. Leach, 2nd K.S.L.I.; educ. Queen's College, Belfast; R. University of Ireland; Lt., R.A.M.C., 14.2.08; Capt. 4.8.11; Major 4.2.20; Semi-final, Army and Navy Boxing Championship (Heavyweight), 1910; Capt., R.A.M.C., 1911; D.A.D.M.S., Mesopotamia, 1914–17; D.A.D.M.S., Base Force D, April, 1916–April, 1917; Army H.Q., 1917–18; N. Command, York, 1919; R. Humane Society's Bronze Medal.

McCOMBE, W. McC. DUGUID- (see Duguid-McCombe, W. McC.).

McCOMBIE, H., D.Sc., Ph.D., M.A. (D.S.O. L.G. 1.1.18); y. s. of late Alex. McCombie; m. Jean, e. d. of Sir J. Craggs; one d.; educ. Universities of Aberdeen, London and Strasbourg; Major; served Europ. War; was Chemical Adviser to the First Army; Controller of the Chemical Factories in the occupied areas in Germany; employed Gas Services, France; is Fellow of King's College, Cambridge; M.C.

McCONAGHEY, M. E. (D.S.O. L.G. 3.6.16); b. 2.6.77; 2nd Lt., R. Sc. Fus., 15.12.97; Lt. 9.10.99; Capt. 22.1.02; Major (Temp. Lt.-Col.), R. Sco. Fus.; S. Africa, 1899–1902; Queen's Medal, 4 clasps; King's Medal, 2 clasps; European War; Despatches. He was killed in action 23.4.17.

McCONAGHY, D. McF. (D.S.O. L.G. 1.1.17); b. in 1887, at Cootamundra N.S.W., Australia; s. of David McConaghy and Mary McConaghy. His brother writes: "He was a volunteer for eight years before the war, and a Captain of 24th Aust. Mil. Forces when war was declared, and left Australia, Aug. 1914, gradually working his way up until his death. The C.M.G. was bestowed upon my brother for services rendered during Lone Pine Campaign; the D.S.O. for Pozières. After this he was Acting Brigadier-General, and later returned to the 54th Battalion in France, where he died of wounds at Villers-Brettoneux 9.4.18."

D. McF. McConaghy.

McCONAGHY, J. G. (D.S.O. L.G. 3.6.16); b. 9.4.79; s. of the late Surg.-Gen. W. McConaghy, I.M.S., and Mary Broderick, d. of Gen. C. Birdwood, I.A.; m. Frances Lucy Alice, d. of W. A. M. Lattey; educ. United Services College, Westward Ho! and Sandhurst; joined the Army 27.7.98; Poona Horse, I.A., 1899; Lt., I.A., 27.10.00; 25th Cavalry, F.F., 1903; Capt. 27.7.07; Major 1.9.15; Regimental Duty, Oct. 1898–Oct. 1914; served Europ. War in Egypt, Gallipoli and France; with H.Q. 2nd Rawalpindi Division, Sept. 1917, to Jan. 1920; in Afghan operations, May to Sept. 1920; Despatches three times; Bt. Lt.-Col. 3.6.19; Serbian White Eagle (with Swords), 4th Class, 15.2.17.

McCONAGHY, W. (D.S.O. L.G. 4.9.18), Major, R.A.M.C. He was killed in action 4.7.18.

McCONNEL, D. F. (D.S.O. L.G. 4.6.17); b. 9.6.93; s. of W. H. McConnel; m. Ruth, d. of Major W. D. Garnett-Botfield, late R.A.; 2nd Lt., R.A., 20.12.12; Lt. 9.6.15; Capt. 20.12.16; Capt. (A/Major), R.F.A.

MACCONNELL, A. L. (D.S.O. L.G. 1.1.18), Major, A. and S. Highrs.

McCONNELL, W. A. (D.S.O. L.G. 1.1.19), Lt., 109th Can. Rgt., 2.2.16; T/Lt.-Col. 27.12.16.

McCORKELL, J. E. (D.S.O. L.G. 3.6.19), Lt., 15th Can. Rgt., 28.10.14.

McCORMACK, P. J. (D.S.O. L.G. 1.1.18), Major, Aust. F.A.

McCORMICK, H. B. (D.S.O. L.G. 29.7.02) (Bar, L.G. 8.3.19) (Details, L.G. 4.10.19) (see "The Distinguished Service Order," from its institution to 31.12.15, by same publishers).

M'CORMICK, JAMES (gazetted as McCormick, James Hanna) (D.S.O. L.G. 27.10.17) (Details, L.G. 18.3.18); b. 2.9.74, in Belfast, Co. Antrim, Ireland; s. of the late Thomas M'Cormick, Water Commissioner, Belfast, and Elizabeth Hanna M'Cormick, of Belfast; educ. Belfast Model Academy; Lt. M'Cormick joined the Imperial Forces 2.11.98, and served in the S. African War, 1899–1902 with the Irish Yeomanry; Queen's and King's Medals and 5 clasps. He went to Canada in 1903; joined the Canadian Militia Cavalry 2.4.08 and took commission at the Royal College of Instruction. In the European War he raised at his own expense the corps known as "M'Cormick's Devils." He became Capt., 2nd Winnipeg Rgt. He reverted to Lieutenant in order to get quickly to France. In the operations at Lens attack of 21.8.17 there had been a hand-to-hand struggle for mastery and fighting amongst the ruined houses and trenches in the streets. The 27th Can. Inf. (City of Winnipeg Rgt.) carried all objectives and finally arrived, led by Lieut. M'Cormick (already wounded) at the railway station. He consolidated the position gained, although there were fearful losses in officers and men. Lt. M'Cormick beat off all enemy counter-attacks and joined up the remnants of the battalion on his left, and was finally wounded in three places; Despatches twice. He became Lt.-Col.

MACCORMICK, K. (D.S.O. L.G. 26.11.17) (Details, L.G. 6.4.18), Major, N.Z. Med. Corps.

MACCORMICK, REV. W. P. G., M.A. (D.S.O. L.G. 1.1.17); b. 14.6.77; s. of late Rev. Canon J. McCormick, D.D., Hon. Chaplain to H.M. The King; m. Miriam, d. of G. H. Shelton, Esq.; two d.; educ. at Llandaff Cathedral School; Exeter School, and St. John's College, Cambridge; Acting C.F. in S. Africa, 1902–3; served throughout Europ. War as Temp. C.F., B.E.F., 1914–19; Guards Division, 1915–17; D.A.C.G., XIVth Corps, 1917–18; A.C.G., Boulogne, 1918–19; gazetted out as Hon. C.F., 1st Class; Vicar of Croydon, 1919; is a member of I Zingari and M.C.C., and played Rugby Football for the Transvaal, 1904 and 1906 and for Blackheath, 1907.

McCOWAN, W. H. (D.S.O. L.G. 1.1.17); b. 6.10.78; 2nd Lt., Cam'n Highrs., 4.1.99; Lt. 27.11.99; Capt. 23.10.05; Major 1.9.15; Bt. Lt.-Col. 3.6.19; Major, Cameron Highlanders, employed Egyptian Army.

McCOWEN, R. B. (D.S.O. L.G. 3.6.18), Cdr., R.N.

McCRACKEN, W. (D.S.O. L.G. 3.6.18); s. of Mr. McCracken, of 13, Lilybank Gardens, Glasgow, W., formerly of Prestwick; educ. Ayr Academy; Major, Arg. and Suth'd Highrs. He went to France in 1914 with the local Territorial Battalion; Despatches.

McCRACKEN, W. J., M.B. (D.S.O. L.G. 18.7.17) (Bar to D.S.O. L.G. 18.1.18) (Details L.G. 25.4.18); s. of Mr. McCracken, of Knocknakiel, Maghera; educ. Queen's University of Belfast (graduated 1913); T/Surgeon, R.N.; was wounded while serving with the R.N.D. on the Gallipoli Peninsula in 1915; Despatches; M.C.

McCRAE, SIR G. (D.S.O. L.G. 1.1.17); b. 1860; m. Eliza Cameron Russell (who died in 1913); three s.; five d.; educ. Edinburgh Lancastrian School; Chairman Scottish Board of Health, from 1919; Vice-President and Chairman of the Local Government Board for Scotland, 1909; D.L., J.P. for County of the City of Edinburgh; M.P. for E. Edinburgh, 1899–1909; Military Member, Edinburgh T.F. Association; Hon. Col., T.F. (V.D.) and Hon Lt.-Col. in the Army; commanded 16th (S.) Batt. The R. Scots.

M'CRAE, J. (gazetted as McCare, J.) (D.S.O. L.G. 1.1.18), Capt. 11.10.16, 14th (S. Otago) Rgt., N.Z.

McCREADY, T. R. (D.S.O. L.G. 11.1.19), T/Lt.-Col., commanding 63rd Battn. M.G.C.; T/Major, Royal Marines; M.C.

McCRIMMON, K. H. (D.S.O. L.G. 18.7.17), Lt., Can. Mil. Forces, 26.10.14; Capt. (A/Major), Can. Inf.; Despatches. His D.S.O. was awarded for gallantry on 9.4.17.

McCROSBIE, H C. (D.S.O. L.G. 3.2.20), T/Capt., Tank Corps.

McCROSTIE, H. C. (D.S.O. L.G. 3.2.20), T/Capt., Tank Corps.

McCUAIG, G. E. (gazetted as McCraig, G. E.) (D.S.O. L.G. 1.1.17) (Bar, L.G. 7.11.18); b. 2.9.85; s. of C. J. McCuaig, of Montreal; educ. McGill College, Montreal; Capt., 5th Cn. Rgt. (R. Highrs. of Canada), 2.7.10; Brig.-Gen., 1st Can. Inf. Brigade; served Europ. War, 1915–18; Despatches thrice; C.M.G. His brother, Lt.-Col. D. R. McCuaig was awarded the D.S.O. in 1915.

McCUBBIN, G. R. (D.S.O. L.G. 27.7.16); b. 18.1.98, in Cape Town; s. of D. A. McCubbin, Chief Architect, S. African Railways, and Lucy McCubbin; educ. King Edward VII. School, Johannesburg, S. Africa; Capt. 1st XI. Football at School; Vice Captain, Cricket; ent. Army 28.2.16; Lt., R.F.C., July, 1917; Staff Capt., R.A.F., 11.4.18; Europ. War; Despatches. His D.S.O. was awarded for gallantry at Lens on 18.6.16.

McCUDDEN, J. H. (D.S.O. L.G. 7.2.18); b. 31.1.81; 2nd Lt. 8.1.01; Lt., I.A. 1.6.03; Capt. 8.1.10; Major, Cavalry, 8.1.16; served Aden, 1903–4; Somaliland, 1908–10; Medal with clasp; Europ. War; Despatches.

McCUDDEN, J. T. B. (D.S.O. L.G. 4.2.18) (Details, L.G. 5.7.18) (Bar, L.G. 18.2.18) (Details—Christian name of Thomas omitted—L.G. 18.7.18), 2nd Lt. (T/Capt.), Gen.List, and R.F.C.; M.C.; V.C.

McCULLAGH, A. C. H., M.B. (D.S.O. L.G. 3.6.19), Capt. (A/Lt.-Col.), 2/2nd (Northumbrian) Fld. Amb., R.A.M.C. (T.F.); M.C.

McCULLAGH, H. R. (D.S.O. L.G. 1.1.19); b. 5.6.81; s. of Dr. T. A. McCullagh, of Bishop Auckland; g.s. of late Rev. T. McCullagh; 2nd Lt., Durham L.I., 3.12.04; Lt. 25.6.98; Capt. 7.1.15; Lt.-Colonel. At the outbreak of war was with his regiment in N. India, and was transferred to France; Despatches twice.

McCULLAGH, W. McK. H., M.B. (D.S.O. L.G. 1.1.18), Capt., R.A.M.C.; M.C.

McCULLOCH, A. J., B.A. (D.S.O. L.G. 26.7.18) (1st Bar, L.G. 16.9.18) (2nd Bar, L.G. 11.1.19); b. 14.7.76; s. of late A. Jameson, Lord Ardwall, Scottish Judge, and Lady Ardwall, of Ardwall, Gatehouse of Fleet (assumed surname of McCulloch, 1892); m. Esmé Valentine, d. of late Colin Mackenzie, I.C.S.; four s.; educ. Edinburgh Academy; St. Andrew's University; New College, Oxford; 2nd Lt., H.L.I., 4.8.00; Lt. 23.4.04; Capt., 7th Dragoon Guards, 18.3.11; Major, 14th Hussars, 31.1.20; Lt.-Colonel 3.6.17; T/Brig.-Gen. 27.8.17; Colonel on the Staff (late H.L.I., 7th Dn. Gds., and 14th Hussars), and Chief Instructor, Staff College, Quetta, from 1919; served S. African War, 1900–2; Despatches; D.C.M.; Queen's Medal, 6 clasps; King's Medal, 2 clasps; Europ. War, 1914–18; commanded 64th Inf. Brigade when it took Grandcourt, France, Aug. 1918; commanded 62nd Inf. Brig., 1919; Despatches thrice; wounded thrice; Bt. Major 3.6.16; Bt. Lt.-Col. 3.6.17; Legion of Honour; D.C.M.

MACDERMOTT, G. A. (D.S.O. L.G. 8.3.19) (Details, L.G. 4.10.19), Capt. (A/Major), 4th Batt. H.L.I., seconded 9th Batt. M.G.C.; M.C.

McDIARMID, J. I. A. (D.S.O. L.G. 1.1.18); b. 29.4.83; 2nd Lt., R.A., 24.12.02; Lt. 24.12.05; Capt. 30.10.14; Adjt., R.A., 1.4.15 to 31.7.15; Bt. Major 1.1.17; Major, R.G.A., 2.8.17.

MACDONALD, A. C. (D.S.O. L.G. 18.8.16); s. of late Hon A. C. Macdonald, of Picton, Nova Scotia, and Amelia Browne de Wolfe; m. Anita Beryl, d. of late W. Walters, M.E., F.R.G.S.; educ. R.M. College of Canada; Governing Director, Macdonald, Gibbs and Co., Engineers, Ltd.; joined the Forces as Capt., R.E., July, 1915; Lt.-Col., Sept. 1915; demobilized May, 1919; Despatches; Serbian Order of White Eagle, 4th Class.

MACDONALD, A. G. (D.S.O. L.G. 3.6.16); b. 6.12.74; 2nd Lt., R. Berks. R., 21.10.93; Lt. 8.4.96; Capt. 14.3.03; Adjt., R. Berks. R., 9.8.03 to 8.8.06; Major 30.4.15; served S. African War, 1900–2; Queen's Medal, 4 clasps; Europ. War; Despatches.

MACDONALD, A. MAC G. (D.S.O. L.G. 22.4.18) (M.C. cancelled and D.S.O. substituted) (Details, L.G. 22.3.18), Lt. (A/Capt.) Sea. Highrs. He was killed in action 22.4.18.

MACDONALD, C. L. (D.S.O. L.G. 1.1.17) (Bar, L.G. 26.9.17) (Details, L.G. 9.1.18), T/Lt.-Col., Manch. R. His Bar was awarded for gallantry on 24.7.17, E. of Ypres.

MACDONALD, D. J. (D.S.O. L.G. 1.1.18) (Bar, L.G. 22.6.18) (2nd Bar, L.G. 15.10.18), Lt.-Col., Canadian Cavalry; C.M.G.; M.C.

MACDONALD, D. R. (D.S.O. L.G. 26.7.18); b. 4.2.84; s. of late D. W. Macdonald; m. Helen, d. of R. M. McMahon; two d.; educ. Harrow; R.M.A., Woolwich; 2nd Lt., R.A., 15.7.03; Lt. 15.7.06; Capt. 30.10.14; Major, R.F.A., 3.7.16; served in France and Belgium, Aug. 1914, to end of war; Despatches twice; twice wounded; M.C.

MACDONALD, E. W. (D.S.O. L.G. 1.1.17) (1st Bar, L.G. 7.11.18) (2nd Bar, L.G. 1.2.19), Major, Can. Inf.; M.C.

McDONALD, G. ST. J. F. (D.S.O. L.G. 1.1.17); s. of the late George Thomas McDonald, of Queensland, and grandson of the late Sir William Fancourt Mitchell, of Bargold, Victoria; Major, R. Aust. Arty. He died, leaving a widow, Erina G. McDonald, of Queenscliff, Australia.

MACDONALD, H. (D.S.O. L.G. 26.8.18); b. 3.5.86; 2nd Lt., Unatt., 29.8.06; 2nd Lt., Ind. Army, 27.10.07; Lt. 29.11.08; Capt. 29.8.15; Bt. Maj. 3.6.17; Despatches.

McDONALD, H. F., B.Sc. (D.S.O. L.G. 14.11.16); b. Fort Qu'Appelle. Sask., 22.11.85; s. of late A. McDonald, Chief Factor, Hudson's Bay Company; m. Marjorie, d. of T. H. Gilmour, K.C., of Winnipeg; educ. Upper Canada College, Toronto; McGill University, Montreal; Lt., 16th Can. Batt. (Can. Scottish), Aug. 1914; Capt. Sept. 1914; Major, Jan. 1916; Lt.-Col. Dec. 1916; Brig.-Gen. Dec. 1917; General Officer Commanding Military District No. 13, H.Q., Calgary, Alberta, Canada; served Europ. War; Despatches twice; seriously wounded at St. Julien, April, 1915, and again at Pozières, Sept. 1916; C.M.G.; Order of St. Anne, 2nd Class, with Swords. His D.S.O. was awarded for gallantry at Pozières on 2.9.16.

MACDONALD, H. S. (D.S.O. L.G. 1.1.18); b. 1.12.88; 2nd Lt., R.A., 18.12.08; Lt. 18.12.11; Capt. 18.12.14; Major 20.5.18; M.C.

MACDONALD, JAMES ALEXANDER (D.S.O. L.G. 3.6.18), Lieut. (A/Major), R.F.A.

McDONALD, JOHN ANGUS (D.S.O. L.G. 1.1.17) (Bar, L.G. 1.2.19), Lt.-Col., 3rd Brig., Can. F.A.

MACDONALD, J. B. L. (D.S.O. L.G. 1.1.18); b. North Uist, Inverness-shire, 22.7.67; joined Can. Exp. Force 19.6.16; Major 26.11.16; Lt.-Col., Jan. 1917; commanding 3rd Batt. Can. Rly. Troops.

McDONALD, J. H. (D.S.O. L.G. 1.2.19), Major, 20th Batt. Aust. Inf. M.C.

MACDONALD, J. L. A. (D.S.O. L.G. 1.1.18), T/Major, R. Scots.

MACDONALD, K. L., M.A. (D.S.O. L.G. 3.6.16); b. 1867; s. of late L. McK. Macdonald and Minna, d. of late J. Mackenzie; m. 1st, Jane Geraldine Lindsay Junius-Stallard, d. of late Junius Smith; 2nd, Marnie, d. of W. H. Caldwell; educ. Edinburgh University; St. John's College, Oxford; J.P.; Hon. Lt., Army; Major, Lovat's Scouts, Yeomanry; formerly Lt., 3rd Batt. Can Highrs.; Lt.-Colonel; served S. Africa, 1899–1901; Queen's Medal, 4 clasps; King's Medal, 2 clasps; Europ. War, 1914–16; Despatches.

McDONALD, M. H. S. (D.S.O. L.G. 15.9.16); b. at Tormore, Skye, Aug, 1879; 2nd s. of the late M. N. McDonald, of Tormore, Skye, and of Dogapore, Sarun, India; better known as Calum McDonald; educ. Inverness College; entered R.N.; has seen a good deal of service at home and abroad, and took part in the Jutland Battle; Despatches (Admiral Jellicoe); Chevalier, Legion of Honour; O.B.E.

MACDONALD, R. H. (D.S.O. L.G. 3.6.19), Lt.-Col., 4th Field Ambulance, Can. A.M.C.

MACDONALD, R. J. (D.S.O. L.G. 1.1.18); b. 29.1.67; 2nd Lt., R.A., 6.7.87; Lt. 6.7.90; Capt. 19.10.97; Major 12.5.06; Lt.-Col., R.G.A., 30.10.14; retired pay 30.10.20.

MACDONALD, R. W. (D.S.O. L.G. 22.12.16); b. 22.4.81; 1st com. 28.7.00; Major, I.A., 1.9.15; transferred to Supernumerary List 23.12.14.

McDONALD, S. (D.S.O. L.G. 14.1.16) (Bar, L.G. 1.1.18) (2nd Bar, L.G. 18.2.18) (Details, L.G. 18.7.18); b. 28.11.77, at Macduff, Banffshire; s. of J. McDonald and Margaret McDonald (*née* Reid); m. Jessie S. Walker, d. of G. Walker, J.P., Harbour Commissioner; one s.; educ. Macduff Public School; Gordon's College, Aberdeen, and Aberdeen University; joined 1/5th Gordon Highlanders, T.F., 1907; served in European War with 5th G. Highrs.; became 2nd in command, and commanded the battalion; was then appointed to command the 6th Seaf. Highrs., and temporarily commanded the 152nd Brigade (51st H. Division); Despatches; twice wounded; C.M.G.

MACDONALD, T. W. (D.S.O. L.G. 3.6.18); b. 10.5.84; m. Mollie, d. of H. Jefferson; 2nd Lt., Bord. R., 3.12.04; Lt. 15.3.07; Capt. 3.11.14; ret. pay 31.7.21; Europ. War, 1914–18; Despatches twice.

MACDONALD, W. B. (D.S.O. L.G. 22.4.19), Comdr. (A/Capt.), R.N.

MACDONELL, J. A. (D.S.O. L.G. 1.1.17), Major, Can. Inf.

McDONNELL, E., M.B. (D.S.O. L.G. 1.1.17); b. 6.2.75; s. of E. McDonnell; educ. Clongowes; Lt., R.A.M.C., 4.12.99; Capt. 4.12.02; Major 4.9.11; Lt.-Col. 28.12.17; T/Col. 2.3.18; S. African War, 1900–2; Queen's Medal, 3 clasps; King's Medal, 2 clasps; Europ. War, Dardanelles (wounded; Despatches).

McDOUGALL, A. (D.S.O. L.G. 18.1.18) (Details, L.G. 25.4.18), Capt., Yeomanry.

MACDOUGALL, A. I. (D.S.O. L.G. 1.1.19); s. of late Col. J. W. Macdougall, R.A., Deputy Commissioner, C.P., India; 2nd Lt., 5th Lancers, 8.2.08; Lt. 22.5.09; Capt. 5.12.14; Bt. Major 3.6.17; 6th Inniskilling Dragoons 23.11.21; Despatches; M.C.

McDOUGALL, K. H. (D.S.O. L.G. 8.3.18), T/Major, Canadian Forestry Corps.

McDOUGALL, W. A. (D.S.O. L.G. 1.1.17); b. 5.6.68; ent. A.V.C. (now R.A.V.C.) 21.6.93; retired 24.9.13; Major, R. of O., 15.12.15; served N.W. Frontier of India, 1897–98; Medal and clasp; Europ. War; Despatches.

MACDOWELL, C. C. (D.S.O. L.G. 1.1.17); b. 12.7.73; s. of late C. W. Macdowell; m. Bertha M. F., d. of late F. Vere-Hopegood; one s.; 2nd Lt., Devon R. Arty., 1891; Capt., 1894; served S. Africa, 1900–1; is Hon. Lt.-Col., 3rd London Yeomanry (Sharpshooters); Europ. War; commanded 281st Brigade, R.F.A., for three years on Western front (Despatches four times; C.M.G.). His elder son, Capt. C. M. V. Macdowell, Black Watch, served in the Europ. War, and died of wounds.

McDOWELL, D. (D.S.O. L.G. 1.1.17); b. 10.7.79; s. of D. McDowell, C.E., and G. N. McDowell; educ. in H.M.S. Conway and H.M.S. Britannia; went to sea as a Naval Cadet in H.M.S. Gibraltar, 1896; Midshipman, 1896; Sub-Lt., 1900; Lt., 1902; Lt.-Cdr., 1910; specialized in Physical Training in R.N. Barracks, Portsmouth, 1906; was Mine-Sweeping during the whole of the war; in command of Speedwell and Aries II.; was notified in French Army Orders, and awarded the French Croix de Guerre with Palm, Nov. 1917; was in command of Delphinium in the Mine Clearance Service, May, 1919; late Senior Officer of Sheerness Mine-Sweeping Trawlers in H.M. Trawler Aries II., attached H.M.S. Actaeon, Sheerness.

MACDOWELL, T. W. (D.S.O. L.G. 10.1.17), Capt., Can. Cavalry. His D.S.O. was awarded for gallantry on 18.11.16, near Petit Maraumont; V.C. (see "The Victoria Cross," by same publishers).

McEACHERN, N. A. (D.S.O. L.G. 18.10.17) (Details, L.G. 7.3.18) (Bar, 1.2.19), Lt., Can. Inf.

McELLIGOTT, A. E. (D.S.O. L.G. 14.11.16); b. 1888; s. of W. N. McElligott and Isabella Esther McElligott (*née* Fairbridge); served with Queen's Westminster Rifles, afterwards 16th Bn. Co. of London R., 1904–11; enlisted 22.10.14; Sergeant 9.11.14; arrived in France with 27th Can. Inf. Bn. 18.9.15; T/Lt., 1916; Capt., 1916; A/Major, Sept. 1916. His D.S.O. was awarded for gallantry at Pozières 16.9.16.

McELROY, F. W. (D.S.O. L.G. 18.2.18) (Details, L.G. 18.7.18), T/2nd Lt., Tank Corps. He died 16.11.18.

McENROY, P. (D.S.O. L.G. 1.1.19); b. 26.3.85; 2nd Lt., Leins. R., 23.2.15 Lt. 5.10.15; Capt. 18.3.17; Despatches; M.C.

McEWAN, C. F. (D.S.O. L.G. 1.1.19), Major, Can. Light Horse.

McEWAN, J. A. (D.S.O. L.G. 4.2.18) (Details, 5.7.18), Major, Infantry, Canadian Force.

M'EWEN, A. B. (D.S.O. L.G. 1.1.17); b. Byron, Ontario, Canada, 23.1.91; s. of R. M'Ewen; m. Marjorie, d. of R. V. Sinclair, K.C., of Ottawa; educ. R. M. College, Canada, and McGill University; Civil Engineer, Canadian Explosives Ltd. Montreal; Subaltern, Canadian Militia, 1910; Capt., 1st Can. Divl. Arty., C.E.F., 1914; went to France, Feb. 1915; Major and O.C., 9th Battery, C.F.A., Aug. 1915. His D.S.O. was awarded for services during the actions at Ypres in April and May, 1915; Festubert and Givenchy, 1915; Bois Grenier, 1915; Ypres, June, 1916; wounded 7.1.16, near Neuve Eglise.

MACEWEN, N. D. K. (D.S.O. L.G. 17.9.17); b. 8.11.81; 2nd Lt., Unattached, 8.1.01; Arg. and Suth'd Hldrs. 9.3.01; Lt. 13.12.04; Capt. 1.2.13; Major 8.1.16; Wing Cdr., R.A.F., late A. and S. Highrs.; served S. African War, 1901–2; Queen's Medal, 5 clasps; European War, 1914–17; Despatches.

MACFARLAN, J. B. (D.S.O. L.G. 1.1.18); b. 6.4.76; 2nd Lt., R.A., 2.11.95; Lt. 2.11.98; Capt. 1.4.01; Major 30.10.14; Lt.-Col., R.F.A. 1.5.21.

MACFARLANE, REV. A. (D.S.O. L.G. 7.2.18); e. s. of late Rev. Mr. Macfarlane, of Muir of Ord. He was Chaplain to a Scottish regiment. He served in France and Mesopotamia.

MACFARLANE, F. A. J. (D.S.O. L.G. 1.1.18), Lt. (T/Capt.), London Rgt.

McFARLANE, G. W. (D.S.O. L.G. 4.6.17), Major, Can. Inf.

MACFARLANE, H. E. (D.S.O. L.G. 11.4.18); b. 5.8.85; 2nd Lt., 19 Hussars, 24.1.06; Lt. 17.10.08; Capt. 17.2.13; Adjt., 19th Hussars, 1913–14–15; Major 9.10.18; 4th Hussars 23.11.21; Bt. Lt.-Col. 24.1.21; Despatches; M.C.

MACFARLANE, R. A. (D.S.O. L.G. 4.6.17) (1st Bar, L.G. 11.1.19) (2nd Bar, L.G. 8.3.19) (Details, L.G. 4.10.19), Lt.-Col., 58th Inf. Batt., 2nd Central Ontario R.

MACFARLANE, W. (D.S.O. L.G. 1.1.18), Major, Glasgow Yeomanry.

MACFARLANE, W. McC. (D.S.O. L.G. 26.9.16); b. 1875; s. of late Lt.-Col. John Macfarlane, M.V.O., D.L., J.P.; m. Leila Campbell, d. of James Macdonald, of Invergare, Row, Dumbartonshire. As T/Lt.-Colonel, H.L.I., he served in the European War, and was killed in action 19.2.17.

W. McC. Macfarlane.

McFEELY, C. M. CRAIG- (see Craig-McFeely, C. M.).

MACFIE, C. (D.S.O. L.G. 3.6.18); b. 4.6.78; 2nd Lt., Sea. Highrs., 17.2.00; Lt. 19.3.01; Capt. 27.6.06; Maj. 1.9.15; retired pay 30.3.20.

MACFIE, T. G. (D.S.O. L.G. 3.10.19), Capt., 4th Batt. S. African Inf.; M.C.

MACFIE, W. C. (D.S.O. L.G. 14.1.16); b. 10.3.74; 2nd Lt., R.E., 27.2.94; Lt. 21.2.97; Capt. 1.4.04; Major 27.2.14; served S. African War, 1899–1902; Despatches; Queen's Medal, 3 clasps; King's Medal, 2 clasps.

McGAVIN, SIR D. J., M.D. (D.S.O. L.G. 16.8.17; Brig.-Genl.; Director-General of Medical Services, New Zealand; served Europ. War, with N.Z. Medical Corps; C.M.G.

McGHEE, A. S. P. (D.S.O. L.G. 3.6.19); b. 11.12.76; 2nd Lt., R.A., 21.3.96; Lt. 21.3.99; Capt. 2.9.01; Lt.-Col. 1.5.21; ret. pay 7.6.21; S. African War, 1900–1; Queen's Medal, 3 clasps; Europ. War; Despatches.

McGHIE, H. B. (D.S.O. L.G. 8.3.20), Eng.-Comdr., Royal Navy.

McGILDOWNY, W. (D.S.O. L.G. 4.6.17); b. 12.7.70; 2nd Lt., R.A., 27.7.89; Capt. 20.9.99; retired pay 22.7.05; retired as Major from S.R. 22.9.06; served Europ. War; Despatches.

McGILLYCUDDY, R. K. (The McGillycuddy of the Reeks) (D.S.O. L.G. 14.1.16); b. 26.10.82; s. of The McGillycuddy of the Reeks and Gertrude Laura, d. of E. H. Hiller; m. Helen Grace, d. of E. Courage; three s.; one d.; ent. R.A. 31.7.02; Lt. 31.7.05; 4th Royal Irish Dn. Gds. 25.8.09; Capt. 3.8.12; served Europ. War from 1914; D.A.A.G., G.H.Q., Br. Armies in France, 12.7.16; Despatches seven times; Bt. Major 3.6.16; Bt. Lt.-Col. 1.1.19.

McGILP, C. (D.S.O. L.G. 1.1.17); b. 12.10.84, at Russell, Bay of Islands, Auckland, N.Z.; s. of Alexander and Mary McGilp; m. at Alexandria, Egypt, 1.12.17, Jeanne Aquilina, d. of the Chevalier C. Aquilina; entered Mil. Forces, 1900; Lt., 1906; Capt., 1909; Major, 1914, N.Z. Field Artillery; served S. African War; Europ. War; mentioned in Sir Ian Hamilton's Despatch (Gallipoli); Despatches for services on the Somme.

McGIVENAY, P. (D.S.O. L.G. 24.9.18), 2nd Lt., Lanc. Fus. He died of wounds 2.6.18.

McGOWAN, T. (D.S.O. L.G. 14.1.16); b. 16.6.82; s. of J. H. McGowan and Annie Fuller McGowan (*née* Marshall); educ. Cheltenham College, and the R.M.A., Woolwich, where he won the Half-Mile and the Billiard Cue; played Hockey for Sussex County, 1902; won the South of Scotland Handicap and Singles at Lawn Tennis, 1909; 2nd Lt., R.F.A., 18.8.00; Lt. 18.8.03; Capt. 20.2.12; Major 15.2.15; A/Lt.-Col. 14.4.18; served Europ. War in France; Despatches; wounded three times; Croix de Guerre.

McGRATH, A. T. (D.S.O. L.G. 1.1.17) (Bar, L.G. 2.4.19) (Details, L.G. 10.12.19); b. 31.8.81; 2nd Lt., R.A., 22.11.99; Lt. 16.2.01; Capt. 21.8.07; Major 30.10.14; Bt. Lt.-Col. 1.1.19.

McGREGOR, J. (D.S.O. L.G. 3.6.19), Major, 3rd Batt. Can. Rly Troops.

McGREGOR, R. S. (D.S.O. L.G. 1.1.18), Major, Aust. A.M.C.

McGUFFIN, C. F. (gazetted as McGuffen) (D.S.O. L.G. 4.6.17), Lt.-Col., Can. A.M.C.

McHARG, A. A. (D.S.O. L.G. 1.2.17), 2nd Lt., R.E., 25.7.93; Lt. 25.7.96; Capt. 1.4.04; Major 25.7.13; Bt. Lt.-Col. 1.1.18; Lt.-Col. 1.1.21.

MACHELL, P. W. (D.S.O. L.G. 3.6.16); b. 5.12.62; s. of the Rev. Canon Machell and the Hon. Mrs. Machell (Emma, sister of the 8th Lord Middleton); m. Countess Valda Gleichen, d. of the late Admiral His Serene Highness Prince Victor of Hohenlohe-Langenburg; one s.; Lt., 56th Rgt., 1882; Capt., 1888; T/Major, 1893; R. of O., 1896; Lt.-Colonel. In 1884–85 he accompanied the Nile Expeditionary Force, and received the Medal with clasp and Bronze Star. Joining the Egyptian Army in 1886, he was in command at the Capture of Fort Khor Mousa, being afterwards awarded the Order of the 4th Class Osmanieh. His remaining services were: Action at Gamaizah; action at Toski, No. 2 Columns (two clasps); capture of Tokar (4th Class Medjidie, clasp to Bronze Star). From 1891 to 1895 he commanded the 12th Sudanese Battalion, and he afterwards filled the posts of Inspector-General of Egyptian Coastguard (1896) and Adviser to the Ministry of the Interior in Egypt (1898–1908); Grand Cordon of the Medjidie, 1902. Returning to England, he served in the capacity of an Alderman of the London County Council from 1912 to 1913, and was made a J.P. for Westmorland. The battalion of the Border Rgt. he commanded was raised, formed and trained by him in 1914, and went to the front in November, 1915. He was mentioned in Despatches. He also had the C.M.G. Colonel Machell, then in command of a battalion of the Border Regiment, was killed while leading his men in the attack of 1.7.16.

MACILWAINE, A. H. (D.S.O. L.G. 2.4.19) (Details, L.G. 10.12.19); b. 27.3.89; s. of A. W. Macilwaine, J.P., of The Manor House, Ferriby, Yorks, and Mary Emily MacIlwaine (*née* Lemprière); m. Joan, d. of late Col. J. Manners Smith, V.C.; one d.; educ. Clifton College; English Rugby Football International; 2nd Lt., R.A., 22.5.12; Lt. 22.5.15; Captain, R.F.A., 8.8.16; served Europ. War in France, Mesopotamia and India, 1914–18; with R.H.A., R.F.A., Trench Mortars, and Staff; Despatches; M.C.; Croix de Guerre with Palm.

MACINTOSH, C. L. S. (D.S.O. L.G. 4.6.17), Capt., Aust. A.M.C.

McINTOSH, J. A. (D.S.O. L.G. 1.1.19), Major, 18th Batt. Can. Inf.

MACINTOSH, S. H. (D.S.O. L.G. 1.1.17), T/Major, North'd Fus.

MACINTYRE, D. E. (D.S.O. L.G. 15.3.16); b. 17.5.85 in Montreal; s. of late D. S. Macintyre and Frances Jane Macintyre (*née* Smith); m. Marjorie, d. of F. Scott; educ. Montreal High School; Lt., 60th Saskatchewan Rifles, June, 1913; volunteered as Lt. with the 28th North-West Battalion in the 2nd Canadian Div. Oct. 1914, and was present at all actions fought by the 2nd Can. Div. from its arrival in France; Capt. 15.10.15; Major 17.7.17; Lt.-Col. His D.S.O. was awarded for one of the earliest trench raids (30–31.1.16) which took place near Wytschaete. He won his M.C. at Courcelette on 26.9.16. From 8.3.16 to 3.10.16 he was Staff Captain (Intelligence), 6th Canadian Infantry Brigade; from 3.10.16 to 13.2.17 he was General Staff Officer, 3rd Grade, 2nd Canadian Division, and from 13.2.17 to 8.6.17 he was Brigade Major of the 4th Canadian Infantry Brigade, and from 8.6.17 to 16.7.17, Brigade Major of the 6th Canadian Infantry Brigade, and from 16.7.17 to 20.11.17 General Staff Officer, 2nd Grade, 2nd Canadian Division, and from 20.11.17 to 6.5.18 General Staff Officer, 1st Grade, 2nd Canadian Division. He was wounded 21.4.18; evacuated to Canada; returned to France, Nov. 1918; commanded 28th Canadian Inf. Bn. from 2.10.18 till demobilization 7.6.19.

MACINTYRE, H. R., M.D. (D.S.O. L.G. 1.2.19), T/Capt. (A/Major), R.A.M.C., att. 29th Field Amb.; M.C.

McIVER, K. I. (D.S.O. L.G. 1.1.19); b. 19.5.86; 2nd Lt., R.A., 21.12.04; Lt. 21.12.07; Capt. 30.10.14; M.C.

McKAIG, J. B. (D.S.O. L.G. 4.6.17) (Bar, L.G. 18.2.18, gazetted as McKaigh) (Details, L.G. 18.7.18), Capt. (A/Lt.-Col.), L'pool Rgt.

MACKAY, A. T. (D.S.O. L.G. 3.6.18), Major, Can. Field Arty.

MACKAY, D. (D.S.O. L.G. 1.1.19), T/Capt. (A/Major), R.F.A.

MACKAY, I. G., B.A. (D.S.O. L.G. 1.1.17) (Bar, L.G. 18.6.17); b. 7.4.82; s. of the Rev. I. Mackay and his wife, Emily Frances; m. Marjorie Evelyn, d. of Brig.-Gen. J. B. Meredith; educ. Newington College, Sydney, and St. Andrew's College, University of Sydney; admitted Emmanuel College, Cambridge; Lt., Commonwealth Military Forces, 1911; served in European War as Capt. and Adjt., 4th Batt., A.I.F., 1914; Major, 1915; Lt.-Col., 1916; T/Brig.-Gen. Oct. 1918, Cdg. 1st Aust. Inf. Brig.; served in Gallipoli, and was wounded at Lone Pine (Despatches); served in France from 1916; Despatches; Bar to D.S.O. awarded for gallantry on 5–6.5.17; C.M.G.; French Croix de Guerre.

MACKAY, J. D. (D.S.O. L.G. 1.1.17); b. 4.8.66; 2nd Lt., R. Dub. Fus., 5.7.99; Lt. 24.2.00; Capt., Middx. R., 12.10.01; Major, Hants R., 19.4.11; Lt.-Col. 13.6.15; retired pay 25.2.20; Nile Exped., 1898; promoted 2nd Lt.; Medal, 2 clasps; British East Africa, 1901; Medal with clasp; East Africa, 1905; clasp; Nandi, 1905–6; Despatches; clasp; Somaliland, 1908–10; Despatches; clasp.

MACKAY, J. K. (D.S.O. L.G. 25.11.16), Lt.-Col., Can. F.A.; served Europ. War; severely wounded. His D.S.O. was awarded for gallantry on 8.10.16 at Courcelette.

McKAY, R. J. (D.S.O. L.G. 26.9.16), 2nd Lt. (T/Capt.), A. and S. Highrs. His D.S.O. was awarded for gallantry on 18.8.16 at High Wood.

McKEAN, F. T. (D.S.O. L.G. 1.1.18); b. 23.2.82; s. of late R. McKean and Isabella McKean, of St. John, N.B.; Lt., Can. Militia, 1906; Capt., 1911; Major; given command on securing Field Officer's Certificate, 1913; sailed in command of H.Q. Company, 2nd Can. Div. Train for France, April, 1915; command of 4th Can. Div. Supply Column, Aug. 1916, and O.C., Canadian Corps Ammunition Park, Jan. 1917.

McKECHNIE, D. W. (D.S.O. L.G. 2.12.18), No. 6 Field Amb., Can. A.M.C.

McKEE, J. (D.S.O. L.G. 17.9.17); b. 23.9.86, in Belfast; s. of the late Samuel McKee and of Janet McKee; educ. Belmont School, and Campbell College, Belfast; commissioned 17.9.14, 14th R. Irish Rifles; Captain 8.12.14. He accompanied the Ulster Division overseas in Sept. 1915, and was for a period in 1916 Second-in-Command of his battalion, with the rank of Acting Major. He was at the front continuously for a year and eight months until wounded in the Messines Battle. His D.S.O. was awarded for gallantry during the victorious advance on the Messines-Wytschaete Ridge on 7.6.17, when a severe wound necessitated the amputation of his left leg above the knee. His only brother, Lt. W. D. McKee, 12th R. Irish Rifles, was killed in action 12.8.17 in Flanders.

J. C. McKenna.

McKEEVER, A. E. (D.S.O. L.G. 4.2.18) (Details, L.G. 5.7.18), Capt., R.F.C. (now R.A.F.), S.R.; assisted Col. Bishop in the organization of the Canadian Air Force. He has a brilliant reputation as a fighting airman; M.C.

MACKENDRICK, W. G. (D.S.O. L.G. 1.1.18), Capt. (A/Lt.-Col.), Can. Engrs.

McKENNA, J. C. (D.S.O. L.G. 19.10.16); b. 4.8.79; s. of Capt. J. McKenna, R.A.; educ. privately, and at the R.M. College, Sandhurst; 2nd Lt., Border R., Aug. 1896; Lt., I.A., Sept. 1901; Capt., Rajputs, I.A.; served Europ. War as Staff Captain, Oct. 1914, to April, 1915; was sent to Mesopotamia, where he served with Gen. Townshend's Force, and was taken prisoner by the Turks.

A. E. G. McKenzie.

McKENZIE, A. E. G., M.A. (D.S.O. L.G. 1.1.17) (Bar, L.G. 11.1.19); b. at Campbelltown, N.B., Canada, 21.1.78; s. of A. McKenzie; m. Charlotte, d. of J. M. Troy; educ. University of New Brunswick; B.A., 1902; M.A., 1904; Bachelor of Civil Law, King's College, 1907; was Adjt. of a Militia Batt. at the outbreak of war; was given command of the 26th (N.B.) Batt., Canadians, 1916. Lt.-Col. McKenzie was killed in action 8.9.18.

MACKENZIE, A. G. (D.S.O. L.G. 1.1.17), Major, N.Z. Force.

MACKENZIE, A. K. (D.S.O. L.G. 15.2.19) (Details, L.G. 30.7.19), Major (T/Lt.-Col.), 1st Batt. Aust. Inf.; M.C.

MACKENZIE, CHARLES (D.S.O. L.G. 25.8.17); b. 25.7.69; 2nd Lt., Bedf. R., 21.12.89; Lt. 5.4.92; Capt., Ind. Army, 21.12.00; Major 21.12.07; Lt.-Col. 21.12.15; retired pay 1.7.20; N.W. Frontier, 1897–98; Medal, clasp; Europ. War; Despatches.

McKENZIE, CYRIL (D.S.O. L.G. 26.7.18), T/Lt. (A/Capt.), E. Lancs. R.

MACKENZIE, C. M. (D.S.O. L.G. 1.1.17), Capt. (T/Lt.-Col.), London R.

C. R. Mackenzie.

MACKENZIE, C. R. (D.S.O. L.G. 25.10.16); b. 3.5.92; s. of Alexander Linton Mackenzie and Marion Patrick Mackenzie; educ. Fonthill, E. Grinstead; Winchester, and Trinity College, Cambridge; Commander Colin Roy Mackenzie joined the Royal Navy on the declaration of war, 1914, as an Assistant Surgeon; was sent to the Spitfire (torpedo destroyer), and remained there for 10 months,

being in several actions with the Cat Fleet. In July, 1915, he joined the R.N.A.S., and did good work till he was killed at Bapaume 24.1.17. He received the Croix de Guerre from the French, and was twice mentioned in Despatches.

MACKENZIE, SIR DUNCAN (D.S.O. L.G. 22.8.18); b. 19.8.59; s. of late D. Mackenzie, of Lion's Bush, Natal; m. Katherine Agnes, d. of late A. Macarthur; educ. Hilton College, Natal; Member of Council of Defence, Union of South Africa; operations in S. Africa, 1897; Medal with clasp; S. African War, 1899–1902; Despatches three times; Queen's Medal, 5 clasps; King's Medal, 2 clasps; C.B.; C.M.G.; Natal Native Rebellion, 1906, in command; Despatches; Medal with clasp; K.C.M.G.; Brig.-Gen., retired list, late Natal Militia Force; V.D.

MACKENZIE, D. F., M.B. (D.S.O. L.G. 1.1.17); b. 26.5.81; s. of late P. W. J. Mackenzie; m. Maud, d. of W. Y. Reilly; one s.; educ. Dover College; Edinburgh University; gained the Diploma of Tropical Medicine at Liverpool University, 1906; Lt., R.A.M.C., 28.1.07; Capt. 28.7.10; Major 28.1.19; served Europ. War; went to France, Sept. 1914, with Indian Exp. Force; was attached to No. 19 British Field Ambulance; was A/Lt.-Colonel, commanding the No. 59 F.A. from Sept. 1916, to May, 1919; Despatches three times.

MACKENZIE, D. S. (D.S.O. L.G. 3.6.18), Major, Aust. A.M.C.

MACKENZIE, D. W. A. D. (D.S.O. L.G. 4.6.17); b. 20.10.89; s. of Major W. R. D. Mackenzie and Maud Evelyn, d. of Gen. Sir G. Higginson, G.C.B.; m. Patience Elizabeth, d. of R. Basil Hoare; one s.; one d.; educ. Eton; Magdalen College, Oxford; played Cricket, Hockey, Football (Association) for his college; 2nd Lt., Sea. Highrs., May, 1911; Lt., Nov. 1913; Capt., May, 1915; T/Major, Feb. 1918; served in India and France with 1st Batt. Seaforth Highlanders; wounded; France, second time from May, 1916; appointed D.A.A.G. in France, July, 1916; Despatches; Chevalier, Order of Leopold (Belgium); Croix de Guerre (Belgian); Mons Star.

MACKENZIE, E. D. (D.S.O. L.G. 1.1.17); b. 22.8.91; s. of late Sir Allan Mackenzie, Bart. of Glennwick, Aberdeenshire; educ. Eton College; joined Scots Guards, 1911; Adjt., 1916; Capt., 1917; Second-in-Command, 2nd Bn. Scots Guards, Dec. 1918–19; served Europ. War; went to France with 1st Batt. Scots Guards 13.8.14; wounded in the Battle of the Aisne 14.9.14; rejoined Batt. March, 1915; wounded Battle of Loos 27.9.15; rejoined Batt., June, 1916; wounded, March, 1918, Forest of Nieppe; Despatches several times.

MACKENZIE, E. R. L. FRASER- (see Fraser-Mackenzie, E. R. L.).

MACKENZIE, F. B. (D.S.O. L.G. 1.1.18), Capt. (T/Major), R. Scots; M.C.

MACKENZIE, F. W. (D.S.O. L.G. 1.1.17), Lt.-Col., R.F.A.

MACKENZIE, G. B. (D.S.O. L.G. 3.6.16); b. 31.1.72; s. of late William Laurence Mackenzie, of Inner Temple; Barrister; educ. Dulwich College; R.M.A., Woolwich; 2nd Lt., R.A., 12.2.92; Lt. 12.2.95; Capt. 1.1.00; Maj. 17.8.12; Bt. Lt.-Col. 18.2.15; Col. 18.2.19; served in New Zealand, Gibraltar, Hong-Kong and Peking; Europ. War; commanded the 1st Siege Battery to fire; Despatches six times; C.B., 1919; C.M.G., 1918; Officier de la Légion d'Honneur; Croix de Guerre.

MACKENZIE, H. G. G., M.A., M.D. (D.S.O. L.G. 3.6.18); b. 1869; s. of Gordon Mackenzie, of Montreal, Canada; educ. Winchester College; Magdalen College, Oxford; Lt.-Col., R.A.M.C. (T.); served Europ. War, 1914; commanded 83rd Field Ambulance; Despatches three times; Assistant Tuberculosis Officer, Charing Cross Hospital.

MACKENZIE, H. J. (D.S.O. L.G. 15.2.17); b. 19.9.78; e. s. of late P. W. J. Mackenzie; m. 1917, Vere, d. of Colonel C. Churchill; one d.; educ. Dover College; 2nd Lt., K.O. Sco. Bord., 26.6.01; Lt., Ind. Army, 26.9.03; Capt. 26.6.10; Major 26.6.16; served S. African War, 1900–1; Queen's Medal, 4 clasps; N.W. Frontier, 1908; Medal, clasp; Europ. War, 1914; Despatches.

MACKENZIE, J. A. (D.S.O. L.G. 14.11.16), Major, 26th Bn. Can. Inf. His D.S.O. was awarded for gallantry 17.9.16, at Courcelette.

MACKENZIE, J. H. (D.S.O. L.G. 1.1.17); b. 2.7.76; s. of late Major H. L. Mackenzie, R.A.; m. 1906, Lorna Gladys, d. of E. Bourne Lucas; one d.; educ. Merchiston Castle School, Edinburgh; R.M.C., Sandhurst; 2nd Lt., R. Scots, 1896; Lt., 1899; Capt., 1903; Adjt., 2nd R. Scots, 1903–6; Major, 1914; Bt. Lt.-Col., 1917; O.C., 11th R. Scots, 1919; served Europ. War; Despatches five times; C.M.G., 1919; Comdr., Order of Avis Portugal; G.S.O.1, Poona District, since, 1920.

MACKENZIE, J. L. (D.S.O. L.G. 1.1.17) (Bar, L.G. 2.4.19) (Details, 10.12.19), Lt.-Col., 1st Brig., Can. Engnrs.

MACKENZIE, J. M. (D.S.O. L.G. 3.6.18); b. 11.5.82; e. s. of J. H. Munro Mackenzie, of Mornisk, Isle of Mull; 2nd Lt., R. Scots, 4.7.03; Lt. 16.5.05; Capt. 28.8.14; Maj. 4.7.18; S. Africa, 1902; Queen's Medal, 2 clasps; Somaliland, 1908–10; Medal, clasp; Europ. War; Despatches.

MACKENZIE, J. P. (D.S.O. L.G. 1.1.17) (Bar, L.G. 26.7.17) (2nd Bar, L.G. 2.4.19) (Details, L.G. 10.12.19), Major, Can. Inf. His first Bar was awarded for gallantry on 28.4.17, at Arleux-en-Geville.

McKENZIE, K. A. (D.S.O. L.G. 3.3.17), Major, Aust. Light Horse Regt.

MACKENZIE, K. McL. (D.S.O. L.G. 14.1.16); b. 25.3.81; joined A.V.C. 4.2.05; Capt. 4.2.10; Major 10.7.15; A/Lt.-Col. 15.6.18 to 9.4.19.

MACKENZIE, K. W., M.B. (D.S.O. L.G. 26.7.18), T/Capt. (A/Lt.-Col.), R.A.M.C.; M.C.

MACKENZIE, L. H. (D.S.O. L.G. 27.5.19), Major Nova Scotia R.

MACKENZIE, L. DE A. (D.S.O. L.G. 1.1.19); first commission, July, 1916; Capt. 15.6.17; Bt. Maj. 1.1.18, Gordon Highrs.; retired pay 29.9.21; M.C.

McKENZIE, L. E. (D.S.O. L.G. 1.1.18), Major, Aust. A.V.C.

W. K. S. Mackenzie.

MACKENZIE, R. C. (D.S.O. L.G. 3.6.18), Major, Can. Inf.

MACKENZIE, R. H. (D.S.O. L.G. 1.1.19), Major R.E. (T.F.).

MACKENZIE, SIR V. A. F., Bart. (D.S.O. L.G. 14.1.16); b. 15.12.82; s. of the late Sir Allen Mackenzie, Bart.; 2nd Lt., Scots Guards, 18.1.02; Lt. 18.2.04; Capt. 3.7.12; Major 18.1.17; M.V.O.; served Europ. War; Despatches.

MACKENZIE, W., M.B. (D.S.O. L.G. 1.1.19), T/Capt., R.A.M.C.

MACKENZIE, W. K. S. (D.S.O. L.G. 1.1.17); b. 7.1.72; s. of Walter Fawkes Mackenzie, M.D., of Sydney; educ. Sydney Grammar School, and University of Sydney; St. John's College, Oxford; B.A.; Barrister-at-Law of the Inner Temple, and New South Wales Bar.; 2nd Lieut., N.S.W. Scottish Rifles Regt., 20.11.98 (which was affiliated to the R. Highrs., 1898); in command of that Regt., 1909–15; appointed to the command of the 19th Batt., A.I.F., 26.4.15; served Europ. War in Gallipoli and France; Despatches; Order of St. Stanislaus, 3rd Class; V.D. (Volunteer Officer's Decoration for 20 years' service).

McKENZIE, WILLIAM SINCLAIR (D.S.O. L.G. 26.3.17) (Details, L.G. 18.7.17), 2nd Lt., Sea. Highrs. He was killed in action 21.4.17.

MACKENZIE, WILLIAM SCOBIE (D.S.O. L.G. 1.1.17), Lt.-Col., R.A.O.C.

MACKESSACK, P., M.B. (D.S.O. L.G. 4.6.17); b. 4.8.72; Lt., R.A.M.C., 28.7.97; Capt. 28.7.00; Major 28.1.09; Lt.-Col. 1.3.15; Col. 28.7.21; retired pay 28.7.21; Despatches.

MACKESY, C. E. R. (D.S.O. L.G. 1.1.17); b. 1861; Lt.-Col., Auckland Mtd. Rifles; served Europ. War, 1915–17; Despatches; C.M.G., 1917; C.B.E., 1919.

MACKESY, J. P. (D.S.O. L.G. 1.1.17); b. 1873; s. of Lt.-General Mackesy; m. 1910, Leila Stewart, of Kingstown; educ. Stonyhurst College; privately; R.M.A., Woolwich; 2nd Lt., R.E., 14.7.91; Lt. 24.7.94; Capt. 1.4.02; Major 24.7.11; Lt.-Col. 24.9.18; served in the Expedition in Sierra Leone Hinterland, 1898–99, including operations in Kissi country at the back of Liberia; was Commander, R.E., at Sierra Leone, 1898–1900 (Medal with clasp); S. African War, 1900–2 (Queen's Medal, 3 clasps; King's Medal, 2 clasps; Despatches); Europ. War; Despatches twice; commanded a Field Coy. for nine months at Ypres, including fighting near Hooge during July, Aug., Sept. 1915; then appointed Commander, R.E., of a Division, and took part in attacks opposite Serre, 1916.

MACKESY, P. J. (D.S.O. L.G. 1.1.18); b. 5.4.83; 2nd Lt., R. Eng., 23.8.02; Lt. 21.3.05; Capt. 23.8.13; Major 23.8.17; Bt. Lt.-Col. 11.11.19 Europ. War; M.C.

MACKIE, G. (D.S.O. L.G. 4.6.17), Capt., R A.M.C.

McKIE, J., M.B. (D.S.O. L.G. 1.2.17), Lt.-Col., R.A.M.C.

MACKIE, J. C. (D.S.O. L.G. 4.6.17); b. 17.4.88; Inspector of Mech. Transport, 3rd Class, 26.10.10; 2nd Class 26.10.16; Capt. 26.10.16.

McKILLOP, A. (D.S.O. L.G. 1.1.19), Maj., 1st Fld. Amb., Aust. Army Med. Corps; M.C.

McKIMM, D. S. A. (D.S.O. L.G. 19.11.17) (Details, L.G. 22.3.18), Lt., Shrops. L.I. (from temp. comm.), 2.8.17; M.C.

McKINERY, J. W. H. (D.S.O. L.G. 26.9.17) (Details, L.G. 9.1.18), Lt.-Col., Labour Batt. Can. Force.

MACKINNON, D. A. (D.S.O. L.G. 4.6.17), Major, Can. Inf.

MACKINNON, E. J. G. (D.S.O. L.G. 11.12.18); b. 11.4.80; s. of Colonel Walter Carr Mackinnon, late Royal Ir. Fus.; m. 1907, Katherine Ethel, 3rd d. of Mr. and Mrs. Rothwell, of St. John's, Newfoundland; one d.; educ. Littlejohns', Greenwich; joined H.M.S. Britannia, July, 1894; went to sea Aug. 1896; Comdr., R.N., 30.6.15; served Europ. War; Despatches; in H.M.S. Druid 11.3.14 to 11.1.15; present at action in Heligoland Bight 28.8.14; 1st Bombardment of Zeebrugge 28.11.14; H.M.S. Myngs 12.1.16 to 23.2.16; Trident 24.2.16 to 23.7.17; Tancred 24.7.17 to 16.1.18; Walker 17.1.18 to 28.1.19; Valkyrie 29.1.19 to 10.1.20; service in Baltic, Sept.–Nov. 1919. His D.S.O. was awarded for services in H.M. Destroyers of the Grand Fleet.

MACKINNON, J. (D.S.O. L.G. 1.1.17), Major, T/Lt.-Col., R.A.M.C.

MACKINNON, L. (D.S.O. L.G. 3.6.19), Major (T/Lt.-Col.), 4th Batt. Gordon Highrs., T.F., att. 1/8th Batt. Lanc. Fus., T.F.

MACKINTOSH, E. E. B. (D.S.O. L.G. 1.1.17); b. 3.11.80; s. of Ernest Alexander and Mary Georgina Frances Mackintosh; educ. Frank Buckland's School, Laleham; Temple Grove, East Sheen; Eton; R.M.A., Woolwich; 2nd Lt., R.E., 28.6.99; Lt. 13.2.02; Capt. 28.6.08; Major 1.4.16; was seconded to the Egyptian Army, 1916; A.D.C. to the Sirdar, and Governor-General of the Sudan, 1908–11; D.A.A.G. on H.Q. Staff, 1911–13; A.A.G., 1913–15; 4th Class Osmanieh; rejoined British Army, 1915, and served with a Field Company, R.E., May, 1915–March, 1916; Staff Officer, R.E., 4th Army (graded D.A.A.G.), March–Dec. 1916; Asst. Engineer-in-Chief, G.H.Q., France, Oct. 1917, to end of war; Despatches twice; Bt. Lt.-Col. 1.1.19; Legion of Honour. He was a member of the winning polo teams, Coldstream Cup, Khartum, 1909, and 60th Rifles Cup, Khartum, 1912.

MACKINTOSH, J. B. (D.S.O. L.G. 3.6.19); b. 5.4.69; 2nd Lt., R.A., 27.7.88; Lt. 7.7.91; Capt. 23.1.99; Maj. 1.3.09; Col. 26.2.20; retired pay 14.2.21; Chitral, 1895; Mohmand F.F. and Tirah, 1897–98; Medal, 2 clasps.

MACKINTOSH, J. K. (D.S.O. L.G. 11.4.18); e. s. of ex-Treasurer John and Mrs. Mackintosh, of Southwood, Inverness; Major, A.S.C. (now R.A.S.C.), T.F.; mobilized at outbreak of war, and saw active service in Gallipoli, Salonika, Egypt and the Holy Land; Despatches twice, and D.S.O. awarded for the military operations culminating in the capture of Jerusalem.

MACKINTOSH, W. A. O. C. (D.S.O. L.G. 1.1.18); b. 22.3.84; 2nd Lt., R.A., 23.12.03; Lt. 23.12.06; Capt. 30.10.14; Major 11.9.18; Bt. Major 1.1.17.

MACKWORTH, G. (D.S.O. L.G. 8.3.18), Cdr., R.N.

MACLACHLAN, A. F. C. (D.S.O. L.G. 31.10.02) (Bar, L.G. 1.1.18), T/Lt.-Col., K.R.R.C.; C.M.G. He was killed in action on 22.3.18 (see "The Distinguished Service Order," from its institution to 31.12.15, by same publishers).

McLACHLAN, J. D. (D.S.O. L.G. 3.6.16); b. 14.2.69; m. Gwendolen Mab, d. of H. C. White, of Havilah, N.S.W.; one d.; educ. Cheltenham College; R.M.C., Sandhurst; 2nd Lt., Cam. Highrs., 25.3.91; Lt. 2.8.92; Capt. 9.5.98; Major 16.12.04; Lt.-Col. 9.3.13; Col. 9.3.17; Nile Expedition, 1898; Egyptian Medal, clasp; Medal; Europ. War from 1914; Brigade Cdr., 1915–17; severely wounded; Despatches thrice; C.B.; C.M.G.; Legion of Honour (Officer); Medal of La Solidaridad (1st Class), Republic of Panama; United States Distinguished Service Medal; was Military Attaché, Washington, 1917–19, with temp. rank of Major-Gen., 1918–19; Col. on Staff, in charge of Administration, Gibraltar, 1920.

R. C Maclachlan.

MACLACHLAN, R. C. (D.S.O. L.G.3.6.16); b. 24.7.72; s. of late Rev. A. N. Maclachlan, Vicar and Patron of Newton Valence, Hants; m. Elinor Mary, d. of J. C. Cox, M.P., of Sydney, N.S.W., and widow of Hon. S. Trench; educ. Cheam School; Eton; Sandhurst; 2nd Lt., Rif. Brig., 8.7.93; Lt. 27.11.95; Capt. 24.4.00; Maj. 26.1.10; Lt.-Col.; served S. African War; Despatches; Queen's Medal, 3 clasps; he commanded the 8th S. Batt. R. Brigade, taking it to France, 1915; T/Brig.-General; severely wounded 29.12.15; Despatches. He was killed in action on 11.8.17.

McLACHLAN, T. (D.S.O. L.G. 16.9.18), T/Capt. (A/Major), North'd Fus.; M.C.

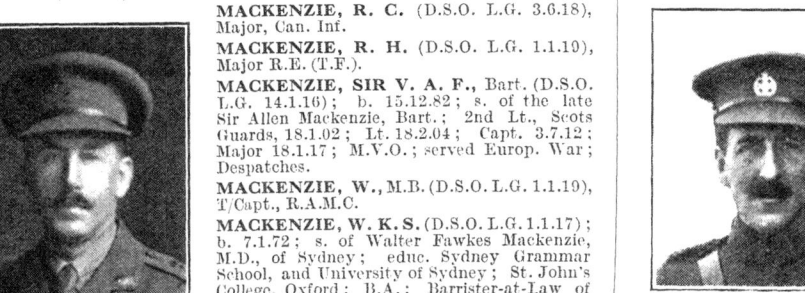

MACLACHLAN, W. K. (D.S.O. L.G. 3.6.18) : s. of ex-Provost MacLachlan, of Helensburgh ; m. a d. of Mrs. M'Dougall, of Craigbank House, Helensburgh ; was on the Clerical Staff at the Head Office in Glasgow of The Turkey Red Dye Co. (Ltd.), and joined up shortly after the outbreak of the war ; was commissioned in the North'd Fusiliers, and became T/Major.

MACLAREN, C. H. (D.S.O. L.G. 14.1.16) ; m. Dorothy Olivia, d. of Lt.-Col. F. White, C.M.G. ; Brig.-Gen., C.R.A., 4th Can. Div., Can. Force ; served Europ. War, 1914–18 ; C.M.G.

MACLAREN, D. R. (D.S.O. L.G. 8.2.19) ; m. Verna, d. of R. H. Harrison ; Major, Can. Air Force ; commanded the 46th Squadron, R.A.F., in France for a year and has 57 German machines to his credit ; was appointed Attaché to the British Air Board ; Director of Air Services, Can. Air Force ; M.C. and Bar ; D.F.C. ; Legion of Honour ; Croix de Guerre.

McLAREN, H. (D.S.O. L.G. 3.6.19) ; s. of late Sir John McLaren, K.B.E. ; m. Edith, d. of late W. Beverley, Barrister-at-Law ; educ. Mill Hill School ; Capt., R.E., T.F. ; served Europ. War, 1915–19, in Gallipoli, Sinai, Palestine and Syria ; M.C., 3rd Class Order of the Nile.

McLARTY, G. A., M.B. (D.S.O. L.G. 1.1.18), T/Capt., R.A.M.C.

McLAUGHLIN, C. E. (D.S.O. L.G. 17.10.19), Lt., R.N. ; deceased.

McLAUGHLIN, L. T. (D.S.O. L.G. 14.11.16) (Bar, L.G. 18.2.18) (Details, L.G. 18.7.18) (2nd Bar, L.G. 1.2.19) ; b. Tyrone, Ontario, Canada, 14.2.79 ; s. of J. W. McLaughlin, ex-Reeve of Barlington ; educ. Bowmanville High School, Ontario ; joined 46th Rgt., Can. Militia, 1898 ; Capt., 1910 ; Major (Junior), 46th Durham Rgt., Sept. 1914 ; Company Commander, 39th Can. Inf. Batt. Can. Exp. Force, Dec. 1914 ; went overseas, June, 1915 ; O.C., 2nd Can. Batt. E. Ontario Rgt., and took part in the fight for Vimy Ridge, April, 1917. His D.S.O. was awarded for gallantry at Pozières on 9.9.16.

MACLEAN, A., M.B. (D.S.O. L.G. 15.9.16) ; b. 10.1.68, at the Manse, Halkirk, Caithness ; s. of the Rev. Alexander Macle n ; educ. George Watson's College, Edinburgh ; Edinburgh University ; joined R.N., Aug. 1889 ; promoted Staff Surgeon, Aug. 1901 ; Fleet Surgeon, Aug. 1905 ; Surgeon Captain 1.6.19 ; served Europ. War ; mentioned in Despatches of Sir J. Jellicoe for the Battle of Jutland.

MACLEAN, C. A. H. (D.S.O. L.G. 1.1.18) ; b. 26.11.74 ; 2nd Lt., Arg. and Suth'd Highrs., 28.12.95 ; Lt. 17.12.97 ; Capt. 28.12.01 ; Bt. Major 21.2.14 ; Maj. 1.9.15 ; Bt. Lt.-Col. 3.6.16 ; Temp. Brig.-Gen. 19.11.17 ; Tirah, 1897–98 ; Medal, clasp.

MACLEAN, C. K. (D.S.O. L.G. 20.7.17) ; only surviving son of the late Major-General Charles Smith Maclean. All General Maclean's sons greatly distinguished themselves in the European and other wars, and one of them, Hector Maclean won the Victoria Cross. Capt. C. K. Maclean, R.N., served at Zeebrugge and with the Destroyer Flotilla of the Harwich Force ; C.B.

MACLEAN, C. T. (D.S.O. L.G. 3.6.19), Lt.-Col., Royal Scots Fus. ; M.C.

MACLEAN, C. W. (D.S.O. L.G. 1.1.18) ; b. 5.3.75 ; s. of Major-Gen. H. H. MacLean, M.P. for Royal Division of New Brunswick in the Canadian Parliament ; 2nd Lt., W.I.R., 10.10.94 ; Lt. 3.4.97 ; Capt., Lanc. Fus., 9.2.00 ; Major, Cam. Highrs., 17.12.14 ; retired pay 19.7.19 ; Lt.-Colonel ; Sierra Leone, 1898–99 ; severely wounded ; Medal, clasp ; Parliamentary Private Secretary to Lt.-Col. L. S. Amery, M.P., Under-Secretary of State for the Colonies.

McLEAN, C. W. W. (D.S.O. L.G. 4.11.15) (1st Bar, L.G. 18.7.17) (2nd Bar, L.G. 18.7.17) ; 1st Bar awarded for gallantry near Arras on 9.4.17 ; 2nd Bar awarded for gallantry at Roeux 13.4.17 ; Major, R.F.A. (see "The Distinguished Service Order," from its institution to 31.12.15, by same publishers).

McLEAN, CHARLES HERBERT (gazetted as Charles Henry) (D.S.O. L.G. 2.4.19) (Details, L.G. 10.12.19), Major, 4th Can. Mounted Rifle Batt.

MACLEAN, I. C. (D.S.O. L.G. 26.9.17) (Details, L.G. 8.1.18), T/Capt., R.A.M.C. ; M.C. He died of wounds 4.4.18.

McLEAN, J. (D.S.O. L.G. 15.2.19) (Details, L.G. 30.7.19), Lt., 42nd Batt. Aust. Inf. ; M.C.

McLEAN, J. B. (D.S.O. L.G. 3.6.16), Major, Aust. A.M.C.

MACLEAN, N. B. (D.S.O. L.G. 3.6.18) ; b. 14.4.83 ; educ. Universities of Toronto and Chicago ; Professor of Mathematics, Manitoba University, from 1910 ; Fellow Royal Astronomical Society of Canada ; Lt.-Colonel, Can. Mil. Forces : served European War, Commanding University of Manitoba Contingent, C.O.T.C., Dec. 1920.

McLEISH, R. S. (D.S.O. L.G. 15.10.18), Major, Aust. Mounted Rcgt.

MACLELLAN, G. P. (D.S.O. L.G. 1.1.17) (Bar, L.G. 16.9.18), Major (ALt.-Col.), R.G.A., att. R.F.A.

McLELLAN, J. (D.S.O. L.G. 8.3.19) (Details, L.G. 4.10.19), Lt. (A/Major), 446th (Northumbrian) Field Co., R.E. ; M.C.

McLENNAN, B. (D.S.O. L.G. 1.1.17) ; s. of late Hugh McLennan, of Montreal, Canada ; Lt.-Col., Quebec Rgt. He was killed in action, aged 49.

McLENNAN, F., M.B. (D.S.O. L.G. 1.1.19) ; b. 29.9.72 ; educ. Aberdeen University ; Lt., R.A.M.C., 25.4.00 ; Capt. 25.4.03 ; Maj. 25.4.12 ; Bt. Lt.-Col. 1.1.17 ; Lt.-Col. 26.12.17 ; Bt. Col. 3.6.19 ; Somaliland, 1902–4 ; Medal, clasp.

MACLEOD, A. G. (D.S.O. L.G. 1.1.18), T/Major, A.S.C. (now R.A.S.C.).

McLEOD, D. (D.S.O. L.G. 1.1.18) ; b. 5.1.69 ; ent. Army 14.6.00 ; Capt. 16.8.05 ; retired 5.1.14 ; Capt. (T/Lt.-Col.), N. Staffs. R., S.R. ; M.C.

McLEOD, D. K. (D.S.O. L.G. 1.1.17) ; b. 19.6.85 ; 2nd Lt., Unatt., 19.8.03 ; 2nd Lt., I.A., 29.11.04 ; Lt. 19.11.05 ; Capt. 19.8.12 ; Major 19.8.18 ; Despatches.

MACLEOD, D. McL. (D.S.O. L.G. 1.1.17). During the sittings of the General Assemblies at Edinburgh, Lt.-Col. D. M. Macleod, D.S.O., S. African Scottish, acted as Senior A.D.C. to the Duke of Atholl, the Lord High Commissioner.

MACLEOD, G. W. (D.S.O. L.G. 14.11.16) (Bar, L.G. 18.1.18) (Details, L.G. 25.4.18), Major, Can. Inf.

McLEOD, J. K. (D.S.O. L.G. 23.5.17), Lt.-Cdr., R.N., 31.12.14. He died 29.9.20.

MACLEOD, J. P. G. (D.S.O. L.G. 2.4.19) (Details, L.G. 10.12.19), Lt., 46th Batt. Can. Inf. (Saskatchewan R.).

MACLEOD, J. S. (D.S.O. L.G. 3.6.19), Lt.-Col., 8th Batt. Durham L.I., T.F., att. 1/8th Batt. Lancs. Fus., T.F.

MACLEOD, M. N. (D.S.O. L.G. 1.1.18), Major, R.E. ; M.C.

MACLEOD, M. W. M. (D.S.O. L.G. 1.1.18) ; b. 25.5.96 ; 2nd Lt., R.A., 17.11.14 ; Lt. 9.6.15 ; Capt., R.G.A., 3.11.17.

MACLEOD, NORMAN (D.S.O. L.G. 25.8.17) ; b. 8.1.79 ; 2nd Lt., 25.1.99 ; Lt., Ind. Army, 15.7.01 ; Capt. 25.1.08 ; Major 1.9.15 ; *p.s.c.*

MACLEOD, NORMAN (D.S.O. L.G. 4.6.17), T/Lt.-Col., Cam. Highrs. ; served Egyptian Exp., 1882–84 (Despatches ; Medal ; Bronze Star) ; Europ. War, 1914–18 ; wounded ; Despatches.

McLEOD, N. MAC D. (D.S.O. L.G. 1.1.18) ; b. 3.9.85 ; 2nd Lt., R.A., 25.7.06 ; Lt. 25.7.09 ; Capt. 30.10.14 ; Major, R.F.A., 13.2.17 ; Bt. Lt.-Col. 25.7.21 ; M.C.

MACLEOD, R. (D.S.O. L.G. 1.1.19) ; b. 13.11.91 ; 2nd Lt., R.A., 23.12.11 ; Lt. 23.12.14 ; Adjt., R.A., 27.11.15 to 17.12.15 ; Capt., R.F.A., 8.8.16 ; M.C.

MACLEOD, R. D. C. (D.S.O. L.G. 3.6.18) ; b. 16.2.79 ; 2nd Lt. (from Impl. Yeo.), Hamps. R., 24.7.01 ; Lt., Ind. Army, 24.10.03 ; Capt. 4.5.10 ; Maj. 4.5.16 ; S. Africa, 1899–1902 ; Queen's Medal, 6 clasps ; King's Medal, 2 clasps ; Tibet, 1903–4 ; Medal ; N.W. Frontier, 1908 ; Medal, clasp.

McLEOD, T. J. (D.S.O. L.G. 17.4.16) ; b. 3.6.70 ; 2nd Lt., K.R.R.C., 29.10.90 ; Lt., Ind. S.C., 26.8.92 ; Capt., Ind. Army, 10.7.01 ; Maj. 29.10.08 ; Lt.-Col. 29.10.16 ; retired pay 30.10.20 ; served Miranzai (2nd) Exp., 1891 (Medal and clasp) ; Waziristan Exp., 1894–95 ; clasp ; N.W.F. of India, 1897–98 ; Mohmand ; Medal with clasp ; Tirah, 1897–98 ; Capture of the Sampagha and Arhanga Passes ; operations in the Bazar Valley 25–30.12.97 ; clasp ; Europ. War ; Despatches.

M'MAHON, F. R. (D.S.O. L.G. 1.1.17) ; b. Wellington, N.Z., 1.11.78 ; s. of Martin M'Mahon and Mary M'Mahon (*née* Dunne) ; m. Alice Joan, d. of Rev. T. Jones, of Manor Park ; three d. ; educ. Clyde Quay School, and St. Patrick's College, N.Z. ; Mining Engineer ; joined King Edward's Horse on their formation 13.8.14 ; commissioned in Shropshire L.I. 24.12.14 ; Capt., R.E., 12.5.15 ; Major 20.10.15 ; went to France 8.1.15 ; gassed at Cambrai, Nov. 1915 ; joined Ministry of Munitions (Aircraft), 1918 ; transferred to Air Ministry, 1920.

MACMAHON, M. (D.S.O. L.G. 4.6.17), A/Lt.-Cdr., R.N.R.

McMASTER, H. (D.S.O. L.G. 1.1.18) ; b. 11.3.87 ; s. of H. D. McMaster, J.P., and Florence McMaster ; d. of Major-General Saxton ; educ. at Tyttenhanger Lodge ; at Rugby ; R.M.A., Woolwich ; entered R.F.A., July, 1907 ; Capt., Oct. 1914 ; Major, July, 1917 ; served Europ. War ; proceeded to Belgium, Aug. 1914 ; took part in the Retreat from Mons ; was severely wounded in the subsequent advance on 15.9.14 ; then trained a new battery and went out in command of it in May, 1915 ; was again seriously wounded on 15.9.16, and was fatally wounded on 29.11.17, dying of his wounds on 2.12.17 ; Despatches several times ; M.C.

McMASTER, R. M. (D.S.O. L.G. 26.11.17) (Details, L.G. 6.4.18), Major, Aust. A.M.C.

MACMICHAEL, H. A. (D.S.O. L.G. 1.1.17) ; b. 15.10.82 ; s. of late Rev. C. MacMichael and Hon. Mrs. MacMichael, of Walpole Grange, Sittingbourne, and nephew of Lord Curzon, of Kedleston ; m. Nesta, d. of Rev. Canon J. Otter Stephens, of 104, Belgrave Road, S.W. ; one d. ; educ. King's Lynn and Bedford Schools ; Magdalene College, Cambridge (Scholar) ; 1st Class Honours in Classics, 1904 ; joined Sudan Civil Service, 1905 ; successively Inspector in Provinces of Kordofan, Blue Nile and Khartum ; Political and Intelligence Officer with Expeditionary Force which reoccupied Darfur, 1916 ; Despatches ; D.S.O. ; Sub-Governor of Darfur Province. He has written "The Tribes of Northern and Central Kordofan."

McMICKING, N. (D.S.O. L.G. 3.6.19) ; b. 3.6.94 ; 2nd Lt., R. Highrs., 17.9.13 Lt. 29.1.15 ; Capt. 17.3.16 ; M.C.

MACMILLAN, ANGUS (gazetted as MacMillar, A.) (D.S.O. L.G. 15.10.18), 2nd Lt., Sea. Highrs., 12.3.16 ; Lt. 12.9.17 ; Capt. 1.4.20.

McMILLAN, ALEXANDER (D.S.O. L.G. 18.7.17), Lt.-Col., R. Can. Dragoons.

MACMILLAN, J., M.B. (D.S.O. L.G. 1.1.19), Capt. (A/Lt.-Col.), R.A.M.C. M.C.

MACMILLAN, J. B. (D.S.O. L.G. 14.11.16) ; b. 14.8.87 ; s. of Police-Sergeant John Macmillan, of Cupar, Fife, who died in 1900 ; educ. Castlehill School, Cupar ; was commissioned 7th Batt. D.C.L.I., 1914 ; Captain before he went to France in 1915 ; awarded the D.S.O. for gallantry at Les Bœufs on 16.9.16 ; passed Senior Officers' Course at Aldershot, March, 1917 ; recommended for Lieut.-Colonelcy ; was Major commanding his battalion when he fell in action, 1½ miles S.W. of the village of Les Rues Vertes, on 30.11.17.

MACMILLAN, R. J. A. (D.S.O. L.G. 2.4.19) (Details, L.G. 10.12.19), Major, R.G.A., T.F.

McMORDIE, S. P. (D.S.O. L.G. 19.8.16), Major, Can. Pioneers.

McMULLEN, D. J. (D.S.O. L.G. 1.1.18) ; b. 27.7.91 ; 2nd Lt., R.E., 20.7.11 Lt. 31.7.13 ; Capt. 26.6.17 ; Bt. Maj. 1.1.19.

McMURCHIE, J. W. (D.S.O. L.G. 8.3.20), A/Lt.-Cdr., R.N.V.R.

McMURTRY, A. O. (D.S.O. L.G. 2.12.18), Major, 4th By., 1st Bde., Can. F.A.

MACNAB, A. A. (D.S.O. L.G. 3.6.19), Major, 3rd N.Z. Rifle Brigade.

MACNAGHTON, B. (D.S.O. L.G. 25.8.17) ; b. 23.12.75 ; s. of late A. H. Macnaghton and Arabella Marie, d. of W. Betts ; m. Hilda, d. of W. G. Lardner ; one d. ; educ. Eton ; 2nd Lt., 12th Lrs., 9.12.96 ; Lt. 11.5.98 ; Capt. 6.9.01 ; Major 6.1.12 ; Lt.-Col. 4.10.15 ; retired pay 19.11.19 ; S. African War, 1899–1902 ; Despatches twice ; Queen's Medal, 6 clasps ; King's Medal, 2 clasps ; N. Nigeria, 1906 ; Medal, clasp ; Europ. War, 1914–17 ; wounded ; Despatches.

MACNAGHTON, R. F. (D.S.O. L.G. 18.1.18) (Details, L.G. 25.4.18) ; s. of R. E. Macnaghton and Mary, d. of F. Berry, Churchdown, Glos. ; Lieut., Can. Infantry ; served Europ. War, 1915–18 ; Despatches.

M'NAMARA, A. E. (D.S.O. L.G. 22.9.16) ; b. 13.2.77 ; s. of late W. M'Namara, of Dundanion, Blackrock, Co. Cork ; educ. Oratory School, Birmingham ; 2nd Lt., R.W. Surrey R., 20.2.97 ; Lt. 2.9.98 ; Capt. 22.1.03 ; Major 1.9.15 ; Col. 31.8.20 ; S. Africa, 1899–1902 ; Despatches twice ; wounded ; Queen's Medal, 5 clasps ; King's Medal, 2 clasps ; Europ. War, 1914–18 ; wounded ; Despatches six times ; Bt. Lt.-Col. 3.6.17 ; Bt. Col. 3.6.19 ; C.M.G. ; Belgian Croix de Guerre. His D.S.O. was awarded for gallantry 14–20.7.16, at Delville Wood and Longueval Village.

McNAUGHT, G. S., B.A. (D.S.O. L.G. 1.1.19) ; b. 16.5.86 ; s. of late G. McNaught ; m. Muriel, d. of C. Mason, J.P. ; one s. ; educ. Liverpool Institute High School ; University of Liverpool ; Temp. 2nd Lt. 14.9.14 ; Temp. Maj. 1.10.16 ; Capt., Ches. R., 19.1.17 ; Asst. Master, H.M.S. Conway, Rock Ferry, 1908–14 ; served with 12th Cheshire Rgt. in France and Salonika, 1915–18 ; with 12th Hants Rgt. in Bulgaria, Dobrudja and Egypt, 1918–19 ; Despatches twice ; Greek Military Cross, 2nd Class.

McNAUGHTON, A. G. L., M.Sc., LL.D. (D.S.O. L.G. 4.2.18) (Details, L.G. 5.7.18) ; b. 1887 ; educ. Lennoxville ; McGill University ; Brig.-Gen., Can. F.A.

McNAUGHTON, F. L. (D.S.O. L.G. 3.6.18); b. 1891; s. of D. N. McNaughton; m. Betty, d. of Rev. A. Pinchard; one s.; educ. Loretto; R.M.A., Woolwich; Capt., R.A.; served Europ. War, 1914–18; wounded; Despatches; Adjt., H.A.C.

McNEE, J. W., M.B. (D.S.O. L.G. 1.1.18), Capt., R.A.M.C., Spec. Res.

MACNEECE, W. F. (D.S.O. L.G. 1.1.17); s. of Col. T. F. MacNeece, of Castle Carey, Co. Donegal; b. 21.8.89; 2nd Lt., R.W. Kent R., 6.2.09; Lt. 2.2.12; Capt. 10.6.15; T/Major; Despatches; D.F.C.

MACNEIL, A. (D.S.O. L.G. 16.8.17); b. 24.8.92, at Inverness, Scotland; s. of Alexander and Grace MacNeil; m. Mary, d. of C. M. Rose; educ. Inverness; joined the Army 29.8.14; Lt., 10th Batt. Aust. Exp. Force, 16.3.16; Despatches twice. His D.S.O. was awarded for gallantry east of Bullecourt 6.5.17.

McNEILE, D. H. (D.S.O. L.G. 8.3.19) (Details, L.G. 4.10.19), Lt.-Col., 19th Lrs., I.A.; b. 6.2.71; 2nd Lt., R.A., 13.2.91; Lt. 13.2.94; Capt., Ind. Army, 10.7.01; Major 13.2.09; Lt.-Col. 13.2.17; retired pay 1.6.20.

McNEILL, A. J. (D.S.O. L.G. 3.6.18); b. 31.5.74; s. of Capt. D. McNeill (of Colonsay), late Scots Greys, and Fanny, d. of Admiral Sir C. Talbot, K.C.B.; m. Lilian, widow of Capt. C. Findlay, Q.O. Cameron Highrs., and d. of late Major-Gen. Sir H. Barron, K.C.M.G.; one s.; educ. Harrow; 2nd Lt., Sea. Highrs., 29.5.95; Capt. 19.3.01; Brigadier-General; retired pay with rank of Major 20.7.10; Col. (T.F.); C.B.; Nile Exped., 1898; Despatches; S. African War, 1899–1900, as A.D.C. to Gen. Gatacre, afterwards in command of Montmorency's Scouts; Despatches twice; Bt. Major; Queen's Medal, 3 clasps; served Europ. War, 1914–18; France, 1915; Gallipoli, 1915, in command 2nd Lovat's Scouts; Egypt, 1916; Brig.-Gen., 1917; Palestine, Syria; Despatches five times; Serbian Order, Karageorge, with Swords; Order of the Nile, 1914–15 Star.

McNEILL, A. N. R., M.B., Ch.B. (D.S.O. L.G. 3.6.18); b. 24.4.86; s. of late Alexander McNeill, J.P.; m. Nora Josephine, d. of Sir C. S. Dawson; Lt., R.A.M.C., 1.8.08; Capt. 1.2.12; Maj. 1.8.20; Second-in-Command, Cavalry Field Ambulance, 1914–16; O.C. of the same, 1916–19; served Europ. War, 1914–18; Despatches; 1914 Star.

McNICOLL, D. G. (gazetted as McNicoll G.) (D.S.O. L.G. 1.1.17); s. of late D. McNicoll. On the outbreak of war he enlisted as a Private, and the following March was given a commission in the E. Yorks. R.; six months later he was transferred to a Service Battalion of the Durham L.I.; received rapid promotion, and in July, 1916, was gazetted to field rank; Despatches. In July he was given command of a Battalion of the R. Fusiliers. He fell mortally wounded while leading his men to the attack, and died of wounds on 20.11.17.

McNISH, R. L. H. (D.S.O. L.G. 24.5.19), Chief Officer, Mercantile Marine; Lt., R.N.R.

McPARLAND, J. F. (D.S.O. L.G. 1.1.18), Major, Can. Field Arty.

McPHERSON, ANDREW (D.S.O. L.G. 13.2.17), Capt., H.L.I. His D.S.O. was awarded for gallantry at Beaumont Hamel on 18.11.16.

McPHERSON, ANGUS (D.S.O. L.G. 27.9.20); b. 25.1.89; 2nd Lt., A. and S. Highrs., 4.2.15; Lt., A. and S. Highrs., 21.1.16; M.C., D.C.M.

MACPHERSON, ALAN DAVID (D.S.O. L.G. 3.6.18); s. of W. C. Macpherson, C.S.I., of Blairgowrie, Perthshire; m. Catharine Richardson Hill, d. of R. C. Hill; educ. Winchester College; R.M.A., Woolwich; 2nd Lt., R.A., 29.7.08; Lt. 29.7.11; Capt. 30.10.14; Major 13.3.18; served European War, 1914–18; Despatches thrice; M.C.

MACPHERSON, ALEXANDER DUNCAN (D.S.O. L.G. 23.11.16); b. Dec. 1877; m. Kathleen, d. of S. Oxley; 2nd Lt., Cam. Highrs., Sept. 1898; Lt., May, 1899; Capt., March, 1903; Adjt., Cam. Highrs., Nov. 1913; served Europ. War; T/Lt.-Col., Nov. 1915; Colonel; Despatches; Bt. Major, June, 1915; C.M.G.

McPHERSON, J. (D.S.O. L.G. 3.6.19), Major, R.F.A., T.F.

MACPHERSON, J. R. (D.S.O. L.G. 8.2.18) (Details, L.G. 18.7.18), T/Capt., Can. Inf. He was killed in action.

MACPHERSON, K. P. (D.S.O. L.G. 3.6.19), Major, 7th Batt. Can. Engrs.

MACPHERSON, L. A. W. (D.S.O. L.G. 8.3.19) (Details, L.G. 4.10.19), Major, 8th Aust. L.H. Regt.; M.C.

McQUARRIE, R. S. (D.S.O. L.G. 3.6.19), Lt.-Col., H.Q., 3rd Brig. N.Z.F.A.

McQUEEN, JOHN ALEXANDER (D.S.O. L.G. 17.10.19), Lt. (A/Lt.-Cdr.), R.N.V.R.

McQUEEN, JOHN ARTHUR (D.S.O. L.G. 4.6.17); b. 15.12.82; 2nd Lt., R.E., 21.12.01; Lt. 7.9.04; Capt. 21.12.12; Major 21.12.16; Despatches; M.C.

McQUEEN, J. D. (D.S.O. L.G. 4.6.17), Lt.-Col., Can. A.M.C.

McQUEEN, N. (D.S.O. L.G. 4.6.17) (Bar, L.G. 7.11.18), Capt. (T/Major), A. and S. Highrs., S.R.

McRAE, H. ST. G. M. (D.S.O. L.G. 1.1.17); b. 10.11.78; s. of late Col. H. N. McRae, C.B.; m. Esmé, d. of R. Craigie Hamilton; two d.; educ. Highgate; entered 3rd Batt. R. Irish (Wexford) Militia, 1899, as 2nd Lt.; joined the 2nd Batt. R. Irish Rgt., 1899; transferred to Indian Army, 1900; joined the 14th Sikhs, and served in China, 1901–2; transferred to the 45th "Rattray's" Sikhs, 1902, and served against the Darwesh Khel Waziris, N.W.F. of India, 1902; raised and commanded the 8th Indian Contingent, serving in Nyasaland, 1907–10; Staff Capt., 32nd (Imperial Service) Inf. Brig., Sept. 1914, and was on service on the Suez Canal, 1914–16; G.S.O., 2/4th Aust. Div., 1916, and went to France; was G.S.O.2, 2nd A.N.Z.A. Corps, B.E.F., France; recalled to India, Aug. 1917; served against Afghans, May–Sept. 1919; Despatches; O.B.E. Major McRae was appointed to command 1/124th Baluchistan Inf., Dec. 1919, and served with them in E. Persia.

MACRAE, J. C. (D.S.O. L.G. 18.8.16); b. 1.9.81; s. of the late J. Macrae, Procurator Fiscal of the Orkneys; m. Adela, d. of Sir C. Mordaunt, 10th Bart.; 2nd Lt., Hants R., 1900; Lt., 1902; Lt., I.A., 1904; Capt., 1909; Major, 1916; served Aden, 1903–4; European War, 1914–17; Mesopotamia; Despatches.

MACRAE, J. N. (D.S.O. L.G. 15.4.16) (Bar, L.G. 7.2.18) (John only as Christian name in gazette of D.S.O.); Qr.-Mr. and Hon. Lt., Sea. Highrs., 25.2.14; Capt. 18.8.15; Bt. Maj. 3.6.16; Maj. 13.12.21; Q.M., Sea. Highrs., 13.9.21. His D.S.O. was awarded for gallantry at Sheikh Said on 7.1.16.

MACREADY, G. N. (D.S.O. L.G. 3.6.18); b. 5.4.91; s. of Sir N. Macready, G.C.M.G.; m. Elizabeth de Noailles, d. of the Duc de Noailles; educ. Cheltenham, and R.M.A., Woolwich; 2nd Lt., R.E., 23.12.10; Lt. 21.12.12; Capt. 23.12.16; served Europ. War, 1914–18; A.A. and Q.M.G., 66th Div., Nov. 1917–May, 1918; A.A. and Q.M.G., Supreme War Council, Versailles, May, 1918–April, 1919; A.A.G., Br. Mil. Mission to Berlin, April–Sept. 1919; Special Mission (to organize Police Force) in Poland, Oct. 1919; Despatches six times; Bt. Major 3.6.17; O.B.E.; M.C.

MACROBERTS, N. DE P. (D.S.O. L.G. 26.9.17) (Details, L.G. 9.1.18); was commissioned R. Sussex R.; commanded a Service Battalion; A/Lt.-Colonel; Despatches; M.C., and two Bars.

MACRORY, F. S. N. (D.S.O. L.G. 1.1.17); b. 13.6.76, at Ardmore Lodge, Limanady, Ireland; s. of late S. M. Macrory; m. Rosa Baigrie Pottinger, d. of the late Lt.-Gen. Pottinger, R.A.; educ. Cheltenham College; ent. Militia, 1896. On outbreak of war entered 12th (S.) Batt. Manchester R. 18.9.14; was transferred to 10th (S.) Batt. R. Innisk. Fus. 22.10.14. He commanded his battalion on 1.7.16 at Thiepval, and during the 1st July Offensive, when the Ulster Division lost so heavily but fulfilled all the tasks allotted to it. He commanded his battalion during the Battle of Messines on 7.6.17, when the Ulster Division, with the 16th Division on its left, captured the important Messines and Wytschaete Ridge. He was a second time mentioned in Despatches, and was seriously wounded on 12.8.17, during the fighting for the Passchendaele Ridge, and was invalided home.

F. S. N. Macrory.

McSHARRY, T. P. (D.S.O. L.G. 4.6.17) (Bar, L.G. 15.10.18). Lt.-Col. McSharry held a Lieutenant's commission in the original Australian Expeditionary Force, and was awarded the M.C. He died of wounds 1.11.17.

McSLOY, J. I. (D.S.O. L.G. 1.1.19), Major, 4th Brig. Can. F.A.

McSWINEY, H. F. C. (D.S.O. L.G. 12.12.19); b. 8.11.86; s. of late Col. E. F. H. McSwiney, C.B., D.S.O., and Ida F., d. of late Col. H. Knaggs, A.M.S.; 2nd Lt. 29.8.06; Lt., I.A., 29.11.08; Capt. 29.8.15; Major 29.8.21.

McTAGGART, M. F. (D.S.O. L.G. 14.1.16) (Bar, L.G. 30.1.20); b. 1.11.74; s. of Capt. W. B. McTaggart (late 14th Hussars); m. Winifred Grace, d. of J. P. Law; educ. Harrow and Sandhurst; 2nd Lt., 5th Lrs., 20.2.95; Capt. 22.9.04; Major 22.5.09; N.W. Frontier, 1897–98; Medal, 2 clasps; Tirah, 1897; clasp; S. Africa, 1899–1900; Queen's Medal, 3 clasps; served Europ. War, first with the 3rd Cav. Brigade; commanded 5th Batt. Gordon Highlanders from June, 1915; was in the Battle of Mons and the Retreat; the Marne, Ypres, the Battle of the Somme, Beaumont Hamel, 3rd Battle of Ypres, Cambrai, etc., etc.; wounded twice; Despatches thrice; Bt. Lt.-Colonel 1.1.18. He was in the English Team in the International Jumping Competition, Horse Show, Olympia, and New York in 1913–14. He has written "Hints on Horsemanship."

McTAGGART, W. B. (D.S.O. L.G. 1.1.18), Major, Can. Field Arty. (deceased).

McTAVISH, D. (D.S.O. L.G. 14.1.16); b. 16.5.79; s. of late Capt. A. B. McTavish; educ. Inverness College. On the outbreak of war he joined the Gordon Highlanders as Lieutenant; became Capt., 1915; was severely wounded at Hulloch.

McVEAN, D. A. D. (D.S.O. L.G. 2.9.09) (Bar, L.G. 27.6.19), Capt., I.S.C. (see "The Distinguished Service Order," from its institution to 31 Dec., 1915, by same publishers).

McVITTIE, C. E. (D.S.O. L.G. 1.1.17), Major (T/Lt.-Col.), A.S.C. (now R.A.S.C.), R. of O.

MACWATT, S. L. (D.S.O. L.G. 1.1.19); b. 8.1.94; s. of Colonel R. C. MacWatt, C.I.E., K.I.H., F.R.C.S., Inspector-General of Civil Hospitals, Punjab, India, and Blanche Mathilde, d. of the late Major-Gen. B. F. Blythe, C.B.; 2nd Lt., R.A., 17.7.14; Lt. 9.6.15; Capt., R.G.A., 3.11.17; M.C.

McWATTERS, H. C. (D.S.O. L.G. 22.12.16); b. 9.10.78; 2nd Lt., Unatt., 27.7.98; 2nd Lt., I.S.C., 12.10.99; Lt. 27.10.00; Capt. 27.7.07; Major 1.9.15; Bt. Lt.-Col. 3.6.17; Punjabis, I.A.; O.B.E.

MADDEN, REV. A. (D.S.O. L.G. 1.2.19), Can. Chaplains' Service, attd. 7th Bn. Can. Infy., Br. Columbia R.; M.C.

MADDEN, J. G. (D.S.O. L.G. 25.8.16); Capt., Manch. Regt.; served Europ. War, 1914–19; wounded; Despatches.

MADOCKS, W. R. N. (D.S.O. L.G. 4.6.17); b. 1870; 2nd s. of late Henry Robarts Madocks and Hon. Anne Amelia; m. 1903, Laura, d. of late Sir Walter Buller, K.C.M.G., F.R.S.; two s.; one d.; educ. R.M.A., Woolwich; Staff Officer, N. Zealand Defence Forces, 1896–99; 2nd Lt., R.A., 25.7.90; Lt. 25.7.93; Capt. 7.2.00; Bt. Maj. 29.11.00; Lt.-Col. 11.1.15; Col. 11.1.19; Temp. Brig.-Gen. 3.11.17; South African War, 1899–1902; Despatches; Queen's Medal, 3 clasps; King's Medal, 2 clasps; served Europ. War; Despatches; C.B.; C.M.G.; Croix de Guerre with Palm; Commandant, N. Wales Infantry Brigade, T.A.; 1920.

MAGAWLY CERATI DE CALRY, V. A. (D.S.O. L.G. 1.1.17), Lt.-Col., Innis. Dragoons; served Europ. War; Despatches; Legion of Honour. He was killed in action near Arras 10.8.17.

MAGEE, A. A. (D.S.O. L.G. 1.1.19), T/Lt.-Col., Quebec Regt.

MAGEE, F. C. (D.S.O. L.G. 14.1.16), Lt.-Col., Can. Arty.

MAGEE, W. E. B. (surname gazetted as Majee) (D.S.O. L.G. 8.3.20), Lieut.-Comdr., R.N.

MAGENIS, G. C. (D.S.O. L.G. 1.1.17), Capt., Aust. Mil. Forces.

MAGILL, R., M.B. (D.S.O. L.G. 4.6.17); m. 1919, Roselle, e. d. of Henry Hind, of Blytheholme, Harrogate; one s.; Major, R.A.M.C. (S.R.); served Europ. War, 1914–17; Despatches.

MAGINN, J. F. (D.S.O. L.G. 4.2.18) (Details, L.G. 5.7.18), 2nd Lt., London Regt.

MAGNIAC, M. (D.S.O. L.G. 3.6.16); b. 27.6.80; 2nd Lt., Lanc. Fus., Aug. 1899; Lt. 16.5.00; Capt. 15.2.04; served Europ. War. He was killed in action 24.4.17.

MAGRATH, M. M. (D.S.O. L.G. 4.6.17); b. 24.5.89; ent. R.A. 18.12.08; served Europ. War; Despatches. He was killed in action 2.8.18.

MAGUIRE, F. A. (D.S.O. L.G. 3.6.18); m. Alma Myee (d. 1919); Col., Aust. A.M.C.; served Europ. War, 1915–18; Despatches.

MAGUIRE, O. H. K. (D.S.O. L.G. 1.10.17), A/Cdr., R.N.

MAHAFFY, KENNETH ARNOLD (gazetted as Mahaffy, Kennett Arnold) (D.S.O. L.G. 26.7.17), A/Major, Can. Inf.; M.C. His D.S.O. was awarded for gallantry at Vimy Ridge 9.4.17.

MAHAR, T. B. J. (D.S.O. L.G. 3.6.19), T/Lt. (T/Capt.), General List; M.C.

MAHON, A. E. (D.S.O. L.G. 27.7.18); b. 1.12.78; 2nd Lt., R. Ir. Fus., 7.3.00; Lt., R. Ir. Fus., 1.12.01; Lt., Ind. Army, 12.2.03; Capt. 7.3.09; Major 1.9.15; Despatches.

MAHON, B. McM. (D.S.O. L.G. 4.6.17); b. 18.2.90; Capt., Ind. Army (from T.F.), 20.2.18; M.C.

MAHON, M. C. J. HARTLAND- (see Hartland-Mahon, M. C. J.).

MAHONY, M. J., M.D., B.Ch. (D.S.O. L.G. 20.10.16) (gazetted as Mahoney); b. 1865; s. of Richard Mahony, of Tramore; educ. St. Vincent's College, Castleknock; N.U.I.; R.U.I.; B.A.O.; late Senior Surgeon, Liverpool Hospital for Cancer and Skin Diseases; Major, R.A.M.C.; served S. African War (Queen's Medal, 4 clasps), as Lieut., King's Liverpool Regt.; Europ. War, 1914–17; Despatches; T.D., 1915. His D.S.O. was awarded for gallantry on 8–9.8.16, at Maltz Horn Ridge.

MAIN, A. K. (D.S.O. L.G. 1.1.17); b. 6.9.81; s. of Col. T. R. Main, C.B., C.M.G.; 2nd Lt., R.A., 18.8.90; Lt. 18.8.03; Capt. 9.10.11; Adjt., 11.10.12 to 29.1.15; Major 28.12.14; Bt. Lt.-Col. 3.6.19.

MAINGUY, R. F. (D.S.O. L.G. 4.6.17); b. 16.10.81; 2nd Lt., R.E., 2.5.00; Lt. 2.5.03; Capt. 2.5.10; Major 2.11.16; ret. pay 30.3.21.

MAINPRISE, C. W., M.R.C.S., L.R.C.P. (D.S.O. L.G. 1.1.17); b. 23.6.73; s. of late W. B. Mainprise, Paymaster-in-Chief, R.N.; educ. Royal Naval School, New Cross; St. Bartholomew's Hospital; Lt., R.A.M.C., 27.7.98; Capt. 27.7.01; Major 27.7.10; Lt.-Col. 1.3.15; served in Tibet Expedition in charge of the only British Field Hospital, 1903–4 (Medal and clasp); present at Delhi Durbar, 1911 (Coronation Medal); Europ. War, in France; commanded an Indian Cavalry Field Ambulance, 1914; Despatches; also a Casualty Clearing Station, 1915; Despatches; in charge of Military Hospital, Curragh, Ireland, 1917; O.C., 80 General Hospital, Salonika, April, 1918; present in offensive against Bulgaria as A.D.M.S., Advanced Base, and after the Bulgar defeat went through to Sofia; A.D.M.S., 16th Corps; took part in Afghan War, 1919 (A.D.M.S.), Peshawar.

MAINWARING, G. R. (D.S.O. L.G. 20.1.21); b. 5.8.85; 2nd Lt. 5.8.05; Lt., Ind. Army, 5.11.07; Capt. 5.8.14; Maj. 5.8.20; Despatches.

MAIR, B. V. (D.S.O. L.G. 26.9.17) (Details, L.G. 9.1.18); b. 30.12.82; 2nd Lt., Manch. R., 22.4.03; Lt. 24.4.07; Capt. 11.12.14; Major 22.4.18; *p.s.c.*; Despatches; M.C.

MAITLAND, A. E. (D.S.O. L.G. 2.4.19) (Details, L.G. 10.12.19); b. 21.11.90; s. of Augustus Wetherall Maitland and Amy Katherine Maitland; m. 1916; Dorothy Margaret Polson; one d.; one s.; educ. Malvern College; R.M.C., Sandhurst; 2nd Lt., Essex Regt., 7.5.10; Lt. 2.1.12; Capt. 6.5.15; served Europ. War; Despatches four times; M.C.

MAITLAND, C. A. S. (D.S.O. L.G. 3.6.16); b. 12.11.74; 2nd Lt., Gord. Highrs., 5.1.01; Lt. 3.2.04; Capt. 1.3.10; Maj. 5.1.16; Bt. Lt.-Col. 3.6.18; *p.s.c.*; C.M.G.; S. African War, 1900–1; Despatches; Queen's Medal, 3 clasps; King's Medal, 2 clasps; Europ. War; Despatches.

MAITLAND, E. M., B.A., F.R.G.S. (D.S.O. L.G. 20.7.17); b. 21.2.80; e. s. of late Arthur Maitland, M.A., J.P.; educ. Haileybury College; Trinity Coll., Cambridge; 2nd Lt., Essex R., 23.5.00; Lt. 26.1.02; Capt., Essex Regt., 13.1.11; Air Bn. R.E. 19.5.11 to 12.5.12; R.F.C. 13.5.12 to 30.6.14; Major, Essex R., 1.9.15; Bt. Lt.-Col. 3.6.16; was gazetted to R.N.A.S., as Wing Comdr.; Wing Capt., 1915; Brig.-Gen. on formation of R.F.A., April, 1918; Air Comn.; served S. African War, 1901–2 (Medal, 4 clasps); Europ. War; C.M.G.; A.F.C., 1919; D.S.M. (American), 1917; Senior Air Ship Officer; took part in R 34's Atlantic crossing, 1919; American Naval Distinguished Service Cross, 1921. He was killed in H.M. Airship R 38, 24.8.21, in the flight trial over Hull, together with other officers, British and American, the crews and scientists.

MAITLAND, F. L. MAKGILL-CRICHTON- (D.S.O. L.G. 3.6.18); b. 7.3.78; 2nd s. of late Maj.-Gen. David Makgill-Crichton-Maitland and Lady Margaret Pleydell-Bouverie, d. of 4th Earl of Radnor; 2nd Lt., Gord. Highrs., 20.5.99; Lt. 12.12.99; Capt. 25.8.04; Maj. 1.9.15; S. African War, 1899–1902; severely wounded; Queen's Medal, 2 clasps; King's Medal, 2 clasps; Europ. War, 1914–17; wounded; Despatches; Croix de Guerre.

MAITLAND, G. R. (D.S.O. L.G. 3.6.18); b. 20.12.82; yr. s. of Sir John Maitland, 5th Bart.; m. 1919, Jean Hamilton, M.B.E., d. of R. Findlay; educ. Cheltenham College; R.M.A., Woolwich; 2nd Lt., R.A., 18.8.00; Lt. 18.8.03; Capt., Ind. Army, 18.8.09; Maj. 1.9.15; Lt.-Col., 1917; ret. pay 3.9.20; S. African War, 1901–2; Queen's Medal, 5 clasps; Europ. War, 1914–18; Despatches thrice; Croix de Guerre (Belgian); M.C.

MAITLAND, M. E. MAKGILL-CRICHTON- (D.S.O. L.G. 1.1.17); b. 1882; s. of Major-Gen. D. M. and Lady Margaret Crichton-Maitland; educ. Eton; R.M.C., Sandhurst; 2nd Lt., Grenadier Gds., 1901; Lt., 1904; Capt., 1910; Major, 1915; T/Lt.-Col. 9.7.16, in command of 1st Batt.; A.D.C. to Governor, New Zealand, 1910 and 1911; served S. African War, 1902 (Medal and clasp); Europ. War, 1914–17; Despatches; wounded; Croix de Guerre.

MAITLAND, O. M. (D.S.O. L.G. 3.6.19), Major, Saskatchewan Regt., att. Can. Engrs., 8th Corps.

MAITLAND, R. C. F. (D.S.O. L.G. 4.6.17); b. 10.10.82; o. s. of Major Reginald Paynter Maitland, late R.A.; m. 1913, Marjorie Agnes Jane, d. of Very Rev. E. Lane; two s.; 2nd Lt., R.A., 4.12.01; Lt. 4.12.04; Capt. 18.9.14; Major 24.11.15; served Europ. War; Despatches.

MAITLAND, W. B. (D.S.O. L.G. 26.9.17) (Details, L.G. 9.1.18), 2nd Lt., G. Highrs.

MAITLAND-EDWARDS, G. (see Edwards, G. Maitland-).

MAITLAND-MAKGILL-CRICHTON, A. G. (see Crichton, A. G. Maitland-Makgill-).

MAITLAND-MAKGILL-CRICHTON, H. C. (D.S.O. L.G. 14.1.16); b. 29.6.80; s. of Andrew Coventry Makgill-Crichton-Maitland; m. 1911, Dorothy Margaret, d. of late Sir Walter Thornburn, of Glenbreck; one d.; educ. Charterhouse; R.M.C., Camberley; 2nd Lt., R. Scots Fus., 16.12.99; Lt. 12.11.00; Capt. 16.6.09; Major 1.9.15; Bt. Lt.-Col. 3.6.18; served S. African War, 1899–1902; severely wounded; Queen's Medal, 4 clasps; Europ. War; Despatches six times; C.M.G.; Officer of the Legion of Honour.

MAJENDIE, B. J. (D.S.O. L.G. 14.1.16); b. 27.4.75; s. of late Rev. A. Majendie; m. Dorothy, y. d. of late G. W. Davidson; educ. Winchester; Sandhurst; joined 60th Rifles 22.1.96; Lt. 1.8.98; Capt. 9.10.01; Major 20.8.12; Lt.-Col., K.R.R.C., 19.7.16; T/Brig.-Gen., Commanding 65th Inf. Brigade, British Salonika Force, 24.4.18 to 23.4.19; Bt. Lt.-Col. 1.1.17; served S. African War, 1899–1902; Queen's Medal, 4 clasps; King's Medal, 2 clasps; Europ. War, 1914–19; Despatches four times; C.M.G., 1918; Officer, Legion of Honour.

MAJENDIE, V. H. B. (D.S.O. L.G. 18.7.17); b. 20.4.86; s. of Rev. H. W. Majendie; m. 1916, Evelyn Margaret Dickson, d. of Colonel C. Dickson King, late R.F.A.; two s.; educ. Winchester; Sandhurst; 2nd Lt., Som. L. Inf., 16.8.05; Lt. 21.12.08; Capt. 10.6.15; Bt. Major 1.1.19; served with W. African Frontier Force in S. Nigeria, 1908–13; Europ. War, 1914–19; Despatches; commanded 1st Batt. Som. L. Inf., 1916–19. His D.S.O. was awarded for gallantry N. of Fampoux 9–16.4.17.

MAKGILL-CRICHTON-MAITLAND-, F. L. (see Maitland, F. L. Makgill-Crichton-).

MAKGILL-CRICHTON-MAITLAND, M. E. (see Maitland, M. E. Makgill-Crichton-).

MALAN, G. S. G. (D.S.O. L.G. 22.8.18), Major, Hanover Commando, S. African Military Forces.

MALCOLM, G. A. (D.S.O. L.G. 1.1.18), Lt.-Col. (T.F. Res.), attd. Lond. Regt.

MALET, SIR H. C., 7th Bart., J.P. (D.S.O. L.G. 4.6.17); b. 21.9.73; s. nephew, 1918; bro. of 5th Bart.; m. 1906, Mildred Laura, d. of Capt. H. S. Swiney; one s.; two d.; 2nd Lt., 8th Hrs., 29.12.00; Capt. 19.10.09; ret. pay 2.4.10; S. Africa, 1899–1902; severely wounded; Queen's Medal, 4 clasps; King's Medal, 2 clasps; Europ. War, as D.A.Q.M.G. and A.Q.M.G.; O.B.E.; Officier du Mérite Agricole; 1914–15 Star; left service with rank of Lt.-Col.

MALING, F. M. (D.S.O. L.G. 12.5.17) (Bar, L.G. 22.6.17), Capt., Mercantile Marine (Lt., R.N.R.).

MALLINSON, S. S. (D.S.O. L.G. 1.1.18); b. 24.4.88; s. of W. Mallinson, J.P.; m. Marjorie Gray, d. of Rev. A. Soothill, B.A.; one s.; one d.; educ. The Leys School, Cambridge; joined H.A.C., Aug. 1914; France, Sept. 1914; commissioned, April, 1915; transferred to R.E. as Captain, Sept. 1916; Major, Dec. 1916; Lt.-Col., March, 1917; Staff of Engineer-in-Chief, G.H.Q., Dec. 1916, to March, 1917; A.D. of Forestry, Armies Group, 1917–19; Despatches three times; M.C.; Officier du Mérite Agricole, 1918; Governor, Leys School, 1920.

MALLOCK, C. H. (D.S.O. L.G. 1.1.17); b. 15.5.78, at Cockington Court, Torquay; s. of the late R. Mallock, formerly M.P., Torquay Division; Lord of the Manor of Cockington and D.L., Devon, and Mary Jones Mallock (*née* Dickson); m. Margaret Iris, d. of John and Lady Grace Bazley-White; three s.; one d.; educ. Horris Hill, Newbury; Winchester College; R.M.A.; 2nd Lt., R.G.A., Jan. 1898; transferred to R.F.A., May, 1901; Capt., 1905; R. of O., 1907; Major 30.10.14; served S. African War from 1901 (Queen's Medal and 4 clasps). He was at the front in Aug. 1914, and continuously until his death on 5.11.17, from wounds received in action in Belgium.

C. H. Mallock.

MALLORY, T. L. (D.S.O. L.G. 1.1.19), Major, R.A.F.

MALONE, J. J. (D.S.O. L.G. 23.5.17), Sub-Lt., R.N.A.S.

MALTBY, P. C. (D.S.O. L.G. 1.1.17), T/Major, R.W.F.

MAN, H. W. (D.S.O. L.G. 3.6.16); b. 14.7.76; 2nd Lt., Hamps. R., 26.2.96; Lt. 26.2.98; Capt. 2.9.03; Major 8.12.14; Bt. Lt.-Col. 3.6.18; R.A.O.C.; C.B.E.; S. African War, 1899–1901; Queen's Medal, 4 clasps; Aden, 1904; Europ. War; Despatches.

MANDLEBERG, L. C. (D.S.O. L.G. 8.3.19) (Details, L.G. 4.10.19); b. 1893; s. of Sir G. C. Mandleberg and Anne Mandleberg (*née* Barnett); m. Marjorie Helen, d. of J. Craig; educ. Harrow; Trinity College, Cambridge; Europ. War; Major, late Lancs. Fus.; Despatches; M.C. and Bar.

MANHARD, W. E. (D.S.O. L.G. 1.1.17), Major, Can. Engrs.

MANIFOLD, J. A., M.B. (D.S.O. L.G. 1.1.18); b. 12.12.84; Lt., R.A.M.C., 30.1.09; Capt. 30.7.12; Major 30.1.21; served Europ. War; Despatches; Bt. of Major for service in E. Africa; was employed as Senior Medical Officer, with acting rank of Lt.-Col.

MANLEY, E. N. (D.S.O. L.G. 26.8.18); b. 27.7.74; 2nd Lt., R.E., 25.7.93; Capt. 1.4.04; Lt.-Col. 1.6.21; ret. pay 8.9.21; N.W. Frontier, 1897–98; Despatches; Medal, 2 clasps; Europ. War; Despatches.

MANN, G. D. (D.S.O. L.G. 14.1.16); b. 28.8.76; s. of Horace Mann and of Mina Mann; educ. Repton; 2nd Lt., R.A., 5.5.00; Lt. 1.5.01; Major 30.10.14; T/Brig.-Gen. 19.10.17; served S. African War, 1902, with I.Y.; Queen's Medal with 2 clasps; employed with W. African Frontier Force, 1905–9; served in W. Africa (N. Nigeria), 1906; Medal with clasp; again employed with W.A.F.F., 1911–18; commanded the Artillery in N. Cameroons, 1915; Despatches; commanded the column operating from Ibi, on Banzo and Jaundi, July, 1915–Feb. 1916; commanded Nigerian Brigade in all fighting, Oct. 1917, to Feb. 1918; commanded British Troops south of Rouma River, in Portuguese E. Africa, Dec. 1917, to Feb. 1918; Despatches three times; Bt. Lt.-Col. 3.6.18; 1914 Star. Two of his brothers were killed in action, one in 1915, and the other in 1916, and his fourth brother was wounded.

MANN, H. U. (D.S.O. L.G. 17.9.17); b. 18.4.90; s. of H. Mann; m. Marjorie Ethel, d. of J. Corbet McBride; educ. Felsted; Capt., London Irish Rifles; served with his regiment and on the Staff in France, 1915–18; Despatches four times; M.C. His D.S.O. was awarded for gallantry, etc., from 22.5.17 to 14.6.17, near Ypres.

MANN, J. (D.S.O. L.G. 1.10.17), of the British India Company; Eng.-Cdr., R.N.R., recently of H.M.S. Angora, Grand Fleet.

MANN, W. E. (D.S.O. L.G. 16.8.17); b. 19.1.85; s. of Sir E. Mann, Bart., and Anna Jane, d. of Paul Bell; m. Sarah Douglas, d. of Sir A. Sprot, Bart.; one s.; educ. Marlborough; R.M.A., Woolwich; 2nd Lt., R.A., 21.12.04; Lt. 21.12.07; Capt. 30.10.14; Maj. 30.9.16; served Europ. War, 1914–17; twice wounded; Despatches. His D.S.O. was awarded for gallantry at Wolverghem, 7.6.17.

MANNERS, C. M. S. (D.S.O. L.G. 19.10.16); b. 24.1.85; s. of Col. R. A. Manners, The Royal Scots; m. Maisie, d. of J. J. Calder; educ. Stonyhurst College; ent. Army 18.1.05; Ind. Army, March, 1906; Lt. 18.4.07; Capt., 104th Wellesley's Rifles, 19.1.14; Major, 1920. He served with Gen. Townshend's Force in Mesopotamia, and was taken prisoner by the Turks; Despatches twice.

MANNING, C. H. E. (D.S.O. L.G. 1.1.17), Lt.-Col., Aust. A.S.C.

MANNING, R. C., B.A., B.A.I. (D.S.O. L.G. 4.6.17); s. of Capt. L. J. Manning, M.B.E., and Mrs. Manning; educ. Chesterfield, Birr, King's County; Portora Royal School, and Trinity College, Dublin; joined Canadian Military Forces, Aug. 1914, as Lance-Corporal, having served in Trinity College O.T.C., and was given a commission on the field for conspicuous bravery in the R.E. (Mining Section); promoted to T/Major, R.E.; was awarded M.C., and several times mentioned in Despatches. He died of wounds in France on 6.9.18.

MANNOCK, E. (D.S.O. L.G. 16.9.18) (1st Bar, L.G. 16.9.18) (2nd Bar, L.G. 3.8.18); Major, R.E., and R.F.C.; V.C.; M.C. (see "The Victoria Cross," by same publishers).

MANSON-BAHR, P. H., M.A., M.D., M.R.C.P., M.R.C.S., D.T.M. and H. Cambs. (gazetted as Bahr, P. H.) (D.S.O. L.G. 4.6.17); b. 26.11.81; s. of L. F. Bahr, Merchant, of Liverpool, and Emily Bahr (*née* Blessig); m. Edith Margaret, d. of Sir P. Manson, G.C.M.G.; two s.; three d.; educ. Rugby; Cambridge; London Hospital; Fellow Royal Society of Tropical Medicine and Hygiene; Fellow Royal Society of Medicine; Lecturer, London School of Tropical Medicine; Physician, Hospital for Tropical Diseases, Endsleigh Gardens; in charge of Stanley Research Expedition to Fiji, 1909; Research Expedition on Sprue, Ceylon, 1912–13; Lt., R.A.M.C., 30.9.14; Capt. 30.9.15;

The Distinguished Service Order 301

Bt. Major 1.1.19; European War, in Gallipoli, Egypt, Palestine, Syria, from Dec. 1915, serving in various capacities up to June, 1919; Despatches twice.

MANTON, L. (D.S.O. L.G. 1.1.18); b. 13.10.87; 2nd Lt., R.E., 20.12.08; Lt. 30.11.08; Capt. 30.10.14; Bt. Major 1.1.21.

MANTON, R. F. (D.S.O. L.G. 17.12.17) (Details, L.G. 23.4.18), Major, Aust. Field Arty.

MAPLESTONE, P. A. (D.S.O. L.G. 17.2.17) (Details, L.G. 23.4.18), Major, Aust. A.M.C.

MARCH, B. O. (D.S.O. L.G. 1.1.19), Capt. (A/Major), R.F.A. (Spec. Res.), att. 158th Art. Brig.; M.C.

MARCHANT, T. H. S. (D.S.O. L.G. 3.6.18); b. 27.10.75; 2nd Lt., 13th Hrs., 13.7.98; Lt. 3.10.00; Capt. 5.5.05; Maj. 1.7.13; Bt. Lt.-Col. 3.6.19; Lt.-Col., 5th D.G., 26.5.21; Temp. Brig.-Gen. 5.9.18 to 15.3.19; S. African War, 1899–1902; Queen's Medal, 4 clasps; King's Medal, 2 clasps; Europ. War; Despatches.

MARCHMENT, A. F. (D.S.O. L.G. 26.7.18); served in the European War; Colonel; O.C., 4th City of London Rgt.; M.C.

MARDON, A. C. (D.S.O. L.G. 15.2.19) (Details, L.G. 30.7.19), Lt.-Col., Royal North Devon Yeomanry, att. 16th Batt. Devon R.

MARE, T. (D.S.O. L.G. 22.8.18), Major, 5th Mtd. Brig. (Supernumerary List), S. African Mil. Forces.

MAREE, C. J. (D.S.O. L.G. 22.8.18), Major, Lydenburg Commando, S. African Mil. Forces.

MARFELL, W. L. (D.S.O. L.G. 1.2.19), Major, 7th Brig. Aust. F.A.

MARGOLIN, E. L. (D.S.O. L.G. 3.6.16), Major, 16th Batt. A.I.F.

MARINDIN, A. H. (D.S.O. L.G. 1.1.18); b. 18.8.68; 2nd Lt., R. Highrs., 7.11.91; Lt. 16.2.96; Capt. 21.10.00; Maj. 24.5.10; Temp. Maj.-Gen. 27.3.18 to 18.3.19; Col. 2.6.19; *p.s.c.*; C.B.; S. Africa, 1899–1900, 1902; Despatches; Queen's Medal, 3 clasps; Europ. War; Despatches; Bt. Lt.-Col. 3.6.16; Bt. Col. 3.6.18.

MARINDIN, C. C. (D.S.O. L.G. 1.1.18); b. 6.7.79; 2nd Lt., R.A., 23.12.18; Lt. 16.2.01; Capt. 16.9.05; Maj., R.G.A., 30.10.14; Aden, 1903–4; Tibet, 1903–4; Medal, clasp; Europ. War; Despatches; Bt. Lt.-Col. 1.1.17.

MARK, A. W. D. (D.S.O. L.G. 17.9.17), T/2nd Lt., North'd Fus.; M.C.

MARK-WARDLAW, W. P. (D.S.O. L.G. 15.2.19), Lt.-Cdr., R.N.

MARKS, A. H. (D.S.O. L.G. 1.1.17), Major, Aust. A.M.C.

MARKS, D. G. (D.S.O. L.G. 3.6.18); b. 20.3.95, at Junee, N.S. Wales; s. of Montague and Elizabeth Marks, of Neutral Bay, Sydney; educ. Sydney; Senior Cadet; 2nd Lt. 30.6.13; 2nd Lt. (provisionally), 29th Inf. (Aust. Rifles), from the Senior Cadets 27.6.14; 2nd Lt., A.I.F., 20.11.14; 2nd Lt., 13th Batt. A.I.F. (Military Order, No. 652 of 1914); wounded, 1915; Lt. 25.3.15; T/Capt. 25.3.15; Capt. 20.1.16; Adjt., 13th Batt., 1.2.16; promoted to Major 11.11.16; Lt.-Col. 5.12.17; M.C.; Despatches three times; White Eagle of Serbia, 5th Class (with Swords). Lt.-Col. D. G. Marks was drowned, aged 24 years, at Palm Beach, Sydney, 25.1.20, in a gallant attempt to save the life of a strange woman (in surf); M.C.

MARKS, W. O. (D.S.O. L.G. 1.1.17); s. of late Dr. Marks, of Cork, and of Mrs. Marks, of 10, Kenilworth Road, Dublin; Lt.-Col., R.A.S.C.

MARKWELL, W. E. (D.S.O. L.G. 3.3.17), Major, Aust. L.H. Rgt. His D.S.O. was awarded for gallantry on 23.12.16, at Magdwaha.

MARPER, G. (D.S.O. L.G. 24.9.18), Capt., Aust. Inf.

MARR, C. W. C. (D.S.O. L.G. 26.8.18), Major, Aust. Engrs.; M.C.

MARR, F. A. (D.S.O. L.G. 3.6.18), Capt., Camb. R.; M.C.

MARR, J. H. (D.S.O. L.G. 3.6.19), T/Capt. (A/Major), R.E.

MARRACK, J. R., M.A., M.B., B.C. (D.S.O. L.G. 4.6.17); b. 26.11.86; s. of late John Read and Mary Marrack; m. Bertha Ada Fitzgerald Whiddington; one s.; educ. Blundell's School, Tiverton; Cambridge University; London Hospital; late University Professor of Pathology, Cambridge University; John Lucas Walker Student, Cambridge University; Beit Memorial Fellow; Fellow St. John's College, Cambridge; Chemical Pathologist, London Hospital; European War from 1914; was serving up to 1919; Despatches; M.C.

J. R. Marrack.

MARRINER, B. L. (D.S.O. L.G. 1.1.18); b. 22.4.88; 2nd Lt., R.A., 23.7.07; Lt. 23.7.10; Capt. 30.10.14; Maj., R.F.A., 20.6.17.

MARRIOTT, E. W. P. V. (D.S.O. L.G. 4.6.17); b. 28.9.73; Lt., R.A.M.C., 28.1.97; Capt. 28.1.00; Major 28.1.09; Lt.-Col. 1.3.15; ret. pay 10.8.19.

MARRIOTT, G. B. (D.S.O. L.G. 25.11.16); b. at Whalley Range, Lancs., 12.1.74; s. of Hail Marriott and Louisa Marriott; educ. Queen Elizabeth's College, Guernsey; enlisted 14th Hussars 1.8.92; served for six years as a Private and N.C.O., and on 15.10.98 was commissioned in the R. Warwicks. Rgt.; Lt. 21.3.00; Capt. 11.7.03; Adjt., Indian Volunteers, Aug. 1912; Major 1.9.15; on Special Service, S. Africa, Dec. 1901, and served in war with M.I.; served with 1st Batt. R. Warwicks. R., Bazar Valley and Mohmand Expeditions, N.W. Frontier of India, 1908; Europ. War; at the front from Aug. 1915, until Armistice, including the Somme, the Ancre, Messines Ridge and the German Offensive of 1918, commanding first the 8th Batt L.N. Lancs Rgt., and later the 1st Batt of his own regiment; Despatches.

MARRIOTT, J. C. O. (D.S.O. L.G. 4.6.17); b. 29.6.95; 2nd Lt., North'n R. 11.11.14; Lt. 10.5.15; Capt. 11.2.17; S. Gds. 20.1.20; Bt. Maj. 3.6.19; Despatches; M.C.

MARRIOTT-SMITH, H. R. W. (see Smith, H. R. W. Marriott-).

MARRYAT, R. (D.S.O. L.G. 1.1.17); b. 13.3.81; 2nd Lt., R.A., 22.11.99; Lt. 16.2.01; Adjt. 1.2.08 to 31.1.11; Capt. 1.4.08; Major 3.10.14; served S. African War, 1901–2; Despatches, L.G. 30.8.01; Queen's Medal, 5 clasps; Europ. War; Despatches.

MARRYATT, J. R. (D.S.O. L.G. 3.6.19); b. 22.9.85; 2nd Lt., R.E., 14.2.04; Lt. 23.12.06; Capt. 30.10.14; Bt. Major 1.1.18; Lt.-Col., Ret. Pay, 11.7.19.

MARRYATT, R. H. (D.S.O. L.G. 3.6.19), Lt. (A/Major), Worcs. R. (S.R.), att. 4th Bn.

MARSDEN, T. R. (D.S.O. L.G. 26.9.16), Capt., Aust. Inf.

MARSH, B. C. (D.S.O. L.G. 22.12.16); s. of Major-Gen. F. H. B. Marsh, Bengal Infantry (son of late Col. H. Marsh and Louisa, d. of Gen. Sir R. H. Cunliffe, 4th Bart.), and Sophia Frederica Augusta (who died in 1918), d. of Colonel R. Taylor; Commander, late R. Indian Marine; Europ. War (Mesopotamia), 1915–17; Despatches; retired 1921.

MARSH, F. G. (D.S.O. L.G. 1.1.19); b. 20.9.75; m. Ursula, d. of J. P. Haslam, J.P., Lancs.; two s.; three d.; 2nd Lt. 22.1.96; Lt. 22.4.98; Capt., I.A., 22.1.05; Major 22.1.14; retired pay; Brig.-Gen. 6.11.21; served N.W. Frontier of India, 1897–98; Medal with 2 clasps; Tirah, 1897–98; clasp; Europ. War, 1914–18; Despatches; Bt. Lt.-Col. 3.6.16; C.M.G.

MARSH, H. E. (D.S.O. L.G. 4.6.17); b. 6.11.65; Lt., R.A., 29.4.85; Capt. 1.4.95; Major 31.12.03; Lt.-Col. 13.3.13; ret. pay 28.5.20.

MARSH, J. F. H. (D.S.O. L.G. 1.1.18), Capt. (A/Lt.-Col.), Hampshire Regt.

MARSHALL, A. (D.S.O. L.G. 26.9.16); b. N.S. Wales 20.5.83; s. of W. H. Marshall, of Wilcania, N.S.W.; m. Winifred Anderson, d. of G. H. English, Naval Architect, of Stockton-on-Tees, Durham; educ. Sydney Grammar School; enlisted as a Bugler, Aust. Exp. Force, 1899; served in China, 1900; Medal and 2 clasps; Somaliland, 1902–4; Medal and clasp; with Australian Naval and Military Exp. Force in New Guinea, 1914; with A.I.F. in Gallipoli, and was granted a commission in the field 8.10.15; landed in France, March, 1916. His D.S.O. was awarded for gallantry on 10 April, and in Aug. 1916, at Bois Grenier. He was promoted to Captain for work in the field at Pozières 26.7.16.

MARSHALL, A. R. (D.S.O. L.G. 1.1.18), Capt. (A/Major), R.E., Spec. Res. M.C.

MARSHALL, C. C. (D.S.O. L.G. 29.10.18); b. 8.1.82; 2nd Lt., R. Lanc. R., 8.5.01; Lt. 19.11.04; Capt. 26.3.13; Maj. 8.5.16.

MARSHALL, C. F. K. (D.S.O. L.G. 1.1.18) (Bar, L.G. 2.12.18); b. 13.10.88; m. Dorothy Margaret, widow of Alan S. Lloyd, M.C., R.F.A.; 2nd Lt., R.A., 11.12.09; Lt. 11.12.12; Capt., R.F.A., 11.12.15; Europ. War, 1914–18, wounded; Despatches; M.C.

MARSHALL, E. H. (D.S.O. L.G. 4.6.17), Lt. (T/Major), R.F.A.

MARSHALL, F. A. J. E. (D.S.O. L.G. 4.3.18) (Details, L.G. 16.8.18); b. 7.1.95; m. Jessie A. (Nan) Munro; joined E. Kent Rgt. 11.8.15; Lt. 1.1.17; served Europ. War; Despatches; M.C.

MARSHALL, F. J. (D.S.O. L.G. 1.1.17); b. 20.8.76; s. of late J. Marshall, Advocate, of Duncrievie, Glenfarg, and Margaret, d. of Rev. J. Champion, of Edale, Derbyshire; m. Alice Maude, d. of late W. Horn, Advocate, of Woodcote, Blackshiels; one s.; four d.; educ. Rugby; R.M.C., Sandhurst; joined Seaf. Highrs. 28.9.95; 2nd Lt. 3.11.97; Capt. 19.3.01; Major 10.6.13; Bt. Lt.-Col. 3.6.16; Lt.-Col. 13.9.18; Bt. Col. 1.1.19; Colonel, Seaf. Highrs.; was T/Brig.-Gen. ; occupation of Crete, 1897; Sudanese Campaign, 1898; S. African War, 1901–2; Europ. War, 1914–18; C.B.; C.M.G.

MARSHALL, REV. G. H., M.A. (D.S.O. L.G. 22.12.16); s. of R. Marshall and Annie Elizabeth Marshall (*née* Gomm); m. a daughter of Rev. G. T. Carruthers, M.A., of Indian Army; educ. University of Manchester (Honours, School of Economics and Political Science); Deacon, 1913; Priest, 1914; served Europ. War, att. XIII. Div. M.E.F.; Gallipoli and Mediterranean Exp. Force, July, 1915, to Jan. 1916; Mesopotamia, Feb.–Aug. 1916; Despatches; attached Guards' Depot at Caterham, Jan. 1917; B.E.F., France, Oct. 1917–March, 1919; Vicar of Shelley, Yorks, 1920.

MARSHALL, H. A. (D.S.O. L.G. 1.1.18); b. 15.4.71; Lt., R.A., 4.3.93; Ins. of Ord. Machinery, 3rd Class, 26.1.99; 2nd Class 4.3.99; 1st Class 4.3.08; Chief Insp. 14.11.20; Lt.-Col., R.A.O.C., 14.11.20.

MARSHALL, H. S. (D.S.O. L.G. 3.6.16); b. 5.3.79; s. of C. Marshall; m. Violet Mabel, d. of J. Attfield; two d.; educ. Eastbourne College; Cooper's Hill (R.I.E.C.); ent. Army; 2nd Lt., R.A., 10.1.00; Lt. 3.4.01; Capt. 10.2.11; Major 16.10.15; was at Gibraltar and Malta till 1904; in India, 1904–14; arrived in India with 90th H.B., Nov. 1914; Egypt and the Dardanelles, with the Artillery of 29th Div., March, 1915; landed Cape Helles, April, 1915; evacuation, 1916; served France from April, 1916.

MARSHALL, J. D., M.R.C.S., L.R.C.P., M.B., Ch.M. (D.S.O. L.G. 1.1.17); b. 5.9.78; s. of Cornelius Marshall, Cotton Manufacturer, of Bolton, and Elizabeth Marshall; m. Dorothy Wilson, R.R.C., d. of the late William Wilson; educ. Bolton High School for Boys; Victoria University, Manchester, qualifying with Honours, 1905; was Senior Resident Officer, Victoria Hospital for Children, S.W., 1907–8. He joined the Army 10.5.15; Regimental Medical Officer to the London Rifle Brigade, and also to the 2nd Batt. The Suffolk Rgt.; Capt., R.A.M.C.; Despatches. His D.S.O. was awarded for Somme operations.

J. D. Marshall.

MARSHALL, J. S. (D.S.O. L.G. 1.2.17); b. 24.2.83; s. of late J. J. Marshall; m. Alice Deborah, d. of Major-Gen. G. Cree; 2nd Lt., Devon R., 3.12.04; Lt. 3.3.07; Capt., Ind. Army, 14.5.13; Major, 35th Sikhs, I.A.; Maj. 14.5.19; S. African War, 1902; Queen's Medal, 2 clasps; Europ. War (E. Africa), 1914–18; Despatches; Bt. Major 3.6.18.

MARSHALL, K. R. (D.S.O. L.G. 4.6.17); b. Toronto; s. of N. G. L. Marshall and Harriette Isabelle, d. of J. Hogg, J.P., of York Mills, Canada; m. Marion Janet, d. of A. Kirkland, of Toronto; one s.; educ. Upper Canada College; Vice-President of Standard Fuel Co., of Toronto, 1906; commissioned 48th Highlanders, 1903; commanded a company, 1912; Lt.-Colonel; went overseas with his battalion in 1st Can. Contingent, Sept. 1914; taken ill on Salisbury Plain and employed in England for some time; went to France as Staff Capt., 12th Can. Inf. Brig., May, 1916; served continuously in the field for 38 months, taking part in many battles, including the last phase of 100 days' semi-open warfare; Despatches three times; C.M.G.

MARSHALL, N. (D.S.O. L.G. 19.11.17) (Details, L.G. 22.3.18) (Bar, L.G. 16.9.18) (2nd Bar, L.G. 1.2.19), Lt.-Col., 54th Batt. Aust. Inf.; M.C.

MARSHALL, W. (D.S.O. L.G. 14.7.16) (Bar, L.G. 1.1.18); b. 10.4.75; s. of late Ellis and Mary Marshall; m. Lylie Horton, d. of late B. M'Grath; three s.; educ. All Saints', Bolton; H.M. Ship Conway, Liverpool; Apprentice, White Star Line Sailing Ship Copley; 3rd Mate, 1894–95; 2nd Mate and 1st Mate, 1895–98; 4th Officer to White Star Liner Cevic, 1899; served in Britannic (Transport 62) as 3rd Officer during S. African War; Sub-Lt., R.N.R., 1900; courses of Gunnery and Torpedo, Excellent and Vernon, 1902–3; afterwards served for twelve months as Lt. in H.M.S. Collingwood; appointed to command in White Star Line, 1911; on outbreak of war was in command of S.S. Afric, outward bound to Australia; taken over as a transport on arrival, and came home under convoy with 1st Contingent of Australian troops; landed troops at Alexandria; Commander, R.N.R., 10.10.14; in command of one of H.M. armed patrol vessels, Jan. 1915; Capt., R.N.R., 5.7.17; R.D.; appointed Special Service.

The Distinguished Service Order

MARSHAM, F. W. BULLOCK- (see Bullock-Marsham, F. W.).

MARSTON, G. S. (D.S.O. L.G. 1.1.19), Capt. (A/Major), R.E. (Spec. Res.); M.C.

MARSTON, J. F. (D.S.O. L.G. 1.1.19); b. 26.6.87; 2nd Lt., R.A., 23.7.07; Lt. 23.7.10; Capt. 30.10.14; Major 1.7.17; Major, R.F.A.; M.C.

MARTEL, G. LE Q. (D.S.O. L.G. 3.6.16); b. 10.10.89; 2nd Lt., R.E., 23.7.09; Lt. 20.12.11; Capt. 23.7.15; Bt. Major 3.6.17; M.C.

MARTELL, A. A. G. (D.S.O. L.G. 15.9.16); b. 3.1.84; m. Susie, d. of W. Colenso; two s.; educ. R.N. Engineering College, Devonport; Eng. Sub-Lt., R.N., 1904; Eng. Lt., 1907; Eng. Lt.-Cdr., 1915; Eng.-Cdr., 1920; H.M.S. Hood; took part in battles of Heligoland, Dogger Bank and Jutland; Despatches for Jutland.

A. A. G. Martell.

MARTELLI, H. DE C. (D.S.O. L.G. 1.1.17), Major (T/Lt.-Col.), R.A.

MARTIN, A. V. P. (D.S.O. L.G. 3.6.18); b. 20.10.80; 2nd Lt., Wilts. R., 5.1.01; Lt. 14.6.03; Capt. 6.4.09; Major 1.9.15; Lt.-Col., ret. pay, 5.5.20; S. African War, 1900-1; Queen's Medal, 5 clasps; Europ. War; Despatches.

MARTIN, B. W. J. H. (D.S.O. L.G. 26.9.17) (Details, L.G. 9.1.18), 2nd Lt., R.F.A.

MARTIN, C. K. CRAUFORD (D.S.O. L.G. 1.1.18), Lt. (T/Capt.), Can. F.A.

MARTIN, C. R. (D.S.O. L.G. 1.1.19), T/Lt.-Col., 20th (Service Batt.), K.R.R.C. (Pioneers).

MARTIN, C. T. (D.S.O. L.G. 4.6.17) (Bar, L.G. 16.9.18); b. 11.12.77; 2nd Lt., High. L.I., 15.5.97; Lt. 11.2.00; Capt. 23.1.07; Major (Actg. Lt.-Col.); S. Africa, 1899-1902; Queen's Medal, 2 clasps; King's Medal, 2 clasps; Europ. War; T/Brig.-Gen., Staff, 151st Inf. Brig., H.L.I. He was killed in action in France 27.5.18; Despatches.

MARTIN, C. W. (D.S.O. L.G. 20.10.16); b. 14.2.78; s. of late J. J. Martin; educ. Wakefield, and Yorkshire College, Leeds; commissioned 1901, I.Y.; served S. African War; in 1914 joined 8th Batt. R. Warwicks. R. as a Captain, and served on the Western Front; afterwards he was seconded for service with the Nigerian Rgt., and served in German E. Africa; Despatches twice. His D.S.O. was awarded for gallantry on 1.7.16, near Serre.

C. T. Martin.

MARTIN, E. B. (D.S.O. L.G. 1.1.18), T/Major (T/Lt.-Col.), R.E.

MARTIN, E. C. DE R. (D.S.O. L.G. 26.9.17) (Details, L.G. 9.1.18); b. 30.3.83; s. of Lt.-Gen. Sir A. R. Martin; m. Winifred Grace Alicia, d. of E. C. P. Hull; one s.; three d.; educ. Wellington; R.M.C., Sandhurst; 2nd Lt., Yorks. L.I., 18.1.02; Lt. 18.4.04; Capt. 18.1.11; Lt.-Col., ret. pay, 1.7.20; Europ. War, 1914-18; Despatches; Bt. Major 3.6.17; C.M.G.

MARTIN, E. E. (D.S.O. L.G. 3.6.18), Lt.-Col., Aust. Inf.

MARTIN, E. F. (D.S.O. L.G. 1.1.17), Lt.-Col., Aust. Mil. Forces.

MARTIN, E. S. D. (D.S.O. L.G. 3.6.18); b. 19.2.94; 2nd Lt., 5th D.G., 5.2.13; Lieut. 18.11.13; Capt., Dragoon Guards, 29.6.16; M.C.

MARTIN, E. T. (D.S.O. L.G. 23.10.19); b. 31.1.88; 2nd Lt., R.A., 18.12.08; Lt. 18.12.11; Capt. 18.12.14; Maj. 3.7.18.

MARTIN-LEAKE, F. (see Leake, F. Martin-).

MARTIN, G. H. (D.S.O. L.G. 14.1.16); b. 15.7.79; m. Mary Augusta, d. of late G. B. Rennie; 2nd Lt., K.R.R.C., 15.10.98; Lt. 7.1.00; Capt. 23.1.05; Adjt., K.R.R.C., 3.9.05 to 2.9.08; Major 1.9.15; served S. African War, 1899-1902; Queen's Medal with 4 clasps; King's Medal with 2 clasps; Europ. War, 1914-18; Despatches; Bt. Lt.-Col. 3.6.17; C.M.G.

MARTIN, G. N. C. (D.S.O. L.G. 2.4.19) (Details, L.G. 10.12.19); b. 23.12.92; 2nd Lt., R.A., 19.7.12; Lt. 9.6.15; Capt. 8.8.16; M.C.

MARTIN, H. (D.S.O. L.G. 4.6.17), T/Capt. (A/Major), R.F.A.

MARTIN, H. G. (D.S.O. L.G. 26.5.19); b. 28.2.89; 2nd Lt., R.A., 25.7.06; Lt. 25.7.09; Capt. 30.10.14; Maj. 12.2.17; O.B.E.

MARTIN, JAMES (D.S.O. L.G. 19.12.17), Chief Officer, Mercantile Marine (Lt., R.N.R.).

MARTIN, JASPER (D.S.O. L.G. 3.6.19); b. 20.7.79; 2nd Lt., R.A., 17.3.00; Lt. 3.4.01; Capt., Ind. Army, 17.3.09; Maj. 1.9.15; M.C.

MARTIN, J. E. B. (D.S.O. L.G. 3.6.19); b. 20.6.59; s. of late Col. A. P. Martin, of Fleetlands, near Fareham, Hants; ent. Army 23.4.81; Capt. 11.6.90; retired 3.2.97; Major; was Lt. Instructor of Musketry at Hythe; Inspector of Musketry in the Eastern District, and later in the Southern District, and Adjt. of the Post Office Volunteers; Equerry to T.R.H. Prince and Princess Christian, 1897; Comptroller of the Household, 1901-14; Controller and Treasurer to H.R.H. Princess Christian; is a Sergeant-at-Arms to the King; attached G.S., 20th Div., Sept. 1914; A.P.M., 20th Div., July, 1915; A.P.M., XIII. Corps, Oct. 1918; A.P.M., 3rd Area, April, 1919; C.V.O.; Companion of the Sword of Sweden; Chevalier of the Order of Leopold of Belgium; Belgian Croix de Guerre.

MARTIN, J. G. (D.S.O. L.G. 1.1.19), T/Major, 8th Bn. North Staffs. Regt.

MARTIN, J. H. (D.S.O. L.G. 3.6.18); b. 12.7.71; 2nd Lt., R. Lanc. R., 16.3.15; Capt. 23.12.17; Lt.-Col., ret. pay, 25.4.20; M.C.

MARTIN, L. T. (D.S.O. L.G. 1.1.18), Lt., Can. Rly. Troops.

MARTIN, O. (D.S.O. L.G. 27.7.18), T/Lt. (Temp. Capt.), Spec. List, att. King's African Rifles.

MARTYN, A. M., B.E. (D.S.O. L.G. 14.1.16); b. 5.6.81, at Armidale, N.S.W., Australia; s. of John Griffin Martyn and Hope Martyn (née Markham) (deceased); m. Stella Godfrey Swifte, d. of late Frank Swifte, of Tasmania; one d.; educ. The Armidale School, and Sydney University; Sydney University Scouts, 2nd Lt., 3.10.03; Lt. 28.1.05; Royal Australian Engrs., Lt. 9.6.06; Capt. 16.5.11; Major 1.6.18; left Australia as O.C., 2nd Field Coy., Engrs., on 21.10.14; Gallipoli Landing, 25.4.15; Lone Pine and Evacuation (C.R.E., 1st Aust. Div., with rank of Lt.-Col. from 19.11.15 till 5.4.18); France: all operations of 1st Aust. Div. up to 5.4.18, including Pozières, Somme, 1916-17; Passchendaele, etc.; C.R.E. Corps Troops, Aust. Corps, 7.7.18 to 7.11.18; operations of Aust. Corps, Somme, 8.8.18, and subsequently; C.E. Aust. Corps, Nov. 1918, to March, 1919, with rank of Temp. Col. from 1.1.19; C.M.G.; Croix de Guerre, France; four times mentioned in Despatches; Brevet Major, R.A.E., 1.12.15; Brevet Lt.-Colonel, R.A.E., 1.1.19.

MARTYN, A. W. (D.S.O. L.G. 25.8.17); b. 9.2.64; entered R.W. Kent R., 8.2.85; Major 2.8.02; ret. pay 19.3.04; Col. 25.2.19; O.B.E.; Soudan, 1885-86; Despatches; Medal; Bronze Star. His D.S.O. was awarded for gallantry at St. Eloi 7.6.17.

MARTYN, D. B. (D.S.O. L.G. 2.12.18), Major, 44th Can. Inf. Batt. N. Brunswick R.; M.C.

MARTYN-NASH, E. J. (see Nash, E. J. Martyn-).

MARTYN, M. C. (D.S.O. L.G. 17.12.17) (Details, L.G. 23.4.18); s. of Dr. Martyn, of Cromer House, Chesterfield Road, Mansfield; Lt.-Col., Sherwood Foresters; M.C.

MARX, J. L. (D.S.O. L.G. 23.3.17); b. 23.4.52; m. Celia, d. of Cdr. G. P. Heath, R.N.; one s.; one d.; ent. R.N., 1865; Cdr., 1888; Capt. 1895; Rear-Admiral, 1906; Vice-Admiral, 1910; Admiral, 1913; served River Niger, 1895 (Medal and clasp); Mombasa, 1895; A.D.C., 1905-6; retired 1913; served in European War as Commander, Capt., R.N.R., and Rear-Admiral afloat; Officer, Legion of Honour; Humane Society's Bronze and Silver Medals; M.V.O.

MASCALL, M. E. (D.S.O. L.G. 4.6.17); b. 28.4.82; 2nd Lt., R.A., 18.8.00; Lt. 4.7.02; Capt. 18.8.13; Major 30.12.15; Despatches; O.B.E.

MASKELL, W. C. (D.S.O. L.G. 17.12.17) (Details, L.G. 23.4.18), Lt. (A/Major), R.F.A.; M.C. He died of wounds 15.12.17.

MASON, C. C. (D.S.O. L.G. 19.11.17) (Details, L.G. 22.3.18), Lt.-Col., Aust. Infy.

MASON, D. H. C. (D.S.O. L.G. 19.8.16) (Bar, L.G. 2.12.18); b. 1883, in Toronto; s. of late H. Mason; educ. Ridley College, St. Catharine's, Ontario, and the University of Toronto (B.A.Sc.); joined the Toronto Rgt. on its formation at the outbreak of the war as a Captain, and came to England, Oct. 1914, with 1st Can. Contingent; became Major, and Lt.-Col. in 1919; was wounded at the 2nd Battle of Ypres, April, 1915, and at the Battle of Zillebeke, June, 1916; again wounded at breaking of Drocourt-Quéant Line, 2.9.18; Despatches twice; O.B.E.

W. C. Maskell.

MASON, D. J. (D.S.O. L.G. 1.1.18), Major R.F.A.

MASON, G. K. M. (D.S.O. L.G. 3.6.16) Bar, 8.3.19) (Details, 4.10.19), b. 26.5.87; s. of Sir W. P. Mason, Bart., and Edith, d. of A. M. Affleck; m. Grace Ellina, d. of N. Keen; one d.; educ. Eton; 2nd Lt., 14th Hrs., 29.8.06; Lt. 14.12.07; Capt. 3.5.12; retired with rank of Lt.-Col.; served Europ. War; was a regimental officer, 10.9.14 to 4.11.14, when he was wounded near Messines, with the 20th and 4th Hussars; served with Signal Service in France 10.5.15 to 15.7.15; served Salonika and Serbia, Nov. 1915 to 4.2.16, as G.S.O.3, 10th Div.; from 11.2.16 to 26.12.16, Brigade Major in Macedonia, and was Second-in-Command of Sherwood Rangers Yeomanry 26.12.16 to 8.1.18 in Palestine, being present at the capture of Jerusalem and of Damascus; torpedoed on journey to Egypt, June, 1917; Lt.-Col. to command Dorset Yeomanry, serving in Palestine 8.1.18 to 2.3.19; wounded.

MASON, H. F. (D.S.O. L.G. 3.6.19), T/Major, R.G.A.

MASON, H. L. (D.S.O. L.G. 27.10.17) (Details, L.G. 18.3.18), Capt., R.F.A., S.R.; M.C.

MASON, J. (D.S.O. L.G. 3.2.20), Capt., R.E.; M.C. He died 24.9.21.

MASON, M. F. (D.S.O. L.G. 1.1.18), Major (T/Lt.-Col.), Suffolk R.

MASON, R. H. MONCK- (see Monck-Mason, R. H.).

MASSEY, F. G. (D.S.O. L.G. 16.9.18) Lt., (A/Major), New Zealand Rifle Brigade; M.C.

MASSIE, A. E. (D.S.O. L.G. 4.6.17), Lt.-Col., Can. A.S.C.

MASSIE, R. F. (D.S.O. L.G. 1.1.18), Major, Can. F.A.

MASSIE, R. J. C. (D.S.O. L.G. 3.6.18), Lt.-Col., Aust. Inf.; Croix de Guerre.

MASSY, C. W. (D.S.O. L.G. 1.1.18); b. 2.5.87; 2nd Lt., R.A., 15.7.03; Lt. 15.7.06; Capt. 30.10.14; Major, R.F.A., 22.11.17; M.C.

MASSY, E. C. (D.S.O. L.G. 1.1.17); b. 5.10.68; m. Grace Mary, d. of late H. A. Burrowes, of Dangan Castle, Co. Meath; one s.; one d.; educ. Cheltenham; R.M.A., Woolwich; ent. R.A. 17.2.88; Lt. 17.2.29; Capt. 31.10.98; Major 26.3.04; Lt.-Col. 3.10.14; retired 1920; Brig.-Gen.; served Tirah Campaign, 1895; was in command of 5th London Territorial Artillery, when war broke out; took them out to France, March, 1915, and was with them at Festubert, Loos, Somme, etc., till promoted T/Brig.-Gen., March, 1917; commanded artillery of 52nd Division and 7th Indian Division in Palestine; Despatches six times; C.B.; C.M.G.

F. G. Massey.

MASSY, H. R. S. (D.S.O. L.G. 4.6.17); b. 5.1.84; s. of late A. W. Massy and Emma Elizabeth Massy (née Stokes); m. Maud Ina Nest, d. of Col. Roch; one s.; one d.; educ. Bradfield College; R.M.A., Woolwich; was First Whip of

Mr. Curwen's Foxhounds, Cumberland, 1913–14; 2nd Lt., R.A., 24.12.02; Lt. 24.12.05; Capt. 30.10.14; Major 22.5.16; served W. Africa, 1907–11; Europ. War; served in Gallipoli, subsequently with the 9th Corps on the Suez Canal; joined 31st Div. in France in 1916; was present at the Somme Battle, the taking of the Vimy Ridge, the German advance against the 3rd Army in March, 1918, and across the Lys in April of that year, and the 2nd Army operations in Belgium immediately preceding the Armistice; Despatches; M.C.

MASSY, S. D. (D.S.O. L.G. 3.6.16); b. 5.4.82; 2nd Lt. 8.1.01; Lt., Ind. Army, 5.9.03; Capt. 8.1.10; Bt. Maj. 3.6.15; Major 8.1.16.

MASTER, E. G. H. (D.S.O. L.G. 8.3.20), Lt.-Cdr., R.N.

MASTER, G. (D.S.O. L.G. 4.6.17); b. 9.9.82; s. of H. Master and the late Mary Jessie Master; m. Alice Mary (Molly), d. of the late Charles Phipps; educ. Bradfield College; 2nd Lt., R.E., 4.2.01; Lt. 4.2.04; Capt. 4.2.11; Adjt., R.E. Troops, 12.10.12–17.12.14; Adjt., R.E., 18.12.14 to 7.10.15; Major 2.11.16; served Europ. War in Belgium, Macedonia and France; C.R.E., 21st Div., July, 1918–March, 1919 (A/Lt.-Col.); Despatches three times; 1914–15 Star.

MASTER, R. CHESTER- (see Chester-Master, R.).

MASTERS, A. C. (D.S.O. L.G. 3.6.19); b. 15.10.88; 2nd Lt., S. Wales Bord., 25.12.09; Lt. 21.7.12; Capt. 28.4.15; M.C.

MASTERS, G. (D.S.O. L.G. 16.9.18); b. 9.7.75; 2nd Lt., R.A., 28.3.00; Lt. 3.4.01; Capt. 30.3.09; Maj., R.F.A., 30.10.14.

MASTERS, J. (D.S.O. L.G. 12.9.19), Major, 16th Rajputs, I.A.; b. 5.10.83; 2nd Lt. 27.8.02; Lt., Ind. Army, 27.11.04; Capt. 27.8.11; Maj. 27.8.17; Abor, 1911–12; Despatches; Europ. War; Despatches.

MASTERSON, T. S. (D.S.O. L.G. 12.3.17), Capt., Gen. List.

MATHER, J. H. (D.S.O. L.G. 21.1.20), T/Major, R.E. (Lt.-Cdr.), R.N.V.R.

MATHER, L. F. S. (D.S.O. L.G. 22.9.16), Major, Aust. Engrs.

MATHERS, D. (D.S.O. L.G. 14.11.16) (Bar, L.G. 17.9.17); b. 24.3.70; educ. Glasgow High School; ent. Army; commissioned R. Scots Rgt. 27.7.01; Lt. 23.1.04; Capt., R. Innis. Fus., 6.1.06; Lt.-Col. 13.7.19; ret. pay 11.11.20; served Chitral, 1895; Medal and clasp; Tochi, 1897–98; clasp; Tirah, 1897–98; Despatches; clasp; D.C.M.; S. African War, 1899–1901; Queen's Medal, 5 clasps; N. and S. Nigeria, 1901–4; Despatches; Medal, 5 clasps; Europ. War; Despatches. His D.S.O. was awarded for gallantry 11.6.17, at Costaverne Line; Bar for action at Messines; O.B.E.; Knight, Legion of Honour.

MATHESON, A. (D.S.O. L.G. 4.6.17), T/Capt., R.E., Spec. Res.

MATHESON, C. G. (D.S.O. L.G. 12.5.17), Lt.-Cdr., R.N.R.

MATHESON, G. MAC L. (D.S.O. L.G. 2.12.18), Capt. (A/Major), 25th Batt. Can. Infy., Nova Scotia Rgt.; M.C.; M.M.

MATHESON, J. C. MAC I. (D.S.O. L.G. 3.6.18); b. 2.10.92; s. of late D. Matheson, of Lochalsh and Glasgow; m. Isa, d. of late A. Gray; one s.; educ. Hutcheson's Grammar School; Glasgow University; Temp. Maj., M.G.C., 24.4.16; Capt., Cam. Highrs., 25.10.17; Major, late Q.O. Cam. Highrs.; served Europ. War, France and Italy; Despatches four times; Champion Heavy-Weight Boxer, Glasgow University O.T.C., 1918.

MATHESON, N. W. (D.S.O. L.G. 2.4.19) (Details, L.G. 10.12.19), Lt. (A/Capt.), R.E., T.F.; M.C.

MATHESON, W. M. (D.S.O. L.G. 16.9.18), Lt. (A/Major), R.F.A.; M.C.

MATHEW-LANNOWE, B. H. H. (D.S.O. L.G. 23.11.16); b. 9.7.72; 2nd Lt., 4th Dragoon Guards, Aug. 1894; Lt., Sept. 1895; Capt., 1902; Adjt., I.Y., 1905–8; Adjt., T.F., 1908–10; Lt.-Colonel, 2nd Dn. Gds., late commanding A. and S. Highrs., T.F.; served Tirah Exp., 1897–98; Medal with 2 clasps; S. African War, 1899–1900; Despatches; Queen's Medal with 2 clasps; Europ. War, 1914–18; Despatches; Bt. Lt.-Col.

MATHEW-LANNOWE, E. B. (D.S.O. L.G. 1.1.17); s. of late Major-General B. H. H. Mathew-Lannowe, R.E.; m. Mary, widow of A. T. Mackenzie and d. of G. Onslow Deane; one d.; Brig.-Gen., The Queen's Rgt., and commanding Tank Corps Training Centre; served N.W. Frontier of India, 1897–98; Medal, 2 clasps; Europ. War, 1914–17; Despatches.

MATHEWS, F. A. V. D. (D.S.O. L.G. 3.6.19), Lt. (A/Major), R.E., T.F.); M.C.

MATHEWSON, F. S. (D.S.O. L.G. 3.6.19), Major, 13th Batt. Can. Inf., Quebec Regt.

MATHIAS, F. M. (D.S.O. L.G. 4.2.18) (Details, L.G. 5.7.18), T/Capt., The Welsh R.

MATHIAS, L. W. H. (D.S.O. L.G. 23.8.18); b. 31.10.90; 2nd Lt., Unatt., 3.9.10; I.A., 26.10.11.; Lt. 3.12.12; Capt. 1.9.15.

MATHIAS, T. G. (D.S.O. L.G. 4.6.17); b. 12.8.78; s. of late Surg.-Major C. Mathias; m. Florence Davies; one s.; educ. Clifton College; R.M.C., Sandhurst; 2nd Lt., Welsh R., 3.8.98; Welsh R. 11.3.00; Welsh R. 30.12.04; Maj. 1.9.15; Europ. War, 1914–17; Despatches; Belgian Croix de Guerre.

MATSON, T. (D.S.O. L.G. 4.6.17), Lt.-Col., Aust. A.V.C.; S. Africa, 1899–1900; Queen's Medal, 5 clasps; Europ. War; Despatches.

MATTHEW, J. S. (D.S.O. L.G. 1.1.17); joined up on outbreak of war, and was afterwards attached to A.S.C.; became Lieutenant-Colonel, seeing service in Salonika and also in Egypt; C.M.G.; was awarded the Serbian Eagle.

MATTHEWS, A. B. (D.S.O. L.G. 19.10.16; b. 20.8.92; s. of Lt.-Col. W. H. Matthews, T.F., D.S.O., and Lena Penelope Matthews (*née* Young); m. Elsie Margaret Lazarus-Barlow; one s.; educ. St. Andrew's, Eastbourne; Oundle; Woolwich, Aug. 1910; 2nd Lt., R.E., 23.12.11; Lt. 24.3.14; Capt., resigned commission 1920; served Europ. War with Gen. Townshend's Force, and was taken prisoner by the Turks at fall of Kut-el-Amara; attached 22nd Co. 3rd Sappers and Miners, Nov. 1914; took part in the original landing at Fao, the capture of Basra (Despatches; M.C.), the first capture of Kut, the Battle of Ctesiphon and the defence of Kut (Despatches twice; D.S.O.); taken prisoner on fall of Kut and interned at Yozgat; Despatches three times; M.C.

MATTHEWS, C. L. (D.S.O. L.G. 3.3.19); b. 27.8.77; 2nd Lt., Durh. L.I., 4.5.98; Lt. 19.2.00; Capt. 22.1.04; Maj. 1.9.15; Bt. Lt.-Col. 10.3.17; S. Africa, 1899–1902; Despatches twice; Queen's Medal, 6 clasps; Europ. War; Despatches.

MATTHEWS, E. A. C. (D.S.O. L.G. 3.6.18); b. 3.8.73; Lt., I.M.S., 27.1.00; Capt. 27.1.03; Maj. 27.7.11; Lt.-Col. 27.7.19; N.W. Frontier, 1908; Medal, clasp; Europ. War; Despatches.

MATTHEWS, J. (D.S.O. L.G. 4.6.17); b. 28.12.71; Lt., R.A.M.C., 17.11.99; Capt. 17.11.02; Major 17.8.11; Lt.-Col. 26.12.17; S. Africa, 1899–1902; Queen's Medal, 3 clasps; King's Medal, 2 clasps; Europ. War; Despatches.

MATTHEWS, L. W. (D.S.O. L.G. 16.9.18), Major, Aust. Inf.

MATTHEWS, R. C. (D.S.O. L.G. 1.1.18); b. 30.6.73; Civ. Vet. Surg., 3 years; Lt., A.V.C., 16.5.03; Capt. 16.5.08; Major 10.7.15; ret. pay, R.A.V.C., 26.2.20; S. Africa; Queen's Medal, 3 clasps; King's Medal, 2 clasps; Europ. War; Despatches.

MATTHEWS, W. H. (D.S.O. L.G. 3.6.16); b. 14.7.64; s. of Marmaduke Matthews and the late Eliza Theodora Matthews (*née* Capper); m. Lexa Penelope, d. of the late A. Young; three s.; educ. Hastings and London University; Lt.-Colonel, 20th Batt. London R.; commissioned as Major in the T.F. on the outbreak of war; went to France in March, 1915, as Second-in-Command, 1/20th London Regt.; was given command of the 1/19th London Regt. during the Battle of Loos, Sept. 1915 (the C.O. of the battalion having been killed early in the assault), and was subsequently gazetted Lt.-Col. as from that date; in May, 1916, the command of the 1/20th London Regt. having become vacant, he was retransferred to and given command of that battalion; Despatches twice.

MATTHEWS, W. R., M.B., M.C. (D.S.O. L.G. 1.1.18); b. 1872; s. of Rev. T. T. Matthews, D.D., of Aberdeen, late of Madagascar; m. A. J. Pemberton; three d.; educ. Grammar School, Aberdeen; Marischal College, Aberdeen University; Surgeon to Hendon College Hospital; late T/Lt.-Col., A.M.S.; late A.D.M.S., 42nd E. Lanc. Div., B.E.F., France; Despatches thrice; holds T.D.

MATURIN, J. W. H. (D.S.O. L.G. 3.6.18); b. 20.5.72; commissioned Lt. A.S.C., 13.8.92; Major 1.4.07; retired pay 19.12.08; Lt.-Col., R.A.S.C., 6.5.19, S. African War, 1899–1902; Queen's Medal, 3 clasps; King's Medal, 2 clasps; Europ. War; Despatches.

MATURIN, R. G. (D.S.O. L.G. 28.1.02) (Bar, L.G. 1.1.18), Lt.-Col., R.A. (see "The Distinguished Service Order," from its institution to 31.12.15, by same publishers).

MAUD, H. (D.S.O. L.G. 1.1.17), T/Major, Gen. List.

MAUDE, A. H., M.A. (D.S.O. L.G. 1.1.17); b. 18.8.85; s. of Edmund Maude, J.P., of Crowborough, and Claudine Ida, d. of J. Pridmore; m. Dorothy Maude, d. of F. Upton; one s.; educ. Rugby; Oriel College, Oxford; B.A., Lit. Hum., 1908; M.A., 1912; Capt., Rugby School Shooting VIII., 1904; and of the Oxford University Shooting VIII. in 1908; entered A.S.C. (now R.A.S.C.), 2nd London Div., T.F., as 2nd Lt., 1909; Lt., 1909; Capt., 1912; Major, 1916; served Europ. War from 1914; Despatches; A/Lt.-Col. commanding 47th (London) Divl. Train, 1918–19, and 59th Divl. Train, 1919.

A. H. Maude.

MAUDE, C. G. (D.S.O. L.G. 3.6.18); b. 4.9.84; 2nd Lt., North'd Fus., 10.2.04; Lt. 3.3.06; Capt., R. Fus., 1.10.12; Bt. Major 3.6.16; Lt.-Col., A.E.C., 1.4.21; O.B.E.; N.W. Frontier, 1908; Medal, clasp; Europ. War; Despatches; M.C.

MAUDE, E. A. (D.S.O. L.G. 25.8.17); b. 10.7.82; 2nd Lt., R. Lanc. R., 8.2.02; Ind. Army 8.5.04; Capt. 6.7.09; Maj. 1.9.15; S. Africa, 1900–2; Queen's Medal, 2 clasps; King's Medal, 2 clasps; Europ. War, Mesopotamia, 1914–17; Despatches.

MAUDE, R. W. (D.S.O. L.G. 3.6.19); b. 1873; y. s. of late Hon. Mrs. Maude, d. of 2nd Baron Sudeley, and Capt. C. H. Maude; younger brother of Cyril Maude; m. Alice Thomson; one s.; educ. Charterhouse; joined Army, 1914; T/Major, Special List.; Major, and was first attached to 2/8th Gurkhas; was A.P.M., Bethune, Dieppe, Rouen, Amiens and Cologne; French Croix de Guerre; Despatches twice. He wrote "The Haymarket Theatre," with Cyril Maude.

MAUGHAN, F. G. (D.S.O. L.G. 14.11.16); b. 25.6.78; s. of Rev. J. A. C. Maughan and Mary, d. of the Rev. R. Sale; m. Grace Collingwood, d. of J. M. Maughan; one s.; educ. Durham School; 2nd Lt., Durham L.I., 4.1.99; Lt. 1.8.00; Capt. 3.5.04; Adjt., Durham L.I., 2.2.08 to 2.2.11; Capt.; Major 1.9.15; served Europ. War, 1914–16; Despatches; Bt. Lt.-Col. 1.1.19; Croix de Guerre (French).

MAUGHAN, J. M. (D.S.O. L.G. 26.9.16), Major, Aust. Inf. His D.S.O. was awarded for gallantry at Pozières on 26–27.7.16.

MAUGHAN, J. ST. A. (D.S.O. L.G. 1.1.17); b. 24.6.81; s. of late J. H. Maughan and Bertha Maughan (*née* St. Aubyn), of Marazion, Cornwall; m. Lilian Edith, d. of late J. Whitworth Hulse; educ. privately; Edinburgh University; Lt., R.A.M.C.; Capt., 1908; Major, 1915; posted on outbreak of war as M.O. to 18th Q.M.O. Hussars; D.A.D.M.S., 2nd Cav. Div.; 46th N. Midland Div., Jan. 1917; Despatches.

MAULE, H. P. G. (D.S.O. L.G. 1.1.18), Lt. (T/Capt.), H.A.C.; M.C.

MAULE, W. H. F., B.A. (D.S.O. L.G. 25.8.16); b. 1889; s. of late Rev. W. Maule; educ. Winchester and Magdalene College, Cambridge; 2nd Lt., N. Lancs. R., 14.9.14; T/Lt. 27.11.14; Capt. 15.8.16; served Europ. War from 1914; wounded once in the Ancre Valley and twice in the Ypres Salient; Despatches twice; M.B.E.

MAULE, W. J. (D.S.O. L.G. 1.1.18); T/Major, Special List.

MAUND, A. C. (D.S.O. L.G. 1.1.18), Lt., Can. Inf. and R.F.C.

MAUNDER, H. A. (D.S.O. L.G. 1.1.19), Major (Temp. Lt.-Col.), Aust. A.S.C.

MAURICE, G. K. (D.S.O. L.G. 3.6.19), Capt. (A/Lt.-Col), R.A.M.C. (T.F.).

MAURICE-JONES, K. W. (D.S.O. L.G. 8.2.18) (Details, L.G. 18.7.18); b. 31.8.98; 2nd Lt., R.F.A., 10.5.16; Lt. 10.11.17.

MAXFIELD, W. E. (D.S.O. L.G. 3.6.18), Major, Can. Mtd. Rifles; S. African War, 1899–1902; Queen's Medal, 4 clasps; King's Medal, 2 clasps; served in European War; when given the D.S.O. he had been in France just on three years, and had seen much fighting, notably at Vimy Ridge and Passchendaele; was wounded April, 1917.

MAXTED, G. (D.S.O. L.G. 4.6.17), Hon. Major (T/Major), Gen. List, A.I.F.

MAXWELL, ALLEN (D.S.O. L.G. 19.11.17) (Details, L.G. 22.3.18), T/Capt. (A/Major), R. Fus.

MAXWELL, ARTHUR (D.S.O. L.G. 24.6.16) (Bar, L.G. 1.1.18), 2nd Lt., 8th Batt. City of London Rgt., T.F.; Capt. 20.1.01; Major; served Europ. War from 1914. His D.S.O. was awarded for gallantry on 21.5.16, near Souchez.

MAXWELL, A. M. (D.S.O. L.G. 25.8.17), Capt., Aust. Infantry. His D.S.O. was awarded for gallantry N.W. of Messines 7–12.6.17; M.C.

MAXWELL, F. A. (D.S.O. L.G. 20.5.98) (Bar, L.G. 25.11.16), Major and Bt. Lt.-Col. (T/Lt.-Col.), 18th Lancers, I.A.; V.C.; C.S.I. (see "The Victoria Cross," by same publishers).

MAXWELL, G. A. P. (D.S.O. L.G. 1.1.17); b. 29.10.85, at Charlottetown, Prince Edward Island, Canada; s. of late W. F. Maxwell, Capt., R.N.; m. Agnes Duncan, d. of S. P. Ruthven; educ. St. Andrew's School, Tenby; Cheltenham College; ent. R.M.A., Woolwich, Sept. 1902; won Benson Memorial

Aquatic Sports Cup and Silver Medal at R.M.A., Woolwich; was Second String in the High Jump for Woolwich in the annual Athletic Sports against Sandhurst, and played in the R.E. Hockey Team, 1904–5, 1905–6, and 1911–12; 2nd Lt., R.E., 4.7.04; Lt. 16.3.07; Capt. 30.10.14; T/Major 25.4.16; T/Lt.-Col. 22.8.16; T/Colonel 2.7.19; D.A.D. of Railway Transport 5.8.14 to 24.4.16; Despatches seven times; Bt. Major 1.1.18; M.C.; M.V.O.; Officer, Order of Leopold of Belgium with Palm; Legion of Honour; French Croix de Guerre with Palm; Belgian Croix de Guerre with Palm; Deputy Chairman, Communications Section, Supreme Economic Council.

MAXWELL, J. (D.S.O. L.G. 1.1.18), Capt. (A/Lt.-Col.), The Rif. Brig. (8th K.R.R.C.); M.C. He died of wounds 4.12.17.

MAXWELL, J. McC. (D.S.O. L.G. 1.1.18); b. 26.1.65; m. Dorothy Frances, d. of the late Baron von Notting; ent. Army 15.2.84; Capt. 1.4.93; Major 15.3.00; Lt.-Col., R.F.A., 20.7.10; Col. 5.1.18; Brig.-Gen. 16.1.18; ret. pay, 1920; served Europ. War, 1914–15; Despatches; C.B.

MAXWELL, R. D. P. (D.S.O. L.G. 1.1.18), T/Lt.-Col., R. Irish Rgt.

MAXWELL-SCOTT, M. R. J. (D.S.O. L.G. 16.2.17); b. 22.10.83; s. of Hon. J. C. and late Mrs. Maxwell-Scott, of Abbotsford; m. Fearga, d. of late Sir N. O'Conor; one s.; educ. Downside and Beaumont Colleges; joined H.M.S. Britannia, 1898; Lt., R.N., 1905; Lt.-Cdr., 1913; Commander; served Europ. War; Despatches; Croix de Guerre.

MAY, E. R. H. (D.S.O. L.G. 8.3.19) (Details, 4.10.19), T/Major, R. Ir. Rifles, att. 1st Batt.

MAY, H. (D.S.O. L.G. 26.9.17) (Details, L.G. 9.1.18); b. 16.2.86; 2nd Lt., R.A., 21.8.15; Lt., R.F.A., 1.7.17; A/Lt.-Col. 9.2.19 to 21.4.19; Despatches; M.C. His D.S.O. was awarded for gallantry on 14–15.7.17, at Boisinghe and Turco Farm.

MAY, J. (D.S.O. L.G. 1.10.17); b. S. Africa, 19.10.78; s. of Staff Cdr. D. J. May, R.N.; m. Mary E., d. of Cdr. D. L. Dixon, R.N.; one s.; joined H.M.S. Britannia, 1892; first went to sea in H.M.S. Raleigh, Flagship on the Cape Station, 1894; Midshipman in H.M.S. St. George at bombardment of Zanzibar, 1895; landed in Benin Exp. from H.M.S. St. George, 1896 (Benin Medal and clasp); on outbreak of war was 1st Lt. of H.M.S. Thetis (Minelayer); A/Cdr., H.M.S. Orvieto (Minelayer), Jan. 1915; in command of H.M.S. Paris (Minelayer), 1916; Despatches.

MAY, L. (D.S.O. L.G. 15.2.19) (Details, L.G. 30.7.19), Major, Aust. A.M.C., att. 11th Batt. Aust. Inf.; M.C.

MAY, R. S. (D.S.O. L.G. 14.1.16); b. 10.8.79; s. of Admiral of the Fleet Sir W. H. May, R.N., G.C.B., G.C.V.O., and Kinbarra Swene, d. of late W. J. Marrow; m. Marguerite Geraldine Ramsay, d. of J. R. Drake; two s.; 2nd Lt., R.F., 3.8.98; Lt. 2.8.99; Capt. 3.11.03; Colonel 3.4.19; Major-General; served S. African War, 1899–1902; Despatches; Bt. Major 4.11.03; Bt. Lt.-Col. 3.6.16; Bt. Col. 1.1.19; C.B.; C.M.G.; Officer, Legion of Honour; Commander, Order of Leopold.

MAYALL, R. C. (D.S.O. L.G. 12.12.19), T/Capt., 11th Bn. North'd Fus.; M.C.

MAYGAR, L. C. (D.S.O. L.G. 4.6.17), Lt.-Col., Australian Light Horse; V.C.; (see "The Victoria Cross," by same publishers).

MAYNARD, P. G. W. (D.S.O. L.G. 1.1.19); b. 9.10.78; 2nd Lt., R. Ir. Rif., 18.10.99; Lt. 1.3.02; Capt. 28.6.08; Maj. 1.9.15; ret. pay 2.1.20; S. African War, 1899–1902; Queen's Medal, 3 clasps; King's Medal, 2 clasps; Soudan, 1912; Soudan Medal, clasps; Europ. War; Despatches.

MAYNE, A. G. O. M. (D.S.O. L.G. 25.8.17); b. 24.4.89; 2nd Lt., Unatt., 9.9.08; I.A., 9.12.09; Lt., I.A., 9.12.10; Capt. 1.9.15; Bt. Major 3.6.19.

MAYNE, H. B. (D.S.O. L.G. 1.1.18); b. 14.5.71; 2nd Lt., R.A., 13.2.91; Lt. 13.2.94; Capt. 18.10.09; Major 21.8.11; Lt.-Col. 1.5.17; Col. 1.5.21.

MEAD, O. H. (D.S.O. L.G. 3.6.19), Lt.-Col., 2nd Batt. Canterbury R., N.Z. Force.

MEAD, S. (D.S.O. L.G. 3.6.18); b. 23.11.82; 2nd Lt., R.A., 21.12.01; Lt. 27.8.04; Capt. 30.10.14; Maj. 1.5.17; served Europ. War; Despatches.

MEADE, G. W. (D.S.O. L.G. 4.6.17; b. 21.12.82; 4th s. of late Warren Meade; m. 1913, May, e. d. of Surgeon-General Howard Todd; educ. Cheltenham College; R.M.A., Woolwich; 2nd Lt., R.A., 21.12.01; Lt. 21.12.04; Capt. 30.10.14; Major 22.1.16: served Europ. War, 1914–19; Despatches four times; Bt. Lt.-Col. 3.6.19; M.C.; Croix de Guerre.

MEADE-WALDO, E. R. (D.S.O. L.G. 3.6.16); b. 17.2.81; e. s. of E. G. B. Meade-Waldo and Ada Coralie, d. of late Rt. Hon. Sir Richard Baggallay; m. Margaret Editha, y. d. of J. H. Gurney; one s.; two d.; educ. Eton; Sandhurst; 2nd Lt., Rif. Brig., 11.8.00; Lt. 21.1.02; Capt. 23.3.10; Maj. 1.9.15; Lt.-Col., Rifle Brigade; served Europ. War, 1914–18; Bde. Machine Gun Officer, 17th Inf. Bde., Sept. 1914–Oct. 1915: Bde. Major, Oct. 1915–Oct. 1916; Corps M.G. Officer, Oct. 1916–Feb. 1917; present at the Aisne, Ypres, Armentières, 1914; Ypres, June, 1915–March, 1916, including Hooge, Aug. 1915; The Somme, Arras, 3rd Battle of Ypres, fighting in March and April, 1918; operations between Ypres and the Scheldt, and many other actions; Despatches thrice; French Croix de Guerre. He was second (beaten by half a head) in the Regimental Light Weight Point-to-Point, 1910, on "Helen."

MEADEN, A. A. (D.S.O. L.G. 14.1.16); b. 15.6.76; Lt., R.A.M.C., 30.1.04; Capt. 30.7.07; Major 1.12.15; served Europ. War; Despatches.

MEADOWS, R. T. (D.S.O. L.G. 4.6.17), Major, R.A.M.C.

MEADOWS, S. M. W., M.R.C.S., L.R.C.P. (D.S.O. L.G. 1.1.18); b. 22.7.76; e. s. of late G. F. W. Meadows; m. 1903, Blanche, o. d. of Staff-Surgeon Sexton, R.N.; one s.; educ. Epsom College; Middlesex Hospital; London University; Lt., R.A.M.C., 1.9.02; Capt. 1.3.06; Maj. 1.6.14; served Europ. War, 1914–19; Officer Commanding, No. 2 Stationary Hospital, late Acting A.D.M.S., Abbeville Area; Assistant Inspector of Drafts and Sanitary Officer, Abbeville; Hon. Life Member, St. John's Ambulance Association; Despatches thrice; 1914 Star; in charge Garrison Dispensary and Military Families' Hospital, Gibraltar.

MEARES, C. F. (D.S.O. L.G. 1.1.18); b. 7.11.80; s. of late Col. George Brooke-Meares; m. 1919, widow of Lt.-Col. Russell, 9th Hodgson's Horse; educ. St. Paul's School; 2nd Lt., R. Ir. Fus., 23.5.00; Lt. 17.2.03; Capt. 16.7.10; Maj. 1.9.15; Bt. Lt.-Col. 3.6.19; served S. African War, 1899–1902; Queen's Medal, 3 clasps; King's Medal, 2 clasps; Europ. War in France; Despatches; Croix de Guerre with Palm.

MEARES, H. M. S. (D.S.O. L.G. 1.1.19); b. 14.4.88; s. of Percy N. Meares, Civil Engineer; m. 1915, Margaret S., d. of late Alexander M. Bredon, M.B., of Scarborough; one d.; educ. Bedford Grammar School; T/Capt. (A/Major), R.E.; served Europ. War, 1914–19; Despatches; M.C.

MEARES, M. (D.S.O. L.G. 1.1.17); b. 5.10.80; s. of Hugh Meares; m. 1907, Erna Murdoch, d. of Alexander Liddell; educ. Isle of Wight College; R.M.A., Woolwich; 2nd Lt., R.A., 22.10.99; Lt. 16.2.01; Capt. 1.6.06; Major 30.10.14; now Major, R.A.O.C.; served S. African War, 1901 (Queen's Medal, 3 clasps); Europ. War; Despatches five times; C.M.G.; Chevalier, Légion d'Honneur.

MEARS, E. L. (D.S.O. L.G. 1.1.17); b. 21.12.72; 2nd Lt., Wilts. R., 19.7.95; Lt. 10.7.95; A.S.C. 1.10.95; Capt. 1.4.00; Major 21.1.08; Lt.-Col., R.A.S.C., 30.10.14; served Europ. War; Despatches.

MEARS, T. I. N. (D.S.O. L.G. 1.1.17); b. 10.9.75; 4th s. of late Capt. A. Mears, Madras Staff Corps; m. 1902, Ethel Scobell, e. d. of Foster J. Bone; one s.; educ. St. Paul's School; 2nd Lt., E. Surr. Regt., 24.3.97; Wilts. R. 15.12.97; A.S.C. 2.1.99; Lt. 20.9.99; Capt. 21.4.01; Major 15.2.13; Lt.-Col., R.A.S.C., 15.7.17; served S. African War, 1899–1900 (Queen's Medal, 3 clasps); Europ. War, 1914–18; Despatches thrice; C.M.G.

MEDCALF, F. G. (D.S.O. L.G. 22.9.16), Capt., Aust. Force.

MEDILL, P. M. (D.S.O. L.G. 7.2.18); b. 15.5.82; 2nd Lt., R.A., 23.7.01; Lt. 21.4.04; Capt. 23.7.14; Maj. 29.9.16; served Europ. War; Despatches.

MEDLICOTT, H. E. (D.S.O. L.G. 3.6.18); b. 24.7.82; 2nd Lt., R.A., 2.5.00; Lt. 2.8.02; Capt., Ind. Army, 2.5.09; Major 1.9.15; Lt.-Col., ret. pay, 17.9.21; S. African War, 1902; Queen's Medal, 2 clasps; Europ. War; Despatches.

MEEKE, REV. H. C., M.A. (D.S.O. L.G. 3.6.18); b. 15.2.72; 4th Class, C.F., 4.1.05; 3rd Class 4.1.15; 2nd Class 3.6.15; served Europ. War; Despatches.

MEIKLE, J. H. (D.S.O. L.G. 3.6.19), Lt.-Col., 256th (Highland Bde.), R.F.A. (T.F.).

MEIKLEJOHN, J. R. C. (D.S.O. L.G. 1.1.17) (Bar, L.G. 11.5.17); b. 11.4.82; 2nd Lt., Bord. R., 18.1.02; Lt. 19.12.03; Capt. 22.8.14; Major 18.1.17; Bt. Lt.-Col. 3.6.19.

MEIKLEJOHN, N. S. (D.S.O. L.G. 27.6.19), Surgeon Lt.-Cdr., R.N.

MEIN, D. B. (D.S.O. L.G. 3.8.20); b. 7.12.89; 2nd Lt., Unatt., 8.9.09; Ind. Army 2.11.10; Lt. 8.12.11; Capt. 1.9.15; served Europ. War; Despatches; M.C.

MEINERTZHAGEN, R. (D.S.O. L.G. 2.2.16); b. 3.3.78; 2nd Lt., R. Fus., 18.1.99; Lt. 8.2.00; Capt. 12.10.04; Major 1.9.15; Bt. Lt.-Col. 3.6.18; served E. Africa, 1904; Medal and clasp; Nandi, 1905–6; Despatches; clasp; Europ. War; Despatches.

MELDON, P. A. (D.S.O. L.G. 3.6.16); b. 18.12.74; e. s. of Sir Albert Meldon; educ. Beaumont College; Dublin University; Professor of Artillery and Tactics at R.M.C., Canada, 1913–14; 2nd Lt., R.A., 28.3.00; Lt. 3.4.01; Capt. 4.2.09; Major 30.10.14; served S. African War, 1900–2 (Queen's Medal, 2 clasps; King's Medal, 2 clasps); Europ. War; Despatches.

MELDRUM, D. R. (D.S.O. L.G. 23.11.16), T/Capt., Gen. List.

MELDRUM, W. (D.S.O. L.G. 1.1.17), Lt.-Col., Wellington Mtd. Rif., N.Z. Force; C.M.G.

MELHUISH, H. M. H. (D.S.O. L.G. 3.6.19); b. 22.9.76; Lt., Ind. Med. Serv., 1.9.02; Capt. 1.9.05; Maj. 1.3.14; Bt. Lt.-Col. 3.6.17.

MELLARD, R. W. (D.S.O. L.G. 4.6.17); b. 6.10.83; Lt., A.V.C., 3.2.06; Capt., R.A.V.C., 3.2.11; Major, 3.2.21; Ass. Dir. of Vety. Services (Salonika), 28th Div., 11.8.15 to 6.7.18.

MELLIN, A. A. (D.S.O. L.G. 1.1.17) (Bar, L.G. 23.3.17), Lt.-Cdr., R.N.

MELLONIE, L. W. (D.S.O. L.G. 1.1.19), T/Capt. (A/Major), 16th Heavy Battery, R.G.A.; M.C.

MELLOR, A. (D.S.O. L.G. 3.6.16) (Bar, L.G. 26.7.18); b. 18.1.80; s. of C. W. Mellor, J.P., late I.C.S.; m. Barbara Janet, d. of late E. A. Smithers; one d.; 2nd Lt., R.A., 3.12.98; Lt. 16.2.01; Capt. 5.12.06; Major 30.10.14; Lt.-Col., late R.H.A., 24.7.20; S. African War, 1899–1902; Queen's Medal, 2 clasps; King's Medal, 2 clasps; Europ. War; Despatches; C.M.G.

MELSOM, A. P. (D.S.O. L.G. 6.4.18), Lt. (A/Lt.-Cdr.), R.N.R.

MELVILL, C. W. (D.S.O. L.G. 1.1.17); b. 5.9.78; s. of late Lt. Teignmouth Melvill, V.C., 24th Rgt., and Mrs. Melvill, of Lanarth, Bournemouth; m. Rita, d. of W. Burnett, of Te Tarata, Dunedin, N.Z., and niece of Sir C. Burnett, K.C.B.; educ. Wellington College; 2nd Lt., S. Lancs. R., 1897; Capt. and Adjt., 1906; on Staff of N.Z. Forces, 1911; Staff College, Camberley, 1913; went to France with S. Lancs. R., Sept. 1914 (wounded); G.S.O. to N.Z. Forces, Gallipoli, 1915; remained till evacuation; Brig. Major, N.Z. Rif. Brig., Egypt; commanded 4th Batt. N.Z. R. Brig., March, 1916 (including Somme), to June, 1917; Commander, 1st N.Z. Inf. Brig. till Feb. 1919; Despatches four times; Officer of Order of the Crown of Belgium, 1917; Croix de Guerre.

MELVILL, T. P. (D.S.O. L.G. 1.1.18); b. 13.2.77; s. of late Lt. Teignmouth Melvill, V.C., 24th Rgt.; 2nd Lt., S.W.B., 14.10.96; Lt. 1.4.98; Capt., 17th Lancers, 27.1.06; Major 24.2.15; served Europ. War; Despatches; Bt. Lt.-Col. 3.6.19; is a Member of the celebrated 17th Lancers Polo Team.

T. P. Melvill.

MENZIES, A. F. (D.S.O. L.G. 18.2.18) (Details, L.G. 18.7.18), T/Lt. (A/Capt.), R. Fusiliers. He was killed in action 4.5.18.

MENZIES, A. H. (D.S.O. L.G. 1.1.17) (Bar, L.G. 16.9.18); b. 15.11.78; s. of J. F. N. Menzies, of Bothwell, Lanarkshire; m. Katharine Robertson Henderson, of Edinburgh; one s.; educ. Blairlodge; served in Volunteer and Territorial Force for 20 years; Lt.-Colonel, H.L.I.; served Europ. War; wounded, Somme, July, 1916; Despatches.

MENZIES, G. F. (D.S.O. L.G. 3.6.16); b. 1.9.61; s. of Gen. W. G. Menzies and Elizabeth, d. of J. H. Burke; educ. Leamington College; Cheltenham; 2nd Lt., S. Lanc. R., 19.12.83 Maj. 5.8.02; ret. 1.9.11; Lt.-Col., Army, 26.9.15; N.W. Frontier, 1897–98; Medal, 2 clasps; China, 1900; Medal clasp; Europ. War, in France, 1915–18, as 2nd-in-command, 8th S. Lancs. R.; commanded 14th Durham L.I. for over 18 months at the front, including six months at the Ypres Salient; present at the gas attack on Ypres 19.12.15; commanded his battalion during Battle of the Somme; 14th Durham L.I. was mainly responsible for the capture of the Quadrilateral; Despatches.

MENZIES, J. (D.S.O. L.G. 4.6.17) (Bar, L.G. 15.10.18), Lt.-Col., High. L. Inf.

MENZIES, J. M. (D.S.O. L.G. 3.6.19), T/Capt. (A/Major), R.G.A.; M.C.

MEREDITH, A. P. O. (D.S.O. L.G. 18.7.17); m. Jean Grahame, d. of late Dr. H. P. Wright, of Ottawa; Major, Can. Inf.

MEREDITH, J. B. (D.S.O. L.G. 1.1.17), Lt.-Col., Aust. Mil. Forces.

MEREDITH, J. C. (D.S.O. L.G. 3.6.18); b. 12.11.86; s. of the late Master of the Rolls in Ireland; 2nd Lt., R.A., 23.5.08; Lt. 23.5.11; Capt. 30.10.14; Despatches three times; Croix de Guerre awarded on the field at Soissons. His D.S.O. was awarded for service in Italy.

MEREDITH, W. R. (D.S.O. L.G. 1.1.19); b. 24.8.82; 2nd Lt., R. Innis. Fus., 22.10.02; Lt. 25.10.05; Capt. 19.2.14; Maj. 22.10.17; Somaliland, 1908–10; Medal, clasp; Europ. War; Despatches.

MERRICK, T. (D.S.O. L.G. 1.1.19), Lt. (A/Major), A/87th Brig., R.F.A.; M.C.

MERRIMAN, A. D. N. (D.S.O. L.G. 3.6.16), Major, Irish Rifles.

MERSEREAU, C. J. (D.S.O. L.G. 8.3.19) (Details, L.G. 4.10.19), Major, 25th Inf. Batt. Nova Scotia R., Can. Mil. Forces.

MESSER, A. A. (D.S.O. L.G. 4.6.17); b. 24.12.63; s. of J. Messer, J.P.; m. Mrs. H. Ellis Hickes, who died in 1911; went to France, Sept. 1914, under B.R.C.S. with an Ambulance Car, serving with the 1st French Cavalry Corps and the 10th French Army; commissioned B.E.F., Feb. 1915; Lt.-Colonel. O.C.G.R. Units on the Directorate of Graves Registration Inquiries and Imperial War Graves Commission since 1919; C.B.E.; Chevalier, Légion d'Honneur.

MESSITER, C. B. (D.S.O. L.G. 11.12.16); b. 28.10.70; s. of late C. A. Messiter and Lucy Ashton, d. of H. M. Bagard; m. 1st, Alice Emma Mary (who died in 1909), d. of C. S. Lindsell, of Holme, Bedfords.; 2nd, Olive Blanche, d. of W. E. Moore; Capt., L. N. Lancs. Rgt.; served S. African War, 1900–2; Queen's Medal, 6 clasps; King's Medal, 2 clasps; Europ. War, 1914–17; Despatches.

METCALFE, C. H. F. (D.S.O. L.G. 1.1.17), Capt. (T/Major), Bedfords. R.

METCALFE, F. E. (D.S.O. L.G. 3.6.16) (Bar, L.G. 26.7.18); s. of F. Metcalfe, of Metcalfe Park, Enfield, Ireland; educ. Malvern; joined 7th Batt. Lincs. R., as Captain; transferred from the Northern Bengal Mounted Rifles Sept. 1914; commanded 7th Batt. Lincs. R.; served Europ. War from June, 1915; Brig.-Gen., Sept. 1918; Despatches six times; C.B.; C.M.G.; Chevalier, Legion of Honour.

METCALFE, F. H. (D.S.O. L.G. 1.1.17); b. 18.2.69; 2nd Lt., R.A., 27.7.88; Lt. 27.7.91; Capt. 25.11.99; Major 19.4.09; Lt.-Col., R.G.A., 1.1.16; served S. African War; Queen's Medal, 4 clasps; King's Medal, 2 clasps; Europ. War; Despatches.

METCALFE, H. C. (D.S.O. L.G. 16.9.18) (Bar, L.G. 16.9.18); b. 9.5.64; 2nd Lt., Northants R., 7.2.85; Capt. 30.5.94; retired 26.11.02; Lt.-Col., S.R.

METCALFE, J. B. (D.S.O. L.G. 16.9.18), Major, Aust. A.M.C.; M.C.

METHUEN, H. C. (D.S.O. L.G. 8.3.18) (Details, L.G. 4.10.19); b. 7.3.85; s. of late Col. C. L. Methuen, 79th Highrs.; m. Nell Gordon, widow of Major A. J. Usborne, R.F.A., and d. of the late Col. Gordon Price, I.M.S.; one s.; one d.; 2nd Lt., Cam. Highrs., 6.12.05; Lt. 1.4.11; Capt. 15.12.14; M.C.

METHUEN, J. A., M.I.Mech.E. (D.S.O. L.G. 11.12.16); b. 1878; s. of J. Methuen; educ. Stirling and Bridge of Allan; went to Rhodesia, 1902; joined Defence Force; commanded local forces in Umtali from 1909; served in S. African Rebellion, 1914; S.W. Campaign, 1915; with 1st Rhodesian Rgt. under Gen. Botha (Croix de Guerre; Despatches); 2nd-in-command, K.R.R.C., Dec. 1915; Lt.-Col. 14.11.16; twice wounded. His D.S.O. was awarded for gallantry at Schwaben Redoubt 16.10.16.

MEURLING, H. F. V. (D.S.O. L.G. 1.1.19), Major (A/Lt.-Col.), 2nd Mounted Machine Gun Brigade, Can. M. Gun Corps; M.C.

MEYER, I. J. (D.S.O. L.G. 22.8.18), Major (Temp. Lt.-Col.), 12th Mounted Rifles, S. African Forces.

MEYLER, H. M. (D.S.O. L.G. 1.1.19); b. 25.6.75; 2nd Lt., Middx. R., 5.5.00; Lt. 26.2.01; resigned 11.2.03; Capt., Border R., from Spec. Res., 2.10.15; M.C.

MEYNELL, F. H. L. (D.S.O. L.G. 1.1.17); b. 14.4.80; s. of late Hon. F. Meynell (Wood) and Lady Mary Meynell; m. Lady Dorothy Legge, d. of the Earl of Dartmouth; two s.; two d.; educ. Eton; J.P.; D.L.; Lt.-Col., 3rd N.M. Brig., R.F.A. (T.A.); Europ. War, 1914–17; wounded in France, at Wancourt 2.5.17; Despatches.

MICHELMORE, W. G. (D.S.O. L.G. 3.6.19), Lieut. (A/Major), R.E.; M.C.

MICHIE, D. K. (D.S.O. L.G. 1.1.18), T/Major, High. Light Inf.

MICKLE, K. A. (D.S.O. L.G. 26.7.17); b. 23.12.85; s. of David Mickle, for many years an Officer in the G.P.O., Melbourne, and Clara Mickle; educ. Queen's College, St. Kilda, Victoria, Australia, and Melbourne University; Capt., R.G.A.; served Europ. War. A newspaper correspondent in the "Melbourne Herald" writes: "Regret will be felt at the announcement of the death of Captain Kenneth Aubrey Mickle, D.S.O., R.G.A., which took place at Marine Parade, St. Kilda. Captain Mickle served for two years in France with the 9th Division of the British Army. He won the D.S.O. as Commanding Officer of the Division's Heavy Trench Mortar Brigade at the Battle of Arras, and was mentioned in Despatches on three occasions. Captain Mickle, at the outbreak of war, held the position of Metallurgist to the Burmah Mines. In 1912 he won the Grimwade Prize at the Melbourne University for original research work. He will be buried with military honours in the Brighton Cemetery. His death followed upon a long illness primarily caused by his being gassed while on active service."

K. A. Mickle.

MICKLEM, C., M.A. (D.S.O. L.G. 1.1.19); b. 1882; s. of L. Micklem; m. Diana, d. of W. Graham Lloyd, J.P.; educ. Wellington College; Hertford College, Oxford; Major; served with R.M.A. Howitzer Brigade in Gallipoli and France, 1915–18; Despatches twice.

MICKLEM, J. (D.S.O. L.G. 20.10.16); b. 13.9.89; s. of Leonard Micklem, of Elstree; m. 1917, Iris, d. of Sir A. T. Dawson, Bart., R.N.; educ. Winchester; 2nd Lt., R. Brig., 1910; Lt., 1911; Capt., 1914; Bt. Major, 1917; T/Lt.-Col., att. Glouc. R., 1915; Brig.-Gen., 1918; served Europ. War; wounded; Despatches four times; M.C. His D.S.O. was awarded for gallantry 1st and 22nd July, 1916, at Ovillers.

MIDDLEMAST, E. L. (D.S.O. L.G. 15.2.19) (Details, L.G. 30.7.19), Major, Fort Garry Horse, Can. Mil. Forces.

MIDDLETON, F. (D.S.O. L.G. 3.6.18), Lt.-Col., R.F.A.

MIDDLETON, S. A. (D.S.O. L.G. 1.1.19), Major, Aust. Mil. Forces.

MIDDLETON, W. H. (D.S.O. L.G. 4.6.17); b. 27.10.78; s. of late H. B. Middleton; m. Percie Vera, d. of late Rear-Admiral A. E. Dupuis; three d.; educ. Charterhouse; Merton College, Oxford; 1st com. Hants. R. 24.1.00; Lt. 12.7.01; Capt. 21.7.05; Major 13.6.15; Bt. Lt.-Col. 1.1.19; served with 1st Batt. Hants R., India, 1900–1; 23rd and 27th Batt. M.I., S. Africa, 1901–2; Hants R., S. Africa and Home, 1902–3; India, Aden, Somaliland and Home, 1903–14; Adjt., Home, 1913–15; France (in command Jan. to Dec. 1916), Nov. 1915, to July, 1917; North'd Fus. in France and Italy (in command, Sept. 1917, to Feb. 1919), July, 1917, to Feb. 1919; Lt.-Col. commanding Depôt, Hants R., Winchester, from Oct. 1919.

MIERS, H. J. (D.S.O. L.G. 15.2.19) (Details, L.G. 30.7.19), Capt. (A/Major), 2nd Batt. Mon. R., att. E. Lanc. R.

MIÉVILLE, A. L. (D.S.O. L.G. 3.6.19), Major (A/Lt.-Col.), Can. Engrs.; M.C.

MIÉVILLE, J. L. (D.S.O. L.G. 28.8.18), Lt.-Cdr., R.N.V.R.

MILBURN, B. (D.S.O. L.G. 20.10.16); mobilized T.F. to 25.11.16 (2 yrs., 60 days); 2nd Lt. (Temp. Capt.), Herts. Regt.; Lt., C. Gds., from T.F., 30.9.15; A/Capt., C. Gds., 7.5.19; Adjt., C. Gds., 7.5.19; served Europ. War; Despatches; M.C. His D.S.O. was awarded for gallantry on 27–28.7.16, at Delville Wood.

MILDRED, S. (D.S.O. L.G. 14.1.16); b. 6.1.72; s. of late W. Mildred; m. Norah, d. of R. Dibdin-Lewis; one d.; educ. St. Paul's School; R.M.A., Woolwich; 2nd Lt., R.E., 6.8.91; Lt. 6.8.94; Capt. 6.8.02; Major 13.11.11; Bt. Lt.-Col. 1.1.17; served R.E. with 4th and 5th Divisions; Europ. War; Despatches; Bt. Lt.-Col.

MILDREN, W. F. (D.S.O. L.G. 17.4.17), Colonel (Hon. Brig.-Gen.), Lond. Regt., T.F.; served Europ. War, 1914–18; Despatches; C.B.; C.M.G.

MILES, A. T. (D.S.O. L.G. 7.2.19), Temp. Major, King's African Rifles; M.C.

MILES, C. G. N. (D.S.O. L.G. 1.1.17); s. of C. S. Miles, of Brisbane; Major, Aust. Arty.; served Europ. War, 1914–18; Despatches.

MILES, E. G. (D.S.O. L.G. 4.6.17); b. 11.8.91; 2nd Lt., K.O.S.B., 3.6.11; Lt. 1.9.14; Capt. 25.1.16; Bt. Major 1.1.19; Despatches; M.C.

MILES, REV. F. J. (D.S.O. L.G. 1.1.17); b. 18.11.69; s. of Stephen Miles, Printing Machine Manufacturer, and Annie Miles; m. Isabella Killick; two sons; the elder, H. F. Miles, was killed in action 8.5.18; educ. West Australian Baptist College; Missionary in Ceylon, 1892 to 1900; held various pastorates in Australia, 1900 to 1914; Senior Baptist Chaplain for five years in Victoria; was appointed Senior Chaplain, Aust. Imp. Force; served Europ. War in Egypt; Canal Defence; through Gallipoli; in France and Flanders, at taking of Pozières; only Padre allowed front line; five days under constant shell fire; three days and nights without a break attending the wounded; 42 days in front line without a break, Bois Grenier Salient, May–June, 1916; at Administrative H.Q., London, from 1917, with quarterly visits of three weeks each to Padres at the front; Despatches; O.B.E.

MILES, L. G. (D.S.O. L.G. 22.9.16); b. 1.5.88; s. of G. H. Miles; m. Joan, d. of S. Gambier-Parry; one d.; educ. Harrow; T/2nd Lt. 1.1.15; Capt., The Black Watch, 8.2.17; served Europ. War, 1914–18; wounded; Despatches. His D.S.O. was awarded for gallantry on 8–10.7.16, at Bernafoy Wood.

MILES, R. (D.S.O. L.G. 26.7.18), Major, N.Z. F.A.; M.C.

MILFORD, E. (D.S.O. L.G. 23.10.19); b. 28.9.78; 2nd Lt., S. Staff. R., 4.5.98; Lt. 4.8.00; Capt. 4.5.07; Ind. Army 15.11.12; Maj. 1.9.15; Lt.-Col. 1.2.21.

MILFORD, E. J. (D.S.O. L.G. 1.1.19), Major, 4th Batt. Aust. F.A.

MILFORD, K. E. (D.S.O. L.G. 3.6.18); b. 9.11.80; 2nd Lt., R.A., 4.5.01; Lt. 4.5.04; Capt. 17.3.14; Major 23.9.15; served Europ. War; Despatches.

MILLAR, C. R. (D.S.O. L.G. 1.1.17); b. 30.12.78; s. of late R. C. Millar; m. Marjorie, d. of late Surgeon-Major G. M. Nixon, I.M.S.; educ. Dublin University; R. College of Surgeons, Ireland; Lt., R.A.M.C., 30.7.04; Capt. 30.1.08; Major 1.7.15; served in Ceylon and Sierra Leone; Europ. War, 1914–17; Despatches.

MILLAR, J. (D.S.O. L.G. 15.10.18); b. 25.1.79; 2nd Lt., R. Highrs., 17.11.14; Lt. 10.5.15; Capt. 27.3.17; Despatches; M.C.

MILLAR, J. McI. (D.S.O. L.G. 2.4.19) (Details, L.G. 10.12.19), Major, 85th Battn. Can. Inf., Nova Scotia Regt.; M.C.

MILLAR, J. W. J. (D.S.O. L.G. 26.11.17) (Details, L.G. 6.4.18), 2nd Lt. (T/Lt., A/Capt.), Notts. and Derby. R.; joined the Army about 1907, and on the outbreak of war was serving with 1st Batt. Sherwood Foresters in India as Machine Gun Sergeant. The unit was despatched to France in Nov. 1914, and was early engaged in the fighting at Neuve Chapelle. During this engagement Sgt. Millar was awarded the D.C.M., and was wounded on three occasions. As C.S. Major on 6.12.16 he was granted a commission "for services in the field," and was posted to the 17th Batt. Sherwood Foresters; A/Capt., Feb. 1917; again wounded July, 1917; D.S.O.; Despatches 7.11.17; Major 6.4.18, and temporary command of 16th Batt. S. Foresters; wounded for the fifth time 16.4.18; was sent home and retired with a gratuity 11.8.19, with hon. rank of Major.

MILLAR, W. J. (D.S.O. L.G. 2.2.16); b. 4.6.66; s. of Major J. S. Millar and C. Millar (*née* Donald); m. M. Tweddle; two s.; one d.; educ. Annan Academy; Heriot College, Edinburgh; joined Dumfriesshire Rifles as Bugler, serving in all ranks in this Corps, its successors, 3rd V.B., K.O.S.B., and 5th K.O.S.B.; Sergt. 7.5.90; 2nd Lt. 10.4.95; Lt. 23.10.95; Capt. 28.3.00; Major 22.6.11; Lt.-Col. 3.12.15; commanded 1/5th K.O.S.B. in Gallipoli, Egypt and Syria, 3/5th, 4th Reserve, and 5th Batt. K.O.S.B. at home; Despatches. His D.S.O. was awarded for services in front of Achi Baba; holds T.D.

MILLEN, L. H. (D.S.O. L.G. 1.1.18) (Bar, L.G. 11.1.19); m. Mary Morison Macfarlane, d. of Mrs. Gavin Scott Macfarlane, of Ottawa; Lt.-Col., 19th Batt. Can. Inf.; 1st Cent. Ont. Rgt.

MILLER, A. B. (D.S.O. L.G. 16.9.18), Temp. Lt., S. Staffs. Regt.

MILLER, A. M. (D.S.O. L.G. 22.9.16); b. 10.9.92, Swaziland, S. Africa; s. of A. M. Miller, J.P., and Beatrice Mary Miller; m. Marion Mary, d. of late T. P. Bagshaw; educ. Rhodes University, S. Africa; Technical College, S. Kensington; commissioned 10.9.14; T/Capt., Cavalry, and R.F.C.; Major, 5th Res., Cav. Rgt. and R.F.C.

MILLER, A. P. (D.S.O. L.G. 18.10.17) (Details, L.G. 7.3.18), Capt., Can. Inf., 1.7.14; M.C.

MILLER, C. F. (D.S.O. L.G. 4.6.17), Temp. Major, Duke of Corn. L. Inf.

MILLER, G. CHRISTIE- (see Christie-Miller, G.).

MILLER, G. R. (D.S.O. L.G. 1.1.19); b. 23.12.74; 2nd Lt., R.A., 23.5.00; Lt. 15.1.02; Capt. 15.1.11; Major 30.10.14; served S. African War, 1899–1900; Queen's Medal, 3 clasps; Europ. War; Despatches.

MILLER, G. S. (D.S.O. L.G. 3.6.18) (Bar, L.G. 15.10.18), Capt. (T/Lt.-Col.), R. War. Rgt.

MILLER, GEORGE WATERSTON, M.B., B.Ch., B.Sc. (D.S.O. L.G. 1.1.18); b. 1874; s. of Dr. J. W. Miller and Alice Miller (*née* Waterston); m. Maria Louisa Gilbert; one s.; one d.; educ. Dundee High School; Edinburgh University; Assistant Professor of Medicine, St Andrews University, 1909–19; Hon. Associate, St. John of Jerusalem in England; 1st V.B.R.H. and Q.R. V.B.R.'s, 1891–98; held combatant commission, 1st V.B.R.H., 1899–1904; Medical Commission, 1st V.B.R.H., 1904–8; 3rd Highland Field Ambulances, R.A.M.C. (T.F.), since 1908; Capt., 1908; Major, 1914; Lt.-Col., 1920, commanding 3rd Highland Field Ambulance;

served in France with 51st Div. from 1915; A/Lt.-Col., commanding 1/2nd H.F. Ambulance, 1918–19; Despatches twice; French Croix de Guerre with Silver Star; T.D.

MILLER, GERARD WILLIAM (D.S.O. L.G. 3.6.19); b. 7.2.95; s. of T. B. Miller, of 12, Savile Row, W.; m. Rosemary, d. of late C. Lacy Thompson; educ. Shrewsbury; R.M.C., Sandhurst; 2nd Lt., L'pool R., 12.8.14; Lt. 12.1.15; Capt. 25.2.20; M.C.; Chevalier de l'Ordre de Léopold; Belgian Croix de Guerre.

MILLER, H. (D.S.O. L.G. 1.1.18), Staff Paymaster (A/Fleet Paymaster), R.N.

MILLER, H. G. B. (D.S.O. L.G. 1.1.18); b. 9.9.80; 2nd Lt., R. Sc. Fus., 24.7.01; Capt. 22.1.12; Bt. Lt.-Col. 1.1.19; Lt.-Col., ret. pay (Res. of Off.), 8.10.21; S. African War, 1899–1901; Queen's Medal, 3 clasps; Europ. War; Despatches; M.C.

MILLER, J. (D.S.O. L.G. 3.6.19), Capt. (A/Lt.-Col.), R.A.M.C.; M.C.

MILLER, J. A. (D.S.O. L.G. 16.9.18); b. 18.2.91; s. of T. Brand Miller; m. Doris S. Freund; educ. Buxton College; Manchester Grammar School; served before the war in 6th Manchester R.; at outbreak of war joined 4th Camerons; commissioned 2nd London R. 16.1.15; Capt. and Adjt.; 2nd-in-command; in command 2/2nd London R., as A/Lt.-Col.; Permanent Capt., T.F., 1918; demobilized 7.2.19; Despatches thrice.

MILLER, J. S. (D.S.O. L.G. 1.1.17), T/Capt., M.G. Corps.

MILLER, L. C. (D.S.O. L.G. 18.7.18), T/Lt. (A/Major), R.G.A. His D.S.O. was awarded for gallantry at Feuchy Chapelle 16–22.4.17.

MILLER, L. W. (D.S.O. L.G. 3.6.18), Major, Mounted Rifles, Can. Force.

MILLER, R. M., M.B., B.C.Camb., M.R.C.S., L.R.C.P. (D.S.O. L.G. 1.1.17); s. of late R. Miller; m. Annie, d. of late T. Mortimer Kelson, Capt., 6th Royal Rgt.; one d.; educ. Cambridge; St. Bartholomew's Hospital; late Senior House Surgeon, Metropolitan Hospital; Senior Casualty Officer, East London Hospital for Children; served Europ. War, 1914–18; Despatches.

MILLER, S. (D.S.O. L.G. 3.6.18), Capt. (A/Lt.-Col.), R.A.M.C.; M.C.

MILLER, T. E. (D.S.O. L.G. 8.3.19) (Details, L.G. 4.10.19), Lt., 8th Inf. Batt. Manitoba R.; M.M.

MILLER, W. (D.S.O. L.G. 3.6.18); b. 30.3.74; 2nd Lt., S. Staff. R., 5.5.00; Lt. 16.12.01; Capt., Midd'x R., 18.2.05; Maj. 1.9.15; Bt. Lt.-Col. 3.6.16; S. African War, 1899–1902; Queen's Medal, 4 clasps; King's Medal, 2 clasps; Europ. War; Despatches.

MILLER, W. A., M.B. (D.S.O. L.G. 24.6.16) (Details, L.G. 27.7.16); b. 1883; s. of late Rev. R. Miller, M.A., F.E.I.S.; educ. Geo. Watson's College; University, Edinburgh; Lt., R.A.M.C., 1911; Capt., 1915; Major, 1917; served Europ. War, 1914–17; Despatches; M.C. and Bar.

MILLER, REV. W. H. L., B.A. (D.S.O. L.G. 1.1.18), C.F., 4th Class, T/C.F., 2nd Class; A. Ch. Dept.

MILLIGAN, H. L. (D.S.O. L.G. 1.1.17), Lt.-Col., Can. Engrs.

MILLIGAN, J. (D.S.O. L.G. 1.1.17), Major, R.F.A.

MILLIGAN, J. W. (D.S.O. L.G. 1.1.18), Major, E. African Supply Corps.

MILLIGAN, R. G. (D.S.O. L.G. 1.1.19), Major, New Zealand F.A.

MILLIGAN, STANLEY LYNDALL (D.S.O. L.G. 1.1.17) (gazetted as Milligan, Stanley Lynall), Major, Aust. Mil. Forces.

MILLIS, C. H. G. (D.S.O. L.G. 24.9.18); b. 1894; s. of C. T. Millis; m. Violet, d. of late H. J. Gifford; one s.; Capt., late The Sherwood Foresters; served Europ. War, 1914–18; Despatches; M.C.

MILLNER, G. E. (D.S.O. L.G. 1.1.18); b. 18.3.84; s. of G. M. Millner and Harriet Mary Millner (*née* Butler); educ. Paris; Heidelberg; joined 24th London R. (The Queen's), 1908; Major; served Europ. War, 1915; Despatches twice; M.C.; commanded 1st Batt. 1917–18.

MILLS, A. J. (D.S.O. L.G. 12.12.19), Lt.-Col., 15th Aust. L.H. Rgt.

MILLS, A. L. S., B.A., B.C.L. (D.S.O. L.G. 18.7.17); b. 27.6.90; s. of the Rt. Rev. W. L. Mills, D.D., LL.D., D.C.L., Bishop of Ontario; educ. Brockville, Ontario, Canada; Merton College, Oxford; McGill University, Montreal; B.A. (Oxon), 1911; Honours, English Literature; B.C.L. (McGill), 1914; 1st Class Honours, Law; Merton College, Oxford, Cricket, Rugger and Lawn Tennis Teams; McGill University Cricket and Lawn Tennis Teams (Capt., 1912–13); Intercollegiate Tennis Champion of Canada; Singles, 1912; Doubles, 1913; Doubles Champion of Province of Quebec, 1914; received commission 20.9.14 in 5th Royal Highlanders of Canada; seconded Oct. 1914, to 24th Canadian Bn. Victoria Rifles of Canada (2nd Cdn. Div.); Major; went to France, Sept. 1915, with 2nd Canadian Division; served at Kemmel, St. Eloi (crater fighting), Ypres, Somme (Courcelette), Bully Grenay (Loos), Neuville St. Vaast (Vimy Ridge) and Fresnoy. His D.S.O. was awarded for gallantry at Vimy Ridge.

A. L. S. Mills.

MILLS, A. M. (D.S.O. L.G. 1.1.17) (1st Bar, L.G. 4.2.18) (Details, L.G. 5.7.18) (2nd Bar, L.G. 8.3.19) (Details, L.G. 4.10.19); b. 13.8.79; 2nd Lt., Devon R., 4.5.01; 2nd Ind. Army 10.10.02; Lt. 1.8.03; Capt. 29.3.10; Major, 18th Lancers, I.A., 29.3.16; served S. African War, 1901–2; Queen's Medal, 3 clasps; Europ. War; Despatches; late commanding S. Batt. Linc. Fus.

MILLS, A. S. (D.S.O. L.G. 18.10.17) (Details, L.G. 7.3.18), Lt. (A/Major), Can. Inf.

MILLS, F., M.I.C.E., M.I.M.E., F.R.G.S., F.Z.S. (D.S.O. L.G. 16.8.17); b. 30.4.72; s. of late F. Mills; m. Winifred Jessie, d. of J. Rice Roberts, M.A., D.L., J.P.; one s.; served in M.I.; Lieutenant's commission in the Federated Malay States, 1902; Capt., 1904; joined 1/6th Batt. R.W.F., as Company Commander, Sept. 1914; Commander of Batt., 1917; Lt.-Col., R.W.F., commanding 6th Batt. R.W.F.; Despatches twice; served at Landing, and for six months in Gallipoli, and for three years in Egypt and Palestine. His D.S.O. was awarded for gallantry in Egypt 26.3.17.

MILLS, G. P. (D.S.O. L.G. 4.6.17); b. 8.1.67; s. of W. D. Mills and Charlotte Elizabeth, d. of Capt. G. Pilkington, R.E.; m. Mary, d. of late W. Larkins; one s.; educ. Liverpool University; joined 5th Batt. Bedfords. R., 1889; Lt., 1891; Capt., 1896; Major, 1903; retired 1906. On outbreak of war appointed 2nd-in-command, 7th S. Batt. Bedfords. R.; served with 18th Div. in France and Flanders, 1914–18 (Despatches thrice; promoted Lt.-Colonel); commanded 54th Inf. Brig., Nov. and Dec. 1917, during operations in Houlthost Forest.

MILLS, J. E. (D.S.O. L.G. 3.6.16); b. 3.11.78; s. of Dr. J. Mills; m. Mildred, d. of E. G. Meredith, of Quebec; three s.; two d.; educ. Guelph Collegiate; Univ. of Toronto; joined Canadian Militia; commissioned 16th Guelph Field Battery, 1899; Permanent Force of Canada, 1903; Capt., 1905; Major, 1911; Lt.-Col., 1915; Col., 1916; R. Can. Horse Artillery, commanding Can. Res. Arty., Shorncliffe; joined Can. Exp. Force, Aug. 1914; served in France 1.2.15 to 30.5.15; in Gallipoli, with 13th Div. from July, and present during evacuation in January; Despatches.

MILLWARD, W. C. (D.S.O. L.G. 27.10.17) (Details, L.G. 18.3.18); b. 6.11.86; s. of Arthur Millward and Sarah Donald Millward (*née* Orr); m. Gladys Irene Vaughan Parcy; one d.; att. 11th Batt. R. Sussex R., 9.9.14; 2nd Lt. 1.11.14; Lt. 10.2.15; Capt. 10.8.15; Major 21.7.16; Lt.-Col. 3.8.16; went to France 15.3.16; served on the Somme, 1916; Ypres Salient, 1916–18; Somme, 1918; Lt.-Col. in command 116th Inf. Brig. 18.3.18 to 29.3.18; wounded; left leg amputated above the knee; retired 26.9.19.

MILMAN, O. R. E. (D.S.O. L.G. 1.1.17); b. 23.4.82; 2nd Lt., R.A., 18.8.00; Lt. 8.9.02; Capt. 18.8.13; Bt. Major 29.11.15; Major 30.12.15.

MILNE, E. O. (D.S.O. L.G. 3.6.16); b. Bundanoon, N.S.W., 8.11.86; s. of Col. E. Milne, J.P., F.R.S., and Emily, d. of J. Cork; left Australia as Lieut. in charge of 1st Aust. Railway Supply Detachment; Major at Anzac, controlling the Army Corps Supplies, and also the Anzac Tramways, and after the evacuation, the Desert Light Railways at Ferry Post and Serapeum, Suez Canal.

MILNE, J. A. (D.S.O. L.G. 25.8.17), Lt.-Colonel, 36th Battalion, Australian Expeditionary Force. His D.S.O. was awarded for gallantry at St. Yves 7–12.6.17. He was killed in action.

MILNE, J. E., M.A., M.D., Ch.M. (D.S.O. L.G. 20.10.16); b. 30.9.68, at Fraserburgh, Aberdeenshire; s. of Capt. James Milne, Mercantile Marine Service, and Jessie Milne (*née* Mitchell), deceased; educ. Old Aberdeen Grammar School; Aberdeen Grammar School; Aberdeen University (M.A., M.B. and C.M. with Honours, 1891; M.D. with Honours, 1894). He applied for a commission in the R.A.M.C. (T.) in April, 1915, and a few days after receiving his commission sailed with Col. Ogston and the Highland Casualty Clearing Station, and subsequently became M.O., King's Liverpool Rgt. "In due course Ellis Milne passed into the Cauldron of the Somme. He established his aid post in the front-line trenches, and went over the parapet to bring in the wounded. He chose the position himself to be near to the men who fell in No Man's Land." Captain Milne was killed in action 22.2.17; mentioned in Sir D. Haig's Despatch, Jan. 1917. His D.S.O. was awarded for gallantry at Guillemont on 31.7.16.

J. E. Milne.

MILNE, T. (D.S.O. L.G. 12.12.19); b. 24.2.82; 2nd Lt. 8.5.01; Lt., Ind. Army, 8.8.03; Capt. 8.5.10; Maj. 8.5.16; N.W. Frontier, 1908; Medal, clasp; Europ. War; Despatches.

MILNER-WHITE, REV. E. M., M.A. (D.S.O. L.G. 1.1.18); b. 23.4.84; s. of Sir H. Milner-White, and 1st wife, Kathleen Lucy (who died in 1890), d. of C. Meeres, M.R.C.S.; educ. Harrow; King's College, Cambridge (Scholar); Cuddesdon Theological College; 1st Class Historical Tripos, Pt. 1., 1905; University Lightfoot Scholar, 1906; 1st Class Historical Tripos, Pt. II., 1907; Deacon, 1908; Priest, 1909; Fellow and Dean of King's College, Cambridge; Chaplain to the Forces, B.E.F., 1914; served with 7th Div.; S.C.F., 7th Div., 1917.

MILSOM, C. F. (D.S.O. L.G. 1.1.18); b. 28.7.81; s. of F. H. Milsom; m. Lucy Gwladys, d. of Sir R. A. Morris, Bart.; two d.; educ. Bath College; Trin. College, Cambridge; 2nd Lt., A.S.C., 25.7.03; Lt. 31.3.05; Capt. 4.5.12; Major 1.8.15; ret. pay, R.A.S.C., 16.1.19; served Europ. War; Despatches thrice.

MILWARD, C. A. (D.S.O. L.G. 4.6.17); b. 20.5.77; 2nd Lt., Unatt., 4.8.97; Lt., I.A., 25.10.00; Capt. 4.8.06; Major, I.A., 4.8.15; Despatches; Bt. Lt.-Col. 4.6.17.

MILWARD, H. M. (D.S.O. L.G. 1.1.17) (Bar, L.G. 1.1.18); b. 22.9.81; s. of late L. M. Milward, J.P.; m. May Braithwayte, d. of A. Heymann, J.P.; educ. Cheltenham College; 2nd Lt., Notts. and Derby. R., 5.1.01; Lt. 12.9.01; Capt. 7.12.08; Maj. 8.5.16; S. African War, 1899–1902; Despatches; Queen's Medal, 3 clasps; King's Medal, 2 clasps; Europ. War, 1914–18; Despatches three times; Bt. Lt.-Col. 1.1.19; Chevalier Légion d'Honneur.

MINAGALL, C. F. (D.S.O. L.G. 1.1.18), Major, Aust. Inf.

MINCHIN, F. F. (D.S.O. L.G. 1.1.18); s. of Major-Gen. F. P. Minchin and the late Margery Minchin; Lt.-Col., R.A.F.; M.C.

MINCHIN, J. B. (D.S.O. L.G. 15.10.18), Lt., Aust. Mil. Forces; M.C.

MINCHIN, T. W. (D.S.O. L.G. 14.11.16), 2nd Lt., G. Guards, S.R. His D.S.O. was awarded for gallantry on 14.9.16, near Ginchy.

MINET, E. C. T. (D.S.O. L.G. 18.10.17) (Details, L.G. 7.3.18), T/Lt. (A/Capt.), M.G. Corps; M.C.

MINOGUE, M. J. (D.S.O. L.G. 3.6.18); b. 23.2.78; 2nd Lt., Manch. R., 3.9.02; Lt. 21.4.04; Capt. 1.4.10; Maj. 24.7.16; S. African War, 1899–1902; Queen's Medal, 5 clasps; King's Medal, 2 clasps; Europ. War; Despatches.

MINNS, A. N. (D.S.O. L.G. 22.12.16); b. 28.3.91; Lt., R.A.M.C., 1.1.17; Capt. 26.3.18; Despatches; M.C.

MINSHALL, T. H. (D.S.O. L.G. 1.1.18), T/Col., Gen. List.

MINSHULL-FORD, J. M. (D.S.O. L.G. 1.1.17); b. 12.5.81; s. of late Capt. Minshull-Ford, J.P., 8th (The King's) Rgt.; m. Dorothy, d. of Sir J. Harmood-Banner, M.P.; one s.; one d.; educ. Twyford School, Winchester; Haileybury; Sandhurst; joined 2nd Batt. R.W. Fus., 1900; Capt., 1st Batt., 1911; Adjt., 4th Batt., 1912; joined 1st Batt. Exp. Force, France, Oct. 1914; commanded 1.11.14–March, 1915; wounded at Neuve Chapelle; Staff, April to Sept. 1915; commanded 1st R.W.F., Sept. 1915–Feb. 1916; Brig.-Gen. 3.2.16; wounded 14.7.16 and 4.6.17; Despatches six times; Bt. Major; Bt. Lt.-Col.; M.C.

MITCHELL, ALEXANDER (D.S.O. L.G. 3.6.19), 13th Aust. L.H. Rgt.

MITCHELL, ARTHUR (D.S.O. L.G. 1.1.18); b. 10.7.76; 2nd Lt., R.A., 21.9.96; Lt. 21.9.99; Capt. 22.1.02; Adjt., R.A., 21.6.12 to 22.3.14; Major, R.G.A., 30.10.14; Despatches.

MITCHELL, A. M. (D.S.O. L.G. 1.1.18) (Bar, L.G. 22.4.18); b. 8.4.78; s. of A. Mitchell, of Leith, and Annie, d. of Alex. Alexander; m. Jessie Mitchell Campbell, d. of W. W. Campbell; two s.; one d.; educ. R. High School, Edinburgh; Blairlodge School, Polmont; joined Volunteers, 1897; 2nd Lt., R.A., 21.9.96; Lt. 21.9.99; Capt. 22.1.02; Major 30.10.14; Lt.-Colonel, commanding

The Distinguished Service Order 307

1/4th Batt. The R. Scots, June, 1917–April, 1919; Lt.-Col. 1.5.21; mentioned in Despatches by Gen. Murray, Egypt, dated 18.3.17, L.G. 16.7.17, and again dated 28.6.17, L.G. 12.1.18.

MITCHELL, C. (D.S.O. L.G. 1.1.18); b. 8.1.83; 2nd Lt., G. Gds., 1.2.07; Lt. 25.12.07; resigned 11.7.08 (R. of O. employed (to 14.7.15) 303 days); Capt., G. Gds., 4.5.15 to 9.7.16; A/Major, Essex R., 1.8.16 to 15.9.16; T/Major 16.9.16; O.B.E.

MITCHELL, C. C. (D.S.O. L.G. 1.1.19); b. 1891; s. of Major H. W. Mitchell; m. Hildred Ruth, d. of late T. J. Blackwell, J.P.; educ. Wellington College; Major, late R.F.A.; served Europ. War (France) from 1914; wounded twice; Despatches; M.C.; retired 1919.

MITCHELL, C. H. (D.S.O. L.G. 3.6.16); b. Canada, 1872; s. of Rev. G. A. Mitchell, B.A.; m. Myra E. Stanton; educ. University of Toronto (B.A.Sc. and C.E.); Brigadier-General; served Europ. War, 1914–19, as G.S.O. (Intelligence) with 1st Can. Div., Can. Corps, 2nd (Imperial) Army, and G.H.Q., British Forces in Italy; Despatches seven times; C.B.; C.M.G.; Officier, Légion d'Honneur, France; Officer, Order of Leopold, Belgium; Croix de Guerre, Belgium and Italy; Order of Crown of Italy.

MITCHELL, C. J. (D.S.O. L.G. 1.1.17); b. 20.9.79; s. of Col. H. L. Mitchell, R.A., and Mary Arabella Susan, d. of C. J. Reynolds; m. Maud Elsie, d. of C. A. Galton, I.C.S.; Major, R. of O., Oxfords. and Bucks. L.I.; served in Europ. War from 1914. He died 16.10.18.

MITCHELL, G. (D.S.O. L.G. 1.1.18), Lt.-Col., N.Z. Inf.

MITCHELL, G. R. (D.S.O. L.G. 1.2.19), Major, Otago Mtd. Rif., XXII. Corps, N.Z. Mounted Troops.

MITCHELL, H. S. (D.S.O. L.G. 9.9.21); b. 5.2.79; 2nd Lt., Midd'x R., 19.5.00; Lt. 12.10.01; Capt. 19.5.09; Maj. 1.9.15; S. African War; Queen's Medal, 4 clasps; Tibet, 1903–4; severely wounded; Medal with clasp; Mohmand country, 1908; Medal, clasp; Europ. War; Despatches.

MITCHELL, J. (D.S.O. L.G. 1.4.20), Observer Officer (Observer), R.A.F.

MITCHELL, J. D. (D.S.O. L.G. 26.7.18); b. 1881; s. of late T. Mitchell, of Chelsea; m. Lisa, 3rd d. of late J. M. Garden, of Aberdeen; one d.; educ. Eastbourne; Mill Hill; Lt.-Colonel, Durham L.I.; served Europ. War, 1914–19; commanded 1st Sherwood Foresters, 1918–19; thrice wounded; Despatches twice; Belgian Croix de Guerre; C.M.G.

MITCHELL, J. H. (D.S.O. L.G. 4.6.17), Lt.-Col. (T/Brig.-Gen.), Can. F.A.

MITCHELL, J. T. R. (D.S.O. L.G. 1.1.17), T/Major, R. Scots. He died of wounds 1.4.18.

MITCHELL, J. W. (D.S.O. L.G. 1.1.18) (Bar, L.G. 1.2.19), 8th Batt. Aust. Inf.

MITCHELL, P. R. (D.S.O. L.G. 3.6.18); b. 14.10.82; 2nd Lt., R.A., 21.12.00; Lt. 21.12.03; Maj., R.G.A., 30.12.15; ret. pay 4.3.21; N.W. Frontier, 1908; Medal, clasp.

MITCHELL, R., M.A., B.L. (D.S.O. L.G. 14.1.16); b. 8.6.73; s. of late R Mitchell, of Logierieve, Aberdeenshire; educ. Gymnasium, Old Aberdeen; Aberdeen University; 2nd Lt., 1st Aberdeenshire (R.E.) Volunteers, Nov. 1900; Capt. (T/Major), 2nd Highland Field Co., R.E., T.F.; served Europ. War, 1915–19; 1914-15 Star; has King Edward's Coronation Medal; T.D.

MITCHELL, T. J., M.B. (D.S.O. L.G. 26.8.18); b. 2.10.82; Lt., R.A.M.C., 1.8.08; Capt. 1.2.12; Bt. Maj. 3.6.16; Maj. 1.8.20.

MITCHELL, W. G. S. (D.S.O. L.G. 1.1.18); b. 8.3.88; 2nd Lt., High. L.I., 17.3.09; Lt. 4.11.11 (R.F.C.); Capt.; M.C.

MITCHELL, W. J. (D.S.O. L.G. 11.1.19); b. 5.3.71; 2nd Lt., N. Lan. R., 28.10.91; Lt. 11.4.93; Capt., Ind. Army, 10.7.01; Maj. 28.10.09; Lt.-Col. 28.10.17; Col. 28.1.21; Temp. Col.-Comdt. 2.6.21; C.M.G.; Chitral, 1895; Medal, clasp; East Africa, 1895–96; Medal; East Africa, 1904; Despatches; Medal, 2 clasps; Europ. War; Despatches.

MITCHELL, W. J. FORBES- (see Forbes-Mitchell, W. J.).

MITFORD, HON. B. T. C. O. FREEMAN- (D.S.O. L.G. 17.3.19); s. of late Lord Redesdale; Capt., R.N.; served Europ. War; Despatches.

MITFORD, J. P. (D.S.O. L.G. 1.2.17); b. 12.6.80; s. of Rev. E. Mitford, M.A., Vicar of Hunmanby, Yorks, and Annie Maria Louisa Mitford (*née* Price); m. Edith, d. of F. W. Tytler; one s.; educ. Haileybury College; 2nd Lt., 1st Dorsets R., 5.1.01; transferred to I.A., 1903; Captain; served in E. Africa Nov. 1914–Jan. 1917; Despatches. His regiment was with Gen. Cleve's Column from Mwanza to Tabora, co-operating with the Belgians. From Feb. 1916, he was in command of the Rgt. in the absence of the Commandant. He won the championship at Poona at the Bombay Presidency Rifle Meeting, 1906, and the Silver Jewel at the Bombay Presidency Rifle Association Meeting at Meerut, 1904.

MOBBS, E. R. (D.S.O. L.G. 1.1.17); s. of Oliver Mobbs, of Northampton; educ. Bedford Modern School. He received permission to raise a company, and so great was his popularity in Northampton, where for six years he had been Captain of the Rugby Football Club, that in a fortnight he got together 250 men, most of them trained athletes. Joining as a Private, he became Captain before the training period was ended, and in May, 1917, was gazetted Lt.-Col. of his battalion. The battalion had its baptism of fire at Loos in 1915, and when Col. Parkin, who was in command, was killed, Capt. Mobbs took charge in a very difficult and trying position. He was wounded in the fighting on the Somme in 1916. He was fatally wounded on 31.7.17, having first completed his 35th year. "Such was his heroic devotion to duty that even when so seriously wounded that he had only ten minutes to live he wrote out map references of the position of the guns which were checking any advance." Col. Mobbs was a great football player. He appeared in all the international matches 1908–9. In 1909–10 he played against Ireland, and was Captain of the England Fifteen which defeated France in Paris. He was a Member of the Committee of the English Rugby Union.

MOBERLY, A. H. (D.S.O. L.G. 3.6.16); b. 3.1.79; 2nd Lt., R.A., 26.2.98; Lt. 16.2.01; Capt. 18.11.03; Maj. 30.10.14; Bt. Lt.-Col. 1.1.18.

MOBERLY, M. (D.S.O. L.G. 26.6.16); b. India, 9.12.77; s. of Col. W. H. Moberly, 40th R. (S. Lancs.), and Mary, daughter of Surg.-Gen. Fraser; m. Katherine Mary, d. of Surg.-Gen. Innes, C.M.; two s.; educ. University College; Inspector-General, Egyptian Camel Transport, Miralei Bey; served Europ. War; T/Major, Egyptian Camel Transport Corps, in 1915, serving in the European War, 1915–17; Miralei Bey, Egyptian Army.

MOBERLY, W. H. (D.S.O. L.G. 18.10.17) (Details, L.G. 7.3.18), 2nd Lt., Oxf. and Bucks. L.I.; Professor, Birmingham University.

MOCATTA, J. E. A. (D.S.O. L.G. 15.9.16), Lt.-Cdr., R.N., 1.10.17; served Europ. War; Battle of Jutland; Despatches.

MODERA, F. S. (D.S.O. L.G. 16.9.18) (Bar, L.G. 15.2.19) (Details, L.G. 30.7.19); Temp. 2nd Lt. 20.3.15; Capt., R. Fus., 7.3.17; Bt. Maj. 3.6.19; M.C.

MOENS, A. W. H. M., F.R.G.S. (D.S.O. L.G. 25.8.17); b. 20.12.79; s. of late S. M. Moens, I.C.S.; m. 1st, Agnes Swetenham, d. of T. Pike, M.D.; 2nd, May, d. of Capt. A. G. Douglas, R.N., and widow of Capt. D. Affleck-Graves, R.E.; educ. Charterhouse; R.M.C., Sandhurst; 2nd Lt., Unatt., 27.7.78; Lt., I.S.C., 13.3.00; Lt., I.A., 23.3.01; Capt. 27.7.07; Major 1.9.15; Col., I.A.; served Somaliland, 1903–4 (Medal and 2 clasps); Europ. War (Mesopotamia), 1915–18; Despatches; Bt. Major 29.11.15; Bt. Lt.-Col. 1.1.17; C.M.G.

MOFFAT, F. J. C. (D.S.O. L.G. 19.11.17) (Details, L.G. 22.3.18); s. of C. C. Moffat, S.S.C., Edinburgh; m. Jean Lesley, d. of J. D. M'Lauchlan; T/Capt., G. Highrs.

MOFFAT, G. B. (D.S.O. L.G. 22.8.18); educ. Methodist College, and Queen's College, Belfast; was one of the Surgeons of the E. Rand Mines; Capt., S. African Medical Corps (wrongly gazetted as Captain, S.A.V.C.), served in France with the Kimberley Rgt., and later in the German S.W. African Campaign.

MOFFAT, G. D. (D.S.O. L.G. 17.1.19), Capt., Mercantile Marine (Lt., R.N.R.).

MOFFAT, H. A. (D.S.O. L.G. 1.2.17), Lt.-Col., S. African Medical Corps.

MOGG, R. J. REES- (see Rees-Mogg, R. J.).

MOHAMMED, EFFENDI SHAHIM (D.S.O. L.G. 4.2.16), El Bimbashi, Egyptian Cavalry.

MOIR, A. J. G. (D.S.O. L.G. 4.6.17); b. 30.11.73; 2nd Lt., R. Scots, 20.5.93; Lt. 23.11.95; Adjt., R. Scots, 20.2.98 to 19.2.02; Capt. 19.7.99; Major 7.8.12; T/Brig.-Gen. 1917–19; Lt.-Col., R. Irish Rgt., 25.8.19; served S. African War, 1899–1902; Despatches twice; Bt. Major 29.11.00; Queen's Medal with 3 clasps; King's Medal with 2 clasps; Europ. War; Despatches; Bt. Lt.-Col. 3.6.16; Bt. Col. 1.1.19.

MOIR, D. F. (D.S.O. L.G. 8.3.18), Cdr., R.N., 30.6.19.

MOIR, H. L. (D.S.O. L.G. 7.11.18) (Bar, L.G. 1.1.19), Major (A/Lt.-Col.), 1/7th Batt. Cheshire Rgt.; S. African War, 1900–2; Queen's Medal, 3 clasps; King's Medal, 2 clasps; Europ. War; Despatches.

MOIR, J. H., M.D. (D.S.O. L.G. 2.4.19) (Details, L.G. 10.12.19), T/Capt. (A/Major), 2nd Batt. North'd Fus.; M.C.

MOIR, M. E. (D.S.O. L.G. 3.6.18); b. 3.8.93; 2nd Lt., R.A., 17.7.14; Lt. 9.6.15; Capt. 3.11.17.

MOIR, R. G. (D.S.O. L.G. 16.9.18); b. 6.6.94; 2nd Lt., A. and S. Highrs., 1.10.14; Lt. 11.5.15; Capt. 11.4.17; M.C.

MOKE-NORRIE, C. W. (D.S.O. L.G. 1.1.19); b. 26.9.93; s. of late Major G. E. M. Norrie; m. Jocelyn Helen, d. of R. H. Gosling; educ. Eton; Sandhurst; 2nd Lt., 11 Hrs., 5.2.13; Lt. 5.8.14; Capt. 25.6.18; Europ. War from 1914; Despatches twice; wounded four times; M.C. and Bar.

MOLESWORTH, H. E. (D.S.O. L.G. 1.1.17); b. 15.12.72; s. of late Major-Gen. H. T. Molesworth, R.A.; m. Eileen Mary Renny-Tailyour; two d.; educ. U.S. College, Westward Ho! R.M. Academy, Woolwich; ent. R.A., 1891; Capt., 1899; Major, 1912; T/Lt.-Col., 1916; Lt.-Col.; served Europ. War; Despatches twice; C.M.G.

MOLLER, P. W. (D.S.O. L.G. 22.8.18), Lt.-Col., Pietersburg Commando, S. African Mil. Forces

MOLLOY, H. T. (D.S.O. L.G. 8.6.20); b. 2.9.82; 2nd Lt. 18.1.02; Lt., Ind. Army, 18.4.04; Capt. 18.1.11; Maj. 18.1.17; N.W. Frontier, 1908; Medal, clasp; Europ. War; Despatches.

MOLLOY, L. G. S. (D.S.O. L.G. 4.6.17), Major, Yeomanry.

MOLONY, W. B. (D.S.O. L.G. 2.12.18), T/Lt.-Col., 9th Batt. R. Lancaster R., att. 4th Batt. Midd'x R.

MOLONY, W. W. (D.S.O. L.G. 4.6.17); 2nd Lt., Conn. Rangers, 15.5.97; Lt. 22.9.99; 2nd Lt., A.S.C., 12.2.00; Lt. 12.2.01; Capt. 13.3.02; Major, R.A.S.C., 5.8.14.

MOLYNEUX, G. M. J. (D.S.O. L.G. 1.2.17); educ. Stonyhurst; Lt.-Colonel, S. African Infy.; served Europ. War, 1915–17; wounded; Despatches; 3rd Class, Order of St. Stanislaus; Croix de Guerre.

MOLYNEUX, P. L. (D.S.O. L.G. 10.6.21); b. 23.7.93; T/2nd Lt. 11.1.15; Lt. 11.10.16; Capt., I.A., 11.10.19.

MOMBER, E. M. F. (D.S.O. L.G. 31.5.16); b. 16.6.88, at Biarritz, France; s. of Frederick Ernest Robert Momber (son of a London Banker) and Eugénie, d. of Capt. Ardoin, of the French Grenadiers de la Garde, a Crimean veteran, holder of the Médaille Militaire, who won the Légion d'Honneur, and lost a leg at the storming of Sebastopol, and was later Commandant of the Emperor Napoleon III.'s Villa Eugénie in Biarritz, and the founder of the town. Educ. Stubbington House; Cheltenham College, being head of both schools; R.M.A., Woolwich; S.M.E., Chatham. He played Rugby Football for R.M.A., Woolwich; S.M.E., Chatham; Captain, Aldershot Command; played for United Services; Army; Hampshire County; rowed for the R.E., Chatham, on the Medway and at Henley, and was also Captain of the Hong-Kong R.C.; rowed races at Hong-Kong and at Canton; in fencing represented R.M.A., Woolwich, and won Sabres Competition (Cadet) at Olympia in 1907; in gymnastics won the Colours for R.M.A., Woolwich, against Sandhurst in 1907, and was the holder of about 40 cups for swimming, field sports, rowing and tug of war. He loved hunting, and rode in Point-to-Point. He was 2nd Lt., R.E., 18.12.07; Lt. 2.5.10; Capt. (T/Major). After leaving S.M.E., Chatham, went to 11th Field Co., Aldershot; to Hong Kong as Adjt., R.E., 1912; returned with 25th Fortress Co., R.E., and landed in France, Dec. 1914; formed and commanded 176th Tunnelling Co., R.E.; was wounded at Vimy Ridge 26.6.16; at Aldershot, commanding Depôt Co. until recovered, and commanded 177th Tunnelling Co. from 12.2.17, preparing and firing Wytschaete-Messines Mines 7.6.17. He died on 20.6.17 of wounds received on the 18th. His General wrote: "His place cannot adequately be filled, for by his death we lose one of our bravest and best officers." His D.S.O. was awarded for gallantry at Vimy Ridge 26 April and 3 May, 1916.

E. M. F. Momber.

MONCK-MASON, R. H. (D.S.O. L.G. 4.6.17); b. 19.12.71; 2nd Lt., R. Munster Fus., 13.8.92; Lt. 13.9.94; Capt. 23.7.01; Major 11.3.13; Lt.-Col. 23.5.15.

MONCKTON-ARUNDELL, HON. G. V. A. (D.S.O. L.G. 4.6.17); b. 24.3.82; e. s. of 7th Viscount Galway; b. 24.3.82; educ. Christ Church, Oxford; 2nd Lt., 1st L.G., 28.9.04; Lt. 3.3.06; Adjt., 1st L.G., 10.11.08 to 9.11.11; Capt. 21.10.11; Major 20.3.16; Bt. Lt.-Col. 1.7.19; O.B.E.; served Europ. War, 1914–18 Despatches.

MONEY, B. M. (D.S.O. L.G. 17.3.19); b. 11.9.80; s. of Rev. G. E. Money, Rector of Byfleet, Surrey; m. Florence, d. of Dr. J. Leale, of Vale House, Guernsey; one s.; one d.; educ. Lambrook, Bracknell; The Grange, Eastbourne; H.M.S. Britannia; Lt., R.N., Feb. 1901; Commander, Jan. 1913; Capt., Jan. 1918. He served in the European War; Acheron (1st Destroyer Flotilla), in command, to Jan. 1916; in actions, Heligoland 28.8.14; bombardment of Zeebrugge 23.11.14; Dogger Bank 24.1.15; sinking of U 12, 10.3.15; Botha (1st and 14th Flotillas), in command, Jan. 1916, to May, 1917; Anzac (14th Flotilla), in command, May, 1917 to Jan. 1918; sinking of U 69, 12.7.17; promoted to Captain, Jan. 1918; Seymour (11th Flotilla), in command of Flotilla, Jan. to Nov. 1918; Despatches twice.

MONEY, E. D. (D.S.O. L.G. 3.6.18); b. 11.3.66; 2nd Lt., Linc. R., 9.5.88; Lt. 14.1.91; Capt. 9.5.99; Maj. 9.5.06; Lt.-Col. 9.5.14; Hon. Brig.-Gen., ret. pay, 31.10.20; C.I.E.; Sazar, 1892; Waziristan, 1894–95; Medal, clasp; Tirah, 1897–98; Medal, clasp; Europ. War; Despatches. He has the C.I.E.

MONEY, E. F. D. (D.S.O. L.G. 1.2.17); b. 18.6.78; s. of late Col. Money, I.A.; m. Frances Marion, d. of late P. A. Young, M.D. Edinburgh; 2nd Lt., Unatt., 20.7.98; 2nd Lt., I.S.C., 28.10.99; Lt., I.A., 20.10.00; Capt. 20.7.07; Major 1.9.18; Lt.-Col., 4th Gurkha Rifles; Despatches.

MONEY, N. C. K. (D.S.O. L.G. 2.2.16); b. 6.12.82; 2nd Lt., R.A., 21.12.01; Lt., Army, 21.3.04; R.A. 1.12.04; Ind. Army 14.3.08; Capt. 21.12.10; 22nd Punjabis, I.A.; T/Major. He died of wounds 6.9.15.

MONEY, N. E. (D.S.O. L.G. 27.9.01) (Bar, L.G. 1.1.18), Major (T/Lt.-Col., Shrops. Yeom. (see "The Distinguished Service Order," from its institution to 31.12.15, by same publishers).

MONIER-WILLIAMS, C. V. (D.S.O. L.G. 1.1.19), Capt. and Bt. Major (A/Lt.-Col.), York and Lancaster Rgt., seconded R.E. Signal Service.

MONROE, H. S. (D.S.O. L.G. 23.3.17); b. 4.11.77; s. of late Rt. Hon. J. Monroe, P.C., Judge of the Law Courts, Ireland, and the late Elizabeth Monroe (*née* Moule); educ. Park House, Southborough; Stubbington House, Fareham; joined H.M.S. Britannia, Jan. 1892, and went to sea as Midshipman, R.N., 15.1.94; Commander 30.6.18; served S. African War; Queen's Medal; was Senior Officer, Number Four Nore Defence Flotilla. For his services in the European War he received the 1914–15 Star, and the French Croix de Guerre with Palm.

MONTAGU, HON. L. S. (D.S.O. L.G. 17.4.17); b. 8.9.83; s. of 1st Baron Swaythling; educ. Clifton; New College, Oxford; is a breeder and owner of racehorses; served Europ. War from 1914; T/Capt., R.M.; Despatches. His D.S.O. was awarded for gallantry at Beaucourt 13–14.11.16.

MONTAGUE, P. J. (D.S.O. L.G. 1.1.18), Major (T/Lt.-Col.), Can. Inf.; M.C.

MONTAGUE-BATES, F. S. (D.S.O. L.G. 1.1.17); b. 8.2.76; s. of F. Montague-Bates; m. Gladys, d. of late H. S. Thomas; one s.; educ. Appledurcombe College, I. of Wight; joined Lumsden's Horse, and served S. African War, 1899–1901; 2nd Lt., E. Surrey Rgt., 4.8.00; Queen's Medal, 4 clasps; Lt. 21.5.02; Capt. 28.7.09; Major 1.9.15; T/Brig.-Gen. 23.9.16; served Europ. War from 1914; Bt. Lt.-Col. 3.6.16; Despatches; C.B.; C.M.G.

MONTEAGLE-BROWNE, E. (D.S.O. L.G. 3.6.16); b. 15.6.78; s. of J. Monteagle-Browne; ent. Army, 1898; served with 1st Batt. R. Irish Fusiliers throughout the S. African War; Queen's and King's Medals with 5 clasps; Major, 10th S. Batt. L. N. Lancs R.; Lt.-Col.; served Europ. War; Despatches.

MONTEFIORE, T. H. SEBAG- (see Sebag-Montefiore, T. H.),

MONTFORD, I. C. (D.S.O. L.G. 3.10.19), Capt. (T/Lt.-Col., Rif. Brig.), S.R.

MONTGOMERY, H. F. (D.S.O. L.G. 1.1.17); b. 6.5.80; 2nd Lt., R. Mar., 1.9.98; Lt. 1.7.99; Adjt., R.M., 2.7.05 to 1.4.09; Capt. 22.4.07; Bt. Major 15.11.12; Major 22.7.16; Bt. Lt.-Col. 3.6.18.

MONTGOMERY, J. W. V. (D.S.O. L.G. 13.2.17); b. Brantford, Canada, W., 1867; s. of late Capt. A. N. Montgomery, J.P., The R. Fusiliers, and the late Istere Alicia Montgomery (*née* Altrutel); m. Flora McDonald Seton, d. of late H. J. Reid; twos.; educ. Repton; Hilton College, Natal; St. Mary's Hospital; joined Natal Carbineers, 1888, as Trooper; Lt., Oct. 1900; Capt., Sept. 1904; Major, Oct., 1908; T/Lt.-Col., Jan. 1915; served S. African War, 1899–1902; Despatches; Queen's and King's Medals, with 6 clasps; Native Rebellion, 1906 (Medal and clasp); Europ. War; commanded 1st M.R. (Natal Carbineers) in S.W. Africa; Despatches; C.M.G.; formed and commanded 6th S. African Infantry for service in E. Africa; Despatches; 1914 Star; regiment presented with King's Colour. Col. Montgomery holds the Volunteer Decoration.

J. W. V. Montgomery.

MONTGOMERY, R. N. V. (D.S.O. L.G. 3.6.19); b. 26.4.84; 2nd Lt., R.A., 4.6.04; Lt. 4.6.07; Capt. 30.10.14; Major, R.H.A. He died on 1.4.19.

MONTGOMERY, T. H. (D.S.O. L.G. 1.1.18), T/Major, A.S.C. (now R.A.S.C.).

MONTGOMERY, W. A. (D.S.O. L.G. 22.9.16), T/Capt., R. Irish Rifles. His D.S.O. was awarded for gallantry at Thiépval on 1.7.16.

MONTGOMERY-SMITH, E. C. (D.S.O. L.G. 26.9.17) (Details, L.G. 9.1.18), Major (T/Lt.-Col.), R.A.M.C.

MOODIE, P. A. (D.S.O. L.G. 16.9.18), Lt., H.L.I.

MOODIE, W. H. (D.S.O. L.G. 1.1.18); b. 22.9.71; s. of W. and Janet E. Moodie, of Quebec; m. Marcella, d. of E. D. Twiss: one s.; two d.; educ. Quebec High School; served in 2nd R.C.R. in S. Africa, 1899–1900; Queen's Medal and 4 clasps. Lt.-Col. Moodie came overseas in 1915, in command of B Company, 1st Can. Pioneers, commanding Battalion 31.3.17; O.C., 9th Batt. Can. Rly. Troops.

MOON, E. R. (D.S.O. L.G. 15.6.17) (Bar, L.G. 16.3.18), Sqn. Cdr., R.N.A.S.

MOON, J. A. (D.S.O. L.G. 15.9.16); s. of G. Moon; m. Ada, d. of J. Simmons; educ. Royal School, Dungannon; Fleet-Surgeon, R.N.; served China War, Boxer Rebellion (Medal); Imperial Red Cross, Japan (Russo-Japanese War, 1904–5); St. Stanislaus of Russia (Battle of Jutland); Surgeon in H.M.S. Victoria when rammed and sunk by H.M.S. Camperdown 22.6.93; Fleet-Surgeon, H.M.S. Benbow and H.M.S. Hercules, Grand Fleet, 1916–17.

MOORE, THE REV. C. W. G., M.A. (D.S.O. L.G. 4.6.17), T/Chaplain, R.N.

MOORE, D. H. (D.S.O. L.G. 1.1.18), Major (T/Lt.-Col.), Aust. F.A.

MOORE, D. T. (D.S.O. L.G. 22.9.16), Major, Aust. Infy.

MOORE, E. D. (D.S.O. L.G. 1.1.18), Major, E. Riding Yeomanry.

MOORE, E. H. M. (D.S.O. L.G. 1.1.18), Major, R.A.M.C.; b. 28.10.77; Lt., R.A.M.C., 30.1.04; Capt. 30.7.07; Maj. 1.7.15.

MOORE, F. H. (D.S.O. L.G. 14.1.16); b. 26.5.76; 2nd Lt., R. Berks. R., 5.9.96; Lt. 22.10.99; Capt. 5.8.04; Major 27.6.15; served S. African War, 1899–1902; Queen's Medal, 3 clasps; King's Medal, 2 clasps; Brig. Major, 149th Inf. Brig., Central Force, Home Defence, B.E.F., 5.8.14 to 16.2.16; G.S.O.2, 23rd Div., B.E.F., Br. Armies in France, 17.2.16 to 16.2.17; G.S.O.2, 5th A.C., Br. Armies in France, 17.2.17 to 14.10.17; G.S.O.1 and T/Lt.-Col., 29th Div., Br. Armies in France, 15.10.17 to 27.12.17.

MOORE, F. W. (D.S.O. L.G. 3.6.19), T/Capt. (A/Major), 12th Field Co., R.E., S.R; M.C.

MOORE, G. A., M.D., B.Ch., B.A.O., B.A. (D.S.O. L.G. 1.1.18); b. 24.3.69; s. of late W. Moore, J.P., M.D., F.R.C.P.I., Physician-in-Ordinary in Ireland to Queen Victoria and King Edward VII.; m. Helena Catherine Georgina, d. of Surg.-General Whitla; three s.; one d.; educ. Charterhouse; Trinity College, Dublin; Specialist in Diseases of Throat, Nose and Ear; previous service 3 years; Capt., R.A.M.C., 27.7.95; Major 27.7.04; Lt.-Col. 1.3.15; Col., A.M.S., 26.12.17; served N.W. Frontier of India, and Tirah Campaign, 1897–98 (Medal and 2 clasps); S. African War, 1899–1902; Queen's Medal, 4 clasps; King's Medal, 2 clasps; Europ. War; Despatches thrice; C.M.G.

MOORE, H. (D.S.O. L.G. 16.9.18), T/Capt. (A/Major), R.A.M.C.; M.C.

MOORE, H. D. (D.S.O. L.G. 4.6.17); b. 4.5.82; m. Vera Critchley-Salmonson; one s.; one d.; 2nd Lt., Suffolk R., 5.1.01; Lt. 23.4.02; Lt., I.A., 29.7.03; Capt. 5.1.10; Major 5.1.16; served Europ. War, 1914–18; Afghanistan Campaign, 1919.

MOORE, H. E. (D.S.O. L.G. 3.6.19); b. 11.2.88; Mob. Spec. Res., 5 years; Capt., R.E., 5.2.21; M.C.

MOORE, H. M. BRETTINGHAM- (see Brettingham-Moore, H. M.).

MOORE, H. R. (D.S.O. L.G. 15.9.16), Lt.-Cdr., R.N., 15.1.16; served Europ. War, Battle of Jutland; Despatches; invested with the Insignia of D.S.O. by the King at sea, June, 1917.

MOORE, L. G. (D.S.O. L.G. 1.1.17) (Bar, L.G. 4.3.18) (Details, L.G. 16.8.18); b. 5.2.86; 2nd Lt., R. Brig., 9.3.10; Lt. 11.11.11; Capt. 30.12.14; Bt. Major 1.1.18; served Europ. War; Despatches; M.C.

MOORE, M. (D.S.O. L.G. 3.6.16); b. 6.2.76; m. Louisa Chichester Hart; two s.; one d.; 2nd Lt., Ches. R., 29.5.95; Lt., A.S.C., 1.1.99; Capt. 1.1.01; Maj. 25.7.12; Lt.-Col. 20.2.17; Col. 20.2.21; S. African War, 1899–1902; Queen's Medal, 6 clasps; Europ. War, 1914–18; Despatches; 1914 Star; C.M.G.

MOORE, N. C. (D.S.O. L.G. 15.2.19), Lt., R.N., 15.7.09; Lt.-Cdr., R.N.

MOORE, R. F. (D.S.O. L.G. 26.7.18), T/Lt. (A/Lt.-Col.), Notts. and Derby. R.; M.C. He was killed in action 30.5.18.

MOORE, R. S. (D.S.O. L.G. 2.12.18), 29th Can. Infy. Batt., Br. Columbia Rgt.

MOORE, W. A. (D.S.O. L.G. 3.3.17); b. 4.4.76; 2nd Lt., R.A., 2.5.00; Lt. 3.4.01; Capt. 28.9.12; Major, R.G.A., 30.12.15, att. Imp. Camel Brigade in Europ. War; Despatches. His D.S.O. was awarded for gallantry at Magdwaha on 23.12.16.

MOORE-GWYN, H. G. (D.S.O. L.G. 3.6.19); b. 7.7.86; s. of J. E. Moore-Gwyn; m. Winifred Gilbertson; educ. Winchester and Sandhurst; 2nd Lt., Rif. Brig., 29.8.06; Lt. 15.4.10; Capt. 5.8.14; served Europ. War, Salonika, 1915–17; Egypt, 1917–18; with Capt. T. O. Jameson, 3rd Batt. R. Brig., he won the final of the Army Rackets Championship (Doubles) in 1922 at Queen's Club; M.C.

MOORHOUSE, H. (D.S.O. L.G. 14.1.16), Lt.-Col., The King's Own (Yorks. L.I.), 4th Batt. (T.); served S. African War; Queen's Medal, 4 clasps; Europ. War; Despatches; Legion of Honour. He also held the Territorial Decoration. Col. Moorhouse fell in action on 9.10.17, and his son, Capt. R. Moorhouse, who was serving in the same regiment, was killed on the same day.

MOORHOUSE, W. N. (D.S.O. L.G. 1.1.19), Lt.-Col., Can. M.G. Corps.

MORANT, E. R. (D.S.O. L.G. 1.1.16) (Bar, L.G. 1.10.17); b. 1874; s. of Admiral Sir George Digby Morant, K.C.B., and Sophia Georgina (who died in 1886), d. of the late Col. Eyres, G. Gds.; m. Daisy Kathleen, d. of F. Grigor; ent. R.N., 1887; Cdr. 31.12.06; A/Capt.; served Chili, 1891; took part in blockade of Venezuela, 1902–3; Europ. War, 1914–18; Despatches.

MORANT, H. H. S. (D.S.O. L.G. 1.1.17) (Bar, L.G. 1.1.18); b. 27.12.70; s. of Lt.-Gen. H. H. Morant and Katherine Selina, d. of F. Locke; m. Helen Isabella, d. of J. C. Straker; 2nd Lt., Durh. L.I., 16.10.89; Lt. 19.11.92; Capt. 9.8.99; Maj. 23.5.10; Lt.-Col. 7.1.19; Nile Exped., 1898; Despatches; 4th Class Osmanieh and Medjidieh; Egyptian Medal, clasp; Medal; Europ. War, 1914–18; wounded four times; raised and commanded 10th D.L.I.; commanded 3rd and 147th Inf. Brigades.

MORDAUNT, O. C. (D.S.O. L.G. 4.6.17); b. 26.5.76; 2nd Lt., Som. L.I., 23.5.00; Lt. 2.8.02; Capt. 22.1.10; Major 1.9.15; Bt. Lt.-Col. 1.1.19; Despatches.

MORDY, A. G. (D.S.O. L.G. 3.6.18), Major, Can. Infy.

MORE, J. C. (D.S.O. L.G. 26.8.18); b. 3.2.83; 2nd Lt., R. Sc. Fus., 18.1.02; Lt., Ind. Army, 18.4.04; Capt. 18.1.11; Maj. 18.1.17; Sikhs, I.A.

MORELL, R. (gazetted as Morrell, R.) (D.S.O. L.G. 4.6.17), Major, Aust. M.G.C.

MORETON, J. A. (D.S.O. L.G. 26.4.18), Sub-Lt., R.N., May, 1896; Lt., Dec. 1898; Cdr. 30.6.09; Capt. 31.12.15. He was one of the earliest Submarine Captains in the British Navy; served in the Indomitable during the early part of the war. Under Admiral Bacon's command he took charge of the new 12 in. gun monitor General Wolfe, which did such good work in the bombardment of the German positions along the Belgian coast. In May, 1918, Capt. Moreton was appointed to command the 15 in. gun monitor Erebus; C.M.G.; Capt. Moreton died from pneumonia contracted while on active service in the Baltic, aged 43.

MORETON, P. C. R. (D.S.O. L.G. 4.6.17); b. 20.1.86; s. of Rev. P. D. Moreton, Vicar of Compton Dundon, Somerton, and Alti Edith, d. of Gen. Sir W. A. Gibb, K.C.B.; Major, late R. Monmouthshire Engineers; served Europ. War, 1914–18; wounded.

MORGAN, B. E. (D.S.O. L.G. 25.8.17); b. 11.6.78; 2nd Lt., Welsh R., 20.5.99; Lt. 14.11.00; I.A. 11.2.01; Capt. 20.5.08; Major 1.9.15.

MORGAN, C. E. (D.S.O. L.G. 27.6.19), Lt.-Cdr., R.N., 1.10.19.

MORGAN, C. R. F. (D.S.O. L.G. 1.1.18); b. 25.3.80; 2nd Lt., A.S.C. (now R.A.S.C.), 16.8.02; Lt. 18.2.04; Capt. 1.1.11; Major 30.10.14; S. African War, 1902; Queen's Medal, 3 clasps; Europ. War; Despatches.

MORGAN, C. W. (D.S.O. L.G. 8.3.19) (Details, L.G. 4.10.19); b. 2.9.89; s. of A. E. Morgan and M. I. Morgan; educ. Queen's College, and Sheffield University; joined the Army 24.9.14; commissioned 12.2.15, 5th (T.) Batt. Welsh R.; became Captain; served Gallipoli (Suvla Bay), Egypt and the Libyan Desert, 1916, and in Palestine, 1917–18; M.C. for gallantry at Beersheba.

MORGAN, D. W. (D.S.O. L.G. 4.2.18) (Details, L.G. 5.7.18); b. 18.12.67; s. of T. and M. Morgan; m. Blanche Amy Morgan; two s.; four d.; educ. Grammar School, Swansea; M.P. (Lab.), Rhondda East, from 1918; Miners' Agent, Rhondda Valley, from 1898; joined 10th Batt. Welsh R. as a Private 5.8.14; commissioned Major; C.B.E. He has published "Compensation Act Treatise;" "Miners' Tables of Wages;" "Hand Book, Safety in Mines."

MORGAN, F. A. S. (D.S.O. L.G. 4.6.17); b. 12.7.77; s. of Rev. J. Parry Morgan; m. Frances Mary, d. of Lt.-Col. F. Willoughby, O.B.E., V.D.; one s.; educ. Fettes College, Edinburgh; ent. R.A., 23.5.00; Lt. 2.11.01; Capt. 23.5.13; Major, R.G.A., 30.12.15; served S. Africa, 1899–1902; severely wounded; Queen's Medal, 3 clasps; King's Medal, 2 clasps; Europ. War, 1914–18; wounded; Despatches thrice; Greek Medal for Military Merit, 3rd Class.

MORGAN, F. J. (D.S.O. L.G. 20.10.16); s. of Rev. E. A. Morgan, Rector of Welborne; m. Phyllis Edwina, d. of late E. Windsor; T/Lt. and T/Capt., Norfolk Rgt.; Captain; served European War, 1914–17; Despatches; M.C. His D.S.O. was awarded for gallantry on 1.7.16, at Montauban Ridge; C.B.E., 1919.

MORGAN, H. DE R. (D.S.O. L.G. 16.9.18); b. 12.3.88; 2nd Lt., E. Kent R., 4.10.10; Lt. 2.3.12; Capt. 4.8.15; Local Lt.-Col. 12.9.19.

MORGAN, H. L. (D.S.O. L.G. 22.1.20), Lt.-Cdr., R.N., 1.4.19.

MORGAN, J. W. M. (D.S.O. L.G. 4.6.17), Lt.-Col., A.S.C. (now R.A.S.C.); b. 25.5.70; 2nd Lt., R. Irish Fus., 2.5.91; Lt., R. Ir. Fus., 26.4.94; Lt., A.S.C. (now R.A.S.C.), 1.10.94; Capt. 1.6.99; Major 3.3.06; Lt.-Col. 30.10.14; served S. African War, 1899–1901; Queen's Medal with 2 clasps; European War; Despatches.

MORGAN, R. W. (D.S.O. L.G. 14.1.16) (Bar, L.G. 20.10.16); b. 17.10.79; s. of late W. T. Morgan, Lt.-Col., K.O.S.B., and Mary Morgan; m. Maud Esther Nathan; educ. Wellington; Sandhurst; joined 1st Batt. S. Staffs. R., 1899; Adjt., 2nd Batt. S. Staffs. R., Dec. 1914; T/Brig.-Gen., 1916; Lt.-Colonel; served S. African War, 1900–2; Queen's Medal, 3 clasps; King's Medal, 2 clasps; served Europ. War, 1914–17; wounded near Richebourg; Despatches; Bt. Lt.-Col.; C.M.G.; Bar to D.S.O. awarded for gallantry on 16.7.16, at Delville Wood; commanding 1st Batt. S. Staffs. R.

MORGAN, W. D. (D.S.O. L.G. 3.6.19); b. 15.12.91; 2nd Lt., R.A., 20.12.12; Lt. 9.6.15; Capt., R.F.A., 20.12.16; served Europ. War; Despatches; M.C.

MORGAN, W. H., A.M.I.C.E. (D.S.O. L.G. 4.6.17); b. 1883; s. of E. F. Morgan; m. Evelyn Mary, d. of W. H. Wright; one s.; Major, R.E., S.R.; served Europ. War, 1915–19; Despatches.

MORGAN-GRENVILLE-GAVIN, HON. T. G. B. (D.S.O. L.G. 4.2.18) (Details, L.G. 5.7.18); b. 28.2.91; 2nd s. of the Baroness Kinloss and Major L. F. H. C. Morgan (who died in 1896); m. Georgina May St. John, d. of A. St. J. Murphy; two d.; educ. Eton; R.M.C., Sandhurst; 2nd Lt., Rif. Brig., 19.11.10; Lt. 25.5.12; Capt. 17.3.15; Lt.-Colonel, The Rif. Brigade; served Europ. War, 1914–16; Bt. Major 1.1.17; Despatches; M.C.; Legion of Honour, N. Russia, 1918–19; succeeded to Langton Estate in Berwickshire, and added Gavin to surname, 1916.

MORGAN-OWEN, LL. I. G. (D.S.O. L.G. 2.2.16); b. 31.3.79; s. of T. Morgan-Owen, M.A., J.P.; m. Ethel Berry, d. of J. B. Walford; one s.; educ. Arnold House, Llandulas; Shrewsbury School; Trinity College, Dublin; joined Carnarvon Militia, 1899; passed into Army as University Candidate; 2nd Lt., 24th S.W.B., 1900; Capt., 1909; Major, 1915; Lt.-Colonel; served S. African War, 1900–2 (Queen's Medal, 3 clasps; King's Medal, 2 clasps); with N. Nigeria M.I., 1905–9; Adjt., 1908–9; Europ. War, 1914–16, including Gallipoli (Brig.-Major, 40th Inf. Brig., 13th Div.), Battle of Sari Bair and the evacuations of Suvla and Helles; Mesopotamia, with 13th Div. as G.S.O.2, including the Capture of Kut and Baghdad; Despatches five times; Bt. Lt.-Col. (after Capture of Baghdad); G.S.O.1, 13th Div., Sept. 1917; C.M.G.

Ll. I. G. Morgan-Owen.

MORGAN-OWEN, M. M. (D.S.O. L.G. 4.3.18) (Details, L.G. 16.8.18); s. of T. Morgan-Owen; Capt. (A/Lt.-Col.) Morgan Morgan-Owen, Essex Rgt., commanded the 10th Rif. Brig. on the Western front, and was awarded the D.S.O. for gallantry at Cambrai. His brother, Lt.-Col. Ll. I. Gethin Morgan-Owen also won the D.S.O., and a third brother, Lt. Garth Morgan-Owen, S.W.B., was killed in action.

MORIARITY, O. E. (D.S.O. L.G. 4.6.17), L/Lt. (T/Capt.), R.F.A. (late Lt., R.G.A., S.R.).

MORIARTY, O. N. (D.S.O. L.G. 25.8.16) (Bar, L.G. 26.9.17) (Details, L.G. 9.1.18); b. 8.11.82; Capt. (from S.R.), R.A., 5.8.14; Maj. 1.5.17; commanding 8th Heavy Battery, R.G.A.; served Europ. War, 1914–17; Despatches twice. His D.S.O. was awarded for gallantry on 3 and 25.7.16, at Mametz Wood, and north of Bazentin-le-Petit; Bar for gallantry on 24.7.17, at Templeux-le-Guerrand.

MORIARTY, T. B. (D.S.O. L.G. 1.1.18); b. 16.9.77; Lt., R.A.M.C., 31.7.05; Capt. 31.1.09; Major 15.10.15; served Europ. War, 1914–17; Despatches.

MORIN, A. H. (D.S.O. L.G. 25.8.17); b. 4.3.70; s. of Henry David Morin, of Cheltenham (s. of John Morin, of Allanton, Dumfries, N.B.); m. Ellen Eaglesome; two s.; educ. Warwick School and R.I.E.C., Cooper's Hill; joined I.A.R.O. when first formed in 1897, and was called out on 15.9.14; had been a Volunteer since 1885, and an Officer since 1893; V.D.; serving in Southern Provinces Mounted Rifles at outbreak of war. On being called out was attached to 2nd Q.V.O. Sappers and Miners as Capt., and proceeded on active service to France in Oct. 1914, with 2nd Field Troop S. and M., attached to 1st Indian Cav. Div.; commanded this unit from 15 June, after fighting round Hooge, and was then transferred with it to Lahore Div. on Neuve Chapelle front; proceeded to Mesopotamia with Indian Corps in Dec. 1915, and was again attached to Cavalry (6th Bde.); relinquished command of Field Troops in Nov. 1916, on appointment as Field Engineer 1st Army Corps, and S.O. to Chief Engineer; Majority 1.9.15; Despatches. He was awarded the D.S.O. for services during period covered by Gen. Maude's Despatches published in L.G. of 14.8.17. Major Morin has the Delhi Durbar Medal.

MORLAND, W. E. T. (D.S.O. L.G. 23.8.18); b. 27.6.82; 2nd Lt., Oxf. L.I., 18.1.02; Lt., Oxf. and Bucks. L.I., 11.8.05; Capt. 22.1.14; Maj. 18.1.17; S. African War, 1902; Queen's Medal, 3 clasps; East Africa, 1908–10; Medal, clasp; Europ. War; Despatches; M.C.

MORLET, C. (D.S.O. L.G. 1.1.19), Major, 13th F.A., Aust. A.M.C.

MORLEY, F. J. (D.S.O. L.G. 26.7.18); b. 14.8.91; 2nd Lt., Dorsets. R., 1.10.14; Capt. (A/Major); served Europ. War from 1914; Despatches; M.C. He died of wounds 24.4.18.

MORLEY, L. ST. H. (D.S.O. L.G. 14.1.16); b. 10.2.76; 2nd Lt., Derby. R., 29.2.96; Lt. 12.12.96; Capt., Notts. and Derby. R., 11.7.00; Major 20.2.14; served S. African War; Queen's Medal with 4 clasps; King's Medal with 2 clasps; Europ. War; Despatches.

MORLIDGE, A. (D.S.O. L.G. 16.9.18), Capt., North'd Fus.

MORPHETT, G. C. (D.S.O. L.G. 22.12.16); b. 23.12.78; 2nd Lt., R. Sussex R., 20.5.99; Lt. 27.6.00; Adjt., R. Sussex R., 1904–7; Capt. 23.1.09; Adjt., R. Sussex R., 1913–15; Major 1.9.15; served S. African War; Despatches; Queen's Medal with 4 clasps; King's Medal with 2 clasps; Europ. War; Despatches; Bt. Lt.-Col. 3.6.17; C.M.G.

MORPHEW, E. M., M.R.C.S., L.R.C.P. (D.S.O. L.G. 1.1.17); b. 28.7.67; educ. University College, London; Capt., R.A.M.C., 30.1.95; Major 30.1.04; Lt.-Col. 20.4.14; Col. 25.4.18; Colonel, late R.A.M.C.; ret. pay, 1921; served in operations on N.W.F. of India, 1897–98, with Tirah Exp. Force; Medal with 2 clasps; S. African War, 1899–1902; Despatches twice; Queen's Medal with 4 clasps; King's Medal with 2 clasps; Europ. War; Despatches; C.M.G.

MORPHY, J. A. (D.S.O. L.G. 1.1.18), Major, Pioneer Batt. Can. Mil. Forces.

MORRELL, J. F. B. (D.S.O. L.G. 1.1.19) (Bar, L.G. 2.4.19) (Details, L.G. 10.12.19); b. 7.9.83; 2nd Lt., R. Lanc. R., 20.11.07; Lt. 1.4.11; Capt. 11.5.15; Bt. Maj. 3.6.17; M.V.O.

MORRIS, A. (D.S.O. L.G. 4.6.17), Capt. (T/Major), R. Fusiliers.

MORRIS, B. M. (D.S.O. L.G. 3.6.19), Major, Aust. F.A.

MORRIS, C. E. (D.S.O. L.G. 12.2.20); b. 16.10.81; 2nd Lt., Hants R., 4.12.01; 2nd Lt., I.A., 23.5.03; Lt. 4.3.04; Capt. 4.12.10; Major, Corps of Guides, 4.12.16; served S. African War, 1902; Queen's Medal, 4 clasps; N.W.F. of India, 1908; operations in the Mohmand country; Medal with clasp; A/Lt.-Col., Corps of Guides, att. 85th Burman Rifles, I.A.; Europ. War; Despatches.

MORRIS, C. H. (D.S.O. L.G. 8.3.19) (Details, L.G. 4.10.19); b. 9.5.85; 2nd Lt., Bedf. R., 3.3.15; Lt., Dorset R., 20.10.16; Capt. Middx. R., 23.12.17; Europ. War; Despatches; M.C.

MORRIS, C. O. (D.S.O. L.G. 22.12.16); b. Camberley, Surrey, 13.1.79; s. of late Col. Augustus Morris, late Commanding 1st Northants R., and Ena Constance, d. of late Surg.-Gen. W. Oxley; m. Hester Elizabeth, d. of the late Mary and General Francis; one s.; two d.; educ. Bedford Grammar School; 2nd Lt., 1st Batt. Northants R., 7.5.98; Lt., Northants R., 27.11.00; I.A. 19.12.01; Supply Trans. Corps, I.A., 1904; Capt. 7.5.07; Major 1.9.15; Asst. Dir. of Supplies and Trans., India, 11.5.19 to 12.6.19; Europ. War; Despatches.

MORRIS, C. R. M., M.B. (D.S.O. L.G. 4.6.17) (Bar, L.G. 1.2.19); b. 10.11.82; Lt., R.A.M.C., 30.1.06; Capt. 30.7.09; Maj. 30.1.18.

MORRIS, E. N. G. (D.S.O. L.G. 1.1.18), Lt., R.N.V.R., att. R.N.A.S.

MORRIS, E. R. (D.S.O. L.G. 1.1.19), Major, 1st Batt. Can. M.G.C.

MORRIS, E. W. (D.S.O. L.G. 3.6.19); b. 8.12.90; 2nd Lt., Conn. Rangers, 4.3.11; Lt. 15.8.14; Capt. (A/Major), 1st Batt. Conn. Rangers (att. 1/4th Batt. Ches. R., T.F.).

MORRIS, F. G. G. (D.S.O. L.G. 12.3.17); b. 8.9.69; 2nd Lt., Border R., 12.3.92; Lt. 30.6.95; Capt. 15.11.01; Major 4.11.12; T/Lt.-Colonel; served S. African War, 1899–1902; Queen's Medal with 5 clasps; King's Medal with 2 clasps. He served in the European War, attached 16th Middlesex Rgt., and was killed in action 17.8.17. His D.S.O. was awarded for gallantry on 27.1.17, south of Le Transloy.

MORRIS, G. A. (D.S.O. L.G. 4.6.17), Lt.-Col., S. African Mil. Forces.

MORRIS, G. M. (D.S.O. L.G. 17.3.17); b. 17.3.68; 2nd Lt., Devon. R., 28.6.90; Lt. 19.5.91; Lt., I.S.C., 7.9.92; Capt., I.A., 28.6.01; Major 28.6.08; Lt.-Col. 28.6.16, Punjabis, I.A.; Bt. Col. 3.6.18; T/Brig.-Gen., Commanding 55th Inf. Brig., Mes. Exp. Force, 2.3.18; C.B.

MORRIS, G. W. S. (D.S.O. L.G. 3.6.16); b. 13.7.79; 2nd Lt., R.A., 14.9.98; Capt. 25.4.06; Maj. 16.11.16; ret. pay 8.7.19; S. African War, 1901; Queen's Medal, 3 clasps; Europ. War; Despatches.

MORRIS, J. (D.S.O. L.G. 4.6.17), Capt. (T/Major), M.G.C.

MORRIS, J. H. (D.S.O. L.G. 1.1.18); b. 24.4.81; 2nd Lt., A.S.C. (now R.A.S.C.), 4.7.03; Lt. 31.3.05; Capt. 7.11.11; Major 30.10.14; Bt. Lt.-Col. 1.1.19; S. African War, 1901–2; Queen's Medal, 4 clasps; Europ. War; Despatches.

MORRIS, R. J. (D.S.O. L.G. 11.12.16), Capt. (T/Major), S. Staffs R.

MORRISEY, T. S. (D.S.O. L.G. 3.6.16); b. St. John, N.B., Canada, 30.8.90; s. of T. L. Morrisey, of Montreal; m. Beatrice Hilda, d. of late J. Coristine; one s.; educ. Abingdon School, Montreal, and St. Alban's School, Brockville; R.M. College, Canada; McGill University, Montreal; commissioned in 13th Can. Batt (The R. Highrs. of Canada), June, 1910; became Major, and at the outbreak of the war served with that unit in France from 15.2.15; later served with 3rd Can. Inf. Brig., Gen. Staff, 3rd Can Div., and as Brig. Major, 8th Can. Inf. Brig. from 13.7.16; Gen. Staff, 1st Can. Div.; G.S.O.1, Can. Exp. Force in Siberia; Despatches twice.

MORRISON, F. L. (D.S.O. L.G. 1.1.18), Colonel, The H.L.I., 5th (City of Glasgow) Batt. (T.); C.B. He died 22.12.17, on active service in Egypt.

MORRISON, F. S. (D.S.O. L.G. 1.1.17); b. 1881; Col., R. Can. Dragoons; served Europ. War, 1914–18; Despatches; C.M.G.; Russian Order of St. Anne.

MORRISON, G. F. (D.S.O. L.G. 1.1.17); b. 16.10.84; s. of C. Morrison, J.P., of Toronto; m. Mabel E., d. of late W. E. Chalcroft; one d.; educ. Harbord Collegiate Institute; late Regimental Adjt., 2nd Queen's Own Rifles, Toronto; Lieutenant-Colonel; served Europ. War; commanded 18th Can. Batt., B.E.F.

MORRISON, J. A. (D.S.O. L.G. 3.6.16); m. 1st Hon. Mary Hill-Trevor, d. of 1st Lord Trevor; one s.; two d.; 2nd, 1920, Dorothy Halton; ent. Army, 1896; Lt., 1898; Capt., late Grenadier Guards; served Sudan, 1898, including Khartum; British Medal; Khedive's Medal, with clasps; S. Africa, 1899–1900; Europ. War, 1914–16; wounded.

MORRISON, W. (D.S.O. L.G. 15.10.18); b. 30.4.81; 2nd Lt., G. Highrs., 9.1.15; Lt. 28.9.15; Capt. 15.6.17; served Europ. War; was Staff Capt., 56th Inf. Brigade, 12.9.16 to 13.12.16; A/Lt.-Col., Sea. Highrs., 1918; A/Lt.-Col., G. Highrs., 1919; Despatches; M.C.; D.C.M.

MORRISON, W. K., M.B. (D.S.O. L.G. 25.8.17); b. 1891; m. Annie Beatrice, d. of late J. Runciman; Capt., R.A.M.C.; served Europ. War (France and Mesopotamia), 1914–17; Retreat from Mons, 1914; wounded at Le Cateau 26.8.14; Despatches twice.

MORRISON-SCOTT, R. C. S. (D.S.O. L.G. 1.1.18), T/Capt. (A/Maj.), R.M.A.

MORROGH, W. F. (D.S.O. L.G. 19.12.22), Capt. (A/Major), Leinster Rgt. and M.G.C.; M.C.

MORSE, H. E. (D.S.O. L.G. 22.1.20), Lt., R.N., 15.10.12.

MORSE, R. V. (D.S.O. L.G. 4.6.17), Major, Mining Section, Aust. Mil. Forces.

MORSHEAD, H. T., F.R.G.S. (D.S.O. L.G. 1.1.17); b. 23.11.82; s. of late R. Morshead, M.A., J.P., of Hurlditch Court; m. Evelyn Templer, d. of H. Widdicombe, of 21, St. George's Square, S.W.; one s.; educ. Winchester

College; R.M.A., Woolwich; 2nd Lt., R.E., 21.12.01; Lt. 3.8.04; Capt. 21.12.12; Major 21.12.16; served in France, 1915–19; Despatches; with Waziristan Field Force, 1920.

MORSHEAD, L. J. (D.S.O. L.G. 4.6.17), Lt.-Col., Aust. Mil. Forces.

MORSHEAD, O. F. (D.S.O. L.G. 26.11.17) (Details, L.G. 6.4.18); b. 1893; s. of late R. Morshead; educ. Marlborough; R.M.A., Woolwich; Magdalene College, Cambridge; Fellow and Librarian, Magdalene College, Cambridge; Asst. Sec. to University Appointments Board from 1920; served Europ. War, 1914–19; in R.E. and on Staff, in France and on Italian Front; Despatches five times; Bt. Major; M.C.; Croce di Guerra.

MORSHEAD, R. H. ANDERSON- (see Anderson-Morshead, R. H.).

MORT, G. M. (D.S.O. L.G. 22.6.18); b. Sydney, N.S.W.; s. of Thomas Sutcliffe and Marianne Elizabeth Mort; m. Sylvia Gertrude, d. of Col. Farquhar Glennie and Edith Glennie; educ. Charterhouse; 2nd Lt., 8th Hrs., 8.9.97; Lt. 4.5.98; Capt. 16.4.01; Maj. 19.10.09; Lt.-Col. 19.10.17; ret. pay 1.11.20; S. African War, 1900–2; Despatches twice; Queen's Medal, 3 clasps; King's Medal, 2 clasps; Europ. War; Despatches twice. His D.S.O. was awarded for the fighting about Montauban in March, 1918. He died 27.12.23.

MORTER, S. P. (D.S.O. L.G. 1.1.18), Lt.-Col., R.F.A.

MORTIMORE, C. A. (D.S.O. L.G. 14.1.16); b. 28.12.75; s. of late A. Mortimore; educ. Uppingham; 2nd Lt., R.F.A., 25.7.00; Lt. 4.7.03; Capt. 24.7.11; Major 21.11.14; Lt.-Col., R.F.A.; served S. Africa, 1900–2; Queen's Medal, 4 clasps; King's Medal, 2 clasps; Europ. War, 1914–18; Despatches; Bt. Lt.-Col. 3.6.18; Légion d'Honneur.

MORTON, F. W. (D.S.O. L.G. 22.8.18), Major, 12th Inf., Pretoria Rgt., S. African Mil. Forces; served Natal Native Rebellion, 1906; Medal and clasp; Europ. War; Despatches.

MORTON, H. (D.S.O. L.G. 3.6.18); b. 16.10.82; 2nd Lt., Notts. and Derby. R., 14.8.16; Lt. 14.2.18; Lt.-Col., ret. pay, 18.7.19; M.C.

MORTON, H. M., M.B. (D.S.O. L.G. 25.8.17); b. 26.8.73; Lt., R.A.M.C., 17.11.99; Capt. 17.11.02; Major 17.5.11; Lt.-Col. 1.3.15; C.B.E.

MORTON, W. A. (D.S.O. L.G. 1.1.19), Major, Aust. A.M.C.

MOSBY, J. E. G. (D.S.O. L.G. 26.7.18), T/Lt., R.A.F.

MOSELEY, A. H. (D.S.O. L.G. 1.1.18), Lt.-Col., Aust. A.M.C.

MOSLEY, H. S. (D.S.O. L.G. 14.1.16); b. 3.2.79; served S. African War, 1901–2; Queen's Medal, 2 clasps; Lt., A.V.C. (now R.A.V.C.), 15.3.02; Capt. 15.4.07; Major 10.7.15; served Europ. War; A.D.V.S., 1st Cav. Div., Br. Armies in France, 1916–17; T/Lt.-Col. and A.D.V.S., 4th A.C., Br. Armies in France, 16.6.17; Despatches; Bt. Lt.-Col. 3.6.16.

MOSLEY, W. H. (D.S.O. L.G. 3.6.19); b. 10.4.83; 2nd Lt., Wilts. R., 19.11.02; Lt. 24.8.04; Capt. 25.1.11; Maj. 19.11.17; M.C.

MOSS, D. W. (D.S.O. L.G. 3.6.19); b. 13.6.81; 2nd Lt., R.A., 6.3.15; Lt. 18.8.16; Major, ret. pay, 29.1.20; M.C.

MOSS, L. B. BOYD- (see Boyd-Moss, L. B.).

MOSS, W. (D.S.O. L.G. 16.9.18), T/Capt., Linc. R.

MOSS-BLUNDELL, F. B. (D.S.O. L.G. 1.1.17); b. 21.9.73; s. of J. S. Moss-Blundell; educ. Rugby; Trinity College, Cambridge; 2nd Lt., 2nd E. Riding Yorks. Rgt., R.G.A. (Volunteers), 1898, and served in this till the formation of the present brigade as a T.F. in 1907; Lt.-Col., 1913, and went to France in command of the Brigade, April, 1915; Colonel, 2nd Northumbrian Brig. He was taken prisoner and sent to Stralsund, where he remained until his release; Despatches several times; C.M.G.

MOSSOP, A. I. (D.S.O. L.G. 1.1.18); was Capt. commanding a Squadron I.Y. in S. African War, 1901–2. In Sept. 1914, he was posted to 11th Batt. R.W.F.; afterwards transferred to 12th Batt. R.W.F., as Major, Second-in-Command, and from end of 1916 took over command of the battalion; transferred to regular list, Oxford and Bucks. L.I., and sent to France; attached to 5th Batt. as Second-in-Command; took part in Arras operations 9.4.17 and onwards; Despatches. He was awarded his D.S.O. for Ypres operations of 31 July and onwards.

MOSTYN-OWEN, R. A. (D.S.O. L.G. 7.11.18), Capt. (A/Lt.-Col.), Rif. Brig.

MOTHERSILL, G. S. (D.S.O. L.G. 1.1.18), Major, Can. A.M.C.

MOUAT, G. E. D. (D.S.O. L.G. 1.2.17); b. Madras, 14.2.79; s. of Col. G. Bridges Mouat, R.A.M.C., of Camilla Lodge, Sutton, Surrey, and Florence Mouat (*née* Mathewes); m. Maud Grace Frances McArthur, d. of Col. E. W. McArthur, R.E.; educ. Eastbourne; Sandhurst; Captain of Sandhurst Association Football Team, 1898; won the Revolver for Gymnastics at Sandhurst, 1898; Lawn Tennis Champion South of India, 1907; Lawn Tennis Champion Mauritius, 1902–3–4–5; played Cricket for Madras Presidency, 1907–8; 2nd Lt., Unatt., 25.1.99; Indian S.C. 10.4.00; Lt., I.A., 25.4.01; Capt. 25.1.08; Major 1.9.15; served on the Staff in E. Africa, 1914–15–16; Despatches; severely wounded.

MOULD, J. (D.S.O. L.G. 25.8.16), A/Capt., Worc. R. His D.S.O. was awarded for gallantry on 15–17.7.16, at Pozières; M.C. He was killed in action 3.9.16.

MOULTON-BARRETT, A. L. (D.S.O. L.G. 3.6.18); b. 15.11.74; 2nd Lt., Dorset R., 1.12.97; Lt. 11.12.99; Capt. 22.3.05; Maj. 15.6.15; Lt.-Col. 20.5.20.

MOULTON-BARRETT, E. M. (D.S.O. L.G. 23.6.15) (Bar, 26.7.18), Major (T/Lt.-Col.), North'd Fus. (see "The Distinguished Service Order," from its institution to 31.12.15, same publishers).

MOULTRIE, H. C. (D.S.O. L.G. 1.1.18); b. 23.9.68; 2nd Lt., R.A., 17.2.88; Lt. 17.2.91; Capt. 19.10.98; Maj. 12.12.08; Col. 5.1.20; ret. pay 22.10.21; Chitral, 1895; Medal, clasp; Tirah, 1897–98; 2 clasps; Europ. War; Despatches.

MOUSLEY, J. H. (D.S.O. L.G. 3.6.16); b. 26.8.85; s. of J. A. Mousley, of Feulan House, Leamington; educ. St. Alban's School; Rugby School; University College, London; joined 1st London R.E. (V.F.) 1.4.04, and later E. Lanc. R.E.; T/Major, Aug. 1914; Major, R.E. (T.F.), 11.6.04; Capt. (from T.F.) 5.2.21; A/Lt.-Col. 4.8.18; served on the Suez Canal Defences from about 26.9.14 to 28.4.15; unit was responsible for all bridges, etc., at Ismailia and Toussoim and defence works at those and other posts; present at Turkish Attack 3.2.15; landed at Gallipoli 12.5.15, and left there on the night of 28–29.12.15; during this period was in the front trenches for five months on end; present at the Battle of Romani, Aug. 1916; entered El-Arish, 5.1.17; left Alexandria 12.2.17 for France; landed in France 2.3.17; assisted in the construction of bridges over the Somme at Bray, near Peronne, and served with his unit in the line at Ronssoy, Havrincourt Wood, Ypres, Nieuport, La Bassée Canal, and in the retreat of March and April, 1918, from Gommecourt, Bucquoy, to Gommecourt Wood, and again in the line at Colincamps until appointed C.R.E. of the IV. Corps Troops 4.8.18, which appointment he held during the advance; Despatches three times; holds T.D.

J. H. Mousley.

MOUTON, W. J. (D.S.O. L.G. 22.8.18), Lt.-Col., S. African Mil. Forces.

MOWAT, A. L. (D.S.O. L.G. 2.4.19) (Details, L.G. 10.12.19); s. of J. G. Mowat; Capt., Duke of Wellington's Rgt.; M.C.

MOWATT, C. R. J. (D.S.O. L.G. 14.1.16); b. 13.12.72; 2nd Lt., North'n R., 2.6.94; Lt. 7.11.97; Capt. 17.3.03; Adjt., North'n R., 1908–11; Major 12.11.14; Lt.-Col. 25.1.21.

MOXON, C. C. (D.S.O. L.G. 1.1.18); b. 4.3.66, at Pontefract; s. of R. Moxon; m. Lucia, d. of Dr. C. Percival; one s.; one d.; educ. Edinburgh Academy; St. Thomas's Hospital, London; 1st comm., 1892; Lt.-Col., Oct. 1912; Hon. Colonel, 5th Batt. K.O.Y.L.I.; served S. African War, 1900–1; Queen's Medal, 3 clasps; Europ. War, 1914–18; Despatches twice; C.M.G.; has T.D.

MOXON, C. S. (D.S.O. L.G. 4.2.18) (Details, L.G. 5.7.18); s. of A. E. Moxon, of Dalton, Huddersfield; Lt. (A/Capt.), W. Riding Rgt.

MOYER, L. C. (D.S.O. L.G. 22.6.18), Major, Can. Rly. Troops.

MOZLEY, B. C., B.A. (D.S.O. L.G. 30.3.16); b. Eton, 7.10.93; s. of late H. W. Mozley, M.A., retired House Master, Eton College, and Clara Magdalene Mozley; educ. Eton College (Foundation Scholar); King's College, Cambridge; 2nd Lt., Dorsets. R., 1914; Lt., Feb. 1915; Capt., Feb. 1916; demobilized Feb. 1919; served Europ. War, 1914–17; left England for B.E.F. 13.7.15, with 6th Dorset Rgt.; wounded, and won D.S.O. during an unsuccessful counter-attack against captured positions on 15–16.2.16; wounded (second time) 2.1.17, near Les Bœufs; Ypres Salient, July, 1915–March, 1916; Armentières, March–April, 1916; Somme Area, July, 1916–Jan. 1917; Despatches.

MOZLEY, E. N. (D.S.O. L.G. 3.6.16); b. 21.5.75; s. of J. R. Mozley and Edith Mozley; m. Annie Campbell, d. of A. Scott; one s.; one d.; 2nd Lt., R.E., 20.9.94; Lt. 20.9.97; Capt. 1.4.04; Maj. 20.9.14; ret. pay 3.12.19; S. African War, 1899–1900; Queen's Medal, 3 clasps; Europ. War, fighting for seven months with A.N.Z.A.C. at Gallipoli, Helles, Suvla Bay, and also in Egypt; Despatches three times; Bt. Lt.-Col. 3.6.18.

MUDIE, T. C. (D.S.O. L.G. 3.6.19); b. 8.10.80; 2nd Lt., R. Scots., 12.8.99; Lt. 7.11.00; Capt. 16.5.05; Maj. 1.9.15; Bt. Lt.-Col. 3.6.18; *p.s.c.*; S. African War, 1899–1902; Queen's Medal, 4 clasps; King's Medal, 2 clasps; Europ. War; Despatches.

MUIR, A. W. (D.S.O. L.G. 2.4.19) (Details, L.G. 10.12.19), T/Capt. (A/Major), 2nd Batt. Northd. Fus.; M.C.

MUIR, H. G. (D.S.O. L.G. 31.5.16), Commander, R.N.R.; R.D.

MUIR, J. (D.S.O. L.G. 1.2.19), Lt. (A/Capt.), 5th Batt. R. Scots, att. 5/6th Batt. T.F.

MUIR, J. B. (D.S.O. L.G. 18.10.17) (Details, L.G. 7.3.18), Lt.-Col., R. Highrs.; served Europ. War, 1914–18; Despatches; Croce di Guerra; Legion of Honour.

MUIRHEAD, J. A. (D.S.O. L.G. 4.6.17); b. 24.5.79; educ. Bedford School; 2nd Lt., R.A., 18.7.00; 2nd Lt., I.S.C., 9.4.02; Lt., I.A., 8.10.02; Capt. 18.7.09; Major 1.9.15; Major (Bt. Lt.-Col.), 1st Lancers, I.A.; served Europ. War, 1914–18; Despatches thrice; Bt. Lt.-Col.; served Afghanistan, 1919; Medal and clasp.

MUIRHEAD, J. R. (D.S.O. L.G. 3.6.19), Major (T/Lt.-Col.), 5th F.A., Aust. A.M.C.

MUIRHEAD, J. S. (D.S.O. L.G. 3.6.18); s. of J. Muirhead; nephew of Lt.-Col. C. L. Spencer, D.S.O., of the Glasgow R.E.; educ. Fettes College, and Oxford, where he graduated with 1st Class Honours. Before the war he was an Officer of the Glasgow R.E.; Major, R.E.; M.C.

MUIRHEAD, MURRAY (D.S.O. L.G. 18.2.15) (Bar, L.G. 8.3.19) (Details, L.G. 4.10.19) (see "The Distinguished Service Order," from its institution to 31.12.15, same publishers).

MULLEN, L. M. (D.S.O. L.G. 4.6.17), Lt.-Col., Aust. Mil. Forces.

MULLER, C. H., M.B. (D.S.O. L.G. 1.2.17), T/Lt.-Col., S. African Med. Corps.

MULLER, F. (D.S.O. L.G. 22.8.18), Major, S.A.E.C.

MULLER, J. (D.S.O. L.G. 3.6.19), Capt. (T/Major and A/Lt.-Col.), Welsh R., Commanding 36th Batt. M.G.C.; M.C.

MULLIGAN, E. N. (D.S.O. L.G. 1.1.18), Major, Aust. Engrs.

MULLINS, A. G. (D.S.O. L.G. 4.6.17); b. 22.11.86, at Grahamstown, S. Africa; s. of late Rev. Canon R. J. Mullins; m. Joan Cicely, d. of J. D. Tyrwhitt-Drake; two d.; educ. St. Andrew's College, Grahamstown; Rhodes University College; Keble College, Oxford; joined Military Forces 27.8.14 (eight years' previous Volunteer Service); Major, S. African Heavy Artillery; served Europ. War in German S.W. Africa from Aug. 1914, first with Imp. L.H., and later with Heavy Artillery; in France and Belgium from April, 1916; Despatches twice.

MULOCK, G. F. A. (D.S.O. L.G. 14.3.16), Cdr., R.N., 30.6.16.

MULOCK, R. H., B.Sc. (D.S.O. L.G. 22.6.16) (Bar, L.G. 26.4.18); b. 11.8.86; s. of W. R. Mulock, K.C., of Winnipeg; m. Edythe, d. of B. Goodman; Graduate in Electrical Engineering, McGill University, Montreal; served Europ. War, 1914–18, 1st Can. Contingent, B.E.F.; Colonel; Lt.-Col., R.A.F.; Member of British Air Board; Chevalier, Legion of Honour; C.B.E.

MULQUEEN, F. J. (D.S.O. L.G. 16.9.18), T/Major, R.E.; M.C.

MULVEY, J. J. (D.S.O. L.G. 1.1.18), Major, S. African Pioneer Batt.

MUNBY, A. M. (D.S.O. L.G. 3.6.18); b. 7.6.82; 2nd Lt., Bord. R., 29.7.03; Lt. 20.10.05; Capt. 16.6.12; Maj. 22.10.17; Lt.-Col., ret. pay, 19.10.21; S. African War, 1901–2, in Mediterranean; Medal; Europ. War; Despatches.

MUNBY, J. E. (D.S.O. L.G. 1.1.17); b. Myton-on-Swale, Yorks, 26.3.81; s. of late E. C. Munby; m. Helena Maud, d. of late J. G. Lyon; educ. Malvern; R.M.C., Sandhurst; joined 1st Yorks. L.I., 1900; raised 6th S. Batt. K.O.Y.L.I. at beginning of European War, and served with it till the end of 1914; Lieut.-Colonel; was Brig.-Major, 83rd Brig., at and near Ypres till May, 1915; with 2nd Batt. K.O.Y.L.I. till July, 1915; with 14th Light Division as G.S.O., 3rd and 2nd Grade, July to Feb. at Ypres, Arras, and on the Somme; D.A.A. and Q.M.G. from 1921; Despatches; Bt. Lt.-Col.; C.M.G.

MUNDY, G. H. B. (D.S.O. L.G. 1.1.19); b. 11.8.60; m. Rose, 9th d. of late Sir Robert Miller Mundy; one s.; one d.; ent. R.N., 1873; Commander, 1896; Capt., 1902; Rear-Admiral, 1912; Vice-Admiral, 1917; Admiral, 1920; served Egyptian War, 1892; Medal; Khedive's Bronze Star; Admiral Superintendent, Pembroke Dockyard, 1908–11; Devonport Dockyard, 1913–16; retired 1917; Vice-Admiral, North Atlantic Convoy, 1917; Despatches; C.B.; M.V.O.

MUNDY, P. R. M. (D.S.O. L.G. 1.2.19); b. 16.7.91; 2nd Lt., S.W.B., 4.3.11; Lt. 18.4.13; Capt. 21.6.15; M.C.

MUNN, F. L. R. (D.S.O. L.G. 20.1.21); M.C.; b. 20.7.89; 2nd Lt. 20.1.09 Lt., Ind. Army, 20.4.11; Capt. 1.9.15.

MUNRO, A. (D.S.O. L.G. 19.11.17) (Details, L.G. 22.3.18), 2nd Lt., Sea. Highrs.

MUNRO, D. C. D. (D.S.O. L.G. 16.9.18); b. 13.12.85, at Cairnie, Aberdeenshire; s. of R. Munro, Farmer, of Aberdeenshire, and Mary Campbell, d. of Dr. Campbell, of Gartly; m. Grace, widow of M. J. Sutton, of Wargrave Manor, Berks, and d. of C. T. Studd and P. L. Studd, d. of W. Stewart, of Belfast; educ. Ruthven Public School, and in Edinburgh; joined R.M.L.I., 30.6.03; Gordon Highrs., Dec. 1903; served Europ. War; D.C.M. for Neuve Chapelle; Medal of St. George of Russia; wounded; 2nd Lt., Gordon Highrs., 4.5.15; Lt. 9.7.16; Capt. 18.7.17; T/Major 22.5.17; T/Lt.-Col. 5.4.18; Despatches; Military Cross for gallantry in the Battle of the Somme. His D.S.O. was awarded for gallantry in action near La Bassée.

MUNRO, E. J. (D.S.O. L.G. 4.6.17), Major, Aust. A.S.C.

MUNRO, W. A. (D.S.O. L.G. 1.1.19), Lt.-Col., 11th Batt. Can. Rly. Troops.

MURCHISON, D. S. (D.S.O. L.G. 1.1.18), Major, N.Z. Mtd. Rifles.

MURCHISON, K. D., M.B. (D.S.O. L.G. 4.6.17), Capt. (A/Lt.-Col.), R.A.M.C., S.R.

MURDIE, R. (D.S.O. L.G. 27.7.16), Capt., 5th Can. Infy. Bn.

MURDOCH, C. (D.S.O. L.G. 16.9.18); s. of late H. H. Murdoch, of Calverley Lodge, Tunbridge Wells; Capt. (T/Lt.-Col.), Yeom., att. Hants R.

MURDOCH, T. (D.S.O. L.G. 1.1.19), Lt.-Col., 1st Pioneer Batt. Aust. Mil. Forces.

MURIEL, J. C. (D.S.O. L.G. 1.1.18); b. 12.9.88; m. Kitty, d. of late W. A. Fitzherbert; one s.; Major, R. Inniskilling Fus.; served Europ. War, 1914–18; Despatches.

MURLIS-GREEN, G. W. (see Green, G. W. Murlis-).

MURPHY, A. D. (D.S.O. L.G. 25.8.17); b. 30.4.90; s. of Lt.-Col. E. W. Murphy, late 2nd Batt. Leinster R.; 2nd Lt., Leins. R., 2.12.11; Lt. 5.3.13; Capt.; Bt.-Major (A/Lt.-Col.), 2nd Batt. Leinster R. As Subaltern and Transport Officer he embarked for France 8.9.14, with the 2nd Batt., which formed part of the 6th Div. of the original Exp. Force; took part in Battle of the Aisne, and later, on 20.10.14, near Lille, and later commanded the battalion. He was killed in action on 6.11.17. His D.S.O. was awarded for gallantry at Wytschaete on 7.6.17. He also had the M.C.

MURPHY, C. F. DE S. (D.S.O. L.G. 1.1.17); b. 1882; s. of Jerome Murphy, of Ashton, Cork; educ. Beaumont; Lt.-Col., late R. Berks. Rgt.; served S. African War; Europ. War, R. Berks. R. and R.F.C. (now R.A.F.); Despatches thrice; M.C.

MURPHY, G. F. (D.S.O. L.G. 4.6.17) (Bar, L.G. 16.9.18), Lt.-Col., Aust. Inf.; C.M.G.

MURPHY, J. J. (D.S.O. L.G. 14.1.16), T/Major, A.S.C. (now R.A.S.C.).

MURPHY, J. L. (D.S.O. L.G. 15.2.19) (Details, L.G. 30.7.19) (Bar, L.G. 2.4.19) (Details, 10.12.19), Major, Manchester R., S.R., att. 2nd Batt.

MURPHY, L., L.R.C.P., L.R.C.S., L.F.P.S. (D.S.O. L.G. 19.10.16); b. 8.10.86; s. of J. Murphy; m. Millicent Fetherstonhaugh; one s.; Lt., R.A.M.C., Feb. 1908; Capt., Aug. 1911; served Europ. War; Mesopotamia, 1915–16; Despatches.

MURPHY, T. J. F. (D.S.O. L.G. 1.1.18) (Bar, L.G. 11.1.19), Lt.-Col., Can. A.M.C.

MURPHY, W. H. (D.S.O. L.G. 18.2.18) (Details, L.G. 18.7.18), Major, London R.

MURPHY, W. R. ENGLISH- (see English-Murphy, W. R.).

MURRAY, HON. A. C. (D.S.O. L.G. 14.1.16); b. 27.3.79; 4th s. of 10th Viscount Elibank and Blanche, d. of E. J. Scott; ent. Army, 1898; Lt.-Colonel, late K.O.S.B.; served China, with International Forces, 1900; Medal; Europ. War, 2nd King Edward's Horse, 1914–16; Despatches; Member of Royal Company of Archers (King's Bodyguard for Scotland); Parliamentary Private Secretary to Under-Secretary of State for India, 1909, and to Sir Edward Grey, Secretary of State for Foreign Affairs, 1910–14; employed Ministry of Munitions (Labour Disputes), 1916; Assist. Mil. Attaché, Washington, 1917 (C.M.G.); Political Intelligence Dept., F.O., 1918; Director, North British Railway Company; on 4.12.18 was re-elected to Parliament as a Coalition Liberal without opposition.

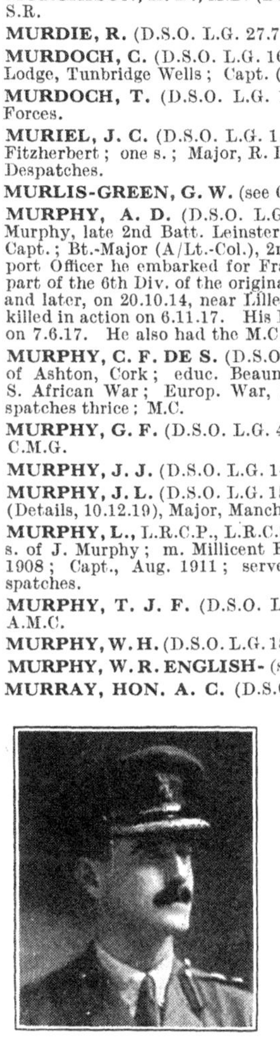

Hon. A. C. Murray.

MURRAY, A. D. (D.S.O. L.G. 1.1.19); b. 30.4.78; s. of late Col. K. D. Murray, D.S.O., R. Irish Fus.; m. Rosamund, d. of late T. Davey; three s.; educ. Haileybury; 2nd Lt., R.A., 24.6.98; Capt. 3.3.04; Lt.-Col., ret. pay 30.10.21; Waziristan, 1901–2; Medal, clasp; Europ. War, 1915–18, in France; severely wounded; Legion of Honour; Croix de Guerre.

MURRAY, A. J. L. (D.S.O. L.G. 11.11.19); b. 25.11.86; s. of A. H. Hallam Murray, M.A., F.S.A., F.R.G.S. (3rd son of John Murray III., Publisher), and Alice M., d. of R. du Cane; m. 3.9.12 in New College Chapel, Oxford, Ellen Maxwell, d. of Rev. W. A. Spooner, D.D., Warden of New College, Oxford, and Frances Wycliffe Goodwin, d. of Harvey Goodwin, Bishop of Carlisle; one s.; three d.; educ. Eton; H.M.S. Britannia; R.N. College; Midshipman, 1903; Lt., 1908; Commander, 1920; served in H.M.S. Agamemnon (Channel Fleet and Dardanelles); Mining School, Portsmouth, and Dwina River Flotilla, N. Russian Campaign, 1919; wounded; Despatches twice; O.B.E.

MURRAY, B. E. (D.S.O. L.G. 14.1.16); b. 10.5.81; s. of late Col. P. H. Murray, Commanding 2nd Shrops. L.I. and 4th Regimental District, and Mary Leaycraft, d. of Hon. S. S. Ingham, of Bermuda; educ. Wellington College; joined 4th Batt. (Militia), 1898; 1st Batt. 18.4.00; Lieut. 15.4.01; Capt., 1910; Major, 1915; Lt.-Colonel; served in India, Somaliland and Uganda, W. Africa; E. Africa and Aden (Medal); Somaliland, 1908 (Medal with clasp); Europ. War, 1914–17; Despatches twice; Bt. Lt.-Colonel 1.1.17; 1914 Star.

MURRAY, C. A. G. O. (D.S.O. L.G. 3.6.18); b. 19.11.87; 2nd Lt., K.O.S.B., 22.2.08; Lt. 17.4.09; Capt. 28.4.15; Bt. Major 3.6.19.

MURRAY, C. M. (D.S.O. L.G. 3.6.18); b. 4.3.77, at Claremont, Cape Colony; s. of C. F. K. Murray, O.B.E., Lt.-Col., S.A.M.C., and Caroline Murray; m. a daughter of H. M. Robertson; one s.; two d.; educ. Diocesan College, Rondebosch; Pembroke College, Cambridge; Capt., S.A.M.C., 24.8.14; Major 15.8.15; 2nd-in-Command of 1st S.A. Field Ambulance; served in G.S.W. African Campaign, with the Northern Force, and subsequently with the 1st S.A. Field Ambulance, attached to S.A. Brigade in the 9th Division; Despatches twice. He was awarded his D.S.O. for gallantry at Passchendaele, Sept.–Oct. 1917; M.C.

MURRAY, D. (D.S.O. L.G. 1.1.19) (Bar, L.G. 2.4.19) (Details, L.G. 10.12.19), T/Capt., Manch. R., att. 21st Batt.

MURRAY, D. D. C. (D.S.O. L.G. 22.8.18), Major, 5th Mounted Brigade (Supernumerary List), S. African Military Forces.

MURRAY, D. N. W., M.D. (D.S.O. L.G. 1.1.17); b. New Zealand, 1876; s. of B. M. Murray, of Scotland; educ. Auckland College and Grammar School; Edinburgh University; Colonel, N.Z. Medical Corps; served S. African War, 1900 (R.A.M.C.); Europ. War from 1914; N.Z. Exp. Force; operations on the Suez Canal, 1915; Gallipoli, 1915; France, 1916; Despatches; C.M.G.

MURRAY, E. M. (D.S.O. L.G. 2.12.18); b. 24.9.86; s. of late Col. R. D. Murray, M.B., I.M.S.; m. Gladys Vivienne, d. of H. H. Woodruff; one d.; educ. Clifton College; R.M.C., Sandhurst; joined 2nd Batt. The Black Watch, 1906; transferred to Q.V.O. Corps of Guides, F.F. (Cavalry), 1909; att. R.F.C. from Sept. 1914, till commissioned in R.A.F., Aug. 1919; Squadron Leader; served France, Egypt, Mesopotamia; Despatches; M.C.

MURRAY, G. A. DELMÉ- (see Delmé-Murray, G. A.).

MURRAY, G. B. (D.S.O. L.G. 19.12.17), Capt., Mercantile Marine (Lt., R.N.R.).

MURRAY, H. P. W. G. (D.S.O. L.G. 15.9.16); b. 8.9.80; s. of Peter Murray, R.N.; m. 1914, Mabel, y. d. of W. Avens; three sons; educ. Portsmouth Grammar School; entered R.N. 15.1.98; Paymaster Commander, 1914; served as Secretary to Senior Officer of International Squadron blockading coasts of Montenegro and Albania, 1913; Secretary to International Commission of Admirals administering Scutari, Albania. At the beginning of the Europ. War was Secretary to Vice-Admiral commanding Channel Fleet, 1914; Secretary to Admiral commanding 1st Battle Squadron and 2nd-in-Command, Grand Fleet, 1914–16; Secretary to Second Sea Lord, Admiralty, 1916–17; Secretary to Commander-in-Chief, Coast of Scotland, 1917–19; Secretary to Commander-in-Chief, Portsmouth, 1919-20; present at Jutland; Despatches; Order of St. Stanislas.

MURRAY, H. W. (D.S.O. L.G. 14.11.16) (Bar, L.G. 18.6.17), Lt.-Col., Aust. Inf.; V.C.; C.M.G.; M.C. (see "The Victoria Cross," same publishers).

MURRAY, JAMES (D.S.O. L.G. 8.3.18); s. of Sir James Murray, D.L., of Glenburnie Park, Aberdeen; Capt., R. Scots.

MURRAY, JOHN, M.A. (D.S.O. L.G. 15.2.19) (Details, L.G. 30.7.19) (Bar, L.G. 3.6.19); b. 12.6.84; s. of John Murray, C.V.O., Head of the Publishing House of John Murray, and of a daughter of William Leslie, of Warthill, Aberdeenshire, late M.P.; m. Lady Helen de Vere, d. of 1st Earl Brassey, G.C.B.; educ. Eton; Magdalen College, Oxford (2nd Class Mod. Hist.); Lt.-Col., Scottish Horse, Commanding 12th Batt. The Royal Scots, 1918–19; served Europ. War, in Gallipoli, Egypt and France; Despatches; Croix de Guerre (Belgium); T.D.; High Sheriff, County of London, 1914; Member of the Westminster City Council; Editor of the "Magdalen College Record."

MURRAY, J. A. S. (D.S.O. L.G. 4.6.17); b. 17.8.69; 2nd Lt., Suff. R., 9.11.89; Lt. 9.4.92; Capt. 19.5.98; Adjt., A.O.D., 18.5.06 to 31.5.07; Major 16.2.11; Lt.-Col. 8.12.14; served S. African War, 1899-1902 (Queen's Medal, 3 clasps; King's Medal, 2 clasps); served Europ. War; Despatches.

MURRAY, J. J. (D.S.O. L.G. 1.2.19), Major, Aust. I.F.; M.C.

MURRAY, J. WOLFE- (D.S.O. L.G. 22.4.19), Comdr. (now Capt.), R.N.

MURRAY, K. D. B. (D.S.O. L.G. 1.1.17); b. 30.10.79; 2nd Lt., R. Muns. Fus., 11.2.99; Lt. 21.10.00; Lt., Ind. Army, 18.6.03; Capt. 11.2.08; Major 1.9.15; served S. African War, 1902 (Queen's Medal, 2 clasps); N.W. Frontier of India, 1908; Medal and clasp; Europ. War; Despatches.

MURRAY, L. (D.S.O. L.G. 1.1.17); b. 29.2.78; 1st commission 25.8.97; Major (Res. of Off.) 21.6.15; Lt.-Col. 15.11.15; retired from E. Surr. R. 3.6.14; served E. Africa, 1901 (Medal, with clasp); W. Africa (Liberia), 1905; Medal with clasp; Europ. War; Despatches.

MURRAY, R. A. WOLFE- (see Wolfe-Murray, R. A.).

MURRAY, R. E. (D.S.O. L.G. 26.4.17) (Bar, L.G. 1.1.18), Lt.-Col., British S. Africa Police. He died 29.6.20.

MURRAY, S. (D.S.O. L.G. 27.7.16), 2nd Lt., 2nd Batt. Rifle Brigade.

MURRAY, S. J. (D.S.O. L.G. 1.1.19); b. 26.8.67; s. of late E. F. Murray, M.I.C.E.; m. Mary Shedden, d. of late C. Evans-Lombe; two s.; one d.; educ. Haileybury; Clifton; R.M.C., Sandhurst; 2nd Lt., Conn. Rang., 11.2.88; Lt. 20.11.89; Capt. 16.8.94; Major 22.9.06; Lt.-Col., 1914; Bt. Col. 3.6.16; Col. 11.12.18; ret. pay, Staff, 1.12.20; served Europ. War, 1914–18, in command of 1st Batt. The Connaught Rangers in Flanders, Mesopotamia, Palestine; wounded twice; Despatches thrice; General Director of Graves Registration Work in three Eastern Theatres, 1919–20.

MURRAY, S. W. (gazetted as Murray, Sydney) (D.S.O. L.G. 27.7.16); b. 2.4.83; s. of late D. F. Murray, of Belfast; m. Maud Mary, d. of J. J. Hatch; one s.; two d.; joined Rif. Brig., 1901; 2nd Batt. S. Africa, 1902; Egypt, 1902–4; 3rd Batt., India, 1904; Aden, 1905; Devonport, 1906–7; Winchester, 1908–9; Physical Trainer, Kerrison School, 1900–12; Cheltenham College, 1912 (College Gym. Championship); Instructor to College; Kerrison School, 1913–14; rejoined Colours 4.8.14; France 19.8.14; engagements, Ligny; Retreat, Compiègne; Marne, Aisne, 1st Battle of Ypres; Albert 1.7.16; Le Transloy; twice wounded; Despatches; three times officially recognized by G.O.C. for gallantry; D.S.O. and D.C.M. (from Private to Major); Company Commander; Member of Military Training Mission to U.S.A., 1917–18; Organizer, Physical Training, Bancrofts School, 1920.

MURRAY, TERENCE DESMOND (D.S.O. L.G. 1.2.19); b. Parramatta, N.S.W., 19.1.91; s. of J. H. P. Murray, C.M.G., Lt.-Governor and Chief Judicial Officer, Papua, and Sybil, d. of Dr. R. L. Jenkins; m. Philippa Chevallier, d. of Lt.-Gen. Sir F. W. Kitchener, K.C.B.; one d.; educ. Beaumont College; Stonyhurst; 2nd Lt., Leins. R., 5.10.10; Lt. 17.4.12; Capt. 1.10.15; served Europ. War, 1914–18, France, Salonika, Palestine; Despatches; M.C.; King's Hundred, Bisley, 1919.

MURRAY, THOMAS DAVID (D.S.O. L.G. 26.1.17); Major, Hamps. R., attd. R. Highrs., temp. attd. Cam. R. He was awarded his D.S.O. for gallantry 13.11.16, at St. Pierre Divion.

MURRAY, W. (D.S.O. L.G. 3.6.19), T/Major, H.L.I., att. R. Scots; M.C.

MURRAY, W. A. (D.S.O. L.G. 4.6.17); b. 21.7.79; 2nd Lt., R.A., 25.4.00; Lt. 3.4.01; Capt. 24.9.09; Major 30.10.14; Bt. Lt.-Col. 1.1.18; served Europ. War; Despatches; C.M.G.

MURRAY, W. G. P. (D.S.O. L.G. 3.6.19); b. 30.5.74; 2nd Lt. 28.1.93; Lt., Ind. S.C., 28.4.95; Capt., Ind. Army, 28.1.02; Maj. 28.1.11; Lt.-Col. 22.1.18; *p.s.c.*; Chitral, 1895; Medal, clasp; Europ. War; Despatches.

MURRAY, W. H. (D.S.O. L.G. 3.6.19), Temp. Major (A/Lt.-Col.), 10th Battn. Scottish Rifles.

MURRAY-LYON, D. M. (D.S.O. L.G. 18.2.18) (Details, L.G. 18.7.18); b. 14.8.90; 2nd Lt., High. L.I., 9.12.11; Lt. 28.3.14; Capt. 1.10.15; Bt. Major, 1.1.19; M.C.

MURRAY-SMITH, W. (D.S.O. L.G. 1.2.17), Lt.-Col., S. African Horse.

MURRAY-THREIPLAND, W. (D.S.O. L.G. 3.6.16); b. 21.12.16; 2nd s. of late W. Scott-Kerr, J.P., D.L.; m. Charlotte Eleanor, y. d. and co-heiress of

W. W. Lewis, D.L., J.P.; one s.; succeeded to the estates of his cousin-german Sir P. Murray-Threipland, Bart.; educ. Fettes College, Edinburgh; Lt., 3rd Batt. R. Highrs., Militia, 1885; 2nd Lt., G. Gds., 28.5.87; Capt. 23.10.98; retired 23.7.02; Captain, 1902; Colonel 26.2.19; ret. 14.12.20; commanding Welsh Guards' Regimental District; late commanded 4th (The Border) Batt. K.O.S.B.; late Major, G. Gds.; served in Sudan Campaign, 1898 (Khartum; Queen's and Khedive's Medals and clasp); S. African War, 1900–2; Queen's and King's Medals with 5 clasps; Europ. War, 1914–16; Despatches.

MURRAY-WHITE, R. S. (D.S.O. L.G. 4.6.17), Capt., Yeomanry.

MURROW, H. LL. (D.S.O. L.G. 1.1.17); b. 31.1.79; 2nd Lt., R.A., 20.5.99; Lt. 16.2.01; Capt. 4.3.06; Major 30.10.14; served S. African War, 1900–2; Queen's Medal, 2 clasps; King's Medal, 2 clasps; Europ. War; Despatches.

MUSGRAVE, A. D. (D.S.O. L.G. 7.2.18); b. 10.3.74; 2nd Lt., R.A., 21.10.93; Lt. 21.10.96; Capt. 28.7.00; Adjt., R.A., 2.6.05 to 15.8.08; Major 14.11.10; Lt.-Col., R.F.A., 1.3.16; Bt. Col. 3.6.16; T/Brig.-Gen., 1917–18.

MUSGRAVE, E. C. (D.S.O. L.G. 3.6.16); b. Argentine Republic, 17.12.72; m. Muriel (who died in 1904), d. of C. Livingston; one d.; educ. R.M. College, Canada; T/Capt., 12th K.R.R.C., 1.10.14; Major, Feb. 1916; A/Lt.-Col. from 1.10.16 to 20.3.17; Major, late 12th Batt. K.R.R.C.

MUSGROVE, G. H. (D.S.O. L.G. 16.9.18); b. Walsall, England, 3.2.82; s. of William and Caroline Musgrove; m. Eva Flett, d. of J. Litster; one s.; educ. Birmingham University; enlisted S. Staffs. R. in 1900, to serve in S. African War (Medal and clasps); joined Victoria Rifle Rgt. (Canada); Lt., 31st Grey Rgt. (Canada), May, 1913; Capt., June, 1914; Major, Feb. 1916; left in command of men from Grey County for 1st Can. Contingent; was absorbed into 48th Highlanders; had his arm badly shattered in the Orchard engagement at Festubert; joined 20th Can. Batt., and was killed in action 28.8.18; Despatches twice.

MUSPRATT, S. F. (D.S.O. L.G. 3.6.16); b. 11.9.78; 2nd Lt., Unatt., 22.1.98; I.S.C. 23.9.99; Capt. 22.1.07; Major 1.9.15; Bt. Lt.-Col. 3.6.17; N.W.F. of India, 1908; operations in the Zakka Khel country; operations in the Mohmand country; Medal with clasp.

MUSSON, E. L. (D.S.O. L.G. 1.1.18); b. 6.7.85; 2nd Lt., Manch. R., 28.1.05; Lt. 12.6.09; Capt. 18.12.14; Despatches; M.C.

MUSTERS, J. N. CHAWORTH- (see Chaworth-Musters, J. N.).

MUTCH, G. (D.S.O. L.G. 12.3.17), 2nd Lt. (Temp. Lt.). Gord. Highrs. He was killed in action 6.7.17.

MYBURGH, P. STAFFORD- (D.S.O. L.G. 1.1.19); b. 12.5.93; s. of R. W. Myburgh and Mary S. Myburgh; m. 1919, Marie-Louise Picard; one d.; educ. Beaumont College, Windsor; 2nd Lt. 19.7.12; Lt. 9.6.15; Capt. 8.7.16; served Europ. War; Despatches four times; wounded four times; M.C., 1915; Croix de Guerre with Palms.

MYLES, E. K., (D.S.O. L.G. 17.3.17) (Details, L.G. 26.4.17), 2nd Lt. Welsh R., att. Worc. R.; V.C. (see "The Victoria Cross," by same publishers).

NADEN, F. (D.S.O. L.G. 26.11.17) (Details, L.G. 6.4.18) (1st Bar, L.G. 16.9.18) (2nd Bar, L.G. 8.3.19) (Details, L.G. 4.10.19), Lt. (A/Major), Ches. R., att. R. Highrs.; joined R.M.; served Ashanti Campaign (Medal); joined Stockport Volunteers; served S. African War; both Medals and clasps for S. Africa; Johannesburg, Orange Free State and Cape Colony; served in France with Territorials (Cheshire Rgt.) from Nov. 1914; won the M.C. and Bar. He was given the command with the rank of Lt.-Col. of a battalion of the Hants R. at the front.

NAGLE, W. J. (D.S.O. L.G. 11.1.19), T/2nd Lt. (A/Capt.), Suff. R.; served Europ. War; Despatches; M.C.

NAISMITH, J. O. (D.S.O. L.G. 4.6.17); b. 25.1.84; s. of the late Rev. R. Naismith and Mary Bertram Naismith; m. 1917, Maria Cecilia, 2nd d. of T. A. Bell; one d.; educ. George Watson's College, Edinburgh, and University, Edinburgh; R.F.A. (Spec. Res.) 30.3.10; Artillery Staff, R.M.A., 13.11.18; Inst., R.M.A., Woolwich, 4.9.20; Capt. (Spec. Res.), A.E.C., 25.11.20; served Europ. War; Despatches three times.

NALL, J. (D.S.O. L.G. 3.6.18); b. 24.8.87; e. s. of Joseph Nall, of Worsley, Lancs; m. 1916, Edith Elizabeth, y. d. of late J. L. Francklin and Hon. Mrs. Francklin; educ. privately; Director of Manchester Chamber of Commerce; Member, National Church Assembly; Member of E. Lancs. County Assocn. (T.F.); joined E. Lancs. Art., T.F., 1906; Staff Capt., R.A., Aug. 1914; served Europ. War, Suez Canal, Gallipoli, France, 1914–18; Despatches, Sinai; wounded; M.P. (U.), Hulme Division of Manchester, from Dec. 1918.

NANSON, G. G. (D.S.O. L.G. 1.1.19), T/Capt. (A/Major), 3rd Siege Battery, R.G.A.; served Europ. War; Despatches; M.C.

NAPER, L. A. D. (D.S.O. L.G. 1.1.18); b. 19.12.77; s. of Lt.-Col. William Dutton Naper, late 11th Foot (Devons.), and Jane W. Naper; m. Laura, Daphne Theodora, d. of Major O. F. T. Annesley, R.H.A.; one s.; one d.; educ. Evelyn's; Haileybury College; 2nd Lt., R.A., 24.6.99; Lieut. 14.2.01; Capt. 10.11.07; Adjt. 1.10.09 to 30.9.12; Major 30.10.14; Lt.-Col. 1.1.21; commanded 1st F.A. Brigade; served S. African War (Queen's Medal, 5 clasps); Europ. War, in France and Macedonia; Despatches twice; 3rd Class Serbian White Eagle with Swords; Caucasus, 1919.

NAPIER, L. E. S. (D.S.O. L.G. 4.5.20), Lt., R.N.; served Europ. War; Despatches.

NAPIER, W. R. (D.S.O. L.G. 2.7.17); b. 13.6.77; o. surv. s. of late Comdr. Lenox Napier and Ellen, 2nd d. of W. B. Buddicom, of Penbeddw Hall, Flints; m. 1902, Florence Maria, e. d. of late James O'Reilly Nugent, of Fareham; one s.; one d.; Capt., R.N.; served Europ. War; Superintendent of the Mining School, Portsmouth. His D.S.O. was awarded for Mine-sweeping.

NAPIER-CLAVERING, N. W. (D.S.O. L.G. 4.6.17); b. 24.12.83; e. s. of F. Napier-Clavering and Elizabeth, d. of T. Cowan; m. 1921, Margaret, d. of T. W. Vigers, of Guernsey; educ. Clifton College; R.M.A., Woolwich; 2nd Lt., R.E., 29.7.08; Lt. 18.8.10; Capt. 30.10.14; Bt. Major 1.1.19; served Europ. War; Despatches.

NARES, J. D. (D.S.O. L.G. 20.2.19), Cdr., R.N.; served Europ. War; Despatches.

NASH, E. J. MARTYN- (D.S.O. L.G. 26.8.18); e. s. of A. J. Nash, a General Manager of the Royal Mail Steam Packet Co., of whose four sons in the Army two have been severely wounded; T/Major, R.A.S.C.; served Europ. War; was a Lt.-Colonel. He was awarded his D.S.O. for Mesopotamia; Despatches.

NASH, G. S. F. (D.S.O. L.G. 29.11.18), Lt.-Comdr. (now Comdr.), R.N.; served Europ. War; Despatches.

NASH, H. E. P. (D.S.O. L.G. 1.1.18) (Bar, L.G. 18.2.18) (Details, L.G. 18.7.18); b. 6.3.89; 2nd Lt., R. Scots, 17.1.91; Lt. 25.4.94; Capt. 21.8.97; Major 8.10.10; Bt. Lt.-Col. 3.6.19; Lt.-Col. 7.8.20; served S. African War, 1899–1901 (Queen's Medal, 4 clasps); Europ. War; Despatches.

NASH, REV. R. H. (D.S.O. L.G. 3.6.18), Chaplain to the Forces, 2nd Class, Army Chaplains' Dept.; served Europ. War; Despatches.

NASMITH, A. P. (D.S.O. L.G. 10.1.17); s. of late Martin A. Nasmith, of Clevehurst, Weybridge; T/Capt., Bord. Regt.; served Europ. War; Despatches. He was awarded the D.S.O. for gallantry on 2.11.16, at Le Transloy. Capt. Nasmith was killed in action on 23.4.17. His two brothers received decorations during the war, Capt. M. Nasmith, R.N., being awarded the V.C. in 1915 and the C.B. in 1920, and Major R. Nasmith, H.L.I., the D.S.O. and M.C.

NASMITH, R. (D.S.O. L.G. 3.6.19); b. 4.4.92; s. of late Martin A. Nasmith; Capt., Highl. L. Inf., 26.7.17; Bt. Major 11.11.19 (Adjt., Tank Corps, 11.6.21; Major, Tank Corps, 6.8.21); served Europ. War, 1914–19; Despatches; M.C.

NATION, J. J. H. (D.S.O. L.G. 4.6.17); b. 5.12.74; s. of late General Sir John L. Nation, K.C.B.; educ. R.M.A., Woolwich; 2nd Lt., R.E., 1.4.95; Lt. 1.4.98; Capt. 1.4.04; Major 30.10.14; Bt. Lt.-Col. 1.1.17; T/Brig.-Gen. 10.11.17 to 14.8.19; Lt.-Col. 1.10.21; served S. African War; Despatches (L.G. 10.9.01); Queen's Medal, 5 clasps; King's Medal, 2 clasps; Europ. War, 1914–18; Despatches six times; C.V.O., 1917; Commander, Légion d'Honneur; French Croix de Guerre; Officer of Order of Leopold of Belgium; Belgian Croix de Guerre; lent for service under the Persian Government under the terms of the Anglo-Persian Agreement, 1919.

NAUNTON, H. P. (D.S.O. L.G. 16.8.17), T/Capt., E. Surrey R.; served Europ. War; Despatches. He was awarded the D.S.O. for gallantry on 24.4.17.

NAYLOR, C. (D.S.O. L.G. 29.8.17) (Bar, L.G. 2.11.17) (2nd Bar, L.G. 22.2.18); b. 12.6.91; e. s. of Wm. Naylor, A.M.I.C.E., F.C.S.; m. 1918, Lilian Margaret, o. d. of Jonathan Jenson; one s.; educ. Preston and Manchester Grammar School; served four years' apprenticeship at sea; joined Leyland Line, 1911, and served as 3rd, 2nd and 1st Officer till 1914; joined R.N.R., serving in H.M.S. Conqueror, 2nd Battle Squadron, till July, 1915; H.M.S. Oropesa, 10th Cruiser Squadron, till Dec. 1915; H.M.S. Q7, engaged on special work; commanded Q7, June, 1917; transferred R.N. with seniority; commanded H.M.S. Polyanthus, 1918; in H.M.S. Dryad; served Europ. War; Despatches; D.S.C. and Bar.

NAYLOR, R. F. B. (D.S.O. L.G. 3.6.19); b. 6.10.89; 2nd Lt., S. Staffs. R., 18.9.09; Lt. 1.4.10; Capt. 26.5.15; Major 1.1.18; served Europ. War; Despatches; M.C.

NEAME, P. (D.S.O. L.G. 14.1.16), Capt., R.E.; V.C. (see "The Victoria Cross," same publishers).

NEEDHAM, H. (D.S.O. L.G. 14.1.16); b. 23.4.76; e. s. of late Lt.-Col. Hon. H. C. Needham, Grenadier Gds.; m. 1902, Violet, d. of late Capt. H. Andrew, 8th Hrs., and Mrs. Yates Brown; educ. privately; 2nd Lt., Glouc. R., 28.3.00; Lt. 2.3.02; Capt. 1.7.09; Bt. Major 3.6.15; Major 1.9.15; Bt. Lt.-Col. 1.1.17; T/Brig.-Gen. 20.9.18 to 23.10.19; Lt.-Col., Worc. Regt., 8.10.21; Bt. Col. 3.6.19; served S. African War, 1899–1900; Queen's Medal, 2 clasps; Europ. War, in France, Egypt, Salonika, Russia; C.M.G.; Legion of Honour; St. Vladimir; U.S. Distinguished Service Medal; 1914 Star.

NEEDHAM, J. G. (D.S.O. L.G. 3.6.18), Lt.-Col., A.S.C.

NEEDHAM, R. A., M.D. (D.S.O. L.G. 14.1.16); b. 31.7.77; s. of late John Needham, Steel Merchant, of Manchester; educ. Owens College; Manchester University; B.Sc., 1897; M.B., 1899; D.P.H.; President, Manchester University Union; Demonstrator in Anatomy, Manchester University, 1900–2; Lt., Ind. M.S., 31.1.03; Capt. 31.1.06; Major 31.7.14; Deputy Director-Gen., Indian Medical Service, 1918; served Europ. War, in France, 1914–16 (Despatches three times); India, 1917–19 (Despatches); C.I.E., 1919; Delhi Durbar Medal, 1911.

NEEDHAM, R. M. B. (D.S.O. L.G. 1.1.18); b. 28.12.79; 2nd Lt., Suff. R., 23.7.02; Lt. 8.4.05; Capt. 24.2.14; Major 11.5.16; Bt. Lt.-Col. 3.6.19.

NEELAND, R. H. (D.S.O. L.G. 1.1.18), Lt., Can. Inf., 9.11.15; served Europ. War; was T/Capt. (A/Lt.-Col.), Can. Labour Corps.

NEELY, G. H. (D.S.O. L.G. 1.2.19); b. 15.7.85; s. of Wm. Valentine and Henrietta Neely; m. Evelyn Margaret, widow of Col. P. Prideaux Budge, D.S.O., R.F.A., d. of Mr. Gibson-Watt; educ. Kilkenny College; Dublin University; University of France; Capt., H.L.I., from T.F., 3.11.17; late O.C., 1st Batt. H.L.I.; served Europ. War from 1915; Despatches; four times wounded; 1914–15 Star; M.C. and Bar.

NEEVES, H. H. (D.S.O. L.G. 18.7.17), T/2nd Lt. (A/Capt.), North'd Fus.; served Europ. War; Despatches; M.C.

NEGUS, R. E. (D.S.O. L.G. 20.10.16); b. 18.7.83; s. of W. Negus, J.P., and Emilie Negus; m. Margaret Smith, d. of W. H. Renwick, J.P.; one s.; educ. Merchant Taylors' School, London, and St. John's College, Oxford; played for Oxford University Lacrosse Club, 1904–5; joined Inns of Court O.T.C., July, 1910; 2nd Lt., Inns of Court O.T.C., 1911; Capt., Aug. 1914; and in April, 1915, joined the King's Shropshire L.I.; Lt.-Colonel commanding 7th Shrops. L.I. from Dec. 1915, to July, 1916; served in France; Despatches twice.

NEILL, D. F. D. (D.S.O. L.G. 1.1.18), Capt. (A/Lt.-Col.), R. of Off., R.E.

NEILL, E. S. (D.S.O. L.G. 3.6.19), T/Major, 38th Batt. R. Fus.

NEILL, F. A. (D.S.O. L.G. 4.6.17); b. 11.11.91; s. of J. Neill; m. Winifred Margaret, d. of the late R. Colver; educ. Wellington College (Salop); commissioned R.E., T.F., 18.4.13; Capt. 6.2.15; Major 1.6.16; Lt.-Colonel; served Europ. War; wounded 23.5.18; Despatches four times; 1914 Star; Croix de Guerre.

NEILL, J. H. (D.S.O. L.G. 1.2.19), N.Z. A.M.C.

NEILL, R. B. (D.S.O. L.G. 1.1.18); b. 22.11.80; s. of P. C. Neill and Gertrude Emeline Neill; m. Katharine Gertrude, d. of J. Sinclair Thomson; one s.; one d.; educ. Christ's College, Christ Church, N.Z.; joined Army 14.9.01; Major, late R. Ir. Fus., S.R.; served S. African War; Queen's Medal and 5 clasps; Europ. War, 1914–18; Despatches three times.

NEILSON, D. F. (D.S.O. L.G. 26.7.18), Lieut. (T/Capt.), Lincs. R.; M.C. He was killed in action in France 16.4.18.

NEILSON, J. B. (D.S.O. L.G. 4.6.17), Lt.-Colonel, 5th Batt. H.L.I.

NEILSON, J. F. (D.S.O. L.G. 24.1.17); b. 27.6.84; 3rd s. of Wm. Neilson, of Arnewood, Kelvinside, Glasgow; m. Helen Vera, d. of W. Cazalet, of Moscow; educ. Uppingham; Sandhurst; 2nd Lt., 10th Hrs., 2.3.04; Lt. 22.10.05; Capt. 3.5.11; Major 15.5.15; Major, late 10th R. Hussars. At outbreak of Europ. War was attached to the Russian Armies; holds Russian Orders of St. Vladimir, St. Stanislas, St. Anne; C.B.E.

NEILSON, WILLIAM (D.S.O. L.G. 3.6.18), Major, Can. Infy.

NEILSON, WILLIAM (D.S.O. L.G. 1.1.19); b. 9.10.81; 2nd s. of William Neilson, of Arnewood, Kelvinside, Glasgow; m. Maud Anson, d. of Henry Anson Harton; three s.; educ. Uppingham; Sandhurst; 2nd Lt., 4th Hrs., 8.5.01; Lt. 1.5.04; Capt. 15.9.09; Major 22.11.15; Lt.-Col. 1.4.18; T/Brig.-Gen., 1918; served Europ. War, 1914–18; Despatches; Bt. Lt.-Col. 1.1.18, late Commanding 4th Q.O. Hussars.

NELLES, L. H. (D.S.O. L.G. 3.6.18) (Bar, L.G. 2.12.18), Lt.-Col., Canadian Inf.

NELSON, G. E. (D.S.O. L.G. 16.8.17); b. 8.12.74; 2nd Lt., Cheshire R., 27.6.15; Lt. 1.7.17; His D.S.O. was awarded for gallantry in Egypt 26.3.17.

NELSON, H. (D.S.O. L.G. 2.2.16) (Bar, L.G. 18.2.18) (Details, L.G. 18.7.18); b. 3.9.75; 2nd Lt., Bord. R., 28.9.95; Lt. 25.2.97; Capt. 19.12.03; Major 28.4.15; Bt. Lt.-Col. 1.1.18; T/Brig.-Gen. 28.11.18 to 29.3.19; Lt.-Col. 18.3.19.

The Distinguished Service Order 313

NELSON, J. W. (D.S.O. L.G. 17.4.16) ; b. 28.5.78 ; 2nd Lt. North'd Fus. 3.1.00 ; Lt. 9.6.00 ; Capt. 28.8.04 ; R.W. Kent R. 3.7.07 ; Major 1.9.15 ; served S. African War, 1899–1902 ; Queen's Medal, 3 clasps ; King's Medal, 2 clasps ; E. Africa, 1904 ; Medal with 2 clasps ; Nandi, 1905–6 ; Despatches ; Europ. War ; Despatches.

NEPEAN, H. D. H. Y. (D.S.O. L.G. 18.1.18) (Details, L.G. 25.4.18) ; b. 27.11.93 ; s. of Col. H. E. C. Nepean ; educ. Tonbridge School ; R.M.C., Sandhurst ; 2nd Lt., Unatt., 14.1.14 ; Ind. Army 10.10.14 ; Lt. 1.9.15 ; Capt. 14.1.18 ; 5th Royal Ghurkhas ; served Europ. War from 1914 ; wounded ; Despatches.

NETHERSOLE, M. H. B. (D.S.O. L.G. 8.2.19), Major, R.A.F.

NEVILE, G. C. (D.S.O. L.G. 1.1.18) ; b. 1.6.80 ; s. of P. S. Nevile, of Skelbrooke Park, Doncaster ; m. Jean, widow of Capt. D. F. P. Wormald ; 1st commission 22.8.00 ; Major 1.4.15 ; retired R.F.A. 11.3.19 ; served Europ. War, 1914–18 ; Despatches.

NEVILL, C. C. R. (D.S.O. L.G. 2.2.16) ; b. 21.1.73 ; ent R. War. Rgt. 21.4.00 ; Lt. 4.1.01 ; Capt. 18.11.08 ; Adjt., 9th Batt. R. War. R., 12.9.14 to 31.8.15 ; Major 1.9.15 ; served S. African War, 1902 ; Queen's Medal ; Europ. War ; Despatches ; O.B.E.

NEVILL, R. A. (D.S.O. L.G. 1.1.18), Lt.-Col., R.E.

NEWBOLD, C. J. (D.S.O. L.G. 4.6.17), T/Capt., R.E.

NEWBOLD, T. C. (D.S.O. L.G. 1.1.18), Major, Notts. and Derby. R. ; served S. African War, 1900–1 ; Queen's Medal with 3 clasps.

NEWCOMBE, E. O. A. (D.S.O. L.G. 1.1.17) ; b. 30.8.74 ; s. of late E. Newcombe, M.I.C.E. ; m. Annie Maria Laura, d. of late Hon. H.L. Courtenay ; one d. ; educ. Bath College ; R.M.A., Woolwich ; 1st commission 25.7.93 ; Major (Res. of Off.) 30.10.14 ; ret. pay, R.E., 24.12.12 ; Traffic Manager, Sudan Govt. Railways ; served Nile Exp., 1897 ; Nile Exp., 1898 ; Despatches ; Battle of Khartum ; 4th Class Medjidie ; 4th Class Osmanieh ; Medal ; S. African War, 1899–1902 ; Despatches ; Queen's Medal with 4 clasps ; King's Medal with 2 clasps ; Europ. War, 1914–17, with Egyptian Army ; Despatches ; Order of the Nile.

NEWCOMBE, S. F. (D.S.O. L.G. 22.1.16) ; b. 9.7.78 ; m. Elsie Chaki, of Constantinople ; one s. ; one d. ; 2nd Lt., R.E., 23.6.98 ; Lt. 14.2.01 ; Capt. 3.6.07 ; Major 30.10.14 ; Lt.-Colonel ; served S. African War, 1899–1900 ; Queen's Medal, 4 clasps ; Europ. War, Gallipoli, 1914–16 ; Despatches ; Bt. Lt.-Col. 3.6.17 ; Legion of Honour ; Order of the Crown of Italy.

NEWELL, E. M., A.M.Inst.C.E. (D.S.O. L.G. 3.6.16), Lt.-Col., R.E., T.F. ; served S. African War, 1901–2 (4th Lanc. R.E. Vols.) ; Queen's Medal with 5 clasps ; Europ. War ; Despatches ; has T.D.

NEWELL, F. W. M. (D.S.O. L.G. 3.6.19), T/Lt.-Col., R.E.

NEWELL, S. M. (D.S.O. L.G. 3.6.16), Major (T/Major, R.E.), R.E., T.F.

NEWILL, J. B. (D.S.O. L.G. 14.9.18), Lt.-Cdr., R.N.

NEWINGTON, H. A. H. (D.S.O. L.G. 14.1.16), Lt. (T/Capt.), 14th Co. of London Batt. The London Rgt., T.F. ; served S. African War, 1901–2 ; Queen's Medal, 4 clasps ; Europ. War ; Despatches.

NEWLAND, H. S. (D.S.O. L.G. 1.1.18), Lt.-Col., Aust. A.M.C.

NEWMAN, C. N. (D.S.O. L.G. 1.1.18), Major, N.Z. F.A.

NEWMAN, C. R. (D.S.O. L.G. 14.1.16) ; b. 24.7.75 ; s. of Major C. C. Newman, late 14th Foot, and Fanny Newman (*née* Walker) ; m. Dorothy Carr ; educ. Clifton College ; 2nd Lt., R.A., 15.6.95 ; Lt. 15.6.98 ; Capt. 14.3.01 ; Major 21.8.11 ; Lt.-Col. 22.3.16 ; Col. 1.1.21 ; served N.W. Frontier of India, 1897–98 ; Medal with clasp ; Tirah, 1897–98 ; clasp ; Europ. War in France, 1914–18 ; Despatches ; Bt. Lt.-Col. 1.1.16 ; Bt. Col. 1.1.19 ; C.M.G.

C. R. Newman.

NEWMAN, J. (D.S.O. L.G. 3.6.18), Major, Aust. Inf.

NEWMAN, T. G. W. (D.S.O. L.G. 14.1.16), Major, 17th (Co. of London) Bn. The London R. (T.F.).

NEWNHAM, C. C. (D.S.O. L.G. 3.6.18) ; b. 15.6.71 ; 2nd Lt., Sco. Rif., 25.3.91 ; Lt. 7.3.94 ; Lt., I.S.C., 4.1.95 ; Capt. 10.7.01 ; Major 25.3.09 ; Bt. Lt.-Col. 1.1.16 ; Lt.-Col. 4.2.16 ; Col. 13.9.19 ; served N.W. Frontier of India, 1897–98 ; Medal with 2 clasps ; Tirah, 1897–98 ; clasp ; S. African War, 1899–1901 ; Queen's Medal with 2 clasps ; Despatches.

NEWSTEAD, B. R. (D.S.O. L.G. 11.1.19) ; b. 29.6.98 ; 2nd Lt., North'd Fus. 7.4.16 ; Lt. 7.10.17 ; Europ. War ; Despatches ; employed with Somaliland Camel Corps 25.6.19.

NEWTH, A. L. W. (D.S.O. L.G. 3.6.19), Capt. (A/Lt.-Col.), 4th Batt. Glouc. R. (T.F.), att. 2/23rd Batt. London R. ; M.C.

NEWTON, C. T. H., M.D., F.R.C.S. (D.S.O. L.G. 1.1.18), Lt.-Col., N.Z. Med. Corps.

NEWTON, F. G. (D.S.O. L.G. 3.6.19) ; b. 5.10.77 ; s. of R. Newton, of Brisbane, Queensland ; m. Kathleen, d. of late F. Verney ; one s. ; two d. ; educ. Brisbane Grammar School ; enlisted in Queensland M.I. as a Private, 1899 ; commission granted on active service, S. Africa, 1900 ; wounded, Aug. 1900 ; A.D.C. to Sir H. Chermside, Private Secretary to Lord Chelmsford ; left Government House and became a Grazier, 1909 ; joined 5th Aust. L.H. Rgt. as Lt., 1914 ; Capt. in Gallipoli, 1915 ; Major, 1916 ; A.A.G., A.I.F., in Egypt with Desert Mounted Corps H.Q. ; Lt.-Col., 1917 ; C.B.E. ; returned to Australia, 1919.

H. Newton.

NEWTON, H. (D.S.O. L.G. 3.6.16) ; b. 24.2.80 ; s. of T. Newton ; m. Beryl Bertha, d. of E. A. Barford, of Luton ; two d. ; educ. Derby School ; Director, Newton Brothers (Derby) Ltd. ; entered 5th Sherwood Foresters, T.F., in 1902 ; commanded an Inf. Company, 5th Notts. and Derby. Rgt., T.F., 1912–15 ; Lt. ; served Europ. War, in France, 1914–17 ; O.C., II. Army R.E. Workshops, 1915–17 ; Member of Trench Warfare Committee ; Deputy Controller, Trench Warfare Dept. ; Chief of Design, Mech. Traction Dept., 1917–19 ; Inventor of Nos. 107 and 110 Fuses (the first wire-cutting fuses ever used by British troops), Newton 6 in. Trench Mortar, Newton Trench Mortar Bomb, Newton Pippin Rifle and Hand-grenades, Ring charge (which employed with the Stokes Mortar reduced prematures and more than doubled the range), Newton Universal Military Tractor, etc., whilst serving with Infantry, R.E., and Artillery Services.

NEWTON, H. L. (D.S.O. L.G. 4.6.17), Lt. (T/Major), R.F.A.

NEWTON, P. I. (D.S.O. L.G. 4.9.18) ; b. 11.6.85 ; 2nd Lt., R.A., 29.7.04 ; Lt. 29.7.07 ; Capt. 30.10.14 ; Despatches.

NEWTON, T. C. (D.S.O. L.G. 3.6.18) ; b. 1.1.85 ; 2nd Lt., R.A., 23.12.03 ; Lt. 23.12.06 ; Capt. 30.10.14 ; Major, R.F.A., 22.7.16 ; Despatches ; O.B.E.

NEWTON-CLARE, E. T., M.A., A.M.I.C.E. (D.S.O. L.G. 12.5.17) ; s. of late E. S. Newton-Clare, M.R.C.S., L.R.C.P., of Calne, Wilts, and Emma Newton-Clare (*née* Honychurch), later Mrs. Haworth ; m. Aileen Marianne Swann, A.R.R.C., d. of Major-Gen. Swann, C.B. ; one s. ; educ. Epsom College, Surrey, and Clare College, Cambridge University ; joined Naval Wing, R.F.C., Jan. 1914 ; Fl. Cdr., R.N.A.S., June, 1915 ; Sqn.-Cdr., R.N.A.S., Dec. 1916 ; Major, R.A.F., 1.4.18 (retired) ; served throughout Siege of Antwerp ; took part in first bomb raid to Cologne, Sept. 1914, under Sqdn.-Comdr. Spenser Grey, D.S.O., and Major Gerrard, C.M.G., D.S.O., etc. ; Dardanelles Campaign, 1915, under Commander Samson ; Dunkerque, R.N.A.S., 1916 and 1917 ; commanded No. 5 Sqdn., No. 5 Wing, R.N.A.S. ; home service end of 1917 to May, 1918 ; commanded 98th Squadron, R.A.F., under General R. E. T. Hogg, June, 1918, to Sept. 1918 ; through Battles of Somme and Second Battle of the Marne, Aug. 1918, in Marshal Joffre's Armée de Manœuvre ; his two brothers are Major H. J. Newton-Clare, O.B.E., R.A.F., and Captain W. S. Newton-Clare, M.B.E., R.A.F. ; he raced at Brooklands with some success in 1912 ; took up flying for fun at Vickers, Brooklands, 1913.

E. T. Newton-Clare.

NIBLETT, H. (D.S.O. L.G. 3.6.16), T/Major, A.S.C.

NICHOLAS, G. M. (D.S.O. L.G. 20.10.16) ; b. 1887 ; e. s. of J. P. Nicholas, of Trafalgar, Victoria, Australia ; m. E. Hilda, y. d. of late Mr. and Mrs. Rix ; Capt., Aust. Inf. ; promoted Major ; served Europ. War. He was killed in action 14.11.16.

NICHOLL, H. I. (D.S.O. L.G. 14.1.16) ; b. 21.2.70 ; s. of late Iltid Nicholl ; m. 1904, Vera, o. d. of Frank Hedges Butler ; one s. ; educ. Eton ; 1st commission 12.3.92 ; Capt. 28.10.99 ; ret. Bradford R. 12.8.08 ; Bt. Major (Res. of Off.) 3.6.16 ; Lt.-Col. 22.6.16 ; served in Expedition, Relief of Chitral, 1895 (Medal and clasp) ; Malakand Relief Force, 1897 (clasp) ; served with Mounted Infantry, S. African War, 1900 (severely wounded ; Queen's Medal, 4 clasps) ; Europ. War, 1914–16 ; Despatches twice.

NICHOLL, V. (D.S.O. L.G. 1.5.18), Sqn.-Cdr., R.N.A.S. ; D.S.C.

NICHOLLS, E. P. (D.S.O. L.G. 16.9.18) ; b. 1883 ; s. of Col. William Nicholls, V.D., of Boothlands, Newdigate, Surrey ; m. 1918, Violet C. Elliott, adopted d. of Capt. and Mrs. R. Elliott Palmer ; one s. ; educ. Malvern ; Brasenose College, Oxford ; served Europ. War, 1914–19 ; Despatches ; T.D.

NICHOLLS, F. (D.S.O. L.G. 2.4.19) (Details, L.G. 10.12.19) ; 3rd s. of Samuel H. Nicholls ; m. 1919, Nellie Hay, e. d. of A. J. Mills ; T/Capt., 20th Batt. Manch. Regt. ; M.C. ; Despatches.

NICHOLLS, S. C. P. (D.S.O. L.G. 3.6.18), Major, New Zealand Staff Corps.

NICHOLLS, W. A. (D.S.O. L.G. 1.1.17) ; b. 14.12.83 ; o. s. of Gen. Sir W. C. Nicholls, K.C.B. ; educ. Cheltenham College ; R.M.A., Woolwich ; 2nd Lt., R.A., 21.12.01 ; Lt. 21.12.04 ; Capt. 30.10.14 ; Major 10.3.16 ; served Europ. War, 1914–19 ; Despatches.

NICHOLSON, B. W. L. (D.S.O. L.G. 27.6.17), Comdr., R.N.

NICHOLSON, E. H. (D.S.O. L.G. 1.1.18) (Bar, L.G. 1.1.19) ; e. s. of late Alfred James Nicholson ; educ. The Towers, Crowthorne ; Winchester ; m. 1912, Ethel Frances, d. of late Cecil Henry ; one s. ; 2nd Lt., R. Fus., Aug. 1900 ; Lt. 12.12.03 ; Capt. 26.4.09 ; Major (A/Lt.-Col.), R. Fus. ; served S. African War ; Queen's Medal ; King's Medal and 5 clasps ; Europ. War, in France and Salonika ; Despatches. He was killed in action 4.10 18. He was the eldest of four brothers, of whom the two youngest, 2nd Lt. Bruce Wills Nicholson, R. Fus., and Sub-Lieut. Victor Wills Nicholson, R.N., gave their lives for their country in 1917.

NICHOLSON, E. J. H. (D.S.O. L.G. 1.1.17) ; b. 17.4.70, at Gravesend, Kent, England ; s. of Lt.-Col. J. S. Nicholson, 108th Regt. ; m. 1896, Anna Beatrice, d. of J. Noblett Taylor ; one s. ; two d. ; educ. Nelson College, New Zealand ; Anglo-French College ; entered the Australian Militia Forces, 1890 ; Capt. 5.9.14 ; Major 26.7.15 ; Lt.-Col. 12.3.16 ; served Europ. War, 1914–18. He was awarded the D.S.O. for special work at the Battle of Pozières, Somme ; services : Gallipoli Campaign from the landing at Gaba Tepe until the evacuation, April 25 to 20.12.15 ; Intelligence Work in Suez Canal Zone, Dec. 1915–Jan. 1916 ; France, April, 1916 ; Despatches, Karageorge ; Bac St. Maur ; Despatches ; Somme Pozières–Mouquet Farm, 1916 ; Ypres, 1916 ; Flers–Longueval, 1916 ; Martinpuich to Bapaume, Feb.–April, 1917 ; Despatches ; Battle of Bullecourt, April–May, 1917 ; Despatches ; Menin Road to Zonnebeke, Sept.–Nov. 1917 ; Despatches ; C.M.G. ; Messines–Wytschaete, Dec. 1917–March, 1918 ; Somme, Ancre defences, April–1.7.18 ; Despatches.

NICHOLSON, F. L. (D.S.O. L.G. 26.8.18) ; b. 16.1.84 ; 2nd Lt., R.W. Surr. R., 18.11.03 ; Ind. Army 23.6.05 ; Lt. 18.2.06 ; Capt. 18.11.12 ; Major 18.11.18 ; Bt. Lt.-Col. 3.5.21 ; Despatches ; M.C.

NICHOLSON, H. B. (D.S.O. L.G. 1.1.18) ; b. 13.11.66 ; ent. Army 11.2.88 ; Capt. 1.1.96 ; Capt. (A/Major), R. of Off., K.R.R.C. ; served Europ. War ; Despatches.

NICHOLSON, J. B. (D.S.O. L.G. 27.6.19), Eng.-Cdr., R.N.

NICHOLSON, R. (D.S.O. L.G. 3.6.19) : b. 8.4.94 ; 2nd Lt., R.A., 7.7.15 ; Adjt., R.A., 14.3.16 ; Lt. 1.7.17 ; served Europ. War ; Despatches ; M.C.

NICHOLSON, R. L. (D.S.O. L.G. 15.9.16) ; b. 29.10.82 ; s. of Charles J. Lindsay Nicholson ; m. Millicent, d. of Colonel Sir A. R. Holbrook, K.B.E., D.L., M.P. ; two s. ; educ. privately ; joined H.M.S. Britannia, 1898 ; specialized in Torpedo and Wireless Telegraphy, and qualified for Naval War Staff ; became Wireless Officer to the Grand Fleet, 1914–17 ; Director of Signal Division, Admiralty Naval Staff ; served Europ. War ; present at action of Jutland Bank ; Despatches ; Officer of Legion of Honour ; Commander of Crown of Italy ; retired 1920 ; Director of Wireless Telegraphs, India.

NICHOLSON, ST. J. R. (D.S.O. L.G. 3.6.18) ; b. 5.7.82 ; 2nd Lt., R.A., 21.12.01 ; Lt. 15.9.04 ; Adjt., R.A., 5.12.11 ; Capt. 30.10.14 ; Major 1.5.17 ; Despatches.

314 The Distinguished Service Order

NICHOLSON, W. C. (D.S.O. L.G. 26.7.18), Capt., Can. M.G.C.; M.C.

NICHOLSON, W. N. (D.S.O. L.G. 3.6.16); b. 10.6.77; educ. Charterhouse; Trinity College, Cambridge; 2nd Lt., Suff. R., 24.1.00; Lt. 21.3.01; Adjt. 30.12.04 to 29.12.07; Capt. 7.5.10; Major 20.4.15; Bt. Lt.-Col. 3.6.17; served S. African War, 1899–1902 (Queen's Medal, 3 clasps; King's Medal, 2 clasps); Europ. War, 1914–18; Despatches; C.M.G.

NICKALLS, C. P. (D.S.O. L.G. 1.1.18), Major, R.F.A.

NICKALLS, P. W. (D.S.O. L.G. 3.6.18), Major, Yeomanry.

NICOL, G. G. (D.S.O. L.G. 4.6.17), Capt. (A/Major), Gordon Highrs., att. R.E.

NICOL-SMITH, A. G. (D.S.O. L.G. 1.1.17); b. 1873; s. of Alex. Smith; m. Agnes Mary, d. of J. Sangster, of Aberdeen; educ. Aberdeen Grammar School; 1st commission, A.S.C. (T.F.), 1908; Major, R.A.S.C.; Bt. Lt.-Colonel; served Europ. War; Despatches four times.

NICOLLS, E. H. J. (D.S.O. L.G. 18.2.18) (Details, L.G. 18.7.18); b. 17.7.86; s. of Major-Gen. O. H. A. Nicolls, Colonel Commandant, R.A.; educ. Cheltenham College; United Service College, Westward Ho!; 2nd Lt., E. Surr. R., 29.5.07; Lt. 16.7.09; Capt. 27.9.14. He served three years in the Militia Art., four years in India, one year in Burma, and three years at a depôt; served Europ. War; Despatches three times; M.C., 1917.

NICOLSON, HON. E. A. (D.S.O. L.G. 21.6.19); b. British Legation, Athens, 1884; s. of Lord Carnock; m. 1919, Katharine, e. d. of Sir Henry Lopes; educ. H.M.S. Britannia; R.N. Staff College, 1913; Comdr., R.N. 31.12.17; War Staff Officer to the Light Cruiser Forces, 1914–19; Légion d'Honneur; St. Anne with Swords; Intelligence Division, Admiralty.

NIMMO, J. S. (D.S.O. L.G. 1.1.18); b. 1.1.78; Lt., A.V.C., 4.2.05; Capt. 4.2.10; Major 10.7.15.

NISBET, D. (D.S.O. L.G. 3.6.19), Capt. (A/Major), 1/5th Bn. S. Lancs. Regt., T.F.; M.C.

NISBET, F. C. (D.S.O. L.G. 14.1.16); b. 18.1.69; s. of Harry Curtis Nisbet and Louisa Margaret Nisbet; educ. Rugby; Sandhurst; 2nd Lt., Glouc. R., 29.3.90; Lt. 21.10.91; Captain 24.2.00; Major 26.11.13; Bt. Lt.-Col. and Bt.-Col.; T/Brig.-Gen. 23.3.18; served S. African War, 1899–1901 (Queen's Medal, 3 clasps); Europ. War, Commander, 2nd Glouc. R., in France, 1915; 84th Inf. Brigade in Macedonia, 1918; Despatches four times; the Serbian Order of Karageorge, 4th Class; served in Turkey, 1919; commanded 1st Glouc. Regt., 1919–21; retired pay, 1921.

NISBET, T. (D.S.O. L.G. 17.3.17); b. 1.12.82; s. of T. M. Nisbet; m. Barbara Frances, d. of late T. Lawson; educ. Fettes College, Edinburgh; R.M.C., Camberley; enlisted in ranks of Imp. Yeom., 1901; Lt. 1.4.01; 2nd Lt., Som. L. Inf., 14.7.01; Ind. Army 16.10.03; Lt., Ind. Army, 9.5.04; Capt. 1.4.10; Major 1.4.16; Bt. Lt.-Col. 3.6.18; Adjt., Bihar Light Horse, 1911–14; served S. African War (Queen's Medal, 5 clasps); Delhi Coronation, Durbar Decoration; Europ. War, served with the Reserve Cavalry, Staff, 13th Brigade, Gallipoli, 1915–16; Mesopotamia, 1916–18; General Maude's Staff and A.A. and Q.M.G., Cavalry Division, Palestine, 1918; A.A. and Q.M.G., 3rd Lahore Division; Special Duty, Somaliland, 1919; Director-in-Chief, Repatriation and Relief of Refugees, Syria and Palestine, 1919; Despatches four times; C.M.G.; Croix de Guerre (France).

NISSEN, P. N. (D.S.O. L.G. 15.2.17); b. 1871; s. of George H. and Lavinia Nissen; m. 1900, Louisa M. Richmond; one d.; educ. Trinity College, North Carolina; Queen's University, Kingston, Canada; Mining Engineer; Member, Institution of Mining and Metallurgy; Inventor of the Nissen Stamp Mill; Inventor of the Nissen Huts and Nissen Steel Tents; Chairman, Nissen Ltd.; T/Capt. (A/Major), R.E.; served Europ. War, 1915–19; Despatches.

NIVEN, H. W. (D.S.O. L.G. 19.8.16) (Bar, L.G. 18.1.18) (Details, L.G. 25.4.18); b. 22.5.76; s. of James Simpson Niven, M.B.; m. 1916, Marie Elizabeth MacAndrew; two s.; educ. Upper Canada College, Toronto; many years an enthusiastic Volunteer; Militiaman in 26th Middlesex L. Inf.; Capt. and Adjt.; joined P.P.C.L.I. as Private, Aug. 1914; became Lieut.; Transport Officer; Capt.; Major; served Europ. War; Despatches five times; M.C.

NIVEN, O. C. (D.S.O. L.G. 3.6.16); b. 1.8.77; e. s. of Cdr. O. B. Niven, R.N.; m. Edith, e. d. of Major C. J. Miller, M.V.O.; four s.; one d.; educ. Portsmouth Grammar School; R.M.A., Woolwich; 2nd Lt., R.A., 23.3.97; Lt. 23.3.00; Capt. 1.2.02; Major 30.10.14; Bt. Lt.-Col. 3.6.18; Lt.-Col. 1.5.21; served Europ. War, in Gallipoli, in command of a heavy battery; serving in command of H.A. Group at captures of Beersheba and Jerusalem, afterwards in command of a brigade in France; Despatches.

NIXON, C. H. F. (D.S.O. L.G. 22.12.16); b. 14.8.84; 2nd Lt., R.W. Surr. R., 4.11.03; Ind. Army 26.8.05; Lt. 4.2.06; Capt. 4.11.12; Major 4.11.18; served Europ. War; Despatches.

NIXON, SIR C. W., Bart. (D.S.O. L.G. 4.2.18) (Details, L.G. 5.7.18); b. 19.4.77; s. of 1st Bart and Mary Agnes, d. of D. E. Blake; s. father, 1914; m. Louise, y. d. of Robert Clery, J.P.; one s.; educ. Beaumont College; Trinity College, Dublin; R.U.I.; M.A. (Hon.); Barrister-at-Law, King's Inn; 2nd Lt., R.A., 28.3.00; Lt. 3.4.01; Capt. 25.3.09; Adjt. 7.5.10 to 30.9.11; Major 30.10.14; served Europ. War, 1914–18; Despatches.

NIXON, E. J. (D.S.O. L.G. 17.9.17); b. 8.1.85; 2nd Lt., R.A., 15.7.03; Lt. 15.7.06; Capt. 30.10.14; Major, R.G.A., 22.11.17; Despatches; M.C.

NIXON, F. B. (D.S.O. L.G. 3.6.18); b. Seafield, Westward Ho! N. Devon, 16.10.80; s. of B. de Courcy and Evelyn Hampton Nixon; educ. United Service College, Westward Ho!; 2nd Lt., 6th Innis. Dns., 18.8.00; Lt. 8.2.02; Adjt., 6th Dns., 1.8.03–31.7.06; Capt. 3.5.07; Major; served S. African War, 1901–2; Queen's Medal with 3 clasps; Europ. War; Despatches twice. He was a Member of his Regimental Team which won the Durbar Tournament.

NIXON, J. A. (D.S.O. L.G. 3.6.16); b. 26.11.79; s. of Major-Gen. A. J. Nixon and Maria Lucy, d. of J. Lawrence; m. Hon. Joan Burdett Money-Coutts; two s.; educ. Wellington College Sandhurst; 2nd Lt., R. Lanc. R., 11.2.99; Lt. 23.2.00; Capt. 19.4.02; Major 1.9.15; Lt.-Col.; Bt. Col.; served S. African War; wounded at action of Spion Kop; Despatches twice; Queen's Medal, 5 clasps; King's Medal, 2 clasps; Europ. War, with 1st Batt. The King's Own Rgt. (France); wounded at Le Cateau; went again to France with the Ulster Division as Brigade Major; appointed to command 1st Batt. The King's Own Rgt.; invalided home, 1917; Despatches; Bt. Lt.-Col. 3.6.19.

NOAKES, C. J. L. (D.S.O. L.G. 29.10.18), Cdr., R.N., 30.6.19.

NOAKES, S. M. (D.S.O. L.G. 11.1.19); b. 26.2.87, in Sydney, N.S.W.; s. of W. M. Noakes, Iron Master, and Jessie Noakes; m. Norah Parkyns, d. of Rev. W. E. Buckland, and great-niece of Frank Buckland, Naturalist; one s.; educ. Sydney, N.S.W.; Onslow Hall, Richmond; R.M.A.; 2nd Lt., R.A., 23.7.07; Lt. 23.7.10; Capt. 30.10.14; Major 22.6.17; Europ. War from 1914; Despatches.

NOBLE, N. D. (D.S.O. L.G. 14.1.16); b. 2.3.81; 2nd Lt., R.E., 28.7.99; Lt. 1.4.02; Capt. 28.7.08; Major 1.4.16; Despatches.

NOBLETT, REV. J. J. (D.S.O. L.G. 8.3.18), T/Chaplain to the Forces.

NOCKOLDS, H. (D.S.O. L.G. 3.6.18); b. 2.5.88, at 117. Goldhawk Rd., Shepherd's Bush; s. of Dr. W. S. Nockolds and Alice Amelia Nockolds; m. Josephine Louisa Wilson; educ. The Grange, Cowes; Dover College; Blundell's School; University College Hospital; was Temp. Hon. Capt., R.A.M.C.; served Europ. War, P.M.O. Friends' Ambulance Unit (British Red Cross Society), from 1914–19, and afterwards O.C., Queen Alexandra Hospital, Dunkirk; Despatches; 1914 Star; Hon. Associate of the Order of St. John of Jerusalem; French Médaille des Epidémiques.

NOEDL, L. (D.S.O. L.G. 1.2.19), 7th Field Co., Aust. Engrs.

NOEL, E. W. C. (D.S.O. L.G. 3.6.19); b. 14.4.86; s. of late Lt.-Col. Hon. E. W. Noel and Ruth, d. of W. H. Lucas; educ. Oratory School, Birmingham; R.M.A., Woolwich; Major, Foreign and Political Dept., Govt. of India; 2nd Lt., R.A., 21.12.04; Lt., R.A., 21.12.07; Ind. Army 15.2.09; Capt., Ind. Army, 21.12.13; C.I.E.

NOEL, H. E. (D.S.O. L.G. 26.3.18) (Details, L.G. 24.8.18), Capt. (A/Major), R.H.A.

NOOTT, C. C. (D.S.O. L.G. 14.1.16); b. 4.9.70; s. of Major F. H. Noott, R.M.L.I.; educ. R.M.A., Woolwich; 2nd Lt., R.A., 15.2.89; Lt. 15.2.92; Capt. 25.5.99; Adjt., R.A., 10.10.06 to 20.4.08; Major 15.7.09; Lt.-Col. 20.4.16; Col. 20.4.20; Europ. War, 1915; wounded; Despatches; C.M.G.

NORBURY, P. F. (D.S.O. L.G. 10.8.21); b. 28.9.79; 2nd Lt., R. Irish Rt., 12.8.99; Lt. 18.9.00; Lt., I.A., 24.6.01; Capt. 12.8.08; Major 1.9.15, 34th Poona Horse, I.A., attd. Political Dept.

NORCOCK, H. L. (D.S.O. L.G. 3.6.18); b. 3.9.77; s. of Lt.-Col. H. J. L. Norcock, R.M. (retired); m. Violet Ramsay, d. of Cdr. Belson, R.N.; two s.; one d.; educ. Mannamead School, Plymouth; Major, late R.A.S.C.; served with Shanghai Volunteer Force during China War (Boxer Rebellion), 1900; China Medal; commission in China, 1914; Lt., R.A.S.C., 1915; Capt., 1915; Adjt., 33rd Div. Train, B.E.F., 1917; Major, 1918; commanded No. 1 Co., 33rd Div. Train, B.E.F., 1918; served with B.E. Forces in France and Belgium continuously from Nov. 1915, to Nov. 1919.

NORMAN, C. C. (D.S.O. L.G. 4.6.17); b. 14.12.77; 2nd Lt., R.W. Fus., 4.1.99; Lt. 12.5.00; Capt. 17.11.06; Adjt., R.W. Fus., 6.4.11 to 18.10.13; Major 1.9.15; Bt. Lt.-Col. 1.1.18; Despatches; served S. African War, 1899–1902; Queen's Medal with 5 clasps; King's Medal with 2 clasps; West Africa (Liberia), 1905; operations of the Kissi F.F. (Medal with clasp); Europ. War; Despatches; C.M.G.

NORMAN, C. L. (D.S.O. L.G. 25.8.17); b. 19.2.76; 2nd Lt., Unatt., 22.1.96; 2nd Lt., I.S.C., 14.3.97; Lt., I.A., 22.4.98; Capt., I.A., 22.1.05; Major 22.1.14; Bt. Lt.-Col. 29.11.15; Bt. Col. 3.6.18; Col. 13.9.19; T/Col. Comdt. 1.1.21; served N.W. Frontier of India, 1897–98; Tirah, 1897–98; clasp; E. Africa, 1903–4; operations in Somaliland; Despatches; Medal with clasp; Europ. War; Despatches. He has the M.V.O.

NORMAN, E. H. (D.S.O. L.G. 3.6.16); b. 5.11.80; s. of P. Norman, LL.D., F.S.A.; m. Isabel, d. of J. W. Philip; one d.; 2nd Lt., R.W. Kent Rgt., 18.4.00; Lt. 29.1.02; Capt. 22.1.06; Major 1.9.16; served in S. Africa; Queen's Medal, 3 clasps; King's Medal, 2 clasps. He went to France early in 1915, and in Sept. took part in the Capture of Loos; was T/Lt.-Col., commanding 1/17th Batt. London Rgt.; O.B.E. 1919.

NORMAN, R. H. (D.S.O. L.G. 11.1.19), Lt., Aust. Mil. Forces; M.C.

NORMAN, W. H. (D.S.O. L.G. 25.8.17); b. 14.6.71; 2nd Lt., R. War. R., 8.10.90; Lt., I.S.C., 2.12.91; Capt., I.A., 10.7.01; Major 8.10.08; Lt.-Col. 4.7.16; Col. 30.4.20; served Isazai Exp., 1892; N.W. Frontier of India, 1897–98; 2 clasps; China, 1900; Europ. War; Despatches; Bt. Col. 3.6.18; C.B.

NORMAN, W. W. (D.S.O. L.G. 1.1.17); b. 1860; s. of Major Gen. Sir F. B. Norman, K.C.B.; m. Violet Anna, d. of late Maj.-Gen. Sir O. R. Newmarch, K.C.S.; educ. Oxford Mil. College; Lt.-Col. 21.12.05; Bt. Col. 21.12.08; retired, I.A., 23.10.12, with rank of Colonel in the Army; served Tirah Campaign, 1897–98; Medal with clasp; Europ. War, 1914–18; Despatches; commanded 21st Batt. Manchester R.

NORMAND, S. R. (D.S.O. L.G. 1.1.18); b. 29.5.75; s. of W. J. Normand and Isabella Normand (*née* Fitzgerald); m. Marie Isabel, d. of Gen. C. Grant; one d.; educ. Fettes College, Edinburgh; R.M.A., Woolwich; 2nd Lt., R.A., 17.11.94; Lt. 17.11.97; Capt. 10.10.00; Adjt., R.A., 1.1.05 to 31.12.07; Major 4.2.21; Lt.-Col.; served S. African War, with Mountain Artillery and Pompoms; Queen's Medal, 5 clasps; King's Medal, 2 clasps; Europ. War, with Coast, Heavy and Siege Artillery; Despatches; Croix d'Officier de la Couronne, Belgium; Croix de Guerre, Belgium.

NORNABELL, H. M. (D.S.O. L.G. 4.6.17); b. 16.10.77; s. of late M. Nornabell; m. Catherine Perle, d. of late G. Van Dyke; two d.; educ. Wellington (Salop); 2nd Lt., R.A., 12.5.00; Lt. 5.11.01; Capt. 14.11.10; Adjt., R.A., 27.12.13 to 29.10.14; Major, R.F.A., 30.10.14; Europ. War in France, 1914; Despatches thrice; O.B.E.

NORRIE, C. M., M.Inst.C.E., F.R.G.S. (D.S.O. L.G. 26.8.18); s. of late W. H. Norrie; m. Gwladys Marjorie Alice Jones, d. of Col. G. Mitton; one s.; one d.; educ. Dundee High School; St. Andrews University; Hydro-Electric Engineer to Vickers Ltd., Westminster, from 1919; A.D. of Works, Mesopotamia Exp. Force; served R.E., 1915–19; Lt.-Colonel.

NORRIE, C. W. MOKE- (see Moke-Norrie, C. W.).

NORRIE, E. C. (D.S.O. L.G. 1.1.18), Lt.-Col., Aust. Infy.

NORRIS, H. (D.S.O. L.G. 14.11.16); b. 2.12.81; s. of R. W. and Sophia Norris (*née* Hughes); m. Hilda Clements; one s.; served with 2nd Batt. The Queen's, in the S. African War, 1901–2; enlisted Europ. War in 31st Batt. Can. Inf. 16.11.14; commissioned Feb. 1916; Captain, Sept. 1916; Can. Infantry; served with 2nd Batt. The Queen's, S. Africa, 1901–2; Europ. War; wounded, St. Eloi, April, 1916. He was awarded the D.S.O. for gallantry at Courcelette on 15.9.16.

NORRIS, S. E. (D.S.O. L.G. 1.1.17); b. at Mudgee, N.S.W., 8.5.74; s. of Major C. G. Norris, late 80th Foot and Australian Local Forces, and Katherine Eliza Norris, d. of Thomas Cadell, of N.S. Wales; m. Mary Cristobel, d. of A. R. Birks, I.C.S.; two d.; 2nd Lt. (from N.S.W. Bushmen), L'pool R., 19.5.00; Lt. 7.1.05; Capt. 4.7.10; Major 1.9.15; T/Lt.-Col., Commanding 4th Batt. The King's Rgt., Jan. to Aug. 1918; served S. African War; Queen's Medal, 4 clasps; King's Medal, 2 clasps; Staff Services in Europ. War; Despatches.

NORSWORTHY, S. C. (D.S.O. L.G. 26.7.17), Capt., Can. Inf., 25.5.15; Major; M.C.

NORTH, C. B. (D.S.O. L.G. 4.6.17), Major, R.E.; M.C.

NORTH, E. B. (D.S.O. L.G. 1.1.17); b. 28.3.69; s. of N. North, J.P., D.L. (late I.A.), and Alicia, d. of Major L. R. J. Versturme, late 18th Hussars; m. Margaret, d. of Hon. J. C. Dundas, Lord Lieutenant of Orkney and Shetland, and the Honourable Alice Louisa, d. of Lord Halifax; one s.; two d.; educ. Stubbington House, Fareham, Hants; 2nd Lt., R. Fus., 5.2.90; Lt. 17.3.92; Capt. 18.1.99; Major 1.4.09; Lt.-Col. 18.5.17; served with Egyptian Army, 1898–99; Despatches; 4th Class Medjidie; British and Egyptian Sudan Medals; 3 clasps; with R. Fus. in S. Africa, 1899–1900; Queen's Medal, 5 clasps; attached Imperial Japanese Army, 1908–9; Europ. War, 1915–18; commanded 4th R. Fus., 1916–17; 10th Batt. The Queen's, 1918; late commanding 3rd R. Fusiliers; Despatches three times; C.M.G.; has 4th Class Medjidie; 1897 Jubilee Medal; King Edward VII. Coronation Medal.

NORTH, H. N. (D.S.O. L.G. 25.8.17); b. 11.6.83; 2nd Lt., R.E., 21.12.00; Lt. 21.12.03; Capt. 21.12.10; Major 2.11.16; Bt. Lt.-Col. 3.6.18; Despatches.

NORTH, O. (D.S.O. L.G. 14.9.18), Lt., R.N.

NORTH, P. W. (D.S.O. L.G. 26.9.17) (Details, L.G. 7.1.18); b. 30.3.71; s. of late North North, of Newton Hall, formerly of Thurland Castle; educ. R.M.C., Sandhurst; ent. Army 17.6.91; Capt. 7.11.00; retired 2.6.09; Lt.-Colonel; served S. African War with M.I., 1899–1901; Despatches; Queen's Medal, 4 clasps; Europ. War, Assistant in Charge of Foreign Military Attachés, 1914; France and Gallipoli, 1915–17; commanded 20th Durham L.I.; wounded twice; Despatches twice; O.C., 3rd R. Berks. R.

NORTHAMPTON, MARQUESS OF (D.S.O. L.G. 3.6.19); b. 6.8.85; s. of 5th Marquess and Hon. Mary Florence Baring (who died 1902), d. of 2nd Lord Ashburton; educ. Eton; Balliol College, Oxford; joined Imp. Yeom.; 2nd Lt., R.H.G., 1908; Lt., 1908; served Europ. War; wounded.

NORTHCOTE, A. F. (D.S.O. L.G. 21.1.20); b. 5.10.31; 2nd Lt., Devon R., 7.5.02; Lt. 14.1.07; Capt. 23.12.14; Major 15.3.17; Despatches.

NORTHCOTE, R. (D.S.O. L.G. 11.1.19), T/2nd Lt., M.G.C.

NORTHCROFT, E. H. (D.S.O. L.G. 3.6.19), Major, N.Z. Field Arty.

NORTHEN, A. (D.S.O. L.G. 3.6.16); b. 24.10.73; 2nd Lt., S. Lanc. R., 29.5.95; Lt. 12.7.98; Capt., S. Lanc. R., 22.1.02; Capt., A.S.C., 1.2.02; Major 28.3.14; Bt. Lt.-Col. 3.6.17; Lt.-Col. 15.12.18; served S. African War, 1899–1902; att. to A.S.C. from 24.7.01; Queen's Medal, 3 clasps; King's Medal, 2 clasps; Europ. War; Despatches; C.B.E.

NORTON, A. E. (D.S.O. L.G. 1.1.18); b. 18.10.77; 2nd Lt. (from Lumsden's Horse), W.I. Rgt., 18.7.00; Lt. 13.2.01; Adjt., W.I.R., 19.3.11 to 18.3.14; Capt. 31.10.13; Major 1.9.15; Bt. Lt.-Col. 3.6.18; served S. African War, 1900; Queen's Medal, 3 clasps; Despatches.

NORTON, C. B. (D.S.O. L.G. 14.1.16); b. 10.4.68; s. of Major-Gen. E. Nugent Norton; m. Charlotte Alexandra, d. of Col. F. R. Begbie; 3 d.; 1st com. 23.8.93; Capt. 12.10.01; retired D.C.L.I. 25.7.08; Lt.-Col., R. of O., 1st Batt. D.C.L.I.; Brig.-Gen.; served operations on N.W. Frontier of India, 1897, with Tirah Exp. Force; Medal with 2 clasps; Europ. War, 1914–18; Despatches; C.M.G.; Legion of Honour.

NORTON, E. F. (D.S.O. L.G. 26.7.18); b. 21.2.84; 2nd Lt., R.A., 24.12.02; Lt. 24.12.05; Capt. 30.10.14; Major 24.4.16; Despatches; M.C.

NORTON, G. P., M.A. (D.S.O. L.G. 14.1.16) (Bar, L.G. 26.7.18); b. 17.8.82; s. of G. P. Norton and Julia Anne Norton (*née* Slade); m. Daisy, d. of T. Naylor; one s.; two d.; educ. Shrewsbury School; Caius College, Cambridge; served Europ. War, 1915–18; Lt.-Col., 5th W. Riding Rgt. (T.F.); commanded 2/10th Manchester Battalion, 4th E. Lancs. R., and 15th W. Yorks. R.; Despatches thrice.

NOSWORTHY, F. P. (D.S.O. L.G. 8.3.18) (Bar, L.G. 16.9.18); b. 21.9.87; 2nd Lt., R.E., 18.12.07; Lt. 2.5.10; Capt. 30.10.14; Bt. Major 1.1.17; T/Lt.-Col., R.E.; M.C.

NOTLEY, W. KILMISTER (gazetted as Notley, W. Kilminster) (D.S.O. L.G. 1.1.18); b. 24.8.80; educ. Sherborne School; T/Lieut.-Colonel, Unatt. List, E.A. Force; served with S. Africa Constabulary, 1901–7; Queen's Medal with 5 clasps; Europ. War, E. Africa, 1914–19; Despatches twice; King's Police Medal; Cavalier St. Maurice and St. Lazarus (Italy); Acting Colonial Secretary and Member Executive Council, Kenya Colony; Commissioner of Police, B.E. Africa, from 1908.

NOTMAN, J. P. (D.S.O. L.G. 4.2.18) (Details, L.G. 5.7.18), 2nd Lt., Seaf. Highrs.

NOTT, J. G. L. PLEYDELL- (see Pleydell-Nott, J. G. L.).

NOTT, T. W. (D.S.O. L.G. 1.1.17), Lt.-Col., The Gloucestershire Rgt., 6th Batt. (T.). He was killed in action 18.4.17.

NOYES, C. R. F. (D.S.O. L.G. 1.5.18), Sqn.-Cdr., R.N.A.S.

NUGEE, G. T. (D.S.O. L.G. 1.1.19); b. 7.7.93; 2nd Lt., R.A., 18.7.13; Lt. 9.6.15; Adjt., R.A., 9.11.15 to 6.10.16; Capt. 18.7.17; Despatches; M.C.

NUGENT, F. H. BURNELL- (see Burnell-Nugent, F. H.).

NUGENT, H. A. (D.S.O. L.G. 1.1.17); b. Brunswick, Victoria, 18.10.87; s. of W. B. Nugent; m. Ivy, d. of late R. B. Paterson; two d.; commissioned in Aust. A.S.C., 1911; Capt., 1914; Major, 12th Aust. A.S.C.; commanded 28th A.S.C. At outbreak of war was appointed to command 15th A.S.C., A.I.F., April, 1915; served Egypt (Suez Canal), June, 1915–March, 1916; promoted to Major and Senior Supply Officer for services rendered after evacuation of Gallipoli; served in France from March, 1916, to the Armistice, Armentières Sector, Battle of the Somme, Ypres, and the Battle of the Ancre; S.S.O., 2nd Aust. Div.; O.B.E.; Despatches thrice.

NUGENT, J. F. H. (D.S.O. L.G. 22.12.16); b. 1.7.89, at Mussourie, India; s. of late J. Nugent, I.C.S., and Florence Nugent (*née* Henslowe); m. Violet Gwendolen, d. of L. G. Cox; educ. Downside School, near Bath; R.M.C., Sandhurst; 2nd Lt., Unatt., 20.1.09; 2nd Lt., I.A., 28.3.10; Lt. 20.4.11; Capt., 28th Punjabis, I.A., 1.9.15; Brig.-Major, 57th Inf. Brig., 30.5.18; served Europ. War in Mesopotamia, Nov. 1915 (wounded, April, 1916; Despatches); Afghanistan, 1919.

NUGENT, W. V. (D.S.O. L.G. 3.6.16); b. 3.12.80; s. of Nicholas and Constance Nugent; g.s. of Sir Oliver Nugent; m. Dorothy Florence, d. of J. S. Rawson, J.P.; two s.; one d.; educ. Pocklington School; R.M.A., Woolwich; 2nd Lt., R.A., 6.1.00; Lt. 3.4.01; Capt. 3.12.10; Major 26.7.15; Bt. Lt.-Col. 1.1.18; Lt.-Colonel; W. Africa (N. Nigeria), 1908; Medal with clasp; served Europ. War. He was awarded the D.S.O. for Topographical Work on Gallipoli Peninsula during Dardanelles Campaign; Despatches five times; C.B.E.; Legion of Honour; Knight of Order of Crown of Italy.

NUNN, R. A. (D.S.O. L.G. 2.11.17), Asst. Paymaster, R.N.R.; D.S.C.

NUNN, R. L. (D.S.O. L.G. 3.6.18), T/Capt. (A/Major), R.E.

NUSSEY, A. H. M. (D.S.O. L.G. 18.8.16); b. in Orange Free State 11.7.80; s. of Joah Nussey and Annie Nussey (*née* Francis); m. Bridget, d. of P. Kelly, of Bloemfontein; joined O.F.S. Civil Service, 1897; served with the Boers in the S. African War, 1899–1902; was on General De Wet's Staff, 1900, and attended the Peace Conference as Staff Officer. He joined the British Army on 9.12.12, becoming a Member of the Permanent Force (Staff), Union of S. Africa Defence Forces; was Private Secretary to General De Wet, Minister of Agriculture, during responsible Government, O.F. State Colony. He served in the Europ. War, and took part in the campaign in German South-West Africa in 1915. He was promoted Brevet Lieutenant-Colonel. He was in German East Africa in the same year, and became on 1.4.16. Chief of Staff, Second Division. He was wounded during the German East African Campaign. On 8.8.16 he became Brigadier-General commanding the 1st South African Mounted Brigade. He was three times mentioned in Despatches (once especially by General Smuts); C.B.E., 1919. He was awarded the D.S.O. for gallantry at Colkissale 3–4–5.4.16; Ufiome 12–13.4.16; Kondoa-Irangi 20.4.16 to 31.5.16.

NUSSEY, W. J. (D.S.O. L.G. 22.8.18), Major, 4th Mtd. Brig., S. African Mil. Forces (Supernumerary List).

NUTT, A. C. R. (D.S.O. L.G. 10.6.20); b. 19.3.73; 2nd Lt., R.A., 16.3.93; Lt. 16.3.96; Capt. 28.5.00; Adjt., R.A., 17.3.05 to 16.3.08; Major 15.3.10; Lt.-Col., R.F.A., 10.11.15; served N.W. Frontier of India, 1897–98; Medal with clasp; Tirah, 1897–98; clasp; Europ. War; Despatches.

NUTT, A. V. (D.S.O. L.G. 1.1.18) (Bar, L.G. 15.10.18), T/Major (A/Lt.-Col.), York and Lancaster R.

NUTT, H. J. (D.S.O. L.G. 1.1.17), Lt.-Col. (Hon. Col.), R. Warwicks. R.

NUTT, N. H. (D.S.O. L.G. 1.1.18), T/Major, Tank Corps.

NUTTALL, C. M. (D.S.O. L.G. 8.8.17); b. 19.1.72; 2nd Lt., R.A., 1.4.92; Lt. 1.4.95; Capt. 19.1.00; Major 29.1.13; Lt.-Col., R.G.A.; served in China, 1900; Medal; Europ. War; Despatches.

NUTTALL, W. F. DIXON- (see Dixon-Nuttall, W. F.).

OAKDEN, T. H. (D.S.O. L.G. 16.9.18), T/2nd Lt., Border R.

OAKLEY, R. (D.S.O. L.G. 14.11.16); b. 27.10.72; s. of G. Oakley; m. Enid Elizabeth, d. of J. N. Graham; 4 d.; educ. Wellington College; 2nd Lt., Sco. Rif., 12.12.94; Lt. 26.4.96; Capt. 25.1.00; Maj. 10.10.13; Lt.-Col. 11.3.19; N.W. Frontier, 1897–98; Medal, 2 clasps; went out to France with original Exp. Force, 1914, with 1st Cameronians; wounded twice; appointed to command 10th Batt. The Queen's Rgt., and took it to France; was transferred as a Battalion Commander to M.G.C., and subsequently commanded 63rd Inf. Brig. In 1919 was given command of 2nd Batt. The Cameronians; Despatches twice.

OAKMAN, W. G. (D.S.O. L.G. 17.12.17) (Details, L.G. 23.4.18), Lt., C. Gds., S.R.

OATES, A. (D.S.O. L.G. 22.9.16), Capt., Aust. Inf.

OATES, J. S. C. (D.S.O. L.G. 18.6.17); s. of Lt.-Col. W. C. Oates, D.S.O.; Capt., Notts. and Derby. R.; M.C.

OATES, W. C. (D.S.O. L.G. 1.1.18); b. 7.7.62; 2nd Lt., R. Muns. Fus., 9.9.82; Capt. 1.4.92; ret. pay 2.8.02; Lt.-Col., late T.F. Res; Burmese Exped., 1885–89; Medal, 2 clasps; S. African War; severely wounded; Queen's Medal, 2 clasps

O'BRIEN, G. (D.S.O. L.G. 4.2.18) (Details, L.G. 5.7.18), 2nd Lt., R. Munster Fusiliers, S.R., att. 1st Inniskilling Fusiliers. He was killed in action 22.3.18.

O'BRIEN, H. E. (D.S.O. L.G. 1.1.18), T/Lt.-Col. (T/Col.), R.E.

O'CARROLL, A. D., M.B. (D.S.O. L.G. 4.6.17); b. 26.11.77; s. of late A. O'Carroll, of Dundrum, Dublin; educ. Clongowes; Catholic University, Dublin; Lt., R.A.M.C., 31.7.05; Capt. 1.3.09; Maj. 31.7.17.

O'CONNELL, REV. M. (D.S.O. L.G. 1.1.17); b. Co. Cork; educ. Maynooth; formerly Asst. Priest, St. Patrick's, Livesey Street, Manchester; served Europ. War, R.C. Chaplain.

O'CONNOR, C. B. (D.S.O. L.G. 17.3.17) (Details, L.G. 26.5.17), 2nd Lt. (A/Capt.), N. Lancs. R.

O'CONNOR, H. WILLIS- (see Willis-O'Connor, H.).

O'CONNOR, J. L. (D.S.O. L.G. 17.9.17), T/Major, A.S.C. (now R.A.S.C.).

O'CONNOR, R. N. (D.S.O. L.G. 16.8.17) (Bar, L.G. 1.2.19); b. 21.8.89; 2nd Lt., Sco. Rif., 18.9.09; Lt. 6.5.11; Capt. 11.3.15; Bt. Maj. 1.1.17; M.C.

ODAM, W. T. (D.S.O. L.G. 1.1.18); s. of late J. Odam, of The Firs, Newborough; educ. at Bridgwater, and in London; came from Ottawa at the outbreak of war, and rejoined his old regiment, the 2nd London Brig., R.F.A.; was transferred to 293rd Brig., R.F.A., with which he went out to France; Lt.-Colonel, R. of O., R.F.A.; Despatches several times.

ODDIE, W. (D.S.O. L.G. 3.6.18) (Bar, L.G. 16.9.18), Lt.-Col., W. Yorks. R.

ODLUM, V. W. (D.S.O. L.G. 23.12.15) (Bar, L.G. 2.12.18), Brig.-Gen; C.B.; C.M.G. (see "The Distinguished Service Order," from its institution to 31.12.15, by same publishers).

O'DONAHOE, D. J. (D.S.O. L.G. 1.1.18), Major, Can. Inf.

O'DONAHOE, J. V. P. (D.S.O. L.G. 4.6.17), Major, Can. Inf.

O'DONNELL, A. B. (D.S.O. L.G. 26.9.16); b. Bombay, India, 20.2.76; s. of Lt.-Col. O'Donnell, O.B.E., late 1st K.D.G. S.A.C., Suffolk Yeom., and Remount Dept., France; educ. The Oratory School, Edgbaston, Birmingham; R.M.C., Sandhurst; 2nd Lt., W.I. Rgt., 13.11.97; served through Timini and Mendi Rising in Sierra Leone; Medal and clasp; resigned commission, Nov. 1900; served Europ. War, first as a Sergeant, Natal L.H., through S. African Rebellion and the German S.W. African Campaign; then went to England and enlisted in 2nd King Edward's Horse; from Aug. 1915, to 2.4.16 in Flanders and France; commissioned 10th (S.) Batt., Royal Warwickshire Regiment; promoted Captain on the field; gazetted 17.8.16, the date on which he was made a prisoner of war; Despatches twice; French Croix de Guerre with Palm. His D.S.O. was awarded for gallantry on 30–31.7.16, at Bazentin-le-Petit.

A. B. O'Donnell.

O'DONOGHUE, R. J. L. (D.S.O. L.G. 1.1.18), T/Major, A.S.C.

OGG, A. C. (D.S.O. L.G. 18.8.16); b. 16.9.78; 2nd Lt., Dorset. R., 7.5.89; Lt. 16.7.00; Capt., Ind. Army, 7.5.07; Major 1.9.15; *p.s.c.*; Europ. War, 1914–17; Mesopotamia.

OGG, W. M. (D.S.O. L.G. 14.1.16); b. 12.1.72; 2nd Lt., R.A., 1.8.93; Lt. 1.8.96; Capt. 1.4.00; Maj. 23.4.14; Lt.-Col. 4.3.18; Loc. Col. 4.8.19; served Europ. War in France; Despatches; Bt. Lt.-Col. 3.6.17; C.M.G.

OGILBY, R. J. L. (D.S.O. L.G. 1.1.18) (Bar, L.G. 7.11.18); b. 27.11.80; s. of late R. A. Ogilby and Helen Sarah, d. of Rev. G. B. Wheeler, Rector, of Ballysax, Co. Kildare; High Sheriff, 1911; J.P.; D.L.; late Lt., 2nd Life Guards; Lt.-Col., R. of O., London Scottish; Europ. War; Belgian Croix de Guerre.

OGILVIE, A. T. (D.S.O. L.G. 15.2.19) (Details, L.G. 30.7.19), Lt.-Col., 14th Brig., Can. F.A.

OGILVIE, S. S. (D.S.O. L.G. 25.8.16) (1st Bar, L.G. 1.1.18) (2nd Bar, L.G. 26.7.18); b. 1884; s. of G. S. Ogilvie and Helen Emmeline, d. of S. Davidson; m. Gladys Mina Henrietta, d. of M. Rooke; two s.; three d.; Lt.-Col., Wilts. R. He was awarded the D.S.O. for gallantry on 6–8.7.16, at Leipzig Salient.

OGILVY, D. (D.S.O. L.G. 1.1.18); b. 14.7.81; 2nd Lt., R.E., 6.1.00; Lt. 6.1.03; Capt. 6.1.09; Major, R.E., 2.11.16; Bt. Lt.-Col. 3.6.19; served S. African War, 1901–2 (Queen's Medal, 5 clasps); E. Africa, Somaliland, 1903–4 (Medal, clasp); Europ. War; Despatches.

OGLE, E. C. (D.S.O. L.G. 4.6.17); b. 26.8.78; 2nd Lt., W.I.R., 11.2.99; Lt. 25.7.00; Capt. 8.7.11; Major 1.9.15; served S. African War, 1901, in St. Helena (Queen's Medal); Europ. War; Despatches.

OGLE, N. (D.S.O. L.G. 25.8.17); b. 17.9.82; 2nd Lt., Unatt., 8.5.01; Ind. Army 3.11.02; Lt., Ind. Army, 4.8.04; Capt. 8.5.10; served Europ. War; Despatches.

O'GORMAN, BERNARD (gazetted as O'Gorman, Bernardine) (D.S.O. L.G. 1.1.18), T/Major, Gen. List.

O'GRADY, D. DE COURCY (D.S.O. L.G. 3.6.19); b. 31.5.81; Lt., R.A.M.C., 30.1.06; Capt. 30.7.09; Maj. 30.1.18. He died 23.12.20.

O'GRADY, S. DE C. (D.S.O. L.G. 4.6.17); b. 27.7.72; e. s. of late Captain S. de C. O'Grady and Charlotte, d. of G. P. Houghton; m. Esther Alice, o. d. of Col. P. D. Vigors; Lt., R.A.M.C., 28.1.98; Capt. 28.1.01; Major 28.1.09; Lt.-Col. 1.3.15; served E. Africa, Somaliland, 1904 (Despatches; Medal, clasp); Europ. War; Despatches; C.M.G.

O'HARA, E. R. (D.S.O. L.G. 3.6.19); b. 6.9.79; eighth s. of C. W. O'Hara, J.P., D.L., of Annaghmore and Cooper's Hill, Co. Sligo; m. Moneen, d. of Capt. W. Bond; one s.; 2nd Lt., A.S.C., 21.2.00; Lt. 1.4.01; Capt. 1.1.06; Maj. 30.10.14; served S. African War, 1900–2; Despatches; Queen's Medal, 3 clasps; King's Medal, 2 clasps; E. Africa, 1903–4; Medal with clasp; Somaliland, 1908–10 (clasp); Europ. War, 1914–18; Bt. Lt.-Col. 3.6.17; C.M.G.; Legion of Honour; Croix de Chevalier; 3rd Class Order of Nadha.

OHLENSCHLAGER, N. A. G. (D.S.O. L.G. 14.9.18), Lieut., R.N.

OHLSON, B. J. (D.S.O. L.G. 8.3.20), R.D.; Cdr., R.N.R.

O'KELLY, A. N. (gazetted as O'Kelley, A. N.) (D.S.O. L.G. 26.7.18), Major (A/Lt.-Col.), King Edward's Horse, seconded Tank Corps; served Europ. War, 1914–18; Despatches.

O'KELLY, E. J. DE PENTHENY- (see De Pentheny-O'Kelly, E. J.).

OLDEN, A. C. N. (D.S.O. L.G. 8.3.19) (Details, L.G. 4.10.19), Major, 10th Aust. Light Horse.

OLDFIELD, A. R. (D.S.O. L.G. 1.1.17); b. 8.1.72; s. of Major-Gen. R. Oldfield, late Commandant, R.A.; m. Muriel, d. of Col. C. C. Gordon; one s.; one d.; educ. Trent College, Nottingham; R.M. Academy, Woolwich; 2nd Lt., R.A., 3.2.91; Lt. 13.2.94; Capt., A.O.D., 14.10.99; Maj. 26.11.10; Bt. Lt.-Col. 3.6.18; Temp. Col. 27.5.16.

OLDFIELD, R. W. (D.S.O. L.G. 3.6.18); b. 6.9.91; s. of Maj.-Gen. R. Oldfield, Col.-Comdt., R.A.; m. Beatrix Albinia, d. of G. E. Wherry, F.R.C.S.; educ. Monkton Combe School, Bath; Pembroke College, Cambridge; 2nd Lt., R.A., 19.7.12; Lt. 9.6.15; Capt. 8.8.16; Bt. Maj. 3.6.19; served Europ. War, France, Italy; Despatches six times; wounded twice; M.C.; 2 bars; Italian Bronze Medal for Valour; Croce di Guerra.

OLDHAM, F. H. L. (D.S.O. L.G. 4.6.17); b. 9.5.76; e. s. of late Ven. Archdeacon A. L. Oldham, D.D.; m. Christabel Josephine, o. c. of T. H. Burd; one s.; four d.; educ. Shrewsbury School; New College, Oxford; 2nd Lt., R.A., 26.5.00; Lt. 7.3.02; Capt. 1.2.11; Maj. 30.10.14; Bt. Lt.-Col. 3.6.18; served Europ. War, in France and Italy; Despatches six times; Order of Saints Maurice and Lazarus (Italy).

OLDHAM, G. M. (D.S.O. L.G. 3.6.16); b. Sept. 1876; entered R.E., Feb. 1897; Bt. Lt.-Col., Jan. 1918; served Europ. War; Despatches.

OLDING, E. A. (D.S.O. L.G. 1.1.18), Major, Aust. Field Arty.

O'LEARY, H. W. D. McCARTHY- (see McCarthy-O'Leary, H. W. D.).

OLIPHANT, H. G. L. (D.S.O. L.G. 25.7.16); b. 22.11.79; e. s. of late Gen. Sir L. J. Oliphant, of Condie and Newton, Perthshire, and the Hon. Monica Mary Oliphant (*née* Gerard); m. Ruth, d. of late Vice-Admiral Sir H. Deacon Barry, K.C.V.O.; one s.; two d.; educ. Beaumont; Capt., R.N.; served Europ. War, in command of Amazon during bombardment of German Army's right wing from coast, 1915 (Despatches); Patrol Work, 1916 (D.S.O.); M.V.O., 1915.

OLIPHANT, P. L. K. B. (D.S.O. L.G. 20.10.16); b. 1867; s. of Philip O. K. B. Oliphant; m. 1901, Laura Geraldine, 2nd d. of F. Bodenham; three s.; one d.; educ. Harrow; 2nd Lt., Rifle Brigade, 1888; Capt., 1895; retired (R. of Off.), 1903; joined Ulster Volunteer Force, 1914; on the formation of the Ulster Division was appointed Second-in-Command of the 11th Batt. R.I. Rifles, subsequently given command of this battalion; served Europ. War; Despatches four times. He was wounded 28.3.18, and died of wounds 8.4.18. He wrote under the pen-name of Philip Laurence Oliphant. His D.S.O. was awarded for gallantry on 1.7.16, at Thiépval Wood.

OLIVER, D. A. (D.S.O. L.G. 22.6.16); b. 9.6.87; s. of Rev. A. Oliver, of Latton Vicarage, Harlow, Essex; educ. The Grange, Folkestone; H.M.S. Britannia; Midshipman, H.M.S. Jupiter and New Zealand; Sub-Lt. in H.M.S. Monmouth in China, 1908–10; Lt., 1910; ent. R.N.A.S., 1912; Fl.-Cdr.; Sqn.-Cdr., 1915; Wing Cdr., R.N.A.S., 1.1.17; took part in Cuxhaven Raid 25.2.14, as Fl.-Cdr. (Despatches); in action off Yarmouth against German Squadron 25.4.16. He was awarded the Italian War Cross; O.B.E., June, 1919.

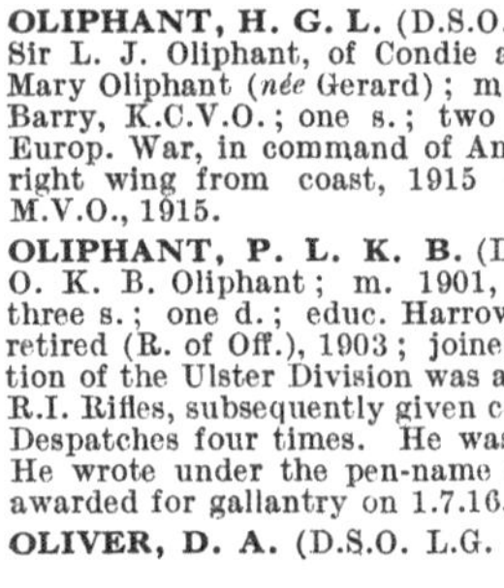

D. A. Oliver.

OLIVER, E. A. (D.S.O. L.G. 1.1.19), Quartermaster and Major, 38th Batt. Can. Inf.

OLPHERT, W. (D.S.O. L.G. 23.3.17) (Bar, L.G. 15.2.19); b. 15.9.79; s. of late W. Olphert; m. 1910, Evelyn Arnold Tennent; one s.; two d.; educ. Bristol Grammar School; H.M.S. Worcester; joined New Zealand Shipping Co., 1895; appointed to R.N.R., 1896; Lieut.-Commander, R.N.R.; remained in service of N.Z. Shipping Co. until Nov. 1914, when called up for active service by Proclamation; D.S.C.

O'NEILL, E. M., M.B. (D.S.O. L.G. 14.1.16); b. 1.10.82; educ. St. Vincent's College, Castleknock; University College, Dublin; Lt., R.A.M.C., 30.1.06; Capt. 30.7.09; Maj. 30.1.18; Despatches.

ONSLOW, C. C. (D.S.O. L.G. 4.6.17); b. 19.9.69; s. of Capt. Hamilton Cranley Onslow and Henrietta Fanny, d. of Major-Gen. J. Forbes Musgrove; m. Sydney Alice Hastings, d. of Sir B. Franklin; two s.; two d.; ent. Bedfords. R. 9.11.89; Lt. 11.8.91; Capt. 1.7.98; Major 3.6.10; Colonel 17.2.20; Temp. Col.-Comdt. 1.1.21; Isazai Exp., 1892; Chitral, 1895 (Medal with clasp); Europ. War, 1914–18; twice wounded; C.M.G.; C.B.E.

ONSLOW, G. M. M. (D.S.O. L.G. 1.1.17), Major, 9th L. Horse, N.S.W. Mtd. Rifles; C.M.G.; V.D.

OPPEN, H. (D.S.O. L.G. 6.4.18), Lt.-Cdr., R.N.R., R.D.

ORD, G. L. (D.S.O. L.G. 1.1.18), Capt. (A/Major), Pioneer Bn. Can. Force.

ORDISH, H. (D.S.O. L.G. 3.6.18), Major, M.G.C.

O'REILLY, C. J., M.D. (D.S.O. L.G. 3.6.19), Capt. (Temp. Major), R.A.M.C.; M.C.

O'REILLY, H. J. M. (D.S.O. L.G. 3.6.19), Lt. (A/Major), R. Ir. Regt.; M.C.

O'REILLY-BLACKWOOD, E. H. (D.S.O. L.G. 3.6.18); b. 1.1.84; 2nd Lt., R.A., 31.7.02; Lt. 31.7.05; Capt. 30.10.14; Maj. 1.5.17.; M.C.

ORGAN, C. A. (D.S.O. L.G. 4.6.17); b. 29.11.81; 2nd Lt., A.S.C., 19.11.02; Lt. 23.8.04; Capt. 1.1.11; Maj. 30.10.14; Bt. Lt.-Col. 3.6.19; Despatches.

ORMEROD, G. M. (D.S.O. L.G. 1.1.17); b. 8.2.79; s. of J. A. Ormerod, M.A., M.D., F.R.C.P., Registrar, R. College of Physicians, London, and Mary Ellen, d. of E. Milner, F.L.S.; m. Mildred Grace, d. and co-heiress of D. G. Ottley; three s.; educ. Rugby; Queen's College, Oxford; 1st com. R.H. and F.A., 1900; Capt., 1909; Asst. C.C., Lancs., 1912; T/Lt.-Colonel, 1915; Europ. War, 1915–18; Despatches twice.

ORMISTON, T. (D.S.O. L.G. 8.8.19), T/Major, 1st Bn. S. African Inf.

ORMOND, D. M. (D.S.O. L.G. 4.6.17) (Bar, L.G. 18.10.17) (Details, L.G. 7.3.18); b. Pembroke, Ontario; s. of D. Ormond; m. Annie Laura Codham; four d.; educ. University of Manitoba; Brig.-Gen., Can. Infy.; served Europ. War, 1915–18; wounded; Despatches three times; C.M.G.; Russian Order of St. Stanislas with Swords; Croix de Guerre.

ORMROD, M. S. (D.S.O. L.G. 1.1.19); b. 9.11.91; 2nd Lt., K.R.R.C., 19.1.12; Lt. 5.8.14; Capt. 14.3.16; Despatches.

T. Ormsby.

ORMSBY, T. (D.S.O. L.G. 3.6.16); b. 30.5.71; s. of late J. Y. Ormsby; m. Lucy Mary, d. of Capt. C. H. Thomson (74th Highlanders); one s.; one d.; educ. St. Columba's College; Sherborne; 2nd Lt., 2nd Batt. S. Stafford Rgt., 18.2.91; Lt. 23.12.92; Capt., A.P.D., 4.11.99; Major 18.2.11; Lt.-Col. 23.8.18; ret. pay 23.3.20; served Europ. War, Egypt, Gallipoli, Salonika, 1914–16; Despatches. He has written "Army Finance as a Military Science."

ORMSTON, E. W. (D.S.O. L.G. 4.6.17), Temp. Capt. (A/Major), R.E.

O'RORKE, THE REV. B. G., M.A. (D.S.O. L.G. 1.1.17); b. 7.4.74; s. of Wm. J. O'Rorke; m. Myra Roberta, d. of late Rev. H. MacDougall; three d.; educ. Nottingham High School; University College, Nottingham; Exeter College, Oxford; B.A., 1887; M.A., 1901; also at the Wycliffe Hall, Oxford; joined the Army 1.8.01; served S. African War, 1901–2 (Queen's Medal 4 clasps); Europ. War, as Chaplain to the Forces (C. of E.); captured at Landrecies by the Germans 26.8.14, and held prisoner for 10 months, 1914–15; Senior Chaplain of the 33rd Division for nine months; Senior Chaplain of the XIth Army Corps for two months; Assistant to the Deputy Chaplain-General, B.E.F.; Despatches; author of "African Missions," 1912; "Our Opportunity in the West Indies," 1913; "In the Hands of the Enemy," 1915. He died at Falmouth on Christmas Day, 1918.

The Rev. B. G. O'Rorke.

O'RORKE, J. M. W. (D.S.O. L.G. 3.6.18); b. 11.12.84; 2nd Lt., Unatt., 24.1.05; Lt. 24.4.07; Capt., Ind. Army, 24.1.14; Maj. 24.1.20.

ORPEN-PALMER, H. B. H. (D.S.O. L.G. 11.4.18); b. 8.9.76; 2nd Lt., R. Irish Fus., 23.8.99; Lt. 24.2.00; Capt. 10.11.06; Major 1.9.15; T/Brig.-Gen. 21.12.17 to 25.3.19; S. African War, 1899–1902; Despatches; Queen's Medal, 4 clasps; King's Medal, 2 clasps; Europ. War; Despatches; Bt. Lt.-Col. 1.1.17 C.M.G.

ORPEN-PALMER, R. A. H. (D.S.O. L.G. 3.6.16); b. 26.12.77; s. of late R. A. H. Orpen-Palmer; m. 1916, Lilian Lucy, d. of John Leland, and widow of late C. B. Irwin; educ. Cheltenham College; Clare College, Cambridge; 2nd Lt., Leins. Regt., 13.7.98; Adjt. 15.8.03 to 14.8.06; Major, Leins. Regt.; served S. African War (Queen's Medal, 3 clasps; King's Medal, 2 clasps); Europ. War; wounded twice; Despatches.

ORR, E. H. (D.S.O. L.G. 22.6.18), Major, New Zealand Force.

ORR, G. M. (D.S.O. L.G. 1.1.18); b. 9.6.76; 2nd Lt. 22.1.96; Lt., Ind. Army, 22.4.98; Capt. 22.1.05; Maj. 22.1.14; Col. 24.4.20; Temp. Col.-Comdt. 12.3.21; *p.s.c.*; Malakand, 1897–98; Medal, 2 clasps; Europ. War; Despatches; Bt. Lt.-Col. 3.6.16; Bt. Col. 3.6.18.

ORR, J. B., M.A., M.D., D.Sc. (D.S.O. L.G. 26.9.17) (Details, L.G. 8.1.18); b. 23.9.80; s. of late R. C. Orr, of Holland Green, Kilmaurs, Ayrshire; m. Elizabeth Pearson, d. of late J. Callum; one s.; two d.; educ. University, Glasgow; Honours; Bellahouston Gold Medallist; Barbour Research Scholar; Director of Rowett Institute for Research in Animal Nutrition, Aberdeen; Research Lecturer in Physiology of Nutrition, University, Aberdeen; served Europ. War, Oct. 1914, to Oct. 1917; R.A.M.C.; M.C.; Despatches; joined Navy as Temp. Surgeon, Nov. 1917.

ORR, N. C. (D.S.O. L.G. 22.7.18); b. 6.8.83; 2nd Lt., Seaf. Highrs., 22.10.02; Lt. 14.1.07; Capt. 22.10.14; Major 22.10.17; Despatches.

OSBORN, L. J. (D.S.O. L.G. 1.1.18), Lt.-Col., R.F.A.

OSBORN, W. L. (D.S.O. L.G. 15.4.16); b. 30.7.71; s. of Lt.-Genl. W. Osborn, I.A.; m. Ethel Marion, d. of late Gen. C. Elgee, 23rd R. Fus.; educ. U.S. College, Westward Ho!; Sandhurst; 2nd Lt., R. Suss. R., 29.11.90; Lt. 10.2.92; Capt. 14.2.99; Adjt., R. Sussex R., 4.9.99 to 3.9.03; Major 13.7.10; Bt. Lt.-Col. 1.1.17; Lt.-Col. 16.11.16; T/Brig.-Gen. 26.7.16 to 9.1.19; served N.W. Frontier of India. 1897–98; Medal, clasp; Tirah, 1897–98; clasp; Tibet, 1904; Europ. War; Despatches six times; C.B.; C.M.G.; Order of Danilo, 3rd Class. He was awarded the D.S.O. for gallantry 3.3.16, at Hohenzollern Redoubt.

OSBORNE, E. O. B. S. (D.S.O. L.G. 23.7.18); s. of Capt. H. B. Osborne, late 53rd Rgt.; m. Joan Marion Herbert, d. of Godfrey C. Chester Master; one s.; educ. The Grange, Folkestone; ent. Britannia, 1897; Lt., 1904; Cdr., 1915; Capt., 1920; Boxer Exp., 1900 (Despatches; early promotion and 4th Order, Crown of Prussia with Crossed Swords); Grand Fleet, 1914–18; Jutland, 1916; Dover Patrol Flag Commander, 1918; Zeebrugge, 1918; Despatches; early promotion.

OSBORNE, G. F. F. (D.S.O. L.G. 4.1.16); b. 6.12.73; s. of G. P. Osborne and Edna Cornelia Osborne (*née* Folger); m. Louisa, d. of W. H. Lockhart-Gordon; one s.; two d.; educ. R.M.C., Kingston, Canada; Deputy Agent, Oudh and Rohilcund Railway, 1913; ent. R.E., 1894; 2nd Lt., R.E., 27.6.94; Lt. 27.6.97; Capt. 1.4.04; Major, R.E., 27.6.14; ret. pay 4.1.20; proceeded to France with the Indian Exp. Force, Aug. 1914; invalided, 1916.

OSBORNE, J. E. (D.S.O. L.G. 30.1.20), T/Lt.-Col., 15th Batt. Can. Inf.

OSBORNE, L. A. (D.S.O. L.G. 16.9.18), Capt., Som. L.I.; Despatches; M.C.

OSBORNE, R. H. (D.S.O. L.G. 3.6.18); b. 30.6.83; m. Cynthia, d. of Lt.-Col. Tom Morris, M.C., Rif. Brig., I.O.; educ. Harrow; 2nd Lt., York and Lanc. R., 22.10.02; Lt. 18.6.04; Capt., 20th Hrs., 14.1.13; 13th Hrs. 23.11.21; Europ. War, 1914–18; Despatches; M.C.; Légion d'Honneur; Bt. Maj. 1.1.18; Bt. Lt.-Col. 14.1.21.

OSBOURNE, G. N. T. SMYTH- (see Smyth-Osbourne, G. N. T.).

OSBURN, A. C. (D.S.O. L.G. 3.6.16) (Bar, L.G. 4.2.18) (Details, L.G. 5.7.18); b. 15.11.76; s. of Francis Osburn, R.N.; m. Sylvia, d. of the Rev. R. Trousdale; educ. King's College; Guy's Hospital; Lt., R.A.M.C., 31.8.03; Capt. 28.2.07; Maj. 28.2.15; S. African War, 1899–1900; Europ. War; Despatches five times.

O'SHAUGHNESSY, C. L. (D.S.O. L.G. 13.2.17) (gazetted O'Shaugnessy for O'Shaughnessy); b. 12.3.89; educ. Burnley and Manchester Schools of Technology; served apprenticeship to Electrical Engineering at Messrs. Simpson and Co., of Hapton, Lancs; joined R.E. as Sapper, March, 1915; commissioned 5.11.15; served in France, Sept.–Dec. 1916; awarded D.S.O. and promoted T/Capt. for service at Grandcourt, Nov. 1916; wounded, Dec. 1916; transferred to M.G.C., May, 1918; France, Belgium and Germany, Aug. 1918, to Sept. 1919; demobilized Sept. 1919; ent. Victoria University, Manchester, Oct. 1919.

O'SHEA, P. J. F. (D.S.O. L.G. 1.2.19), Capt., Aust. A.M.C.; M.C.

O'SHEA, T. (D.S.O. L.G. 3.6.16); b. 2.1.56; 1st commission 10.1.94; retired K.R.R.C. 2.1.11; Qr.-Mr. and Hon. Major, 9th London R. (T.F.); served in Burma, 1891; Medal with clasp; S. African War, 1902; Despatches (L.G. 29.7.02); Queen's Medal, 2 clasps; Europ. War, 1914–18; Despatches twice; 1914 Star.

OSLER, S. H. (D.S.O. L.G. 4.6.17), Major (T/Lt.-Col.), R. Can. Engrs.

OSMOND, C. F. (D.S.O. L.G. 18.7.17), Capt. (A/Lt.-Col.), H.A.C.

OSTROROG, S. J. (D.S.O. L.G. 3.6.19), T/Lt.-Col., R.A.

O'SULLEVAN, J. J. (D.S.O. L.G. 14.1.16); b. March, 1879; s. of late R. O'Sullevan; m. Vera, d. of Sir J. Henry; educ. privately; Blackrock College, Co. Dublin; joined the Cape Mounted Rifles, 1898; assisted in suppressing a Native Rising in Pondoland, 1899; served S. African War, being gazetted to 2nd Batt. Northants Regt. for gallantry in the field at Wepener; Second-in-Command of French's Scouts; Despatches; twice wounded. In 1903 joined the Barotzeland Police in N. Rhodesia; Captain, 1905; commanded in Barotzeland and N.W. Rhodesia till 1909; seconded to command the North-Eastern Rhodesian Constabulary as Major; served Europ. War as Second-in-Command of the European and Native Troops of the Mobile Column at Shuckmansbury, German S. Africa; the campaign in South-West Africa; served Tanganyika, North-East Rhodesia, on the German East African Border; commanded No. 2 Mobile Column, Rhodesian Forces; posted to the command of the Allied Forces (Belgian and British), and fought a number of successful actions in Northern Rhodesia and German E. Africa (Despatches three times); wounded and invalided home, 1915. In April, 1916, he commanded the 19th Cheshires in France; posted to command (11th Service) Battn. Sherwood Foresters, 23rd Division, taking part in the severe fighting on the Somme (again wounded and gassed). During General Gordon's absence he commanded the 69th Inf. Bdge., 23rd Div.; appointed Commandant, Ballykinlar Command Depôt, 29.4.17; Resident Magistrate, Killarney.

OSWALD, K. A. (D.S.O. L.G. 17.12.17) (Details, L.G. 23.4.18), Major (A/Lt.-Col.), R.W. Surrey Rgt.

J. P. H. Ouchterlony.

OUCHTERLONY, J. P. H. (D.S.O. L.G. 4.6.17); b. 10.6.84; 2nd Lt., R.E., 21.12.01; Lt. 3.8.04; Capt. 21.12.12. He was killed in action 8.6.17.

OUTERBRIDGE, L. C. (D.S.O. L.G. 1.1.19) Major. 75th Battn. Can. Inf.

OVERTON, G. C. R. (D.S.O. L.G. 1.1.18); b. 8.10.66; 2nd Lt., R. Fus., 15.3.93; Capt. 27.9.99; ret. pay 8.6.10; Maj., Res. of Off., 1.9.15; Lt.-Col., Army, 6.6.16; S. African War, 1899–1902; Despatches; Queen's Medal, 5 clasps; King's Medal, 2 clasps; Europ. War; Despatches.

OVEY, D. (D.S.O. L.G. 1.1.17), Major, Rifle Bgde.

OVEY, R. L. (D.S.O. L.G. 14.1.16), Major, Oxf. and Bucks. L. Inf. (T.F.).

OWEN, A. D. (D.S.O. L.G. 17.9.17); b. 2.9.77; 2nd Class Inspector of Mechanical Transport 1.10.07; 1st Class 19.5.15; Hon. Maj. 1.7.17; served Europ. War; Despatches.

OWEN, C. H. W. (D.S.O. L.G. 14.1.16); b. 26.10.72; s. of George Wells Owen, M.I.C.E.; m. Marjorie, d. of Colonel S. E. Craster, R.E.; one s.; one d.; educ. Marlborough; 2nd Lt., R.A., 12.2.92; Lt. 12.2.95; Capt. 1.1.00; Major 2.9.12; Lt.-Col. 1.5.17; ret. pay 1.11.21; served Nile Expedition, 1898 (Despatches twice; Egyptian Medal); Europ. War, 1914–18; C.M.G.; Mil. Order of Savoy.

OWEN, D. C. (D.S.O. L.G. 4.6.17); b. 17.12.80; 2nd Lt., Middx. R., 4.5.01; Lt. 24.9.02; Capt. 26.8.09; Maj. 4.5.16; S. African War, 1902; Queen's Medal, 3 clasps; Europ. War; Despatches.

OWEN, G. (D.S.O. L.G. 31.5.16), Temp. Capt., 15th Bn. R.W. Fus. He was awarded the D.S.O. for gallantry on 27.5.16, at Piccanton.

OWEN, H. B., M.B. (D.S.O. L.G. 1.1.18), Temp. Capt., Uganda Medical Service.

OWEN, L. C. (D.S.O. L.G. 1.1.18); b. 15.9.87; 2nd Lt., R.E., 23.7.07; Lt. 2.5.10; Capt. 30.10.14; Bt. Maj. 3.6.19.

OWEN, LL. I. G. MORGAN- (see Morgan-Owen, Ll. I. G.).

OWEN, M. M. MORGAN, (see Morgan-Owen, M. M.).

OWEN, R. A. MOSTYN- (see Mostyn-Owen, R. A.).

OWEN, S. LL. (D.S.O. L.G. 3.6.16); b. 27.2.72; s. of late Dr. Lloyd Owen, of Southsea; educ. Portsmouth Grammar School; R.M.A., Woolwich; 2nd Lt., R.E., 13.2.91; Lt. 13.2.94; Capt. 13.2.02; Maj. 13.2.11; Lt.-Colonel 24.9.18; ret. pay 1.5.21; served S. African War, 1899–1902; Despatches, 2 Medals, 7 clasps.

OWEN, W. H. (D.S.O. L.G. 3.6.18), Comdr. (A/Capt.), R.N.R.

OWEN, W. LL. (D.S.O. L.G. 8.3.19) (Details, L.G. 4.10.19), Capt. and Bt. Major (Temp. Lt.-Col.), 5th Bn. Liverpool Regt. (T.F.), Commanding 11th Bn. R.W. Surrey R.; M.C.; Despatches.

OWSTON, L. V. (D.S.O. L.G. 3.3.17); b. 10.2.83; 2nd Lt., 3rd D.G., 26.3.02; Lt. 8.8.06; Capt. 3.4.12; Maj. 26.3.19; served Europ. War; Despatches.

OXENHAM, N. H. (D.S.O. L.G. 1.1.18), T/Major, M.G.C.

OZANNE, H. (D.S.O. L.G. 17.4.17), Major, R.M.L. Inf. His D.S.O. was awarded for gallantry on 17.2.17.

PACE, T. G. (D.S.O. L.G. 3.6.18), T/Major, A.S.C. (now R.A.S.C.).

PACKE, E. C. (D.S.O. L.G. 1.1.17); b. 14.11.77; s. of late Rev. W. J. Packe, M.A.Oxon., of Stretton Hall, Leicester, and Glenn Hall, Leicester, and Vicar of Feering, Essex; m. Olivia Rachel Nora, d. of late C. Maclean, J.P., D.L.; three s.; one d.; educ. Haileybury College; Magdalene College, Cambridge; B.A.; 2nd Lt., R. Fus., 18.10.99; Lt. 12.1.01; Adjt., 3rd Batt. R. Fus., 1905–8; Capt. 5.5.07; Major 1.9.15; Lt.-Col., ret. pay, 3.12.21; served S. African War, 1899–1900; Relief of Ladysmith, including operations on Tugela Heights (wounded; Queen's Medal, 3 clasps); Europ. War, 1914–17; Despatches thrice; O.B.E.

PACKE, W. V. (D.S.O. L.G. 3.6.16), Major, R.F.A., S.R.

PADWICK, H. B. (D.S.O. L.G. 26.3.17), T/Surg., R.N.

PAGE, C. A. S. (D.S.O. L.G. 26.7.18); b. 2.3.80; 2nd Lt., Middx. R., 26.6.01; Lt. 6.3.03; Capt. 14.12.10; Maj. 8.5.16; ret. pay 18.5.20; S. African War, 1900–2; Queen's Medal, 3 clasps; King's Medal, 2 clasps; Europ. War; Despatches; Bt. Lt.-Col. 3.6.19.

PAGE, C. F. G. (D.S.O. L.G. 3.6.16), Bt. Lt.-Col., R.G.A.

PAGE, C. H. (D.S.O. L.G. 26.7.18), T/Major, Notts. and Derby. R.

PAGE, C. M., M.B., F.R.C.S. (D.S.O. L.G. 1.1.19); b. Sept. 1882; m. Helen, d. of Sir T. W. Holderness, Bart., G.C.B.; one s.; two d.; educ. Westminster School; St. Thomas's Hospital; Gold Medal, London University, M.S., 1908; Capt., R.A.M.C., S.R.; S.M.O., British Red Cross Society's Detachment in Turkey, 1912–13; served with B.E.F. in France, Aug. 1914–Jan. 1919; Surgeon Specialist, 1915–16; with 29th Div. 1917; O.C. a Field Ambulance of 32nd Div., 1918; promoted A/Lt.-Col., March, 1918; Despatches three times.

PAGE, F. (D.S.O. L.G. 23.6.15) (Bar, L.G. 13.2.17), Major (T/Lt.-Col.), Herts R. (see "The Distinguished Service Order," from its institution to 31.12.15).

PAGE, G. F. (D.S.O. L.G. 25.11.16); b. 23.3.94; m. Gereth Margaret, d. of Percy E. Wheeler, of Hans Place, S.W.; one s.; one d.; educ. Harrow; Sandhurst; joined 2nd Lancs. Fus. 15.2.13; Lt. 2.1.15; Capt. 15.2.16; Le Cateau; Retreat from Mons; Aisne; Marne; Retreat from Serbia, 1915; British offensives, Doiran, Macedonia front, 1916–17; served Europ. War; Despatches thrice; Serbian White Eagle, 4th Class, with Swords; 1914 Star.

PAGE, G. F. L. L. (D.S.O. L.G. 17.5.18) (Bar, L.G. 29.11.18), Cdr., R.N., 31.12.18. He died 27.10.20.

PAGE, H. H., (D.S.O. L.G. 1.1.19), Major, Aust. Mil. Forces; M.C.

PAGE, L. F. (D.S.O. L.G. 1.1.17) (1st Bar, L.G. 3.6.18) (2nd Bar, L.G. 2.12.18); b. 17.12.84; s. of H. J. Page and A. E., d. of Capt. Winchester Jones, 60th Rifles; m. Rose Laura Whitehouse; one d.; educ. Berkhamsted School; went to Canada, 1903; commissioned in 35th Central Alberta Horse; joined 5th Can. Batt., Aug. 1914; went to France, Feb. 1915; served continuously from that time as Lt., Capt. and Major (2nd-in-command) of 5th Batt.; given command of 50th Can. Batt., March, 1916; Bt. Lt.-Colonel, Lord Strathcona's Horse.

PAGE, L. M. S. (D.S.O. L.G. 1.1.17); b. 23.2.79; 2nd Lt., A.S.C., 22.5.00; Lt. 1.6.01; Capt. 1.2.05; Maj. 30.10.14; Bt. Lt.-Col., R.A.S.C., 3.6.19; S. African War, 1899–1902; Queen's Medal, 5 clasps; Europ. War; Despatches.

PAGET, SIR A. W. (D.S.O. L.G. 4.6.17); b. 20.3.52; 2nd s. of late Gen. Lord Alfred Henry Paget, C.B., 5th s. of 1st Marquis of Anglesey; m. Viti, d. of Rt. Hon. Sir W. MacGregor, K.C.M.G.; one d.; ent. R.N., 1865; Capt., 1896; Rear-Admiral, 1906; Vice-Admiral, 1911; Senior Officer, Coast of Ireland, 1908–11; Admiral; K.C.B.; K.C.M.G.; T/Capt., R.N.R.; served Egyptian War, 1882 (Medal; Khedive's Star); Eastern Sudan, 1884–85; Suakim, 1888; Despatches; promoted Commander; clasp; 3rd Class Medjidie.; Naval Attaché to Paris, Petrograd and Washington, 1896–99; China, 1900–1; Officer, Legion of Honour. He died 17.6.18.

PAGET, B. C. T. (D.S.O. L.G. 1.1.18); b. 15.9.87; s. of late F. Paget, Bishop of Oxford, and Helen Beatrice, d. of late Very Rev. R. W. Church, Dean of St. Paul's; m. Winifred Nora, d. of Sir John Paget, 2nd Bart.; one s.; educ. Shrewsbury School; 2nd Lt., Oxf. and Bucks. L.I., 13.11.07; Lt. 19.11.10; Capt. 10.6.15; Bt. Maj. 3.6.17; M.C.

PAGET, C. W. (D.S.O. L.G. 3.6.16); b. 19.10.74; s. of Sir G. E. Paget, Bart., D.L., and Sophia, who died in 1913, d. of Col. C. Holden; m. Lady Alexandra Louisa Godolphin Osborne, 4th d. of the 9th Duke of Leeds; Lt.-Col., late R.E.; served Europ. War; Despatches; C.M.G.

PAGET-TOMLINSON, W. (D.S.O. L.G. 2.4.19) (Details, L.G. 10.12.19); b. 1.3.77; 2nd Lt., 7th Hrs., 19.9.00; Lt. 27.7.02; Capt. 12.4.10; Maj. 23.7.19; ret. pay 24.7.20; S. African War, 1901–2; Queen's Medal, 5 clasps.

PAIGE, C. J. M. (D.S.O. L.G. 8.3.19) (Details, L.G. 4.10.19), T/2nd Lt. (A/Capt.), 11th Batt. R.W. Surrey Rgt.; M.C.

PAIGE, C. P. (D.S.O. L.G. 19.12.22), Major (A/Lt.-Col.), 109th Inf., I.A.

PAIN, J. H. F. (D.S.O. L.G. 1.1.19), Major (2nd Batt. A.I.F.), Aust. Forces; M.C.

PAINE, D. D. (D.S.O. L.G. 3.6.18), Major, Aust. A.S.C.

PAINTER, G. W. A. (D.S.O. L.G. 4.6.17); b. 24.2.93; s. of Brig.-Gen. A. C. Painter, C.M.G., and Amy Caroline (who died in 1895), d. of late Thomas Whistler Smith, of Glenrock, Sydney, N.S.W.; m. Kathleen Hay Lannoy, d. of Col. J. L. Tweedie, D.S.O.; one d.; educ. Malvern College; R.M.A., Woolwich; 2nd Lt., R.G.A., 19.12.13; Lt. 19.6.15; Adjt., R.A., 10.1.16 to 21.10.16; Capt. 3.11.17; served Europ. War, in France and Belgium, March, 1915–July, 1919.

PALLANT, H. A. (D.S.O. L.G. 26.9.17) (Details, L.G. 9.1.18), Capt., R.A.M.C.; M.C. His D.S.O. was awarded for gallantry on 11.7.17, Nieuport Bains.

PALLANT, S. LUIS (gazetted as Luis-Pallant, S.) (D.S.O. L.G. 1.1.17); b. 26.7.78; s. of T. Pallant, A.M.Inst.C.E.; educ. Ramsgate; France; Guy's Hospital; 2nd Lt., R.A.M.C., 31.8.03; Capt. 28.2.07; Maj. 28.2.15; Bt. Lt.-Col. 1.1.18.

PALLIN, S. F. G., F.R.C.V.S. (D.S.O. L.G. 1.1.17); b. 8.12.78; Lt., A. Vety. Corps; Capt. 16.5.08; Major 10.7.15; S. African War, 1901–2; Queen's Medal, 5 clasps.

PALLIN, W. A., F.R.C.V.S. (D.S.O. L.G. 4.6.17); b. 16.6.73; Capt., A.V.C., 5.10.03; prev. serv. 7 years; Maj. 6.1.12; Lt.-Col., R.A.V.C., 1.4.21; China, 1900; Medal; Europ. War; Despatches; C.B.E.

PALLOT, E. G. (D.S.O. L.G. 3.6.18), Eng.-Cdr., R.N., 29.10.14.

PALMER, A. (D.S.O. L.G. 15.7.19), Lt. (T/Capt.), 6th Batt. North'd Fus., T.F.

PALMER, A. E. G. (D.S.O. L.G. 4.6.17); b. 26.3.86; s. of Lt.-Cdr., C. B. Palmer, R.N., retired; m. Jeanne Léonie, d. of M. Baratoux; educ. Eton; 2nd Lt. 4.5.07; Lt. 23.11.10; Capt. 8.3.15, Green Howards; served Europ. War, 1914–18; Despatches; M.C.

PALMER, A. J. (D.S.O. L.G. 4.6.17); s. of late S. Palmer; m. Catita, d. of late Lt.-Col. H. C. Lyle; Lt.-Col., R. Glouc. Hussars; T.D.; J.P.; High Sheriff of Gloucestershire; served Europ. War, Egypt, Gallipoli, from 1914; Despatches; Order of White Eagle, 4th Class.

PALMER, H. B. H. ORPEN- (see Orpen-Palmer, H. B. H.).

PALMER, H. R. (D.S.O. L.G. 3.6.18); b. 26.5.66; Lt., R.A., 17.2.86; Capt. 30.9.96; Maj. 7.9.04; Lt.-Col., R.G.A., 30.10.14; ret. pay 30.4.20.

PALMER, H. W. T. (D.S.O. L.G. 3.6.18); b. 21.2.86; s. of late Major-Gen. H. W. Palmer, C.B. (74th Highrs. and 90th L.I.), and Margaret Dartnell, d. of late J. Tuthill; educ. Wellington College; R.M.A., Woolwich; 2nd Lt., R.E., 31.8.05; Lt. 23.3.08; Capt. 30.10.14; served Europ. War in France, Belgium and Germany, 1914–18; served in 5th Co., R.E., 2nd Div.; commanded 73rd Field Co., R.E., 15th (Scottish) Division; commanded 1st Field Squadron, R.E., 1st Cav. Div.; Despatches.

PALMER, L. R. (D.S.O. L.G. 15.9.16), Cdr., R.N., 30.6.19.

PALMER, REV. R. (D.S.O. L.G. 1.1.18); s. of late J. Palmer; educ. Fettes College, Edinburgh; Cambridge University; ordained 1903; Hon. Chaplain to the Forces; served S. African War, R. Irish Rgt., 1900–2; S.S.O.M.I.; C.F.; Europ. War from 1916; Despatches; M.C.

PALMER, R. A. H. ORPEN- (see Orpen-Palmer, R. A. H.).

PALMER, R. H. (D.S.O. L.G. 1.1.17), Major, Can. Inf.

PALMER, R. L. (D.S.O. L.G. 15.10.18); b. 1.12.83; 2nd Lt., R.A., 24.12.02; Lt. 24.12.05; Capt. 30.10.14; Maj. 24.5.16; M.C.

PANET, A. E. (D.S.O. L.G. 4.6.17); b. Quebec, 13.12.67; s. of late Col. C. E. Panet; m. Corinne, d. of the late Sir H. E. Taschereau, P.C.; one s.; one d.; educ. R.M.C., Kingston, Canada; entered the Can. Forces, 28.7.88; Lt. 28.7.91; Capt. 28.7.99; Major 4.7.08; Lt.-Col. 25.7.16; T/Brig.-Genl. 27.1.17; served in Waziristan, 1894–95 (Medal with clasp); Europ. War from 1915; Despatches; C.B.; C.M.G.; Belgian Croix de Guerre; Bt. of Colonel 3.6.18; French Croix de Guerre.

PANET, E. DE B. (D.S.O. L.G. 14.1.16), Major, R. Can. Arty.

PANK, C. H. (D.S.O. L.G. 4.2.18) (Details, L.G. 5.7.18); b. 4.4.76; s. of J. L. Pank, D.L., J.P., of New Barnet, Herts; m. Dorothy Annie, d. of late W. Priestley Offord D'Arcy; one s.; two d.; educ. Haileybury College; gazetted to 3rd Middlesex R.V., 1893; Lt.-Col., May, 1917; served continuously from that time; transferred to T.F. on its formation; commanded 2/10th Middlx. Rgt., Gallipoli (Suvla Bay), Aug.–Dec. 1915; Egpyt, Dec. 1915–July, 1916; 8th Middlx. R., France, Aug. 1917–Feb. 1919; C.M.G.

PANNALL, C. (D.S.O. L.G. 8.3.19) (Details, L.G. 4.10.19); b. 6.4.79; 2nd Lt., R.W. Surr. R., 27.10.15; Lt. 1.7.17; Capt., Yorks. R., 23.3.21; Bt. Maj. 24.3.21; M.C.

PANTON, H. F., M.C., M.B. (D.S.O. L.G. 26.11.17) (Details, L.G. 6.4.18); b. 5.12.85; s. of G. A. Panton, F.R.S.E.; m. Honor Mary, d. of Conway Lowe; one s.; educ. Trinity College, Glenalmond; Edinburgh University; M.B.; Ch.B.; commissioned R.A.M.C. 20.7.12; Capt. 30.3.15; Bt. Maj. 3.6.17; M.C.

PAPILLON, P. R., M.A., B.C.L. (D.S.O. L.G. 20.10.16); s. of P. O. Papillon and Emily Caroline, d. of late Very Rev. T. Garnier, B.C.L., Dean of Lincoln, and Lady Caroline Garnier; m. Constance Lauretta, d. of J. W. Roseby; one s.; two d.; educ. Winchester; University College, Oxford; J.P.; 3rd R. Sussex Rgt., 1889–1904; Capt. and Hon. Major, 9th R. Sussex R., 21.9.14 to 2.2.15; Capt., 13th Essex R., 2.2.15 to 22.3.17; Hon. Lt.-Col. in Army; served S. African War; Despatches; Queen's Medal, five clasps; Europ. War, 1914–16; Despatches.

PARBURY, K. (D.S.O. L.G. 4.6.17); b. 22.8.84; 2nd Lt., R.A., 21.12.04; Lt. 21.12.07; Capt. 30.10.14; Maj. 1.11.16.

PARDOE, T. K. (D.S.O. L.G. 1.1.18); b. 19.7.73; 2nd Lt., Worc. R., 5.5.00; Lt. 6.2.01; Capt. 5.9.08; Maj. 26.10.15; Lt.-Col., ret. pay, 22.10.20; S. African War, 1899–1902; Queen's Medal, 3 clasps; King's Medal, 2 clasps.

PARGITER, L. L. (D.S.O. L.G. 7.11.18); b. 3.5.85; s. of E. H. Pargiter; m. Marjorie, d. of C. A. Horn; 2nd Lt., Midd'x R., 27.5.08; Lt. 9.3.11; Capt. 11.12.14; Adjt., 1914, Midd'x Rgt.; Europ. War from 1914; Despatches thrice; Bt. Major 3.6.19.

PARISH, F. W. (D.S.O. L.G. 26.7.18); b. 20.5.84; 2nd Lt., K.R.R.C., 3.8.04; Lt. 13.2.08; Capt. 3.11.14; Maj. 11.7.18. He died 13.10.21; M.C.

PARK, G. W. A. (D.S.O. L.G. 16.9.18), T/Capt., E. Yorks. R.

PARK, J. D. (D.S.O. L.G. 1.1.18), Major, R.E.

PARKER, A. C. (D.S.O. L.G. 1.1.18), T/Capt. (Local Lt.-Col.), Spec. List.

PARKER, G. A. (D.S.O. L.G. 10.1.17); b. 19.12.92; 2nd Lt. from S.R., North'n R., 24.3.13; Capt., North'n R. and R.F.C.; M.C.

PARKER, G. H. I. (D.S.O. L.G. 12.12.19), Lt.-Cdr., R.N., 30.9.11.

PARKER, H. (D.S.O. L.G. 3.6.19); s. of J. Parker. He mobilized as Junior Captain in the Preston Territorials; Major, 1/4th Batt. N. Lancs. Rgt., T.F.

PARKER, H. S. W. (D.S.O. L.G. 1.1.19), Major, 6th Art. Brig., Aust. F.A.

PARKER, J. S. (D.S.O. L.G. 21.4.17); b. 16.6.77; s. of J. E. Parker and Marion Frances Parker (*née* Sandbach); m. Linda Mary Olivia, d. of Rev. L. Davies; one s.; educ. Weybridge; H.M.S. Britannia; ent Navy, 1891; present at taking of Port Arthur and Wei-Hei-Wei during Chinese-Japanese War, 1894–95; Lt., 1899; Lt.-Cdr. 1.10.07; sunk in H.M.S. Aboukir 22.9.14, and interned in Holland four days; in command of H.M.S. Harrier, Downs and Mediterranean, Oct. 1914–Sept. 1918; present at loss of H.M.S. Russell, April, 1916; engaged with Submarine 23.2.17, and saved crew and French troops from S.S. Dorothy (D.S.O.; Croix de Guerre avec Palmes); salved Transport Kingstonian from Cape Granitola, May and June, 1917; retired 1920.

PARKER, P. E. (D.S.O. L.G. 15.2.19) (Details, L.G. 30.7.19), Capt., R.N., 31.12.18.

PARKER, W. (D.S.O. L.G. 1.1.17), Major (T/Lt.-Col.), London Rgt.

PARKER, W. A. (D.S.O. L.G. 1.2.19), Capt., 5th Batt. Scottish Rifles, T.F.

PARKER, W. M. (D.S.O. L.G. 26.8.18); b. 14.6.75; s. of late Col. W. Parker; m. Dorothy Margaret, d. of late F. Buszard, M.D., J.P.; educ. Queen Elizabeth College, Guernsey; 2nd Lt., Northants R., 7.12.95; Lt. 9.4.98; Capt., A.S.C., 1.2.02; Maj. 5.8.14; Lt.-Col. 10.8.20; Col. 4.2.21; Colonel, R.A.S.C.; Tirah Exp., N.W.F. of India, 1897–98; Medal and three clasps; Europ. War, War Office, Gallipoli, Salonika, Egypt, Mesopotamia, France; Despatches five times; Bt. Col. 11.8.20; C.M.G.

PARKER, W. N., M.D., L.R.C.P., M.R.C.S. (D.S.O. L.G. 1.1.17); b. Gt. Gonerby, Lincs, 26.2.60; s. of W. Parker, Landed Proprietor and Farmer; m. Ellen Maude (who died 1910), d. of late Rev. Canon Dorman; two d.; educ. Grantham Grammar School; London Hospital; was posted to a battalion, Border R., and accompanied it in action in Flanders at Vimy and on the Somme.

PARKES, W. (D.S.O. L.G. 8.3.19) (Details, L.G. 4.10.19), T/Major (A/Lt.-Col.), 8th Batt. Glouc. R.; M.C.

PARKIN, F. L. (D.S.O. L.G. 16.9.18), Major (T/Lt.-Col.), Yorks. L.I., att. W. Riding Rgt.

PARKIN, J. F. (D.S.O. L.G. 4.9.18); b. 29.4.82; 2nd Lt., A.S.C., 1.5.01; Lt. 1.5.02; Capt., Ind. Army, 1.5.10; Maj. 1.5.16.

PARKINSON, G. S. (D.S.O. L.G. 1.1.18); b. 1.10.80; Lt., R.A.M.C., 1.8.08; Capt. 1.2.12; Maj. 1.8.20

R. F. Parkinson.

PARKINSON, R. F. (D.S.O. L.G. 1.1.18), Lt.-Col., Can. Inf.

PARKINSON, T. W. (D.S.O. L.G. 14.1.16); b. 8.7.80; 2nd Lt., York. and Lanc. R., 30.8.99; Lt. 2.2.01; Capt. 12.3.07; Maj. 29.8.15; S. African War, 1900–2; Queen's Medal, 5 clasps; King's Medal, 2 clasps; Europ. War; Despatches; Lt.-Col., Commanding 15th Welsh Rgt. (Carmarthenshire Batt.).

PARKS, E. J. (D.S.O. L.G. 3.6.19), Major (T/Lt.-Col.), 16th Batt. Aust. Inf.; M.C.

PARMINTER, R. H. R. (D.S.O. L.G. 25.8.17); b. 28.3.93; s. of late Major W. G. Parminter; m. Muriel, d. of J. H. Davis; 2nd Lt., Manch. R., 5.2.13; Lt. 15.9.14; Capt. 1.10.15; Bt. Maj. 3.6.19; M.C.

PARNELL, G. L. (D.S.O. L.G. 8.3.18), Cdr., R.N., 31.12.12.

PARR, V. H. (D.S.O. L.G. 18.10.17) (Details, L.G. 7.3.18), T/Capt., R. Innis. Fusiliers; M.C.

PARRY, C. F. P. (D.S.O. L.G. 1.1.17); b. 19.6.70; s. of late Major-General F. W. B. Parry, of the Cheshire Rgt., and of Mrs. Parry, of Verlands, Windsor; 2nd Lt., R.A., 14.2.90; Lt. 14.2.93; Capt. 3.2.00; Maj. 20.7.07; Lt.-Col., 34th Brig., R.A.; Despatches several times. He was killed in action 20.8.18.

PARRY, D. B. (D.S.O. L.G. 18.6.17), retired 3rd D.G.; Major (A/Lt.-Col.), London Rgt., and M.G.C. His D.S.O. was awarded for gallantry on 7.4.17, near Ypres. He was killed in action 24.3.18.

PARRY, J. L. R. (D.S.O. L.G. 1.2.19) M,ajor, 50th Batt. Can. Infy., Alberta Rgt.

PARRY, P. E. LANGWORTHY- (see Langworthy-Parry, P. E.).

PARRY, R. A. (D.S.O. L.G. 14.1.16), Capt., Suffolk R., T.F.

PARRY, R. ST. P. (D.S.O. L.G. 28.8.18), M.V.O.; Capt., R.N.

PARRY, T. H., B.A., LL.B. (D.S.O. L.G. 16.8.17); b. 1881; s. of T. Parry, J.P.; educ. Alyn Grammar School, Mold; University College, Aberystwyth; Christ's College, Cambridge (B.A., LL.B., Honours); Barrister; M.P., Flint Burghs, 1913; Flint County from 1918; Subaltern in 5th R.W.F. (T.) at outbreak of war; Capt., 1/5th R.W.F., 1914; Major, June, 1916; Lt.-Col., Commanding 5/6th R.W.F.; served Europ. War, Gallipoli, Egypt, Palestine, from 1914; wounded at Suvla Bay; invalided home, but returned to Egypt, Sept. 1916; was three times wounded in the Battle of Gaza, March, 1917 (D.S.O.); again rejoined his unit 1.9.17; Despatches.

PARSON, G. (D.S.O. L.G. 4.6.17) (Bar, L.G. 1.1.18; under name Parsons, G.), Major, British S. African Police; mentioned in Despatches 1.1.18 by Lt.-Gen. Van Deventer.

PARSONS, A. E. B. (D.S.O. L.G. 25.5.23), Maj., 2nd Batt. 12th Frontier Force, I.A.; O.B.E.

PARSONS, B. E. T. (D.S.O. L.G. 2.4.19) (Details, L.G. 10.12.19), Major, 2/4th Batt. Hants Rgt., T.F.

PARSONS, C. (D.S.O. L.G. 1.1.17); b. 8.12.70; s. of late Maj.-Gen. C. Parsons; educ. Dover College; 2nd Lt., The Queen's R., 4.2.91; Capt. 9.10.99; ret. pay 5.1.07; Lt.-Col., Res. of Off., 2.1.20; N.W. Frontier, 1897–98; Medal, clasp; Tirah, 1897–98; clasp; S. African War, 1899–1902; Queen's Medal, 3 clasps; King's Medal, 2 clasps; Europ. War; rejoined 1914; Brigade Major with B.E.F. to 1915; D.A.A. and Q.M.G. of a Div., B.E.F., Nov. 1915–17; Despatches three times; Bt. Lt.-Col., The Queen's Rgt., R. of O.

PARSONS, D. (D.S.O. L.G. 1.1.17); b. 29.2.72; m. Frances May, d. of Capt. R. B. Needham, R.N. (retired); one d.; 2nd Lt., North'n R., 1.10.95; Lt., A.S.C., 29.9.96; Capt. 18.11.00; Maj. 3.9.10; Lt.-Col., Res. of Off., 24.2.15; retired pay 10.9.20; served W. Africa, 1898 (Medal and clasp); S. African War, 1899–1902; Queen's Medal and 6 clasps; King's Medal and 2 clasps; Europ. War, 1914–18. He was Senior Supply Officer, 6th Division, in 1914; O.C., 39th Divisional Train, 1915–18; in the former Division served on the Aisne and Armentières Sectors; in the latter, Ypres and Somme Sectors for two years, nine months. He was given the Bt. of Lt.-Col., Jan. 1915; promoted Lt.-Col., 1915; was created a C.M.G.; received the Mons Star; 1914 clasp; Despatches four times.

PARSONS, H. M. (D.S.O. L.G. 11.4.18), Major, Aust. Light Horse.

PARSONS, J. L. ROWLETT (D.S.O. L.G. 1.1.17); b. 1876; s. of late Major W. Parsons and Annie, d. of Capt. J. L. Bolton; m. Minnie Burns, d. of late J. D. Weldon; one s.; one d.; educ. University of Toronto; B.A.; Colonel, Canadian Mil. Forces, 1913; served Europ. War; Major, 28th Batt. Can. E.F., Oct. 1914; Despatches four times; C.M.G.; Croix de Guerre (French); Légion d'Honneur (Chevalier).

PARSONS, J. S. (D.S.O. L.G. 3.6.18), Lt. (T/Major), R.E.

PARSONS, J. W. (D.S.O. L.G. 4.6.17); S. African War, 1899–1900; Queen's Medal, clasp; Europ. War; Despatches; Major, Aust. Light Horse Rgt.

PARSONS, WILLIAM FORSTER (D.S.O. L.G. 4.6.17); b. 11.6.79; 2nd Lt., R.A., 23.6.98; Lt. 16.2.01; Capt., Jan. 1906; Adjt., R.A., 28.4.06 to 23.3.09; Major 30.10.14; Lt.-Col. 1.10.18; C.M.G.

PARSONS, WILLIAM FREDERIC (D.S.O. L.G. 4.6.17); b. 10.11.79; s. of Hon. R. C. Parsons and Agnes Elizabeth, d. of late J. F. La Trobe Bateman, F.R.S.; m. Clara Helena, d. of Hon. E. G. Strutt; one s.; one d.; 2nd Lt., R.A., 20.5.99; Capt. 15.10.07; retired pay 20.5.14; Bt. Lt.-Col. 1.1.19; Lt.-Col., R. of O., 25.2.19; C.M.G.

PARTRIDGE, LL. (D.S.O. L.G. 26.8.17); b. 27.3.78; 2nd Lt., 3rd Dragoon Guards, 4.1.99; Capt. 27.7.01; retired pay 26.2.08; Major, Pembroke Yeomanry, att. Welsh Rgt.; served Europ. War; Despatches; Order of the Nile.

PASCOE, J. S. (D.S.O. L.G. 4.6.17); b. 17.10.77; Lt., R.A.M.C., 31.1.05; Capt. 31.7.08; Major 15.10.15; served S. African War, 1900–1; Queen's Medal, 4 clasps; Europ. War; Despatches. He died 29.12.20.

PASK, I. A. J. (D.S.O. L.G. 26.9.16); b. 15.3.81; only s. of A. T. Pask, a Writer of some note in the Eighties, and during the war a civilian prisoner in Germany; 2nd Lt., R.A., 4.12.01; Lt. 6.6.04; Capt., R.G.A.; A/Major, 102nd Brig., R.F.A.; Despatches; M.C.; His D.S.O. was awarded for gallantry in July and Aug. 1916, at Montauban. Capt. Pask was killed in action on 1.9.16.

PASKE, G. F. (D.S.O. L.G. 4.6.17), Major, Oxf. and Bucks. L.I., S.R.

PATCH, F. R. (D.S.O. L.G. 25.8.17); b. 7.1.68; s. of Col. R. Patch and Frances Maria Patch (*née* Lloyd); 2nd Lt., R.A., 23.7.87; Lt. 23.7.90; Capt. 25.12.97; Maj. 22.9.06; Lt.-Col. 1.2.15; Col. 1.2.19; Temp. Colonel-Cmdt. 1.1.21; served Miranzai, 1891; Despatches; wounded; Isazai, 1892; Chitral, 1895; 2 Medals, 2 clasps; S. Africa, 1899–1902; Despatches twice; Bt. Major 26.11.00; Queen's and King's Medals, 8 clasps; Europ. War (Mesopotamia), 1915–18; Despatches; C.M.G.; C.B.

PATERSON, A. A. A. (D.S.O. L.G. 3.6.18), T/Capt., R.F.A.; M.C.

PATERSON, A. G. (D.S.O. L.G. 25.8.17) (Bar, L.G. 3.2.20); b. 1.7.88; s. of late Rev. J. M. Paterson, of Srinagar, Kashmir; m. Sybil Irene, d. of A. J. Webb; educ. Wellington; R.M.C., Sandhurst; 2nd Lt., K.O. Sco. Bord., 22.2.08; Lt. 15.9.09; Capt. 28.4.15; K.O.S.B., att. Tank Corps; Europ. War, in Gallipoli, Mesopotamia and N. Russia; Despatches four times; Bt. Major 3.6.19; M.C.; Order of St. Stanislaus.

PATERSON, ALEXANDER THOMAS (D.S.O. L.G. 3.6.18) (Bar, L.G. 11.1.19), Major, Can. F.A.

PATERSON, ALEXANDER THOMAS (D.S.O. L.G. 3.6.19), Lt.-Col., 39th Batt. Aust. Inf.; M.C.

PATERSON, A. W. S. (D.S.O. L.G. 1.1.17); b. 28.2.78; 2nd Lt., Som. L.I., 16.2.98; Lt. 7.1.00; Capt. 26.2.04; Maj. 1.9.15; S. African War, 1899–1902; Queen's Medal, 5 clasps; King's Medal, 2 clasps.

PATERSON, D. (D.S.O. L.G. 3.6.19), Major, 3rd Highland Brigade, R.F.A., T.F.

PATERSON, E. (D.S.O. L.G. 27.9.01) (Bar, L.G. 22.6.18), Bt.-Col., 6th Inniskilling Dragoons (see "The Distinguished Service Order," from its institution to 31.12.15, same publishers).

PATERSON, G. R. S. (D.S.O. L.G. 8.3.19) (Details, 4.10.19), T/Major, H.L.I.; M.C.

PATERSON, R. W. (D.S.O. L.G. 26.9.17) (Details, L.G. 9.1.18); commanded 6th Batt. (The Fort Garry Horse of Winnipeg), Aug. 1914–March, 1915; took over the command of the Fort Garry Horse in France in Feb. 1916, and during the intervening period he was O.C., The Canadian Cavalry Depôt in England. When in command of the Fort Garry Horse he took part in the operations which led to the German Retreat from Peronne to Havrincourt in March, 1917; was at Passchendaele in Oct. 1917, and at the first and second battles of Cambrai on 20 and 30.11.18. He commanded the 3rd Cav. Div. Mounted Detachment; rearguard to the 5th Army and the French, from 21 to 28.3.18 (St. Quentin to Compiègne), and for his services at the Battle of Bois des Essarts and Porquerecourt on 26.3.18 was presented with the Croix de Guerre by General Pelle, and mentioned in his Despatches. He commanded the Canadian Cavalry Brigade at Moreuil Wood and Rifle Wood, in front of Amiens, on 30.3.18 and 1.4.18. He took part in the Second Battle of Amiens from 8 to 12.8.18, and in the advance to Le Cateau from 8 to 10.10.18; Despatches five times. He was wounded in one of the series of gallant actions in which the Canadian Cavalry Brigade figured, following the German attack south of the Somme. He was promoted to the rank of Brig.-Gen. with command of the Canadian Cavalry Brigade. His D.S.O. was awarded for gallantry on 8–9.7.17, east of Ascension Farm.

PATERSON, T. G. F., M.B. (D.S.O. L.G. 25.8.17); b. 6.12.76; Lt., I.M.S., 29.1.02; Capt. 29.1.05; Maj. 29.7.13; Bt. Lt.-Col. 1.1.19; I.M.S. 29.7.21.

PATESHALL, H. E. (D.S.O. L.G. 1.1.18); b. 20.7.79; 2nd Lt., East York. R., 11.2.99; Lt. 17.1.00; Capt. 10.10.08; ret. pay 25.3.14; Major, R. of O., 8.1.16; S. African War, 1900–2; Queen's Medal, 3 clasps; Europ. War; Despatches.

PATON, M. P., M.B. (D.S.O. L.G. 1.1.19), T/Capt. (A/Major), R.A.M.C.; M.C.

PATON, W. D. (D.S.O. L.G. 23.5.17); b. 13.8.74; s. of Major J. Paton; ent. Navy, 1888; Cdr., 1907; served River Gambia, 1894 (Medal, clasp); M.V.O., 1908; Europ. War, 1914–17; promoted to Captain, 1915, commanding H.M.S. Erin.

PATRICK, W. J. C. KENNEDY-COCHRAN- (see Kennedy-Cochran-Patrick, W. J. C.).

PATTENSON, E. C. TYLDEN- (see Tylden-Pattenson, E. C.).

PATTERSON, A. F. I. (D.S.O. L.G. 17.9.17); b. 22.3.91; Lt., R.A.M.C., 1.1.17; Capt. 6.4.18.

PATTERSON, JOHN (D.S.O. L.G. 1.2.17); b. 19.7.82; 2nd Lt., R.A., 23.7.01; Lt. 9.3.04; Capt. 23.7.14; Maj. 17.7.16.

PATTERSON, JOHN (D.S.O. L.G. 4.5.17), T/Major, E. African Pay Corps.

PATTERSON, J. W. (D.S.O. L.G. 14.11.16); b. 18.4.83; s. of Mervyn S. Patterson; m. Dorothy, d. of late Rev. E. Ekin, M.A.; educ. Queen's University, Belfast; T/2nd Lt., R.E., 16.1.15; T/Lt., May, 1916; A/Capt., Nov. 1917; A/Major, July, 1918; Demobilized, Jan. 1919; served Europ. War in France and Belgium in 1915–16–17–18. His D.S.O. was awarded for gallantry near Ginchy 10–11.9.16.

PATTERSON, W. R. (D.S.O. L.G. 25.11.16), T/Major, Can. Mtd. Rifles. His D.S.O. was awarded for gallantry on 15.9.16, at Pozières.

PATTINSON, L. A. (D.S.O. L.G. 3.6.19), Major (A/Lt.-Col.), R. Fus. I. Force (France); M.C.; D.F.C.

PATTISSON, J. H. (D.S.O. L.G. 29.10.18); b. 26.5.82; 2nd Lt., Essex R., 18.1.02; Lt. 7.5.04; Capt. 26.11.13; Maj. 18.1.17; S. African War, 1902; Queen's Medal, 4 clasps.

PAUL, C. T. S. (D.S.O. L.G. 22.9.16); b. 18.11.81; s. of W. S. Paul; educ. Clifton College; 2nd Lt., R.A., 19.12.00; Lt. 19.12.03; Capt. 16.8.12; Major (A/Lt.-Col.), R.A., 45th Brigade. His D.S.O. was awarded for gallantry at Laventie, 16–18.7.16. He was killed in action at Ypres 31.7.17.

PAUL, J. K. (D.S.O. L.G. 4.6.17), Capt. (T/Major), Aust. Arty.

PAUL, J. W. B. (D.S.O. L.G. 1.1.19), T/Major (T/Lt.-Col.), Labour Corps.

PAUL, W. (D.S.O. L.G. 4.2.18) (Details, L.G. 5.7.18), 2nd Lt. (A/Capt.), W. Yorks. R.; M.C. He died on 1.2.17.

PAULIN, S. (D.S.O. L.G. 15.2.19) (Details, L.G. 30.7.19), Lt.-Col., 11th Fld. Amb., Can. A.M.C.

PAULL, J. H. (D.S.O. L.G. 4.6.17), T/Major (T/Lt.-Col.), General List. He died 23.10.20.

PAUNCEFORT-DUNCOMBE, SIR E. P. D., Bart., M.A. (D.S.O. L.G. 1.1.18); b. 6.12.85; s. of 2nd Bart and Flora, d. of Sir A. Matheson, 1st Bart.; educ. Eton; Trinity College, Cambridge; Major, R. Bucks. Hussars, T.F. Reserve; Hon. Attaché at H.M. Embassy at Madrid, 1908–9; served Europ. War, 1914–18; with regt. in England and Egypt until July, 1915; Military Landing Officer at A.N.Z.A.C., July–Oct. 1915; A.D.C. to G.O.C., 15th Scottish Div., March, 1916–Feb. 1917; G.S.O.3, 15th Scottish Div., Feb.–Aug. 1917; Bgde. Major to 105th Inf. Bgde., Aug. 1917–Dec. 1918.; Croix de Guerre.

PAWLETT, F. (D.S.O. L.G. 1.2.19), Lt.-Col., Sask. R., Can. Forces.

PAXTON, A. N. (D.S.O. L.G. 11.4.18), Major (A/Lt.-Col.), R.E.; b. 3.4.83; 2nd Lt., R.E., 21.12.01; Lt. 6.8.04; Capt. 21.12.12; Major 21.12.16; M.C.

PAYNE, D. W. (D.S.O. L.G. 1.1.18); b. 5.12.82; 2nd Lt., R.A., 24.12.02; Lt. 24.12.05; Capt. 30.10.14; Maj., R.G.A., 30.7.17; M.C.

PAYNE, F. G. (D.S.O. L.G. 4.6.17), T/Major, M.G.C.

PAYNE, H. G. (D.S.O. L.G. 1.1.18), T/Capt., General List.

PAYNE, J. E. L. (D.S.O. L.G. 2.12.18), T/Capt., 10th Batt. W. Riding Rgt.; M.C.

PAYNE, L. H. (D.S.O. L.G. 18.1.18) (Details, L.G. 25.4.18); b. 5.11.88; s. of Hon. H. J. M. Payne; m. Ruby, d. of A. Bessell; one s.; one d.; Major; Second-in-Command, 40th Batt. Aust. Inf.; served Europ. War with A.I.F., France; Despatches twice.

PAYNTER, G. C. B. (D.S.O. L.G. 2.12.14.) (Bar, L.G. 2.12.18) (see "The Distinguished Service Order," from its institution to 31.12.15, same publishers).

PAYNTER, W. P. (D.S.O. L.G. 1.1.17); b. 13.12.72; 2nd Lt., R.A., 12.5.00; Lt. 20.9.01; Capt. 17.10.10; Maj. 30.10.14.

PEACE, A. G. (D.S.O. L.G. 31.5.16); b. 7.8.85; s. of late A. Peace; J.P., of Bridgwater; m. Maud, d. of Gen. C. H. Scafe, R.M.; two s.; two d.; educ. St. Peter's School, Weston-super-Mare; Northwood Park, Winchester; joined Britannia, Sept. 1900; Midshipman, 1902; Sub-Lt., 1905; Lt., 1907; Lt.-Cdr., 1915; Cdr., 31.12.18; served in Jupiter, 1902; Ariadne, 1902–5; Nith, 1906–7; in command of Torpedo Boat 101, 1907–8; Inflexible, 1908–10; in command of Torpedo Boat 051 in 1910; in command of Torpedo Boat 109 in 1910–12; in command of Mermaid, 1912–14; Irresistible, 1914; in command of Torpedo Boat No. 22, 1914–15; in command of Acorn, 1915–16; in command of Ready from 1916; Despatches.

PEACH, C. W. KEIGHLY- (see Keighly-Peach, C. W.).

PEACOCKE, W. J. (D.S.O. L.G. 24.6.16) (Bar, L.G. 1.1.18), T Lt.-Col., 9th Batt. R. Innis. Fusiliers. His D.S.O. was awarded for gallantry north of Thiepval Wood on 7–8.5.16.

PEAL, W. E. (D.S.O. L.G. 1.1.19), Lt.-Col., R.F.A., T.F.

PEARCE, L. F. (D.S.O. L.G. 15.2.19) (Details, L.G. 30.7.19), Major, 4th Batt. Can. M.G. Corps; M.C.

PEARD, C. J. (D.S.O. L.G. 16.9.18), Capt., Somerset L.I.

PEARKES, G. R. (D.S.O. L.G. 11.1.19), Lt.-Col., Can. Forces; V.C.; M.C. (see "The Victoria Cross," by same publishers).

PEARLESS, C. W. (D.S.O. L.G. 4.6.17); b. 14.2.72; 2nd Lt., S. Wales Bord., 19.11.92; Lt. 24.10.93; Capt. 23.11.98; Maj. 26.3.12; Bt. Lt.-Col. 3.6.16; Bt. Col. 3.6.19; Col. 22.6.21; *p.s.c.*; C.M.G.; S. African War, 1901–02; Queen's Medal, 3 clasps; King's Medal, 2 clasps; European War, 1914–18; Despatches; C.M.G.

PEARSE, R. G. (D.S.O. L.G. 8.3.19) (Details, L.G. 4.10.19); s. of W. Pearse, of Modbury; joined the Public Schools Battalion shortly after the outbreak of war, and received his commission in the following year, serving with the Sherwood Foresters. Capt. Pearse also was awarded the M.C.

PEARSE, S. A. (D.S.O. L.G. 1.1.17); s. of Major E. O. Pearse, J.P., D.L., of Bryn Celyn, Beaumaris, Anglesey, and Jane Elizabeth, d. of H. Williams; educ. Marlborough College; passed into 1st Batt. Welsh R. (from Militia), 1884; ent. Indian Army, 1887; retired as Major, 1904; served Burmese War, 1885–89; Medal, 2 clasps; in command Stonyhurst College O.T.C., 1909–14; joined 9th (S.) Batt. E. Lancs. R., as 2nd-in-command, 1914; served in France and Salonika; Lt.-Col. of 9th Batt., Dec. 1915–Sept. 1916; severely wounded; Despatches; Lt.-Col. Army, retired 27.2.19.

PEARSON, A. G. (D.S.O. L.G. 8.2.18) (Details, L.G. 18.7.18); b. 28.6.89; s. of late G. F. Pearson and late Marion de Hauteville Pearson; m. E. Sylvia Craven; two s.; one d.; educ. Uppingham; Trinity College, Cambridge; B.A.; University commission into R. Berks. R., 1911; Spec. Res., 1913; Captain.

PEARSON, B. L. (D.S.O. L.G. 25.8.17), T/Lt. (A/Capt.), Yorks. Rgt.; M.C. His D.S.O. was awarded for gallantry at Hill 60, 7.6.17.

PEARSON, H. D. (D.S.O. L.G. 1.1.18); b. 17.2.73; 2nd Lt., R.E., 22.7.92; Lt. 22.7.95; Capt. 1.7.03; Maj. 22.7.12; Bt. Lt.-Col. 1.1.19; ret. pay 25.5.19; Tirah, 1897–98; Medal, 2 clasps; China, 1900; Despatches twice; Medal, clasp; Soudan, 1912; Soudan Medal, clasp. He died 28.12.22.

PEARSON, HAROLD LESLIE (D.S.O. L.G. 4.6.17), Capt. (T/Major), R.F.A.

PEARSON, HENRY LAURENCE (D.S.O. L.G. 26.8.18), T/Major (T/Col.), R.E.

N. G. Pearson.

PEARSON, J. H. (D.S.O. L.G. 16.9.18), T/Major, Notts. and Derby. Regt.; M.C.

PEARSON, N. G. (D.S.O. L.G. 16.9.18); b. 30.9.84; s. of Henry John and Laura Kate Pearson, of Bramcote, Notts; m. Kathleen Mary, d. of Rev. E. R. J. Nicolls, of Trowell Rectory, Notts; two s.; one d.; educ. Aysgarth; Olivia Mount School, Scarborough; Charterhouse; enlisted as Private in 9th Sherwood Foresters 31.8.14; promoted to Lance-Sergeant; commissioned as 2nd Lt. 19.11.14, in 12th Sherwood Foresters (Pioneers); Adjt. 31.12.14; T/Lt., March, 1915; T/Capt., May, 1916; T/Major, 6th S.W.B. Pioneers, 30.11.17; Lt.-Col., Commanding 2/16th London Rgt. (Q.W.R.), 30.9.18; went overseas 29.8.15; Despatches twice; M.C.

PEARSON, R. W. (D.S.O. L.G. 18.1.18) (Details, L.G. 25.4.18), Capt., Can. Infantry; M.C.

PEARSON, T. W. (D.S.O. L.G. 1.1.18), Major (A/Lt.-Col.), R.F.A.

T. W. Pearson.

PEARSON, V. L. N. (D.S.O. L.G. 3.6.18); b. 3.12.80; s. of late Lt.-Col. J. Pearson, R. Ir. Regt., and A.P.D.; m. Lilian J., d. of late Rev. A. J. Wilson; educ. Weymouth College; King's School, Worcester; 2nd Lt., Middx. R., 27.7.01; Lt. 8.9.03; Capt. 24.3.11; Maj. 24.7.16; Temp. Brig.-Gen. 10.5.17 to 28.10.18; S. African War, 1899–1902; Queen's Medal, 3 clasps; European War, Flanders, France, Salonika, Egypt and Palestine; Despatches four times; Bt. Lt.-Col. 1.1.18.

PEARSON, W. J., M.B. (D.S.O. L.G. 3.6.18), T/Capt., R.A.M.C.; M.C.

PEASE, E. R. (D.S.O. L.G. 26.7.17), Capt. (A/Major), Can. Inf. His D.S.O. was awarded for gallantry at Vimy Ridge, 9–28.4.17.

H. E. Pease.

PEASE, H. E. (D.S.O. L.G. 25.8.16); b. 1889, at Dunedin, N.Z.; s. of Major A. J. Pease, of Southport, and grandson of late E. T. Pease, J.P., of Darlington; m. Hon. Cynthia Chaloner, d. of Lord Gisborough; educ. The Priory, Malvern; Malvern College; Malvern Shooting VIII., 1908; Temp. 2nd Lt., Durham L.I., 22.9.14; Capt., Durh. L.I., 12.12.16; Temp. Lt.-Col.; served Europ. War, in France from Aug. 1915; Despatches; wounded Oct. 1916. His D.S.O. was awarded for gallantry on 7 and 10.7.16, at Bailiff Wood, which was described as follows: "On the 7th July this Officer led the Battalion in the attack on the enemy trenches near Point X.16.b.1.7. He showed great gallantry and set a fine example of dash and bravery; it was greatly owing to his efforts that the hostile trench was captured. With characteristic energy he worked at the consolidation. On 8 July patrols of his company pushed out to the high ground point X.13.d.8.1, and the redoubt here was occupied and consolidated, and Bailiff Wood patrolled. The night of the 8th the Battalion was brought into reserve, and the next day Captain Pease was sent off with one company and one platoon to occupy the trench running from point X.10.a.1.3. to point X.16.б.1.5 and the N.E. and S.W. corners of Bailiff Wood. Contrary to expectations, the enemy were found in strength, and it was not possible to occupy more than three-fourths of the above-named trench, but most excellent work was done in consolidating the parts occupied, and Captain Pease hung on, in spite of an enemy counter-attack, which, though repulsed, threatened at the time to have most serious consequences. Captain Pease's action undoubtedly largely assisted the successful capture of Contalmaison."

PEASE-WATKIN, E. H. P. (D.S.O. L.G. 13.2.17); b. 21.8.83; 2nd Lt., R.A., 15.7.03; Lt. 15.7.06; Capt. 30.10.14; Maj. 10.7.16.

PEAT, P. S. (D.S.O. L.G. 7.6.18), Lt., R.N.R.

PEBERDY, C. E. V. K. (D.S.O. L.G. 8.3.19) (Details, L.G. 4.10.19); b. 8.3.94; joined T.F., Aug. 1914; Lt., W. York. R., 5.11.17; M.C.

PECK, A. H. (D.S.O. L.G. 4.3.18) (Details, L.G. 16.8.18), T/Capt., Gen. List, and R.F.C.; M.C.

PECK, A. M. (D.S.O. L.G. 10.5.17), Capt., R.N.

PECK, C. H. (D.S.O. L.G. 3.6.18), T/Capt. (A/Major), R.F.A.; M.C.

PECK, C. W. (D.S.O. L.G. 4.6.17) (Bar, L.G. 11.1.19), Lt.-Col., 16th Batt. Can. Inf., Manitoba Rgt.; V.C. (see "The Victoria Cross," same publishers).

PECK, E. G., M.A., M.R.C.S., L.R.C.P. (D.S.O. L.G. 25.11.16); educ. Cambridge; St. George's Hospital; Fellow, Medical Society of London; served Europ. War, 1914–17; Lt.-Col., R.A.M.C.; wounded; Despatches three times. His D.S.O. was awarded for gallantry at Thiépval on 30.9.16.

PECK, H. R. (D.S.O. L.G. 25.8.17); b. 7.10.74; s. of late P. W. Peck; m. Kathleen Dulcibella, d. of late Colonel C. Hore, C.M.G.; one s.; 2nd Lt., R.A., 17.11.94; Lt. 17.11.97; Capt. 14.11.00; Maj. 20.4.11; Lt.-Col. 17.4.16; Col. 20.4.20; Temp. Brig.-Gen. 4.8.17 to 30.5.19; served S. African War, 1899–1902; severely wounded; Despatches twice; Bt. Major; Queen's Medal, 4 clasps; King's Medal, 2 clasps; Bt. Maj. 22.8.02; Europ. War, 1915–18; Gallipoli and Mesopotamia; Despatches five times; C.M.G.; Bt.-Colonel 1.1.18.

PECK, J. H. (D.S.O. L.G. 4.6.17), Lt.-Col., Aust. Forces.

PECK, S. C. (D.S.O. L.G. 1.1.17); b. 2.9.71; 2nd Lt., R.A., 26.5.00; Lt. 25.12.01; Capt. 26.5.13; Major 30.12.15; Bt. Lt.-Col. 1.1.18; Northern Nigeria, 1903; Medal, clasp; Europ. War; Despatches.

PEDDIE, T. A. (D.S.O. L.G. 26.11.17) (Details, L.G. 6.4.18); b. 20.10.92; Temp. 2nd Lt. 16.9.14; 2nd Lt., Linc. R., 16.6.15; Lt. 2.10.16.

PEDLER, G. H. (D.S.O. L.G. 1.2.17), T/Major, S. African A.S.C.

PEEBLES, A. W. (D.S.O. L.G. 23.5.17); b. 8.1.80; s. of late W. B. Peebles, J.P., M.D., Ch.M.Dublin; m. Alice Kathleen, d. of late S. R. Fetherstonhaugh; ent. Navy, 1894; Lt., 1904; Lt.-Cdr., 1913; Commander, 1916; M.V.O., 1901; served Europ. War, 1914–17; Commander of the Order of the Redeemer; Letter of Appreciation from the Lords of Admiralty for salvage of H.M.S. Peony ashore on the Turkish coast, 1916.

PEEBLES, H. W. (D.S.O. L.G. 4.6.17); b. 24.12.77; s. of late Col. T. Peebles, Devonshire Rgt., and Mrs. Peebles (*née* Chiappini); m. G. Davies, of Wrexham; one s.; educ. Cheltenham College; Army and Colonial Civil Service; Major, Ret. List, R.A.S.C.; served S. African War, 2½ years as a Trooper; severely wounded; Queen's Medal, 4 clasps; King's Medal, 2 clasps; Somaliland Campaign, 1902–4; Medal, 2 clasps; Despatches twice; Europ. War, France, Oct. 1914–Oct. 1917; Despatches four times; Bt. Major, June, 1920.

PEEBLES, W. C. (D.S.O. L.G. 1.1.18) (Bar, L.G. 3.6.18), Lt.-Col., T.F. Reserve; D.L.; Europ. War, 1914–18.

PEEK, SIR W., Bart. (D.S.O. L.G. 7.2.18); b. 9.10.84; s. of 2nd Bart. and Hon. Augusta Louisa Brodrick, d. of 8th Viscount Midleton; m. 1913, Edwine Warner, d. of the late W. H. Thornburgh; one s.; educ. Eton; Trinity College, Cambridge; Capt., Royal 1st Devon Yeomanry; served Europ. War, 1914–18; Despatches.

PEEL, B. G. (D.S.O. L.G. 19.10.16); b. 26.12.81; 2nd Lt., Som. L.I., 18.4.00; Lt. 18.7.02; Capt., Ind. Army, 8.2.09; Maj. 1.9.15; S. African War, 1900; Queen's Medal, 4 clasps; Europ. War.

PEEL, E. J. R. (D.S.O. L.G. 18.2.15) (Bar, L.G. 16.9.18), Brig.-Gen., ret. pay; C.M.G. (see "The Distinguished Service Order," from its institution to 31.12.15, by same publishers).

PEEL, E. T. (D.S.O. L.G. 3.6.18), T/Lt. (T/Lt.-Col.), Wilts. Rgt.; M.C.

PEEL, H. (D.S.O. L.G. 1.1.18), Capt. (Brig.-Major), 8th (City of London Batt.) The London Rgt. (Post Office Rifles); M.C. He was killed in action 24.3.18.

PEEL, J. (D.S.O. L.G. 4.2.18) (Details, L.G. 5.7.18); b. 17.8.91; 2nd Lt., R. Fus., 27.6.17; Lt. 27.12.18; ret. pay 11.6.19; M.M.

PEEL, HON. S. C. (D.S.O. L.G. 4.6.17); b. 3.6.70; 3rd s. of 1st Viscount Peel; m. Lady Delia Spencer, d. of 6th Earl Spencer; educ. Eton; New College, Oxford; late Fellow of Trinity; Lt.-Col., Beds. Yeom.; T.D.; served S. African War, 1900; Queen's Medal, 6 clasps; Europ. War, 1914–18; Despatches; M.P., Uxbridge Div., from 1918; Financial Adviser to Foreign Office, 1918; Member of British Delegation, Peace Conference, Paris, 1919.

PEEL, W. E. (D.S.O. L.G. 1.1.18); b. 1882; m. Alice Dalrymple, d. of Major-General W. C. Hunter-Blair; two s.; two d.; Lt.-Colonel, Camel Transport Corps; served Europ. War, 1914–18; Despatches thrice.

PEEL, W. R. (D.S.O. L.G. 4.6.17) (Bar, L.G. 16.9.18) (2nd Bar, L.G. 2.4.19) (Details, L.G. 10.12.19), T/Major, Yorks. R.

PEGLER, S. J. (D.S.O. L.G. 26.9.17) (Details, L.G. 8.1.18), T/2nd Lt., Rifle Brigade.

PEIRS, H. J. C., B.A. (D.S.O. L.G. 3.6.16) (Bar, L.G. 26.9.17) (Details, L.G. 9.1.18) (2nd Bar, L.G. 16.9.18); b. 1.2.86; s. of H. V. Peirs and Charlotte Sophia, d. of J. R. Paull; educ. Charterhouse, and New College, Oxford (Honours, Law Final); 2nd Lt., 3rd Batt. Queen's R.W. Surrey Rgt., March, 1906; retired 1912; rejoined as Capt., 8th Queen's; became T/Major, and served from 1914–19; wounded three times; Despatches twice; C.M.G.

PEIRSE, N. M. DE LA P. BERESFORD- (see Beresford-Peirse, N. M. de la P.).

PEIRSON, G. (D.S.O. L.G. 3.6.19), T/Capt., Gen. List; M.C.

PELHAM, HON. D. R. H. (D.S.O. L.G. 3.6.16); b. 1872; 4th s. of 3rd Earl of Yarborough; m. Evelyn Elizabeth, d. of M. A. Waldo-Sibthorp; educ. Eton; R.M.C., Sandhurst; joined 10th Hussars, 1894; Major, Res. of Officers, late 10th Hussars, March, 1919; served S. Africa, 1899–1902; Despatches; Queen's Medal, 4 clasps; King's Medal, 2 clasps; went to France in the Reserve of Officers, and served in 1914 with 10th Hussars, and in 1915–16 with the Aust. Light Horse in Egypt, and in 1918–19 was with H.Q. Cavalry Corps in France.

PELLING, A. J. (D.S.O. L.G. 1.1.18), T/Capt.; M.C.; R.E.

PELLY, REV. D. R. (D.S.O. L.G. 1.1.18); b. 20.2.65; s. of the late Canon R. P. Pelly; m. Verena Noélie, d. of Rev. G. W. Herbert; three s.; one d.; educ. Harrow; Emmanuel College, Cambridge; Chaplain to the Forces for the duration of the war; Corps Chaplain of XII. Corps.

PELLY, E. G. (D.S.O. L.G. 7.2.18); b. 1889; m. Isobel Amy Fowler; educ. Charterhouse; Trinity College, Cambridge; Lt.-Col., late R.A.S.C.; M.C.

PELLY, R. T. (D.S.O. L.G. 14.1.16) (Bar, L.G. 2.4.19) (Details, L.G. 10.12.19); b. 30.7.81; s. of Rev. Canon Raymond Percy Pelly (deceased) and Alice Schaffalitsky Pelly; m. Moriet Elsie Maxwell Creagh, d. of Major-Gen. A. G. Creagh, C.B., and great-niece of late F.M. Viscount Wolseley; two d.; educ. Haileybury; joined Imperial Yeomanry, 1899; served Boer War, 1900–1 (Queen's S.A. Medal and 4 clasps); L.N. Lancs. Regt., 1901–15; Hampshire Regt., 1915; Commanded 8th R. Irish Rifles in France, Jan.–July, 1916, including Battle of Somme; Commander, P.P.C.L.I., May–Dec. 1915, and again July, 1916, including 2nd Battle of Ypres and Battle of Somme; Brevet Majority and one mention in Despatches awarded for services rendered while commanding the 8th R. Irish Rifles. His D.S.O. and two mentions in Despatches were awarded for services rendered while commanding P.P.C.L.I.; Despatches seven times; Bt. Lt.-Col. 1.1.18; T/Brig.-Gen. 16.5.17 to 13.4.19; C.B.; C.M.G.

PELTZER, A. (D.S.O. L.G. 3.6.19), T. Major (A/Lt.-Col.), 9th Batt. E. Lancs. Rgt.

PEMBERTON, G. H. (D.S.O. L.G. 17.12.17); b. 16.7.97; 2nd Lt., Lan. Fus., 24.11.15; Lt. 1.7.17; M.C.

PEMBERTON, H. C. (D.S.O. L.G. 27.6.19), T/Capt., 20th Batt., att. 16th Batt., Lanc. Fus.

PEMBERTON, R. T. (D.S.O. L.G. 1.1.17); b. 26.5.88; s. of Talbot and Mary Louisa Pemberton; m. Alice Emmeline, d. of A. S. Denham; joined the 1st Volunteer Batt. S. Staffs. Regt. as a Private on 6.2.06; promoted Corporal, and on the formation of the T.F. transferred as a Sergeant to the 8th Batt. R. Warwicks. Regt.; commissioned in the N. Midland Div. S. & T. Column; Lieut. 28.6.10; Captain 1.2.11; Major 11.2.15; mobilized 4.8.14; Despatches twice.

PEMBERTON, S. (D.S.O. L.G. 25.8.17); s. of late Lt.-Col. S. E. Pemberton, R.F.A., and Emily Marion Pemberton; m. Winifred Katharine Carew, d. of Col. Carew Smyth; educ. Marlborough College; R.M.A., Woolwich; 2nd Lt., R.E., 31.7.02; Lt. 31.7.05; Capt. 31.7.13; Bt. Major 3.6.16; Major 31.7.17; Europ. War; joined 12th Indian Division as Major and Company Commander, 12th Field Company, 2nd Q.V.O. Sappers and Miners, in Mesopotamia 18.3.15, and proceeded with General Gorringe's Column for the Relief of Ahwaz and subsequent operations on the Karkheh River, April and May, 1915; mentioned in Despatches by Sir John Nixon; in June and July he took part in operations on the Euphrates, leading to the capture of Nasiriyeh; Despatches (Sir J. Nixon); M.C.; joined Tigris Corps in same capacity, Jan. 1916, and served throughout the Relief of Kut operations until Kut fell in April, 1916; Despatches (Sir P. Lake); Bt. Major. His company served with 14th Indian Div. operations in Dahra Bend; the crossing of the Tigris 23.2.17, and operations leading to the fall of Baghdad 3.3.17; Despatches (Sir S. Maude); operations in Jebel Hamrin until 2.11.17; G.S.O.2, 7th Meerut Div., and went with it to Egypt; Brig. Major, 162nd Inf. Brig., 54th Div.; operations leading to the rout of the Turkish Army and conquest of Palestine and Syria, until Oct. 1918; Despatches (Sir E. Allenby), Jan. 1919; G.S.O.2, 3rd Lahore Div., Oct. 1919; remained in Palestine until June, 1919.

E. A. Penfold.

PENDER, E. P. U. (D.S.O. L.G. 8.3.18), Lt.-Cdr., R.N., 1.10.16.

PENDER, H. D. DENISON- (see Denison-Pender, H. D.).

PENFOLD, E. A., M.B. (D.S.O. L.G. 1.1.17); b. Portsmouth, 1866; s. of Alfred Penfold, of H.M. Dockyard, Portsmouth; m. Ada, d. of late R. Dixon, of Grove Park, Kent; two s.; two d.; educ. Preparatory Schools at Portsmouth and Pembroke; The Grammar School, Portsmouth; Edinburgh University; St. Thomas's Hospital; M.B.; C.M.; passed as Surgeon into the R.N., 1891; Staff Surgeon, 1899; Fleet Surgeon, 1907; Surgeon Commander, 1918; Surgeon Captain 14.9.19; served in H.M S. Goldfinch in Australia and

New Zealand; with R.M., Plymouth, 1897–99; in H.M.S. Crescent, N. America and West Indies; in H.M.S. Aurora and Highflyer, training ships for Naval Cadets; in H.M.S. Terrible when escort to Prince and Princess of Wales, in India, 1905–6; H.M.S. Hindustan, 1907–12; since the war has served in Depôt Ship for Destroyer Flotillas, and later in the Grand Fleet, H.M.S. Barham; present at the Battle of Jutland (Despatches; recommended for early promotion; D.S.O.); Order of St. Stanislaus, 2nd Class (with Swords). He has written "A Battleship in Action" (Journal of the Royal Naval Medical Service). Since Jan. 1918, has served as S.M.O., attached to the Plymouth Division, R.M.L.I.; appointed to H.M.S. Vivid as P.M.O., R.N. Barracks, Devonport, 4.11.19.

PENHALE, J. J. (D.S.O. L.G. 3.6.18), Lt.-Col., Can. F.A.

PENN, B. H. (D.S.O. L.G. 1.1.18); b. 17.2.83; 3rd Class Inspector of Ordnance Machinery 14.3.08; 2nd Class 19.9.20; Capt. 1.7.17; T/Major 7.2.21.

PENNANT, D. H. (D.S.O. L.G. 26.1.17); b. 1.9.90; s. of W. Pennant; m. Nan, d. of Rev. T. Davies, of St. Clears; educ. Llandaff Cathedral School; Cardiff Medical School; London Hospital; M.R.C.S.; L.R.C.P.; Capt., late R.A.M.C., att. 162nd Brig. R.F.A., 1915–17; Despatches twice.

PENNELL, R. (D.S.O. L.G. 26.9.17) (Details, L.G. 8.1.18) (Bar, L.G. 19.11.17) (Details, L.G. 22.3.18); b. 28.2.85; 2nd Lt., K.R.R.C., 29.9.15; Lt. 23.2.17; Capt., Oxf. and Bucks. L.I., 10.8.21.

PENNINGTON, H. S. W. (D.S.O. L.G. 1.1.17), T/Major, A.S.C. (now R.A.S.C.).

PENNINGTON, R. (D.S.O. L.G. 10.1.17), 2nd Lt., Linc. Rgt.

PENNY, F. S., M.B. (D.S.O. L.G. 1.1.18); b. 4.12.69; s. of W. Penny; educ. Crewkerne Grammar School (Scholar); King's College, London; three scholarships; several prizes; Capt., Cricket XI.; M.R.C.S.; L.R.C.P.; M.B.; D.P.H.; Lt., R.A.M.C., 28.1.98; Capt. 28.1.01; Maj. 28.7.09; Lt.-Col. 1.3.15; operations Sierra Leone, 1898 (Medal with clasp); S. Africa, 1902; Queen's Medal and 2 clasps; served Europ. War from 1914; Despatches four times; C.M.G.

PENNYCUICK, J. A. C. (D.S.O. L.G. 9.12.14) (Bar, L.G. 18.7.17), Capt., R.E. (see "The Distinguished Service Order," from its institution to 31.12.15, by same publishers).

PENNYMORE, P. G. (D.S.O. L.G. 14.1.16): b. 7.12.69; s. of Col. P. G. Pennymore, J.P., V.D. (retired), and Lucy Ann Pennymore (who died in 1902); m. Mabel, d. of J. Fowler; Lt.-Col., late 2nd Batt. Monmouths. R.; served Europ. War, 1914–16; B.E.F. 5.11.14 to 7.7.15; D.S.O. for 2nd Battle of Calais (Ypres); Despatches twice; has T.D. and King Edward's Coronation Medal.

P. G. Pennymore.

PENSE, H. E. (D.S.O. L.G. 3.6.18), Major, Can. Infy.

PENTON, B. C. (D.S.O. L.G. 3.6.19), Major (A/Lt.-Col.), 25th Punjabis, I.A., Commanding 1/152nd Punjabis, I.A.

PEPLER, E. (D.S.O. L.G. 1.1.18), Major, Can. Engrs.

PEPLOE, H. (D.S.O. L.G. 3.6.19); b. 19.9.89; Temp. 2nd Lt. 23.8.14; Temp. Lt. 20.1.15; Capt., R.W. Kent R., 1.7.16; served Europ. War from 1914: Despatches.

PEPYS, C. (D.S.O. L.G. 2.4.19) (Details, 10.12.19); b. 11.8.92; Temp. 2nd Lt. 26.8.14; 2nd Lt., Devon R., 26.5.15; Lt. 1.7.17; M.C.

PEPYS, W. (D.S.O. L.G. 8.3.18); b. 8.8.76; 2nd Lt., 19th Hussars, 20.2.97; 13th Hussars, 2.3.98; Major and Hon. Lt.-Col., Yeomanry, R. of O., late Hussars; S. African War, 1899–1902; Despatches; Queen's Medal, 5 clasps; King's Medal, 2 clasps; Europ. War; Despatches.

PERCEVAL, C. P. W. (D.S.O. L.G. 4.6.17); b. Christchurch, N.Z., 11.6.90; s. of Sir Westby Brook Perceval, K.C.M.G., and Jessie, d. of Hon. J. Johnston, M.L.C., of Wellington, N.Z.; educ. Wimbledon College; R.M.A., Woolwich; 1st Comm., R.A., 23.12.10; Lt. 23.12.13; Capt. 8.8.16; A.D.C. to G.O.C., R.A., 3rd Div., Aug. 1914; served Gallipoli, April, 1915; commanded a Battery of New Army in France, 1916; A/Major, Jan. 1917–19; Adjt., R.H.A., July, 1919; Despatches twice; wounded; 1914 Star.

PERCIVAL, A. E. (D.S.O. L.G. 16.9.18) (Bar, L.G. 21.1.20); b. 26.12.87; Temp. 2nd Lt. 12.9.14; Capt., Essex R., 1.10.16; Bt. Maj. 1.1.19; O.B.E.; M.C.

PERCIVAL, E. (D.S.O. L.G. 20.10.16); b. 20.6.90; Lt., R.A.M.C., 25.7.13; Capt. 30.3.15; M.C.

PERCIVAL, J. (D.S.O. L.G. 1.1.17), Lt.-Cdr., R.N.R.; A/Director of Nigeria Marine, 1914; King's Harbour-Master, Duala, 1914; Director of Nigeria Marine at Lagos since Dec. 1914.

PERCIVAL, P. R. P. (D.S.O. L.G. 26.4.18) (Bar, L.G. 21.6.18), Lt.-Cdr. 31.12.16.

PERCY, SIR J. S. J. (D.S.O. L.G. 3.6.16) (gazetted as Baumgartner, J. S. J.), Lt.-Col., East Lancs. R.; K.B.E.; C.B.; C.M.G.; served Chitral, 1895; medal with clasp; S. African War; both medals and 6 clasps; Europ. War from 1914; Bt. Lt.-Col.

PERCY, LORD W. R. (D.S.O. L.G. 4.6.17); b. 17.5.82; 2nd s. of 7th Duke of Northumberland; educ. Oxford; B.A.; called to Bar, Inner Temple, 1906; Colonel, late Grenadier Guards.

PEREIRA, A. B. P. (D.S.O. L.G. 26.3.17); b. 7.8.86; 2nd Lt., Suff. R., 4.5.07; Lt. 22.1.10; Capt., R.A.S.C., 30.10.14; Bt. Maj. 1.1.18.

PERKINS, G. F. (D.S.O. L.G. 8.3.18); b. 8.4.84; m. Nora Shuttleworth; 2nd Lt., Hamps. R., 22.4.03; Lt. 4.10.05; Capt. 9.8.11; Bt. Maj. 18.2.15; Bt. Lt.-Col. 1.1.19.

PERKINS, H. R. (D.S.O. L.G. 2.12.18), T/Capt., 13th Batt. Welsh Rgt.; M.C.

PERKS, R. C. (D.S.O. L.G. 26.9.16), T/2nd Lt., W. Riding Rgt. He was killed in action 27.10.18.

PERROTT, R. B. (D.S.O. L.G. 22.8.18), Capt. (T/Major), S. African Railway Rgt.

PERRY, B. H. H. (D.S.O. L.G. 1.1.19); b. 22.11.84; s. of late Henry Perry, of Torcrest, Torquay; 2nd Lt., R. Scots, 23.5.06; Lt. 11.4.09; Capt. 4.12.14; Bt. Major 3.6.19; M.C. He died 27.2.21, after serving through the Great War.

PERRY, E. L. (D.S.O. L.G. 25.8.17); b. 28.6.72; Lt., Ind. Med. Serv. (Bengal), 29.1.96; Capt. 29.1.99; Maj. 29.7.07; Lt.-Col. 29.7.15; N.W. Frontier, 1897; Despatches twice; Waziristan, 1901–2; Medal, clasp; Europ. War; Despatches.

PERRY, K. M. (D.S.O. L.G. 19.8.16) (Bar, L.G. 15.2.19) (Details, L.G. 30.7.19); b. 1884; s. of Col. A. B. Perry, B.A., B.Sc., C.M.G., Commissioner, Can. Mounted Police, and Emma Durante Perry (*née* Meikle); educ. McGill University; joined Can. Active Militia, 10.12.10; Capt., Can. Exp. Force; Major 1.1.16; Lt.-Col. 12.5.18, 87th Batt. Can. Gren. Gds.; served Europ. War from 1914; Despatches twice. His D.S.O. was awarded for gallantry on 13.6.16, at Sanctuary Wood.

PERRY, N. D. (D.S.O. L.G. 3.6.18), Major, Central Ontario Rgt., Can. Forces.

PERRY, S. LL. (D.S.O. L.G. 7.11.18), Lt.-Col., Aust. Inf.; M.C.

PERSSE, D. F. (D.S.O. L.G. 5.10.18), Lt., R.N.

PERSSE, R. (D.S.O. L.G. 3.6.18); b. 6.12.79; Cmdg. Imp. Yeo., ret. pay, 10.8.02; Temp. Capt. 19.11.14; Capt., S. Staff. R., 29.3.16; S. African War, 1901; severely wounded; Despatches; Europ. War; Despatches; M.C.

PERTWEE, H. G. (D.S.O. L.G. 11.11.19); b. 28.7.93; s. of H. A. Pertwee, M.I.M.E., and Minnie Kate Pertwee; m. Carmen Waddon-Martyn; educ. Gresham's School, Holt; joined the Navy 15.7.11; Paymaster Lieut. 15.1.17; served Europ. War, on the Staff of Rear-Admiral Stoddard, 1914–15 (including the Falklands action); on the Staff of Rear-Admiral Tyrwhitt, 1915–18, including Arethusa and other ships in the Harwich Force, and on the Staff of Commodore Comely, British Caspian Expedition, as Secretary, 1918–19. He fought several actions with the Bolshevist Squadron, having control of battery of guns in Flagship H.M.S. Kruger. In Dec. 1919, he was awarded the 3rd Class Order of St. Anne for helping General Denikin, Dec. 1919.

PERY, HON. E. C. (D.S.O. L.G. 26.7.18); b. 16.10.88; s. of 3rd Earl of Limerick and Isabella, d. of J. de Colquhoun; half brother of 4th Earl of Limerick; educ. Eton; New College, Oxford; B.A.; 1st commission, Feb. 1909; Major, City of London Yeomanry, June, 1916; served Europ. War from 1914; wounded; Despatches; G.S.O.3, 1917 (France). His D.S.O. was awarded for services rendered in March, 1918, in the field while Brigade Major, 92nd Inf. Bde., France, during the Somme Retreat; all in connection with the rallying, extrication and organization of troops during the retreat near Ervillers (north of Bapaume) and Ayette, under fire; served with Regiment in Egypt, Sinai and Gallipoli (Suvla Bay) with 2nd Mounted Division, 1915 (1914 on East Coast Defence); served as Regtl. and Staff Officer in France, 1916–19; Despatches.

PERY-KNOX-GORE, A. F. G. (D.S.O. L.G. 1.1.17); b. 1.9.80; 2nd Lt., A.S.C., 26.11.02; Lt. 15.11.04; Capt. 31.5.11; Maj., R.A.S.C., 30.10.14; Bt. Lt.-Col. 3.6.19; Europ. War from 1914; Despatches.

PERY-KNOX-GORE, I. C. (D.S.O. L.G. 3.6.18); b. 15.9.86; 2nd Lt., R.A., 18.12.07; Lt. 18.12.10; Capt. 30.10.14; Major, R.F.A., 26.11.17; Adjt., R.A., 9.6.20; M.C.

PESHALL, REV. C. J. E. (D.S.O. L.G. 23.7.18); s. of Rev. S. Peshall, of Oldbarrow, Warwickshire; m. Beatrice, d. of L. Docker; one s.; educ. Haileybury College; Pembroke College, Cambridge; Chaplain, R.N., 1908; Chaplain, H.M.S. Repulse from 1921; has served in H.M.S. Black Prince, Encounter, St. George and Cornwallis; present in Vindictive attack by night on Zeebrugge, April, 1918.

PETER, F. H. (D.S.O. L.G. 11.1.19) (Bar, L.G. 1.2.19); b. 8.7.80; 2nd Lt., R.W.F., 26.3.16; Lt. 26.9.17; Capt. 25.10.18; M.C.

PETERS, C. A. (D.S.O. L.G. 1.1.18), Lt.-Col. (T/Col.), Can. A.M.C.

PETERS, J. W. P. (D.S.O. L.G. 14.1.16); educ. Winchester; R.M.C., Sandhurst; Major, R. of O., 7th Dragoon Gds.; served Chin Lushai Exp., 1889–90 (Medal with clasp); Hazara Exp., 1891 (clasp); S. African War, 1900–2; Queen's Medal, 4 clasps; King's Medal, 2 clasps; Europ. War, 1914–16; Despatches four times; O.B.E.; 1915 Medal.

PETERSON, A. J. (D.S.O. L.G. 25.8.16) (Bar, L.G. 26.9.17) (Details, L.G. 8.1.18) (2nd Bar, L.G. 1.2.19), T/Capt. (A/Major), R.F.A. His D.S.O. was awarded for gallantry on 15.7.16, at Pozières.

PETERSON, F. H. (D.S.O. L.G. 22.6.17), Lt., R.N.R.; D.S.C.

PETERSON, W. G. (D.S.O. L.G. 3.6.18); b. 8.11.86; s. of late Sir W. Peterson, K.C.M.G.; educ. Eastbourne College; McGill University, Montreal; Trinity College, Oxford; M.A.; Harvard University; Lt., 5th Rgt., R.H.C., 1910; Lt., The R. Can. Rgt. (Permanent Force), 1912; Bt. Capt., 1917; Major, 73rd Batt. R. Highrs. of Canada, 1915; served Europ. War from 1914; Despatches; wounded.

PETRE, H. A. (D.S.O. L.G. 22.12.16); b. 12.6.84; s. of S. H. Petre and Elise, d. of W. E. Sibeth; g.s. of Hon. H. W. Petre, of The Manor House, Writtle; educ. Mount St. Mary's College, Chesterfield; took up Aviation, 1910; went to Australia to found Australian Flying Corps, Dec. 1912; Squadron Commander, R.A.F.; served in Mesopotamia, 1915–16; Despatches five times; M.C.; transferred from Aust. F.C. to R.A.F., 1918.

PETRE, R. L. (D.S.O. L.G. 25.8.17); b. 28.11.87; s. of F. Loraine Petre, O.B.E., and Maud Ellen, d. of Rev. W. C. Rawlinson; educ. Downside College; Sandhurst; joined S.W.B. 22.2.08; Lt. 22.12.10; Capt. 24.1.15; Bt. Major 3.6.18; served Siege and Capture of Tsingtau, 1914; Despatches; throughout Gallipoli Campaign, 1915 (Despatches; M.C.); Mesopotamia and Capture of Baghdad, 1916–18 (Despatches; D.S.O.); Afghanistan, 1919.

PETRE, W. R. G. (D.S.O. L.G. 1.10.17); b. Dec. 1873; s. of late Sir G. G. Petre, K.C.M.G., C.B.; m. Agnes Marie, d. of late Capt. Cadic, of Rennes, France; four s.; three d.; educ. Royal Naval Academy, Gosport; Midshipman, 1889; Sub-Lt., 1894; Lt., 1896; Commander, 1907; Capt., June, 1915; served Persian Gulf, 1897 (thanks of Indian Govt.); Europ. War; Despatches.

PETRIE, D. P. (D.S.O. L.G. 26.9.17) (Details, L.G. 9.1.18), Lt., Sc. Rifles, S.R. His D.S.O. was awarded for gallantry on 31.7.17, east of Ypres.

PETRIE, P. C. (D.S.O. L.G. 15.2.19) (Details, L.G. 30.7.19), Major, D/245th W. Riding Brig., R.F.A., T.F.; M.C.

PETTY, W. (D.S.O. L.G. 1.1.18); b. 1875; s. of late Rev. W. Petty, of Kendal, Westmorland, Vicar of St. Peter's, Ealing; m. Helen, d. of late Lt.-Col. H. A. Walford, 20th Hussars; two s.; educ. St. Paul's School; Corpus Christi College, Cambridge; B.A.; Lt.-Colonel, late 9th Seaf. Highrs., 1914–19; commanding, April, 1917–Aug. 1918; served S. Africa, 1901–2; Queen's Medal, 5 clasps; Europ. War; Despatches.

PEVERELL, T. H. (D.S.O. L.G. 30.1.20)., Capt, 1/4th Batt. Seaf. Highrs.; M.C.

PEYTON, T. H., (D.S.O. L.G. 1.1.17); b. 15.5.84; s. of J. H. Peyton, J.P.; m. Joyce Mary, d. of J. Taylor, J.P.; educ. Trinity College, Dublin; M.A.; M.D.; B.Ch.; B.A.O.; D.P.H.; L.M.; Chief Tuberculosis Officer and Deputy County Medical Officer, Cheshire County Council; Lt.-Col. (retired), R.A.M.C.; Europ. War, 1914–18; Despatches; Greek Military Cross with Star, 1918.

PHELAN, E. C., M.B. (D.S.O. L.G. 1.1.18); b. 16.2.81; Lt., R.A.M.C., 30.7.06; Capt. 30.1.10; Maj. 30.7.18; M.C.

PHELAN, F. R. (D.S.O. L.G. 1.1.19), Major, 87th Batt. Can. Inf.; M.C.

PHILIP, G. M. (D.S.O. L.G. 25.8.17), T/Lt., North'd Fus.; M.C.

PHILIPS, J. L. (D.S.O. L.G. 25.8.17); b. 6.8.78; 2nd Lt., R.A., 28.3.00; Lt. 3.4.01; Capt. 2.6.09; Major 30.10.14; Lt.-Col., R.H.A.; served Europ. War, France, Mesopotamia and Palestine, 1914–18; Despatches; Bt. Lt.-Col. 1.1.18; M.C.

322 The Distinguished Service Order

PHILLIMORE, R. H. (D.S.O. L.G. 3.6.18); b. 19.6.79; 2nd Lt., R.E., 23.6.98; Lt. 17.4.01; Capt. 23.6.07; Maj. 29.3.15; Lt.-Col. 3.6.19.

PHILLIPS, A. E. (D.S.O. L.G. 1.1.19), T/Major, 7th (S.) Batt., R.W. Kent Rgt.

PHILLIPS, C. G. (D.S.O. L.G. 3.6.19), Capt. (T/Lt.-Col.), W. Yorks. Rgt., and 3/2nd K. African Rifles; M.C.

PHILLIPS, E., M.B. (D.S.O. L.G. 3.6.19), Lt., R.A.M.C., 31.7.14; Capt. 30.3.15; M.C.; D.A.D.M.S., India, 13.8.19.

PHILLIPS, E. C. M. (D.S.O. L.G. 30.1.20), Major (A/Lt.-Col.), Bedfords. and Herts. Rgt.; T.F.

PHILLIPS, E. S. (D.S.O. L.G. 1.1.19); b. 21.10.76; 2nd Lt., R.A., 16.5.00; Lt. 8.7.01; Capt. 16.5.13; Major, R.G.A., 30.12.15.

PHILLIPS, F. (D.S.O. L.G. 1.1.19), T/Capt. (T/Major), Gen. List.; M.C.

PHILLIPS, F. A. (D.S.O. L.G. 22.6.18); b. 11.4.72; s. of P. S. Phillips, J.P.; m. Ruth Ives; one s.; one d.; educ. Rossall; Exeter College, Oxford (Oxford University Cricket XI., 1892–95); Secretary to the Wye Board of Conservators and Wye Fisheries Association; Director of Wolseley Sheep Shearing Machine Co., Birmingham; Major, late Montgomery Yeomanry; served S. African War, with Montgomery Yeomanry, 1900–1; Europ. War, with Montgomery Yeomanry and 1/4th London R., as Second-in-Command; Despatches.

PHILLIPS, F. R. (D.S.O. L.G. 4.6.17); b. 23.1.77; s. of late F. Phillips; m. Dorothy, d. of late Major W. Barrett, J.P., D.L., and widow of Major Elmhirst Luard, D.S.O., The Norfolk Rgt.; one d.; 2nd Lt., R.A., 12.5.00; Lt. 11.5.01; Capt. 12.5.13; Maj. 30.12.15; Lt.-Colonel, R.A.; Europ. War, 1914–18; Despatches; Bt. Lt.-Col., 1.1.19.

PHILLIPS, H. P. (D.S.O. L.G. 11.1.19), Major, 3rd Aust. Pioneer Batt.; M.C.

PHILLIPS, J. C. SPENCER- (see Spencer-Phillips, J. C.).

PHILLIPS, N. C. (D.S.O. L.G. 4.6.17), Capt., L.N. Lancs. Rgt., S.R. (A/Lt.-Col.); M.C.

PHILLIPS, O. F. (D.S.O. L.G. 1.1.17), Lt.-Col., Aust. Artillery.

PHILLIPS, P. E. (D.S.O. L.G. 19.12.17) (Bar, L.G. 29.11.18), Lt.-Cdr., R.N., 15.10.17.

PHILLIPS, W. E. (D.S.O. L.G. 1.1.19); b. 3.1.93; Capt., Leins. R. (from T.F.), 25.2.17; M.C.

PHILLPOTTS, B. S. (D.S.O. L.G. 1.1.17); b. 18.2.75; s. of J. S. Phillpotts, formerly Headmaster of Bedford School, and Mrs. Phillpotts; educ. Bedford School; R.M.A., Woolwich; 2nd Lt., R.E., 1.4.95; Lt. 1.4.98; Capt. 1.4.04; went to the front with a field company in Sept. 1915. In 1916 he was appointed C.R.E. of a division with the rank of Lieutenant-Colonel. He was twice mentioned in Despatches. He was wounded 2.9.17, and died of his wounds two days later.

PHILPOT, D. (D.S.O. L.G. 18.7.17) (Bar, L.G. 8.3.19) (Details, 4.10.19), Capt. (A/Major), Can. Inf. His D.S.O. was awarded for gallantry at Vimy Ridge 9.4.17.

PHIPPS, C. F. (D.S.O. L.G. 3.6.16); b. 4.9.71; s. of Col. R. W. Phipps, late R.A.; m. Margaret Alice, d. of E. Hellard; educ. Charterhouse; R.M.A., Woolwich; 2nd Lt., R.A., 30.11.91; Lt. 30.11.94; Capt. 21.12.99; Maj. 29.5.12; Lt.-Col. 1.5.17; Col. 18.2.19; served S. African War, 1901–2; Queen's Medal and 3 clasps; N.W. Frontier of India, 1908; Medal and clasp; Europ. War, 1914–18; Despatches; Bt. Lt.-Col. 18.2.15.

PHIPPS, C. J. (D.S.O. L.G. 1.1.19); b. 20.11.93; s. of Rev. Canon C. O. Phipps, C.T.F., and Mrs. Phipps, of Lee Vicarage, Bucks; educ. Cordwalles School; Winchester; R.M.C., Sandhurst; 2nd Lt., 1st King's (Liverpool Rgt.), on 12.9.13. He went out to France on 12.8.14 with his battalion, which was in the 6th Brigade and the 2nd Division, and he served during the whole four and a half years of the war, being twice wounded, first at the end of Aug. 1914, during the Mons Retreat, in the Battle of Villers-Cotteret, and next on 3.3.15, near Givenchy. He became Brigade Signalling Officer in 1916, and in March, 1917, O.C., 2nd Div., Signal Co. He was three times mentioned in Despatches, and had the M.C. He was Lt. (T/Capt.) (A/Major), and died of pneumonia 19.2.19. His younger brother, Lieut. Charles Percy Phipps, of the Oxford and Bucks L.I., was killed in action on 19.7.16.

C. J. Phipps.

PHIPPS, H. R. (D.S.O. L.G. 1.1.18); b. 10.9.74; s. of Col. R. W. Phipps, late R.A., and the late Anne Elizabeth Phipps, d. of J. Daniell, M.D.; m. Lorna, d. of Neill Graeme Campbell (Auchindarroch) and Maude Georgina, d. of Sir W. Bovill, K.C., Lord Chief Justice of Common Pleas; two s.; one d.; educ. Temple Grove School, East Sheen; Wellington College, Berks; R.M.A., Woolwich; 2nd Lt., R.A., 21.10.93; Lt. 21.10.96; Capt. 28.7.00; Maj. 14.11.10; Lt.-Col. 1.3.16; ret. pay 22.5.20; S. African War, 1899–1900; Queen's Medal, 2 clasps; Soudan, 1904; Egyptian Medal, clasp; served Europ. War, in Belgium, 1914–18; wounded 20.10.14, at Ypres; Despatches; 1914 Star.

PHIPPS, J. H., M.B., M.R.C.S., L.R.C.P. (D.S.O. L.G. 1.1.17); s. of late G. C. Phipps, M.D., of Manchester; educ. Rossall School; Owens College, and Guy's Hospital; was commissioned in the Commonwealth Military Forces in 1903; became Lt.-Col., Aust. A.M.C., and served in the European War.

PHIPSON, E. S., M.B. (D.S.O. L.G. 2.2.16); b. 10.3.84; Lt., Ind. Med. Serv., 1.8.08; Capt. 1.8.11; Maj. 1.2.20.

PHYTHIAN-ADAMS, W. J. (D.S.O. L.G. 1.1.18), T/Major, R. Fus.; M.C.

PICKARD, J. A. A. (D.S.O. L.G. 1.1.18); b. 23.7.85; s. of late Rev. H. Adair Pickard, of Oxford, H.M. Inspector of Schools, and Catharine Pickard, of Airedale; m. Angela Mary, d. of A. Conyers Baker and Mary Abercromby Baker; educ. O.P.S., Oxford; Rugby; R.M.A., Woolwich; Director, Tramways and Road Services Branch, Traffic Department, Ministry of Transport; commissioned R.E., 1904; transferred to Special Reserve, 1911; Capt. 1914; Major, 1918; Lt.-Colonel, late R.E.; went to France, Aug. 1914, with 8th Co., R.E.; appointed Assistant Railway Construction Engineer, First Army, March, 1917; appointed Assistant Director, Light Railways, G.H.Q., Oct. 1917. He was awarded the D.S.O. for services in connection with the organization of railways in the Forward Area; Despatches four times.

PICKERING, C. J. (D.S.O. L.G. 14.1.16); b. 26.4.80; m. Eileen Rosetta Lane-Long, d. of R. W. C. Reeves, J.P., D.L.; two s.; educ. Mill Hill School; 2nd Lt., W. Rid. R., 26.4.00; Lt. 1.2.02; Capt. 16.10.09; Major 1.9.15; *p.s.c.*; Europ. War, 1914–18; severely wounded; Despatches; Bt. Lt.-Col. 1.1.18; C.M.G.

PICKERING, E. W. (D.S.O. L.G. 1.1.17); b. 3.1.82; s. of J. Pickering, J.P. and Emily Pickering, d. of J. Greaves; m., Evelyn Joyce Morton, d. of J. E. Shaw; one s.; educ. Tettinhall College; M.P. (Co. U.), Dewsbury, from Dec. 1918; 2nd Lt., R.F.A., 16.3.11; Lt. 16.9.13; Capt. 29.8.16; Major 2.1.15; Lt.-Colonel; served Europ. War, in France and Belgium; Despatches twice.

E. W. Pickering.

PICKERING, F. A. U. (D.S.O. L.G. 1.1.17); b. 2.8.81; 2nd Lt., 2nd Dragoons, 5.1.01; Lt. 15.11.01; Capt. 10.4.11; S. African War, 1901–2; Queen's Medal, 4 clasps; Europ. War. He was killed in action when commanding a battalion of the Rifle Brigade 23.12.17.

PICKFORD, P. (D.S.O. L.G. 24.9.18); s. of Mrs. A. Pickford: Headmaster of N. Walsham School; Major, Oxf. and Bucks. L.I.; M.C.

PIDSLEY, W. G. (D.S.O. L.G. 3.6.18); b. 19.8.92; s. of T. G. Pidsley; m. Bertha May, d. of C. Wreford; Mobd. Terr. Force from Aug. 1914; Lt., A.E.C., 15.6.20; Capt. 1.4.21.

PIERCEY, J. G. (D.S.O. L.G. 3.6.18), Lt.-Col., Can. F.A.

PIERSON, C. E. (D.S.O. L.G. 3.6.19), Major, A/307th (S.M.) Brig., R.F.A.; T.F.

PIGG, N. B. (D.S.O. L.G. 8.3.19) (Details, L.G. 4.10.19), T/Lt. (A/Capt.), 1st Batt. North'd Fus.; M.C.

PIGGOTT, F. S. G. (D.S.O. L.G. 1.1.17); b. 18.3.83; s. of Sir F. T. Piggott and Mabel Waldron, d. of late J. W. Johns, J.P., D.L.; m. Jane, d. of late W. James Smith, J.P.; two s.; educ. Cheltenham College; R.M.A., Woolwich; 2nd Lt., R.E., 4.2.01; Lt. 4.2.04; Adjt., R.E. (Gibraltar, 1906–8); Capt. 4.2.11; Major 2.11.16; *p.s.c.*; specially employed in Tokyo during Russo-Japanese War, 1904–6; served in Egypt and France during Europ. War; Despatches five times; Bt. Lt.-Col. 1.1.19; has 4th Class Order of the Rising Sun; Officer, Legion of Honour; Officer of the Order of Leopold; 3rd Class Order of the Sacred Treasure; French Croix de Guerre with two Palms; Belgian Croix de Guerre; attached to Crown Prince of Japan during visit to England, 1921 (3rd Class Order of the Rising Sun); G.S., War Office, 1920–21; Military Attaché to H.B.M. Embassy, Tokyo.

PIGOT, R. (D.S.O. L.G. 20.10.16); b. 2.5.82; s. of Sir G. Pigot, 5th Bart. of Patshull, and Alice, d. of Sir J. T. Mackenzie, 1st Bart., of Glen Muick; m. Norah Beatrice Oakley, d. of C. Reginald Hargreaves; three d.; 2nd Lt., Rif. Brig., 4.12.01; Capt. 23.12.11; Lt.-Col. (Res. of Off.) 23.4.17; Bt. Lt.-Col., Rif. Brig.; Brig.-Gen. (retired) 30.7.19; S. African War, 1902; Queen's Medal, 3 clasps; served Europ. War, 1914–18; T/Adjt. to R.F.C., Aug. 1914; rejoined his Regt., Sept.; Adjt., 3rd Bn. The Rifle Brigade, June to March, 1915; O.C., 3rd Bn. The Rifle Brigade, March, 1915–July, 1917; O.C., 11th Tank Bn., July, 1917–Sept. 1918; G.O.C., 6th Tank Brigade, Sept. 1918; Despatches five times; Bt. Major; Bt. Lt.-Col.; M.C. His D.S.O. was awarded for gallantry at Guillemont on 21.8.18.

R. Pigot.

PIGOTT, G. A. ROYSTON- (see Royston-Pigott, G. A.).

PIGOTT, J. R. W. SMYTH- (see Smyth-Pigott, J. R. W.).

PIGOTT, W. M. ROYSTON- (see Royston-Pigott, W. M.).

PIJPER, S. W. (D.S.O. L.G. 22.8.18), Col.-Commandant, 5th Mtd. Brig., S. African Forces.

PIKE, F. O. (D.S.O. L.G. 4.6.17); b. 1851; s. of late Capt. T. W. R. Pike, R.N.; m. d. of late Judge Pohlman, of Melbourne; Vice-Admiral, retired, 1911; served Europ. War with R.N.R.; C.M.G. He died 5.4.21.

PIKE, W. (D.S.O. L.G. 2.2.16); b. 28.9.81; 2nd Lt., R. Innis. Fus., 5.1.01; Lt. 4.6.02; Capt. 13.1.10; S. African War, 1901–2; Queen's Medal, 2 clasps. He was reported missing, Aug. 1915; reported killed 9.5.16.

PILCHER, C. H. (D.S.O. L.G. 8.3.20); b. 1877; s. of H. C. Pilcher; m. Catherine Moraitinis, g.d. of Aristide Moraitinis, Prime Minister and Regent of Greece; one s.; one d.; educ. Stubbington House; H.M.S. Britannia, Dartmouth; Captain, R.N.; Commander (2nd-in-command) of H.M.S. St. Vincent, 1915–17; present at Battle of Jutland (promoted Captain); at Admiralty, 1917–18; commanded H.M.S. Dauntless, 1919–21; employed in Baltic; Despatches; D.S.O.

PILCHER, W. S. (D.S.O. L.G. 1.1.17); b. 1888; s. of late H. D. Pilcher; educ. Eton; 2nd Lt., G. Gds. (from S.R.), 24.10.08; Lt. 1.4.10; Capt. 30.1.15; Bt. Major 1.1.18; Europ. War; Despatches four times; specially employed, British Mission, Warsaw, Poland, 1920–21.

PILE, F. A. (D.S.O. L.G. 1.1.18); b. 14.9.84; e. s. of Sir T. D. Pile, 1st Bart., and Caroline Maude, d. of J. M. Nicholson, J.P., of Dublin; m. Vera Millicent, d. of Brig.-Gen. Lloyd; two s.; 2nd Lt. 29.7.04; Lt. 29.7.07; Capt. 30.10.14; Major 26.8.16; Lt.-Col., R.F.A.; served Europ. War, 1914–18; Despatches Bt. Lt.-Col. 3.6.19; M.C.

PILKINGTON, G. R. (D.S.O. L.G. 1.1.17); b. 15.4.81; 6th s. of late Col. R. Pilkington, C.B., M.P., and Louisa, d. of A. Sinclair; m. Margery, d. of W. Frost; one s.; one d.; educ. Clifton; Trinity College, Cambridge; Major, S. Lancs. R.; served Europ. War, 1914–17.

PILKINGTON, W. N. (D.S.O. L.G. 3.6.16) (Bar, L.G. 16.9.18); b. 26.7.77 s. of late Col. R. Pilkington, C.B., and Louisa, d. of A. Sinclair; educ. Clifton College; Trinity College, Cambridge; Captain of the Cambridge University XV., 1898, and played for England the same year, while he also ran for Cambridge *v.* Oxford "first string" in the 100 yards; gazetted to 1/5th S. Lancs. Regt., 1900; Lt.-Col. to command the Batt. June, 1920; served Europ. War from 1914; Despatches twice.

PIM, D. C., M.B. (D.S.O. L.G. 25.8.17), Capt., R.A.M.C., S.R.

PINCHING, M. C. C. (D.S.O. L.G. 14.1.16); b. 25.10.81; s. of late Capt. A. Pinching; m. Mrs. R. Warner; one d.; educ. Wellington College; 2nd Lt., 2nd D.G., 5.12.00; Lt. 8.6.01; Adjt., 1903–6; Capt. 3.4.07; Major 1.11.14; S. African War, 1901–2; Queen's Medal, 5 clasps. He went to France with the original Exp. Force, and was twice wounded. After two years and eight months' active service in France he died in a military hospital in London 20.4.17.

PINKNEY, E. W. R. (gazetted as Pinkney, E. W. P.) (D.S.O. L.G. 1.1.17), Lt.-Col., A.S.C. (now R.A.S.C.).

PINSENT, J. R. (D.S.O. L.G. 1.1.18); b. 12.8.88; s. of R. A. Pinsent, President, Law Society, 1918–19; m. Kathleen May, d. of Col. E. G. Boyce; one s.; educ. Winchester; R.M.A., Woolwich; 2nd Lt., R.E., 6.8.09; Lt. 23.1.12; Capt. 6.8.15; served Europ. War, 1914–18; Despatches three times; Legion of Honour for services at the Battle of the Somme. His D.S.O. was awarded for services in connection with the Battle of Ypres; Bt. Major 3.6.19, for services during the last nine months of the war.

PINWILL, W. R. (D.S.O. L.G. 1.1.18); b. 9.10.73; 2nd Lt., L'pool R., 20.5.93; Lt. 15.1.96; Capt. 21.3.00; Maj. 1.9.15; Bt. Lt.-Col. 1.1.16; *p.s.c.*; S. African War, 1899–1902; Despatches; Queen's Medal, 3 clasps; King's Medal, 2 clasps; Europ. War; Despatches; Bt. Lt.-Col. 1.1.16.

PIPER, S. H. (D.S.O. L.G. 1.1.19), 2nd Lt. (T/Major), 9th Batt. Notts. and Derbys. R.

PIPON, R. H. (D.S.O. L.G. 26.7.17) (Bar, L.G. 26.7.18); b. 17.1.82; 2nd Lt. 8.1.01; R. Fus. 9.3.01 Lt. 4.5.04; Capt. 3.6.10; Maj. 8.1.16; Somaliland, 1908–10; Medal, clasp; Europ. War; Despatches; M.C.

PIRIE, W. B. (D.S.O. L.G. 1.1.16); b. 10.3.88; s. of Martin Henry Pirie and Lilian Frances Pirie (*née* Campbell); m. Leonora Stafford; four s.; educ. Eton; H.M.S. Britannia; ent. Navy, 1902; Submarines, 1907; Commander, R.N. (retired); took command of Submarine "H," at Montreal, May, 1915; in charge of first four submarines to cross Atlantic; operations in Sea of Marmora, Sept. 1915 (D.S.O.); Adriatic, 1916 (Cavalier St. Maurice and St. Lazarus).

PITCHER, D. LE G. (D.S.O. L.G. 1.1.19); b. Naini Tal, U.P., India, 31.8.77; s. of Col. D. G. Pitcher and Rose, d. of Capt. J. C. Evison, R.N.; educ. Sedbergh School; Geneva University; Sandhurst; 2nd Lt., 24th Rgt. (S.W.B.), 16.2.98; Lt. 10.1.00; Adjt., 1904; Capt. 16.2.07; Major 1.9.15; Temp. Brig.-Gen. 1.4.16; Air Commodore, R.A.F.; Asst. Inspector, Imp. Service Troops, Central India, 1910–11; Pilot's Certificate, Royal Aero Club, No. 125, 1911; served with Central India Horse in Central Persia, 1911–13; joined Central Flying School, 1914; attached to R.F.C., and posted to B.E.F., France, Aug. 1914; Asst. Commandant, C.F.S., April, 1915; Commandant, Dec. 1915; Wing Commander, B.E.F., France, March, 1916; Despatches; Mons Star; Bt. Lt.-Col. 1.1.17; Bt. Col. 3.6.19; C.M.G.; C.B.E.; Officer, Order of St. Maurice and St. Lazarus; Legion of Honour; Controller of Technical Design to the Air Board; in 1908 he was Tutor to the Maharajah of Holkar.

PITKEATHLY, J. S. (D.S.O. L.G. 7.2.18), T/Major, Special List, C.V.O.

PITMAN, C. R. S. (D.S.O. L.G. 17.3.17) (Details, L.G. 18.6.17); b. Bombay, 19.3.90; s. of C. E. Pitman, C.I.E., and Lucy Maude, d. of late D. Cargill; educ. Royal Naval School, Eltham; Blundell's School, Tiverton; R.M.C., Sandhurst; King's India Cadet; 2nd Lt. 8.9.09; Lt., 27th Punjabis, 8.12.11; Capt. 1.9.15; retired 14.2.21; served in Egypt, 1914–15; France, 1915; Mesopotamia, 1916–17–18; Palestine, 1918–19–20. He was awarded the M.C. (L.G. 22.9.16), and his D.S.O. was awarded for a raid by night below Kut, in Mesopotamia, which had to cross a broad river in high flood. Owing to the strong current only six of the twelve boats reached their objective, but in spite of reduced numbers and heavy fire he, being in command, reorganized his party and inflicted much damage on the enemy, bringing back two trench mortars, motor gun belts and other booty. He was mentioned in Despatches by Sir Percy Lake, and later by Sir Stanley Maude. He is a Member of the Bombay Natural History Society, and a Member of the British Ornithologists' Union.

PITMAN, J. D. (D.S.O. L.G. 1.1.18), Capt. (A/Major), Can. Ordnance Corps.

PITTS, A. T., M.R.C.S., L.D.S. (D.S.O. L.G. 26.7.18) (Bar, L.G. 3.6.18); b. 3.3.81; s. of Alfred and Alice Mary Pitts; m. Alexandra Dorothy, d. of the late Capt. A. McCarthy, Bengal Staff Corps; one d.; educ. Aske's School, Hatcham; entered the Army 23.7.14; Capt. (A/Lt.-Col.), R.A.M.C., S.R.; went to France as O.C., Sanitary Section, 2nd Cav. Div., 25.12.14; 2nd-in-command, 4th Cavalry Field Amb., 2nd Cavalry Division, 4.7.16; O.C., 4th Cav. Fld. Amb., 8.10.17 to 12.5.19; A/Lt.-Col. 12.12.17; Despatches twice.

PLACE, C. G. M. (D.S.O. L.G. 17.12.17) (Details, L.G. 23.4.18); b. 2.11.86; s. of G. W. Place, I.C.S. (retired); m. Anna Margaret, d. of late W. A. Stuart-William, P.W.D., India; one s.; one d.; educ. St. Columba's College, Rathfarnham; Trinity College, Dublin; served Europ. War. from 1914; T. Capt. (A/Major), E. Surrey Rgt.; Despatches; M.C.

PLANCK, O. B. F. (D.S.O. L.G. 1.1.18), T/Major, A.S.C. (now R.A.S.C.).

PLANT, E. C. P. (D.S.O. L.G. 1.1.17) (Bar, L.G. 18.7.17); s. of Lt.-Col. C. F. Plant; m. Oona, d. of the late J. Hunter Brown; Major, Aust. Military Forces. His D.S.O. was awarded for gallantry at Bullecourt 3.5.17.

PLATT, F. C. (D.S.O. L.G. 29.11.18), Lt.-Comdr., R.N. 30.7.15.

PLAYFAIR, I. S. O. (D.S.O. L.G. 1.1.18); b. 10.4.94; 2nd Lt., R.E., 18.7.13; Lt. 9.6.15; Capt. 3.11.17; Bt. Maj. 3.6.19; M.C.

PLAYFAIR, T. A. J. (D.S.O. L.G. 4.6.17), Capt. (T/Major), Aust. Arty.

PLEYDELL-BOUVERIE, HON. S. (D.S.O. L.G. 1.1.17); b. 1877; s. of 5th Earl of Radnor; m. Edith Dorothy, d. of A. Vickers; four s.; educ. Harrow; Engineer; Director, Phœnix Assurance Co. Ltd.; Lt.-Col., R.F.A. (T.); served Europ. War, 1914–17, commanding Ammunition Column, R.A., at the front; Despatches thrice.

PLEYDELL-NOTT, J. G. L. (D.S.O. L.G. 1.1.17); b. 5.5.71; s. of late Capt. J. Nott, R.N. (son of Major-Gen. G. Nott, I.A.), and Elizabeth, d. of Rev. H. Brownrigg, M.A., Rector of Wicklow; m. Winefred, d. of late H. S. Poole; one d.; educ. Mr. Backhouse's Military Academy, Dublin; 2nd Lt., Wicklow R.G.A. Militia, March, 1888; Capt., 1891; retired 1901; Wicklow Artillery, S.R.; T/Major, R.G.A., 9.10.14; transferred to Mech. Trans. A.S.C. as T/Major, April, 1915; Capt., A.S.C., S.R.; served with B.E.F. continuously; A/Major, R.A.S.C., S.R.; Despatches twice; Bt. Major 3.6.19.

PLIMPTON, K. A. (D.S.O. L.G. 1.1.17); b. 12.11.84; 2nd Lt., E. Yorks. R., 2.3.04; Lt. 20.4.07; Capt. 28.9.14; Bt. Maj. 3.6.18; Lt.-Col., ret. pay, 20.8.21.

PLOWDEN, R. A. A. (D.S.O. L.G. 11.4.19), Cdr., R.N., 30.6.19.

PLUMMER, E. W. (D.S.O. L.G. 14.1.16); b. 23.3.71; s. of Lt.-Col. H. Plummer, late 7th R. Fusiliers; m. Mary Dorothy, d. of Mrs. Brooke-Smith and widow of Major L. C. Hill, M.C., R.F.A.; one d.; educ. St. Michael's College; R.M.A., Woolwich; 2nd Lt., R.A., 13.2.91; Lt. 13.2.94; Capt. 13.2.00; Maj. 16.8.08; Lt.-Col. 15.3.15; ret. pay 1.7.20; served in India, 1891–1900; Adjt., Midlothian Vol. Arty. 1901–6; served Europ. War; Despatches twice; Russian Order of St. Anne; Belgian Croix de Guerre; Mons Star.

PLUMMER, M. V. (D.S.O. L.G. 2.4.19) (Details, L.G. 10.12.19), Major, 51st Howitzer Battery, 13th Brig. Can. F.A.

PLUMMER, T. H. (D.S.O. L.G. 1.1.18), Major, R.G.A., S.R.

PLUNKETT, J. F. (D.S.O. L.G. 1.1.18) (Bar, L.G. 4.2.18) (Details, L.G. 5.7.18) (2nd Bar, L.G. 2.12.18); b. 7.3.77; 2nd Lt., R. Innis. Fus., 23.5.15; Lt., R. Irish Rgt., 22.11.15; Capt., R. Dub. Fus., 23.12.17; Bt. Maj. 3.6.19; Major, E. Lan. Rgt., 12.10.20; M.C.; D.C.M.

PLUNKETT-ERNLE-ERLE-DRAX, HON. R. A. R. (D.S.O. L.G. 17.5.18); b. 28.3.80; s. of 17th Baron Dunsany and Ernle Elizabeth Louisa Maria Grosvenor, d. of Col. F. A. P. Burton, Coldstream Guards (assumed by Royal Licence, 1916, additional names of Ernle-Erle-Drax); m. Kathleen, d. of Quintin Chalmers, M.D.; two d.; educ. Cheam School; H.M.S. Britannia; went to sea, 1896; Lt., 1901; Cdr., 1912; Captain 30.6.16; served afloat in the Grand Fleet from 1914 onwards; present on board H.M.S. Lion at the Heligoland Action, Dogger Bank and Jutland; Despatches; promoted to be Captain; Russian Order of St. Stanislas (2nd Class) with Swords, 1916. His D.S.O. was awarded for services when commanding H.M.S. Blanche. He has written "The Modern Officer of the Watch." Director of R.N. Staff College, Greenwich, from 1919.

POCOCK, F. P. (D.S.O. L.G. 23.7.18), Surgeon Lieutenant, R.N.; M.C. and Bar. He was mortally wounded near the Escault Canal 29.9.18, while tending the wounded of the Drake Battalion, R.N.D., to which he was attached. His brother, Lieutenant C. A. F. Pocock, R. Warwicks. Rgt., was killed in action near Fresnoy, 8.5.17, aged 30.

POCOCK, M. R. (D.S.O. L.G. 7.2.18); b. 17.5.76; 2nd Lt. 22.1.96; Lt., Ind. Army, 4.7.98; Capt. 22.1.05; Major (A/Lt.-Col.) 22.1.14; East Africa, 1903–4; Medal, 2 clasps; N.W. Frontier, 1908; Despatches; Medal, clasp. He was killed in action 5.11.17.

POCOCK, P. F. (D.S.O. L.G. 23.8.18); b. 5.12.71; 2nd Lt., L'pool R., 25.3.91; Lt., I.S.C., 6.7.92; Capt., I.A., 10.7.01; Major 25.3.09; Lt.-Col. 25.3.17; Col. 23.7.20; served E. Africa, 1903–4; operations in Somaliland; action at Jidballi; Medal, 2 clasps; N.W. Frontier of India, 1908; operations in the Mohmand country; operations in the Zakka Khel country; Despatches; Medal with clasp; Europ. War; Despatches.

PODMORE, H. (D.S.O. L.G. 31.5.16); b. 21.11.87, at Charney Hall, Grange-over-Sands; s. of Mr. and Mrs. George Podmore. From his father's school, Charney Hall, he gained the top Scholarship at Rugby School. There he was head of Collins's House; got his "flannels" at Football, and was in the Cricket XXII. and the Running Eight. From Rugby he gained a Classical Exhibition at Trinity College, Oxford, and was the first holder of the Lees Knowles Leaving Exhibition from Rugby. He took a First Class in "Mods," and a Third in Greats. It had been his great desire to get back to his old school, and on leaving Oxford he gladly accepted a Mastership at Rugby, and became an Officer in the O.T.C. On the outbreak of war he applied for a commission, and in Sept. 1914, was gazetted to the 6th Northamptons (then under the command of Col. Ripley, also an O.R.), and got his company just before the end of the year. In July, 1915, he went out to France. His D.S.O. was awarded for gallantry on 12–13.4.16, north-east of Carnoy. He was wounded at Trônes Wood in July, 1916, and was gazetted Major the same month. He was three times mentioned in Despatches, and was again wounded in Aug. 1917, and returned to the front in Dec. Lt.-Col. Podmore had only been in command of his new battalion (the 12th Middlesex) eight days, when he was killed by an accidental explosion of ammunition, 31.12.17.

H. Podmore.

POË, J. H. L. (D.S.O. L.G. 3.6.19); b. 21.11.78, in Armagh, Ireland; s. of Capt. J. Hill Poë, J.P., D.L., of Nenagh, Tipperary; m. Frida Mary Lees; one d.; educ. Cheltenham College, etc.; 2nd Lt., W. India Rgt., May, 1899; Lt., July, 1900; Capt., Oct. 1913; Major 1.9.15; Major, E. Lancs. Rgt., 27.8.21; T/Lt.-Col. 18.4.16–28.8.19; Despatches three times.

POE, W. S. (D.S.O. L.G. 3.6.18); b. 24.6.78; s. of the late Admiral Sir E. Poe, G.C.V.O.; m. Joan Rosina, d. of Col. C. P. Boyd, of Crofton House, Titchfield, Hants; 2nd Lt., R. Mar., 1.9.96; Lt., R.M. Art., 1.7.97; Capt. 18.2.04; Maj. 23.9.15; Paymaster, R. Mar., 9.10.20; served with Naval Brigade in S. Africa, 1899–1900; Queen's Medal, 3 clasps; Europ. War, 1914–18; severely wounded; Despatches; Bt. Lt.-Col. 1.1.19.

POLAND, A. (D.S.O. L.G. 20.9.18), Lt.-Cdr., R.N., 15.3.17.

POLLARD, A. M. (D.S.O. L.G. 1.1.18); b. 7.11.80; Lt., R.A.M.C., 1.8.08; Capt. 1.2.12; Maj. 1.8.20.

POLLARD, C. A. (D.S.O. L.G. 14.1.16), Capt. (T/Major), 2nd Co. of London (Howitzer) Battery, R.F.A. (T.F.).

POLLARD, J. H. W. (D.S.O. L.G. 3.6.19); b. 13.5.66; m. Clare Evelyn (who died in 1917), d. of G. H. Low, Can. Rifles); educ. Repton; Sandhurst; ent. Army 25.8.86; Lt. 15.9.86; Capt. 31.7.95; Major 13.6.06; Lt.-Col. 31.1.15; Colonel 31.1.19; Burma, 1887–89; Medal with clasp; Chin Lushai Exp., 1890 (clasp); Isazai Exp., 1892; Waziristan, 1894–95 (clasp); Chitral, 1895 (Medal with clasp); S. Africa, 1899–1902 (Despatches; Queen's Medal, 4 clasps; King's Medal, 2 clasps); E. Africa, 1902–4 (Despatches; Medal with clasp); Europ. War, 1914–18; Despatches seven times; Bt. Colonel; C.M.G.; C.B.

POLLARD, W. F. (D.S.O. L.G. 22.2.18), Lt.-Cdr. (A/Cdr.), R.N.R., R.D.

POLLARD-LOWSLEY, H. DE L. (D.S.O. L.G. 3.6.16); b. 20.4.77; s. of Lt.-Col. B. Lowsley, R.E., and Mrs. A. M. Lowsley; m. on 6.5.11, in Salisbury Cathedral, Sylvia Janet Penrose, d. of Brig.-Gen. C. Penrose, C.B., C.M.G., R.E.; one s.; two d.; educ. Foster's (Stubbington House, Fareham), 1889–90; Cheltenham College, 1890–94; R.M.A., Woolwich, 1894–95; passed 1st from Woolwich into R.E. in 1895, obtaining Pollock Medal and prizes for Mathematics, Fortification, Topography and Electricity; obtained Fowke Medal at Chatham, 1898; 2nd Lt., R.E., 21.12.95; Lt. 21.12.98; Capt. 21.12.04; Major 30.10.14; Adjt., R.E., 16.11.14; Bt. Lt.-Col. 3.6.17; Lt.-Col. 15.2.22; service: Chatham, 1896–98; Malakand, India, Q.V.O. Sappers and Miners, 1898–99; joined P.W.D., 1899; Executive Engineer, P.W.D., 1904; O.C., C.P. Camps, Delhi Durbar, 1902–3; U. Secy., C.P., P.W.D., 1911–13; O.C., C.P. Camps, Delhi Durbar, 1911–12; U. Secy. to Govt. of India, P.W.D., 1914; Adjutant, 11th Div., 1914–15; O.C., 91st Field Coy., R.E., 1915–16; S.O.R.E., I. Corps, 1916; C.R.E., 37th Div., 1916; present at Battles of Loos (1915), Somme (1916), Ancre (1916); Despatches five times; C.I.E. awarded for work on Famine and Irrigation in India; C.M.G.; Asst. to Engineer-in-Chief, G.H.Q., France, 1918–19; Chief Engineer and Secretary to Govt. in P.W.D., Central Provinces, India, 1920.

POLLITT, G. P., M.Sc., Ph.D. (D.S.O. L.G. 1.1.17) (1st Bar, L.G. 18.7.17) (2nd Bar, L.G. 2.4.19) (Details 2nd Bar, L.G. 10.12.19); b. 23.8.78; s. of J. S. Pollitt; educ. Bruges; Manchester University; Zürich Polytechnic; Director, Brunner, Mond and Co. At outbreak of war enlisted as Despatch Rider, and served with original Exp. Force in that capacity; commissioned rank Nov. 1914, first in Intelligence Corps, then in R.E.; subsequently Lt.-Col. Commanding 11th Batt. Lancs. Fus.; Despatches four times; 1914 Star. His 1st Bar was awarded for gallantry 12–17.5.17, at Bullecourt.

POLLOCK, C. E., M.R.C.S., L.R.C.P. (D.S.O. L.G. 1.1.17); b. 25.4.68; s. of A. R. Pollock, of Greenhill, Paisley; educ. Wellington College; Guy's Hospital; Capt., R.A.M.C., 30.1.96 (previous service 3 years); Major 30.7.04; Lt.-Col. 1.3.15; Col. 26.12.17; took part in operations on the N.W. Frontier of India, 1897–98, with Tirah Exp. Force; Medal, 2 clasps; served S. African War, 1902; Queen's Medal, 2 clasps; Europ. War from 1914; Despatches; C.B., 1921; C.B.E., 1919.

POLLOCK, H. A. (D.S.O. L.G. 3.6.19), Major, 5th Batt., att. 12th Batt., R. Scots Fus., T.F.

POLLOCK, H. B. (D.S.O. L.G. 4.3.18) (Details, L.G. 16.8.18) (Bar, L.G. 8.3.19) (Details, L.G. 4.10.19); s. of late J. G. Pollock and Mrs. Pollock; served Europ. War from 1914; wounded; Despatches, and retired as Commander, R.N.V.R.

POLLOCK, J. A. (D.S.O. L.G. 15.2.19) (Details, L.G. 30.7.19); b. 3.4.82; 2nd Lt., Oxf. L.I., 5.1.1; Lt., Oxf. and Bucks. L.I., 1.7.04; Capt. 22.1.10; Maj. 1.9.15; Lt.-Col., ret. pay, 10.1.20; S. African War, 1900–2; Queen's Medal, 2 clasps; King's Medal, 2 clasps; Europ. War; Despatches.

POLLOCK, W. (D.S.O. L.G. 1.1.19), T/Major, 465th Battery, 65th Brig., R.F.A.

POLLOK, R. V. (D.S.O. L.G. 1.1.18); b. 14.2.84; s. of late John Pollok, D.L., and g.s. of 4th Lord Clanmorris; 2nd Lt., 15th Hrs., 28.3.03; Lt. 24.11.06; Capt. 12.12.14; Irish Guards 7.6.15; Major 14.5.18; served Europ. War; wounded; Despatches; C.B.E.

POLLOK-M'CALL, J. B. (D.S.O. L.G. 11.4.18); 2nd s. of late R. M. Pollok-Morris, of Craig, Kilmarnock; b. 6.2.70; m. Frances, d. of F. M'Call, of Lochbrae; one s.; educ. Harrow; Oxford; Sandhurst; 2nd Lt., The Black Watch, 4.3.91; Capt., 1900; Major 25.8.09; retired 5.10.10; commanded 5th Batt. R. Scots Fusiliers, 1912–15; Brig.-Gen., R. of O.; served S. African War, 1899–1902; Queen's Medal, 3 clasps; King's Medal, 2 clasps; Tibet Exp., 1904; Despatches; Medal with clasp; Europ. War, command of 1/5th R.S.F. Batt.; Despatches five times; C.M.G.; Brigade Commander, Gallipoli, Palestine and France 14.8.15 to 7.6.19; Order of the Nile, 3rd Class; D.L. and J.P., Ayrshire.

POMEROY, E. J. (D.S.O. L.G. 7.2.19); b. 5.5.71; 2nd Lt., W.I.R., 15.3.93; Lt. 9.11.94; Capt. 4.1.99; Maj. 8.7.15; Lt.-Col. 8.7.19; S. African War, 1900–2; Queen's Medal, 3 clasps; King's Medal, 2 clasps; Europ. War; Despatches.

PONSONBY, D. G. (D.S.O. L.G. 25.8.17); b. 12.4.86; 2nd Lt., W.I.R., 16.8.05; Lt. 16.11.07; Capt., Ind. Army, 16.8.14; Maj. 16.8.20.

PONSONBY, H. C. (D.S.O. L.G. 3.6.18); b. 8.4.83; s. of late C. H. Ponsonby and Hon. Mary Sophia Eliza Plunkett, d. of 16th Baron Dunsany; 2nd Lt., K.R.R.C., 22.10.02; Lt. 9.10.07; Capt. 12.10.14; Maj. 22.10.17; served Europ. War, 1914–18; Despatches; Bt. Maj. 3.6.17; M.C.

POOLE, G. R. (D.S.O. L.G. 3.6.19); b. 17.1.68; s. of Rev. Canon Poole, D.D.; Lt., R.M.A., 1.9.85; Capt. 19.6.96; Bt. Maj. 1.9.06; Major 1.7.08; Bt. Lt.-Col. 1.9.13; Lt.-Col. 9.2.16; 2nd Colonel Commandant, R.M.A., 2.7.20; Col.-Comdt. 3.10.21; served S. Africa, 1901; Europ. War, 1914–17; Despatches; C.M.G.; Aide-de-Camp to H.M. the King 3.10.21.

POOLE, G. S. (D.S.O. L.G. 4.2.18) (Details, L.G. 5.7.18), Major, Yeomanry.

POOLE, H. R. (D.S.O. L.G. 14.1.16); b. 12.5.77; 2nd Lt., R.A., 19.6.99; Lt. 16.2.01; Capt. 29.3.06; Major 30.10.14; ret. pay 17.11.21; O.B.E.; S. African War, 1900–2; Queen's Medal, 5 clasps; King's Medal, 2 clasps; Europ. War; Despatches; O.B.E.

POOLE, I. M. C. (D.S.O. L.G. 22.12.16); b. 23.2.78; s. of late Lt.-Col. M. Conway Poole, Burmah Commission; m. Hazel, d. of late Major R. Johnston, A.P.D.; one s.; one d.; educ. Malvern College; Unatt. List., I.S.C., 22.1.98; Lt., Ind. Army, 22.4.00; Capt. 22.1.07; Maj. 1.9.15; S. and T. Corps; Europ. War; served France, Meerut Div., I.E.F. (A.), 1914–15; Mesopotamia, 1915–16; A.D.T., Tigris A.C.; Despatches.

POOLE, J. S. (D.S.O. L.G. 15.2.17); b. 16.9.96; 2nd Lt., K.R. Rif. C., 11.11.14; Lt. 1.8.15; Capt. 17.2.17.

POOLE, L. T. (D.S.O. L.G. 26.7.18); b. 21.4.88; Lt., R.A.M.C., 26.7.12; Capt. 30.3.15; M.C.

POOLE, R. (D.S.O. L.G. 22.8.18), Capt., S. African Engrs.; M.C.

POOLL, J. A. BATTEN- (see Batten-Pooll, J. A.).

POPE, A. T. (D.S.O. L.G. 22.2.18), Capt., Mercantile Marine (Lt., R.N.R.).

POPE, E. A. (D.S.O. L.G. 1.1.17); b. 23.11.75, at Dorchester, Dorset; s. of Alfred Pope, J.P., F.S.A., and Mary Elizabeth, d. of A. Whiting; m. Sybil Aline, d. of Lt.-Col. C. Briggs, J.P., D.L.; educ. Winchester College; entered the Militia, June, 1894; 3rd. Batt. Welsh Rgt.; Capt., 1898; Major, 1913; T/Lt.-Col., April, 1915; Lt.-Col., April, 1917; served S. African War, 1899–1902; Queen's Medal, 2 clasps; King George's Coronation Medal; raised, trained and commanded in France 12th Batt. S.W.B., 119th Brigade; Temp. Lieut.-Col.; wounded April, 1917; Lieut.-Col. to command 3rd S.R. Batt. Welch Rgt., 22.4.17; took over command Nov. 1917; J.P.; Despatches. He died 9.4.18.

POPE, E. B. (D.S.O. L.G. 24.9.18); b. 20.4.90; Temp. 2nd Lt. 6.1.15; 2nd Lt., Glouc. R., 6.10.15; Lt. 1.7.17.

POPE, F. (D.S.O. L.G. 1.1.17); b. 8.12.74; 2nd Lt. 1.12.97; Capt. 23.1.05; ret. pay, North'n R., 22.11.13.

POPE, R. K. C. (D.S.O. L.G. 1.1.19), Lt.-Cdr. 13.12.17.

POPE, S. B. (D.S.O. L.G. 3.6.16); b. 9.2.79; s. of Professor J. Pope; educ. St. Paul's School; Christ's College, Cambridge; 2nd Lt., R. Ir. R., 4.5.01; Lt., Ind. Army, 4.8.03; Capt. 4.5.10; Maj. 4.5.16; *p.s.c.*; served N.W. Frontier of India, 1908 (Medal with clasp); Europ. War, France, 1914–17; Palestine, 1918; Despatches four times; Bt. Lt.-Col. 1.1.19; Bt. Col. 3.5.21; Légion d'Honneur (Croix de Chevalier), April, 1917.

POPE, V. V. (D.S.O. L.G. 31.5.16); b. 30.9.91; 2nd Lt., N. Staff. R., 4.12.12; Lt. 1.10.14; Capt. 24.3.16; Bt. Maj. 1.1.18; M.C. His D.S.O. was awarded for gallantry near Wolverghem 29–30.4.16.

POPHAM, E. L. (D.S.O. L.G. 17.10.17); b. 14.12.76; 2nd Lt. 20.1.97; Lt., Ind. Army, 20.4.99; Capt. 20.1.06; Maj. 20.1.15; Bt. Lt.-Col. 3.6.18.

POPHAM, F. J. (D.S.O. L.G. 2.12.18); b. 4.2.71, at Portreath, Cornwall; s. of the Rev. V. W. Popham and C. H., d. of Rev. W. Gilbee; educ. Bedford School; 2nd Lt., 2nd County of London Yeomanry, 1907–12; 2nd Lt., 10th Batt. R. Fus., Sept. 1914; Capt., April, 1915; Major, 10th Batt. L.N. Lanc. Rgt., May, 1916; Lt.-Col., 2/5th K.O.R.L. Rgt., Aug. 1918; Europ. War from 1914. His D.S.O. was awarded for action on 29.8.18, in the Capture of Rennecourt in the advance on Cambrai; Despatches.

PORCH, C. P. (D.S.O. L.G. 26.3.17) (Bar, L.G. 18.7.17); b. 25.1.73; 2nd Lt., East Surrey Regt., 25.2.93; Capt. 13.11.01; retired 5.3.10; Lt.-Col., R. of O., 12.11.20; S. African War, 1899–1902; Despatches; Queen's Medal, 4 clasps; King's Medal, 2 clasps; Europ. War; Despatches. His Bar to the D.S.O. was awarded for gallantry north-east of Arras 9–14.4.17.

PORTAL, C. F. A. (D.S.O. L.G. 18.7.17) (Bar, L.G. 26.7.18); s. of E. R. Portal, formerly Master of the Craven Hounds; m. Joan Margaret, d. of Sir C. G. Welby; Squadron Leader, R.A.F.; served Europ. War, 1914–18; Despatches; M.C. His five brothers also served in the Great War.

PORTAL, J. L. (D.S.O. L.G. 4.6.17); b. 13.4.86; s. of E. R. Portal and Rose Leslie, d. of late J. N. Napier; m. Violet Eleanor, d. of Major T. S. Baldock, C.B.; educ. Eton College; 2nd Lt., Oxf. and Bucks. L.I., 23.5.06; Lt. 7.4.09; Capt. 17.5.15.

PORTAL, M. (D.S.O. L.G. 3.6.18), T/Major, Remount Service.

PORTAL, W. R. (D.S.O. L.G. 26.11.17) (Details, L.G. 6.4.18); b. 1885; e. s. of Sir W. W. Portal, 2nd Bart.; m. Lady Louise Rose Mary Kathleen Virginia Cairns, o. c. of 2nd Earl Cairns; educ. Eton; Christ Church, Oxford; Lt.-Col., late Life Guards; served Europ. War; M.V.O., 1918.

PORTEOUS, N. (D.S.O. L.G. 3.6.19), T/Capt. (A/Major), R.E.; M.C.

PORTER, C. G. (D.S.O. L.G. 4.6.17), Capt. (A/Major), Can. Infy.

PORTER, C. L. (D.S.O. L.G. 1.1.18); b. 4.6.72; 2nd Lt., E. Kent R., 21.1.93; Lt. 25.10.95; Capt. 24.11.99; Maj. 16.3.12; Bt. Lt.-Col. 1.1.17; Bt. Col. 3.6.19; C.M.G.; Chitral, 1895; Medal, clasp; N.W. Frontier, 1897–98; clasp; Europ. War; Despatches.

PORTER, H. C. M. (D.S.O. L.G. 14.11.16); b. 27.10.82; s. of H. R. M. Porter (late 1st R. Dragoons) and Justine Henriette Porter (*née* Ross); educ. Eton; Sandhurst; 2nd Lt., K.R. Rif. C., 8.5.01; Lt. 16.5.05; Capt. 5.8.14; Maj. 8.5.16; S. African War; Queen's Medal, 2 clasps; Europ. War, att. to Army Cyclists' Corps and M.G. Corps, and commanding 9th Batt. K.R.R.C.; Despatches five times; Bt. Lt.-Col. 1.1.18; twice wounded. His D.S.O. was awarded for gallantry at Delville Wood on 15.9.16.

PORTER, J. H. (D.S.O. L.G. 1.1.18) (Bar, L.G. 16.9.18), Capt. (A/Lt.-Col.), N. Staffs. Rgt., T.F.

PORTER, W. G., F.R.C.S., M.B., Ch.B., B.Sc. (D.S.O. L.G. 4.6.17); b. 2.3.77, at Kumbhakonam, India; s. of William Archer Porter, Fellow of Peterhouse College, Cambridge, 3rd Wrangler, Barrister-at-Law of Lincoln's Inn, and Secretary to the late Maharajah of Mysore, and Mary Margaret Welsh, d. of the late Rev. Daniel James Welsh; m. Gwenllian Mary, d. of J. M. Cotterill, M.B., C.M., F.R.C.S., s. of the late Bishop of Edinburgh and M. J. Wynne Jones, d. of the Ven. Archdeacon Wynne Jones, of Treiorwerth Valley, Anglesey; educ. Edinburgh Academy; Edinburgh University; was a Specialist in Diseases of the Ear, Nose and Throat. As a Medical Student he was a Member of the University Cadet Corps, and he went to S. Africa as a Corporal in the R.A.M.C.; Queen's Medal with clasps; Surgeon-Lieutenant, 1st Lowland Brig., R.F.A. (T.) (formerly Midlothian Brig., R.G.A.), 16.7.07; 2nd Lt. 3.1.08; A/Major, 1917; Captain, 2nd City of Edinburgh Battery. His Brigade (1st Lowland) was sent to France, Oct. 1915. The original 2nd C. of E. Battery was attached to 86th Army F.A. Brigade at the time when Major Porter was killed. They had been in action in many parts of the line from Suzanne in the south to near Ypres in the north. On 14 March, 1917, Major Porter was slightly wounded. He was in hospital for a month, and then had three weeks' sick leave, and only returned to France on 28th May, and was killed on 8.6.17. He was mentioned in Despatches.

W. G. Porter.

POSTON, W. J. LL. (D.S.O. L.G. 14.1.16); b. 13.8.81; s. of George James Poston, J.P., and Nina Phyllis Poston (*née* Pearse), of Bishopsford, Mitcham, Surrey; m. 1st, Nellie (who died 17.2.09), d. of R. A. Pfungst; 2nd, Marjorie Blanche, widow of late Lt.-Col. E. T. F. Hood, D.S.O., R.F.A., and d. of E. Dalglish; educ. Malvern College (Cricket XI.; Racquet Pair; played for R.A. Cricket and Racquets); 2nd Lt., R.A., 5.5.00; Lt. 5.6.01; Capt. 23.4.10; Maj. 30.10.14; Bt. Lt.-Col. 3.6.19; gazetted to 134th Batty. R.F.A., 5.5.00; posted to "V" Batty. R.H.A. Dec. 1900; transferred to "D" Batty. R.H.A., Meerut, India, 1904; promoted Captain, and posted to England, April, 1910; seconded for service with Egyptian Army, Dec. 1910; served in Anuak Patrol, Southern Sudan, 1912; mentioned in Despatches; awarded 4th Class Mejidieh and Sudan Medal, 1912; appointed Hd. Qr. Staff, E.A., D.A.A.G., 1912 to Sept. 1914; posted to Home Establishment, and served in France and Belgium, Oct. 1914, to March, 1919; commanded 48th, 22nd, C/51st Batty. R.F.A.; "I" Batty. R.H.A.; Brigade Major, R.A., 12th Division and 2nd Aust. Division; commanded 29th Brigade, R.F.A., and brought it to England; commanding 73rd Batty. R.F.A.; Despatches twice; 1914 Star. His D.S.O. was awarded for Battle of Loos, action in Hohenzollern Redoubt, 26.9.15.

W. J. Ll. Poston.

POTT, D. (D.S.O. L.G. 25.8.17); b. 24.2.88; s. of Col. William Pott, of Springfields, Steyning, Sussex; educ. Wellington College; 2nd Lt., R. Muns. Fus., 6.10.06; Lt. 6.1.09; Capt., Ind. Army, 1.9.15; N.W. Frontier, 1908; Medal, clasp; Europ. War, 1914–18; Despatches; M.C.

POTT, E. H. (D.S.O. L.G. 4.6.17); b. 1880; s. of Col. William Pott, of Springfields, Steyning, Sussex; m. Louisa Medora Hermione, d. of late Hon W. A. Vanneck and sister of Lord Huntingfield; one d.; educ. Wellington College; 2nd Lt. 8.1.01; Lt., Ind. Army (1st D.Y.O. Lancers), 23.4.05; Capt. 8.1.10; Major 8.1.16; S. African War, 1901–2; Queen's Medal, 5 clasps; Europ. War, 1914–17; Despatches; Staff Captain, Secunderabad Brigade, April, 1915, and served in the 2nd Indian Cavalry Division at the 2nd Battle of Ypres, May, 1915; G.S.O.3, 1st Army, Oct. 1915; Brigade Major, 58th Infantry Brigade, 15th March, 1915, to July, 1917, and was with the 19th Division at the Battle of the Somme (La Boiselle, Bazentin-le-Petit) and the Ancre, Nov. 1916, to Feb. 1917; Wytschaete and Messines Ridge, June, 1917; Despatches twice.

The Distinguished Service Order 325

POTTER, C. F. (D.S.O. L.G. 3.6.16); b. 26.5.81; s. of late W. Furniss Potter, of Arundel Lodge, Ilkley, Yorks; m. 1920, Ann Janet Baird (who died in 1920), widow of F. G. Linn; 2nd Lt., R.A., 6.1.00; Lt. 3.4.01; Capt. 5.5.08; Maj. 30.10.14; Lt.-Col. 1.7.21; *p.s.c.*; served S. African War, 1902; Queen's Medal and four clasps; Europ. War from 1914; wounded; Despatches; Bt. Lt.-Col. 3.6.17; C.M.G.

POTTER, C. K. (D.S.O. L.G. 26.9.17) (Details, L.G. 9.1.18) (Bar, L.G. 16.9.18), Major (A/Lt.-Col.), N. Lancs. Rgt.; S. African War, 1901–2; Queen's Medal, 3 clasps; Europ. War; Despatches; M.C.

POTTER, HERBERT CECIL (Christian name altered to Herbert from Hubert, L.G. 18.2.18) (D.S.O. L.G. 1.1.17); b. 10.10.75; m. d. of late Rev. Moule Griffith; one d.; 2nd Lt., L'pool R., 29.2.96; Lt. 2.3.99; Capt. 5.12.00; Maj. 1.9.15; Bt. Lt.-Col. 1.1.16; Bt. Col. 3.6.18; Temp. Col. Comdr. 17.7.21; served S. African War, 1901–2; Queen's Medal and 3 clasps; Sudan, 1908; Medal and clasp; 4th Class Osmanieh; Europ. War, 1914–18; Despatches; C.M.G.

POTTER, J. (D.S.O. L.G. 27.7.16); b. 25.8.94; s. of William Manuel Potter and Mary Potter; educ. at Southborough; at Tunbridge Wells, Kent, and at Clifton College, and joined the R.A.M.C. on 4.8.14; commissioned in the 1st S. Staffs. Rgt., Dec. 1915; served on Western front; Despatches. His D.S.O. was awarded for gallantry at Mametz on 1.7.16. He died of wounds on 24.7.16.

POTTER, J. W. (D.S.O. L.G. 8.3.19) (Details, L.G. 4.10.19), Lt. (A/Capt.), 1/5th Batt., att. 1/6th Batt., Notts. and Derby. Rgt., T.F.

POTTER, K. M. (D.S.O. L.G. 25.8.17); b. 25.4.82; 3rd s. of late W. Furniss Potter and of Mrs. Furniss Potter; educ. Marlborough College, and passed into Woolwich at the end of 1899; 2nd Lt., R.F.A., 23.7.01; Lt. 23.7.04; Capt. 23.7.14; Major 15.11.15. His D.S.O. was awarded for gallantry on the night of 1.6.17, and he was killed in action on 8.7.17.

POTTER, W. A. (D.S.O. L.G. 1.1.17); s. of late Tom Potter, J.P.; m. Margaret, d. of J. Forman; two d.; Lt.-Colonel, R.A.S.C., T.F.; served Europ. War, 1914–18.

POTTINGER, ELDRED CHARLES (D.S.O. L.G. 1.1.18) (Christian name corrected to Eldred for Edward); b. 28.5.68; commissioned R.A. 23.7.87; Maj. 10.12.02; retired 4.3.17; China, 1900; S. African War, 1902; Queen's Medal, 3 clasps; Europ. War; Despatches.

POTTS, J. (D.S.O. L.G. 18.7.17), T/2nd Lt. (A/Capt.), Durham L.I. His D.S.O. was awarded for gallantry on 22.4.17, at Hill 70, near Loos.

POUNTNEY, F. S. (D.S.O. L.G. 3.6.18), Capt. (A/Lt.-Col.), London Rgt.

POUPORE, A. G. (D.S.O. L.G. 4.6.17), Major, Can. Infantry.

POW, J. (D.S.O. L.G. 1.1.17), Colonel, N.Z. Rifle Brigade; Organizing Secretary of the New Zealand Returned Soldiers' Association.

POWELL, A. H. (D.S.O. L.G. 4.6.17), Capt., Aust. A.M.C.

POWELL, A. T. (D.S.O. L.G. 1.1.18), Major, Can. Infy.

POWELL, D. W. (D.S.O. L.G. 2.12.18); b. 8.7.78; 2nd Lt., North'n Rgt., 17.2.00; Lt. 11.3.03; Capt. 1.12.08; Major 1.9.15; A/Lt.-Col. 15.8.17.

POWELL, E. B. (D.S.O. L.G. 1.1.18); b. 11.6.78; 2nd Lt., Rif. Brig., 18.10.99; Lt. 1.8.00; Capt. 23.1.05; Maj. 15.6.15; *p.s.c.*; S. African War; Queen's Medal, 6 clasps; King's Medal, 2 clasps.

POWELL, E. D. (D.S.O. L.G. 3.6.18); s. of the late E. F. Powell (Wyndsor, Co. Mayo) and Mrs. Powell, of 33, Addison Court Gardens, Kensington; m. Gwennie, d. of the late William Ireland de Courcy Wheeler, President of the Royal College of Surgeons, Dublin. He was a Graduate of Trinity College, Dublin, where he qualified as a Civil Engineer. In the first year of the war he returned from employment in Ceylon to join the Army, and was commissioned in the R.E. in May, 1915. During three and a half years of active service his professional ability and personal bravery were given recognition. He was promoted Captain in 1916; was twice mentioned in Despatches, and received the Military Cross for his gallantry in action in 1917. In 1918 he was promoted Major, and awarded the D.S.O. Major Powell was reported "wounded and missing" on 1.9.18, and was later presumed to have been killed near Bethune on that date.

POWELL, E. E. (D.S.O. L.G. 1.1.18); b. 3.11.64; Capt., R.A.M.C., 31.1.91; Maj. 31.1.03; Lt.-Col. 26.9.16; Bt. Col. 1.1.19; ret. 3.11.21; Chitral, 1895; Medal, clasp; S. African War, 1900–2; Queen's Medal, 3 clasps; King's Medal, 2 clasps; Europ. War; Despatches.

POWELL, G. (D.S.O. L.G. 16.9.18); s. of T. Powell, of Worksop; 2nd Lt., Notts. and Derby Rgt.

POWELL, H. E. (D.S.O. L.G. 3.6.18), Capt. (T/Major), A.V.C. (now R.A.V.C.). His D.S.O. was awarded for services in the advance in Palestine when with the Veterinary Service in the Egyptian Exp. Force.

POWELL, H. LL. (D.S.O. L.G. 11.1.19), Lt.-Col., 215th Brig., R.F.A., T.F.

POWELL, JAMES (D.S.O. L.G. 27.6.19), Lt.-Cdr., R.N.

POWELL, JOHN, B.A., M.B., B.Ch. (D.S.O. L.G. 3.6.18) (Bar, L.G. 26.7.18); b. 30.7.76; s. of J. C. Powell and Susan Margaret Powell (*née* Prentice); m. Elsie Kate Barrass; one s.; one d.; educ. Cambridge (priv. school); Trinity College, Dublin; Lt., R.A.M.C., 25.4.00; Capt. 25.4.03; Maj. 25.1.12; Lt.-Col. 26.12.17; Bt. Col. 3.6.19; S. African War, 1900–2; Queen's Medal, 3 clasps; King's Medal, 2 clasps; European War, Egypt, France; Despatches three times; 4th Class Order of Osmanieh; 3rd Class Order of the Nile; M.C.

POWELL, J. E. (D.S.O. L.G. 4.6.17); b. 23.10.75; Lt., R.A.M.C., 31.8.03; Capt. 28.2.07; Maj. 28.2.15; China, 1900; Europ. War; Despatches.

POWELL, P. L. W. (D.S.O. L.G. 3.6.16); b. 24.4.82; s. of Col. L. L. Powell; m. Maud M. Wells-Dymoke; educ. privately; Sandhurst; 2nd Lt., Unatt., 8.1.01; Lt. 10.3.04; Capt. 15.5.11; Maj. 8.1.16; *p.s.c.*; served S. African War, 1901–2; Queen's Medal, 2 clasps; Europ. War, Aug. 1914–18; Despatches; Bt. Lt.-Col. 3.6.18; C.B.E.

POWELL, R. ff. (D.S.O. L.G. 14.1.16); b. 16.5.80; s. of Commander R. ff. Powell, R.N., and Annie Powell (*née* Watson); m. Alice Katharine Beatrix, d. of G. Shedden, J.P.; three s.; one d.; educ. Wellington College; 2nd Lt., R.A., 8.9.00; Lt. 8.9.03; Capt. 1.4.12; Maj. 9.4.15; Europ. War, in France, from Aug. 1914, serving through Mons, Marne, the Aisne, Ypres, Festubert, Loos, on the Somme, etc.; Despatches.

POWELL, RANDOLPH MACHATTIE (D.S.O. L.G. 1.1.18); s. of late H. W. Powell, and g.s. of late R. Machattie, M.D., of Bathurst, N.S. Wales; m. Clara Carew, M.B.E., widow of C. J. Tetley, of La Chacra, Ameghino, Buenos Aires, and Ledge Hill, near Farnham, Surrey, and d. of Lt.-Col. Corry-Smith; T/Major, R.G.A.; Bt. Lt.-Col.; served Europ. War, 1914–18; Despatches; Order of Crown of Italy.

POWELL, ROBERT MONTAGU (D.S.O. L.G. 1.1.17); b. 19.5.81; 2nd Lt., R.A., 6.1.00; Lt. 3.4.01; Capt. 6.5.08; Maj. 11.6.15; Bt. Lt.-Col. 3.6.18; S. African War, 1901–2; Queen's Medal, 5 clasps; Europ. War; Despatches.

POWELL, W. B. (D.S.O. L.G. 23.10.19); b. 28.2.86; ent. Middlesex R. 14.9.87; Lt. 10.3.89; Capt. 14.9.98; Major 14.9.05; Lt.-Col. 14.9.18; retired 5.5.20, late Gurkha Rifles; served Europ. War, Mesopotamia, 1914–16; C.M.G.

POWELL, W. H. (D.S.O. L.G. 1.1.17); b. 1.3.88; 2nd Lt., R.A., 22.12.14; Lt. 8.8.16; Actg. Maj.

POWELL-EDWARDS, H. I. (see Edwards H. I. Powell-).

POWER, J. J. (D.S.O. L.G. 1.1.18), Major, Aust. A.M.C.

POWER, M. S. (D.S.O. L.G. 1.1.17), T/Major, S. African Medical Corps.

POWER, R. E. (D.S.O. L.G. 4.2.18) (Details, L.G. 5.7.18); b. 22.5.74; 2nd Lt., E. Kent R., 21.10.93; Lt. 17.3.97; Capt. 24.2.00; Capt. 4.8.14; Bt. Maj. 3.6.19; Chitral, 1895; Medal, clasp; N.W. Frontier, 1897–98; clasp; Aden, 1904; S. Nigeria, 1905–6; Europ. War; Despatches.

POWER, T. (D.S.O. L.G. 1.1.18), Major, M.L.B.

POWERS, T. E. (D.S.O. L.G. 1.1.17), Major, Can. Divisional Signal Company.

POWLES, C. G. (D.S.O. L.G. 3.6.16); b. 1872; m. Jessie Mary Richardson; educ. Wellington College, N.Z.; served S. African War, 1900–1; Queen's Medal, 4 clasps; served Europ. War, 1914–18, as Major (T/Lt.-Col.), Staff Corps, N.Z. Imp. Force; C.M.G.

POWNALL, H. R. (D.S.O. L.G. 1.1.18); b. 19.11.87; s. of C. A. W. Pownall; m. Lucy Loutit, widow of Capt. J. Gray, 36th Sikhs, and d. of late William Henderson and Mrs. Henderson, of Aberdeen; educ. Rugby School; R.M.A., Woolwich; 2nd Lt., R.A., 20.12.06; Lt. 20.12.09; Capt. 30.10.14; Major, R.F.A., 31.3.17; served Europ. War, "A" Battery, R.H.A., from Oct. 1914; commanded "C" Battery, 91st Brig., R.F.A., from Jan. 1915; Bde. Major, R.A., 17th Div., from April, 1917; Despatches twice; M.C.

POYNTZ, H. S. (D.S.O. L.G. 1.1.17); b. 17.9.77; s. of late Major W. H. Poyntz, R.M.L.I., and Henrietta Emily Stainton Poyntz; m. Hilda Gwendoline, d. of A. Thackeray; one s.; one d.; educ. Eastbourne College; 2nd Lt., Bedfords. Rgt., 20.5.99; Lt. 8.4.00; Capt. 13.1.07; Major 18.5.15; Bt. Lt.-Col. 1.1.19; S. African War, 1899–1902; Queen's Medal, 3 clasps; King's Medal, 2 clasps; Europ. War; commanded the 2nd Batt. Bedfordshire Regt. from Nov. 1915, to April, 1917 (returned home sick), and from Dec. 1917, to April, 1918; Despatches twice; Captain of Army Football Team (Association), 1907; played Cricket for Somerset County from 1905–13.

POYSER, K. E. (D.S.O. L.G. 1.1.17); Barrister-at-Law; served Europ. War; Capt., Yorks. L.I.; A/Lt.-Col., L.N. Lancs. Rgt.; Despatches.

PRAGNELL, T. W. (D.S.O. L.G. 1.1.17); b. 12.1.83; s. of late G. W. Pragnell; m. Ida, d. of Rt. Hon. Sir W. J. Goulding, Bart.; one s.; one d.; 2nd Lt., Border Rgt., 1900; 2nd Lt., 4th Hussars, 26.3.02; Lt. 1.2.05; Capt. 24.2.12; Major 9.4.18; Lt.-Col., 4th Hussars; served operations in N. Nigeria, 1911; Europ. War, 1914–18; Despatches; Bt. Lt.-Col. 3.6.19.

PRANCE, R. C. (D.S.O. L.G. 14.1.16); b. 19.2.82; 2nd Lt., R.A., 2.5.00; Lt. 3.4.01; Capt. 13.2.10; Maj. 30.10.14; S. African War, 1902; Queen's Medal, 4 clasps; Europ. War, France, Salonika, Egypt; Despatches.

PRATT, A. C. (D.S.O. L.G. 1.1.17); b. 13.5.74; s. of J. Pratt, D.L.; educ. Harrow; 2nd Lt., R. Scots.; Capt. 3.11.02; ret. pay 20.8.13; S. African War, 1900–2; Despatches; Queen's Medal, 3 clasps; King's Medal, 2 clasps; Europ. War from 1914; T/Lt.-Col., R. Inniskilling Fusiliers. He died of wounds 16.8.17.

PRATT, A. G. (D.S.O. L.G. 14.1.16); b. 3.6.72; s. of late Rev. T. A. C. Pratt, of West Harling Rectory, Norfolk; educ. Bradfield College; 2nd Lt., 1st Batt. Essex R., 26.4.93; Lt. 8.7.97; Capt. 9.10.00; Major 5.5.15; Lt.-Col., ret. pay, 6.5.20; served S. African War, 1899–1902, as Adjt., 1st Batt.; twice severely wounded; Despatches twice; Queen's Medal with 6 clasps; King's Medal with 2 clasps; Bt. Maj. 29.11.00; Europ. War, 1914–17; on the Staff and in command of 2nd Batt. Essex Rgt.; severely wounded, Oct. 1917; Despatches twice; Bt. Lt.-Col. 1.1.17.

PRATT, A. W. (D.S.O. L.G. 1.2.19), Major, 116th Batt. Can. Inf., 2nd Central Ontario Rgt.

PRATT, D. H. (D.S.O. L.G. 18.2.18) (Details, L.G. 18.7.18); b. 7.10.92; 2nd Lt., R. Ir. Regt., 20.9.11; Lt. 15.4.14; Capt. 1.10.15; M.C.

PRATT, O. S. (D.S.O. L.G. 3.6.18), T/Major, Midd'x Rgt.

PRATT, R. E. B. (D.S.O. L.G. 1.1.17); b. 5.2.82; 2nd Lt., R.E., 2.5.00; Lt. 2.5.03; Capt. 31.10.11; Maj. 2.11.16.

PRECHTEL, A. F. (D.S.O. L.G. 1.1.17), Lt.-Col., R.F.A.

PREEDY, F. (D.S.O. L.G. 1.1.17); b. 17.4.87; s. of late F. Preedy; m. Mary Caroline, d. of late A. S. Orlebar; educ. The Grange, Crowborough; Dover College; R.M.A., Woolwich; 2nd Lt., R.E., 20.12.06; Lt., R.E., 6.1.09; Capt., R.E., 30.10.14; served Europ. War, France, from 1914; Despatches six times; Bt. Major 3.6.16; M.C.

PREESTON, N. P. R. (D.S.O. L.G. 3.6.18); b. 7.12.80; 2nd Lt., R.A., 22.11.99; Lt. 16.2.01; Capt. 1.4.08; Maj. 30.10.14; Bt. Lt.-Col. 3.6.19; Lt.-Col. 6.4.21; S. African War, 1899–1901; Queen's Medal, 2 clasps; Europ. War; Despatches.

PRENDERGAST, N. H. (D.S.O. L.G. 29.11.19); b. 7.11.86; 2nd Lt., Unatt., 24.1.06; I.A., 6.4.07; Lt. 24.4.08; Capt. 24.1.15; Major 24.1.21; served N.W. Frontier of India, 1908; operations in the Mohmand Country; Medal with clasp.

PRENTICE, R. E. S. (D.S.O. L.G. 3.6.16); b. 17.2.72; s. of R. R. Prentice; m. Violet Rosabelle, d. of Brig.-Gen. J. H. S. Craigie, late H.L.I.; one s.; two d.; educ. Loretto School, Musselburgh; 2nd Lt., H.L.I., 7.12.92; Lt. 16.8.95; Capt. 1.8.00; Adjt., 2nd H.L.I., 1901–5; Maj. 4.9.12; Lt.-Col. 4.11.19; Temp. Brig.-Gen. 16.7.16; served Indian Frontier Campaign, 1897–98; Medal with clasp; Europ. War, 1914–18; Bde. Major, 2nd Bde., B.E.F., Feb. to April, 1915; Bde. Commander, 188th Brigade, B.E.F., July, 1916; wounded; Despatches five times; Bt. Lt.-Col. 1.1.17; C.B.; C.M.G. He has King Edward VII.'s Coronation Medal; appointed to command 1st Batt. H.L.I. on 11.11.19.

PRENTIS, W. S. (D.S.O. L.G. 15.2.19) (Details, L.G. 30.7.19); b. 5.8.70; 2nd Lt., Oxf. L.I., 21.9.89; Lt. 2.5.92; Capt. 21.9.00; Maj. 21.9.07; Lt.-Col. 21.9.15; Col. 12.9.19; ret. pay 26.10.21; China, 1900; Medal; Europ. War; Despatches.

PRESCOTT, A. E. (D.S.O. L.G. 1.1.18), Lt.-Col., R.E.; served Europ. War from 1916; Despatches; Legion of Honour.

PRESCOTT-DECIE, C. (D.S.O. L.G. 4.6.17); b. 4.8.65; s. of Col. R. Prescott-Decie; m. Margaret Elizabeth, d. of late Major F. H. de Vere, R.E., and widow of F. Joyce; educ. Clifton College; R.M.A., Woolwich; Lt., R.A., 29.4.85; Capt. 1.4.95; Major 29.6.00; Lt.-Col. 1.4.12; Colonel 1.4.16; Brig.-General, ret. pay, 1.4.20; served S. African War, Actions of Colenso, Spion Kop, Vaal Kranz and Relief of Ladysmith; Queen's Medal, 2 clasps; commanded Artillery of 1st Indian Division at Peshawar, 1915; operations against Frontier tribes, actions of Shabkadr, Sept. and Oct. 1915; served Europ. War, 1916–17; commanded Artillery, 4th Div., in France; severely wounded.

PRESCOTT-WESTCAR, W. V. L. (D.S.O. L.G. 14.11.16); b. 18.9.82; s. of C. W. Prescott-Westcar, of Stoke Park, Herne, Kent; educ. Wellington College; Sandhurst; 2nd Lt., Unatt., 8.1.01; 2nd Lt., Rif. Brig., 9.3.01; Lt. 1.4.04; Capt. 8.12.10; Major 8.1.16; served S. African War, 1901–2; Queen's Medal, 3 clasps; Europ. War, with Rifle Brigade, and the 10th Rifle Brigade and the M.G.C.; wounded; Despatches. His D.S.O. was awarded for gallantry at Guillemont, on 3.9.16.

W. V. L. Prescott-Westcar.

PRESTON, C. O'D. (D.S.O. L.G. 1.1.18); b. 17.9.86; s. of Sidney and Amy Preston; m. Aimée Marguerite Maitland-Kirwan; one s.; educ. Malvern; R.M.A., Woolwich; 2nd Lt., R.A., 20.12.06; Lt. 20.12.09; Capt. 30.10.14; Maj. 6.4.17; served Europ. War, 1914–18; Despatches.

PRESTON, SIR E. H., Bart. (D.S.O. L.G. 1.1.19); b. 17.9.88; s. of 3rd Bart. and Mary Hope, d. of late E. L. Clutterbuck, of Hardenhuish Park, Wilts; succeeded brother as 5th Bart., 1918; m. Margaret, d. of late B. Bond-Cabbell, of Cromer Hall, Norfolk; 2nd Lt., R. Suss. R., 11.12.09; Lt. 26.4.11; Capt. 11.12.15; Bt. Maj. 1.1.18; ret. pay 9.7.19; served Europ. War, 1914–18; Despatches; M.C.

PRESTON, E. M. (D.S.O. L.G. 15.2.19) (Details, L.G. 30.7.19), Lt., Can. Infantry, 87th Batt. Quebec R.; M.M.

PRESTON, J. (D.S.O. L.G. 26.11.17) (Details, L.G. 6.4.18); b. 1894; s. of T. Preston, of Coatbridge, Lanark; enlisted 1914; Lt., Sc. Rifles, 1916; served Europ. War; twice wounded.

PRESTON, HON. R. M. P. (D.S.O. L.G. 4.6.17) (Bar, L.G. 27.10.17) (Details, L.G. 18.3.18); b. 12.8.84; s. of the late Viscount Gormanston, G.C.M.G.; brother of 15th Viscount; m. Belle, d. of late F. H. Hamblin; two s.; two d.; educ. Oratory School; R.M.A., Woolwich; formerly Lt., R.A.; Lt.-Colonel, R.H.A.; served Europ. War, 1914–18; Despatches five times. He has written "The Desert Mounted Corps," 1921.

PRESTON, W. J. P. (D.S.O. L.G. 22.12.16); b. 11.6.73; s. of late Surgeon-Genl. A. F. Preston, K.H.P., A.M.S.; m. Ina, d. of late Rt. Hon. Sir C. Nixon, 1st Bart., P.C., M.D., Vice-Chancellor of the National University of Ireland; one s.; educ. St. Helen's College, Southsea; R.M.C., Sandhurst; 2nd Lt., 2nd Batt. Middx. Rgt., 31.8.92; Lt. 1.12.94; Capt., Ind. Army, 31.8.01; Major 31.8.10; Lt.-Col. 31.8.18; served Europ. War in Mesopotamia, in temporary command of 97th Deccan Inf.; severely wounded; Despatches; Afghanistan and Indian Frontier, 1919; with Baluchistan Field Force; O.B.E.

PRESTON-WHITE, R. P. (D.S.O. L.G. 4.6.17), T/Major (A/Lt.-Col.), Somerset L.I.

PRETOR-PINNEY, C. F. (D.S.O. L.G. 1.1.17); b. 1864; eldest s. of late Col. F. W. Pretor-Pinney; m. Phyllis Julia, d. of Vincent Stuckey; educ. Eton; Cambridge; commissioned in the Rifle Brigade, and before the S. African War he had retired with the rank of Captain, but rejoined on the outbreak of that war, and saw considerable service (Queen's Medal, 3 clasps). At the conclusion of peace he retired with the rank of Major, and rejoined the Rifle Brigade, 1914, being gazetted Captain, and soon afterwards promoted Major. In Oct. 1914, he was appointed to the command of a battalion of that regiment, and in July, 1915, took it to the front. A year afterwards he was wounded. He resumed the command of his battalion at the front in Feb. 1917. Lt.-Colonel Pretor-Pinney died on 28.4.17, of wounds received four days previously.

PRETORIUS, H. S. (D.S.O. L.G. 22.8.18), Major, 4th Mounted Brigade, Supernumerary List, S. African Forces.

PRETORIUS, N. J. (D.S.O. L.G. 22.8.18), Lt.-Col., Western Transvaal Ruiters, S. African Forces.

PRETORIUS, P. J. (D.S.O. L.G. 25.11.16) (Bar, L.G. 17.12.17) (Details, L.G. 23.4.18), Major, E. African Protectorate Forces, att. Intelligence Dept.

PRETTEJOHN, N. K. (D.S.O. L.G. 22.8.18), Major, Supernumerary List, S. African Forces.

PRIAULX, G. K. (D.S.O. L.G. 18.6.17); b. 15.9.77; 2nd s. of O. de L. Priaulx; educ. at Harrow and Sandhurst; commissioned 60th Rifles 23.2.98; Lt. 21.10.99; Capt. 22.1.02. He fought through the S. African War, 1899–1902 (Despatches twice; Queen's Medal, 6 clasps; King's Medal, 2 clasps). He went to France in Aug. 1914, and was dangerously wounded in Sept. of that year, and again in Sept. 1915, at Loos, when he was in command of his battalion. After his recovery he was appointed to the command of another battalion, and in March, 1917, won the D.S.O. Lt.-Col. Priaulx was killed in action on 25.3.18.

PRICE, C. B. (D.S.O. L.G. 8.3.19) (Details, L.G. 4.10.19), Major, 14th Inf. Batt. Quebec R., Can. Forces; D.C.M.

PRICE, E. E. (D.S.O. L.G. 26.3.18) (Details, L.G. 24.8.18), Lt., R. Can. Dragoons; M.C.

PRICE, F. P. HOWELL- (see Howell-Price, (F. P.).

PRICE, I. H., M.A., LL.D. (D.S.O. L.G. 24.1.17); b. 18.3.66; s. of James Price, M.A., and Frances Alicia Price (*née* Peebles); m. Margaret Emily, d. of late G. Kinahan, D.L.; six sons; two daughters; the 2nd son, Lt. Ernest Dickenson Price, R.I.R., was killed in action in France, 19.1.16; educ. Trinity College, Dublin. He joined the Army 5.8.14; T/Major, Special List, retiring with the Bt. of Lt.-Colonel.

PRICE, J. HOWELL- (see Howell-Price, J.).

PRICE, O. G. HOWELL- (see Howell-Price, O. G.).

PRICE, O. LL. (D.S.O. L.G. 4.6.17); b. 24.4.77; 2nd Lt., R.A., 23.3.97; Lt. 23.3.00; Capt. 31.1.02; Maj. 30.10.14; Lt.-Col. 1.5.21.

PRICE, P. Ll. HOWELL- (see Howell-Price, P. Ll.).

PRICE, R. B., M.B. (D.S.O. L.G. 22.6.18); b. 19.12.85; Lt., R.A.M.C., 26.7.12; Capt. 30.3.15.

PRICE, T. E. (D.S.O. L.G. 22.6.17), Lt., R.N.R.; D.S.C.

PRICE, T. H. F. (D.S.O. L.G. 1.1.17); b. 29.6.69; s. of Sir J. Frederick Price, K.C.S.I., and Alice, d. of Hon. H. D. Phillips, Member of Council, Fort St. George, Madras; m. Lurline May, d. of Hon. H. Moses, M.L.C., Sydney, N.S.W., and widow of Major J. A. Higgon, Pembrokeshire Yeomanry and R.W.F.; 2nd Lt., D.C.L.I., 15.3.93; Lt. 20.5.96; Capt. 8.7.01; Major 18.9.12; Lt.-Col. 5.2.18; Brig.-Gen., retired pay, 12.1.21; served Tirah Exp., 1897–98; Medal, 2 clasps; S. African War, 1902; Queen's Medal, 2 clasps; Europ. War from 1914; Despatches; Bt. Lt.-Col. 18.2.15; C.M.G.

PRICE, T. R. (D.S.O. L.G. 17.4.17); b. 15.9.94; s. of Rev. T. J. Price, B.A.; educ. Kingswood School, Bath; Temp. Lt. 15.7.16; Lt., North'n R., 16.12.16; served in France; Despatches; thrice wounded, Loos, 1915; Somme, 1917, and German advance, 1918; M.C. and Bar; seconded to Tank Corps.

PRICE, T. R. C. (D.S.O. L.G. 1.1.17); b. 2.8.75; s. of late Col. T. Price, C.B.; m. Dorothy, d. of Sir Henry Verey; two s.; one d.; educ. Melbourne; R.M.C., Sandhurst; 2nd Lt., R.W. Kent R., 10.10.94; Lt. 27.5.96; Capt., Ind. Army, 10.10.03; Maj. 10.10.12; W. Gds. 10.5.15; Lt.-Col. 14.12.20; Temp. Brig.-Gen. 6.8.18 to 14.4.19; *p.s.c.*; Commanding 1st Batt. Welsh Guards; served N.W. Frontier Campaign, 1897–98; Medal, clasp; Tibet Exp., 1903–4; Medal; G.S., Army H.Q. of India, 1913–14; served Europ. War, in France, on General Staff, with Batt., and in command 114th Inf. Brig., 1914–19; Despatches; C.M.G.; Bt. Lt.-Col. 1.1.18; Chevalier, Légion d'Honneur. He is a tournament polo player and winner of races in India across country.

PRICE-WILLIAMS, H. (D.S.O. L.G. 16.9.18); b. 23.10.92; s. of S. Price-Williams, M.Inst.C.E.; m. Constance Maud, d. of W. C. Crawshay; educ. Repton; R.M.A., Woolwich; passed out of Woolwich at the top of the Artillery List, and obtained the Tombs Memorial Scholarship; 2nd Lt., R.A., 19.7.12; Adjt., R.A., 1.4.15–15.10.17; Lt. 9.6.15; Capt. 8.8.16 (9th Battery); was at Landrecies and the Aisne, and was badly wounded at Ypres on 21.10.14; M.C. His D.S.O. was awarded for re-establishing communication with his battery on 23.8.14 at Mons. The following is an extract from a letter from his Commanding Officer: ". . . how you managed to re-establish communication that was broken during the action at Givry, near Mons, when your battery was detailed with the 5th Brigade. I must congratulate you on having performed your duty with much courage and credit."

PRICHARD, H. V. HESKETH- (see Hesketh-Prichard, H. V.).

PRICHARD, W. C. H. (D.S.O. L.G. 1.1.18); b. 10.11.83; 2nd Lt., R.E., 21.12.01; Lt. 24.9.04; Capt. 21.12.12; Maj. 21.12.16; Bt. Lt.-Col. 3.6.19.

PRIDEAUX, H. H., M.A. (D.S.O. L.G. 3.6.18); b. 19.1.78; s. of Sir W. S. Prideaux, of Goldsmith's Hall, E.C.2, and Catharine, d. of the late Rev. J. V. Povah, Minor Canon of St. Paul's; educ. Eton; Trinity College, Oxford; Ranks, 3rd Norfolk Rgt., Aug. 1914–Jan. 1915; Lt. 10.1.15; Capt., 3rd (S.R.) Batt. North'd Fusiliers, 26.2.15; Major, North'd Fus.; served Europ. War; in France and Belgium from July, 1915, to July, 1919; Staff Capt., 9th Inf. Brig., March–31.10.16; D.A.A.G., 2nd Anzac (afterwards XXII. Corps), 1.11.16–8.7.19; Despatches thrice; M.C.; Belgian Croix de Guerre.

PRIDEAUX-BRUNE, D. E. (D.S.O. L.G. 18.7.17) (Bar, L.G. 26.7.18); b. 18.6.91; s. of Col. C. R. Prideaux-Brune, D.L., J.P., and the Hon. Katharine Cecilia, d. of 1st Baron Brabourne; m. Cecely Alice, d. of Sir P. Grey Egerton, Bart.; one d.; educ. Eton; R.M.C., Sandhurst; 2nd Lt., Rif. Brig., 4.3.11; Lt. 1.2.13; Capt. 10.5.15; Bt. Maj. 3.6.16; Despatches.

PRIDGEON, A. F. (D.S.O. L.G. 7.2.18); b. 19.2.61; Hon. Commission, 14th Hrs., 16.1.01; Hon. Lt.-Col. Qr.-Mstr., ret. pay, 1.1.19; S. African War, 1899–1902; Despatches; Queen's Medal, 7 clasps; King's Medal, 2 clasps; D.C.M.

PRIDHAM, G. R. (D.S.O. L.G. 1.1.17); b. 4.10.72; s. of late Col. F. Pridham m. Mignonne Muriel Maude, d. of late C. L. B. Cumming, I.C.S., and widow of Major John Chrystie, R.G.A.; one d.; 2nd Lt., R.E., 12.2.92; Lt. 12.2.95; Capt. 12.2.03; Maj. 12.2.12; Lt.-Col. 31.7.20; Tirah Exp., 1897–98; Medal, clasp; China, 1900; Europ. War; Despatches; O.B.E.; Bt. Lt.-Col. 8.11.15.

PRIDIE, E. D. (D.S.O. L.G. 15.10.18); s. of Dr. J. F. Pridie. At the outbreak of war Capt. Pridie held a temporary commission in the King's Own R. Lancs. Rgt. He went to France in July, 1915, and after 18 months' service he was invalided home. In March, 1918, he was sent to Mesopotamia. The troopship in which he was travelling was torpedoed, and after some considerable time in the water he was picked up by a destroyer. His D.S.O. was awarded for gallantry and devotion to duty in connection with operations to the north of Baghdad in April, 1918.

PRIESTLEY, J. H., B.Sc., F.L.S. (D.S.O. L.G. 4.6.17); b. Tewkesbury, 5.10.83; s. of J. E. Priestley, Headmaster of Tewkesbury Grammar School, and Henrietta, d. of William Rice; m. Marion Ethel, d. of R. A. Young; educ. Tewkesbury Grammar School; University College, Bristol; Professor of Botany, University of Leeds, from 1911; Lt. 15.1.12, when he was attached to the Leeds O.T.C.; served from Aug. 1914, with B.E.F., as Capt., T.F., Unattached List; on G.S. (Intelligence), Aug. 1915–Jan. 1919; demobilized 25.1.19; Despatches twice; Croix de Chevalier de la Couronne (Belgium).

PRIESTMAN, J. H. T. (D.S.O. L.G. 26.9.17) (Details, L.G. 9.1.18); b. 22.7.85; 2nd Lt., Linc. R., 29.11.05; Lt. 8.10.10; Capt. 4.8.14; Bt. Maj. 1.1.19; *p.s.c.*

PRINCE, P. (D.S.O. L.G. 1.1.18); b. 18.10.82; 2nd Lt., Shrops. L.I., 18.1.02; Lt. 15.9.06; Capt. 5.8.14; Maj. 18.1.17; S. African War, 1902; Queen's Medal, 4 clasps; Europ. War; Despatches.

PRINCE, P. E. (D.S.O. L.G. 26.8.18); b. 27.4.82; 2nd Lt., R.E., 18.8.00; Lt. 18.8.03; Capt. 18.8.10; Maj. 2.11.16.

PRING, B. V. (D.S.O. L.G. 8.3.19) (Details, L.G. 4.10.19); b. 8.5.85; m. Ethel Lilian, d. of C. Roberts; three d.; educ. St. Luke's College, Exeter; 2nd Lt., K.O.Y.L.I., 10.11.14; A/Capt., K.O.Y.L.I., att. 2nd Batt.; Despatches; M.C. and Bar.

PRINGLE, H. G. (D.S.O. L.G. 1.1.17); b. 1876; m. Mrs. Ridley, widow of Capt. C. N. Ridley, Yeomanry; one d.; 2nd Lt., R.A., 21.3.96; Lt. 21.3.99; Capt. 20.1.02; Maj. 5.10.12; Lt.-Col. 3.1.17; Col. 8.2.19; *p.s.c.*; served China, 1900; N. Nigeria, 1901–2; Medal and clasp; Europ. War, 1914–17; Despatches; Order of Aviz of Portugal; Rising Sun of Japan; Bt. Lt.-Col. 3.1.17.

PRINGLE, R. N. (D.S.O. L.G. 4.6.17), Major (A/Lt.-Col.), S. African Forces; S. African War, 1900–1; Queen's Medal, 3 clasps; Europ. War; Despatches.

PRIOR, B. H. L. (D.S.O. L.G. 4.6.17) (Bar, L.G. 26.7.18); served S. African War, 1900–1; Queen's Medal, 4 clasps; Europ. War; Despatches.

PRIOR, E. R. S. (D.S.O. L.G. 1.1.18), T/Major (A/Lt.-Col.), S. Lancs. R.; M.C. He was reported missing 25.5.18, and his death was later accepted.

PRIOR, G. E. R. (D.S.O. L.G. 15.2.19) (Details, L.G. 30.7.19); b. 2.12.85; 2nd Lt., Devon. R., 23.5.06; Lt. 18.11.09; Capt. 6.5.15; Bt. Maj. 3.6.18; M.C.

PRIOR, H. A. S. (D.S.O. L.G. 3.6.16), T/Major, Yorks. Rgt., S. Batt.

PRIOR, J. H. (D.S.O. L.G. 27.9.01) (Bar, L.G. 16.9.18), Major, R.E., S.R. (see "The Distinguished Service Order," from its institution to 31.12.15, by same publishers).

F. C. R. Prior-Wandesforde.

PRIOR-WANDESFORDE, F. C. R. (D.S.O. L.G. 19.11.17) Bar, L.G. 22.3.18); b. 23.10.97; s. of R. H. Prior-Wandesforde, J.P., D.L., Capt. (Hon.), R.F.A., of Castlecomer House, Co. Kilkenny, and Kirklington Hall and Hipswell Lodge, Yorks, and of Florence Jackson

Prior-Wandesforde, d. of the late Rev. W. F. Prior, of Halifax, Nova Scotia; educ. at Mourne Grange, Co. Down, Ireland; Rugby School; was in the Rugby Shooting VIII., 1913, when Rugby won the Rapid Firing at Bisley and was 2nd for the Ashburton Shield; was in the Rugby VIII. again in 1914; passed the entrance examination into Cambridge, June, 1915, but, instead of taking up residence, volunteered for active service and joined the Cadet Corps at St. John's Wood, London, 28.5.16; T/2nd Lieut., R.F.A., 10.9.16; was granted a regular commission in June, 1917; Lt. 10.1.19; T/Capt., May, 1918.

PRITCHARD, C. G. (D.S.O. L.G. 1.1.17); b. Mussoorie, 10.8.71; s. of late Lt.-Gen. Sir Gordon Douglas Pritchard, K.C.B., Col.-Commandant, R.E., and late Agnes Maria, d. of W. H. Cox, J.P.; m. Edith, d. of Rev. J. Ellershaw; educ. Temple Grove, East Sheen; Malvern College; R.M.A., Woolwich; ent. R.A. 23.11.91; Lt. 23.11.94; Capt. 4.12.99; Major 16.12.11; Lt.-Col. 1.5.17; Col., R.G.A., 31.8.20; trained a new Heavy Battery, and took it to France 10.7.15, and served in France continuously from that date; Temp. Brig.-General, commanding Corps Heavy Artillery, 3.7.17; Brig.-General, Royal Artillery, in M.G.R.A.'s Office, G.H.Q., France, April, 1918, to Jan. 1919; G.O.C., R.A. Corps, Jan. to April, 1919; Brig.-Gen. commanding Corps Heavy Artillery, April to 2.11.19; Brevet Col. 1.1.18; Despatches twice; C.M.G.; Commander of the Order of the Crown of Belgium with Palm; Belgian Croix de Guerre; American Distinguished Service Medal.

PRITCHARD, R. B. (D.S.O. L.G. 16.9.18), T/Capt., North'd Fusiliers; M.C. He died of wounds 26.4.18.

PRITTIE, HON. H. C. O'C. (D.S.O. L.G. 3.6.16); b. 19.7.77; e. s. of 4th Baron Dunalley; m. Beatrix Evelyn, d. of J. N. Graham; two s.; educ. Harrow; Trinity College, Cambridge; 2nd Lt., Rif. Brig., 4.5.01; Lt. 4.7.04; Capt. 15.2.11; Maj. 4.5.16; ret. pay 25.7.19; S. African War, 1902; Queen's Medal, 3 clasps; served Europ. War, 1914–16; Despatches.

PROBYN, H. M. (D.S.O. L.G. 17.9.17), 2nd Lt. (T/Capt.), R. War. R., and R.F.C.

PROCKTER, P. W. (D.S.O. L.G. 1.1.18), Lt. (T/Major), A.S.C. (now R.A.S.C.).

PROCTOR, A. H., M.D. (D.S.O. L.G. 26.8.18); b. 21.1.79; Lt., Ind. Med. Serv., 1.9.04; Capt. 1.9.07; Maj. 1.9.15.

PROCTOR, A. W. BEAUCHAMP- (see Beauchamp-Proctor, A. W.).

PROCTOR, W. H. (D.S.O. L.G. 26.9.16), T/Lt.; Capt., L.N. Lancs. Rgt. He was killed in action 24.4.17.

PROFEIT, C. W., M.B. (D.S.O. L.G. 1.1.17); b. 23.8.70; educ. Aberdeen University; M.B.; C.M.; Capt., R.A.M.C., 29.1.98; prev. serv. three years; Major 29.10.06; Lt.-Col. 1.3.15; Col. 26.12.17; S. African War, 1899–1902; Queen's Medal, 6 clasps; King's Medal, 2 clasps; European War; C.M.G.; C.S.I.

PROWER, J. M. (D.S.O. L.G. 14.1.16) (Bar, L.G. 1.1.18); b. Quebec, Canada, 8.3.85; s. of Lt.-Col. J. E. Prower, R.E., and Adèle Thérèse Prower (*née* Kimber); m. (1st), Una Catherine Corse Scott (who died 16.4.15), d. of Major John Corse Scott, 2nd Goorkhas, and Eugenia Scott (*née* Money); two d.; (2ndly), Ella Sylvia, d. of L. Mundy, of Kensington; educ. Bedales School, Petersfield, Hants; joined Donegal R.G.A. (M.), March, 1902, as 2nd Lieutenant; 1st Hampshire Regt., Dec. 1905, as 2nd Lieutenant; Lieutenant, June, 1907; resigned commission Dec. 1910; joined 31st British Columbia Horse, Dec. 1911, as Captain; 8th Canadian Battn. on mobilization, Valcortier Camp, 10.8.14, as Captain; to Western front with 8th Canadian Inf. Batt. 10.2.15; promoted Major 26.5.15; Brigade Major, 2nd Canadian Inf. Bde., 15.9.15; Lieut.-Col. and to command 8th Canadian Battn. 3.8.16; Despatches five times; mentioned in Notes to Sir Max Aitkin's publication, "Canada in Flanders."

PROWSE, C. B. (D.S.O. L.G. 3.6.16); b. 23.6.69; 2nd Lt., Som. L.I., 12.10.93; Lt. 27.6.96; Adjt., Som. L.I., 16.11.00 to 15.11.04; Capt. 14.8.01; Major 21.4.14; served S. African War, 1899–1902; Despatches three times; Queen's Medal, 5 clasps; King's Medal, 2 clasps; Europ. War; Despatches (L.G. 19.10.14 and 30.11.14); Bt. Lt.-Col. 3.11.14. When Temp. Brig.-Gen., 11th Inf. Brig., he died of wounds 1.7.16.

PROWSE, W. B. (D.S.O. L.G. 4.6.17), Major, Can. Arty.

PRYCE, C. AP R. (D.S.O. L.G. 4.6.17); b. India, 1876; s. of Col. D. D. Pryce, I.A.; m. Ellen Mary, widow of Lt. R. F. Morkill, W. Yorks. R., and d. of late T. L. Wilkinson; educ. Trinity College, Glenalmond; Major, late R.F.A.; served in B.S.A. Police (Medal, Mashona Rebellion, 1897); Natal Police; Imp. Light Horse; S. African Constabulary; served S. African War; Queen's Medal, 2 clasps; King's Medal, 2 clasps; transferred from Can. Artillery to R.F.A., 1915; European War, France, 1915–June, 1917; wounded; Despatches thrice.

PRYCE, H. E. AP R. (D.S.O. L.G. 4.6.17); b. 30.11.74; m. Alice Louisa, d. of R. F. H. Pughe; 2nd Lt. 16.1.95; Lt., Ind. Army, 16.4.97; Capt. 16.1.04; Maj. 16.1.13; Bt. Lt.-Col. 3.6.16; Bt. Col. 1.1.19; Col. 19.4.20; Temp. Col.-Comdt. 1.1.21; *p.s.c.*; Tibet, 1903–4; Medal; European War, 1914–17; Despatches; C.M.G.

PRYCE-JONES, H. M. (D.S.O. L.G. 4.6.17); b. 1878; s. of late Sir P. Pryce-Jones and Eleanor, Lady Pryce-Jones (who died in 1914), d. of E. R. Morris; m. Marion Vere, d. of late Lt.-Col. Hon. Lewis Payan-Dawnay; two s.; educ. Eton; Trinity College, Cambridge; 2nd Lt., C. Gds., 9.8.99; Capt. 16.2.09; Major 17.7.15; Lt.-Col. (Res. of Off.), ret. pay, 21.4.20; served in S. Africa, 1899–1902 (Despatches twice; Queen's Medal, 6 clasps; King's Medal, 2 clasps); N. Nigeria, 1904–5; served Europ. War; several Staff appointments; Bt. Lt.-Col. 1.1.19; M.C.; M.V.O.; Despatches six times.

PRYER, A. A. (D.S.O. L.G. 4.6.17); b. 22.5.91; Lt., A.V.C., 31.7.14; Capt. 3.9.15; Bt. Maj. 3.6.19.

PRYNNE, H. V., F.R.C.S., L.R.C.P. (D.S.O. L.G. 1.1.17); b. 26.11.69; educ. Middlesex Hospital; Capt. 29.1.97; previous service three years; Maj. 29.10.05; Lt.-Col. 1.3.15; Col. 26.12.17; retired as A.D.M.S. 26.10.19; China, 1900; Despatches; Medal, clasp; European War; Despatches.

PRYOR, P. HOLLAND- (see Holland-Pryor, P.).

PRYOR, T. (D.S.O. L.G. 7.2.18), Lt. (T/Major), I.A., R. of O.

PRYOR, W. M. (D.S.O. L.G. 18.6.17) (Bar, L.G. 3.6.19); b. Nov. 1880; s. of late M. R. Pryor, D.L., of Weston Park, Herts; m. Ethne Philippa, d. of Sir N. Moore, Bart., M.D.; three s.; educ. Eton; Trinity College, Cambridge; gazetted 5.10.14; Capt., 1st Herts. Rgt.; went to France, Sept. 1916; Despatches; Bt. Major; Italian Bronze Medal.

PUCKLE, B. H. (D.S.O. L.G. 1.1.17), T/Major, M.G.C.

PUDDICOMBE, T. P., M.B., M.R.C.S., L.R.C.P., M.B., B.S., D.P.H. (D.S.O. L.G. 4.6.17); b. 1877; s. of late R. Puddicombe; m. Violet Mabel, d. of M. E. Baxter; one s.; educ. Devon County School; King's College, and St. Thomas's Hospital, London; Lt.-Col., R.A.M.C. (T.); late O.C., 25th Field Amb.; served France 5.11.14 to 10.5.19; Despatches; M.C.

PUDSEY, D. (D.S.O. L.G. 1.1.18); b. 21.7.76; s. of late Col. H. F. Pudsey and Mrs. Pudsey; 2nd Lt., R.A., 12.5.00; Capt. 12.5.13; ret. pay 27.12.13; Maj. 16.11.15; was on the outbreak of the war attached to the late Lord Kitchener's Staff as Interpreter in China. He at once rejoined the Army, and was placed in charge of the British Legation Guard at Pekin. A few months later he carried Despatches to Petrograd, on his way to England. He was put to train batteries in England, and then proceeded with the R.F.A. to France, and later to Salonika; Despatches twice.

PUGH, D. C. (D.S.O. L.G. 4.6.17); ret. T.F. 13.12.05; V.D.; Lt.-Col., R.G.A.

PUGH, M. P. (D.S.O. L.G. 16.9.18), T/Lt. (A/Capt.), R. Berks. Rgt.; M.C.

PULLEN, E. F. (D.S.O. L.G. 16.9.18), Major, Can. Rly. Troops.

PULLEYNE, R. I. (D.S.O. L.G. 7.8.18), Lt., R.N.; D.S.C. He was killed in action on 20.7.18.

PULLIBLANK, J. B. (D.S.O. L.G. 23.5.17), Eng.-Cdr., R.N., 1.9.17.

PULLING, E. L. (D.S.O. L.G. 5.12.16), Fl. Sub.-Lt., R.N.A.S. He was killed in action on 2.3.17.

PUMPHREY, A. (D.S.O. L.G. 4.6.17); s. of T. E. Pumphrey, J.P. He served in the European War; became T/Capt., April, 1916, and was killed in action 21.9.17.

PURDON, W. B., M.B., B.Ch., R.U.I., D.P.H. (D.S.O. L.G. 1.1.17); b. 28.11.81; s. of late R. Purdon; m. Dorothy Myrtle, d. of W. Coates; one s.; educ. Queen's College, Belfast; Rugby Football, Ireland and Army; Lt., R.A.M.C., 28.1.07; Capt. 28.7.10; Maj. 28.1.19; served Europ. War, 1914–17; Despatches; M.C.

PURDY, J. S. (D.S.O. L.G. 25.8.17), Lt.-Col., Aust. A.M.C. His D.S.O. was awarded for gallantry at Ploegstraet Works 6–12.6.17.

PUREY-CUST, R. B. (D.S.O. L.G. 1.1.18); b. 22.4.88; 2nd Lt., R.A., 18.12.07; Lt. 18.12.10; Capt. 30.10.14; Maj. 26.11.17; M.C.

PURSER, L. M., M.B. (D.S.O. L.G. 1.1.17); b. at Tobago, W. Indies, 6.10.75; s. of William Allen and Catherine Anne Purser; m. Hilda Mary Inglis; educ. Galway Grammar School, and Trinity College, Dublin; Lt., R.A.M.C., 25.4.00; Capt. 25.4.03; Maj. 25.4.12; Lt.-Col. 26.12.17; S. African War, 1900–2; Queen's Medal, 3 clasps; King's Medal, 2 clasps; Europ. War, Oct. 1914–Sept. 1916, France; severely wounded; Despatches three times.

PURSER, M. (D.S.O. L.G. 26.11.17) (Details, L.G. 6.4.18), Lt.-Col., Aust. Infy.

PURVES, R. B., M.B., F.R.C.S. (D.S.O. L.G. 6.9.18). He served in the European War as Major, R.A.M.C., T.F.

PURVIS, E. R. (D.S.O. L.G. 2.4.19) (Details, L.G. 10.12.19), Major, 47th Batt. Can. Inf., W. Ontario Rgt.

PURVIS, J. H. (D.S.O. L.G. 3.6.16); b. 4.4.66; s. of late John Purvis and of Mina Purvis (*née* Berry); m. Agatha, d. of late Lt.-Gen. John Sprot, of Riddell, Roxburgh; one s.; one d.; educ. Cheltenham College; Caius College, Cambridge; joined H.L.I. from Fife Artillery Militia 16.5.88; Capt. 7.1.95; Lt.-Col. 10.7.15; commanded 16th Batt. M.I. in S. Africa, 1901–2; Despatches; Bt. Major 22.8.02; Queen's Medal, 4 clasps; retired 19.10.07; rejoined Sept. 1914, and appointed to command 12th Service Batt. H.L.I., July, 1915; commanded the Battalion at the attack on Loos and Hill 70, 25.9.15; Despatches. In 1915 Lt.-Col. (then Major), J. H. Purvis won the National Hunt Steeplechase at Cheltenham on Martial IV.

PUTTICK, E. (D.S.O. L.G. 1.1.18), Major, N.Z. Rif. Brigade.

PYE, C. R. A., M.B., Ch.B. (gazetted as Pye, John Van der Byl) (D.S.O. L.G. 11.5.17); b. in N.S. Wales, 1890; educ. Sydney University. On outbreak of war he was Captain of Aust. Inf. and served at Anzac with the Australian Infantry, and earned the highest praise from the Australian Commander. Lt.-Col. Pye was killed in action, aged 27 years.

PYE, K. W. (D.S.O. L.G. 1.1.17); b. 12.9.82; 2nd Lt., R.E., 21.12.01; Lt. 1.4.04; Capt. 21.12.12; Maj. 21.12.16; ret. pay 12.2.20.

PYE-SMITH, C. D., M.B., F.R.C.S. (D.S.O. L.G. 16.8.17) (Bar, L.G. 17.12.17) (Details, L.G. 23.4.18); s. of late J. W. Pye-Smith, formerly Mayor of Sheffield. He joined the Army in 1914; Capt., late R.A.M.C. (was T/Lt.-Colonel); Europ. War; Despatches; M.C.

PYM, REV. T. W., M.A. (D.S.O. L.G. 4.6.17); b. 1885; s. of late Rt. Rev. W. R. Pym, Bishop of Bombay; m. Dora Olive, d. of late W. Ivens; educ. Bedford School; Trinity College, Cambridge; Head of Cambridge House, Camberwell, from 1919; formerly Chaplain at Trinity College, Cambridge, and Assistant Chaplain-General to the Third Army in France; served Europ. War from 1914; Despatches three times.

PYMAN, C. K. L. (D.S.O. L.G. 15.10.18) (Bar, L.G. 1.2.19), Major, 5th (att. 12th) Can. Batt. Saskatchewan Rgt. He was killed in action on 10.8.18, and his brother, Ronald Lee Pyman, Lieut., 1st Middlesex Rgt., was killed in action in France 3.5.17.

PYMAN, G. L. (D.S.O. L.G. 4.6.17), T/Capt., Yorks. L.I.

PYNE, F. S., B.A. (D.S.O. L.G. 4.6.17); educ. Blundell's School, Tiverton; Pembroke College, Cambridge; B.A., Math. Tripos, 1907; University Commission, R.F.A., 18.12.07; Lt. 18.12.10; Capt. 30.10.14; Maj. 22.10.17; served Europ. War in France, 1914–17; Mons Medal.

PYOTT, I. V. (D.S.O. L.G. 15.12.16); b. Dundee, 31.8.95; educ. Grey Institute, S. Africa; Watson's College, Edinburgh; lived mostly in S. Africa; came to England, Feb. 1916, and enlisted in the M.M.G.C. (Tanks); joined R.F.C. (now R.A.F.), June, 1916; destroyed Zeppelin off Hartlepool, Durham, 27.11.16, for which he was awarded the D.S.O.

QUIBELL, A. H. (D.S.O. L.G. 24.1.17); b. 15.3.94; s. of O. Quibell, J.P.; educ. Magnus Grammar School, Newark, and Leys School, Cambridge; Member of Nottingham Rugby Team; joined T.F. 26.10.11, on leaving school at 17 years of age; Lt., 8th Sherwood Foresters, 1.4.14; T/Capt. 1.10.14; made Permanent 1.1.16; Adjt. 26.4.16–20.1.18; served in France 27.2.17–18.4.18.

QUICK, B. (D.S.O. L.G. 3.6.18), Lt.-Col., Aust. A.M.C.

QUIGLEY, F. G. (D.S.O. L.G. 22.6.18), T/Capt., R.F.C. (now R.A.F.); M.C.

QUILLER-COUCH, B. B. (D.S.O. L.G. 3.6.19), A/Major, R.A.; M.C. He died 6.2.19.

QUINNE, J. (D.S.O. L.G. 1.10.17), Eng. Lt.-Cdr., R.N.R.

QUIRK, D. (D.S.O. L.G. 1.1.17); b. 24.3.87; s. of Rev. Canon J. F. Quirk, M.A., J.P., and Dora, d. of late Rev. W. H. Parson; m. Ella Gladstone, d. of late G. R. Leyland; educ. Pocklington School, E. Yorks; 2nd Lt., 8th (S.) Batt. York and Lancaster Rg., 1914; Adjt., 1914–16; Major 1.7.16; Lt.-Col., late Commanding 8th (S.) Batt. K.O.Y.L.I.; previously commanded temporarily 9th (S.) Batt. York and Lancaster Rgt. and 11th (S.) Batt. Notts. and Derby. Rgt.; Commandant of 23rd Divisional School; went out to France 27.9.15, as Capt. and Adjt., 8th Batt. York and Lanc. R.; commanded 8th K.O.Y.L.I. from 1.3.17; Despatches four times; C.M.G.; Italian Croce di Guerra.

RADCLIFFE, A. DELMÉ- (see Delmé-Radcliffe, A.).

RADCLIFFE, SIR P. P. DE B. (D.S.O. L.G. 3.6.16); b. 9.2.74; s. of late General Sir W. Pollexfen Radcliffe, K.C.B., and Lady Radcliffe, d. of the late Hon. P. de Blaquiere; m. Râhmêh Theodora, d. of late Sir J. Swinburne, Bart., of Capheaton, and widow of late R. Walrond; educ. Winchester College; R.M.A., Woolwich; 2nd Lt., R.A., 4.10.93; Lt. 4.10.96; Capt. 26.7.00; Major 17.10.10; Lt.-Col. 1.1.16; Maj.-Gen. 3.6.18; served with "G" Battery, R.H.A., in S. Africa, 1899–1900; Despatches; Queen's Medal, 3 clasps; Europ. War, France, 1914–18; Despatches six times; C.B.; K.C.M.G.; Bt. Lt.-Col. 3.6.15; Bt. Col. 1.1.17.

RADCLIFFE, S. R. (D.S.O. L.G. 11.4.18); b. 29.5.84; 2nd Lt., R.A., 24.12.02; Lt. 23.12.06; Major, R.F.A. He died 30.4.18.

RADCLYFFE, C. R. (D.S.O. L.G. 3.6.18), T/Major, A.S.C., att. Tank Corps.

RADDALL, T. H. (D.S.O. L.G. 3.6.18), Major, Can. Inf.

RADFORD, E. G. (D.S.O. L.G. 1.1.17), Major, Aust. M.G.C.

RADFORD, N. H. (D.S.O. L.G. 26.11.17) (Details, L.G. 6.4.18), T/Lt. (A/Capt.), R.W.F.; M.C.

RADICE, A. H. (D.S.O. L.G. 1.1.18); b. 17.9.73; s. of A. Hampden Radice; g.s. of Col. Evasio Radice, of the Piedmontese Artillery, Private Secretary to Charles Albert of Savoy, Chargé d'Affaires for the first Italian Government and Member of the Italian Parliament; m. Sheila, d. of Col. Alister Jamieson, F.G.S.), Ind. Army, retired; one s.; one d.; educ. Bedford School; Sandhurst; 2nd Lt., Glouc. R., 21.10.93; Lt. 26.5.97; Capt. 2.6.03; Major 1.9.15; Lt.-Col., ret. pay, 29.1.21; served S. African War, 1899–1900; Queen's Medal, 3 clasps; Europ. War, 1914, Mons to Ypres as Adjt., 1st Gloucestershires (wounded 1st Battle of Ypres); Commanding 14th Batt. Glouc. R., and 11th Batt. S.W.B., France; wounded Pilckem Ridge; Chief Instructor, Interpreter, G.H.Q. Schools, Italy; Despatches four times; Croce di Guerra.

RAE, G. B. L. (D.S.O. L.G. 3.6.19), Major, 10th Batt. L'pool R., T.F., att. 17th Batt. Manch. R., T.F.

RAE, J. (D.S.O. L.G. 3.6.18), Capt. (A/Major), A.V.C. (now R.A.V.C.), S.R.; M.C.

RAE, W., M.A., B.L. (D.S.O. L.G. 14.1.16); b. 15.1.83; s. of W. Rae, M.A.; educ. Aberdeen Grammar School and University; late Lt.-Col., Can. Exp. Force; Major, Seaforth Highrs. of Canada (Can. Militia); Capt., 16th Batt. Can. Scottish on mobilization, 1914; 2nd-in-command, 3rd Can. Inf. Batt., 1915; Major 11.10.14; Commanding 4th Can. Inf. Batt., 1916–17; afterwards G.S.O.1, Can. Corps H.Q.; Europ. War from 1914; Despatches four times; Croix de Guerre (French).

RAFFERTY, R. A. (D.S.O. L.G. 4.6.17), Major, Aust. Mil. Forces.

RAIKES, D. T. (D.S.O. L.G. 18.2.18) (Details, L.G. 18.7.18); b. 1897; y. s. of late R. T. Raikes; educ. Radley College; Merton College, Oxford; Oxford VIII., 1920; Major, late Tank Corps; served Europ. War, 1916–18; Despatches; M.C.; Bar.

RAIKES, G. T. (D.S.O. L.G. 22.9.16) (1st Bar, L.G. 4.2.18) (Details, 5.7.18) (2nd Bar, L.G. 16.9.18); b. 7.4.84; 4th s. of late Robert Taunton Raikes and Rosa Margaret, d. of H. W. Cripps, Q.C.; educ. Radley College; Sandhurst; 2nd Lt., S.W. Bord., 10.10.03; Lt. 25.5.07; Capt. 30.4.14; Maj. 10.10.18; employed with Egyptian Govt., 1913–15; served Europ. War, 1914–18; Despatches; Bt. Major 1.1.18; Bt. Lt.-Col. 3.6.19. His D.S.O. was awarded for gallantry at Beaumont Hamel.

RAIKES, L. T. (D.S.O. L.G. 14.1.16); b. 9.5.82; e. s. of late R. T. Raikes, of Treberfydd; m. Marion Eva, d. of A. C. Hankin; three s.; two d.; educ. Radley College; R.M.A., Woolwich; ent. Army 2.5.00; Lt. 3.4.01; Capt. 13.2.10; Maj. 30.10.14; A/Lt.-Col., 1917–19; served Europ. War, 1914–18; came to France from India 7.11.19 with Lahore Division; served in 64th Bty. R.F.A. until Jan. 1915, when he was posted to command 94th Bty. R.F.A.; was present at Battle of Neuve Chapelle, March, 1915; Second Battle of Ypres, April, 1915; Richebourg, May, 1915; Ypres 2.6.16 (wounded, shell shock); Battle of the Somme 4.8.16–11.10.16.

RAIKES, R. H. T. (D.S.O. L.G. 25.10.16) (Bar, L.G. 22.6.17); b. 23.8.85; 5th s. of late R. T. Raikes, of Treberfydd; m. Ida Guinevere, d. of late D. Evans; two s.; educ. Radley; ent. R.N., 1900; Submarine Service, 1908; in 1913 was appointed to H.M.S. Defence; rejoined Submarine Service, Aug. 1915; Commander 30.6.17; served Europ. War, 1914–17; Despatches; Chevalier, Legion of Honour, June, 1917. His D.S.O. was awarded when in command of Submarine E 54, for sinking German submarine U C 7, 21.8.16. His Bar to D.S.O. was awarded for sinking German Submarine U 81, 1.5.17.

RAIKES, W. T. (D.S.O. L.G. 3.6.19); b. 4.7.92; s. of late Robert Taunton Raikes; educ. Radley College; Merton College, Oxford; joined Army, S.W.B., 16.8.14; Capt. 11.5.15; Capt. (T/Lt.-Col.), S.W.B. (S.R.); Commanding 25th Batt. M.G.C.; served Europ. War; Despatches twice; awarded M.C., Cambrai Battle, 20–30.11.17; Bar to M.C., Battle of Lys, 10–11–12.4.18.

RAIMES, A. L. (D.S.O. L.G. 16.9.18); b. 9.11.85; s. of late F. Raimes; educ. The Leys School, and King's College, Cambridge; Major, 5th Durham L.I.; served in Flanders, 1915–18; Despatches.

RAINSFORD-HANNAY, A. G. (D.S.O. L.G. 1.1.17); b. 9.11.82, at Malta; s. of Col. R. W. Rainsford-Hannay, D.L., J.P.; m. Muriel Erskine, d. of W. Austin; educ. Wellington College; R.M.A.; 2nd Lt., R.E., 21.12.01; Lt. 26.6.04; Capt. 21.12.12; Maj. 21.12.16; served as Commanding Royal Engineer in the expedition against Ali Dinar, 1916; proceeded to France in April, 1918; captured at Croanne on 27 May, while in command of a Field Coy.; Despatches; 4th Class Order of the Nile.

RAINSFORD-HANNAY, F. (D.S.O. L.G. 1.1.17); b. St. Thomas Mount, Madras, 28.4.78; s. of Col. R. W. Rainsford-Hannay, late R.A., and late Helen Jane, d. of J. Brancker; m. Dorothea Letitia May, d. of Sir W. F. Maxwell, Bart., of Cardoness; one s.; educ. Wellington College; R.M.A., Woolwich; Football Fifteens, 1894–96; 2nd Lt., R.A., 23.3.97; Lt. 23.3.00; Capt. 26.3.02; Maj. 16.5.14; Lt.-Col. 1.7.17; *p.s.c.*; served S. African War, 1899–1902; Pieter's Hill, Relief of Ladysmith, Laing's Nek, Belfast, various actions in Transvaal, O.R.C., and Cape Colony; Batteries, 21st Battery, R.F.A.; "R" Battery, R.H.A.; 86th Battery, R.F.A.; R.H.A. Mounted Rifles, Dec. 1901, to May, 1902; actions in O.R.C. and Western Transvaal; wounded at Geluk Farm 23.8.00. Col. Rainsford-Hannay wrote: "At Geluk Farm my section of 21st Battery, R.F.A., was in action, and my father was paying me a visit. He came up to the position just when three men had been hit, and assisted in carrying up ammunition until the casualties had been replaced. This is, or was rather, a well-known story." He was awarded the Queen's Medal, 6 clasps; King's Medal, 2 clasps; Despatches twice; Europ. War, Aug. 1915–18; Brig. Major, R.A., 24th Div., Loos, 1915; commanded 89th Army Brig., R.F.A., 1.7.15, Somme; wounded, March, 1916; commanded 86th Army, Brig. R.F.A., Serre, March, 1917; Arras, April, 1917; Messines, June, 1917; Ypres, 1.7.17 to 19.10.17; Instructor, School of Gunnery, Salisbury, Nov. 1917–March, 1918; Commanded 169th Army Brig., Hangard Wood and Gentilles, 24–26.4.18; Despatches; C.M.G.

RAINSFORD-HANNAY, J. (D.S.O. L.G. 14.1.16); b. 4.9.79; 2nd s. of Col. R. W. Rainsford-Hannay; m. Evelyn Gordon Forbes; two s.; one d.; educ. Wellington; Sandhurst; 2nd Lt. 7.9.98; Lt. 23.5.00; Capt. 5.10.04; Major 1.9.15 2nd Batt. R.W. Surrey Rgt.; served S. African War, 1899–1902; Queen's Medal, 3 clasps; King's Medal, 2 clasps; Europ. War, 1914–16; Despatches; Hon. Sec., Army Rugby Union.

RAIT-KERR, R. S. (D.S.O. L.G. 1.1.18); b. 13.4.91; s. of S. Rait-Kerr, of Rathmoyle, Edenderry, King's Co.; m. Helen Margaret, d. of F. Metcalfe; one d.; educ. Arnold House, Llandulas; Rugby; R.M.A., Woolwich; 2nd Lt., R.E., 23.12.10; Lt. 21.12.12; Capt. 23.12.16; sailed for France with 3rd Lahore Division, Aug. 1914; wounded, Neuve Chapelle, 1914; returned to France, June, 1915, to Sept. 1917; commanded a Field Squadron, R.E.; M.C.; Adjt., 3rd R. Sappers and Miners, 1918–20; played Cricket for Rugby, R.M.A., R.E., Bombay Presidency and Free Foresters; played Football for R.M.A. and R.E.

RALPH, A. C. (D.S.O. L.G. 26.8.18); b. 3.5.69; s. of A. E. Ralph, J.P.; m. Winifred Mabel, d. of E. Goodall, of Calcutta; one s.; educ. Sutton Valence School; R.M.C., Sandhurst; 2nd Lt., 2nd Batt. The King's (Liverpool) Rgt., 22.8.88; Lt. 23.6.90; Ind. Army 11.8.90; Capt. 22.8.99; Maj. 22.8.06; Lt.-Col. 22.8.14; Colonel 6.7.19; retired pay 11.12.20; served N.W. Frontier of India, 1897–98; Medal and clasp; Mesopotamia, 1915–19; Despatches thrice; commanded 1/4th (P.A.V.'s) Rajputs, 1915–20.

RALPH, E. M. (D.S.O. L.G. 1.1.18), Lt.-Col., Aust. Gen. List.

RALSTON, A. W., B.A., LL.B. (D.S.O. L.G. 1.1.17); b. 27.11.85; s. of A. G. Ralston, K.C., and Mary Emily, d. of Sir W. Windeyer; educ. Sydney Grammar School; University of Sydney; joined Aust. Naval and Military Exp. Force as Capt., 1914; Lt.-Col. Commanding Sydney University Scouts; present at capture of Rabaul, Herbertshohe, Madang, Quieta, and in command of expedition to southern end of New Ireland; joined A.I.F., March, 1915, as Major; in Gallipoli, 1915, to evacuation, becoming 2nd-in-command of 19th Batt. in Oct. 1915; in France from March, 1916; promoted Lt.-Col. and to command 20th Batt. 16.6.16; 2nd Aust. M.G. Batt. March, 1918–Aug. 1919; Despatches four times; C.M.G.

RALSTON, G. H. (D.S.O. L.G. 4.6.17), Lt.-Col., F. Arty.

RALSTON, J. L. (D.S.O. L.G. 26.9.17) (Details, L.G. 9.1.18) (Bar, L.G. 15.2.19) (Details, L.G. 30.7.19), Major, Can. Inf. His D.S.O. was awarded for gallantry from 26.6.17 to 1.7.17 south of Sonchez River.

RALSTON, W. H. (D.S.O. L.G. 25.8.17); b. 27.3.83; 2nd Lt. 18.1.02; Lt., Ind. Army, 9.5.04; Capt. 18.1.11; Maj. 18.1.17; Bt. Lt.-Col. 3.6.19; M.C.

RAMBAUT, G. M. (D.S.O. L.G. 1.1.18); b. 1.3.88; s. of Dr. A. A. Rambaut, F.R.S., Radcliffe Observer, Oxford, and Emily Rambaut, *née* Longford; m. Gladys Evelyn, d. of A. Vansittart Frere; one d.; educ. Westminster; Christ Church, Oxford; Assistant Master, Shrewsbury School, 1910–14; Commissioned Territorial Artillery, Jan. 1911; Capt., late R.F.A.; served in France 1.3.15 to 30.11.17; three times wounded; Despatches.

RAMPLING, R. (D.S.O. L.G. 20.9.18), Eng. Lt.-Cdr., R.N.

RAMSAY, HON. A. R. M. (D.S.O. L.G. 14.3.16); b. 29.5.81; s. of 13th Earl of Dalhousie and Ida, d. of 6th Earl of Tankerville; m. 1919, H.R.H. Princess Victoria Patricia Helen Elizabeth, d. of Duke of Connaught; one s.; educ. R.N. College, Dartmouth; entered R.N. in 1896; promoted Captain 30.6.19; served Europ. War, first as Gunnery Officer of the battle cruiser Indefatigable, and from 1915–19 on the Staff of Admiral de Robeck; in Dardanelles, 1914–15, and in the Grand Fleet; Despatches; Naval Attaché in Paris till 1922; in Nov. 1922, he assumed command of the light cruiser Dunedin.

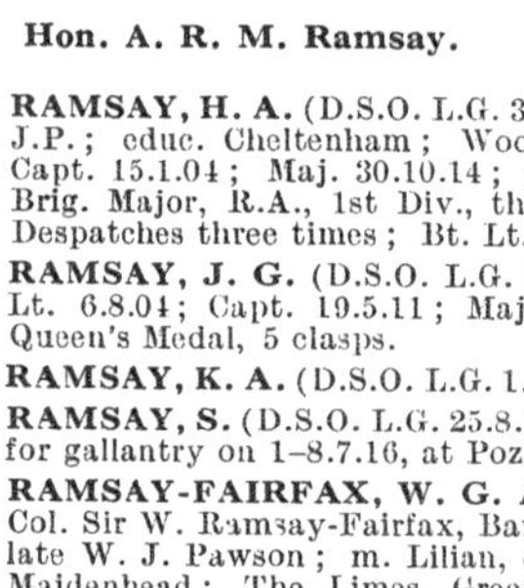

Hon. A. R. M. Ramsay.

RAMSAY, F. W. (D.S.O. L.G. 14.1.16); b. 10.12.75; s. of Brig.-Gen. W. A. Ramsay (late 4th Q.O. Hussars); 2nd Lt., Midd'x R., 15.5.97; Lt. 24.2.00; Capt. 29.3.01; Maj. 1.9.14; Col. 2.6.19; Temp. Maj.-Gen. 14.6.18 to 17.3.19; served S. African War, 1901–2; Queen's Medal, 5 clasps; Europ. War, France and Flanders, 1914–18; Bt. Lt.-Col. 3.6.16; Despatches; Bt. Col. 1.1.19; C.B.; C.M.G.

RAMSAY, H. A. (D.S.O. L.G. 3.6.16); b. 20.12.78; s. of late Capt. J. Ramsay, J.P.; educ. Cheltenham; Woolwich; 2nd Lt., R.A., 26.2.98; Lt. 16.2.01; Capt. 15.1.04; Maj. 30.10.14; *p.s.c.*; Lt.-Col., R.A.; served Europ. War as Brig. Major, R.A., 1st Div., then on H.Q. Staff of Third Army; wounded; Despatches three times; Bt. Lt.-Col. 3.6.18.

RAMSAY, J. G. (D.S.O. L.G. 1.1.18); b. 11.8.80; 2nd Lt., Cam'n Highrs.; Lt. 6.8.04; Capt. 19.5.11; Maj. 5.1.16; O.B.E.; S. African War, 1901–2; Queen's Medal, 5 clasps.

RAMSAY, K. A. (D.S.O. L.G. 1.1.18), Capt. (A/Lt.-Col.), Can. Rly Troops.

RAMSAY, S. (D.S.O. L.G. 25.8.16), T/Lt., N. Lan. R. His D.S.O. was awarded for gallantry on 1–8.7.16, at Pozières Wood. He died of wounds 3.6.17.

RAMSAY-FAIRFAX, W. G. A. (D.S.O. L.G. 13.2.17); b. 1876; s. of late Col. Sir W. Ramsay-Fairfax, Bart., of Maxton, Roxburghshire, and Mary, d. of late W. J. Pawson; m. Lilian, d. of late H. Rich; two s.; educ. Cordwalles, Maidenhead; The Limes, Greenwich; H.M.S. Britannia, 1890; Lt., R.N.; resigned 1901; Commander, R.N. Emergency List, and Lieut.-Colonel; joined XXXth Rgt., I.Y., 1902; served S. African War with rank of Captain; Medal and clasps; served with Abyssinian Army, co-operating with British Somaliland F.F., 1903–4 (Medal and clasp); Europ. War at Sea with R.N.D., and with the Tank Corps in France; C.M.G.; promoted T/Brig.-General; Despatches four times; holds the Bronze Medal of the R. Humane Society. The D.S.O. was awarded for gallantry 13–15.11.16, north of the Aisne.

RAMSBOTTOM, G. O. (D.S.O. L.G. 4.6.17) (Bar, L.G. 2.4.19) (Details, L.G. 10.12.19), Temp. Lt.-Col., 22nd Batt. Manch. R.

RAMSDEN, A. G. F. (D.S.O. L.G. 24.9.18), Capt. (A/Major), R.F.A., S.R.

RAMSDEN, R. E. (D.S.O. L.G. 15.2.17); b. 21.11.75; s. of R. Ramsden and Elizabeth Frances, d. of J. S. Salmon, of Bagdale, Jamaica; 2nd Lt., R.A., 2.11.95; Lt. 2.11.98; Capt. 23.11.01; Maj. 15.5.12; Lt.-Col. 9.9.16; ret. pay 9.3.21; served S. African War, 1899–1900; Despatches; 2 Medals, 6 clasps; Europ. War, 1914–17.

RAMSDEN, V. B. (D.S.O. L.G. 26.7.18) (Bar, L.G. 2.4.19) (Details, L.G. 10.12.19); b. 25.3.88; 2nd Lt., S. Wales Bord., 22.2.08; Lt. 18.3.11; Capt. 24.1.15; Bt. Maj. 3.6.19; M.C.

RANDALL, E. A. H. (D.S.O. L.G. 3.6.18), Major, Aust. Arty.

RANDOLPH, A. F. (D.S.O. L.G. 1.1.17); b. 12.4.65; m. Constance Mary, sister of Sir G. A. A. L. St. J. Mildmay, 7th Bart., and widow of J. A. B. Wallington; entered Army 23.8.84; Maj. 21.12.01; ret. Midd'x R. 22.2.05; Lt.-Col., R. of O., Suffolk R.; served Europ. War, 1914–17; Despatches; C.M.G.

RANKIN, G. J. (D.S.O. L.G. 11.4.18) (Bar, L.G. 8.3.19) (Details, L.G. 4.10.19), Major, 4th Aust. L.H. Rgt.

RANKIN, J. S. (D.S.O. L.G. 1.1.18) (Bar, L.G. 1.2.19), Major, 46th Batt. Can. Inf., Sask. Rgt.

The Distinguished Service Order 329

RANSOME, A. L. (D.S.O. L.G. 1.1.18) (Bar, L.G. 16.9.18); b. 29.8.83; 2nd Lt., Dorset. R., 19.12.03; Lt. 1.4.06; Capt. 17.2.12; Bt. Maj. 1.1.16; Bt. Lt.-Col. 1.1.19; *p.s.c.*; M.C.

RANSON, W., F.R.C.S., L.R.C.P., L.R.C.S., L.R.F.P.S. (D.S.O. L.G. 1.1.17); b. 1870; s. of J. F. Ranson and Anna Maria, d. of J. J. Wilson; m. Florinda Maude Richardson; one s.; educ. Bradfield College, Edinburgh; St. Thomas's Hospital; Colonel, R.A.M.C.; served Europ. War from 1914; Despatches twice; specially promoted Dec. 1917; O.C., 3rd Northumbrian Field Amb., 50th Div.; O.C., 47th Casualty Clearing Station, 5th Army; O.C., 30th General Hospital, A.D.M.S. No. 1 Army Area.

RAPSON, G. F. E. (D.S.O. L.G. 24.9.18), Capt. (A/Lt.-Col.), Wilts. R.; 2nd Lt., Midd'x R., 10.10.14; Capt., Wilts. R., 25.2.15; Bt. Maj. 1.1.19; Adjt., Hong-Kong Defence Corps, 26.3.20.

RASHLEIGH, P. (D.S.O. L.G. 3.6.18); b. 9.7.81; 2nd Lt., R.A., 19.12.00; Lt. 14.3.03; Capt. 19.12.13; Maj. 30.12.15; Major, R.G.A.

RASHLEIGH, R. N. (D.S.O. L.G. 26.7.17); b. 29.4.88; 2nd Lt., R.A., 23.7.07; Lt. 23.7.10; Capt. 30.10.14; Major 11.7.17. His D.S.O. was awarded for gallantry at Metz-en-Couture, 4.4.17; M.C.

RATCLIFFE, W. C. (D.S.O. L.G. 8.3.19) (Details, L.G. 4.10.19) (Bar, L.G. 8.3.19) (Details, L.G. 4.10.19); b. 31.7.84; Temp. Capt. 8.2.15; Capt., North'n R., 1.10.16; Capt. (T/Major), North'n R., att. 9th Batt. Yorks. L.I.

RATHBONE, H. E. F. (D.S.O. L.G. 4.6.17); b. 12.1.79; s. of J. Rathbone; m. Violet Cranston; two s.; one d.; educ. Harrow; 2nd Lt., R.E., 23.6.98; Lt. 29.3.01; Capt. 3.6.07; Maj. 15.12.14; served Europ. War; Despatches twice.

RATHBORNE, C. E. H. (D.S.O. L.G. 17.1.19) (Bar, L.G. 16.12.19), Wing-Cdr., R.N.A.S. (Capt., R. Marine Light Inf., now Lt.-Col., R.A.F.).

C. E. H. Rathborne.

RATSEY, H. E. (D.S.O. L.G. 7.2.18), T/Major (T/Lt.-Col.); Colonel, R.E.; C.B.E.

RATTRAY, J. G. (D.S.O. L.G. 14.1.16); b. 15.1.67; s. of A. Rattray and Jan, d. of W. Tennant; m. Emily, d. of A. Wallace, of Mt. Forest, Ontario; one d.; educ. High School, Park Hill, Ontario; Normal School, Ottawa, Ontario; Lt., 12th Manitoba Dns., 1906; commanded 20th Border Horse, 1910; joined 1st Can. Contingent, Aug. 1914; organized 10th Can. Inf. Batt. at Valcartier, Sept. 1914; served Europ. War, 1914–18; Lt.-Colonel, O.C., 10th Can. Inf. Batt.; C.M.G.

RATTRAY, M. MAC G., M.B. (D.S.O. L.G. 4.6.17); b. 21.9.69; Lt., R.A.M.C., 28.1.97; Capt. 28.1.00; Maj. 28.10.08; Lt.-Col. 1.3.15.

RAWLENCE, M. (D.S.O. L.G. 7.2.18); b. 8.9.85; 2nd Lt., R.E., 21.12.04; Lt. 23.6.07; Capt. 30.10.14.

RAWLING, C. G. (D.S.O. L.G. 1.1.18); b. 16.2.70; 2nd Lt., Som. L.I., 10.10.91; Lt. 1.2.96; Capt. 14.8.01; Maj. 27.11.13; N.W. Frontier, 1897–98; Medal, clasp; Tibet, 1903–4; Medal, clasp; Bt. Lt.-Col. (Temp. Brig.-Gen.); C.M.G.; C.I.E. He was killed in action 28.10.17.

RAWLINGS, H. C. (D.S.O. L.G. 8.3.20), Cmdr., R.N.

RAWLINSON, A. (D.S.O. L.G. 8.3.19) (Details, L.G. 4.10.19), T/Lt.-Col., R.G.A.; C.M.G.

RAY, J. (D.S.O. L.G. 18.7.17), Major, Aust. F.A. His D.S.O. was awarded for gallantry on 15.4.17, at Lagnicourt.

RAY, M. B., M.D., C.M. (D.S.O. L.G. 1.1.17); s. of R. Ray; m. Edith Charlotte Frances, d. of Lord Henry Cholmondeley and widow of Capt. R. E. Heaven, M.D., C.M.; educ. Lancaster; Edinburgh University; Fellow of the Royal Society of Medicine; A/Lt.-Col., R.A.M.C. (T.F.); served with B.E.F. as Lt.-Col., R.A.M.C. (T.F.), in command of No. 3 Casualty Clearing Station, 41 Stationary Hospital; acted as S.M.O., Amiens; Despatches.

RAY, R. A. (D.S.O. L.G. 3.6.18); b. 20.12.73; 2nd Lt., R. Lanc. R., 4.9.01; Lt. 9.5.06; Capt. 3.9.14; Maj. 4.9.16; S. African War, 1900–1.

RAYMER, R. R., M.A. (D.S.O. L.G. 3.6.16); b. 1.11.70; s. of late Capt. R. Raymer, Inspector of Army Schools; m. Ethel, d. of late Capt. E. G. Peyton, 106th L.I.; one s.; educ. Farnham Grammar School; Trinity College, Dublin; Capt., Jersey Militia, 1904; Major, 1910; Col., May, 1919; late 5th Batt. S. Staffs. R. (T.F.); commanded 1/5th Batt. S. Staffs. R., 1915–16; 10th Batt. Duke of Wellington's Rgt., 1916–17; 10th Officer Cadet Batt. Jan.–May, 1918; 5th S.W.B., Oct. 1918–June, 1919; served with 1st Batt. Leic. R. in S. African War, 1901–2; Queen's Medal with 5 clasps; Europ. War, 1915–18; Despatches four times; wounded; C.M.G.

RAYMOND, E. D. (D.S.O. L.G. 17.9.17); b. 2.5.81; 2nd Lt., Essex R., 18.4.00; Lt., Army, 18.7.02; Capt., Ind. Army, 18.4.09; Major 1.9.15; M.C.; S. African War, 1900–2; Queen's Medal, 3 clasps; King's Medal, 2 clasps.

RAYMOND, E. H. B. (D.S.O. L.G. 14.1.16); b. 6.9.68; 2nd Lt., R. Scots, 23.3.89; Capt. 12.8.96; ret. pay 9.9.08; Maj., Res. of Off., 1.9.15; S. African War; Queen's Medal, 3 clasps; King's Medal, 2 clasps; Europ. War; Despatches.

RAYNER, F. (D.S.O. L.G. 24.1.17), Capt. (T/Lt.-Col.), Notts. and Derbys. Regt.

RAYNER, W. B. F. (D.S.O. L.G. 3.6.16); b. 20.5.79; 2nd s. of late E. Rayner, and nephew of Admiral of the Fleet Sir William May; m. Eileen, d. of late J. Fitzgerald; two s.; two d.; educ. Eton; ent. 2nd Batt. R. Fus. 18.10.99; Lt. 2.1.01; Capt. 5.5.07; Maj. 1.9.15; retired R. Fus. 4.5.19; served S. African War, 1899–1902; Relief of Ladysmith, including action at Colenso; operations on Tugela Heights (14–27.2.00) and action at Pieter's Hill; operations in Natal, March–June, 1900; operations in Transvaal, Dec. 1900–Jan. 1901; operations in Cape Colony Feb. 1901–March, 1902; Queen's Medal, 5 clasps; King's Medal, 2 clasps; Adjt., 1st Batt. R. Fus., 1907–10; Adjutant, 1st London Rgt. (T.F.), 1914–15; Brigade Major, 23rd Inf. Brig., 1915–16; G.S.O.2, 1916; served during Europ. War, Malta, Sept. 1914, to Feb. 1915; France from March, 1915; G.S.O., 1916; action of Fromattes, May, 1915; Bridoux, Sept. 1915, and Battle of the Somme, July, 1916; Despatches twice; 1914–15 Star.

W. B. F. Rayner.

RAYNOR, C. A. (D.S.O. L.G. 23.10.19); b. 6.12.89; 2nd Lt., Unatt., 8.9.09; I.A., 24.10.10; Lt. 8.12.11; Capt. 1.9.15; M.C.

RAYNSFORD, R. M. (D.S.O. L.G. 3.6.19); b. 19.5.77; s. of Lt.-Col. F. M. Raynsford, I.A.; m. Daphne Mildred, d. of Col. W. W. Pemberton, I.A.; two s.; one d.; educ. Highgate School; R.M.C., Camberley; 2nd Lt., Leinster R., 8.9.97; Lt. 3.2.00; Capt. 27.5.03; Maj. 1.9.15; S. African War, 1900–2; Queen's Medal, 3 clasps; King's Medal, 2 clasps; Europ. War, 1914–18, in Salonika and France; Commanded 5th Connaught Rangers and 10th Devons., and served on Staff, G.H.Q., France, as D.A.D. General of Transportation; Despatches. He has written "Officers' Requirements in India," and (with Major R. A. H. Orpen-Palmer) "Officers' Mess Accounts."

REA, C. P. (D.S.O. L.G. 3.6.18), T/Capt. (A/Major), R. Scots Fus.

REA, J. G. G. (D.S.O. L.G. 1.1.18), Capt., Yeomanry.

READ, G. A. (D.S.O. L.G. 1.1.18), Lt.-Col., Aust. Inf.

READ, H. E. (D.S.O. L.G. 26.7.18); b. 4.12.93; s. of the late Herbert and Eliza Read; m. Evelyn, d. of A. Roff; educ. Crossley's School, Halifax; University of Leeds, where he was in the O.T.C.; joined Army, 1914; 2nd Lt., Yorks. Regt., 16.1.15; Lt., Yorks. Regt., July, 1917; Captain; served Europ. War 1915 to 1918, in France and Belgium; Despatches; M.C.

READ, H. S. (D.S.O. L.G. 3.6.19), Lt. (A/Major), 1/20th Batt. London R.; M.C.

READ, JAMES JOHN (gazetted as Read, John James) (D.S.O. L.G. 1.1.17), Capt. (T/Major), R.F.A.

READ, R. O. CREWE- (see Crewe-Read, R. O.).

READ, R. V. (D.S.O. L.G. 3.6.19), Capt. (T/Major), Essex Regt.; M.C.

READE, A. (D.S.O. L.G. 26.7.18), T/Major, S. Lancs. R.; M.C.

READMAN, J. J. (D.S.O. L.G. 3.6.16); b. 6.11.84; 2nd Lt., 2nd Dns., 2.3.04; Lt. 2.11.09; Capt. 4.11.11; Maj. 2.10.19.

READY, J. M. (D.S.O. L.G. 4.3.18) (Details, L.G. 16.8.18), 2nd Lt. (T/Capt.), R. Berks. R.; M.C.

REASON, C. H. (D.S.O. L.G. 1.1.18), Major (T/Lt.-Col.), Can. A.M.C.

REAY, T. (D.S.O. L.G. 4.6.17), T/Major, North'd Fus.

REBSCH, W. K. (D.S.O. L.G. 3.6.16); b. 29.8.85; 2nd Lt. 29.10.05; Lt., Ind. Army, 13.11.06; Capt. 13.8.13; Bt. Maj. 3.6.19; Maj. 13.8.19; Despatches.

REDE, R. L'E. M. (D.S.O. L.G. 21.6.18), Cdr., R.N.

REDFERN, J. G. (D.S.O. L.G. 3.6.18), Capt., E. Yorks. Regt.

REDHEAD, C. M. (D.S.O. L.G. 1.1.18), Lt.-Cdr. (A/Capt.), R.N.R.

REDMOND, R. M. (D.S.O. L.G. 3.6.19), Major, 87th Batt. Can. Inf., Quebec R.

REDMOND, W. A. (D.S.O. L.G. 18.10.17) (Details, L.G. 7.3.18); b. 1886; o. s. of late John Redmond (Chairman of Irish Parliamentary Party) and Johanna d. of late James Dalton, of N.S. Wales; educ. Clongowes; Trinity College, Dublin; called to Irish Bar, 1910; Gray's Inn, 1921; M.P., Tyrone, 1910–18; M.P. (N.), Waterford, from March, 1918; Captain, late Irish Guards; served European War.

REED, A. DAYRELL (D.S.O. L.G. 12.5.17), Lieut., R.N.R.

REED, A. E. (D.S.O. L.G. 24.9.18); b. 29.3.88, at Clunes, Victoria, Australia; s. of George Effingham Reed and the late Annie Reed; m. yr. d. of Lieut.-Col. J. J. Hanley, V.D., and Mrs. Hanley, of Brighton, Victoria, Australia; educ. Ballarat College, Australia; joined Victorian Rifles, Commonwealth Military Forces, Sept. 1907; obtained a commission 10.10.10; Lieut., A.I.F., Feb. 1915; Capt., A.I.F., 16.5.15; Major, A.I.F., 1.1.18; left Australia 16.7.15; served in Gallipoli; invalided 1.12.15; served in France from 26.3.16; Despatches. Major Reed was in S.S. Southland when it was torpedoed in the Ægean Sea 2.9.15, *en route* for Gallipoli.

REED, C. (D.S.O. L.G. 22.12.16); b. 10.8.79; s. of late Talbot Baines Reed; m. Marion Ethel, d. of late Lt.-Col. E. A. Pemberton, R.A.; three d.; educ. Haileybury College; joined R.G.A. 9.8.99; Lt. 16.2.01; Capt. 12.5.06; Major 30.10.14; served with 26th (Jacob's) Mountain Battery, 1900; Indian Ordnance Dept., 1908; went to France as D.A.D. of Ordnance Services, Meerut Division, Sept. 1914; Mesopotamia, Dec. 1915–Jan. 1917; A.D. of Ordnance Services (Provision), Mesopotamia Expeditionary Force, 1917; Bt. Lt.-Col. 3.6.18; Order of White Eagle, 4th Class, Serbia.

C. Reed.

REED, W. L. (D.S.O. L.G. 11.11.19), Engr., Sub-Lt., R.N.R.

REES, E. T. (D.S.O. L.G. 3.6.18), T/Major (A/Lt.-Col.), S.W.B.; M.C.

REES, J. G. (D.S.O. L.G. 18.1.18) (1st Bar, L.G. 26.3.18) (Details, L.G. 25.4.18) (2nd Bar, L.G. 15.2.19) (Details, L.G. 30.7.19); b. 22.11.84; s. of W. T. Rees and Alice Rachel, d. of late W. Powell; educ. Clifton; Rugby; R.M.C., Sandhurst; High Sheriff of Radnorshire, 1915; Deputy Lt. of Breconshire; entered 13th Hussars, Aug. 1904; Adjt., 13th Hrs., 1910 to 1912; Capt., 1910; resigned commission Dec. 1913; Major, Welsh Horse (from R.O.O.), Aug. 1914; Lt.-Col., Welsh Horse; served Europ. War; Despatches.

REES, T. W. (D.S.O. L.G. 15.2.19) (Details, L.G. 30.7.19); b. 12.1.98; 2nd Lt., Unatt., 15.11.15; Ind. Army 18.11.15; Capt., Ind. Army, 15.11.19; M.C.

REES-MOGG, R. J. (D.S.O. L.G. 1.1.17); b. 4.9.78; 2nd Lt., R. Ir. Regt., 4.1.99; Lt. 31.5.00; Capt. 26.8.04; Maj. 16.3.15; Lt.-Col., ret. pay, 10.8.20; Soudan, 1908; Egyptian Medal, clasp; 4th Class Medjidieh; Soudan, 1910; Soudan Medal, clasp; served Europ. War; Despatches.

REEVE, J. T. W. (D.S.O. L.G. 1.1.19); b. 1.4.91; s. of W. Reeve; m. Sybil Alice, d. of Sir G. Agnew; 2nd Lt., Rif. Brig., 5.10.10; Lt. 23.3.12; Capt. 15.3.15; Capt., Rifle Brigade; served Europ. War from 1914; Despatches.

REEVES, R. C. (D.S.O. L.G. 1.1.18); b. 13.3.78; 2nd Lt., R.A., 26.5.00; Lt. 15.3.02; Capt. 24.2.11; Maj. 30.10.14.

REID, A. D. (D.S.O. L.G. 4.6.17); b. Edinburgh, 2.2.82; s. of William Thomas Reid, J.P., and Margaret Grieg, d. of James Grey; educ. Westminster; R.M.C., Sandhurst; Lt., Ind. Army, 28.10.02; ret. 26.4.09; rejoined on outbreak of war; became Major, Royal Innis. Fus., Feb. 1915, and went to France; appointed to command a battalion of the Royal Irish Rifles, with which he fell in the advance 31.7.17; Despatches; Silver Medal of Italy.

A. D. Reid.

REID, A. K. (D.S.O. L.G. 3.6.19), Major, 9th Batt. H.L.I.; M.C.; T.F.

REID, C. (D.S.O. L.G. 26.9.18); s. of W. A. Reid, J.P., of Aberdeen; educ. Aberdeen University; Major; commanded (A/Lt.-Col.) 8/10th Batt. G. Highrs., 1917; Despatches thrice.

REID, C. S. (D.S.O. L.G. 1.1.18); b. 23.8.79; 2nd Lt., R.E., 7.7.99; Lt. 13.2.02; Capt. 7.7.08; Maj. 1.4.16; served S. African War, 1901–2; Queen's Medal, 3 clasps; Europ. War; Despatches.

REID, D. W. (D.S.O. L.G. 26.7.18), T/Capt. Seaf. Highrs.; M.C.

REID, F. J. (D.S.O. L.G. 3.6.16); b. 25.3.77; 2nd Lt., R.M., 1.1.96; Lt., R.M., 1.1.97; 2nd Lt., A.S.C., 2.10.99; Lt. 2.10.00; Capt. 15.7.01; Major 30.9.13; Lt.-Col., R.A.S.C., 15.2.18; served S. African War, 1900–2; Queen's Medal, 3 clasps; King's Medal, 2 clasps; Europ. War; Despatches; C.B.E.

REID, F. M. (D.S.O. L.G. 4.6.17); b. 17.6.49; 6th s. of late William Reid and late Louisa Margaret Reid; m. Katharine Elizabeth Julia, e. d. of Colonel George William Holmes Ross, late 92nd Highrs.; educ. Harrow; Ensign by purchase, 71st Foot, The H.L.I., 8.7.68; Lieutenant by purchase, Aug. 1870; Capt. March, 1878; Major, 1885; 2nd-in-command, Nov. 1890, 1st Bn. The H.L.I.; Lt.-Col. in command, Nov. 1894; Bt. Col. to command 7th Bn. Linc. R. 6.9.14; transferred to 13th (S.B.) The Worcs. R. 3.5.15; raised 34th R. Fus. 3.4.16; served Kandia, 1898; Despatches; Bt. Col. and year extension of command; Europ. War; Despatches twice. He was 66 years of age when he went to France in command of the 34th Labour Batt. The R. Fusiliers.

REID, G. E. (D.S.O. L.G. 26.7.17); b. London, Ontario, Canada, 1.12.93; s. of G. M. Reid; m. Lewisa McGregor, d. of J. W. MacDonald; educ. McGill University, Montreal; joined Can. Forces 14.10.14, and obtained his commission in 3rd Batt. Toronto Regt.; promoted Major; served Europ. War; Despatches twice (L.G. 1.1.16 and 1.1.17); Chevalier of the Legion of Honour. His D.S.O. was awarded for gallantry at Farbus Wood 9.4.17.

REID, G. R. M. (D.S.O. L.G. 1.1.19), Major, R.A.F.; M.C.

REID, H. A. (D.S.O. L.G. 26.9.18), T/Major, R.E.; M.C.

REID, H. G. (D.S.O. L.G. 4.6.17); b. 6.6.81; 2nd Lt., A.S.C., 21.3.00; Lt. 1.4.01; Capt. 1.2.05; Maj. 30.10.14; served S. African War, 1901–2; Queen's Medal and 5 clasps; Europ. War, 1914–18; S. Russia, 1919; Bt. Lt.-Col. 1.1.16; Despatches; C.B.E.; C.M.G.

REID, J. G. (D.S.O. L.G. 26.7.18); b. 13.5.78; s. of late J. A. Reid, M.D.; m. Morag, d. of late J. Macmillan; educ. Ontario Public and High Schools; Bishop Ridley's College; served Europ. War, 1915–18; Lt.-Colonel, Reserve; 2nd-in-command, Canadian Overseas Construction Corps; Despatches.

REID, N. (D.S.O. L.G. 3.6.19), Lt. (A/Capt.), R.F.A., S.R., att. 40th Div. Trench Mortar Battery; M.C.

REID, N. S. (D.S.O. L.G. 25.8.16); b. 19.12.92, at El Nido, Port Orotava, Teneriffe, Canary Islands; s. of Thomas Miller, British Vice-Consul, Port Orotava, and Lisette Reid; m. Clara Louisa Kestin; one s.; educ. Sir William Borlase's School, Gt. Marlow; Lt., Oxford. and Bucks. L. Inf., 1913; Capt. 1.6.16; served abroad, March, 1915–Aug. 1917; wounded at Ypres, Aug. 1917; M.C.; Despatches twice. His D.S.O. was awarded for gallantry on 23.7.16, at Pozières.

REID, R. S. (D.S.O. L.G. 1.1.19), Major, 5th Field Co., Aust. Engrs.

REID-KELLETT, A. (D.S.O. L.G. 1.1.19), T/Major, S.W.B., att. 6th Batt.; M.C.

REILLY, H. L. (D.S.O. L.G. 19.10.16); b. 18.10.86; s. of Col. B. L. P. Reilly, Ind. Army, and Mrs. E. Reilly; m. Alice Isabel Hathorn; two s.; educ. Bedford Grammar School; 2nd Lt. 5.8.05; Lt., Ind. Army, 5.11.07; Capt. 5.8.14; attd. R.F.C., Aug. 1914; Squadron Leader, R.A.F.; served Indian Frontier, Mohmand Exp., 1908; Medal, clasp; Europ. War (France, Egypt and Mesopotamia), 1914–15; Despatches; Bt. Maj. 3.6.15; was taken prisoner by the Turks.

REILLY, N. E. (D.S.O. L.G. 3.8.20); b. 30.12.83; 2nd Lt., Unatt., 27.8.02; Lt., Ind. Army, 27.11.04; Capt. 27.8.11; Maj. 27.8.17; Despatches.

REINOLD, B. E. (D.S.O. L.G. 11.4.19), Cdr., R.N.; Destroyers.

REIRDON, W. R. (D.S.O. L.G. 1.1.18), Major, Can. F.A.

RENDALL, F. H. S. (D.S.O. L.G. 14.1.16); b. 22.11.79; 2nd Lt., D.C.L. Inf., 20.5.99; Lt. 7.6.00; Capt. 6.8.04; Major 1.9.15; served S. African War, 1899–1902; Queen's Medal, 6 clasps; King's Medal, 2 clasps. He died of wounds on 9.7.16.

RENDALL, H. E. (D.S.O. L.G. 12.12.18); b. 1888; s. of late E. D. Rendall, late of Charterhouse, Godalming; m. Nora Kathleen, d. of W. W. Ellis; one s.; Lt.-Cdr., R.N.; served Europ. War from 1914; Despatches; Russian Order of St. Stanislaus with Swords for services in N. Russia, 1918.

RENDELL, H. T. (D.S.O. L.G. 1.1.18), Lt. (T/Major), A.S.C., S.R.

RENNIE, R. (D.S.O. L.G. 14.1.16); b. 15.12.62; s. of late W. Rennie; m. Marion, d. of late W. Ross; one s.; educ. Toronto; Brig.-Gen., Queen's Own Rifles, Canada,; M.V.O., 1910; left Canada, Aug. 1914, in command Toronto Batt. 3/1st Can. Div., afterwards in charge of 4th Inf. Bde., 2nd Can. Div.; in command Bramshott Camp, 1918; served Europ. War, 1914–18; C.B.; C.M.G.

RENNIE, W. B. (D.S.O. L.G. 3.6.19), T/Major (T/Lt.-Col.), Spec. List; M.C.; Lt.-Col., Gen. List, ret. pay.

RENNISON, A. J., B.A. (D.S.O. L.G. 23.11.16); b. 3.11.76; s. of late Ven. Archdeacon Rennison, of Navan, Co. Meath; m. Norah Gertrude, d. of late Col. J. B. Backhouse, C.B., The Buffs; one s.; one d.; educ. privately; Trinity College, Dublin; 1st com. in A.S.C. 22.5.00; Lt. 22.8.02; transferred to S. and T. Corps, Ind. Army, 18.4.09; Capt. 22.5.09; Major 1.9.15; served Europ. War from 1914; Despatches twice; 1914 Star; Bt. Major.

RENNY-TAILYOUR, J. W. (D.S.O. L.G. 18.8.16); b. 20.5.81; s. of late Col. H. W. Renny-Tailyour and late Emily Rose, d. of J. Wingfield Stratford; educ. Wellington College; R.M.A., Woolwich; 2nd Lt., R.A., 2.5.00; Lt. 3.4.01; Capt. 8.2.10; Major 30.10.14; served Europ. War, in Mesopotamia, 1914–17; Despatches thrice; Croix de Guerre. He was invalided to India in May, 1917; given command 16th Bgde. N.W. Frontier of India; commanded this Brigade during Afghan War, 1919; Despatches.

RENTON, R. H. LINDSAY- (see Lindsay-Renton, R. H.).

RETTIE, W. J. K. (D.S.O. L.G. 1.1.17); b. 24.7.68; 2nd Lt., R.A., 7.2.88; Lt. 17.2.91; Capt. 8.9.98; Maj. 16.3.04; Lt.-Col. 30.10.14; retired pay 30.4.20; served Europ. War, 1914–18; Despatches.

REVELL, J. W., A.M.I.C.E. (D.S.O. L.G. 1.1.18) (Bar, L.G. 26.7.18), Major, late R.E.; served Europ. War, 1914–18; Despatches.

REWCASTLE, G. L. D. (D.S.O. L.G. 25.11.16); b. 15.11.90, at South Shields; s. of C. L. D. Rewcastle and C. E. Rewcastle; m. Annie Douglas Sweeney; served four years in Territorial Force in 4th North'd Howitzer Bde.; enlisted R.G.A. 27.11.14; 2nd Lt., R.G.A. (S.R.), 18.10.15; Lt., R.G.A., 1.7.17; Capt., R.G.A., 23.8.17; Major, R.G.A., 11.3.18; served Europ. War; wounded; Despatches; M.C. His D.S.O. was awarded for gallantry on 7.8.16, at Trônes Wood; left Army of Occupation, Germany, June, 1919, and was appointed Assistant Commissioner of Police, Southern Nigeria.

REYNE, G. VAN ROSSUM (D.S.O. L.G. 19.10.16); b. 29.3.86; s. of Major J. F. Reyne, 37th Foot; educ. Wellington College; R.M.C., Sandhurst; 2nd Lt. 5.8.05, being att. 2nd Ches. Regt., until posted to the 76th Punjabis 7.12.06; Lt., Ind. Army, 5.11.07; Adjt. 1.1.14; Capt. 5.8.14; Major, Ind. Army, 5.8.20; served Europ. War, in Egypt and Mesopotamia, and with General Townshend's Force in Kut; Despatches three times (L.G. 5.4.16, L.G. 13.7.16, L.G. 19.10.16). He was taken prisoner of war by the Turks at the fall of Kut, and liberated on the signing of the Armistice with Turkey. He is M.V.O.

REYNOLDS, A. B. (D.S.O. L.G. 3.6.19); b. 12.3.79; e. s. of Sir Alfred Reynolds and Emily Margaret, d. of late A. Boyd, J.P.; 2nd Lt., 12th Lrs., 23.5.00; Lt. 3.9.02; Capt. 22.8.08; Maj. 12.12.14; late Lt.-Col. North'd Hrs.; S. African War, 1901–2; Despatches; Queen's Medal, 3 clasps; Europ. War from 1914; Despatches.

REYNOLDS, C. E. (D.S.O. L.G. 14.11.16); b. 21.4.87, at Bobcaygeon, Ontario; s. of Charles C. Reynolds, Farmer of 1,000 acres in Dewdner, B.C., Canada, and of Emma Reynolds; educ. Owen Sound, Ontario; joined the Army 20.9.14; promoted Lieutenant, Can. Inf.; served Europ. War; Despatches; M.C. His D.S.O. was awarded for gallantry on 26.9.16, at Courcelette.

REYNOLDS, C. H. (D.S.O. L.G. 3.6.19); b. 23.8.83; 2nd Lt., R.A., 15.7.03; Lt. 15.7.06; Capt. 30.10.14; Maj. 1.3.18; M.C.

REYNOLDS, D. W. (D.S.O. L.G. 12.12.19); b. 5.8.84; 2nd Lt., York. and Lanc. R., 5.2.08; Lt. 1.6.09; Capt. 10.9.14; Maj. 10.9.21; Capt. (A/Lt.-Col.), York and Lancaster R., commanding 2/2nd K.A. Rifles.

REYNOLDS, SIR JAMES P., Kt. (D.S.O. L.G. 4.6.17); b. 16.2.65; 3rd s. of Francis William Reynolds and Clare Reynolds; m. 1892, Elizabeth Emelia (Leila), d. of Nicholas R. and Elizabeth Rosbell; three s.; five d.; educ. Ushaw, Durham; Fort Augustus Abbey, N.B.; President of the Liverpool Cotton Association, 1907; D.L., J.P., for the county of Lancaster; joined 3rd West Lancs. Bde., R.F.A. (T.), 23.9.96; Lieut.-Col; took command of this Bde. 6.1.09, until 30.9.16; the Brigade went out to France 30.9.15, with the 2nd Canadian Division, being in the line at Kemmel until Dec. 1916; merged into the 55th West Lancs. Division, Jan. 1916; in the line at Beaumetz. Despatches twice; Coronation Medal and T.D.; 1914–15 Medal; Chairman, National Society for Prevention of Cruelty to Children, Liverpool Outer District; Father Berry's Homes for Destitute Children.

REYNOLDS, L. L. C., M.R.C.S., L.R.C.P. (D.S.O. L.G. 14.11.16) (Bar, L.G. 26.9.17) (Details, L.G. 9.1.18); b. 11.5.82; s. of L. W. Reynolds, J.P.; m. Elizabeth Bianca Weber; one s.; one d.; educ. Epsom College; Guy's Hospital; D.L., Bucks; joined Bucks. Batt. Oxf. and Bucks. L.I., 1901; Lt.-Col. 3.6.16; Commanding Bucks. Batt. Oxf. and Bucks. L.I., since 1916; served Europ. War from 1914; French Croix de Guerre avec Palmes; Italian Silver Medal for Valour, 1918; Despatches five times. His D.S.O. was awarded for gallantry 23.7.16, at Les Ovillers.

RHOADES, W. (D.S.O. L.G. 3.6.18) (Bar, L.G. 11.1.19), Lt.-Col., 5th Bn. Can. Inf., Quebec R.; served S. African War, 1900; Queen's Medal, 5 clasps; Europ. War; Despatches.

RHODES, F. W. (D.S.O. L.G. 14.11.16); b. 11.12.88; s. of G. W. Rhodes; m. Kate Olive Inions; educ. The City of London School; Lt., late King's Shrops. L.I.; served during Europ. War, 1914–18; served with King's African Rifles, 1917; Despatches. His D.S.O. was awarded for gallantry on 15.9.16, at Gird Trench.

RHODES, G. D. (D.S.O. L.G. 1.1.17); b. Victoria, B.C., Canada, 18.7.86; s. of H. Rhodes; m. M. J. Topping; one s.; educ. Trinity College School, Port Hope, Canada; R.M.C., Kingston, Canada; commissioned in R.E. 27.6.07; Lt. 6.1.09; Capt. 30.10.14; Adjt. to Rly. Construction Troops in France, 1914–15; Capt. and Bt. Major, Commanding Rly. Cons. Coy., Peninsula, and Salonika, 1915–16; T/Major, 1916; T/Lt.-Col., 1916; A.D. of Railways, Salonika; Brig.-Gen., 1919; served Europ. War from 1914; Despatches thrice; Bt. Major 3.6.18; C.B.E.; Legion of Honour (Officer), Order of Redeemer (Greek).

RHODES, J. P. (D.S.O. L.G. 1.1.18); b. 19.7.84; elder s. of Sir G. Rhodes, Bart., and Margaret Catherine, d. of J. Phillips; m. Elsie, d. of Lt.-Col. G. A. Maclean Buckley, C.B.E.; one s.; educ. Harrow; R.M.A., Woolwich; F.R.G.S.; ent. R.E. 23.3.04; Lt. 23.12.06; Capt. 30.10.14; Bt. Maj. 3.6.19; Lt.-Col., ret. pay, 9.1.20; served Europ. War, 1914–18; Bt. Major; Croix de Guerre.

RHODES, S. (D.S.O. L.G. 24.9.18), Capt. (A/Lt.-Col.), York and Lancaster R.

RHYS-DAVIDS, A. P. F. (D.S.O. L.G. 27.10.17) (Details, L.G. 18.3.18), 2nd Lt. R.F.C., S.R.; M.C. He was killed in action 27.10.17.

RICARDO, H. G. (D.S.O. L.G. 1.1.17); b. 23.6.60; e. s. of late H. D. Ricardo, of Gatcombe, and Ellen, d. of Ven. W. Crawley, Archdeacon of Monmouth; m. Adela, d. of late J. P. Cobbold, M.P., of Ipswich; three d.; educ. Winchester; entered R.A., 1879; retired with rank of Major, April, 1897; rejoined (after 18 years' service) as Lt.-Col., R.F.A., Dec. 1914; served Europ. War, 1914–17, in command of 92nd Bde. R.F.A.; Despatches twice.

RICARDO, W. F. (D.S.O. L.G. 4.6.17); b. 1868; s. of late F. Ricardo; m. Nora, d. of late I. Bell, U.S. Plenipotentiary at The Hague; educ. Eton; Major, retired, late R. Horse Guards; Lt.-Col., Leic. Yeomanry; S. African War, 1899–1900; Queen's Medal, 3 clasps; served Europ. War.

RICE, B. A. MC H. (D.S.O. L.G. 26.8.18); b. 7.2.76; 2nd Lt., Som. L.I., 5.9.96; Lt., Ind. Army, 5.12.98; Capt. 5.9.05; Maj. 5.9.14; Lt.-Col. 25.8.19; ret. pay 7.9.20; N.W. Frontier, 1897–98; Medal, clasp.

RICE, C. E. (D.S.O. L.G. 4.6.17) (Bar, L.G. 18.7.17), Major (T/Lt.-Col.), Yeom. (Cdg. Bn. R. Fus.). His Bar was awarded for gallantry at Monchy-le-Preux on 10.4.17.

RICE, G. D. (D.S.O. L.G. 26.8.18); b. 12.6.83; 2nd Lt., R. Muns. Fus., 19.10.01; Lt., Ind. Army, 19.1.04; Capt. 19.10.10; Maj. 19.10.16; S. African War, 1901, in Mediterranean; Medal; Europ. War; Despatches.

RICE, W. V. (D.S.O. L.G. 1.1.16), Lt.-Cdr., R.N., 30.6.17); served Europ. War, 1914–18; D.S.C. From 1918 he was Executive Officer and Second-in-Command in the Fantome, which was surveying in Australian waters. He was then appointed to a similar position in the Beaufort.

RICE-JONES, A. P. (D.S.O. L.G. 18.2.18) (Details, L.G. 18.7.18), T/Lt. (A/Capt.), R.E.; Major.

RICH, C. E. F. (D.S.O. L.G. 14.1.16); b. 1871; m. Violet Cecile Anne, d. of late Admiral H. C. St. John; one s.; one d.; educ. Winchester; Lt.-Colonel, Lincs. R., R. of O.; Governor of H.M. Borstal Institution from 1920; served S. African War, 1902; Medal and 2 clasps; Europ. War from 1914; Despatches five times; Bt. Lt.-Col.; Croix de Guerre (France) with Palm; Order of Redeemer and Order of Merit, Greece, with Palm.

RICH, E. E. (D.S.O. L.G. 1.1.18); b. 14.5.84; 2nd Lt., R.A., 24.12.02; Lt. 24.12.05; S. African War, 1902; Queen's Medal, 4 clasps; Europ. War; Despatches. He was killed in action 1.12.17.

RICHARDS, C. E. M. (D.S.O. L.G. 3.6.19); b. 29.4.88; Capt. (from Mob. Spec. Res.), East Lanc. R., 2.10.15; M.C.

RICHARDS, D. J. R. (D.S.O. L.G. 16.8.17); b. 5.11.90; 2nd Lt., R.A., 23.12.10; Lt. 23.12.13; Capt. 8.8.16; M.C. His D.S.O. was awarded for gallantry on 5.4.17.

RICHARDS, F. H. (D.S.O. L.G. 4.6.17); b. 26.12.90; 2nd Lt., R.A., 23.12.10; Lt. 23.12.13; Capt. 8.8.16.

RICHARDS, F. W. (D.S.O. L.G. 2.4.19) (Details, L.G. 10.12.19), T/Capt. (A/Major), 105th Co., R.E.; M.C.

RICHARDS, H. A. D. (D.S.O. L.G. 1.1.17); b. 16.2.74; s. of Rev. A. J. Richards, of Farlington, Havant, Hants; m. Helen Dorothy, d. of R. L. Parker; one d.; educ. Charterhouse; joined 1st Batt. R. Sussex Rgt. 6.6.96; Lt., A.S.C., 1.1.99; Capt. 1.1.01; Maj. 7.10.12; Lt.-Col. 1.4.17; ret. pay 1.10.21; served S. African War, 1899–1902; Despatches twice; Bt. Major 26.6.02; Queen's and King's Medals, 5 clasps; Europ. War; Despatches four times; C.M.G.; Belgian Croix de Guerre.

RICHARDS, J. F. G., M.R.C.S., L.R.C.P., M.B., B.S. (D.S.O. L.G. 1.1.18); b. 1887; s. of J. G. Richards; educ. Wellington College, N.Z.; Guy's Hospital; Sir George Grey Scholar, Victoria College, University of N.Z.; Gold Medal in Surgery, Guy's Hospital; Capt., R.A.M.C.; served Europ. War, 1914–18; 1914 Star.

RICHARDSON, A. J. (D.S.O. L.G. 20.10.16); b. 19.7.62; s. of late C. Richardson and Mary, d. of William Reeves, Bishop of Down; m. Emily, d. of late Rev. A. Armitage, of Breckenbrough, Cheltenham; three s.; one d.; educ. Haileybury College; R.M.C., Sandhurst; joined E. Yorks. R. 9.9.82; Lt.-Col. 15.8.07; served Burmese War, 1885–87, commanding a M.I. Coy.; helped to raise and train 1st Batt. W.A.F.F., 1897; served W. Africa, 1897–98; Medal and clasp; South Africa, 1900–2; 2 Medals and 4 clasps; retired 15.8.11, on completing his command of a battalion. When war began was called out to command 1st Hull Batt.; in the Somme Battle commanded the 8th Batt. S. Lancs. R. The D.S.O. was awarded for gallantry from Aug.–Sept. 1916.

A. J. Richardson.

RICHARDSON, A. N. (D.S.O. L.G. 3.6.19), T/Major, 39th Batt. M.G.C.; M.C.

RICHARDSON, A. R. (D.S.O. L.G. 25.8.17), Lt.-Col., London Regt. His D.S.O. was awarded for gallantry north-west of Bullecourt 16.6.17.

RICHARDSON, A. W. C. (D.S.O. L.G. 15.2.17); b. 11.5.87; s. of J. C. Richardson; m. Agnes Mackay, d. of A. Thackeray, J.P.; one s.; one d.; educ. Denstone College, Staffs; 2nd Lt., Bedf. R., 11.12.07; Lt. 17.7.09; Capt., Beds. and Herts. R., 9.8.13; Major 1.1.18; *p.s.c.*; served Europ. War, 1915–18; Bt. Major.

RICHARDSON, G. C. (D.S.O. L.G. 1.1.18) (Bar, L.G. 16.9.18): b. 18.7.84; 2nd Lt., R.A., 29.7.04; Lt. 29.7.07; Major 9.7.16; ret. pay 29.7.19; M.C.

RICHARDSON, H., M.D. (D.S.O. L.G. 11.4.18), Major (T/Lt.-Col.), R.A.M.C.

RICHARDSON, H. MC K. W. (D.S.O. L.G. 1.1.18), T/Major, N.Z. Rif. Brig.; S. African War, 1901–2; Queen's Medal, 4 clasps; Europ. War; Despatches; M.C.

RICHARDSON, J. D. (D.S.O. L.G. 1.1.18), Major, Aust. L.H. Rgt.

RICHARDSON, JAMES JARDINE (D.S.O. L.G. 25.8.17) (Bar, L.G. 2.4.19) (Details, L.G. 10.12.19); b. 26.2.73; 2nd Lt., 11th Hrs., 5.10.92; Lt. 18.7.94; Capt. 19.3.01; Maj. 28.3.08; Lt.-Col., 13th Hrs., 1.7.17; N.W. Frontier, 1897–98; Medal, clasp; S. African War, 1899–1902; Queen's Medal, clasp; King's Medal, 2 clasps; Europ. War; Despatches.

RICHARDSON, JOHN JAMES (D.S.O. L.G. 14.11.16), Lt., 18th Bn. Canadian Infantry. His D.S.O. was awarded for gallantry on 15.9.16 at Courcelette.

RICHARDSON, M. E. (D.S.O. L.G. 25.8.16); b. 22.8.78; s. of M. Richardson; m. Olive Katherine, d. of W. A. Soames; two s.; one d.; educ. Charterhouse; Trinity College, Cambridge; B.A.; 2nd Lt., 23.5.00, 20th Hussars (in India); Lt. 3.12.01; Capt. 12.10.06; Major 20.5.14; Lt.-Col. 27.3.18; T/Brig.-Gen., late 20th Hussars; retired 16.7.21; served S. African War, 1902; Medal and 2 clasps; served with 20th Hussars from Battle of Mons till Dec. 1915; then commanded 26th North'd Fus. in France till Feb. 1918; for one month commanded 11th E. Suffolk Rgt.; Temp. Brig.-Gen., 175th Brig., in France; Despatches four times; Legion of Honour, Croix de Chevalier; 1914 Star and Bar; took over command 20th Hussars, April, 1919. His D.S.O. was awarded for gallantry south of La Boiselle 1.7.16, when he was wounded.

RICHARDSON, N. G. STEWART- (see Stewart-Richardson, N. G.).

RICHARDSON, R. C. (D.S.O. L.G. 6.4.18), Lt.-Cdr., R.N.

RICHARDSON, R. W. (D.S.O. L.G. 1.4.19), Lt.-Cdr. (A/Cdr.), R.N.

RICHEY, F. W. (D.S.O. L.G. 3.6.19); b. 21.8.75; 2nd Lt., R.A., 15.6.95; Lt. 15.6.98; Capt. 12.2.01; Maj. 30.10.14; Lt.-Col. 1.5.21.

RICHMOND, G. W., A.M.I.C.E. (D.S.O. L.G. 18.6.17); b. 8.7.88; s. of R. Richmond, C.A., J.P.; educ. Berkhamsted School; Finsbury Technical College; A.M.I.C.E.; Gas Engineer; Capt., R.E., S.R.; served Europ. War, 1914–18; Despatches.

RICHMOND, J. D., M.B. (D.S.O. L.G. 4.6.17); b. 4.10.77; Lt., R.A.M.C., 31.8.03; Capt. 28.2.07; Maj. 28.2.15; O.B.E.

RICHMOND, J. MAC D. (D.S.O. L.G. 1.1.18), Major, N.Z. Field Arty.; M.C.

RICHMOND, L. (D.S.O. L.G. 1.2.19), T/2nd Lt., 12th Batt. Ches. R.

RICKARDS, G. A. (D.S.O. L.G. 1.1.18); s. of A. G. Rickards, K.C., V.D., and Elinor Frances, d. of C. Butler; m. Stella Evelyn, d. of Lt.-Col. H. G. Ricardo D.S.O., late R.A.; educ. Eton; R.M.A., Woolwich; 2nd Lt., R.F.A., 25.7.06; Lt. 25.7.09; Capt. 30.10.14; Major, R.H.A., 19.3.17; served Europ. War (France), May, 1915–April, 1919; Despatches twice; M.C.; Order of Aviz, Portugal, 2nd Class.

RICKETTS, P. E. (D.S.O. L.G. 1.1.17); b. 5.3.68; s. of George Ricketts, C.B.; m. Lilian Caroline, d. of late Lt.-Gen. H. Morant; educ. Winchester Coll.; R.M.C., Sandhurst; 2nd Lt., Devon R., 22.8.88; Lt. 17.6.90; Capt., I.A. 22.8.99; Major 3.4.08; Lt.-Col. 3.4.16; 18th K.G.O. Lancers 3.4.20; served Chitral, 1895; Despatches; Medal with clasp; N.W. Frontier of India, 1897–98; clasp; Tirah, 1897–98; clasp; M.V.O., 1914; Europ. War, 1914–17 Despatches twice; dangerously wounded Battle of the Somme.

RICKMAN, A. W. (D.S.O. L.G. 1.1.17) (Bar, L.G. 16.9.18); b. 25.9.74; s. late Lt.-Gen. W. Rickman and Mary Pulsford Rickman; m. Muriel Joicey Fulton; educ. Winchester College; entered Army 26.5.97; Capt. 22.4.01; ret. pay 16.9.09; Lt.-Col., Spec. Res., North'd Fus.; served S. African War, 1899–1902; Queen's Medal and 3 clasps; King's Medal and 2 clasps; Europ War, 1914–18; wounded twice; Despatches four times.

RICKWOOD, H. G. (D.S.O. L.G. 3.6.19), T/Major (A/Lt.-Col.), 9th Bn. S. Lanc. R.; M.C.

RIDDEL, D. O., M.B. (D.S.O. L.G. 25.11.16), Temp. Capt., R.A.M.C. His D.S.O. was awarded for gallantry on 7.10.16 at Destremont Farm, Le Sars.

RIDDELL, A. (D.S.O. L.G. 25.8.17); b. 2.4.82; 2nd Lt., Essex R., 18.1.02; Lt. 22.4.04; Capt., Ind. Army, 18.1.11; Maj. 18.1.17; S. African War, 1902; Queen's Medal, 4 clasps; Europ. War; Despatches.

RIDDELL, C. C. (D.S.O. L.G. 25.8.17); b. 1887; s. of T. W. G. W. Riddell and Virginia Eleanor Consett, d. of M. Consett Stephen; educ. C. of E. Grammar School, Melbourne; University of Melbourne (Trinity College); B.Sc.; B.M.E.; Major, Aust. Engrs.; served Europ. War from 1914; Despatches twice. His D.S.O. was awarded for gallantry at Messines 7–8.6.17.

RIDDELL, E. P. A. (D.S.O. L.G. 11.12.16) (1st Bar, L.G. 26.9.17) (Details, L.G. 9.1.18) (2nd Bar, L.G. 26.7.18); b. 23.5.75; s. of late J. G. Riddell, of Felton Park and Swinburne Castle, Northumberland, and his 2nd wife, Victoria Henrietta, d. of P. Purcell; m. Frances Hygnia, d. of late F. J. Sumner; 2nd Lt., North'd Fus., 21.2.00; Lt. 9.6.00; Capt. 9.2.05; Maj., Rif. Brig., 1.9.15; Temp. Brig.-Gen. 2.10.17; served S. Africa, 1901–2; Queen's Medal, 3 clasps; Europ. War, 1914–18; Bt. Lt.-Col. 1.1.18; C.M.G.

RIDDELL, R. B. (D.S.O. L.G. 1.1.18); b. 1.4.72; 2nd Lt., R.A., 28.3.92; Lt. 28.3.95; Capt. 3.1.00; Maj. 22.11.12; Lt.-Col. 1.5.17; Col. 1.5.21; S. African War, 1899–1902; Despatches; Bt. Maj. 29.11.00; Queen's Medal, 6 clasps; King's Medal, 2 clasps; served Europ. War; Despatches.

RIDDICK, J. G. (D.S.O. L.G. 1.1.19), Major (A/Lt.-Col.), R.E., T.F.

RIDEAL, J. G. E. (D.S.O. L.G. 4.6.17), Capt. (T/Maj), York and Lancs. Rgt.

RIDGWAY, J. H. (D.S.O. L.G. 1.1.17); b. 3.8.75; 2nd Lt., N. Staff. R., 21.4.00; Lt. 6.12.00; Capt. 14.3.09; Lt.-Col., comdg. a battn. of the York and Lancs. Regt.; S. African War, 1900–2; Queen's and King's Medals, 4 clasps; Europ. War; Despatches. He was killed in action 24.4.17. With the exception of three months' sick leave he had been at the front since Sept. 1914.

RIDGWAY, T. (D.S.O. L.G. 3.6.19), Capt. (A/Lt.-Col.), 1/4th Batt. R.G.A., att. 72nd Army Brig., R.F.A.; M.C.

RIDLER, R. H. (D.S.O. L.G. 3.6.19), Capt., 25th Batt. London R., att. 11th Batt. Som. L.I., T.F.

RIDLEY, B. W. (D.S.O. L.G. 8.3.19) (Details, L.G. 4.10.19), T/Major (A/Lt.-Col.), 29th Batt. Durham L.I. (formerly E. Lancs. R.); M.C.

RIDLEY, C. A. (D.S.O. L.G. 14.11.16); b. Nov. 1897; s. of L. C. Ridley; educ. Dr. Roscoe's, Harrogate; St. Paul's London; Sandhurst; commissioned in R. Fusiliers, 1915; Capt., R. Fus., att. R.F.C. (now R.A.F.) (Flight Commander); took Pilot's Certificate, June, 1915; went to France immediately afterwards, and was wounded in aerial combat over the German lines on a Morane Parasol Machine (M.C.); returned to France, July, 1916, and when his machine was wrecked, escaped with valuable information; was decorated on the field by Gen. Haig (D.S.O.); Despatches four times, and on his return had a private audience of the King; Gold Medal from the Lord Mayor for bringing down Zeppelin L 15, 31.3.16, with another officer.

RIDLEY, J. C. T. E. C. (D.S.O. L.G. 1.1.17), Major, Aust. Lt. Horse.

RIDLEY, J. J. C. (D.S.O. L.G. 8.3.18), Lt.-Cdr., R.N.

RIDOUT, J. Y. H. (D.S.O. L.G. 3.6.18); b. 6.5.78; 2nd Lt., R.A., 19.6.99; Lt. 16.2.01; Capt. 29.3.06; Maj. 30.10.14; Bt. Lt.-Col. 1.1.19; served China, 1900; Europ. War; Despatches.

RIGBY, W. (D.S.O. L.G. 4.5.17), Capt., R. of O., late R.I. Rifles, and E. African Police.

RIGG, E. H. (D.S.O. L.G. 3.6.16) (Bar, L.G. 3.6.18) (2nd Bar, L.G. 1.2.19); b. 8.12.80; s. of Rev. W. H. Rigg; m. Clara Benita, d. of late Rev. J. H. Douglas; 2nd Lt., Yorks. L.I., 6.12.99; Lt. 26.1.01; Capt. 17.6.06; Maj. 1.9.15.

RIGG, G. S. (D.S.O. L.G. 26.7.17), 2nd Lt. (T/Lt.), York and Lanc. R., S.R. His D.S.O. was awarded for gallantry at Roeux 16.5.17. He was killed in action 31.7.17.

RIGG, W. G. (D.S.O. L.G. 1.1.16), Lt.-Cdr. (A/Cdr.), R.N.

RIGGALL, H. W. (D.S.O. L.G. 1.1.18), Major (T/Lt.-Col.), Aust. F.A.

RILEY, H. J. (D.S.O. L.G. 18.7.17) (Bar, L.G. 11.1.19) (2nd Bar, L.G. 8.3.19) (Details, L.G. 4.10.19), Lt.-Col., 27th Batt. Can. Inf. His D.S.O. was awarded for gallantry on 4.4.17 at Farbus.

RIPLEY, B. (D.S.O. L.G. 1.1.18), Lt.-Col., Can. Rly. Troops.

RISK, C. E. (D.S.O. L.G. 3.6.19), Lt.-Col., R.M.L. Inf. (Mediterranean).

RISLEY, C. G. (D.S.O. L.G. 1.1.17); b. 8.10.81; 2nd Lt., R.A., 23.7.01; Lt. 23.7.04; Ind. Army 4.2.05; Capt., Ind. Army, 23.7.10; Maj. 23.7.16.

RISPIN, D. E. A. (D.S.O. L.G. 1.1.18), Major, Can. Inf.

RITCHIE, C. F. (D.S.O. L.G. 8.3.19) (Details, L.G. 4.10.19); b. 12.10.88, at Three Rivers, Prov. of Quebec, Canada; s. of Arthur Dudley Ritchie and Rosina Ritchie; m. Frances, d. of late Mr. and Mrs. L. E. Dodwell, of Montreal; one s.; one d.; educ. Three Rivers, High School; joined 3rd Regt., Victoria Rifles of Canada, as a Private, Oct. 1910; Lieut., Can. Militia, 10.6.14; Lieut., 24th Can. Bn. V.R.C., C.E.F., 26.10.14; Capt. 10.5.15; Major 4.10.16; Lt.-Col. 17.10.17; served Europ. War; Despatches; M.C. 17.9.16.

RITCHIE, THE HON. H. (D.S.O. L.G. 1.1.18) (Bar, L.G. 1.2.19); m. Ella, d. of R. C. Priestley; T/Major, 11th Bn. Sc. Rifles (att. 1st R.W. Surrey Regt.). He died of wounds 28.10.18.

RITCHIE, M. B. H, (D.S.O. L.G. 14.1.16); b. 26.7.82; s. of late Rev. R. Ritchie, Rector of St. Mary's, Inverurie, N.B.; m. Sydney d'Abzac, d. of late Rev. A. Crofton, formerly Vicar of Giggleswick; educ. Aberdeen University; M.B.; Ch.B.; joined R.A.M.C. 31.7.05; Capt. 31.1.09; Major 15.10.15; served in India and on Mohmand Expedition, 1908; Despatches; Medal, clasp; Europ. War, in Medical Charge, 29th Brig., R.F.A., from commencement until Jan. 1915, when appointed D.A.D.M.S., 3rd Corps; Despatches four times; M.C.; O.B.E.

RITCHIE, N. M. (D.S.O. L.G. 25.8.17); b. 29.7.97; 2nd Lt., R. Highrs., 16.12.14; Lt. 2.10.15; Capt. 19.11.17.

RITCHIE, THEODORE FRANCIS, M.B. (D.S.O. L.G. 1.1.17), Maj. (T/Lt.-Col.), R.A.M.C.; b. 16.6.76; Lt., R.A.M.C., 27.6.01; Capt. 27.6.04; Maj. 27.3.13; Lt.-Col., ret. pay, 18.8.20; S. African War, 1901–2; Despatches; Queen's Medal, 5 clasps; Europ. War; Despatches.

RITCHIE, THOMAS FRASER (D.S.O. L.G. 14.1.16); b. 31.8.75; s. of late T. Ritchie, of Halifax, N.S.; educ. Canada; joined Manchester Rgt., 18.4.00; Lt. 5.1.01; Capt. 18.9.07; transferred to Somerset L.I. 20.5.08; Major 1.9.15; served in S. African War, 1901–2; Queen's Medal, 5 clasps; Europ. War; Despatches.

RITSON, J. A. S. (D.S.O. L.G. 27.10.17) (Details, L.G. 18.3.18) (Bar, L.G. 26.7.18), Capt. (T/Lt.-Col.), Durham L.I.; M.C.

RITZEMA, T. P. (D.S.O. L.G. 3.6.19), T/Lt.-Col., R.F.A., att. 66th (E. Lancs.) Div., Amm. Column, R.F.A.; T.F.

RIVIS, T. C. L. (D.S.O. L.G. 3.6.18); b. 12.3.78; 2nd Lt., R. Innis. Fus., 4.1.99; Lt., A.S.C., 12.2.01; Capt. 27.8.02; Maj. 5.8.14; Lt.-Col. 1.1.21; S. African War, 1900–2; Queen's Medal, 4 clasps; King's Medal, 2 clasps.

ROACHE, J. G. (D.S.O. L.G. 4.6.17), T/Lt.-Col., Rifle Bde.

ROBERTON, J. B. W. (D.S.O. L.G. 1.2.19), T/Capt., 11th Batt. North'd Fusiliers.

ROBERTS, A. C. (D.S.O. L.G. 14.1.16); b. 2.3.70; 2nd Lt., R. Fus., 17.12.90; Lt. 26.6.92; Capt. 16.11.98; Major 16.11.07; Brig.-Gen. (80th Inf. Bde.), R. Fus.; served S. African War, 1902; Queen's Medal, 4 clasps; Europ. War; Despatches; C.M.G. He died on 17.5.17.

ROBERTS, A. H. (D.S.O. L.G. 1.1.17); b. 24.2.78; 2nd Lt., A.S.C., 19.6.01; Lt. 19.6.02; Capt. 1.5.07; Maj. 30.10.14; Bt. Lt.-Col. 3.6.19; O.B.E.; S. African War, 1900–2; Queen's Medal, 7 clasps; Europ. War; Despatches.

ROBERTS, A. M. (D.S.O. L.G. 5.10.18); b. 1.2.86; s. of the late Rev. George Edward Roberts; m. Caroline Elizabeth, widow of Lt.-Col. C. Worthington, The Buffs; educ. Greenhall, Belper; The Limes, Greenwich; H.M.S. Britannia; joined R.N. 7.5.02; Lt.-Cdr., R.N.; seniority in rank 30.6.17; served as Lieut. in H.M.S. Odin in Persian Gulf, June, 1910, to Aug. 1912; Naval General Service Medal; Naval Persian Gulf clasp; Europ. War, as Lieut., H.M.S. Neptune, in the Battle of Jutland; Commander, H.M.S. Jackal, in the Adriatic; Despatches; wounded; 1914–15 Star; played Rugby and Association for H.M.S. Britannia, 1902–3.

ROBERTS, C. A. G. (D.S.O. L.G. 17.5.18), Cdr., R.N.R., R.D.

ROBERTS, E. A. (D.S.O. L.G. 7.2.18); b. 15.1.79; s. of the late Rev. A. J. Roberts, formerly Vicar of Tidsbrook; Lt., I.M.S., 30.1.04; Capt. 30.1.07; Maj. 1.7.15; Bt. Lt.-Col. 1.1.19. He died 5.9.21, in Madras.

ROBERTS, F. E. (D.S.O. L.G. 14.1.16); b. 13.9.78; s. of late C. Roberts, M.R.C.S.; m. Gladys Helen, d. of W. E. Whitehouse; two d.; educ. Malvern; St. George's Hospital; M.R.C.S.; ent. R.A.M.C. 31.1.05; Capt. 31.7.08; served five years in Malta; Major 15.10.15; served Europ. War, 1914–18, in France and Egypt; Despatches thrice.

ROBERTS, G. (D.S.O. L.G. 8.3.19) (Details, L.G. 4.10.19), T/Capt. (A/Major), A/123rd Brig. R.F.A.; M.C.

ROBERTS, H. (D.S.O. L.G. 15.2.19) (Details, L.G. 30.7.19), Lt. (A/Capt.), 2nd Bn. R. Sussex R.; M.C.

ROBERTS, H. C. (D.S.O. L.G. 4.6.17), T/Capt., Intelligence Corps.

ROBERTS, J. (D.S.O. L.G. 27.6.17), Cdr., R.N.R., R.D.

ROBERTS, J. P. (D.S.O. L.G. 16.9.18), T/Capt. (A/Major), M.G.C.; M.C.

ROBERTS, P. T. (D.S.O. L.G. 26.11.17) (Details, L.G. 6.4.18), Capt., Aust. Inf.

ROBERTS, R. J. A. (D.S.O. L.G. 31.5.16); Temp. Capt., The Welsh R. His D.S.O. was awarded for gallantry at Colvin Craters, Moated Grange Section, 5–6.5.16. He died of wounds 22.9.17.

ROBERTS, S. R. H. (gazetted as Roberts, S. R.) (D.S.O. L.G. 1.1.17); b. 15.11.74; s. of William and Caroline Roberts, of Ararat, Victoria; educ. Grammar School, Stawell, Victoria; J.P.; commissioned Goldfields Infantry Rgt., 1899; Lt.-Col.; V.D.; O.C., 2/11th Inf. Aust. Mil. Forces; commanded Squadron, Aust. L.H., S. African War, 1902; served Egypt, 1914–15, including Gallipoli, 1915; France, Belgium, 1916–18; Despatches twice.

ROBERTS, W. B. (D.S.O. L.G. 1.2.17); b. 10.3.79; s. of late Colonel H. B. Roberts, R.M.A., who served in the Crimea, and won the Legion of Honour; m. (1st), Jessie Honor Cassanda, d. of Canon P. F. Gell (died 1907); one s.; (2nd), Geraldine Blanche, d. of Colonel R. E. Sullivan, Ind. Army; one d.; educ. Freiburg, Germany; Sandhurst; 2nd Lt., Unatt., 25.1.99; Ind. S.C. 25.3.00; Lt., Ind. Army, 25.8.01; Capt. 25.1.08; Major 1.9.15; served in Somaliland, 1902–4; Despatches; Medal with clasp; Europ. War, in E. Africa; Despatches.

ROBERTS, W. H. (D.S.O. L.G. 26.8.18); b. 21.9.82; 2nd Lt., R.E., 23.7.01; Lt. 1.4.04; Capt. 23.1.12; Maj. 2.11.16; M.C.

ROBERTSON, A. (D.S.O. L.G. 3.6.16), Capt. (T/Major), R.E. (T.F.).

ROBERTSON, A. B. (D.S.O. L.G. 23.11.16); b. 26.4.78; s. of late W. B. Robertson, J.P.; m. Annie Clare Carmichael, d. of Major J. R. Cruden; two s.; one d.; 2nd Lt., Cam'n Highrs., 4.1.99; Lt. 14.10.99; Capt. 26.4.05; Maj. 1.9.15; *p.s.c.*; served S. African War, 1900–2; Queen's Medal and 4 clasps; King's Medal and 2 clasps; Europ. War, including Egypt, 1914–18; Despatches; Bt. Lt.-Col. 3.6.17; C.M.G.; 4th Class White Eagle, Serbia; Chevalier, Legion of Honour.

ROBERTSON, B. H. (D.S.O. L.G. 3.6.19); b. 22.7.96; s. of F.M. Sir William Robertson, Bart., G.C.B., G.C.M.G., K.C.V.O., D.S.O., and Mildred Adelaide, d. of late Lt.-Gen. T. C. Palin, Bombay Staff Corps; 2nd Lt., R.E., 17.11.14; Lt. 23.12.15; Capt. 3.10.17; Capt., R.E.; served Europ. War, 1914–19; Despatches; M.C.

ROBERTSON, C. C. (D.S.O. L.G. 1.1.17); b. 24.4.71; 2nd Lt., R.A., 25.7.90; Maj. 5.5.98; ret. pay 4.9.12; Bt. Lt.-Col. 1.1.18; Lt.-Col., Res. of Off., 9.5.19; West Africa, 1898; Medal, clasp; S. African War, 1900–2; Queen's Medal, 4 clasps; King's Medal, 2 clasps; Europ. War; Despatches.

ROBERTSON, C. MC L. (D.S.O. L.G. 1.1.18), Lt.-Col., R.F.A. (For over two years in command of a divisional ammunition column.)

ROBERTSON, D. E. (D.S.O. L.G. 27.9.20); b. 22.12.79; 2nd Lt., Leins. R., 19.5.00; Lt. 11.6.02; Capt. 3.5.09; Maj. 1.9.15; Bt. Lt.-Col. 1.1.19.

ROBERTSON, D. W. (D.S.O. L.G. 11.1.19), T/2nd Lt., 1st Batt. K.R.R.C.; M.C.

ROBERTSON, F. A. (D.S.O. L.G. 1.1.19), Major, 12th Siege B'y. Can. G.A.

ROBERTSON, F. M. B. (D.S.O. L.G. 1.1.18); b. 4.7.76; 2nd Lt., Black Watch, 3.8.98; Lt. 12.12.99; Capt. 8.12.03; Maj. 25.2.15; Lt.-Col., ret. pay, 28.8.20; S. African War, 1901–2; Queen's Medal, 4 clasps.

ROBERTSON, G. MC M. (D.S.O. L.G. 3.6.18) (1st Bar, L.G. 11.1.19) (2nd Bar, L.G. 15.2.19) (Details, L.G. 30.7.19); b. 7.7.91; s. of late W. Shirras Robertson, P.W.D., Indian Government. He comes from Aberdeen; 2nd Lt., N. Staff. R., 25.3.11; Lt. 22.8.14; Capt. 23.3.16; Bt. Maj. 1.1.19.

ROBERTSON, G. R. G. (D.S.O. L.G. 16.9.18); b. 6.10.87; s. of late G. Robertson; m. Hilda Mary, d. of C. T. Stuart; educ. Rossall; Major, R.F.A.; T.D.; served Europ. War, 1914–18; Despatches several times.

ROBERTSON, H. C. H. (D.S.O. L.G. 4.6.17), Capt., Aust. Light Horse Rgt.

ROBERTSON, J. C. (D.S.O. L.G. 4.6.17); b. 24.10.78; educ. Toowoomba Grammar School, Queensland; Commanding 11th Inf. Batt. Commonwealth Mil. Forces before the War; joined A.I.F. 20.8.14; Brig.-Gen., Commanding 7th Inf. Brig., Commonwealth Military Forces; served Europ. War, 1915–16; landing at Gallipoli with covering brigade 25.4.15; wounded; Despatches seven times; C.M.G.; served in France, 1916–18; C.B.; D.S.O.

ROBERTSON, J. FORBES- (see Forbes-Robertson, J.).

ROBERTSON, J. J. (D.S.O. L.G. 10.1.17), Capt. (Temp. Major), Seaforth Highlanders. His D.S.O. was awarded for gallantry on 13.11.16, at Beaumont Hamel.

ROBERTSON, J. R. (D.S.O. L.G. 1.1.19); b. 21.6.80; 2nd Lt., R. Berks. R., 20.5.05; Lt. 9.3.09; Capt., Beds. and Herts. R., 7.5.13.

ROBERTSON, N. B. (D.S.O. L.G. 1.1.17); b. 12.8.82; s. of late F. Ewart Robertson and of Mrs. F. Ewart Robertson; 2nd Lt., R.A., 23.7.01; Lt. 23.7.04; Major, R.F.A. He was killed in action on 30.11.17.

ROBERTSON, N. R. (D.S.O. L.G. 3.6.18), Major, Can. Engrs.

ROBERTSON, R. T. C., M.B. (D.S.O. L.G. 18.1.18) (Details, L.G. 25.4.18), Capt. (A/Lt.-Col.), R.A.M.C., S.R.

ROBERTSON, W. (D.S.O. L.G. 1.1.17); b. 21.10.72; s. of late W. Robertson; m. Winnifred, d. of J. Russell; three s.; educ. Sedbergh School; R.M.A., Woolwich; ent. R.E. 22.7.92; Lt. 22.7.95; Capt. 22.7.1903; Major 22.7.12; Colonel 31.8.20; served in India for 10 years with 2nd Q.V.O. Sappers and Miners; Adjutant for five years, Chitral Relief Exp. 1895; N.W. Frontier of India, 1897–98; Tirah; Despatches twice; Medal and four clasps; went to France with 5th Corps as G.S.O.2, Dec. 1914; severely wounded near Ypres, March, 1915; France again July, 1916, G.S.O.1, H.Q., 2nd Army; T/Lt.-Col.; Oct. 1918–Jan. 1919, T/Brig.-Gen., G.S. at G.H.Q., B.E.F.; Despatches five times; Bt. Lt.-Col. 3.6.17; Bt. Col. 3.6.18; Croix d'Officier de la Légion d'Honneur; Croix d'Officier de l'Ordre de Léopold; Order of the Crown of Italy; Belgian Croix de Guerre.

ROBERTSON, W. C. (D.S.O. L.G. 1.1.18); b. 9.6.82; 2nd Lt., R.A., 15.5.01; Lt. 22.2.04; Capt. 15.5.14; Maj. 27.4.16.

ROBERTSON-EUSTACE, R. W. B. (D.S.O. L.G. 1.1.18); b. 11.1.70; educ. Shrewsbury School; Capt., R. of O. and S.R., Unatt. List, from 1904; formerly Capt., 4th Batt. S. Staffs. R.; retired with rank of Major after Europ. War; served S. African War with Can. M.R. and A.S.C.; Queen's Medal with 6 clasps; appointed to E.A. Police, 1904; served Europ. War, in British and German E. Africa, 1914–18; 1914 Star.

ROBINS, T. E., B.A. (D.S.O. L.G. 1.1.19); b. Philadelphia, U.S.A., 31.10.84; s. of late Major R. P. Robins, U.S. Army, and Mary, d. of late T. de la Roche Ellis; m. Mary St. Quintin, d. of late P. Wroughton, D.L., of Woolley Park, Berks; one d.; educ. privately; University of Pennsylvania, U.S.A.; Christ Church, Oxford; was the first Rhodes Scholar from State of Pennsylvania to Oxford University, 1904–07; mobilized with City of London Yeom. 4.8.14, and served overseas in M.E.F. and E.E.F., April, 1915–Jan. 1921; Provost-Marshal, E.E.F. (Egypt and Palestine), Feb. 1919, to Jan. 1921; Despatches twice.

ROBINSON, A. C. (D.S.O. L.G. 1.1.18); b. 1.1.80; s. of late Col. Wellesley Robinson, C.B.; m. Doris Lilian, d. of A. Barrett; 2nd Lt., A.S.C., 2.5.00; Lt. 1.6.01; Capt. 1.8.06; Maj. 30.10.14; Bt. Lt.-Col. 3.6.19; S. African War, 1901–2; Queen's Medal, 5 clasps; East Africa, 1903–4; Medal, clasp.

ROBINSON, A. C. H. (D.S.O. L.G. 26.9.17) (Details, L.G. 9.1.18), T/2nd Lt., Yorks. L.I.

ROBINSON, A. T. (D.S.O. L.G. 1.1.17); b. June, 1872; y. s. of the late Major-General D. G. Robinson, the third son, out of six in the Army, who has died on service; m. Winifred Marjorie, d. of Mrs. Appleyard, of Claygate; 2nd Lt., E. Surrey Rgt., 2.6.94; Lt. 24.7.97; Capt. 28.4.03; T/Major 21.2.12; employed with W.A.F.F. 6.2.09 to 8.8.13; Major, April, 1915. He was appointed to the command of a battalion of the Oxfords. and Bucks. L.I. He was seriously wounded at Ypres in Feb. 1915, and for his services in command of a battalion on an Eastern front he was awarded the D.S.O. and the Croix de Guerre. He died of wounds on an Eastern front on 11.5.17.

ROBINSON BEVERLEY, B. (D.S.O. L.G. 1.1.17), T/Lt.-Col., Yorks. L.I.

ROBINSON, D. G. (D.S.O. L.G. 14.1.16); b. 25.5.78; 2nd Lt., Suff. R., 7.5.98; Lt. 24.2.00; Ind. Army, 30.8.00; Capt. 7.5.07; Maj. 1.9.15; Lt.-Col. 1.2.21.

ROBINSON, D. L. (D.S.O. L.G. 15.10.18), T/Capt. (Tank Corps), Lt., R.M.

ROBINSON, EDWARD HEATON (D.S.O. L.G. 1.1.17); b. 4.2.68; Lt., R.A., 18.5.02; Insp. of Ord. Mach., 3rd Class, 1.4.96; 2nd Class 18.5.98; 1st Class 18.5.07; Chief Insp. 2.11.17; Lt.-Col. 28.11.17; S. African War, 1900–1; Despatches; Queen's Medal, 4 clasps.

ROBINSON, ERNEST HAROLD (D.S.O. L.G. 26.11.17) (Details, L.G. 6.4.18), T/Capt., Shrops. L.I.; M.C.

ROBINSON, F. (D.S.O. L.G. 4.6.17) (Bar, L.G. 16.9.18); b. 28.12.84; Mob. Terr. Force from Aug. 1914, to Dec. 1916; Capt., R. Innis. Fus. 1.11.16.

ROBINSON, F. L. (D.S.O. L.G. 5.4.19), Sqn.-Cdr., R.N.A.S.; M.C.

ROBINSON, FREDERICK WILFRED (D.S.O. L.G. 3.6.18), Major, M.G.C.; M.C.

ROBINSON, FREDERICK WILLIAM (D.S.O. L.G. 22.2.18), Lt. (A/Lt.-Cdr.), R.N.R.

ROBINSON, FREDERICK WINWOOD (D.S.O. L.G. 1.1.17); b. 26.7.77; s. of late Col. H. J. Robinson and Mrs. Robinson, of Moorwood, Cirencester. He passed out of Woolwich into R.A. 17.2.00; Lt. 3.4.01; Capt. 12.9.08; Major 30.10.14; S. African War, 1901–2; Queen's Medal, 3 clasps; Europ. War; Despatches, 1914. He died of wounds 18.4.17. A mural tablet to his memory was erected by the officers and men of his battery (130th Battery R.F.A.), in Bagendon Church, Gloucestershire.

ROBINSON, THE REV. G. L. (D.S.O. L.G. 8.3.18), T/Chaplain to the Forces.

The Distinguished Service Order 333

ROBINSON, G. ST. G. (D.S.O. L.G. 8.3.19) (Details, L.G. 4.10.19); b. 2.4.87; s. of St. G. C. W. Robinson and Isabella Robinson (*née* Carson), sister of Lord Carson; m. Eva Suzanne, d. of late A. Hadra; one d.; educ. Malvern; Sandhurst; 2nd Lt., Northants R., 4.5.07; Lt. 12.4.09; Capt. 16.9.14; went to France, Aug. 1916; A/Adjutant to 1st Northamptonshire Regt., Sept.–Nov. 1914, until wounded at Ypres on 11.11.14; Adjutant to 1st Northamptonshire Regt., from April until Oct. 1915; 2nd-in-command to 1st Northamptonshire Regt., April–July, 1917; commanded 1st Northamptonshire Regt. from July, 1917, until April, 1919; mentioned in Despatches twice; M.C.; played Association Football for Malvern College, 1904–5; played Association Football for Sandhurst, 1906; represented Sandhurst against Woolwich, Athletic Sports, 1906; played Hockey for Army *v.* Navy, 1913–14; played Rugby Football United Services, Devonport, 1911–12.

ROBINSON, H. A. (D.S.O. L.G. 11.12.16) (Bar, L.G. 27.10.17) (Details, L.G. 8.3.18); s. of N. Robinson, of Frankton Grange; m. Dorothy Beryl, d. of H. Brumell; Lt.-Col., late R. Fus.; served Europ. War; Croix de Guerre.

ROBINSON, H. B. (D.S.O. L.G. 12.12.19), Cdr., R.N.

ROBINSON, H. H., M.R.C.S., L.R.C.P. (D.S.O. L.G. 25.8.16); educ. Owens College, Manchester (M.R.C.S., L.R.C.P., London); was Senior House Surgeon of Southport Infirmary, later House Surgeon of the Infirmary, Burton-on-Trent, and subsequently Honorary Medical Officer of Birkenhead Children's Hospital. He served in the Europ. War from 1914, as T/Capt., R.A.M.C. He was drowned on 4.5.17.

ROBINSON, H. ROWAN- (see Rowan-Robinson, H.).

ROBINSON, H. T. K. (D.S.O. L.G. 4.6.17) (Bar, L.G. 17.12.17) (Details, L.G. 23.4.18) (2nd Bar, L.G. 16.9.18), Lt.-Col., R. Sussex R. (att. 13th Batt.). He was killed in action on 26.4.18.

ROBINSON, J. A. (D.S.O. L.G. 26.5.17), Major, Aust. Infy.

ROBINSON, J. A. P. (D.S.O. L.G. 1.1.8); b. 5.12.74; 2nd Lt., R.A., 5.6.95; Lt. 15.6.98; Capt. 15.2.01; Maj. 30.10.14; Lt.-Col., R.G.A., 1.5.21; S. African War, 1900–2; Queen's Medal, 3 clasps; King's Medal, 2 clasps; Aden, 1903; Europ. War; Despatches.

ROBINSON, J. P. B. (D.S.O. L.G. 4.6.17); b. 30.5.81; s. of Rev. A. D. J. Robinson (deceased) and Sara Elizabeth Robinson (*née* Bowring); m. Ethna Henrietta Pauline Hackett, d. of the Dean of Limerick; one s.; one d.; educ. Westminster School; R.M.C., Sandhurst; 2nd Lt., R. Dub. Fus., 11.8.00; Lt. 27.7.04; Capt. 4.2.11; Maj. 1.9.15; S. African War, 1899–1902; Queen's Medal, five clasps; Aden, 1903; Europ. War, 1914–17; Despatches several times; C.M.G.

ROBINSON, J. R. ROWAN- (see Rowan-Robinson, J. R.).

ROBINSON, L. (D.S.O. L.G. 18.2.18) (Details, L.G. 18.7.18), Lt. (A/Maj.), R.E.

ROBINSON, L. J. W. (D.S.O. L.G. 1.1.17); b. 2.5.82; m. Daphne Phillips; 2nd Lt., R.A., 18.8.00; Lt. 18.8.03; Capt. 10.8.12; Maj. 16.5.15; served Europ. War; Despatches; wounded.

ROBINSON, P. G. (D.S.O. L.G. 15.2.17); b. 11.2.82; s. of E. Robinson; educ. Clifton College; 2nd Lt., R.A., 19.12.00; Lt. 19.12.03; Capt. 8.3.13; Major 27.7.15; Lt.-Col., ret. pay, 18.10.19.

ROBINSON, S. W. (D.S.O. L.G. 1.1.17); b. 25.10.71; 2nd Lt., R.A., 5.7.90; Lt. 25.7.93; Capt. 9.10.99; Maj. 25.4.11; Bt. Lt.-Col. 1.1.16; Lt.-Col. 1.5.17; Bt. Col. 3.6.18; Col. 2.3.21; Temp. Brig.-Gen. 28.10.16 to 8.8.19; N.W. Frontier, 1897–98; Medal, 2 clasps; Tirah, 1897–98; clasp; S. African War, 1901–2; Queen's Medal, 3 clasps; N.W. Frontier, 1908; Medal, clasp.

ROBINSON, T. C. (D.S.O. L.G. 1.1.18); s. of late Col. A. J. Robinson, of Clitheroe Castle; Major (T/Lt.-Col.), 4th E. Lancs. Rgt.; served in Egypt and Gallipoli under his brother, Col. F. D. Robinson, of Clitheroe, and subsequently received a Staff appointment as D.A.A.G. He later served in Palestine.

ROBINSON, T. T. H., M.B. (D.S.O. L.G. 1.1.19); b. 17.11.80; Lt., R.A.M.C., 30.1.06; Capt. 4.10.09; Major 30.1.18 (A/Lt.-Colonel). He is the well-known Dublin University and Irish International Rugby half-back.

ROBINSON, W. P. (D.S.O. L.G. 1.1.17); b. 27.10.77; 2nd Lt., R. Muns. Fus., 23.4.02; Lt., A.S.C., 9.6.04; Capt. 1.1.11; Maj. 30.10.14; O.B.E.; S. African War, 1900–2; Queen's Medal, 4 clasps; King's Medal, 2 clasps.

ROBSON, F. W. (D.S.O. L.G. 25.11.16); s. of T. Robson; Lt.-Col., Yorkshire Regt. (5th Batt., T.F.). His D.S.O. was awarded for gallantry on 15.9.16, at Martinpuich. He was killed in action March, 1918.

ROBSON, H. M. (D.S.O. L.G. 25.10.16), Lt.-Cdr., R.N., 30.7.18.

ROBSON, J. C. (D.S.O. L.G. 1.1.19), Major, R.F.A., T.F.

ROBSON, L. (D.S.O. L.G. 7.4.16); b. 1855; s. of late T. W. and Margaret Robson; m. 1st, Mary Isbel (who died in 1899), d. of W. Ritchie; 2nd, Jenny (who died 1909), d. of G. Redhead; 3rd Sarah, d. of G. Pollard; educ. Lilburne School, Sunderland; served in Volunteer Force from 1870, and T.F. from its formation; Lt.-Col., late Durham R.G.A., V.D.; commanded Durham R.G.A. and C.R.A., Tees Garrison, 1910–18; commanded the batteries at Hartlepool, Dec. 1914, when three German cruisers bombarded the Hartlepools; Despatches three times; C.M.G.; J.P.; D.L.; ex-Mayor of the County Borough of W. Hartlepool.

ROBSON, S. (D.S.O. L.G. 3.6.19), Major, 10th By. 4th Brig., Can. F.A., att. 5th Can. Div., Arty.

ROCH, H. S. (D.S.O. L.G. 1.1.17); b. 18.8.76; s. of late Surgeon-Gen. S. Roch and Agnes Roch; m. Marjorie (who died in 1919), d. of late R. H. Power; educ. King's College Hospital, London; M.R.C.S., L.R.C.P.; joined R.A.M.C. 17.11.99; Capt. 17.11.00; Major 17.5.11; Lt.-Col. 1.3.15; served S. African War, 1899–1902; with Buller's force in Natal; present at Spion Kop, Tugela Heights, Laing's Nek and Relief of Ladysmith; later M.O. to Gorringe's Column in Cape Colony from Jan. 1901, to June, 1902; Queen's and King's Medals, 8 clasps; Adjutant, West Riding Territorial Force R.A.M.C. School of Instruction (Leeds), April, 1908, to Oct. 1911; served Europ. War; D.A.D.M.S., 28th Division, Dec. 1914, to Nov. 1915; D.A.D.M.S., 7th Division, Nov. 1915, to Sept. 1916; D.D.M.S., 2nd Cavalry Division, Sept. 1916, to Dec. 1917; A.D.M.S., 36th (Ulster) Division (Temporary Colonel), from Dec. 1917; Despatches several times; C.M.G.; C.B.E.; S. Russia, 1919; 2nd Class St. Anne with Swords.

ROCHE-KELLY, E. (D.S.O. L.G. 17.9.17); b. 11.4.81; s. of Michael Roche-Kelly; m. Kathleen Mary, d. of Col. J. M. F. Shine, C.B., A.M.S.; one s.; one d.; educ. Downside College, near Bath; 2nd Lt., Unatt., 8.1.01; 2nd Lt., R. Irish R., 9.3.01; Lt. 14.10.03; Capt. 1.6.09; Major 8.1.16; Adjt., R. Irish R., 1909–12; served S. African War, 1901–2; Queen's Medal and 5 clasps; Europ. War, 1914–18; commanded a battalion; M.C.; Chevalier, Legion of Honour.

ROCHFORT, H. BOYD- (see Boyd-Rochfort, H.).

ROCHFORT, R. A. (D.S.O. L.G. 18.1.18) (Details, L.G. 25.4.18); b. 9.5.79; 2nd Lt., R. Innis. Fus., 15.4.15; Lt. 3.3.16, R. War. Rgt.; Capt. 17.2.17; M.C.

ROCKE, C. E. A. S. (D.S.O. L.G. 1.1.18); b. 7.9.78; m. Elizabeth, d. of Hon. L. M. Iddings; educ. Sandhurst; 2nd Lt., E. Surr. R., 3.8.98; Lt. 26.5.00; Capt. 3.8.07; Ind. Army 18.7.09; Maj., Ir. Gds., 14.2.16; Lt.-Col., ret. pay, 23.12.20; served S. African War, 1899–1902; Queen's Medal, 5 clasps; King's Medal, 2 clasps; Europ. War, 1914–17; wounded; Despatches thrice; Kaisar-i-Hind; Chevalier, Légion d'Honneur; Military Attaché, British Embassy, Rome, from 1918.

RODD, W. J. P., M.I.M.E. (D.S.O. L.G. 26.8.18); b. 15.1.79; Ins. of Ord. Mach., 3rd Class, 19.5.00; 2nd Class 19.5.06; 1st Class 19.5.15; Maj., R.A.O.D., 1.7.17.

RODDICK, J. A. (D.S.O. L.G. 3.6.19), Lt. (A/Major), 1/10th Batt. L'pool R., T.F., att. 13th Batt. W. Riding R.; M.C.

RODERICK, W. D. (D.S.O. L.G. 2.4.19) (Details, L.G. 10.12.19), T/2nd Lt. (A/Capt.), 14th Batt. R.W. Fus.; M.C.

RODGERSON, A. P. (D.S.O. L.G. 18.1.18) (Details, L.G. 25.4.18); b. 11.5.92; 2nd Lt. 6.9.11; Lt., Ind. Army, 6.12.13; Capt. 6.9.15.

RODOCANACHI, T. E. (D.S.O. L.G. 18.6.17), Capt., Oxf. and Bucks. L.I. (Lt., Hampshire Rgt., S.R.). His D.S.O. was awarded for gallantry on 9.4.17, south-east of Arras; M.C.

ROE, C. G. HENDERSON- (see Henderson-Roe, C. G.).

ROE, W. F., L.R.C.P.I., L.R.C.S.I. (D.S.O. L.G. 14.1.16); b. 4.5.71; s. of W. Roe, M.D., F.R.C.P.I., F.R.C.S.I., and Ellen Roe (*née* Carter); m. Emma, d. of late B. Ormsby; one d.; educ. Wesley College, Dublin; R. College of Surgeons, Ireland; R. City of Dublin Hospital; Volunteer Bloomsbury Rifles, 1903 (Queen Victoria Rifles (Amalgamated), T.F.); Major, 1915; T/Lt.-Col., 1916; served Europ. War from 1914; Despatches twice.

ROFFEY, H. B. (D.S.O. L.G. 1.1.18); b. 16.6.75; 2nd Lt., Lanc. Fus., 7.12.95; Lt. 6.4.98; Capt. 25.1.00; Major (T/Lt.-Col.), Lancs. Fus., att. 2/5th Linc. R.; S. African War, 1899–1902; Queen's Medal, 5 clasps; King's Medal, 2 clasps; served Europ. War. He was killed in action 15.4.18.

ROFFEY, M. H. (D.S.O. L.G. 1.1.18), T/Major, Welsh R.

ROGERS, A. L. (D.S.O. L.G. 3.6.18), T/Capt. (A/Major), R.F.A.

ROGERS, C. R. DE W. (D.S.O. L.G. 8.3.19) (Details, L.G. 4.10.19); b. 17.10.94; 2nd Lt., Leins. R., 24.1.14; Lt. 16.5.15; Capt. 1.1.17.

ROGERS, D. T. (D.S.O. L.G. 1.1.17), Major, Australian Artillery. He died of wounds. He was a member of the first Contingent of the Australian Expeditionary Force.

ROGERS, H., M.B. (D.S.O. L.G. 4.6.17); b. 15.9.76; Lt., R.A.M.C., 27.6.01; Capt. 27.6.04; Maj. 27.6.13.

ROGERS, H. H. (D.S.O. L.G. 1.1.17); b. 20.1.58; s. of R. Rogers; m. Fanny Rose, d. of late J. Gibbs, C.S.I., C.I.E.; one s.; one d.; educ. Sherborne; R.M.A., Woolwich; ent. R.A., 1878; retired through ill health, 1894; re-employed in R.F.A., Jan. 1915, and went out to France in May with the 9th Division; Lt.-Col., Dec. 1915, and transferred to 7th Division; Despatches twice.

ROGERS, H. P. (D.S.O. L.G. 3.6.19), T/Major (A/Lt.-Col.), 23rd Batt. R. Fus.

ROGERS, HENRY SCHOFIELD (D.S.O. L.G. 1.1.17); b. 29.6.69; s. of late Col. H. C. Rogers, Can. Militia; m. Aileen Mary, d. of late J. E. O'Conor, C.I.E.; one s.; one d.; educ. R.M.C., Kingston, Canada (Gold Medal, General Proficiency; Sword of Honour, Military Subjects); commissioned R.E. 27.6.89; Lt. 27.6.92; Major, R.E., retired, 5.12.08; Lt.-Col., R. of O., late R.E.; served Tirah Exp., 1897–98 (Medal, 3 clasps); Mahsud Waziri Blockade, 1899–1901 (clasp and thanks of Punjab Govt.); served in France, 1915–19; Despatches four times; C.M.G.; promoted Lt.-Col., R. of O., on retirement 19.3.19.

ROGERS, HUGH STUART (D.S.O. L.G. 3.6.16); b. 5.4.78; 2nd Lt., Shrops. L.I., 23.5.00; Lt. 11.2.02; Capt. 9.1.10; Bt. Maj. 3.6.15; Maj. 1.9.15; Bt. Lt.-Col. 1.1.18; Temp. Brig.-Gen. 27.10.18; C.M.G.

ROGERS, J. B. (D.S.O. L.G. 18.7.17) (Bar, L.G. 2.12.18), Lt.-Col., 3rd Batt. Can. Inf.; M.C. His D.S.O. was awarded for gallantry at Vimy Ridge 9.4.17.

ROGERS, J. S. Y., M.B., C.M. (D.S.O. L.G. 14.1.16) (Bar, L.G. 26.9.17) (Details, L.G. 9.1.18); b. 21.6.68; s. of J. S. Rogers; m. Mary Louisa Pattullo; educ. Stanley House, Crieff; Edinburgh University, 1889; Lt.-Col., R.A.M.C. (T.), att. 4th Black Watch; Territorial Officer in 4th Black Watch for 21 years; T.D., 1915. The D.S.O. and Bar were awarded for gallantry at Neuve Chapelle, Festubert and on 25.9.15.

ROGERS, R. P. (D.S.O. L.G. 1.1.18), Major, Can. Engrs.

ROGERS, V. (D.S.O. L.G. 1.1.17); only son of Rev. J. H. Rogers, Vicar of Timaru, N.Z.; Major, N.Z. Field Artillery. He was killed at the front. He came over with the first New Zealand contingent and had been wounded twice. His Commanding Officer writes: "I feel his death personally more than that of any other of my officers. He sailed with me in the battery as a Second Lieutenant, served with me in Egypt, the Sinai Peninsula, Gallipoli, where, though a Subaltern, he commanded the battery with great skill and courage. He came here in command of the battery as Captain, until we went into the Somme. . . . There he did extraordinarily well. . . ."

ROGERS, V. B. (D.S.O. L.G. 1.1.19), T/Capt., Gen. List; M.C.

W. F. Rogers.

ROGERS, W. F. (D.S.O. L.G. 4.6.17); b. 20.11.90; 2nd Lt., R.A., 19.7.12; Capt. (A/Major), R.F.A. He was killed in action 19.5.17.

ROGERS, W. L. Y. (D.S.O. L.G. 1.1.18); b. 20.9.78; 2nd Lt., R.A., 28.3.00; Lt. 3.4.01; Capt. 5.6.09; Maj. 30.10.14; Bt. Lt.-Col. 1.1.19.

ROGERS-TILLSTONE, E. M. (D.S.O. L.G. 3.6.19), Lt. (A/Major), R.F.A., S.R.; M.C.

ROLFE, C. N. (D.S.O. L.G. 22.2.18) (Bar, L.G. 8.3.20); b. 1884; s. of C. W. N. Rolfe; m. Sybil Katherine, O.B.E., d. of Admiral Sir Cecil Burney, and widow of Lt. A. C. Gotto, R.N.; one d.; Lt.-Cdr., R.N., retired 1920; served Europ. War, 1914–18; Despatches.

ROLFE, H. N. (D.S.O. L.G. 3.6.18), Capt., R.N.

ROLLAND, A. (D.S.O. L.G. 3.6.16); b. 6.3.71; 2nd Lt., R.E., 14.2.90; Lt. 14.2.93; Capt. 14.2.01; Maj. 14.2.10; Bt. Lt.-Col. 3.6.17; Lt.-Col. 14.7.18; Bt. Col. 1.1.19; Temp. Brig.-Gen. 29.11.17; China, 1900; Medal.

ROLLESTON, J. P. (D.S.O. L.G. 6.4.18); ent. R.N.; Vice-Admiral, retired, 1919; served Europ. War, 1914–18; Despatches.

ROLLO, G. (D.S.O. L.G. 1.1.17) (Bar, L.G. 26.7.18), T/Lt.-Col., L'pool Rgt.

ROLLS, N. T. (D.S.O. L.G. 1.1.18), T/Major (A/Lt.-Col.), R.W. Surrey Rgt.

ROLLS, S. P. A. (D.S.O. L.G. 1.1.17); b. 20.8.85; 2nd Lt., Dorset R., 28.1.05; Lt. 25.5.07; Capt. 16.6.12; *p.s.c.*; M.C.

ROLSTON, J. M. (D.S.O. L.G. 1.2.19), Major (A/Lt.-Col.), 2nd Batt. Can. Engrs.

ROMANES, J. G. P. (D.S.O. L.G. 25.11.16) (Bar, L.G. 26.3.18) (Details, L.G. 24.8.18); b. 12.1.84; s. of late G. J. Romanes, F.R.S., and Ethel, d. of late Andrew Duncan; educ. Charterhouse; R.M.C., Sandhurst; ent. Army 24.1.03; Lt. 27.10.04; Capt. 26.6.13; Major 24.1.18; served Europ. War; commanded 1/7th Cameronians; Despatches thrice; Croix de Chevalier; Légion d'Honneur; Bt. Lt.-Col. 1.1.19. His D.S.O. was awarded for gallantry in Egypt on 4.8.16.

ROME, C. L. (D.S.O. L.G. 26.7.18) (Bar, L.G. 1.2.19); b. 30.10.78; s. of late C. Rome, of Queensland, Australia; m. Phyllis, d. of H. Illingworth; two s.; educ. Harrow; 2nd Lt., 11th Hussars, 16.11.98; Lt. 3.10.00; Capt. 18.3.05; Maj. 30.5.19; Bt. Lt.-Col. 3.6.19; 3rd D.G. 14.11.19; served S. African War with I.Y., 1902; Queen's Medal and 2 clasps; Adjt., Lovat's Scouts, 1914–15; T/Lt.-Col., 3rd Dn. Gds., 1918–19; Despatches.

ROME, C. S. (D.S.O. L.G. 1.1.18); b. 14.1.75; m. Hon. Grace Lovdenne Blyth, 2nd d. of 1st Lord Blyth; two s.; 2nd Lt., 11th Hrs., 28.9.95; Lt. 25.10.99; Capt. 18.3.05; Maj. 29.9.16; Bt. Lt.-Col. 3.6.17; Lt., 2nd D. Gds., 24.9.20; Temp. Brig.-Gen. 12.4.17; served Tirah Campaign, 1897; Medal and clasp; S. African War, 1900–2; Queen's Medal and 4 clasps; King's Medal and 2 clasps; Europ. War, 1914–18; Despatches; C.M.G.

RONALD, H. (D.S.O. L.G. 16.9.18), Capt., Aust. Inf.

RONEY-DOUGAL, A. R. (D.S.O. L.G. 1.1.19); b. 14.1.87; 2nd Lt., R.A., 23.7.07; Lt. 23.7.10; Capt. 30.10.14; Bt. Maj. 3.6.17; Maj. 22.6.17; M.C.

ROOKE, C. P. (D.S.O. L.G. 1.1.17), Major, Middlesex Rgt.

ROOKE, E. H. (D.S.O. L.G. 1.1.18); b. 20.10.75; 2nd Lt., R.E., 3.11.94; Lt. 3.11.97; Capt. 1.4.04; Maj. 30.10.14; Bt. Lt.-Col. 11.11.19; Lt.-Col. 21.6.21; served Europ. War, 1914–18; Despatches; C.M.G.

ROPER, E. R., B.A., LL.B. (D.S.O. L.G. 1.1.18); b. 30.10.85; s. of late Rev. T. Roper, of Kroonstad, Orange Free State, and Mary Roper; m. Gladys Frances, d. of F. W. Farrow; educ. Kingswood College, Grahamstown; Victoria College, Stellenbosch; Diocesan College, Rondebosch; Maynard Scholar and Ebden Prizeman, University of Cape of Good Hope; 2nd Lt., Cape Garrison Artillery, April, 1909; Capt., Cape Garrison Artillery, 22.10.12; T/Capt., R.F.A., 17.10.15; T/Major, R.F.A., 21.12.17; Brigade Major, R.A., 9.9.18–20.4.19; served S. African Rebellion, 1914; German S.W. Africa, 1914–15; Egypt, 1916; France and Belgium, 1916–17; Italy, 1917–18; France and Belgium, 1918; Army of the Rhine, 1919; wounded three times; Despatches; M.C.; French Croix de Guerre.

RORIE, D., M.D., C.M., D.P.H. (D.S.O. L.G. 4.6.17); b. Edinburgh, 17.3.67; s. of late G. L. Rorie; m. Margaret Elizabeth, d. of late J. W. Miller, M.D.; one s.; one d.; educ. Aberdeen Collegiate School; Aberdeen and Edinburgh Universities; J.P.; Hon. Assoc. Order of the Hospital of St. John of Jerusalem; mobilized as Capt., R.A.M.C. (T.F.), at outbreak of war; Major, Sept. 1914; Bt. Lt.-Col.; Colonel, A.M.S., T.A. Reserve; T.D.; A.D.M.S., 51st Div., in the Field, Dec. 1917; Despatches; Bt. Lt.-Col.; Chevalier, Légion d'Honneur.

RORKE, H. V. (D.S.O. L.G. 11.5.17), Major (A/Lt.-Col.), Can. Infy. His D.S.O. was awarded for gallantry on 17.1.17, north-east of Calonne.

ROSCOE, B. W. (D.S.O. L.G. 1.1.17), Major, Can. Mtd. Rifles.

ROSE, A. M., M.B. (D.S.O. L.G. 1.1.17); b. 14.8.78; 2nd Lt., R.A.M.C., 31.7.05; Capt. 31.1.09; Maj. 15.10.15.

ROSE, SIR H. A. (D.S.O. L.G. 1.1.17); b. 1875; s. of late Hugh Rose, of Kilravock Lodge, Edinburgh, and Margaret Robertson Rose (*née* Anderson); m. Mary, d. of late R. Weir, J.P., D.L., of Edinburgh; one s.; two d.; educ. Harrow; Trinity College, Cambridge; J.P.; Director of Land Settlement, Scotland, 1920; original commission, 1893, 5th V.B. The R. Scots; rejoined Army as Major, 2nd i/c 15th Bn. The Royal Scots; proceeded to France, Jan. 1916; commanded 25th Bn. Northumberland Fusiliers in Somme, returning to command 15th Bn. R.S. on 6.7.16; invalided 26.4.17; Hon. Lt.-Colonel; Despatches.

ROSE, H. A. L. (D.S.O. L.G. 1.1.17); b. 30.5.82; s. of late Hugh Rose; educ. Wellington College; 2nd Lt., Sussex Arty., 19.7.99; 2nd Lt., R.F.A., 4.5.01; Lt. 4.5.04; Capt. 17.3.14; Major, 1916. He served at the front from 15.8.14, until his death in action on 18.4.18, when serving as Brigade Major, R.A., to his Division; Despatches three times; 1914 Star; Belgian Croix de Guerre.

ROSE, J. G. (D.S.O. L.G. 17.4.17), Colonel, S. African Service Corps, formerly O.C., Mechanical Transport; served S. African War, 1900–2; Queen's Medal, 5 clasps; Europ. War; Despatches.

ROSE, J. M. (D.S.O. L.G. 14.9.18); Lt., R.M. Art., 1.9.82; Capt. 1.9.93; Bt. Maj. 1.9.03; Maj. 8.8.04; Bt. Lt.-Col. 1.9.10; Lt.-Col. 2.10.11; Col., ret. pay, 1.7.19. He acted as D.A.A.G. of the Marines, March, 1908–Oct. 1911; served Europ. War; Despatches.

ROSE, R. A. DE B. (D.S.O. L.G. 14.1.16) (Bar, L.G. 27.7.18); b. 9.5.77; s. of Surg.-Gen. H. J. Rose, A.M. (who died 2.6.15); m. Vera Lambert, d. of Dr. J. A. Turner, C.I.E.; educ. Dover College; 2nd Lt., Worcesters. R., from 3rd E. Surrey Rgt., 4.4.00; Lt. 28.7.00; Capt. 14.4.04; Maj. 1.9.15; served S. African War, 1899–1902; Queen's Medal, 3 clasps; King's Medal, 2 clasps; employed with the Gold Coast Rgt., W.A.F.F., 21.4.06 to 21.8.10; returned to duty with British Regiment in 1910, returning as Second-in-Command, Gold Coast Regiment, 4.10.11. When the Great War broke out Major Rose was gazetted to the command of the Gold Coast Regiment 4.9.14. He commanded this regiment throughout the Cameroon Campaign, and was mentioned in General Dobell's Despatch on its successful conclusion. Major Rose was then sent to command the same regiment in German East Africa (Despatches; D.S.O.; Bt. Lt.-Col. 1.1.17), and on 10.1.17 he was posted in command of 3rd E. African Brigade; Bar to D.S.O.; C.M.G.; Croix d'Officier, Legion of Honour.

R. A. de B. Rose.

ROSENTHAL, SIR C., A.R.I.B.A. (D.S.O. L.G. 3.6.18); b. N.S. Wales, 12.2.75; m. Harriet Ellen Burston, of Melbourne, Victoria; three s.; joined Militia Forces in Australia, 1903, and served continuously from that time; left Australia with A.I.F., Sept. 1914; served through Gallipoli Campaign as O.C., 3rd Field Artillery Brigade, 1st Aust. Div. (twice wounded; Despatches; C.B.); served in France and Belgium, at Armentières, Ypres, Somme, Bullecourt, Messines, as C.R.A., 6th Aust. Division (wounded at Somme; Despatches twice; C.M.G.); as G.O.C., 9th Aust. Inf. Brigade; served at Passchendaele, Hangard, Villers-Bretonneux and Morlancourt (gassed at Passchendaele); Despatches twice; Belgian Croix de Guerre; as G.O.C., 2nd Aust. Div., served at Villers-Bretonneux, and in final Allied advance, including capture of Mt. St. Quentin (wounded at Villers-Bretonneux); Despatches twice; K.C.B.; French Croix de Guerre avec Palme; Officier, Légion d'Honneur. Major-General Sir C. Rosenthal commanded A.I.F. Depôts in U.K., Feb.–Sept. 1919.

ROSHER, J. B., B.A., LL.B. (D.S.O. L.G. 4.2.18) (Details, L.G. 5.7.18) (Bar, L.G., 18.2.18) (Details, L.G. 18.7.18); b. 29.6.90; s. of G. B. Rosher and Eleanor Rosher; educ. Charterhouse; Trinity College, Cambridge; rowed in Cambridge University Eight, 1909–10–11; President, C.U.B.C., 1910–11; 2nd Lt., 1914; Lt., Nov. 1914; Capt., Sept. 1915; Major, Aug. 1916; Lt.-Col., Aug. 1917, Durham L.I.; served Europ. War, in France, 1915–19; commanded 14th S. Batt. Durham L.I., 1917–18; Despatches four times. His D.S.O. was awarded at Cambrai 22.11.17, for capture of Cantaing; Bar to D.S.O. was awarded at Cambrai 3.12.17, for defence of Marroing; M.C. was awarded at Ypres, 1916.

ROSKRUGE, F. J. (D.S.O. L.G. 15.6.17), Engr.-Cdr., R.N., 2.7.12; O.B.E.

ROSOMAN, R. R. (D.S.O. L.G. 31.7.19), Cdr., R.N., 23.4.18.

ROSS, ALEXANDER (D.S.O. L.G. 18.7.17) (Bar, L.G. 16.9.18); b. Forres, Scotland, 2.12.80; s. of Adam Simpson and Grace Ross; m. Harriet Beatrice, d. of late J. Scott; educ. Saskatchewan; gazetted Lieut., 95th Saskatchewan Rifles, 28.9.08; Capt., 1910; Major 31.3.12; served Europ. War; posted Canadian Exp. Force as Capt. 23.10.14; Major 1.1.15; Lieut.-Col., and to command 28th Battalion, Canadian Inf., Saskatchewan Regt., 21.9.16; promoted Brig.-Gen., and to command 6th Inf. Brigade 2.10.18; Despatches seven times; C.M.G. His D.S.O. was awarded for gallantry on 9.4.17 at Thelus.

ROSS, A. J. (D.S.O. L.G. 3.6.16) (Bar, L.G. 8.8.17); b. 6.7.81, at Allahabad, U.P., India; s. of G. E. A. Ross, K.C., and Mary Louisa Ross (*née* Hodgkinson); educ. South Kensington Preparatory School; Malvern College, and R.M.A., Woolwich, where he did well in Gymnastics and Games; 2nd Lt., R.E., 2.5.00; Lt. 2.5.03; Capt. 2.5.10; Bt. Major, 1915; Major 2.11.16. In 1901 he went to India and served there in Sappers and Miners, and as Garrison Engineer, Kurram Valley, on the N.W. Frontier until 1911, when he was seconded for service in the Egyptian Army. On the outbreak of war he reverted to the British Army, and was employed by the Intelligence Department in the Sinai Desert. In 1915 he served with the Flying Corps as Observer in the campaign against the Senussi Arabs. Having qualified as a Pilot at home, he returned to Egypt as Flight-Commander, and for his services on the Hedjaz Mission (from end 1916, to March, 1917) he was sent home on promotion to Squadron-Commander. In July, 1917, he was sent to command a Training Squadron at Thetford, Norfolk, and there he was killed on 2 Aug., when flying with a pupil. In the "Times" of 22.6.16 he is mentioned three times, viz.: By Sir A. Wilson, and twice by General Maxwell. He had the Order of the Nile and Bar (4th Class) from the Sultan of Egypt in 1916. The Bar to his D.S.O. was awarded a week after his death. A friend in Egypt wrote: "He was one of the best all-round men I ever met, excelling in everything he took up, but he remained one of the simplest and most unspoilt. A charming companion, most unselfish and good-natured, he was beloved wherever he went."

A. J. Ross.

ROSS, A. M. (D.S.O. L.G. 2.2.16); b. 9.3.79; 2nd Lt., W. Yorks. R., 11.2.99; Lt. 1.8.00; Capt. 11.6.09; Maj. 1.9.15; S. African War, 1899–1902; Queen's Medal, 2 clasps; King's Medal, 2 clasps; Europ. War; Despatches; Bt. Lt.-Col. 1.1.17; C.M.G.

ROSS, D. (D.S.O. L.G. 1.2.19); s. of the late Mr. and Mrs. David Ross, and husband of Margaret M. Ross; Lt. (A/Capt.), A. and S. Highlanders; M.C. He was killed in action on 6.11.18.

ROSS, G. W. (D.S.O. L.G. 22.12.16); b. 6.6.78; s. of Col. Sir E. Ross, C.S.I.; m. Clare Josephine, d. of Lt.-Col. Welman, I.A.; one s.; educ. Clifton College; commissioned 22.1.98; Lt., Ind. Army, 22.4.00; Capt. 22.1.07; Maj. 1.9.15; served in India with 2nd Q.V.O., Rajput L.I.; China Campaign, 1900–2; entered Military Finance Dept. 1903; Europ. War, in Mesopotamia, Nov. 1914–March, 1916 (D.S.O.).

ROSS, H. (D.S.O. L.G. 3.8.20); b. 17.4.69; 2nd Lt., Som. L.I., 31.5.90; Lt. 24.4.92; Capt. 31.5.01; Maj. 31.5.08; Lt.-Col. 31.5.16; Col. 13.2.20; Temp. Col. Comdt. 1.1.21; C.I.E.; Tirah, 1897–98; Medal, 2 clasps; Somaliland, 1903; Medal, clasp.

ROSS, H. C. E. (D.S.O. L.G. 25.11.16); b. 23.6.84; 2nd Lt., S. Gds., 1.2.07; Lt. 20.2.10; Capt. 28.1.15; Maj. 28.5.20; served Europ. War, 1914–18; wounded thrice; Despatches; Croix de Guerre; Croce di Guerra. His D.S.O. was awarded for gallantry on 15.9.16, at Guillemont.

ROSS, J. (D.S.O. L.G. 4.6.17), Major, late Canadian Infantry; served S. African War, 1900–2; Queen's Medal; Europ. War, 1915–19; Despatches.

ROSS, J. A. (D.S.O. L.G. 24.6.16) (Details, L.G. 27.7.16), Major, 24th Can. Inf. Batt. Mr. Walter Ross, President of the Brown Ranche Co. Ltd., of Lethbridge, Alberta, Canada, wrote on 27.3.17: "Major John Alexander Ross was reported wounded and missing on the 17.9.16, since which time no word of him has been received. Until the war is over I am not in position to give authentic information as to his performances. I know he was three times mentioned in Despatches, got the D.S.O. for some fighting about St. Eloi, and would have been 23 years old on his next birthday."

ROSS, J. M. (D.S.O. L.G. 1.1.17) (Bar, L.G. 1.1.18); b. 1878; Lt.-Col. (T/Brig.-Gen.), Can. Inf.; S. African War, 1899–1900; Queen's Medal, 2 clasps; Europ. War, 1914–18; Despatches; C.M.G.

ROSS, L. (D.S.O. L.G. 1.1.17); b. Montreal, 26.11.78; m. Katherine K. Cameron; one s.; educ. Montreal High School; Lt.-Colonel commanding a Canadian Battalion; Lt., 13th Scottish Light Dragoons, 1904; Capt., 29th Saskatchewan L.H., 1911; Major, 50th Gordon Hghrs., 1913; served Europ. War, 1914–17; Major, 16th Can. Scottish Batt. (wounded), 1915; raised and commanded 67th Can. Batt. Western Scots, 1916–17; Despatches.

ROSS, M. N. (D.S.O. L.G. 26.7.17) (Bar, L.G. 15.2.19) (Details, L.G. 30.7.19), Lt.-Col., Can. F.A. His D.S.O. was awarded for gallantry at Vimy Ridge 9–28.4.17.

ROSS, R. C. (D.S.O. L.G. 14.1.16) (Bar, L.G. 17.4.17); b. 28.6.82; 2nd Lt., E. Surr. R., 11.8.00; Lt. 9.7.02; Capt., Ind. Army, 11.8.09; Maj. 1.9.15; S. African War, 1901–2; Queen's Medal, 5 clasps; Europ. War; Despatches; Bt. Lt.-Col. 3.6.18.

ROSS, R. K. (D.S.O. L.G. 1.1.18); b. 23.8.93; s. of Brig.-Gen. R. J. Ross, C.B., C.M.G., and Frances Cecilia Caroline Ross (*née* Knox); educ. Cheltenham College; R.M.C., Sandhurst; 2nd Lt., R.W. Surr. R., 5.2.13; Lt. 15.9.14; Capt. 18.10.15; Europ. War, 1914–18; Despatches thrice; M.C.

ROSS, R. P. (D.S.O. L.G. 1.10.17), Wing-Commander, R.N.A.S.

ROSS, S. G. (D.S.O. L.G. 2.12.18), Major, 6th Field Amb. Can. A.M.C.; M.C.

ROSS, T. G. (D.S.O. L.G. 1.1.17), Lt.-Colonel, Aust. A.M.C.

ROSS-SKINNER, H. (D.S.O. L.G. 18.2.18) (Details, 18.7.18); b. 14.1.96; s. of Sir Harry Ross-Skinner and Annie Janet, d. of late J. Milne, of Aberdeen; educ. Ardvreck, Crieff, Perthshire, and Glenalmond, Perthshire; 2nd Lt., H.L.I., 11.11.14; Lt. 17.5.15; Capt. 11.2.17. His D.S.O. was awarded for Defence of Moeuvres; M.C. for Battle of the Somme, 1916.

ROSS-TAYLOR, M. (see Taylor, M. Ross-).

ROSSI-ASHTON, C. G. (D.S.O. L.G. 2.12.18), T/Capt. and Bt. Major (A/Major), 7th Batt. Tank Corps.

ROTHERFORD, R. W. (D.S.O. L.G. 3.6.19), T/Capt., Gen. List; M.C.

ROTHSCHILD, G. F. (gazetted as Rothschild, G.) (D.S.O. L.G. 1.1.19), 13th Batt. (gazetted as 12th) R. Sussex R., att. 2/10th Batt. London Rgt.; M.C.

ROTHWELL, R. S. (D.S.O. L.G. 17.10.17); b. 18.1.82; m. Gwendoline Marion Allardice; 2nd Lt., R.A., 19.12.00; Lt. 14.2.03; Capt. 19.12.13; Major 30.12.15.

ROTHWELL, W. E. (D.S.O. L.G. 1.1.18); b. 4.1.79; 2nd Lt., R. Garr. R., 27.9.02; Lt. 9.12.03; Capt., R. Innis. Fus., 21.2.12; Maj. 8.1.16; served Europ. War from 1914; Despatches; O.B.E.

ROUND, H. C. (D.S.O. L.G. 16.8.17); b. 7.5.96; s. of Francis R. Round, C.M.G., J.P. for Essex, and F. Emily Round, d. of J. Jolliffe Tufnell; educ. at Felsted, Essex, and Marlborough College, where he had been a Cadet Lieutenant in the School O.T.C. He was in the Marlborough Hockey XI. of the seasons 1913–14 and 1914–15, when he was Captain of his House. He became 2nd Lt., Rifle Brigade, 4.12.15; Lt. 21.2.17; Capt., May, 1917. In Aug. 1916, he joined his battalion at the front ,and in his first month's service won the M.C. He was killed in action 14.8.17. His Colonel wrote: " . . . There can be few boys who have got a D.S.O. and M.C. before the age of 21, and done such splendid work before being killed." His D.S.O. was awarded for gallantry in front of Vis Enartois on 3.5.17. His brother, Lt. A. F. H. Round, 2nd Batt. Essex Regt., died on 5.9.14 of wounds received on 26.8.14. Another brother, Capt. J. Murray Round, M.C., Essex Rgt., was reported missing in the "Times" of Nov. 1916.

ROUSSOUW, P. J. (D.S.O. L.G. 22.8.18), Major, Rustenburg Commando (Van Tonder's Horse), S. African Mil. Forces.

ROUTH, G. M. (D.S.O. L.G. 26.6.16); b. 18.6.82; 2nd Lt., R.A., 21.12.00; Lt. 21.12.03; Capt. 21.12.13; Maj. 30.12.15.

ROUX, P. D. A. (D.S.O. L.G. 22.8.18), Lt.-Col., 12th Mtd. Rifles, S. African Forces.

ROW, R. A. (D.S.O. L.G. 1.1.18), Lt.-Col., N.Z. Inf.

ROWAN, G. (D.S.O. L.G. 3.6.19), Lt. (A/Major), 1/7th Batt. R. Highrs., T.F., att. 254th Tunn. Co., R.E.; M.C.

ROWAN-HAMILTON, G. B. (D.S.O. L.G. 4.6.17); b. 5.7.84; m. Phyllis Frances Agnes, d. of Lord Blackburn; two s.; 2nd Lt., R. Highrs., 23.3.04; Lt. 9.11.06; Capt. 17.9.14; *p.s.c.*; served Europ. War, 1914–18; Despatches; deferred Bt. Lt.-Colonel; M.C.

ROWAN-ROBINSON, H. (D.S.O. L.G. 2.2.16); b. Gibraltar 4.5.73; m. Evelyn Russell Bowlby; two s.; educ. King's School, Canterbury; ent. R.A. 15.2.92; Lt. 15.2.95; Capt. 3.1.00; Major 14.9.12; Lt.-Col. 1.5.17; Colonel 1.5.21; *p.s.c.*; Temp. Brig.-Gen. 28.12.18 to 19.6.19; served S. African War, 1901–2; Queen's Medal, 4 clasps; Europ. War; wounded twice; Despatches six times; C.M.G.; Belgian Croix de Guerre; French Croix de Guerre (twice).

ROWAN-ROBINSON, J. R. (D.S.O. L.G. 23.11.16); b. 25.1.76; 2nd Lt., Leic. R., 5.5.00; Lt. 11.12.01; Capt. 5.5.09; Ind. Army 30.9.09; Maj. 1.9.15; S. African War, 1901–2; Queen's Medal, 4 clasps; King's Medal, 2 clasps; Europ. War; Despatches; Bt. Lt.-Col. 3.6.18.

ROWBOTHAM, J., B.Sc., A.M.I.C.E. (D.S.O. L.G. 19.11.17) (Details, L.G. 22.3.18) (Bar, L.G. 26.7.18); b. Buenos Aires, Argentine, 1892; s. of J. M. Rowbotham, M.B.E., M.I.C.E., and Globina Rowbotham (*née* Buchanan); m. Edith May, d. of late J. Henning; one d.; educ. London University; B.Sc.; Lt.-Col., H.L.I.; served Europ. War, 1914–18; wounded; Despatches; M.C.

ROWCROFT, C. H. (D.S.O. L.G. 3.6.19); b. 2.3.72; 2nd Lt., R.A., 19.2.92; Lt., R.A., 19.2.95; I.S.C. 15.11.96; Capt. 10.7.01; Major 20.2.10; Lt.-Col. 19.2.18.

ROWE, R. H. (D.S.O. L.G. 1.1.19); b. 12.7.83; s. of late Lt.-Col. H. Rowe; educ. Wellington College; R.M.A., Woolwich; commissioned R.A. 31.7.02; Lt. 31.7.05; Capt. 30.10.14; Major, R.G.A., 1.5.17; served Bermudas and W. Indies, with Nigeria Rgt. (Native Inf.), 1907; Northern Hinterland Exp.; operations against Abini and operations against the Munchis, Cameron Exp. Force, 1914, with Major-General Sir Charles Dobell as Chief of Administrative Staff; France with 11th E. Lancs. and 31st Div., 1916; commanded Howitzer Battery at Battles of Vimy, Messines and Flanders; Brig. Major, Corps Heavy Artillery, in Nieuport Sector and Battles of Armentières and Hazebrouck; Russia, 1918, where he took part in landing on the Murman Coast; Despatches thrice; Bt. Major 3.6.16; M.C.

ROWE, S. G. (D.S.O. L.G. 1.1.18), Major, Aust. F.A.

ROWE, W. B. (D.S.O. L.G. 1.1.18); b. 29.5.83; 2nd Lt., R. Art., 31.7.02; Lt. 31.7.05; Capt. 30.10.14; Maj., R.G.A., 1.5.17.

ROWLAND, R. H. (D.S.O. L.G. 1.1.19), T/Major, 8th (S.) Batt. R.W. Surrey R.

ROWLANDS, H. (D.S.O. L.G. 2.4.19) (Details, L.G. 10.12.19), Lt. (A/Capt.), 2nd Batt. London R.; M.C.

ROWLANDSON, M. G. D. (D.S.O. L.G. 4.9.18); b. 3.8.78; 2nd Lt. 22.1.98; Lt., Ind. Army, 22.4.00; Capt. 22.1.07; Maj. 1.9.15; Lt.-Col. 1.2.21; Col. 1.8.21; *p.s.c.*; Waziristan, 1901–2; Medal. clasp; Zakka Khel country, 1908; Medal, clasp; Europ. War; Despatches; Bt. Lt.-Col. 3.6.16.

ROWLETTE, L. M., L.R.C.P.I. and L.M., L.R.C.S.I. and L.M. (D.S.O. L.G. 27.7.16); b. 6.4.90; Temp. Lt., 8.9.15; Capt. 8.3.19; R.A.M.C. (attd. 1st Bn. Welsh Guards); served Europ. War; Despatches; M.C. His D.S.O. was awarded for gallantry in the vicinity of Ypres 22.7.16.

ROWLEY, F. G. M. (D.S.O. L.G. 1.1.18); b. 4.1.66; s. of Thomas Rowley, of De Beauvoir, Guernsey, and Emily Rowley; m. Agnes Mary, d. of late Capt. J. D. Travers, Leic. R., and widow of Capt. E. Lonsdale, R. Fus.; educ. Elizabeth College, Guernsey, and R.M.C., Sandhurst; Lt., Middlesex Rgt., 30.1.86; Capt. 21.2.95; Major 12.12.03; Lt.-Col. 1.9.14; Col. 1.9.18; Brig.-Gen., ret. pay, 27.9.18; served Europ. War, 1914–18; saw no active service till Aug. 1914; 2nd-in-command of 1st Middlesex Regt. at beginning of war; commanded 1st Bn. during retreat after Battle of Le Cateau; promoted Lt.-Col. on 1.9.14; Brigadier-General 13.6.16; commanded 56th Brigade in Somme and Ancre battles in 1916; commanded 107th Brigade in 1917 (March to June); commanded 138th Brigade from June, 1917, to 20.4.19; took part in battles of Mons and Le Cateau, also fight at Néry, and was with Battalion during retreat and subsequent advance to Marne and Aisne; wounded in 1st Battle of Ypres 29.10.14; took part in Battle of Loos, 1915, battles on Somme in July, 1916, battles of Ancre in Oct. and Nov. 1916; battle for Loos in June, 1917; Despatches six times; Brig.-Gen. retired 27.9.18; C.B.; C.M.G.; Comdt., Ceylon Defence Force.

ROYLE, R. G. (D.S.O. L.G. 3.6.18), T/Capt. (A/Major), K.O.Y.L.I. His brother, Lt. W. Royle, was killed at the Somme in July, 1916, and two other brothers joined the R.F.C. He went out to France in the spring of 1915, and was wounded in the same year, and in 1917 was injured in a bomb explosion.

ROYSTON-PIGOTT, G. A. (D.S.O. L.G. 14.1.16); b. 18.12.74; s. of late G. W. Royston-Pigott, F.R.S., and Agnes Royston-Pigott; educ. Sandhurst; 2nd Lt., North'n R., 20.2.95; Lt. 23.2.98; Capt. 30.3.03; Major 15.3.15; S. African War, 1899–1902; Queen's Medal, 4 clasps; King's Medal, 2 clasps. Major Royston-Pigott went to the front as second-in-command of the 1st Batt. Northamptonshire Rgt., in May, 1915, and with this battalion took part in the operations at Loos, becoming T/Lt.-Colonel 14.7.15. He was mentioned in Despatches. On 16.2.16 he was given command of a battalion of the Worcestershire Rgt., and he was killed in action at La Boisselle 3.7.16.

ROYSTON-PIGOTT, W. M. (D.S.O. L.G. 1.1.17); b. 8.2.81; s. of late G. W. Royston-Pigott, F.R.S., and Agnes, d. of Rev. J. Mitton; m. Dorothy Kathleen, d. of late Robert Clarke, I.C.S.; one s.; educ. Charterhouse; Trinity College, Cambridge; 2nd Lt., Suff. R., 23.2.01; Lt., Suff. R., 26.4.02; 2nd Lt., A.S.C., 1.4.05; Lt., A.S.C., 1.4.06; Capt. 23.2.12; Major, R.A.S.C., 30.10.14; Lt.-Col. ret., R.A.S.C., 29.7.21; served Europ. War, in Flanders, 1914, and on the Staff in Gallipoli, Serbia and Macedonia, 1915–18; Despatches; Legion of Honour.

RUCK, O. L. (D.S.O. L.G. 3.6.19); b. 6.9.81; 2nd Lt., Bedfordshire Rgt., 23.4.02; I.A. 8.7.03; Lt. 23.7.04; Capt. 23.4.11; Major 23.4.17; served S. African War, 1900–1; Queen's Medal, 4 clasps; N.W. Frontier of India, 1908; operations in the Mohmand country; Medal, clasp; Europ. War; Despatches.

RUDKIN, C. M. C. (D.S.O. L.G. 30.1.20), T/Lt.-Col., R.F.A.

RUDKIN, G. F., M.R.C.S., L.R.C.P. (D.S.O. L.G. 23.11.16); b. at Teignmouth, S. Devon, 9.11.80; s. of late G. M. A. Rudkin; m. Norah Watkins; one s.; educ. Blundell's School, Tiverton; London Hospital; Lt., R.A.M.C., 28.1.07; Capt. 28.7.10; Major 28.1.19; He commanded a Field Ambulance with the Salonika Army, and became T/Lt.-Colonel in 1916.

RUEL, W. G. (D.S.O. L.G. 1.2.17); b. 12.1.80; 2nd Lt., York. and Lanc. R., 20.1.00; Lt. 12.10.01; Capt., Ind. Army, 20.1.09; Maj. 1.9.15; S. African War, 1899–1902; Queen's Medal, 4 clasps; King's Medal, 2 clasps; Europ. War; Despatches.

RUNDALL, C. F. (D.S.O. L.G. 4.2.18) (Details, L.G. 5.7.18); b. 25.6.71; 2nd Lt., R.E., 13.2.91; Lt. 13.2.94; Capt. 15.11.01; Maj. 13.2.11; Lt.-Col. 24.9.18; C.M.G.

RUNDLE, F. P. (D.S.O. L.G. 1.2.17); b. 13.10.71; 2nd Lt., R.E., 14.2.90; Lt. 14.2.93; Capt. 14.2.01; Maj. 14.2.10; Bt. Lt.-Col. 1.1.18; Lt.-Col. 10.7.18; C.M.G.; N.W. Frontier, 1897–98; Tirah, 1897–98; Europ. War; Despatches.

RUNDLE, M. (D.S.O. L.G. 1.1.18), Engr.-Cdr., R.N., 1.7.09.

RUNGE, C. H. S. (D.S.O. L.G. 3.6.18), T/Capt., Gen. List; M.C.

RUSH, F. C. (D.S.O. L.G. 8.3.18), Major, N. Brunswick Rgt., Canadian Force.

RUSH, W. W. (D.S.O. L.G. 22.8.18), Major (T/Lt.-Col.), 5th Rgt., S. African Permanent Force.

RUSHBROOKE, W. P. H. (D.S.O. L.G. 25.11.16); b. 19.6.88; s. of Capt. W. H. Rushbrooke, a Count of Rome, and Margaret Mary, d. of H. F. Whyte; educ. Oratory School, Birmingham; 2nd Lt., North'd Fus., 3.4.09; Lt. 23.12.11; Capt. 28.3.15; Europ. War, 1914–17, in France and Salonika; commanded 2nd Batt. D.C.L.I. from 12.5.18 to 2.7.18, in Salonika and the Caucasus. His D.S.O. was awarded for gallantry on 10.9.16, and he was mentioned in Despatches.

RUSHTON, H. W. (D.S.O. L.G. 4.6.17); b. 7.8.67; 2nd Lt., R.E., 23.7.87; Lt. 23.7.90; Capt. 22.5.98; Maj. 1.4.06; Lt.-Col. 30.10.14; ret. pay 15.1.20.

RUSSELL, A. (D.S.O. L.G. 1.1.18) (Bar, L.G. 16.9.18); b. 24.3.80; 2nd Lt., R. Eng., 18.4.15; Lt. 26.6.17; Capt. 6.8.20.

RUSSELL, B. A. (D.S.O. L.G. 17.12.17) (Details, L.G. 23.4.18), T/Capt., Glouc. R.

RUSSELL, B. B. (D.S.O. L.G. 1.1.18); b. 25.8.59; 2nd Lt., R.E., 18.12.78; Bt. Col. 1.10.07; Col. 1.10.09; ret. pay (Ind. pen.), 23.10.12; Somali Coast, 1890; Chitral, 1895; Medal, clasp; Europ. War; Despatches.

RUSSELL, C. B. (D.S.O. L.G. 3.6.18), Major, Can. Engrs.

RUSSELL, G. B. (D.S.O. L.G. 25.8.16); b. 2.8.95; 2nd Lt. (from Mob. Spec. Res.), Wilts. R., 3.12.14; Lt. 28.1.15; Capt. 1.1.17; employed with Egyptian Army 9.12.21. His D.S.O. was awarded for gallantry on 6 and 7.7.16, in the Leipzig Salient.

RUSSELL, G. G. (D.S.O. L.G. 4.2.18) (Details, L.G. 5.7.18), Lt.-Col., King Edward's Horse, S.R.

RUSSELL, G. H. (D.S.O. L.G. 3.8.20); b. 2.10.82; 2nd Lt., Unatt., 27.7.02; I.A. 9.1.04; Lt. 27.11.04; Capt. 27.8.11; Maj. 27.8.17.

RUSSELL, H. J. (D.S.O. L.G. 1.1.17); b. 26.10.72; 2nd Lt., Dorset R., 19.7.93; Lt., A.S.C., 29.3.96; Capt. 1.4.00; Major 6.6.08; Lt.-Col. 30.10.14; ret. pay 30.4.20; S. African War, 1899–1902; Despatches; Queen's Medal, 4 clasps; King's Medal, 2 clasps; Europ. War; Despatches.

RUSSELL, JAMES COSMO (D.S.O. L.G. 1.1.17); b. 18.10.78; s of Rev. H. C. Russell, of Wollaton Rectory, Nottingham; 2nd Lt., 4th Hrs., 20.5.99; Lt. 4.12.00; Ind. Army 10.5.02; Capt. 20.5.08. He was Lt.-Colonel commanding a battalion of Cameron Highlanders when he was killed in action on 31.7.17.

James Cosmo Russell.

RUSSELL, JOHN CANNON (D.S.O. L.G. 3.6.19), Major, R.E. (T.F.).

RUSSELL, N. H. C. (D.S.O. L.G. 1.1.18); b. 26.12.79; entered Army 26.6.01; Capt. 15.2.10; ret. pay, 4th Hrs., 5.4.11; S. African War, 1901–2; Queen's Medal, 5 clasps; Europ War; Despatches.

RUSSELL, R. T. (D.S.O. L.G. 17.3.17) (Details, L.G. 18.6.17); s. of S. B. Russell, of Gosmore, Hitchin; m. Ethel Frances Hatch, M.B.E., d. of H. Hatch; 2nd Lt., Ind. Army, R. of O.

RUSSELL, V. C. (D.S.O. L.G. 26.7.18); b. 14.2.96; s. of S. A. Russell; m. Mabel Hannah, d. of A. Brewster; 2nd Lt., 2nd Suff. R., 20.10.15; Lt. 18.6.17; served Europ. War, 1914–18; Despatches twice; M.C.

RUSSELL, W. C. P. (D.S.O. L.G. 1.1.17); b. 28.6.79; 2nd Lt., R.A., 4.3.99; Lt. 16.2.01; Capt. 12.4.04; Maj. 30.10.14.

RUSSELL, W. K. (D.S.O. L.G. 1.1.17); b. 2.8.73; 2nd Lt., R.E., 10.2.93; Lt. 10.2.96; Capt. 10.2.04; Maj. 10.2.13; Lt.-Col. 1.1.21; C.M.G.

RUSSELL, W. M. (D.S.O. L.G. 1.1.18). He has retired with rank of Major in the Army.

RUSSELL-BROWN, C. (D.S.O. L.G. 3.6.16); b. 11.4.73; 2nd Lt., R.E., 22.7.92; Lt. 22.7.95; Capt. 22.7.03; Maj. 22.7.12; Lt.-Col. 4.10.20; S. African War, 1899–1900; severely wounded; Despatches; Queen's Medal, 3 clasps; Europ. War; Despatches; Bt. Lt.-Col. 3.6.15.

RUST, W. T. C. (D.S.O. L.G. 1.1.18), Major, A.S.C. (now R.A.S.C.).

RUSTON, A. H. (D.S.O. L.G. 8.3.19) (Details, L.G. 4.10.19), T/Major, M.M.G.C.

RUTHERFORD, E. M. C. (D.S.O. L.G. 17.3.19), Cdr., R.N., 31.12.14.

RUTHERFORD, N. C. (D.S.O. L.G. 17.9.17); b. 14.3.82; s. of J. J. Rutherford, M.D.; m. Alice Maud Mary, d. of Sir J. Roberts, Bart., of Saltaire; three s.; three d.; educ. University of Edinburgh; London Hospital; M.B.; F.R.C.S.; late Commissioner of Medical Services, Ministry of National Service; T/Lt.-Col., R.A.M.C., T.F.; served B.E.F. 14.3.15–27.9.17; Despatches. His D.S.O. was awarded for gallantry on 6 and 8.6.17, near Ypres.

RUTHVEN, HON. A. G. A. HORE- (see Hore-Ruthven, The Hon. A. G. A.).

RYALLS, H. D. (D.S.O. L.G. 20.10.16); b. 19.6.87; s. of H. J. and Frances Maud Ryalls; educ. Birkenhead School; enlisted in 10th Batt. L'pool Rgt. (L'pool Scottish) 5.8.14, having had two years' previous experience in 4th Batt. Cheshire Rgt. (T.F.); joined B.E.F., Nov. 1914, and saw service with L'pool Scottish until 30.3.15, when he returned to England for commission in 16th Batt. Cheshire R. This Batt. left for France 31.1.16; Capt., late O.C., 52nd Batt. Cheshire Rgt. His D.S.O. was awarded for gallantry on 17–18.7.16.

RYAN, A. W. (D.S.O. L.G. 4.6.17); b. 20.12.80; 2nd Lt., R.A., 15.11.14; Lt. 9.6.15; Capt. 3.11.17.

RYAN, C. F. M. N. (D.S.O. L.G. 3.6.18), Capt., R.E.; M.C.

RYAN, D. G. J. (D.S.O. L.G. 25.8.15) (Bar, L.G. 12.2.20), Capt. and Bt. Major, 1/6th Gurkha Rifles, I.A. (see "The Distinguished Service Order," from its institution to 31.12.15, by same publishers).

RYAN, E. (D.S.O. L.G. 14.1.16); b. Templehill, Co. Cork, 29.9.73; s. of Thomas Ryan; educ. Queen's College, Cork, and Edinburgh University; Lt., R.A.M.C., 29.1.01; Capt. 29.1.04; Major 29.1.13; served S. African War, 1901–2; Queen's Medal, 5 clasps; Europ. War, Retreat from Mons; Battle of Aisne, Sept.–Oct. 1914; 1st Battle of Ypres, 1914; Battle of Loos, 1915; Somme, 1916; served in France from Aug. 1914, to 5.4.19; M.O. on Personal Staff of C.-in-C. Lord Haig, K.T., etc., from Sept. 1916, to April, 1919; Despatches seven times; Bt. Lt.-Col. 1.1.17; C.M.G.; Legion of Honour; L'Etoile de Roumania.

RYAN, E. J. W. (D.S.O. L.G. 15.2.19) (Details, L.G. 30.7.19), Major. 102nd Batt. Can. Inf.

RYAN, H. T. (D.S.O. L.G. 1.1.18); b. 17.8.76; Lt., A.V.C., 22.7.03; Capt. 22.7.08; Major 10.7.15; Lt.-Col., ret. pay, R.A.V.C., 4.12.19.

RYAN, R. S. (D.S.O. L.G. 3.6.18); b. 6.5.84; 2nd Lt., R.A., 21.12.04; Lt. 21.12.07; Capt. 30.10.14; Bt. Maj. 1.1.16; Bt. Lt.-Col. 3.6.19.

RYBOT, N. V. L. (D.S.O. L.G. 17.4.16); b. 7.1.76; 2nd Lt. 5.8.96; Lt., Ind. Army, 3.4.99; Capt. 5.8.05; Maj. 5.8.14; ret. pay 6.12.20; Tibet 1903–4; Medal, clasp; Europ. War; Despatches.

RYCROFT, A. R. H. (D.S.O. L.G. 7.11.18); b. 1876; s. of late C. A. W. Rycroft and Edith Maud, d. of late Capt. H. Barnes, R.N.; m. Violet, d. of late Capt. W. Kevill-Davies, 17th Lancers, of Marsh Court, Leominster; one d.; Major, Yeomanry, attd. Tank Corps; served S. African War, 1899–1900; Queen's Medal, 3 clasps; Europ. War, 1914–18; wounded; Despatches.

RYCROFT, J. N. O. (D.S.O. L.G. 1.1.18); b. 22.2.92; s. of Major-Gen. Sir W. H. Rycroft, K.C.B., K.C.M.G., and G. R., only d. of the late F. N. Menzies, of Menzies; m. Elizabeth Mildred, d. of Sir Ralph Anstruther; educ. Eton and Sandhurst; 2nd Lt., R. Highrs., 20.9.11; Lt. 28.4.14; Capt. 1.10.15; Adjt., 1st Batt. Black Watch; A.D.C., 1914–15; commanded 12th Batt. H.L.I., 1918; served Europ. War; Bt. Major 3.6.19; M.C.; Belgian Croix de Guerre.

RYDER, T. E. (D.S.O. L.G. 3.6.19), Major, 7th Siege By. Can. Garr. Art.; M.C.

RYE, H. B. TONSON- (see Tonson-Rye, H. B.).

RYRIE, H. S. (D.S.O. L.G. 16.9.18); b. 23.3.78, at Coolringdon, Cooma, New South Wales, Australia; s. of David and Ellen Eliza Ryrie; educ. The King's School, Parramatta; joined the Australian Forces in Sept. 1914; Capt. (T/Major), 6th Light Horse Rgt.; served Europ. War; severely wounded.

SADLEIR-JACKSON, L. W. DE V. (D.S.O. L.G. 27.9.01) (Bar, 16.9.18) (see "The Distinguished Service Order," from its institution to 31.12.15, by same publishers).

SADLER, A. (D.S.O. L.G. 4.6.17), Temp. Major, A.S.C., now R.A.S.C.

SADLER, H. K. (D.S.O. L.G. 4.6.17); b. 18.11.77; s. of late T. Sadler; m. Clarice Laurence, d. of late L. Hancock; educ. Eton; Christ Church, Oxford; ent. Army, 2nd Lt., R.A., 22.8.00; Lieut. 22.8.03; Capt. 1.3.12; Adjt., R.A., 1913–15; Major, R.F.A., 15.3.15; Commanding 25th Battery, R.F.A.; served Europ. War, 1914–18; Despatches six times; M.C.

SADLER, R. M. (D.S.O. L.G. 3.6.19), Lt.-Col., 17th Batt. Aust. Inf.; M.C.

SAGAR, A. L. (D.S.O. L.G. 11.1.19); m. Kathleen Mary, d. of F. Weekes; Capt., late 13th Batt. K.R.R.C.

SAINT, E. T. (D.S.O. L.G. 16.9.18), Lt.-Col., Cambs. R. He died of wounds 29.8.18.

ST. AUBYN, E. G. (D.S.O. L.G. 11.1.19), Capt. (A/Lt.-Col.), K.R.R.C., S.R., att. 2nd Batt.

ST. CLAIR, G. J. P. (D.S.O. L.G. 1.1.17); b. 29.6.85; s. of Hon. L. M. St. Clair; m. Charlotte Theresa Orme, d. of Major A. C. Little; three d.; educ. R.M.A., Woolwich; 2nd Lt., R.A., 29.8.04; Lt. 29.7.07; Capt. 30.10.14; Major, R.H.A., 25.9.16; served Europ. War, 1914–17; wounded; Despatches.

ST. CLAIR, W. H. (D.S.O. L.G. 1.1.17), Major, Aust. Arty.

ST. CLAIR, W. L. (D.S.O. L.G. 1.1.18); b. 22.6.82; 2nd Lt., R.A., 21.12.01; Lt. 5.10.04; Capt. 30.10.14; Major R.F.A., 23.2.16. He died 23.2.20.

ST. HILL, A. A. (D.S.O. L.G. 1.1.18); b. 1.3.73; 2nd Lt., W. Rid. R., 28.12.95; Lt. 9.2.99; Capt. 1.2.02; Major 9.10.14; served W. Africa, 1900 (slightly wounded; Despatches (L.G. 8.3.01); Medal, clasp); Europ. War; Despatches. He was killed in action 27.10.18.

ST. JOHN, E. F. (D.S.O. L.G. 1.1.17) (Bar, L.G. 16.9.18); b. 27.2.79; s. of late Hon. and Rev. E. T. St. John and Hon. Mrs. E. T. St. John, of Bletsoe, Aboyne, Aberdeenshire; m. Henrietta Frances, d. of late J. A. Dalmahoy, M.V.O., W.S.; educ. Harrow School; R.M.A., Woolwich; joined R.A. 26.2.98; 2nd Lt. 16.2.01; Capt. 14.11.05; Adjt., R.A., 28.3.08 to 17.5.09; Major 30.10.14; Lt.-Colonel 24.7.18; served S. African War, 1899–1902; Despatches; Queen's Medal, 4 clasps; Europ. War; Despatches four times; C.M.G.; Croix de Guerre avec Palme.

ST. JOHN, F. O., F.R.G.S. (D.S.O. L.G. 25.8.17); b. British Legation, Caracas, Venezuela, 16.10.86; s. of Sir F. R. St. John, K.C.M.G., and Isabella Annie, d. of Hon. J. T. Fitzmaurice; educ. Ascham School, Bournemouth; served two years in the ranks; 2nd Lt., R. Scots, 9.10.12; Lt. 15.7.13; Capt. 21.8.15; Royal Corps of Signals; served Europ. War; Despatches; M.C.

F. O. St. John.

ST. JOHN, R. S. (D.S.O. L.G. 25.8.17); b. 15.1.76; s. of R. F. St. A. St. John and Julia Louise, d. of Rev. W. Churchill; m. Edwardine Annie Georgina, d. of late Capt. L. A. Jourdier, 20th French Dragoons; 2nd Lt., Unatt., 22.1.96; Ind. S.C. 11.4.97; Lt. 22.4.98; Capt. 22.1.05; Major 22.1.14; Bt. Lt.-Col. 3.6.16 (T/Brig.-Gen. 21.6.17 to 31.12.20); Bt. Lt.-Col. 3.6.19; Colonel, I.A., 23.4.20; served Europ. War, 1914–18; Despatches; Bt. Col., C.I.E., 1919; Japanese Order of the Sacred Treasure; India and China Medals; Serbian Order of Karageorge, with Crossed Swords.

ST. JOHN, R. J. HARRIS- (see Harris-St. John, R. J.).

ST. JOHN, ST. A. O. (D.S.O. L.G. 12.12.19), Lt.-Cdr., R.N.

ST. JOHN, W. HARRIS- (see Harris-St. John, W.).

ST. JOHN, W. E. (D.S.O. L.G. 1.1.18) (Bar, L.G. 4.3.18) (Details, L.G. 16.8.18), Major, Yeomanry.

ST. LEGER, S. E. (D.S.O. L.G. 14.1.16); b. 18.3.68; s. of F. Y. St. Leger; educ. Cambridge; 2nd Lt., R. Ir. Regt., 29.1.90; Lt. 12.8.91; Capt. 5.2.96; Major 12.3.08; Lt.-Col. 19.2.17; Colonel 29.2.21; served with M.I. in S. African War; Queen's Medal and 5 clasps; Europ. War, 1914–17; Despatches; C.M.G.; C.V.O.

SALE, G. G. (D.S.O. L.G. 2.4.19) (Details, L.G. 10.12.19), T/Lt. (A/Capt.), 179th Tunn. Co., R.E.; M.C.

SALE, J. C. (D.S.O. L.G. 27.10.17) (Details, L.G. 18.3.18), T/Capt., R.A.M.C.; M.C.

SALISBURY, A. G. (D.S.O. L.G. 4.6.17) (Bar, L.G. 16.9.18), Lt.-Col., Aust. Mil. Forces; C.M.G.

SALKELD, H. Y. (D.S.O. L.G. 4.3.18) (Details, L.G. 16.8.18); b. 22.10.81; 2nd Lt., R. Mar., 1.9.99; Lt., R.N., 1.7.00; 2nd Lt., Unatt., 25.8.04; Ind. Army 28.9.05; Capt. 28.7.09; Major 1.9.15.

SALMON, R. (D.S.O. L.G. 6.4.18), Lt.-Cdr. (A/Cdr.), R.N.R.

SALMOND, SIR W. G. H. (D.S.O. L.G. 3.3.17); b. 1878; s. of Maj.-Gen. Sir W. Salmond, K.C.B., R.E., and Emma Mary, d. of W. F. Hoyle; brother of Air Vice-Marshal Sir J. M. Salmond, K.C.B., C.M.G., D.S.O.; m. Margaret, d. of W. Carr, of Ditchingham Hall, Norfolk; one s.; Air Vice-Marshal, R.A.F., late R.A.; served S. African War, 1899–1902; Queen's Medal, seven clasps; China, 1900; Medal; Europ. War, 1914–18; K.C.M.G.; C.B.; Despatches; Orders of the Nile and St. Saviour of Greece.

SALT, H. F. (D.S.O. L.G. 1.1.18); s. of late Sir T. Salt, 1st Bart.; m. Phyllis Dulce, d. of late Major E. D. Cameron, R.A.; one d.; educ. Cooper's Hill; joined Army 10.1.00; Lt. 3.4.01; Capt. 1.9.08; Major 30.10.14; Bt. Lt.-Col. 3.6.18; Colonel 3.6.19; D.D. of Remounts, Army H.Q., India; served Europ. War, Gallipoli (Suvla Bay), Salonika, Palestine and Syria; Despatches; Bt. Lt.-Col., 1918; Bt. Col. 1919; C.M.G.; Order of the Nile, 3rd Class.

SALT, SIR T. A., Bart. (D.S.O. L.G. 24.1.17), of Standing and Weeping Cross, Co. Stafford; b. 8.1.63; s. of Sir T. Salt, 1st Bart., and Helen, d. of J. L. Anderdon, of Chislehurst; m. Elinor Mary, d. of Sir H. A. Wiggin, 2nd Bart.; two s.; one d.; educ. Clifton; Oriel College, Oxford; Sandhurst; 1st commission 25.8.86; Adjt., 11th Hussars, 1890–94; Major 2.11.02; retired, 11th Hrs., 7.5.04; served W. Coast of Africa, 1887–88; Despatches; Medal with clasp; N.W. Frontier of India, 1897; Medal with clasp; S. Africa, att. to 7th Dragoon Guards, 1902; Medal with 2 clasps; Europ. War, 1914–19; Despatches; 1914 Star; Order of the Nile, 4th Class; J.P. and D.L., Co. Stafford; High Sheriff, 1909. His D.S.O. was awarded for the Irish Rebellion; since then served on Doiran front in Macedonia, and during operations of latter part of 1917 in Palestine.

SAMPSON, B. (D.S.O. L.G. 1.1.19), Lieut., Aust. Mil. Forces, 1.7.15.

SAMPSON, F. C., M.B. (D.S.O. L.G. 14.1.16) (Bar, L.G. 15.2.19) (Details, L.G. 30.7.19); b. 14.10.79; m. Mary D. Woodhouse, R.R.C., Q.A.I.M.N.S.; educ. Clongowes; Catholic University, Dublin; Lt., R.A.M.C., 31.7.05; Capt. 31.1.09; Major 15.10.15; Major, R.A.M.C.; Lt.-Col., 91st Field Amb., 32nd Division; served Europ. War, 1914–16; Despatches twice; Bt. Major.

SAMSON, C. R. (D.S.O. L.G. 23.10.14) (Bar, L.G. 23.1.17), Commander, R.N.; C.M.G. (see "The Distinguished Service Order," from its institution to 31.12.15, by same publishers).

SAMUEL, F. A. (D.S.O. L.G. 1.1.17), T/Major, R. Welsh Fus.

SAMUEL, F. D. (D.S.O. L.G. 1.1.17) (Bar, L.G. 26.9.17) (Details, L.G. 9.1.18), Lt.-Col., London R.

SAMUEL, H. T. (D.S.O. L.G. 3.6.19), Major (A/Lt.-Col.), R.A.M.C., T.F., commanding 170th Indian Combined Field Amb.

SANDARS, S. E. (D.S.O. L.G. 1.2.19), Capt. (A/Lt.-Col.), R.F. (S.R.), att. 3rd Batt. London R.; M.C.

SANDAY, W. D. S. (D.S.O. L.G. 20.10.16); b. 1883; s. of S. S. Sanday, of Paddington Hall, Cheshire; m. Mary, d. of A. H. Brodrick; Lt.-Col., R.F.C. (now R.A.F.); served Europ. War, 1914–17; Despatches twice; M.C.

SANDAY, W. H. (D.S.O. L.G. 1.1.19), Major, Aust. Mil. Forces; M.C.

SANDEMAN, G. R. (D.S.O. L.G. 3.6.18); b. 20.10.82; 2nd Lt., Border R., 28.1.03; Lt. 14.1.05; Capt. 29.10.14; Major 22.10.17; Despatches; M.C.

SANDERS, A. R. C. (D.S.O. L.G. 3.6.16) (Bar, L.G. 2.12.18); b. 20.1.77; 2nd Lt., R.E., 18.1.97; Lt. 15.1.00; Capt. 18.1.06; Major and Bt. Lt.-Col.; T/Brig.-Gen., R.E.; served N.W. Frontier of India, 1908; Medal with clasp; Europ. War; C.M.G.; Legion of Honour. He was killed in action 20.9.18.

SANDERS, G. H. S. (D.S.O. L.G. 8.3.18), Eng. Lt.-Cdr., R.N.

SANDERS, H. J. (D.S.O. L.G. 1.2.19); s. of late H. W. Sanders, of The White House, Blackwell, Worcestershire; m. Winifred Ada, d. of J. S. Motion; Lt. (A/Capt.), 1/24th Batt. London R.; M.C.

SANDERS, R. E. (D.S.O. L.G. 3.6.18), T/Major (A/Lt.-Col.), A.S.C.

SANDERS, W. C. (D.S.O. L.G. 15.9.16); b. 23.2.68; s. of W. T. Sanders, late of H.M. Civil Service; Eng. Cdr. R.N.; served Europ. War, Battle of Jutland; Despatches.

SANDERS, W. E. (D.S.O. L.G. 14.9.17), Lt.-Cdr., R.N.R. V.C. (since killed) (see "The Victoria Cross," by same publishers).

SANDERS, W. O. S. (D.S.O. L.G. 3.6.19); b. 21.8.76; 2nd Lt., R.A., 21.9.96; Lt. 21.9.99; Capt. 21.12.01; Major 30.10.14; Lt.-Col. 1.5.21; Major, 324th Siege By. R.G.A.

SANDERSON, A. (D.S.O. L.G. 1.1.19), Major, 3rd Tunnelling Corps, Aust. R.E.; M.C.

SANDERSON, A. E. (D.S.O. L.G. 16.9.18); b. 1.4.86; 2nd Lt., Oxf. L. Inf., 16.8.05; Lt. 20.1.08; Capt. 25.7.14; Bt. Major, Oxf. and Bucks. L.I. 1.1.18.

SANDERSON, C. (D.S.O. L.G. 30.3.16); b. 8.3.88; s. of John Richard Sanderson; m. 1917, Agnes, d. of Mr. and Mrs. Farmistir, of Dundee; educ. Tudhoe National School; The Dundee Training College of Hygiene and Physical Training; 2nd Lt., 1st. Batt. Gord. Highrs., March, 1916; served Europ. War; Despatches; wounded and gassed, 1916, and returned to France; awarded French Military Cross; Russian Cross of St. George. He was killed in action 18.6.17. His D.S.O. was awarded for gallantry on 3.3.16, at Ypres-Comines Canal.

C. Sanderson.

SANDERSON, W. D. (D.S.O. L.G. 14.1.16); b. 28.8.68; ent. Army 17.1.91; Lt. 13.7.92; Capt. 10.8.98; Major 8.7.08; Lt.-Col.; Colonel 14.9.18; retired pay, late L.N. Lancs. R., 24.12.18; served Nile Exp., 1898 (Medal and clasp); S. African War, 1899–1901; Despatches; Queen's Medal and 6 clasps; Europ. War, 1914–18; Despatches; C.M.G.

SANDES, E. W. C. (D.S.O. L.G. 23.10.19); b. 13.2.08; s. of late Col. H. T. T. Sandes, R.A.; m. Sylvia Mary, d. of late F. Sneyd-Kynnersley; one s.; Professor of Civil Engineering, Thomason Engineering College, Roorkee, India; 2nd Lt., R.E., 22.11.99; Lt. 24.7.02; Capt. 22.11.08; Major, R.E., 30.7.16; served Europ. War, Mesopotamia, 1914–16, and was in the besieged garrison of Kut-el-Amarah; M.C.

SANDFORD, A. B. (D.S.O. L.G. 3.6.18), Lt., A.F.A., 1.9.14; Major, Aust. F.A.

SANDFORD, D. A. (D.S.O. L.G. 2.2.16) (Bar, L.G. 16.9.18); b. 1882; s. of late Ven. E. G. Sandford, Archdeacon of Exeter, and Ethel, d. of Gabriel Poole; m. Christine, d. of H. S. Lush; one d.; 2nd Lt., R.A., 18.8.00; Lt. 22.5.02; Capt. 18.8.13; Major 30.12.15; Bt. Lt.-Col., R.G.A., 3.6.19; served Sudan, 1910; Medal and clasp; Europ. War, 1914–18; wounded; Despatches; Legion of Honour.

SANDILANDS, H. R. (D.S.O. L.G. 4.6.17); b. 7.8.76; 2nd Lt., North'd Fus., 22.1.98; Lt. 17.3.00; Capt. 18.6.01; Major 1.9.15; Bt. Lt.-Col. 1.1.19; Lt.-Col. 5.11.21; served S. African War, 1899–1902 (Despatches (L.G. 10.9.01); Queen's Medal, 2 clasps; King's Medal, 2 clasps); N.W. Frontier of India, 1908 (Medal with clasp); Europ. War; Despatches.

SANDILANDS, P. (D.S.O. L.G. 1.2.19); b. 6.2.78; 2nd Lt., R. Mar., 1.1.97; Lt. 1.1.98; Capt. 16.3.05; Major 21.10.15; Major (A/Lt.-Col.), 1st. R.M.L.I. Batt.

SANDILANDS, V. C. (D.S.O. L.G. 1.1.17); b. 8.2.78; 2nd Lt., Sco. Rif., 16.2.98; Lt. 3.5.99; Capt. 20.5.03; Major, Sc. Rifles, 1.9.15; served Europ. War, 1914; Despatches.

SANDO, L. C. (D.S.O. L.G. 3.6.18), Capt., A.A.S.C., 9.12.12; Major, Aust. A.S.C.

SANDYS, E. T. F. (D.S.O. L.G. 22.9.16); b. 9.1.76; 2nd Lt., W.I.R., 5.9.96; Lt. 22.12.97; Adjt. 13.6.00 to 12.6.04; Capt., W.I.R., 5.11.00; Midd'x R. 25.3.05; Major, Sept. 1915; T/Lt.-Col.; served in Sierra Leone, 1898–99, Kare Expedition; Europ. War; Despatches. He died of wounds 14.9.16.

SANFORD, G. A. (D.S.O. L.G. 3.6.19); b. 23.11.83; s. of Major E. A. Sanford, of Triley Court, Abergavenny; m. Violet, d. of Rev. R. Jardine; one s.; one d.; educ. Wellington College; joined 20th Hussars, 22.4.03; Lt. 28.7.06; Capt. 9.9.11; Adjt. 16.10.12 to 15.10.15; Major 9.12.17; Major, D.G., 23.11.21; served Europ. War, in France and Belgium, 1914–18; severely wounded; Despatches twice.

SANGSTER, P. B. (D.S.O. L.G. 3.6.16), 2nd Lt., Unatt., 28.11.94; 2nd Lt., I.S.C. 22.2.96; Capt. 28.11.03; Major 28.11.12; Lt.-Col. 7.8.16; Col. 3.5.20; served Tirah Campaign, 1897–98; Medal with 2 clasps; Europ. War; Despatches; C.M.G.

SANKEY, C. E. P. (D.S.O. L.G. 22.6.15) (Bar, L.G. 8.3.19) (Details, L.G. 4.10.19), Lt.-Col. R.E. (see "The Distinguished Service Order," from its institution to 31.12.15, by same publishers).

SANSOM, W. I. S. (D.S.O. L.G. 10.6.20), Major, 4th Batt. Can. M.G.C.

SARGEAUNT, P. R. (D.S.O. L.G. 26.9.17) (Details, L.G. 9.1.18), Capt. (A/Major), R.G.A.

SARGENT, A. E. E. (D.S.O. L.G. 1.1.17); b. 22.5.78; 2nd Lt., Derby R., 18.4.00; Lt., Notts. and Derby. R., 6.12.00; Ind. Army 30.1.03; Capt. 18.4.09; Major 1.9.15; served E. Africa, 1902–4; operations in Somaliland; Medal with clasp.

SARGENT, J. (D.S.O. L.G. 4.6.17); b. 8.2.81; 2nd Lt., Lan. Fus., 24.7.01; Lt. 14.10.04; Capt. 5.8.14; Major 8.5.16; Bt. Lt.-Col. 3.6.18; served S. African War, 1899–1901; Queen's Medal, 3 clasps; Europ. War; Despatches.

SARGENT, P. W. G., M.A., M.B., F.R.C.S. (D.S.O. L.G. 1.1.17); b. 1873; e. s. of E. G. Sargent, of Clifton; m. 1907, May Louise, d. of late Sir Herbert Ashman, Bart.; one s.; one d.; educ. Clifton; St. John's College, Cambridge; St. Thomas's Hospital; joined the Army, 1914; served Europ. War, 1914–18; Despatches twice; C.M.G., 1919.

SARGON, A. I. (D.S.O. L.G. 26.5.19), Lt., Ind. Army (from Ind. Army Res. of Off.), 8.10.16; Capt. 8.10.19; Capt., I.A., R. of O., att. 114th Mahrattas.

SARSON, E. V. (D.S.O. L.G. 1.1.18); b. 15.2.78; 2nd Lt., R.A., 28.3.00; Lt. 3.4.01; Capt. 19.4.09; Major, R.F.A., 30.10.14.

SASSE, C. D. (D.S.O. L.G. 20.10.15) (Bar, L.G. 1.2.19), Major (T/Lt.-Col.), Aust. Mil. Forces (see "The Distinguished Service Order," from its institution to 31.12.15, by same publishers).

SAUNDERS, A. (D.S.O. L.G. 8.3.18), Engr. Cdr., R.N.

SAUNDERS, A. L. (D.S.O. L.G. 7.11.18), Capt. (A/Major), Manitoba Rgt., Can. Inf.; M.C.

SAUNDERS, C. G. (D.S.O. L.G. 3.6.18), Major, Can. A.V.C.

SAUNDERS, H. C. (D.S.O. L.G. 14.1.16); b. 19.4.80; m. 1903, Edith Lydia Beckley, d. of Augustus Beckley, L.D.S., of Brighton; one d.; educ. Brighton Grammar School; joined R.E., T.F., 1.1.04; Capt. 28.1.08; Major 1.6.16; Bt. Lt.-Col. 4.1.19; served Europ. War, France, Salonika; Despatches three times; 1914–15 Star; T.D.; Greek Military Cross (2nd Class).

SAUNDERS, H. C. R. (D.S.O. L.G. 1.1.17); b. 28.4.82; s. of Arthur Rich Saunders, M.B., F.R.C.S., and Emma Louise, d. of James Cecil Phillipps, M.D.; m. 1915, Dorothy May, d. of Brig.-Gen. C. P. Triscott, C.B., C.M.G.; one s.; educ. Clifton College; 2nd Lt., E. Yorks. R., 29.11.05; Lt. 24.4.09; Capt. 30.10.14; served in Somaliland, 1910–11(Medal); Europ. War, served in France from Jan. to Feb. 1915, when he was wounded and invalided home; appointed to command the Officers' Training School at Tynemouth, with temp. rank of Major; rejoined the 1st Batt. of his Regt. in France, Oct. 1915, as Second-in-Command, and promoted A/Lt.-Col. 1.7.16, and when the Commanding Officer was killed on the Somme, he was appointed to command 1st Battalion. He commanded it through the whole of the fighting on the Somme during the summer of 1916; was invalided home, and reverted to the rank of Temp. Major; rejoined 1st Batt. of his regiment in France in Feb. 1917, and remained with it as Second-in-Command until appointed Chief Instructor in III. Corps School, April, 1917. In March, 1918, appointed to command a Battalion formed from the Schools to hold a section of the line during big German offensive; Despatches; reported missing, and afterwards killed in action 30.5.18.

H. C. R. Saunders.

SAUNDERS, J. LL. (D.S.O. L.G. 4.6.17), Major, New Zealand Force.

SAUNDERS, M. (D.S.O. L.G. 17.10.17); b. 9.11.84; s. of Col. M. W. Saunders; m. Marjory, d. of Francis Bacon; educ. Malvern College; R.M.A., Woolwich; 2nd Lt., R.F.A., 23.12.03; Lt., R.A., 23.12.06; Lt., I.A., 12.11.07; Capt. 23.12.12; Major, Sikhs, I.A., 23.12.18; Lt.-Colonel 1.1.19; Staff Capt., 2nd R. Naval Brigade, 1914; operations in Belgium and Siege of Antwerp; operations in Gallipoli, 1915, from first landing to evacuation; G.S.O.3 in Egypt to March, 1916; Brig. Major, Eastern Persian Field Force to April, 1917; G.S.O.2 and Intelligence Officer with Major-Gen. Dunsterville's Mission through N.W. Persia to the Caucasus, 1918; G.S.O.1, Caucasus Section, G.H.Q., Br. Salonika Force, 1919; wounded; Despatches four times; Bt. Lt.-Colonel.

SAUNDERS, R. (D.S.O. L.G. 28.8.18), Commander, R.N.V.R.

SAUNDERS, R. G. F. (D.S.O. L.G. 3.6.16); b. 1882; s. of late F. W. Saunders, B.A., and Edith, d. of late A. Watson; m. Ottilie, d. of late N. Schmit, of Luxembourg; educ. St. Paul's School; entered the P. and O. Service, 1899; Lt., A.S.C., 1914; Capt., 1914; Major, 1915; late T/Major, A.S.C. (now R.A.S.C.); served S. African War, with Paget's Horse, 1901–2; Queen's Medal with 5 clasps; returned to the P. and O. Service; served Europ. War from Nov. 1914; Despatches four times.

R. G. F. Saunders.

SAUNDERS, R. P. (D.S.O. L.G. 1.1.19), Major, 19th Batt. Can. Inf.; M.C.

SAUNDERS, W. J. T. (D.S.O. L.G. 6.4.18), Cdr., R.N.

SAVAGE, A. J. (D.S.O. L.G. 3.6.18); b. 17.6.74; 2nd Lt., R.E., 25.7.93; Lt. 25.7.96; Capt. 1.4.04; Major 25.7.13; Bt. Lt.-Col. 3.6.19; Lt.-Col. 1.1.21; S. African War, 1900–2; Queen's Medal, 2 clasps; King's Medal, 2 clasps; Europ. War; Despatches.

SAVAGE, G. T. (D.S.O. L.G. 1.1.17); b. 8.9.83; 2nd Lt., A.S.C., 23.8.03; Lt. 1.5.04; Capt. 1.1.11; Major, R.A.S.C., 30.10.14.

SAVAGE, H. M. (D.S.O. L.G. 18.1.18) (Details, L.G. 25.4.18) (Bar, L.G. 3.6.19), Major, Can. F.A.

SAVAGE, P. J. (D.S.O. L.G. 22.9.16), Capt. (T/Major), Aust. Engrs.

SAVAGE, V. W. (D.S.O. L.G. 1.1.19), Capt., A.A.M.C., 23.11.14.

SAVIGE, S. G. (D.S.O. L.G. 8.3.19) (Details, L.G. 4.10.19), Capt., Aust. Mil. Forces; M.C.

SAVILE, C. R. U. (D.S.O. L.G. 14.1.16); b. Bermuda 5.12.81; s. of Brig.-Gen. W. C. Savile, C.B., D.S.O., and Helen Vernon, d. of W. Ruxton, of Ardee House, Co. Louth; m. Katherine Gladys Ritchie; educ. Wellington College; Sandhurst; 2nd Lt., Unatt., 8.1.01; joined R. Fus. 9.3.01; Lt. 26.4.04; Capt. 21.2.10; Major 8.1.16; Nigeria R., W.A.F.F., 1905–10; operations N. Nigeria, 1906 (Medal and clasp); Brig. Major, Nigeria R., 1911–16; Cameroon Exp., 1914–16; France, 1917; O.B.E., 1919.

C. R. U. Savile.

SAVILE, L. W. (D.S.O. L.G. 1.1.17); b. 12.9.80; s. of late Col. Henry B. O. Savile, C.B., R.A.; m. Jeanie Letitia Kathleen, d. of late Henry Litton; one s.; educ. Clifton College; R.M.A., Woolwich; 2nd Lt., R.A., 22.11.99; Lt. 16.2.01; Capt. 1.4.08; Lt.-Col. 1.4.21; served Europ. War, in France; Despatches three times; French Croix de Guerre with Palm; commanded 152nd Brigade, R.F.A., July, 1918, to April, 1919.

SAVILL, S. R. (D.S.O. L.G. 1.2.19); s. of P. Savill, of Carr End, Reigate; m. Sybilla Morris, d. of W. Dorling; Lt.-Col., 1/16th Batt. London R.; M.C.

SAVORY, A. K. M. C. W. (D.S.O. L.G. 1.1.17); b. 24.6.82; s. of Rev. A. Wordsworth Savory, M.A.; m. B. K. N. Molineux; three s.; one d.; educ. Wellington College; 2nd Lt., 3rd Lincs. R., 1900; Lt., 1905; Adjt., 1907–10; resigned commission 1911; T/Capt., 13th E. Yorks. R., Nov. 1914; T/Major and 2nd-in-command, Jan. 1915 (Despatches); T/Lt.-Col. commanding a Batt., March, 1917; Seniority, Aug. 1916; commanding E. Lancs. Rgt. till June, 1919; subsequently 117th Inf. Brig.

SAVORY, K. S. (D.S.O. L.G. 22.6.16) (Bar, L.G. 29.8.17), Fl. Lt., R.N.A.S.

SAWERS, W. C. (D.S.O. L.G. 1.1.19), Major, Aust. A.M.C.

SAWYER, G. H. (D.S.O. L.G. 3.6.16) (Bar, L.G. 24.9.18); b. 18.5.82; 2nd Lt., R. Berks. R., 8.5.01; Lt. 11.11.03; Capt. 1.8.10; Major 8.5.16; served S. African War, 1901–2; Queen's Medal with 3 clasps; Europ. War; Despatches.

SAWYER, L. (D.S.O. L.G. 11.12.16); b. 3.6.95; T/Major, York and Lanc. R. His D.S.O. was awarded for gallantry at Le Sars.

SAXBY, C. G. (D.S.O. L.G. 1.1.17); 3rd s. of Mr. and Mrs. Saxby, of Remuera, Auckland, N.Z.; educ. Wanganui Collegiate School; Captain, New Zealand Mounted Rifles, May, 1915; promoted Major and Lt.-Col.; served S. African War; Medal, 5 clasps; Europ. War, in Gallipoli and France; Despatches.

SAYE, K. N. (D.S.O. L.G. 8.3.18), T/Capt. (A/Major), R.E.

SAYER, A. C. (D.S.O. L.G. 3.6.19), Major, Sussex Yeom., att. 16th Batt. R. Sussex R.; M.C.

SAYER, H. (D.S.O. L.G. 1.1.19), Capt., Sussex Yeomanry; M.C.

SCAFE, W. E. (D.S.O. L.G. 3.6.16); b. 7.11.78; s. of late Gen. C. H. Scafe, R.M.; m. Elizabeth Mary, d. of late J. R. Shirreff, of Joradah, Bengal; one s.; educ. St. Paul's School, London; R. Naval School, Eltham; 2nd Lt., 3rd Batt. Devon Rgt. (Militia), 1897; 2nd Lt., Devonshire Rgt., 2.8.99; Lt. 12.11.00; Capt. 22.1.07; Major 1.9.15; Bt. Lt.-Col. 3.6.17; served S. African War, 1899–1902; Queen's Medal with 2 clasps; King's Medal with 2 clasps; Europ. War; C.M.G.

SCAIFE, A. J. P. (D.S.O. L.G. 1.1.19), Major, R.G.A. (T.F.), 187th Siege Battery.

SCALE, J. D. (D.S.O. L.G. 12.3.17); b. 27.12.82; 2nd Lt., R. War. R., 8.5.01; Ind. Army 15.6.03; Lt. 8.8.03; Capt. 8.5.10; Major 8.5.16.

SCALES, J. L. (D.S.O. L.G. 26.11.17) (Details, L.G. 6.4.18), Lt., Aust. Inf.

SCAMMELL, A. G. (D.S.O. L.G. 3.6.16), Major, R.F.A. (T.F.).

SCANLAN, J. J. (D.S.O. L.G. 3.6.18) (Bar, L.G. 16.9.18), Major (T/Lt.-Col.), Aust. Inf.

SCARLETT, F. R. (D.S.O. L.G. 1.10.17); b. 1875; s. of late Col. W. J. Scarlett, 5th Dragoon Guards and Catherine Henrietta, d. of J. Low; m. Dora, d. of J. Blakiston-Houston; three s.; Capt., R.N., 1914; Wing Capt., R.N.A.S., 1915; Brig.-Gen., R.A.F., 1918; Air Commodore; C.B., 1919.

SCARLETT, H. ASHLEY- (D.S.O. L.G. 18.2.18) (Details, L.G. 18.7.18), Capt. T/Major), R. of O., R. Fus.

SCARLETT, HON. H. R. (D.S.O. L.G. 14.1.16); b. 25.11.78; s. of late Lt.-Col. L. J. Y. C. Scarlett and Bessie Florence, d. of E. Gibson and niece and adopted daughter of Sir Percy Shelley, 3rd Bart.; and brother of 6th Baron Abinger; m. Marjorie, d. of J. McPhillamy, of Blair Athol, Bathurst, N.S.W.; three s.; educ. Bath College; 2nd Lt., R.A., 26.5.00; Lt. 25.3.02; Capt. 1.4.11; Adjt., R.A., 22.1.14 to 29.10.14; Major 30.10.14; Lt.-Col., R.A.; served S. African War; Queen's and King's Medals, 5 clasps; Europ. War, 1914–18; Bt. Lt.-Col. 1.1.19; Despatches several times.

SCEALES, G. A. M'L. (D.S.O. L.G. 1.1.17); b. 5.7.78; m. Evelyn Lily May, d. of A. P. Macewen and widow of Brig.-Gen. H. B. Kirk, 91st A. and S. Highrs.; one s.; educ. Charterhouse; Sandhurst; joined Princess Louise's 91st A. and S. Highrs., 18.5.98; Lt. 12.12.99; Adjt., A. and S. Highrs., 1.4.08; Capt. 28.4.09; Major 1.9.15; Adjt., 1908–11; retired pay, 1921; Lt.-Colonel; served with this battalion continuously till Europ. War, including S. African Campaign, 1899–1902; Queen's Medal, clasps; King's Medal, clasps; went to France with batt., Dec. 1914; commanded 4th Black Watch, 1915; amalgamated 4th and 5th Black Watch, 1916–Dec. 1917; Despatches thrice; Bt. Lt.-Col. 1.1.18; commanded 14th Batt. Tank Corps, and Brig.-Gen., commanding 1st Tank Brigade, Dec. 1917–1919; commanded 5th (Regular) Tank Batt.; Member of Royal Company of Archers, King's Body Guard for Scotland.

SCHOMBERG, H. ST. G. (D.S.O. L.G. 3.6.18); b. 24.8.86; 2nd Lt., E. Surr. R., 8.7.08; Lt. 26.1.10; Capt. 15.2.15; Bt. Major 1.1.18.

SCHOMBERG, R. C. F., B.A. (D.S.O. L.G. 22.12.16) (Bar, L.G. 11.1.19); b. 19.9.80; s. of R. B. Schomberg; educ. Oratory School; New College, Oxford; joined 1st Seaf. Highrs. 4.12.01; Lt. 17.8.03; Capt. 15.3.13; Major 4.12.16; Bt. Lt.-Col. 3.6.19; served Indian Frontier Exp., 1908; Europ. War; severely wounded twice; Despatches; Bt. Lt.-Col. Commandant, Singapore Volunteer Corps.

SCHUSTER, L. R. (D.S.O. L.G. 1.1.18); b. 20.10.79; s. of late Louis Schuster, of Fulwood Park, Cheshire; m. Audrey Bruce, d. of A. C. Bruce-Pryce; one s.; one d.; educ. Malvern College; Sandhurst; Staff College; 2nd Lt., L'pool R., 1.2.99; Lt. 21.3.00; Adjt. 20.7.05 to 19.7.08; Capt. 14.8.09; Major 1.9.15; served S. African War, 1899–1902; Queen's Medal, 4 clasps; King's Medal, 2 clasps; Europ. War, 1915–18; served on G.S. in France, Salonika, Egypt, Palestine; Despatches four times.

SCLATER, J. (D.S.O. L.G. 1.1.18), Lt.-Col., Can. Inf.

SCOBELL, S. J. P. (D.S.O. L.G. 14.1.16); b. 26.9.79; s. of late S. G. T. Scobell and Edith Scobell (*née* Palairet); m. Cecily Maude Hopkinson; one s.; one d.; educ. Winchester; Sandhurst; joined 1st Batt. Norfolk Rgt., in India, 12.8.99; Lt. 29.8.00; Capt. 24.1.06; Adjt., Norf. R., 28.11.07 to 27.11.10; Major 1.9.15; Lt.-Colonel; went to Somaliland with a British M.I. Company, 1903–4 (Medal with clasp); served Europ. War; Despatches seven times; Bt. Lt.-Col. 1.1.18; C.M.G.

SCOONES, G. A. P. (D.S.O. L.G. 4.6.17); b. 25.1.93; s. of Major Fitzmaurice Scoones, late R.F.; m. Angela Maud, d. of Rev. S. R. A. Buller, R.D.; one d.; educ. Wellington College; R.M.C., Sandhurst; 2nd Lt., Unatt., 20.1.12; Ind. Army 8.3.13; Lt. 20.4.14; Capt. 20.1.16; M.C.

SCOTHERN, A. E., M.A. (D.S.O. L.G. 1.1.18); b. 12.9.82; m. Joyce E. F. Pilling; educ. St. John's College, Oxford; played Association Football for Oxford and England; Headmaster, Redditch Secondary School, Worcestershire; T/Major (A/Lt.-Col.), Notts. and Derby. R.; served Gallipoli, Egypt, France and Belgium; Despatches six times; C.M.G.

SCOTT, A. (D.S.O. L.G. 1.1.19), Capt., 1/7th Batt. Arg. and Suth. Highrs.; M.C.

SCOTT, A. A. (D.S.O. L.G. 3.6.18), Lt.-Cdr., R.N.

SCOTT, A. F. S. (D.S.O. L.G. 14.1.16); b. 14.4.68; ent. R.A. 17.2.88; Lt. 17.2.91; Capt. 18.5.98; Major 9.8.07; Lt.-Col. 18.8.15; T/Brig.-Gen. 19.2.17 to 7.6.17; Brig.-Gen., R.A. Heavy Artillery, 13th A.C., Br. Armies in France, 19.2.17 to 7.6.17.

SCOTT, C. A. (D.S.O. L.G. 22.12.16); b. Sambalpur, C.P., India, 22.9.79; s. of Col. T. A. Scott, I.A.; m. Violet Eveline Walker; one s.; one d.; educ. Victoria College, Jersey; H.M.S. Conway; served five years in Merchant Service; joined the R. Indian Marine as Sub-Lt., 1901; Lt.-Cdr.; was commanding R.I.M.S. Comet on the outbreak of war, Aug. 1914; Asst. Marine Transport Officer, Mesopotamia, Jan. 1915–Sept. 1916; Acting Port Officer at Aden.

SCOTT, C. A. R. (D.S.O. L.G. 1.1.17); b. 17.7.63; 2nd Lt. 23.2.85; Major 29.11.03; h.p., late S. Wales Bord., 26.9.09; A/Lt.-Col., R.A.; served S. African War; Queen's Medal, 2 clasps; Europ. War; Despatches.

SCOTT, C. W. (D.S.O. L.G. 14.1.16); b. 1.4.75; s. of late W. H. Scott, J.P.; educ. Charterhouse; R.M.A., Woolwich; 2nd Lt., R.A., 17.11.94; Lt. 17.11.97; Capt. 28.1.01; Major 21.7.11; Lt.-Col. 24.4.16; served S. African War. 1899–1902; Queen's Medal with 5 clasps; King's Medal with 2 clasps; Europ. War, in command of 71st Battery, 2nd Division; was A.D. of Artillery, G.H.Q., Br. Armies in France, 1916–18; T/Brig.-Gen., Staff, 1918; Bt. Col. 1.1.18; C.M.G.

SCOTT, E., M.B. (D.S.O. L.G. 1.1.17), T/Capt., R.A.M.C.

SCOTT, EDWARD IRWIN CHARLES (D.S.O. L.G. 1.1.18) (gazetted as Scott, E. Irvine C.), Major, Aust. Pioneer Batt.

SCOTT, REV. CANON F. G., M.A., D.C.L., F.R.S.C. (D.S.O. L.G. 7.11.18); b. Montreal 7.4.61; s. of late W. E. Scott, M.D., Professor of Anatomy, McGill University, for nearly 40 years, and Elizabeth Scott, *née* Sproston; m. Amy, d. of late G. Brooks; six s.; one d.; educ. Montreal High School; Proprietary School; McGill; Bishop's College, Lennoxville; King's College, London; Deacon, 1884; Priest, 1886; Rector of St. Matthew's, Quebec, from 1899; Canon of Quebec Cathedral from 1906; late Senior Chaplain, 1st Can. Div., B.E.F.; wounded; Despatches four times; C.M.G.; Sandford Gold Medal, R. Canadian Humane Society.

SCOTT, F. W. A. (D.S.O. L.G. 11.4.18), Lt.-Col., Dorsetshire Regt.

SCOTT, G. (D.S.O. L.G. 3.6.19), Major (T/Lt.-Col.), 6th Batt. Lancs. Fus., T.F., commanding 75th Batt. M.G.C.

SCOTT, G. B. (D.S.O. L.G. 11.8.17); b. 27.10.75; s. of Lt.-Col. Hopton Bassett Scott; m. Amy Blanche, d. of G. F. de Caen, J.P.; educ. United Service College, Westward Ho! 2nd Lt., Unatt., 22.1.96; Ind. S.C. 1.4.97; Lt., Ind. Army, 22.4.98; Capt. 22.1.05; Major 22.1.14; served N.W. Frontier of India, Waziristan, 1901–2; Medal with clasp; E. Africa, Somaliland, 1903–4; Medal, 2 clasps; Commandant of N. Waziristan Militia, 1914–18; in command when an attack on Miranshah by the Afghan tribe of Zadrans was driven off on 29–30.11.14; commanded columns of Militia which, working in conjunction with the Bannu Brigade, drove off further Zadran attacks on 10 Jan. and 26.3.15; served Waziristan, 1917; Despatches.

SCOTT, H. L. (D.S.O. L.G. 25.8.17) (Bar, L.G. 10.8.21); b. 6.4.82; 2nd Lt., Dorset R., 18.1.02; Ind. Army 8.7.03; Lt. 18.4.04; Capt. 18.1.11; Major 18.1.17; Bt. Lt.-Col. 3.6.19; M.C.

SCOTT, H. ST. G. S. (D.S.O. L.G. 29.10.15) (Bar, L.G. 17.3.17) (Details, L.G. 26.5.17), Capt. (T/Major), Gurkha Rifles, I.A. (see "The Distinguished Service Order," from its institution to 31.12.15, by same publishers).

SCOTT, JOHN, M.B. (D.S.O. L.G. 26.3.18); b. 28.6.86; Lt., Ind. Med. Serv., 28.1.11; Capt. 28.1.14; Bt. Lt.-Col. 1.1.19.

SCOTT, JOHN (D.S.O. L.G. 3.6.19); b. 1887; m. Sybil Hewitt; Major; Adjt., 2nd Highland Brig., R.F.A., T.F.; served Europ. War from 1914.

SCOTT, J. C. (D.S.O. L.G. 3.6.16); b. 18.1.79; s. of late Capt. J. Creagh Scott, R.M.L.I., of Crevagh, Co. Clare, and Mary Scott (*née* Fergusson); m. Sybil, d. of Col. Sir H. Oldham, K.C.V.O.; one d.; educ. Radley College; joined 1st A. and S. Highrs., 1899; 2nd Lt., Arg. and Suth'd Highrs., 18.10.99; Lt. 28.5.01; Capt. 20.5.09; Adjt. 1.4.11 to 31.3.14; Major 1.9.15; served S. African War; 2 Medals, with five clasps; seriously wounded; served Europ. War; twice wounded; Croix de Guerre (French) avec Etoile d'Or; Despatches six times; temporarily commanded 2nd A. and S. Highrs., May–Aug., 1916, in the Battle of the Somme, and again Jan.–April, 1917; temp. commanded 5/6th R. Scots Fus., April–May, 1916; G.H.Q. Staff, France, and Corps Staff, France; O.B.E.

SCOTT, J. D. (D.S.O. L.G. 1.1.18), Capt. (A/Lt.-Col.), R. Irish Rgt. (att. 2nd Batt.). He was killed in action on 21.3.18.

SCOTT, JOHN WILFRED (D.S.O. L.G. 22.4.19), Cdr., R.N., 31.12.15.

SCOTT, JOHN WILLOUGHBY (D.S.O. L.G. 1.1.17); b. at Ramleh, in Egypt, 25.1.79; s. of late Sir John Scott, formerly Judicial Adviser to the Khedive of Egypt; m. 1916, Madelaine E., e. d. of Canon Worsley, Vicar of Evenley, Northamptonshire; educ. Rugby; R.M.A., Woolwich; 2nd Lt., R.G.A., 1897; Capt., 1905; retired 1908, and read for the Bar; joined the Oxfordshire Hussars, 1908; Major, 1914; Lt.-Col., 1916; served S. African War; twice mentioned in Despatches; Queen's Medal, 3 clasps; King's Medal, 2 clasps; Europ. War, in France; Despatches; wounded, 1916; returned to France, and was killed in action 23.4.17. At the time of his death Lt.-Col. Davies-Evans wrote to Lady Scott: "It is with the deepest grief I write to tell you of Col. Scott's death. He died bravely leading the attack on April 23, shot dead instantaneously through the head."

John Willoughby Scott.

SCOTT, J. W. L. (D.S.O. L.G. 1.1.18); b. 30.1.83; Lt., R.A.M.C., 30.1.06; Capt. 30.7.09; Major, R.A.M.C., 30.1.18; served Europ. War, 1914–18; Despatches.

SCOTT, M. A. (D.S.O. L.G. 1.1.18), Capt. (T/Major), Can. M.G.C.

SCOTT, M. R. J. MAXWELL- (see Maxwell-Scott, M. R. J.).

SCOTT, O. A. (D.S.O. L.G. 3.6.18); b. 1893; m. Hermione Monica, d. of W. Ferrand; H.M. Diplomatic Service; T/Major; served with Hants R.; Europ. War, 1914–18; Despatches.

SCOTT, R. A. (D.S.O. L.G. 5.10.18), Eng. Lt.-Cdr. (A/Eng.-Cdr.), R.N.R., R.D.

SCOTT, R. C. S. MORRISON- (see Morrison-Scott, R. C. S.).

SCOTT, R. H. (D.S.O. L.G. 1.1.17), T/Major, R. Innis Fus.

SCOTT, T. H., M.B. (D.S.O. L.G. 11.1.19); b. 5.9.83; Lt., R.A.M.C., 28.1.07; Capt. 28.7.10; Major 28.1.19; A/Lt.-Col. 28.1.17; M.C.

SCOTT, W. (D.S.O. L.G. 8.2.18) (Details, L.G. 18.7.18), R. Irish Fus., S.R.; M.C.

SCOTT, W. D. (D.S.O. L.G. 17.9.17), T/Major, H.L.I.; M.C. His D.S.O. was awarded for gallantry on 10–11.7.17, at Nieuport.

SCOTT, W. H. (D.S.O. L.G. 16.5.16) (Bar, L.G. 8.3.19) (Details, L.G. 4.10.19); b. 1881; m. Rosamund, d. of late W. J. Carter; Lt.-Col., late 9th L.H. Rgt. Aust. Imp. Force; served Europ. War, 1914–18; C.M.G. His D.S.O. was awarded for gallantry at Sinai Peninsula 11–13.4.16.

SCOTT, W. J. R. (D.S.O. L.G. 10.1.17); b. Bingara, N.S. Wales, 21.6.88; s. of D. H. Scott; m. Jean Marguerite, d. of H. Mitchell; educ. Sydney Grammar School; joined A.I.F. 31.12.14; 1st appointment 5.5.15; Major, 19th Aust. Inf. Batt.; went to Gallipoli 20.8.15; to Sinai Peninsula, Jan. 1916; to France, April, 1916. His D.S.O. was awarded for gallantry during the attack on Flers 14.11.16.

SCOTT-ELLIOT, W. (D.S.O. L.G. 1.1.18); b. 13.3.73; 2nd Lt., 11th Hrs., 12.12.94; Lt. 26.1.98; Capt., A.S.C., 1.2.02; Major, R.A.S.C., 22.7.14; served N.W. Frontier of India, 1897–98; Medal with clasp; Europ. War; Despatches.

SCOTT-HOPKINS, R. (see Hopkins, R. Scott-).

SCRIMGEOUR, G. C. (D.S.O. L.G. 16.9.18), Lt. (A/Capt.), R.F.A.; M.C.

SCROGGIE, J. A. (D.S.O. L.G. 3.6.19); b. 4.8.90; s. of William Thomson Scroggie; m. 1915, Catherine Bewick; educ. Dundee, Scotland; joined the Canadian Inf. as a Private 9.11.14; Lt. 14.5.16; Capt. 5.11.16; Major 15.6.18; Lt.-Col. 6.1.19; served Europ. War, in France; Despatches; wounded twice; M.C.; 2 bars; Médaille Militaire (France).

SCULLY, THE REV. V. J. (D.S.O. L.G. 8.3.18); b. April, 1876; educ. College of Canons Regular of the Laseran; Priest, 1899; temp. commission as C.F., June, 1915; 3rd Class, Dec. 1916; Despatches twice; wounded, Nov. 1917; relinquished commission March, 1919; Médaille du Roi Albert, 1920.

SCULLY, V. M. B. (D.S.O. L.G. 8.3.19) (Details, L.G. 4.10.19); b. 2.7.81; Capt. (from Spec. Res.), Bord. R., 29.3.15; Temp. Lt.-Col., 5th Bn. Conn. Rang. 9.2.16; h.p. 25.5.20; O.B.E.

SEAGRAM, T. O. (D.S.O. L.G. 1.1.17); b. 27.8.72; s. of late Lt.-Col. J. H. Seagram; educ. Bath College; R.M.A., Woolwich; 2nd Lt., R.A., 11.8.93; Lt. 11.8.96; Capt. 29.6.00; Major 2.7.10; Lt.-Col. 17.1.16; T/Brig.-Gen. 13.9.18; served Europ. War (France), 1914–18; once wounded; C.M.G.; late commanding 10th Brig., R.F.A., Colchester.

SEAGRIM, A. H. (D.S.O. L.G. 1.1.19); b. 14.2.83; 2nd Lt., Sco. Rif., 5.1.01; 2nd Lt., Ind. Army, 4.11.02; Lt. 5.4.03; Capt. 20.2.09; Leins. Regt. 27.10.11; Major 8.5.16.

SEARIGHT, H. ff., F.R.G.S. (D.S.O. L.G. 1.1.18); b. 9.6.75; m. Lilian Martinho; one s.; educ. Charterhouse; R.M.C., Sandhurst; joined 1st (King's) Dragoon Guards, 1895; Major, R. of O; served S. African War, 1901–2; Queen's Medal with 5 clasps; N. Nigeria, 1905–6; commanded M.I., N. Nigeria, 1906–9; Despatches; Medal and clasp; Reserve of Officers, 1910–14; served Europ. War, France; Despatches.

SEARLE, F. (D.S.O. L.G. 1.1.18), Colonel, late Tank Corps; served Europ. War, 1914–18; Despatches; C.B.E.

SEARS, H. B. (D.S.O. L.G. 11.12.18); b. 15.9.80; s. of R. H. Sears; m. May, d. of late Dr. C. C. Skardon; educ. Oundle, and R.N.E. Coll., Keyham; Eng. Lt.-Cdr., R.N., 1.7.19; served in Grand Fleet Flotilla, H.M.S. Defender, 1st Flotilla, to Feb. 1915; H.M.S. Raider, 15th Flotilla, to Aug. 1918; Despatches.

SEATH, G. H. (D.S.O. L.G. 14.3.16); s. of late Capt. Seath; m. Eleanor, d. of late Capt. E. M. Dayrell, R.N.; educ. Victoria College, Jersey; R.N. College, Greenwich; 2nd Lt., R.M.L.I., 1.9.05; Lt. 1.7.06; Capt. 1.9.15; Major 1.1.18; posted to Chatham Division, 1907; served H.M.S. Africa, 1908–11; H.M.S. St. George, 1911; H.M.S. Implacable, 1912–14, and was in Implacable at X Beach landing 25.4.15 to 1.5.15; landed as left flank Observation Officer at Helles, 1 May, and left Peninsula on night of 8.1.16; Despatches; served with Salonika Army, March, 1916, to Oct. 1918; Brevet Majority; Despatches; appointed R.N. College, Greenwich, 13.1.19; commanded Naval Battery, Stavros.

SEBAG-MONTEFIORE, T. H. (D.S.O. L.G. 3.6.18); b. 8.11.87; 4th s. of late Arthur Sebag-Montefiore, of East Cliff Lodge, Ramsgate, Kent; m. Irene Catherine, d. of Leonard Cohen; 2nd Lt., R.A., 25.7.06; Lt. 25.7.09; Capt. 30.10.14; Major, R.H.A., 2.2.17; served Europ. War; Despatches; M.C.

SEBASTIAN, E. G. (D.S.O. L.G. 3.3.17); b. 2.8.92; s. of Lewis Boyd Sebastian, of Lincoln's Inn, Barrister-at-Law, and Harriet Maria, his wife; educ. Rottingdean; Winchester; University College, Oxford; Student of Lincoln's Inn; Liveryman of the Skinners' Co., London; 2nd Lt., E. Kent Regt., Oct. 1914; Lieut., Oct. 1915; served Europ. War, in France and Salonika. Lieutenant Sebastian had two brothers serving in the Army, one of whom was awarded the M.C., also another brother serving in the R.N.

SECKHAM, D. T. (D.S.O. L.G. 1.1.17); b. 1.5.73; 1st commission 29.5.95; Capt. 20.6.00; retired Lan. Fus. 2.7.10; Major (T/Lt.-Col.), S. Staffs. Regt., Spec. Res.; served S. African War, 1899–1900; Queen's Medal, 3 clasps; Europ. War; Despatches.

SEDDON, E. MC M. (D.S.O. L.G. 4.6.17); b. 24.12.67; 2nd Lt., R.A., 17.2.88; Lt. 17.2.91; Capt. 18.4.98; Major 10.2.07; Lt.-Col., 129th H.B., R.G.A. He was killed in action 24.6.17.

SEDGWICK, F. R. (D.S.O. L.G. 14.1.16); b. Bombay, 5.7.76; s. of late R. B. Sedgwick; m. Madeline Louise, d. of late W. L. Jennings, M.P., of Stockport; one s.; one d.; educ. Uppingham School; R.M.A., Woolwich; ent. R.A. 26.3.96; Lt. 21.3.99; Capt. 15.1.02; retired in 1913; became Major; Lt.-Col. 4.8.17; Lt.-Col., R.F.A., half-pay, 1921; served S. African War; Medal and 4 clasps; W. African Frontier Force, 1901–5; was called up on mobilization; served Europ. War; wounded; Despatches four times; Bt. Lt.-Col. 1.1.18; C.M.G.

SEGRAVE, W. H. E. (D.S.O. L.G. 7.3.99) (Bar, L.G. 4.3.18) (Details, L.G. 16.8.18) (2nd Bar, L.G. 26.7.18), Major (A/Lt.-Col.), H.L.I. (see "The Distinguished Service Order," from its institution to 31.12.15, by same publishers).

SELBY, C. W. (D.S.O. L.G. 4.6.17); b. 22.8.83; s. of C. E. M. Selby; educ. R.M.A., Woolwich; ent. R.F.A. 24.12.02; Lt. 24.12.05; Capt. 30.10.14; Major 22.5.16; appointed R.H.A., 1909; Lt.-Col., R.H. and R.F.A.; Gold Staff Officer at the Coronation of King George V., 1911 (Coronation Medal); served Europ. War, 1914–18; Despatches four times; Bt. Lt.-Col. 3.6.19; M.C.; French Croix de Guerre; Belgian Croix de Guerre; appointed Inter-Allied Military Commission of Control for Austria, 1920.

SELBY, E. R. (D.S.O. L.G. 3.6.19), Major (A/Lt.-Col.), 8th Field Ambulance, Can. A.M.C.

SELIGMAN, H. S. (D.S.O. L.G. 1.1.17); b. 14.7.72; 2nd Lt., R.A., 17.10.92; Lt., R.A., 17.10.95; Capt. 18.4.00; Major 17.12.09; Bt. Lt.-Col. 18.2.15; Lt.-Col. 24.9.15; Bt. Col. 1.1.18; served S. African War, 1900; Queen's Medal, 3 clasps; Europ. War, 1914–18; Despatches.

SELLAR, T. B. (D.S.O. L.G. 1.1.18); b. 2.3.65; s. of late T. Sellar; m. Evelyn, d. of late L. P. Pugh, J.P., D.L.; educ. Fettes; 1st commission 29.12.88; Major 15.1.08; retired K.O. Sco. Bord. 3.5.13; T/Lt.-Col. in command 8th Bn. K.O. Sco. Bord.; served Chitral, 1895; Medal with clasp; N.W. Frontier of India, 1897–98; clasp; Tirah, 1897–98 (clasp); S. Africa, 1899–1900; Queen's Medal, 4 clasps; Europ. War, 1914–17; Despatches; C.M.G.; Order of St. Michael and St. Lazarus (Chevalier).

SELMES, J. C. (D.S.O. L.G. 18.1.18) (Details, L.G. 25.4.18.); Major, Aust. F.A.

SELOUS, F. C. (D.S.O. L.G. 26.9.16); m. Marie Catherine Gladys, d. of Rev. Canon Maddy, of Down Hatherley; educ. Rugby and abroad; was in the Rugby School Volunteers in 1868, and was present at a Review by Queen Victoria in Windsor Great Park. Before he was 20 he went to S. Africa, and in Matabeleland obtained from Lobengula the right to shoot elephants. His career as a Big Game Hunter is, of course, well known, and altogether he killed nearly 1,000 head of big game, 33 specimens of which are in the Natural History Museum at S. Kensington. His biggest lion stood 4 ft. 6 in. in height, but, owing to the difficulties of transport, he never succeeded in bringing a whole elephant to England. He spent several years in Mashonaland, helping to map the country, and in 1890 acted as Guide to the British South Africa Company's Expedition. In 1892 he returned to England and wrote "A Hunter's Wanderings in Africa." In 1893 he took part in the first Matabele War—he was a Guide in the expedition organized by Mr. Cecil Rhodes—and during the years that followed was chiefly occupied in shooting and hunting, extending his wanderings even to Asia. When nearly 60 years of age he joined Mr. Roosevelt in a big game hunting expedition, and later had a visit from Mr. Roosevelt at Worplesdon. He wrote also "Travel and Adventure in South-East Africa," "Sunshine and Storm in Rhodesia," and "Sport and Travel East and West," and among his other works are "Recent Hunting Trips in British North America," 1907; "African Nature Notes and Reminiscences," 1908. In 1914 Mr. Selous joined a service battalion of the R. Fusiliers; became Lieut., Feb. 1915; Capt. Aug. 1915. With a draft of his regiment he joined the forces of General Smuts for the campaign in German E. Africa, quickly came under the observation of his Commanding Officer, was mentioned in Despatches, and awarded the D.S.O. He fell on 4.1.17, while leading the attack on Bhobeho. Though wounded he continued to encourage his men in the advance till he fell, shot dead. His elder son, Capt. F. H. B. Selous, M.C., R.W. Surrey Rgt., att. R.F.C., was reported missing on 4.1.18, and was later on reported killed in action on that date, aged 19.

SEMMENS, J. N. (D.S.O. L.G. 3.6.18), Major, Can. Inf.

SENIOR, E. (D.S.O. L.G. 1.2.19), Major, 5th Batt. W. Riding R., T.F.

SENIOR, H. W. R. (D.S.O. L.G. 26.8.18); b. 13.9.66; Lt., Leins. R., 25.8.86; Ind. Army 5.7.88; Capt. 25.8.97; Major 25.8.04; Lt.-Col. 25.8.12; Colonel 1.12.17; T/Brig.-Gen. 5.2.20 to 19.5.20; C.B.; C.I.E.

SETH-SMITH, H. G. (D.S.O. L.G. 1.1.18); b. 13.6.85; 2nd Lt., A.S.C., 16.8.05; Lt. 18.8.07; Capt., R.A.S.C., 5.8.14; Adjt. 27.5.16 to 30.10.16.

SETTLE, R. H. N. (D.S.O. L.G. 1.1.18); b. Cairo, Egypt, 19.5.92; s. of Lt.-Gen. Sir Henry H. Settle, K.C.B., D.S.O., and Lady Settle; educ. Wivenford; Eton; Sandhurst; 2nd Lt., 19th Hussars, 3.9.10; Lt. 27.1.13; Capt. 5.5.15; Bt. Major 16.3.19; he went with his regiment to France in Aug. 1914; was severely wounded at Mons, and during convalescence studied machine-guns; on his return to France he was appointed to command a Machine-Gun Squadron, later a Machine-Gun Battalion; was reported missing 24.3.18, and later said to have been killed in action on that date at Cléry-sur-Somme. He was wounded four times; mentioned three times in Despatches; M.C.; 1914 Star.

R. H. N. Settle.

SEWELL, E. P., M.R.C.S., L.R.C.P., M.B., B.C., D.P.H. (D.S.O. L.G. 3.6.16); b. 23.2.74; s. of Rev. H. D. Sewell, of Headcorn, Kent; m. Zébée Maud, d. of late Lt.-Col. A. Crombie, C.B., I.M.S.; two d.; one s.; educ. Monkton Combe School; Pembroke College, Cambridge; St. Bartholomew's Hospital; commissioned R.A.M.C., 25.4.00; Capt. 25.4.03; Major 27.4.11; D.D.M.S., 21st Army Corps, Feb. 1918; Lt.-Colonel 1.3.15 Europ. War, 1914–18, in Egypt; C.M.G., 1919; Despatches twice.

SEWELL, H. S. (D.S.O. L.G. 23.6.15) (Bar, L.G. 18.1.18) (Details, L.G. 25.4.18), Major (A/Lt.-Col.), Dragoon Guards (see "The Distinguished Service Order," from its institution to 31.12.15, by same publishers).

SEYMOUR, A. G. (D.S.O. L.G. 1.1.17); b. 21.9.75; s. of late G. E. Seymour; m. 1907, Ellen Mary, d. of R. C. Bucknall; two s.; educ. Eton; Sandhurst; joined R. Scots Greys, 1896; 2nd Lt., 2nd Dns., 25.3.96; Lt. 23.3.98; Capt. 22.5.01; Major 19.8.11; Lt.-Col. 6.7.19; served S. African War, 1899–1901; Despatches; Medal, 4 clasps; Europ. War, in France, 1914–18; Despatches; wounded; Bt. Lt.-Col., 1918.

SEYMOUR, C. (D.S.O. L.G. 14.3.16); b. 17.3.76; s. of late Alfred Seymour and Jessie Madeleine, d. of Hon. W. Macdougall, C.B., of Toronto; m. Auriel Dorothy, d. of R. Quin; educ. Temple Grove, East Sheen; Eastman's, Stubbington; in H.M.S. Britannia; entered R.N., 1889; Capt. 31.12.15; served Europ. War, 1914–17, in Gallipoli; Despatches twice; afterwards serving on the Admiralty Naval Staff till June, 1918, when he was given command of the Southern Patrol Force.

SEYMOUR, C. H. N. (D.S.O. L.G. 14.1.16); b. 11.11.74; e. s. of late Lord Albert Seymour, 2nd s. of the 5th Marquess of Hertford, and late Sarah, d. of Capt. J. M. Napier, 62nd Regt.; m. 1905, Mary Adelaide, e. d. of William Morton Philips; one s.; educ. Charterhouse; 2nd Lt., K.R.R.C., 15.9.97; Lt. 30.8.99; Capt. 7.1.02; Major 1.9.15; served S. African War, 1899–1902; Queen's Medal, 4 clasps; King's Medal, 2 clasps; Durbar Medal; Europ. War, as Coy. Com. with 8th K.R.R.C. until Dec. 1915, then commanded various service battalions of K.R.R.C. and Rifle Brig.; severely wounded, Feb. 1916; returned to France Jan. 1917; Despatches twice; 1914–15 Star.

C. H. N. Seymour.

SEYMOUR, E. (D.S.O. L.G. 1.1.17); b. 10.2.77; m. Lady Blanche Frances Conyngham, d. of 4th Marquess Conyngham; one s.; one d.; educ. Eton; ent. Army, 1897; Capt., 1904; Grenadier Guards (retired 1908); Major; served Nile Exp., 1898; S. African War, 1900–2; Europ. War, 1914–18; Despatches; O.B.E., 1919; M.V.O., 1901; was Comptroller of the Household to H.R.H. the late Duchess of Albany.

SEYMOUR, E. F. E. (D.S.O. L.G. 1.1.18); b. 7.5.82; 2nd Lt., Unatt., 8.1.01; 2nd Lt., R. Dublin Fus., 9.3.01; Lt. 7.6.06; Capt. 1.3.12; Major 8.1.16; Despatches; O.B.E.; served S. African War, 1901–2; Queen's Medal with 5 clasps; Aden, 1903; operations in the interior.

SEYMOUR, H. (D.S.O. L.G. 1.1.17), (Bar, L.G. 11.12.18), Cdr., R.N., 30.6.15.

SEYMOUR, LORD H. C. (D.S.O. L.G. 3.6.16) (Bar, L.G. 2.12.18); b. 18.5.78; brother of 7th Marquess of Hertford; m. Lady Helen Frances Grosvenor, d. of 1st Duke of Westminster; one d.; 2nd Lt., G. Gds., 20.5.99; Lt. 3.2.00; Capt. 27.4.07; Major 11.9.14; Bt. Lt.-Col. 1.1.17; Lt.-Col., Grenadier Guards, 1.9.19; served S. African War, 1900–2; Queen's Medal, 3 clasps; King's Medal, 2 clasps; Cameroons, 1914; severely wounded; Bt. Lt.-Col.; Europ. War, in France, 1915; Lt.-Col. Commanding 4th Batt. G. Gds., 1916; Brig.-Genl. Commanding 3rd Guards Brigade, 1917; severely wounded; Despatches four times; Croix d'Officier, Légion d'Honneur.

SEYMOUR, R. F. (D.S.O. L.G. 15.9.16); b. 6.1.86; s. of late Sir Horace Seymour, K.C.B., and Elizabeth Mary, d. of Col. Frederick Romilly; entered Britannia, Sept. 1900; Midshipman 15.1.02; Sub-Lieut. 15.3.05; Lt. 15.12.06; Flag-Lt. to Rear-Admiral David Beatty, Flag in H.M.S. Lion, 1.3.13; Commander, R.N., June, 1912; served Europ. War, 1914–19, on personal staff of Admiral Sir David Beatty, including battles of Heligoland, Dogger Bank and Jutland Bank; promoted to Commander, 1917; C.M.G.

SEYS, R. C. (D.S.O. L.G. 1.1.18); b. 30.10.83; 2nd Lt., R.A., 24.12.02; L. 24.12.05; Capt. 30.10.14; Major 14.6.17. He died 10.4.21.

SHAHIM, EL BIMBASHI MOHAMMED EFFENDI (see Mohammed, S. E. El Bimbashi).

SHAKESPEAR, A. T. (D.S.O. L.G. 1.1.18); b. 15.9.84; 2nd Lt., R.E., 23.10.03; Lieut. 31.8.06; Capt. 30.10.14; M.C.

SHAKESPEAR, G. F. C. (D.S.O. L.G. 1.1.18); b. 31.10.89; 2nd Lt., Unatt., 8.9.09; Ind. Army, 31.10.10; Lt. 8.12.11; Capt. and Bt. Major, I.A. He died 24.2.19; M.C.

SHANAHAN, D. D. (D.S.O. L.G. 1.1.17); b. 11.4.63; s. of J. Shanahan and Joan Shanahan (*née* Davis); m. Henrietta (who died in 1919), d. of late J. Young; educ. Blackrock College, Dublin; R. College of Surgeons, Ireland, and Trinity College, Dublin; Capt., R.A.M.C., 31.1.91; Bt. Major 22.8.02; Major 31.1.03; Lt.-Col. 5.2.13; Col. 26.12.17; Colonel, late R.A.M.C.; served N.W. Frontier of India, 1897; S. African War, 1899–1902; severely wounded; Despatches; Bt. Major; went with Exp. Force to France, Aug. 1914 (Despatches); proceeded to Gallipoli; in July, 1915, took part in landing at Suvla (Despatches); after the evacuation of Gallipoli returned to France; took part in the Battle of the Somme (Despatches; D.S.O.); in the taking of Messines Ridge; the operations in Belgium, ending with the taking of Paschendaele; Despatches; C.M.G.; A.D.M.S., A. Div., in France.

SHANAHAN, M. (D.S.O. L.G. 25.11.16), Major, Aust. Light Horse Regt.

SHANLY, C. N. (D.S.O. L.G. 3.6.16); Lt.-Col., Can. Army Pay Corps. He died Oct. 1916.

SHANNON, H. J. (D.S.O. L.G. 1.1.18), Major, Aust. Light Horse Regt.

SHANNON, W. BOYD- (D.S.O. L.G. 2.5.16); b. 1.9.74; s. of Edmund John Shannon; m. Flora Gertrude, d. of Lt.-Col. Stratton-Thompson, Deputy Lieutenant of the City of London; gazetted to Yorks. Regt., 1895; retired 1902; Capt., R. of O.; rejoined 1914; Major, Dec. 1914; second-in-command of a battalion; served S. African War, 1902; Queen's Medal, 2 clasps; Europ. War; Despatches; wounded.

SHANNON, W. J. (D.S.O. L.G. 3.6.16) (Bar, L.G. 18.7.17); b. 27.4.76; 2nd Lt., 16th Lrs., 7.3.00; Lieut. 3.10.00; Capt. 11.5.14; Adjt. 11.5.14 to 31.8.14; Major 22.2.15; served S. African War, 1900–2; Queen's Medal, 2 clasps; King's Medal, 2 clasps; Europ. War; C.M.G.

SHARLAND, A. A. (D.S.O. L.G. 26.9.17) (Details, L.G. 9.1.18); b. 27.11.83; 2nd Lt., Manch. Regt., 22.4.03; Lt., E. Lanc. Regt., 4.5.07; Capt., E. Lanc. R., 14.5.13; Major 22.4.18, E. Lancs R. His D.S.O. was awarded for gallantry on 31.7.17, east of Ypres.

SHARP, M. J. R. (D.S.O. L.G. 14.9.17), Engineer Lt.-Comdr., R.N.

SHARP, R. R. (D.S.O. L.G. 16.9.18), 2nd Lt. (A/Capt.), R.F.A. (Spec. Res.); M.C.

SHARPE, A. G. M. (D.S.O. L.G. 16.9.18); b. 16.8.84; 2nd Lt., R. Berks. R., 18.11.03; Lt. 20.5.06; Capt. 10.4.12; Bt. Major 1.1.18; O.B.E.

SHARPE, C. S. (D.S.O. L.G. 1.1.18); b. 28.8.83; 2nd Lt., York and Lanc. R., 23.4.02; Lt. 10.4.04; Capt. 6.4.12; Major 23.4.17.

SHARPE, G. L. (D.S.O. L.G. 3.6.19), Capt. (A/Major), 5th Batt. W. Riding Rgt., T.F., att. Army Cyclists' Corps.

SHARPE, S. S. (D.S.O. L.G. 1.1.18), Lt.-Col., Can. Inf.

SHARPE, W. J. (D.S.O. L.G. 3.6.18), Major, Can. Cav.

SHARPE, W. MC C. (D.S.O. L.G. 1.1.19), T/Major, 317th Siege By., R.G.A.

SHAW, A. D. MC I. (D.S.O. L.G. 2.12.18), T/Capt., 1st Batt. R. Sc. Fus.

SHAW, A. L. B. (D.S.O. L.G. 3.6.19), Major, 1/8th Batt. Lancs. Fus., T.F.

SHAW, C. G. (D.S.O. L.G. 1.1.17), Lt.-Col., Aust. A.M.C.

SHAW, D. P. (D.S.O. L.G. 2.12.18), T/Major, 6th Batt. Dorsets. R.

SHAW, F. V. (D.S.O. L.G. 3.6.19), T/Major, R.F.A.; M.C.

SHAW, G. D. A. (D.S.O. L.G. 1.1.17); b. Motihari, India, 1.9.82; s. of late F. A. Shaw; m. Philippa, d. of H. H. Arnold; one d.; educ. Charterhouse; Woolwich; ent. R.A., 31.7.02; Lt. 31.7.05; Capt. 3.10.14; Major, R.F.A., 13.4.16; served France with Exp. Force, Aug. 1914; wounded at Ypres; returned to France, July, 1915; Salonika, Nov. 1915; France, 1918; wounded; Despatches; was Army and Navy Featherweight and Lightweight Champion for 1904, 1905 and 1907.

SHAW, H. M. D. (D.S.O. L.G. 1.1.19); b. 5.6.78; 2nd Lt., Unatt., 27.7.98; Ind. S.C. 19.10.99; Lt., Ind. Army, 20.10.00; Major 20.7.07; Major 1.9.15; Lt.-Col. 1.11.21.

SHAW, J. A. (D.S.O. L.G. 1.1.17); educ. Bowmanville, Ontario; 2nd Q.O. Rifles of Canada, 1891; commissioned Can. A.S.C., 1902; enlisted O.S. Service, Nov. 1914; reached England 10.4.15; France, as Senior Supply Officer, 2nd Canadians, 10.9.15; transferred to Imp. Cavalry, 2nd Indian Division, as O.C., A.S.C., Nov. 1916; transferred as O.C., 5th Can. Divl. Train, March, 1917.

SHAW, J. T. (D.S.O. L.G. 2.4.19) (Details, L.G. 10.12.19), T/Lt. (A/Capt.), Yorks. R., att. 8th Batt.

SHAW, L. D., M.B. (D.S.O. L.G. 4.6.17) (Bar, L.G. 26.7.18), T/Capt. (A/Lt.-Col.), R.A.M.C. He died 21.3.21.

SHAW, R. (D.S.O. L.G. 18.7.17), Lt. R. War. R. (Spec. Res.). He was killed in action 24.8.17.

SHAW, R. M. (D.S.O. L.G. 1.1.19), Major, R.F.A. (T.F.), A/24th (West Riding) Bgde.; M.C.

SHAW, W. (D.S.O. L.G. 1.1.18), T/Major, A.S.C.

SHAW, W. M. (D.S.O. L.G. 14.1.16); b. 19.4.82; y. s. of late James J. Shaw, K.C.; educ. St. Columba's College, Rathfarnham; 2nd Lt., R.A., Dec. 1900; Lt., Dec. 1903; Capt., April, 1913; Major, July, 1915; served Europ. War; Despatches. His D.S.O. was awarded for gallantry 27.9.16, at Martinpuich. He was killed in action 28.5.17.

SHAW-STEWART, B. H. (D.S.O. L.G. 1.1.17); b. 8.12.77; s. of late Major-Gen. J. H. M. Shaw-Stewart, g. s. of 5th Bart. and Mary C. B., d. of late Gen. G. C. Collyer, R.E.; m. Vera, d. of W. H. Caldwell; one s.; educ. Marlborough; R.M.A., Woolwich; 2nd Lt., R.A., 23.12.97; Lt. 28.12.00; Capt. 24.1.05; Major 30.10.14; Lt.-Col., R.A., 3.7.18; served Europ. War, 1914–18; Despatches; C.M.G.

SHEA, A. G. (D.S.O. L.G. 25.8.17); b. 23.6.80; 2nd Lt., Unatt., 25.1.99; Ind. Army 21.4.00; Lt. 6.4.03; Capt. 25.1.08; Major 1.9.15; Bt. Lt.-Col. 3.5.21; served China, 1900; Medal, clasp; N.W. Frontier of India, 1902; Europ. War; Despatches.

SHEA, A. W. (D.S.O. L.G. 3.6.18), Surg.-Major, Notts. and Derby. Regt.

SHEA, H. F., M.B. (D.S.O. L.G. 1.1.18); b. 26.1.73; Lt., R.A.M.C., 14.11.00; Capt. 18.11.03; Major 14.11.12; served S. African War, 1899–1902; Queen's Medal, 3 clasps; King's Medal, 2 clasps; Europ. War; Despatches.

SHEARER, G. W. (D.S.O. L.G. 3.6.18) (Bar, L.G. 1.2.19), Major, 11th By., 3rd Brig., Can. F.A.

SHEARMAN, C. E. G. (D.S.O. L.G. 1.1.18); b. 1.5.89; 2nd Lt., Bedford. R., 6.11.09; Lt. 1.3.11; Capt. 15.12.14; M.C.

SHEARMAN, T. (D.S.O. L.G. 1.2.19), Capt. (A/Major), 5th Batt. Yorks. L.I., T.F.

SHEBBEARE, R. A. (D.S.O. L.G. 1.1.18), T/Major, A.S.C. (now R.A.S.C.).

SHEDDEN, J. A. (D.S.O. L.G. 8.3.19) (Details, L.G. 4.10.19), Lt. (A/Major), 7th Batt. Scottish Rifles; M.C.

SHEEHAN, G. F. (D.S.O. L.G. 4.6.17); b. 22.12.74; Lt., R.A.M.C., 29.1.01; Capt. 29.1.04; Major 29.1.13; Bt. Lt.-Col. 1.1.19; served S. African War, 1901–2; Queen's Medal, 3 clasps; Europ. War; Despatches.

SHEFFIELD, W. G. F. (D.S.O. L.G. 3.2.20), Capt. (T/Major), Midd'x R., S.R., and M.G.C.

SHEKLETON, A. (D.S.O. L.G. 11.4.18), T/Lt.-Col., R. Muns. Fus., and R.F.C.

SHELDON, C. D. (D.S.O. L.G. 4.6.17), Lt. (T/Capt.), R.E. (Spec. Res.).

SHELDON, J. (D.S.O. L.G. 8.3.19) (Details, L.G. 4.10.19), Lt., 2nd Batt. Notts. and Derby. Regt.; M.C.

SHELLARD, E. (D.S.O. L.G. 20.10.16), Capt. (T/Major), 1/4th Bn. Glouc. R. (T.F.).

SHELLSHEAR, J. L. (D.S.O. L.G. 1.1.18), Lt.-Col., Aust. F.A.

SHELTON, R. (D.S.O. L.G. 1.1.17), Bt. Lt.-Col. R.A.S.C.

SHELTON, R. H. (D.S.O. L.G. 17.4.17); s. of G. H. Shelton; m. Gladys Margaret, d. of late J. Kaufmann, of Barcelona: one s.; late Lt.-Com., R.N.V.R.; served Europ. War, 1914–17; wounded; Despatches.

SHEPHARD, G. S. (D.S.O. L.G. 4.6.17); b. in Madras, 1885; 2nd s. of Sir Horatio and Lady Shephard; educ. Summerfields; Eton; Sandhurst; obtained a commission in R. Fus., 1905; he was a Staff College Graduate. In July, 1912, he joined R.F.C., and flew over to France with the first five squadrons 13.8.14; Capt., Royal Fus., 16.1.13; T/Major and Squad.-Comdr., R.F.C., 1.12.14; Bt. Major and Bt. Lt.-Col., and commanded a Brigade, R.F.C.; served Europ. War; Despatches five times; M.C.; Legion of Honour. He was killed in an aeroplane accident in France 19.1.18.

SHEPHERD, A. E. D.S.O. L.G. 3.6.18), Lt.-Col. (T/Col.), Aust. A.M.C.

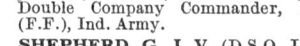

A. S. Shepherd.

SHEPHERD, A. S. (D.S.O. L.G. 17.9.17), 2nd Lt., R.F.C., S.R.; M.C. He was killed in action 20.7.17.

SHEPHERD, C. I. (D.S.O. L.G. 17.3.17) (Details, L.G. 18.6.17); b. 14.1.84; s. of late Major A. L. Shepherd, 4th Punjab Inf., P.F.F.; m. (1st), Edith Ivy (who died in 1911), d. of H. G. Reid, Punjab Police; (2nd) Evelyn Flora, d. of late H. Villiers Margary, of Ceylon; educ. Bedford Grammar School; Sandhurst; 2nd Lt., Unatt., 27.8.02; att. to the Queen's; joined Ind. Army, 53rd Sikhs, F.F., 19.1.04; Lt. 27.11.04; Capt. 27.8.11; Major 27.8.17; served Mohmand Exp., N.W. Frontier of India, 1908; Adjt. of Regt., 1910–13; served with Imp. Service troops in Egypt, 1914–15, and with own regiment in Mesopotamia, 1916–17; on Staff in Egypt, 1918; Double Company Commander, 53rd Sikhs (F.F.), Ind. Army.

SHEPHERD, G. J. V. (D.S.O. L.G. 4.6.17); b. 15.2.87; 2nd Lt., R.E., 17.2.06; Lt. 28.7.08; Capt. 30.10.14; Bt. Major 1.1.19.

SHEPHERD, N. F. (D.S.O. L.G. 1.1.19); b. 2.9.89; Lt., Sco. Rif., 25.7.16; Capt. 21.7.21.

SHEPHERD, W. K. O. (D.S.O. L.G. 4.6.17), Major, R.F.A.

SHEPPARD, E. (D.S.O. L.G. 14.11.16); b. 26.6.78; e. s. of late Rev. Canon Edgar Sheppard, and brother of Rev. H. R. L. Sheppard, Vicar of St. Martin-in-the-Fields, W.C., from 1914; m. Isobel, d. of Col. Sir George Hastings, M.D., V.D., and Alice, d. of late W. P. Frith, R.A., C.V.O.; 2nd Lt., Manch. R., 27.7.01; 19th Hrs. 7.12.01; Lt. 2.3.03; Capt. 1.6.12; G. Gds. 5.1.16; Major, ret. pay, G. Gds., 1921; served Europ. War, 1914–16; Despatches; M.C.

SHEPPARD, E. G. (D.S.O. L.G. 4.6.17), T/Major, R.E. (Capt., R.E., T.F.); M.V.O.

SHEPPARD, H. C. (D.S.O. L.G. 23.11.16); b. 23.7.69; s. of late Col. T. D. Sheppard, and brother of Col. G. S. Sheppard, C.M.G., I.A., and Vice-Admiral T. D. L. Sheppard, C.B., M.V.O.; 2nd Lt., R.A., 13.11.89; Lt. 13.11.92; Capt. 3.1.00; Major 20.9.06; Lt.-Col. 30.10.14; Brig.-Gen., late R.A.; served W. Africa, 1899 (Benin Territories), and also 1900 (Ashanti); Despatches; S. African War, 1900; Queen's Medal, 3 clasps; Europ. War, 1914–18; Bt. Col.; C.B.; C.M.G.

SHEPPARD, J. J. (D.S.O. L.G. 3.6.19), Lt. (A/Major), 1/19th Batt. London R.; M.C.

SHEPPARD, R. O. (D.S.O. L.G. 4.6.17); b. 9.11.81; 2nd Lt., R.A., 18.8.00; Lieut. 19.8.02; Capt. 25.6.13; Major 8.12.14.

SHEPPARD, W. T. (D.S.O. L.G. 3.6.18); b. 28.8.79; 2nd Lt., R.A., 22.6.01; Lt. 2.5.04; Capt. 25.1.11; Major 8.12.14; Bt. Lt.-Col. 3.6.19; Major (T/Lt.-Col.), A.O.D. (now R.A.O.C.).

SHERBROOKE, H. G. (D.S.O. L.G. 21.9.17), Cdr., R.N.

SHERBROOKE, N. H. C. (D.S.O. L.G. 4.6.17); b. 8.4.80; s. of Rev. H. N. Sherbrooke (Incumbent of Portman Chapel, W., from 1878 to 1891), and Lady Lilias Charlotte Sherbrooke, e. d. of 1st Earl Cairns; m. Cicely Morton, y. d. of Rev. John Mansel-Pleydell (Vicar of Sturminster Newton, 1898 to 1915); one s.; two d.; educ. Winchester; R.M.A., Woolwich; 2nd Lt., R.A., 14.9.98; Lt. 16.2.01; Capt. 20.6.06; Adjt., R.A., 1.10.12 to 21.1.14; Major 30.10.14; Bt. Lt.-Col. 3.6.19; served S. African War; Queen's Medal, 5 clasps; King's Medal, 2 clasps; Europ. War; Despatches three times.

SHERBROOKE, R. L. (D.S.O. L.G. 26.9.17) (Details, L.G. 9.1.18); b. 1885; s. of late Cdr. W. Sherbrooke, R.N., and great-nephew and godson of late Viscount Sherbrooke (Robert Lowe); m. Eileen Cecil, d. of J. R. McLaren; one s.; educ. Malvern College; gazetted to 2nd Batt. The Sherwood Foresters 23.5.06; Lt. 30.9.06; Capt. 21.1.15; Bt. Major 3.6.16; served Europ. War with 1st Batt. The Sherwood Foresters, 1914–18, and with M.G.C. from 1918; commanded 1st S. Foresters, 8th, 1st Res., and 4th Batt. M.G.C., 1915–20; twice wounded; 1914 Star; Despatches five times; Bt. Major.

The Distinguished Service Order 341

SHERER, J. D. (D.S.O. L.G. 1.1.17); b. 18.1.70: 2nd Lt., R.A., 15.2.89; Lt. 15.2.92; Capt. 14.8.99; Major 8.9.09; Lt.-Col. 9.5.16; T/Brig.-Gen. 20.9.18 to 13.4.19 (local Col. 13.4.20 to 8.5.20); Col. 9.5.20; C.M.G.

SHERINGHAM, C. J. DE B., B.A. (D.S.O. L.G. 1.2.19); b. 12.2.83; s. of late Rev. W. A. Sheringham and Elizabeth Frances, d. of late Rev. H. G. de Bunsen; educ. Winchester College; Christ Church, Oxford (B.A., Honours; 2nd Class Arabic); commissioned Highrs. of Canada, Aug. 1914; Capt., April, 1915; with 43rd Exp. Batt.; transferred to 5th Q.O. Cam. Highrs.; Staff Capt., 1917; Brig. Major, Dec. 1917; Lt.-Col. Commanding 8th Batt. Somerset L.I., Aug. 1918; served in France and Belgium from 1915; wounded; Despatches four times; M.C.

SHERLOCK, D. J. C. E. (D.S.O. L.G. 4.6.17); b. 6.6.79; s. of D. Sherlock; educ. Beaumont College; Clongoweswood College; joined Army, R.A., 17.3.00; Lt., April, 1901; Capt. 25.9.08; Major 30.10.14; Bt. Lt.-Col., R.F.A., 3.6.19; served in R.H. and R.F.A.; Europ. War, from 17.8.14; Chevalier, Légion d'Honneur; Croix de Guerre.

SHERMAN, E. C. (D.S.O. L.G. 4.6.17), T/Major, A.S.C.

SHERSTON, J. R. V. (D.S.O. L.G. 1.1.18); b. 2.10.88; s. of late Lt.-Col. J. Sherston, D.S.O., Rif. Brig.; 2nd Lt., Unatt., 17.8.07; Ind. Army 12.11.08; Lt. 17.11.09; Capt. 1.9.15; Bt. Major, 11th Lancers, I.A., 1.1.20; served Europ. War, 1914–18; Despatches; M.C.; Third Afghan War, 1919; Bt. Major; Medal with clasp.

SHERWOOD, O. C. (D.S.O. L.G. 4.6.17), Major and Bt. Lt.-Col., ret. pay, late R.A.O.C.

SHERWOOD-KELLY, J. (D.S.O. L.G. 2.2.16), Major, Norfolk Regt.; V.C.; Lt.-Col. retired (see "The Victoria Cross," by same publishers).

SHEWELL, E. F. (D.S.O. L.G. 25.8.17); b. 8.5.77; s. of late Rev. F. Shewell; m. (1st) Frances, d. of late J. Greene; one s.; (2nd) Dorothy, twin daughter of Mrs. A. W. F. Baird; one s.; 2nd Lt., R.A., 1.9.97; Lt. 1.9.00; Adjt. 8.7.17 to 7.7.07; Capt. 4.7.04; Major 30.10.14; Lt.-Col., R.F.A., 20.3.18; served S. African War, 1899–1902; Queen's Medal and 3 clasps; King's Medal and 2 clasps; Europ. War (Mesopotamia), 1915–18; Despatches; C.M.G.

SHIEL, F. R. A. (D.S.O. L.G. 18.7.17), Capt. (A/Major), R.F.A.

SHINER, H. (D.S.O. L.G. 26.7.18), Lt. (A/Major); M.C.

SHINKWIN, I. R. S. (D.S.O. L.G. 4.6.17); b. 29.9.76; s. of late Col. R. S. Shinkwin, 59th Rgt. of Foot, and of a daughter of Rev. F. Wall, D.D.; m. Susan Digby (who died in 1918), d. of E. D. Berkeley, I.S.O.; one s.; educ. Cheltenham College; 2nd Lt., A.S.C., 21.2.00; Lieut. 1.4.01; Capt. 7.1.03; Major, R.A.S.C., 5.8.14; Lt.-Col. 5.1.21.; Lt.-Col. Commanding R.A.S.C., Palestine; C.M.G.

SHOOK, A. M. (D.S.O. L.G. 1.1.18), Fleet Cdr., R.N.A.S.; D.S.C.

SHORE, J. L. (D.S.O. L.G. 30.1.20); b. 8.9.80; 2nd Lt., Ches. R., 21.2.00; Lt. 7.2.01; Capt. 19.12.06; Major 1.9.15; served Europ. War; Legion of Honour, 5th Class; Despatches.

SHORLAND, J. W. (D.S.O. L.G. 15.2.19) (Details, L.G. 30.7.19), T/2nd Lt., Hants R., att. 2/4th Batt. T.F.

SHORROCK, J. (D.S.O. L.G. 11.1.19), 2nd Lt., A.I.F.

SHORT, H. G. R. BURGES- (See Burges-Short, H. G. R.).

SHORTHOSE, W. J. T. (D.S.O. L.G. 1.1.18), Capt. (T/Major), S. Staffs. R. and K.A.R.

SHOUBRIDGE, C. A. G. (D.S.O. L.G. 27.6.19); b. 6.8.74; 2nd Lt., Norf. R., 10.10.94; Lieut. 6.1.97; Ind. Army 19.4.98; Capt. 10.10.03; Major 10.10.12; Lt.-Cdr. 11.9.19; served N.W. Frontier of India; Medal with clasp; Europ War; Despatches.

SHOVE, H. W. (D.S.O. L.G. 2.11.17); b. 1886; m. Guinevere, d. of G. A. E. Wren; four d.; Lt.-Cdr., R.N.; served Europ. War from 1914; Despatches.

SHRUBSOLE, P. J. (D.S.O. L.G. 27.6.19); son of Charles Baldock Shrubsole; educated at Sir Joseph Williamson's School, Rochester; Royal Naval Engineering College, Keyham; joined R.N. in 1892; served in H.M.S. Majestic from 1897–1901; in the flagship of Admirals Sir Harry Stephenson, Sir Harry Rawson and Sir Arthur Wilson in the Channel Fleet; was in H.M.S. Fox, 1901–3; Medal for service with the Naval Brigade in Somaliland; Instructor at R.N.E.C., Keyham, 1904–6; Europ. War; present at the Battle of Coronel; Despatches; also in the return engagement at the Falkland Islands (again mentioned in the Commodore's Despatches); promoted Eng.-Cdr., 1.9.15. His D.S.O. was awarded for valuable work in H.M.S. Calypso.

SHUTE, J. J. (D.S.O. L.G. 3.6.16); b. in Liverpool; s. of J. J. and Mary E. Shute; educ. privately; Catholic Institute, Liverpool; joined 1st V.B. King's (Liverpool Rgt.), now 5th King's Liverpool Rgt. (T.F.), 1895, and went to France as 2nd-in-command, Feb. 1915; Lt.-Col., Commanding 5th Liverpool Rgt. (T.F.); actions of Neuve Chapelle, Richebourg, Givenchy, and on the Somme, Ypres, La Bassée; Despatches four times; C.M.G.

SHUTTLEWORTH, D. I. (D.S.O. L.G. 3.6.19); b. 23.8.76; 2nd Lt., Unatt., 5.8.96; Ind. S.C. 3.10.97; Lt. 5.11.98; Capt. 5.8.05; Major 5.8.14; Bt. Lt.-Col. 3.6.17; Temp. Brig.-Gen. 22.3.19; C.B.E.

SIDNEY, H. (D.S.O. L.G. 4.6.17); b. 1879; s. of late H. Sidney, J.P., of Cowpen Hall, Northumberland, and 2nd wife, Frances Elizabeth, d. of W. H. Hobkirk, M.D.; m. Adèle, d. of late J. McCulloch, of Yongala, S. Australia; one d.; educ. Stonyhurst College; 2nd Lt., North'd Hussars, 1905; Lt.-Col., 1920; T.D.; late commanding North'd Hussars; in France with Regt., Oct. 1914–Dec. 1917; twice wounded; Despatches thrice.

SIFTON, C. (D.S.O. L.G. 2.12.18); Major, 4th Brig., Can. F.A.

SIFTON, W. V. (D.S.O. L.G. 11.1.19), Major, 4th Batt. Can. Mtd. Rif., 1st Cent. Ont. Rgt.

SILCOX, L. E. (D.S.O. L.G. 3.6.19), Major, 11th Batt. Can. Rly. Troops.

SILLS, J. H. (D.S.O. L.G. 1.1.18), Major, Can. Inf.

SILVER, J. P., M.B. (D.S.O. L.G. 1.1.17), Lt.-Col., late R.A.M.C.; served N.W. Frontier of India, 1897–98; Medal with 2 clasps; Europ. War, 1914–17; Despatches twice.

SIM, G. E. H. (D.S.O. L.G. 25.8.16); b. 15.8.86; m. a daughter of B. Dale; two d.; 2nd Lt., R.E., 13.2.06; Lt. 21.7.08; Capt. 30.10.14; Bt. Major 3.6.18; Europ. War, 1914–18; Despatches thrice; Bt. Major, 1918; M.C.; Order Wen Hu, 5th Class, 1919. His D.S.O. was awarded for gallantry at High Wood on 20.7.16.

SIMCOX, C. T. (D.S.O. L.G. 1.1.17), T/Major, D.C.L.I.

SIME, A. W. H. (D.S.O. L.G. 26.7.18), T/2nd Lt., M.G.C.; M.C.

SIMMONDS, T. (D.S.O. L.G. 11.1.19); T/Sub-Lt. Drake Batt. R.N.V.R.; M.C.; D.C.M.

SIMMONS, C. D. (D.S.O. L.G. 6.4.18), Lt. (A/Cdr.), R.N.R.

SIMMONS, J. A. (D.S.O. L.G. 16.9.18), T/Major, Ches. R.; M.C.

SIMMONS, W. G. (D.S.O. L.G. 8.3.19) (Details, L.G. 4.10.19), T/Capt., 7th Batt. R.W. Surrey R.; M.C.

SIMNER, P. R. O. A. (D.S.O. L.G. 1.1.17) (Bar, L.G. 30.1.20), T/Lt.-Col., 10th Batt. W. Yorks. R.

SIMONDS, C. B. (D.S.O. L.G. 1.1.18); b. 15.4.67; 1st com. 16.9.85; Major 31.1.04; retired R.A. 27.5.11; Major, R. of O., R.G.A.; served S. African War, 1899–1902; Despatches; Queen's Medal, 3 clasps; King's Medal, 2 clasps; Europ. War; Despatches.

SIMONDS, J. DE L. (D.S.O. L.G. 1.1.17); b. 7.5.84; s. of the late L. de L. Simonds; educ. Summerfields, Oxford, and Winchester, which he entered in 1897 as first on the roll of scholars. He went to Woolwich in 1901, and joined the R.G.A. 15.7.03; Lt. 15.7.06; Capt. 30.10.14; A/Major. He served in Malta and Hong Kong. He was in India when war broke out, and proceeded thence with a mountain battery to the front in Dec. 1914, where he served almost continuously up to 21.4.17, when he was killed in action. His D.S.O. was awarded for services while acting as artillery liaison officer with the R.F.C.

SIMPSON, A. F. (D.S.O. L.G. 2.12.18), Capt., 28th Can. Inf. Batt. Sask. R., Can. Mil. Forces.

SIMPSON, C. (D.S.O. L.G. 12.12.19), Eng. Lt.-Cdr., R.N., 1.8.17.

SIMPSON, C. N. (D.S.O. L.G. 4.6.17); b. 11.4.56; s. of late Maj.-Gen. W. H. R. Simpson, R.A.; joined R.A. 28.1.75; Lt.-Col., R.F.A., 10.7.00; Bt. Col. 10.2.04; retired 6.3.07, with rank of Colonel in the Army; rejoined 1914, and raised 53rd Brig., R.F.A., at Aldershot; took over command of 5th Div. A.C. in France, Feb. 1915, and served with that unit and 34th D.A.C.; Despatches three times.

SIMPSON, G. S. (D.S.O. L.G. 23.11.16), Major (T/Lt.-Col.), R.F.A., T.F.

SIMPSON, H. C. (D.S.O. L.G. 14.1.16); b. 24.4.79; s. of Robinson Henry and Kathleen Elizabeth Simpson; educ. at Tonbridge; ent. R.A. 22.12.98; Lt. 16.2.01; Capt. 25.8.06; Adjt., R.A., 1.9.09 to 31.12.09; Major 30.10.14; Lt.-Col. 1.1.21; served S. African War, 1899–1902; Queen's Medal and 3 clasps; King's Medal and 2 clasps; Europ. War, 1914–18; Despatches eight times; Bt. Lt.-Col. 1.1.18; C.M.G.; Croix de Guerre; Order of Danilo.

SIMPSON, J. G. (D.S.O. L.G. 3.6.19); b. 1.1.88; s. of J. C. Simpson, M.D., C.M., of Glasgow, and Helen Beath, d. of late J. Gray, M.D.; m. Florence, d. of late J. Pinion; two d.; educ. Warriston School, Moffat; Loretto School, Musselburgh; joined 3rd Spec. Res. Batt. Q.O. Cam. Highrs., 1912; Capt. in Regular Army (Q.O. Cam. Highrs.), 1915; served in France, 1915–17; Italy, 1917–19; Despatches five times; M.C.

SIMPSON, L. S., B.A., A.M.Inst.C.E. (D.S.O. L.G. 4.6.17); educ. Cambridge University; Colonel, late R.E.; served Europ. War, 1914–17; Despatches; C.B.E.

SIMPSON, P. J., F.R.C.V.S. (D.S.O. L.G. 3.6.18), Capt. (T/Lt.-Col.), A.V.C. (now R.A.V.C.).

SIMPSON, R. M. (D.S.O. L.G. 2.12.18), Col., Can. A.M.C., A.D. of M.S., 2nd Can. Div.

SIMPSON, S. H. (D.S.O. L.G. 29.8.17) (Bar, L.G. 22.2.18), Cdr., R.N., 30.6.19.

SIMPSON, W. (D.S.O. L.G. 12.12.19), Qr.-Mr. and Capt., K.O.S.B.; M.C.; D.C.M.

SIMPSON, W. A. J. (D.S.O. L.G. 1.1.18), T/Lt.-Col., R.F.A.; M.C.

SIMPSON, W. G. (D.S.O. L.G. 3.6.18); b. 1876; s. of late Col. S. Simpson, R.A.; m. Evelyn, d. of late Rev. A. Rasch; one d.; joined R. Marines, 1895; retired 1910, as Captain; served N. China, 1900 (China Medal); Lt.-Col., 24th London R. The Queen's, 1910–18; Col., T.F. Res.; served Europ. War, 1915; Despatches four times; C.M.G.; Commander, Order of Avis.

SIMSON, G. B. SPICER- (see Spicer-Simson, G. B.).

SIMSON, J. R. (D.S.O. L.G. 1.1.18); b. 21.11.79; 2nd Lt., H.L.I., 23.5.00; Lt. 26.4.02; Capt. 23.9.11; Major (T/Lt.-Col.), H.L.I., att. K.O.S.B. He served in the Europ. War, and died of wounds 9.11.17.

SIMSON, W. A. (D.S.O. L.G. 14.1.16); b. 1872; s. of W. H. Simson and Jessie Ada Simson (*née* Smith); m. Louise, d. of late E. L. Du Barry, of Norfolk, Virginia; educ. Halifax High School; joined Can. Mil. Forces, Feb. 1901; came over with the 1st Can. Contingent; Colonel, 1st Divl. Train; served Europ. War, 1914–18; Despatches twice; C.M.G.; 1914–15 Star.

SINCLAIR, I. M. R. (D.S.O. L.G. 8.3.19) (Details, L.G. 4.10.19), Major, 13th Batt. Quebec R.; M.C.

SINCLAIR, J. L. (D.S.O. L.G. 14.3.16), Lt., R.N.R. His D.S.O. was awarded for services in Gallipoli.

SINCLAIR, J. N. (D.S.O. L.G. 3.6.16); b. 11.10.80; 2nd Lt., R.A., 5.5.00; Lt. 13.6.01; Capt. 13.5.10; Major 30.10.14; A/Lt.-Colonel. He served in the Europ. War, and was killed in action 24.3.18.

SINCLAIR, THE REV. P., M.A. (D.S.O. L.G. 1.1.18); was ordained to the parish of Urquhart, Elgin, N.B., 1894; was a T.F. Chaplain attached to the Morayshire Seaforths before the war, and was on service from Aug. 1914, as a Senior Divisional Chaplain.

SINCLAIR, W. C. C. (D.S.O. L.G. 30.1.20), Major, 1/4th Batt. R. Scots., T.F.

SINEL, W. C. (D.S.O. L.G. 2.12.18), Major, 2nd Batt. Auckland Rgt.

SINGLE, C. V. (D.S.O. L.G. 3.6.19), Major (T/Lt.-Col.), Aust. A.M.C., Cdg. 4th L.H. Field Amb.

SKEFFINGTON-SMYTH, R. C. E. (D.S.O. L.G. 4.6.17); b. 27.12.64; s. of late E. R. Skeffington-Smyth and Hon. Gertrude Valentine, d. of 1st Baron Castletown; m. Beatrix Louisa Virginia Tollemache, d. of late Rt. Hon. T. E. Taylor, M.P., of Ardgillan Castle, Dublin; educ. Eton; 1st com. 25.11.85; served in Central Africa, 1896–98; S. African War, 1899–1902; Nigeria, 1903, 1906–7; Europ. War, 1914–18; Major, C. Gds., 4.3.03; ret. C. Gds. 8.10.10; Lt.-Col., Army, 5.8.14.

SKEIL, A. P. (D.S.O. L.G. 1.2.19), Capt. (T/Major), R. Sc. Fus.; M.C.

SKELTON, D. S., M.R.C.S., L.R.C.P., D.P.H. (D.S.O. L.G. 2.2.16); b. 8.8.78; s. of George William and Marie Skelton (*née* Sheridan); m. Charlotte Nancy, d. of M. G. Rooper; one s.; educ. Shrewsbury School; Bonn; London Hospital; Lt., R.A.M.C., 1.9.02; Capt. 1.3.06; Major 1.3.14; served S. Africa; Queen's Medal and 5 clasps; Somaliland, 1908–10; Medal and clasps; Europ. War, 1914–18; D.A.D.M.S., 13th Division, 1915–17; Despatches; Bt. Lt.-Col. 3.6.17.

SKELTON, R. W. (D.S.O. L.G. 15.9.16), Engr. Cdr., R.N., 26.12.18; served Europ. War, Battle of Jutland; Despatches; C.B.; C.B.E.

SKEY, C. O. (D.S.O. L.G. 18.2.18) (Details, L.G. 18.7.18), T/Capt., R. Fus.; M.C.

SKINNER, A. B. (D.S.O. L.G. 1.1.18); b. 13.10.79; s. of Col. G. Skinner, D.S.O.; m. Agnes Dorothy, d. of late D. M. McKechnie; 2nd Lt., Unatt., 25.1.99; 2nd Lt., I.S.C., 13.4.00; Capt. 25.4.01; Major 1.9.15.

SKINNER, E. J. (D.S.O. L.G. 3.6.16); b. 11.9.76; m. Emmeline Louisa, d. of late T. W. Miles, P.W.D., India; one s.; educ. Bedford School; Balliol College, Oxford; 2nd Lt., R.A., 28.3.00; Lt. 3.4.01; Capt. 4.2.09; Major, R.H.A., 3.6.18; served S. African War, 1901–2; Queen's Medal, 2 clasps; Europ. War, France, 1914–18; Despatches five times; Bt. Lt.-Col. (L.G. 3.6.18).

SKINNER, E. W. (D.S.O. L.G. 1.1.18), Hon. Major, Linc. R.

SKINNER, H. ROSS- (see Ross-Skinner, H.).

SKINNER, H. T. (D.S.O. L.G. 26.6.16); b. 15.4.77; 2nd Lt., Hants R., 23.11.98; Lt. 24.3.00; Lt., I.A., 19.11.00; Capt. 23.11.07; Major 1.9.15; served in Waziristan, 1901–2; Medal with clasp.

SKINNER, P. C. B. (D.S.O. L.G. 1.1.17); b. 10.2.71; 2nd Lt., North'n R., 6.4.91; Lt. 8.11.93; Capt. 15.6.01; Major 7.2.12; Lt.-Col. 2.6.15; Col. 2.6.19; T/Col. Comdt. 1.1.21; Col., Northants Rgt.; served S. African War, 1900–2; Queen's Medal and 4 clasps; King's Medal and 2 clasps; Europ. War, 1914–18; Despatches; Bt. Colonel 3.6.18; C.B.; C.M.G.; Croix de Guerre.

SKINNER, W. B., M.B. (D.S.O. L.G. 1.2.17), Lt.-Col., S. African Med. C.

SKIRROW, A. G. W. (D.S.O. L.G. 4.6.17), T/Major, Gen. List.

SLADDEN, C. E., B.A. (D.S.O. L.G. 8.3.19) (Details, L.G. 4.10.19); b. 1890; s. of J. Sladden; m. Alice Amelia, M.B.E., d. of Rev. A. E. Brown-Constable, late Indian Ecclesiastical Establishment; one s.; educ. Christ Church, Brecon; Christ Church, Oxford (Exhibitioner); 2nd Class Honours Mathematical Moderations, 1910; 2nd Class Honours Chemistry, 1912; Assistant Master (Science), Eton College; gazetted to 9th (S.) Batt. The Worcesters. Rgt., 26.8.14; Capt., Dec. 1915; Major, Feb. 1917; served with this unit in Gallipoli, Egypt, Mesopotamia, Persia and Caucasus, 1915–19; M.C.

SLADE, A. J. (D.S.O. L.G. 1.2.19), Capt., 50th Batt. Can. Inf., Alberta R.

SLADE, E. C. (D.S.O. L.G. 22.9.16), Lt.-Col., Glouc. R.; (T.) M.C. His D.S.O. was awarded for gallantry near Ovillers 16–17.7.16. He was killed in action 4.5.18.

SLADE, H. A. (D.S.O. L.G. 26.9.17) (Details, L.G. 9.1.18), T/Capt., Rif. Brig.; M.C.

SLADEN, D. B. C. (D.S.O. L.G. 1.1.19); b. Melbourne, Australia, 25.11.81; s. of Douglas Brooke Wheelton Sladen and his 1st wife, Margaret Isabella (who died in 1919), d. of Robert Muirhead, of The Grampians, Victoria, Australia; m. Eleanor Thorold Dinorbin Hughes; one s.; one d.; educ. St. Paul's School; ent. R.G.A. from Cornwall and Devon Miners (Royal Miners), R.G.A., 1902; Major from Spec. Res. 31.3.18; served in France and Palestine with Heavy Artillery from 1915; commanded 96th Brig. R.G.A., 1918; Despatches; Bde. Major, R.A. Northern Command.

SLADEN, G. C. (D.S.O. L.G. 14.1.16) (Bar, L.G. 20.10.16); b. 11.6.82; s. of late Col. Sir E. Sladen; m. Mabel Ursula, d. of Sir A. E. Orr-Ewing, 3rd Bart.; one d.; educ. Eton; 2nd Lt., R. Brig., 19.10.02; Lt. 8.3.05; Capt. 3.10.11; Major 18.5.16; Bt. Lt.-Col. 1.1.17; T/Brig.-Gen., 1916–19; served S. African War, 1899–1902; slightly wounded; Despatches; Queen's Medal with 2 clasps; King's Medal with 2 clasps; Europ. War; T/Lt.-Col., 5th Batt. R. War. R., 1915–16; commanded 143rd Inf. Brig., Br. Armies in France, 2.9.16 to 1.3.17; C.B.; C.M.G.; M.C.; Order of St. Stanislas with Swords; Italian Croce di Guerra. The Bar to his D.S.O. was awarded for gallantry on 16.7.17, near Ovillers.

SLANE, J. C. F. (D.S.O. L.G. 1.1.18), Lt.-Col., Aust. Inf.

SLANEY, T. B. (D.S.O. L.G. 1.1.19), Major, 8th Bde. Aust. Field Arty.

SLATER, H. A. (D.S.O. L.G. 16.9.18); s. of J. E. Slater; Lt., Notts. and Derby. R.

SLATER, H. E. (D.S.O. L.G. 26.11.17) (Bar, L.G. 6.4.18), Lt., Aust. Inf.

SLATER, J. M. (D.S.O. L.G. 2.12.18), Capt. (A/Major), 1/4th Batt. R. Scots (T.F.).

SLAUGHTER, R. J. (D.S.O. L.G. 2.2.16); b. 28.4.74; s. of W. E. Slaughter; educ. St. Augustine's College, Ramsgate; St. Mary's College, Oscott; commissioned from Lt., Volunteer Service Company of the Buffs into S. Lancs. Rgt., 1900; transferred to R.A.S.C., 1901; Lt., 1901; Capt., 1905; Major, 1914; Lt.-Col.; served S. African War, 1900–2; Queen's and King's Medals; served Europ. War in Gallipoli, May–Dec. 1915; Despatches twice; Egyptian Exp. Force, 1916; Battle of Romani, Aug. 1915; France, 1917; Despatches four times; Bt. Lt.-Col.; C.M.G.

SLAYTER, E. W., M.B., C.M. (D.S.O. L.G. 1.1.18); b. 15.1.69; s. of late Dr. W. B. Slayter, of Halifax, N.S.; m. Florence Mary, d. of late J. J. Richardson; two s.; two d.; educ. Germany; Dalhousie College, Nova Scotia; Edinburgh University; ent. A.M.S., 1892; Capt. 27.7.95; Major 27.7.04; Lt.-Col. 31.12.14; Col. 26.12.17; A.D. of M.S. (Rawal Pindi District); served Tochi Valley Expeditionary Force, 1897; Medal and clasp; S. African War, 1899; Queen's Medal with 2 clasps; Europ. War, 1914–18; Despatches six times; C.M.G.

SLINGSBY, T. W. (D.S.O. L.G. 2.4.19) (Details, L.G. 10.12.19); b. 6.3.76; 2nd Lt., E. Kent R., 29.2.96; Shrops. L.I. 25.3.96; Lt., I.A., 3.2.99; Capt. 1.3.05; Major, 22nd Cav., I.A., 1.3.14; served N.W. Frontier of India, Waziristan, 1901–2; Medal with clasp; Europ. War; Despatches.

SLOAN, A. T. (D.S.O. L.G. 4.6.17), T/Capt. (A/Major), R.F.A.

SLOGGETT, A. J. H. (D.S.O. L.G. 1.1.18); b. 4.5.82; s. of Lt.-Gen. Sir A. Sloggett, K.C.B., K.C.M.G., K.C.V.O., and Helen (Lady of Grace, St. John of Jerusalem), d. of J. R. Boyson, late Solicitor-General, of Madras; m. Gabrielle, d. of late Monsieur de Lebois, of Roubaix, France; two d.; educ. Temple Grove; Harrow; R.M.C., Sandhurst; 2nd Lt., Unatt., 8.1.01; 2nd Lt., 1st Batt. Rif. Brig. 13.3.01; Lt. 14.5.04; Adjt., Rif. Brig., 15.12.07 to 14.12.10; Capt. 22.1.11; Major 8.1.16; Despatches; served S. African War, 1900–2; Medal, 4 clasps; Europ. War, 1914–18; Brig.-Major and commanding a Batt. Rif. Brig.; 1914 Star; Despatches; Army Champion, Racquets Singles, 1920.

SMALES, W. C. (D.S.O. L.G. 3.6.16); b. 27.8.79; Lt., R.A.M.C., 30.1.06; Capt. 30.7.09; Major 30.1.18; Bt. Lt.-Col. 3.6.19; served Europ. War, 1914–17; Despatches; Bt. Lt.-Col. 3.6.16.

SMALL, E. A. (D.S.O. L.G. 21.1.20), T/Lt., Gen. List.

SMALLEY, E. (D.S.O. L.G. 1.1.17); b. 9.5.77; s. of A. Smalley; m. Lilian, d. of T. H. Bowman, D.Sc.; one s.; four d.; educ. Chorlton High School, Manchester, and in Belgium and Germany; 2nd Lt., 20th Batt. Manchester R., Dec. 1914; Capt. 9.12.14; Major 5.3.15; Lt.-Col. and appointed to command his Battalion 2.7.16; served in France from 6.11.15, and went through the Somme Offensive, 1916; was wounded 15.4.16. He played Lacrosse for England, 1900–1–2.

SMALLMAN, A. B., M.D., Ch.M., D.P.H. (D.S.O. L.G. 14.1.16); b. 1.12.73; s. of Samuel Smallman and Sarah Jane Smallman (*née* Rowley); m. Alice Florence, d. of late R. G. Duncan; two s.; educ. Manchester Grammar School; Owens College, Manchester; graduated M.B., Ch.M. Victoria; M.B., London, 1903; M.D., Victoria University of Manchester, 1913; Civil Surgeon, S. African War, 1900–2; Queen's Medal, 3 clasps; King's Medal, 2 clasps; ent. R.A.M.C. 1.9.02; Capt 1.3.06; Major 1.3.14; Lt.-Col., retired pay, 1920; Balkan War, 1912–13, with the Turkish Forces; Bt. Major 10.5.13; Europ. War, 1914–18; Despatches five times; C.B.E.

SMART, B. A. (D.S.O. L.G. 2.11.17) (Bar, L.G. 21.9.18), Lt. (Hon. Capt.), Sea Patrol, R.A.F.

SMART, E. K. (D.S.O. L.G. 3.6.19), Major, 10th Brig., Aust. F.A.; M.C.

SMART, G. E. (D.S.O. L.G. 1.1.19); b. 9.1.81; 2nd Lt., R.A., 2.5.00; Lt. 3.4.01; Capt. 22.11.12; Major, R.G.A., 30.12.15.

SMART, M., M.D., Ch.M. (D.S.O. L.G. 4.6.17); b. 1878; s. of late J. Smart, R.S.A., R.S.W.; educ. Watson's College, Edinburgh; University, Edinburgh; Edinburgh College of Surgeons; Fellow, R. Society of Medicine; Commander, R.N.V.R.; served S. African War; served Europ. War from 1914, at Admiralty; North Sea; Chief of Staff to Admiral in Command of Gunboats on Belgian Canals, 1914; attached 1st Army in France, 1915; commanded Gunboat Flotilla, Dardanelles, 1915–16; in command of all Motor Launches in Ægean, 1916–17; Salonika (Despatches; D.S.O.; Order of St. Charles of Monaco); S.N.O., Trinidad, W. Indies, 1918–19; command of H.M. Naval Station, Trinidad, W. Indies, 1918; commanded flotilla of motor launches which made the passage from England to Mudros.

SMEATHMAN, L. F. (D.S.O. L.G. 1.1.18); b. 31.5.80; s. of L. Smeathman and Frances Anne, d. of Rev. J. Graves, Vicar of Great Missenden, Bucks; m. Helen Joyce, d. of Sir C. Longmore, K.C.B., V.D., T.D.; educ. Rugby; served in Hertfords. Rgt. (T.F.), 1910–16; Capt. 1914; Lt.-Colonel; commanded 2/1st Batt. Herts. R., 13.5.16–28.9.16; served in France with 1st Herts. Rgt. (T.F.), 5.11.14; B.E.F., two and three-quarter years; wounded at Loos 25.9.15; home until Sept. 1916; Lt.-Col. Commanding 2/1st Herts. R.; to France, Commanding 9th R.W.F., Sept. 1916, to 30.1.19; wounded 8.11.18; Despatches four times; M.C.

SMELLIE, J. H. (D.S.O. L.G. 1.2.17), Hon. Lt.-Col., Rly. Corps, Uganda.

SMELTZER, A. S. (D.S.O. L.G. 18.2.18) (Details, L.G. 18.7.18) (Bar, L.G. 7.11.18); b. 31.12.81; 2nd Lt., E. Kent Rgt., 13.10.15; Lt. 1.7.17; T/Lt.-Col. Commanding 6th Batt. E. Kent Rgt., 9.6.17; M.C.

SMILES, W. D. (D.S.O. L.G. 11.8.17) (Bar, L.G. 17.5.18), Lt.-Cdr., R.N.V.R. He was with Commander M. Blackwood in his Q Boat adventures.

SMIT, B. J. J. (D.S.O. L.G. 1.2.17), Lt.-Col., S. African Horse.

SMITH, A. DIGBY- (see Digby-Smith, A.).

SMITH, A. D. THORNTON- (see Thornton-Smith, A. D.).

SMITH, A. E. (D.S.O. L.G. 22.6.18), Lt. (A/Major), R.F.A.; M.C.

SMITH, A. F. G. (D.S.O. L.G. 1.1.18) (gazetted as Smith, A. F.); b. 9.12.90; s. of late Col. Granville R. F. Smith, C.B., C.V.O., and Lady Blanche Smith; m. Hon. Monica Crossley, d. of Baron Somerleyton; two d.; educ. Eton; Sandhurst; joined Coldstream Guards, 3.9.10; Lt. 1.4.12; Capt. 17.7.15; Adjt., 3rd Batt. C. Gds., Sept. 1914–Nov. 1915; Staff, Nov. 1915–Aug. 1917; T/Lt.-Col. 24.3.19; served Europ. War, 1914–18; wounded thrice; M.C.; Croix de Guerre.

SMITH, A. G. B. (D.S.O. L.G. 30.1.20); b. 14.6.66; 1st com. 29.8.85; Lt.-Col. 25.8.14; retired R. Scots. Fus. 18.2.19; served Burmese Exp., 1886; Medal and clasp; N.W. Frontier of India, 1897–98; action at the Ublan Pass 27.8.97; severely wounded; Medal with clasp; Europ. War; Despatches.

SMITH, A. G. NICOL- (see Nicol-Smith, A. G.).

SMITH, A. J. (D.S.O. L.G. 15.2.19) (Details, L.G. 30.7.19), 2nd Lt., 1st Batt. Border R.; D.C.M.

SMITH, B. A. (D.S.O. L.G. 15.2.19) (Details, L.G. 30.7.19); s. of Robert Smith; m. Hon. Rhona Margaret Ada Hanbury Tracy, d. of 4th Baron Sudeley; two s.; one d.; educ. Eton; Trinity College, Cambridge; Major, S. Notts. Hussar Yeomanry; Lt.-Col. Commanding 8th Batt. S. Foresters; served in Egypt, Gallipoli and Salonika; commanded 23rd Batt. Midd'x Rgt., 41st Div. in France; M.C.

SMITH, C. A. (D.S.O. L.G. 7.4.16); b. 9.6.77; s. of Samuel Smith; educ. Christ's College, Finchley; joined the R.N.D. 25.9.14 as 2nd Lt., and became Lt., R.N.V.R. He served in the Europ. War; was wounded 21.7.15; mentioned in Despatches by Sir D. Haig 30.4.16; won the D.S.O. south of Verlorenhoek in April, 1916. His Father writes: "He came to England to receive his decoration from the King early in June, 1916, and returned about the 7th June. On the 9th June he organized a raiding party to destroy an Observation Post just north of Ypres into No Man's Land, where the Germans surrounded them, and my son was wounded. He has not been heard of since." Maj.-Gen. Sir W. E. Ironside (then a Lieut.-Col.), said, in a letter dated 9.4.16: "I can assure you that he has earned his distinction several times over. Always jolly, he was welcomed by everybody. The dangerous work which he was daily carrying out with explosives was just suited to his temperament. I used to tell him that I should have to chain him down." He was presumed to have been killed in action 9.6.16.

SMITH, C. D. PYE- (see Pye-Smith, C. D.).

SMITH, THE VERY REV. MONSIGNOR C. W. (D.S.O. L.G. 4.6.17); b. 3.2.73, at Oxford; s. of Frederick Augustus and Louisa Smith; educ. Beaumont College, Old Windsor; Chaplain to the Forces from 24.4.15; Assistant Principal Chaplain, 4th Army H.Q., from 30.11.16; Despatches five times; C.B.E. Monsignor Smith is the composer of the children's play, "Snowdrop and the Seven Little Men," produced at the Court Theatre, London.

SMITH, C. W. J. (D.S.O. L.G. 1.2.17); b. 15.12.81; s. of late Johnstone and of Alicia Fanny Emma Smith; educ. Bedford Grammar School; 2nd Lt., Unatt., 28.7.00; I.S.C. 7.10.01; Lt., I.A., 28.10.02; Capt. 28.7.09; Major, 29th Punjabis, I.A., 1.9.15; served N.W. Frontier of India, Waziristan, 1901–2; Medal with clasp; Europ. War, East Africa, from 1915; Despatches.

SMITH, D. K. (D.S.O. L.G. 4.6.17); b. 24.5.83; s. of Rev. A. Kirke Smith, of Boxworth Rectory, Cambridge; m. Mary Ellen Beadle; one s.; two d.; educ. Haileybury College; joined Territorial R.A., 1908; Lt.-Colonel; served Europ. War, in France, 1914–17; Despatches.

SMITH, D. V. (D.S.O. L.G. 14.1.16); b. 18.5.78; s. of Frederick Smith; m. Nora. d. of late C. J. Webb; educ. at Uppingham, and in France, and in 1900 was commissioned in The London Rgt. (R. Fusiliers), T.F., becoming Captain in 1901. He went to the front in March, 1915; was gazetted Major in the same month, and took part in the battles of Festubert, the Somme, Loos, Combles, and other engagements; T/Lt.-Col. to command his battalion, June, 1916; Lt.-Col., Dec. 1916. He was wounded 1.10.16, but returned to the front in Feb. 1917, to take up the command of his battalion. He died at Rouen on 13.4.17, from the effects of wounds received in action four days previously in the Battle of Arras.

SMITH, D. W. A. (D.S.O. L.G. 1.1.18), Major, Aust. L.H. Rgt.

SMITH, E. C. MONTGOMERY- (see Montgomery-Smith, E. C.).

SMITH, F. W. (D.S.O. L.G. 4.6.17), T/Lt.-Col. Commanding Battalion, Welsh Rgt. (Hon. Lieut., Yeomanry).

SMITH, G. A. (D.S.O. L.G. 3.6.16); s. of late R. Smith, J.P., and late Jessie Smith; educ. Aberdeen Grammar School and University; 2nd Lt., 1st V.B. Gordon Highrs., 1900; passed into T.F. on change of organization; Major, 1913, and was Junior Major, 4th Batt. G. Highrs., on mobilization; went to France with Batt., Feb. 1915, as Second-in-Command; was wounded in attack on Y Wood, near Hooge, Sept. 1915 ; from Dec. 1915, till Oct. 1916, in command of 8th K.O.R.L. Rgt. ; he saw much service at the Bluff, St. Eloi, and in the Somme battles of Delville Wood, Guillemont, etc. He was again wounded 16.8.16, in an attack on Guillemont ; from Oct. 1916, to Oct. 1917, he was in charge of the Territorial Records at Rouen. He then joined the 5th G. Highrs., and took part in the Retreat at St. Quentin ; from that time he commanded the Batt. until he was killed by a shell on 28.7.18, while assisting the French, west of Rheims.

SMITH, G. E. (D.S.O. L.G. 1.1.17) ; b. 6.8.68 ; s. of late A. Smith, F.R.S. ; educ. Winchester ; ent. R.E., 1888 ; Capt., 1899 ; Major, 1907 ; Lt.-Col., 1915 ; Bt. Col., 1919 ; Col., 1920 ; Brig.-General ; Director of Surveys, E. African Protectorate, 1906–10 ; C.M.G., 1909 ; served S. African War, 1901–2 ; Queen's Medal, five clasps ; Europ. War, 1914–18 ; Croix d'Officier, Légion d'Honneur ; served at Boulogne as C.R.E., Aug. 1914, to Aug. 1917 ; served in Italy, Nov. 1917, to May, 1919, as Director of Works and Brig.-Gen. ; mentioned five times in Despatches during the war. He won the Fencing Officers' R.M. Tournament, 1890 ; Curled twice for England *v.* Scotland whilst Member of Prince's Curling Club.

SMITH, G. E. S. (D.S.O. L.G. 1.1.19) ; s. of Col. Sir George Smith, of Treliske, Truro ; Lt.-Col. Commanding 1/4th Batt. D.C.L.I. (T.F.) ; Despatches twice. For 15 months the Batt. was in India, taking the place of a regular battalion. The Cornishmen took their part in defeating the enemy in Syria and Palestine.

SMITH, G. M. SPENCER- (see Spencer-Smith, G. M.).

SMITH, HENRY (D.S.O. L.G. 27.6.17.), Lt.-Cdr. (A/Cdr.), R.N.R.

SMITH, HENRY (D.S.O. L.G. 15.10.18), Lt., E. Yorks. Rgt.

SMITH, H. BROKE- (D.S.O. L.G. 19.10.16) ; b. 13.3.75 ; s. of Surg.-Gen. P. Broke-Smith, A.M.S. ; educ. Clifton College, and R.M.A., Woolwich ; 2nd Lt., R.A., 17.11.94 ; Lt. 17.11.97 ; Capt. 1.1.01 ; Adjt., 1910 ; Major 22.4.11 ; Lt.-Col. 19.4.16 ; served Europ. War ; was with Gen. Townshend's Force in Mesopotamia, commanding 63rd Batt. R.F.A., and was captured by the Turks at the surrender of Kut-el-Amara in April, 1916.

SMITH, H. C. HYDE- (D.S.O. L.G. 4.6.17) (Bar, L.G. 26.7.18) ; b. 26.7.80 ; 2nd Lt., Sc. Rifles, 21.2.00 ; Lt. 3.4.03 ; Capt. 12.3.12 ; Major 1.9.15.

SMITH, H. D. ST. A. (D.S.O. L.G. 1.1.18), Major, Can. Engrs.

SMITH, H. F. (D.S.O. L.G. 22.6.16) ; b. 11.1.75 ; educ. Porstmouth ; R.N.E.C., Devonport ; R.N. College, Greenwich ; ent. R.N., July, 1894 ; Asst. Engr. ; served in H.M.S. Blonde, and took part in the suppression of the Mendi Rising of 1898 ; African Medal and Sierra Leone clasp ; promoted to Engr.-Lt. 1.7.99 ; Engr.-Cdr. 1.7.11 ; served Europ. War from 1914 in H.M.S. Suffolk, North Atlantic Patrol, and in H.M.S. Renown, 1st Battle Cruiser Squadron ; Chevalier, Legion of Honour.

SMITH, H. F. E. (D.S.O. L.G. 17.9.17), Capt., K.R.R.C. ; S.R.

SMITH, H. G. SETH- (see Seth-Smith, H. G.).

SMITH, HUBERT HAMILTON (D.S.O. L.G. 22.12.16) ; b. 5.3.78 ; 2nd Lt., Glouc. R., 7.5.98 ; Lt., Glouc. R., 24.2.00 ; I.A. 16.4.02 ; Capt. 7.5.07 ; Major 1.9.15 ; Lt.-Col., I.A., 1.2.21 ; served S. African War, 1899–1901 ; Despatches ; Queen's Medal, 3 clasps ; Europ. War ; Despatches ; Bt. Lt.-Col. 3.6.18.

SMITH, HUMPHREY HUGH (D.S.O. L.G. 21.4.17), Capt., R.N., 30.6.15.

SMITH, H. R. W. MARRIOTT- (D.S.O. L.G. 3.6.16) ; b. 1.8.75 ; s. of Col. W. Marriott-Smith, C.B.E., R.A., and Alice Mary, d. of J. H. Ley, of Trehill, Devon ; m. Dorothy Herbert, d. of Herbert Smith, J.P. ; educ. Elstree ; Repton (Exhibitioner, 1889 ; Scholar, 1890) ; R.M.A., Woolwich ; 2nd Lt., R.A., 2.11.95 ; Lt. 2.11.98 ; Capt. 9.10.01 ; Adjt., R.A., 6.4.03 to 15.4.06 ; Major 28.9.13 ; Lt.-Col. 21.8.16 ; Col. 21.8.20 ; served Nile Exp. and Battle of Omdurman, 1898 ; 2 Medals, clasp ; S. African War, 1899–1902 ; Despatches ; Queen's Medal, 3 clasps ; King's Medal, 2 clasps ; Europ. War, 1914 ; battles of the Marne, the Aisne and the First Battle of Ypres, and in the Dardanelles, July, 1915, to evacuation in Jan., when he was in H.M.S. Russell ; wounded ; Battles of the Somme (wounded) and of Arras ; Despatches ; D.D. of Armaments in India, Sept. 1919. He has written " History of the 13th Battery, R.F.A."

H. R. W. Marriott-Smith.

SMITH, H. SOMERVILLE- (see Somerville-Smith, H.).

SMITH, H. W. T. (D.S.O. L.G. 2.2.16) ; b. 26.3.74 ; 2nd Lt. (from I. Yeom.) 26.5.00 ; Lt. 1.1.02 ; Capt. 26.5.13 ; Adjt., R.A., 1.6.14–18.8.15 ; Major 30.12.15 ; served S. African War, 1900 ; Queen's Medal with clasp ; Europ. War ; Despatches ; Bt. Lt.-Col. 3.6.18.

SMITH, I. M. (D.S.O. L.G. 1.1.19) ; b. 29.1.84 ; 2nd Lt., Som. L.I., 22.10.02 ; Lt. 20.5.05 ; Capt. 11.8.14 ; Major 22.10.17 ; Despatches ; M.C.

SMITH, I. P. (D.S.O. L.G. 1.1.18) ; b. 25.1.90 ; 2nd Lt., R.A., 23.12.09 ; Lt. 23.12.12 ; Capt. (A/Major), R.G.A. He was killed in action on 30.11.17.

SMITH, J. G. (D.S.O. L.G. 3.6.16) ; b. 13.9.73, at Inverallan, Grantown-on-Spey ; s. of the late John Smith, who was for 50 years factor on the Seafield Estates ; m. Maud, d. of W. Mackay, LL.D., of Inverness ; two s. ; educ. George Watson's College, Edinburgh ; Edinburgh University ; J.P. and Member of County Councils, Inverness and Elgin ; Chairman of three School Boards ; Factor for the Strathspey estates of the Seafield Trustees ; joined 3rd V.B. Seaf. Highrs., 1891 ; commissioned 1898 ; mobilized with 6th S. Highrs. on 4.8.14, as 2nd-in-command ; embarked for France 1.5.15 ; Lt.-Colonel Commanding 6th Seaf. Highrs., T.D., for 14 months, and on Staff of 2nd and 3rd Armies in France ; served Europ. War, 1915–18 ; Despatches twice ; T.D.

SMITH, J. H. (D.S.O. L.G. 20.10.16) ; joined the Rifle Brigade from the Militia, Nov. 1914 ; T/Capt., June, 1915 ; served Europ. War ; Despatches ; M.C. He died of wounds 29.8.17.

SMITH, L. A. (D.S.O. L.G. 7.2.18) ; b. 8.11.70 ; 2nd Lt., R.A., 14.2.90 ; Lt. 14.2.93 ; Capt. 3.2.00 ; Major 11.12.07 ; Lt.-Col. 17.12.14 ; T/Brig.-Gen., 1917–19.

SMITH, RT. REV. M. L., D.D. (Bishop of Hereford) (D.S.O. L.G. 1.1.17) ; b. 4.7.69 ; s. of J. A. Smith, Dean of St. David's, and Charlotte Isabella, d. of Rev. Canon Henry Linton ; m. Kathleen Dewe, d. of T. Mathews, of St. John's College, Cambridge ; one s. ; one d. ; educ. Repton and Hertford College, Oxford (Oxford Trial Eights, 1890–91) ; T/Chaplain to the Forces, 3rd Class, A/Chaplains' Dept., 9.4.15 ; went to France 7.11.15 ; Battle of the Somme, July and Oct. 1916 ; Battle of Arras, April, 1917 ; 3rd Battle of Ypres, July, 1917 ; Chaplain to a Brig., 1915–16 ; Senior Chaplain, C.E., 30th Div., 1916–17 ; Despatches ; Bishop of Hereford, 1920.

J. H. Smith.

SMITH, M. S. SPENCER- (see Spencer-Smith, M. S.).

SMITH, P. J. (D.S.O. L.G. 16.9.18), 2nd Lt., Aust. Inf.

SMITH, P. W. L. BROKE- (see Broke-Smith, P. W. L.).

SMITH, R. (D.S.O. L.G. 1.1.17) (Bar, L.G. 18.6.17), Col. (T/Brig.-Gen.), Aust. Infy.

SMITH, R. A. (D.S.O. L.G. 16.9.18) (Bar, L.G. 15.2.19) (Details, L.G. 30.7.19), T/Lt.-Col., 13th Batt. R. Fus. ; M.C.

SMITH, R. K. (D.S.O. L.G. 26.3.18) (Details, L.G. 24.8.18), Lt. (A/Capt.), Wilts. R., S.R. ; M.C.

SMITH, SIDNEY (D.S.O. L.G. 1.1.17) ; b. 8.5.86 ; s. of Sidney Smith ; m. Winifred, d. of Dr. H. Poole Berry, of The Priory, Grantham ; educ. Lowestoft College ; ent. R.F.A., T.F., 1910 ; at outbreak of war was commanding a Territorial Howitzer Battery ; seconded to R.F.C. in 1915 ; in France as an Observer, April to Aug. 1915 ; afterwards became Pilot, and was in France as Flight Commander, and eventually as Squadron Commander from March, 1916 ; Despatches ; Squadron Leader, A.F.C. ; Croix de Guerre with Palms ; Wing Commander, R.A.F., 1921.

SMITH, SUTTON (D.S.O. L.G. 14.7.16) ; b. 1868 ; s. of A. J. Smith ; educ. Thames Nautical Training College ; H.M.S. Worcester, and joined R.N., 1895 ; promoted to Capt. for war services, and reverted to retired list, Aug. 1919 ; served Europ. War, 1914–18 and was engaged in mine-sweeping the whole period, and in clearing the seas of mines afterwards ; Croix de Guerre.

SMITH, SYDNEY (D.S.O. L.G. 3.6.19), Capt. (A/Major), C/276th (W. Lancs.) Brig., R.F.A., T.F. ; M.C.

SMITH, S. B., M.D. (D.S.O. L.G. 4.6.17) ; b. 12.12.72 ; Lt., R.A.M.C., 29.11.00 ; Capt. 29.11.03 ; Major 29.8.12 ; Lt.-Col. 15.10.18 ; served N.W. Frontier of India, 1908 ; operations in the Mohmand country ; Medal with clasp ; O.B.E.

SMITH, S. C. W. (D.S.O. L.G. 23.10.19), Capt., E. Surrey R., S.R., and R.A.F.

SMITH, S. F. (D.S.O. L.G. 3.6.19), Lt.-Col., Can. Light Horse.

SMITH, T. G. L. LUMLEY- (see Lumley-Smith, T. G. L.).

SMITH, T. M. O. CATTERSON- (see Catterson-Smith, T. M. O.).

SMITH, THOMAS OSWALD (gazetted as Smith, Tristram Oswald) (D.S.O. L.G. 4.6.17), Lt. (A/Lt.-Col.) ; commanded a Batt. L.N. Lancs. R. ; wounded.

SMITH, W. (D.S.O. L.G. 1.1.18), Major (T/Lt.-Col.), Aust. Provost Corps.

SMITH, W. C. (D.S.O. L.G. 15.2.19) (Details, L.G. 30.7.19) (Bar, L.G. 1.1.19) ; b. 4.1.88 ; s. of T. Smith, of Oudtshoorn, S. Africa ; m. Dorothy, d. of E. E. Bentall, and widow of Lt. Eric Westmacott, R.N. ; educ. Repton ; commissioned 1914 ; Lt., Northants Rgt. ; A/Lt.-Colonel, K.R.R.C., ; went to France, May, 1915 ; joined 1st Batt. K.R.R. in France, Dec. 1916 ; 2nd-in-command, 1st King's Rgt., Aug. 1917 ; Commanding Officer of the 1st King's Rgt., March, to May, 1918 ; 17th Batt. R. Fus., June, 1918–April, 1919 ; battles fought in Loos, Somme, Ancre, Cambrai, March retirement, 1918, Canal du Nord and Cambrai ; Commanding Officer, 20th K.R.R. Light Division, British Army of the Rhine ; Despatches three times ; M.C.

SMITH, W. E. (D.S.O. L.G. 6.4.18), Cdr. (A/Capt.), R.N.R., R.D.

SMITH, W. G. (D.S.O. L.G. 2.4.19) (Details, L.G. 10.12.19) ; Lt. (A/Major), R.E. ; M.C.

SMITH, W. MURRAY- (see Murray-Smith, W.).

SMITH, W. M. (D.S.O. L.G. 4.6.17) ; b. 27.4.69 ; s. of F. P. Smith, of Barnes Hall, Sheffield, and Margaret Scott, d. of Rev. A. Gatty, D.D., Vicar of Ecclesfield, Sheffield ; m. The Lady Mabel Florence Harriett Wentworth Fitzwilliam, d. of Earl Fitzwilliam ; educ. Charterhouse ; joined Q.O. Yorks. Dragoons, Jan. 1893 ; Lt.-Col., June, 1914 ; Col. 4.8.18 ; T.D. ; commanded Regiment from 1914, serving in France from July, 1915 ; operations on Somme and Ancre, July, 1916, to March, 1917 ; won II. Corps Chargers' Steeplechase 6.1.17, at Crecy, France.

SMITH, W. P. A. HATTERSLEY- (see Hattersley-Smith, W. P. A.).

SMITH, W. S. (D.S.O. L.G. 1.1.18), Capt., R.F.A.

SMITH, W. W. CUNNINGHAME- (see Cunninghame-Smith, W. W.).

SMITHARD, R. G. (D.S.O. L.G. 2.12.18) ; b. 11.6.91 ; in ranks, 16 days ; T/2nd Lt. 25.9.14 ; T/Lt. 19.12.14 ; T/Capt. 25.9.15 ; T/Major 1.9.16 ; Capt., Shrops. L.I., 1.11.16 ; T/Lt.-Col., 7th Batt. Shrops. L.I., 31.5.18 to 27.6.19 ; M.C.

SMITHWICK, A. R. (D.S.O. L.G. 17.4.18) ; b. 3.4.87 ; s. of S. P. Smithwick, late Chancellor of St. Brigid's Cathedral, Kildare, and Caroline Anne Smithwick (*née* Webb) ; m. Kathleen, d. of Sir David Wilson, K.C.M.G. ; one d. ; educ. Skelsmergh House School, Margate ; Northwood Park, Winchester ; H.M.S. Britannia (Jan. 1902) ; Sub-Lt., R.N., 30.7.06 ; Lt. 30.10.07 ; Commander 31.12.19 ; landed as a Midshipman from H.M.S. Andromeda at Shanghai, Christmas, 1905, for the protection of the European Settlement ; served as Sub-Lt. in H.M.S. Dreadnought, 1908 ; Lt. (Watchkeeper) in H.M.S. Victorious, 1908 ; Lt., H.M.S. Formidable, 1909 ; qualified as Navigating Officer in 1910, and served as such in H.M.S. Pergamus, 1911 ; Swift, 1912–13 ; Sappho, 1914–15 ; Roxburgh, 1916–17–18 ; Malaya, 1918–19. His D.S.O. was gazetted under heading, " In Action with Enemy Submarines." Details of Occurrence : H.M.S. Roxburgh, having turned over an American Homeward Bound Convoy to the Destroyer Escort, proceeded at 18 knots. At 11.30 p.m., whilst running through banks of fog, sighted a submarine on the surface, nearly ahead. Being the Officer in Charge on the Bridge, rammed and sank what eventually proved to be U 89. No survivors were picked up.

SMOLLETT, A. P. D. TELFER- (see Telfer-Smollett, A. P. D.).

SMYTH, A. D. D. (D.S.O. L.G. 17.5.18), Lt.-Cdr., R.N., 31.12.16.

SMYTH, C. E. R. HOLROYD- (see Holroyd-Smyth, C. E. R.).

SMYTH, G. A. (D.S.O. L.G. 1.1.18) ; b. 14.2.71 ; 2nd Lt., R.A., 1.2.91 ; Lt. 13.2.94 ; Capt. 13.2.00 ; Major 30.6.08 ; Lt.-Col., R.F.A., 25.2.15.

SMYTH, G. B. F. (D.S.O. L.G. 11.11.14) (Bar, L.G. 18.7.17), Capt. and Bt. Major (A/Lt.-Col.), R.E., att. K.O.S.B. (see " The Distinguished Service Order." from its institution to 31.12.15, by same publishers). His Bar was awarded for gallantry east of Arras 3.5.17.

SMYTH, G. J. WATT- (D.S.O. L.G. 1.1.18) ; b. 29.3.74, at Lahore, India ; s. of John Watt Smyth, Bengal Civil Service, and Annabella Charlotte, d. of Hon. H. O'Brien ; m. Florence Mabel, d. of H. T. Layers ; two s. ; educ. Wellington College and R.M.A. ; 2nd Lt., R.E., 27.2.94 ; Lt. 27.2.97 ; Capt. 1.4.04 ; Major 27.2.14 ; T/Lt.-Col. 18.5.16 ; served Europ. War ; Despatches twice.

SMYTH, G. O. S. (D.S.O. L.G. 16.9.18) ; b. 27.1.90 ; 2nd Lt., R.A., 23.12.09 ; Lt. 23.12.12 ; Capt., R.F.A. ; served Europ. War ; Despatches ; Bt. Major 3.6.19 ; M.C. He was killed in Ireland 13.10.20.

SMYTH, H. (D.S.O. L.G. 1.1.18); b. 9.6.66; Lt., Ches. R., 30.1.86; Capt. 4.5.95; Major 16.9.08; Lt.-Col. 7.5.15; served Chin Lushai Exp., 1889–90; operations on N.W.F. of India, 1897–98, with Tirah Exp. Force; Despatches; Medal with 2 clasps; Europ. War; Despatches.

SMYTH, H. E. (D.S.O. L.G. 4.6.17); b. Sialkot, India, 4.5.84; s. of Col. E. W. Smyth, C.B., and Katharine Ellen, d. of late T. E. Heath, J.P.; m. Kathleen, d. of Aubrey Robinson; one s.; educ. R.M.A., Woolwich; first commissioned R.G.A. 24.12.02; Lt. 24.12.05; Capt. 30.10.14; Major 16.6.17; transferred to R.A.O.C., 1918; served Europ. War from 1915; Despatches four times; O.B.E.

SMYTH, H. H. (D.S.O. L.G. 16.2.17), Captain, R.N., 31.12.14; C.M.G.

SMYTH, R. C. SKEFFINGTON- (see Skeffington-Smyth, R. C.).

SMYTH, R. R. (D.S.O. L.G. 4.6.17); b. 8.12.75: 2nd Lt., Leinster R., 5.1.01; Lt. 3.1.03; Capt. 1.4.10; Major 1.9.15; T/Lt.-Col. 2.8.18; served S. African War, 1899–1902; Queen's Medal with 3 clasps; King's Medal with 2 clasps; Europ. War; Despatches; C.M.G.

SMYTH, T. (D.S.O. L.G. 27.7.18), Lt.-Col., S.A.M.C.

SMYTH, V. G. (D.S.O. L.G. 3.6.19); b. 11.10.92; 2nd Lt., R.A., 23.12.11; Lt. 23.12.14; Capt., R.G.A., 8.8.16; served Europ. War from 1914; Despatches.

SMYTH, W. (D.S.O. L.G. 3.6.19), T/Capt. (A/Major), 122nd Field Co., R.E.; M.C.

SMYTH-OSBOURNE, G. N. T. (D.S.O. L.G. 1.1.17); b. 6.9.77; s. of late J. Smyth-Osbourne, of Ash, Co. Devon, and Eliza Cotton, d. of Col. Prior; m. Gladys, d. of Sir Leslie Porter; educ. Eton; R.M.C., Sandhurst; D.L., Co. Devon; 2nd Lt., Devon. R., 11.5.98; Lt. 9.10.99; Capt. 8.3.02; Major 1.9.15; served S. African War, 1899–1902; Despatches twice; Queen's Medal, 2 clasps; King's Medal, 2 clasps; Europ. War from 1914; served in France and N. Russia, 1914–20; T/Brig.-Gen., Oct. 1918; Bt. Major 3.6.15; Bt. Lt.-Col. 3.6.17; C.B.; C.M.G.

SMYTH-PIGOTT, J. R. W. (D.S.O. L.G. 24.11.15) (Bar, L.G. 1.10.17), Lt.-Col., R.A.F. (see "The Distinguished Service Order" from its institution to 31 Dec. 1915, same publishers).

SMYTHE, R. B. (D.S.O. L.G. 1.1.17), Lt.-Col., N.Z. Signal Corps.

SMYTHE, R. C. (D.S.O. L.G. 1.1.18); b. 10.2.79; s. of Capt. R. A. Smythe and Frances, d. of late Sir A. Bellingham, Bart.; m. Cecile Isabel Caroline, d. of late Major F. Munn; one s.; 2nd Lt., R. Innis. Fus., 7.3.00; Lt. 4.5.01; Capt. 13.1.07; Adjt., R. Innis. Fus., 13.1.07 to 12.1.10; Major 1.9.15; served S. African War, 1900–2; Queen's Medal and 4 clasps; King's Medal and 2 clasps; Europ. War, 1914–18; Despatches; C.M.G.

SMYTHE, R. E. (D.S.O. L.G. 1.2.19), Major, 58th Batt. Can. Inf., 2nd Cent. Ontario Rgt.; M.C.

SNAPE, J. (D.S.O. L.G. 3.6.18), Lt. (A/Major), S. Staffs. R., att. H.A.C.; M.C.

SNELL, A. E. (D.S.O. L.G. 1.1.17), Col., Can. A.M.C.; served Europ. War, 1914–18; Despatches; C.M.G.

SNEPP, E. (D.S.O. L.G. 26.8.18); b. 3.5.86; s. of Rev. E. H. Snepp and Clara Snepp; m. Mildred Sturge, d. of E. A. Hitchens, J.P.; one s.; educ. Rossall; Driver (Voluntary) with Duchess of Westminster's Hospital at Le Touquet; 2nd Lt., A.S.C., Dec. 1914, in France; O.C., 348th Coy. (M.T.), R.A.S.C., July, 1915, England; O.C., 729th Coy. (M.T.), R.A.S.C., Mesopotamia; O.C., No. 1 (M.T.) Column, R.A.S.C., Mesopotamia and Persia; Despatches; Lt.-Colonel, O.C., 369th (M.T.) Coy. R.A.S.C., Fulham.

SNEYD, R. S. (D.S.O. L.G. 1.1.16); b. 1882; s. of late G. E. Sneyd; m. Harriet Rose Mary, d. of E. S. Fursdon; Cdr., R.N., 31.12.14; Capt. 23.4.18; served Europ. War, 1914–18; Despatches; promoted; Croix de Guerre; Legion of Honour; Order of Leopold of Belgium.

SNOW, H. W. (D.S.O. L.G. 3.6.16); b. 10.4.79; 1st com. 2.5.99; Capt. 30.5.04; retired R.W. Kent Rgt. 20.5.14; served Europ. War, 1914–17; R. of O.; Major, R. of O., 1.9.15; Bt. Lt.-Col. 1.1.18; ret. pay with rank of Lt.-Col. in the Army; Despatches; C.M.G.; Legion of Honour.

SNOW, W. R. (D.S.O. L.G. 22.4.18), Lt. (T/Major), R.F.C. (now R.A.F.), S.R.; M.C.

SNOWDON, H. S. K. (D.S.O. L.G. 3.6.18); b. 8.3.79; 2nd Lt., R.A., 23.6.98; Lt. 16.2.01; Capt. 10.2.04; Major, R.G.A., 30.10.14.

SOAMES, A. A. (D.S.O. L.G. 3.6.18); b. 11.6.82; s. of W. A. Soames, of Moor Park, Farnham; m. Marjorie, d. of Richard Combe and Lady Constance Combe; educ. Eton; Sandhurst; 2nd Lt., Unatt., 8.1.01; K.R.R.C. 23.3.01; Lt. 23.1.05; Capt. 28.1.13; Major 8.1.16; T/Lt.-Col., 1917; served S. Africa, 1901–2; Queen's Medal and clasps; Europ. War, 1914–18; Salonika Front, 1916–18; commanding 7th Wilts. R., and 3rd K.R.R.C., Russia; having volunteered, was attached as 2nd-in-command, 45th Batt. R.F., in Archangel Relief Force; Despatches.

SOLA, P. (D.S.O. L.G. 21.6.19), Capt., Mercantile Marine; Lt. R.N.R.

SOLE, D. M. A. (D.S.O. L.G. 1.1.17); b. 3.5.83; s. of late Rev. W. A. Sole, Rector of Cruswell, Malmesbury, Wilts, and Mrs. W. A. Sole (*née* Preston). By his first wife he had one d., and married 2ndly Lilian May, d. of R. H. Story; one s. educ. Cheltenham College; 2nd Lt., Worc. R., 19.10.01; Lt. 14.4.04; resigned 12.12.06; Capt., Border R., 7.4.16; Bt. Major 3.6.18; served S. African War; Queen's Medal and 2 clasps; Europ. War; T/Lt.-Col., commanding 10th Batt. Worc. R., 4.7.16 to 12.1.19. His D.S.O. was awarded for commanding Batt. through action at Bazentin-le-Petit 22.7.16, and Despatches for services in 1915 and 1916, and for commanding Battalion through first 10 days of the Somme Battle; owned and hunted a pack of beagles, 1903–6 in Ireland and later in England; well known as a Breeder of Fox Terriers.

SOLLY-FLOOD, R. E. (D.S.O. L.G. 2.5.16); b. 11.12.77; s. of late Sir F. Solly-Flood, K.C.B.; m. Marguerite, d. of late Major Connellan, of Coolmore, Thomastown; one s.; one d.; educ. Eton; ent. Rif. Brigade from Eton 5.4.99; Lt., Rif. Brig., 24.4.00; Capt. 28.7.04; Adjt., Rif. Brig., 15.9.10 to 14.9.13; Major 15.6.15; Colonel 27.1.22; served South African War, 1899–1902; Despatches; Queen's Medal, 5 clasps; King's Medal, 2 clasps; Europ. War from landing at Gallipoli 8.8.15 to evacuation of Helles; Despatches; G.S.O.1; Bt. Lt.-Col. 1.1.17; Bt. Col. 3.6.19; commanded 82nd Brig., 27th Div., Salonika, Jan. 1918; Despatches; C.M.G.; Order of the Serbian White Eagle, 4th Class, with Swords; Officer, Legion of Honour.

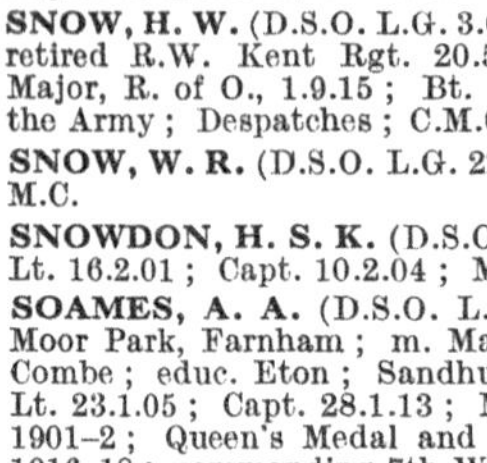

Baron Somers.

SOMERS, BARON (Sir A. H. T. Somers Cocks, Bart.) (D.S.O. L.G. 3.6.19); b. 20.3.87; s. of late Capt. H. H. Somers Cocks, Coldstream Guards, and Blanche Margaret Standish, d. of Major Herbert Clogstoun, V.C., R.E.; 6th Baron; succeeded great-uncle, 1899; m. Daisy Finola, d. of late Capt. B. Meeking; educ. Mulgrave Castle; Charterhouse; New College, Oxford; 2nd Lt., 1st Life Guards, 19.12.08; Lt. 20.12.08; Capt., resigned 21.10.11; Capt. 13.11.14; served Europ. War, 1914–18; Capt. (T/Lt.-Col.), 1st Life Guards, att. Tank Corps; 1914 Star; M.C. His D.S.O. was awarded for commanding a Tank Battalion during the latter stages of the war. Winner, with Hon. J. J. Astor, of Military Doubles Racket Championship, March, 1908.

SOMERSET, H. R. S. F. DE V. (D.S.O. L.G. 18.2.18) (Details, L.G. 18.7.18); b. 3.3.98; s. of H. C. S. A. Somers Somerset; educ. Eton; Sandhurst; 2nd Lt., C. Gds., 20.10.15; Lt. 25.10.15; served Europ. War, att. R.A.F.; Despatches.

SOMERSET, HON. N. F. (D.S.O. L.G. 2.4.19) (Details, L.G. 10.12.19); b. 27.7.83; 2nd Lt., Glouc. R., 3.9.13; Lt. 3.11.14; Capt. 4.6.21; served Europ. War; Despatches; Bt. Major 2.7.21; M.C.

SOMERVAIL, W. F. (D.S.O. L.G. 1.1.18), Capt., The Cameronians (Scottish Rifles); M.C. He was killed in action on 4.10.18.

SOMERVILLE, G. C. (D.S.O. L.G. 1.1.17); b. 1878; m. Brenda Elsie, d. of late J. Holland; one d.; educ. Brisbane Grammar School; Sydney University; Lt.-Col., Staff, Aust. Mil. Forces; served Europ. War, 1914–18; severely wounded; Despatches thrice; C.M.G.

SOMERVILLE, H. F. (D.S.O. L.G. 1.1.17); b. 25.5.81; 2nd Lt., Rif. Brig., 11.8.00; Lt. 5.11.01; Capt. 8.7.08; Major 1.9.15.

SOMERVILLE, H. G. C. (D.S.O. L.G. 11.12.18); s. of late Lt.-Col. T. H. Somerville, D.L., a Crimean Veteran, and Adelaide, d. of the late Admiral Sir Josiah Coghill, 3rd Bart., and g.d. of the late Charles Kendal Bushe, Chief Justice of Ireland. One of Capt. H. G. C. Somerville's sisters is Miss Edith Œ. Somerville (Author, and M.F.H., West Carbery Foxhounds, 1903–8, and again 1912–19). He entered the Royal Navy and became Captain 30.6.14. He was in command of one of the two monitors (H.M.S. Earl of Peterborough) in the Adriatic, where he had some severe fighting, and did excellent work in shelling the bridges over the Piave, for which he was also decorated by the Italian Government.

SOMERVILLE, J. A. H. B. (D.S.O. L.G. 3.6.19); b. 23.3.84; 2nd s. of late Capt. B. A. Somerville; educ. R.M.A., Woolwich; 2nd Lt., R.A., 24.12.02; Lt. 24.12.05; Capt. 30.10.14; Major 13.7.17; served Europ. War from 1914; Despatches.

SOMERVILLE, J. F. (D.S.O. L.G. 14.3.16); b. 1882; s. of A. F. Somerville; m. Mary Kerr, d. of Col. T. Ryder Main; one s.; one d.; ent. R.N., 1898; Commander 31.12.15; served on the Staff of Vice-Admiral de Robeck during the landing of the Mediterranean Expeditionary Force in Gallipoli on 25–26.4.15, and was mentioned in Admiral de Robeck's Despatch; was subsequently appointed to the Vernon.

SOMERVILLE, R. S. (D.S.O. L.G. 18.6.17), Capt., Aust. Inf.; M.C.

SOMERVILLE, W. A. T. B. (D.S.O. L.G. 18.2.15) (Bar, L.G. 26.11.17) (Details, L.G. 22.3.18); Major and Bt. Lt.-Col., R. Lanc. R.

SOMERVILLE, W. J. (D.S.O. L.G. 4.6.17), T/Capt. (A/Major), R.E.

SOMERVILLE-SMITH, H. (D.S.O. L.G. 3.6.19), T/Lt. (A/Major), D/113th Army Brigade, R.F.A.; M.C.

SOMMERVILLE, C. (D.S.O. L.G. 1.1.19), Capt. N.Z. Field Arty.

SOMMERVILLE, F. A. (D.S.O. L.G. 17.4.18), Cdr., R.N., 31.12.18.

SOMMERVILLE, J. A. (D.S.O. L.G. 16.8.17), Capt. 21.1.16, 6th (Manawatu) Mounted Rifles, N.Z. Mil. Forces. His D.S.O. was awarded for gallantry in Egypt on 27.3.17.

SOPPER, E. (D.S.O. L.G. 3.6.19); b. 2.4.86; 2nd Lt., 17th Lancers, 16.8.05; Lt. 4.8.06; Capt. 16.9.13; G.S.O.3, 26th Div., New Armies, Br. Salonika Force, 15.2.16–27.12.16; T/Major, att. 6th Batt. Leic. R., when D.S.O. was awarded; M.C.

SOREL, W. L. (D.S.O. L.G. 4.6.17), T/Major (A/Lt.-Col.), A.S.C. (now R.A.S.C.).

SOTHEBY, H. G. (D.S.O. L.G. 1.1.18); b. 9.11.71; s. of late Admiral Sir E. S. Sotheby, K.C.B.; Lt.-Col., R. of O.; M.V.O.; served S. Africa, 1900–1; Queen's Medal, 2 clasps; Europ. War, 1914–19; commanded 10th Batt. A. and S. Highrs. 1915–19; 1914 Star; French Croix de Guerre.

SOUTER, H. M. W. (D.S.O. L.G. 4.4.16); b. 30.10.72; s. of late Sir F. Souter, K.C.S.I., C.I.E.; educ. Clifton; R.M.C., Sandhurst; joined Manchester R. 18.5.92; Lt., Manch. R., 31.7.95; Lt., I.S.C., 19.12.96; 14th Bengal Lancers, I.A., 1897; Capt. 10.7.01; Major 18.5.10; Lt.-Col. 14.11.16; commanded 1916–20; Colonel Commandant; served Tibet, 1903–4; Despatches; Medal and clasp; N.W.F., 1911; wounded; Despatches; Medal and clasp; N.W. Frontier, 1911; wounded; Despatches; Europ. War, France, Gallipoli, Egypt and Mesopotamia, from 1914; Despatches; C.M.G.; Croix de Guerre avec Palme; commanded 9th Inf. Brig., Waziristan F.F., 1921.

SOUTHAM, L. A. C. (D.S.O. L.G. 4.6.17), Lt.-Col., R.F.A.

SOUTHEY, M. V. (D.S.O. L.G. 3.6.19), Major, 1st Fld. Amb. Aust. A.M.C.

SOUTRY, T. LL. B. (D.S.O. L.G. 1.1.17); b. 23.3.78; 2nd Lt., R. Irish Rifles, 18.10.99; Lt. 1.3.02; Capt. 28.6.08; Major 1.9.15; served S. African War, 1899–1902; Despatches; Queen's Medal with 3 clasps; King's Medal with 2 clasps; Europ. War; Despatches.

SOWERBY, M. E. (D.S.O. L.G. 3.6.16), Capt. (T/Major), R.E.

SOWREY, F. (D.S.O. L.G. 4.10.16); b. at Gloucester 25.8.93; s. of J. Sowrey, Deputy Chief Inspector of Inland Revenue, Somerset House, and of Susan Sowrey (*née* Chambers), of Sandringham; educ. King's College School, Wimbledon; King's College, London University; Caius College, Cambridge; was commissioned in the R. Fusiliers, Aug. 1914; transferred to R.F.C., Jan. 1916; Flight Commander, R.F.C., 1.12.16; became Capt., R.F.C. (as did his two brothers); was promoted to Major, R. Fusiliers, and to Squadron Leader, R.A.F. He served with his regiment in France, July to Dec. 1915; was gassed and slightly wounded in the Battle of Loos, Sept. 1915. His D.S.O. was awarded for the destruction single-handed of Zeppelin L 32, which fell in flames at Billericay, Essex, on the night of 23.9.16. He had been "up" on the night when Cuffley became famous, and his friend Lieutenant Robinson was the first to congratulate him on his success in bringing down the second Zeppelin.

SPAIGHT, T. H. L. (D.S.O. L.G. 3.6.18); b. 7.12.79; s. of Col. W. F. Spaight, retired R.E.; m. Effie, d. of A. Colson, M.I.C.E.; one d.; educ. Malvern; R.M.A., Woolwich; 2nd Lt., R.E., 25.6.99; Lt. 31.12.01; Capt. 25.6.08; Major 22.10.15; served Mohmand Exp., N.W. Frontier of India, 1908; Medal and clasps; Europ. War, 1914–18; 1914–15 Star; Despatches twice.

SPAN, H. J. B. (D.S.O. L.G. 1.1.19); b. 9.9.70; 2nd Lt., Welsh R., 1.3.90; Lt. 6.1.92; Capt. 11.3.00; Major 22.5.07; Lt.-Col. 28.11.16, 1st Batt. Welsh R.; S. African War, 1902; Queen's Medal with 2 clasps; Europ. War; Despatches.

SPARKES, W. M. B. (D.S.O. L.G. 3.6.16) (Bar, L.G. 1.1.18); b. 9.10.72; Lt., R.A.M.C., 29.11.00; Capt. 29.11.03; Major 29.8.12; Lt.-Col. 13.10.18.

SPARKS, H. C. (D.S.O. L.G. 19.8.16); b. 1874; s. of late E. A. Sparks; educ. Repton School; ent. London Scottish (later forming 1/14th Batt. London Rgt., London Scottish), Feb. 1900; 1st com. 20.12.14; Major (2nd-in-command)

5.10.16; seconded and att. Third Army H.Q., France, 2.6.17–9.1.19; Lt.-Col. 2.6.17; trans. to Reserve, Colonel (L.G. 18.7.19); Despatches twice; Mons Star; C.M.G.; M.C.; Croix de Guerre avec Palme. His D.S.O. was awarded for gallantry on 1.7.16, south of Hébuterne.

SPARLING, A. W. (D.S.O. L.G. 26.7.17) (1st Bar, L.G. 2.12.18) (2nd Bar, L.G. 1.2.19), Lt.-Col., 1st Batt. Can. Inf., W. Ontario Rgt.

SPARLING, H. C. (D.S.O. L.G. 4.6.17), Lt.-Col., Can. Inf.

SPARROW A. A. H. HANBURY- (see Hanbury-Sparrow, A. A. H.).

SPARROW, R., F.R.G.S., F.Z.S. (D.S.O. L.G. 15.10.18); b. 10.6.71; s. of late Basil and Julia Sparrow; m. Cecily Mabel. d. of Major B. C. Garfit and widow of Capt. H. P. L. Heyworth, N. Staffs. R.; educ. Wellington College; Sandhurst; 2nd Lt., 7th Dragoon Guards, 12.3.92; Lt. 8.5.95; Capt. 15.4.99; Major 26.8.03; Lt.-Col. 24.12.14; Col. 24.12.18; retired 1920; Remount Dept., S. Africa, 1899–1901; served S. African War, 1899–1902; Despatches; Queen's Medal, 3 clasps; King's Medal, 2 clasps; Europ. War, in France, from 13.10.14 to 11 11.1918; 1914 Star; Despatches twice; C.M.G.; late commanding 7th (Princess Royal's) Dragoon Guards.

SPEEDING, J. H. (D.S.O. L.G. 1.1.19), Major, R.G.A., att. 283rd Siege Battery.

SPEER, F. S. LITCHFIELD (see Litchfield-Speer, F. S.).

SPEIR, K. R. N. (D.S.O. L.G. 3.6.18), T/Lt.-Col., R.E.

SPENCE, G. O. (D.S.O. L.G. 1.1.17); b. 1879; s. of H. G. Spence, J.P.; educ. Uppingham; J.P., N.R. Yorks.; D.L., Co. of Durham; Lt.-Col., 5th Batt. Durham L.I., 1910; Colonel; T.D.; served Europ. War, 1914–18; wounded; Despatches thrice; C.B.

SPENCE, R. (D.S.O. L.G. 15.9.16), Engr.-Cdr., R.N.

SPENCE-COLBY, C. J. H. (gazetted as Spence-Jones, C. J. H.) (D.S.O. L.G. 4.2.18) (Details, L.G. 5.7.18); b. 1873; s. of late Very Rev. H. D. M. Spence-Jones, of Pantglas, Carmarthenshire (assumed by Royal Licence the name of Spence-Colby, 1920); m. Aline Margaret, d. of J. V. Colby, D.L., J.P., of Ffynone, Pembrokeshire; late Capt., Rif. Brigade; one s.; one d.; educ. Harrow; D.L. and J.P., Co. Carmarthen; Lt.-Col. Commanding Pembrokeshire Yeom. from 1914; Colonel 1918; T.D.; served throughout S. African War of 1899–1902; Adjt., 1st M.I., and afterwards as A.D.C. to Inspector-Genl., M.I.; Despatches; Europ. War; commanded Pembrokeshire Yeomanry, also 24th Batt. (Pembroke and Glam. Yeo.), Welsh Rgt.; Despatches four times; C.M.G.

SPENCER, C. L. (D.S.O. L.G. 1.1.18), Lt.-Col., R.E.

SPENCER, F. E. (D.S.O. L.G. 16.9.18); b. 25.7.81; s. of Lt.-Col. C. F. H. Spencer, late R. Innis. Fus., and Emily, d. of late W. Ball; m. Augusta, d. of Col. A. Tracey, late R.A.; one s.; one d.; educ. Dover College; R.M.A., Woolwich; 2nd Lt., R.A., 2.5.00; Lt. 3.4.01; Capt. 22.11.12; Major 30.12.15; served China Exp. Force, 1900–1 (Medal); Tibet F.F. (advance to Lhasa), 1904 (Medal and clasp); Mekran F.F., 1911; served with R.F.A.; Europ. War, 1914–18, in France and Belgium (last 15 months A/Lt.-Col., R.F.A.); Despatches five times; M.C.

SPENCER, G. E. (D.S.O. L.G. 11.1.19); b. 5.4.89; s. of J. F. and Sarah Maria Marion Spencer; m. Irene May Milnes; two s.; educ. Leeds Modern School; Bank Accountant; joined ranks 2/5th Buffs (E. Kent Rgt.); gazetted to K.O. Yorks. L.I. as 2nd Lt.; Captain; served with them as Specialist Battalion Bombing Officer; Brigade Lewis Gun Officer; Platoon Commander; Company Commander; M.C.

G. E. Spencer.

SPENCER, J. (D.S.O. L.G. 2.4.19) (Details, L.G. 10.12.19), T/2nd Lt. (A/Capt.), 17th Batt. R. Fus.; M.M.

SPENCER, J. A. W. (D.S.O. L.G. 11.4.18); b. 1881; m. Eleanor Georgiana, d. of W. Peel; one s.; educ. Harrow; R.M.C., Sandhurst; Lt.-Col., The Rifle Brigade; served Europ. War from 1914; Despatches; C.M.G.; Legion of Honour.

SPENCER, N. (D.S.O. L.G. 8.3.19) (Details, L.G. 4.10.19), Lt.-Col., 31st Inf. Batt. Alberta R., Can. Mil. Forces. He comes from Medicine Hat, and is M.L.A.

SPENCER, R. A. (D.S.O. L.G. 4.6.17); b. 14.12.88; s. of late Lt.-Col. A. C. Spencer; educ. St. Clare, Walmer; Wellington College; R.M.A., Woolwich; appointed to R.F.A. 23.7.09; Lt. 23.7.12; Capt. 23.7.15; Major 2.10.18, R.F.A.; commanded a battery R.F.A. in France, 1916–19; Despatches twice.

SPENCER-PHILLIPS, J. C., M.A. (D.S.O. L.G. 4.6.17); s. of late J. Spencer-Phillips and Mary Spencer-Phillips (*née* Borgnis); m. Hermione Rose Lucas, d. of late Rev. Canon J. Hammond, M.A., LL.B.; two s.; two d.; educ. Winchester; New College, Oxford; J.P., Essex; joined T.F., 1911; Captain, R.A.S.C., T.F.

SPENCER-SMITH, G. M. (D.S.O. L.G. 4.6.17); b. 4.6.81; 2nd Lt., R.A., 19.12.00; Lt. 19.12.03; Capt. 27.1.13; Major, R.H.A., 22.7.15.

SPENCER-SMITH, M. S. (gazetted as Spencer-Smith, M.) (D.S.O. L.G. 1.1.19); b. 1881; s. of Rev. S. C. Spencer-Smith, of Kingston Vicarage, Dorset; m. Penelope, d. of Rev. A. Delmé Radcliffe; two s.; one d.; educ. Eton; New College, Oxford; Partner in H.S. Lefevre & Co., 16 Bishopsgate, E.C.; Director, Bank of England; joined Army, Aug. 1914; served in K.R.R.C., and on Staff of Canadian Corps Heavy Artillery; promoted Lt.-Colonel, and employed as A.A. and Q.M.G., Murmansk, 1918; Despatches; M.C.

SPENDER, W. B. (D.S.O. L.G. 1.1.19); b. 6.10.76; 1st com. 18.6.97; ret. R.G.A. 13.8.13; Major, R. of O., 30.10.14; Bt. Lt.-Col. 3.6.17; retired with rank of Lt.-Col., Army; M.C.

SPENS, H. B., B.A., LL.B. (D.S.O. L.G. 1.1.18) (Bar, L.G. 16.9.18); b. 1.1.85; s. of J. A. Spens; m. Margaret Emily, d. of J. A. Black; two s.; one d.; educ. Rugby (Scholar and Head of School); King's College, Cambridge (Scholar); B.A.Cantab.; LL.B. Glasgow; Lt.-Colonel commanding 5th Bn. Cameronians (Scottish Rifles, T.F.); served Europ. War; wounded in Gallipoli; commanded 5th Scottish Rifles in France from Aug. 1917.

SPEYER, A. W. (D.S.O. L.G. 1.1.18), T/Capt., Gen. List, late W. York. R., S.R.

SPICER, F. F. F. (D.S.O. L.G. 2.4.19) (Details, L.G. 10.12.19); b. 25.4.93; 2nd Lt., 12th Lrs., 10.6.14; Lt. 21.9.15; Capt. 21.1.21.

SPICER, L. D. (D.S.O. L.G. 11.1.19); b. 22.3.93; s. of Rt. Hon. Sir A. Spicer, Bart.; m. Iris, d. of late Wm. Pallett Cox; educ. Rugby School; Trinity College, Cambridge; T/Commission in the Army, Sept. 1914; T/Capt., July, 1916; Brig. Major, April, 1918; served Europ. War; M.C. and Bar.

SPICER-SIMSON, G. B. (D.S.O. L.G. 31.5.16); b. 15.1.76, at Hobart, Tasmania; s. of Frederick John Simson and Dora Mary Simson (formerly Spicer); m. Amy Elizabeth, d. of Edmund and Phœbe Baynes-Reed, of Victoria, B.C., Canada; one s.; educ. Ecole Casimir Delavigne, Havre, France; Brudergemeine Schule, Neuwied, Rhine Province, Germany; Stubbington House, England; H.M.S. Britannia 15.10.90; Midshipman, 1892; Sub-Lieut., 1896; Lieutenant, 1898; Lieut.-Comdr., 1906; Acting Comdr., 1915; Commander, 1915; Acting Captain, 1918; served China, 1900 (Medal); Director of Surveys, Gambia, 1910; specially promoted for success in action with the German gunboat Kingani, which was incorporated in H.M. Fleet under the name of Fifi; expression of appreciation of services from the Lords Commissioners of the Admiralty and High Commissioners of S. Africa for successfully bringing armed boats to Lake Tanganyika, Jan. 1916, and a like expression of appreciation for the capture of the Kingani. He received also an autograph letter from the Governor-General of Belgian Congo, thanking him for the great services which he rendered to the Colony and the Allied cause; served as Assistant Director of Naval Intelligence and Naval Delegate to the Peace Conference, Paris; created Commandeur de l'Ordre de la Couronne, and awarded the Croix de Guerre by H.M. the King of the Belgians; F.R.G.S; F.R.C.I.

SPICKERNELL, F. T. (D.S.O. L.G. 15.9.16); b. 21.12.85; s. of F. Spickernell; educ. King's School, Canterbury; ent. Navy, 1903; Paymaster Commander; Secretary to Rear-Admiral, Commanding 1st Battle Cruiser Squadron, 1913–14; to Vice-Admiral Commanding Battle Cruiser Fleet, 1914–16; was appointed Secretary to the Commander-in-Chief, Grand Fleet, when Sir David Beatty succeeded Sir John Jellicoe in Nov. 1916; received the C.B., April, 1919.

SPILLER, D. W. L. (D.S.O. L.G. 26.7.17) (Bar, L.G. 16.9.18); b. 2.8.77; 2nd Lt., R.A., 1.9.97; Lt. 1.9.00; Capt. 10.10.04; Adjt., R.A., 20.4.05 to 28.11.06; Major 30.10.14; Lt.-Col., R.F.A., 25.3.18; served S. African War, 1899–1902; Queen's Medal with 5 clasps; King's Medal with 2 clasps; Europ. War; Despatches. His D.S.O. was awarded for gallantry on 5–6.6.17, near Ypres.

SPINKS, C. W. (D.S.O. L.G. 1.1.17); b. 9.11.77; s. of J. C. Spinks, of Victoria, B.C.; m. Marguerite Stuart, d. of R. H. Coleman, of Toronto; three d.; 2nd Lt., R.A., 28.3.00; Lt. 3.4.01; Capt. 4.2.09; Major 30.10.14; Lt.-Col., Royal Field Artillery, 20.9.16; Director of Ordnance Services, Egyptian Army; served N. Nigeria, 1903; Kano-Sokoto Campaign (Despatches; Medal with clasp); again 1903–4, operations in the Bassa Province against the Okpotos (Despatches; clasp); Sudan, 1912, against Bier and Annak tribes (Medal with clasp); Europ. War, 1914–18; Gallipoli and Egypt; served in Hedjar-Arab Forces, 1916; Despatches; E.E.F., 1918; O.B.E. He has the Order of the Nile, 4th Class.

SPITTLE, G. H. (D.S.O. L.G. 4.6.17), T/Major, R.E. (late R.M.).

SPONG, C. A. T. (D.S.O. L.G. 3.6.19); b. 1.10.93; 2nd Lt., R.A., 19.12.13; Lt. 9.6.15; Capt., R.G.A., 3.11.17.

SPOONER, A. H. (D.S.O. L.G. 18.2.15) (Bar, L.G. 26.7.18), Major and Bt. Lt.-Colonel, Lanc. Fusiliers; C.M.G. (see "The Distinguished Service Order," from its institution to 31.12.15, by same publishers).

SPOONER, C. C. (D.S.O. L.G. 25.8.16); b. 27.11.91, at Aldershot; s. of Major W. B. Spooner (deceased), A.V.D., and Mrs. W. B. Spooner, of Lockeridge, Marlborough, Wilts; m. Madoline Wish, d. of W. Holland, D.L., J.P.; one s.; educ. Felsted School and R.M.C.; 2nd Lt., Essex R., 20.9.11; joined the 2nd Batt. (Pompadours) at Bordon; Lt. 2.5.12; Capt. 6.5.15; proceeded with Bn. to France on 30.5.15 During the summer of 1915 the 12th Div. held the line east of Ploegsteert until relieved on 26 Sept., when it took part in the fighting at Loos and in particular the attack on the Hohenzollern Redoubt and the Quarries near Hulluch on 13 Oct.; promoted Temp. Major 16.10.15; served continuously with Bn. as Adjutant, being in the line at Givenchy and east of Vermelles in turn during winter 1915–1916; moved to Somme area in June, 1916, and took part in opening stages of the Somme Battle at Ovillers-La Boiselle until invalided to England on 7.7.16; from 29.9.16 to 20.8.18 was Officer of Coy. of Gentleman Cadets at the R.M.C.; rejoined Expeditionary Force, France, on 12.9.18; twice mentioned in Despatches.

SPOONER, E. J. (D.S.O. L.G. 21.6.19); b. Winchester 22.8.87; s. of J. D. Spooner; educ. West Downs, Winchester; H.M.S. Britannia; ent. R.N.; Midshipman, Jan. 1903; Lt.-Cdr. 30.1.17.

SPOWERS, A. (D.S.O. L.G. 22.12.16); 2nd Lt., E. Lanc. R., S.R.; M.C.

SPRENGER, L. F. (D.S.O. L.G. 26.11.17) (Details, L.G. 6.4.18); b. 13.11.92, at St. Mark's, Cape Colony, S. Africa; s. of Major C. F. Sprenger, Cape Mounted Rifles (killed in action, Siege of Wepener, S. African War, 1899–1902), and Mary Ellen Sprenger; educ. South African College School, Cape Town; Lord Williams' School, Thame, Oxon; Sandhurst; joined S. African Military Forces, 13.11.13; Major, S. African Infantry, 1.12.14; M.C.

SPREULL, A. (D.S.O. L.G. 4.6.17); b. 10.8.77; s. of Andrew Spreull, F.R.C.V.S., and Jeanie Harvey Spreull; m. Effie, d. of J. M. Andrew; eight children; educ. Dundee High School; New Veterinary College, Edinburgh; R. Veterinary College, London; Trooper, Fife and Forfar Yeomanry, 1.6.97; served S. African War; Despatches; Queen's Medal, 4 clasps; 2nd Lt., R.A.V.C., T.F., 18.6.04; Capt., June, 1909; Lt.-Colonel; served in France and Belgium, Aug. 1915–April, 1919; D.A.D. of Veterinary Supplies, 5th Division; A.D.V.S., 8th Corps; Despatches twice.

A. Spreull.

SPRING, F. G. (D.S.O. L.G. 18.7.17); b. 25.7.78; s. of late Col. F. W. M. Spring, R.A.; m. Violet Maud, d. of A. C. Turnbull; educ. Blundell's School, Tiverton; 2nd Lt., Linc. R., 7.5.98; Lt. 3.1.00; Adjt., Linc. R., 16.11.04 to 15.11.07; Capt. 5.11.05; Major 16.4.15; Lt.-Col., Lincolns. Rgt.; served S. African War, 1900–2; Queen's Medal and 3 clasps; King's Medal and 2 clasps; Europ. War, 1914–18; Despatches five times; Bt. Lt.-Col. 1.1.18; Brig.-Gen.; C.M.G.

SPRING, T. C. (D.S.O. L.G. 26.11.17) (Details, L.G. 6.4.18); b. 6.2.82; 2nd Lt., Hants R., 3.9.02; Lt. 21.9.04; Capt. 24.3.11; Major 8.1.16; served S. African War, 1900–2; Queen's Medal with clasp; King's Medal with 2 clasps; Aden, 1903; operations in the interior; Europ. War; Despatches.

SPROT, A. W. R. (D.S.O. L.G. 3.6.18); b. 5.1.83; 2nd Lt., A. and S. Highrs., 17.7.01; Adjt., A. and S. Highrs., 1.4.05 to 31.3.08; Lt. 16.7.07; Capt. 4.9.13; Major 17.7.16; served S. African War, 1902; Queen's Medal, 3 clasps; Europ. War; T/Lt.-Col. from Dec. 1916; T/Lt.-Col., Tank Corps, from 9.11.17 to 8.5.19.

SPRY, C. A. N. HUME- (see Hume-Spry, C. A. N.).

SPRY, W. E. HUME- (see Hume-Spry, W. E.).

SPURRELL, W. J., B.A. (D.S.O. L.G. 16.9.18); b. 19.1.93; s. of Dr. W. D. Spurrell; m. Violet, d. of G. A. Tonge; one s.; educ. Gresham's School; Lincoln College, Oxford; Major, late Norfolk R.; M.C.

SPURRIER, G. S. (D.S.O. L.G. 14.1.16), T/Major, A.S.C. (now R.A.S.C.).

SQUIRE, R. H. E. HUTTON- (see Hutton-Squire, R. H. E.).

SQUIRES, E. K. (D.S.O. L.G. 22.12.16); b. 18.12.82, at Poona, India; s. of late Rev. R. A. Squires, formerly Rector of St. Peter, St. Albans, and the late Elizabeth Anne, d. of C. B. Ker; m. Sylvia, d. of late Sir H. Risley, K.C.I.E.; two d.; educ. Eton; R.M.A., Woolwich; 2nd Lt., R.E., 17.1.03; Lt. 21.9.05; Capt. 17.1.14; Major 2.1.18; posted to India, 1905; served for nine years in 3rd Sappers and Miners; served Europ. War with Indian Exp. Force, in France, Oct. 1914–15; wounded at Givenchy, Dec. 1914; with the Mesopotamia Exp. Force, 1916–18; twice wounded; Despatches five times; M.C.; operations against Afghanistan, 1919.

STABLE, R. H. (D.S.O. L.G. 16.8.17); b. 2.8.93; 2nd Lt., Unatt., 22.1.13; 2nd Lt., I.A., 11.3.14; Lt. 22.4.15; Capt. 22.1.17.

STACEY, G. A. (D.S.O. L.G. 14.1.16), Capt., Feb. 1905; T/Major, 2nd (City of London) Batt. The London R. (R. Fusiliers). He was killed in action on 11.10.16.

STACK, G. H. (D.S.O. L.G. 14.1.16); b. 1.8.79; s. of R. Theodore Stack, M.D., F.R.C.S.I. and Charlotte, d. of the late H. Thompson, M.D.; 2nd Lt., R.E., 23.6.98; Lt. 1.4.01; Capt. 23.6.07; Major 26.1.15; S. African War, 1901–2; Queen's Medal with 2 clasps; Europ. War; Despatches; Bt. Lt.-Col. 3.6.17. He went to France Sept. 1914 with the Lahore Div.; served in France and Belgium as Field Engineer 1914-15, being present at 1st and 2nd Battles of Ypres, the Battles of Festubert, Neuve Chapelle and many other engagements. He accompanied his Division to Mesopotamia and took part in the battles which culminated in the capture of Kut and Baghdad. He later accompanied his Division to Palestine and took part in Gen. Allenby's victorious campaign and died in that country 16.9.19.

STACK, W. J. (D.S.O. L.G. 3.6.18), Major, Aust. A.M.C.

STACY, B. V. (D.S.O. L.G. 4.6.17) (Bar, L.G. 1.2.19), Lt.-Col., Aust. Military Forces; served Europ. War, 1915–17; Despatches; C.M.G.

STAFFORD, J. (D.S.O. L.G. 1.1.18), Major, N.Z. Veterinary Corps.

STAFFORD, R. S. H., B.A. (D.S.O. L.G. 20.10.16) (Bar, L.G. 26.7.18); b. 22.2.90; educ. Temple Grove; Haileybury (Scholar); Jesus College, Cambridge (Exhibitioner); B.A. (2nd Class Honours), 1912; Egyptian Civil Service, 1913; K.R.R., 1915; Lt.-Colonel, late K.R.R.; served Europ. War, 1914–18; Despatches four times; M.C.

STAFFORD-MYBURGH, P. (see Myburgh, P. Stafford-).

STAIR (J. J.), EARL OF (D.S.O. L.G. 30.1.20); b. 1.2.79; s. of 11th Earl and Susan Harriett, d. of Sir J. Grant-Suttie, 6th Bart.; m. Violet Evelyn, d. of Col. Harford; four s.; two d.; educ. Harrow and Sandhurst; 2nd Lt., Scots Guards, 16.2.98; Lt. 11.10.99; Capt. 17.6.03; Major 24.1.14; Lt.-Col. (retired), Scots Guards; served S. African War, 1900–2; Queen's Medal with 5 clasps; King's Medal with 2 clasps; Europ. War from 1914; Despatches; J.P., D.L., Wigtownshire; A/Brigadier, R. Company of Archers, King's Bodyguard, Scotland.

STAIRS, P. B. (D.S.O. L.G. 15.2.19) (Details, L.G. 30.7.19), Lt.-Can. F.A.

STALLARD, C. F. (D.S.O. L.G. 8.3.19) (Details, L.G. 4.10.19), T/Major, 23rd Batt. Midd'x R., att. 15th Batt. Hants R.; M.C.

STALLARD, S. F. (D.S.O. L.G. 23.11.16); b. 1873; s. of Major-Gen. S. Stallard; m. Violet Kathleen, d. of Brooke Mockett; one s.; one d.; 2nd Lt., R.A., 11.8.93; Lt. 11.8.96; Capt. 29.6.00; Adjt., R.A., 7.1.05 to 19.1.08; Major 3.7.10; Lt.-Col. 6.2.16; Col. 6.2.20; served S. African War (Queen's Medal); Europ. War; France and Mesopotamia; Despatches twice; C.M.G.; Croix de Guerre; 1914 Star.

STALLARD, S. (D.S.O. L.G. 1.1.18), Capt. (T/Lt.-Col.), London R.

STAMFORD, A. R. (D.S.O. L.G. 1.1.18); b. 9.5.82; m. Grace Madeline, d. of Capt. T. H. Dymoke; two d.; educ. Birkbeck College; Student of Mechanical Engineering till 1905; gained Whitworth Exhibition, 1903; ent. Army 1905; Capt., 1911; Major, R.A.O.C., 10.5.18; A/Inspector of Ordnance Machinery, 1st Class, 8.10.18; served Europ. War, in France, Belgium and Mesopotamia, Aug. 1914 to Nov. 1918; Despatches.

STANBROUGH, L. K. (D.S.O. L.G. 3.6.16); b. 27.8.74; s. of Rev. M. E. Stanbrough; m. Doris, d. of late Major-Gen. T. B. M. Glascock, I.A.; educ. Charterhouse; R.M.A., Woolwich; 2nd Lt., R.A., 17.11.94; Lt. 17.11.97; Capt. 10.10.00; Major 30.10.14; Lt.-Col., R.G.A., 21.2.21; served Europ. War, 1914–16; Despatches.

STANDING, REV. G. (D.S.O. L.G. 8.3.18), Asst. Principal Chaplain and T/C.F., 1st Class; M.C.

STANFORD, A. W. (D.S.O. L.G. 3.6.19), Lt. (A/Major), R.F.A. (S.R.), att. 92nd By. 17th Brig.; M.C.

STANFORD, C. E. C., M.B., B.Sc. (D.S.O. L.G. 1.1.17), Surg.-Cdr. 11.2.15.

STANHOPE (J. R. S.), EARL (D.S.O. L.G. 4.6.17); b. 11.11.80; s. of 6th Earl and Evelyn, d. of late R. Pennefather and Lady Emily Hankey; m. Lady Eileen Browne, d. of 6th Marquess of Sligo; late Capt., G. Gds.; Lt.-Col., R. of O.; late Major, 4th Batt. R. W. Kent R.; T/Lt.-Col. in the Army, 1918–19; served S. African War, 1902; Queen's Medal, 2 clasps; with 1st Batt. G. Gds. in France from Nov. 1914; G.S.O., March, 1915, to May, 1918; Despatches twice; M.C.; Parliamentary Secretary to War Office, 1918.

STANISTREET, H. D. C. (D.S.O. L.G. 8.3.18), Lt.-Cdr., R.N., 15.11.17.

STANLEY, E. A. B. (D.S.O. L.G. 20.2.19); b. 2.9.82; s. of Major E. Stanley, N. Staffs. R.; m. Lilian Gertrude Hunter, d. of J. H. Rodwell; one s.; one d.; educ. H.M.S. Britannia; joined R.N. 15.1.97; Sub.-Lt. 15.1.02; Lt. 31.3.04; Commander, 31.12.17; served China War; Relief of Pekin; medal and clasp; Europ. War, 1914–18; Despatches for evacuation of Helles; Order of the Nile; M.V.O.

STANLEY, F. (D.S.O. L.G. 4.6.17); b. 20.7.71; 2nd Lt., R.A., 1.9.91; Lt. 1.9.08; Capt. 2.3.04; Adjt., R.A., 1.8.11 to 21.3.13; Major 30.10.14; Lt.-Col., R.F.A., 12.12.17; served S. African War, 1899–1901; Queen's Medal with 4 clasps; Europ. War; Despatches.

STANLEY, F. E. C. (D.S.O. L.G. 1.1.19), Major, R.F.A., T.F.

STANLEY, HON. F. W. (D.S.O. L.G. 1.1.17); b. 27.5.78; s. of 16th Earl of Derby; m. Lady Alexandra Louise Elizabeth Acheson, d. of 4th Earl of Gosford; one s.; two d.; educ. Wellington; Sandhurst; late Capt., 10th Hussars; Bt. Lt.-Col., R. of O.; served S. Africa, 1899–1902; severely wounded; Queen's Medal, 6 clasps; King's Medal, 2 clasps; Europ. War, 1914–18; Extra A.D.C. to Viceroy at Delhi Durbar, 1903.

STANLEY, H. P. (D.S.O. L.G. 16.8.17), Capt. (A/Major), Canadian Infy.

STANLEY, J. L. (D.S.O. L.G. 18.7.17), T/2nd Lt., W. Yorks. R.

STANLEY, HON. O. H. (D.S.O. L.G. 1.1.18); b. 23.10.79; s. of 4th Baron Sheffield; m. Lady Kathleen Thynne, d. of the Marquess of Bath; one s.; 1st com. 23.12.98; Capt. 5.12.06; retired R.A. 28.1.14; Major, R. of O., R.A.; Lt.-Colonel; S. African War, 1899–1902; Queen's Medal with 2 clasps; served Europ. War; Despatches.

STANLEY, R. A. (D.S.O. L.G. 3.6.18), Major, Aust. Engrs.

STANLEY, W. A. (D.S.O. L.G. 1.1.18), T/Major, M.G.C.

STANLEY-CLARKE, A. C. L. (D.S.O. L.G. 1.1.18) (Bar, L.G. 26.7.18); b. 30.6.86; 2nd Lt., Sc. Rifles., 6.3.09; Lt. 6.6.10; Capt. 11.3.15; A/Lt.-Col., 1916; T/Lt.-Col., 1916–18, 1918–19.

STANLEY-CLARKE, A. E. (see Clarke A. E. Stanley-).

STANLEY-DAVIES, O. (see Davies, O. Stanley-).

STANNUS, T. R. A. (D.S.O. L.G. 17.9.17), Major (A/Lt.-Col.); S.R. Leins. R. retired. He died of wounds 17.6.17.

STANSFIELD, W. (D.S.O. L.G. 1.1.18), Lt.-Col., Aust. A.S.C.

STANTON, H. A. S. (D.S.O. L.G. 14.1.16); b. 3.3.80; s. of Francis Robert Stanton, Capt., The R. Scots, and Margaret Ann Stanton (*née* Chambers); m. Frances May, d. of Col. Sir W. Foster, 3rd Bart., and Aileen Foster (*née* Portman); two s.; one d.; educ. Radley College; 2nd Lt., Worcesters. Militia, 1898; 2nd Lt., R. Scots, 21.4.00; Lt. 20.2.02; Capt. 8.3.09; T/Lt.-Col., 1916; Major 1.9.15; served S. African War, 1901–2; Queen's Medal with 5 clasps; Europ. War, France, 1915–17, Battles of the Somme and the Ypres Salient; Despatches twice; severely wounded.

H. A. S. Stanton.

STANWAY, W. H. (D.S.O. L.G. 27.7.16) (M.C. cancelled and D.S.O. substituted, L.G. 5.8.16.) (Bar, L.G. 26.1.17); b. 13.8.81; 2nd Lt., R.W.F., 28.10.14; Lt. 21.5.15; Capt. 30.12.16; served Europ. War from 1914; Bt. Major 1.1.18; Bt. Lt.-Col. 3.6.19.

STARNES, F. (D.S.O. L.G. 14.11.16), Major, Canterbury Rgt., N.Z. Mil. Forces; O.B.E.

STAUNTON R. K. LYNCH- (see Lynch-Staunton, R. K.).

STAYNER, R. W. (D.S.O. L.G. 1.1.18), Can. Mtd. Rif.; M.C.

STEARN, J. H. (D.S.O. L.G. 18.7.17), T/Lt., Durham L.I. He was killed in action 3.12.17.

STEBBING, N. A., M.A. (D.S.O. L.G. 1.1.17); b. 14.1.79; s. of W. Stebbing; m. Gladys, d. of Rev. C. de Havilland, Rector of Crux Easton, Hants; one d.; educ. Rugby; St. Andrews University; direct commission into R.F.A. from University, 1900; Major, 1914; served in France, 1916–19.

STEDALL, L. P. (D.S.O. L.G. 18.1.18) (Details, L.G. 25.4.18), Major, Yeomanry

STEEL, F. M. (D.S.O. L.G. 4.6.17), Major, Can. Infy.

STEEL, M. R. (D.S.O. L.G. 3.6.18), T/Capt., North'd Fus.; M.C.

STEELE, A. (D.S.O. L.G. 1.1.17), Major, Aust. M.G.C.

STEELE, J. McC. (D.S.O. L.G. 2.4.19) (Details, L.G. 10.12.19) (Bar, L.G. 1.1.19); b. 9.3.70; s. of late Gen. Sir T. M. Steele, G.C.B.; m. Sybil, d. of W. J. Mure, C.B.; two s.; one d.; educ. Eton; Sandhurst; 2nd Lt., Coldstream Guards, 29.10.90; Lt. 24.6.96; Adjt., C. Gds., 29.12.96 to 28.12.00; Capt. 1.4.99; Major 28.10.06; Lt.-Col. 17.7.15; Colonel 1.1.17; Colonel, Commanding 2nd Guards Brigade; served S. African War, 1899–1901; Despatches twice; Bt. Major 29.11.00; Queen's Medal, 7 clasps; served Europ. War from 1914; Despatches seven times; Bt. Colonel 1.1.17; C.B.; C.M.G.; Croix de Guerre; Croce di Guerra.

STEELE, R. C. (D.S.O. L.G. 17.12.17) (Details, L.G. 23.4.18), 2nd Lt., R.F.C. (now R.A.F.), Spec. Reserve.

STEELE, W. J., M.Inst.C.E. (D.S.O. L.G. 1.1.18); educ. Hendon, Sunderland; Major, R.E.; served Europ. War, 1914–18; Despatches.

STEENKAMP, W. E. (D.S.O. L.G. 22.8.18), Major, Ermelo "B" Commando, S. African Mil. Forces.

STEEVENSON, J. R. (D.S.O. L.G. 3.6.18); b. 1.5.81; s. of late R. H. Steevenson; m. Muriel Theodora, d. of D. A. Quiggin; Lt., A.V.C., 16.5.03; Capt. 16.5.08; Major, R.A.V.C., 10.7.15; served S. African War, 1902; Queen's Medal with 4 clasps; Europ. War; Despatches.

STEIN, O. F. (D.S.O. L.G. 22.6.18), Lt. (A/Capt.), G. Gds.

STENHOUSE, H. W. (D.S.O. L.G. 14.1.16); b. 5.12.79; 2nd Lt., E. Yorks. R., 3.8.98; Lt. 21.10.99; Capt., North'd Fus., 26.3.04; Capt., The Queen's R.W. Surrey R., 20.5.08; Major 1.9.15; served S. African War, 1900–2; severely wounded; Despatches; Queen's Medal with 3 clasps; King's Medal with 2 clasps; Europ. War, D.A.A.G., 5.8.14 to 20.11.14; G.S.O.2 11.10.15. He was G.S.O. Div. H.Q. when he was killed in action on 26.6.16; Despatches.

STENHOUSE, J. R. (D.S.O. L.G. 3.2.20), Lt., R.N.R.; D.S.C.

STENNETT, H. M. (D.S.O. L.G. 14.1.16); b. 2.8.77; s. of late H. J. Stennett; m. Lydia Amy Dorothy, 2nd d. of late J. Robertson-Reid; one d.; Lt.-Colonel Commandant, Rhodesia Police; served S. African War; Queen's and King's Medals, 5 clasps; Chevalier, Order of Leopold II., 1910; Europ. War, in Campaign against German S.W. Africa and German East Africa; Despatches.

STEPHEN, J. H. (D.S.O. L.G. 1.1.19), Major (A/Lt.-Col.), R.A.M.C. (T.F.).

STEPHENS, H. F. (D.S.O. L.G. 3.6.18), T/Major (86th Brig.), R.A.; M.C. He died of wounds on 14.10.18.

STEPHENSON, A. (D.S.O. L.G. 1.1.18), Lt.-Colonel, late 9th R. Scots; fought through Europ. War, 1914–18, and escaped without a wound; Despatches; C.M.G.; M.C.

STEPHENSON, D. C. (D.S.O. L.G. 4.6.17); b. 11.10.87; s. of late Lt.-Col. K. Stephenson, R.H.A.; educ. at Ludgrove; Eton; R.M.A., Woolwich; 2nd Lt., R.F.A., 18.12.07; Lt. 18.12.10; Capt. 30.10.14; Major, R.H.A., Dec. 1917. He went to France in Aug. 1914, and served there till the day of his death. In June, 1917, he was blown up in his dug-out at night, and had severe concussion, but insisted on returning to his battery before he was really recovered. Except for this two months at home he served continuously at the front. He was all through the Retreat from Mons, battles of the Marne and Aisne, the First Battle of Ypres, and took part in almost every important action of the war. Major Stephenson (Z Battery, R.H.A.) was killed instantaneously by a shell on 23.3.18; Despatches twice; M.C.

STEPHENSON, H. K. (D.S.O. L.G. 1.1.18); b. 1865; s. of late Sir H. Stephenson; m. Francis, d. of late Major W. G. Blake, D.L., J.P.; four s.; four d.; educ. Rugby; Lt., 4th W. York Vol. Arty., 1886; transferred to T.F., 1908;

The Distinguished Service Order 347

Lt.-Col. Commanding 4th W.R. (How.) Brig., R.F.A. (T.F.), 1915; served Europ. War, in France and Belgium, 1915–18; Despatches thrice; V.D.; J.P.; LL.D.; M.P. (Co. L.), Park Div. of Sheffield, from 1918; Lord Mayor of Sheffield, 1908–9, and 1910–11; Master Cutler, 1919–20; Pro-Chancellor, University of Sheffield, from 1910.

STEPHENSON, M. B. (D.S.O. L.G. 16.9.18), Capt., 3rd Batt. E. York. R. S.R.; M.C.

STEPHENSON, R. (D.S.O. L.G. 4.6.17), T/Lt.-Col., S. Staffs. R. (formerly North'd Fus.).

STEPHENSON-FETHERSTONHAUGH, A. J. (D.S.O. L.G. 1.1.19), Capt. (T.Major), Worc. R., S.R.; M.C.

STEPNEY, C. C. HERBERT- (see Herbert-Stepney, C. C.).

STERICKER, A. W. (D.S.O. L.G. 1.1.17); b. 4.10.79; 2nd Lt., D.C.L.I., 12.8.99; Lt. 18.11.00; Capt. 16.12.04; Adjt., D.C.L.I., 4.5.10 to 3.5.13; Major 1.9.15; served S. African War, 1899–1902; Despatches; Queen's Medal, 6 clasps; King's Medal, 2 clasps; Europ. War; Despatches.

STERLING, G. P. (D.S.O. L.G. 15.10.18), T/Capt., North'd Fus.; M.C. He was killed in action 27.10.18.

STERNDALE-BENNETT, W. (D.S.O. L.G. 26.1.17) (Bar, L.G. 18.7.17); s. of Rev. J. Sterndale Bennett, for some years Headmaster of Derby School; T/Lt., R.N.V.R. His D.S.O. was awarded for gallantry on 13.11.16, at Beaucourt. He died of wounds on 7.11.17.

STEVEN, J. F., M.B. (D.S.O. L.G. 14.1.16), T/Lt., R.A.M.C.

STEVENS, A. C. J. (D.S.O. L.G. 1.1.17); b. 1.3.75; 2nd Lt., R.E., 17.12.94; Lt. 17.12.97; Capt. 1.4.04; Major 30.10.14; Lt.-Col. 21.7.21; served China, 1900; Medal; Europ. War; Despatches.

STEVENS, C. M. H. (D.S.O. L.G. 1.1.17); b. Gibraltar 26.11.81; s. of Colonel Stevens; m. Dorothea Leila Janvrin; educ. R.M.A., Woolwich; joined R.F.A., 2.5.00; Lt. 3.4.01; Capt. 24.2.10; Adjt., R.A., 1913–14; Adjt., 29th Brig., R.F.A., 1915–17; Major 3.10.14; G.S.O.2, R.A., XIII. Corps, 1917; commanded 46th Brig., R.F.A., 1918; Brig. Major, Lowland (9th) Divl. Artillery.

STEVENS, G. A. (D.S.O. L.G. 14.1.16); b. 23.10.75; s. of Col. G. M. Stevens; educ. Victoria College, Jersey; Eastman's R.N. Academy; Appledurcombe College, I.W.; enlisted R. Scots Greys, 1894; commissioned R. Fus. 2.11.98; Lt. 9.10.99; Capt. 10.9.04; Major 1.9.15; Bt. Lt.-Col. 1.1.17; served W. Africa, 1900; operations in Ashanti; Europ. War; T/Lt.-Col., Dec. 1915, to command 6th Durham L.I.; commanded 2nd Royal Fusiliers from July, 1916, till promoted Brig.-Gen., Nov. 1917, to command 90th Inf. Brig.; Brevet Lieut.-Col. 1917; created C.M.G.; Belgian Croix de Guerre; six times mentioned in Despatches; also Waziristan Field Force, 1920, expedition against Mahsuds.

STEVENS, H. L. (D.S.O. L.G. 2.2.16); b. 7.2.73; 2nd Lt. (from Local Mil. Forces, Natal), R. Berks. R., 19.5.00; Lt. 15.1.02; Adjt., R. Berks. R., 9.8.06 to 3.11.08; Capt., Welsh R., 9.2.10; Major 1.9.15; T/Lt.-Col. 1.10.17; operations in Mashonaland; Medal; S. African War, 1899–1900; Queen's Medal, 2 clasps; Europ. War, Dardanelles, Mesopotamia; Despatches.

STEVENS, H. R. G. (D.S.O. L.G. 1.1.17); b. 4.5.83; 2nd Lt., R.A., 21.12.00; Lt. 1.9.03; Capt. 21.12.13; Adjt., R.H., 16.6.15 to 30.12.15; Major, R.G.A., 30.12.15; Bt. Lt.-Col. 3.6.19.

STEVENS, H. W. (D.S.O. L.G. 12.12.19); b. 19.10.74; 1st com. 7.3.94; Capt. 22.3.02; retired S.W.B. 26.10.12; Major, ret. pay, R. of O., late S.W.B.; served S. African War, 1900–2; Queen's Medal, 3 clasps; King's Medal, 2 clasps; E. Africa, 1902–4; Medal; operations in Somaliland; action at Jidballi; Medal with 2 clasps; Nandi, 1905–6; clasp; E. Africa (Somaliland), 1908–10; clasp; Europ. War; Despatches.

STEVENS, L. M. (D.S.O. L.G. 1.1.17); b. 27.2.80; educ. Winchester; 2nd Lt., Worc. R., 12.8.99; Lt. 21.2.00 Capt. 17.3.03; Adjt., Worc. R., 23.11.04 to 22.11.07; Major 28.7.15; T/Brig.-Gen. 4.6.18 to 13.8.18; Lt.-Col., Worcesters. R.; served S. African War, 1900–2; Queen's Medal and 2 clasps; King's Medal and 2 clasps; Europ. War, 1914–18; Despatches; Bt. Lt.-Colonel 3.6.18.

STEVENS, P. R. (D.S.O. L.G. 5.4.19), Cdr., R.N., 30.6.16.

STEVENSON, D. F. (D.S.O. L.G. 26.7.18), Lt. (T/Capt.), Yeomanry, and R.A.F.; M.C.

STEVENSON, G. H., M.B. (D.S.O. L.G. 4.6.17), Capt., R.A.M.C.

STEVENSON, G. I. (D.S.O. L.G. 1.1.19); b. 8.3.82; s. of George Stevenson and Margaret Ann Stevenson (*née* Ingram); educ. Brunswick College, Brunswick, Melbourne, Victoria; landed in Australia, 1888; served S. African War, 1901–2, as Trooper in Prince of Wales' Light Horse and 4th Batt. Aust. Commonwealth Horse; Queen's Medal, 5 clasps; joined A.I.F. on 15.8.14 as Capt., 6th Battery, Field Artillery, and landed at Cape Helles (Gallipoli) beginning of May, 1915; commanded Battery at end of May; proceeded to Anzac middle of Aug., and commanded 6th Battery there until the evacuation, 1915; returned to Egypt; Lieut.-Colonel; Despatches; C.M.G., 1915; served in France and Belgium, 1916–18.

STEVENSON, H. I. (D.S.O. L.G. 22.6.18) (Bar, L.G. 15.2.19) (Details, L.G. 30.7.19), Lt.-Col., Fort Garry Horse, Can. Mil. Force.

STEVENSON, P. H. (D.S.O. L.G. 1.1.17), Capt. (A/Lt.-Col.), K.O.S.B., S.R.

STEVENSON, W. S., M.A. (D.S.O. L.G. 3.6.19); b. 21.3.92; s. of late W. S. Stevenson; m. Mary June, d. of D. Angus, of Chile; one s.; educ. George Watson's College; University of Edinburgh; graduated with Honours, 1914; served Europ. War; A. and S. Highrs. and G.S.; T/Major, Gen. List; Despatches four times; M.C.; French Croix de Guerre.

STEWARD, C. K. (D.S.O. L.G. 1.1.18); b. 12.9.92; 2nd Lt., S.W.B., 20.9.11; Lt. 11.3.14; Capt. 9.10.15; G.S.O.3, 1st Army, B.E.F., Br. Armies in France, 5.1.16 to 24.6.16; G.S.O.3, 2nd Div., Br. Armies in France, 25.6.16 to 10.9.16; Brig. Major, 143rd Inf. Brig., Br. Armies in France, 11.9.16 to Aug. 1917; M.C.

STEWART, A. C. (D.S.O. L.G. 27.6.19); b. Bangalore, 27.12.72; s. of late Gen. Sir R. C. Stewart, K.C.B.; educ. Marlborough; R.M.C., Sandhurst; gazetted 52nd Oxfords. L.I., 27.1.92; transferred to Q.V.O. Corps of Guides 21.3.93; Capt. 10.7.01; Major 27.1.10; Lt.-Col. 27.1.18; Lt.-Colonel, Commanding Q.V.O. Corps of Guides, Cavalry; served Burma, 1892 (Medal and clasp); Chitral Relief Force, 1895; Medal and clasp; N.W. Frontier, India, 1897–98; clasp; S. African War; Queen's Medal and 3 clasps; Europ. War, 1914–18, France, Gallipoli, Egypt, Palestine and Mesopotamia; Despatches three times.

STEWART, A. E. (D.S.O. L.G. 1.1.17), Lt.-Col., N.Z. Rifle Brigade.

STEWART, A. F. (D.S.O. L.G. 23.10.19); b. 9.4.79; 2nd Lt., Unatt., 25.1.99; I.S.C. 12.4.00; Lt., I.A., 12.12.02; Capt. 25.1.08; Major 1.9.15; Lt.-Col. 28.9.18.

STEWART, A. J. (D.S.O. L.G. 26.9.17) (Details, L.G. 9.1.18), Capt., R. Highrs.

STEWART, A. L. (D.S.O. L.G. 1.1.18); s. of James Stewart, Solicitor, of Donegall Street, Belfast; T/Major, M.G.C. He was killed in action on 4.10.17.

STEWART, B. H. SHAW- (see Shaw-Stewart, B. H.).

STEWART, C. J. T. (D.S.O. L.G. 14.11.16) (Bar, L.G. 11.1.19), Major, P.P.C.L.I.

STEWART, D. (D.S.O. L.G. 1.1.17); b. 23.11.75; s. of Major A. F. Stewart, 6th Dragoons; m. 1st, Mabel Elizabeth Ponsonby (who died 1913); two d.; 2nd, Eileen Cecilia Ponsonby; one s.; 2nd Lt., R.A., 26.7.99; Lt. 16.2.01; Capt. 3.3.08; Major 30.10.14; Lt.-Colonel 1.1.21; served W. Africa (N. Nigeria), 1901; Despatches; W. Africa (S. Nigeria), 1901–2; Aro Exp. Medal with clasp; Europ. War, 1914–18; Despatches.

STEWART, D. B. (D.S.O. L.G. 3.6.16); b. 19.11.71; 2nd Lt., R.A., 25.7.90; Lt. 25.7.93; Capt. 13.2.00; Major 1.4.08; Lt.-Col. 13.2.15; Brig.-Gen., R.A. 66th Div., Br. Armies in France, 13.6.17 to 11.9.17.

STEWART, F. N., M.D. (D.S.O. L.G. 26.7.18), T/Capt., R.A.M.C.; M.C.

STEWART, HUGH, M.B. (D.S.O. L.G. 4.6.17); b. 15.4.81; Lt., R.A.M.C., 31.7.05; Capt. 31.1.09; Major (T/Lt.-Col.), att. 94th F.A.; M.C. He was killed in action 12.4.18.

STEWART, HUGH (D.S.O. L.G. 4.6.17) (Bar, L.G. 1.1.18); b. 1884; s. of late Rev. J. Stewart; m. Alexandrina Kathleen (who died in 1920); d. of W. Johnston; one s.; educ. Fettes College, Edinburgh; Edinburgh University; Trinity College, Cambridge; Professor of Classics, Canterbury College, University of N. Zealand; volunteered with the N.Z. Forces, Aug. 1914, as Lt. in Canterbury Rgt.; became Colonel; in Gallipoli, April–Dec. 1915 (M.C.; Croix de Guerre with Palm); went to France, April, 1916; commanded 2nd Batt. Canterbury Rgt., N.Z.E.F., 1916–18.

STEWART, H. A. (D.S.O. L.G. 1.1.18), Major, Can. A.S.C.

STEWART, JAMES CAMPBELL (D.S.O. L.G. 1.1.17) (Bar, L.G. 19.11.17) (Details, L.G. 22.3.18), Lt.-Col., Aust. Infantry.

STEWART, JAMES CROSSLEY (D.S.O. L.G. 3.6.18), Lt.-Col., Can. F.A.

STEWART, JOHN (D.S.O. L.G. 3.6.19); b. 21.5.69; 1st com. 22.11.02; ret. R. Highrs. 21.5.14; Major, R. of O., 29.1.17; T/Lt.-Col., R. Highrs.

STEWART, JOHN (D.S.O. L.G. 30.1.20), Lt., H.L.I., S.R., att. 16th Batt.

STEWART, J. H. (D.S.O. L.G. 30.1.20); s. of A. Y. Stewart, M.D., of Waterford; m. Nan, d. of J. M. Dickson; late Capt., 15th Batt. R. Ir. Rifles; M.C.

STEWART, J. L., M.B. (D.S.O. L.G. 26.7.18), T/Capt., R.A.M.C.; M.C.

STEWART, J. M. Y. (D.S.O. L.G. 1.1.18), Lt.-Col., Aust. A.M.C.

STEWART, J. S. (D.S.O. L.G. 1.1.17); b. Brampton, Ontario, 8.5.77; m. Jean Chesney M'Clure; educ. Brampton Public and High Schools; Honour Graduate, Trinity University, Toronto; served as Private, Strathcona's Horse, S. Africa, 1900–1; Queen's Medal, 4 clasps; appointed O.C., 7th Brig., C.F.A., 10.3.15; came to France, Jan. 1916; wounded in France; C.M.G.; Despatches; Croix de Guerre; Brig.-Ben., Dec. 1917; C.R.A., 3rd Can. Div.

STEWART, P. D. (D.S.O. L.G. 27.10.17) (Details, L.G. 18.3.18); b. 11.9.76; 2nd Lt., S. Lanc. R., 20.5.99; G. Highrs. 4.11.99; Lt. 10.10.00; Capt., G. Highrs., 1.1.06; Adjt., G. Highrs., 1908–11; Capt., 3rd Dn. Gds., 2.10.12; served S. African War, 1899–1902; Queen's Medal with 4 clasps; King's Medal with 2 clasps; Europ. War; Despatches.

STEWART, R. D. FALCONAR- (see Falconar-Stewart, R. D.).

STEWART, W. M. (D.S.O. L.G. 1.1.18); b. 27.8.75; s. of J. R. Stewart, M.A.; m. Frances Alice Debnam, d. of late Maj.-Gen. Collis, C.B., Col., 21st Punjabis; two s.; one d.; educ. Charterhouse; 2nd Lt., W. Riding R., 28.9.95; Cam'n Highrs. 4.12.95; Lt. 19.5.98; Capt. 6.6.00; Major 12.2.15; served Nile Exp., 1898; Battle of the Atbara; Egyptian Medal with clasp; Medal; S. African War, 1900–2; twice slightly wounded; Despatches; Queen's Medal with 3 clasps; King's Medal with 2 clasps; Europ. War; Despatches three times; Bt. Lt.-Col. 3.6.19; C.M.G.

STEWART, W. N. (D.S.O. L.G. 4.6.17); s. of late J. Stewart, at one time Member for Greenock, and Mrs. Stewart; educ. Evelyn's, Hillingdon; Eton; served with the Lothian and Border Horse through the S. African War; Despatches; Queen's Medal with 5 clasps. He left his ranch in British Columbia on hearing that war was declared and joined his Yeomanry at Haddington. After some months he went to the front as second-in-command of an Indian Cavalry Rgt. Later he was transferred first to the N. Somerset Yeomanry, and later to the North'd Fusiliers; in July, 1917, he was given command of a battalion of the Leicesters. Rgt. He was present at the 2nd Battle of Ypres, at Loos, where he was wounded, and on other of the chief battlefields since. Lt.-Col. W. N. Stewart was killed in action on 22.3.18. His brother, Colonel Ian Stewart, C.M.G., D.S.O., wrote: "They tell me his battalion worshipped him and all mourn his loss."

STEWART, W. P. (D.S.O. L.G. 14.1.16); b. 1887; s. of C. G. Stewart, J.P., of Davo, Fordown; m. Jessie Edith, d. of late Cdr. T. E. Cochrane, R.N.; one s.; one d.; educ. Stonyhurst; R.M.C., Sandhurst; joined 1st H.L.I., 1907; Capt., 1915; served in India and in Europ. War in Egypt, Sept.–Oct. 1914; then in France; Brig. Major, 193rd Brig., serving in England from May, 1916, to Feb. 1917. He returned to the Western front until April, 1918, when he was wounded a second time; Brig. Major, 201st Inf. Brig., Nov. 1917–Oct. 1918.

STEWART, W. R. (D.S.O. L.G. 1.1.18); b. 7.2.88; 2nd Lt., Rif. Brig., 24.6.08; Lt. 3.3.11; Capt. and Bt. Major (T/Lt.-Col.), Rif. Brig.; M.C. He was killed in action on 8.4.18.

STEWART-DAWSON, N. G. (D.S.O. L.G. 18.11.19), Fl.-Lt., R.A.F.; D.S.C.

STEWART-RICHARDSON, N. G. (D.S.O. L.G. 11.4.18); b. 23.10.81; s. of Sir J. T. Stewart-Richardson, 14th Bart., late Capt., Seaf. Highrs; Major (A/Lt.-Col.), late N. Irish Horse; served S. African War, 1901–2; Medal, 5 clasps; Europ. War.

STEYN, P. (D.S.O. L.G. 14.11.16); b. 1890; educ. S. African College, Cape Town; Capt., 8th Bedfordshire Rgt. At outbreak of war joined Gen. Botha's forces and served through the German S.W. African Campaign; then joined B.E.F., France; severely wounded on the Somme. His D.S.O. was awarded for gallantry at Guillemont on 15.9.16.

STEYN, W. H. (D.S.O. L.G. 22.8.18), Major (T/Lt.-Col.), 14th Dismounted Rifles (Karroo Schutters), S. African Mil. Forces.

STIBBARD, C. C. (D.S.O. L.G. 21.1.20), Lt. (T/Lt.-Col.), Can. Inf., Manitoba R.

STICKNEY, J. E. D. (D.S.O. L.G. 2.4.19) (Details, L.G. 10.12.19), Capt. (A/Major), 2/4th Batt. York and Lancaster R., T.F.; M.C.

STIDSTON, C. A. A., M.D. (gazetted as Stidson) (D.S.O. L.G. 4.2.18) (Details, L.G. 5.7.18), Major (T/Lt.-Col.), R.A.M.C.

STILLWELL, W. D. (D.S.O. L.G. 26.7.18) (Bar, L.G. 3.6.18); b. 7.6.81; 2nd Lt., R.A., 6.1.00; Lt. 3.4.01; Capt. 11.4.08; Adjt., R.A., 1.10.11 to 29.10.14; Major 30.10.14; Lt.-Col., R.F.A., 24.6.21.

STILWELL, W. B. (D.S.O. L.G. 17.4.16); b. 2.4.80; s. of late J. P. Stilwell, J.P.; m. Blanche, d. of late W. Lipscomb, J.P.; one s.; one d.; educ. Eton; Magdalen College, Oxford; Lt.-Col., 4th Hants Rgt.

STIRKE, H. R. (D.S.O. L.G. 18.2.18) (Details, L.G. 18.7.18), T/Major, R. Dublin Fus.

STIRLING, A. D., M.B., Ch.B., D.P.H. (D.S.O. L.G. 1.1.18); b. 8.6.86; s. of late Rev. A. Stirling; educ. Arbroath High School; University College, Dundee; St. Andrews University; ent. R.A.M.C. 30.1.09; Capt. 30.7.12; Major 30.1.21; served Europ. War, France and Italy, 1914–19; wounded; Despatches four times; M.C.; Portuguese Military Order of Avis.

STIRLING, C. R. H. (D.S.O. L.G. 1.1.18) (Bar, L.G. 18.2.18) (Details, L.G. 18.7.18); b. 3.2.94; 2nd Lt., Sc. Rifles, 5.2.13; Lt. 15.9.14; Capt. (A/Lt.-Col.), 2nd Batt. Sc. Rifles; M.C. He died in hospital at Rouen on 29.5.18, of wounds received on 24.3.18.

STIRLING, J. A. (D.S.O. L.G. 4.2.18) (Details, L.G. 5.7.18); b. 20.9.81; e. s. of late P. Stirling, of Kippendavie, and Margaret Mary, d. of Rear-Admiral J. Leith.; Lt.-Col.; Bt. Major, R. of O., Scots Guards; retired; M.C.

STIRLING, W. (D.S.O. L.G. 1.1.17); b. 15.3.76; 2nd Lt., R.A., 1.3.96; Lt. 21.3.99; Capt. 8.1.02; Adjt., R.A., 28.5.06 to 21.10.06; 19.9.07 to 3.2.08 and 10.11.08 to 20.10.11; Major 26.8.12; Lt.-Col. 30.12.16; Col., R.F.A., 30.12.20; Despatches; C.M.G.

STIRLING, W. A. (D.S.O. L.G. 1.1.18); b. 5.8.83; s. of late Gen. Sir William Stirling, K.C.B., Colonel-Commandant, R.A.; m. Louie, d. of late J. V. Faber, K.C.D., Consul-General for Denmark; one s.; one d.; educ. Wellington College; R.M.A., Woolwich; commissioned in R.F.A. 24.12.02; Lt. 24.12.05; Capt. 30.10.14; Major 24.4.16; seconded to S. Nigeria Rgt., W.A.F.F., 1907–9; took part in Niger-Cross River Exp.; Adjt., 3rd N. Mid. Brig., R.F.A. (T.), 1912–15; proceeded to France, Feb. 1915; commanded Battery, 18th Div., Oct. 1915, to Feb. 1917; Brig. Major, R.A., 18th Div., Feb. 1917–March, 1919; Army of the Rhine, March–April, 1919; Despatches; M.C.

STIRLING, W. F. (D.S.O. L.G. 28.1.02) (Bar, L.G. 8.3.19) (Details, L.G. 4.10.19), Major, R. of O., R. Dublin Fus.; M.C. (see "The Distinguished Service Order," from its institution to 31.12.15, by same publishers).

STIRLING-COOKSON, C. S. (D.S.O. L.G. 1.1.19); b. 24.3.87; 2nd Lt. (from S.R.), K.O.S.B., 16.12.08; Lt. 1.4.11; Capt. 3.5.15; Despatches; M.C.

STITT, A. D. (D.S.O. L.G. 1.1.18), Major, N.Z. Inf.; M.C.

STITT, W. H. (D.S.O. L.G. 16.9.18), T/Capt., R. Irish Fus., att. R. Dublin Fus.; M.C.

STOBART, H. M. (D.S.O. L.G. 1.1.18), Capt. (Hon. Lt.-Col.), T/Lt.-Col., Yeomanry.

STOCKDALE, G. V., M.B. (D.S.O. L.G. 25.11.16); b. 21.10.87; s. of late T. Stockdale; educ. Leeds Grammar School; Leeds University; gazetted Lieut., R.A.M.C. (S.R.), 7.8.14; Capt. 1.4.15; A/Major 4.1.18–12.2.19; demobilized 30.4.20, and granted rank of Major; served continuously with 11th Div. from 28.8.14–12.2.19, and was present at all the engagements in which the Division took part; i.e., the landing at Suvla, 6–7.8.15; also the evacuation of Suvla (acting at that time as O.C., 24th Fd. Amb.); in Egypt, Feb.–July, 1916, on Suez Canal Defences; in France and Belgium, July, 1916–Feb. 1919; Battles of Somme, 1916; 3rd Battle of Ypres, 1917; in Battles north of Cambrai and up to the Armistice in 1918; Despatches. His D.S.O. was awarded for gallantry and devotion to duty 26.9.16 to 2.10.16, at Thiépval.

STOCKINGS, G. M. (D.S.O. L.G. 1.1.19), T/Major (A/Lt.-Col.), Yorks. L.I.

STOCKLEY, C. H. (D.S.O. L.G. 23.10.19); b. 12.2.82; 2nd Lt., Unatt., 8.5.01; Ind. Army 6.11.02; Lt. 10.10.04; Capt. 8.5.10; Major, 22nd Punjabis, I.A., 8.5.16; served E. Africa (Somaliland), 1908–10; Medal with clasp; Europ. War; Despatches; M.C.

STOCKLEY, E. N. (D.S.O. L.G. 1.1.17) (Bar, L.G. 16.9.18); b. 25.9.72; s. of Col. G. W. Stockley, R.E.; m. Elsie Shewell, d. of Lt.-Col. H. F. Cooper, R.M.; three s.; one d.; educ. Wellington College; R.M.A., Woolwich; 2nd Lt., R.E., 24.7.91; Lt. 24.7.94; Capt. 24.7.02; Major 24.7.11; Lt.-Col. 24.9.18; present at Battle of Maizar, 1897, and with Tochi Field Force, 1897 (Indian Frontier Medal with clasp); Europ. War; formed and commanded 77th Field Co., R.E., and served with it in France, July–Oct. 1915; Temp. Lt.-Col., May, 1916; Battle of the Somme, 1916; Battle of Messines Ridge, 1917; served with Italian Exp. Force, Nov. 1917–Feb. 1918; 2nd Battle of the Somme, 1918; T/Brig.-Gen. 19th Corps, June, 1918, and served with that Corps in the final advance of the Allied Armies; Despatches five times; C.M.G.; Légion d'Honneur; Croix de Guerre; Bt. Lt.-Col. 1.1.18; Bt. Col. 3.6.19; T/Brig.-Gen. 6.6.18. His D.S.O. was awarded for services in 1st Battle of the Somme; Bar for services on 24. and 25 March, at Biefvilliers, near Bapaume.

STOCKS, H. L. (D.S.O. L.G. 1.1.17), T/Major, R. Scots; reported as wounded and missing on 1.7.16; was subsequently presumed killed in action.

STOCKS, J. L., M.A. (D.S.O. L.G. 3.3.17); b. 26.10.82; 6th s. of Ven. J. E. Stocks, D.D., Archdeacon of Leicester; m. Mary Danvers, d. of R. D. Brinton, M.D.; one s.; two d.; educ. Rugby; Corpus Christi College, Oxford; T/Lt., K.R.R.C., Nov. 1914; Capt., Feb. 1915; served with 13th (S.) Batt. in France, July, 1915, to Nov. 1916; with No. 19 O.C.B., Pirbright, 1917–18; Oxford University Hockey XI. (Capt., 1904–5); has played Hockey for England. His D.S.O. was awarded for gallantry 13 to 16.11.1916, at Beaucourt.

STOCKWELL, C. V. (D.S.O. L.G. 1.1.18) (Bar, L.G. 2.12.18), Major, Can. F.A.

STOCKWELL, H. (D.S.O. L.G. 27.6.17), Lt.-Cdr. (A/Cdr.), R.N.R., R.D.

STODART, D. E. (D.S.O. L.G. 21.9.18), Capt. (T/Major), R.A.F., D.F.C.

STOKER, H. H. G. D. (D.S.O. L.G. 22.4.19), Lt.-Cdr., R.N.

STOKES, A. M.D., F.R.C.S. (D.S.O. L.G. 1.1.18), T/Capt., R.A.M.C.

STOKES, A. W. (D.S.O. L.G. 11.4.18), Major (T/Lt.-Col.), R.E.; M.C.

STOKES, C. B. (D.S.O. L.G. 3.6.19); b. 27.10.75; 2nd Lt., E. Kent R., 28.9.95; Lt. 28.7.97; Lt., Ind. Army, 7.10.97; Capt. 28.9.04; Major 28.9.13; Bt. Lt.-Col. 3.6.18; Lt.-Col. 28.9.21; served N.W. Frontier of India, 1897–98; Medal, clasp; Europ. War; Despatches; C.I.E.; O.B.E.

STOKES, H. W. P. (D.S.O. L.G. 3.6.18); b. 15.1.78; 2nd Lt., A.S.C., 22.5.00; Lt. 1.6.01; Capt. 1.10.04; Major, R.A.S.C., 30.10.04; served S. African War, 1901–2; Queen's Medal with 3 clasps; Europ. War from 1914; Despatches; Legion of Honour (5th Class).

STOKES, J. G. (D.S.O. L.G. 16.8.17), Capt., London R.; M.C. His D.S.O. was awarded for gallantry near Zillebeke 10–15.6.17.

STOKES, O. M. F. (D.S.O. L.G. 20.2.19), Cdr., R.N., 31.12.16.

STOKES, R. S. G. (D.S.O. L.G. 4.6.17), T/Major, R.E.; M.C.

STOKOE, T. R. (D.S.O. L.G. 1.1.17); b. 5.5.72; 1st com. 17.12.92; Lt.-Col. 17.4.16; retired D.C.L.I. 30.3.19; op. on N.W. Frontier of India, 1897–98; with Tirah Exp. Force; Medal with 2 clasps; S. African War, 1900–2; Queen's Medal with 3 clasps; King's Medal with 2 clasps.

STONE, A. (D.S.O. L.G. 22.6.18); 2nd s. of Edward Stone; T/Lt.-Colonel, Lanc. Fus.; served Europ. War; Despatches. He was killed in action 2.10.18. Col. Stone was a well-known rifle shot. He also played football for Cambridge and for Kent.

STONE, C. R. (D.S.O. L.G. 3.6.18); b. Eton, 19.9.82; s. of late Rev. E. D. Stone; m. Alice, d. of J. Wilson, and widow of W. M. Chinnery; educ. Eton; Christ Church, Oxford; Private, 16th Midd'x., 1914; commissioned 22nd R. Fus., 1915; Major, 2nd-in-command, 1917; A.D.C. to G.O.C., 2nd Div., 1918; Despatches four times; M.C.

STONE, J. H. (D.S.O. L.G. 3.6.18); b. 21.7.79; 2nd Lt., R.A., 26.5.00; Lt. 23.4.02; Capt. 12.4.11; Major, R.A.O.C., 8.12.14; T/Lt.-Col. 5.8.16; S. African War, 1899–1902; Queen's Medal with 2 clasps; King's Medal with 2 clasps.

STONE, P. V. P. (D.S.O. L.G. 1.1.17); b. 29.9.83; s. of P. G. Stone and Frances M. B. Stone (*née* Powys); educ. Blundell's; Sandhurst; 2nd Lt., Norfolk R., 18.1.02; joined 2nd Batt. in S. Africa, 1902; Lt. 28.11.04; Capt. 11.3.09; Bt. Major 3.6.16; Bt. Lt.-Col. 3.6.17; T/Brig.-Gen. 14.2.17; served S. African War; Queen's Medal and 4 clasps; Army Revolver XX., 1904; seconded for service with 2nd N. Nigeria Rgt., W.A.F.F., 1905–10; Munshi and Hadeija Expeditions; O.C., Benue Patrol, 1906 (Medal and clasp); joined 1st Batt. Norfolk Rgt. in Flanders, Nov. 1914; wounded at Hill 60, April, 1915; Despatches; in command of 1st Norfolk Rgt., Dec. 1915–Feb. 1917; Despatches; wounded near Arras, March, 1916; Bt. Major; Despatches, and promoted T/Lt.-Col., June, 1916; Battle of Somme, Longueval, Delville Wood, Falfemont Farm, Morval, July–Oct. 1916; Despatches; Brig.-Gen. Commanding 17th Inf. Brig., Feb. 1917; Battle of Arras, Liévin (wounded April, 1917); Despatches; Bt. Lt.-Col.; Battle of Messines, June, 1917; Third Battle of Ypres, July–Sept. 1917; Despatches; 2nd Battle of the Somme, March–April, 1918; Despatches; C.M.G.; Chevalier, Legion of Honour.

STONE, R. G. (D.S.O. L.G. 17.5.18), Lt.-Cdr., R.N., 31.12.09; 3rd s. of Edward Stone, whose second son, Lt.-Col. A. Stone, was also awarded the D.S.O.

STONE, R. G. W. H. (D.S.O. L.G. 3.6.19); b. 16.1.90; 2nd Lt., R.E., 23.12.09; Lt. 23.1.12; Adjt. 29.9.15 to 16.1.17; Capt., R.E., att. H.Q., 32nd Inf. Brig., 23.12.15; served S. African War, 1902; Queen's Medal; Europ. War; Despatches; M.C.

STONE, W. A. C. (D.S.O. L.G. 16.9.18), T/Capt. (A/Major), R.F.A.; M.C.

STONEY, G. J. L. (D.S.O. L.G. 16.9.18); b. 15.6.84; 2nd Lt., Worc. R., 20.5.05; Lt. 5.2.08; Capt. 22.10.14; M.C.

STONEY, H. H. (D.S.O. L.G. 1.1.18); b. 12.3.86; 2nd Lt., N. Staff. R., 16.8.05; Lt. 11.9.08; Capt. 11.11.14; Europ. War; Despatches; Bt. Major 1.1.19.

STOOKS, C. S. (D.S.O. L.G. 13.2.17); b. 24.11.75; s. of late Rev. C. D. Stooks and Alice Louisa Stooks, d. of late C. Sumner, and g.d. of Bishop Sumner, of Winchester; m. Eileen Alberta, d. of late Col. G. A. Strover, Burma Commission; educ. Cheltenham College; 2nd Lt., S.W.B., 28.9.95; Lt., S.W.B., 8.4.97; transferred to I.A. (20th Madras Inf.), 14.2.99; 5th Light Inf., 1901; Capt. 28.9.04; Major 28.9.13; Lt.-Col. 28.9.21; served in China with 31st Burma L.I., 1901; in Egypt with 62nd Punjabis, 1914–15; in Cameroons, with 5th L.I., 1915–16; in E. Africa with 5th L.I., 1916; wounded.

C. S. Stooks.

STOPFORD-TAYLOR, R., M.B., Ch.M., F.R.C.S.E. (D.S.O. L.G. 4.6.17); b. Liverpool, 7.3.84; s. of late G. G. S. Stopford-Taylor, M.D., and Ann Alice Stopford-Taylor; m. Marion Gertrude, d. of late W. Buckley, J.P.; educ. Epsom College; Liverpool University; Thelwall College Fellow and Holt Fellow in Pathology, Liverpool University, 1910–12; Capt., R.A.M.C., T.F.; mobilized Aug. 1914; Gallipoli 25.4.15 to Jan. 1916; Egypt, Jan.–March, 1916; France, March, 1916–March, 1918; invalided home; Overseas Service all done in the 29th Div., with the 1/1st W. Lancs. Field Amb., R.A.M.C., T.F.; Despatches.

STORDY, R. J. (D.S.O. L.G. 26.6.16), T/Lt.-Col., A.V.C. (now R.A.V.C.).

STOREY, C. E. (D.S.O. L.G. 11.5.17), Temp. Lt., M.G. Corps.

STOREY, H. I. (D.S.O. L.G. 15.2.17) (Bar, L.G. 8.3.19) (Details, L.G. 10.4.19); b. 20.2.79; 2nd Lt., Devon. R., 20.5.99; Lt. 24.2.00; Capt. 19.5.04; Major 1.9.15; T/Lt.-Col. Commanding 9th Batt. Devons. R., 13.9.15 to 20.2.20; S. African War, 1899–1902; Queen's Medal, 6 clasps; King's Medal, 2 clasps; Europ. War; Despatches.

STORK, E. S., M.B. (D.S.O. L.G. 18.6.17). His D.S.O. was awarded for gallantry on 11.4.17, at Monchy.

STORR, H. (D.S.O. L.G. 15.2.17); e. s. of H. Storr; b. 8.7.75; 1st com. 28.9.95; Major 21.1.11; retired Middx. R. 6.3.12; Major (T/Lt.-Col.), R. of O.; served S. African War, 1899–1902; Despatches; Queen's Medal, 6 clasps; King's Medal, 2 clasps; Europ. War; Despatches. Major Storr died of pneumonia, following upon wounds received in action, on 15.8.18.

STORR, L. P. (D.S.O. L.G. 4.2.18) (Details, L.G. 5.7.18), T/Major, L'pool R.

STORRIE, W. (D.S.O. L.G. 18.10.17) (Details, L.G. 7.3.18), 2nd Lt., H.L.I., Spec. Res.

STORY, P. F. (D.S.O. L.G. 1.1.17) (Bar, L.G. 15.2.19) (Details, L.G. 30.7.19); b. 6.5.73, at Meerut, India; s. of Lt.-Col. P. C. Story (late Cameronians) and Emily Priscilla Rebecca Story (*née* Chapman), both deceased; educ. The School, Windermere; Highgate School, and in France and Germany; ent. Army 9.10.14; demobilized with rank of Lt.-Col.; Commanded 96th Field Coy. R.E.; then appointed C.R.E., 50th Div., and finally C.R.E., 6th Corps, after the Armistice; served in France with 96th Fd. Coy., R.E., 20th Div., from July, 1915, to April, 1918, and was with them in Laventie Area in 1915; in Ypres Salient early in 1916; the Somme to May, 1917; Salient, July to Oct. 1917; Cambrai, attack and defence, 1917; retreat 5th Army, March, 1918; as C.R.E., 30th Divn. in advance of 2nd Army in Sept. 1918; C.R.E., Corps Troops, 6th Corps, Cologne, early in 1919.

STOURTON, HON. E. P. J. (D.S.O. L.G. 1.1.17); b. 24.3.80; s. of 23rd Baron Mowbray; educ. Beaumont; Ampleforth; 2nd Lt., Yorks. L.I., 8.4.00; Lt. 18.3.01; Capt. 4.9.06; Major 1.9.15; Lt.-Col., Yorks. L.I.; served S. African War, 1900–2; Bt. Lt.-Col. 3.6.19; Queen's Medal, 3 clasps; King's Medal, 2 clasps; Europ. War, 1914–18; Despatches five times; wounded twice; M.C.

STOUT, P. W. (D.S.O. L.G. 16.8.17), T/Lt. (A/Capt.), M.M.G.C. His D.S.O. was awarded for gallantry in Egypt 26–27.3.17.

STOUT, T. D. M., M.B., M.S., F.R.C.S. (D.S.O. L.G. 4.6.17); b. 25.7.85; s. of Hon. Sir R. Stout; m. Agnes I. Pearse; educ. Wellington College, N.Z.; Guy's College and Hospital; Lt.-Col., N.Z. Med. Corps; O.B.E.

STRANACK, C. E. (D.S.O. L.G. 1.1.17); b. Rawal Pindi, India, 21.11.82; s. of E. F. and G. E. Stranack (*née* Harington); m. Violet, d. of E. Millar; two s.; educ. Cheltenham College; commissioned 21.12.01; Lt. 21.12.04; Capt. 30.10.14; Major 13.2.16; Lt.-Col., R.F.A.; posted to "O" Battery, R.H.A.

The Distinguished Service Order 349

(Rocket Troop), and went to France with 8th Div., Nov. 1914; Adjt., 33rd Brig., R.F.A., 1915; served on Staff to 1918; Despatches five times; Bt. Lt.-Col. 3.6.18; Belgian Croix de Guerre, 1918; Chevalier, Legion of Honour, 1919.

STRANGE, F. G. (D.S.O. L.G. 3.6.19), Major, 1/1st Berks. Yeom., att. 101st Batt. M.G.C.

STRANGE, J. S. (D.S.O. L.G. 26.9.17) (Details, L.G. 8.1.18), T/Capt., Welsh R.; M.C. His D.S.O. was awarded for gallantry on 31.7.17, and 1 and 2.8.17, at Steenbeck.

STRANGE, L. A. (D.S.O. L.G. 8.2.19); b. 27.7.91; 2nd Lt., Dorset R., 30.7.14; Lt. 23.1.15; Capt. 1.1.17; Lt.-Col., R.A.F.; served Europ. War; Despatches; M.C.; D.F.C.

STRATTON, F. J. M. (D.S.O. L.G. 1.1.17) (third Christian name gazetted Martin for Marrian); b. 16.10.81, at Birmingham; s. of late Stephen Samuel Stratton; educ. King Edward's Grammar School, Five Ways; The Mason University College, Birmingham; Gonville and Caius College, Cambridge 3rd Wrangler, 1904; Isaac Newton Student, 1905; Smith's Prizeman, 1906; Fellow, 1906; Capt. (T.F.), C.U. O.T.C., 1910–14; Signal Service, R.E., 1914–19; Bt. Lt.-Col. (R.E.), 1.1.19; served Europ. War; Despatches five times; Chevalier, Legion of Honour, 1918.

STREATFEILD, G. E. S. (D.S.O. L.G. 4.6.17), T/Capt., R.E.

STREATFEILD, H. S. J. (D.S.O. L.G. 4.6.17); b. 1886; s. of Col. Sir H. Streatfeild, K.C.; m. Dorothy, d. of Sir D. Cooper, 2nd Bart.; one s.; educ. Sandhurst; late Grenadier Guards; Lt.-Col., Commanding 2/23rd Batt. London Rgt.

STREATFEILD-JAMES, R. (D.S.O. L.G. 25.11.16); b. 6.11.90; s. of Charles Streatfeild-James; educ. Berkhamsted; 2nd Lt., E. Surr. R., 5.10.10; Lt. 1.12.13; Capt. 18.3.16; served Europ. War; wounded at Lindenhoek, near Kemmel, 10.3.15, and on the Somme 20.9.15; was in the fighting at Longueval, Delville, Leuze Wood; was wounded in the Capture of Morval, on the Somme, 25.9.16, and died of his wounds 2.10.16. His D.S.O. was awarded for gallantry 25.9.16, at Morval.

STREET, A. H., A.M.Inst.C.E. (D.S.O. L.G. 3.6.18), Major, late R.G.A.; served Europ. War, 1914–18; Despatches.

STREET, F. (D.S.O. L.G. 1.1.19), Maj. (T. Lt.-Col.), 30th Batt. Aust. Mil. Forces.

STREET, H. (D.S.O. L.G. 14.1.16); b. 6.3.80; 2nd Lt., Unatt., 17.1.00; Ind. S.C. 21.3.01; Lt., Ind. Army, 17.4.02; Capt. 17.1.09; transferred to Devons. Regt.; Major 1.9.15; Bt. Lt.-Col. 1.1.18; served on N.W. Frontier of India, Waziristan, 1901–2; Medal, clasp; N.W. Frontier of India, 1902, during operations against Khel Waziris; Europ. War; Despatches.

STRETCH, E. A. (D.S.O. L.G. 22.12.16), Capt., R. Welsh Fus.

STREVENS, H. (D.S.O. L.G. 3.6.18), Capt. (A/Lt.-Col.), R. War. R., employed Devons. R.; M.C.

STRIEDINGER, O. (D.S.O. L.G. 4.6.17); b. 26.4.75; 2nd Lt., R. Berk. R., 20.2.95; A.S.C. 1.1.98; Lt., A.S.C., 1.1.99; Capt. 1.1.01; Major 3.4.12; Lt.-Col., R.A.S.C., 7.11.16; Col. 7.11.20; served S. African War, 1899–1902; Queen's Medal, 5 clasps; King's Medal, 2 clasps; Europ. War; Despatches.

STRINGER, C. H. (D.S.O. L.G. 26.7.18); b. 10.4.86; Lt., R.A.M.C., 29.7.10; Capt. 29.1.14.

STRODE-JACKSON, A. N. S. (D.S.O. L.G. 4.6.17) (1st Bar, L.G. 18.7.17) (2nd Bar, L.G. 13.5.18) (3rd Bar, L.G. 2.12.18), s. of Morton S. Jackson, asst. secretary, Board of Inland Revenue; m. Dora B., d. of late W. A. Mooney, U.S.A.; 2nd Lt. Sept., 1914; T/Lt., Dec. 1914; T/Capt., Sept., 1916; Capt. N. Lancs. Rgt., 1.7.16; A/Lt.-Col., August, 1917; served Europ. War and was wounded. Won the mile for Oxford at University Sports three consecutive years; won 1,500 metre race at Olympic Games, Stockholm, 1912; in 1913 visited America with combined Oxford and Cambridge Athletic team.

STRONG, A. D. (D.S.O. L.G. 14.1.16); b. 10.3.75; s. of late Major-Gen. D. M. Strong, C.B., and M. L. Strong; m. Eleanor Constance, d. of C. S. Colvin, C.S.I.; two d.; educ. Bedford Grammar School; 2nd Lt., Unatt., 16.1.95; Ind. S.C. 27.7.96; Lt. 16.8.97; Capt., I.A., 16.1.04; Major, 10th D.C.O. Lancers, Hodson's Horse, 16.1.13; Lt.-Col., 10th D.C.O. Lancers, Hodson's Horse, I.A., 16.1.21; served N.W.F. of India; Medal and clasp; Europ. War; with Jodhpur Imperial Service Lancers in France from Sept. 1914, to April, 1918, and then in Mesopotamia and in the Afghan operations; Despatches three times; Bt. Lt.-Col. 3.6.18; Despatches (Afghan War); R. Humane Society's Medal; Coronation Medal. His D.S.O. was awarded for counter-attack on German trenches at Festubert.

STRONG, F. E. K. (D.S.O. L.G. 1.1.17) (Bar, L.G. 8.3.18), Cdr., R.N., 30.6.13.

STRONG, G. M. (D.S.O. L.G. 8.3.18), T/Major, Can. Forestry Corps.

STRONGE, H. C. T. (D.S.O. L.G. 3.6.19); b. 24.2.91; 2nd Lt., E. Kent R., 5.10.10; Lt. 8.5.12; Capt. 16.9.15; Capt. (A/Lt.-Col.), E. Kent Rgt., Commanding 7th Batt.; M.C.

STROVER, M. R. (D.S.O. L.G. 1.1.18); b. 17.4.82; 2nd Lt., R.A., 18.8.00; Lt. 17.4.02; Capt. 18.8.13; Major, R.G.A., 30.12.15; served N.W. Frontier of India, 1908; operations in the Mohmand country; engagement of Kargha; Medal with clasp; Europ. War; Despatches.

STRUDWICK, S. G. (D.S.O. L.G. 15.2.19) (Details, L.G. 30.7.19), Lt. (A/Major), R.F.A., S.R., att. B. 78th Brigade; M.C.

STRUTT, E. L. (D.S.O. L.G. 1.1.18); b. 1874; s. of late Hon. A. Strutt; m. Florence Nina, d. of John Hollond; educ. Beaumont College, Windsor; Innsbruck University; Christ Church, Oxford; Major, R. Scots, S.R.; Lt.-Colonel; served S. African War, 1900–2; Despatches; Queen's Medal and 4 clasps; King's Medal and 2 clasps; Europ. War from 1914; wounded; Despatches four times; C.B.E.; Croix de Guerre with four Palms; Chevalier and Officer of Legion of Honour; Chevalier of Order of Leopold; Officer of Star of Roumania; 1914 Star and clasp.

STUART, B. (D.S.O. L.G. 3.6.19); b. 1.7.87; 2nd Lt., R.A., 14.1.15; Lt. 28.4.17; Lt. (A/Major), D. 77th Brig., R.F.A.

STUART, C. G. (D.S.O. L.G. 8.3.20), Lt.-Cdr., R.N., 1.4.17; D.S.C.

STUART, G. E. M. (D.S.O. L.G. 3.6.19), Lt.-Col., Aust. A.M.C., Cdg. 3rd L.H. Field Amb.

STUART, G. F. (D.S.O. L.G. 4.2.18) (Details, L.G. 5.7.18), Lt., W. Yorks. R.; Despatches.

STUART, G. R. BURNETT- (see Burnett-Stuart, G. R.).

STUART, K. (D.S.O. L.G. 1.1.19), Major, 7th Batt. Can. Engrs.; M.C.

STUART P. VILLIERS- (see Villiers-Stuart, P.).

STUART, R. N. (D.S.O. L.G. 23.3.17), Lt., R.N.R.

STUART, W. (D.S.O. L.G. 29.10.18), Lt., Yeom. and M.G.C.

STUBBER, R. HAMILTON- (see Hamilton-Stubber, R.).

STUBBS, G. C. (D.S.O. L.G. 1.1.17) (Bar, L.G. 17.9.17); b. 19.11.82; 2nd Lt., Suff. R., 10.10.03; Lt. 21.5.06; Adjt. 1.11.09 to 31.10.12; Capt. 2.3.14; Bt. Major 1.1.18; Temp. Brig.-Gen. 17.9.18 to 2.4.19 Major 10.10.18 Bt. Lt.-Col. 3.6.19. His Bar was awarded for gallantry from 14 to 19.6.17, east of Monchy.

STUBBS, J. W. C., M.B., B.Ch., B.A.O. (D.S.O. L.G. 3.6.19); b. 30.5.91; s. of W. C. Stubbs, M.A., and Mary, d. of J. G. Gibbon, LL.D.; educ. Portora, and Trinity College, Dublin; Lt., R.A.M.C., 30.1.14; Capt. 30.3.15; A/Lt.-Col., 1918–19; served throughout Europ. War; Despatches twice; M.C.

STUDD, F. C. R. (D.S.O. L.G. 1.1.18); b. 9.2.81; 2nd Lt., E. Kent R., 11.8.00; Lt. 16.4.03; Capt. 21.10.11; Major (T/Lt.-Col.), E. Kent R.; Aden, 1904; operations in the interior; Europ. War; Despatches. He was killed in action on 13.4.18.

STUDD, M. A. (D.S.O. L.G. 1.1.19); b. 29.9.87; 2nd Lt., R.A., 18.12.07; Lt. 18.12.10; Capt. 30.10.14; Major, R.F.A., 2.12.17; Adjt. 25.9.20 to 31.12.21; served Europ. War; Despatches; M.C.

STUDD, R. G. (D.S.O. L.G. 15.2.19); m. Lady Kathleen Smith, d. of late Earl of Leitrim, and widow of late G. K. Smith, C. Gds.; educ. H.M.S. Britannia; Cordwalles, Maidenhead; Midshipman, 1905; Sub-Lt., 1908; Lt., 1910; Lt.-Commander 30.9.18; qualified as Gunnery Specialist, 1915; Lt.-Cdr., 1918; served Europ. War, Aug. 1914, to Jan. 1915, H.M.S. Agamemnon; Sept. 1915, to Armistice in H.M.S. General Wolfe, a monitor in Dover Patrol; Croix de Guerre.

STUDDERT, R. H. (D.S.O. L.G. 26.11.17) (Details, L.G. 6.4.18); b. 20.11.90; 2nd Lt., R.A., 23.7.10; Lt. 23.7.13; Adjt., R.A., 27.8.14 to 27.10.14; Capt. 23.7.16; Bt. Major 1.1.17; M.C.

STUDHOLME, J., M.A. (D.S.O. L.G. 1.1.17); b. Horarata, N.Z., 10.10.63; s. of J. Studholme, of Merevale, Christchurch, and Auckland, N.Z.; m. 1st, Alexandra, d. of the late Archbishop Thomson, of York; three s.; 2nd, Katherine G., d. of late Sir C. C. Bowen. K.C.M.G.; educ. Christ's College, N.Z.; Christ Church, Oxford; commanded the Ashburton Mounted Rifles (N.Z.), and was 2nd-in-command of the 8th S. Canterbury Rgt.; Major, 1908; Lt.-Colonel; served Europ. War from 1915; A.A.G., N.Z. Exp. Force; C.B.E.

STURDEE, V. A. H. (D.S.O. L.G. 1.1.17); b. 16.4.90; s. of Col. A. H. Sturdee; m. Edith Georgina, d. of F. J. Robins, of Melbourne; one s.; educ. Church of England Grammar School, Melbourne; 2nd Lt., Aust. Engrs. (Militia), 1908; transferred to R. Aust. Engrs. (Regular), 1911; seconded to 1st Aust. Divl. Engrs., Aug. 1914, as Lt. and Adjt.; Capt., Jan. 1915; took part in Landing and Evacuation of Anzac; Major to command 8th Field Coy., R.E., July, 1915; served in Egypt, Sinai and France; G.S., G.H.Q., B.E.F., France, March–Nov. 1918; Bt. Lt.-Colonel; O.B.E.

STURMY-CAVE, W. (see Cave, W. Sturmy-).

STURROCK, W. D., M.D. (D.S.O. L.G. 11.1.19), Capt. (T/Major), R.A.M.C., T.F.

STURT, M. A. S. (D.S.O. L.G. 1.1.18), T/Major, R.A.S.C.

STYLES, A. G., LL.B. (D.S.O. L.G. 19.8.16); b. Winnipeg, 5.10.91; s. of W. G. Styles; educ. St. John's College, Winnipeg; University of Manitoba; ent. Can. Militia, 1908; commissioned in 95th Saskatchewan Rifles, 1913; posted from 95th Sask. Rifles as Lieut. to 28th N.W. Batt. on mobilization, Oct. 1914; served Europ. War, 1914–17; promotion to Major, July, 1916; Despatches twice; Brig. Major, 7th Can. Inf. Brig. His D.S.O. was awarded for gallantry 6.6.16, at Hooge, Belgium.

SUGARS, H. S. (D.S.O. L.G. 26.7.17.), T/Capt., R.A.M.C.; M.C.

SUGDEN, J. E. (D.S.O. L.G. 22.9.16); s. of late R. Sugden; joined R. Irish Rifles as Lt. and Quartermaster, Oct. 1914. A year afterwards he obtained his Captaincy, and later was appointed Adjutant of the battalion. He was killed in action 28.9.16. His D.S.O. was awarded for gallantry north of Thiépval 1–2.7.16. Capt. Sugden was a prominent Rugby Union Football player.

SUGDEN, R. E. (D.S.O. L.G. 3.6.16) (Bar, L.G. 17.12.17) (Details, L.G. 23.4.18); b. Aug. 1871; s. of R. Sugden; m. Norah, d. of W. H. Wayman; two s.; one d.; educ. Marlborough College; retired Feb. 1920, with Hon. rank of Brig.-Gen.; served S. African War with Imp. Yeom. from 1900–2; Europ. War, 1914; Lt.-Col., W. Riding Rgt.; Despatches six times; C.M.G., 1919; played Football for Yorks, 1895–96.

SULIVAN, H. E. (D.S.O. L.G. 15.9.16), Capt., R.N., 30.6.17.

SULLIVAN, G. A. (D.S.O. L.G. 14.1.16); b. 3.3.80; 2nd Lt., Oxf. and Bucks. L.I., 6.12.99; Lt. 11.1.01; Capt. 28.12.08; Major; served S. African War, 1900–2; Queen's Medal with 4 clasps; King's Medal with 2 clasps; Europ. War; Despatches; Bt. Lt.-Col. 3.6.19.

SUMMERHAYES, J. O., M.R.C.S., L.R.C.P. (D.S.O. L.G. 1.1.17); s. of W. Summerhayes, M.D.; b. 1869; m. Lucy Alexa Heathcote, d. of late R. G. Currie; educ. Yarmouth Grammar School; Major, R.A.M.C., T F.; served as Lt.-Col., 1/1st S. Midland Field Arty.; Europ. War, 1914–18; Despatches.

SUMMERS, FRANK (D.S.O. L.G. 1.1.17); served Matabeleland in Charter Coy. Police, 1893; S. Africa in E. Kent Yeom., 1900; Despatches; Medal, 2 clasps; Europ. War, R.N. Div., Belgium and France; Despatches; D.S.C.; Dardanelles, R.N.A.S.; with Tanks, France, 1916–17; Despatches; D.S.O.; Lt., R.M., 1914; Capt. and Adjt., 1915; transferred to M.G.C. Heavy Branch, April, 1916; Major, June, 1916; Lt.-Col., Tank Corps, Nov. 1916. His only child, Midshipman C. H. G. (Jerry) Summers, R.N., H.M.S. Indefatigable, was killed in action on 31.5.16, in the Battle of Jutland.

SUMMERS, FREDERICK, (D.S.O. L.G. 3.6.19), T/Major (A/Lt.-Col.), R.E.; M.C.

SUMPTER, G. (D.S.O. L.G. 24.9.18); b. 19.9.91; 2nd Lt., R.A., 20.7.11; Lt. 20.7.14; Capt., R.F.A., 8.8.16; A/Major 14.3.17; M.C.

SUTCLIFFE, A. W. (D.S.O. L.G. 8.3.19) (Details, L.G. 4.10.19), Capt. (A/Major), 3rd Batt. Border R., att. 1st Batt.; M.C.

SUTCLIFFE, R. D. (D.S.O. L.G. 26.7.18), Capt. (A/Major), London R.

SUTER, R. N. (D.S.O. L.G. 7.8.18), Cdr., R.N., 30.6.18.

SUTHER, P. (D.S.O. L.G. 16.5.16); b. 5.11.73; s. of Gen. C. C. Suther, R.M.A., retired; m. Margaret Russell Hunter; 2nd Lt., R.A., 16.6.93; Lt. 16.6.96; Capt. 1.4.00; Major 15.4.14; Lt.-Col. 1.3.18; Despatches; Bt. Lt.-Col. 1.1.17; C.M.G.; Officier, Order of Leopold; Croix de Guerre (Belgian); Croix de Guerre (French); Chief Instructor, School of Artillery.

SUTHERLAND, A. O. (D.S.O. L.G. 23.10.19); b. 21.12.79; 2nd Lt., Border R., 20.1.00; Lt. 15.11.01; I.A. 17.7.03; Capt. 20.1.09; Major, 22nd Punjabis, I.A., 1.9.15; served S. African War, 1899–1900; Queen's Medal, 4 clasps; Europ. War; Despatches.

SUTHERLAND, D. M. (D.S.O. L.G. 1.2.19), Lt.-Col., W. Ontario Rgt., Can. Mil. Forces, att. 52nd Batt. Can. Inf., Manitoba R.

SUTHERLAND, H. W. (D.S.O. L.G. 3.6.19), T/Major, 7/8th Batt. K.O.S.B.

SUTHERLAND, JAMES, M.I.C.E. (D.S.O. L.G. 1.2.17); s. of late Mackay Forbes Sutherland and Elizabeth, d. of late Capt. W. Campbell, 46th Rgt.; m. d. of late Major H. Dawson; educ. Cooper's Hill; joined Indian Public Works Dept., 1888; volunteered for active service, Aug. 1914; Lt.-Colonel, R.E.; served with E. African Exp. Force, Oct. 1914–March, 1918, and afterwards in Mesopotamia till the end of the war.

SUTHERLAND, JOHN (D.S.O. L.G. 11.1.19), Major, 116th Batt. Can. Inf., 2nd Cent. Ont. R.

SUTHERLAND, R. O. (D.S.O. L.G. 25.8.17); b. 1.10.81; 2nd Lt., Norf. R., 4.12.01; Lt. 28.11.04; I.A. 1.11.05; Capt., 4.12.10; Major 4.12.16.

SUTHERLAND, T. D. (D.S.O. L.G. 26.9.17) (Details, L.G. 9.1.18) (Bar, L.G. 2.4.19) (Details, L.G. 10.12.19), T/Capt., 6th Batt. Lincs. R.; M.C.

SUTTIE, H. F. GRANT- (see Grant-Suttie, H. F.).

SUTTON, A. C. (D.S.O. L.G. 4.6.17), Major, Pioneer Batt. Can. Mil. Forces.

SUTTON, B. E. (D.S.O. L.G. 26.9.17) (Details, L.G. 9.1.18), 2nd Lt. (T/Capt.), Yeomanry and R.F.C. (now R.A.F.); M.C. His D.S.O. was awarded for gallantry between Langemarck and Boisinghe, during July and Aug. 1917.

SUTTON, F., F.R.G.S. (D.S.O. L.G. 3.6.16); b. 4.7.78; s. of late Dr. J. R. H. Sutton; 2nd Lt., R.A., 4.3.99; Lt. 16.2.01; Capt. 13.4.04; Major 30.10.14; A/Lt.-Col. 24.7.17 to 8.11.17; served South African War, 1900–1, with Heavy Artillery; Queen's Medal, 3 clasps; British Mountain Artillery, 1902–4; Adjutant, 2nd South Midland Brigade, R.F.A., 1906–11; British Mountain Artillery, 1911–13; Europ. War, in Royal Field Artillery, April, 1915, France; Ypres Salient, July, 1915, to March, 1916. He was awarded the D.S.O. for operations at Bluff, Feb. and March, 1916; France, March, 1916 onwards; Battles of Somme and Ancre, 1916; operations in France and Belgium, 1917; Member, Army Polo Committee.

F. Sutton.

SUTTON, G. W. (D.S.O. L.G. 26.7.18); b. 10.1.93; s. of late C. W. Sutton; educ. Kersal School; 2nd Lt., 8th Lancs. Fus. (T.F.). from Manchester University O.T.C., Aug. 1914; Lt., 1915; Capt., 1916; Adjt., 8th Lancs. Fus.; served Europ. War, Egypt, 1914–15; Gallipoli, 1915 (wounded); Sinai Peninsula, 1916; France, 1917–18; severely wounded; Despatches.

SUTTON, W. M. (D.S.O. L.G. 1.1.19), Capt. and Bt. Major (T/Lt.-Col), Som. L.I.; M.C.

SUTTON-NELTHORPE, O. (D.S.O. L.G. 1.1.19); b. 5.6.88; 2nd Lt., Rif. Brig., 6.10.06; Lt. 27.10.10; Capt. 5.8.14; T/Lt.-Col. 4.5.18; Europ. War; Bt. Major 1.1.18; M.C.

SVENSSON, R., M.B. (D.S.O. L.G. 1.1.19), T/Capt. (A/Lt.-Col.), R.A.M.C., 102nd Field Ambulance; M.C.

SWABEY, G. T. C. P. (gazetted as Swabey, G. T. C.) (D.S.O. L.G. 14.3.16), Capt., R.N., 30.6.18.

SWAINSON, J. L. (D.S.O. L.G. 3.6.16); b. 22.3.77; 2nd Lt., Lan. Fus.; 6.12.99; Lt. 16.5.00; Capt., Lan. Fus., 14.10.04; D.C.L.I. 20.5.08; Major, served S. African War, 1899–1902; Queen's Medal, 4 clasps; King's Medal, 2 clasps; Europ. War; Despatches. He died of wounds 9.8.16.

SWAN, W. G. (D.S.O. L.G. 1.1.19), T/Major, 2nd Batt. Can. Rly. Troops.

SWANN, H. L. A. (D.S.O. L.G. 1.1.18), T/Major, A.S.C. (now R.A.S.C.).

SWEENY, R. L. C. (D.S.O. L.G. 1.2.17); b. 21.11.78; s. of Col. J. F. Sweeny (retired), and A. M. Sweeny (*née* Fielding); m. Hilda Elmes, d. of late G. Lumgair, Collector of Customs, Mauritius; one s.; two d.; educ. Montreal, Quebec, and R.M. College, Kingston, Ontario, Canada; 2nd Lt., Unatt. List, I.A., 2.8.99; I.S.C. 28.11.00; Lt. 2.11.01; Capt. 2.8.08; Major, S. and T. Corps, I.A., 1.9.15; on field service in Jubaland, B.E. Africa, March–July, 1914; in E. Africa, Oct. 1914–May, 1917; Despatches twice; D.S.O.; M.C.; Egyptian Exp. Force, June–Dec. 1918; operations against Afghanistan, May–Nov. 1919; operations in Waziristan, Nov. 1919–June, 1920; O.B.E.

SWEET, E. H. (D.S.O. L.G. 25.8.17); b. 1.6.71; 2nd Lt., R. Irish Rgt., 9.4.92; Lt., R. Ir. R., 27.3.94; I.S.C. 10.7.96; Capt. 10.7.01; Major 9.4.10; Lt.-Col. 1.1.17; served N.W. Frontier of India, 1897–98; operations on the Samana during Aug. and Sept. 1897; Medal; Tirah, 1897–98; clasp; operations in the Abor country, 1911–12; Medal with clasp; Europ. War; Despatches; C.M.G.

SWEET, F. (D.S.O. L.G. 11.1.19), T/Major, R.W. Fusiliers, att. 13th Batt.

SWEET, R., M.B., Ch.B. (D.S.O. L.G. 22.12.16); b. Lamlash, Isle of Arran, N.B., 12.6.87; s. of J. B. Sweet, J.P.; educ. Rothesay Academy; Glasgow University; commissioned as Lt., I.M.S., 25.1.13; Capt. 1.9.15; served France with Indian Exp. Force, 1914–15; Mesopotamia, 1916–17; Despatches.

SWEET, R. T. (D.S.O. L.G. 19.10.16); b. 27.3.92; only child of late H. E. Sweet and Mrs. Sweet, of Bella Vista, Parkstone Road, Poole; 2nd Lt., Unatt., 6.9.11; I.A. 2.12.12; Lt. 6.12.13; Captain, 2/7th Gurkha Rifles. He died, aged 26.

SWELL, A. E. (D.S.O. L.G. 31.5.16), 2nd Lt. (T/Lt.), 1st Batt. Northamptons. R. His D.S.O. was awarded for gallantry at Maroe 28–29.4.16.

SWEMMER, I. V. (D.S.O. L.G. 22.8.18), Lt.-Col., Botha's Hogevald Ruiters, S. African Mil Forces.

SWENY, W. F. (D.S.O. L.G. 1.1.17); b. 25.6.73; s. of Col. G. A. Sweny, late R. Fus.; m. (1st) Gladys Cole (who died in 1913), d. of late R. H. Metge; two s.; (2nd) Kathleen Prudence Eirene, widow of Capt. W. Blackett, and d. of B. F. Bagenal; educ. Wellington College; Trinity College School; R.M.C., Kingston, Canada; joined R. Fus. 27.9.93; Lt. 4.5.97; Capt. 9.10.99; Major 25.5.10; Bt. Lt.-Col. 3.6.15; Brig.-Gen. retired, 1920; served Egyptian Army, 1902–6; commanded the Arab Batt.; Senior Inspector, Bahr-el-Ghazel, during 1906 incident; commanded 2nd M. Inf., S. Africa, 1911–13; att. Can. Militia, 1914; A.A.G., 1st Can. Contingent, at Valcartier; commanded 2nd S. Lancs. R., 2nd E. Yorks. Rgt., 4th R. Fus. and 61st, 72nd and 41st Inf. Brigades, France; three times wounded; Despatches five times; Bt. Lt.-Col.; C.M.G.; Officier, Légion d'Honneur.

SWIFT, A. E. (D.S.O. L.G. 14.1.16); b. at Quebec, 30.1.70; s. of H. Swift and of Mrs. Swift (*née* Williams); educ. Lennoxville College; joined the Military Forces, Nov. 1899; served S. African War; Despatches twice; Queen's and King's Medals; Europ. War; commanded 2nd Can. Inf. Batt. in France; Brig.-Gen., 14th Can. Inf. Brig., 3.11.16; subsequently served in Liberia. He was formerly a prominent Canadian Athlete.

SWIFT, N. C. (D.S.O. L.G. 26.7.18); s. of Dr. Swift, of Adelaide, S. Australia; educ. St. Peter's College, Adelaide; came to England, April, 1915, and was commissioned in the E. Lancs. R. He went to France, Oct. 1915, and was wounded at Contalmaison in Aug. 1916. Returning to France in Oct. 1916, he was wounded again in Jan. 1917, but went out a third time in Oct. In Dec. he was awarded the M.C. when he was Captain in command of a company, and in the following month he was awarded a Bar. He was severely wounded on 27.3.18, while (as A/Major, att. 2nd Bn. R. Lancs. R.) commanding his battalion in a counter-attack, and died the next day in a casualty clearing station, aged 22.

SWINBURNE, T. A. S. (D.S.O. L.G. 15.3.16); b. 20.12.86; s. of Lt.-Col. Swinburne, R.M.A., and Mrs. Swinburne, of Pontop Hall, Durham, and 23, Eaton Place, S.W.; educ. Rugby and Woolwich; 2nd Lt., R.E., 20.12.05; Lt. 25.6.08; Capt. (A/Major) (2 Field Co.), R.E. He served for six years in the 3rd Sappers and Miners in India, and saw service in the Persian Gulf. Reverting to home service, he was quartered at the Curragh during the spring of 1914, and was one of the officers who chose to risk his commission rather than coerce Ulster. On the outbreak of war he sailed with the first Exp. Force, and had nearly four years' fighting from the Retreat from Mons up till nearly the end of the war. He was killed in action on 1.4.18.

SWINTON, C. W. (D.S.O. L.G. 1.1.18); b. 25.9.72; 2nd Lt., R.A., 23.3.92; Lt. 23.3.95; Capt. 3.1.00; Major 9.11.12; Lt.-Col. 1.5.17; Col. 1.5.21; served N.W. Frontier of India, 1902; operations against the Darwesh Khel Waziris; Europ. War; Despatches; C.M.G.

SWITHINBANK, C. W. (D.S.O. L.G. 3.6.18); s. of the Rev. H. Swithinbank, of Wonston, Hants; Cdr., R.N., 30.6.18.

SWORD, D. C. D. (gazetted as Sword, D. C.) (D.S.O. L.G. 1.1.17); b.4.2.81; s. of late A. B. D. Sword; m. Eileen Edith, d. of Sir W. F. Alexander, Bart.; one s.; joined Lanark Militia, 1900; commissioned Scottish Rifles 11.5.01; Lt. 23.11.04; Capt. 1.2.13; Major 1.9.15; Major, 2nd Sc. Rifles, March, 1916; Brig. Major, Sc. Rifles and Highland L.I. Brigade from 1920; served S. African War; Queen's Medal and 5 clasps; Europ. War; Despatches.

SWORDER, K. F. (D.S.O. L.G. 22.6.17), Lt.-Cdr., R.N.

SYDENHAM, E. V. (D.S.O. L.G. 3.6.18), Major, R. War. R.

SYDNEY-TURNER, C. G. R. (D.S.O. L.G. 3.6.16); b. 22.3.83; s. of Alfred Noxon Sydney-Turner, M.R.C.S., J.P.; m. 1907, Edith Mary, d. of H. W. Bartram, of Melbourne; one s.; educ. All Hallows, Honiton; Clayesmore, Enfield; 2nd Lt., A.S.C., 7.12.01; Lt. 1.1.03; Capt. 10.11.06; Major, R.A.S.C., 30.10.14; Bt. Lt.-Col. 3.6.19; served Europ. War, in Egypt, the Mediterranean, France, Italy, 1914–18; Despatches four times; O.B.E., 1919; Legion of Honour (Officer); the Crown of Belgium (Officer); Belgian Croix de Guerre.

SYER, J. M. (D.S.O. L.G. 1.1.18), Major, Can. F.A.

SYKES, A. C., F.R.G.S., A.M.I.E.E. (D.S.O. L.G. 7.2.18); b. 26.5.91; s. of late A. Sykes; m. Lorna Evelyn, d. of E. Stanier; one s.; educ. Wellington College; R.M.A., Woolwich; 2nd Lt., R.E., 22.12.10; Lt. 21.12.12; Capt. 23.12.16; transferred to Royal Corps of Signals 8.3.21; Despatches five times; O.B.E.

SYKES, A. R. (D.S.O. L.G. 11.1.19), T/Major, L'pool R.; M.C.

SYKES, C. A. (D.S.O. L.G. 4.6.17); b. 21.9.71; 2nd Lt., R.A., 27.7.89; Lt. 27.7.93; Capt. 1.1.00; Major 16.5.06; Lt.-Col. 30.10.14; Brig.-Gen., late R.F.A.; served Uganda, 1900–2; Queen's Medal and 4 clasps; King's Medal and 2 clasps; Europ. War, 1914–18; Despatches; C.M.G.

SYKES, F. B. (D.S.O. L.G. 8.11.15) (Bar, L.G. 11.1.19), Bt. Lt.-Col., R.F.A., T.F. (see "The Distinguished Service Order," from its institution to 31.12.15, by same publishers).

SYME, G. A. (D.S.O. L.G. 4.6.17), T/Capt. (T/Major), R.E.; M.C.

SYMES-THOMPSON, A. H. (D.S.O. L.G. 27.7.18); b. 7.11.76; m. Florisse, widow of Major M. C. Dobson, R.F.A., and d. of Sir H. Sloley; one d.; 2nd Lt., R.A., 22.10.97; Lt. 22.10.00; Capt. 23.1.05; Adjt. 20.6.06 to 7.1.13; Major 3.8.15; served S. African War, 1899–1902; Queen's Medal and 6 clasps; King's Medal and 2 clasps; Europ. War (E. Africa), 1914–18; Despatches.

SYMON, F. (D.S.O. L.G. 4.6.17), Lt.-Col., N.Z. Artillery; served Europ. War, 1914–17; Despatches; C.M.G.

SYMON, J. A. (D.S.O. L.G. 26.9.17) (Details, L.G. 9.1.18), Lt. (A/Capt.), Cam. Highrs.

SYMONDS, G. (D.S.O. L.G. 4.6.17), T/Lt.-Col., R.F.A.

SYMONDS, W. F. J. (D.S.O. L.G. 1.1.18), Major (A/Lt.-Col.), London R. He died of wounds 24.4.18.

SYNGE, M. (D.S.O. L.G. 1.1.17); b. 25.4.81; y. s. of late Joshua Sing, J.P.; m. 1899, Beatrice Ellen, d. of late Sir W. W. Cooper; one s.; three d.; educ. Shrewsbury; Christ Church, Oxford; 2nd Lt., Unatt., 28.11.94; Ind. S.C. 21.2.96; Lt., Ind. Army, 28.2.97; Capt. 28.11.03; Major 28.11.12; Lt.-Col. 28.11.17; served N.W. Frontier of India, 1897–98; Medal with clasp; Tibet, 1903–4; Medal with clasp; operations in the Abor country, 1911–12; Medal with clasp; C.I.E., 1919, for operations in E. Persia; Europ. War, 1914; Despatches twice.

SYNNOTT, A. H. S. HART- (see Hart-Synnott, A. H. S.).

SYNNOTT, W. T. (D.S.O. L.G. 4.6.17); b. 15.7.77; s. of T. Synnott, of Innismore, Co. Dublin; m. Gwendoline Hermione, d. of Capt. Keown-Boyd; educ. Stonyhurst; ent. R.A. 23.12.97; Capt. 17.3.05; retired 28.12.12; Major, R.A., 1915; Bt. Lt.-Col., ret. pay, late R.G.A.; served S. African War, 1899–1902; Queen's Medal, 4 clasps; King's Medal, 2 clasps; Europ. War; Despatches thrice; Bt. Lt.-Col.

SZULEZEWSKI, O. (D.S.O. L.G. 11.8.17), Lt., R.N.V.R. He died 26.10.17.

TABERER, T. C. M. (D.S.O. L.G. 17.12.17) (Details, L.G. 23.4.18), b. at Salisbury, Rhodesia, 17.9.97; s. of H. M. Taberer and Ethel Mary Taberer (*née* Platt); educ. St. Andrew's College, Grahamstown, S. Africa; Clifton College; Trinity College, Oxford; joined the Army 31.3.16; Lieut. 3rd Hampshire Regt. 6.8.16.; A/Captain; D.S.O. awarded for Tower Hamlets, Menin Road, Sept. 26–27th, 1917. The attack was made in a very heavy mist, when direction was very difficult without a compass. Lt. Taberer's Company Commander was killed almost immediately and Lt. Taberer took command. After having captured his first objective, he went on to the final objective and captured it with his Company. He arrived there with forty-five other ranks, and during that night and the next day repelled three counter-attacks; Despatches.

T. C. M. Taberer.

TABUTEAU, G. G. (D.S.O. L.G. 11.1.19); b. 19.10.81; Lt., R.A.M.C., 31.1.05; Capt. 31.7.08; Major 15.10.15; Major (A/Lt.-Col.), No. 1 Field Amb., R.A.M.C.

TAGG, E. J. B. (D.S.O. L.G. 1.1.18); b. 29.8.85; s. of James and Alice Tagg; m. Helen, d. of Robert Morton Findlay, of Johannesburg; 3 d.; educ. Dover College; 2nd Lt., R. Mar., 1.9.04; Lt. 1.7.05; Capt. 1.9.15; Durh. L. Inf. 23.5.18; Bt. Major 3.6.19; served Europ. War; Despatches four times; Croix de Guerre with Palms; Mérite Agricole.

TAILYOUR, J. W. RENNY- (see Renny-Tailyour, J. W.).

TAIT, J. (D.S.O. L.G. 4.6.17), Capt. (T/Major), R. Scots.

TALBOT, C. P. (D.S.O. L.G. 13.9.15) (Bar, L.G. 2.11.17), Cdr., R.N. (see "The Distinguished Service Order," from its institution to the 31st Dec. 1915, same publishers).

TALBOT, D. H. (D.S.O. L.G. 3.6.18); b. 17.6.82; 2nd Lt., Unatt., 8.1.01; 17th Lrs., 8.3.01; Lt. 1.6.04; Capt. 9.5.06; Major 24.2.19; Bt. Lt.-Col. 3.6.19; served S. African War, 1901–2; Queen's Medal, 3 clasps; Europ. War; Despatches; M.C.

TALBOT, G. J. F. (D.S.O. L.G. 4.6.17); b. 6.1.57; 1st commission 25.1.77; Major 20.3.95; retired R.A. 6.1.05; served S. African War, 1900; Despatches (L.G. 10.9.01); Queen's Medal, 2 clasps; Europ. War; Despatches.

TALBOT, H. F. G. (D.S.O. L.G. 14.3.16); b. 24.2.74; s. of Major Henry Charles Talbot (late 43rd Foot); m. Susan Blair Athol, d. of W. Allison; one s.; one d.; educ. Stubbington House; in H.M.S. Britannia; joined R.N., Jan. 1889; Capt. 30.6.14; served in the British Soudan Campaign, 1898; 2 Medals, Khartoum clasp; Despatches; S. African War, in H.M.S. Gibraltar as Flag-Lieutenant to Admiral Sir Arthur Moore, 1901–2; Queen's Medal; Persian Gulf Gun-running Blockade, 1912–13, commanding H.M.S. Perseus; Naval General Service Medal (Persian Gulf clasp); Europ. War; given command of H.M.S. Majestic at the Dardanelles, until she was sunk; in charge of one of the beaches at Cape Helles; Beach Master at Suvla Bay; given command of Swiftsure; Despatches; in 1917 commanded H.M.S. Birkenhead in the North Sea; invalided for six months; in Dec. 1919, was appointed to command the Royal Naval College, Osborne. He died 3.7.20.

TALLENTS, G. E. (D.S.O. L.G. 2.5.16); b. 31.7.83; s. of Geoffrey Tallents; educ. Wellington; 2nd Lt., Lan. Fus., 18.1.02; Lt. 11.3.05; Adjt. 4.5.11 to 3.5.14; Capt. 26.12.14; Major 18.1.17; Europ. War, 1914–18; Despatches twice.

TALLENTS, H. (D.S.O. L.G. 4.6.17), Capt. (T/Major), Yeomanry.

TAMBLYN, D. S. (D.S.O. L.G. 1.1.18), Capt. (T/Lt.-Col.), A.V.C.

TAMPLIN, R. J. A. (D.S.O. L.G. 14.11.16); b. 24.11.81; s. of Robert Tamplin; m. Gladys G., d. of J. G. M'Entagart; two d.; educ. King's Coll., London; joined the 6th Bn. Connaught Rangers, 1914; Adjt.; T/Lt.-Col., Connaught Rangers; Europ. War, 1914–18, in France; Despatches; wounded on Somme; was commanding 9th R. Irish Fus. at cessation of hostilities. His D.S.O. was awarded for gallantry at Guillemont 3.9.16.

TANCRED, T. A. (D.S.O. L.G. 8.3.18); b. 16.7.67; educ. R.M.A., Woolwich; Lt., R.A., 17.2.86; Capt. 15.6.96; Major 13.7.04; Lt.-Col. 25.5.14; T/Brig.-Gen. 18.8.15 to 28.5.18; Bt. Col. 1.1.16; Colonel 25.5.18; T/Maj.-Gen. 7.7.18 to 11.5.19; Major-General 17.8.21; with Bechuanaland Border Police, 1893–1906; served Matabeleland, 1893–94; China, 1900 (Medal); Europ. War, 1914–17; C.B.; C.M.G.

TANDY, E. N. (D.S.O. L.G. 4.6.17); b. 1879; s. of Surg.-Col. E. O. Tandy; m. Brenda Moncrieff, d. of late A. Laing; educ. Wellington, and R.M.A.; served S. Africa, 1899–1902; Despatches; Queen's Medal, 4 clasps; King's Medal, 2 clasps; Europ. War, 1914–18; Despatches; Legion of Honour; Croix de Guerre; C.M.G.; Belgian Croix de Guerre.

TANDY, H. G. H. (D.S.O. L.G. 11.8.17), Lt.-Cdr., R.N.

TANDY, M. O'C. (D.S.O. L.G. 7.2.18); b. 17.11.73; m. Mabel, e. d. of late James Dillon; two s.; two d.; educ. Tonbridge; R.M.A., Woolwich; 2nd Lt., R.E., 25.7.93; Lt. 25.7.96; Capt. 1.4.04; Major 25.7.13; Lt.-Col. 1.1.21; served in Aden Hinterland, 1902–4; Europ. War, 1914–18; Despatches; O.B.E.; Afghan War, 1919.

TANNER, A. G. (D.S.O. L.G. 1.2.19), T/Capt. (A/Lt.-Col.), R. Fus., att. 10th Batt.; M.C.

TANNER, G. (D.S.O. L.G. 2.4.19) (Details, L.G. 10.12.19), Major, 1/7th Batt. W. Riding R., T.F.

TANNER, R. M. (D.S.O. L.G. 22.8.18), Major, 7th Mtd. Brig. (1st Mtd. Rif.), S. African Mil. Forces.

TANNER, W. E. C. (D.S.O. L.G. 1.1.18); b. 1875; m. Isobel Erskine; two s.; educ. Hilton Coll., Natal; Lt.-Col., S. African Inf.; Lt., 1903, Nat. Carbineers; South African War; Queen's and King's Medals; Zululand Rebellion, 1906; German S.W. Campaign, 1915–18; Europ. War; C.B.; C.M.G.

TAPP, J. H. W. (D.S.O. L.G. 15.2.19) (Details, L.G. 30.7.19); b. 19.10.67; 1st commission 16.2.87; Major 19.3.02; Bt. Major 29.11.00; retired R.A. 21.11.03; R. of O., att. H.Q., 230th (N.M.) Brig., R.F.A., T.F.; served S. African War, 1899–1900; Despatches (L.G. 8.2.01; L.G. 10.9.01); Bt. of Major; Queen's Medal, 5 clasps; Europ. War; Despatches.

TARLETON, F. R. (D.S.O. L.G. 15.10.18); b. 24.1.77; 2nd Lt., R. War. R., 21.4.00; Lt. 17.2.01; R. Highrs. 20.5.08; Capt. 15.5.09; Major 1.9.15; served S. African War, 1901–2; Queen's Medal; E. Africa (Somaliland), 1908–10; Medal; clasp; Europ. War; Despatches.

TASSIE, L. G. (D.S.O. L.G. 16.9.18), Major, Aust. A.M.C.

TATE, A. W. (D.S.O. L.G. 1.1.19), Capt. (Temp. Major) (A/Lt.-Col.), Royal Highrs. (Spec. Res.), att. 41st Battn. M.G.C.

TATE, G. W., M.B. (D.S.O. L.G. 1.2.17); b. 20.11.66; educ. Dublin Univ.; commissioned 28.7.91; Colonel, R.A.M.C., 26.12.17; retired 12.11.19; served Sierre Leone, 1898–99; Medal and clasp; S. African War, 1901–2; Queen's Medal and 5 clasps; Europ. War, 1914–18; C.M.G.

TATHAM, F. S. (D.S.O. L.G. 4.6.17), Temp. Major, General List (Lt.-Col.), Reserve of Officers, S. African Defence Forces.

TATTERSALL, E. H. (D.S.O. L.G. 22.4.18); b. 28.2.97; 2nd Lt., 5th D.G., 26.1.16; Lieut. 26.7.17.

TATTERSALL, P. C. P. (D.S.O. L.G. 16.8.17), Capt., London R. His D.S.O. was awarded for gallantry in Egypt 19.4.17. He was accidentally drowned 28.7.17.

TATTERSALL, THE REV. T. N. (D.S.O. L.G. 4.6.17), Temp. Chaplain to the Forces, 2nd Class, Army Chaplains' Dept.

TAUNTON, A. J. S. (D.S.O. L.G. 18.7.17); b. 17.8.88; s. of Capt. R. A. Taunton, M.C.; educ. Cheltenham Coll.; Manitoba University; Major, Can. Inf.; Europ. War, 1916–19; Despatches; wounded.

TAYLER, F. L. (D.S.O. L.G. 8.3.19) (Details, L.G. 4.10.19); b. 1.7.83; m. Kathleen Edythe, d. of H. S. Wildeblood, late P.W.D., India; two s.; educ. Marlborough Coll.; Sandhurst; 2nd Lt., Wilts. R., 22.10.02; Ind. Army 16.7.04; Lt. 22.1.05; Capt. 22.10.11; R.F.C. 13.8.16 to 23.7.17; Major, Ind. Army, 22.10.17; served in Mesopotamia, 1915; France, 1916–17; Baluchistan, 1918; Palestine, 1918–19; Khyber, 1920; Despatches twice.

TAYLER, H. P. B. (D.S.O. L.G. 4.6.17), Temp. Maj., General List (late A.S.C.).

C. L. O. Tayleur.

TAYLEUR, C. L. O. (D.S.O. L.G. 30.3.16); b. 28.4.91; 2nd Lt., R.F.A., 23.12.10; Lt. 23.12.13; Capt. 8.8.16.

TAYLOR, A. C. (D.S.O. L.G. 26.9.16), Temp. 2nd Lt., Midd'x Regt. His D.S.O. was awarded for gallantry 28–29.7.16, near Pozières.

TAYLOR, A. E. (D.S.O. L.G. 3.6.18), Major, Inf.

TAYLOR, A. J. (D.S.O. L.G. 1.2.17), Lt.-Col., S. African Inf.

TAYLOR, B. M. (D.S.O. L.G. 1.1.18), Temp. 2nd Lt. (A/Capt.), D. of Corn.'s L. Inf. He was killed in action 6.11.17; M.C.

TAYLOR, B. W. (D.S.O. L.G. 14.1.16); b. 31.1.81; 2nd Lt., R.A., 2.5.00; Lt. 3.4.01; Capt. 1.4.10; Adjt., R.A., 4.8.13 to 29.10.14; Major 30.10.14. He died on 8.4.16 of wounds received in action 8.3.16.

TAYLOR, C. L. (D.S.O. L.G. 1.1.18); b. 23.10.73; educ. Harrow; 2nd Lt., S.W.B., 7.3.94; Lt. 14.11.96; Adjt. 18.3.97 to 4.11.99; Capt. 21.2.06; Major 1.11.14; Bt. Lt.-Col. 3.6.19; Lt.-Col. 16.11.20; served South African War, 1899–1902; Queen's Medal, 3 clasps; King's Medal, 2 clasps; Europ. War, 1914–18; Despatches.

TAYLOR, C. W. H. (D.S.O. L.G. 1.1.19); b. 1880; m. Margaret Edith Syra, e. d. of Col. H. W. Jameson; one d.; educ. Eton and Cambridge; Major, Royal W. Kent Regt.

TAYLOR, F. A. (D.S.O. L.G. 11.1.19), Lt., Can. Light Horse.

TAYLOR, F. G. (D.S.O. L.G. 18.7.17), Major, Can. Rifles.

TAYLOR, G. J. S. (D.S.O. L.G. 1.1.18); b. 2.1.77; 2nd Lt., R.A., 4.3.99; Lt. 16.2.01; Capt. 5.7.07; Major 30.10.14.

TAYLOR, G. P., M.B. (D.S.O. L.G. 1.1.18) (Bar, L.G. 7.11.18); b. 10.8.86; Lt., R.A.M.C., 30.1.09; Capt. 30.7.12; Major 30.1.21; M.C.

TAYLOR, G. V. (D.S.O. L.G. 3.6.19), Capt., Norf. R., 1.1.21; M.C.

TAYLOR, H. (D.S.O. L.G. 26.7.18), Lieut., Aust. Inf.

TAYLOR, H. B. (D.S.O. L.G. 1.1.18), Major, Aust. F.A.

TAYLOR, H. J. (D.S.O. L.G. 1.1.18); b. 4.5.81; m. Eveleen, 2nd d. of late Major Carter O'Neal; one d.; educ. Wellington; 2nd Lt., Durh. L. Inf., 4.12.01; Lt. 19.10.04; Capt. 21.9.14; Major 4.12.16; served South African War; Queen's Medal, 3 clasps; Europ. War; 1914 Star; Despatches.

TAYLOR, H. J. COX- (see Cox-Taylor, H. J.).

TAYLOR, J. A. C. (D.S.O. L.G. 26.7.18), Capt., Manch. R.

TAYLOR, K. C. C. (D.S.O. L.G. 15.3.16); e. s. of A. Dumbar Taylor, of Vancouver; educ. Royal Military College, Kingston, Canada; Major, 29th Can. Inf. Bn.; served Europ. War. He was killed in action 12.9.16.

TAYLOR, L. M. (D.S.O. L.G. 6.3.19), T/Major, 4th Batt. Yorks. L.I., T.F.; M.C.

TAYLOR, L. R. E. W. (D.S.O. L.G. 3.6.18); b. 18.1.82; 2nd Lt., R.A., 2.5.00; Lt. 3.4.01; Capt. 22.11.12; Major 30.12.15; served Europ. War, R.G.A., 1914–18; Despatches thrice.

TAYLOR, M. G. (D.S.O. L.G. 3.6.16); b. 31.5.81; m. Winifred Anderson, d. of S. J. Thacker; one s.; educ. St. Mark's, Windsor; R.M.A., Woolwich; 2nd Lt., R.E., 2.5.00; Lt. 2.5.03; Capt. 2.5.10; Bt. Major 3.6.16; Major 2.11.16; Bt. Lt.-Col. 3.6.17; T/Brig.-Gen. 26.2.18; Bt. Col. 3.6.19; Col. 17.8.20; Europ. War, 1914–18; Despatches; C.M.G.

TAYLOR, M. ROSS-, M.D. (D.S.O. L.G. 4.6.17), Capt. (A/Lt.-Col.), R.A.M.C.

TAYLOR, N. C. (D.S.O. L.G. 22.12.16); b. 2.12.82; 2nd Lt., R.A., 19.12.00; Lt., R.A., 19.8.03; Ind. Army 3.7.05; Capt. 12.12.09; Major 19.12.15.

TAYLOR, R. STOPFORD-, M.B., F.R.C.S. (see Stopford-Taylor, R.).

TAYLOR, S. C. (D.S.O. L.G. 18.7.17); b. 2.6.72; 1st commission 17.12.92; Capt. 21.10.99; ret. Yorks. L. Inf. 15.7.11; Major (Temp. Lt.-Col.), retired pay, (R. of Off.), Yorks. L. Inf., Spec. Res; Brig.-Gen. (att. Staff), 93rd Inf. Bde.; served during operations on N.W. Frontier of India, 1897–98; Medal, 2 clasps; S. African War, 1899–1902; Despatches; Queen's Medal, 4 clasps; King's Medal, 2 clasps; Europ. War; Despatches. His D.S.O. was awarded for gallantry on 3.5.17, at Gavrelle. He died of wounds 11.10.18.

T. E. H. Taylor.

TAYLOR, S. S. (D.S.O. L.G. 1.2.17); b. 1875; Lt.-Col., S. African F. Artillery; served Europ. War, 1916–18; C.M.G.; Croix de Guerre; Despatches.

TAYLOR, T. E. H. (D.S.O. L.G. 11.1.19); b. 6.7.88; s. of the late Rev. T. Taylor; m. Alexandra Clare, y. d. of late Brabazon Campbell, Esq.; one d.; educ. Tipperary Grammar School; Campbell College, Belfast; 2nd Lt., R. Ir. R., 16.12.08; Lt. 22.12.09; Capt. 11.12.14; Bt. Major 1.1.18; served Europ. War; Despatches four times; Greek Military Cross (2nd Class). His D.S.O. was awarded for gallantry during assault by the 82nd Inf. Bde. on the fortified Roche-Noir Bulgar Salient on 1.9.18; M.C. for the 2nd Battle of Ypres.

N. McD. Teacher.

TAYLOR, T. G. (D.S.O. L.G. 1.1.17); b. 1.3.85; s. of Thomas and Maria Mona Taylor; m. Josephine Margaret, d. of Robert J. Lang; four s.; educ. Harrow and Oxford; 2nd Lt., R. Highrs., 29.8.06; Lt. 6.1.09; Capt., Gordon Highrs., 11.12.14; Bt. Lt.-Col. 1.1.18; served Europ. War, 1914–18; in France 1915-18 with 9th Batt. Gordon Highrs., of which he took command 30.10.16; Battle of Loos, '15, Somme, '16, Arras, '17; 3rd Battle of Ypres; gassed at Arras; wounded; Despatches four times.

TEACHER, N. McD. (D.S.O. L.G. 14.1.16); b. 23.1.78; s. of late Donald Teacher; m. Dorothy, e. d. of late Joseph Hone; one s.; educ. Clifton; Sandhurst; 2nd Lt., R. Sco. Fus., 16.2.98; Lt. 13.11.99; Capt. 12.12.04; Major 1.9.15; served S. African War, 1899–

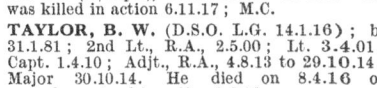

1902; Queen's Medal, 5 clasps; King's Medal, 2 clasps; employed with Egyptian Army, 1904–13; 3rd Class Medjidieh; 3rd Class Osmanieh, being Military Secretary to the Sirdar the last year and half of his service; Europ. War; Despatches four times. He was killed in action 26.9.17.

TEALE, J. W. (D.S.O. L.G. 31.5.16), Temp. Major, R. Mar.

TEALL, G. H. (D.S.O. L.G. 1.1.18); b. 24.10.80; m. Josephine, d. of late Robert C. Burrell, J.P.; two d.; educ. Dulwich Coll., and St. John's College, Cambridge; 2nd Lt., R. Garr. R., 4.2.03; Lt., Linc. R., 15.12.06; Capt. 9.1.14; Major 4.7.18; served Europ. War, 1914–18; Despatches four times; Croix de Guerre.

TEBBUTT, A. H. (D.S.O. L.G. 4.6.17), Lt.-Col., Aust. A.M.C.

TEICHMAN, O., M.A., M.R.C.S.Eng., L.R.C.P.Lond., F.R.G.S. (D.S.O. L.G. 3.6.18); b. 1.11.80; s. of E. Teichman; m. Edith Henrietta, d. of late William Harbord; three s.; educ. Aldenham; Repton; Caius College, Cambridge; St. Bartholomew's Hospital (House Physician); joined R.A.M.C. (T.F.), 1911; served Europ. War, with Worcestershire Yeomanry, 1915, in Egypt and Gallipoli; wounded on Chocolate Hill, Suvla Bay; 1916, Sinai Peninsula; present at Battle of Romani; wounded near Katia; 1917, Palestine; battles of Rafa, Gaza I. and II., Beersheba, Khuweilfe, Sheria (Huj), Balin; advance on Jerusalem; 1918, Palestine, Jordan Valley, Es Salt Raid; also 1918, Italy; present at Battle of Papadopoli, Piave, attached to 22nd Bde., 7th Div.; Despatches thrice; M.C.; Croix de Guerre with Palm; Croce di Guerra, Italy; 1914–15 Star; Winner of Heavy-Weight Race, West Kent Hunt Point-to-Point Steeplechases, 1905 and 1906.

O. Teichman.

TELFER-SMOLLETT, A. P. D. (D.S.O. L.G. 1.1.19); b. 12.8.84; 2nd Lt., High. L. Inf., 9.4.04; Lieut. 1.7.08; Capt. 27.9.14; Bt. Major 3.6.17; Despatches (L.G. 19.10.14); M.C.

TEMPERLEY, A. (D.S.O. L.G. 1.1.17), Major, N. Fus.

TEMPERLEY, A. C. (D.S.O. L.G. 3.6.16); b. 31.8.77; m. Madeline, d. of late Walter Whitehead, F.R.C.S.; educ. Sherborne; Queens' College, Cambridge; 2nd Lt., North'd Fus., 23.5.00; Lt. 2.9.01; Capt. 18.12.07; Capt., Norfolk Regt., 20.5.08; Major 1.9.15; Bt. Lt.-Col. 1.1.18; served S. African War, 1901–2; Queen's Medal, 5 clasps; Mohmand Exp., 1908; Medal; Europ. War, 1914–18; Despatches eight times; Bt. Lt.-Colonel; C.M.G.

TEMPERLEY, E. (D.S.O. L.G. 16.9.18), Major (Lt.-Col.), Northumberland Fus.

TEMPEST, E. V. (D.S.O. L.G. 2.4.19) (Details, L.G. 10.12.19), Lt., 1/6th Batt. W. Yorks. R., T.F.; (Int. Officer), 146th Inf. Brig.; M.C.

TEMPEST, R. S. (D.S.O. L.G. 1.1.17); b. 1876; m. Valerie Arthur, e. d. of late A. L. Glover; educ. at the Oratory School and Stonyhurst Coll.; 2nd Lt., S. Gds., 4.5.98; Lt. 28.3.00; Capt. 12.3.04; Adjt., S. Gds., 1.7.04 to 30.1.07; Regt. Adjt. 3.2.14 to 4.8.14; Major 28.10.14; Bt. Lt.-Col. 3.6.16; Lt.-Col. 15.5.19; Bt. Col. 3.6.19; T/Brig.-Gen. 2.9.17 to 12.6.19; S. Africa, 1900–2; Queen's Medal; King's Medal; Despatches twice; Europ. War, 1914–18; wounded; Despatches five times; Croix de Guerre with Palms; C.M.G.

TEMPEST, W. J. (D.S.O. L.G. 13.10.16); b. 22.1.91; 2nd s. of Wilfrid F. Tempest and his 2nd wife, Florence Helen, o. d. of Vincent L. O'Rourke; educ. Stonyhurst College; H.M.S. Worcester; 2nd Lt., General List, R.F.C.; served Europ. War, 1914–17; Despatches; M.C., 1917. His D.S.O. was awarded for destruction of a Zeppelin at Potters Bar 1.10.16.

W. J. Tempest.

TEMPLE, R. D. (D.S.O. L.G. 1.1.18); b. 27.12.80; s. of Lt.-Col. Sir R. C. Temple, Bart.; m. Katherine Marjorie, d. of F. de la F. Williams; one s.; entered Army, 1900; Col., Worc. Regt.; served S. African War, 1901–2; Queen's Medal, 4 clasps; Europ. War, 1914–18; Despatches.

TEMPLE-GORE-LANGTON, HON. E. A. G. (D.S.O. L.G. 22.2.18); b. 5.4.84; 3rd s. of 4th Earl Temple of Stowe; educ. Stubbington House, and H.M.S. Britannia; ent. Roy. Navy, 1900; Comdr., R.N.; retired 1911; rejoined 1914; served Europ. War, Mine-sweeping Flotilla, 1914–19.

TEMPLETON, C. P. (D.S.O. L.G. 4.6.17), Capt., Can. A.M.C.; C.B.E.

TENISON, W. P. C. (D.S.O. L.G. 1.1.17); b. 25.6.84; e. s. of Col. William Tenison; m. Olive Leonora, d. of late C. L. Mackenzie and Baroness Wesselenyi; two d.; educ. Marlborough, and R.M.A., Woolwich; 2nd Lt., R.A., 15.7.03; Lt. 15.7.06; Capt. 30.10.14; Major 26.6.16; served Europ. War, 1914–17.

TENNANT, J. (D.S.O. L.G. 3.6.18), Capt. (T/Major), S. Lanc. Regt., att. Army Cyclists' Corps.

TENNANT, J. E. (D.S.O. L.G. 3.8.18); b. 12.10.90: m. Georgina Helen, d. of Lt.-Gen. Sir George Kirkpatrick; educ. R.N. College, Osborne, and Dartmouth; Midshipman, 1908; 2nd Lt., Sco. Gds., 1.2.12; Lt., Sco. Gds., 7.8.12; R.F.C. 12.9.14 to 31.3.18; Capt. Sco. Gds., 15.9.15; Bt. Major 10.3.17; Lt.-Col.; served Europ. War, 1914–16; Mesopotamia, 1916–18; Despatches five times; M.C.; Legion of Honour.

TENNANT, M. F. (D.S.O. L.G. 2.12.18), Lt., Scots. Guards, S.R.

TERROTT, C. R. (D.S.O. L.G. 4.6.17) (Bar, L.G. 15.10.18); b. 26.8.78; 2nd Lt., 6th Dns., 2.12.99; Lt. 16.10.00; Capt. 17.3.06; Adjt. 11.8.09 to 11.8.11; Major 12.8.11; Bt. Lt.-Col. 3.6.19; Lt.-Col. 3.11.21; served S. African War, 1900–2; Queen's Medal, 4 clasps; King's Medal, 2 clasps; Europ. War; Despatches.

TERRY, C. H. M. IMBERT- (see Imbert-Terry, C. H. M.).

TERRY, H. B. IMBERT- (see Imbert-Terry, H. B.).

TETLEY, C. H. (D.S.O. L.G. 17.12.17) (Details, L.G. 23.4.18); b. 30.1.77; s. of C. F. Tetley and Alice Margaret Tetley (*née* Atkinson); m. Evelyn Gertrude, d. of Frank Vandeleur; one s.; one d.; educ. Harrow; Trinity College, Cambridge; 2nd Lt. 11.4.96; Lt. 2.12.96; Capt. 7.12.01; Major 9.9.11; Lt.-Col., W. Yorks. R., 1.6.16; served Europ. War; Despatches three times; 1914–15 Star; T.D. His D.S.O. was awarded for services on 9.10.17, at Passchendaele.

TETLEY, F. E. (Christian names gazetted as Frank Eric for Francis Eric) (D.S.O. L.G. 4.6.17), Major, Linc. R.

THACKER, H. C. (D.S.O. L.G. 3.6.18); b. 16.9.70; s. of late Maj.-Gen. Thacker, I.A.; educ. Upper Canada Coll.; R.M. Coll. of Canada; Colonel, R. Can. Art.; served S. Africa, 1899–1900; Queen's Medal, 3 clasps; Russo-Jap. War, 1904–5, att. Japanese Army; Jap. Medal; Order of Sacred Treasure, 4th Class; Europ. War, 1914–18; C.B.; C.M.G.

THACKERAY, C. B. (D.S.O. L.G. 3.6.16); b. 20.12.75; 3rd s. of Sir E. T. Thackeray, V.C., K.C.B.; m. Adeline, o. d. of late William I. Ritchie, Board of Education; one s.; one d.; educ. Dulwich; R.M.A., Woolwich; 2nd Lt., R.A., 2.11.95; Lt. 2.11.98; Capt. 16.11.01; Major 9.5.12; Lt.-Col. 28.8.16; served S. African Campaign (Queen's Medal with 5 clasps), 1901–2; France, with VIIIth Division, Nov. 1914, to Sept. 1915, in command of 5th Battery, 45th Brigade, R.F.A., including Battle of Neuve Chapelle 9 to 13.3.15 (mentioned in Despatches), and actions near Fromelles 9.5.15 (slightly wounded) and 25.9.15, near Bois Grenier (severely wounded; Despatches, June, 1916); returned to duty (home service), Dec. 1916; foreign service, April, 1917; Turkey, 1919–20.

THACKERAY, E. F. (D.S.O. L.G. 25.11.16); b. 1870; s. of Col. Sir E. T. Thackeray, V.C., K.C.B.; m. Linda, d. of late Baron Von Wutzburg; two d.; Lt.-Col., S. African Infantry; served Chitral, 1895; Matabele Rebellion, 1896; S. Africa, 1899–1902; Europ. War, 1914–16; C.M.G.; Croix de Guerre with Palms. His D.S.O. was awarded for gallantry at Delville Wood 18.7.16.

THACKERAY, F. S. (D.S.O. L.G. 1.1.17); b. 25.2.80; e. s. of late Alexander Thackeray, J.P.; m. Leila May, e. d. of Oliver William Warner, J.P.; educ. Charterhouse; Oriel College, Oxford; 2nd Lt., H.L.I., 4.12.01; Lt. 7.11.07; Capt. 18.12.12; Major 4.12.16; Europ. War, France, 1914–17; commanded 9th Batt. R. Dublin Fus. from 13.3.16. He afterwards commanded the 2/7th Duke of Wellington's Regiment, 29th Bn. Durham L.I., 2nd Bn. Highland L.I. and 229th Infantry Brigade; Brevet Lieutenant-Colonel 1.1.19; Despatches five times; wounded twice; M.C.

THATCHER, G. G. (D.S.O. L.G. 18.1.18) (Details, L.G. 25.4.18); b. 20.10.73; Major (A/Lt.-Col.), R.G.A., att. R.F.A.; previous full pay service 14.10.93 to 1.2.10; ret. pay 2.2.10; recalled, R. of O., 5.7.17; 2 years, 314 days; Major, R.G.A., 16.11.15; A/Lt.-Col. 21.9.16 to 10.3.18.

THELLUSSON, THE HON. H. E. (D.S.O. L.G. 14.1.16); b. 7.7.76; s. of 5th Baron Rendlesham; 2nd Lt., R.A., 3.6.99; Lt. 16.2.01; Capt. 9.11.07; Major, R.G.A., 30.10.14.

THEOBALD, A. C. L. (D.S.O. L.G. 14.1.16); b. 21.8.77; educ. Harrow; 2nd Lt., R.A., 6.10.00; Lt. 6.10.03; Capt. 26.4.12; Major 21.4.15.

THESIGER, HON. E. R. (D.S.O. L.G. 3.6.19); b. 1874; s. of 2nd Baron Chelmsford; m. Pearl, d. of J. Coupland; Major (T/Lt.-Col.), Surrey Yeom., Commanding 10th Batt. R.W. Kent R.; served S. African War, 1900–2; Queen's Medal, 3 clasps; King's Medal, 2 clasps; Europ. War; Despatches. He was formerly a Page of Honour to Queen Victoria.

THEWLES, H. A. (D.S.O. L.G. 4.6.17); b. 20.9.79; 2nd Lt., E. Kent R., 14.5.04; Lt. 1.3.07; Capt. 9.5.14; Major 15.2.17; Bt. Lt.-Col. 3.6.18.

THICKNESSE, F. W. (D.S.O. L.G. 4.6.17); b. 8.5.86; s. of Rev. Prebendary F. N. Thicknesse, Rector of St. George's, Hanover Square; educ. Winchester College (Scholar); passed 2nd into Woolwich; 2nd Lt., R.A., 20.12.06; Lt. 20.12.09; Capt., R.G.A., 30.10.14; A/Major, R.G.A. (122nd H.B.); was on the Staff at Hong-Kong on the outbreak of war, and was thus unable to reach France till May, 1915. He was twice mentioned in Despatches, and had commanded his battery of heavy guns for about fifteen months. He died of wounds received while reconnoitring for an O.P. beyond Zonnebeke 19.10.17.

THIN, E. G. (D.S.O. L.G. 1.1.19), Lt.-Col., 10th Batt. L'pool R. (T.F.).

THOM, J. G. (D.S.O. L.G. 18.7.17), T/Major (A/Lt.-Col.), G. Highrs.; M.C. His D.S.O. was awarded for gallantry near Arras on 11.4.17.

THOMAS, A. E. W. (D.S.O. L.G. 26.9.17) (Details, L.G. 9.1.18); b. 21.8.96; s. of Ernest Thomas; educ. Malvern; Cambridge; 2nd Lt. (T/Capt.), R.W. Kent R.; served Europ. War from 1915; Despatches; M.C.; four times wounded. His D.S.O. was awarded for gallantry on 17.7.17, near Monchy-le-Preux.

THOMAS, A. F. (D.S.O. L.G. 3.6.18); b. 4.11.79; 2nd Lt., Manch. R. (from Imp. Yeom.), 23.4.02; Lt. 17.2.04; Capt. 1.12.14; Major, Manch. R., 20.1.17; R. Corps of Signals 24.11.20.

THOMAS, G. GWYN- (see Gwyn-Thomas, G.).

THOMAS, A. N., M.B. (D.S.O. L.G. 4.6.17); b. 7.8.80; Lt., I.M.S., 27.7.07; Capt. 27.7.10; Major 27.7.19.

THOMAS, B. (D.S.O. L.G. 1.1.18), T/Major, Glouc. R.

THOMAS F. S. WILLIAMS- (see Williams-Thomas F. S.).

THOMAS, G. (D.S.O. L.G. 14.11.16); b. 19.7.71; 2nd Lt., Devon. R., 4.3.91; Lt., Devon R., 23.11.94; I.S.C. 25.5.95; Capt., I.A., 10.7.91; Major 4.3.09. His D.S.O. was awarded for gallantry at Flers on 15.9.16.

THOMAS, G. C. (D.S.O. L.G. 4.6.17), Hon. Major, S.W.B.

THOMAS, G. I. (D.S.O. L.G. 26.9.17) (Details, L.G. 9.1.18); b. July, 1893; s. of late John Thomas (Pencerdd Gwalia), Harpist to late Queen Victoria and late King Edward, and Joan Francis, d. of W. Denny; educ. Cheltenham College; R.M.A., Woolwich; 2nd Lt., R.A., 30.12.12; Lt. 9.6.15; Capt. 20.12.16; Adjt., R.A., 20.1.20; Europ. War from 1914; Despatches; M.C. and Bar.

THOMAS, H. M. (D.S.O. L.G. 1.1.18); b. 26.1.70; 2nd Lt., R.A., 15.2.89; Lt. 15.2.92; Capt. 9.10.99; Major 5.4.05; Lt.-Col. 30.10.14; served S. African War; Despatches; Bt. Major 29.11.00; Queen's Medal with 4 clasps; King's Medal with 2 clasps; served Europ. War; Despatches; Bt. Col. 3.6.18; C.M.G.

THOMAS, H. ST. G. (D.S.O. L.G. 4.6.17); b. 23.4.62; 2nd s. of General Sir F. W. Thomas, K.C.B.; m. 1st, Elsie Harriott (d. 1912); 2nd, Rose, widow of late H. D. Solomon, of Johannesburg; one d.; educ. King's School, Rochester; Lt., R. Sussex R., 14.5.84; Capt., I.S.C., 2.11.86; Major 14.5.02; Lt.-Col. 16.5.09; retired 20.2.19; served Egypt, 1884–85; Medal, clasp; Khedive's Star; Burma, 1885; Medal, 3 clasps; Sikkim, Thibet Mission Escort, 1904–5; Medal, clasp; Europ. War, 1915–18; in command 9th Batt. North'd Fus. 6.9.14; Despatches twice; 1914–15 Star.

THOMAS, J. H., M.B. (D.S.O. L.G. 1.1.18), Capt., R.A.M.C.

THOMAS, L. R. (D.S.O. L.G. 25.8.17), T/Major, A.S.C. (now R.A.S.C.); Lt., Unatt. List.

THOMAS, R. H. (D.S.O. L.G. 1.1.19); b. 23.4.77; 2nd Lt., R.E., 21.6.96; Lt. 21.6.99; Capt. 21.6.05; Major 30.10.14.

THOMAS, S. F. (D.S.O. L.G. 1.1.19), T/Major (A/Lt.-Col.), 6th Batt. Shrops. L.I.

THOMAS, W. E. (D.S.O. L.G. 2.12.18), Lt. (T/Major), E. Yorks. R. He died of wounds 4.11.18. M.C.

THOMAS, W. LL. (D.S.O. L.G. 26.5.19), T/Major, 2nd Batt. Br. W. India R.; M.C.

THOMAS-EVELYN, R. (D.S.O. L.G. 15.2.19) (Details, L.G. 30.7.19), T/2nd Lt., att. Manch. R., 12th Batt.; M.C.

The Distinguished Service Order 353

THOMPSON, A. C. (D.S.O. L.G. 1.1.18), T/Lt.-Col., R. Dublin Fus.

THOMPSON, A. E., M.D. (D.S.O. L.G. 3.6.19), T/Capt., R.A.M.C., att. 8th Batt. York and Lancaster Rgt.; M.C.

THOMPSON, A. G., M.B. (D.S.O. L.G. 1.1.17); b. 24.5.67; educ. Edinburgh University; Capt., R.A.M.C., 27.7.95; Major 27.7.04; Lt.-Col. 1.3.15; Col. 13.9.18; served S. African War, 1902; Queen's Medal with 2 clasps; Europ. War, 1914–18; Despatches; Bt. Col. 1.1.19; C.M.G.

THOMPSON, A. H., SYMES- (see Symes-Thompson, A. H.).

THOMPSON, ARNOLD JOHN (D.S.O. L.G. 3.6.18), Lt. (T/Capt.), S. Gds.; M.C.

THOMPSON, AUBREY JULIAN (D.S.O. L.G. 4.6.17); b. 17.7.73; 2nd Lt., R.A., 4.1.94; Lt. 4.1.97; Capt. 7.5.00; Major 30.10.14; Lt.-Col., R.G.A., 31.10.18.

THOMPSON, C. E. (D.S.O. L.G. 1.1.18), T/Lt. (T/Capt.), S. Lancs. R.; M.C.

THOMPSON, C. W. (D.S.O. L.G. 3.6.19), Lt.-Col., 14th Field Amb., Aust. A.M.C.

THOMPSON, CECIL H. F. (gazetted as Thompson Cyril H. F.) (D.S.O. L.G. 1.1.18), Major, London R.

THOMPSON, E. V. (D.S.O. L.G. 1.1.19), Major, 33rd Battery, 9th Brig. Can. F.A.

THOMPSON, F. V. (D.S.O. L.G. 3.6.16); b. 26.4.80; s. of late Gen. C. Thompson, I.S.C.; m. Evelyn R. Mackay; educ. Bedford Grammar School; R.M.A., Woolwich; 2nd Lt., R.E., 23.3.99; Lt. 1.10.01; Capt. 23.3.08; Adjt., R.E., 14.11.14; Major; served S. African War, 1901–2; Queen's Medal, 5 clasps; Europ. War; took out a Signalling Company to France, 1914; served on the Staff of a division; then Brig. Major, and afterwards attached to the Staff of an Army Corps; subsequently he was given command of a battalion of the Essex Rgt. He was mentioned in Despatches three times. Colonel Thompson was killed in action 14.10.17.

THOMPSON, G. E. (D.S.O. L.G. 20.10.16), 2nd Lt., 2/15th Batt. London R.

THOMPSON, H. (D.S.O. L.G. 31.5.16); b. 17.11.81, at Derry; s. of William Gamble Thompson and Eliza Thompson (née Reid); m. Sophia, d. of J. S. Hepburn; two d.; educ. Ardvreck; Crieff, and Fettes College, Edinburgh; 2nd Lt., R. Sc. Fus., 4.12.01; Lt. 14.6.05; Capt. 22.1.12; Adjt. from Jan. 1914; Major, July, 1916; served S. African War, 1902; Queen's Medal with 3 clasps; afterwards with his Regt. in India, Burma and S. Africa. At the beginning of the European War he was Adjutant to the 4th R.S.F., and went with his battalion to Gallipoli, where he won the Croix de Guerre. He was at the evacuation of Cape Helles, and went in command of the battalion to Egypt. His D.S.O. was awarded for gallantry at Duidar on the Sinai Peninsula 23.4.16. At the Battle of Gaza 19.4.17 he received the fatal wounds of which he died in hospital at El Arish 22.4.17.

H. Thompson.

THOMPSON, H. C. ST. J. (D.S.O. L.G. 17.12.17) (Details, L.G. 23.4.18); b. 4.12.87; s. of H. St. J. O. Thompson and Lilian Mary, d. of J. H. and A. G. Steinmetz; educ. Stone House, Broadstairs; Eton; 2nd Lt., Corps of Interpreters, 8.9.14, att. Indian Cavalry Corps in France; commissioned 4th Batt. C. Gds., S.R.; regular commission, C. Gds., 8.6.15; transferred into 2nd Batt. 6.10.16; A/Capt. 6.8.17. His D.S.O. was awarded for gallantry in the advance to Broembeck; Despatches. He was mortally wounded at Gouzeaucourt 30.11.17, dying a few minutes later.

THOMPSON, J. G. (D.S.O. L.G. 3.6.18), Capt., L'pool R.; M.C.

THOMPSON, J. G. COULTHERD (gazetted as Thompson, J. G. Coulthered) (D.S.O. L.G. 1.1.18), Major, R.F.A.

THOMPSON, J. T. C. (D.S.O. L.G. 3.6.18); s. of late Sir John Thompson, Prime Minister of Canada; Lt.-Colonel, Can. Infy. He was wounded in July, 1917.

THOMPSON, R. (D.S.O. L.G. 8.3.19) (Details, L.G. 4.10.19), Lt.-Col., 1/1st Yorks. Dragoons.

THOMPSON, R. J. C. (D.S.O. L.G. 14.1.16); b. 1.8.80; s. of R. P. Thompson and Caroline Thompson (née Gwatkin); m. Juliette, d. of late Commandant Cottin de Melville, Chevalier de la Légion d'Honneur; one s.; educ. Marlborough; St. Thomas's Hospital; Lt., R.A.M.C., 31.1.05; Capt. 31.7.08; Major 15.10.15; Europ. War, 1914–18; Despatches; C.M.G.

THOMPSON, R. L. B. (D.S.O. L.G. 1.1.17); b. 23.11.74; s. of Col. R. Thompson, C.B., R.E., and Fanny Maud, d. of Rev. A. H. Brereton; m. Louise, d. of P. P. Vassallo; one s.; one d.; educ. Mannamead School, Plymouth; R.M.A., Woolwich; 2nd Lt., R.E., 10.2.93; Lt. 10.2.96; Capt. 10.2.04; Major 10.2.13; Bt. Lt.-Col. 3.6.15; Lt.-Col. 22.11.20; served Europ. War; Despatches thrice; C.M.G.

THOMPSON, R. M. (D.S.O. L.G. 18.1.18) (Details, L.G. 25.4.18), Can. Field Arty.; M.C.

THOMPSON, S. J. (D.S.O. L.G. 1.1.17), Capt. (T/Major), R.F.A.

THOMPSON, T. A. L. (D.S.O. L.G. 16.9.18), Lt. (A/Capt.), North'd Fus.; M.C.

THOMPSON, T. J. C. C. (D.S.O. L.G. 16.8.17); commissioned through the Queen's University (Belfast) O.T.C., and gazetted to Special Reserve of R. Irish Fus. 25.3.15; became Captain; saw severe fighting at Ypres in 1917; was twice wounded; twice mentioned in Despatches. His D.S.O. was awarded for gallantry on the Messines-Wytschaete Ridge 7.6.17. He was killed in action 24.3.18.

T. A. L. Thompson.

THOMPSON, W. D. B. (D.S.O. L.G. 16.9.18), Lt., Durham L.I.; M.C.

THOMPSON, W. G. (D.S.O. L.G. 4.6.17); b. 13.4.71; s. of William Thompson and Julia Ann Thompson (née Hunt); m. Annette Wilhelmina Bryant, d. of T. H. Bryant; two d.; educ. Marlborough College; 2nd Lt., R.A., 16.2.93; Lt. 16.2.96; Capt. 21.5.00; Major 13.2.10; Lt.-Col. 7.11.15; Brig.-General, R.A.; served N.W.F. India, 1897–98; Medal and 3 clasps; S. Africa, 1899–1900; wounded; Despatches; Queen's Medal and 2 clasps; Europ. War (France), 1914–18. His D.S.O. is thought to have been awarded for work during the winter campaign, 1916–17, with 3rd Australian Division when acting C.R.A.; Despatches for the Somme, Aug. 1916; C.M.G.; Russian Order of St. Anne; President of R.A. Coaching Club, Aldershot. He has had many trips after big game in India.

W. G. Thompson.

THOMPSON, W. I., M.B. (D.S.O. L.G. 1.1.18); b. 14.3.80; Lt., R.A.M.C., 30.7.06; Capt. 30.1.10; Major 30.7.18.

THOMPSON, W. J. (D.S.O. L.G. 31.5.16); b. 1877; s. of E. Thompson; m. Mary Olive, d. of Rev. S. E. Rowe, of Pietermaritzburg; educ. Kendal Grammar School; 2nd Lt., Northern M. Rifles, 1905; Capt., Transvaal Cycle Corps, 1905; Maj. 1908; Major (2nd. in-command), 7th S.A. Infantry from Nov-1915; Lt.-Col., Commanding 7th S.A. Inf., March, 1917; served German S.W. Africa Campaign with Rand Light Infantry from 1914. His D.S.O. was awarded for gallantry on 11–12.3.16.

THOMPSON, W. M. (D.S.O. L.G. 18.12.17); b. 18.11.69; s. of late Col. H. M. Thompson, 82nd Rgt.; m. Frances Helen, d. of late Rev. C. Bull; one s.; one d.; educ. Westminster School; R.M.A.; 2nd Lt., R.E., 3.3.89; Lt. 3.3.92; Capt. 19.7.99; Major 14.11.08; Lt.-Col. 31.12.16; retired pay, 1921; Europ. War, Gibraltar, Dardanelles, and on Home Defence; Despatches twice.

W. J. Thompson.

THOMPSON, W. W. (D.S.O. L.G. 19.11.17) (Details, L.G. 22.3.18), Lt. (A/Capt.), Can. Inf.

THOMS, N. W. B. B. (D.S.O. L.G. 25.8.17), Major, New Zealand Force; M.C.

THOMSON, A. C. (D.S.O. L.G. 1.1.19), Lt.-Col., late R.E.; served Europ. War, 1914–19; Despatches; Order of Leopold; Croix de Guerre.

THOMSON, A. F. (D.S.O. L.G. 23.11.16); b. 7.9.80; 2nd Lt., R.A., 23.12.98; Lt. 16.2.01; Capt. 13.4.07; Major 30.10.14; Bt. Lt.-Col. 1.1.18; Lt.-Col. 1.1.21.

THOMSON, A. H. G. (D.S.O. L.G. 4.6.17); b. 12.8.69; 2nd Lt., Norf. R., 29.11.90; Lt., I.S.C., 15.5.93; Capt., I.A., 10.7.01; Major 29.11.08; Lt.-Colonel, 30th Punjabis, I.A.; served operations in Chitral, 1895; Medal with clasp; N.W. Frontier of India, 1897–98; clasp; Tirah, 1897–98; clasp; Europ. War; Despatches. He died in India 28.18, of pneumonia.

THOMSON, A. L. (D.S.O. L.G. 11.1.19); b. 18.2.89; s. of Lt.-Col. W. B Thomson, R.A.M.C. (retired); educ. King's School, Canterbury (represented School in Cricket and Rugby Football 1905-07); R.M.C. Sandhurst; 2nd Lt., R. Sussex R. 6.2.09; Lt. 14.10.10; Capt. 10.6.15; A/Lt.-Col., commanding 7th Batt. R. Sussex R.; served N. W. Frontier operations, 1915-16, slightly wounded; Despatches.

THOMSON, A. T. (D.S.O. L.G. 25.11.16), T/Major, Can. Inf.

THOMSON, C. B. (D.S.O. L.G. 11.4.18); b. 13.4.75; 2nd Lt., R.E., 28.3.94; Lt. 28.3.97; Capt. 1.4.04; Major 28.3.14; Bt. Major 2.4.04; T/Brig.-Gen. 2.6.18; operations in S. Africa, 1896; Medal; S. African War, 1899–1902; Despatches; Queen's Medal with 3 clasps; King's Medal with 2 clasps; Balkan Campaign, 1912–13, att. to the Serbian Forces; 2 Serbian Medals; Europ. War; Despatches; C.B.E.

THOMSON, C. G. (D.S.O. L.G. 1.1.17); b. 4.5.74; Lt., R.A.M.C., 3.8.01; Capt. 3.8.04; Major 3.5.13.

THOMSON, C. P., M.D. (D.S.O. L.G. 3.6.16); b. 22.1.79; Lt., R.A.M.C., 31.1.05; Capt. 31.7.08; Major 15.10.15.

THOMSON, D. (D.S.O. L.G. 3.6.19), Capt. (A/Major), R.F.A.; M.C.

THOMSON, E. C. O. (D.S.O. L.G. 1.1.17), Cdr., Roy. Navy, 31.12.16; served Europ. War, 1914–18; Despatches.

THOMSON, E. L. (D.S.O. L.G. 3.6.19), Major (A/Lt.-Col.), York and Lancaster R. (S.R.), att. 9th Batt. North'd Fus. (Lt., ret. pay, late Norfolk R.); S. African War, 1902; Queen's Medal, 3 clasps; Europ. War; Despatches.

THOMSON, GEORGE (D.S.O. L.G. 1.1.18) (Bar, L.G. 26.7.18); b. 27.8.90; m. Dorothy Dundas, d. of late Capt. R. C. Freeman; one d.; Capt., Yorks. L.I., 11.5.17; served Europ. War, 1914–18; Despatches; wounded; M.C.; Croix de Guerre.

THOMSON, GEORGE (D.S.O. L.G. 1.1.19), Temp. Major, 12th Battn. R. Ir. Rifles.

THOMSON, G. E. (D.S.O. L.G. 22.6.18), Lt. (T/Capt.), Gen. List.; M.C. He died 23.5.18.

THOMSON, H. G. (D.S.O. L.G. 19.10.16), Major, R.F.A.

THOMSON, H. W., M.D. (D.S.O. L.G. 3.6.18), Lt.-Col., R.A.M.C.

THOMSON, J. A. R. (D.S.O. L.G. 16.9.18), Lt.-Col., Yorks. Regt.; M.C.

THOMSON, J. F. (D.S.O. L.G. 3.6.19); b. 30.10.80; 2nd Lt., N. Staff. R., 19.10.01; Lt. 20.11.05; Capt. 1.9.14; Major 6.5.16; att. 36th Batt. North'd Fus.; S. African War, 1899-1901; Despatches; Queen's Medal, 2 clasps; Europ. War; Despatches.

THOMSON, J. N. (D.S.O. L.G. 3.6.19); b. 25.12.88; 2nd Lt., R.A., 27.7.09; Lt., R.A., 23.7.12; Capt., R.A., 23.7.15; Adjt. 8.8.15 to 14.3.16; Major 1.10.18; Major, R.F.A.; M.C.

THOMSON, N. A. (D.S.O. L.G. 3.6.16); b. 1.4.72; 2nd Lt., Sea. Highrs., 9.4.92; Lt., Sea. Highrs., 3.3.95; Capt., Sea. Highrs., 23.1.09; Lt.-Col., Sea. Highrs., 23.12.17 to 3.4.21; Colonel 4.4.21; served Nile Expedn., 1898; Battles of the Atbara and Khartoum; wounded; S. Africa, 1899–1902; Despatches; Queen's Medal, 3 clasps; King's Medal, 2 clasps; Europ. War, 1914–18; Despatches; C.M.G.; Bt. Lt.-Colonel 3.6.17; Bt. Col. 3.6.19.

A 23

THOMSON, R. G. (D.S.O. L.G. 3.6.16); b. 4.4.78; s. of Major-Gen. D. Thomson, R.E.; m. Florence Lucy, y. d. of Major-Gen. W. E. Delves Broughton, Bengal Staff Corps; one s.; two d.; educ. Cheltenham Coll.; R.M.A.; 2nd Lt., R.A., 23.6.98; Lt., R.A., 16.2.01; Capt. 14.11.05; Major, R.A., 30.10.14; Lt.-Col. 21.8.18; served Europ. War, 1914–18; C.M.G.

THOMSON, V. H. (D.S.O. L.G. 3.6.18), Major, R. of O., R.F.A.; M.C.

THORBURN, W. (D.S.O. L.G. 3.6.19), Lt.-Col., 1/8th Batt. R. Scots. T.F.

THORNE, A. F. A. N. (D.S.O. L.G. 14.1.16) (1st Bar, L.G. 18.2.18) (Details, L.G. 18.7.18) (2nd Bar, L.G. 2.12.18); b. 20.9.85; e. s. of Augustas Thorne; m. Hon. Margaret Douglas Pennant, d. of 2nd Baron Penrhyn; three s.; two d.; educ. Mulgrave, near Whitby; Eton; Sandhurst; 2nd Lt., G. Gds., 2.3.04; Lt., G. Gds., 30.8.05; Capt. 22.3.13; Major 30.9.15; served Europ. War; Despatches seven times; C.M.G.

THORNEYCROFT, G. E. M. (D.S.O. L.G. 1.1.18); b. 4.12.83; 2nd Lt., R.A., 24.12.02; Lt., R.A., 24.12.05; Capt., R.A., 30.10.14; Major, R.A., 20.5.16.

THORNHILL, C. J. M. (D.S.O. L.G. 1.1.18) (Bar, L.G. 11.1.19); b. 4.10.83; 2nd Lt., York. and Lanc. R., 18.1.02; I.A. 19.12.02; Lt. 18.4.04; Capt. 18.1.11; Major 18.1.17; served Europ. War; Despatches; Bt. Major 1.1.17; Bt. Lt.-Col. 3.6.18.

THORNHILL, C. M. (D.S.O. L.G. 25.8.17); b. 5.2.85; 2nd Lt., Unatt., 29.8.06; 2nd Lt., I.A., 22.10.07; Lt. 29.11.08; Capt. 29.8.15; M.C.

THORNHILL G. BADHAM (see Badham-Thornhill, G.).

THORNHILL, J. E. (D.S.O. L.G. 14.1.16); b. 7.4.80; educ. Cheltenham Coll.; 2nd Lt., Sco. R., 6.12.99; transferred Seaforth Highrs. 20.12.99; Lt., Seaforth Highrs., 21.1.01; Capt., Seaforth Highrs., 24.2.06; Adjt., T.F., 15.3.13 to 8.2.16; Major 1.9.15; served S. African War, 1900–2; Queen's Medal, 3 clasps; King's Medal, 2 clasps; Europ. War; Despatches. He died 2.10.18.

THORNLEY, G. S. (D.S.O. L.G. 15.6.17), Cdr., R.N., 30.6.18.

THORNLEY, J. H. (D.S.O. L.G. 26.7.17), Major, Can. Engrs. His D.S.O. was awarded for gallantry on 16.5.17, north of Scarfe River.

THORNTHWAITE, F. (D.S.O. L.G. 1.1.19), Major, 5th D.A.C., Aust. F.A.; M.C.

THORNTON, G. ST. L. (D.S.O. L.G. 2.2.16); b. 21.3.81; 4th s. of Henry Edward Thornton, his mother being d. of Pascoe St. Leger Grenfell and sister of Field-Marshal Lord Grenfell, G.C.B., etc.; educ. Tyttenhanger; Winchester; entered Woolwich, Jan. 1899; 1st commission in R.F.A. 2.1.00; Lt., R.A., 3.4.01; Capt., R.A., 5.10.08; Adjt. 29.10.09 to 28.10.12; Major 30.10.14; Lt.-Col., Nov. 1916; in command of a brigade; served S. African War, 1901–2; Queen's Medal, 5 clasps; India, present at Delhi Durbar; Europ. War, in the retreat from Mons to the Marne; wounded at Ypres; served at Gallipoli (Despatches; wounded); left England for France, June, 1916; fought at Ypres, Messines and elsewhere; invalided home, 1917. He died 4.2.18.

THORNTON, L. H. (D.S.O. L.G. 14.1.16); b. 21.12.73; s. of Rev. John Thornton, of Betchworth, Surrey; m. Kathleen, d. of Col. Doncaster, late Black Watch; one s.; one d.; educ. Marlborough; 2nd Lt., Rif. Brig., 6.3.95; Lt. 19.7.97; Capt. 5.2.01; retired with rank of Capt., and employed as Adjt., Cambridge University Officers' Training Corps, 1908–14; Major; Lt.-Col.; Colonel; served Tochi Valley Expedn.; Medal and clasp; S. Africa, 1902; Queen's Medal, 3 clasps; Europ. War, 1915–18; C.M.G.

THORNTON, N. S. (D.S.O. L.G. 3.6.18), Lt. (T/Major), Rif. Bdge. (att. 7th Bn.); M.C. He died on 10.4.18 at 2nd Stationary Hospital, Abbeville, of wounds received in action while in command of his Regiment on 4 April.

THORNTON, REV. S. A. L. (D.S.O. L.G. 13.2.17); b. 1871; s. of late M. McNeil Thornton; ordained, 1896; served Europ. War; Naval Chaplain's Dept., att. R. Dublin Fus.; Despatches twice.

THORNTON-SMITH, A. D. (D.S.O. L.G. 26.7.17), T/Lt. (A/Capt.), K.R.R.C., att. 12th Bn. He was killed in action 16.8.17.

THORNYCROFT, C. M. (D.S.O. L.G. 14.1.16); b. 6.8.79; e. s. of C. E. Thornycroft, J.P.; m. Vida Maude, 2nd d. of late G. W. Deakin; educ. Eton; Sandhurst; 2nd Lt., Manch. Regt., 12.8.99; Lt., Manch. Regt., 16.5.00; Capt. 5.2.03; Major (S.R.); Lt.-Col.; served S. Africa, 1900–2; Despatches; Queen's Medal, 3 clasps; King's Medal, 2 clasps; Europ. War, 1914–18; Despatches thrice; C.B.E.

THOROLD, R. S. GRANT- (see Grant-Thorold, R. S.).

THOROWGOOD, A. P. N. (D.S.O. L.G. 17.5.18); b. 19.1.84; s. of Frank Napier Thorowgood; m. Agnes Henrietta, d. of Sir Philip Watts, K.C.B., F.R.S., etc.; one s.; two d.; educ. St. Michael's, Westgate-on-Sea; H.M.S. Britannia; joined Roy. Navy 15.1.00; Sub-Lt. 19.1.03; Lt. 30.9.08; Comdr. 31.12.17; served Europ. War; present at Heligoland Bight action in H.M.S. Arethusa 28.8.14; Dogger Bank 24.1.15; air raid on Cuxhaven 25.12.14; Battle of Jutland 31.5.16, in H.M.S. Gloucester; Despatches; 1914–15 Star.

THORP, A. (D.S.O. L.G. 1.1.17); b. 23.10.73; s. of Charles William Thorp, M.D., F.R.C.S., L.R.C.P., of Dobroyd, Tormorden, Lancs., and Edith, d. of F. Spencer; m. Edith May, d. of late W. H. Petrie; one s.; one d.; educ. Bedford County School (afterwards known as Elstow School); R.M.A., Woolwich; 2nd Lt., R.A., 4.3.93; Lt. 4.3.96; Capt. 22.2.00; Major 15.3.14; Lt.-Col.; served in India and Burma in R.F.A., R.G.A., and Indian Mountain Artillery from 1893 to 1901; passed through the Gunnery Staff Course in 1903, and served with the R.G.A. in Malta, 1903–7, as Instructor in Gunnery, and in the Indian Mountain Artillery in India and Burma, 1908–14. At the outbreak of war he was commanding the R.G.A. Depôt at Plymouth, but took over a battery of Field Artillery in the New Armies in May, 1915, and proceeded to France in July, 1915; in December of that year was given command of a brigade, holding that appointment till his death. He was present in many actions, and in the March retreat his brigade formed part of the Fifth Army, and afterwards, from August onwards, he was continually in heavy fighting. He was five times mentioned in Despatches, and created a C.M.G. He was killed in action at Boursies, near Le Cateau, on 30.10.18. His General wrote of him: "Ever since our advance in August last he has excelled himself, and the success of the 18th Div. Artillery has been greatly due to him."

THORP, A. H. (D.S.O. L.G. 1.1.18); b. 5.9.69; m. Ethel Mary Muriel, o. d. of W. Benton, of Texas, U.S.A.; educ. Bath Coll.; R.M.A.; 2nd Lt., R.A., 27.7.88; Lt. 27.7.91; Capt. 17.2.99; Major 5.5.09; Lt.-Col. 7.4.16; Europ. War; Despatches four times; C.M.G.

THORP, H. W. B. (D.S.O. L.G. 14.1.16); b. 14.10.79; educ. Harrow; Sandhurst; 2nd Lt., K.O. Yorks. L.I., 7.5.98; Lt. 26.7.99; Capt. 15.5.05; Major 1.9.15; Bt. Lt.-Col. 3.6.18; served Somaliland, 1901 and 1902–4; Despatches; Medal, 3 clasps; S. Africa, 1901–2; Queen's Medal, 3 clasps; Europ. War, 1914–18; Despatches six times.

THORP, J. C. (D.S.O. L.G. 1.1.18); b. 30.3.63; 1st com. 14.2.83; Lt.-Col. 1.8.06; ret. A.O.D. 27.1.12; Lt.-Col., R. of O., A.O.D., now R.A.O.C.; served Burmese Exp., 1885–87; Medal with clasp; Europ. War; Despatches.

THORPE, E. I. DE S. (D.S.O. L.G. 1.1.17); b. 10.9.71; 2nd Lt., Bedf. R., 20.2.92; Lt. 14.11.93; Capt. 28.10.99; Major 21.9.12; Lt.-Col., Bedf. and Herts. R., 16.10.17; served operations on the Niger, 1897; Despatches; Medal with clasp; Europ. War; Despatches; Bt. Lt.-Col. 18.2.15; C.M.G.

THORPE, G. (D.S.O. L.G. 18.2.15) (Bar, L.G. 15.2.19) (Details, L.G. 30.7.19); Colonel, Argyll and Sutherland Highlanders; C.M.G. (see "The Distinguished Service Order," from its institution to 31.12.15, by same publishers).

THORPE, HAROLD (D.S.O. L.G. 1.1.17), Major and Bt. Lt.-Col. (T/Lt.-Col.), Yeomanry.

THREIPLAND, W. MURRAY- (see Murray-Threipland, W.).

THRING, A. L. (D.S.O. L.G. 22.8.18), Lt.-Col., Vrijstaatse Schutters (1st Rgt.), S. African Mil. Forces.

THRUSTON, B. J. (D.S.O. L.G. 14.1.16); b. 2.1.85; 2nd Lt., Linc. R., 29.10.10; Lt., Linc. R., 28.11.11; employed with W.A.F.F. 26.2.13; Capt. (T/Major), W.A.F.F. (Lincoln R.); served Europ. War from 1914; Despatches; Legion of Honour (5th Class). He died 22.11.18.

THUNDER, S. H. J. (D.S.O. L.G. 15.2.17); b. 23.3.79; s. of H. B. D. Thunder, late 58th Foot; m. Ethel, e. d. of David Tidmarsh; two s.; educ. Fort Augustus, Inverness-shire; 2nd Lt., North'n R., 21.4.00; Lt. 4.4.03; Capt. 21.8.09; Major 1.9.15; served Europ. War, 1914–18; Despatches six times; C.M.G.; M.C.; Bt. Lt.-Colonel 1.1.18.

THURN, B. B. VON B. IM (see Im Thurn, B. B. von B.).

THURSTAN, N. M. C. (D.S.O. L.G. 1.1.16), Cdr., R.N., 30.6.16.

THURSTON, L. V. (D.S.O. L.G. 1.1.17); b. 28.6.81; y. s. of Hugh Kingsmill Thurston; educ. St. Bart.'s Hosp.; Lt., R.A.M.C., 30.7.04; Capt. 30.1.08; Major 1.7.15; served Europ. War, 1914–16; Despatches.

THWAITES, A. H. (D.S.O. L.G. 1.1.18), Lt.-Col., Aust. A.M.S.

THWAITES, G. (D.S.O. L.G. 1.1.17); b. 4.11.77; 2nd Lt., A.S.C. (now R.A.S.C.), 1.5.01; Lt. 1.5.02; Capt. 1.5.06; Major 30.10.14; served S. African War, 1902; Queen's Medal, 4 clasps; Europ. War; Despatches. He was drowned on 29.5.17.

THWAYTES, H. D. (D.S.O. L.G. 2.12.18) (Bar, L.G. 2.4.19) (Details, L.G. 10.12.19); b. 3.6.89, in Guernsey, Channel Isles; s. of Col. Henry James Thwaytes (Retired) and Alice Maud Thwaytes; m. Mary, d. of R. Robertson, M.D., J.P.; educ. Warwick School, Warwick; St. Helen's College, Southsea; R.M.C., Sandhurst; played Association Football for R.M.C., Sandhurst v. R.M.A., Woolwich, 1908; 2nd Lt., Dorset R., 8.9.09; Lt. 6.12.11; Capt. 14.1.15; T/Lt.-Col., Dorset R., 26.4.18 to 14.5.19; joined 1st Batt. Dorset R. in France on 3.1.15 as a Company Commander; was wounded on 20.4.15, adjacent to Hill 60; rejoined in France 3.10.15; promoted A/Major and 2nd-in-command 22.5.16 on the Somme; commanded 1st Batt. from 1.7.16 to 15.8.16; invalided to England 26.9.16; rejoined as 2nd-in-command, Dec. 1917; in command 11.4.18 to May, 1919. His D.S.O. was awarded for gallantry and ability during the attack on Damery and Parvilliers on 11.8.18, whilst commanding 1st Batt. Dorsets. R.; Bar to D.S.O. awarded for services whilst commanding 1st Batt. Dorsets. R. on 4.11.18 for the successful crossing of the Sambre Canal at Ors.

H. D. Thwaytes.

THYNNE, LORD A. G. (D.S.O. L.G. 1.1.17); b. 1873; s. of the 4th Marquess of Bath and brother of the 5th Marquess; educ. Eton and Balliol College, Oxford; ent. R. Wilts. Yeomanry about 1898; Lt.-Colonel; served with 1st Batt. I.Y. in S. Africa, and on the Staff, 1900–2; Despatches twice; Queen's Medal, 4 clasps; King's Medal, 2 clasps; was Secretary to the Lt.-Governor, Orange River Colony, 1902–5; served with Somaliland Field Force, 1903–4, as Reuter's Special Correspondent (Medal and clasp), and on the outbreak of the Europ. War he went to the front with the Wilts. Yeomanry, in which he was a Major; in 1916 he was made Lieutenant-Colonel commanding a battalion of the Wilts. Rgt., and was mentioned in Despatches in Jan. 1917, and again in Dec. of the same year. He was killed in action on 14.9.18.

TILLARD, A. T. (D.S.O. L.G. 8.3.20), Cdr., R.N.

TILLARD, E. D. (D.S.O. L.G. 1.2.17); b. 22.7.80; e. s. Charles Tillard; m. Molly, 3rd d. of G. E. McNeely; educ. Malvern Coll. and R.M.A.; 2nd Lt., R.E., 20.8.99; Lt. 1.4.02; Capt. 30.8.08; Major 30.4.16; served Somaliland, 1902–4; Medal and clasp; Europ. War; Despatches.

TILLETT, A. (D.S.O. L.G. 1.1.18), Lt. (A/Lt.-Col.), Devon. R.; M.C. He died of wounds, 2.12.17.

TILLIE, W. K. (D.S.O. L.G. 16.9.18); b. 1887; m. Victoria Helen, e. d. of Arnold Royle, C.B.; two s.; educ. Charterhouse; 1st commission, Dec. 1914, 8th R.W. Kent Regt.; T/Lt.-Col., M.G.C., Nov. 1917; served Europ. War; Despatches six times; M.C.

TILLOTSON, J. E. (D.S.O. L.G. 4.2.18) (Details, L.G. 5.7.18), Temp. 2nd Lt., W. York Regt.

TILLSTONE, E. M. ROGERS- (see Rogers-Tillstone, E. M.).

TILLY, J. C. (D.S.O. L.G. 3.6.19); b. 27.1.88; 2nd Lt., W. York. R., 11.12.09; Lt. 23.1.11; Capt. 7.12.14; Capt. (A/Lt.-Col.), W. Yorks. R.; commanding 10th Batt. Tank Corps; M.C.

TILNEY, N. E. (D.S.O. L.G. 1.1.17); b. 2.3.72; 2nd Lt., R.A., 19.3.92; Lt., R.A., 19.3.95; Capt., R.A., 15.3.00; Major, R.A., 25.9.09; Lt.-Col. 29.8.15; served China, 1900; Medal; Europ. War; Despatches.

TILNEY, R. H. (D.S.O. L.G. 4.6.17); b. 11.2.66; s. of Col. Robert J. Tilney, C.B.; m. Frances Mary, d. of Rev. A. G. Barber; two sons; one d.; educ. Eton; Brasenose College, Oxford; Col., Duke of Lancaster's Own Yeomanry, 1889; served Europ. War, in France; Despatches twice; Croix de Guerre (French), 1917; presented by the French President at Péronne, 1.4.17.

TIMBRELL, T. (D.S.O. L.G. 17.9.17); 2nd Lt., Unatt., 30.7.99; Ind. S.C. 12.6.00; Lieut., Ind. Army, 20.10.00; Capt. 20.7.07; Major, 1.7.15; served China, 1900; Medal; operations in the Abor Country, 1911–12; Medal and clasp; Europ. War; Despatches.

TIMINS, THE REV. F. C. (D.S.O. L.G. 4.6.17); T/Chapl. to the Forces.

TIMMIS, R. S. (D.S.O. L.G. 16.9.18), Major, Can. Cavalry.

TIPPET, A. G. (D.S.O. L.G. 17.11.17), Lt.-Cdr., R.N.

TOBIN, H. S. (D.S.O. L.G. 8.3.19) (Details, L.G. 4.10.19), Lt.-Col., 29th Inf. Batt. Br. Columbia R.

TOBIN, H. W. (D.S.O. L.G. 18.8.16); b. 17.9.79; 2nd Lt., R.A., 23.12.98; Lt., R.A., 16.2.01; Lt., I.A., 9.1.03; Capt. 23.12.07; Major 1.9.15; T/Lt.-Col. 14.11.19; served E. Africa, 1902–4; operations in Somaliland; Medal with clasp; Europ. War; Despatches; O.B.E.

TOD, D. (D.S.O. L.G. 16.9.18), T/Lt. (A/Capt.), M.M.G.C.

TODD, A. G. (D.S.O. L.G. 23.11.16); b. 9.1.71; Capt., A.V.C., 5.10.03; Bt. Major 18.1.11; Major 2.4.13; Lt.-Col. 15.10.21; served S. African War, 1899–1902; Queen's Medal, 7 clasps; King's Medal, 2 clasps; Europ. War; Despatches; Bt. Col. 16.10.21; C.B.E.

TODD, C. W. (D.S.O. L.G. 25.11.16); s. of late W. A. Todd, J.P.; ent. Gloucester Artillery, 1896; retired with the rank of Capt., 1912; rejoined on outbreak of war; T/Capt., R.F.A.; served in France from spring of 1915; invalided home with trench fever, returning to the front only four weeks before he was killed in action on 4.8.17, aged 39.

TODD, G. J. (D.S.O. L.G. 29.8.17), Capt., R.N., 30.6.15.

TODD, T. J. M. (D.S.O. L.G. 19.4.01) (Bar, L.G. 1.1.18), Lt.-Col., Aust. L.H. Regt. (see "The Distinguished Service Order," from its institution to the 31st Dec. 1915, same publishers).

TOLERTON, R. H. (D.S.O. L.G. 3.6.19), Capt. (A/Lt.-Col.), 1/23rd Batt. London R.; M.C.

TOLFREY-CHRISTY, W. E. (see Christy, W. E. Tolfey-).

TOLL, F. W. (D.S.O. L.G. 1.1.17) (Bar, L.G. 26.11.17) (Details, L.G. 6.4.18); b. 18.1.72; s. of B. Toll; married as 2nd wife, M. L. Berry; one s., Frederick Vivian (killed in action in Gallipoli); one d.; educ. Brisbane; Cadet, Queensland Forces, 1888; Lt.-Col., Aust. Mil. Forces; served S. Africa, 5th Queensland Impl. Bushmen; Despatches four times; Queen's Medal, 5 clasps; King's Medal, 2 clasps; Col. Auxy. Officers' Decoration; Europ. War, New Guinea, 1914; Egypt, France; Despatches.

TOLLEMACHE, HON. D. P. (D.S.O. L.G. 3.6.19); b. 12.1.84; s. of late Hon. L. P. Tollemache, and brother of 3rd Baron Tollemache; 2nd Lt., 7th Hrs., 22.10.02; Lt. 10.2.06; Capt. 9.10.11; Bt. Major 3.6.16; Major, Oct. 1919.

TOLLEMACHE, E. D. H. (D.S.O. L.G. 3.6.19); b. 1.6.85; 2nd Lt., C. Guards, 16.8.05; Lt. 21.12.07; Capt. 4.2.15; Bt. Major 1.1.15; Major 27.3.20; M.C.

W. S. N. Toller.

TOLLER, W. S. N. (D.S.O. L.G. 14.1.16), Major, Leic. R., T.F.

TOLLEY, H. G. (D.S.O. L.G. 19.11.17) (Details, L.G. 22.3.18), Major, Aust. Engrs.

TOLLWORTHY, F. G. (D.S.O. L.G. 3.6.19), Lt. (A/Major), 1st Batt. London R., att. 2/2nd Batt.; M.C.

TOMBAZIS, J. L. (D.S.O. L.G. 8.3.19) (Details, L.G. 4.10.19), 2nd Lt., 2nd Batt. Notts. and Derby. R.; M.C. He was killed in action 8.10.18.

TOMES, C. T. (D.S.O. L.G. 1.1.18); b. 28.8.82; 2nd Lt., R. War. R., 8.5.01; Lt. 8.2.05; Adjt., R. War. R., 27.9.10 to 26.9.13; Capt. 14.12.12; Major 8.5.16; served N.W.F. of India, 1908; operations in the Mohmand country; Medal and clasp; Europ. War; Despatches; M.C.

TOMKINSON, F. M. (D.S.O. L.G. 1.1.17) (Bar, L.G. 18.7.17), Capt. (T/Lt.-Col.), Worc. R. His Bar was awarded for gallantry 12–13 April, at Roussoy, and 25–26.4.17, at Guillemont Farm.

TOMKINSON, H. A. (D.S.O. L.G. 4.6.17) (Bar, L.G. 26.7.18); b. 19.6.81; 2nd Lt., Unatt., 8.1.01; 1st Dns. 9.3.01; Lt. 27.6.01; Capt. 22.12.08; Adjt., 1st Dns., 22.12.08 to 11.9.11; Major 23.5.15; Lt.-Col. 21.12.19; S. African War, 1902; Queen's Medal, 5 clasps; Europ. War; Despatches.

TOMKINSON, L. (D.S.O. L.G. 22.12.19), Squadron Leader, R.A.F. (N. Russia); A.F.C.

TOMKINSON, W. (D.S.O. L.G. 3.6.19), Major, 10th Brig. Aust. F.A., att. H.Q., Aust. Divl. Arty. Brig.

TOMLIN, J. L. (D.S.O. L.G. 1.1.18); b. 23.4.86; s. of late Capt. B. Tomlin, King's Dragoon Guards; m. Gertrude Faulkner; one d.; educ. King's School, Canterbury; R.M.A., Woolwich; 2nd Lt., R.E., 14.8.06; Lt. 22.11.08; Capt. 30.10.14; Bt. Major 1.1.19; Major, R. C. of Signals, 11.6.21; Signal Service, Aldershot, and in France.

TOMLINSON, L. W. (D.S.O. L.G. 25.11.16); b. Pietermaritzburg, 21.6.72; s. of late G. A. and M. Tomlinson; m. (1st) Amy (who died in 1904), d. of late C. G. Levy, J.P.; (2nd) Ethel Bradley, d. of W. H. Harris; two d.; educ. Pietermaritzburg College; Capt., 3rd S. African Inf.; served in Boer War; Zululand Rebellion; Great War; German S. W. Africa; with S. African Brig., France. His D.S.O. was awarded for gallantry on 15.7.16, at Delville Wood.

TOMLINSON, P. S. (D.S.O. L.G. 3.6.19); b. 11.11.84; Lt., R.A.M.C., 30.1.09; Capt. 30.7.12; Bt. Major 1.1.18; Major 30.1.21.

TOMLINSON W. PAGET- (see Paget-Tomlinson, W.).

TOMORY, D. M. (D.S.O. L.G. 1.1.18), Major, S. African Medical Corps.

TONG, T. B. (D.S.O. L.G. 16.9.18), T/Lt. (A/Capt.), Welsh R.

TONKIN, F. C. (D.S.O. L.G. 11.1.19), T/Lt. (T/Capt.), E. Yorks. R., att. 7th Batt.; M.C. He died of wounds 4.11.18.

TONSON-RYE, H. B. (D.S.O. L.G. 16.9.18) (Bar, L.G. 15.2.19) (Details, L.G. 30.7.19); b. 1.2.82; 2nd Lt., R. Munster Fus., 4.5.01; Lt. 29.3.06; Adjt., R. Munster Fus., 16.9.08 to 15.9.11; Capt. 14.9.13; Major 6.9.15; served S. African War, 1901–2; Queen's Medal and clasp; N.W.F. of India, 1908; Medal, clasp; Europ. War; Despatches.

TOOGOOD, C. G. (D.S.O. L.G. 17.3.17) (Details, L.G. 18.6.17); b. 23.8.93; T/2nd Lt., 18.12.14 to 15.8.17; Lt., Army, 18.9.16; I.A. 16.8.17; Capt. 18.9.19.

TOOP, F. H. (D.S.O. L.G. 27.7.16); b. 22.2.88; 2nd Lt., Glouc. R., 15.12.14; Lt. 22.3.11; T/Capt., 14th Batt. Glouc. R.

TOOTH, S. A. (D.S.O. L.G. 1.1.19), Major, 6th Aust. L.H. Rgt.

TOPP, C. B. (D.S.O. L.G. 11.1.19), Capt. (A/Major), 42nd Batt. Can. L.I., Quebec R.; M.C.

TORKINGTON, O. M. (D.S.O. L.G. 3.6.18); b. 28.4.80; 2nd Lt., Sco. Rif., 24.6.99; Lt. 29.1.00; Capt., 9.3.08; Major 1.9.15.

TORR, W. W. T., (D.S.O. L.G. 15.2.17); b. 7.7.90; s. of Rev. Canon W. E. Torr; m. Enid Milnes, d. of Rev. Canon H. D. Burton; educ. Harrow; Sandhurst; 2nd Lt., W. Yorks. R., 20.4.10; Lt. 10.1.12; Capt. 21.12.14; Europ. War, in France, from 1915; Despatches four times; Bt. Major 1.1.18; M.C.; Croix de Guerre.

TORRANCE, P. V. (D.S.O. L.G. 15.10.18), Major, Cav. Can. Force.

TORRANCE, W. S. (D.S.O. L.G. 3.6.18), Eng.-Cdr., R.N., 7.3.15.

TORRENS, G. L. (D.S.O. L.G. 3.6.16) (Bar, L.G. 26.7.18); b. 12.12.87 at Bangalore, India; s. of C. P. Torrens, Land Records, Burma, and Eleanor Alice Torrens (*née* Gow); m. Phyllis Mary, d. of Capt. C. Greenwood, late Border R., of Oaklands, Grange-over-Sands, and Beechgrove, Harrogate; one s.; educ. Coombe Florey Rectory, near Taunton, Somerset, and R.M.C., Camberley; 2nd Lt., W.I.R., 20.4.10; Lt. 8.7.11; Capt., W.I.R., 20.4.16; Capt., Lan. Fus., 30.1.18; A/Lt.-Col., 1917–19. He organized and led a counter-attack on the Bluff (Ypres-Comines Canal), which the enemy had captured after the explosion of a mine 14.2.16, and was congratulated by Divisional and Corps Commanders for bravery; served with 1st D.C.L.I. (attached) from April to Sept. 1910; 2nd Lt.; Lt., W.I.R., 8.7.11; Jamaica and Sierra Leone, W.A.; Capt. and Adjt., 10th Lan. Fus., 8.9.14; embarked with Batt. 15.7.15, and served continuously with it in France; T/Major, 2nd-in-command, 10th Lan. Fus., 13.8.15; mentioned in Despatches.

TORTISE, H. J. (D.S.O. L.G. 16.9.18) (Bar, L.G. 3.6.18), T/Capt. (A/Major), R.W. Surrey Rgt.

TOSTEVIN, H. B. (D.S.O. L.G. 15.9.16), Eng.-Cdr., R.N., 1.1.19.

TOTTENHAM, C. L. (D.S.O. L.G. 7.8.18), Lt., R.N.R. He died 27.10.18.

TOVELL, R. W. (D.S.O. L.G. 1.1.19); b. 9.3.90, in Victoria, Australia; s. of C. E. Tovell, of Melbourne, and Mary Ann Tovell (*née* Mitchell); enlisted in A.I.F. 25.4.15; 1st com. 5.7.15; Lt. 12.10.15; Capt. 27.5.16; Major 22.10.17, 4th Aust. Pioneer Batt.; Brig. Major, 4th Aust. Inf. Brig., 19.2.18; Despatches twice.

TOVEY, G. S. (D.S.O. L.G. 14.1.16); b. 29.9.75; s. of late Col. H. Tovey, R.E.; 2nd Lt., R.A., 21.3.96; Lt. 21.3.99; Capt. 20.1.02; Adjt., R.A., 27.2.05 to 26.2.08; Major 1.1.13; Lt.-Col. 2.2.17; ret. pay, 1921; served S. African War; Despatches; Queen's Medal with 3 clasps; King's Medal with 2 clasps; Europ. War, 1914–18; Bt. Lt.-Col. 1.1.17; Despatches; C.M.G.

TOVEY, J. C. (D.S.O. L.G. 10.7.19), Cdr., R.N., 30.6.16.

TOWER, C. E. (D.S.O. L.G. 1.1.18), Rear Admiral, R.N.

TOWL, P. G. (D.S.O. L.G. 1.2.19), Capt., 37th Batt. Aust. Mil. Forces.

TOWNSEND, E. N. (D.S.O. L.G. 30.1.20); b. 4.7.71; 2nd Lt., W. Rid. R., 4.9.15; Lt. 16.2.98; Capt. 22.2.01; Major 6.3.12; served S African War, 1899–1901; dangerously wounded; Queen's Medal, 6 clasps; Europ. War. Despatches.

TOWNSEND, F. O. (D.S.O. L.G. 17.9.17), 2nd Lt. (T/Capt.), Ind. Army, R. of O.

TOWNSEND, J. N. (D.S.O. L.G. 1.1.17), Major, R. War. R., T.F., retired; Egyptian Exp., 1882; wounded; Medal; Bronze Star; Sudan Exp., 1885; Suakin; action at Tofrek, 2 clasps; Sudan, 1885–86; Frontier Field Force; S. African War, 1900–2; Queen's Medal, 4 clasps; King's Medal, 2 clasps; Europ. War; Despatches.

TOWNSEND, M. D. (D.S.O. L.G. 3.6.18); b. 1.6.87; 2nd Lt., R.A., 18.12.07; Lt. 18.12.10; Capt. 30.10.14; Major 31.10.17.

TOWSEY, F. W. (D.S.O. L.G. 1.1.18); b. 6.10.64; s. of Capt. G. W. Towsey, R.N.; m. Florence Harriet, d. of Lt.-Gen. Fisher, R.A.; one s.; educ. Rugby; Lt., W. Yorks. R., 25.11.85; Capt. 16.11.92; Adjt., W. Yorks. R., 15.2.94–14.2.98; Major 23.2.04; Lt.-Col. 7.3.14; Col. 7.3.18; Brig.-Gen. retired; served Lushai Exp., 1892; Medal; Ashanti Exp., 1896; Ashanti Star; Europ. War, 1914–18; T/Brig.-Gen., 1915–19; Despatches; C.M.G.; C.B.E.

TOZER, C. J. (D.S.O. L.G. 1.1.18), Major, R.A.M.C.

TRACY, G. C. (D.S.O. L.G. 3.6.18); b. 27.9.76; 2nd Lt., W.I.R., 4.3.99; Lt. 25.7.00; Capt. 31.12.08; Major 1.9.15; S. African War, 1901; served in St. Helena; Queen's Medal; Europ. War; Despatches.

TRAILL, E. F. T. (D.S.O. L.G. 1.1.18); b. 10.5.78; 2nd Lt., R. Innis. Fus., 24.1.00; Lt., R. Innis. Fus., 13.4.01; 2nd Lt., A.S.C., 1.5.01; Lt., A.S.C., 1.5.02; Capt. 30.4.06; Major, R.A.S.C., 30.10.14; Queen's Medal, 3 clasps; King's Medal, 2 clasps; Europ. War; Despatches.

TRAILL, H. E. O'B. (D.S.O. L.G. 14.11.16); b. 3.11.76; 2nd Lt., R.A., 28.3.00; Lt. 3.4.01; Capt. 28.5.10; Major 26.6.15; S. African War, 1901–2; Queen's Medal, 5 clasps; Europ. War; Despatches. His D.S.O. was awarded for gallantry at Longueval and elsewhere 19.7.16 to 4.9.16.

TRAILL, J. C. M. (D.S.O. L.G. 26.11.17) (Details, L.G. 6.4.18), Capt., Aust. Inf.; M.C.

TRAILL, R. F. (D.S.O. L.G. 16.9.18); b. 22.2.81; 2nd Lt., Worc., 7.5.02; Lt. 18.1.05; Capt. 18.9.14; Major 7.5.17.

TRAILL, W. H. (D.S.O. L.G. 1.1.17); b. 24.11.71; 2nd Lt., E. Lanc. R., 17.12.92; Lt. 10.10.95; Capt. 11.9.01; Major 10.9.14; ret. pay, 1921; Lt.-Col., late E. Lancs. R.; served Tirah, 1897–98; Medal and clasp; Europ. War, 1914–18; Despatches; C.M.G.; Bt. Lt.-Col.

TRAILL, W. S. (D.S.O. L.G. 14.1.16); b. 28.3.68; s. of late A. Traill, Provost of Trinity College, Dublin, and Catherine Elizabeth, d. of Capt. Stewart Moore, of Ballydivity, Co. Antrim, who fought in the Battle of Waterloo; m. Selena Margaret, d. of late C. Frizell; three s.; educ. Birney's, Gosport; Trinity College, Dublin; D.L., Co. Antrim; 2nd Lt., R.E., 29.3.90; Lt. 29.3.93; Capt. 29.3.01; Major 29.3.10; Lt.-Col. 31.7.18; retired 1919; served Waziristan, N.W. Frontier of India, 1894–95 (Medal and clasp); Tirah, N.W. Frontier, 1897–98 (Medal and 3 clasps); Europ. War, 1915; Despatches thrice; Croix de Guerre. He has the Durbar Medal, 1911.

TRAVERS, H. C. (D.S.O. L.G. 23.11.16); b. 26.1.76; 2nd Lt., R.A., 28.3.00; Lt. 3.4.01; Capt. 19.1.10; Major 8.12.14; Despatches; Bt. Lt.-Col. 1.1.18; C.B.E.

TRAVERS, R. J. A. (D.S.O. L.G. 3.6.16) (Bar, L.G. 1.1.18), Major, Aust. Mil. Forces.

TREASE, R. E. (D.S.O. L.G. 26.7.17); s. of late G. Trease and of Mrs. Trease. Prior to the war he was in the R.H.A., and he early gained a commission in the R.F.A.; was wounded three times; awarded the Military Cross; mentioned in Despatches, and recommended for the V.C. He was in Queen's Hospital, Sidcup, for his 19th operation when he contracted influenza. He died on 5.12.18.

TREDENNICK, J. P. (D.S.O. L.G. 14.1.16); b. 14.10.79; s. of Capt. W. R. Tredennick; 2nd Lt., R. Dublin Fus., 18.4.00; Lt. 14.7.04; Capt. 7.6.10; Major 1.9.15; S. African War, 1900–2; Queen's and King's Medals; Aden Hinterland Exp., 1903; W. Africa (S. Nigeria), 1905–6; commanded 18th London R. (London Irish), Sept. 1915–Dec. 1916; G.S., G.H.Q., Home Forces, Feb. 1917, to May, 1918; D.A.A.G., 63rd (R.N.) Div., 22.9.18.

TREHARNE, D. E. (D.S.O. L.G. 3.6.19). Capt. (A/Major, R.F.A.), T.F., att. 265th Brig. R.F.A.

TRELEAVEN, G. W. (D.S.O. L.G. 2.4.19) (Details, L.G. 10.12.19), Major, 4th Field Amb., Can. A.M.C.; M.C.

TRELOAR, G. D. (D.S.O. L.G. 26.9.17) (Details, L.G. 9.1.18), Lt. (A/Capt.), Coldstream Gds., S.R. His D.S.O. was awarded for gallantry on 31.7.17, at Pilckem Ridge.

TREMBLAY, T. L. (D.S.O. L.G. 1.1.17), Brig.-Gen., Can. Infantry ; served Europ. War, 1914–18 ; Despatches ; C.M.G. ; M.C. ; Legion of Honour.

TREMLETT, E. (D.S.O. L.G. 26.7.17), T/Lt., M.G.C. His D.S.O. was awarded for gallantry at Bullecourt 3.5.17.

TRENCH, C. F. (D.S.O. L.G. 25.8.16) ; b. 29.7.85 ; s. of C. O'H. Trench, D.L., of Clonfort, Co. Galway ; educ. Charterhouse ; R.M.C., Sandhurst ; 2nd Lt., Unatt., 18.1.05 ; 2nd Lt., I.A., 6.3.06 ; Lt. 18.4.07 ; Capt. 18.1.14 ; Major 18.1.20 ; served in 7th Hariana Lancers with the Mesopotamian Exp. Force, Aug. 1915, to Oct. 1916, including the First Battle of Kut, the Battle of Ctesiphon and subsequent retreat, and afterwards with Gen. Aylmer's attempted Relief of Kut ; Despatches several times ; served two years as G.S.O.2, Derajat Brigade, N.W. Province, India, including operations against Afghanistan and the N.W. Frontier tribes, 1919.

TRENCH, D. LE P. (D.S.O. L.G. 4.6.17) ; b. 25.5.82 ; s. of Col. and Mrs. Stewart Trench ; passed out of Woolwich into R.A. 21.12.00 ; Lt. 21.12.03 ; Capt. 21.12.13 ; Major, Sept. 1915 ; in Feb. 1917, he was appointed to the Staff as D.A.A.G. He was mentioned in Despatches, and awarded the M.C. He was killed in action 27.8.17. A Memorial Service for him and for Brig.-Gen. Malcolm Peake, C.M.G., who was killed by the same shell, was held at Holy Trinity Church, Brompton.

TRENCH, J. F. CHENEVIX- (Chenevix-Trench, J.F.).

TRENCH, L. CHEVENIX- (see Chevenix-Trench, L.).

TRENT, G. A. (D.S.O. L.G. 3.6.19) ; b. 1.9.70 ; 2nd Lt., North'n R., 3.5.90 ; Lt. 24.10.92 ; Capt. 22.9.99 ; Adjt., North'n R., 1905–8 ; Major 18.3.11 ; Lt.-Col. 30.3.15 ; Col. 30.3.19 ; served N.W. Frontier, India, 1897–98 ; severely wounded ; Medal, 2 clasps ; Europ. War, 1914–17 ; Despatches ; C.M.G. ; Chevalier, Legion of Honour.

TRESTRAIL, A. E. Y., M.A. (D.S.O. L.G. 8.3.19) (Details, L.G. 4.10.19) ; b. 1876 ; s. of Major A. B. Trestrail, M.B.E., V.D., J.P. ; m. Margaret Spiers, d. of A. S. Cunningham ; two s. ; educ. Amersham Hall School ; Christ's College, Cambridge ; Major, late the Cheshire Rgt. ; served Europ. War from 1914 ; Despatches.

TREW, E. F. (D.S.O. L.G. 4.6.17) ; b. 7.12.79 ; 2nd Lt., R.M., 1.1.98 ; Lt. 1.1.99 ; Capt. 1.4.07 ; Major 17.6.16 ; Brig.-Gen. retired, 1920, late R.M.L.I. ; served Europ. War, Egypt and Palestine ; Despatches ; C.M.G. ; Bt. Lt.-Colonel.

TREW, W. M. (D.S.O. L.G. 18.7.17), Major, Aust. Inf. His D.S.O. was awarded for gallantry on 3.5.17, at Bullecourt.

TRIMBLE, J. B. O. (D.S.O. L.G. 1.1.18) ; b. 8.8.81 ; 2nd Lt., Unatt., 8.1.01 ; E. Yorks. R., 9.3.01 ; Lt. 19.3.04 ; Capt. 18.12.12 ; Major 8.1.16 ; served S. African War, 1901–2 ; Queen's Medal, 4 clasps ; M.C. ; Europ. War ; Despatches

TRIMMER, P. H. (D.S.O. L.G. 22.2.18), Cdr., R.N., 30.6.14.

TRIPP, D. O. H. (gazetted as Tripp, D. O.) (D.S.O. L.G. 30.3.16) ; b. 21.11.90 ; s. of C. Howard Tripp ; educ. Derby School ; Dunchurch Hall, near Rugby ; Stubbington House, Fareham, and Rugby School. He played regularly for the Harlequins as Full Back ; commissioned Dec. 1914, and joined the L.N. Lancs. Rgt. at Felixstowe ; left for France 30.9.15 ; was four times wounded ; T/Capt. 19.4.16. He was killed in action at High Wood on 18.8.16.

TRIPP, W. H. L. (D.S.O. L.G. 4.6.17) ; b. July, 1881 ; 2nd Lt., R.M.A., 1.1.99 ; Lt. 1.1.00 ; Capt. 1.1.10 ; Major 6.6.17.

TRIST, L. H. (D.S.O. L.G. 1.1.19), Capt. (A/Lt.-Col.), Lincs. R., S.R. ; M.C.

TROBRIDGE, F. G. (D.S.O. L.G. 1.1.18), T/Major, Gen. List.

TROLLOPE, H. C. N. (D.S.O. L.G. 1.1.19) ; b. 17.2.96 ; 2nd Lt., Suff. R., 12.8.14 ; Lt. 11.12.14 ; Capt. 1.1.17 ; Despatches ; M.C.

TROLLOPE-BELLEW, F. D. (see Bellew, F. D.).

TRON, REV. M. (D.S.O. L.G. 26.11.17) (Details, L.G. 6.4.18) ; b. 1885 ; m. F. Bulmer ; educ. Alexandra Grammar School, Gateshead ; King's College, London ; joined Bush Brotherhood, W. Australia, for three years ; Rector of Dwellingup, 12 months ; commissioned as Chaplain to Australian Troops, Sept. 1914 ; served Egypt and Gallipoli, proceeding to France after evacuation ; transferred to English Army ; served with Artillery ,R.W. Surrey Rgt., and North'd Fus. ; Despatches thrice ; M.C. ; 2 Bars ; Chaplain to 2nd Lincs. Rgt. ; is Rector of Rushock, Worcesters. ; won 10-mile open, Essex, 1905 ; Norfolk, 1907.

TROTMAN-DICKENSON, REV. L. G. (see Dickenson, The Rev. L. G.).

TROTTER, C. T. (D.S.O. L.G. 4.6.17), Capt., Can. Engrs.

TROTTER, H. L. (D.S.O. L.G. 1.1.18), Major, Can. Engrs.

TROUP, A. G. (D.S.O. L.G. 3.6.18) ; b. 2.6.79 ; m. Victoria Louisa, d. of His Honour Judge A. B. Ellicott ; one d. ; 2nd Lt., R.M.A., 1.9.96 ; Lt. 1.7.97 ; Capt. 27.4.03 ; Major 23.9.15 ; Bt. Lt.-Col. 30.6.16 ; Lt.-Col., R.A.S.C., T.F. ; served Europ. War, 1914–18 ; Despatches thrice.

TROUSDELL, A. J. (D.S.O. L.G. 3.6.19) ; b. 22.5.80 ; 1st com. 11.12.09 ; 2nd Lt., retired, R. Ir. Fus. 13.3.12 ; Capt. R. Irish Fus., Spec. Res. ; M.C.

TROWER, R. G. (D.S.O. L.G. 1.1.17) ; b. at Sydney, Australia, 14.7.82 ; s. of Herbert Arthur Trower and Agnes Trower (*née* Dickinson) ; m. Elizabeth Claridge, d. of A. W. McCune, of New York ; educ. Park House, Southborough ; Loretto, Scotland ; Lt., 9th Border Regt., Jan. 1915 ; Lt., Tunnelling Compy., R.E., France, May, 1915 ; Capt., Oct. 1915 ; commanding Company, Oct. 1915 ; Major 1.1.16 ; M.C.

TROYTE, G. J. ACLAND- (see Acland-Troyte, G. J.).

TROYTE-BULLOCK, C. J. (D.S.O. L.G. 14.11.16) ; b. 17.5.67 ; s. of late G. Troyte and his 2nd wife, Alice, d. of Sir G. E. Welby-Gregory, Bart. ; m. Joan Acland, d. of L. Harper ; educ. Charterhouse ; 1st com. 10.10.91 ; Major 26.8.13 ; retired with rank of Lt.-Col. in the Army 23.1.19 ; served Europ. War, 1914–18 ; posted to command of 7th (S.) Batt. Som. L.I. (13.9.14) on its formation ; in France from July, 1915, remaining in command until the end of June, 1918 ; present at Laventie, Fleurbaix, 1915, Ypres, 1916 ; Battle of the Somme, 1916–17 ; Guillemont (3.9.16) ; Despatches three times ; Bt. Lt.-Col. 1.1.19 ; Lt.-Col. Commanding 4th Batt. Dorsets. Rgt.

TRUMAN, C. M. (D.S.O. L.G. 1.1.17) ; b. 26.10.80 ; s. of late Maj.-Gen. Truman ; m. Marslie, d. of Col. and Hon. Mrs. Tom Wood ; 2nd Lt., 12th Lancers, 21.2.00 ; Lt. 17.4.01 ; Adjt., 12th Lancers, 1.11.06 to 31.10.09 ; Capt. 25.3.08 ; Major 3.11.14 ; Lt.-Col. 4.9.21 ; served S. African War, 1901–2 ; Queen's Medal, 5 clasps ; Europ. War ; Despatches ; Bt. Lt.-Col. 1.1.18.

TRUMP, F. J. (D.S.O. L.G. 1.1.17) ; s. of late H. V. Trump, J.P. ; joined 1st Batt. Monmouthshire Rgt., T.F., in 1900 ; went to S. Africa, and on the outbreak of war returned and rejoined his old battalion, going to the front in Oct. 1915 ; in Dec. 1916, he was given command of a batt. of the S. Staffs. R., which he continued to command with great success until he was killed in action on 2.12.17, aged 45. Lt.-Col. Trump was awarded the Croix de Guerre.

TUCK, G. L. J. (D.S.O. L.G. 1.1.18) (Bar, L.G. 16.9.18) ; b. 26.11.89 ; e. s. of Rev. F. J. Tuck ; educ. Eton ; King's College , Cambridge (M.A.) ; Capt. (Temp. Major), Unatt. List, att. Suff. R. ; served Europ. War, 1914–19 ; Despatches four times ; twice wounded ; C.M.G. ; Legion of Honour.

TUCKEY, E. C. (D.S.O. L.G. 4.2.18) (Details, L.G. 5.7.18), 2nd Lt., R.F.A. (Spec. Res.).

TUDOR, E. O. (D.S.O. L.G. 14.5.20), Cdr., R.N.

TUDOR, L. P. O. (D.S.O. L.G. 18.7.17) (Bar, L.G. 1.2.19), Major, Can. Inf.

TUDWAY, L. C. P. (D.S.O. L.G. 12.7.19), Lt., R.N. ; D.S.C.

TUFFLEY, V. E. (D.S.O. L.G. 1.2.19), Lt., 2/10th Batt. London R. He died of wounds 7.9.18.

TUFTON, HONBLE. J. S. R. (D.S.O. L.G. 14.1.16) ; b. 8.11.73 ; e. s. and heir of 1st Baron Hothfield ; m. Lady Ierne Hastings, d. of 13th Earl of Huntingdon ; two s. ; two d. ; Major, R. Sussex R. ; served S. African War, 1901–2 ; Queen's Medal, 5 clasps ; Europ. War, 1914–19 ; Order Leopold ; Croix de Guerre.

TUKE, G. F. S. (D.S.O. L.G. 1.1.17) ; b. 7.2.76 ; e. s. of late Capt. Stratford Tuke, R.N. ; m. May, d. of Henry Langan ; one s. ; 2nd Lt., R.A., 4.3.99 ; Lt., R.A., 16.2.01 ; Capt., R.A., 5.12.05 ; Adjt., R.A., 20.5.13 to 29.10.14 ; Major 30.10.14 ; served S. African War, 1899–1902 ; Despatches twice ; Queen's Medal, 3 clasps ; King's Medal, 2 clasps ; Europ. War, 1914–18 ; Despatches twice.

TULLOCH, D. F. (D.S.O. L.G. 1.1.18) ; b. 21.4.70 ; 2nd Lt., R.A., 27.7.89 ; Lt. 27.7.92 ; Capt. 20.9.99 ; Major 21.10.10 ; Lt.-Col., R.A., 1.8.16 ; served in China ; Medal, clasp ; Europ. War ; Despatches.

TULLOCH, E. (D.S.O. L.G. 4.6.17), Temp. Capt. (Temp. Major), R.E.

TURLE, C. E. (D.S.O. L.G. 11.12.18), Cdr., R.N.

TURNBULL, D. O. (D.S.O. L.G. 4.6.17), Temp. Capt. (Temp. Major), A.V.C.

TURNBULL, F. K. (D.S.O. L.G. 2.12.18) ; b. 1885 ; y. s. of late Andrew Turnbull, of Hawera, N.Z. ; m. Winifred Sydney, o. d. of Harry Bayly ; educ. Univ., New Zealand ; Major, 1st Bn. Well. R., New Zea. Force ; served Europ. War, 1914–19 ; Despatches thrice ; M.C.

TURNBULL, G. O. (D.S.O. L.G. 14.1.16) ; b. 21.7.77 ; s. of Major-Gen. P. S. Turnbull ; m. Dora Amy, d. of Gen. Sir Edmund Elles ; educ. Merchiston School, Edinburgh ; 2nd Lt. (Unatt.), 22.1.98 ; 2nd Lt., Ind. S.C., 26.3.99 ; Lt., Ind. Army, 24.4.00 ; Capt., Ind. Army, 22.1.07 ; Major 1.9.15 ; served Tirah Exp., 1897–98 ; Medal, clasp ; Europ. War, 1914–18 ; Despatches.

TURNBULL, J. A. (D.S.O. L.G. 4.6.17) ; b. 9.10.79 ; Lt., R.A.M.C., 30.1.04 ; Capt., R.A.M.C., 30.7.07 ; Major 1.7.15 ; served N.W. Frontier of India, 1908 ; Medal with clasp ; Europ. War ; Despatches.

TURNBULL, R. J. (D.S.O. L.G. 20.7.17), Lt., R.N.R. ; D.S.C.

TURNER, A. C. (D.S.O. L.G. 3.6.18), Major, R.A.M.C.

TURNER, A. C. F., M.D. (D.S.O. L.G. 18.6.17) ; s. of A. J. Turner, M.D. ; educ. St. Thomas's Hospital ; Capt. (T/Major), R.A.M.C. ; served Europ. War, 1914–18 ; Despatches twice. His D.S.O. was awarded for gallantry on 12–14.3.17, at Bucquoy.

TURNER, A. G. B. (D.S.O. L.G. 25.8.17) ; b. 20.5.66 ; 2nd Lt., W. Rid. R., 5.2.87 ; Devon R. 26.2.87 ; Lt., Ind. S.C., 6.5.89 ; Capt. 5.2.98 ; Major 5.2.05 ; Lt.-Col., Ind. Army, 5.2.13 ; served N.W. Frontier of India, 1897–98 ; Medal with clasp ; China, 1900 ; Europ. War ; Despatches.

TURNER, A. M. (D.S.O. L.G. 14.1.16) ; b. 30.8.79 ; s. of Sir Montagu Cornish Turner, Chairman of Chartered Bank of India, Australia and China ; m. Oliver Beatrice Carr ; one s. ; one d. ; educ. Winchester ; Merton, Oxford ; 2nd Lt., 1st D. Gds., 14.3.00 ; Lt., 1st D. Gds., 10.10.00 ; Capt. 21.4.06 ; Major 9.9.14 ; served S. African War, 1901–2 ; Queen's Medal, 5 clasps ; Europ. War, 1914–19, in France and Palestine ; Despatches twice.

TURNER, CHARLES (gazetted as Turner, Canning) (D.S.O. L.G. 1.1.18), Major, T/Lt.-Col., Leic. R., S.R. ; served S. Africa, 1902 ; Queen's Medal, 3 clasps ; Europ. War ; Despatches.

TURNER, C. E. (D.S.O. L.G. 11.12.16), Capt. (T/Major), Glos. Yeomanry.

TURNER, C. G. R. SYDNEY- (see Sydney-Turner, C. G. R.).

TURNER, C. H. (D.S.O. L.G. 14.1.16) ; b. 30.6.76 ; Lt., R.A.M.C., 30.1.04 ; Capt., R.A.M.C., 30.7.07 ; Major, R.A.M.C., 1.7.15 ; Bt. Lt.-Col., R.A.M.C., 3.6.18 ; served Europ. War ; Despatches.

TURNER, EDWARD GEORGE (D.S.O. L.G. 17.9.17) ; b. 8.7.87 ; Lt., A.V.C., 5.1.10 ; Capt., R.A.V.C., 5.1.15.

TURNER, ERNEST GILBERT (D.S.O. L.G. 26.9.16), 2nd Lt., Royal Scots. His D.S.O. was awarded for gallantry on 10.7.16 at Ovillers. He was killed in action 12.4.17.

TURNER, E. V. (D.S.O. L.G. 1.1.17) ; b. 31.12.72 ; 2nd Lt., R.E., 22.7.92 ; Lt., R.E., 22.7.95 ; Capt., R.E., 22.7.03 ; Bt. Major, R.E., 23.7.03 ; Major, R.E., 22.7.12 ; Bt. Lt.-Col., R.E., 3.6.15 ; Bt. Colonel 3.6.18 ; Colonel, R.E., 31.8.20 ; served W. Africa, 1897–98 ; Despatches ; Medal, clasp ; S. African War, 1899–1902 ; Despatches ; Queen's Medal, 4 clasps ; King's Medal, 2 clasps ; Europ. War ; Despatches.

TURNER, G. F. B. (D.S.O. L.G. 3.6.19) ; b. 30.3.76 ; 2nd Lt., R.A., 26.5.00 ; Lt., R.A., 4.3.02 ; Capt., R.A., 11.2.11 ; Major, R.A., 30.10.14.

TURNER, J. A. (D.S.O. L.G. 18.7.17), Lt. (T/Lt.-Col.), The R. Scots ; M.C. He was killed in action 26.7.18.

TURNER, J. E. (D.S.O. L.G. 1.1.17) ; b. 24.8.80 ; 2nd Lt., Sco. Rif., 20.1.00 ; Lt., Sco. Rif., 1.4.03 ; Capt., Sco. Rif., 17.4.10 ; Major 1.9.15 ; Bt. Lt.-Col. 1.1.18 ; served S. African War, 1899–1902 ; Queen's Medal, 2 clasps ; King's Medal, 2 clasps ; Europ. War ; Despatches ; C.M.G.

TURNER, J. F. (D.S.O. L.G. 26.8.18) ; b. 24.4.81 ; 2nd Lt., R.E., 6.1.00 ; Lt., R.E., 6.1.03 ; Capt., R.E., 6.1.09 ; Major, R.E., 6.9.16 ; Bt. Lt.-Col., R.E., 15.11.19 ; served N.W. Frontier of India, 1908 ; Medal with clasp ; Europ. War ; Despatches.

TURNER, J. R. (D.S.O. L.G. 7.11.18), Major, R. Scots Fus.

TURNER, R. (D.S.O. L.G. 19.4.01) (Bar, L.G. 15.2.19) (Details, L.G. 30.7.19) (see "The Distinguished Service Order," from its institution to 31.12.15, by same publishers).

TURNER, R. A. (D.S.O. L.G. 1.1.18) ; b. 25.7.89 ; 2nd Lt., R.E., 4.9.09 ; Lt., R.E., 23.1.12 ; Capt., R.E., 4.9.15 ; Bt. Major, R.E., 1.1.19 ; M.C.

TURNER, R. B. (D.S.O. L.G. 4.6.17), T/Lt.-Col., S. African Defence Force ; C.M.G.

TURNER, R. G., F.R.C.S. (D.S.O. L.G. 1.2.17) ; b. 5.2.70 ; Capt., Ind. Med. Serv., 29.7.96 ; Major, Ind. Med. Serv., 30.1.05 ; Lt.-Col., Ind. Med. Serv., 30.1.13 ; Colonel, Ind. Med. Serv., 15.8.21 ; served Waziristan Expedition, 1894–95 ; Medal with clasp ; Uganda, 1897–98 ; Medal, 2 clasps ; China, 1900 ; Medal ; Europ. War ; Despatches ; C.M.G.

TURNER, R. L. (D.S.O. L.G. 1.2.19), Major, Can. Inf., Manitoba Rgt.

TURNER, R. R. (D.S.O. L.G. 25.10.16); b. 13.10.85; s. of Thomas Turner; m. Isabel, d. of James Fisher; two s.; one d.; educ. Dulwich College; joined R.N., 1900; Lt., 1906; joined Submarine Service; served in H.M.S. Argyll, 1912 to 1914; Comdr., 1917; served Europ. War, being at the outbreak of the war Commander on C15; in command of D3, Oct. 1914; commanded E23, Jan. 1916.

TURNER, R. V. (D.S.O. L.G. 8.3.19) (Details, L.G. 4.10.19); b. 12.5.82; 2nd Lt., Unatt., 8.1.01; Durh. L. Inf. 9.3.01; Lieut., Durh. L. Inf., 24.5.02; Capt., Durh. L. Inf., 7.4.14; Major, Durh. L. Inf., 8.1.16; served S. African War, 1901–2; Queen's Medal, 3 clasps; Europ. War; Despatches.

TUXFORD, G. S. (D.S.O. L.G. 8.3.19) (Details, L.G. 4.10.19) (Bar, L.G. 1.1.19); b. 7.2.70; educ. Wellingborough Grammar School, Northants; Brig.-Gen., Sask. R., commanding Can. Inf. Brigade, 1916–19; served Europ. War, 1914–19; Despatches eight times; C.B., 1917; C.M.G., 1916; Legion of Honour, Croix d'Officier.

TWEED, L. T. (D.S.O. L.G. 1.2.19), Major, Can. Engrs.

TWEEDIE, J. L. F. (D.S.O. L.G. 1.1.17) (Bar, L.G. 16.9.18); s. of Col. M. Tweedie; b. 19.11.72; 2nd Lt., Glouc. R., 4.4.00; Lt. 2.6.03; Capt. 14.1.11; Major 1.9.15; served S. African War, 1899–1901; Medal with 2 clasps.

TWEEN, A. S. (D.S.O. L.G. 20.10.16), Temp. Major, 10th Batt. Essex R. He was killed in action 23.3.18. His D.S.O. was awarded for gallantry on 19–21.7.16, at Delville Wood.

TWIDALE, W. C. E. (D.S.O. L.G. 1.1.17); b. 7.10.77; 2nd Lt., R.A., 1.9.97; Lt. 1.9.00; Adjt., R.A., 1902–5; Capt. 30.10.14; Major 20.2.18; served S. African War, 1899–1902; Despatches; Queen's Medal, 5 clasps; King's Medal, 2 clasps; Europ. War, 1914–18; Despatches; C.M.G.

TWISLETON-WYKEHAM-FIENNES, N. I. E. (D.S.O. L.G. 11.1.19); b. 28.3.76; 2nd Lt., R.A., 8.9.00; Lt. 8.9.03; Capt. 23.4.12; Major, R.F.A., 10.4.15.

TWISS, C. C. H. (D.S.O. L.G. 1.1.18), T/Capt. (A/Major), E. Yorks. R.

TWISS, E. K. (D.S.O. L.G. 1.1.17); b. 9.11.82; 2nd Lt., Devon R., 24.7.01; Lt., Devon R., 10.12.03; I.A. 19.4.05; Capt. 24.7.10; Bt. Major 3.6.16; Major 24.7.16.

TWISS, F. A. (D.S.O. L.G. 1.1.17); b. 5.5.71; ent. R.A. 13.2.91; Lt. 13.2.94; Capt. 21.10.99; Adjt. 1901–6; Major 27.9.11; Lt.-Col. 1.5.17; T/Brig.-Gen., 1918–19; served N.W. Frontier of India, 1897–98; Medal, 2 clasps; Tirah, 1897–98; clasp; S. African War, 1901–2; Queen's Medal, 5 clasps; M.V.O., 1905; Europ. War; Despatches; C.M.G.

TWISS, H. W. F. (D.S.O. L.G. 3.6.18); b. 20.11.79; 2nd Lt., Devon R., 11.2.99; Lt. 24.2.00; Adjt. 6.12.03 to 9.2.06; Capt. 11.2.08; Ind. Army 10.2.09; Major, Ind. Army, 1.9.15; served S. African War, 1899–1902; severely wounded; Despatches; Queen's Medal with 3 clasps; King's Medal with 2 clasps; Europ. War; Despatches.

TYLDEN-PATTENSON, E. C. (D.S.O. L.G. 26.8.18); b. 10.12.71; 2nd Lt., R.E., 12.2.92; Lt. 12.2.95; Capt. 17.1.03; Major 12.2.12; operations in Chitral, 1895; Medal with clasp; N.W. Frontier of India, 1897–98; Tochi; clasp; China, 1900; Despatches; Medal; N.W. Frontier of India, 1908; operations in the Mohmand country; Medal with clasp; operations in the Abor country, 1911–12; Despatches; Bt. Lt.-Col. 6.6.12; Europ. War; Despatches.

TYLDEN-WRIGHT, W. R. (D.S.O. L.G. 3.6.18); b. 17.10.80; 2nd Lt., Manch. R., 4.5.01; Lt., Manch. R., 30.11.01; 3rd Hussars 17.5.02; Capt. 24.10.11; served S. African War, 1900–2; Queen's Medal, 3 clasps; King's Medal, 2 clasps; Europ. War; Despatches; Bt. Major 3.6.19.

TYLER, A. M. (D.S.O. L.G. 4.6.17); b. 22.4.66; Lt., R.A., 16.9.85; Capt. 13.11.95; Major 16.3.04; Lt.-Col. 6.8.13; Col., R.G.A., 6.8.17.

TYLER, R. M. (D.S.O. L.G. 4.6.17); only s. of Major-General Trevor Tyler, C.B., and Ada, d. of Edward Perkins; Lt.-Col., Durham L.I.; Chevalier, Legion of Honour; Croix de Guerre with Palm. He died of pneumonia following influenza at the Field Ambulance Hospital, Rheinbach, near Bonn, Germany, on 26.2.19, aged 41.

TYNAN, J. (D.S.O. L.G. 16.5.16); b. 9.1.78; 2nd Lt., Wilts. R., 14.11.15; Lt. 31.5.17; Capt., York and Lanc. R., 25.10.18; His D.S.O. was awarded for gallantry on 8–9.4.16, at Ferme Cour, St. d'Avoue.

TYNDALE, W. F., M.D. (D.S.O. L.G. 1.1.18); b. 11.5.74; s. of Wentworth R. Tyndale, M.B.; m. Ethel Margaret McEwan; two s.; two d.; educ. St. George's Hospital; Lt., R.A.M.C., 1.9.02; Capt. 1.5.06; Major 1.3.14; Bt. Lt.-Col. 3.6.19; served S. Africa, 1899–1902; Despatches; Queen's Medal, 3 clasps; Europ. War, 1914–18; Despatches; C.M.G.

TYNDALL, H. S. (D.S.O. L.G. 1.2.17); b. 16.7.75; 2nd Lt., Unatt., 16.1.95; Ind. S.C. 29.3.96; Lt., Ind. Army, 16.4.97; Capt. 16.1.04; Major 16.1.13; Lt.-Col. 16.1.21; served N.W. Frontier of India, 1897–98; Medal with 2 clasps; Europ. War; Despatches.

TYRRELL, G. G. M., F.R.C.S. (D.S.O. L.G. 12.12.19); b. 10.11.76; o. s. of late George Tyrrell; m. Eva, 7th d. of 16th Baron St. John of Bletsoe; one s.; one d.; educ. Charterhouse; 2nd Lt., 5th Lancers, 15.11.99; Lt. 20.11.00; Capt. 16.5.08; retired with rank of Lt.-Col., 1920; served S. African War, 1899–1901; Europ. War, 1915–19; Despatches thrice; Chevalier, Legion of Honour, 1919.

TYRRELL, W., M.B. (D.S.O. L.G. 1.1.18) (Bar, L.G. 26.7.18); s. of Alderman Tyrrell, of Belfast; educ. Belfast University; Capt., R.A.M.C., from S. Res., 6.2.18; A/Lt.-Col.; M.C. He was on active service from the first week of the war.

TYRRELL, W. G. (D.S.O. L.G. 4.6.17); b. 6.6.82; 2nd Lt., R.E., 24.6.03; Lieut., R.E., 31.12.05; Capt., R.E., 24.6.14; Bt. Major 3.6.18; Major 24.6.18; Bt. Lt.-Col. 3.6.19.

TYRWHITT, F. ST. J. (D.S.O. L.G. 14.1.16); b. 30.8.78; s. of Cdr. Philip N. Tyrwhitt; 2nd Lt., Worc. R., 27.10.00; Lt., Worc. R., 21.12.01; Capt., Worc. R., 17.11.04; Adjt. 17.11.07 to 20.12.10; Major 26.10.15; served S. African War, 1900; Queen's Medal with 4 clasps; Europ. War; Despatches four times.

TYRWHITT, SIR REGINALD YORKE, K.C.B. (D.S.O. L.G. 3.6.16); b. 1870; s. of late Rev. Richard St. John Trywhitt; m. Angela, 2nd d. of late Mathew Corbally, J.P.; one s.; two d.; educ. Oxford; H.M.S. Britannia, Aug. 1883; Lt., 1894; Commander, 1903; Capt., 1908; Commodore, 1st Class, 1915; Rear Admiral 2.12.19; as Lieut., H.M.S. Cleopatra, landed with party at Nicaragua, 1894; in command of Destroyer Flotillas of First Fleet, 1913; served Europ. War, and commanded the Harwich Force throughout entire war; Despatches; C.B., 1914; K.C.B., 1917; Commander of Legion of Honour, 1916; an Officer of the Order of Savoy, 1917; Croix de Guerre with Palms; created a Baronet, 1919, and received grant £10,000 for services rendered during the war; received the Freedom of the Cities of Oxford and Ipswich, and D.C.L., Oxford University; appointed Senior Naval Officer, Gibraltar, July, 1919.

TYSOE, W. (D.S.O. L.G. 16.9.18), Temp. 2nd Lt., Bed. R.

TYSON, E. J. (D.S.O. L.G. 26.9.17) (Details, L.G. 9.1.18), Major (T.F.), R.F.C.; M.C. He died of wounds 11.3.18.

TYTLER, H. C. (D.S.O. L.G. 27.7.18); b. 26.9.67; Lt., Manch. Regt., 30.1.86; Ind. S.C., 9.11.87; Capt., Ind. Army, 30.1.97; Major, Ind. Army, 30.1.04; Lt.-Col., Ind. Army, 22.5.11; Col., Ind. Army, 2.7.16; Temp. Brig.-Gen. 19.1.19; Major-Gen. 4.9.20; served Sikkim Exp., 1888; Despatches; Medal with clasp; N.E. Frontier of India, Lushai, 1890; services acknowledged by the Government; N.W. Frontier of India, Waziristan, 1901–2; Medal with clasp; served Europ. War; C.B.; C.M.G.; C.I.E.

TYTLER, J. F. FRASER- (see Fraser-Tytler, J. F.).

TYTLER, N. FRASER- (see Fraser-Tytler, N.).

UBSDELL, T. R. (D.S.O. L.G. 1.1.18), Major, R. of O., late R.A.; served S. African War, 1901; Queen's Medal, 5 clasps; Europ. War.

ULRICH, T. F. (D.S.O. L.G. 1.1.17) (Bar, L.G. 1.2.19); b. 10.12.88; s. of A. C. T. Ulrich, of Melbourne; educ. Wesley College, Melbourne; Lt.-Col., Aust. Mil. Forces; served Europ. War, 1914–18; O.C., 6th Batt. A.I.F., previously 2nd-in-command of 8th Batt.

UMFREVILLE, R. B. (D.S.O. L.G. 25.8.17); m. Georgina Florence, d. of late E. Heron-Maxwell-Blair; T/Lt.-Col., late Glouc. Rgt.; served Europ. War, 1914–17; C.M.G. His D.S.O. was awarded for gallantry at Wytschaete 7–8.6.17.

UNDERWOOD, J. P. D. (D.S.O. L.G. 3.6.16); b. 25.1.82; s. of the late Capt. C. F. W. Underwood, formerly of Lomesby Hall, near Brigg, Lincolnshire; m. Rosina, d. of R. C. Watts, J.P.; educ. Lancing College; 2nd Lt., N. Lanc. R., 17.9.02; Lt. 4.3.05; Capt. 8.10.14; Maj. 2.2.17; served S. African War with I.Y., 1900–2; Adjt., 9th Batt. I.Y., 1.1.02 to 31.7.02; Queen's Medal, 2 clasps; King's Medal, 2 clasps; served with W.A.F.F., Nigeria, 1910–20; O.C., 5th Bn. Nigeria R. Mtd. Inf., 1917–18; O.C., 4th Bn., Nig. R. from 1.1.19; with Nig. R. under Gen. Sir Charles Dobell in German Cameroons as a Company Commander in Col. Hayworth's Column.

UNIACKE, E. W. P. (D.S.O. L.G. 24.6.16); s. of Capt. H. T. Uniacke and Isabella Uniacke (*née* Fortescue); educ. Charterhouse; Lt.-Col., 2nd King Edward's Horse, att. 8th R. Irish Fusiliers; with Imp. Yeo. went through ranks attaining rank of Capt.; served S. African War; Queen's and King's Medals; Commissioner, S. Nigeria, 1904–09; Europ. War, 1914–18, with 2nd King Edward's Horse and 8th R. Irish Fus.; Despatches twice. His D.S.O. was awarded for gallantry at Hulloch 27.4.16.

UNIACKE, G. L. (D.S.O. L.G. 18.1.18) (Details, L.G. 25.4.18) (Bar, L.G. 1.1.18); Capt. and Bt. Major (T/Lt.-Col.), R. of O., R. Lancaster R., and 2nd Nigeria R.; served S. African War, 1900; Queen's Medal, 5 clasps; Europ. War.

UNSWORTH, G. (D.S.O. L.G. 11.4.19), Lt.-Cdr. (A/Cdr.), R.N.R.; D.S.C.

UNTHANK, J. S. (D.S.O. L.G. 1.1.18); b. 19.7.75; s. of C. W. J. Unthank; m. Ione Eleanor, d. of late C. Bewicke; two d.; 2nd Lt., Durh. L.I., 9.12.96; Lt. 23.11.98; Capt. 24.5.02; Maj. 1.9.15; served S. African War, 1899–1902; Queen's Medal and 5 clasps; Europ. War, 1914–18; Despatches.

UPTON, W. A. (D.S.O. L.G. 4.2.18) (Details, L.G. 5.7.18), T/2nd Lt., Wilts. R.

URMSTON, A. G. B. (D.S.O. L.G. 1.1.17); b. 6.11.60; Lt., R. Marines, 1.9.80; Capt. 10.3.90; Major 11.2.99; ret. pay 18.11.03; served S. African War, 1899–1900; Despatches; Bt. Lt.-Col. 2.5.00; Queen's Medal, 3 clasps; Europ. War.

URQUHART, H. M. (D.S.O. L.G. 18.7.17) (Bar, L.G. 11.1.19); Lt.-Col., R. of O., Canadian Militia; extra Aide-de-Camp to the King; M.C. His D.S.O. was awarded for gallantry at Farbus 9.4.17.

URQUHART, J. A. B. (D.S.O. L.G. 1.1.18); s. of J. Urquhart; served during the whole war; Capt. (Staff Capt.), Heavy Artillery; Despatches three times.

URWICK, F. D. (D.S.O. L.G. 26.3.18) (Details, L.G. 24.8.18), Major, Somersets. L.I.

USSHER, R. (D.S.O. L.G. 12.7.19), Lt.-Cdr., R.N., 30.4.16.

UTTERSON, A. T. LE M. (D.S.O. L.G. 1.1.17); b. 10.4.86; 2nd Lt., Leic. R., 25.4.06; Lt. 4.9.08; Capt. 18.5.13.

UTTERSON, H. K. (D.S.O. L.G. 15.3.16); b. 8.11.77; 2nd Lt., Dorset R., 8.9.97; Lt. 1.12.99; Capt. 22.3.05; Major; served African War, 1899–1902; Queen's Medal, 5 clasps; King's Medal, 2 clasps; Europ. War; Despatches. He was killed in action 10.8.18.

UTTERSON-KELSO, J. E. (D.S.O. L.G. 26.7.18) (Bar, L.G. 1.2.19); b. 16.5.93; 2nd Lt., R. Sco. Fus., 4.9.12; Lt. 24.10.14; Capt. 25.12.15; M.C.

UZIELLI, T. J. (D.S.O. L.G. 8.3.18); b. 10.10.82; s. of late T. Uzielli and Mrs. Uzielli; m. Georgina Marie, d. of D. F. Mackenzie, and widow of Bt. Lt.-Col. W. A. de C. King, D.S.O., R.E.; educ. Marlborough College; R.M.C., Sandhurst; 2nd Lt., The King's Own Regt., 22.10.02; Lt. 22.1.07; Capt. 22.10.14; Maj. 22.10.17; Col. ret. pay, 10.8.19; served Europ. War, 1914–18; Despatches five times; M.C.; Legion of Honour; Bt. Maj. 1.1.17; Bt. Lt.-Col. 1.1.19.

VACHER, C. C. B. (D.S.O. L.G. 15.9.16); b. 3.10.86; s. of Sydney Vacher and Janet Vacher (*née* Dumas); m. 24.3.17, Dorothy Byron Kelsey; one s.; educ. H.M.S. Britannia; R.N. College, Greenwich; Lt., R.N., 30.1.08; Lt.-Comdr. 30.1.16; served Europ. War from 1914 under Rear Admiral Tyrwhitt in Harwich Force, in H.M.S. Undaunted and Canterbury; present at Cuxhaven, Dogger Bank, Jutland.

VALENTINE, J. (D.S.O. L.G. 4.6.17); b. 22.8.87; s. of the late James Valentine, Manager, Northern Assurance Co., and Mrs. Valentine, d. of the late John Chambers Roe; m. Louisa Eileen Knox, d. of Major-General G. W. Knox, C.B., and Lady Sybil Knox, sister of the Earl of Lonsdale; educ. Dulwich; joined the R.F.C., Aug. 1914; Lieutenant-Colonel, R.F.C.; took part in the Europ. Circuit of 1911; only British Competitor to complete the course; flew in the "Circuit of Britain" "Daily Mail" race round England; took part in the "Military Trials" on Salisbury Plain, 1912; was the first man to fly over Paris; Legion of Honour (Chevalier) 8.11.15, for services rendered to the French Government. His D.S.O. was awarded for good work in Russia; Cross of Stanislaus, 1st Class; Order of St. George, 4th Degree (Russian), for distinction in the fights at Tarnopol and Tremboviay in July, 1917. As a consequence of the strenuous work and privations borne by him he died at Kieff 7.8.17.

VALLINGS, REV. G. R., M.A. (D.S.O. L.G. 1.1.18); b. Bishop's College, Calcutta, 4.3.67; s. of Rev. F. R. Vallings; m. Mary Gertrude, d. of R. Orr; one s.; one d.; educ. St. Edmund's, Canterbury; St. Edmund's, Salisbury; Worcester College, Oxford; Hon. Canon of Cumbrae; Rector of St. John the Baptist, Perth; C.F., 1915; S.C.F., C.E., 1917; D.A.C.G., 5th Corps.

VANDELEUR, C. B. (D.S.O. L.G. 30.1.20); b. 28.3.67; 2nd Lt., Sco. Rifles, 5.2.87; Lt. 22.6.91; Capt. 23.12.96; Bt. Major 22.8.02; Major 10.10.05; Lt.-Col. 11.3.15; served S. African War, 1899–1902; Despatches; Queen's Medal, 4 clasps; King's Medal, 2 clasps; Europ. War; Despatches.

VANDELEUR, T. B. (D.S.O. L.G. 1.1.17); b. 27.7.77; 2nd Lt., R. Irish Rgt., 27.7.01; Lt. 6.2.04; Adjt., R. Ir. Rgt., 1906–9; Capt. 28.8.09; Major 27.7.16; Bt. Lt.-Col. 3.6.18; served S. African War, 1900–2; Queen's Medal, 4 clasps; King's Medal, 2 clasps; Sudan, 1910; operations in S. Kordofan; Sudan Medal, clasp; Europ. War; Despatches.

VAN DEN BERG, J. W. H. G. H. (D.S.O. L.G. 4.6.17), Capt. (A/Major), Can. Inf.

VAN DER BYL, J. (D.S.O. L.G. 11.5.17); b. 11.10.78; educ. Wellington College; 2nd Lt., 8th Hrs., 7.5.98; Lt. 5.7.99; Capt. 9.11.01; Maj. 19.10.13; Lt.-Col. 1.11.20; S. African War, 1900–2; Despatches twice; Queen's Medal, 5 clasps; King's Medal, 2 clasps; Europ. War; 1914 Star; Despatches. He has the Delhi Durbar Medal.

VAN DER KISTE, F. W. (D.S.O. L.G. 1.1.17); b. 11.5.75; s. of late Capt. W. Van der Kiste (84th Rgt.) and S. M. van der Kiste (*née* Harding); m. Evelyn G., d. of late Gen. R. Y. Shipley, C.B., R. Fus.; four s.; educ. Trinity College School, Stratford-on-Avon; R.M.A., Woolwich; commissioned R.A. 17.11.94; Lt. 17.11.97; Capt. 10.10.00; Major 30.10.14; Lt.-Col., R.G.A., 6.1.21; Europ. War, from Sept. 1914, France and Salonika; Despatches twice.

VANDERSLUYS, C. H. (D.S.O. L.G. 4.6.17), Major, Can. Inf.

VANDERWATER, R. (D.S.O. L.G. 14.11.16); b. 6.1.89; s. of C. H. Vanderwater; educ. Stirling High School; Albert College, Belleville, Ontario; first commission 9.9.08; Lt.-Col., Argyle L.I., Ontario. His D.S.O. was awarded for gallantry on 9.9.16 at Pozières.

VAN DER WESTHUIZEN, P. B. (D.S.O. L.G. 22.8.18), Lt.-Col., 17th Mtd. Rifles, S. African Forces.

VAN DE VENTER, D. J. C. B. (D.S.O. L.G. 22.8.18), Col., 4th Mtd. Brig. (10th Dismounted Rifles), S. African Forces.

G. P. Vanier.

VANIER, G. P. (D.S.O. L.G. 11.1.19), Major, 22nd French Batt. Can. Inf., Quebec R.; M.C.

VANNER, J. C. (D.S.O. L.G. 26.7.18), T/Capt., Leic. R.; M.C. He died 19.3.19.

VAN NIEKIRK, L. (D.S.O. L.G. 22.8.18), Lt.-Col., Marico Commando, S. African Mil. Forces.

VANRENEN, G. R. (D.S.O. L.G. 12.9.19); b. 24.11.68; 2nd Lt., R. War. R., 11.2.88; Lt. 31.7.89; Capt., Ind. Army, 11.2.99; Maj. 11.2.06; Lt.-Col. 11.2.14; ret. pay 5.10.20; served N.W. Frontier, 1897–98; Medal, clasp; Europ. War; Despatches.

VAN RENSBURG, M. J. J. (D.S.O. L.G. 22.8.18), Lt.-Col., Wolmaranstad Commando, S. African Mil. Forces.

VAN RYNEVELD, SIR H. A., B.A., B.Sc., A.C.G.I. (D.S.O. L.G. 1.1.19); b. Orange Free State, 2.5.91; s. of D. J. Van Ryneveld, J.P.; m. Miss Collard, of Croydon; educ. Grey College School, and Grey University College, S. Africa; Imperial College, University of London; commissioned Loyal North Lancashire Rgt. 2.9.14; transferred R.F.C., April, 1915; Lt.-Col., R.A.F.; Colonel; Director, S. African Air Force, from 1921; served Egypt (Western Frontier and Palestine), Oct. 1915–June, 1916; Salonika, June–Nov. 1916; R.F.C. (Home Defence), Nov. 1916, to March, 1917; B.E.F., March, 1917–Feb. 1919; S.A. Liaison at Air Ministry with R.F.C. and R.A.F.; K.B.E., 1920; Despatches six times; M.C.; 1915 Star; Order of Nile (4th Class); Legion of Honour; Croix de Guerre (Belgian); flew from London to Cape Town, via Cairo, 1920.

VANSITTART, E. (D.S.O. L.G. 30.1.20); b. 19.4.56; first commission 10.9.75; Col. 10.9.06; Unemp. Supy. List, Ind. Army, 19.4.13, late commanding 8th Batt. R.W. Kent Rgt.; served Mahsud Waziri Expedition, 1881; Hazara Expeditions, 1888 and 1891; Medal, clasp; N.W. Frontier and Tirah, 1897–98; Medal, 3 clasps; Europ. War.

VAN SOMEREN, W. V. L. (D.S.O. L.G. 18.2.18) (Details, L.G. 18.7.18), T/Major, R. Fus.; M.C.

VAN STRAUBENZEE, A. W. (D.S.O. L.G. 4.6.17) (Bar, L.G. 22.6.18); b. 18.3.84; 2nd Lt., R.A., 31.7.02; Lt. 31.7.05; Capt. 30.10.14; Maj., R.H.A., 13.4.16.

VAN TONDER, R. J. P. (D.S.O. L.G. 22.8.18), Col. Commandant, Rustenburg Commando (Van Tonder's Horse).

VAN VELDEN, D. O. (D.S.O. L.G. 27.7.18), T/Lt.-Col., Gen. List.; Lt.-Col., S. African Defence Force.

VAN ZYL, J. A. (D.S.O. L.G. 22.8.18), Lt.-Col. (T/Col. Commandant), Kalahar, Horse, S. African Forces.

VAN ZYL, J. S. (D.S.O. L.G. 22.8.18), Lt.-Col., 20th Mounted Rifles (Graaf Reinet Ruiters), S. African Forces.

VAN ZYL, K. J. (D.S.O. L.G. 22.8.18), Major, Carnarvon Commando, S. African Forces.

VARLEY, O. (D.S.O. L.G. 15.2.19) (Details, L.G. 30.7.19); s. of late J. W. Varley; T/Capt., 7th Batt. E. Yorks. R.; M.C.

VASEY, G. A. (D.S.O. L.G. 3.6.18), Major, Aust. Arty.

VAUGHAN, A. O. (D.S.O. L.G. 1.1.19), Major (T/Lt.-Col.), Labour Corps.

VAUGHAN, E. (D.S.O. L.G. 4.6.17); b. 20.10.66; 2nd Lt., Manch. R., 10.11.88; Lt. 10.9.90; Capt. 1.11.97; Maj. 17.2.04; Lt.-Col. 1.9.16; Col. 1.9.20; served S. African War, 1899–1902; Despatches twice; Bt. Maj. 22.8.02; Queen's Medal, 5 clasps; King's Medal, 2 clasps; Europ. War; C.M.G.

VAUGHAN, E. J. F. (D.S.O. L.G. 3.6.16); b. 7.8.75; s. of Lt.-Col. E. H. Vaughan, late Devons. R.; educ. Winchester; joined Devons. R. from Militia, 1896; 2nd Lt., Devon R., 9.12.96; Lt. 28.12.98; Capt. 13.7.01; Maj. 1.9.15; Colonel 31.8.20; Brig.-Gen., ret. pay, 10.12.21; served S. African War, 1899–1902; Despatches; Queen's Medal, 5 clasps; King's Medal, 2 clasps; with Egyptian Army for nine years; took part in Beir Patrol, 1912 (Sudan Medal and clasp); 3rd Class Osmanieh; 4th Class, Medjidie; served Europ. War as Adjt., S.R. Batt. Devons. R., 1914; then D.A.A. and Q.M.G., Base, Egypt; commanded 2/4th R.W. Kent Rgt. at Gallipoli; Despatches; A.A. and Q.M.G., 27th Div., B.S.F.; Despatches; Bt. Lt.-Col. 3.6.17; Croix de Guerre; A.Q.M.G., 12th Corps, B.S.F.; D.A. and Q.M.G., 12th Corps; Despatches; Bt. Col. 3.6.19; Order of White Eagle, 3rd Class; D.A. and Q.M.G., Allied Forces, Constantinople; C.M.G.

VAUGHAN, E. N. E. M. (D.S.O. L.G. 20.10.16); b. 19.11.78; s. of late E. Vaughan and Mary Celeste, d. of Hon. G. L. Vaughan; m. Hilda Winifred, d. of N. H. Mander; one s.; one d.; educ. Beaumont College, Old Windsor; R.M.C., Sandhurst; 2nd Lt., G. Gds., 7.5.98; Capt. 23.1.05; retired 10.5.13; Major, R. of O., G. Gds.; served S. African War; wounded; Europ. War, 1914–18; Despatches.

VAUGHAN, E. W., M.B. (D.S.O. L.G. 3.6.19); b. 25.8.82; Lt., R.A.M.C., 1.8.08; Capt. 1.2.12; Maj. 1.8.20; M.C.

VAUGHAN, P. E. (D.S.O. L.G. 22.9.16); b. 25.3.76; s. of the late Capt. Herbert Vaughan, 68th Foot; educ. United Services College, Westward Ho!; m. Marjorie Bennett; two s.; 2nd Lt., York and Lanc. R., 26.8.96; Capt. 23.1.05; ret. pay, Worc. R., 21.12.10; Maj., Spec. Res., Worc. R.; employed with Egyptian Army, 1904–9; served S. African War, 1899–1902; Despatches; Queen's Medal, 6 clasps; King's Medal, 2 clasps. His D.S.O. was awarded for gallantry on 10.7.16 at Contalmaison.

VAUGHAN-WILLIAMS, H. W. (D.S.O. L.G. 4.6.17), Lt.-Col., S. African Medical Corps.

VELLACOTT, P. C. (D.S.O. L.G. 1.1.17), T/Major, S. Lan. Rgt.; served Europ. War; Brig. Major, Inf. Brig.; was a prisoner of war in Germany.

VENABLES, J. D. (D.S.O. L.G. 1.2.17); s. of H. Venables; m. Margaret, d. of late Lt.-Gen. Sir H. Le Gezt Bruce, K.C.B., R.A.; 2nd Lt., R.W. Fus., 11.5.01; Lt. 2.11.04; Capt. 9.9.11; Major 11.5.16.

VENN, G. W. C. (D.S.O. L.G. 14.7.16), Lt.-Cdr. (A/Cdr.), R.N.R.

VENN-ELLIS, S. G. (see Ellis, S. G. Venn-).

VENNING, F. E. W. (D.S.O. L.G. 25.8.17); b. 26.1.82; 2nd Lt., 8.5.01; Lt., Ind. Army, 8.8.03; Capt. 8.5.10; Maj. 8.5.16; Bt. Lt.-Col. 1.1.19.

VENNING, J. A. (D.S.O. L.G. 22.8.18), Major, S. African Field Post and Telegraph Corps.

VERCOE, H. R. (D.S.O. L.G. 26.7.18), Capt., Auckland Rgt., N.Z. Forces; D.C.M. Capt. Vercoe is the grandson of a great Maori chief who fell in fighting against us in the Battle of Gate Pa.

VEREY, H. E. (D.S.O. L.G. 3.6.18), T/Lt. (A/Major), Gen. List.

VERMAAS, P. A. (D.S.O. L.G. 22.8.18), Major, Calvinia-Kenhardt Commando, S. African Forces.

VERNEY, SIR H. C. W., Bart., M.A. (D.S.O. L.G. 1.1.18); b. 7.6.81; s. of 3rd Bart. and Margaret Maria, d. of Sir John Hay Williams and Lady Sarah, d. of 1st Earl Amherst; m. Lady Rachel Bruce, d. of 9th Earl of Elgin; four s.; two d.; educ. Harrow; Balliol College, Oxford; was M.P. (L.) for N. Bucks, 1910–18; Lt.-Colonel; served Europ. War, 1915–18.

VERNEY, L. M., F.R.C.V.S. (D.S.O. L.G. 1.1.18); b. 2.6.78; Lt., A.V.C. (now R.A.V.C.), 3.9.04; Capt. 3.9.09; Maj. 10.7.15.

VERNON, A. J. (D.S.O. L.G. 1.1.19); b. 16.6.85; 2nd Lt., R. Ir. Fus., 4.11.14; Lt. 5.11.15; Temp. Lt.-Col. 1.1.19; M.C.

VERNON, G. C. F. HARCOURT- (see Harcourt-Vernon, G. C. F.).

VERNON, H. A. (D.S.O. L.G. 20.10.16); b. 5.12.79; s. of the late H. C. E. Vernon, I.C.E. (y. s. of Col. G. A. Vernon, Coldstream Guards, of Harefield Park, Uxbridge) and Helen Mayne Vernon, d. of Gen. John Liptrott, Bengal Staff Corps; m. Maud Valerie, d. of Major-Gen. James G. Turner, C.B., and Blanche Rose Turner (*née* Boileau); one s.; educ. Wellington College; Sandhurst; Winner of Kadir Cup on chestnut Australian gelding Fireplant; 2nd Lt., K.R.R.C., 11.4.00; Lt. 9.5.01; Capt. 23.11.10; Major 1.9.15; Lt.-Col., R.C. of Signals, 28.6.20; T/Brig.-Gen. 3.9.17 to 29.9.18; joined 2nd Batt. K.R.R.C., June, 1900, at Ingogo, Natal; served S. African War, 1900–1; Queen's Medal, clasp; went with Battalion to India, 1901; A.D.C. to General Sir Beauchamp Duff, G.C.B., etc. (C.-in-C. in India), from Feb. 1914, to outbreak of war; landed in Marseilles, Nov. 1914, in command of Indian Cavalry Corps Signal Squadron; received Légion d'Honneur (Chevalier), Nov. 1915; appointed 2nd-in-command, 1st Batt. K.R.R.C., Dec. 1915; appointed to command 23rd Batt. R. Fusiliers, Jan. 1916 (T/Lt.-Col.); actions with Battalion, Delville Wood 27.7.16; Beaumont Hamel, Nov. 1916; Miraumont; Grevillers, etc., Feb. and March, 1917; Arras, April and May, 1917; ordered to Egypt to command a Brigade, May, 1917. On arrival, there being no vacancy, appointed Aug. 1917, to command 2/5th Hants Territorials; appointed to command 158th (Welsh) Brigade, E.E.F., Sept. 1917; Despatches twice; Bt. Lt.-Col. 3.6.18. His D.S.O. was awarded for gallantry at Delville Wood on 27.7.16; Order of the Nile (Class 3).

H. A. Vernon.

VERNON, H. V. (D.S.O. L.G. 1.1.18), Lt.-Col., Aust. F.A.; S. African War, 1899–1900; Queen's Medal, 3 clasps.

VERRETT, H. B. (D.S.O. L.G. 19.8.16); b. Loretteville, Quebec, 9.2.74; s. of J. A. Verrett and E. Verrett (*née* Bacon); m. Irène Forbes; educ. Levis College; Laval University, Quebec; Lt. in The Governor-General's Foot Guards, Ottawa, 1906–8; Capt., 1908; Major, 1915; came to England with 2nd Batt. 1st Can. Contingent, as Capt., 1914; promoted Major in the Field, 1915, and Lt.-Col., 1916; Despatches; Asst. Deputy Postmaster General, Ottawa, Canada, from 1911.

VESEY, I. L. B. (D.S.O. L.G. 4.6.17); b. 11.8.76; s. of late Major-Gen. G. H. Vesey and Constance, d. of G. Marshall; m. Geraldine, d. of late Vice-Admiral F. J. Foley; two s.; 2nd Lt., The Queen's Regt., 20.2.97; Lt. 20.10.98; Capt. 22.1.03; Maj. 1.9.15; Temp. Maj.-Gen. 3.6.19; p.s.c.; served Europ. War; C.M.G.; Officer, Legion of Honour, and of the Order of the Crown; St. Michael and Lazarus; Croix de Guerre; C.B., 1921; Bt. Lt.-Col. 3.6.16; Bt.-Col. 3.6.18.

VIBART, N. M. (D.S.O. L.G. 12.12.19); b. 13.12.93; s. of Col. E. D. H. Vibart, late 15th Bengal Cavalry, and Isabella Louisa Vibart (formerly Horn); 2nd Lt., R.E., 1.4.14; Lt. 9.6.15; Capt. 3.11.17; served Europ. War, 1914–18; wounded twice; Despatches three times; M.C. and Bar.

VICARS, D. O. (D.S.O. L.G. 16.8.17), Lt., Can. Inf.

VICARY, A. C. (D.S.O. L.G. 3.6.18) (Bar, L.G. 11.1.19); b. 1888; m. Kathleen Hamilton, d. of late F. Hilton Green, J.P.; one d.; educ. Newton College; R.M.A., Woolwich; 2nd Lt., Glouc. R., 8.2.08; Lt. 14.1.11; Capt. 3.11.14; A/Lt.-Col., 1917–19; served Europ. War from 1914; Despatches six times; M.C.; Bt. Maj. 1.1.17; Knight of Legion of Honour.

VICCARS, J. E. (D.S.O. L.G. 3.6.18), Major, Leic. R.

VICKERMAN, H., M.Sc., A.M.I.C.E. (D.S.O. L.G. 1.1.18); b. 1880; s. of C. R. Vickerman, Wellington, N.Z.; m. Arabella Colquhoun, d. of H. A. Morrow; educ. Auckland Grammar School; N.Z. University; Major, N.Z. Mil. Forces; served Europ. War, 1915–18; Despatches.

VICKERS, G. E. (D.S.O. L.G. 1.1.18); b. 2.5.64; Manch. R. 5.2.02; Hon. Capt., Manchester R., 5.2.12; Lt.-Col. 3.6.18; ret. 22.7.19; served S. African War, 1900–2; Queen's Medal, 3 clasps; Europ. War; Despatches.

VICKERS, S., B.A. (D.S.O. L.G. 1.2.19); b. 13.6.81; s. of C. W. Vickers, M.R.C.S., L.R.C.P., D.P.H., and A. Vickers (*née* Stansfeld); m. Mary Eadson; five d.; educ. Blundell's School, Tiverton; Caius College, Cambridge; Major, commanding 2nd Devon Battery, 3rd Wessex Brig., R.F.A., T.A.; served Europ. War, India, France and Egypt from 1914; severely wounded.

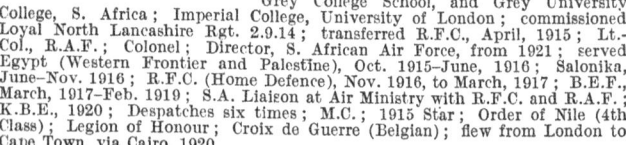

VICKERS, W. (D.S.O. L.G. 3.6.18), Major, Aust. A.M.C.

VICKERY, C. E. (D.S.O. L.G. 31.10.02) (Bar, L.G. 2.4.19) (Details, L.G. 10.12.19), Major and Bt. Lt.-Col., R.F.A. (see "The Distinguished Service Order," from its institution to 31.12.15, by same publishers).

VICKRESS, W. H. (D.S.O. L.G. 4.6.17), T/Major, A.S.C. (now R.A.S.C.).

VIDAL, A. C. (D.S.O. L.G. 18.4.16); b. 2.5.80; m. Kathleen O'Donohoe; Lt., R.A.M.C., 31.7.05; Capt. 29.8.09; Maj. 28.2.18; served Europ. War, 1914–16.

VIGNOLES, W. A. (D.S.O. L.G. 18.7.17) (Bar, L.G. 16.9.18), T/Lt.-Col., North'd Fus. His D.S.O. was awarded for gallantry on 28.4.17, near Arras.

VIGORS, M. D. (D.S.O. L.G. 8.3.19) (Details, L.G. 4.10.19); b. 18.11.86; s. of C. D. Vigors, (late Ceylon Civil Service); m. Daphne Stewart, d. of J. Wilson; one s.; educ. Wellington College; 2nd Lt. 24.1.06; Lt. 24.4.08; Capt. 24.1.15; 9th Hodson's Horse, Ind. Army; M.C.

VILLIERS, HON. A. G. CHILD- (see Child-Villiers, Hon. A. G.).

VILLIERS, C. W. (D.S.O. L.G. 23.11.16); b. 1873; m. Lady Kathleen Mary Cole, d. of 4th Earl of Enniskillen; one s.; two d.; educ. Eton; Lt.-Col., C. Gds. Reserve; one of H.M.'s Body Guard for Scotland; served Europ. War from 1914; Despatches four times; C.B.E.; Order of Redeemer of Greece; Serbian Order of White Eagle with Swords; French Croix de Guerre with Palm.

VILLIERS, E. H. (D.S.O. L.G. 26.5.19); b. 1881; s. of Rt. Hon. Sir F. H. Villiers and Virginia Katharine, d. of Eric Carrington Smith; educ. Wellington; Capt., late H.L.I.; served Europ. War from 1914; Despatches.

VILLIERS, O. G. G. (D.S.O. L.G. 1.1.18); b. 1886; s. of late Rev. H. M. Villiers and 2nd wife, Charlotte Louisa Emily, d. of Hon. F. W. Cadogan; m. Aleen Judith, d. of Rev. H. V. Heber Percy; one d.; educ. Harrow; Major, R.A.F.; served Europ. War, 1914–18; Légion d'Honneur; Croix de Guerre.

VILLIERS, P. F. (D.S.O. L.G. 1.1.17); b. 1884; s. of late Rev. H. M. Villiers; m. Evelyn, d. of E. Webb; one d.; educ. Harrow; Sandhurst; joined 14th Hussars, 1905; seconded to King's African Rifles, 1909; resigned commission, 1912; Major, Can. Inf., 1915; served Somali Exp., 1910; served Europ. War, 1914–17; joined Gordon Highlanders of Canada, 1914; served in 1st Can. Division until end of war; Despatches; Order of Danilo of Montenegro.

VILLIERS-STUART, P. (D.S.O. L.G. 1.1.18); b. 27.4.79; 5th s. of late H. W. Villiers-Stuart, D.L., M.P. for Waterford, 1882–86; m. Constance Mary, d. of late J. Fielden, D.L., J.P.; one d.; educ. Charterhouse; R.M.C., Sandhurst; 2nd Lt., R. Fus., 4.5.75; Lt. 27.9.99; Capt. 10.9.04; Maj. 1.9.15; served Europ. War; Brig. Major, 30th Brig., Suvla Bay, 1915, and Allied Exp. to Serbia; British Military Representation to Bulgaria, 1918; Despatches thrice; Chevalier de la Légion d'Honneur. His D.S.O. was awarded for the capture of a Bulgarian position on the Struma 15.5.17.

VINCE, A. N. (D.S.O. L.G. 1.1.17), T/Lt.-Col., L'pool Regt.; served S. African War, 1901–2; Queen's Medal, 5 clasps; Europ. War; Despatches. He was killed in action 21.3.18.

VINCE, W. B. (D.S.O. L.G. 18.2.18) (Details, L.G. 18.7.18), Private Secretary to the Postmaster-General from 1920; served Europ. War, London Rgt., 1914–18; Despatches; M.C.

VINEN, H. N. (D.S.O. L.G. 3.6.19); b. 30.7.83; 2nd Lt., Glouc. R., 4.7.03; Lt. 12.4.06; Capt. 6.5.14; Maj. 3.5.17; served S. African War, 1902; Queen's Medal, 3 clasps.

VINER, E. (D.S.O. L.G. 3.6.19), T/Major, 24th Batt. Manch. Regt.

VINEY, C. F. B. (D.S.O. L.G. 1.1.18), Capt. (T/Major), S. African Mtd. Rifles.

VINEY, H. G. (D.S.O. L.G. 1.1.17), Major, Aust. L.H. Rgt.

VINEY, T. E. (D.S.O. L.G. 1.1.16), Fl. Sub-Lt., R.N. He was shot down in an air raid 26.5.16.

VIPOND, C. W. (D.S.O. L.G. 1.1.19), T/Lt.-Col., 9th Field Amb., Can. A.M.C.

VISSER, P. F. (D.S.O. L.G. 22.8.18), Lt.-Col., Potchefstroom "B" Commando, S. African Forces.

VIVIAN (G. C. B.), BARON (D.S.O. L.G. 3.6.18); b. 21.1.78; s. of 3rd Baron and Louisa, d. of R. G. Duff; m. (1st) Barbara, d. of W. F. Fanning; one s.; one d.; (2nd) Nancy, M.B.E., widow of Adrian Rose, R. Horse Guards, d. of E. Lycett Green; one s.; one d.; educ. Eton; late Major, 1st Devon Yeom.; served S. Africa, 1900–1 (severely wounded; Queen's Medal, 4 clasps); Europ. War; Chevalier, Legion of Honour; Officer, Order of Leopold; French Croix de Guerre; Belgian Croix de Guerre.

VIVIAN, HON. O. R. (D.S.O. L.G. 18.10.17) (Details, L.G. 7.3.18); half-brother of 2nd Baron Swansea; m. Hon. Winifred Hamilton, d. of 1st Baron Holm Patrick; one d.; educ. Eton and Trinity College, Cambridge; Lt.-Col., Cdmg. 6th Batt. The Welsh Regiment; M.V.O.; T.D.; Despatches.

VIVIAN, V. (D.S.O. L.G. 14.1.16); b. 1880; m. Lady Aline Mary Seymour Dawson-Damer, d. of 5th Earl of Portarlington; Asst. Mil. Attaché, Paris, from 1920; Lt.-Col.; 2nd Lt., G. Gds., 12.8.99; Lt. 28.11.00; Capt. 14.9.07; Maj. 31.10.14; p.s.c.; served S. African War, 1899–1902; Queen's Medal, 3 clasps; King's Medal, 2 clasps; Europ. War, 1914–18; Despatches; D.S.O.; Bt. Lt.-Col. 1.1.17; C.M.G.; M.V.O. in 1905.

VON TREUENFELS, C. O. (D.S.O. L.G. 16.8.17), Lt. (T/Capt. and A/Major), H.A.C., attd. R.F.A. His D.S.O. was awarded for gallantry at Armentières 8.6.17.

VORSTER, P. W. (D.S.O. L.G. 22.8.18), Lt.-Col., Krugersdorp Commando S. African Forces.

VOWLES, A. S. (D.S.O. L.G. 22.9.16), Capt., Aus. Inf.

VYVYAN, A. V. (D.S.O. L.G. 14.3.16); b. 1875; s. of late Col. R. O. Vyvyan; m. Frances Claire, d. of late Gen. Sir Æneas Perkins, K.C.B., R.E., R.N.; Air Vice-Marshal, commanding Coastal Area; served in Punitive Naval Expedition against the King of Benin, 1897; Medal and clasp; served Dardanelles, 1914–15, as Beach Master at Anzac; C.B.; Legion of Honour; St. Anne; Rising Sun; American Distinguished Service Medal; Grand Cordon of the Redeemer.

WACE, E. G. (D.S.O. L.G. 3.6.16); b. 19.11.76, at Poona, India; s. of Major-Gen. R. Wace, C.B., R.A., and Gertrude Mary, d. of the late Major Candy, C.S.I.; m. Evelyn Mabel Hayward, d. of Col. G. H. Sim, C.B., C.M.G., R.E.; one s.; three d.; educ. Marlborough; Woolwich; 2nd Lt., R.E., 11.1.96; Lt. 11.1.99; Capt. 11.1.05; Major 30.10.14; Bt. Lt.-Col., June, 1918; T/Brig.-Gen. 1.9.18–14.11.19; served Europ. War as G.S.O., G.H.Q., B.E.F., and with the 15th and 32nd Divisions, later as Deputy Director of Labour, and then as Controller of Labour (T/Brig.-Gen.), G.H.Q., B.E.F., 1918–19; Despatches; C.B.

WADDY, R. H. (D.S.O. L.G. 3.6.18); b. 8.2.86; 2nd Lt., Som. L.I. 29.8.06; Lt. 21.12.08; Capt. 10.6.15; A/Lt.-Col., W. Yorks. Rgt., 24.9.17.

WADE, E. W., M.B. (D.S.O. L.G. 3.6.18); b. 14.10.89; m. Winifred Alexander; Capt., R.A.M.C., 30.3.15; A/Lt.-Col.; Despatches; M.C.

WADE, H., M.D., F.R.C.S. (D.S.O. L.G. 11.4.18), T/Lt.-Col., R.A.M.C.

WADE, H. O., LL.B. (D.S.O. L.G. 1.1.17); b. 1869; s. of J. H. Wade; m. (1st) Alice Lilian (who died in 1905), d. of J. R. Vaizey; two s.; one d.; (2nd) Eileen Lucy, d. of J. W. Rawson-Ackroyd; three s.; educ. Bradford; Trinity College, Cambridge (LL.B.); Colonel, W. Yorks. Rgt.; served Europ. War, from 1914; Despatches twice.

WADE, T. S. H. (D.S.O. L.G. 1.1.17); b. 22.5.69; 2nd Lt., Lanc. Fus., 24.4.89; Lt. 22.4.91; Capt. 6.4.98; Major 3.11.03; Lt.-Col. 22.3.16; T/Brig.-Gen. 20.10.17; served operations in German S.W. Africa, 1906–7; att. to German Forces; Europ. War; Despatches; Bt. Lt.-Col. 1.1.16.

WADLEY, E. J. (D.S.O. L.G. 14.1.16); b. 5.1.80; s. of T. Wadley; m. Nancy, d. of P. Ryan; one s.; Lt., A.V.C., 16.5.03; Capt. 16.5.08; Major 10.7.15; Lt.-Col., late R.A.V.C.; served S. African War, 1901–2; Queen's Medal, 5 clasps; Europ. War, 1914–18; Despatches; C.B.E.; Bt. Lt.-Col. 3.6.18; retired pay, 1920.

WADSWORTH, W. R. (D.S.O. L.G. 15.2.19) (Details, L.G. 30.7.19), Major, 14th Batt. Aust. Inf.; M.C.

WAGGETT, E. B., M.B. (D.S.O. L.G. 1.1.18), Major, R.A.M.C.

WAGSTAFF, C. M. (D.S.O. L.G. 2.2.16); b. 5.3.78, at Calcutta; s. of P. Wagstaff, of Berkhamsted, Herts; m. Rosabel, d. of Col. E. Thelwall, late R.M.A.; three s.; ent. Army 23.6.97; Capt. 23.6.06; Major 30.10.14; Col. 21.4.21; Col. on the Staff, N. Command, India; served N.W. Frontier, India, 1908 (Medal with clasp); Europ. War, 1914–18; Despatches; Bt. Lt.-Col. 1.1.17; Bt. Col. 3.6.19; C.M.G.; C.I.E.; Croix de Guerre with two Palms; D.S.M. (United States of America); Order of the Couronne (Commandeur), Belgium; Order of the Crown of Italy (Commendation).

WAINEWRIGHT, A. R. (D.S.O. L.G. 1.1.18); b. 16.9.74); 2nd Lt., R.A., 17.11.94; Lt. 17.11.97; Capt. 15.12.00; Major 20.4.11; Lt.-Col. 18.4.16; Colonel 18.4.20; Brig.-Genl., R.A., 9th Division, Br. Armies in France, 9.4.18; Despatches; C.M.G.

WAIT, H. G. K. (D.S.O. L.G. 3.6.16); b. 8.2.71; s. of late W. K. Wait; m. Helen Mary Lothian, d. of late Gen. Sir L. Nicholson, K.C.B.; 2nd Lt., R.E., 27.7.89; Lt. 27.7.92; Capt. 1.4.00; Major 9.6.09; Lt.-Col. 1.6.17; Col. 1.6.21; Europ. War, 1914–18; C.B.E.

WAITE, C. W. (D.S.O. L.G. 3.6.18); elder son of G. H. Waite; T/Major, 11th E. Yorks. Rgt. He was taken prisoner by the Germans, and died 31.1.19. His brother, Lt. G. Norman Waite, was twice wounded; Despatches.

WAITE, W. C. N. (D.S.O. L.G. 4.6.17), Lt.-Colonel, Aust. Mil. Forces; Despatches; M.C.

WAITHMAN, R. H. (D.S.O. L.G. 1.1.18); b. 7.11.76; 2nd Lt., R. Sussex Rgt., 20.2.97; Lt. 14.2.99; Capt. 3.2.05; Major 1.9.15; Despatches; Bt. Lt.-Col. 3.6.19.

WAKE-BOWELL, R. H. (D.S.O. L.G. 9.1.18); b. 11.2.83; s. of late Rev. W. Bowell, M.A., and the late Sophia Bowell (*née* Jones); m. Dulcinea Mary Charlton, d. of late Capt. Charlton; one s.; one d.; educ. St. John's School, Leatherhead, Surrey; joined Can. Exp. Force, 15.12.15; Lt. retired pay; D.S.O. for attack on Cité du Moulin; Despatches in Sept. 1917, and subsequently for patrol work in front of Hulloch and St. Elie; gassed and wounded.

WAKEFIELD, N. (D.S.O. L.G. 1.1.19), T/Lt. (A/Major), R.F.A.

WAKEFIELD, T. M., F.R.G.S. (D.S.O. L.G. 1.1.17); b. 22.2.78; s. of Lt.-Col. T. Wakefield, late I.S.C., and Margaret Maria, d. of Lt.-Col. H. F. Waddington, late I.S.C.; educ. King William's College, I. of Man; R.M.A., Woolwich; 2nd Lt., R.G.A., 1.9.97; Lt. 1.9.00; Capt. 20.3.02; Major 30.10.14; Lt.-Colonel 20.1.22; took part in Boxer Rebellion, 1900; Relief of Peking; Despatches; American Order of the Dragon; Past Dist. Gd. Dir. Ceremonies, H.-K. and S. China, 1914; served Europ. War; Despatches thrice.

WALBY, H. C. (D.S.O. L.G. 11.1.19), Lt. (A/Capt.), 4th Batt. N. Staffs. R., att. 9th Batt. Yorks. L.I.; M.C.

WALCH, J. C. (D.S.O. L.G. 1.1.17); b. 19.6.75; 2nd Lt. (from Local Mil. Forces, Tasmania), R.A., 23.5.00; Lt. 19.11.01; Adjt., R.A., 20.8.10 to 26.9.13; Capt. 24.12.10; Major 30.10.14; T/Lt.-Col., R.A., 16.9.18; served S. Africa, 1900 (Queen's Medal with 4 clasps); Europ. War; Despatches.

WALDO, E. R. MEADE- (see Meade-Waldo, E. R.).

WALES, J. (D.S.O. L.G. 8.3.20), A/Lt.-Cdr., R.N.R.

WALKEM, H. C. (D.S.O. L.G. 3.6.18), Major 1.10.14, 4th Rgt., R. Highlanders of Canada; Lt.-Col., Can. Pioneers; M.C.

WALKER, A. (D.S.O. L.G. 16.9.18), Capt. and Bt. Major, R.A.M.C.

WALKER, A. D. (D.S.O. L.G. 3.6.18); b. 3.7.79; 2nd Lt., R.E., 23.12.98; Lt. 25.7.01; Capt. 23.12.07; Major (A/Lt.-Col.); served Tibet, 1903–4; slightly wounded; operations at and around Gyantse; March to Lhassa; Medal with clasp; served Europ. War. He was killed in action 26.3.18.

A. D. Walker.

WALKER, A. L. (D.S.O. L.G. 3.6.18), Major, Can. Inf.; M.C.

WALKER, B. J. (D.S.O. L.G. 3.6.18), T/Lt.-Col., R. Sussex R.

WALKER, CHARLES ERNEST (D.S.O. L.G. 4.6.17); b. 6.8.82; 2nd Lt., R.A., 4.12.01; Lt. 4.12.04; Capt. 18.9.14; Major 6.12.15; M.C.

WALKER, CECIL EDWARD, (D.S.O. L.G. 12.12.19), Major, R.A.; M.C.

WALKER, C. E. FORESTIER- (see Forestier-Walker, C. E.).

WALKER, C. W. G. (D.S.O. L.G. 7.2.18); b. 2.7.82; 2nd Lt., Unatt., 27.8.03; I.A. 20.12.02; Lt. 27.11.04; Capt. 27.8.11; Major 27.8.17; Bt. Lt.-Col. 1.1.19.

WALKER, E. W. (D.S.O. L.G. 16.8.17); b. 1892; only s. of late Rev. W. Greaves Walker, Rector of Knockin, and of Mrs. Walker, of Oswestry; educ. Heswell; Charterhouse; Oxford; belonged to the Charterhouse and Oxford O.T.C. He volunteered the day after war was declared; commissioned in the T.F., became Capt., R. W. F., and saw service at Suvla Bay, returning home after the evacuation with typhoid. He rejoined his battalion and fought in the First Battle of Gaza in March, 1917, where he won his D.S.O. After the battle of Gaza he was invalided home with malarial fever. Capt. Walker rejoined his battalion, and was killed in action 6.11.17. His D.S.O. was awarded for gallantry in Egypt 26.3.17.

WALKER, F. W. (D.S.O. L.G. 19.11.17) (Details, L.G. 22.3.18), Capt., 4th Batt. London R., T.F.; retired; Despatches.

WALKER, G. (D.S.O. L.G. 23.11.16); b. in India 5.2.69; s. of late Major G. R. Walker, R.E.; m. Louisa Elinor, d. of late Major-General W. Weldon; educ. Wellington College; R.M.A., Woolwich; 2nd Lt., R.E., 27.7.88; Lt. 27.7.91; served in India with 3rd (Bombay) Sappers and Miners, West Africa; Capt. 27.7.99; Major 26.3.08; Lt.-Col. 1.4.16; Europ. War, 1914–18; present at Mons, Le Cateau, Marne, Aisne, Ypres (1 and 2); also served in Macedonia; Bts. of Lt.-Col. (18.2.15) and Colonel (1.1.18); T/Brig.-Genl. 3.11.18; Commander; T/Col. Comdr. 19.2.21; Star of Roumania; Despatches five times.

WALKER, G. G. (D.S.O. L.G. 1.1.18), T/Capt. (A/Major), R.G.A.; M.C.

WALKER, H. W. (D.S.O. L.G. 1.1.17); b. 20.10.82; s. of A. Walker; educ. Marlborough College; R.M.A., Woolwich; 1st com., R.H.A., 31.7.02; Lt. 31.7.05; Capt. 30.10.14; Major 18.4.16; A.D.C. to G.O.C., 1st Div., 1906–7; served Europ. War, 1914–17; Despatches twice.

WALKER, JAMES (D.S.O. L.G. 3.6.16); commissioned in E. Riding of Yorks. Yeomanry from formation of Regiment by the late Lord Wenlock; Major, late E. Riding Yeom. and R.F.A.; T/Lt.-Col. Commanding 32nd Div. Ammunition Column, R.F.A., from 1916; served Europ. War, 1914–17; Despatches.

WALKER, JAMES (D.S.O. L.G. 26.7.18) (Bar, L.G. 3.6.18); b. 19.3.79; s. of John Ely Walker, J.P., and Mary Elizabeth Walker (*née* Firth); educ. Huddersfield College; Mill Hill School; joined the Army, March, 1906 (Volunteer Force), W. Riding Regt. He was a Territorial Officer (Capt.) on outbreak of war; went to France with 1/4th West Riding, 49th Division, in April, 1915; promoted Major, June, 1916; Acting Lt.-Col., Sept. 1917; Brevet Lt.-Col., June, 1919; Lt.-Col., Feb. 1920; served continuously in France and Belgium from 1915 to end of war; in Germany from Dec. 1918, to April, 1919; mentioned Despatches seven times; served with 1/4th West Riding, 49th Division, from mobilization; then with 1/5th West Riding (2nd-in-command); afterwards with 1/5th West Riding, in command; transferred to command 5th West Riding, 62nd Division; Légion d'Honneur; Croix de Guerre, Belgium; promoted Brevet Lt.-Col.

WALKER, JAMES (D.S.O. L.G. 1.1.17), Capt., R. of O., Aust. Mil. Forces, Unatt. List.; Hon. Lt.-Col. 1.2.16; V.D.; Despatches.

WALKER, J. McC. (D.S.O. L.G. 8.3.19) (Details, L.G. 4.10.19), T/2nd Lt., R. Highrs.

WALKER, J. T. (D.S.O. L.G. 1.1.19), T/Major, 317th Siege Battery, R.G.A.; M.C.

WALKER, J. W. (D.S.O. L.G. 11.4.18), Lt.-Col. (T/Brig.-Gen.), R.F.A.

WALKER, M. G. E. (D.S.O. L.G. 3.6.19); b. 4.9.84; s. of late E. O. Walker, C.I.E.; educ. St. Paul's School; R.M.A., Woolwich; 2nd Lt., R.A., 29.7.04; Lt. 29.7.07; Capt. 30.10.14; ent. Army, 1904; Capt., R.A.; served Europ. War, 1914–18, commanding a heavy battery, 1917; also on Gen. Staff, and as Brig. Major, Heavy Artillery, 8th Army Corps, Br. Armies in France 23.9.18; 1914 Star with Bar.

WALKER, P. (D.S.O. L.G. 8.3.19) (Details, L.G. 4.10.19), Major, Manitoba R., Can. Mil. Forces.

WALKER, P. L. E. (D.S.O. L.G. 27.6.19); b. 8.6.83; 2nd Lt., 7th Hussars, 19.8.03; Lt. 12.2.10; Capt. 10.3.13; A/Lt.-Col., W. Riding Rgt., 19.1.18; A/Lt.-Col., 7th Hussars; commanding E. Lan. Rgt., 18.10.18; Despatches.

WALKER, R. S. (D.S.O. L.G. 3.6.16); b. 16.4.71; 2nd Lt., R.E., 25.7.90; Lt. 25.7.93; Capt. 25.7.01; Major 25.7.10; served S. African War, 1900–2; Despatches twice; Queen's Medal, 4 clasps; Lt.-Col., R.E. (VI. Corps H.Q.), He was killed in action on 30.9.18.

WALKER, R. S. FORESTIER- (see Forestier-Walker, R.S.).

WALKER, S. J. (D.S.O. L.G. 3.6.18), Major, Aust. F.A.

WALKER, T. H. (D.S.O. L.G. 1.1.19), Major (A/Lt.-Col.), R.F.A., T.F.

WALKER, T. M. (D.S.O. L.G. 15.10.18), Major, R.F.A.

WALKER, T. P. (D.S.O. L.G. 3.6.18); b. 1858; m. Gertrude Elizabeth, d. of C. H. Marten; one s.; two d.; Midshipman, Modeste; served with Laroot Field Force during operations against Malays, 1875–76; Perak Medal and clasp; Member of Naval Intelligence Dept., 1896–99; A.D.C. to King Edward VII., 1907–8; retired, 1911; Admiral appointed an Assessor under the Supreme Court of Judicature Act to attend Admiralty Appeals in House of Lords, also an Assessor to attend investigations into Shipping Casualties; served on active service afloat as Capt., R.N.R., 1914–19.

WALKER, V. D. (D.S.O. L.G. 8.3.19) (Details, L.G. 4.10.19), T/2nd Lt., 34th Batt. M.G.C.; M.M.

WALKER, W. H. (D.S.O. L.G. 1.1.17); b. 18.1.83; s. of J. Walker, Vet. Surg., of Alton, Hants; educ. Eggars Grammar School, Alton; R. Veterinary College, London; Lt., A.V.C., 3.2.06; Capt. 3.2.11; Major, R.A.V.C., 3.2.21; served in India, 1907 to 1909; served in Sudan with Egyptian Army, 1909 to 1914; on service 1913 in Sudan against Annuak Tribe; on leave from Sudan on outbreak of war, and returned to British Service at own request; Comdg. No. 4 Vety. Hospital from March, 1915; before that served in France with 8th Division; Despatches twice.

WALKER, W. K. (D.S.O. L.G. 18.1.18) (Details, L.G. 25.4.18) (Bar, L.G. 7.11.18); s. of Rev. Canon Walker, D.D.; Lt.-Col., M.G.C.; M.C.

WALLACE, C. H. (D.S.O. L.G. 1.1.19); b. 21.7.86; 2nd Lt., R.A., 25.7.06; Lt. 25.7.09; Capt. 30.10.14; Major 13.2.17; served Europ. War in Egypt and Salonika; Despatches.

WALLACE, C. J. (D.S.O. L.G. 1.1.18); b. 6.2.90; s. of Lt.-Col. H. R. Wallace; 2nd Lt., H.L. Inf., 5.10.10; Lt. 19.3.13; Capt. 17.5.15; Bt. Major 1.1.17; served throughout the war (1) with the 2nd Batt. H.L.I. until appointed Brig. Major, 68th Brig.; (2) G.S.O.2, Irish Div.; (3) G.S.O.2, 3rd Army (Sir Julian Byng); G.S.O.2 after Armistice, Highland Div., Army of the Rhine; served in operations (including Mons and the Battle of Loos) from Aug. 1914, till the end of the war; was nominated for the Staff College, and served as Adjt., 1st Batt., in Egypt; Despatches five times; O.B.E. (Mil. Div.); M.C.; Croix de Guerre with Palm; Bt. Major at the age of 26.

WALLACE, C. W. (D.S.O. L.G. 23.10.19); b. 24.11.84; 2nd Lt., Unatt., 9.1.04; Ind. Army 2.4.05; Lt. 9.4.06; Capt. 9.1.13; retired 9.1.21; served N.W. Frontier of India, 1908; Medal, clasp; Europ. War; Despatches.

WALLACE, E. C. LL. (D.S.O. L.G. 27.7.18); b. 14.10.75; 2nd Lt., Unatt., 14.8.95; Ind. S.C. 14.12.96; Lt., Ind. Army, 14.11.97; Capt., Ind. Army, 14.8.04; Major 4.8.13; served China, 1900; Medal with clasp; Europ. War; Despatches.

WALLACE, F. C. (D.S.O. L.G. 1.1.19), Lieut. (Temp. Capt.), Royal Ir. Rifles (Spec. Res.); M.C.

WALLACE, G. P. (D.S.O. L.G. 1.2.17), Temp. Major, S. African Def. Force and R.F.C.

WALLACE, H. R. (D.S.O. L.G. 3.6.16); b. 31.8.61; s. of late Capt. H. R. Wallace, G. Highrs.; m. (1st) Matilda Marion Christie (who died in 1905), d. and heiress of late A. Campbell, of Cammo, Midlothian; (2nd) Isabel M., widow of C. R. Duke, of Glasgow, and d. of late W. R. Arthur; three s.; one d.; educ. Cheltenham College; Convener of County of Ayr; Hon. Sheriff Substitute for the County; J.P.; D.L.; Lt.-Col., late commanding Res. Garrison Batt. Suffolk Rgt., 10th Gordon Highrs.; Lt.-Col., retired 1918; served Europ. War, 1914–18; Despatches twice; Lt.-Col. Wallace and his three sons were all at the Battle of Loos, and came out of that action alive. He is fond of shooting and fishing, and in early days, hunting and polo. Perhaps it was a sporting achievement to have 1914–15 Star. He stuck it during period of training first 100,000, and the subsequent campaign at the age of 53 to that of 57, with a crocked heart, without being sick.

H. R. Wallace.

WALLACE, J. T. (D.S.O. L.G. 3.6.18), 2nd Lt., R.A., 23.12.03; Lt., R.A., 23.12.06; Capt., R.A., 30.10.14; Major, R.A., 31.7.16; Despatches; M.C.

WALLACE, R. B., M.B. (D.S.O. L.G. 4.6.17), Temp. Capt., R.A.M.C.

WALLER, H. W. L. (D.S.O. L.G. 3.6.18); b. 3.7.86; 2nd Lt., R.A., 23.5.06; Lt., R.A., 23.5.09; Capt., R.A., 30.10.14; Major, R.A., 17.1.17; Despatches; M.C.

WALLER, J. H. DE W. (D.S.O. L.G. 1.1.18), Temp. Capt., R.E.

WALLER, R. DE W. (D.S.O. L.G. 3.6.19); b. 28.5.03; 2nd Lt., R.A., 23.7.01; Capt., R.A., 5.5.04; Ind. Army 22.5.09; Capt., Ind. Army, 22.7.10; Major 23.7.16.

WALLER, R. J. R. (D.S.O. L.G. 3.6.16), Capt., R.A., att. Nigeria R.

WALLINGER, E. A. (D.S.O. L.G. 3.6.16); b. 11.6.75; s. of W. H. Arnold Wallinger, of Hare Hall, Essex; m. Irene, d. of H. Benn, J.P., of Bradford, and Holcombe Hall, Dawlish, S. Devon; one s.; one d.; educ. Clare College, Cambridge; ent. R.F.A., 1900; Capt., 1912; Major, 1915; T/Lt.-Col., 1919–20; went to France with 4th Div., B.E.F., Aug. 1914; severely wounded at the Battle of the Aisne, Sept. 1914; Intelligence Section, G.S., G.H.Q., France, 1915–19; Despatches four times; Chevalier, Legion of Honour; French Croix de Guerre avec Palme; Belgian Croix de Guerre avec Palme; Officier de l'Ordre de la Couronne, Belgium.

WALLINGER, J. A. (D.S.O. L.G. 14.1.16); b. 1872; s. of W. H. A. Wallinger, Indian Forest Service (retired); Indian Police, att. Gen. Staff; entered the Service, 1895; att. Gen. Staff, 1914; T/Major, Spec. List; Despatches; C.I.E.

WALLIS, H. M. (D.S.O. L.G. 3.6.19), Capt., Quebec R., Seconded to 4th Can. Inf. Brig.

WALMESLEY, C. T. J. G. (D.S.O. L.G. 3.6.19); b. 1881; s. of late H. J. Walmesley; m. (1st) Mary (who died in 1918), d. of Col. Druitt, R.E.; one s.; one d.; (2nd) Dorothy Mary, d. of Capt. J. G. Mayne, O.B.E.; one d.; educ. Beaumont College, Old Windsor; ent. 17th Lancers, 1898; left 1904; Lt.-Col., O.C., Berks. Yeom.; served in Gallipoli one year; went to France with Naval Div. as D.A.P.M., May, 1916; A.P.M. to R.N.D., 63rd R.N.D.; M.C.

WALSH, C. H. (D.S.O. L.G. 3.6.19); b. 15.9.85; 2nd Lt., Con. Rangers, 20.3.07; Lt. 6.10.09; Capt. 17.12.14; A/Lt.-Col.; Despatches; M.C.

WALSH, J. (D.S.O. L.G. 18.2.18) (Details, L.G. 18.7.18); b. 25.2.85; 2nd Lt., L'pool R., 30.1.16; Lt., Innis. Fus., 15.10.16; Capt., North'd Fus., 25.10.18; Bt. Major 1.1.19; went to France with the "Contemptibles," and was through the fighting on the Western front from that time; was Second in Command of the Footballers' Battalion of the Middlesex Rgt. for nearly 12 months, then Lt.-Col. commanding a Batt. The Essex R.; won his D.S.O. at Cambrai.

J. Walsh.

WALSH, R. H. (D.S.O. L.G. 26.7.17); b. 7.12.84; 2nd Lt., R.A., 21.12.04; Lt., R.A., 21.12.07; Capt., R.A., 30.10.14; Major, R.A., 1.11.16; M.C.

WALSH, R. K. (D.S.O. L.G. 26.9.16); b. 25.12.73; s. of late Surg.-Gen. T. Walsh, A.M.S., and Mary Letitia, d. of late Lt.-Gen. R. Knox, of Grace Dieu, Co. Dublin; educ. Beaumont; R.M.C., Sandhurst; 2nd Lt., R. Scots Fus., 10.10.94; Lt. 24.2.97; Capt. 9.12.00; Major 18.2.15; Adjt., R. Scots. Fus., 6.6.03 to 5.6.06; Bt. Lt.-Col., R. Scots Fus., 3.6.17; served S. African War, 1901–2; Queen's Medal, 4 clasps; Europ. War, 1914–18; Despatches five times; C.B.; C.M.G.

WALSH, R. S. (D.S.O. L.G. 2.12.18), Lt., 4th Batt. G. Highrs., T.F., Seconded 11th Batt. Tank Corps; M.M.

WALSH, R. W. W. (D.S.O. L.G. 4.6.17), Capt., Aust. A.M.C.

WALSH, T. A. (D.S.O. L.G. 11.1.19) (Bar, L.G. 1.2.19); b. 4.7.82; s. of late Col. H. A. Walsh, C.B.; m. Winifred, d. of Col. S. H. Woodhouse; one d.; educ. Repton School; 2nd Lt., Somerset L.I., 1901; Lt. 1.4.04; Capt. 21.4.14; Major 1.9.14; Lt.-Col., late Som. L.I.; served with Egyptian Army 1908–10; Sudan G.S. Medal; joined B.E.F. as Adjt., 1st Batt. H.A.C., Nov. 1914; commanded 12th North'd Fus., and subsequently 9th K.O. Yorks. L.I.; three times wounded; Despatches; 1914 Star.

WALSHE, F. W. H. (D.S.O. L.G. 1.1.17); b. 26.7.72; m. Hilda Louise, d. of Rev. G. C. Carter; one s.; two d.; educ. R.M.A., Woolwich; ent. R.A., 1892 (Tombs Memorial Scholarship); 2nd Lt., R.A., 22.7.92; Lt. 22.7.95; Capt. 6.4.00; Adjt., R.A., 14.5.01 to 31.3.03; Major 10.10.09; Lt.-Col. 11.9.15; Bt. Colonel 3.6.18; T/Brig.-Gen.; served Europ. War in Gallipoli, Egypt and France; Despatches; Legion of Honour; C.M.G., 1919; Bt. Colonel; A.D.C. to the King.

WALSTAB, J. (D.S.O. L.G. 4.6.17), Lt.-Col., Aust. I.F.

WALTER, B. (D.S.O. L.G. 14.1.16), 2nd Lt., R.A., 2.5.00; Lt., R.A., 3.4.01; served Europ. War; Despatches. Major Walter died of wounds 16.9.16.

WALTER, F. E. (D.S.O. L.G. 14.1.16); b. 10.3.76; 2nd s. of J. H. Walter; m. Myrtle Evelyn, d. of Charles Orde; educ. Eton; 1st commission, Norfolk R., 16.9.97; retired 1913; rejoined 1914; Major 1.9.15; served S. African War, 1900–2; Queen's Medal, 3 clasps; King's Medal, 2 clasps; Europ. War, 1914–16; Despatches; wounded.

WALTERS, H. DE L. (D.S.O. L.G. 1.1.18); b. 13.10.68; Major, R.A., 5.8.14; previous service (full pay) 17.2.88 to 2.12.10; Europ. War; Lt.-Col. 31.3.18; Despatches.

WALTERS, R. H. (D.S.O. L.G. 1.1.16); b. 1874; s. of H. H. Walters; m. Evelyn Mayura, C.B.E., d. of C. W. Engleheart; one d.; educ. St. Bernard's, Woking; Stubbington; H.M.S. Britannia; Midshipman, 1890; Lt., 1894; qualified as Torpedo Lieut., 1899; Cdr., 1904; Capt., R.N., retired; Commanding R. Australian Naval College, Jervis Bay; served in H.M.S. Doris and Gibraltar at Cape of Good Hope Station (S. African Medal); served Europ. War, 1914–17; Despatches.

R. H. Walters.

WALTON, C., Assoc.Inst.C.E. (D.S.O. L.G. 3.6.16); b. 16.2.78; 2nd Lt., R.E., 25.7.97; Lt. 25.7.00; Capt. 25.7.06; Major 30.10.14; Bt. Lt.-Col., R.E., 1.1.18; served Europ. War, 1914–18; Despatches; Bt. Lt.-Col.; Legion of Honour.

WALTON, L. A. (D.S.O. L.G. 16.8.17), T/2nd Lt., Welsh R.; M.C. His D.S.O. was awarded for gallantry at Villiers Plœnich on 24.4.17.

WALWYN, C. L. T. (D.S.O. L.G. 1.1.17); b. 20.4.83; s. of Col. Walwyn, late R. Welsh Fus.; m. Jean Cowland; educ. Wellington College; ent. R.F.A. 24.12.02; Lt. 24.12.05; Capt. 30.10.14; Major, R.H.A., 20.4.16; served S. African War from 1900; Queen's Medal, 2 clasps; Europ. War, 1914–18; Despatches thrice; O.B.E.; M.C.

WALWYN, H. T. (D.S.O. L.G. 15.9.16), Cdr., R.N.

WANDESFORDE, F. C. R. PRIOR- (see Prior-Wandesforde, F. C. R.).

WANLISS, H. B. (D.S.O. L.G. 27.7.16); b. Ballarat, Victoria, Australia, 11.12.91; o. s. of Newton Wanliss; nephew of Sir William Irvine, K.C.M.G., Chief Justice of the State of Victoria, Australia, and of Lt.-Colonel D. S. Wanliss, C.M.G., who commanded the 5th Australian Division at the landing in Gallipoli; educ. Ballarat College; Hawkesbury Agricultural College, N.S. Wales; enlisted A.I.F. 28.4.15; 2nd Lt. 16.7.15; left Australia 29.12.15; was assigned to the 14th Australian Infantry Battalion in Egypt; promoted Lieut. 10.4.16; Capt., March, 1917; served Europ. War in France. Soon after his arrival he was severely wounded during a successful trench raid, the first made by the Fourth Australian Division in France. He was the first Australian subaltern to win the D.S.O. in the Great War, which was awarded on 27.7.16 for gallantry in the Bois Grenier District; Adjutant, 14th Batt. from 4.1.17 to July, 1917; present at the battles of Bullecourt and Messines; appointed to command A Company of his old Battalion. He was killed in action on 26.9.17, in the attack on Polygon Wood, just when his company, which he led with great dash and judgment, had gained its objective. Sir John Monash praised him very highly, and said that Australia would deplore his loss, but his fine example would embellish the glorious history of his country.

H. B. Wanliss.

WANNELL, G. E. (D.S.O. L.G. 3.6.16); b. 12.5.82; s. of late Rev. G. F. W. Wannell; m. Hilda, d. of S. Johnson; educ. Oundle School; 2nd Lt., Bedfords. Yeom. and 18th Hussars, 1900; Lt., 1904; att. Indian Cavalry, 1904–5; resigned commission, 1905; commissioned W. Australian L.H., 1907–8; att. Depot, Sherwood Foresters, Derby; 9th Duke of Wellington's Rgt., Oct. 1914; Major, Dec. 1915; Lt.-Col. 31.1.16, late 9th Batt. Duke of Wellington's Rgt.; served S. African War; Queen's Medal, 5 clasps; King's Medal, 2 clasps; Europ. War; commanded Battalion after gas attack at Ypres 19.12.15; Despatches thrice.

WANSBROUGH, C. C. (D.S.O. L.G. 4.6.17) (Bar, L.G. 16.8.17); b. 1878; s. of late Rev. C. E. Wansbrough; m. Rose, d. of late J. Russell; Major, Can. Inf.; served Europ. War, 1915–17; Despatches. His D.S.O. was awarded for gallantry on 9.4.17, east of Neuville St. Vaast.

WARBURTON, A. (D.S.O. L.G. 1.1.19), Lt. (T/Capt.), 1/6th Batt. L'pool R., T.F.; M.C.

WARBURTON, G. (D.S.O. L.G. 22.6.17), Lt.-Cdr., R.N.

WARBURTON, G. EGERTON- (see Egerton-Warburton, G.).

WARBURTON, W. M. (D.S.O. L.G. 1.1.17); b. 7.6.77; s. of late Col. W. P. Warburton, C.S.I.; m. (1st) Yda Frances (who died in 1907), d. of the late Col. J. P. D. Vanrenen; (2nd) Muriel Frances, d. of late W. J. Henderson; two d.; educ. Wellington College; R.M.A., Woolwich; commission in R.A.; 2nd Lt., R.A., 23.3.97; 1st Lt. 23.3.00; Capt. 1.4.02; Adjt., R.A., 10.4.07 to 6.3.10; Major 8.6.14; Lt.-Col. 21.7.17; went to France Sept. 1914, in command of 110th Battery, R.F.A., 6th Div.; in Dec. 1915, sent to command 160th Bde., R.F.A., 34th Div., and held this command until Dec. 1919; present at Aisne, Armentières, 1914; Ypres, 1915; Somme, 1916; Arras, Ypres, 1917; Oulchy le Chateau, Ypres, 1918; Germany 1919; Despatches four times; C.M.G.; Croix d'Officier, Legion of Honour, and Croix de Guerre with Palm.

W. M. Warburton.

WARD, A. (D.S.O. L.G. 4.6.17); b. 1.2.66; 2nd Lt., Leic. R., 4.5.87; Lt., I.S.C., 21.3.90; Capt., Ind. Army, 17.10.99; Major 18.10.05; Lt.-Col. 12.12.13; served Burmese Expedition, 1887–89; Medal with clasp; Hazara Expedition, 1891; clasp; Miranzai (2nd) Expedition, 1891; clasp; Tirah, 1897–98; Europ. War; Despatches.

WARD, A. B., M.B. (D.S.O. L.G. 1.1.18), Lt.-Col., S. African Medical Corps.

WARD, C. H. DUDLEY- (see Dudley-Ward, C. H.).

WARD, C. P. (D.S.O. L.G. 3.6.19), Major, 72nd Siege Battery, S. African Horse Artillery, att. R.G.A.

WARD, C. W. (D.S.O. L.G. 20.10.16); b. 1878; s. of Rev. J. R. Ward, of Pudlestone, Hereford, and Richmond, Natal; educ. Christ's Hospital; joined 3rd K.O.R.L., Jan. 1915; went to France, July, 1915, to join 2nd Wilts. R.; served in France; A/Capt. 22.2.16; wounded 9.4.17.

WARD, E. B. (D.S.O. L.G. 3.6.19); b. 30.10.78; 2nd Lt., D.C.L.I., 21.4.00; Lt. 12.4.02; Capt. 17.3.10; Major 1.9.15; A/Lt.-Col.; served S. African War, 1899–1920; Queen's Medal, 3 clasps; King's Medal, 2 clasps; Europ. War; Despatches.

WARD, E. F. (D.S.O. L.G. 13.2.17); b. 21.6.70; s. of late Lt.-Col. B. E. Ward and 2nd wife, Charlotte Eugenia, d. of S. G. Smith; 1st commission 25.5.92; retired K.R.R.C. 15.6.07; Major, R. of O., 18.1.17; served Europ. War, 1914–17; Despatches.

WARD, G. B. C. (D.S.O. L.G. 3.6.18); b. 4.11.75; s. of late Maj.-Gen. Sir E. W. Ward, K.C.M.G.; m. Beatrice Constance Charlotte, d. of late Hon. C. L. Butler; one d.; 2nd Lt., S.W.B., 25.3.96; Lt., S.W.B., 24.11.97; Capt. 2.3.07; Major 1.9.15; Lt.-Col., late S.W.B.; served S. African War, 1900; Queen's Medal, 3 clasps; Europ. War, 1914–18; Despatches thrice; Bt. Major; French Croix de Guerre.

C. W. Ward.

WARD, H. M. A., M.A. (D.S.O. L.G. 1.1.18); b. May, 1884; s. of Col. A. J. H. Ward, O.B.E., V.D., D.L.; m. Kathleen, d. of Lt.-Col. W. C. Underwood, 4th Hussars; two s.; one d.; educ. Felsted School; Clare College, Cambridge; joined Territorials, Oct. 1904 (Essex and Suffolk R.G.A.), 1914–16; raised 200th Siege Battery, July, 1916; D.S.O.; played Hockey for Essex, 1903–6; won Eastern Counties Lawn Tennis Championship, 1908; Cambridge Seniors, Cricket and Football.

WARD, J., L.R.C.P., M.R.C.S. (D.S.O. L.G. 1.1.18); b. 15.11.78; s. of late J. S. Ward; m. (1st) Isabella Frances (deceased), d. of late H. Wilton, D.I.R.I.C., Co. Antrim; (2nd) Eva, d. of late H. B. Willis, of Tunbridge Wells; educ. Chesterfield Grammar School; University College, Sheffield; Lt., R.A.M.C. (T.F.), 1906; mobilized 14.8.14; Capt., R.A.M.C., T.F.; Major 9.10.14; A/Lt.-Col. 15.6.15 to demobilization 18.4.19; served Europ. War in France, Dec. 1914–Dec. 1915; Salonika, Dec. 1915–Oct. 1918; Despatches thrice; C.M.G.; Commander, St. Sava, Serbia.

WARD, J. C. (D.S.O. L.G. 25.8.17), Temp. Major, R.E. (Lt.-Cdr., Royal Indian Marines); M.B.E.

WARD, J. H. (D.S.O. L.G. 26.7.18), Capt. (A/Lt.-Col.), R.A.M.C., S.R.; M.C.

WARD, L. E. S. (D.S.O. L.G. 2.2.16) (Bar. L.G. 1.1.18); b. 7.8.75; 2nd Lt., Oxf. L.I., 1.12.97; Capt., 1903; retired Oxf. and Bucks. Light Inf. 8.1.13; Major 1.9.15 (Res. of O.); Lt.-Col.; employed with K.A.R., 1902–7 and 1908–12; served Tirah Exp., 1897–98; Medal, 2 clasps; Nandi Exp., 1905–6; Medal and clasp; Somaliland, 1908–10; Despatches; clasp; Europ. War, 1915–18; Despatches; C.M.G.

WARD, R. (D.S.O. L.G. 2.12.18), Lt. (T/Capt.), 9th Batt. Manch. R., T.F.; M.C.

WARD, R. M'G. BARRINGTON- (see Barrington-Ward, R. M'G.).

WARD, RONALD OGIER (gazetted as Ward, Robert Ogier), F.R.C.S., M.Ch. (D.S.O. L.G. 3.6.19); b. 6.3.86; s. of A. O. Ward; educ. Magdalen College School, and Queen's College, Oxford; St. Bartholomew's Hospital; served as Surgeon with British Red Cross in Balkan War, 1912–13; Europ. War, 1914–18; Capt. (A/Major), H.A.C.. att. R.F.A., T.F.; Despatches; M.C.

J. H. Ward.

WARD, V. M. BARRINGTON- (see Barrington-Ward, V. M.).

WARDE-ALDAM, W. ST. A., B.A. (D.S.O. L.G. 4.6.17); b. 10.5.82; s. of W. W. Warde-Aldam, of Frickley Hall, Yorkshire, and Sarah Julia, d. of Rev. W. Warde, of Hooton Pagnell; m. Clara, d. of late G. Macavoy; educ. Eton; Trinity College, Cambridge; 2nd Lt., C. Gds., 4.6.04; Lt., C. Gds., 14.11.06; Capt., C. Gds., 15.10.13; Bt. Major, C. Gds., 3.6.19; Major 2.11.19; Bt. Lt.-Col. 4.6.19; Lt.-Col. 30.11.21; served Europ. War, 1914–18; Despatches; Legion of Honour.

WARDELL, H. (D.S.O. L.G. 25.8.17), Lt.-Col., late R.W. Surrey Rgt.; served Europ. War, 1914–17; Despatches. His D.S.O. was awarded for gallantry at St. Eloi 7.6.17. He lost an eye in the Messines fighting.

WARDEN, H. F. (D.S.O. L.G. 1.1.17); b. 10.3.71; s. of late T. F. Warden; m. Frances Muriel, d. of late H. A. Hamshaw; two d.; educ. Haileybury College; Sandhurst; 2nd Lt., The Queen's Rgt., 9.10.90; Lt. 11.9.92; Capt. 20.10.98; Major 2.3.13; Lt.-Col. 5.11.18; late commanding 1st Batt. The Queen's Rgt., retired 1920; served S. African War; twice wounded; Queen's Medal, 5 clasps; King's Medal, 2 clasps; Despatches twice; Europ. War; Despatches twice.

WARDEN, H. L. (D.S.O. L.G. 4.2.18) (Details, L.G. 5.7.18) (Bar, L.G. 16.9.18), Lt.-Col., E. Surrey Rgt.

WARDEN, J. W. (D.S.O. L.G. 10.1.17), Capt., 6th Regt. (Canada), 15.1.14; Despatches; O.B.E.

WARDEN, ST. L. S. (D.S.O. L.G. 16.3.18), Cdr., R.N.

WARDER, R. O. (D.S.O. L.G. 15.3.16); b. 16.1.85; e. s. of J. W. H. Warder; m. Dallas Elise Gedge; one d.; educ. King Edward High School, Birmingham; Major, R.F.A.; served Europ. War, 1914–16; Despatches.

WARDLAW, W. P. MARK- (see Mark-Wardlaw, W. P.).

WARDLE, M. K. (D.S.O. L.G. 26.7.18); b. 17.2.88; 2nd Lt., Leic. R., 13.10.09; Lt., Leic. R., 25.10.11; Capt., Leic. R., 13.2.15; M.C.

WARDLE, T. E. (D.S.O. L.G. 22.6.16); b. 9.1.77; s. of Henry Wardle, M.P. for S. Derbyshire, 1885–92; D.L. for Derbyshire; educ. Cheam School; in H.M.S. Britannia; entered R.N., Aug. 1900; Naval Secretary to the Ordnance Board, 1910–12; served Europ. War; Commander, H.M.S. Crescent, Flagship of Rear-Admiral D. R. S. Sinclair, M.V.O., Aug. to Nov. 1914; Commander, H.M.S. Calyx, Nov. 1914, to March, 1915; Capt., H.M.S. Alcantara, April, 1915, to Feb. 1916; Assistant to the Director of Naval Intelligence, March, 1916, to Oct. 1917; Capt., H.M.S. Lowestoft, Dec. 1917, to Feb. 1918; Captain, H.M.S. Dreadnought, Flagship of Vice-Admiral Sir Dudley R. G. De Chair, K.C.B., M.V.O.; Captain, H.M.S. London, May to June, 1918; Captain H.M.S. Danae, June, 1918; Despatches.

WARE, F. B. (D.S.O. L.G. 1.1.17), Capt., 7th Regt. (Canada), 1.10.10 ; Major, Can. Inf.

WARE, G. W. W., M.B. (D.S.O. L.G. 1.1.18) ; m. Marie, d. of late Eloi Lambert, of Liége ; Lt., R.A.M.C., 31.1.09 ; Major, R.A.M.C., 15.10.15 ; served Europ. War, 1914–18 ; Despatches ; Order of St. Maurice and St. Lazarus of Italy ; Legion of Honour.

WARING, A. H. (D.S.O. L.G. 4.6.17) ; b. 28.11.71 ; s. of Henry R. Waring and Mrs. A. Waring, of Palma-de-Mallorca, Balearic Islands, Spain ; m. Isabel Frank Fenella, d. of the late Lt.-Col. Francis M. Salmond, R. Scots Fus. ; 3 sons ; educ. St. George's College, Weybridge ; University College and Hospital, London ; Lt., R.A.M.C., 29.1.96 ; Capt. 29.1.99 ; Major 29.1.08 ; Lt.-Col. 1.3.15 ; Colonel 15.10.18 ; served Europ. War ; Despatches twice ; 1914 (Mons) Star ; Commander of the Military Order of Avis (Portugal).

WARING, H. A. (D.S.O. L.G. 1.1.18) ; b. 20.3.82 ; 2nd Lt., R.W. Kent Regt., 30.5.04 ; Capt. 26.3.13 ; Major 17.12.16 ; Bt. Lt.-Col. 3.6.19 ; Lt.-Col., The Queen's Own (R.W. Kent Rgt.) ; served in Mediterranean with Militia during S. African War, 1901 ; Medal ; Europ. War, 1914–18 ; Despatches ; Bt. Lt.-Col.

WARING, J. (D.S.O. L.G. 1.1.17) ; b. 12.10.81 ; s. of late Lt.-Col. H. Waring ; m. Bertha Grace, d. of late Capt. J. Woon ; one s. ; educ. Oxford Military College, Cowley ; Cheltenham ; R.M.A., Woolwich ; 2nd Lt., R.G.A., 2.5.00 ; Lt. 3.4.01 ; Capt. 29.1.13 ; Adjt., R.A., 8.4.15 to 29.12.15 ; Major 30.12.15 ; Bt. Lt.-Col. 1.1.19 ; served with B.E.F. in France, with Heavy Artillery since 9.12.14 ; Brig. Major, V. Corps, Heavy Artillery, March, 1916–April, 1917 ; Lt.-Col. for Counter Batteries, V. Corps, April, 1917 ; Despatches twice ; Bt. Lt.-Col.

WARK, B. A. (D.S.O. L.G. 3.6.18), Major, Aust. Inf. ; V.C. (see "The Victoria Cross," same publishers).

WARMAN, C. W. (D.S.O. L.G. 26.9.17) (Details, L.G. 9.1.18), 2nd Lt., Gen. List., R.F.C. ; M.C.

WARNER, E. C. T. (D.S.O. L.G. 4.6.17) ; b. 4.1.86 ; e. s. of Sir Courtenay Warner, Bart., and Lady Leucha Diana Maude, d. of 1st Earl de Montalt ; m. Hon. Nesta Douglas Pennant, half-sister of 3rd Baron Penrhyn ; educ. Eton ; Christ Church, Oxford ; 2nd Lt. 1.2.07 ; Lt. 7.8.09 ; Capt. 28.1.15 ; Bt. Major 3.6.18 ; 2nd-in-command, 1st Batt. Scots Guards, 1918 ; served Europ. War, 1914–18 ; Despatches seven times ; 1914 Star ; M.C. ; Croix de Guerre (France) ; Order of Danilo (Montenegro) ; Order of Avis (Portugal) ; steered Oxford University Eight, 1904.

WARNER, F. A. (D.S.O. L.G. 23.5.17), Lt.-Cdr., R.N. He was killed in action 23.12.17.

WARNER, K. C. H. (D.S.O. L.G. 3.6.19), Major, 2/1st Kent Cyclists' Batt., T.F., att. 7th Batt. York and Lancaster R.

WARNER, T. L. (D.S.O. L.G. 19.11.17) (Details, L.G. 22.3.18) ; s. of late Charles Warner, of Leicester Abbey ; T/Major, Leic. R. He died of wounds 27.12.17, at a casualty clearing station, aged 23.

WARREN, L. E. (D.S.O. L.G. 1.1.18) ; b. 7.10.08 ; 2nd Lt., R.A., 26.6.99 ; Lt., R.A., 16.2.01 ; Capt., R.A., 1.12.07 ; Major 30.10.14 ; served S. African War, 1901–2 ; Queen's Medal, 5 clasps ; Europ. War ; Despatches.

WARREN, W. H. F. (D.S.O. L.G. 17.5.18), Comdr., R.A.N. He has since died.

WARRENDER, H. V. (D.S.O. L.G. 3.6.16) ; b. 14.9.68 ; s. of late Sir G. Warrender, 6th Bart., of Lochend, and Helen, d. of Sir H. Hume Campbell, 7th Bart., of Marchmont ; educ. Eton ; Sandhurst ; joined G. Gds., 1889 ; retired 1897 ; joined Civil Service Rifles, T.F., on outbreak of Europ. War ; served im France, 1914–18 ; Lt.-Col., commanded 1st Batt. Civil Service Rifles ; resigned commission, 1920.

WARRENS, E. R. C. (D.S.O. L.G. 1.1.18), Major, R.F.A.

WARTON, R. B. (D.S.O. L.G. 1.1.17) ; b. 22.12.82 ; 2nd Lt., R.A., 31.7.02 ; Lt. 31.7.05 ; Capt. 30.10.14 ; Major 9.4.16.

WARWICK, H. B. (D.S.O. L.G. 1.1.17) ; b. 10.3.79 ; 2nd Lt., R.A., 10.1.00 ; Lt. 3.4.01 ; Capt. 10.2.11 ; Major 8.12.14 ; Bt. Lt.-Col. 3.6.19 ; substantive rank retained on permanent appointment to the A. Ord. Dept., now R.A.O.C. ; served S. African War, 1899–1902 ; Queen's Medal, 3 clasps ; King's Medal, 2 clasps ; Europ. War ; Despatches.

WARWICK, P. H. (D.S.O. L.G. 1.1.18) ; b. 19.3.80 ; s. of late R. H. Warwick, of Burgage Manor, Southwell, Notts ; m. Dulcie Joan, d. of T. Warner Turner, of Langwith Lodge, Mansfield, Notts ; one d. ; one s. ; educ. Charterhouse ; Hertford College, Oxford ; joined S. Notts. Hussars, 1901 ; A/Lt.-Col., 100th Batt. M.G.C., Dec. 1918 ; served Europ. War ; Lt.-Colonel.

WASHINGTON, B. G. (D.S.O. L.G. 11.11.19), Capt., R.N. ; C.M.G. His D.S.O. was awarded for gallantry, Caspian Sea, 1918–19.

WASS, A. E. (D.S.O. L.G. 3.2.20) ; b. 6.3.83 ; 2nd Lt., 8th Hrs., 22.12.14 ; Lt., 8th Hrs., 1.7.17 ; A/Lt.-Col., Cdg. Bn. R. Bgde., 11.6.18 to 30.6.18 ; Despatches ; M.C.

WASSELL, C. E. (D.S.O. L.G. 1.1.18), Lt.-Col., Aust. A.M.C.

WATERHOUSE, T. F. (D.S.O. L.G. 8.3.18) ; b. 1865 ; s. of late T. Waterhouse, of Sedgley, Staffs ; m. Harriette Mander, d. of H. Mander Jackson ; two d. ; an Officer in S. Staffs. Rgt. from 1889 ; in command of 1/6th S. Staffs R. during Europ. War ; Despatches thrice ; commanding 6th S. Staffs. 1920 ; D.L. Co. of Stafford.

WATERS, A. H. S. (D.S.O. L.G. 3.6.18), Major, 218th Field Co., R.E. ; V.C. ; M.C. (see "The Victoria Cross," by same publishers).

WATERS, J. D., B.A. (D.S.O. L.G. 13.5.18) ; b. 1889 ; m. Lettice, d. of 2nd Baron Newton, and widow of Capt. J. Egerton-Warburton, Scots Guards ; Lt.-Colonel Waters commanded 10th Batt. R. Fus. in France, Europ. War, from 1914 ; Despatches four times ; 1914–15 Star.

P. L. Watkin-Williams.

WATKIN, E. H. P. PEASE- (see Pease-Watkin, E. H. P.).

WATKIN - WILLIAMS, P. L., F.R.C.S., L.R.C.P. (D.S.O. L.G. 19.8.16) ; s. of late Sir C. J. Watkin-Williams ; m. Ellin Margaret, d. of G. T. Skilbeck ; one s. ; two d. ; educ. Middlesex Hospital ; Deputy Commissioner of Medical Services, S.W. Region, Ministry of Pensions ; Major, R.A.M.C. ; served Europ. War, 1914–18. His D.S.O. was awarded for gallantry on 1.7.16, at Montauban.

WATKINS, G. D. (D.S.O. L.G. 26.9.17) (Details, L.G. 9.1.18) ; s. of Councillor Watkins, of Brynmawr ; Capt., R.A.M.C. ; Despatches ; M.C.

WATKINS, G. R. S. (D.S.O. L.G. 22.6.17) (Bar, L.G. 19.12.17), Lt.-Cdr., R.N.

WATKINS, J. W. (D.S.O. L.G. 26.7.18) ; s. of W. Watkins ; m. Ethel Mary Price, d. of J.J. Price ; T/Lt. (A/Lt.-Col.), Lancs. Fus. ; M.C.

WATKINS, O. F. (D.S.O. L.G. 26.6.16) ; b. Allahabad, 23.12.77 ; s. of Ven. O. D. Watkins ; m. W. A. Baillie-Grohman ; two d. ; educ. Marlborough ; Oxford ; served S. African War, 1900–1 ; in S.A. Constabulary, 1902–4 ; Transvaal Civil Service, 1904–7 ; B.E.A. Protectorate Service, 1908 ; District Commissioner, B.E. Africa ; during Europ. War, Director of Military Labour in operations against German E. Africa ; Despatches thrice ; C.B.E.

WATKINS, P. S. (D.S.O. L.G. 4.6.17) ; b. 8.4.78 ; 2nd Lt., R.E., 29.7.97 Lt., R.E., 9.7.00 ; Capt., R.E., 29.7.06 ; Major, R.E., 30.10.14.

WATLING, F. W. (D.S.O. L.G. 1.1.17) ; b. 9.7.69 ; 2nd Lt., R.E., 17.2.88 ; Lt. 17.2.91 ; Capt. 17.2.99 ; Major 3.4.07 ; Lt.-Col. 12.8.15 ; served N.W.F. of India, 1897 (severely wounded) ; Medal with 2 clasps ; Despatches 5.11.97 Europ. War ; C.B.E.

WATSON, A., M.B. (D.S.O. L.G. 17.3.17) (Details, L.G. 26.4.17) ; b. 7.3.87 ; s. of late Rev. W. Watson, of Kiltearn, Ross-shire ; Lt., R.A.M.C., 30.1.14 ; Capt. 30.3.15 ; Despatches. He died at Tembura, Southern Sudan.

WATSON, A. A. (D.S.O. L.G. 1.1.17) ; s. of Andrew Watson and Isabella Watson (*née* Small) ; m. Jessie Mathews ; educ. Galashiels Academy ; The Institution School, Edinburgh, and Edinburgh University ; Lt., R.A.M.C., 1885 ; Capt. 1888 ; Major 1900 ; Lt.-Col. 1905 ; A/Colonel 1918 ; served S. Africa, 1900–2 ; Despatches ; Queen's Medal, 2 clasps ; King's Medal, 2 clasps ; Europ. War from 4.8.14 to end of war ; Despatches four times ; C.M.G. ; Mons Star.

A. A. Watson.

WATSON, A. C. (D.S.O. L.G. 11.4.18) ; b. 14.3.84 ; 2nd Lt., 17th Hrs., 4.1.03 ; Lt., 17th Hrs., 7.4.06 ; Capt., 17th Hrs., 11.10.11 ; Despatches.

WATSON, A. W. H. (D.S.O. L.G. 3.6.19), T/Capt., Gen. List (late 9th Batt. K.R.R.C.) M.C.

WATSON, B. C. (D.S.O. L.G. 4.6.17), Cdr., R.N.

WATSON, C. B. GRAHAM- (see Graham-Watson, C. B.).

WATSON, C. H. (D.S.O. L.G. 4.6.17) ; b. 14.1.70 ; Lt., I.M.S., 26.1.97 ; Capt. 28.1.00 ; Major 28.1.09 ; Lt.-Col. 28.1.17 ; served N.W. Frontier of India, 1897–98 ; Medal, 2 clasps ; N.W. Frontier of India, 1908 ; Medal with clasp ; Europ. War ; Despatches.

WATSON, C. N. (D.S.O. L.G. 26.9.17) (Details, L.G. 9.1.18) (Bar, L.G. 26.7.18), T/Major (A/Lt.-Col.), L'pool R. ; Despatches.

WATSON, C. S. M. C. (D.S.O. L.G. 1.2.17) ; b. 25.2.81 ; 2nd Lt., R.E., 2.5.00 ; Lt., R.E., 2.5.03 ; Capt. 2.5.10 ; Major 2.11.16 ; served S. African War, 1901–2 ; Queen's Medal, 5 clasps ; Europ. War ; Despatches ; O.B.E.

WATSON, C. V. (D.S.O. L.G. 1.1.19) (Bar, L.G. 2.4.19) (Details, L.G. 10.12.19), Lt.-Col., 58th Batt. Aust. Inf.

WATSON, D. P., M.B. (D.S.O. L.G. 3.6.18) ; b. 22.10.75 ; Lt., R.A.M.C., 31.8.03 ; Capt. 28.2.07 ; Major 28.2.15 ; served S. African War, 1902 ; Queen's Medal, 4 clasps ; Despatches.

WATSON, D. S. (D.S.O. L.G. 3.6.19), Major, 1/5th Batt. Som. L.I., T.F. ; served S. African War, 1900–1 ; Queen's Medal, 4 clasps ; Europ. War ; Despatches.

WATSON, E. V. (D.S.O. L.G. 3.6.19) ; b. 4.12.80 ; 2nd Lt., R.A., 4.12.01 ; Lt. 30.6.04 ; Capt. 30.10.14 ; Major 1.5.17 ; Major, R.G.A., Commanding 428th Battery, R.F.A.

WATSON, F. B. (D.S.O. L.G. 4.6.17) ; b. Sept. 1884 ; s. of late Rear-Admiral Burges Watson and Marie Thérèse Watson (*née* Fischer), of Sydney, N.S. Wales ; m. Sybil Mona, d. of late Major H. Holden ; educ. Private School (Ashdown House, Forest Row) ; H.M.S. Britannia ; Midshipman 1900 ; Sub-Lt. 1903 ; Lt. 1905 ; Lt.-Cdr. 1913 ; Cdr. 1914 ; played Rugby Football for Navy *v.* Army, 1908–11.

WATSON, F. S. (D.S.O. L.G. 26.7.18) ; b. 2.5.80 ; 2nd s. of late Col. John Whaley Watson, Political Agent, Kathiawar, India ; educ. Haileybury ; 2nd Lt., R.A., 22.11.99 ; Lt. 16.2.01 ; Capt. 6.0.06 ; Major, R.G.A., 30.10.14 ; served S. African War ; Queen's Medal, 3 clasps ; Europ. War ; Despatches twice. He died at Boullens on 2.5.18, his 38th birthday, of wounds received the previous day. His brother, Capt. C. R. Watson, Indian Infantry, was killed in action in Mesopotamia in April, 1916, and another brother, Major G. E. B. Watson, D.S.O., M.C., R.H.A. was also killed in action on 29.8.18.

WATSON, G. E. B. (D.S.O. L.G. 4.6.17) ; third s. of late Col. J. W. Watson ; educ. Wellington College and the R.M.A., Woolwich ; commissioned in the R.F.A., 1906, joining a R.F.A. Battery in India ; selected for R.H.A. in 1914 ; went to France with the First Expeditionary Force, and was present at the Retreat from Mons. He then trained a battery of R.F.A. in England, and returned with it to France. Subsequently he was given command of a battery of R.H.A., and fell on 29.8.18 while leading it into action, aged 33 ; M.C. His elder brother, Major F. S. Watson, D.S.O., M.C., died of wounds, and his youngest brother, Capt. C. R. Watson, was killed in action.

WATSON, H. F. (D.S.O. L.G. 3.6.18) ; b. 25.7.76 ; s. of late J. Watson, of Darling Point, Sydney, Australia ; m. Margery Stanley, d. of late A. S. Marks ; Major, Aust. Inf. ; served Europ. War, 1915–18 ; Despatches ; M.C.

WATSON, H. N. G. (D.S.O. L.G. 15.7.19) ; b. 9.9.85 ; 2nd Lt., A.S.C., 8.12.09 ; Lt. 8.12.12 ; Adjt., A.S.C., 8.8.14 to 15.6.15 ; Capt., R.A.S.C., 8.12.15 ; Bt. Lt.-Col. 3.6.19.

WATSON, H. W. M. (D.S.O. L.G. 14.1.16) (Bar, L.G. 18.2.18) (Details, L.G. 18.7.18) ; b. 13.8.81 ; s. of late Major-Gen. J. K. Watson, 60th Rifles, and Alice, d. of Col. Pears ; m. Lydia Gladys (*née* Adams), widow of Hon. P. Hore-Ruthven ; two d. ; educ. Winchester ; joined Militia, 7th K.R.R., in 1899 ; 2nd Lt., K.R.R.C., 4.8.00 ; Lt. 26.6.01 ; Capt. 23.1.11 ; Major 1.9.15 ; Bt. Lt.-Col., K.R.R., 3.6.18 ; served S. Africa, 1900–2 ; Queen's Medal, 3 clasps ; King's Medal, 2 clasps ; served Europ. War, 1914–18, including St. Eloi, Ypres Salient and Cambrai ; Gallipoli, 1915 ; evacuation of Suvla ; Egypt, 1915 ; in command 2/4th Queen's R.W. Surrey Rgt., 1916 ; 1st K.R.R.C., 1916–17 ; twice wounded ; C.M.G. ; Bt. Lt.-Col.

WATSON, O. C. S. (D.S.O. L.G. 26.7.17), Lt.-Col., 1st County of London Yeomanry, V.C. (see "The Victoria Cross," same publishers).

WATSON, R. A. (D.S.O. L.G. 3.6.19) ; b. 6.7.89 ; 2nd Lt., R.A., 29.11.14 ; Lt., R.A., 9.6.15 ; Capt. 3.11.17 M.C.

WATSON, R. H. M. (D.S.O. L.G. 1.1.19); b. 23.1.79; s. of late Rev. A. Watson, M.A.; m. Vera Hope Innes; one s.; educ. Cheltenham College; R.M.A., Woolwich; 2nd Lt., R.A., 23.12.98; Lt. 16.2.01; Capt. 26.3.04; Major 3.10.14; A/Lt.-Col., 1917; served 10 years in China with local Indian Artillery; Europ. War in France and Italy, commanding 61st Siege Battery and 15th Brigade; Despatches thrice; 1914 Star with Bar; Order of Leopold; Order of the Crown of Italy; Croix de Guerre.

WATSON, R. J. N. (D.S.O. L.G. 15.6.17) (Bar, L.G. 1.1.19), Cdr., R.N.

WATSON, S. (D.S.O. L.G. 3.6.19); b. 25.2.91; Capt., Cheshire Regt., 19.1.17; Capt. (T/Major and A/Lt.-Col.), Ches. R., att. 12th Batt.; Despatches; M.C.

WATSON, S. H. (D.S.O. L.G. 1.1.19), Major, 2nd Art., Div. Signal Co., Aust. Engineers; M.C.

WATSON, S. T. (D.S.O. L.G. 14.11.16); b. 27.7.79; s. of late R. Twells Watson; m. Winifred Mary (who died in 1919), d. of F. Baring-Gould; educ. New College, Eastbourne; Army, 2nd R.W. Surrey Rgt., 7.3.00; Lt. 20.2.02; Capt. 22.1.11; Major 1.9.15; served S. African War, 1900–2; Queen's Medal, 2 clasps; King's Medal, 2 clasps; Europ. War, 1914–17.

WATSON, S. W. (D.S.O. L.G. 4.6.17), Capt. (A/Major), Can. Inf.

WATSON, T. H. (D.S.O. L.G. 3.6.18), Capt., Worc. R.; T/Lt.-Col. commanding the 1st Sherwood Foresters; M.C. He was killed in action before St. Quentin on 23.3.18, aged 25.

WATSON, W. H. L. (D.S.O. L.G. 3.6.19), T/Major, 4th Tank Carrier Co., Tank Corps; D.C.M.

WATSON, W. W. (D.S.O. L.G. 28.8.18), Cdr., R.N.V.R.

WATT, D. M. (D.S.O. L.G. 8.5.15) (Bar, L.G. 1.1.18); Col. (Hon. Brig.-Gen.), I.A. (ret.) (see "The Distinguished Service Order" from its institution to 31 Dec. 1915, same publishers).

WATT-SMYTH, G. J. (see Smyth G. J. Watt-).

WATTS, A. G. (D.S.O. L.G. 28.8.18), Cdr., R.N.V.R.

WATTS, B. (D.S.O. L.G. 1.1.17); b. 7.4.72; s. of J. Watts; m. Lily, d. of E. S. Thomasson, F.R.G.S.; one d.; educ. Sheffield; London Hospital; Lt., R.A.M.C., 28.1.98; Capt. 28.1.01; Major 28.10.09; Lt.-Col. 1.3.15; with B.E.F. in France from Aug. 1914, serving with 5th, 55th and 29th Divisions; A.D.M.S. of a Division with T. rank of Colonel, Sept. 1916; Despatches twice.

WATTS, B. A. G. (D.S.O. L.G. 3.6.16), Major, R. Aust. Garr. Art. He was killed in action 10.4.17.

WATTS, R. A. B. P. (D.S.O. L.G. 3.2.20); b. 20.4.87; 2nd Lt., Som. L.I., 4.5.07; Lt. 17.8.09; Capt. 10.6.15.

WAUHOPE, G. B. (D.S.O. L.G. 15.10.18); b. 9.5.82; m. Violet Adelaide, widow of Capt. M. Crawshay, 5th Dn. Gds.; one d.; educ. Charterhouse; Sandhurst; 2nd Lt., Lan. Fus., 11.8.00; Lt. 1.3.02; Capt., York and Lan. R., 1.9.11; Major 1.9.15; Bt. Col., York and Lancaster R., 1.1.19; retired pay, 1921; served Sudan, 1912; Medal and clasps; Europ. War, 1914–18; Despatches.

WAY, B. I., F.R.G.S. (D.S.O. L.G. 1.1.17); b. Denham Place, Bucks, 9.7.69; s. of late B. H. W. Way and Isabel, d. of late Rev. H. H. Way, of Alderbourn, Fulmer, Bucks; educ. Eton; Sandhurst; J.P., Bucks; joined 1st N. Staffs. R. at Cape Town 3.5.90, and went with it to Mauritius and experienced the great hurricane of 1902, when over 1,500 lives were lost; Capt. 16.10.99; Lt.-Col., late 4th N. Staffs. R.; was in Malta, 1893–95, and Egypt, 1895; served Dongola Exp., 1896; Br. and Sudan Medal and 4th Class Medjidie. He served in India, 1897–1903, and retired in 1905 to join the 4th N. Staffs. Regt.; in command of Batt., 1912, and on outbreak of war went with it to Guernsey. He commanded 8th E. Yorks. R., Aug. 1915; went to France, Sept. 1915; severely wounded at Loos; rejoined 8th E.Y.R., March, 1916; took part in attack on Longueval, 1916, and was again wounded; Despatches twice.

WAY, G. O. (D.S.O. L.G. 4.6.17), Capt., N. Staffs. R. (Spec. Res.).

WAY, J. (D.S.O. L.G. 1.1.18); b. 21.10.76; 2nd Lt., R.A., 23.5.00; Lt. 10.10.01; Capt. 23.5.13; Major 30.12.15; served S. African War, 1899–1902; Queen's Medal, 4 clasps; King's Medal, 2 clasps; Europ. War; M.C.; Despatches.

WAY, L. F. K. (D.S.O. L.G. 3.6.19); b. 20.4.85; s. of H. Way; m. (1st) Gladys Elizabeth Mary (who died in 1919), d. of Rev. C. H. V. Pixell, M.A.; one s.; one d.; (2nd), 1920, Margaret Amy, widow of Capt. L. T. Watson, 1st Batt. Worc. R.; educ. St. Bartholomew's Hospital; Lt., R.A.M.C., 29.7.10; Capt. 29.1.14; Lt.-Col., R.A.M.C.

L. F. K. Way.

WAYMAN, H. R. B. (D.S.O. L.G. 1.1.18), Temp. Major (A/Lt.-Col.), Northumberland Fus.

WAYTE, A. B. (D.S.O. L.G. 1.1.18); b. 2.5.82; s. of late G. H. Wayte, J.P., and Annie, d. of late Sir J. Paxton, M.P.; educ. Repton; joined 2nd Batt. Sherwood Foresters, 27.7.01; Adjt., 14th Batt. S. Foresters, Oct. 1914; Lieut. 14.2.06; Capt. 25.10.10; Major 25.6.16; served S. African War with Berks. I.Y.; Queen's and King's Medals; commanded 1st Batt. S. Foresters at battles of Festubert and operations near Bois Grenier, 1915; commanded 11th Batt. S. Foresters at Battle of Messines, 1917; commanded 1/5th The King's Own (R.L.R.) at 3rd Battle of Ypres, July and Sept. 1917; commanded 166th Inf. Brig., Oct. and Nov. 1917; commanded 1/5th The King's Own (R. Lanc. R.) at Battle of Cambrai, 1917, and during the offensive by the Germans at Givenchy, April, 1918; Despatches twice.

WEAVER, C. Y. (D.S.O. L.G. 1.2.19), Major (A/Lt.-Col.), 49th Batt. Can. Inf., Alberta Rgt.

WEBB, A. H. (D.S.O. L.G. 14.1.16); b. 1873; s. of Capt. H. J. Webb, late 11th Rgt.; m. Evelyn Dorothea, d. of H. Brady, Deputy Accountant-General, R.N.; one s.; three d.; educ. privately; R.M.A., Woolwich; 2nd Lt., R.A., 10.8.92; Lt., R.A., 10.8.95; Capt., R.A., 1.2.00; Major 1.1.14; Lt.-Col., R.G.A., 9.6.17; served S. African War, 1899–1900; Queen's Medal with 3 clasps; Europ. War; C.M.G.

WEBB, E. N., Assoc.M.Inst.C.E. (D.S.O. L.G. 1.2.19); b. 1889; educ. New Zealand University; Chief Magnetician with Australasian Antarctic Exp. 1911–14; served Europ. War (Egypt and France), 1915–19; Despatches; M.C.

WEBB, G. A. C. (D.S.O. L.G. 1.1.17); b. 7.10.69; s. of Rev. A. C. Webb, M.A., of Dysartgallen, Queen's Co.; m. Hilda Hyneley, d. of Lt.-Col. Schreiber; two s.; educ. Chard; R.M.C., Sandhurst; 2nd Lt., 1st Batt. R. Munster Fus., 29.3.90; Adjt. for three and a half years until joined Egyptian Army; Capt. 1.11.98; Bt. Major 29.1.02; retired 28.6.05; rejoined Aug. 1914; Bt. Lt.-Col. 1.1.18; served Nile Exp.; Medal, clasp and 4th Class Medjidie; S. African War; commanded Rimington's Guides, later Damant's Horse; dangerously wounded, 1901; Despatches; Queen's Medal, 5 clasps; Bt. Major; rejoined from R. of O. on outbreak of, and served in, Europ. War, 1914–18; Despatches twice; Bt. Lt.-Col.

WEBB, M. E., F.R.I.B.A. (D.S.O. L.G. 11.4.18); b. 1880; s. of Sir Aston Webb; m. Dorothea, d. of E. Besant; educ. Marlborough; Pembroke College, Cambridge; served in R.E. in Europ. War from 1914, Suvla, Serbia, Salonika and Palestine; M.C.; President, Architectural Association, 1914 and 1919.

WEBB, R. H. (D.S.O. L.G. 4.9.18), Lt.-Col., West Ontario Regt., Can. Forces; M.C.

T. P. Webb.

WEBB, T. P. (D.S.O. L.G. 20.9.18), Lt.-Cdr., R.N.R.

WEBB, W. E. (D.S.O. L.G. 1.1.18); b. 27.12.55; served first in K.O.S.B., 1874–1903; commissioned 8.6.92; Capt., 1902; Major; Lt.-Col.; served Afghan War, 1878–80 (Medal); Chin Lushai Exp., 1889 (Medal and clasp); S. African War, 1900–2; Despatches; Queen's Medal, 3 clasps; King's Medal, 2 clasps; Europ. War, 1914–18; wounded; Despatches four times; 1914 Star; 1st London Scottish Secretary from 1906; also Quartermaster, 1914; Freeman, Royal Burgh of Dumfries.

WEBB, W. F. R. (D.S.O. L.G. 25.11.16); b. 12.3.83; s. of Major W. W. Webb, M.D., Indian Medical Service; educ. Portsmouth and Sandhurst; 2nd Lt., Bedfords. R., 8.5.01; I.A. 11.10.02; Lt. 8.8.03; Capt. 8.5.10; Major 8.5.16; served N.W. Frontier of India, 1902; operations against Darweshi Khel Waziris, N.W.F. of India, 1908; operations in Mohmand country; Medal with clasp; Europ. War; Despatches four times; O.B.E.; Afghanistan, 1919. His D.S.O. was awarded for gallantry 15.9.16, at Delville Wood.

WEBB-BOWEN, H. E., A.M.I.E.E., A.M.I.Mech.E. (D.S.O. L.G. 3.6.18) b. 1882; s. of late B. Ince Webb-Bowen; m. Gladys, d. of W. J. Crampton, of Southsea; educ. St. Paul's School; City and Guilds of London Technical College; served with London Electrical Engineers (V.) in S. Africa, 1901–2; Medal and 5 clasps; served London Electrical Engineers (T.), 1914–16; Salonika, 1916–19; Serbian White Eagle with Cross Swords; C.M.G. He has the T.D.

WEBB-BOWEN, W. I. (D.S.O. L.G. 4.6.17); b. 26.7.82; 2nd Lt., M'sex Regt., 27.7.01; Lt. 10.11.03; Capt. 6.3.12; Bt. Major 4.9.12; Major 27.7.16; T/Brig.-Gen. 2.4.18.

WEBB-JOHNSON, A. E., F.R.C.S., M.B., Ch.B., F.Z.S. (D.S.O. L.G. 3.6.16); s. of late S. Johnson, M.D., and Julia, d. of late J. Webb; m. Cecilia Flora, d. of late D. G. MacRae; educ. Victoria University of Manchester; late Col., A.M.S.; Consulting Surgeon, B.E.F., France; Capt., R.A.M.C., T.F.; att. to University of London O.T.C.; served Europ. War from 1914; Despatches three times; C.B.E.; Knight of Grace, St. John of Jerusalem.

WEBBER, N. W. (D.S.O. L.G. 3.6.16); b. 22.2.81; s. of late H. Webber; m. Maud, d. of G. Critchley-Salmonson; two s.; one d.; educ. Bradfield; Woolwich; joined R.E. 25.6.99; Lt. 31.12.01; Capt. 25.6.08; Major 15.11.15; Bt. Lt.-Col. 1.1.17; Bt. Col. 3.6.19; T/Brig.-Gen. 14.3.18; Col. 1920; served S. African War, 1901–2; Queen's Medal, 4 clasps; Europ. War, 1914–18; Despatches; Bt. Major; Bt. Lt.-Col.; Bt. Col.; C.M.G.; Chevalier, Legion of Honour; Croix de Guerre.

WEBBER, A. B. INCLEDON- (see Incledon-Webber, A. B.).

WEBER, W. H. F. (D.S.O. L.G. 3.6.16); b. 13.8.75; s. of late Sir Hermann Weber, F.R.C.P.; educ. Stoke House, Slough; Charterhouse; R.M.A., Woolwich; m. Benita, d. of Reginald Douglas Thornton, J.P., D.L.; two s.; 2nd Lt., R.A., 17.11.94; Lt. 17.11.97; Capt. 25.1.01; Adjt., R.A., 27.4.05 to 24.11.05; Major 21.7.11; Lt.-Col. 24.4.16; Colonel 24.4.20; served S. African War, 1899–1900; Despatches (L.G. 10.9.01); Queen's Medal, 6 clasps; Europ. War; wounded 13.10.15; Despatches; C.M.G.

WEBSTER, A. E. (D.S.O. L.G. 12.5.17), Capt. (Lieut., R.N.R.).

WEBSTER, J. A. (D.S.O. L.G. 8.3.19) (Details, L.G. 4.10.19); s. of late J. Webster; m. Constance, d. of Richard and Lady Constance Combe; one s.; educ. St. Bees, Cumberland, and privately; Magdalen College, Oxford; Asst. Secretary to Air Ministry from 1919; served Europ. War from 1914 in 8th London Rgt., and as Brig. Major, 53rd Inf. Brig.; Bt. Major, 1917; Despatches; Italian Order of St. Maurice and St. Lazarus.

WEBSTER, J. R. (D.S.O. L.G. 26.11.17) (Details, L.G. 6.4.18); e. s. of late J. M. Webster; Lt.-Col., The Sherwood Foresters; M.C. He was killed in action 22.3.18.

WEBSTER, J. T. V. (D.S.O. L.G. 27.6.19), Paymaster Lt.-Cdr., R.N.

WEBSTER, W., M.D., C.M. (D.S.O. L.G. 1.1.17); b. 24.8.65; s. of W. Webster; educ. Middleton, Manchester; University of Manitoba; commissioned 1901 in Can. Militia; mobilized No. 4 Can. Field Ambulance, 2nd Can. Div., and in command from 5.11.14; Colonel, formerly commanding No. 4 Can. Field Amb.

WEBSTER, W. H. (D.S.O. L.G. 12.3.17), 2nd Lt., Lond. R. He was killed in action 10.2.17.

WEDD, W. B. (D.S.O. L.G. 1.1.19), Major, 1st Cent. Ont. R., Can. Mil. Force M.C.

WEDGBURY, E. (D.S.O. L.G. 2.4.19) (Details, L.G. 10.12.19), T/2nd Lt., Glouc. R., att. 1/8th Batt. Worcesters. R.; M.C.; D.C.M.; M.M.

WEDGWOOD, G. H. (D.S.O. L.G. 26.7.18); b. 19.6.76; second s. of late Lawrence and of Emma E. Wedgwood; m. Dorothy H., youngest d. of Walter Salmond and Mrs. Salmond, O.B.E., of Newton Old Hall, Alfreton; educ. Pembroke School, Southbourne; Newcastle High School (Staff); Clifton College; 2nd Lt., York and Lanc. R., 4.5.98; Lt. 20.6.00; Capt. 14.6.05; Major 1.5.15; Lt.-Col. 22.9.20; served S. African War, 1899–1902; Queen's Medal, 6 clasps; King's Medal, 2 clasps; served Europ. War; left Jubbalpore with 28th Div. in 1st Batt. for England, Nov. 1914; landed in France 15.1.15; wounded; served in Egypt and France to Nov. 1916; trench fever; A/Lt.-Col., 6th Yorkshires, 1917; T/Lt.-Col., 8th Duke of Wellington's, 1917; transferred to 6th Manchesters, till May, 1918; T/Brig.-Gen. commanding 126th Inf. Brig. till Sept. 1918; Despatches twice; M.C.; 1914–15 Star.

WEEKES, H. W. (D.S.O. L.G. 14.1.16); b. 1.3.70; s. of late Rev. W. J. Weekes, at one time Precentor of Rochester Cathedral; m. Katherine, d. of late Rev. Chancellor Harman, Cork Diocese; one d.; educ. King's School, Rochester; R.M.A., Woolwich; 2nd Lt., R.E., 27.7.88; Lt., R.E., 27.7.91; Capt. 27.7.99; Adjt. 1.11.00 to 31.10.04; Major 1.10.07; Lt.-Col. 15.11.15; Col. 15.11.19; served in M.W.D. and Sappers and Miners, India, 1891–97; took part in expedition for relief of Chitral; Medal and clasp; Brig. Major and Secretary, S.M.E., Chatham, 1910–15; served in France with 1st Div. and as C.R.E., 51st Div. Despatches twice O.B.E.

WEEKS, R. M. (D.S.O. L.G. 1.1.18), Capt., S. Lanc. R.; M.C.

WEIR, D. L. (D.S.O. L.G. 15.4.16) (Bar, L.G. 8.3.19) (Details, L.G. 4.10.19); b. 21.9.85; 2nd Lt., Leic. R., 6.7.07; Lt., Leic. R., 4.5.10; Capt. 2.5.14; Capt. (A/Lt.-Col.), Leic. R., att. 1st Batt. W. Yorks. R.; M.C. He died 21.10.21. His D.S.O. was awarded for gallantry on 13.1.16, in Mesopotamia.

WEIR, F. V. (D.S.O. L.G. 2.12.18), Major, 1st Aust. L.H.R.

WEIR, J. G. (D.S.O. L.G. 1.1.19), Lt.-Col., 2nd Batt. Can. M.G. Corps; M.C.

WEIR, S. P. (D.S.O. L.G. 1.1.17); b. 23.4.66; s. of A. Weir, of Aberdeen; m. Rosa, d. of J. Wadham; one s.; one d.; educ. Norwood Public School; ent. Surveyor General's Dept., 1879; Public Service Commissioner, 1917; enlisted in Militia Force, 1885; 1st com., 1890; Capt., 1893; Major, 1904; Lt.-Col., 1908; Col., 1913; Brig.-Gen., 1921; V.D.; commanded 19th Inf. Brig., 1912; 10th A.I.F., 1914; commanded Batt. at landing at Gallipoli 25.4.15, and in France, July and Aug. 1916; Despatches; Russian Order of St. Anne.

WEISBURG, H. (see Whitehill, H.).

WELCH, H. E. (D.S.O. L.G. 19.11.17) (Details, L.G. 22.3.18) (Bar, L.G. 18.2.18) (Details, L.G. 18.7.18); m. Miss Maude, of Senaghan Park, Enniskillen; Lt.-Col., Shrops. L.I.; served S. African War, 1899–1902; Queen's Medal, 3 clasps; King's Medal, 2 clasps; Europ. War; Despatches. He was killed in action 29.3.18.

WELCH, H. L. ST. V. (D.S.O. L.G. 4.6.17), Major, Aust. A.M.C.

WELCH, J. B. ST. V. (D.S.O. L.G. 1.1.17), Lt.-Col., Aust. A.M.C.

WELCH, M. KEMP- (see Kemp-Welch, M.).

WELCH, R. H. (D.S.O. L.G. 11.1.19); b. 26.3.95; 2nd Lt., R. Lanc. Regt., 11.6.15; Lt., R. Lanc. Regt., 14.9.16.

WELDON, E. S. (D.S.O. L.G. 3.6.19); b. 6.1.77; 2nd Lt., Dorset Regt., 4.5.98; Lt. 4.2.00; Capt. 29.4.05; Major 1.9.15; A/Lt.-Col.; served S. African War, 1899–1902; Queen's Medal, 4 clasps; King's Medal, 2 clasps; Europ. War; Despatches.

WELDON, H. W. (D.S.O. L.G. 15.2.19) (Details, L.G. 30.7.19); b. 2.11.78; 2nd Lt., Leins. Regt., 9.12.99; Lt. 4.4.01; Capt. 23.1.04; Adjt., Leins. Regt., 4.4.12 to 3.10.15; Major 1.9.15; served S. African War, 1902; Queen's Medal, 4 clasps; Europ. War; Despatches.

WELDON, K. C. (D.S.O. L.G. 1.1.17); b. 25.4.77; 2nd Lt., R. Dub. Fus., 17.2.00; Lt. 28.5.02; Capt. 22.1.09; Major 1.9.15; Bt. Lt.-Col. 3.6.19; served S. African War, 1902; Queen's Medal, 4 clasps; Europ. War; Despatches.

WELLS, A. G. (D.S.O. L.G. 4.6.17); b. 10.11.82; Lt., R.A.M.C., 4.2.08; Capt. 4.8.11; Major 4.2.20.

WELLS, B. C. (D.S.O. L.G. 1.1.18), Major (A/Lt.-Col.), Essex R.

WELLS, G. K. (D.S.O. L.G. 8.3.19) (Details, L.G. 4.10.19); b. 28.2.89; 2nd Lt., K.R.R.C., 23.3.16; Lt. 23.9.17; Despatches; M.C.

WELLS, L. F., B.Sc., M.Inst.C.E., Assoc.Inst.T. (D.S.O. L.G. 11.4.18); b. 20.10.77; s. of L. B. Wells, M.Inst.C.E.; m. Edith Mabel, d. of Brig.-Gen. Sir E. Raban, K.C.B., K.B.E.; educ. Blundell's School, Tiverton; Victoria University, Manchester; 2nd Lt. 8.2.00; Capt. 30.8.02; Major 1.6.16; Lt.-Col., R.E. (T.F. Res.); T.D.; served in Egypt and on the Suez Canal, 1914–15; Gallipoli, 1915; Sinai, Palestine and France from 1916; Despatches five times; Bt. Lt.-Col. 3.6.19; Serbian Order of Kara George with Swords, 4th Class.

WELLS, L. V. (D.S.O. L.G. 14.1.21), Cdr., R.N.

WELLS, J. S. COLLINGS- (see Collings-Wells, J. S.).

WELLS, R. P. COLLINGS- (gazetted as Wells, R. P.) (see Collings-Wells, R. P.).

WELLS-HOOD, W. (see Hood, W. Wells-).

WELMAN, A. E. P. (D.S.O. L.G. 23.7.18) (Bar, L.G. 28.8.18); b. 1893; s. of Col. A. P. Welman; m. Eileen, d. of Lt.-Cdr., G. R. Maltby, and of the late Hersey Maltby, d. of late Admiral Sir G. Elliot; Lt., R.N.; served Europ. War in command of Coastal Motor Boat Flotilla operating upon the Belgian coast, and during Blocking Operations against Zeebrugge and Ostend; Despatches; D.S.C.; Croix de Guerre; Legion of Honour.

WELSH, W. M. M. O'D. (D.S.O. L.G. 1.1.19); b. 3.7.88; 2nd Lt., R.A., 23.7.07; Lt. 23.7.10; Capt. 30.10.14; Major, R.F.A., 12.7.17; M.C.

WENYON, H. J. (D.S.O. L.G. 18.10.17) (Details, L.G. 7.3.18) (Bar, L.G. 16.9.18), T/Major (A/Lt.-Col.), R.W. Kent R.

WERE, H. H. (D.S.O. L.G. 1.1.17); b. 8.3.65; s. of N. Were; m. Kathleen, d. of late S. Creagh Sandes; educ. Kelly College, Tavistock; Sandhurst; joined E. Lancs. R., 1885; 1st commission 7.2.85; Capt., 1893; Major, E. Lancashire Rgt., 23.9.05; retired 12.2.13; served Europ. War, 1916–17; Despatches twice.

WERNICKE, F. P., M.B. (D.S.O. L.G. 26.8.18); b. 19.4.81; Lt., I.M.S., 1.2.06; Capt. 15.12.13; Major, Ind. M.S., 1.2.18.

WESSEL, J. A. (D.S.O. L.G. 22.8.18), Capt., Lichtenburg Commando, S. African Mil. Force.

WEST, A. H. D. (D.S.O. L.G. 1.1.17) (Bar, L.G. 1.2.19); b. Longford, Ireland, 27.12.77; s. of late Rev. H. M. West; m. Harriet Laura, d. of Rev. Canon E. Chichester and the Hon. Mrs. Chichester, of Dorking; educ. Haileybury College; R.M.A., Woolwich; ent. Army 19.1.98; Lt. 19.1.01; Capt. 27.10.05; Major 30.10.14; Bt. Lt.-Col. 1.1.18; Lt.-Col., R.H.A., 24.7.18; served S. African Campaign, 1900–2; severely wounded; Despatches; Queen's and King's Medals; Europ. War, 1914–18; Despatches four times; holds R. Humane Society's Silver Medal.

WEST, C. S. (D.S.O. L.G. 17.4.17); b. 22.4.86, at Temple Michael Rectory, Longford, Ireland; s. of the late Rev. H. M. West; educ. St. Clare, Walmer, and H.M.S. Britannia; joined R.N., 1902; served in Channel Squadron, 1902 to 1903; in the China Squadron, 1903 to 1905; was invalided from 1905 on his return from China till 1908; entered Trinity College, Cambridge, 1911, taking a 2nd Class in the History Tripos; volunteered for service immediately on the outbreak of war; was gazetted Lieut., R.N.V.R., 25.8.14, and promoted Lieut.-Comdr.; went with the Hawke Battalion, R.N.D., to Antwerp; was interned in Holland; he, with two others, succeeded in escaping in disguise, thus avoiding having to give parole, May, 1915; he went to Gallipoli as 2nd-in-command of the Collingwood Battalion; wounded 4 June. After three weeks for recovery in Alexandria he returned to Gallipoli and served (as Second-in-Command) with Howe Battalion till the evacuation of Gallipoli. In May, 1916, he went to France with same Battalion, to the command of which he was afterwards appointed; he took part in the operations at Arras, Gavrelle, Angres, Ancre, etc.; Despatches. He was killed in action 30.12.17.

WEST, F. G. (D.S.O. L.G. 1.1.17), Major (T/Lt.-Col.), R.A.

WEST, R. A. (D.S.O. L.G. 1.1.18) (Bar, L.G. 7.11.18), Capt., Yeomanry; V.C. (see "The Victoria Cross," by same publishers.)

WEST, R. M., M.D. (D.S.O. L.G. 4.6.17), Major (T/Lt.-Col.), R.A.M.C.

WESTCAR, W. V. L. PRESCOTT (see Prescott-Westcar, W. V. L.).

WESTERN, B. C. M. (D.S.O. L.G. 22.9.16) (Bar, L.G. 1.1.18); b. 25.6.86; s. of late Rev. W. T. Western; m. Phyllis Beatrice, adopted d. of Sir T. Western, 3rd Bart.; one d.; educ. Haileybury; Sandhurst; 2nd Lt., E. Lan. Regt., 9.10.07; Lt. 7.1.11; Capt. 9.9.14; Bt. Major 1.1.17; Major, late E. Lancs. R.; served Europ. War, 1914–17; Despatches three times; twice wounded. His D.S.O. was awarded for gallantry on 10.7.16, at Contalmaison.

WESTLEY, J. H. S. (D.S.O. L.G. 3.6.16); b. 10.9.82; 2nd Lt., York. R., 18.1.02; Lt. 1.11.04; Capt. 20.1.11; Major 18.1.17; served S. African War, 1902; Queen's Medal, 4 clasps; Europ. War, 1914–18; Despatches; C.M.G.

WESTMACOTT, G. P. (D.S.O. L.G. 14.1.16); b. 7.4.80; s. of late P. G. B. Westmacott; m. Effie Marion, d. of A. Gibson, of Burrungwiroolong, Goulburn, N.S.W.; one d.; educ. Eton; Major, late North'd Fus, 9th Batt., and 5th Fus.; A/Lt.-Col., 1916–17; served S. African War, 1899–1902; wounded; Queen's Medal, 3 clasps; King's Medal, 2 clasps; Europ. War, 1914–18; wounded; Despatches; Mons Star, 1914–15.

WESTMACOTT, G. R. (D.S.O. L.G. 4.2.18) (Details, L.G. 5.7.18); b. 16.7.91; s. of Maj.-Gen. Sir R. Westmacott, K.C.B., D.S.O., and Rose Margaret, d. of Maj.-Gen. F. J. Caldecott, C.B.; m. Edith Victoria Blanche Winn, d. of 2nd Baron St. Oswald; two s.; educ. Eton; Christ Church, Oxford; played Football, Racquets and Fives for Eton; represented Oxford *v.* Cambridge at Real Tennis, 1913; joined G. Gds. at outbreak of war; Captain; was wounded, March, 1915; served with the battalion at Cuinchy, Neuve Chapelle, Third Battle of Ypres, Bourlon Wood, Gouzeaucourt, Battle of Arras (1918) and Mt. Kemmel; Croix de Guerre.

WESTMINSTER, THE DUKE OF (D.S.O. L.G. 28.3.16); b. 19.3.79; s. of Victor Alexander, Earl Grosvenor and Countess Grosvenor (*née* Lady Sibell Mary Lumley), who m. 2ndly the late G. Wyndham, M.P.; grandson of 1st Duke; succeeded grandfather 1899; m. 1st Constance Edwina, C.B.E., d. of late W. C. Cornwallis-West; m. 2ndly, Violet Mary Geraldine Rowley, d. of Sir William Nelson, first bart.; educ. Eton; served S. African War as A.D.C. to Lord Roberts, 1899-1900; Despatches; Queen's Medal, 5 clasps; European War from 1914; Despatches. D.S.O. awarded for services with armoured cars in the Senussi Campaign under Sir William Peyton.

WESTMORE, H. G. G. (D.S.O. L.G. 1.1.17); b. 1870; s. of R. G. Westmore; Captain in Steamers of Bristol City Line, 1906–14; Lt. in H.M.S. Amphitrite and Sutlej, in China Station, 1904–6; Lt.-Cdr., R.N.R., H.M.S. Macedonia, Falkland Battle, 6.8.14–1.2.15; commanded H.M.S. Hecate, patrol and mine-sweeper, 10.3.15 to 1.10.16; commanded H.M.S. Q 17, 5.10.16 to 27.4.17. His D.S.O. was awarded for destroying submarines in English Channel 24.10.16; Commander, R.N.R., R.D.

WESTMORLAND, H. C. (D.S.O. L.G. 16.9.18) (Bar, L.G. 15.2.19) (Details, L.G. 30.7.19); b. 7.12.93; s. of Lt.-Col. H. G. Westmorland, late 37th Foot; educ. Wellington College; Sandhurst; 2nd Lt., Hants Rgt., 3.9.13; Lt. 31.10.14; Capt. 3.3.16. At Cricket he represented Colchester Garrison and his Battalion. Playing for his unit in 1914, his top score was 106 not out against the United Services at Colchester. With a score of 18 out of a possible 20 he gained second prize at 500 yards in the Eastern Command Championship Rifle Meeting in 1914. In the Europ. War, with the 4th Division, he commanded a platoon at the Battle of Le Cateau, the Retreat, the Battles of the Marne and Aisne; was severely wounded; rejoined the 1st Batt. Hants Rgt. at Hamel on the Ancre, and serving again in the 1st Div. From 3.11.15 he commanded a company as T/Capt.; on 29.4.16 he was again wounded, and in June, 1917, went again to France, to the 2nd Batt. The Hants Rgt. in the 29th Div., commanding a company in the Ypres Sector till the offensive of Aug. 1917; took part in the Battle of Langemarck (Despatches); 2nd-in-command of the Battalion until he took over command at Passchendaele, March, 1918, and commanded it until March, 1919; slightly wounded again in Aug. 1918; French Croix de Guerre.

WESTON, C. H., LL.B. (D.S.O. L.G. 1.1.18); b. 29.12.79; s. of late T. S. Weston, of Christ Church, N.Z.; educ. Christ Church Grammar School; Canterbury College (LL.B.); N.Z. University; Lt.-Col., N.Z. Inf.; served Europ. War, 1915–17; Despatches.

WESTON, J. L. (D.S.O. L.G. 1.1.17); b. 28.1.82; s. of John and Margaret Louisa Weston; m. Ella Esther, d. of late D. Lynch, Q.C., Dublin; three d.; educ. Clifton College; 5th T. Dublin Fus., 1900–1; 2nd Lt., 1st R. Inns. Fus., 26.6.01; Lt. 27.1.04; 2nd Lt., A.S.C., 1.10.04; Lt. 1.10.05; Capt. 21.1.11; Major, R.A.S.C., 30.10.14; Bt. Lt.-Col., R.A.S.C., 3.6.19; served S. African War, 1900–2, with 5th R. Dublin Fus.; Europ. War, in France, on Staff, 51st (Highland) Division; Despatches thrice; Bt. Lt.-Col.

WESTON, S. V. P. (D.S.O. L.G. 17.4.17) (1st Bar, L.G. 18.2.18) (Details, L.G. 18.7.18) (2nd Bar, L.G. 26.7.18), Capt. (T/Lt.-Col.), R. Berks. R.; Brig.-Gen.; served Europ. War; M.C.; French and Belgian Croix de Guerre.

WESTON, W. J. (D.S.O. L.G. 4.6.17); b. 3.7.81; Lt., R.A.M.C., 31.7.05; Capt. 31.1.09; Major 15.10.15.

WESTROP, S. A. (D.S.O. L.G. 16.8.17); b. 20.5.93; s. of Arthur W. Westrop; m. Eileen Maria, d. of Dr. and Mrs. Alton; educ. Bridgeworth Grammar School, Shropshire, and Birmingham University; 2nd Lt. 1.9.14; Lieut., Feb. 1915; Capt. 15.11.15; Major 14.7.16; served Europ. War, France, from 15 May; Despatches; M.C., 1916. His D.S.O. was awarded for gallantry at Roeux Village 3 and 12.5.17.

WESTROPP, F. M. (D.S.O. L.G. 1.1.18); b. 6.2.70; 2nd Lt., R.E., 15.2.89; Lt. 15.2.99; Capt. 15.2.00; Major 27.8.08; Lt.-Col. 13.8.16; served N.W. Frontier of India, 1897–98; Medal, 2 clasps; Tirah, 1897–98; Europ. War; Despatches.

WETHERALL, H. E. DE R. (D.S.O. L.G. 18.10.17) (Details, L.G. 7.3.18); b. 22.2.89; yr. s. of late Major Wetherall, C. Gds.; 2nd Lt., Glouc. Regt., 22.5.09; Lt., Glouc. Regt., 1.11.11; Capt., Glouc. Regt., 10.5.15; M.C.

WETHERED, H. L. (D.S.O. L.G. 1.1.17); b. 10.11.77; s. of Rev. F. T. Wethered, Vicar of Hurley; m. Eileen, d. of late Col. Dominick Brown, D.L., of Co. Mayo; one s.; 2nd Lt., E. Lan. R., 8.9.97; Lt. 26.11.99; Capt. 22.1.08; Major 8.12.14; Lt.-Col., R.A.O.C.; served S. African War, 1899–1902; Queen's Medal, 4 clasps; King's Medal, 2 clasps; Europ. War; C.M.G.

WETHERED, J. R. (D.S.O. L.G. 3.6.16); b. 26.11.73; s. of Rev. F. T. Wethered, Vicar of Hurley; m. Dorothy, d. of Brig.-Gen. H. S. FitzGerald, C.B.; one d.; educ. Radley; joined (2nd Lt.) Gloucestershire Rgt. 19.7.93; Lt. 8.2.97; Adjt. 12.7.02–11.7.05; Capt. 12.7.02; Major 11.5.16; Bt. Lt.-Col. 1·1.18; Lt-Col. 4.6.21; served throughout S. African War; Queen's Medal, 4 clasps; King's Medal, 2 clasps; Europ. War, 1914–18; Despatches five times; C.M.G.; Bt. Lt.-Col.

WETHERILT, W. A. (D.S.O. L.G. 2.4.19) (Details, L.G. 10.12.19), T/2nd Lt., R. Berks. R., att. 1/4th Batt. T.F.

WHAIT, J. R., M.B. (D.S.O. L.G. 3.6.18), Lt.-Col., R.A.M.C.

WHALLEY, F. M.D. (D.S.O. L.G. 1.1.18), Major (T/Lt.-Col.), R.A.M.C.; went to France with the West Riding Division in 1915 as D.A.D. of M.S.; was later given command of a Field Ambulance with temp. rank of Lt.-Col., and was twice mentioned in Despatches. He has a long association with the Territorial Forces in Leeds.

WHALLEY, P. R. (D.S.O. L.G. 26.9.17) (Details, L.G. 9.1.18); b. 29.9.81; 2nd Lt., Unatt., 8.1.01; Worc. R., 9.3.01; Lt. 26.4.02; Capt., Worc. R., 8.1.10; Major 8.1.16; Lt.-Col. 1.1.19; served S. African War, 1901–2; Queen's Medal, 5 clasps.

S. L. Whatford.

WHATFORD, S. L. (D.S.O. L.G. 4.6.17) (Bar, L.G. 1.1.18); b. 23.7.79; 2nd Lt., Yorks. R., 15.1.02; Lt. 1.10.04; Capt. 9.10.10; Major 23.1.16; served Europ. War; Despatches; Bt. Lt.-Col. 1.1.19. He was killed in action 30.8.19.

WHATTON, S. M. DE H. (D.S.O. L.G. 3.6.19); b. 10.5.91; 2nd Lt., R.A. (from Spec. Res.), 11.8.14; Lt. 9.6.15; Adjt., R.A., 17.12.15 to 25.1.17; Capt. 3.11.17; A/Major, C/23rd Brig.; served Europ. War; R.F.A.; Despatches; M.C.

WHEAL, S. (D.S.O. L.G. 26.9.17) (Details, L.G. 9.1.18); b. 1.8.82; 2nd Lt., E. Lanc. R., 29.10.16; Lt. 29.4.18.

WHEATLEY, C. M. (D.S.O. L.G. 1.1.17); b. 1.8.70; s. of late Col. M. J. Wheatley, C.B., R.E.; educ. Marlborough; joined 2nd Essex R., 1900; rejoined Essex R., 1914, as Major; served S. African War, 1900–2; Europ. War; Despatches.

WHEATLEY, L. L. (D.S.O. L.G. 20.5.98) (Bar, L.G. 8.3.19) (Details, L.G. 4.10.19), Bt. Lt.-Col. (see "The Distinguished Service Order," from its institution to 31.12.15, by same publishers).

WHEATLEY, P. (D.S.O. L.G. 4.6.17); b. 29.5.71; s. of Lt.-Col. W. F. Wheatley; 2nd Lt., R.A., 16.5.91; Lt. 16.5.94; Capt. 13.2.00; Major 29.11.00; Lt.-Col. 10.4.15; Brig.-Gen., R.A., retired pay; served S. African War, 1899–1901; Despatches; Queen's Medal and 7 clasps; Bt. Major; Europ. War, 1914–18; Despatches; C.M.G.

WHEATLEY, W. P. R. (D.S.O. L.G. 25.8.17); b. 6.11.78; 2nd Lt., Middx. R., 4.12.01; Lt., Army, 4.3.04; Midd'x R. 21.12.04; Capt., Army, 4.12.10; I.A. 10.7.11; Major 4.12.16; served E. Africa, 1903; operations in Somaliland; action ta Judballi; Medal with 2 clasps; Europ. War; Despatches.

WHEELDON, F. L. (D.S.O. L.G. 17.9.17), T/2nd Lt., E. Lancs. R. His D.S.O. was awarded for gallantry on 10–12.7.17, between Oppy and Gavrelle.

WHEELER, C. (D.S.O. L.G. 26.7.17); b. 13.9.84; s. of J. Wheeler; m. Winifred Ethel, d. of W. Freeman; educ. West Buckland School, Devon; Keble College, Oxford; Assistant Master, Wellington College, Berks; Hon. Lt.-Colonel, 7th (S.) Batt. Oxf. and Bucks. L.I., Sept. 1914–March, 1918; commanded 11th (S.) Batt. Worc. R.; Despatches twice; Greek M.C. He has had published "The Memorial Record of the 7th (S.) Batt. The Oxfordshire and Buckinghamshire Light Infantry."

WHEELER, REV. F. H. (D.S.O. L.G. 8.3.18); b. 9.5.78; s. of C. Wheeler; m. Dorothy Osborne, d. of J. Scott; two s.; educ. London University; ent. Congregational Ministry, 1903; Army Chaplain, in France, 3.5.15; Chaplain to Warwick Brigade (143rd); promoted Jan. 1917, D.A. Principal Chaplain, on posting to 2nd Corps; saw service at Messines, Somme, Ypres Salient, Occupation Army, Cologne; transferred to Royal Air Force, April, 1919; relinquished commission 31.1.20; Hon. Chaplain to the Forces; Despatches three times. His D.S.O. was awarded for gallantry in the field, Somme and Ypres Salient. He was the first Congregational Minister to win the D.S.O.

WHELAN, J. F., M.B. (D.S.O. L.G. 7.2.18); b. 1.3.73; Lt., R.A.M.C., 14.11.00; Capt. 14.11.03; Major 14.8.12; Lt.-Col. 2.6.18; served Europ. War; Despatches.

WHELDON, W. P., M.A., LL.B. (D.S.O. L.G. 1.1.18; s. of late Rev. T. J. Wheldon, of Bangor, and Mary Elinor Wheldon (*née* Powell); m. Megan, d. of Hugh Edwards; two s.; educ. Friars School, Bangor; Oswestry High School; U.C.N.W.; St. John's College, Cambridge; enlisted Inns of Court O.T.C., Sept. 1914, and gazetted to 14th R.W.F., Dec. 1914; T/Major; served in France with the Battalion, Dec. 1915–Nov. 1918, and as 2nd-in-command, July, 1916; Secretary and Registrar of the University College of North Wales, Bangor, from 1920.

WHETHAM, A. C. BODDAM- (see Boddam-Whetham, A. C.).

WHETHAM, E. K. BODDAM- (see Boddam-Whetham, E. K.).

WHETHAM, P. (D.S.O. L.G. 22.6.18), T/Major (A/Lt.-Col.), Manch. R.

WHETHAM, S. A. BODDAM- (see Boddam-Whetham, S. A.).

WHETHERLEY, W. S. (D.S.O. L.G. 1.1.18); b. 4.2.79; s. of late Lt.-Col. W. Whetherley; m. Marjorie Isabel, d. of late E. W. Holmes; two s.; one d.; educ. Uppingham; Sandhurst; 2nd Lt., 7th Dragoon Guards, 3.8.98; Lt. 3.6.99; Capt. 15.6.03; Adjt., 7th D.G., 22.5.05 to 31.5.08; Major, 19th Hussars, 16.1.18; Lt.-Col. 3.6.19; Lt.-Col., late 19th (Royal) Hussars, retired pay, 1921; served S. African War, 1899–1902; Queen's Medal and 5 clasps; King's Medal and 2 clasps; Europ. War, 1914–18; Despatches; Bt. Lt.-Col. 3.6.19.

WHIGHAM, R. D. (D.S.O. L.G. 2.5.16); b. 31.1.73; 2nd Lt., Lanc. Fus., 19.5.00; Lt. 10.7.01; K.O.S.B. 20.5.08; Capt. 21.5.08; Major 1.9.15; employed with W.A.F.F., 1901–6; 1907–12, and after 1916; served S. Nigeria, 1901–6; Medal, 5 clasps; Europ. War, 1914–18; Despatches twice.

WHINNEY H. F. (D.S.O. L.G. 3.6.16); b. 6.2.78; 2nd Lt., R. Fus., 5.5.00; Lt. 9.4.02; Capt. 16.11.09; Major 1.9.15; served Europ. War; Despatches; O.B.E.

WHISTLER, A. H. (D.S.O. L.G. 2.11.18); b. 30.12.96; 2nd Lt., Dorsets. R., 19.7.16; Lt. 12.1.18; served Europ. War; employed under Air Ministry 1.4.18; Despatches; D.F.C.

WHITAKER, A. P. D. (D.S.O. L.G. 1.1.18); b. 8.11.85; 2nd Lt., A.S.C., 24.1.06; Lt. 4.1.08; Capt., R.A.S.C., 5.8.14.

WHITAKER, H. C. (D.S.O. L.G. 2.12.18), Lt., 72nd Batt. Can. Inf.; Br. Columbia R.

WHITCOMBE, R. H. (D.S.O. L.G. 1.1.17), Major, retired, R.A.S.C., T.F.; served S. African War, 1900–1; Queen's Medal with 4 clasps; Europ. War; Despatches.

WHITE, ALFRED (gazetted as Arthur) (D.S.O. L.G. 8.3.19) (Details, L.G. 4.10.19), Capt. (A/Lt.-Col.), 4th Bn. E. Surrey R., att. 1/5th Bn. S. Staffs. R., T.F.

WHITE, A. C. (D.S.O. L.G. 1.1.17), T/Major, Yorks. L.I.

WHITE, A. K. G. (D.S.O. L.G. 14.1.16); b. 2.1.81; 2nd Lt., R.A., 19.12.00; Lt. 19.12.03; Capt. 26.8.12; Major 8.7.15.

WHITE, C. E. H. (D.S.O. L.G. 29.11.18), Lt.-Cdr., R.N.

WHITE, CHARLES RAMSAY (D.S.O. L.G. 3.6.18), Major, 3rd Batt. Yorks. R.; served S. African War, 1900–2; Queen's Medal with 2 clasps; King's Medal with 2 clasps.

WHITE, CHARLES RICHARDSON, F.R.C.S., L.R.C.P. and S., M.D., etc. (D.S.O. L.G. 1.1.18); b. 25.4.73; educ. Daniel Stewart's College, Edinburgh; Edinburgh University; joined Volunteers, 1903; transferred to Territorials when latter were formed; Lt.-Col., R.A.M.C. (T.F.), T.D.; commanded Welsh Casualty Clearing Station from April, 1915, taking it out to Suvla, July, 1915; served continuously in Gallipoli, Egypt, Sinai Peninsula and Palestine June, 1918; then transferred to France at his own request; demobilized March 1919; Despatches twice.

WHITE, D. A. (D.S.O. L.G. 3.6.18), Major, Can. F.A.

WHITE, E. S. (D.S.O. L.G. 3.6.18); b. 15.11.88; s. of W. W. White; educ. Felsted; Sandhurst; Capt. and Bt. Major, R.A.S.C.

WHITE, F. A. K. (D.S.O. L.G. 1.1.18); b. 9.12.73; 2nd Lt., R.E., 25.7.93; Lt. 25.7.96; Capt. 1.4.04; Major 25.7.13; Bt. Lt.-Col. 1.1.17; served Europ. War; Despatches; C.M.G.

WHITE, REV. E. M. MILNER- (see Milner-White, Rev. E. M.).

WHITE, G. F. C. (D.S.O. L.G. 1.1.17); b. 4.8.82; s. of late G. F. White; m. Violet, d. of late Capt. N. P. Stewart, J.P., of Bangor, N. Wales; one s.; educ. Giggleswick; R.M.A., Woolwich; 2nd Lt., R.G.A., 21.12.00; Lt. 21.9.03; Capt. 21.12.03; Major 30.12.15; Adjt., R.A., 7.1.20; Adjt. to Welsh R.G.A., 1913–16; went to France, Feb. 1916, commanding 35th Heavy Battery; Brigade Major, Heavy Artillery, April, 1918–19; Officer of the Belgian Order of the Crown; Belgian Croix de Guerre, 1919.

WHITE, G. H. A. (D.S.O. L.G. 3.6.16); b. 3.11.70; s. of F. A. White; m. Beatrice, d. of late D. R. de Chair, and widow of J. T. Studley; educ. Eton; R.M.A., Woolwich; 2nd Lt., R.A., 25.7.90; Lt. 25.7.93; Capt. 13.2.00; Major 1.4.08; Lt.-Col. 12.2.15; Bt. Col., Jan. 1917; Col. 12.2.19; T/Col. Comdt. 1.1.21; served in India, 1895–98, with U Battery, R.H.A. (The Eagle Troop); served S. African War, 1899–1900 (U Battery, R.H.A.); took part in the Relief of Kimberley and Battles of Paardeberg and Driefontein (Queen's Medal, 4 clasps); returned to England on promotion in Dec. 1900; served in various parts of England and Ireland, mostly with R.H.A.; commanded Riding Establishment, R.A., at Woolwich, 1910–13; went out to front in Great War in command of K. Battery, R.H.A., 7th Cavalry Brigade, in Oct. 1914; present during operations of 3rd Cav. Div. and 7th Div., including 1st Battle of Ypres; commanded a Brigade, R.F.A., in 2nd Battle of Ypres; appointed to command 7th Brig., R.H.A., 1st Cav. Div. in July, 1915; appointed C.R.A., 30th Div., with rank of T/Brig.-Gen., April, 1916; present with 30th Div. at Battle of the Somme, July, 1916, and again in Oct. and Nov. 1916; Despatches three times.

WHITE, H. (D.S.O. L.G. 3.6.19), T/Lt. (A/Capt.), 7th Batt. Royal Irish Rgt.; M.C.

WHITE, H. A. D. (D.S.O. L.G. 3.6.18), Major (T/Lt.-Col.), Aust. Light Horse.

WHITE, H. F. (D.S.O. L.G. 25.8.17), Major, Aust. Infy. His D.S.O. was awarded for gallantry at St. Yves 7–12.6.17.

WHITE, H. H. R. (D.S.O. L.G. 13.2.17); b. 9.2.79; s. of late Maj.-Gen. H. G. White; m. Florence Geraldine, d. of late Sir John Arnott, 1st Bart.; two s.; educ. Rugby; Sandhurst; 2nd Lt., 60th Rifles, 1898; resigned commission, 1908; T/Major; resigned Temp. Commission, 1919; served S. African War, 1901–2; Queen's Medal, 4 clasps; Somaliland, 1903–4; severely wounded at Jidballi; Adjt., 1st Mounted Corps (Medal and 2 clasps); Adjt., 25th Batt. R. Fus., March, to Sept. 1915; served E. Africa, May, 1915–March, 1917; Despatches; O.B.E.; Nyassaland and Portuguese E. Africa, 1918; High Sheriff, Co. Donegal, 1912.

WHITE, J. A. G. (D.S.O. L.G. 3.6.19), Major, H.Q., 2nd Brig. Can. Engineers; M.C.

WHITE, J. B. (D.S.O. L.G. 1.1.18), Lt.-Col. (T/Col.), Can. Forestry Corps.

WHITE, J. D. (D.S.O. L.G. 26.9.17) (Details, L.G. 9.1.18); b. 4.11.84; mobilized T.F. to 17.12.20, 6 yrs., 135 days; Capt., R.E., 1.7.20; M.C.

WHITE, J. R. (D.S.O. L.G. 4.6.17); b. 20.10.75; 2nd Lt., R.E., 15.3.95; Lt. 15.3.98; Capt. 1.4.04; Adjt., R.E., 5.8.14 to 7.2.15; Major 30.10.14; Bt. Lt.-Col. 3.6.15; served Europ. War; Despatches.

WHITE, M. FITZG. G. (D.S.O. L.G. 4.6.17); b. 7.12.87; s. of Col. J. Grove White, C.M.G.; m. Bernice Agnes, d. of F. W. Parlane; educ. St. Andrew's College, Grahamstown; Wellington College; R.M.A., Woolwich; 2nd Lt., R.E., 18.12.07; Lt. 2.5.10; Capt. 30.10.14; served in France from May, 1915, in 54th Field Co., 7th Div.; on G.S., XIII. Corps, G.H.Q., France and War Office; Despatches four times; O.B.E.; Bt. Major 1.1.18; Legion of Honour.

WHITE, N. B. (D.S.O. L.G. 1.1.18), T/Lt. (A/Capt.), Gen. List.

WHITE, O. W. (D.S.O. L.G. 1.1.17); b. 29.6.84; 2nd Lt., W.I.R., 10.10.03; Lt. 3.12.04; Dorset R. 29.12.06; Adjt., Dorset R., 8.6.10 to 7.6.13; Capt. 17.2.12; Bt. Major 3.6.19.

WHITE, HON. R. (D.S.O. L.G. 1.1.18); b. 26.10.61; 4th s. of 2nd Baron Annaly and Emily, d. of J. Stuart; educ. Eton; Trinity College, Cambridge; joined 23rd R.W. Fus., 1882; Major (R. of O.) 29.11.00; Hon. Brig.-Gen., R. of O; served Nile Campaign, 1884–85 (Staff); Medal with clasp; Khedive's Star; Staff Officer, Rhodesia Horse, 1894; served S. African War (Staff of 6th Div.), 1900; Despatches; Medal with 5 clasps; Bt. Major; raised and commanded 10th Batt. R. Fusiliers from the Stock Exchange, Aug. 1914; served in France, 1915–18; Despatches six times; C.M.G.; Bt. Col.; twice wounded; Brig.-Gen. commanding 184th Inf. Brig., France, 1916–18.

WHITE, R. B. L. BAZLEY- (see Bazley-White, R. B. L.).

WHITE, R. F. (D.S.O. L.G. 20.4.20); b. 21.12.80; 2nd Lt., Essex R., 11.8.00; Lt. 16.4.02; Capt. 23.1.11; Major 1.9.15; served S. African War, 1901–2; Queen's Medal, 5 clasps; E. Africa, 1904; Medal and 2 clasps; Europ. War; Despatches.

WHITE, R. K. (D.S.O. L.G. 3.6.18); b. 1.10.79; Lt., I.M.S., 1.2.05; Capt., I.M.S., 1.2.08; R.A.M.C. 11.7.10; Major 15.10.15.

WHITE, R. L. (D.S.O. L.G. 14.1.16); b. 29.6.75; 2nd Lt., R.W. Kent R., 5.5.00; Lt. 16.7.02; Capt. 25.12.07; Major 1.9.15; Major, R.W. Kent R.; served Europ. War, 1914–16.

WHITE, R. P. PRESTON- (see Preston-White, R. P.).

WHITE, R. S. MURRAY- (see Murray-White, R. S.).

WHITE, S. P. R. (D.S.O. L.G. 16.3.18), Lt., R.N.R.; D.S.C.

WHITE, W. (D.S.O. L.G. 8.3.19) (Details, L.G. 4.10.19), T/Major, 15th Batt. H.L.I.; M.C.

WHITE, W. J. (D.S.O. L.G. 8.3.19) (Details, L.G. 4.10.19), Capt., 28th Inf. Batt. Sask. R.; M.C.

WHITE, W. L. (D.S.O. L.G. 18.6.17), T/Capt. (A/Major), R.F.A.

WHITE, W. N. (D.S.O. L.G. 14.1.16); b. 10.9.79; s. of W. N. White; m. Evelyn Laura, d. of Sir Gilbert Carter, K.C.M.G.; three s.; educ. Malvern College; joined 4th Sherwood Foresters, 1900; transferred to A.S.C. 7.12.01; Lt. 1.1.03; Capt. 10.11.08; Major, R.A.S.C., 30.10.14; Lt.-Col. 3.6.19; Lt.-Col., R.A.S.C., late D.A.D. of Transport; served S. African War; Queen's Medal, 4 clasps; Europ. War, 1914–16; Despatches twice; has King George's Coronation Medal; Hants County Cricket Team, 1907–14; Army Team for four years; Captained Army Association Football Team, 1901–2.

WHITE, W. O. (D.S.O. L.G. 3.2.20), Major, Eastern Ontario Rgt., Can. Mil. Forces; M.C.

WHITEHEAD, C. M. (D.S.O. L.G. 1.2.19), T/Capt., R. Lancaster Rgt.; M.C.; mentioned in Despatches by Gen. Milne for Salonika; Croix de Chevalier.

WHITEHEAD, E. L'E. (D.S.O. L.G. 1.1.18); b. 4.9.70; 2nd Lt., R.A. 26.7.90; Lt. 25.7.93; Capt. 9.10.99; Adjt., R.A., 6.11.08 to 26.4.11; Major 27.4.11; Lt.-Col. 1.5.17.

WHITEHEAD, H. F. (D.S.O. L.G. 1.1.18) (Bar, L.G. 26.7.18); b. at Inverness, and educated at the Academy there; joined as a Trooper, and became Lt.-Col. in command of the 1/4th Batt. R. Berks Rgt. (T.F.) on the Italian Front. He was awarded the Croix de Guerre with Palms for gallant and devoted service with the 12th Army Corps and the French Forces; severely wounded at the Battle of the Somme; commanded his battalion at the Battle of Passchendaele. His Bar was awarded for gallantry during the critical days of the Battle of St. Quentin.

WHITEHEAD, J. (D.S.O. L.G. 3.6.16); b. 18.1.80; s. of late Lt.-Col. E. Whitehead; m. a daughter of Sir Arthur Fell; educ. R.M.C., Sandhurst; 2nd Lt., R.W. Kent R., 12.8.99; I.S.C. 29.10.01; Lt., I.A., 12.11.01; Capt. 12.8.08; Major 1.9.15; Col. 5.7.20; Europ. War; Despatches; Bt. Lt.-Col. 1.1.17; Legion of Honour.

WHITEHEAD, J. H., M.R.C.S., L.R.C.P. (D.S.O. L.G. 1.2.17); b. 1.10.69; s. of W. Whitehead; m. Maude, d. of F. N. Lowe; two d.; educ. St. Peter's Grammar School, Thanet; Upper Canada College, Toronto; University London (Charing Cross Hospital); passed into A.M.S., 1894; resigned, 1896; rejoined 1899; served S. African War; Queen's and King's Medals and 4 clasps; transferred to S.A. Constabulary, 1901, with rank of Capt.; retired 1904; served through S.A. Rebellion, 1914, as Capt., S.A.M.C.; Colonel, 1916; retired Dec. 1919; commanded 8th Mounted Brigade Field Amb. in German W. Africa Campaign; S.M.O., L. of C., Northern Force, German S.W. Africa; Despatches; in 1915 was S.M.O., Potchefstroom; went to S.E. Africa in command of 4th Field Amb., and S.M.O., 3rd Brig.; A.D.M.S., 2nd Div. (Gen. Van Deventer's), 1.4.16; Despatches; returned to S. Africa 1.4.17; A.D.M.S., Durban.

WHITEHEAD, J. J. (D.S.O. L.G. 4.6.17), T/Major (A/Lt.-Col.), Manch. R.

WHITEHEAD, T. H. (D.S.O. L.G. 2.12.18), T/Capt., 13th Batt. R. Fus.; M.C.

WHITEHEAD, W. J. (D.S.O. L.G. 1.1.17), Lt.-Col., London R.

WHITEHILL, H. (gazetted as Weisburg, H.—name changed) (D.S.O. L.G. 1.1.19), Major (A/Lt.-Col.), A. and S. Highrs., att. 2/16th Batt. London R.; served S. African War, 1900–1; Queen's Medal, 4 clasps; Europ. War; Despatches.

WHITEHOUSE, P. H. (D.S.O. L.G. 2.4.19) (Details, L.G. 10.12.19), Lt.-Col., 1/8th Batt. R. War. R., T.F.

WHITELEY, P. (D.S.O. L.G. 1.2.17), Major, S. African Pay Corps.

WHITFELD, L. C. (D.S.O. L.G. 1.1.17), Capt. (T/Major), Aust. A.V.C.

WHITFIELD, REV. J. L. (D.S.O. L.G. 8.3.18), T/Chapl. to the Forces.

WHITFIELD, P. (D.S.O. L.G. 5.10.18), Cdr., R.N., 30.6.16; O.B.E.

WHITHAM, J. L. (D.S.O. L.G. 16.9.18); b. 7.10.81; m. Olive, widow of E. P. C. Young, and d. of G. R. Le Pays; one s.; one d.; Lt.-Col.; served S. African War, 1902; Aust. Commonwealth Horse; Queen's Medal; S.A.C., 1902–4; Tasmanian Volunteers, 1898–1902; Aust. Permanent Forces from 1910; Europ. War from 1914; C.M.G.

WHITLEY, SIR E. N. (D.S.O. L.G. 1.1.18), Colonel, Commanding R.A., W. Riding Div., T.F.; served Europ. War, 1914–18; Despatches; C.M.G.; C.B.; K.C.B.; T.D.

WHITMARSH, A. J. (D.S.O. L.G. 1.2.19), T/Capt., att. E. Kent Rgt.

WHITMORE, F. H. D. C. (D.S.O. L.G. 1.1.17); b. 1872; s. of late T. C. D. Whitmore, late Capt., R.H.G., and Louisa M. E., d. of Sir W. E. Cradock Hartopp, 3rd Bart.; m. Violet F. E., d. of late Sir W. H. Houldsworth, 1st Bart.; educ. Eton; Lt.-Col. commanding Essex Yeom., 1915–18; Lt.-Col. comdg. 10th (P.W.O.) R. Hussars, 1918–19; T.D.; J.P.; D.L.; served Europ. War from 1914; Despatches four times; C.M.G.

WHITRIDGE, M. W. (D.S.O. L.G. 27.7.18), T/Major (A/Lt.-Col.), K.A. Rifles.

WHITTAKER, G. W. (D.S.O. L.G. 13.2.17), T/Sub-Lt., R.N.V.R.

WHITTALL, H. (D.S.O. L.G. 23.11.16), T/Lt., Gen. List., formerly R.M.

WHITTALL, P. F. (D.S.O. L.G. 4.6.17) (Bar, L.G. 16.9.18); b. 15.7.77; s. of late Fleet Paymaster J. Whittall, R.N.; m. Mary Gwendolen Dalzell, d. of Mr. Justice Green, of Nigeria; educ. Felsted; joined R.E. in ranks, 1896; served S. African War, 1899–1900; Queen's Medal, 3 clasps; commissioned Lincs. Rgt., 1902 to R. of O.; served Europ. War with R.E. from 1915; Lt.-Colonel; Despatches four times; 1914–15 Star; French Croix de Guerre.

WHITTING, E. LE G. (D.S.O. L.G. 1.1.18); b. 5.9.81; s. of Rev. W. H. Whitting, M.A., Rector of Stower Provost and Todber, Dorset; m. Doris, d. of J. Macpherson Lawrie, M.D., J.P., D.L.; two s.; educ. King's Choir School, Cambridge; Aldenham School; 2nd Lieut., R.G.A., 18.8.00; Lt. 17.4.02; Capt. 18.8.13; Major, R.G.A., 30.12.15; Adjt., R.A., 28.1.20 to 2.11.20; served N.W. Frontier of India (Mohmand), 1908; Medal with clasp; Egypt (Suez Canal), 1915; Despatches twice; M.C.; France, 1916–18; Despatches twice.

E. Le G. Whitting.

WHITTINGHAM, C. H. (D.S.O. L.G. 4.6.17); b. 1873; Colonel, late Durham L.I.; Inspector-General of Prisons, Egypt; served Nile Exp., 1898; Egyptian Medal and clasp; Medal; S. African War, 1899–1902; Queen's Medal and 6 clasps; King's Medal and 2 clasps; Europ. War, including Egypt, 1914–18; Despatches; C.M.G.; C.B.E.; 2nd Class Nile; Order of the White Eagle of Serbia, 4th Class; 4th Class Osmanieh.

WHITTINGTON, A. R. (D.S.O. L.G. 1.1.18), T/Major, A.S.C. (now R.A.S.C.).

WHITTY, A (D.S.O. L.G. 14.1.16), Qr. Mr. and Hon. Major, Worc. R.

WHITTY, N. I. (D.S.O. L.G. 4.6.17); b. Corowa, Australia, 8.9.85; s. of late H. T. Whitty; m. Lilian Margaret, d. of J. H. E. Garrett; one s.; educ. Clifton College; Sandhurst; joined Queen's Own R.W. Kent R. 24.1.06; Lt. 21.1.09; Capt. 19.9.14; served Europ. War, in France, from Aug. 1915; Despatches thrice; Bt. Major 3.6.16.

WHITWILL, M. (D.S.O. L.G. 26.7.18), Lt. (A/Major), R.E.; M.C.

WHITWORTH, H. (D.S.O. L.G. 13.2.17); b. 6.2.84; 2nd Lt., Yorks. L.I., 9.5.15; Lt. 1.1.17.

WHITWORTH, J. H. (D.S.O. L.G. 22.6.18); s. of late John and Marion Whitworth; Major, The Manchester Rgt.; 6th Batt. (Territorial); M.C. He died on Easter Sunday morning (31.3.18) of wounds, received in action near Dampierre, 26 March. His younger brother died 14.9.18 of wounds received in action two days earlier.

J. H. Whitworth.

WHITWORTH, W. J. (D.S.O. L.G. 8.3.18), Cdr., R.N., 30.6.18.

WHYTE, J. B. (D.S.O. L.G. 3.6.18), Major, N.Z., A.S.C.

WHYTE, J. H. (D.S.O. L.G. 8.11.15) (Bar, L.G. 1.1.18), Lt.-Col., Wellington Mtd. Rifles, N.Z. Force (see "The Distinguished Service Order," from its institution to 31.12.15, by same publishers).

WHYTE, R. (D.S.O. L.G. 3.6.19), Capt. (A/Lt.-Col.), 2/14th Batt. London R.; M.C.

WHYTE, W. H. (D.S.O. L.G. 1.1.18); b. 10.3.80; s. of John Joseph Whyte, J.P., D.L.; educ. Stonyhurst College; Saint Edmund's, Old Hall; 2nd Lt., R. Dub. Fus., 3.3.00; Lt. 3.5.06; Capt. 5.10.14; Major 9.9.15; Lt.-Col. (R. of O.) 19.11.19; joined 4th R. Dublin Fus., then 1st R. Dublin Fus.; served in S. African War, 1900–1; operations in the Transvaal; Queen's Medal, 5 clasps; served with 1st Batt. during Occupation of Crete in 1903; subsequently in Egypt and India; posted 6th R. Dublin Fus. 5.10.14; served with battalion in Gallipoli, 1915; wounded; Despatches; commanded 6th R. Dublin Fus. during operations in Serbia, 1915; wounded; awarded Serbian White Eagle; subsequently served in Macedonia; wounded; Despatches twice; commanded 6th R. Dublin Fus. in Egypt and Palestine, 1917; commanded 6th R. Dublin Fus. in France, 1918.

WICKENS, R. C. (D.S.O. L.G. 17.12.17) (Details, L.G. 23.4.18), Major, Field Arty., N.Z. Force.

WICKHAM, J. C. (D.S.O. L.G. 14.1.16); b. at Simla, India, 23.6.86; s. of late Col. C. B. Wickham, R.A.; educ. Cheltenham College; R.M.A., Woolwich; 2nd Lt., R.E., 22.7.04; Lt. 23.3.07; Capt. 30.10.14; served Europ. War; Despatches twice; severely wounded in June, 1916.

WICKHAM, T. E. P. (D.S.O. L.G. 27.9.01) (Bar, L.G. 1.1.18), Major, R.A. (see "The Distinguished Service Order," from its institution to 31.12.15, by same publishers).

WIDDOWSON, E. A. (D.S.O. L.G. 3.6.18), Major, N.Z. Forces; M.C.

WIDDRINGTON, B. F. (D.S.O. L.G. 23.11.16); b. 14.9.74, at Newton Hall, Northumberland; s. of S. F. Widdrington (deceased) and Cecilia, d. of the late Capt. E. G. Hopwood; m. Clothilde Enid, d. of late E. Onslow Ford, R.A.; two s.; educ. Winchester College; Sandhurst; 2nd Lt., K.R.R.C., 24.1.94; Lt., 1897; Capt., 1901; Major, 1911; Bt. Lt.-Col., Jan. 1917; retired 2.4.19 with rank of Brig.-Gen.; commanded a Batt., 60th Rifles, from Sept. 1914 (in India) to May, 1916; brought Batt. from India to England, Oct. 1914, and to France, Oct. 1914; wounded at St. Eloi 4.3.14; to Macedonia, Nov. 1915, with Batt., which formed part of the 80th Brig., 27th Div.; appointed Brig.-Gen. in command of 81st Inf. Bde., 27th Div.; in command of 81st Bde. and other troops, which were the first to cross the River Struma and defeat the Bulgars; took part in the final attacks on and victories over the Bulgars, Aug. and Sept. 1918, and advanced into Bulgaria. He had served continuously abroad, mostly in India, from 1898 to 1918; Despatches eight times; C.M.G.; Order of the Holy Redeemer, 3rd Class. He belongs to the same family as one of the heroes of Chevy Chase:

> "For Widdrington my heart was wo
> That ever he slain should be,
> For when his legs were hewn in two
> He knelt and fought on his knee."

WIECK, G. F. G. (D.S.O. L.G. 4.6.17), Major, Aust. Light Horse Regt.

WIENHOLT, A. (D.S.O. L.G. 15.10.18), Capt., E. African Force; M.C.

WIENHOLT, W. H. M. (D.S.O. L.G. 4.6.17) (Bar, L.G. 26.9.17) (Details, L.G. 9.1.18), T/Major, N. Lanc. R.

WIGAN, J. T. (D.S.O. L.G. 3.6.16); b. 31.7.77; only s. of Charles Wigan; m. Aline, e. d. of H. W. Henderson; one s.; educ. Rugby; was for five years Adjt., Berks. Yeomanry; Brig.-Gen.; served S. African War; Queen's Medal; King's Medal, 4 clasps; Europ. War, in command of the Berkshire Yeomanry in Gallipoli, Gaza, Jerusalem; Despatches four times; wounded at Suvla Bay, 1915; C.M.G.

J. T. Wigan.

WIGGIN, E. A. (D.S.O. L.G. 1.1.17); b. 26.11.67; 4th s. of late Sir Henry Wiggin, 1st Baronet, of Metchley Grange, Harborne; m. Emily Margaret, d. of Arthur Keen; one s.; educ. Clifton; Sandhurst; Lt., 13th Hussars, 29.8.85; Capt. 12.11.90; Adjt. 11.4.95 to 13.5.96; Major 18.12.11; retired 2.4.19 with hon. rank of Brig.-Gen.; served S. African War 1899–1902; Despatches three times; Queen's Medal, 3 clasps; Bt. Major; Bt. Lt.-Col. 22.8.02; Europ. War; Despatches; Croix d'Officier, Legion of Honour.

WIGGIN, W. H. (D.S.O. L.G. 23.11.16) (Bar, L.G. 18.2.18) (Details, L.G. 18.7.18); s. of A. H. Wiggin, of Bordesley Hall, Alvechurch; Major, Yeomanry.

WIGHTMAN, J. (D.S.O. L.G. 3.6.18), T/Major, E. Surrey Regt.; M.C. He died of wounds 9.4.18.

WIGHTON, E. (D.S.O. L.G. 14.1.16); b. 19.8.76, at St. John's, Newfoundland; s. of late Col. Wighton, R.A.; m. Muriel, d. of late Capt. A. Pinhey, R.A.; educ. Bedford Grammar School; R.M.A., Woolwich; 2nd Lt., R.A., 2.11.95; Lt. 2.11.98; Capt. 9.7.01; Adjt. 20.9.04 to 21.1.12; Major 30.10.14; Bt. Lt.-Col. 3.6.18; Lt.-Colonel 1.5.21; served S. Africa, Feb.–May, 1900; Queen's Medal with clasp; China, 1900; Medal; Officer Commanding R.A.; Legation Guard, Peking, Sept. 1901–May, 1902; served Europ. War, 1914–18; 1914 Star; Bt. Lt.-Col.

WIGGLESWORTH, H. E. P. (D.S.O. L.G. 21.4.17), Flt. Sub-Lt., R.N.A.S.

WIGRAM, E. (D.S.O. L.G. 12.1.16); b. 16.4.77; s. of late H. Wigram, Madras Civil Service; brother of Col. Clive Wigram, C.B., C.S.I., M.V.O., and Col. K. Wigram, C.B., C.S.I., C.B.E., D.S.O.; educ. Fosters; Stubbington, Hants; joined Britannia, Sept. 1891; Lieut. 3.12.00; Comdr. 31.12.12; Capt., R.N.,

30.6.15; served Europ. War; Falkland Islands, Dardanelles and Belgian Coast, 1914-18; Despatches; C.M.G.; 1914 Star; Croix de Guerre with Palm (French); Order of Leopold Officer; Belgium.

WIGRAM, K. (D.S.O. L.G. 1.1.17); b. 5.12.75; s. of late H. Wigram, Indian Civil Service; educ. Winchester; Sandhurst; 2nd Lt., Unatt., 22.1.96; Ind. S.C. 29.3.97; Lt. 22.4.98; Capt. 22.1.05; Major 22.1.14; Bt. Lt.-Col. 3.6.16; Lt.-Col. 2.4.20; Bt. Col. 1.1.18; Temp. Brig.-Gen.; Colonel 28.4.20; Commandant, 2nd Batt. King Edward's Own Gurkha Rifles; served N.W. Frontier, 1897-98; Medal with clasp; Tirah, 1897-98; clasp; N.W. Frontier, Waziristan, 1901-2; clasp; Thibet; March to Lhasa, 1903-4; Medal with clasp; Europ. War, 1914-18; Despatches; C.B.; C.B.E.; C.S.I.

WIGRAM, R. S. J. (D.S.O. L.G. 2.7.17), Cdr., R.N.

WILBERFORCE, H. H. (D.S.O. L.G. 1.1.18), Capt. (T/Lt.-Col.), A.S.C. (now R.A.S.C.).

WILBERFORCE, W. (D.S.O. L.G. 1.2.19); b. 22.11.85; 2nd Lt., R.W. Kent R., 16.8.05; resigned 11.11.08; R. of O. recalled 17.1.17; Capt., R.W. Kent R., 18.1.17; M.C.

WILBRAHAM, B. H. (D.S.O. L.G. 14.1.16); b. 15.8.80; s. of late H. Wilbraham, of Oldhead, Westport, Co. Mayo, and the late Lady Marian Wilbraham (née Browne), d. of the 2nd Marquess of Sligo; m. Bernice, d. of J. Segrave, of Tasmania, and widow of Arthur R. Browne; one d.; educ. Marlborough; R.M.A., Woolwich; commissioned R.E. 29.11.99; Lt. 6.8.02; Capt. 22.11.08; Major 8.8.16; in Egyptian Army, 1908-10; served in S. African War, 1901-2; Queen's Medal, 5 clasps; Europ. War, 1914-18.

B. H. Wilbraham.

Bt. Lt.-Col. 1.1.19 (Tank Corps 30.9.20); Queen's Medal, 6 clasps.

WILCOX, E. A. C. (D.S.O. L.G. 3.6.18), Major, Can. Inf.

WILD, W. H. (D.S.O. L.G. 16.5.16); b. 6.6.74; 2nd Lt., Northumberland Fus., 29.5.95; Lt. 10.3.97; Capt. 19.5.00; Adjt., May, 1900, to May, 1904; Major 1.9.15; Bt. Lt.-Col. 1.1.19.

WILDBLOOD, E. H. (D.S.O. L.G. 1.1.18) (Bar, L.G. 3.6.18); b. 2.5.78; in ranks Roberts' Horse, 142 days; 2nd Lt., Leins. R., 19.5.00; Lt. 11.6.02; W. African R. 21.3.03 to 4.10.04; Capt. 3.5.09; Major 1.9.15; Queen's Medal, 6 clasps.

WILDE, L. C. (D.S.O. L.G. 4.6.17), Major, Manch. Regt.

WILDE, R. C. (D.S.O. L.G. 26.11.17) (Details, L.G. 6.4.18); b. 30.12.88; s. of Wilton Gough Wilde, J.P., and Mrs. Wilde; educ. Bispham Lodge School; entered the Army, Jan. 1915 (in ranks); 2nd Lt., 9th Batt. King's L'pool R., Jan. 1916; Lt. 1.7.17; became Capt.; served Europ. War; Despatches; M.C.

WILDER, A. S. (D.S.O. L.G. 8.3.19) (Details, L.G. 4.10.19), Major, Wellington Mtd. Rif. R., N.Z. Mil. Forces; M.C.

WILDER-NELIGAN, M. (D.S.O. L.G. 25.8.16) (Bar, L.G. 7.11.18), Lt.-Col., Aust. Inf.; C.M.G.; D.C.M.

WILDING, H. G. (D.S.O. L.G. 3.6.18) (Bar, L.G. 2.12.18), Major, 7th Battery, N.Z. Field Arty.

WILES, H. J. (D.S.O. L.G. 16.9.18), Lt., Aust. Infantry.

WILEY, C. J. (D.S.O. L.G. 1.1.17), Capt. (T/Lt.-Col.), R. Irish Rifles; served S. African War, 1901; Queen's Medal, 5 clasps; Europ. War; Despatches.

R. C. Wilde.

WILFORD, A. L. (D.S.O. L.G. 15.2.17); b. 22.11.81; s. of Colonel Edmund Percival Wilford, Glos. Regt.; m. Audrey, d. of B. Simons; one d.; educ. Elizabeth College, Guernsey; 2nd Lt., Unatt., 28.7.00; Ind. Army 11.10.01; Lt. 6.4.03; Capt. 28.7.09; Lt.-Col. 1.7.17; served Europ. War; Despatches. He died of wounds.

WILFORD, E. E. (D.S.O. L.G. 1.1.17); b. 13.1.76; 2nd Lt., E. York. R., 5.9.96; Lt. 15.6.98; Ind. Army 12.10.98; Capt. 5.8.05; Major 5.9.14; Lt.-Col. 1.2.21; served Europ. War; wounded.

WILGAR, W. P. (D.S.O. L.G. 4.6.17); b. Coburg, Ontario, 9.3.77; s. of J. Wilgar and Maria Wilgar (née Sykes); m. Emilie Stewart, d. of E. Low, of Ottawa; one s.; educ. Queen's University, Kingston; Professor of Civil Engineering (Faculty of Applied Science), Queen's University, Kingston; Lt.-Colonel, R. of O.; joined Exp. Force for Europ. War, 1915; commanded 10th Field Co., C.E., and 10th Batt. C.E.

WILKENS, J. (D.S.O. L.G. 18.8.16), Major, 1st S. African Horse. His D.S.O. was awarded for gallantry at Solkissale 4-6.4.16; Kondoa Irangi, 17-19.4.16.

WILKINS, C. F. (D.S.O. L.G. 1.1.18); b. 30.4.90; 2nd Lt., R. Ir. Rif., 6.3.15; Lt., R. Ir. Rif., 28.11.15; Adjt., R. Ir. Rif., 23.1.17 to 5.3.18; served S. African War; Queen's Medal, 6 clasps; King's Medal, 2 clasps; Europ. War; Despatches; M.C.

WILKINSON, A. M. (D.S.O. L.G. 20.10.16) (Bar, L.G. 26.5.17); b. 21.11.91; m. Lina Rachel, d. of J. A. Snell, Clifton; educ. Repton; Oriel College, Oxford (Association Football Blue, 1914); Major, Hants R. and R.F.C.; served Europ. War, 1914-17; Despatches twice; in charge of No. 3 Aerial Fighting School, 1918-19. His D.S.O. was awarded for gallantry on 31.8.16, near Villers.

WILKINSON, C. L. (D.S.O. L.G. 1.1.17); 2nd s. of late George Wilkinson; educ. Mr. Wilkinson's Preparatory School, Newcastle; Shrewsbury School; Neuchâtel University, Switzerland; 1st commission (T.F.), March, 1906; appointed to the command of a battery in Oct. 1914; Major, R.F.A.; served Europ. War; wounded, Battle of Arras; Despatches; returned to the Western front, Nov. 1917; Major Wilkinson died of wounds 7.4.18.

WILKINSON, C. R. (D.S.O. L.G. 3.6.19); b. 9.5.77; 2nd Lt., Unatt., 20.1.97; 2nd Lt.,

A. M. Wilkinson.

WILKINSON, C. W. (D.S.O. L.G. 13.2.17); b. 8.10.68; 2nd Lt., R.E., 27.7.88; Lt. 27.7.91; Capt. 27.9.99; Major 2.3.08; Lt.-Col. 1.4.16; Col., R.E., 1.4.20; served N.W. Frontier of India, 1897-98; Medal and clasp; Europ. War, 1914-18; C.M.G.; Despatches.

WILKINSON, G. H. (D.S.O, L.G. 3.6.18); b. 14.4.78; 2nd Lt., S. Lan. R., 4.4.00; Lt. 11.4.02; Capt. 11.2.09; Ind. Army 26.1.12; Major 1.9.15; served S. African War, 1900-2; Queen's Medal, 3 clasps; Europ. War; Despatches.

WILKINSON, H. B. DES VŒUX (D.S.O. L.G. 1.1.17); b. 18.10.70; s. of late Major H. C. Wilkinson; m. Bridget, d. of late Col. C. Blencowe Cookson, C.B.; educ. Cheam School; Wellington College; R.M. College, Sandhurst; joined the Durham L.I. 9.1.92; Lt. 29.7.94; Capt. 11.11.99; Major 29.2.12; Bt. Lt.-Colonel 3.6.17; served S. African War; Despatches; Queen's Medal and 5 clasps; Europ. War, in France, from 1914; Despatches thrice; C.B.E.; Bt. Lt.-Col.

WILKINSON, H. V. (D.S.O. L.G. 1.1.18); e. s. of E. H. Wilkinson; m. Aileen, e. d. of late Thomas Monaghan; T/Major, M.G.C.; served Europ. War; Despatches.

WILKINSON, J. S. (D.S.O. L.G. 27.7.18); b. 30.9.84; 2nd Lt., Notts. and Derby. R., 7.2.06; Lt. 16.11.07; Capt. 21.1.15.; M.C.

WILKINSON, L. F. GREEN- (see Green-Wilkinson, L. F.).

WILKINSON, R. (D.S.O. L.G. 2.2.16); b. 21.9.77; m. Irene Rosalind, d. of Fleet-Surgeon E. J. Butler, R.N.; three s.; educ. Eton; joined Glouc. R. from 3rd Bedfords. R. (Militia), 1896; 2nd Lt., Glouc. R., 9.12.96; Lt. 12.12.98; Adjt. 12.7.05 to 11.7.08; Capt. 13.10.05; Major 1.9.15; served S. African War; Queen's and King's Medals; Adjt., 2nd Glouc. R., 1905-08; served Europ. War, 1915-16, first in Gallipoli, as Adjt. of and then in command of 7th Gloucesters. R.; Despatches; commanded an Officer Cadet Batt., 1916; commanded 1/4th Glouc. Rgt., 1917.

WILKINSON, S. J. (D.S.O. L.G. 14.1.16); b. 27.8.77; yr. s. of late Major H. C. Wilkinson, 82nd Regt.; m. Gladys Mary, yr. d. of J. D. Rowlands; one s.; educ. Wellington College; joined Militia 30.8.99; 2nd Lt., W. Yorks. R., 21.4.00; Lt. 12.12.01; Capt. 5.3.10; Major 1.9.15; Lt.-Col., Nov. 1915; given command of 19th (Pioneer) Batt. Welsh Regt.; transferred at own request to command 10th Batt. S.W. Borderers; served S. African War, 1899-1900; Queen's Medal, 3 clasps; on 10.9.95 saved life from drowning at Folkestone, and received the Testimonial of the Royal Humane Society; Europ. War from April, 1915; Despatches. He was killed in action 8.7.16 in Caterpillar Wood on the east of Mametz village, at the First Battle of the Somme.

WILKINSON, W. D. (D.S.O. L.G. 12.3.17), T/Capt., York. R.; M.C.

WILKINSON, W. T. (D.S.O. L.G. 27.9.01) (Bar, L.G. 26.7.18), Major and Bt. Lt.-Col., K.O.S.B. (see "The Distinguished Service Order," from its institution to 31.12.15, by

S. J. Wilkinson.

same publishers).

WILKS, G. L. (D.S.O. L.G. 8.3.18); b. 3.3.95; s. of T. Wilks, J.P.; m. Joan Louise, d. of Col. F. Searle, C.B.E., D.S.O.; Lt.-Col., R.M.A., seconded Tank Corps; served Europ. War, 1914-18; Despatches.

WILL, R. R. (D.S.O. L.G. 16.9.18), Capt. (A/Major), R.F.A.

WILLAN, G. T., B.A., M.R.C.S.Eng., L.R.C.P.Lond. (D.S.O. L.G. 1.1.17); b. 1.2.75; s. of George Thomas Willan, Surgeon; educ. Oakham School; Cambridge University; Guy's Hospital; Lieut., R.A.M.C., 3.4.09; Capt., R.A.M.C., 3.10.12; served Europ. War, in France and Salonika; Despatches; invalided to England 4.10.18; appointed to command 302nd Field Ambulance 8.11.18.

WILLAN, R. H. (D.S.O. L.G. 3.6.16); b. 6.9.82; 2nd s. of Col. F. Willan; m. Violet, d. of late Brig.-Gen. Eyre Crabbe, C.B., G. Gds.; two s.; educ. Eton; 2nd Lt., K.R.R.C., 7.5.02; Lt. 10.2.07; Capt. 14.9.14; Major 18.1.17; Royal Corps of Signals, 1920; Despatches; Bt. Lt.-Col. 1.1.19; served Europ. War; Military Cross.

WILLANS, H. (D.S.O. L.G. 3.6.18); b. 1892; s. of late J. T. Willans; educ. Aldenham; 2nd Lt., Bedfordshire Rgt., 1914; Capt., R. of O., Bedfords. R.; served in France, 1914-18; Italy, 1917; M.C.; Despatches twice; 1914 Star; wounded; Adjt., 1st Batt. Bedfords. Rgt., 1915-17; Staff Capt., 15th Inf. Brig., 1914-17; M.C.

WILLCOCK, R. (D.S.O. L.G. 3.6.19), Capt. (A/Major), 42nd Batt. Can. Inf., Quebec R.; M.C.

WILLCOCKS, J. L. (D.S.O. L.G. 1.1.18); b. 5.1.93; s. of Gen. Sir J. Willcocks, G.C.B., G.C.M.G., K.C.S.I., D.S.O., and Winifred, d. of Col. G. A. Way, C.B.; m. Muriel Kathleen, d. of late Col. Gordon Price; one d.; educ. Cheltenham College; 2nd Lt., R. Highrs. 14.2.12; Lt. 16.5.14; Capt. 1.10.15; Major; served Europ. War, 1914-18; Despatches three times; M.C.

WILLCOX, H. B. D. (D.S.O. L.G. 1.1.18); b. 30.4.89; 2nd Lt., Notts. and Derby. R., 20.12.11; Adjt., Notts. and Derby. Regt., 21.9.14 to 21.3.16; Lt., Notts. and Derby. R., 21.11.14; Capt., Notts. and Derby. R., 1.10.16; M.C.

WILLETS, C. R. E. (D.S.O. L.G. 26.7.17), Major, Can. Infy.

WILLETT, F. W. B. (D.S.O. L.G. 14.1.16); b. 3.3.78; 2nd Lt., R. Suss. R., 15.5.97; Lt. 22.2.99; Capt. 1.6.05; Major 6.9.15; served S. African War, 1900-2; Queen's Medal, 4 clasps; King's Medal, 2 clasps; Europ. War; Despatches.

WILLIAMS, A. B. (D.S.O. L.G. 3.6.19), Major, 5th Battery, 2nd Brig., N.Z. Field Arty.

WILLIAMS, ALFRED ERNEST (D.S.O. L.G. 16.8.17), Colonel, late 4th Batt. R. War. R.; Additional A.D.C. to the King 7.8.20; served S. African War, 1900-1; operations in Orange River Colony, May to 29.11.00; Queen's Medal with 3 clasps; Europ. War. His D.S.O. was awarded for gallantry at Messines Ridge 7.6.17.

WILLIAMS, AUBREY ELLIS (D.S.O. L.G. 15.2.19) (Details, L.G. 30.7.19), b. 9.5.88; 2nd Lt., S.W.B., 9.10.07; Lt. 9.6.09; Capt. 22.10.14; Adjt., S.W.B., 4.2.15 to 12.9.15; Bt. Major 1.1.18; Europ. War; Despatches; M.C.

WILLIAMS, A. J., F.R.C.V.S. (D.S.O. L.G. 26.8.18); b. 7.11.76; Capt., A.V.C., 5.10.03; Major, R.A.V.C., 6.7.13; Lt.-Col. 1.12.21; served S. African War, 1899–1902; Queen's Medal, 4 clasps; King's Medal, 2 clasps; Tibet, 1903–4; Medal; Sudan, 1908; Egyptian Medal with clasp; Europ. War; Despatches.

WILLIAMS, A. S., M.R.C.S., L.R.C.P. (D.S.O. L.G. 2.11.16); b. 17.12.78; y. s. of late Major-Gen. H. E. T. Williams; educ. Cheltenham College; St. Bartholomew's Hospital; Lt. 30.1.06; Capt. 30.7.09; Major, R.A.M.C., 30.1.18; served Europ. War, in France, 1914–18; made prisoner. His D.S.O. and also Gold Life-Saving Medal of Order of St. John were awarded for services at prisoners' camp, Gardelegen, Germany, during typhus epidemic, 1915.

WILLIAMS, C. A. N. (D.S.O. L.G. 22.6.16), Eng. Lt.-Cdr., R.N.R.

WILLIAMS, C. R. (D.S.O. L.G. 2.4.19) (Details, L.G. 10.12.19); b. 18.2.81; 2nd Lt., R. Munster Fus., 23.5.06; Lt. 2.8.08; Capt. 28.11.14; M.C.

WILLIAMS, C. V. MONIER- (see Monier-Williams, C. V.).

WILLIAMS, D. BROCK- (see Brock-Williams, D.).

WILLIAMS, E. H. W. (D.S.O. L.G. 26.7.18); b. 21.3.84; s. of C. H. B. Williams; m. Florence Jane Brett; one d.; educ. Rugby; Sandhurst; 2nd Lt., 10th Hussars, 9.3.03; Lt. 13.6.04; Capt. 7.5.08; Major 15.5.15; served under I.G., Cavalry, Egypt and Palestine, Sept. 1916–Sept. 1917, as Hotchkiss Machine Gun Expert; 2nd-in-command, 10th R. Hussars, Sept. 1917–March, 1918; wounded March, 1918; O.C., 10th R. Hussars from March, 1919. His D.S.O. was awarded for mounted charge at Colezy, 24.3.18, with a detachment of 10th Hussars, Royal Dragoons and 3rd Dragoon Guards; Despatches; served British Upper Silesian Force, 1921; won Punjab Army Cup at Rawalpindi, 1906, with Lohengrin, and C.T.C. Steeplechase, 1909, with Cravat; Governor's Cup, Lahore, 1909, with Promise; rode 31 winning races on bay Arab, Pasha.

WILLIAMS, E. J. (D.S.O. L.G. 4.6.17), Lt.-Col., Can. A.M.C.

WILLIAMS, E. M. (D.S.O. L.G. 1.1.18), Aust. Light Horse Rgt.

WILLIAMS, F. S. (D.S.O. L.G. 18.2.18) (Details, L.G. 18.7.18), Lt., R.E.

WILLIAMS, G. A. S. (D.S.O. L.G. 1.1.18), Major, S. Staffs. R. (Spec. Res.).

WILLIAMS, G. D. (D.S.O. L.G. 8.3.20), A/Lt.-Cdr., R.N.R.

WILLIAMS, G. N. (D.S.O. L.G. 1.1.18), T/Lt.; T/Lt.-Col., S. African Forces.

WILLIAMS, G. W. (D.S.O. L.G. 3.6.18), T/Capt. (A/Major); M.C.; R.E.

WILLIAMS, HENRY JAMES (D.S.O. L.G. 1.1.18), Major, Aust. A.M.C.

WILLIAMS, HENRY JOHN (D.S.O. L.G. 4.6.17); b. 11.7.70; 2nd s. of late E. A. G. Williams; educ. Uppingham; 2nd Lt., 1st D.G., 4.3.91; Lt., 1st D.G., 1.3.93; Capt. 13.9.98; Major 14.6.06; Lt.-Col., 1st D.G., 14.6.18; served S. African War, 1901–2; Queen's Medal, 5 clasps; Europ. War; Despatches twice; Arab rising, Mesopotamia, 1920; Order of Iron Crown, Austria; 3rd Class Order of Franz Joseph (Austria).

WILLIAMS, H. LLOYD- (see Lloyd-Williams, H.).

WILLIAMS, H. M. (D.S.O. L.G. 1.1.18); b. 9.6.79; Lt., A.V.C., 4.2.05; Capt. 4.2.10; Major, A.V.C.; S. African War, 1877–78–79; Despatches; Medal with clasp; Europ. War; Despatches. He was killed in action on 23.12.17.

WILLIAMS, HENRY PROSSER (D.S.O. L.G. 7.6.18), Paymaster Lt.-Cdr., R.N., 21.8.15.

WILLIAMS, H. PRICE- (see Price-Williams, H.).

WILLIAMS, H. W. VAUGHAN- (see Vaughan-Williams, H. W.).

WILLIAMS, J. (D.S.O. L.G. 26.9.17) (Details, L.G. 9.1.18), T/Major, R. Welsh Fus. His D.S.O. was awarded for gallantry on 1.8.17, at Pilckem.

WILLIAMS, J. C. M. (D.S.O. L.G. 1.1.17), Capt., R.F.A.

WILLIAMS, J. H. (D.S.O. L.G. 26.5.19), 2nd Lt., Unatt., 20.1.12; I.A. 8.3.13; Lt. 20.4.14; Capt. 20.9.15; Capt., 1/10 Gurkha Rifles.

WILLIAMS, J. W. (D.S.O. L.G. 23.3.17); s. of late H. Williams; m. Elsie Dunkin, d. of late H. G. G. Zoller; Cdr., R.N.R.; served Europ. War. He has an Italian decoration for relief work in connection with the great earthquake at Messina.

WILLIAMS, L. G. (D.S.O. L.G. 18.8.16); b. 12.10.78; 2nd Lt., N. Staffs. R., 17.10.00; I.A. 14.4.02; Capt. 17.10.09; Major 17.10.15; Bt. Lt.-Col. 3.6.17; Col. 1.8.21; Despatches; C.M.G.; served S. African War, 1900–1; Queen's Medal and 4 clasps; Europ. War (Mesopotamia), 1914–16; Despatches; Legion of Honour.

WILLIAMS, P. L. WATKIN-, (see Watkin-Williams, P. L.).

WILLIAMS, R. (D.S.O. L.G. 16.8.17), Capt., Flying Corps. His D.S.O. was awarded for gallantry at Gaza 20.5.17.

WILLIAMS, R. C. (D.S.O. L.G. 3.6.16); b. at Muttra, India, 2.2.80; s. of late G. R. C. Williams, late I.C.S.; m. Mary Frances Elizabeth, d. of late C. N. Draper; two d.; educ. Elizabeth College, Guernsey; 2nd Lt., R.A., 25.6.99; Lt. 16.2.01; Capt. 21.11.07; Major 30.10.14; Lt.-Col., R.F.A., 1.1.21; served S. Africa, 1901–2; Queen's Medal, 4 clasps; S. Nigeria, 1906; Medal with clasp; Europ. War, 1914–18; Gallipoli, Egypt, France; wounded four times; Despatches four times; C.M.G. and Croix de Guerre.

WILLIAMS, REV. R. C. L. (D.S.O. L.G. 1.1.18); b. 26.7.81; s. of A. C. Williams and Marian Williams (*née* Jarrett); educ. St. Lawrence College; Peterhouse, Cambridge; Ordained 1905; ent. Army Chaplains' Dept., 1907; Chaplain of the Duke of York's Royal Military School from 1912; Asst. Chaplain-General.

WILLIAMS, R. D. (D.S.O. L.G. 11.1.19), T/Major, 13th Batt. Welsh R.

WILLIAMS, R. J. (D.S.O. L.G. 19.11.17) (Details, L.G. 22.3.18), T/2nd Lt. (A/Capt.), Welsh R.

WILLIAMS, R. LL. (D.S.O. L.G. 26.7.18), T/Capt., R.A.M.C.; M.C.

WILLIAMS, S. H. (D.S.O. L.G. 4.6.17), T/Capt. (A/Major), R.F.A.

WILLIAMS, S. J. (D.S.O. L.G. 3.6.18), Capt. (A/Major), A.V.C. (now R.A.V.C.).

WILLIAMS, T. (D.S.O. L.G. 1.2.19), 4th Aust. Light Horse Rgt.

WILLIAMS, T. G. (D.S.O. L.G. 3.6.19); b. 5.4.92; s. of Thos. Edward and Ida Marling Williams; m. Muriel Pelham, d. of late E. H. Aldborough Maekley; educ. Enfield Grammar School; Hawarden County School; Moravian College; Neuwied-on-Rhine; commissioned T.F. 14.12.14; Lt., 1/7th King's Liverpool Rgt., 1915; Capt., 1916; Major, 1917; Lt.-Colonel; demobilized, March, 1919; resigned commission, 1920, and granted rank of Lt.-Colonel; served Europ. War, France, May, 1915, till Armistice; M.C.

WILLIAMS, T. I. C. (D.S.O. L.G. 4.6.17), Major, Aust. Arty.

WILLIAMS, T. R. (D.S.O. L.G. 4.6.17), Major, Aust. Engrs.

WILLIAMS, V. P. B. (D.S.O. L.G. 22.3.19), Major (T/Lt.-Col.), 4th Cav., I.A.; b. 30.10.81; 2nd Lt., Unatt., 8.1.01; 2nd Lt., I.A., 15.4.02; Lt. 12.10.03; Capt. 8.1.10; Major 8.1.16; Bt. Lt.-Col. 3.6.19.

WILLIAMS, W. E. (D.S.O. L.G. 16.9.18), Capt. (A/Lt.-Col.), Middlesex R.

WILLIAMS, W. P. BRADLEY- (see Bradley-Williams, W. P.

WILLIAMS-FREEMAN, A. P. (D.S.O. L.G. 3.6.18); b. 21.2.77; 2nd Lt., D.C.L.I., 20.2.97; Lt. 31.1.99; Capt. 11.4.04; Major (A/Lt.-Col.), 1.9.15; operations on N.W. Frontier of India, 1897–98, with Tirah Exp. Force; Medal with 2 clasps; Europ. War; Despatches; O.B.E.

WILLIAMS-FREEMAN, F. A. P. (D.S.O. 23.10.14) (Bar, L.G. 14.1.21), Lt.-Cdr., R.N. (see "The Distinguished Service Order," from its institution to 31.12.15, by same publishers).

WILLIAMS-THOMAS, F. S. (D.S.O. L.G. 30.1.20), Major, Worcesters. Yeomanry; M.C.

WILLIAMSON, A. J. (D.S.O. L.G. 3.6.18); b. 30.8.84; s. of late J. Williamson, J.P.; m. Cecil Isobel, d. of Dr. J. D. Burnett; one s.; educ. Aberdeen University; mobilized as Lieut., R.A.M.C. (T.F.), with 4th London Field Ambulance on 5.8.14; served with this unit in France and Belgium till demobilized in 1919; appointed Acting Lieut.-Col. in command of 4th London Field Amb. 16.12.16, and remained in command till demobilized; 1914–15 Star; Despatches twice.

WILLIAMSON, H. N. H. (D.S.O. L.G. 27.9.20), Major, R.F.A.; M.C.

WILLIAMSON, J. D. (D.S.O. L.G. 6.4.18), Eng.-Cdr., R.N.R.

WILLIS, A. U. (D.S.O. L.G. 8.3.20), Lt.-Cdr., R.N., 15.11.17.

WILLIS, H. G., M.B. (D.S.O. L.G. 26.7.18), T/Capt. (A/Major), R.A.M.C.; M.C.

WILLIS, M. H. S. (D.S.O. L.G. 3.6.16), Capt., Suffolk R. (att. Nigeria R.).

WILLIS, S. G. R. (D.S.O. L.G. 4.6.17); b. 24.8.77; 2nd Lt., R.A., 23.3.97; Lt. 23.3.00; Capt. 3.2.04; Major 1.10.14; Lt.-Col. 1.10.17.

WILLIS, W. J. (D.S.O. L.G. 4.6.17), Hon. Major, Aust. Inf. Batt.

WILLIS-O'CONNOR, H. (D.S.O. L.G. 1.1.19), Major, E. Ontario R., Can. Mil. Forces.

WILLISON, A. C. (D.S.O. L.G. 8.3.19) (Details, L.G. 4.10.19): b. 2.1.96; 2nd Lt., 1st Batt. Notts. and Derby. R., 4.5.15; Lt. 6.7.16; served Europ. War, 1914–19; Despatches; M.C.

WILLOCK, F. G. (D.S.O. L.G. 1.1.18), Lt.-Col., R.F.A.

WILLOUGHBY, D. V. (D.S.O. L.G. 25.8.17); b. 6.2.82; 2nd Lt., R. Sc. Fusiliers, 11.8.00; Lt., I.A., 19.12.02; Capt. 11.8.09; Major 1.9.15; Bt. Lt.-Col. 3.6.19.

WILLOUGHBY, SIR J. C., Bart. (D.S.O. L.G. 4.6.17); b. 20.2.59; s. of 4th Bart. and 2nd wife, Maria Elizabeth, d. of T. Fawkes, of Hemley House, Staffs; educ. Eton; Trin. Coll., Camb; Lt., 3rd Batt. Oxford Light Infantry, 1879; 2nd Lt., 6th Dragoon Guards, and entered R. Horse Guards, 1880; Major 18.1.95; served Egyptian Exp., 1882; Battle of Tel-el-Kebir; Medal with clasp; Bronze Star; Sudan Exp., 1884–85; Nile; employed on Transport Duties; Despatches; clasp; Second-in-Command of forces of Imperial British South Africa Co., Matabeleland, 1890–91; Matabeleland Conquest, 1893 accompanied Dr. Jameson, C.B., into the Transvaal, 1896; served S. African War, 1899–1900; was in Ladysmith with Cavalry Headquarter Staff during the siege, and appointed Major under General Hunter in command of the transport of the flying column for the relief of Mafeking, also employed on the Intelligence Department; Queen's Medal, 2 clasps; Despatches; served Europ. War, 1914–17; T/Major, A.S.C. (now R.A.S.C.); Despatches. He died on 16.4.18.

WILLOUGHBY-OSBORNE, D'A. (D.S.O. L.G. 4.6.17); b. 28.4.82; 2nd Lt., R.A., 24.5.02; Lt. 24.5.05; Capt. 30.10.14; Major, R.F.A., 28.2.16. Before the war he was serving with the W. African F.F.

WILLS, C. S. (D.S.O. L.G. 20.7.17), Capt., R.N., 31.12.12; C.M.G.

WILLSALLEN, T. L. (D.S.O. L.G. 18.2.18) (Details, L.G. 18.7.18), Major, Australian Light Horse Rgt.

WILLSON, E. (D.S.O. L.G. 3.6.18); b. 11.1.78; 2nd Lt., R.A., 15.11.14 Lt. 9.6.15; Capt., R.G.A., 3.11.17.

WILLYAMS, E. N. (D.S.O. L.G. 4.6.17); b. 14.2.91; s. of H. J. Willyams and Margaret, d. of late J. Jowitt; m. Beatrice Jean Blewett, R.R.C., late C.A.M.C.; e. d. of late Coleman and Mary Blewett, of Toronto, Canada; educ. Eton; R.M.C., Sandhurst; 2nd Lt., D.C.L.I., 5.10.10; Lt. 12.6.12; Capt. 22.12.15; served Europ. War, 1914–18.

WILMER, G. H. (D.S.O. L.G. 11.4.18); b. 3.12.83; 2nd Lt., Essex Rgt., 7.5.02; Lt. 14.3.05; Adjt., Essex Rgt., 2.9.09 to 1.9.12; Capt. 26.11.13; Majo 7.5.17; Bt. Lt.-Col. 11.11.19; M.C.

WILMOT, THEODORE EARDLEY- (see Eardley-Wilmot, Theodore).

WILMOT, TREVOR EARDLEY- (see Eardley-Wilmot, Trevor).

WILSON, A. D. (D.S.O. L.G. 11.5.17), Major, Can. Infy.

WILSON, A. E. J. (D.S.O. L.G. 1.1.18); b. 26.12.79; 2nd Lt., North'd Fus., 20.12.99; Lt. 9.6.00; Capt. 30.5.04; Capt., Somerset L.I., 20.5.08; Major 1.9.15; S. African War, 1901–2; Queen's Medal, 3 clasps; Europ. War; Despatches; Bt. Lt.-Col. 3.6.19; Despatches.

WILSON, A. G. B. (D.S.O. L.G. 11.11.19), Lt., R.N., 30.3.15.

WILSON, A. H. (D.S.O. L.G. 14.1.16); b. 24.7.69; 2nd Lt. 9.11.89; Lt. 31.10.91; Capt. 1.9.98; Major 14.1.09; retired E. Surrey Rgt. 17.3.09; Major, R. of O.

WILSON, A. H. H. (D.S.O. L.G. 1.1.17); b. 10.9.73; s. of R. Hutton Wilson; m. Edith Alice, d. of Lt.-Gen. Sir H. S. G. Miles; one s.; two d.; educ. Charterhouse; joined Wilts. R. 21.10.93; Lt. 16.10.95; Capt. 9.2.00; Bt. Major 23.7.10; Bt. Lt.-Col. 29.11.15; Colonel 29.11.19; served S. African War, 1899–1902; Queen's Medal with 4 clasps; King's Medal with 2 clasps; France, 1915–18.

WILSON, ALEXANDER MORETON (D.S.O. L.G. 1.1.17); b. 24.9.82 2nd Lt., A.S.C., 7.12.01; Lt. 1.1.03; Capt. 10.11.06; Major, R.A.S.C., 30.10.14 Bt. Lt.-Col. 1.1.19.

WILSON, ARTHUR MITCHELL (D.S.O. L.G. 7.11.18), Lt.-Col., Aust. A.M.C.

WILSON, A. R. G. (D.S.O. L.G. 8.3.19) (Details, L.G. 4.10.19); b. 13.11.84 s. of Major-Gen. Sir A. Wilson, K.C.B.; m. Violet Alice, d. of Lt.-Col. H. Morland and the late Lady Alice Morland; one s.; one d.; 2nd Lt., A. and S. Highrs., 19.10.04; Lt. 31.1.08; Capt. 21.3.14; Bt. Major 3.6.19.

WILSON, A. T. (D.S.O. L.G. 17.4.16); b. 18.7.84; s. of Ven. J. M. Wilson, D.D., F.G.S., Canon of Worcester and Sub-Dean, and his 2nd wife, Georgina Mary Talbot; educ. Clifton College; Sandhurst (King's Medal; Sword of Honour); 2nd Lt., Unatt., 19.8.03; 32nd Sikh Pioneers, I.A., 18.12.04; Lt. 19.11.05; Capt. 19.8.12; Major 19.8.18; Deputy Chief Political Officer, Indian Exp. Force "D," 1915; Deputy Civil Commissioner, 1916; Officiating Civil Commissioner and Officiating Political Resident in the Persian Gulf, 1918; Despatches; C.I.E.; C.S.I.; C.M.G.

WILSON, B. T. (D.S.O. L.G. 4.2.18) (Details, L.G. 5.7.18); b. Toronto, 12.12.85; s. of Alexander Wilson and Mary Louise Wilson (*née* Barker); m. Florence Erica, d. of J. R. Starkey, M.P.; educ. Clifton; R.M.A., Woolwich; 2nd Lt., R.E., 12.8.05; Lt. 8.3.08; Capt. 30.10.14; Adjt., R.E., 30.9.16 to 21.1.17; Bt. Major 3.6.17; Major 31.10.18; served Europ. War, 1914–18;

served Egypt, battles on Suez Canal, Gallipoli, France, Italy; Despatches three times; Italian Silver Medal for Military Valour. He has the Delhi Durbar Medal, 1911.

WILSON, C. E. (D.S.O. L.G. 8.8.17); b. 9.3.73; s. of Maj.-Gen. Sir C. W. Wilson, K.C.B., K.C.M.G., etc., and Lady Wilson (Olivia) (*née* Duffin) (both deceased); m. Beryl Marie, d. of Col. W. Hunter Little; one d.; educ. Clifton College; R.M.C., Sandhurst; 1st commission, E. Lancs. R., 21.10.93; Major 8.1.16; retired E. Lancs. Rgt. 30.13.10; Colonel, late E. Lancs. R., R. of O; served Sudan Campaign, 1898 and 1899; attached to Egyptian Army, South African Campaign, 1900–2; Egyptian Army and Sudan Government; held following appointments: Governor and Officer Comdg., Sennar Province; Governor, Khartum Province; Governor to O.C., Red Sea Province; from July, 1916, British Military and Political Representative in the Hedjaz. His D.S.O. was awarded for services connected with the Arab Revolt; C.M.G.; Grand Cordon; Order of El Nadha, 2nd Class Order of the Nile; Officer, Legion of Honour; 3rd Class Medjidieh.

WILSON, C. S. (D.S.O. L.G. 3.6.19); b. 13.12.67; Lt., R.E., 24.7.86; Capt. 31.12.96; Major 14.4.05; Lt.-Col. 27.8.13; Bt. Col. 1.1.16; C.B.; C.M.G.; served S. African War; Queen's Medal, 3 clasps; King's Medal, 2 clasps; Europ. War; Despatches.

WILSON, D. C. (D.S.O. L.G. 1.1.18); b. 8.5.85; 2nd Lt., R.A., 27.7.05; Capt. 27.7.08; Major 30.10.14; Lt.-Col. 23.11.16.

WILSON, D. H. (D.S.O. L.G. 1.1.18), T/Capt. (T/Lt.-Col.), Gen. List (deceased).

WILSON, E. B. (D.S.O. L.G. 3.6.19), T/Major (A/Lt.-Col.), 6th Batt. Yorks. L.I., att. 34th Batt. London R.

WILSON, F. (D.S.O. L.G. 14.1.16); b. 23.1.77; s. of James and Agnes Clara Wilson; educ. Bedford Grammar School; entered the Army, June, 1900; Lt., 1901; Capt. 1905; Major, 1911; Lt.-Col., 1st East Anglian Field Co., R.E., T.F.

WILSON, F. O'B. (D.S.O. L.G. 14.1.16); entered the Royal Navy, subsequently transferring to the E. African Mounted Rifles; Capt.

WILSON, G. (D.S.O. L.G. 4.6.17); b. 25.4.69; s. of late Capt. R. Wilson of Cambuskenneth Abbey, Stirling, Scotland; m. Letitia, d. of R. Moneypenny; two s.; three d.; ent. K.O.R.L. Rgt.; commissioned 24.2.00; Capt., 1910; Major, 1915; Lt.-Col., 1919; foreign service includes Malta, 1895 to 1897; Hong Kong, 1898; Singapore, 1899–1900; Malta, 1901–3; India, 1903–5; Burma, 1905–8, and India, 1908 to 1913; served in the Great War with the 1st Batt. The King's Own Royal Lancaster Regt. from 4.8.14 to 21.1.18, continuously; in the Retreat from Mons and the advance to the Aisne, including the 1st Battle of the Marne, the Aisne, the 1st, 2nd and 3rd Battles of Ypres, the 1st and 2nd Battle of the Somme; mentioned in Despatches three times; He was awarded the D.S.O. for distinguished conduct in action; 1914 Star.

WILSON, G. F. W. (D.S.O. L.G. 20.7.17), Lt.-Cdr., R.N., 29.2.16.

WILSON, G. L. (D.S.O. L.G. 18.10.17) (Details, L.G. 7.3.18); s. of John Wilson; served Europ. War; Lt.-Col., 8th A. and S. Highlanders; M.C. He died at 20th General Hospital, Dannes Camiers, on 16.2.19, and was buried at Etaples.

WILSON, G. T. B. (D.S.O. L.G. 1.1.17); s. of Adam Wilson and Grace, d. of J. Brand, of Lala Shaafia, Tangier, Morocco; m. Louisa Adelaide, d. of R. K. Masterton; one s.; one d.; joined Kent Artillery Militia, 1887; 1st H.L.I., 1891; retired pay, 1908; Lt.-Col., 4th A. and S. Highrs., 1912; Col., retired from S.R.; Bt. Lt.-Col., R. of O., H.L.I.; served S. African War; Despatches; Queen's Medal, 4 clasps; Europ. War, Gallipoli, Sinai Peninsula and France, 1914–18; in command of a battalion in France, 1917–18; Despatches twice; 3rd Class Stanialaus with Cross Swords.

WILSON, H. D. (D.S.O. L.G. 12.3.17), Major, R.F.A., T.D., of Bolton-le-Sands, Lancs.

WILSON, H. G. (D.S.O. L.G. 1.1.19), Major (A/Lt.-Col.), 1/5th Batt. Lincs. R. (T.F.).

WILSON, H. M. (D.S.O. L.G. 1.1.17); b. 5.9.81; 2nd Lt., Rif. Brig., 10.3.00; Lt. 18.3.01; Capt. 2.4.08; Major 1.9.15; Bt. Lt.-Col. 1.1.19; S. African War, 1900–1, with Imp. Yeomanry; Queen's Medal, 4 clasps.

WILSON, H. R. (D.S.O. L.G. 3.6.18), Major, R.F.A.

WILSON, L. C. (D.S.O. L.G. 1.1.19); b. 1871; educ. Brisbane Grammar School; Brig.-Gen., late 3rd L.H. Brig., A.I.F.; served S. Africa, 1900–1; Queen's Medal, 5 clasps; Europ. War from 1914; Despatches five times; C.B.; C.M.G.; Croix de Guerre.

WILSON, M. F. F. (D.S.O. L.G. 17.5.18); b. 22.6.86, at Gravesend; s. of M. F. Wilson, M.I.C.E., and Florence May, d. of the late Ven. Archdeacon Badnall, of the Cape; m. Catherine Gladys, d. of the late Col. P. H. Murray, K.S.L.I.; one d.; educ. Castlemount, Dover; Winchester College; Britannia, Sept. 1901; Commander, R.N., 30.6.19; served in H.M.S. Drake, Grand Fleet, outbreak of war till April, 1915; H.M.S. Abercrombie, Dardanelles, May, 1915, to May, 1917; H.M.S. Calypso, Grand Fleet, June, 1917, to Armistice; H.M.S. Calypso, Baltic, Nov. 1918, to Jan. 1919, when that ship, with others, commanded by Capt. B. S. Thesiger, C.B., C.M.G., captured the Bolshevik destroyers Spartak and Avtroill, off Reval. His D.S.O. was awarded for action between 6th Light Cruiser Squadron and German light cruisers in Heligoland Bight 17.11.17.

WILSON, SIR M. R. H., Bart. (D.S.O. L.G. 3.6.18); b. 25.8.75; s. of 3rd Bart. and Georgina Mary, d. of R. T. Lee; m. Hon. Barbara Lister, d. of 4th Baron Ribblesdale; three s.; ent. 10th R. Hussars 26.5.97; Lt. 22.1.99; Capt., 1902; Major 7.5.08; Lt.-Col., retired 7.8.12; served S. African War, 1899–1902; Queen's Medal, 3 clasps; King's Medal, 2 clasps; Military Secretary to Commander-in-Chief, India, 1909; C.S.I., 1911; served Egypt from 1915; M.P. (U.), Bethnal Green, from 1914.

WILSON, N. M. (D.S.O. L.G. 17.4.16); b. 6.4.84; s. of A. M. Wilson, O.B.E.; m. Violet Freddie, d. of late Lord Charles Edward Fitzroy and Hon. Ismay Mary Helen Augusta, d. of 3rd Baron Southampton; one d.; 2nd Lt., R.W.F., 20.4.04; Lt. 20.7.05; Capt., I.A., 29.4.13; Major 20.4.19; served Europ. War, 1914–16; Despatches; Bt. Major 1.1.17.

WILSON, N. R. (D.S.O. L.G. 1.1.19), Major, 2nd Batt. Canterbury R., N.Z. Mil. Force; M.C.

WILSON, N. Y. (D.S.O. L.G. 2.4.19) (Details, L.G. 10.12.19), T/Capt., 11th Batt. North'd Fus.; M.C.

WILSON, P. H. (D.S.O. L.G. 3.6.16); b. 18.8.74; m. Faith, d. of F. Priestman, D.L., J.P.; one s.; b. 18.8.74; 2nd Lt., R.A., 23.5.00; Lt. 10.1.02; Capt. 10.1.11; Major 30.10.14; Bt. Lt.-Col. 1.1.19; served S. African War, 1899–1902; Despatches; Queen's Medal, 5 clasps; King's Medal, 2 clasps; Europ. War, 1914–17. He has the R. Humane Society's Medal.

WILSON, P. N. W. (D.S.O. L.G. 26.9.17) (Details, L.G. 9.1.18) (Bar, L.G. 16.9.18); b. 28.2.86; 2nd Lt., R. Fusiliers, 24.1.06; Lt. 1.10.08; Capt. 26.11.14; M.C.

WILSON, P. P. (D.S.O. L.G. 26.7.18), Major, 7th Batt. Durham L.I.; served S. African War, 1902; Queen's Medal, 2 clasps; Europ. War; Despatches.

WILSON, R. A. (D.S.O. L.G. 1.1.19), Major, 6th Batt. 2nd Art. Brig., N.Z. Field Arty. (att. from R.G.A.).

WILSON, R. C. (D.S.O. L.G. 26.8.18); b. 26.12.82; 2nd Lt., Ches. Rgt., 8.5.01; Lt., I.A., 19.4.04; Capt. 8.5.10; Major, 114th Mahrattas, 8.5.16; Bt. Lt.-Col. 3.6.17; Col. 11.12.20.; M.C.

WILSON, R. E. (D.S.O. L.G. 16.5.16); b. 15.4.84; 2nd Lt., R.A., 15.7.03; Lt. 15.7.06; Capt. 30.10.14; Major 14.11.17. His D.S.O. was awarded for gallantry at Birtaniyeh, Mesopotamia.

WILSON, R. G. H. (D.S.O. L.G. 7.2.19), T/Major, K.A.R.; M.C.

WILSON, T. CARNS- (see Carns-Wilson, T.).

WILSON, T. N. F. (D.S.O. L.G. 3.6.19); b. 20.3.96; educ. West Downs, Winchester; Winchester College; R.M.C., Sandhurst; 2nd Lt., K.R.R.C., 11.11.14; Lt. 23.7.15; Capt. 11.2.17; Adjt., 1st Batt. K.R.R.C.; served Europ. War from 1914; Despatches; M.C.

WILSON, W. C. (D.S.O. L.G. 4.11.15) (Bar, L.G. 4.6.17), Bt. Major, Leic. R.; O.B.E.; M.C. (see "The Distinguished Service Order," from its institution to 31.12.15, by same publishers).

WILSON, W. D. (D.S.O. L.G. 18.1.18) (Details, L.G. 25.4.18), Major, Can. F.A.

WILSON, W. E. (D.S.O. L.G. 16.8.17); s. of W. Wilson; m. Elena, d. of T. C. Clarke, of Buenos Ayres; one d.; Major, Essex R.; served Europ. War; Despatches. His D.S.O. was awarded for gallantry at Gaza, Egypt, 26.3.17.

WILSON, W. H. (D.S.O. L.G. 1.1.17); s. of late Col. T. Wilson, C.B.; m. Florence Kerr, d. of late D. Fernie; educ. Wellington College; commissioned in the Auxiliary Force, 1885–1902, retiring with the rank of Major; joined R.F.A. with rank of Major, shortly after outbreak of War; Despatches.

WILSON, W. T. (D.S.O. L.G. 15.2.19) (Details, L.G. 30.7.19), T/Capt (A/Major), 256th Tunn. Co., R.E.; M.C.

WILSON-CHARGE, J. A. (D.S.O. L.G. 22.9.16), Capt. (T/Major), R. Warwicks. Rgt. His D.S.O. was awarded for gallantry on 27.7.16, near Pozières.

WILSON-FITZGERALD, F. W. (see Fitzgerald, F. W. Wilson-).

WILSON-JOHNSTON, W. E. (D.S.O. L.G. 22.12.16); b. 27.10.78; 2nd Lt., Unatt., 27.7.98; Lt., I.S.C., 19.10.99; Capt. 27.10.00; Major 27.7.07; Lt.-Col. 1.9.15; Bt. Lt.-Col. 3.6.18; C.I.E.

WILTON, E. A. (D.S.O. L.G. 1.1.18), Major, Aust. M.G.C.

WILTSHIRE, A. R. L. (D.S.O. L.G. 3.6.18), Lt.-Col., Australian Infy.; M.C.

WILTSHIRE, H. W., M.D. (D.S.O. L.G. 3.6.18); b. 2.5.79; s. of Alfred Wiltshire, M.D., F.R.C.P., and Kate Wiltshire (*née* Waterlow); educ. Cheltenham College; Clare College, Cambridge; King's College Hospital; T/Lt., R.A.M.C., 13.8.14; T/Capt., June, 1915; T/Major, July, 1916; Despatches three times; O.B.E.; Order of St. Sava of Serbia, Aug. 1918.

WINCH, G. B. (D.S.O. L.G. 1.1.18); s. of late G. Winch; m. Gertrude Dale, d. of the late T. Uzielli; educ. Charterhouse; Trinity College, Cambridge. He joined the H.A.C. in 1905; in 1913 he was commissioned in the 5th London Brigade; in March, 1915, he went to France and fought at Givenchy, Festubert, La Bassee and Loos, at which latter place he commanded his battery; in 1916–17 he was home for seven months' training a battery, and during this period he obtained his majority; in Feb. 1917, he went to the front again; was mentioned in Despatches, and was awarded the D.S.O. for gallantry in the field at Langemarck, in Dec. of that year. He died on 9 April, 1918, of wounds.

WINDER, J. H. R., M.D. (D.S.O. L.G. 1.1.18); b. 13.8.72; Lt., R.A.M.C., 27.2.01; Capt. 27.2.04; Major 27.2.13; served S. African War, 1900–2; Queen's Medal with clasp; Europ. War; Despatches.

WINDER, M. G., M.R.C.S., L.R.C.P. (D.S.O. L.G. 1.1.17); b. 4.11.76; educ. St. Bartholomew's Hospital; Lt., R.A.M.C., 31.1.03; Capt. 31.7.06; Major 1.9.14; Lt.-Colonel; served S. African War, 1901–2; Europ. War; Despatches; Bt. Lt.-Col. 1.1.18.

WINGATE, B. F., M.R.C.S., L.R.C.P. (D.S.O. L.G. 1.1.17); b. 16.7.75; educ. St. Mary's Hospital; Lt., R.A.M.C., 17.11.99; Capt. 17.11.02; Major 17.11.11; Lt.-Col. 26.12.17; served S. African War, 1900–2; Queen's Medal, 5 clasps; King's Medal, 2 clasps; Europ. War, 1914–17; Despatches.

WINGATE, G. H. F. (D.S.O. L.G. 1.1.18); b. 17.1.73; 2nd Lt., R. Scots., 21.1.93; Lt. 24.7.95; Capt. 19.7.99; Bt. Major 29.11.00; Major 5.4.11; served S. African War, 1899–1902; Queen's Medal, 3 clasps; King's Medal, 2 clasps; Europ. War; T/Brig.-Gen., Comdg. 78th Infy. Brigade, Salonika Force; Despatches; Bt. Lt.-Col. 1.1.17; Lt.-Col. 27.5.21.

WINGFIELD, HON. M. A. (D.S.O. L.G. 3.6.16); b. 21.6.83; s. of 7th Viscount Powerscourt, K.P.; m. Sybil Frances, d. of late F. D. Leyland; one s.; one d.; educ. Charterhouse; Sandhurst; joined Rif. Brig. 22.10.02; Lt. 3.7.07; Capt. 1.2.13; Bt. Major 18.2.15; Major 22.10.17; Bt. Lt.-Col. 1.1.17; Col. 1.1.21; T/Brig.-Gen. 1.12.18 to 28.2.19; served in Malta, 1904–6; India, 1908–10; Staff Coll., Cambridge, 1911–12; Secy., Mil. Manœuvres Commn., War Office, 1914; served as D.A.A. and Q.M.G., 3rd A.C., H.Q., in Europ. War (Belgium and France), 1914–15; as A.A. and Q.M.G. on Staff of 7th Div., Sept. 1915–17; A.Q.M.G., Staff of 2nd Army; served in Italy, Nov. 1917–March, 1918; D.A. and Q.M.G., 11th Army (T/Brig.-Gen.), Nov. 1918, to March, 1919; Despatches seven times; Bt. Major 18.2.15; Bt. Lt.-Col. 1.1.17; C.M.G.; Brevet Majority awarded for services on the Staff of the 3rd Army Corps during the Retreat from Compiègne and the battles of the Marne, the Aisne and Ypres–Armentières. His D.S.O. was awarded for services on the Staff of the 7th Division at the Battle of Loos; Brevet Lt.-Colonelcy awarded for services on the Staff of the 7th Division throughout the Battle of the Somme; French and Belgian Croix de Guerre; Legion of Honour; Ordre de la Couronne, Belgium; Order of the Crown of Italy.

WINGFIELD, REV. W. E. (Lt.-Col.) (D.S.O. L.G. 1.1.17); s. of late Capt. R. Wingfield, 52nd L.I.; m. Elizabeth Mary, d. of late G. J. Trench; two s.; two d.; educ. Wellington; Ridley Hall, Cambridge; R.M.A., Woolwich; commissioned R.A., 1886; retired 1907; Deacon, 1909; Priest, 1911; Curate of St. Paul, Portman Square, 1911–13; recalled from R. of O., 1914; served 3½ years overseas in Europ. War; promoted Lt.-Col. in Gallipoli; wounded in France, 1918; Despatches three times; Rector of Broome, Norfolk, from 1920.

WINSER, C. R. P. (D.S.O. L.G. 25.8.16) (Bar, L.G. 26.7.18); b. 29.6.80; s. of Rev. C. J. Winser, M.A., of Lullingworth, Painswick, and A. C. C. Winser, d. of Sir R. Kettle, Bart.; m. Ada, d. of late W. Bouch; two children; educ. Denstone, Staffs; joined the Army, Nov. 1899; was when Europ. War broke out a Captain in the Reserve of Officers; Lt.-Col. and Brig.-Gen., R. of O., S. Lanc. R.; served S. African War 1900–2; Queen's Medal, 4 clasps; wounded; Europ. War; Despatches several times; C.M.G.; won Hoghunters' Cup, 1907; Master, Lahore Hounds, 1906–7; Official Umpire, Ranelagh, 1914; Breeder of Pedigree Percheron Horses.

WINSLOE, H. E. (D.S.O. L.G. 15.2.17); b. 14.11.73; s. of late Col. R. W. C. Winsloe, C.B., late Commander, 21st R. Scots Fus.; m. Aileen Marie Constance Venables; educ. University College School; Dover College; R.M.A., Woolwich; 2nd Lt., R.E., 22.7.92; Lt. 22.7.95; Capt. 22.5.03; Major 22.7.12; served Tirah, 1897–98; Medal with clasp; N.W.F. of India, 1908; Zakka Khel Exp.; Medal with clasp; Europ. War; Despatches; three or four times in connection with advance on Amara, June, 1916 ; action of Ess Sinn, Sept. 1916 ; Ctesiphon, Nov. 1916 ; Siege of Kut, Dec. 1916–April, 1917 ; Bt. Lt.-Col. 3.6.16 ; C.M.G.

WINTER, C. B. (D.S.O. L.G. 22.12.16); b. 16.1.69 ; s. of W. H. Winter ; m. May Cooper ; two d. ; educ. Derby School ; Wren and Gurney's ; joined 2nd Linc. R., 1.3.90 ; Lt. 30.3.92 ; I.S.C. 9.6.92 ; 25th Punjabis, 1893 ; Capt. 1.3.01 ; Major 1.3.08 ; Lt.-Col. 1.3.16 ; Colonel, late 112th Rgt., I.A., retired June, 1920 ; served Isazar Exp., 1892 ; D.A.Q.M.G. to Sir J. Nixon's Staff in Mesopotamia, April, 1915 ; served on as A.Q.M.G. until invalided in April, 1919 ; Despatches ; Bt. Col. 3.6.18 ; C.M.G.

WINTER, E. A. (D.S.O. L.G. 1.1.18) (Bar, L.G. 26.7.18) ; s. of late J. Winter ; m. Mary Madeline Jung ; two d. ; joined H.M. Forces, 1914 ; Lt.-Col. ; demobilized 27.11.19 ; served with 23rd Batt. R. Fus., 1914–19 ; commanded the Batt., 1917–19 ; Despatches thrice ; M.C.

WINTER, G. C. (D.S.O. L.G. 8.3.20) ; Cdr., R.N. ; O.B.E.

WINTER, O. DE L'E. (D.S.O. L.G. 8.11.15) (Bar, L.G. 26.7.17), Colonel, R.F.A., C.B., C.M.G. (see " The Distinguished Service Order," from its institution to 31.12.15, by same publishers).

WINTER, W. O. (D.S.O. L.G. 1.1.19) ; b. 24.2.91 ; 2nd Lt., R.E., 23.12.10 ; Lt. 21.12.12 ; Captain. He died at Douai 30.11.18.

WINTER-EVANS, A. (D.S.O. L.G. 16.8.17), Lt.-Col., N.Z. Infantry. He was killed in action 12.10.17.

WINTERBOTHAM, H. ST. J. L. (D.S.O. L.G. 14.1.16) ; b. 5.2.78 ; s. of Rev. Canon R. Winterbotham ; m. Daisy, d. of G. Stocking ; two s. ; two d. ; educ. Fettes College, Edinburgh ; R.M.A., Woolwich ; 2nd Lt., R.E., 23.12.97 ; Lt. 23.12.00 ; Capt. 23.12.06 ; Major 30.10.14 ; served S. African War, 1899–1900 ; Queen's Medal, 3 clasps ; Europ. War, 1914–18 ; to France, Oct. 1914, as O.C., Ranging Section, R.E. ; Maps, 3rd Army, 1915–17 ; att. G.S., G.H.Q., 1917 to end of war ; Despatches thrice ; Bt. Lt.-Col. 1.1.17 ; C.M.G. ; Officer, Legion of Honour; American D.S. Medal ; Victoria Medal, R. Geographical Society, 1920.

WINTERBOTTOM, A. D. (D.S.O. L.G. 15.10.18) ; b. 11.5.85 ; 2nd Lt., 5th Dragoon Guards, 27.5.08 ; Lt. 1.4.11 ; Capt. 28.4.16.

WINTERSCALE, C. F. B. (D.S.O. L.G. 3.6.18) ; b. 9.6.79 ; Lt., Shrops. L.I., 22.9.06 ; Capt. 5.8.14 ; Major 18.1.17 ; Bt. Lt.-Col. 3.6.19 ; S. African War, 1901–2 ; Queen's Medal, 5 clasps ; Europ. War ; Despatches.

WINTLE, C. E. H. (D.S.O. L.G. 26.5.19) ; b. 4.5.71 ; 2nd Lt., Suff. R., 16.12.96 ; Army 16.3.99 ; Capt., Army, 16.12.05 ; Capt., Ind. Army, 18.11.10 ; Major 16.12.14 ; Bt. Lt.-Col. 3.6.17 ; Lt.-Col., 114th Mahrattas, I.A., 29.3.18 ; Col. 5.10.20 ; served Waziristan, 1894–95 ; Medal ; clasp.

WISDOM, E. A. (D.S.O. L.G. 3.6.16) ; b. 1869 ; s. of Francis William Wisdom and Mary Wisdom (*née* Cameron) ; m. Agnes Bell, d. of F. B. Jackson ; educ. at Inverness and Edinburgh ; joined the Commonwealth Military Forces, 1901, and subsequently Brig.-Gen. He was M.L.A., W. Australia ; served in Gallipoli to the evacuation. He also served in the Sinai Peninsula, Feb. 1916, and in France from 1916 ; Despatches several times ; C.B. ; C.M.G. ; Order of Danilo, 3rd Class. The D.S.O. was awarded for services in Gallipoli, particularly as Staff Officer to the O.C. Rear Guard during the evacuation. This Rear Guard was known as the " Diehards," as it was not expected that any of them would get away.

WISDOM, F. A. (D.S.O. L.G. 1.1.19), Major, Aust. Mil. Forces ; M.C.

WISE, A. D. (D.S.O. L.G. 10.6.21) ; b. 12.6.84 ; 2nd Lt., R.W. Surrey Rgt., 27.5.03 ; Lt. 17.10.05 ; Capt. 27.5.12 ; Major, I.A., 27.5.18.

WISE, J. (D.S.O. L.G. 2.12.18), 25th Batt. Can. Infy., Novia Scotia Rgt. ; M.C.

WISE, P. K. (D.S.O. L.G. 4.6.17) ; b. 17.4.85 ; 2nd Lt., Wilts. R., 3.12.04 ; Lt., Army, 3.3.07 ; I.A. 5.3.09 ; Capt., 7th D. Gds., 15.9.14 ; Capt., R. Warwicks. R., 1.2.15 ; T/Lt.-Col. 5.12.16 to 31.3.18 ; Despatches ; C.M.G.

WISTANCE, W. A. (D.S.O. L.G. 17.12.17) (Details, L.G. 23.4.18), Lt.-Colonel, The S. Staffs. Rgt., 5th Batt. (Territorial). He was killed in action 25.4.18 ; M.C.

WITHAM, A. (D.S.O. L.G. 1.5.18) (Details, L.G. 18.7.18) ; b. 6.2.80 ; 2nd Lt., R.A., 27.9.14 ; Lt. 9.6.15 ; Capt., R.F.A., 29.3.18 ; A/Major 25.8.18 ; served S. African War, 1899–1902 ; Queen's Medal, 5 clasps ; King's Medal, 2 clasps ; Europ. War ; Despatches. His M.C. was cancelled and a D.S.O. substituted.

WITHER, H. G. BIGG- (see Bigg-Wither, H. G.).

WITHERS, ROBERT BRYSON (gazetted as Withers, Rupert Bryson) (D.S.O. L.G. 3.6.18) ; b. 26.9.90 ; 2nd Lt., R.A., 23.7.10 ; Lt. 23.7.13 ; Capt., R.G.A., 23.7.16 ; A/Major 29.3.17.

WITHYCOMBE, W. M. (D.S.O. L.G. 1.1.18) ; b. 8.5.69 ; 2nd Lt., Yorks. L.I., 10.11.88 ; Lt. 23.4.90 ; Capt. 2.10.95 ; Bt. Major 22.8.02 ; Major 14.6.04 ; Lt.-Col. 1.9.14 ; Col. 1.9.18 ; T/Brig.-Gen. 20.10.15 ; served S. African War, 1899–1902 ; Despatches twice ; Bt. Major 22.8.02 ; Queen's Medal, 4 clasps ; King's Medal, 2 clasps ; Europ. War ; Despatches ; C.B. ; C.M.G.

WITTS, E. F. B. (D.S.O. L.G. 3.6.18), T/Major, Glouc. Rgt.

WITTS, F. H. (D.S.O. L.G. 3.6.19) ; b. 22.2.87 ; Lt., Irish Gds., 7.6.15 ; Capt. 19.8.16 ; Despatches ; M.C.

WITTS, F. V. B. (D.S.O. L.G. 25.8.17) ; b. 30.1.89 ; 2nd Lt., R.E., 23.7.07 ; Lt. 6.1.09 ; Capt. 30.10.14 ; Bt. Major 3.6.19 ; Despatches ; C.B.E. ; M.C.

WODEHOUSE, P. G. (D.S.O. L.G. 17.5.18) ; s. of late Rev. P. J. Wodehouse and 2nd wife, Marion Bryan, d. of Rev. G. J. Wallas ; b. 1883 ; m. Beaujolais Theresa Constance, d. of A. G. Ridout ; two d. ; Cdr., R.N. ; served Europ. War, 1914–18 ; Despatches ; Order of the Crown of Italy.

WOLFE-MURRAY, J. (see Murray, J. Wolfe-).

WOLFE-MURRAY, R. A. (D.S.O. L.G. 26.7.18) ; b. 2.6.89 ; 2nd Lt., S. Lan. R., 9.3.10 ; Lt. 4.9.12 ; Capt. 10.6.15 ; Bt. Major 3.6.18 ; M.C.

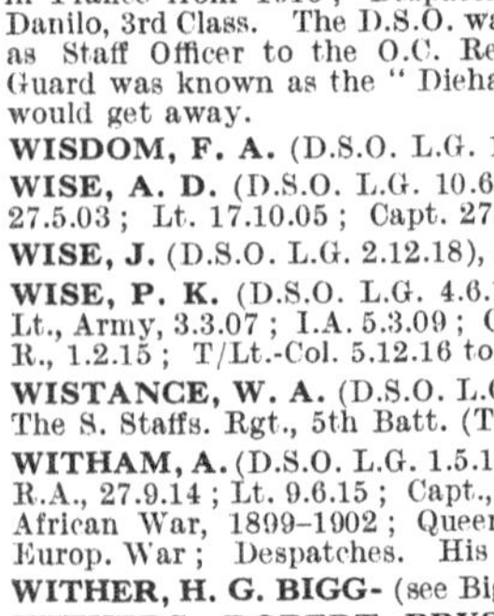

R. A. Wolfe-Murray.

WOLFF, A. J., F.R.G.S., F.R.A.S. (D.S.O. L.G. 2.2.16) ; b. 1.9.73 ; s. of A. H. Wolff and Jean Johnston Wolff (*née* Crawford) ; m. Norah Gladys, d. of Dr. Platt ; educ. Merchiston ; R.M.A., Woolwich ; 2nd Lt., R.E., 10.2.93 ; Lt. 10.2.96 ; Capt. 13.1.04 ; Major 10.2.13 ; Lt.-Col. 22.10.20 ; served S. African War, 1899–1902 ; Queen's Medal, 3 clasps ; King's Medal, 2 clasps ; Europ. War with 13th Div. in France, Gallipoli, Egypt and Mesopotamia ; Despatches thrice. His D.S.O. was awarded for landing at Gallipoli Peninsula 6.8.15 and following dates with 13th Division.

WOLLASTON, F. H. A. (D.S.O. L.G. 14.1.16) ; b. 7.5.79 ; s. of F. Wollaston ; educ. Eton ; 2nd Lt., Rif. Brig. (from Militia), 18.10.99 ; Lt. 24.10.00 ; Capt. 27.2.05. On the outbreak of the European War he was in India, and he joined his regiment in Belgium in March, 1915. At the end of the year he was transferred to the Salonika Army, where he served for eight months. Major Wollaston was mentioned in Despatches for his services on the Western front and awarded the D.S.O. ; was subsequently promoted to Lieutenant-Colonel commanding a battalion of the Suffolk Rgt. in Egypt, where he commanded his regiment in the Battle of Gaza and the subsequent advance in Palestine, and was a third time mentioned in Despatches. He was killed by a German bomb in the air raid on London 7.3.18, on his way back to Palestine the next day to resume command of his Regt. after three weeks' leave.

WOOD, C. B. (D.S.O. L.G. 25.8.17) ; b. 6.5.58 ; 1st com. 11.5.78 ; Major 19.2.96 ; retired Sc. Rifles 26.10.98 ; Lt.-Col., R. of O., 18.10.02 ; served S. African War, 1899–1900 ; Queen's Medal, 3 clasps ; promoted Lt.-Col., R. of O. ; Europ. War ; Despatches.

WOOD, C. J. F. (D.S.O. L.G. 3.6.18), Cdr., R.N., 30.6.18.

WOOD, C. M. A. (D.S.O. L.G. 4.6.17) ; b. 2.4.73 ; 2nd s. of late F.M. Sir Evelyn Wood, V.C., G.C.B., G.C.M.G. ; m. Olive Mary de Bathe, d. of Major H. Miles, late R.A. ; educ. Beaumont College ; abroad ; R.M.C., Sandhurst ; 2nd Lt., North'd Fus., 19.11.92 ; Lt. 15.5.96 ; Adjt., North'd Fus., 17.12.99–16.12.00 ; Capt. 17.2.00 ; Major 14.10.10 ; Bt. Lt.-Col. 1.4.15 ; Col. 1.4.19; employed Egyptian Army, 1894–95 ; served Nile Exp., 1898 ; Battle of Khartoum ; Despatches ; Medal ; 4th Class Medjidie ; Egyptian Medal and clasp; occupation of Crete, 1898 ; served S. African War, 1899–1900 ; Despatches; Queen's Medal with 3 clasps ; A.A.G., War Office, 1915–16 ; served Europ. War, 1914–18 ; Despatches ; Bt. Lt.-Col. ; C.M.G. ; Chevalier, Legion d'Honneur.

WOOD, E. (D.S.O. L.G. 4.6.17) ; b. 28.9.71 ; 2nd Lt., K.O.S.B., 2.6.94 ; 2nd Lt., A.S.C., 1.4.96 ; Lt. 1.4.97 ; Capt. 1.1.01 ; Major 9.6.11 ; Lt.-Col., R.A.S.C., 1.1.16 ; Despatches ; O.B.E. ; operations in Chitral, 1895 ; Medal, clasp ; S. African War, 1899–1902 ; Queen's Medal, 4 clasps ; King's Medal, 2 clasps.

WOOD, E. A. D.S.O. L.G. 1.1.17) (Bar, L.G. 26.9.17) (Details, L.G. 9.1.18) (2nd Bar, L.G. 16.9.18) (3rd Bar, L.G. 12.12.19), T/Lt.-Col. (T/Brig.-Gen.), Shrops. L.I. ; C.M.G.

WOOD, E. J. M. (D.S.O. L.G. 25.8.17) ; b. 5.2.67 ; Lt., E. Surrey Rgt., 25.8.86 ; I.S.C. 28.1.88 ; Capt., I.A., 25.8.97 ; Major 25.8.04 ; Lt.-Col. 25.8.12 ; T/Brig.-Gen. 21.5.18.

WOOD, H. G. W. (D.S.O. L.G. 24.9.18), Capt., Worc. R.

WOOD, H. R. (D.S.O. L.G. 4.6.17), T/Major (A/Lt.-Col.), Welsh R.

WOOD, J. (D.S.O. L.G. 1.1.18), T/Lt.-Col., R.A.M.C.

WOOD, J. B. (D.S.O. L.G. 26.7.18), T/Capt., G. Highrs. ; M.C.

WOOD, J. H. (D.S.O. L.G. 1.1.19), Major (A/Lt.-Col.), 2nd Field Amb., Can. A.M.C.

WOOD, L. (D.S.O. L.G. 4.6.17) ; b. 9.3.80 ; 2nd Lt., R.A., 22.12.14 ; Lt., R.F.A., 8.8.16 ; A/Major, R.A., from 25.9.16.

WOOD, M. D. (D.S.O. L.G. 2.2.16) ; b. 22.2.73 ; 2nd Lt., W. Yorks. Rgt., 21.10.93 ; Lt. 20.2.95 ; Capt. 24.11.00.

WOOD, W. F., M.B. (D.S.O. L.G. 18.6.17), Capt., R.A.M.C., S.R., att. Hussars. His D.S.O. was awarded for services on 11–14.4.17 at Monchy.

WOOD, W. S. (D.S.O. L.G. 16.8.17), Major, Can. Inf.

WOODCOCK, F. A. (D.S.O. L.G. 3.6.18), T/Capt. (A/Lt.-Col.), R.F.A.

WOODCOCK, J. B. H. (D.S.O. L.G. 3.6.19), Major, Pembroke Yeom., att. 24th Batt. Welsh Rgt., T.F.

WOODCOCK, W. J. (D.S.O. L.G. 1.1.18), Capt. (T/Lt.-Col.), Lan. Fus., S.R. ; Capt., R. of O., late Lanc. Fus.

WOODHEAD, B. M. (D.S.O. L.G. 22.8.18), Capt., 2nd. S. African Inf. (Duke of Edinburgh's Own Rifles).

WOODHOUSE, H. K. S. (D.S.O. L.G. 1.1.17), Capt. (T/Major), L'pool Rgt.

WOODHOUSE, J. D. F. (D.S.O. L.G. 11.1.19), Capt. (A/Major), 14th Hrs. ; b. 10.1.81 ; 2nd Lt., 14th Hussars, 11.2.03 ; Lt. 26.8.05 ; Capt. 6.4.08.

WOODHOUSE, J. W. (D.S.O. L.G. 17.9.17), T/Capt., R.F.C., Spec. Res. ; M.C.

WOODHOUSE, P. R., M.B. (D.S.O. L.G. 1.2.19), T/Capt. (A/Major), 9th Field Amb., R.A.M.C. ; M.C.

WOODLEY, R. N. (D.S.O. L.G. 1.1.17) ; b. 12.9.75 ; s. of late F. W. Woodley, J.P., D.L., and Jane Woodley (*née* Mason) ; educ. St. Fauthnan's College ; Lt., R.A.M.C., 29.1.01 ; Capt. 29.1.04 ; Major 29.10.12 ; Colonel ; served S. African War, 1900–2 ; Queen's Medal, 5 clasps ; Europ. War, 1915–18, France and Belgium ; A.D.M.S., 1st Cav. Div., B.E.F. ; Despatches twice.

WOODMAN, H. E. (D.S.O. L.G. 18.6.17) ; b. 21.9.93, at Gawler, S. Australia ; s. of Eustace Vincent and Charlotte Jane Woodman, of Dungog, N.S. Wales ; educ. Primary Central School, Broken Hill, N.S. Wales ; Prince Alfred College, Adelaide, S. Australia ; awarded Royal Humane Society's Medal for attempt to save life at Silverton, N.S. Wales, 1.1.07 ; awarded Gold Medal for Swimming Championship at Broken Hill, N.S. Wales ; awarded Gold Medal, best all-round athlete, Prince Alfred College, S. Australia ; joined Australian Military Forces as Private 17.8.14 ; Lt. 28.1.16 ; served overseas as Capt., 4th Batt. 1st Inf. Brig., A.I.F., 18.10.16 ; Major 5.7.18 ; Despatches thrice. His D.S.O. was awarded for gallantry at Boursies on 15.4.17. The following is extracted from a letter from General Birdwood : " I know what gallantry and skill you displayed in the defence of your position in the heavy German attack, and that your personal energy and determination were largely responsible for our success in holding that village. Your action, too, in counter-attacking a very large body of Germans, whom you held up until reinforcements arrived, was indeed valuable, ensuring, as it did, our holding on to the high ground overlooking Boursies."

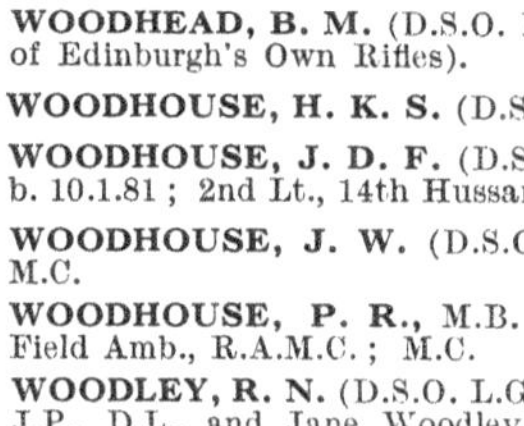

H. E. Woodman.

WOODRUFFE, J. S. (D.S.O. L.G. 16.9.18) ; b. 2.2.79 ; 2nd Lt., R. Sussex Rgt., 20.5.99 ; Lt. 12.6.00 ; Capt. 14.6.08 ; Major 1.9.15 ; served S. African War, 1900–2 ; slightly wounded ; Queen's Medal, 2 clasps ; King's Medal, 2 clasps ; Europ. War ; Despatches ; O.B.E.

WOODS, A. G. (D.S.O. L.G. 1.1.19), T/Capt., 2nd Brig. Tank Corps ; M.C.

WOODS, A. R. W. (D.S.O. L.G. 15.9.16) (Bar, L.G. 11.8.17), Capt., R.N. 30.6.19.

WOODS, REV. A. W. (D.S.O. L.G. 1.1.18), Can. Chaplains' Service.

WOODS, B. J. G. (D.S.O. L.G. 14.1.16); b. 1872; s. of Major H. B. Woods, late R.M.L.I., and Annie, d. of late Major-Gen. J. Pickard, R.M.L.I.; m. Lilian Rose, d. of late Staff Surgeon T. Conry, R.N.; educ. Mannamead School, Plymouth; 2nd Lt., Worc. R., 21.4.00; Lt. 2.1.01; 2nd Lt., A.S.C., 1.5.01; Lt., A.S.C., 1.5.02; Capt. 1.2.05; Major, R.A.S.C., 30.10.14; served Natal Mounted Police, 1891–94; S. Africa, 1901–2; Queen's Medal, 4 clasps; Europ. War, 1914–18; Despatches.

B. J. G. Woods.

WOODS, H. K. (D.S.O. L.G. 15.2.19) (Details, L.G. 30.7.19); b. 5.9.77; 2nd Lt., S. Lanc. R., 16.3.98; Lt. 11.11.99; Capt. 4.6.04; Major 14.9.14; Bt. Lt.-Col. 1.1.16; Lt.-Col., Tank Corps, 1.8.19; T/Brig.-Gen. 2.11.18 to 22.9.19; served S. African War, 1899–1902; Despatches; Queen's Medal, 5 clasps; King's Medal, 2 clasps; Europ. War; Despatches.

WOODS, J. P. S. (D.S.O. L.G. 22.8.18), Lt.-Col. (Active Citizen Force), 2nd Mounted Rifles (Natal Carbineers).

WOODS, M. (D.S.O. L.G. 1.1.17), Capt. T/Major), S. Lanc. R.

WOODS, P. J. (D.S.O. L.G. 1.1.17); b. 23.9.80; s. of late H. Woods and Emily Catherine Woods (*née* Puleston), g.d. of Sir J. Puleston; m. Florence Edith, d. of S. Blacker-Quin; one d.; educ. R. Academical Institution, Belfast; Belfast School of Art; Lt., 9th (W. Belfast) R. Irish Rifles; Capt., Nov. 1914; Major, Sept. 1915; 2nd-in-command, Dec. 1915; Lt.-Col., Jan. 1917; Colonel, 1919; served S. African War, in Baden Powell's Force, S. African Constabulary; Europ. War, Battle of Somme, July, 1916; commanded 19th Res. Batt. R. Irish Rifles, Jan. to June, 1918; volunteered for N. Russia; landed there June, 1918; transferred to Gen. List; formed, organized and led the Koralian Rgt. against Germans and White Finns in Koralia, Aug. 1918 (C.M.G.); commanding the Koralian Rgt. and Allied Forces, Kem and Koralia, N. Russia, till evacuated 3.10.19; appointed to G.S. Lithuanian Army, as Inspector of Forces, Kovno District, Nov. 1919.

WOODS, P. W. (D.S.O. L.G. 1.1.18) (Bar, L.G. 1.2.19), Lt.-Col., Aust. Inf.; M.C.

WOODS, W. T. (D.S.O. L.G. 1.1.18), Capt., Manch. R.; M.C.

WOODSIDE, W. A. (D.S.O. L.G. 25.8.17); b. 26.7.71; Lt., R.A.M.C., 27.7.99; Capt. 27.7.02; Major 27.7.11; Lt.-Col. 1.3.15; served S. African War, 1900–2; Despatches; Queen's Medal, 4 clasps; King's Medal, 2 clasps; Europ. War; Despatches.

WOODWARD, H. J. (D.S.O. L.G. 23.5.17) (Bar, L.G. 22.1.20), Lt.-Cdr., R.N., 31.8.15.

WOODWARD, L. C. (D.S.O. L.G. 18.2.18) (Details, L.G. 18.7.18); s. of G. M. Woodward; m. Annie Hind; educ. Nottingham High School; ent. Notts. R.H.A.; volunteered and served in the European War as T/Major, R.F.A.; Despatches twice. He died of wounds 3.9.18.

WOODWARD, W. E. (D.S.O. L.G. 6.4.18), Capt., R.N., 31.12.16.

WOOLCOCK, A. R. (D.S.O. L.G. 1.1.18), Lt.-Col., Aust. Infy.

WOOLLETT, H. W. (D.S.O. L.G. 16.9.18), T/Capt., Gen. List., att. R.A.F.; M.C.

WOOLMARENS, J. F. (D.S.O. L.G. 22.8.18), Capt. (T/Major), 4th Permanent Battery (S.A.M.R.).

WOOLMER, E. (D.S.O. L.G. 3.6.18), Major, Lan. Fus.; M.C.

WOON, E. W. (D.S.O. L.G. 13.2.17), Major, S. African Infantry.

WOOSTER, F. C. (D.S.O. L.G. 3.6.19), Lt.-Col., 13th Field Amb., Aust. A.M.C.

WOOTTEN, G. F. (D.S.O. L.G. 4.6.17); b. Sydney, N.S.W., 1.5.93; s. of W. F. Wootten and L. Wootten (*née* Old); m. Muriel, d. of J. Kirwan Bisgood, of Roehampton; one s.; ent. R.M. College of Australia, Duntroon, June, 1911; graduated Aug. 1914; Lieutenant, posted to 1st Batt.; did duty as Acting Adjt.; then posted as Machine Gun Officer; embarked 18.10.14 at Sydney; disembarked Egypt 10.12.14; embarked at Alexandria, April, 1915; Gallipoli Peninsula 25 April (landing) to night 19–20.12.15; one of "C" Party (last to leave) in evacuation; promoted Captain, May, 1915, and made Adjt., 1st Batt., A.I.F.; later Brigade Machine Gun Officer, 1st Inf. Brig.; then commanded "D" Company, 1st Batt.; transferred to 3rd Batt., A.I.F., 10.12.15; 2nd-in-command to assist in evacuation; Staff Captain, 8th Aust. Inf. Brig., Feb. 1916, and proceeded to France; G.S.O.3, 3rd Aust. Div. (Gen. Monash's Staff), July, 1916; Brig. Major, 9th A.I. Brig., Sept. 1917; Passchendaele, Oct.; G.S.O.2, 5th Aust. Div., Dec. 1917; Villers Bretonneux and offensive, Aug. to Oct.; Amiens, through Hindenburg Line, 1918; Staff College, Camberley, March to Dec. 1920; *p.s.c.*; returned to Australia, March, 1920; Despatches five times; Bt. of Major; Major, Aust. Mil. Forces, Feb. 1916.

WOOTTEN, H. E. (D.S.O. L.G. 4.6.17), T/Lt.-Col., Border Rgt.

WORDSWORTH, R. J. (D.S.O. L.G. 1.1.18), Major, Notts. and Derby. R.

WORGAN, R. B. (D.S.O. L.G. 1.1.17); b. 4.3.81 at Arah, Bengal; 5th s. of John Berney and Bertha Elizabeth Worgan; educ. Bedford School; Sandhurst; 2nd Lt., A.S.C., 21.2.00; Lt. 1.4.01; served S. African War, 1900–2; Queen's Medal, 2 clasps; King's Medal, 2 clasps; transferred to Indian Army 17.10.05, and joined the 20th Deccan Horse; became A.D.C. to Sir Arthur Lawley, Governor of Madras, 1907–8; Capt. 1.2.09; under orders of Lord Carmichael, of Skirling, raised and commanded the Body Guard of the 1st Governor of Bengal, 1912–13; Major, I.A., 1.9.15; Lt.-Col. 4.4.21; T/Brig.-Gen. 2.10.17 to 2.9.18; served Europ. War from 1914; commanded the 9th (S.) Bn. The Cheshire Regt.; commanded the 173rd Inf. Brigade, 1917–18; recalled to India in Aug. 1918, and commanded the Mounted Troops, Aden, 1919; commanded 62nd Inf. Bde. during Afghan War and Waziristan Campaign, 1919–20; appointed Military Secretary to H.R.H. the Prince of Wales for his tour in India in winter, 1920–21; on cancellation of tour appointed Military Secretary to H.R.H. the Duke of Connaught during his tour in India in winter, 1920–21; Bt. Major 3.6.16; Brevet Lt.-Col. 1.1.18. He has the C.V.O.

WORRALL, P. R. (D.S.O. L.G. 1.1.18); b. 2.5.80; s. of late W. H. Worrall; m. Agnes M. M., d. of Sir P. Mostyn, Bart.; four s.; two d.; educ. Haileybury; 2nd Lt., Devon Rgt., 4.12.01; Lt. 14.12.04; Capt. 28.10.14; Major 4.12.16; served S. Africa, 1902; Queen's Medal and four clasps; Europ. War, in France, Gallipoli and Italy, 1914–18; Despatches; Bt. Lt.-Col. 1.1.19; M.C.

WORRALL, R. (D.S.O. L.G. 11.1.19) (Bar, L.G 1.2.19), Lt.-Col., 14th Batt. Can. Inf., Quebec R.; M.C.

WORRALL, S. H. (D.S.O. L.G. 1.1.18); b. 20.12.81; 1st com., 2nd Lt., Border, R., 11.8.00; Lt. 27.8.02; Capt. 22.1.12; Major 1.9.15; retired Border Regt. 1.4.19, with rank of Lt.-Col., Army; S. African War, 1900–2; Queen's Medal, 5 clasps; Europ. War; Despatches.

WORSLEY, F. A. (D.S.O. L.G. 17.11.17) (Details, L.G. 22.3.18) (Bar, L.G. 17.10.19); b. 1872; s. of H. T. Worsley; educ. Fendalton High School, N.Z.; Capt. of S.Y. Endurance in Shackleton's South Pole Expedition; navigated Shackleton's boat from Elephant Island to S. Georgia; Chief Navigator in the Quest, 1921; Commander, R.N.R., R.D.; served Europ. War from 1916; commanded two mystery ships, one gunboat, H.M.S. Cricket, one monitor (No. 24); Despatches; Director of Arctic Equipment and Transport, Archangel Front, N. Russia.

WORSLEY, F. P. (D.S.O. L.G. 4.6.17) (Bar, L.G. 17.12.17) (Details, L.G. 23.4.18); b. 23.8.74; 2nd Lt., W. Yorks. Rgt., 20.2.95; Lt. 8.12.87; Capt. 10.1.02; retired W. Yorks. Rgt. 5.3.10; served N.W. Frontier of India, 1908; operations in the Mohmand country; Europ. War; Despatches; Bt. Major, R. of O., 1.1.16; Lt.-Col., Army, 31.10.16.

F. P. Worsley.

WORSLEY, H. B. (D.S.O. L.G. 17.5.18), Lt.-Cdr., R.N., 31.12.12.

WORSLEY, R. H. W. (D.S.O. L.G. 15.2.17); b. 1.11.86; 2nd Lt., K.O.S.B., 27.9.05; Lt. 16.10.07; Capt. 1.9.14.

WORSLEY, R. S. (D.S.O. L.G. 2.5.16); b. 7.9.79; s. of Major-Gen. Richard Worsley, I.A. and Ethel Meaborn Worsley; educ. Wellington Coll. and Sandhurst; 2nd Lt., A.S.C., 21.2.00; Lt. 1.4.01; Capt. 9.7.04; Major 7.10.14; Lt.-Col.; served S. African War, 1900–2; Queen's Medal, 3 clasps; King's Medal, 2 clasps. In 1913 att. Egyptian Army; served Europ. War from 1914; Despatches; early in 1915 he landed with the Exp. Force in Gallipoli, where he served till the following September; also took part in Exp. to Darfur; Despatches three times; Bt. Lt.-Col. and thanks of the Sirdar. He was drowned 4.5.17.

WORSLEY, S. J. (D.S.O. L.G. 1.2.19), Capt. 4th Batt. N. Staffs R.; M.C.

WORSNOP, C. B. (D.S.O. L.G. 10.1.17), Major, Can. Inf. His D.S.O. was awarded for gallantry on 10.11.16, at Courcelette.

WORTHAM, H. C. W. H. (D.S.O. L.G. 3.6.18); b. 28.3.78; 2nd Lt., R. Irish Fus., 20.5.99; Lt. 24.2.00; Capt. 10.9.06; Adjt., R. Irish Fus., 18.1.12 to 17.1.15; Major 1.9.15; Bt. Lt.-Col. 1.1.17; Lt.-Col. 14.3.21; served S. African War, 1899–1902; Queen's Medal, 3 clasps; King's Medal, 2 clasps; Europ. War; Despatches; C.M.G.

WORTHINGTON, C. S. (D.S.O. L.G. 2.2.16) (Bar, L.G. 2.4.19) (Details, L.G. 10.12.19) (Major, Manch. R., T.F. See Amendment, L.G. 21.2.16), Lt.-Col., 6th Batt. Manch. R., T.F., att. 5th Batt. Dorsets. R.

WORTHINGTON, F., M.B. (D.S.O. L.G. 14.1.16) (Bar, L.G. 1.1.18); b. 15.6.80: Lt., R.A.M.C., 4.2.08; Capt. 4.8.11; Major 4.2.20; M.C.; O.B.E.

WORTHINGTON-WILMER, G. R. (D.S.O. L.G. 1.1.17), Major, Scottish Rifles, empl. Egyptian Army.

WOULFE-FLANAGAN, E. M. (D.S.O. L.G. 1.1.17); b. 4.11.70: 2nd Lt., E. Surrey Rgt., 8.9.00; Lt. 18.7.02; Capt. 4.8.09; Major 1.9.15; served S. African War, 1899–1902; Queen's Medal, 6 clasps; Europ. War, from 1914; Despatches; C.M.G.; Legion of Honour.

WOULFE-FLANAGAN, R. J. (D.S.O. L.G. 26.5.19); b. 24.8.68; 2nd Lt., R.W. Kent Rgt., 26.6.89; Lt. 23.12.92; Capt. 28.1.99; Major 4.3.08; Lt.-Col. 14.3.16; Bt. Col. 1.1.19; Col. 14.3.20; served S. African War. 1900–2; Despatches; Queen's Medal, 3 clasps; King's Medal, 2 clasps.

WRAITH, E. A. (D.S.O. L.G. 4.6.17), Lt.-Col., 1st N. Midland Field Amb., R.A.M.C.; served S. African War, 1900–1, as Civil Surgeon; Europ. War; Despatches.

WRATHALL, W. P. (D.S.O. L.G. 16.9.18), Capt. R. Highrs.; M.C.

WRAY, E. M. G. (D.S.O. L.G. 26.3.18) (Details, L.G. 24.8.18); b. 16.6.94; 2nd Lt., Essex R.; Lt. (from T.F.), Middx. R., 27.8.19.

WRAY, F. (D.S.O. L.G. 14.3.16); b. 25.9.73; s. of late G. O. Wray, LL.D., Vicar of Brockenhurst, Hants; educ. Bedford School; R.N. School, New Cross; passed into Britannia, 1886; promoted Lieut., 1894; promoted Commander, 1904; Capt., 1911; Flag Commander to Lord Charles Beresford, 1905–8; commanded H.M.S. Foresight, 1909–10; commanded H.M.S. Defence, 1913–14; H.M.S. Talbot, 1915; H.M.S. Drake, 1916–17; H.M.S. Berwick and Cæsar, 1918. His D.S.O. was awarded for services in command of Talbot in Gallipoli operations.

WRAY, H. C. (D.S.O. L.G. 4.6.17); b. 11.12.78; s. of C. H. Wray, J.P.; m. Vessie, d. of late J. A. Philipson; one s.; one d.; educ. Haileybury; Christ Church, Oxford; joined R.F.A. 26.5.00; Lt. 31.3.02; Captain 1.4.11; Major 30.10.14; T/Lt.-Col., 1918; ret. pay, 1921; Major, 6th (N. Midland) Brig., since 1921; served Europ. War, in France for three years; Despatches twice; retired pay, 1921

WRIGHT, A. (D.S.O. L.G. 8.3.19) (Details, L.G. 4.10.19), Lt. (A/Capt.), 2/2nd Batt. London R.; M.C.

WRIGHT, A. E. H. (D.S.O. L.G. 8.3.20), Lt.-Cdr., R.N.

WRIGHT, A. J. (D.S.O. L.G. 3.6.19), Lt. (T/Capt.), 1/4th Batt. Northants R., T.F.; M.C.

WRIGHT, A. R., M.B. (D.S.O. L.G. 1.1.18); b. 25.2.81; Lt., R.A.M.C., 1.8.08; Capt. 1.2.12; Major 1.8.20; Bt. Lt.-Col. 1.8.20.

WRIGHT, C. V. R. (D.S.O. L.G. 3.6.18); b. 7.3.64; 1st commission 7.2.85; Major 2.12.05; retired S.W.B. 6.3.12; Lt.-C 30.4.16; served Expedition Tamaku Country, W. Africa, 1892; Medal with clasp; West Africa, 1897–99; Gold Coast clasp; Europ. War; Despatches.

WRIGHT, E. T. L. (D.S.O. L.G. 3.6.18); b. 13.7.80; 2nd Lt., 14th Hussars, 12.8.99; retired as Captain; served Europ. War as T/Major (A/Lt.Col.), A.S.C. (now R.A.S.C.).

WRIGHT, G. J. HORNSBY- (see Hornsby-Wright, G. J.).

WRIGHT, G. M. H. (D.S.O. L.G. 3.6.18); b. 17.1.86; 2nd Lt., R. Irish Fusiliers, 16.1.07; Lt. 12.2.09; Capt. 14.9.14; Bt. Major 3.6.19; M.C.

WRIGHT, H. H. (D.S.O. L.G. 1.1.18); b. 17.9.83; 2nd Lt., R. Irish Rgt., 4.6.04; A.S.C. 2.4.06; Lt., A.S.C., 4.6.07; Capt. 5.8.14; Major, R.A.S.C., 15.12.18.

WRIGHT, H. L. (D.S.O. L.G. 4.6.17); b. 12.12.82; 2nd Lt., R.E., 2.4.02; Lt. 14.3.05; Capt. 2.8.13; Major 2.8.17; R. Corps of Signals 24.11.20.

WRIGHT, N. I. (D.S.O. L.G. 4.6.17), Capt. (T/Lt.-Col.), North'd Fus.

WRIGHT, P. L. (D.S.O. L.G. 3.6.19), Capt., Oxf. and Bucks L.I.; M.C.

WRIGHT, R. (D.S.O. L.G. 25.11.16), T/Capt., The King's Own Yorks. L.I. He died of wounds 17.8.17.

WRIGHT, R. P., M.D., C.M. (D.S.O. L.G. 1.1.17); b. Montreal, 5.10.82; s. of J. A. Wright; m. Helen Frances Murphy; educ. Montreal High School; McGill University; Specialist to the G.S.C., Drummond Street Hospital,

Montreal; qualified commission in C.A.M.C. (Militia), 1908; T/Major, 1914; Major, 1st Can. Field Amb., B.E.F.; O.C., 1st Can. Field Amb., France; Lt.-Col., Sept. 1915; Col. 22.7.17; Despatches twice; C.M.G.; French Croix de Guerre (Argent).

WRIGHT, S. C. (D.S.O. L.G. 3.6.18), Capt. (A/Major), R.F.A.

WRIGHT, T. J. (D.S.O. L.G. 4.6.17); b. 24.6.80; Lt., R.A.M.C., 31.8.03; Capt. 28.2.07; Major 28.2.15.

WRIGHT, W. (D.S.O. L.G. 3.6.18), Capt. (T. Major), R.A.F.

WRIGHT, W. D. (D.S.O. L.G. 1.1.18), Bt. Col., R.W. Surrey Rgt.; V.C.; C.M.G.; M.C. (see "The Victoria Cross," by same publishers).

WRIGHT, W. G., L.R.C.P.I. and L.M., L.R.C.S.I. and L.M. (D.S.O. L.G. 1.1.17); b. 1883; s. of W. M. A. Wright; m. Phyllis May, d. of Maj.-Gen. A. A. Sutton; educ. R. College of Surgeons of Ireland; Major, R.A.M.C.; served Europ. War, 1914–17; Despatches; Bt. Major; Croix de Guerre.

WRIGHT, W. O. (D.S.O. L.G. 1.1.18), Major, R. Lanc. R.

WRIGHT, W. R. TYLDEN- (see Tylden-Wright, W. R.).

WRIGHTON, E. (D.S.O. L.G. 2.4.19) (Details, L.G. 10.12.19), Lt., 4th Batt. North'd Fus., T.F., att. 10th Batt.

WRIGHTSON, E. G. (D.S.O. L.G. 22.2.18); b. 25.8.79; s. of Professor J. Wrightson, Principal, College of Agriculture, Downton, Salisbury, and Maria Isabel Wrightson (*née* Hulton); m. Rose Frances, d. of E. Y. Western; one s.; one d.; educ. Littlejohn's; H.M.S. Worcester; served in Mercantile Marine until 1910; floated Manchu S.S. Co., 1911, and traded in China, 1915–19; H.M. Navy as Lt.-Cdr., R.N.R.; Commander, H.M.Y. Zaza and H.M. Special Service Ship Merops.

WROTTESLEY, F. R. (D.S.O. L.G. 17.7.19), Cdr., R.N.

WROUGHTON, A. O. B. (D.S.O. L.G. 1.1.18); b. 29.10.72; Lt., R.A.M.C., 28.1.99; Capt. 28.1.02; Major 28.10.10; Lt.-Col. 1.3.15; served S. African War, 1899–1902; Queen's Medal, 6 clasps; King's Medal, 2 clasps; Europ. War; Despatches.

WYATT, E. R. C. (D.S.O. L.G. 1.1.17); b. 27.4.80; s. of Rev. J. L. Wyatt, M.A., and E. I. Wyatt, d. of late Bishop Caldwell, of Tinnevelly, India; m. Barbara Elizabeth, d. of Rev. A. W. Booker; one d.; educ. Cheltenham; Sandhurst; 2nd Lt., Unatt., 25.1.98; I.S.C. 15.4.00; Lt., I.A., 25.4.01; Capt. 25.1.08; Major 1.9.15 (106th Hazara Pioneers); Bt. Lt.-Col. 22.3.22; served Somaliland, 1902–4; Europ. War, 1914–17; Despatches thrice.

WYATT, G. N. (D.S.O. L.G. 11.4.18); b. 11.10.77; 2nd Lt., R.A., 23.3.97; Lt. 23.3.00; Capt. 4.2.04; Major 10.10.14; Lt.-Col. 4.10.17; Tirah, 1897–98; operations in the Bara Valley 7–14.12.97; Medal, 2 clasps; Europ. War; Despatches.

WYATT, L. J. (D.S.O. L.G. 3.6.16); b. 14.9.74; s. of J. M. G. Wyatt; m. Marion Jessie, d. of W. Sloane; two d.; educ. King's College, London; 2nd Lt., Prince of Wales's N. Staffs. R., Dec. 1895; Lt. 27.11.97; Capt., May, 1901; Major 6.3.12; Bt. Lt.-Col. 3.6.17; Bt. Colonel 1.1.21; served Dongola Exp., 1896; Medals; S. African War, 1900–2; Despatches; Medals; Europ. War, 1914–18; Despatches; Chevalier, Legion d'Honneur; Lt.-Col., 1/4th Yorks. and Lancs. R., 1915–17; T/Brig.-Gen., 1918.

WYLD, H. W. (D.S.O. L.G. 14.3.16); b. 4.6.82; s. of Rev. C. N. Wyld, of Salisbury; m. Eleanor, d. of Ven. Archdeacon Carpenter, of The Close, Salisbury; two s.; educ. Holyrood House, Bognor; Britannia; Commander, R.N., 30.6.19; Midshipman, Majestic, 1898; Illustrious, 1899–1901; Sub-Lt., Zebra, 1902–3, and then Royal Sovereign; Lt., 1904; served H.M.S. Pomone and Proserpine in E. Indies during Somali Campaign; H.M.S. Hindustan, 1907–9; in command successively of H.M. Torpedo Boat 35, H.M.S. Nith, Afridi, Pincher; served during whole of Gallipoli Campaign, including sweeping inside Dardanelles during landing, and subsequently flanking duties at Anzac; Nereide, 1916–19, Adriatic and Black Sea.

WYLD, J. W. G. (D.S.O. L.G. 1.1.18); b. 6.1.96; 2nd Lt., Oxf. and Bucks. L.I., 15.8.14; Lt. 10.6.15; Capt. 1.1.17; Bt. Major 11.11.19; M.C.

WYLIE, J. P., B.A. (D.S.O. L.G. 17.4.17); b. 20.5.88; s. of Rt. Hon. Mr. Justice Wylie, P.C., and Mrs. Wylie (*née* Price), of The Elms, Blackrock, Co. Dublin; m. Barbara, d. of Capt. and Mrs. Jeffrey Clark; one s.; educ. Private School; Trinity College, Dublin; 2nd Lt., Unatt., 8.9.09; I.A. 1.11.11; Lt., I.A., 8.12.11; Notts. and Derby. Rgt. 28.3.14; Capt. 12.4.16; A/Major 25.12.16; served Europ. War, 1914–15, France; wounded twice, 1915; Dardanelles, 1916; Egypt, 1916–17; France, wounded slightly and gassed, 1917; Egypt (Palestine); Varsity Junior Eight (Rowing), Trin. Coll., Dublin, 1907; Varsity Golf Team, Trin. Coll., Dublin, 1906.

WYLIE, J. S. (D.S.O. L.G. 22.8.18), Lt.-Col. (T/Col.), 4th Inf. Brig. (1st Inf. S. African Mil. Forces; M.V.O., V.D.

WYLLY, G. G. E. (D.S.O. L.G. 1.1.18), Major, Q.V.O. Corps of Guides, I.A.; V.C. (see "The Victoria Cross," by same publishers).

WYMAN, R. (D.S.O. L.G. 3.6.16), Major, Auckland Mounted Rifle Rgt., N.Z. Mil. Forces.

WYNFORD (P. G.), LORD (D.S.O. L.G. 4.6.17); b. 27.8.71; s. of 5th Baron and Edith Anne, d. of M. H. Marsh, of Ramridge, Andover, Hants; m. Hon. Eva Lilian Napier, only child of 2nd Baron Napier, of Magdala; three d.; 1st com. 14.2.90; Capt., retired R.H.A., 21.4.06; Major, R. of O., 3.10.14; Lt.-Col., Army, 26.3.19; served Europ. War, 1914–18.

WYNNE, F. G. (D.S.O. L.G. 26.9.16); b. 7.11.85; 2nd Lt. (from Militia), L.N. Lancs. Rgt., 20.7.07; Lt. 5.10.10; Adjt., 8th Batt. L.N. Lancs. Rgt., 18.9.14; Major, L.N. Lancs. Rgt., att. 1st Wilts. Rgt. He was killed in action on 10.4.18. Major Wynne's D.S.O. was awarded for gallantry at Ovillers on 10.7.16.

F. G. Wynne.

WYNNE, H. E. S. (D.S.O. L.G. 14.1.16); b. 4.1.77; s. of Bt. Major W. R. C. Wynne, R.E.; m. Katherine Hart, d. of Rev. D. W. Kennedy; one s.; one d.; educ. Uppingham; R.M.A.; 2nd Lt., R.A., 21.9.96; Lt. 21.9.99; Capt. 1.2.02; Major 12.9.13; Lt.-Col. 11.6.17; served with 62nd Battery, R.F.A., S. African War, 1899–1901; dangerously wounded; Despatches; Queen's Medal, 5 clasps; on mobilization, Aug. 1914, became Brigade Major, Highland Divisional Artillery, T.F.; went to France with 51st (Highland) Division, April, 1915; transferred to command 62nd Brigade, R.F.A., in March, 1916; Despatches; C.M.G.

WYNNE, R. O. (D.S.O. L.G. 1.1.17) (Bar, L.G. 16.9.18); b. 12.6.92, at Moss Vale, N.S.W. Australia; s. of the late H. J. Wynne and of Cecil Marion Wynne (afterwards Mrs. Matthews); educ. Marlborough College (Shooting Eight, 1907–10); Clare College, Cambridge (rowed in the College 1st Lent and May boats, 1913–14); 2nd Lt., 3rd (Spec. Res.) Batt. Bedfords. Rgt., 15.8.14; Lt.-Col., late 2nd Bedfords. Rgt.; served in France and Flanders for four years. His D.S.O. was awarded for fighting in Trônes Wood 11 and 12 July, and at Maltz Horn Ridge, near Guillemont, by the Somme, 30 July, 1916; was at Second Battle of Ypres, Loos, the Somme, Arras, Third Battle of Ypres, 1917, and in the fighting during the German offensive near St. Quentin, 21–28.3.18, when he won the Bar to his D.S.O. whilst A/Major in command of his Batt. He also fought at Ypres during the German offensive of April and May, 1918, and in the British offensive round about Le Cateau in Oct. and Nov. 1918.

WYNNE-EDWARDS, R. M. (D.S.O. L.G. 11.1.19), T/Capt., 13th Batt. R.W.F.; M.C.; Bar.

WYNNE-EYTON, C. S. (D.S.O. L.G. 1.1.18), T/Major, Gen. List, and R.F.C.

WYNTER, C. P. (D.S.O. L.G. 12.2.20); b. 12.7.69; 2nd Lt., Suffolk Rgt., 17.1.91; Lt., I.S.C., 19.9.93; Capt., I.A., 10.7.01; Major 17.1.09; Lt.-Col., 52nd Sikhs, 24.5.16.

WYNTER, G. C. (surname gazetted as Winter) (D.S.O. L.G. 8.3.20), Cdr., R.N., 30.6.18; O.B.E.

WYNTER, H. D. (D.S.O. L.G. 3.6.18), Lt.-Col., Aust. Gen. List.

WYNTER, J. R. (D.S.O. L.G. 31.5.16); b. 6.10.85; s. of Col. W. Wynter (son of Rev. P. Wynter, D.D., of Oxford University) and Anne, d. of H. Rawson; educ. Wellington College; R.M.C., Sandhurst; gazetted as 2nd Lt. to Unatt. List, I.A., 5.8.05; I.A. 6.12.06; appointed to 52nd Sikhs, F.F.; Lt. 5.11.07; Capt. 5.8.14; Major, 1920; served with 59th Rifles, F.F., in France, Jan.–Dec. 1915; in Mesopotamia, Jan.–Mar. 1916; wounded; Despatches. His D.S.O. was awarded for gallantry on 8.3.16, at Dijaileh Redoubt.

YALLAND, R. R. (D.S.O. L.G. 3.6.18); b. 2.2.86; 2nd Lt., Leic. R., 16.1.07; Lt. 13.11.08; Capt. 1.11.13.

YARDLEY, J. H. R. (D.S.O. L.G. 23.11.16), Capt., R. Inniskilling Fusiliers, S.R.; served S. African War, 1902; Europ. War; Despatches.

YARDLEY, J. W., B.A. (D.S.O. L.G. 3.6.16); b. 17.7.58; s. of the late J. Yardley, of Chesterfield Lodge, Staffs; educ. Repton; Trinity College, Cambridge; R.M.C., Sandhurst; 2nd Lt., 6th Inniskilling Dragoons, 10.5.82; Capt. 26.10.87; retired 2.8.99; Lt.-Col., R. of O., 18.10.02. He served in the Bechuanaland Expedition, 1884–85; in Zululand, 1888; was A.D.C. to the Governor of Natal, 1887–90. When the Inniskilling Dragoons went to S. Africa Capt. Yardley rejoined the Regiment from a shooting expedition in India, commanding A Squadron from 13.4.00 until 16 Oct. following, when he was wounded. On the night of 11 May Capt. Yardley commanded the escort when Major Hunter Weston attempted a raid on the railway communication, north of Kroonstadt. On 19 May Capt. Yardley took A Squadron with orders to reconnoitre the railway to Honing Spruit and report on its condition. This he accomplished after a good deal of fighting. When, during the advance on Johannesburg the Inniskillings seized Elandsfontein, Major (now Lord) Allenby and Capt. Yardley narrowly escaped being killed by one of our own shells. After he was wounded Captain Yardley wrote "With the Inniskilling Dragoons in South Africa," a book to which Major F. R. Burnham, the celebrated American Scout, referred when giving details of his own career for this work. Lieut.-Colonel Yardley served in the European War as D.D. Remounts with Cavalry Corps, 4th and 5th Armies; was mentioned in Despatches, and created a C.M.G. in 1918; subsequently he was District Remount Officer, Gloucestershire. A member of the National Hunt Committee, he was Sporting Editor of the Cavalry Journal; a well-known cross-country rider, polo player, and rider to hounds. He died on 28.11.20, greatly regretted by his countless friends.

J. W. Yardley.

YATES, C. McG. (D.S.O. L.G. 1.1.18); b. 27.12.81; 2nd Lt., R.A., 15.5.01; Lt. 4.3.04; Capt. 15.5.14; Major 9.5.16.

YATES, F. B. (D.S.O. L.G. 11.11.19), Eng.-Lt. (A/Eng.-Lt.-Cdr.), R.N.

YATES, H. P. (D.S.O. L.G. 23.11.16); b. 6.10.74; s. of Gen. H. P. Yates, C.B., late R.A.; m. Gertrude, d. of late Gen. H. A. Sarel, late 9th and 17th Lancers; two s.; educ. Newton College, S. Devon; 2nd Lt., S. Wales Bord., 9.12.96; Lt. 25.6.98; Capt. 19.6.07; Maj. 1.9.15; proceeded to Gallipoli as Adjt., 4th S.W.B.; promoted T/Lt.-Col., 6th King's Own Rgt., in 1915; proceeded to Mesopotamia; Bt. Lt.-Colonel 3.6.16; Order of St. Anne, 3rd Class.

YATES, J. A. (D.S.O. L.G. 26.8.18); b. 4.11.83; s. of Col. H. T. S. Yates, late R.A.; m. Ada Margaret, d. of J. L. Lushington; three s.; 2nd Lt., Leic. R., 3.9.02; Lt., Ind. Army, 9.10.07; Capt. 21.12.10; Maj., 103rd Mahrattas, 21.12.16; served S. African War, 1900–2; Queen's Medal and 3 clasps; Europ. War (Mesopotamia), 1915–18; C.I.E.

YATES, R. (D.S.O. L.G. 3.6.19), T/Capt. (A/Major), 183rd Tunnelling Co., R.E.; M.C.

YATES, R. J. B. (D.S.O. L.G. 1.1.18); b. 4.3.83; 2nd Lt., N. Lanc. R., 8.5.01; Lt. 26.4.04; Capt., Ind. Army, 8.5.10; Maj. 8.5.16.

YATES, W. T. (D.S.O. L.G. 18.7.17), Capt., Aust. Infy.

YATMAN, A. H. (D.S.O. L.G. 1.1.19); b. 1.7.74; 2nd Lt., Som. L.I., 6.3.95; Lt. 10.8.98; Capt. 16.7.03; Maj. 27.11.14; Bt. Lt.-Col. 1.1.17; Lt.-Col. 8.7.20; S. African War, 1899–1902; Queen's Medal, 5 clasps; King's Medal, 2 clasps; Europ. War; Despatches.

YEATS-BROWN, A. M. (D.S.O. L.G. 23.5.17), Cdr., R.N., 30.6.10.

YEHYA, MOHAMMED BEY SADEK (D.S.O. L.G. 4.9.18), El Mir (Colonel), Egyptian Army.

YEOMANS, J. C. (D.S.O. L.G. 8.3.19) (Details, L.G. 4.10.19); s. of late A. Yeomans, of Gilgoin, N.S. Wales; m. Norma, d. of C. J. Dillon, of Murrumbarra, N.S.W.; educ. Sydney Grammar School; Lt., 30th Batt., A.I.F.; served Europ. War, 1916–18.

YONGE, P. C. (D.S.O. L.G. 3.6.18); b. 29.5.77; s. of Rev. D. N. Yonge; m. Doris Evelyn, d. of Rev. J. S. Barrass; one s.; one d.; educ. Forest School, Walthamstow; Lt.-Col., The Essex Rgt.; served Europ. War, 1914–18; Despatches.

YOOL, G. A. (D.S.O. L.G. 3.6.18); b. 15.10.76; 2nd Lt., S. Staff. R., 5.5.00; Lt. 24.6.02; Capt. 22.4.09; Maj. 1.9.15. attached Lincolns

YORK, R. L. (D.S.O. L.G. 1.1.18), Major, R.F.A.

YORKE, P. G. (D.S.O. L.G. 1.1.19); b. 9.1.82; 2nd Lt., R.A., 21.12.00; Lt. 21.12.03; Capt. 21.12.13; Maj. 11.9.15.

YORKE, R. M. (D.S.O. L.G. 1.1.17); b. 22.10.74; s. of late J. R. Yorke, M.P., and 2nd wife, Sophia Matilda, d. of Baron Vincent de Tuyll de Serooskerken; m. Hon. Muriel Fanny Herschell, d. of 1st Baron Herschell; two d.; 2nd Lt., 11th Hrs., 6.3.95; Capt. 18.3.05; ret pay 12.9.06; served Europ. War, 1914–18; Major (T/Lt.-Col.), Yeomanry; C.M.G.

YOUDEN, H. A. (D.S.O. L.G. 3.6.18), Major, Aust. Inf.

YOUNG, B. (D.S.O. L.G. 22.8.18), Major, 10th Inf. (Witwatersrand Rifles), S. African Forces.

YOUNG, C. E. (D.S.O. L.G. 26.7.18), Capt., Aust. Infy.

YOUNG, C. R. (D.S.O. L.G. 8.3.19) (Details, L.G. 4.10.19), T/Capt., R.A.M.C. att. 1st Batt. Shrops. L.I.; M.C.

YOUNG, E. HILTON, M.A. (D.S.O. L.G. 11.1.19); b. 20.3.79; s. of Sir George Young, 3rd Bart., of Formosa Place, Cookham, and Alice Eacy, d. of E. Kennedy, M.D.; m. Lady Scott, widow of the famous Arctic Explorer; educ. Eton; Trinity College, Cambridge; called to Bar, Inner Temple, 1904; Financial Editor of " Morning Post," 1910–14; M.P. (L.), Norwich, from 1915; Financial Secretary to the Treasury, 1921; Lt., R.N.V.R., and appointed to H.M.S. Iron Duke, Aug. 1914; Naval Mission in Serbia, 1915; Obilich Medal (Semendria, Oct. 1915) and Karageorge Order, 4th Class with Swords; H.M.S. Centaur (Harwich), 1916; actions of 22 Jan. and 11 May, 1917, etc.; R.N. Siege guns on Flemish front, 1917 (D.S.C. and Croix de Guerre); served in Vindictive at Zeebrugge Mole, 1918 (severely wounded and special promotion to Lt.-Cdr.); in command of armoured train in Archangel Campaign. His D.S.O. was awarded for services in action.

YOUNG, G. B. W. (D.S.O. L.G. 3.6.18), Capt., R.N., 31.12.15.

YOUNG, HARVEY GORDON, M.B. (D.S.O. L.G. 18.1.18) (Details, L.G. 25.4.18); s. of J. B. Young, of Toronto; educ. Toronto University; was on Staff of Toronto General Hospital before coming overseas as Capt., Can. A.M.C., and M.O. of an Alberta unit.

YOUNG, HENRY GEORGE (D.S.O. L.G. 25.8.17); b. 7.3.70; 2nd Lt., R. Fus., 8.10.90; Lt. 2.3.92; I.S.C. 25.11.92; Capt., I.A., 10.7.01; Maj. 8.10.08; Lt.-Col. 8.10.16; Col. 9.5.20; Brig.-Gen., ret. pay, 10.8.21; C.I.E., Chitral, 1895; Medal, clasp; N.W. Frontier, 1897–98; clasp; S. African War, 1902; Queen's Medal, 2 clasps; Europ. War; Despatches; C.I.E.

YOUNG, H. N. (D.S.O. L.G. 1.1.17) (Bar L.G. 15.10.18); b. 18.10.82; 2nd Lt. 8.1.01; Lt. 13.1.04; Capt. 1.4.10; served S. African War, 1901–2; Queen's Medal, 5 clasps; N. Nigeria, 1906. He was killed in action 25.10.18.

YOUNG, H. W. (D.S.O. L.G. 8.3.19) (Details, L.G. 4.10.19); 3rd surv. s. of late Rev. H. S. Young, of Wallands Court, Stokechurch, Oxon; m. Constance, y. d. of late Brig.-Gen. H. D. Findlay; Capt. (T/Major), 116th Mahratta L.I. Ind. Army.

YOUNG, J., M.D., F.R.C.S. (D.S.O. L.G. 1.1.19); b. 1883; m. Eva, widow of Capt. G. H. Harvey-Webb, R.A.M.C.; two s.; one d.; educ. Heriot's School and University, Edinburgh; M.B., with 1st Class Honours, 1905; M.D., with Gold Medal, 1910; late Lt.-Col., R.A.M.C.; served in Gallipoli, Egypt, Palestine and France, 1915–19; Despatches twice; He wrote " With the 52nd Division in Three Continents."

YOUNG, J. A. (D.S.O. L.G. 16.9.18), T/Major, R.F.A.; M.C.

YOUNG, J. D. (D.S.O. L.G. 3.6.19), Major, 52nd Batt. Can. Inf., Manitoba R.; M.C.

YOUNG, J. D. S. (D.S.O. L.G. 1.2.19), T/Lt., 10th Batt. A. and S. Highrs.; M.C.

YOUNG, J. H. (D.S.O. L.G. 1.1.19); b. 12.5.88; 2nd Lt., Arg. and Suth'd Highrs., 21.3.08; Lt. 1.4.10; Capt. 12.12.14; M.C.

YOUNG, J. H. B. (D.S.O. L.G. 2.4.19) (Details, L.G. 10.12.19), T/Lt. (A/Capt.), 10th Batt. Ches. R., att. 9th Batt.; M.C.

YOUNG, J. MAC L. (D.S.O. L.G. 3.6.18); b. 13.4.80; 2nd Lt., R. Lanc. R., 5.5.00; Lieut. 1.10.01; Capt. 23.11.07; Adjt., R. Lanc. R., 11.8.08–10.8.11; Major 8.1.16; served Europ. War; Despatches.

YOUNG, JULIAN MAYNE (D.S.O. L.G. 4.6.17); b. 6.8.72; s. of Col. G. G. Young, I.S.C.; m. Gwendoline Mary, d. of G. H. B. Young; two d.; educ. Repton; 2nd Lt., Lanc. Fus., 20.5.93; Lt. 24.3.96; Capt., A.S.C., 1.1.01; adjt., 1908–10; Major 1.1.11; Lt.-Col. 15.10.15; Colonel, R.A.S.C., 31.8.20; T/Brig.-Gen. 17.11.17; served S. African War, 1899–1901; Queen's Medal, 5 clasps; Europ. War, 1914–17; Bt. Col. 3.6.19; Despatches three times; Order of St. Maurice and Lazarus; C.M.G.

YOUNG, K. (D.S.O. L.G. 26.9.17); s. of Mark P. Young; T/2nd Lt., Lincs. Rgt.; served Europ. War; Despatches.

YOUNG, REV. S. D., M.A. (D.S.O. L.G. 4.6.17); b. 7.5.84; y. s. of O. W. Young, F.S.I., of Liverpool; educ. Downside School; Christ's College, Cambridge; Priest, Roman Catholic Church; Member of Benedictine Community, Downside Abbey; Temp. Chaplain to the Forces 1.2.15; 3rd Class 16.11.16; served Europ. War; Despatches three times; O.B.E.

YOUNG, T. F., Assoc. M.Inst.C.E. (D.S.O. L.G. 15.2.19) (Details, L.G. 30.7.19), Major, R.E.; served Europ. War, 1914–19; Despatches.

YOUNG, W. A., M.D. (D.S.O. L.G. 1.1.17); educ. Universities of Edinburgh, Dublin, Cambridge; University College, London; M.D.; D.P.H., R.C.P.S.; late R.A.M.C.; served Europ. War, 1914–18.

YOUNG, W. H. (D.S.O. L.G. 1.1.17); b. 7.2.70; s. of late Major-Gen. C. M. Young, R.A.; m. Marguerite, d. of G. Bolden, late 15th R.; one s.; two d.; educ. U.S. College, Westward Ho!; 2nd Lt., E. York. R., 23.3.89; Lt. 5.8.91; Capt. 27.11.97; Maj. 29.4.08; Lt.-Col. 15.5.15; ret. pay 18.6.19; S. African War, 1900–2; Despatches twice; Bt. Maj. 22.8.02; Queen's Medal, 3 clasps; King's Medal, 2 clasps; Europ. War; Bt. Lt.-Col. 18.2.15; Despatches three times.

YOUNG, W. McK. (D.S.O. L.G. 1.1.17), Major, Aust. Forces.

YOUNGER, A. A. S. (D.S.O. L.G. 1.1.18); b. 3.6.81; m. Marjorie Rhoda Halliley; two s.; educ. Wellington College; 2nd Lt., R.A., 17.3.00; Lt. 3.4.01; Capt. 21.10.08; Major 30.10.14; served Europ. War, 1914–18; Despatches.

YOUNGER, J., B.A. (D.S.O. L.G. 15.2.19) (Details, L.G. 30.7.19); b. 19.5.80; s. of Sir G. Younger, Bart., of Leckie, Stirlingshire, and Lucy, d. of late E. Smith, M.D., F.R.S.; m. Maud, d. of Sir J. Gilmour, Bart., of Lundin and Montrose; two s.; two d.; educ. Winchester; New College, Oxford; commissioned in 1901; Lt.-Col., Fife and Forfar Yeomanry; T.D.; served Europ. War with Fife and Forfar Yeomanry in Gallipoli and Egypt, and then in command of the 14th Battalion, The Black Watch, in Palestine and France, until wounded in Sept. 1918; mentioned in Sir Archibald Murray's Despatch from Egypt in July, 1916, for services as Staff Officer, Khargeh Column, West Force, and again in 1919 for services in command of 14th Battalion, The Black Watch, in France during summer and autumn, 1918; rowed Oxford University VIII., 1901 and 1902.

YOUNGER, L. (D.S.O. L.G. 3.6.19), Capt., Alberta Rgt., Can. Mil. Forces; M.C.

YOUNGHUSBAND, H. (D.S.O. L.G. 2.2.16); b. 13.10.75; 2nd Lt., Bedf. R., 10.2.00; Lt. 11.1.01; Capt. 10.10.08. He was killed in action 20.4.16.

YUILL, H. H., M.Sc. (D.S.O. L.G. 4.6.17); b. 1886; s. of H. W. Yuill, of Truro, Nova Scotia; m. Winifred, d. of T. A. Baker; one s.; educ. McGill University, Montreal; M.Sc.; Lt.-Col., R.E.; served Europ. War from 1914; Despatches four times; M.C.; Croix de Guerre; Montenegrin Medal for bravery; late Comptroller of Mines, First Army, B.E.F.

YULE, G. U. (D.S.O. L.G. 1.1.17); b. 17.11.81; 2nd Lt., R.E., 18.8.00; Lt. 18.8.03; Capt. 18.8.10; Major, R.E.; served at Aden, 1903–4, during operations in the Interior; Europ. War; Despatches. He died 22.12.18.

ZIEGLER, C. L. (D.S.O. L.G. 25.8.17); b. 27.6.84; 2nd Lt., R.A., 23.12.03; Lt. 23.12.06; ret. pay 16.3.12; Maj., R.A. (S.), 21.10.17; finally retired 13.5.21.

www.ingramcontent.com/pod-product-compliance
Lightning Source LLC
Chambersburg PA
CBHW080916230426
43668CB00014B/2136